Y0-BCT-671

COMMERCIAL TRANSACTIONS UNDER THE UNIFORM COMMERCIAL CODE AND OTHER LAWS

Fifth Edition

Donald B. King
Professor of Law
Saint Louis University

Calvin Kuenzel
L. Leroy Highbaugh, Sr. Professor of Law
Stetson University

Bradford Stone
Professor of Law
Stetson University

W.H. Knight, Jr.
Professor of Law
University of Iowa

CASEBOOK SERIES

1997

MATTHEW BENDER

QUESTIONS ABOUT THIS PUBLICATION?

For questions about the **Editorial Content** appearing in this volume or reprint permission, please call:

Michael Bruno, J.D. at .... (800) 252-9257 (ext. 2518)
Outside the United States and Canada please call .... (212) 448-2000

For assistance with shipments, billing or other customer service matters, please call:

Customer Services Department at .... (800) 533-1646
Fax number .... (518) 487-3584

LIBRARY OF CONGRESS CATALOGING-IN-PUBLICATION DATA

King, Donald Barnett.
Commercial transactions under the uniform commercial code / Donald B. King, Calvin A. Kuenzel, Bradford Stone, W.H. Knight, Jr. — 5th ed.
p. — (Analysis and skills series) (Cases and materials series)
Includes Index.
ISBN 0-8205-2766-1
1. Sales—United States—States—Cases. 2. Negotiable instruments—United States—States—Cases. 3. Security (Law) —United States—States—Cases. I. Kuenzel, Calvin A. II. Stone, Bradford, 1929– . III. Title. IV. Series. Cases and materials.
KF915.Z95K45 1997 96-29996
346.7307'2—dc21 CIP

MATTHEW BENDER

MATTHEW BENDER & CO., INC.
Editorial Offices
2 Park Avenue, New York, NY 10016-5675 (212) 448-2000
201 Mission St., San Francisco, CA 94105-1831 (415) 908-3200

PREFACE

In 1968, a small group of authors edited one of the first Uniform Commercial Code casebooks. This text was also one of the first casebooks published by Matthew Bender. Subsequent editions were published in 1974, 1981, and 1987. As this current group of authors edit this fifth edition, our goal our goal has remained constant.

"We have designed this casebook to be the best possible teaching tool for commercial law."

This edition, centering primarily around recent developments in caselaw and code revisions, carries forward several precepts developed over the years:

1. Ample material is given to permit each professor who uses the book to cover not only basics, but to have the option to go beyond if he or she wishes.

2. In the "to read" notations, the most recent code section cites are given that relate to each topic and each subtopic. Any older cites contained in cases are noted as well within the cases. In addition, the "to read" notations include cites to the convention on the International Sale of Goods as well for those who wish to use it.

3. There is not only a look at individual code sections, but the "to read" cites also contain reference to sections which are related to, substantiate, or seem contrary to, the major section under discussion. The student is encouraged to integrate the code into a single fluid body of law, rather than learning random legal principles.

4. The professor is given an opportunity to concentrate teaching on either the code itself or the caselaw, or both, to whatever degree seems best. The book also furnishes a comprehensive framework of commercial law which allows the professor to incorporate his own problems and other handouts.

5. Faculty may use individualized teaching techniques concentrating in either a caselaw or a problem approach, or both.

6. Modern and up-to-date cases are stressed, but some historical landmarks are mentioned in text or notes. Almost all of the principal cases have been decided within the last decade.

7. An effort has been made to include "cutting edge" cases. Not only can one see conflicting trends which have emerged in regard to some sections of the code, but one can also explore the direction the law is taking. We have tried to select cases that have interesting fact patterns, that involve interesting personalities of our times, or that include other factors that promote easier understanding of the subject matter

8. Illustrations of some of the major commercial documents in each area of the law are included, as well as some diagrams. These inclusions should give students a better appreciation of the documents used in practice and discussed in the cases.

9. Introductory and historical text is used throughout the text so as to form an easy bridge to learning the particular subject.

The editors recognize that many professors will use only parts of the casebook in accordance with the scope of their course and time and number of credits allotted them. Some may want to use a few of the chapters later as a basis for an advanced commercial law seminar as well. Again, our emphasis is one of material flexibility and user–friendliness.

Donald King
Calvin Kuenzel
Bradford Stone
W. H. Knight

DEDICATION

To our families and everyone else who has endured this effort.

Donald King

Calvin Kuenzel

Bradford Stone

W.H. Knight, Jr.

TABLE OF CONTENTS

Chapter 1

AN INTRODUCTORY VIEW

Chapter 2
SCOPE: SUBJECT MATTER OF THE CONTRACT FOR SALE

Chapter 3
THE CONTRACT FOR SALE

Chapter 4
PROPERTY INTERESTS

Chapter 5
WARRANTY/PRODUCTS LIABILITY

Chapter 6

PERFORMANCE

Chapter 7
REMEDIES

Chapter 8

RIGHTS OF THIRD PARTIES: GOOD FAITH PURCHASE OF GOODS

Chapter 9

LEASES OF GOODS

Chapter 10

DOCUMENTARY TRANSACTIONS

Chapter 11

NEGOTIABLE INSTRUMENTS: INTRODUCTION AND SCOPE, CONSEQUENCES OF NEGOTIABILITY

Chapter 12

REQUIREMENTS FOR OBTAINING RIGHTS GREATER THAN THOSE OF AN ASSIGNEE

Chapter 13
LIABILITY OF THE PARTIES

Chapter 14

BANKS AND THE CHECK COLLECTION PROCESS

Chapter 15

THE ROLE OF BANKS IN WIRE TRANSFERS

Chapter 16

AN INTRODUCTION TO SECURED TRANSACTIONS

Chapter 17
PERFECTION

Chapter 18
PRIORITIES

Chapter 19
DEFAULT

Chapter 20
SECURITY INTERESTS IN BANKRUPTCY

Chapter 21

PROBLEMS OF ADVANCED SCOPE

Chapter 22

INVESTMENT SECURITIES

Chapter 23

LETTERS OF CREDIT

CHAPTER 1

AN INTRODUCTORY VIEW

§ 1.01 Historical Development

In some law schools, there are separate courses for Sales, Negotiable Instruments, Payment Systems, and Secured Transactions. In others, combinations of these are taught in a course called Commercial Transactions. Regardless, some history gives one a better perspective of the particular course, and it seems desirable to see part of that picture within the overall development of commercial law.

A broader perspective of various aspects of commercial law (Sales, Negotiable Instruments and Payment Systems, and Secured Transactions) as practiced today can be gained through a short review of its historical development. Some of the commercial law principles of today may be seen in past developments. This approach reveals how commercial law became a part of the common law, of how commercial law was placed into uniform acts, of what gave rise to the formulation of the Uniform Commercial Code (U.C.C.), the role of the U.C.C. in modern commercial law, and other statutes and laws that supplement the U.C.C., and the development of an international commercial law of sales.

The basic framework of modern commercial law is found in the U.C.C. The U.C.C. embraces the major fields of commercial law: Sales, Commercial Instruments and Payment Systems, and Secured Transactions. It also covers letters of credit, bulk sales, bills of lading, warehouse receipts, and investment securities. The basic principles are set forth in the provisions of the U.C.C. and underlying policies are explained in the U.C.C. comments. This basic framework is not static; several major parts are being revised and new subjects added.

In addition to the U.C.C., other statutes and caselaw developments govern the practice of commercial law. For example, some consumer-oriented statutes affect manufacturers, sellers, and financiers. Product liability is reflected not only in the U.C.C., but also in the Restatement of Torts and caselaw. The effect of Negotiable Instruments on cutting of consumer defenses and curtailing consumer rights in regard to default through late payments and repossession led to special consumer statutes. Government regulations also may be applicable. International conventions, customs, and rules likewise may be pertinent and are a part of the recent continuing history of commercial law.

PROBLEM 1.1

One of your senior partners is on a panel of the American Historical Society. The main speaker has proposed as his topic "Commercial Law Then and Now: Old Problems in New Containers." While the speech is not yet available, he would like your opinion on the pertinent part of this subject matter and some ideas supporting it and some opposing. He would like an opinion after you have read Chapter 1 and another after you have finished the course.

PROBLEM 1.2

Another senior partner is concerned about the various commercial laws which apply to the firm's clients. The firm represents:

(1) businesses in states with the traditional U.C.C. (*e.g.*, Article 3 and 4 on Negotiable Instruments).

(2) ones with the Revised U.C.C. adopted in a number of states (*e.g.*, Articles 3 & 4 Negotiable Instruments, Article 2A on Leasing and 4A Electronic Transfers).

(3) businesses that want to be advised as to possible proposals for change that may be made in law in the next several years (*e.g.*, Revision of U.C.C. Articles and other laws).

(4) businesses that deal with businesses in other countries (*e.g.*, Convention on the International Sale of Goods; other internationally proposed or adopted conventions, such as the Convention on International Bills of Exchange and International Promissory Notes and other international principles).

In responding to these issues, what laws and sources are you dealing with primarily? In what way can the firm be prepared to handle these matters? In some situations, its clients may have the "upper hand" in the negotiations; in others they will not. Should this make a difference? What should they be concerned about in regard to possible long range changes? Should the firm back any law reforms — and should they be on a state, federal, or international level? Your senior partner would like a preliminary opinion after you have read Chapter 1 and a final one when you have finished the course.

[A] Early Commercial Law

As tribes and early kingdoms developed, there undoubtedly was some contract and commercial law. Indeed, reference to contract law is found in the Babylonian Empire. Negotiable notes were found in Phoenician times. However, greater development of commercial law is found with the Roman Empire. Although some ideas came from the Grecian era, the Roman law established rules of contracts and of the marketplace. In terms of secured interest, the pledge of goods or property was paramount.

Another source of commercial law is found among the early merchants whose trade transcended national borders. A set of maritime laws developed concerning transportation of goods and remedies of parties, which determined duties and risks in such trade, and contributed to the overall commercial law concepts of insurance that developed from maritime trade. The merchants, dealing with others from considerable distances, also developed concepts such as negotiability of commercial paper.

In early England, the primary emphasis of the King's law was upon property and incidents of the feudal system. The commercial law, to the extent that it existed, was to be found in other forums: manor courts, fair courts, and town courts. Some cases involved matters related to negotiable paper. Customs among merchants and financiers also contributed to the emerging law of sales and negotiable paper.

With the increase of trade during the early 1300's, large commercial fairs became more frequent. These were attended by merchants from different parts of England and foreign lands and served as a convenient forum for promoting trade both between merchants and between merchants and persons able to afford the commodities offered. The importance of these fairs should not be underemphasized in relation to the commerce of the times. Much of the internal and foreign trade of England was carried on at such fairs. These fairs were established by special grant from the King and were, in effect, a grant to establish marketplaces. To handle disputes which arose there, courts were established at the fairs. These courts, picturesquely called "Piedpoudre" courts after the "dusty feet" of the merchants, quickly dispensed justice. The following excerpt from the court of St. Ives in 1319 illustrates the swift settlement of disputes:

> John of Honing was attached to answer Roger of Stanton in a plea of covenant. And whereof he complains that whereas the said John sold to the said Roger a last of red herring for nine marks of silver, to wit, on Monday after the feast of St. Gregory the Pope last past in the villa of St. Ives, and thereof showed him three kemps of good herring and assured him that all the residue of the said herring was similar to the said three kemps, and the said Roger gave him a God's penny in confirmation of the said bargain; nevertheless, after receiving the said herring, the said Roger found that the whole residue of the said herring was unlike the first three kemps, and was mixed with stickiebacks and with putrid herring. Wherefore, he says that he is injured and has damage to the value of 60s, and therefore he produces suit. And the said John comes and denies tort and force etc., and says that he broke no covenant with him, as the said Roger has alleged against him. And he craves that this be inquired, and the said Roger does likewise. Therefore, it is ordered that the bailiff cause a good inquest to come, etc. And the inquest comes and says that the said John broke the covenant with him (Roger) to his damage 40d. Therefore, it is awarded that the said Roger recover against him the said 40d. and that the said John be in mercy 6d pledge (for the fine), Thomas of Ellington.

Certain towns became commercial centers, and courts similar to the fair courts were established which handled disputes arising out of commercial transactions. In addition to the legislation by fair and town courts, a certain degree of regulation was undertaken at the same time by guilds over their own crafts. These guilds were not only concerned with members, but also the quality and sale of goods.

[B] Common Law

For centuries, the common law concerned itself primarily with property law. Even by the 12th century, a simple promise not under seal wasunenforced in the common-law courts. In the 13th and 14th centuries the emphasis of the common law courts continued to be on property law, with some developments in tort law. Despite the lack of interest in commercial law disputes during this early period of the common law, the common-law courts entered the field in the 1400's and 1500's.

In the several centuries during which the common law took jurisdiction over commercial law, the assimilation of the commercial law of the past occurred. It was not an easy transition, however, because of the common law judges' hostility toward commercial law principles. The adjustment of the common law toward the concept of negotiability, for example, was a gradual one.

In the 1500's, Dutch goldsmiths began to issue checks to those who deposited gold with them. They also collected and canceled debts on the written orders of their customers. In England, the practice took hold in the 1600's and goldsmith notes or receipts were issued promising to pay the customer or another. Also, the customers could write the goldsmith directing him to pay another — an early type of check. Goldsmiths or banks also sent these checks by messenger to other banks when asked to by their customers. When the messengers decided to meet for a drink at a mid-town cafe and simply exchange the checks there, the first bank "clearinghouse" developed.

Lord Mansfield, a Scottish lawyer who became an English judge, aided in the adjustment of common law to commercial needs from 1756 onward. In contrast to other judges of his time, he was more receptive to the needs of those engaged in commerce. During his ascendancy as Chief Justice, Lord Mansfield designed several innovations to make the legal system more compatible with commercial requirements, earning him an enduring reputation as the "father of commercial law." He established, for example, a special "jury," a set of advisors, to aid him in making decisions relating to commercial law. The commercial jury tended to increase the confidence of the commercial community in the common law. He also attempted to formulate principles of commercial law out of the chaos of mercantile custom. One of Lord Mansfield's landmark decisions utilizing merchant law did away with the doctrine of consideration in special settings. He dealt with letters of credit and negotiable instruments such as drafts. During these years, the pledge of property for a loan continued as one of the primary forms of secured transactions. But also it became recognized with the mortgaging of real property for loans or sales that there also could be personal property mortgages as well — a type of security interest.

With the steady growth of case law during the 1800's, commentators began to recognize aspects of commercial law as being distinct subject areas. In 1847, in England, one of the first books relating to sales and commercial law was published. In 1866, an English lawyer named Chalmers compiled a digest of some of the English commercial law cases. His digest of the Law of Negotiable Instruments was published in 1878. A decade later, he drafted the English Bills of Exchange Act, thus solidifying negotiable instruments law. In 1882 it was enacted in England and subsequently enacted throughout the British empire. Interestingly, Chalmers had been in India earlier, and his digest was based on some of the Indian code.

In 1868, a well-known treatise, Benjamin on Sales, was published. Judah Benjamin was an American lawyer who served as Secretary of State for the Confederacy, and then fled to England and there did his writing. By 1875, the second edition was published and contained reference to American decisions as well as to the French Civil Code. The Sale of Goods Act also was drafted by Chalmers and enacted in 1893. One of the primary new ideas which developed throughout the 1800's was that of implied warranties, and the number of cases in the field of commercial law generally continued to grow.

The continued growth of commercial enterprises, larger populations to consume more goods and technology combined with mass production made commercial law increasingly important. Not only were there more sales, but the use of credit came to be used on a large scale. Negotiable instruments and several types of secured transactions became used even more. Various state laws and caselaw developed.

[C] Uniform Acts

In the United States, the movement for codification of the law had both successes and reversals during the latter portion of the 1800's. Codification in the area of commercial law did not occur until the very end of that century, but when it did occur, Negotiable Instruments law was put into statutory form. The Negotiable Instruments Act closely followed the English Bills of Exchange. In 1896, the Uniform Negotiable Instruments Law was drafted under the auspices of the Commissioners on Uniform State Laws. This was to be followed by the Uniform Sales Act in 1906, and a series of other uniform acts in succeeding years:

Uniform Law	Approved by Commissioners	No. of States Adopting
Negotiable Instruments Law	1896	48
Uniform Sales Act (Amended in 1922)	1906	34
Uniform Warehouse Receipts Act	1906	48
Uniform Stock Transfer Act	1909	48
Uniform Bills of Lading Act	1909	31
Uniform Conditional Sales Act	1918	10
Uniform Trust Receipts Act	1933	32

Another development took place during the same time period in both the commercial and consumer realms. The potential and desirability of using credit started to become a part of the psychological and economic milieu of the times. The enactment of the uniform laws in some states also encourages the use of credit. With these developments come the greater use of negotiable instruments and secured transactions in a variety of forms.

[D] Diversity

Despite the efforts of the Commissioners on Uniform State Laws, uniformity was not achieved, partially due to the scattered and haphazard pattern of adoptions by states of the different uniform acts. Twenty-eight years after its approval by the Commissioners, the Negotiable Instruments Act was finally adopted in all 48 states. Uniformity also was impaired by divergent judicial decisions on various provisions. By 1948, 75 sections out of a total of 198 sections of the Uniform Negotiable Instruments Act were subject to conflicting court decisions. The Sales Act also was not being uniformly construed by the courts.

In addition, a number of courts were construing the commercial legislation in a somewhat narrow and mechanical fashion. Some of the real commercial needs and underlying policy considerations were being ignored. Further, there seemed to be a need for commercial decency, backed by sanction of law, in the performance of obligations. The diversity and uncertainty of the law, together with commercial needs, gave rise to a demand for a recodification of commercial law.

§ 1.02 The Uniform Commercial Code

It is, of course, difficult to set the precise point of origin of any major development of law. To some, the origin of the Uniform Commercial Code might be placed in the movement for codification and the early Field-Carter debates which took place in newspaper and magazine articles. David Dudley Field was a prominent New York attorney in the 1830s who argued that legal principles should be codified so everyone could understand them. Carter also was a prominent New York attorney; he believed law should be left to develop only through caselaw and was bitterly opposed to codification. Others might single out the growth of the Uniform Acts as the origin of the U.C.C. The more contemporary and perhaps more particularized point of origin, however, which has been singled out by a number of commentators is the late nineteen thirties and nineteen forties.

In 1938, a proposal had been sponsored by the Merchants Association of New York City for a federal sales act to govern all interstate sales transactions. In response to this indication of inadequacies in the Uniform Sales Act, the National Conference of Commissioners on Uniform State Laws undertook revision of the Uniform Sales Act it had originally prepared in 1906.

A revision of the Uniform Negotiable Instruments Law, originally prepared in 1896, was then also under consideration.

Growing dissatisfaction with the variety of laws and filing requirements for secured transactions made this another area ripe for reform.

In 1940, the National Conference adopted a proposal to prepare a Uniform Commercial Code, embracing a modernization and coordination of the Uniform Sales Act, the Uniform Negotiable Instruments Law, the Uniform Bills of Lading Act, the Uniform Warehouse Receipts Act, and all other Uniform Acts in the field of commercial law, with new provisions where no uniform acts existed on important and closely related commercial problems. The American Law Institute joined in the undertaking the following year, and in 1942 participated in discussions of the draft Revised Sales Act as a proposed sales chapter of the prospective Code. In 1945, work on the enlarged project was begun. (Report of Association of the Bar of the City of New York, Comm. On Uniform State Laws, May 9, 1950)

Between 1945 and 1952, a great number of drafts and redrafts of parts of the proposed Code were prepared by a reporting staff supervised by an Editorial Board. They were considered successively by advisory groups of judges, lawyers, and law teachers, and by the Council of the American Law Institute and the Commercial Acts Section and the Property Acts Section of the National Conference of Commissioners on Uniform State Laws, and then by the general membership of the two organizations. In preparing the several redrafts, the reporting and advisory groups also consulted with individuals and organizations in business and banking circles in many parts of the country who had come forward with criticisms. The first complete draft of the Code was released in May 1949. Judge Goodrich, Chairman of the U.C.C. Editorial Board described the subsequent development:

> A final text of the proposed Code was completed in September, 1951, and was also approved at that time by the House of Delegates of the American Bar Association. A final text edition was issued in November, 1951. Thereafter, a number of amendments were adopted by the sponsoring organizations in May and September, 1952. Following this action, an official edition was prepared with explanatory comments, and was published as the 1952 Official Text and Comments Edition.
>
> . . .[A] relatively few months after the New York Law Revision Commission's report was made public in 1956 the Editorial Board of the U.C.C. recommended the adoption of a great many amendments to meet criticisms and suggestions which had been received from the New York Revision Commission and other committees and agencies. These amendments were subsequently approved both by the National Conference of Commissioners on Uniform State Laws and the American Law Institute. The Code as thus amended was published under the title "1957 Official Edition."
>
> This version of the Code was enacted by Massachusetts in the fall of 1957 and by Kentucky in the spring of 1958.

(Goodrich, Forward to the Official Edition, U.C.C. (1959)).

By the mid-1960s, the Code had been enacted throughout the nation. The law of sales was primarily embodied in Article 2 of the U.C.C. Negotiable Instruments law was set forth in Articles 3 and 4. The law of Secured Transactions was in Article 9. A U.C.C. Committee reviewing Article 9 (Secured Transactions) suggested some amendments which became part of a new official 1972 edition. In 1977, some amendments were made to Article 8 on Investment Securities (uncertificated stock transfers) were added to its coverage. In the 1980's, individual states were enacting these changes into their law. Since the Code was first enacted in the mid-1960's, a number of cases relating to its provisions have been decided. Thus, there is a body of caselaw interpreting various provisions of the U.C.C. Some of the cases represent diverse interpretations. Discussions of caselaw development under the Code through court interpretations are found in some court opinions rendered in the 1980s, and are contained in this casebook.

A "Permanent Editorial Board" for the U.C.C. continues to review the Code, caselaw, and proposals for amendment of the U.C.C. This Board was established by the American Law Institute and Commissioners for Uniform State Laws, which had formulated and urged enactment of the U.C.C. Article 6 on Bulk Transfers has been revised. A new payments law for electronic transfers also was proposed by the Articles 3-4-8 Committee with a report to the Board; an American Bar Association committee also studied the matter. There were Amendments to Articles 3 and 4 and an Article 4A for Electronic Transfers. Article 2A on "leasing" was added.

In addition to the Code becoming the law of the land, other aspects of commercial law developed in the 1960's, 1970's and 1980's and 1990's. There were important developments relating to products liability, credit cards and electronic funds transfer, consumer protection, bankruptcy and letters of credit. Since these subjects are a part of modern commercial law, and fill gaps in the law not covered by the Code, this book contains some cases and materials relating to them.

The drafters of the Uniform Commercial Code were primarily concerned with a Code for the United States. Foreign representatives were excluded from the drafting process, even though at times the law of other countries was noted. Nevertheless, Article 9 (Secured Transactions) has been enacted in some Canadian provinces. In light of a new interest in comparative commercial law in recent decades, some studies have been made of Code concepts, such as unconscionability, as they exist in other countries. It is most likely that the interest in comparative commercial and consumer law will accelerate into the coming century.

The Uniform Commercial Code remains the law throughout the United States. 1999 will mark the fiftieth anniversary of its formulation. Although there will be some Amendments and even added Articles, the basic framework of the U.C.C. will remain. The student and lawyer of today with knowledge of the U.C.C. and comparable international commercial law will be well equipped to deal with commercial law into the new 21st century.

§ 1.03 The Uniform Commercial Code: Subsequent Development

The mass production and new technologies of the earlier part of the century seemed dwarfed by the later ones following World War II. Even more consumers and an even more relaxed attitude toward using credit created more production and business than ever. The last psychological barriers which some earlier generations had to the use of credit fell. New ways of doing business also brought about many changes in the Uniform Commercial Code. In addition, a vast increase in commercial activity was necessary to satisfy the needs of a growing population and new international markets. This engendered even more use of sales contracts, negotiable instruments, and security interests. Article 2A on leasing has been enacted in nearly all the states in the U.S. Consequently, a new chapter, 9A, has been added to these materials dealing with leases of goods. In addition, where similar provisions in Article 2, dealing with goods, appear in Article 2A, the parallel section citations to the lease material now appear with the Article 2 provisions.

Article 3 on commercial paper was revised along with parts of Article 4 on bank deposits and collections. Some states have adopted these provisions. A new Article 4A, entitled Funds Transfers, has been approved and enacted throughout the nation.

It was recommended by the Commissioners of Uniform State Laws and the American Law Institute that Article 6 on Bulk Transfers be repealed. However, for those states still wishing to regulate bulk sales, a revised version of the article was provided. A majority of the states considering the matter have voted for repeal.

[A] Law Reform Oversight

PROBLEM 1.3

What position would you support if you were a member of the ALI attending this session mentioned in the following discussion?

As a member of the legal profession, what would be your view as to the handling of law reform? Should it be left to the ALI and the Commissioners for Uniform State Laws? Why or why not?

One of the purposes of the Uniform Commercial Code was to make uniform the law among the various jurisdictions (U.C.C. § 1-102(2)(c)). One can easily see how the legislative reaction of the various jurisdictions to this flurry of reform legislation can impact substantially on this purpose of uniformity. One reaction to the problem was the possible creation of a Law Reform Oversight Committee and the matter was raised at the 1990 meeting of the American Law Institute, and appears in the Record of Proceedings.

> *Donald Barnett King (Mo.):* One thing I would like to raise at this point is the matter of this whole amendment process in the sense that what you have here, in these few years, is an amending of a number of articles of the Uniform Commercial Code. While this is desirable and while this meeting should proceed to consider the matters at hand, it seems to be that The American Law Institute must appoint a special committee on commercial law reform, a long-range committee that can deal with what is happening and what will happen as history has shown us in the past — what will happen, in regard to this whole amendment process. . ..
>
> Through the nation, there is a lack of uniformity that is occurring. We now face the greatest lack of uniformity possible. That is, we are revising, at this point, parts of Article 3 and Article 4, and the states, as they look at these amendments, will indeed not enact them uniformly. They will be enacted over a period of varying years.
>
> We have also Article 2, which is being revised by Dick Speidel and some others; that, too, will go through the same process of lack of uniformity. Article 2A will go through the same thing. Someone told me there may be an Article 2B proposed by a couple of lawyers who want licensing included. Article 5 is being revised; Boris Kozolchyk, among others, is working on that. Article 9 is going through further revisions; Article 8, also.
>
> I make a motion that The American Law Institute appoint a special long-range committee on commercial law reform, because it seems to me that this is most crucial. It should be a committee with some representatives of the Permanent Editorial Board, both ALI and states, but it should be with other independent members of The American Law Institute.
>
> I think we want to keep the same process because The American Law Institute has done a magnificent job, but we have to consider varying alternatives, including federal enactment,

in part, or other alternatives for making the law reform process more efficient. Otherwise, this Institute will be proposing uniform laws amending every single article, knowing that 50 states will not enact them uniformly.

Opposition to the proposal for a special long-range committee on commercial law reform was quickly voiced.

> Mr. Carlyle C. Ring, Jr. (Va.): I am from the National Conference of Commissioners on Uniform State Laws, a partner in this process of the Uniform Commercial Code. . . .
>
> [I] think that any committee of The American Law Institute really has got to coordinate with the other bodies, and that is the point I think I am trying to make. I would hope that the Council, if this were favorably accounted upon, would take into account these inner relationships and hopefully conclude — and maybe this body should conclude — that the Permanent Editorial Board is really the right vehicle (pp. 386-387).

[B] Possible Federal Enactment

PROBLEM 1.4

As an aide to one of the U.S. Senators from your state, you have been asked to look into the possible federal enactment of the U.C.C. or portions of it. Thus, there would be a Federal Sales Act, a Federal Negotiable Instruments Act and a Federal Security Interest Act. Present the arguments *pro* and *con* and make your recommendation to the Senator. He has given you a copy of an excerpt from an article dealing with federal enactment:

> Another possible way of dealing with this lack of uniformity is through federal enactment of commercial law. The U.C.C. could be enacted on the federal level so that national law could deal with commercial matters. Indeed, by trying to promote a uniform law on a state by state basis, the A.L.I. and the Commissioners indirectly acknowledge this fact. State by state enactment reaches the same goal as federal enactment. The A.L.I. should have no problem formulating an appropriate plan since it can propose legislation on either a state or federal level. The Commissioners should find it implied in their powers to promote the best commercial law for each state, whether through federal or state action. Clearly, uniformity is desirable and practical; federal enactment promotes uniformity in state law. The state can act voluntarily by appointing commissions, drafting acts, and entrusting those acts to federal enactment.
>
> Commercial laws should not be decided on a state by state basis. Those laws do not inherently reflect a strong state interest or command state enactment. Indeed, laws that regulate the flow of goods and commercial transactions over state lines should be considered national in character. The states have little interest in the massive number of goods flowing over their boundaries or even those that are part of a national economy. Because some states might feel the need for greater consumer protection than others, those states can enact special legislation to provide such protection. In any event, the basic national framework of the commercial law should be the same.
>
> The federal government clearly has the power to enact a federal law on commercial matters including leasing through the interstate commerce clause. That clause covers both transactions that involve crossing state boundaries and those that have an indirect economic impact. Under relevant case law, localized activity, although only remotely and indirectly affecting interstate commerce, is enough to allow federal enactment.

The case involving a farmer who raised extra wheat locally for his own local use is a good illustration of the broad federal constitutional power. Similarly, the federal government regulated a family owned restaurant, Ollie's Barbecue, although it served food only to local customers. Though not enacted for commercial purposes, the civil rights statute is constitutional since it falls within the purview of the interstate commerce clause. Undoubtedly, laws on commercial activity such as leasing fall within the interstate commerce clause power; its inclusion is constitutionally justified more easily than in the examples above. Commercial activity is national in character. More importantly, federal power was designed to promote federal regulation of commercial activity. Federal and state courts generally have concurrent jurisdiction over issues of federal law, by implication of Article III of the United States Constitution, unless Congress expressly states otherwise. Also by congressional act, federal court jurisdiction over U.C.C. issues could be negated, leaving it solely to the state courts if so desired.

King, *Major Problems With Article 2A: Unfairness, "Cutting Off" Consumer Defenses, Unfiled Interests, and Uneven Adoption*, 43 Mercer Law Rev. 869 at 873-74 (1992).

§ 1.04 International Commercial Law

[A] Uniform International Commercial Law

PROBLEM 1.5

Your senior partner is a member of an International Academy which is discussing the matter of uniformity under the convention for the International Sale of Goods. Such discussions also may be applicable to the International Unification of Negotiable Instruments and Secured Transactions. He has looked at the educational, structural, and broad principles proposals mentioned in the next several pages and seeks your views on this matter.

There also has been work toward a uniform international commercial law, which has included efforts of UNIDROIT (International Institute for Unification of Private Law in Rome), the Hague Conference on Private International Law and UNICITRAL (United Nations Commission on International Trade Law in Vienna) over many years. American representatives involved with these efforts were experts in the U.C.C. In 1980, a diplomatic conference of sixty-two nations approved the United Nations Convention on Contracts for the International Sales of Goods. It is often referred to as the Vienna Convention or the International Sales Convention (ISC), or the Convention on the International Sale of Goods (C.I.S.G.).

This International Sales Convention applies to sales transactions between parties in different nations. It does not apply to contracts for services, consumer sales, negotiable paper, or certain miscellaneous sales involving aircraft, ships, electricity, or auctions. Parties may by contract exclude the application of the convention, terms of the contract generally prevail over provisions of the convention if they conflict. Part I (Articles 1-13) governs the scope of applications of ISC and sets forth rules of interpretation, such as good faith and trade usage.

Part II (Articles 14-24) deals with the making of the contract. This includes matters relating to offers, acceptances, and "acceptances" which deviate from the offer.

Part III (Articles 25-88) covers rights, obligations, and remedies of the parties. This includes what constitutes the seller's delivery, place and time for delivery, handing over of documents, quality or warranty of goods, and right to cure performance before or after the date of delivery.

It also includes the buyer's rights and duties of examination and giving notice and the buyer's basic obligations of payment. Risk of loss or damage to the goods, anticipatory breach, fundamental breach, and installment contracts are covered. Seller and buyer remedies and damages also are in this Part.

Part IV (Articles 89-101) deals with certain reservations permitted to nations choosing them, and with steps for bringing the Convention into force.

By early 1987, the ISC had been ratified by over ten nations, including the United States, effective January 1, 1988. As adopted by the United States the ISC is applicable to transactions between businesses that are located in different countries.

By mid-1994, thirty-seven nations had ratified the United Nations Convention on Contracts for the International Sales of Goods (CISG). We have provided in this casebook citations to CISG sections that parallel similar provisions in Article 2.

[B] International Bills of Exchange and International Promissory Notes

In 1988, the General Assembly of the United Nations called for nations to adopt this new Convention. It pointed out that the circulation of negotiable instruments facilitates international trade and finance. This Convention would be a part of the progressive harmonization and unification of international trade law. However, there was far less success in regard to the adoption of this Convention.

[C] Uniformity of International Commercial Law

In May of 1992, UNICITRAL celebrated its twenty-fifth anniversary with a congress to review possible further needs and possibilities regarding international commercial law. One of the major problems with the global adoption of commercial laws is the problem of diverse court interpretations. Several proposals have been made in that regard.

[1] Informational Measures

Secretary of UNICITRAL, Gerald Hermann, suggested at the 25th Anniversary Conference that there be publication of uniform law texts and related materials, *e.g.*, Register of Texts, Official Records, Book on UNICITRAL, Yearbooks comprising regular documentation, Status of Conventions and Brochures with explanatory notes ("ten-pagers") entitled "Case Law on UNICITRAL Texts." He also suggested organization or co-sponsorship of regional or national seminars, congresses or similar programs, briefing of visiting lawyers or business representatives, training of interns, hosting of scholars, and other educative measures. The analysis of court interpretation of UNICITRAL texts and possible recommendations for uniform interpretation also was mentioned.

[2] Structural Measures

[i] International Uniform Law Court

Professor Louis Sohn proposed an International Uniform Laws Court at the UNICITRAL Anniversary Conference.

> The rapid growth in international trade is accompanied by a constant increase in the number of international uniform laws and of international conventions establishing uniform rules for one important area after another. A parallel increase in litigation before domestic courts and

commercial arbitral tribunals has resulted in inconsistent decisions and conflicting interpretations of the same uniform law or common conventional rule in different countries. This leads often to forum shopping and a conduct of litigation in an inconvenient forum with limited access to facts and witnesses. Each conflicting decision results also in diminishing the value of the uniform law or conventional rule, and the laborious effort to reach agreement on them is often wasted.

Establishment of stricter jurisdictional rules might cut down forum shopping but would not prevent discrepancy in interpretation. The only adequate remedy would be to establish an international court composed of legal experts with experience in preparation, application of interpretation of uniform laws and uniform conventional rules. It would perform in the field of private international law (in the broad sense of this phrase) the same function as is being performed by the International Court of Justice in the field of public international law. States might be willing to accept its jurisdiction for all, or at least some, international agreements establishing uniform laws or common rules to which they are parties. If some States are not willing to go that far, they might agree to least to resort to the Court when national tribunals of different countries render conflicting interpretations of a uniform text. The modalities of such a procedure might parallel the practice of the Supreme Court of the United States in case of conflicting decisions of Circuit Appeal Courts and a similar practice is developing in the European Community's judicial system. Many other problems of jurisdiction, composition and procedure would have to be solved, but the trail has been blazed by many interesting proposals and reports. The approach envisaged in this paper is preferable to the establishment of special tribunals for a variety of topics, as it would avoid the excessive cost of maintaining simultaneously a constantly increasing number of tribunals for one topic after another. Once established, a general tribunal for the interpretation of uniform laws and rules would be able to develop techniques enabling it to deal with even the most difficult or most specialized subjects. Such a tribunal is long overdue, and its establishment would constitute an important contribution to the United Nations Decade of International Law.

[ii] International Commercial Law Court

At that same Conference, Professor Donald King supported Professor Sohn's proposal, but also proposed an interim measure in the event the International Court for Uniform Treaties was not effectuated. An International Commercial Law Court could be created with jurisdiction primarily over the International Sale of Goods Act, the International Bills of Exchange and International Promissory Notes Convention and other UNICITRAL developed commercial laws. It also could handle some cases of conflicting interpretation of general international commercial principles by national arbitration bodies or courts if that seemed desirable. This would entail much less funding and effort. Because conflicting case decisions in the various countries on these international commercial provisions would be slow to arise, such a court would have to meet only a couple of months each year. The judges could be law professors, judges, governmental and UNICITRAL officials, and distinguished retired members of the legal profession. As the work of the International Commercial court grows over the years, the positions can be made full-time ones.

[iii] Development of Broad International Principles

The development of broad general principles of contract and of business ethics also would aid in the uniform interpretation of the Convention. As noted by Professor Sono of Japan at the UNICITRAL 25th Anniversary Conference:

In the field of the settlement of international commercial disputes, the success of UNICITRAL's activities on international commercial arbitration was fortunate as they coincided with the period of the formation and expansion of globalized economic activity in the 1970s. The flexibility of arbitration often enables arbitrators to maneuver away from those not-so-helpful national laws particularly for the settlement of disputes of complex modern contracts. And, through arbitral awards, there is a phenomenon of a resurgence of the rule of reason at a delocalized level away from the legal positivism and traditional dogma.

For complex transactions which were seldom heard of in the past, there is a tendency to resort to "the general principle of law," "lex mercatoris," or "the principle of good faith and fair dealing" particularly through arbitration clauses. During the Congress, I was told personally from a reliable source that 5 to 10 percent of the disputes which are submitted to arbitration now contain such clauses. The person who provided me with this information said "only 5 to 10 percent," but to me it is an extremely significant percentage. Yet, the contents of these principles are still far from certain. However, it is interesting to note in this context that international bodies such as UNICROIT and E.C. are presently undertaking to elaborate their contents more concretely in the form of principles of international contract law under the influence of the Vienna Sales Convention which continues to make a valuable contribution to reorient the traditional dogma-oriented jurisprudence beyond the area of sales. The International Law Association also started to elaborate global contract principles interestingly through its Committee on International Commercial Arbitration.

As Professor King also indicated, a need may soon be felt for the establishment of a global court of commerce initially for cases where resort has been made in arbitration to a national or international lex mercatoria or to general principles of contract law. At this Congress, we already heard a suggestion of Professor Sohn for the establishment of an international tribunal to interpret uniform legal texts.

[iv] International Restatement of General Principles

In 1994, UNIDROIT issued a set of General Principles for International Sales Law. This was the work of almost 15 years by international experts. It seems quite possible that it will become recognized as an international "law merchant."

[v] Internationalization of Security Interests

In 1994, the final draft of an International Convention on Security Interests in Mobile Equipment under the auspices of UNIDROIT was produced, with subsequent reports in 1995. This is an attempt to internationalize one aspect of secured transactions.

During this same time, studies of creating a security interest law and system for the NAFTA countries was undertaken by the National Law Center of Inter-American Free Trade.

An international-national electronic filing system with more certain identification of debtors also has been proposed (See King, Secured Transactions 4-15 (1995)). It is pointed out that the present state filing systems, which necessitate the use of writings and physical filing of financing statements, were developed before the development of new technology when such writings and filings were necessary. It urges that these systems are now obsolete, and should be scrapped, and replaced with "International-National Electronic Filing (INEF)." International electronic systems, like the Internet, make information easily accessible through a home or office computer virtually anywhere in the world. The Internet would make searches for information on security interests and filing easier and would not be constrained by state boundaries. These electronic networks make the establishment of a major national filing office unnecessary, although an overall supervisor might be in order. Combined with INEF, a system of more certain identification of debtors (CID) would eliminate more filing problems. Such an identification system should be compatible with electronic filing, possibly using Social Security numbers or tax identification numbers. Similar certain identification could be established for other countries when international expansion of the system seemed feasible.

§ 1.05 Construction and Interpretation

Read: U.C.C. § 1-102 and Comments.

Read also: CISG Art. 7.

Commercial law, as contrasted with other legal subjects, has its own unique principles of interpretation. While each of these three points could be explored at great length, some summary statements with brief excerpts from King, The New Conceptualism of the U.C.C. (1968), pp. 8-10, 99-103 (footnotes omitted) on the nature of the Code, the relationship of parties, and rejection of past concepts are sufficient to illustrate the U.C.C. methodology.

[A] Nature of the Code

PROBLEM 1.6

Some persons maintain that the "nature of the Code" is only an idealized method of interpretation and that in a common law system the courts will continue to emphasize case law development and caselaw interpretation of the Code. The Code, they say, is no different than an ordinary statute. What do you think in this regard? Consider the following excerpt along with the common law training of judges.

> The U.C.C. is a Code — not an ordinary statute — and the principles of its interpretation are different.
>
> "True" codes, systematic and comprehensive in nature, differ significantly from ordinary statutory legislation in terms of the methodology of interpretation. For one thing, a code is to be viewed by any court confronted by it as a document which is self-explanatory. The court is to look to the codified principle and its underlying purposes and policies rather than any technicalities of prior case law. Where a gap may occur, or in an unforeseen situation, the court must look to the other principles contained in the code for its answer. This may be contrasted with other statutory law where the common law or former case law is dealt with instead. Under the U.C.C., the pre-Code caselaw should not be used either for purposes of interpretation or for the solving of new problems. This same principle applies even as to case decisions interpreting provisions of the Code itself. Other courts, while recognizing such opinions as having some persuasive value, should still look to the Code itself and its qualities for the answers. As one commentator has stated, a code "remains at all times its own best evidence of what it means; cases decided under it may be interesting, persuasive, cogent, but each new case must be referred for decision to the undefiled code text." This is to be distinguished from a statute which has been interpreted over a space of time in a series of judicial opinions which have themselves "become part of the statutory complex." This view is reiterated by another authority, who emphasizes the fact that the doctrine of stare decisis should not be used in applying the Code. As he states, it may be hoped. . .that its application

> will be less vigorous here, that the courts will more readily return to the statutory text for their answers. . . . [C]ases construing the Code should be given the highest credit, but it should not be forgotten that the code itself is its own best evidence of what it means. Thus, the Code by its very nature dictates a return of itself and its purposes for interpretation and requires this methodology of construction.
>
> In civil law jurisdictions, such methodology has long been used. One authority on civil law has emphasized that this new code methodology "represents a remarkable advance in the history of American law." As he points out, where the text of the Code falls short of deciding the controversy, the Code may "itself be developed or 'applied to promote its underlying reasons, purposes and policies.' "

King, *supra,* at 8-10.

[B] Relationships and Circumstances

In deciding U.C.C. cases, it has been said the courts should give consideration to the relationship of the parties affected by the transaction.

> In most instances, the relationship will manifest itself in terms of the more immediate parties to a transaction, since it is primarily their relationship which will be the subject of litigation. In some instances, however, particularly those where the rights of creditors, good faith purchasers, or purchasers in the ordinary course of business have come into conflict with the rights of one of the immediate parties, other individuals may become involved. Then too, in the sales of many goods, members of the buyer's family or other persons who come into contact with the goods may become involved. Finally, where a particular class of persons is significantly affected through a number of transactions, the relationship may be more extensive and involve questions of social values.

The court also should look in U.C.C. cases to circumstances in the overall setting and at several levels:

> The first is related to the particular circumstances involved in the particular transaction between the parties; this would include specific facts surrounding the transaction and such matters as course of performance and course of dealing. The second includes elements such as custom, trade usage, and any other relevant external commercial circumstances. The third includes the relationship of the particular setting to the entire social setting, comprising commercial and non-commercial factors.[1]

King, *supra*, 99-103.

Is this an ideal or can courts look to the relational factors in deciding cases? On what levels? Should courts take into account the entire social setting?

[C] Rejection of Past Concepts

The U.C.C. drafters rejected some concepts developed in pre-Code caselaw. The U.C.C. emphasizes a functional approach to commercial problems, rather than applying past sets of rules based solely on logic. Thus the U.C.C. rejects some concepts "even though these concepts have been deeply implanted within sales and contract law." In many cases, these concepts were developed during an early period of the law in which there was a distinct tendency to define

---

legal concepts in somewhat "visible" terms. This approach, for example, permitted the "pigeon-holing" of legal actions. Even though scholars often pierced portions of the rationalizations underlying these intangible, but terminologically visible theories, the theories continued to thrive throughout the years and affected the results of numerous cases.

As Professor William D. Hawkland (author of books and articles on the U.C.C. and a member of the Permanent Editorial Board) noted, "The technical 'ribbon matching' approach of contract law is foreign to most buyers and sellers, and its rules that an acceptance can never vary an offer, that telegraphic offers must be accepted by telegraphic acceptances, and the like, often have frustrated the reasonable expectations of businessmen." Karl Llewellyn (Chief Reporter of the U.C.C., professor, and author of well known writings in commercial law and jurisprudence) dissected and exposed the artificial concept of "title" which controlled cases for years. He pointed out that it was mythical, illusive, and unsatisfactory for settling commercial disputes. Questions formerly decided by a mechanistic determination of title passage (logical analysis based on rules designed to ascertain intent) are now to be determined "in terms of step by step performance or non-performance under the contract for sales and not in terms of whether or not title to the goods has passed." King, *supra,* at 99-103.

In regard to negotiable instruments, the drafters centered on eliminating many of the controversies that centered around some of the old NIL provisions. Clarification was sought through the use of the new U.C.C. provisions and words. There were not, however, major reformulations of concepts.

In regard to secured transactions, there was a major reformulation of concept. Rather than the diverse concepts and rationale that was found among the various security devices, such as chattel mortgages, conditional sales, trust receipts, bailment leases, and field warehousing, the drafters created a new single unified concept known as the "security interest." Here too, the drafters respected the concept of "title" as having an importance in regard to the rights and obligations of the parties.

[D] Application by Analogy

PROBLEM 1.7

The Teddy Roosevelt University has contracted with several companies and is experiencing some problems with them. The University counsel has consulted you as to whether the U.C.C. or analogy could be utilized in regard to them:

(1) The contract with Bigger Foods for managing the cafeteria and providing meals has resulted in poor quality food and student protests.

(2) The contract with Flowers Landscapes to make flower beds and maintain them on campus has not been satisfactory and a campus that once had a variety of flowers all spring, summer and fall and was a joy to walk through is much more bleak with only a few blooming at a time.

(3) The law firm that drafted those two contracts did not provide for a number of things and contingencies.

University counsel is convinced that it would win on warranty of merchantability-type principles, but not on negligence. What is your advice?

In addition to understanding the unique manner in which courts should construe the U.C.C., it is also important to know that courts may sometimes apply the U.C.C. by analogy to commercial law cases outside the scope of the Code.

In applying the Code by analogy, the court may apply U.C.C. principles to a transaction not technically covered by the Code, on the basis that those principles should be more broadly applied; or it may analogize the transaction not technically covered to the transactions covered and thus bring the former within the U.C.C. coverage. In some cases, the court may be faced with applying a principle found in one U.C.C. Article to transactions covered by another U.C.C. Article.

§ 1.06 Underlying Principles

A basic principle of the Code drafters was that custom and trade usage should be looked to in solving commercial disputes. Courts should look to trade usage in interpreting contracts and a trade usage may actually be recognized as a term of the contract by the court.

Another basic principle of the Code drafters was that parties to a commercial transaction should act within ethical standards. Good faith in performance of contracts, and not making unconscionable ones, may seem to be an idealized, ethical goal. But it is much more—it is set forth expressly in the Code. Failure to exercise good faith in the performance or enforcement of a contract constitutes a breach of contract. A court may strike or modify an unconscionable term in a contract or it may hold the entire contract to be unenforceable. This has been described as the "new business ethic." If one doubts that these standards will be applied, a look at the ever increasing flow of Code cases on this matter may dispel doubt.

[A] Custom and Trade Usage

Read: U.C.C. § 1-205.

Read also: CISG Art. 9.

PROBLEM 1.8

Your client, The Black Top Company, is a seller of asphalt. As a seller, it makes bids to buyers who are in the contract and asphalt business. Your client is supplied the asphalt by one of the giant oil companies, Exaco. In the Exaco contract with Black Top, there is an express term that made the price Exaco's current posted price. There also is a trade usage that a supplier of asphalt, like Exaco, would not apply a price increase to a buyer, like Black Top, for amounts the buyer needed to satisfy bids it had already submitted to others. With the change of Exaco's management, it refused to give Black Top this price protection on some asphalt that Black Top had submitted bids on. Instead Exaco insisted on the written contract terms of the current posted price.

Should the court treat the concept of trade usage? What are the perimeters of trade usage in regard to the type of business involved? What were the geographical boundaries? What was the course of performance involved? Was this even stronger than the trade usage? Does the failure to follow trade usage or course of performance reflect a lack of good faith in the performance of the contract?

NOTES

(1) While the contract may seem to cover issues that may arise, it is sometimes custom and trade usage that becomes determinative. *Torstenson v. Melcher*, 195 Neb. 764, 241 N.W.2d 103

(1976), involved the sale of a "breeder" bull. Defendant, who was in the cattle business, sent a sale catalogue to prospective buyers, including the plaintiffs. The catalogue contained the following notice: "All animals are guaranteed to be without known defects. Animal failing to breed after trial of six months may be returned to the seller if in good condition. The seller reserves the right to try said animal for six months and if it proves a breeder to return it to the station of the buyer at his expense. If animal proves a non-breeder, a satisfactory exchange will be made or the purchase price will be refunded."

The plaintiffs purchased the bull, named H.M. Silver Domino 10. When H. M. Silver Domino 10 was turned into an 80-acre pasture with 32 of the plaintiffs' stock cows, he covered the cow herd well, but in later weeks, the plaintiff noticed the cows continued to recycle.

The bull was given a field semen test. A veterinarian, Doctor Dierks, reported that the bull was capable of breeding, and Melcher asked the plaintiffs to try him for a longer time.

Doctor Dierks suggested that the bull be rested for approximately 2 weeks before running him back in with the cow herd. Plaintiffs immediately turned the bull back in with the cows. They continued to be dissatisfied with the bull's performance, and on December 11, 1972, the bull was returned to the defendant.

Tests conducted by Doctor Stevens, another veterinarian, on January 5, 1973, indicated that 17 of the plaintiffs' 32 cows had been impregnated. About January 10, 1973, a different bull was turned in with the cows. All but one of the remaining cows were settled thereafter in one cycle.

In the trial, the defendant introduced evidence to the effect that 32 cows would be too many for a two-year-old bull to cover, and that a reduction in fertility could result from overuse. Plaintiff's evidence was that placing the bull with 32 cows would be within acceptable limits.

The issue at trial centered around the meaning to be attached to the term "breeder," contained in the catalogue warranty set out above. There was evidence that a normal bull should impregnated from 50 to 75 percent of the healthy cows he bred in each heat cycle, and that 95 percent of the cows should be settled within 3 months. There was also testimony that an animal settling 10 cows in a lifetime could technically be termed a "breeder."

After citing U.C.C. §§ 2-315 and 2-316(3)(c), the appellate court reviewed contested instruction (No. 14) of the trial court: "The jury is instructed that under the facts in this case an implied warranty of fitness for breeding purposes may be excluded by the usage of the trade in question, and that before the jury shall consider whether or not the implied warranty of fitness stated in Instruction No. 13 is breached, the jury shall consider and determine whether or not the implied warranty of fitness has been excluded by the usage of the purebred Hereford cattle trade. In the event the jury shall find the implied warranty of fitness has been excluded, then the jury shall disregard all instructions with regard to damages, for breach of the alleged and implied warranty of fitness for breeding purposes."

Plaintiffs contend that trade usage excluding the implied warranty of fitness was not properly presented by the pleadings or the evidence, so that any instruction allowing the jury to find the warranty excluded was erroneous.

The answer filed by the defendant in this case alleged: "That said written warranty is in accord with the custom and usage of the cattle trade in the community where the sale was made. That by custom (of) the trade in breeding animals there is no implied warranty of fitness for particular purpose in the case of sale of a bull." The court then cited U.C.C. § 1-205(6) and found no unfair surprise. It also found "sufficient evidence in the record to support instruction 14. The testimony of the field representative of the American Hereford Association indicated that he had observed no other warranties in his extensive experience in the trade. This evidence is sufficient to submit the issue to the jury."

It then noted plaintiff's other contention that the evidence was "insufficient to support the verdict and judgment."

> Their argument is essentially that the bull could not be found to be a "breeder" since in the cattle business a bull that settles roughly half a 32-cow herd, as this one did, will not be considered acceptable. We believe the question of the bull's status as a "breeder" was properly submitted to the jury. In addition to the plaintiff's evidence that 95 percent of their herd should have been settled, there was testimony that a bull which settles 50 percent of the healthy cows he breeds may be considered a "breeder." There was also a question as to whether the bull was turned in with too many cows. One of the experts, from a semen test, said he would not expect any problem in pasture breeding with 25 females. While we may have some question on the result herein, the trial was held in a farm and ranch community. It was a question of fact for the jury. We are bound by its determination.

The verdict for the defendant was affirmed.

Consider how trade usage was used in this case. Was it for interpretation of the contract term "breeder bull"? Was it to supply a disclaimer of warranties? Or both? Do the experts agree on the trade usage? How can the jury decide what is the trade usage? Is it trade usage with the community, the state, or the cattle raising industry?

(2) See *Columbia Nitrogen Corp. v. Royster Co.*, 451 F.2d 3(4th Cir. 1971), where the court noted that extrinsic evidence may be introduced to explain or supplement a written contract despite any apparent ambiguity.

> Royster manufactures and markets mixed fertilizers, the principal components of which are nitrogen, phosphate and potash. Columbia is primarily a producer of nitrogen, although it manufactures some mixed fertilizer. For several years Royster had been a major purchaser of Columbia's products, but Columbia had never been a significant customer of Royster. In the fall of 1966, Royster constructed a facility which enabled it to produce more phosphate than it needed in its own operations. After extensive negotiations, the companies executed a contract for Royster's sale of a minimum of 31,000 tons of phosphate each year for three years to Columbia, with an option to extend the term. The contract stated the price per ton, subject to an escalation clause dependent on production costs.
>
> Columbia assigns error to the pretrial ruling of the district court excluding all evidence on usage of the trade and course of dealing between the parties. It offered the testimony of witnesses with long experience in the trade that because of uncertain crop and weather conditions, farming practices, and governmental agricultural programs, express price and quantity terms in contracts for materials in the mixed fertilizer industry are mere projections to be adjusted according to market forces.
>
> Columbia also offered proof of its business dealings with Royster over the six-year period preceding the phosphate contract. Since Columbia had not been a significant purchaser of Royster's products, these dealings were almost exclusively nitrogen sales to Royster or exchanges of stock carried in inventory. The pattern which emerges, Columbia claimed, is one of repeated and substantial deviation from the stated amount or price, including four

instances where Royster took none of the goods for which it had contracted. Columbia offered proof that the total variance amounted to more than $500,000 in reduced sales. This experience, a Columbia officer offered to testify, formed the basis of an understanding on which he depended in conducting negotiations with Royster.

The District Court held that the evidence should be excluded. It ruled that "custom and usage or course of dealing are not admissible to contradict the express, plain, unambiguous language of a valid written contract, which by virtue of its detail negates the proposition that the contract is open to variances in its terms."

The Court of Appeals reversed, admitting evidence of trade usage and course of performance. Citing U.C.C. § 1-102, the court stated that any extrinsic evidence "shall be liberally construed and applied to promote its underlying purposes and policies," which include "the continued expansion of commercial practices through custom, usage and agreement of the parties." The court in Columbia Nitrogen further stated that U.C.C. § 2-202, when read in conjunction with U.C.C. § 1-205(4), resulted in a test of admissibility which is "not whether the contract appears on its face to be complete in every detail, but whether the proffered evidence of course of dealing and trade usage reasonably can be construed as consistent with the express terms of the agreement."

PROBLEM 1.9

Suppose Honest Jake, a car dealer, sells a used car to Mrs. Buckless. In order to finance the transaction, Jake also signed an installment contract and a bank note with Mrs. Buckless. The bank required there be insurance on the car and handled the obtaining of the policy. Shortly after, Mrs. Buckless was in a car accident. The insurance company covered the accident, but then canceled the policy because Mrs. Buckless was a poor risk.

The bank did not give any notice of cancellation to Honest Jake. A short time later, Mrs. Buckless was in another accident, and this time the car was demolished. Since Mrs. Buckless is unable to make the rest of the payments on the car, the bank now sues Honest Jake for the money due on the contract and note. If there had been insurance on the car, this would have covered the total payment for it and nothing would have been owed on it by Honest Jake. Honest Jake asserts that there was a custom in the trade for the bank to give notice to him that Mrs. Buckless's insurance was canceled. The bank asserts that any custom was waived when Jake signed the contract and negotiable note that both stated that Jake expressly waives all notices and agrees his liability is absolute.

As attorney for Honest Jake, what arguments can you use that will prevail over the contract clause? What expert witnesses will you use to prove custom? Would it be easier to prove either trade usage or course of dealing? Even if one of these is established, can it prevail over the express waiver of notice clause?

NOTE

In a case similar to the Problem, *Provident Tradesman Bank Trust Co. v. Pemberton*, 24 D&C.2d 720, *aff'd*, 196 Pa. Super. 180, 173 A.2d 780 (1959), the court held that the waiver of all notices did not include those notices mandated by trade usage. Any waiver of those, said the court, must be specific. The court quoted from Comment 2 to U.C.C. § 2-202.

[B] Merchant/Non-Merchant Dichotomy

PROBLEM 1.10

One of your clients, a prosperous stockbroker, Robert Rich, made so much money that he decided to become a "gentleman" farmer. He bought a farm fifty miles outside of town which has a hundred areas for planting. Mr. Rich hires the planting and combining and trucking to a local grain company which pays for each truckload delivery. This year the company claims it has discovered that his grain, while not being useless, is of low quality. He refuses to return any of the payments and asserts that he is not a merchant of grain, knows nothing about it, spends virtually none of his time on farming, and is not responsible for the quality of the grain.

PROBLEM 1.11

Robert Rich also had thirty Beefalo (cross between cows and buffalo) which he decided he would sell. He entered into a oral contract with another farmer over a drink at the local country tavern. The farmer wrote a brief letter confirming the sale, but Mr. Rich never replied to it and now wants more money than agreed since the price of Beefalo has suddenly risen. Is Mr. Rich a merchant, and therefore under the merchant reply exception [§ 2-201(2)]?

NOTES

(1) What type of professionalism or expertise is the court looking for generally to determine if a party to a contract is a merchant? What evidence should it find relevant? What effect, if any, does the fact that someone has other businesses have upon the result? When would other farmers selling grain be merchants and in what circumstances would they not be merchants? What affect does the definition of merchant have on the legal issue(s)?

(2) Is a farmer with a lessee's interest in cattle a "merchant" within the meaning of the Code (provided that the farmer-lessee in possession of the property has the power to transfer ownership to a buyer in the ordinary course of business)? See *Bauer v. Curran*, 360 N.W.2d 88 (Iowa 1984), in which the court held that whether a farmer is a "merchant" is an issue of fact, not of law, and therefore a question for the trier of fact. The *Bauer* court outlined three basic forms of merchant status:

> Merchant status is said to take three forms: The first is transactional in nature: The seller is a dealer in the type of goods involved in the questioned transaction. The second form involves the merchant who holds himself out as having some skill or knowledge focusing on the specific transaction and goods involved. The third revolves around the principal-agent relationship. See Article, *Is He or Isn't He a Merchant? The Farmer, Part I*, 82 Com. L.J. 155, 1 56-57 (May 1977).
>
> The Iowa court has held that a farmer, in order to be a merchant, must be:
>
> > (1) [A] dealer who deals in goods of the kind involved, or (2) he must by his occupation hold himself out as having knowledge or skill peculiar to the practices or goods involved in the transaction, or (3) he must employ an agent, broker or other intermediary who by his occupation holds himself out as having knowledge or skill peculiar to the practices or goods involved in the transaction.
>
> In the immediate case Carl Davidson, a farmer, leased approximately 100 head of cattle from plaintiff in the spring of 1979. Davidson did not receive title to the cattle and did not have any

authority to transfer them. In the fall of 1980, Davidson sold sixteen cow-calf pairs to Curran. Curran later sold these cow-calf pairs through defendant Russell Sale Co. Mr. Curran at no time attempted to discover whether Davidson actually owned the cattle. The relevant section of the Iowa Code (section 554.2403(2)) provides:

> Any entrusting of possession of goods to a merchant who deals in goods of that kind gives him power to transfer all rights of the entrustor to a buyer in ordinary course of business.

The evidence provided a sufficient basis for a decision either way on Davidson's status. Prior to the sale in question, there was evidence that Davidson had bought, sold, and leased cattle. One year, for example, Davidson leased approximately twenty head of cattle from another individual and in addition had entered into a lease-purchase agreement with a Clearview Cattle Company. Matthew Bauer, the individual who had leased the present cattle to Davidson, testified that although he had engaged in a large number of transactions in buying and selling cattle in the area, he had never seen or met Davidson prior to 1980 when they entered into the lease agreement in question.

Most other cattle sales involving Davidson were said by him to be merely attempts to cull his herd, and, while Davidson had earlier sold part of these cattle leased from plaintiff Bauer, he had done so under Bauer's name and at his direction. Davidson appears to have only occasionally bought or sold cattle.

While other factors tended to support a finding that Davidson may have been a merchant, our question is not whether there was evidence to support a finding the jury did not make but whether reasonable minds could have drawn different inferences from the facts. We conclude they could and that the issue was therefore properly submitted to the jury.

[C] Good Faith

Read: U.C.C. §§ 1-203, 1-201(19), 2-103(1)(b), 2-309(3).

Read also: U.C.C. § 2A-103(2); CISG Art. 7(1).

PROBLEM 1.12

Although your client had a written agreement to buy Gulfcoast Marina at a fixed price from the Standard Oil Company, the Standard now denies that there is a contract. When asked to acknowledge that there was a contract and fulfill its obligation, Standard's Sales officer laughed and said "See you in court." This denial of the contract caused serious damages for Gulfcoast Marina. Can your client successfully assert that this denial of a contract is in violation of good faith? Can you successfully argue for both compensatory and punitive damages?

PROBLEM 1.13

In a contract between the Green Company and the Red Company a price was set for the first two shipments, and a contract term that said the parties would later negotiate a price as to the third shipment. The Red Company maintains that the price for that third shipment must be the maximum price allowed by the contract and has refused to negotiate on it. As the counsel for Green, what is your strategy?

NOTE

(1) The case of *Seaman's Direct Buying Serv. v. Standard Oil,* decided by the *California Supreme Court*, 36 Cal. 3d 752, 206 Cal. Rptr. 354, 686 P.2d 1158 (Cal. 1984), involved a

situation similar to that in Problem 1.12. Standard Oil denied the existence of a contract, Seaman's sued, and the court stated the major issue:

> For breach of contract the jury awarded compensatory damages of $397,050. For tortious breach of the implied covenant of good faith and fair dealing, they awarded $397,050 in compensatory damages and $11,058,810 in punitive damages.

The court went on to note:

> While the proposition that the law implies a covenant of good faith and fair dealing in all contracts is well established, the proposition advanced by Seaman's — that breach of the covenant always gives rise to an action in tort — is not so clear. In holding that a tort action is available for breach of the covenant in an insurance contract, we have emphasized the "special relationship" between insurer and insured, characterized by elements of public interest, adhesion, and fiduciary responsibility. No doubt there are other relationships with similar characteristics and deserving of similar legal treatment.
>
> When we move from such special relationships to consideration of the tort remedy in the context of the ordinary commercial contract, we move into largely uncharted and potentially dangerous waters. Here, parties of roughly equal bargaining power are free to shape the contours of their agreement and to include provisions for attorney fees and liquidated damages in the event of breach. They may not be permitted to disclaim the covenant of good faith but they are free, within reasonable limits at least, to agree upon the standards by which application of the covenant is to be measured.[2] In such contracts, it may be difficult to distinguish between breach of the covenant and breach of contract, and there is the risk that interjecting tort remedies will intrude upon the expectations of the parties. This is not to say that tort remedies have no place in such a commercial context, but that it is wise to proceed with caution in determining their scope and application.
>
> For the purposes of this case it is unnecessary to decide the broad question which Seaman's poses. Indeed, it is not even necessary to predicate liability on a breach of the implied covenant. It is sufficient to recognize that a party to a contract may incur tort remedies when, in addition to breaching the contract, it seeks to shield itself from liability by denying in bad faith and without probable cause, that the contract exists.
>
> It has been held that a party to a contract may be subject to tort liability, including punitive damages, if he coerces the other party to pay more than is due under the contract terms through the threat of a lawsuit, made "without probable cause and with no belief in the existence of the cause of action." There is little difference, in principle, between a contracting party obtaining excess payment in such manner, and a contracting party seeking to avoid all liability on a meritorious contract claim "justified expectations" are established, "good faith" requires the parties to act "reasonably" in light of those expectations.
>
> In commercial contracts which lack those characteristics, the expectations and purposes of the parties necessarily differ from those of insurer and insured. Thus, the requirements of good faith in a commercial contract are different than the requirements imposed on an insurer. While those requirements are probably less stringent in a commercial context, *they definitely exist.*

[2] California's Commercial Code section 1102 prohibits disclaimer of the good faith obligation, as well as the obligations of diligence, reasonableness and care, but provides that "the parties may by agreement determine the standards by which the performance of such obligations is to be measured if such standards are not manifestly unreasonable."

Certain expectations derive from assumptions so basic to the very notion of a contract that they are shared by virtually all contracting parties. Foremost among these is the expectation that a breaching party will compensate the other party for losses caused by the breaching party's failure to perform. The availability of contract damages, in turn, supports the equally fundamental assumption that breach is a foreseeable and, in most situations, acceptable possibility.

Indeed, the assumption that parties may breach at will, risking only contract damages, is one of the cornerstones of contract law. "[I]t is not the policy of the law to compel adherence to contracts, but only to require each party to choose between performing in accordance with the contract and compensating the other party for injury resulting from a failure to perform. This view contains an important economic insight. In many cases it is uneconomical to induce the completion of the contract after it has been breached." (Posner, Economic Analysis of Law (1972) p. 55.) In most commercial contracts, recognition of this economic reality leads the parties to accept the possibility of breach, particularly since their right to recover contract damages provides adequate protection.

For example, one party to a contract may decide to breach if it concludes that the market will bring a higher price for its product than that set forth in the contract. In commercial contracts, the risk of such a breach is widely recognized and generally accepted. "[I]ntentional, willful, selfishly induced breach[es] of contract [are] often an anticipated, expected and encouraged reality of commercial life." (Diamond, *The Tort of Bad Faith Breach of Contract: When, If At All, Should It Be Extended Beyond Insurance Transactions?* (1981) 64 Marq. L. Rev. 425, 438).

When the breaching party acts in bad faith to shield itself entirely from liability for contract damages, however, the duty of good faith and fair dealing is violated.

This type of conduct violates the non-breaching party's justified expectation that it will be able to recover damages for its losses in the event of a breach. The expectation must be protected. Otherwise, the acceptance of the possibility of breach by the contracting parties and by society as a whole may be seriously undermined.

There is no danger that permitting tort recovery for bad faith denial of the existence of a valid commercial contract will make every breach of contract a tort. First, the vast majority of contract breaches in the commercial context do not involve this type of bad faith conduct.

Second, "it [is] well established in this state that if the cause of action arises from a breach of a promise set forth in the contract, the action is ex contractu, *but if it arises from a breach of duty growing out of the contract it is ex delicto*." (Emphasis added.) Thus, tort "[l]iability is imposed not for a bad faith breach of the contract, but for failure to meet the duty. . .included within the implied covenant of good faith and fair dealing." There are many situations in which a defendant's actions may sound both in tort and contract. The fact that overlapping remedies may exist in some situations does not make every breach of contract a tort.

Similarly, an attempt to avoid any liability for contract damages may involve a discrete course of conduct or it may be indistinguishable from the breach of contract itself. "Breach of the covenant provides the injured party with a tort action for "bad faith," notwithstanding that the acts complained of may also constitute a breach of contract.

It is a well-established principle of law that the parties' reasonable expectations should govern the determination of what conduct constitutes a tortious breach of the implied covenant of good faith and fair dealing. Application of that principle is fully warranted here. The duty of good faith and fair dealing was violated because a party attempted to avoid all liability for a contract breach by denying, in bad faith, the very existence of the contract. Such conduct violates the nearly universal expectation that the injured party will be compensated for losses caused by the breaching party's failure to perform. This tort remedy was recognized by this court in its earlier decisions involving the implied covenant of good faith and fair dealing. Those decisions should be the basis for the holding here.

II.

A breach of contract may also constitute a tortious breach of the covenant of good faith and fair dealing in a situation where the possibility that the contract will be breached is not accepted or reasonably expected by the parties.

This could happen, for example, if at the time of contracting, the parties expressly indicate their understanding that a breach would be impermissible. Or, it could happen if it were clear from the inception of the contract that contract damages would be unavailable or would be inadequate compensation for a breach. Under these circumstances, a breach of the contract could well constitute a tortious breach of the duty of good faith and fair dealing.

These are just a few examples. If a plaintiff can show that, under the circumstances or characteristics of his contract, he was justified in expecting that the other party would not breach, then a voluntary breach by that party could well constitute a violation of the duty to deal fairly and in good faith.

On this record, there is ample evidence to support the conclusion that the parties' reasonable expectations did not include the possibility of breach. Standard was repeatedly informed that Seaman's needed a "binding commitment." Throughout the negotiations, there was an emphasis on the need for such a commitment and for a stable relationship between Seaman's and its supplier. Standard knew that Seaman's lease, and, to some extent, the entire marina development depended on these factors. Under these circumstances, it would be reasonable to conclude that the parties' justified expectations did not include the possibility of breach.

Under this cause of action, no independent showing of bad faith should be required. Where the possibility of breach was not reasonably expected at the inception of the contract, the voluntary breach of an acknowledged contract is in itself a violation of the duty to deal fairly and in good faith.

Standard's breach did not take the form of a refusal to perform under the terms of an acknowledged contract. Instead, Standard denied the existence of the contract to the federal agency and subsequently refused to stipulate to its existence. This action was tantamount to a denial. Those denials constituted anticipatory breaches of the contract.

In this setting, the simple fact that a breach occurred will not support tort recovery without a showing of bad faith. Just as a denial of the existence of a binding contract provides the basis for tort liability only upon a finding of bad faith, a contract breach predicated upon such a denial will support tort recovery on the theory of unexpected and unacceptable breach only if the denial is found to have been made in bad faith.

III.

The trial court failed to include a bad faith requirement in its instruction on the duty to refrain from denying the existence of a binding contract. This failure constituted error. Recovery will lie in tort if the denial was made in bad faith.

Standard's denial of the existence of the contract to the federal agency and the subsequent refusal to stipulate were anticipatory breaches of the contract. Neither the breach nor the underlying resistance to an assertion of contract liability is a tort if undertaken in good faith. In this case, however, Standard did not deny that a contract existed until it had been ordered by the federal government to supply fuel to Seaman's. Moreover, Standard did not make its denials forthrightly as a defense to an action for breach of contract. It used them as a trump card in its final attempt to avoid all liability for nonperformance The timing and the intended effect of both denials tend strongly to establish that they were made in bad faith.

I would affirm the judgment for Seaman's for breach of contract and breach of the duty of good faith and fair dealing.

(2) In *City Builders Supply Co. v. National Gypsum Co.*, 39 U.C.C. Rep. 826 (D. Mass. 1984), plaintiffs and defendant entered into a distributorship agreement. The agreement, entered into during September, 1979, contained no termination clause. Under the agreement, defendant would extend credit for and furnish vinyl siding and other merchandise.

On September 25, 1980, defendant advised plaintiff that it was pleased with plaintiff's performance and raised its credit limit from $125,000 to $200,000. In further praising plaintiff's performance and indicating many more profitable years for each company, defendant again raised the credit limit on December 22, 1980, to $300,000.

On January 8, 1981, defendant canceled the distributorship agreement, after secretly negotiating an agreement with a new distributor. Plaintiffs alleged that this was a breach of the duty of good faith in two respects: first, that the termination without notice was an unfair trade practice, and second, that the sale of $200,000 worth of goods to plaintiff without disclosing the impending termination was also a breach of good faith.

The district court adopted the Magistrate's Recommendation in favor of summary judgment for defendant on the first issue since plaintiff failed to prove damages. The court, however, denied defendant's motion for summary judgment on the second issue because of the defendant's "duplicitous" actions of praising plaintiff's performance and increasing its credit line while simultaneously planning to terminate the distributorship agreement.

(3) In *Goldstein v. S. & A. Restaurant Corp.*, 42 U.C.C. Rep. 81 (D.D.C. 1985), plaintiff and defendant had entered an agreement whereby plaintiff would buy meat from defendant, process it, and then distribute it to defendant's retail restaurants. Between April 1 and June 19, 1981, S. & A. paid Goldstein approximately $3.2 million for the processing and distribution of the meat. Largely due to his decision to divert funds to his real estate ventures, Goldstein fell behind between $1.15 and $ 1.5 million in his payments for the meat.

After a series of negotiations involving such things as post-dated checks and a $1 million, 30-day note, Goldstein and S & A. finally negotiated a new agreement containing a 10-day notification in the event of cancellation by either party. In October, 1981, S. & A. gave Goldstein 10 days' notice and canceled the agreement.

The district court found that the series of agreements signed by Goldstein, a sophisticated businessman, and the justifiable insecurity on the part of S. & A. occasioned by the large debt were sufficient to defeat any allegations by Goldstein of duress or bad faith by S. & A.

(4) In *First National Bank in Libby v. Twombly*, 39 U.C.C. Rep. 1192 (Mont. 1984) defendant had negotiated a secured loan with the Bank. When it became apparent that there would be difficulty in paying the note at maturity, one of the Bank officers agreed to transform the note into an installment loan. The original note came due while this officer was on vacation, whereupon the Bank withdrew $2,865 from Twombly's checking account, leaving a balance of $1.65, without first notifying Twombly.

The Montana Supreme Court held that the lower court erred by not submitting punitive damages to the jury. The court reasoned that punitive damages may be recoverable where the duty to exercise good faith is imposed by law rather than by the contract itself.

(5) Compare *Weyerhauser Co. v. Godwin Bldg. Supply,* 253 S.W.2d. 625 (1979). In *Weyerhauser* defendant asserted that Weyerhauser said it would "provide unlimited ninety percent (90%) conventional financing at locally competitive rates [up to] forty thousand dollars ($40,000) per house." However, the contractual agreement only provided that Weyerhauser would "assist dealer in arranging interim and permanent mortgage financing for Weyerhauser Registered Homes." Weyerhauser subsequently refused to provide financing as agreed and argued that "it had no duty to provide financing but only to assist in arranging financing." Without reference to the U.C.C. section on good faith which is pertinent and would have supported its decision, the court found that it is

> a basic principle of contract law that a party who enters into an enforceable contract is required to act in good faith and to make reasonable efforts to perform his obligations under the agreement. "Good faith and fair dealing" are required of all parties to a contract; and each party to a contract has the duty to do everything that the contract presupposes that he will do to accomplish its purpose.

The court went on to say that there was sufficient evidence for a jury to find that Weyerhauser had failed to make reasonable efforts to assist Godwin in obtaining financing; the jury verdict against Weyerhauser for $100,000 was upheld.

(6) In *Riveridge Associates v. Metropolitan*, 774 F. Supp. 897 (D.N.J. 1991), the issue of lack of good faith in bringing the action was raised. In that case, Riveridge had borrowed $11.5 million from its partner, Metropolitan. It alleged in an action against Metropolitan that the latter had refused to allow pre-payment of the loan and that this refusal was in violation of their agreement and a violation of fiduciary duties. The court granted a summary judgment in favor of Metropolitan, finding no law, fiduciary or otherwise, that would permit such pre-payment. Metropolitan counterclaimed that Riveridge had acted in bad faith in bringing this groundless claim and action. Riveridge's motion to dismiss, viewing the alleged facts in the most favorable light for Metropolitan, was denied by the court. It noted that while the case would have to be tried on this point, if bad faith of Riveridge's were shown, then Riveridge would be liable for all counsel fees and punitive damages. It also noted that while Riveridge's suit might not be deemed frivolous under Rule N, this was not proper standard to be used in judging its good faith or lack thereof.

[D] Unconscionability Theory

PROBLEM 1.14

Your client needs some high speed diamond cutting equipment, to replace its current equipment which suddenly broke, in order to prepare for the New York Annual Jewelry Fair starting the next day. The salesman for the Belgium seller does not mention or point out the disclaimer clause in a printed standardized contract which is signed hastily in order to assure immediate air shipment. The cutting equipment arrives the next morning, but after two days breaks down. The Belgium company points out the disclaimer and refuses to fix the machine or return the payment. Your client wishes to argue that the disclaimer is unconscionable. What other facts do you need to know? Can your client argue unconscionability?

Read: U.C.C. §§ 2-302, 2-719(3).

Read also: U.C.C. §§ 2A-108, 2A-503(3); CISG Art. 4(a).

Section 2-302 of the U.C.C. sets forth the principle of unconscionability.

What is an "unconscionable" term? What criteria are to be used? What factors does the comment suggest be taken into account? How are these to be determined? Is the comment statement on "economic" strength clear? To what degree, if any, does this factor enter it?

The question of what constitutes unconscionability was raised in the New York Revision Commission studies. A reply was made by the late Karl Llewellyn, who had served as the Chief Reporter for the U.C.C.

Llewellyn, 1 N.Y. Law Rev. Comm. Rep., 177-178 (1954)

The same is true of the much controverted section on unconscionability. What now goes on—and this is a thing that I can't prove in any speech like this, and it would take an awful long time to bring the cases and gather them to show what now goes on—is that there is a practice among business lawyers to do a thing that no intelligent engineer would think of doing. I can't understand it. I never have understood it, but I observe that it is there.

Business lawyers tend to draft to the edge of the possible. Any engineer makes his construction within a margin of safety, and a wide margin of safety, so that he knows for sure that he is getting what he is gunning for. The practice of business lawyers has been, however—it has grown to be so in the course of time—to draft, as I said before, to the edge of the possible.

Let me rapidly state that I do not find that this is desired by the business lawyers' clients. In all the time that I have been working on this Code, and before, one of the more striking phenomena has been to me that the lawyers insist on having all kinds of things that their clients don't want at all.

This kind of thing does not make for good business, it does not make for good counseling, and it does not make for certainty. It means that you never know where you are, and it does a very bad thing to the law indeed. The bad thing that it does to the law is to lead to precedent after precedent in which language is held not to mean what it says and indeed what its plain purpose was, and that upsets everything for everybody in all future litigation.

We believe that if you take this and bring it out into the open, if you say, "When it gets too stiff to make sense, then the court may knock it out," you are going to get a body of principles of construction instead of principles of misconstruction, and the precedents are going to build up so that the language will be relied upon and will be construed to mean what it says.

We believe further that this particular section is safeguarded to a curious degree. Have you gentlemen really looked it over to see how carefully safeguarded it is to lead into principles of true construction?

The section is 2-302, and the first thing that happens is that it is taken completely out of the realm of the jury. Anything that is done under this section is going to make precedent, and the precedents can be recorded and the precedents can accumulate and guide. That is No. 1.

If the court finds the contract or any clause of the contract to be unconscionable, it may refuse to enforce the contract or may strike any unconscionable clauses and enforce the contract as if the stricken clause had never existed. That is court action, and it is reviewable. That is No. 1, and it makes precedents and guides.

Secondly, in order that we may not be left to the untutored imagination of courts that don't know the situation, in order that cases where very careful insistence, for example, upon very exact performance is reasonable because that is the way business has to be done in that trade, you have the second provision which allows all kinds of background to be presented to instruct the court. We count this, therefore, by no means as a section which threatens certainty. We regard it instead as a section which greatly advances certainty in a now most baffling, most troubling, and almost unreckonable situation.

Llewellyn, THE COMMON LAW TRADITION[3]

370, 371 (1960)

And the true answer to the whole problem seems, amusingly, to be one which could occur to any court or any lawyer, at any time, as readily as to a scholar who had spent a lifetime on the subject-though I doubt if it could occur to anyone without the inquiry and analysis in depth which we owe to the scholarly work.

The answer, I suggest, is this: Instead of thinking about "assent" to boiler plate clauses, we can recognize that so far as concerns the specific, there is no assent at all. What has in fact been assented to, specifically, are the few dickered terms, and the broad type of the transaction, and but one thing more. That one thing more is a blanket assent (not a specific assent) to any not unreasonable or indecent terms the seller may have on his form, which do not alter or eviscerate the reasonable meaning of the dickered terms. The fine print which has not been read has no business to cut under the reasonable meaning of those dickered terms which constitute the dominant and only real expression of agreement, but much of it commonly belongs in.

The queer thing is that where the transaction occurs without the fine print present, courts do not find this general line of approach too hard to understand: thus in the cases Prausnitz gathers, in regard to what kind of policy an oral contract for insurance contemplates; nor can I see a

[3] Copyright © 1960 by Little Brown & Co. Reprinted by permission.

court having trouble, where a short memo agrees in due course to sign "our standard contract," in rejecting an outrageous form as not being fairly within the reasonable meaning of the term. The clearest case to see is the handing over of a blank check: no court, judging as between the parties, would fail to reach for the circumstances, in determining whether the amount filled in had gone beyond the reasonable.

Why, then, can we not face that fact where boiler-plate is present? There has been an arm's-length deal, with dickered terms. There has been accompanying that basic deal another which, if not on any fiduciary basis, at least involves a plain expression of confidence, asked and accepted, with a corresponding limit on the powers granted: the boiler plate is assented to en bloc, "unsight, unseen," on the implicit assumption and to the full extent that (1) it does not alter or impair the fair meaning of the dickered terms when read alone, and (2) that its terms are neither in the particular nor in the net manifestly unreasonable and unfair. Such is the reality, and I see nothing in the way of a court's operating on that basis, to truly effectuate the only intention which can in reason be worked out as common to the two parties, granted good faith. And if the boiler-plate party is not playing in good faith, there is law enough to bar that fact from benefiting it. We had a hundred years of sales law in which any sales transaction with explicit words resulted in two separate contracts for the one consideration: that of sale, and the collateral one of warranty. The idea is applicable here, for better reason: any contract with boiler-plate results in two severable contracts: the dickered deal, and the collateral one of supplementary boilerplate.

Rooted in sense, history, and simplicity, it is an answer which could occur to anyone.

King, NEW CONCEPTUALISM OF THE UNIFORM COMMERCIAL CODE: ETHICS, TITLE, AND GOOD FAITH PURCHASE[4]

In contemporary society, however, an even more important factor may be that of time. One of the parties to the contract may not feel that he has the time or the energy to devote to a full reading of a lengthy form contract. Were he to devote such time to the reading and understanding of each term of every transaction into which he entered, a substantial portion of his life might be spent in the reading of form contracts rather than in the use of articles being purchased. It is not unrealistic to say that many individuals, even those with considerable education, find that they do not have the time to search through contracts for hidden disclaimers or other limitations of remedy.

King, THE TORT OF UNCONSCIONABILITY: A NEW TORT FOR NEW TIMES

23 Saint Louis U. L.J. 124 (Conclusion) (1979)[5]

The tort of unconscionability exists now and need only be recognized by the courts. Unconscionable acts or practices have been severely condemned by courts and recognized as contributing to social problems and injustice. Even though the courts have not explicitly recognized unconscionability as a tort, there is an adequate basis in statutes, dicta and reason for doing so.

Unconscionable acts and conduct also are recognized as a legal wrong by consumer protection statutes and hence clearly satisfy the tort definition of a legal wrong. Since this legislation already deems unconscionable conduct a legal wrong, it is in effect acknowledging the tort of unconscionability although not expressly doing so. The Uniform Consumer Credit Code recognizes that unconscionable conduct is a legal wrong and may exist in several ways: in the making of unconscionable terms or provisions, in the conduct inducing debtors to enter into such transactions, or in unconscionable terms. The Model Consumer Credit Act, the Uniform Consumer Sales Act, and the New York City Consumer Protection Law, also recognize that unconscionable acts or conduct are legal wrongs.

Unconscionable conduct and practices cause considerable harm to the individual. This may encompass not only payments which he has made, but also other expenses that he has incurred. In addition, the unconscionable conduct frequently creates mental and emotional suffering for its victim. It also may create an added legal obstacle to recovery where there is a very real legal right and may require the incurring of otherwise unneeded additional legal expenses. . . .

As a matter of public policy it would seem that persons who suffer harm from the unconscionable conduct of others should be permitted to recover compensation for that harm. Indeed, they are allowed to do so in most other situations unless there is a legal reason to deprive them of compensation for the harm. Further, since unconscionability is already recognized as a legal wrong, they are being given "a right without a remedy" to the extent that their harm is not compensated.

Recognition of the tort of unconscionability has several major advantages for the consumer. One is that he is compensated for all of the harm which he has suffered, rather than simply having the contract declared unenforceable. Another is that he is placed in a more strategic position for effectuating a fair settlement. Punitive damages for this tort in some situations would further the consumer's action and have a broader impact as well. If the only detriment that the seller may suffer in a court case is that the contract will be declared unconscionable and hence unenforceable, he has nothing to lose turning down the consumer's claims and fighting the case all the way. On the other hand, if the seller is confronted with the tort of unconscionability which carries with it more compensatory damages and possible punitive damages, a settlement is more likely. Still another advantage of the tort of unconscionability is that it may serve as the basic cause of action in a class action suit or an injunction proceeding which will simultaneously benefit many consumers.

In our society some manufacturers and sellers have engaged in deliberate and outrageous unconscionable practices which have affected millions of people. Although one may invoke unconscionable concepts in regard to a particular contract clause or a particular transaction, this is insufficient. It is necessary that unconscionable acts and conduct be recognized as a tort so as to permit persons to recover for all of the harm they have suffered and to promote the courts to assess punitive damages when proper. If this is done, and the injunctive remedy also is utilized, many of the unconscionable practices of manufacturers and sellers may be restricted. The new tort of unconscionability may be a significant tool for achieving consumer justice.

PROBLEM 1.15

Your client, Green Dwarf, is a small produce company operating in Hidden Valley. It needs some machinery to process its pea crop. It purchases some farm machinery which turns out to be very inadequate, squashing all the peas. The seller's standard form printed contract contains a disclaimer of all warranties clause in bold print and a disclaimer of consequential damages in small print. The seller of the machinery points to the disclaimers and denies any legal liability. What arguments can your client make? On what basis?

PROBLEM 1.16

Your client has sold some computerized equipment to a Canadian publisher in Toronto. After four months the equipment has a serious problem requiring major repair. Your client's contract was a standard form printed one with an italicized disclaimer clause as to any defects or other problems occurring after three months. The Canadian firm refuses to make any further payments, and asserts that the disclaimer clause is unconscionable. The printed contract has no provision as to what law shall be applicable. What other facts do you need? What is your advice?

ADAMS v. AMERICAN CYANAMID CO.

Nebraska Court of Appeals
21 U.C.C. Rep Serv 2d 962, 498 N.W.2d 577 (1992)

This appeal arises from an action based on theories of strict liability and breach of warranty of merchantability under the Uniform Commercial Code. William Timothy "Tim" Adams and Carol Adams brought suit against American Cyanamid Company, and Panhandle Cooperative Association for damages sustained to a crop of edible beans which was lost after a herbicide manufactured by American Cyanamid was applied to the Adamses' field [a limitation of remedies clause in the contract was held unconscionable]. The jury awarded a judgment for the Adamses in the amount of $193,500 against American Cyanamid. American Cyanamid appeals. We affirm in part, and in part reverse and remand for a new trial.

The defendant first claims that the trial court erred by not holding a conscionability hearing on its limitation of remedy.

Guaranteed Foods v. Rison, 207 Neb. 400, 407, 229 N.W.2d 507, 512 [30 U.C.C. Rep Serv 1248] (1980), states that "the issue of unconscionability must be pleaded in order to be considered by the court." The issue of unconscionability was raised in the Adamses' reply to the defendant American Cyanamid's answer.

Limitations of remedies are governed by § 2-719(3), which states that "[c]onsequential damages may be limited or excluded unless the limitation or exclusion is unconscionable." Section 2-302 requires that the trial court make a conscionability determination for contracts in general; however, § 2-719 is silent on the issue.

We believe that the requirement that an unconscionability hearing be held under § 2-302 also applies to determinations of whether limitations of remedies are unconscionable under § 2-719(3). However, § 2-302(2) requires only that a party be afforded a reasonable opportunity to be heard. So long as sufficient evidence has been adduced concerning the commercial setting, purpose, and effect of the clause or contract, it is not necessary that a special hearing be held to determine whether a limitation of remedies is unconscionable. Rather, the issue may be raised at any time in the proceeding. In the case at bar, sufficient evidence had been adduced concerning the enforceability of the exclusion of consequential damages. The defendant had a reasonable opportunity to request a hearing on the issue of the enforcement of the provision excluding consequential damages. It never requested a hearing.

The defendant claims that it was error for the trial court not to address the unconscionability of the exclusion. Since the issue is likely to arise again on remand, we provide direction for the lower court by determining in advance whether American Cyanamid's limitation of remedies is unconscionable.

The concept of conscionability is not defined by the Code. The supreme court has quoted with approval from the comments to § 2-302: "The basic test is whether in the light of the general commercial background and the commercial needs of the particular trade or case, the clauses involved are so one-sided as to be unconscionable *under the circumstances existing at the time of the making of the contract. . .* " (Emphasis in original.) *T.V. Transmission v. City of Lincoln,* 220 Neb. 887, 896, 374 N.W.2d. 49 (1985).

Although the test is stated in *T.V. Transmission,* we have not found a Nebraska case that has applied it. Accordingly, we must determine how the concept of unconscionability is to be applied. The Code's concept of unconscionability developed in the context of consumer transactions. Since our concern here is solely with a commercial contract, we must determine how the concept applies in a commercial setting.

Generally, the issue of unconscionability is divided into substantive unconscionability and procedural unconscionability. "Substantive unconscionability involves those cases where a clause or term in the contract is alleged to be one-sided or overly harsh, while procedural unconscionability relates to impropriety during the process of forming a contract." *Schroeder v. Fageol Motors,* 86 Wash.2d 256, 260, 544 P.2d 20, 23 [18 U.C.C. Rep. Serv. 584] (1975). Generally, a contract is not substantively unconscionable unless the terms are grossly unfair under the circumstances as they existed at the time the contract was formed. See *Guthmann v. La Vida Llena*, 103 N.M. 506, 709 P.2d 675 (1985). An often-quoted formulation of substantive unconscionability is the following:

> "In determining reasonableness or fairness, the primary concern must be with the terms of the contract considered in light of the circumstances existing when the contract was made. The test is not simple, nor can it be mechanically applied. The terms are to be considered 'in the light of the general commercial background and the commercial needs of the particular trade or case.' Corbin suggests the test as being whether the terms are 'so extreme as to appear unconscionable according to the mores and business practices of the time and place.' "

Williams v. Walker-Thomas Furniture Company, 350 F.2d 445, 450 [2 U.C.C. Rep. Serv 955] (D.C. Cir.1965). Accordingly, to determine whether a contract clause is substantively unconscionable, a court asks "whether under the circumstances existing at the time of making of the contract, and in light of the general commercial background and commercial needs of a particular case, clauses are so one-sided as to oppress or unfairly surprise one of the parties." *Barnes v. Helfenbein,* 548 P.2d 1014, 1020 (Okla. 1976).

In the present case, the limitation of consequential damages clause would leave the herbicide user without any substantial recourse for his loss. "One-sided agreements whereby one party is left without a remedy for another party's breach are oppressive and should be declared unconscionable." *Durham v. Ciba-Geigy Corp.,* 315 N.W.2d 696, 700 [33 U.C.C. Rep Serv 588] (S.D. 1982). *See, also, Campbell Soup Co. v. Wentz,* 172 F.2d 80 (3d Cir. 1948). We conclude that the provision excluding consequential damages is substantively unconscionable. The remaining question, therefore, is whether there is evidence of procedural unconscionability. The factors involved in determination of procedural unconscionability have been formulated in *American Nursery v. Indian Wells,* 115 Wash.2d 217, 797 P.2d 477 [12 U.C.C. Rep Serv 2d

928] (1990). In *American Nursery,* the court stated that a clause excluding damages may be found to be conscionable when "the general commercial setting indicates a prior course of dealing or reasonable usage of trade as to the exclusionary clause." *Id.* at 223, 797 P.2d at 481. Otherwise,

> [u]nconscionability is determined in light of all the surrounding circumstances, including (1) the manner in which the parties entered into the contract, (2) whether the parties had a reasonable opportunity to understand the terms of the contract, and (3) whether the important terms were hidden in a maze of fine print.

Id. at 222, 797 P.2d at 481. None of the factors is conclusive; rather, unconscionability is determined under the totality of the circumstances.

Although the evidence supports the conclusion that there is a trade practice among chemical firms related to excluding consequential damages, we find it unreasonable to impose the trade practice on the Adamses. In selecting Prowl herbicide, Adams was merely following the advice of Johnson. He was not independently assessing the risks involved in the use of particular chemicals; and the use of middlemen, as in the case at bar, appears to be a common trade practice in the agricultural industry.

Therefore, we examine the totality of the circumstances. In this case, Adams was in no position to bargain with American Cyanamid. Johnson testified that all herbicide manufacturers place the same disclaimers on their products. Moreover, Adams testified that he did not receive the label containing the exclusion until he had problems with his crops. Even if we disregard the fact that Adams may not have received the contract terms at the time of purchase, the language of the exclusion is not such as to be immediately understandable by a layperson such as Adams. The exclusion specifically excludes "indirect" damages, but allows direct damages without specifying the extent of such damages.

This is a situation where the Adamses had no alternative other than to accept the manufacturer's exclusion. The undisputed evidence is that Adams could not purchase any manufacturer's herbicide without such an exclusion. The Adamses were not in a position to bargain with the defendant for more favorable terms than those set out in the preprinted label. Nor were they in a position to test the effectiveness of the herbicide prior to purchase. As Adams expected, the herbicide he purchased killed the weeds in his crop. However, quite unexpectedly and unfortunately, the herbicide also destroyed his crop.

If the evidence is believed, to permit the defendant to escape all consequential responsibility by inserting a limitation of consequential damage clause, as in this case, would leave a farmer without any substantial recourse for his loss. We conclude that under the circumstances presented here, the exclusion is procedurally unconscionable. Having found the exclusion both substantively and procedurally unconscionable, we decline to enforce it.

NOTES

(1) In *A & M Produce Co. v. FMC Corp.,* 186 Cal. Rptr. 114, 135 Cal. App. 3d 473 (1982), decided by the California Court of Appeals, Fourth District, the owner of a small business signed a form contract for the purchase of tomato processing equipment.

Mr. Abatti was informed by Mr. Walker and Mr. Isch of FMC Corporation (FMC) that their equipment was so fast that no hydrocooler was necessary and they bid $15,299.55 for the weightsizer. Mr. Abatti signed a "field order" and made a $5,000 deposit. After plans (including a 20-foot extension of Mr. Abatti's building) were drawn up by FMC's engineers, FMC mailed

Mr. Abatti a form contract with a total price of $32,041.80. The contract contained a disclaimer of warranty in bold print and a disclaimer of consequential damages in smaller print. He signed the contract and returned it with a down payment. The equipment never functioned properly.

The court noted that the principal question involved was:

Whether the trial court erred in concluding that FMC's attempted disclaimer of warranties and exclusion of consequential damages was unconscionable and therefore unenforceable. Before we can answer that question however, we must first concern ourselves with the nature of the unconscionability doctrine.

The Uniform Commercial Code does not attempt to precisely define what is or is not "unconscionable." Nevertheless, "[u]nconscionability has generally been recognized to include an absence of meaningful choice on the part of one of the parties together with contract terms which are unreasonably favorable to the other party." (*Williams v. Walker-Thomas Furniture Company*, (DC Cir 1965) 350 F.2d 445, 449 fn omitted.) Phrased another way, unconscionability has both a "procedural" and a "substantive" element.

The procedural element focuses on two factors: "oppression" and "surprise." "Oppression" arises from an inequality of bargaining power which results in no real negotiation and "an absence of meaningful choice." "Surprise" involves the extent to which the supposedly agreed-upon terms of the bargain are hidden in a prolix printed form drafted by the party seeking to enforce the disputed terms. Characteristically, the form contract is drafted by the party with the superior bargaining position.

Of course the mere fact that a contract term is not read or understood by the non-drafting party or that the drafting party occupies a superior bargaining position will not authorize a court to refuse to enforce the contract. Although an argument can be made that contract terms not actively negotiated between the parties fall outside the "circle of assent" which constitutes the actual agreement, commercial practicalities dictate that unbargained for terms only be denied enforcement where they are also substantively unreasonable. No precise definition of substantive unconscionability can be proffered. Cases have talked in terms of "overly-harsh" or "one-sided" results. One commentator has pointed out, however, that "unconscionability turns not only on a 'one-sided' result, but also on an absence of 'justification' for it," which is only to say that substantive unconscionability must be evaluated as of the time the contract was made. The most detailed and specific commentaries observe that a contract is largely an allocation of risks between the parties, and therefore that a contractual term is substantively suspect if it reallocates the risks of the bargain in an objectively unreasonable or unexpected manner. But not all unreasonable risk reallocations are unconscionable; rather, enforceability of the clause is tied to the procedural aspects of unconscionability (see ante), such that the greater the unfair surprise or inequality of bargaining power, the less unreasonable the risk reallocation which will be tolerated.

Although there is little California precedent directly on point, the importance of both the procedural and substantive elements of unconscionability finds support by analogy in the recent decision by the California Supreme Court.

[The court discussed a California case where a music promoter booked concerts for a group using a standard form contract prepared by the musicians' union providing that all disputes were to be settled by an arbitrator selected by the union. The court found that this was a contract of adhesion since virtually all prominent musicians were in the union. Although the promoter was not surprised by the arbitration clause, the court held it unconscionable since it did not meet the "minimum levels of integrity" that are required for arbitration clauses.]

With these considerations in mind, we must now determine whether the trial court in this case was correct in concluding that the clauses in the FMC form contract disclaiming all warranties and excluding consequential damages were unconscionable. In doing so, we keep in mind that while unconscionability is ultimately a question of law, numerous factual inquiries bear upon that question. The business conditions under which the contract was formed directly affect the parties relative bargaining power, reasonable expectations, and the commercial reasonableness of the risk allocation as provided in the written agreement. To the extent there are conflicts in the evidence or in the factual inferences which may be drawn therefrom, we must assume a set of facts consistent with the court's finding of unconscionability if such an assumption is supported by substantial evidence.

Turning first to the procedural aspects of unconscionability, we note at the outset that this contract arises in a commercial context between an enormous diversified corporation (FMC) and a relatively small but experienced farming company (A & M). Generally, ". . .courts have not been solicitous of businessmen in the name of unconscionability." This is probably because courts view businessmen as possessed of a greater degree of commercial understanding and substantially more economic muscle than the ordinary consumer. Hence, a businessman usually has a more difficult time establishing procedural unconscionability in the sense of either "unfair surprise" or "unequal bargaining power."

Nevertheless, generalizations are always subject to exceptions and categorization is rarely an adequate substitute for analysis. With increasing frequency, courts have begun to recognize that experienced but legally unsophisticated businessmen may be unfairly surprised by unconscionable contract terms and that even large business entities may have relatively little bargaining power, depending on the identity of the other contracting party and the commercial circumstances surrounding the agreement. This recognition rests on the conviction that the social benefits associated with freedom of contract are severely skewed where it appears that had the party actually been aware of the term to which he "agreed" or had he any real choice in the matter, he would never have assented to inclusion of the term.

Both aspects of procedural unconscionability appear to be present on the facts of this case. Although the printing used on the warranty disclaimer was conspicuous, the terms of the consequential damage exclusion are not particularly apparent, being only slightly larger than most of the other contract text. Both provisions appear in the middle of the back page of a long preprinted form contract which was only casually shown to Abatti. It was never suggested to him, either verbally or in writing, that he read the back of the form. Abatti testified he never read the reverse side terms There was thus sufficient evidence before the trial court to conclude that Abatti was in fact surprised by the warranty disclaimer and the consequential damage exclusion. How "unfair" his surprise was is subject to some dispute. He certainly had the opportunity to read the back of the contract or to seek the advice of a lawyer. Yet as a factual matter, given the complexity of the terms and FMC's failure to direct his attention to them, Abatti's omission may not be totally unreasonable. In this regard, the comments of the Indiana Supreme Court in *Weaver v. American Oil Company,* 276 N.E.2d 147-148 (Ind. 1972) are apposite:

> The burden should be on the party submitting [a standard contract] in printed form to show that the other party had knowledge of any unusual or unconscionable terms contained therein.

The principle should be the same as that applicable to implied warranties, namely that a package of goods sold to a purchaser is fit for the purposes intended and contains no harmful materials other than that represented.

Here, FMC made no attempt to provide A & M with the requisite knowledge of the disclaimer or the exclusion. In fact, one suspects that the length, complexity and obtuseness of most form contracts may be due at least in part to the seller's preference that the buyer will be dissuaded from reading that to which he is supposedly agreeing. This process almost inevitably results in a one-sided contract.

Even if we ignore any suggestion of unfair surprise, there is ample evidence of unequal bargaining power here and a lack of any real negotiation over the terms of the contract. Although it was conceded that A & M was a large-scale farming enterprise by Imperial Valley standards, employing five persons on a regular basis and up to fifty seasonal employees at harvest time, and that Abatti was farming some 8,000 acres in 1974, FMC Corporation is in an entirely different category. The 1974 gross sales of the Agriculture Machinery Division alone amounted to $40 million. More importantly, the terms on the FMC form contract were standard. FMC salesmen were not authorized to negotiate any of the terms appearing on the reverse side of the preprinted contract. Although FMC contends that in some special instances, individual contracts are negotiated, A & M was never made aware of that option. The sum total of these circumstances leads to the conclusion that this contract was a "bargain" only in the most general sense of the word.

Although the procedural aspects of unconscionability are present in this case, we suspect the substantive unconscionability of the disclaimer and exclusion provisions contributed equally to the trial court's ultimate conclusion. As to the disclaimer of warranties, the facts of this case support the trial court's conclusion that such disclaimer was commercially unreasonable. The warranty allegedly breached by FMC went to the basic performance characteristics of the product. In attempting to disclaim this and all other warranties, FMC was in essence guarantying nothing about what the product would do. Since a product's performance forms the fundamental basis for a sales contract, it is patently unreasonable to assume that a buyer would purchase a standardized mass-produced product from an industry seller without any enforceable performance standards. From a social perspective, risk of loss is most appropriately borne by the party best able to prevent its occurrence.

Rarely would the buyer be in a better position than the manufacturer/seller to evaluate the performance characteristics of a machine.

In this case, moreover, the evidence establishes that A & M had no previous experience with weight-sizing machines and was forced to rely on the expertise of FMC in recommending the necessary equipment. FMC was abundantly aware of this fact. The jury here necessarily found that FMC either expressly or impliedly guaranteed a performance level which the machine was unable to meet. Especially where an inexperienced buyer is concerned, the seller's performance representations are absolutely necessary to allow the buyer to make an intelligent choice among the competitive options available. A seller's attempt, through the use of a disclaimer, to prevent the buyer from reasonably relying on such representations calls into question the commercial reasonableness of the agreement and may well be substantively unconscionable. The trial court's conclusion to that effect is amply supported by the record before us.

As to the exclusion of consequential damages, several factors combine to suggest that the exclusion was unreasonable on the facts of this case. Consequential damages are a commercially recognized type of damage actually suffered by A & M due to FMC's breach. A party ". . . should be able to rely on their existence in the absence of being informed to the contrary . . ." This factor is particularly important given the commercial realities under which the contract was executed. If the seller's warranty was breached, consequential damages were not merely "reasonably foreseeable"; they were explicitly obvious. All parties were aware that once the tomatoes began to ripen, they all had to be harvested and packed within a relatively short period of time.

Another factor supporting the trial court's determination involves the avoidability of the damages and relates directly to the allocation of risks which lies at the foundation of the contractual bargain. It has been suggested that "[r]isk shifting is socially expensive and should not be undertaken in the absence of a good reason. An even better reason is required when to so shift is contrary to a contract freely negotiated." But as we noted previously, FMC was the only party reasonably able to prevent this loss by not selling A & M a machine inadequate to meet its expressed needs. "If there is a type of risk allocation that should be subjected to special scrutiny, it is probably the shifting to one party of a risk that only the other party can avoid."

In summary, our review of the totality of circumstances in this case, including the business environment within which the contract was executed, supports the trial court's determination that the disclaimer of warranties and the exclusion of consequential damages in FMC's form contract were unconscionable and therefore unenforceable. When non-negotiable terms on preprinted form agreements combine with disparate bargaining power, resulting in the allocation of commercial risks in a socially or economically unreasonable manner, the concept of unconscionability as codified in Uniform Commercial Code § 2-302 and § 2-719, subdivision (3), furnishes legal justification for refusing enforcement of the offensive result.

The majority affirmed the trial court finding of unconscionability. There was also a short concurring opinion which stated:

Facts fly as "thick as autumnal leaves that strow the brooks of Vallombrosa," in support of the trial court's conclusion these contract clauses were oppressive, contrary to oral representations made to induce the purchase, and unreasonably favorable to the party with a superior bargaining position. No experienced farmer would spend $32,000 for equipment which could not process his tomatoes before they rot and no fair and honest merchant would sell such equipment with representations negated in its own sales contract.

(2) In *Industralease Automated & Scientific Equip. Corp. v. R.M.E. Enterprises, Inc.*, 396 N.Y.S.2d 427 (1977), the court considered the issue of whether disclaimers of express or implied warranties are unconscionable under circumstances where the equipment fails to operate. In Industralease, defendant picnic grove owner-operator entered into a lease for the use of rubbish incinerators. Plaintiff subsequently informed defendant that the initial lease was "no good" and asked that he sign "new papers." The new lease contained an unqualified disclaimer of express and implied warranties. The incinerators were delivered and installed properly but did not "then or thereafter work." Defendant then demanded removal of the incinerators from his property, but plaintiff refused to accede and insisted upon timely receipt of the monthly payments. The trial court held that the disclaimer of warranties was not unconscionable as a matter of law. On appeal, the court found that the new contract which eliminated the warranties was entered into

under an "atmosphere [of] haste and pressure" which was "clearly pervasive." The court also found that since the summer season for defendant's operations had already begun, defendant was clearly disadvantaged at this point in the bargaining. The court also explicitly refused to "divorce entirely" events which occur after the time of the making of the contract, even though it recognized that U.C.C. § 2-302 applied only to the time of making of the contract. The court held that the disclaimer of warranties was unconscionable under the circumstances and that the express warranties to the defendant concerning the incinerators had been breached. Judgment for defendant was affirmed.

PROBLEM 1.17

Your senior partner is on the Permanent Editorial Board of the American Law Institute, which has been asked by the Director to consider whether the Article 2 section on unconscionability should be revised so as to parallel the Article 2A unconscionability section. While much of § 2A-108 follows § 2-302, it does contain this addition:

> (2) With respect to a consumer lease, if the court as a matter of law finds that a lease contract or any clause of a lease contract has been induced by unconscionable conduct or that unconscionable conduct has occurred in the collection of a claim arising from a lease contract, the court may grant appropriate relief.

In addition, it provides that if the court finds unconscionability, the court shall award the lessee attorney fees. In subsection 4, the court may award the lessor attorney fees if it decides that the lessee knew the claim was groundless. Your senior partner asks for your opinion on the matter. He also gives you an article with the excerpt that follows:

> In paragraph 3 of the section on unconscionability, the drafters seem to encourage an attack on unfair and unconscionable lease terms by providing that if one prevails on the unconscionability claim, he or she shall also prevail as to attorney fees. Without this provision, many attorneys might never take an unconscionability case because the amounts involved are often not great enough to justify participation on their part. by assuring attorney fees, paragraph 3 makes it practical for lawyers to attack the unfair contract or lease clauses.
>
> Unfortunately, paragraph 4(b) of the same section destroys the possibility of attacks on unfair clauses by placing the risk of huge attorney fees for the other side on the consumer. This paragraph deals the "death blow" to unconscionability claims. Indeed, it makes the other three sections virtually meaningless. While paragraph 4(b) may seem logical to some on the surface, its impact is disastrous.
>
> Paragraph 4(b) provides that if a judge deems any unconscionability claim to be groundless, then attorney fees may be assessed against the party raising it. "Groundless" is so nebulous and uncertain that it makes it risky for consumers to assert unconscionability. The term is not defined in either the text or comments, and what is "groundless" to one person may not seem so to another. For example, one might view the lease clause as harsh, one-sided, and unconscionable, while another might justify it on the basis of the lessor's need to discipline lessees or to avert any possible risks; one might view the unread and hidden standard form lease clause as "unfair surprise," while another might say consumers have a duty to read the entire contract.
>
> If an attorney asserts a new theory of unconscionability, a judge unfortunately might find it to be groundless. As pointed out in the American Law Institute ("A.L.I.") discussion, would

the judges have held the assertion by Brandeis and Warren of the right of privacy as a new theory groundless? Some judges might have! Yet this theory eventually became a major part of the law.

The doctrine of unconscionability has only been used in the last several decades and may still undergo considerable development. In this regard, a number of theories are likely to be asserted and accepted by the courts in the coming years. Also, unconscionability could be recognized in an increasing number of situations. Nevertheless, in this period of uncertainty and development, some courts will hesitate to find unconscionability. Many judges may be conservative and see the unconscionability claim as "groundless." In a fair number of unknown cases, paragraph 4 will indeed be evoked against the party raising unconscionability with a most serious impact.

From King, *Major Problems with Article 2A: Unfairness, "Cutting Off" Consumer Defenses, Unfiled Interests, and Uneven Adoption*, 43 Mercer L. Rev. (1992).

§ 1.07 Further Developments: The Next Millennium

While future developments are never certain, various trends and developments make their occurrence most probable. Reform of the Uniform Commercial Code in several major aspects will take place in the near future. There is already a new U.C.C. Article 5 on Letters of Credit, now contained in the new official text of the code (1995). The work on U.C.C. Article 2 is continuing and the revision of it should be completed around 1998. In addition, Article 2B on the Licensing of Information is proceeding ahead in its draft stages. It also should be promulgated in the official text of the U.C.C. in the next several years. A new section 402A on Strict Liability for Defective Products is also in the process of being formulated.

PROBLEM 1.18

Your law professor in commercial law has been asked to give a talk at a "millennium conference." He has asked you as his research assistant to assist him in formulating some ideas and also in filling out some points of his:

(1) The major reforms of the U.C.C. will finally be in place. With the previous revisions of Articles 3 and 4 on Negotiable Paper and Article 5 on Letters of Credit, the promulgated revised Article 2 on Sales and the new Article 2A on Licensing of Technology will complete current revision efforts. As the states enact them into law, there will be one or two decades without much further activity in this regard. Gradually, of course, there will be some case law interpretation taking place.

(2) The whole area of services will require a review. The Sale of Goods will become proportionately less important and the sale of services will gain. There will need to be a look at that entire area and its relationship to the principles found in the U.C.C.

(3) There will be more comparisons made with the laws of other countries and with developing international standards. Courts will cite the laws and cases in other countries for their persuasive value. Law reform organizations will also undertake more comparative studies and base some of their revisions on developments abroad.

(4) Commercial law attorneys will be more conversive with both U.S. and comparative laws. Many will spend some of their time in offices in the U.S., but also more time travelling or serving in branch offices abroad.

(5) There will be a greater use of mediation and arbitration in solving commercial disputes. In addition, there may be some special commercial courts established to facilitate the settling of disputes.

(6) An international commercial law court, similar to that proposed by Professor King in § 1.04, will be established to oversee court interpretations of the Convention on the International Sale of Goods and other developing commercial law principles.

Please give these matters some thought and also note any ideas of your own.

CHAPTER 2

SCOPE: SUBJECT MATTER OF THE CONTRACT FOR SALE

§ 2.01 Applicability of U.C.C. Article 2—Transactions Included and Excluded

Read: U.C.C. §§ 2-102 (see § 9-206(2)), 2-105, 2-106 (see § 2-304), 2-107, 2-314(1)).

Read also: U.C.C. §§ 2A-102, 2A-103(1)(j) and (h) and (e) and (g), 1-201(37), 9-102(2), 2A-104 (1990); CISG Arts. 1-6, 10, 95.

Article 2 of the Uniform Commercial Code is entitled "Sales." Section 2-102 makes it clear that Article 2 deals with goods: "Unless the content otherwise requires, this Article applies to transactions in goods. . ." The Code does not define "transaction." Arguably, a transaction is broader than a "sale," and therefore includes leases and other arrangements relating to goods which are not technically sales.

Section 2-106 offers a definition of "sale": "A 'sale' consists in the passing of title from the seller to the buyer for a price." Section 2-105 defines "goods": " 'Goods' means all things. . . which are movable at the time of identification to the contract other than the money in which the price is to be paid, investment securities (Article 8) and things in action."

As to the application of the Code by analogy, see § 1.03[D] above and U.C.C. §§ 1-102 Comment 1, 2-105 Comment 1 (last paragraph), and 2-313 Comment 2. See also, Proposed Final Draft of U.C.C. Article 2A Leases.

[A] Goods or Services

PROBLEM 2.1

Your client, Robert Rich, recently entered into a contract with the Olympia Pool Company for construction of a pool with a diving board which the company then built. While engaged in diving, Robert fell from the side of the diving board and was badly injured. Robert asserted that the skid resistant material built into the surface of the top of the diving board stopped one inch short of each edge. This condition, he claims, made the board defective. The Olympia Pool Company denies any liability. Is the U.C.C. applicable to this transaction? What possible arguments or theories can be used by the parties in regard to this point? Which do you think will prevail?

NOTE

Two major tests, the "Predominant" factor test and the "Gravamen" test have been used by the courts. These were discussed in the *Anthony Pools* case: (295 Md. 285, 455 A.2d 434, 35 U.C.C. Rep. 498, 1983):

> Here, Anthony undertook the construction of an in ground, steel reinforced, gunite swimming pool with hand finished plaster surfacing, tile trim and coping. The Sheehans were not buying steel rods, or gunite, or plaster or tiles. The predominant factor, the thrust, the purpose of the contract was the furnishing of labor and service by Anthony, while the sale of the diving board was incidental to the construction of the pool itself. The question thus resolves itself into whether the predominant purpose test, which we applied in *Burton* for the purpose of determining whether the U.C.C. statute of limitations governed that transaction, should be applied to determine whether the sale of the diving board, included in the Anthony Sheehans transaction, carries an implied warranty of merchantability under § 2-314.
>
> Were the predominant purpose test mechanically to be applied to the facts of this case, there would be no quality warranty implied as to the diving board. But here the contract expressly states that Anthony agrees not only to construct the swimming pool, but also to sell the related equipment selected by the Sheehans. The Sheehans are described as "Buyer." The diving board itself is not structurally integrated into the swimming pool. Anthony offered the board as an optional accessory, just as Anthony offered the options of purchasing a pool ladder or a sliding board. When identified to the contract, the diving board was movable. See CL § 2-105. The board itself remains detachable from its support, as reflected by a photograph in evidence. The diving board, considered alone, is goods. Had it been purchased by the Sheehans in a transaction distinct from the pool construction agreement with Anthony, there would have been an implied warranty of merchantability.
>
> A number of commentators have advocated a more policy-oriented approach to determining whether warranties of quality and fitness are implied with respect to goods sold as part of a hybrid transaction in which service predominates. See Farnsworth, *Implied Warranties of Quality in Non-Sales Cases,* 57 Colum. L. Rev. 653 (1957); Comment, *Sale of Goods in Service-Predominated Transactions,* 37 Fordham L. Rev. 115 (1968); Note, *Products and the Professional; Strict Liability in the Sale-Service Hybrid Transaction,* 24 Hastings L.J. 111(1972); Note, *Contracts for Goods and Services and Article 2 of the Uniform Commercial Code,* 9 Rut-Cam L.J. 303 (1978); Comment, *Sales-Service Hybrid Transactions. A Policy Approach,* 28 Sw L.J. 575 (1974). To support their position, these commentators in general emphasize loss shifting, risk distribution, consumer reliance and difficulties in the proof of negligence. These concepts underlie strict liability in tort.
>
> A leading case applying a policy approach in this problem area is *Newmark v. Gimbel's Incorporated,* 54 N.J. 585,258 A.2d 697(1969). There the patron of a beauty parlor sued for injury to her hair and scalp allegedly resulting from a lotion used in giving her a permanent wave. Because the transaction was viewed as the rendering of a service, the trial court had ruled that there could be no warranty liability. The intermediate appellate court's reversal was affirmed by the Supreme Court of New Jersey which reasoned in part as follows (*Id.,* at 593, 258 A.2d at 701):
>
> > The transaction, in our judgment, is a hybrid partaking of incidents of a sale and a service. It is really partly the rendering of service, and partly the supplying of goods for a

> consideration. Accordingly, we agree with the Appellate Division that an implied warranty of fitness of the products used in giving the permanent wave exists with no less force than it would have in the case of a simple sale. Obviously in permanent wave operations the product is taken into consideration in fixing the price of the service. The no-separate-charge argument puts excessive emphasis on form and downgrades the overall substance of the transaction. If the beauty parlor operator bought and applied the permanent wave solution to her own hair and suffered injury thereby, her action in warranty or strict liability in tort against the manufacturer-seller of the product clearly would be maintainable because the basic transaction would have arisen from a conventional type of sale. It does not accord with logic to deny a similar right to a patron against the beauty parlor operator or the manufacturer when the purchase and sale were made in anticipation of and for the purpose of use of the product on the patron who would be charged for its use. Common sense demands that such patron be deemed a customer as to both manufacturer and beauty parlor operator. [Citations omitted.]

The court was careful to limit its holding to commercial transactions, as opposed to those predominantly involving professional services. *Id.* at 596-97, 258 A.2d at 702-703.

1 R. Anderson, Uniform Commercial Code (1970), § 2-102:5 at 209 refers to *Newmark* as illustrative of a possible trend in the law and states:

> It is probable that a goods-services transaction will come to be subjected to Article 2 of the Code insofar as the contractor's obligations with respect to the goods themselves are involved, at least where the goods involved could have been purchased in the general market and used by the plaintiff-customer.

A warranty of fitness for particular purpose under § 2-315 of the U.C.C.was implied in *Worrell v. Barnes,* 87 Nev. 204, 484 P.2d 573 (1971). In that case a contractor was engaged to do some carpentry work and to connect various appliances in the plaintiff's home to an existing liquified petroleum gas system. The appliances were not supplied by the contractor. Suit was for damage to the plaintiff's home resulting from a fire. The plaintiff produced evidence that the fire was caused by a defective fitting installed by the contractor which had allowed propane to escape. Dismissal of the plaintiff's claims, based on the Nevada version of strict liability in tort and based on implied warranty, was reversed. The court reasoned that, because it had held that the contractor had sold a product so as to bring into operation the doctrine of strict liability, "so also must we deem this case to involve 'goods' within the purview of the Uniform Commercial Code." *Id.* at 208, 484 P.2d at 576.

1 W. Hawkland, Uniform Commercial Code Series (1982), § 2-102:04, at Art. 2, p 12 has suggested what might be called a "gravamen" test in light of the decision in *Worrell.* He writes:

> Unless uniformity would be impaired thereby, it might be more sensible and facilitate administration, at least in this grey area, to abandon the "predominant factor" test and focus instead on whether the gravamen of the action involves goods or services. For example, in *Worrell v. Barnes,* if the gas escaped because of a defective fitting or connector, the case might be characterized as one involving the sale of goods. On the other hand, if the gas escaped because of poor work by Barnes the case might be characterized as one involving services, outside the scope of the U.C.C..

In this state, the provisions of CL § 2-316.1(1) and (2) reflect an implicit policy judgment by the General Assembly which prevents the mechanical application of the predominant purpose test to cases like the one under consideration. Subsection (1) states that § 2-316, dealing in part with the manner in which an implied warranty of merchantability may be excluded or modified, does not apply to "consumer goods. . . services, or both." Under subsection (2) language "used by a seller of consumer goods and services" to exclude or modify implied warranties is unenforceable. The hybrid transaction is covered by, or at least embraced within, those terms.

Under the predominant purpose test, as applied by a majority of the courts, a hybrid transaction must first be classified as a sale of goods in order for there to be U.C.C. based, implied warranties on the goods included in the transaction. If goods predominate and they are consumer goods, an all or nothing classification of the instant transaction under the predominant purpose test would mean there could be no U.C.C. based, implied warranties on the diving board.

The gravamen test of Dean Hawkland suggests the vehicle for satisfying the legislative policy. Accordingly, we hold that where, as part of a commercial transaction, consumer goods are sold which retain their character as consumer goods after completion of the performance promised to the consumer, and where monetary loss or personal injury is claimed to have resulted from a defect in the consumer goods, the provisions of the Maryland U.C.C. dealing with implied warranties apply to the consumer goods, even if the transaction is predominantly one for the rendering of consumer services.

Thus the diving board which Anthony sold to the Sheehans as part of the swimming pool construction contract carried an implied warranty of merchantability under CL § 2-314.

PROBLEM 2.2

Your client, Educational Resources Inc., recently decided to modernize in several ways:

1. it contracted to have its office system computerized and every person's office now has a computer supposedly appropriate for each person's type of work;
2. it contracted for a computer system connecting the main office with the branch operating as to office matters and inventory supplies;
3. it has joined Internet, an information system;
4. it has purchased a software system which is supposedly designed to produce educational tests which Educational Resources can sell.

None of these systems are working satisfactory and it wished to sue for breach of contract. What other facts do you need to know? Would the U.C.C. be applicable?

GEOTECH ENERGY CORP. v. GULF STATES

Court of Appeals of Texas, Houston (14th Dist.)
788 S.W.2d 386 (1990)

CANNON, JUSTICE.

Geotech Energy Corporation [Geotech] appeals from a judgment on the jury's verdict in favor of Gulf States Telecommunications [Gulf States] in a breach of contract case. Geotech alleges the trial court erred (1) by submitting an instruction concerning substantial performance, (2) by refusing to submit an issue on mitigation of damages, (3) by denying Geotech's motion for continuance, (4) by refusing to submit an issue on the effect of reciprocal promises, (5) in awarding damages based on insufficient evidence, and (6) by submitting an issue on bad faith filing of a Deceptive Trade Practices Act claim. We affirm the judgment of the trial court.

On June 27, 1986, Geotech and Gulf States signed a contract. Under the terms of the contract Gulf States was to install a used OKI Spectrum 100A telephone system; Geotech was to arrange for payment to Gulf States through a third-party leasing company. Geotech negotiated a lease agreement with its usual leasing company, Corporate Funding. When Geotech signed a certificate of acceptance for the telephone system, Corporate Funding was then to pay Gulf States.

The equipment was installed and the necessary software written by Chuck Toney, vice president of Gulf States. After a few problems were corrected, the system was verbally accepted by Joel Brown of Geotech. Both Brown and Linda McNaspy, vice president of Geotech, assured Gulf States the certificate of acceptance would be signed by Michael Reedy, one of Geotech's owners, who was in California at the time and the person to whom the certificate was sent.

The record reflects that when Reedy returned from California he was unhappy with the appearance of the telephone, because they did not look sufficiently "high tech." Geotech then began a series of meritless complaints about the phone system. Toney made daily calls at Geotech to attempt to correct the alleged problems. Eventually Gulf States offered to remove the OKI system and replace it with an alternate one, if an inspection by a neutral third-party found it to be defective. Geotech refused to allow such an inspection.

Ultimately, Geotech had the system dismantled and refused to pay Gulf States. Gulf States sued for breach of contract. Geotech answered and counterclaimed against Gulf States for violations of Tex. Bus. & Com. Code Ann. §§ 17.41-17.826 (Vernon 1987 & Supp. 1990) [more commonly referred to as the Deceptive Trade Practices Act, or DPTA].

Geotech's first point of error contends the trial court erred by including an instruction on substantial performance in the jury's charge. Since Geotech raised no objection to the language of the instruction given, we are only concerned with the question of whether an instruction on substantial performance was proper in this case.

Geotech argues the doctrine of substantial performance is inapplicable because this case is controlled by Chapter 2 of Tex. Bus. & Com. Code Ann. (Vernon 1968 & Supp. 1989) [more commonly referred to as the Uniform Commercial Code, or the U.C.C.]; alternatively, it contends that the doctrine is strictly limited to cases involving breach of construction or employment contracts. We disagree with both propositions.

Chapter Two of the U.C.C., by its express terms, applies only to contracts involving the sale of goods. Tex. Bus. & Com. Code Ann. §§ 2.102, 2.106 (Vernon 1968). The contract before us does not fall within its scope.

Appellant concedes the contract involves both goods and services. When faced with such a hybrid contract we must determine whether the essence of the contract is the sale of materials or services. Obviously telephone equipment, the hardware, is a necessary component for the installation of telephone services. However, the hardware alone would be useless to a buyer. The record reveals the telephone system in question is a very sophisticated model. A significant degree of expertise on the part of Gulf States' representative, Chuck Toney, was necessary to install the hardware. Further, even with the equipment installed, Toney's services in writing the software were essential to make the phone system operable and to customize it to meet Geotech's specific needs. The contract itself is written as a contract for service: "Gulf States shall perform and/or deliver services on the Customer's premises. . . ." Since the essence of this contract is services, not goods, it does not fall within the scope of the U.C.C.

Even if we assume, *arguendo*, that the contract essentially involves goods, the U.C.C. does not apply because the contract does not provide for the sale of goods to Geotech. Section 2-106 of the U.C.C. specifies that a sale "consists in the passing of title from the seller to the buyer for a price." Geotech opted to lease the equipment through a third-part leasing company instead of purchasing it outright. The record reveals Geotech asserted there was no sale, that Geotech would never own the equipment; rather, the leasing company would own it. By Geotech's own admission, title would never pass to it, so no sale was to occur.

Geotech asserted during oral argument that it would have had an option to buy the equipment at the end of the lease term, and that the lease agreement with Corporate Funding assigned to appellant all of Corporate Funding's rights against Gulf States. We note that the copy of the lease agreement between Geotech and Corporate Funding in the record does not contain a purchase option. Further, Geotech did not bring this action as assignee of Corporate Funding's rights. In fact, though its contract with Gulf States required Geotech to enter into a binding lease agreement, Geotech's pleadings refer to the lease as "the proposed lease" and assert that Corporate Funding returned it to Geotech stamped "void" after Geotech refused to sign the certificate of acceptance. Geotech cannot meet the U.C.C. requirement for the passage of title by claiming supposed rights created by an instrument that Geotech has previously asserted is void as a result of its own actions.

Since the U.C.C. is inapplicable, the trial court correctly applied common law principles to the case. Geotech contends that Texas law limits consideration of substantial performance to those cases involving breach of construction and employment contracts. However, a review of the case law reveals that substantial performance is applied to a broad range of contract cases. [cases cited:] (upheld jury finding of substantial performance of a contract for the right of first refusal to purchase property); (applied doctrine to an oil-field drilling contract); (upheld jury finding of substantial compliance with a contract for sale of crops).

Geotech has cited no authority excepting their agreement with Gulf States from the general principles of contract law, which include the doctrine of substantial performance. Gulf States plead full performance, which supports the submission of an instruction on substantial performance. Since both the pleadings and the evidence supported submission of an instruction on substantial performance, the trial court did not err. Point of error number one is overruled.

COMMUNICATIONS GROUPS, INC. v. WARNER COMMUNICATIONS

Civil Court of the City of New York, New York County
138 Misc.2d 80, 527 N.Y.S.2d 341 (1988)

LEONARD N. COHEN, JUDGE.

Plaintiff Communications Groups, Inc. ("CGI") moves to dismiss defendant Warner Communications, Inc.'s ("Warner") first through third counterclaims which are identical to defendant's second through fourth affirmative defenses, respectively, pursuant to CPLR 3211(a)(1), (a)(7) and (b).

This action arises out of an alleged breach of a written agreement dated July 18, 1986 for the licensing, installation and servicing of a certain computer software package (the "Agreement"). Subsequently, the parties entered into two subcontract for additional software and related hardware. As per the Agreement, defendant paid 50% of the amount due upon signing the Agreement. The remaining 50% was to be paid upon installation of the software. It is undisputed that defendant has not paid this remaining amount due under the Agreement.

The complaint, dated October 23, 1987, sets forth three causes of action for breach of contract to recover payment in the total amount of $16,650.00 still due and owing from defendant to plaintiff. Defendant does not dispute nonpayment, but defendant's Answer asserts four affirmative defenses and three counterclaims: breach of an implied warranty of fitness of the computer software for defendant's specified known purposes; breach of an express and/or implied warranty of merchantability of the software system and the good working order of its system and repair services; and the breach of contract in failing to provide support service to keep the system operational and in good working order.

As to the counterclaims alleging implied warranties of merchantability and fitness for a specified known business purpose, the movant, CGI, contends that the Agreement provided for a software system or package which was neither for a tangible and movable product or goods nor a transaction for a sale or lease of either services or goods. Rather, CGI claims the Agreement was a license for computer software as an intangible service for limited use by defendant of "copyrightable information" and for the acquisition of the "abstract right" only "to listen" as with music on a record or disk. As a consequence, CGI argues that since implied warranties of fitness for a particular purpose or merchantability are remedies exclusively for contracts of the sale of goods and because the Agreement herein is not such a transaction of goods, the implied warranty counterclaims lack merit and cannot be maintained either under common law or under the Uniform Commercial Code (U.C.C.).

Moreover, movant contends that even if the contract was for a sale of goods or a lease of goods, the contract, by its terms, provides for an express disclaimer of any implied warranties of fitness and merchantability.

As for the third counterclaim, movant characterizes this claim as a breach of express warranties of the good working order and adequate support services of the computer software. Movant contends that such express warranties are lacking under the terms of the Agreement. Movant argues that any prior or subsequent oral promises or warranties which may have been made by movant cannot be considered part of the agreement based on the parol evidence rules under common law and the U.C.C.

The threshold issue presented is whether the software computer package or system provided for under the Agreement involved a transaction of "goods" as defined under U.C.C. 2-105(1) to mean "all things (including specially manufactured goods) which are movable at the time of identification to the contract for sale . . . ."

A review of the Agreement, the sole documentary and evidentiary matter submitted on these motion papers, shows that the computer software referred to therein is not defined. Nor have either of the parties in their motion papers articulated the precise form of the instant software. Software, however, is a widely used term and has several meanings. [cases cited] (software includes programs and computer language listings); (software includes magnetic cards or paper cards programmed to instruct the computer); (software refers to programs used in the computer); see generally, *Note, Computer Programs As Goods Under The U.C.C.*, 77 Mich. L. Rev. 1149 (1979).

Regardless of the software's specific form or use, it seems that computer software, generally, is considered by the courts to be a tangible, and movable item, not merely an intangible idea or thought and therefore qualifies as a "good" under Article 2 of the U.C.C. Moreover, U.C.C. Sec. 1-102 provides that the Act shall be liberally construed and applied to promote its underlying purposes and policies.

Here, the Agreement clearly provides, in part, for the installation by CGI of its specially designed software equipment for defendant's particular telephone and computer system, needs and purposes. This equipment is expressly listed on schedules annexed and made a part of the Agreement. Said schedules clearly reflect installation by CGI of identifiable and movable equipment such as recording, accounting and traffic analysis and optimizations, modules, buffer, directories and an operational user guide and other items. A review of the counterclaim allegations shows that a software computer system and equipment were designed for defendant's special and unique known needs to store data relating to thousand of defendant's monthly telephone calls and to process and print this data on defendant's main computer frame so that defendant's operations would prove more time and labor efficient. Although the ideas and concepts of the CGI designed software system remained its intellectual and copyrightable property under the Agreement, the court finds in the context of the case law and the U.C.C. that the contract terms clearly provided for a transaction of computer software equipment involving movable, tangible and identifiable products or goods and not solely intangible ideas and services and, in fact, such goods were installed by CGI for defendant's special purposes. Therefore, the first and second counterclaims are not dismissable on the ground of an exclusive contractual intangible services transaction as urged by movant.

The next issue raised by movant is that the contractual transaction failed to constitute either a sale or lease but merely was a license to use and service the software, therefore precluding defendant from relying on the common law of the U.C.C. implied warranties of merchantability (U.C.C. Sec. 2-314) and fitness for a particular known purpose (U.C.C. 2-315).

The court finds that the Agreement clearly constituted a lease for the use of CGI's goods despite the terms expressed therein of a "license to use" CGI "proprietary" software for the payment of a one-time perpetual license fee in accordance with attached pricing schedules. The Agreement, although labelled a license agreement, is clearly analogous to a lease for chattels or goods. The movant has not addressed nor presented a distinction, factually or legally, between a license to use goods from an ordinary lease to use goods. Plaintiff's argument is based on an alleged contractual license to provide intangible services which, as hereinabove, the court rejects. Therefore, the court finds the Agreement clearly is a lease for the use of plaintiff's goods, despite the contractual label of a "license."

The law is clear that common law rights exist to state a cause of action or counterclaim for breach of implied warranties of merchantability and/or fitness for a particular known purpose involving the lease of chattels or goods without reliance on the U.C.C. The cases cited by movant suggesting the non-existence of common law rights of implied warranties are inapposite as they involve the provision of contractual services as distinguished form products and goods as found hereinabove.

Therefore, the defendant has sufficiently stated in its first and second counterclaims a common law breach of implied warranties under a contractual lease of goods. However, these counterclaims allege a purchase and sale of the software products. In this regard the contract specifically provided that the CGI software was to be its sole and exclusive property and upon termination of the agreement the defendant would return the software to CGI. Thus, CGI contends the transaction was not a sale within the meaning of U.C.C. Sec. 2-106 (U.C.C. 2-401) as no title passed from seller to buyer for a price and therefore defendant is precluded from asserting U.C.C.'s implied warranties.

However, New York courts have liberally construed the meaning of "transaction" under U.C.C. 2-102, choosing to analyze the underlying facts of the agreement at issue in determining whether it sufficiently resembles a sale.

Courts in this jurisdiction have consistently applied Article 2 of the U.C.C. to the leasing of chattels. Even if the lessor retains title to the goods, where the contract price of a lease is as large as the sales price of the same item, the transaction is analogous to a sale and will be covered by U.C.C.

Therefore, the analysis used by the courts in this jurisdiction to determine whether or not a lease sufficiently resembles a sale so as to bring it within the scope of the U.C.C. may be applicable to the Agreement herein. Although the Agreement specifically provides that plaintiff will retain title to the software, the Agreement appears to have no term and, in fact, is referred to as a "perpetual license." The economic effect of the Agreement is unclear from the sole submitted documentary evidence of the Agreement itself. Despite the Agreement spelling out the fee to be paid by defendant to plaintiff for use of the software, the court lacks information as to the actual value of the software. *But see* Note, op. cit. 77 Mich. L. Rev. 1149, 1156. ("The economic result of a software loan is indistinguishable from a software sale. The price is apt to be the same in either case," *citing United States Leasing Corp., supra.*)

Neither party has submitted an affidavit by a person with knowledge of the transaction at issue nor is the intent of the parties and surrounding circumstances of the whole transaction between the parties clear from the Agreement alone as to whether this transaction was a sale or only a lease of computer software goods. In the context of the case law, as hereinabove, the contractual retention of title to the goods by CGI in and of itself is not determinative of whether this lease transaction resembled a sale for U.C.C. applicability. There are factual triable issues raised in this regard and therefore dismissal of the implied warranty counterclaims for a sale for failure to sufficiently state a counterclaim of affirmative defense is not warranted. The court for purposes of this type of motion must accept the facts as alleged in the counterclaim as true. Here there is a sufficient showing to support legally cognizable counterclaims for the breach of implied warranties of fitness and merchantability for a sale of goods within the scope of the U.C.C.

Finally, as the first and second counterclaims, the CGI contention that the Agreement contains an express and/or implied disclaimer of implied warranties lacks merit. The contractual provision relied on by CGI in this regard fails to alert or call to defendant's attention the exclusion of any warranty of merchantability or fitness for a particular known purpose but relates solely to CGI's maintenance, service and repair obligations for the software systems. Nor does this clause use the words "merchantability," "fitness," "disclaimer," "as is," "warranty," or "all faults."

The courts look to the relevant sections of the U.C.C., and even movant refers to the U.C.C., to test the validity of warranty disclaimers. The above words or other commonly understood language must be set forth in the contract, specifically and conspicuously, to call attention to the exclusion of warranties and make plain that there is no implied warranty in order to validate the exclusion of implied warranties. U.C.C. Sec. 2-316 and Sec. 1-201(10); Therefore the plaintiff's motion to dismiss the first and second counterclaims is denied.

Turning to that branch of the motion to dismiss the defendant's third counterclaim for failure to sufficiently state a cause of action, movant characterizes it as a claim for breach of an express warranty for a "good working order software system and for adequate support services." However, a review of the allegations of this counterclaim shows that it is clearly based on a breach of contract. The Agreement expressly states the CGI will provide "maintenance services" after installation of the system for the "reparation of any failure, malfunction, defects or non-conformity in CGI Software which prevents such CGI software from performing in accordance with the specifications, documentation and criteria set forth in this agreement and any attachments thereto." The Agreement further provides that "The liability of CGI for damages or expenses arising in connection with the failure of CGI software to perform in accordance with its specifications shall be limited to the return of any payments made by the Customer or the actual amount of said damages and expenses, whichever is less."

The court finds that the allegations in the third counterclaim sufficiently set forth a cognizable legal claim for breach of that portion of the Agreement as stated above which clearly imposed a duty on CGI to provide maintenance support services for the adequate functioning and operation of the system. It is noted that no affidavits or other evidence has been submitted relating to the specifications and criteria to be applied for the software operational performance. This appears to raise triable factual issues as to the merits of the alleged contractual breach. It is further noted that there is no explicit language in the Agreement that it is the complete and exclusive statement between the parties. Therefore, plaintiff's branch of the motion to dismiss the third counterclaim is denied.

Accordingly, the plaintiff's motion is denied in its entirety.

PROBLEM 2.3

Your senior partner is a member of the Advisory Board of the Article 2 Revision Committee. Questions have come up as to whether licensing of technology and sale or leasing of computer systems and specialized software should be covered by Article 2. This method would be used rather than having a separate Article 2B for computer or technology law.

He has just heard that the Reporter of Revised Article 2 has included this subject matter into Revised Article 2 with a hub-spoke approach, *e.g.*, some of Article 2 general principles will apply to these just as to all sales of goods (the Hub); others will be fashioned to cover specific peculiar facets of this subject matter (the Spokes). Should he support or oppose this development? At what stages: drafting, debate on floor of ALI, proposal before state legislatures?

[B] Hub-Spoke

The "Hub-Spoke" concept has been described by Professors Nimmer and Speidel in a discussion paper:

Statement of the Idea

The "hub and spoke" idea argues that there are basic contract law principles that apply across all of the types of transactions that might be viewed as commercial transfers of personal property. These principles can be stated separate and apart from contract law applies only to specific types of transactions (*e.g.*, lease, sale license) or particular types of property (*e.g.*, goods, intangibles, services). By stating these basic principles as an identifiable body of contract law rules independent of particular types of transactions, one can facilitate the coordination and symmetry of the current drafting process and establish a more flexible base for inclusion of additional commercial transactions within the Article 2 contract law structure.

In a "hub and spoke" configuration, the general transactional principles would form the "hub" provisions of the revised Article 2. As discussed in more detail below, "hub" provisions include many current Article 2 rules about contract formation and interpretation. Important issues in defining these principles involve (1) delineating which contract law rules should be in this general law hub and (2) specifying the scope of applicability for the hub provisions.

The "spoke" provisions consist of contract law rules that are particularly applicable to specific types of transactions. These could be placed in sub-parts of revised Article 2, defined to apply specifically to the particular subject matter. Thus, for example, one could conceive of current Article 2A as a form of "spoke" applicable to leases. There would be a spoke applicable to sales of goods and a spoke applicable to transfers involving intangibles, including software contracts. Future decisions might include additional spokes to cover transactions in other types of personal property or services as economic and other considerations justify such action.

Excerpts from a memorandum responding by Professor King to this approach and elaborating on it follows:

This approach [Hub-Spoke] permits us to set forth certain basic principles of contract law in Article 2 of the Uniform Commercial Code and to subsequently also set forth from this Hub from these principles in the spokes from other fields of law such as computer software and services law. The scope and importance of this is clearly evident with the increased technological developments and the greater emphasis on service law. Indeed these fields may well eventually surpass the field of sale of goods in terms of economic activity and lawyers' professional activity. It appears that software contracts and some intangible services are to be covered. But what about services? Are services generally to be covered? Now? Or at some distant future time?

"Issue Hub" Approach

It seems to me that the hubs or components of the hub should be thought of in terms of issues when drafting the law. This gives us the necessary flexibility to ask what principles should be set forth in Article 2 of the U.C.C. and also whether they should be set forth in one of the spokes or other fields. It also permits the law to progress and be adopted by states that feel a more progressive or liberal law may be advisable. The *Issue-Hub* component approach would set forth the Hub or its components in terms of an issue rather than in terms of a principle, although certainly there my be alternative statements of principle. For example, a hub may be the issue of the Statute of Frauds (or the issue of a writing). Another hub issue might be the issue of consideration: should there be the requirement of consideration or no consideration necessary? Another might be in terms of the parol evidence rule: should there be a parol evidence rule or not? The value of the *issue-hub* approach is that it permits us to take an issue such as the Statute of Frauds and state it in the sense of whether it is any longer advisable? Indeed, the drafting committee and Reporter for Article 2 are advocating the abolishment of the Statute of Frauds for the sale of goods. Yet it is quite possible that in one of the spokes for one of the specialized subjects it might be retained. In terms of something like the consideration requirement, the *issue-hub* approach permits us to reevaluate that particular requirement and offer alternatives in regard to it, as mentioned in the *dual hub* approach.

While I realize drafters often think of issues while drafting principles, this *issue-hub* approach forces us to do so and to think in terms of alternate possibilities.

Hollow Hubs

Following the *issue-hub* approach, some of the hubs or components of the hub will be *hollow hubs*. The earlier example of Statute of Frauds is case in point. In Article 2, where it will be most probably abolished, it becomes a *hollow hub*, yet it may be part of the spoke of some specialized area of law such as suretyship law, services, or software law. Or it may be that the central *hollow hub* of abolishing the Statute of Frauds will also find it abolished in some of the spokes, if not all.

Dual Hubs

Some of the hubs may be *dual hubs*. For example, take the issue of the parol evidence rule. There may be an Alternative A of the Article 2, which is a continuation of the parol evidence rule in only a slight modified form. There may well be, however, an Alternative B for states to adopt if they want to do away with the parol evidence rule. The same is true for "consideration." Indeed, in Article 2 there are so many inroads on, and modifications of, consideration that it would be relatively easy to do away with it. On the other hand, it might be an important part of one of the fields covered by a spoke of the wheel.

Extent Hubs

The *issue-hub* approach also permits us to have *extent hubs*. There may be some principles of law such as unconscionability or good faith which are so agreed upon that they need not be offered as *dual hubs*. The extent of them, however, may be a matter of concern. For example, good faith is a core type hub because it is a well accepted principle. The extent of that hub may be different in regard to the different spokes. Even in regard to the basic field of sale of goods, there is a question of whether the U.C.C. good faith principle is sufficient. In some countries good faith is being extended to create pre-contractual liability and it is most likely that the question will continue to arise in regard to the good faith requirement of the Code and also in the caselaw.

Domestic-International Hubs

It seems to me that we should try to make the *issue-hubs* which will be placed in to the Uniform Commercial Code compatible with the International hubs that have been developed. In this regard, the wheels should be interchangeable, rather than subjecting our attorneys to two different size hubs. The Convention on International Sale of Goods principles should be generally compatible with the domestic ones and vis-a-versa. In this regard, an *issue-hub* such as consideration should be compatible with the international convention. At the very least it should be a *dual hub* which permits states to adopt an Alternative compatible with the convention. Likewise, parol evidence, Statute of Frauds, good faith, etc. should be basically compatible. This does not mean that they need to be identical, but that we not have them so different that they are not interchangeable or subject to later harmonization or international efforts or uniformity.

Multi-Wheel Hubs

If we think of the hub-spoke concept as containing various hub principle components, then it seems to me that the hubs must be multi-wheel ones. When one thinks of hubs, one often thinks of the old fashioned wagon with four wheels; instead we may be thinking of the "eighteen wheeler" type modern truck. The number of wheels, of course, can be ascertained or decided upon only after our discussion, but we should be open to having a number of hubs so as to create sufficient uniformity both between the U.C.C. and the other fields and also in the international arena.

NOTES ON OTHER AREAS

(1) *Blood Transfusions.* An area of difficulty has been the furnishing of blood by hospitals for transfusions to patients. Recipients of transfusions not infrequently contract homologous serum hepatitis, a serious but usually nonfatal disease, from a virus in the transfused blood. While the patient is generally charged a specific sum for each unit of blood, the courts have frequently refused to apply sales concepts to these transactions, but have instead characterized the furnishing of blood as a service instead of a "sale." The difference, as we shall see in our later discussion of warranty and strict products liability, is that instead of being able to recover from the hospital upon the relatively strict liability of the sales warranty, the patient is forced to allege and prove negligence. Moreover, charitable and governmental tort immunity may, in some jurisdictions, shield hospitals from actions based upon negligence. Logically, the nonsale view is indefensible. But most courts, seeking to protect hospitals from liability, have viewed public policy as justifying this result. A leading case is *Perlmutter v. Beth David Hospital,* 308 N.Y. 100, 123 N.E.2d 792 (1954). When a few courts began to hold the furnishing of blood to be a sale and to impose liability for breach of warranty, state legislatures responded to hospital pressures by enacting statutes declaring the furnishing of blood not to be a sale and to be free from implied warranties. See Fla. Stat. Ann. § 672.316(5) and (6)(Supp. 1985):

> (5) The procurement, processing, storage, distribution, or use of whole blood, plasma, blood products, and blood derivatives for the purpose of injecting or transfusing the same, or any of them, into the human body for any purpose whatsoever is declared to be the rendering of a service by any person participating therein and does not constitute a sale, whether or not any consideration is given therefor; and the implied warranties of merchantability and fitness for a particular purpose are not applicable as to a defect that cannot be detected or removed by a reasonable use of scientific procedures or techniques.
>
> (6) The procurement, processing, testing, storing, or providing of human tissue and organs for human transplant, by an institution qualified for such purposes, the rendering of a service; and such service does not constitute the sale of goods or products to which implied warranties of merchantability or fitness for a particular purpose are applicable. No implied warranties exist as to defects which cannot be detected, removed, or prevented by reasonable use of available scientific procedures or techniques.

(2) *Serving of Food. Niskey v. Childs Co.,* 135 A. 805 (N.J. Court of Errors and Appeals 1927), stated the pre-Code general rule that serving food to be immediately consumed on the premises was not a sale of goods but a service. Therefore, no warranty could be implied. Cf. U.C.C. § 2-314(1).

(3) *Electricity as "Goods."* Should a sale of electricity by a utility company be characterized as a sale of "goods" so as to bring Article 2 into play in the relationship between the utility

and its customers? Two recent decisions have reached opposite conclusions. Electricity was held to be "goods" in *Hedges v. Public Service Co. of Indiana,* 396 N.E.2d 933 (Ind. App. 1979), but an opposite result was reached in *Navarro County Electric Cooperative Inc., v. Prince,* 640 S.W.2d 399 (Texas 1982).

(4) *Computer Programs as "Goods." Computer Programs as Goods,* 77 Mich. L. Rev. 1149 (1979).

(5) *Money as "Goods."* Does U.C.C. Article 2 apply to the following: A contracts to purchase from B a rare Liberty Head nickel for $750. See U.C.C. § 2-105; cf. §§ 9-105(1)(h), 9-304(1), 9-305.

(6) *Transactions Excluded.* U.C.C. § 2-102 excludes secured transactions from Article 2 and does not impair or repeal statutes regulating sales to consumers, farmers or other specified classes of buyers. See U.C.C. § 9-206(2); Uniform Consumer Credit Code and see, e.g., Utah Code Ann. 4-24-20 (from Utah Livestock Brand and Anti-theft Act):

> Livestock sold at market to be brand inspected — Proceeds of sale may be withheld — Distribution of withheld proceeds — Effect of receipt of proceeds by department
>
> (1) No livestock shall be sold at any livestock market until after they have been brand inspected by the department. Title to purchased livestock shall be furnished the buyer by the livestock market.
>
> (2) Upon notice from the department that a question concerning the ownership of consigned livestock exists, the operator of the livestock market shall withhold the proceeds from the sale of the livestock for a period of 60 days to allow the consignor of the questioned livestock to establish ownership. If the owner or consignor fails within the 60 days to establish ownership to the satisfaction of the department, the proceeds of the sale shall be transmitted to the interested person or to the department as appropriate. Receipt of the proceeds by the department relieves the livestock market from further responsibility for the proceeds.

See *Pugh v. Stratton*, 22 Utah 2d 190, 450 P.2d 463 (1969) (former Utah Code section of this title governed, not Article 2 of the U.C.C.).

[C] Goods or Real Property

Read: U.C.C. §§ 2-105(1), 2-107.

PROBLEM 2.4

Your client owns a small piece of land. Unfortunately, it has a layer of clay just inches below ground level and nothing will grow on it. Fortunately, the Potters Company wants the clay and is willing to purchase it at a high price. Thus, your client's bad fortune has turned out for the good. You are asked to draw up the contract. Will this be governed by the U.C.C.? Does it matter who actually removed the clay as to whether this U.C.C. applies?

PROBLEM 2.5

Your client, August Mellon III, has a large farm. He is a "gentleman farmer" and engages primarily the activities of the "Fox Hunt Society." While some of the family wealth has been used up with these and similar activities, he has the good fortune of having several businesses interested in contracting with him. One is a timber company that wishes to cut some trees in the forested part of the farm. Another is a mining company that wishes to strip-mine a part of his land for coal, but promises to later re-landscape it. The third company wishes to establish some oil pumps at various points on his land, but this will not interfere with the general use of the land. All three are agreeable to not beginning operations until after the fox hunting season. Will these contracts be covered by the U.C.C.? What are the distinctions and rationale? Is it sound or should the code be revised?

NOTES

(1) S owned and operated a sod farm. B entered into an oral contract with S to purchase S's entire crop of sod. B was to remove the sod. Held: a sale of goods within U.C.C. §§ 2-105(1) and 2-107(2). Consequently, the Code Statute of Frauds (§ 2-201) was applicable. See *Barron v. Edwards, 45 Mich. App. 210, 206 N.W 2d 508, 12 U.C.C. Rep. 671(1973).*

(2) A timber lease stated in part: "I, [Lessor], do lease all of my workable timber for turpentine on all lands owned or controlled by me to [Lessee], for a period of five years for a percentage of 30% of each and every dipping . . ." Held: "There is no merit in [Lessee's] contention that the instrument . . . purported to lease or sell only the turpentine itself and thus constituted a contract for the sale of personalty under the Uniform Commercial Code. . . . This writing purported to lease the trees themselves, not merely the product thereof, and therefore was a lease of realty." *Newton v. Allen,* 220 Ga. 681, 141 S.E.2d 417, 2 U.C.C. Rep. 770 (1965).

§ 2.02 Territorial Application of U.C.C. Article 2

Read: U.C.C. §§ 1-105(2), 2A-105, 2A-106; CISG Art. 6.

PROBLEM 2.6

A farmer in Mississippi agrees to sell two thousand head of cattle to a buyer in Tennessee. The buyer is to pick the cattle up at the farm. The farmer-seller and the buyer concluded the transaction on the Delta Queen, a historic paddlewheel steamboat which was docked at Saint Louis, Missouri at that time. Some of the cattle were defective, and the buyer wishes to sue under Tennessee law; the seller asserts that under a special Mississippi Law the U.C.C. warranty of merchant is made inapplicable at this time of transaction. Which law controls?

PROBLEM (Optional-CISG) 2.7

Samson Industries of Michigan entered into a contract to supply logging trucks to the Hudson Bay Timber Company of Canada. There is now a dispute under the contract and a question of whether the U.C.C. enacted in Michigan or the CISG is applicable. In the contract, which had been drafted by Samson, there is a provision that the "law of Michigan" is to be applied. Samson contends that the law of Michigan is the Michigan U.C.C. Hudson Bay contends that the law of Michigan in this setting is the CISG since it is a federal treaty and automatically becomes the law of Michigan for international transactions such as this one. What would be your decision as the judge in this case? Would it make any difference if the case were brought in federal or state court?

CHAPTER 3

THE CONTRACT FOR SALE

§ 3.01 Introduction

Sale of goods law is generally part of the law of contracts. Thus, unless displaced by the U.C.C., the general law of offer and acceptance, consideration, capacity to contract, etc., is applicable. See U.C.C. § 1-103; Restatement, Second, Contracts §§ 9-81(1981). See also, CISG Arts. 14-24.

The law relating to contract formation, consideration and capacity to contract, etc., is given thorough treatment in the first year course in Contracts. This chapter will summarize the Code's effect on this general law.

PROBLEM 3.1

One of your senior partners is on a Law Reform Committee for your jurisdiction. She asks you what you know of contracts and sales law and whether you think there are any major legal doctrines or rules that need changing. While she would like a more detailed response later, she needs a preliminary opinion from you now. She also is interested in whether you have read or thought of any new ideas that merit consideration for law reform.

§ 3.02 Formation of the Contract for Sale

[A] Formation in General

Read: U.C.C. § 2-204.

Read also: U.C.C. § 2A-204; CISG Art. 14, see Art. 55.

Article 2 of the Code, in recognition that commerce depends upon the creation of contracts, has been written to encourage parties to form contracts and to encourage the courts to uphold the creation and existence of contracts whenever the acts of the parties make this rationally supportable. Formality and strictness of interpretation of the parties' words or conduct are minimized. Thus U.C.C. § 2-204 provides that a contract for sale of goods "may be made in any manner sufficient to show agreement." It is not fatal to the existence of a contract that the time of its making is uncertain, or that one or more terms of the agreement have been left open, so long as the intent to contract exists and there is a basis for granting a remedy in case of breach. As to open terms, see U.C.C. §§ 2-305 through 2-311.

It has been proposed that there is a major shift in contract law, much of it surrounding formation:

The new model of contracts consists of five major parts:

I. A contract is primarily a relationship of parties recognized by law. This requires analysis of the setting and the particular relationship in the transaction. Parts of the relationship which are not agreed upon are imposed by law and constitute the "law made" part of the contractual relationship.

II. Agreement is often to a general transaction. Rather than a specific agreement or dovetailing of consensual points, there is only the generalized consent. This spark of generalized consent allows the law to find and enforce a much more thorough and detailed "law made" relationship.

III. A legal framework of reasonableness and fairness is imposed by the law to create the major part of the contract. Principles of trade usage, course of dealing, and course of performance, and Code gap-filling provisions constitute important aspects of contract; good faith, unconscionability and gap-filling terms of reasonableness are also imposed by law. The part drawn from these various sources may be termed "law made," as contrasted to "consensual." In some consumer situations, the contract terms to be used have already been agreed upon previously by a trade association or company negotiating with a consumer representative such as a consumer "ombud" or Ministry of Justice or Attorney General. The making of the contract in this manner before the parties ever actually enter into it, is the "law-made" aspect.

IV. With the generalized consent and the "law made" contract legally enforceable, a contract exists at a very early point in practically all contract situations. In situations where the parties continue to develop the relationship by developing and agreeing on more specific terms, it is in the context of an already existing contractual relationship created by the earlier spark of consent and law made obligations. They are further refining their contract under a legal obligation which is already enforceable.

V. Consideration should no longer be viewed as a major aspect of contract law. Consideration or its substitute can almost always be found, making consideration an over-emphasized part of contract law which should no longer be required. Indeed, the primary question should not be whether there is consideration, but whether there is a relationship which should be recognized.

The new model then is comprised primarily of "relationship" and standards of "reasonableness" and "fairness" which are "law made" and imposed by operation of law. No longer should contracts be viewed as primarily consensual and agreement on specific terms is not necessary. Consideration should no longer be a part of contract law.[1]

[B] Form Contracts Generally

Consider the following new approach:

PROPOSED "REALITY THEORY"

The approach advocated by this article that "dickered upon" or actually agreed upon terms constitute the contract is relatively simple; it is also consistent with true contract theory and with reality and fairness as well. This approach may be called the "Reality Theory" because it recognizes realities without imposing legal fiction. This theory could also be given a more detailed title of the "Only Agreed Upon Terms are Part of the Contract."

---

[1] King, *Death of Contracts, Part One*, 7 J. Con. L. 256 (1994).

Under the proposed theory, only those terms which have been specifically agreed upon by the seller and the buyer are part of the contract. Where there has been an exchange of purchase orders and acknowledgment forms, it is only those particular terms the parties have agreed upon that become part of that contract. This is generally the agreement on the price, the types of goods, and the time and place of delivery. The numerous fine print clauses on the back of the order form, acknowledgment form, or invoice of the seller are simply not part of the contract. If it is a printed form contract signed by both parties, the same approach is taken. It is those specifically negotiated and agreed upon terms that are part of the contract. This is consistent with Karl Llewellyn's analysis of "dickered" terms of a contract. In reality, the only contract between the parties is that dickered upon or the actually agreed upon terms. Thus, if the parties have discussed and negotiated the price of the goods, then this is an agreed term which is part of the contract. If they have discussed delivery of the goods, this, too, is an agreed upon term. All of the terms in the printed form contract which have not been discussed are not a part of the contract.

Thus, the numerous additional terms found in the mass of fine print which was unread and undiscussed by the parties have no legal effect. The large body of printed form contract clauses fails to have any legal significance; instead they simply stand as statements of what the party using them would desire or an initial position which it would like to have, but nothing more. This theory is one which is in line with reality. It is entirely consistent with contract theory which requires mutual assent to the terms of the contracts. They are recognized as making the contract from a meeting of the wills or a meeting of the minds, and clauses not agreed upon are simply not part of the contract. Importantly, there is a contract formed by this meeting of minds in the decision to enter into the general transaction. This also is consistent with the Uniform Commercial Code emphasis on viewing the contract as less of an "entity" or "thing," and instead looking to the relationship of the parties and the overall setting.

It may be asked: If the contract terms in the printed form contract are meaningless and unenforceable by the courts, how will a number of issues covered by them be decided? The answer is that the law with its emphasis on finding a contract from the relationship of the parties and the overall surrounding circumstances already provides for such gaps to be filled in. The Uniform Commercial Code in supporting more general agreements allows a number of terms that are missing to be filled in by the courts. It allows for this in regard to contract formation, contract formalities, contract content, contract performance, and contract remedies. There is a framework of rights or imposition of a legal status upon the parties.

If there is a trade usage which is reasonable and followed by different merchants and known to both, then that may become part of the contract. In the case of merchant transactions, this may be an important gap filler. If the transaction is between a merchant and a consumer, the consumer is generally unaware of trade usages and would not be bound. Further, he is not a member of that trade or engaged in the creation and use of such practices and should not be bound to them. Even if he were, the trade usage would still have to be in good faith and not unconscionable, and would have to conform to consumer protection laws.

The main terms not agreed upon will be filled in by the courts by looking to the Uniform Commercial Code "gap filler terms" found in Part 3 of Article 2. These relate to situations where the parties have not agreed upon things such as price, delivery, payment, and quality of goods, and warranty. These have been discussed in other books and articles at more length.

King, *Standard Form Contracts: A New Perspective*, 1991 Comm. L. Annual 137, 156-8.

[C] Firm Offers

Read: U.C.C. § 2-205.

Read also: U.C.C. § 2A-205; CISG Arts. 15-17.

When an offer is received by the offeree, it is advantageous to the offeree to know how long the offer will be kept open to afford him time in which to decide whether to accept. Where the offer contemplates a complex contract, the offeree may be required to spend much time and effort in determining whether to accept. Prior to the Code, an offer once made might be freely withdrawn by the offeror at any time prior to acceptance unless made irrevocable by a collateral agreement supported by consideration. Rarely, exceptions might also be made through application of the doctrine of promissory estoppel.

U.C.C. § 2-205 modifies prior law to permit a merchant, by means of a signed writing, to make an offer irrevocable, without consideration, for a period of up to three months. This section is intended to relieve the parties of the necessity of forming a collateral contract to keep the offer open. Note that U.C.C. § 2-205 does not prevent the parties from entering into an agreement, supported by consideration, to keep the offer open, and that if they do so, they may agree that the offer remains open for a period of more than three months.

[D] Construing the Offer: Bilateral or Unilateral Contract?

Read: U.C.C. § 2-206.

Read also: U.C.C. § 2A-206(2); CISG Art. 18(3).

The offeree must determine what action upon his part will constitute an acceptance. If the offer by its terms contemplates a bilateral contract, then the offeree will accept by making a promise, in writing or orally. If a unilateral contract is contemplated, then acceptance is through performance of the requested act. The offeree may experience difficulty in ascertaining whether a particular offer contemplates a bilateral contract or a unilateral one. Under pre-Code law, an inappropriate response by the offeree might well result in a failure to form any contract. Code § 2-206 permits acceptance to be made "in any manner and by any medium reasonable in the circumstances" unless the offer unambiguously indicates otherwise; and an order or offer for goods for prompt or current shipment may be accepted either by a promise to ship or by shipment. Note that U.C.C. § 2-206(1)(b) is not without possible complication, however, in that the offeree may accept by the act of shipping non-conforming goods, which results in the seeming anomaly that the very act of acceptance which creates the contract also constitutes a breach of the contract.

[E] Additional Terms in Acceptance or Confirmation

Read: U.C.C. § 2-207.

Read also: CISG Art. 19.

PROBLEM 3.2

Your firm has a number of clients who are sellers and who send their own acknowledgment forms with their own terms in response to any order received. You have been asked for a general position memorandum in regard to the validity of these for contract formation and for effectiveness of special terms contained only in the acknowledgment form. You have been asked to discuss this in light of:

1. current law
2. existing and proposed theories
3. proposed revision to U.C.C. § 2-207

Basic contract law holds that the acceptance must mirror the offer exactly; if the purported acceptance varies in any respect from the offer, then it is not an acceptance, but a counter-offer. In recognition that modern commercial contracts are customarily created through the use of printed forms, with one form often coming from the offeror and a different form coming from the offeree, with the result that frequently there is some disparity in the forms, Code § 2-207(1) provides that a "definite and seasonable expression of acceptance or a written confirmation" operates as an acceptance and a contract is formed, even if it contains terms different from or in addition to those in the offer. U.C.C. § 2-207(2) provides rules for how these additional terms are to be treated; they are "proposals for additions to the contract" and as between merchants may become a part of the contract itself if they do not materially alter the contract and no objection is made by the offeror within a reasonable time. U.C.C. § 2-207(3) seeks to preserve even those exchanges of writings which do not establish a contract, so long as the parties' conduct evidences a belief that they have a contract.

In a report for the Permanent Editorial Board on proposed amendments to Article 2 of the U.C.C., recommendations relating to U.C.C. § 2-207 "Battle of the Forms" were summarized as follows:

> Although the Study Group recommends that § 2-207 be revised, not all agree [on] the form of the revision . . . . For some, that proposed revision is too elaborate and complex. Most of the Study Group favor what might be called a "lean and mean" revision that focuses upon the key issue, under what circumstances should standard form terms which materially alter the standard terms (or "default" rules) of Article 2 be included in the agreement of the parties?[2]

PEB Study Group: *Uniform Commercial Code, Article 2 Executive Summary*, 46 Bus. Law. 1869, 1878-9 (1991) (referred to subsequently as "PEB Study Group Report").

[F] The Reality of the "Battle of the Forms"[3]

The "battle of the forms" has long received the attention of legal commentators and practitioners. Frequently an order form sent by one company ordering goods will contain a number of fine print clauses. Commonly, this is answered by an acknowledgment, confirming receipt of the order and notification that the goods will be sent, but also containing numerous other printed terms. Quite often the printed terms on the two forms, each drafted by respected attorneys with different interests in mind and seeking to gain the greatest advantage for their clients, will conflict with each other. Karl Llewellyn has noted that in such contracts the attorneys often go much further than the businessmen in seeking to gain a one-sided advantage.

---

[2] Study Group member Robert Weeks articulates the "lean and mean" approach to include in the contract "only those provisions as to which the writings agree, leaving the other terms of the contracts to be determined by the rules of Article 2, including course of business, usage of trade and course of performance." An alternate approach is to repeal § 2-207 and deal with the problem of standard forms in other provisions of Article 2, as they become relevant. Comments of Professor John Honnold, ALI Sales Consultants Meeting, Philadelphia, Pa., Nov. 16, 1990. The Study Group reserved judgment on Professor Honnold's suggestion.

[3] Excerpt from King, *New Perspective on Standard Form Contracts: A Subject Revisited,* Commercial Law Annual pp 91,92 (1993).

Each attorney seeks to have his form control the other. This is done through the "grand defensive" clause and the "grand offensive" clause. The "grand defensive" clause simply states that all the terms mentioned in the order form shall control. The "grand offensive" term in the other answering form simply states that all of its terms shall be controlling. In using the "grand offensive" and the "grand defensive" clauses, each seeks to control the situation.

In terms of the Code, if there is no such clause then the additional term becomes part of the contract provided it is not a material one or is not one objected to subsequently by the other party. In terms of forms which use the "grand defensive" and "grand offensive" clauses, it is the solution of the Code to cancel out each of the extra boilerplate and the terms that have not been agreed upon are viewed as being conditional and are "knocked out" by the other's objecting clause. This is pointed out in the comments.

Thus the Code already has accomplished in a large number of cases, though indirectly, the solution proposed by the Reality Theory. However, the Code does this through an artificial deeming of these conflicting terms to be objections to each other's terms. The Reality Theory is much more direct and simple. It views these terms as never having been agreed upon and hence never part of the contract. In the large number of transactions where the attorneys are alert in using such offensive and defensive clauses, the Reality Theory is already working in effect. It is primarily in those cases where one side is not represented by an attorney who is clever enough to use such terms that the results would differ.

[G] Sale by Auction

Read: U.C.C. § 2-328.

Read also: CISG Art. 2(b).

A sale by auction is complete when the auctioneer so announces by the fall of the hammer. Such a sale is with reserve unless the goods are explicitly put up without reserve. (In an action with reserve, the auctioneer may withdraw the goods at any time until he announces completion of the sale.) U.C.C. § 2-326(1),(2).

[H] Home Solicitation Sale

Federal Regulations 16 CFR Part 429 (Cooling Off Period for Door-to-Door Sales) alter the traditional contract concepts of offer, acceptance and repudiation by affording buyers in door-to-door consumer credit sales a limited right to cancel a sale during a cooling-off period ending midnight of the third business day after the date of the transaction. See also Uniform Consumer Credit Code §§ 2.501 *et seq.* (1968), 3.501 *et seq.* (1974).

§ 3.03 Consideration

Read: U.C.C. §§ 2-106(1), 2-304(1), 2-205, 2-209; see § 2-203.

Read also: U.C.C. §§ 2A-103(l)(j), 2A-205, 2A-208, see § 2A-203; CISG Arts. 1(1), 30, 53.

The law relating to consideration as a necessary element of a contract generally receives thorough treatment in the first-year Contracts course. Under the Sales article of the Uniform Commercial Code consideration remains an essential element of a contract for sale. This is made explicit in U.C.C. § 2-106(1): "A 'sale' consists in the passing of title from the seller to the buyer for a price." And U.C.C. § 2-304(1)provides "The price can be made payable in money or otherwise."

The Code has abolished the need for consideration in two areas: firm offers (U.C.C. § 2-205) and modification of contract (U.C.C. § 2-209). Section 2-205 states that a signed written offer by a merchant to buy or sell goods which gives assurance that it will be held open is not revocable for lack of consideration, during the time stated or, if no time is stated, for a reasonable time.

Section 2-209(1) provides that a contract for the sale of goods may be modified by agreement without the necessity of consideration being given. This section represents, then, a departure from the common law of contracts, which requires consideration for a modification to be binding. The section places two limitations upon the power to modify by agreement: under U.C.C. § 2-209(2), if the original agreement was in writing and signed and excluded modification or rescission of the contract except by another signed writing, the contract may be modified or rescinded only by such a signed writing; and under U.C.C. § 2-209(3), if the contract as modified is within the Statute of Frauds, then modification must be accomplished in accordance with the requirements of U.C.C. § 2-201.

Further, U.C.C. § 2-203 abolishes any special effect which affixing a seal to a writing evidencing a sales contract may have had; a seal no longer makes a contract for sale binding without consideration.

PROBLEM 3.3

One of the senior professors has proposed a conference of law professors and practitioners to discuss "Should the requirement of consideration be abolished in regard to Sales Contracts?" He shows you an excerpt from a letter set forth below that he recently received from another professor who is advocating that the doctrine of consideration be abolished. He has asked you as a young professor what arguments you would make on both sides of this issue? Also what do you think in terms of this possible change?

> It may well be that consideration should be removed from the law as a contract requirement. As pointed out, it has been eroded away by case law, substitute reliance, and the Code. In business transactions it is nearly always present, serves no usefulness, and has almost no impact on the law generally. Outside of the contracts classroom where it may be given a few weeks of attention, consideration is indeed academic!
>
> Interestingly, in the Convention for the International Sale of Goods, there is no requirement of consideration for the formation of a contract. This is not a matter of validity and therefore is not left to domestic law. It should be remembered that to the extent that the Convention is now part of United States law there already has been the abolition of consideration! While this development has been given little or no attention, it may affect a large number of contracts. It means that already the United States has moved significantly in ending consideration as a contractual requirement. It might be said that, combined with the dilution previously mentioned, consideration has realistically been buried already, even though memories of it remain.
>
> It does not currently appear that any major change will be made in the revised Article 2 on Sales in the Code. While this writer has advocated that a general section be added which would abolish the requirement of consideration, it is quite possible that the longstanding affinity of the American legal profession for the doctrine of consideration is too great. Also, with the present Code exceptions already dispensing with it in a number of situations discussed, it may be felt that there is no need to abolish it. A counter-argument is that this would make its

abolition even easier, would do away with its occasional mischiefs, and make the Uniform Commercial Code more consistent with the International Sale of Goods Convention.

King, *Reshaping Contract Theory and Law: Death of Contracts II Part Two: Ending Consideration and Beginning New Performance and Remedies*, 8 J. of Contracts Law 16 (1995).

§ 3.04 Statute of Frauds

Read: U.C.C. §§ 2-201, 2-209(3), 2-326(4), 8-319; see §§ 9-203, 1-206.

Read also: U.C.C. § 2A-201; CISG Arts. 11-13, see Arts. 29, 96.

Background

In 1671, in Old Marston, Oxfordshire, England, defendant Egbert was sued by plaintiff John over an alleged oral promise by Egbert to sell to John a fighting cock named Fiste. John's friend, Harold, claimed he overheard the "deal" and by that dubious means John won, though in fact there apparently was no deal. In 1676, courts did not allow parties to a lawsuit to testify, so Egbert could not testify to rebut Harold's story. Compounding the problem was the fact that courts then could not throw out jury verdicts manifestly contrary to the evidence. So, in response to the plight of the Egberts of this world and to the recurring mischief of the Johns, as well as to combat possible "fraude and perjurie" by the Harolds, Parliament passed in 1677 a "statute of frauds" which required that certain contracts for the sale of goods be in writing to be enforceable.[4]

PROBLEM 3.4

Also Arte, a famous painter, orally agreed to appear on a television fund-raising program for the non-profit Friends of History Society and paint, before the camera, a picture of the Saint Louis Gateway Arch. Arte was then to donate the painting to the Society to be sold to raise funds. The Society alleges that defendant estimated the picture would be worth $25,000. Some pre-program parties and interviews with Arte were thrown by the Society, and considerable newspaper publicity concerning the coming event ensued. When Arte refused at the last moment to appear, the program was canceled and suit was brought by the Society. Among other things, Arte argues that this contract was for a sale of goods in excess of $500 and was, therefore, within the Statute of Frauds (U.C.C. § 2-201). Your client is the Historical Society. What are your possible arguments? What do you thinks Arte's counsel will argue? Who do you think will win? Why?

NOTES AND QUESTIONS

(1) *Writing Signed by Defendant.* The following is an example of a minimal form of contract for sale sufficient to satisfy U.C.C. § 2-201(1) of the Statute of Frauds. It is from 12 West's Legal Forms at § 4.1-Form 1 (2d ed. 1985) and states:[5]

[4] From J. White & R. Summers, Handbook of the Law.

Buyer and seller hereby contract for the sale of 10,000 gallons of 100 octane gasoline.

[Signed]______Buyer

[Signed]______Seller

The Comment to the form observes:

> Where a writing is required to satisfy the statute of frauds, the writing must (1) identify the parties, (2) indicate that a contract for sale was made, (3) describe the goods which are the subject of the sale, (4) specify the quantity of goods involved and (5) be signed by the party against whom enforcement is sought. The writing in § 4. 1-Form 1 meets these minimal requirements.
>
> Obviously a number of important contract terms are not spelled out in this writing (§ 4. 1-Form 1) but this does not matter for purposes of satisfying the statute of frauds. Once the statute of frauds has been satisfied, a court can enforce the contract because the terms which are left open by the writing can be supplied by parol evidence of agreement between the parties on such terms (U.C.C. § 2-202) or if not agreed upon, the provisions of the Code will fill out the necessary additional terms of the contract. (U.C.C. § 2-204(3)). For example, if the price was not agreed upon by the parties, the price of gasoline will be a reasonable price at the time for delivery (U.C.C. § 2-305). Similarly, the time for delivery of the gasoline will be within a reasonable time after contracting (U.C.C. § 2-309). The place for delivery of the gasoline will be the seller's place of business (U.C.C. § 2-308). The gasoline must be tendered in a single delivery (U.C.C. § 2-307). Payment is due at the time and place at which buyer receives the gasoline (U.C.C. § 2-310).

Would the following language on a scrap of paper satisfy the statute? "Sold 10,000 gal. J.D. (initialed)."

(2) *Writing in Confirmation of Future Agreement. Martco, Inc. v. Doran Chevrolet, Inc.,* 632 S.W. 2d 927, 33 U.C.C. Rep. 1619 at 1620-21 (Texas 1982) states:

> The writing in question is on Doran Chevrolet stationery and is signed by Craig Arledge, apparently a sales agent for Doran. The memo is entitled: "Price Worksheet" and indicates that it is a "Competitive Equalization Request." It includes a quantity term (24), but indicates that it is for bid purposes: the only date on the memo is labeled "Bid Opening Date." The affidavit of Martco's own Vice-President confirms that this writing is not in confirmation of the contract but, in fact, formed the basis on which he later claims to have placed an order for the truck chassis. The writing clearly contemplates a contract to be made in the future. The facts and circumstances surrounding these events merely confirm that the writing is not a confirmation of a pre-existing agreement, but constitutes an offer for an agreement that was not entered into until much later, if at all. Our inquiry is whether such a writing will satisfy the statute of frauds. [The Court recites U.C.C. § 2-201(1).] The statute requires that the writing be sufficient to indicate that a contract has been made. Although we are directed to no Texas case, authorities in other jurisdictions uniformly interpret this phrase to disqualify writings which contain "futuristic" language as not confirmatory of a contract already in existence.

(3) *Tape Recording as Writing. Ellis Canning Co. v. Bernstein,* 348 F. Supp. 1212, 11 U.C.C. Rep. 443 at 453-4 (D. Col. 1972) states:

> We hold that when the parties agreed to the tape recording of the oral agreement, that tape recording satisfies the requirements of 63 CRS 155-8-319. This conclusion we reach by taking

into account the fact that "the purpose of the statute is to prevent fraud and perjury in the enforcement of obligations depending for their evidence on the unassisted memory of witnesses," 37 CJS Statute of Frauds, § 1, p 513. Moreover,'63 CRS 155-1-201, the definition section of the U.C.C. says:

> (46) "Written" or "writing" includes printing, typewriting, or any other intentional reduction to tangible form.

We think and we hold that when the parties to an oral contract agree that the oral contract shall be tape recorded, the contract is "reduced to tangible form" when it is placed on the tape. We do not overlook the requirement for signature contained in the statute, but the clear purpose of this is to require identification of the contracting party, and where, as here, the identity of the oral contractors is established, and, in fact, admitted, the tape itself is enough. So, we hold that even if the signed correspondence were insufficient to get around the statute [which it isn't], the tape recording of the oral contract would be a "reduction to tangible form" under the provisions of the U.C.C. Probably the opposite result would be required under historical statutes of frauds which do not contain the tangible form language of this somewhat unusual definition of the word "written." However, under this statute, we think that the tape recorded agreement meets its requirements.

Contra, see *Roos and Aloi,* 487 N.Y.S.2d 637 (1985) (Tape recording of an oral agreement for the sale of stock did not constitute a "writing" within the meaning of § 8-319 Statute of Frauds). Cf. U.C.C. §§ 2-201, 8-319, see § 8-113 (1994).

(4) The definitional section of the U.C.C. also sets the general standard for what mailrooms "should do":

> An organization exercised due diligence if it maintains reasonable routines for communicating significant information to the person conducting the transaction and there is reasonable compliance with the routines.

U.C.C. §1-201(27). In one case, *Thomson Printing Machinery Co. v. B.F. Goodrich Co.*, 714 F.2d 744 (7th Cir. 1983), the question arose as to whether a letter sent to the company generally containing a purchase order and check, without specifying any particular company official's name, was sufficient notice. The court noted: One cannot say that Goodrich's mailroom procedures were reasonable as a matter of law: if Goodrich had exercised due diligence in handling Thomson Printing's purchase order and check, these items would have reasonably promptly come to Ingram Meyers' attention. First, the purchase order on its face should have alerted the mailroom that the documents referred to a purchase of used printing equipment. Since Goodrich had only one surplus machinery department, the documents' "home" should not have been difficult to find. Second, even if the mailroom would have had difficulty in immediately identifying the kind of transaction involved, the purchase order had Tomson Printing's phone number printed on it and we think a "reasonable routine" in these particular circumstances would have involved at some point in the process a simple phone call to Thomson Printing. Thus, we think Goodrich's mailroom mishandled the confirmatory writings. This failure should not permit Goodrich to escape liability by pleading nonreceipt. See Williston on Sales, supra, §14-8 at 284-85.

We note that the jury verdict for Thomson Printing indicates that the jury found as a fact that the contract had in fact been made and that the Statute of Frauds had been satisfied. Also, Goodrich acknowledges those facts about the handling of the purchase order which we regard as determinative of the "merchants" exception question. We think that there is ample evidence to support the jury findings both of the existence of the contract and of the satisfaction of the Statute.

The district court, in holding as a matter of law that the circumstances failed to satisfy the Statute of Frauds, was impressed by James Thomson's dereliction in failing to specifically direct the purchase order and check to the attention of Ingram Meyers or the surplus equipment department. We agree that Thomson erred in this respect, but, for the reasons we have suggested. Goodrich was at least equally derelict in failing to find a "home" for the well-identified documents. Goodrich argues that in the "vast majority" of cases it can identify checks within a week without contacting an outside party; in the instant case, therefore, if Goodrich correctly states its experience under its procedures, it should presumably have checked with Thomson Printing promptly after the time it normally identified checks by other means—in this case, by its own calculation, a week at most. Under the particular circumstances of this case, we therefore think it inappropriate to set aside a jury verdict on Statute of Frauds grounds.

(5) U.C.C. Article 2A, Leases, has a Statute of Frauds section modeled on § 2-201. The Draft substitutes $1,000 for $500 and does not adopt the "merchant's exception" of § 2-201(2). See § 2A-201.

(6) *Admissions.* In *Garrison v. Piatt*, 113 Ga. App. 74, 147 S.E.2d 374 (1966), the court held that a general demurrer (a motion to dismiss for failure to state a cause of action) could not be sustained on the grounds that the alleged sales contract for a house trailer for a price in excess of $500 was within the Statute of Frauds.

Prior to enactment of U.C.C. § 2-201(3)(b), a defendant could both admit the contract and simultaneously insist on the benefit of the Statute of Frauds. The U.C.C., however, permits enforcement of the contract if the defendant admits it at trial.

A general demurrer must admit, for the purposes of the demurrer only, that all facts in the petition are true—including the existence of the contract. Dismissal at this stage would deprive plaintiff of the opportunity to have the defendant admit the contract otherwise during the course of the trial.

Also, R. Henson, The Law of Sales 6 (1985) observes, "An admission in testimony, even if involuntary, that involves facts which establish the existence of a contract as a matter of law should satisfy the requirements of the statute. If the existence of a contract is denied in testimony and is not otherwise admitted, then it would appear that the statute is not complied with, even though the judge does not find the testimony credible. This gives even an unconvincing liar a break. Query whether the exception for an 'or otherwise in court' admission should not be found in such a case."

(7) *Partial Performance.* In *Williamson v. Martz,* 29 Northumb. L.J. 32 Pa. D. & C.2d 33 (Pa. Court of Common Pleas 1956), defendant paid $100 down on an oral contract for $1,600 for two 200-gallon vats to be manufactured by plaintiff. When finished, defendant refused to accept delivery or make further payments. Plaintiff then sold the vats for $800 and sued for the balance. The court rejected plaintiff's argument that payment of the $100 took the contract out of the Statute of Frauds and held that the complaint failed to state a cause of action since the Statute of Frauds was apparent on the face of the petition. See U.C.C. § 2-201(3)(c).

R. Henson, The Law of Sales 7 (1985), notes that:

> [T]here is a problem with partial payments made by buyers and accepted by sellers when the goods have not been delivered. If the quantity of goods allegedly covered by the oral contract

can be apportioned so that the goods paid for can be delivered, that would not be difficult case. If the down payment is small and the item or items allegedly covered rather expensive, the problem is acute. One solution is to say that an enforceable contract results if the down payment is less than the cost of any one item. Another solution is to enforce the contract at least to the extent of one unit, which may be all that the contract involves as in the case of such goods as automobiles. The statutory language is reasonably susceptible to either reading.

(8) *Article 2 Proposed Revisions.* Section 2-201. No Formal Requirements. A contract or modification *of a contract* under this Article is enforceable *whether* or not there is a writing signed or *record* authenticated by a party against whom enforcement is sought, even if the contract or modification is *not* capable of performance within one year of its making.

Reporter's Notes — Revised Section 2-201 was approved by the Drafting Committee on March 6, 1993.

PROBLEM 3.5

Your senior partner has just received a copy of the Proposed Article 2 revision. It eliminates the Statute of Frauds! He asks you whether as a member of the American Law Institute he should support or oppose this and reasons therefore. What is your advice?

PROBLEM 3.6

One of your colleagues who is also a young professor has asked you whether you would support her position that the parol evidence rule is generally ineffective because of the many caselaw doctrines used to get around it, and the U.C.C. allowance for trade usage and consistent additional terms, and the cases where courts allow it to show that a word or term which appears to mean one thing can really mean another when either trade usage or course of dealing are used. She also believes that the rule often is asserted so as to prevent companies from being responsible for the oral contemporaneous statements of their own salespersons! She has asked for your opinion on these matters. She also wonders how she might go about trying to reform the law in this regard.

NOTES

(1) See *Omac, Inc. v. Southwestern Machine & Tool Works, Inc.*, Georgia Court of Appeals 189 Ga. App. 39, 374 S.E.2d 829 (1988):

BENHAM, J. Appellant and appellee entered into an agreement whereby appellee manufactured and sold to OMAC certain specified parts made from materials supplied by OMAC. Appellee filed suit to recover monies owed it, and appellant counterclaimed. A jury returned a verdict in favor of appellee, and appellant appeals, contending the trial court erred in charging the jury on the principles espoused in OCGA §§ 11-601; 11-602; and 11-2-606.

The contested instructions are part of the Sales Article of the Uniform Commercial Code which appellant contends is inapplicable because there was no sale involved. "A 'sale' consists in the passing of title from the seller to the buyer for a price." OCGA §11-2-106(1). "Article 2 of the Uniform Commercial Code is expressly limited to transactions involving the sale of goods. [OCGA §11-2-102][A] 'contract for services and labor with an incidental furnishing of equipment and materials' is not a transaction involving 'the sale of goods' and is not controlled by the [U.C.C.]. [Cits.]" *W.B. Anderson Feed & C. Co. v. Ga. Gas Distrib.*, 164

Ga. App. 96 [34 U.C.C. Rep Serv 1509] (296 S.E.2d 395) (1982). The record does not contain a contract outlining the parties' duties and responsibilities, but appellee certified that the work performed by it was done on materials supplied by appellant and conformed to blueprints and revisions. The prices quoted (and presumably charged) by appellee for its work were based upon appellant's supplying the materials. In essence, appellee agreed to perform a service, making appellant's material into the parts appellant needed. Because it used materials supplied by appellant, appellee's prices reflected only the labor cost of making the parts appellant ordered. Inasmuch as appellee sold a service and not goods to appellant, the U.C.C. was inapplicable and the trial court erred in giving the charges excepted to.

Judgment reversed. McMurray, P.J., and Pope, J., concur.

(2) *King Industries, Inc. v. Worlco Data Systems, Inc.,* United States District Court, ED Va. 736 F Supp 114 (1989).

At oral argument, plaintiff's counsel stated that plaintiff's business is in the construction trade, as opposed to retail carpet sales, and that plaintiff relied upon the representations of a Worlco sales agent who stated that the "builder's package" software was compatible with plaintiff's needs; that is, the sale of carpeting and floor covering in the construction trade. Plaintiff's counsel further stated that plaintiff has been unable to use the computer system because it does not comport with plaintiff's business needs.

Defendants Worlco and Copelco argue that plaintiff's claim for breach of express and implied warranties fails as a matter of law because of the disclaimer clauses in both agreements. The disclaimer in the Worlco contract is on the front page of that agreement above the signature line. The disclaimer, in capital letters, states:

> WDS MAKES NO WARRANTY OF ANY KIND, EXPRESS OR IMPLIED, INCLUDING WITHOUT LIMITATION WARRANTIES OF MERCHANTABILITY OR FITNESS FOR A PARTICULAR PURPOSE.

In *Hoover Universal, Inc. v. Brockway Imco, Inc.,* 809 F.2d 1039 [3 U.C.C. Rep. Serv. 2d 46] (4th Cir.1987), the Fourth Circuit addressed the effect of a merger clause on the admissibility of extrinsic evidence. In *Hoover,* the buyer of industrial equipment alleged that the seller had misrepresented the cavitation capacity of its equipment. *Hoover,* 809 F.2d at 1041. The misrepresentation was contained in a handout which summarized certain technical data in connection with the equipment. *Id.* The handout had been given to plaintiff's representatives prior to entering the contract. *Id.* The plaintiff alleged in its complaint that the handout created an express warranty. *Id.*

The Fourth Circuit began its analysis by noting that the written contract between the parties contained an enforceable disclaimer clause disclaiming warranties of merchantability, condition or fitness for a particular purpose. *Id.* at 1041-42. The contract also contained a well-drafted merger clause. *Id.* at 1043. The court also noted that the cavitation capacity of the seller's equipment was not mentioned in the final written contract between the parties. *Id.* at 1041. The Fourth Circuit found that the district court did not commit error in finding that the contract between buyer and seller was the "complete and exclusive statement" of their agreement. Accordingly, the Fourth Circuit held that because of the detailed nature of the contract, including the well-drafted merger clause, the Virginia parol evidence rule precluded the admission of the handout in an effort to establish an express warranty.

An effectively worded merger clause can have the same effect as a disclaimer. J. White & R. Summers, Uniform Commercial Code, §12-4 (3d ed. 1988). The *Worlco* contract contains a merger or integration clause, in capital letters above the signature line, which provides:

ALL TERMS AND CONDITIONS WRITTEN ON THE REVERSE SIDE HEREOF AND ON THE FACE HEREOF, INCLUDING SCHEDULE A HERETO, CONSTITUTE THE COMPLETE AND BINDING CONTRACT WHEN ACCEPTED BY WDS. THIS ORDER EXPRESSLY LIMITS ACCEPTANCE TO SUCH TERMS AND CONDITIONS PROPOSED BY THE BUYER ARE REJECTED.

Plaintiff argues that despite the integration clause, the contact is not complete because it contains no description of the "builder's package" and therefore evidence of consistent additional discussions is admissible.

The court finds, however, that the parol evidence rule precludes the admission of oral statements which contradict the terms of a written disclaimer. *Hill v. BASF Wyandotte Corp.*, 696 F.2d 287, 291 [35 U.C.C. Rep Serv 91] (4th Cir. 1982). In *Hill*, a farmer brought suit for breach of warranty and misrepresentation against the manufacturer of an agricultural herbicide. The plaintiff farmer alleged that a sales agent for defendant manufacturer had made false oral representations upon which plaintiff relied to his detriment. Each of the cans of herbicide purchased by plaintiff contained a disclaimer of express and implied warranties. The Fourth Circuit found that the oral representations made by defendant's sales agent were not admissible to vary the terms of sale and warranty on the product label. Additionally, most courts hold that when a disclaimer of warranties is contained in an integrated agreement, parol warranties are "contradictory" within the meaning of parol evidence rule and are therefore inadmissible. J. White & R. Summers, Uniform Commercial Code, § 12-4 n.2 (3d ed. 1988).

Accordingly, this court finds that even if the oral representations made by Worlco's representative became the "basis of the bargain" and therefore constituted an express warranty, those oral statements would not be admissible to contradict or vary the disclaimer of express warranties clause contained in the integrated agreement between Worlco and plaintiff. This parol evidence would be admissible, however, in a properly pleaded fraud in the inducement claim. See, *George Robberecht Seafood, Inc. v. Maitland Bros. Co.*, 220 Va. 109, 255 S.E.2d 682, 683 [26 U.C.C. Rep Serv 669] (1979).

§ 3.05 Terms, Construction and Interpretation of the Contract for Sale

Read: U.C.C. § 1-201(3),(11),(42); §§ 2-202, 1-205, 2-208.

Read also: U.C.C. §§ 2A-103(1)(k) and (1), 2A-202, 1-205, 2A-207; CISG Arts. 8 and 9.

Contracts for sale of goods may contain a variety of terms. U.C.C. § 1-201(3),(11),(42); see § 2-106(1). More common terms relate to description, quantity, quality, price, payment, delivery, inspection, warranties, remedies, risk of loss, circumstances excusing performance, etc.

Please study the following "General Contract for Sale of Goods" and "Check List of Terms to be Included in Contracts for the Sale of Goods."

General Contract for Sale of Goods[6]

[Name of seller], of [address], agrees to sell and [name of buyer], of [address], agrees to buy ______ tons of [describe or identify goods] at $ ________ per ton to be delivered by [name of seller] to [name of buyer] at [address] on or before [date]. In consideration of the premises and of the mutual benefits to each party, it is further agreed as follows:

1. *Description.* The goods subject of this sale and which the seller shall deliver to the buyer and for which the buyer shall pay shall conform to the following specifications:

[here list specifications]

2. *Warranty.* The seller warrants that the goods shall meet the specifications described herein. The foregoing warranty is exclusive, and is in lieu of all other warranties, whether written, oral or implied, including the warranty of merchantability and the warranty of fitness for a particular purpose.

3. *Delivery.* Delivery shall be on or before [date] and shall be to buyer at the seller's place of business. Seller agrees to furnish the facilities and at his cost to load the goods on trucks furnished by the buyer.

4. *Packaging.* Buyer shall give the seller instructions for the packaging of the goods not less than 48 hours prior to the date of delivery, and the reasonable cost of such packaging shall be charged to the buyer.

5. *Title.* Title shall remain with the seller until delivery and actual receipt thereof by the buyer.

6. *Risk of loss.* Identification shall take place on the packaging of the goods, and the risk of loss shall pass on such identification.

7. *Price and time of payment.* The price of the goods shall be $ ____ per ton, and shall be paid at the time of delivery and at the place of delivery in bank draft or cashier's check or certified check.

8. *Inspection.* Inspection shall be made by the buyer at the time and place of delivery.

9. *Claims.* Buyer's failure to give notice of any claim within ______ days from the date of delivery shall constitute an unqualified acceptance of the goods and a waiver by the buyer of all claims with respect thereto.

10. *Remedies.* Buyer's exclusive remedy and seller's limit of liability for any and all losses or damages resulting from defective goods or from any other cause shall be for the purchase price of the particular delivery with respect to which losses or damages are claimed plus any transportation charges actually paid by the buyer.

11. *Assignment and delegation.* Buyer may not assign its rights or delegate its performance hereunder without the prior written consent of the seller, and any attempted assignment or delegation without such consent shall be void.

12. *Choice of law.* This contract is to be construed according to the laws of, and under the Uniform Commercial Code as adopted by, the State of ______.

13. *Integration of contract.* This document constitutes the full understanding of the parties, and no terms, conditions, under standings or agreement purporting to modify or vary the terms

[6] Adapted from 12 West's Legal Forms § 17.2-Form 8 (2d ed. 1985); copyright © West Publishing Company, reprinted with permission.

of this document shall be binding unless hereafter made in writing and signed by the party to be bound.

Signed and sealed in triplicate this ________ day of ________, 19______

Buyer Seller

Check List of Terms to Be Included in Contracts for the Sale of Goods[7]

Each contract must be tailored to suit the particular transaction but the following check list sets forth terms or items which may be necessary or useful.

a. Description of the parties (§§ 2-103, 2-104).

b. Description of the goods.

   (1) Quantity (§ 2-201).

   (2) Quality (§§ 2-313, 2-314, 2-315).

   (3) Manner of selection (§§ 2-311(2), 2-501).

c. Warranties.

   (1) Title (§ 2-312).

   (2) Quality (§§ 2-313, 2-314, 2-315).

   (3) Disclaimer of warranties (§ 2-316).

   (4) Limitation of liability for breach of warranty (§ 2-719).

d. Title to the goods (§ 2-401).

e. Risk of loss and insurance (§§ 2-303, 2-501, 2-509, 2-510).

f. Seller's obligation to tender delivery of the goods.

   (1) Time of delivery (§§ 2-309, 2-503).

   (2) Place of delivery (§§ 2-308, 2-319 through 2-324,[8] 2-503, 2-504).

   (3) Manner of delivery (§§ 2-311(2), 2-503).

      (a) Delivery in single or several lots (§ 2-307).

      (b) Shipment under reservation (§§ 2-310(b), 2-505).

      (c) Delivery on condition (§ 2-507(2)).

   (4) Seller's right to cure improper tender (§ 2-508).

g. Buyer's obligation to accept goods (§ 2-507).

   (1) Buyer's right to inspect the goods before acceptance (§§ 2-513, 2-606).

   (2) Buyer's right to reject goods (§ 2-601).

      (a) Manner of rejection (§ 2-602).

      (b) Obligation to state reasons for rejection (§ 2-605).

---

[7] From B. Stone, Uniform Commercial Code in a Nutshell, pp. 42-44; copyright © 1995 West Publishing Company, reprinted with permission.

[8] [Abbreviated mercantile terms, such as F.O.B., F.A.S., C.I.F., etc. are often used in contracts involving the shipment of goods.-Ed.]

(c) Obligation to care for rejected goods (§§ 2-603, 2-604).

(3) Buyer's obligation to notify seller of breach discovered after acceptance (§ 2-607).

(4) Buyer's right to revoke his acceptance (§ 2-608).

h. Buyer's obligation to pay for goods (§§ 2-507, 2-606).

(1) Price (§ 2-305).

(2) Medium of payment (§§ 2-304, 2-511).

(3) Time of payment (§ 2-310).

(4) Obligation to pay before inspection of the goods (§ 2-512).

i. Remedies of seller (§ 2-703).

j. Remedies of buyer (§§ 2-711, 2-714).

k. Signature of parties (§ 2-201).

l. Miscellaneous provisions.

(1) Duration and termination of contract term (§§ 2-106(3), 2-309(2)).

(2) Provision forbidding parol modification (§§ 2-202, 2-209).

(3) Provision relating to waiver of rights by course of performance (§§ 2-208, 2-209).

(4) Delegation of performance (§ 2-210).

(5) Assignment of rights (§§ 2-210, 9-318(4)).

(6) Output and requirements clauses (§ 2-306).

(7) Sale on approval terms (§§ 2-326, 2-327).

(8) Sale or return (§§ 2-326, 2-327).

(9) Consignment sale terms (§§ 1-201(37), 2-326).

(10) Seller's rights on buyer's insolvency (§ 2-702).

(11) Buyer's rights on seller's insolvency (§ 2-502).

(12) Preservation of goods in dispute (§ 2-515).

(13) Right to adequate assurance of performance (§ 2-609).

(14) Installment contract provisions (§ 2-612).

(15) Force majeure (§§ 2-613 through 2-616).

(16) Liquidated damages (§ 2-718).

(17) Proof of market price (§§ 2-723, 2-724).

(18) Clause shortening the statute of limitations period (§ 2-725).

(19) Acceleration clauses (§ 1-208).

(20) Choice of law clause (§ 1-105).

Construction and Interpretation. The principal problems of construction and interpretation are twofold: (1)(a) what did the parties agree to, and (b) what legal meaning is to be placed thereon;

and (2)(a) what things did the parties fail to agree to, and (b) what will the law supply as "gap-fillers" to round out the contract?

What Parties Agreed to and Legal Meaning. The Code adopts a parol evidence rule in U.C.C. § 2-202 which provides that certain agreed written terms may not be contradicted by evidence of prior agreements or contemporaneous oral agreements. Also, U.C.C. § 1-205(3) provides that a course of dealing[9] between parties and any usage of trade[10] in the vocation or trade in which they are engaged or of which they are or of should be aware give particular meaning to and supplement or qualify terms of an agreement.[11] Further, U.C.C. § 2-208(1) provides that where the contract for sale involves repeated occasions for performance by either party with knowledge of the nature of the performance and opportunity for objection to it by the other, any course of performance accepted or acquiesced in without objection shall be relevant to determine the meaning of the agreement. As Comment 1 to U.C.C. § 2-208 states:

> The parties themselves know best what they have meant by their words of agreement and their action under that agreement is the best indication of what that meaning was. This section thus rounds out the set of factors which determines the meaning of the "agreement."[12]

Further, the Code has rules to determine the meaning of certain terms, for example: output or requirements terms (§ 2-306(1)), exclusive dealing terms (§ 2-306(2)), terms relating to assignment of the contract (§ 2-210(3), (4)); mercantile terms, e.g., F.O.B. (§ 2-319 et seq.); auction with or without reserve terms (§ 2-328(3)); sale on approval and sale of return terms (§§ 2-326, 2-327); option to accelerate "at will" term (§1-208).

Of course, not all terms upon which parties have agreed will necessarily have legal consequences. § 1-201(3), (11). For example, the Code's obligation of good faith in the performance or enforcement of every contract may prevent enforcement of certain terms or agreements. §§1-203, 1-201(19), 2-103(1)(b); see e.g., § 2-209(1) and Comment 2. Further, good faith, diligence, reasonableness and care prescribed by the Code may not be disclaimed by agreement. § 1-102(3) and Comment 3. Also, if a court as a matter of law finds a contract or any clause of the contract to have been unconscionable at the time it was made, the court may: (1) refuse to enforce the contract, or (2) enforce the remainder of the contract without the unconscionable clause, or (3) so limit the application of any unconscionable clause as to avoid any unconscionable result. § 2-302(1); see §§ 2-309(3), 2-719(3).

Parties Failure to Agree and "Gap-Fillers." Where the parties have entered into a contract but have failed to agree on some of the terms (see U.C.C. § 2-204(3)), the Code provides "gap-fillers" to supply the omitted terms. Remember that the Code defines "agreement" to mean the bargain of the parties in fact as found in their language or by implication from other circumstances

[9] U.C.C. § 1-205(1) states:

> A course of dealing is a sequence of previous conduct between the parties to a particular transaction which is fairly to be regarded as establishing a common basis of understanding for interpreting their expressions and other conduct.

[10] U.C.C. § 1-205(2) provides:

> A usage of trade is any practice or method of dealing having such regularity of observance in a place, vocation or trade as to justify an expectation that it will be observed with respect to the transaction in question. The existence and scope of such a usage are to be proved as facts. If it is established that such a usage is embodied in a written trade code or similar writing the interpretation of the writing is for the court.

[11] See Comment 1 to § 1-205.

[12] See U.C.C. § 2-202(a) and Comment 2.

including course of dealing or usage of trade or course of performance as provided in U.C.C. §§ 1-205 and 2-208. U.C.C. § 1-201(3).

The Code gap-fillers include: U.C.C. §§ 2-305 (open price term), 2-306 (output, requirements and exclusive dealings), 2-307 (delivery in single or several lots), 2-308 (place for delivery), 2-309 (absence of specific time provisions), 2-310 (open time for payment), and 2-311 (options and cooperation respecting performance). In addition, other Code provisions will yield to the contrary agreement of the parties, e.g., U.C.C. §§ 2-401(passing of title), 2-509 (risk of loss), 2-513 (buyer's right to inspection). Note that some Code provisions state that they cannot be varied by contrary agreement, e.g., U.C.C. §§ 1-102(3) and (4), 1-105(2), 1-204, 2-210(2), 2-318, 2-718(1).

In summary, the terms of a contract for sale may be supplied by (1) express language of the parties; (2) course of dealing, usage of trade and course of performance; (3) gap-filling rules of the Code (and general law).

The PEB Study Group Report contains the following comments:

Terms of Delivery

> Article 2 contains extensive treatment of the context and effect of certain terms of delivery. See §§ 2-319 through 2-324. CISG does not deal with these terms, leaving them to the parties' agreement or such sources as the INCOTERMS or the ICC.
>
> The Study Group discussed whether Article 2 should follow the lead of CISG in this matter, particularly those terms involving international transportation. If that lead were sound, the delivery terms would be deleted from Article 2 and the parties would be free to provide them by contract or to select other alternatives, such as the INCOTERMS. Such a recommendation, however, would be premature without a study of Article 2's current terms, a comparison with those terms used in international trade, and a consideration of how to obtain a continuing, proper mesh between what Article 2 does and does not do and other alternatives.

46 Bus. Lawyer 1869, 1881 (1991).

CHAPTER 4

PROPERTY INTERESTS

§ 4.01 Introduction

In Chapter 3, entitled "The Contract For Sale," we were reminded that U.C.C. Article 2 applies contract law principles to the sale of goods. In this chapter, we see that in certain instances, property principles may be applicable.

The Code recognizes four property interests in goods, namely (1) title, (2) special property, (3) insurable interest, and (4) security interest. Further, the Code deals with the question of risk of loss. This is historically closely related to property interests in goods. These matters are discussed in this chapter.

§ 4.02 Title

Read: U.C.C. § 2-401, see § 2-327(1)(a).

Read also: U.C.C. § 2A-302; CISG Arts. 4(b), 30.

A sale of goods is fundamentally a transaction which brings about a transfer of the property interest in the goods from a seller to a buyer. Section 2-106(1) states, "A 'sale' consists in the passing of title from the seller to the buyer for a price." Given this view of the sale transaction, it is not surprising that pre-Code law, including the Uniform Sales Act (U.S.A.), not only stressed the importance of the passage of title, but also used this concept to solve numerous other problems which arose in the course of the sale. "Has title passed?" was the crucial question in ascertaining the rights and remedies of the parties to the sale contract. For example, U.S.A. § 22 stated in part: "Unless otherwise agreed, the goods remain at the seller's risk until the property therein is transferred to the buyer, but when the property therein is transferred to the buyer the goods are at the buyer's risk." Another example is found at U.S.A. § 66 which reads: "Where the property in the goods has passed to the buyer and the seller wrongfully neglects or refuses to deliver the goods, the buyer may maintain any action by law to the owner of goods of similar kind when wrongfully converted or withheld."

Section 2-401 of the Code abandons the title concept as being the test of the rights, obligations, and remedies of the parties. This abandonment is described by Duesenberg and King as "The single most important conceptual distinction between Article 2 and either the common law or the Uniform Sales Act."[1] Duesenberg and King hasten to point out, however, that the abandonment of the title theory will not bring about a "great purge of the past" or "shocking changes in results achieved under pre-Code law."[2] Instead, while the reasoning of counsel and

[1] See the Comment to U.C.C. § 2-101.

[2] Duesenberg & King, Sales and Bulk Transfers Under the Uniform Commercial Code § 8.01.

judges must necessarily be altered, the outcome of sales controversies will not be radically different.

If title is no longer important in determining the rights of the parties to the sales contract, then why do we have U.C.C. § 2-401 with its elaborate distinctions?

NOTES AND QUESTIONS

(1) *Sales tax. State of Alabama v. Delta Airlines, Inc.,* 356 So. 2d 1205, 23 U.C.C. Rep. 1156 (Ala. Civ. App. 1978), states in part:

> Alabama sales tax applies only to sales that are "closed" within the State. Sections 40-23-1(a)(5),-2(1), Code of Alabama (1975). For tax purposes, sales are closed when title to the goods passes to the purchaser. *Hamm v. Continental Gin Co.,* 276 Ala 611, 165 So. 2d 392(1964); *State v. Altec, Inc.*, 46 Ala App 450, 243 So. 2d 713(1971). Actual delivery is of great importance in determining when title passes. *State v. Communication Equip. & Contr. Co.,* 335 So. 2d 123 (Ala Civ App 1976). Title passes, unless otherwise explicitly agreed, at the time and place of completion of performance by physical delivery of the goods. Section 7-2-401(2), Code of Alabama (1975). Under the stated facts, delivery of a meal, if at all, occurs outside Alabama and is in interstate commerce. Delta has no contractual obligation to deliver a meal at all. It maintains possession until actually served. Therefore, the trial court did not improperly conclude that the alleged sale was closed and title passes at the time of delivery without the State and was not subject to Alabama sales tax.

Compare Undercofler v. Eastern Airlines, Inc., 221 Ga. 824,147 S.E.2d 436, 3 U.C.C. Rep. 352 (1966), in which the court held that, while an airline's sale of meals to its passengers is a taxable event:

> such sale occurs when the ticket, the cost of which includes the price of the meal, is purchased. . . . The fact that actual delivery of the meal does not occur until later does not prevent perfection of its sale at the time of purchase of the ticket. . . . [T]he sale is complete when the ticket is bought.

(2) *Criminal Law.* "Whoever . . .steals . . .any . . .thing of value of the United States . . .[s]hall be fined not more than $10,000 or imprisoned not more than ten years, or both." 18 U.S.C. § 641. "Suppose the United States contracts for sale of scrap metal to a buyer. Before delivery of the scrap by the U.S. to buyer, X steals the scrap. Issue: At the time of the stealing was the scrap any thing of value of the United States, *i.e.*, did the U.S. still own or have title to the scrap?" B. Stone, Uniform Commercial Code in a Nutshell 51 (2d ed. 1984).

In a similar vein, Kentucky Revised Statutes § 514.030 (theft by unlawful taking or disposition) provides in part:

> A person is guilty of theft by unlawful taking or disposition when he unlawfully . . .[t]akes or exercises control over movable *property of another* with intent to deprive him thereof. [Emphasis added.]

(3) *Voidable title.* U.C.C. § 2-403(1) states that a person with voidable title has power to transfer a good title to a good faith purchaser for value. This is discussed in Chapter 8 below.

§ 4.03 Special Property

Read: U.C.C. §§ 2-401(1), 2-501(1). Cf. U.C.C. § 2A-217 Comment.

When the contract for sale has proceeded to the point that certain goods are designated by the parties as those to which the contract refers, it is important to recognize that the buyer has some interest in the goods. Under pre-Code law, the act of designating the goods was described as "appropriating them to the contract," and thereafter goods were called "ascertained goods." (See Uniform Sales Act §§ 17-20.) U.C.C. § 2-401(1)(first sentence) and U.C.C. § 2-501(1) use the term "identification" of goods to the contract, and the goods are spoken of as "identified." Generally, identification occurs when goods are designated by the seller as goods to which the contract refers. See U.C.C. § 2-501(l)(b).

The buyer obtains a "special property" by identification of goods. The incidents of this special property are summarized (see U.C.C. § 2-401 Comment 3):

1. *Buyer's Right to Goods on Seller's Insolvency.* A buyer who has paid a part or all of the price of goods in which he has a special property may on making and keeping good a tender of any unpaid portion of their price recover them from the seller if the seller becomes insolvent within ten days after receipt of the first installment on their price. U.C.C. §§ 2-711(2)(a), 2-502. This is discussed at § 7.04[D][1] below.
2. *Buyer's Right to Replevy the Goods.* The buyer has a right of replevin for goods identified to the contract (identification is the event which gives rise to buyer's special property) if after reasonable effort he is unable to cover for such goods. U.C.C. §§ 2-711(2)(b), 2-716(3). This is discussed at § 7.04[D][2] below.
3. *Rights of Seller's Creditors Against Sold Goods.* Generally, rights of unsecured creditors of the seller with respect to goods which have been identified to a contract for sale are subject to the buyer's rights to recover the goods under U.C.C. § 2-502 and U.C.C. § 2-716 summarized in the two preceding paragraphs. This is discussed at § 8.02.
4. *Suit Against Third Parties for Injury to Goods.* Where a third party so deals with goods which have been identified to a contract for sale as to cause actionable injury to a party to that contract, a right of action against the third party is in the party to the contract who has a special property in the goods. U.C.C. § 2-722(a). This is discussed at § 7.07[D] below.
5. *Rights of Good Faith Purchasers.* Certain good faith purchasers, *e.g.*, buyers in the ordinary course of business, may get better title to goods than their transferors had. Will these greater rights arise at the time the goods are identified (which gives rise to a special property) or delivered? See discussion at § 8.02 below.

§ 4.04 Insurable Interest

Read: U.C.C. § 2-501.

Black's Law Dictionary 720 (5th ed. 1979) defines "insurable interest":

> Such a real and substantial interest in specific property as will prevent a contract to indemnify the person interested against its loss from being a mere wager policy. Such an interest as will make the loss of the property of pecuniary damage to the insured. . . . Generally, an "insurable interest" exists where insured derives pecuniary benefit or advantage by preservation and continued existence of property or would sustain pecuniary loss from its destruction.[3]

[3] Copyright © 1979 by West Publishing Co. Reprinted by permission.

Under the Code, a buyer obtains an insurable interest in goods (as well as a special property) by their identification. U.C.C. § 2-501(1). Special property is discussed at § 4.03 above.

Suppose goods are identified to a contract for sale but remain in the possession of seller. Buyer does not yet "own" the goods since seller has not completed his performance with reference to the physical delivery of the goods. U.C.C. § 2-401(2) discussed at § 4.02 above. Further, risk of loss has not passed to the buyer since buyer has not taken physical possession of the goods. U.C.C. § 2-509(3) discussed at § 4.06 below. Nevertheless, U.C.C. § 2-501(1) states that buyer has an insurable interest in the identified goods. What "pecuniary loss" will buyer sustain from destruction of the goods?

Seller retains an insurable interest so long as title to or any security interest in the goods remains in him. U.C.C. § 2-501(2). See *St. Paul Fire and Marine Insurance Co. v. Toman,* set forth below.

The principal significance of the insurable interest relates to the law of insurance, not the U.C.C. The Code, however, does recognize that a party to a contract for sale of goods with an insurable interest can sue third parties for injury to the goods. See U.C.C. § 2-722.

PROBLEM 4.1

Your client, William Works, recently bought a weekend retreat in the country with an old farm house and also a log barn. While imbued with the "Puritan" work ethic, William has decided he will not spend his weekends raising cattle. He is pleasantly surprised when Gable Gunther comes along and offers to buy the barn for his "historical village" which is a few miles away. Gunther has obtained many historical buildings throughout the country. William sells Gabe the barn and immediately heads for town to celebrate; Gabe returns home. That very day lightning strikes the barn and it burns completely down. William's insurance company, the Fireman's Mutual, refuses to pay on the basis that William no longer had an insurable interest.

Does the U.C.C. apply? Does William still have an insurable interest?

NOTES

(1) In a case similar to Problem 4.1, *St. Paul Fire and Marine Insurance Co. v. Toman,* 351 N.W.2d 146 (1984), the court noted:

> In a newspaper display advertisement Toman advertised his public auction for September 23, 1981. Among the items listed for sale was a 24-foot by 40-foot house which was to be removed from Toman's farmstead. Prior to the auction sale, the auctioneer announced that the house had to be removed under terms negotiated by the buyer and Toman.
>
> Van Collins was the successful bidder at the sale. He purchased the residence for $3,250.00, and issued his check to the auctioneer for that amount. No written document evidencing a sale was issued to Van Collins by the auctioneer.
>
> On September 26, 1981, the house had been completely destroyed by fire. Insurer's policy of insurance covering loss by fire of Toman's property insured the residence for $28,000.00.
>
> Insurer admits that if it is liable under the policy, it is liable for the payment of the full amount of the $28,000.00 since the policy was a "valued policy."
>
> Insurer claims, however, that Toman no longer had an insurable interest in the house at the time of the fire loss and that the risk of the loss had passed to Van Collins. Toman contends he did have an insurable interest and payment under the policy provision should be effected.

The trial court concluded that the risk of loss had not yet passed to Van Collins; that there had been no "tender of delivery" as required by SDCL 57A-2-509(3); and, that the sale of the house was a sale of "goods" to which SDCL 57A-2-107(2) of the Uniform Commercial Code applied.

Insurer claims that at the time of the sale the house constituted real property and that title had passed to Van Collins, thereby negating any insurable interest in Toman. Insurer points out that SDCL 5 7A-2-107(1) provides that where "materials [are] to be removed from realty [it] is a contract for the sale of goods . . .if they are to be severed by the seller[,] but until severance a purported present sale thereof which is not effective as a transfer of an interest in land is effective only as a contract to sell." Insurer contends that this represented a contract for the sale of an interest in real property to which U.C.C. provisions have no application. Insurer insists that this conclusion is correct in view of the trial court's finding that title had passed to Van Collins. Such a conclusion is not warranted on an examination of the record. There is no document of any kind entered into evidence indicating a conveyance from Toman to Van Collins of an interest in real property.

Insurer further claims that because the sale of an interest in land was made the provisions of the Uniform Vendor and Purchaser Risk Act, particularly SDCL 43-26-7, are applicable and dispositive of Toman's claim of an insurable interest in the house. However, since we conclude that the sale of the house was not a sale of an interest in land, this contention is without merit.

It is important to note at this juncture that the concept of title under the U.C.C. is of decreased importance.

> No longer is the question of title of any importance in determining whether a buyer or a seller bears the risk of loss. It is true that the person with title will also (and incidentally) often bear the risk that the goods may be destroyed or lost; but the seller may have title and the buyer the risk, or the seller may have the risk and the buyer the title. In short, title is not a relevant consideration in deciding whether the risk has shifted to the buyer.

R. Nordstrom, Handbook of the Law of Sales, 393 (1970) quoted in *Martin v. Melland's Inc.*, 283 N.W.2d 76, 79 (ND 1979). The prevailing view is that the passage of title is not a final determining factor. Under the risk of loss provisions of the U.C.C. the courts should determine the rights of the parties.

Insurer contends that the sale was one for "goods" or personal property for the purpose of determining passage of title and then argues that the provisions of the Uniform Vendor and Purchaser Risk Act should be used to determine the risk of loss. This is a clear contradiction in legal theory. Simply put, insurer has failed to provide evidentiary support in the record and the settled law to support its claim that the sale of an interest in real property resulted when Toman's house was sold.

The provisions of SDCL 57A-2-1 07(2) provide that the sale of "other things attached to realty and capable of severance without material harm thereto. . .is a contract for the sale of goods. . .whether the subject matter is to be severed by the buyer or by the seller even though it forms part of the realty at the time of contracting, and the parties can by identification effect a present sale before severance." Here it is undisputed that Toman and Van Collins mutually identified the property being sold. It was in fact sold at the public auction sale on September 23, 1981.

SDCL 57A-2-501(2) recognizes that "[t]he seller retains an insurable interest in goods so long as title to or any security interest in the goods remains in him and where the identification is by the seller alone he may until default or insolvency or notification to the buyer that the identification is final substitute other goods for those identified." In addition SDCL 57A-2-509(3) provides:

> In any case not within subsection (1) or (2), the risk of loss passes to the buyer on his receipt of the goods if the seller is a merchant; otherwise the risk passes to the buyer on tender of delivery.

No one contends Toman as the seller was a "merchant" as defined in SDCL 57A-2-1 04(1). Further, it is clear that Toman never made the "tender of delivery" of the house as required by SDCL 57A-2-509(3). Van Collins knew that Toman was occupying the house at least on a part-time basis; he further knew from the auctioneer's announcement that the removal of the house would have to be negotiated with Toman since Toman not only used the house occasionally, but also retained personal property in it. We agree with the trial court that Toman had an insurable interest, SDCL 58-10-8, in the house at the time of the fire loss and payment by the insurer should be made pursuant to the terms of its policy of insurance.

The trial court awarded Toman prejudgment interest on the $28,000.00 principal sum from September 26, 1981, the date of the fire. Toman is entitled to prejudgment interest only from the date of the refusal of the claim since there was no showing that insurer was dilatory in conducting an investigation of the claim. We note that the summons and complaint was served Toman on December 31, 1981, less than ninety days after the fire loss. Since there was no other evidence about the refusal of the claim, we fix the date of refusal as of December 31, 1981. Interest shall begin to accrue from that date.

Accordingly, the judgment is affirmed in the principal sum with modification only as to the prejudgment interest.

(2) In the case just discussed, the Court states, *inter alia*, "We agree with the trial court that Toman had an insurable interest, SDCL 58-10-8, in the house at the time of the fire loss. . ." This statute reads:

> *58-10-8. Insurable interest in property defined.* "Insurable interest" as used in §§ 58-10-7 and 58-10-9 means any actual, lawful, and substantial economic interest in the safety or preservation of the subject of the insurance free from loss, destruction, or pecuniary damage or impairment.

Further, SDCL 58-10-7 states:

> *58-10-7. Insurance of property—Insurable interest required.* No contract of insurance of property or of any interest in property or arising from property shall be enforceable as to the insurance except for the benefit of persons having an insurable interest in the things insured as at the time of the loss.

See U.C.C. § 2-501(3).

(3) The Uniform Vendor and Purchaser Risk Act, particularly SDCL 43-26-7, and referenced in the case, states as follows:

> *43-26-7. Transfer of subject matter of contract for purchase and sale of realty—Destruction without fault of vendor—Taking by eminent domain—Payment of purchase price.* If, when either the legal title or the possession of the subject matter of the contract has

> been transferred, all or any part thereof is destroyed without fault of the vendor or is taken by eminent domain, the purchaser is not thereby relieved from a duty to pay the price, nor is he entitled to recover any portion thereof that he has paid.

§ 4.05 Security Interest

Read: U.C.C. §§ 1-201(37), 9-113 Comment 1.

" 'Security interest' means an interest in personal property or fixtures which secures payment or performance of an obligation. . . . The special property interest of a buyer of goods [see § 4.03 above] on identification of such goods to a contract for sale under U.C.C. § 2-401is not a 'security interest,' but a buyer may also acquire a 'security interest' by complying with Article 9." U.C.C. § 1-201(37). Secured transactions creating security interests are dealt with at Chapters 15-20 below.

Security interests can arise under U.C.C. Article 2 Sales, *e.g.*, (1) the rights of a shipper-seller to exercise control over goods in the hands of a carrier when he ships "under reservation" pursuant to U.C.C. § 2-505 (see Chapter 10 below); (2) rights of a buyer who rejects non-conforming goods to hold and resell them if he has paid a part of the price or incurred certain expenses pursuant to U.C.C. § 2-711(3) (see § 7.04[B] below). See U.C.C. § 9-113 Comment 1.

§ 4.06 Risk of Loss

Read: U.C.C. §§ 2-509, 2-510, 2-327(see 2-326(1)), 2-303, 2-319 through 2-322, 2-324; see §§ 2-501 Comment 4, 2-709(1)(a), 7-204, 7-309.

Read also: U.C.C. §§ 2A-219, 2A-220, 2A-221, 2A-529(1)(a); CISG 66-70, see Arts. 25 and 36(1).

PROBLEM 4.2

Your client, Susan Santiago runs a jewelry shop in Oaxaca, Mexico. She agreed to purchase watches from Karen Karinol who operated a wholesale business in Miami. The contract stipulated "Oaxaca Mexico via Belize." There were no provisions allocating risk of loss while the watches were in possession of the carriers and no shipment terms such as FOB or C&F. The shipping cartons were opened in Belize for a customs inspection and no watches were contained therein! Karen's insurance company refuses to pay and Karen refuses to replace the watches. Your client Susan has no insurance covering these watches. Who has the risk of loss? Suppose Karen asks you what shipment term she should put into future contracts? Also she asks what are the meanings of various shipment terms she has encountered in some of her other contracts.

NOTES

In a similar case, *Pestana v. Karinol Corp.,* 367 So. 2d 1096 (1979), the court noted:

> There are two types of sales contracts under Florida's Uniform Commercial Code wherein a carrier is used to transport the goods sold: a shipment contract and a destination contract. A shipment contract is considered the normal contract in which the seller is required to send the subject goods by carrier to the buyer but is not required to guarantee delivery thereof at a particular destination. Under a shipment contract, the seller, unless otherwise agreed, must: (1) put the goods sold in the possession of a carrier and make a contract for their transportation

as may be reasonable having regard for the nature of the goods and other attendant circumstances, (2) obtain and promptly deliver or tender in due form any document necessary to enable the buyer to obtain possession of the goods or otherwise required by the agreement or by usage of the trade, and (3) promptly notify the buyer of the shipment. On a shipment contract, the risk of loss passes to the buyer when the goods sold are duly delivered to the carrier for shipment to the buyer. §§ 672.503 (Official U.C.C. comment 5), 672.504, 672.509(1), Fla Stat (1977).

A destination contract, on the other hand, is considered the variant contract in which the seller specifically agrees to deliver the goods sold to the buyer at a particular destination and to bear the risk of loss of the goods until tender of delivery. This can be accomplished by express provision in the sales contract to that effect or by the use of delivery terms such as F.O.B. (place of destination). Under a destination contract, the seller is required to tender delivery of the goods sold to the buyer at the place of destination. The risk of loss under such a contract passes to the buyer when the goods sold are duly tendered to the buyer at the place of destination while in the possession of the carrier so as to enable the buyer to take delivery. The parties must explicitly agree to a destination contract; otherwise the contract will be considered a shipment contract. §§ 672.31 9(1)(b), 672.503 (Official U.C.C. comment 5), 672.509(1), Fla Stat (1977).

Where the risk of loss falls on the seller at the time the goods sold are lost or destroyed, the seller is liable in damages to the buyer for non-delivery unless the seller tenders a performance in replacement for the lost or destroyed goods. On the other hand, where the risk of loss falls on the buyer at the time the goods sold are lost or destroyed, the buyer is liable to the seller for the purchase price of the goods sold. [U.C.C. § 2-709(1)(a).]

In the instant case, we deal with the normal shipment contract involving the sale of goods. The defendant Karinol pursuant to this contract agreed to send the goods sold, a shipment of watches, to the plaintiff's decedent in Chetumal, Mexico. There was no specific provision in the contract between the parties which allocated the risk of loss on the goods sold while in transit. In addition, there were no delivery terms such as F.O.B. Chetumal contained in the contract.

All agree that there is sufficient evidence that the defendant Karinol performed its obligations as a seller under the Uniform Commercial Code if this contract is considered a shipment contract. Karinol put the goods sold in the possession of a carrier and made a contract for the goods' safe transportation to the plaintiff's decedent; Karinol also promptly notified the plaintiff's decedent of the shipment and tendered to said party the necessary documents to obtain possession of the goods sold.

The plaintiff Pestana contends, however, that the contract herein is a destination contract in which the risk of loss on the goods sold did not pass until delivery on such goods had been tendered to him at Chetumal, Mexico—an event which never occurred. He relies for this position on the notation at the bottom of the contract between the parties which provides that the goods were to be sent to Chetumal, Mexico. We cannot agree. A "send to" or "ship to" term is a part of every contract involving the sale of goods where carriage is contemplated and has no significance in determining whether the contract is a shipment or destination contract for risk of loss purposes. As such, the "send to" term contained in this contract cannot, without more, convert this into a destination contract.

It therefore follows that the risk of loss in this case shifted to the plaintiff's decedent as buyer when the defendant Karinol as seller duly delivered the goods to the defendant freight forwarder American under a reasonable contract of carriage for shipment to the plaintiff's decedent in Chetumal, Mexico. The defendant Karinol, its agent the defendant American, and its insurer the defendant Fidelity could not be held liable to the plaintiff in this action. The trial court properly entered judgment in favor of all the defendants herein.

Affirmed.

PROBLEM 4.3

Jason sells a hundred thousand pounds of "St. Louis" style barbecue pork ribs to Eckrich, delivery to be effected by a transfer of the ribs from Jason's account in an independent warehouse to Eckrich's account in the same warehouse — which is to say without the ribs actually being moved. On January 13, Jason's phoned warehouse and requested that the ribs be transferred to Eckrich's account. Warehouse noted the transfer on its books immediately and mailed a warehouse receipt which was received by Eckrich on January 24. On January 17 the ribs were destroyed (not barbecued) by a fire at warehouse. Who suffers the risk of loss?

NOTES

(1) In the case from which the problem is drawn, *Jason Foods Inc. v. Peter Eckrich & Sons, Inc.*, 774 F.2d 214 (1985), the court noted that the underlying policies of U.C.C. risk of loss, *i.e.* control and ability to insure, were not helpful:

> [L]et us shift now to the plane of policy. The Code sought to create a set of standard contract terms that would reflect in the generality of cases the preferences of contracting parties at the time of contract. One such preference is for assignments of liability—or, what amounts to the same thing, assignments of the risk of loss—that create incentives to minimize—the adverse consequences of untoward events such as (in this case) a warehouse fire. There are two ways of minimizing such consequences. One is to make them less painful by insuring against them. Insurance does not prevent a loss—it merely spreads it—but in doing so it reduces (for those who are risk averse) the disutility of the loss. So if one of the contracting parties can insure at lower cost than the other, this is an argument for placing the risk of loss on him, to give him an incentive to do so. But that as we have seen is not a factor in this case; either party could have insured (or have paid the warehouse to assume strict liability for loss or destruction of the goods, in which event the warehouse would have insured them), and so far as the record shows at equal cost.
>
> The other method of minimizing the consequences of an unanticipated loss is through prevention of the loss. If one party is in a better position than the other to prevent it, this is a reason for placing the risk of loss on him, to give him an incentive to prevent it. It would be a reason for placing liability on a seller who still had possession of the goods, even though title had passed. But between the moment of transfer of title by Jason's and the movement of receipt of the warehouse receipt by Eckrich, neither party to the sale had effective control over the ribs. They were in a kind of limbo, until (to continue the Dantesque image) abruptly propelled into a hotter region. With Jason's having relinquished title and Eckrich not yet aware that it had acquired it, neither party had an effective power of control.
>
> But this is not an argument for holding that the risk of loss shifted at the moment of transfer; it is just an argument for regarding the parties' positions as symmetrical from the standpoint

of ability either to prevent or to shift losses. In such a case we have little to assist us besides the language of subsection (b) and its surrounding subsections and the U.C.C. comments; but these materials do point pretty clearly to the conclusion that the risk of loss did not pass at the moment of transfer.

(2) The court then decided the case:

> When did it pass? Does "acknowledgment" means receipt, as in the surrounding subsections of § 2-509(2), or mailing? Since the evidence was in conflict over whether the acknowledgment was mailed on January 17 (and at what hour), which was the day of the fire, or on January 18, this could be an important question—but in another case, Jason's waived it. The only theory it tendered to the district court, or briefed and argued in this court, was that the risk of loss passed either on January 13, when the transfer of title was made on the books of the warehouse, or at the latest on January 14, because Eckrich knew the ribs would be transferred at the warehouse sometime between January 10 and 14. We have discussed the immateriality of the passage of title on January 13; we add that the alternative argument, that Eckrich knew by January 14 that it owned the ribs, exaggerates what Eckrich knew. By the close of business on January 14 Eckrich had a well-founded expectation that the ribs had been transferred to its account; but considering the many slips that are possible between cup and lips, we do not think that this expectation should fix the point at which the risk shifts. If you were told by an automobile dealer from whom you bought a car that the car would be delivered on January 14, you would not take out insurance effective that day, without waiting for the actual delivery.
>
> Finally, Jason's argument from trade custom or usage is unavailing. The method of transfer that the parties used was indeed customary but there was no custom or usage on when the risk of loss passed to the buyer.
>
> *Affirmed.*

(3) *Passage of Risk of Loss on Buyer's Receipt of Goods.* In *Hughes v. Al Green Inc.*, 65 Ohio St.2d 110, 418 N.E.2d 1355, 31 U.C.C. Rep. 890 (1981), buyer of an automobile paid a down payment and took immediate possession. Before leaving the dealership, buyer signed a purchase contract and an application for certificate of title. En route from the dealership to her home, buyer was involved in a collision and the automobile was substantially damaged. Under U.C.C. § 2-509(3), the risk of loss for the damage passed to the buyer on receipt of the goods, since seller was a merchant. Buyer, however, pointed to the Ohio Certificate of Title Act, RC § 4505.04, which provides:

> No person acquiring a motor vehicle from the owner thereof, whether such owner is a manufacturer, importer, dealer, or otherwise, shall acquire any right, title, claim, or interest in or to said motor vehicle until such person has had issued to him a certificate of title to said motor vehicle, or delivered to him a manufacturer's or importer's certificate for it; nor shall any waiver or estoppel operate in favor of such person against a person having possession of such certificate of title, or manufacturer's or importer's certificate for said motor vehicle, for a valuable consideration.
>
> No court in any case at law or in equity shall recognize the right, title, claim, or interest of any person in or to any motor vehicle sold or disposed of, or mortgaged or encumbered, unless evidenced:
>
> (A) By a certificate of title or a manufacturer's or importer's certificate issued in accordance with sections 4505.01 to 4505.19, inclusive, of the Revised Code.

(B) By admission in the pleadings or stipulation of the parties.

Buyer's argument was that the car dealer was in breach of contract because when the certificate of title was issued in buyer's name and ownership of the automobile thereby legally transferred to her, the dealer no longer possessed that for which she bargained, i.e., an undamaged automobile.

The court held that risk of loss passed to buyer on receipt of goods per U.C.C. § 2-509(3) and that the Certificate of Title Act was irrelevant to the issue of risk of loss.

The court stated:

> This provision [U.C.C. § 2-509] represents a significant shift away from the prior importance of the concept of title in determining the point at which risk of loss passes from the seller to the buyer. Under the common law, not only did title to the contract goods determine risk of loss, but it also determined the issues of the buyer's right to the goods (through replevin), the seller's right to the purchase price, and the right to proceed against tortfeasors. Under the U.C.C., however, "[e]ach provision . . .with regard to the rights, obligations, and remedies of the seller, the buyer, purchasers, or other third parties applies irrespective of title to the goods except where the provision refers to such title." RC 1302.42 (U.C.C. § 2-401).
>
> Thus, as noted in Nordstrom, Sales, Section 130, at page 393:
>
> > [T]here is. . .one principle which applies to all risk of loss problems. This principle is summarized in one sentence from the Comments:
> >
> > > The underlying theory of these sections on risk of loss is the adoption of the contractual approach rather than an arbitrary shifting of the risk with the "property" in the goods.
> >
> > No longer is the question of title of any importance in determining whether a buyer or a seller bears the risk of loss. It is true that the person with title will also (and incidentally) often bear the risk that the goods may be destroyed or lost; *but the seller may have title and the buyer the risk*, or the seller may have the risk and the buyer the title. In short, title is not a relevant consideration in deciding whether the risk has shifted to the buyer. (Emphasis added.)
>
> Similarly, in 3A Bender's Uniform Commercial Code Service, Section 8.03, it is stated, at page 8-21, that U.C.C. § 2-509 (RC 1302.53):
>
> > sets forth a contractual approach, as distinguished from the property concept of title, to solving the issues arising when goods are damaged or destroyed. The section focuses on specific acts, such as tender of delivery by the seller, or receipt of the goods or of documents representing the goods by the buyer. Title is relevant under this section only if the parties provide that risk of loss shall depend upon the location of title.
>
> In the instant cause, the appellant-buyer had received possession of the automobile as partial execution of a merchant-seller's obligations under a purchase contract. Thus, unless other statutory provisions make RC 1302.53 inapplicable, the appellant, as a buyer in receipt of goods identified to a contract, must bear the loss of the car's value resulting from the collision.
>
> RC 1302.53 does not conflict with RC 4505.04 [the Certificate of Title Act]. The purpose of the Certificate of Title Act is to prevent the importation of stolen motor vehicles, to protect Ohio bona fide purchasers against thieves and wrongdoers, and to create an instrument

evidencing title to, and ownership of, motor vehicles. (Citations omitted). The Act was not adopted to clarify contractual rights and duties, as was RC Chapter 1302.

As stated in *Grogan Chrysler-Plymouth, Inc. v. Gottfried,* (1978), 59 Ohio App. 2d 91, 94-95, 392 N.E.2d 1283:

> RC 4505.04 was intended to apply to litigation where the parties were rival claimants to title, i.e., ownership of the automobile; to contests between the alleged owner and lien claimants; to litigation between the owner holding the valid certificate of title and one holding a stolen, forged or otherwise invalidly issued certificate of title; and to similar situations. (Citations omitted.)

In cases decided prior to the adoption of the Uniform Commercial Code, the Certificate of Title Act was properly consulted in determining whether a buyer or seller bore the risk of loss or could proceed against third-party tortfeasors because determination of those issues was dependent, under the common law, upon a finding of ownership. With ownership no longer being determinative, RC 4505.04 is irrelevant to the issue of risk of loss, and thus does not conflict with a U.C.C. risk of loss analysis.

(4) *Transfer of Title and Risk Under the U.S.A.* Uniform Sales Act § 22 said in part: "[T]he goods remain at the seller's risk until the property therein is transferred to the buyer, but when the property therein is transferred to the buyer the goods are at the buyer's risk. Also, U.S.A. § 19 Rule 1 said: "Where there is an unconditional contract to sell specific goods, in a deliverable state, the property in the goods passes to the buyer when the contract is made."

These provisions were applied in *Radloff v. Bragmus,* 214 Minn. 130, 7 N.W.2d 491 (1943), where plaintiff Radloff on November 9, 1940, sold his flock of turkeys (about 100 hens and 600 toms) to Bragmus. Removal was to be made by Bragmus Nov. 13. On Nov. 11 a blizzard destroyed some 330 of the turkeys and those not destroyed were damaged. The court held that title (and risk) passed to the buyer on Nov. 9 when the contract was made. The goods were "in a deliverable state" on Nov. 9. There was nothing further for plaintiff to do "for the purpose of putting them into a deliverable state." (The counting, weighing and grading of the turkeys were purely matters of routine and of simple computation.)

When would risk of loss pass under the U.C.C.? What policy considerations are relevant? See U.C.C. §§ 2-401, 2-509 and Comment 3.

(5) *Sale on Approval.* In *First Coinvestors, Inc. v. Coppola,* 388 N.Y.S.2d 833, 20 U.C.C. Rep 884 (D. Suffolk City 1976), a coin collector (buyer) submitted an order for certain coins from a coin dealer through a mail order coin collecting club. The dealer mailed the coins to the buyer by registered mail, return receipt requested, on a "sale on approval" basis. See U.C.C. § 2-326(1)(a). The receipt was signed by an unknown person who presumably stole the coins. Held: Risk of loss does not pass to a buyer on a sale on approval until he accepts the goods under U.C.C. § 2-606. Hence, the dealer-seller bore the risk of loss. U.C.C. §§ 2-509(4), 2-327(1)(a).

§ 4.07 Risk of Loss: Breach Settings

Read: U.C.C. § 2-510; see §§ 2-501, 2-508, 2-606, 2-608; cf. § 9-207(2)(b).

PROBLEM 4.4

Prestige Motors delivered a new Jeep Cherokee to your client without the required undercoating. The jeep was returned to Prestige later that day so the coating could be applied. The car was stolen from Prestige's premises and never recovered. Prestige denies any responsibility and says that its insurance company also will not pay. It says your client should have taken out insurance coverage which would cover the theft. What is your argument and position?

NOTE

In a similar case to the fact pattern of the above Problem, *Jakowski v. Carole Chevelet, Inc.*, the court noted:

> Given the undisputed facts the operation of § 2-510(1) is inescapable. The goods failed to conform, the buyer never accepted them and the defect was never cured. Accordingly, the risk of loss remained on the seller and judgment is granted for plaintiff. A further note on the law is in order.
>
> It is possible to conjure up a host of hypotheticals leading to seemingly perverse results under § 2-510. The section has been the subject of some scholarly criticism. See *e.g.*, White & Summers, *supra,* § 5.5 at 187. Williston, *The Law of Sales in the Proposed Uniform Commercial Code,* 63 Harv. L. Rev. 561, 583 (1950).
>
> The fact is, however, that those courts considering it have had little difficulty in applying it as written. [Cases cited.]
>
> The rule is simple enough: under NJSA 1 2A: 2-510(1) where goods fail to conform to the contract of sale, the risk of loss remains on the seller until the buyer accepts the goods or until the seller cures the defect. In the aforecited cases, such was the result even though in all of them the goods were still in the buyer's possession at the time of their destruction.
>
> For present purposes it is adequate to hold simply that where a seller obtains possession of the goods in an effort to cure defects in them so as to comply with his end of the bargain, he is under a contractual duty to redeliver them to the buyer. In failing to do so, he has breached the contract.

§ 4.08 Warranty of Title

Read: U.C.C. § 2-312.

Read also: U.C.C. § 2A-211; CISG Arts. 41-44.

PROBLEM 4.5

Your client has just contracted to purchase a modern printing press machine from the News Now Company for $100,000. Your client hopes to resell it to the Current Times Company for $150,000. A computer mechanic, who has his own independent repair services, has filed a $9000 mechanic lien against it.

Your client has asked News Now to pay the mechanic which it had hired and remove the lien. It refuses to do so saying his services were unsatisfactory and it had to hire another mechanic to fix it.

Your client also knows that Current Times will not purchase the machine from it if there is a lien outstanding.

What is your advice to your client?

NOTES

(1) 2 Hawkland, Uniform Commercial Code Series § 2-312:02 (1984), states in part:[4]

> [T]here may be situations where the seller has the power, but not the right, to convey a perfect title to the goods that may expose the buyer unreasonably to the claim of a third person to ownership. In those cases, there is a breach of warranty of title, even though the buyer has the legal ability to defeat the third-party claim. Such a situation might arise, for example, under section 2-403 where a third party delivers goods to a merchant for repair. If the merchant is in the business of selling goods of the kind, he had the power to sell the entrusted goods to a buyer in the ordinary course free and clear of the third party's ownership rights. This new rule is one which many third parties might not be aware of or understand and some third parties might proceed against the buyer in the ordinary course, even though they could not win a lawsuit if he could establish that status. That being the case, the buyer should be able to revoke acceptance, or sue for breach of warranty of title on the ground that the transfer was not rightful. The test is not whether the buyer can win a lawsuit against third-party claimants, but whether he is unreasonably exposed to such a suit.

U.C.C. § 2-403 is discussed at Chapter 8, "Rights of Third Parties-Good Faith Purchase."

Compare the Hawkland quote above with U.C.C. § 3-417 Comment 9.

(2) In *Sunseri v. RKO-Stanley Warner Theaters, Inc.*, 248 Pa Super 111, 374 A.2d 1342 (1977), the following language in a bill of sale for recreational equipment was held insufficiently specific to exclude the warranty of title:

> It is expressly understood and agreed that seller shall in nowise be deemed or held to be obligated, liable, or accountable upon or under guaranties [sic] or warranties, in any manner or form including, but not limited to, the implied warranties of title, merchantability. . .

Note that the warranty of title is not designated as an "implied" warranty, and hence is not subject to U.C.C. § 2-316(3) which deals with the exclusion or modification of implied quality warranties (see Chapter 5 below). Disclaimer of the warranty of title is governed by U.C.C. § 2-312(2), which requires either specific language or the described circumstances. See Comment 6 to U.C.C. § 2-312.

(3) In *Catlin Aviations v. Equilense Corp.*, 626 P.2d 857 (1981), the court said:

> Buyer argues although an aggrieved buyer must mitigate damages, such is inapplicable where the seller has the duty to uphold its warranty of title. However there is no evidence in the record that buyer informed seller of its potential sale and unless the cloud was removed quickly the sale would be lost. Without such knowledge seller should not be held to account for its inaction, especially when buyer could have mitigated easily, quickly and reasonably, and saved its potential sale. We agree with the trial court under the facts of the case in its refusal to grant consequential damages.

---

[4] Copyright © 1984 by American Law Institute. Reprinted by permission.

CHAPTER 5

WARRANTY/PRODUCTS LIABILITY

§ 5.01 Introduction

Read: U.C.C. §§ 2-313, 2-314, 2-315, 2-316, 2-317, 2-318 and Restatement of Torts (Second), § 402A.

Read also: U.C.C. §§ 2A-210, 2A-212 through 2A-216; CISG Arts. 35-40, see Arts. 27, 44.

There is "much more than meets the eye" in sales contracts. A part of the "contract" is found in advertising sales talk, brochures, booklets, and tags which may constitute express warranties. Another part consists of the standards set by implied warranties under the U.C.C., the obligations imposed by the strict liability of § 402A of the Restatement of Torts Second, or federal legislation. Caselaw also has expanded these obligations.

§ 5.02 Historical Development

Some warranty law is found in the time of the fair courts in the thirteenth and fourteenth centuries; the examples in Chapter 1 relating to the defective herring, p. 3 *supra*, reflects this development.

Later, the common law courts predominated and warranty law went through a new development. In the 1600's, it was necessary to use special language to create a warranty. In *Chandelor v. Lopus,* 1 Jac. 1, 79 Eng. Rep. 3 (1625), the plaintiff asserted that the defendant being a goldsmith, and having skill in jewels and precious stones, had a stone which he affirmed to Lopus to be a bezar-stone, and sold it to Lopus for one hundred pounds; but it was not a bezar-stone.

The court held that "the bare affirmation that it was bezar-stone, without warranting it to be so, is no cause for action; and although he knew it to be no bezar-stone, it is not material; for every one in selling his wares will affirm that his wares are good, or the wares which he sells is sound; yet he does not warrant them to be so, it is no cause of action."

In the late 1700's and early 1800's, implied warranties were developed. While it appears that implied warranty as a cause of action was being argued in the mid-1700's, it was not until 1815 in the case of *Gardiner v. Gray*, 4 Camp. 144, 171 Eng. Rep. (1815), that the cornerstone for the establishment of the implied warranty of merchantability was laid. In that case, the buyer purchased 12 bags of waste silk which was of such an inferior quality that it was not saleable under the denomination of "waste silk." The judge was of the opinion

> [t]hat under such circumstances, the purchaser has a right to expect a saleable article answering the description in the contract. Without any warranty, this is an implied term in every such contract. Where there is no opportunity to inspect the commodity, the maxim of *caveat emptor* does not apply. He cannot without a warranty insist that it shall be of any particular quality

> of fineness, but the intention of both parties must be taken to be that it shall be saleable in the market under the denomination mentioned in the contract between them. The purchaser cannot be supposed to buy goods to lay them on a dunghill. The question then is whether the commodity purchased by the plaintiff be of such a quality as can be reasonably brought into the market to be sold as waste silk? The witnesses describe it as unfit for the purposes of waste silk, and of such a quality that it cannot be sold under that denomination.

The development of warranty law may be viewed as a pendulum which has swung back and forth — at times favoring the buyer, at times the seller. In its earliest period, it appears to have favored the buyer. Whether it be in the manor court, the church court, or the fair courts, it afforded him some protection. It was not, of course, sophisticated in concept, and practical difficulties of protection also were present.

In the period of *caveat emptor*, the shift was decidedly in favor of the seller. It is somewhat questionable, however, how strong this doctrine was.

With the rebirth of warranty in the late 1700's, the pendulum seemed to swing again, giving the buyer protection against defective goods.

With the establishment of implied warranties, the pendulum began to swing at a slightly faster pace. From the initial protection given the buyer, with the use of disclaimers and the emphasis placed on the "privity" doctrine, it swung to the seller. As some courts began to find reasons to circumvent the then-used disclaimers, the pendulum swung back toward the buyer. The seller, however, merely improved the wording of the disclaimer to take into account the judicial decisions. From disclaimer to circumvention to disclaimer — from seller to buyer to seller — began the pattern. With the assault of the courts on the doctrine of "privity" and their more critical view of "disclaimers," the pendulum has come back somewhat in favor of protecting the buyer against defective products. For the small buyer or consumer, in many instances, there are practical difficulties of securing adequate protection.

The "pendulum" model is somewhat of an oversimplification of legal phenomena since some of the periods of favoring the buyer or seller overlapped. Also, of course, jurisdictional variations existed. Nevertheless, it is helpful in understanding the broader movement of the law in this field. The U.C.C. represented a compromise, permitting the pendulum to swing in favor of the buyer with its warranty sections, and in favor of the seller with its disclaimer section. Its provision on privity also represented only a slight swing toward the buyer, while remaining primarily neutral. It was with § 402A of the Restatement of Torts Second, which eliminated disclaimer and privity as defenses, that the pendulum swung toward the buyer. But, as seen later, the U.C.C. rather than § 402A may apply in some cases involving commercial buyers and sellers.

Warranties also are included in Article 2A on leasing. The drafters noted that:

> All of the express and implied warranties of the Article on Sales (Article 2) are included (Sections 2A-210 through 2A-216, revised to reflect differences in lease transactions). The lease of goods is sufficiently similar to the sale of goods to justify this decision. Further, many courts have reached the same decision.

In the mid-1990s, a proposal was drafted and is under consideration in the ALI for the reformulation of § 402A of the Restatement of Torts Second.

§ 5.03 Express Warranties

Read: U.C.C. § 2-313.

Read also: U.C.C. § 2A-210; CISG Art. 35(1), (2)(c), (3) and Arts. 36-40.

PROBLEM 5.1

Your firm is "fortunate" to represent some well known actors and entertainers. One day Brian Keith (once played on TV) comes to the firm with a problem. It seems that even though plaintiff belonged to the Waikiki Yacht Club, had attended a sailing school, had joined the Coast Guard Auxiliary and had sailed on many yachts in order to ascertain his preferences, he had not previously owned a yacht. He attended a boat show in Long Beach during October 1978 and looked at a number of boats, speaking to sales representatives and obtaining advertising literature. In the literature, the sailboat which is the subject of this action, called an "Island Trader 41," was described as a seaworthy vessel. In one sales brochure, this vessel is described as "a picture of sure-footed seaworthiness." In another, it is called "a carefully well-equipped, and very seaworthy live-aboard vessel." Brian says he relied on representations in the sales brochures in regard to the purchase and that he and a sales representative also discussed desire for a boat which was ocean-going and would cruise long distances. Being a cautious individual, Brian asked his friend Buddy Ebsen (who played Jed on the Beverly Hillbillies on TV) who was involved in a boat building enterprise, to inspect the boat. Mr. Ebsen and one of his associates, both of whom had extensive experience with sailboats, observed the boat and advised plaintiff that the vessel would suit his stated needs. A deposit was paid on the boat, a purchase contract was entered into, and optional accessories for the boat were ordered. After delivery of the vessel, a dispute arose in regard to its seaworthiness. The seller refuses to accept the boat back and refuses to return the deposit. What are Brian's rights? What defenses will the Seller raise? Who should win? Why? (See *Keith v. Buchanan,* 220 Cal. Rptr. 392, 42 U.C.C. Rep. 386 (1985).)

NOTES

(1) In *Szajna v. General Motors Corp., 40 U.C.C. Rep. 77 (Ill. App. 1985)*, plaintiff filed a class action suit against defendant General Motors (GMC). In his complaint, plaintiff argued that the trade name "1976 Pontiac Ventura" was a description of the car which created an express warranty that the car would have component parts of a particular kind and quality. The court found that "the use of a trade name, alone, [cannot] be extended to encompass a 'description' of the component parts therein." Compare Szajna to *Kilbourn v. Henderson*, 65 So.2d 533 (1953), where the court affirmed the finding of a breach of express warranty where the car advertised as a "1940 Mercury" was found to have a motor manufactured several years before 1940.

(2) In *Slyman v. Pickwick Farms,* 39 U.C.C. Rep. 1630 (Ohio 1984),the court held that a description given by the seller, or adoption by seller of a third party's opinion, which is a part of the "basis of the bargain," will create a warranty under U.C.C. § 2-313.

David Slyman, plaintiff, attended the Scioto-Tattersalls and Ohio Harness Horse Breeders, Inc. yearling sale. Plaintiff purchased five horses, all consigned by Pickwick Farms. One of the colts, named Masterpoint, purchased for $4,200, occasionally exhibited symptoms of difficulty in breathing. Prior to bids being accepted, a veterinarian, at the request of Pickwick Farms, read the following statement over the public address system:

> This animal at very rare intervals will make a slight noise on expiration of air. This is due to the so-called false nasal folds being very slightly more softer than normal. The true nasal openings and nasal cavities are normal in size and in no way is the animal's breathing affected.

A few days after accepting delivery of Masterpoint, William Smith, the trainer, notified plaintiff that the horse was having difficulty breathing and that its training would have to cease.

Plaintiff notified Pickwick Farms, by letter, of the problem and requested that his purchase money plus expenses be returned. Plaintiff also had Masterpoint examined by Dr. Catherine Kohn, a doctor and associate professor of Equine Medicine and Surgery at Ohio State University. Dr. Kohn's examination revealed that Masterpoint's breathing problem was a result of a congenital defect of the ventral meatus and, as a result, Masterpoint could not race in his present condition.

The *Slyman* court, at 39 U.C.C. Rep. 1635-6, stated that:

> As far as the origin of the statement is concerned, regardless of the fact that the description was formulated by a third party, and not by the seller, the statement may still be found to be part of the basis of the bargain and, therefore, constitutes an express warranty. "[T]he seller need only introduce it into the bargaining process so that it becomes part of the basis of the bargain. . ." The major factor to be considered when dealing with a statement originating from a third party is whether or not the description or statement in question became a part of the basis of the bargain. The origin of the statement is not important so long as it is the seller who introduces it into the bargaining process. In the instant case, Knappenberger examined Masterpoint on October 12, 1979 and prepared his evaluation of the horse at the request of Pickwick Farms. It was Pickwick who introduced the statement into the bargaining process by having it read aloud before the sale of the horse. As such, the description given by [Pickwick's veterinarian] concerning the horse's respiratory condition at the time of the sale constituted an express warranty.

(3) Warranties in writing in consumer sales must comply with the provisions of the Magnuson-Moss Act. See § 5.10[A], *infra.*

§ 5.04 Implied Warranties

[A] Merchantability

Read: U.C.C. § 2-314.

Read also: U.C.C. §§ 2A-212, 1-205(1990); CISG. Art. 35(1), (2)(a) and (d) and (3) and Arts. 36-40.

PROBLEM 5.2

Your firm is representing Sara Mayflower, who suffered serious injury from a fish bone which lodged in her throat while eating fish chowder at the Clipper Ship Restaurant. At a small social gathering of several of the firm's members and spouses, the general topic of fish chowder is mentioned. One of the wives mentions that she has an excellent fish chowder recipe her great-grandmother, Mrs. John Standish, used. Another said she has several recipe books with "fish chowder" in them. One of your partners remembers having read about fish chowder in *The House of the Seven Gables* by Hawthorne. Is this conversation of any importance to your case?

NOTES

The courts have split on the issue of liability for injuries suffered from substances in food consumed in a restaurant. Two distinct lines of authority have emerged, the "foreign-natural" test and the "reasonable expectations" test. Although both theories are usually applied to objects found in food, they are also applicable to cases of chemical contamination, such as food poisoning. In *Battiste v. St. Thomas Dining Club,* United States District Court, DVI (1979), plaintiff brought suit for damages resulting from ciguatera fish poisoning contracted after she consumed a fish dinner served by defendant. In addition to an assumption of risk defense, defendant also pleaded that ciguatera fish poisoning is a natural, latent condition in fish; thus, the seller is not liable under the implied warranties in U.C.C. §§ 2-314 and 2-315.

The "reasonable expectations" test holds that "it is a question for the trier of fact whether a buyer could reasonably expect to find the substance in the food consumed" whereas the "foreign-natural" test will bar a buyer from recovery as a matter of law "where the substance in the food which causes the injury was'natural' to the food served." *Battiste.* The court ruled that the "reasonable expectations" was the better choice, finding that this test was more consistent with Restatement (Second) of Torts § 402A (1965).

[B] Fitness for a Particular Purpose

Read: U.C.C. § 2-315, cf. § 2-314(2)(c); see § 2-317.

Read also: U.C.C. § 2A-213, cf. § 2A-212(2)(c), see § 2A-215 (1990); CISG Art. 35(2)(b), (3) and Arts. 36-40.

PROBLEM 5.3

Two farmers, Richard Warren and James Perry came to your law office in regard to some defective cabbage seed they purchased. The facts and evidence thus far may be summarized as in the statement below. What type of warranties could be asserted? If fitness for particular purpose is asserted, how would it be articulated? Can you have more than one type of warranty from the same facts and can you assert more than one theory?

FACTS OF PROBLEM

In August 1979, plaintiff Richard Warren went to W.S. Clark and Sons and spoke with Murry Fulcher. Mr. Fulcher informed plaintiff that there was a shortage of RioVerde and A-C 5 seed, and offered to sell plaintiff "Sanibel" seed instead. Plaintiff testified as follows:

> So I asked him did he know if these cabbage would winter over or had any experience with them, because I had never heard of this type cabbage.

Mr. Fulcher then called the New York seed company that sold the seed. Plaintiff testified:

> I asked Mr. Fulcher to ask the man or the woman, whoever it was he was talking to, to be sure to ask him if these cabbage seed would winter over in eastern North Carolina, specifically Carteret County, the area I was concerned with. Mr. Fulcher asked this question and assured me that these cabbage would winter over and do as good, if not better, than the AC 5 or the Rio Verde. Therefore, based upon this conversation and the information Mr. Fulcher had received, I ordered 20 pounds of the Sanibel seeds.
>
> . . . .

> I told Mr. Fulcher that if he didn't really know anything about it and he was not sure of these Sanibel seeds, not to even order them, that I would wait and get Florida plants, what I know I could make a crop with. And he stated these cabbage would be all right. Therefore we ordered the seed.

Plaintiff also testified about a later conversation with Mr. Fulcher, in which the following interchange occurred:

> I said, "Monk, now are you sure, absolutely sure, have no doubt in your mind that these seeds are going to do well in eastern North Carolina and Carteret County?" And Mr. Fulcher replied to me, said, "I'll guarantee this seed will be as good, if not better, than the AC 5's or the Rio Verde."

Plaintiff planted the seed on 28 September and transferred the plants to fields in January, 1980. In early March, plaintiff observed that the plants "were beginning to look funny." Plaintiff informed Mr. Fulcher of the plants' unusual appearance and his concern that the cabbage was going to "run up." Plaintiff testified:

> I told him, I said, "Now, Monk, if there's any doubt in your mind at this point, I have still got time to order plants from Florida and still raise a crop." He said, "No," said, "I don't think you have anything to worry about," said, "that's the way these cabbage grow." He said, "They grow funny and different than your other type cabbage."

As a result of this conversation, plaintiff did not order plants from Florida. More than 50 per cent of the cabbages he raised from Sanibel seed went to seed and were thus unmarketable. Plaintiff James Perry testified as follows:

> I asked Monk, I said, "Monk, Richard told me you found some cabbage seed," and he said, "Yes, I couldn't find any Rio Verde or AC 5 but I found a cabbage called Sanibel that I believe will grow just as good a crop if not better than the AC 5 or the Rio Verde, and the only stipulation on them is you can't put them quite as far apart as you do the Rio Verde or they will get big on you and if they get too big you can't market them." So I said, "Murry, you know the type of weather we have in Carteret County." He said, "Jimmy, I believe these cabbage is going to be the cabbage of the future for you boys. You put more plants per acre and I believe they will produce more." I said, "Okay, I want you to order me five pounds."

Mr. Perry also testified to a later conversation with Mr. Fulcher:

> I called him and I told him, I said, "Monk, these cabbage don't look right," and I said, "Now we still got time to get the cabbage plants out of Florida." And I said, "What are you thinking about?" He said, "Jimmy, I think that's the way to go. I wouldn't worry with them. I believe they'll be all right." So I didn't do anything.

NOTES

(1) In *El Fredo Pizza, Inc. v. Roto-Flex-Oven Co.*, 261 N.W.2d 358 (1978), plaintiff needed to purchase a new pizza oven for a new El Fredo branch store. Plaintiff negotiated with Roto-Flex, and entered into a contract on September 1, 1973, whereby plaintiff purchased a "Pizza Oven Special" for his new restaurant.

The oven was installed on October 22, 1973, and problems developed immediately. After the oven continued to malfunction plaintiff replaced it with one from a different vendor. The El Fredo court's holding follows:

Roto-Flex contends that the evidence was insufficient to submit the issue of implied warranty of fitness of the oven for a particular purpose to the jury because the evidence did not show that Center Street Pizza had relied on Roto-Flex' skill or judgment in purchasing the oven. Two implied warranties provided for in the Uniform Commercial Code are relevant to this case. Under section 2-314, U.C.C., a warranty that the goods shall be merchantable is implied in a contract for their sale if the seller is a merchant with respect to goods of that kind. In order for goods to be merchantable under section 2-314, they must be at least such as are fit for the ordinary purposes for which such goods are used. Under this implied warranty, no reliance upon the seller need be shown. Under section 2-315, U.C.C., a warranty of fitness for a particular purpose is implied where the seller at the time of contracting has reason to know any particular purpose for which the goods are required and that the buyer is relying on the seller's skill or judgment to select or furnish suitable goods. . . .

Roto-Flex' argument essentially is that Center Street Pizza did not rely on Roto-Flex' skill or judgment in buying the oven, but relied on the judgment of Fred Lennon, who recommended the Roto-Flex oven because his experience with a similar oven had been favorable. This argument misses the mark. Comment 1 to section 2-315, U.C.C., provides that whether or not the warranty of fitness for a particular purpose arises in any individual case is basically a question of fact to be determined by the circumstances of the contracting. Under this section the buyer need not bring home to the seller actual knowledge of the particular purpose for which the goods are intended or of his reliance on the seller's skill and judgment, if the circumstances are such that the seller has reason to realize the purpose intended or that the reliance exists. The buyer, of course, must actually be relying on the seller. If anything, the fact that Center Street Pizza went to Roto-Flex, to purchase an oven because of Lennon's knowledge of past success with a similar oven underscores the fact that Center Street Pizza was relying on Roto-Flex skill to furnish suitable goods for its business. The testimony indicated that Roto-Flex ovens are custom built for Roto-Flex customers, and Roto-Flex was aware of the particular purpose for which the oven was required in this case. Under the circumstances of this case, the evidence was clearly sufficient to raise the factual question of reliance under section 2-315, U.C.C., and it was proper to submit that question to the jury.

Affirmed as modified. [Modifications were to the amount of damages only.—Ed.]

(2) Questions of reliance may arise in U.C.C. § 2-315 cases. The court in *Keith v. Buchanan*, *supra* Problem 5.1, discussed this matter:

II. Implied Warranty

Appellant also claimed breach of the implied warranty of fitness for a particular purpose in regard to the sale of the subject vessel. An implied warranty of fitness for a particular purpose arises when a "seller at the time of contracting has reason to know any particular purpose for which the goods are required and that the buyer is relying on the seller's skill or judgment to select or furnish suitable goods," which are fit for such purpose. The Consumer Warranty Act makes such an implied warranty applicable to retailers, distributors, and manufacturers. An implied warranty of fitness for a particular purpose arises only where (1) the purchaser at the time of contracting intends to use the goods for a particular purpose, (2) the seller at the time of contracting has reason to know of this particular purpose, (3) the buyer relies on the seller's skill or judgment to select or furnish goods suitable for the particular purpose, and (4) the seller at the time of contracting has reason to know that the buyer is relying on such skill and judgment.

The reliance elements are important to the consideration of whether an implied warranty of fitness for a particular purpose exists. "If the seller had no reason to know that he was being relied upon, his conduct in providing goods cannot fairly be deemed a tacit representation of their suitability for a particular purpose. And if the buyer did not in fact rely, then the principal justification for imposing a fitness warranty disappears." The major question in determining the existence of an implied warranty of fitness for a particular purpose is the reliance by the buyer upon the skill and judgment of the seller to select an article suitable for his needs.

The trial court found that the plaintiff did not rely on the skill and judgment of the defendants to select a suitable vessel, but that he rather relied on his own experts. "Our sole task is to determine 'whether the evidence, viewed in the light most favorable to [respondent], sustains [these] findings.' Moreover, 'in examining the sufficiency of the evidence to support a questioned finding an appellate court must accept as true all evidence tending to establish the correctness of the finding as made, taking into account, as well, all inferences which might reasonably have been thought by the trial court to lead to the same conclusion.' [Citations.] If appellate scrutiny reveals that substantial evidence supports the trial court's findings and conclusions, the judgment must be affirmed."

A review of the record reveals ample evidence to support the trial court's finding. Appellant had extensive experience with sailboats at the time of the subject purchase, even though he had not previously owned such a vessel. He had developed precise specifications in regard to the type of boat he wanted to purchase. He looked at a number of different vessels, reviewed their advertising literature, and focused on the Island Trader 41 as the object of his intended purchase. He also had friends look at the boat before making the final decision to purchase. The trial court's finding that the buyer did not rely on the skill or judgment of the seller in the selection of the vessel in question is supported by substantial evidence.

§ 5.05 Privity

Read: U.C.C. § 2-318.

Read also: U.C.C. §§ 2-607(5), 2A-216, see § 2A-516(4), see also § 2A-209 (1990); CISG Arts. 1(1), and 2(a), 4 and 5.

PROBLEM 5.4

Your law firm represents Mrs. Redblood and plans to appeal. The essential facts are these: Mr. Redblood died on the operating table on March 9, 1976, during open-heart surgery because the heart-lung machine allegedly pumped air into his aorta instead of blood. One of the defenses which the lower court upheld was that there was a lack of privity as to the machine manufacturer, the distributor who sold the machine, the hospital and the doctor held that the hospital and doctors were the ultimate purchasers of the machine, not Mr. Redblood. What causes of action should have been brought? Is privity a valid defense? Should the court make an exception to privity and on what basis?

PROBLEM 5.5

Your client, a restaurant customer, was injured by a defective container of drain opener that came open and splashed on her when it fell from a shelf in the restaurant. The customer was denied recovery by the restaurant under an implied warranty theory because, as a bystander, she had no contractual privity. What is your analysis? Your reply? Your recommendations?

NOTES

(1) In a case similar to the Problem 5.4, the court made the following observations concerning privity:

> Similar issues have been previously addressed by the supreme court, but this application to operating room equipment appears to be a case of first impression. Title 12 OS 1981 §§ 2-314 and 315, provide an implied warranty of fitness and merchantability of goods for their ordinary use. Section 2-318 limits the warranty to "any natural person who is in the family or household of his buyer or who is a guest in his home. . . ." This limitation has been termed a "horizontal" extension of the warranty. See *Hardesty v. Andro Corp.-Webster Div.*, Okla., 555 P.2d 1030 (1976), in which the court refused to permit recovery by the owner of a construction project against the manufacturer of defective air conditioner parts. That decision turned on "lack of privity" between the manufacturer and the ultimate purchaser. It was later declared to be an erroneous decision in *Old Albany Estates, Ltd. v. Highland Carpet Mills, Inc.*, Okla., 604 P.2d 849 (1979), wherein the court declared the ultimate purchaser of defective goods is entitled to recover from the manufacturer for breach of an implied warranty of merchantability regardless of lack of "privity" between it and the manufacturer. the court determined that the ultimate purchaser is properly within the ambit of the "vertical" chain of sale and is entitled, as a mater of policy, to Code protection.
>
> The protection afforded to the purchaser of defective carpet in Old Albany is an extension of rulings previously made applicable to buyers of pre-packaged edibles.
>
> "Horizontal" protection, *i.e.*, remedy for those other than the purchaser, has been strictly limited to the statutory confines of the family, invitees, and household of the purchaser under § 2-318.

In a separate opinion, one of the judges made the following suggestion:

> I would also like to point out what I feel is a major flaw in our law pertaining to actions for breach of warranty that possibly our supreme court or the legislature may want to consider. That flaw comes about as to items sold which the purchaser itself will never use as intended, but which will only be "used" by purchaser's patients, clients or customers. This case, in my opinion, is a classic example of what I refer to. The "purchaser" of the heart-lung machine, be it hospital, doctor, clinic, etc., will never be the "consumer" or "user" that would be damaged by a defective machine, but only the unconscious patient will be the party affected. The cases referred to in the main opinion refer to the so-called "vertical" and "horizontal" chain for determining whether a party can maintain an action for breach of warranty. One must be in the "vertical" chain to maintain the action.
>
> I submit that we need a "diagonal" chain as an exception. The diagonal chain would be an exception wherein the item purchased is one referred to above that virtually no person in the vertical chain would ever be the user/consumer of. Such items normally would be part

of service related occupations or professions where the purchaser buys the item to use on persons other than the purchaser. I would therefore suggest the "diagonal" exception to the cases permitting only "purchasers" in the vertical chain to maintain an action for breach of warranty. Until such exception is recognized or legislated a "warranty" on such items is virtually meaningless. The purchaser (and those in the vertical chain) will never be the ultimate user/consumer of the item. Because the "user consumer" is not in the vertical chain no action for breach of warranty could be maintained by any person — thus any warranty is meaningless.

(2) Can a seller of consumer goods who has given an express warranty limit or exclude consequential damages by the inclusion of an express disclaimer within the contract?

In *Collins v. Uniroyal, Inc.*, 315 A.2d 30 (NJ 1973), Uniroyal, included the following disclaimer: "This Guarantee does not cover consequential damage, and the liability of the manufacturer is limited to repairing or replacing the tire. . . . No other guarantee or warranty, express or implied, is made." The decedent, an entertainer, who with his family traveled extensively throughout the country performing a knife-throwing act, was killed in an automobile accident. Decedent had purchased five new tires for his station wagon from a Uniroyal distributor. While traveling on Interstate Highway 80, in their vehicle laden with personal belongings and "paraphernalia of their act," the right rear tire failed, resulting in loss of control of the vehicle which subsequently rolled over. Decedent died of injuries received in the accident.

Uniroyal argues that the court erred in allowing evidence of Uniroyal's advertisements, and by disallowing the jury to consider the limitation of damages provision of the warranty.

The pertinent language of the warranty is as follows:

The new U.S. Royal Master tire with wrap-around tread and pin stripe (1/2 inch) whitewall design is of such quality and reliability that U.S. Rubber Tire Company makes the following Guarantee:

LIFETIME—Every such U.S. Royal Master tire of our manufacture, bearing our name and serial number, other than "seconds," is guaranteed to be free from defects in workmanship and material for the life of the original tread without limit as to time or mileage.

ROAD HAZARD—In addition, every such U.S. Royal Master tire, when used in normal passenger car service, is guaranteed during the life of the original tread against blowouts, cuts, bruises, and similar injury rendering the tire unserviceable. Tires which are punctured or abused, by being run flat, improperly aligned, balanced, or inflated, cut by chains or obstructions on vehicle, damaged by fire, collision or vandalism, or by other means, and "seconds" are not subject to the road hazard provision of this Guarantee.

If our examination shows that such a U.S. Royal Master tire is eligible for adjustment under either the Lifetime or Road Hazard provision of this Guarantee, we will repair it or provide a new U.S. Royal Master tire at a fractional price computed on percentage of wear of original tread depth and then current U.S. suggested exchange price as follows: [There follows a rate chart and several additional paragraphs not relevant here.]

The jury also had before it copies of Uniroyal tire advertisements used during 1966, received in evidence over the objection of defense counsel. Mrs. Collins testified without objection that about a month before the purchase her husband had shown her a Uniroyal advertisement and had indicated his intent to buy the product. The jury could have inferred from these proofs that the advertisement was like the ones in evidence and that decedent relied upon it when he bought the tires. More importantly, the advertisement helped to explain the scope and intent of the "road hazard" part of the warranty which guaranteed for the life of the original tread every Royal Master tire, when used in normal passenger car service, against blowouts, cuts, bruises, and similar injury rendering the tire unserviceable. Although the term was not defined, the advertisements reflected defendant's concept of what normal passenger car service included. They extolled the virtues of the tire, containing statements such as:

> If it only saves your life once, it's a bargain.
>
> . . . It could pay off some day. The day you hit a pothole at 70 miles an hour.
>
> The day you sweep around a tricky, rain-slicked curve. The day it's 90 degrees in the shade and you have to go 600 miles in a hurry. The day you pick up a nail and it's three in the morning. You're getting a brute of a carcass that's so strong, you can practically forget about blowouts.

The court held that in the case of breach of warranty the recovery of consequential damages is permitted. N.J.S.A. 12A:2-714(3). Although consequential damages may be limited or excluded absent unconscionability, "the limitation of consequential damages for injury to the person in the case of consumer goods is prima facie unconscionable." N.J.S.A. 12A:2-719(3).

(3) The PEB Study Group Report contains the following comments:

> *F. Privity and Related Warranty Issues*
>
> In view of the criticisms of the treatment of consumer issues, there was "substantial sentiment" in the Study Group to retreat from two earlier recommendations, namely that Alternative A to § 2-318 and § 2-719(3) be deleted from Article 2. Both of these provisions dealt with personal injuries caused by a breach of warranty and it was our view that remedies for these injuries should be left to the law of torts. On reflection, this imposes an undue restriction upon the options of individuals injured by unmerchantable or defective goods. Thus, buyers and others injured in person or property by a breach of warranty should be able to recover under Article 2, but they should be subject to the same limitations as buyers who suffer only commercial loss, e.g., privity, notice, disclaimers, and statute of limitations, unless those limitations have been modified in the interest of consumers.
>
> The Study Group spent considerable time discussing the "privity" issue and how it should be analyzed.

46 Bus. Lawyer 1869, 1880 (1990).

§ 5.06 Disclaimer

Read: U.C.C. §§ 2-316, 1-201(10); see §§ 2-719, 2-302.

Read also: U.C.C. §§ 2A-108, 2A-214, 2A-503; CISG Arts. 4(a), 6, 7(1), 8(2), 35(2) and (3).

NOTES

(1) *Conspicuous.* One court analyzed this requirement: There is no dispute that the language contained in the contract was in this case sufficient to waive all implied warranties. The issue is whether the disclaimer was "conspicuous." Section 1201(10) [Cal. Comm. Code]. Basic/Four points out that it disclaimed the implied warranties not once but twice, and that the disclaimers were written in italicized print, in contrast to the regular print used on the rest of the contract. Nevertheless, the disclaimers are not conspicuous. In *Dorman v. International Harvester Co.*,

120 Cal. Rptr. 516 (Cal. App. 1975), the California court of appeals noted that under pre-Code California law, disclaimers of warranty are strictly construed, and, applying the code, it found that an attempted disclaimer written in only slightly contrasting print and without a heading adequate to call the buyer's attention to the disclaimer clause was not effective. That decision controls in this case. The two disclaimers in the Office Supply-Basic/Four contract are on the reverse sides of the first two pages of the contract. They are not positioned close to the buyer's signature line. The contracts are printed on pale green paper and the disclaimers are set forth in print which, although italicized, is only slightly contrasting with the remainder of the contract. There are no headings noting the disclaimers of warranty. Since there is only "some slight contrasting set-off" and there is "only a slight contrast with the balance of the instrument," the disclaimers are not conspicuous.

If the disclaimer is not conspicuous, does knowledge of it make it effective?

(2) *Knowledge.* Consider the following testimony:

James Bruno testified during his deposition taken on November 3, 1980, that before he purchased the Basic/Four system, he spent approximately two months comparing it with other systems, and that he drew up a written comparison of the Basic/Four and Qantel systems, including their guarantees: Basic/Four, 90 days; and Qantel had one year. He read the back of the contract before he signed it, when he received the contract from Basic/Four he made out a list of questions to ask Basic/Four before signing and one subject on his list was the ninety-day guarantee and before he signed he showed the warranty provision in the contract to someone he knew in the data processing field. He discussed the warranties with Basic/Four before signing and tried to have them modified:

Q: Did you read the provisions of the warranty?

A: Yes.

Q: And did you discuss those provisions with Basic/Four, or with someone from Basic/Four?

A: Yes.

Q: And what was said to you about those provisions?

A: That that was the condition that I had to accept.

Q: All right. And was that discussion before or after the contract was signed?

A: I would say before.

A: . . . .

Q: . . . did you call up Darryl Bannister, for example, and say I want to buy this system but I refuse to agree to the warranty provisions in the contract?

A: Well, I argued with him, but it was to no avail. Nothing.

He also was aware of the warranty limitations before he signed the contract.

Q: Well, were you aware of the provisions of that warranty before you signed the contract?

A: That there were limitations?

Q: That there are limitations to the warranty? Were you aware of that?

A: Certainly.

Q: You were?

A: Yes.

(3) The PEB Study Group Report contains the following comments: p. 168

E. Disclaimer of Warranty

The Study Group agreed in the Preliminary Report that § 2-316 should be revised and placed this revision in the category that justified appointing a Drafting Committee. See Part III(5). After further consideration, the Study Group makes two additional recommendations for revision and retreats from a recommendation made earlier. Rec. A2.2(13).

The additional recommendations for change involve consumer protection and are drawn from the Magnuson-Moss Warranty Act.

First, we recommend that the implied warranty of merchantability should not be disclaimable under § 2-316(2) when the seller makes a written warranty that is subject to MMWA. This is the effect under federal law and there is no good reason why state law should not be the same. Under this recommendation, a revision of the definition of "consumer" in Article 2 would be required.

Second, if a written warranty subject to the MMWA is made, Article 2 should require the same disclosure as that required by federal law. A written warranty which disclaims or limits warranties and provides agreed remedies should clearly and conspicuously state the nature and, perhaps, the effect of the agreement.

The retreat is from our earlier recommendation that a disclaimer should be effective if the buyer knew or had reason to know about it, even though the statutory requirements of form, § 2-316(2), were not met. The Study Group. . . .

46 Bus. Lawyer 1869, 1879-80 (1991).

(4) The New York court in *Rice v. R.M. Burritt Motors, Inc.*, 477 N.Y.S.2d 278 (1984), held that a vehicle sold subject to an as is clause would not be "as is," but rather "as it should be." The plaintiff in *Rice* purchased a vehicle on August 22, 1983. Plaintiff discovered that the heater-defroster unit was inoperable in October of 1983. Defendant in this case did not dispute plaintiff's factual claims, but relied on the traditional interpretation of the contractual "as is" clause. Plaintiff argued that New York State Law gives consumers "additional protection as to used motor vehicles, this being the warranty of serviceability." New York State Law mandates that a dealer furnish the customer a certificate which indicates that the vehicle is in compliance with § 417 of the Vehicle and Traffic Law. 15 NYCRR 78.1 3(c)(9) requires that "all 1964 and later model vehicles must be equipped with a front windshield defrosting device in good working order. . ."

Former law and the apparent intent of the framers of the Uniform Commercial Code was that if one purchases a used car "as is," one gets the car "as is" and one may not be heard to complain, at least in terms of contract, that the vehicle is not what the purchaser in retrospect feels it should have been. Thus, "as is" used to mean "as is."

Now, however, the "warranty of serviceability" which has existed for some time is apparently recognized by the courts as something more than simply a restatement of the implied warranties of merchantability which can be excluded by "as is" clauses. Thus a sale of a used vehicle in New York State "AS IS" no longer means "as is" — but rather it now means "as it should be" under the Vehicle and Traffic Law and the Commissioner's regulations. Whether this be good or bad, it is now certainly the case.

(5) As to unconscionable warranty disclaimers, see Chapter One at § 1.06[D].

§ 5.07 Strict Liability

Read: CISG Arts. 2(a), 5.

[A] Restatement[1]

RESTATEMENT OF TORTS SECOND § 402A

SPECIAL LIABILITY OF SELLER OF PRODUCT FOR PHYSICAL HARM TO USER OR CONSUMER.[2]

(1) One who sells any product in a defective condition unreasonably dangerous to the user or consumer or to his property is subject to liability for physical harm thereby caused to the ultimate user or consumer, or to his property, if

(a) the seller is engaged in the business of selling such a product, and

(b) it is expected to and does reach the user or consumer without substantial change in the condition in which it is sold.

(2) The rule stated in Subsection (1) applies although

(a) the seller has exercised all possible care in the preparation and sale of his product, and

(b) the user or consumer has not bought the product from or entered into any contractual relation with the seller.

See Reporter's Notes

Caveat:

The Institute expresses no opinion as to whether the rules stated in this Section may not apply

(1) to harm to persons other than users or consumers;

(2) to the seller of a product expected to be processed or otherwise Substantially changed before it reaches the user or consumer; or

(3) to the seller of a component part of a product to be assembled.

Comment b of § 402A describes its history:

b. *History.* Since the early days of the common law those engaged in the business of selling food intended for human consumption have been held to a high degree of responsibility for their products. As long ago as 1266 there were enacted special criminal statutes imposing penalties upon victualers, vintners, brewers, butchers, cooks, and other persons who supplied "corrupt" food and drink. In the earlier part of this century this ancient attitude was reflected in a series of decisions in which the courts of a number of states sought to find some method of holding the seller of food liable to the ultimate consumer even though there was no showing of negligence on the part of the seller. These decisions represented a departure from, and an exception to, the general rule that a supplier of chattels was not liable to third persons in the absence of negligence or privity of contract. In the beginning, these decisions displayed considerable ingenuity in evolving more or less fictitious theories of liability to fit the case. The various devices included an agency of the intermediate dealer or another to purchase for

[1] 1964-65 current version. For proposed changes being considered by ALI, see. pp. 5-49.

[2] Copyright © 1968 by American Law Institute. Reprinted by permission.

the consumer, or to sell for the seller; a theoretical assignment of the seller's warranty to the intermediate dealer; a third party beneficiary contract; and an implied representation that the food was fit for consumption because it was placed on the market, as well as numerous others. In later years the courts have become more or less agreed upon the theory of a "warranty" from the seller to the consumer, either "running with the goods" by analogy to a covenant running with the land, or made directly to the consumer. Other decisions have indicated that the basis is merely one of strict liability in tort, which is not dependent upon either contract or negligence.

Recent decisions, since 1950, have extended this special rule of strict liability beyond the seller of food for human consumption. The first extension was into the closely analogous cases of other products intended for intimate bodily use, where, for example, as in the case of cosmetics, the application to the body of the consumer is external rather than internal. Beginning in 1958 with a Michigan case involving cinder building blocks, a number of recent decisions have discarded any limitation to intimate association with the body, and have extended the rule of strict liability to cover the sale of any product which, if it should prove to be defective, may be expected to cause physical harm to the consumer or his property.

Comment c deals with theories underlying § 402A.

c. On whatever theory, the justification for the strict liability has been said to be that the seller, by marketing his product for use and consumption, has undertaken and assumed a special responsibility toward any member of the consuming public who may be injured by it; that the public has the right to and does expect, in the case of products which it needs and for which it is forced to rely upon the seller, that reputable sellers will stand behind their goods; that public policy demands that the burden of accidental injuries caused by products intended for consumption be placed upon those who market them, and be treated as a cost of production against which liability insurance can be obtained; and that the consumer of such products is entitled to the maximum of protection at the hands of someone, and the proper persons to afford it are those who market the products.

The comments to § 402A also deal with contributory negligence and assumption of risk.

n. *Contributory negligence.* Since the liability with which this Section deals is not based upon negligence of the seller, but is strict liability, the rule applied to strict liability cases (see § 524) applies. Contributory negligence of the plaintiff is not a defense when such negligence consists merely in a failure to discover the defect in the product, or to guard against the possibility of its existence. On the other hand the form of contributory negligence which consists in voluntarily and unreasonably proceeding to encounter a known danger, and commonly passes under the name of assumption of risk, is a defense under this Section as in other cases of strict liability. If the user or consumer discovers the defect and is aware of the danger, and nevertheless proceeds unreasonably to make use of the product and is injured by it, he is barred from recovery.

Parties covered by § 402A are termed users or consumers, and are described in the comments:

I. *User or consumer.* In order for the rule stated in this Section to apply, it is not necessary that the ultimate user or consumer have acquired the product directly from the seller, although the rule applies equally if he does so. He may have acquired it through one or more intermediate dealers. It is not even necessary that the consumer have purchased the product at all. He may be a member of the family of the final purchaser, or his employee, or a guest at his table, or a mere donee from the purchaser. The liability stated is one in tort, and does not require any contractual relation, or privity of contract, between the plaintiff and the defendant.

"Consumers" include not only those who in fact consume the product, but also those who prepare it for consumption; and the housewife who contracts tularemia while cooking rabbits for her husband is included within the rule stated in this Section, as is also the husband who is opening a bottle of beer for his wife to drink. Consumption includes all ultimate uses for which the product is intended, and the customer in a beauty shop to whose hair a permanent wave solution is applied by the shop is a consumer. "User" includes those who are passively enjoying the benefit of the product, as in the case of passengers in automobiles or airplanes, as well as those who are utilizing it for the purpose of doing work upon it, as in the case of an employee of the ultimate buyer who is making repairs upon the automobile which he has purchased.

The following comment to § 402A describes some of the basic differences between warranty and strict liability in tort:

m. "*Warranty.*" The liability in this Section does not rest upon negligence. It is strict liability, similar in its nature to that covered by Chapters 20 and 21. The basis of liability is purely one of tort.

A number of courts, seeking a theoretical basis for the liability, have resorted to a "warranty," either running with the goods sold, by analogy to covenants running with the land, or made directly to the consumer without contract. In some instances this theory has proved to be an unfortunate one. Although warranty was in its origin a matter of tort liability, and it is generally agreed that a tort action will still lie for its breach, it has become so identified in practice with a contract of sale between the plaintiff and the defendant that the warranty theory has become something of an obstacle to the recognition of the strict liability where there is no such contract. There is nothing in this Section which would prevent any court from treating the rule stated as a matter of warranty" to the user or consumer. But if this is done, it should be recognized and understood that the "warranty" is a very different kind of warranty from those usually found in the sale of goods, and that it is not subject to the various contract rules which have grown up to surround such sales.

The rule stated in this Section does not require any reliance on the part of the consumer upon the reputation, skill, or judgment of the seller who is to be held liable, nor any representation or undertaking on the part of that seller. The seller is strictly liable although, as is frequently the case, the consumer does not even know who he is at the time of consumption. The rule stated in this Section is not governed by the provisions of the Uniform Sales Act, or those of the Uniform Commercial Code, as to warranties; and it is not affected by limitations on the scope and content of warranties, or by limitation to "buyer" and "seller" in those statutes. Nor is the consumer required to give notice to the seller of his injury within a reasonable time after it occurs, as is provided by the Uniform Act. The consumer's cause of action does not depend upon the validity of his contract with the person from whom he acquires the product, and it is not affected by any disclaimer or other agreement, whether it be between the seller and his immediate buyer, or attached to and accompanying the product into the consumer's hands. In short, "warranty" must be given a new and different meaning if it is used in connection with this Section. It is much simpler to regard the liability here stated as merely one of strict liability in tort.

The following chart illustrates some of the differences between Warranty and Strict Liability.[3]

	Warranty of Merchantability § 2-314	Strict Liability in Tort Restatement, Second, Torts § 402A
1. Condition of goods giving rise to liability	Not merchantable, e.g., not fit for ordinary purpose. 2-314(1), (2)(c).(1).	Defective condition unreasonably dangerous. § 402A
2. Character of defendant	Must be seller who is a merchant with respect to goods of that kind. §§ 2-314(1), 2-104(1).	Must be seller who is engaged in the business of selling such a product § 402A (1)(a).
3. Reliance	No explicit requirement. Such warranty "taken for granted." § 2-314 and Comment 11; see, however, § 2-316(3)(b).	No requirement of "any reliance on the part of the consumer upon the reputation, skill or judgment of the seller." § 402A Comment m.

[3] Excerpt from B. Stone, Uniform Commercial Code in a Nutshell, pp. 74-75; Copyright © 1995, West Publishing Co. Reprinted with permission.

4. Disclaimer	Limitation of consequential damages for injury to the person in the case of consumer goods is prima facie unconscionable. §§ 2-316 (4), 2-719(3), 2-302; but see § 2-316(1)-(3).	Cause of action not affected by any disclaimer or any other agreement. § 402A Comment m.
5. Notice	Buyer must within a reasonable time after he discovers or should have discovered any breach notify seller of breach or be barred from any remedy. Reason of rule to defeat commercial bad faith not to deprive a good faith consumer of his remedy. § 2-607(3) (a) and Comments 4 and 5.	Consumer not required to give notice to seller of his injury within a reasonable time after it occurs § 402A Comment m.
6. Causation	Buyer may recover consequential damages <u>resulting</u> from seller's breach including injury to person or property <u>proximately resulting</u> from any breach of warranty §§ 2-714, 2-715(2)(b) and Comment 5, § 2-314 Comment 13, see § 2-316 (3)(b) and Comment 8.	Seller subject to liability for physical harm <u>caused</u> § 402A(1); see Comment n <u>Contributory negligence</u> Comment p <u>Further process ing or substantial chance;</u> Comment q <u>Component parts;</u> see also Comments g, h, j.
7. Protected persons	Any person who may reasonably be expected to use, consume or be affected by the goods. § 2-318 Alternative C.	Ultimate user or consumer § 402(1), (2)(b) and Comment I.
8. Protected injuries	Injuries to person listed in 7 above or his property. § 2-318 Alternative C and Comment 3; cf. Alternative B.	Physical harm to ultimate user or consumer, or to his property. § 402A(1).
9. Statute of limitations	Four years from tender of delivery. § 2-725(1), (2).	State law varies, e.g. three years from injury.

[B] Caveats to Restatement (Second) of Torts § 402A

The drafters of U.C.C. § 402A included a "Caveat" limiting its coverage in several ways. One of these dealt with parties injured by the defective products:

> o. *Injuries to non-users and non-consumers.* Thus far the courts, in applying the rule stated in this Section, have not gone beyond allowing recovery to users and consumers, as those terms are defined in Comment l. Casual bystanders, and others who may come in contact with the product, as in the case of employees of the retailer, or a passer-by injured by an exploding bottle, or a pedestrian hit by an automobile, have been denied recovery. There may be no essential reason why such plaintiffs should not be brought within the scope of the protection afforded, other than that they do not have the same reasons for expecting such protection as the consumer who buys a marketed product; but the social pressure which has been largely responsible for the development of the rule stated has been a consumer's pressure, and there is not the same demand for the protection of casual strangers. The Institute expresses neither approval nor disapproval of expansion of the rule to permit recovery by such persons.

The following article excerpts discuss this caveat and also give insight into the Restatement processes.

King and Neville, THE BYSTANDER'S RIGHT UNDER STRICT LIABILITY DOES EXIST: A CALL FOR REFORM OF THE RESTATEMENT
25 St. Louis L.J. 543, 546 (1981)[4]

The reason given by the Institute for excluding bystanders is appalling. There is no attempt by the drafters to logically judge whether to include bystanders. Rather the decision to exclude is placed upon grounds that are not logically relevant. Of course bystanders do not have the same reasons for expecting protection from the product as a consumer. However the idea that a bystander does not use or purchase a product, and does not have a consumer's expectation of a reasonably safe product, does not change the fact that he is injured by defective products which are near him or which cause injury to him. Generally, the expectation rationale relating to purchasers is not realistically or judicially sound. In many situations purchasers or users are not consciously examining the safety features of the product when buying or using it. Rather the safety features of the product are quite often only thought of when an accident occurs. Further, the expectations of purchasers and users are not the crucial basis underlying strict liability.

The Restatement position reflects a view of the law from a political pressure perspective, rather than justice. The fact that consumers as a group are more organized and have sought changes in the law should hardly exclude other who are logically entitled to protest from receiving it. The fact that there is not a strong outcry of demand for the protection of "casual strangers" does not justify the failure to extend protection to them which is caused by reason of the defective product.

The term "casual strangers" used by the Institute almost indicates that they are not so important and perhaps should not have been present. Yet in most cases the bystander is legitimately engaged in his own activities when he is injured by the defective product. Furthermore that injured individual is just as important as the injured individual who is a consumer or user and it is just as difficult, if not more difficult, for the bystander to bear the loss which is a central policy behind § 402A. It is perhaps unfortunate that there is not a "National Association of Bystanders" to put pressure on the Institute for such protection!

The underlying reason why the Institute did not include bystanders in their protection is to be found in its view of its function and the dearth of case law in 1965. When the section was being considered by the Institute, no cases could be found which held in favor of protecting a bystander injured by defective products. In a major survey of cases, the Columbia Law Journal found no support for bystander recovery. Many members of the Institute had believed that the Restatement must reflect the principles found in the majority of the cases. A few members were amenable to looking at trends of cases portending future development in some situations; they would weigh with such trends the desirability of action and consideration of policy. But in 1965 there was not a majority of cases reflecting bystander protection; there was not a trend; there was not a single case! Some persons in the Institute involved with the formulation of § 402A did not feel it was possible to extend recovery under that section to bystanders without even one case to support such a proposition.

The illogic of not covering bystanders was noted in the discussion on the floor of the Institute in the 1965 annual meeting by Witman Knapp, a member from New York. The Reporter, William Prosser, agreed with Knapp's logic but stated that he felt unjustified in broadening the rule since the only cases of strict liability coverage at that time were in terms of consumers or users. A motion was made by Knapp to change the caveat to read that the "Institute expresses approval of the expansion of the rule to permit recovery by such persons." As Professor Wechsler, Director of Institute, who presided over the discussion at the time has said "the motion was defeated, primarily I think on the ground that it was inappropriate in the Restatement (and especially in a caveat) to take a position, without decisional support, that a rule should be extended." Such a view of the function of the Restatement, in the opinion of the Director, is "unfortunate." It should be noted that at this time the views of the Institute as to its function were in a state of flux and that under current views there might have been a chance for such an inclusion of bystanders. Equally unfortunate is the failure to clearly articulate this reason in the comments to the § 402A caveat since this would undoubtedly lead to the Institute's position of neutrality, leaving it up to the courts to extend strict liability coverage.

CONCLUSION

The court decisions overwhelmingly support recovery by the bystander against the seller or manufacturer of a defective product. These decisions are ample in number and of sufficient geographic spread to make this rule applicable throughout the nation. In addition, the courts have had a sufficient number of years to deal with the problem and to reach these conclusions. The reasoning of the courts is sound and reflective of the underlying basis of the Restatement § 402A.

Policy considerations support extending strict liability coverage to bystanders. Risk spreading is just as possible in regard to the bystander as it is for buyers, consumers and users. Deterrence of less than quality production is likewise similar. The need for protecting innocent victims who are unable to bear the burden of loss individually is present.

Authorities who have written on the question of whether strict liability for defective products should extend to bystanders favor such coverage. The illogic of not doing so and the carry-over of the "dead-hand of privity" to include bystanders have been discussed. The commentators generally recognize that the policies underlying strict liability support coverage of bystanders and that the trend of cases favors them.

U.C.C. Alternatives B and C have been adopted by a number of states. These are broadly worded to include not only consumers and users, but those affected by the product and can be applied to cover bystanders. While these Code provisions deal with warranty rather than strict liability, both theories concern defective products liability. Both warranty and strict liability often are raised in a suit by the injured party against the manufacturer or seller of the defective product and the result should be consistent. Furthermore, the policies behind eliminating such privity type requirements and extending such liability to injuries of bystanders are the same for warranty and strict liability in tort; consistency of the law in regard to the elimination of the privity for bystanders is desirable.

It remains only now for the American Law Institute to amend this portion of the Restatement and recognize that fact. In the meantime, bystanders and third persons injured by defective products have been given protection by the courts and this should be recognized in future cases. The right of the bystander exists!

Two other caveats to § 402A by the American Law Institute are explained in the following comments:[5]

p. *Further processing or substantial change.* Thus far the decisions applying the rule stated have not gone beyond products which are sold in the condition, or in substantially the same condition, in which they are expected to reach the hands of the ultimate user or consumer. In the absence of decisions providing a clue to the rules which are likely to develop, the Institute has refrained from taking any position as to the possible liability of the seller where the product is expected to, and does, undergo further processing or other substantial change after it leaves his hands and before it reaches those of the ultimate user or consumer.

It seems reasonably clear that the mere fact that the product is to undergo processing, or other substantial change, will not in all cases relieve the seller of liability under the rule stated in this Section. If, for example, raw coffee beans are sold to a buyer who roasts and packs them for sale to the ultimate consumer, it cannot be supposed that the seller will be relieved of all liability when the raw beans are contaminated with arsenic, or some other poison. Likewise the seller of an automobile with a defective steering gear which breaks and injures the driver, can scarcely expect to be relieved of the responsibility by reason of the fact that the car is sold to a dealer who is expected to "service" it, adjust the breaks, mount and inflate the tires, and the like, before it is ready for use. On the other hand, the manufacturer of pigiron, which is capable of a wide variety of uses, is not so likely to be held to strict liability when it turns out to be unsuitable for the child's tricycle into which it is finally made by a remote buyer. The question is essentially one of whether the responsibility for discovery and prevention of the dangerous defect is shifted to the intermediate party who is to make the changes. No doubt there will be some situations, and some defects, as to which the responsibility will be shifted, and others in which it will not. The existing decisions as yet throw no light upon the questions, and the Institute therefore expresses neither approval nor disapproval of the seller's strict liability in such a case.

---

[5] Copyright © 1968 by American Law Institute. Reprinted by permission.

q. *Component parts.* The same problem arises in cases of the sale of a component part of a product to be assembled by another, as for example a tire to be placed on a new automobile, a brake cylinder for the same purpose, or an instrument for the panel of an airplane. Again the question arises, whether the responsibility is not shifted to the assembler. It is no doubt to be expected that where there is no change in the component part itself but it is merely incorporated into something larger, the strict liability will be found to carry through to the ultimate user or consumer. But in the absence of a sufficient number of decisions on the matter to justify a conclusion, the Institute expresses no opinion on the matter.

§ 5.08 Interaction of Warranty and Strict Liability

Read: CISG Arts. 2(a), 5.

PROBLEM 5.6

Your client, Interstate Movers, a major trucking company, recently purchased twenty Transnational Company "20 wheeler" trucks (and trailers). These are longer than the current "18 wheelers" and can haul more freight. Unfortunately, the twenty transnational trucks were defective in several respects. The motor size was not sufficient to pull the larger trucks up many hills and mountain pass highways; the wheels were made with defective metals; and the design of the coupling of the truck cabs and trailers were defective. The Interstate Company has suffered considerable losses in regard to these defects in the sense of repairs, lost days of use, need to take longer routes in some situations, and compensation to customers for delays.

Transnational has refused to remedy these problems or compensate Interstate in anyway. It points to the disclaimers in the contract, which appear to meet U.C.C. disclaimer standards. What theories can you use in regard to these losses?

PROBLEM 5.7

Another of your clients, Robert Roader, recently bought a Transnational "twenty wheeler" with the same defects. On one of his "runs" he was badly injured when one set of wheels broke loose causing the truck to crash. Transnational denies any liability based on its disclaimer. What theories can be used and what type of losses can be recovered?

NOTES

(1) In *Sanco Inc. v. Ford Motor Co.*, 579 F. Supp. 893 (1984), the court noted:

"Economic loss" designates the diminution in the value of a product and consequent loss of profits because the product is inferior in quality and does not work for the general purposes for which it was manufactured and sold. See Comment, *Manufacturers' Liability to Remote Purchasers for "Economic Loss" Damages-Tort or Contract?*, 114 U. Pa. L. Rev. 539, 541(1966). Some definitions further limit economic loss to costs of repair and replacement of the product and consequent loss of profits — "without any claim of personal injury or damage to other property." Note, *Economic Loss in Products Liability Jurisprudence*, 66 Colum. L. Rev. 917, 918 (1966). For reasons which will appear hereafter, we believe that economic loss is better defined without this limitation.

The only indication of the way Indiana courts would view the issue of whether such losses should be recoverable in a negligence action is provided in *Babson Bros. Co. v. Tipstar Corporation*, 446 N.E.2d 11 (Ind. App. 1983) (transfer denied August 31, 1983), where the Indiana Court of Appeals cited with approval the leading case in Illinois, *Moorman Mfg. Co. v. National Tank Co.*, 435 N.E.2d 443 (Ill. 1982), holding that economic losses cannot be recovered in a tort action. The *Babson* court, however, went on to affirm an award of lost profits as consequential damages for negligently performed services. This apparent contradiction renders that decision of limited value to our inquiry.

Since our effort to determine whether the Indiana law of negligence is compatible with recovery of economic losses has not been aided by any other opinions of Indiana courts, we have referred to decisions from other jurisdictions and to the works of scholarly commentators to determine the better rule of law.

The majority of jurisdictions which have considered this issue have not permitted the recovery of economic loss in a negligence action.

Dean Prosser summarized the majority rule with respect to recovery of economic losses as follows:

> There can be no doubt that the seller's liability for negligence covers any kind of physical harm, including not only personal injuries, but also property damage to the defective chattel itself, as where an automobile is wrecked by reason of its own bad brakes, as well as damage to any other property in the vicinity. But where there is no accident, and no physical damage, and the only loss is a pecuniary one, through loss of the value or use of the thing sold, or the cost of repairing it, the courts have adhered to the rule . . .that purely economic interests are not entitled to protection against mere negligence, and so have denied the recovery.

W. Prosser, *Handbook on the Law of Torts*, § 101 at 665 (4th ed 1971).

One of the most fully articulated discussions of the considerations underlying this rule is found in [Chief] Justice Traynor's majority opinion in *Seely v. White Motor Co.*, 63 Cal. 2d 9, 45 Cal. Rptr. 17, 403 P.2d 145 (1965). In *Seely* the plaintiff sought to recover lost profits and a refund of the purchase price of a defective truck. The California Supreme Court ruled that such damages, although recoverable in a breach of warranty action, were not recoverable in strict liability in tort. The following passage from the majority opinion is pertinent to this case:

> The distinction that the law has drawn between tort recovery for physical injuries and warranty recovery for economic loss is not arbitrary and does not rest on the "luck" of one plaintiff in having an accident causing physical injury. The distinction rests, rather, on an understanding of the nature of the responsibility a manufacturer must undertake in distributing his products. He can appropriately be held liable for physical injuries caused by defects by requiring his goods to match a standard of safety defined in terms of conditions that create unreasonable risks of harm. He cannot be held for the level of performance of his products in the consumer's business unless he agrees that the product was designed to meet the consumer's demands. A consumer should not be charged at the will of the

> manufacturer with bearing the risk of physical injury when he buys a product on the market. He can, however, be fairly charged with the risk that the product will not match his economic expectations unless the manufacturer agrees that it will. Even in actions for negligence, a manufacturer's liability is limited to damages for physical injury and there is no recovery for economic loss alone.

45 Cal. Rptr. at 23, 403 P.2d at 151 (Citations omitted).

We think that the rule embraced by the majority of the jurisdictions is sound for the reasons articulated by [Chief] Justice Traynor in *Seely*. A tort action traditionally presupposes that the plaintiff has been exposed to an unreasonable risk of injury to his person or his property. Qualitative defects which merely disappoint the buyer's expectations of the product's performance do not expose the user or his property to any risk of physical harm. When a product does not perform as expected, the buyer's remedy should be governed by the rules of contract, which traditionally protect expectation interests.

We are aware that this argument loses some of its appeal when the plaintiff is an ordinary consumer faced with the usual "take-it-or-leave-it" disclaimed warranties from all of the potential sellers. The effect of these disclaimers is that a consumer may have purchased a worthless product and yet be left without a remedy. In his dissent in *Seely* Justice Peters recognized this problem and suggested that consumer buyers in particular should have a tort cause of action to cover purely economic losses.

However, the consumer is not entirely remediless in such situations. The Uniform Commercial Code has several provisions which provide courts with room for the exercise of judicial discretion to ensure that substantial justice results in particular cases. See Ind Code 26-1-2-302 and Ind Code 26-1-2-719(3) concerning unconscionable clauses and contracts, and Ind Code 26-1-1-203 imposing a general obligation of good faith. The fact that courts are reluctant to invoke these provisions does not justify the application of tort theory to resolve a problem of sales law.

Imposing tort liability on a manufacturer, and thus increasing the cost of doing business, is justified when a product causes personal injury or even when it causes damage to itself or other property under circumstances in which the absence of personal injury is merely fortuitous, such as when an object explodes but does not inflict personal injuries on anyone. Society has a great interest in spreading the cost of such injuries. We believe, however, that the Supreme Court of Indiana would concur in the opinion of most courts that when a plaintiff has suffered only economic loss, as first above defined, the societal interest in cost spreading is insufficient to justify requiring "the consuming public to pay more for their products so that a manufacturer can insure against the possibility that some of his products will not meet the . . . needs of some of his customers." *Seely v. White Motor Co.*, 403 P.2d at 151.

Justice Traynor stated another reason why subjecting a manufacturer to liability under a tort theory for economic loss is inappropriate: it would encroach on the decision of the legislature to enact the carefully articulated sales provisions of the Uniform Commercial Code. Ind Code 26-1-2-101 to 26-1-2-725. See *Seely v. White Motor Co.*, 403 P.2d 145,150. Thus, in the present case, if a negligence cause of action were available, Sanco could recover despite any effective disclaimer of warranty under Ind Code 26-1-2-316, or any failure of Sanco to adhere to the notice requirements of Ind Code 26-1-2-607.

We agree that this result would represent an unwarranted extension of the traditional boundaries of tort law into an area that our legislature, by enactment of the Uniform

Commercial Code, has provided with a finely tuned mechanism for dealing with the rights of parties to a sales transaction with respect to economic losses. We are confident that the Supreme Court of Indiana would view unfavorably any encroachment of tort law on the sales scheme of the Uniform Commercial Code.

Finally, we note that the Restatement (Second) of Torts, § 395 (1965) is in apparent agreement with the majority rule. The Restatement states that a manufacturer is to be liable for "physical harm" caused by its negligence in the manufacture of a chattel dangerous unless carefully made. That section, however, does not extend the manufacturer's liability to encompass purely economic loss.

As indicated above, however, not every instance of damage to the defective product itself is a case of economic loss. Sometimes such damage is properly characterized as physical harm susceptible to tort recovery. In some such circumstances it is difficult to determine which theory of recovery is appropriate. The line between tort and contract must then be drawn "by analyzing the interrelated factors such as the nature of the defect, the type of risk, and the manner in which the injury arose." Although this analysis sometimes demands fine line drawing, the proper view of the distinction between tort and contract theories requires that the line be drawn, even in close cases.

Two cases decided by the Alaska Supreme Court illustrate the difference in types of damage and the necessity of distinguishing between tort and warranty causes of action. In *Morrow v. New Moon Homes, Inc.*, 548 P.2d 279 (Alaska 1976), the plaintiff purchased a mobile home and proceeded to occupy it. He soon discovered that the roof leaked continually and that it had numerous other defects. He sued the manufacturer under a strict liability theory to recover for the defects. The Alaska Supreme Court noted that the defects merely reduced the value of the product below the price actually paid for it. The defects did not create a situation potentially dangerous to persons or other property; they only disappointed the buyer's expectations of the product's performance. The court therefore refused to allow Morrow to proceed under a strict liability in tort theory and instead relegated him to his rights under contract theory embodied in the Uniform Commercial Code.

In contrast, fire destroyed a mobile home in *Cloud v. Kit Manufacturing Co.*, 563 P.2d 248 (Alaska 1977). Padding stored under the mobile home had been ignited by a heating unit mounted under the structure to keep pipes from freezing. The fire did not result in personal injury and damaged only the mobile home. However, the fire was a sudden event which reduced the product's value in a manner entirely different than in *Morrow*. The defect in *Cloud* created a situation potentially dangerous to persons or other property and the loss occurred as a result of that danger. Recovery in tort was therefore held to be appropriate, even though the damage was confined to the product itself.

It may therefore be said, as a general rule, that when damage is sudden and calamitous, resulting from an occurrence hazardous to human safety, recovery may be had in tort, but damage resulting merely from deterioration, internal breakage, depreciation, failure to live up to expectation, and the like, will be considered economic loss, as to which recovery may be had only on a contract theory.

Although the revised definition refers to "economic losses" without defining them, and fails to make clear whose property is referred to in the first sentence, we believe that a fair construction of the act, as amended, would lead to precisely the result which we have elaborated in the foregoing pages. The new definition would not, of course, have any retroactive effect but does tend to show that the Indiana legislature and this court are in agreement as to the distinction which we have attempted to make clear as to what type of defect does, and what does not, properly give rise to an action in tort for damage caused to the defective property itself, and for consequential damages approximately caused by sudden, major damage.

(2) *Sanco, Inc.*, appealed but the appellate court affirmed at 7871 F.2d 1081(7th Cir. 1985). The appellate court found that Indiana's enactment of the U.C.C. precluded recovery for purely economic interests in a negligence action. Court cites: (Court denied recovery of lost profits and refund of purchase price in a strict liability case, although they would be recoverable in a breach of warranty action). The appellate court in *Sanco* also found that the warranty booklets formed a part of the sale agreement as a matter of law since the warranty disclaimers were known by the president of Sanco to be the routine and only way in which Ford warranted its trucks and engines.

(3) In *Salt River Project Agricultural Improvement & Power v. Westinghouse Elec. Corp.*, 694 P.2d 198 (Ariz. 1984), the Arizona Supreme Court dealt with the issue of whether tort law or contract law is to govern claims arising from the malfunction of a product. In December 1971, Salt River Project (SRP) purchased and accepted for commercial operation a gas-turbine generator unit from Westinghouse, to be installed at the Kyrene Power Plant in Tempe, Arizona. In April 1972, SRP notified Westinghouse that the generator had a number of problems, including "frequent computer malfunctions" with the one-word P-50 control computer. SRP further suggested that "an improvement could be made if there was a means of operating the turbine manually." Westinghouse wrote to SRP and advised them that Westinghouse was developing a device (LMC) which "would permit manual operation of . . .gas turbine plants during maintenance of the [P-50]." On March 2, 1973, SRP sent a standard purchase order to Westinghouse. The purchase order contained SRP's standard boilerplate "terms and conditions" which included the following:

> 1. Acceptance of Purchase Order. . . . Acceptance of this Purchase Order must be made on its exact terms and if additional or different terms are proposed by Seller such response will constitute a counter-offer, and no contract shall come into existence without Buyer's written assent to the counter-offer. Buyer's acceptance or payment for material shipped shall constitute acceptance of such material subject to the provisions herein, only, and shall not constitute acceptance of any counter-offer by Seller not assented to in writing.

On March 15, 1973, Westinghouse responded to SRP's purchase order with a standard acceptance form of its own, which stated: "Your order has been entered as our general order number as shown above." The form also referred the purchaser to the reverse side where Westinghouse's "terms and conditions" of the sale were printed as follows:

TERMS AND CONDITIONS

> The conditions stated below shall take precedence over any conditions which may appear on your standard form, and no provisions or condition of such form except as expressly stated herein, shall be binding on Westinghouse.
>
> WARRANTY—. . .Westinghouse warrants that the products sold hereunder shall be of the kind and quality described in this quotation and shall be free of defects in workmanship or materials . . . THIS WARRANTY . . . IS EXCLUSIVE AND IN LIEU OF ANY WARRANTY OF MERCHANTABILITY, FITNESS FOR PURPOSE, OR OTHER WARRANTY OF QUALITY, WHETHER EXPRESS OR IMPLIED. (Emphasis in original.)

> LIMITATION OF LIABILITY—Neither party shall be liable for special, indirect, incidental or consequential damages. The remedies of the Purchaser set forth herein are exclusive, and the liability of Westinghouse with respect to any contract or sale or anything done in connection therewith, whether in contract, in tort, under any warranty or otherwise, shall not, except as expressly provided herein, exceed the price of the product or part on which such liability is based.

The LMC was delivered to SRP's Kyrene plant in February 1974. Westinghouse employees assisted in the installation and testing of the LMC. On May 16, 1976, an accident destroyed the rotating blades in sections one through four of the gas turbine unit. Damages were calculated to be in excess of $1.9 million. SRP alleges that the accident was a result of an explosion and fire due to a malfunction in the LMC unit. In the alternative, SRP alleged that Westinghouse breached an implied warranty of fitness.

With respect to the "battle of the forms" the court held that Westinghouse prevailed since SRP had "accepted the LMC device nearly a year later without protesting any of the terms in the Westinghouse boilerplate." The rationale behind this result is that the U.C.C. recognizes that merchants may merely exchange forms without ever "engaging in actual negotiations concerning a knowledgeable allocation of risks." The court also rejected SRP's assertions that Westinghouse's boiler-plate "terms and conditions" were unconscionable, stating that, "although a commercial purchaser is not doomed to failure in pressing an unconscionability claim, . . . findings of unconscionability in a commercial setting are rare."

SRP then contended that even if relief were unavailable under the U.C.C., it still may proceed against Westinghouse under a tort doctrine of strict liability. In determining whether SRP can invoke a strict liability theory, the court turned to the question of whether SRP's claim was a "claim governed by tort law, or a contract claim governed by the U.C.C., or partly one and partly the other."

The Westinghouse court emphasized the policy considerations which underlie contract and tort law.

Strict liability "is not based upon traditional concepts of fault," *Reader v. General Motors Corp.*, 107 Ariz. 149, 154, 483 P.2d 1388, 1393 (1971), but is imposed in an attempt to make the products safer.

> The "prophylactic" factor of preventing future harm has been quite important in the field of torts. The courts are concerned not only with compensation of the victim, but with admonition of the wrongdoer. When the decisions of the courts become known, and defendants realize that they may be held liable, there is of course a strong incentive to prevent the occurrence of the harm. Not infrequently one reason for imposing liability is the deliberate purpose of providing that incentive. . . . [T]he manufacturer who is made liable to the consumer for defects in a product will do what can be done to see that there are no such defects.

Thus, preventing accidents by deterring the distribution of unsafe products is one of the prime goals of tort law.

A basic policy of contract law, on the other hand, is to preserve freedom of contract and thus promote the free flow of commerce. This policy is best served when the commercial law permits parties to limit the redress of a purchaser who fails to receive the quality of product he expected. When a defect renders a product substandard or unable to perform the functions for which it was manufactured, the purchaser's remedy for disappointed commercial expectations is through contract law.

Division One of the Arizona Court of Appeals has aptly summarized the difference between tort and contract:

> [T]he rationale for making a distinction is that traditional contract remedies are designed to redress loss of the benefit of the bargain while tort remedies are — designed to protect the public from dangerous products.
>
> In making the determination of whether a claim to recover damages alleged to have been caused by a defect in the goods is governed by the doctrine of strict liability or by the U.C.C., the court outlined three relevant factors to be considered. These factors are (1) the nature of the product defect that caused the buyer's loss, (2) the manner in which the loss occurred, and (3) the type of loss for which redress is sought.
>
> The type of product that will trigger tort liability is one which is defective in a way that poses an unreasonable danger to those who use or consume it. In contrast, the type of product defect contemplated by the U.C.C. is a qualitative one; the Code provides that a merchant impliedly warrants that his goods are "merchantable," that is, fit for the ordinary purposes for which such goods are used.
>
> Though the manner in which loss occurs will not often be determinative, in a particular case it may be relevant. In discussing this factor, courts have distinguished between losses resulting from a sudden accident and those occurring from a slow process of deterioration.
>
> These courts have allowed tort recovery only in instances where an accident has occurred and have relegated the plaintiff to commercial remedies where the property loss was of a non-accidental nature and where, for example, there was "no evidence of violence, fire, collision with external objects, or other calamity."
>
> In discussing the type of loss or damage, the court utilized the hypotheticals:
>
> A few hypotheticals will be useful to illustrate the problems to be addressed in determining whether certain types of loss should be recoverable in tort or under the U.C.C. In all five hypotheticals, a new LMC unit with an unreasonably dangerous and undiscovered defect was installed in the previously purchased turbines. Subsequently the LMC malfunctioned, causing the losses and damage illustrated below.
>
> At Plant # 1, the defect caused the LMC to malfunction at a time when the plant engineer was aloft on a catwalk inspecting one of the turbines controlled by the LMC. The force of the resulting explosion (accident) knocked the engineer to the floor, injuring him.
>
> At Plant #2, the same malfunction affected only one turbine, which accidentally caught on fire and was completely destroyed.
>
> At Plant #3, the defect caused the LMC to malfunction and burn. The fire department responded quickly, so none of the turbines or other property located near the LMC was damaged in the accident.
>
> At Plant #4, the plant engineer discovered the defect in the LMC and was able to shut down the turbines and replace the LMC before any damage occurred. However, the LMC replacement cost to SRP is $50,000, including shutdown, start-up and testing costs.
>
> At Plant #5, during a peak demand period, the LMC malfunctioned and failed to start all four of the gas turbines. The plant was down for twenty-four hours. As a result, SRP could

not deliver electricity to its numerous commercial and residential users. SRP not only lost all the profits anticipated from the sales to those consumers but must replace the LMC and faces lawsuits by some of its large commercial users.

By unanimous authority, the personal injuries suffered by the engineer at Plant #1 and the property damage at Plant #2 are recoverable in a strict tort liability action. Restatement (Second) of Torts § 402A. The defect was unreasonably dangerous to person or property and caused accidental damage to other property.

There is a split in authority on whether to allow recovery in tort for physical harm to or destruction of only the defective product itself, the situation at Plant #3. The defect was unreasonably dangerous and caused an accident. However, the only "loss" was the product itself. No person or other property was damaged. Cases which have held such losses not recoverable in tort have done so on the rationale that the aggrieved buyer has lost only the benefit of his bargain, that the loss is purely economic, and that the buyer therefore may seek redress only through the U.C.C. Courts which have allowed tort recovery for such losses generally have done so on a policy basis, reasoning that a manufacturer's responsibility to market safe products should not depend on the fortuity of whether the full extent of the unreasonable danger posed — personal injury or damage to property other than the defective product — has actually occurred. It is in the realm of this direct property damage that we believe the unreasonably dangerous nature of the product defect and the occurrence of the loss in a sudden, accidental manner would tip the balance in favor of strict tort liability even though the damage fortuitously was confined to the product itself. *Russell v. Ford Motor Co., supra; Berg v. General Motors Corp., supra.* However, where the loss to a defective product alone occurs in such a way as to pose no unreasonable danger of harm to person or other property, then U.C.C. remedies will generally be appropriate and exclusive for recovery of the damage to the defective product itself.

The majority rule holds that economic losses such as those at Plants #4 and #5 are not recoverable in tort. There was no accident; the danger remained latent, even though the loss is attributable to a defect that could have become unreasonably dangerous. The loss is only economic in nature. The rule denying recovery in tort for such losses had its genesis in *Seely v. White Motor Co., supra,* and has been applied by courts to deny tort recovery for repair and replacement costs, as well as lost profits.

The immediate case was remanded for further proceedings not inconsistent with this opinion.

(4) In *Vaugh v. General Motors Corp.*, 102 Ill. 2d 432 (1984), the court considered the interaction of tort liability for economic loss and the legislative scheme of the U.C.C. Defendant contended that product liability law was developed to overcome problems of privity of contract. Defendant also contended that where privity is not a problem and where the purchaser is not injured, the General Assembly intended that the rights of the parties be determined by the Uniform Commercial Code (§ 1-101 *et seq.*). In ruling that economic damages were recoverable under tort theory the court stated:

> "There can be no doubt that the seller's liability for negligence covers any kind of physical harm, including not only personal injuries, but also property damage to the defective chattel itself, as where an automobile is wrecked by reason of its own bad brakes." Prosser, *Torts* Sec. 101, at 665 (4th ed. 1971).

91 Ill. 2d 69, 86.

The court thus rejected the argument that recovery must be under the U.C.C. only.

(5) In *Santor v. A.M. Karagheusian, Inc.*, 44 N.J. 52, 207 A.2d 305 (1965), the court upheld recovery under strict liability for "economic loss" to the extent that the defect caused the product to diminish in value. The case involved a consumer purchase of a defective carpet. The manufacturer of the carpet had asserted the defense of lack of privity. The court noted that a cause of action based on strict liability in tort and that this liability was not subject to such a defense, since that cause of action arose simply from marketing the product. The court thereby recognized consumer rights to the economic loss resulting from the goods being defective under strict liability, rather than limiting consumer rights to only U.C.C. warranties.

(6) In questions of recovery for the economic loss caused the buyer when the product turns out to be defective, some courts have distinguished between situations where the product defect causes "violent" damage to the product as opposed to deterioration of the product. In the former, these courts would allow recovery under Restatement of Torts, Second, § 402A; in the latter they would not allow a U.C.C. § 402-A action, but only a U.C.C. warranty action which is subject to privity and disclaimer defenses. In a Missouri case, a car was bought new; after only 23,500 miles there was a heater core rupture that allowed coolant to escape, causing severe damage to the engine. The court of appeals said that in order to claim damages under § 402A there must be a violent occurrence causing damage and that here there was not. Warranty law, not strict liability, governed.

§ 5.09 Special Problems

[A] Design

A defect in design of a product may cause harm, giving rise to a product liability action. The following notes indicate some of the problems that may arise.

NOTES

(1) In *Bowman v. General Motors Corporation*, 427 F.Supp. 234 (E.D. Pa. 1977), plaintiff suffered extremely serious and disfiguring burns when his 1966 Oldsmobile Toronado burst into flames after being struck in the rear by another vehicle. The front of the vehicle which struck Mr. Bowman's vehicle underrode the Toronado's rear bumper and pierced its fuel tank. Plaintiff's crashworthiness allegation is that the Toronado was not designed to minimize the risk of injury to the vehicle's occupants in the event of accident. Factually, plaintiff's case rests on the following claims of defective design: (1) the fuel tank was positioned too close to the rear bumper; (2) the angle of the rear bumper invited a striking vehicle to underride it, thus exposing the fuel tank to trauma; and (3) openings in the Toronado's structure (especially the plenum drain) unnecessarily allowed flames to invade the passenger cabin.

Plaintiff founded his design defect claim upon Restatement (Second) of Torts, § 402A. Section 402A of the Restatement provides:

> One who sells any product in a defective condition unreasonably dangerous to the user or consumer . . .is subject to liability for physical harm thereby caused to the ultimate user.

The *Bowman* court, with reference to Professor Henderson's article, *Judicial Review of Manufacturer's Conscious Design Choices: The Limits of Adjudication*, 73 Colum. L. Rev. 1531, 1548 (1973), wrote:

> At one end of the spectrum are risks of harm which originate in the inadvertent failure of the design engineer to appreciate adequately the implications of the various elements of his design, or to employ commonly understood and universally accepted engineering techniques to achieve the ends intended with regard to the product. At the other end of the spectrum are risks of harm which originate in the conscious decision of the design engineer to accept the risks associated with the intended design in exchange for increased benefits or reduced costs which the designer believes justify conscious acceptance of the risks.

427 F. Supp. at 241.

In order for a trier of fact to determine the existence of a "defect," the only standard alluded to in § 402A is that of "unreasonably dangerous." The *Bowman* court concluded that in a conscious design choice case, where the trade-off among safety, utility, and cost is weighed against that which is acceptable to the consumer, "defect" should be defined in terms of "unreasonableness of danger."

(2) In developing the balancing test in *Bowman* the court relied heavily upon the works of Dean Wade [Court's footnote 18] in which

> Dean Wade proposed a set of criteria by which the reasonableness of product danger can be measured, which reflects a . . .realization that all products involve some degree of danger; and that what is being censured is the manufacturer's failure to strike a proper balance between design safety and social desire for utility and aesthetics. They include:
>
> (1) The usefulness and desirability of the product — its utility to the user and to the public as a whole.
>
> (2) The safety aspects of the product — the likelihood that it will cause injury, and the probable seriousness of the injury.
>
> (3) The availability of a substitute product which would meet the same need and not be as unsafe.
>
> (4) The manufacturer's ability to eliminate the unsafe character of, the product without impairing its usefulness or making it too expensive to maintain its utility.
>
> (5) The user's ability to avoid danger by the exercise of care in the use of the product.
>
> (6) The user's anticipated awareness of the dangers inherent in the product and their avoidability because of general public knowledge of the obvious condition of the product, or of the existence of suitable warnings or instructions.
>
> (7) The feasibility, on the part of the manufacturer, of spreading the loss by setting the price of the product or carrying liability insurance. [footnote omitted]

Wade, *On the Nature of Strict Tort Liability Products*, 44 Miss. L. J. 825 837-38 (1973).

Professor Fisher [sic] has also suggested some factors which could be used in a balancing test:

> In deciding when to impose strict liability courts should consider, in light of the facts of the particular case, the merits of the policies underlying strict liability and balance these

considerations against countervailing factors. Some of the factors that should be considered are as follows:

I. Risk Spreading

A. From the point of view of consumer.

1. Ability of consumer to bear loss.

2. Feasibility and effectiveness of self-protective measures.

a. Knowledge of risk.

b. Ability to control danger.

c. Feasibility of deciding against use of product.

B. From point of view of manufacturer.

1. Knowledge of risk.

2. Accuracy of prediction of losses.

3. Size of losses.

4. Availability of insurance.

5. Ability of manufacturer to self-insure.

6. Effect of increased prices on industry.

7. Public necessity for the product.

8. Deterrent effect on the development of new products.

II. Safety Incentive.

A. Likelihood of future produce improvement.

B. Existence of additional precautions that can presently be taken.

C. Availability of safer substitutes.

Fischer, *The Meaning of Defect*, 39 Mo. L. Rev. 339, 359 (1974).

In appropriate cases other factors listed by Wade and/or Fischer [sic] could be incorporated into the unreasonably dangerous charge.

Bowman, 427 F. Supp. at 234.

[B] Comparative Negligence and Strict Liability

PROBLEM 5.8

The plaintiff had the duty of operating a planing machine in the course of his employment. The blades of the machine were protected by a metal guard which was designed to close after the board being planed had cleared the cutterhead. A board slipped out of the plaintiff's hand and he reached down to catch it as it fell. The guard plate had not covered the blades as it should have and his hand engaged the blades, resulting in the loss of two fingers and severe laceration of others.

The plaintiff alleged that the planing machine was defective and unreasonably dangerous and that inadequate warning of the danger had been given and that there is breach of warranty and strict liability. The defendant asserts a percentage of fault should be assessed against the plaintiff that his negligence had contributed to his injury.

You are counsel for the plaintiff. What arguments will you make?

You are the judge. What is your decision on this issue?

NOTES

(1) In *Correlia v. Firestone Tire & Rubber Co.*, 446 N.E. 2d 1033 (1983), involving the issue of whether contributing negligence should be considered in a strict liability § 402A action, the court noted:

> As Restatement (Second) of Torts § 402A, comment n, indicates, actions for strict liability are not actions in negligence. The defendant may be liable "even though he has exercised all possible care in the preparation and sale of the product. . . ."
>
> If the comparative negligence statute does not literally apply, the question remains whether its underlying principles should be given effect by judicial adoption. This is the course of action most strongly urged by Firestone. We decline to take such action. To do so would be to meld improperly the theory of negligence with the theory of warranty as expressed in G.L. c. 106, §§ 2-314–2-318, and thereby to undercut the policies supporting these statutes.
>
> Simply stated, the policy of negligence liability presumes that people will, or at least should, take reasonable measures to protect themselves and others from harm. This presumption justifies the imposition of a duty on people to conduct themselves in this way. A person harmed by one whose conduct "falls below the standard established by law for the protection of others against unreasonable risk" may recover against the actor. However, if the injured person's unreasonable conduct also has been a cause of his injury, his conduct will be accounted for in apportioning liability or damages.
>
> Strict liability is justified on a much different basis.
>
> On whatever theory, the justification for the strict liability has been said to be that the seller, by marketing his product for use and consumption, has undertaken and assumed a special responsibility toward any member of the consuming public who may be injured by it; that the public has the right to and does expect, in the case of products which it needs and for which it is forced to rely upon the seller, that reputable sellers will stand behind their goods; that public policy demands that the burden of accidental injuries caused by products intended for consumption be placed upon those who market them, and be treated as a cost of production against which liability insurance can be obtained; and that the consumer of such products is entitled to the maximum of protection at the hands of someone, and the proper persons to afford it are those who market the products.
>
> Recognizing that the seller is in the best position to ensure product safety, the law of strict liability imposes on the seller a duty to prevent the release of "any product in a defective condition unreasonably dangerous to the user or consumer," into the stream of commerce. This duty is unknown in the law of negligence and it is not fulfilled even if the seller takes all reasonable measures to make his product safe. The liability issue focuses on whether the product was defective and unreasonably dangerous and not on the conduct of the user or the seller. Given this focus, the only duty imposed on the user is to act reasonably with respect to a product which he knows to be defective and dangerous. When a user unreasonably proceeds

to use a product which he knows to be defective and dangerous, he violates that duty and relinquishes the protection of the law. It is only then that it is appropriate to account for his conduct in determining liability. Since he has voluntarily relinquished the law's protection, it is further appropriate that he be barred from recovery. The absolute bar to the user for breach of his duty balances the strict liability placed on the seller. Other than this instance, the parties are not presumed to be equally responsible for injuries caused by defective products, and the principles of contributory or comparative negligence have no part in the strict liability scheme. Given this focus, the user's negligence does not prevent recovery except when he unreasonably uses a product that he knows to be defective and dangerous. In such circumstances, the user's conduct alone is the proximate cause of his injuries, as a matter of law, and recovery is appropriately denied. In short, the user is denied recovery, not because of his contributory negligence or his assumption of the risk but rather because his conduct is the proximate cause of his injuries.

The policies of negligence and warranty liability will best be served by keeping the spheres in which they operate separate until such time as the Legislature indicates how and to what extent they should be melded. The standards of care and the duties are well defined in each sphere. The comparative negligence statute defined no standard of behavior and imposed no duty not previously recognized under the traditional theories of contributory negligence. It merely adjusted the manner in which unreasonable conduct which caused injury would be treated in a negligence action. There is no reason to presume that by passage of the comparative negligence statute the Legislature intended to merge negligence liability with warranty liability. Even if we were convinced that some restructuring of the Massachusetts law of warranty was necessary, we ordinarily would leave that restructuring to the Legislature, given the wide variety of possible solutions it might reasonably adopt.

Restatement (Second) of Torts § 402A, comment n (1965), states the essence of our position. To paraphrase and elaborate on that comment, we conclude that the plaintiff in a warranty action under G.L. c. 106, § 2-314, may not recover if it is found that, after discovering the product's defect and being made aware of its danger, he nevertheless proceeded unreasonably to make use of the product and was injured by it. No recovery by the plaintiff shall be diminished on account of any other conduct which might be deemed contributorily negligent.

(2) Consider the following from *Lippard v. Houdaville Indus., Inc.*, 715 S.W.2d 491 (Mo. Supr. Ct. 1986):

Products liability law, essentially, is to socialize the losses caused by defective products.

Inasmuch as negligence is not an element of a products liability case, we have consistently held that the claimant's contributory negligence does not operate as a bar to recovery.

Gustafson v. Benda, supra, introduced the concept of comparative fault into Missouri negligence law.

. . . .

The respondent argues eloquently, however, that the rule of comparative fault is a fair one in products liability cases just as in negligence cases, that it gives product users a motive for being more careful, and that it states a good rule for decision. Authorities in other states are divided on the point. We therefore make the choice for ourselves, based on our doctrines of products liability, as expounded in our numerous cases.

We conclude that there should be no change in the Missouri common law rule, as established in the *Keener* opinion that the plaintiff's contributory negligence is not at issue in a products liability case. It should neither defeat nor diminish recovery. The defendant may sometimes make use of the plaintiffs alleged carelessness in support of arguments that the product is not unreasonably dangerous, or that the alleged defects in a product did not cause the injury, but these are traversing claims not appropriate for instruction. If the defective product is a legal cause of injury, then even a negligent plaintiff should be able to recover.

. . . .

The judgment is reversed and the cause is remanded with directions to enter judgment for the plaintiff for the full amount of damage determined by the jury.

(3) In the *Lippard* case, *supra*, the defendants raise an assumption of risk defense, but the court found no evidence in support of this defense. If it had, what would have been the result? Would this be desirable?

(4) How should assumption of risk, in the sense of choosing to encounter a known risk, be treated in states which adopt comparative fault? In the Uniform Comparative Fault Act, it is treated as "fault."

PROBLEM 5.9

You are a member of the legislature. The courts of your state have followed the rational of the *Correlia* case and the *Lippard* case. You are now asked to consider on a bill which would make warranty and strict liability actions subject to comparative fault.

If you are for it, what arguments would you make?

If you oppose it, what arguments?

You are a legislator who has heard arguments both ways. Which way do you vote?

NOTES

(1) The determination of whether the comparative negligence doctrine should apply to products liability cases may ultimately be decided by state legislatures. After the *Lippard* case, the Missouri legislature enacted the following:

Section 36.

1. Contributory fault, as a complete bar to plaintiff's recovery in a products liability claim, is abolished. The doctrine of pure comparative fault shall apply to products liability claims as provided in this section.

2. Defendant may plead and prove the fault of the plaintiff as an affirmative defense. Any fault chargeable to the plaintiff shall diminish proportionately the amount awarded as compensatory damages but shall not bar recovery.

3. For purposes of this section, "fault" is limited to:

(1) The failure to use the product as reasonably anticipated by the manufacturer;

(2) Use of the product for a purpose not intended by the manufacturer;

(3) Use of the product with knowledge of a danger involved in such use with reasonable appreciation of the consequences and the voluntary and unreasonable exposure to said danger;

(4) Unreasonable failure to appreciate the danger involved in use of the product or the consequences thereof and the unreasonable exposure to said danger;

(5) The failure to undertake the precautions a reasonably careful user of the product would take to protect himself against dangers which he would reasonably appreciate under the same or similar circumstances; or

(6) The failure to mitigate damages.

(2) The trend in states with applicable statutes is to apply comparative negligence principles to strict liability and implied warranty actions. The court in *Fiske v. MacGregor*, 464 A.2d 719 (R.I. 1983), noted that:

> Our decision today to apply comparative negligence principles to strict liability and implied warranty is well supported by other jurisdictions. [The court cites cases in Kansas, Alaska, California and Florida.]
>
> The state of Mississippi, which has the same comparative-negligence statute as our own, has had that statute interpreted by a federal court to allow its application to strict-liability claims. Moreover, there are jurisdictions that have applied comparative negligence principles to strict-liability claims despite the presence of comparative-negligence statutes that are limited by their terms to actions for negligence. (held that Strict liability in torts is the equivalent of negligence per se; therefore, application of comparative negligence in such cases would be appropriate); contra (held that the comparative negligence statute did not apply to strict-liability cases because it is confined by its term to actions for negligence; however, the court further held that strict liability is a judicially created doctrine to which the principle of comparative causation will apply); (held that phrase, "in an action. . .for negligence" should not be read literally so as to refer only to traditional negligence tort actions). Fortunately, because of the broad language in our comparative negligence statute, we do not need to engage in any such creative analysis. Nonetheless, the existence of these cases can only lend support to our decision.

Fiske, 464 A.2d at 728.

(3) The rationale behind the trend to apply comparative negligence principles to strict liability actions is founded on the desire for a fair and equitable result. In *Fiske v. MacGregor, supra*, the court stated:

> If the comparative-negligence statute only applied to negligence actions, a defendant manufacturer found liable in strict liability or implied warranty could not have the damages apportioned because of plaintiff's culpable conduct. Ironically, defendant manufacturers found liable in negligence would have the damages apportioned, despite the fact that their conduct was clearly more culpable than the conduct of those defendants found liable in strict liability or implied warranty. We believe that the just outcome of a case should not be determined by adroit pleading or semantical distinctions. A defendant's culpability is the basis for an award of damages, whether that culpability is denominated negligence, strict liability, or breach of warranty. Similarly, a plaintiff's culpable conduct is the basis for an apportionment of those damages. In the present case there is a finding of fact by the jury in regard to plaintiff's culpability which cannot be dismissed by adverting to semantics.

464 A.2d at 728.

(4) In *Gagnon v. Dresser Industries Corp.*, 344 N.W.2d 582 (Mich. 1984), plaintiff argued that a defense of comparative negligence did not apply to his action under a theory of implied warranty. Plaintiff based his allegation on U.C.C. § 2-314 (MCL 440.2314; MSA 19.2314).

The court in *Gagnon* noted that plaintiff's implied warranty theory was not contractual in nature, but a products liability action as defined by MCL 600.2945; MSA 27A.2945. The court held that comparative negligence is a defense to any claim of inadequate safety devices. "Accordingly, given that plaintiff's claim is contractual in nature . . .comparative negligence was . . .applicable regardless of whether the claim is characterized as a products liability action for breach of implied warranty on the one hand, or a claim of inadequate safety devices on the other."

PROBLEM 5.10

Your firm handles a number of products liability cases for a variety of clients (though always avoiding conflicts of interest). These include manufacturers, metal sellers, and consumers who have suffered personal or economic injury. Your senior partner is aware of the proposed § 402A revision and asks your opinion as to how each of these client groups may be affected? Also should he vote for or against the proposal at the ALI annual meeting?

§ 1 Commercial Seller's Liability for Harm Caused by Defective Products

(a) One engaged in the business of selling products who sells a defective product is subject to liability for harm to persons or property caused by the product defect.

(b) A product is defective if, at the time of sale, it contains a manufacturing defect, is defective in design, or is defective because of inadequate instructions or warnings.

Comment:

a. History. The Section states a rule of tort liability applicable to commercial sellers of products. The types of products defects referred to in § 1(b) are defined in § 2. The liability established in this Section draws on both warranty law and tort law. Historically, the focus of products liability law was on manufacturing defects. A manufacturing defect is a physical departure from a product's intended design that poses risks of harm to persons or property. Typically manufacturing defects occur in only a small percentage of units in a product line. Courts early began imposing liability without fault on product sellers for harm caused by such defects. When holding a seller liable for harm caused by manufacturing defects even though all possible care had been exercised by the seller in the preparation and marketing of the product, courts relied on the concept of warranty, in connection with which fault has never been a prerequisite to liability.

The imposition of liability for manufacturing defects has a long history in the common law. As early as 1266, criminal statutes imposed liability upon victualers, vintners, brewers, butchers, cooks, and other persons who supplied contaminated food and drink. By the early 1960s, American courts recognized that a seller of any product having a manufacturing defect should be liable in tort for harm caused by the defect regardless of the plaintiff's ability to maintain a traditional negligence or warranty action. Liability would attach even if the manufacturer's quality control in producing the defective product was reasonable. Furthermore, it had been held that a plaintiff need not be in direct privity with the defendant seller to bring an action. A cause of action in tort for defectively manufactured products, recognized by American courts since the early 1960s, merges the concept of implied warranty, in which negligence is not required, with the concept of negligence in tort, in which contractual privity is not required.

Questions of design defect and defects based on inadequate instructions or warnings arise when the specific product unit conforms to the intended design but the intended design itself, or its sale without adequate instructions or warnings, renders the product not reasonably safe. If these forms of defect are found to exist, then every unit in the same product line is potentially defective. See § 2, Comments c and d. Liability for design defects and for defects based on inadequate instructions or warnings occurred relatively infrequently until the late 1960s and early 1970s. A number of limited-duty rules made recovery for such defects, especially design defects, difficult to obtain. Following the erosion of these restrictive rules, courts sought to impose liability without fault for design defects and defects due to inadequate instructions or warnings, accepting the invitation of § 402A of the Restatement, Second, of Torts. It soon became evident that § 402A, created to deal with liability for manufacturing defects, could not readily be applied to cases of design defects or defects based on inadequate instructions or warnings. A product unit that fails to meet the manufacturer's own design specifications thereby fails to perform its intended function and is, almost by definition, defective. However, when the product unit meets the manufacturer's own design specifications it is necessary to go outside those specifications to determine whether the product is defective.

Sections 2(b) and (c) and 4(b)(2), (3), and (4) recognize that the rule developed for manufacturing defects is inappropriate for the resolution of claims of defective design and defects based on inadequate instructions or warnings. The latter categories of cases require determinations that the product could have reasonably been made safer by a better design or instruction or warning. Sections 2(b) and (c) and 4(b)(2), (3), and (4) rely on a reasonableness test traditionally used in determining whether an actor has been negligent. See Restatement, Second, Torts §§ 291-293. Nevertheless, many courts insist on speaking of liability based on the standards described in §§ 2(b)(2) and (3) and 4(b)(2), (3), and (4) as being "strict."

Several factors help to explain this rhetorical preference. First, in many cases dealing with design defects, if the product causes injury while being put to a reasonably foreseeable use, the seller is held to have known of the risks that attend such use. See § 2, Comment *i*. Second, some courts have sought to limit the defense of comparative fault in certain products liability contexts. In furtherance of this objective, they have avoided characterizing the liability test as based in negligence, thereby affording freedom to fashion comparative or contributory fault doctrine in a more restrictive fashion. See § 7, Comment *d*. Third, some courts are concerned that a negligence standard might be too forgiving of a small manufacturer who might be excused for its ignorance of risk or for failing to take adequate precautions to avoid risk. Negligence, which focuses on the conduct of the defendant-manufacturer, might allow a finding that a defendant with meager resources was not negligent because it was too burdensome for the defendant to discover some risks or to design or warn against them. Strict liability language, which focuses on the product rather then the conduct of the manufacturer, may help make the point that a defendant is held to the standard of knowledge available to the relevant manufacturing community at the time the product was manufactured. Finally, the liability of nonmanufacturing sellers in the distributive chain is strict. It is no defense that they acted reasonably and were not aware of a defect in the product, be it manufacturing, design, or failure to warn.

Thus, "strict products liability" is a term of art that reflects the judgment that products liability is a discrete area of tort law which borrows piecemeal from negligence and warranty. It is not fully congruent with classical tort or contract law. Rather than perpetuating confusion spawned by existing doctrinal categories, §§ 1 and 2 define the liability for each form of defect in functional terms. As long as the functional criteria are met, courts may utilize the doctrines of negligence, strict liability, or the implied warranty of merchantability, or simply define liability in the functional terms set forth in the black letter. See § 2, Comment *j*.

b. *Product sellers*. The rule stated in this Section applies not only to sales transactions but also to other forms of product distribution that are the functional equivalent of product sales. Commercial lessors of products for consumer use are thus liable for injuries caused by defective products that they lease to consumers. The rule in this Section also applies to housing, although sales of real property historically have not been within the ambit of product sales. Providers of services unaccompanied by products are not product sellers. See the rules governing providers of services who provide or install products while performing their services.

c. *One engaged in the business of selling*. The rule stated in this Section applies only to commercial sellers who are engaged in the business of selling or distributing the type of product that harmed the plaintiff. The rule does not apply to an occasional seller of such products. Thus, it does not apply to one who occasionally sells jam or other foodstuffs to neighbors, nor does it apply to the noncommercial private owner of an automobile who sells it to another.

It is not necessary that the seller be engaged exclusively or even primarily in selling the type of product that injured the plaintiff. Thus the rule applies to a motion picture theater that sells popcorn or ice cream, either for consumption on the premises or in packages to be taken home.

A service station that does mechanical repair work on cars may also sell tires and automobile equipment. Such sales are subject to the rule in this Section. However, the rules does not cover occasional sales outside the regular course of business (frequently referred to as "casual sales"). Thus, an occasional sale of surplus equipment by a business does not fall within the ambit of this rule. Whether the defendant is a commercial seller is ordinarily a question of law to be determined by the court.

d. *Harm to persons or property*. The rule stated in this Section applies only to harm to persons or property, commonly referred to as personal injury and property damage. In this context, property damage does not include harm to the product itself. See rules governing emotional upset, for economic loss.

§ 7 Apportionment of Liability Between Negligent Plaintiff and Seller of a Defective Product

When the conduct of the plaintiff combines with a product defect to cause harm to the plaintiff's person or property and the plaintiff's conduct fails to conform to an applicable standard of care, liability for harm to the plaintiff is apportioned between the plaintiff and the product seller pursuant to the applicable rules governing apportionment of liability.

Comment:

a. Rationale. The rules governing apportionment of liability are frequently referred to as the rules governing "comparative responsibility" or "comparative fault." Those rules impose on users and consumers responsibility they should bear for safe product use and consumption. The premise is that it would be unfair to impose the costs of substandard plaintiff conduct on manufacturers, who will be impelled to pass on those costs to all users and consumers, including those who use and consume products safety and reasonably. See § 2, Comment a. Shifting injury costs to plaintiffs who properly should bear those costs is not considered to significantly diminish a manufacturer's incentive to produce and sell reasonably safe products. Theoretically, a manufacturer might reduce the level of its investment in product safety to take into account its reduced exposure by reason of comparative responsibility. However, such a calculation would be entirely speculative on the manufacturer's part. Hence, any diminished incentive effect is likely to be insignificant.

b. Conduct of the plaintiff. The applicable rules of apportionment of liability vary among jurisdictions. Some states have adopted "pure" comparative fault. Others follow some variant of modified comparative fault. The apportionment of liability principles as they have developed in each jurisdiction should be applied to products liability cases. With respect to whether special exceptions should be made in products liability cases for certain categories of plaintiff conduct, see Comment d.

Illustration:

1. Roger was driving his car manufactured by the ABC Motor Co. when he noticed the temperature light flashing. The instruction manual warned drivers that when the temperature light flashes it is a sign that the car is seriously overheating and that the car should be brought to a stop and the motor shut off. The overheating in this instance was caused by a hose that was defective at the time of sale by ABC and was leaking coolant. Roger had not read the instruction manual and paid no attention to the flashing temperature light. He continued driving for 30 minutes. The overheating of the car was so intense that it brought about an electrical fire in the car causing Roger serious personal injury. Roger's conduct in failing to read the manual and failing to pay attention to the flashing temperature light may be considered by the trier of fact to be negligent conduct warranting a reduction of Roger's recovery against ABC based on the percentage of fault attributed to him.

c. Misuse, alteration, and modification. When plaintiff's misuse, alteration, or modification of a product constitutes substandard plaintiff conduct, and that conduct combines with a product defect to bring about harm to the plaintiff, liability is apportioned between plaintiff and the product defendant under the rule of this Section.

Illustration:

ABC Machine Tools, Inc. manufactures and sells pelletizer machines, which draw strands of plastic into position for cutting into very small pellets. The pelletizer comes equipped with a removable guard. It is necessary periodically to dismantle the guard so that the inside of the machine can be cleaned. Fred, an employee, removed the guard on an ABC pelletizer to perform the cleaning but neglected to reinstall it. Fred resumed operation of the machine without the guard. Shortly thereafter a strand of plastic caught his hand and pulled it into the rollers of the machine. Fred lost four fingers. Fred alleges that the pelletizer should have been equipped with an interlock mechanism that would have prevented it from operating without the safety guard in place. On the evidence presented, a trier of fact may conclude that the pelletizer was defectively designed and also that Fred's failure to replace the safety guard was a foreseeable alteration of the machine. The trier of fact may also find that Fred's conduct in failing to reinstall the safety guard and operating the machine without the guard constitute negligent conduct on his part that should reduce his recovery based on the percentage of fault attributed to him.

d. Particular forms of plaintiff conduct. Some decisions hold that when the plaintiff's negligence consists in the failure to discover a product defect, there should be no reduction of damages on the basis of apportionment of liability. The premise is that a consumer has a right to expect a defect-free product and should not be burdened with a duty to inspect for defects. Other decisions hold that apportionment of liability is inappropriate where the product lacked a safety feature that would protect against the risk that resulted in the injury in question. The premise is that liability should not be diminished when the plaintiff engages in the very conduct that the product design should have prevented. On the other hand, some decisions hold that assumption of the risk should be a complete defense to a products liability action, not merely a basis for apportionment of liability.

Section 7 states that all forms of plaintiff's failure to conform to applicable standards of care should be presented to the trier of fact for the purpose of apportioning liability between the plaintiff and the product seller. How much responsibility to attribute to a plaintiff will vary with the circumstances. When the plaintiff's conduct is failure to discover a defect, or inattention to a danger that should have been eliminated by a safety feature, a trier of fact may decide to allocate little or no responsibility to the plaintiff. Conversely, when the plaintiff voluntarily and unreasonably encounters a risk, the trier of fact may decide to attribute all or a substantial percentage of responsibility to the plaintiff. All forms of plaintiff misconduct should be the subject of apportionment by the trier of fact. The relative innocence or seriousness of plaintiff's fault should be taken into account by the trier of fact in apportioning liability between the plaintiff and the product seller, but should not serve automatically to absolve the plaintiff from fault or bar the plaintiff from recovery.

Several justifications support the position that plaintiff fault should not be separated into discrete categories. Recognition of such special categories tends to result in either a plaintiff being absolved from responsibility or being completely barred from recovery. The litigation becomes involved in competing efforts to fit plaintiff's conduct into one or another of the categories. This, in turn, spawns appellate litigation seeking precise definition of the category boundaries. That effort has proven costly and largely futile. By and large, the trier of fact should be able fairly to assess the appropriate percentages of responsibility in the circumstances of a case. Such fact-sensitive evaluations are better adapted to apportioning liability that is reliance on discrete categories of plaintiff conduct. Courts always retain the power to review whether the percentage of responsibility assigned to a plaintiff is unreasonable.

Another significant reason to eschew separate categories of plaintiff conduct is that products liability cases often involve parties other than the plaintiff and the product seller, who are either joined by the plaintiff or impleaded by the defendant for contribution purposes. Establishing special categorical rules governing the apportionment of liability between the plaintiff and the product seller creates difficulties when the fault of other parties must be taken into account. These non-seller parties can legitimately insist that plaintiff's fault be determined in assessing their liability. Using different systems for allocating liability, one for the plaintiff and product seller and another for plaintiff and non-seller parties, makes it difficult to adjudicate such a case in a coherent and consistent manner.

§ 8 Disclaimers, Litigations, Waivers, and Other Contract-Based Defenses to Products Liability Claims for Harm to persons.

Disclaimers and limitations of remedies by product sellers, waivers by product purchasers, and other similar contractual exculpations, oral or written, do not bar or reduce otherwise valid products liability claims for harm to persons.

Comment:

a. Effect of contract defenses on products liability tort claims for harm to persons. A commercial seller of a product is not permitted to escape liability for harm to persons through limiting terms in a contract governing the sale of a product. It is presumed that the plaintiff lacked sufficient information, bargaining power, or bargaining position necessary to execute a fair contractual limitation of rights to recover. For a limited exception to this general rule, see Comment d. The rule in this Section applies only to "product sellers," a term defined to include only sellers of new products. See the rule governing sellers of used products and whether they may rely on disclaimers, waivers, and other contractual defenses.

b. Distinguishing disclaimers from warnings. This Section invalidates disclaimers and contractual exculpations of liability by sellers of new products when they are raised to bar or limit claims by plaintiffs for personal injury. Disclaimers should be distinguished from warnings. Warnings usually convey specific information to the buyer about avoiding risk in using the product. In some cases warnings inform the consumer of risks that cannot be avoided. Both types of warnings provide consumers with valuable information concerning the risks attendant to using the product. A product sold with reasonable instructions or warnings may be nondefective. See § 2, Comments f, g, and h. Disclaimers attempt contractually to avoid liability for defective products. For the reasons set forth in Commend a, courts refuse to enforce disclaimers to deny recovery for personal injury caused by new products that were defective at the time of sale.

c. Effect of disclaimers on claims for harm to property or for economic loss. See the effect of disclaimers on tort claims for defect-caused harm to property or for economic loss.

d. Waiver of rights in non-adhesive contracts. The rule in this Section applies to cases in which commercial product sellers attempt to disclaim or otherwise limit their liability to persons who are presumed to lack information and bargaining power adequately to protect their interests. This Section does not address whether consumers, especially when represented by consumer groups or intermediaries, with full information and sufficient bargaining power, may contract with product sellers to accept curtailment of liability for concomitant benefits, or whether such consumers might be allowed to agree to substitute alternative dispute resolution mechanisms in place of traditional adjudication. When such contracts are accompanied by alternative non-tort remedies that serve as an adequate quid pro quo for reducing or eliminating rights to recover in tort, especially when authorized by statute, persuasive argument support giving effect to such agreements. Such contractual arrangements raise policy questions different from those raised by this Section and require careful consideration by the courts.

§ 5.10 Proposed Federal Legislation

PROBLEM 5.11

Your senior partner also is interested in how this particular proposed federal legislature will affect the firm's clients. It would override and replace state law products liability. Please advise as to how manufacturers, retail sellers, and consumers will be affected. He also asks you whether he should as a matter of professional responsibility and good citizenship support such legislation.

H.R. 10 104th Congress, 1st Session to reform . . . product liability law

(1) GENERAL RULE. — Except as provided in paragraph 2, in a product liability action, a product seller shall be liable to a claimant for harm only if the claimant establishes that —

(A)(i) the product which allegedly caused the harm complained of was sold by the product seller,

(ii) the product seller failed to exercise reasonable care with respect to the product, and

(iii) such failure to exercise reasonable care was a proximate cause of the claimant's harm,

(B)(i) the product seller made an express warranty applicable to the product which allegedly caused the harm complained of, independent of any express warranty made by the manufacturer as to the same product,

(ii) the product failed to conform to the warranty, and

(iii) the failure of the product to conform to the warranty caused the claimant's harm, or

(C) the product seller engaged in intentional wrongdoing as determined under applicable State law and such intentional wrongdoing was a proximate cause of the harm complained of by the claimant.

For purposes of subparagraph (A)(ii), a product seller shall not be considered to have failed to exercise reasonable care with respect to a product based upon an alleged failure to inspect a product where there was no reasonable opportunity to inspect the product in a manner which would, in the exercise of reasonable care, have revealed the aspect of the product which allegedly caused the claimant's harm.

(2) SPECIAL RULE — In a product liability action, a product seller shall be liable for harm to the claimant caused by such product as if the product seller were the manufacturer of such product if —

(A) the manufacturer is not subject to service of process under the laws of the State in which the claimant brings the action, or

(B) the court determines that the claimant would be unable to enforce a judgment against the manufacturer.

CHAPTER 6

PERFORMANCE

§ 6.01 Rights and Obligations of the Parties

[A] In General

Read: U.C.C. § 2-301.

Read also: U.C.C. § 2A-103(1)(j); CISG Arts. 30, 53.

Generally, the obligation of a seller of goods is to transfer and deliver them, and that of a buyer is to accept and pay for them. See U.C.C. §§ 2-301, 2-503, 2-606, 2-310. Buyer has a right to inspection of goods. U.C.C. § 2-513. Buyer's rights on improper delivery include the right to reject the goods. U.C.C. § 2-601. Seller may have a right to cure an improper tender or delivery. U.C.C. § 2-508. These and other rights and obligations will be explored in this Chapter.

[B] Good Faith

Read: U.C.C. § 1-203.

Read also: CISG Arts. 7(1), 60(a), 65.

Every contract within the Uniform Commercial Code imposes an obligation of good faith in its performance. U.C.C. § 1-203. Such obligation may not be disclaimed. U.C.C. § 1-102(3). Good faith is discussed in Chapter 1 at § 1.04[C].

PROBLEM 6.1

S contracts to sell 600 pens to *B; B* has the option of choosing styles and colors desired but *B* refuses to so choose. What remedies has *S*? U.C.C. § 2-311, *see* § 2-305(3).

[C] Right to Unimpaired Expectation of Proper Performance

Read: U.C.C. §§ 2-609, 2-610, 2-611.

Read also: U.C.C. §§ 2A-401, 2A-402, 2A-403; CISG Arts. 71, 72, see Arts. 25-27.

Adequate Assurance of Performance. Section 2-609(1) states: "A contract for sale imposes an obligation on each party that the other's expectation of receiving due performance will not be impaired." Comment 1 observes: "The section rests on the recognition of the fact that the essential purpose of a contract between commercial men is actual performance and they do not bargain merely for a promise, or for a promise plus the right to win a lawsuit and that a continuing sense of reliance and security that the promised performance will be forthcoming when due, is an important feature of the bargain. If either the willingness or the ability of a party to perform declines materially between the time of contracting and the time for performance, the other party is threatened with the loss of a substantial part of what he has bargained for." See U.C.C. §§ 2-210(5), 2-311(3), 2-611(2), 2-612(2).

Anticipatory Repudiation. Comment 1 to U.C.C. § 2-610 reads: "With the problem of insecurity taken care of by the preceding section [U.C.C. § 2-609, Right to Adequate Assurance of Performance] . . ., anticipatory repudiation [U.C.C. § 2-610] centers upon an overt communication of intention or an action which renders performance impossible or demonstrates a clear determination not to continue with performance."

CREUSOT-LOIRE INTERNATIONAL, INC. v. COPPUS ENGINEERING CORP.

United States District Court, Southern District of New York
585 F. Supp. 45, 39 U.C.C. Rep. 186 (1983)

CANNELLA, DISTRICT JUDGE. Plaintiff's motion for summary judgment is granted.

BACKGROUND

Plaintiff commenced this diversity action alleging breach of contract and warranty. Simply stated, in January 1979, plaintiff purchased five type DG-26 fanmix burners [the "burners"] from defendant for installation in an ammonia plant in Kutina, Yugoslavia. According to plaintiff in February 1981, before the burners were installed, it learned that serious problems developed concerning the operation of similar burners manufactured by defendant in ammonia plants in Syria and Sri Lanka. Thereafter, plaintiff claims it sought reasonable assurances from defendant that its burners would perform satisfactorily. Plaintiff asserts that defendant repudiated its contract by failing to give adequate assurances, thus, justifying plaintiff's revocation and its demand for rescission. Plaintiff now moves for summary judgment contending that defendant is liable for the purchase price of the burners plus plaintiff's incidental damages.

FACTS

Plaintiff is a wholly-owned subsidiary of Creusot-Loire, S.A. ["Creusot-Loire"], a French manufacturing and engineering concern. Creusot-Loire Enterprises ["CLE"] is a contracting subsidiary of Creusot-Loire. CLE is the project engineer for the ammonia plants in Yugoslavia and Syria. The design process engineer for all three ammonia plants—Yugoslavia, Syria and Sri Lanka—is M.V. Kellogg ["Kellogg"], an American engineering firm with affiliated offices in Europe. As design process engineer, Kellogg designated defendant's burners for the auxiliary steam boiler in all three plants.

In the fall of 1978, plaintiff sent Kellogg's burner specifications to defendant. In response, defendant mailed plaintiff both technical specifications and price information on the burners. Defendant expressly warranted that the burners were capable of continuous operation using heavy fuel oil with combustion air preheated to 260 degrees Centigrade. Defendant further guaranteed that this warranty would extend for one year from the start-up of the plant but not exceeding three years from the date of shipment.

After receiving several technical clarifications, on January 3, 1979 plaintiff issued a purchase order for the burners. Subsequently, the purchase order was amended on two occasions to include additional components. Plaintiff paid $175,586 for the burners and additional parts. In November 1979, the burners were shipped to Yugoslavia. The Kutina plant originally was scheduled for start-up in 1981, however, for reasons not pertinent to the instant motion, the plant will not be operational until the end of 1983.

In 1981 after the burners were shipped, plaintiff became aware of operational difficulties with the burners at the Syrian and Sri Lankan ammonia plants. With respect to the Sri Lankan plant,[1] it became clear that the burners overheated when using heavy fuel oil with combustion air preheated to 316 degrees C. Moreover, as plaintiff later learned, efforts to modify the burners proved futile. Indeed, even when the operating conditions at Sri Lanka were substantially relaxed, the burners still failed to function properly. In May 1981, Kellogg terminated defendant's attempts to rectify the problems with the Sri Lankan burners and replaced them with a competitor's burner which apparently satisfied all performance specifications.

In February 1981, plaintiff wrote to defendant expressing its concern that the burners purchased for Yugoslavia, like the Sri Lankan burners, would be unable to perform satisfactorily. In June 1981, defendant told plaintiff that the problems with the Syrian burners were being resolved. Defendant, however, did not inform plaintiff of the difficulties experienced in Sri Lanka. In September 1981, defendant suggested to plaintiff several modifications in the burners. These modifications were necessary to insure that the Yugoslavian operational specifications could be met. Defendant also indicated that plaintiff would be billed for these modifications.

In response, plaintiff demanded proof that the burners delivered to Yugoslavia would satisfy the contract specifications. Thereafter, on November 6, 1981, defendant informed plaintiff that it had no experience operating burners under conditions comparable with the specifications for the Yugoslavia plant. Defendant suggested, however, that plaintiff consider altering the contract specifications with respect to the preheat temperature and the type of fuel. Defendant did not disclose that the same modifications proved unsuccessful in Sri Lanka.

In December 1981, after Kellogg withdrew its approval for installing defendant's burners, representatives from CLE, Kellogg and defendant met in London. At this meeting, the difficulties with the Sri Lankan burners were discussed. In addition, Kellogg informed defendant that the decision to withdraw prior approval for the Yugoslavian burners was based on the problems encountered at Sri Lanka. CLE also requested that defendant take back the burners and refund the purchase price to plaintiff. Defendant declined this request. On December 15, 1981, plaintiff also demanded that defendant take back the burners.

On December 23, 1981 and again on January 13, 1982, representatives of plaintiff and defendant met in New York. At these meetings, plaintiff stated that it would accept the burners only if defendant provided contractual and financial assurances of performance. Plaintiff requested that defendant extend its contractual guarantee because of a delay in the start-up of the Yugoslavian plant and that defendant post an irrevocable letter of credit for the purchase price of the burners. Defendant refused this request and plaintiff's further demand for a refund.

---

1 . . .Apparently there is no dispute that the specifications for the Syrian plant were less onerous than the specifications for the Sri Lankan and Yugoslavian plants because the Syrian burners used light weight fuel without combustion air being preheated.

Defendant's correspondence and internal memoranda reveal that it was less than candid with plaintiff. For example, in May 1981 defendant knew that the modifications it would propose in September to plaintiff proved unsuccessful in Sri Lanka. Moreover, after suggesting the modifications, defendant failed to tell plaintiff that the modifications met with limited success under conditions less rigorous than those specified for Yugoslavia.[2] Further, defendant's documents recognize that the representations in its technical offering were misleading because they failed to disclose that defendant had no experience with preheated Kellogg burners. Finally, the documents disclose that from at least September 1981, defendant decided to stall or delay plaintiff's efforts to obtain assurances and to cajole plaintiff into purchasing burners from a competitor.

DISCUSSION

To grant the instant motion, the court must be convinced, after viewing the facts and circumstances in a light most favorable to defendant, that no genuine issues exist for trial. . . . Moreover, merely because a "factual dispute *may* exist, without more, is not sufficient to overcome a convincing presentation by the moving party." *Quinn v. Syracuse Model Neighborhood Corp.*, 613 F.2d 438, 445 (2d Cir. 1980) (emphasis in original). Plaintiff contends that defendant's failure to give adequate assurances after plaintiff learned that the burners probably could not perform as warranted constitutes a repudiation, thus, justifying plaintiff's revocation and demand for a refund. Defendant, on the other hand, argues that summary judgment is inappropriate because (1) the burners substantially conformed to contract specifications; (2) plaintiff's request for assurances was unreasonable; (3) plaintiff did not revoke its acceptance within a reasonable time; and (4) defendant needs further discovery.[3]

As defendant correctly observes, because the Yugoslavian burners were never installed, to establish that these burners did not conform to specifications, plaintiff must show that the Yugoslavian and Sri Lankan specifications and operating conditions were similar and that the Sri Lankan burners did not perform satisfactorily. After reviewing the record, the court concludes that defendant has not raised a genuine question of fact in this area.

First, defendant's documents reveal the scope of the problems encountered with the Sri Lankan burners and defendant's inability to correct them. Moreover, defendant's assertion that the Sri Lankan burners operated at ninety-three percent capacity does not raise a material question of fact. This capacity only was attained for a short period of time and under conditions less rigorous than that contracted for at either Sri Lanka or Yugoslavia.

Second, the court agrees with plaintiff that the operating specifications for Sri Lanka and Yugoslavia were sufficiently similar to give plaintiff reasonable grounds for insecurity. Three of defendant's employees have stated or represented that the operating conditions for the

[2] . . .The telexes relied upon by defendant indicate that the Sri Lankan burners were operating (1) at 50 to 90% capacity; (2) with significant down-time for repairs and adjustments; and (3) at preheat temperatures less than that called for in the specifications. . . . There is no dispute that defendant did not make these facts known to plaintiff.

[3] Initially, defendant cross-moved for summary judgment or, alternatively, to add CLE as a party-plaintiff. In essence, defendant asserted that CLE was the real party-in-interest and that plaintiff suffered no damages. Further, defendant claimed that it was necessary to add CLE as a party to avoid multiple litigation. Relying on Fed R Civ P 17 and the language of the contract, plaintiff in response argued that it rather than CLE is the proper party to bring this action. In addition, plaintiff obtained an assignment from CLE for all claims it may have had against defendant. . . . Upon receiving a copy of this assignment, defendant withdrew its motion. Neither party disputes the applicability of New York law to this action.

Yugoslavian and Sri Lankan plants are similar; thus, the court finds unpersuasive defendant's sales engineer's claim that the two plants are different. While the court recognizes that several technical differences between the two plants' specifications exist, defendant has failed to demonstrate the materiality of these differences to the determination of the instant motion. Indeed, with respect to the preheating requirement, the record shows that the burners could not perform adequately at temperatures below that required for Yugoslavia.[4]

Turning to defendant's claim that plaintiff's request for assurances was unreasonable, the court notes that defendant promised to do more than just deliver the burners. The contract plainly states that defendant was obligated to provide burners which would operate under certain conditions. The present record establishes that plaintiff was justified in seeking assurances that the burners were able to meet the Yugoslavian operating specifications. As the Official Comment to NYUCC § 2-609 (McKinney 1964) recognizes, a buyer of precision parts has reasonable grounds for insecurity "if he discovers that his seller is making defective deliveries of such parts to other buyers with similar needs." *Id.*, Comment 3. As stated previously, defendant's own documents indicate that the burners delivered to Sri Lanka did not conform to specifications; thus plaintiff was justified in seeking assurances from defendant.

With respect to defendant's claim that the assurances sought by plaintiff were unreasonable, the court initially observes that after being asked for technical assurances in February, defendant did not respond until September,[5] thereby heightening plaintiff's suspicions. . . . Further, the court finds that the assurances later sought by plaintiff—an extension of contractual guarantee and the posting of a letter of credit—were not unreasonable in light of the circumstances. First, plaintiff's contention that its demand for a letter of credit comported with accepted international business practice is not seriously contested.[6] Second, the record demonstrates that defendant's stalling and lack of candor forced plaintiff to request security in the form of a letter of credit as an extension of the warranty. Third, while it understands that defendant bargained for a contract that included a limited warranty, in view of the strategy adopted to meet plaintiff's demand for assurances, the court concludes that plaintiff's request to extend its warranty also was reasonable. Thus, defendant's failure to provide any assurances save its statement that the burners would work if installed, constitutes a repudiation of the contract. NYUCC § 2-609(4). . . .

Defendant's claim that plaintiff did not timely revoke its acceptance is also without merit. What constitutes a reasonable time for plaintiff to revoke its acceptance depends upon the nature, purpose and circumstances of the case. NYUCC § 1-204(2) (McKinney 1964). While case law indicates that as a matter of law revocation within the warranty period, which occurred in this case, is timely, see *White Devon Farm v. Siahl*, 88 Misc 2d 961, 965, 389 NYS2d 724, 727-28 (Sup Ct 1976), the evidence establishes that plaintiff timely revoked its acceptance. After plaintiff sought assurances in February 1981, it did not receive an answer until September. Moreover, defendant's September response indicates that further assurances were forthcoming. Thus, it was

[4] . . ."Combustion air temperature had to be limited to 150 deg C and they could not reach target 316 deg C, or problems mounted".

[5] While defendant did communicate with plaintiff before its September 8 telex, nothing in these communications can be construed as providing reasonable assurances that the Yugoslavian burners would meet contract specifications.

[6] Defendant's reliance on paragraph seven of Peter Horstmann's affidavit to raise a question of fact in this regard is misplaced. Horstmann's affidavit does not indicate that the request for a letter of credit failed to comport with "commercial standards," rather, the affidavit indicates that defendant disputed the basis upon which plaintiff sought the letter of credit. Thus, plaintiff's claim that its demand for a letter of credit was consistent with international business dealings stands unrefuted. . . .

not until November that plaintiff learned that defendant had no experience with burners operating under "Yugoslavian-like" conditions and that it was unlikely that the burners could satisfy the contract specifications. Accordingly, the court concludes that any delay in revoking acceptance occurred because plaintiff reasonably relied on defendant's assurances that the burners would work. Moreover, it is clear that after it learned that defendant had been less than candid with its assurances, plaintiff revoked its acceptance within a reasonable time. Finally, as plaintiff correctly observes, defendant has not shown that it was prejudiced by this alleged delay.

Defendant further argues that plaintiff's motion must be denied because defendant needs more discovery. In response, plaintiff contends that defendant (1) has knowledge of all the facts and circumstances relevant to the instant motion, and (2) declined to seek the information allegedly pertinent to its defense of the instant motion during the discovery period established by the court. Because the court finds merit to both these arguments, the application for further discovery is denied.

The court finds unavailing defendant's protestation that it had no knowledge of the operation of the Sri Lankan burners. Similarly, defendant's claim that it has no information concerning the workings of the Yugoslavian plant or the relationship between plaintiff, CLE and Kellogg as it relates to this action is belied by defendant's own evidence. Moreover, as stated previously, at least three of defendant's employees acknowledged the similarities between the Yugoslavian and Sri Lankan plants; thus, further discovery in this area is unwarranted.

Defendant's failure to seek either informally or by motion information it now claims is necessary also militates against ordering further discovery. Several avenues of discovery were available to defendant to obtain information from plaintiff CLE or Kellogg. Defendant, however, declined to do so. Accordingly, it would be inequitable for the court, at this time, to order further discovery.

Plaintiff claims that it is entitled to recover the price it paid for the burners as well as incidental damages. Plaintiff asserts that this is an appropriate measure of damages because the burners are of no value to it. Thus, plaintiff claims it is entitled to a full refund which represents the difference between the value of the burners as accepted and the value of the burners if they meet the contract specifications. *City of New York v. Pullman Inc.*, 662 F.2d 910, 916 [31 U.C.C. Rep 1375] (2d Cir 1981), *cert. denied*, 454 US 1164 (1982); see NYUCC § 2-714(2) (McKinney 1964). Initially, the court observes that defendant does not seriously dispute the *amount* of money plaintiff seeks to recover.[7] Moreover, nothing in the present record justifies a smaller award because defendant failed to replace the burners or give adequate assurances. See *Tokio Marine & Fire Insurance Co. v. McDonnell Douglas Corp.*, 617 F.2d 936, 941 (2d Cir 1980). With respect to incidental damages, it is clear that the transportation, inspection and storage costs incurred by plaintiff are recoverable, NYUCC § 2-715(1) (McKinney 1964). In addition, as was the case with plaintiff's other claim for damages, defendant does not dispute the amount. Accordingly, the court concludes that plaintiff is entitled to recover damages in the sum of $242,335.58.

. . . .

---

7. . .Defendant initially claimed that CLE, not plaintiff; incurred the loss but did not dispute the amount sought.

CONCLUSION

In accordance with the foregoing, plaintiff's motion for summary judgment is granted.

Plaintiff is awarded the sum of $242,335.58 and shall submit a proposed judgment forthwith because the court finds that there is no just reason for delay. This is done without prejudice to plaintiff seeking further incidental and consequential damages unknown at this time.

Plaintiff's and defendant's applications for attorneys' fees are denied.

OPTIONAL QUESTION

How would *Creusot-Loire* be resolved under CISG Articles 71 and 72?

§ 6.02 Seller's Obligation to Deliver

Read: U.C.C. §§ 2-301, 2-507(1).

Read also: U.C.C. §§ 2A-508(1), 2A-509(1); CISG Arts. 30-34.

Seller's basic obligation is to tender delivery of conforming goods to buyer. U.C.C. §§ 2-301, 2-507(l), 2-503(1); §§ 2-601(a), 2-106(2), 2-511(l). "Tender" connotes such performance by the tendering party as puts the other party in default if he fails to proceed in some manner. See U.C.C. § 2-503 Comment 1 and § 2-301.

Significance of Tender. If seller duly tenders conforming goods and buyer does not accept them (U.C.C. § 2-606), buyer is in breach; if seller does not duly tender delivery of conforming goods, seller is in breach. U.C.C. § 2-507(1); see §§ 2-703, 2-601(a), 2-612(3), 2-711.[8] Seller's and buyer's damages may be measured by the market price at the time and place for tender (U.C.C. § 2-708(1)), or the market price as of the place for tender (U.C.C. § 2-713(2)). A cause of action under the Statute of Limitations may accrue when tender of delivery is made. U.C.C. § 2-725(2).[9] The risk of loss may pass to the buyer on tender of delivery. U.C.C. § 2-509(3).[10]

PROBLEM 6.2

In the absence of agreement (§ 1-201(3)) otherwise:

1. What is the time and place for tender and delivery?
2. Are specifications or arrangements relating to shipment at the seller's or buyer's option?
3. Is delivery to be made in a single lot or several lots?

---

[8] Buyer generally will have the right to inspect the goods before payment or acceptance. U.C.C. § 2-513. (Unless otherwise agreed, payment is due at the time and place at which the buyer is to receive the goods. U.C.C. § 2-310(a).) Inspection, acceptance and payment are discussed at § 6.03, below.

[9] Damages are discussed at Chapter 7, below.

[10] Risk of loss is discussed at § 4.06, above.

See U.C.C. §§ 2-307, 2-308, 2-309, 2-311.

Manner of Tender. Tender of delivery requires that (1) the seller put and hold conforming goods at the buyer's disposition and (2) give the buyer any notification reasonably necessary to enable the buyer to take delivery. Study U.C.C. § 2-503(1). The manner of tender of delivery (1) where goods are to be delivered by carrier or (2) where goods are in the possession of a bailee and are to be delivered without being moved, are explored below.

PROBLEM 6.3

What are the tender of delivery requirements in the following cases:

1. In a "shipment" contract? U.C.C. § 2-503(2).
2. In a "destination" contract? U.C.C. § 2-503(3).
3. Where the following mercantile terms are used: "F.O.B. Seller City"; or "F.O.B. Buyer City"; or, "C.I.F. Buyer City?"[11] U.C.C. §§ 2-319 through 2-325. Documents of Title are discussed in Chapter 10.

HALSTEAD HOSP., INC. v. NORTHERN BANK NOTE CO.

United States Court of Appeals
680 F.2d 1307, 33 U.C.C. Rep. 1665 (10th Cir. 1982)

SETH, CHIEF JUDGE.

---

[11] Where goods were sold "F.O.B. Cambridge, Massachusetts," Massachusetts was the place of delivery for conflict of laws purposes. *Travenol Laboratories, Inc. v. Zotal, Ltd.*, 394 Mass. 95, 474 N.E.2d 1070, 40 U.C.C. Rep. 487(1985).

In international transactions, note "Incoterms" codified by the International Chamber of Commerce. For information contact: ICC Publishing Company, Inc., 156 Fifth Avenue, New York, NY 10010.

In any contract or communication involving agricultural commodities within the scope of the Perishable Agricultural Commodities Act, 7 U.S.C. §§ 499a-499s, certain trade terms and definitions are construed in accordance with 7 C.F.R. § 46.43. *See, e.g.*, such terms as "Shipping-point inspection," "Shipping-point inspection final," etc.

Halstead Hospital, Inc. commenced a diversity suit alleging breach of contract by the failure of Northern Bank Note Company to deliver printed bond forms in time for a bond closing in New York City. Trial was to the district judge and Halstead obtained a judgement. . . .

Halstead is a nonprofit corporation with its principal place of business in Halstead, Kansas. Northern is an Illinois corporation with a nationwide business of printing bonds and other securities. Northern's principal place of business is located near Chicago. Halstead planned new Hospital facilities to be financed by industrial revenue bonds. A New York City law firm was retained to serve as bond counsel and agent in the bond offering. Halstead's bond counsel on behalf of the Hospital placed an order with Northern by telephone for the printing of bonds. A subsequent letter from bond counsel to Northern confirmed the order and stated that the bond closing was scheduled for December 18, 1975. Northern in turn accepted the order, and by letter stated, "[W]e will complete our work for shipment December 16." The parties agreed that the bonds were to be at the Signature Company in New York on December 17 so that they could be inspected and signed prior to the formal closing on December 18.

Northern printed the bonds and boxed them in four separate cartons. Northern arranged for a common carrier or courier to pick up the four cartons on the afternoon of December 16 and deliver them to New York the next morning. However, one of the boxes of bonds did not arrive in New York until after December 18, 1975. This delay necessitated cancellation of the December 18 closing.

As to the contract matter the parties agree that it is governed by the Uniform Commercial Code. The basic question is whether the contract to provide the bonds was a destination contract requiring shipment and timely delivery by the defendant at a particular place (U.C.C. § 2-503(3), K.S.A. § 84-2-503(3)) or a shipment contract which required only that the goods be put on a carrier with no further responsibility on the seller. Recognizing that a shipment contract is regarded as normal and a delivery contract is viewed as variant (U.C.C. § 2-503, Official Comment 5, K.S.A. § 84-2-503), the trial court concluded that the Halstead-Northern contract was a destination contract. We agree with the trial court's determination that the contract was a destination contract.

Northern's pivotal role in arranging for the delivery of the bond forms to a specific location in New York City, the Signature Company, indicates that the parties intended a destination contract. Furthermore, the obvious deadline provided by the closing date, accepted by Northern, created an obligation beyond placing the bonds on a common carrier. Northern paid the carrier it had selected for its services. The "Carrier" was apparently a courier. The trial court's finding that Northern breached its contract with Halstead when it failed to deliver the fourth box of bond forms in time for the scheduled closing in New York is supported by the evidence.

[Ruling of district court is affirmed.]

PROBLEM 6.4

S agrees to sell certain goods to *B*. The goods are stored in *W* warehouse. It is anticipated that *B* will not immediately remove the goods from *W* but rather B anticipates leaving them in storage for a period. *W* has issued to *S* a warehouse receipt engaging to deliver the goods "to *S*." What is the manner of S's tender of delivery?" What if the warehouse receipt read "to the order of *S*?" U.C.C. §§ 7-104, 2-503(4). *See North Dakota Public Service Commission v. Valley Farmers Bean Association, 365 N.W.2d 528, 40 U.C.C. Rep. 1847 (1985)* (§ 2-503(4)(a) involves a situation in which a bailee merely holds possession of the goods and the sales transaction occurs between a seller and buyer *unrelated* to the bailee. In this case *buyer* is also the bailee who has physical possession of the goods).

NOTE

Proposed U.C.C. § 2-503(d)(1) clarifies § 2-503(4)(a) by requiring that the seller procure an acknowledgment by the bailee *to the buyer* of the buyer's right to possession of the goods.

PROBLEM 6.5

S sold and delivered nonmerchantable quality goods to *B*. *S* asserts that U.C.C. § 2-725 provides: (1) An action by *B* for breach of contract must be commenced within four years after the cause of action occurred. (2) A cause of action accrues when the breach occurs. (3) A breach of warranty occurs when *tender of delivery* is made. Since B did not commence its action within the four years, B's claim is barred by the statute of limitations. U.C.C. § 2-725(1), (2).

B contends that there was never a proper tender of delivery and therefore the limitations period of § 2-725 has never expired. *B* bases this argument on § 2-503(1) which states, "Tender of delivery *requires* that the seller put and hold *conforming* goods at the buyer's disposition." [Emphasis added.] In this respect, § 2-106(2) provides that goods are conforming to the contract "when they are in accordance with the obligations under the contract." Here, the goods did not conform and, consequently, the statute has not run.

As *S*'s counsel, kindly counter this argument. What would be the consequence if the court bought *B*'s position? See U.C.C. § 2-503 Comment 1.

NOTES

(1) See *Eades Commodities, Inc. v. Hoeper*, 825 S.W.2d 34, 17 U.C.C. Rep. 2d 771 (Mo. App. 1992) (seller's delivery of grain to buyer excused when buyer refused to accept deliveries due to limited storage capacity; also, seller called in advance for delivery time which was denied them).

(2) *Mercantile Terms. In re Isis Foods, Inc.*, 38 BR 48, 38 U.C.C. Rep. 1134 (WD Mo. 1983): According to buyer's purchase order, shipment was to be made "F.O.B. St. Louis. St. Louis was the destination of the shipment and the location of the buyer. Held: " 'F.O.B. St. Louis' in the purchase order is clear and unequivocal in its importing a 'destination' contract under which the duty to pay arises as of the terms of receipt of the shipment. . . . Any contrary or additional terms then unilaterally laid down by [seller] in its invoice could only become provisions of the

contract if they were accepted by [buyer]." 38 U.C.C. Rep. at 1136. U.C.C. §§ 2-319, 2-503, 2-507; see § 2-207.

Steuber Co., Inc. v. Hercules, Inc., 646 F.2d 1093, 31 U.C.C. Rep. 508, 510-11(5th Cir. 1981):

> The Uniform Commercial Code has codified the well-settled principles of commercial law relating to C.I.F. contracts. A contract containing the phrase C.I.F. plus a destination requires the seller to deliver goods meeting the contract description on an appropriate carrier, obtain prepaid bills of lading and appropriate insurance certificates for the goods, and then tender these documents plus an invoice to the buyer. Upon tender of these documents, the buyer must pay the full C.I.F. price to the seller. Delivery and possession of conforming goods then becomes a matter between the buyer and the carrier and/or insurer of the goods, but the seller's involvement in the transaction is at an end. In other words, under C.I.F. terms, the buyer pays on delivery of documents; the risk of loss during shipment and the responsibility for delivery and unloading of the goods are for the buyer. However, terms or conditions agreed to by the parties must control over the general reference to C.I.F. contained on the face of the document. This fact is recognized, not only in the commentary but also the express language, "unless otherwise agreed," of the sections of the Uniform Commercial Code. [See U.C.C. §§ 2-320, 2-504.]

(3) *Delay in Shipping. In Harlow & Jones, Inc. v. Advance Steel Co.*, 424 F. Supp. 770, 21 U.C.C. Rep. 410 (E.D. Mich. 1976). Advance contracted to buy steel from Harlow to be imported from a West German mill for shipment C.I.F. during "September-October." The first two shipments were accepted and paid for. The third shipment was shipped from Antwerp on November 14 and arrived in Detroit on November 27. On October 29, Advance by letter canceled because of "late delivery." (According to an accepted steel importing trade usage, shipment in "September-October" meant delivery in October-November.) Thus the situation: seller breached a contractual shipment term but still managed to make timely delivery. The court cited an Ohio case (*Van Decker Packing Co. v. Armour and Co.*, 184 NE 2d 548 (Ohio Ct of Comm Pl 1967)) which noted that delivery time, not shipment time, was the primary concern of the parties and that a delay in shipment was therefore not of such material importance as to justify buyer's cancellation. The court then remarked:

> U.C.C. [§§] 2-320 and 2-504 have not really departed from nor modified traditional contract doctrine regarding shipment contracts. A material delay in shipment has traditionally been required before a buyer under a C.I.F. agreement is allowed to cancel his order, and a merely technical delay or a delay which is later cured by timely delivery has never by itself justified cancellation. . . .

Compare U.C.C. § 1-201(38).

(4) *Contract for Successive Performances But Indefinite in Duration.* Such a contract is valid for a reasonable time but, unless otherwise agreed, may be terminated at any time by either party. U.C.C. § 2-309(2), (3). But see Federal and state legislation: 15 U.S.C. § 1221 *et seq.* (Chapter 27—Automobile Dealer Suits Against Manufacturers—The policy behind enactment of this chapter was to correct abuses of arbitrary termination and nonrenewal of dealer's franchises by automobile manufacturers. *Blenke Bros. v. Ford Motor Co.*, 203 F. Supp. 670 (D.C. Ind. 1962)); Mich. Comp. Laws Ann. § 445. 1561 et seq. (Fair Trade and Business—Motor Vehicles) (445.1580 is captioned, "Termination, failure to renew or discontinuance of dealer agreement for other than good cause; action and damages"). See Comment, *Franchise Termination and Nonrenewal*, 26 S.D.L. Rev. 321(1981).

§ 6.03 Buyer's Right to Inspect and Obligation to Accept and Pay

Read: U.C.C. §§ 2-301, 2-310, 2-507, 2-511, 2-512, 2-513, 2-606.

Read also: U.C.C. §§ 2A-515, 2A-516; CISG Arts. 35(3), 38, 53-60.

Inspection. Unless otherwise agreed, "where goods are tendered or delivered . . .the buyer has a right before payment or acceptance to inspect them." U.C.C. § 2-513(1). The buyer does not have a right to inspect the goods before payment of the price when the contract provides for delivery C.O.D. or for payment against documents. U.C.C. § 2-513(3), see § 2-512.

Acceptance. "If the seller has made a tender which in all respects conforms to the contract, the buyer has a positive duty to accept U.C.C §§ 2-602 Comment 3, 2-507(1).[12] In some instances, buyer will be obligated to accept goods even though they are nonconforming. *See, e.g.,* U.C.C. § 2-504 (postamble), see also § 2-326(1).[13]

Payment. "Unless otherwise agreed payment is due at the time and place at which the buyer is to receive the goods." U.C.C. § 2-310(a). Unless otherwise agreed, tender of payment is a condition to the seller's duty to tender and complete any delivery, tender of delivery is a condition to the buyer's duty to pay for them. U.C.C. §§2-511(1) and Comment 2, 2-507(1). The requirement of payment against delivery has no application to the great body of commercial contracts which carry credit terms. U.C.C. § 2-511 Comment 1. In such instances the buyer need not tender payment as a condition to the seller's duty to tender and complete delivery.

An early case involving a buyer's right of inspection where payment is due at the time and place buyer is to receive the goods is *Imperial Products Co. v. Capitol Chemical Co.*, 187 App. Div. 599, 176 N.Y.S. 49 (1919). Here, B agreed to purchase and accept from S one car of standard quality white naphthalene flakes in barrels at a certain price per pound, f.o.b. West Elizabeth, N.J., prompt shipments from S's plant at Birmingham, Ala. The question involved was whether B had the right to inspect the goods shipped to it by S pursuant to the agreement of sale. The court stated:

> In this case there was no agreement that the shipment should be made "collect on delivery" nor was there any agreement that the buyer would pay the purchase price by sight draft to be attached to the bill of lading. No terms of payment were specified in the agreement between the parties. Under such a contract, delivery and payment are concurrent obligations. [*Cf.* U.C.C. §§ 2-310(a), 2-507(1), 2-511(1) and Comment 1.] This is very different from payment of the purchase price by sight draft with bill of lading attached. In the first, the buyer has the right of inspection to ascertain whether the goods are in conformity with the contract, when the seller tenders delivery, before he is required to accept and pay for the goods. In the latter, payment is a condition precedent to delivery, and hence inconsistent with the right of

[12] " 'Acceptance' . . .means that the buyer, pursuant to the contract, takes particular goods . . .as his own, whether or not he is obligated to do so, and whether he does so by words, action, or silence when it is time to speak." U.C.C. § 2-606 and Comment 1. See U.C.C. § 2-607(2) and (4).

[13] Discussion of the "perfect tender rule" and exceptions is found below at § 6.04, Buyer's Rights on Improper Delivery.

inspection. . . . Inasmuch as there was no provision in the agreement between the parties inconsistent with the right of inspection before acceptance and payment, the seller could not deprive the buyer of that right by adopting a method of collection not provided in the agreement. . . .

PROBLEM 6.6

Resolve *Imperial Products* case assuming the Uniform Commercial Code is applicable. *See* U.C.C. §§ 2-310 and Comments, 2-513 and Comment 2, *see* § 2-503 Comment 2.

PROBLEM 6.7

Chapman was the prime contractor for the plumbing work in the construction of a dormitory for Pacific Lutheran University. On January 10, Chapman purchased from Cervitor Kitchens four kitchen units to be installed in the dormitory for a price of $1,284, f.o.b. job site. On May 4 Chapman received from Cervitor four kitchen units enclosed in shipping crates. The units were not inspected. Chapman's manager then caused the units enclosed in their shipping crates to be stored in a separate room at the dormitory then under construction.

About August 5, Chapman removed the units from the crates and installed them without further inspection in the dormitory. Shortly thereafter it was determined by the University architect that the units were of poor quality and did not comply with specifications. The defects included chipped and rough edges on the stove sections which did not fit properly with the adjoining surface, poorly fitted doors, a poorly installed aluminum panel along one side of the unit, and inadequate hinges on the refrigerator section. Consequently, Chapman rejected the units and caused them to be shipped back to Cervitor who refused to accept them. They were then stored and ultimately sold for storage charges.

Cervitor contends that Chapman waited too long to inspect and reject the units and his installation of the units without inspection further precludes him from rejecting them. Chapman asserts that it was well known by both parties: (1) that the units were to be installed in a building then under construction; (2) that Cervitor knew that the units would not be installed until the building had reached the proper stage of completion; (3) that it would have been uneconomical and would have exposed the units to unnecessary risk of damage to have unpacked them until just before installation.

The question is whether Chapman must be deemed to have accepted the kitchen units because of his failure to inspect and reject them for a period of approximately 3 months after delivery and because of his installation of the units without prior inspection and rejection. *See* U.C.C. §§ 2-513, 2-601, 2-602(1), 2-606; *Cervitor Kitchens, Inc. v. Chapman*, 513 P.2d 25, 13 U.C.C. Rep. 458 (Wash. 1973).

NOTES

(1) *Inspection v. Examination.* " 'Inspection' under [§ 2-513] has to do with the buyer's check-up on whether the seller's *performance* is in accordance with a contract previously made and is not to be confused with the 'examination' of the goods or of a sample or model of them at the *time* of *contracting* which may affect the warranties involved in the contract." [Emphasis added.] (*See* U.C.C. § 2-316(3)(b).) U.C.C. § 2-513 Comment 9. See *E.L.E.S.C.O. v. Northern States Power Co.*, 370 N.W.2d 700 (Minn. App. 1985). *Cf.* CISG Arts. 35(3), 38, 58.

(2) *Sufficiency of Tender of Payment.* In *Armfield v. Poretsky Mgmt., Inc.*, 39 U.C.C. Rep. 883, 884 (D.C. 1984), the court observed:

> The use of checks in today's economy is so common as to spawn a belief that there is a right to pay by check. Yet a check is not legal tender and a debtor pays by check only at the sufferance of the creditor. Where the creditor objects to the use of a check, the debtor must pay in legal tender—cash. [The court cited U.C.C. § 2-511(2).]

For discussion of payment by check in a "cash sale" transaction, see U.C.C. §§ 2-507(2), 2-511(3) and § 7.03 entitled, "Seller's Remedies (1) on Discovery of Buyer's Insolvency, (2) in a " 'Cash Sale.' "

(3) *Payment Against Documents of Title.* The sales contract may require the buyer to pay the price before he inspects the goods. The typical example of this is where delivery is COD or where the buyer is required to pay against documents, such as an order bill of lading. As we shall see later in greater detail, this practice is one solution to one of the great dilemmas in dealings between parties who either do not quite trust one another or are unwilling to rely upon the other's fulfillment of the contractual obligation in unquestioned fashion. The seller wants to be assured of payment before he will relinquish the goods to the buyer; if he delivers without payment he may end up getting no payment at all, or at best payment only after a long delay. Also, the unpaid seller who has delivered the goods is particularly vulnerable to claims on the part of the buyer that the goods are defective or otherwise fail to conform to the contract—accompanied of course, by a demand that there be a corresponding deduction from the balance due on the purchase price. The buyer, on the other hand, does not want to pay for goods unless he has some assurance that conforming goods actually will be delivered to him. He may find that after he has paid the price the seller will turn a deaf ear to his claims that the goods do not conform. If the parties are in the same locality, the buyer may inspect the goods at the seller's place of business and ascertain that they are indeed the goods he has contracted to purchase before he pays for them and secures delivery. Likewise, the seller can be assured of payment before he delivers the goods to the buyer.

But if the parties are dealing at a distance and the goods must travel by carrier, some further arrangements must be made. The seller wants to be protected against the possibility that he will ship goods to Desolation, North Dakota only to have them refused there on the basis of some minor alleged discrepancy from the sale contract terms. The buyer, on the other hand, wants to assure himself that the goods he pays for do conform to the contract—to the buyer in Desolation a cause of action against the seller in Moosetrack, Maine may have little value.

Some compromise is necessary. It may be reached through the seller's shipment of the goods under an order bill of lading, which bill of lading will be turned over to the buyer upon payment of a draft for the sale price. Here, the seller is assured of payment before the goods will be delivered to the buyer. The buyer is assured that goods will be delivered—because the carrier has issued its bill of lading describing the goods generally. However, the buyer will not be certain that the goods conform to the sale contract before paying for them, because he will not have opportunity to inspect the goods. Either he will pay for the goods before they arrive, precluding inspection before payment, or will not be permitted by the carrier to inspect after arrival, in accordance with the terms of the bill of lading: "The surrender of this Original ORDER Bill of Lading properly indorsed shall be required before the delivery of the property. Inspection of property covered by this bill of lading will not be permitted unless provided by law or unless permission is indorsed on this original bill of lading or given in writing by the shipper." Thus, to a degree, the buyer is buying a pig in a poke. Yet the seller continues to bear the risk that the buyer, when the draft for the purchase price is presented to him for payment, will not pay it, leaving the seller with a carload of goods at Desolation, North Dakota. One solution is to use a documentary letter of credit. See Chapter 10, below, entitled "Documentary Transactions."

§ 6.04 Buyer's Rights on Improper Delivery: Reject or Accept

[A] Rejection or Acceptance

Read: U.C.C. §§ 2-601 through 2-607.

Read also: U.C.C. §§ 2A-509 through 2A-512, 2A-514 through 2A-516; CISG Arts. 45-52, 81-84 (see Arts. 49, 25-27), 86-88.

U.C.C. § 2-601 states in part: "[I]f the goods or the tender of delivery fail in any respect to conform to the contract, the buyer may (a) reject the whole; or (b) accept the whole . . ." This is often referred to as the "perfect tender rule." The policy considerations underlying this rule are stated by Professors Braucher and Riegert: (1) buyer should not be required to guess at his peril whether a breach is material, (2) proof of materiality would sometimes require disclosure of buyer's private affairs (e.g., secret formulas or processes).[14]

The perfect tender rule is, however, subject to certain limitations or exceptions, summarized as follows:[15]

1. In a shipment contract, failure to make a proper contract for transportation or to notify buyer is a ground for rejection only if material delay or loss ensues. U.C.C. § 2-504.

2. Where an agreed manner of delivery becomes commercially impracticable, a commercially reasonable substitute must be tendered and accepted. U.C.C. § 2-614(1).

3. In an installment contract, a buyer may not reject any installment which is non-conforming if the non-conformity does not substantially impair the value of that installment. U.C.C. § 2-612(2).

---

[14] R. Braucher & R. Riegert, Introduction to Commercial Transactions 305-6 (1977).

[15] B. Stone, Uniform Commercial Code in a Nutshell 93-94 (4th ed. 1995). Copyright © by West Publishing Co. Reprinted by permission.

4. There may be an enforceable agreement that buyer will accept goods even though there is a non-conformity. U.C.C. § 2-601.

5. Course of dealing, usage of trade, course of performance and the obligation of good faith may afford some leeway. U.C.C. §§ 1-205, 2-208, 1-203, 2-508 Comment 4, 2-106 Comment 2.

Further, the perfect tender rule is undercut by:

6. Seller in appropriate circumstances has the right to cure an improper tender or delivery. U.C.C. § 2-508. This is discussed at [§ 6.05, below].

7. Buyer, if he does not meet certain procedural requirements, *e.g.*, timely notice of rejection, will have accepted the goods. U.C.C. §§ 2-602(1), 2-606(1)(b). Buyers frequently will accept by not timely rejecting. [See this § 6.04[A], below.]

8. Buyer, after accepting, may revoke his acceptance (which gives buyer the same rights as if he had rejected them), but only if the non-conformity *substantially* impairs the value of the goods to buyer. U.C.C. § 2-608. Other requirements for revocation of acceptance are discussed [at § 6.04[C], below].

The "perfect tender rule" in Proposed § 2-601 has been preserved, but rejection is subject to the seller's expanded power to cure under Proposed § 2-508.

BORGES v. MAGIC VALLEY FOODS, INC.

Idaho Supreme Court
616 P.2d 273, 29 U.C.C. Rep. 1282 (1980)

SHEPARD, J. This is an appeal from a judgment following a jury verdict which awarded plaintiffs-respondents Borges and G & B Land and Cattle Company $12,832.00 for potatoes received by defendant-appellant Magic West pursuant to a contract with respondents. We affirm.

In 1975, respondents grew and harvested approximately 45,000 c.w.t. of potatoes, which were stored in a cellar near Buhl, Idaho. Magic West inspected those potatoes and, although their inspection indicated that some contained a "hollow heart" defect, Magic West agreed to purchase them for $3.80 per c.w.t. "Hollow heart" indicates a vacant space in the middle of the potato. The purchase contract provided that "if internal problems develop making these potatoes unfit for fresh pack shipping, this contract becomes null and void." It was agreed that the cost of transporting the potatoes from the storage cellar to the processing plant would be borne by Magic West. Examination of the potatoes by State inspectors would occur at the plant to determine that the number of potatoes affected by the hollow heart defect did not exceed the limit prescribed for shipping under the fresh pack grade.

The potatoes were transported to the processing plant, where more than 30,000 c.w.t. were processed and shipped under the fresh pack grade. In March, 1976, State inspectors declared the remaining 4,838.77 c.w.t. of potatoes unfit for the fresh pack grade because of the increased incidence of hollow heart condition.[16] On March 31, 1976, the parties met to discuss the problem of the remaining potatoes and it was apparently agreed that Magic West should attempt to blend them with other potatoes of a higher grade in the hope that such a blend would meet fresh pack grade standards. That experiment failed and Magic West, without notifying the respondents, processed the remaining 4,838.77 c.w.t. of potatoes into flakes and sold them for $1.25 per c.w.t. The evidence in the record disclosed that the remaining potatoes could not be removed from the processing plant without destroying at least one-third of the potatoes.

Respondents demanded the contract price of $3.80 per c.w.t. for the potatoes sold as flakes. Magic West refused, and instead offered to pay $1.25 per c.w.t. This action resulted. The jury returned a general verdict to the respondents of $12,832.00 and the trial court also awarded $6,975.00 as and for attorney fees and costs to the respondents.[17]

Magic West's basic contention is that the 4,838.77 c.w.t. of potatoes were clearly defective and that they were never accepted. It is claimed that when Magic West processed the potatoes into flakes and sold them for $1.25 per c.w.t., they were only following respondents' instructions.

The potatoes in the instant case were clearly movable at the time they were identified in the contract, IC § 28-2-105, and, hence, were "goods" within the purview of the Idaho Uniform Commercial Code, IC §§ 28-2-101 to -2-725, and the dispute is governed by the provisions of the Uniform Commercial Code.

It is clear and undisputed that Magic West had the responsibility of transporting the potatoes from the storage cellar to the processing plant and that State inspection would occur at the plant. It is also clear that the 4,838.77 c.w.t. of potatoes, unable to make the fresh pack grade, did not conform to the contract and gave Magic West the right of rejection. IC § 28-2-601(a). Also, it is not disputed that when Magic West determined that the potatoes would not meet fresh pack grade, Magic West so notified the respondents and met with them to determine what disposition should be made of the potatoes. The record is unclear as to precisely what was decided at that March 31, 1976 meeting, but respondents apparently approved of Magic West's proposal to blend the defective potatoes with those with higher quality in an attempt to meet the fresh pack grade. However, it is clear that no agreement on price was reached at that meeting.

A buyer must pay the contract rate for any goods accepted. IC § 28-2-607(1). Generally, a buyer is deemed to have accepted defective goods when, knowing of the defect, he resells the goods without notifying the seller. See White & Summers, Uniform Commercial Code, §8-2 (2d ed 1980); 67 Am Jur2d Sales (1973). A buyer accepts goods whenever he does any act inconsistent with the seller's ownership. IC §28-2-606(1)(c). Respondents assert that Magic West's processing of the remaining potatoes into flakes and the subsequent sale constituted acts inconsistent with the respondents' ownership.

---

[16] There were also potatoes still in storage which Magic West never paid for due to the hollow heart problems. There is no dispute with regard to those potatoes. Respondents eventually sold them for $3.00 per c.w.t. to be used as french fries. There were also 702 c.w.t. of defective potatoes in transit to the plant on March 31, 1977. The respondents agreed to accept $1.25 per c.w.t. for those potatoes from Magic West.

[17] Both parties agreed that the jury had apparently awarded respondents the full contract price of $3.80 per c.w.t. for the potatoes in dispute. If no deductions were made, a jury award of $3.80 per c.w.t. would have resulted in a jury verdict of $18,387.32 [$3.80 x 4838.77]. Obviously, some deductions were made although they are not apparent from the record and were not explained or challenged by counsel. For purposes of this appeal, we assume, as counsel do, that the jury awarded $3.80 per c.w.t. for the potatoes in dispute.

Magic West argues, however, that their processing of the potatoes into flakes and their subsequent sale did not constitute an acceptance, but rather was a permissible resale under the provisions of either IC § 28-2-603(1) or IC § 28-2-604. [The court cites IC §§ 28-2-603(l) and 28-2-604.] [Read U.C.C. §§ 2-603(1), 2-604; see § 2-602(2).]

We note that both IC § 28-2-603(1) and IC §28-2-604 were given in their entirety as instructions to the jury. We find it unclear from the record whether the respondents had agents or a place of business at the "market of rejection." Also, the duty to resell under IC § 28-2-603(1) is triggered by an absence of instructions from a seller. Here, given the state of the record and its lack of clarity and the conflicting evidence, the jury could have reasonably found that the respondents did instruct Magic West to attempt to blend the potatoes, but did not instruct them to process the potatoes into flakes. While IC § 28-2-604 allows a buyer an option to resell rejected goods if the seller gives no instructions within a reasonable time after the notification of rejection, the jury could have reasonably found that respondents' instructions were only to blend the potatoes in hope of accomplishing fresh pack grade and that Magic West's processing of the potatoes into flakes and subsequent resale thereof was a precipitate action taken before the lapse of a reasonable time within which respondents could give further instructions.

In addition, even if a reasonable time had elapsed, thus permitting Magic West to resell the potatoes, the jury properly could have concluded that processing of the potatoes by Magic West was an acceptance rather than a resale. There was no evidence presented either of an attempt to resell the potatoes in the bins to an independent third party, or of the value of the potatoes in the bins, less damage caused by removal, should it have been effected. Absent any evidence that the \$1.25 per c.w.t. offered by Magic West was the highest value obtainable for the potatoes, Magic Valley's use of the potatoes in the ordinary course of its own business (presumably for profit) was an act inconsistent with the seller's ownership, and constituted an acceptance of the goods. IC § 28-2-606(1)(c).

The jury was adequately and correctly instructed regarding the provisions of IC § 28-2-603(1) and IC § 28-2-604, which constituted Magic West's theory of its duty or option of resale because of an absence of instructions from respondents. The jury was at liberty to reject Magic West's theory of defense based on substantial, albeit conflicting, evidence that Magic West's resale of the potatoes after processing them into flakes constituted an acceptance and Magic West was hence liable for the full contract price.

We have examined appellants' remaining assignments of error and find them to be without merit.

Affirmed. Costs to respondents.

NOTES

(1) *Use After Rejection as Acceptance.* J. White & R. Summers, Uniform Commercial Code § 8-2 at 352 (3d ed. 1988), observe: "[T]here may be cases in which continued use is inevitable (for instance, a carpet nailed to the floor), and in such cases use should not be regarded as

inconsistent with seller's ownership" [under U.C.C. § 2-606(l)(c)]. *See, e.g., Garfinkel v. Lehman Floor Covering Co., 302 N.Y.S.2d 167, 6 U.C.C. Rep. 915 (1969)* (carpet on floor of buyer's house). Of course, one may have trouble drawing a line between those cases where the buyer must use the goods (*e.g.*, a rug) and those where it would be very convenient but not necessary for him to do so (*e.g.*, commuting by "rejected" car rather than by bus). Cases involving the rejection of motor homes, the revocation of acceptance of motor homes, or both, have been especially difficult to classify. The courts have come to divergent conclusions. [*See, e.g., Twin Lakes Mfg. v. Coffey, 281 S.E.2d 864, 32 U.C.C. Rep. 770 (1981)*]."

(2) *Payment as Acceptance.* In *Klockner, Inc. v. Federal Wire Mill Corp.*, 663 F.2d 1370, 32 U.C.C. Rep. 1097, 1107 (7th Cir. 1981), the court stated that seller would have been justified in believing that full payment ($504,853.98) made after arrival of the goods and five days after a meeting between the parties constituted acceptance under U.C.C. § 2-606(1)(a). (The court noted that buyer attempted to cancel purchase order 5836 *following* the precipitous decline in rod prices.) See U.C.C. § 2-512(2).

(3) *Reasonable Time for Rejection.* Rejection of goods must be within a reasonable time after their delivery or tender and is ineffective unless buyer seasonably notifies seller. U.C.C. § 2-601(2). When the buyer fails to make an effective rejection under U.C.C. § 2-602(1), acceptance of the goods occurs. U.C.C. § 2-606(1)(b). In *Bowlin's Inc. v. Ramsey Oil Co., Inc.*, 662 P.2d 661, 36 U.C.C. Rep. 1110, 1123 (N.Mex. 1983), the court quoted White and Summers:

> [F]our "circumstances" which will always have relevance to the determination of whether a reasonable time has passed before the buyer took his action to reject or revoke:
>
> (1) the difficulty of discovering the defect,
>
> (2) the terms of the contract,
>
> (3) the relative perishability of the goods, and
>
> (4) the course of performance after the sale and before the formal rejection[.]

White and Summers, Uniform Commercial Code § 8-3 (3d ed. 1988), also comment:

> The obvious policies behind the notice provisions are to give the seller an opportunity to cure, to permit seller to assist the buyer in minimizing the buyer's losses, and to return the goods to seller early, before they have substantially depreciated. If the seller can step in and cure the difficulty and so save the sale and prevent several months' lost profit that the buyer might otherwise suffer, the policy has been fulfilled. Even if seller's inspection discloses that the goods are defective and he agrees to take them back, the entire loss from the transaction may be minimized by early action, because the seller may be able to resell the goods to another party shortly after the sale at a higher price than the goods would command after they had depreciated over a period of time.

In *Bowlin's,* the provision of the contract for the purchase of gasoline which provided a two-day period after each delivery for buyer to report any shortages was not unconscionable under U.C.C. § 2-302 in light of the fact that the buyer had established by memo to its gasoline outlets a procedure to verify the quantities of gasoline delivered *within* the two-day period.

(4) *Particularize Reasons for Rejection.* It is important that the buyer state with particularly all defects which are ascertainable by reasonable inspection when he gives notice of rejection. A buyer that does not do so runs the risk of being precluded from relying on unstated defects

to justify the rejection where the seller could have cured the defect if notified thereof. U.C.C. § 2-605(l)(a). 12 West's Legal Forms § 9.9-Form 6 (2d ed. 1985) illustrates:[18]

[*Date*]

Seller Company

[*Address*]

We have rejected the goods which you have delivered to us today under our contract dated [*date*].

We have rejected the goods for the following reasons among others: (1) the goods, which are of a seasonal character were delivered ______ days later than the date set forth in our contract; (2) the quantities for the various colors ordered do not conform to those set forth in our contract, there being shortages in quantity as to some colors and overages as to quantities in other colors; and (3) the goods are of quality number 2, whereas the contract calls for quality number 1.

Kindly advise as to disposition of these goods.

Buyer Company

By ______________________________

(5) *Acceptance and Rejection Under the Perishable Agricultural Commodities Act.* The Act, 7 U.S.C. § 499a *et seq*., is intended to prevent agricultural commodities from becoming distress merchandise and to protect sellers, who often are at a great distance from a buyer. Accordingly, in certain instances, a buyer's remedy is by recovery of damages from a seller and not by rejection of a shipment. See 7 C.F.R. § 46.43 which construes certain trade terms, for example:

> (m) "F.o.b. acceptance final" or "Shipping point acceptance final" means that the buyer accepts the produce at shipping point and has no right of rejection. Suitable shipping condition does not apply under this trade term. The buyer does have recourse for a material breach of contract, providing the shipment is not rejected. The buyer's remedy under this type of contract is by recovery of damages from the seller and not by rejection of the shipment.

[B] Notice of Breach

Read: U.C.C. § 2-607(3), (5), (6).

Read also: U.C.C. § 2A-516(3)-(5); CISG Arts. 27, 39, 40, 44.

Article 2 of the U.C.C. has many provisions where notification is necessary or desirable. *See, e.g.*, 13 West's Legal Forms Chs. 18-23 (2d ed. 1985). Here, we look particularly at § 2-607(3)(a) which states that "[w]here a tender has been accepted the buyer must within a reasonable time after he discovers or should have discovered any breach notify the seller of breach or be barred from any remedy." This provision was considered in *Eastern Air Lines v. McDonnell-Douglas*

---

[18] Copyright © 1985 by West Publishing Co. Reprinted by permission.

Corp., 532 F.2d 957 (5th Cir. 1976). The jury awarded Eastern damages of approximately 25 million dollars against McDonnell Douglas for breach of contract to deliver jet aircraft. The Fifth Circuit found error and reversed, ruling that the question of timely and adequate notice under U.C.C. § 2-607 should have been submitted to the jury.

CITY OF WICHITA, KAN. v. U.S. GYPSUM, CO.

United States District Court, District of Kansas
828 F. Supp. 851, 23 U.C.C. Rep.2d 96 (1993)

BELOT, DISTRICT JUDGE.

This matter is before the court on the joint motion of defendants for partial summary judgment; summary judgment; and the motion of plaintiff for partial summary judgment. The City of Wichita ("the City") brings this action to recover damages for the costs of removing asbestos from two City buildings—the Century II Civic Cultural Center ("Century II"), and the Wichita Public Library. Plaintiff seeks recovery against defendant U.S. Gypsum Company as the manufacturer of asbestos products used in the construction of both buildings. Plaintiff alleges that asbestos products manufactured by the remaining two defendants—U.S. Mineral Products Company and Asbestospray—were used in the construction of the Public Library. Plaintiff seeks recovery under theories of negligence, strict liability, implied warranty, and fraud for defendants' alleged misrepresentations as to the characteristics and health hazards associated with their products. Plaintiff also seeks punitive damages.

* * * *

1. *Partial Summary Judgment*

Defendants seek partial summary judgment on plaintiff's claims based upon negligence, strict liability, and implied warranty.

A. *Negligence and Strict Liability*

* * * *

B. *Implied Warranty*

Defendants seek summary judgment on plaintiff's claim of breach of implied warranty, arguing that plaintiff failed to give defendant notice of the claimed breach.

The parties agree that K.S.A. § 84-2-607 is applicable to plaintiff's implied warranty claim. Under this statute, "the buyer must within a reasonable time after he discovers or should have discovered any breach notify the seller of breach or be barred from any remedy; . . . ." *Id.* § 84-2-607(3)(a). The Kansas Comment makes clear that under this provision, "the buyer may waive any claim for defect against the seller by failing to give notice to the seller of any defect." As defendants observe, notice of the alleged breach has been held to be a condition precedent to suit, and the burden is on the party claiming the breach to plead and prove notice within a reasonable time. *Dold v. Sherow*, 220 Kan. 350, 351-52, 552 P.2d 945, 947 (1976). However, this general rule has its exceptions.

The Kansas Court of Appeals has recognized three general purposes served by the notice requirement:

> First, notice provides the seller a chance to correct any defect. Second, notice affords the seller an opportunity to prepare for negotiation and litigation. Third, notice provides the seller a safeguard against stale claims being asserted after it is too late for the manufacturer or seller to investigate them.

Carson v. Chevron Chem. Co., 6 Kan. App. 2d 776, 784, 635 P.2d 1248, 1255 (1981) (citations omitted; quoting *Prutch v. Ford Motor Co.*, 618 P.2d 657, 661 (Colo. 1980)). "[T]he rule of requiring notification is designed to defeat commercial bad faith, not to deprive a good faith consumer of his remedy.' " *Dold*, 220 Kan. at 352, 552 P.2d at 948 (quoting comment 4 to Official U.C.C. Comment).

Plaintiff concedes that prior to filing suit, it did not give notice to defendant. Plaintiff argues, however, that this is not fatal to its claim.

The court agrees. Kansas law requires the court to focus on the purposes of giving notice under the totality of the circumstances. In *Smith v. Stewart*, 233 Kan. 904, 914, 667 P.2d 358, 366 (1983), the Kansas Supreme Court considered whether K.S.A. § 84-2-607(3) was an "absolute bar" to a plaintiff who failed to give pre-suit notice of an alleged breach of express warranty. 233 Kan. at 910, 667 P.2d at 363. The court quoted favorably from several sources indicating that pre-suit notice is not required in all cases. For example, *"[a] comparably strict application of the notice requirement . . .may not be appropriate in a case involving a consumer's claim of breach.'* " 233 Kan. at 912, 667 P.2d at 365 (emphasis supplied by *Stewart* court; quoting *Armco Steel Corp. v. Isaacson Struct. Steel*, 611 P.2d 507, 513 n.15 (Alaska 1980)). Thus, "[t]he defendant's lawyer whose client is sued *not by merchant-buyer but by a consumer*, especially by a consumer who suffered personal injury or property damage, should not rely heavily on a lack of notice defense.' " *Stewart*, 233 Kan. at 913, 667 P.2d at 366 (emphasis added; quoting White & Summers, Uniform Commercial Code § 11-10, at 423 (2d ed. 1980)). In addition, *Stewart* also recognized that "[a] commonly utilized exception to the requirement of giving notice of the defect within a reasonable time is involved in situations where the defective produce has caused personal injury." 233 Kan. 912, 667 P.2d at 365. In these cases, courts typically require no pre-suit notice, because the damage has already been done, and notice would not serve the purpose of allowing the seller to cure the defect. *Id.* at 913, 667 P.2d at 365 (quoting *Maybank v. Kresge Co.*, 302 N.C. 129, 134, 273 S.E.2d 681 (1981)). *See also Graham v. Wyeth Laboratories*, 666 F.Supp. 1483, 1500 (D.Kan.1987) (filing of lawsuit sufficient notice in personal injury action). Because "none of the purposes of the notice within a reasonable time requirement of K.S.A. § 84-2-607(3)(a) [were] served by blind adherence to the generally appropriate 'condition precedent' concept," 233 Kan. at 914, 667 P.2d at 366, the *Stewart* court concluded that plaintiff's express warranty claim was not barred for failure to give pre-suit notice of the defect. Thus, *Stewart* interprets pre-suit notice as a "requirement" only to the extent that notice would serve the underlying purpose of this "condition precedent." *See also Unified Sch. Dist. No. 500 v. U.S. Gypsum Co.*, 788 F.Supp. 1173, 1176 (D.Kan.1992).

As applied to the facts of this case, the court finds that notice prior to filing suit would have accomplished none of the purposes of K.S.A. § 84-2-607(3)(a). The defect in this case is not restricted to a single instance of improper performance of an otherwise safe product. As alleged in this case and numerous other asbestos-contamination cases across the country involving these same defendants, the defect *is* the product, not because it fails to perform its function as a fire retardant, but rather because it presents a health hazard. Defendants have disputed the health hazard allegation from the outset of this litigation, and it is highly doubtful that defendants would have utilized earlier notice to cure a defect that they vigorously contend, here and elsewhere, does not even exist.[19] Defendants do not suggest otherwise. Moreover, defendants have not alleged or demonstrated any prejudice to their litigation posture as a result of plaintiff's failure to give earlier notice. Finally, it is significant that plaintiff is not a merchant-buyer, but a consumer, to whom the notice requirement does not strictly apply.

Thus, as to this issue, the court finds no material facts in substantial controversy, Fed.R.Civ.P. 56(d), and concludes as a matter of law that plaintiff's failure to give presuit notice does not bar its implied warranty claim.

* * *

NOTES AND QUESTIONS

(1) Do you agree with the court's analysis? See U.C.C. § 1-102 Comment 1 (text accompanying *Fiterman v. J.N. Johnson & Co.* citation). Note that Proposed U.C.C. § 2-606(c)(1) adds the language: "However, a failure to give proper notice does not bar the buyer from any remedy that does not prejudice the seller."

(2) *Timeliness of Notice. In Mazur Bros. & Jaffe Fish Co., Inc.*, 3 U.C.C. Rep. 419 (VACAB 1965), Appellant-seller sought recovery of the purchase price of raw shrimp ordered and received by a Government hospital (buyer). The shrimp was inspected by buyer's inspector at seller's plant then delivered to buyer on July 23. On July 24 buyer cooked the shrimp and noticed an unwholesome odor and a discoloration. On July 29 buyer notified seller by telephone and telegram that the shrimp were rejected because unfit for service to patients. In sustaining seller's appeal the Board said:

> Conversion of virtually the entire order of shrimp from a raw to a cooked state in preparation for service to patients far exceeded the testing necessary for inspection purposes. This alteration of the product rendered it incapable of return to Appellant in the condition in which it had been delivered, and in our opinion constituted an act of dominion inconsistent with Appellant's ownership. . . . In addition, we believe the Government's delay of five days in notifying Appellant of the rejection was unreasonable because of the perishable nature of the commodity and must therefore be regarded as an additional act of implied acceptance. Appellant was a local supplier and could have been notified of any defects the same day they were discovered. Prompt rejection is necessary in order that the contractor may have a fair opportunity to show that the supplies complied with the contract or to correct any deficiencies. . . . Under the facts of this case Appellant had no opportunity to do either.

---

[19] As indicated in part III, *infra*, U.S. Gypsum has declined to admit that it manufactured the asbestos material found in the Public Library. It seems doubly doubtful that Gypsum would have agreed to cure the alleged defect.

. . . .

As an additional defense the Government contends that Appellant breached an implied warranty that the shrimp would be of merchantable quality, suitable for cooking, and fit for service to hospital patients. Under the Universal [sic] Commercial Code and the Universal [sic] Sales Act such a warranty exists where the seller is a dealer in the goods described and is aware of the purposes for which they are required by the buyer. U.C.C. Secs 2-314, 2-315; USA, Sec 15. Both the Code and the Sales Act provide, however, that the seller shall not be liable under an implied warranty if the buyer, after acceptance, fails to give notice of a breach within a reasonable time after its discovery. U.C.C. Sec 2-607. The hospital's failure in this case to give reasonable notice of rejection after performing an act of acceptance thus stands as a bar to the Government's defense of breach of warranty.

We find no basis under the facts of law for the Government's rejection of the shrimp and conclude that Appellant is entitled to payment in full.

(3) Contractual Time Limitation. In *Q. Vandenberg & Sons, N.V. v. Siter, 204 A.2d 494, 2 U.C.C. Rep. 383 (Pa. 1964),* a Netherlands seller sued defendants (buyers) for the balance of the purchase price of certain tulip and hyacinth bulbs; defendants in Pennsylvania counterclaimed for breach of warranty that bulbs were sound and healthy. The contract provided: "The seller warrants the goods to be sound and healthy at the time of shipment but does not otherwise warrant flowering or other planting, growing or forcing results. . . . All claims hereunder shall be deemed waived unless presented within eight (8) days after receipt of the goods." The goods were delivered on October 18, 1960. Defendants offered testimony that most of the bulbs were planted shortly thereafter; about a month later some of the unplanted bulbs were examined and broken open and found by "Mr. Rotteveel, the expert" to be worthless; the defective character of the remaining bulbs could not be discovered until flowering time shortly before Easter 1961. Plaintiff objected to the reception of any testimony as to occurrences more than eight days after delivery. Should defendants' evidence be admitted? See U.C.C. §§ 2-607(3)(a), 1-204.

(4) *Content of Notice.* In *Mountain-Aire Refrigeration & Air Conditioning Co., Inc. v. General Electric Co.*, 703 P.2d 577,41 U.C.C. Rep. 1304, 1308 (Arizona 1985), the court quoted White & Summers on the sufficiency of the notice requirement:

Finally, what constitutes sufficient notice under § 2-607(3)(a)? How explicit must it be? May it be oral? Must it threaten litigation? Quite clearly the drafters intended a loose test; a scribbled note on a bit of toilet paper will do:

The content of the notification need merely be sufficient to let the seller know that the transaction is still troublesome and must be watched. There is no reason to require that the notification which saves the buyer's rights under this section must include a clear statement of all the objections that will be relied on by the buyer, as under the section covering statements of defects upon rejection (Section 2-605). Nor is there reason for requiring the notification to be a claim for damages or of any threatened litigation or other resort to a remedy. The notification which saves the buyer's rights under this Article need only be such as informs the seller that the transaction is claimed to involve a breach, and thus opens the way for normal settlement through negotiation.

Under this comment, it is difficult to conceive of words which, if put in writing, would not satisfy the notice requirement of 2-607. Indeed, a letter containing anything but the most exaggerated encomiums would seem to tell that the transaction "is still troublesome and must be watched." [J. White & R. Summers, Uniform Commercial Code § 11-10 at 484 (3d ed. 1988).

The content of a possible notice of discovery of breach is illustrated by 13 West's Legal Forms § 21.13-Form 2:[20]

[*Date*]

Seller Company

[*Address*]

We hereby notify you that you have breached our agreement dated [*date*] for our purchase from you of 10,000 precision steel fittings, to be delivered to us in one lot on [*date*], in the following respects:

(1) The delivery was twenty (20) days subsequent to that specified in the contract, which has occasioned a readjustment of our production schedule at considerable expense;

(2) The quantities shipped, based upon a tentative count, are 1500 units less than the contract amount;

(3) Express and implied warranties of quality and fitness for purpose have been breached in that a spot-check has disclosed the following defects among a substantial number of the units inspected:

(a) rust spots,

(b) uneven surfaces,

(c) improper threading.

Our hurried inspection in the one day that has elapsed since delivery has disclosed these breaches. We are continuing our inspection and will promptly advise you of any additional breaches which we intend to assert.

Buyer Company

By ______________________________

(5) *Magnuson-Moss Warranty Act.* The Act, in 15 U.S.C. § 2304, sets forth federal minimum standards for "full" warranty. Generally, a warrantor can not impose any duty (*other than notification*) upon any consumer as a condition of securing remedy of any consumer product which malfunctions, is defective, etc. See U.C.C. §§ 2-602(1), 2-607(3)(a), 2-608(2).

(6) *Strict Liability in Tort.* Restatement (Second) of Torts § 402A, Comment m states in part:

> The rule stated in this Section is not governed by the provisions of the Uniform Sales Act, or those of the Uniform Commercial Code, as to warranties; and it is not affected by limitations on the scope and content of warranties, or by limitation to "buyer" and "seller" in those statutes. Nor is the consumer required to give notice to the seller of his injury within a reasonable time after it occurs, as is provided by the Uniform Act.

[C] Revocation of Acceptance

Read: U.C.C. § 2-608, see § 2-607(2).

[20] Copyright © 1985 by West Publishing Co. Reprinted by permission.

Read also: U.C.C. 2A-517; see § 2A-516(2); CISG Arts. 45, 49, 81-84 (see Arts. 25-27).

COLONIAL DODGE, INC. v. MILLER

Michigan Supreme Court
420 Mich. 452, 362 N.W.2d 704, 40 U.C.C. Rep. 1 (1984)

KAVANAGH, J. This case requires the court to decide whether the failure to include a spare tire with a new automobile can constitute a substantial impairment in the value of that automobile entitling the buyer to revoke his acceptance of the vehicle under MCL 440.2608; MSA 19.2608.

We hold it may and reverse.

On April 19, 1976, defendant Clarence Miller ordered a 1976 Dodge Royal Monaco station wagon from plaintiff Colonial Dodge which included a heavy-duty trailer package with extra wide tires.

On May 28,1976, defendant picked up the wagon, drove it a short distance where he met his wife, and exchanged it for her car. Defendant drove that car to work while his wife returned home with the new station wagon. Shortly after arriving home, Mrs. Miller noticed that their new wagon did not have a spare tire. The following morning defendant notified plaintiff that he insisted on having the tire he ordered immediately, but when told there was no spare tire then available, he informed the salesman for plaintiff that he would stop payment on the two checks that were tendered as the purchase price, and that the vehicle could be picked up from in front of his home. Defendant parked the car in front of his home where it remained until the temporary ten-day registration sticker had expired, whereupon the car was towed by the St. Clair police to a St. Clair dealership. Plaintiff had applied for license places, registration, and title in defendant's name. Defendant refused the license plates when they were delivered to him.

According to plaintiff's witness, the spare tire was not included in the delivery of the vehicle due to a nation-wide shortage caused by a labor strike. Some months, later, defendant was notified his tire was available.

Plaintiff sued defendant for the purchase price of the car. On January 13, 1981, the trial court entered a judgment for plaintiff finding that defendant wrongfully revoked acceptance of the vehicle. The Court of Appeals decided that defendant never accepted the vehicle under MCL 440.2606; MSA 19.2606 of the Uniform Commercial Code and reversed. 116 Mich App 78, 85; 322 NW2d 549; 34 UCCRS 123 (1982). On rehearing, the Court of Appeals, noting the trial court found the parties had agreed that there was a valid acceptance, affirmed the trial court's holding there was not a substantial impairment in value sufficient to authorize defendant to revoke acceptance of the automobile.

Defendant argues that he never accepted the vehicle under MCL 440.2606; MSA 19.2606, claiming mere possession of the vehicle is not sufficient according to the U.C.C. Plaintiff contends defendant did accept the vehicle by executing an application for Michigan title and driving the vehicle away from the dealership. The trial court stated "[t]he parties agree that defendant Miller made a valid acceptance of the station wagon under § 2.606 of the Uniform Commercial Code. . . ."[21]

We are not persuaded that, had the matter been contested in the trial court, a finding of acceptance would be warranted on this record. However, since defendant did not submit the question to the trial judge, but in effect stipulated to acceptance, we will treat the matter as though there was acceptance.

We are satisfied defendant made a proper revocation under MCL 440.2608(1)(b); MSA 19.2608(1)(b). This section reads:

. . . .

Plaintiff argues the missing spare tire did not constitute a substantial impairment in the value of the automobile, within the meaning of MCL 440.2608(1); MSA 19.2608(1). Plaintiff claims a missing spare tire is a trivial defect, and a proper construction of this section of the U.C.C. would not permit defendant to revoke under these circumstances. It maintains that since the spare tire is easy to replace and the cost of curing the nonconformity very small compared to the total contract price, there is no substantial impairment in value.

However, MCL 440.2608(1); MSA 19.2608(1) says "[t]he buyer may revoke his acceptance of a lot or commercial unit whose non-conformity substantially impairs its value *to him*. . . . (Emphasis added.) Number two of the Official Comment to MCL 440.2608; MSA 19.2608 attempts to clarify this area. It says that

> [r]evocation of acceptance is possible only where the nonconformity substantially impairs the value of the goods to the buyer. For this purpose the test is not what the seller had reason to know at the time of contracting; the question is whether the nonconformity is such as will in fact cause a substantial impairment of value to the buyer though the seller had no advance knowledge as to the buyer's particular circumstances.

We cannot accept plaintiff's interpretation of MCL 440.2608(1); MSA 19.2608(1). In order to give effect to the statute, a buyer must show the nonconformity has a special devaluing effect on him and that the buyer's assessment of it is factually correct. In this case, the defendant's concern with safety is evidenced by the fact that he ordered the special package which included special tires. The defendant's occupation demanded that he travel extensively, sometimes in excess of 150 miles per day on Detroit freeways, and often in the early morning hours. Mr. Miller testified that he was afraid of a tire going flat on a Detroit freeway at 3 a.m. Without a spare, he testified, he would be helpless until morning business hours. The dangers attendant upon a stranded motorist are common knowledge, and Mr. Miller's fears are not unreasonable.[22]

---

[21] The basis for the statement by the trial court appears to be the argument in defendant's brief to the trial court, which stated: "Mr. Miller contends that the provisions of MCLA 440.2608(1) and (b) have been clearly met due to the fact that he accepted the vehicle in question . . ." The first opinion of the Court of Appeals, 116 Mich App 78, 85, held that the trial court clearly erred in finding acceptance. However, on rehearing the plaintiff pointed out the statement cited above and the Court of Appeals found a valid acceptance. 121 Mich. App. 466; 328 N.W.2d 678 (1982).

[22] [Judge Deming, in the first opinion of the Michigan Court of Appeals, 116 Mich.App. 78, 82, 322 N.W.2d 549 (1982), remarked:

> We take judicial notice of the fact that Detroit area freeways and expressways have been the scene of violent crime and that many citizens justifiably fear automobile breakdowns while traveling on the expressways and the danger attendant thereto.—Ed.]

We hold that under the circumstances the failure to include the spare tire as ordered constituted a substantial impairment in value to Mr. Miller, and that he could properly revoke his acceptance under the U.C.C.

That defendant did not discover this nonconformity before he accepted the vehicle does not preclude his revocation. There was testimony that the space for the spare tire was under a fastened panel, concealed from view. This out-of-sight location satisfied the requirement of MCL 440.2608(1)(b); MSA 19.2608(1)(b) that the nonconformity be difficult to discover.

MCL 440.2608(2); MSA 19.2608(2) requires that the seller be notified of the revocation of acceptance and that it occur within a reasonable time of the discovery of the nonconformity. Defendant notified plaintiff of his revocation the morning after the car was delivered to him. Notice was given within a reasonable time.

Plaintiff argues that defendant failed to effectively revoke acceptance because he neglected to sign over title to the car to plaintiff.

Defendant, however, had no duty to sign over title absent a request from plaintiff that he do so. Under MCL 440.2608(3); MSA 19.2608(3), "[a] buyer who so revokes has the same rights and duties with regard to the goods involved as if he had rejected them." And a buyer who has rejected goods in his possession "is under a duty . . .to hold them with reasonable care at the seller's disposition for a time sufficient to permit the seller to remove them; but the buyer has no further obligations with regard to the goods. . . ." MCL 440.2602(1)(b) and (c); MSA 19.2602(1)(b) and (c). Defendant's notice to plaintiff and holding of the car pending seller's disposition was sufficient under the statute, at least in the absence of evidence that defendant refused a request by the plaintiff to sign over title.

Plaintiff contends defendant abandoned the vehicle, denying it any opportunity to cure the nonconforming tender as prescribed in MCL 440.2508; MSA 19.2508. We find that defendant's behavior did not prevent plaintiff from curing the nonconformity. Defendant held the vehicle and gave notice to the plaintiff in a proper fashion; he had no further duties.

Reversed.

RYAN, J. (dissenting). I dissent.

While I agree that MCL 440.2608(1)(b); MSA 19.2608(1)(b) establishes what is essentially a subjective test to measure the buyer's authority to revoke an acceptance of nonconforming goods, the requisite impairment of the value of the goods to the buyer must be *substantial.* It is not sufficient that the nonconformance be worrisome, aggravating, or even potentially dangerous. It must be a nonconformity which diminishes the value of the goods to the buyer to a substantial degree. The mere possibility that the new car in this case would have a flat tire in the early hours of the morning in an unsafe area of the City of Detroit, leaving its driver with no spare tire, although real, is unlikely. In all events, it is not a possibility which can reasonably be said to elevate the absence of a spare tire, a temporary deficiency easily remedied, to the level of a "substantial impairment" of the value of the new automobile for its ordinary use as a motor vehicle.

Consequently, I would reverse the judgment of the Court of Appeals and affirm the finding of the trial court on this issue.

BOYLE, J. (dissenting). I disagree with the conclusion reached by the majority for the reasons stated by Judge Cynar in his dissent in the Court of Appeals. 116 Mich App 78, 87; 322 NW2d

549 (1982) (Cynar, P.J., dissenting). I agree with Judge Cynar's analysis of the law of substantial impairment and its application to the facts in this case. As he succinctly summarized:

> A buyer may properly revoke acceptance where the nonconformity substantially impairs its value. The existence of such nonconformity depends on the facts and circumstances of each case. *Jorgensen v. Pressnall*, 274 Or 285; 545 P.2d 1382 (1976). The determination of substantial impairment has been made from the buyer's subjective view, considering particular needs and circumstances. See Summers & White, Handbook of the Law Under the Uniform Commercial Code (2d ed), § 8-3, p 308; committee Comment 2 to MCL 440.2608; MSA 19.2608. An objective approach was utilized in *Fargo Machine & Tool Co. v. Kearney & Trecker Corp.*, 428 F Supp 364 (ED Mich, 1977), and an objective and subjective test was employed in *Jorgensen, supra.*
>
> The purpose of the requirement of substantial impairment of value is to preclude revocation for trivial defects or defects which may be easily corrected. . . .
>
> The trial judge's determination that the temporarily missing spare tire did not constitute a substantial impairment in value under either the subjective or objective test was not clearly erroneous.

Therefore, I do not agree that defendant Miller properly rejected the vehicle, and I would affirm the trial court's finding on that issue.

CAVANAGH, J., concurs.

NOTES AND QUESTIONS

(1) Both Michigan Court of Appeals opinions and a dissent referenced *Zabriskie Chevrolet, Inc. v. Smith*, 99 N.J. Super. 441, 240 A.2d 195, 5 U.C.C. Rep. 30 (1968). Here, buyer (B) signed a purchase order form on February 2 for a "brand-new car that would operate perfectly." B made a $124 deposit followed by a check representing the balance of the purchase price. In the evening of February 10, B's wife took delivery of the car. En route home, about 2-1/2 miles away, and after having gone about 7/10 of a mile from the showroom, the car stalled at a traffic light, stalled again within another 15 feet and again each time the vehicle was required to stop. When about half-way home the car could not be driven in "drive" gear at all, and B's wife was obliged to then propel the vehicle in "low-low" gear at a rate of about five to ten miles per hour, its then maximum speed. In great distress, B's wife was fearful of completing the journey home and called B, who thereupon drove the car in "low-low" gear about seven blocks home. B immediately called his bank (which was open in the evening), stopped payment on the check given in payment, and called S to notify them that they had sold him a "lemon," that he had stopped payment on the check and that the sale was canceled. The next day S sent a wrecker to B's home, brought the vehicle to its repair shop and after inspection determined that the transmission was defective. S replaced the transmission with another one removed from a vehicle then on S's showroom floor, notifying B thereafter of what had been done. B refused to take delivery of the vehicle as repaired and reasserted his cancellation of the sale. S sued on the check and the purchase order for the balance of the purchase price, and B counterclaimed for return of his deposit.

In rendering judgment for B the court said, *inter alia*:

> [W]e hold that the vehicle. . .was substantially defective and constituted a breach of the contract and the implied warranty of merchantability [U.C.C. § 2-314]. . . . It is clear that a buyer does not accept goods until he has had a "reasonable opportunity to inspect." [U.C.C. § 2-606(l).] Defendant [B] sought to purchase a new car. He assumed . . .that his new car, with the exception of very minor adjustments, would be mechanically new and factory-furnished, operate perfectly, and be free of substantial defects. . . . How long the buyer may drive the new car under the guise of inspection of new goods is not an issue in the present case. It is clear that defendant [B] discovered the non-conformity within 7/10 of a mile and minutes after leaving plaintiff's [S's] showroom. Certainly this was well within the ambit of "reasonable opportunity to inspect". . . . [D]efendant never accepted the vehicle.
>
> Even if defendant [B] had accepted the automobile tendered, he had a right to revoke [acceptance] under [U.C.C. § 2-608]: "(1) The buyer may revoke his acceptance of [goods] whose non-conformity *substantially impairs its value* to him. . . ."
>
> [The court related that B properly rejected the car under U.C.C. §§ 2-601 and 2-602.]

(2) In assessing U.C.C. §§ 2-601, 2-602 and 2-608 it should be evident that it is more difficult for a buyer to revoke acceptance of goods than to have rejected them. Why this is the case is stated in J. White & R. Summers, Uniform Commercial Code § 8-4 (3d ed. 1988):

> [First],. . .the longer the buyer has the goods, the higher the probability that the alleged defect was caused by him or aggravated by his failure properly to maintain the goods. Secondly, the longer the buyer holds the goods (if he uses them), the greater the benefit he will have derived from them. All of these factors support a rule which makes it difficult for the buyer who has once accepted to cast the goods and attendant loss from depreciation and market factors back on the seller.

(3) *Continued Use After Revocation of Acceptance*. In *McCullough v. Bill Swad Chrysler-Plymouth, Inc.*, 449 N.E.2d 1289, 36 U.C.C. Rep. 513, 518-20 (1983), the court said:

> In ascertaining whether a buyer's continued use of an item after revocation of its acceptance was reasonable, the trier of fact should pose and divine the answers to the following queries: (1) Upon being apprised of the buyer's revocation of his acceptance, what instructions, if any, did the seller tender the buyer concerning return of the now rejected goods? (2) Did the buyer's business needs or personal circumstances compel the continued use? (3) During the period of such use, did the seller persist in assuring the buyer that all nonconformities would be cured or that provisions would otherwise be made to recompense the latter for the dissatisfaction and inconvenience which the defects caused him? (4) Did the seller act in good faith? (5) Was the seller unduly prejudiced by the buyer's continued use?
>
> It is manifest that, upon consideration of the aforementioned criteria, appellee [buyer] acted reasonably in continuing to operate her motor vehicle even after revocation of acceptance. First, the failure of the seller to advise the buyer, after the latter has revoked his acceptance of the goods, how the goods were to be returned entitles the buyer to retain possession of them. . . . Appellant [seller], in the case at bar, did not respond to appellee's request for instructions regarding the disposition of the vehicle. Failing to have done so, appellant can hardly be heard now to complain of appellee's continued use of the automobile.
>
> Secondly, appellee, a young clerical secretary of limited financial resources, was scarcely in position to return the defective automobile and obtain a second in order to meet her business

and personal needs. A most unreasonable obligation would be imposed upon appellee were she to be required, in effect, to secure a loan to purchase a second car while remaining liable for repayment of the first car loan.

Additionally [third], appellant's successor (East), by attempting to repair the appellee's vehicle even after she tendered her notice of revocation, provided both express and tacit assurances that the automobile's defects were remediable, thereby, inducing her to retain possession. Moreover [fourth], whether appellant acted in good faith throughout this episode is highly problematic, especially given the fact that whenever repair of the car was undertaken, new defects often miraculously arose while previous ones frequently went uncorrected. Both appellant's and East's refusal to honor the warranties before their expiration also evidences less than fair dealing.

Finally [fifth], it is apparent that appellant was not prejudiced by appellee's continued operation of the automobile. Had appellant retaken possession of the vehicle pursuant to appellee's notice of revocation, the automobile, which at the time had been driven only 12,000 miles, could easily have been resold. Indeed, the car was still marketable at the time of trial, as even then the odometer registered less than 35,000 miles. In any event, having failed to reassume ownership of the automobile when requested to do so, appellant alone must bear the loss for any diminution of the vehicle's resale value occurring between the two dates.

[U.C.C. § 2-711(3)] provides an additional basis for appellee's retention after revocation of the automobile. A buyer who possesses, as appellee does in the instant action, a security interest in the rejected goods may continue to use them even after revoking his acceptance. . . . Consequently, appellee's continued use of the defective vehicle was a permissible means of protecting her security interest therein.

In *Computerized Radiological Services v. Syntax Corp.*, 786 F.2d 72, 42 U.C.C. Rep. 1656 (2d Cir. 1986), buyers of CAT scanner continued to use it for some 22 months after the letter of revocation. The court said:

The continued use of goods is inconsistent with the seller's ownership and may be found to constitute an acceptance. U.C.C. § 2-606(1)(c). If so, such use would be at odds with a revocation of acceptance and could be held to have invalidated an earlier attempt at revocation. *Gasque v. Mooers Motor Car Co.*, 227 Va. 154, 313 S.E.2d 384 (1984) (buyer cannot use automobile after revocation).

CRS argues, however, that continued use for a reasonable period of time to allow buyers to seek an alternative or to avoid substantial hardship may be allowed. *Minsel v. El Rancho Mobile Home Center, Inc.*, 32 Mich. App. 10, 188 N.W. 2d 9 (1971) (use of mobile home for six weeks after revocation while searching for another dwelling held reasonable); *Fablok Mills, Inc. v. Cocker Machine & Foundry Co.*, 125 N.J. Super. 251, 310 A.2d 491(1973) (continued use of machines reasonable where seller is only manufacturer and alternative is going out of business).

Under the U.C.C., a buyer who revokes acceptance rather than relying solely upon an action for breach of warranty must begin the search for replacement goods with reasonable dispatch and may not put off purchase until a seller offers ideal financial terms. CRS' desultory search for another scanner simply belies its revocation claim, much as the long delay in the hope of avoiding personal liability implies that CRS continued to use the Syntex scanner because continued use was more advantageous than the existing alternatives. CRS' extended use of the defendant's scanner thus invalidates the purported revocation of acceptance.

(4) *Offset for Buyer's Use.* In *Johnson v. General Motors Corp., Chevrolet Motor Division, 233 Kan. 1044, 668 P.2d 139, 36 U.C.C. Rep. 1089,1097-98 (1983)*, the buyers revoked acceptance of a pickup truck. The principal issue was whether the trial court erred in allowing a setoff from the purchase price of the truck for the buyers' continued use of the truck after the buyers' revocation of acceptance. The court said:

> The purpose of allowing revocation after acceptance is to restore the buyer to the economic position the buyer would have been in if the goods were never delivered. . . . After revocation of acceptance any significant use by the buyer should allow the seller to recover from the buyers restitution for the fair value of any benefit obtained resulting from such use. . . . The proper setoff is the value of use of the goods received by the buyer after his revocation of acceptance.
>
> [GMC introduced into evidence a Federal Highway Administration booklet entitled, "Cost of Owning Automobiles and Vans 1982." The booklet] stated the cost of owning and operating a similar vehicle to the truck purchased by the buyers is calculated at 33.2 cents per mile. After deduction of maintenance, gas and oil, parking and tolls, insurance and state and federal taxes, expenses the buyers have already paid, the booklet concluded the original vehicle cost to operate is 10.7 cents per mile. Since buyers drove the vehicle 14,619 miles at 10.7 cents per mile after revocation, the setoff would be $1,564.23. From the evidence presented in this case, GMC is entitled to the sum of$1,564.23 as a setoff for the buyers' use of the truck after revocation of acceptance.

In *Stridiron v. I.C., Inc.*, 578 F.Supp. 997, 37 U.C.C. Rep. 1568, 1575 (D. Virgin Islands 1984), the court said:

> Even though offset seems to be inconsistent with 11A VIC § 2-608 which precludes revocation where there has been a substantial change in the condition of the goods, many courts and commentators have recognized and permitted sellers to offset the purchase price returned to revoking buyers in order to reflect the use of the goods made by the buyers. See G. Priest, *Breach & Remedy for the Tender of Non-Conforming Goods Under the U.C.C.: An Economic Approach*, 91 Harv. L. Rev. 960 (1978); . . .Although we recognize that there is authority to award an offset, we cannot say that the trial court erred by refusing to do so.

State "lemon laws" may provide for offset. *See, e.g.*, New York General Business Law § 198-a. Under subdivision (c)(1), any refund from the manufacturer or dealer may be reduced by:

> an allowance for the consumer's use of the vehicle in excess of the first twelve thousand miles of operation pursuant to the mileage deduction formula defined in paragraph four of subdivision (a) of this section, and a reasonable allowance for any damage not attributable to normal wear or improvements.

Paragraph four of subdivision (a) reads:

> "Mileage deduction formula" means the mileage which is in excess of twelve thousand miles times the purchase price, or the lease price if applicable, of the vehicle divided by one hundred thousand miles.

[D] Installment Contracts

Read: U.C.C. § 2-612.

Read also: U.C.C. § 2A-510; CISG Art. 73, see Arts. 25-27, 81-84.

An "installment contract" is one which requires or authorizes the delivery of goods in separate lots to be separately accepted. U.C.C. § 2-612(1). See the references to U.C.C. § 2-612in U.C.C. §§ 2-703 (Seller's Remedies in General), 2-711(1) (Buyer's Remedies in General). Remedies are discussed in the next chapter. Under Proposed U.C.C. § 2-611, the definition has been revised to include installment contracts by operation of law (§ 2-307) and clarify that an installment contract exists where the delivery of goods is in separate lots to be separately accepted even though payment is not in installments.

TRANS WORLD METALS, INC. v. SOUTHWIRE CO.

United States Court of Appeals
769 F.2d 902, 41 U.C.C. Rep. 453 (2nd Cir. 1985)

Jon O. Newman, Circuit Judge: This appeal requires us to resolve an expensive dispute arising out of the repudiation of a long-term commodity supply contract. Southwire Company ("Southwire") appeals from a judgment of the District Court for the Southern District of New York (Charles E. Stewart, Jr., Judge) entered in this diversity action following a four-week jury trial. The jury awarded plaintiffs Trans World Metals, Inc., Trans-World Metals & Co., Ltd., and Trans World Metals, Ltd. (collectively "Trans World") approximately $7.1 million in damages. Southwire challenges the finding that it is liable to Trans World under the contract, the measure of damages awarded to Trans World, and various rulings by the District Court. We affirm.

BACKGROUND

On April 7, 1981, Trans World and Southwire negotiated by telephone for the purchase and delivery in 1982 of approximately $20.4 million of aluminum. The parties confirmed the contract by exchanging unsigned, standard form documents: Trans World sent Southwire both a confirming telex and a similarly worded "sales contract"; Southwire sent Trans World a "purchase contract confirmation." The contract documents reflect an agreement for the sale and delivery of twelve thousand metric tons of primary aluminum at an average price of $.77 per pound. The "delivery time" clause of the Trans World sales contract and the "shipment schedule" clause of the Trans World telex both state that delivery shall occur "[a]t the rate of 1000 mt [metric tons] per month from January 1982 through December 1982." The Southwire purchase contract confirmation indicates that the quantity and "expected date" under the agreement is 2,205,000 lbs. (one thousand metric tons) "Per Month." The standard printed form on the reverse side of the purchase contract confirmation indicates, in the "Delivery" clause, that "Time is hereby made of the essence, any late delivery shall be a default, and Seller shall be fully responsible for any cost occasioned Buyer thereby."

Also pertinent to the delivery obligation is the following clause in the Trans World sales contract:

> Delivered Railhead, usual midwest U.S.A. destinations *as per buyer's instructions, which are to be submitted no later than the 15th of the month of shipment*. Any tonnage not released by that date is to be invoiced on the last day of month on net 30 days terms.

(Emphasis added.) The purchase contract confirmation contained similar language.

The Southwire purchase contract confirmation contained a "termination" clause with the following provision regarding untimely delivery:

> (a) Buyer may, by written notice of default, cancel this contract in whole or in part if:
>
> (1) Seller fails to make timely delivery, time being of the essence; or
>
> (2) Seller fails to comply with any provision thereof; and
>
> Seller fails to cure such failure within ten (10) days, or such longer period as may be specified in the notice, from the date of receiving the notice.

Pursuant to the delivery terms of the contract, Southwire sent Trans World several delivery instruction "releases" during January 1982. Trans World shipped about three-fourths of the first month's one thousand metric tons of aluminum during January. The remaining one-fourth of the first one thousand tons of metal was shipped between February 1 and February 11, 1982. On February 17, 1982, representatives of Trans World attended a meeting at Southwire's request in Carrollton, Georgia, at which Southwire sought to extend the length of the contract to two years without altering the total quantity of aluminum to be delivered. The parties did not discuss the late delivery of the aluminum ordered in January. Southwire sent no delivery instruction releases to Trans World after January 1982.

Between April 1981, when the contract was negotiated, and March 1982, the price of aluminum fell dramatically. On March 4, 1982, Southwire sent Trans World a telex repudiating the entire contract, pursuant to the termination clause of the purchase contract confirmation. The telex stated:

> Pursuant to [the termination clause] of our contract . . .Southwire Company hereby notifies you of default in your performance of said contract and cancels the same because of your failure to make timely delivery of material called for by said contract.
>
> Please advise us how to dispose of material you have late shipped, which we hold for your instruction.

The "failure to make timely delivery" refers to shipments to be made during the first month of the twelve-month contract. The "late shipped" material consists of the $419,232.84 worth of aluminum shipped by Trans World in early February 1982.

On May 3, 1982, Trans World brought suit in New York state court against Southwire for breach of the aluminum supply contract.[23] Southwire removed the action to federal court and unsuccessfully sought to transfer the case to Georgia. At the conclusion of the trial the jury answered special interrogatories in addition to rendering a general verdict in favor of Trans World. The jury found that the parties had entered into a contract but that the "time is of essence" and "termination" clauses of Southwire's "purchase contract confirmation" were not a part of the

[23] Southwire had earlier brought a similar action against Trans World in the Northern District of Georgia. The day after repudiating the supply contract, Southwire field suit seeking a declaratory judgment that the contract was of no force and effect. The District Court for the Northern District of Georgia dismissed for lack of personal jurisdiction. The Eleventh Circuit reversed that judgment after the action in the Southern District of New York had gone to trial. See *Southwire Co. v. Trans World Metals & Co., Ltd.*, 735 F.2d 440 (11th Cir. 1984).

contract. The jury could not agree whether the aluminum shipments made in early February were timely but found that, even if the shipments were late, they were accepted by Southwire and that there was no substantial impairment of the value either of any particular shipment or of the contract as a whole. The jury awarded Trans World total damages of $7,122,141.84, consisting of $6,702,529.00 for repudiation of the remaining purchase obligations of the contract and $419,232.84 for shipments accepted without payment by Southwire in February.[24] The District Court applied the New York prejudgment interest rate and awarded Trans World $1,304,804.88 in prejudgment interest, for a total of $8,426,946.72. The District Court denied Southwire's motions for judgment notwithstanding the verdict and for a new trial. This appeal followed.

DISCUSSION

I.

Southwire challenges the jury's finding that it is liable for repudiation of the contract, arguing that the District Court should have ruled as a matter of law that Trans World breached the contract by failing to complete the first month's shipments in January. Southwire argues, in essence, that the deliveries made in February violated the "delivery" and "termination" clauses of its purchase contract confirmation and therefore that it was error for the District Court to permit Trans World to introduce evidence regarding trade practices in order to show that the February deliveries were timely. Even if we ignore the jury's finding that the "time is of the essence" and "termination" clauses were not part of the contract between the parties, Southwire's argument fails.

First, because the provisions governing the timing of delivery are somewhat ambiguous, the District Court correctly admitted parol evidence regarding the contract meaning of the terms. See *Rose Stone & Concrete, Inc. v. County of Broome*, 429 N.YS.2d 295, 296 (3d Dep't 1980) ("[T]rade terms may be shown by parol evidence to have acquired a meaning by usage."); cf. *Long Island Airports Limousine Service Corp. v. Playboy-Elsinore Associates*, 739 F.2d 101, 103-04 (2d Cir. 1984) (non-U.C.C. case; parol evidence admissible when contract susceptible of at least two fairly reasonable meanings); *Schering Corp. v. Home Insurance Co.*, 712 F.2d 4, 9 (2d Cir. 1983) (same). The contract provides for delivery at a rate of 1,000 metric tons per month, but the apparent certainty of this provision is undermined by the provision regarding delivery instructions from the buyer. It is not self-evident from reading both provisions whether 1,000 metric tons are to be delivered precisely within each calendar month or whether some part of each month's shipment may be delivered in the following month so long as it is shipped within a reasonable time after receipt of delivery instructions. At a minimum the delivery provisions were permissibly "explained or supplemented" by evidence of trade usage. N.Y.U.C.C. Law § 2-202(a) (McKinney 1964); see . . . N.Y.U.C.C. Law § 1-205(3).

Second, the termination clause in Southwire's purchase contract confirmation explicitly affords Trans World a right to cure "within ten (10) days. . .from the date of receiving [written] notice" of default. Southwire provided no written notice of default before March 4, when it sent Trans World the telex repudiating the contract. Because Trans World had cured any potential default by completing all requested deliveries before the period for cure expired, the contract does not permit Southwire to terminate on the basis of the shipments made in February.

[24] The component figures total $380 less than the aggregate figure awarded by the jury. The discrepancy has not been noticed by the parties, which we take to be a waiver of any complaint.

Finally, the Uniform Commercial Code offers Southwire no ground to repudiate the contract. The agreement at issue is an "installment contract" within the meaning of N.Y.U.C.C. Law § 2-612(1) because it "requires or authorizes the delivery of goods in separate lots to be separately accepted." Therefore, Southwire may treat a late shipment of one installment as a breach of the entire contract only if the "default with respect to one or more installments substantially impairs the value of the whole contract." *Id.* § 2-612(3). The jury's finding, not challenged by Southwire on appeal, that there was no substantial impairment of the value of either the shipments received in February or the contract as a whole supports the ultimate finding that Southwire breached the contract. The District Court properly refused to overturn the jury verdict against Southwire.

II. & III.

[The court evaluated the damage award per U.C.C. § 2-708. With respect to fixed price contracts, the court observed: "Because Trans World accepted the risk that prices would rise, it is entitled to benefit from their fall." 41 U.C.C. Rep. at 461.]

. . . .

We have considered Southwire's remaining claims and find them to lack merit. The judgment of the District Court is affirmed.

§ 6.05 Seller's Right to Cure

Read: U.C.C. §§ 2-508, 2-608(1)(a).

Read also: U.C.C. §§ 2A-513, 2A-517(1)(a); CISG Arts. 34, 37, 48, see Art. 46.

T.W. OIL, INC. v. CONSOLIDATED EDISON CO. OF NEW YORK, INC.

New York Court of Appeals
443 N.E.2d 932, 35 U.C.C. Rep. 12 (1982)

FUCHSBERG, J. In the first case to wend its way through our appellate courts on this question, we are asked, in the main, to decide whether a seller who, acting in good faith and without knowledge of any defect, tenders nonconforming goods to a buyer who properly rejects them, may avail itself of the cure provision of § 2-508 (subd [2]) of the Uniform Commercial Code. We hold that, if seasonable notice be given, such a seller may offer to cure the defect within a reasonable period beyond the time when the contract was to be performed so long as it has acted in good faith and with a reasonable expectation that the original goods would be acceptable to the buyer.

The factual background against which we decide this appeal is based on either undisputed proof or express findings at trial term. In January 1974, midst the fuel shortage produced by the oil embargo, the plaintiff (then known as Joc Oil, USA, Inc.) purchased a cargo of fuel oil whose sulfur content was represented to it as no greater than 1%. While the oil was still at sea en route to the United States in the tanker MT Khamsin, plaintiff received a certificate from the foreign refinery at which it had been processed informing it that the sulfur content in fact was .52%. Thereafter, on January 24, the plaintiff entered into a written contract with the defendant (Con Ed) for the sale of this oil. The agreement was for delivery to take place between January 24 and January 30, payment being subject to a named independent testing agency's confirmation of quality and quantity. The contract, following a trade custom to round off specifications of sulfur content at, for instance, 1%, .5% or .3%, described that of the Khamsin oil as .5%.[25] In the course of the negotiations, the plaintiff learned that Con Ed was then authorized to buy and burn oil with a sulfur content of up to 1% and would even mix oils containing more and less to maintain that figure.

When the vessel arrived, on January 25, its cargo was discharged into Con Ed storage tanks in Bayonne, New Jersey.[26] In due course, the independent testing people reported a sulfur content of. 92%. On this basis, acting within a time frame whose reasonableness is not in question, on February 14 Con Ed rejected the shipment. Prompt negotiations to adjust the price failed; by February 20, plaintiff had offered a price reduction roughly responsive to the difference in sulfur reading, but Con Ed, though it could use the oil, rejected this proposition out of hand. It was insistent on paying no more than the latest prevailing price, which, in the volatile market that then existed, was some 25% below the level which prevailed when it agreed to buy the oil.

The very next day, February 21, plaintiff offered to cure the defect with a substitute shipment of conforming oil scheduled to arrive on the SS Appolonian Victory on February 28. Nevertheless, on February 22, the very day after the cure was proffered, Con Ed, adamant in its intention to avail itself of the intervening drop in prices, summarily rejected this proposal too. The two cargos were subsequently sold to third parties at the best price obtainable, first that of the Appolonian and, sometime later, after extraction from the tanks had been accomplished, that of the Khamsin.[27]

There ensued this action for breach of contract,[28] which, after a somewhat unconventional trial course, resulted in a non-jury decision for the plaintiff in the sum of $1,385,512.83, essentially the difference between the original contract price of $3,360,667.14 and the amount received by the plaintiff by way of resale of the Khamsin oil at what the court found as a matter of fact was a negotiated price which, under all the circumstances,[29] was reasonably procured in the open market. To arrive at this result, the trial judge, while ruling against other liability theories advanced by the plaintiff; which, in particular, included one charging the defendant with having failed to act in good faith in the negotiations for a price adjustment on the Khamsin oil (Uniform Commercial Code, § 1-203), decided as a matter of law that Uniform Commercial Code § 2-508(subd [2]) was available to the plaintiff even if it had no prior knowledge of the nonconformity. Finding that in fact plaintiff had no such belief at the time of the delivery, that

[25] Confirmatorily, Con Ed's brief describes .92% oil as "nominally" 1% oil.

[26] The tanks already contained some other oil, but Con Ed appears to have had no concern over the admixture of the differing sulfur contents. In any event, the efficacy of the independent testing required by the contract was not impaired by the commingling.

[27] Most of the Khamsin oil was drained from the tanks and sold at $10.75 per barrel. The balance was retained by Con Ed in its mixed form at $10.45 per barrel. The original price in January had been $17.875 per barrel.

[28] The plaintiff originally also sought an affirmative injunction to compel Con Ed to accept the Khamsin shipment or, alternatively, the Appolonian substitute. However, when a preliminary injunction was denied on the ground that the plaintiff had an adequate remedy at law, it amended its complaint to pursue the latter remedy alone.

[29] These circumstances included the fact that the preliminary injunction was not denied until April so that, by the time the Khamsin oil was sold in May, almost three months had gone by since its rejection.

what turned out to be a .92% sulfur content was "within the range of contemplation of reasonable acceptability" to Con Ed, and that seasonable notice of an intention to cure was given, the court went on to hold that plaintiff's "reasonable and timely offer to cure" was improperly rejected (*sub nom Joc Oil USA, Inc. v. Consolidated Edison Co. of NY*, 107 Misc 2d 376 [Shanley N. Egeth, J.]). The Appellate Division having unanimously affirmed the judgment entered on this decision, the case is now here by our leave.

In support of its quest for reversal, the defendant now asserts that the trial court erred (a) in ruling that the verdict on a special question submitted for determination by a jury was irrelevant to the decision of this case, (b) in failing to interpret Uniform Commercial Code, § 2-508(subd [2]) to limit the availability of the right to cure after date of performance to cases in which the seller knowingly made a nonconforming tender and (c) in calculating damages on the basis of the resale of the nonconforming cargo rather than of the substitute offered to replace it. For the reasons which follow, we find all three unacceptable.

. . . .

II

We turn then to the central issue on this appeal: Fairly interpreted, did subdivision 2 of § 2-508 of the Uniform Commercial Code require Con Ed to accept the substitute shipment plaintiff tendered? In approaching this question, we, of course, must remember that a seller's right to cure a defective tender, as allowed by both subdivisions of § 2-508, was intended to act as a meaningful limitation on the absolutism of the old perfect tender rule, under which, no leeway being allowed for any imperfections, there was, as one court put it, just "no room for the doctrine of substantial performance" of commercial obligations (*Mitsubishi Goshi Kaisha v. J. Aron & Co., Inc.*, 16 F2d 185, 186 [Learned Hand, J.]).

In contrast, to meet the realities of the more impersonal business world of our day, the Code, to avoid sharp dealing, expressly provides for the liberal construction of its remedial provisions (§1-102) so that "good faith" and the "observance of reasonable commercial standards of fair dealing" be the rule rather than the exception in trade (see § 2-103 subd [1], par [b]), "good faith" being defined as "honesty in fact in the conduct or transaction concerned" (Uniform Commercial Code, § 1-201, subd [19]). As to § 2-508 in particular, the Code's Official Comment advises that its mission is to safeguard the seller "against surprise as a result of sudden technicality on the buyer's part" (Uniform Commercial Code, § 2-106, Official Comment 2).

Section 2-508 may be conveniently divided between provisions for cure offered when "the time for performance has not yet expired" (subd [1]), a pre-Code concept in this State, and ones which, by newly introducing the possibility of a seller obtaining "a further reasonable time to substitute a conforming tender" (subd [2]), also permit cure beyond the date set for performance. In its entirety the section reads as follows: [The court quotes U.C.C. § 2-508.]

Since we here confront circumstances in which the conforming tender came after the time of performance, we focus on subdivision (2). On its face, taking its conditions in the order in which they appear, for the statute to apply (1) a buyer must have rejected a non-conforming tender, (2) the seller must have had reasonable grounds to believe this tender would be acceptable (with or without money allowance) and (3) the seller must have "seasonably" notified the buyer of the intention to substitute a conforming tender within a reasonable time.[30]

In the present case, none of these presented a problem. The first one was easily met for it is unquestioned that, at .92%, the sulfur content of the Khamsin oil did not conform to the .5% specified in the contract and that it was rejected by Con Ed. The second, the reasonableness of the seller's belief that the original tender would be acceptable, was supported not only by unimpeached proof that the contract's .5% and the refinery certificate's .52% were trade equivalents, but by testimony that, by the time the contract was made, the plaintiff knew Con Ed burned fuel with a content of up to 1%, so that, with appropriate price adjustment, the Khamsin oil would have suited its needs even if, at delivery, it was, to the plaintiff's surprise, to test out at .92%. Further, the matter seems to have been put beyond dispute by the defendant's readiness to take the oil at the reduced market price on February 20. Surely, on such a record, the trial court cannot be faulted for having found as a fact that the second condition too had been established.

As to the third, the conforming state of the Appolonian oil is undisputed, the offer to tender it took place on February 21, only a day after Con Ed finally had rejected the Khamsin delivery and the Appolonian substitute then already was en route to the United States, where it was expected in a week and did arrive on March 4, only four days later than expected. Especially since Con Ed pleaded no prejudice (unless the drop in prices could be so regarded), it is almost impossible, given the flexibility of the Uniform Commercial Code definitions of "seasonable" and "reasonable," to quarrel with the finding that the remaining requirements of the statute also had been met.

Thus lacking the support of the statute's literal language, the defendant nonetheless would have us limit its application to cases in which a seller *knowingly* makes a nonconforming tender which it has reason to believe the buyer will accept. For this proposition, it relies almost entirely on a critique in Nordstrom, Law of Sales (§105), which rationalizes that, since a seller who believes its tender is conforming would have no reason to think in terms of a reduction in the price of the goods, to allow such a seller to cure after the time for performance had passed would make the statutory reference to a money allowance redundant.[31] Nordstrom, interestingly enough, finds it useful to buttress this position by the somewhat dire prediction, though backed by no empirical or other confirmation, that, unless the right to cure is confined to those whose nonconforming tenders are knowing ones, the incentive of sellers to timely deliver will be undermined. To this it also adds the somewhat moralistic note that a seller who is mistaken as to the quality of its goods does not merit additional time (Nordstrom, *loc cit*). Curiously, recognizing that the few decisions extant on this subject have adopted a position opposed to

---

[30] Essentially a factual matter, "seasonable" is defined in Uniform Commercial Code, § 1-204(subd [3]) as "at or within the agreed time or if no time is agreed at or within a reasonable time." At least equally factual in character, a "reasonable time" is left to depend on the "nature, purpose and circumstances" of any action which is to be taken (Uniform Commercial Code, § 1-204, subd [2]).

[31] The premise for such an argument, which ignores the policy of the Code to prevent buyers from using insubstantial remediable or price adjustable defects to free themselves from unprofitable bargains (Hawkland, Sales and Bulk Sales, 120-122), is that the words "with or without money allowance" apply only to sellers who believe their goods will be acceptable with such an allowance and not to sellers who believe their goods will be acceptable without such an allowance. But, since the words are part of a phrase which speaks of an otherwise unqualified belief that the goods will be acceptable, unless one strains for an opposite interpretation, we find insufficient reason to doubt that it intends to include both those who find a need to offer an allowance and those who do not.

the one for which it contends, Con Ed seeks to treat these as exceptions rather than exemplars of the rule (*e.g., Wilson v. Scampoli*, 228 A2d 848 [goods obtained by seller from their manufacturer in original carton resold unopened to purchaser; seller held within statute though it had no reason to believe the goods defective]; *Appleton State Bank v. Lee*, 33 Wis 2d 690 [seller mistakenly delivered sewing machine of wrong brand but otherwise identical to one sold; held that seller, though it did not know of its mistake, had a right to cure by substitution]).[32]

That the principle for which these cases stand goes far beyond their particular facts cannot be gainsaid. These holdings demonstrate that, in dealing with the application of § 2-508 (subd [2]), courts have been concerned with the reasonableness of the seller's belief that the goods would be acceptable rather than with the seller's pre-tender knowledge or lack of knowledge of the defect (*Wilson v. Scampoli, supra;* compare *Zabriskie Chevrolet, Inc. v. Smith*, 99 NJ Super 441).

It also is no surprise then that the aforementioned decisional history is a reflection of the mainstream of scholarly commentary on the subject (*e.g.*, 1955 Report of NY Law Rev Comm, p 484; White and Summers, Uniform Commercial Code [2d ed], § 8-4, p 322; . . .

White and Summers, for instance, put it well, and bluntly. Stressing that the Code intended cure to be "a remedy which should be carefully cultivated and developed by the courts" because it "offers the possibility of conforming the law to reasonable expectations and of thwarting the chiseler who seeks to escape from a bad bargain" (*supra*, at 322, 324), the authors conclude, as do we, that a seller should have recourse to the relief afforded by Uniform Commercial Code, § 2-508(subd [2]) as long as it can establish that it had reasonable grounds, tested objectively, for its belief that the goods would be accepted (*ibid.*, at 321). It goes without saying that the test of reasonableness, in this context, must encompass the concepts of "good faith" and "commercial standards of fair dealing" which permeate the Code (Uniform Commercial Code, §§1-201, subd [19]; 1-203; 2-103, subd [l], par[b]).[33]

III

As to the damages issue raised by the defendant, we affirm without reaching the merits. . . .

For all these reasons, the order of the Appellate Division should be affirmed, with costs.

---

[32] The only New York case to deal with this section involved a seller who knowingly tendered a "newer and improved version of the model than was actually ordered" on the contract delivery date. The court held he had reasonable grounds to believe the buyer would accept the newer model (*Bartus v. Riccardi*, 55 Misc 2d 3).

[33] Except indirectly, on this appeal we do not deal with the equally important protections the Code affords buyers. It is as to buyers as well as sellers that the Code, to the extent that it displaces traditional principles of law and equity (U.C.C. § 1-103), seeks to discourage unfair or hypertechnical business conduct bespeaking a dog-eat-dog rather than a live-and-let-live approach to the marketplace (*e.g.*, U.C.C. §§ 2-314, 2-315, 2-513, 2-601, 2-608). Overall, the aim is to encourage parties to amicably resolve their own problems (*Ramirez v. Autosport*, 88 NJ 277, 285; compare Restatement, Contracts, 2d, Introductory Note to Chapter 10, p 194 [". . . the wisest course is ordinarily for the parties to attempt to resolve their differences by negotiations, including clarification of expectations [and] cure of past defaults . . ."]). See also U.C.C. § 2-605 Comment 2—Ed.]

PROBLEM 6.8

On September 5, Gappelberg (B) purchased a large screen Advent television set from The Video Station owned by Landrum (S). B paid $2,231.25 in cash and was allowed a $1,500 credit on the trade-in of his old set. B immediately experienced numerous and different problems with the new set. S and Alpha Omega, the authorized repair agency, made several house calls in an effort to repair the set. On September 26, the set totally ceased operating. B allowed the television set to be removed from his home, but refused offers to make further repairs on the set, saying he simply wanted his money and his old set returned to him. S felt he was in no position to return the old set, as he had promised it as a prize for a promotional sweepstakes, and offered B another Advent as replacement. B refused to accept the substitute and brought suit against S for return of his consideration.

The trial court held that B had duly revoked acceptance under U.C.C. § 2-608: (1) B accepted the TV without knowledge of the defects (which were discovered later); (2) B revoked acceptance within a reasonable time after the defects were discovered and before any change in the condition of the set occurred not caused by such defects; (3) B timely notified S of the revocation; (4) the set's faulty convergence (thereby causing color shadowing around the screen's images), the constant projection of a red dot on one corner of the screen when the set was in operation, and the complete power failure of the set, were each defects which substantially impaired the set. Nevertheless, the trial court concluded that revocation of acceptance was subject to S's right to cure under U.C.C. § 2-508. Consequently, the court denied relief to B because B prevented S from curing the nonconforming goods by B's refusal to accept a replacement Advent set.

On appeal what is S's argument that it has the right to cure after revocation of acceptance? See U.C.C. § 2-608(3). As B's counsel, what is your argument that S does *not* have the right to cure after B has revoked acceptance. Could you distinguish between cure by *repair* and cure by *replacement*? *See Gappelberg v. Landrum*, 654 S.W.2d 549 (Tex. App. 1983), 666 S.W.2d 88 (Tex. 1984).

NOTES

(1) Proposed U.C.C. § 2-508 expands the seller's right to cure to include cases where acceptance is rightfully revoked. Cure will not be available if acceptance was revoked because the seller had failed seasonably to cure a nonconformity that the buyer assumed would be cured. Proposed § 2-607(c) modifies § 2-608(3) by stating that a buyer who justifiably revokes acceptance has the same rights and duties, with regard to the goods involved under §§ 2-603 and 2-604, as if they had been rejected. Would these proposed sections change the analysis or result of Problem 6.8?

(2) With respect to cure, *Zabriskie Chevrolet, Inc. v. Smith*, 5 U.C.C. Rep. 30 at 42 (1968), cited at § 6.04[C] Notes and Questions (1), states:

> The "cure" intended under . . .the Code does not, in the court's opinion, contemplate the tender of a new vehicle with a substituted transmission, not from the factory and of unknown

lineage from another vehicle in plaintiff's possession. It was not the intention of the Legislature that the right to "cure" is a limitless one to be controlled only by the will of the seller. A "cure" which endeavors by substitution to tender a chattel not within the agreement or contemplation of the parties is invalid.

(3) See *Olmstead v. General Motors Corp., Inc.,* 500 A.2d 615, 619 (Del. Super. 1985):

Though neither the Federal nor State laws specify how many failed attempts at repair are necessary before a buyer is justified in revoking acceptance, it would appear from caselaw that at a minimum there must be more than one or two attempts, or there must be an outright refusal to repair.

See also Travalio, *The U.C.C.'s Three "R's": Rejection, Revocation and (The Seller's) Right to Cure,* 53 Cin. L. Rev. 931 (1984) (strong policy reasons support seller's right to cure following revocation of acceptance).

(4) *Federal Magnuson-Moss Warranty Act.* With respect to "full" warranties under the Act, see 15 U.S.C. § 2304(a)(1) and (4).

(5) *State Automobile/Consumer Goods "Lemon Laws."* Illustrative of such a law is the Missouri statute at V.A.M.S. § 407.560 *et seq.*

§ 6.06 Preserving Evidence of Goods in Dispute

Read: U.C.C. § 2-515.

NOTE

The purpose of U.C.C. § 2-515 is "[t]o meet certain serious problems which arise when there is a dispute as to the quality of goods and thereby perhaps to aid the parties in reaching a settlement . . ."; "to afford either party an opportunity for preserving evidence . . . and thereby to reduce the uncertainty in any litigation, and in turn perhaps, to promote agreement." U.C.C. § 2-515 Comments 1 and 2. When litigation has been commenced, the applicable rules of procedure govern discovery, including inspections. *See Fenway Cambridge Motor Hotel, Inc. v. American Contract Designers, Inc. v. Milliken & Co.,* 39 U.C.C. Rep. 1263 (D. Mass. 1984).

§ 6.07 Excuse of Performance

Read: U.C.C. §§ 2-613 (see U.C.C. § 2-509), 2-614, 2-615, 2-616; see U.C.C. § 2-311(3)(a).

Read also: U.C.C. §§ 2A-221, 2A-404, 2A-405, 2A-406; CISG Arts. 79, 80, see Art. 27.

The Code contains three sections which state general principles relieving the seller from full performance of his contractual obligations.[34] They can be rationalized within the law of contracts in several ways. They can be explained under language of excuse, impossibility, impracticability, or even implied promise or condition. The most accurate way, however, to explain these sections is to consider the risks which the parties shifted by their agreement.[35]

Section 2-615, Excuse by Failure of Presupposed Conditions, states in subsection (a) that delay in delivery or non-delivery is not a breach of seller's duty under a contract for sale "if performance as agreed has been made impracticable by the occurrence of a contingency the non-occurrence

[34] U.C.C. §§ 2-613, 2-614, 2-615.

[35] R. Nordstrom, Handbook of the Law of Sales § 107 at 324 (1970).

of which was a basic assumption on which the contract was made." The issue of "commercial impracticability" as a basis for excusing performance can arise in many situations including those (1) where costs to seller have increased and (2) where there is a crop failure. *See* U.C.C. § 2-615 Comments 3 and 4.

Increased cost. In Publicker Industries, Inc. v. Union Carbide Corp., 17 U.C.C. Rep. 989 (E.D. Pa. 1975), the defendant Union Carbide had contracted in 1972 to sell ethanol in specified quantities over a three year period to the plaintiff. The price was set by a formula, adjusted annually to reflect the seller's cost for raw materials, and subject to a ceiling on adjustment increases. The raw materials were derivatives of natural gas; their price soared beginning in 1973. The seller's costs for ethanol rose from 21.2 cents a gallon in 1973 to 37.2 cents per gallon in mid-1974. The ceiling contract sales price was then 26.5 cents per gallon. The seller's loss of 10.7 cents per gallon led to a projected aggregate loss of $5.8 million. The court refused to relieve the seller. It found that the ceiling provision constituted an intentional allocation of the "risk of a substantial and unforeseen rise in cost" to the seller. It based this finding in part on the twenty-five percent rise in prices by OPEC in 1971 which made future cost increases highly foreseeable.

Other commonly cited cases, where seller's performance was not excused, include: *Eastern Air Lines, Inc. v. Gulf Oil Corp.*, 415 F. Supp. 429 (S.D. Fla. 1975) (increase of price of jet fuel); *Iowa Elec. Light & Power Co. v. Atlas Corp.*, 467 F. Supp. 129 (N.D. Iowa 1978), *rev'd. on other grounds*, 603 F.2d 1301 (8th Cir. 1979) *cert. denied*, 445 U.S. 911 (1980) (increase of price of uranium); *Maple Farms, Inc. v. City School Dist.*, 352 N.Y.S.2d 784 (1974) (radical increase in milk costs); *Transatlantic Financing Corp. v. United States*, 363 F.2d 312 (D.C. Cir. 1966) (increased costs to carrier shipping goods via Cape of Good Hope upon closing of Suez Canal).

A particularly noteworthy case is *Aluminum Company of America v. Essex Group, Inc.*, 499 F. Supp. 53, 29 U.C.C. Rep. 1 (W.D. Pa. 1980). Here, ALCOA and Essex were parties to a long term toll conversion *service contract* where Essex would supply ALCOA with alumina which ALCOA would convert into molten aluminum that would be picked up by Essex for further processing. The price provisions of the contract contained an escalation formula which indicated that: (1) $.03 per pound of the original price escalated in accordance with changes in the Wholesale Price Index — Industrial Commodities (WPI) and (2) $.03 per pound escalated in accordance with an index based on the average hourly labor rates paid to ALCOA employees at a designated plant. The price term also included a cap. Assisting in the preparation of this formula was economist Alan Greenspan. The WPI did not take into account subsequent material increases in energy costs and the contract became unprofitable to ALCOA who stood to lose $75 million over the life of the contract. ALCOA sought relief on the basis of commercial impracticability because the non-occurrence of an extreme deviation of the WPI was a basic assumption on which the contract was made. *See* Restatement, Second, Contracts §§ 261, 265, 266. The court did not excuse ALCOA's performance, rather, it reformed the contract and fashioned its alternative price schedule. For a critique, see Dawson, *Judicial Revision of Frustrated Contracts: The United States,* 64 B.U.L. Rev. 1 (1984); *cf.* Speidel, *Court-Imposed Price Adjustments Under Long-Term Supply Contracts,* 76 Nw.U.L. Rev. 369 (1981).

Crop failure. Study Comments 4, 5 and 9 to U.C.C. § 2-615 and the following case.

ALIMENTA (U.S.A.), INC. v. CARGILL INCORPORATED

United States Court of Appeals
861 F.2d 650, 7 U.C.C. Rep.2d 1100 (11th Cir. 1988)

NESBITT, DISTRICT JUDGE:

In July 1980, Alimenta (U.S.A.), Inc. ("Alimenta") entered into seven contracts with Cargill, Incorporated ("Cargill") under which Cargill promised to deliver to Alimenta shelled, edible peanuts. The peanut crops were still in the field at the time the contracts were entered into. Later that summer there was a drought, the severity of which is disputed, which reduced the peanut crop yield.

Due to the decrease in the crop yield, Cargill notified Alimenta that it would proceed under U.C.C. § 2-615,[36] that is, Cargill would allocate deliveries of the 1980 peanut crop among its customers, distributors of peanuts with whom they had contracted. Alimenta was advised that it would receive approximately 65% of the peanuts for which they had contracted. Alimenta accepted their allocated share of the peanuts, but later filed suit for breach of contract against Cargill alleging that Cargill acted in bad faith in opting to proceed under Section 2-615. At trial the jury rendered a verdict for Defendant Cargill.

I.

At the inception of the trial, the trial court granted Cargill's motion *in limine* thus barring Alimenta from referring to Cargill's size in any respect.[37] Alimenta urges the exclusion of this evidence was error entitling Alimenta to a new trial because the excluded evidence of Cargill's size and financial resources was relevant to the issue of commercial impracticability. This Court has previously stated that the standard by which impracticability should be judged is an objective one, *Alimenta (U.S.A.), Inc. v. Gibbs Nathaniel (Canada) Ltd.*, 802 F.2d 1362 (11th Cir. 1986). Commercial impracticability under Section 2-615 focuses upon the "the reasonableness of the expenditure at issue, not upon the ability of a party to pay the commercially unreasonable expense." *Asphalt International, Inc. v. Enterprise Shipping Corp.*, 667 F.2d 261 (2nd Cir. 1981); *Transatlantic Financing Corp. v. United States,* 363 F.2d 312, 319 n. 13 (D.C. Cir. 1966) ("the issue of impracticability should no doubt be 'an objective determination of whether the promise can reasonably be performed rather than a subjective inquiry into the promisor's capability of performing as agreed.' "). Under this objective standard, the focus of the impracticability analysis is upon the nature of the agreement and the expectations of the parties, not to the size and financial ability of the parties. The fact that Cargill has grain elevators in Minnesota and barges on the Mississippi is irrelevant to the contract at issue and the expectations of the parties with respect to that contract. Cargill's net sales or net worth has no bearing upon the reasonableness of Cargill's decision to allocate production of peanuts. Accordingly, the trial court was correct in excluding evidence as to Cargill's size inasmuch as such evidence was not relevant to the issue of impracticability.

[36] Section 2-615 of the Uniform Commercial Code provides as follows: [Read § 2-615.]

[37] Cargill is a large agriprocessing and trading company based in Minneapolis, Minnesota. Cargill had between 30 and 40 billion dollars in sales in 1980.

This objective standard applies to both parties. A dealer opting under U.C.C. § 2-615 may not represent itself to the jury as a small company beset by circumstances with which it does not have the financial resources to contend. Just as Alimenta was barred from portraying Cargill as a large company who could have financially met its obligations, Cargill could not portray itself as a small company. The statements made by Cargill addressed the contracts at issue and the expected profits at the time of contracting and not, as Alimenta contends, the size of the Cargill peanut business. Thus Cargill did not improperly mislead the jury as to the issue they were to resolve: whether or not their performance was made impracticable by the crop failure.[38]

II.

The District Court held that under Georgia law, in order to preclude reliance on the allocation remedy of O.C.G.A. § 11-2-615, the seller need expressly assume a greater obligation in the contract. This Court had previously dealt with this issue in *Alimenta (U.S.A.), Inc. v. Gibbs Nathaniel (Canada) Ltd.,* 802 F.2d 1362 (11th Cir. 1986):

> In this diversity action we are bound by the Georgia Supreme Court's interpretation of this statute:
>
> We therefore construe Code Ann. Sec. 109A-2-615 to mean that in order for there to be an expectation to and an exemption from the rule of allocation applicable to a contract of sale, such a contract must contain an affirmation provision that the seller will perform the contract even though the contingencies which permit an allocation might occur.

Mansfield Propane Gas Co., Inc. v. Folger Gas Company 231 Ga. 868, 870, 204 S.E.2d 625, 628 (1974).

> Since neither of the contracts contained such an affirmative provision, Gibbs was entitled to allocate if it could satisfy the jury by a preponderance of the evidence that the occurrence of the contingency (drought) was not reasonably foreseeable when the contracts were entered into and that performance as agreed was made impractical thereby. Obviously, its burden entailed the production of persuasive factual evidence.

Gibbs, 802 F.2d at 1363-64. As required under *Erie R.R. Co. v. Tompkins*, 304 U.S. 64, 58 S.Ct. 817, 82 L.Ed. 1188 (1938), the trial court sitting in diversity applied the law of Georgia. Inasmuch as this court is bound by the law of Georgia and prior opinions of this court, plaintiff's lengthy arguments citing authority and rationale of other jurisdictions are without effect.

III.

Alimenta raises three separate errors relating to the trial court's failure to make factual findings as a matter of law, apparently contending that the court should have directed a verdict in their favor. In reviewing the district court's decision to deny a motion for directed verdict, the evidence must be viewed in a light most favorable to the prevailing party. *Prudential Insurance Company of America v. Schreffler*, 376 F.2d 397, 399 (5th Cir. 1967). This court cannot delve into any conflicts of the evidence, but must assume that all such conflicts have been resolved by the jury in favor of the prevailing party. *Id.; Russell v. Baccus*, 707 F.2d 1289, 1292 (11th Cir. 1983).

---

[38] Cargill has expected $3,000,000.00 in profits. Projected loses after the drought reduced the crop yield amou to $47,000,000.00.

A. Foreseeability of the Peanut Crop Failure

Alimenta first argues that the issue of foreseeability of crop failure should not have gone to the jury. We find that there was sufficient evidence to submit this case to the jury. First, the evidence demonstrated that for the twenty years preceding the 1980 crop there had been a surplusage of domestic peanuts. Secondly, there was evidence that pre-harvest forward sales contracts are customary in the peanut industry. This contracting practice reflects the need to sufficiently schedule production to comport with the capacity of peanut shelling plants. In this manner, such contracts enable production capacity to be pre-committed and deliveries of the plant's output can be scheduled throughout the harvest season. The shelling plant can run more economically; the peanuts are shipped rather than stored; and the plant generated a steady cash flow from sales. Thirdly, improved agronomic and irrigation methods contributed to the industry's expectations of a continued surplusage of peanuts. There was evidence that the shortage of peanuts in 1980 was unprecedented and unforeseen by many if not all experts. The unforeseeability was also demonstrated by the effect of the drought on the peanut market prices: price of peanuts increase often exceeded one dollar per pound. In view of the evidence introduced during trial, it was proper for the trial court to submit the issue of the foreseeability of the crop failure to the jury for its determination.

B. Fairness of Peanut Allocation under § 2-615

Alimenta contends the trial court erred by refusing to rule as a matter of law that Cargill's allocation to its distributors of the available peanuts was both unfair and unreasonable. O.C.G.A. § 11-2-615 provides that the seller may allocate in any manner which is fair and reasonable. Upon a review of the record it appears that there was sufficient evidence to submit this issue to the jury. *See Cosden Oil & Chemical Co. v. Carl O. Helm Aktiengesellschaft*, 736 F.2d 1064 (5th Cir. 1984).

C. Seasonable Notice

Thirdly, Alimenta claims that the trail court erred by refusing to rule as a matter of law that Cargill failed to give reasonable notice of its intention to allocate the peanuts under O.C.G.A. § 11-2-615. Section 11-2-615(c) provides that "the seller must notify the buyer seasonably that there will be delay or non-delivery and, when allocation is required under paragraph (b) of this Code section, of the estimated quota thus made available for the buyer." O.C.G.A. § 11-2-615(c). Action is taken seasonably when it is taken within a reasonable time period, O.C.G.A. § 11-1-204(3), and the reasonable time for taking any action depends upon the nature, purpose and circumstances of such action, O.C.G.A. § 11-1-204(2). From a review of the record in this case there was sufficient evidence to submit the issue of seasonable notice to the jury for determination.

IV.

Alimenta charges as error the trial court's refusal to give its instruction on the definition of good faith. In addition to the definition of good faith stated in the commercial code, Alimenta requested the following:

> This obligation applies in determining whether Cargill acted in good faith in its dealings with customers prior to the time Cargill notified Alimenta of its intention to allocate, whether Cargill

acted in good faith in making its decision to allocate, whether Cargill acted in good faith in deciding to discontinue all efforts to acquire peanuts as of November 12, 1980, and whether Cargill acted in good faith in dividing up peanuts among its customers.

In evaluating the instructions given to the jury, we consider the charges given as a whole. *Lacaze v. Olendorff*, 526 F.2d 1213, 1220, *reh'g en banc granted*, 526 F.2d 1223 (5th Cir. 1976). The instructions given are reviewed in light of the evidence given, the pleadings in the cause and the arguments presented to counsel. *See First Virginia Bankshares v. Benson*, 559 F.2d 1307, 1316 (5th Cir. 1977). To determine whether the trial court was in error in refusing to give Alimenta's particular instruction, we look to whether the jury was misled by the instructions given and whether the jury understood the issues. *See id.* We find that the requested charge by Alimenta was mere surplusage, redundant to the charges given by the court on O.C.G.A. §§ 11-2-615 and 11-2-616. The jury was instructed that Cargill had to prove that they had allocated in a fair and reasonable manner, that the law requires good faith on the part of Cargill, and that Cargill could allocate only if the crop failure was not reasonably foreseeable by commercial standards. While a general instruction as to the definition of good faith, *i.e.,* honesty in fact, O.C.G.A. § 11-2-203 [§ 1-203—Ed.], may have been helpful to the jury, the failure to give such a charge, viewing the instructions as a whole, was not error.

For these reasons, the rulings of the District Court are hereby *affirmed.*

Suppose in *Alimenta* buyer either wants all the peanuts ordered or no peanuts; it does not want an allocation. What, if anything, can buyer do? *See* U.C.C. § 2-616.

NOTES

(1) *Excuse of Buyer's Performance. In International Minerals & Chemical Corp. v. Llano, Inc.*, 770 F.2d 879, 41 U.C.C. Rep. 347 (10th Cir. 1985), IMC (buyer) (owner of a potash mine and processing facility) was obligated to buy natural gas from Llano (seller) under a "take or pay" requirements contract. Subsequently, the New Mexico Environmental Improvement Board (EIB) promulgated Regulation 508 which limited emissions from potash processing equipment. There was no technically suitable way for buyer to comply with EIB's Regulation 508 without shutting down the gas-powered boilers with the concomitant decrease in natural gas consumption. Held: Performance by buyer was excused when made impracticable by having to comply with a supervening governmental regulation. See U.C.C. § 2-615 and Comments 9 and 10. *Cf.* CISG Art. 79.

As to impracticability of performance under a fixed price contract to purchase pinto beans where there was a radical drop in market price, see *Lawrence v. Elmore Bean Warehouse, Inc.*, 702 P.2d 930, 41 U.C.C. Rep. 358 (Idaho App. 1985).

(2) *Substituted Performance. In Jon-T Chemicals, Inc. v. Freeport Chemical Co.,* 704 F.2d 1412, 36 U.C.C. Rep. 154 (5th Cir. 1983), John-T (buyer) agreed to buy several thousand short tons of phosphoric acid from Freeport (seller). When the Chicago area (buyer's location) was crippled by severe snowstorms, the railroad embargoed shipments from seller into Chicago. Under the *force majeure* clause seller's performance was excused by "adverse weather condition . . .or any contingency or delay or failure or cause beyond the reasonable control of Seller." 36 U.C.C. Rep. at 157; see U.C.C. § 2-615. As to substituted performance the court said:

> The sales agreement between Jon-T and Freeport expressly provided that delivery of the phosphoric acid was to be made by *rail unless otherwise agreed.* On its face, this language expresses the intention of the parties who negotiated and entered into the contract that delivery was to be by rail unless both parties *mutually* agreed to make delivery by another carrier. It was thus not error for the district court to decline to instruct the jury that Freeport should have considered delivery by truck when delivery by rail became impossible.
>
> Despite the provisions of the contract terms, Jon-T argues that since the parties did not contract to make delivery by *rail only* then Texas Business and Commerce Code, § 2.614 imposes a duty upon the seller to tender delivery by a commercially reasonable substitute. This contention might have merit were there no contract between the parties relating to the manner of delivery and the absence of such an agreement created a vacuum or an apparent ambiguity; however, the parties' agreement to deliver the acid by rail *unless otherwise agreed* does not create a gap for the relevant provisions of the Code to fill.
>
> . . . .
>
> To summarize, we hold that (i) Freeport was not required to seek an alternative method of delivery under the contract, (ii) the force majeure clause in the contract excused Freeport's obligation to deliver the balance of the acid under the contract. . . .

36 U.C.C. Rep. at 158,59,61.

(3) *Casualty to Identified Goods.* In *Emery v. Weed, 494 A.2d 438, 41 U.C.C. Rep. 115 (Pa. Super. 1985),* buyer signed an agreement on June 7 to purchase from seller for $25,000 a Chevrolet "Pacer Corvette," serial number 1Z87L85901303, and paid $10,000 toward the purchase price. On June 27, July 12, August 10 and September 28, he made additional payments totaling $2,229.90. On or about November 5 the Pacer Corvette was stolen from seller's premises. On November 15 buyer died. Father, as his son's administrator, sought to cancel his son's agreement for the purchase of the Pacer and demanded a refund of the $12,229.90 paid toward its purchase. The court affirmed for buyer's father and stated that all the requirements of U.C.C. § 2-613 were satisfied: (1) the Pacer Corvette "suffer[ed] casualty without fault of either party" prior to delivery to the buyer, (2) the casualty was "total" and occurred "before the risk of loss [had] pass[ed] to the buyer" [U.C.C. § 2-509(3)], (3) "the contract requir[ed] for its performance goods identified [see U.C.C. § 2-501] when the contract [was] made." As to the requirement of identification the court observed:

> Quite apart from its identification in the agreement by serial number, the Pacer was identified by being removed from the display showroom, after the agreement was signed, and being covered and locked. From this it may be inferred that there was "a meeting of the minds as to the particular or actual goods designated."

41 U.C.C. Rep. at 121.

CHAPTER 7

REMEDIES

§ 7.01 Remedies Generally

Read: U.C.C. § 1-106.

Read also: CISG Art. 74.

Make Aggrieved Party Whole. In examining Article 2 remedies set forth in this Chapter, consider whether the Code drafters have achieved "the end that the aggrieved party may be put in as good a position as if the other party had fully performed." U.C.C. § 1-106(1). Further, observe that Article 2 "rejects any doctrine of election of remedy as a fundamental policy and thus the remedies are essentially cumulative in nature and include all of the available remedies for breach." U.C.C. § 2-703 Comment 1; cf. §§ 2A-508 Comment 2, 2A-523 Comment 1. For example, in *Tinker v. De Maria Porsche Audi, Inc.*, 459 So. 2d 487, 37 U.C.C. Rep. 1519 at 1528 note 8 (Fla. App. 1984), it was noted:

> Although not made an issue in this case we note that Section 672.721 [U.C.C. § 2-721, discussed at § 7.07[C], *infra*], Florida Statutes (1981), the Florida version of the Uniform Commercial Code, provides that in an action based on material misrepresentation or fraud, neither rescission of the contract nor rejection or return of the goods bars or is deemed inconsistent with a claim for damages or other remedies. The comment to the Uniform Commercial Code following this section states that an action for rescission does not bar other remedies (such as damages) unless the circumstances make the remedies incompatible. This provision is a change from pre-Code Florida law which required a defrauded buyer to make a choice between the remedies of rescission and damages.
>
> Maintaining a suit in equity to obtain rescission of a sales agreement induced by fraud does not necessarily preclude plaintiff from later suing for damages or other relief inconsistent with rescission if rescission is inadequate, unavailable or useless. . . .

Waiver of Remedies. "Any claim or right arising out of an alleged breach can be discharged. . .without consideration by a written waiver or renunciation signed and delivered by the aggrieved party." U.C.C. § 1-107; see §§ 1-207, 2-720.

§ 7.02 Seller's Remedies for Breach by Buyer

Read: U.C.C. §§ 2-703, 2-709(1)(a).

Read also: U.C.C. §§ 2A-523, 2A-532; CISG Art. 61.

Buyer breaches its obligations under the sales contract when it: (1) wrongfully rejects goods, (2) wrongfully revokes acceptance of goods, (3) fails to make a payment due on or before delivery, or (4) repudiates. Seller's remedies in such instances are indexed in U.C.C. § 2-703. Where buyer accepts and retains the goods, but fails to make payment due after delivery, see U.C.C. § 2-709(1)(a). With regard to rejection, acceptance and revocation of acceptance, see U.C.C. §§ 2-601 through 2-608. These matters are discussed above at § 6.04, Buyer's Rights on Improper Delivery.

[A] Cancellation

Read: U.C.C. §§ 2-703(f), 2-106(3) and (4); cf. § 2-711(1).

Read also: U.C.C. §§ 2A-523(1)(a), 2A-103(1)(b) and (z), cf. § 2A-508(1)(a); CISG Arts. 64, 25-27, 81-84, cf. 49.

A case which draws a distinction between "termination and cancellation" is *Camfield Tires, Inc. v. Michelin Tire Corp.*, 719 F.2d 1361(8th Cir. 1983). There, tire manufacturer (Michelin) had a dealership contract with plaintiff dealer (Camfield). The court said:

> Camfield, the district court found from the record, was chronically in debt to Michelin and "substantially in breach of the dealership agreement as early as January of 1980." When Michelin canceled in April of 1980, the account remained unpaid, more than half of it over 180 days.
>
> Camfield argues that . . . its agreement with Michelin did not allow Michelin to terminate the contract until after the first anniversary date of the contract and upon 120 days written notice. Camfield further argues that under U.C.C. § 1-102(3) which permits parties to vary by agreement provisions of the U.C.C., the contract's termination provision supersedes Michelin's power to cancel under Section 2-703. We disagree. The U.C.C. explicitly draws a distinction between "termination" and "cancellation."
>
> "Termination" occurs when either party pursuant to a power created by agreement or law puts an end to the contract *otherwise than for its breach*. . . . "Cancellation" occurs when either party puts an end to the contract for breach by the other and its effect is the same as that of "termination" except that the canceling party also retains any remedy for breach of the whole contract or any unperformed balance.
>
> N.Y.U.C.C. § 2-106 (McKinney 1964) (emphasis supplied). Thus, the contract's limitation applies only to the "termination" remedy, not to a party's right to cancel for breach by the other party.

[B] Take Action as to the Goods

[1] Withhold or Stop Delivery

Read: U.C.C. §§ 2-703(a) and (b), 2-705.

Read also: U.C.C. §§ 2A-523(1)(c) and (d), 2A-525(1), 2A-526; CISG Arts. 58(2), 64, 71, 72.

BUTTS v. GLENDALE PLYWOOD CO.

United States Court of Appeals
710 F2d 504, 36 U.C.C. Rep. 545 (9th Cir. 1983)

NORRIS, CIRCUIT JUDGE.

The question presented by this appeal is whether Glendale Plywood Co. (Glendale) had the right to stop a shipment of plywood to Summit Creek Plywood Company (Summit Creek) after Summit Creek resold the plywood to a third party and ordered its destination changed. The district court held that, under § 2-705 of the Uniform Commercial Code,the redirection of a shipment at the order of a buyer, without the seller's knowledge, constitutes a reshipment that cuts off the seller's right to stop the goods in transit. We affirm.

I

Summit Creek ordered two railroad carloads of lumber from Glendale Plywood in March, 1978. On April 15, Glendale was instructed to ship the cars to "Summit Creek Forest Products, Murray, Utah." On April 17, Glendale shipped the cars. The railroad issued a [straight (nonnegotiable)] bill of lading showing Glendale as the shipper, Summit Creek as the consignee, and Summit Creek at Murray, Utah as the destination. On April 19, while the goods were in transit, Summit Creek sold its interest in the lumber to Davidson Lumber Sales (Davidson). At the request of Summit Creek, the railroad changed the waybills to show Summit Creek as the shipper, Davidson as the consignee, and Davidson at Murray, Utah as the destination. Summit Creek then sold this account receivable from Davidson, and others, to Walter E. Heller Western, a factoring agent.

The railroad, following Summit Creek's instructions, sent the cars on their way to Davidson at Murray. On April 28, having learned that Summit Creek might be insolvent and before the cars had reached Murray, Glendale ordered the railroad to stop both cars. The railroad complied with Glendale's orders and Glendale then sold the lumber directly to Davidson. The lumber was delivered to Davidson at Murray on May 3.

On May 3, Summit Creek was adjudicated a bankrupt. Thereafter, Summit Creek's trustee in bankruptcy sued Glendale, claiming it had no right to stop the shipment. The bankruptcy court held for Glendale. The district court reversed, holding that Glendale was not allowed to stop the shipment and that Summit Creek, not Glendale was entitled to payment from Davidson. Glendale appeals. The only issue on appeal is whether, under § 2-705 of the Uniform Commercial Code, Glendale had the right to stop the shipment while it was in transit.

II

Section 2-705 of the Uniform Commercial Codeprovides that: [the Court quotes § 2-705(1), (2)(a)-(c)] . . . The dispute in this case is whether the railroad's redirection of the cars from Summit Creek to Davidson at Summit Creek's request constituted a reshipment which cut off Glendale's right to stop delivery under § 2-705(2)(c). The legal question we must thus decide is whether a re-routing of a shipment from a purchaser to a subpurchaser (a buyer from the original purchaser) upon the instructions of the purchaser and without the knowledge of the seller should constitute a reshipment under § 2-705(2)(c). We hold that it should.

The purpose of § 2-705(2)(c) is to protect transactions between original buyers and subpurchasers. See *Interlake, Inc. v. Kansas Power & Light Co.*, 79 Ill App 3d 679, 685-86, 34 Ill Dec 954, 959, 398 NE2d 945, 950, 28 U.C.C. Rep 689, 695-96 (1979). Section (2)(c) protects a subpurchaser from being affected by disputes between the buyer and the seller by ensuring that the goods he orders are delivered regardless of the financial condition of his seller (the original buyer). Whether the original seller has knowledge of the transaction between his buyer and the sub-purchaser has no effect on the subpurchaser's need for protection. To read into § 2-705 a requirement of seller knowledge or permission for reshipment would endanger subpurchasers and discourage resale transactions of the sort conducted here.[1]

Moreover, defining reshipment as the point at which the seller's right to stop shipment ceases provides a time at which the rights of all parties are fixed. Disputes between sellers, buyers, and subpurchasers as to whether permission was ever granted or what the seller intended in his grant of permission, which would result if the seller's permission was required to reship, are avoided.

We find unpersuasive Glendale's argument that the rule we adopt today will cause sellers to demand payment before shipment in order to ensure that they will be paid. While it is true that our interpretation of § 2-705 gives the buyer the power, by reshipping, to cut off the seller's right to stop shipment, the seller's right to stop transit is cut off once the goods are received by the buyer in any event. In most instances the seller has not been paid at this point and still runs the risk of being unable to collect. Yet sellers have not, as a response, shipped only on a C.O.D. basis. There is no reason to believe that they will begin demanding prepayment under our interpretation of § 2-705(2)(c).[2]

The interpretation of § 2-705 adopted by the district court is consistent with the goals of predictability in commercial transactions and providing protection for buyers and sellers alike. The judgment is thus affirmed.

PROBLEM 7.1

In *Butts* what if the railroad had issued a negotiable bill of lading wherein the plywood was "Consigned to ORDER of Summit Creek Plywood Company" and Glendale retained possession of the bill. How would this affect the analysis and outcome of the case? *See* U.C.C. §§ 2-705, 7-104, 7-303.

---

[1] Glendale argues that, while § 2-705 is designed to protect subpurchasers, the subpurchaser here needed no protection because he was able to buy the goods directly from the seller when shipment was stopped. It is true that the subpurchaser in this case was able to mitigate his damages by buying from the seller (though we do not know at what price). However, that may not be the situation in other cases, for example when the subpurchaser has already paid his seller (the buyer). To allow the seller to stop transit after the buyer has made a bargain with a subpurchaser forces the shipment to the subpurchaser to be delayed and the subpurchaser to renegotiate his deal, possibly at a higher price, through no fault of his own. Moreover, an interpretation of § 2-705 that would allow a seller in a rising market to stop transit of the goods and resell them to the subpurchaser at a higher price would allow the seller, merely by claiming a fear of buyer insolvency, to deprive the buyer of the benefit of an advantageous bargain with the subpurchaser. Such a result would be both inequitable and inconsistent with the goals of protection of the contractual rights of all the parties.

[2] Glendale also contends that it is inequitable to establish a rule under which a buyer, without the seller's knowledge, can cut off the seller's right to stop shipment by merely shipping the goods to a third party. While it is true that a buyer can cut off the seller's right to collect by reshipment, to do so he has to sell the goods to someone else and give up the right to receive and use them. If he only has them shipped to himself at another location, his action would be a mere diversion which would not rise to the status of a reshipment, U.C.C. § 2-705 Official Comment 3, and would not cut off the seller's rights.

[2] Identify Goods to the Contract or Salvage Unfinished Goods

Read: U.C.C. §§ 2-703(c), 2-704.

Read also: U.C.C. §§ 2A-523(1)(b), 2A-524; CISG Art. 77.

MODERN MACHINERY v. FLATHEAD COUNTY

Montana Supreme Court
656 P2d 206, 36 U.C.C. Rep. 395 (1982)

HARRISON, JUSTICE.

Plaintiff brought this action for breach of contract in the Eleventh Judicial District in Flathead County. A jury trial commenced in Kalispell, Montana, on February 24, 1982. On February 26, 1982, the jury returned a verdict awarding plaintiff $10,000. Plaintiff and defendant appeal from the judgment entered upon the jury's verdict.

On or about July 30, 1979, the Flathead County commissioners issued a call for bids for the purchase of a jaw-type rock crusher to be used by the Flathead County road department. The commissioners received three bids in response to the call, one from plaintiff in the amount of $305,725 and two from another Kalispell distributor, Westmont; one for $201,193 and the other for $200,870. On August 22, 1979, the day the bids were opened, the commissioners voted to take the bids under advisement pending recommendation of the county road department. Representatives from the road department and Commissioner Frank Guay then flew to Cedar Rapids, Iowa, with plaintiff's agent, Jim Fox, to view plaintiff's crusher. Commissioner Guay and the representatives from the road department were impressed with features contained on plaintiff's crusher which were not available on Westmont's models.

On September 14, 1979, the commissioners met with members of the road department and Jim Fox to discuss the crusher bids. The road department recommended that the commissioners purchase plaintiff's crusher. Commissioner Guay then made a motion to accept the road department's recommendation. The motion was seconded by Commissioner Joan Deist. The motion was recorded in the minutes of the meeting as follows:

> Motion to Guay to accept the Road Department's recommendation to purchase gravel crusher from Modern Machinery for $305,725. The only other bid being received having been for used power plant generator contained in a second unit not attached to the crusher itself, thereby creating operational problems. Motion seconded by Joan A. Deist, motion carried. Note: Mel Wollan votes no on crusher bid as the lower bid for a jaw crusher was very adequate and a savings of $100,000.

Everyone in attendance at the meeting who testified at the trial felt that the county was going to eventually purchase plaintiff's crusher. On September 17, the following Monday, an attorney representing Westmont delivered a letter to commissioner Frank Guay which requested that the award to plaintiff be vacated or he would seek to enforce Westmont's rights in the matter by whatever means permitted by law. Guay then called Jim Fox in Missoula and told him if the crusher had been ordered from the factory, to have the order stopped.

On Wednesday, Fox and another representative for plaintiff, Larry Exe, met Guay in Helena, Montana, to discuss the crusher. Guay testified at trial that he again told Fox and Exe to stop order on the crusher if it had, in fact, been ordered. Fox and Exe testified that the meeting in Helena was mainly to discuss the political ramifications to Guay should the sale be completed. After the meeting in Helena, Exe called the factory to see how far they had progressed on the order. Exe told the factory to let him know how much expense would be incurred if plaintiff was to stop order on the crusher at that time. That was the last contact plaintiff had with the factory concerning a stop order on the crusher.

Fox, Guay and Exe then met with Assistant County Attorney, Charles Kuether, at the Flathead County commissioner's office. Again, Guay told plaintiff's representatives not to order the crusher. Guay stated that the bid award was not final until the clerk and recorder's office issued a letter accepting plaintiff's bid and rejecting all other bids. A second meeting with Kuether followed attended by Fox, Exe, Guay and plaintiff's attorney. Again, Guay stated the bid award was not final until the clerk and recorder's office issued notice of the successful bid. Plaintiff's counsel requested a letter directing plaintiff to either order or stop order on the crusher. Guay refused to draft such a letter stating that since the commissioners had not formally ordered the crusher it was not necessary to rescind an order. That was the last meeting between plaintiff and the commissioner's office.

On November 11, 1979, plaintiff tendered the crusher to Flathead County pursuant to the statement in the call for bids that delivery must be within forty-five days from date of order. The county refused to accept delivery of the machine. On November 20, 1979, the commissioners met and issued a letter to plaintiff stating they had decided to reject all bids received in response to its call for bids on the rock crusher. Plaintiff subsequently transported the crusher to Tempe, Arizona, where it was finally sold. On December 11, 1979, plaintiff filed a complaint in the District Court of the Eleventh Judicial District, in and for the County of Flathead, against Flathead County alleging breach of contract. After a jury trial commencing February 24, 1982, the jury returned a verdict in favor of plaintiff assessing damages in the amount of $10,000. Plaintiff then filed this appeal and defendant cross-appeals.

The substance of the appeals is as follows:

1. Whether there was a valid contract.
2. Whether the jury was properly instructed on the measure of damages.
3. Whether the jury verdict was supported by substantial credible evidence.

[The court held that there was a valid contract not barred by the Statute of Frauds.]

The next issue is whether the jury was properly instructed on the measure of damages. First, plaintiff argues the giving of court's instruction No. 7 was in error. The instruction states:

> If you find that the Plaintiff is entitled to damages, you may award any of the following: 1) Lost net profits; 2) Incidental damages such as expenses incurred in the transportation of goods after the buyer's breach.

The measure of damages when a buyer wrongfully rejects or revokes acceptance of goods is governed by the Uniform Commercial Code. Section 30-2-703, MCA, states: "Where the buyer wrongfully rejects or revokes acceptance of goods. . .the aggrieved seller may: (d) resell and recover damages as hereinafter provided (30-2-706); (e) recover damages for nonacceptance (30-2-708). . . ." Pursuant to § 30-2-706, MCA: "the seller may recover the difference between the resale price and the contract price together with any incidental damages . . . less expenses saved in consequence of the buyer's breach." Pursuant to § 30-2-708, MCA: "the measure of damages for nonacceptance or repudiation by the buyer is the difference between the market price at the time and place for tender and the unpaid contract price together with any incidental damages . . . less expenses saved in consequence of the buyer's breach," or "If the measure of damages provided in subsection (2) is inadequate to put the seller in as good a position as performance would have done, then the measure of damages is the profit . . . which the seller would have made from full performance by the buyer together with any incidental damages . . ., due allowance for costs reasonably incurred and due credit for payments or proceeds of resale."

We find court's instruction no. 7 was not a correct statement of the law as stated by the U.C.C. The possible measures of damages under the U.C.C. are not stated in permissive language, but rather, are mandatory and specifically state the amount of recoverable damage depending upon the remedy seller has pursued. The District Court's use of the words "may award any of the following" in instruction no. 7 implied to the jury that they were not required by law to award specific damages. Thus, the giving of the District Court's instruction no. 7 was in error as being in contradiction of the U.C.C.

Plaintiff also claims the giving of the following instruction was in error:

> A party who alleges that it has been damaged by the breach of contract by another party is bound to exercise reasonable care and diligence to avoid loss and to minimize its damage. A party may not recover for losses which could have been prevented by reasonable efforts on its part.

We find the giving of this instruction was in error. In this case a method of mitigating damages is addressed by § 30-2-704(2), MCA. The section states:

> Where the goods are unfinished an aggrieved seller may in the exercise of reasonable commercial judgment for the purposes of avoiding loss and of effective realization either complete the manufacture and wholly identify the goods to the contract or cease manufacture and resell for scrap or salvage value or proceed in any reasonable manner.

This section is better understood by looking to the Official Comment [2] to § 30-2-704(2), MCA:

> Under this Chapter the seller is given express power to complete manufacture or procurement of goods for the contract unless the exercise of reasonable commercial judgment as to the facts as they appear at the time he learns of the breach makes it clear that such action will result in a material increase in damages. The burden is upon the buyer to show the commercially unreasonable nature of the seller's action in completing manufacture.

Here, Commissioner Guay expressed concern about the contract at an early date, but the board of commissioners refused to repudiate the contract. The county has power to contract, and its contracts are the contracts of its board of county commissioners, not of the individual members thereof. Commissioner Guay did not have the authority to individually revoke the contract, and when plaintiff asked that the board take some action, it refused. Thus, plaintiff was acting in a commercially reasonable manner to fulfill its obligation under the contract. If plaintiff had not delivered the crusher within forty-five days, it would have breached the contract and exposed itself to legal liability. Had the board taken some action at an early date, plaintiff could have mitigated its damages under § 30-2-704, MCA. The District Court's instruction unfairly placed the entire burden to mitigate damages upon plaintiff whereas the comments to § 30-2-704, MCA, state: "the burden is upon the buyer [Flathead County] to show the commercially unreasonable nature of the seller's action in completing manufacture." Thus, the giving of the court's instruction was in error.

The last issue is whether the jury verdict was supported by substantial credible evidence. As stated above, the measure of damages is governed by § 30-2-706, MCA, and § 30-2-708, MCA. Under § 30-2-706, MCA, the damages would be the contract price ($305,725) plus incidental damages less the resale price ($186,499.86) and expenses saved in consequence of the buyer's breach. Under § 30-2-708(2) the damages would be plaintiff's anticipated profit ($78,879.56) plus incidental damages less credit for payments made or proceeds of resale. Using either section in this instance the record shows plaintiff's damages were far in excess of $10,000 and there is no substantial credible evidence which can support the jury verdict.

We affirm the case as to county's liability and judgment is reversed and the case is remanded to the District Court for a hearing on damages by following the applicable statutes.

NOTE

Comment 1 to U.C.C. § 2-704 reads:

> This section gives an aggrieved seller the right at the time of breach to identify to the contract any conforming finished goods, regardless of their resalability, and to use reasonable judgment as to completing unfinished goods. It thus makes the goods available for resale under the resale section [U.C.C. § 2-706, see § 2-708] the seller's primary remedy, and in the special case in which resale is not practicable, allows the action for the price [U.C.C. § 2-709(1)(b)] which would then be necessary to give the seller the value of his contract. [*Cf.* U.C.C. §§ 2A-527, 2A-528, 2A-529. CISG Arts. 62, 75, 76.]

U.C.C. §§ 2-706, 2-708 and 2-709 are discussed at § 7.02[C] immediately below.

[C] Recover Monies

[1] Resell and Recover Damages

Read: U.C.C. §§ 2-703(d), 2-706; cf. § 2-712.

Read also: U.C.C. §§ 2A-523(1)(e), 2A-527, cf. § 2A-518; CISG Arts. 61(1)(b), 74, 75.

APEX OIL CO. v. THE BELCHER CO. OF NEW YORK, INC.

United States Court of Appeals
855 F.2d 997 (2d Cir. 1988)

WINTER, CIRCUIT JUDGE

This diversity case, arising out of an acrimonious commercial dispute, presented the question whether a sale of goods six weeks after a breach of contract may properly be used to calculate resale damages under Section 2-706 of the Uniform Commercial Code, where goods originally identified to the broken contact were sold on the day following the breach. Defendants The Belcher Company of New York, Inc. and Belcher New Jersey, Inc. (together "Belcher") appeal from a judgment, entered after a jury trial before Judge McLaughlin, awarding plaintiff Apex Oil Company ("Apex") $432,365.04 in damages for breach of contract and fraud in connection with an uncompleted transaction for heating oil. Belcher claims that the district court improperly allowed Apex to recover resale damages and that Apex failed to prove its fraud claim by clear and convincing evidence. We agree and reverse.

BACKGROUND

Apex buys, sells, refines and transports petroleum products of various sorts, including No. 2 heating oil, commonly known as home heating oil. Belcher also buys and sells petroleum products, including No. 2 heating oil. In February 1982, both firms were trading futures contracts for No. 2 heating oil on the New York Mercantile Exchange ("Merc"). In particular, both were trading Merc contracts for February 1982 No. 2 heating oil—*i.e.*, contracts for the delivery of that commodity in New York Harbor during that delivery month in accordance with the Merc's rules. As a result of that trading, Apex was short 315 contracts, and Belcher was long by the same amount. Being "short" one contract for oil means that the trader has contracted to deliver one thousand barrels at some point in the future, and being "long" means just the opposite—that the trader has contracted to purchase that amount of oil. If a contract is not liquidated before the close of trading, the short trader must deliver the oil to a long trader (the exchange matches shorts with longs) in strict compliance with Merc rules or suffer stiff penalties, including disciplinary proceedings and fines. A short trader may, however meet its obligations by entering into an "exchange for physicals" ("EFP") transaction with a long trader. An EFP allows a short trader to substitute for the delivery of oil under the terms of a futures contract the delivery of oil at a different place and time.

Apex was matched with Belcher by the Merc, and thus became bound to produce 315,000 barrels of No. 2 heating oil meeting Merc specifications in New York Harbor. Those specifications required that oil delivered in New York Harbor have a sulfur content no higher than 0.20%. Apex asked Belcher whether Belcher would take delivery of 190,000 barrels of oil in Boston Harbor in satisfaction of 190 contracts, and Belcher agreed. At trial, the parties did not dispute that, under this EFP, Apex promised it would deliver the No. 2 heating oil for the same price as that in the original contract—89.70 cents per gallon—and that the oil would be lifted from the vessel *Bordeaux*. The parties did dispute, and vigorously so, the requisite maximum sulfur content. At trial, Belcher sought to prove that the oil had to meet the New York standard of 0.20%, while Apex asserted that the oil had to meet only the specifications for Boston Harbor of not more than 0.30% sulfur.

The *Bordeaux* arrived in Boston Harbor on February 9, 1982, and on the next day began discharging its cargo of No. 2 heating oil at Belcher New England, Inc.'s terminal in Revere, Massachusetts. Later in the evening of February 10, after fifty or sixty thousand barrels had been offloaded, an independent petroleum inspector told Belcher that tests showed the oil on board the *Bordeaux* contained 0.28% sulfur, in excess of the New York Harbor specification. Belcher nevertheless continued to lift oil from the ship until eleven o'clock the next morning, February 11, when 141,535 barrels had been pumped into Belcher's terminal. After pumping had stopped, a second test indicated that the oil contained 0.22% sulfur—a figure within the accepted range of tolerance for oil containing 0.20% sulfur. (Apex did not learn of the second test until shortly before trial.) Nevertheless, Belcher refused to resume pumping, claiming that the oil did not conform to specifications.

After Belcher ordered the *Bordeaux* to leave its terminal, Apex immediately contacted Cities Service. Apex was scheduled to deliver heating oil to Cities Service later in the month and accordingly asked if it could satisfy that obligation by immediately delivering the oil on the *Bordeaux*. Cities Service agreed, and that oil was delivered to Cities Service in Boston Harbor on February 12, one day after the oil had been rejected by Belcher. Apex did not give notice to Belcher that the oil had been delivered to Cities Service.

Meanwhile, Belcher and Apex continued to quarrel over the portion of the oil delivered by the *Bordeaux*. Belcher repeatedly informed Apex, orally and by telex, that the oil was unsuitable and would have to be sold at a loss because of its high sulfur content. Belcher also claimed, falsely, that it was incurring various expenses because the oil was unusable. In fact, however, Belcher had already sold the oil in the ordinary course of business. Belcher nevertheless refused to pay Apex the contract price of $5,322.200.27 for the oil it had accepted, and it demanded that Apex produce the remaining 48,000 barrels of oil owing under the contract. On February 17, Apex agreed to tender the 48,000 barrels if Belcher would both make partial payment for the oil actually accepted and agree to negotiate as to the price ultimately to be paid for that oil. Belcher agreed and sent Apex a check for $5,034.997.12, a sum reflecting a discount of five cents per gallon from the contract price. However, the check contained an endorsement stating that "[t]he acceptance and negotiation of this check constitutes full payment and final settlement for all claims" against Belcher. Apex refused the check, and the parties returned to square one. Apex demanded full payment; Belcher demanded that Apex either negotiate the check or remove the discharged oil (which had actually been sold) and replace it with 190,000 barrels of conforming produce. Apex chose to take the oil and replace it, and on February 23 told Belcher that the 142,000 barrels of discharged oil would be removed on board the *Mersault* on February 25.

By then, however, Belcher had sold the 142,000 barrels and did not have an equivalent amount of No. 2 oil in its entire Boston terminal. Instead of admitting that it did not have the oil, Belcher told Apex that a dock for the *Mersault* was unavailable. Belcher also demanded that Apex either remove the oil *and* pay terminalling and storage fees, or accept payment for the oil at a discount of five cents per gallon. Apex refused to do either. On the next day, Belcher and Apex finally reached a settlement under which Belcher agreed to pay for the oil discharged from the *Bordeaux* at a discount of 2.5 cents per gallon. The settlement agreement also resolved an unrelated dispute between an Apex subsidiary and a subsidiary of Belcher's parent firm, The Coastal Corporation. It is this agreement that Apex now claims was procured by fraud.

After the settlement, Apex repeatedly contacted Belcher to ascertain when, where and how Belcher would accept delivery of the remaining 48,000 barrels. On March 5, Belcher informed Apex that it considered its obligations under the original contract to have been extinguished, and that it did not "desire to purchase such a volume [the 48,000 barrels] at the offered price." Apex responded by claiming that the settlement did not extinguish Belcher's obligation to accept the 48,000 barrels. In addition, Apex stated that unless Belcher accepted the oil by March 20, Apex would identify 48,000 barrels of No. 2 oil to the breached contract and sell the oil to a third party. When Belcher again refused to take the oil, Apex sold 48,000 barrels to Gill & Duffus Company. This oil was sold for delivery in April at a price of 76.25 cents per gallon, 13.45 cents per gallon below the Belcher contract price.

On October 7, 1982, Apex brought this suit in the Eastern District, asserting breach of contact and fraud. The breach-of-contract claim in Apex's amended complaint contended that Belcher had breached the EFP, not in February, but in March, when Belcher had refused to take delivery of the 48,000 barrels still owing under the contract. The amended complaint further alleged that "[a]t the time of the breach of the Contract by Belcher the market price of the product was $.7625 per gallon," the price brought by the resale to Gill & Duffus on March 23. In turn, the fraud claim asserted that Belcher had made various misrepresentations—that the *Bordeaux* oil was unfit, and unusable by Belcher, and that consequently Belcher was suffering extensive damages and wanted the oil removed—upon which Apex had relied when it had agreed from the *Bordeaux.* Apex asserted that as a result of the alleged fraud it had suffered damages of 2.5 cents per gallon, the discount agreed upon in the settlement.

The case went to trial before Judge McLaughlin and a jury between February 3 and February 13, 1986. As it had alleged in its pleadings, Apex asserted that its breach-of-contract claim was based on an alleged breach occurring *after* February 11, 1982, the day Belcher rejected the oil on board the *Bordeaux*. Judge McLaughlin, however, rejected this theory as a matter of law. His view of the case was that Belcher's rejection of the *Bordeaux* oil occurred under one of two circumstances: (i) either the oil conformed to the proper sulfur specification, in which case Belcher breached; or (ii) the oil did not conform, in which case Apex breached. Judge McLaughlin reasoned that, if Belcher breached on February 11, then it could not have breached thereafter. If on the other hand Apex breached, then, Judge McLaughlin reasoned, only under the doctrine of cure, *see* N.Y.U.C.C. § 2-508 (McKinney 1964), could Belcher be deemed to have breached. Apex, however, waived the cure theory by expressly disavowing it (perhaps because it presumes a breach by Apex). Instead, Apex argued that, regardless of whether the *Bordeaux* oil had conformed, Belcher's refusal throughout February and March 1982 to accept delivery of 48,000 barrels of conforming oil, which Belcher was then still demanding, had constituted a breach contract. Judge McLaughlin rejected this argument, which he viewed as simply "an attempt to reintroduce the cure doctrine."

In a general verdict, the jury awarded Apex $283,752.94 on the breach-of-contract claim, and $148,612.10 on the fraud claim, for a total of $432,365.04. With the addition of prejudgment interest, the judgment came to $588,566.29.

Belcher appeals from this verdict. Apex has not taken a cross-appeal from Judge McLaughlin's dismissal of its post-February 11 breach theories, however. The parties agree, therefore, that as the case comes to us, the verdict concerning the breach can be upheld on the theory that, if Belcher breached the contract, it did so only on February 11, 1982, and that the oil sold to Gill & Duffus on March 23 was identified to the broken contract.

DISCUSSION

[Here the court cited U.C.C. § 2-706 and italicized the following in subjection (2): *The resale must be reasonably identified as referring to the broken contract. . . ."*]

Belcher's principal argument on appeal is that the district court erred as a matter of law in allowing Apex to recover resale damages under Section 2-706. Specifically, Belcher contends that the heating oil Apex sold to Gill & Duffus in late March of 1982 was not identified to the broken contract. According to Belcher, the oil identified to the contract was the oil aboard the *Bordeaux*—oil which Apex had sold to Cities Service on the day after the breach. In response, Apex argues that, because heating oil is a fungible commodity, the oil sold to Gill & Duffus was "reasonably identified" to the contract even though it was not the same oil that had been on board the *Bordeaux*. We agree with Apex that, at least with respect to fungible goods, identification for the purposes of a resale transaction does not necessarily require that the resold goods be the exact goods that were rejected or repudiated. Nonetheless, we conclude that as a matter of law the oil sold to Gill & Duffus in March was not reasonably identified to the contract breached on February 11, and that the resale was not commercially reasonable.

Resolving the instant dispute requires us to survey various provisions of the Uniform Commercial Code. The first such provision is Section 2-501, which defines "identification" and states in pertinent part:

[The court recites U.C.C. § 2-501(1)(a) and (b).]

The *Bordeaux* oil was unquestionably identified to the contract under Section 2-501(1)(b), and Apex does not assert otherwise. Nevertheless, Apex argues that Section 2-501 "has no application in the context of the Section 2-706 resale remedy," because Section 2-501 defines identification only for the purpose of establishing the point at which a buyer "obtains a special property and an insurable interest in goods." N.Y.U.C.C. § 2-501. This argument has a facial plausibility but ignores Section 2-103, which contains various definitions, and an index of other definitions, of terms used throughout Article 2 of the Code. With regard to "[i]dentification," Section 2-103(2) provides that the "definition[] applying to *this Article*" is set forth in Section 2-501. *Id.* § 2-103 (emphasis added).

Section 2-501 thus informs us that the *Bordeaux* oil was identified to the contract. It does not end our inquiry, however, because it does not exclude as a matter of law the possibility that a seller may identify goods to a contract, but then substitute, for the identified goods, *identical* goods that are then identified to the contract.

. . .

Belcher relies upon Section 2-706's statement that "the seller may resell the *goods concerned,*" N.Y.U.C.C. § 2-706(1) (emphasis added), and upon Section 2-704, which states that "[a]n aggrieved seller . . . may . . . identify to the contract conforming goods *not already identified* if at the time he learned of the breach they are in his possession or control." *Id.* § 2-704(1) (emphasis added). According to Belcher, these statements absolutely foreclose the possibility of reidentification for the purpose of a resale. Apex, on the other hand, points to section 2-706's statement that "it is not necessary that the goods be in existence or that any or all of them have been identified to the contract before the breach." *Id.* § 2-706(2). According to Apex, this language shows that "[t]he relevant inquiry to be made under Section 2-706 is whether the resale transaction is reasonably identified to the breached contract and not whether the goods resold were originally identified to the contract."

None of the cited provisions are dispositive. First, Section 2-706(1)'s reference to reselling "the goods concerned" is unhelpful because those goods are the goods identified to the contract, but which goods are so identified is the question to be answered in the instant case. Second, as to Section 2-704, the fact that an aggrieved seller may identify goods "not already identified" does not mean that the seller may not identify goods as substitutes for previously identified goods. Rather, Section 2-704 appears to deal simply with the situation described in Section 2-706(2) above, where the goods are not yet in existence or have not yet been identified to the contract. Belcher thus can draw no comfort from either Section 2-704 or Section 2-706(1). Third, at the same time, however, Section 2-706(2)'s reference to nonexistent and nonidentified goods does not mean, as Apex suggests, that the original (pre-breach) identification of goods is wholly irrelevant. Rather, the provision regarding nonexistent and nonidentified goods deals with the special circumstances involving anticipatory repudiation by the buyer. *See* N.Y.U.C.C. § 2-706 comment 7. Under such circumstances, there can of course be no resale remedy unless the seller is allowed to identify goods to the contract after the breach. That is obviously not the case here.

. . .

[F]ungible goods resold pursuant to section 2-706 must be goods identified to the contract, but need not always be those *originally* identified to the contract. In other words, at least where fungible goods are concerned, identification is not always an irrevocable act and does not foreclose the possibility of substitution.

. . .

Nevertheless, as [§ 2-706] expressly states, "[t]he resale must be *reasonably* identified as referring to the broken contract," and "every aspect of the sale including the method, manner, time, place and terms must be commercially reasonable." N.Y.U.C.C. § 2-706(2) (emphasis added). Moreover, because the purpose of remedies under the Code is to put "the aggrieved party . . . in as good a position as if the other party had fully performed," *id.* § 1-106(1), the reasonableness of the identification and of the resale must be determined by examining whether the market value of, and the price received for, the resold goods "accurately reflects the market value of the goods which are subject of the contract." *Servbest*, 82 Ill. App.3d at 671, 37 Ill. Dec. at 952, 403 N.E.2d at 8.

. . .

[A]n example of an unreasonable identification and resale would be to claim as a resale the sale of goods located where they would have a significantly lower value than the originally identified goods. For example, had Apex purported to identify and resell 48,000 barrels of No. 2 oil contained in a storage tank in the Virgin Islands, where heating oil is presumably less useful and valuable than in Boston, while simultaneously delivering the same amount to Cities Service in Boston, the identification and resale would be unreasonable.

The most pertinent aspect of reasonableness with regard to identification and resale involves timing. As one treatise explains:

> [T]he object of the resale is simply to determine exactly the seller's damages. These damages are the difference between the contract price and the market price at the time and place when performance should have been made by the buyer. The object of the resale . . . is to determine what the market price in fact was. *Unless the resale is made at about the time when performance was due it will be of slight probative value, especially if the goods are of a kind which fluctuate rapidly in value.* If no reasonable market existed at this time, no doubt a delay may be proper and a subsequent sale may furnish the best test, though confessedly not a perfectly exact one, of the seller's damage.

4 R. Anderson, Anderson on the Uniform Commercial Code § 2-706:25(3d ed. 1983); *see also Servbest*, 82 Ill. App.3d at 671, 37 Ill. Dec. at 952, 403 N.E.2d at 8. The issue of delay between breach and resale has previously been addressed only in the context of determining commercial reasonableness where the goods resold are the goods originally identified to the broken contract. However, the principles announced in that context apply here as well.

> What is . . .a reasonable time [for resale] depends upon the nature of the goods, the condition of the market and other circumstance of the case; its length cannot be measured by any legal

yardstick or divided into degrees. Where a seller contemplating receives a demand from the buyer for inspection under the section of [sic] preserving evidence of goods in dispute, the time for resale may be appropriately lengthened.

N.Y.U.C.C. § 2-706 comment 5. . . .

Here, Apex's delay of nearly six weeks between the breach on February 11, 1982 and the purported resale on March 23 was clearly unreasonable, even if the transfer to Cities Service had not occurred. Steven Wirkus, of Apex, testified on cross-examination that the market price for no. 2 heating oil on February 12, when the *Bordeaux* oil was delivered to Cities Service, was "[p]robably somewhere around 88 cents a gallon or 87." (The EFP contract price, of course, was 89.70 cents per gallon.) Wirkus also testified on redirect examination that the market price fluctuated throughout the next several weeks:

Q: Sir, while you couldn't remember with particularity what the price of oil was on a given day four years ago, is it fair to say that prices went up and down?

A: Definitely that's fair to say.

Q: From day-to-day?

A: Yes.

Q: Towards the end of February prices went down?

A: That's correct.

Q: Then in early March it went back up?

A: In early March, yes.

Q: Then they went back down again towards the middle of March; isn't that correct?

MR. GILBERT: I object to the form of this, your Honor, on redirect.

THE COURT: Yes.

Q: Did they go back down in mid March, Mr. Wirkus?

A: My recollection, yes.

Q: In late March what happened to the price?

A: Market went back up.

Moreover, Wirkus testified that, on March 23, in a transaction unrelated to the resale, Apex purchased 25,000 barrels of No. 2 oil for March delivery at 80.50 cents per gallon, and sold an equivalent amount for April delivery at 77.25 cents per gallon. Other sales on March 22 and 23 for April delivery brought similar prices: 100,000 barrels were sold at 76.85 cents, and 25,000 barrels at 76.35 cents. The Gill & Duffus resale, which was also for *April* delivery, fetched a price of 76.25 cents per gallon—some eleven or twelve cents below the market price on the day of the breach.

In view of the long delay and the apparent volatility of the market for No. 2 oil, the purported resale failed to meet the requirements of Section 2-706 as a matter of law. The delay unquestionably prevented the resale from "accurately reflect[ing] the market value of the goods." *Servbest*, 82 Ill. App.3d at 671, 37 Ill. Dec. at 952, 403 N.E.2d at 8. Indeed, in the analogous context of the securities markets (which are arguably not much more liquid or volatile than today's centralized and computerized commodities markets), we have upheld a district court's conclusion that thirty days was a maximum time for the commercially–reasonable resale of securities after the breach of a tender offer. [Citation.]

Nor do we find Apex's delay justified on any other ground. Apex does not assert, for example, that "the time for resale [should] be appropriately lengthened" because Belcher sought an "inspection . . .[to] preserv[e] evidence of [the] goods in dispute," N.Y.U.C.C. § 2-706 comment 5; Belcher of course made no such request, and Apex immediately disposed of the *Bordeaux* oil in any event. Apex's only asserted justification, which the district court accepted in denying Belcher's motion for judgment notwithstanding the verdict, was that the delay was caused by continuing negotiations with Belcher. We find that ruling to be inconsistent with the district court's view that Belcher's breach, if any, occurred on February 11. The function of a resale was to put Apex in the position it would have been on that date by determining the value of the oil Belcher refused. The value of the oil at a later date is irrelevant because Apex was in no way obligated by the contract or by the Uniform Commercial Code to reserve 48,000 gallons for Belcher after the February 11 breach. Indeed, that is why Apex's original theory, rejected by the district court and not before us on this appeal, was that the breach occurred in March.

The rule that a "resale should be made as soon as practicable after . . .breach," *Bache*, 339 F.Supp. at 352 should be stringently applied where, as here, the resold goods are not those originally identified to the contract. In such circumstances, of course, there is a significant risk that the seller, who may perhaps have already disposed of the original goods without suffering any loss, has identified new goods for resale in order to minimize the resale price and thus to maximize damages. That was not the case in *Servbest*, for example, where the resale consisted of the first sales made after the breach. *See* 82 Ill. App.3d at 675, 37 Ill. Dec. at 955, 403 N.E.2d at 11. Here, by contrast, the oil originally identified to the contract was sold the day after the February 11, 1982 breach, and no doubt Apex sold ample amounts thereafter in the six weeks before the purported resale. . . . Because the sale of the oil identified to the contract to Cities Service on the next day fixed the value of the goods refused as a matter of law, the judgment on the breach-of-contract claim must be reversed.

We turn finally to Apex's fraud claim. [The court held that the reliance element of fraud was not established in view of the acknowledgment by Apex's president that he did not believe Belcher's misrepresentations.]

Reversed.

NOTES

(1) The case of *Afram Export Corp. v. Metallurgiki Halyps, S.A.*, 772 F.2d 1358, 41 U.C.C. Rep. 1709 (7th Cir. 1985), involved U.C.C. § 2-706. The pertinent portion of the court's opinion states:

> Afram Export Corporation, the plaintiff, is a Wisconsin corporation that exports scrap metal. Metallurgiki Halyps, S.A., the defendant, is a Greek corporation that makes steel. In 1979, after a series of trans-Atlantic telephone and telex communications, the parties made a contract through an exchange of telex messages for the purchase by Metallurgiki of 15,000 tons of clean shredded scrap, at $135 per ton, F.O.B. Milwaukee, delivery to be made by the end of April. Metallurgiki apparently intended to use the scrap to make steel for shipment to Egypt,

pursuant to a contract with an Egyptian buyer. Afram agreed to pay the expenses of an agent of Metallurgiki—Shields—to inspect the scrap for cleanliness before it was shipped.

The scrap for the contract was prepared, in Milwaukee, by Afram Metal Processing Company. Both Afram Metal Processing and the plaintiff Afram Export are wholly owned subsidiaries of Afram Brothers. All three are Wisconsin corporations, and have the same officers and directors. Unless otherwise indicated, when we say "Afram" we mean "Afram Export."

Shields arrived to inspect the scrap on April 12. He told Afram that the scrap was clean but that Metallurgiki would not accept it, because the price of scrap had fallen. Sure enough, Metallurgiki refused to accept it. Afram brought this suit after selling the scrap to other buyers. Metallurgiki unsuccessfully challenged the court's jurisdiction over it, then filed a counterclaim alleging that Afram had broken the contract and had thereby made it impossible for Metallurgiki to fulfill its contract with the Egyptian purchaser.

After a bench trial, the district judge gave judgment for Afram for $425,149 and dismissed the counterclaim. Metallurgiki has appealed from the judgment for Afram, and Afram has cross-appealed, contending that the judge should have given it the full damages it sought—$483,750—plus incidental damages of $40,665, prejudgment interest, the cost of a so-called public sale, and attorney's fees for defending against the counterclaim.

. . . .

This completes our consideration of Metallurgiki's appeal and we turn to Afram's cross-appeal. Afram claims that it sold all of the scrap rejected by Metallurgiki at a public sale on June 15, 1979, and that its damages should therefore be based on the price of that sale, which was $102.75 per ton. The district judge disagreed. He found that two-thirds of the scrap had been sold at a substantially higher price to Luria Brothers on June 4 ($118—actually somewhat less, because Afram defrayed some freight costs) and the other third to International Traders on September 15 at a price of $103. Afram points out that the sale on June 4 actually was made by its affiliate, Afram Metal Processing Company, and further argues that since all Afram scrap is sold from the same pile in Milwaukee it is arbitrary to treat the first sale after the breach of contract as the cover transaction, rather than the sale that Afram designated as that transaction.

We agree with the district judge that the sale on June 4 was a cover transaction, even though the nominal seller was a different corporation from the plaintiff. Not only are both corporations wholly owned subsidiaries of another corporation, not only do all three corporations have the same officers and directors, but the record indicates substantial commingling of assets and operation of the three corporations as a single entity. Shortly after Metallurgiki's rejection, Zeke Afram, an officer of both Afram Export (the party to the contract with Metallurgiki) and Afram Metal Processing (the nominal owner of the scrap sold on June 4), called Luria Brothers and explained that he had extra scrap for sale because of a buyer's breach; apparently he did not bother to indicate which Afram corporation he was calling on behalf of. The June 4 sale followed shortly. The conversation and the timing of the sale are powerful evidence that the breach enabled the sale—that it would not have occurred but for the breach—and hence that the revenue from the sale must be subtracted from the contract price to determine Afram's loss.

But this does not dispose completely of the issue of the cover price. If the sale on June 15 was "made in good faith and in a commercially reasonable manner," it fixed Afram's damages on the remaining one-third of the scrap. U.C.C. § 2-706(1), Wis. Stat. § 402.706(1). The question may seem less than earthshaking since the June sale price and the September sale price which the district court used as the cover price for the remaining third were only 25 per ton apart. But the bona fides of the June 15 sale casts additional light on the intercorporate relations of the Afram group and hence on the proper interpretation of the sale to Luria Brothers. In any event, the district judge was entitled to find that neither condition in § 2-706(1) was satisfied. . . . The June 15 "sale" was about a pure a bookkeeping transaction—as empty of economic significance—as can be imagined. It consisted of a transfer of the scrap on the books of one affiliated corporation to the books of another. The transferor and transferee were not only under common ownership but were operated as if they were limbs of a single organism. The scrap itself was not moved; it remained on the scrap heap till sold later on. No invoice or check for the sale was produced at trial. The inference that the sale was designed simply to maximize the enterprise's damages, leaving it free to resell the scrap at higher prices later on, is overpowering. The sale of the scrap three months later to International Traders at a (slightly) higher price provided better evidence of what the enterprise actually lost, so far as the scrap not sold to Luria Brothers is concerned, by Metallurgiki's breach of contract.

(2) *Person in Position of Seller.* In *Hart v. Sims*, 702 F.2d 574, 35 U.C.C. Rep. 1517 (5th Cir. 1983), an art dealer had become responsible for the balance of the purchase price of a painting on behalf of her principal. Held: She was a "person in the position of a seller," and entitled to remedies available to a seller, *e.g.*, those under U.C.C. § 2-706. U.C.C. § 2-707.

(3) Under proposed § 2-706, except where a buyer with a security interest in the seller's goods sells the goods under § 2-711, notice is no longer required for a private resale under § 2-706(b).

[2] Recover Damages for Non-Acceptance or Repudiation

Read: U.C.C. §§ 2-703(e), 2-708; see §§ 2-723, 2-724, 2-503; cf. § 2-713.

Read also: U.C.C. §§ 2A-523(1)(e), 2A-528, 2A-507, cf. § 2A-519(1) and (2); CISG Arts. 61(1)(b), 74, 76.

Comment 2 to U.C.C. § 2-706 states in part: "Failure to act properly under this section deprives the seller of the measure of damages here provided [difference between resale price and contract price] and relegates him to that provided in Section 2–708." In *Apex*, above, how would damages be calculated under § 2-708(1)?

PROBLEM 7.2

Seller contracts to sell certain goods to buyer for $10,000. Buyer repudiates. In accordance with U.C.C. § 2-706, Seller resells the goods to X for $8,000. Under U.C.C. § 2-708(1), however, the market price for the goods at the time and place for tender is $6,000. Seller wishes to recover damages based on the 2-708(1) formula rather than that under 2-706. May it do so? *See* §§ 1-106, 2-712 Comment 3. *See also*, *Tesoro Petroleum Corp. v. Holborn Oil Company, Ltd.*, 547 N.Y.S.2d 1012 (1989).

UNION CARBIDE CORP. v. CONSUMERS POWER CO.

United States District Court
636 F.Supp. 1498, 1 U.C.C. Rep.2d 1202 (E.D. Mich. 1986)

JOINER, DISTRICT JUDGE.

This dispute arises out of a contract between Union Carbide Corporation ("Union Carbide") and Consumers Power Company ("Consumers") for the purchase of large quantities of residual fuel oil. Plaintiff Union Carbide alleges that Consumers breached this contract by refusing to accept further deliveries of the oil. Both parties have filed motions asking this court to determine the appropriate measure of damages to be applied if a breach is determined to have occurred.

FACTUAL BACKGROUND

The facts of the case which are relevant to these motions are largely agreed upon. There are two major contracts involved: one between Union Carbide and Consumers, and the other between Petrosar Limited ("Petrosar") and Union Carbide. On September 5, 1980, Union Carbide and Consumers entered into a contract whereby Union Carbide would deliver, and Consumers would purchase, 10,000 barrels of residual fuel oil per day until December 31, 1987. Union Carbide's oil supplier was Petrosar.

After the contract was signed, and deliveries begun, there was a dramatic drop in the price of residual fuel oil which was not passed through to Consumers. Thus, Consumers was paying prices well in excess of the market price for the oil it received from Union Carbide. In late 1981, Consumers announced that it would refuse to take any further deliveries of residual fuel oil after December 31, 1981. Union Carbide made sporadic efforts to resell the oil Consumers refused until August 27, 1982. Union Carbide then canceled the contract under the terms of Uniform Commercial Code (U.C.C.) § 2-703(f) [Mich. Comp. Laws. Ann. § 440.2703]. In lieu of accepting further deliveries of oil previously sold to Consumers, Union Carbide paid Petrosar to keep the oil. These payments were called residual oil reduction payments (RORP). They continued making these payments until July 1, 1983, when Union Carbide and Petrosar terminated their contract.

The pricing mechanism for the Union Carbide-Consumers contract insured that Union Carbide was guaranteed to profit on each barrel of oil that Consumers accepted. Using the price Union Carbide paid to Petrosar as a base, Consumers' price was calculated by multiplying the base price by a fixed percentage and adding in certain fixed costs. The net result was that Consumers always paid Union Carbide more per barrel than Union Carbide paid to Petrosar, with the difference between these two prices amounting to a certain net profit.

The second contract involved in this case is Union Carbide's 1974 contract with Petrosar to purchase 27,000 barrels of residual fuel oil per day. Since it had no use for the oil in its own operations, Union Carbide sought to dispose of it through resale contracts or on the spot market.

In addition to the Consumers contract, Union Carbide had contracted with Niagara Mohawk Power and Light (Mohawk) for the resale of 5,000 barrels per day. As noted above, Union Carbide terminated its contract with Petrosar on July 1, 1983. Union Carbide's termination of its Petrosar contract was the result of many factors, only one of which was Consumers' refusal to accept further deliveries of residual fuel oil after 1981. As a result of its decision to end this contract, Union Carbide negotiated a settlement of its contractual obligations with Petrosar. The terms of this settlement required Union Carbide to assign the Mohawk contract to Petrosar and pay it approximately $20 million (Canadian).

There is no dispute over the measure of damages to be applied for all shipments of oil which Union Carbide resold. Both parties agree that U.C.C. § 2-706(1) dictates that damages for this oil should be measured by the difference between the resale price and the contract price plus allowable incidental damages minus expenses saved in consequence of the buyer's breach.

The parties disagree over the proper measure of damages to be applied for the oil which Consumers refused that Union Carbide did not attempt to resell. This includes the oil identified to the Consumers' contract which Union Carbide paid RORP to Petrosar to not deliver to it plus the amount of oil that would have been identified to the Consumers' contract if Union Carbide had not terminated its contract with Petrosar. While the parties concur that U.C.C. § 2-708 applies, they differ over which section of that provision should be utilized.

The text of § 2-708 provides that: [the Court quotes U.C.C. § 2-708].

Union Carbide claims that the appropriate measure of damages is governed by section 1 (market price differential). It urges that the court award market price damages. These were estimated at oral argument to amount to approximately $120 million (U.S.).

Consumers responds that section 2 (lost profits) damages are more appropriate in this case because they give Union Carbide what it would have received if the contract had been performed. Consumers believes that market price damages would greatly overcompensate Union Carbide for the riskless role it assumed in this contract. It says this would violate U.C.C. § 1-106. Lost profit damages were estimated at oral argument to amount to $30 million (U.S.).

LEGAL ANALYSIS

Turning first to the language of the statute, the court must interpret the first phrase of § 2-708(2), which says: "If the measure of damages provided in subsection (1) is *inadequate* to put the seller in as good a position as performance would. . ." The key to understanding this passage's meaning is the word "inadequate."

Union Carbide claims that the language of the statute supports reading inadequate to mean insufficient. Thus, whenever market price damages undercompensate the seller (relative to contract performance), the seller can, under Union Carbide's interpretation, elect lost profits damages. This reading of the statute ignores the question of what measure of damages is appropriate where market price damages greatly over-compensate the seller vis-a-vis what it would receive if the contract had been performed. Presumably, Union Carbide would claim the seller somehow deserved this exorbitant award as the premium for standing ready to perform in the face of the buyer's breach.

This position is contrary to the clear intention of the U.C.C. that remedies should place the parties in the same position as if the contract had been performed. U.C.C. § 1-106, for example, provides that the remedies of the U.C.C. should be ". . .liberally administered to the end that the aggrieved party may be put in as good a position as if the other had performed . . ." and that neither penal, special, nor consequential damages be awarded except where specifically provided by law. This court is reluctant to endorse any position that runs counter to this policy.

Instead, the court believes that inadequate should be interpreted to mean incapable or inadequate to accomplish the stated purpose of the U.C.C. remedies of compensating the aggrieved person but not overcompensating that person or specially punishing the other person. The measure of damages provided in section 1 will be incapable of putting the seller in as good a position as performance whenever it does not fairly measure the damages suffered by the aggrieved party. This interpretation is more flexible in that it provides the damages under section 1 can be too great or too small.

Moreover, the language of 2-708(2) states the seller should be put in "as good as" a position as performance would have done. "As good as" does not include better than. The statute should not authorize awards of damages which put the seller in a better position than performance would have put them. This view is supported by the policy behind U.C.C. § 1-106, discussed above.

Existing case law supports the court's reading of the statute. There is no Michigan case law which addresses this issue. However, since the U.C.C. is intended to be interpreted uniformly across the country, it is appropriate to look to the decisions of other courts in other states for guidance. The Fifth Circuit has examined a factual situation very similar to this one and held that U.C.C. § 2-708(2) applies when the buyer can prove that damages under 2-708(1) would overcompensate the seller. *Nobs Chemical, USA, Inc. v. Koppers Co., Inc.*, 616 F.2d 212 (5th Cir. 1980).

Nobs Chemical involved a suit by the disappointed sellers of 1000 metric tons of cumene (a colorless oily hydrocarbon used as an additive for high-octane gasoline) against the breaching buyer. The sellers had not yet actually purchased, or contracted in a binding fashion to purchase, the cumene. They had contacted their manufacturer in Brazil and arranged to get the cumene with another shipment of 3000 tons that they had ordered for some clients.

In district court, the seller requested market price damages under 2-708(l). The buyer objected that these damages would overcompensate the seller and asked the court to award lost profits. The district court awarded lost profits and the Court of Appeals affirmed.

The Court of Appeals relied on White and Summers treatise on the U.C.C. J. White and R. Summers, Uniform Commercial Code (1st Ed. 1972). The court examined White and Summers' analysis of section 2-708, saying:

> Professors White and Summers, recognizing that § 2-708(b) [§ 2-708(2)] is not the most lucid or best-drafted of the sales article sections, decided that the drafters of the Uniform Commercial Code intended subsection (b) to apply to certain sellers whose losses would rarely be compensated by the subsection (a) [§ 2-708(1)] market price-contract price measure of damages, and for these sellers the lost profit formula was added in subsection (b). One such type of seller is a "jobber," who, according to the treatise writers, must satisfy two conditions: "[f]irst, he is a seller who never acquires the contract goods. Second, his decision not to acquire those goods after learning of the breach was not commercially unreasonable. . . ."
>
> . . . .
>
> The plaintiffs argue, however, that in this case the measure of damages under subsection (a) would adequately compensate them and therefore, according to the terms of subsection (a), subsection (b) does not control. This is an intriguing argument. It appears that the drafters

> of § 2708(a) did not consider the possibility that recovery under that section may be more than adequate. White & Summers, *supra*, § 7-12, at 232-233. It is possible that the code drafters intended subsection (a) as a liquidated damage clause available to a plaintiff-seller regardless of his actual damages. There have been some commentators who agree with this philosophy. . . . But, this construction is inconsistent with the code's basic philosophy, announced in Tex. Bus. & Com. Code Ann. § 1.106(a) (Vernon), which provides "that the aggrieved party may be put in as good a position as if the other party had fully performed" but not in a better posture. White & Summers, *supra*, § 7-12, at 232.
>
> . . . .
>
> Moreover, White and Summers conclude that statutory damage formulas do not significantly affect the practices of businessmen and therefore "breach deterrence," which would be the purpose of the statutory liquidated damages clause, should be rejected in favor of a standard approximating actual economic loss. White & Summers, *supra*, § 7-12, at 232. No one insists, and we do not think they could, that the difference between the fallen market price and contract price is necessary to compensate the plaintiffs for the breach. Had the transaction been completed, their "benefit of the bargain" would not have been affected by the fall in market price, and they would not have experienced the windfall they otherwise would receive if the market price-contract price rule contained in § 2-708(a) is followed. Thus, the premise contained in § 1.106 is a strong factor weighing against application of § 2.708(a).[3]

Id. at 215-216. (citations to the official text of the U.C.C. added). The figures referred to in footnote 3 showed that lost profits damages amounted to $95,000 (U.S.), while market price damages would have come to approximately $300,000 (U.S.).

Union Carbide can be described as a middleman or jobber in this case, at least for the period in which it did not accept the residual fuel oil which it had contracted to sell to Consumers. As the middleman between Petrosar and Consumers, Union Carbide's role was simply to get the oil, transport it to Consumers and receive its guaranteed profit. Once it stopped reselling the oil identified to the Consumers' contract, Union Carbide's decision not to acquire further quantities of oil from Petrosar was a commercial reasonable one. Thus, for the period of time in which Union Carbide claims it should be awarded market price damages, it was a middleman.

This court agrees with the *Nobs Chemical* court that allowing section 1 damages where they overcompensate the plaintiff is equivalent to awarding liquidated damages to Union Carbide. This would be inconsistent with the code's basic philosophy as expressed in U.C.C. § 1-106(1). Neither does this court believe that breach deterrence justifies granting such a disproportionate award.

Most importantly, this court finds that here, as in *Nobs Chemical*, had the transaction between Union Carbide and Consumers been completed, Union Carbide's "benefit of the bargain" would not have been affected by changes in the market price of oil. The price formula which set the contract price paid by Consumers tracked the price that Union Carbide paid to Petrosar. No matter what happened to Petrosar's prices, Union Carbide could pass through the change in prices to Consumers. It was guaranteed its fixed profit on the contract and no more. Any windfall gains

---

[3] White and Summers condition forcing the damage formula of subsection (b) on the plaintiff-seller. They would require the defendant to prove that the measure of damages in subsection (a) would overcompensate the plaintiff. We do not find this to be a problem here, as the figures themselves refute any contention that the market price-contract rule is anything but over-adequate compensation for the plaintiffs. White & Summers, *supra*, § 7-12, at 232-233.

that might arise from rapid price changes would be realized by Petrosar, not Union Carbide. For this court to fundamentally alter this allocation of contractual benefits between the parties by giving Union Carbide vastly greater returns than were provided for by its contract with Consumers would fly in the face of the U.C.C.'s basic premises and be manifestly unjust. In short, Union Carbide was guaranteed a riskless, fixed profit under the terms of the contract and they should not receive the benefit of price fluctuations whose risk they did not assume.

Finally, the court finds that market price damages will overcompensate Union Carbide. By overcompensation, the court means that Union Carbide would receive greatly more than the riskless benefit of the bargain they would have received if the contract had been performed.[4] At oral argument, the court heard uncontested evidence that Union Carbide would have earned approximately $30 million (U.S.) if the contract had been performed. These were its lost profits. Its damages under the market price measure of damages would be four times as great, or roughly $120 million (U.S.).[5] This is sufficient to establish overcompensation.

Union Carbide relies on the Second Circuit's decision in *Trans World Metals, Inc. v. Southwire Company*, 769 F.2d 902 (2d Cir.1985), to support its argument that it should be able to elect market price damages if it prefers them. This court finds that *Trans World* is distinguishable.

In that case, Southwire, the buyer, repudiated a short-term supply contract for the provision of aluminum that it had entered into with Trans World, the seller. The contract ran from January to December, 1982. It was negotiated in April of 1981. Between that time and March 1982, the price of aluminum dropped dramatically. Southwire repudiated the entire contract in March 1982, alleging that the supplies for February had been delivered late in violation of a "time-is-of-the-essence" clause. The jury held for Trans World in special interrogatories finding that the "time-is-of-the-essence" clause was not part of the contract and therefore the repudiation was a total breach. The court of appeals held that the jury's findings were supported by the evidence. They then reviewed the alleged errors of the district court.

The court considered the defendant's argument that the award of contract price damages overcompensated the plaintiff-seller. It held that market price damages should be awarded. *Id.* at 907.

The court was unconvinced that Trans World would be overcompensated by the award of damages under 2-708(1). They believed that the parties had consciously assumed different risks of price variations: Southwire assumed the risk that prices would fall and Trans World assumed the risk that the price would rise. It would deny Trans World the benefit of its bargain if they were not allowed to gain from the drop in prices.

The *Trans World* court distinguished the *Nobs Chemical* decision. They said the seller in *Nobs Chemical* was a middleman who had fixed its supply price prior to entering into the contract with the buyer Koppers Company. The seller had therefore protected itself against the risk of market price fluctuations and it would have been unfair to allow them to reap a riskless benefit. This was not the case in *Trans World* because the parties had expressly bargained for the allocation of the risk of price changes.

Similarly in this case, the focus of the decision must center on the fundamental allocation of risk between the parties. The price mechanism in the contract insured that Union Carbide

---

[4] The court does not imply that this same standard of overcompensation would apply if Union Carbide bore the risks of price fluctuations.

[5] In *Nobs Chemical*, the Fifth Circuit found that market price damages three times greater than lost profits were overcompensation: 616 F.2d at 216, n. 3.

could pass through all of its costs to Consumers. This means Union Carbide, the middleman, assumed no risk of price changes. *Trans World* is therefore inapplicable; *Nobs Chemical* should be applied instead.

One other matter should be resolved. Under U.C.C. § 2-708(2), Union Carbide is entitled to incidental damages. Counsel for Consumers represented at oral argument that the RORP payments which Union Carbide made to Petrosar would fall within the rubric of incidental damages. Consumers' counsel further stated that Union Carbide's payments to Petrosar in settlement of its contractual obligations with them would be incidental damages at least to the extent they can be apportioned to the loss of the Consumers contract. The court finds that U.C.C. § 2-710 defining a seller's incidental damages can be reasonably interpreted to cover these costs. They are commercially reasonable expenses incurred by the seller as a result of the buyer's breach.

In summary, the limited applicability of this decision should be reemphasized. The seller in this case was a middleman who assumed none of the risks of price variations. The contract provided that the seller would be guaranteed a profit on all goods accepted by the buyer. Moreover, the buyer proved that market price damages would overcompensate the seller. Given these limiting facts, the court holds that the seller's damages should be calculated under § 2-708(2).

So Ordered.

NOTES AND QUESTIONS

(1) Proposed U.C.C. § 2-703 states that it is subject to § 2-701. Section 2-701(c) states that Article 2 remedies must be liberally administered to put the aggrieved party in as good a position as if the other party had fully performed. If those remedies fail to place the aggrieved party in that position, damages may be awarded measured by the loss resulting in the ordinary course of events from the breach as determined in any manner which is reasonable. Thus, courts may protect not only the expectation interest but reliance and restitution interests where appropriate.

Proposed § 2-701(e) reinforces the idea that the rights and remedies provided by Article 2 are cumulative. But the subsection goes on to say that a court may deny or limit a remedy if it would put an aggrieved party in a substantially better position than if the other party had fully performed.

Proposed § 2-708(a) measures damages based on market price in two ways: (1) for breach other than repudiation, damages are the "contract price less the market price of comparable goods at the time and place for tender;" (2) for breach by repudiation, damages are "the contract price less the market price of comparable goods prevailing at the place for tender and at the time when a commercially reasonable period after the seller learned of the repudiation has expired."

Proposed § 2-708(b) measures damages based on other than market price, including (1) lost profits (including reasonable overhead) resulting from the breach determined in any reasonable manner (plus incidental and consequential damages, less expenses avoided) and (2) reasonable unreimbursed expenditures made in preparing for or performing the contract. A seller may choose this remedy rather than market price damages unless the choice puts it in a substantially better position than full performance under § 2-701(e).

(2) How would Proposed §§ 2-701, 2-703 and 2-708 affect the analysis and result of *Union Carbide*?

R. E. DAVIS CHEMICAL CORP. v. DIASONICS, INC.

United States Court of Appeals
826 F.2d 678 (7th Cir. 1987)

[Davis contracted to purchase a piece of medical diagnostic equipment from Diasonics. Subsequently, Davis wrongly refused to take delivery of the equipment. Diasonics later resold the equipment to a third party for the same price at which it was to be sold to Davis. Davis sued Diasonics asking for restitution of its $300,000 downpayment under U.C.C. § 2-718(2); Diasonics claimed that it was entitled to an offset under § 2-718(3). Diasonics' position was that it was entitled to lost profits as a "lost volume seller" under U.C.C. § 2-708(2). The district court held that Diasonics was limited to recovering damages under §2-706. Diasonics appealed.]

We consider . . .Diasonics' claims that the district court erred in holding that Diasonics was limited to the measure of damages provided in 2-706 and could not recover lost profits as a lost volume seller under 2-708(2). Surprisingly, given its importance, this issue has never been addressed by an Illinois court, nor, apparently, by any other court construing Illinois law. Thus, we must attempt to predict how the Illinois Supreme Court would resolve this issue if it were presented to it. Courts applying the laws of other states have unanimously adopted the position that a lost volume seller can recover its lost profits under 2-708(2). Contrary to the result reached by the district court, we conclude that the Illinois Supreme Court would follow these other cases and would allow a lost volume seller to recover its lost profit under 2-708(2).

. . .

Article 2 contains four provisions that concern the recovery of a seller's general damages (as opposed to its incidental or consequential damages): 2-706 (contract price less resale price); 2-708(1) (contract price less market price); 2-708(2) (profit); and 2-709 (price). The problem we face here is determining whether Diasonics' damages should be measured under 2-706 or 2-708(2). To answer this question, we need to engage in a detailed look at the language and structure of these various damage provisions.

The Code does not provide a great deal of guidance as to when a particular damage remedy is appropriate. The damage remedies provided under the Code are catalogued in section 2-703, but this section does not indicate that there is any hierarchy among the remedies. One method of approaching the damage sections is to conclude that 2-708 is relegated to a role inferior to that of 2-706 and 2-709 and that one can turn to 2-708 only after one has concluded that neither

2-706 nor 2-709 is applicable.[6] Under this interpretation of the relationship between 2-706 and 2-708, if the goods have been resold, the seller can sue to recover damages measured by the difference between the contract price and the resale price under 2-706. The seller can turn to 2-708 only if it resells in a commercially unreasonable manner or if it cannot resell but an action for the price is inappropriate under 2-709. The district court adopted this reading of the Code's damage remedies and, accordingly, limited Diasonics to the measure provided in 2-706 because it resold the equipment in a commercially reasonable manner.

The district court's interpretation of 2-706 and 2-708, however, creates its own problems of statutory construction. There is some suggestion in the Code that the "fact that plaintiff resold the goods [in a commercially reasonable manner] does *not* compel him to use the resale remedy of § 2-706 rather than the damage remedy of § 2-708." Harris, *A Radical Restatement of the Law of Seller's Damages: Sales Act and Commercial Code Results Compared*, 18 Stan.L.Rev. 66, 101 n. 174 (1965) (emphasis in original). Official comment 1 to 2-703, which catalogues the remedies available to a seller, states that these "remedies are essentially cumulative in nature" and that "[w]hether the pursuit of one remedy bars another depends entirely on the facts of the individual case." *See also State of New York, Report of the Law Revision Comm'n for 1956*, 396-97 (1956).[7]

Those courts that found that a lost volume seller can recover its lost profits under 2-708(2) implicitly rejected the position adopted by the district court; those courts started with the

[6] Evidence to support this approach can be found in the language of the various damage sections and of the official comments to the U.C.C. *See* § 2-709(3) ("a seller who is held not entitled to the price under this Section shall nevertheless be awarded damages for non-acceptance under the preceding section [§ 2-708]"); U.C.C. comment 7 to § 2-709 ("[i]f the action for the price fails, the seller may nonetheless have proved a case entitling him to damages for non-acceptance [under § 2-708]"); U.C.C. comment 2 to § 2-706 ("[f]ailure to act properly under this section deprives the seller of the measure of damages here provided and relegates him to that provided in Section 2-708"); U.C.C. comment 1 to § 2-704 (describes § 2-706 as the "primary remedy" available to a seller upon breach by the buyer); *see also Commonwealth Edison Co. v. Decker Coal Co.*, 653 F.Supp. 841, 844 (N.D. Ill.1987) (statutory language and case law suggest that "§ 2-708 remedies are available only to a seller who is not entitled to the contract price" under § 2-709); Childres & Burgess, *Seller's Remedies: The Primacy of U.C.C. 2-708(2)*, 48 N.Y.U.L.Rev. 833, 863-64 (1973). As one commentator has noted, 2-706

> is the Code section drafted specifically to define the damage rights of aggrieved reselling sellers, and there is no suggestion within it that the profit formula of section 2-708(2) is in any way intended to qualify or be superior to it.

Shanker, *The Case for a Literal Reading of U.C.C. Section 2-708(2) (One Profit for the Reseller)*, 24 Case W.Res. 697, 699 (1973).

[7] U.C.C. comment 2 to 2-708(2) also suggests that 2-708 has broader applicability than suggested by the district court. U.C.C. comment 2 provides:

> This section permits the recovery of lost profits in all appropriate cases, which would include all standard priced goods. The normal measure there would be list price less cost to the dealer or list price less manufacturing cost to the manufacturer.

The district court's restrictive interpretation of 2-708(2) was based in part on U.C.C. comment 1 to 2-704 which describes 2-706 as the aggrieved seller's primary remedy. The district court concluded that, if a lost volume seller could recover its lost profit under 2-708(2), every seller would attempt to recover damages under 2-708(2) and 2-706 would become the aggrieved seller's residuary remedy. This argument ignores the fact that to recover under 2-708(2), a seller must first establish its status as a lost volume seller.

The district court also concluded that a lost volume seller cannot recover its lost profit under 2-708(2) because such a result would negate a seller's duty to mitigate damages. This position fails to recognize the fact that, by definition, a lost volume seller cannot mitigate damages through resale. Resale does not reduce a lost volume seller's damages because the breach has still resulted in its losing one sale and a corresponding profit.

assumption that 2-708 applied to a lost volume seller without considering whether the seller was limited to the remedy provided under 2-706. None of those courts even suggested that a seller who resold goods in a commercially reasonable manner was limited to the damage formula provided under 2-706. We conclude that the Illinois Supreme Court, if presented with this question, would adopt the position of these other jurisdictions and would conclude that a reselling seller, such as Diasonics, is free to reject the damage formula prescribed in 2-706 and choose to proceed under 2-708.

Concluding that Diasonics is entitled to seek damages under 2-708, however, does not automatically result in Diasonics being awarded its lost profit. Two different measures of damages are provided in 2-708. Subsection 2-708(1) provides for a measure of damages calculated by subtracting the market price at the time and place for tender from the contract price.[8] The profit measure of damages, for which Diasonics is asking, is contained in 2-708(2). However, one applies 2-708(2) only if "the measure of damages provided in subsection (1) is inadequate to put the seller in as good a position as performance would have done. . . ." Ill.Rev.Stat. ch. 26, para. 2-708(2) (1985). Diasonics claims that 2-708(1) does not provide an adequate measure of damages when the seller is a lost volume seller. To understand Diasonics' argument, we need to define the concept of the lost volume seller. Those cases that have addressed this issue as one that has a predictable and finite number of customers and that has the capacity either to sell to all new buyers or to make the one additional sale represented by the resale after the breach. According to a number of courts and commentators, if the seller would have made the sale represented by the resale whether or not the breach occurred, damages measured by the difference between the contract price and market price cannot put the lost volume seller in as good a position as it would have been in had the buyer performed.[9] The breach effectively cost the seller a "profit," and the seller can only be made whole by awarding it damages in the amount of its "lost profit" under 2-708(2).

We agree with Diasonics' position that, under some circumstances, the measure of damages provided under 2-708(1) will not put a reselling seller in as good a position as it would have been in had the buyer performed because the breach resulted in the seller losing sales volume. However, we disagree with the definition of "lost volume seller" adopted by other courts. Courts awarding lost profits to a lost volume seller have focused on whether the seller had the capacity to supply the breached units in addition to what it actually sold. In reality, however, the relevant questions include, not only whether the seller could have produced the breached units in addition to its actual volume, but also whether it would have been profitable for the seller to produce both units. Goetz & Scott, *Measuring Sellers' Damages: The Lost-Profits Puzzle,* 31 Stan.L.Rev. 323, 332-33, 346-47 (1979). As one commentator has noted, under

[8] There is some debate in the commentaries about whether a seller who has resold the goods may ignore the measure of damages provided in 2-706 and elect to proceed under 2-708(1). Under some circumstances in the contract-market price differential will result in overcompensating such a seller. *See* J. White & R. Summers, Handbook of the Law under the Uniform Commercial Code § 7-7, at 271-73 (2d ed. 1980); Sebert, *Remedies Under Article Two of the Uniform Commercial Code: An Agenda for Review*, 130 U.Pa.L.Rev. 360, 380-83 (1981). We need not struggle with this question here because Diasonics has not sought to recover damages under 2-708(1).

[9] According to one commentator,

> Resale results in loss of volume only if three conditions are met: (1) the person who bought the resold entity would have been solicited by plaintiff had there been no breach and resale; (2) the solicitation would have been successful; and (3) the plaintiff could have performed that additional contact.

Harris, *supra*, text accompanying n.7, at 82 (footnotes omitted).

> the economic law of diminishing returns or increasing marginal costs[,] . . .as a seller's volume increases, then a point will inevitably be reached where the cost of selling each additional item diminishes the incremental return to the seller and eventually makes it entirely unprofitable to conclude the next sale.

Shanker, *supra* at 705. Thus, under some conditions, awarding a lost volume seller its presumed lost profit will result in overcompensating the seller, and 2-708(2) would not take effect because the damage formula provided in 2-708(1) does place the seller in as good a position as if the buyer had performed. Therefore, on remand, Diasonics must establish, not only that it had the capacity to produce the breached unit in addition to the unit resold, but also that it would have been profitable for it to have produced and sold both. . . .

One final problem with awarding a lost volume seller its lost profits was raised by the district court. This problem stems from the formulation of the measure of damages provided under 2-708(2) which is "the profit (including reasonable overhead) which the seller would have made from full performance by the buyer, together with any incidental damages provided in this Article (Section 2-710), due allowance for costs reasonably incurred and due credit for payments or *proceeds of resale.*" (emphasis added). The literal language of 2-708(2) requires that the proceeds from resale be credited against the amount of damages awarded which, in most cases, would result in the seller recovering nominal damages. In those cases in which the lost volume seller was awarded its lost profit as damages, the courts have circumvented this problem by concluding that this language only applies to proceeds realized from the resale of uncompleted goods for scrap. *See, e.g., Neri*, 30 N.Y.2d at 399 & n. 2, 334 N.Y.S.2d at 169 & n.2, 286 N.E.2d at 314 & n. 2; *see also* J. White & R. Summers, Handbook of the Law under the Uniform Commercial Code § 7-13, at 285 ("courts should simply ignore the 'due credit' language in lost volume cases") (footnote omitted). Although neither the text of 2-708(2) nor the official comments limit its application to resale of goods for scrap, there is evidence that the drafters of 2-708 seemed to have had this more limited application in mind when they proposed amending 2-708 to include the phrase "due credit for payments or proceeds of resale." We conclude that the Illinois Supreme Court would adopt this more restrictive interpretation of this phrase rendering it inapplicable to this case.

We therefore reverse the grant of summary judgment in favor of Davis and remand with instructions that the district court calculate Diasonics' damages under 2-708(2) if Diasonics can establish, not only that it had the capacity to make the sale to Davis as well as the sale to the resale buyer, but also that it would have been profitable for it to make both sales. Of course, Diasonics, in addition, must show that it probably would have made the second sale absent the breach.

. . .

NOTES

(1) On remand, the district court found that Diasonics' profit would have been $453,050. (The contract price was $1,500,000.) The 7th Circuit held that the method of calculating damages was not unreasonable. 924 F.2d 709 (1991).

(2) The Reporter's Notes to proposed § 2-708 states that no attempt was made to provide a detailed solution to the lost volume problem. Whether a seller is a lost volume seller and the measure of lost profits if it is, are left to the courts.

[3] Recover the Price

Read: U.C.C. §§ 2-703(e), 2-709; cf. § 2-716(3).

Read also: U.C.C. §§ 2A-523(1)(e), 2A-529, cf. § 2A-521(3); CISG Arts. 61(1)(a), 62; see Arts. 28, 78, cf. Art. 45(1).

SCHUMANN v. LEVI

United States Court of Appeals
728 F.2d 1141, 38 U.C.C. Rep. 131 (8th Cir. 1984)

Before LAY, CHIEF JUDGE, AND ROSS AND MCMILLIAN, CIRCUIT JUDGES.

PER CURIAM.

[Pursuant to an auction sale, Schumann (plaintiff-appellee) sold some items of personal property, including a Bobcat loader, to Levi (defendant-appellant). Levi breached the contract to buy and Schumann rejected Levi's offer of settlement. United States Magistrate Boline entered a judgment for Schumann, awarding him the price of the Bobcat plus interest. Levi appeals, arguing that the magistrate erred in ordering specific performance of the contract and in his calculation of pre-judgment interest.]

Specific Performance/Action for the Price

The pertinent part of the magistrate's order states:

CONCLUSIONS OF LAW

1. That defendant entered into a valid contract with plaintiff on March 14, 1981 to purchase a Bobcat loader, backhoe attachment and trailer for the sum of $11,600.00, and that defendant has breached the contract.

2. That plaintiff is entitled to specific performance to obtain the benefit of his bargain.

3. That plaintiff is entitled to the sum of $11,600.00 because of the breach of contract.

4. That plaintiff suffered additional damages consisting of interest costs from March 15, 1981 through October 7, 1981 in the amount of $851.09 less the reasonable rental for machinery in the amount of 300.00.

5. That plaintiff is not entitled to an award of punitive and exemplary damages.

ORDER FOR JUDGMENT

1. That plaintiff is awarded $11,600.00 plus interest in the amount of $551.09.

2. That plaintiff shall tender possession and title of the Bobcat loader, backhoe attachment and trailer to defendant at the time defendant satisfies this judgment.

Appellant contends that the magistrate ordered specific performance of the contract, and that this was in error. Citing cases that speak specifically to the traditional division of law and equity, appellant argues that under the doctrine of election of remedies, specific performance was unavailable to plaintiff because he only brought a legal claim for damages. In response, appellee argues that specific performance is not the issue here; he claims that the court awarded him his legal remedy of the price pursuant to Minn Stat § 336.2-709 (1966). That section reads in pertinent part: [the court quotes U.C.C. § 2-709(1)(b), (2)].

The facts as found by the magistrate meet the requirements for recovery of the price. Appellant failed to pay the price when it was due. The goods were identified to the contract, and appellee presented evidence of his unsuccessful attempts to resell. Appellee's contention that he was awarded his legal remedy is persuasive. The equitable remedy of specific performance and the Uniform Commercial Code's action for the price are virtually identical, and the court's order appears to be a judgment for the price.

Appellant also argues that the magistrate abused his discretion in awarding Schumann the price because his complaint did not allege an action for the price or cite the Minnesota statute. Schumann's complaint alleged a breach of contract, and in his prayer for damages, he asked for "an amount necessary to compensate for his loss of bargain." Because a trial court must grant the relief to which a prevailing party is entitled, the court can award such relief, even though the party has not demanded it: Fed. R. Civ. P. 54(c). . . . Here, the parties stipulated to the breach of contract prior to trial and proceeded to litigate the damages issues. As stated above, the evidence adduced at trial provided the support for an award of the price.

. . . .

For the foregoing reasons, the magistrate's judgment is affirmed in part and reversed and remanded in part.

NOTES

In *Rowland Meledandi, Inc. v. Kohn*, 7 U.C.C. Rep. 34 (N.Y. Civ. Ct. 1969), buyer ordered a custom-made suit from seller. Seller cut the pattern in accordance with the buyer's particular measurements and specifications, ordered the cloth, and on receipt of the latter, cut it, along with the lining. Buyer then stopped payment on his $100 check. The court said:

> When [seller] learned that payment had been stopped on [buyer's] check, it treated this as a repudiation and ceased further work on the suit (on which it had spent no more than six hours, including several hours selling time). Nonetheless, [seller] seeks to recover the full contract price, relying, inter alia, on § 2-704 of the U.C.C. That section must be read in conjunction with §§ 2-709 and 2-708. When a seller, in the process of manufacturing goods which are not resalable when finished, elects to cease manufacture on the buyer's repudiation, the seller does not have an action for the full purchase price (see Bender U.C.C. Service, Vol. 3, Sales & Bulk Transfer sec. 13.07(4) p. 13-85. . . . He does retain his action for damages (U.C.C. § 2-709(3)).

U.C.C. § 2-704 is discussed at § 7.02[B][2], *supra*.

SWIFT & CO. v. REXTON, INC.

Connecticut Supreme Court
187 Conn. 540, 447 A.2d 9, 34 U.C.C. Rep. 558 (1982)

PER CURIAM.

The single issue presented by this appeal is the sufficiency of the evidence relied upon by the trial court in ruling for the plaintiff in an action to recover the purchase price of goods allegedly sold to the defendants.

From the evidence presented at trial, the trial court could reasonably have found the following facts. From November, 1977, through September, 1978, the plaintiff, Swift and Company (hereinafter Swift), sold goods in the form of meat products to the defendant, Rexton, Inc. d/b/a Chicago Beef and Provision Company (hereinafter Rexton), on an open account basis. The plaintiff's witness, a salesman with Swift for 27 years, testified that because Rexton was his account, he visited and sold it products on a regular basis. In his capacity as a salesman, he prepared invoices at the time orders were taken from which a ledger card was prepared for each account, including Rexton. These ledger cards were periodically updated by Swift, indicating dates, charges, credits and balances due. All charges by the plaintiff and payments by the defendant were included on the ledger cards.

The ledger cards for the Rexton account from November 4, 1977, to September 21, 1978, were introduced as evidence by the plaintiff. The second to last entry, showing a payment of $300, left a balance due Swift of $8728.04. The last entry, however, marked "J/E" for journal entry, indicated a credit of $8728.04 and left the balance column blank. The plaintiff's witness testified that this last entry was an accounting procedure utilized to clear the ledger and suspend the account as a prerequisite to collection proceedings by Swift's legal department.

In this appeal from the judgment of the trial court rendered against it in the amount of $8728.04, the defendant asserts that the findings of fact were unsupported by sufficient competent evidence. We disagree.

When a buyer accepts goods and fails to tender payment when due, the seller may recover the purchase price. General Statutes § 42a-2-709(1)(a). As prerequisites to recovery, therefore, a seller must establish acceptance by the buyer of goods sold and delivered, as well as the failure of the buyer to fulfill his payment obligation.

In the ordinary civil action, while the plaintiff must establish every element of a claim by a fair preponderance of the evidence, there need not be direct evidence of each material fact. It is sufficient if the evidence presented establishes circumstances "from which logical and reasonable inferences of other material facts can be fairly drawn." Moreover, the plaintiff's evidence need not be so overwhelming that every other possible result is excluded; it is sufficient if the evidence "induces in the mind of the trier a reasonable belief that it is more probable than otherwise that the fact in issue is true."

It is the province of the trier of fact to weigh the evidence presented and determine the credibility and effect to be given the evidence. On appellate review, therefore, we will give the evidence the most favorable reasonable construction in support of the verdict to which it is entitled.

Viewed within these principles, the evidence, although scant, supports the judgment rendered by the trial court. The plaintiff's witness testified that as a salesman for Swift he sold the defendant products on a regular basis, from which invoices and subsequently ledger cards were prepared. The ledger cards show charges and payments made against and by the defendant. From this uncontroverted evidence it is reasonable and logical to infer the sale, delivery and acceptance of the plaintiff's goods by the defendant. Moreover, the final balance due of $8728.04 as shown on the ledger cards, although disputed, reasonably establishes the failure by the defendant to tender payment to the plaintiff. Thus, on the foregoing facts and reasonable inferences therefrom, we conclude that the judgment of the trial court was adequately supported by the evidence presented.

There is no error.

NOTES

(1) Would U.C.C. § 2-606(1)(b) be of relevance in this case?

(2) U.C.C. § 2-709(1)(a) states that seller may recover the price of conforming goods lost or damaged within a commercially reasonable time after risk of their loss has passed to the buyer. Risk of loss is discussed at § 4.06, *supra*. See U.C.C. § 2-509.

[4] Incidental Damages

Read: U.C.C. § 2-710.

Read also: U.C.C. § 2A-530; CISG Art. 74.

At § 7.02, we have been evaluating seller's remedies for breach by buyer. In particular, § 7.02[C][1] discussed that the seller may recover the difference between the resale price and the contract price "together with any incidental damages allowed . . ." U.C.C. § 2-706, cf. § 2A-527(2).

Section § 7.02[C][2] recited that the measure of damages for non-acceptance or repudiation by the buyer is the difference between the market price and the unpaid contract price "together with any incidental damages. . . ." U.C.C. § 2-708(1). Further, U.C.C. § 2-708(2) states the measure of damages as the profit which the seller would have made "together with any incidental damages. . . ." *Cf.* U.C.C. § 2A-528(1) and (2).

Section § 7.02[C][3] explained that when the buyer fails to pay the price as it becomes due, the seller may recover the price in enumerated circumstances, "together with any incidental damages . . ." U.C.C. § 2-709(1), *cf.* U.C.C. § 2A-529(1).

Because Section 2-710 [Seller's Incidental Damages] does not include recovery for consequential damages, it is not surprising that some courts may be willing to include that which might be considered consequential damages within the "or otherwise resulting from the breach" language of § 2-710. Representative cases are surveyed below.

In *Bulk Oil (U.S.A.), Inc. v. Sun Oil Trading Co.*, 697 F.2d 481, 35 U.C.C. Rep. 23 (2d Cir. 1983), seller contracted to sell $4,000,000 worth of fuel oil to buyer. Seller bought the oil from a third party supplier and financed the transaction by borrowing almost all the cost from Chase Manhattan Bank. Buyer accepted delivery of the oil from seller but refused to pay. After the breach, seller incurred further interest charges on the Chase loan which it paid on a monthly basis. The court held that seller's post breach interest payments to Chase were incidental damages.

In *Ernst Steel Corp. v. Horn Construction Division, Haliburton Co.,104 A.D.2d 55, 481 N.Y.S.2d 833, 40 U.C.C. Rep. 145 at 152-3 (1984)* the court commented:

> In an appropriate case a seller is entitled to recover commercially reasonable finance and interest charges incurred as a result of a buyer's breach as a proper item of incidental damages (see Uniform Commercial Code, § 2-710; *Neri v. Retail Mar. Corp.*, 30 NY2d 393 [10 U.C.C. Rep 950]). For the most part, however, interest expenses have only been awarded to sellers for indebtedness specifically identified to goods intended for resale to the breaching party and who, as a result of the breach, cannot repay the loans (*see, e.g., Bulk Oil [USA], Inc. v. Sun Oil Trading Co.*, 697 F2d 481; *Intermeat, Inc. v. American Poultry, Inc.*, 575 F2d 1017; *Neri v. Retail Mar. Corp., supra; Hoffman v. Stoller*, 320 NW2d 786, 792; *Gray v. West*, 608 SW2d 771, 781). In the case of *Atlas Concrete Pipe, Inc. v. Roger J. Au & Son, Inc.* (467 F Supp 830, rev'd 668 F2d 905) relied upon by the trial court, interest expenses were awarded. Although in that case there was no proof of a loan specifically covering the contract goods, the seller proved instead that it was virtually insolvent and had financed fully 100% of its operations. While there is no requirement in the code that interest expenses must be identified to indebtedness specifically covering the contract goods, where a seller cannot link the claimed damages to the contract it clearly has a more difficult burden of proof.

In *S.C. Gray Incorporated v. Ford Motor Company*, 92 Mich. App. 789, 286 N.W.2d 34 (1979), Gray sought to recover for interest it paid on loans taken out to maintain the business when Ford failed to pay the money Gray claimed was due. The court concluded (1) that the interest paid fell within the category of consequential damages, not incidental damages, and (2) that the U.C.C. does not allow a seller to recover consequential damages, U.C.C. §§ 1-106(1), 2-710. The court quoted the *Petroleo Brasileiro* case, which was cited in court's footnote 6 to *Bulk Oil (U.S.A.) v. Sun Oil Trading Co., supra*.

The difference between incidental and consequential damages was highlighted in *Petroleo Brasileiro, SA v. Ameropan Oil Corp*, 14 U.C.C. Rep. 661, 667 (E.D.N.Y., 1974), wherein the court stated:

> While the distinction between the two is not an obvious one, the Code makes plain that incidental damages are normally incurred when a buyer (or seller) repudiates the contract or wrongfully rejects the goods, causing the other to incur such expenses as transporting, storing, or reselling the goods. On the other hand, consequential damages do not arise within the scope of the immediate buyer-seller transaction, but rather stem from losses incurred by the nonbreaching party in its dealings, often with third parties, which were a proximate result of the breach, and which were reasonably foreseeable by the breaching party at the time of contracting.

In *Afram Export Corp. v. Metallurgiki Halyps, S.A.*, 772 F.2d 1358, 41 U.C.C. Rep. 1709 (1985), seller was allowed prejudgment interest. The court observed at 41 U.C.C. Rep. 1716-18:

> Looking first to general principles, we point out that while at one time a plaintiff in a contract suit could obtain an award of prejudgment interest only if the suit was for a fixed amount, as in a suit to collect a promissory note, this is no longer required; it is nowadays quite enough that the amount of damages be ascertainable by reference to an objective standard of value, such as market value where "readily ascertainable." . . . In other fields of law, too, courts increasingly award prejudgment interest, noting for example that a failure to award such interest gives defendants an incentive to prolong litigation. . . .

The Wisconsin cases seem generally in accord with the position outlined above, though we can find no case on point. Provided that there is "a reasonably certain standard of measurement by the correct application of which [the party who breaks the contract] can ascertain the amount he owes," prejudgment interest will be awarded, *Dahl v. Housing Authority*, 54 Wis. 2d 22, 31, 194 N.W.2d 618, 623 (1972), unless the damage claim is "substantially inflated," *Wyandotte Chemicals Corp. v. Royal Electric Mfg. Co*, 66 Wis. 2d 577, 586, 225 N.W.2d 648, 653 (1975). Afram [seller] passes this two-part test (the second part of which may be special to Wisconsin). The test of ready ascertainability is satisfied by so much of Afram's claim as seeks simply the difference between the contract price, a fixed amount, and the market value at the date of breach. [See U.C.C. § 2-708(1).]

. . . .

What must give us pause through is the statement in *Congress Bar & Restaurant* that, "As long as there is a genuine dispute about the amount that is due, the insurer should not have to pay interest until the amount has been determined and judgment entered thereon." 42 Wis. 2d at 71, 165 N.W.2d at 417. Like all judicial language, however, this must be read in context. The case involved fire damage which proved difficult to estimate, and as mentioned the plaintiff's estimate was way too high. There was no contract price to provide a lodestar. The court in *Congress Bar & Restaurant* quoted approvingly the statement made in many Wisconsin opinions that "before interest can be recovered the amount claimed must be fixed or determined *or readily determinable*," . . .and the words we have italicized described this case.

See also North American Foreign Trading Corp. v. Direct Mail Specialist, 697 F.2d 163 (S.D.N.Y. 1988).

In *Nobs Chemical, U.S.A., Inc. v. Koppers Co.*, 616 F.2d 212 (5th Cir. 1980), seller contracted to sell cumene (an additive for high-octane motor fuel) to buyer. Buyer breached the contract. Seller was forced to pay its Brazilian supplier an extra $25 per ton when the price per ton increased because its total order with the supplier was reduced from 4,000 metric tons to 3,000 because of buyer's breach. The court affirmed the district court and decided this lost quantity discount amounted to consequential damages and therefore not recoverable.

See also Atlanta Paper Box Co. v. Whitman's Chocolates, 23 U.C.C. Rep. 2d 361, 844 F. Supp. 1038 (E.D. Pa. 1994). (When buyer cancelled a million dollar order for candy boxes and seller brought suit alleging that this decreased the value of seller's business, and thereby caused a potential purchaser of seller's business to withdraw its offer, this was clearly an impermissible attempt to obtain consequential damages); *Jelen & Son, Inc. v. Brandimere*, 801 P.2d 1182, 13 U.C.C. Rep. 2d 344 (Colo. 1990). (Absent other statutory or contractual provisions to the contrary, attorney's fees are not incidental damages under U.C.C. § 2-710).

Of particular interest is *Associated Metals & Minerals Corp. v. Sharon Steel Corp.*, 590 F. Supp. 18, 39 U.C.C. Rep. 892 (S.D.N.Y. 1983), where the seller sought to recover interest for delayed payment of the purchase price by the buyer. The court allowed recovery of the interest as consequential damages. It recognized that consequential damages are not awarded to seller under § 2-710, but it applied the common law of Pennsylvania to award consequential damages under § 1-103 and Restatement, Second, Contracts § 347, which gives "the injured party" incidental or consequential loss caused by the breach. See U.C.C. §1-106(1): "Consequential damages . . .may not be had except as specifically provided in this Act *or by other rule of law*." [Emphasis added.]

NOTE

Proposed § 2-710 is captioned, "Seller's Incidental and Consequential Damages." The consequential damages provision is drafted to parallel § 2-715(2)(a) (Proposed § 2-715(b)(1)).

—

§ 7.03 Seller's Remedies (1) on Discovery of Buyer's Insolvency, (2) in a "Cash Sale" Transaction

Read: U.C.C. § 2-702, cf. § 2-502; §§ 2-507(2), 2-511(3).

Read also: U.C.C. §§ 2A-523(1)(c), 2A-525, cf. 2A-522; CISG Arts. 81(2), 84(2).

Discovery of Buyer's Insolvency. Section 2-702(2) provides in part: "Where the seller discovers that the buyer has received goods on credit while insolvent he may reclaim the goods upon demand made within ten days after the receipt . . ." This right to reclaim is subject to the rights of certain good faith purchases under U.C.C. § 2-403. See U.C.C. § 2-702(3). See discussion at Chapter 8, Rights of Third Parties: Good Faith Purchase of Goods.

Cash Sale Transaction. L. Vold, The Law of Sales § 29 (2d ed. 1959) summarizes the common law:[10]

> Technical cash sales at common law differ from ordinary sales. In technical cash sales the property interest does not pass until the price is paid. Example: over-the-counter cash deal in the old-fashioned retail store. Such a deal involves no credit. The goods are handed over in exchange for the price then paid at about the same time.
>
> . . . .
>
> Cumbersome details often make exactly simultaneous exchange of goods for price impossible. . . . The delay that is involved may not exceed what the practical circumstances require for exchanging goods for price paid. If so, the parties often treat this exchange as if it were "substantially simultaneous." Where the parties have done so, the courts, seeking justice between the parties, often treat the deal the same way. . . .
>
> Waiver of expected cash payment may be shown in various ways: agreement or usage showing giving of credit; permitting the buyer without objection after delivery to retain the goods for a considerable time; failure promptly to reclaim possession.
>
> Where payment is made by check, Vold at § 30 observes:
>
> Our American authorities commonly treat payment by check as only conditional payment until cashed. Receiving the buyer's check for the price therefore does not waive cash payment. Making and receiving payment here includes not only the issue of the check but its cashing at the drawee bank. The routine time involved in check collection is thus included in the time that is treated as "substantially simultaneous." Payment by check thus usually is not regarded as an extension of credit for the time needed to cash the check.
>
> Suppose on the other hand, the seller takes a promissory note for the price, or a postdated check. What then? This clearly amounts to an extension of credit. It thereby waives immediate cash payment.

A no-fund check will "bounce." It will not be paid on presentation at the drawee bank. If paid by mistake in the first instance, it will promptly be charged back to the holder on discovery

[10] Copyright © by West Publishing Co. 1959. Reprinted by permission.

of this mistake. Such a check therefore not only is not completed payment when given but never becomes completed payment.

On this basis American common law usually holds, in cases of this kind, that the goods still belong to the seller; that is, unless the seller is shown to have accepted the check itself as absolute payment.

Vold summarizes:

> Payment by check, unless otherwise agreed, is usually treated as merely conditional payment until the check is cashed. In technical cash sale deals, therefore, though the goods be delivered, the property interest does not pass until the check is cashed. If the check "bounces," the unpaid seller can reclaim his goods.

How is the "cash sale" transaction handled under the Code? See U.C.C. §§ 2-507(2) and Comment 3, 2-511(3) and Comments 4-6 and PEB Commentary No. 1, U.C.C. § 2-507(2) (March 10, 1990). See also U.C.C. § 2-403(1)(b) and (c) and Chapter 8, Rights of Third Parties: Good Faith Purchase of Goods.

IN RE CHARTER CO.

United States Bankruptcy Court, Middle District of Florida
52 BR 263, 42 U.C.C. Rep. 192 (1985)

GEORGE L. PROCTOR, BANKRUPTCY JUDGE.

The amended complaint in this adversary proceeding sets forth two factually related but theoretically distinct claims for relief, *i.e.* reclamation and constructive trust, both arising from a sale of crude oil by Pratt to the defendant Charter Crude Oil Company (CCOC). A trial was held on April 18, 1985, and the parties have submitted post-trial briefs. The facts as stipulated lead the court to conclude that Charter International Oil Company (CIOC) is merely a nominal party, and references to "the defendant" throughout the text of the opinion will be to CCOC. The essential facts are subject to a stipulation entered into by the parties, and we will draw on that stipulation, as well as evidence adduced at trial, for our summary of the material facts.

Prior to April 20, 1984, the defendant had, on a regular basis, purchased crude oil from leases operated by the plaintiff. Throughout this course of dealing, the defendant only was responsible for payment for oil it purchased. Between April 3 and April 14, 1984, crude oil with a value of $32,410.41 was produced by Pratt and delivered for the account of the defendant to Mobil Oil Corporation. Between April 15 and April 18, 1984, crude oil with a value of $73,594.98 was delivered in the same manner.

On April 24, 1984, Pratt sent the defendant notice of reclamation as to all of the oil delivered on or after April 3, 1984.

The defendant and Mobil Oil Corporation had entered into the exchange agreement whereby Mobil was to purchase oil from the defendant in November 1983. The plaintiff was not a party to this agreement.

On or about April 3, 1984, Larry Golden, president of the defendant, sent the plaintiff a letter, which appears to be a form letter sent to all operators and producers with which the defendant had a business relationship. The letter appears to be intended to amplify on an announcement that had been made publicly by the defendant on April 2, 1984, to no longer "run crude oil on a sustained basis . . .at the Houston division." The second paragraph of the letter reads in pertinent part as follows:

> As to the impact this has on the operations, organization, and financial condition of the Crude Oil Gathering Company, we anticipate that there will be no changes. This segment of our business continues to be one in which we take great pride and anticipate continuing for many years to come.

Delivery of the crude oil was made from trucks operated by Pratt via either trucks leased by Mobil or via the facilities of Mobil Pipe Line Company and was not in the custody or possession of CCOC at any time.

On April 16, 1984, the Charter Company and various of its subsidiaries including the defendant filed in this court for protection under Chapter 11 of the Bankruptcy Code. On May 8 and 18, 1984, the defendant billed Mobil in the amount of $109,540.00 for the subject crude oil. No payment pursuant to the contract has been made; rather, pursuant to the court's order of February 21, 1985, granting relief from the automatic stay and allowing offset of mutual debts in the bankruptcy cases to which this adversary proceeding is related, Mobil has placed the funds in a segregated interest bearing account and has agreed to distribute it as provided by court order or agreement of the parties. It is undisputed that, to the extent that state law governs the outcome of this proceeding, Kansas law applies.

Section 546[(c)] of the Bankruptcy Code defines the rights of reclaiming creditors where the defaulting buyer has filed for bankruptcy protection. It provides in pertinent part that

> . . . the rights and powers of a trustee under sections 544(a), 545, and 549 of this title are subject to any statutory or common-law right of a seller that has sold goods to the debtor, in the ordinary course of such seller's business, to reclaim such goods if the buyer has received such goods while insolvent, but — (1) such a seller may not reclaim any such goods unless such seller demands in writing reclamation of such goods before ten days after receipt of such goods by the debtor. . . .

Uniform Commercial Code § 2-702(2) as adopted in Kansas provides [the Court quotes U.C.C. § 2-702(2)].

Subsection (3) makes the seller's right to reclaim subject to

> . . . the rights of a buyer in the ordinary course of business or other good faith purchaser or lien creditor under this chapter.[11]

By agreement of the parties, the issue of the alleged insolvency of the defendant has been reserved for a separate trial at a later time.

We first must confront the issues created by the debtor's nonpossession of the goods at the time of the reclamation demand or indeed at any time. The defendants treat as dispositive their non-possession at the time of reclamation, citing case law to the effect that where the goods sought to be reclaimed are not in the hands of the buyer at the time reclamation is sought there is nothing to reclaim and thus that remedy is foreclosed. Cases which treat possession by the

[11] [This is the 1962 version of U.C.C. § 2-702(3). In 1966 § 2-702(3) was amended to delete "or lien creditor."—Ed.]

buyer as an absolute prerequisite to the right of reclamation have generally not arisen in the factual context of the defaulting buyer, by agreement, *never* having had possession of the goods; they rather appear to arise from the situation in which the buyer had possession but relinquished it to a third party before a timely reclamation demand. This court does not specifically disavow but is unwilling to adopt the sweeping proposition that non-possession by the defaulting buyer at the time of reclamation demand is *invariably* a bar to reclamation. The case law makes abundantly clear, however, that if the goods sought to be reclaimed are not in the hands of the buyer and are in the hands of a good faith purchaser, no reclamation remedy can lie.

Had there been no bankruptcy, the plaintiff would have been able to pursue any rights created by state law, i.e. principally, if not exclusively, the provisions of U.C.C. § 2-702. In the context of bankruptcy, the reclaiming seller would have no rights against a debtor-in-possession exercising the rights of a trustee, but for the provision of § 546(c). Section 546(c), however, places a crucial limitation on a reclaiming seller's pursuit of state law reclamation rights. According to its plain language, no reclamation is to be had unless the seller has made a reclamation demand before ten days after receipt of the goods. The state law with which § 546(c) was drafted to harmonize sets forth *two* sets of circumstances under which a seller may reclaim from an insolvent buyer — the seller may make timely demand or the demand may be excused where a written misrepresentation as to the debtor's solvency has been made by the debtor. The plaintiff urges that the letter from Mr. Golden of February 21, 1984, constitutes such a written misrepresentation and that § 546 permits use of the written misrepresentation-as-to-solvency route to reclamation. The case law and this court's unambivalent reading of § 546(c) do not support the plaintiff's position. *In re Gibson Distributing Co.*, 40 B.R. 767 (Bkrtcy.W.D.Tex.1984), *In re L.T.S., Inc.*, 32 B.R. 907(Bkrtcy.D.Idaho 1983), and *In re Ateco Equipment*, 18 B.R. 917(Bkrtcy.W.D.Pa 1982) have all held that the § 546 requirement for written demand for reclamation within ten days is absolute and cannot be waived on the ground of the buyer's written misrepresentation as to solvency. Our conclusion that, as a matter of law, any written misrepresentation as to solvency is immaterial determines that we need not consider whether Mr. Golden's letter constituted such a misrepresentation. Thus failure to make a timely reclamation demand in itself cuts off the plaintiff's rights in the oil delivered more than 10 days before demand was made.

With respect to that oil for whose reclamation a timely demand *was* made, U.C.C. § 2-702 provides that the reclaiming seller's rights are cut off by the rights of a good faith purchaser. We must determine then, with respect to that portion of the oil for which the plaintiff made a timely reclamation demand, whether Mobil was a good faith purchaser. The plaintiff contests good faith purchaser status on Mobil's part in that, 1) it alleges knowledge on Mobil's part of the defendant's insolvency prior to the plaintiff's reclamation demand, and, 2) because Mobil has, rather than actually paying for the oil, placed the agreed-upon price in a segregated fund subject to this court's order. The facts as stipulated do not suggest that Mobil intended to be other than a buyer in the ordinary course of business. We can find that Mobil is not a good faith purchaser if and only if some additional fact stipulated or shown has the legal effect of affirmatively disqualifying Mobil for good faith purchaser status.

The vast majority of published cases which address the rights of the reclaiming seller vis-a-vis those of a third party concern themselves with a lien creditor of the debtor and are not applicable in this instance. The case most factually analogous to that before us appears to be *In re Coast Trading Co., Inc.*, 31 B.R. 667(Bkrtcy.D.Ore. 1982). There, three growers sold grain to Coast which in turn sold it to Ralston Purina. Ralston "did not pay for the grain as it was in doubt as to which party was entitled to payment," *Id.* at 668. Ralston did later pay the agreed upon price into the registry of the bankruptcy court pursuant to an interpleader action which it filed, i.e. it followed a course of behavior similar to that of Mobil in the instant case. The Coast court holds that "[w]hether the ultimate purchaser has yet paid for the goods . . .is clearly immaterial," *Id.* A finding of good faith purchaser status on Ralston's part is clearly implicit in the slightly earlier language, "[i]f the buyer, before reclamation, has already sold the goods to *a good faith purchaser for value*, there is nothing to reclaim as the seller cannot demand a return of the goods from the ultimate purchaser." (*Id.*, emphasis added). The *Coast* court clearly, in predicating its ultimate holding on good faith purchaser status, did not believe that mere non-payment of the purchase price by the ultimate purchaser does negate good faith status where, as the facts in *Coast* and the case before us indicate, it cannot be said that the ultimate purchaser has received, or attempted to receive, a windfall.

We see no merit in the position that Mobil is not in good faith because of some knowledge it may have had of financial instability of the defendant's part—the facts indicate no reason to believe that Mobil sought any unfair advantage or expected to be anything other than a buyer for value in the ordinary course of business. Thus we find Mobil Oil to be a good faith purchaser. Its good faith purchaser status cuts off reclamation rights which the plaintiff would otherwise have to oil delivered within ten days before the reclamation demand.

Our holding in favor of the defendant on the statutory reclamation count of the amended complaint renders moot for this particular adversary proceeding the issue of the defendant's solvency at the time of receipt of the goods.

The second count of the plaintiff's amended complaint urges that this is an appropriate instance for imposition of a constructive trust. It is apparent to this court, however, that it was the intent of the drafters of the Uniform Commercial Code to create U.C.C.-based reclamation as the exclusive remedy to sellers to insolvent defaulting buyers. As we have discussed *supra* it was equally clearly the intent of Congress to further limit the rights of such parties in a bankruptcy context by the restrictions of 11 U.S.C. § 546. We cannot reconcile with such strictly limited statutory remedies, the concept that recourse may be had to a vaguely defined equitable remedy.

. . . .

For the reasons set forth above, a judgment in favor of the defendant on both counts will be entered with this opinion.

Final judgment for defendants and order directing turnover of property of the estate

Ordered as follows:

1. Judgment is hereby entered in favor of the defendants on both counts of the amended complaint;

2. Mobil Oil Corporation holds funds which, by the terms of this judgment, become property of the bankruptcy estate and it appearing that those funds have been held in an interest bearing account and that Mobil Oil Corporation asserts no interest in the funds other than that of a stakeholder, Mobil shall forthwith turnover to the debtor-in-possession all principal and interest so held.

NOTES

Section 546(c) of the Bankruptcy Code, 11 U.S.C. § 546(c), reads in full:

(c) Except as provided in subsection (d) of this section, the rights and powers of a trustee under sections 544(a), 545, 547, and 549 of this title are subject to any statutory or common-law right of a seller of goods that has sold goods to the debtor, in the ordinary course of such seller's business, to reclaim such goods if the debtor has received such goods while insolvent, but—

(1) such a seller may not reclaim any such goods unless such seller demands in writing reclamation of such goods

(A) before 10 days after receipt of such goods by the debtor; or

(B) if such 10–day period expires after the commencement of the case, before 20 days after receipt of such goods by the debtor; and before ten days after receipt of such goods by the debtor; and

(2) the court may deny reclamation to a seller with such a right of reclamation that has made such a demand only if the court—

(A) grants the claim of such a seller priority as a claim of a kind specified in section 503(b) of this title; or

(B) Secures such claim by a lien.

PROBLEM 7.3

On May 20, Braxton Motor Company sold and delivered to Richard Taggart a new brown four-door Cadillac for a cash price of $29,864.30. Taggart paid Braxton by a check dated May 20. Before the check cleared, Taggart moved the car out of town. On June 1 the check was returned to Braxton for lack of sufficient funds.

Meanwhile, Taggart owed Citizens Bank $30,000 pursuant to two promissory notes. He defaulted on the notes and the bank brought suit in the Placer County Superior Court and secured judgment against Taggart for an amount in excess of $30,000. A writ of execution was issued and on July 15 the Placer County Sheriff levied on the Cadillac registered in Taggart's name. Braxton was unable to locate the Cadillac until notified by the Placer County Sheriff that the vehicle had been seized.

Braxton asserts a cash seller's reclamation rights under U.C.C. §§ 2-507(2) and 2-511(3). Citizens Bank concedes that an unpaid cash seller prevails over an attaching lien creditor. But it asserts that Braxton waived its reclamation rights by not demanding reclamation within ten days after the receipt of the Cadillac by Taggart. Bank's authority is Comment 3 to § 2-507 (1989) which reads in part: "The provision of this Article for a ten day limit within which the seller may reclaim goods delivered on credit to an insolvent buyer [§ 2-702(2)] is also applicable here."

Who prevails, Braxton or Citizens Bank? See § 2-507 Comment 3 (1990) and PEB Commentary No. 1, dated March 10, 1990; *Citizens Bank of Roseville v. Taggart*, 143 Cal. App. 3d 318, 191 Cal. Rptr. 729, 36 U.C.C. Rep. 529 (1983).

NOTES

(1) Proposed § 2-702 combines in one place the right of a seller to reclaim goods delivered to a buyer (1) in a cash sale where payment is not made or (2) in a credit sale where the buyer was insolvent. The credit sale provision follows essentially present § 2-702(2); the cash sale provision is: "If payment is due and demanded on delivery to the buyer, a seller may reclaim the goods delivered upon demand made within a reasonable time after the seller discovers or should have discovered that payment was not made."

(2) U.C.C. § 2-403 is discussed at Chapter 8, Rights of Third Parties: Good Faith Purchase of Goods.

§ 7.04 Buyer's Remedies for Breach Where Goods Not Accepted or Acceptance Justifiably Revoked

Read: U.C.C. § 2-711.

Read also: U.C.C. § 2A-508, CISG Art. 45.

The remedies dealt with in this section are those available to a buyer who has not accepted the goods or who has justifiably revoked his acceptance. These remedies are indexed in U.C.C. § 2-711, cf. § 2A-508.

The remedies available to a buyer with regard to goods finally accepted appear in the next section, § 7.05, and at U.C.C. § 2-714, Buyer's Damages in Regard to Accepted Goods. See U.C.C. § 2-711Comment 1.[12] Cf. §§ 2A-508(3) and (4), 2A-519(3) and (4).

For discussion of rejection, acceptance and revocation of acceptance, see § 6.04, Buyer's Rights on Improper Delivery, and U.C.C. §§ 2-601 through 2-608. Cf. §§ 2A-509 through 2A-512, 2A-514 through 2A-517.

The buyer's right to proceed as to all goods when the breach is as to only some of the goods is determined by the section on breach in installment contracts, U.C.C. §§ 2-612, cf. § 2A-510. See § 6.04[D] above. As to partial acceptances, see U.C.C. § 2-601(c). U.C.C. § 2-711Comment 1.

[A] Cancellation

Read: U.C.C. §§ 2-711(1), 2-106(3) and (4); cf. § 2-703(f).

---

[12] Simply, the buyer's remedies for breach of the sale contract by the seller fall into two functional categories: those remedies available where the buyer does not receive and retain the goods, as where seller fails to deliver, or where buyer rejects or revokes acceptance; and those remedies available where the buyer has received and retained the goods. The first category is contained in § 2-711; the second in § 2-714.

Read also: U.C.C. § 2A-508(1)(a), 2A-103(1)(b) and (z), 2A-505(1)-(3), cf. § 2A-523(1)(a); CISG Arts. 49, 25-27, 81-84, cf. Art. 64.

ROYCO, INC. v. COTTENGIM

Florida District Court of Appeal
427 So. 2d 759, 35 U.C.C. Rep. 465 (1983)

SHARP, J.

Royco, Inc., d/b/a Uncle Roy's Mobile Home Sales, appeals from a judgment, entered after a non-jury trial, which allowed the Cottengims (purchasers of a mobile home from Royco) to cancel a contract for the purchase of a mobile home and to recover the sums they had paid Royco. The trial court ruled the Cottengims had not accepted the mobile home; Royco had materially breached the sales contract; and the Cottengims could cancel the contract under § 672.711, Florida Statutes (1981), even though they had an adequate remedy at law (damages). We affirm.

The trial court found Royco had breached the sales contract in three respects: failure to provide a mobile home with a beamed living room ceiling, as in the model shown to the purchasers when they ordered the home; failure to provide ceramic tile in the bathrooms, as in the model they were shown; and failure to provide a 36 inch-wide entry door to the mobile home. Mr. Cottengim is physically handicapped, and his wheelchair requires 36 inches for passage — a fact made known to Royco's salesman. The record is also clear that Royco refused to remedy these defects after the mobile home was delivered to the Cottengims, although it was given adequate time and opportunity to do so.

Although some pre-Code Florida cases held that rescission was not an available remedy to a buyer if the breach was curable by an award of damages, the rule is clearly otherwise under § 672.711. It provides: [the court quotes U.C.C. § 2-711(1)]. This section imposes no condition or qualification on the buyer's right to cancel the contract where he rightfully rejects or justifiably revokes acceptance. He is no longer required to bring an equitable action for rescission, and, as part of that remedy, prove that damages are an inadequate remedy.

Affirmed.

[B] Recover Price Paid; Security Interest in Rejected Goods

Read: U.C.C. § 2-711(1) and (3), see § 2-706, especially (6).

Read also: U.C.C. § 2A-508(1)(b) and (5); CISG Art. 81, 84.

U.C.C. § 2-711(1) allows the buyer to recover so much of the price as has been paid. Subsection (3) is intended to make it clear that the buyer may hold and resell rejected goods if he has paid part of the purchase price or incurred expenses of the type specified. U.C.C. § 2-711 Comment 3.

IN RE ADAMS PLYWOOD, INC.

United States Bankruptcy Court, Western District of Tennessee
48 BR 719, 41 U.C.C. Rep. 830 (1985)

WILLIAM B. LEFFLER, BANKRUPTCY JUDGE.

Champion Building Products ("Champion") purchased from Adams Plywood, Inc. ("Debtor") 708 sheets of one-fourth inch four-by-eight natural birch plywood along with 61 sheets of one-fourth inch four-by-eight red oak plywood. Champion paid the Debtor $6,656.93 upon delivery of the plywood. On August 22, 1984, nine days after delivery, Champion inspected the plywood and exercised its right to reject all the goods because they did not conform to the contract. Tenn. Code Ann. § 47-2-601. Champion returned the plywood to the Debtor on August 22, 1984, the same day that the Debtor filed a Chapter 11 Petition in Bankruptcy. The plywood was sold or otherwise disposed of before this matter was filed with this Court.

Champion is now before this court by virtue of what it calls a "Petition to Require Debtor to Relinquish in and Return Equipment to Petitioner." In this petition, Champion prays for the following: an injunction against the Trustee selling or otherwise disposing of goods; an order allowing Champion to reclaim the goods; an order allowing Champion's claim for $6,656.93, including $2,218.98 in attorney fees.[13]

Champion takes the position that it has a right to reclaim the goods pursuant to 11 U.S.C. § 546(c).[14] The court finds that Champion's position is without merit. Section 546(c) grants the right of reclamation to a *seller* of goods. Champion is clearly a buyer that exercised its right to reject the goods. Therefore, Section 546(c) is unavailable to Champion.

The remedies available to Champion once it discovered that the goods shipped by the Debtor did not conform to the contract are found at Tenn. Code Ann. § 47-2-711. Section 47-2-711(3) reads in pertinent part as follows:

---

[13] This should have been filed as an adversary proceeding pursuant to Bankruptcy Rule 7001.

[14] Champion sent a written demand for reclamation of the plywood within ten days after the Debtor received the plywood. Section 546(c) states as follows:

(c) Except as provided in subsection (d) of this section, the rights and powers of a trustee under sections 544(a), 545, and 549 of this title are subject to any statutory or common-law right of a seller of goods that has sold goods to the debtor, in the ordinary course of such seller's business, to reclaim such goods if the debtor has received such goods while insolvent, but—

(1) such a seller may not reclaim any such goods unless such seller demands in writing reclamation of such goods before ten days after receipt of such goods by the debtor; and

(2) the court may deny reclamation to a seller with such a right of reclamation that has made such a demand only if the court—

(A) grants the claim of such a seller priority as a claim of a kind specified in section 503(b) of this title; or

(B) secured such claim by a lien.

(3) On rightful rejection . . .of acceptance a buyer has a security interest in goods *in his possession* or control for any payments made on their price and any expenses reasonably incurred in their inspection, receipt, transportation, care and custody and may hold such goods and resell them in like manner as an aggrieved seller.

(Emphasis added.)

Champion could have protected itself by properly exercising its remedies under Tenn. Code Ann. § 47-2-711. Under § 47-2-711(3), Champion could have rejected the plywood yet kept the goods and maintained a security interest in the goods. By sending the plywood back to the Debtor, Champion is left with a mere unsecured claim against the Debtor in the amount of $6,656.93.

Although the result reached by the Court in this case seems inequitable at first glance, when one views the case in the context of the entire bankruptcy proceeding and from the perspective of all the other creditors involved, the holding can be justified.

There are two principal goals underlying the Bankruptcy Act. The first goal is to ". . . relieve the honest debtor from the weight of oppressive indebtedness and permit him to start afresh . . ." *Local Loan Co. v. Hunt*, 292 U.S. 234, 244 (1934). The other principal goal is to provide for equitable distribution of a debtor's estate among all his creditors . . . .

Therefore, under the particular facts and circumstances of the case, the court must hold that Champion holds an unsecured claim against the Debtor in the amount of $6,656.93.

[C] Recover Money Damages

[1] Cover and Have Damages

Read: U.C.C. §§ 2-711(1)(a), 2-712; cf. § 2-706.

Read also: U.C.C. §§ 2A-508(1)(c), 2A-518, 2A-520, cf. § 2A-527, CISG Arts. 75, 77.

MARTELLA v. WOODS

United States Court of Appeals
715 F.2d 410, 36 U.C.C. Rep. 1200 (8th Cir. 1983)

BRIGHT, CIRCUIT JUDGE.

James H. Woods, Jr., d/b/a Chaumiere Farms, appeals the judgment of the district court awarding Fred H. Martella, Robert M. Berry, Robert M. Lee and William J. Mouren, d/b/a Arkavalley Farm $43,248 in damages for cover and $64,529.60 in damages for the nondelivery of certain heifers. Arkavalley Farm cross-appeals, arguing that the district court erred in failing to award $ 129,391.50 in damages for lost profits. For the reasons outlined below, we affirm on the merits, but reverse and remand to the district court for recomputation of damages.

I. Background.

On or about December 2, 1976, Woods and Ralston Purina Company, d/b/a Arkavalley Farm, executed the "Arkavalley Farm Heifer Growing Contract." The contract provided that Woods would purchase from Arkavalley Farm an unspecified number of three and four month-old heifers. Woods would feed these heifers and allow them to breed with bulls furnished by Arkavalley. The contract also provided that when these heifers reached approximately 24 to 30 months of age Woods would sell them back to the Arkavalley Farm at a price determined by the weight of each heifer. The then-pregnant heifers would be used to replace the less productive heifers in Arkavalley's dairy farm.[15]

Pursuant to this contract, Woods purchased 190 Holstein heifer calves from Arkavalley. Woods expected that the calves would reach 900 pounds between 18 and 19 months of age. At that time, the parties expected to place the heifers with a bull. Waiting until the calves reached 900 pounds before breeding them would benefit both parties because Woods could produce heavier bred heifers thereby obtaining the maximum contract price of 48 cents per pound and Arkavalley would receive replacement heifers capable of producing more milk than could smaller heifers.

Problems arose, however, because the heifers did not grow fast enough. None of the first 36 heifers ultimately placed with bulls reached 900 pounds between 18 and 19 months of age. Indeed, 34 of the 36 heifers did not reach 900 pounds until they were 22 months or older.

Between March 26 and May 8, 1979, Woods sold 41 bred heifers to Arkavalley. These heifers averaged slightly more than 30 months of age.

In April of 1979, Ralston Purina sold Arkavalley Farm to Martella, Berry, Lee and Mouren, and assigned them its interest in the 1976 contract.

On May 5, 1979, Woods informed Arkavalley that, because the heifers were not progressing normally and were causing the Chaumiere Farm to lose money, he was going to sell the heifers. Arkavalley offered Woods 46 cents per pound for the 144 heifers.[16] Woods rejected this offer. Woods then proceeded to sell the remaining 144 heifers, which were supposed to have been sold to the dairy, to third persons.

To compensate for the heifers that Woods failed to supply, Arkavalley purchased 50 pregnant heifers from third parties. Arkavalley then sued Woods in federal district court for breach of contract. Arkavalley contended that Woods breached the contract by failing to resell 144 of the 186 heifers to Arkavalley Farm. Woods failed to dispute that his sale of the 144 heifers to third parties did not conform to the requirements of the contract. Rather, Woods argued in the district court that the contract was rescinded by failure of consideration. Woods asserted that no consideration for the contract existed because Arkavalley breached expressed and implied warranties concerning the quality of the heifers provided to him.

---

[15] Specifically, the contract provided in pertinent part:

1. Feeder [Woods] will purchase from Dairy [Arkavalley Farm] a mutually agreeable number of replacement heifers weighing approximately 200 pounds. . . .

. . . .

3. Feeder will transport these replacement heifers to his farm . . .where Feeder will care for and raise them, allow them to breed with the bull(s) furnished by Dairy. . . .

4. When these heifers reach approximately 24-30 months of age, Feeder will sell these heifers back to the Dairy using the following formula:

1. Those heifers weighing less than 1,100 pounds at forty (40) cents per pound.

2. Those heifers weighing over 1,100 pounds but less than 1,200 pounds at forty-four (44) cents per pound.

3. Those heifers weighing over 1,200 pounds at forty-eight (48) cents per pound.

[16] As we noted earlier in the text, Woods purchased 190 heifer calves from Arkavalley. One calf died and three others were viewed as unfit and sold on the open market. Between March 26 and May 8, 1979, Woods sold 41 bred heifers to Arkavalley. Woods also resold to Arkavalley a single "freemartin," which is a heifer incapable of reproduction. Thus, by mid-May 1979, Woods still had 144 of the original 190 heifers purchased from Arkavalley.

The district court found that: (1) the assignment of the contract from Ralston Purina to Martella, Berry, Lee and Mouren was effective because it did not materially change the duties, burdens or risks of Woods; (2) Arkavalley made no express warranties as to the quality of the heifers Woods purchased; (3) there existed no implied warranties as to the calves because it is impossible to determine the growth and breeding potential of heifer calves at three or four months of age, when they were purchased by Woods; (4) the fact that the heifers had grown slowly and thus were incapable of being dairy replacement heifers at 24 to 30 months of age was not a condition precedent to Woods' performance of the contract, making the contract unenforceable; and finally, (5) the contract was not, therefore, rescinded because of failure of consideration.

On the issue of damages, the district court: (1) awarded Arkavalley $43,248 in damages for cover; (2) awarded Arkavalley $64,529.60 in damages for nondelivery; and (3) determined that Arkavalley was not entitled to damages for lost profits.

On appeal, Woods urges that the district court erred in: (1) concluding that no express or implied warranties of the quality of the heifer calves existed; (2) concluding that growth of the heifers and their development into dairy replacement heifers within the time frame specified in the contract was not a condition precedent; (3) concluding that the conduct of the parties did not demonstrate mutual rescission of the contract; and (4) awarding damages. . . .

II. Discussion.

A. The Merits.

After a careful review of the briefs and record in this case, we conclude that the district court did not err in any of its rulings on the merits. However, the district court's award of damages presents more substantial questions, and it is to those issues we now turn.

B. Damages for Cover.

The district court found that Arkavalley had partially covered Woods' breach by purchasing 50 heifers at $63,088. The court observed that the contract price for the 50 heifers would have been $19,840. The district court concluded that the difference, $43,248, was recoverable as cover costs by Arkavalley. The court rejected Woods' argument that the 50 replacement heifers purchased by Arkavalley were not like-kind substitutes for the heifers Woods had sold to third parties. The court stated that "[i]t is irrelevant what the state of the heifers was when defendant Woods sold them to third parties." We disagree.

The Uniform Commercial Code, as adopted in Missouri, provides: [the court quotes U.C.C. § 2-712].

Section 400.2-712 allows a buyer the right to purchase reasonable substitutes and recover the difference between the cost to obtain the substitute goods and the contract price. To recover under this section, the buyer must act in good faith and in a reasonable manner in purchasing substitute goods, and the goods must be a like-kind substitute. However, the buyer may not utilize cover to put himself in a better position than he would have been had the contract been performed. . . .

We note initially that the contract did not require Woods to deliver pregnant heifers of a certain weight and quality to Arkavalley. The contract merely required Woods to sell and Arkavalley to buy those heifers between 24-30 months of age.[17] Therefore, a breach of that contract only

[17] We note that specifically the contract did not require Woods to deliver to Arkavalley pregnant heifers. The contract provided that "Feeder will transport these replacement heifers to his farm . . .where Feeder will care for and raise

permits Arkavalley to cover with the quality and size of heifers Woods was obligated to sell Arkavalley. The 50 heifers purchased by Arkavalley were not like-kind substitutes for the heifers Woods sold to third parties. The district court found that Arkavalley covered by purchasing 50 pregnant heifers, weighing between 1,100 to 1,200 pounds each. In contrast, the evidence establishes that, at best, only a third of the 144 heifers Woods sold to third parties could have been pregnant. The district court found, for example, that only 84 of the 190 heifers Woods possessed had been bred with Arkavalley bulls. Moreover, according to the district court's findings, the average weight of the 50 heifers Arkavalley purchased as cover was 1,100 to 1,200 pounds, which was substantially higher than Woods' 144 heifers. As the district court found, only 110 of Woods' 144 heifers weighed 900 pounds or more.

Arkavalley was only entitled to cover what Woods had to sell. By purchasing heifers seven and a half to eight months pregnant, weighing 1,100 to 1,200 pounds, Arkavalley placed themselves in a better position than they would have been had Woods resold his heifers to them. Arkavalley's cover was not a reasonable like-kind substitute for Woods' heifers. Accordingly, we determine that the district court erred in awarding cover damages.

[The case is continued and concluded at § 7.04[C][2] immediately below.]

NOTES

(1) In *Dangerfield v. Markel*, 278 N.W.2d 364, 26 U.C.C. Rep. 419 (N.D. 1979), seller breached a contract to deliver chipping potatoes to buyer. Buyer completed "covering" the contract on March 21, 1973, which was 38 days after the date of breach. During the first 18 days of this cover period, the buyer's purchases averaged $4.41 per cwt. During the remaining 20 days, the buyer's purchases averaged over $5.41 per cwt., with many purchases made at $6.00 per cwt. Seller argues that 38 days for the buyer to cover in a rapidly rising market is improper under U.C.C. § 2-712; therefore U.C.C. § 2-713 should have been used to compute damages. Held: for buyer. He covered in good faith and without unreasonable delay under U.C.C. § 2-712.

The court cited *Farmer's Union Co-op of Mead v. Flamme Bros.*, 196 Neb. 699, 245 N.W.2d 464 (1976), where the Supreme Court of Nebraska was presented with a similar situation in which the seller argued that the buyer should not have been allowed to cover a breached corn contract over a 15-day period in a rising market. The Nebraska court rejected the argument:

---

them, allow them to breed with the bull(s) furnished by the Dairy . . . ." Thus, the plain language of the contract imposes upon Arkavalley the responsibility for breeding the heifers, and merely requires Woods to permit breeding. Indeed, Charles N. Brock, who had been the director of operations at Arkavalley Farms from 1969 to 1979, stated during direct examination:

Q What was your understanding with respect to these one hundred and forty-four heifers, if some of them were not bred?

[Brock] Under the terms of the contract, we always took the heifers back, whether they were bred or not.

Q If they were not bred, what did Arkavalley do with them, if anything?

[Brock] We would breed them.

Arkavalley does not argue on appeal that Woods thwarted or in any way hampered Arkavalley's attempt to impregnate the heifers.

In the case at bar, the appellee did not go into the market and buy corn specifically to cover the contracts, but appellee did continue buying corn from its members, as was its normal practice until the three contracts were fulfilled. The trial court determined, as inherent in its verdict and judgment for appellee, that appellee did "cover" the contract "without unreasonable delay," and under all the circumstances of this case, we affirm the trial court's judgment. Appellee did between the dates of January 2 and January 15, 1974, purchase over 111,000 bushels of corn and applied such purchases to the unfulfilled contracts. The comment following section 2-712, U.C.C., is particularly applicable to this case. That comment states, in part: "2. The definition of 'cover' under subsection (1) envisages a series of contracts or sales, as well as a single contract or sale; . . . and contracts on credit or delivery terms differing from the contract in breach, but again reasonable under the circumstances. The test of proper cover is whether at the time and place the buyer acted in good faith and in a reasonable manner, and it is immaterial that hindsight may later prove that the method of cover used was not the cheapest or most effective."

The offended party is not bound by hindsight, and the practice used by appellee might have resulted in lower damages if the price over the time period had declined. Instead, the price fluctuated and the net result was that the damages were slightly higher than if the entire volume of corn had been purchased on January 2, 1974, at the $2.32 price. Appellee acted in good faith and made the 'cover' purchases without unreasonable delay, within the meaning of the Uniform Commercial Code. 196 Neb. at 706, 245 N.W.2d at 468. The court also noted White and Summers's comment on U.C.C. § 2-712:

If 2-712 is to be the remedy used by more aggrieved buyers than any other remedy, then the courts must be chary of finding a good faith buyer's acts unreasonable. The courts should not hedge the remedy about with restrictions in the name of "reasonableness" that render it useless or uncertain for the good faith buyer. Indeed, one may argue that the courts should read very little substance into the reasonableness requirement and insist only that the buyer proceed in good faith. A question a lawyer might put to test his client's good faith under 2-712 is this: "How, where, and when would you have procured these goods if you had not been covering and had no prospect of a court recovery from another?" If the client can answer truthfully that he would have spent his own money in the same way, the court should not demand more.

J. White & R. Summers, Handbook of the Law under the Uniform Commercial Code, at p. 178.

(2) U.C.C. § 2-712(l) provides that cover must be "without unreasonable delay" and that the purchase of substitute goods must be "reasonable." As seen in the foregoing cases, where the buyer has covered, the seller will often raise one or both of these reasonableness questions. Professors White and Summers lament that the Code furnishes little guidance. After quoting U.C.C. § 1-204(2) that "What is a reasonable time for taking any action depends on the nature, purpose and circumstances of such action," they continue:

The drafters have hardly left us with a solid basis upon which to predict whether a given act was or was not "reasonable"; each new sentence of the Comment is like an additional bucket of muck thrown into a quagmire. Of course the drafters were not dummies, and their vagueness was doubtless purposeful.

J. White & R. Summers, Uniform Commercial Code § 6-3 at 246 (3d ed. 1988).

[2] Recover Damages for Non-Delivery or Repudiation

Read: U.C.C. §§ 2-711(1)(b), 2-713; see §§ 2-723, 2-724, 2-503; cf. § 2-708.

Read also: U.C.C. §§ 2A-508(1)(c), 2A-519(1) and (2), 2A-507, 2A-520, cf. § 2A-528; CISG Arts. 45(1)(b), 76, 77.

MARTELLA v. WOODS

United States Court of Appeals
715 F2d 410, 36 U.C.C. Rep. 1200 (8th Cir. 1983)

[This case is continued from § 7.04[C][1] immediately above.]

C. Damages for Nondelivery.

The district court also awarded Arkavalley $64,529.60 in damages for Woods' failure to deliver 94 of the 144 heifers. This award represented the difference between the fair market price, at the time of the breach, of 89 pregnant heifers and 5 non-pregnant heifers, and the contract price. After a careful review of the record and briefs in this case, we conclude that the district court erred in awarding nondelivery damages.

Missouri law provides for damages for nondelivery: [the Court recites U.C.C. § 2-713].

The contract merely required Woods to sell and Arkavalley to buy those heifers between 24-30 months of age. Therefore, a breach of that contract only permits recovery of the difference between the lower contract price and the higher market price of those heifers Woods was obligated but did not sell to Arkavalley. As we noted earlier, the evidence establishes that only a third of the 144 heifers Woods sold to third parties could have possibly been pregnant, and only 110 of Woods' 144 heifers weighed 900 pounds or more. Accordingly, we remand to the district court for a recomputation of damages based on the difference between the contract price and the market price for those heifers Woods had previously sold to third parties as of the time Arkavalley learned of the breach.

III. Conclusion

We affirm the district court's decision on the merits. . . . However, we conclude that the district court erred in calculating damages for cover [U.C.C. § 2-712] and nondelivery [U.C.C. § 2-713]. We determine that Arkavalley is entitled to damages only for the difference between the fair market price of the 144 heifers Woods sold to third parties and the lesser contract price, said differential to be determined as of the time that Arkavalley learned of the breach.

We observe that there exists some evidence in the record regarding the fair market price of the 144 heifers Woods sold to third parties. The district court, however, did not engage in any substantial factfinding on this issue. Accordingly, on remand, the district court may, at its discretion, hold a new hearing for additional factfinding before proceeding to recalculate damages.

Affirmed in part, reversed in part, and remanded to the district court for proceedings consistent with this opinion.

Read: U.C.C. §§ 2-610, 2-713.

Read also: U.C.C. §§ 2A-402, 2A-519(1) and (2); CISG Arts. 71, 72, 76, 25-27, 81-84.

COSDEN OIL & CHEMICAL CO. v. KARL O. HELM AKTIENGESELLSCHAFT

United States Court of Appeals
736 F.2d 1064, 38 U.C.C. Rep. 1645 (5th Cir. 1984)

Reavley, Circuit Judge.

We must address one of the most difficult interpretive problems of the Uniform Commercial Code—the appropriate time to measure buyer's damages where the seller anticipatorily repudiates a contract and the buyer does not cover. The district court applied the Texas version of Article 2 and measured buyer's damages at a commercially reasonable time after seller's repudiation. We affirm, but remand for modification of damages on another point.

I. Case History

This contractual dispute arose out of events and transactions occurring in the first three months of 1979, when the market in polystyrene, a petroleum derivative used to make molded products, was steadily rising. During this time Iran, a major petroleum producer, was undergoing political turmoil. Karl O. Helm Aktiengesellschaft (Helm or Helm Hamburg), an international trading company based in Hamburg, West Germany, anticipated a tightening in the world petrochemical supply and decided to purchase a large amount of polystyrene. Acting on orders from Helm Hamburg, Helm Houston, a wholly-owned subsidiary, initiated negotiations with Cosden Oil & Chemical Company (Cosden), a Texas-based producer of chemical products, including polystyrene.

Rudi Scholtyssek, general manager of Helm Houston, contacted Ken Smith, Cosden's national sales coordinator, to inquire about the possibility of purchasing quantities of polystyrene. Negotiating over the telephone and by telex, the parties agreed to the purchase and sale of 1250 metric tons[18] of high impact polystyrene at $.2825 per pound and 250 metric tons of general purpose polystyrene at $.265 per pound. The parties also discussed options on each polystyrene type. On January 18, 1979, Scholtyssek met with Smith in Dallas, leaving behind two purchase confirmations. Purchase confirmation 04 contained the terms for high impact and 05 contained the terms for general purpose. Both confirmations contained the price and quantity terms listed above, and specified the same delivery and payment terms. The polystyrene was to be delivered during January and February in one or more lots, to be called for at Helm's instance. Confirmation 04 specified that Helm had an option for an additional 1000 metric tons of high impact, and

[18] One metric ton equals approximately 2,204.5 pounds.

confirmation 05 expressed a similar option for 500 metric tons of general purpose. The option amounts were subject to the same terms, except that delivery was to be during February and March. The options were to be declared, at the latest, by January 31, 1979.

On January 22, Helm called for the first shipment of high impact under order 04, to be delivered FAS at a New Jersey port to make a January 29 shipping date for a trans-Atlantic voyage. On January 23, Helm telexed Cosden to declare the options on purchase orders 04 and 05, designating the high impact option quantity as order 06 and the general purpose option quantity as order 07. After exercising the options, Helm sent purchase confirmations 06 and 07, which Cosden received on January 29. That same day Helm Houston received confirmations 04 and 05, which Smith had signed.

Cosden shipped 90,000 pounds of high impact polystyrene to Helm on or about January 26. Cosden then sent an invoice for that quantity to Helm Houston on or about January 31. The front of the invoice stated, "This order is subject to the terms and conditions shown on the reverse hereof." Among the "Conditions of Sale" listed on the back of the invoice was a force majeure provision. Helm paid for the first shipment in accordance with the agreement.

As Helm had expected, polystyrene prices began to rise in late January, and continued upward during February and March. Cosden also experienced problems at two of its plants in late January. Normally, Cosden supplied its Calumet City, Illinois, production plant with styrene monomer, the "feed stock" or main ingredient of polystyrene,[19] by barges that traveled from Louisiana up the Mississippi and Illinois Rivers to a canal that extended to Cosden's plant. Due to the extremely cold winter of 1978-79, however, the Illinois River and the canal froze, suspending barge traffic for a few weeks. A different problem beset Cosden's Windsor, New Jersey, production plant. A new reactor, used in the polystyrene manufacturing process, had recently been installed at the Windsor plant. A manufacturing defect soon became apparent, however, and Cosden returned the reactor to the manufacturer for repair, which took several weeks. At the time of the reactor breakdown, Cosden was manufacturing only general purpose at the Windsor plant. Cosden had planned on supplying Helm's high impact orders from the Calumet City plant.

Late in January Cosden notified Helm that it was experiencing problems at its production facilities and that the delivery under 04 might be delayed. On February 6, Smith telephoned Scholtyssek and informed him that Cosden was canceling orders 05, 06, and 07 because two plants were "down" and it did not have sufficient product to fill the orders. Cosden, however, would continue to honor order 04. Smith confirmed the cancellation in a letter dated February 8, which Scholtyssek received on or about February 12. After Helm Hamburg learned of Cosden's cancellation, Wolfgang Gordian, a member of Helm's executive board, sent an internal memorandum to Helm Houston outlining a strategy. Helm would urge that Cosden continue to perform under 04 and, after receiving the high impact polystyrene, would offset amounts owing under 04 against Helm's damages for nondelivery of the balance of polystyrene. Gordian also instructed Helm Houston to send a telex to Cosden. Following instructions, Scholtyssek then requested from Cosden "the relevant force majeure certificate" to pass on to Helm Hamburg. Helm also urged Cosden to deliver immediately several hundred metric tons of high impact to meet two February shipping dates for which Helm had booked shipping space.

---

[19] Styrene monomer comprises approximately 90% of high impact polystyrene and a larger percentage of general purpose polystyrene.

In mid-February Cosden shipped approximately 1,260,000 pounds of high impact to Helm under order 04. This shipment's invoice, which also included the force majeure provision on the reverse side, specified that Helm owed $355,950, due by March 15 or 16. After this delivery Helm requested that Cosden deliver the balance under order 04 for shipment on a vessel departing March 16. Cosden informed Helm that a March 16 delivery was not possible. On March 15, citing production problems with the 04 balance, Cosden offered to sell 1000 metric tons of styrene monomer at $.41 per pound. Although Cosden later lowered the price on the styrene monomer, Helm refused the offer, insisting on delivery of the balance of 04 polystyrene by March 31 at the latest. Around the end of March, Cosden informed Scholtyssek by telephone that it was canceling the balance of order 04.

Cosden sued Helm, seeking damages for Helm's failure to pay for delivered polystyrene. Helm counterclaimed for Cosden's failure to deliver polystyrene as agreed. The jury found on special verdict that Cosden had agreed to sell polystyrene to Helm under all four orders. The jury also found that Cosden anticipatorily repudiated orders 05, 06, and 07 and that Cosden canceled order 04 before Helm's failure to pay for the second 04 delivery constituted a repudiation. The jury fixed the per pound market prices for polystyrene under each of the four orders at three different times: when Helm learned of the cancellation, at a commercially reasonable time thereafter, and at the time for delivery.

The district court, viewing the four orders as representing one agreement, determined that Helm was entitled to recover $628,676 in damages representing the difference between the contract price and the market price at a commercially reasonable time after Cosden repudiated its polystyrene delivery obligations and that Cosden was entitled to an offset of $355,950 against those damages for polystyrene delivered, but not paid for, under order 04.

II. Time for Measuring Buyer's Damages

Both parties find fault with the time at which the district court measured Helm's damages for Cosden's anticipatory repudiation of orders 05, 06, and 07.[20] Cosden argues that damages should be measured when Helm learned of the repudiation. Helm contends that market price as of the last day for delivery — or the time of performance — should be used to compute its damages under the contract-market differential. We reject both views, and hold that the district court correctly measured damages at a commercially reasonable point after Cosden informed Helm that it was canceling the three orders.

Article 2 of the Code has generally been hailed as a success for its comprehensiveness, its deference to mercantile reality, and its clarity. Nevertheless, certain aspects of the Code's overall scheme have proved troublesome in application. The interplay among §§ 2.610, 2.711, 2.712, 2.713, and 2.723, Tex Bus & Com Code Ann (Vernon 1968), represents one of those areas, and has been described as "an impossible legal thicket." J. White & R. Summers, Uniform Commercial Code § 6-7 at 242 (2d ed 1980). The aggrieved buyer seeking damages for seller's anticipatory repudiation presents the most difficult interpretive problem.[21] Section 2.713 describes the buyer's damages remedy:

---

[20] The damages measurement problem does not apply to Cosden's breach of order 04, which was not anticipatorily repudiated. The time Helm learned of Cosden's intent to deliver no more polystyrene under 04 was the same time as the last date of performance, which had been extended to the end of March.

[21] The only area of unanimous agreement among those that have studied the Code provisions relevant to this problem is that they are not consistent, present problems in interpretation, and invite amendment.

Buyer's Damages for Non-Delivery or Repudiation

(a) Subject to the provisions of this chapter with respect to proof of market price (Section 2.723), the measure of damages for non-delivery or repudiation by the seller is the difference between the market price *at the time when the buyer learned of the breach* and the contract price together with any incidental and consequential damages provided in this chapter (Section 2.715), but less expenses saved in consequence of the seller's breach.

(Emphasis added).

Courts and commentators have identified three possible interpretations of the phrase "learned of the breach." If seller anticipatorily repudiates, buyer learns of the breach:

(1) When he learns of the repudiation;

(2) When he learns of the repudiation plus a commercially reasonable time; or

(3) When performance is due under the contract.

See, e.g., *First National Bank of Chicago v. Jefferson Mortgage Co.*, 576 F2d 479 (3d Cir 1978); *Cargill, Inc. v. Stafford*, 553 F2d 1222 (10th Cir 1977); J. White & R. Summers § 6-7 at 240-52; Note, U.C.C. § 2-713: *Anticipatory Repudiation and the Measurement of an Aggrieved Buyer's Damages*, 19 Wm & Mary L Rev 253 (1977).

We would not be free to decide the question if there were a Texas case on point, bound as we are by Erie to follow state law in diversity cases. We find, however, that no Texas case has addressed the Code question of buyer's damages in an anticipatory repudiation context. Texas, alone in this circuit, does not allow us to certify questions of state law for resolution by its courts. . . .

Fredonia Broadcasting Corp. v. RCA Corp., 481 F2d 781(5th Cir 1973) (*Fredonia I*), contains dicta on this question. The court merely quoted the language of the section and noted that the time for measuring market price — when buyer learns of the breach — was the only difference from pre-Code Texas law.[22] *Id.* at 800. . . . We have found no Texas case quoting or citing *Fredonia I* for its dicta on damages under § 2.713. Although *Fredonia I* correctly stated the statutory language, it simply did not address or recognize the interpretive problems peculiar to seller's anticipatory repudiation.[23]

Since *Fredonia I*, four Texas courts have applied § 2.713 to measure buyer's damages at the time he learned of the breach. In all of these cases the aggrieved buyer learned of the breach at or after the time of performance.

Two recent Texas cases indicate that appropriate measure for buyer's damages in the anticipatory repudiation context has not been definitively decided. In *Aquamarine Associates v. Burton Shipyard*, 645 SW2d 477 (Tex App-Beaumont 1982), affd, 659 SW2d 820 (Tex 1983),

[22] Before Texas adopted the Code, its courts applied the traditional time-of-performance measure of damages in repudiation cases. By interpreting the time buyer learns of the breach to mean a commercially reasonable time after buyer learns of the repudiation, we depart from pre-Code law, although in a different manner than suggested by the dicta of *Fredonia I*. This panel, however, is not bound by dicta of a previous panel.

[23] In *Fredonia I*, the buyer, a television station, brought contract claims against the seller of broadcasting equipment. Fredonia claimed that delays in delivery and delivery of defective equipment by RCA caused Fredonia to miss its initial broadcast date and to suffer interruptions in broadcasting service. The jury found that RCA repudiated the contract by several acts or omissions — the same acts that supported other jury findings that RCA breached the contract. The *Fredonia I* court reversed the judgment on both the breach and repudiation claims. On remand, since Fredonia's contract claims were precluded by terms of the contract, the case was tried on a fraud theory. . . .

seller anticipatorily repudiated its obligation to construct and deliver ships. After seller learned of the repudiation, it covered by contracting with another party to complete the vessels. Since buyer covered under § 2.712, the jury's answer to the section 2.713 damages issue was properly disregarded. Referring to comment 5 of § 2.713, however, the Texas Court of Civil Appeals cited two cases that measured buyer's damages for anticipatory repudiation at different times. *Id.* at 479 & n 8. *Cargill, Inc. v. Stafford*, 553 F2d 1222 (10th Cir 1977), held that buyer's damages for anticipatory repudiation should be measured at a commercially reasonable time after he learned of the repudiation if he should have covered, and at the time of performance if buyer had a valid reason for failure or refusal to cover. *Id.* at 1226-27. In *Ralston Purina Co. v. McFarland*, 550 F2d 967 (4th Cir 1977), the court measured buyer's damages at the market price prevailing on the day seller anticipatorily repudiated. *Id.* at 971. The two citations in *Aquamarine* reveal uncertainty concerning the applicable time for measuring damages.

Hargrove v. Powell, 648 SW2d 372 (Tex App-San Antonio 1983, no writ), also indicates that the interpretation of § 2.713 in an anticipatory repudiation case has not been settled in Texas. In referring to the hypothetical case of seller's repudiation, the *Hargrove* court cited *Cargill* and Professor Anderson's article, which presents the argument that "time when the buyer learned of the breach" means the time for performance or later. *Id.* at 377; see Anderson, *supra*.

We do not doubt, and Texas law is clear, that market price at the time buyer learns of the breach is the appropriate measure of § 2.713 damages in cases where buyer learns of the breach at or after the time for performance. This will be the common case, for which § 2.713 was designed. See Peters, *Remedies for Breach of Contracts Relating to the Sale of Goods Under the Uniform Commercial Code: A Roadmap for Article Two*, 73 Yale LJ 199, 264 (1963). In the relatively rare case where seller anticipatorily repudiates and buyer does not cover, see Anderson, *supra*, at 318, the specific provision for anticipatory repudiation cases, § 2.610, authorizes the aggrieved party to await performance for a commercially reasonable time before resorting to his remedies of cover or damages.[24]

In the anticipatory repudiation context, the buyer's specific right to wait for a commercially reasonable time before choosing his remedy must be read together with the general damages provision of § 2.713 to extend the time for measurement beyond when buyer learns of the breach. Comment 1 to § 2.610 states that if an aggrieved party "awaits performance beyond a commercially reasonable time he cannot recover resulting damages which he should have avoided." This suggests that an aggrieved buyer can recover damages where the market rises during the commercially reasonable time he awaits performance. To interpret § 2.713's "learned of the breach" language to mean the time at which seller first communicates his anticipatory repudiation would undercut the time that § 2.610 gives the aggrieved buyer to await performance.

The buyer's option to wait a commercially reasonable time also interacts with § 2.611, which allows the seller an opportunity to retract his repudiation. Thus, an aggrieved buyer "learns of the breach" a commercially reasonable time after he learns of the seller's anticipatory repudiation. The weight of scholarly commentary supports this interpretation. See J. Calamari & J. Perillo, Contracts § 14-20 (2d ed 1977); Sebert, *Remedies Under Article Two of the Uniform Commercial Code: An Agenda for Review*, 130 U Pa L Rev 360, 372-80 (1981); Wallach, *Anticipatory Repudiation and the U.C.C.*, 13 U.C.C.LJ 48 (1980); Peters, *supra*, at 263-68.

Typically, our question will arise where parties to an executory contract are in the midst of a rising market. To the extent that market decisions are influenced by a damage rule, measuring

[24] Section 2.610 provides: [the court recites U.C.C. § 2-610].

market price at the time of seller's repudiation gives seller the ability to fix buyer's damages and may induce seller to repudiate, rather than abide by the contract. By contrast, measuring buyer's damages at the time of performance will tend to dissuade the buyer from covering, in hopes that market price will continue upward until performance time.

Allowing the aggrieved buyer a commercially reasonable time, however, provides him with an opportunity to investigate his cover possibilities in a rising market without fear that, if he is unsuccessful in obtaining cover, he will be relegated to a market-contract damage remedy measured at the time of repudiation. The Code supports this view. While cover is the preferred remedy, the Code clearly provides the option to seek damages. See § 2.712(c) [U.C.C. § 2-712(3)] & comment 3. If "[t]he buyer is always free to choose between cover and damages for non-delivery," and if § 2.712 "is not intended to limit the time necessary for [buyer] to look around and decide as to how he may best effect cover," it would be anomalous, if the buyer chooses to seek damages, to fix his damages at a time before he investigated cover possibilities and before he elected his remedy. *See id.* comment 2 & 3; *Dura-Wood Treating Co. v. Century Forest Industries, Inc.*, 675 F2d 745, 754 (5th Cir), cert. denied, 459 US 865, 103 S Ct 144, 74 L Ed 2d 122 (1982) ("buyer has some time in which to evaluate the situation"). Moreover, comment 1 to § 2.713 states, "The general baseline adopted in this section uses as a yardstick the market in which the buyer would have obtained cover had he sought that relief." See § 2.610 comment 1. When a buyer chooses not to cover, but to seek damages, the market is measured at the time he could have covered-a reasonable time after repudiation. See §§ 2.711 & 2.713.

Persuasive arguments exist for interpreting "learned of the breach" to mean "time of performance," consistent with the pre-Code rule. See J. White & R. Summers, *supra*, § 6-7; Anderson, *supra*. If this was the intention of the Code's drafters, however, phrases in § 2.610 and § 2.712 lose their meaning. If buyer is entitled to market-contract damages measured at the time of performance, it is difficult to explain why the anticipatory repudiation section limits him to a commercially reasonable time to await performance. See § 2.610 comment 1. Similarly, in a rising market, no reason would exist for requiring the buyer to act "without unreasonable delay" when he seeks to cover following an anticipatory repudiation. See § 2.712(a) [U.C.C. § 2-712(1)].

The interplay among the relevant Code sections does not permit, in this context, an interpretation that harmonizes all and leaves no loose ends. We therefore acknowledge that our interpretation fails to explain the language of § 2.723(a) insofar as it relates to aggrieved buyers. We note, however, that the section has limited applicability — cases that come to trial before the time of performance will be rare. Moreover, the comment to § 2.723 states that the "section is not intended to exclude the use of any other reasonable method of determining market price or of measuring damages. . . ." In light of the Code's persistent theme of commercial reasonableness, the prominence of cover as a remedy, and the time given an aggrieved buyer to await performance and to investigate cover before selecting his remedy, we agree with the district court that "learned of the breach" incorporates § 2.610's commercially reasonable time.[25]

[25] We note that two circuits arrived at a similar conclusion by different routes. In *Cargill, Inc. v. Stafford*, 553 F2d 1222 (10th Cir 1977), the court began its discussion of damages by embracing the "time of performance" interpretation urged by Professors White and Summers. *Id.* at 1226. Indeed, the court stated that "damages normally should be measured from the time when performance is due and not from the time when the buyer learns of repudiation." *Id.* Nevertheless, the court

> conclude[d] that under § 4-2-713 a buyer may urge continued performance for a reasonable time. At the end of a reasonable period he should cover if substitute goods are readily available. If substitution is readily available

VI. "Cover" as a Ceiling

At trial Cosden argued that Helm's purchases of polystyrene from other sources in early February constituted cover. Helm argued that those purchases were not intended to substitute for polystyrene sales canceled by Cosden. Helm, however, contended that it did cover by purchasing large amounts of high impact polystyrene from other sources late in February and around the first of March. Cosden claimed that these purchases were not made reasonably and that they should not qualify as cover. The jury found that none of Helm's purchases of polystyrene from other sources were cover purchases.

Now Cosden argues that the prices of polystyrene for the purchases that Helm claimed were cover should act as a ceiling for fixing market price under § 2.713. We refuse to accept this novel argument. Although a buyer who has truly covered may not be allowed to seek higher damages under § 2.713 than he is granted by § 2.712, see § 2.713 comment 5; J. White & R. Summers, *supra*, § 6-4 at 233-34, in this case the jury found that Helm did not cover. We cannot isolate a reason to explain the jury's finding: it might have concluded that Helm would have made the purchases regardless of Cosden's nonperformance or that the transactions did not qualify as cover for other reasons. Because of the jury's finding, we cannot use those other transactions to determine Helm's damages.

NOTES AND QUESTIONS

(1) Proposed U.C.C. § 2-711 states that it is subject to § 2-701. Section 2-701(c) states that Article 2 remedies must be liberally administered to put the aggrieved party in as good a position as if the other party had fully performed. If those remedies fail to place the aggrieved party in that position, damages may be awarded measured by the loss resulting in the ordinary course of events from the breach as determined in any manner which is reasonable. Thus, courts may protect not only the expectation interest but reliance and restitution interests where appropriate.

> and buyer does not cover within a reasonable time, damages should be based on the price at the end of that reasonable time rather than on the price when performance is due.

Id. at 1227. The *Cargill* court would employ the time of performance measure only if buyer had a valid reason for not covering.

In *First Nat'l Bank of Chicago v. Jefferson Mortgage Co.*, 576 F2d 479 (3d Cir 1978), the court initially quoted with approval legislative history that supports a literal or "plain meaning" interpretation of New Jersey's § 2-713. Nevertheless, the court hedged by interpreting that section "to measure damages within a commercial reasonable time after learning of the repudiation." *Id.* at 492. In light of the unequivocal repudiation and because cover was "easily and immediately . . .available . . .in the well-organized and easily accessible market," *id.* at 493 (quoting *Oloffson v. Coomer*, 11 Ill App 3d 918, 296 NE2d 871(1973)), a commercially reasonable time did not extend beyond the date of repudiation.

We agree with the *First National* court that "the circumstances of the particular market involved should determine the duration of a 'commercially reasonable time.' " 576 F2d at 492; see Tex Bus & Com Code § 1.204(b). In this case, however, there was no showing that cover was easily and immediately available in an organized and accessible market and that a commercially reasonable time expired on the day of Cosden's cancellation. We recognize that § 2.610's "commercially reasonable time" and § 2.712's "without unreasonable delay" are distinct concepts. Often, however, the two time periods will overlap, since the buyer can investigate cover possibilities while he awaits performance. See Sebert, *supra*, at 376-77 & n 80.

Although the jury in the present case did not fix the exact duration of a commercially reasonable time, we assume that the jury determined market price at a time commercially reasonable under all the circumstances, in light of the absence of objection to the form of the special issue.

Proposed § 2-701(e) reinforces the idea that the rights and remedies provided by Article 2 are cumulative. But the subsection goes on to say that a court may deny or limit a remedy if it would put an aggrieved party in a substantially better position than if the other party had fully performed.

Under proposed § 2-713 the measure of market damages for the buyer depends upon the type of breach by the seller. For breach other than by repudiation, the measure is that provided by present § 2-713(1). For breach by repudiation, the measure is that provided in proposed § 2-708(a)(2), that is, damage is the "market price for comparable goods prevailing at the time when a commercially reasonable period after the seller learned of the repudiation has expired less the contract price" determined at the place stated in subsection (b). Under (b) market price is determined at the place for tender; in case of rejection after arrival or revocation of acceptance, it is determined at the place of arrival.

(2) How would Proposed §§ 2-701, 2-711 and 2-713 affect the analysis and result of *Cosden Oil*?

[D] Reach the Goods Themselves

[1] Recover Identified Goods on Seller's Insolvency

Read: U.C.C. §§ 2-711(2)(a), 2-502, see § 2-501; cf. § 2-702.

Read also: U.C.C. §§ 2A-508(2)(a), 2A-522, 2A-217, cf. § 2A-525(2); CISG Arts. 45(1)(a), 46(1), 28, cf. Art. 62.

IN RE CSY YACHT CORP.

United States Bankruptcy Court, Middle District of Florida
42 BR 619, 39 U.C.C. Rep. 879 (1984)

Alexander L. Paskay, Chief Judge.

This is a Chapter 11 case and the matter under consideration is an objection by the Debtor, CSY Yacht Corporation (CSY) to claim number 72 filed by Alan R. Jaegar and Katherine Jaegar (Jaegars). The claim under challenge was filed as a priority claim in the amount of $900 and as secured in the amount of $39,100. CSY does not object to the priority claim asserted under § 507(a)(5) of the Bankruptcy Code nor to the allowance of an unsecured claim for $37,000, but does object to the claim as secured. The Jaegars claim secured status of this claim on the basis that they have a special property interest in CSY's materials, supplies and parts inventory pursuant to Fla Stat § 672.502 (1981).

The matter came on for hearing and the parties, by stipulation, created the record through submission of depositions. The facts as adduced from the record as created and pertinent to resolution of the matter may be summarized as follows:

At the time pertinent to the transaction under consideration, CSY was engaged in the business of manufacturing and selling sailing yachts. The Jaegars became interested in purchasing a yacht from CSY after attending a sailing school conducted by one of CSY's affiliates. Before executing the sales contract, the Jaegars paid an initial deposit of $1,000 to CSY in August of 1980 and a second deposit of $4,000 on February 5, 1981 toward the purchase of a 44 foot cutter to be constructed by CSY for a total purchase price of $176,111. On February 24, 1981, the Jaegars executed the sale purchase agreement with CSY and pursuant to the agreement paid an additional $35,000 towards the purchase price of the yacht.

CSY was in poor financial condition and by the spring of 1981 following the receipt of the Jaegars' $35,000, CSY ceased constructing any new yachts. The Jaegars' yacht was one of several yachts which were never started.

On August 28, 1981, CSY filed its petition for relief pursuant to Chapter 11 of the Bankruptcy Code. While operating as a debtor in possession, CSY completed the yachts which were already under construction at the time of the commencement of the case and then proceeded to sell its unneeded inventory. Notice of Sale was sent to all interested parties and creditors of CSY. The Notice provided that the items would be sold free and clear of all liens and any liens or claims against the items sold would attach to the proceeds of the sale. In February, 1982, the sale was concluded.

The Jaegars did not file their claim contending a secured position until March 29, 1982. It is without dispute that the Jaegars do not have a security agreement nor did they file a financing statement pursuant to § 679.302 in order to perfect a security interest under Article 9 of the U.C.C. as adopted in this state by Florida Statute § 679.101. The basis for the Jaegars' asserted secured claim is based on paragraph 14 of the sales and purchase agreement which provides as follows:

> The boat and all materials, engines and equipment attached to the boat or any material in the possession of the builder and designated for use on the boat shall become the property of the purchaser upon the payment of the first installment. The boat and all the materials, engines and equipment in the possession of the builder shall be subject to a lien in favor of the builder as against the purchaser. In the event of any rejection of any materials or equipment by the purchaser, title to such goods will revest in the builder.

It is Jaegars' position that they have a right to recover goods from CSY as an insolvent seller under Fla Stat § 672.502 and that this right was transferred to the proceeds of the sale under the notice of the sale. Fla Stat § 672.502 provides as follows: [the Court quotes U.C.C. § 2-502].

In order for a buyer to recover goods in the seller's possession after the seller has become insolvent, several elements must be present. The buyer must (1) have a special property interest in the goods under Fla Stat 672.501; (2) have paid part or all of the purchase price; and (3) keep good a tender of any unpaid portion of the purchase price. Additionally, the seller must become insolvent within ten days following the receipt of the first installment of the purchase price. 3A Bender's Uniform Comm Code Serv, § 14.03[2] (1983).

There is no dispute that the Jaegars paid part of the purchase price or that they were willing to keep good a tender for the remaining balance. The only issues to be resolved are whether the Jaegars have a special property interest in the goods and whether CSY became insolvent within ten days of receiving the $35,000 installment.

In order to determine if the Jaegars have a special property interest in the goods, it is necessary to refer to Fla Stat § 672.501 (1)(a) and (b) which provides as follows: [the Court quotes U.C.C. § 2-501(a) and (b)].

According to Fla Stat § 672.501, the buyer obtains a special property interest when the goods are identified. In the present case the Jaegars contracted to purchase a yacht to be built in the future. Pursuant to paragraph 14 of that contract, the boat and all materials, engines and equipment attached to the boat would become property of the Jaegars upon payment of the first installment. Since construction of the boat never commenced there were obviously no materials, engines or equipment attached to the boat.

As noted earlier, Paragraph 14 of the contract further provides that any materials designated for use on the boat shall become property of the Jaegars upon payment of the first installment. The Jaegars contend that this provision is inconsistent with Paragraph 3(b) which requires the installment to be paid at least 30 days prior to construction of the hull, unless CSY designated the materials to be incorporated into the boat from its inventory when it received the first installment.

Paragraph 3(b) merely requires that 30% of the purchase price be paid before construction will begin. Identification is governed by paragraph 14 which occurs when the materials were "designated" by CSY Nothing in the record indicates that the materials were set aside or ever designated for the Jaegars' yacht.

In the alternative, the Jaegars take the position that the materials and inventory of CSY constitute a tangible bulk and that reference to the materials in the contract is for an undivided share of the fungible bulk which is sufficient to establish identification for purposes of U.C.C. § 2-501. In support of their position, the Jaegars rely on Comment 5 of U.C.C. § 2-501 which provides as follows:

> 5. Undivided shares in an identified fungible bulk, such as grain in an elevator or oil in a storage tank, can be sold. The mere making of the contract with reference to an undivided share in an identified fungible bulk is enough under subsection (a) to effect an identification if there is no explicit agreement otherwise.

The Jaegars' reliance on Comment 5 is misplaced. The contract did not refer to an identified fungible bulk such as 35,000 pounds of fiberglass and resin. Rather, the contract explicitly referred to those materials "designated" for use on the Jaegars' yacht. As a result, this court is satisfied that the Jaegars' contention is without merit.

In light of the foregoing, the court is satisfied that the materials were never identified so as to create a special property interest pursuant to U.C.C. § 2-501. As a result, the Jaegars cannot recover any property from CSY under U.C.C. § 2-502.

This being the case, it is unnecessary to address the question of whether CSY became insolvent within ten days after it received the $35,000 installment from the Jaegars.

A separate final judgment will be entered in accordance with the foregoing.

NOTE

The scope of proposed § 2-502 has been expanded. Under revised § 2-502 a pre-paying buyer can recover identified goods, whether or not conforming, from a seller, whether or not insolvent, who repudiates or fails to deliver upon making and keeping a tender of full performance.

[2] Obtain Specific Performance or Replevy the Goods

Read: U.C.C. §§ 2-711(2)(b), 2-716; see §§ 2-306, 2-501; cf.§ 2-709(1)(b).

Read also: U.C.C. §§ 2A-508(2)(b), 2A-521, 2A-217, cf. § 2A-529(1)(b); CISG Arts. 45(1)(a), 46(1), 28, cf. Art. 62.

SEDMAK v. CHARLIE'S CHEVROLET, INC.

Missouri Court of Appeals
622 S.W.2d 694, 31 U.C.C. Rep. 851 (1981)

SATZ, J.

This is an appeal from a decree of specific performance. We affirm.

In their petition, plaintiffs, Dr. and Mrs. Sedmak (Sedmaks), alleged they entered into a contract with defendant, Charlie's Chevrolet, Inc. (Charlie's), to purchase a Corvette automobile for approximately $15,000.00. The Corvette was one of a limited number manufactured to commemorate the selection of the Corvette as the Pace Car for the Indianapolis 500. Charlie's breached the contract, the Sedmaks alleged, when, after the automobile was delivered, an agent for Charlie's told the Sedmaks they could not purchase the automobile for $15,000.00 but would have to bid on it.

The trial court found the parties entered into an oral contract and also found the contract was excepted from the Statute of Frauds. The court then ordered Charlie's to make the automobile "available for delivery" to the Sedmaks.

Charlie's raises three points on appeal: (1) the existence of an oral contract is not supported by the credible evidence; (2) if an oral contract exists, it is unenforceable because of the Statute of Frauds; and (3) specific performance is an improper remedy because the Sedmaks did not show their legal remedies were inadequate. . . .

[T]he record reflects the Sedmaks to be automobile enthusiasts, who, at the time of trial, owned six Corvettes. In July, 1977, "Vette Vues," a Corvette fancier's magazine to which Dr. Sedmak subscribed, published an article announcing Chevrolet's tentative plans to manufacture a limited edition of the Corvette. The limited edition of approximately 6,000 automobiles was to commemorate the selection of the Corvette as the Indianapolis 500 Pace Car. The Sedmaks were interested in acquiring one of these Pace Cars to add to their Corvette collection. In November, 1977, the Sedmaks asked Tom Kells, sales manager at Charlie's Chevrolet, about the availability of the Pace Car. Mr. Kells said he did not have any information on the car but would find out about it. Kells also said if Charlie's were to receive a Pace Car, the Sedmaks could purchase it.

On January 9, 1978, Dr. Sedmak telephoned Kells to ask him if a Pace Car could be ordered. Kells indicated that he would require a deposit on the car, so Mrs. Sedmak went to Charlie's and gave Kells a check for $500.00. She was given a receipt for that amount bearing the names of Kells and Charlie's Chevrolet, Inc. At that time, Kells had a pre-order form listing both standard equipment and options available on the Pace Car. Prior to tendering the deposit, Mrs. Sedmak asked Kells if she and Dr. Sedmak were "definitely going to be the owners." Kells replied, "yes." After the deposit had been paid, Mrs. Sedmak stated if the car was going to be theirs, her husband wanted some changes made to the stock model. She asked Kells to order the car equipped with an L82 engine, four speed standard transmission and AM/FM radio with tape deck. Kells said that he would try to arrange with the manufacturer for these changes. Kells was able to make the changes, and, when the car arrived, it was equipped as the Sedmaks had requested.

Kells informed Mrs. Sedmak that the price of the Pace Car would be the manufacturer's retail price, approximately $15,000.00. The dollar figure could not be quoted more precisely because

Kells was not sure what the ordered changes would cost, nor was he sure what the "appearance package" — decals, a special paint job — would cost. Kells also told Mrs. Sedmak that, after the changes had been made, a "contract" — a retail dealer's order form — would be mailed to them. However, no form or written contract was mailed to the Sedmaks by Charlie's.

On January 25, 1978, the Sedmaks visited Charlie's to take delivery on another Corvette. At that time, the Sedmaks asked Kells whether he knew anything further about the arrival date of the Pace Car. Kells replied he had no further information but he would let the Sedmaks know when the car arrived. Kells also requested that Charlie's be allowed to keep the car in their showroom for promotional purposes until after the Indianapolis 500 Race. The Sedmaks agreed to this arrangement.

On April 3, 1978, the Sedmaks were notified by Kells that the Pace Car had arrived. Kells told the Sedmaks they could not purchase the car for the manufacturer's retail price because demand for the car had inflated its value beyond the suggested price. Kells also told the Sedmaks they could bid on the car. The Sedmaks did not submit a bid. They filed this suit for specific performance.

Mr. Kells' testimony about his conversations with the Sedmaks regarding the Pace Car differed markedly from the Sedmaks' testimony. Kells stated that he had no definite price information on the Pace Car until a day or two prior to its arrival at Charlie's. He denied ever discussing the purchase price of the car with the Sedmaks. He admitted, however, that after talking with the Sedmaks on January 9, 1978,[26] he telephoned the zone manager and requested changes be made to the Pace Car. He denied the changes were made pursuant to Dr. Sedmak's order. He claimed the changes were made because they were "more favorable to the automobile" and were changes Dr. Sedmak "preferred." In ordering the changes, Kells said he was merely taking Dr. Sedmak's advice because he was a "very knowledgeable man on the Corvette." There is no dispute, however, that when the Pace Car arrived, it was equipped with the options requested by Dr. Sedmak.

Mr. Kells also denied the receipt for $500.00 given him by Mrs. Sedmak on January 9, 1978, was a receipt for a deposit on the Pace Car. On direct examination, he said he "accepted a five hundred dollar ($500) deposit from the Sedmaks to assure them the first opportunity of purchasing the car." On cross-examination, he said: "We were accepting bids and with the five hundred dollar ($500) deposit it was to give them the first opportunity to bid on the car." Then after acknowledging that other bidders had not paid for the opportunity to bid, he explained the deposit gave the Sedmaks the "last opportunity" to make the final bid. Based on this evidence, the trial court found the parties entered into an oral contract for the purchase and sale of the Pace Car at the manufacturer's suggested retail price.

Charlie's first contends the Sedmaks' evidence is "so wrought with inconsistencies and contradictions that a finding of an oral contract for the sale of a Pace Car at the manufacturer's suggested retail price is clearly against the weight of the evidence." We disagree. The trial court chose to believe the Sedmaks' testimony over that of Mr. Kells and the reasonableness of this belief was not vitiated by any real contradictions in the Sedmaks' testimony. Charlie's examples of conflict are either facially not contradictory or easily reconcilable.

Although not clearly stated in this point or explicitly articulated in its argument, Charlie's also appears to argue there was no contract because the parties did not agree to a price. The

[26] According to Kells' testimony, both Mr. and Mrs. Sedmak visited Charlie's on January 9, 1978. Mrs. Sedmak testified only she visited Charlie's on that date.

trial court concluded "[t]he price was to be the suggested retail price of the automobile at the time of delivery." Apparently, Charlie's argues that if this were the agreed to price, it is legally insufficient to support a contract because the manufacturer's suggested retail price is not a mandatory, fixed and definite selling price but, rather, as the term implies, it is merely a suggested price which does not accurately reflect the market and the actual selling price of automobiles. Charlie's argument is misdirected and, thus, misses the mark.

Without again detailing the facts, there was evidence to support the trial court's conclusion that the parties agreed the selling price would be the price suggested by the manufacturer. Whether this price accurately reflects the market demands on any given day is immaterial. The manufacturer's suggested retail price is ascertainable and, thus, if the parties choose, sufficiently definite to meet the price requirements of an enforceable contract. Failure to specify the selling price in dollars and cents did not render the contract void or voidable. . . . See also, § 400.2-305 RSMo 1978. As long as the parties agreed to a method by which the price was to be determined and as long as the price could be ascertained at the time of performance, the price requirement for a valid and enforceable contract was satisfied. See . . .§ 400.2-305 RSMo 1978. This point is without merit.

Charlie's next complains that if there were an oral contract, it is unenforceable under the Statute of Frauds. . . .

. . . .

We hold, therefore, that where, as here, there is no dispute as to quantity, part payment for a single, indivisible commercial unit validates an oral contract under § 400.2-201(3)(c) RSMo 1978.

Finally, Charlie's contends the Sedmaks failed to show they were entitled to specific performance of the contract. We disagree. Although it has been stated that the determination whether to order specific performance lies within the discretion of the trial court, this discretion is, in fact, quite narrow. When the relevant equitable principles have been met and the contract is fair and plain, "specific performance goes as a matter of right." Here, the trial court ordered specific performance because it concluded the Sedmaks "have no adequate remedy at law for the reason that they cannot go upon the open market and purchase an automobile of this kind with the same mileage, condition, ownership and appearance as the automobile involved in this case, except, if at all, with considerable expense, trouble, loss, great delay and inconvenience." Contrary to defendant's complaint, this is a correct expression of the relevant law and it is supported by the evidence.

Under the Code, the court may decree specific performance as a buyer's remedy for breach of contract to sell goods "where the goods are unique or in other proper circumstances." § 400.2-716(l) RSMo 1978. The general term "in other proper circumstances" expresses the drafters' intent to "further a more liberal attitude than some courts have shown in connection with the specific performance of contracts of sale." § 400.2-716, U.C.C., Comment 1. This Comment was not directed to the courts of this state, for long before the Code, we, in Missouri, took a practical approach in determining whether specific performance would lie for the breach of contract for the sale of goods and did not limit this relief only to the sale of unique goods. *Boeving v. Vandover*, 218 SW2d 175 (Mo App 1945). In *Boeving*, plaintiff contracted to buy a car from defendant. When the car arrived, defendant refused to sell. The car was not unique in the traditional legal sense but, at that time, all cars were difficult to obtain because of war-time shortages. The court held specific performance was the proper remedy for plaintiff because a new car "could not be obtained elsewhere except at considerable expense, trouble or loss, which cannot be estimated in advance and under such circumstances [plaintiff] did not have an adequate remedy at law." *Id.* at 177-178. Thus, *Boeving* presaged the broad and liberalized language of § 400.2-716(1) and exemplifies one of the "other proper circumstances" contemplated by this subsection for ordering specific performance. § 400.2-716, Missouri Code Comment 1. The present facts track those in *Boeving*.

The Pace Car, like the car in *Boeving*, was not unique in the traditional legal sense. It was not an heirloom or, arguably, not one of a kind. However, its "mileage, condition, ownership and appearance" did make it difficult, if not impossible, to obtain its replication without considerable expense, delay and inconvenience. Admittedly, 6,000 Pace Cars were produced by Chevrolet. However, as the record reflects, this is limited production. In addition, only one of these cars was available to each dealer, and only a limited number of these were equipped with the specific options ordered by plaintiffs. Charlie's had not received a car like the Pace Car in the previous two years. The sticker price for the car was $14,284.21. Yet Charlie's received offers from individuals in Hawaii and Florida to buy the Pace Car for $24,000.00 and $28,000.00 respectively. As sensibly inferred by the trial court, the location and size of these offers demonstrated this limited edition was in short supply and great demand. We agree, with the trial court. This case was a "proper circumstance" for ordering specific performance.

Judgment affirmed.

NOTES

(1) In *Schweber v. Rallye Motors, Inc*, 12 U.C.C. Rep. 1154 (N.Y. Sup. Ct. 1973), buyer sought specific performance and an injunction to restrain seller from selling or transferring to a third party a 1973 Rolls Royce Corniche auto. The court believed the circumstance of the case justified the relief of specific performance, citing U.C.C. § 2-716(1), "where the goods are unique, *or in other proper circumstances*." *Cf. Bander v. Grossman,* 611 N.Y.S.2d 985, 23 U.C.C. Rep. 2d 1159 (1994) where buyer contracted to purchase a rare Astin-Martin automobile. The court held that it would be inequitable and improper to grant specific performance in the form of a constructive trust upon the proceeds of the sale of the auto to a third party.

In *Scholl v. Hartzell*, 33 U.C.C. Rep. 951 (Pa. Ct. Com. Pl. 1981), the court stated that although a 1962 Chevrolet Corvette may be considered by many a collector's item, it is not one of the unique goods contemplated by U.C.C. § 2-716(1). Also, buyer did not allege he was unable to cover; accordingly, buyer's action did not lie in replevin per U.C.C. § 2-716(3).

In *Tatum v. Richter*, 373 A.2d 923 (Md. 1977), Richter contracted to purchase a 1971 Ferrari Daytona coupe for $17,500, paying more than $15,000 down in the form of a personal check for $7,500 and a bank cashier's check for $7524.10. Both checks referred to the 1971 Ferrari by its serial number. When the car arrived in the hands of the dealer, excuses were made for nondelivery. Richter secured possession of the car in a replevin action. "Once the car was identified to the contract, § 2-716(3), Richter had a right of replevin, because he was unable to effect cover, and there was no other way to protect himself against the loss of his deposit." 373 A.2d at 926. *See also, King Aircraft Sales, Inc. v. Lane*, 846 P.2d 550, 22 U.C.C. Rep. 2d 515 (Wash. App. 1993) (The airplanes, although not necessarily unique, were rare enough to make the ability to cover virtually impossible).

(2) The energy crisis, with its attendant shortages of commodities such as oil and natural gas and unprecedented price increases, resulted in threats by suppliers to cease deliveries, particularly under contracts entered into at a time when the suppliers failed to foresee the magnitude of price increases. The courts have been willing to grant specific performance of these contracts, not because the goods are unique, but because of "other proper circumstances," *i.e.*, that "chaos and irreparable damage" would result, or that it would be difficult or impossible to find another supplier willing to enter into a long-term supply contract. *See, e.g., Laclede Gas Co. v. Amoco Oil Co.*, 522 F.2d 33 (8th Cir. 1975); *Iowa Electric Light & Power Co. v. Atlas Corp.*, 467 F. Supp. 129 (N.D. Iowa 1978); *Eastern Air Lines, Inc. v. Gulf Oil Corp.*, 415 F. Supp. 429 (S.D. Fla. 1975); *Missouri Public Service Co. v. Peabody Coal Co.*, 583 S.W.2d 721 (Mo. App. 1979); compare *Columbia Gas Transmission Corp. v. Larry H. Wright, Inc.*, 443 F. Supp. 14 (S.D. Ohio 1977).

(3) U.C.C. § 2-716(2) states: "The decree for specific performance may include such terms and conditions as to payment of the price, damages, or other relief as the court may deem just." In *Iowa Electric Light & Power Co. v. Atlas Corp.*, 467 F. Supp. 129, 135 (N.D. Iowa 1978), an action resulting from an enormous increase in the market price of uranium concentrate ("yellowcake"), the court at first indicated that this section "would allow this court to equitably adjust the price of the disputed U308." In a supplemental opinion the court reversed itself, declaring that this section does not permit the court "to adjust the price in favor of seller to balance the equities of specific performance." 467 F. Supp. at 138.

(4) Under proposed § 2-716(a), a court may order specific performance if the parties have expressly agreed in the contract for sale. *Cf.* CISG Articles 28 and 46.

§ 7.05 Buyer's Remedies Where Goods Finally Accepted

[A] Buyer's Damages for Breach

Read: U.C.C. § 2-714; see § 2-607(1).

Read also: U.C.C. §§ 2A-508(3) and (4), 2A-519(3) and (4), 2A-520, see § 2A-516(1); CISG Arts. 50, 74.

WINCHESTER v. McCULLOCH BROTHERS GARAGE, INC.

Alabama Supreme Court
388 So. 2d 927 30 U.C.C. Rep. 212 (1980)

TORBERT, CHIEF JUSTICE.

This is a breach of warranty case under the Alabama version of the Uniform Commercial Code. The facts in this case are stated in the dissenting opinion of Mr. Justice Faulkner and need not be repeated.

Code 1975, §§ 7-2-316(4), -719(1), provides that a seller may contractually limit his buyer's remedies for breach of warranty. The warranty given by the defendants in this case was the type typically given — the vehicle warranty expressly limited the buyer's remedy to repair or replacement of defective parts and disclaimed liability for incidental and consequential damages. As a result of the limitation sanctioned by § 7-2-719, the jury must find that the limited warranty failed of its essential purpose before it can proceed to award damages other than as provided in the limited warranty. See Code 1975, § 7-2-719(2).

Since testimony revealed that the cost to repair the Jeep was around $1,200, we believe that the jury concluded the warranty failed of its essential purpose. Furthermore, we find the facts reasonably support the jury's conclusion. Where a seller refused to honor its own limited warranty, that warranty may properly be found to fail by reason of § 7-2-719(2).

Because the jury presumably found the contractual remedy ineffective, the buyer is entitled to other remedies provided in the Code. Code 1975, § 7-2-714(2), (3), sets down the general rule in breach of warranty cases: [the court quotes U.C.C. § 2-714(2), (3)]. According to the statute, damages are normally the difference between the value of the goods as warranted and the value as delivered, plus incidental and consequential damages.

The purchase price is evidence of the value of the goods as warranted. However, it is often difficult to ascertain the value of the goods as delivered. For this reason, where the goods are repairable, cost to repair is a useful measure of the difference in values. See J. White & R. Summers, Handbook of The Law Under The Uniform Commercial Code § 10-2(1972) [§10-2 (2d ed. 1980)].

Under the authority of §§ 7-2-714(3), -715, plaintiff buyer may also claim consequential damages. Evidence adduced at trial shows the plaintiff spent $1,000 for an expert witness. Here, however, expenses of trial preparation are not consequential damages.

Plaintiff also produced evidence that the reasonable rental value of an automobile was $15 per day, but plaintiff did not rent an automobile. He borrowed an automobile for two days, and then he purchased a substitute means of transportation. Although the plaintiff's purchase of the replacement automobile may have been more than was reasonably required at the time, plaintiff chose to buy the substitute car. Recovery for consequential damages is allowed only to the extent the buyer suffers actual damage, and since the plaintiff borrowed, then bought, another car, the rental cost of a substitute car is not an item of damage.

Applying the foregoing rules to this case, it is apparent the jury verdict was excessive. We recognize the amount of damages is left largely to the jury, but the jury may not ignore the statutory standards by which to measure plaintiff's damages. In the unlikely event the truck could not be repaired and had no salvage value, the difference in the value of the truck as accepted and its value as warranted can be no more than $8,225, the cost of the truck. Since no includable consequential damage was shown, the total award could not exceed $8,225, and the jury award of $20,000 was certainly improper.

The trial judge recognized the impropriety of the jury award and ordered a new trial unless the plaintiff consented to remittitur. Under the facts, his order was undoubtedly not an abuse of discretion; The order is due to be affirmed.

Affirmed.

MADDOX, ALMON, SHORES, EMBRY AND BEATTY, JJ., concur.

FAULKNER, J., with whom JONES, J., concurs, dissents.

FAULKNER, JUSTICE (dissenting).

This is an appeal from a judgment of the Circuit Court of Lawrence County granting a motion for new trial unless Winchester remitted $15,100 of a jury verdict of $20,000 damages awarded him in a suit for breach of warranty of a Jeep motor vehicle. I would reverse and render.

In February, 1978, James Winchester traded a 1978 Chevrolet four-wheel drive vehicle with one of the McCulloch brothers, owners of McCulloch Brothers Jeep dealership in Decatur, for a 1978 Jeep Honcho vehicle. He paid, in cash the day of the sale, the difference in price between the two vehicles, $485.00. This vehicle was used to drive back and forth to work each day, a trip between Hillsboro and Decatur. Mr. Winchester owned no other automobile.

On March 4, while driving the Jeep, having only 692 miles on it, Winchester felt a hard jolt and the Jeep fell down in the rear. It pulled to the left-hand side of the road and ran off the road into a ditch and hit a mailbox. He finally got it straightened up and went directly up the ditch. While the Jeep was being removed by the wrecker, he noticed that the rear leaf spring on the driver's side had broken completely loose from where it was attached to the frame and was hanging loose. The drive shaft had come out of the Jeep, having been broken at the universal joint and having slipped out of the transmission. The vehicle was taken to Moulton and after McCulloch Brothers was called and Hoss McCulloch was told of the problem, the Jeep was taken to McCulloch Brothers dealership. After talking with McCulloch Brothers later, he was told the North Alabama adjuster had told them not to fix the Jeep. He called the adjuster in Nashville and the factory in Detroit and received no satisfaction. Two days after this incident in which the Jeep was wrecked, Winchester purchased a 1975 car and paid $2,556.00 for it in order to have a car to drive to work. Rental cost of a car would have been $15.00 a day and at the time of the trial, 435 days after the wreck, rental could have been $6,525.00.

On May 18, Winchester filed suit against the McCulloch Brothers, AMC, American Motors Sales Corporation, and Jeep Corp., for breach of warranty. The complaint was later amended to include a count under the Alabama Extended Manufacturers Liability Doctrine. At trial Winchester presented expert testimony that the leaf spring was defectively made. The jury returned a verdict for Winchester in the amount of $20,000.00. Defendants filed a motion for new trial and in the alternative for judgment notwithstanding the verdict, asserting that the excessive verdict exhibited bias against the defendants and the damages were not supported by the evidence. The trial judge ordered a remittitur as to all defendants in the amount of $15,000.00 or a new trial. Winchester initially accepted the remittitur, believing the amount remitted was to be $4,900.00, but later struck consent to the remittitur and appeals.

The sole issue before this Court is whether the trial judge abused his discretion by ordering the remittitur.

The evidence shows the following proof relating to damages: Winchester purchased the Jeep for $8,225.00. To pay this, he traded in a Chevrolet, and paid $485.00 cash. Two days after the accident, Winchester bought another automobile for $2,556.00. He introduced evidence that the fair rental value of a vehicle was $15.00 per day, and he claimed loss of 435 days $6,525.00 The cost to repair the Jeep was estimated to be $1,200.00. (It was never repaired.) Winchester paid a metallurgist $1,000.00 to testify as an expert witness at the trial.

Section 7-2-714, Code 1975, provides that the measure of damages for breach of warranty is the difference at the time and place of acceptance between the value of the goods accepted, and the value they would have had if they had been as warranted. Here, the only evidence presented as to the value of the Jeep when accepted was its purchase price. The Court of Civil Appeals held that the purchase price of personal property is admissible as going to the value of the property, and in the absence of other evidence, it is sufficient. In *Riley v. Ford Motor Company,* 442 F.2d 670 (1971), the Fifth Circuit permitted evidence of purchase price as going to the value, but there the owner testified that the property made the basis of a breach of warranty action was useless to him.

Because there was no evidence of value introduced other than the purchase price of the Jeep, we take that as a starting point to assess damages. The purchase price was $8,225.00, and it was obviously useless in its present condition at the time of the trial. In fact it was sitting on jacks — none of the defendants would agree to repair it. Therefore, I would find that the purchase price is an element of damages. Next, Winchester, when he had no automobile to go to his place of employment, had to buy another vehicle as a substitute means of transportation. I opine that this is another element of damages. Cf. *Riley*, where substitute transportation was permitted as an element of damages.

I would hold that Winchester's damages should be $10,781.00 instead of $4,900.00 as found by the trial judge. With this award he would be placed in the same economic condition as he was in at the time he purchased the Jeep.

JONES, J., concurs.

NOTES

(1) Several states have enacted automobile "lemon laws." Note particularly Mich.Comp.Laws Ann. § 257.1403, subsection (1):

> (1) If a defect or condition which was reported to the manufacturer or new motor vehicle dealer pursuant to section 2 continues to exist and the new motor vehicle has been subject to a reasonable number of repairs as determined under subsection (3), the manufacturer shall within 30 days have the option to either replace the new motor vehicle with a comparable replacement motor vehicle currently in production and acceptable to the consumer or accept return of the vehicle and refund to the consumer the full purchase price including the cost of any options or other modifications installed or made by or for the manufacturer, and the amount of all other charges made by or for the manufacturer, less a reasonable allowance for the consumer's use of the vehicle not exceeding 10 cents per mile driven at the time of the initial report of the same defect or conditions or 10%, of the purchase price of the vehicle, whichever is less, and less an amount equal to any appraised damage that is not attributable to normal use or to the defect or condition. A reasonable allowance for use is that amount directly attributable to use by the consumer and any previous consumer prior to his or her first report of a defect or condition that impairs the use or value of the new motor vehicle to the manufacturer, its agents, or the new motor vehicle dealer. Whenever a vehicle is replaced or refunded under the provisions of this section, in those instances in which towing services and rental vehicles were not made available without cost to the consumer, the manufacturer shall also reimburse the consumer for those towing costs and reasonable costs for a comparable rental vehicle that were incurred as a direct result of the defect or condition.

(2) *See Davis Industrial Sales, Inc. v. Workman Construction Co.,* 856 S.W.2d 355, 21 U.C.C. Rep. 2d 607 (Mo. App. 1993) (Section 2-714(2) formula is the difference between the value

of goods as accepted and the value of goods as warranted. Value of forklift in the condition warranted was its sales price of $8,400; cost of repair was $3,500. A useful objective measurement of the difference in values is the cost of repair or replacement).

(3) The court in *Nelson v. Logan Motor Sales, Inc.*, 370 S.E.2d 734 at 737 (W.Va. 1988) remarked:

> Our ruling in *Mountaineer Contractors* is in accord with the generally accepted view that the damage formula provided in Code, 46-2-714(2) "works fairly smoothly where the buyer replaces the defective goods. The cost of repair is strong evidence of the difference between the value they would have had if they had been as warranted . . . . In most cases damages can be determined based on estimates of what it would cost to repair or replace." 3 W. Hawkland, U.C.C. Series § 2-174:04 and cases cited therein (1984).

(4) *But see Santor v. A and M Karagheusian, Inc.*, 207 A.2d 305, 2 U.C.C. Rep. 599 (N.J. 1965) (defective carpeting — purchase price $14 per square yard; salvage value $3 to $4 per square yard. Measure of damages: difference between price paid and actual market value of defective carpeting at the time buyer knew or should have known that it was defective).

HILL v. BASF WYANDOTTE CORP.

Supreme Court of South Carolina
311 S.E.2d 734 (1984)

LITTLEJOHN, JUSTICE:

This case comes before us as a certified question from the United States District Court, District of South Carolina.

The question presented is as follows:

> Given the distinction between (1) actual or direct and (2) consequential damages as set forth in §§ 36-2-714 and 36-2-715 of the South Carolina Code of Laws, 1976, as amended, what is the measure of actual damages in a herbicide failure case where there is a valid limitation of consequential, special or indirect damages?

This is a breach of warranty case involving an alleged herbicide failure which caused crop damage.

Plaintiff Hill (Farmer) purchased a quantity of the herbicide, Basalin, from a retail distributor. Basalin is manufactured by defendant BASF Wyandotte Corporation (BWC).

Among other things, to each can of Basalin there were attached the following statements:

1) "BWC" warrants that this product conforms to the chemical description on the label and is reasonably fit for the purpose referred to in the Directions for Use subject to the inherent risks to above.

2) In no case shall "BWC" or the Seller be liable for consequential, special or indirect damages resulting from the use or handling of this product, and

3) Read "CONDITIONS OF SALE AND WARRANTY" before buying or using. If terms are not acceptable, return product at once, unopened.

Farmer alleges that he used Basalin on approximately 1,450 acres of soybeans and another herbicide, Treflan, on approximately 200 acres. He further alleges that although there was a severe drought that year, the Treflan treated crops were significantly better than the Basalin crops both in quality and yield per acre.

Farmer initially brought suit in United States District Court on oral and written warranties for damages. A jury awarded him $207,725.00. BWC appealed and the Fourth Circuit Court of Appeals reversed and remanded the case, holding that only the written warranties on the labels of the product apply and that the limitation of remedies quoted above is valid. *Hill v. BASF Wyandotte Corp.*, 696 F.2d 287 (4th Cir. 1982).

In footnote 6 the court stated:

> We express no opinion as to whether under subsections (1) and (2) of § 36-2-714 and on the evidence that may be adduced on retrial the appropriate measure of damages would be the purchase price of the herbicide or some other measure.

This question was certified to us by the trial court after remand.

Ordinarily, *S.C. Code Ann.* § 36-2-714(2) (1976) is controlling as the measure of damages in a breach of warranty case. This section provides:

> (2) The measure of damages for breach of warranty is the difference at the time and place of acceptance between the value of the goods accepted and the value they would have had if they had been as warranted, *unless special circumstances show proximate damages of a different amount.* (Emphasis added.)

We find that the formula in this subsection is inapplicable to a herbicide failure case. This formula is most appropriate where the nonconforming good can be repaired or replaced and value (both as warranted and as accepted) can be defined with certainty.

A herbicide failure is a latent defect in the product. There is no reasonable way a farmer can determine in advance whether a herbicide will perform as warranted. Discovery of the problem must await the development of the crop at which time it is usually too late to correct.

The value of a herbicide as warranted is difficult to define. Price and value are not equivalents. From the farmer's perspective, the value of the herbicide is a healthy crop at maturity. In the manufacturer's viewpoint, the value is its selling price.

The value as accepted is equally uncertain and difficult to define. There is no market for such goods and thus no market price. If anything, it has a negative value.

In our view, the inability of a court to ascertain with certainty the value of goods both as warranted and as accepted creates a special circumstance within the meaning of § 36-2-714(2). It is this special circumstance which removes cases of this type from the § 36-2-714(2) measure of damages into subsection (1).

Subsection (1) provides: [The court cites U.C.C. § 2-714(1).]

Official Comment 2 to § 36-2-714 indicates that subsection (1) is applicable in breach of warranty cases.

It has consistently been held by this Court that the measure of actual damages, in cases similar to this, is the value the crop would have had if the product had conformed to the warranty less the value of the crop actually produced, less the expense of preparing for market the portion of the probable crop prevented from maturing. [Citations.] We hold this formula to be appropriate in the present case.

BWC has argued that this formula includes lost profits and that lost profits are a consequential damage barred by the limitation of remedies on the cans of Basalin. We disagree.

In *W.R. Grace and Co., supra*, it was noted that the ". . .destruction or loss of a mature crop, which has a realizable value in excess of the cost of harvesting, processing and marketing, results in a monetary loss to the owner, regardless of whether the farming operation would, otherwise, have been profitable."

If the measure of damages we have adopted includes an element of lost profits, such inclusion is merely coincidental as the measure covers the direct loss resulting in the ordinary course of events from the alleged breach of the warranty. See, § 36-2-714(1).

The foregoing is the order of this Court.

LEWIS, C.J., and NESS, GREGORY and HARWELL, J.J., concur.

NOTES

(1) "Special circumstances" under § 2-714(2) have also been found where after acceptance of defective goods by the buyer, the seller has repaired some of the defects. Thus, in *Stutts v. Green Ford, Inc.*, 267 S.E.2d 919, 926 (N.C.App. 1980), the court said:

> [T]he date of acceptance preceded the time when numerous repairs were made in full compliance with the warranty. At the end of the warranty period, the only nonconformity of which plaintiff complains and of which there is evidence of defective parts or workmanship is the oil leakage. Under the special facts of this case, we hold, then, that an appropriate measure of damages would be the difference in the fair market value of the truck in its condition at the time and place of acceptance, increased by the value of repairs and replacements made in compliance with the warranty, and its fair market value had it been as warranted. . . . This, in effect, would permit plaintiff to recover damages compensating him for the loss in value due to the persistent oil problem, while preventing him from receiving windfall damages for defects which were subsequently successfully repaired.

(2) *Nelson v. Logan Motor Sales Inc.*, 370 S.E.2d 734 at 378 note 8 (W.Va. 1988), points out other "special circumstances":

> Examples of true "special circumstances" cases, where the formula was found wholly inadequate and other means of proving damages were approved are: *Hirst v. Elgin Metal Casket Co.*, 438 F. Supp. 906 (D.C.Mont.1977) (Damages for breach of expressed warranty for a "leak-proof casket" are the pain and suffering of the decedent's relatives when viewing a moldy corpse upon exhumation); *Baden v. Curtiss*, 380 F. Supp. 243 (D.C.Mont.1977) (Damages

for breach of implied warranty of merchantability of defective bull semen are the value of the first calf crop that would have been produced.)

(3) Reported decisions are legion in which counsel for buyer, having successfully crossed the hurdles of proving the existence of a warranty and the breach thereof by seller, has then failed to marshal sufficient evidence to prove damages. Typical language appears in *Chrysler Corp. v. Marinari*, 177 Ga. App. 304, 42 U.C.C. Rep. 1310 at 1311-12 (1985), where the court said with regard to damages:

> With regard to the award of compensatory damages for breach of warranty, appellant [seller] contends that the evidence was not sufficient to authorize the jury's verdict of "the estimated $4,000.000. . . ."
>
> "The measure of damages for breach of warranty is the difference *at the time and place of acceptance* between the value of the goods accepted and the value they would have had if they had been as warranted. . . ." (Emphasis supplied.) OCGA § 11-2-714(2). Appellee [buyer] did testify as to the purchase price of the van, and, thus, he established *one* of the two figures for calculating the amount of damages recoverable for breach of warranty. However, a review of the transcript reveals that appellee's testimony failed further to establish the second figure, which is "the value of the vehicle delivered in a defective condition." The evidentiary basis upon which the jury obviously arrived at its "estimated" verdict is a portion of appellee's testimony concerning the difference between the "as warranted" value and the actual value of the allegedly defective van *at the approximate time of trial,* some years *after* the time of original delivery and acceptance. The transcript reveals no competent evidence of the value of the van in its defective state *at the time and place of delivery*. When the entirety of appellee's testimony is considered, it is clear that he was *never* able to establish any value for the van at the time and place of delivery except that value indicated by the price that he paid for it. In order to recover for breach of warranty, it was necessary for appellee to produce evidence of the actual value of the *defective* van at the time of delivery. In the absence of such evidence, it was error to enter judgment on the jury's award of compensatory damages for the breach of warranty count.
>
> . . . .
>
> *Judgment reversed.*

The burden to prove damages is not, however, insuperable. "The damage award need not be absolutely exact; a reasonable estimate based on relevant data is sufficient to support an award." *District Concrete Co., Inc. v. Bernstein Concrete Corp.*, 418 A.2d 1030, 1038 (D.C. Ct. App.1980).

[B] Deduction of Damages From Price

Read: U.C.C. § 2-717.

Read also: U.C.C. § 2A-508(6); CISG Arts. 45(1)(a), 50.

PROBLEM 7.4

In April-May 1993, Forsythe Racing, Inc. entered into an oral agreement with Hector Rebaque and his son under which the son was to serve as a race driver for an Indy-type race car owned by Forsythe for the 1993 Indy Car World Series. Forsythe agreed to provide the equipment and support staff for the racing team. Forsythe asserted that Rebaque agreed to furnish it in turn with $675,000 in sponsorship funds for the 1993 season. Rebaque maintained that he was obligated to furnish only $500,000. The amount actually paid to Forsythe by Rebaque was $500,000.

On July 19, 1993, Rebaque purchased in Italy a Lamborghini sports car. It was shipped from Italy on July 27, 1993. Prior to the automobile's arrival in the United States, Rebaque and Forsythe orally agreed that Forsythe would purchase the automobile from Rebaque for $72,000.

On June 2, 1993, Forsythe paid Rebaque $36,000 toward the purchase price. Upon the automobile's arrival in the United States, Forsythe took immediate possession. On August 2, 1993, Forsythe issued a check to Rebaque for the $36,000 balance owing on the sales agreement. Forsythe stopped payment on the check. It never paid the balance of $36,000 to Rebaque. Forsythe withheld the balance due as a $36,000 credit against an amount it believed Rebaque owed to it under the sponsorship agreement. Despite repeated requests, Forsythe refused either to complete payment or to relinquish the Lamborghini.

Rebaque filed suit against Forsythe to recover the $36,000 balance due on the automobile. Forsythe, in an attempt to set off the amount it alleged Rebaque owed it under the sponsorship agreement, filed a counterclaim against Rebaque seeking $175,000. It claimed that its liability for the balance of the automobile purchase agreement would be more than offset by the damages it claimed under the sponsorship agreement.

On March 20, 1995, Rebaque moved for summary judgment in the amount of $36,000 (plus prejudgment interest), arguing that Forsythe had no right to set off its debt to him against its claim against him because such set-off was prohibited by U.C.C. § 2-717. Forsythe also moved for summary judgment in its favor as to seeking declaratory relief to confirm its right to assert a set-off. It further argued that any judgment — or at a minimum any enforcement of judgment — should await trial of its counterclaim seeking $175,000 against Rebaque.

On May 15, 1995, the trial court entered judgment for Rebaque for $36,000 (plus prejudgment interest) and ordered Rebaque to furnish and execute all documents necessary for registration and domestication of the automobile by Forsythe. The court found that there was no just cause to delay its order.

On May 23, 1995, Forsythe moved for modification of the May 15 order by deletion of the finding making that order immediately enforceable. It argued that it would be inequitable to permit Rebaque to immediately collect his judgment against it — while its claim against him remained pending — since Rebaque was a nonresident alien without assets in the United States sufficient to satisfy any judgment which might be ultimately entered against him. In its motion Forsythe offered to post a letter of credit or set aside sufficient funds under court supervision to ensure payment to Rebaque of any net judgment which might be entered in his favor. The court denied this motion to modify.

Forsythe on appeal argues that the trial court improperly refused to allow a set-off from the automobile purchase price based on its claim under the sponsorship agreement. What result? *See Rebaque v. Forsythe Racing Inc.*, 480 N.E.2d 1338, 42 U.C.C. Rep. 222 (Ill. App. 1985); *see also*, *Berdex International, Inc. v. Milfico Prepared Foods, Inc.*, 630 N.E.2d 998, 23 U.C.C. Rep. 2d 1167 (Ill. App. 1994).

§ 7.06 Buyer's Incidental and Consequential Damages

Read: U.C.C. § 2-715.

Read also: U.C.C. § 2A-520; CISG Arts. 45(1)(b), 74, 77, 78.

At § 7.04, we evaluated remedies available to a buyer who has not accepted the goods or who has justifiably revoked his acceptance. In particular, § 7.04[C][1] recited buyer's right to cover and to recover from seller as damages the difference between the cost of cover and the contract price "together with incidental or consequential damages." U.C.C. § 2-712. Section 7.04[C][2] recited buyer's right to recover damages for non-delivery or repudiation by the seller measured by the difference between the market price and the contract price "together with any incidental and consequential damages." U.C.C. § 2-713. Cf. U.C.C. §§ 2A-518, 2A-519(1) and (2).

Further, at § 7.05, we evaluated the remedies available to a buyer with regard to goods finally accepted. In particular, § 7.05[A] recited buyer's measure of damages as the difference between the value of the goods accepted and the value they would have had if they had been as warranted. Also, in a proper case "any incidental and consequential damages . . .may . . .be recovered." U.C.C. § 2-714. Cf. U.C.C. § 2A-519(3) and (4).

In this section we evaluate buyer's incidental and consequential damages under U.C.C. § 2-715.

HORIZONS, INC. v. AVCO CORP

United States Court of Appeals
714 F2d 862, 36 U.C.C. Rep. 1207 (8th Cir. 1983)

Ross, Circuit Judge.

This diversity action was instituted by Horizons, Inc. alleging a breach of express and implied warranties of fitness for an ordinary purpose and fitness for a particular purpose in connection with the purchase by Horizons of an airplane engine which was remanufactured by Avco Corporation. Horizons claimed that it suffered ordinary, incidental and consequential damages as a result of backfiring which occurred in the engine shortly after installation. Following a bench trial, the district court found that Avco had breached an implied warranty of merchantability and awarded Horizons $9,974.37 in general damages, $619.84 in incidental damages, and $56,265.00 in consequential damages. Horizons cross-appeals alleging that the failure to award damages for the cost of "cover" was error.

Horizons is a South Dakota corporation in the business of providing aerial photographic and photogrammetric services, including topographic surveying and mapping. Avco does not sell its remanufactured engines directly to the public, but does so only through its authorized domestic distributors. Aviation Sales, Inc. of Denver, Colorado, is an authorized distributor of Avco engines. James Spell, president of Horizons, contacted purchasing an Avco remanufactured engine for one of its company airplanes. Aviation Sales advised Spell that Horizons would be better off to order the engine through an Avco "fixed base operator," such as Casper Air Service, a dealer located in Casper, Wyoming. In December of 1977, Horizons ordered an Avco engine from Casper Air Service for a price of $12,767.00.

Robert Collett, Horizons' pilot, installed the engine in a Cessna 310 aircraft owned by Horizons about mid-June of 1978. After the engine was installed and ground-tested, Horizons' personnel attempted to operate the aircraft. A series of mechanical failures and breakdowns occurred primarily because of backfiring in the engine. Horizons notified Avco, in writing, of the engine malfunctions. In order to correct the backfiring problems, Horizons incurred numerous expenses and ultimately had to overhaul the engine. The district court found that expert testimony established that there was a defect in the valve train which existed at the time the engine was remanufactured and was not caused by normal engine wear.

The district court held that an award of consequential damages was proper because Aviation Sales was the ostensible agent of Avco who had "reason to know" of the requirements of Horizons' business and the knowledge of an agent is imputed to the principal under South Dakota law. The district court found that in 1977 and 1978, Horizons had sufficient contract work available to occupy the aircraft on every available flight day. Horizons lost eleven flight days (57.7 hours) in 1978 due to the defective condition of the Avco engine. The court found that consequently, Horizons was unable to complete its 1978 contracts and was forced to utilize flight days in late 1978, 1979 and 1980 to complete those contracts. The court held that the evidence at trial established, to a reasonable degree of certainty, that had Horizons been able to complete flights on those days it would have received net earnings of $56,265.00, which was then awarded as consequential damages for the "down time" experienced by the aircraft during repair of the defective valve train.

On appeal, Avco contends that the district court erred in its award of consequential damages and also in its computation of the proper amount of consequential damages. Horizons, as cross-appellant, contends that the district court erred in failing to award damages for the cost of "cover." We find that the district court correctly awarded consequential damages but failed to award the proper amount of such damages. We also find that the district court correctly denied an award of damages for the cost of "cover." We accordingly affirm in part and reverse in part.

The district court based its determination that an award of consequential damages was proper in this case upon SD Codified Laws Ann § 57A-2-715(2)(a), providing as follows [the Court quotes U.C.C. § 2-715(2)(a)].

Avco alleges that the district court erred when it found that Avco had "reason to know" of Horizons' requirements. Avco traced the reasoning of the district court as finding: (1) that Horizons communicated its requirements to Aviation Sales; (2) Aviation Sales was the ostensible agent[27] of Avco; and (3) that knowledge of Horizons' requirements are imputed to Avco, the principal, under South Dakota law, thereby giving Avco "reason to know" as required under the statute. Avco argues that each of the three steps in the district court's reasoning is flawed and allowed an erroneous award of consequential damages. We disagree.

Avco contends that the first step of the court's analysis is erroneous because Horizons never put on evidence that it actually communicated its requirements to anyone at Aviation Sales. Avco alleges that the district court should not have relied on the fact that Horizons' president, James Spell, habitually explained the nature of Horizons' business to people that he spoke to on the telephone. Avco argues that such testimony does not establish that Spell actually told Aviation Sales of its business requirements. We conclude that the district court's finding that Avco had

27 Agency is ostensible when by conduct or want of ordinary care the principal causes a third person to believe another, who is not actually appointed, to be his agent. SD Codified Laws Ann § 59-1-5.

knowledge of Horizons' requirements is not clearly erroneous under Fed R Civ P 52(a). The record in this case fully supports the court's finding and demonstrates that, at every level of the transaction, knowledge of Horizons' business use of its airplane engines was either communicated to or previously known by Avco. We find three instances of communication to Avco of Horizons' requirements. First, Avco sent mailings to Horizons' business address which identified Horizons as an aerial photographer. Second, it is doubtful that James Spell departed from his habit of identifying himself and his company's line of work when he talked to Aviation Sales about purchasing the engine. Third, Casper Air Service, the Avco dealer which sold the engine to Horizons, had previously modified Horizons' plane for aerial photography. Thus, it is clear that Avco knew, both directly from its own mailing list and indirectly through its distributors, of Horizons' business requirements.

In *Lewis v. Mobil Oil Corporation*, 438 F2d 500, 510-11 [8 U.C.C. Rep 625] (8th Cir 1971) we held that

> [w]here a seller provides goods to a manufacturing enterprise with knowledge that they are to be used in the manufacturing process, it is reasonable to assume that he should know that defective goods will cause a disruption of production, and loss of profits is a natural consequence of such disruption. Hence, loss of profits should be recoverable under those circumstances.

We find the analysis in *Lewis* controlling in this case. Avco provided Horizons, a company it knew through its own mailing list to be an aerial photographer, with a remanufactured engine to be used in its photograph business. It is now unreasonable for Avco to contend that it was unaware that a defective engine could disrupt Horizons' photograph business and cause a loss of profits.

Since we have previously held that Avco had "reason to know" of Horizons' requirements because of Horizons' presence on Avco's own mailing list, we deem it unnecessary to reach the district court's findings that Aviation Sales was the ostensible agent of Avco and its knowledge is thereby imputed to Avco.

The district court awarded Horizons $56,265.00 in consequential damages as compensation for the value of productive capacity lost during the engine's down time. Horizons calculated its lost production claim by utilizing a formula approved in *Clark v. International Harvester Co.*, 581 P2d 784, 805 (Idaho 1978). To arrive at the total claim amount of $56,265.00, Horizons multiplied the contract payment rate per square mile times the number of square miles the aircraft could have covered with the engine functioning properly and subtracted from that figure the operation costs of the plane and the cost of materials. Horizons did not deduct the overhead expense of maintaining the film processing personnel as it felt that this was a cost incurred by Horizons without the benefit of income to meet the expenses during the down time. Although Horizons was ultimately paid the full contract price for both of its contracts which had to be completed at a later date due to the engine's down time, the district court found that 57.7 hours of productive time lost can never be recovered in a company which has sufficient work to keep busy on every available flight day. The district court viewed this loss as similar to the loss suffered by a volume seller: even though the goods are later purchased by another, the supply is endless and a loss of profits has still occurred. We agree with the district court that a loss of profits has occurred. However, we disagree with the amount of consequential damages suffered by Horizons.

In general, expected profits of a commercial business are too remote, speculative and uncertain to permit a recovery of damages for their loss. *Cargill, Inc. v. Taylor Towing Service, Inc.*, 642 F2d 239, 241 (8th Cir 1981). Proof of lost profits must be sufficient to remove the question of profits from the realm of speculation and conjecture. *Rogers v. Allis-Chalmers Credit Corp.*, 679 F2d 138, 142 (8th Cir 1982). The burden of proving the extent of loss incurred by way of consequential damage is on the plaintiff but mathematical precision is not required, only that the loss can be shown in a manner reasonable under the circumstances. *Karlen v. Butler Mfg. Co.*, 526 F2d 1373, 1380 (8th Cir 1975). The sufficiency of the evidence of lost profits is dependent upon whether the financial information contained in the record is such that a just or reasonable estimate can be drawn. *Cargill, supra*, 642 F2d at 241. The law in South Dakota concerning recovery of lost profits mirrors the position taken by the Eighth Circuit. See *Drier v. Perfection, Inc.*, 259 NW2d 496 (SD 1977); *Olson v. Aldren*, 170 NW2d 891 (SD 1969).

In reviewing the consequential damage award, we are convinced that the amount of loss suffered by Horizons was not calculated in a manner reasonable under the circumstances. However, because of the quality of the financial information contained in the record, we feel that a just and reasonable estimate can be drawn by adopting reasonable accounting procedures on gross receipts and expenses for the year of 1978.

Trial Exhibit 67 discloses that in 1978 Horizons' gross receipts amounted to $402,239.12, while expenses amounted to $348,792.00. This results in a net profit of $53,447.12 for the year 1978. This figure includes payment in full on the two contracts which had to be completed at a later date due to the defective engine. Thus, it seems grossly excessive to award Horizons $56,265.00 for 57.7 hours of lost flying time when they only made $53,447.12 for a total of 855.05 hours of flying time in 1978. We find that the most reasonable method of calculating Horizons' loss of profits is to employ a rate of average hourly profit. In 1978 Horizons flew 855.05 hours and made a net profit of $53,447.12. Thus, Horizons' 1978 average hourly profit was $62.51. In multiplying the average hourly profit and the 57.7 hours of down time, we find that the amount of Horizons' loss of profits is $3,606.83. Although this is a far cry from the original award of $56,265.00, we find it quite reasonable considering that the two contracts which had to be completed at a later date were not completely profitable ventures for Horizons. In sum, we hold that Horizons is entitled to $3,606.83 in consequential damages.

On cross-appeal, Horizons contends that the district court erred in failing to award damages for the cost of "cover" incurred when Horizons purchased substitute engines to use during the period of down time. The district court held that Horizons could not recover its claim for the cost of "cover" as Horizons had never rejected or revoked its acceptance of the Avco engine. We agree.

SD Codified Laws Ann § 57A-2-711(1)(a) provides that: [the court cites § 57A-2-711(1)(a)]. Thus, the district court was correct in finding that Horizons was not entitled to damages for the cost of "cover."

In summary, we affirm the district court's decision to award consequential damages and deny the claim for the cost of "cover." However, we reverse the amount of the consequential damage award and order that the total damage award be reduced to $14,201.04.

NOTES

(1) This case may bring to mind *Hadley v. Baxendale*, 9 Exch. 341, 156 Eng. Rep. 145 (1854). Illustration 1 to Restatement, Second, Contracts § 351(1981) is based on Hadley and reads:[28]

> A, a carrier, contracts with B, a miller, to carry B's broken crankshaft to its manufacturer for repair. B tells A when they make the contract that the crankshaft is part of B's milling machine and that it must be sent at once, but not that the mill is stopped because B has no replacement. Because A delays in carrying the crankshaft, B loses profit during an additional period while the mill is stopped because of the delay. A is not liable for B's loss of profit. That loss was not foreseeable by A as a probable result of the breach at the time the contract was made because A did not know that the broken crankshaft was necessary for the operation of the mill.

(2) *Duracote Corp. v. Goodyear Tire & Rubber Co.*, 2 Ohio St. 3d 160, 443 N.E.2d 184, 35 U.C.C. Rep. 471, 472-73 (1983), quotes as follows:

> Professors White and Summers have observed that U.C.C. § 2-715(2). . ."imposes two restrictions on the recovery of consequential damages in addition to the foreseeability requirement: they must be reasonably ascertainable, and the plaintiff cannot recover for losses he reasonably could have prevented." White & Summers, Uniform Commercial Code (2 Ed 1980), 396, § 10-4.

See, e.g., *Prutch v. Ford Motor Co.*, 618 P.2d 657, 29 U.C.C. Rep. 1507 (Colo. 1980) (The court reasoned that plaintiffs, in deciding to continue farming with the knowledge that their Ford tractor, plow, disc harrow and hay baler might continue to malfunction, actually mitigated their losses. This they were required to do by U.C.C. § 2-715(2)(a). Their decision to try to produce at least part of a normal crop, rather than no crop at all, was required by their duty to lessen, rather than increase, their damages).

(3) It is clear from the outcome in numerous cases that consequential damages are often difficult to establish. Occasionally the courts will give some concrete indication of how difficult the task may be. Thus, in *Farmers Mutual Exchange of Baxley, Inc. v. Dixon*, 146 Ga. App. 663, 247 S.E.2d 124, 126 (1978), where plaintiff sought consequential damages in the form of lost profits from lost crops, the court said:

> In the present case there is no uncertainty that the alleged cause of damage was defective seed corn. If plaintiffs can establish by comparison to corn crops grown on land in the same planted field, with the same soil, the same brand of seed, fertilized and cultivated in the same manner, and planted at the same time and under identical weather conditions, then the damages would not be too speculative and conjectural for a jury to determine.

(4) In *Tremco, Inc. v. Valley Aluminum Products Corp.*, 831 S.W.2d 156, 18 U.C.C. Rep.2d 168 (Ark. App. 1992), seller sold window assembly gaskets to buyer, a manufacturer of window

---

assemblies. Buyer had contacted to provide window assemblies to Win-Wall, Inc., a glazing subcontactor, for two commercial buildings. The gaskets were defective and buyer sought recovery for consequential damages. Held: For buyer: (1) substantial evidence was introduced as to loss of profits and amount of loss so as to support an award of consequential damages, and (2) award of damages for cost of replacing gaskets was not speculative. Note regarding lost profits: Win-Wall's president testified that he had refused to allow buyer the opportunity to bid on subsequent projects and that buyer would receive no further business as long as the gasket problem existed. The president listed ten contracts he had awarded since the gasket incident totaling $1,408,000, which required materials of the kind supplied by buyer. He was "very confident" that he would have sublet at least half of them to buyer but for the problem experienced with the gaskets.

DAKOTA GRAIN CO., v. EHRMANTROUT

Supreme Court of North Dakota
502 N.W.2d 234, 23 U.C.C. Rep.2d 402 (1993)

LEVINE, JUSTICE.

. . . .

During the Spring of 1989, Ehrmantrout orally agreed to sell [to Dakota Grain Co., Inc. (the Elevator)] some of his Lenn variety hard red spring wheat. The Elevator intended to sell this wheat to other farmers for seeding and insists that Ehrmantrout was informed that the wheat would be used as seed. Ehrmantrout claims that he was neither told nor had reason to believe that the Elevator intended to resell his wheat for seed. Ehrmantrout delivered four truck loads of spring wheat to the Elevator in April 1989.

In early May 1989, the Elevator manager asked Ehrmantrout if he would agree to sell more of his spring wheat to the Elevator. Ehrmantrout agreed and on May 9, 1989, he delivered to the Elevator two truck loads of wheat, totaling 629.49 bushels. The Elevator cleaned this wheat and sold about 585 bushels of it to four different farmers for seeding. The farmers planted the seed, but none of the crops matured. It was ultimately determined that the wheat planted by the four farmers was not Lenn spring wheat, but a winter wheat which, by its nature, will not produce a crop when seeded during the spring of the year. The Elevator paid the four farmers a total of $22,201 as damages for selling them winter wheat to seed instead of spring wheat. The Elevator then filed this action for damages against Ehrmantrout, alleging various theories of recovery, including breach of contract, breach of warranty, negligence and fraud.

The parties made this case much more complex and confusing than was necessary by trying the case on mixed principles of tort and contract law. Yet, this is a classic breach of warranty case, resolvable by application of Chapter 41-02, N.D.C.C., our codification of the Article 2—Sales provisions of the Uniform Commercial Code. Despite the lack of clarity in the parties' presentation of their respective legal theories, the trial court's analysis was close to the mark and, in fact, its resolution of the case, except for some ambiguity in its findings regarding consequential damages, is in accord with Chapter 41-02, N.D.C.C.

The trial court concluded that Ehrmantrout breached his oral sale contract with the Elevator by delivering winter wheat instead of Lenn spring wheat. Using comparative fault principles, the court concluded that Ehrmantrout was 51 percent responsible and the Elevator was 49 percent responsible for the consequential damages arising from the sale of the wheat to the four farmers for spring seeding. The trial court entered judgment awarding the Elevator $125.90 in general damages, representing the difference in the value of the spring wheat Ehrmantrout contracted to sell the Elevator and the value of the winter wheat that he actually delivered to the Elevator. In addition, the trial court awarded the Elevator consequential damages of $11,332.51, representing 51 percent of the total damages incurred by the Elevator in its settlement with the four farmers. Ehrmantrout filed a post-trial motion to amend the trial court's findings of fact, conclusions of law and judgment and filed an alternative motion for a new trial. These post-trial motions were denied by the court, and Ehrmantrout appealed.

Ehrmantrout asserts on appeal that the trial court erred by not specifying what act or omission by Ehrmantrout constituted negligent conduct. The parties unnecessarily complicated this case by using negligence terminology to describe Ehrmantrout's breach of his express warranty to deliver Lenn spring wheat. Under the Uniform Commercial Code, a bargain that includes a description of the goods to be sold creates an express warranty that the goods will conform to that description. Section 41-02-30(1)(b), N.D.C.C. [U.C.C. § 2-313(1)(b)]. The contract is breached when the delivered goods do not conform to the description, irrespective of whether the seller acted negligently or otherwise. Section 41-02-93(1), N.D.C.C. So, the seller's negligence, or lack of negligence, is not relevant to the question of whether the seller breached his or her express warranty to delivery conforming goods. . . .

Ehrmantrout also asserts that the trial court's findings that Ehrmantrout delivered to the Elevator winter wheat instead of spring wheat and that the wheat purchased by the four farmers was wheat sold to the Elevator by Ehrmantrout are not supported by the evidence. We disagree. . . .

Ehrmantrout also asserts that the trial court erred in awarding consequential damages in this case. The appropriate measure of damages for a breach of warranty is set forth under Section 41-02-93(2) and (3), N.D.C.C. [U.C.C. 2-714(2) and (3)]: . . .

The trial court awarded general damages to the Elevator of $125.90 based upon a 20 cent per bushel difference in value between the spring wheat for which Ehrmantrout was paid and the winter wheat that he actually delivered (629.49 bushels delivered X $.20 per bushel price difference = $125.90). Section 41-02-93(2), N.D.C.C. Ehrmantrout does not object to this award of general damages.

However, Ehrmantrout does object to the court's award of consequential damages. In awarding consequential damages, the trial court compared the "fault" of Ehrmantrout and the Elevator that caused those damages and apportioned them accordingly. Before we discuss the elements necessary to award consequential damages, we must first determine whether the court erred in applying comparative fault principles here.

Our comparative fault law, Chapter 32-03.2, N.D.C.C., defines the term "fault" to include "breach of warranty . . .and failure to exercise reasonable care to avoid an injury or to mitigate damages." Section 32-03.2-01, N.D.C.C. Under Section 32-03.2-03, N.D.C.C., "fault" is expressly defined to mean "product liability or *breach of warranty* for product defect." (Emphasis added.) So, under this section pure comparative fault applies in a breach of warranty action and damages are diminished in proportion to the amount of contributing fault of the person recovering the damages. Section 32-03.2-03, N.D.C.C.

Clearly the, the trial court did not err in comparing fault for purposes of awarding consequential damages in this case. *See Peterson v. Bendix Home Systems, Inc.,* 318 N.W.2d 50 (Minn. 1982) (comparative fault applies to consequential damages in a breach of warranty action).

Ehrmantrout also argues that in awarding consequential damages, the trial court did not first determine whether those damages were foreseeable by Ehrmantrout and, if foreseeable, whether the Elevator could reasonably have prevented them. Consequential damages are defined under 41-02-94(2), N.D.C.C. [U.C.C. 2-715(2)]:

> "2. Consequential damages resulting from the seller's breach include:
>
> a. Any loss resulting from general or particular requirements and needs of *which the seller at the time of contracting had reason to know and which could not reasonably be prevented by cover or otherwise;* and
>
> b. Injury to person or property proximately resulting from any breach of warranty." (Emphasis added.)

Under this provision, the primary factor for awarding consequential damages is whether the losses were foreseeable by the seller at the time he or she entered the contract. *Schneidt v. Asbey Motors, Inc.* 248 N.W.2d 792 (N.D. 1976); White & Summers, Uniform Commercial Code § 10-4(1988). The Official Comment to this section of the Uniform Commercial Code is instructive:

> "Subsection (2) operates to allow the buyer, in an appropriate case, any consequential damages which are the result of the seller's breach. The 'tacit agreement' test for the recovery of consequential damages is rejected. Although the older rule at common law which made the seller liable for all consequential damages of which he had 'reason to know' in advance is followed, the liberality of that rule is modified by refusing to permit recovery unless the buyer could not reasonably have prevented the loss by cover or otherwise." Uniform Commercial Code (U.L.A.) Section 2-715 p.418 (1989).

Following the requirements of this uniform provision on consequential damages, the Idaho Supreme Court upheld an award of consequential damages under factual circumstances nearly identical to those in this case. *Nezperce Storage Co. v. Zenner,* 105 Idaho 464, 670 P.2d 871 (1983). The Zenners, wheat farmers in Idaho, agreed to sell spring wheat to Nezperce but instead delivered winter wheat, which was subsequently resold to farmers, who planted it in the springtime and experienced complete crop failures. Nezperce paid for the farmers' damages and then sued the Zenners for reimbursement. The court, based upon a jury verdict, required the Zenners to reimburse Nezperce. In making this award of consequential damages, the court concluded that there was evidence supporting the jury's finding that the Zenners had reason to know that the wheat they sold Nezperce was intended to be resold as wheat seed.

The same analysis for awarding consequential damages applies in this case. As a prerequisite to awarding consequential damages against Ehrmantrout in favor of the Elevator, one must find that Ehrmantrout either knew or had reason to know when he entered the contract, that the spring wheat was going to be resold as seed. Unfortunately, the trial court's findings on this issue are unclear.

In its findings of fact, the court stated that prior to delivering the wheat, "Ehrmantrout brought a sample of the grain to Dakota Grain to be germination tested." Ehrmantrout's testimony indicates that he was aware that the only reason for doing a germination test was to determine whether the grain was useable for seed. The court also found that the Elevator manager "called Ehrmantrout and told him the germination was acceptable and that he could use the wheat," and that Ehrmantrout orally contracted with the Elevator on or about May 9, 1989, "to deliver two loads of Lenn spring wheat, which was subsequently to be sold to local farmers for seeding purposes." The implication of these findings is that Ehrmantrout either knew or had reason to know that the wheat he was selling to the Elevator was intended to be resold as seed.

However, in its order denying the post-trial motions, the court made the following relevant statements:

> "While there certainly is some evidence that [Ehrmantrout] knew or reasonably should have known that the [Elevator] intended to resell his wheat as seed wheat, I did not find that such evidence was sufficient to prove by a preponderance that Ehrmantrout had such personal knowledge. . . . [B]y the application of comparative negligence, the [Elevator] has already been 'penalized' for its inability to prove that Ehrmantrout actually knew or should have known that the wheat involved was intended for resale as seed stock."

These seemingly inconsistent statements by the trial court on this issue leave unresolved the question of whether Ehrmantrout either knew or should have known when he entered the contract, that his wheat was intended to be resold by the Elevator for seed. The resolution of that question is the key element in determining whether an award of consequential damages is appropriate in this case. So, we must remand this case for clarification of the court's findings on this issue.

Ehrmantrout argues that the Elevator's actions are the sole cause of the consequential damages and the trial court erred in apportioning fault. The apportionment of fault for purposes of awarding consequential damages only becomes an issue in this case if the trial court finds that Ehrmantrout either knew or had reason to know that his wheat was intended to be resold for seed. In the absence of that finding, it would be inappropriate for the court to award consequential damages. Section 41-02-94(2)(a), N.D.C.C. [U.C.C. § 2-715(2)(a)].

If, however, the court does find that Ehrmantrout had reason to know that the wheat was intended to be resold for seed, then the second element, *i.e.*, whether the Elevator could have reasonably prevented the consequential damages, must be resolved because it, too, is a prerequisite to awarding consequential damages. Section 41-02-94(2)(a), N.D.C.C. We conclude that the court's findings with regard to this element of consequential damages are clear and that on remand the court does not have to redetermine this issue. The trial court found that the Elevator was 49 percent responsible for the consequential damages and deducted that percentage from the award of consequential damages. The court stated in its memorandum opinion, that the elevator "failed to take reasonable measure [sic] to mitigate or reduce to a minimum the losses which eventually resulted." In discussing the Elevator's failure to mitigate, the court stated that, "there was no testing of any kind of the wheat delivered on May 9." Unless reasonable persons could not disagree, the court's allocation of fault is a finding of fact that will not be overturned on appeal, unless we are convinced that the court has made a mistake. *See Jones v. Ahlberg*, 489 N.W.2d 576 (N.D.1992). We conclude that the trial court's finding of 49 percent causation of the consequential damages by the Elevator is not clearly erroneous.

We affirm the trial court's determination that Ehrmantrout breached his contract with the Elevator and the court's award of $125.90 in general damages. However, we hold that, as a necessary element of consequential damages, the Elevator was required to prove that Ehrmantrout either knew or should have known when he entered the contract, that his wheat was intended to be resold by the Elevator for seed. The trial court's findings on this key element are unclear and need to be clarified in order to resolve the consequential damages issue. Accordingly, we reverse the award of consequential damages and remand for clarification of the findings and a redetermination on that issue.

Affirmed in part, reversed in part, and remanded.

VANDE WALLE, C.J., and NEUMANN, SANDSTROM AND MESCHKE JJ., concur.

NOTES AND QUESTIONS

(1) E. Farnsworth, Contracts § 12.17 at 931-33 (2d ed. 1990), comments on the requirements of *foreseeability* and *certainty* (footnotes omitted):

> Sometimes a court is confronted with a large damage claim that seems greatly disproportionate to the modest consideration received by the party in breach. It may not seem just to require the party in breach to pay for all loss caused by the breach, even though that loss was foreseeable and has been proved with reasonable certainty. . . .
>
> For a time many courts overtly used the tacit agreement test to justify their refusal to award damages to the full extent of the loss in such cases. . . . However, the tacit agreement test has now generally been discarded and no longer affords a vehicle for limiting recovery in such cases.
>
> Nevertheless, there remains a judicial reluctance to impose on a contracting party liability in an amount greatly disproportionate to the consideration received. . . . Courts have covertly expressed their reluctance by so applying the test of foreseeability as to find that what was foreseeable becomes "unforeseeable." They have also shown their reluctance by a particularly rigorous application of the requirement of certainty. Use of the requirements of foreseeability and certainty as surrogates for some other principle, however, has not contributed to clarity in dealing with this problem. What is the principle for which these limitations are surrogates?
>
> Restatement Second § 351(3) gives the following answer: "A court may limit damages for foreseeable loss by excluding recovery for loss of profits, by allowing recovery only for loss incurred in reliance, or otherwise if it concludes that in the circumstances justice so requires in order to avoid disproportionate compensation.". . .Section 351(3). . .invites the court to make a frank evaluation of the proper allocation of risks in determining what justice requires.

In *Native Alaskan Reclamation and Pest Control, Inc. v. United Bank Alaska*, 685 P.2d 1211 (Alaska 1984), action was instituted against a bank for breach of a loan agreement made by a corporation in connection with a plan to purchase and convert planes for use in fire fighting. The court held that damages were recoverable if the corporation's inability to obtain replacement financing and resulting loss of profit were foreseeable as a probable result of the bank's breach at the time of contracting. Restatement, Second, Contracts § 351(1). On remand, though, the court stated that the trial court should reconsider its award in light of § 351(3) (a court may limit damages for foreseeable loss if in the circumstances justice so requires).

Proposed U.C.C. § 2-715(2)(a) conforms to Restatement, Second, § 351: The seller must still have reason to know at the time of contracting of the particular needs or requirements of the buyer. In addition the seller must have reason to know that the loss would "probably result from the breach" and the court has power, where justice requires, to limit disproportionate consequential loss.

(2) *Injury to Person or Property*. U.C.C. §§ 2-714(3) and 2-715(2)(b) allow recovery of consequential damages resulting from seller's breach and include injury to person or property proximately resulting from any breach of warranty. This is discussed in Chapter 5 at § 5.08, Interaction of Warranty and Strict Liability.

(3) *Incidental Damages*. U.C.C. §§ 2-714(3) and 2-715(1) set forth buyer's incidental damages. Cf. U.C.C. § 2-710. The following are recent noteworthy cases: *Frank B. Bozzo, Inc. v. Electric Weld Division of Spang Industries, Inc.*, 498 A.2d 895, 42 U.C.C. Rep. 213 (Pa. 1985) (buyer of steel mesh could recover prejudgment interest as an incidental damage resulting from the seller's breach if the interest represented a reasonable expense incident to the delay); *Fast v. Southern Offshore Yachts*, 587 F. Supp. 1354, 38 U.C.C. Rep. 1569 (Conn. 1984) (buyer entitled to incidental damages in the form of statutory interest on the monies paid by him running from the date of breach through judgment); *Happy Dack Trading Co., Ltd. v. Agro-Industries, Inc.*, 602 F. Supp. 986, 41 U.C.C. Rep. 1718 (S.D.N.Y. 1984) (buyer may recover as incidental damages expenses reasonably incurred in inspection of goods rightly rejected; thus, where plaintiff intermediate buyers had sent a representative to the People's Republic of China to investigate claims of nonconformity made by the ultimate buyer, plaintiff intermediate buyers were entitled to the travel and testing expenses incurred by the representative); *Devore v. Bostrom*, 632 P.2d 832, 31 U.C.C. Rep. 984 (Utah 1981) (allowed as incidental damages in an action revoking acceptance of a new car which seller refused to repair were expenses associated with car insurance, license plates, lost wages and interest on the purchase price of the automobile; attorney's fees were not allowable (with dissent)).

In *Ohline Corp. v. Granite Mill*, 849 P.2d 602, 21 U.C.C. Rep.2d 49 (Utah App. 1993), seller agreed to sell window shutters to buyer to be used in remodeling suites at the Las Vegas Hilton. Seller was late in delivering the shutters and buyer had to pay $9405 in overtime pay to install the shutters before an August 4 deadline buyer had with Hilton. Held: Buyer was entitled to recover from seller the overtime charges, regardless of whether the overtime damages were considered incidental or consequential damages under U.C.C. § 2-715.

PROBLEM 7.5

You represent Heat Treater Inc., a firm which manufactures and heat treats bolts, nuts and reinforcing rods. Heat Treater sold and delivered to Essex Auto Co., an automobile manufacturer, 50,000 bolts for use in steering mechanisms of Essex automobiles. One bolt is used in each steering mechanism. The price of the 50,000 bolts is 4 cents each, or a total of $2,000.

When the bolt sale was made, Heat Treater's sales manager recognized that if defects appeared in the bolts after they were installed in the automobiles, a recall of Essex automobiles might occur pursuant to the National Traffic and Motor Vehicle Safety Act. For this reason, pains were taken to ensure that due care was exercised in the manufacture of the bolts. However, at the time of the sale Heat Treater was unable: (1) to assess the magnitude of the risk that defects might appear in the bolts and that a recall would occur; (2) to purchase insurance against losses which might ensue if recall did occur; (3) to add to the price of the bolts sold to Essex an amount commensurate with the risk; (4) to spread the risk among all buyers of Heat Treater bolts; or (5) to set aside and deduct from corporate taxable income a fund to pay any recall expenses which might occur. At the same time, when the sale was made, Heat Treater dealt rather informally with Essex Auto Co., and no attempt was made to allocate the risks, whether by warranty disclaimer, limitation of damages or otherwise.

After the 50,000 Essex automobiles containing Heat Treater bolts were manufactured and sold to consumers, it was discovered that some of the bolts were defective, causing a dangerous condition. The result was that the 50,000 vehicles were recalled pursuant to the Act, at a cost to Essex Auto Co. of $820,000.

Essex has now brought suit against Heat Treater for the $820,000 in recall expenses. What defenses, if any, can you raise for Heat Treater? Could (should) Restatement, Second, Contracts § 351(3) and proposed § 2-715(2)(a), cited in Note (1) above, affect the outcome of the Essex suit?

See B. Stone, *Recovery of Consequential Damages for Product Recall Expenditures*, 1980 B.Y.U.L. Rev. 485. See also, *Taylor & Gaskin v. Chris-Craft Industries*, 732 F.2d 1273, 38 U.C.C. Rep. 858 (6th Cir. 1984) (expenses of recall of defective fuel tanks which buyer had installed in power boats were recoverable as consequential damages); *Upjohn Co. v. Rachelle Laboratories, Inc.*, 661 F.2d 1105, 32 U.C.C. Rep. 747 (6th Cir. 1981) (cost to buyer of drug tablet recall and lost sales of drug tablets before recall were recoverable as damages).

§ 7.07 Remedies Applicable to Sellers and Buyers

[A] Liquidated Damages

Read: U.C.C. §§ 2-718, 2-719(1), 2-302; see § 1-106.

Read also: U.C.C. §§ 2A-504, 2A-108; CISG Arts. 4(a), 6.

An early U.C.C. case was *Denkin v. Sterner*, 10 Pa. D.&C.2d 203, 1 U.C.C. Rep. 173 (Pa. 1956). Here defendants (buyers) agreed to purchase from plaintiff (seller) certain refrigerated cases and equipment for a food market. Buyers by letter canceled the order before delivery of any of the goods. Judgment was entered for the full amount of the purchase price. The court observed the sales agreement and stated:

> Perusal of the agreement disclosed some peculiar features which would indicate that it was undoubtedly prepared by the sellers. In paragraph 16 it provides: "This agreement may be canceled by seller at any time before delivery of the property to purchaser," but nowhere in the agreement is there any similar right extended to the purchaser. On the contrary, paragraph 11 provides: "In the event of default by purchaser, seller shall have the following rights in addition to any and all other rights under the Uniform Commercial Code and/or any other applicable law." Then follows the authority to enter judgment in replevin for the goods in question and also the authority to enter judgment for the full amount of the unpaid purchase price plus interest and costs, with 15 percent added for attorney's fees.
>
> Why anyone would sign such a biased and one-sided agreement is difficult to understand. . . .

While there seems little doubt from the depositions taken under the rule issued in this case that plaintiff is entitled to damages, for defendants admit that they canceled the agreement because they found out after checking that they could buy more equipment for less money elsewhere, yet it also seems evident under all the circumstances that to permit plaintiff to recover the full amount of the purchase price without showing what goods, if any, have been identified to the contract, what goods were standard items and readily salable and what goods had actually been specially manufactured prior to the cancellation by defendants, as well as what goods have been or can be readily resold, would be in effect "unreasonably large liquidated damages" and, therefore, unconscionable and void.

. . . .

We therefore hold that the judgment in this case should be opened to permit defendants to defend as to the amount due plaintiff. Incidentally, it would seem that well-intentioned counsel, informed of all the actual pertinent facts involved, might be in a much better position to resolve this question than would the customary 12 good men and true [jury].

A liquidated damages term which takes into account the elements to be considered as set forth in U.C.C. § 2-718(1) is illustrated by 12 West's Legal Forms § 15.1 — Form 1 (2d ed. 1985):[29]

Inasmuch as the failure of the seller to deliver the quantity of commodities specified herein, in accordance with the terms of this agreement will, because of the urgent need for the commodities by the buyer, arising from the present emergency conditions, cause serious and substantial damages to the buyer, and it will be difficult, if not impossible to prove the amount of such damages, the seller agrees to pay to the buyer, [amount] as liquidated damages for failure to deliver, which sum is computed as follows:

[*number*] cents per pound for [*identify or designate article*];

[*number*] cents per pound for [*identify or designate article*];

[*etc.*]

The sum is agreed upon as liquidated damages and not as a penalty. The parties hereto have computed, estimated and agreed upon the sum as an attempt to make a reasonable forecast of probable actual loss because of the difficulty of estimating with exactness the damages which will result.

STOCK SHOP, INC. v. BOZELL & JACOBS, INC.

New York Supreme Court, New York County
126 Misc. 2d 95, 481 N.Y.S.2d 269, 39 U.C.C. Rep. 1295 (1984)

SAXE, J.

[29] Copyright © 1985 by West Co. Reprinted by permission.

In this motion for summary judgment, I am asked to decide whether an unusual liquidated damage clause in a contract is valid or instead, a penalty.

The underlying facts are these: On three occasions during November and December 1979, the plaintiff delivered to defendant 697 stock photographs for the defendant's consideration for possible use as part of a slide show for one of its advertising clients. The photographs depicted various cities, and other points of interest in the United States. It appears that 39 of the 40 photographs that the defendant agreed to license were never returned. The plaintiff argues that each of the 39 photographs has a value of at least $1,500. The principal basis for this contention lies in paragraph "3" of the delivery memoranda between the parties which states:

> The monetary damage for loss or damage of an original color transparency or photograph shall be determined by the value of each individual photograph. Recipient agrees however, that the reasonable minimum value of such tort or damaged photographs or transparency shall be no less than fifteen hundred ($1,500.00) dollars.

The plaintiff claims that this clause is a proper liquidated damage provision and that they are entitled to summary judgment in an amount representing the total number of photographs not returned multiplied by $1,500.00.

The defendant's main argument is that even if it is liable for the non-return of 39 photographs, the $1,500 per photograph liquidated damage demand bears no relationship to the actual or fair or reasonable value of the photographs and is therefore a penalty.

In early English legal history, parties used penal bonds to secure performance of a contract. Upon a breach, the entire amount of the bond was due immediately, regardless of the actual damages suffered (S. Williston, Contracts, 3d Ed § 774 (1961)). Courts sitting in equity, however, had jurisdiction to intervene and mitigate the harsh results where the breach did not cause any actual damage (*Id*).

American courts recognized the parties' right to set damages in advance of a breach, and distinguished valid clauses from penalties. These courts allowed recovery where the parties had attempted to reasonably estimate in advance the damages that might result from a breach. *United States v. Bethlehem Steel Co.*, 205 US 105 (1907).

In contrast, where the preset damages were "disproportionate to the damage which could have been anticipated from breach of the contract, and which [were] agreed upon in order to enforce performance. . ." (*Bignall v. Gould*, 119 US 495 (1886)), the court labeled the clause an "unenforceable penalty." *Caesar v. Rubinson*, 174 NY 492 (1903).

The controlling principle of law is contained in § 2-718(1) of the Uniform Commercial Code ("U.C.C.") which reads:

> Damages for breach by either party may be liquidated in the agreement but only at an amount which is reasonable in the light of the anticipated or actual harm caused by the breach, the difficulties of proof of loss, and the inconvenience or nonfeasibility of otherwise obtaining an adequate remedy. A term fixing unreasonably large liquidated damages is void as a penalty.

The first sentence of subdivision (1) of U.C.C. § 2-718 focuses on the situation of the parties both at the time of contracting and at the time of breach. So, a liquidated damage provision will be valid if reasonable with respect to either (1) the harm which the parties anticipate will result from the breach at the time of contracting or (2) the actual damages suffered by the nondefaulting party at the time of breach (*See, Equitable Lumber Corp. v. IPA Corp.*, 38 NY2d 516 (1976)).

The plaintiff contends that the $1,500 per photograph liquidated damage provision is an industry wide standard or custom. The defendant disputes this. But, the fact remains that even assuming that his amount is accepted throughout the industry, U.C.C. § 2-718(1) requires that an examination be made to determine the reasonableness of the sum from the aspect of anticipated harm determined at the time of entry into the contract or actual harm determined at the time of breach.

The plaintiff has not made a successful demonstration under either prong of this test. The $1,500 per photograph figures may bear no relationship to the actual value of a photograph which (a) may never have generated any past revenue; (b) is neither unique or novel, and (c) may be able to be duplicated by the photographer who submitted the photograph.

In terms of assessing the reasonableness of the anticipated harm, depending upon the nature and quality of the photograph, an amount required for the loss of one or more of them would, of necessity, vary. I conclude, therefore that the liquidated damage provision is invalid because it is not reasonable with respect to the anticipated or actual harm.

Alternatively, the provision in question is indefinite, rendering it unenforceable. The $1,500 figure is a minimum value and permits the plaintiff to prove a greater value if disposed to do so. There is therefore, no true liquidation of damages since the plaintiff is given the option to disregard the liquidated sum and sue for actual damages. Such a clause is invalid. *Jarro Building Industries Corp. v. Schwartz*, 54 Misc 2d 13.

In *Jarro*, the so-called liquidated damage clause permitted the plaintiff to recover 25% of the total agreed contract price but also afforded the plaintiff the option to disregard the clause and sue for damages if they exceeded the amount stipulated. The court had no trouble finding this clause invalid noting that a valid liquidated damages provision must fix the damages in advance and be for a sum certain.

But here, the clause under scrutiny operates a bit more subtly. It establishes a minimum recovery with the option to seek more by way of a suit for actual damages. A similar clause was invalidated in *Dalston Const. Corp. v. Wallace*, 26 Misc 2d 698, 214 NYS2d 19 (Dist Ct Nassau Co, 2nd Dist 1960), where the court said:

> A liquidated damage clause must always be examined rather closely. The policy of the law is to approve such clauses where they are reasonable. The underlying purpose is to permit parties to look to the future, anticipate that there may be a breach and make a settlement in advance. This implies two things: (1) that the amount specified be a fixed amount and (2) that both parties be bound to that amount. The clause here does not disclose a fixed amount. In essence it fixes a minimum which must be paid by the home owner to the contractor, but leaves the door wide open to him to prove actual damage in addition to the so-called liquidated damage. This is no settlement at all and it permits the contractor to have his cake and eat it too.

214 NYS2d at 193.

The clause here would allow the plaintiff to have its cake and eat it too. Accordingly, it is no liquidated damage clause at all and therefore, plaintiffs motion for summary judgment is denied. Settle order.

BAKER v. INTERNATIONAL RECORD SYNDICATE, INC.

Texas Court of Appeals
812 S.W.2d 53, 15 U.C.C. Rep.2d 875 (1991)

ENOCH, C.J. The opinion of this court issued April 15, 1991 is withdrawn. This is the opinion of the court. Jeff Baker, d/b/a/ Jeff Baker Photography (Baker), appeals a judgment rendered in his favor in a breach of contract case. The trial court determined that a liquidated damages provision was unenforceable and awarded damages to Baker based on jury findings. We reverse the trial court's judgment and render judgment for Baker.

International Record Syndicate (IRS) hired Baker to take photographs of the musical group Timbuk-3. Baker mailed thirty-seven "chromes" (negatives) to IRS via the business agent of Timbuk-3. When the chromes were returned to Baker, holes had been punches in thirty-four of them. Baker sued for the damages to these chromes. The trial court submitted the issues of actual damages and attorney's fees to the jury. The jury found $15,000 in actual damages and $5000 for attorney's fees. The trial court rendered judgment awarding $51,000 in actual damages and $5000 for attorney's fees. The damage award was pursuant to a liquidated damages clause, which set damages at $1500 per chrome. The trial court later modified the judgment, awarded Baker the $15,000 actual damages found by the jury, and eliminated the attorney's fee award.

Liquidated Damages

The provision printed on Baker's invoice states: "[r]eimbursement for loss or damage shall be determined by a photograph's reasonable value which shall be no less than $1500 per transparency." A liquidated damages clause is meant to be the measure of recovery in the event of nonperformance or breach of a contract. . . . The determination of whether a contractual clause is enforceable as a liquidated damages provision or void as a penalty is a question of law. . . .

The Uniform Commercial Code provides:

[Read U.C.C. § 2-718(1).]

Under Texas law, a liquidated damages provision will be enforced when the court finds (1) the harm caused by the breach is incapable or difficult of estimation, and (2) the amount of liquidated damages is a reasonable forecast of just compensation. . . . This might be termed the "anticipated harm" test. The party asserting that a liquidated damages clause is, in fact, a penalty provision has the burden of proof. . . . Evidence related to the difficulty of estimation and the reasonable forecast must be viewed as of the time the contract was executed.

Baker testified that he had been paid as much as $14,000 for a photo session, which resulted in twenty-four photographs and that several of these photographs had also been resold. Baker further testified that he had received as little as $125 for a single photograph. Baker also testified he once sold a photograph for $500. Subsequently, he sold reproductions of the same photograph three additional times at various prices; the total income from this one photo was $1500. This particular photo was taken in 1986 and was still producing income in 1990. Baker demonstrated, therefore, that an accurate determination of the damages from the loss of a single photograph is virtually impossible.

Timbuk-3's potential for fame was an important factor in the valuation of the chromes. At the time of the photo session, Timbuk-3's potential was unknown. In view of the inherent difficulty in determining the value of a piece of art, the broad range of values and long-term earning power of photographs, and the unknown potential for fame of the subject, $1500 is not an unreasonable estimate of Baker's actual damages.

Additionally, liquidated damages must not be disproportionate to actual damages. If the liquidated damages are shown to be disproportionate to the actual damages, then the liquidated damages can be declared a penalty and recovery limited to actual damages proven. . . . This might be called the "actual harm" test. The burden of proving this defense is upon the party seeking to invalidate the clause. *Id.* The party asserting this defense is required to prove the amount of the other party's actual damages, if any, to show that the actual loss was not an approximation of the stipulated sum. . . .

While evidence was presented that showed the value of several of Baker's other projects, this was not evidence of the value of the photographs in question. The evidence clearly shows that photographs are unique items with many factors bearing on their actual value. Each of the thirty-four chromes may have had a different value. Proof of this loss is difficult; where damages are real but difficult to prove, injustice will be done the injured party if the court substitutes the requirements of judicial proof for the parties' own informed agreement as to what is a reasonable measure of damages. The evidence offered to prove Baker's actual damages lacks probative force. IRS failed to establish Baker's actual damages as to these particular photographs.

Even assuming that the jury's findings as to damages are an accurate assessment, we do not agree that that sum is so disproportionate to the stipulated sum so as to abrogate the parties' agreement. Consequently, we conclude that the facts and circumstances of this case require that we reach a decision contrary to the one made by the trial court. We sustain Baker's first point of error and hold that the liquidated damages clause is enforceable.

. . . .

We reverse the judgment of the trial court. We render judgment for Baker in the amount of $51,000 for actual damages and $5000 for attorney's fees.

NOTES

(1) In *Grumman Flexible Corp. v. City of Long Beach*, 505 F. Supp. 623, 31 U.C.C. Rep. 1248 (E.D. N.Y 1980), a contract for purchase of buses contained a liquidated damages provision whereby a charge of $35 per day per bus was to be assessed if the total contract price per bus was not paid within a twenty-day time frame. Held: The provision was consistent with U.C.C. § 2-718(1). "The court . . .finds that the liquidated damages mandated by said agreement are reasonable under the circumstances."

(2) A liquidated damage clause may make a "lease" one intended as security. U.C.C. §§ 1-201(37), 2A-103(1)(j), 9-102(2). See *In re Zerkle Trucking Co.*, 132 B.R. 316 (Bkrtcy, S.D.W.Va. 1991) (Equipment leases with "terminal rent adjustment clauses" (TRAC) were leases intended for security, and not true leases, where agreement provided creditor a guarantee of receiving on default the full cost of equipment plus its anticipated profit).

(3) Proposed U.C.C. § 2-718(a) deletes the word "actual" from 2-718(1) (first sentence), and deletes the second sentence. Proposed subjection (a) goes on to say that in consumer contracts a term fixing unreasonably large or small liquidated damages is unenforceable. The last sentence states that if a liquidated damage term is unenforceable, the aggrieved party has the remedies provided in Article 2. In sum, proposed § 2-718 increases the chances that an otherwise conscionable liquidated damage clause will be enforceable in a commercial contract.

PROBLEM 7.6

Buyer ordered a quantity of wood from Seller for $895 and made a down payment in the amount of $400. Seller accepted the order. There was no understanding with respect to liquidated damages. Three weeks later — and before the wood was delivered — Buyer canceled the order, *i.e.*, repudiated the contract.

Buyer institutes a small claims action for return of the $400 down payment. Is Buyer entitled to recover the down payment or any part thereof? *See* U.C.C. § 2-718 and *Feinberg v. J. Bongiovi Contracting*, 442 N.Y.S.2d 399, 32 U.C.C. Rep. 139 (1981).

NOTE

Proposed U.C.C. § 2-718(b) and (c) has deleted the 20%/$500 formula of § 2-718(2).

WENDLING v. PULS

Kansas Supreme Court
610 P2d 580, 28 U.C.C. Rep. 1362 (1980)

HERD, J.

This is a civil action to recover damages for breach of an oral contract for the purchase and sale of cattle. The case was tried to the court which rendered judgment for the plaintiff-appellee seller [Wendling] in the amount of $14,755.02. . . .

Appellants' second issue is as follows: after Wendling accepted and cashed a down payment check of $1000, can he claim damages in excess of that sum in light of KSA 84-2-718 or in light of the custom and usage in the cattle trade?

Appellants argue custom and usage in the livestock industry considers all down payments on livestock purchase contracts to be liquidated damages, thereby eliminating the need for a specific agreement.

We held in *McSherry v. Blanchfield*, 68 Kan 310, 75 Pac 121 (1904), that custom and usage cannot be shown to create a contract where none existed, but rather its use is restricted to the explanation of technical or trade terms in a contract. This court went on to point out that it must first be shown either that the other party had knowledge of such a custom or that the knowledge among those in the business or industry was so notorious as to furnish a presumption that the other party had knowledge of it. These principles have often been applied.

In *Radio Station KEH Co. v. Local No. 297*, 169 Kan at 603, we discussed the standard of proof required in custom and usage cases as follows:

> The requisites of a good custom must all be established by evidence which is clear and convincing.

The trial court found the evidence of custom and usage was insufficient to show such a custom exists in the cattle trade. We find the appellants failed to meet the required standard of proof and we will not disturb the trial court's findings and conclusions of law as to this issue.

KSA 84-2-718 provides parties to a sales contract may agree to a reasonable amount of liquidated damages in the event of breach. That statute states: [the Court quotes U.C.C. § 2-718].

Appellants argue "if the contract provides for a down payment but not for liquidation of damages, this section [KSA 84-2-718] in effect liquidates them." Appellants argue they are entitled to a refund of their down payment in excess of $500, except that Wendling can offset any damages he proves he has the right to recover. Appellants claim that Wendling may take only $952.70. They arrive at this figure by subtracting $500 [they claim Wendling would keep $500 of the original $1000, pursuant to KSA 84-2-718(2)(b)], from $1452.70, a figure they claim represents the true difference between the market price on the date of delivery and the contract price. They measure the date of delivery from August 23, 1973, rather than September 21, 1973. We do not agree with this construction of KSA 84-2-718. First, there is no written agreement between the parties regarding the amount of liquidated damages to be recovered in the event of breach by the parties. The down payment check itself does not serve as a clear agreement and there is no evidence the parties intended it to indicate a firm agreement regarding damages. Second, we agree that where a seller withholds delivery of the goods because of a buyer's breach, the buyer is entitled to restitution of his down payment, pursuant to KSA 84-2-718(2)(a), or, in the absence of an agreement, pursuant to the formula set forth in KSA 84-2-718(2)(b). The appellants seem to have overlooked, however, the next section of the statute which states the buyer's right to restitution is subject to offset to the extent the seller establishes "(a) a right to recover damages under the provisions of this article other than subsection (1)." The seller in this case has his remedy under KSA 84-2-708. The entire down payment must be applied to the amount recovered pursuant to that statute. In this case, we have already determined the date upon which to base the seller's damages. That date is September 21, 1973, rather than August 23, 1973.[30] Therefore, appellants' proposed recovery formula will not stand. This issue is without merit.

[B] Contractual Modification or Limitation of Remedy

Read: U.C.C §§ 2-719, 2-302; cf. §§ 2-316, 7-204(2), 7-309(2).

Read also: U.C.C. §§ 2A-503, 2A-108, Cf. § 2A-214; CISG Arts. 4(a), 6, 8(2).

IN RE FEDER LITHO-GRAPHIC SERVICES, INC.

United States Bankruptcy Court, Eastern District of Michigan
40 BR 486, 39 U.C.C. Rep. 495 (1984)

George Brody, Bankruptcy Judge.

On March 16, 1978, Rockwell International Corporation (Rockwell) entered into a contract to sell a Miehle Roland Four Color Offset Press to Feder Litho-Graphic Services, Inc. (debtor) for $381,970.[31] Feder Litho-Graphic Services made a down payment of $50,000, and granted Rockwell a security interest to secure the payment of the balance due under the contract. The contract provided for some warranties and excluded others. The warranties and exclusions were as follows:

> WARRANTY: Seller warrants for a period of twelve (12) months from date of initial shipment that new Machinery erected under Seller's supervision is free from defects in material and workmanship at the date of shipment.
>
> THERE IS NO WARRANTY OF MERCHANTABILITY THERE ARE NO WARRANTIES WHICH EXTEND BEYOND THE DESCRIPTION ON THE FACE HEREOF. THERE ARE NO WARRANTIES EXPRESS OR IMPLIED OR ANY AFFIRMATION OF FACT OR REPRESENTATION EXCEPT AS SET FORTH HEREIN.
>
> REMEDY: Seller's sole responsibility and liability and Purchaser's exclusive remedy under this agreement shall be limited to the repair or replacement at Seller's option, of part or parts, not so conforming to the warranty. . . .
>
> DAMAGES: In no event shall Seller be liable for damages of any nature, including incidental, consequential damages, including but not limited to any damages resulting from nonconformity, defect in material or workmanship, services provided or delay of shipment for whatever reason.

On December 22, 1980, Feder Litho-Graphic Services, Inc. filed a chapter 11 proceeding. At the time of the filing of the petition in bankruptcy, the debtor was in default on the payments required under the purchase agreement. Rockwell, accordingly, moved to have the stay vacated to permit it to recover the press, which secured its obligation. Feder counterclaimed, alleging

---

30 [The court found defendants breached the contract when they failed to take delivery of the cattle on or before September 21, 1973. Plaintiffs damages were computed, pursuant to KSA 84-2-708 to be the difference between the contract price computed as to the weight of the cattle on September 21 ($50,533.59) and the fair market value of the cattle on that date ($34,849.08), plus plaintiffs incidental damages incurred in the way of freight costs ($70.51), but less the amount of the down payment tendered by the defendants ($1,000.00).

28 U.C.C. Rep. at 1366-7.-Ed.]

31 Rockwell entered into the contract with David Feder individually. Thereafter, the business was incorporated.

that Rockwell breached its repair warranty and, therefore, the debtor was entitled to recover damages for such breach and additionally to recover consequential damages for lost profits resulting from the breach.[32]

Rockwell denies that it failed to repair the machine, but contends that even if the repair warranty was breached, such breach would not reinstate the consequential damage remedy. To facilitate the progress of the case and in the interest of economy, the parties agreed to submit prior to trial the question whether an exclusion of consequential damages clause survives if a limited remedy fails of its essential purpose. In deciding the preliminary question submitted, the court will assume that the limited repair remedy was breached but that the failure to repair was not willful—that the failure was due to Rockwell's inability to satisfactorily repair the machine.

Initially it is necessary to decide whether Michigan or Illinois law governs the construction of the contract. Subject to certain conditions, the Uniform Commercial Code, adopted in both Illinois and Michigan, permits parties to a contract covered by the Code to designate the law to govern the rights and duties expressed in the agreement. U.C.C. § 1-105(1).[33] The contract provided that the "agreement shall be governed by the laws of the state of Illinois.". . .Accordingly, the contract is to be construed by reference to Illinois law.

The basic provisions of Illinois' U.C.C. governing the merits of this controversy are not in dispute.[34] The debtor and Rockwell agree that parties to a contract of sale may "limit or alter the measure of damages recoverable," § 2-719(1)(a), and that "[c]onsequential damages may be limited or excluded unless the limitation or exclusion is unconscionable," § 2-719(3). Nor is there any question that if the exclusion of consequential damages is unconscionable the court may disregard the exclusionary clause. § 2-302(1). Finally the parties recognize that "[w]here circumstances cause an exclusive or limited remedy to fail of its essential purpose, remedy may be had as provided in this act." § 2-719(2).

The debtor does not contend that the exclusion of consequential damages was unconscionable when the contract was negotiated. The debtor's sole contention is that since Rockwell failed to repair the press, the limited remedy of repair failed of "its essential purpose" and, therefore, by virtue of § 2-719(2), it may recover not only damages for breach of the warranty to repair[35] but may also recover consequential damages despite the contract provision excluding such recovery.

The debtor's argument is simplistic, isolates § 2-719(2) to the exclusion of other related provisions, and is contrary to existing construction of Illinois law. Courts applying Illinois law have consistently held that the failure of a limited remedy to repair does not automatically nullify a contractual provision excluding consequential damages as a remedy. . . .[36]

---

[32] The case was converted to Chapter 7 on August 23, 1982, and the press was sold pursuant to court order for $315,000.

[33] Section 1-105(1) of the U.C.C. reads in pertinent part: "[W]hen a transaction bears a reasonable relation to this state and also to another state or nation the parties may agree that the law either of this state or of such other state or nation shall govern their rights and duties." U.C.C.§ 1-105(1).

[34] Actually, the U.C.C. of every state has essentially the same provisions. However, not all states have reached the same result as to the construction to be given these provisions.

[35] The measure of damages for breach of warranty to repair is the difference between "the value of the goods accepted and the value they would have had if they had been as warranted." § 2-714(2).

[36] For an analysis of the cases dealing with this issue, see Eddy, *On "Essential Purposes" of Limited Remedies: The Metaphysics of U.C.C. Section 2-719(2)*, 65 Calif. L. Rev. 28 (1977).

These holdings harmonize the statutory provisions that relate to this controversy. The Code was intended to encourage and facilitate the allocation of risks associated with the sale of goods. "By limiting the warranties available and the remedies under the warranties, parties are able to provide a consensual allocation of risks in accordance with sound business practices." *AES Technology Systems Inc.*, 583 F2d at 939. Courts, therefore, absent circumstances that warrant their intrusion, ought not to "rewrite contracts by ignoring parties' intent; rather, [they should] interpret the existing contract as fairly as possible when all events did not occur as planned." *Id.* at 941. "The limited remedy of repair and a consequential damages exclusion are two discrete ways of attempting to limit recovery for breach of warranty. The Code, moreover, tests each by a different standard. The former survives unless it fails of its essential purpose, while the latter is valid unless it is unconscionable." *Chatlos Systems, Inc.*, 635 F2d at 1086 (citations omitted). No reason exists, therefore, to hold, "as a general proposition, that the failure of the limited remedy provided in the contract, without more, invalidates a wholly distinct term in the agreement excluding consequential damages. The two are not mutually exclusive." *Id.* Whether the preclusion of consequential damages as a remedy is to be nullified when a limited warranty fails "depends upon the circumstances involved." *Id.* Essentially, the question "narrows to the unconscionability of the buyer retaining the risk of consequential damages upon the failure of the essential purpose of the exclusive repair remedy." *Id.* at 1087. *See also Adams v. J.I. Case Co.*, 125 Ill. App 2d 388,261 NE2d 1(1970). Absent the presence of factors that make the exclusion of consequential damages unconscionable at the inception of the contract or in its performance, the buyer's recovery for the breach of a warranty to repair is limited to the damages flowing from the breach of such warranty.

The cases construing Illinois law relied upon by the debtor, *Adams v. J.I. Case Co.*, 125 Ill App 2d 388, 261 NE2d 1 (1970); *Custom Automated Machinery v. Penda Corp.*, 537 F Supp 77 (D ND Ill 1982); *KKO, Inc. v. Honeywell -Inc.*, 517 F Supp 892 (D ND Ill 1981), do not support the debtor's position. In *Adams*, the court did refuse to give effect to the contract provision excluding consequential damages when the warranty to repair clause was breached, but did so only because the complaint alleged facts "that would constitute a repudiation by the defendants of their obligations under the warranty, that repudiation consisting of their wilful failure or their careless and negligent compliance." 261 NE2d at 7-8. The court made it clear that had the sellers "reasonably complied with their agreement contained in the warranty they would be in a position to claim the benefits of their stated limited liability and to restrict plaintiff to his stated remedy." *Id.* at 7.

The contract in *Penda* did not expressly exclude consequential damages. Therefore, the court had no reason to, and did not, address the question presented here.

Honeywell also offers no aid to the debtor. *Honeywell* does not hold, as the debtor maintains, that the breach of a limited warranty automatically entitles a buyer of goods to recover consequential damages when the contract specifically excludes such damages. *Honeywell* merely holds, as this court now holds, that, although consequential damages are not automatically recoverable, "factual circumstances may permit an award of consequential damages where a remedy has failed its essential purpose, notwithstanding an exclusion clause." 517 F Supp at 898.

. . .

An order consistent with this opinion has been previously entered.

NOTES AND QUESTIONS

(1) The court in *Middletown Concrete Products, Inc. v. Black Clawson Co.*, 802 F. Supp. 1135 at 1151-52 (D. Del. 1992) comments:

> The courts from various jurisdictions are divided on the issue of whether a clause disclaiming liability for consequential damages is automatically ineffective when a repair and replacement remedy has failed of its essential purpose. Some courts have read subsection (2) and (3) of § 2-719 as being interdependent, thus permitting recovery of consequential and incidental damages when a limitation of remedy contained in a contract has failed of its essential purpose. [Citations.] Special Project, *Article Two Warranties in Commercial Transactions: An Update*, 72 Cornell L.Rev. 1159, 1307 (1987) (noting a majority of cases have concluded that the failure of an exclusive remedy voids the consequential damages exclusion when an exclusive remedy fails).
>
> These "interdependent" courts find support for their position in the straightforward application of § 2-719(2) which reads, "[w]here circumstances cause an exclusive or limited remedy to fail of its essential purpose, the remedy may be had as provided in this chapter." Focusing solely on the language of subsection (2), the interdependent courts conclude that when a limited remedy fails of its essential purpose, the plain language of subsection (2) entitles plaintiff to consequential and incidental damages as remedies available "in this chapter."
>
> Further support for this position is found in the comments to § 2-719. Comment 1 to Iowa's equivalent of § 2-719, for instance, reads in pertinent part, "[U]nder subsection (2), where an apparently fair and reasonable clause because of circumstances fails in its purpose or operates to deprive either party of the substantial value of the bargain, it must give way to the general remedy provisions of this Article." Since consequential and incidental damages are permitted under the general remedy provisions of the Iowa Code, it can be argued they are, therefore, permitted when the limited remedy of repair and replace fails of its essential purpose. Explaining the underlying assumptions of this approach, one student commentator has observed, interdependent courts "conclude that the parties intended the validity of the consequential damage exclusion to depend on the effectiveness of the limited remedy; if the limited remedy fails, so does the consequential damage exclusion." Murtagh, *U.C.C. Section 2-719: Limited Remedies and Consequential Damage Exclusions,* 74 Cornell L.Rev. 359, 369 (1989).
>
> Other courts, however, have reached different conclusions based on the language in subsection (3). [Citations.] Subsection (3) reads, "Consequential damages may be limited or excluded unless the limitation or exclusion is unconscionable. Limitation of consequential damages for injury to the person in the case of consumer goods is prima-facie unconscionable but limitation of damages where the loss is commercial is not." The courts relying on subsection (3) view it as "independent" from subsection (2). Accordingly, these "independent" courts "see no reason to hold, as a general proposition, that the failure of the limited remedy provided in the contract, without more, invalidates a wholly distinct term in the agreement excluding

consequential damages. The two are not mutually exclusive." [Citation.] That the two subsections are independent is supported by the Code which tests each by a different standard: a limited remedy of repair or replace survives under subsection (2) unless it fails of its essential purpose; a limitation of consequential damages survives under subsection (3) unless it is unconscionable. Because the tests for the two subsections are different, the "independent" courts conclude the two subsections are wholly distinct.

Further support for this approach can also be found in the comments to § 2-719. Comment 1 to the Iowa equivalent of § 2-719 reads, "Under this section parties are left free to shape their remedies to their particular requirements and reasonable agreements limiting or modifying remedies are to be given effect." . . . Consistent with this sentiment, independent courts have concluded the purpose of § 2-719 is to encourage and facilitate allocation of risk between contracting parties. . . . Accordingly, independent courts will not preclude a limitation of consequential damages unless it is unconscionable. . . .

Having weighed both positions, the Court concludes the latter line of cases is more thoroughly reasoned and consistent with the general purposes of the Uniform Commercial Code. . . . According to Professors James White and Robert Summers, the cases treating the two subsections as independent,

> seem most true to the Code's general notion that the parties should be free to contract as they please. When the state intervenes to allocate the risk of consequential loss, we think it more likely that the loss will fall on the party who cannot avoid it as the lowest cost. This is particularly true when a knowledgeable buyer is using an expensive machine in a business setting. It is the buyer who operates the machine, adjusts it, and understands the consequences of its failure. Sometimes flaws in such machines are inherent and attributable to the seller's faulty design or manufacture. But the fault may also lie in buyer neglect, inadequate training and supervision of the operators or in intentional use in ways forbidden by the seller. Believing the parties to know their own interests best, we would leave the risk allocation to the parties.

(2) In *Rudd Construction Equipment Co., Inc. v. Clark Equipment Co.*, 735 F.2d 974, 38 U.C.C. Rep. 873 (6th Cir. 1984), Rudd purchased a tractor shovel from Clark. The machine was destroyed by a fire caused by fluid from a ruptured hydraulic hose which ignited upon contact with heat from the turbochargers. (The hose was part of the original equipment of the machine.) The contract for sale had provisions (1) disclaiming warranties (with exceptions) (2) limiting remedies to replacing or repairing defective parts and (3) excluding liability for consequential damages. Held: Repair-replace and consequential damages exclusion clauses were ineffective to limit liability; buyer was entitled to the net replacement value of the machine. "[W]here the failure of a part of the machine has resulted directly in the loss of the whole, the machine is considered 'one big defective part.' " 38 U.C.C. Rep. at 876. Alternatively, "any limitation which would deny this recovery would also fail of its essential purpose under [U.C.C. § 2-719(2)]." *Id.*

(3) See *Adams v. American Cyanamid Co.*, 498 N.W.2d 577, 21 U.C.C. Rep.2d 962 (Neb. App. 1992) (conspicuous requirement imposed by U.C.C. § 2-316(2)for warranty disclaimers should be read into § 2-719 for remedy limitations); cf. *American Dredging Co. v. Plaza Petroleum, Inc.*, 799 F.Supp. 1335, 18 U.C.C. Rep.2d 1101 (E.D. N.Y. 1992) (U.C.C. § 2-719 provides that parties to a contract may agree to exclude consequential damages so long as the limitation is not unconscionable, but it does not require that the clause be conspicuous. Conspicuousness, however, is a factor to consider when determining unconscionability).

(4) The Magnuson-Moss Federal Warranty Act applies to written warranties as to "consumer products." 15 U.S.C. § 2301 et seq.; 16 C.F.R. 700. Generally, the act does not affect state law regarding consequential damages for injury to the person or other injury. § 2311 (b)(2). However, under § 2304(a)(3), a "warrantor may not exclude or limit consequential damages for breach of any written or implied warranty on such product, unless such exclusion or limitation conspicuously appears on the face of the warranty." Further, 16 CFR § 701.3(a)(8)(see § 2302(a)) requires disclosure of any exclusions of or limitations on relief such as incidental or consequential damages, accompanied by the following statement:

> Some states do not allow the exclusion or limitation of incidental or consequential damages, so the above limitation or exclusion may not apply to you.

(5) Proposed U.C.C. § 2-719(b) clarifies the effect when an agreed, exclusive remedy fails of its essential purpose: The aggrieved party has remedies provided in Article 2 to the extent that the agreed remedy has failed, but agreed remedies outside the scope of and not dependent on the failed agreed remedy are enforced as provided in § 2-719. Under subsection (c) a limitation or exclusion of consequential damages for commercial loss is presumed to be conscionable. Subsection (d) provides special rules for consumer contracts, e.g., if an exclusive remedy fails of its essential purpose, the consumer buyer may revoke acceptance, obtain a refund or replacement of the goods from the seller. A term limiting or excluding consequential damages is inoperative unless the seller proves by clear and convincing evidence that the buyer understood and expressly agreed to the term. Exclusion or limitation of consequential damages for injury to the person is unconscionable as a matter of law.

[C] Remedies for Fraud

Read: U.C.C. § 2-721.

Read also: § 2A-505(4) and (5); CISG Art. 4(a).

PROBLEM 7.7

Tinker purchased for investment purposes a used Jaguar automobile from DeMaria who orally represented to Tinker, prior to making the sale, that the Jaguar was in good operating condition, was powered by its original engine, and had never been involved in a major collision. Tinker relied on these representations and DeMaria intended for Tinker to act on the representations.

Tinker had problems with the Jaguar immediately after its purchase. In addition to the misrepresentation with respect to the automobile's operating condition at the time of purchase, it was not powered by its original engine when sold, had previously been involved in a major collision and was considered a total loss by its previous owner's insurance company. DeMaria knew of and concealed the true history of the automobile which constituted intentional misrepresentation.

Tinker seeks to obtain recision of the sales agreement induced by DeMaria's intentional misrepresentation (fraud) and seeks in addition to recover consequential damages for loss of its investment. DeMaria asserts that the state's fraud law requires defrauded Tinker to make a choice between the remedies of recision and damages. May Tinker rescind *and* have damages? See U.C.C. §§ 1-103, 2-608, 2-711, 2-715, 2-721 and *Tinker v. DeMaria Porsche Audi, Inc.*, 459 So. 2d 487, 37 U.C.C. Rep. 1519 (Fla. App. 1984). See also, *South Hampton Co. v. Stinnes Corp.*, 733 F.2d 1108, 38 U.C.C. Rep. 1137 (5th Cir. 1984).

[D] Who Can Sue Third Parties for Injury to Goods?

Read: U.C.C. § 2-722.
Read also: U.C.C. § 2A-531; CISG Art. 4.

INTERNATIONAL HARVESTER CREDIT CORP v. VALDEZ

Washington Court of Appeals
42 Wash. App. 189, 42 U.C.C. Rep. 337 (1985)

MUNSON, J.

International Harvester Credit Corporation (International) appeals a summary judgment in favor of Santiago Valdez. The sole issue is whether the holder of a security interest in a motor vehicle is barred from bringing suit against a tortfeasor, who had destroyed the secured vehicle, after the tortfeasor's settlement with the registered owner. We answer in the affirmative.

In 1980, David Valle purchased a used truck tractor and potato bed for $14,375.84. He made a substantial down payment and received a trade-in allowance; the remainder of the purchase price was financed by the seller, who assigned the contract to International. Valle was to make four payments, due in July and December 1981 and 1982 respectively. International's perfected security interest was shown on the certificate of title. See RCW 62A.9-302; RCW 46.12.095.

In October 1981, the tractor was involved in a collision with a truck owned by Santiago Valdez and driven by his employee. The tractor was apparently damaged beyond repair. Valdez's insurance carrier paid Valle approximately $14,000 in full settlement of his property damage claim. Neither Valdez nor his insurance carrier had actual knowledge of the security interest; neither contacted the Department of Licensing to examine the certificate of title.

Valle failed to make the 1982 payments, totaling approximately $4,000. International first learned of the accident and settlement when it began its collection effort.

International commenced this action against Valdez for the damages to its security interest. The trial court granted summary judgment for Valdez, stating: (1) Valdez had no duty to protect International's security interest and (2) International's suit was barred by Valdez's settlement in full with Valle. International appeals.

We assume arguendo that Valdez was responsible for the 1981 accident. Initially, both the debtor and secured party have a cause of action against the tortfeasor who damages the secured property. RCW 62A.2-722;[37] . . .

In *Stotts v. Puget Sound Traction, Light & Power Co., supra*, the court noted a tortfeasor with actual notice of security interest in the damaged property could protect himself by bringing in the secured party as an additional party. However, the court went on to hold the secured party had waived his right to recover by appearing as a witness on the debtor's behalf and not seeking to formally intervene. Neither Stoss [sic] nor articles 2 and 9 of the Uniform Commercial Code speak to whether a settlement between the debtor and tortfeasor releases the tortfeasor from liability to the secured party. See 69 Am. Jur. 2d Secured Transactions, § 267 at 97 (1973); Weinberg, *Secured Party's Right to Sue Third Persons for Damage to or Defects in Collateral*, 81 Com. L.J. 445 (1976).

---

[37] RCW 62A.2-722 provides: [the Court quotes U.C.C. § 2-722].

The majority rule is that only one cause of action arises out of the tortfeasor's misconduct; therefore settlement in full between the tortfeasor and debtor for all property damage, absent fraud or collusion, bars a subsequent suit by the secured party.

International vigorously argues the certificate of title constituted constructive notice to Valdez of its security interest. Thus, Valdez had a duty to notify International of the accident, and include it as a party to any settlement of the claim.

Nationwide Ins. Co. v. Bank of Forest, 368 S.2d 1273 (Miss. 1979), supports International's position. There it was held the tortfeasor's insurer acted without reasonable prudence when it settled with the owner of the other vehicle without first checking the certificate of title. Therefore, the secured party was entitled to maintain an action, subsequent to the settlement, against the tortfeasor and her insurer to recover the amount of its lien. The court reasoned the purpose of the Mississippi Motor Vehicle Title Law was to establish a central source of information regarding motor vehicle titles, affording protection to the public, including secured parties. The court referred to statutes which provide the certificate of title constitutes prima facie evidence of the facts appearing on it, and that notation on the certificate of title is the exclusive method of perfecting a security interest.

Nationwide, at 1276, rejected the majority rule, stating:

> We acknowledge the rule but do not think it persuasive. The numerous business and credit transactions directly related to motor vehicles are common knowledge. The protection of business through registration of title under the Motor Vehicle Title enactment, in our opinion, outweighs the barring of either a mortgagor or mortgagee from bringing suit against a tortfeasor who has settled with either one or the other with total disregard for the lien rights of others. We think the very purpose of the Motor Vehicle Title Law was to afford a central place and a designated official so that essential information concerning title to motor vehicles might be readily available to anyone with legitimate needs therefor. It seems to us that ordinary prudence, at the very minimum, would require a cursory investigation of title before an owner was paid the full value of the vehicle, less salvage value, in settlement of a claim. Had this been done both the Bank of Forest and Nationwide would have been protected.

However, the court restricted its holding to cases where the collateral has been destroyed:

> The present factual situation does not permit discussion of the many claims that might arise from minor accidents, "fender benders," which, it is contended, might inundate the motor vehicle comptroller's office with multiple inquiries, thereby disturbing its normal business activities. Moreover, the repair of a vehicle as distinguished from a sale for salvage has the likelihood of maintaining the value of the security and thereby protecting the lien rather than obliterating it. We presently speak only to facts wherein a vehicle was demolished leaving the residue of salvage value only.

Nationwide, at 1275.

We adopt the majority rule for the following reasons. First, the purpose of the Certificate of Title Act is to protect secured parties as those parties are identified and defined in the Uniform Commercial Code. See RCW 46.12.005; RCW 46.12.095 (procedure for protecting security interest in motor vehicle). Official Comment 1, RCW 62A.9-303 states that the result of perfecting a security interest is that the secured party is protected against *creditors, transferees*, and creditors' representatives in insolvency. Tortfeasors are not among those given record notice of properly perfected security interests.

Second, RCW 62A.2-722 contemplates one settlement in which the settling party holds the proceeds in trust for the secured party to the extent of the outstanding obligation. The underlying rationale is that the debtor has the right to possession and is entitled to recover the full amount of damage. Thus, a tortfeasor would not necessarily have a duty to join the secured party even if he had actual notice of the security interest. But cf. . . . (where tortfeasor's insurer assured secured party that settlement would not affect his rights, tortfeasor estopped from raising settlement with debtor as bar to subsequent action by secured party). This comports with the common law of bailment and the public policy favoring compromise and settlement.

In applying the above concepts to the facts presented here, we conclude the tortfeasor, Valdez, did not owe any duty to the secured party, International. First, International's perfection of its security interest in the tractor did not provide Valdez or his insurer with notice of that interest. Neither Valdez nor his insurer was required to ascertain whether there were any liens upon Valle's tractor prior to the settlement of the claim. Official Comment 1, RCW 62A.9-303. Moreover, International's contract does not obligate Valle to give the secured party notice of any damage to the collateral. International is seeking to impose a higher duty upon Valdez than it imposed upon its own debtor, Valle.

Second, Valle and not International was in possession of the tractor at the time the accident occurred. Valle was not in default and, in fact, made one payment after the accident. Valdez's wrongful act created only once cause of action for property damage, and Valle as vendee was entitled to recover for the full value of the damage. *Universal Credit Co. v. Collier, supra; Ellis v. Snell, supra*; RCW 62A.2-722.

The judgment is affirmed.

NOTES

(1) *Security Interest Under Article 2 Sales*. In *Johnson v. Conrail-Amtrak Federal Credit Union, 37 U.C.C. Rep. 933 (D.C. Super. 1983)*, the court asserted that any security interest, whether it is a security interest which arises by a security agreement under Article 9, or a security interest by virtue of Article 2, is a security interest within U.C.C. § 2-722 so as to justify suit by the secured party against the third person tortfeasor. See U.C.C. §§ 2-703(a), 9-113 and Comment 1; see also § 4.05 Security Interest.

(2) *Special Property*. In *Ross Cattle Co. v. Lewis, 415 So. 2d 1030, 34 U.C.C. Rep. 913 (Miss. 1982)*, Lewis contracted to sell identified cattle to Ross. Lewis then sold some of the animals through Cow Palace, Inc., an auction sales corporation. With respect to Ross's rights against Cow Palace, and its officers Delony and Reeves, the court said:

> In substance, § 75-2-722 [U.C.C. § 2-722], provides for a cause of action against a third person who deals with goods that have been identified to a contract in such a way as to cause an actionable injury to a party to the contract. The right of action is given to either the seller or the buyer who has title to or a security interest in, or a special property or insurable interest in the goods. 67 Am Jur 2d, Sales § 236 (1973). The effect of § 75-2-722 is that third parties

will be liable for conversion, physical damage to goods, or interference with the buyer's rights in goods. Mississippi Code Annotated § 75-2-103 (1972) defines a buyer as a person who buys or contracts to buy the goods.

Upon the evidence we think Ross had a right of action under this section against Cow Palace, Delony, and Jim Reeves. There can be no doubt that Ross had a special property interest in the animals because the company had contracted to buy them and the animals had been identified to the contract.[38]

. . . .

The plain black letter language of § 75-2-722 means that Ross having a "special property" interest in the animals has a right of action against the third parties (Cow Palace, Delony, and Jim Reeves) because they were "converting" the animals after they were shown or given knowledge of Ross's contract vesting in Ross the special property interest in the animals. These three defendants/appellees, with full knowledge of Ross's claim against the animals, actively and knowingly aided and abetted Lewis in disposing of the animals contrary to his contract with Ross.

See § 4.03 Special Property.

[E] Statute of Limitations

Read: U.C.C. § 2-725; see §§ 2-313, 2-314, 2-315, 2-503.

Read also: U.C.C. § 2A-506; see §§ 2A-210, 2A-212, 2A-213; Convention on the Limitation Period in the International Sale of Goods (1974 and 1980 Protocol of Amendment).

NEW ENGLAND POWER CO. ET AL. v. RILEY STOKER CORP.

Massachusetts Appeals Court
20 Mass. App. Ct. 25, 477 N.E.2d 1054, 40 U.C.C. Rep. 1735 (1985)

PERRETTA, J.

In 1969, the plaintiffs (referred to herein, in the singular, as NEP) entered into two contracts with the defendant (Riley) for the design, manufacture, and installation of two boilers for NEP's facilities at Salem and Brayton Point (Fall River). A detailed description of the boilers is unnecessary. It is sufficient to state, as did NEP in its amended complaint, that "[b]oilers such as these are technologically complex and sophisticated and . . .are entirely dissimilar from the small, residential or commercial units with which the public is generally familiar." Almost as soon as the boilers were put into use, it became apparent that they suffered from serious defects. Then began an extended period, from 1972 through 1976, during which Riley, working along with independent consultants and engineers retained by NEP, made repeated but unsuccessful attempts to repair the boilers. By 1978, Riley was no longer participating in any repair attempts. On March 11, 1980, NEP brought this action, alleging breaches of warranties and of promises to repair, as well as negligence. Riley affirmatively pleaded that the action was time-barred under GL c 106, § 2-725(1), and c 260, § 2A, and moved for summary judgment. NEP appeals from

[38] Under Miss Code Ann § 75-2-501 identification of goods occurs when existing goods are designated or agreed upon as the goods to which the contract refers, which happened in the instant case at the time the contract was signed.

the judgment entered on Riley's motion and argues that its action was not commenced beyond the time allowed by those statutes and, in the alternative, that Riley is estopped by its conduct from asserting that defense. We affirm.

I. Breaches of Warranties[39]

If NEP were to commence timely its action for breaches of warranties under the contract, it was required by GL c 106, § n 2725(1), as appearing in St 1957,c 765, § 1, to bring its action "within four years after the cause of action has accrued." Paragraph (2) of § 2-725 provides, in full: [the Court quotes U.C.C. § 2-725(2)].[40]

When Riley tendered delivery of the boilers is the issue in dispute. By way of definition, GL c 106, § 2-503(1), as appearing in St 1957, c 765, § 1, provides that tender of delivery "requires that the seller put and hold conforming goods at the buyer's disposition." The judge found that the Salem and Brayton Point boilers were put into "commercial use" on August 24, 1972, and December 18, 1974, respectively, and concluded that delivery had to have been completed prior to March, 1976.[41] Suit was commenced on March 11, 1980.

NEP argues that there was no tender of delivery prior to March of 1976 and that, in fact, delivery has never been tendered. As support for this contention, NEP extracts two sentences from the first paragraph of the official comment to GL c 106, § 2-503: "The term 'tender' is used in this Article in two different senses. In one sense it refers to 'due tender' which contemplates an offer coupled with a present ability to fulfill all the conditions resting on the tendering party and must be followed by actual performance if the other party shows himself ready to proceed."[42] Uniform Laws Comment, GL c 106, § 2-503, Ann Laws of Mass, at 69. Defining tender as "due tender," NEP argues that there was no tender of delivery within the meaning of § 2-725(2), because when the boilers were "delivered," both Riley and NEP knew that they were defective and had to be repaired. Extending this theory, NEP takes the position that since the boilers are still defective, there has been no tender of delivery.

---

[39] Counts one and seven of the amended complaint allege breaches of express and implied warranties under the two contracts of sale, count one as to Salem, count seven as to Brayton Point. The arguments in NEP's brief are diffuse and scattered, but, as we understand them, NEP now argues only as to implied warranties. Its claims based on breaches of express warranties under those contracts have been transformed, as will be seen *infra*, to claims of breaches of promises to repair, as alleged in counts two and eight. . . .

[40] We are not dealing with warranties as to future performance. (See *e.g.*, *Mittasch v. Seal Lock Burial Vault, Inc.*, 42 AD2d 573 [NY 1973], where the court held that the statement that the casket and burial vault "will give satisfactory service at all times" was a warranty which explicitly extended to future performance.) Were we, NEP would have no claim, since it does not argue express warranties, and "an implied warranty, by its very nature cannot explicitly extend to future performance. . . .

[41] In its brief, NEP states that in the utility industry the term "commercial use" means that the boiler is generating steam and that the term is "strictly a financial and rate-making consideration unrelated to compliance or non-compliance with the contract." This contention would be material and in dispute only if we accept NEP's definition of "tender of delivery," which, as will be seen, *infra*, we do not.

[42] That paragraph continues: "Unless the context unmistakably indicates otherwise this is the meaning of'tender' in this Article and the occasional addition of the word 'due' is only for clarity and emphasis. At other times it is used to refer to an offer of goods or documents under a contract as if in fulfillment of its conditions, even though there is a defect when measured against the contract obligation. *Used in either sense, however, 'tender' connotes such performance by the tendering party as puts the other party in default if he fails to proceed in some manner.*" (Emphasis added.)

A similar, if not identical, argument was unsuccessfully made in *Standard Alliance Indus. v. Black Clawson Co.*, 587 F2d 813, 819 (6th Cir 1978),[43] i.e., that "tender" of new, highly complex machinery should not be held to have occurred until the machine is made to operate properly. We also do not accept this claim, for to do so would "extend the statute of limitations indefinitely into the future since a defect at the time of delivery would prevent proper 'due tender' from taking place until it was corrected." *Id. See also Ontario Hydro v. Zallea Sys., Inc.*, 569 F Supp 1261, 1267 (D Del 1983) ("If the court were to apply the phrase ['due tender'] as [the plaintiff] suggests, then until the seller tenders conforming goods, the limitation period provided in § 2-725 would never apply. This would circumvent the very purpose of § 2-725, which . . .is to provide a finite period in time when the seller knows that he is relieved from liability for a possible breach of contract for sale or breach of warranty"). We conclude that the definition of tender of delivery urged by NEP is inconsistent with the purpose of § 2-725(2), as well as with the final sentence of the first paragraph of the official code comment to § 2-503. *See* note 6, *supra*.

We are not dissuaded from our conclusion by NEP's argument that acceptance of "due tender" as the controlling definition is compelling where the seller and buyer acknowledge at the time of delivery that the goods are defective. We see no reason to apply a more rigorous rule to an unwitting buyer than to a fully informed one. Simply put, although knowledge may be relevant to a buyer's acceptance of goods, see GL c 106, § 2-607, it is irrelevant to the running of the time period set out in § 2-725, except where, unlike here, there is a warranty as to future performance.

II. PROMISES TO REPAIR.[44]

Both contracts entered into in 1969 contain the following clause:

> Notwithstanding the other continuing obligations of the Contractor under this Agreement, the Contractor shall repair and make good, without cost to the Purchaser, any damages, defects or faults resulting from imperfect or defective work done or unsound or improper materials furnished by the Contractor which develop during the period of one year (or during a longer period if so stipulated in the specifications) from date of the certification by the Engineer that the work has been completed.

NEP argues that language constitutes "a promise rather than a warranty," and that this cause of action could not have accrued until Riley, in 1978, refused or failed to repair the boilers. However, promises to repair or to replace are generally viewed as specifications of a remedy rather than as an independent or separate warranty. See *Standard Alliance Indus. v. Black Clawson Co.*, 587 F2d at 818 n 10; *Ontario Hydro v. Zallea Sys., Inc.*, 569 F Supp at 1266-1267; *Centennial Ins. Co. v. General Elec. Co.*, 74 Mich App 169, 171-172 (1977); *Commissioners of Fire Dist. No. 9 v. American La France*, 176 NJ Super 655, 573 (1980); *Owens v. Patent Scaffolding Co.*, 77 Misc 2d 992, 998-999 (1974), rev'd on other grounds, 50 AD2d 866 (NY 1975). Those cases instruct that when there are a warranty and a promise to repair, the remedy of first resort is the promise to repair. If that promise is not fulfilled, then the cause of action is the underlying breach of warranty.

[43] Cases from jurisdictions other than Massachusetts deal with the relevant parts of § 2-725 of the Uniform Commercial Code which are in a form identical to those found in GL c 106.

[44] Counts two and eight of the amended complaint speak in terms of breaches of express warranties. NEP now couches its claims in terms of promises distinct from warranties.

The reasoning is sound and particularly pertinent here, where NEP's argument seems structured to avoid the consequences of its failure timely to commence suit. As pointed out in *Centennial Ins. Co. v. General Elec. Co.*, 77 Mich App at 172: "Plaintiff's argument is in essence that by failing to remedy its first breach, the defendant committed a second breach, giving rise to a brand new cause of action and starting anew the limitations period. The fallacy of this approach is apparent. If we adopted plaintiff's position, limitations periods could be extended for virtually infinite time. We doubt that the Legislature intended such a result." It follows from this that what we have stated in part one of this option is applicable to NEP's claims of breaches of the promises to repair.

III. TOLLING AND ESTOPPEL.

NEP next contends that Riley's repeated efforts to repair and assurances that the boilers would be fixed either tolled the running of § 2-725(1) or estopped Riley from relying upon it as a defense.

a. Tolling. Whether repeated repair efforts toll the running of § 2-725(1) depends upon our tolling statutes, as found in GL c 260, §§ 7 through 12, since § 2-725 "does not alter the law on tolling of the statute of limitations. . . ." GL c 106, § 2-725(4), as appearing in St 1957, c 765, § 1. There is nothing in our tolling statutes which would allow NEP to commence suit as late as sometime in 1982, in other words, four years after Riley ceased its efforts to repair the boilers. Nor is it open to us to enlarge upon those statutes.[45] See *Del Grosso v. Board of Appeal of Revere*, 330 Mass 29, 32(1953), and cases therein cited.

b. Estoppel. If NEP is to escape the consequence of its lack of diligence in bringing its action, it must be by way of proof that Riley wrongfully lulled NEP into the delay. See *White v. Peabody Constr. Co.*, 386 Mass 121, 134 (1982) ("[E]stoppel would require proof that the defendants made representations they knew or should have known would induce the plaintiffs to put off bringing a suit and that the plaintiffs did in fact delay in reliance on the representations"). The judge concluded that the facts alleged by NEP to estop Riley, even if proved, were insufficient as matter of law because: (1) NEP made no allegation of fraud or misrepresentations by Riley which would show that Riley "purposely prolonged the time for repairs beyond the running of the statute of limitations"; (2) any assurance given by Riley that the boilers would be fixed did not rise to the level of "lulling" NEP into "foregoing suit"; and (3) "both parties are large corporations with equal access to legal advice."

There are no rigid criteria to apply in determining whether a defendant's conduct was such as to give rise to an estoppel. The test, if it can be so called, is that the "doctrine of estoppel is not applied except when to refuse it would be inequitable." We think it appropriate then, when looking to the facts offered by NEP to show an estoppel, that they be viewed in the context in which they took place, *i.e.*, "Here . . .we have two corporate behemoths, well able to look out for themselves. . . ."

NEP contends that whether it was lulled into inaction by Riley presents a material factual dispute. The conduct NEP relies upon is correspondence between NEP and Riley in 1974. NEP wrote to Riley suggesting that arbitration would be a reasonable course of action "at this time." NEP's letter pointed out: "While arbitration is not the nicest place to end up, it seems preferable

[45] NEP relies upon *Colorado-Ute Elec. Assn. v. Envirotech Corp.*, 524 F Supp 1152, 1155-1156 (D Col 1981), for the proposition that repair efforts generally toll § 2-725(1). However, there the court cited and relied upon *Kniffin v. Colorado Western Dev. Co.*, 622 P2d 586 (Col App 1980), as indicative of Colorado's acceptance of the theory that repair efforts operate to toll the running of a limitation period.

to an open-break between our companies, and the unpleasant events that will inevitably follow . . . ." Riley responded, and swiftly, that Riley and NEP were more competent than an arbitrator to analyze the problems with the boilers. Riley added that it "has in the past and will in the future stand behind all of its warranties" and that "[s]hould there be design deficiencies, Riley. . .corrects them without further cost to the customer." Riley pointed out that there were "major questions" as to whether problems with the boilers were in fact caused by improper operation rather than any design deficiencies. The letter concluded with Riley voicing "concerns" of its own regarding NEP's failure to release certain monies owed to Riley.

Reading this correspondence as favorably as possible to NEP, we do not see how, in the absence of distortion, Riley's statements could give rise to an estoppel.[46] When we couple these statements with Riley's repeated efforts to repair (1972 through 1976, when the efforts tapered off; they ceased altogether by 1978), NEP's argument loses rather than gains force. The undisputed facts show that it was Riley's position from the outset that it would repair the boilers and that it continuously tried to do so. NEP does not allege that Riley's repair efforts were insincere or a mere pretext, only that they were unsuccessful.

That NEP may have behaved in a commercially reasonable manner in relying upon Riley's efforts (in the belief that because Riley designed, manufactured, and installed the boilers, it was best able to repair them) does not become material until it is first shown that Riley engaged in some conduct, such as insincere effort, which would make it unfair to allow Riley to rely upon § 2-725(1). We do not view the fact of honest, genuine repair efforts, standing alone, as sufficient basis for application of the doctrine of estoppel. In our view, to conclude otherwise would be to hold that repair efforts toll § 2-725.

Judgment affirmed.

NOTES AND QUESTIONS

(1) *Tender of Delivery*. With respect to a breach of warranty, proposed U.C.C. § 2-725(c)(1)[Alternative 1] provides that a claim for relief accrues when the seller has tendered delivery of *nonconforming* goods. Further, Subsection (c)(2) states that if a warranty expressly extends to performance of the goods after delivery, a claim for relief accrues thereafter when the buyer discovers or should have discovered the breach. Subsection (c)(3) provides that if the seller, after delivery, attempts to conform goods to the contract and fails, the period of limitation is tolled during the time of the attempt.

[46] NEP also relies upon oral statements alleged by NEP's general purchasing agent by way of affidavit to have been made by Riley in response to the purchasing agent's complaints that if the boilers were not fixed, litigation would be commenced. The purchasing agent set out Riley's response as, "Riley repeatedly assured me that it would repair the boilers and that litigation was not necessary." It does not appear from the judge's memorandum of decision that he took these statements into account. He was, however, free to disregard them. Conspicuously missing from the affidavit are any factors to show who from Riley gave these assurances.

(2) *Warranty of Future Performance.* Compare the "tender of delivery" rule with the "discovery of the breach" rule of U.C.C. § 2-725(2). Which rule do you prefer from seller's standpoint; from buyer's? Now read the following excerpt.

Nationwide Insurance Co. v. General Motors Corporation/ Chevrolet Motor Division, 625 A.2d 1172, 21 U.C.C. Rep.2d 277 (Pa. 1993), held that GM's automobile warranty which provided that the dealer would repair or make adjustments to the automobile for the first 12 months or 12,000 miles, whichever came first, was a warranty which explicitly extended to future performance of the automobile and the cause of action accrued at the time the breach of warranty was or should have been discovered, rather than the date of delivery of the automobile, even though GM claimed that the commitment was not a warranty but an undertaking to repair or replace. See U.C.C. § 2-725(2). A dissent observed:

> Here, the promise to repair or adjust defective parts for 12 months or 12,000 miles. This is not the same as a promise that the car and its parts will remain free of defects for 12 months or 12,000 miles. The latter promise "explicitly extends to future performance of the goods;" the former promise does not.

With respect to implied warranties the majority stated:

> Although we find the express warranty to explicitly extend to future performance of the goods, we cannot find that the implied warranties of merchantability and fitness for a particular purpose so extend. The warranty contains the following language: "ANY IMPLIED WARRANTY OF MERCHANTABILITY OR FITNESS FOR A PARTICULAR PURPOSE APPLICABLE TO THIS CAR IS LIMITED IN DURATION TO THE DURATION OF THIS WRITTEN WARRANTY." We do not read this language as explicitly extending the terms of any implied warranties, because the document states that any implied warranties are of a duration *no longer than* that of the express warranty and not that they are of a duration *equal to* that of the express warranty. The quoted language does not create implied warranties, because such warranties are created not by contract language but by operation of law in certain circumstances. *See* [U.C.C. §§ 2-314, 2-315]. The legal effect of the quoted language is merely to limit the protection that the law might otherwise impose. Therefore, it cannot be read as the type of language that "explicitly extends to future performance" for purposes of § [2-725(2)]. In addition, the great weight of authority takes the position that an implied warranty, by nature, cannot "explicitly" extend to future performance.

But a dissent stated:

> I would hold that the implied warranties of merchantability and fitness for a particular purpose also extend to the future performance of the vehicle because these implied warranties are expressly linked temporally to the express warranty by the [above] language contained in the express warranty at issue.

See *Tittle v. Steel City Oldsmobile GMC Truck, Inc.*, 544 So.2d 883 (Ala. 1989) (New car limited warranty which covered "any repairs and needed adjustments to correct defects in material or workmanship" was warranty to repair, and not warranty extending to future performance).

(3) *Proposed U.C.C. § 2-725(c).* Proposed § 2-725(c) [Alternative 1] is summarized at Notes and Questions (1) above. Alternative 2 states that if a breach of warranty occurs, a claim for relief accrues when the buyer discovers or should have discovered the breach. The Reporter's Notes state that § 2-725(c) provides a choice for the Drafting Committee in breach of warranty cases between the tolling principle now found in § 2-725(2) and a discovery principle, *i.e.*, the

cause of action does not accrue until the buyer "discovers or should have discovered the breach." Which Alternative would you recommend to the Drafting Committee and why?

(4) *Tolling*. West's Ann.Cal.Civ.Code § 1795.6 (Tolling or expiration of warranty period during time of repairs) states that every warranty period relating to an implied or express warranty accompanying a sale of consumer goods (bought for personal, family or household purposes) selling for $50 or more shall be automatically tolled for the period as set forth in the statute. See also, *e.g.*, Mich.Comp.Laws Ann. § 440.2313b (Express warranty, extension of period for repaired goods).

As to tolling of the statute for mental incapacity, see *Curlee v. Mock Enterprises Inc.*, 173 Ga. App. 594, 327 S.E.2d 736, 41 U.C.C. Rep. 63 (1985); as to tolling of the statute for fraudulent concealment in a personal injury case, see *Freiberg v. Atlas Turner, Inc.*, 1984 WL 178948, 37 U.C.C. Rep. 1592 (D. Minn. 1984).

See Proposed U.C.C. § 2-725(c)(3)[Alternative 1] at Notes and Questions (1) above.

(5) *Tort versus Contract*. A recurrent question arising in actions for defective goods is whether the cause of action arises in tort or in contract. If the action can be characterized as tort, whether on the basis of negligence or strict liability, the statute of limitations will often be only two or three years, but the statute will not begin to run until the plaintiff has been injured by the defect. If the action is a contract action, on the other hand, U.C.C. § 2-725 will apply, the period of limitation will be four years (unless shortened by agreement), but the statute will begin to run upon breach of the sale contract, which will normally occur when tender of delivery is made. Some courts have permitted the plaintiff to characterize the action as tort or contract through allegations in the complaint. See, *e.g., Cochran v. Buddy Spencer Mobile Homes Inc.*, 618 P.2d 947 (Okla. 1980); *Colvin v. FMC Corp.*, 43 Ore. App. 709, 604 P.2d 157 (1979). Other courts have held that all personal injury actions arising from defective products must be treated as tort actions. See, *e.g.,Witherspoon v. General Motors Corporation*, 535 F. Supp. 432, 33 U.C.C. Rep. 583 (WD. Mo. 1982). The Delaware Supreme Court, on the other hand, has held that enactment of the U.C.C. sales provisions preempted the entire field of sales cases, and therefore strict tort liability has no application. *Cline v. Prowler Industries of Maryland, Inc.*, 418 A.2d 968, 29 U.C.C. Rep. 461 (Del. 1980). Accordingly, the four-year statutory period of U.C.C. § 2-725is applicable in all actions arising from the sale of goods. *Johnson v. Hockessin Tractor, Inc.*, 420 A.2d 154, 29 U.C.C. Rep. 477 (Del. 1980). (For a catalogue of the different approaches taken to this question by the various state and federal courts, see *Ogle v. Caterpillar Tractor Co.*, 716 P.2d 334, 42 U.C.C. Rep. 1668 (Wyo. 1986)).

In *R. W. Murray Co. v. Shatterproof Glass Corp.*, 697 F.2d 818, 35 U.C.C. Rep. 477 (8th Cir. 1983), it was held that the U.C.C. § 2-725 four-year statute of limitations applied to an implied warranty action by a remote purchaser for economic loss arising in the sale of goods. The court at 35 U.C.C. Rep. 487, note 9, observed:

> We do not believe this result is in conflict with the recent decision in *Witherspoon v. General Motors Corp.*, 535 F. Supp. 432 (WD Mo 1982). *Witherspoon* did not address the question of the statute of limitations applicable in Missouri to an implied warranty suit by a remote purchaser for *economic loss*. Instead, the court held only that under Missouri law an action for *personal injuries* arising out of a breach of an implied warranty is not governed by the four year Uniform Commercial Code statute of limitations, but by the five year statute of limitations for actions for personal injuries not arising on contract and not otherwise enumerated. See Mo Ann Stat § 516.120 (Vernon 1952).

For discussion of strict liability and interaction of warranty and strict liability, see §§ 5.07 and 5.08, *supra.*

(6) *Products Liability Action.* Some states have adopted a statute of limitations for "products liability actions," that is, those which involve injuries to person or property. For example, Mich. Comp. Laws Ann. § 600.2945 defines such action:

> As used in . . .section 5805, "products liability action" means an action based on any legal or equitable theory of liability brought for or on account of death or injury to person or property caused by or resulting from the manufacture, construction, design, formula, development of standards, preparation, processing, assembly, inspection, testing, listing, certifying, warning, instructing, marketing, advertising, packaging, or labeling of a product or a component of a product.

Mich. Comp. Laws Ann. § 5805(1) and (9) sets forth the relevant period of limitations:

> (1) A person shall not bring or maintain an action to recover damages for injuries to persons or property unless, after the claim first accrued to the plaintiff or to someone through whom the plaintiff claims, the action is commenced within the periods of time prescribed by this section.
>
> . . . .
>
> (9) The period of limitations is 3 years for a products liability action. However, in the case of a product which has been in use for not less than 10 years, the plaintiff, in proving a prima facie case, shall be required to do so without benefit of any presumption.

For discussion of product liability statutes, see §§ 5.09 and 5.10, *supra.*

(7) *Privity.* If the doctrine of privity of contract has been abolished, so that a consumer may bring a breach of warranty action against the manufacturer, does the statute of limitations begin to run when the manufacturer tenders delivery of the goods to the wholesaler or retailer, or when the consumer receives tender of delivery from the retailer? *Patterson v. Her Majesty Industries, Inc.*, 450 F. Supp. 425, 23 U.C.C. Rep. 1198 (E.D. Pa. 1978), gives the latter answer, reasoning that maximum protection should be accorded the ultimate user.

In *Heller v. U.S. Suzuki Motor Corp.*, 64 N.Y.2d 407, 488 N.Y.S.2d 132, 477 N.E.2d 434, 40 U.C.C. Rep. 917 (1985), distributor Suzuki sold a motorcycle to Bakers on March 30, 1978, who transferred it to retailer Moroney, who in turn, sold it to plaintiff on April 21, 1979. Plaintiff was injured July 7, 1979, and brought suit against Suzuki on February 15, 1983, for breach of warranty that the motorcycle was safe, merchantable and fit for its intended use. (Note that New York had adopted Alternative B to U.C.C. § 2-318. Also note that the tort causes of action were barred by the three-year statute of limitations.) The court held that under U.C.C. § 2-725, the cause of action against distributor Suzuki accrued on the date the party charged tendered delivery of the product to Bakers (March 30, 1978), not on the date some third party (Moroney) sold it to plaintiff (April 21, 1979). Thus plaintiff's failure to commence the action within the four-year period from March 30, 1978, barred his action against Suzuki. (*See also Rissew v. Yamaha Motor Co., Ltd.*, 493 N.Y.S.2d 78, 41 U.C.C. Rep. 1740 (1985).)

For discussion of privity, see § 5.05, *supra.*

(8) *Reduction of Period of Limitation.* U.C.C. § 2-725(1) provides: "By the original agreement the parties may reduce the period of limitation to not less than one year but may not extend it." See *Burroughs Corporation v. Suntogs of Miami, Inc.*, 472 So. 2d 1166, 41 U.C.C. Rep.

498 (Fla. 1985) (effect of § 95.03, Florida Statutes, which provides: "Any provision in a contract fixing the period of time within which an action arising out of the contract may be begun at a time less than that provided by the applicable statute of limitations is void.").

CITY OF WOOD RIVER v. GEER-MELKUS CONSTRUCTION COMPANY, INC.

Supreme Court of Nebraska
444 N.W.2d 305 (1989)

WITTHOFF, DISTRICT JUDGE.

This is an appeal from an order of the Hall County District Court finding the third-party action of Geer-Melkus Construction Company, Inc., and United States Fidelity & Guarantee Company (Geer-Melkus) against Geo. A. Hormel & Company (Hormel) was barred by the statute of limitations.

FACTS

Appellant Geer-Melkus contracted with the City of Wood River to construct a waste water treatment facility. Appellee Hormel manufactured and supplied the rotating media aeration system for the facility. The media system was delivered on or about September 14, 1976, and the plant became operational in the summer of 1977. In the following years, many repairs were made to the media system, and in December 1982 the system broke down completely and could not be repaired.

Wood River filed an action for breach of contract against Geer-Melkus on July 6, 1981. With the court's consent, on December 22, 1981, Geer-Melkus filed a third-party complaint against Hormel, alleging that if it was found liable to Wood River, Hormel was liable to it for breach of warranty.

Specifically, Geer-Melkus complained (1) Hormel warranted the rotating media aeration system would, without further modification, provide a minimum of 22,000 square feet of biological support media in each of the first two stages and 33,000 square feet in the final two stages, for a total of 110,000 square feet of biological support media; (2) Geer-Melkus installed the waste water treatment facility in exact accordance with the plans and specifications; (3) the waste water treatment facility was made operational on or about July 27, 1977; (4) the media rotary disk unit deteriorated and shifted on its shaft; (5) the deterioration and shifting subsequently caused damage to the bearings of the shaft and the shaft itself; (6) the shifting and deterioration required Wood River to replace portions of the waste water treatment system; and (7) the deterioration and shifting were contrary to the specifications for the fixed media rotating disk unit. Geer-Melkus attached, and incorporated by reference, a copy of Wood River's petition as an exhibit to their third-party complaint, and alleged that

> if the allegations of the Plaintiff's Petition are found to be true and if the Plaintiff recovers a judgment against the Defendants and Third Party Plaintiffs, the Third Party Defendant would be liable to the Defendants and Third Party Plaintiffs for the entire amount of the Plaintiffs [sic] claim against them for the reason that said allegations constitute a breach of the Third Party Defendant's express warranty set forth in paragraph 8 hereof.

On February 12, 1982, Hormel filed a demurrer, based primarily upon the statute of limitations defense, which the court overruled. Hormel filed an answer to the third-party complaint on March 5, 1982, admitting it manufactured and supplied the rotating system and stating the system was delivered on February 12, 1978. Hormel raised as affirmative defenses that (1) the action was barred by the statute of limitations; (2) the amount of the claim exceeded the coverage of the warranty; (3) Wood River failed to properly operate and maintain the system; (4) Hormel was not notified of the alleged breach of warranty; and (5) the warranty expired on February 12, 1978. Geer-Melkus filed a reply, alleging the statute of limitations had not run because they were asking for indemnity.

Hormel then moved for summary judgment, once again asserting the statute of limitations. The motion for summary judgment was overruled.

On November 12, 1985, a separate trial was held on the issue of the statute of limitations. At trial, Hormel demurred ore tenus, which demurrer the court also overruled. At the conclusion of this trial, the judge ruled the statute of limitations was tolled because of repairs and replacements made by Hormel.

Trial on the merits was held on October 28, 1986. The court found for Wood River and against Geer-Melkus in the amount of $57,379.54 on the original petition. On the third-party petition, the court found for Hormel and against Geer-Melkus, holding that the third-party action was barred by the statute of limitations. Pursuant to statute, the court allowed attorney fees of $19,000 to Wood River against Geer-Melkus. Geer-Melkus appeals the court's ruling on their third-party complaint and Hormel cross-appeals the earlier failures to dismiss the action.

ASSIGNMENTS OF ERROR ON APPEAL

Geer-Melkus assigns as error (1) the trial court's failure to direct a verdict in favor of Geer-Melkus and against Hormel at the close of the evidence; (2) the trial court's entry of judgment generally in favor of Hormel and against Geer-Melkus; (3) the trial court's failure to enter judgment against Hormel on the theory of indemnity; (4) the trial court's finding, after the trial on merits, that Geer-Melkus' claim was barred by Neb. U.C.C. § 2-725 (Reissue 1980), and reversing its previous finding in favor of Geer-Melkus following a separate trial on the issue of the statute of limitations; and (5) the trial court's failure to determine Neb.Rev.Stat. § 25-224(3) (Reissue 1985) applied to Geer-Melkus' claim.

On cross-appeal, Hormel claims the trial court erred (1) in overruling Hormel's demurrer and (2) in denying Hormel's demurrer ore tenus and admitting evidence at trial on the nature of the statute of limitations issue, over Hormel's objection.

LOSS OF JURISDICTION BY THE
DISTRICT COURT TO MODIFY
ITS OWN ORDERS

The term of court ended after the trial on the statute of limitations and the court's ruling against Hormel. Geer-Melkus claims the court was therefore without authority to modify this ruling after the trial on the merits.

. . . .

[Discussion.]

In conclusion, the district court had jurisdiction to modify its earlier orders on the statute of limitations issue.

ISSUE OF INDEMNITY RAISED BY
THE PLEADINGS

Before we can determine whether the statute of limitations bars Geer-Melkus' third party claim, we must determine whether Geer-Melkus seeks damages on a breach of warranty or seeks indemnification. Geer-Melkus does not specifically ask for "indemnity," but, instead, asks for damages for breach of warranty. The third-party complaint specifically set forth the problems with the "rotating media aeration system" manufactured by Hormel. It incorporated Wood River's petition and all its allegations. Finally, the third-party complaint alleged that if Wood River recovered a judgment against Geer-Melkus, Hormel would be liable to Geer-Melkus for the entire amount of Wood River's claim because of the expressed warranty.

While the term "indemnity" is not specifically used,

> [t]he essential character of a cause of action or the remedy of relief it seeks, as shown by the allegations of the complaint, determines whether a particular action is one at law or in equity, unaffected by conclusions of the pleader or what the pleader calls it, or the prayer for relief.

Waite v. Samson Dev. Co., 217 Neb. 403, 408, 348 N.W.2d 883, 887 (1984); *Brchan v. The Crete Mills*, 155 Neb. 52 N.W.2d 333 (1952).

Even if the pleading mistakenly identified a cause of action, the right to recover under the facts alleged is not affected.

> In order to decide the form of the redress, whether contract or tort, it is necessary to know the source or origin of the duty or the nature of the grievance. Attention must be given to the cause of the complaint; in other words, the character of the action must be determined from what is asserted concerning it in the petition in the cause. It is not important what the plaintiff calls his action. If he does attempt to identify it and is mistaken, that is immaterial. This is the rationale of the code provision that a petition is a statement of facts constituting a cause of action in ordinary and concise language.

Fuchs v. Parsons Constr. Co., 166 Neb. 188, 192, 88 N.W.2d 648, 651 (1958).

It is evident from the pleadings Geer-Melkus claims that (1) appellant Geer-Melkus purchased the rotary system from Hormel; (2) Hormel manufactured the same to meet certain specifications; (3) the system did not meet those specifications; and (4) if Geer-Melkus suffered damages because of the failure of Hormel to fulfill its contractual obligation, they would look to Hormel for payment of their loss. The third-party complaint sets out specifically what Hormel's aeration system did wrong. A duty to indemnify will always arise out of another more basic obligation whether it arises on contract or tort. Although Utah chose to bring sales indemnification actions within § 2-725 of the Uniform Commercial Code, the Utah Supreme Court identified an allegation of a breach of warranty as raising the issue of indemnification.

> Perry argues that [§ 2-725] does not apply because his action is in reality one for indemnity, not one for breach of warranty. We consider this argument in the context of the undeniable fact that the subject matter of this entire lawsuit is the sale of goods, which will be governed where applicable by the Utah version of the Uniform Commercial Code. . . . *The underlying action was for breach of contract, and the amended third-party complaint alleges only a cause of action for breach of warranty. It nowhere mentions indemnity. Nonetheless, we look to the substance of Perry's claim, regardless of what he chose to call it.*

(Emphasis supplied.) *Perry v. Pioneer Wholesale Supply Co.*, 681 P.2d 214, 217 (Utah 1984).

Hormel cannot claim that it did not understand the theory upon which the third-party complaint was predicated or that it had no warning in time to defend itself. The motion for leave to file a third party complaint against Hormel specifically stated that "a rotating media aeration system manufactured by George A. Hormel & Co. was defective and was not merchantable and if such allegations are true these Defendants would be entitled to indemnification from George A. Hormel & Co."

In addition thereto, the reply filed by Geer-Melkus specifically addressed § 2-275 and alleged that it did not apply

> for the reason that under the substantive law of the State of Nebraska the periods of limitation set forth in the foregoing statues, if applicable in the instant case, do not start to run upon a claim for indemnity until such time as the indemnitee's liability has been fixed and discharged.

Therefore, the third-party complaint raised an indemnification cause of action.

APPLICABILITY OF § 2-725 TO INDEMNIFICATION CAUSES OF ACTION

All parties agree the sale which is the subject matter of the third-party complaint is a sale of goods within the meaning of the Uniform Commercial Code. As such, the original contract and warranty were covered by the statute of limitations of contracts for sale.

In examining the statute and the proposed scope of the statute, it should be noted that any action for breach of contract must be commenced within 4 years after the cause of action has accrued. The statute further specifically defines accrual of a cause of action by saying that the breach occurs when a tender of delivery is made, except where a warranty specifically extends to future performance of the goods, and discovery of the breach must await time of such performance. In this case the warranty did not specifically extend to future performance.

We have not previously addressed the question of whether the limitation set out in § 2-725 applies to an indemnity claim. Other jurisdictions have split on the issue.

Georgia, Utah, Illinois, and Idaho have held indemnity claims are controlled and limited by § 2-725. [Citations.] These jurisdictions view the strict application of § 2-725 as necessary to avoid the problem of unending litigation.

> The four-year statute applicable to the indemnity theory does not apply in this case because a sale of goods occurred in 1974 with observable defects (if any), and any cause of action against Third-Party Defendants arose at that time. Otherwise, anyone buying defective goods could resell them before or after the statute had run, and upon being sued for the original defects, file a third-party complaint for indemnity and thus defeat the policy of repose underlying the statute of limitation.

Perry v. Pioneer Wholesale Supply Co., 681 P.2d 214, 217 n. 1 (Utah 1984).

Maryland, New Hampshire, Missouri, Maine, North Carolina, and New York have ruled indemnity claims do not come under the time limitation found in § 2-725. [Citations.] These jurisdictions follow the reasoning advanced by the New York Court of Appeals in *McDermott v. City of N.Y., supra* 50 N.Y.2d at 216-17, 406 N.E.2d at 462, 428 N.Y.S.2d at 646:

> Conceptually, implied indemnity finds its roots in the principles of equity. It is nothing short of simple fairness to recognize that "[a] person who, in whole or in part, has discharged a duty which is owed by him but which as between himself and another should have been discharged by the other, is entitled to indemnity" (Restatement, Restitution, § 76). To prevent unjust enrichment, courts have assumed the duty of placing the obligation where in equity it belongs. [Citations.]

In deciding the statute of limitations question was governed by the indemnity rule rather than the contract or warranty rule, the Maryland Court of Special Appeals stated:

> In approaching this issue, both sides have focused their attention on when limitations begins to run in an action for indemnification and have given but scant consideration to the nature of the indemnity claim actually made by appellant. As to the limitations question, we think that appellant is correct in her view that an action for indemnification accrues and the limitations period commences not at the time of the underlying transaction but when the would-be indemnitee pays the judgment arising from the underlying transaction. That seems to be the majority view, and it is certainly in keeping with the nature of an indemnity action.

(Citations omitted.) *Hanscome v. Perry, supra* 75 Md.App. at 614, 542 A.2d at 425.

In applying the Missouri rule, the U.S. District Court used the same rationale. In *City of Clayton v. Grumman Emer. Prod.,* [576 F. Supp. 1122 (E.D. Mo. 1983)], the issue was which party was financially responsible for cracks in a firetruck frame. The firetruck was purchased by the city from Howe Fire Apparatus Co., Inc., which was subsequently merged into Grumann Emergency Products, Inc. The frame was manufactured by The Warner and Swayse Company. Clayton sued Grumman as the successor in interest to Howe, which brought in Warner and Swayse as third party defendants. Warner and Swayse responded by pleading the statute of limitations.

> Although Grumman raises the issue of the future performance exception to § 2-725, the Court need not address that question. Counts I and III of Grumann's third-party complaint state causes of action for indemnity based on breaches of express and implied warranties. The statue of limitations for indemnity does not start to run until the indemnitee is found liable to a third party. *See Simon v. Kansas City rug Co.,* 460 S.W.2d 596, 600 (Mo.1970). Therefore, Grumman's claims for indemnity from Warner are not time barred. This result does not imprudently enlarge the statute of limitations for breach of warranty. A party who buys and

then resells a product is not in a position to discover the latent defect within the warranty's limitation period because the product is in the hands of the consumer during that time. Only when the consumer sues the retailer does the retailer gain notice of the latent defect. *See Walker Manufacturing Co. v. Dickerson, Inc.*, 619 F.2d 305, 310 (4th Cir.1980) (North Carolina U.C.C. law).

City of Clayton, supra at 1127.

Nebraska has long held a claim for indemnity accrues at the time the indemnity claimant suffers loss or damage. *City of Lincoln v. First Nat. Bank of Lincoln,* 67 Neb. 401, 93 N.W. 698 (1903).

In *Waldinger Co. v. P & Z Co., Inc.*, 414 F.Supp. 59 (D.Neb. 1976), the trial court held the underlying statute of limitations dealing with political subdivision tort claims did not apply to actions seeking contribution or indemnification. Waldinger Co. instituted an action on January 16, 1976, against P & Z, Metropolitan Utilities District of Omaha, and the City of Omaha, alleging negligence proximately resulting in the collapse of a slurry trench wall which surrounded the Omaha-Douglas Civic Center. On May 3, 1976, the City of Omaha filed a third-party complaint against Hawkins Construction Company, Leo A. Daly Company, and Omaha-Douglas Public Commission for indemnification or contribution. Thereafter, the commission moved to dismiss the third-party complaint for failure to file a tort claim pursuant to the Political Subdivisions Tort Claims act, Neb.Rev.Stat. § 23-2401 et seq. (Reissue 1974). The commission argued that any claims not filed within 1 year of the injury were extinguished.

In interpreting Nebraska law on contribution and indemnity, the trial court held:

> These decisions are based on sound equitable principles. Contribution and indemnification are inchoate rights which do not arise until one tort feasor has paid more than his share of the damages or judgment. A plaintiff may sue one tort feasor or he may join all tort feasors in one suit. He may also wait more than a year to file his suit. To accept the Commission's argument that the claim for contribution or indemnification arises when the injury is incurred would allow plaintiff to choose which defendant would bear the burden by simply filing his lawsuit after the one year statute of limitations has run. The defendant joint tort feasor, having no prior knowledge of a claim, would be unable to file a claim prior to being joined in the lawsuit.

Waldinger Co. v. P & Z Co., Inc., supra at 60.

The reasoning in *McDermott, Hanscome,* and *City of Clayton* is consistent with Nebraska law. If we were to adopt the opposite position, a party who might have a claim for indemnification would have to bring his action before the underlying claim was brought to avoid the running of the statue of limitations. Therefore, we hold § 2-725 does not apply where a party is seeking indemnification.

The present case is a classic example of the inequity which would result from adopting the theory advanced by Hormel. Geer-Melkus could not have brought their cause of action for indemnity until the original suit was brought by Wood River on July 6, 1981. The statute of limitations on the indemnity action would have expired on December 14, 1980. Geer-Melkus would be left with no recourse under these circumstances.

It is generally recognized that the party seeking indemnification must have been free of any wrongdoing, and its liability is vicariously imposed. Therefore, it should recover from another. [Citations.] In this case, the product was manufactured and sold by Hormel. The evidence in the record indicates any problems with the product were directly attributable to Hormel, not to Geer-Melkus.

The trial court found that the statute of limitations questions was resolved by *Grand Island School Dist. #2 v. Celotex Corp.*, 203 Neb. 559, 279 N.W.2d 603 (1979). This action was to recover damages arising from a leaky roof installed upon a junior high school. The school district sued the general contractor, the architect, the subcontractors, and various and sundry bonding companies. One of the defendants was dismissed on a demurrer and the others on motions for summary judgment, on the basis that the various statutes of limitations had run. Because none of the defendants were liable, there was no issue of indemnity.

Geer-Melkus asserts the proper statute governing limitation of this action is Neb.Rev.Stat. § 25-224 (Reissue 1985). In the event § 25-224 were deemed applicable, subsection (3) removes the limitation on indemnity claims. We therefore need not address the question of whether the third-party complaint comes within § 25-224.

For the foregoing reasons, we find the statute of limitations does not bar the third-party complaint brought by Geer-Melkus.

CONCLUSION

The trial court's findings that the pleadings and evidence establish that Geer-Melkus Construction Company, Inc., and United States Fidelity & Guarantee Company's claim was for a breach of warranty and not for a claim of indemnification and that the claim was barred by the statute of limitations, § 2-275, are reversed. As noted above, the uncontroverted evidence establishes that the loss was directly attributable to Hormel. The action is therefore remanded with instruction to enter judgment against Hormel.

Reversed and remanded with direction.

NOTES AND QUESTIONS

(1) Proposed U.C.C. § 2-725(c)[Alternative 2] provides that if a breach of warranty or *indemnity* occurs, a claim for relief accrues when the buyer discovers or should have discovered the breach. How would this affect the *Wood River* case? Cf. U.C.C. § 2A-506(2)(second sentence).

(2) Statutes that address the question of indemnity include West's Ann.Cal.Civ.Code § 1792:

> Unless disclaimed in the manner prescribed by this chapter, every sale of consumer goods that are sold at retail in this state shall be accompanied by the manufacturer's and the retail seller's implied warranty that the goods are merchantable. The retail seller shall have a right of indemnity against the manufacturer in the amount of any liability under this section.

Further, § 1795.7 (Liability of manufacturer; extension upon tolling of warranty period) states:

> Whenever a warranty, express or implied, is tolled pursuant to Section 1795.6 as a result of repairs or service performed by any retail seller, the warranty shall be extended with regard to the liability of the manufacturer to a retail seller pursuant to law. In such event, the

manufacturer shall be liable in accordance with the provisions of Section 1793.5 for the period that an express warranty has been extended by virtue of Section 1795.6 to every retail seller who incurs obligations in giving effect to such express warranty. The manufacturer shall also be liable to every retail seller for the period that an implied warranty has been extended by virtue of Section 1795.6, in the same manner as he would be liable under Section 1793.5 for an express warranty. If a manufacturer provides for warranty repairs and service through its own service and repair facilities and through independent repair facilities in the state, its exclusive liability pursuant to this section shall be to such facilities.

See discussion of tolling at Notes and Questions (4) following the New England Power Co. case, *supra*.

§ 7.08 Punitive Damages

Read U.C.C. § 1-106

Traditionally, punitive damages were not allowed by the courts in breach of contract cases. However, in recent years, punitive damages have played an increasingly important role in contract and other commercial law cases. In some cases throughout this casebook, you may note that the damages asserted or given include punitive damages.

Some courts have required that in addition to breach of contract, there be an independent tort show such as fraud. Others have simply allowed punitive damages because the circumstances so warrant (*e.g.*, bad faith, outrageous conduct) and note it as an exception to the traditional rule. The basic code section on remedies, § 1-106, generally is viewed as permitting punitive damages under the "otherwise in law" part. Caselaw has established the doctrine of punitive damages over many decades.

The student of commercial law will find punitive damages in cases where there has been intentional and outrageous conduct by one of the parties. Willfulness or wanton reckless disregard of others are elements of the requirement of intentionalness, There may be various degrees of outrageousness. Some of these will involve sales contracts. Punitive damages also arise in other areas. For example, it may arise in regard to the wrongful dishonor of a customer's checks in Article 3, or in regard to a wrongful repossession under a security agreement in Article 9.

PROBLEM 7.8

A.R. Jones, a car dealer for the Fuji Car Company, often receives some of its luxury "Diamond" cars with minor scratches on a fender incurred during shipment. It is able to repaint these without it being noticed and has the approval of the Fuji Company on doing this. It does not tell the customer and generally it is never noticed.

Mr. Robert Rich has found out that this happened to a Diamond car he recently purchased from A.R. Jones Company.

Suppose you are representing Mr. Rich. What damages would you assert? What evidence would be relevant? What dollar amount would you suggest as appropriate?

PROBLEM 7.9

Suppose you are representing A.R. Jones Company with the facts as stated above. What arguments and damages would you anticipate ? What are your arguments?

PROBLEM 7.10

The A.R. Rich Company also sells s streaking Star sports car with the "Rocket" engine. Out of rocket engines, Fuji substitutes one of its other car engines which is used in the Diamond car. This engine has just as much horsepower, as much quality, and a similar design. It advises A.R. Jones company not to mention this to customers.

You have been consulted by A.R. Jones. What is your advice? What are the possible damages? What are Fuji Company's possible damages? Suppose the Fuji Company carries out this plan and you represent a Streaking car buyer. What damages and what amount would you assert?

NOTES

(1) In a U.S. Supreme Court case with facts similar to Problem 7.8, *BMW of North America, Inc. v. Gore*, 116 S. Ct. 1589 (1996), it was held that the state had a legitimate interest in allowing punitive damages but that the gross excessiveness violated elementary fairness as reflected in due process. For the undisclosed minor repainting of the new car ($ 600 on a $ 40,000 car) the jury assessed compensated damages of $ 4,000 and $ 4 million in punitive damages. The Alabama Supreme Court had reduces punitive damages to $ 2 million. The U.S. Supreme Court found this to be excessive. It looked at:

(1) the degree of reprehensibility,

(2) the disparity of harm or potential harm suffered and the punitive damage award,

(3) the difference between this remedy and civil penalties in comparable areas.

It found no evidence of deliberate false statements or concealment with improper motive.

Three justices in a concurring opinion noted the difficulties in ascertaining just when the punitive damage amount is excessive and exceeds the state's legitimate interests, but that this award lies in the line's far side.

(2) How does one measure the degree of outrageousness or reprehensibility? Can you devise some standards?

(3) One of the purposes of punitive damages is to punish or "slap" the wrongdoer to such an extent that it takes notice and revises its practices. It has long been recognized that the more wealthy the company involved, the harder the "slap" necessary. A very wealthy company is not hurt as badly y a couple million dollar punitive damage award. Evidence of a company's net worth is often brought into such cases for this very purpose. The Supreme Court in the *Gore* case noted that there was no evidence that a more modest sanction would not be sufficient to motivate BMW to make full disclosure thereafter.

(4) Some states require that a part of punitive damage awards (*e.g.*, one half) go the state or a special state government fund to help others. Should this make a difference in evaluating the amount?

CHAPTER 8

RIGHTS OF THIRD PARTIES: GOOD FAITH PURCHASE OF GOODS

§ 8.01 Introduction

The general common law rule was that where goods were sold by a person who was not the owner, and who did not sell them under the authority or with the consent of the owner, the buyer acquired no better title to the goods than the seller had.[1] This rule is reflected in the maxims: Nemo dare protest quod non habet (No man can give that which he has not), Nemo dat qui non habet (He who hath not cannot give), etc. To this rule there were exceptions, notably (1) the doctrine of market overt;[2] and (2) estoppel — the owner of the goods by his conduct may be precluded from denying the seller's authority to sell.[3]

The classic case of *O'Connor's Administratrix v. Clark*, 170 Pa. 318, 32 A. 1029 (1895), is illustrative. There, O'Connor owned a wagon. Tracy, a piano mover, with the knowledge and consent of O'Connor had his name and occupation printed upon the side of the wagon to create the public impression that he was the owner as follows: "George Tracy-Piano Mover" and proceeded to use the same. Thereafter, Tracy, without the knowledge and consent of O'Connor, the owner of the wagon, sold the wagon to Clark. O'Connor sought to recover possession of the wagon from Clark. In holding for Clark the court stated:

> While the soundness of the general rule of law that a vendee of personal property takes only such title or interest as his vendor has and is authorized to transfer cannot for a moment be doubted, it is not without its recognized exceptions. One of these is where the owner has so acted with reference to his property as to invest another with such evidence of ownership, or apparent authority to deal with and dispose of it, as is calculated to mislead, and does mislead, a good-faith purchaser for value. In such cases the principle of estoppel applies, and declares that the apparent title or authority, for the existence of which the actual owner was responsible, shall be regarded as the real title or authority, at least so far as persons acting on the apparent title or authority, and parting with value, are concerned. Strictly speaking, this is merely a special application of the broad equitable rule that, where one of two innocent persons must suffer loss by reason of the fraud or deceit of another, the loss should fall upon

---

[1] See Uniform Sales Act § 23(1) at note c below.

[2] The English Sale of Goods Act § 22(1) provided: "Where goods are sold in market overt, according to the usage of the market the buyer acquires a good title to the goods provided he buys them in good faith and without notice of any defect or want of title on the part of the seller." This doctrine has not been recognized in the United States.

[3] Uniform Sales Act § 23(1) stated:

> [W]here goods are sold a person who is not the owner thereof, and who does not sell them under the authority or with the consent of the owner, the buyer acquires no better title to the goods than the seller had, unless the owner of the goods is by his conduct precluded from denying the seller's authority to sell.

him by whose act or omission the wrongdoer has been enabled to commit the fraud. Assuming, in this case, that a jury, under the evidence, should find — as we think they would be warranted in doing — that such marks of ownership were placed on the property by direction of O'Connor, the real owner, as were not only calculated to deceive, but actually intended to deceive, the public, and that by reason thereof and without any fraud or negligence on his part, the defendant was misled into the belief that Tracy was the real owner, and he accordingly bought and paid him for the property, can there be any doubt, as between the real owner and the innocent purchaser, that the loss should fall upon the former, by whose act Tracy was enabled to thus fraudulently sell and receive the price of the property? We think not. In *Bannard v. Campbell*, . . . a well-considered case, involving substantially the same principle it was held that to create an estoppel by which an owner is prevented from asserting title to and is deprived of his property by the act of a third person, without his assent, two things must concur: (1) The owner must have clothed the person assuming to dispose of the property with the apparent title to or authority to dispose of it. (2) The person alleging the estoppel must have acted and parted with value upon the faith of such apparent ownership or authority, so that he will be the loser if the appearances to which he trusted are not real.

ANDERSON CONTRACTING CO., INC. v. ZURICH INSURANCE CO.

Florida District Court of Appeal
448 So. 2d 7, 38 U.C.C. Rep. 108 (1984)

BARFILED, J.

Anderson Contracting Company, Inc. (Anderson) appeals a summary judgment in favor of Zurich Insurance Company (Zurich) in which Zurich was awarded immediate possession of property. . . . We affirm the summary judgment for Zurich.

The issues raised on this appeal are whether the trial court erred in (1) failing to apply the law of Louisiana in determining the property rights of the parties; (2) granting a motion for summary judgment in favor of defendants on their respective "counterclaims" when no notice of hearing on the motion was given to plaintiff; and (3) granting a summary judgment as to Zurich simultaneously with the filing of the counterclaim and motion for summary judgment thereon. We find no merit in Anderson's arguments as to issues (2) and (3). As to issue (1), our affirmance of the trial court's holding that Florida law applies is based on the public policy of Florida.

Each of the appellees, Zurich and Fireman's Fund, insured a Caterpillar tractor. Both of the tractors were stolen in Texas and were sold to Southeast Equipment Company (Southeast), a Louisiana company which sells used heavy equipment. Southeast subsequently sold both tractors to Ring Power Corporation (Ring Power), which sells new and used heavy Caterpillar equipment. Ring Power had the tractors transported to Florida where they were sold to Anderson. The insurance companies paid the claims on the stolen tractors. When the tractors were found in Florida, this litigation ensued.

Anderson argues that, under the rule of comity, the trial court should have applied Louisiana law, which Anderson asserts would require the true owner to reimburse the subsequent purchaser upon recovery of the stolen property. Comity does not require Florida public policy to be supplanted by foreign law. Comity is not a rule of law, but of practice, convenience and expediency. Where it would be contrary to the statutory law or contravene some established and important policy of the forum state, it is not applied; (New Hampshire's law enforcing "other insurance" clauses in auto policies contrary to Florida public policy against such clauses); (contract not to compete repugnant to Florida's public policy, therefore unenforceable in Florida); (waiver of homestead exemption as to debt contrary to policy of Florida's exemption laws); (both concerned with gambling debts unenforceable in Florida). [Citations omitted.]

It has generally been held by Florida courts that the old English common law principle of title acquired by purchase and sale in open market does not apply in this country and that, in the absence of some intervening principle of estoppel, one cannot convey a better title than he has and conversely, one cannot claim a better title than he, in fact, receives. [Citations omitted.]

Where an owner has voluntarily parted with possession of his chattel, even though induced by a criminal act, a bona fide purchaser can acquire good title, under the theory that where one of two innocent parties must suffer because of the wrongdoing of a third person, the loss must fall on the party who by his conduct created the circumstances which enabled the third party to perpetuate the wrong. [Citations omitted.] However, no such estoppel argument can be advanced against an owner of property that is stolen and subsequently sold to an innocent purchaser. It is the public policy of Florida that one in possession of stolen property, even if he has innocently purchased it from a "dealer," has no possessory or ownership right to the property as against the rightful owner from whom the property was stolen, since the dealer could convey no better title than he received from the thief.

Affirmed.

NOTE

Study U.C.C. § 2-403(1)(first sentence) and Comment 1.

PROBLEM 8.1

One night Carr stole 24 bales of cotton from a gin where the cotton had been processed and tagged. All the cotton was owned by Lineburger. Early the next morning Carr carried the cotton to Warehouse and after weighing had a receipt issued "to the order of Carr" and delivered to him. Carr took the receipt to a nearby town where he indorsed and delivered it to Hodge who purchased it in good faith. Carr then disappeared and has not since been located.

Lineburger discovered the theft and determined the location of the cotton and the existence of the receipt in the hands of Hodge. Both Lineburger and Hodge demand the cotton from

Warehouse and Warehouse interpleads. Who is entitled to the cotton, Lineburger or Hodge? See U.C.C. § 7-503(1).

§ 8.02 Entrusting

Read: U.C.C. § 2-403(2) and (3); see §§ 2-702(3), 7-205, 9-307(1).

Read also: U.C.C. §§ 2A-304(2), 2A-305(2), 2A-103(3)(§ 2-403(3)); CISG Arts. 1(1), 4(b).

A common law case which dealt with entrustment is *Levi v. Booth, 58 Md. 305 (1882)*. In this case, plaintiff was the owner of a diamond ring. He placed the ring in the hands of De Wolff, a dealer and trader in jewelry, for the purpose of obtaining a match for it, or failing that to get an offer for it. There was nothing to show that it was given to De Wolff for any other purpose or that he was in any manner authorized to sell it. Subsequently, De Wolff sold the ring to Levi who was a good faith purchaser. In holding for plaintiff-owner the court said:

> [I]t is very clear, upon the principles that we have already stated, that the *bare possession* of goods by one, though he may happen to be a *dealer* in that class of goods, does not clothe him with power to dispose of the goods as though he were owner, or as having authority as agent to sell or pledge the goods, to the preclusion of the right of the real owner. If he sells *as owner* there must be some other *indicia* of property than mere possession. There must . . . be some act or conduct on the part of the real owner whereby the party selling is clothed with the apparent ownership, or authority to sell, and which the real owner will not be heard to deny or question to the prejudice of an innocent third party dealing on the faith of such appearances. If it were otherwise, people would not be secure in sending their watches or articles of jewelry to a jeweller's establishment to be repaired, or cloth to a clothing establishment to be made into garments.

PROBLEM 8.2

How would *the Levi v. Booth* case be resolved under U.C.C. § 2-403(2), assuming Levi to be a buyer in ordinary course of business?

THORN v. ADAMS

Court of Appeals of Oregon
125 Or. App. 257, 865 P.2d 417 (1993)

LEESON, JUDGE.

Defendant purchased a car in 1989. On April 15, 1992, her son-in-law, Richard, took the car to Gateley's Fairway Motors (Gateley's), a car dealership that also performed repairs. As defendant's authorized agent, Richard requested an estimate of the car's value, and left it for repairs. Several days later, plaintiff saw the car on Gateley's lot, next to several cars for sale. Gateley's allowed her to take the car for a test drive, and later sold it to her. Gateley's never informed plaintiff that it had no authority to sell the car, nor did it indicate that the car was anything other than inventory.

When Richard learned of the sale, he demanded that plaintiff return the car. She refused, and brought this action for an injunction requiring defendant to deliver the certificate of title to her. She also sought damages for conversion, based on defendant's refusal to surrender the certificate of title. Defendant counterclaimed for an order requiring plaintiff to surrender possession of the car, or, in the alternative, to require plaintiff to pay defendant the reasonable market value of the car.

Both parties moved for summary judgment. The trial court denied defendant's motion and granted plaintiff's motion. It ordered defendant to surrender the certificate of title and to take such other actions as reasonably necessary to register the vehicle in plaintiff's name.

Summary judgment should be granted only when there is no genuine issue of material fact and the moving party is entitled to judgment as a matter of law. [Citation.] The parties agree that there is no genuine issue of material fact. The only dispute in which party was entitled to judgment as a matter of law.

Plaintiff bases her claim of legal ownership on ORS 72.4030, the provision of the Oregon Uniform Commercial Code commonly known as the "entrustment principle." ORS 72.-4030(3) provides:

[Read U.C.C. § 2-403(2).]

Under ORS 72.4030(4),

[Read U.C.C. § 2-403(3).]

Plaintiff contends that defendant entrusted the car to Gateley's, which was a merchant that dealt in goods of that kind, and, therefore, that Gateley's had the power to transfer all rights in the car to her as a buyer in the ordinary course of business.

Defendant concedes that the entrustment principle gives merchants the power to pass good title even when the merchant has no authority to sell the goods, but argues that that principle does not apply. She contends that ORS 803.094(1) provides the exclusive method for transferring legal title to a vehicle that has a certificate of title. That statute provides, in part:

> "Except as otherwise provided in this section, *upon the transfer of any interest* shown on an Oregon certificate of title any person whose interest is released, terminated, assigned or transferred, shall release or assign that interest on the title certificate." (Emphasis supplied.)

Nothing in the plain language of the statute describes or limits the methods that may be used to transfer an interest shown on an Oregon certificate of title. Rather, the statute describes what must be done *once the transfer has occurred.* By its terms, ORS 803.094(1) does not prevent or invalidate a transfer of interest that takes place under ORS 72.4030(3).[4]

---

[4] The result would be different under two former statutes, which explicitly described the methods for transferring *any* interest in a vehicle. *Former* ORS 481.405 provided, in part:

> "(1) . . . To transfer title *or any interest* in a motor vehicle, trailer or semitrailer issued a certificate of title under this chapter, the transferor shall sign the certificate and fill in any information required by the division in the appropriate places on the certificate." (Emphasis supplied.)

Former ORS 481.405 was repealed effective January 1, 1986. Or Laws 1983, ch. 338, § 978. It was replaced by *former* ORS 803.095, which provided, in part:

Defendant argues that, even if the entrustment principle of ORS 72.4030 applies, plaintiff still was not entitled to judgment as a matter of law, because she was not a buyer in the ordinary course of business. According to ORS 71.2010(9),

> "[b]uyer in ordinary course of business" means a person who in good faith and without knowledge that the sale to the person is in violation of the ownership rights . . . of a third party in the goods buys in ordinary course from a person in the business of selling goods of that kind . . . .

Good faith is defined as "honesty in fact in the conduct or transaction concerned." ORS 71.2010(19).

Defendant argues that plaintiff could not have acted with honesty in fact, because no legal title can be conveyed at the time of the purchase without a concurrent transfer of the certificate of title. She contends that plaintiff was put on notice that there was something unusual in the transaction when she failed to obtain a certificate of title at the same time she purchased the vehicle.

We disagree. Nothing in the motor vehicle statutes required plaintiff to take possession of the certificate of title at the moment she purchased the car in order to acquire legal title.[5] Absent such a requirement, plaintiff's "failure" to obtain the certificate of title at the moment that she purchased the car is not unreasonable, and does not put plaintiff on notice that the transaction was "unusual." Defendant provides no other support for her contention that plaintiff was not a buyer in the ordinary course of business.

Finally, defendant argues that it is unfair to place motor vehicle owners at the mercy of the entrustment principle. That choice was made by the legislature when it adopted ORS 72.4030(3), which mirrors section 2-402(3) of the Uniform Commercial Code. 1 Bailey, Oregon Uniform Commercial Code § 2.92 (2d ed. 1990). The entrustment principle promotes one of the basic goals of commerce:

> "In most cases the equities between the entruster-owner and the buyer in the ordinary course are equal, and the balance is tipped in favor of the latter because that frees the marketplace and promotes commerce. This goal, called 'security of transactions[,]' is an ideal of the commercial law. The protection of property rights . . . is not an ideal of the commercial law. . . . On the assumption that both the entruster and buyer have been equally victimized by the dishonesty of the merchant-dealer, section 2-403(2) resolves the issue so

---

"This section establishes the procedures for transferring title *or an interest in a vehicle* for which the division has issued a certificate of title. . . . Except as provided in ORS 803.110, the following procedures are for the described type of transfer of an interest:

"(1) Transfer of title *or any interest in a vehicle* requires completion of . . . the following:

"(a) The transferor shall sign the certificate of title in the appropriate place provided on the certificate." (Emphasis supplied.)

Former ORS 803.095 was repealed by Oregon Laws 1989, chapter 148 section 20, and the present version of ORS 803.094 was added. Or Laws 1989, ch. 148, § 2.

[5] We are not persuaded by defendant's citation to cases from other jurisdictions whose statutes are different. For example, defendant cites *Ballard v. Associates* Investment Co., 368 S.W.2d 232, 233-34 (Tex. Civ. App. 1963), in which the court applied the then existing Texas certificate of title act, which provided that "no title to any motor vehicle shall pass or vest" until the transfer of the certificate of title occurred. We are equally unpersuaded by defendant's citation to *Ellsworth v. Worthey*, 612 S.W.2d 396, 400 (Mo. App. 1981), in which the court cited several pre-U.C.C. cases and concluded that Kansas law provided that the sale of a used vehicle without concurrent delivery of the signed certificate was "fraudulent and void."

as to free the marketplace, rather than protect the original owner's property rights." 2 Hawkland, U.C.C. Series § 2.403:07 (1992).

The trial court did not err in granting plaintiff's motion for summary judgment and in denying defendant's motion.

Affirmed.

PROBLEM 8.3

Big Knob Volunteer Fire Department contracted to purchase a fire truck from Hamerly Custom Productions. (Hamerly was in the business of assembling component parts into fire trucks.) Big Knob paid $48,000 toward the purchase price of $51,836. Subsequently, Hamerly ordered a chassis for the truck from Lowe & Moyer who reserved a security interest in the chassis. Hamerly began work on transforming the chassis into a fire truck and painted Big Knob's name on the cab. However, Hamerly neither paid Lowe & Moyer for the chassis nor did it complete and deliver the truck to Big Knob.

Lowe & Moyer seeks possession of the chassis pursuant to its rights under the default provisions of U.C.C. § 9-503. Big Knob seeks possession of the fire truck because it was unable to effect cover for the truck. *See* U.C.C. § 2-716(3).

Big Knob asserts that, as a buyer in ordinary course of business, it takes free of the security interest created by Hamerly in favor of Lowe & Moyer. *See* U.C.C. § 9-307(1). The issue arises as to the point at which a person becomes a buyer in ordinary course of business. Is it when:

(1) *title* to the truck passes to buyer? *See* U.C.C. §§ 2-106(1), 2-401?

(2) the truck is *delivered* to Big Knob? See predecessor Uniform Trust Receipts Act § 9(2) which protected "a buyer in the ordinary course of trade" defined as a person "to whom goods are sold and *delivered.*"

(3) the truck is *identified* to the contract? (Hamerly painted Big Knob's name on the cab.) See U.C.C. §§ 2-501, 2-716(3), 2-401 Comment 3 and Point 3 of Cross References.

See Big Knob Volunteer Fire Co. v. Lowe & Moyer Garage, Inc., 487 A.2d 953, 40 U.C.C. Rep. 1691 (1985).

PROBLEM 8.4

Bailor delivers several tons of grain to Warehouse who not only stores grain but also sells it. Warehouse issues to Bailor a warehouse receipt engaging to deliver "to the order of Bailor." Bailor signs and delivers the receipt to Adams who takes by "due negotiation." Warehouse sells and delivers the grain to Baker who buys in the ordinary course of business. Is Adams or Baker entitled to the goods? See U.C.C. § 7-205.

NOTES AND QUESTIONS

(1) *Merchant as Buyer in Ordinary Course of Business.* In *Sherrock v. Commercial Credit Corp.*, 290 A.2d 648, 10 U.C.C. Rep. 523 (Del. 1972), car-dealer Sherrock agreed to purchase

two automobiles from Dover Motors. Held: a merchant-buyer may be a buyer in ordinary course of business (BOCB) under U.C.C. § 9-307(1); this section is not limited to consumer buyers. BOCB means a person who in *good faith* buys in ordinary course. U.C.C. § 1-201(9) and (19). With respect to U.C.C. Article 2, " 'good faith' in the case of a merchant means honesty in fact and the observance of reasonable commercial standards of fair dealing in the trade." U.C.C. § 2-103(1)(b). Clearly, a merchant BOCB under § 2-403(2) must observe reasonable commercial standards of fair dealing. Is the merchant BOCB of U.C.C. § 9-307(1) required to observe these standards? The court in *Sherrock, supra,* said: "We find no basis anywhere for the conclusion that the drafters of the Code intended to make it permissible to 'cross-over' to Article 2 for the definition of the term 'good faith' as incorporated by reference in Article 9." Should we not direct the Court's attention to U.C.C. § 1-102 Comment 1?

(2) *Seller in Possession.* Entrusting of possession of goods to a merchant who deals in goods of the kind includes any acquiescence in retention of possession by the merchant. U.C.C. § 2-403(2), (3). In *Metalworking Machinery Co., Inc. v. Fabco, Inc.*, 17 Ohio App. 3d 91, 477 N.E.2d 634 (1984), East Coast sold a metalworking machine to Metalworking, who never picked it up. Later, Yoder purchased the same machine from East Coast. (East Coast was a manufacturing company and the machine was not sold by East Coast in the ordinary course of its business.) Subsequently, Yoder sold the machine to Fabco. Held: Money judgment for Metalworking against Fabco. Per U.C.C. § 2-403(2) and (3), the machine was not left in possession of a merchant who dealt in goods of that kind and machine was not sold in ordinary course of East Coast's business. (Further, money judgment was granted to Fabco against Yoder.)

See also U.C.C. § 2-503(4)(b).

(3) *Warranty of Title under* U.C.C. § 2-312. 2 Hawkland, Uniform Commercial Code Series § 2-312:02 (1992) states in part:

> [T]here may be situations where the seller has the power, but not the right, to convey a perfect title to the goods that may expose the buyer unreasonably to the claim of a third person to ownership. In those cases, there is a breach of warranty of title, even though the buyer has the legal ability to defeat the third-party claim. Such a situation might arise, for example, under section 2-403 where a third party delivers goods to a merchant for repair. If the merchant is in the business of selling goods of the kind, he had the power to sell the entrusted goods to a buyer in the ordinary course free and clear of the third party's ownership rights. This new rule is one which many third parties might not be aware of or understand and some third parties might proceed against the buyer in the ordinary course, even though they could not win a lawsuit if he could establish that status. That being the case, the buyer should be able to revoke acceptance, or sue for breach of warranty of title on the ground that the transfer was not rightful. The test is not whether the buyer can win a lawsuit against third-party claimants, but whether he is unreasonably exposed to such a suit.

Cf. U.C.C. § 3-416 Comment 3. Warranty of title is discussed in Chapter 4, Property Interests.

(4) See U.C.C. §§ 2A-304(2), 2A-305(2)(entrusters to merchants lose to "lessees in the ordinary course of business").

§ 8.03 Voidable Title

Read: U.C.C. §§ 2-403(1), 2-702(3); cf. § 3-404(a).

Read also: U.C.C. §§ 2A-304(1) and (3), 2A-305(1) and (3); CISG Arts. 1(1), (4)(b).

A leading common law case with respect to voidable title is *Phelps v. McQuade*, 220 N.Y. 232, 115 N.E. 441 (1917). In this case, Walter J. Gwynne falsely represented to plaintiffs that he was Baldwin J. Gwynne, a man of financial responsibility. Relying on the truth of this statement, plaintiffs delivered to him upon credit a quantity of jewelry. Gwynne in turn sold it to defendant, who bought it without notice of any defect in title and for value. Learning of the deception practiced upon them, the plaintiffs began an action in replevin to recover the goods. The court stated as follows:

> The only question before us is whether under such circumstances, the vendor of personal property does not retain title thereto after he has parted with possession thereof. . . . Where the vendor of personal property intends to sell his goods to the person with whom he deals, then title passes, even though he be deceived as to that person's identity or responsibility. Otherwise it does not. It is purely a question of the vendor's intention.
>
> The fact that the vendor deals with the person personally rather than by letter is immaterial, except in so far as it bears upon the question of intent.
>
> Where the transaction is a personal one, the seller intends to transfer title to a person of credit, and he supposes the one standing before him to be that person. He is deceived. But in spite of that fact his primary intention is to sell his goods to the person with whom he negotiates.
>
> Where the transaction is by letter the vendor intends to deal with the person whose name is signed to the letter. He knows no one else. He supposes he is dealing with no one else. And while in both cases other facts may be shown that would alter the rule, yet in their absence, in the first, title passes; in the second, it does not. Two cases that illustrate the distinction are [1] *Edmunds v. Merchants' Dispatch Transportation Company*, 135 Mass. 283, and [2] Cundy v. Lindsay, 3 App. Cas. 463.

Id. at 234-5.

> In *Cundy v. Lindsay*, one Blenkarn, signing himself Blenkiron & Co., bought goods by letter of Lindsay & Co. The latter shipped the goods to Blenkiron & Co. They knew of the firm of Blenkiron & Son; believed the letter came from that firm and that the goods were shipped to it. Blenkiron & Son were the persons with whom Lindsay & Co. intended to deal and supposed they were dealing. Under those circumstances it was held that, although Blenkiron obtained possession of the goods, he never acquired title thereto.
>
> In *Edmunds v. Merchants' Transportation Company*, a swindler, representing himself to be one Edward Pape, personally bought goods of the plaintiff on credit. The court held that the title passed. "The minds of the parties met and agreed upon all the terms of the sale, the thing sold, the price and time of payment, the person selling and the person buying. The fact that the seller was induced to sell by fraud of the buyer made the sale voidable, but not void. He could not have supposed that he was selling to any other person; his intention was to sell to the person present, and identified by sight and hearing; it does not defeat the sale because the buyer assumed a false name, or practised any other deceit to induce the vendor to sell."
>
> . . .

(The Court held for defendant.)

NOTES AND QUESTIONS

Simply, if plaintiff dealt personally with the impostor (face to face), the impostor acquired voidable title and could pass good title to a good faith or bona fide purchaser. If plaintiff dealt with the impostor through the mails, the impostor acquired void title (no title) and could not pass good title even to a bona fide purchaser. Query: Does U.C.C. § 2-403(1)(a) recognize this distinction?

SHERIDAN SUZUKI, INC. v. CARUSO AUTO SALES, INC.

New York Supreme Court, Erie County
110 Misc. 2d 823, 442 N.Y.S.2d 957, 32 U.C.C. Rep. 1127 (1981)

JOSEPH J. SEDITA, JUSTICE.

The court finds itself in the position of having to choose where to place the burden of loss as between two apparently innocent parties. The basic facts of this case are essentially not in dispute. Only the application of the law to those facts is in serious question. Both parties have moved for summary judgment. To the best of this court's knowledge, this is a case of the first impression in New York State.

On May 26, 1981, the plaintiff, Sheridan Suzuki, Inc., (hereinafter Suzuki) "sold" a motorcycle to one Ronald Bouton. Incident to this sale they gave him possession of the motorcycle, a signed bill of sale marked paid in full and registration of the vehicle in said Bouton's name. Additionally, they filed an application for an original Certificate of Title (pursuant to requirements of Article 46 of the New York State Vehicle and Traffic Law). Said certificate was never received by Bouton. Its processing in Albany was interrupted when they were notified by Suzuki of subsequent developments. In return for the subject motorcycle, the plaintiff was given Bouton's check for $3,559.44 in satisfaction of the purchase price. Said check was later dishonored. Bouton has disappeared from the area.

On May 27,1981, (one day after the initial sale), Bouton offered to sell the vehicle to Caruso Auto Sales, Inc. (hereinafter Caruso). After examining the papers that Bouton had "in hand," but before Bouton had received the Certificate of Title from Albany, Caruso "purchased" the motorcycle from Bouton for $2,000.00. Bouton gave Caruso possession of the motorcycle, signed over the registration and assured Caruso that he would transfer the Certificate of Title upon receipt of the title documents from the State. Before accepting the transaction, Caruso had called Suzuki and they had confirmed Bouton's assertion of prior purchase (not yet having notice of the dishonored check). Justice Norman Stiller has granted a preliminary order placing the motorcycle with Suzuki pending a determination of the legal issues raised here.

To unravel and resolve the controversy presented here, we must examine closely the fabric of law designed to regulate these types of relationships.

At common law, a thief could pass no title whatsoever to stolen goods.

However, § 2-403(2) of the Uniform Commercial Code supplanted the common law rule as to goods received "in exchange for a check which is later dishonored . . ." or "delivery was criminal law."[6] This motorcycle was transferred as part of a transaction involving a bad check, rather than as a result of a direct larceny or burglary and therefore it cannot be asserted that any title received by a "bona fide purchaser for value" would be void. The law is clear that a person receiving goods incident to a transaction involving a dishonored check and a fraud receives only voidable title, at best.[7] (See U.C.C. § 2-403, *supra.*) A "bona fide purchaser for value" can receive good title from a person with "voidable" title under the Uniform Commercial Code.

The crucial question at this point becomes the effect of the State Uniform Vehicle Certificate of Title Act (hereinafter UVCTA) on the species of "title" received by Bouton. The courts have an obligation to give effect to all acts of the legislature and to avoid interpretations which result in a conflict between statutes. Where a general statute and a more particular statute overlap, the courts will usually give greater effect to the more particularized statute.

This court takes note of the fact that the Uniform Commercial Code establishes a general rule for commercial transactions. The Uniform Vehicle Certificate of Title Act does not seek to abrogate the U.C.C., but merely seeks to add additional requirements for transactions involving this unique area of "goods," due to unique problems of fraud and theft experienced with motor vehicles. Section 2113(c) of the UVCTA expressly states in part:

> . . . a transfer by an owner is not perfected so as to be valid against third parties generally until the provisions of this section . . . have been complied with.

Section 2105 of the UMVTA sets forth the procedures for making an application for the first Certificate of Title. This section makes clear that the requirements of this act are more than ministerial record keeping. The commissioner is required to make a "quasi-judicial" determination as to ownership. (See section 2105(d) of the UMVTA.)

"Title" under this act is not an automatic result once the bureaucratic process is triggered, but is a result of a *determination* of the Department after examining the documents submitted to it. The process of obtaining title is not complete, and the provisions of this statute are not fully complied with until the Department is satisfied that title was in the alleged owner/applicant.

Since the Department suspended the issuance of a title certificate due to its knowledge of the fraud perpetrated herein, the voidable "title" received by Bouton was never perfected as required by the statute (sec 2113, (c), cited *supra*) and could not be successfully passed to a "bona fide purchaser for value." The object of this section is clearly to effectuate the intent of the UVCTA, which is to make transfers of improperly obtained motor vehicles more difficult by requiring a "perfected" title before a successful transfer of a vehicle can be made. An interpretation which

[6] [The Court undoubtedly intended to cite U.C.C. § 2-403(1)(b) and (d).—Ed.]

[7] [For a discussion of seller's right to reclaim goods exchanged for a check which was later dishonored, see Chapter 7, Remedies, at § 7.03; see U.C.C. §§ 2-507(2), 2-511 (3).—Ed.]

avoids this requirement would in effect "extract" the "teeth" built into this legislation and circumvent its clear purpose.

If Bouton had obtained a valid Certificate of Title, his title would have still been voidable, but would have been "perfected" according to the requirements of the law. He could then have successfully passed good title to a "bona fide purchaser for value." (As for example in *White v. Pike*, 240 Iowa 596, 36 N.W.2d 761, where the perpetrator of the fraud had obtained a Certificate of Title in addition to the other usual indicia of ownership.)

Since Bouton never had a perfected title, he could not pass good title to Caruso.

Defendant alleges that Suzuki is equitably estopped from denying Caruso's title because of Suzuki's representation that Bouton had properly received ownership of the vehicle in question. Caruso alleges that he relied upon those representations to his detriment. Equitable estoppel, however, does not operate to create rights which are nonexistent. It may only operate to preclude the denial of a right claimed otherwise to have arisen.

Since Bouton never received the Certificate of Title, he never had perfected title as required under New York Law to enable him to transfer good title. Caruso therefore never got any legal title or right to the vehicle, and therefore has no claim to assert in seeking equitable estoppel against Suzuki's claim.

Buyers who purchase from a seller who does not have a Certificate of Title, do so at their own risk. Caruso took that risk in the hope of making a substantial profit by obtaining a brand new $3,500.00 motorcycle for $2,000.00. The risk he took backfired, and this court cannot protect him from his loss. The law is clear and intended to protect society against exactly the type of fraud perpetrated herein. The duty of this court is to enforce the express mandate of that law.

Accordingly, plaintiff's motion for summary judgment is granted and defendant's motion for summary judgment is denied.

NOTES AND QUESTIONS

(1) In *Kotis v. Nowlin Jewelry*, Inc., 844 S.W.2d 920 (Tex. App. 1992), Nowlin sold a Rolex watch to Sitton who paid with a forged check. Sitton then sold the watch to Kotis. Held: For Nowlin. While Sitton acquired voidable title under U.C.C. § 2-403(1), Kotis was not a good faith purchaser.

(2) *Goods Subject to Certificate of Title.* R. Henson, The Law of Sales 103 (1985) comments (footnotes omitted):

> When the goods sold are subject to a certificate of title, as motor vehicles would be in most states, then the application of Section 2-403 is somewhat less clear. The problems basically arise in sales of used vehicles when the seller may not have had "title" and so may be held unable to convey good title to a purchaser, no matter what the purchaser paid and without regard to good faith. It is possible to conclude that Section 2-403 is subject to the operation of the state's certificate of title law [the *Sheridan Suzuki* case, *supra,* is cited], or it may be

found that Section 2-403 controls; but this seems unlikely in a state having a certificate of title law specifically covering the problem.

In *Inmi-Etti v. Aluisi*, 492 A.2d 917, 40 U.C.C. Rep. 1612 (Md. Ct. Spec. App. 1985), Appellant Inmi-Etti purchased a new car. Butler converted the car, obtained a certificate of title in his name from the State of Maryland and sold it to car-dealer Pohanka. Inmi-Etti sued Pohanka for conversion. In holding for Inmi-Etti the court said:

> Under the undisputed facts of the present case Butler possessed void title when Pohanka dealt with him. Although the record simply is not sufficient for us to decide whether Butler actually stole the appellant's vehicle, it is undisputed that the appellant at no time made a voluntary transfer to Butler. Thus, Pohanka obtained no title, and its sale of the vehicle constituted a conversion of the appellant's property. We believe the above analysis sufficient to impose liability upon Pohanka. We will nevertheless answer certain of Pohanka's collateral arguments.
>
> . . . .
>
> Implicit in all that we have said so far is the fact that Butler did not obtain title (voidable or otherwise) merely from the fact that he was able to convince the Motor Vehicle Administration to issue a certificate of title for the automobile to him. Although "[a] certificate of title issued by the Administration is prima facie evidence of the facts appearing on it," Md Code (1977, 1984 Repl Vol), § 13-107 of the Transportation Article, the erroneous issuance of such a certificate cannot divest the title of the true owner of the automobile.
>
> Likewise, we find unpersuasive Pohanka's argument that since Butler had possession of the automobile and a duly issued certificate of title in his name, Pohanka should be protected as a "good faith purchaser for value" under § 2-403 of the Commercial Law Article, *supra.* Such status under that section of the Uniform Commercial Code is relevant in situations where the seller (transferor) is possessed of voidable title. It does not apply to the situation presented by the instant case where the seller had no title at all.
>
> . . . .

Cf. U.C.C. §§ 2A-304(3), 2A-305(3).

(3) *Seller's Right to Reclaim Under U.C.C. § 2-702.* Section 2-702(2) states in part: "Where the seller discovers that the buyer has received goods on credit while insolvent he may reclaim the goods upon demand made within ten days of the receipt." Subsection (3), however, states: "The seller's right to reclaim under subsection (2) is subject to the rights of a buyer in ordinary course or other good faith purchaser [or lien creditor (1962 Code)] under this Article (Section 2-403). . . ."

For discussion see Chapter 7, Remedies, at § 7.03. As to seller's rights against buyer's trustee in bankruptcy, see Bankruptcy Code § 546(c).

(4) *Secured Party and Lien Creditor as Good Faith Purchaser.* A person with a voidable title has power to transfer a good title to a good faith *purchaser* for value. U.C.C. § 2-403(1). "Purchaser" means a person who takes by "purchase," *i.e.*, any . . . voluntary transaction creating an interest in property." U.C.C. § 1-201(32), (33). A U.C.C. Article 9 secured party has engaged in a voluntary transaction (U.C.C. § 9-102(2)) creating an interest (security interest, § 1-201(37)) in property. See U.C.C. § 9-103 Comment 7 (third paragraph). See *Genesee Merchants Bank & Trust Co. v. Tucker*, 143 Mich. App. 339, 372 N.W.2d 546, 42 U.C.C. Rep. 150 (1985) (unpaid

cash seller's right to reclaim goods from buyer subordinate to "floating lien" of buyer's secured creditor); *In re Misco Supply Co.*, 42 U.C.C. Rep. 150 (Mich. 1986) (secured parties which had "floating lien" on debtor's inventory and after-acquired property were good faith "purchasers" for "value").

Lien creditors (creditors who have acquired a lien on the property involved by attachment, levy or the like, U.C.C. § 9-301(3)) are not "purchasers" and consequently cannot qualify as "good faith purchasers for value." U.C.C. § 2-403(1). A "purchaser" is involved in a voluntary transaction; an attaching or levying creditor is involved in an involuntary transaction. The debtor whose property is seized by the sheriff cannot be said to have given his assent. This result reflects the common law position that "a creditor as such is not protected against latent equities against the judgment debtor and that he stands in all respects in the shoes of the judgment debtor." S. Riesenfeld, Creditors' Remedies and Debtors' Protection 130 (4th ed. 1987). The rationale for the common law position is well stated in *Oswego Starch Factory v. Lendrum*, 57 Iowa 573, 10 N.W. 900(1881), with respect to the rights of an attaching creditor:

> The title of the property was not divested by the attachment, but remained in the vendees. The seizure conferred upon the creditors no right to the property as against plaintiff other or different from those held by the vendee. The sole effect of the seizure was to place the property in the custody of the law, to be held until the creditors' claims had been adjudicated and the property could be sold on execution. They parted with no consideration in making the attachment, and their condition as to their claims were in no respect changed. Their acts were induced by no representation or procurement originating with plaintiff which would in law or equity give them rights to the property as against plaintiff. Plaintiff's right to rescind the sale inhered in the contract and attached to the property. It could not be defeated except by a purchaser for value without notice of fraud. . . .
>
> Our position is simply this, that as an attaching creditor parts with no consideration, and does not change his position as to his claim, to his prejudice, he stands in the shoes of the vendee. . . . The innocent purchaser for value occupies a different position, and his rights are, therefore, different.

See *Citizens Bank of Roseville v. Taggart*, 143 Cal. App. 3d 318,191 Cal. Rptr. 729, 36 U.C.C. Rep. 529 (1983) (bank as lien creditor did not have status of good faith purchaser for value; its rights in an auto on which it had levied were subordinate to the reclamation rights of the unpaid seller. Bank had not given value for the auto nor had it relied on the ostensible ownership or voidable title of the debtor to the auto).

See U.C.C. §§ 2-402, 2A-301, 2A-307, 2A-308.

§ 8.04 A Note on Bulk Transfers

Former Article 6 of the Uniform Commercial Code dealt with what were termed "bulk transfers"—defined as a transfer in bulk and not in the ordinary course of business of a major part of the inventory of an enterprise whose principal business is the sale of merchandise from stock. Former U.C.C. §§ 6-102, 6-103. The purpose of Article 6 was to protect the unsecured creditors of such enterprises against the possibility that the owner might suddenly and without notice sell out and disappear, leaving the unsecured creditors without any recourse against the purchaser of the business. To this end, Article 6 required that when a bulk transfer occurred, a schedule of property to be transferred and a list of the seller's creditors must be prepared, and notice of the proposed transfer must be sent to the seller's creditors at least ten days before the buyer takes possession of the goods, or pays for them. See former U.C.C. §§ 6-104 through 6-107. The transfer was ineffective against any creditor of the seller unless the notice was given. Former U.C.C. § 6-104. It is important to note that Article 6 did not protect the seller's creditors by requiring that the buyer pay them, or that the seller use the purchase price for their benefit. The article was primarily a notice provision.

Under the 1989 Code Article 6 was renamed "Bulk Sales." Alternative A repealed Article 6; Alternative B revised Article 6. The Comment to revised § 6-101 recites the major changes from former Article 6, e.g., buyer's noncompliance does not render the sale ineffective, rather, the liability of a noncomplying buyer is for damages. Most states thus far have chosen Alternative A.

CHAPTER 9

LEASES OF GOODS

§ 9.01 Introduction

Read: Forward to Article 2A and U.C.C. § 2A-101 Comment.

Article 2A deals with leases. U.C.C. §§ 2A-102, 2A-104. A lease is defined as "a transfer of the right to possession and use of goods for a term in return for consideration, but a sale . . . or retention or creation of a security interest is not a lease." U.C.C. §§ 2A-103(1)(j) and Comment (j), 1-201(37), 2-106(1), 9-102(2).

Chapters 1 through 8 deal with sales of goods: contract formation, warranties, performance, remedies, and rights of third parties. Throughout these chapters there are references to analogous lease provisions. Consequently, it is anticipated that discussion of leases will be made in association with their sales counterpart.

One area for discussion in this chapter involves warranties with respect to the "finance lease." Read U.C.C. §§ 2A-210 through 2A-216, then proceed to § 9.02 immediately below.

§ 9.02 Warranties in Finance Leases

Read: U.C.C. §§ 2A-103(1)(g), 2A-209, 2A-407, 9-206(1).

IN RE O.P.M. LEASING SERVICES

United States Bankruptcy Court, Southern District of New York
21 B.R. 993 (1982)

BURTON R. LIFLAND, BANKRUPTCY JUDGE.

This matter is before the Court on the Motion of LaSalle National Bank ("LaSalle") for summary judgment pursuant to Bankruptcy Rule 756 and Rule 56 of the Federal Rules of Civil Procedure to dismiss the claim of the State of West Virginia, Department of Finance and Administration ("West Virginia"), and to recover judgment as to liability on LaSalle's counterclaim for accelerated rents.

I. STATEMENT OF FACTS

The instant adversary proceeding within this Chapter 11 case concerns a set of 22 leases of computer equipment (the "Equipment Schedules") by O.P.M. Leasing Services, Inc. ("OPM"), the debtor herein, to plaintiff West Virginia. Pursuant to three security agreements (the "Security Agreements") and three agreements captioned "Consent and Agreement," 19 of these leases are now pledged to defendant LaSalle as security for OPM's indebtedness under three notes held by LaSalle.

West Virginia commenced this adversary proceeding on August 19, 1981 against James P. Hassett as Reorganization Trustee of OPM ("the Trustee"), OPM, LaSalle, International Business Machines Corporation ("IBM") and Computer Equipment Services Corporation ("CES"). The complaint seeks a turnover of $107,252.36, plus accrued interest, from the OPM estate to IBM and CES ("the Maintenance Providers") for maintenance payments which OPM is alleged to have failed to provide, a declaration that the Equipment Schedules have been terminated and an order of the Bankruptcy Court enjoining the Maintenance Providers from terminating maintenance on the hardware pending resolution of the adversary proceeding.[1]

The basis which West Virginia has asserted for this relief is OPM's alleged breach of the Equipment Schedules in its failure to make monthly payments of maintenance fees directly to defendants IBM and CES on 20 of the 22 Equipment Schedules (the "Maintenance Providers"). According to West Virginia's pleadings, this breach by OPM terminates LaSalle's rights as assignee to receive lease payments. Alternatively, West Virginia asserts in its pleadings that LaSalle's purported knowledge of OPM's breach prevents it from claiming that the Equipment Schedules have not terminated.

LaSalle's answer denies all of the material allegations of the complaint and alleges as an affirmative defense that the terms of the Consent and Agreements executed by West Virginia bar West Virginia's claim. LaSalle also asserts in a counterclaim that beginning in March, 1981, West Virginia failed to make the full amount of lease payments under the Equipment Schedules assigned to LaSalle. LaSalle gave written notice of West Virginia's default and of its election to accelerate the balance of assigned lease payments pursuant to Section 12.2 of the Master Lease. Accordingly, LaSalle seeks judgment herein on its counterclaim in the amount of $2,115,388.30, although LaSalle's present motion seeks judgment on liability only.

The reply of West Virginia to LaSalle's counterclaim denies all its material allegations and asserts nine affirmative defenses. These defenses include sovereign immunity under the Tenth and Eleventh Amendments and under West Virginia law, waiver by LaSalle of its right to accelerate rent payments, full payment of all rentals due to LaSalle and that LaSalle is bound by its assignor's default in making maintenance payments.

The Trustee has also contemporaneously moved to reject the 19 leases which were assigned to LaSalle.[2] LaSalle opposes this motion to reject based on its concern that its security interest in the lease payments will not be adequately protected if West Virginia's absolute and unconditional promise to pay rents is not fully enforced.

The Agreements Governing the Transactions at Issue

The rights and duties of each of the three parties to the computer leases at issue herein are specified in the Master Lease as well as in the Equipment Schedules, the Security Agreements and the Consents and Agreements.

West Virginia, as lessee, and OPM, as lessor, are parties to the Master Lease dated March 28, 1980. Each Equipment Schedule incorporates all of the terms and conditions of the Master

[1] West Virginia and the Maintenance Providers entered into a stipulation in the adversary proceeding that the Maintenance Providers would continue to provide maintenance on the hardware pending resolution of the adversary proceeding in exchange for West Virginia's continued remittance of current maintenance payments. This stipulation was so ordered by the Bankruptcy Court on October 9, 1981.

[2] In the Trustee's motion to reject the 19 assigned leases, he also moved to assume the three unassigned leases. That portion of this motion relating to assumption only was the subject of a Stipulation of Settlement between West Virginia and the Trustee which was So Ordered by this Court on June 29, 1982.

Lease. The Master Lease and each Equipment Schedule are to be construed in accordance with New York law.

Section 5.3 of the Master Lease between OPM and West Virginia contains detailed provisions regarding assignments of Equipment Schedules by OPM. Section 5.3(ii) provides that OPM's "assignee shall not be obligated to perform any of the obligations of (OPM) under any Equipment Schedule other than [OPM's] obligation not to take any action to disturb Lessee's quiet and peaceful possession of the Equipment." In Section 5.3(iii) the parties agree that "(l)essee's obligation to pay directly to such assignee the amounts due from lessee under any Equipment Schedule . . . shall be *absolutely unconditional* and shall be payable whether or not any Equipment Schedule is terminated by operation of law, any act of the parties or otherwise." (emphasis added) ("the hell or high water clause"). In Section 5.3(iv), OPM and West Virginia is to pay all amounts due under any Equipment Schedule to OPM's assignee "notwithstanding any defense, offset or counterclaim whatever whether by reason of breach of such Equipment Schedule or otherwise which it may or might now or hereafter have as against Lessor (Lessee reserving its right to have recourse directly against Lessor on account of any such counterclaim or offset)" ("the waiver of defenses clause"). Section 14 of the Master Lease provides that the lessee's unconditional obligation to an assignee continues "until all amounts . . . shall have been paid in full."

Each Equipment Schedule obligates OPM to reimburse West Virginia for monthly maintenance charges actually paid by West Virginia under West Virginia's separate maintenance agreements with the Maintenance Providers for the leased equipment. However, Paragraph 4(a) of each Equipment Schedule provides that OPM's obligation to pay for maintenance of the equipment leased to lessee "shall in (no) manner diminish, impair or otherwise affect any of Lessee's obligations under this Equipment Schedule, including, without limitation, the payment of all monthly rental payments. . . ." Thus, by the terms of these Schedules, West Virginia specifically agreed that any breach of OPM's maintenance obligations shall not affect West Virginia's duty to make monthly lease payments.

The three Security Agreements, identical in form, assign as security to LaSalle OPM's interest in 19 of OPM's 22 Equipment Schedules.[3] Each Security Agreement provides for the assignment of all of West Virginia's monthly lease payments to LaSalle.[4] According to these Security Agreements, LaSalle may demand payment or delivery of and shall receive and collect all money under the assigned Equipment Schedules and apply the funds to OPM's indebtedness. Furthermore, according to Section 1.08 of these Security Agreements, upon a default by West Virginia under the Master Lease, LaSalle is entitled to exercise all of OPM's rights under the assigned Equipment Schedules, but is not thereby to assume any of OPM's obligations to West Virginia.

In each Consent and Agreement, West Virginia acknowledges and consents to OPM's assignment of Equipment Schedules to LaSalle. West Virginia also agrees therein to make all

---

[3] By these three Security Agreements, LaSalle originally held a security interest in 20 of the Equipment Schedules. However, a letter agreement dated August 29, 1980 released LaSalle's security interest in Equipment Schedule No. 1-02 and the computer equipment leased to West Virginia thereunder. LaSalle continues to hold a security interest in the remaining 19 Equipment Schedules.

[4] The 22 Equipment Schedules were classified as "Series A" (5 Schedules), "Series B" (4 Schedules), "Series C" (10 Schedules), and "Unclassified" (3 Schedules). LaSalle transferred funds to OPM in consideration of assignment of OPM's interest in these Schedules as follows:

Series A—June 10, 1980/Series C—August 28, 1980

Series B—August 28, 1980/Unclassified—Never Assigned

monthly lease payments to LaSalle "without abatement, reduction, counterclaim or offset . . . as a result of any breach of any obligation of OPM." *See* Affidavit of Ray H. Camp in support of LaSalle's Summary Judgment Motion ("Camp Affidavit"), Exhibits 9, 10 and 11 at 2.

In addition, opinions from the office of the highest legal officer of West Virginia as to the enforceability of the Equipment Schedules were provided on two occasions. The Deputy Attorney General wrote that the Equipment Schedules and Consents and Agreements each constituted "a legal, valid and binding instrument enforceable in accordance with its terms against (West Virginia)". He qualified this opinion only by asserting: "My opinion is qualified to the extent that the remedies available to enforce your rights under the Transactional Documents may be limited by bankruptcy, insolvency and other laws respecting creditors' rights and remedies generally." *See* Camp Affidavit, Exhibit 5, at 3, Exhibit 7 at 13.

West Virginia concedes having made no monthly lease payments during March, April, May and June 1981. Following these four successive months of default, on July 3, 1981, LaSalle gave West Virginia written notice of its default and of LaSalle's election to accelerate the balance of lease payments. It was not until after LaSalle's notice of acceleration in July 1981 that West Virginia made lease payments on the assigned Equipment Schedules totalling $160,125.00 for the months of March, April and May 1981. LaSalle contends that this amount was less than the properly corresponding amount of West Virginia's lease obligation.[5]

II. ISSUES PRESENTED

The issues presented by LaSalle's motion for summary judgment on its counterclaim and by West Virginia's cross-motion to dismiss LaSalle's counterclaim are:

(1) Whether West Virginia can validly assert that it is immune from LaSalle's counterclaim for accelerated rents because it chooses to invoke its sovereign immunity;

(2) Whether there remain any material issues of fact in dispute so as to preclude summary judgment in favor of LaSalle or whether LaSalle may be granted judgment as a matter of law on its counterclaim for accelerated rentals;

(3) Whether the clause in the Master Lease between OPM and West Virginia creating West Virginia's "absolutely unconditional" obligation to pay rents to OPM's assignee (LaSalle) shall be given full force and effect as a matter of law despite OPM's breach of its maintenance payments obligation.

For the reasons hereinafter stated we grant LaSalle summary judgment on its counterclaim for accelerated rentals and deny West Virginia's motion to dismiss this counterclaim.

III. DISCUSSION OF LAW

A. *Waiver of Sovereign Immunity*

West Virginia contends that LaSalle's counterclaim is not cognizable in this Court because it chooses to invoke its sovereign immunity to this counterclaim. For the reasons hereinafter

[5] West Virginia has failed to make any lease payments since the commencement of this adversary proceeding in August 1981. However, it has made "use and occupancy" payments into an escrow fund at the rate of $61,100 (exclusive of maintenance) per month retroactively and $86,060 (inclusive of maintenance) per month pursuant to an escrow order by this court dated December 11, 1981.

stated, this Court holds that West Virginia has irrevocably waived its sovereign immunity by initiating these proceedings.

[Extensive discussion omitted.]

B. *Merits of LaSalle's Counterclaim*

1. *Hell and High Water Clause*

LaSalle contends that it is entitled to summary judgment as to West Virginia's liability on LaSalle's counterclaim for accelerated rental payments[6] pursuant to Rule 56 of the Federal Rules of Civil Procedureas adopted in bankruptcy matters by Bankruptcy Rule 756. West Virginia contends that LaSalle is not entitled to judgment as a matter of law because there are material issues of fact in dispute as to whether LaSalle took its assignment of rents from OPM in good faith without notice of claims or defenses. For the reasons hereinafter detailed, we grant summary judgment to LaSalle on its counterclaim as to West Virginia's liability.

This holding is based on our view that under New York law, which applies pursuant to the terms of the Master Lease, the plain meaning of West Virginia's absolutely unconditional promise to make rental payments to OPM must be given full force and effect as a matter of law. *See, e.g., Breed v. Insurance Co. of North America*, 46 N.Y.2d 351, 385, N.E.2d 1280, 413 N.Y.S.2d 352 (1978); *Laba v. Carey*, 29 N.Y.2d 302, 277 N.E.2d 641, 327 N.Y.S.2d 613 (1971); *Luna Park Housing Corp. v. Besser*, 38 A.D.2d 713, 329 N.Y.S.2d 332 (2d Dep't 1972).

This "hell or high water" provision contained in Section 5.3 (iii) of the Master Lease provides:

> (iii) (West Virginia's) obligation to pay directly to such assignee the amounts due from Lessee under any Equipment Schedule (whether as rent or otherwise) shall be *absolutely unconditional* and shall be payable whether or not *any* Equipment Schedule is terminated by operation of law, any act of the parties or otherwise . . . (emphasis added).[7]

In essence, this unequivocal provision mandates that regardless of any remedies West Virginia may invoke against OPM, including a defense or claim as to OPM's default in paying the Maintenance Providers, West Virginia may not terminate LaSalle's unconditional right to payment. West Virginia was well aware of this unconditional right to payment of rentals when it executed the Consent and Agreements to the assignments by OPM to LaSalle. *See* Camp Affidavit, exhibits 9, 10 and 11. In addition, the Attorney General of West Virginia gave his express written approval to the content of the Master Lease between OPM and LaSalle, including this hell and high water clause. *See* Camp Affidavit, Exhibit 5 at 3, and Exhibit 7 at 3.

To deny this clause its full force and effect would effectively reconstruct the contract contrary to the intent of the parties, which reconstructions would be impermissible. *See, e.g., Rodolitz*

---

[6] LaSalle is fully entitled to accelerate the rentals due it from West Virginia upon West Virginia's default pursuant to Section 12.2 of the Master Lease. In addition, it informed West Virginia in writing of its intention to accelerate although it was not obligated to give such notice pursuant to Section 12.2.

[7] In addition, Section 4(a) of the Equipment Schedules, the source of OPM's maintenance obligations to West Virginia, contains another express limitation on West Virginia's remedies for any failure by OPM to make maintenance payments. It provides:

> (West Virginia) covenants and agrees that nothing contained in this Section 4(a) shall in any manner diminish, impair or otherwise affect any of (West Virginia's) obligations under this Equipment Schedule, including, without limitation, the payment of all monthly rental payments . . . (OPM) shall indemnify and hold (West Virginia) harmless in respect of any losses suffered by (West Virginia) by reason of a failure to pay (maintenance charges). . . .

v. Neptune Paper Products, Inc., 22 N.Y.2d 383, 386, 239 N.E.2d 628, 630, 292 N.Y.S.2d 878, 881 (1968).

Moreover, it is a well-settled principle that "parties to a contract are given broad latitude within which to fashion their own remedies for breach of contract . . . . It follows that contractual limitations upon remedies are generally to be enforced unless unconscionable".[8] *Wilson Trading Corp. v. David Ferguson, Ltd.*, 23 N.Y.2d 398, 404, 244 N.E.2d 685, 687, 297 N.Y.S.2d 108, 111-112 (1968).

More specifically, courts have uniformly given full force and effect to "hell and high water" clauses in the face of various kinds of defaults by the party seeking to enforce them. *National Equipment Rental v. J. & I. Carting*, Inc., 73 A.D.2d 666, 423 N.Y.S.2d 205 (2d Dep't 1979); *Dixie Groceries, Inc. v. Albany Business Machines*, 156 Ga.App. 36, 274 S.E.2d 81, 83 (1990). *See also First National Bank of Atlanta v. Harrison*, 408 F.Supp. 137, 140 (N.D. Ga. 1975), *aff'd*, 529 F.2d 1350 (5th Cir. 1976).[9]

The courts in all of the above-cited cases held that clauses containing unconditional promises are strictly enforceable as a matter of law. In so doing, they have found summary judgment in favor of the lessor or its assignee because no facts submitted or to be submitted by the lessee opposing summary judgment are in any way relevant to the lessee's unequivocal liability based on these hell and high water provisions.[10]

In *National Equipment Rental, supra*, the court, faced with a lessor's failure to file a criminal complaint against an alleged thief of the equipment at issue, held that the lessor's inaction did

---

[8] Even considering the law of the State of West Virginia (although West Virginia does not expressly dispute in its submissions to this Court that the rights and liabilities of the parties are governed by the law of the State of New York), the hell and high water clause herein is not illegal or unconscionable as West Virginia urges.

West Virginia has cited and this court has found no West Virginia Statute or other provision proscribing double payments by West Virginia. Also West Virginia has misconstrued the effect of a rejection of these leases would not terminate the Equipment Schedules and require the turnover of the equipment. Such a rejection merely constitutes a breach of the lease. *See* Code Section 365(g) Supp. IV 1980. Counsel for the Trustee and LaSalle, recognizing this point, expressly waiving rights, declared that they have absolutely no interest in retrieving the equipment while at the same time requiring West Virginia to pay rent for it. *See* Transcript of Oral Argument on the instant motions at pp. 40, 75-76.

Moreover, if West Virginia is required to make double maintenance payments, these payments are a foreseeable consequence flowing form the structure of the maintenance payments contracts. West Virginia and OPM structured the arrangement in such a way as to make West Virginia directly liable to the Maintenance Providers while making OPM liable to West Virginia for reimbursement of these payments. However, the Maintenance Providers were not made a party to OPM's agreement to reimburse West Virginia. By not making the Maintenance Providers a party to this agreement, West Virginia left itself vulnerable to the possibility of double payments.

Furthermore, the highest legal officer of the State of West Virginia expressly approved the content of these leases. The Attorney General's Office declared each of them "a legal, valid and binding instrument enforceable in accordance with its terms. . . ." Camp Affidavit, Ex 5 at 3, Ex 7 at 3.

[9] In addition, commentators have echoed the strict enforceability of these hell or high water clauses. *See, e.g.*, R. Contino, Legal and Financial Aspects of Equipment Leasing Transactions, 29, 87-88 (1979), where the author states:

> Finance leases frequently contain a "hell or high water" rent commitment. Under this type of obligation, a lessee is required to *unconditionally* pay the full rent when due. He is not permitted to make any deduction even though he has a legitimate claim against the lessor for money owed. This is not as bad as it sounds for a lessee, since he can still bring a lawsuit against the lessor for any claims. *Id.* at 29.

[10] In addition, conspicuous disclaimers of warranty, like hell and high water clauses, have served as the basis for decisions enabling equipment lessors to collect lease paymentsnotwithstanding the merchantability of these products. *See, e.g., Glenn Dick Equipment Co. v. Galey Construction*, Inc., 97 Idaho 216, 541 P.2d 1184 (1975); *Bakal v. Burroughs Corp.*, 74 Misc.2d 202, 205, 343 N.Y.S.2d 541 (N.Y. Sup. Ct. 1972).

not constitute a defense as a matter of law to the lessee's obligation to pay rent unconditionally. Similarly, in *Dixie Groceries, supra*, the Georgia court held that such a clause in an equipment lease remains inviolate as a matter of law, even where facts submitted by the lessee show a failure by the lessor to repair or maintain the equipment.[11]

The essential practical consideration requiring liability as a matter of law in these situations is that these clauses are essential to the equipment leasing industry. To deny their effect as a matter of law would seriously chill business in this industry because it is by means of these clauses that a prospective financier-assignee of rental payments is guaranteed meaningful security for his outright loan to the lessor. Without giving full effect to such clauses, if the equipment were to malfunction, the only security for this assignee would be to repossess equipment with substantially diminished value. *See Contino, supra*, at 87; B. Fritch and A. Reitman, Equipment Leasing -Leveraged Leasing, 131-32 (1977).

Further justification for giving full force and effect to the hell and high water clause herein is found in the fact that OPM is a finance lessor, not a merchant lessor. Courts have distinguished between these two types of equipment lessors in determining whether a lessor's obligation to make payments is separate and apart from the maintenance and performance of the equipment. In the instant case, the lessor involved is a finance lessor whose only service is to provide funds and who is not merchant lessor. A merchant lessor is one who deals in goods and holds itself out as having specialized knowledge about the design, operation and repair of the chattel leased. *See Patriot General Life Insurance v. CFC Investment Co.*, —Mass. App.—, 420 N.E.2d 918 (1981). Since OPM only provided the financing for the lease to West Virginia and thus is a finance lessor, West Virginia had no independently justifiable reason to rely upon OPM for any technical judgment or to hold OPM responsible for the making of maintenance payments on its behalf. *See id.*

Accordingly, whether a bad faith assignment or an assignment on notice of default in maintenance payments took place is irrelevant in deciding this summary judgment motion because of the inclusion of a hell and high water clause in the Master Lease. Thus, under Rule 56(c), as applied in bankruptcy matters by Rule 756, West Virginia has failed to demonstrate a genuine issue of material fact and the case is ripe for summary judgment. *See Leasing Services Corporation v. Justice and Childers*, 673 F.2d 70 (2d Cir. 1982).

The argument advanced by West Virginia against summary judgment concerning facts to be raised by it imputing notice of lack of good faith to LaSalle is misplaced; such facts could only perhaps have relevance absent a hell and high water clause. West Virginia has apparently confused the hell and high water provision with the waiver of defenses clause which was also included in the Master Lease, Section 5.3(iv).[12] If only a waiver of defense clause were present, then, pursuant to Uniform Commercial Code Section 9-206,[13] this court would have to examine the

---

[11] In like fashion, the court in *Luna, supra*, found summary judgment based on the plain meaning of an unequivocal apartment lease provision. Furthermore, the court, in *First National Bank of Atlanta, supra*, held that the parol evidence rule barred the introduction of facts concerning an alleged oral contract in the face of an unconditional promissory note.

[12] This clause waiving defenses which West Virginia could have asserted against OPM absent an assignment to LaSalle is contained in Section 5.3(iv) of the Master Lease. It states:

> Lessee shall pay all amounts due from Lessee under any Equipment Schedule (Whether as rent or otherwise) to such assignee, notwithstanding any defense, offset or counterclaim whatever, whether by reason of breach of such Equipment Schedule or otherwise which it may or might now or hereafter have as against Lessor. . . .

[13] Uniform Commercial Code Section 9-206 provides in relevant part:

sufficiency of the facts raised by West Virginia concerning LaSalle's purported lack of good faith and notice of default in taking the assignment. However, here, the hell and high water clause renders West Virginia liable as a matter of law irrespective of any inference raised as to notice or good faith.[14]

Accordingly, this court grants summary judgment on liability only in favor of LaSalle on its counterclaim for accelerated rentals.

2. *The Result Absent Hell and High Water*

Even absent this Court's granting full force and effect to the hell and high water clause in the Master Lease, West Virginia's merely conclusory allegation that LaSalle took the assignment in bad faith and with notice of default is insufficient to raise a triable issue of fact because West Virginia has failed to plead the facts constituting alleging fraud and notice with the specificity required by Rule 56(c). Thus, under Section 9-206 of the Uniform Commercial Code,West Virginia's contractual waiver of all defenses to LaSalle's counterclaim for rental payments, including the waiver of its defense of default in maintenance payments, is enforceable.

The thrust of West Virginia's Rule 3(g) statement[15] and other affidavits in opposition to summary judgment[16] is that at the time these assignments of rent were made, LaSalle either knew or should have known that OPM had defaulted on payments to the Maintenance Providers. Such knowledge, either actual or imputed, is alleged by West Virginia to constitute bad faith which, under U.C.C. § 9-206(1), permits West Virginia to assert a defense to LaSalle's counterclaim for accelerated rentals.

> [1] [A]n agreement by a buyer or lessee that he will not assert against an assignee any claim or defense which he may have against the seller or lessor is enforceable by an assignee who takes his assignment for value, in good faith, and without notice of a claim or defense, except as to defenses of a type which may be asserted against a holder in due course of a negotiable instrument under the Article on Commercial Paper. U.C.C. § 9-206 (McKinney 1964).

[14] Our holding as to the full force and effect of the hell and high water clause as a matter of law is intended to be the law of the case on this issue. The only objection raised to the Trustee's motion to reject the 19 unassigned leases is raised by LaSalle and concerns the adequacy of protection of LaSalle's security interest in the rental payments absent full enforcement of the hell and high water clause. Accordingly, there appears to be no longer any impediment to the Trustee's motion to reject.

[15] Local Rule 3(g) provides:

> (g) Upon motion for summary judgment to Rule 56 of the Federal Rules of Civil Procedure, there shall be annexed to the notice of motion a separate, short and concise statement of the material facts as to which the moving party contends there is no issue to be tried. Failure to submit such a statement constitutes grounds for denial of the motion. The papers opposing a motion for summary judgment shall include a separate, short and concise statement of the material facts as to which it is contended that there exists a genuine issue to be tried.
>
> All material facts set forth in the statement required to be served by the moving party will be deemed to be admitted unless controverted by the statement required to be served by the opposing party. Local Rule 3(g), Rules for the Southern District of New York (1980).

[16] This Rule 56 motion was fully argued, briefed and marked "submitted" as ripe for determination by the Court on May 20, 1982. None of the parties requested leave of the court to submit post-submission papers or memoranda. Notwithstanding the consensual yield to this court's determination of a mature motion, West Virginia on June 30, 1982, more than one month after this court undertook deliberation, and six months after the original notice of motion, filed an additional affidavit with the court clerk with the apparent intention of raising belated issues of fact. The submission was without application to, or leave of, the court and is in violation of Rule 3(c)(3) of the Civil Rules of the District Court for the Southern District of New York. Accordingly, the affidavit is outside the scope of this Court's consideration.

Rule 56(e) of the Federal Rules of Civil Procedure provides in relevant part:

> When a motion for summary judgment is made and supported as provided in this rule, an adverse party may not rest upon the mere allegations or denials of his pleading, but his response, by affidavits or as otherwise provided in this rule, must set forth specific facts showing that there is genuine issue for trial. If he does not so respond, summary judgment, if appropriate, shall be entered against him.
>
> Fed. R. Civ. P. 56(e).

LaSalle flatly denies having had any knowledge of OPM's default and any lack of good faith on its part. Rule 56(e) requires West Virginia to come forward with affirmative proof of specific facts to contradict this denial by LaSalle. As the court in *Applegate v. Top Associates, Inc.*, 425 F.2d 92 (2d Cir. 1970), stated: "To avoid summary judgment . . . a plaintiff must do more than whet the curiosity of the court; he must support vague accusations and surmise with concrete particulars." *Id.* at 96. *See also Maiorana v. MacDonald*, 596 F.2d 1072, 1080 (1st Cir. 1979); *Donnelly v. Guion*, 467 F.2d 290, 293 (2d Cir. 1972); *Radio City Music Hall Corp. v. United States*, 135 F.2d 715, 718 (2d Cir. 1943). West Virginia has failed completely in presenting such concrete particulars regarding its vague and illusory allegations of bad faith and notice.

West Virginia's affidavits are utterly devoid of any specific facts establishing LaSalle's actual knowledge of OPM's default in complying with the terms of the maintenance agreement.[17] The bare assertion that a dispute exists over the state of mind of a litigant is not *ipso factor* a reason to deny summary judgment. *See Feick v. Fleener*, 653 F.2d 69 (2d Cir. 1981); *Markowitz v. Republic National Bank of New York*, 651 F.2d 825, 828 (2d Cir. 1981); *S.E.C. v. Research Automation Corp.*, 585 F.2d 31, 33-34 (2d Cir. 1978). "Courts, refusing to exalt form over substance, cannot be awed by procedural specters and cannot be swayed by feigned issues." *Feick*, 653 F.2d at 77. *See also Quinn v. Syracuse Model Neighborhood Corp.*, 613 F.2d 438, 445 (2d Cir. 1980); *Applegate v. Top Associates, Inc.*, 425 F.2d at 96.

Similarly, a general innuendo alleging bad faith which points to no particular facts on which to ground the charge is no defense to a motion for summary judgment. *See* Fed. R. Civ. P. Rule 56(e); *Applegate v. Top Associates, Inc.*, 425 F.2d at 96; *In re Carnegie Industries, Inc.*, Bkrtcy. S.D.N.Y., 8 B.R. 983, 986-87, 24 C.B.C. 39; 6 Moore's Federal Practice 56.22(1) at 1324-25 (1982). West Virginia's vague assertion that LaSalle is somehow guilty of bad faith raises no genuine issue as to any material fact to preclude summary judgment. West Virginia's pointing to the general fact that OPM was involved in pyramid schemes without specific reference and without relating such fact to LaSalle is absolutely irrelevant here. *See id.*

Additionally, West Virginia argues that because LaSalle had the right to inspect OPM's books and records under the LaSalle-OPM agreements, knowledge of the default to the Maintenance

---

[17] With regard to constructive or imputed knowledge, that the Attorney General of West Virginia not only gave his approval to the content of the lease between West Virginia and OPM but also approved the assignment to LaSalle after the alleged default, militates against a finding of imputed knowledge and bad faith on the part of LaSalle. Such an imputing of knowledge cannot occur because the only circumstance which could impute bad faith is that LaSalle took the assignment two months after OPM first defaulted on its maintenance payments. This circumstance is greatly overshadowed by the Attorney General's approvals. The Court in *Credit Alliance Corp. v. David O. Crump Sand & Fill Co.*, 470 F. Supp. 489 (S.D.N.Y. 1979), similarly found summary judgment in favor of an equipment lessor although knowledge of default in maintenance could have been imputed from the circumstances. The Court in *Credit Alliance* found that given actual evidence that the lessee had unequivocally acknowledged in writing the complete and satisfactory delivery of the equipment, any knowledge of default that could have been imputed circumstantially was irrelevant. *Id.* at 492.

Providers should be imputed to LaSalle. . . . [T]his imputing of knowledge is greatly overshadowed by West Virginia's express approval of an assignment after the alleged default by OPM. In addition, this argument presupposes the existence of a duty to investigate upon the assignee who takes for value. In *Bankers Trust Co. v. Litton Systems, Inc.*, 599 F.2d 488 (2d Cir. 1979), a lessee of certain equipment similarly sought to impose upon the lessor's secured lender a duty to investigate into matters collateral to the assigned rental payments. In refusing to impose such a duty on the assignee, Second Circuit Judge Moore stated:

> [T]he holder in due course is protected not because of his praiseworthy character, but to the end that commercial transactions may be engaged in *without elaborate investigation of the process leading up to the contract or instrument* and in reliance on the contract rights of one who offers them for sale or to secure a loan. 599 F.2d at 494 (emphasis added). *See also* Gilmore, *The Commercial Doctrine of Good Faith Purchase*, 63 Yale L.J. 1057 (1954).

Although *Litton* involved a claim of bribery against the lessor rather than a default in a contract term as alleged herein, this rationale applies equally here.

Moreover, the opinion letter from the West Virginia Attorney General as to the validity of the rental payments to OPM coupled with West Virginia's execution of Consent and Agreements to the assignment to LaSalle satisfied whatever duty of inquiry LaSalle may have had insofar as OPM's obligations to West Virginia were concerned.

Since West Virginia has presented no specific facts demonstrating the alleged bad faith of LaSalle sufficient to defend against this motion for summary judgment under Rule 56(e), LaSalle is entitled to judgment on its claim for rent as a matter of law.[18]

Accordingly, LaSalle's motion for summary judgment as to West Virginia's liability for accelerated rental payments is granted.[19] West Virginia's cross motion to dismiss the counterclaim is denied.

In addition, in view of our holding affirming West Virginia's independent, absolutely unconditional liability to LaSalle, the rejection by the Trustee of the 19 leases assigned to LaSalle has no effect upon LaSalle's remedies against West Virginia in the event West Virginia defaults.

[18] West Virginia also attempts to raise two other kinds of factual issues in its Rule 3(g) statement and affidavits. First, it states in conclusory terms that there is a factual issue as to whether or not LaSalle took an assignment of the net or gross rentals (including maintenance payments). However, West Virginia submits no facts to support its allegations that only net rentals were assigned to LaSalle. Indeed, the terms "gross" and "net rentals" are found in none of the agreements at issue herein. Moreover, in each Security Agreement, OPM assigns as security "all of its estate, right, title, interest, claim and demand in . . . *the rental payments and rental installments* . . . *damages and other moneys* (with certain exceptions not here pertinent) from time to time payable to or receivable by OPM under the Equipment Schedules. . . ." West Virginia not only received notice of these assignments, but expressly consented to them in each Consent and Agreement it executed. *See* Camp Affidavit, Exs 9, 10 and 11. Accordingly, this court finds from the Security Agreements that gross rentals were assigned to LaSalle.

Second, West Virginia attempts to raise an issue as to the possible waiver by LaSalle of its assignment from OPM by the means of collection of the rentals. However, all parties agreed in open court at the oral argument on this Motion that they were participants in a pass-through mechanism by which West Virginia would forward checks to OPM who would then endorse them directly over to LaSalle. Thus, there can be no issue as to the waiver of the assignment by the mode of rent collection. *See* Transcript of Argument at 22-23.

[19] The defense West Virginia has raised of lack of appropriations with which to pay a judgment against it is legally insufficient. LaSalle is entitled to a judgment on its counterclaim regardless of whether, as a practical matter, funds can be obtained to satisfy it.

Thus, LaSalle's security interest in the lease payment is fully protected. Therefore, the Trustee's motion to reject these 19 leases is granted.

Settle an order in conformity with this opinion.

NOTES AND QUESTIONS

(1) How would this case be decided assuming Article 2A is applicable? (Observe that the case is referenced in Comment 6 to § 2A-407.)

(2) *Consumer Finance Leases*. With regard to cutting off consumer defenses, King, *Major Problems With Article 2A: Unfairness, "Cutting Off" Consumer Defenses, Unfiled Interests, and Uneven Adoption*, 43 Mercer Law Rev. 869 at 878-80 (1992), observes:[20]

> One may understand why the drafters did not want to place positive liability for damages due to loss or injury from defective goods on the finance lessor; however, whether the financier remains subject to the buyer's defense that the goods are defective with regard to making payments is unclear. Can the buyer cease to make payments on the basis that the goods are defective? If the consumer must still make payments, then his or her defenses have been cut off just as effectively as they were under the old "holder in due course" doctrine. Under the former circumstances, the financier of the transaction purchases commercial paper, while in the lease situation, the financier holds a different piece of paper, a lease, over the head of the consumer. If adequate consumer protection is to exist, the results should be the same.
>
> . . . .
>
> Why leave the matter to even the slightest doubt or to the courts' interpretation? An amendment is in order, and it might read:
>
> Consumer Defenses Preserved
>
> No consumer shall be barred from raising any defense he or she has based on the quality or performance of the goods or based on the signing of legal documents against the finance lessor or any other party.
>
> If a state has already adopted Article 2A or wants to cover this matter separately, it can pass a special consumer protection statute:
>
> Consumer Protection Against Depriving Consumers Of Their Defenses by Finance Leasing
>
> No consumer shall be barred from raising against a finance lessor any defense to payment he or she might have concerning the goods or signing of legal documents. All rights preserved against holders in due course of commercial paper or contracts shall be applicable likewise to finance lessors.
>
> The federal government could also enact a similar statute.

[20] Copyright © 1992 by Donald King. Reprinted with permission of the author.

CHAPTER 10

DOCUMENTARY TRANSACTIONS

§ 10.01 Documents of Title

[A] Introduction

Read: U.C.C. § 1-201(15), (6), (45); §§ 7-102(1)(d) and (e), 7-104.

Goods are often shipped or stored at certain stages of the contract for sale. Goods may be delivered to a carrier for shipment, or may be stored at a warehouse. In these situations, the carrier or warehouseman has the relationship of a bailee for the shipper or storer. The bailee-carrier will issue a bill of lading (bill). Likewise, the bailee-warehouseman will issue a warehouse receipt (receipt).

The bill or receipt serves two purposes: (1) the bill or receipt is a receipt for the goods received by the issuer (carrier or warehouseman); (2) the bill or receipt serves as evidence of the contract for shipment in the case of the carrier, or as evidence of the contract for storage in the case of the warehouseman. In addition, if the bill or receipt is negotiable, two additional aspects are manifested. Because of the negotiable quality, (1) the person in possession of the bill or receipt is entitled to receive, hold and dispose of the bill or receipt and the goods it covers (the concept of merger or "symbolism" whereby the possessor of the paper controls the right to that which the paper represents); (2) a good faith purchaser of the bill or receipt may acquire greater rights to the bill or receipt and the goods it covers than the purchaser's transferor. This latter aspect of negotiability is evaluated in Chapter 11 et seq. with respect to negotiable instruments.

Accordingly, U.C.C. Article 7, which deals with documents of title, involves an application of the law of bailments and the law of negotiable instruments.

Bailment. The three basic tenets of bailment are:

1. A bailment results when the bailee is in lawful possession of goods but the bailee does not have title to them. U.C.C. § 7-102(1)(a).

2. The bailee generally has a duty to exercise ordinary care toward the goods. U.C.C. §§ 7-204, 7-309.

3. Upon termination of the bailment, the bailee is under a duty to deliver the goods either to the bailor or otherwise in accordance with the bailor's instruction. Such delivery may be excused, for example, (a) if the bailed goods are delivered to a person with paramount rights to the goods, or (b) if the bailed goods are taken pursuant to legal process such as a levy or attachment, or (c) if the goods are damaged or destroyed notwithstanding bailee's exercising the proper degree of care.

U.C.C. § 7-403. Further, the bailee may be entitled to a possessory lien for storage or transportation charges. U.C.C. §§ 7-209, 7-307.

Document as negotiable instrument. A negotiable bill of lading or warehouse receipt is analogous to a promissory note under Article 3 Negotiable Instruments. Article 3 paper involves a promise to pay money "to order" or "to bearer." U.C.C. §§ 3-104(a), 3-109, 3-412. Article 7 paper involves a promise to deliver identified goods to "order" or "to bearer." U.C.C. §§ 7-104, 7-403. Appreciation of this similarity will be of assistance in studying both Articles 3 and 7. There is, however, one important distinction: Article 3 paper does not cover any particular money, but Article 7 paper purports to cover identified goods. U.C.C. § 1-201(15).

Also, a delivery order under Article 7 is analogous to a draft (*e.g.*, check) under Article 3. A draft is an order by a drawer to a drawee to pay money to a payee. A delivery order is an order by a bailor (*e.g.*, seller) to a bailee (*e.g.*, warehouse) to deliver goods to a deliveree (*e.g.*, buyer). U.C.C. §§ 3-103(a)(2) and (3), 3-104(e), 7-102(1)(b) and (d).

U.C.C. Article 7 has replaced the Uniform Bills of Lading Act, the Uniform Warehouse Receipts Act and the Uniform Sales Act. U.C.C. §§ 10-102(1), 10-104(1). Note, however, paramount federal law (§ 7-103), the Federal Bills of Lading Act (F.B.L.A.), 49 U.S.C. §§ 80101 et seq. (1994), which in § 80102 states the applicability of the Act:

> This chapter applies to a bill of lading when the bill is issued by a common carrier for the transportation of goods —
>
> (1) between a place in the District of Columbia and another place in the District of Columbia;
>
> (2) between a place in a territory or possession of the United States and another place in the same territory or possession;
>
> (3) between a place in a State and a place in another State;
>
> (4) between a place in a State and a place in the same State through another State or a foreign country; or
>
> (5) from a place in a State to a place in a foreign country.

Further, it should be borne in mind that federal legislation, such as the Interstate Commerce Act,[1] the Carriage of Goods by Sea Act,[2] the United States Warehouse Act,[3] etc., may also have an application to the shipment or storage of goods.

Peruse the forms on the following pages. Can you tell why they are negotiable or non-negotiable (aside from their being labeled as such)? Is the delivery order negotiable? Cf. U.C.C. §§ 3-104, 7-104.

---

[1] 49 U.S.C. § 11707.

[2] 46 U.S.C. § 1300 *et seq.*

[3] 7 U.S.C. § 241 *et seq.*

UNIFORM STRAIGHT BILL OF LADING
ORIGINAL—NOT NEGOTIABLE—DOMESTIC

Shipper's No.________
Agent's No.________

GATEWAY TRANSPORTATION CO., INC.

RECEIVED, subject to the classifications and tariffs in effect on the date of the issue of this Bill of Lading.

From ________, Date ________, 196____

At ________ Street, ________ City, ________ County, ________ State

[illegible]

Consigned to ________ Street, ________ City,

Destination ________ County, ________ State

Routing ________

Delivering Carrier ________ Vehicle or Car Initial ________ No. ________

Collect On Delivery $ ________ and remit to: ________

Street ________ City ________ State

C. O. D. charge to be paid by { Shipper □ Consignee □

No. Packages	Description of Articles, Special Marks, and Exceptions	Weight (Subject to Cor.)	Class or Rate	Check Col.

[illegible]

(Signature of Consignor)

If charges are to be prepaid, write or stamp here, "To be Prepaid."

Received $ ________

to apply in prepayment of the charges on the property described hereon.

Agent or Cashier

Per

(The signature here acknowledges only the amount prepaid.)

Charges Advanced:

$

[illegible]

________ Shipper, ________ Agent

Per ________ Per ________

Permanent Address of Shipper: ________ Street, ________ City, ________ State

Form 10-1: Uniform Straight Bill of Lading

(Uniform Domestic Order Bill of Lading adopted by Carriers in Official, Southern, Western and Illinois Classification territories, March 15, 1922, as amended August 1, 1930, and June 15, 1941.)

UNIFORM ORDER BILL OF LADING
(ORIGINAL)

Shipper's No.________

Agent's No.________

RECEIVED, subject to the classifications and tariffs in effect on the date of the issue of this Bill of Lading.

at____19____

from____

the property described below, in apparent good order, except as noted (contents and condition of contents of packages unknown), marked, consigned, and destined, as indicated below, which said compar (the word company being understood throughout this contract as meaning any person or corporation in possession of the property under the contract) agrees to carry to its usual place of delivery at sai destination, if on its own road or its own water line, otherwise to deliver to another carrier on the route to said destination. It is mutually agreed, as to each carrier of all or any of said property over all o any portion of said route to destination, and as to each party at any time interested in all or any of said property, that every service to be performed hereunder shall be subject to all the conditions no prohibited by law, whether printed or written, herein contained, including the conditions on back hereof, which are hereby agreed to by the shipper and accepted for himself and his assigns.

The surrender of this Original ORDER Bill of Lading properly indorsed shall be required before the delivery of the property. Inspection of property covered by this bill of lading will not permitted unless provided by law or unless permission is indorsed on this original bill of lading or given in writing by the shipper.

____

(Mail or street address of consignee—For purposes of notification and

Consigned to ORDER of____

Destination____________________State of____________________County of____________________

Notify____

At____________________State of____________________County of____________________

Route____

Delivering Carrier____________________Car Initial____________________Car No.____________________

NO. PACKAGES	DESCRIPTION OF ARTICLES, SPECIAL MARKS AND EXCEPTIONS	* WEIGHT (Subject to Correction)	CLASS OR RATE	CHECK COLUMN

Subject to Section 7 of conditions, if this shipment is to be delivered to the consignee without recourse on the consignor, the consignor shall sign the following statement:

The carrier shall not make delivery of this shipment without payment of freight and all other lawful charges.

____

(Signature of Consignor.)

If charges are to be prepaid, write or stamp here, "To be Prepaid."

Received $____________________

to apply in prepayment of the charges on the property described hereon.

____

Agent or Cashier

Per____________________

(The signature here acknowledges only the amount prepaid).

Charges Advanced.

$____________________

* If the shipment moves between two ports by a carrier by water, the law requires that the bill of lading shall state whether it is "carrier's or shipper's weight."

NOTE—Where the rate is dependent on value, shippers are required to state specifically in writing the agreed or declared value of the property.

The agreed or declared value of the property is hereby specifically stated by the shipper to be not exceeding

____________________per____________________

This is to certify that the above articles are properly described by name and are packed and marked and are in proper condition for transportation according to the regulations prescribed by the Interstate Commerce Commission.

1

The fibre boxes used for this shipment conform to the specifications set forth in the box maker's certificate thereon, and all other requirements of the Uniform Freight Classification.

____________________Shipper ____________________Agent

Per____________________ Per____________________

Permanent post-office address of shipper.

6K 698 Rediform

(This Bill of Lading is to be signed by the shipper and agent of the carrier issuing same.)

Form 10-2: Uniform Negotiable Bill of Lading

Sec. 1. (a) The carrier or party in possession of any of the property herein described shall be liable as at common law for any loss thereof or damage thereto, except as hereinafter provided.

(b) No carrier or party in possession of all or any of the property herein described shall be liable for any loss thereof or damage thereto or delay caused by the act of God, the public enemy, the authority of law, or the act or default of the shipper or owner, or for natural shrinkage. The carrier's liability shall be that of warehouseman, only, for loss, damage, or delay caused by fire occurring after the expiration of the free time allowed by tariffs lawfully on file (such free time to be computed as therein provided) after notice of the arrival of the property at destination or at the port of export (if intended for export) has been duly sent or given, and after placement of the property for delivery at destination, or tender of delivery of the property to the party entitled to receive it, has been made. Except in case of negligence of the carrier or party in possession (and the burden to prove freedom from such negligence shall be on the carrier or party in possession), the carrier or party in possession shall not be liable for loss, damage, or delay occurring while the property is stopped and held in transit upon the request of the shipper, owner, or party entitled to make such request, or resulting from a defect or vice in the property, or for country damage to cotton, or from riots or strikes.

(c) In case of quarantine the property may be discharged at risk and expense of owners into quarantine depot or elsewhere, as required by quarantine regulations or authorities, or for the carrier's dispatch at nearest available point in carrier's judgment, and in any such case carrier's responsibility shall cease when property is so discharged, or property may be returned by carrier at owner's expense to shipping point, earning freight both ways. Quarantine expenses of whatever nature or kind upon or in respect to property shall be borne by the owners of the property or be a lien thereon. The carrier shall not be liable for loss or damage occasioned by fumigation or disinfection or other acts required or done by quarantine regulations or authorities even though the same may have been done by carrier's officers, agents, or employees, nor for detention, loss, or damage of any kind occasioned by quarantine or the enforcement thereof. No carrier shall be liable, except in case of negligence, for any mistake or inaccuracy in any information furnished by the carrier, its agents, or officers, as to quarantine laws or regulations. The shipper shall hold the carriers harmless from any expense they may incur, or damages they may be required to pay, by reason of the introduction of the property covered by this contract into any place against the quarantine laws or regulations in effect at such place.

Sec. 2. (a) No carrier is bound to transport said property by any particular train or vessel, or in time for any particular market or otherwise than with reasonable dispatch. Every carrier shall have the right in case of physical necessity to forward said property by any carrier or route between the point of shipment and the point of destination. In all cases not prohibited by law, where a lower value than actual value has been represented in writing by the shipper or has been agreed upon in writing as the released value of the property as determined by the classification or tariffs upon which the rate is based, such lower value plus freight charges if paid shall be the maximum amount to be recovered, whether or not such loss or damage occurs from negligence.

(b) As a condition precedent to recovery, claims must be filed in writing with the receiving or delivering carrier, or carrier issuing this bill of lading, or carrier on whose line the loss, damage, injury or delay occurred, within nine months after delivery of the property (or, in case of export traffic, within nine months after delivery at port of export) or, in case of failure to make delivery, then within nine months after a reasonable time for delivery has elapsed; and suits shall be instituted against any carrier only within two years and one day from the day when notice in writing is given by the carrier to the claimant that the carrier has disallowed the claim or any part or parts thereof specified in the notice. Where claims are not filed or suits are not instituted thereon in accordance with the foregoing provisions, no carrier hereunder shall be liable, and such claims will not be paid.

(c) Any carrier or party liable on account of loss of or damage to any of said property shall have the full benefit of any insurance that may have been effected upon or on account of said property, so far as this shall not avoid the policies or contracts of insurance: Provided, That the carrier reimburse the claimant for the premium paid thereon.

Sec. 3. Except where such service is required as the result of carrier's negligence, all property shall be subject to necessary cooperage and baling at owner's cost. Each carrier over whose route cotton or cotton linters is to be transported hereunder shall have the privilege, at its own cost and risk, of compressing the same for greater convenience in handling or forwarding, and shall not be held responsible for deviation or unavoidable delays in procuring such compression. Grain in bulk consigned to a point where there is a railroad, public or licensed elevator, may (unless otherwise expressly noted herein, and then if it is not promptly unloaded) be there delivered and placed with other grain of the same kind and grade without respect to ownership (and prompt notice thereof shall be given to the consignor), and if so delivered shall be subject to a lien for elevator charges in addition to all other charges hereunder.

Sec. 4. (a) Property not removed by the party entitled to receive it within the free time allowed by tariffs, lawfully on file (such free time to be computed as therein provided), after notice of the arrival of the property at destination or at the port of export (if intended for export) has been duly sent or given, and after placement of the property for delivery at destination has been made, may be kept in vessel, car, depot, warehouse or place of delivery of the carrier, subject to the tariff charge for storage and to carrier's responsibility as warehouseman, only, or at the option of the carrier, may be removed to and stored in a public or licensed warehouse at the place of delivery or other available place, at the cost of the owner, and there held without liability on the part of the carrier, and subject to a lien for all freight and other lawful charges, including a reasonable charge for storage.

(b) Where nonperishable property which has been transported to destination hereunder is refused by consignee or the party entitled to receive it, or said consignee or party entitled to receive it fails to receive it within 15 days after notice of arrival shall have been duly sent or given, the carrier may sell the same at public auction to the highest bidder, at such place as may be designated by the carrier: Provided, That the carrier shall have first mailed, sent, or given to the consignor notice that the property has been refused or remains unclaimed, as the case may be, and that it will be subject to sale under the terms of the bill of lading if disposition be not arranged for, and shall have published notice containing a description of the property, the name of the party to whom consigned, or, if shipped order notify, the name of the party to be notified, and the time and place of sale, once a week for two successive weeks, in a newspaper of general circulation at the place of sale or nearest place where such newspaper is published: Provided, That 30 days shall have elapsed before publication of notice of sale after said notice that the property was refused or remains unclaimed was mailed, sent, or given.

(c) Where perishable property which has been transported hereunder to destination is refused by consignee or party entitled to receive it, or said consignee or party entitled to receive it shall fail to receive it promptly, the carrier may, in its discretion, to prevent deterioration or further deterioration, sell the same to the best advantage at private or public sale: Provided, That if time serves for notification to the consignor or owner of the refusal of the property or the failure to receive it and request for disposition of the property, such notification shall be given, in such manner as the exercise of due diligence requires, before the property is sold.

(d) Where the procedure provided for in the two paragraphs last preceding is not possible, it is agreed that nothing contained in said paragraphs shall be construed to abridge the right of the carriers at its option to sell the property under such circumstances and in such manner as may be authorized by law.

(e) The proceeds of any sale made under this section shall be applied by the carrier to the payment of freight, demurrage, storage, and any other lawful charges and the expense of notice, advertisement, sale, and other necessary expense and of caring for and maintaining the property, if proper care of the same requires special expense, and should there be a balance it shall be paid to the owner of the property sold hereunder.

(f) Property destined to or taken from a station, wharf, or landing at which there is no regularly appointed freight agent shall be entirely at risk of owner after unloaded from cars or vessels or until loaded into cars or vessels, and, except in case of carrier's negligence, when received from or delivered to such stations, wharves, or landings shall be at owner's risk until the cars are attached to and after they are detached from locomotive or train or until loaded into and after unloaded from vessels.

Sec. 5. No carrier hereunder will carry or be liable in any way for any documents, specie, or for any articles of extraordinary value not specifically rated in the published classifications or tariffs unless a special agreement to do so and a stipulated value of the articles are indorsed hereon.

R47

Uniform Order Bill of Lading (Reverse)
(Sec. 1-5)

Sec. 6. Every party, whether principal or agent, shipping explosives or dangerous goods, without previous full written disclosure to the carrier of their nature, shall be liable for and indemnify the carrier against all loss or damage caused by such goods, and such goods may be warehoused at owner's risk and expense or destroyed without compensation.

Sec. 7. The owner or consignee shall pay the freight and average, if any, and all other lawful charges accruing on said property; but, except in those instances where it may lawfully be authorized to do so, no carrier by railroad shall deliver or relinquish possession at destination of the property covered by this bill of lading until all tariff rates and charges thereon have been paid. The consignor shall be liable for the freight and all other lawful charges, except that if the consignor stipulates, by signature, in the space provided for that purpose on the face of this bill of lading that the carrier shall not make delivery without requiring payment of such charges and the carrier, contrary to such stipulation, shall make delivery without requiring such payment, the consignor (except as hereinafter provided) shall not be liable for such charges. Provided, that, where the carrier has been instructed by the shipper or consignor to deliver said property to a consignee other than the shipper or consignor, such consignee shall not be legally liable for transportation charges in respect of the transportation of said property (beyond those billed against him at the time of delivery for which he is otherwise liable) which may be found to be due after the property has been delivered to him, if the consignee (a) is an agent only and has no beneficial title in said property, and (b) prior to delivery of said property has notified the delivering carrier in writing of the fact of such agency and absence of beneficial title, and, in the case of a shipment reconsigned or diverted to a point other than that specified in the original bill of lading, has also notified the delivering carrier in writing of the name and address of the beneficial owner of said property; and, in such cases the shipper or consignor, or, in the case of a shipment so reconsigned or diverted, the beneficial owner, shall be liable for such additional charges. If the consignee has given to the carrier erroneous information as to who the beneficial owner is, such consignee shall himself be liable for such additional charges. On shipments reconsigned or diverted by an agent who has furnished the carrier in the reconsignment or diversion order with a notice of agency and the proper name and address of the beneficial owner, and where such shipments are refused or abandoned at ultimate destination, the said beneficial owner shall be liable for all legally applicable charges in connection therewith. If the reconsignor or diverter has given to the carrier erroneous information as to who the beneficial owner is, such reconsignor or diverter shall himself be liable for all such charges.

If a shipper or consignor of a shipment of property (other than a prepaid shipment is also the consignee named in the bill of lading and, prior to the time of delivery, notifies, in writing, a delivering carrier by railroad (a) to deliver such property at destination to another party, (b) that such party is the beneficial owner of such property, and (c) that delivery is to be made to such party only upon payment of all transportation charges in respect of the transportation of such property, and delivery is made by the carrier to such party without such payment, such shipper or consignor shall not be liable (as shipper, consignor, consignee, or otherwise) for such transportation charges but the party to whom delivery is so made shall in any event be liable for transportation charges billed against the property at the time of such delivery, and also for any additional charges which may be found to be due after delivery of the property, except that if such party prior to such delivery has notified in writing the delivering carrier that he is not the beneficial owner of the property, and has given in writing to such delivering carrier the name and address of such beneficial owner, such party shall not be liable for any additional charges which may be found to be due after delivery of the property; but if the party to whom delivery is made has given to the carrier erroneous information as to the beneficial owner, such party shall nevertheless be liable for such additional charges. If the shipper or consignor has given to the delivering carrier erroneous information as to who the beneficial owner is, such shipper or consignor shall himself be liable for such transportation charges, notwithstanding the foregoing provisions of this paragraph and irrespective of any provisions to the contrary in the bill of lading or in the contract of transportation under which the shipment was made. The term "delivering carrier" means the line-haul carrier making ultimate delivery.

Nothing herein shall limit the right of the carrier to require at time of shipment the prepayment or guarantee of the charges. If upon inspection it is ascertained that the articles shipped are not those described in this bill of lading, the freight charges must be paid upon the articles actually shipped.

Where delivery is made by a common carrier by water the foregoing provisions of this section shall apply, except as may be inconsistent with Part III of the Interstate Commerce Act.

Sec. 8. If this bill of lading is issued on the order of the shipper, or his agent, in exchange or in substitution for another bill of lading, the shipper's signature to the prior bill of lading as to the statement of value or otherwise, or election of common law or bill of lading liability, in or in connection with such prior bill of lading, shall be considered a part of this bill of lading as fully as if the same were written or made in or in connection with this bill of lading.

Sec. 9. (a) If all or any part of said property is carried by water over any part of said route, and loss, damage or injury to said property occurs while the same is in the custody of a carrier by water the liability of such carrier shall be determined by the bill of lading of the carrier by water (this bill of lading being such bill of lading if the property is transported by such water carrier thereunder) and by and under the laws and regulations applicable to transportation by water. Such water carriage shall be performed subject to all the terms and provisions of, and all the exemptions from liability contained in the Act of the Congress of the United States, approved on February 13, 1893, and entitled "An act relating to the navigation of vessels, etc.," and of other statutes of the United States according carriers by water the protection of limited liability, as well as the following subdivisions of this section; and to the conditions contained in this bill of lading not inconsistent with this section, when this bill of lading becomes the bill of lading of the carrier by water.

(b) No such carrier by water shall be liable for any loss or damage resulting from any fire happening to or on board the vessel, or from explosion, bursting of boilers or breakage of shafts, unless caused by the design or neglect of such carrier.

(c) If the owner shall have exercised due diligence in making the vessel in all respects seaworthy and properly manned, equipped, and supplied, no such carrier shall be liable for any loss or damage resulting from the perils of the lakes, seas, or other waters, or from latent defects in hull, machinery, or appurtenances whether existing prior to, at the time of, or after sailing, or from collision, stranding, or other accidents of navigation, or from prolongation of the voyage. And, when for any reason it is necessary, any vessel carrying any or all of the property herein described shall be at liberty to call at any port or ports, in or out of the customary route, to tow and be towed, to transfer, trans-ship, or lighter, to load and discharge goods at any time, to assist vessels in distress, to deviate for the purpose of saving life or property, and for docking and repairs. Except in case of negligence such carrier shall not be responsible for any loss or damage to property if it be necessary or is usual to carry the same upon deck.

(d) General Average shall be payable according to the York-Antwerp Rules of 1924, Sections 1 to 15, inclusive, and Sections 17 to 22, inclusive, and as to matters not covered thereby according to the laws and usages of the Port of New York. If the owners shall have exercised due diligence to make the vessel in all respects seaworthy and properly manned, equipped and supplied, it is hereby agreed that in case of danger, damage or disaster resulting from faults or errors in navigation, or in the management of the vessel, or from any latent or other defects in the vessel, her machinery or appurtenances, or from unseaworthiness, whether existing at the time of shipment or at the beginning of the voyage (provided the latent or other defects or the unseaworthiness was not discoverable by the exercise of due diligence), the shippers, consignees and/or owners of the cargo shall nevertheless pay salvage and any special charges incurred in respect of the cargo, and shall contribute with the shipowner in general average to the payment of any sacrifices, losses or expenses of a general average nature that may be made or incurred for the common benefit or to relieve the adventure from any common peril.

(e) If the property is being carried under a tariff which provides that any carrier or carriers party thereto shall be liable for loss from perils of the sea, then as to such carrier or carriers the provisions of this section shall be modified in accordance with the tariff provisions, which shall be regarded as incorporated into the conditions of this bill of lading.

(f) The term "water carriage" in this section shall not be construed as including lighterage in or across rivers, harbors, or lakes, when performed by or on behalf of rail carriers.

Sec. 10. Any alteration, addition, or erasure in this bill of lading which shall be made without the special notation hereon of the agent of the carrier issuing this bill of lading, shall be without effect, and this bill of lading shall be enforceable according to its original tenor.

Uniform Order Bill of Lading (Reverse)
(Sec. 6-10)

NOT-NEGOTIABLE WAREHOUSE RECEIPT

NEW YORK TERMINAL WAREHOUSE CO.

INCORPORATED

MAIN OFFICE: [address]

ISSUED AT

RECEIVED FROM

FOR ACCOUNT OF

IN WAREHOUSE AT

DEPOSITOR | WHSE. No.______

RECEIPT HOLDER | RECEIPT No.______

DATE______

In apparent good order, except as noted, the following property. The Warehouseman, at his discretion, will treat property of a like kind or character as fungible. Property will be delivered to the above Receipt Holder or in accordance with the above Receipt Holder's instructions.

LOT No.	QUANTITY	UNIT	SAID TO BE OR TO CONTAIN	MARKS

NOT-NEGOTIABLE

The Warehouseman's liability shall not exceed the following value as declared by the Depositor

UNIT: TOTAL VALUE:

Storage and other charges as per contract with the Depositor, the provisions of which will be disclosed to the holder hereof upon request to the Warehouseman.

Location of goods is not given for insurance purposes and the Warehouseman disclaims all liability for error or insufficiency of the location shown.

Values shown hereon are declared by the Depositor and the Warehouseman disclaims all responsibility therefor.

The New York Terminal Warehouse Co., Incorporated, certifies its only relationship to the Depositor is that of a Warehouseman and it has no financial interest in the property covered by this receipt, except it claims a lien for all lawful charges for the storage, handling and preservation of the property.

NEW YORK TERMINAL WAREHOUSE CO.

Incorporated

CANCELLED

By.______

RECORD OF DELIVERIES AND BALANCES ON HAND

DATE	DELIVERY ORDER No.	QUANTITY DELIVERED	BALANCE	
		BALANCE F'WARD		

Form 10-3: Not-Negotiable Warehouse Receipt

NEGOTIABLE WAREHOUSE RECEIPT

NEW YORK TERMINAL WAREHOUSE CO.

INCORPORATED

MAIN OFFICE [address]

ISSUED AT

RECEIVED FROM

FOR ACCOUNT OF

IN WAREHOUSE AT

DEPOSITOR

RECEIPT HOLDER

WHSE. No.

RECEIPT No.

DATE

In apparent good order, except as noted hereon, the following described property to be delivered to bearer upon payment of all storage, handling and other charges due, and the surrender of this warehouse receipt properly endorsed. The property described hereon shall be subject to the conditions noted hereon.

LOT No.	QUANTITY	UNIT	SAID TO BE OR TO CONTAIN	MARKS

NEGOTIABLE

The Warehouseman's liability shall not exceed the following value as declared by the Depositor:

UNIT: TOTAL VALUE:

Storage and other charges, as per contract with the Depositor, the provisions of which will be disclosed to the holder hereof, upon request to the Warehouseman.

Location of goods is not given for insurance purposes and the Warehouseman disclaims all liability for error or insufficiency of the location shown.

Values shown hereon are declared by the Depositor and the Warehouseman disclaims all responsibility therefor.

The New York Terminal Warehouse Co., Incorporated, certifies its only relationship to the Depositor is that of a Warehouseman and it has no financial interest in the property covered by this receipt, except it claims a lien for all lawful charges for the storage, handling and preservation of the property.

NEW YORK TERMINAL WAREHOUSE CO.

CANCELLED

By. Authorized Signature

By. Authorized Signature

RECORD OF DELIVERIES AND BALANCES ON HAND

DATE	DELIVERY ORDER No.	QUANTITY DELIVERED	BALANCE	
		BALANCE F'WARD		

Form 10-4: Negotiable Warehouse Receipt

DELIVERY ORDER

NEW YORK TERMINAL WAREHOUSE CO., Inc.

(Control Office) ....

WAREHOUSE ADDRESS..........

WHSE. No..........

DATE.......... 19 ...

No. (this form) ....

You are hereby authorized to deliver to .... the following described property, covered by warehouse receipts assigned to or held by us. You are hereby released from all liability for same.

SAID TO BE OR CONTAIN	UNIT	LOT NO.	QUANTITY	DEPOSITOR'S DECLARED VALUE	
				UNIT	EXTENSION
TOTAL QUANTITY				TOTAL DECLARED VALUE	

The values stated hereon are as declared by the depositor and the Warehouseman disclaims any responsibility therefor.

Date.......... 19......

Receipt of the above described property in good order is hereby acknowledged.

....

By.......... *Title*..........

Yours truly,

....
Receipt Holder

By.......... Title..........
Authorized Signature

Date signed:..........

430/440 D

Form 10-5: Delivery Order

[B] Bailee's Delivery Obligation

Read: U.C.C. §§ 7-403, 1-201(20), 7-104.

Bailee-carrier or warehouseman must deliver the bailed goods to a "person entitled under the document." In the case of a non-negotiable document, this means:

1. The person to whom delivery is to be made by the terms of a non-negotiable document. Example: S delivers goods to C carrier who engages on the bill of lading to deliver the goods "to B." C fulfills its delivery obligation by delivering the goods to B.

2. The person to whom delivery is to be made pursuant to written instructions under a non-negotiable document. Example: S delivers goods to W warehouse who engages on the warehouse receipt to deliver the goods "to S." S issues a written order (delivery order) directed to W to deliver the goods "to B." W fulfills its delivery obligation by delivering the goods to B. See U.C.C. § 7-403(1), (4) and the Uniform Straight Bill of Lading, the Non-Negotiable Warehouse Receipt and the Delivery Order forms located in the introduction to this chapter above.

In the case of a negotiable document of title, the "holder" is the "person entitled under the document" to whom the bailee must deliver the goods. Upon delivery, the holder must surrender the negotiable document covering the goods. A "holder" is "the person in possession [of the negotiable document] if the goods are deliverable to bearer or to the order of the person in possession." U.C.C. § 1-201(5),(20). Example: *S* delivers goods to *C* carrier who engages on the bill of lading to deliver the goods "to the order of *S*." *S* indorses the bill (by signing *S*'s name) and sends it to buyer through bank collection channels. C fulfills its delivery obligation by delivering the goods to holder B who must surrender the bill. See U.C.C. § 7-403(l), (3), (4) and the Uniform Order Bill of Lading form located in the introduction to this chapter above.

The requirement that the holder of the negotiable document must surrender it in order to obtain the goods is a manifestation of the "merger" or "symbolism" attribute of negotiability previously discussed. Accordingly, a bailee who has issued a negotiable document will never (or hardly ever) deliver the goods without surrender of the document. This conclusion is reflected on a negotiable bill which will state: "The surrender of this original order bill of lading properly indorsed shall be required before the delivery of property covered by the bill." Cf. U.C.C. §§ 7-403, 3-601, 3-602(a), 3-301, 3-501(b)(2); see § 7-601; cf. §§ 3-309, 8-405.

Several consequences occur when a document is utilized in a commercial transaction. This is particularly true if the document is negotiable. The following is a catalogue of the several provisions of U. C. C. Articles 2, 7 and 9 which deal with documents of title:

1. Passing of title — § 2-401(2), (3)(a).
2. Risk of loss — §§ 2-509(l)(a), (2)(a) and (c); 2-503(4)(b) and Comment 6; cf. § 3-414(f).
3. Seller's delivery obligation — §§ 2-503(2), 2-504(b); 2-503(3)-(5); cf. §§ 2-511(3). See § 2-319 et seq.
4. Buyer's obligation to accept and pay — §§ 2-310(a)-(c), 2-319(4), 2-320(4), 2-321(1) and (3), 2-505, 2-507(1), 2-511(1) and Comment 1.
5. Buyer's right to inspection of goods — §§ 2-513(1) and (3)(b); see § 2-310(a)-(c) and Comments 1 and 4, §§ 2-505, 2-320 Comments 1 and 12.
6. Buyer's right of rejection on improper delivery — §§ 2-601, 2-503.

7. Stoppage of delivery in transit — § 2-705(2)(d); see §§ 2-705(3)(c) and (d), 7-501(1) and (2), 7-504(4).

8. Seller's remedies in a cash sale transaction — §§ 2-507(2), 2-511(3).

9. Buyer's right of replevin — § 2-716 and Comment 5, § 2-505.

10. Diversion — § 7-303.

11. Lost or missing documents — § 7-601; cf. §§ 3-309, 8-405.

12. Attachment of goods covered by documents — § 7-602, cf. § 8-112; see §§ 2-503(4)(b), 7-504(2)(a).

13. Secured transactions — §§ 9-105(1)(f), 9-305, 9-304(2) and 3.

An important use of this document of title is its utilization as a device to secure payment of the purchase price to seller. This is pointed out by the following excerpt:[4]

Secure payment of purchase price: exchange of goods or document for price. In instances Seller may be unwilling to deliver goods to Buyer without receiving payment. Likewise, Buyer may be unwilling to pay for goods before receiving them. Thus they can agree that at the time and place for delivery they will simultaneously exchange the goods for the purchase price. See §§ 2-310(a), 2-507(1), 2-511(1). If Seller and Buyer are at a great distance, an intermediary (*e.g.*, postman, truck driver) may deliver the goods in exchange for the price and remit the monies to Seller, *i.e.*, a C.O.D. transaction. Or, the terms of the sales agreement may provide for "sight draft against order bill of lading" or "payment against documents" or "shipment under reservation." See § 2-505(1)(a) re reservation of a security interest in the goods. This documentary sale is outlined thus:

(1) Seller delivers the goods to Carrier and Carrier issues to Seller a seller's [shipper's] order bill:

Consigned to ORDER OF *Seller*

Notify *Buyer*

(2) Seller draws a sight draft[5] on Buyer stating in part:

At Sight

Pay to the order of *Seller*

Five Thousand and no/100. . . . . . . .Dollars

To: Buyer

(signed) Seller

Seller indorses the draft in blank or "Pay Seller City Bank, for collection"; Seller indorses the bill of lading in blank. See §§ 3-205, 1-201(20), 7-501(1). The draft and bill are then delivered to Seller City Bank for collection.

(3) Seller City Bank forwards the draft and bill to Buyer City Bank. See § 4-501 et seq. re collection of documentary drafts.

---

[4] Excerpt from B. Stone, Uniform Commercial Code In A Nutshell, pages 321-324; copyright © 1995 West Publishing Company, reprinted with permission.

[5] [Simply, the draft is an order made by seller addressed to buyer to pay the amount of the draft to the order of seller. It is a sight draft and, consequently, it is payable on demand. U.C.C. §§ 3-104(a) and (e), 3-108(a).—Ed.]

(4) Buyer City Bank notifies Buyer that the draft and bill have arrived. Buyer pays the draft and the draft and bill are delivered to Buyer.[6] See § 3-501(b)(2).

(5) Buyer is now the *holder* of the bill of lading since Buyer is in possession of a document issued to order and indorsed in blank. § 1-201(20). Buyer is the "person entitled under the document" to whom Carrier must deliver the goods. § 7-403(4). Thus Buyer surrenders the bill to Carrier and receives the goods. § 7-403(3). See §§ 2-310(b) and (c), 2-513(3)(b).

(6) Buyer City Bank transmits the proceeds (*e.g.*, by transfer(s) of bank credits) to Seller City Bank.

(7) Seller City Bank remits the proceeds to Seller (*e.g.*, by crediting Seller's account).

The above may be diagramed thus:

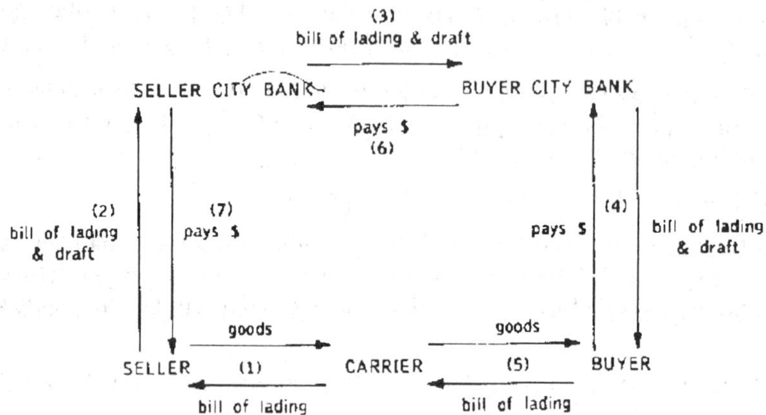

Use of "order bills" may be impeded by the fact that the goods may arrive at destination before the documents. Thus, the Code provides that bills may be issued at destination, thereby arriving before the goods. See § 7-305 and Comment re destination bills.

A non-negotiable document can reserve possession of goods as security thus: Suppose Carrier issued a non-negotiable bill "to Seller" (not "to the order of Seller"). Seller is the "person entitled under the document" to whom Carrier must deliver the goods. While the non-negotiable bill need not be surrendered, Carrier will not deliver to anyone (*e.g.*, Buyer) until it receives written instructions from Seller (a delivery order) to deliver to Buyer. Seller will not so instruct until Buyer has made satisfactory arrangements to pay for the goods. § 2-505(1)(b); see § 7-403(1), (3), (4).

---

6 [In the event that Buyer will be given a period, *e.g.*, sixty days, in which to pay for the goods, the above procedure may be followed except that the draft, which may be referred to as a trade acceptance, will mature sixty days after delivery of the goods to Buyer rather than at sight. In this case Buyer will "accept" the draft (similar to a drawee-bank certifying a check) at Buyer City Bank instead of paying for the goods. Acceptance is Buyer's agreement to pay the draft upon maturity. See U.C.C. §§ 3-409(a), 3-413. Seller may then discount (sell) this draft to its bank. Thus Seller will receive the purchase price of the goods minus a modest discount—the difference reflecting the bank's charges—without having to wait for the draft to mature.—Ed.]

PROBLEM 10.1

Pillsbury (Seller) contracted to sell a quantity of corn to WJM Co. (Buyer), a supplier of chicken feed, for $51,207.80, F.O.B. Toledo, Ohio. Seller delivered the corn to Grand Trunk Eastern (Carrier) on October 28, 1994, and made a reasonable contract for its carriage to Buyer in Lewiston, Maine. Carrier issued to Seller a negotiable bill of lading wherein the corn was consigned "to the order of [Buyer]." (Seller retained possession of the bill of lading.) The corn arrived in Lewiston on November 7. Despite the fact that Buyer neither presented the bill of lading nor paid for the corn, Carrier released the corn to Buyer on November 12.

Did Carrier breach its obligation to Seller to deliver the corn to a person entitled under the bill of lading to receive the corn pursuant to the F.B.L.A.?; pursuant to the U.C.C. (assuming an intrastate shipment to Cincinnati)?

[Note: F.B.L.A. § 80110(a) and (b) (1994) provides:

(a) *General rules.* — Except to the extent a common carrier establishes an excuse provided by law, the carrier must deliver goods covered by a bill of lading on demand of the consignee named in a nonnegotiable bill or the holder of a negotiable bill for the goods when the consignee or holder —

(1) offers in good faith to satisfy the lien of the carrier on the goods;

(2) has possession of the bill and, if a negotiable bill, offers to indorse and give the bill to the carrier; and

(3) agrees to sign, on delivery of the goods, a receipt for delivery if requested by the carrier.

(b) *Persons to whom goods may be delivered.* — Subject to section 80111 of this title, a common carrier may deliver the goods covered by a bill of lading to —

(1) a person entitled to their possession;

(2) the consignee named in a nonnegotiable bill; or

(3) a person in possession of a negotiable bill if —

(A) the goods are delivered to the order of that person; or

(B) the bill has been indorsed to that person or in blank by the consignee or another indorsee.]

PROBLEM 10.2

The facts enumerated in Problem 10.1 continue: On November 12, Buyer presented carrier with an *order shipment bond* which purported to indemnify and hold Carrier harmless against all loss, damages, liability and costs by reason of Carrier delivering the corn to Buyer without surrender of proper documentation.

On November 24, Seller tendered the bill of lading and draft-invoices for collection to Lewiston Bank. After notice, Buyer failed to pay, and the bill of lading and draft-invoices were returned to Seller.

Seller next notified Carrier to ship the corn to another customer. In turn, Carrier, who had already delivered the corn to Buyer, demanded payment from Buyer as an alternative to proceeding upon the order shipment bond. Buyer paid Seller in full for the goods on February 6, 1995. Seller then sent the bill of lading to Carrier, who released its claims against the order shipment bond. On March 2, 1995, Buyer filed its petition under Chapter 11 of the Bankruptcy Code.

The Trustee in Bankruptcy alleges that the payment made to Seller on February 6 constituted a voidable preference under Section 547(b) of the Bankruptcy Code. This section provides that the Trustee may avoid a transfer of an interest of Buyer in property (Buyer's payment to Seller) if the transfer is: (1) for the benefit of Seller, (2) for or on account of an antecedent debt, (3) made while Buyer was insolvent, (4) made on or within 90 days before the date of the filing of the bankruptcy petition, and (5) one that enables Seller to receive more than Seller would receive in a Chapter 7 liquidation of the estate.

While bankruptcy is beyond the scope of our study, suffice it to say that the possibility is real that the Trustee may avoid the payment by Buyer to Seller. If this occurs, what recourse, if any, has Seller against Carrier or upon the order shipment bond? What is the counseling point for Seller the next time this situation arises? *See*, *In re Hillcrest Foods, Inc.*, 40 BR 360, 38 U.C.C. Rep. 1195 (1984).

NOTES AND QUESTIONS

Excuses to Bailee's Delivery Obligation. U.C.C. § 7-403(1)(a) through (g) enumerates excuses to the bailee's duty to deliver the goods to the "person entitled under the document." See also U.C.C. § 7-603. Subsection (l)(a) excuses delivery to a person entitled under the document where delivery of the goods is to a person whose receipt was rightful as against the claimant. Comment 2 illustrates:

> The principal case covered by subsection (1)(a) is delivery to a person whose title is paramount to the rights represented by the document. For example, if a thief deposits stolen goods in a warehouse and takes a negotiable receipt, the warehouseman is not liable on the receipt if he has surrendered the goods to the true owner, even though the receipt is held by a good faith purchaser. See Section 7-503(1). . ..

Under subsection (1)(b), damage to or delay, loss or destruction of the goods for which the bailee is not liable excuses delivery to a person entitled under the document. See U.C.C. §§ 7-204, 7-309. In *World Products, Inc. v. Central Freight Service, Inc.*, 222 F. Supp. 849 (N.J. 1963), Hurricane Donna struck the Metropolitan New York area. The tide waters of the Hudson River rose about four feet above the mean high water mark and flooded defendant's warehouse, ruining plaintiff's pipe fittings. The court held that the evidence established that the warehouseman was negligent in storing plaintiff's goods in its warehouse extending partly over the river without taking sufficient precautions to insure that the high tides caused by severe storm, such as the hurricane which resulted in damage to plaintiff's goods, would not cause flooding of the warehouse. Even though the hurricane qualified as act of God, defendant's negligence was a substantial factor in causing damage to the merchandise.

The court concluded:

> On the question of damages, plaintiff has presented evidence that the replacement value of the damaged goods was $41,434.13. In addition, plaintiff adds freight and labor charges, and deducts salvage value, resulting in a total claim of $40,622.17. Defendant contends that its liability, if any, is limited under section 10(f) of the warehouse receipt, to $26,271.00, which is derived from the base storage rate of $.07 per cwt. and the weight of 75,060 lbs. listed on defendant's delivery order for the 1688 damaged cartons "returned for salvage" (500 x $.07 x 750.6).
>
> Plaintiff argues that the limitation of liability in section 10(f) is not binding on it for the reason that said section was not specifically called to plaintiff's attention by defendant. See *Henningsen v. Bloomfleld Motors, Inc.*, 32 N.J. 358, 396-397,161 A.2d 69, 75 A.L.R.2d 1(1960). However, *Henningsen* and the cases cited therein deal with situations where the seller has an unfair bargaining advantage over the buyer. Such cases have no application where both parties are business corporations, engaged in a commercial relationship with one another over an extended period of time, and where the contract fairly spells out the limitation of liability and contains a provision for extra charges if an excess value is declared. Such a reasonable contractual limitation of warehouseman's liability is not invalid under New Jersey law, in the absence of fraud or a violation of public policy. See *Henningsen v. Bloomfleld Motor, Inc., supra; Siliesh v. South Orange Storage Corp.*, 14 N.J. Super. 205, 81 A.2d 502 (1951); N.J.S.A. 12A:7-204(2), 12A:2-719(3). Therefore, the Court finds that defendant's liability in this case is limited to $26,271.00.

222 F. Supp. 852-53.

[C] Rights Acquired by "Due Negotiation"

Read: U.C.C. §§ 7-104, 7-501 through 7-504.

The classic case of *Weil Bros. v. Keenan*, 180 Miss. 697, 178 So. 90 (1938), illustrates rights acquired by "due negotiation." There Warehouse received from Chris Keenan 5 bales of cotton for storage and issued to him its standard negotiable receipt which stated that the cotton would be delivered to "Chris Keenan or bearer." On October 5, Keenan was induced by fraud to entrust the receipt to Spencer. Spencer had told Keenan that he, Spencer, had a buyer for the cotton. Further, he said that if Keenan would give him the receipt, he would sell the cotton and the receipt and would return with the money realized from the sale. Spencer never returned but rather on the same day sold the receipt, unindorsed, to Weil Bros., Inc. (Weil) who bought it in the usual ordinary course of business and who had no reason to be suspicious of Spencer.

When Spencer didn't return, Keenan began making investigations. He found out that he had been defrauded and that the receipt was in the hands of Weil. Both Keenan and Weil demand the cotton from Warehouse and Warehouse interpleads.

The court determined that Weil bought the cotton from Spencer in good faith and for value and that Weil was entitled to retain the warehouse receipt and the cotton.

PROBLEM 10.3

Resolve *Weil Bros. v. Keenan* under the U.C.C., assuming Weil took by "due negotiation." See U.C.C. §§ 7-104, 7-501 through 7-504.

Comment 1 to U.C.C. § 7-501 explains the rationale for the extraordinary rights acquired by the holder by "due negotiation":

> In general this section is intended to clarify the language of the old acts and to restate the effect of the better decisions thereunder. An important new concept is added, however, in the requirement of "regular course of business or financing" to effect the "due negotiation" which will transfer greater rights than those held by the person negotiating. The foundation of the mercantile doctrine of good faith purchase for value has always been, as shown by the case situations, the furtherance and protection of the regular course of trade. The reason for allowing a person, in bad faith or in error, to convey away rights which are not his own has from the beginning been to make possible the speedy handling of that great run of commercial transactions which are patently usual and normal.

In certain instances, however, the document of title to goods will be defeated even though "duly negotiated." Comment 1 to U.C.C. § 7-503 observes:

> In general it may be said that the title of a purchaser by due negotiation prevails over almost any interest in the goods which existed prior to the procurement of the document of title if the possession of the goods by the person obtaining the document derived from any action by the prior claimant which introduced the goods into the stream of commerce or carried them along that stream. A thief of the goods cannot indeed by shipping or storing them to his own order acquire power to transfer them to a good faith purchaser . . . .

Also, rights of a holder by "due negotiation" may be defeated: (1) where two or more documents are issued by different issuers which represent the same goods (U.C.C. § 7-503(2) and (3)), or where two or more documents are issued by the same issuer which represent the same goods (U.C.C. § 7-402). Title to fungible goods under a warehouse receipt may be defeated where the goods are sold to a buyer in ordinary course of business (U.C.C. § 7-205; cf. §§ 2-403(2), 9-307(1)).

Note that the rights of a holder by "due negotiation" are comparable to the rights of a "holder in due course" of negotiable instruments under U.C.C. Article 3. These rights are discussed at Chapters 11 and 12. Also note that a "protected purchaser" of an investment security under Article 8 has rights comparable to a "holder in due course" under Article 3 and a holder by "due negotiation" under Article 7. See U.C.C. §§ 3-306, 8-303.

[D] Non-Receipt or Misdescription of Goods or Alteration of Document

Read: U.C.C. §§ 7-203, 7-301, see 7-502(1)(c); Read also: §§ 7-208, 7-306.

A warehouseman or carrier who issues a document of title when no goods have been received (or the goods are misdescribed) may have a liability to a purchaser who relies upon the description of the goods in the document. Such liability may be disclaimed by such language as "said to contain." U.C.C. §§ 7-203, 7-301; cf. § 3-305(b).

An altered document of title leaves the document enforceable according to its original tenor. In certain instances a purchaser may treat an insertion as authorized. U.C.C. §§ 7-208, 7-306; cf. §§ 3-407(c), 3-406, 3-115.

§ 10.02 Letters of Credit

In our discussion above concerning the documentary sale we saw that an important use of the document of title (*e.g.*, bill of lading) was its utilization as a device to secure payment of the purchase price to the seller. This was done by a correspondent bank in the buyer's city exchanging the negotiable bill to buyer for payment of the purchase price. Review this transaction at § 10.01[B] above.

While the documentary sale gives the seller assurance that the buyer in a distant city will not be able to obtain the goods without paying for them, there is still a significant risk for the seller. What if the buyer refuses to honor the draft drawn upon him by the seller? The seller, of course, will still control the goods, but the goods are now probably in the buyer's city. The seller may suffer heavy losses in seeking to sell the goods located there. The seller wants assurances *before* it ships that someone responsible has assumed the payment obligation. This is where the letter of credit is utilized.

Study 1995 Revised U.C.C. §§ 5-102(a)(10) and 5-103(a), then proceed to Chapter 23, entitled "*Letters of Credit*."

CHAPTER 11

NEGOTIABLE INSTRUMENTS: INTRODUCTION AND SCOPE, CONSEQUENCES OF NEGOTIABILITY

§ 11.01 Introduction and Scope

Read U.C.C. Article 3 Prefatory Note and §§ 3-101, 3-102, 3-308.

The following five chapters introduce the student to that part of commercial law which is variously known as "Bills and Notes," as "Negotiable Instruments," or as "Commercial Paper." The choice of terms is not of particular importance. The term "Bills and Notes" indicates that this area of the law treats bills of exchange (three-party paper which includes the draft and the check) and promissory notes (two-party paper). U.C.C. § 3-104 also specifically provides for the inclusion of certificates of deposit within the provisions of Article 3. The Uniform Negotiable Instruments Law (NIL) was the basic pre-Code statute. Under its terms, investment securities were members of the same family, but it was an unhappy marriage. The Uniform Commercial Code treats negotiable securities separately. U.C.C. § 3-102(a) provides that the Article does not apply to investment securities.

Chapter 14 deals with Uniform Commercial Code Article 4, Bank Deposits and Collections. A consideration of material dealing with Article 9, Secured Transactions, begins in Chapter 16. U.C.C. § 3-102(b) states that Article 3 provisions are subject to both Article 4 and Article 9 provisions.

Articles 3 and 4 were part of the original U.C.C. first issued in 1949 and with a few changes adopted throughout the United States by the mid-nineteen sixties. This traditional version remained in effect until 1990, when the American Law Institute and the Commissioners on Uniform State Laws approved the Revised Articles 3 and 4.

There also is an excellent description of the appointing of Reporters and the various interests involved in the formation of Article 3 and 4 and the Revisions by Professor Edmond Rubin in an article "*Efficiency Equity, and Proposed Revision of Articles 3 and 4*" in 42 Alabama Law Review 551, 557 (1991):

> The current effort to revise Articles 3 and 4 began in the 1970s, as credit cards and electronic fund transfers became major payment mechanisms. The collection process for these mechanisms, and their use by business, was unregulated and remains so until this day. Their use by individuals, however, was regulated by federal consumer legislation: the 1970 amendments to the Truth in Lending Act for credit cards, and the Electronic Fund Transfer Act. Against the background of this legislation and the promise of further technological changes in the check collection system, the ALI decided to revise Articles 3, 4 and 8. In 1977, it appointed Professor Hal Scott of Harvard Law School as the reporter for this effort.

Professor Rubin then notes that the New York Clearinghouse associates, "perceiving that the effort to meld check, credit card, and electronic fund transfer law would impose some of the consumer protection features of the federal legislation on the checking system . . . reacted with its accustomed fury." With this opposition, the project ended.

It was in 1985 that new efforts were undertaken. Professor Rubin describes this in the following manner. "The new draft would cover only two areas: first, the subject matter of existing Articles 3 and 4, and second, wholesale electronic fund transfers — that is, transfers that did not fall under the Electronic Fund Transfer Act. The sponsors agreed that the balance between banks and consumers in Articles 3 and 4 — the balance that Beutel attacked as class legislation and Gilmore said he did not have the heart to defend — would not be changed. Geoffrey C. Hazard, Jr., Director of the ALI, on March 28, 1990, made the following statement in the Foreword to the Proposed Draft:

> The text here is a comprehensive revision of Article 3 of the Uniform Commercial Code, together with amendments to article 4 that are necessary to accommodate this revision. The work is a major product of efforts commenced a decade ago with the Payments Code, efforts which also led to Article 4A, approved by the Institute last year. In the course of the deliberations in the Payments Code project, it became evident that a revision of Article 3 was required but that the general structure of the present Article should be retained. On that premise, it was also necessary to make changes in Article 4 as well.
>
> The possibility remains open that further and more extensive revisions will be necessary in Article 4. This possibility depends on consideration now being given to further adjustment of the respective spheres of state law and federal law in the regulation of transactions involving checks. It has seemed prudent to go forward with the present revisions in Article 4 to accommodate revision of Article 3, even though article 4 may require further revision in the foreseeable future. At any given time the law on this subject has to be maintained as a coherent whole.
>
> The present project, like the Institute's other work on the U.C.C., is a joint effort with the National Conference of Commissioners on Uniform State Laws under the aegis of the Permanent Editorial Board for the Uniform Commercial Code. The Institute expresses its satisfaction with the continued success of this collaboration. We also express our appreciation to the Reporters, Professors Robert L. Jordan and William D. Warren, for their technical competence, their drafting skill, and their endurance.

There was the suggestion made by some persons present (Professors Henry Bailey, Robert Riegert, and Donald King), who argued at the ALI meeting that the numbering of sections should be kept as nearly the same as possible for the benefit of lawyers, judges, professors and law students. However, the Reporter chose not to alter the draft in this regard, stating that "anyone who is familiar with the present Article 3 would very quickly recognize the old sections in the new Article 3." *See* p. 382 of ALI Proceedings (1990). *See also* the "Table of Disposition of Sections in Former Article 3" at the end of the Prefatory Note to (Revised) Article 3.

There are a variety of methods of organizing the material dealing with negotiable instruments. The problem is presenting the various concepts which apply to all types of paper while highlighting the unique characteristics of the basic types of instruments. This chapter attempts to introduce the consequences of negotiability, as distinguished from the law of assignment of contracts rights, which was discussed in the basic course in Contracts. Chapter 12 deals with the requirements of a negotiable instrument, the requirements for becoming a holder in due course, the defenses to which even a holder in due course is subject, and concludes with an examination of some recent limitations imposed upon such holders of consumer paper. Chapter 13 directs your attention to the liability of various parties to negotiable instruments. Chapter 14 examines some problems in the bank collection process, and also introduces the basic principles found in Article 4 that deal with the relationship between a bank and its customers. Chapter 15 examines the role of banks in wire transfers. (Article 4A)

A few words of encouragement or assistance may be appropriate for the student beginning the study of Bills and Notes, once referred to by Dean Prosser as a "truly dismal subject." First, courts sometimes refer in successive sentences to the ABC Bank, the payor bank and the drawee, all the while talking about the same party. It helps to get the parties straight in your mind.

Second, Thorstein Veblen said that the more that jargon and technical language are involved in an endeavor, the more we may assume that the endeavor is essentially make-believe. And it is probably worse than that. This material is not about real life. It is about the symbols of real life. Caution to the reader. The world of symbols is not the same as the world of reality. As with other legal material, once you realize that we're dealing only with concept, you've taken an important step.

Third, many Negotiable Instrument cases raise a variety of problems dealing with a number of Code sections, only one of which (assuming Negotiable Instruments materials can be organized) should be considered at the time. Sometimes editing can alleviate some of this problem, and consequently, parts of the same opinion may show up at different places in these chapters. In the main, however, it appears that most courts do not write opinions for the benefit of editors of classroom materials, and consideration of some issues will be postponed. You should remember that you do not have to learn it all in one day. Another word of caution to those individuals who do use the "one day" approach to their legal studies, and reserve the day before the examination for that activity. This material is highly unsusceptible to that approach.

Fourth, Negotiable Instruments not as difficult as some upperclasspersons would lead you to believe.

§ 11.02 Consequences of Negotiability

Read: U.C.C. §§ 3-305, 3-306, 3-308.

Amos owes Barry the sum of $100 for services rendered. In the economic sense, Barry has something of value. In the legal world, Barry has the power to initiate a suit against Amos which will result ultimately in execution being levied against the assets of Amos to the extent of permitting Barry to have $100. An economic asset should be transferable. Assume that Barry wishes to realize on this asset. Is it possible to transfer this asset to Chester? What does Chester get? The willingness of Chester to pay value for this asset of Barry's, and the amount of value which Chester will pay for this asset are dependent upon the answers to these questions. A full appreciation of the consequences of negotiability requires a comparison between negotiability and nonnegotiability.

Assume Amos's duty to pay Barry $100 is due and owing in thirty days. Barry could transfer this asset to Chester presently under modern law. It would, of course, be an assignment of a chose in action. What would Chester get? Under well-accepted principals of law, Chester, the assignee, would get what Barry had. That is, at the end of thirty days Chester would have the power to sue Amos in contract for $100. This also means, however, that Chester would have to plead and prove the elements of Barry's cause of action against Amos. (Earlier in the development of the common law, Chester was further hampered in enforcing Barry's right against Amos in that Chester was required to sue in Barry's name. The common law did not recognize the free alienability of a chose in action.) It also follows that Chester's rights against Amos would be subject to any conditions, defenses, or counterclaims which Amos might have had against Barry. An assignee gets no better rights than his assignor. It does not require much contemplation to realize that the law of assignment of choses in action is not well-suited to endowing Barry's economic asset with present liquidity.

Now let us assume that Amos executes a negotiable promissory note to the order of Barry for $100, payable in thirty days. What does Chester get when Barry transfers this instrument to Chester for value in a transfer which qualifies as a negotiation? The answer to this question should illustrate the full consequences of negotiability. It is helpful to discuss what Chester gets in terms of procedural consequences of negotiability and substantive consequences of negotiability.

The basic consequence of executing a negotiable instrument is that the instrument now represents a promise (or order) to pay money which is separated from the transaction out of which the promise (or order) to pay arose. Suit on the promise to pay is considerably simplified. Chester, as holder of a negotiable instrument, simply attaches the instrument to his complaint, alleges that the instrument was executed by Amos, alleges further that the instrument was transferred to Chester, and that it has not been paid. It is not necessary, as is true if suing as assignee of a chose in action generally, for the complaint to allege and prove the transaction out of which the promise arose and that there was consideration. Additionally, where one sues on a negotiable instrument attached to the complaint, the signature need not be proved unless specifically denied (U.C.C. § 3-308(a)) and if the validity of the signatures is admitted or proved, and there is compliance with subsection (a), a plaintiff producing the instrument is entitled to enforce the instrument under U.C.C. § 3-301, unless the defendant proves a defense or claim in recoupment. U.C.C. § 3-308(b).

FAVORS v. YAFFE

Texas Court of Civil Appeals
605 S.W.2d 342, 31 U.C.C. Rep. 154 (1980)

JUNELL, J.

Appellee Paul E. Yaffe, plaintiff in the court below, sued James E. Favors and his wife, Zoe W. Favors, on a promissory note. The note had been sold and assigned to Yaffe by the original payee, against whom the Favors alleged the defense of fraud in the inducement. Yaffe claimed the status of holder in due course of the note. A jury trial resulted in a verdict favorable to defendants. The trial court granted Yaffe's motion for judgment notwithstanding the verdict and rendered judgment for Yaffe in the amount due on the note. Favors and wife appeal contending that the alleged fraud perpetrated upon them by the original payee, as shown by the evidence and found by the jury, precludes Yaffe from becoming a holder in due course and, thus, the judgment n.o.v. was improper. We affirm.

In October, 1971, the Favors were in New Orleans, Louisiana, when they were approached by a person promoting the sale of land in Arizona. The salesman represented to the Favors that the land could be purchased with a money back guarantee whereby the vendor, Cochise College Park, Inc., would refund the total purchase price to the Favors if, upon their on-site inspection of the property in Arizona, they wished to back out. Mr. Favors testified that upon that representation he and his wife purchased the property. On October 27, 1971, they executed a deed of trust to Cochise College Park, Inc., and a promissory note in the face amount of $4,844.28 payable in 84 monthly installments. On the same date the Cochise representative, James Martin, executed and delivered to the Favors the "Money Back Guarantee And Exchange Privilege" which was good for six months as long as the mortgage was not in default. Favors testified that in January or February of 1972 he and his wife traveled to Arizona to inspect the property in order to exercise the refund provision and get their money back. Favors testified that the representative then offered to extend the "Money Back Guarantee" for another year and to try to sell their tract and share the profit with the Favors, to which they agreed and continued making the monthly payments.

Unknown to the Favors, Cochise had sold and assigned their promissory note to Paul Yaffe on November 8, 1971, twelve days after the purchase. Yaffe testified that he had purchased two notes from Cochise at a discount for an investment through an investment broker in his hometown, Cleveland, Ohio. He stated that at the time of purchase he had seen no documents other than the note and the mortgage, had no knowledge of any money back guarantee and would not have purchased the notes had he been aware of it. He testified that he had no knowledge of any default, dishonor, claim or defense against the note, and that he had purchased it for value and in good faith. The Favors were informed that Cochise was in bankruptcy and made a refund demand on the bankruptcy court in January, 1973. They continued making payments on the note until April, 1973. In March, 1974, Yaffe began his collection effort from which this suit resulted.

Every note holder is presumed to be a holder in due course of the instrument absent evidence to the contrary. A holder in due course of a negotiable instrument is a holder who takes the instrument for value, in good faith and without notice of any dishonor, default, defense or claim to it on the part of any person. Tex Bus & Com Code Ann § 3.302 (Tex U.C.C. 1968). A holder in due course takes the instrument free from all claims and all defenses of any party to the instrument with whom he has not dealt except, among other exceptions here not relevant, such misrepresentation as has induced the maker to sign the instrument without knowledge of, or opportunity to discover, its character or its essential terms. Tex Bus & Com Code Ann § 3.305 (Tex U.C.C. 1968). When the signatures on an instrument are admitted, the production of the instrument entitles the holder to recover on it unless the defendant establishes a defense. Tex Bus & Com Code Ann § 3.307(b) (Tex U.C.C. 1968). Thus, Yaffe is presumed to be a holder in due course of the note absent proof to destroy that status. He is entitled to recover on the note if the Favors produced no proof to negate the existence of the elements set out in § 3.302.

The misrepresentation inducing the maker to sign, of which the Code speaks in § 3.305 above, is not present in this case. There was no testimony, and the Favors never claimed, that they signed the promissory note thinking that it was some other type of document or that they did not understand its terms. That type of misrepresentation is the only one in which the subsequent transfer of the note to a holder in due course would not protect the new holder from a fraud defense. It is not present here, thus, Yaffe took the instrument free of any other defense of fraud if he is a holder in due course.

In order to overcome the holder's claim of good faith taking, the defendant would have to show that the purchaser had actual knowledge of facts and circumstances which would amount to bad faith. Even if the defendant proved that the purchaser had knowledge of the fact that the note was signed and returned for an executory promise, or accompanied by a separate agreement, unless the defendant could show that the purchaser had notice that a claim or defense had arisen from the terms thereof, such knowledge by the purchaser is not "notice that a defense or claim [has arisen]" under the Code. Tex Bus & Com Code Ann § 3.304(d)(2) (Tex U.C.C. 1968).

After the defendant shows that a defense to the note exists, the person claiming holder in due course status has the burden to establish that he is in all respects a holder in due course. Tex Bus & Com Code Ann § 3.307(c) (Tex U.C.C. 1968). Thus, when the Favors raised the defense of fraud, Yaffe was obliged to go forward with proof to establish that he is a holder in due course. Upon establishing himself as such, that status shelters him from any defense to the note which the Favors could otherwise successfully assert against a holder who is not a holder in due course.

The statement of facts from the trial below reflects that Yaffe testified unequivocally regarding his holder in due course status. Under cross examination he never deviated from his statements of good faith taking for value, producing the canceled check with which he purchased the notes. Though his unfamiliarity with the technical terminology was demonstrated, his testimony was clear, direct and not contradicted. The Favors' proof was only to the issue of the fraud in the inducement defense; they offered no proof to assail Yaffe's status as a holder in due course.

The Texas Supreme Court has held that a directed verdict can be proper based on the uncontradicted testimony of a party to the lawsuit when reasonable minds can draw only one conclusion from the evidence. The court in *Collora v. Navarro*, 574 SW2d 65 (Tex 1978), held that in that situation it is the duty of the appellate court to determine whether there is any evidence of probative force to raise fact issues on the material questions presented.

We hold that because the Favors did not contradict Yaffe's testimony, and because Yaffe's testimony is clear, direct and positive on the relevant details of the transaction, there was no evidence of probative force to raise a fact issue on holder in due course status which required jury determination. It is only in this situation, when a directed verdict would have been proper, that the granting of a motion for judgment n.o.v. can be upheld. Thus, the trial court did not err in entering judgment for Yaffe, the holder in due course, notwithstanding the jury's failure to find that Yaffe was a holder in due course.

All of appellants' other points are overruled; the judgment is affirmed.

NOTES AND QUESTIONS

(1) While over half of the States have enacted the 1990 amendments to articles 3 and 4, since the enactments are not retroactive, there are few cases considering the new statutes. For students in States where there has been no adoption of the 1990 amendments, these "old" cases are still "good law." For students in States where the 1990 Code is in effect, there is an opportunity to consider the possible impact of the new legislation. For instance, in relation to *Favors v. Yaffe, see* U.C.C. §§ 3-308, 3-305(b).

One should compare the pleading and proof required of the plaintiff in the *Favors* case with that required if the plaintiff were suing as an assignee of the payee's rights. Would the defendant be in any better position in that situation? How important is the placing of the burden of proof? Notice what gets to the jury and what does not in the *Favors* case. As one might expect, many cases involving suits on negotiable instruments are decided on pure questions of law. The student is invited to notice the extent to which summary judgment or some similar proceeding is successfully used in cases throughout this part of the materials.

When an obligation to pay money is evidenced by a negotiable instrument, magic things begin to happen to what was previously a simple chose in action. All of a sudden, the obligation begins to partake of many of the characteristics of personal property. The obligation is now transferred from person to person by physical delivery plus, where appropriate, an indorsement. It is helpful to constantly keep in mind the fact that the obligation now becomes wedded to the piece of paper upon which it is written. And it is with respect to the transfer of this piece of paper that the real substantive advantage or consequence of negotiability makes itself felt.

The general notion of "negotiability" of an economic asset is not unique to a negotiable instrument.[1] However, the development of the law of negotiability reached its earliest and best form in the context of commercial paper. Negotiability means that the right kind of transferee may take better rights than his transferor. This is a startling exception to the basic tenet of the common-law system, "No one can give what he does not have."

Certain purchasers take better rights than their transferors had, in that the obligation to pay has been separated from the contract out of which the obligation arose. Assume Amos's promise to pay $100 to Barry in thirty days was in exchange for Barry's promise to deliver a cow. Assume that the promise to pay is on a negotiable instrument and Barry transfers to Chester who qualifies as the right kind of transferee (holder in due course). Chester may enforce the promise of Amos even though Barry neglects to deliver the cow. Thus, as seen in *Favors v. Yaffe*, the qualifying purchaser takes free of contract defenses.

Additionally, the instrument has special characteristics as personal property. Assume Barry indorsed the instrument but a thief stole it and sold it to innocent Chester. Can Chester successfully resist Barry's suit to reclaim the instrument?

An early English case determined that a good-faith purchaser of negotiable instruments takes free of claims of ownership. In *Miller v. Race*, 98 Eng. Rep. 398 (K.B. 1758), plaintiff purchased a "Bank-note" which had been stolen from the mails. When the plaintiff delivered the note to the bank for payment, the defendant refused either to pay it or return it because the prior owner had reported its theft. The jury found a verdict for the plaintiff, but the judge reserved for the full Bench the question, "Whether, under the circumstances of this case, the plaintiff had sufficient property in this Bank-note to entitle him to recover in the present action?" Lord Mansfield equated the Bank-note with money as currency in that "The true owner cannot recover it; after it has been paid away fairly and honestly upon a valuable and bona fide consideration." He indicated that the fallacy of the defendant's argument was in comparing Banknotes, "[T]o what they do not resemble, and what they ought not to be compared to, viz. to goods, or to securities, or documents for debts." By the time of *Peacock v. Rhodes*, 99 Eng. Rep. 402 (K.B. 1781), the principle of *Miller v. Race* had been extended to other types of commercial instruments.

In *Watkins v. Sheriff of Clark County*, Nevada, 453 P.2d 611, 6 U.C.C. Rep. 517 (1969), the Nevada Supreme Court reversed Watkins' conviction for obtaining money under false pretenses.

1 See Gilmore, *Commercial Doctrine of Good Faith Purchase*, 63 Yale L.J. 1057 (1954), particularly at 1057-1062.

The Silver Slipper Gambling Hall & Saloon issued its payroll check for $ 185.59 to Mrs. Reggie Bluiett, an employee, who endorsed it in blank and left it on the dresser in her home. The following day she learned that the check was missing along with other items of property. On that day Freddie Watkins purchased two tires from Western Auto with Mrs. Bluiett's payroll check. The tires cost $73.21 and Watkins received the balance in cash. Watkins was subsequently charged with having obtained money under false pretenses from Joseph H. Hudson, the owner of Western Auto.

The court stated:

> An essential element of this statutory offense is that the accused intend to cheat or defraud the person from whom the money is obtained. Case law imposes the additional requirement that the person from whom the money is obtained sustain injury or damage. Western Auto did not incur injury or damage since it was a holder in due course, having given value, in good faith and without notice of any claim to the instrument on the part of any person. NRS 104.3302. Theft is not a defense against a holder in due course. NRS 104.3305. Western Auto was protected against the claim of the rightful owner. It received a valid, enforceable payroll check and was not damaged. Accordingly, the statutory offense charged to Watkins was not committed by him and his petition for habeas corpus must be granted. We, therefore, reverse the district court and order that Freddie Watkins be released from custody or restraint upon this particular charge. The state may charge Watkins with whatever offense is warranted by the evidence in its possession.

(2) In *Williams v. Stansbury*, 649 S.W.2d 293, 36 U.C.C. Rep. 879 (Texas 1983) the court stated:

> With certain exceptions not material to the present case, a holder in due course takes an instrument free from all legal and equitable claims by any person to the instrument. Tex Bus & Com Code Ann § 3.305. The adverse claims, against which a holder in due course is protected, are not limited to claims of ownership, but embrace rights acquired through legal process such as garnishment. We hold the garnishment of a debt represented by a promissory note does not affect the rights of a holder in due course, even though the garnishment is prior to the negotiation.[2]

See U.C.C. §§ 3–601(b), 3–602(b), 3-301,

(3) The student may wish to speculate upon what theory legal title comes to the good-faith purchaser. Can the thief have legal title? If not, how does the purchaser get legal title? Where is it until someone can assert *Miller v. Race* (N.1 *supra*). May we assume that our endeavors are essentially make-believe?

---

[2] The general rule is once a writ of garnishment has been served, a judgment-debtor may not by assignment dispose of the funds in the hands of the garnishee. An exception to this rule arises when the underlying debt in the hands of the garnishee has been suspended by the issuance of a negotiable instrument that has not fully matured. The reasons for this exception are explained in 1 E. Cook, Creditors' Rights in Texas § 3.37(a) (2d ed. 1981) at 133:

> Such favored treatment is given to the holder in due course not simply to protect good-faith purchase but also, and even more importantly, to serve the greater need of certainty in commercial dealings. Granting the right to cut off various defenses to a holder in due course gives the purchaser of commercial paper confidence that it will be enforceable and, therefore, worth the amount that it purports to be worth.

CHAPTER 12

REQUIREMENTS FOR OBTAINING RIGHTS GREATER THAN THOSE OF AN ASSIGNEE

§ 12.01 Introduction

To restate the underlying premise of the law of negotiable paper: When we have a special kind of paper (a negotiable instrument) and we transfer it in an appropriate way (by negotiation) to a properly qualified transferee (holder in due course) the result is that the transferee takes free and clear of certain defenses and claims of ownership. It should be obvious to the student by now that the terms "negotiable instrument," "negotiation," and "holder in due course" are key words of art to this area of the law. In this chapter we will give consideration to each of these concepts plus examine the matter of what defenses of the obligor are "cut off" by a holder in due course and what defenses are still available to the obligor even though a transferee attains holder in due course status. We begin by focusing on what the requirements are for an instrument *to be* negotiable.

§ 12.02 Requirements of a Negotiable Instrument

Read: U.C.C. § 3-104.

The natural starting place in the coverage of the law of negotiable commercial paper is the investigation of the question of what types of commercial paper qualify for the procedural and substantive advantages of negotiability as outlined above and as investigated more in depth in the later sections of this chapter. The common-law development proceeded from one type of paper to another; that is, some of the consequences of negotiability were attributed to particular types of commercial paper at various times. During the seventeenth and eighteenth centuries, the common-law courts were slowly recognizing and accepting, as principles of the common law, certain features of the law merchant. At one stage, the courts recognized that the transferee of a foreign bill of exchange could sue in his own name. But when an indorsee sued the maker of a promissory note, declaring "upon the custom of merchants as upon a bill of exchange,[1] Chief Justice Holt refused recovery, stating that "the notes in question are only an invention of the Goldsmiths in Lombard Street, who had a mind to make a law to bind all those that did deal with them. . . ." It took an Act of Parliament to extend the same privilege to the note.[2]

By the end of the nineteenth century, courts began to generalize the requirements of negotiability, and this approach was put in statutory form in the English Bills of Exchange Act of 1882.[3] Crawford's draft of the Uniform Negotiable Instruments Law in 1895 used the same

[1] *Buller v. Crips*, 87 Eng. Rep. 793 (Q.B. 1704).

[2] 3 & 4 Anne, c. 9, § 1 (1704), referred to as the "Statute of Anne."

[3] 45 & 46 Vict.,c.61.

approach. (N.I.L. § 1: "An instrument to be negotiable must conform to the following requirements: . . .") The corresponding section of the U.C.C. is § 3-104. It might be noted that the statutes have determined that a formal test rather than a functional test be used to determine negotiability. (Cf. U.C.C. § 8-102 as the definition of what constitutes a security for the purposes of Article 8.) One may speculate how well a formal test works over a period of time as compared with a functional test. It is often argued that there is a direct correlation between a formal test and a functional test. That is, if the functional test would ask what type of instruments pass the commerce in the credit market, the suggested answer is that only instruments which are unconditional, certain, and marketable pass this test. The purchaser of commercial paper needs to know by looking at the instrument that it represents an easily enforced, uncomplicated promise to pay. The purchaser wants to purchase only on the credit standing of the obligor or his transferor and not on facts and circumstances outside the instrument. Thus, it has been said that the negotiable instrument must be a "courier without luggage."

[A] Signed Writing

Read: U.C.C. §§ 3-104(1)(a), 3-103(a)(6) and (9), 1-201(39) and (46).

U.C.C. § 3-104, Comment 1, states an instrument is either a promise or order. A promise is a written undertaking to pay money signed by the party undertaking to pay. An order is a written instruction to pay money signed by the party giving the instruction. Thus, the term "negotiable instrument" is limited to a signed writing that orders or promises payment of money.

The requirement of a writing has raised few problems. In Herbert, The Uncommon Law 201 (Metheun & Co., 6th ed. 1948), *Board of Inland Revenue v. Haddock,* or the Case of the Negotiable Cow, reports a classic case (fictional) where a check written on the side of a cow in red ink is good. (It is reported that the cow "appeared to resent endorsement and adopted a menacing posture.") The problem of a signature requirement, and particularly whether a printed signature is good, is discussed in various cases, *infra.*

[B] Words of Negotiability

Read: U.C.C. §§ 3-104(a)(1) and (c), 3-109.

Both N.I.L. § 1 and former U.C.C. § 3-104(1)(d) required that a negotiable instrument "be payable to order or to bearer." Prior to the Uniform Acts, there was a question as to the necessity of the so-called "magic" words of negotiability. Analytically, the reason for the requirement is explainable in that the obligor has indicated by the use of the term "to order of" or "payee or order," as well as by using "pay to bearer" that the obligor contemplates transfer and enforcement of the obligation by either someone authorized by the payee or by a bearer of the instrument.

FIRST INVESTMENT COMPANY v. ANDERSON

Utah Supreme Court
621 P.2d 683 (1980)

MAUGHAN, JUSTICE:

Plaintiff, the transferee of the payee of two promissory notes, initiated this action to recover the unpaid balance from the makers, the defendants. The trial court found the notes were not negotiable instruments; plaintiff was not a holder in due course; and there was a failure of consideration on the part of the payee. Defendants were awarded a judgment of no cause of action. Plaintiff appeals therefrom. The judgment of the trial court is affirmed; costs are awarded to defendants.

On September 6, 1965, defendants entered into a franchise agreement with Great Lakes Nursery Corporation, hereinafter identified as the "Nursery," a Wisconsin corporation. Defendants, as the franchisees, were to grow and sell nursery stock and Christmas trees. The Nursery was to provide and to deliver 65,000 trees as planting stock for the purchase price of $9,500.00. The franchisor, the Nursery under the agreement was to provide the number, size, and variety therein specified, as well as to furnish replanting stock; chemicals, fertilizers, and other articles to be used in the production and sale of the trees; to root prune the trees; to provide technical training and supervision necessary for the planting, sheering, pruning, marketing and sale and other technical information affecting the growth, production, harvest and sale of the trees.

Contemporaneously with the franchise agreement, the defendants, as makers, executed two promissory notes, with the Nursery as payee; each in the amount of $6,412.00. The note recited:

> For value received, Robert Andersen of Nephi, Utah, promises to pay to Great Lakes Nursery Corp. at Waukesha, Wisconsin six thousand four hundred twelve dollars payable as follows: $ 100 per month beginning Oct. 1, 1965 for 24 months and then $ 111.30 per month for 36 months including interest computed at 7% per annum added to the principal amount of $4,750.00.
>
> This note may be prepaid with adjustment of interest at any time.

If this note is in default, the holder, after 60 days written notice to the undersigned, may declare the face of the note due and payable if the default is not remedied within 60 days after notice.

Robert Andersen

Franchisee

Donna Andersen

This note is received in full payment for the trees described in Article III-A (Planting Stock) of the Santa's Forest Franchise Agreement.

Great Lakes Nursery Corporation

William Skaife

Prior to the delivery of any trees to defendants, the Nursery transferred the note to plaintiff on September 20, 1965. The following was written on the reverse side of the note:

> For value received, the undersigned does hereby endorse, sell, assign and transfer with full recourse the within note and mortgage to First Investment Company or order, and authorize it to do every act and thing necessary to collect and discharge the same.
>
> September 20, 1965.
>
> *William Skaife*
>
> Great Lakes Nursery Corp.

Defendants were notified by plaintiff of the transfer of the note by a letter dated September 28, 1965. Defendants made payments of $ 1,350.00 on each of these notes between April 2, 1966, and January 7, 1967. In response to plaintiff's demand, the Nursery made payments on each note in the sum of $ 1,033.30 as of August, 1968. In December, 1969, plaintiff applied $1,780.80 on each of the notes from a trust fund established under agreements between the plaintiff and the Nursery in 1964 and 1965.

During 1967, defendants made no further payments on their notes for the reason that the Nursery had failed to perform in accordance with the franchise agreement. In their answer, defendants pleaded a failure of consideration as an affirmative defense. The trial court found there was a failure of consideration on the part of the Nursery for the following reasons: It did not furnish the number, size and variety of trees specified in the agreement; it did not furnish the replanting stock; it did not furnish any chemicals, fertilizers and other articles; it did not root prune the trees; and it did not provide technical training, supervision, and information. There is substantial evidence in the record to sustain the findings.

Prior to discussing plaintiffs points on appeal, it should be observed that the Uniform Negotiable Instruments Act, Title 44, U.C.A. 1953, is controlling in regard to the issues, since the notes were executed and transferred prior to December 31, 1965, the effective date of the Uniform Commercial Code (70A-10-101, U.C.A. 1953, as amended) and the time of repeal of the N.I.L. (70A-10-102(1)).

Hereafter, all statutory references are to the currently repealed N.I.L., Title 44, U.C.A. 1953, unless otherwise indicated.

On appeal, plaintiff contends it was a holder in due course, and as such held the instrument free of any defenses available to prior parties among themselves, § 44-1-58. Defendants prevailed before the trial court on the ground the notes were not negotiable, and failure of consideration was a defense against any person not a holder in due course, § 44-1-29.

The primary issue is whether the two promissory notes were negotiable. Section 44-3-1 provides:

> A negotiable promissory note within the meaning of this title is an unconditional promise in writing made by one person to another, signed by the maker, engaging to pay on demand, or at a fixed or determinable future time, a sum certain in money, *to order or to bearer*. . .[Emphasis added.]

Section 44-1-1 provides:

An instrument to be negotiable must conform to the following requirements:

(4) It must be payable to order or to bearer;. Section 44-1-9 provides:

An instrument is payable to order where it is drawn payable to the order of a specified person, or to him or his order. . .

Under both the N.I.L. and the U.C.C. (70A-3-104(1)(d)), one of the requirements to qualify a writing as a negotiable instrument is that it contain the time-honored "words of negotiability," such as "pay to the order" or "pay to the bearer." The mere promise to pay, absent the magic words "payable to order or to bearer" renders the note nonnegotiable, and the liability is determined as a matter of simple contract law.[4]

In the instant case, the notes were payable simply to the payee, and were not payable to the order of the payee or to the payee or its order and were thus not negotiable instruments. Since the notes were not negotiable, the transfer by the Nursery to plaintiff must be deemed an assignment, and the assignee (plaintiff) stood in the shoes of the assignor and took subject to existing equities and defense.

Significantly, the trial court found that the notes and franchise agreement constituted one integrated contract. This finding is substantiated by the recital concerning consideration in the note, and the absence of words of negotiability. Where there is a failure of consideration under a bilateral contract consisting of a breach by the assignor, such failure is a good defense to an action by the assignee whether it occurred before or after the assignment. Such a defense, although acquired after notice of the assignment, is based on a right of defendant inherent in the contract by its terms. Therefore, where payments under an executory contract are assigned, the debtor may set up failure of the assignor to fulfill his part of the contract though such failure occurs after the assignment, for the assignor cannot give another a larger right than he has himself. The trial court did not err in its ruling that failure of consideration constituted a valid defense to plaintiff's action.

NOTES

(1) What result if the note had been made payable to the "order" of Great Lakes Nursery Corporation? Note that more than one matter affecting negotiability may show up on the same

[4] *von Frank v. Hershey National Bank*, 269 Md. 138, 306 A.2d 207, 210-211(1973); 11 Am.Jur.2d, Bills and Notes, § 105, p. 144, § 108, p. 147; 58 A.L.R. 1005, Anno.: When instrument deemed payable to order within Uniform Negotiable Instruments Act. It should be observed that if the U.C.C. were applicable, the notes in the instant case would be within the purview of§ 70A-3-805, which provides: "This chapter applies to any instrument whose terms do not preclude transfer and which is otherwise negotiable within this chapter but which is not payable to order or to bearer, except that there can be no holder in due course of such an instrument." Under 70A-3-408, failure of consideration is a defense against any person not having the rights of a holder in due course. However, in certain aspects a "nonnegotiable instrument" which is within § 70A-3-805 is not treated as a simple contract but as a negotiable instrument, except there can be no holder in due course and thus the provisions in that regard cannot apply. See 3 Anderson, Uniform Commercial Code (2d Ed.), § 3-805:1, pp. 154-155.

instrument. For example, in *von Frank v. Hershey National Bank*, cited by the *Anderson* court in the footnote, that court stated:

> Under the Maryland U.C.C., to be negotiable, an instrument must, among other requirements, "be payable to order or to bearer." (§ 3-104(1)(d)) The absence of these magic words renders a note non-negotiable. Here, the notes in question contain just a "promise to pay to the Hershey National Bank" the amount due. However, § 3-805 entitled "instruments not payable to order or to bearer" specifies that:
>
> > This subtitle *applies* to any instrument whose terms do not include transfer and *which is otherwise negotiable within this subtitle* but which is not payable to order to the bearer, except that there can be no holder in due course of such an instrument. (Emphasis added.)
>
> The official comments to this section indicate that:
>
> > This section covers the "non-negotiable instrument." As it has been used by most courts, this term has been a technical one of art. It does not refer to a writing, such as a note containing an express condition, which is not negotiable and is entirely outside of the scope of this Subtitle and to be treated as a simple contract. It refers to a particular type of instrument which meets all requirements as to form of a negotiable instrument except that it is not payable to order or to bearer.
>
> Thus, while these notes could still be governed by the Code even though they lack words of negotiability, they must meet all other "requirements as to form of a negotiable instrument" except for that.

(2) The Code drafters essentially keep most of the requisites found in the former commercial paper definition: an unconditional promise to pay, a sum certain (fixed amount), of a definite time, to order or bearer. However, they do tighten some of the requirements, while expanding on the definitions in other regards. For example, if an instrument other than a check is not made payable to "bearer or order," then it falls completely outside of Article 3 under the Revisions. Under the traditional Code, an instrument which lacks these words "to order or bearer" may still be considered as commercial paper, even though there may be no holder in due course. The Revisions eliminate even this limited inclusion of promissory notes, drafts, and other commercial paper with magic words missing in the general scope of Article 3.

In regard to checks, the Revisions become more liberal. Under revised Section 3-104(c), such a check is governed by Article 3. There can be a holder in due course of the check that meets all of the requirements for negotiability, except for the statement "to order or bearer." The drafters state that this is based on the belief that it is good policy to treat checks that are payment instruments as negotiable instruments, whether or not they contain the words "to the order of." While these are almost always on pre-printed forms, the drafters point out that in the past some credit unions use check forms that do not contain such quoted words. The absence of those words could be easily overlooked and should not affect the rights of holders who pay money or give credit for such checks without being aware of it. Thus while there is some tightening of the requirements for commercial paper generally, there is a loosening of the requirements for checks.

One may question why the magic words of "order" or "bearer" need be retained at all for commercial paper. There could be the rule that unless labelled as "Non-Negotiable," commercial paper would be viewed as negotiable. Indeed the possibility of using such words if one wishes to avoid negotiability is recognized in the revision text and comments. The omission of words "order" or "bearer" is generally inadvertent when it occurs in promissory notes or drafts or other similar instruments; nothing is gained by insisting on those magic words and defeating the original expectations of the parties. The drafters indicate a fear that without such magic words, it may be argued by some that ordinary contracts or leases would be asserted as negotiable. While they implicitly recognize that this would be unlikely and that courts could distinguish, they think it might be a "litigation ploy." This, however, seems unlikely and would not seem to outweigh needs of justice where such magic words are unthinkingly left out. Many businessmen and even some lawyers are unaware of this requirement until it is pointed out to them. Yet under the revisions, the magic of Merlin will continue through the centuries to be present in regard to commercial paper other than checks.

[C] Unconditional Promise or Order

Read: U.C.C. §§ 3-104(a), 3-103, 3-106; see § 3-117.

The requirement that the instrument must contain an unconditional promise or order should not be confused with the separate requirement that the instrument be payable to order or to bearer. See § 12.02[B], Words of Negotiability, *supra*.

It should be obvious that certain instruments may look like negotiable instruments, but fail for lack of a promise or order to pay. Thus, the classic I.O.U. is not a negotiable instrument for it does not include a promise to pay. See *Shearer v. Shearer*, 84 Colo. 234, 269 P. 19 (1928). See U.C.C. § 3-103, Comment 3. What constitutes an express promise to pay is not clear. There is some reluctance on the part of the courts to imply a promise, but there are a number of cases finding a promise on what seems at best ambiguous language. It must be remembered too, even though the instrument does not qualify as a negotiable promissory note, suit may be had on a promise using the writing as evidence.

NOTES AND QUESTIONS

(1) In *Booker v. Everhart*, 240 S.E.2d 350, 24 U.C.C. Rep. 165, (1978), the North Carolina Supreme Court considered the following note:

October 30, 1972 Winston-Salem
$ 150,000.00 North Carolina

INSTALLMENT NOTE

FOR VALUE RECEIVED, I, KOYT WOODWORTH EVERHART, JR., do hereby promise to pay to JANE CARTER EVERHART or her order, ONE HUNDRED FIFTY THOUSAND and No./100-Dollars ($150,000.00) in lieu of a property settlement supplementing that certain *Deed of Separation and Property Settlement*, dated May 1, 1972, the terms of which are incorporated herein by reference. That, as of the signing of said document, JANE CRATER EVERHART was not aware of the extent of property interests of KOYT WOODWORTH F. EVERHART, JR. nor was she represented by counsel at said time. That in order to prevent involvement in litigation and dissolution of assets, KOYT WOODWORTH EVERHART, JR. does hereby promise to pay to JANE CRATER EVERHART or her order, the sum of ONE HUNDRED FIFTY THOUSAND and No/l00-Dollars (150,000.00); the terms and conditions of said note are as follows. . .

Is the Everhart note negotiable?

The North Carolina court stated:

To incorporate a separate document by reference is to declare that the former document shall be taken as part of the document in which the declaration is made, as much as if it were set out at length therein.

By incorporating into the note in question the Deed of Separation and Property Settlement, the parties made the note "subject to" any and all possible conditions contained in those prior documents. Under 25-3-105(2)(a), this renders the promise to pay the sum certain conditional. Whether or not the documents incorporated contained any such conditions or contingencies is a matter beside the point. *United States v. Farrington*, 172 F. Supp. 797 (DC Mass 1959). The essential point is that all of the essential terms of the note in question cannot be ascertained from the face of the instrument itself. Because separate documents have been made a part of the note by its express terms, the promise contained therein is conditional, and the note nonnegotiable.

See U.C.C. §§ 3-106(a)(ii), (iii); (b)(i).

(2) The *Farrington* case, 172 F. Supp. 797 (D.C. Mass. 1959), cited by the *Booker* court, was decided under the NIL, but the court suggested that the result would be the same under the U.C.C.. The opinion suggests that there are two ways to approach the problem of an unconditional promise. One way is to examine any document to which there is a reference in the note to determine if there is anything in such document which will condition the promise to pay in the note. The second way to test the conditional nature of the promise is to examine the words on the face of the note and to determine from the use of the words on the note whether a look at the referred to document is necessary. Under this test, the use of words on the face of the note becomes crucial. Thus, a statement that the note is "subject to," "conditioned upon," or "restricted to," would destroy negotiability, while a statement that the note was "pursuant to," "issued in conjunction with," or "as per" would not generally condition the promise.

(3) In *Holly Hill Acres, Ltd. v. Charter Bank of Gainesville*, 314 So. 2d 209, 17 U.C.C. Rep Serv 144 (Fla 1975), the Florida court held that, under § 3-105(2)(a) of the U.C.C., a promissory note which incorporated by reference the terms of the mortgage securing it did not contain the unconditional promise to pay required by § 3-104(1)(b). The note in that case said: "The terms of said mortgage are by this reference made a part hereof." In the course of its opinion, that court noted that this is not a mere reference to the mortgage or agreement on which the note is based. ". . .[S]uch reference in itself does not impede the negotiability of the note. There is, however a significant difference in a note stating that it is 'secured by a mortgage' from one which provides, 'the terms of said mortgage are by this reference made a part hereof.'. . ."

(4) Query, a note with the phrase, "payable in accordance with." Query, a check with the phrase, "Upon acceptance pay to the order of."

On September 8, 1977, Citizens Insurance Company of America (hereinafter Citizens), issued a check for $4,450 payable to its named insured, Ann Moss, following a report that her automobile had been stolen. The instrument was drawn on the First National Bank of Howell (hereinafter First National). Appearing on the face of the instrument was the following language, the interpretation of which forms the basis of this controversy: "Upon acceptance pay to the order of." On September 9, 1977, Ms. Moss endorsed the instrument and transferred it to Standard who paid full value and in so doing acted in good faith. Thereafter, the instrument was presented by Standard to First National for payment.

Subsequent to issuing this draft, Citizens became aware that Ms. Moss' report of a stolen automobile was fraudulent. Based on that fact, Citizens requested First National to stop payment on the draft in question. The draft, which had been forwarded to First National by Standard, was returned to Standard stamped "stop payment." This "stop payment" order was received by Standard after it had paid the money to Ms. Moss. Standard then instituted this action in the 46th Judicial District Court to recover payment on the instrument.

Standard contended that since it was a holder in due course, it took the draft free of any personal defenses Citizens asserted. Citizens responded that the draft in question was not a negotiable instrument, and, therefore, Standard was precluded from becoming holder in due course. The focal point of the controversy revolved around the language on the face of the instrument: "Upon acceptance pay to the order of." Citizens asserted that the language was not an unconditional promise or order to pay as required by MCL § 440.3104(1)(b), MSA § 19.3104(1)(b). Citizens argued that the language on the instrument made payment conditional upon acceptance of the drawee bank, First National. Standard urged that the instrument was negotiable under the U.C.C., as the quoted language referred only to acceptance by the payee-claimant, Ann Moss—in settlement of her insurance claim against Citizens. The trial court agreed with Standard and granted summary judgment in its favor.

The question raised upon appeal is whether the trial court erred in finding that an instrument bearing the phrase, "Upon acceptance pay to the order of. . ." is negotiable. Citizens argues that the word "acceptance" is a term of art which is specifically defined in the Uniform Commercial Code. MCL § 440.3410, MSA § 1 9.3410. In light of that definition, acceptance may only be consummated by the drawee, and, consequently, payment of the note was conditional, precluding negotiability and, thus, precluding Standard from becoming a holder in due course. If Standard was not a holder in due course, the defense of fraud in the inducement would be available against Standard. Citizens further argues that Standard could have avoided any loss had it withheld payment to Ann Moss until the instrument had been accepted by First National.

In opposition, Standard argues that the "upon acceptance" language on the face of the instrument refers to acceptance by Ann Moss as the insured claimant and payee. Her acceptance of the instrument from Citizens was in settlement of a prior claim, and, therefore, MCL § 440.3410, MSA § 19.3410 is inapplicable, in that it relates only to acceptance by a drawee bank. Since the "upon acceptance" language referred to the underlying transaction which gave rise to the instrument, Standard contends that the negotiability of the instrument is not affected by this language.

Defendant's contention that the term "acceptance" must be construed within the narrow parameters of the U.C.C. is not persuasive. Recognition that "[t]echnical construction of negotiable instrument law should not be favored," was the standard before the adoption of the U.C.C.. In view of the policy of the U.C.C. "to encourage the free circulation of negotiable paper," Official Comment 1 to MCL § 440.3118, MSA § 19.3118, we feel this strict construction is still disfavored.

We, therefore, find that the document in question was not made conditional by the Insertion of the language "Upon acceptance pay to the order of." The technical construction of the term "acceptance" argued by defendant is not reasonable in light of the factual situation. The principles that the instrument is to be read as a whole, the entire fact situation surrounding its execution scrutinized, and any ambiguity construed against the maker, lead to the conclusion that this instrument was negotiable. Summary judgment was properly granted in plaintiff's favor. GCR 1963,117.2(3). We affirm.

Standard Federal Savings & Loan Ass'n. v. Citizens Insurance Co., 297 N.W.2d 656, 30 U.C.C. Rep. 228 (1980).

See U.C.C. § 3-409.

(5) Former U.C.C. § 3-105(2)(b) stated that a promise or order was not unconditional if the instrument stated that it was to be paid out of a particular fund or source subject to exceptions found in § 3-105(1)(f),(g) and (h). The general rule was that if the promise to pay was supported by less than the entire general credit of the obligor, then it was not unconditional. Thus, where the obligor promised to pay "out of my corn account" the obligation was conditional upon there being credits in the corn account.

UCC § 3-106(b)(ii) states that a promise or order is not made conditional because payment is limited to resort to a particular fund or source. Comment 1 to the section states, "This reverses the result of former Section 3-105(2)(b). There is no cogent reason why the general credit of a legal entity must be pledged to have a negotiable instrument. Market forces determine the marketability of instruments of this kind. If potential buyers don't want promises or orders that are payable only from a particular source or fund, they won't take them, but Article 3 should apply." Desirable? Consider the following:

> Nevertheless, the cherished belief in the sacrosanct nature of formal requisites serves, as do most legal principles, a useful function. The problem is what types of paper shall be declared negotiable so that purchasers may put on the nearly invincible armor of the holder in due course. The policy in favor of protecting the good faith purchaser does not run beyond the frontiers of commercial usage. Beyond those confines every reason of policy dictates the opposite approach. The formal requisites are the professional rules with which professionals are or ought to be familiar. As to instruments which are amateur productions outside any concept of the ordinary course of business, or new types which are just coming into professional use, it is wiser to err by being unduly restrictive than by being over liberal.

Gilmore, *The Commercial Doctrine of Good Faith Purchase*, 63 Yale L.J. 1057, 1068-69.

(6) Former U.C.C. § 3-105(1)(g) indicated that if the instrument was issued by a government or governmental agency or unit, it was not conditional even though it limited payment to a particular fund or the proceeds of a particular source. Could a few dishonest officials bankrupt an entire town?

Florida Statutes § 673.104(4)(1991) provides: "No warrant issued by the Comptroller of the State of Florida directing the treasurer to pay a sum certain shall be a negotiable instrument within the meaning of this chapter." *See, State of Florida v. Family Bank of Hallandale*, 623 So.2d 474, 20 U.C.C. Rep. 1273, 21 U.C.C. Rep.2d 665 (Fla. 1993).

[D] Fixed Amount of Money With Other Charges

Read U.C.C. §§ 3-104(a), 3-107, 3-112, 1-201(24); see § 3-114.

CONSTITUTION BANK AND TRUST COMPANY v. ROBINSON

Supreme Court of Connecticut
179 Conn. 229,425 A.2d 1268 (1979)

PETERS, ASSOCIATE JUSTICE.

This case concerns the foreclosure of a mortgage given as security for a promissory note containing a variable interest rate. The plaintiff Constitution Bank and Trust Company brought an action for damages, strict foreclosure, possession of the mortgaged premises, reasonable attorney's fees and a deficiency judgment against the defendant Bertram Robinson, trustee of the Mar-Bar Realty Trust, and against two other defendants. The plaintiff moved successfully for summary judgment on the issue of liability, and, after further proceedings in the trial court, a judgment was rendered in its behalf for strict foreclosure and for attorney's fees in the amount of $10,000. The defendant has taken a timely appeal contesting: (1) the enforceability of the note and mortgage; (2) the property of the order of strict foreclosure rather than foreclosure by sale; and (3) the justification for the calculation of attorney's fees.

The underlying facts are not in dispute, and establish that the defendant Robinson, as trustee for the Mar-Bar Realty Trust, executed, on April 23, 1975, a promissory note in the amount of $200,000, secured by a mortgage on real property in Enfield. The note became due two years later and is concededly in default, only $5000 in principal amount ever having been repaid. The mortgage conveyed an interest in property subject to an outstanding long-term commercial lease with an option to purchase; the present value of the mortgaged property depends upon appraisals of the value of the stream of income produced by the lease and the value of the reversionary interest upon the termination of the lease.

The defendant's principal argument on this appeal is that the promissory note and the mortgage that secures it are unenforceable because the note calls for interest in terms so vague as to make the whole note uncertain, indefinite and void. The note stipulates that

> [i]nterest on the unpaid principal balance shall accrue from the date hereof and shall be payable for each calendar quarter on the last day of such calendar quarter with the first payment due June 30, 1975. Each payment of interest shall be at a per annum rate or rates equal to one and one-half(1-1/2) per cent over the prime rate of the payee in effect from time to time during such calendar quarter. On default or after maturity, interest as hereinbefore provided or at the rate of fifteen (15) per cent per year, whichever is higher, shall be payable hereunder.

Whatever the defects, if any, in the articulation of the interest rate in the note before us, we should take note of the draconian remedy that the defendant is seeking to invoke. The defendant, ignoring the fact that he has since 1975 enjoyed the use of the principal sum that was borrowed, of which he still owes $195,000 totally apart from the contested interest, would have us declare the whole transaction so lacking in mutuality, so illusory, as to avoid any liability whatsoever. That is a misreading of the law of contracts. Even contracts considerably more executory than the present contract, even contracts with substantial unilateral rights of cancellation or of termination, are not totally void for lack of mutuality once there has been some performance that makes up for possible defects in the consideration. See *Gurfrin v. Werbelovsky*, 97 Conn. 703, 706, 118 A. 32 (1922); cf. *Sylvan Crest Sand & Gravel Co. v. United States*, 150 F.2d 642 (2d Cir. 1945); 1A Corbin, Contracts §§ 162, 163 (1963). The note and mortgage are therefore at least embraceable in the amount of the unpaid principal and the stipulated post-maturity interest of 15 percent.

The defendant's attack on the variable interest rate is equally unpersuasive. Variable interest rates are a device to allow borrowers and lenders to accommodate to fluctuations in the cost of money. Long-term lending could accommodate to these fluctuations without a variable interest rate if the parties employed an arrangement of revolving credit, in which short-term or demand instruments were at regular intervals replaced by new notes at then current interest rates. Such an arrangement would involve no indefiniteness or uncertainty but would entail substantial transaction costs. Without some form of accommodation to fluctuating monetary costs, banking institutions would be hard pressed to respond competitively to the problems created . . .during periods of tight money.

PROBLEM 12.1

Resolve *Constitution Bank v. Robinson* under the Uniform Commercial Code. *See* U.C.C. § 3-112 and Comment 1.

FIRST NATIONAL BANK OF GRAYSON v. WHALEY

West Virginia Supreme Court of Appeals
284 S.E.2d 618, 32 U.C.C. Rep. 1149 (1981)

McGraw. J.

The First National Bank of Grayson, Kentucky (hereinafter the Kentucky bank), appeals from a final order of the Circuit Court of Cabell County, entered on October 14, 1980, which denied the Kentucky bank's recovery of a reasonable attorney's fee in this action. The court below concluded that the payment of attorneys' fees violates the public policy of the State of West Virginia, and it is from this ruling that the Kentucky bank appeals. . ..

One provision of the note stated: "Each maker, comaker, endorser, surety, and guarantor hereof jointly and severally agrees to pay this note and guarantees payment hereof and waives demand, presentment, protest and notice of dishonor . . .and agrees in case of default to pay all cost of collection, including all reasonable attorney's fees and legal expenses.". . .

The circuit court found that $900 was a reasonable attorney's fee but denied the Kentucky bank judgment in any amount on the ground that such award was contrary to the public policy of the State of West Virginia.

The sole error alleged by the appellant Kentucky bank is that the court below erred in denying it the right to recover all costs of collection, including reasonable attorneys' fees and legal expenses, as provided by the promissory note which was executed by the defendants.

The first question which this court must resolve is whether to apply the law of West Virginia or that of Kentucky to determine what obligation, if any, exists for the payment of attorneys' fees. The note in question here was, without dispute, entered into in Kentucky, the duties it obligated the Kentucky company to perform were to be performed in Kentucky, and the plaintiff; the Kentucky bank, is a resident of Kentucky. Under West Virginia's traditional conflicts of law principles, Kentucky law controls the validity and enforceability of the note in question In this action we must, therefore, turn to the law of Kentucky to determine whether attorneys' fees are recoverable.

In reference to this second issue, we note that the case law in Kentucky is replete with the proposition that promissory notes requiring the payment of reasonable attorneys' fees upon default are not enforceable. In *Mammoth Cave Productions Credit Association v. Geralds*, 551 SW2d 5 (Ky 1977) the court noted that the case law in Kentucky has uniformly held unenforceable as contrary to public policy provisions requiring the debtor to pay attorneys' fees arising as the result of the debtor's default. In *Riley v. West Kentucky Production Credit Association, Inc.*, 603 SW2d 916 (Ky 1980) the court again stated that a long line of cases hold that provisions of a note proporting to agree that attorneys' fees may be recovered against the debtor are invalid as against public policy. That court went on to find that the provisions of the Uniform Commercial Code do nothing to change this policy.

It is clear from these cases that Kentucky has a longstanding policy of denying any requirement that the defaulting debtor be required to pay attorneys' fees and, since Kentucky law is governing in this case, this court must dismiss the Kentucky bank's appeal.

PROBLEM 12.2

Resolve *First National Bank v. Whaley* under the Uniform Commercial Code. *See* U.C.C. § 3-104(a).

HAZEN v. COOK

Supreme Court of Oregon
646 P.2d 33 (1982)

MEMORANDUM.

Plaintiffs sued on a promissory note which provided for recovery of "reasonable attorney's fees" in an action to collect the debt. The trial court found that the note was usurious and entered judgment that the defendants pay the amount of the note to the State of Oregon for use of the Lane County School Fund pursuant to former ORS 82.120(5). The Court of Appeals reversed and remanded for entry of judgment in favor of plaintiff 55 Or. App. 66, 637 P.2d 195 (1981). The court denied the demand of both parties for attorney fees. 56 Or. App. 407, 642 P.2d 318 (1982). Plaintiffs petition for review of this denial. We allow the petition for review and reverse.

ORS 20.096 provides that the prevailing party, defined as "the party in whose favor final judgment or decree is rendered," is entitled to attorney fees in any action or suit to enforce a contract that provides for such fees to one of the parties.[5] After the mandate of the Court of

[5] ORS 20.096:

(1) In any action or suit on a contract, where such contract specifically provides that attorney fees and costs incurred to enforce the provisions of the contract shall be awarded to one of the parties, the prevailing party, whether that party is the party specified in the contract or not, at trial or on appeal, shall be entitled to reasonable attorney fees in addition to costs and disbursements.

. . .

Appeals to enter a judgment in favor of plaintiffs for the principal amount due under the note, plaintiffs were the prevailing party within the meaning of ORS 20.096(5). They therefore were entitled to reasonable attorney fees. *U.S. Nat'l Bank v. Smith*, 292 Or. 123, 637 P.2d 139 (1981).

The decision of the Court of Appeals is reversed and remanded for further proceedings consistent with this opinion.

NOTE

Notice the omission in U.C.C. § 3-104(a) of former U.C.C. § 3-106(1)(d), (e).

PROBLEM 12.3

One of your clients purchased two promissory notes without realizing discrepancies in them. In one, the handwritten number is $50,000, but on the other line it is typed in as five thousand dollars. On the other, the handwritten number is $20,000, but the typed number is $2,000. What advice can you give?

[E] And No Other Promise

Read: U.C.C. § 3-104(a)(3).

It is stated in U.C.C. § 3-106(b)(ii) that a promise is not made conditional because payment is limited to resort to a particular fund or source. The justification for this rule was stated as being that market forces determine the marketability of instruments of this kind and if potential buyers don't want promises that are payable only from a particular source, they won't take them, but Article 3 should apply.

Should the same reasoning apply to a promise to "pay $1,000 and deliver 10 cords of wood?" If so, why so? If not, why not?

WOODWORTH v. THE RICHMOND INDIANA VENTURE

Ohio Court of Common Pleas, Franklin County
13 U.C.C. Rep.2d 1149 (1990)

JOHNSON, J.

This matter is before the court on plaintiff's motion for partial summary judgment and defendant Signet Bank's motion for summary judgment. On December 18, 1987, plaintiff executed a promissory note in which he promised to pay to the order of The Richmond Indiana Venture, A Limited Partnership or holder the sum of $655,625.00. The promissory note was given to pay part of the deferred portion of plaintiff's investment in the partnership. The promissory

(5) As used in this section and ORS 20.097 "prevailing party" means the party in whose favor final judgment or decree is rendered.

note was subsequently assigned or negotiated to defendant, Signet Bank. Plaintiff is in default on the promissory note having failed to make payments that fell due on July 1, 1989 and July 1, 1990. Plaintiff filed this action on November 2, 1989.

The standard for granting summary judgment is clear. On a motion for summary judgment, the moving party bears the burden of demonstrating that no genuine issue of material fact exists and that it is entitled to judgment as a matter of law. The court will construe the evidence most strongly in favor of the party against whom the motion for summary judgment is made.

In order to be negotiable, a promissory note must be a signed, unconditional promise to pay a sum certain in money which is payable on demand or at a definite, stated time. The note must be payable to order or bearer and contain no other promise, order, obligation, or power given by the maker except as authorized by §§ 1303.01 to 1303.78, inclusive, of the Revised Code. R.C. § 1303.03; U.C.C. § 3-104.

The policy under pre-Code law was that instruments should be as concise as possible and free from collateral engagements. As noted above, the Code continues this policy by mandating that the unconditional promise to pay not be cluttered by other promises, orders, obligations, or powers unless otherwise authorized.

The promissory note at issue contains the following term:

> The undersigned agrees that, in the event any payment due pursuant to the terms of this note be not timely made, at the option of the Partnership, the undersigned shall retroactively lose any interest in the Partnership from the date hereof and the Partnership shall have no obligation to account for any payments theretofore made by the undersigned, and that this remedy is in addition to other remedies afforded by the Partnership Agreement.

This term is clearly a promise by the maker resulting in a forfeiture of his partnership interest and payments in the event of default. The term is more than a mere reference to the partnership agreement, a recitation of security, or an agreement to protect collateral; it is a forfeiture provision in addition to other remedies under the referenced partnership agreement.

In *Pacific Finance Loans v. Goodwin* (1974), 41 Ohio App. 2d 141 [16 U.C.C. Rep Serv 750], the court held that the requirement of an unconditional promise to pay is contravened by a term providing for the repossession of collateral by a seller without judicial process. The case sub judice is analogous since the term at issue is a forfeiture without resort to judicial process.

Nothing in R.C. § 1303.04 or § 1303.11 authorizes the forfeiture term at issue. Based on the above analysis, the court finds that the negotiability of this promissory note is doubtful. Where there is doubt, the decision should be against negotiability. Official Code Comment 5 to U.C.C. § 3-104; R.C. § 1303.03. Since the promissory note is not negotiable, defendant Signet Bank cannot claim the status of a holder in due course and is subject to ordinary contract defenses that plaintiff may assert.

Having considered the pleadings and memoranda filed herein, the court finds that plaintiff has fulfilled his burden. Accordingly, plaintiff's motion is sustained. Defendant's motion is denied. Counsel for plaintiff shall prepare an appropriate entry.

[F] On Demand or At a Definite Time

Read: U.C.C. §§ 3-104(a)(2), 3-108, see §§ 1-208, 3-113.

IN RE ESTATE OF BALKUS

Wisconsin Court of Appeals
361 N.W.2d 593, 42 U.C.C. Rep. 877(1985)

NETTESHEIM, J.

Ann Vesely appeals from a judgment denying her claims against the estate of her brother, James T. Balkus. Vesely claims that she is entitled to payment on deposit slips and promissory notes found amongst Balkus's possessions because, as a holder in due course, she takes them free from the defenses asserted by the personal representative of the estate. We conclude the deposit slips are not negotiable instruments and, therefore, Vesely is not a holder in due course. We also conclude that the promissory notes are subject to the personal representative's defense of nondelivery because Vesely is not a holder in due course. Finally, we reject Vesely's claim of constructive delivery.

James T. Balkus died intestate on December 4, 1983. Shortly after his death, Vesely examined Balkus's personal property and discovered six deposit slips from a savings account maintained by Balkus. On each slip was a handwritten notation:

Payable to Ann Balkus Vesely on P.O.D. The full amount and other deposits.[6]

Each slip was dated and signed by Balkus. Both parties treated "P.O.D." as meaning payable on death." Vesely also found two promissory notes, both of which were made payable to her order. Each note was in the amount of $6000 and provided for five percent interest.[7] One note was dated March 23, 1961 and tile other was dated July 10, 1963.

Vesely filed claims against Balkus's estate requesting payment on the deposit slips and the promissory notes. The circuit court disallowed Vesely's claims.

On appeal, Vesely argues that both the deposit slips and the promissory notes are negotiable instruments under Wisconsin's Uniform Commercial Code (UCC), chs. 401-409, Stats. Vesely further argues that under the U.C.C. she is a holder in due course of the instruments and therefore takes the instruments free from the defenses asserted by the personal representative. We reject these arguments.

Vesely's arguments require this court to apply certain sections of the U.C.C. to the fact situation presented. The application of a statute to a particular set of facts presents a question of law. As such, we owe no deference to the trial court's conclusion.

DEPOSIT SLIPS

We first address Vesely's contention that the endorsed deposit slips are negotiable instruments. Section 403.104(1), Stats., defines a negotiable instrument: [the Court cites U.C.C. § 3-104(1)].

---

[6] Some of the deposit slips contained a slightly different notation:

"Payable to Ann Balkus Vesely on P.O.D. The full amts. & other succeeding deposits."

[7] Vesely apparently loaned Balkus $ 12,000 in the early 1960's.

We conclude that the endorsed deposit slips are not negotiable instruments because they fail to meet the requirement that the writing be payable at a definite time. Section 403.109(2), Stats., states that an instrument which is "payable upon an act or event uncertain as to time of occurrence is not payable at a definite time." The 1961 Report of the Wisconsin Legislative Council indicates that § 403.109(2) "[m]akes post obituary notes non-negotiable, even after the death has occurred." See Wis. Stats. Ann. § 403.109 (West 1964). See also Official U.C.C. Comment, *id.; Robert v. Faulkner*, 660 S.W.2d 463, 466-67 (Mo. Ct. App. 1983).[8]

Because the "payable on death" term of the deposit slips makes the instrument payable upon an event uncertain as to the time of occurrence, *i.e.*, the date of Balkus's death, the endorsed deposit slips are not payable at a definite time and are therefore not negotiable instruments. In order to qualify as holder in due course, Vesely must hold a negotiable instrument. See § 403.302 and § 403.305, Stats. Vesely, thus, is not a holder in due course.[9]

NOTES AND QUESTIONS

(1) U.C.C. § 3-108 states that instruments payable on demand include those payable at sight or on presentation and those in which no time for payment is stated. When sued on the instrument in the latter instance, would the maker be allowed to defend based on an alleged parole agreement between maker and payee under which the note was not to mature until some indefinite time in the future determined by certain other ventures of the maker and payee? Would it matter if the plaintiff was the payee, as opposed to an assignee or a holder in due course? See Comment 1(a) to the statement of the parole evidence rule found in U.C.C. § 2-202. See *Schekter v. Michael*, 194 So. 2d 641 (Fla. 1966).

In *Ferri v. Sylvia*, 214 A.2d 470 (R.I. 1965), the trial court in a suit between maker and payee of a negotiable promissory note, payable "within ten (10) years after date" ruled the phase ambiguous, permitted testimony of the parties as to their intention, and found that the parties intended that the payee could have the balance at any time due her. The Supreme Court of Rhode Island reversed, reasoning that § 3-109(1)(a) provided that an "on or before" date was a definite time, equating "within" with "on or before," and concluding that the parties had by their writing agreed on a due date which could not be varied by parole evidence. What is the flaw in the Supreme Court's reasoning?

(2) The most obvious reason for the definite time requirement is that a commercial instrument is not readily marketable unless the putative purchaser can ascertain the due date of the instrument. One will find that the discount rate (that percentage which a purchaser will subtract from the

---

[8] Vesely cites *Sheldon v. Blackman*, 188 Wis. 4, 205 N.W. 486 (1925), in support of her contention that "payment on death" represents a definite time and therefore the deposit slips are negotiable instruments. *Sheldon*, however, was decided before Wisconsin adopted the U.C.C.. Both the Legislative Council's report and the Official U.C.C. Comments indicate that the U.C.C. changed prior law in which instruments payable upon death were considered negotiable See Wis. Stats. Ann. § 403. 109 (West 1964).

[9] The Circuit court also denied Vesely's claim to the savings account proceeds, reasoning that: (1) if considered a gift, it was incomplete because the slips were not delivered; (2) if considered a testamentary bequest, it did not meet the requirements of a will, and (3) Vesely was not named as an owner or beneficiary in the bank's records regarding the savings account. Vesely does not challenge these determinations on appeal and relies solely on her argument that she is a holder in due course of a negotiable instrument. As these determinations are not challenged, we do not address them.

Given our conclusion that the endorsed deposit slips do not meet the requirements of § 403.104(l)(c), Stats., we do not consider whether the deposit slips meet the other requirements of § 403.104(1).

face value of the paper in determining what he shall pay) depends, *inter alia*, on the time remaining until maturity. Obviously, a purchaser will shy away from paper where there is no indication of when the debt is to be liquidated. There is another good reason why the form of a note should show its due date with certainty in order to qualify as negotiable paper. As will be seen, one of the requirements of a holder in due course (that protected purchaser who takes free and clear of prior defenses and claims of ownership) is that he take the instrument before maturity. How can one know if he will have protected purchaser status unless he is able to determine the maturity (due date) of the instrument from an examination thereof?

Some uncertainty is introduced into the definiteness of maturity by permitting acceleration and extension. This is an exception, however, which past commercial usage has sanctioned as a necessity. Certainty does give way where there is an evident need for some uncertainty. Many obligors would refuse to execute instruments of indebtedness if they were not afforded the privilege of prepayment. U.C.C. § 3-108(b)(i)).

(3) Former U.C.C. § 3-109(1) states that an instrument is payable at a definite time if by its terms it is payable "(c) at a definite time subject to any acceleration." Comment 4 to this section states:

> 4. . . . So far as certainty of time of payment is concerned a note payable at a definite time but subject to acceleration is no less certain than a note payable on demand, whose negotiability never has been questioned. It is in fact more certain, since it at least states a definite time beyond which the instrument cannot run. Objections to the acceleration clause must be based rather on the possibility of abuse by the holder, which has nothing to do with negotiability and is not limited to negotiable instruments. That problem is now covered by Section 1-208.

Subsection (1)(c) means the certainty of time of payment and the negotiability of the instrument are not affected by any acceleration clause, whether acceleration is at the option of the maker or the holder, or automatic upon the occurrence of some event, and whether it is conditional or unrestricted. Of course if the terms under which acceleration is permitted are uncertain, the instrument may fail as a contract although it doesn't fail in negotiability.

U.C.C. § 1-208 clarifies the objection to an acceleration clause based on the possibility of abuse by the holder in stating:

> Option to accelerate at will. A term providing that one party or his successor in interest may accelerate payment or performance or require collateral or additional collateral "at will" or "when he deems himself insecure" or in words of similar import shall be construed to mean that he shall have power to do so only if he in good faith believes that the prospect of payment or performance is impaired. The burden of establishing lack of good faith is on the party against whom the power has been exercised.
>
> The comment to this section provides:
>
> The increased use of acceleration clauses either in the case of sales on credit or in time paper or in security transactions has led to some confusion in the cases as to the effect to be given to a clause which seemingly grants the power of an acceleration at the whim and caprice of one party. This Section is intended to make clear that despite language which can be so construed and which further might be held to make the agreement void as against public policy or to make contract illusory or too indefinite for enforcement, the clause means that

the option is to be exercised only in the good faith belief that the payment or performance is impaired.

(4) The brief Official Comment to U.C.C. § 3-108 states that section 3-108 is a restatement of former Section 3-108 and Section 3-109.

PROBLEM 12.4

Your senior partner is on a bar association committee charged with formulating standards for international negotiable promissory notes. He has asked you what requisites would you require for a note to be negotiable? One committee member has suggested that a note to be negotiable must carry a conspicuous label NEGOTIABLE promissory note. What is your opinion on this point?

§ 12.03 "Holder," as in Holder in Due Course

[A] Issuance, Transfer and Negotiation

Read: U.C.C. §§ 3-105, 3-201, 3-202, 3-203, 3-301; see § 1-201(14) and (20).

"Issue" means the first delivery of an instrument by the maker or drawer, whether to a holder or nonholder, for the purpose of giving rights on the instrument to any person (U.C.C. § 3-105). "Delivery" is defined in § 1-201(14) as meaning a voluntary transfer of possession. An instrument is "transferred" when it is delivered by a person other than its issuer for the purpose of giving to the person receiving delivery the right to enforce the instrument. § 3-203(a). Transfer of an instrument, whether or not the transfer is a "negotiation," vests in the transferee any right of the transferor to enforce the instrument. § 3-203(b). Former § 3-201 did not define "transfer." § 3-203(a) defines transfer by limiting it to cases in which possession of the instrument is delivered for the purpose of giving to the person receiving delivery the right to enforce the instrument.

According to Comment 1 to § 3-203, although transfer of an instrument might mean in a particular case that title to the instrument passes to the transferee, that result does not follow in all cases. The right to enforce the instrument and ownership of the instrument are two different concepts. Ownership rights in instruments may be determined by principles of the law of property, independent of Article 3, which do not depend upon whether the instrument was transferred under § 3-203.

"Negotiation" means a transfer of possession, whether voluntary or involuntary, of an instrument by a person other than the issuer to a person who thereby becomes a holder. § 3-201. Except for "remitter" paper (see § 3-103(a)(11)), instruments payable to identified persons require delivery of the instrument plus indorsement by the holder. Instruments payable to bearer may be negotiated by transfer of possession alone. (Read Comment 1 to § 3-201.)

IN RE ESTATE OF BALKUS

[The facts and first part of the opinion appear in § 12.02[F], *supra*].

Promissory Notes

Holder in Due Course

We now turn to Vesely's arguments concerning the promissory notes she found in Balkus's possessions after his death. Vesely claims the notes are negotiable instruments and she is a holder in due course, taking the notes free from the defense of nondelivery asserted by the personal representative.

A holder in due course is a holder who takes an instrument for value, in good faith, and *without notice* that the instrument is overdue or has been dishonored or *of any defense against or claim to it* on the part of any person. Sec. 403.302(1), Stats. As payee of the notes, Vesely can be a holder in due course. See 403.302(2). A payee who acquires the status of a holder in due course is, however, the exception rather than the rule. *Saka v. Sahara-Nevada Corp.*, 558 P2d 535, 536 [20 U.C.C. Rep 958] (Nev. 1976). "Where the payee is an immediate party to the underlying transaction, under normal circumstances he cannot claim this status [holder in due course] because he necessarily knows of any defenses to the contract." *Id.* See also *Courtesy Financial Services, Inc. v. Hughes*, 424 So.2d 1172, 1175 (La. Ct. App. 1982).

Here, as payee of the notes, Vesely necessarily had notice and knowledge of the personal representative's defense of nondelivery because the notes were never delivered to her. Vesely's claim as a holder in due course therefore fails.

Constructive Delivery

Since Vesely is not a holder in due course of the notes and thus takes the notes subject to the defenses asserted by the personal representative, see § 403.306, Stats., we now look to the defense of nondelivery asserted by the personal representative It is undisputed that Balkus did not physically deliver the notes to Vesely. She argues, however, that a letter she received from Balkus in August 1974 constituted constructive delivery of the notes. The letter, in pertinent part, stated:

> Also you will get & shall I say I will bequeath to you all my other junk in my apt. such as tools, radios, TV sets, clothing, clothes and also the money I owe you. I have $6000 in govt. bonds made out in your name & the banker told me, nobody could take it away from you. I also have 2 judgment notes made out to you for the amt. of money I borrowed from you in 1961 & 1962. That should take care of the interest I was supposed to pay you but I didn't.

We reject Vesely's claim that this letter constituted constructive delivery of the notes.

The trial court found that Balkus retained dominion and control of the notes and that be "simply never gave up ownership." These findings are not clearly erroneous. See § 805. 17(2), Stats.

The general rule is that a promissory note has no effect unless it is delivered. The U.C.C. defines delivery of an instrument as the "voluntary transfer of possession." Sec. 401.201(14). A constructive delivery may be sufficient. *Casto* at 729. A constructive delivery occurs only when the maker indicates an intention to make the instrument an enforceable obligation against him or her by surrendering control over it and intentionally placing it under the power of the payee or a third person.

Balkus never surrendered control nor transferred possession of the notes. It is undisputed that the notes were found in Balkus's possessions after his death. The notes were never placed under the control of Vesely or any other third party. We therefore reject Vesely's argument that the letter served as constructive delivery of the notes.

PROBLEM 12.5

Noble, of Noble Petroleum Company, ordered the defendant bank to draw a cashier's check in the sum of $16,216.00 payable to the plaintiff and to draw that amount from Noble company's account with the defendant. Later that same day, Noble again called defendant and spoke to the same officer that he had before, Meredith. He informed Meredith that Noble Petroleum Company was being placed in bankruptcy involuntarily. As the cashier's check had been typed up, signed by Meredith as vice-president of defendant, a debit slip drawn upon Noble Petroleum Company's account, which was still on his desk, Meredith had a credit slip countering the debit slip prepared and had the cashier's check cancelled. All of this was done the same day and the cashier's check never left the possession of the defendant. Does the plaintiff have an interest in the cashier's check?

See Rex Smith Propane, Inc. v. National Bank of Commerce, 372 F. Supp. 499 (N.D. Tex. 1974).

Would there be a difference if the parties had been dealing with a certified check? *See* U.C.C. § 3-409(a).

[B] Special and Blank Indorsements

Read: U.C.C. §§ 3-204, 3-205, 3-109, 3-110; see §§ 3-206, 3-207, 4-205.

All indorsements are either special or blank and also either restrictive or nonrestrictive. These classifications are important in discussing what constitutes negotiation.

An indorsement is special when it "identifies a person to whom it makes the instrument payable." (U.C.C. § 3-205) The following are special indorsements:

"Pay to the order of John Jones
Henry Smith,"

"Pay John Jones
Henry Smith,"

"Pay John Jones, without recourse
Henry Smith."

In these indorsements, John Jones is the indorsee and Henry Smith is the indorser. The last indorsement is special and qualified. The others are special and unqualified. Indorsements are in blank when they do not name the indorsee. (U.C.C. § 3-205(b)) An indorsee or other holder may convert a blank indorsement into a special indorsement (U.C.C. § 3-205(c)). Note that the change from blank to special does not affect the indorser's liabilities.

It is necessary to pay attention to special indorsements inasmuch as further negotiation of an instrument is impossible without the indorsement of any special indorsee. Thus, with respect to the following chain of indorsements, only Jones can qualify as a holder, hence as a holder in due course:

"Pay John Jones or order
Henry Smith,

Pay Able Baker,

Robert Brown,

Sam Stranger."

An instrument payable to bearer needs no indorsement for negotiation. Under pre-Code law, there was a split of authority on the question of whether a subsequent special indorsement would change bearer paper to order paper. There was also a split of authority on the question of whether order paper was converted to bearer paper for all time by a subsequent blank indorsement. The Code adopts the general position that the form of the last indorsement controls what is required for further negotiation. See U.C.C. § 3-205(c).

ASIAN INTERNATIONAL, LTD. v. MERRILL LYNCH, PIERCE, FENNER AND SMITH, INC.

Louisiana Court of Appeal
435 So. 2d 1958, 37 U.C.C. Rep. 171 (1983)

CARTER, J.

This is an appeal by Asian International, Ltd. from a summary judgment in favor of Merrill Lynch, Pierce, Fenner and Smith, Inc.

On March 30,1982, Asian International, Ltd. (Asian) filed suit against Merrill Lynch, Pierce, Fenner and Smith, Inc. (Merrill Lynch), Ben F. Fort, Jr. (Fort), and H. Grady Smith, Jr. (Smith) alleging defendants' liability, individually and in solido, for tortious conversion of a $200,000.00 check and for damages for the loss of corporate opportunity resulting from such tortious conversion.

The dispute among the parties arises from the following facts. On or about July 28, 1981, Cathay Trading Corporation delivered to Asian a check made payable to Asian International, Ltd. in the amount of $200,000.00, in full payment for ten separators sold by Asian to Cathay. Smith, the president of Asian, and Edmund C. McCallum, treasurer of Asian, subsequently endorsed said check to the order of Fort, in payment of an alleged loan obligation owed by Asian to Fort. Fort then deposited the endorsed check in his account with Merrill Lynch. Merrill Lynch credited the funds to Fort's account and received payment from the payor bank.

Merrill Lynch filed a motion for summary judgment claiming it was a holder in due course of the check and asserting that, as such, it took the instrument free from all claims, including those asserted by Asian.

The trial court granted the motion for summary judgment in favor of Merrill Lynch and dismissed Asian's suit. The trial court based its judgment upon finding that there were no genuine issues of material fact and that Merrill Lynch was a holder in due course as a matter of law.

Asian appeals with the following specifications of error:

(1) The trial court erred in holding, as a matter of law, that Merrill Lynch sustained the burden of proving its status as a holder in due course; and

(2) The trial court erred in finding that there were no genuine issues of material fact.

Specification of Error No. 1

The first issue is whether Merrill Lynch sustained its burden of proving its status as a holder in due course as a matter of law. La RS 10:3-302(1) defines a holder in due course as: [the court cites U.C.C. § 3-302(l)].

The status of a holder in due course is significant to the extent that as such he takes the instrument free from all claims to it on the part of any person and all defenses of any party to the instrument with whom the holder has not dealt, with minor exceptions. La RS 10:3-305.

In order for one to enjoy the status of a holder in due course, the four elements of La RS 10:3-302(1) must exist simultaneously during possession of the negotiable instrument. La RS 10:3-307(3) and the corresponding comments in the Uniform Commercial Code (U.C.C.) indicate that the person claiming the rights of a holder in due course must sustain his burden by affirmative proof of all elements.

Holder

Any person who asserts rights of a holder in due course must first prove that he is a "holder." A holder is "a person who is in possession of. . .an instrument, drawn, issued, or endorsed to him or to his order or bearer or in blank." La RS 10:1-201.

Negotiation is the process by which the transferee of an instrument becomes a holder. La RS 10:3-202(1). The comments to that article in the U.C.C. indicate that negotiation is a special form of transfer, the importance of which lies in the fact that it makes the transferee a holder. Stated another way, an endorsement by a holder of an instrument payable to order is necessary for a negotiation of the instrument, for only by a negotiation may a third party become a holder of the instrument. *Developments in the Law, 1980-1981: Banking Law*, 42 La L Rev 330 (1982).

In the present case, the $200,000.00 check was delivered to Fort with the following endorsement:

Asian International, Ltd.

s/n H. Grady Smith, Jr.

s/n Edmund C. McCallum

for deposit to

order of

Ben F. Fort, Jr.

In order for Merrill Lynch to become a holder of the instrument, the instrument had to be negotiated. Negotiation required an endorsement by Fort.

When Fort presented the check for deposit to his Merrill Lynch account, a Merrill Lynch employee wrote "pay to: Merrill Lynch, Pierce, Fenner and Smith" on the instrument. The endorsement on the check prior to deposit appeared as follows:

Asian International, Ltd.

s/n H. Grady Smith, Jr.

s/n Edmund C. McCallum

pay to:

Merrill Lynch, Pierce, Fenner and Smith

for deposit to

order of

Ben F. Fort, Jr.

The check was then deposited into Fort's account.

Under La RS 10:4-205(1), a depositary bank which has taken an item for collection may supply any endorsement of the customer which is necessary to title unless the item contains the words "payee's endorsement required" or the like. In the absence of such a requirement, a statement placed on the item by the depositary bank to the effect that the item was deposited by a customer or credited to his account is effective as the customer's endorsement. This provision was designed to speed up collections by eliminating any necessity to return to a non-bank depositor any items he may have failed to endorse.

La RS 10:1-201 defines a bank as any person engaged in the business of banking. The receiving of deposits and issuing bills and notes has been defined as engaging in the banking business. (See *Rosenblum v. Anglin*, 135 F.2d 512, 9th Cir 1943). It was also held in the above cited case that although the banking business involves more than the accepting and paying out of deposits, an institution which exercises only these two functions may be carrying on a "banking business," if these things are done as a regular business. Under this definition, we find La RS 10:4-205(l) applicable to Merrill Lynch, even though Merrill Lynch is not a bank incorporated under the provisions of Title 6 of the Louisiana Revised Statutes. Since Merrill Lynch provided Fort with a general securities and a checking account, much like that provided by a depositary bank to its depositing customer, the relationship between Merrill Lynch and Fort is analogous to that of a bank and its customer.

Merrill Lynch supplied the required endorsement which was effective as the customer's endorsement, and the check was thereby negotiated to Merrill Lynch. Therefore, we find that Merrill Lynch was a holder as envisioned by La RS 10:3-302(1).

QUESTIONS

Was Merrill Lynch a "bank"? *See* former U.C.C. §§ 1-201(4), 4-105. Is Merrill Lynch a "bank" today? *See* U.C.C. § 4A-105(a)(2).

STRICKLER v. MARX

Virginia Supreme Court
10 VLR 443, 22 U.C.C. Rep.2d 237 (1993)

COMPTON J.

The dispositive question in this appeal is whether, under the circumstances of this case, the transferee of two checks qualified as a "holder," within the meaning of the Uniform Commercial Code (U.C.C.), so as to entitle the transferee to recover on the instruments.[10]

In March 1991, appellee James H. Marx, Sr., filed a motion for judgment against appellant Maynard Strickler seeking recovery in the amount of $11,840 with interest. This sum represents the total of two checks made in November 1981 by the defendant and eventually transferred to the plaintiff.

Following a July 1992 bench trial, the court below, in a letter opinion, ruled in favor of the plaintiff. We awarded the defendant an appeal from the October 1992 order entering judgment in favor of the plaintiff in the amount claimed.

The facts relating to the dispositive question are not in dispute. In 1981, the plaintiff, a resident of Alexandria, provided financing for a business enterprise conducted in Charlottesville by one Charles W. Davis, also known as Chuck Davis. Prior to his association with Davis, the plaintiff had incorporated Energy Technology Corporation. Davis operated A-1 Body Shop, also known as A-1 Car Body Shop, one of the entities falling under the corporate umbrella of Energy Technology Corporation. The plaintiff and Davis were also associated in another corporation that plaintiff had created, which was engaged in the used car rental business in Charlottesville.

In November 1981, defendant Stricker, a farmer living in the Charelottesville area, performed automobile repair work for Davis. Davis owed defendant money from an earlier incident in which Davis was convicted of larceny from defendant and defendant was awarded a money judgment against him.

During 1981, defendant occasionally advanced funds to Davis to meet his payroll at the end of a week so that Davis could stay in business and repay defendant the prior obligation. In the fall of 1981, defendant often left Charlottesville on weekends to officiate college football games. On these weekends, defendant would give Davis a personal check, signed and payable to A-1, and allow Davis to fill in the amount needed to meet the payroll. Davis would cash the check and repay defendant after the weekend. These transactions resulted in Davis filling in the checks for $200.00 to $300.00

[10] The General Assembly made numerous changes in the U.C.C. effective January 1, 1993. Acts 1992, ch. 693. The events giving rise to this controversy predated those changes. Thus, this appeal is decided under the pre-1993 version of the applicable statutes and the cases interpreting those statutes.

On November 27, 1981, a Friday, defendant left Charlottesville to officiate a game. He gave Davis a signed check payable to the order of "A-1 Body Shop," completed except for the amount, and drawn on defendant's account at National Bank and Trust Company. When defendant returned on the following Monday, Davis asked for another check to replace the first check, stating "he messed the check up, but the bank give him the money, but he had to replace the check." On that day, November 30, 1981, defendant gave Davis another signed check payable to the order of "A-1 Car Body Shop," completed except for the amount, and drawn on defendant's account at National Bank.

Davis filled in the amount of $4,860.00 on the first check and the amount of $6,980.00 on the second check. He presented the checks to Albermarle Bank & Trust Company, where he had an account, after indorsing each, "Pay To The Order of Albermarle Bank & Trust Co. Charlottesville, Va. For Deposit Only Chuch [sic] Davis Body Shop." Apparently, Davis was given immediate credit for the checks.

The checks subsequently were dishonored by National Bank and returned to Albermarle bank because defendant had insufficient funds in his National Bank account to pay them. Defendant routinely maintained a balance in that account of no more than $500.00. Because Davis had withdrawn the funds from his Albermarle account, the subsequent charge by Albermarle Bank resulted in an overdraft on Davis's [sic] account.

In December 1981, plaintiff learned, either from Davis or Albermarle Bank, that the two checks had "bounced." Subsequently, plaintiff and Davis executed a note payable to Albermarle Bank for approximately $15,000 to cover the amount of the checks plus other sums owed the bank by A-1. The plaintiff, who had no prior legal obligation to the bank, executed the note to protect his interest as a creditor of Davis's business.

In the spring of 1983, plaintiff paid the note without any contribution from Davis and Albermarle Bank delivered the dishonored checks to plaintiff. In addition to Davis's original indorsement, the checks carried the indorsement, "Pay Any Bank, P.E.G." by Albermarle Bank. No other indorsement, except that of the Federal Reserve System, appears on the checks.

In the meantime, defendant learned of the resulting overdrafts by notice from National bank. He contacted Davis to find out "what was going on." Davis stated that the funds had been used to pay A-1's bills and "some outstanding debts in gambling." Davis told defendant, "I will take care of it . . .right now." Based on this representation, and after verifying with Albermarle Bank that "Mr. Davis and Mr. Marx had taken care of it," defendant took no further action. Subsequently, defendant realized that Albermarle Bank had obtained judgments against him in the amounts of the checks. These judgments were marked satisfied when plaintiff paid the amount of the note to Albermarle Bank.

In 1985, A-1's business failed. The plaintiff testified that he "got an assignment of the assets of A-1" from the trustee in bankruptcy. No written assignment was presented in evidence nor was there testimony of the details of such assignment.

Subsequently, this action ensued against defendant only. The whereabouts of Davis is unknown. In the motion for judgment, plaintiff alleged that he "is the assignee and transferee of all assets, including claims and causes of actions, of Energy Technology Corporation, trading as A-1 Car Body Shop and A-1 Body Shop." Reciting that defendant "drew, uttered and delivered" the checks, which were "returned marked 'insufficient funds,' " and not paid by defendant's bank, plaintiff asked for judgment against defendant. The broad allegations of the motion for judgment were narrowed at trial.

At trial, the parties and the court agreed that the central issue in the case was whether the plaintiff qualified as a "holder" under the U.C.C. For example, plaintiff's counsel stated that "we concede he's not a holder in due course . . .he's a holder because he gave value. I think that a creditor that gets a cause of action on a check [has] given value. So, I think he's a holder." In addition, plaintiff's counsel stated: "He's a holder for value though. Your Honor, and we think that that puts the burden on Mr. Strickler to establish defenses." Also, at the conclusion of the evidence, the trial judge stated that the "turning point" in the case is whether plaintiff is "a holder of these two checks, and is [in] a valid position to seek to collect." The judge further said, "It's simply a matter of law under the Uniform Commercial Code, whether or not Mr. Marx can collect on these two checks." The defendant took the position that plaintiff was not a "holder." Alternatively, defendant asserted that even if the plaintiff was a "holder," defendant had established the defenses of lack of consideration and material alteration of the instruments.

The trial court, in ruling for the plaintiff, implicitly decided that the plaintiff was a "holder," although the court did not discuss the issue in the letter opinion. Instead, the court discussed its rulings that defendant had failed to prove lack of consideration or material alteration. We do not reach the question whether defendant established those defenses because we conclude that the trial court erred in ruling that the plaintiff was a "holder."

Under the provisions of the U.C.C. effective at the time of this controversy, the right of a party to payment of an instrument depended "upon his status as a holder. Code § 8.3-301." *Lambert v. Barker*, 232 Va. 21, 24, 348 S.E.2d 214, 216 [2 U.C.C. Rep. Serv 2d 527] (1986). (§ 8.3-301 has been replaced by § 8.3A-301 [U.C.C. Revised § 3-301].) The U.C.C. defined "Holder" as "a person who is in possession of . . .an instrument . . .drawn, issued or indorsed to him or to his order or to bearer or in blank." Former Code § 8.1-201(20) (now amended). "A transferee may become a holder of order paper only by 'negotiation,' that is, by indorsement and delivery, and the indorsement must be by or on behalf of a person who is himself a holder." *Becker v. Nat'l Bank & Trust Co.*, 222 Va. 716, 720, 284 S.E.2d 793, 795 [32 U.C.C. Rep Serv 1983] (1981) (interpreting former Code § 8.3-202(1) now, with changes, § 8.3A-201 [U.C.C. Revised § 3-201]). "A transfer of an order instrument without a necessary indorsement is not a negotiation." Virginia Comment to former Code § 8.3-202(1), citing *Citizens Bank and Trust Co. v. Chase*, 151 Va. 65, 69, 144 S.E. 464, 965 (1928).

In the present case, we hold that the plaintiff was not a "holder" of the checks, which were order paper, because they had not been indorsed to him or to his order or to bearer or in blank. The checks carried Davis's indorsement to Albermarle Bank and Albermarle Bank's indorsement, "Pay Any Bank, P.E.G." According to former Code § 8.4-201(2), "After an item has been indorsed with the words 'pay any bank' or the like, only a bank may acquire the rights of a holder (a) until the item has been returned to the customer initiating collection; or (b) until the item has been specially indorsed by a bank to a person who is not a bank." (The form of § 8.4-201(2) has been amended.) The plaintiff, as transferee of the checks, did not qualify as a "holder" under either (a) or (b).

At trial, the plaintiff argued that he was a "holder" simply because he received an "assignment" of A-1's assets. *Becker* demonstrates that this argument has no merit. In that case, we focused on whether a bank was a "holder" when the instruments had been transferred by mere assignment. We held that because the entity that transferred notes to the bank took them by mere assignment and not through indorsement, the entity was not a "holder" and thus could not "negotiate" the notes so as to permit its transferee, the bank, to qualify as a "holder." 222 Va. at 721, 284 S.E.2d at 795-96.

Here, as the defendant argues, the essential components of negotiation were not fulfilled by proper indorsements on the instruments. Simple delivery of the checks to the plaintiff did not give him the status of a "holder," entitling him to the remedies of the U.C.C. The so-called "assignment" did not suffice as a substitute for indorsement. "An indorsement must be written by or on behalf of the holder and on the instrument or on a paper so firmly affixed thereto as to become a part thereof." Former Code § 8.3-202(2) (now repealed).

Consequently, the judgment in favor of the plaintiff will be reversed and final judgment will be entered here in favor of the defendant.

PROBLEM 12.6

The Court apparently decided *Strickler v. Marx* under the former Code. What result today? *See* § 3-301. Who is a "person entitled to enforce" an instrument? Read the Official Comment.

§ 12.04 "In Due Course," as in Holder in Due Course

[A] Requirements—Introduction

Read: U.C.C. § 3-302.

Section 52 of the NIL adopted the contemporary case-law approach to the determination of what characteristics determined a holder in due course. The taker must be a holder who took an instrument (a) complete and regular on its face, (b) before maturity, (c) in good faith, (d) for value, and (e) without notice of a defense or claim. Under the U.C.C., the requirement that the instrument was complete and regular is reduced to a requirement that the instrument does not bear apparent evidence of forgery or alteration or is otherwise so irregular or incomplete as to call into question its authenticity. The requirement of taking before maturity is similarly and properly phrased, under the Code, in terms of a requirement that there be no notice that the instrument is overdue (§ 3-304). Thus, with all of the gloss given the test under the Code sections immediately following U.C.C. § 3-302, the requirements of holding in due course can be reduced to: (a) for value, (b) in good faith, and (c) without notice. It is obvious that the holder in due course is the negotiable instruments version of the bona fide purchaser. One of the "thought-questions" to keep in mind in the following materials is why not simply say that a bona fide purchaser of a negotiable instrument cuts off defenses and claims of recoupment (§ 3-305) or property rights (§ 3-306).

[B] For Value

Read: U.C.C. §§ 3-302(a)(2)(i), 3-303, 4-211, 4-210; see § 3-302(d) and (e); cf. § 1-201(44).

ASIAN INTERNATIONAL, LTD. v. MERRILL LYNCH, PIERCE, FENNER & SMITH, INC.

[The facts and first part of the opinion appear in § 12.03[B], *supra*.]

Value

A person gives "value" for rights if he acquires them in return for the extension of immediately available credit. La RS 10:1-201. Although appellant does not assert that Merrill Lynch did not take the instrument for value, the facts of the case affirmatively show that upon deposit of the check Fort was given immediate credit for $200,000.00, the full amount of the check. Therefore, we find that Merrill Lynch gave value for the instrument.

[See former U.C.C. § 3-303.]

EUROPEAN ASIAN BANK, A.G. v. G. CROHN & CO.

United States Court of Appeals
769 F.2d 93, 41 U.C.C. Rep. 850 (2nd Cir. 1985)

LUMBARD, CIRCUIT JUDGE:

In this diversity case, G. Crohn & Company ("Crohn") appeals from a March 26, 1985 judgment of the Southern District of New York, after a bench trial before Charles L. Brieant, J., granting plaintiff bank recovery of $292,445.42 plus interest on a bill of exchange. Crohn claims 1) that the district court erred in finding that European Asian Bank, A.G. ("Eurasbank") had become a holder in due course when it purchased a bill of exchange from third-party defendant H. Khemchand Kundamal Enterprises (HK), Ltd. ("Kundamal"), and 2) that Crohn had received no valid consideration when it accepted the bill, or, in the alternative, that Crohn should have been relieved of liability anyway due to Kundamal's breach of promised performance. The parties agree that New York law governs this case.

Because we believe that Judge Brieant's finding that Eurasbank gave credit to Kundamal when it purchased the bill of exchange was not clearly erroneous, see Fed. R. Civ. P. 52(a), we agree that Eurasbank became a holder in due course, and thereby was entitled to payment on the bill of exchange regardless of any defenses Crohn might have derived from its agreement with Kundamal. Consequently, we affirm the judgment.

I.

Shlomo Sulimani, Crohn's chief executive officer, had engaged in the diamond business for 46 years, and, since 1962, had traded in Indian diamonds. The Kundamal family, which he had known for 25 years, had purchased some 100 shipment of diamonds from Crohn. In July 1983, in a telephone conversation with Hiro Panjabi, a member of the Kundamal family in Hong Kong, Sulimani agreed to purchase from Kundamal a shipment of full cut and single cut polished Indian diamonds. Kundamal would ship the diamonds from Bombay to New York. At the same time, Panjabi would send Crohn an invoice and a bill of exchange for 645,290 Swiss francs payable to Eurasbank, Kundamal's Hong Kong bank. Sulimani agreed to sign and accept the bill once it arrived and thereby to obligate Crohn to pay Eurasbank the specified amount 180 days after acceptance.

Eurasbank purchased the bill of exchange from Kundamal on July 13, 1983. A Collection Order form from Eurasbank, dated July 13, 1983, shows that Kundamal instructed Eurasbank to apply the amount of the bill to certain "trust receipts" that Kundamal owed to Eurasbank and which the district court found to be antecedent debts. According to these instructions, the bank would give credit to Kundamal's account and retire Kundamal's outstanding debts.

The bank's accounting treatment of the credit given to Kundamal is less than crystal clear. Eurasbank produced as evidence a page from a monthly statement used to report movements in an account. This exhibit indicates that, on July 13, 1983, Eurasbank *credited* Kundamal's account by 645,270 Swiss francs, the full amount of the bill of exchange. An exhibit introduced by Crohn, which shows a similar page from a second monthly statement, indicates that on the same date, Eurasbank *debited* a second Kundamal account in the same amount. Hans Kaebe, manager of the bank's bills department, described this entry as a "bookkeeping requirement."

Six days later, on July 19, 1983, the bank made additional *debits*, totalling the full 645,270 Swiss francs, this time to the "trust receipts" as Kundamal had instructed on the Collection Order form. These debits appear on the monthly statement exhibit introduced into evidence by Eurasbank. However, the "bookkeeping requirement" for these additional debits is not shown in the record. No corresponding credit appears on the second account, and Kaebe testified that the debit in that account has continued through the present.

The diamonds arrived in New York before the invoice and the bill of exchange. Kundamal instructed Eurasbank to direct its New York correspondent bank, Algemene Bank Nederland ("ABN"), to release the diamonds to Crohn upon receipt of the latter's written undertaking to accept later the bill of exchange.

On July 18, 1983, Sulimani, on Crohn's behalf, signed a promissory note payable to ABN in Swiss francs for the same amount as the bill of exchange. This note was intended to serve as a temporary substitute for the bill. Sulimani gave the note to ABN, which released the diamonds.

Two days later, on July 20, 1983, the day after Eurasbank had entered the additional debits in Kundamal's "trust receipt" accounts, Crohn received the diamonds and the invoice. Sulimani inspected the diamonds and immediately rejected them as non-conforming goods. The district court found that the diamonds had half the value that Sulimani had expected.

Sulimani telephoned Hiro Panjabi in Hong Kong. They agreed that Sulimani would return the diamonds to Hiro's brother, Anoop Panjabi, who headed the Kundamal operation in New York. Hiro Panjabi promised to "take care" of the ABN note.

Hiro Panjabi then contacted his brother in New York, and on July 21st the latter gave to Sulimani a promissory note for $305,824.65 (the U.S. dollar equivalent of Crohn's Swiss franc note to ABN) due on January 15, 1984, three days prior to the due date on the ABN note. Anoop Panjabi accepted Crohn's return of the diamonds at that time.

Neither Crohn nor Kundamal informed Eurasbank or ABN that Crohn had returned the diamonds. On or about August 2,1983, ABN presented the bill of exchange to Crohn for acceptance. Sulimani again telephoned Hiro Panjabi who continued to promise to satisfy Kundamal's debts to Eurasbank in Hong Kong if Crohn signed the bill of exchange which was payable to Eurasbank.

About August 6th, Sulimani signed and accepted the bill. Eurasbank still had no knowledge that Crohn had returned the diamonds and did not learn of Crohn's accepting the bill until three months later on November 4, 1983.

Kundamal's promissory note to Crohn was due January 15, 1984. Crohn's payment on the bill of exchange was due the next month on February 6, 1984. Shortly before Kundamal's note matured, Kundamal requested Crohn to extend the due date for sixty days to March 15,1984. Crohn agreed, and received a similar extension from Eurasbank on the bill. Thus, Crohn remained able to collect on Kundamal's promissory note prior to the due date of the bill.

About March 15, 1984, Kundamal failed to honor its promissory note. Crohn, in turn, failed to honor the bill of exchange when it became due.

Although Eurasbank could have reversed the credits it had given to Kundamal, the bank never did reverse the credits. But, even so, reversing the credits would have been futile because in May or June of 1984, Kundamal became insolvent.

II.

We agree with Judge Brieant that Eurasbank became a holder in due course.

The obligor on a bill of exchange may assert against a person who purchases the bill any defenses he may have against the bill's drawer unless the purchaser has the rights of a holder in due course. See N.Y. U.C.C. § 3-306 (McKinney 1964). A holder in due course is a holder who takes the instrument for value, in good faith and without notice that it is overdue or has been dishonored or of any defense against or claim to it on the part of any person. See N.Y. U.C.C. § 3-302(1) (McKinney 1964). The parties do not dispute that Eurasbank took the bill in good faith and without notice of any claims or defenses. Crohn argues only that Eurasbank gave no value.

Judge Brieant found that Eurasbank had given value when it credited Kundamal's account and applied the credit to retire the outstanding balances on Kundamal's antecedent debts, which took the form of "trust receipts." This transaction complied with one of the Uniform Commercial Code's definitions of taking for value which states that "[a] holder takes the instrument for value. . .when he takes the instrument in payment of or as security for an antecedent claim against any person whether or not the claim is due." N.Y. U.C.C. § 3-303(b) (McKinney 1964). A bank can give value by taking a securing interest in an instrument. See N.Y. U.C.C. § 4-209 (McKinney 1964). A bank has taken a security interest "in case of an item deposited in an account to the extent to which credit given for the item has been withdrawn or applied." N.Y. U.C.C. § 4-208(1)(a) (McKinney 1964).

Crohn, however, argues that Eurasbank gave no value when it credited Kundamal's account because it simultaneously debited a second account in the same amount, and thereby immediately reinstated the outstanding obligations. This debit on the second account remains, and was not reversed when Eurasbank later applied the credit to the "trust receipt" accounts.

Judge Brieant concluded that this remaining debit entry, as a "bookkeeping requirement," could have shown "an asset account for an outstanding sight draft," representing the funds Eurasbank could collect from Crohn. Although it would have been preferable for the district court to have had a more complete set of accounting entries with a more explicit explanation of their significance, we find that the evidence is more supportive than not of Judge Brieant's determination. Consequently, we cannot say that his finding that Eurasbank applied the credit to Kundamal's antecedent debts was clearly erroneous. See Fed. R. Civ. P 52(a).

Crohn also argues that Eurasbank gave no value because it applied only a provisional credit to the antecedent debts. Printed language on the reverse of the bank's Collection Order form states that:

> . . .it is understood that such credit is conditional and is subject to collection and receipt by [the bank] of the requisite number of dollars; in the absence of such receipt and collection by [the bank], the undersigned [*i.e.*, Kundamal] will, upon [the bank's] demand reimburse [the bank] for the amount so advanced plus the agreed rate of interest for the time outstanding.

Judge Brieant found that such language made conditional the credit which Eurasbank applied to the antecedent debts. So, Crohn argues that, under *Marine Midland Bank-New York v. Graybar Electric Co.*, 41 N.Y.2d 703, 363 N.E.2d 1139, 395 N.Y.S.2d 403 (1977), which states that "the giving of a provisional credit is not a parting with value under the Uniform Commercial Code," *id.* at 712, 363 N.E.2d at 1145, 395 N.Y.S.2d at 409, Eurasbank should not have been found to be a holder in due course.

The holding in *Marine Midland* does not require us to decide against the bank in this case, because in *Marine Midland*, the bank could reverse the credit at any time, and, in fact did reverse the credit, *id.* at 712, 363 N.E.2d at 1145, 395 N.Y.S.2d at 409, whereas, Eurasbank could not have reversed the credit given to Kundamal until Crohn had defaulted on the bill of exchange.

In *Marine Midland*, a bank withdrew a check deposited into its client's lockbox and unilaterally gave a credit to its client's account which it then applied unilaterally by way of setoff to its client's antecedent debts. Upon forwarding the check to the drawee bank for payment, the bank learned that the client's customer had issued a stop payment on the check. The bank then reversed the credit and reinstated the debts. Meanwhile, the bank's client had filed for bankruptcy. The bank then sued the client's customer for payment and argued that it had become a holder in due course when it applied the credit to its client's antecedent debts. See *id.* at 706-707, 363 N.E.2d at 1144, 395 N.Y.S.2d at 405-406.

Because the bank in *Marine Midland* could and did reverse the credit, it had neither bound itself to accept the credit risk of its client's customer nor "made available" to its client the benefits of the credit. "Under this analysis the bank is in no worse position than any other creditor," the Court of Appeals observed, "and the bank's unilateral agreement to take the credit for the indebtedness, conditioned on payment of the check for which the credit was given, is recognized for what it was—an attempt to recoup its losses." 41 N.Y.2d at 713, 363 N.E.2d at 1146, 395 N.Y.S.2d at 410.

Unlike the bank in *Marine Midland*, Eurasbank did not unilaterally apply the credit to Kundamal's outstanding obligations. Indeed, Kundamal had expressly instructed the bank to use the credit in that manner. The printed language on the back of the Collection Order form does not say that Eurasbank had a unilateral right to reverse the entries at any time. At best, the language suggests that Kundamal's customer's default on the bill of exchange was a condition precedent to the bank's seeking recourse against the bill's drawer, Kundamal. In this context, the printed language merely expressed the rights which Eurasbank already would have been able to exercise under the Uniform Commercial Code. See N.Y. U.C.C. § 3-413(2) (McKinney 1964) (unless drawing without recourse, drawer remains liable for payment on dishonored draft); N.Y. U.C.C. § 3-507(2) (McKinney 1964) ("holder has upon dishonor an immediate right of recourse against drawers or indorsers"). Under provisions which seek to protect transferees and to encourage commercial transactions, it would make little sense if, to become a holder in due course, a transferee must discharge the transferor's obligation.

In essence, to become a holder in due course by applying a credit to antecedent debts, the holder must have agreed to expose itself to the credit risk of the party obligated on the instrument taken in payment of the antecedent debts. As the bank in *Marine Midland*, when it first extended the credits, retained the right unilaterally to reverse the credits, it had refrained from exposing itself to the credit risk of its client's customer. Thus, the position of the bank in *Marine Midland* did not necessitate according it full protection under the Uniform Commercial Code's provisions for a holder in due course. See § 3-303 Official Comment 3. Had the bank learned that the item was not likely to be paid, it would not have had to sue on the instrument but could have rescinded the transaction at will. See *id.*

In contrast, Eurasbank did replace Kundamal with Crohn as the primary party to whom it looked to repay the debts originally owed by Kundamal. Had Eurasbank learned that the Crohn-Kundamal deal had gone amiss, it could not have revoked the credits at will, but still would have to wait for Crohn's default, and thereby incur further risk of non-payment by either Crohn or Kundamal.

By applying a credit, which Eurasbank could not reverse at will, to reduce antecedent debts, Eurasbank's transaction had the same practical effect, on the question of its being a holder in due course, as if the bank had made the credit available for "withdrawal as of right," see N.Y. U.C.C. § 4-208(1)(b) (McKinney 1964); N.Y. U.C.C. § 4-213(4) (McKinney 1964), and thereby gave the right to Kundamal, itself, to draw down upon the credit and to apply the proceeds to retire the "trust receipts."

As we agree with the district court that Eurasbank became a holder in due course and is entitled to payment from Crohn regardless of Crohn's defenses, see N.Y. U.C.C. § 3-305 (McKinney 1964), we need not consider whether there is any merit to those defenses.

Crohn must be content with what relief it may obtain from Judge Brieant's default judgment in Crohn's favor against Kundamal.

Affirmed.

NOTES AND QUESTIONS

(1) Payee indorses and deposits a check to its account in bank. When will bank have given value for the check? If bank allows payee to withdraw the funds relating to the check it will have paid value. To determine when payee has withdrawn the funds the U.C.C. adopts the "first in, first out" rule. A bank gives value for purposes of holder in due course to the extent that it has a security interest in the item and it has a security interest when credit is given for the deposited item has been withdrawn using a FIFO rule. *See* U.C.C. §§ 4-210(a)(1) and (b), 4-211.

(2) Negotiable instruments are generally purchased at a discount. Even though the discount may be quite large, the purchaser has nonetheless given value. There may be inquiry into the

amount of value paid for a particular note where the disparity between the sum paid and the face value of the instrument raises a question of the good faith of the purchaser. Generally, it is no bar to holding in due course that one purchases knowing that the maker is insolvent. A holder is a holder in due course to the extent that he gives value where he has not given all of the contracted-for value.

Suppose that note has face value of $1000, and is sold to a holder in due course for $900, but the latter pays only $300 of the $900. What is the holder in due course's interest in the instrument? There are two measures which give different results.

Amount test	Percent test
Holder has paid $300 in Actual amount and this is his interest.	Holder has paid $300 of the $900 due, or one-third. Therefore, one-third of $1000 is $333.33 which is his interest.

Under former U.C.C. § 3-303, it was not clear which should be used; a number of courts used the "amount test;" a few used the "percent test." The revisions use the latter. *See* U.C.C. § 3-302(d) and Comment 6, Case #6.

(3) A matter of some consequence to you personally, as an attorney, was raised in *O.P. Ganjo, Inc. v. Tri-Urban Realty Co.*, 108 N.J. Super. 517, 261 A.2d 722 (1969). The Court stated:

> Under N.J. S.A. 12A: 3-303(a) "A holder takes the instrument for value (a) to the extent that the agreed consideration has been performed. . . ." Official comment 3 emphasizes that "an executory promise to give value is not itself value. . . ." I find no New Jersey authority directly in point. In *Korzenik v. Supreme Radio, Inc.*, 347 Mass. 309, 197 N.E.2d 702 (Sup. Jud. Ct. 1964), plaintiff attorney received two notes "as a retainer for legal services to be performed." Plaintiff's client had obtained them by means of fraud in the inducement which would not constitute a valid defense against a holder in due course. Massachusetts' highest court ruled that a retainer is an executory promise to give value, and therefore plaintiff failed to satisfy this holder in due course requisite. However, as one legal commentator has noted, "though the plaintiff under Section 3-303(a) might have given value to the extent that he had actually performed the executory promise and *thus have been a holder in due course to that extent*, he failed to prove how much value five days' work represented." Willier and Hart, Bender's Uniform Commercial Code Service, Case Annotations (1969). *See* U.C.C. § 3-303(a)(1), 3-302(d).

[C] Before Maturity

Read: U.C.C. §§ 3-302(a)(2)(iii); 3-304.

RICHARDSON v. GIRNER

Arkansas Supreme Court
282 Ark. 302, 668 S.W.2d 523 (1984)

PURTLE, JUSTICE.

The trial court dismissed appellant's suit against appellees for collection of a $5,000 promissory note. The court held that the appellant was not a holder in due course and took the note by assignment subject to the defense of set-off by the makers against an intervening assignee.

Appellant argues: 1) the trial court erred in finding appellant was not a holder in due course; 2) the court erred in finding that appellant took the note without the rights of a holder in due course, and; 3) it was error to refuse to bar the appellees' set-off claim. We disagree with all three arguments.

The appellee executed a $5,000 promissory note to First Realty Corporation on September 25, 1980. Monthly payments on the note were to commence on January 15, 1981. A schedule was printed on the back of the note. The note was assigned by First Realty to Imran Bohra in exchange for property. On July 27, 1981, Bohra transferred the note to his attorney, F. Eugene Richardson, in payment for legal services rendered by Richardson. Prior to this assignment, appellees filed suit against Bohra for an accounting and for default on the purchase of certain properties. The chancery court entered a decree against Bohra in favor of the appellees on April 26, 1982. On July 27, 1981, when appellant took the promissory note in assignment for legal services there was no entry of any payment on the back of the note.

The primary issue before us is whether appellant took the note without notice that it was overdue or was otherwise subject to defense on the part of any holder prior to appellant. Arkansas Stat. Ann. § 85-3-302 (Add. 1961), defines a holder in due course to be one who in good faith takes an instrument for value and without notice that it is overdue or has been dishonored or is subject to any defense against or claim to it on the part of any person. The facts in this case clearly reveal that at the time appellant acquired the note no payments had been entered in the schedule on the back of the note. Six payments should have been made at the time of the transfer to appellant. Appellant found out during the meeting with Bohra, at the time of the assignment, that the note was past due. Appellant argues that the note was not declared to be in default until after he contacted the maker. It is not necessary to have the holder of the note declare that it is in default when this fact is obvious in other ways. Unless a person is a holder in due course the note is subject to all valid claims to it on the part of any person, and all defenses, counterclaims and set-offs. Arkansas Stat. Ann. § 85-3-306 (Add.1961).

QUESTIONS

What result under U.C.C. § 3-304(b)(1)?

What is the basis for requiring that before one can become a holder in due course he must take the instrument without notice that it is overdue?

What is the basis for the distinction in § 3-304(c) between default in the payment of principal and default in the payment of interest? *See* Official Comment 2.

[D] In Good Faith and Without Notice

Read: U.C.C. §§ 3-302(a)((1) and (2)(ii) and (iv)-(vi)), (b), (c)(ii) and (f); § 3-103(a)(4)(1)(7); § 3-307; see §§ 1-201(25)-(27), 3-103(a)(4).

FUNDING CONSULTANTS, INC. v. AETNA CASUALTY & SURETY CO.

Connecticut Supreme Court
447 A.2d 1163, 34 U.C.C. Rep. 591 (1982)

PETERS, J.

In this suit on a promissory note, the dispositive issue is whether a maker of a note may introduce expert testimony to challenge the good faith of a person seeking to enforce the note as a holder in due course. The plaintiff, Funding Consultants, Inc., brought an action, initially only against the defendant Aetna Casualty and Surety Co., Inc., but ultimately also against the defendant Benjamin C. Preisner,[11] as co-makers of a promissory note in the amount of $68,000. Aetna Casualty, in the interim, had impleaded Preisner by a third party complaint alleging that Aetna Casualty as surety was entitled to indemnification from Preisner if Aetna Casualty were held liable to Funding Consultants. See General Statutes § 52-102a; Practice Book § 117. After a trial to a jury, judgments were rendered in favor of the plaintiff against both defendants, and in favor of the third party plaintiff against the third party defendant. Only the appeal of Preisner as defendant and third party defendant is being pursued in this court.[12]

The present action is a suit on a promissory note which was given to Paul King, Jr. in connection with the 1974 sale of the Paul King, Jr. Insurance Company to the defendant Preisner. On this note, hereinafter the Preisner note, Preisner and Aetna Casualty were co-makers, although Aetna Casualty's status was that of an accommodation party for Preisner. The Preisner note was a $68,000 non-interest bearing negotiable instrument calling for four equal installments to be paid annually beginning on November 1, 1975, and ending on November 1, 1978.

King sold the Preisner note to the plaintiff Funding Consultants, Inc. on January 18, 1975, for $5000 cash and a promissory note. This note, hereinafter the Funding note, was a $35,000 noninterest bearing negotiable instrument calling for four equal installments to be paid at bi-monthly intervals beginning on March 20, 1975, and ending on September 20, 1975.

The defendant Preisner, after formal demand, refused to make any payments on the Preisner note because, he alleged, the execution of the note had been induced by fraudulent misrepresentations about the financial condition of the Paul King, Jr. Insurance Company. The plaintiff Funding Consultants thereupon, on December 1, 1975, in reliance upon an acceleration clause contained

[11] The substituted complaint is, on its face, ambiguous in its designation of the parties defendant. In its opening paragraph it describes only Aetna Casualty as a defendant, while in another paragraph it alleges notification of "the defendants." The record as a whole, however, makes it clear that the substituted complaint made Preisner a co-defendant. The parties at trial and on this appeal have treated Preisner as a co-defendant, and the judgment rendered on the plaintiff's complaint awards the plaintiff a recovery against "the defendants" Aetna Casualty and Preisner. Preisner's status as co-defendant is not affected by the fact that he was made a party by the plaintiff pursuant to the provisions of General Statutes § 52-102a and Practice Book § 117.

[12] The defendant Aetna Casualty took a timely appeal from the judgment rendered against it, but withdrew that appeal before this case was heard for oral argument. Insofar as Preisner is appealing from the judgment against him on the substituted complaint, his status as co-defendant allows pursuit of his appeal even though Aetna Casualty has withdrawn. The extent to which Preisner is appealing from the judgment on the third party complaint is more perplexing. No separate issue has been raised in the briefs concerning Preisner's obligation to indemnify Aetna Casualty. At the trial, the parties stipulated that any judgment against Aetna Casualty would also be a judgment against Preisner. We will assume, for the purposes of this appeal, that our resolution of the issues arising pursuant to the underlying complaint will serve to resolve the appeal concerning the third party complaint.

in the Preisner note, declared the whole amount of that note to be then due and payable. This litigation ensued.[13]

At the trial, the plaintiff sought to recover on the Preisner note as a holder in due course. Only a holder in due course may enforce a negotiable instrument without regard to the maker's assertion of a personal defense such as fraud in the inducement. General Statutes § 42a-3-305(2); see E. Peters, A Negotiable Instruments Primer (2d Ed 1974) § I, pp 33-34; White & Summers, Uniform Commercial Code (2d Ed 1980) § 14-9. Evidence of the existence of a personal defense does, however, shift to the holder of the instrument the burden of proving his due course status. General Statutes § 42a-3-307(3); cf. *Hartford National Bank & Trust Co. v. Credenza*, 119 Conn 368, 370, 177A 132 (1935) (under pre-Uniform Commercial Code law); see Peters, op. cit., § J, p 34. That burden requires the holder to prove his taking of the instrument "(a) for value; and (b) in good faith; and (c) without notice that it is overdue or has been dishonored or of any defense against or claim to it on the part of any person." General Statutes § 42a-3-302; see Peters, loc. cit.; White & Summers, op. cit., § 14-6.

In order to establish its due course status, the plaintiff relied on the testimony of its president, Richard R. Splain. When the good faith of the plaintiff's purchase was put into issue, Splain testified that he had little knowledge about or experience in the purchase of negotiable instruments.[14] The defendant sought to counter this testimony by offering, as an expert witness, Michael Schaeffer of the Connecticut Bank & Trust Company to testify that the plaintiff had given inadequate consideration for its purchase of the Preisner note. Such testimony would furnish some evidence, according to the defendant, that Splain had testified untruthfully about the good faith of the plaintiff's purchase. The plaintiff objected to admission of the testimony as irrelevant and prejudicial. After a hearing, the trial court sustained the plaintiffs objection on the ground of prejudice.

The case was submitted to the jury with one special interrogatory. In response to that interrogatory, the jury found the plaintiff to be a holder in due course with respect to the Preisner note. The defendant's appeal has assigned the exclusion of the expert testimony as error.[15]

The disagreement of the parties on this appeal is a narrow one. On the one hand, the defendant concedes that the standard of good faith under the Uniform Commercial Code is, as it was under the prior Negotiable Instruments Law, a subjective standard. "Good faith," as used in General Statutes § 42a-3-302(l)(b), is defined in General Statutes § 42a-1-201(19) as "honesty in fact

[13] It is of passing interest to note that the record reveals that the Funding note equally fell into immediate default. On March 20,1975, before the due date of the first installment of the Preisner note, the plaintiff informed King that the payment schedule on the Funding note was being readjusted to coincide with the payment schedule on the Preisner note, so that "[i]f payment is not received on your note, no payments will be made by Funding Consultants, Inc." The Funding note in turn was assigned by King to five insurance companies to whom he was indebted. These insurance companies subsequently recovered a judgment on the Funding note against the plaintiff in the amount of $48,071.47. *Middlesex Mutual Ins. Co. v. Funding Consultants, Inc.*, Superior Court Judicial District of New Haven, Docket No. 145988. In the present litigation, in order to collect on that judgment, the five insurance companies were permitted to intervene as additional parties plaintiff.

[14] Since the parties have certified only part of the transcript to this court, we do not know what other evidence to prove or to disprove the plaintiff's good faith was before the jury. Although the plaintiff's default on its own negotiable promissory note would not impair its capacity to be a holder for value; see General Statutes § 42a-3-303(c); its early repudiation of that note might be some indication of notice of a defense on the Preisner note.

[15] In the alternative, the defendant has also assigned as error a procedural irregularity in the amendment of the jury's verdict.

in the conduct or transaction concerned." Both the language of other sections of the Code[16] and the Code's drafting history[17] incontrovertibly demonstrate that this standard is one that imposes no duty of due care on the holder. The test is honesty in fact rather than negligence. On the other hand, the plaintiff does not dispute that application of this test calls for the factfinder to determine the inferences appropriately to be drawn from all of the evidence, including testimony "regarding the relationship between the plaintiff and the [transferor of the negotiable instrument], and the circumstances surrounding the purchase of this paper. . .." A defendant who wishes to overcome the plaintiffs own testimony in support of its good faith perforce must introduce evidence to contradict the plaintiff's assertions of honesty in fact. See *Favors v. Yaffe*, 605 SW2d 342, 345 (Tex Civ App 1980).

The issue that does divide the parties, here as in the trial court, is what evidence is admissible to test the holder's subjective good faith. In order to decide whether a holder of an instrument acted in good faith, the trier of fact must determine the intent or state of mind of the party concerned. As in other determinations concerning intent, the trier is entitled to consider not only the testimony of the interested party but also evidence of surrounding circumstances that interentially illuminate his honesty in fact in view of his actual knowledge. "Although mere negligence or failure to make the inquiries which a reasonably prudent person would make does not of itself amount to bad faith, if a party fails to make an inquiry for the purpose of remaining ignorant of facts which he believes or fears would disclose a defect in the transaction, he may be found to have acted in bad faith." Similarly, if a party pays for an instrument an amount far less than its face value, such evidence is a factor that a trier may reasonably consider in weighing whether a purchase was made in good faith. The sale of an instrument at a substantial discount may in fact have alerted a prospective purchaser to a possible defense to which he may not willfully close his eyes. See 2 F. Hart & W. Willier, Commercial Paper under the Uniform Commercial Code § 11.04, pp 11-21 through 11-22 (1982). We therefore hold that the defendant was entitled to introduce evidence in this case to show that there was such inadequacy of

[16] Compare, in Article 3, General Statutes § 42a-3-406, which requires a payor to pay an instrument "in good faith and in accordance with the reasonable commercial standards of the drawee's or payor's business." Compare, in Article 2, General Statutes § 42a-2-103(1)(b), which requires a merchant to satisfy a standard of good faith which means "honesty in fact and the observance of reasonable commercial standards of fair dealing in the trade." Good faith is similarly elaborated to include not only honesty in fact but also observance of reasonable commercial standards in provisions of Articles 7 and 8 concerning a bailee's dealings with documents of title; General Statutes § 42a-7-404; and an agent's dealings with investment securities. General Statutes § 42a-8-318. Since the recurrent insistence, in these other sections of the Uniform Commercial Code, on the additional requirement of"observance of reasonable commercial standards" cannot be disregarded as surplusage, good faith alone cannot properly be read to include such a requirement.

[17] The Uniform Commercial Code, although officially promulgated by the American Law Institute and the National Conference of Commissioners on Uniform State Laws in 1951, continued thereafter to undergo drafting revisions. In 1952, the proposed Uniform Commercial Code required in § 3-302(l) (b) that a holder in due course take a negotiable instrument "in good faith including observance of the reasonable commercial standards of any business in which the holder may be engaged." American Law Institute, Uniform Commercial Code, 1952 Official Text Edition. Four years later, the language "including . . .engaged" was deleted, with a comment that the intent of the deletion was "to make clear that the doctrine of an objective standard of good faith, exemplified by the case of *Gill v. Cubitt*, 3 B & C 466 (1824), is not intended to be incorporated in Article 3." American Law Institute, Uniform Commercial Code, 1956 Recommendations, p 103. See White & Summers, Uniform Commercial Code (2d Ed 1980) § 14-6.

consideration that this factor, among others, should have been weighed by the jury in its determination of the plaintiffs good faith.[18]

Even if evidence of inadequacy of consideration is generally admissible, the question still remains whether the particular evidence offered by this defendant was sufficiently probative so that it should not have been excluded. The plaintiff had bought a $68,000 noninterest bearing note. The expert testimony was offered by the defendant to show what a commercial bank would have paid for the Preisner note and what the effective rate of return on the plaintiff's investment would have been. It is not an answer to this offer of proof that the plaintiff's president had testified about his inexperience with the purchase of negotiable paper and his ignorance of the practices and procedures of commercial banks. The jury might have chosen to disregard some or all of this testimony. The expert's evidence would have provided the jury with some basis for assessing the present value of both the Preisner note and the Funding note. It is not unreasonable to offer a lay jury expert assistance in the proper calculation of values that are not obvious on the face of the instruments to be compared. The proffered evidence was relevant because it would have enabled the jury to make a more accurate assessment of whether the plaintiff took the Preisner note in good faith.

The trial court's decision to exclude the expert testimony impliedly agreed with the defendant that the testimony would have been relevant since the court made its determination on the ground that the testimony was too prejudicial to be admissible. The only basis advanced by the plaintiff for the finding of prejudice is the argument that evidence about mathematical projections by a commercial bank would unfairly bring into play the objective criteria of good faith which the Uniform Commercial Code has repudiated. As we have noted above, there is no inherent inconsistency between a subjective standard of good faith and a reasonable inquiry into the actual known circumstances surrounding a purchase of negotiable paper. The price actually paid, the present value of the instrument actually bought, are elements which may be considered in determining a holder's good faith. Although in most instances admission of expert testimony and questions of relevancy and prejudice rest within the sound discretion of the trial court, in this case the court's action was clearly erroneous. Because exclusion of the expert testimony kept admissible evidence from the jury, the defendant is entitled to a new trial.

Having decided that the trial court's evidentiary ruling requires a new trial on the merits, we need not address the defendant's alternate ground of appeal. That issue concerned an alleged procedural irregularity in the formal amendment of the jury's verdict. Since such an irregularity is unlikely to recur on retrial, we need not consider its consequences.

There is error, the judgment is set aside, and the case is remanded for a new trial in accordance with this opinion.

NOTES AND QUESTIONS

(1) U.C.C. § 3-103(a)(4) adds "the observance of reasonable commercial standards of fair dealing" to the definition of "good faith" as found in Article 1, the definition applicable to former Article 3. Could we say that the more things change, the more they remain the same"

---

[18] We note that other courts have critically examined allegations of good faith, especially when the holder of a promissory note seeks to enforce that note against a consumer. See *Unico v. Owen*, 50 NJ 101,116, 232 A.2d 405 (1967); Gilmore, *The Good Faith Purchase Idea and the Uniform Commercial Code: Confessions of a Repentant Draftsman*, 15 Ga L Rev 605, 619(1981); White & Summers, Uniform Commercial Code (2d Ed 1980) § 14-8. Although the present transaction does not involve a consumer debtor, it does involve the unitary purchase of a negotiable promissory note rather than the commercial transfer of large numbers of banking items such as checks. Cf. Gilmore, *Formalism and the Law of Negotiable Instruments,* 13 Creighton L Rev 441 (1979).

(2) Do you believe Justice Peters thought she was citing primary authority when she cited A Negotiable Instruments Primer by E. Peters?

PROBLEM 12.7

Your firm advises the Second National Bank which wishes to know the effect of the new "good faith" standard in the Code. Should it do anything in regard to these so as to be more certain of following the law and avoiding liability?

SEINFELD v. COMMERCIAL BANK & TRUST CO.

Florida District Court of Appeal
405 So. 2d 1039, 32 U.C.C. Rep. 1137 (1981)

SCHWARTZ, JUDGE.

In unjustified reliance on the representations of a lady friend named Rachel Wolfson that they would not be negotiated, Barry Seinfeld gave her three checks, totalling $160,000, payable to the order of Wolfson's corporation, Yahalomit, Inc. Predictably enough, Wolfson almost immediately deposited the checks to the corporate account at the Commercial Bank & Trust Co., the present appellee. Although that account was then in an overdraft position of some $57,000, Wolfson requested that the checks be given immediate clearance. This was granted at once, notwithstanding that Commercial had no prior acquaintance with Seinfeld, and did not ask Seinfeld's bank, Great American, the status of the account upon which the checks were drawn, an inquiry which would have revealed a balance of about $2,000. Commercial then credited the overdrawn balance and permitted Wolfson to make additional withdrawals against the checks in the total sum of $157,402.09. When the checks were dishonored by Great American for insufficient funds, Commercial sued Seinfeld for that amount plus interest, alleging that it had become a holder in due course of the instruments. Seinfeld's amended answer denied this and asserted his non-liability on the checks essentially on the ground of fraud in the inducement.[19] This appeal is from a summary final judgment entered in the bank's favor. We reverse on a holding that the bank did not carry its required statutory and procedural burden conclusively to establish its status as a holder in due course with the consequent right to recover on the checks as a matter of law.

When the summary judgment was entered the trial court had before it Seinfeld's affidavit and deposition which basically described the circumstances under which he wrote the checks and the status of his bank account. On the other side, the bank supported its motion with a single affidavit, that of Robert Singleton, the vice-president in charge of operations at the branch office where Wolfson's account was located. The affidavit recounted the series of events concerning

[19] It is clear that fraud in the inducement is a personal defense of the maker which is not available against a holder in due course. Section 673.305, Florida Statutes (1979).

the presentation, immediate clearance and crediting of the checks which has been described. As to the bank's knowledge of the surrounding circumstances and its own role in the transactions, Singleton, who was not shown to have met with Wolfson or otherwise to have personally participated in the decision-making process, stated only,

Affiant, upon personal knowledge, as well as information and belief states that between June 13, 1980 and June 19, 1980, the Bank had no knowledge, nor was it put on notice by any third party that the subject checks would not be honored upon presentment; that any person, including the maker, had any defense or claim against the payee effecting the validity or enforceability of the subject instruments; and the Bank at all times acted and intended to act honestly and in good faith with respect to the instruments in question.

This portion of the affidavit was obviously an attempt to track the statutory requisites of a holder in due course[20] that he take the instrument "in good faith," § 673.302(1)(b), Florida Statutes (1979)—which is in turn defined as "honesty in fact in the conduct or transaction concerned," § 671.201(19)—and "without notice. . ..of any defense against or claim to it on the part of any person." Section 673.302(l)(c).[21]

As the party claiming that it was a holder in due course, the bank had the burden affirmatively to establish that this was the case. Section 673.307(3), Florida Statutes (1979). In moving for summary judgment on that issue, moreover, it was required conclusively to establish the nonexistence of a genuine issue of material fact, *Holl v. Talcott*, 191 So 2d 40 (Fla 1966), concerning its good faith in paying on the instruments and lack of notice of Seinfeld's defenses to them. It is clear that the general statements in the affidavit, which are framed in terms only of conclusions of law, do not satisfy that burden. In addition, since as the bank correctly contends, the issue of both "good faith," see *Baraban v. Manatee National Bank of Bradenton*, 212 So 2d 341 (Fla 2d DCA 1968); and lack of notice, § 671.201(25) Florida Statutes (1979) are based upon the bank's subjective knowledge and state of mind, the failure to submit the testimony of those employees who actually dealt with Wolfson concerning these facts made it impossible, on the face of the matter, for the movant to sustain its position on these questions.

Furthermore, while we might agree with the bank that, standing alone, neither its indulgence of a chronically overdrawn depositor, *St. Cloud National Bank & Trust Co. v. Sobania Construction Co., Inc.*, 302 Minn 71, 224 NW2d 746 (1974) nor its failure to observe the normal commercial practices of waiting for the checks to clear and determining the balance in Seinfeld's account before paying on them might not have been sufficient evidence of "bad faith," see *Frantz v. First National Bank of Anchorage* [584 P2d 1125 (Alaska 1978)]; *Exchange National Bank of Winter Haven v. Beshara*, 236 So 2d 198 (Fla 2d DCA 1970), the coexistence of all these factors raises at least a reasonable inference that the bank acted as precipitately and "foolishly" as it did in order to attempt to shift to Seinfeld its own probable loss from Wolfson's machinations—an intent and motivation which demonstrate the antithesis of good faith. It is true that the Florida version of the holder in due course provision of the U.C.C. does seem to protect the objectively stupid so long as he is subjectively pure of heart.[22] See *Frantz v. First National*

[20] Section 673.302(1) provides in its entirety:. . .

[21] The third requirement, that a holder take the instrument "for value," § 673.302(1)(a), was clearly satisfied by the bank's payments and credits upon the checks, even though they were initially taken for collection. Sections 674.208(1)(a), 674.209, Florida Statutes (1979); *Exchange National Bank of Winter Haven v. Beshara*, 236 So 2d 198 (Fla 2d DCA 1970).

[22] The notion of a bank as Parsifal may strike one as the quintessential paradox.

Bank of Anchorage, supra; J. White & R. Summers, Uniform Commercial Code § 14-6 (2d ed 1980); compare, *Potter Bank & Trust Co. v. Massey*, 11 Misc 2d 523, 171 NYS2d 27 (Sup Ct 1958) (applying original U.C.C. § 3-302(1)(b) requirement of "good faith *including observance of the reasonable commercial standards of any business in which the holder may be engaged.*") But playing dumb is not the same as being dumb. A mere protestation of one's own innocence is not enough conclusively to demonstrate that this is really true when the trier of fact could find from the admitted circumstances that something more than simple mindedness lay behind the conduct in question.

Surely, the "circumstances of the holder's taking the checks were [not] free of all doubt" so as to permit the summary disposition rendered below. It is therefore reversed and the cause remanded for further consistent proceedings.

NOTE AND QUESTION

While it is said that under former U.C.C. we had a "subjective" test of good faith (sometimes referred to as "white heart and empty head") and now we have an "objective" test ("red lights ahead"), would this conceptual distinction make much difference if the litigant claiming to be a holder in due course couldn't get a motion for summary judgment granted?

ASIAN INTERNATIONAL, LTD. v. MERRILL LYNCH, PIERCE, FENNER AND SMITH, INC.

[The facts and the first part of the opinion appear in § 12.03[B], *supra*, and § 12.04[B], *supra*.]

Good Faith

Good faith is defined as honesty in fact in the conduct or transaction concerned. La RS 10:1-201. Good faith is determined on a reasonableness standard, in that the facts must be such as would necessarily put a reasonable person on inquiry to ascertain the true facts.

Appellant contends that Merrill Lynch was not in good faith when it took the instrument because of the questionable corporate authority of Smith and McCallum to endorse the check on behalf of Asian.[23] Although these allegations may be pertinent as between the immediate parties (Smith, McCallum, and Asian), they do not affect third parties who take the instrument because the signatures are presumed to be authorized. La RS 10:3-307(1) (b). Appellant, however, offered no facts to prove that Merrill Lynch lacked the requisite good faith at the time it took the instrument. The deposition of a Merrill Lynch employee, however, reveals that the check was taken by Merrill Lynch in good faith, and there is no controverting evidence in the record. Therefore, we find that Merrill Lynch took the instrument in good faith.

[23] Appellant argues that presentment of the check to Merrill Lynch without an accompanying corporate resolution, in light of the fact that such was standard practice in the industry, adversely affected Merrill Lynch's good faith. However, Title 10 of the Louisiana Revised Statutes imposes no such duty.

Without Notice of Claims or Defenses

La RS 10:1-201 provides that: [the Court cites U.C.C. § 1-201(25)].

Appellant alleges no particular facts, other than lack of authority of Smith and McCallum as officers of Asian to endorse checks, that Merrill Lynch had notice of existing claims or defenses. However, when the effectiveness of a signature is put at issue, the signature is presumed to be authorized and does not affect third parties who take the instrument. La RS 10:3-307(1)(b); La RS 10:3-403. Appellant asserted no other facts to prove that Merrill Lynch knew or should have known that a claim or defense existed. Merrill Lynch established by uncontroverted testimony that it took the $200,000.00 check with no notice of any claim or defense. Therefore, we find that Merrill Lynch took the check without notice of any claim or defense to the check on the part of any person.

The trial court held, and we agree, that Merrill Lynch took the instrument as a good faith holder, for value, and without notice of any claim to it and that Merrill Lynch is a holder in due course, entitled to judgment as a matter of law.

QUESTION

Did the former Code provide for a definition of "good faith" that was "determined on a reasonableness standard, in that the facts must be such as would necessarily put a reasonable person on inquiry to ascertain the true facts?"

ARCANUM NATIONAL BANK v. HESSLER

Ohio Supreme Court
433 N.E.2d 204, 33 U.C.C. Rep. 604 (1982)

Appeal from the Court of Appeals for Darke County.

Appellant, Kenneth Hessler, was in the business of raising hogs for the John Smith Grain Company. John Smith Grain Company or J & J Farms, Inc., would deliver hogs to appellant and require appellant to sign a promissory note payable to John Smith Grain Company to cover the cost of the hogs and feed. Without the knowledge or consent of appellant, John Smith Grain Company would then sell the note to appellee, Arcanum National Bank. Appellee would credit the John Smith Grain Company with the face amount of the note and open a commercial loan account for appellant. The first such transaction, according to the bank's records, was August 28, 1974. The hogs were usually sold by J & J Farms, Inc. to Producer's Livestock Association, and a portion of the proceeds were applied to satisfy appellant's note and loan account. Appellant received a flat fee and a share of the net profits.

On January 4, 1977, appellant signed a promissory note payable to John Smith Grain Company for hogs delivered on that date. J & J Farms, Inc. had previously mortgaged the hogs to Producer's

Livestock Association. Accordingly, in its separate findings of fact and conclusions of law, the trial court found appellant received no consideration for the note.

Appellant signed his name and was advised by C. North, Jr., an officer and director of both John Smith Grain Company and J & J Farms, Inc., to sign his wife's name, Carla Hessler, on the note; appellant then placed his initials U.C.C., after her name. John Smith Grain Company as payee assigned this note to appellee, Arcanum National Bank.

In early 1977, Producer's Livestock Association took the hogs from appellant's farm because of the serious financial difficulties of John Smith Grain Company. John Smith Grain Company was later placed in receivership, and no funds were available to pay appellee bank for appellant's note.

Appellee bank sued appellant and Carla Hessler in the Common Pleas Court of Darke County to collect the face amount of the note, viz., $ 16,800. Appellee's motion to dismiss Carla Hessler was granted.

Also in the separate findings of fact and conclusions of law, the trial court found the relationship between appellee bank, John Smith Grain Company and J & J Farms, Inc. was not an arm's length relationship. Appellee bank supplied John Smith Grain Company with blank note forms, provided the company with the interest rate to be charged, and customarily purchased the company's commercial paper. At the time it purchased appellant's first note, appellee bank ran its own credit check on appellant. The president of John Smith Grain Company, H.K. Smith, was also one of appellee bank's directors. An officer and director of John Smith Grain Company, C. North, Jr., was also an officer and director of J & J Fais, Inc. During the period between November, 1976 and January, 1977, at the time appellant signed the note, the executive vice-president of appellee bank, B. Henninger, was visiting John Smith Grain Company several times a week to advise the officers on business practices. During that time, John Smith Grain Company's financial condition was failing.

The trial court held appellee was a holder in due course of the note, and appellant's defense of want of consideration could not be asserted against appellee. The Court of Appeals affirmed.

This cause is now before this court pursuant to the allowance of a motion to certify the record.

KRUPANSKY, J.

The sole issue in this case is whether appellee is a holder in due course who takes the note free from appellant's defense of want of consideration.

I.

Appellant contends appellee has not established holder in due course status because appellee took the instrument with notice of a defense against it. We agree.

The requirement that the purchaser take the instrument without notice of a claim or defense in order to qualify as a holder in due course is explained, under the heading of "Notice to Purchaser," at RC § 1303.33 (U.C.C. § 3-304), which provides in relevant part: [the Court cites U.C.C. § 3-304(1)(a)].

Whether a transferee has taken an instrument with notice of a defense depends upon all the facts and circumstances of a particular situation and is generally a question of fact to be determined by the trier of fact. One situation when a bank was denied holder in due course status was found in *First National Bank of Linton v. Otto Huber and Sons, Inc.*, 394 F Supp 1284

(DC SD 1975). This case held the bank had notice of a defense because of an ambiguity involving the due date; the note was considered irregular on its face. Similarly, when a transferee receives a note which is blank except for the maker's signature, the note is irregular on its face. The transferee takes with notice of a defense and is therefore not a holder in due course of the note.

In the case sub judice, the trial court, sitting as fact finder, weighed the evidence of the relationship between appellee and appellants and reasoned: "The defect on the promissory note is that the signature of Carla Hessler was added by Kenneth Hessler and, since the Arcanum National Bank handled the Hesslers' personal finances,[24] it should have noticed that there was a defect on the face of the instrument. . . . The note also bears the initials 'K.H.' indicating that Kenneth Hessler had signed Carla Hessler's name." Accordingly, the trial court specifically found "this 'irregularity' does call into question the validity of the note, the terms of the note, the ownership of the note or create an ambiguity as to the party who is to pay the note." Thus, the trial court, while specifically finding appellee took the note with notice of a defense, nonetheless erroneously held appellee bank qualified as a holder in due course.

We hold, therefore, when the trier of fact finds a transferee took a note with notice of a defense, the legal conclusion which follows from such finding is the transferee cannot benefit from holder in due course status and the maker may assert all valid defenses. Since the fact finder in this case specifically found appellee bank took the note with notice of a defense, appellee cannot qualify as a holder in due course.

II.

Appellant also contends, in essence, appellee bank failed in its burden of proving holder in due course status because appellee failed to establish it took the note in good faith as required under RC § 1303.31(A)(2) [UCC § 3-302(1)(b)].

"Good faith" is defined as "honesty in fact in the conduct or transaction concerned." RC § 1301.01(S) [UCC § 1-201(19)]. Under the "close connectedness" doctrine, which was established by the Supreme Court of New Jersey in *Unico v. Owen,* 50 NJ 101, 232 A.2d 405 (1967), a transferee does not take an instrument in good faith when the transferee is so closely connected with the transferor that the transferee may be charged with knowledge of an infirmity in the underlying transaction. The rationale for the close connectedness doctrine was enunciated in *Unico*, at pages 109-110, as follows:

> In the field of negotiable instruments, good faith is a broad concept. The basic philosophy of the holder in due course status is to encourage free negotiability of commercial paper by removing certain anxieties of one who takes the paper as an innocent purchaser knowing no reason why the paper is not sound as its face would indicate. it would seem to follow, therefore, that the more the holder knows about the underlying transaction, and particularly the more he controls or participates or becomes involved in it, the less he fits the role of a good faith purchaser for value; the closer his relationship to the underlying agreement which is the source of the note, the less need there is for giving him the tension-free rights considered necessary in a fast-moving, credit-extending world.

Soon after the decision in *Unico* was reached, the close connectedness doctrine was adopted by Ohio courts. Headnote No. 2 in *American Plan Corp. v. Woods*, 16 Ohio App. 2d 1, 4500 2d 2 (1968), announced the following:

---

[24] The record indicates appellee had a signature card on Mr. and Mrs. Hessler, and that Carla Hessler is left-handed and Kenneth Hessler is right-handed.

A transferee of a negotiable note does not take in "good faith" and is not a holder in due course of a note given in the sale of consumer goods where the transferee is a finance company involved with the seller of the goods, and which has a pervasive knowledge of factors relating to the terms of the sale.

Similarly, in *Security Central Nat'l Bank v. Williams*, 52 Ohio App. 2d 175, 6 N.E.2d 167 (1976), a finding that the transferee did not take the note in good faith was justified when the transferee-bank was alerted to the possibility that the underlying transaction which generated the note was not a completely above-board transaction.

According to White and Summers, noted authorities on the Uniform Commercial Code, the following five factors are indicative of a close connection between the transferee and transferor:

> (1) Drafting by the transferee of forms for the transferor; (2) approval or establishment or both of the transferor's procedures by the transferee (*e.g.*, setting the interest rate, approval of a referral sales plan); (3) an independent check by the transferee on the credit of the debtor or some other direct contract between the transferee and the debtor; (4) heavy reliance by the transferor upon the transferee (*e.g.*, transfer by the transferor of all or substantial part of his paper to the transferee) and; (5) common or connected ownership or management of the transferor and transferee. White & Summers, Uniform Commercial Code 481 (1972).

An analysis of the above factors in relation to the facts of this case, as set forth in the trial court's findings, reveals an unusually close relationship between appellee bank (the transferee), the John Smith Grain Company (the transferor-payee) and J & J Farms, Inc.

Appellee provided John Smith Grain Company with the forms used in the transaction and supplied the interest rate to be charged. At the time of the purchase of the first note, appellee bank ran an independent credit check on appellant. There is evidence of a heavy reliance by John Smith Grain Company upon appellee bank insofar as it was customary for the grain company to transfer substantially all of its commercial paper to appellee bank. There was not only a common director of appellee and John Smith Grain Company, but also common directors or management between John Smith Grain Company and J & J Farms, Inc. H.K. Smith was a director of appellee bank and the president and director of John Smith Grain Company. C. North, Jr., was an officer and director of both John Smith Grain Company and J & J Farms, Inc. John Milton Smith was officer and director of John Smith Grain Company and officer of J & J Farms, Inc. In addition, the trial court found that B. Henninger, the executive vice-president of appellee who had previously been employed by John Smith Grain Company, frequented John Smith Grain Company several times a week between November 1976 and January 1977 to advise the officers of John Smith Grain Company on business practices. During that time, John Smith Grain Company was experiencing serious financial difficulties.

The facts of this case clearly indicate such close connectedness between appellee bank and John Smith Grain Company as to impute knowledge by appellee bank of infirmities in the underlying transaction. The trial court specifically found, in its separate findings of fact and conclusions of law, the relationship between appellee bank and J & J Farms was not an arm's length relationship. In spite of this finding, the trial court erroneously concluded "the facts do not permit the court to void the holder in due course protections under these circumstances."

The trial court, however, missed the point. Not only do the facts indicate appellee bank was aware of the impending bankruptcy of John Smith Grain Company, but they also show appellee has reason to know of a fatal infirmity in the underlying transaction, viz., there was no consideration given by John Smith Grain Company for the note. C. North, Jr., an officer and director of both John Smith Grain Company and J & J Farms, Inc., obtained appellant's signature and advised appellant to sign his wife's name on the note. As an officer and director of J & J Farms, Inc., C. North, Jr., undoubtedly was aware that at the time he obtained appellant's signature, the hogs had already been mortgaged by J & J Farms, Inc. It is well-established in Ohio a corporation can act only through its officer and agents, and the knowledge of the officers of a corporation is at once the knowledge of the corporation. *The First Nat'l Bank of New Bremen v. Burns*, 88 Ohio St 434 (1913). If North, as officer and director of both John Smith Grain Company and J & J Farms, Inc., knew there was no consideration for the note, then such knowledge is imputed to both corporations. Thus, H.K. Smith, as president and director of John Smith Grain Company, had ample reason to know of the failure of consideration; and since H.K. Smith was also a director of appellee bank, his knowledge is imputed to appellee bank.

The executive vice-president of appellee bank, B. Henninger, who had previously been employed by John Smith Grain Company, was also in close contact with John Smith Grain Company at the time appellant signed the note. According to the trial court's conclusions, at the time appellant's signature was obtained on the note, B. Henninger was meeting several times a week with the officers of John Smith Grain Company to advise them on business practices. At that time, the officers of John Smith Grain Company included H.K. Smith, who was also a director of appellee bank, and C. North, Jr., who was also an officer and director of J & J Farms, Inc.

Given these facts, one cannot conclude with absolute certainty that appellee bank had actual knowledge of the failure of consideration. As appellant correctly states in his brief, however, the doctrine of close connectedness was developed in part because of the difficulty of proving the transferee's actual knowledge of problems in the underlying transaction. The doctrine allows the court to imply knowledge by the transferee when the relationship between the transferee and transferor is sufficiently close to warrant such an implication. Under the circumstances of this case, we find the relationship between appellee bank and John Smith Grain Company was so entwined that it was error for the trial court not to apply the doctrine of close connectedness to find appellee bank failed to carry its burden of proving good faith.

If we accept the trial court's findings of fact and apply the close connectedness doctrine, we can reach only one conclusion, viz., appellee bank did not take the note in good faith.

Upon either one or both of the above reasoned theories, *i.e.*, (1) notice of a defense and (2) close connectedness doctrine, we find the Court of Appeals erred in affirming the trial court's finding that appellee bank was a holder in due course. The judgment of the Court of Appeals is, therefore reversed.

Judgment reversed.

FIRST ALABAMA BANK OF GUNTERSVILLE v. HUNT

Alabama Court of Civil Appeals
402 So.2d 992, 31 U.C.C. Rep. 151 (1981)

HOLMES, J. This case is governed by Article III of Alabama's Uniform Commercial Code, §§ 7-3-101 et seq., Code of Ala 1975.

The First Alabama Bank of Guntersville sued Hunt on a promissory note. The trial court found that on the basis of pertinent uncontroverted evidence, First Alabama Bank was barred from holder in due course status by § 7-3-302(3)(c), Code of Ala 1975, and entered a directed verdict in favor of Hunt. First Alabama Bank appeals and we reverse.

The dispositive issue is whether § 7-3-302(3)(c), Code of Ala 1975, applies to the facts of this case.

The record reveals the following facts:

In August of 1974, Hunt pursuant to a contract for the sale and purchase of two residential lots executed a promissory note payable to Fitts and Rodgers. Fitts and Rodgers were real estate developers who, in addition to selling two lots to Hunt, sold residential subdivision lots to several individuals. Like Hunt, these individuals paid for their lots by giving Fitts and Rodgers promissory notes.

In December of 1974, Fitts and Rodgers sold the Hunt note and nine to thirteen other notes to First Alabama Bank. At trial the president of First Alabama Bank testified to the effect that, while the bank had dealt with Fitts and Rodgers in the past, this was the only time the bank had purchased promissory notes from them. There was no evidence as to whether Fitts and Rodgers had sold notes to other purchasers.

As indicated above, the trial court found that First Alabama Bank was barred from holder in due course status by § 7-3-302(3)(c), Code of Ala 1975, and entered a directed verdict in favor of Hunt. Apparently, the trial court found that First Alabama Bank purchased the note as part of a bulk transaction not in regular course of business of the transferor, here Fitts and Rodgers. This determination was based on the uncontroverted evidence that First Alabama Bank purchased ten to fourteen notes at one time and that this was the only time Fitts and Rodgers sold notes to First Alabama Bank.

First Alabama Bank contends through counsel that the trial court erred in its interpretation of § 7-3-302(3)(c). We agree.

Section 7-3-302(3)(c) provides:

A holder does not become a holder in due course of an instrument:

. . ..

(c) By purchasing it as part of a bulk transaction not in regular course of business of the transferor.

Since the key phrase "bulk transaction not in regular course of business of the transferor" is not defined by the Uniform Commercial Code, the scope of § 7-3-302(3)(c) cannot be readily ascertained from the face of the statute. However, Comment 3 of the Official comments to § 7-3-302(3)(c) does provide guidance in determining this Code section's field of operation. Comment 3 in pertinent part states:

> Subsection (3) is intended to state existing case law. It covers a few situations in which the purchaser takes the Instrument under unusual circumstances which indicate that he is merely a successor in interest to the prior holder and can acquire no better rights. . .
>
> Subsection (3)(c) applies to bulk purchases lying outside of the ordinary course of business of the seller. It applies, for example, when a new partnership takes over for value all of the assets of an old one after a new member has entered the firm, or to a reorganized or consolidated

corporation taking over in bulk the assets of a predecessor. It has particular application to the purchaser by one bank of a substantial part of the paper held by another bank which is threatened with insolvency and seeking to liquidate its assets.

From Comment 3 we find that § 7-3-302(3)(c) has narrow field of operation limited to bulk transfers incident to the cessation, liquidation, or reorganization of the transferor's business where the circumstances indicate that the transferee is a mere successor in interest to the transferor. Stated differently, a bulk transfer of notes incident to the cessation, liquidation, or reorganization of the transferor's business to a person who is merely a successor in interest to the transferor is not a transfer in the regular course of business of the transferor. This type of transaction is to be distinguished from transactions wherein the transferor sells or pledges notes to obtain cash funds for use in his business. The latter type of transaction is one which would be in the ordinary course of business, *Third National Bank in Nashville [v. Hardi-Gardens Supply of Illinois, Inc.*, 350 F Supp 930 (MD Tenn 1974)]; *Pugatch [v. David's Jewelers*, 278 NYS2d 759 (1967)], and which would be in the regular course of business regardless of whether the transaction was the transferor's first or fortieth.

In the instant case there is no evidence indicating that the sale of the notes to First Alabama Bank was incident to the cessation, liquidation, or reorganization of Fitts and Rodgers' real estate development business, nor is there evidence of circumstances indicating that First Alabama Bank is a mere successor in interest to Fitts and Rodgers.

As stated above, the fact that the sale of the notes to First Alabama Bank was a one time occurrence is not dispositive of the question of whether or not the transaction was in the ordinary course of business. We find that the learned trial judge misinterpreted § 7-3-302(3)(c) and that, by relying on the fact that the transaction was a one time occurrence, it erred in entering a directed verdict in favor of Hunt.

DESMOND v. FEDERAL DEPOSIT INSURANCE CORP.

United States District Court, District of Massachusetts
798 F. Supp. 829, 20 U.C.C. Rep.2d 196 (1992)

WOODLOCK, DISTRICT JUDGE.

The facts of this case press against the limits of federal common law and statutory protections afforded the Federal Deposit Insurance Corporation (FDIC)when it takes over failed banking institutions. As banks continue to fail in troubled economic times, the FDIC, invoking protections carved out by the courts and Congress, has adopted an aggressive stance in meeting the claims and defenses asserted by borrowers from the failed institutions the FDIC is required to supervise. In this case, it is necessary to address the nature and extent of any protections shielding the FDIC when borrower allegations of duress are at issue.

The case arises out of a series of loan transactions entered into by Robert Desmond and the Eliot Savings Bank ("Eliot"). Desmond appeared to be defaulting on a series of bank loans and began negotiating a restructuring of those loans in late 1988. Desmond alleges that Eliot, citing a potential conflict of interest, maliciously forced Desmond's attorney to withdraw at a crucial time during the negotiations and then coerced Desmond into signing an oppressive forbearance agreement. Desmond sued, and the FDIC, which took over for the failing Eliot, counterclaimed on the loans. The FDIC has moved for summary judgement on the Complaint and on its Counterclaims. Because there remain factual issues relevant to certain of the claims and counterclaims, I will grant the FDIC's motion only in part.

II. THE FEDERAL ESTOPPEL DOCTRINE

The principal thrust of the FDIC's motion is that Desmond's claims and defenses are barred by the doctrine of federal estoppel announced in *D'Oench, Duhme & Co. v Federal Deposit Ins. Corp.*, 315 U.S. 447, 62 S. Ct. 676, 88 L. Ed. 956 (1942) and codified by 12 U.S.C. § 1823(e). Because the estoppel doctrine lies at the core of this lawsuit, it warrants close examination. In *D'Oench*, a borrower defaulted on bonds he had previously sold to a bank. In an apparent effort to inflate its assets prior to a bank examination, the bank then accepted a promissory note from the borrower with the understanding that the bank would never try to collect on the note. That understanding was indicated on the receipts for the notes, but was not memorialized as part of the bank's official records. *Id.* at 454, 62 S. Ct. at 678. When the FDIC later attempted to enforce the note, the Supreme Court rejected the borrowers's defense that he had agreed with the bank that the note would not be called for payment. This unrecorded understanding violated a federal policy of protecting the FDIC against "secret agreements." *Id.* at 461, 62 S.Ct. at 681. The Court described the basic test for this doctrine of estoppel as involving a determination:

> whether the note was designed to deceive the creditors or the public authority, or would end to have that effect. It would be sufficient in this type of case that the maker lent himself to a scheme or arrangement whereby the banking authority on which [the FDIC] relied in insuring the bank was or was likely to be misled.

Id. at 460, 62 S.Ct. at 681. The Court thus acted to estop borrowers from avoiding repayment to the FDIC by pleading unofficial "arrangements or schemes" that tend to misrepresent the actual value of a bank's assets.

The First Circuit has interpreted the *D'Oench* doctrine to bar defenses or claims that derive from "secret agreements that tend to make the FDIC susceptible to fraudulent arrangements." *Timberland Design, Inc. v. First Service Bank for Sav.,* 932 F.2d 46, 48 (1st Cir. 1991). In order to "lend himself" to such a scheme, the borrower need not intend to defraud, and is sufficiently at fault simply by failing to reduce the agreement pled in defense to writing. *Id.* at 48-49. Moreover, *D'Oench* estoppel is not limited to defenses to FDIC actions, but also operates to bar affirmative claims which are similarly premised on "secret" agreements. *Id.* at 49.

Congress codified this estoppel doctrine in 12 U.S.C. § 1823(3).[25] The codification reads as follows:

> No agreement which tends to diminish or defeat the interest of the [FDIC] in any asset acquired by it under this section or section 11 [12 U.S.C. § 1821], either as security for a

[25] This section was amended by the Financial Institutions Reform, Recovery, and Enforcement Act of 1989 (FIRREA), which applied the section to the FDIC when it acts as receiver. *See Timberland Design, Inc. v. Federal Deposit Ins. Corp.*, 745 F.Supp. 784, 788 (D. Mass. 1990), *aff'd, Timberland Design, Inc. v. First Service Bank for Sav.*, 932 F.2d 46 (1st Cir. 1991).

loan or by purchase or as receiver of any insured depository institution, shall not be valid against the [FDIC] unless such agreement—

(1) is in writing,

(2) was executed by the depository institution and any person claiming an adverse interest thereunder, including the obligor, contemporaneously with the acquisition of the asset by the depository institution,

(3) was approved by the board of directors of the depository institution or its loan committee, which approval shall be reflected in the minutes of said board or committee, and

(4) has been, continuously, from the time of its execution, an official record of the depository institution.

The statute thus enforces the *D'Oench* doctrine by requiring that any "agreement" that might diminish the value of an asset acquired by the FDIC be formally recorded as part of a bank's official records. For the purposes of the instant motion, the problem lies in determining in a principled way what constitutes an "agreement" within the meaning of the statute.

The Supreme Court shed light on the meaning of that term in a recent case recognizing broad applicability for § 1823(e). In *Langley v. Federal Deposit Inc. Corp.*, 484 U.S. 86, 108 S.Ct. 396, 98 L.Ed.2d 340 [5 U.C.C. Rep. Serv. 2d 1] (1987), to finance the purchase of land, the petitioners borrowed money from an FDIC insured bank and executed a note, mortgage, and personal guaranty in consideration for the loan. When the petitioners failed to pay an installment due on the note, the bank sued, and the petitioners counterclaimed, asserting both as a defense and as part of their affirmative claim fraudulent inducement. They alleged that the note had been procured by the bank's misrepresentations about the acreage of the property, its mineral content, and the absence of mineral leases on the land. These misrepresentations were not reflected in the records of the bank or the documents executed by the borrowers. 484 U.S. 86, 88, 108 S. Ct. 396, 399-400, 98 L. Ed. 2d 340 (1987).

The Court held that § 1823(e) barred the fraudulent statement claim in the circumstances of this transaction. Justice Scalia interpreted the bank's oral promises about the size and nature of the land as a warranty whose truthfulness "was a condition to performance of [petitioners'] obligation to repay the loan." *Id.* at 91, 108 S.Ct. at 401. As such, the bank's alleged misrepresentations were part of the parties' "bargain" and within the scope of "agreement" as that term is used in § 1823(e). "Agreement," in other words, embraces conditions to payment of promissory notes, including the truthfulness of a warranted fact, such as the size of land to be purchased. *See id.* at 92, 108 S.Ct. at 401-402. Because the borrowers neglected to include the warranty and condition in the note, they were barred by the statute.

In making this assessment, the Supreme Court identified two essential purposes of § 1823(e). First, by requiring that side agreements be recorded properly, the statute permits federal and state banking authorities to rely confidently on a bank's records in evaluating the worth of the bank's assets. Second, the contemporaneousness and board approval requirements ensure "mature consideration of unusual loan transactions by senior bank officials, and prevent fraudulent insertion of new terms, with the collusion of bank employees, when a bank appears headed for failure." *Id.* at 92, 108 S.Ct. at 401. I bear these two policies in mind as I assess the FDIC's claims of estoppel in this case.

IV. THE HOLDER IN DUE COURSE DOCTRINE

The FDIC argues alternatively that Desmond's defenses and claims are defeated by the federal holder in due course doctrine developed by courts contemporaneously with the passage of § 1823(e). *See* Memorandum of Reasons Why Motion for Summary Judgment on Complaint Should be Granted at 14-18. The First Circuit recently explored the history of this somewhat imprecise doctrine by citing the Eleventh Circuit's seminal holding that

> [A]s a matter of federal common law, the FDIC has a complete defense to state and common law fraud claims on a note acquired by the FDIC in the execution of a purchase and assumption transaction, for value, in good faith, and without actual knowledge of the fraud at the time the FDIC entered into the purchase and assumption agreement.

604 Columbus Avenue Realty Trust at 1350 (quoting *Gunter v. Hutcheson*, 647 F.2d 682, 873 (11th Cir.), *cert. denied*, 459 U.S. 826, 103 S.Ct. 60, 74 L.Ed.2d 63 (1982)). The court then noted that other Circuits have expanded the federal holder in due course doctrine to bar in the appropriate circumstances not only claims of fraud, but all personal defenses against the FDIC. *Id.: see, e.g., Campbell Leasing, Inc. v. Federal Deposit Ins. Corp.*, 901 F.2d 1244, 1248 [12 U.C.C. Rep Serv 2d 138] (5th Cir. 1990). A number of courts imply that § 1823(e) itself vests the FDIC with holder in due course status, *see, e.g., Meyer*, 755 F.Supp. at 12, but the First Circuit treats the doctrine as the creature of federal common law and as affording protections different from the federal estoppel doctrine. *See 604 Columbus Avenue Realty Trust* at 1349-50; *see also Federal Deposit Ins. Corp. v. Wood*, 758 F.2d 156, 159 [40 U.C.C. Rep Serv 937] (6th Cir.), *cert. denied*, 474 U.S. 944, 106 S. Ct. 308, 88 L. Ed. 2d 286 (1985) (holder in due course doctrine is not authorized by § 1823(e), but is "part of the federal common law").

The essential purpose behind this broad protection for the FDIC when it holds negotiable instruments is to facilitate purchase and assumption transactions. As the First Circuit has explained, when the FDIC takes over for a failed bank, it generally either liquidates the bank or engages in a purchase and assumption transaction.[26] The latter tack is favored, because "it avoids the specter of closed banks and the interruption of daily banking services." *604 Columbus Avenue Realty Trust* at 1349 (citation omitted). In other words, by transferring the failed bank's healthy assets to a viable banking institution, the purchase and assumption transaction promotes financial stability and avoids the delays inherent in the process of liquidation. However, this transactional method puts a premium on speed and efficiency, and the holder in due course doctrine is designed to permit the FDIC rapidly to scan the failed bank's books and records to assess its own potential losses. *See id.* Unencumbered by the possibility of personal defenses, the FDIC as a holder in due course can rely on the failed bank's notes as representing transferrable or collectible assets.

---

[26] In a purchase and assumption transaction,

> . . . the FDIC, in its capacity as receiver, sells the bank's healthy assets to the purchasing bank in exchange for the purchasing bank's promise to pay the failed bank's depositors. In addition, as receiver, the FDIC sells the'bad' assets to itself acting in its corporate capacity. With the money it receives, the FDIC-receiver then pays the purchasing bank enough money to make up the difference between what it must pay out to the failed bank's depositors, and what the purchasing bank was willing to pay for the good assets that it purchased. The FDIC acting in its corporate capacity then tries to collect on the bad assets to minimize the loss to the insurance fund. Generally, the purchase and assumption must be executed in great haste, often overnight.

604 Columbus Avenue Realty Trust at 1337 (quoting *Timberland*, 932 F.2d at 48).

Of course, to enjoy this considerable protection, the FDIC must first meet the requirement of holder in due course status. *604 Columbus Avenue Realty Trust* does not precisely define how this determination is made—although it does suggest that, in the case of fraud, the FDIC must be a good faith purchaser for value without knowledge of the fraud—but prior decisions of the First Circuit have looked to state law to determine whether the FDIC is a holder in due course in a given situation. *See Federal Deposit Ins. Corp. v. Grupo Girod*, 869 F.2d 15, 17 (1st Cir. 1989) (looking to Puerto Rican law in assessing whether the FDIC might be a holder in due course). Other circuits have held that the FDIC may enjoy holder in due course status even if it does not satisfy the technical requirements of such status under state law. *See Campbell*, 901 F.2d at 12149; *Wood*, 759 F.2d at 158. I need not enter this thicket, however, because the FDIC is stripped of this protective shield for two other reasons in the instant case.

First, the FDIC becomes a holder in due course only with respect to negotiable instruments. *See New Connecticut Bank*, 132 B.R. at 208, 209 [16 U.C.C. Rep Serv 2d 438]; *Sunbelt Savings, FSB Dallas, Texas v. Montross*, 923 F.2d 353, 356 [13 U.C.C. Rep Serv 2d 792] (5th Cir.), reinstated and remanded, 944 F.2d 227, 228 (5th Cir. 1991) (en banc) (taking no position on the negotiability of variable interest rate notes). In *New Connecticut Bank*, Judge Tauro looked to U.C.C. §§ 3-104 and 3-106 and relevant case law to determine whether variable interest rate notes qualified as negotiable instruments containing a promise to pay a "sum certain." 132 B.R. at 208-9. He held that, because the interest rates could only be determined by an external and variable standard, the notes were non-negotiable and prevented the FDIC from enjoying the "blanket protection of a holder in due course." *Id.* Desmond's notes in this case are similarly subject to variable interest rates; they are all payable at interest rates dependent on "the rate of interest announced from time to time by the First National Bank of Boston . . .as its base rate." *See* Exhibits C,E,F,G, and I attached to Linderman Affidavit. They too are subject to an external and variable standard for calculating interest. Moreover, the other documents in the FDIC's possession—the Desmond Guaranty, and the forbearance and security agreements—are all premised on the obligations contained in the notes and thus are equally non-negotiable. *See Federal Deposit Ins. Corp. v. Percival*, 752 F.Supp. 313, 324-325 [14 U.C.C. Rep Serv 2d 355] (D. Neb. 1990) (FDIC held not a holder in due course with respect to a guaranty agreement, which does not contain unconditional promise to pay a sum certain and is not payable on demand or at time certain and is therefore non-negotiable). Thus, because the FDIC holds only non-negotiable instruments, it is not entitled to the protections afforded a holder in due course.

Second, the thrust of the First Circuit's most recent pronouncement is that the FDIC is not entitled to holder in due course status in the absence of a purchaser and assumption transaction. *See 604 Columbus Avenue Realty Trust* at 1352-53. Where the FDIC is concerned only with liquidation, the policies of maintaining uninterrupted banking services and executing a rapid purchase and assumption based on the bank's books do not apply. *See id.* In this case, it appears from the record that the FDIC has chosen to liquidate Eliot rather than to sell its healthy assets to a purchasing bank and consummate a purchase and assumption transaction. Even if it held negotiable instruments, this posture would deprive the FDIC of the protections of a holder in due course under *604 Columbus Avenue Realty Trust*. Thus, both because it holds variable interest rate notes and has not pursued the purchase and assumption path, the FDIC cannot benefit from the federal common law holder in due course rule.

§ 12.05 Payee as Holder in Due Course

Read U.C.C. § 3-302 Comment 4.

IN RE ESTATE OF BALKUS

[The facts and opinion appear in §§ 12.02[F], *supra*, 12.03[A], *supra*.]

QUESTION

Could the payee, Vesely, ever be a "holder," let alone a "holder in due course?" Were these notes ever issued?

COURTESY FINANCIAL SERVICES, INC. v. HUGHES

Louisiana Court of Appeals
424 So. 2d 1172, 35 U.C.C. Rep. 1551 (1982)

SHORTESS, J.

Courtesy Financial Services, Inc. (plaintiff) filed suit against John A. Hughes and Teresa Hughes (defendants) for $ 1,025.43, the unpaid balance due on a promissory note executed for the purchase price of a used car. Finding that plaintiff was not a holder in due course, and that defendants established a failure of consideration in that the car was defective, the trial judge dismissed plaintiff's suit.

On October 13, 1978, defendants purchased a used 1976 Plymouth Fury Station Wagon from Security Motors. Paul A. Crumrin, Jr., handled the transaction both as salesman for Security Motors and as loan officer for plaintiff. One month after the sale, defendants experienced problems with the brakes and replaced them. During the two years that defendants drove the car, numerous other problems arose: the ceiling liner inside the car fell out and emitted a musty smell; the gas tank rusted and leaked; the water pump went out; the radiator overheated; the electrical system shorted and the brake lights ceased to function; the heater, air conditioner and power steering went out, etc. As the various problems arose, defendants attempted to repair the car themselves. However, they finally "gave up the ghost" in June of 1980. Since that time, the car has been sitting in defendants' front driveway.

Defendants' last payment was made on July 1, 1980. Payments stopped because breakdowns were causing defendants to be late for work, and because defendants felt that they were "getting further and further in the hole trying to keep the car running." Prior to July 1, 1980, defendants continued to make payments even though they were both out of work. Defendants paid approximately $2,502.06, the difference between the amount financed ($3,527.49) and the amount sued upon ($1,025.43) before they ceased making payments. When payments were made, defendants informed plaintiff that they were having problems with the car. In fact, defendants asked plaintiff for a loan of $600.00 so they could get repair work done. In response to plaintiff's suit, defendants raised the affirmative defense of failure of consideration, asserting that the car was defective, rendering it totally unfit for normal use.

Plaintiff says that: (1) the trial judge erred in entering judgment based on the defense of failure of consideration, and (2) the trial judge erred in finding that the plaintiff was not a holder in due course.

In a suit on a promissory note by a payee against the maker, the plaintiff will be given the presumption that the instrument was given for value received unless the maker casts doubt upon the consideration. Once the maker has cast doubt upon the issue of consideration, the burden shifts to the payee to prove consideration by a preponderance of the evidence.

Defendants testified as to the various malfunctions in the car and cast doubt on the issue of consideration. Plaintiff did not offer any evidence to rebut the testimony of defendants or to establish that consideration was given. Whether defendants' testimony alone was sufficient to cast doubt on the issue of consideration was a question of fact which the trial judge, by judging the credibility of the witnesses, was most competent to determine. The trial judge found that:

> Defendants have presented evidence, largely uncontradicted, of an impressive array of defects and malfunctions for even a two-year old used automobile. This court is persuaded that, taken as a whole, they manifest a failure of consideration.

We agree with the conclusion of the trial court that a failure of consideration existed.

Although the original payee on the note, plaintiff claims the status of holder in due course, and thus an exemption from the defense of failure of consideration. [The Court cites U.C.C. § 3-307(3).]

Plaintiff says that La RS 10:3-302(2) gives a payee the status of a holder in due course.[27] However, said provision only states that a "payee *may* be a holder in due course." La RS 10:3-302(2) (emphasis added). Although a payee may be a holder in due course, said status is not automatic. When the payee deals with the maker through an intermediary (remitter) and does not have notice of defenses, such an isolated payee may take as a holder in due course. In most instances, however, a payee will not be a holder in due course because said payee will usually have notice of defenses and claims by virtue of the fact that he has dealt directly with the maker. In order for a payee to be a holder in due course, all of the basic requirements must be met. A holder in due course is a holder who takes the instrument (1) for value, (2) in good faith, and (3) without notice that the instrument is overdue or has been dishonored or of any defense or claim affecting the instrument. La RS 10:3-302. Thus, a payee who is an immediate party to the transaction is not automatically entitled to holder in due course status.

In this case, Security Motors, the vendor, and plaintiff were owned by the same person and occupied the same building. Paul A. Crumrin, Jr., the branch manager for plaintiff, testified that he handled the sale both as salesman for Security Motors and also as loan officer for plaintiff, as he was employed by both corporations. The trial court correctly found that plaintiff, a payee who was an immediate party to the transaction, was not entitled to holder in due course status.[28] Thus, defendants may properly assert the defense of failure of consideration.[29]

---

[27] Prior to the enactment in 1975 of Title 10 of the La Revised Statutes, a payee was not entitled to holder in due course status. La RS 7:52; See *Republic Finance of Gramercy, Inc. v. Davis*, 289 So 2d 891 (La App 4th Cir 1974).

[28] Contra, *Ford Motor Credit Co. v. Williams*, 225 So 2d 717 (La App 1st Cir 1969). In this case, the plaintiff was not the named payee on the note, but took the note by endorsement. In addition, a sufficient connection between the plaintiff and the vendor was not proven.

[29] A Federal Trade Commission regulation requires that notice be given that the holder of a consumer credit contract is subject to all claims and defenses which the debtor could assert against the seller. 16 CFR 433.1, 433.2. However, it is the inclusion of the required language that prevents a subsequent holder from becoming a holder in due course. *Capital Bank and Trust Co. v. Lacey*, 393 So 2d 668 (La 1980). Even if the present transaction was a consumer credit transaction, plaintiff is not automatically precluded from being a holder in due course because the requisite notice did not appear on the face of the instrument. See also, *Jefferson Rank and Trust Co. v. Stamatiou*, 384 So 2d 388 (La 1980).

Failure of consideration is a defense to an action by one who does not have the rights of a holder in due course. La RS 10:3-306(c), La RS 10:3-408. Since defendants cast doubt upon the issue of consideration, and plaintiff did not meet its burden of proving consideration by a preponderance of the evidence, the trial judge correctly dismissed plaintiff's claim. *Brashears v. Williams* [294 So. 2d 246 (La App 1st Cir 1974)]. Because plaintiff is not entitled to the rights of a holder in due course, the personal defense of failure of consideration can be used to defeat plaintiff's claim. La RS 10:3-306(c); La RS 10:3-408; *Fisher v. Childs Inv. Co., Inc.*, 411 So 2d 1180 (La App 4th Cir 1982), *writ denied*, 416 So 2d 115 (La 1982).

Accordingly, this appeal is affirmed at defendants' costs.

NOTE

Read Official Comment 4 to U.C.C. § 3-302 for a discussion of a number of circumstances where a payee may qualify as a holder in due course.

§ 12.06 Shelter Doctrine

Read U.C.C. §§ 3-203(b), 3-308(b).

PIPER v. GOODWIN

United States Court of Appeals
20 F.2d 216, 23 U.C.C. Rep 2d 466 (6th Cir. 1994)

Per Curiam.

Pursuant to Tennessee's version of the Uniform Commercial Code, the plaintiff sued three individual defendants for collection on two promissory notes. The jury found in favor of the plaintiff and the district court entered a judgment against the defendants on the notes, together with interest and attorney fees. Five issues have been raised on appeal. After reviewing these issues, we find no error and affirm.

I.

This appeal arises out of a complex series of real estate transactions. The plaintiff, Paul Piper, Jr., brought a lawsuit to collect on two promissory notes, both of which were made by the Rivergrove Development Company, Inc. Piper came into possession of these notes by way of an assignment from Ronald K. Moore. Piper claimed that two of the defendants, C. Eugene Goodwin and Daniel P. Goodwin, were liable because they were alter egos of then-insolvent Rivergrove Development and the other defendant, A.S. Hart, was independently liable as an endorser of one of the notes. The facts leading up to this lawsuit are set out below.

In 1978, Moore purchased a large tract of undeveloped land in suburban Memphis, Tennessee. At that time, he intended to build homes on the property for him and his friend Piper. Part of this tract was later subdivided by a partnership owned by Moore and Piper.

In June 1983, Hart approached Moore, stating that he wanted to sell lots in the subdivision but, because he did not have a brokerage license, he would have to hold the lots in his own name. Moore sold three lots to Hart, including one of the lots relevant to this case—lot 8. In return, Moore took a note from Hart in the amount of $45,000 which was secured by a first deed of trust on lot 8.

Later that month, Hart informed Moore that Eugene Goodwin wanted to purchase the remaining lots in the subdivision. Moore received from Hart a proposed contract for the purchase of these lots which included the other lot relevant to this case—lot 9. The contract listed Goodwin Development Company, Inc. as the purchaser.

The closing occurred on July 7, 1983. With respect to lot 9, Moore took a note from Goodwin Development in the amount of $55,000, which was secured by a first deed of trust. As part of this sale, Eugene Goodwin loaned money to Goodwin Development, for which he received a second deed of trust on lot 9 in the amount of $15,000. Both Moore's and Eugene Goodwin's trust deeds contained provisions by which each agreed to subordinate their mortgages to construction loans.

Eugene Goodwin then decided that he did not want to be involved in the building of these properties, so he sold his interest in Goodwin Development to Hart. Eugene Goodwin, who still held the second deed of trust on lot 9, also began to worry about whether his second mortgage would be repaid. Adding to his fears was the fact that the subordination clause contained in this deed precluded any control he might have exercised over a third party builder.

In early January 1984, a builder was found—Eugene Goodwin's son, Daniel. According to Daniel Goodwin's testimony, he "overheard" his father and Hart talking at the Goodwin's family business office about finding a builder for the subdivision. Daniel Goodwin expressed his interest in this project and was selected. Hart also informed Daniel Goodwin that a few days earlier, Hart had filed a charter for a corporation known as Rivergrove Development Company, Inc., with the Tennessee Secretary of State. The corporation had not been used, and Hart offered to sell the corporation to Daniel Goodwin. A short time later, this sale occurred.

On January 9, 1984, Daniel and Eugene Goodwin signed two contracts of sale relating to lots 8 and 9, with Hart as seller of lot 8 and Goodwin Development as seller of lot 9.[30] Daniel and Eugene Goodwin were listed as the purchasers of both lots, and there was no reference to Rivergrove Development in either sales contract. In return, Rivergrove Development gave a $45,000 promissory note to Hart for lot 8 and a $55,000 promissory note to Goodwin Development for lot 9. These notes were then negotiated to Moore: the $45,000 note was endorsed by Hart and the $55,000 note was endorsed by Hart on behalf of Goodwin Development. These two notes replaced the notes Moore had been holding that were made by Hart and Goodwin Development.

On January 30, 1984, Rivergrove Development executed two notes payable to Eugene Goodwin in the amount of $275,000 each. These notes represented construction loans from Eugene Goodwin to Rivergrove Development. As part of this transaction, Rivergrove Development used some of the funds to pay off Eugene Goodwin's second deed of trust on lot 9. Moreover, because this was a "construction loan," the subordination clause kicked in and Moore's first mortgage on lot 9 was reduced to a second mortgage.

Between January and June 1984, there was some clearing and footings were dug on lots 8 and 9, but the work terminated, according to Daniel Goodwin's testimony, when funding stopped.

[30] The sale contract for lot 9 contains an error as to the seller. At the time of the contract, Goodwin Development had title to lot 9; however, the contract lists A.S. Hart as the seller. This mistake might stem from Hart's ownership of Goodwin Development.

Although neither Daniel Goodwin nor Rivergrove Development were in default on Eugene Goodwin's construction loan at that time, Eugene Goodwin stopped funding the project and foreclosed on lots 8 and 9. A foreclosure sale was held and Eugene Goodwin, the sole bidder, obtained title to both properties for about $90,000. Moore's second deed on lot 9 was extinguished. A short time later, Rivergrove Development was insolvent and the State of Tennessee revoked its charter.

On January 13, 1988, Moore filed a lawsuit as the holder of the notes against Eugene Goodwin, Daniel Goodwin, and Hart. This suit was filed in the Chancery Court of Shelby County, Tennessee. At this time, Moore was in financial trouble, and Piper agreed to loan him $400,000. Moore later realized that he would not be able to repay Piper, so they reached an agreement whereby Moore assigned all of his assets to Piper in repayment of the loan.[31] Both Moore and Piper testified that it was their understanding that this assignment included the two notes made by Rivergrove Development. Moore also testified that at the time of the assignment he did not have possession of the notes because they were in the court's records, but at a later date the notes were delivered to Piper through Piper's attorney.

Piper filed this lawsuit on May 18, 1989, and the suit brought in Chancery Court by Moore was dismissed. The case was tried before a jury. At the close of the proof, the district court granted Piper's motion for a judgment against Hart on the promissory note that he had endorsed. The jury returned a verdict in favor of Piper and, based on this verdict, the court found against Eugene Goodwin and Daniel Goodwin on the notes, in the amounts of $45,000 and $59,125, respectively, together with prejudgment interest and attorney fees. The defendants then appealed.

The defendants argue that Piper was not a holder of the notes when he commenced this action and, thus, he had no legal right to seek their collection. Relying on Tenn. Code Ann. § 47-3-202, the defendants contend that because both notes are payable to order, to be negotiated to Piper the notes had to have been delivered to him and endorsed by Moore. The defendants maintain that the evidence is questionable as to whether Moore delivered the notes to Piper and, at a minimum, it is clear that neither note was endorsed by Moore. Therefore, the defendants argue, because the notes were not negotiated to Piper, he is not a holder and cannot bring this action.

Even if we were to assume the defendants' interpretation of § 47-3-202 is correct, it does not resolve this matter. The facts of this case are better analyzed under Tenn Code Ann. § 47-3-201, which provides:

47-3-201. Transfer—Right to endorsement.—

(1) Transfer of an instrument vests in the transferee such rights as the transferor has therein, except that a transferee who has himself been a party to any fraud or illegality affecting the instrument or who as a prior holder had notice of a defense or claim against it cannot improve his position by taking from a later holder in due course.

---

[31] The assignment letter executed by Moore states:

Ron K Moore and ARK, Inc., a Tennessee corporation wholly owned by Ron K. Moore, in consideration of the cancellation of all debts due and owing to Paul P. Piper, Jr. from Ron K. Moore n the principal sum of $400,000.00, do hereby transfer and assign, without recourse, any and all their interest in and to any and all causes of action, whether now existing or accruing hereafter, that they may have as against A.S. Hart, C. Eugene Goodwin, Joseph Russell, Carl Paterson, E.F. Trading Co., Inc., Guardian Trading Co., Rivergrove Development Co., Inc. and Daniel Goodwin, relating to any and all transactions of any nature whatsoever occurring between Assignors and any of the aforesaid named individuals and/or business entities.

(2) A transfer of a security interest in an instrument vests the foregoing rights in the transferee to the extent of the interest transferred.

(3) Unless otherwise agreed any transfer for value of an instrument not then payable to bearer gives the transferee the specifically enforceable right to have the unqualified endorsement of the transferor. Negotiation takes effect only when the endorsement is made and until that time there is no presumption that the transferee is the owner.

This provision is often referred to as the "shelter rule," and in circumstances similar to the one before us, Tennessee courts, and other courts interpreting similar provisions, have held that an assignee does have the rights of the assignor, notwithstanding the absence of a proper negotiation.

In *Martin v. Martin*, 755 S.W.2d 793 (Tenn. Ct. App. 1988), the plaintiff, an assignee of a note, brought an action against the payors for the alleged unpaid balance of the note. On appeal, the defendants argued that the assignee did not have standing to sue on this note. The court referred to Tenn. Code Ann. § 47-3-201 and found that since the assignor did not have possession of the note, it could not have transferred or negotiated the note to the plaintiff. The court conceded that because of this fact, the plaintiff was not a holder of the note. Nevertheless, the court held that the plaintiff had received an assignment of a cause of action on the underlying obligation of the payors to the assignor. Thus, the court found the plaintiff could maintain this action.

The facts before us are similar to those in *Martin*. When Moore assigned his assets to Piper, he did not have possession of the notes because they we with the court in which he had previously filed the related lawsuit. Without possession of the notes, Moore could not transfer or negotiate them to Piper; however, as in Martin, Piper did receive an assignment of the cause of action on the underlying notes. Therefore, we find Piper can bring this claim.

Moreover, the case before us is even stronger than the one in *Martin*, because unlike in *Martin*, there is evidence that the notes themselves were transferred to Piper. We believe the assignment of Moore's assets to Piper and Moore's delivery of the notes to Piper's attorney constitutes a transfer as intended by § 47-3-201's shelter rule. *See* Black's Law Dictionary 1342 (5th ed. 1979) (defining transfer as "every mode, direct or indirect, absolute or conditional, voluntary or involuntary, of disposing of or parting with property or with an interest in property").

In *Schwegmann Bank & Trust Co. v. Falkenberg*, 931 F.2d 1081 [14 U.C.C. Rep Serv 2d 795] (5th Cir. 1991), the court had to determine whether the plaintiff was entitled to holder in due course rights. The court concluded that, pursuant to the shelter rule, the transferee of a holder in due course acquires all the rights of the holder in due course as long as the transferor was not personally involved in any fraud or illegality, and the transferee was not a prior holder who had notice of a defense or claim against the instrument. *Id.* at 1083. Similarly, in *American National Bank & Trust Co. v. St. Joseph Valley Bank*, 389 N.E.2d 379, 383 [26 U.C.C. Rep Serv 1174] (Ind. Ct. App. 1979), the court observed that the shelter rule "allows a transferee a possible betterment of his own position by assuming the status of his transferor. Thus, a transferee may claim the rights of a holder if he proves that his transferor was a holder." *See also Fidelity Bank, Nat'l Ass'n v. Avrutick*, 740 F. Supp. 222, 235 [12 U.C.C. Rep. Serv. 2d 1101] (S.D.N.Y. 1990) ("the transferee itself need not be a holder in due course in order to assert the rights of a holder in due course."); *B.L. Nelson and Assoc. v. Sunbelt Sav.*, 733 F.Supp. 1106, 1112 (N.D. Tex. 1990) ("The clear import of these cases is that assignees of the FSLIC are entitled to the protected status that the corporation itself enjoys, including holder in due course status.").

These cases are consistent with the Uniform Commercial Code's [1990] version of the shelter rule, [Revised] § 3-203. Comment 2 to [Revised] § 3-203 states that "transfer vests in the transferee any right of the transferor to enforce the instrument 'including any right as a holder in due course.' If the transferee is not a holder because the transferor did not indorse, the transferee is nevertheless a person entitled to enforce the instrument under [Revised] § 3-301 if the transferor was a holder at the time of transfer. Although the transferee is not a holder, under subsection (b) the transferor obtained the rights of the transferor as holder." More significantly, Comment 1 to Tenn. Code Ann. § 47-3-201 states: "Any person who transfers an instrument transfers whatever rights he has in it. The transferee acquires those rights even though they do not amount to 'title.' "

Here, it is undisputed that Moore was a holder of the notes made by Rivergrove Development. Because he transferred these notes to Piper, Piper obtained all of the rights that Moore had as a holder. This includes the right to bring a cause of action to recover on the notes. Accordingly, we hold that Piper can bring this claim.

§ 12.07 Rights of a Holder in Due Course

Read U.C.C. §§ 3-305, 3-306; see § 3-601(b).

U.C.C. § 3-305(a)(1) sets forth what are referred to as "real" defenses. Real defenses, as contrasted with "personal" ("unreal"?) defenses, are those which may be asserted even as against a holder in due course. The theory of the real defense is that there is some defect or infirmity which destroys the basic efficacy of the obligation represented on the instrument. That is, a real defense is a defense which renders the obligation, not merely unenforceable, but nugatory or void. These real defenses are set out in U.C.C. § 3-305(2)—infancy, fraud in the factum (sometimes referred to as fraud in the execution), discharge in bankruptcy and any incapacity, duress or illegality that renders the obligation a nullity. Notice that, to a great extent, matters which result in a "nullity" are not determined by the Uniform Commercial Code. Rather, they are left for determination under the laws of the particular jurisdiction. Thus, usury, gambling, etc., may be a real or personal defense, depending upon the law of the particular state.

We suspect that you have already noticed that each of the cases in this chapter have raised a defense concerning matters contained in either U.C.C. §§ 3-305(a)(1) or 3-305(a)(2) and how crucial the distinction between these two sections is. The defenses of failure of consideration and fraud in the inducement predominate in these cases, and you will notice that holders in due course take free of these defenses. *See* U.C.C. § 3-301(b).

IN RE ESTATE OF BALKUS

[The facts and opinion appear in §§ 12.02[F], *supra*, 12.03[A], *supra*.]

Assuming Holder in Due Course Status

Alternatively, even assuming Vesely is a holder in due course, we reject her argument that she takes the notes free from all defenses. Section 403.305, Stats., outlines the rights of a holder in due course:

To the extent that a holder is a holder in due course he takes the instrument free from:

(1) All claims to it on the part of any person; and

(2) *All defenses of any party to the instrument with whom the holder has not dealt except.* . . [Emphasis added.]

A holder in due course, therefore, does not take an instrument free from the defenses of any party to the instrument with whom the holder has dealt. Balkus, as maker of the notes, was a party to the instrument and the personal representative stands in his place. See generally § 857.01 and § 857.03, Stats.

Here, Vesely dealt with Balkus. She loaned him $ 12,000. He wrote a letter to her indicating that he had notes in his possession which would pay her back. There were no other parties involved in making the notes nor any transfer of the notes to a third party. Under § 403.305, Stats., therefore, Vesely cannot take the notes free from the personal representative's defense of nondelivery because she dealt with Balkus.

FEDERAL DEPOSIT INSURANCE CORP. v. MEYER

United States District Court for the District of Columbia
755 F. Supp. 10, 13 U.C.C. Rep 2d 1154 (1991)

PRATT, DISTRICT JUDGE.

Background

The Federal Deposit Insurance Corporation ("FDIC") brings this action to collect on promissory notes signed by certain former partners of the law firm of Finley, Kumble, Wagner, Heine, Underberg, Manley, Myerson & Casey ("Finley Kumble").[32] The promissory notes secured loans that the National Bank of Washington ("NBW") made in 1986 to the Finley partners to enable them to purchase stock in the Merchant Bank of California. After Finley Kumble declared bankruptcy, certain of the Finley partners defaulted on their loans and NBW filed lawsuits in the Superior Court for the District of Columbia against defendants to collect on their promissory notes.

On August 10, 1990, the Office of the Comptroller of the Currency declared the NBW insolvent, closed the bank, and appointed the Federal Deposit Insurance Corporation ("FDIC") as receiver. The FDIC then removed these cases to federal court on September 7, 1990 and moved for summary judgment against each defendant on the grounds that the Federal Deposit Insurance Act of 1950, § 13(3), 64 Stat. 889, as amended, 12 U.S.C. § 1823(e) (hereinafter § 1823(e)) provides special protections for the FDIC which bar all of the Finley partners' defenses as a matter of law.

---

32 Also included as defendants were employees of professional corporations that were partners of Finley Kumble. All defendants will collectively be referred to as the Finley partners.

Twenty of the Finley partners now oppose the FDIC's motion. First, they argue that § 1823(e) does not bar their defense of economic duress. Second, they argue that § 1823(e) is not rationally related to the furtherance of a legitimate governmental objective and therefore violates the due process clause of the fifth amendment. There are no genuine issues of material fact. For the reasons set forth below, this court finds that neither of the arguments of defendants has merit and that the FDIC is entitled to summary judgment against each of the 20 defendants as a matter of law.

Discussion

I. Defendants' Defense of Economic Duress

The Finley partners argue that the FDIC's motion for summary judgment should be denied because their defense of economic duress survives the effects of § 1823(e). They concede that § 1823(e) operates to place the FDIC in the position of a holder in due course, taking promissory notes free of personal defenses. They argue, however, that § 1823(e) does not extinguish real defenses set forth in the Uniform Commercial Code ("U.C.C.") and that their economic duress defense constitutes such a real defense.

Defendants are correct that § 1823(e) bars personal defenses but not real defenses. The section provides that an agreement or condition[33] "which tends to diminish or defeat the interest of the Corporation" shall not be enforceable against the FDIC unless it meets a number of specific requirements. 12 U.S.C. § 1823(e). As the Supreme Court explained in *Langley v. FDIC*, a real defense renders an instrument entirely void, leaving no interest that could be "diminish[ed] or defeat[ed]." 484 U.S. 86, 93-94 [5 U.C.C. Rep Serv 2d 1] (1987). In contrast, personal defenses render a note voidable but not void. A bank holding a voidable note has and can transfer to the FDIC voidable title, which is enough to constitute "interest" in the note within the meaning of § 1823(e). *See id.* at 94.

Thus, if the Finley partners' economic duress defense constitutes a real defense, then their promissory notes were void from the beginning. Asserting such a real defense could not "diminish or defeat" any interest of the FDIC because the FDIC did not have any interest to start with. On the other hand, if the Finley partners' economic duress defense is a personal defense, then the FDIC received voidable title to the promissory notes from the NBW, which constitutes "interest" under § 1823(e). Asserting a defense against this interest, therefore, would "diminish or defeat" an interest of the FDIC, and § 1823(e) would prevent the defendants from asserting the defense.

The main legal question, then, is whether economic duress is a personal defense that rendered NBW's title to the promissory notes voidable, or a real defense that rendered its title entirely void. The Finley partners suggest that duress of any nature constitutes a real defense, citing U.C.C. § 3-305(2)(b) and several cases from outside of the District of Columbia. A careful reading of the U.C.C. and its Official Commentary reveals that it does not make such a blanket classification.

First, § 3-305(2)(b) provides that holders in due course take free of all defenses except for "(b) *such* other incapacity, or duress, or illegality of the transaction, as renders the obligation of the party a nullity." (emphasis added). The words "such" and "as" indicate that the section is not stating that any type of duress renders an obligation to be a nullity. Rather, it suggests

[33] The courts have interpreted the word "agreement" broadly to include all conditions and defenses. *See Langley v. FDIC*, 484 U.S. 86, 90-93 [5 U.C.C. Rep Serv 2d 1] (1987).

that only those types of duress that are so severe as to render it a nullity stand as exceptions to the rule that holders in due course take free of defenses.[34]

Of course, the question left open is what type of duress is severe enough to render it a nullity. Neither U.C.C. § 3-305(2)(b) nor the Official Comment attempt to establish a rule governing which types of duress render a transaction void as opposed to merely voidable. Instead, Official Comment 6 declares that "[a]ll such matters are therefore left to the local law." Further supporting this point is the commentary of Chancellor William D. Hawkland on U.C.C. § 3-305(2)(b): "Unlike the case of infancy, these three defenses [incapacity, duress, illegality] may be raised only if *state* statutory or case law makes the transaction void from the outset and not merely voidable." Hawkland U.C.C. Series § 3-305:05 (emphasis added). Finally, as defendants acknowledge when they cite *Sind v. Pollen*, 356 A.2d 653 (D.C. 1976) for the District Court of Columbia's test for duress, federal courts follow state law precedent when deciding legal issues, which are not precluded by federal law, in the context of § 1823(e) cases. *See Federal Sav. and Loan Ins. Corp. v. Ziegler*, 680 F. Supp. 235, 237 (E.D. La. 1988) ("In order for duress to vitiate consent, the duress must be 'of such a nature as to cause a reasonable fear of unjust and considerable injury to a party's person, property, or reputation.' La. Civ. Code Ann. art. 1959."); cf. *FDIC v. Turner*, 869 F.2d 270, 273-75 [8 U.C.C. Rep Serv 2d 1094] (6th Cir. 1989) (applying § 47-3-305 and § 47-3-406 of the Tennessee Code to determine whether defendant could raise defense of fraud in factum, a real defense, rather than merely fraud in the inducement, a personal defense).

The Finley partners do not cite any precedent from the District of Columbia that supports the view that economic duress renders a transaction void. In fact, they point out that in *Ozerol v. Howard University*, 545 A.2d 638, 643 (D.C. 1988), the D.C. Court of Appeals quoted § 175 of the Restatement (Second) of Contracts which states that duress by threat (rather than by physical compulsion) renders a contract voidable rather than void. Although that case fails to distinguish between void and voidable contracts,[35] it calls attention to the Restatement's distinction between the two categories:

> Duress takes two forms. In one, a person physically compels conduct that appears to be a manifestation of assent by a party who has no intention of engaging in that conduct. The result of this type of duress is that the conduct is not effective to create a contract (§ 174). In the other, a person makes an improper threat that induces a party who has no reasonable alternative to manifesting his assent. The result of this type of duress is that the contract that is created is voidable by the victim (§ 175).

Restatement (Second) of Contracts, Introductory Note, Ch. 7, Topic 12.

The District of Columbia explicitly followed this distinction in *Williams v. Amann,* 33 A.2d 633, 634 (D.C. 1943). In that case, the Municipal Court of Appeals for the District of Columbia

34 Official Comment 6 supports this view of the words "such" and "as" in U.C.C. § 3-305(2)(b). The first sentences state: "Duress is a matter of degree. An instrument signed at the point of a gun is void, even in the hands of a holder in due course. One signed under threat to prosecute the son of the maker may be merely voidable, so that the defense is cut off." Clearly, the section is not placing all types of duress in the same category.

35 The case focuses on the definition of duress—"an improper threat by the other party that leaves the victim no reasonable alternative"— and holds that a threat to withhold money due under the contract is not duress because the victim has the alternative of pursuing a legal remedy rather than giving in to the duress. Although some of the language of the opinion sounds applicable to the case at bar, this court does not reach the issue of whether the Finley partners have alleged adequate facts to constitute duress at all, but assumes arguendo that they have done so.

stated that "[w]hatever duress may have existed at the time of the execution of the contract was that which operated only upon the mind of the appellant and did not involve physical compulsion. Therefore, the contract was voidable only; not void." 33 A.2d 633, 634 (D.C. 1943). Given the fact that *Williams* and *Ozerol* both support the modern Restatement view, and that no D.C. cases have been found that hold to the contrary, the correct conclusion is that in the District of Columbia physical compulsion is the only type of duress that can render a transaction entirely void.

The Finley partners do not allege that they were physically compelled to sign the promissory notes in question. They themselves labeled their defense as "economic" duress, and the substance of their allegations are that they signed the notes because of the threat that their wages and standing in the firm would decrease if they refused. Such economic duress does not reach the level of physical compulsion capable of rendering a transaction entirely void. Thus, NBW held at least voidable title to the promissory notes when the FDIC took over as receiver. Such voidable title constitutes an "interest" of the FDIC that § 1823(e) protects from being diminished or defeated. Thus, defendants' economic defense duress is not valid against the FDIC.

CASANOVA CLUB v. BISHARAT

Connecticut Supreme Court
458 A.2d 1, 35 U.C.C. Rep. 1207 (1983)

PETERS, J.

The principal question in this case is the extent to which the Connecticut policy against the enforcement of gambling debts serves to shield a debtor from his obligation to pay checks issued in a foreign country where such debts are not illegal. The plaintiff; The Casanova Club, brought an action against the defendant Victor H. Bisharat, the drawer of nine dishonored checks in the total amount of 6350£. The defendant replied with an answer and a special defense relying on General Statutes § 52-553.[36] Once the pleadings were closed, the parties filed cross motions for summary judgment. The plaintiff appeals from the denial of its motion for summary judgment and the granting of the defendant's motion.

The underlying facts are undisputed. The defendant, while in Great Britain in early 1976, became a member of the plaintiff, The Casanova Club, a British corporation operating a legal gambling casino in London. Gambling at the plaintiff club was carried on through the use of gambling chips redeemable at the club in local currency at any time. The defendant, over a period

[36] [General Statutes] Sec 52-553. Wagering Contract Void. All wagers, and all contracts and securities whereof the whole or any part of the consideration is money or other valuable thing won, laid or betted, at any game, horse race, sport or pastime, and all contracts to repay any money knowingly lent at the time and place of such game, race, sport or pastime, to any person so gaming, betting or wagering, or to repay any money lent to any person who, at such time and place, so pays, bets or wagers, shall be void, provided nothing herein contained shall affect the validity of any negotiable instrument held by any person who acquired the same for value and in good faith without notice of illegality in the consideration.

of several months, signed, as drawer, nine bearer checks totalling 6350£ to obtain from the plaintiff an equivalent amount of gambling chips, all of which he gambled and lost. His checks, presented for payment to the designated drawee, Hartford National Bank, were returned to the plaintiff with the notation "unpaid for reason: insufficient funds." The plaintiff, as holder of these dishonored checks, then brought the present action against the defendant pursuant to General Statutes § 42a-3-413(2).[37] The defendant maintains an office in this state.

The trial court concluded that the defendant was entitled to prevail on his motion for summary judgment because of "the State's long standing public policy against gambling and a statute prohibiting the enforcement of claims arising out of gambling transactions." [General Statutes § 52-553] This public policy against the enforcement of gambling debts outweighed, according to the trial court, the principle of conflicts of law which generally favors enforcement of contracts if valid where made.

The plaintiff has raised three grounds of error in support of its argument that it, and not the defendant, was entitled to summary judgment as a matter of law. The plaintiff maintains that it was entitled to recover: (1) because of rights conferred by article 3 of the Uniform Commercial Code, § 42a-3-101 et seq.; (2) because the action is not one to enforce a gambling debt; and (3) because there is no violation of Connecticut public policy. The plaintiff has made no claim that a genuine issue as to a material fact makes this case inappropriate for disposition by summary judgment. We find no error.

I

The plaintiff's claims under our negotiable instruments law are governed by principles set down by the Uniform Commercial Code. Under the Code, a drawer, a person who issues checks, engages that, upon their dishonor and due notice of such dishonor, he will pay their face amount to their holder. General Statutes § 42a-3-413(2). A drawer is not, however, absolutely liable, and may interpose defenses to his liability. General Statutes § 42a-3-307(2). Once the drawer has "shown that a defense exists," a person claiming the rights of a holder in due course has the burden of establishing his due course status. General Statutes § 42a-3-307(3). Even a holder in due course, however, does not take checks free of the defenses of a party to the checks with whom the holder has dealt. General Statutes § 42a-3-305(2). *See generally* White & Summers, Uniform Commercial Code (2d Ed 1980) §§ 13-9, 14-9, 14-10.

Applying these statutory mandates to the present case, we conclude that the plaintiff; either as a holder or a holder in due course, can recover the face amounts of the nine checks issued by the defendant only if the defendant cannot establish his defense of illegality. It is undisputed that there was direct dealing between the plaintiff and the defendant with regard to the gambling transactions out of which the checks arose. In the present circumstances, therefore, the plaintiff's reliance on the policy of promoting unencumbered transferability of negotiable instruments is misplaced, since the Uniform Commercial Code, in cases of direct dealing between immediate parties, expressly subjects even due course holders to real and personal defenses. The law of negotiable instruments therefore provides no basis for overturning the judgment rendered by the trial court.

---

[37] General Statutes § 42a-3-4 13(2)provides:

Contract of Maker, Drawer and Acceptor. . . . (2) The drawer engages that upon dishonor of the draft and any necessary notice of dishonor or protest he will pay the amount of the draft to the holder or to any endorser who takes it up. The drawer may disclaim this liability by drawing without recourse.

II

The plaintiff's second claim of error is that enforcement of these checks is not illegal because their issuance does not fall within the prohibitions of General Statutes § 52-553. The plaintiff argues that these checks neither represent "contracts . . . whereof the whole or any part of the consideration is money or other valuable thing won, laid or betted, at any game . . . or pastime nor contracts . . . of such game . . . or pastime, to any person so gaming, betting or wagering, or to repay any money lent to any person who, at such time and place, so pays, bets or wagers." Because the defendant received gambling chips for his checks, rather than cancelled I.O.U.'s for debts incurred while gambling, the plaintiff maintains that the checks are not wagering contracts. We do not agree.

It is true that the defendant had no contract to gamble, and was under no other obligation to do so. In theory he was free at any time to convert his gambling chips either to local currency or to some other equivalent of cash. In fact, however, the transaction as a whole was designed to enable him to gamble at the plaintiff club. No evidence has been presented that suggests either a temporal or a geographic gap between his acquisition of gambling chips and his use of them at the gaming tables. Under these circumstances, it is reasonable to presume that the opportunity to gamble was part of the consideration for the furnishing of gambling chips to the defendant. In the alternative, the defendant's conditional engagement to make good any check that his bank dishonored may also be considered a contract to repay moneys knowingly lent by the plaintiff to enable the defendant to gamble.

The plaintiff might have made a stronger argument that § 52-553 does not apply had the plaintiff properly invoked the statutory proviso that protects "the validity of any negotiable instrument held by any person who acquired the same for value and in good faith without notice of illegality in the consideration." Although in its appellate brief the plaintiff maintains that "there could be no 'notice of illegality' to taint the negotiability and enforceability of the checks," the absence of notice is raised in none of the pleadings in the trial court. A notice question ordinarily raises a question of fact inappropriate for resolution by summary judgment. Having failed to raise the issue of notice in the trial court, having indeed consistently insisted that this case is ripe for summary judgment, the plaintiff cannot for the first time in this court rely on an argument depending upon an unconceded factual assertion on which it bears the burden of proof. Cf. General Statutes § 42a-3-307(3). Without some basis in the record to support its statement that it acquired the defendant's checks "without notice of illegality in the consideration," the plaintiff cannot invoke the exculpatory proviso of § 52-553.

III

The plaintiff's final claim of error is that the defendant's purchase of gambling chips is not so offensive to Connecticut public policy as to bar suit on the checks that he issued. In part, this claim merely reiterates the proposition, which we have already rejected, that the defendant's purchase of chips was severable from any gambling debt or contract, and thus not forbidden by our statute. The plaintiff further suggests that our public policy against gambling, which we have acknowledged to be "ancient and deep-rooted"; *Ciampittiello v. Campitello*, 134 Conn 51, 56, 54 A2d 669 (1947); has become so attenuated that it should not be applied to bar recovery for a transaction valid under British law.

It is undisputed that the gambling activities that took place at the plaintiff's casino were legal under the laws of Great Britain.[38] Had the plaintiff pursued its claim to judgment in Great Britain, our courts could have permitted recovery on that judgment here. See *Hilton International Co. v. Arace*, 35 Conn Sup 522, 527-30, 394 A.2d 739 (1977).

It is equally clear that our General Assembly has made substantial inroads into the public policy against gambling. The legislature has sanctioned activities such as lotteries; General Statutes § 12-568; off-track and parimutuel betting; General Statutes §§12-571 and 12-572; and jai alai frontons; General Statutes § 12-573a. None of these statutes, however, permits gambling on credit, and that is the vice at which the underlying statutes forbidding wagering contracts; General Statutes §§ 52-553 and 52-554; are particularly directed.

In effect, the plaintiff urges that these judicial and legislative developments should lead us to reconsider *Ciampittiello v. Campitello, supra*, 56-57, in which we held that our prohibition against gambling was so deeply rooted in our public policy that we would not enforce a gambling contract despite its validity in Rhode Island, where the debt had been incurred. We decided *Ciampittiello* in accordance with the then prevalent analysis of the Restatement (First), Conflict of Laws § 612 (1934); Goodrich, Conflict of Laws (2d Ed 1938) § 103; and 6 Williston, Contracts (Rev Ed 1938) § 1792, that required deference to the law of a contract's making unless the contrary law of the forum invoked "some prevalent conception of good morals, some deep-rooted tradition of the common weal." *Loucks v. Standard Oil Co.*, 224 NY 99, 111, 120 NE 198 (1918) (Cardozo, J.). We recognize that there is now scholarly support for a different form of analysis. According to the Restatement (Second), Conflict of Laws § 202(1) (1971), the effect of illegality is to be determined by the law of the state that has, in accordance with the standards of the Restatement (Second), Conflict of Laws § 188, the most significant relationship to the parties and to the transaction. Compare General Statutes § 42a-1-105(1); see also Weintraub, Commentary on the Conflict of Laws, c 7 (1971). If that analytic model were adopted, the public policy of the forum state would no longer be dispositive. We note also that some courts in other jurisdictions have re-examined their positions in similar cases to allow out-of-state gambling debts to be enforced.

The present record provides no occasion for a searching reappraisal of *Ciampittiello*. Because of the parties' decision to move for summary judgment, We lack a factual basis for application of the criteria that the Restatement (Second), Conflict of Laws would require us to apply, were we to adopt that analytic model. Nor are we prepared, on the present state of the evidence, to reconsider *Ciampittiello* were we to continue to follow the criteria of the Restatement (First). A case in which the plaintiff has failed to show that it lacked notice of the illegality of the questioned transactions under Connecticut law is, in any event, an unsuitable vehicle for far reaching exploration of public policy. In short, the plaintiff has failed to demonstrate that the judgment of the trial court was in error.

QUESTION

Notice that the Casanova Club was not a holder in due course because of its notice of defenses, and also under U.C.C. § 3-305(2) was considered to have dealt with Bisharat. What result if the action had been brought by a bank that had cashed the checks for the Casanova Club?

---

[38] The defendant has not pursued its preliminary statement of issues in opposition to the appeal, namely that the record contains no evidence that gambling obligations are enforceable in Great Britain. The trial court in its memorandum of decision "noted that gambling activities to which reference is made herein are legal in Great Britain."

SANDLER v. EIGHTH JUDICIAL DISTRICT COURT OF NEVADA

Nevada Supreme Court
614 P.2d 10, 29 U.C.C. Rep. 1546 (1980)

BATJER, J.

Nevada National Bank filed suit against Jerrold Sandler to recover the proceeds from several checks written by Sandler. Sandler wrote the checks on a Maryland bank account to John Hutchings and others for gambling and to cover gambling losses incurred by Sandler, and by Hutchings in Sandler's behalf, during private "freeze out" games of "21." The checks were all negotiated to Nevada National Bank. The district judge denied Sandler's motion for summary judgment. Sandler petitions this court for a writ of mandamus to compel the district judge to grant Summary judgment in his favor.

A writ of mandamus will issue to compel entry of a summary judgment when there is no genuine issue as to any material fact and the movant is entitled to judgment as a matter of law. In this case it is undisputed that the checks were drawn by Sandler to engage in gambling or delivered to John Hutchings for the express purpose of engaging in gambling ventures. As a matter of law, checks drawn for the purpose of gambling are void and unenforceable in this state.

Nevada National Bank seeks to avoid the defense that the checks are void and unenforceable (Statute of 9 Anne, C 14, § l) by claiming to be a holder in due course immune to that defense. NRS 104.3305 provides that a holder in due course takes an instrument free from: "2. All defenses of any party to the instrument with whom the holder has not dealt except:. . .(b) Such other incapacity, or duress, or illegality of the transaction, as renders the obligation of the party a nullity[.]" A holder in due course is not immune to real defenses; that is, those defenses which render the check, and the underlying obligation created thereby, entirely void. *Bankers Trust Co. v. Litton Systems*, 599 F.2d 488 (2d Cir 1979); White & Summers, Uniform Commercial Code § 1410 at 487-488. Because the Statute of Anne renders the checks herein void ab initio, the defense may be asserted against Nevada National Bank. *Pacific National Bank v. Hernreich*, 398 SW2d 22 l (Ark 1966). Therefore, summary judgment in favor of Sandler must be granted.

NOTE

Bankers Trust Co. v. Litton Systems, 599 F.2d 488 (2d Cir. 1979), cited by the Nevada Supreme Court, involved a question of the New York commercial bribery statute. You may recall the problem from *Sirkin v. Fourteenth Street Store*, 124 App. Div. 384, 108 N.Y.S. 830 (1908), and

McConnell v. Commonwealth Pictures Corp., 7 N.Y.2d 465, 166 N.E.2d 494, 199 N.Y.S.2d 483 (1960), as these cases show up in a number of Contracts casebooks. The federal court indicated an examination of the language in the New York decisions on the enforceability of bribery-induced contracts suggested that New York courts held such contracts to be "void." Nonetheless, the court concluded that under New York law a holder in due course could treat a contract induced by illegal bribery as merely voidable. The court stated:

> [I]t would be poor policy for courts to transform banks and other finance companies into policing agents charged with the responsibility of searching out commercial bribery committed by their assignors. We doubt that denying recovery to holders in due course would have an appreciable effect on the frequency of commercial bribery. Moreover, the holder in due course concept embodies important policies which must be weighed against the policy of holding void contracts induced by bribery. To paraphrase Professor Gilmore, the holder in due course is protected not because of his praiseworthy character, but to the end that commercial transactions may be engaged in without elaborate investigation of the process leading up to the contract or instrument and in reliance on the contract rights of one who offers them for sale or to secure a loan. Gilmore, *The Commercial Doctrine of Good Faith Purchase*, 63 Yale L.J. 1057 (1954); Abrogation of the rights of a holder in due course is not warranted in this case.

KEDZIE & 103rd CURRENCY EXCHANGE, INC. v. HODGE

Illinois Supreme Court
619 N.E.2d 732, 21 U.C.C. Rep. 2d 682 (1993)

FREEMAN, J.

We consider here whether a holder in due course of a check is precluded from payment as against the drawer where the check was given in exchange for contract services for which the provider was required to be, but was not, a licensed plumber. We conclude such a claim is not precluded.

BACKGROUND

Pursuant to a written "work order," Fred Fentress agreed to install a "flood control system" at the home of Eric and Beulah Hodge of Chicago for $900.00. In partial payment for the work, Beulah Hodge drafted a personal check payable to "Fred Fentress—A-OK Plumbing" for $500 from the Hodges' joint account at Citicorp Savings.

The system's components were not delivered to the Hodge's home as scheduled. And, when Fentress failed to appear on the date set for installation, Eric Hodge telephoned him to announce the contract "cancelled." Hodge also told Fentress that he would order Citicorp Savings not to pay the check Fentress had been given.

Records of Citicorp Savings confirm acknowledgement of a stop-payment order entered the same day.

Nevertheless, Fentress presented the check at the Kedzie & 103rd Street Currency Exchange (Currency Exchange), endorsing it as "sole owner" of A-OK Plumbing, and obtained payment. However, when the Currency Exchange later presented the check for payment at Citicorp Savings, payment was refused in accordance with the stop-payment order.

The Currency Exchange, alleging it was a holder in due course (*see* Ill. Rev. Stat. 1989, ch. 26, par. 3-302), then sued Beulah Hodge, as drawer of the check, and Fentress for the amount stated. Hodge, in turn, filed a counterclaim against Fentress. Hodge also moved to dismiss the Currency Exchange's action against her (*see* Ill. Rev. Stat. 1989, ch. 110, par. 2-619). The disposition of Hodge's motion gives rise to this appeal.

Hodge asserted a defense provided by § 3-305 of the Uniform Commercial Code (U.C.C.) (Ill. Rev. Stat. 1989, ch. 26, par. 3-305). Under that section, the claim of a holder in due course of a negotiable instrument may be barred based on "illegality of the transaction." (Ill. Rev. Stat. 1989, ch. 26, par. 3-305(2)(b).) Hodge contended Fentress was not a licensed plumber as was required under the Illinois Plumbing License Law (*see* Ill. Rev. Stat. 1989, ch. 111, pars. 1101 through 1140). The director of licensing and registration of the Chicago department of buildings and the keeper of plumbing licensing records of the Illinois Department of Public Health provided affidavits supporting that contention. Hodge asserted that, because Fentress was in violation of the Illinois Plumbing License Law, his promised performance under the contract gave rise to the requisite "illegality" to bar the Currency Exchange's claim for payment.

The circuit court granted the motion and dismissed the Currency Exchange's action against Hodge. The appellate court, with one justice dissenting, affirmed. (234 Ill. App. 3d 1017 [19 U.C.C. Rep Serv 2d 814].) Pursuant to Supreme Court Rule 315(a) (134 Ill. 2d R. 315(a)), we allowed the Currency Exchange's petition for leave to appeal.

The legal sufficiency of the Currency Exchange's action, including the allegation that it possesses the check as a holder in due course, is admitted by Hodge's motion. The reason asserted for dismissal—"illegality" grounded upon noncompliance with a statutory licensure requirement—was raised properly as affirmative matter and supported by affidavit.

The Illinois Plumbing License Law requires that all plumbing, including "installation . . . or extension" of "drains," be performed by plumbers licensed under the Act. (Ill. Rev. Stat. 1989, ch. 111, pars. 1102(5), (8), 1103.) The affidavits establish that Fentress was not licensed either by the City of Chicago or the State of Illinois. That failure is a violation of the Illinois Plumbing License Law and is punishable as a misdemeanor. Ill. Rev. Stat. 1989, ch. 111, pars. 1103, 1128.

Hodge therefore carried the burden of going forward.

No counteraffidavit was supplied. For purposes of the motion, the fact that Fentress was not a licensed plumber is deemed admitted. No other matter was presented to refute the defense.

No material fact remains to be resolved. The question is simply whether Hodge is entitled, as a matter of law, to a judgment of dismissal n view of the defense asserted under U.C.C. § 3-305.

"Illegality" under § 3-305

Section 3-305 provides, in relevant part:

"[A] holder in due course . . .takes the instrument free from

> . . .
>
> (2) all defenses of any party to the instrument with whom the holder has not dealt except
>
> . . .
>
> (b) . . . illegality of the transaction, as renders the obligation of the party a nullity." (Ill. Rev. Stat. 1989, ch. 26, par. 3-305.)

The concern is whether noncompliance by Fentress with the Illinois Plumbing License Law gives rise to "illegality of the transaction" with respect to the contract for plumbing services so as to bar the claim of the Currency Exchange, a holder in due course of the check initially given Fentress.

The issue of "illegality" arises "under a variety of statutes." In view of the diverse constructions to which statutory enactments are given, "illegality" is, accordingly, a matter "left to the local law." Even so, it is only when an obligation is made "entirely null and void" under "local law" that "illegality" exists as one of the "real defenses" under § 3-305 to defeat a claim of a holder in due course. In effect, the obligation must be no obligation at all. If it is "merely voidable" at the election of the obligor, the defense is unavailable.

Historically, this court has recognized "illegality" to arise only in view of legislative declaration affecting both the underlying contract or transaction and the instrument exchanged upon it. A contract or transaction which is void must certainly negate the obligation to pay arising from it as between the contracting parties. But, unless an instrument memorializing the obligation is also made void, an innocent third party who has no knowledge of the circumstances of the initial contract or transaction may yet claim payment of it against the drawer or maker.

Thus, "illegality" has been held to defeat the claims of holders in due course in cases involving contracts of a gaming nature or for retirement of gambling debts. Owning to a deep-seated hostility toward nongovernmental-sanctioned gambling, our legislature has declared that any instrument associated with such activity is void, independent of the status of who may possess it. The absence of similar legislative declaration as for an instrument given upon a usurious contract must account, in part, for the conclusion that usury has not been held to give rise to "illegality" as a defense against a holder in due course.

That the existence or absence of legislative declaration controls the issue was recognized by our appellate court in *McGregor v. Lamont* (1922), 225 Ill. App. 451, a case involving circumstances similar to those here. John T. Lamont was the maker of a note used to pay for shares of stock issued by the Corn Belt Farmers' Cooperative Association (Association). Lamont's note subsequently came into the possession of Robert Roy McGregor, a holder in due course. When Lamont failed to pay on the note, McGregor filed suit and obtained a judgment against him.

Lamont moved to vacate the judgment. Lamont asserted that the purchase of the shares of stock was void under the Illinois Securities Law because the Association had not complied with its requirements. Because the transaction was void, Lamont concluded, the note given in payment must also be void despite McGregor's status as a holder in due course.

The appellate court noted that the Illinois Securities Law did, indeed, make transactions for the sale of shares of stock void based on noncompliance with the Law's requirements. But the court noted that only the "sale and contract of sale" of shares of stock were expressly made void, not instruments exchanged upon such contracts. Absent legislative declaration making such instruments void, the court declined to recognize a defense to McGregor's action for payment on the note.

The same rule obtains in New Jersey. In *New Jersey Mortgage & Investment Corp. v. Berenyi* (App. Div. 1976), 140 N.J. Super. 406, 356 A.2d 421 [8 U.C.C. Rep Serv 825], a holder in due course of an note was permitted to maintain a claim for its payment even though the note had been initially obtained by a corporation in a transaction which violated an injunctive order. No statute rendered the note void, and the holder in due course had no knowledge or notice of the injunction. But in *Westervelt v. Gateway Financial Service* (Ch. Div. 1983), 190 N.J. Super. 615, 464 A.2d 1203 [37 U.C.C. Rep Serv 805], the "illegality" defense was held to bar the claim of a holder in due course of a secondary mortgage and note because New Jersey's Secondary Mortgage and Loan Act specifically made void "[a]ny obligation on the part of the borrower arising out of a secondary mortgage loan." *Westervelt* involved what *Berenyi* did not: applicability of a direct statutory expression that an instrument, itself, arising from a particular contract or transaction was void.

Several other jurisdictions also find reason to draw a distinction between the voidness of a negotiable instrument and the underlying contract or transaction upon which it is exchanged. (See Annot., 80 A.L.R.2d 465, 472-75 (1961) (summarizing several state decisions in which holders in due course were permitted to claim payment of instruments executed in favor of foreign corporations doing business in states without complying with local licensing requirements).) Although recognition of that distinction is not universal (*see Wilson v. Steele* (1989), 211 Cal. App. 3d 1053, 259 Cal. Rptr. 851 (holding that "illegality" need only be present in the underlying contract between an unlicensed contractor and the drafter of a negotiable instrument to bar the claim of a holder in due course)), we are convinced it remains the better rule.

A plaintiff is precluded from recovering on a suit involving an illegal contract because the plaintiff is a wrongdoer. (*See Bankers Trust Co. v. Litton Systems, Inc.* (2d Cir. 1979), 599 F.2d 488, 492 [26 U.C.C. Rep Serv 513] (citing the Restatement of Contracts and Restatement (Second) of Contracts).) Enforcement of the illegal contract makes the court an indirect participant in the wrongful conduct. *See Litton*, 599 F.2d at 493.

But a holder in due course is an innocent third party. Such a holder is without knowledge of the circumstances of the contract upon which the instrument was initially exchanged. (Ill. Rev. Stat. 1989, ch. 26, par. 3-302(1)(c) (defining a holder in due course, in part, as a holder who is "without notice . . .of any defense against or claim to [the instrument] on the part of any person").) The same rationale that precludes recovery by a wrongdoing plaintiff is inapplicable in determining such a holder's right to claim payment. Enforcement of that claim does not sully the court.

The holder in due course concept is intended to facilitate commercial transactions by eliminating the need for "elaborate investigation" of the nature of the circumstances for which an instrument is initially exchanged or of its drafting. If "illegality" means simply negation of the initial obligation to pay, a holder in due course enjoys no more protection than a party to the original contract or transaction. The "real" defense of "illegality" is reduced to a "personal" one.

It is, therefore, not enough simply to conclude that the initial obligation to pay arising from a void contract or transaction is void. Negation of that obligation as between the contracting parties has little bearing on whether a holder in due course of an instrument arising from the contract or transaction should nevertheless be permitted to make a claim for payment.

The "local law" of this state has been formulated upon this court's recognition, in cases predating the U.C.C., of legislative prerogative regarding negotiable instruments. In adopting the U.C.C. and, in particular, § 3-305, our legislature chose to confer upon a holder in due course of a negotiable instrument considerable protection against claims by persons to it. Our legislature also continues to declare certain obligations void because of the circumstances of the agreements from which they arise and without regard to the status of who may claim ownership (subjecting "[a]ny obligation" made void by reason of gambling to be "set aside and vacated" by any court). The selective negation of obligations reflects a legislative aim to declare what will and will not give rise to "illegality" in cases now governed by the U.C.C.. As legislative direction indicates which obligations are always void, legislative silence indicates when the protection afforded a holder in due course must be honored.

We therefore reaffirm, today, the view this court has consistently recognized in cases predating the U.C.C.. Unless the instrument arising from a contract or transaction is, itself, made void by statute, the "illegality" defense under § 3-305 is not available to bar the claim of a holder in due course.

CONCLUSION

To determine whether Hodge is entitled to a judgment of dismissal, we need not engage in an analysis aimed at characterizing the contract between Fentress and the Hodges. Whether the underlying contract should be considered void because Fentress was not licensed as required by the Illinois Plumbing License Law is not dispositive of the Currency Exchange's right, as a holder in due course, to claim payment of the check. It is relevant only to determine whether the Illinois Plumbing License Law provides that any obligation arising from a contract for plumbing services made in violation of its requirements is void. It does not.

For the reasons stated, the judgments of the appellate and circuit courts are reversed, and the cause is remanded to the circuit court for further proceeding. Judgments reversed; cause remanded.

McMorrow, J., took no part in the consideration or decision of this case.

Bilandic, J., dissenting.

EXCHANGE INTERNATIONAL LEASING CORP. v. CONSOLIDATED BUSINESS FORMS CO., INC.

U.S. District Court, Western District of Pennsylvania
462 F. Supp 626, 25 U.C.C. Rep. 1383 (1978)

Diamond, District Judge.

Plaintiff, Exchange International Leasing Corporation, (hereinafter Exchange) brought the instant suit to recover rental payments from defendant, Consolidated Business Forms, (hereinafter

Consolidated) arising out of defendant's leasing of a Phillips business computer. Plaintiff is the named lessor of said computer by virtue of an assignment from the original lessor, third party defendant, Northern Leasing and Financial Corporation, (hereinafter Northern).

It has been established through the ruling on a prior motion for summary judgment filed by plaintiff that the aforesaid assignment conferred upon plaintiff the status of a holder in due course under §3-302 of the Uniform Commercial Code (hereinafter U.C.C.), 12A PS §3-302 and that the defendant's only plausible defense was misrepresentation under §3-305(2) (c) of the U.C.C., 12A PS §3-305 (2)(c). The matter now before the court is plaintiff's second motion for summary judgment in which it claims that no genuine issue of misrepresentation exists. For the reasons set forth below, we conclude that there is no genuine issue of a material fact regarding the misrepresentations defense and that the defendant was not the victim of misrepresentation within the meaning of §3-305(2)(c) and, therefore, grant the motion.

The facts relevant to the disposition of this matter may be summarized as follows: After several weeks of discussion and correspondence with fourth party defendant, Benchmark Systems, Inc. (hereinafter Benchmark), a Pittsburgh area sales representative for third party defendant, Phillips Business Systems, Inc. (hereinafter Phillips), Consolidated decided to acquire a Phillips computer. Because Consolidated was not in a position to purchase the $25,000.00 computer outright, a 66-month lease-purchase was arranged. Northern Leasing, not Phillips or Benchmark, was the lessor of the equipment under a lease signed on November 22, 1974. The lease contained a common waiver-of-defense clause, which stated essentially that rental obligations were not conditioned on the fulfilling of any express or implied warranties. Northern assigned the lease to Exchange in April, 1975. Exchange subsequently instituted this suit alleging that shortly after the assignment Consolidated defaulted in its rental payments.

Consolidated filed an answer in which it claimed that its rental obligations had been excused by the breach of certain performance guarantees made to it by Benchmark during negotiations. In ruling on an earlier motion for summary judgment by Exchange, however, Judge Knox of this court ruled that this defense was not available to Consolidated, since Exchange was a holder in due course within the meaning of §3-302 of the U.C.C. and that therefore, Consolidated could only avail itself of the defenses enumerated in §3-305 of the U.C.C. Of those §3-305 defenses, the one contained in subsection (2)(c) dealing with misrepresentation was raised by Consolidated. Exchange had also sought summary disposition of the §3-305(2)(c) defense, but Judge Knox denied summary judgment in that regard for the reason that the record was insufficient to permit the conclusion that no genuine issue of material fact existed as to the §3-305(2)(c) claim.

Following the denial of summary judgment, Exchange incorporated into the record the deposition of one James E. Spohn, Chairman of the Board of Consolidated. Spohn was the Consolidated representative who negotiated for the acquisition of the Phillips computer and who also signed the lease with Exchange's predecessor in interest, Northern. Exchange then filed the instant motion for summary judgment, contending that Spohn's deposition sufficiently augmented the record to remove any genuine issue of fact concerning misrepresentation under §3-305(2) (c).

In order to rule on the instant motion we must consider (1) the meaning of "misrepresentation" under §3-305(2)(c); (2) the factual basis in support of the allegations of misrepresentation relied on by Consolidated; and (3) whether or not there exists a genuine issue of a material fact which if true would constitute a defense.

Turning first to the meaning of "misrepresentation," §3-305(2)(c) states:

To the extent that a holder is a holder in due course he takes the instrument free from

. . . .

(2) all defenses of any party to the instrument with whom the holder has not dealt except

. . . .

(c) such misrepresentation as has induced the party to sign the instrument with neither knowledge nor reasonable opportunity to obtain knowledge of its character or its essential terms. . .

Thus, to establish the defense, one must not only have had no knowledge of a document's character or essential terms, but also have had no "reasonable opportunity" to acquire such knowledge. Comment 7 to §3-305 elaborates by stating that in determining what constitutes a "reasonable opportunity" factors such as the age, intelligence, and business experience of the signator, his ability to read English, and the representations made to him and his reason to rely on them are to be considered.[39]

The reported Pennsylvania decisions interpreting §3-305(2)(c) while the in number are nonetheless uniform in holding that only fraud in the factum, as opposed to fraud in the inducement, is a defense under §3-305. This view is in accord with comment 7 and also the view expressed by certain scholars in the area.

As comment 7 notes, the classic example of fraud in the factum is that of a person who is tricked into signing a note on the pretense that it is a mere receipt of some sort. Pennsylvania is apparently hesitant to expand the defense and afford relief to less obvious victims. For example, in *Reading Trust Co. v. Hutchison*, 35 D & C2d 790 (1964), defendants agreed to permit a company to install and demonstrate a water softening machine in defendant's home in order to promote sales to defendants' neighbors. The defendants signed a document which was represented by the company to be a bond securing against damage to the equipment. In reality, the document was a note securing the purchase price of the equipment. The court refused to hold that defendants had been the victims of misrepresentation within the purview of § 3-305(2)(c), for the reason that defendants had established no basis from which it could be concluded that they had reason to rely on the statements of the company's representative and, that they had the opportunity, time, and ability to read the document before signing it. For a contra view, see *American Plan Corp. v. Woods*, 16 Ohio App. 2d 1, 240 NE2d 886 (1968).

With the foregoing in mind we consider the specific misrepresentations relied on by Consolidated. In its brief Consolidated contends that "Mr. Spohn was precluded from examining the contents of the agreement by the representations made to him" by employees of Phillips and Benchmark. Although defendant's brief does not disclose the specifics of those representations, Spohn's deposition indicates that they were in the nature of assurances that the computer would be removed with a complete refund if it failed to function properly. Spohn testified that the Benchmark representative with whom he was most actively involved, the person who suggested the lease arrangement and who was present for its signing, one Steve O'Connor, "assured me at all times that the guarantee was in force." Spohn referred to two other statements "guaranteeing" the computer, both of which were made shortly after he initially approached Benchmark in regard to a possible purchase. One statement was made orally at a trade show by the president of Benchmark, while the other was contained in a promotional brochure signed by another officer of Benchmark.

[39] The complete text of comment 7 is as follows: [the Court cites Official Comment 7].

Assuming without deciding that the statements referred to by Spohn could form the basis of a misrepresentation, nevertheless the court is of the opinion that genuine issue exists as to the presence of a §3-305(2)(c) defense. For, even if it be true that Spohn did not have actual knowledge of the essential terms of the lease,[40] it can hardly be said that he lacked a "reasonable opportunity" to acquire that knowledge an essential element of a §3-305(2)(c) defense. Spohn testified unequivocally that O'Connor in no way prevented him from reading the instrument before he signed it, that he could have read the document in its entirety had he so desired, and that he was not busy or otherwise distracted at the time of execution. Spohn further testified that he read part of the lease but simply chose not to read the "fine print" because he had trust in O'Connor.

The court notes that while the waiver of defenses clause was not in bold-face print, it was not inconspicuously buried in the document either. It appeared on the cover page of the lease immediately between the identification of the transaction and the signatory portions of the instrument. The court further observes that there were three "fine print" clauses on the cover sheet and that, of the three, the waiver-of-defense clause was the most prominent. Considering all of these factors, the court concludes that there is no genuine issue of fact concerning the reason for Spohn's ignorance of the essential character and terms of the instrument which he executed on behalf of Consolidated. It was purely a matter of his choice not to read that which was readily and conveniently available for him to read.

Consolidated argues for a contrary result by emphasizing that portion of comment 7 which states that in determining what constitutes a "reasonable opportunity" one is to consider the representation made to the signator and "his reason to rely on them or to have confidence in the person making them." The court does not find this argument persuasive because it simply ignores the other facts to be considered in determining whether one had reasonable opportunity to obtain knowledge of the instrument's character and essential terms. When these other factors; viz., age, intelligence, business experience, ability to read the document, necessity for acting speedily, are considered in the light of Spohn's deposition it is clear that there is no legal justification for the blind reliance which Spohn contends he had on the statements of O'Connor.

An appropriate Order will be entered granting plaintiff's motion for summary judgment.

Because the matter of discharge is treated separately, it may appear that discharge would be a formidable defense. However, U.C.C. § 3-602 makes it very clear: DISCHARGE IS A PERSONAL DEFENSE!

[40] Several times throughout the course of his deposition Spohn states that he did not know the character of the document either. He indicates that he was under the impression that it constituted an installment purchase arrangement between Consolidated and Phillips. It is clear from the deposition, however, that such an erroneous impression was not the result of a misrepresentation by Benchmark or Phillips. For in all their communications with Spohn, both Benchmark and Phillips termed the arrangement a lease and nothing more. Finally, Spohn admits that he nonetheless "assumed" it was really a purchase from Phillips, since he was under the impression that an enforceable guarantee could exist only if the transaction were a purchase. Thus, it is clear that the only matter of which Spohn may have been misinformed or misled was of an "essential term"; namely, continued viability of the Phillips warranty.

FIRST NATIONAL BANK v. ROB-GLEN ENTERPRISES, INC.

New York Supreme Court, Appellate Division
101 A.D.2d 848, 476 N.Y.S.2d 161 (1984)

MEMORANDUM BY THE COURT.

In an action to recover on a series of promissory notes, defendants appeal from a judgment of the Supreme Court, Nassau County, dated January 7, 1983, which, *inter alia*, granted plaintiff's motion for summary judgment, denied defendants' cross motion to dismiss the complaint or alternatively for summary judgment in their favor, and awarded plaintiff $52,211.77.

Judgment affirmed, with costs.

The promissory notes in question were executed by defendant Rob-Glen Enterprises, Inc. on September 9, 1976 and delivered to the Dolly Cam Corp. in return for a loan of $46,000. At the same time, the individual defendants executed identical guarantees of payment for each of the notes waiving presentment, demand, protest, notice of protest and notice of dishonor. Shortly thereafter, on September 27, 1976, prior to their maturity, Dolly Cam endorsed these same notes in blank and delivered them to plaintiff's predecessor pursuant to a general loan and security agreement, as security for past and future debts.

A holder in due course of a negotiable instrument is one who takes the instrument for value in good faith without notice that it is overdue or has been dishonored or of any defense against it or claim to it on the part of any person (Uniform Commercial Code, § 3-302, subd.[1]).

Plaintiff established that it was a holder in due course of the notes in question, having taken them from the Dolly Cam Corp. as security for an antecedent debt (Uniform Commercial Code, § 3-303, subd. [b]), and absent any viable defense was entitled to recover payment on the notes. We agree with Special Term that defendants' claimed defense of payment or accord and satisfaction is without merit. The payment to a third party, nonowner, nonholder of the notes and purported discharge of the obligation in bankruptcy proceedings involving that third party are without effect. In order to effect a discharge of the debt payment, satisfaction must be made to the holder of the instrument (Uniform Commercial Code, § 3-603).

We have examined defendants' other contentions and find them to be equally without merit.

NOTE

See U.C.C. § 3-302(b) and Comment 3. § 3-305(a)(1)(iv) and the last paragraph of Comment 1. An obligor is given a discharge from obligor's debts under the federal Bankruptcy Code. 11 U.S.C.A. §§ 727, 523, 524.

§ 12.08 Use of Third Party Claims as Defenses

Read: U.C.C. § 3-305(c) and Official Comment 4

FEDERAL DEPOSIT INSURANCE CORP. v. MOORE

United States District Court, South Carolina
488 F. Supp. 493, 24 U.C.C. Rep. 176 (1978)

CHAPMAN, DISTRICT JUDGE.

After the American Bank and Trust (AB&T) was closed by the South Carolina State Board of Bank Control in 1974, the plaintiff, Federal Deposit Insurance Corporation (FDIC) was appointed by the Board to act as receiver for the bank. As receiver the FDIC proceeded to liquidate the bank and, as part of the liquidation, it sold a number of assets including some negotiable instruments to itself. Subsequently, FDIC instituted a number of lawsuits. A large number of suits were instituted by FDIC as the corporate owner of the negotiable instruments to collect from the parties liable thereon. The instant case is one of those suits. In its capacity as receiver FDIC instituted an action in federal court seeking a declaratory judgment that it was the owner of all choses in action against the officers and directors of the bank for nonfeasance or malfeasance which may have caused damages to the bank. Since the bank was wholly owned by a holding company, American Bank and Trust Shares (ABTS), FDIC also sought a declaration that it was the owner of all choses in action against the officers and directors of ABTS. The shareholders of ABTS were subsequently made parties defendant in the declaratory judgment action and they counterclaimed alleging in substance that, under state law, the FDIC became receiver illegally and through fraud and asked that the appointment of FDIC as receiver be revoked and that the sale of AB&T assets by FDIC to itself be rescinded. The district court determined that FDIC was the sole owner of the choses in action against the officers and directors of both AB&T and ABTS, indefinitely stayed the trial of the counterclaim, and permitted FDIC to proceed with its case against the officers and directors as soon as practicable. The Fourth Circuit vacated this ruling in *Federal Deposit Ins. Corp. v. American Bank Trust Shares, Inc.*, 558 F.2d 711 (4th Cir. 1977), and required the district court to resolve the issues raised by the counterclaim before trying FDIC's action against the officers and directors.

FDIC instituted the present case seeking to reduce to judgment the balance due on a promissory note executed by defendant in the principle amount of $275,000.00 and payable in full on March 22, 1975. This note had been purchased by the FDIC from the receivership of AB&T. In his answer, defendant denies any liability to FDIC on the note through a number of defenses. The FDIC has conveniently catalogued the various defenses under three headings; the Purchase and Assumption defenses, the Extension defenses, and the Residency and Indebtedness defenses. The Purchase and Assumption defenses include the following claims made by defendant: (1) the FDIC, as receiver, acted beyond the scope of its authority in liquidating AB&T, (2) the FDIC violated its own enabling act when it became receiver of AB&T and commenced liquidation proceedings, (3) the FDIC's takeover of AB&T was in violation of the Constitutions of the United States and of the State of South Carolina, (4) the FDIC did not have authority to purchase the note from the AB&T receivership. The Extension defenses involve an oral agreement between the defendant and FDIC in which the FDIC agreed to extend the time for payment to March, 1977, if defendant would pay $ 150,000 and furnish security for the remainder satisfactory to FDIC. The Residency and Indebtedness defenses relate to defendant's general denial of the residency paragraph of the complaint and to the paragraph of the complaint which sets forth the defendant's execution of the note, its face amount, and the payment date.

Presently before the Court are two motions. The first was made by defendant and seeks a stay of all proceedings until the district court decides the issues raised by the counterclaim in FDIC's declaratory judgment action in accordance with the Fourth Circuit opinion in *Federal Deposit Ins. Corp. v. American Bank Trust Shares, Inc., supra*. Defendant argues in support of his motion that, since the legality of FDIC's receivership is at issue in both cases and since this issue was first raised in the counterclaim to the declaratory judgment action, the present case should be stayed so as to prevent an unnecessary duplication of discovery expenses.

It should first be noted that a stay of this action is not mandated by the Fourth Circuit's opinion in the ABTS case. That case dealt with the FDIC's litigation against corporate officers and directors in its capacity as receiver, not the FDIC's litigation to collect notes it sold to itself. It is true that defendant has raised issues similar to those raised by the shareholders of ABTS. However, the fact that defendant has raised these issues does not mean that the issues are relevant in the instant case. For the reasons stated below, this Court finds that the issues relating to the legality of FDIC's receivership do not affect FDIC's attempts to collect the negotiable instruments it purchased from the receivership. Accordingly, the motion to stay is denied.

Also presently before the Court is FDIC's motion for summary judgment. The FDIC has, through the affidavits and pleadings, established a prima facie case of liability on the note and the motion for summary judgment essentially questions the validity and sufficiency of the defenses. With respect to the Purchase and Assumption defenses, FDIC argues that defendant lacks standing to question the legality of FDIC's receivership and that the defendant is impermissibly collaterally attacking the state court order approving the receivership. This argument has merit. Defendant has no standing to complain about FDIC's acquisition of AB&T's assets. The only party which has standing to make such a complaint is either AB&T or its shareholders. FDIC acquired the note being sued upon from AB&T and is presently the "holder" of said note. See S.C. Code Ann. § 36-1-201(20) (1976). If FDIC illegally acquired its status as a holder then AB&T might be a third party with a claim against the instrument. Defendant, however, as a party liable on the instrument, cannot assert such illegality as a defense to a suit on the note. As stated in S.C. Code Ann. § 36-3-306(d)(1976), "The claim of any third person to the instrument is not otherwise available as a defense to any party liable thereon unless the third person himself defends the action for such party." Furthermore, if defendant satisfies the note through a payment to FDIC he will not risk incurring double liability by becoming liable to AB&T in the event the sale to FDIC is set aside. Defendant will be discharged in accordance with S.C. Code Ann. § 36-3-603(1)(1976) which provides that "[t]he liability of any party is discharged to the extent of his payment or satisfaction to the holder even though it is made with knowledge of a claim of another person to the instrument. . .." The FDIC also correctly argues that the Purchase and Assumption defenses constitute an impermissible collateral attack on the state court order approving the take-over of AB&T by the FDIC.

After reviewing the pleadings and affidavits on file and, after considering the applicable law, this Court finds that no genuine issue exists as to any material fact and that the FDIC is entitled to judgment as a matter of law. The defendant has asserted a counterclaim in which he seeks damages from the plaintiff for the alleged breach of the oral contract to extend payment on the note. Since this oral contract is within the statute of frauds, it is unenforceable and the FDIC is also awarded summary judgment on the counterclaim.

---

§ 12.09 Problems of Consumer Paper

Read: U.C.C. §§ 3-302(g), 3-106(d). See §§ 9-206(1), 2A-407, 2A-103(1)(e) and (g) and (j), 9-109(1).

In the usual consumer transaction, the consumer who wishes to purchase on credit is asked to execute a negotiable promissory note payable to the dealer and a security agreement giving the dealer a security interest in the article sold. Of course, nowadays it is seldom anticipated that the dealer will finance the consumer's purchase of the item. A financing agency, either a finance company or equally, of late, a bank, will generally have a continuing relationship with the dealer which provides for purchase of the consumer paper (note plus security agreement) by the financing agency. Thus, the consumer obligation ends up in the hands of a third party who would like to be treated as a holder in due course. The financing agency does not want to be required to police the dealer's performance as would be the case if consumer defenses could be raised as against the financing company transferee.

A consumer financing situation can, in form and theory, look exactly like a commercial financing transaction. Even where a seller and buyer of commercial or industrial goods are dealing with a bank for financing of the purchase price, there may be an agreement that the bank will be a transferee of the resulting obligation to pay. In the commercial setting there is no policy reason why the bank should not be insulated from the performance aspects of the sales transaction. To the contrary, all parties recognize that the bank's function is financing and the seller's function is providing the object of the sale. Thus, the intimacy of the bank's relationship to the executory contract is irrelevant to the legal question of the holder in due course status of the bank, absent actual knowledge of fraud on the part of the seller. However, modern merchandising methods involving the sale of consumer goods, as will be evident from examining the following cases, call into question the assumption that the financing and the selling aspects of the three-party transaction should or can be separated.

ARCANUM NATIONAL BANK v. HESSLER

[The opinion appears in § 12.04[D], *supra*.]

COURTESY FINANCIAL SERVICES, INC. v. HUGHES

[The opinion appears in § 12.05, *supra*.]

NOTES

Legislation has responded to the problems of transfer of consumer paper in a variety of ways. Contrast the effectiveness and result of the following provisions. Also consider the impact of the provisions on limiting the effectiveness of waiver of defense clauses under U.C.C. § 9-206.

(1) From the Connecticut Home Solicitation Sales Act, 1967 PA. No. 749:

Sec. 5.

(a) Any note or other evidence of indebtedness given by a buyer in respect of a home solicitation sale shall be dated not earlier than the date of the agreement or offer to purchase. Any transfer of a note or other evidence of indebtedness bearing the statement required by subsection (b) of this section shall be deemed an assignment only and any right, title or interest which the transferee may acquire thereby shall be subject to all claims and defenses of the buyer against the seller arising under the provisions of this act. (b) Each note or other evidence of indebtedness given by a buyer in respect of a home solicitation sale shall bear on its face a conspicuous statement as follows: THIS INSTRUMENT IS BASED UPON A HOME SOLICITATION SALE, WHICH SALE IS SUBJECT TO THE PROVISIONS OF THE HOME SOLICITATION SALES ACT. THIS INSTRUMENT IS NOT NEGOTIABLE. (c) Compliance with the requirements of this section shall be a condition precedent to any right of action by the seller or any transferee of an instrument bearing the statement required under subsection (b) of this section against the buyer upon such instrument and shall be pleaded and proved by any person who may institute action or suit against a buyer in respect thereof. (d) A promissory note payable to order or bearer and otherwise negotiable in form issued in violation of this section may be enforced as a negotiable instrument by a holder in due course according to its terms.

(2) From The New York Retail installment Sales Act, N.Y. Pers. Prop. Law § 403(3)(a):

3. No contract or obligation shall contain any provision by which:

(a) The buyer agrees not to assert against an assignee a claim or defense arising out of the sale, but it may contain such a provision as to an assignee who acquires the contract, obligation or obligation together with any related note in good faith and for value and who has no notice of the facts giving rise to the claim or defense within ten days after such assignee mails to the buyer, at his address shown on the contract or obligation, notice of the assignment, indicating or containing in the notice or in an enclosure with the notice:. . .

(3) From Florida Statutes § 516.31 (1993):

Consumer protection; certain negotiable instruments restricted; assigns subject to defenses.

(1) SCOPE. This section shall apply to every consumer credit transaction and contract in which any form of credit is extended to an individual to purchase or obtain goods or services for use primarily for personal, family, or household purposes.

(2) RESTRICTION ON CERTAIN NEGOTIABLE INSTRUMENTS AND INSTALLMENT CONTRACTS. A holder or assignee of any negotiable instrument or installment contract, other than a currently dated check, which originated from the purchase of certain consumer goods or services is subject to all claims and defenses of the consumer debtor against the seller of those consumer goods or services. A person's liability under this section may not exceed the amount owing to the person when the claim or defense is asserted against the person.

(4) From Missouri Revised Statutes § 408.405 (1974):

The rights of a holder or assignee of an instrument, account, contract, right, chattel paper or other writing other than a check or draft, which evidences the obligation of a natural person as buyer, lessee, or borrower in connection with the purchase or lease of consumer goods or services, are subject to all defenses and setoffs of the debtor arising from or out of such sale or lease, notwithstanding any agreement to the contrary, only as to amounts then owing and as a matter of defense to or setoff against a claim by the holder or assignee; provided, however, with respect to goods only, the rights of the debtor under this section may be asserted to the seller at the address at which he did business at the time of the sale and must be so asserted within ninety days after receipt of the goods.

(5) From the rules of the Federal Trade Commission, 16 CFR §433.2:

In connection with any sale or lease of goods or services to consumers, in or affecting commerce as "commerce" is defined in the Federal Trade Commission Act, it is an unfair or deceptive act or practice within the meaning of Section 5 of that Act for a seller, directly or indirectly, to:

(a) Take or receive a consumer credit contract which fails to contain the following provision in at least ten point, bold face type:

NOTICE

ANY HOLDER OF THIS CONSUMER CREDIT CONTRACT IS SUBJECT TO ALL CLAIMS AND DEFENSES WHICH THE DEBTOR COULD ASSERT AGAINST THE SELLER OF GOODS OR SERVICES OBTAINED PURSUANT HERETO OR WITH THE PROCEEDS HEREOF. RECOVERY HEREUNDER BY THE DEBTOR SHALL NOT EXCEED AMOUNTS PAID BY THE DEBTOR HEREUNDER,

or,

(b) Accept, as full or partial payment for such sale or lease, the proceeds of any purchase money loan (as purchase money loan is defined herein), unless any consumer credit contract made in connection with such purchase money loan contains the following provision in at least ten point, bold face type:

NOTICE

ANY HOLDER OF THIS CONSUMER CREDIT CONTRACT IS SUBJECT TO ALL CLAIMS AND DEFENSES WHICH THE DEBTOR COULD ASSERT AGAINST THE SELLER OF GOODS OR SERVICE OBTAINED WITH THE PROCEEDS HEREOF. RECOVERY HEREUNDER BY THE DEBTOR SHALL NOT EXCEED AMOUNTS PAID BY THE DEBTOR HEREUNDER.

See U.C.C. § 3-106(d), Comment 3; U.C.C. § 3-302(g), Comment 7.

(6) Consider the effect of each of these rules, if applicable, in the following case.

HARDEMAN v. WHEELS, INC.

Court of Appeals of Ohio, Warren County
565 N.E.2d 849 (1988)

PER CURIAM.

On April 27, 1985, plaintiff-appellant, Lori Hardeman, purchased an automobile from defendant-appellee, Wheels, Inc. ("Wheels"). Hardeman signed financing papers but was not informed of either the length or terms of the agreement. Wheels subsequently sold Hardeman's loan to defendant-appellee, Chrysler Credit Corporation ("Chrysler").

Before she made any payments on the contract, Hardeman discovered that Wheels had charged her in excess of the agreed-upon sticker price, that Wheels had induced her into purchasing a $500 warranty she did not need, and that she received less than the agreed-upon amount for a trade-in on a used automobile.

Hardeman notified Chrysler of these problems and when negotiations failed, Hardeman filed suit against Wheels and Chrysler. Prior to trial, Hardeman paid $2,299.99 on the contract, leaving an unpaid balance of $10,245.41 due to Chrysler.

During trial before a jury, the trial court granted Hardeman directed verdicts on her following claims: breach of contract and warranties; violations of the Ohio Consumer Sales Practices Act ("CSPA"), R.C. Chapter 1345; and fraud, deceit and misrepresentation.

The issue of damages was submitted to the jury which found Wheels liable for $5,000 actual damages for breach of contract, fraud and violations of the CSPA. The jury further found that Wheels had committed three statutory violations of the CSPA, for which Hardeman was entitled to $200 for each violation. Hardeman was awarded treble damages on both the actual damages and the CSPA statutory violations. The jury also awarded punitive damages of $750,000. The trial court issued a judgment entry in favor of Hardeman for $771,200.

Because Wheels was insolvent, it could only pay $1,185 towards the judgment. Hardeman subsequently sought to set off the judgment against the amount she owed Chrysler. Hardeman also sought a determination of Chrysler's liability regarding her judgment against Wheels.

In an opinion dated July 29, 1987, the trial court ruled that Chrysler, as the assignee of the contract, was not a holder in due course and that Hardeman could set off both the actual damages and statutory damages totaling $5,600 from the balance she owed Chrysler. On the other hand, the court held that neither the treble damages nor punitive damages were subject to a setoff.

Hardeman subsequently filed a motion for attorney fees and expenses, requesting $7,695 in attorney fees and $1,681.48 in expenses. The trial court awarded fees of $1,750 and expenses of $888.50 and ruled that neither could be set off against the balance owed to Chrysler.

Hardeman appeals and submits the following assignments of error for review:

First Assignment of Error

The trial court erred to the prejudice of plaintiff-appellant in its findings that plaintiff's judgment against defendant Wheels, Inc. may not be entirely used to set off the amount owed by the plaintiff to defendant Chrysler Credit Corporation on its retail installment sales contract.

Second Assignment of Error

The trial court abused its discretion in awarding attorney fees under R.C. 1345.09 in the amount of $1,750.00 where plaintiff's attorney was forced to spend more than 83 hours preparing a case for two different trial dates, report conferences with the trial court, pretrial conferences with the trial court, pretrial motions, discovery, motions to compel discovery, and preparation of testimony and testimony of an expert witness, an actual trial, post-trial motions and memoranda and hearings.

Third Assignment of Error

The trial court erred to the prejudice of plaintiff-appellant in its finding that plaintiff's attorney fees and costs judgment against defendant Wheels, Inc. is not a "claim" that may be used to set off the amount owed by the plaintiff to defendant Chrysler Credit Corporation on its retail installment sales contract.

For her first assignment of error, Hardeman argues that she should be permitted to set off the full amount of her judgment against the balance she owes on the contract to Chrysler. Hardeman claims that since Chrysler is not a holder in due course, it is subject to all claims and defenses which she could assert against Wheels.

Hardeman's contract with Wheels contained the following language:

NOTICE

"ANY HOLDER OF THIS CONSUMER CREDIT CONTRACT IS *SUBJECT TO ALL CLAIMS AND DEFENSES WHICH* THE DEBTOR COULD ASSERT AGAINST THE SELLER OF GOODS OR SERVICES OBTAINED PURSUANT HERETO OR WITH THE PROCEEDS HEREOF. RECOVERY HEREUNDER BY THE DEBTOR SHALL NOT EXCEED AMOUNTS PAID BY THE DEBTOR HEREUNDER." (Emphasis added.)

This language is required by a trade regulation rule promulgated by the Federal Trade Commission which effectively banned the utilization of the holder-in-due-course doctrine in consumer credit cases. *See* Section 433.2(a), Title 16, C.F.R. The issue to be decided in this assignment of error is whether the phrase "all claims" as used in Section 433.2(a), Title 16, C.F.R. encompasses Hardeman's claims for punitive and treble damages in addition to actual damages. Hardeman argues that the anti-holder-in-due-course provisions of the federal regulation entitled her to set off the entire $771,200 judgment she obtained against Wheels against the amount she still owes Chrysler under the contract.

One commentator has observed that the purpose of Section 433.2, Title 16, C.F.R. is:

"[B]ased on [a] simple public policy determination: as between an innocent consumer and a third party financier, the latter is generally in a vastly superior position (1) to return the cost to the seller, where it properly belongs, (2) to exert an influence over the behavior of the seller in the first place, and (3) to the extent the . . . [financier] cannot return the cost (as in the case of fly-by-night dealers), to "internalize" the cost by spreading it among all consumers as an increase in the price of credit. . .." 2 Fonseca, Handling Consumer Credit Cases (3 Ed. 1987) 703, Section 24:1.

Thus, the holder of a retail installment contract assigned under such a notice pursuant to the federal regulation is subject to any claim or defense the debtor could assert against the original seller of the goods, provided the claim or defense is one arising out of or connected with the original transaction.

Section 433.2, Title 16, C.F.R. precludes the separation of the buyer's duty to pay for goods or services from the seller's reciprocal duty to perform as promised. *Fonseca, supra.*

In *Thomas v. Ford Motor Credit Co.* , 48 Md. App. 617, 429 A.2d 277 (1981), a Maryland court of appeals held that the assignee of a contract containing the language of the federal regulation can be sued directly by the debtor. However, the regulations's final sentence limits the debtor's recovery to amounts paid by the debtor under the contract. *Id.* Thus, although the regulation limits the amount of the recovery, it does not preclude the debtor from asserting a claim against the holder of the contact. *Id.*

Hardeman asserts that since the regulation subjects Chrysler to all "claims," she may set off or deduct all damages, including the treble damages and punitive damages, since they are claims which she has against Wheels resulting from Wheels' breach of the contract.

The trial court permitted Hardeman to deduct or set off her actual damages but not the treble damages or punitive damages. Treble damages awarded under the CSPA are punitive and designed to prevent or discourage certain activities or misconduct. In addition, since punitive damages are assessed as punishment and not compensation, a positive element of conscious wrongdoing is always required.

We agree with the trial court that Chrysler should not be punished for the culpability of Wheels to the extent that Chrysler should be held accountable for such damages of a purely punitive nature. There is obviously no conscious wrongdoing or misconduct on the part of Chrysler in the case at bar. The onerous burden of paying a potentially extensive statutory and common-law punitive award rendered against a culpable merchant should not be imputed to an innocent assignee of the contract. It is enough that these holders such as Chrysler are denied the advantage of being a holder in due course and are subject to any actual and compensatory damages suffered by the innocent purchaser. This is penalty enough for accepting business from dishonest merchants.

We conclude that the trial court did not err in denying Hardeman's request to set off the treble and punitive damages against Chrysler. The first assignment of error is therefore overruled.

In her second assignment of error, Hardeman claims that the trial court abused its discretion by not awarding the full amount of attorney fees and expenses Hardeman requested under the CSPA.

R.C. 1345.09 provides that a violation of the CSPA entitled a consumer to, among other things, the following relief:

> (F) The court may award to the prevailing party a reasonable attorney's fees limited to the work reasonably performed, if either of the following apply:

. . . .

(2) The supplier has knowingly committed an act or practice that violates this chapter.

In construing R.C. 1345.09, we held in *Brooks v. Hurst Buick-Pontiac-Olds-GMC, Inc.* (1985), 23 Ohio App. 3d 85, 23 OBR 150, 491 N.E.2d 345, that the statute calls for the award of "reasonable" attorney fees. In reviewing such an award, we further noted that:

> "It is well-settled that where a court is empowered to award attorney fees by statute, the amount of such fees is within the sound discretion of the trial court. Unless the amount of fees determined is so high or so low as to shock the conscience, an appellate court will not interfere. The trial judge which participated not only in the trial but also in many of the preliminary proceedings leading up to trial has an infinitely better opportunity to determine the value of services rendered by lawyers who have tried a case before him than does an appellate court." *Id.* at 91, 23 OBR at 155, 491 N.E.2d at 351-52.

In exercising its discretion in the award of such fees and expenses, the trial court may make an award based upon the actual value of the necessary services.

We have reviewed the record and Hardeman's motion for fees and expenses. We cannot say that the trial court abused its discretion by not granting the requested fees. The trial court was obviously in a better position to determine what actual services were necessary in the case at bar and their reasonable value. The amount awarded by the trial court is neither so low nor so high as to warrant or justify our interference with that decision.

Having found no abuse of discretion, we therefore conclude that the second assignment of error is without merit and is accordingly overruled.

In her final assignment of error, Hardeman submits that the attorney fees and costs are "claims" under Section 433.2, Title 16, C.F.R. which she may set off against the balance owed to Chrysler under the contract.

The federal regulation permits the injured party to assert all claims against the holder or assignee of an installment loan contract. It is Hardeman's position that equity should permit her to set off her attorney fees and expenses as such a claim. The provisions of R.C. 1345.09 permit the award of attorney fees against a supplier who knowingly violates the CSPA. *Brooks, supra.* Chrysler clearly was not the supplier in this matter nor was it involved in effecting or soliciting consumer transactions. Chrysler is clearly subject to Hardeman's claims for actual and statutory damages designed to compensate the injured party. However, Chrysler should not be subject to claims or defenses which encompass penalties specifically designed to be assessed against the supplier, rather than the assignee, for the supplier's statutory or common-law infractions. We find no error in the trial court's refusal to grant Hardeman's request to set off the attorney fees and costs against Chrysler's claim for the balance of the contract.

The third assignment of error is hereby overruled.

Judgment affirmed.

---

§ 12.10 Credit Cards

SOCIETY NATIONAL BANK v. KIENZLE

Ohio Court of Appeals
11 Ohio App.3d 178, 463 N.E.2d 1261 (1983)

STILLMAN, JUDGE.

Defendant credit cardholder appeals from a municipal court judgment in favor of plaintiff credit card issuer for alleged authorized transactions involving defendant's credit card. Defendant urges error in the trial court's: (1) refusal to dismiss the case for want of prosecution; (2) hearing of the action without subject matter jurisdiction; and (3) rendering defendant liable for money damages in excess of a federally imposed maximum. Since we agreed with defendant's assertion that he could be liable only for the maximum imposed by the federal statute, we modify the trial court's judgment accordingly.

Defendant testified at trial that he was issued a single Mastercard charge card from plaintiff. He stated that after incurring a large charge bill, he decided to cease using the card until he reduced his indebtedness. Defendant asserted that he did not use the card for approximately eight months, and that he telephoned plaintiff to notify it of his credit card's apparent theft after he discovered a cash advance on his monthly statement which he did not make.

The testimony of plaintiff's employee acknowledged defendant's telephone notification of his stolen credit card. This witness testified regarding the procedures implemented to protect against further unauthorized use of the stolen card. She stated that even though the card was listed as stolen in the bank bulletins, charges were incurred without being charged back to the respective merchant's account. The witness further stated that defendant's account had a balance due and owing of $2,431.18. Bank records indicated that defendant owed $354.54 prior to his discovery of the unauthorized cash advance.

Defendant's further testimony implicated his estranged wife as the alleged thief of his card. Plaintiff contended at trial that her use of the card was authorized. Testimony by defendant and plaintiff's employee established defendant's credit limit to be $1,000, yet evidence exhibited that $4,057.76 was charged to defendant's account.

II

Defendant's third alleged error asserts that at most, he was liable only to the extent mandated by the Federal Truth in Lending Act, Section 1601 et seq., Title 15, U.S. Code. We agree.

Section 1643, Title 15, U.S. Code, states:

> (a)(1) A cardholder shall be liable for the unauthorized use of a credit card only if—
>
> (A) the card is an accepted credit card;

(B) the liability is not in excess of $50;

(C) the card issuer gives adequate notice to the cardholder of the potential liability;

(D) the card issuer has provided the cardholder with a description of a means by which the card issuer may be notified of loss or theft of the card, which description may be provided on the face or reverse side of the statement required by section 1637(b) of this title or on a separate notice accompanying such statement;

(E) the unauthorized use occurs before the card issuer has been notified that an unauthorized use of the credit card has occurred or may occur as the result of loss, theft, or otherwise; and

(F) the card issuer has provided a method whereby the user of such card can be identified as the person authorized to use it.

(2) For purposes of this section, a card issuer has been notified when such steps as may be reasonably required in the ordinary course of business to provide the card issuer with the pertinent information have been taken, whether or not any particular officer, employee, or agent of the card issuer does in fact receive such information.

(b) In any action by a card issuer to enforce liability for the use of a credit card, the burden of proof is upon the card issuer to show that the use was authorized or, if the use was unauthorized, then the burden of proof upon the card issuer to show that the conditions of liability for the unauthorized use of a credit card, as set forth in subsection (a) of this section, have been met.

(c) Nothing in this section imposes liability upon a cardholder for the unauthorized use of a credit card in excess of his liability for such use under other applicable law or under any agreement with the card issuer.

(d) Except as provided in this section, a cardholder incurs no liability from the unauthorized use of a credit card.

Thus, a cardholder is liable for a limited amount if certain conditions are met and if the use of the credit card was unauthorized. Pursuant to Sections 1643(b), (c) and (d), Title 15, U.S. Code, ". . .the burden of proof is upon the card issuer to show that the use was authorized or, if the use was unauthorized, then the burden of proof is upon the card issuer to show that the conditions of liability for the unauthorized use of a credit card, as set forth in subsection (a) of this section, have been met." Section 1643(b), Title 15, U.S. Code; *First National City Bank v. Mullarkey* (1976), 87 Misc.2d 1, 2, 385 N.Y.S.2d 473. Accordingly, the initial determination is whether the use of a credit card is unauthorized. *Transamerica Ins. Co. v. Standard Oil Co.* (N.D. 1982), 325 N.W.2d 210, 213. ". . .The test for determining unauthorized use is agency, and State agency law must be used to resolve this issue." *Transamerica Ins. Co. v. Standard Oil Co., supra,* at 214.

In Ohio, a husband is not answerable for the acts of his wife unless the wife acts as his agent or he subsequently ratifies her acts. 28 Ohio Jurisprudence 2d 227, Husband and Wife, Section 100. In this case, there was no evidence introduced that defendant's wife acted as his agent, or that he ratified her conduct. Indeed, the transcript reveals that defendant notified plaintiff immediately after his discovery of someone else using his credit card. The transcript is devoid of any other evidence of agency or ratification. Thus, plaintiff failed in its burden of proof.

Further, if plaintiff fails to prove that the card use was authorized, defendant must elicit facts which prove the factors delineated in Section 1643(a), Title 15, U.S. Code. Based upon the testimony and evidence adduced at trial, we conclude that defendant has met the burden of proof in regard to Section 1643(A), Title 15, U.S. Code, and we must reduce the judgment rendered to the maximum delineated in that subsection, *i.e.*, fifty dollars.

Judgment modified, and affirmed as modified.

NOTE

What is the status of the holder in due course doctrine in bank credit card transactions? 15 U.S.C.A. § 1666i provides: Assertion by cardholder against card issuer of claims and defenses arising out of credit card transaction; prerequisites; limitation on amount of claims or defenses

> (a) Subject to the limitation contained in subsection (b) of this section, a card issuer who has issued a credit card to a cardholder pursuant to an open end consumer credit plan shall be subject to all claims (other than tort claims) and defenses arising out of any transaction in which the credit card is used as a method of payment or extension of credit if (1) the obligor has made a good faith attempt to obtain satisfactory resolution of a disagreement or problem relative to the transaction from the person honoring the credit card; (2) the amount of the initial transaction exceeds $50; and (3) the place where the initial transaction occurred was in the same State as the mailing address previously provided by the cardholder or was within 100 miles from such address, except that the limitations set forth in clauses (2) and (3) with respect to an obligor's right to assert claims and defenses against a card issuer shall not be applicable to any transaction in which the person honoring the credit card (A) is the same person as the card issuer, (B) is controlled by the card issuer, (C) is under direct or indirect common control with the card issuer, (D) is a franchised dealer in the card issuer's products or services, or (E) has obtained the order for such transaction through a mail solicitation made by or participated in by the card issuer in which the cardholder is solicited to enter into such transaction by using the credit card issued by the card issuer.
>
> (b) The amount of claims or defenses asserted by the cardholder may not exceed the amount of credit outstanding with respect to such transaction at the time the cardholder first notifies the card issuer or the person honoring the credit card of such claim or defense. For the purpose of determining the amount of credit outstanding in the preceding sentence, payments and credits to the cardholder's account are deemed to have been applied, in the order indicated, to the payment of: (1) late charges in the order of their entry to the account; (2) finance charges in order of their entry to the account; and (3) debits to the account other than those set forth above, in the order in which each debit entry to the account was made.

(Pub. L. 90-321, Title I, § 170, as added Pub. L. 93-495, Title III, § 306, Oct. 28, 1974, 88 Stat. 1515.)

PROBLEM 12.8

Your client, a prominent businessperson who lives in St. Louis, recently purchased a laptop computer on a business trip to New York City. Two days later, the computer malfunctions and the client notifies the computer seller. The seller refuses to fix it or to return the client's money. The client has notified the credit card company in writing, but it refuses to recredit the bill on the basis that the seller is more than 100 miles away from the client buyer's residence as mentioned in the federal statute. What advice would you give and what action would you recommend the client take?

PROBLEM 12.9

Assume that you are the attorney for the credit card company in the situation in Problem 12.8. What advice would you give, what action should it take, and what are its liabilities?

IZRAELEWITZ v. MANUFACTURERS HANOVER TRUST CO.

New York City Civil Court
120 Misc. 2d 125, 465 N.Y.S. 2d 486 (1983)

IRA B. HARKAVY, JUDGE.

As the texture of the American economy evolves from paper to plastic, the disgruntled customer is spewing its wrath upon the purveyor of the plastic rather than upon the merchant.

Plaintiff George Izraelewitz commenced this action to compel the Defendant bank Manufacturers Hanover Trust Company to credit his Mastercharge account in the amount of $290.00 plus finance charges. The disputed charge, posted to Plaintiff's account on July 16, 1981, is for electronic diagrams purchased by Plaintiff via telephone from Don Britton Enterprises, a Hawaii-based mail order business.

On September 9, 1981 Plaintiff advised Defendant bank, Manufacturers Hanover Trust Company (Trust Company), that the diagrams had been unsuitable for his needs and provided Defendant with a UPS receipt indicating that the purchased merchandise had been returned to Don Britton. Defendant's Customer Service Department credited Plaintiff's account and waived finance charges on the item. Trust Company subsequently proceeded to charge back the item to the merchant. The merchant refused the charge back through The 1st Hawaii Bank, and advised Defendant bank of their strict "No Refund" policy. Don Britton also indicated that Plaintiff, during the course of conversation, had admitted that he was aware of this policy. On April 1, 1982 Defendant advised Plaintiff that his account would be redebited for the full amount. At two later dates, Plaintiff advised Trust Company of said dispute, denied knowledge of the "No Refund" policy and stated that the goods had been returned. The Trust Company once again credited Plaintiff's account and attempted to collect from Don Britton. The charge back was again refused and Plaintiff's account was subsequently redebited.

Bank credit agreements generally provide that a cardholder is obligated to pay the bank regardless of any dispute which may exist respecting the merchandise. An exception to this rule arises under a provision in the Truth in Lending Law which allows claimants whose transactions exceed $50.00 and who have made a good faith attempt to obtain satisfactory resolution of the problem, to assert claims and defenses arising out of the credit card transaction, if the place of the initial transaction is in the same state or within 100 miles of the cardholder. Consumer Credit Protection Act, 15 U.S.C.A. § 1666i.

It would appear that Plaintiff is precluded from asserting any claims or defenses since Britton's location exceeds the geographical limitation. This assumption is deceiving. Under Truth in Lending the question of where the transaction occurred (*e.g.*, as in mail order cases) is to be determined under state or other applicable law. Truth in Lending, 12 CFR, § 226.12(c). Furthermore, any state law permitting customers to assert claims and defenses against the card issuer would not be preempted, regardless of whether the place of the transaction was at issue. In effect, these federal laws are viewed as bare minimal standards.

In *Lincoln First Bank, N.A. v. Carlson*, 103 Misc.2d 467, 426 N.Y.S.2d 433 (1980), the court found that:

> [T]he statement that a card issuer is subject to all defenses if a transaction occurred less than 100 miles from the cardholder's address, does not automatically presume a cardholder to give up all his defenses should the transaction take place at a distance of greater than 100 miles from the mailing address. *Id.* at 436.

The facts at bar do not warrant a similar finding. Whereas in *Lincoln, supra*, the cardholder's defense arose due to an alleged failure of the card issuer itself to comply with statutory rules, the Defendant herein is blameless. The geographical limitation serves to protect banks from consumers who may expose them to unlimited liability through dealings with merchants in faraway states where it is difficult to monitor a merchant's behavior. These circumstances do not lend the persuasion needed to cast-off this benefit.

Considering, arguendo, that under the Truth in Lending Act, Plaintiff was able to assert claims and defenses from the original transaction, any claims or defenses he chose to assert would only be as good as and no better than his claim against the merchant. Accordingly, Plaintiff's claim against the merchant must be scrutinized to ascertain whether it is of good faith and substantial merit. A consumer cannot assert every minuscule dispute he may have with a merchant as an excuse not to pay an issuer who has already paid the merchant.

The crux of Plaintiff's claim, apparently, is that he returned the diagrams purportedly unaware of merchant's "No Refund" policy. The merchant contends that Plaintiff admitted that he knew of the policy and nonetheless used deceptive means to return the plans; in that they were sent without a name so they would be accepted; were not delivered to an employee of the company; were not in the original box; and showed evidence of having been xeroxed.

"No Refund" policies, per se, are not unconscionable or offensive to public policy in any manner. Truth in Lending Law "[n]either requires refunds for returns nor does it prohibit refunds in kind." Truth in Lending Regulations, 12 CFR, § 226.12(e). Bank-merchant agreements, however, usually do contain a requirement that the merchant establish a fair policy for exchange and return of merchandise.

To establish the fairness in Don Britton's policy, the strength of the reasons behind the policy and the measures taken to inform the consumer of it must necessarily be considered. Don Britton's rationale for its policy is compelling. It contends that printing is a very small part of its business, which is selling original designs, and "once a customer has seen the designs he possesses what we have to sell." Britton's policy is clearly written in its catalog directly on the page which explains how to order merchandise. To compensate for not having a refund policy, which would be impractical considering the nature of the product, Britton offers well-advertised backup plans with free engineering assistance and an exchange procedure, as well, if original plans are beyond the customer's capabilities. The Plaintiff could have availed himself of any of these alternatives which are all presumably still open to him.

On the instant facts, as between Plaintiff and the Defendant bank, Plaintiff remains liable for the disputed debt, as he has not shown adequate cause to hold otherwise.

Judgment for Defendant dismissing the complaint.

UNIVERSAL BANK v. McCAFFERTY

Court of Appeals of Ohio, Summit County
624 N.E.2d 358 (1993)

COOK, PRESIDING JUDGE.

Universal Bank ("Universal") appeals the trial court's judgment that James E. McCafferty's ("McCafferty") liability on a credit card contract with Universal was $50. We affirm.

In April 1991, McCafferty applied for and received a Mastercard credit card from Universal. Objecting to the family having another credit card, McCafferty's wife returned the cards to Universal. McCafferty then called Universal and asked them to reissue the card but to send it to a different address. McCafferty gave Universal his friend's address and Universal sent the card and the personal identification number for the automatic teller machines to that address. After telling his friend that the card would be coming in the mail, McCafferty asked the friend to notify him upon its arrival. McCafferty's friend, however, did not notify him when the card came but instead used it for purchases and cash advances totaling $3,800.

Universal then called McCafferty and inquired as to when payment would be made. McCafferty told Universal that he would pay them when his friend paid him. McCafferty's friend never paid him and Universal sued McCafferty to recover the credit card charges. The trial court found that the credit card charges were unauthorized and awarded Universal $50 on the credit card contract.

Universal appeals, assigning two errors.

Assignment of Error No. 1

"The trial court errored [*sic*] in not finding that apparent authority existed for the use of the credit card and therefore defendant-appellee was liable."

"In any action by a card issuer to enforce liability for the use of a credit card, the burden of proof is upon the card issuer to show that the use was authorized . . . ." Section 1643(b), Title 15, U.S. Code. Section 1643(a), Title 15, U.S. Code limits the liability of a credit cardholder for the unauthorized use of the credit card to $50.

"Unauthorized use" is defined in Section 1602(o), Title 15, U.S. Code as "a use of a credit card by a person other than the cardholder who does not have actual, implied, or apparent authority for such use and from which the cardholder receives no benefit." Thus, the issue is whether the use of the credit card is authorized or unauthorized and state agency law must be used to answer this issue. *Society Natl. Bank v. Kienzle* (1983), 11 Ohio App. 3d 178, 182, 11 OBR 271, 275, 463 N.E.2d 1261, 1265, quoting *Transamerica Ins. Co. v. Standard Oil Co.* (N.D. 1982), 325 N.W.2d 210, 213-214.

Universal contends that McCafferty and his friend had an agency relationship based on apparent authority. Apparent authority is not established by the conduct of the agent, but by acts of the principal which cloak the agent with apparent power to bind the principal. Universal claims that McCafferty's act of requesting that the credit card be sent to his friend's address clothed his friend with apparent authority.[41] We disagree. While McCafferty authorized Universal to send the card to his friend's address, that did not authorize use of the card by the addressee. The mere authorization to mail a credit card to a certain address cannot be expanded to encompass the apparent authorization to charge on that credit card. Based on the record before this court, no act of McCafferty can be said to have facilitated a mistaken belief that the friend was authorized to use his credit card; therefore, the trial court did not err in finding that the charges on McCafferty's credit card were unauthorized.

Universal's first assignment of error is overruled.

Assignment of Error No. II

"The trial court errored [*sic*] in not finding the defendant-appellee ratified Wade's acts in using the card, therefore leading to defendant-appellee's liability."

With this assignment of error, Universal contends that the trial court erred in not finding that McCafferty ratified the charges that his friend made. The record presented by Universal includes nothing regarding a ratification argument. Unless the record shows that an argument was presented to the trial court, we cannot consider it. A presumption of validity attends the trial court's action and it is the appellant's responsibility to provide this court with an adequate record to support the claimed errors. *Volodkevich, supra.* Thus, this issue is not properly before this court.

The second assignment of error is overruled.

The judgment of the trial court is affirmed.

---

[41] Universal also asserts that McCafferty lied to them by telling them that the address he was giving them was his business address when in reality it was his friend's address. Universal, however, failed to provide this court with a record to support its version of the substantive facts of this case and we, therefore, must consider the findings of the court the only facts of this case. App. R. 9(B); *Volodkevich v. Volodkevich* (1989), 48 Ohio App. 3d 313, 314, 549 N.E.2d 1237, 1238. The trial court's judgment entry did not make any reference to Universal's claim that McCafferty told Universal that the address was his business address; therefore, we will not address that issue.

CHAPTER 13

LIABILITY OF THE PARTIES

§ 13.01 Introduction

Read: Prefatory Note to Article 3.

For the purposes of this book, long-term credit instruments are those which mature more than ninety days after issue. Naturally, such an arbitrary classification has no legal relevance to the type of instrument involved. However, under this rough classification, the dominant long-range credit device is the promissory note. The varieties of promissory notes are many. The demand promissory note is common, being used where the contemplated period of payment is indefinite but brief. However, the demand promissory note is sometimes used with the intention of not liquidating for some time. If such is the case, the parties do not contemplate further transfer of the instrument. It is not an instrument which is usually bought and sold in the credit market.

Of the more common types of long-term promissory notes, mention might be made of a few by way of example. Many long-term obligations are either sufficiently secured by collateral or by the undoubted solvency of the obligor as to be readily saleable. A corporation might issue and sell five-year interest-bearing promissory notes in order to obtain temporary capitalization funds. (Some of these instruments might qualify as investment securities under Article 8.) It is desirable to draft such notes so as to be negotiable. There is also a definite market in real estate mortgage notes. Even though the mortgage note is a long-term note, and even though it refers to the mortgage which stands as security, the note almost always qualifies as a negotiable instrument. It is generally accepted that the negotiability of the note is imparted to the mortgage. This means that the security of the mortgage belongs to the holder of the note. Furthermore, if the holder of the note qualifies as a holder in due course so as to enforce the note free of defenses, then he may also realize on the mortgage free of these defenses. As noted in Chapter 12, the use of the installment promissory note with a "purchase money security interest" (U.C.C. § 9-107) in the financing of the purchase of goods has become a definite feature of the economy. The note, if properly drafted so as to separate it from the accompanying security agreement, and if not subject to some pro-consumer rule, is negotiable.

Before we discuss the liability of various parties (makers, drawers, indorsers, etc.), some rules of general application should be discussed.

§ 13.02 Signatures

Read: U.C.C. §§ 3-401, 3-402, 3-403, 3-406, 1-201(39) and (43).

The question of signatures, per se, seldom gives problems. Students tend, however, to forget the efficacy of the use of stamps or printing as signatures. The key is not the unique movement of a human arm, but the intent of the person causing a signature to be made. One can direct his agent to set his "Auto-pen" to subscribing promissory notes and there is no question of the efficacy of the resulting John Hancocks. *See* Comment 2, U.C.C. § 3-401.

"And in witness that it was sooth He bit the wax with his foretooth."[1]

GREYHOUND LINES, INC. v. FIRST STATE BANK OF ROLLINGSTONE

Minnesota Court of Appeals
366 N.W.2d 354, 40 U.C.C. Rep. 1757 (1985)

CRIPPEN, J.

Appellant bank appeals from a summary judgment in favor of respondent Greyhound. The trial court found that the appellant drawee bank accepted a check payable to Greyhound, based upon the preprinted name and logo, the signing of the check and parol evidence.

FACTS

Respondent Greyhound Lines, Inc., sued appellant First State Bank of Rollingstone, on a check drawn to Greyhound by B.C. Dahl in the amount of $9,730.44. Appellant drawee bank dishonored the check because Dahl's account had insufficient funds.

Lou Hodnik, a supervisor for Greyhound, stated in an affidavit that B.C. Dahl, a commission agent for Greyhound in Winona, presented him with the check to cover amounts due to Greyhound on his May, 1983 report. Hodnik told Dahl that he would not take the check unless it was confirmed for funds by the bank. Dahl later brought back the check signed by Duane Klein, the vice-president of bank. Hodnik called the bank and talked to Klein, who assured him that the funds were in the bank. Hodnik further stated that because he knew Klein was a vice-president of the bank, and because Klein was at the bank when Hodnik spoke to him, he "understood he signed the check for the Bank." He "relied upon Mr. Klein's representation as an officer of the Bank that the Bank would pay the check."

The district court granted summary judgment in favor of respondent, and appellant brought this appeal.

ISSUE

1. Whether the presence on a check of a bank's printed name and logo identifying it as the drawee bank "names the person represented" by an agent of the bank who signs his own name to the check.

2. Whether Min Stat § 336.3-403(2)(b) can be used to impose liability on a principal.

---

[1] Quoted in *Sterling v. Park*, 129 Ga. 309, 58 S.E. 828 (1907).

3. Whether undisputed statements that the funds are in the bank and the bank will pay the check are sufficient as a matter of law to establish that the agent accepted a check on behalf of his principal.

ANALYSIS

The trial court granted a motion for summary judgment under Minnesota Rules of Civil Procedure 56.03. Upon review, this court must determine:

> (1) whether there are any genuine issues of material fact and (2) whether the trial court erred in its application of the law.

Betlach v. Wayzata Condominium, 281 NW2d 328, 330 (Minn. 1979). Here, neither party contends that a genuine issue of material fact exists, and the sole argument of appellant is that the trial court erred as a matter of law. This court is not bound upon review by the trial court's determination of a question of law. *Miles v. City of Oakdale*, 323 NW2d 51, 55 (Minn. 1982).

1.

The liability of a drawee bank as an acceptor is governed by statute. Minn Stat § 336.3-409(1) (1984) provides: . . .[the Court cites U.C.C. § 3-409(1)].

Minn. Stat. § 336.3-410(1) (1984) provides: . . .[the Court cites U.C.C. § 3-410(1)].

An agent or other representative may make a signature for a principal. Minn. Stat. § 336.3-403(1).

The principal's name must also appear on the check in order to find it liable, because "[n]o person is liable on an instrument unless his signature appears thereon." Minn. Stat. § 336.3-401(1) (1984).

> This rule precludes the application of the agency doctrine of undisclosed principal to obligations on negotiable paper, and implements the principle that the nature, scope, and terms of the obligations on such paper must be certain and determinable from the instrument itself.

Id. Minnesota Code Comment.

In order to conclude that the bank accepted the check, we must first find that the bank signed the check.

> A signature is made by use of any name, including any trade or assumed name, upon an instrument, or by any word or mark used in lieu of a written signature.

Minn Stat § 336.3-401(2) (1984). The only place in which the name of the principal, the bank, appears on the check is in the lower left hand side, where its name, address and logo appear in a preprinted form.

The bank argues that it is not named on the check because its name is not "associated" with the vice-president's signature, which was below the drawer's signature on the lower right hand side of the check. We disagree. In *St. Croix Engineering Corp. v. McLay*, 304 NW2d 912 (Minn. 1981), the court found the principal was named where the principal's name, address, and logo appeared in the upper left hand corner of the check. *Id.* at 914. The court in *Wurzburg Brothers, Inc. v. Coleman*, 404 So 2d 334 (Ala 1981), interpreted a U.C.C. § 3-403(2)(b) requirement that an instrument "names the person represented" to allow examination of the entire face of the instrument:

The language of the section indicates that the entire face of the instrument may be given attention when discovering who is liable on the instrument.

Id. at 336.

Appellant contends that if the bank's name on a check constitutes a naming, any signature on a check will raise a question of possible acceptance by the bank. However, Minn Stat § 336.3-404 (1) (1984) renders an unauthorized signature ineffective except against the one who actually signed it. Parol evidence may be used if necessary to prove or deny the authority of one to sign for another. U.C.C. § 3-403Official Comment 1 (1962).

We hold that the bank's printed name and logo on the check were sufficient to name it as principal of an agent, to determine if the agent accepts the check for the bank when he signs the instrument.

2.

The trial court used parol evidence, along with information from the face of the check, to impose liability upon a principal for the agent's signature.

Minn Stat § 336.3-403(2) (1984), provides: [the Court quotes § 336.3-403(2)].

If a party sues an agent on a check which names the principal and is signed by the agent, and the agent did not indicate his representative capacity, the agent may overcome the presumption of personal liability by parol evidence, in litigation between the immediate parties. *St. Croix*, 304 NW2d at 914. Whether parol evidence may be used to hold the principal liable has not been decided in Minnesota.

In general, the commercial code indicates that obligations on negotiable paper should be certain and determinable from the instrument itself. Minn Stat § 336.3-40 1(1) Minnesota Code Comment. Our holding here, which applies only to dealings between the immediate parties, does not disturb this general rule.

The general limits on the use of parol evidence do not apply as between the parties. "[A]s between the original parties and those having notice of the facts relied upon as constituting a defense, the consideration and the conditions under which the note was delivered may be shown."

Study of a note and the circumstances surrounding execution of an instrument is appropriate to determine the liability of the principal, as between the immediate parties. *First Security Bank v. Fastwich, Inc.*, 612 SW2d 799 (Mo App 1981). In *First Security Bank*, a bank obtained judgment against a defendant corporation on a note. On appeal, it was argued that parol evidence was not admissible to fix liability upon a corporate principal as a maker of a promissory note, and that such evidence is admissible under § 3-403(2)(b) of the Uniform Commercial Code only to show whether an agent is personally liable. The court held:

[Appellants'] convoluted argument, if given credence, would produce the anomalous result of permitting Comment 2 of the Uniform Commercial Code Comment to Section 400.-3-403, *supra*, to be used as a shield to protect an agent from personal liability on a promissory note by permitting the admission of parol evidence and as a weapon to defeat fixing liability upon a principal as a maker of a promissory note by excluding parol evidence."

Id. at 806.

In the circumstances here, we conclude the trial court correctly used parol evidence.

3.

The undisputed facts as set forth in the affidavit of Lou Hodnik and on the face of the check are sufficient as a matter of law to hold that the appellant accepted the check, Minn Stat § 336.3-409(1), and that the bank is liable on the check.

DECISION

As between the immediate parties to negotiation of a check, liability of a principal may be established by studying circumstances surrounding execution of the check, together with study of the face of the instrument. The trial court correctly recognized and applied this rule of commercial law.

Affirmed.

NOTES AND QUESTIONS

(1) *See* U.C.C. § 3-409(a), particularly the second sentence.

(2) What result in *Greyhound Lines* today? *See* U.C.C. § 3-402(a) and Comment 1.

BANKERS TRUST CO. v. JAVERI

New York Supreme Court, Appellate Division
39 U.C.C. Rep. 1346 (1984)

PER CURIAM.

Order, Supreme Court, New York County (B. McM. Wright, J.), entered March 21, 1984 denying plaintiff's motion for summary judgment in lieu of complaint, is unanimously reversed, on the law, with costs, and plaintiff's motion for summary judgment pursuant to CPLR § 3213 is granted, and judgment is directed to be entered in favor of plaintiff against defendant for $169,000.45, together with interest and costs.

Plaintiff Bankers discounted three promissory notes for the payee and credited the payee's account therefor. The notes not having been paid at maturity, plaintiff sues defendant Javeri individually. The notes are all signed in the corporate name K & J Diamond Imports, Inc. and on the next line appears defendant Javeri's signature. Javeri says that he signed only in a representative capacity and is thus not personally obligated on the notes.

U.C.C. § 3-403(2) provides: . . .[the Court quotes U.C.C. § 3-402(a), (b)].

Each note here sued on "names the person represented [the corporation] but does not show that the representative [Javeri] signed in a representative capacity." Thus, Javeri is personally obligated unless he can come within the clause "except as otherwise established between the immediate parties." But that clause is inapplicable because this lawsuit is not "between the immediate parties." Plaintiff Bankers is not an immediate party but a transferee, indeed a holder in due course.

The affidavits establish that Bankers is a holder in due course having discounted the notes for a customer and credited the customer's account. There is no evidence that Bankers had any notice of any defense or of any claim that defendant Javeri was signing only in a representative capacity. See U.C.C. § 3-302. Even as between immediate parties, the "undisclosed intention" of a signer that he is not to be individually responsible is insufficient to defeat liability under U.C.C. § 3-403(2)(b).

Furthermore, in two previous actions by Bankers against the corporate signer, it was adjudicated that Bankers was a holder in due course of these notes. Defendant is collaterally estopped, precluded, to question the determination in those actions that Bankers was a holder in due course. Although not nominally a party to the earlier actions, defendant was in privity with the corporate defendant in those actions within the meaning of the res judicata rules because defendant was the president of the corporation and actively participated in the defense of those actions, and thus had a full and fair opportunity to contest the issue.

Order filed.

NOTES AND QUESTIONS

(1) *See* U.C.C. § 3-402(a) and (b). Notice the distinction in (b)(2) between holders in due course and "any other person."

(2) In some jurisdictions, so-called "dead man statutes" prevent introduction of oral testimony by a surviving party to a transaction "upon a claim, or demand" against the decedent's estate. Certain jurisdictions apply the statute to defense of an action brought on behalf of an estate. See McCormick on Evidence 65. In *Bell v. Dornan*, 203 Pa. Super. 562, 201 A.2d 324, 2 U.C.C. Rep. 189 (1964), the judgment note was signed "Chet B. Earle Inc., James G. Dornan." The plaintiff was the executrix of the payee and defendant-Dornan was not permitted to testify that he signed in a representative capacity because of the dead man statute.

(3) *Negligence in Signing*. The Revisions to the Code include a major change in § 3–406. The change is one which involves the concept of comparative negligence and is more in accord with general trends in modern tort law. It remains a section labeled "Negligence Contributing to Forged Signature or Alteration of the Instrument," and the basic negligence premise is maintained. A person whose failure to exercise ordinary care substantially contributes to an alteration of an instrument is precluded from asserting that there was an alteration or forgery against a person that in good faith pays the instrument or takes it for value. Thus, there is a continuation of the negligence concept which has been brought into the law of commercial paper.

However, the revision goes on to provide in subsection (b) "if the person asserting the preclusion fails to exercise ordinary care in paying or taking the instrument and that failure substantially contributes to loss, the loss is allocated between the person precluded and the person asserting the preclusion according to the extent to which the failure of each to exercise ordinary care contributed to the loss." Thus, a comparative negligence standard is introduced into the law of commercial paper which did not previously exist. The drafters state in Comment 4 of the proposed amendment that "Subsection (b) differs from present Section 3–406 in that it adopts a concept of comparative negligence. If the person precluded under subsection (a) proves that the person asserting the preclusion failed to exercise ordinary care and that failure contributed to the loss, the loss may be allocated between the two parties on a comparative negligence basis." Clearly the standard of comparative negligence is brought in where both parties are negligent. Is the standard of the Traditional Code or the Revised Code preferable? What problems may arise with the latter?

(4) In *Pollin v. Mindy Mfg. Co.*, 236 A.2d 542 (Pa. Super. 1967), the corporate name "Mindy Mfg. Co., Inc." appeared in the lower righthand corner of a payroll check, followed by two blank lines. The president of the company simply signed his name "Robert I. Apfelbaum" under the printed company name. When the checks were later dishonored, Apfelbaum was sued personally. The court stated that it was not likely that a "check showing two lines under the imprinted corporate name indicating the signature of one or more corporate officers would be accepted by any reasonably prudent person as a fully executed check of the corporation. . . . It is common to expect that a corporate name placed upon a negotiable instrument in order to bind the corporation as a maker, especially when printed on the instrument will be accompanied by the signatures of officers authorized by the bylaws to sign the instrument." The inference was that in this context, the signature manifested its "representative capacity."

(5) Where two blank lines appear under the corporate name, are two signatures required? See *New Waterford Bank v. Morrison Buick, Inc.*, 38 Pa. D. & C.2d 371, 3 U.C.C. Rep. 426 (1965). *See* U.C.C. § 3-403(b).

PROBLEM 13.1

ARIZONA AUTO AUCTION, INC. No 5650
2701 W. THOMAS RD. TELEPHONE 269-6271
PHOENIX, ARIZONA 85009
91-0001/1221

CAR NO.	DESCRIPTION	SELLING PRICE	COMM.	DEDUCT OTHER	NET AMOUNT
88A	75 Olds 98 HT 4D 140496	2900.00	50.00		2850.00

CHECKS MUST BE CLEARED THROUGH CONSIGNOR'S BANK

PAY TWO THOUSAND EIGHT HUNDRED FIFTY AND NO/100 DOLLARS

DATE 10/21/77 AMOUNT $ 2850.00

TO THE ORDER OF CENTRAL MOTORS CO.

ARIZONA AUTO AUCTION, INC.
[signature]

FIRST NATIONAL BANK OF ARIZONA
31ST AVE. & INDIAN SCHOOL PHOENIX

⑆1221⑉0001⑆ 0622⑉18585⑈ ⑈0000285000⑈

Is J.M. Cook, who signed this check without indicating her representative capacity, personally liable on the obligation evidenced by the check? *See Valley National Bank v. Cook*, 665 P.2d 576, 35 U.C.C. Rep. 578 (1983). U.C.C. § 3-402(c).

PROBLEM 13.2

Your firm advises the Second National Bank which wishes to know the effect of the new "reasonable care" definition in the Code. Specifically, SNB asked whether it should it do anything differently so as to be more certain of following the law and avoiding liability.

PROBLEM 13.3

Your firm represents the First State Bank. You have been asked to write a memo on its liability in the following situations which have arisen. Assume first that the bank can show reasonable care on paying the checks. However, then also do another analysis of the same setting and assume the bank may have lacked reasonable care in paying the checks. It seems that attorneys for eash of the customers involved may question whether the bank exercised sufficient care in the checking of identification and in the checking of the signature. Also, if it appears that there is comparative negligence present, what percent should the bank be responsible or liable for? What strategy or procedures would you recommend for the bank?

The bank is confronted with having cashed forged checks arising out of the following circumstances:

1. One of its customers always carried several blank checks in his wallet. While in a out–of–town business trip, he spent a night drinking in some rather disreputable night clubs. The next say when he woke up in his hotel room the customer found that his wallet was missing. Although he notified the bank immediately, two checks had already been forged and cashed for $4,000 and $6,000.

2. A prominent business customer always keeps several checks in an unlocked desk drawer. These were apparently stolen, forged, and cashed before the customer noticed they were missing. These checks were cashed for $500 and $1,000.

3. Another customer, a judge, carried her checkbook in her briefcase while attending a judges conference. The judges left their briefcases in the conference room while going to lunch after it was announced that the conference room would be locked. At the end of the conference that afternoon, the judge reached into her briefcase to get a check to pay for some additional materials which were being made available at that time. She found the checkbook was missing and immediately notified the bank. At the time the judge gave notice, one of her checks had been cashed for $7,000.

PROBLEM 13.4

Suppose you are the attorney representing clients mentioned in the above problem. Do you believe that they have been negligent? Is there comparative negligence, and if so, to what degree? What strategy and means can you use to have your clients' accounts recredited for the amount of the forged checks?

SERNA V. MILANESE, INC.

District Court of Appeal of Florida, Third District
643 So. 2d 36, 24 U.C.C. Rep. 980 (1994)

NESBITT, JUDGE.

Jose Serna appeals a final summary judgment in an action filed by Milanese, Inc. (Milanese) to collect on dishonored checks. We affirm.

Milanese sold clothing to Jemaros Investments, Inc. d/b/a/ Natalia Boutique (Jemaros). Jose Serna, president of Jemaros, paid for the goods by check. Serna signed the checks, which were imprinted with the corporate name, but did not indicate his representative capacity. Following Jemaros' payment for certain merchandise by checks later dishonored, Milanese filed a multi-court action against Jemaros and Serna.[2] The count against Serna sought recovery for the dishonored checks tendered to Milanese. There is no contention that Serna was not authorized to sign the checks.

Milanese sought summary judgment restating the complaint's dishonored check allegations against Jemaros and Serna. In support of its motion, Milanese filed an affidavit of its president stating that Jemaros and Serna issued the dishonored checks. The trial court granted Milanese's motion and pursuant to section 68.065, Florida Statutes (1991)[3] ordered Serna to pay treble the face amount of the checks.

Section 673.403, Florida Statutes (1991), which was in effect when Serna signed the dishonored checks, provides: (The Court cites U.C.C. 3-403(2).

During the pendency of the suit this statute was repealed and replaced by the legislature with section 673.4021, Florida Statutes (1993), effective January 1, 1993. Section 673.4021 provides in part:

> (3) If a representative signs the name of the representative as drawer of a check without indication of the representative status and the check is payable from an account of the represented person who is identified on the check, the signer is not liable on the check if the signature is an authorized signature of the represented person.

Serna argues that the newly created statute operates retrospectively[4] to relieve him of personal liability for treble damages under section 68.065. We disagree.

---

[2] Serna, as part of the credit application to Milanese, executed an individual guaranty "for any indebtedness incurred by virtue of any and all credit extended" to Jemaros by Milanese. Milanese die not seek recovery for the dishonored checks pursuant to Serna's personal guaranty. The trial court, on a separate count, awarded Milanese damages against Serna, under Serna's personal guarantee, for merchandise for which Jemaros did not remit payment. We affirm that portion of the judgment.

[3] Section 68.065 provides, in pertinent part: (1) In any civil action brought for the purpose of collecting a check . . .the payment of which was refused by the drawee because of the lack of funds, and where the maker or drawer fails to pay the amount owing, in cash, to the payee within 30 days following a written demand . . .the maker or drawer shall be liable to the payee, in addition to the amount owing upon such check . . .for damages of triple the amount so owing.

[4] Some courts and commentators differentiate between "retroactive" and "retrospective" applications. The former refers to the application of a new law or case to matured rights, that is, to a case that has gone to final judgment. The latter term refers to application of a new law or case to pending controversies. *See Joyner v. Monier Roof Tile, Inc.*, 784 F.Supp. 872, 874 n.3 (S.D. Fla. 1992). We use the term "retrospective: in this opinion to refer to those non-final controversies concurring pre-amendment conduct."

Statutes that create new rights or take away existing rights, as opposed to furthering existing rights, are substantive in nature and may not be applied retroactively. It is well established in Florida that statutory changes which are substantive in nature are presumed to operate prospectively unless the legislature expressly manifests a contrary intention. *Meek v. Layne-Western Co.*, 624 So. 2d 345, 347 (Fla. 1st DCA 1993).

In *Meek*, the court rejected retroactive application of an amended statute that reduced a claimant's wage loss benefits when applied to a wage loss claim that occurred before the amendment. The *Meek* court reasoned that when substantive legislation changes the amount of relief available under the statute, or creates a new quantum of relief, application of such legislation to an injury that occurred before the amendment will be viewed as retroactive, and thus forbidden.

Section 673.4021 is not merely a procedural section that changes the method by which a payee can enforce his or her rights. Rather, the section substantively alters rights available to the payee, and should be prospectively applied only, absent an express legislative pronouncement that it should be retroactively applied.[5] The legislature did not provide this express intention for section 673.4021 in Chapter 92-82, section 62, at 819, Laws of Florida.

Serna signed the dishonored checks in July and August of 1992. Milanese's substantive right to collect treble damages on the worthless checks under section 673.403(2) arose in September, 1992, when it brought suit to enforce its right. The legislature created section 673.4021, effective January 1, 1993. The final judgment granting treble damages in favor of Milanese was rendered one month later, on February 3, 1993. If the statute were retrospectively applied, all the benefits to which Milanese was entitled under section 673.403 in 1992 would be effectively eradicated mid-litigation in 1993, dramatically reducing Milanese's options for recovering its undisputed damages.

We therefore find section 673.4021 confers substantive rights and thus cannot be retrospectively applied to this case. Retrospective application of section 673.4021(3) would eliminate the substantive right and remedy available to Milanese under sections 68.065 and 673.403(2).

Accordingly, the order under review is affirmed.

GERSTEN, J., concurs.

BASKIN, JUDGE (dissenting).

I am unable to agree with the majority opinion for two reasons. First, I disagree with the majority's conclusion that section 673.403(2), Florida Statutes (1991), governs this case rather than 673.4021(3), Florida Statutes (Supp. 1992). Second, I find the majority fails to address the issue concerning whether the record reflects unresolved genuine issues of material fact regarding Jose Serna's signing capacity, even under section 673.403. I conclude that genuine issues of material fact remain unresolved and would reverse the summary judgment and remand for further proceedings.

Reviewing section 673.403(2) and section 673.4021(3), I find that the latter statute governs. Section 673.4021(3) does not diminish the substantive rights and remedies of Milanese, Inc. to collect treble damages on the dishonored checks. Milanese may still pursue a claim against Serna,

[5] The United states Supreme Court by an 8-1 vote recently held that several of the 1991 amendments to the federal civil rights laws do not apply to conduct that occurred before their enactment. The opinions endorse a strong presumption against retroactivity of statutes that impair rights a party possessed when he acted, or impose new duties with respect to transactions already completed. *Landgraf v. USI Film Products*, — U.S. —, 114 S. Ct. 1483, 128 L. Ed. 2d 229 (1994); *Rivers v. Roadway Express, Inc.*, — U.S. —, 114 S. Ct. 1510, 128 L. Ed. 2d 274 (1994).

individually, to recover on the checks. The new statute has merely eliminated the statutory presumption that Serna is liable individually. The elimination of the presumption where, as here, a person signs a corporate check without indicating a representative status does not take away a vested right: Milanese does not have a vested right in a method of procedure.

In *Alamo Rent-A-Car, Inc. v. Mancusi*, 632 So. 2d 1352 (Fla. 1994), the court discussed the substantive and procedural or remedial nature of legislation, stating:

> A substantive statute is presumed to operate prospectively rather than retrospectively unless the Legislature clearly expresses its intent that the statute is to operate retrospectively. This is especially true when retrospective operation of a law would impair or destroy existing rights. Procedural or remedial statutes, on the other hand, are to be applied retrospectively and are to be applied to pending cases.
>
> As we stated in *Benyard v. Wainwright,* 322 So. 2d 473, 475 (Fla. 1975), substantive law prescribes duties and rights and procedural law concerns the means and methods to apply and enforce those duties and rights.

Consequently, I would hold that section 673.4021(3) is procedural or remedial in nature as it merely changes the means employed in redressing an injury and thus may be applied retrospectively.

Under section 673.4021(3), Serna is not personally liable on the checks if the statutory criteria are met, absent evidence of an agreement to the contrary. § 671.102(3), Fla.Stat. (1993). On the other hand, under section 673.403(2), Florida Statutes (1991), Serna is personally liable on the checks, unless the immediate parties establish evidence to the contrary, and the transaction meets the statutory requirements. The statute does not abrogate Milanese's substantive right to collect on the checks or to receive treble damages under section 68.065; or relocates the burden of proof by shifting the presumption in favor of the agent. "Burden of proof requirements are procedural in nature. The procedural rights granted by the act could be abrogated retroactively because 'no one has a vested right in any given mode of procedure.' " *Walker & LaBerge, Inc. v. Halligan*, 344 So.2d 239, 243 (Fla. 1977) (citations omitted) (*quoting Ex Parte Collett*, 337 U.S. 55, 71, 69 S.Ct. 944, 953, 93 L.Ed. 1207, 1217 (1949)); "[T]he statute does not operate to impair rights vested before enactment, create new obligations for the parties in a pre-existing legal relationship or impose new penalties on conduct which occurred before enactment." *Oakbrooke Assocs., Ltd. v. Insurance Comm'r of State of Cal.*, 581 So. 2d 943, 946 (Fla. 5th DCA 1991). Thus, section 673.-4021(3) should be applied to the case before this court.[6]

As to whether the trial court properly granted summary judgment in favor of Milanese under section 673.403(2), I find that Milanese failed to carry its burden of proving that no material fact issues remain unresolved.

> [T]he burden of proving the absence of a genuine issue of material fact is upon the moving party. Until it is determined that the movant has successfully met this burden, the opposing party is under no obligation to show that issues do remain to be tried.

[6] The statute is remedial in nature in that it "give[s] effect to the acts and contracts of individuals according to their expressed intention." *Oakbrooke Assocs.,* 581 So.2d at 945 (quoting *In Aloma Square, Inc.*, 116 B.R. 827(M.D. Fla. 1990)). The statute was designed to remedy cases in which the representative was held responsible on a corporate check based on some evidence that the person receiving the check was not aware of the signatory's representative status. The Uniform Commercial Code Comment following section 673.4021 states, in part, that "[v]irtually all checks used today are in personalized form which identify the person on whose account the check is drawn. In this case, nobody is deceived into thinking that the person signing the check is meant to be liable. This subsection is meant to overrule cases decided under former Article 3 such as *Griffin v. Ellinger*, 538 S.W.2d 97 (Texas 1976)."

> This means that before it becomes necessary to determine the legal sufficiency of the affidavits or other evidence submitted by the party moved against, it must first be determined that the movant has successfully met his burden of proving a negative, *i.e.*, the non-existence of a genuine issue of material fact. He must prove this negative conclusively. The proof must be such as to overcome all reasonable inferences which may be drawn in favor of the opposing party.

Holl v. Talcott, 191 So. 2d 40, 43 (Fla. 1966) (citations omitted). Here, Milanese's affidavit and other evidence failed to establish the absence of factual issues. Pursuant to section 673.403(2)(b), Derna is personally obligated "[e]xcept as otherwise established between the immediate parties. . .." Milanese's affidavit asserts that Jemaros Investments Inc., *and* Serna signed the checks. That assertion confirms the existence of a material fact issue rather than establishing the absence of such issue. Furthermore, the record contains an individual guaranty signed by Serna in which he agreed to pay individually for goods upon Jemaros' failure to remit payment. There would be no need for an individual guaranty promising payment if Serna signed the checks and remitted payment in an individual capacity. The adoption of Milanese's contention that Serna signed the checks individually would render the individual guaranty meaningless. *Cf. Tampa Bay Economic Dev. Corp. v. Edman*, 598 So. 2d 172, 174 (Fla. 2d DCA 1992) ("For a corporation to guarantee its own debt would add nothing to its existing obligation and would be meaningless."); *Central Nat'l Bank of Miami v. Muskat Corp. of Am., Inc.*, 430 So.2d 957 (Fla. 3d DCA 1983) (same). Instead of demonstrating the nonexistence of triable issues, the individual guaranty signed by Serna creates a material fact issue as to whether Serna signed the checks in his individual capacity. I conclude that Milanese did not carry its burden of proving the nonexistence of genuine triable issues of material facts.

For these reasons, I would reverse and remand for further proceedings.

§ 13.03 Liability of the Maker or the Issuer of Cashier's Check

Read: U.C.C. §§ 3-412, 3-411, 3-104(e) and (g), 3-103(5) and (6) and (9) and Comment 2, 3-116(a); see § 3-204(a) (first sentence).

EVENSON v. HLEBECHUK

North Dakota Supreme Court
305 N.W.2d 13, 32 U.C.C. Rep. 154 (1981)

Erickstad, C.J.

The defendants, David and Janice Hlebechuk, appeal from a summary judgment entered against them by the District Court of Cass County contending that they should have been allowed to present parol evidence concerning a promissory note issued by them to plaintiff William Evenson. We affirm the summary judgment entered by the district court.

It is undisputed that Evenson was employed by the Hlebechuks to sell a twelveplex apartment building in Casselton, North Dakota. A purchaser, Darwin Jacobson, was procured by Evenson. An earnest money receipt and agreement was entered into between Jacobson and the Hlebechuks. Jacobson paid $12,500 as a down payment. The Hlebechuks were to carry a contract for deed for the balance of $237,500 for a term of 20 years with a balloon payment due at the end of two years. At the end of this period, Jacobson had an option for an additional two-year period to pay the balloon.

On June 1, 1977, when the sale was consummated, the Hlebechuks executed a promissory note to Evenson in the amount of $12,500 "for services rendered by the payee to the makers in connection with the sale" of the apartment.[7] Subsequently, Jacobson failed to make any payments and in lieu of a foreclosure deeded the apartment building back to the Hlebechuks. Evenson demanded payment under the promissory note and the Hlebechuks refused to pay. They assert that the note was to become payable only if the balloon payment was made by Jacobson. Evenson contended that the promissory note was clear and unambiguous and that any parol evidence which contradicts the note is excluded by the parol evidence rule. The trial court, after receiving briefs and holding a hearing, entered summary judgment for Evenson. The Hlebechuks assert the following issues on appeal:

I.

> Whether the written contract of the parties, as evidenced by an Earnest Money Agreement and a Promissory Note executed by the parties, is ambiguous and uncertain as to Defendants' obligation to pay Plaintiff his real estate commission for the sale of real property.

II.

> Whether parol evidence is admissible to show the oral agreement of the parties subjecting Plaintiff's real estate commission to a condition precedent that the purchaser make the deferred payments on a Contract for Deed with the Defendants, when that parol agreement was the inducing cause of a Promissory Note and an integral part of the consideration for the Promissory Note.

7

"PROMISSORY NOTE
"$12,500.00
Fargo, North Dakota
June 1, 1977

"Two years after date, for value received, the undersigned, David R. Hlebechuk and Janice B. Hlebechuk, husband and wife, promise to pay to the order of William E. Evenson, at Fargo, North Dakota, the sum of Twelve Thousand Five Hundred and no/l00ths Dollars ($12,500.00), with interest from date hereon at the rate of 9–3/4% per annum. The several makers, signers, guarantors and endorsers hereof hereby waive presentment, demand, notice of dishonor and protest and consent that the time of payment may be extended or this note renewed without affecting their liability thereon.

"The makers hereof reserve the privilege of prepaying this note in whole or in part at any time.

"This note is given in consideration for services rendered by the payee to the makers in connection with the sale of real property located in Casselton, North Dakota, under the terms of a certain Contract for Deed bearing this date between the makers and Darwin Jacobson. The due date of this note may he accelerated by the payee to the date of full performance of the said contract by Darwin Jacobson. The aforesaid Contract for Deed contains an option on the part of said Darwin Jacobson to extend the date of final performance under the contract to June 1,1981. If the date of final performance under said Contract for Deed is extended, the makers hereof reserve the right to extend the due date of this note for an additional time up to June l, 1981, said option must he exercised by the makers hereof in writing addressed to the payee and deposited in the United States mail on or before May 1, 1979."

III.

Whether parol evidence is admissible to establish that a Promissory Note given for the commission on a sale of realty by the payee was delivered on the express condition that it was to be operative only when the purchaser made the deferred payments on the purchase price.

IV.

Whether Summary Judgment was appropriate under the circumstances of the present case.

I. Scope of Review

On appeal from a summary judgment, we review the evidence in the light most favorable to the party against whom the summary judgment was granted. The summary judgment will be upheld only if it appears that there is no genuine issue of any material fact and that the moving party is entitled to judgment as a matter of law.

II. Admission of Parol Evidence

The district court determined that "[t]he promissory note together with the asserted earnest money contract and the asserted Contract for Deed are clear, certain and unambiguous on their face," and that parol evidence was not admissible.

A. Ambiguous Contract

The Hlebechuks assert that the written agreement of the parties concerning the real estate commission is ambiguous and that parol evidence is admissible to explain the true meaning of the terms of the agreement.

The promissory note falls under the commercial paper chapter of North Dakota's Uniform Commercial Code as it is a negotiable instrument. § 41-03-04, NDCC. As required by Section 41-03-04, the note (a) was signed by the makers, the Hlebechuks; (b) contained an unconditional promise to pay a sum certain, $ 12,500 at 9–3/4% interest; (c) is payable at a definite time; and (d) is payable to the order of William Evenson. § 41-03-04, NDCC. Thus, the note is governed by the Uniform Commercial Code. [NDCC § 41-03-04 is U.C.C. § 3-104. Ed.]

The parol evidence rule of Section 9-06-07, NDCC, also is applicable as a general principle of law to supplement the U.C.C. § 41-01-03, NDCC. [U.C.C. § 1-103. Ed.]

Section 9-06-07, NDCC, provides:

9-06-07. Written contract supersedes oral negotiations.—The execution of a contract in writing, whether the law requires it to be written or not, supersedes all the oral negotiations or stipulations concerning its matter which preceded or accompanied the execution of the instrument.

We have previously held that "[t]his is a legislative enactment, in part, of the parol evidence rule. . .. This is not an evidentiary or interpretive rule, but rather one of substantive law." Parol evidence is admissible, however, when the writing is ambiguous. Whether or not the writing is ambiguous is a question of law for the court to determine.

The district court considered the earnest money receipt and agreement between Jacobson and the Hlebechuks in reaching its determination that the writing was not ambiguous. At the bottom of this writing there is a handwritten note after the printed statement "OWNER'S CLOSING INSTRUCTIONS AND AGREEMENT TO PAY COMMISSION" which simply states "Deferred with Balloon." This portion of the earnest money receipt and agreement is not signed by any of the parties. The Hlebechuks contend that when this writing is interpreted and construed together with the promissory note it raises an ambiguity. We disagree.

The district court properly construed the promissory note and the earnest money receipt and agreement together as they were both executed as part of the same transaction and contained terms relating to the commission to be paid. § 41-03-19, NDCC [U.C.C. § 3-119].

Even when the writings are construed together, however, they are not ambiguous. The promissory note provides that the commission may be deferred if Jacobson exercised his option to extend payment of the balloon two years. The earnest money receipt and agreement states the same thing in a short-hand manner. As there is no ambiguity in these writings, that exception to the parol evidence rule does not apply.

B. Oral Agreement as Inducing Contract

The Hlebechuks next assert that parol evidence is admissible when an oral agreement is the inducing cause of the written contract.

Evenson argues that this issue was not raised in the trial court. Our review of the briefs on the motion for summary judgment and the transcript of the hearing confirms Evenson's contention.

In *Mattis v. Mattis*, 274 NW2d 201, 204 (ND 1979), we said:

> . . .ordinarily on appeals to this court the record must reflect that the appellant brought all matters necessary for the disposition of the issues raised on appeal before the trial court or that they were improperly excluded by the court; and that all issues raised on appeal were presented to the trial court but were not resolved in accordance with law. The appeal process is designed to review action taken by the trial court. It is not designed to give the appellant an opportunity to develop different strategy or theories. The appellant is bound by the record he made.

Accordingly, this issue is not appropriately before us on this appeal.

C. Parol Evidence of a Condition Precedent

The Hlebechuks final assertion is that parol evidence is admissible to show that the note was delivered on a condition precedent that it was to become operative only when the balloon payment was made.

The district court in its memorandum opinion said:

> The Defendants urge that they should be able to show intrinsic evidence that a condition precedent was to happen (full payment) before the note is operative. Amendment of Defendants' Answer to specifically plead this will not change the parol evidence rule. Neither will it come under any exception to the rule. It still results in an attempt to alter the terms of a written document which is clear, certain and unambiguous on its face.

In *Mattco, Inc. v. Mandan Radio Ass'n, Inc.*, 224 NW2d 822, 825 (ND 1974) we said:

> North Dakota recognizes that a condition precedent under appropriate circumstances may be a prerequisite to the existence of a contract. Section 9-01 -II, NDCC, defines a "condition precedent" as—

> . . .[A] condition which is to be performed before some right dependent thereon accrues or some act dependent thereon is performed.
>
> On several occasions, this Court has considered the matter of conditions precedent, their existence and legal effect.

224 NW2d at 825.

> The existence of a condition precedent may be considered an exception to the rule or a situation where the rule has no application. Parol testimony is admissible to prove a condition precedent to the legal effectiveness of a written agreement, *if the condition does not contradict the express terms of such written agreement.*

224 NW2d at 825 (concurring opinion by Johnson). A condition precedent cannot be used to contradict express terms of a written contract.

It is also the established law in North Dakota that promissory notes may be subject to conditions precedent. Parol evidence is admissible to prove the existence of a condition precedent to the effectiveness of the writing. *Id.*

We agree with the reasoning used by the Supreme Court of Idaho in deciding *Ventures, Inc. v. Jones*, 623 P2d 145 (Idaho 1981). In that case, the court held that the law prior to enactment of the U.C.C. regarding the admissibility of parol evidence to prove a condition precedent to a negotiable instrument was equally applicable to post U.C.C. cases. 623 P2d at 149. In that case, the court said:

> Thus, even before the enactment of the Uniform Commercial Code, it was the rule in Idaho that where promissory notes are given subject to conditions upon their delivery, observance of those conditions is essential to the validity of the notes and that the annexing of such conditions to the delivery is not an oral contradiction of the written obligation. . . .
>
> The theory behind the cases cited above is that when a note is delivered subject to a condition, it does not become enforceable until the condition has been fulfilled. This theory has continued application in the code in IC § 28-3-306(c) [which is similar to § 41-03-36, NDCC], which lists the defense of nonperformance of any condition precedent as available against one not a holder in due course.

623 P2d at 149.

The Supreme Court of Idaho was discussing delivery for a special purpose but used the law concerning conditional delivery.

Evenson contends that such parol evidence contradicts the unconditional promissory note and is inadmissible. We agree. Although there may be conditions precedent to negotiable instruments, this is not such a case as the condition precedent alleged by the Hlebechuks conflicts with the terms of the note. Such a conflict does not arise simply because a condition precedent would make the unconditional promissory note unenforceable; rather, the condition precedent is so inconsistent with the note as to require it to be in writing.

In this case, the note does more than just establish a definite due date as all negotiable instruments must. The note contains four conceivable times for payment: (1) the note may be paid on the due date, two years after June 1, 1977; (2) the note may be prepaid at any time by the Hlebechuks; (3) the note may be accelerated by Evenson at any time that Jacobson renders full performance of the contract for deed; and (4) the note may be extended to June 1, 1981, if Jacobson chooses to exercise his option to extend the due date of the balloon payment under the contract for deed. It appears that all eventualities contemplated for payment of the note were included by the parties. Had the parties intended payment of the balloon payment as a condition precedent, it would have been easy to have so included it in the note. Having not done so, they cannot attempt to do so now through parol evidence, for to permit that would be to permit evidence of a condition precedent which is inconsistent with the other terms of the note relevant to payment.

The condition precedent alleged by the Hlebechuks is so inconsistent with the terms of the note that oral evidence concerning it was properly excluded.

III. Summary Judgment

The note itself is clear, certain, and unambiguous. As there were no issues of material fact, the motion for summary judgment was properly granted by the district court.

The summary judgment is affirmed.

NOTE

For the rules governing presentment and dishonor of a note, *see* U.C.C. §§ 3-501(a) and 3-502(a). *See* § 13.07, *infra.*

For the Statutes of Limitations relating to notes *see* U.C.C. § 3-118(a) and (b). *See* § 13.11, *infra.*

LOUIS FALCIGNO ENTERPRISES, INC. v. MASSACHUSETTS BANK & TRUST CO.

Massachusetts Appeals Court
436 N.E.2d 993, 34 U.C.C. Rep. 206 (1982)

DREBEN, J.

The question before us is whether a bank which has issued a treasurer's or cashier's check may, when sued by the payee, assert as defenses claims of its customer arising out of the underlying transaction for which the treasurer's check was delivered by the bank's customer to the payee. We hold that in the circumstances of this case the bank may not assert such defenses and that summary judgment was properly entered for the plaintiff the payee of the cashier's check.

An affidavit of the bank's customer filed by the defendant indicates that the dispute between the customer and the plaintiff relates to a license given by the plaintiff to the customer to exhibit a championship boxing match on closed circuit television. Prior to the telecast, the plaintiff demanded payment in the form of a bank check for expenses amounting to $47,305. When the customer claimed the expenses were not then due, the plaintiff indicated that it would not transmit the necessary signals for the telecast unless the bank check was delivered. As a result of the plaintiff's threat, and because it had already incurred substantial expenses, the customer delivered the check as demanded. After the telecast, the customer prevailed upon the bank to dishonor the check.

The customer's affidavit also alleges that, despite its repeated protests, the plaintiff refused to make adjustments. Because of the plaintiff's "misrepresentations," the customer sustained losses in excess of $50,000. The alleged misrepresentations related to receipts of prior matches, to the availability of certain facilities, and to the number of spectators who would buy tickets on the evening of the match.

The defendant also filed an affidavit of its president appending a letter of the customer, the body of which is set forth in the margin.[8] The affidavit refers to the letter as a "written indemnification agreement."

These affidavits establish that, unlike the situation in *Travi Constr. Corp. v. First Bristol County Natl. Bank*, — Mass App —, 405 NE2d 666, the defense asserted is not that of the bank but is a defense of the customer. Moreover, the defense relates to the underlying transaction and is not a "claim . . .to the instrument." See GL c 106, § 3-306(d), and § 3-603(1), both inserted by St 1957, c 765, § 1.

No cases have been cited to us and we have found none which allow this kind of contract defense of its customer to be asserted by a bank where the bank is the sole obligor on the instrument. See GL c 106, § 3-802(1)(a). Compare *Leo Syntax Auto Sales, Inc. v. Peoples Bank & Sav. Co.*, 6 Ohio Misc 226, 215 NE2d 68 (Ct CP 1965), the only case found allowing the bank to raise such defenses; in that case the purchaser as endorser of the check was also liable on the instrument. To the contrary, the authorities seem in accord in holding that a bank may not raise such a contract defense on a cashier's check. They reach this result, however, by different routes, as the Uniform Commercial Code (Code) does not deal specifically with defenses to cashier's checks. See generally Lawrence, *Making Cashier's Checks and Other Bank Checks Cost-Effective: A Plea for Revision of Articles 3 and 4 of the Uniform Commercial Code,* 64 Minn L Rev 275 (1980).

Some cases hold flatly that a cashier's check may not be dishonored. *E.g., State ex rel. Chan Siew Lai v. Powell*, 536 SW2d 14, 16 (Mo 1976); *Abilities, Inc. v. Citibank, N.A.*, App Div, 449 NYS2d 242 (1982); see also *Moon Over the Mountain, Ltd. v. Marine Midland Bank*, 87 Misc 2d 918, 386 NYS2d 974 (NY Civ Ct 1976); *National Newark & Essex Bank v. Giordano,* 111 NJ Super 347, 351-352, 268 A2d 327 (1970). One rationale given for these cases is that the check is drawn by the bank on itself and is accepted by the mere act of issuance. See GL c 106, § 3-41 3(1).

Other cases treat cashier's checks like ordinary negotiable instruments under the Code. They point out that while some defenses of a third party may be available, both under the Code and prior law,[9] only claims to the instrument and not defenses to the underlying transaction may be asserted by the bank. This is true even where the third party defends the lawsuit. See GL c 106, § 3-306(d); *Fulton Nat'l Bank v. Delco Corp.*, 128 Ga App 16, 19, 195 SE2d 455 (1973) (bank draft). Compare *Deones v. Zeches*, 212 Minn 260, 264, 3 NW2d 432 (1942) (claim that

[8] "Please stop payment on your treasurers check No. 032615 in the amount of $47,305.00 to Lou Falcigno Enterprises, Inc., issued Wednesday, October 1, 1980.

"The reason for this stop payment is that the goods and services ordered and agreed upon were not delivered as agreed upon.

"I agree to hold this bank harmless and also agree to indemnify this bank against any loss arising from the stop payment."

[9] *Prouty v. Roberts*, 6 Cush 19, 20 (1850). *Nichols v. Somerville Sav. Bank*, 333 Mass 488, 490-491, 132 NE2d 158 (1956). Sutherland, *Article Three: Commercial Paper*, 1957 Ann Survey of Mass Law 24, 29-30.

title to the instrument had not passed). An extensive discussion of jus tertii, the use of the rights of third persons as a defense, is contained in Note, *Blocking Payment on a Certified, Cashier's, or Bank Check,* 73 Mich L Rev 424, 428-435, 436-439 (1974).

See also White & Summers, Uniform Commercial Code 682 & n 113 (2d ed 1980); Note, *Personal Money Orders and Teller's Checks: Mavericks Under the U.C.C.*, 67 Colum L Rev 524, 547-548 (1967); Benson, *Stop Payment of Cashier's Checks and Bank Drafts Under the Uniform Commercial Code*, 2 Ohio NUL Rev 445, 460 (1975); Wallach, *Negotiable Instrument Is: The Bank Customer's Ability to Prevent Payment on Various Forms of Checks*, 11 Ind L Rev 579, 592 (1978); Lawrence, *supra* at 304-316. Some authorities would apply the full scope of GL c 106, § 3-306(d), to cashier's checks and would, therefore, permit as a defense claims on account of the underlying transaction which are serious enough to give rise to the right of rescission. See GL c 106, § 3-306, U.C.C. comment 5; *First Natl. Bank v. Associates Inv. Co.*, 140 Ind App 394, 398, 221 NE2d 684 (1966); Fox, *Stopping Payment on a Cashier's Check*, 19 BCL Rev 683, 692 (1978). Contrast Lawrence, *supra* at 316-320.[10]

We think it plain that the policy in favor of reliability of bank checks requires a rule that the bank be precluded from raising the contract defenses claimed here on behalf of its customer. See *Travi Constr. Corp. v. First Bristol County Natl. Bank*, — Mass App at —, 405 NE2d 666; *State ex rel. Chan Siew Lai v. Powell*, 536 SW2d at 16; *National Newark & Essex Bank v. Giordano*, 111 NJ Super at 351-352, 268 A2d 327. Thus, even if we were to accept the defendant's invitation and reject an absolute rule against dishonor of cashier's checks where claims of a remitter are involved, we would, in any event, not permit defenses broader than those permitted under GL c 106, § 3-306(d).[11] Since the customer's claims do not fall within that section of § 3-603, the plaintiff must prevail.[12]

Judgment affirmed.

QUESTION

What result in *Louis Falcigno Enterprises* today? *See* U.C.C. § 3-305(d) and Comment 4.

---

[10] Another rule for cashier's checks has been suggested by one commentator, namely, "the finality of payment" rule of the Code. GL c 106, § 3-418. See Brady on Bank Checks § 20.12, at 20-30 through 20-31 (5th ed 1979), cited in *Travi Constr. Corp. v. First Bristol County Natl. Bank*, — Mass App at — —, & n 3, Mass App Ct Adv Sh (1980) at 1120-1121 & n 3, 405 NE2d 666. Cf. *Rockland Trust Co. v. South Shore Natl. Bank*, 366 Mass 74, 78, 314 NE2d 438 (1974). See also Lawrence, *supra* at 288. We note that the uncontroverted allegation in the plaintiff's affidavit as to its expenditures based on the issuance of the bank check brings the plaintiff within the final payment rule suggested by Brady.

[11] The defendant concedes that if the plaintiff is a holder in due course, the bank may not assert the customer's contract defenses. it argues, however, that there is a question of material fact as to whether the plaintiff is a holder in due course. We need not consider that question since we hold that even if the plaintiff is not a holder in due course so that c 106, § 3-306, and not c 106, § 3-305, is applicable, the defenses claimed do not fall within § 3-306(d). Different views have been expressed as to whether a payee who receives a bank check from a remitter who claims failure of consideration is a holder in due course. Compare *Fulton Natl. Bank v. Delco Corp.*, 128 Ga App at 18, 195 SE2d 455 and Kock, *Commercial Law*, 25 Mercer L Rev 49, 60 (1974) (not a holder in due course) with Note, 67 Colum L Rev at 547, Benson, *supra* at 459 & 460, and 6D U.C.C. Rep-Dig (MB) § 3-306 at 2-886.24(1981) (suggesting payee may in such a case be a holder in due course).

[12] In those cases where the claims of a customer fall within GL c 106, § 3-306(d), the last sentence of that section provides that "[t]he claim of any third person to the instrument is not otherwise available as a defense to any party liable thereon unless the third person himself defends the action for such party."

Also *see* U.C.C. § 3-411for the consequences of a refusal to pay a cashier's check.

HOTEL RIVIERA, INC. v. FIRST NATIONAL BANK & TRUST CO.

United States Court of Appeals
768 F2d 1201, 41 U.C.C. Rep. 363 (10th Cir. 1985)

MOORE, J.

This is an appeal from the denial of a motion for reconsideration of the trial court's order granting summary judgment to the appellee. The underlying action was brought to enforce payment of a cashier's check issued by the appellee, First National Bank and Trust Company of Oklahoma City, Oklahoma (Bank), and endorsed by the payee to the appellant, Hotel Riviera, Inc. (Hotel). When the check was presented for payment, the Bank dishonored it having discovered the check had been paid for with forged instruments. In the trial court, the Bank argued the Hotel was not a holder in due course, thereby permitting the Bank to assert the personal defense of failure of consideration. The trial court allowed the defense, entered judgment for the Bank, and denied the Hotel's motion for rehearing. We reverse.

The question presented is whether the Hotel, as endorser [sic; endorsee] without knowledge of the underlying fraud of the purchaser of the cashier's check, is subject to the Bank's defense. Even though the Hotel agrees it is not a holder in due course because it accepted the endorsement of the cashier's check in satisfaction of a gambling debt, the issue turns upon the-nature of a cashier's check and consideration of whether the Hotel is otherwise an innocent party to the transaction.

The record shows that the cashier's check was issued to Richard K. Pemberton, a Bank customer, who deposited to his own account two checks drafted by his employer and ostensibly issued to two of the employer's customers. Prior to deposit, Pemberton forged the endorsements of the customers. Pemberton's bank account was initially credited with the amount of the forged checks, $480,000, and then debited with the amount of the cashier's check, $250,000.

After being issued the cashier's check, Pemberton flew to Las Vegas, Nevada, where he set out to gamble at the Hotel's casino. To finance this effort, Pemberton offered the check to the Hotel in exchange for credit in the casino. Though the Hotel had a policy against acceptance of checks without verification, it eventually agreed to a late night acceptance of this check conditioned upon certain requirements irrelevant here. As soon as possible the next day, and while Pemberton was still in the casino, a Hotel employee called the Bank to verify the check. The Hotel was informed that the name of the payee, the amount of the check, and its number were accurate. The Hotel was also told that there were no outstanding stop orders and that the check had not been reported lost or stolen. With this verification, on January 6, the Hotel deposited the cashier's check in its own bank for collection.

On January 8, the Bank was notified of Pemberton's forged endorsements of his employer's checks and of the resultant dishonor of those checks by the employer's bank. Then, in turn, the Bank dishonored the cashier's check, prompting this suit.

Our analysis hinges on the nature of a cashier's check. We note that although there is some judicial disparity in the perception of instruments of this genre, we have said that a cashier's check is an indebtedness of a bank which is accepted—as that term is applied by the Uniform Commercial Code (U.C.C. or Code)—upon its issuance. Accordingly, the issuing bank's liability on the instrument is governed by the Code.

Under most circumstances, acceptance by a bank constitutes a promise to honor the check upon presentment, U.C.C. § 3-410; Okla. Stat. tit. 12A, § 3-410 (1963); but we and other courts have recognized an exception to that general rule. Although not specifically provided in the Code, banks have been allowed to countermand cashier's checks when presented by a holder who has participated in some act of fraud which has led to or caused the original issuance of the cashier's check. Lawrence, *Making Cashier's Checks and Other Bank Checks Cost-Effective: A Plea for Revision of Articles 3 and 4 of the Uniform Commercial Code*, 64 Minn. L. Rev. 275 (1980). Underlying this exception is the unassailable equity that no one should profit from fraudulent acts. Yet, that equity has never been applied in the context of this case.

The question we face here is whether the endorsee who neither participated in nor knew of the fraudulent procurement of the cashier's check should bear the burden of the fraudulent actor. The Bank argues for the affirmative because the check was endorsed in payment of a gambling debt, rendering the endorsement void under the laws of Nevada. Assuming only for the sake of argument the contention is sound, the Hotel's concession that it is not a holder in due course moots the point. However, it is arguable whether Nev. Rev. Stat. § 1.030 (1957), which makes gambling debts unenforceable, would apply to transactions in which the maker of the instrument (here the Bank) was not a party to the gambling transaction.

Thus, if the purpose for which Pemberton endorsed and negotiated the check is significant, it is significant only in relation to whether the Hotel came into possession of the check with knowledge of its "defects."[13] Since that point is conceded, however, we need only consider whether the Hotel can nonetheless demand payment of the check under Article 3 of the U.C.C.

We believe the reason for allowing a defrauded bank to defend against a demand for payment made by a culpable holder does not obtain here. There is a relationship between the acts of a holder who procures the issuance of a check by fraud and the loss resultantly sustained by an innocent bank. No similar relationship exists here. It is true the Hotel accepted the check in payment of a gaming debt; yet, that acceptance was not the cause of the Bank's injury. The forged endorsements of the checks deposited by Pemberton in payment of the cashier's check, coupled with the Bank's subsequent issuance of its own check without verification of the deposit, caused the injury. The Hotel had no part in prompting that injury, and its subsequent acceptance of the endorsement by Pemberton is irrelevant to the Bank's loss.[14] Since the cashier's check

---

[13] Since the "defect" had nothing to do with the issuance of the cashier's check, and could only be asserted against the endorsement, the concession is perplexing in the context of this suit.

[14] The trial court concluded that the Hotel's acceptance of the check placed the Hotel in the same position as a payee whose fraud caused the issuance of the check. We respectfully suggest the logic is faulty as between the Bank and the innocent endorsee. This is especially true when, as here, the endorsee obtains the issuing bank's verification of the check prior to its unconditional acceptance and the endorsee's change of position.

was accepted on issuance, the Bank cannot be allowed to escape the effect of its acceptance on the ground that the endorsement was nullified because it was made in payment of a gambling debt. That result is both a non sequitur and an intentional avoidance of the clear import of U.C.C. § 4-303(1)(a); Okla. Stat. tit. 12A, § 4-303(1)(a)(1963).[15]

This holding does not deny the effect of Nevada law regarding the enforceability of instruments given in satisfaction of gambling debts, nor does it ignore the concept of allowing the assertion of personal defenses. It does, however, recognize the peculiar nature of a cashier's check and effects the purpose of such an instrument. In commercial circles, cashier's checks have the aura of cash. Whether that aura bears scrutiny in the law is irrelevant here. It is important only that there is a universal commercial reverence for cashier's checks which is the product of the issuing bank's promise of payment. While the U.C.C. speaks in general terms about the acceptance of cashier's checks upon issuance, any attempt to exclude that consequence must have some logical relationship to the law of negotiation established and relied upon in the Code. While the relationship is manifest when a fraudulent purchaser attempts to negotiate a cashier's check, the logic fails in the case of an endorsee who has done nothing to cheat the issuing bank. *Whitehead v. American Security & Trust Co.*, 285 F.2d 282 (D.C. Cir. 1960) (en banc).[16] In short, the personal defense of failure of consideration is inapplicable to the instant transaction.

The judgment of the District Court is reversed with directions to enter judgment in favor of the appellant.

QUESTION

What result in *Hotel Riviera* today? See U.C.C. § 3-302, Comment 4, Case #1.

MERITOR v. DUKE

Virginia Circuit Court, Nineteenth Judicial Circuit
22 U.C.C. Rep.2d 833 (1993)

WILLIAMS, J.

This case was tried before the court on April 28, 1993, and is now before the court for decision. Based upon the evidence, the arguments of counsel, and the memoranda filed, the court makes the following findings.

[15] That section provides: [the Court quotes § 4-303(1)(a)].

[16] Although Whitehead involved a "treasurer's check," a cashier's check and treasurer's check are equivalent.

FACTS

The facts are set out in the parties' briefs, memoranda, pleadings and by stipulation. Briefly stated, John V. Duke (hereinafter "Duke") was a customer of Meritor Savings, FA (hereinafter "Meritor"). On February 6, 1992, Duke appeared at Meritor and requested that the bank issue a teller's check[17] in the amount of $19,115.98 to PST, Ltd. drawn from funds in Duke's savings account. A check was then issued by Meritor, drawn on its account with the Federal Home Loan Bank of Atlanta (hereinafter "FHLB"). The check was delivered to the payee by Duke. On February 7, 1992, Duke reappeared at Meritor and requested that the bank issue a stop payment order on the same check. In consideration for issuing the order, Meritor required Duke to execute an indemnity agreement dated February 7, 1992. Meritor issued the stop payment order to FHLB and recredited Duke's account for the amount of the check. FHLB dishonored the check when presented by the payee. Sometime thereafter, an attorney notified Meritor and demanded that Meritor honor the dishonored check. On February 25, 1992, Meritor issued a replacement check drawn on its account with FHLB in the amount of $19,190.11, payable to PST, Ltd. On February 27, 1992, Meritor placed a hold on $10,859.38, which was the balance of Duke's funds in his account with Meritor, and made a written demand on Duke for the remainder of the loss. When Duke refused to pay Meritor, this lawsuit followed.

Meritor argues that the check issued by it on behalf of Duke was analogous to a certified or cashier's check, and was not subject to countermand under the Virginia Uniform Commercial Code, Virginia Code §§ 8.1-101 et seq. (1950, as amended). According to Meritor, it agreed to issue a stop payment order as an accommodation to its customer, but, because the check is a cash equivalent, Meritor was "compelled" to honor the same when presented by the payee. Finally, Meritor asserts that the indemnity agreement releases it from all liability arising from the stop payment order, and was intended to protect the bank from the very thing that occurred in this case.

In response, Duke argues that the check issued by Meritor was a teller's check, not a cashier's check. The distinction is significant in that the former is more like an ordinary check under the Code. Duke avers that like an ordinary check, a teller's check is subject to a stop payment order by the customer because it is not accepted upon issuance. Thus, Duke maintains that Meritor was not obligated or compelled to honor the check upon presentment by the payee because it had not yet been accepted or certified. With regard to the indemnity agreement, Duke contends that Meritor either breached the contract by failing to perform as promised or is not entitled to indemnification because Duke's performance was discharged by Meritor's failure to satisfy a condition precedent, that is stopping payment of the check.

CONCLUSIONS OF LAW

I. WHETHER THE TELLER'S CHECK ISSUED BY MERITOR AT THE REQUEST OF DUKE OBLIGATED MERITOR TO PAY ON THE INSTRUMENT OVER A SUBSEQUENT STOP PAYMENT ORDER.

In order to determine whether the teller's check issued by Meritor was an unconditional promise to pay by Meritor, it is necessary to determine the nature of the check involved in the present case. By definition, a check drawn by a bank upon itself is a cashier's check. In effect, the bank

[17] The check at issue in this case has been referred to as an "official," "bank," or "teller's" check. The court will use the term "teller's" check in this opinion.

is the drawer and the drawee. Commercially, a cashier's check, unlike an ordinary check, operates as an assignment of funds and is treated as a cash equivalent or substitute. *Swiss Credit Bank v. Virginia Nat'l Bank–Fairfax*, 538 F.2d 487 [19 U.C.C. Rep Serv 603] (4th Cir. 1976). The issuing bank is not free to refuse payment on such a check when it is presented for payment by the payee. *Id.* Further, under Va. Code § 8.4-403, a cashier's check is not subject to countermand because it is deemed "accepted" by the mere act of its issuance. "Acceptance" is the "*drawee's* signed engagement to honor the draft as presented." Va. Code § 8.3-410(1). In the case of a cashier's check, the *drawee* is the issuing bank and the drawer.

However, a teller's check is distinguishable from a cashier's check. It is a check drawn by a bank on its account in another bank. For purposes of the Virginia Uniform Commercial Code, a "bank carrying an account with another bank" is a "customer." Va. Code § 8.4-103(1)(e). The drawer bank as the customer may stop payment on its check prior to acceptance or certification. Va. Code § 8.4-403(1). As such, the drawer bank's liability is not governed by Va. Code § 8.3-411 in that it was not "accepted" upon issuance by the drawer/customer bank like a cashier's check.

In the present case, Duke purchased a teller's check from Meritor. Meritor issued a check drawn on its account with the Federal Home Loan Bank of Atlanta ("FHLB"). At the request of Duke, Meritor agreed to issue a stop payment order on the check as a customer with FHLB. In accordance with the stop payment order, FHLB dishonored the check when presented for payment by the payee. Despite Meritor's arguments to the contrary, the court concludes that the check issued by Meritor was a teller's check that was not accepted or certified upon issuance or by the drawee, and was subject to countermand.

In support of its position, Meritor relies primarily on *Guaranty Fed. Sav. & Loan v. Horseshoe Operating*, 748 S.W.2d 519 [6 U.C.C. Rep. Serv. 2d 774] (Tex. App. Dallas 1988), *rev'd on other grounds*, 793 S.W.2d 652 [1 U.C.C. Rep. Serv. 2d 261] (Tex. 1990)[18] in which the court applied the "cash equivalent" theory to teller's checks. In that case, a payee sued the drawer bank that stopped payment on a teller's check at the request of its customer. The court held that the drawer of the teller's check had no right to stop payment because "business of this state is transacted with such checks with the expectation that they do represent cash." *Id.* at 525. The court looked to other jurisdictions, found two different approaches to the treatment of teller's checks, and concluded that because the evidence in that case indicated that Guaranty considered the teller's check to be the equivalent of cash, the teller's check was accepted for payment when issued and was not subject to countermand. But several jurisdictions have disagreed, finding a teller's check and a cashier's check to be two distinct negotiable instruments. *Lo Monaco v. Belfior*, 175 A.D.2d 59, 572 N.Y.S.2d 315 [15 U.C.C. Rep Serv 2d 991] (A.D. 1st Dept.1991); *Fur Funtastic, Ltd. v. Kearns*, 104 Misc.2d 1030, 430 N.Y.S.2d 27 [29 U.C.C. Rep Serv 960] (NY City Civ. Ct.1980); *Rubin v. Walt Whitman Fed. Sav. & Loan Assoc.*, 21 U.C.C. 610 -21 Fed Rules Evid Serv 610] (N.Y. Sup.App.T. 1977); *Bruno Collective Fed. Sav. & Loan Assoc.*, 147 N.J.Super. 115, 370 A.2d 874 (1977); *Fulton Nat. Bank v. Delco Corp.*, 128 Ga. App. 16, 195 S.E.2d 455 [12 U.C.C. Rep Serv 302] (1973).

Although there is no guiding precedent in Virginia on this issue, the court finds that the check issued by Meritor on its account with FHLB has the characteristics of an ordinary check, not a cashier's or certified check.

---

[18] It is interesting to note that on appeal, one of the issues presented to the Texas Supreme Court was whether a bank which issues a teller's check may assert defenses (including its customers' defenses) to payment. The court held that banks could assert their customers' defenses if the payees were holders and not holders in due course. The court remanded the matter for the determination of the status of Horseshoe as a holder in due course.

Upon dishonor, PST, Ltd., as a holder, may have a right of recourse against Meritor as the drawer of the teller's check. a. Code § 8.3-507. However, a mere holder takes the instrument subject to any defenses that a party would have on a simple contract. Va. Code § 8.3-305. Assuming that Duke had a valid defense to PST's entitlement to payment, Meritor could have raised Duke's defense in an action on the instrument by PST, Ltd. *Fulton Nat. Bank v. Delco Corp.*, 128 Ga. App. 16, 195 S.E.2d 455 [12 U.C.C. Rep Serv 302] (1973). In addition, Meritor did not prove that the attorney who allegedly demanded payment was a holder in due course. Nor is there any evidence that PST, Ltd. enjoyed the status of a holder in due course.

Because the teller's check issued by Meritor at the request of Duke was not an unconditional promise to pay by Meritor under the Virginia Uniform Commercial Code, Meritor was not compelled to honor it upon presentment by the payee.

. . . . . .

In the case at bar, the court has already determined that Meritor was not under a legal obligation to unconditionally honor the teller's check when presented for payment. Instead, Meritor made a voluntary payment not contemplated by the indemnity agreement. Meritor may have had a good faith belief in a potential liability on the check as the drawer. But because Meritor failed to notify Duke of the payee's demand and to give Duke an opportunity to defend the claim on his or Meritor's behalf, Meritor is not entitled to indemnity from Duke for the payment of the teller's check.

For the foregoing reasons, the court renders judgment in favor of the defendant.

§ 13.04 Liability of the Drawer

Read: U.C.C. §§ 3-414, 3-103(a)(3) and (6), 3-503.

Up to this point, we have been examining the promissory note or what is often called two-party paper. Now we turn our attention to the standard instrument used in commercial transactions for short-term credit, the draft, which is three-party paper. It is true that the draft, particularly the bank draft, is also used as a payment or transmission of funds device. However, the law of the draft is the same whether it is used for short-term credit or for payment. The next chapter will investigate more fully the special characteristics of the check, which in our American economy is the principal payment device.

The draft, when it qualifies as an unconditional order to pay a sum certain in money on demand or at a definite time (U.C.C. § 3-104(a); see § 3-104(e) for the definition of a draft), is a negotiable instrument. As such, the previous materials and problems discussing negotiability, problems of transfer, and rights of holders and holders in due course are relevant to three-party paper, as well as to two-party paper.

The draft is very likely the oldest form of a negotiable instrument. It very probably developed as a consequence of continental trading and served the function of reducing the necessity of transporting gold and other valuable commodities over robber-threatened overland-routes or over pirate-infested waters in vessels which were not immune to storm. Suppose that Hugh de Beaufort were traveling from London to Genoa to purchase Italian luxuries. He might learn that Jason of Whitinsby had recently sold wool to a Genoese merchant, Antonio. Hugh and Jason would undoubtedly both profit if neither had to risk a gold shipment. It is not too difficult to imagine that Hugh traveled to Genoa with a minimum of gold on his person and with a simple piece of paper on which Jason has written, as follows: "My Esteemed Antonio: Please to permit me to introduce your good self to my friend, the bearer of this, Hugh de Beaufort. Having received value of him, please pay to him the 100 Marks which you have to my account and may God be with you and yours. Your Obed't, etc., Jason of Whitinsby." The form of the present draft (bill of exchange) evidences its origin in the form of a letter. The drawee (addressee) is generally indicated in the lower left corner, and the drawer signs in the lower right corner.

One standard use of the draft is as a short term credit device representing the purchase price of commercial goods. The buyer may wish to purchase on thirty-day credit so that he may pay for the goods out of the proceeds of their resale. The seller, however, wishes to have the price at time of delivery. A bank will therefore be extending credit to buyer and the draft affords a convenient device for these purposes. When seller is ready to deliver the goods to buyer, he will draw a draft on buyer for the purchase price of the goods, payable in thirty days, and name himself or the bank as payee. Seller's bank will forward the draft to buyer's bank, who, acting in accordance with a prior agreement, will present for acceptance to the buyer. Once the buyer accepts the draft, the bank will forward the purchase price to the seller. This basic transaction is often coupled with the use of the bill of lading which increases the security of all parties while the paper work is proceeding.

Merchants refer to this standard transaction as a shipment, payment by draft with bill of lading attached.

EUROPEAN ASIAN BANK, A.G. v. G. CROHN & CO.

[The opinion appears in § 12.04[B], *supra.*]

The materials in the next chapter will include a more specific investigation of the consequences of the use of the check. However, it is helpful to introduce the check at this point to discuss the drawer's liability. A check is defined as a demand draft in which the drawee is a bank (U.C.C. § 3-104(f)). The check is a payment device. The drawer will maintain a deposit relation with a bank. The check is an order upon the drawee-bank to transfer part of that deposit to the payee of the check or to the payee's nominee. The check is almost never drawn or issued where there are not sufficient funds on deposit. It is a crime in many States to draw a check on insufficient funds. Thus, the use of the check is devoid of any credit implications.

If a check is not presented for payment or given to a depositary bank for collection within 30 days after its date, and the drawee suspends payment, and because of the suspension the drawer is deprived of funds maintained with the drawee to cover payment of the check, the drawer to the extent deprived of funds may discharge its obligation to pay the check by assigning to the "person entitled to enforcing the check the rights of the drawer against the drawee with respect to the funds." U.C.C. §§ 3-414(f), 3-301. After the passage of the 30 day period, the risk of the drawee's insolvency passes from the drawer to the payee of other holder. The existence of federal bank deposit insurance minimizes the risk. *See* U.C.C. § 3-414, Comment 6.

APOLLO SAVINGS & LOAN CO. v. STAR BANK

Court of Appeals of Ohio, Hamilton County
90 Ohio App.3d 536, 530 N.E.2d 13 (1993)

PER CURIAM.

Roy C. Bradley of Bradley and Associates drew two checks on an account at the Provident Bank. The two checks were made payable to Mankin and Associates for $18,538.88, and Marketing Masters for $21.967. Both checks were deposited in the payees' accounts at Star Bank, which indorsed them and forwarded them to Provident Bank for presentment. Star allowed Mankin and Associates and Marketing Masters to withdraw the funds from the accounts even though the checks had not been cleared by Provident. After Mankin and Associates and Marketing Masters withdrew the funds, Provident dishonored both checks and returned them to Star. Star, in turn, filed a claim against Roy C. Bradley and Bradley and Associates for the amount due on the dishonored checks.

The trial court entered summary judgment for Star, and Bradley and Associates brings this appeal. Appellant argues that the trial court erred by granting summary judgment because (1) its drawer's contract was preempted by federal law; (2) Star violated sections of the Code of Federal Regulations; (3) Star certified the checks; (4) the trial court did not have subject-matter jurisdiction over the dispute; (5) Star violated its duty of good faith; and (6) the trial court wrongly considered an affidavit that contained inadmissible evidence under Civ.R. 56(E). The assignments of error are not well made.

A trial court may grant summary judgment when no genuine issues of material fact remain in dispute, and the moving party is entitled to judgment as a matter of law. In this case, the record contains no evidence of any disputed material facts—the parties agree that appellant drew two checks, which were indorsed by Star and dishonored by Provident. Consequently, the only issue is whether Star is entitled to judgment as a matter of law. The relevant law in this case states that, when Provident dishonored the two checks, appellant, on its drawer's contract, was bound to "pay the amount of the draft to the holder or to any indorser who [took] it up." R.C. 1303.49(B) and 1303.57(A)(2); White & Summers, Uniform Commercial Code (2d Ed.1980) 501-503, Section 13-9 (explaining U.C.C. 3-413[2] and 3-502, the analogs to R.C. 1303.49[B] and 1303.57[A][2]).

In the first assignment of error, appellant argues that its duty to pay on a drawer's contract is preempted by the Expedited Funds Availability Act ("EFAA"). Generally, a state law, like

R.C. 1303.49, may be preempted by federal legislation when Congress evidences intent to preempt or there is an actual conflict between the two provisions. *Silkwood v. Kerr-McGee Corp.* (1984), 464 U.S. 238, 248, 104 S.Ct. 615, 621, 78 L.Ed.2d 443, 452.

Regarding Congressional intent, the federal statute does not expressly preempt R.C. 1303.49. See generally, Section 229.20, Title 12, C.F.R. (state laws that have longer "hold" times for depositors are preempted). In addition, because R.C. 1303.49 and the EFAA deal with entirely different banking subjects, Congress has not shown an implied intent to preempt by pervasively occupying the field of drawers' contracts. See, generally, *Pacific Gas & Elec. Co. v. State Energy Resources Conservation Dev. Comm.*, 461 U.S. 190, 203-204, 103 S.Ct. 1713, 1722, 76 L.Ed.2d 752, 764-765 (1983) (implied intent). Specifically, R.C. 1303.49 codifies the drawer's duty to pay holders and indorsers. White & Summers, *supra*, at 501-503, Section 13-9 (explaining U.C.C. 3-413[2], the analog to R.C. 1303.49[B]). By contrast, the EFAA addresses the problem of a person who "deposits a check, waits a few days, and then writes several checks to pay some bills—only to have those checks returned as unpayable because of "uncollected funds.' " S.Rep. No. 100-19, 100th Cong., 1st Sess. (1987) 25, reprinted in 2 U.S.Code Congressional & Adm.News (1987) 489, 515.

Not only has Congress not shown express or implied intent to preempt R.C. 1303.49, but the drawer's contract does not conflict with the EFAA. First, it is physically possible to comply with the drawer's contact and the hold times of the EFAA—appellant need only pay for the dishonored checks. Second, R.C. 1303.49 does not frustrate the purpose of the EFAA. See, generally, S. Rep. No. 100-19, *supra*; Rubin, *Uniformity, Regulation, and the Federalization of State Law: Some Lessons from the Payment System (1989),* 49 Ohio St. L.J. 1251, 1257-1261 (EFAA preempts state laws related to dishonor, return, final settlement, indorsement, notice of dishonor, and excuse for delay). Therefore, because the EFAA does not evidence an intent to preempt and there is no conflict with R.C. 1303.49, the first assignment of error is overruled.

In appellant's second assignment of error, it argues that Star violated Sections 229.12 and 229.13(b), Title 12, C.F.R. Appellant reasons that if Star had held the funds until the checks were returned by Provident, Star would not have had to sue appellant to recover its losses. Because the regulations control the bank's hold time on deposits, even if Star violated the provisions, it would be liable to the payees—Mankin and Associates and Marketing Masters—not the drawer. Section 229.21, Title 12, C.F.R. Therefore, Star's compliance with Sections 229.12 and 229.13(b), Title 12, C.F.R. is irrelevant to this dispute, and the assignment of error is overruled.

In the third assignment of error, citing R.C. 1303.47(A), appellant argues that it is not liable on its drawer's contract because Star certified the checks. The record, however, contains no evidence that Star certified the checks. Consequently, the assignment of error is overruled.

Appellant maintains, in its fourth assignment of error, that the Hamilton County Court of Common Pleas did not have subject-matter jurisdiction in this action because Star is a federally chartered bank. When the legislature has the power to create a court, it also has the power to define that court's jurisdiction. *Tumey v. Ohio*, 273 U.S. 510, 47 S.Ct. 437, 71 L.Ed. 749 (1927). The legislature in Ohio created the court of common pleas and gave it subject-matter jurisdiction over all civil cases. R.C. 2305.01. Therefore, because the trial court entered summary judgment against appellant on a violation of an Ohio statute, it had subject-matter jurisdiction over this dispute. The assignment of error is overruled.

In its fifth assignment of error, appellant claims that Star violated its requirement of good faith by not posting information about funds' availability as required by section 229.18, Title

12, C.F.R. Under R.C. 1304.03 and 1301.01(S), Star has a duty of good faith to its customers "in the conduct or transaction concerned." The federal posting regulations deal with the bank's duties to depositors, not drawers of checks. Therefore, even if the bank did not post the information required by Section 229.18, Title 12, C.F.R., it would not have concerned the transaction in which appellant was involved. As a result, the argument is not well made, and the assignment of error is overruled.

. . ..

All of appellant's assignments of error are without merit. Therefore, the entry of summary judgment is affirmed.

Judgment affirmed.

SHANNON, P.J., HILDEBRANDT and GORMAN, JJ., concur.

SMART v. WOO

Virginia Circuit Court, Richmond
20 U.C.C. Rep.1288 (1993)

JOHNSON, J.

This is a declaratory judgment action brought by the administrator of the estate of William D. Yee. The administrator seeks (1) a declaration that the defendant, S. Hing Woo, is not entitled to receive any part of the estate to satisfy a check in the amount of $80,000 which was given to her by Yee before his death, but which was never cashed; (2) a judgment against Woo for $44,600, plus interest, representing the amount received by Woo from two other checks given to her by Yee and cashed by Woo after Yee's death; and (3) a declaration that Woo has no interest in certain securities and bank accounts which were listed in Yee's name at his death, but to which Woo claims to have made significant cash contributions. In her amended cross-bill, Woo seeks a declaration that (1) she is entitled to receive $80,000 from Yee's estate to satisfy the $80,000 check given her by Yee; (2) she is entitled to keep the $44,600 obtained by her when she cashed the other two checks given to her by Yee; and (3) she has an interest in the aforementioned securities and bank accounts listed only in Yee's name. The parties have submitted trial briefs, and an ore tenus hearing was held on February 4.

William D. Yee died on March 29, 1989. He was, and Woo is, of Chinese ancestry, a fact the court mentions only because of what Woo claims are important cultural traditions and superstitions which support certain of her positions in this case. Yee and Woo were lovers, and had been for nearly twenty years. They often lived together, and held themselves out as husband and wife, Yee even giving Woo a wedding band which she wore. Woo's family also treated Yee as though he were Woo's husband, Woo's mother giving Yee birthday and New Year's presents normally reserved, according to Woo, for sons-in-law under Chinese tradition.

On the other hand, Yee had little or no contact with his own family, most of whom lived in New York and Canada. In fact, testimony from Woo and others indicated that there were ill feelings between Yee and his family growing out of a dispute over his grandfather's property after the grandfather's death in or around 1973. Apparently, Yee had no "family feelings" toward his own family after that time.

Yee and Woo worked at the Waikiki Restaurant on Midlothian Turnpike, a business which Woo's father had set in motion prior to his death around 1975 or 1976. On March 27, 1989, two days before his death, Yee called Woo at the restaurant and told her he felt "terribly bad," that he had a "heaviness" in his chest, and that he believed he would die. That night, he came to the restaurant and gave her two checks—one for $42,700 drawn on an account at Signet Bank, and one for $80,000 drawn on an account at Central Fidelity Bank. At the time he gave her the checks, he told her that if he died, he wanted her to be taken care of; he wanted her to be provided for. On March 28, 1989, one day before his death, Yee gave Woo a third check, this one for $1,900, and drawn on a different account at Central Fidelity. At the time he gave her the check, Yee was "sweating all over", and said he felt "terribly bad." As noted, Yee died the next day. After Yee's death, Woo cashed the $42,700 check and the $1,900 check. The $80,000 check was never cashed.

1. The Checks

With regard to the three checks which Yee gave to Woo, the obvious question is whether they constitute valid gifts causa mortis; that is; gifts given in contemplation of death. Such gifts are specifically recognized in Virginia:

> A gift causa mortis is a gift of personal property made by a party in the expectation of death, the imminent, and upon the essential condition that the property shall belong fully to the donee in case the donor dies as anticipated leaving the donee surviving him, and the gift is not in the meantime revoked.

King v. Merryman, 196 Va. 844, 855, 86 S.E.2d 141 (1955).[19]

In order to be a valid gift causa mortis, several things are necessary. Obviously, the intent to make a gift must be present. In addition, three other elements are required:

> Briefly stated, the essential attributes of a gift causa mortis are: (1) It must be of personal property; (2) the gift must be made in the last illness of the donor, while under the apprehension of death as imminent, and subject to the implied condition that if the donor recover of the illness, or if the donee die first, the gift shall be void; and (3) possession of the property given must be delivered at the time of the gift to the donee, or to some one for him, and the gift must be accepted by the donee.

Johnson v. Colley, 101 Va. 414, 416, 44 S.E. 721 (1903).

After considering the elements set out above, and applying them to the evidence presented in this case, I hold that no valid gifts causa mortis were made.

First, the court has no problem finding that Yee fully intended to make a gift of money to Woo. The testimony of Woo and her sister, which the court finds perfectly credible, easily establishes that Yee intended to give Woo the funds represented by the three checks in question.

---

[19] As noted in *King*, there are two kinds of gifts; gifts inter vivos and gifts causa mortis. As was true in *King*, Woo makes no claim of gifts inter vivos here.

When he gave her the checks, he told her that he wanted her to be taken care of; he wanted her to be provided for. The checks were given to her for that purpose.

The court also finds that the checks were given to Woo by Yee under the apprehension that death was imminent. . ..

The court also makes the obvious finding that the subject of the alleged gift—money—is personal property. Accordingly, two of the three elements of a gift causa mortis set out in *Johnson v. Colley, supra,* are met. Also met is the required element of intent. The gifts fail, however, because delivery of the checks did not constitute delivery of the object of the gifts themselves; that is, the money in the bank.

The Virginia Supreme Court has never had occasion to consider whether a check can be the proper subject of a gift causa mortis, and the cases cited by the administrator dealing with bills of exchange, bonds and passbooks are inapposite.[20] In each of those cases, some factual consideration led the court to question, and eventually find absent, the required intent on the part of the decedent to make a gift in praesenti, one of the necessary elements of a gift cause mortis. Here, the court has specifically found that the necessary intent was present. Still, no gifts causa mortis were made.

As was stated in *Johnson v. Colley,* an essential element of a gift causa mortis is that "possession of the property given must be delivered at the time of the gift to the donee, or to some one for him, and the gift must be accepted by the donee." 101 Va. at 416. Section 3-409(1) of the Uniform Commercial Codeprovides:

> A check or other draft does not of itself operate as an assignment of any funds in the hands of the drawee available for its payment, and the drawee is not liable on the instrument until he accepts it.

Va. Code § 8.3-409(1).

Thus, while three checks were delivered by Yee to Woo, no *money* was delivered. And since no *money* was delivered, no *money* can be claimed by Woo as a gift causa mortis.

Woo argues that the above provision of the Uniform Commercial Code is not controlling because that provision is intended only to protect banks. I disagree. As is pointed out in American Jurisprudence's treatment of the subject, the Uniform Commercial Code provision cited above is a basis for "[t]he general rule supported now by nearly all the cases on the subject . . .that the donor's check, prior to acceptance or payment by the bank, is not the subject of a valid gift either inter vivos or causa mortis." 38 Am.Jur.2d, Gift, § 65 (1968). See also A.L.R.2d 594, 596 ("While there are a few cases to the contrary, and limitations have been recognized in some instances, the general rule appears to be that the donor's own check is not the subject of a valid gift, either inter vivos or causa mortis, prior to acceptance or payment by the bank.").

The reasons for the general rule are several. First, in accordance with the literal language of § 3-409(1) of the Uniform Commercial Code, no assignment of funds takes place until the check is paid, and assignment of the funds is necessary to delivery. Second, until the check is paid, the donor retains dominion and control over the funds; that is, he or she can issue a stop-payment order. Since a gift cause mortis requires the donor to relinquish all further dominion and control over the subject of the gift, a retention of the power to stop payment defeats the gift. Third,

---

[20] *See Gardner v. Moore's Administrator,* 122 Va. 10, 94 S.E. 162 (1917); *Norris v. Barbour,* 188 Va. 723, 51 S.E.2d 334 (1949); and *King v. Merryman, supra.*

since a check is nothing more than the drawer's command to his or her agent (the drawee) to pay money, such command ceases at the drawer's death. Thus, the check is revoked prior to payment, and the gift is not complete. See 38 Am. Jur.2d, *supra*, at 877.[21]

Fourth, and somewhat related to the second reason, is the fact that until the check is paid, the donor may intentionally *or inadvertently* defeat the gift by any number of acts, such as by writing another check on the same account. Indeed, such an occurrence happened here. When Woo cashed the $1,900 check at Central Fidelity, an overdraft in the amount of $250.07 was created. Does this mean that Yee intended a gift of only $1,649.93; that is, $1,900 minus $250.07? Or did he intend that his estate make up the difference? Suppose there was only $1 in the account when the check was presented for payment? Suppose Yee gave out three checks each for $1,900; which one is the *real* gift causa mortis? As was stated in *Quarles v. Fowlkes*, *supra*:

> Gifts causa mortis are not favored in law. They are a fruitful source of litigation, often bitter, protracted and expensive. They lack all those formalities and safeguards which the law throws around wills, and create a strong temptation to the commission of fraud and perjury. Lord Hardwick declared, more than a hundred years ago, that it was a pity the statute for the prevention of frauds and perjuries did not set aside all such gifts. Justinian was so justly apprehensive of fraud with respect to them that he required them to be made in the presence of five witnesses. If the law limited such gifts to articles of small value, and required the gift to be executed in the presence of disinterested witnesses, they would be less objectionable. But if large estates, amounting to thousands of dollars, may be thus disposed of, and the title of the donee supported mainly by his own testimony, and that of near relatives, the public feeling of security may well be startled.
>
> Unfortunately, the common law has not adopted any of these precautions. It does not require the gift to be executed in the presence of any stated number of witnesses; nor does it limit the amount of property that may be thus disposed of. *But it does require clear and unmistakable proof, not only if an intention to give, but of an actual gift, perfected by as complete a delivery as the nature of the property will admit of. It not only requires the delivery to be actual and complete, such as deprives the donor of all further control and dominion, but it requires the donee to take and retain possession til the donor's death.* Although the delivery may have been at one time complete, yet this will not be sufficient, unless the possession be constantly maintained by the donee. If the donor again has possession, the gift becomes nugatory and public policy requires these rules to be enforced with great stringency, otherwise the wholesome safeguards of our testamentary laws become useless. It is far better that occasionally a gift of this kind fail, than that the rules of law be so relaxed as to encourage fraud and perjury.

147 Va. at 506-07 (quoting *Hatch v. Atkinson*, 56 Me. 324, 326-27 (96 Am. Dec. 464) (emphasis added)).

While this court is not concerned with any possible commission of fraud in this case, and while adhering to the majority rule may seem harsh in light of Yee's obvious intent to make a gift, the dangers inherent in relaxing the rule require, as stated in *Quarles v. Fowlkes*, that the rule be stringently enforced.

Woo argues that the court should consider her testimony and that of others that under Chinese tradition, wills are not often made, and people often give property shortly before death instead

[21] This is true even though the drawee bank is not liable for cashing a check of a deceased drawer under certain conditions. *See* U.C.C. § 4-405(Va. Code § 8.4-405).

of writing wills. One reason for this, according to Woo and her witnesses, is a belief that by writing a will, a person "courts death." This argument, however, even if accepted by the court, goes only to Yee's intent to make a gift, something the court has expressly found. It has nothing to do with delivery of the subject of the gift itself.

Finally, Woo argues that even if all the technical requirements of a gift cause mortis are not met, the court should use its equitable powers to declare a constructive or resulting trust in her favor. This should occur, according to Woo, because even if there was a technical failure of delivery, Yee's intent was so obvious, and his love for Woo so strong, that it would be unjust to allow Yee's relatives, with whom Yee had had so little contact, and to whom there was probably lingering hostility, to inherit his money. While the court appreciates Woo's argument and sympathizes with her predicament, the argument must be rejected. Specifically, if Woo's argument in this regard were accepted, this court would be eliminating one of the essential elements of a gift cause mortis—delivery. If, as Woo argues, intent to make a gift cause mortis can overcome lack of delivery simply by calling the gift a constructive or resulting trust, there is no point in talking about the essential elements of a gift cause mortis in the first place. Those elements, however, do exist, and intend *and* delivery are equally necessary. The presence of one cannot make up for the absence of the other. Both must exist, as well as the other elements required. Because the necessary element of delivery was not present here, no gift—whether called a gift cause mortis or anything else—occurred. Woo is not entitled to any part of the estate to satisfy the $80,000 check, and she must repay to the estate the $44,600 received when she cashed the other two checks.

. . .. . .

A copy of an order consistent with this opinion, and which I have entered today, is enclosed.

ORDER

This cause came on February 4, 1993, to be heard on its merits. And the court having heard the evidence and arguments of counsel, it is ordered as follows:

1. Defendant S. Hing Woo is entitled to no part of the estate of William D. Yee, a/k/a. Dun Wai Yee, to satisfy that certain check in the amount of $80,000 given to Woo by Yee before Yee's death, and drawn on Central Fidelity Bank.
2. Defendant S. Hing Woo is entitled to no part of the aforesaid estate in satisfaction of her claim of any portion of securities or other accounts listed solely in Yee's name at Yee's death.
3. Judgment is entered in favor of the estate of Willaim D. Yee, a/k/a. Dun Wai Yee, against S. Hing Woo in the amount of $44,600, plus interest at the rate of 9% per annum from March 29, 1989, until paid.
4. Defendant shall pay to plaintiff the costs of this proceeding.

The objections of the defendant to this order are noted.

PROBLEM 13.5

Assume Yee was in good health at the time he delivered the checks to Woo and had been killed in an automobile accident on March 29, 1989. What result? *See* U.C.C. § 3-408.

§ 13.05 Liability of the Indorser

Read: U.C.C. §§ 3-415, 3-204(a) and (b), 3-502, 3-503; see § 3-117.

Former U.C.C. § 3-102(1)(d) defined a "secondary party" as a "drawer or endorser." According to Comment 2 of U.C.C. § 3-414: "Under revised Article 3, notice of dishonor is necessary only with respect to indorser's liability. The liability of the drawer of an unaccepted draft is treated as a primary liability. Under former Section 3-102(1)(d) the term 'secondary party' was used to refer to a drawer or indorser. The quoted term is not used in revised Article 3."

While the Code apparently abjures the term "secondary party" it is still a useful concept in describing "liability" of a party to an instrument that is "conditional" on the occurrence of certain events. Thus, for example, an indorser of a check is liable under its contract of secondary liability under U.C.C. § 3-415(a), and is discharged if the check is not presented for payment, or given to a depository bank for collection, within 30 days after the day the indorsement was made. (U.C.C. § 3-415(e) and Comment 4.)

The conditions are discussed in more detail in § 13.07, *infra*.

BRANNONS NUMBER SEVEN, INC. v. PHELPS

Oklahoma Court of Appeals
665 P.2d 860, 36 U.C.C. Rep. 225 (1983)

MEANS, J.

This is an appeal by the defendant, Robert Phelps, from an order of the trial court which granted summary judgment in favor of the plaintiff; Brannons Number Seven.

The issues involved are (1) whether Brannons, as the holder of two insufficient payroll checks, was required to give notice of dishonor to Phelps as the endorser, and (2) whether a disputed notice of dishonor is a substantial material fact precluding the granting of summary judgment.

We answer both questions in the affirmative and reverse.

The basic facts are not in dispute. Phelps was in the employment of Jet Service Company. Jet issued two payroll checks to Phelps in the amounts of $454.49 and $350.05. Brannons, a grocery store, cashed the two checks for Phelps. Phelps had endorsed the two checks, placing his telephone number on the back of each check, below his endorsement. Phelps received the proceeds from the checks. Upon presentment by Brannons to the drawee bank, notice of dishonor due to insufficient funds in the drawer's account was given to Brannons.

Brannons, by way of affidavit attached to its motion for summary judgment, states that it "requested Robert Phelps to pay Plaintiff [Brannons]" the sums of the two checks. Attached to Phelps' response to Brannons' motion for summary judgment is his affidavit which states that Brannons never requested him to pay the sums of the checks "by either verbal or written demand."

Again in Phelps' answers to Brannons' request for admissions, Phelps denied that Brannons requested him to pay the sums of the checks.

The trial court granted plaintiff Brannons summary judgment for the sum of $804.64, plus attorneys' fees and costs.

I.

The requirement of notice of dishonor to an endorser is clear.

Title 12A OS 1981 § 3-501 (2)(a), stated that unless notice is excused under §3-511:

(a) notice of any dishonor is *necessary to charge* any endorser; (emphasis added)[22]

The contractual duties and liabilities of an endorser and holder when an uncertified check passes between the parties are found in 12A OS 1981 § 3-414(1). . .. [The Court quotes U.C.C. § 3-414(1).] The holder's rights are stated in 12A OS 1981 § 3-507(2). . .. [The Court quotes U.C.C. § 3-705(2).]

An endorser's liability is contingent and does not become fixed unless and until the holder complies with the requirement of notice of dishonor. This notice is an element of Brannons' cause of action and Brannons thus has the burden of proving that it gave notice.

II.

The affidavits, briefs and exhibits to the pleadings relied upon by the trial judge in granting summary judgment present a substantial controversy as to a material fact as to whether notice of dishonor of the checks was given to the endorser Phelps. Assuming arguendo, that requesting payment by Phelps of the checks in question constituted notice of dishonor, Phelps denies that such a request occurred. This presents a question of fact to be proved by Brannons to the satisfaction of the trier of facts before recovery is permissible.

Reversed and remanded for trial on the issue of notice of the dishonor.

QUESTION

Would a summary judgment in the *Brannons* case be appropriate today?

---

[22] Uniform Commercial Code Comment 2, 12A OSA 1963 § 3-501, relating to this provision, states in part:

The words "necessary to charge" are retained from the original Act. They mean that the necessary proceeding is a condition precedent to any right of action against the drawer or indorser.

FIRST VALLEY BANK v. FIRST SAVINGS & LOAN ASSN. OF CENTRAL INDIANA

Indiana Court of Appeals
412 N.E.2d 1237, 32 U.C.C. Rep. 145 (1980)

BUCHANAN, C.J.

CASE SUMMARY

First Valley Bank (Bank) brings a consolidated appeal from eighteen separate summary judgments in three different courts, all holding the Bank liable as an endorser with recourse of mortgage notes which the Bank had assigned to First Savings & Loan Association of Central Indiana (Association), claiming real estate mortgage notes are not negotiable instruments, that there was a genuine issue of material fact as to recourse against it, that an unsolicited form of judgment should not have been used and attorneys fees were improperly awarded.

We affirm.

FACTS

Throughout the decade 1960 to 1969, the Bank, then doing business as Twin City State Bank in Gas City, Indiana, made loans secured by real estate mortgages. In that same period, the Bank sold to the Association, then doing business as First Savings & Loan Association of Madison County, some six million dollars worth of those mortgages. It appears that such sales were made at least once in every year from 1962 to 1968.

The transfer of the mortgages was accomplished by an assignment in the following words:

FOR VALUE RECEIVED, the undersigned TWIN CITY STATE BANK, hereby sells, transfers, sets over and assigns to the ANDERSON LOAN ASSOCIATION, its entire right, title, and interest in and to each and all of the following described bona fide mortgages executed to or held by the under-signed, all prior mortgages held by the assignor having been fully paid and released, together with all of tile promissory notes and any other indebtedness thereby secured which said mortgages are hereinafter described and identified by the names of the mortgagors, the dates of execution, and the amounts of the original loans, the book and page of recordings in Grant County, Indiana, and the exact principal balances due on each at this transfer date as follows: [a list then followed]

The promissory notes secured by the mortgages were endorsed:

We hereby assign the within note to First Savings & Loan Ass'n.

[Date]

Twin City State Bank

/s/ Donald F. Hundley

Donald F. Hundley, Pres.

Under a separate agreement, the Bank continued to service the loans for the Association. The Bank did not carry any indication on its books that the notes were negotiated with or without recourse, and the Bank repeatedly informed the examiners of the State Department of Financial Institutions that the Bank had no liabilities that did not appear on its books, and that the Bank had not guaranteed any obligation, except as noted on its books. In the course of the examination of the Bank conducted in 1969, the Department of Financial Institutions transmitted to the Association a list of the real estate mortgages which the Association had purchased from the Bank. The Department asked that the list be verified, and that the Association "Indicate how each loan was purchased as to RECOURSE, REPURCHASE or WITHOUT RECOURSE agreement." The Association's answer to this request contained nothing that was responsive to the question on recourse. In his deposition, the president of the Association said that he did not know the answer to that question, and simply forwarded copies of a mortgage assignment and the servicing agreement, in the hope that this would satisfy the Department.

At least thirty-five of these mortgages became delinquent, and over a period running from June 12, 1972, to January 9, 1973, the Association filed complaints in the eighteen cases before us in the Grant Circuit Court seeking foreclosure of the mortgages, and judgment on the notes. In all but the first few cases, the Association named the Bank as a defendant, on the theory that the Association had recourse against the Bank as an endorser of the notes; the first few complaints did not mention the Bank, but were amended to do so. All eighteen cases were revenued, as follows: Six to the Tipton Circuit Court; seven to the Miami Circuit Court; and five to the Wells Circuit Court.

With respect to the Bank, all of these cases were disposed of by summary judgment in favor of the Association. In all cases, it was found that the Bank had endorsed the mortgage notes without qualification, and that its liability to the Association was governed solely by the applicable law of negotiable instruments. As to those mortgage notes which were transferred after July 1, 1964, the applicable law was § 3-414(1) of the Indiana Uniform Commercial Code (UCC). Ind Code 1971, § 26-1-3-414(1). As to notes transferred before that date, the applicable law was § 66 of the Indiana Uniform Negotiable Instruments Law (NIL). Indiana Annot Statutes § 19-507 (Burns, 1950). Judgments were therefore entered in the Association's favor in the amount of the unpaid balance on the mortgage notes, plus "interests, taxes, insurance, attorney fees and other accrued costs as provided in" the notes and mortgages.

The findings of fact, conclusions of law, and entries of judgment were in most of the cases entered by forms supplied to the courts by the Association. The findings and judgments of the trial courts in these cases are therefore identical, with the exceptions of names, dates, dollar amounts, and citations to the U.C.C. and NIL. These details were supplied by the Association, and the forms were signed by the three respective judges. Nothing in the record indicates that any of the trial judges solicited proposed findings of fact and conclusions of law from either party.

ISSUES

The Bank presents four issues: . . ..

2. Did the Bank present a genuine issue of material fact by presenting to the court evidence that it did not intend that its endorsement of the notes should give the Association recourse against it?

The contentions of the parties will be dealt with as each issue is resolved. . . . .

Issue Two

Did the Bank present a genuine issue of material fact by presenting to the trial court evidence that it did not intend that its endorsement of the notes should give the Association recourse against it?

Parties' Contentions

The Bank believes that the transferor of a mortgage note transfers without recourse, unless he and his transferee explicitly agree otherwise. It says that by presenting certified records of the State Department of Financial Institutions that the Association never said that it had recourse against the Bank; and by displaying to the court the form of the endorsement on the notes, and the form of the transfer of the mortgages themselves, the Bank had shown probative evidence to contest the issue of recourse. Further, the Bank claims that it had raised the defense of estoppel against the Association when it showed that the Association did not respond when asked by the State Department of Financial Institutions about recourse on the mortgage notes.

The Association points out that the endorsement on the notes is an unqualified endorsement, and that both the NIL and the U.C.C. imply as a matter of law that an unqualified endorser contracts to pay the instrument upon dishonor by the maker; and that the Bank has presented no evidence which the law could recognize as showing anything else. As for the claim of estoppel, the Association says that the facts which the Bank has alleged do not even arguably make out an estoppel.

Conclusion

The Bank did not present a genuine issue of material fact as to its intention in endorsing the notes without recourse.

The contract of an endorser is implied in law, unless the endorser takes the simple step of clearly indicating otherwise in his endorsement.

It is elementary that an unqualified endorser is liable upon the instrument, if the maker defaults. Section 3-414(1) of the U.C.C. phrases it thusly: . . .[the Court quotes U.C.C. § 3-414(1)j.] Sections 38 and 66 of the NIL are to the same effect. Indiana Statutes Annotated §§ 19-309, 507 (Burns 1950).

The Bank correctly reminds us that as between an endorser and his immediate endorsee, the transaction is to be viewed as a whole, as an ordinary contract. U.C.C. § 3-119(1) says that "[a]s between the obligor and his immediate obligee . . .the terms of an instrument may be modified or affected by any other written agreement executed as a part of the same transaction. . .." This is but a codification of the law in Indiana before the U.C.C.

What all this means is that in determining the obligations between the Bank and the Association, we are to look not only to the Bank's endorsements, but also to the contemporaneously executed contracts assigning the mortgages. Even so, we do not think that the endorsements and the contracts show that there is a genuine issue of material fact as to the objective intent of the Bank and the Association that the mortgage notes should be transferred without recourse.

Because the phrase "without recourse" appears nowhere in either the contracts or the endorsements, the Bank must show that the language it did use in transferring the notes was to the same effect as an endorsement without recourse. U.C.C. § 3-414(1); NIL § 38, Indiana Statutes Annotated § 19-309 (Burns 1950). The Bank argues that the language of assignment used in both the endorsement of the note and in the contracts that assigned the mortgages, operated merely as an assignment of the title to the notes, and does not carry the contract of an endorser.

Such is not the case in Indiana. It is true that in some jurisdictions, an endorsement containing language such as "we hereby assign the within note," or, "we hereby assign all right, title and interest in the within note," would operate merely to transfer title to the instrument, without engaging that the endorser would pay the note upon dishonor.

In *Bond*, one of two copayees of a promissory note endorsed upon the note, "I sine [sic] over my interest on the within note to" his copayee. *Bond v. Holloway* is distinguishable from the case at bar on three points: *first*, the court evidently decided that the commercial law of Indiana at the time permitted it to examine the subjective intention of the endorser to determine that he meant merely to assign the instrument. Both the NIL and the U.C.C. greatly curtail our ability to do this. We are, for instance, required to deem a person an endorser who has signed an instrument in an ambiguous capacity. NIL § 17, Indiana Statutes Annotated § 19-117(6); U.C.C. § 3-402. And we must say that recourse is available against such an endorser, unless he plainly indicates otherwise. NIL § 38, Indiana Statutes Annotated § 19-309; U.C.C. § 3-414(1).

Second, *Bond v. Holloway* in fact states a very narrow rule. Assuming without deciding that *Bond v. Holloway* survives as law after the passage of NIL and the U.C.C., it speaks only to the rare instances in which one copayee of a negotiable instrument signs over to his copayee his part-interest in the instrument. As that transaction would make the instrument more merchantable, and would likely be done in exchange for consideration that is not strictly related to the face value of the instrument, there is logic in favor of a special rule for assignments between copayees that does not exist in the usual case in which one holder endorses the whole instrument over to another.

Finally, it appears that the controlling precedent of the Supreme Court at the time of *Bond v. Holloway* (1897) was that in general, words of assignment in an endorsement of a negotiable instrument did not affect the character of the endorsement; the undertaking to pay the instrument upon dishonor was made regardless. This, in fact, was the rule in a majority of states as to words of assignment under the Negotiable Instrument Law. *See Fay v. Witte* (1933), 262 NY 215, 186 NE 678; Contra, *Fecko v. Tarczinski* (1937), 281 Mich 590, 275 NW 502. (Words assigning "right, title and interest" *in a note constitute an endorsement without recourse, in deference to controlling Michigan precedent*; but mere words of assignment amount to an unqualified endorsement.).

Thus, the Uniform Commercial Code merely reenacts the prior law in Indiana when it says, "Words of assignment . . .and the like accompanying an endorsement do not affect its character as an endorsement." U.C.C. § 3-202(4).

The endorsements and the assignment contracts therefore presented no issue of material fact, for by law their language was unambiguous. The language on the backs of the notes was, by NIL § 17 and U.C.C. § 3-402, part of an endorsement; the terms of the assignment contracts were offered as showing the Bank's contract of endorsement. These writings contained nothing which Indiana law recognizes as being of the same import as the phrase "without recourse." The writings were unqualified endorsements of the notes, and unambiguously so. There being no ambiguity in the writings, the parole evidence rule forbade the trial courts' pursuing the matter further. The facts being undisputed indeed, indisputable, it was proper for the courts to grant the Association's motion for summary judgment.

NOTES AND QUESTIONS

Words of assignment used by an indorser can create at least three possible problems.

1. The problem in the principal case relating to the liability of the endorser to the indorsee. Compare former U.C.C. § 3-414(1) with U.C.C. § 3-415(b).

2. What is the extent of the warranty on transfer of the instrument by the indorser to indorsee? Compare former U.C.C. §§ 3-417(2)(d) & (3) with U.C.C. § 3-416(4) and Comment 1. The comments to § 333 of the Restatement of Contracts, 2d, state that the warranties of an assignor of contractual rights are similar to one who transfers a negotiable instrument without indorsement. Unlike the indorser of commercial paper an assignor is not liable for defaults of the obligor and does not warrant his solvency.

3. Can a transferee-indorsee become a holder in due course? Compare former U.C.C. § 3-202(4), Comments 5 and 6, with U.C.C. § 3-202(4) in the Table of Disposition of Sections in Former Article 3. *See* U.C.C. § 3-204(a).

§ 13.06 Liability of Maker or Acceptor of a Draft Payable at a Bank

Read: U.C.C. §§ 3-501(a)(1), 3-502(a)(2),(d), 4-106; *see* § 3-414(f) and Comment 6.

In *Binghampton Pharmacy v. First National Bank*, 131 Tenn. 711, 176 S.W. 1038 (1915), the makers of a note payable at a bank claimed that they had been discharged because the holder of the note had failed to present the note to the bank for payment at its maturity and the bank subsequently failed. The defense was based upon the wording of the NIL § 87 which provided: "Instrument Payable at Bank Equivalent to What. Where the instrument is made payable at a bank, it is the equivalent to an order to the bank to pay the same from the account of the principal debtor thereon."

The court rejected the makers' argument, stating:

> Presentment for payment is not necessary to charge the maker of a note. No duty to one primarily liable on a note is breached by a failure to present the instrument for payment. Such an omission is not laches, and affords the maker no ground for complaint. By the very terms of the statute, the holder of a note is relieved of any such obligation in so far as the maker is concerned.
>
> We think that section 87, declaring an instrument payable at a bank the equivalent of an order on the bank, was only intended to settle the vexing question of the bank's right, without

specific authority, to pay such an instrument and charge same to the account of the principal debtor. Prior to the Act of 1899, in Tennessee and elsewhere, the fact that a note was made payable at a bank did not, without more, confer authority upon the bank to pay the note, when presented there at maturity by the holder, out of funds standing on deposit to the credit of the maker. A contrary rule obtained in many States. See discussion of the case in *Grissom v. Bank*, 87 Tenn., 350, 10 S.W., 774, 3 L.R.A., 273, 10 Am. St. Rep., 669.

Section 87 authorizes a bank, at which an instrument is made payable, to pay same for the account of the principal debtor. To that extent all instruments payable at a bank are orders on the bank designated. The language used in this section, however, must not be so expanded as to destroy other provisions of the act.

The Uniform Commercial Code appears more enthusiastic about the position of a maker of a domiciled note when there are funds available at the bank on maturity of the note and the bank subsequently goes under. *See Mandel v. Sedrich*, 3 U.C.C. Rep. 526 (N.Y. Sup. Ct. 1966), where the court stated:

> The third separate defense alleges that the note was presented at a bank other than the bank stated in the original note and "at a date long after the payment date of the note given by defendant to plaintiff." If the note be considered for purposes of this defense as having been made payable at a specified bank, then presentment for payment at that bank is necessary (U.C.C. § 3-501[1][c], but under § 3-501[i][c] hereinabove cited, failure to make presentment discharges the defendant herein as maker "only as stated in § 3-502(1)(b)," that is to say, only where the maker who, because of insolvency of the payor bank occurring during the period of delay in presentment, is deprived of funds maintained with the payor bank to meet the note, and the maker thereupon executes a written assignment, to the holder of the note, of his rights against the payor bank with respect to said funds. These conditions and circumstances are not alleged in the third defense herein. According the said defense is insufficient on its face.

Former U.C.C. § 3-121 dealing with instruments payable at banks attempted to deal with NIL § 87 by providing alternatives that States could choose between. Alternative A provided:

> A note or acceptance which states that it is payable at a bank is the equivalent of a draft drawn on the bank payable when it falls due out of any funds of the maker or acceptor in current account or otherwise available for such payment.

Alternative B provided:

> A note or acceptance which states that it is payable at a bank is not of itself an order or authorization to the bank to pay it.

The comments to the section stated that in the former instance the bank was not only authorized but ordered to make payment out of the account of the maker or acceptor when it fell due, and was expected to do so without consulting him. Under Alternative B, the instrument was treated as merely designating a place of payment and the bank's only function was to notify the maker or acceptor that the instrument had been presented, and ask for instructions.

U.C.C. § 4-106(b) retains the alternative approach indicated above. Under Alternative A, as a "draft drawn on a bank" the liability of a maker of a "domiciled" note would appear to be that of a "drawer" and the obligation provisions of U.C.C. § 3-414 would apply. Since a "domiciled" note in all probability would not be payable on demand, the "check" provision of U.C.C. § 3-414(f) would not apply. Rather, if the bank has suspended payments, U.C.C. § 3-414(b)(i) would appear applicable.

Domiciling an instrument also has an advantage in dealing with the "good note" problem.

PROBLEM 13.6

Maker is willing to execute a note with a very high rate of interest but only for 90 days. How can he protect himself from holder who thinks this was a great investment and decides to hold the note and not present it for payment until shortly before the Statute of Limitations runs? See U.C.C. § 3-603.

§ 13.07 Obligation of Drawer or Indorser Detailed

Read: U.C.C. §§ 3-501 through 3-505, 4-212, 4-301(c).

Sections 13.04 and 13.05 *supra* which dealt with the contracts of drawers and indorsers respectively, indicated that liability of these parties requires dishonor of the instrument that they signed. Loosely speaking, an instrument is dishonored when a presentment for payment or acceptance is made and the instrument is not paid or accepted. Because these acts must occur before there is liability, we speak of the liability as "conditional" or "secondary." The other condition to their liability is that, in many situations, due notice of the dishonor is required. The necessity of satisfying any or all of these conditions by or on behalf of a person entitled to enforce the instrument can depend upon a variety of things (*e.g.*, the nature of the instrument, is it being presented for payment of acceptance, where and when it is being presented, are we interested in the liability of a drawer or of an indorser).

"Presentment" means a demand made by or on behalf of a person entitled to enforce an instrument (i) to *pay* the instrument made to the drawee or a party obliged to pay the instrument (*e.g.*, maker) or, in the case a note or accepted draft payable at a bank, to the bank, or (ii) to accept a draft made to the drawee. See U.C.C. § 3-501(a). Presentment either may be made at the *place* of payment and must be made at the place of payment if the instrument is payable at a bank in the United States. It may be made by any commercially reasonable means (*e.g.*, oral, written or electronic) and is effective when the demand for payment or acceptance is received. U.C.C. § 3-501(b)(1).

Upon demand of the person to whom presentment is made, the person making the presentment must (i) exhibit the instrument, (ii) give reasonable identification, and (iii) sign a receipt on the instrument for any payment made, or surrender the instrument if full payment is made. U.C.C. § 3-501(b)(2). The party to whom the presentment is made, may, without dishonoring the instrument (i) return the instrument for lack of a necessary indorsement, or (ii) refuse payment or acceptance for failure of the presentment to comply with the terms of the instrument, an agreement of the parties, or other applicable law or rule. U.C.C. § 3-501(3).

U.C.C. § 3-504(a) lists certain circumstances where presentment for payment or acceptance will be excused. They are (i) if the person entitled to present the instrument cannot with reasonable diligence make presentment; (ii) if the maker or acceptor has repudiated an obligation to pay the instrument, or is dead, or in insolvency proceedings; (iii) if by the terms of the instrument presentment is not necessary to enforce the obligation of indorsers or the drawer (As indicated in Comment 2 to § 3-502, in the great majority of cases presentment and notice of dishonor are waived with respect to notes.); (iv) if the drawer or indorser whose obligation is being enforced has waived presentment or otherwise has no reason to expect or right to require that the instrument be paid or accepted; or (v) if the drawer instructed the drawee not to pay or accept the draft, or the drawee was not obligated to the drawer to pay the draft.

With respect to notes, a demand note is dishonored if presentment is duly made to the maker and the note is not paid on the day of presentment. U.C.C. § 3-502(a)(1). A note payable at a definite time is dishonored if it is not paid on the day it becomes payable. U.C.C. § 3-502(a)(3). As stated in Comment 3: "If the note is not paid on its due date it is dishonored. This allows holders to collect notes in ways that make sense commercially without having to be concerned about a formal presentment on a given day."

However, if a time note is payable at or through a bank, or by its terms requires presentment, then presentment is required. U.C.C. § 3-502(a)(2).

U.C.C. § 3-502(b) deals with dishonor of unaccepted drafts other than documentary drafts. A check duly presented for payment over the counter is dishonored if the payor bank does not pay the draft on the day of presentment. U.C.C. §§ 502(b)(2), 3-501(b)(4). A check presented for payment through the check collection system is dishonored if the payor bank makes timely return of the check or sends timely notice of dishonor or nonpayment (or becomes accountable for the amount of the check). U.C.C. § 3-502(b)(1) and Comment 4.

A draft payable on a date stated in the draft (a time draft) is dishonored if presentment for payment is made and payment is not made on either the day the draft becomes payable or the day of presentment, whichever is later. A holder of a time draft has a choice of presenting the draft for acceptance before the payable date to establish whether the drawee is willing to assume liability by accepting. If the draft is not accepted when presented, dishonor occurs. U.C.C. § 3-302(b)(3) and Comment 4.

A time draft, which is payable on elapse of a period of time after sight or acceptance, must be presented to start the running of the time period. It is dishonored if presented for acceptance and it is not accepted on the day of acceptance. U.C.C. § 3-502(4).

U.C.C. § 3-502(c) deals with the dishonor of documentary drafts and they are handled similarly to other unaccepted drafts (excluding checks) under U.C.C. § 3-502(b)(2), (3) and (4), except that payment or acceptance may be delayed without dishonor until no later than the close of the third business day following presentment. The drawee is given this extended period with regard to documentary drafts to examine the documents.

With regard to drafts that have been accepted, if the draft is payable on demand, it is dishonored if presentment for payment is duly made to the acceptor and it is not paid on the day of presentment. This is similar to the rule regarding demand notes in § 3-502(a)(1). If not payable on demand, the accepted draft is dishonored if the presentment for payment is duly made and payment is not made on the day it becomes payable or the day of presentment, whichever is later. This is a rule similar to that of time note under U.C.C. § 3-502(a)(2).

The other condition, notice of dishonor, is always a condition to the liability of an indorser. U.C.C. § 3-503(a), 3-415(a), (c). Notice of dishonor is no longer relevant to the liability of a drawer. Drawers are entitled to have the draft presented to the drawee and dishonored before they are liable to pay the instrument but no notice of dishonor need be made as a condition of liability. U.C.C. § 3-503(a) and Comment 1. There is an exception to this latter generalization however. The obligation of the drawer stated in § 3-414(d) may not be enforced unless the drawer is given notice of dishonor. § 3-414(d) covers the situation of a draft accepted by an acceptor other than a bank. If the latter subsequently dishonors the draft, the drawer liability is transformed into the liability of an indorser, and drawer's liability cannot be enforced unless given notice of the dishonor. U.C.C. § 3-414(d) and Comment 4.

Notice of dishonor may be given by any person. It may be given by any commercially reasonable means (*e.g.*, oral, written, electronic means) and is sufficient if it reasonably identifies the instrument and indicates that the instrument has been dishonored or has not been paid or accepted. See U.C.C. § 1-201(26). Return of an instrument given to a bank for collection is sufficient notice of dishonor. U.C.C. § 3-503(b).

In the case of an instrument taken for collection by a collecting bank, notice of dishonor must be given by the bank before midnight of the next banking day following the banking day which the bank receives notice of dishonor of the instrument. This is really an exceptional rule for in every other instance, notice of dishonor must be given within 30 days following the day on which dishonor occurs. U.C.C. § 3-503(c) and Comments.

Notice of dishonor is excused in only two situations: if by the terms of the instrument notice is not necessary to enforce the obligation of a party to pay the instrument, or if the party whose obligation is being enforced waived notice of dishonor or presentment. U.C.C. §§ 3-504(b), 3-503(a)(ii). Delay in giving notice of dishonor is excused if the delay was caused by circumstances beyond the control of the person giving the notice and that person exercised reasonable diligence after the cause of the delay ceased to operate. U.C.C. §§ 3-504(c), 3-503(c).

---

§ 13.08 Liability of Transferors—Transfer Warranties

Read: U.C.C. §§ 3-416, 4-207.

You will remember from the Sales materials in this volume that the transfer of goods carries with them certain warranties. You should remember from your Contracts course that the assignment of non-negotiable contract rights carry with that transfer certain warranties. The transfer of commercial paper likewise carries with it certain warranties. These two sections spell out these warranties and to whom they run. U.C.C. §§ 3-416 and 4-207 deal with warranties on transfer of the instrument and are usually referred to as such.

Transfer warranties are to be distinguished from presentment warranties found in U.C.C. §§ 3-417 and 4-208. Keep in mind that Article 3 rules are subject to the provisions of Article 4. As most presentment warranty problems have occurred in the check collection process, these warranties will be considered in Chapter 14, *infra*.

UNION BANK v. MOBILLA

Court of Common Pleas, Erie County, Pa.
43 Erie Co. Leg. J. 45 (1959)

LAUB, J.

This is a complaint in assumpsit for breach of warranty to which the defendant filed an answer containing new matter and a counterclaim. The plaintiff filed a reply, then moved for judgment on the pleadings. It is this latter action which is before us now.

On January 15, 1958, the defendant, a used car dealer, represented to the plaintiff that he had sold a used Ford automobile to one Theresa Piotrowski of 650 East 24th Street. For finance purposes, he exhibited an installment sales contract and a judgment note allegedly signed by Theresa Piotrowski as maker. There was nothing on the face of either instrument to indicate that the signatures had not been placed there by the maker or that either had been signed by someone else acting in the maker's behalf. . . . The note which was payable to defendant was endorsed by him "without recourse" and the security agreement, which was in defendant's favor as a seller of a chattel, was assigned to the bank. Both instruments, as well as the title to the vehicle in question, were turned over to the bank as part of the finance transaction.

. . .After default the bank importuned both the purported maker and the defendant to discharge the obligation but without avail, the maker having denied executing either document or having bought the vehicle from the defendant. In consequence, plaintiff instituted this action, alleging that defendant is guilty of a breach of warranty, and as part of its action, alleging a written warranty in the security agreement "that the above instrument is genuine and in all respects what it purports to be." Plaintiff also claims upon an implied warranty of the genuineness of the note.

The defendant in his answer admits that he endorsed the note and assigned the security agreement to the plaintiff. He also admits that the maker did not sign either document. It is his defense, however, that Theresa Piotrowski's signature was affixed by an authorized agent named Edward Rogalia and that he (the defendant) is not liable in any event because his endorsement of the note was "without recourse." He also contends that plaintiff may not recover, as an item of damage, the fifteen percent collection of attorney's fees provided for in the warranty to confess judgment.

We can see no merit whatever in the defenses offered and consider that plaintiff is entitled to the judgment which it seeks. The defendant's conception of the litigation as being a suit against an endorser who signed "without recourse," misses the point. Plaintiff is not suing on the note, but, as noted above, is claiming upon a breach of warranty. If it were true that the suit was against the defendant on the sole basis that he was an endorser, there might be some value to the defenses offered, but the pleadings reveal an entirely different situation. As the pleadings now stand, it is admitted on the record that the defendant in writing warranted the security agreement to be all that it purported to be, and it is clear that it was not. Further, the admission that defendant endorsed the note as part of his finance dealings with the plaintiff and that the note was not signed by the maker is a clear admission of a breach of the implied warranty which accompanies situations of this character. While no statute is required to establish the common sense conclusion that one who presents a document for discount or otherwise, impliedly warrants its genuineness when he accepts a consideration for its transfer, the Uniform Commercial Code has such a provision. In Section 3-417(2)(a) of that Act (Act 1953, April 6, P.L. 3, 12APS 3-417(2)(a)) it is provided that the transferor of an instrument for consideration warrants among other things, that all signatures are genuine or authorized. This certainly does not imply that a transferor, with knowledge that a signature is not that of the person it purports to belong to and there is no qualifying or descriptive language indicating that the signature was made by someone other than the maker, may remain silent and suppress such knowledge to the detriment of the transferee.

. . . . .

Warranting the signature, or warranting that an instrument is all that it purports to be are important elements for the protection of a transferee in situations of this kind. The confession of judgment clause in the note was a very real and substantial element in the transaction. If there was an impediment to the entry of judgment, not disclosed to the transferee, it suffered material harm when it accepted the note on faith. A judgment note, not of sufficient validity to support a judgment obtained under its warrant, would, under such circumstances, be no security to the plaintiff; particularly where the endorsement was without recourse. . ..

While there is no contest over the circumstances that the note was in default and that the unpaid balance of the debt was as noted above, defendant particularly denies plaintiff's right to recover the fifteen percent of the principal and interest if placed in the hands of an authority for collection as provided for in the warranty to confess judgment. Had the note been genuine and available for entry into judgment by the plaintiff, there is not question but that the attorney's fee, if reasonable, would be an acceptable item of collection. The defendant does not maintain that the percentage is too high, but denies liability solely upon the ground that the provisions of the warrant cannot be made effective against an endorser without recourse. It is his view that, even though we were to conclude that the plaintiff might recover on the face of the debt, we cannot allow the item in question because the matters in the warrant are not referable to an endorser. While this position might be true if the defendant's theory of the litigation was correct, *i.e.*, that this is a suit upon the note, we do not regard it as correct in view of the real nature of the controversy.

Attorney's fees stipulated for in a warrant of attorney are not costs; they are a part of the judgment and belong to the plaintiff. *Harper v. Consolidated Rubber Co.*, 284 Pa. 444, 448. Thus, the plaintiff was entitled under the defendant's warranty to have a security instrument of such validity that it could recover the amount due it by the tenor of the instrument itself. The defendant could easily have defeated the collection of attorney's fees by paying the debt when due, or even by tendering a reasonable fee less than fifteen percent when the matter was placed in the hands of council and before litigation was instituted (*Cunningham v. McCready*, 219 Pa. 594), but this defendant did not choose to do. Having once forced plaintiff into litigation of the magnitude of this action, the item of collection fees became a substantial element of plaintiff's damage. Consequential damages are frequently allowed in cases of implied warranties (*Campbell v. G.C. Murphy Co.*, 122 Pa. Superior Court, 342, 343) and there is no reason why the rule should be different where the suit is on both an express and an implied warranty. The provision for collection fees contained in the warrant does not make that item collectible against defendant as an endorser, but being an integral portion of the protective mechanism of the instrument and an essential part of the debt due the plaintiff, it becomes an item of damage when the warranty as to the instrument's genuineness is breached.

. . . . .

And now, to wit, April 9, 1959, judgment is entered on the pleadings in favor of the plaintiff and against the defendant in the sum of $1,701.30 being the balance unpaid on the debt of $1,396.97, with interest at 6% from April 15, 1958, and 15% added for attorney's collection fees, and the prothonotary is directed to enter judgment accordingly on the judgment docket.

QUESTIONS

1. Do the warranties made by an unqualified indorser under U.C.C. § 3-415(a) differ from those made by a qualified indorser under U.C.C. § 3-415(b)?

2. What is the measure of damages where the indorser is sued on his warranty as compared with the measure of damages where the suit is on the indorsement contract? What other differences can you outline as to the holder's rights on the contract and in warranty?

GREAT LAKES HIGHER EDUCATION CORP. v. AUSTIN BANK OF CHICAGO

United States District Court, ND Illinois
837 F.Supp. 892, 22 U.C.C. Rep.2d 858 (1993)

Memorandum Opinion and Order

Marovich, District Judge.

Plaintiffs Great Lakes Higher Education Corporation ("Great Lakes") and First Wisconsin National Bank of Milwaukee ("First Wisconsin") filed a five count complaint against Defendant Austin Bank of Chicago ("Austin") alleging breach of warranty (810 ILCS 5/4-207), negligence in the presentment of certain checks (810 ILCS 5/4-202), breach of warranty to a third party beneficiary (810 ILCS 5/4-207), conversion (810 ILCS 5/3-420) and common law negligence. Pursuant to Fed.R.Civ.P. 12(b)(6), Austin filed a motion to dismiss the entire complaint for failure to properly plead damages and to dismiss counts II through V for not alleging valid causes of action. For the reasons below, we grant Austin's motion to dismiss Counts II through V and require that Plaintiffs replead Count I.

FACTUAL BACKGROUND

For the purposes of this motion to dismiss, the Court accepts as true the following factual allegations taken from Plaintiffs' complaint. Great Lakes is a Wisconsin not-for-profit corporation with its principal place of business in Madison, Wisconsin. First Wisconsin is a national bank with its principal place of business in Milwaukee, Wisconsin. Great Lakes was a customer of First Wisconsin and maintained a bank account there. Austin is a state bank with its principal place of business in Chicago, Illinois.

Between October 1990 and January 1992, Great Lakes, as servicer, issued 224 checks (the "checks") drawn against lender's funds in the account of Great Lakes at First Wisconsin, payable to the order of various payees. The checks were issued to the payees as loan proceeds pursuant to a student loan application submitted by each payee who was certified by the InterAmerican Business Institute ("IBI") located in Chicago, Illinois. Shortly after the issuance of each check, it was presented for payment to Austin Bank without the endorsement of the named payee. Austin Bank accepted each check for purposes of collection and forwarded each check to First Wisconsin for that purpose. Austin received payment from First Wisconsin in the face amount of each check even though the endorsement signature of the payee was not on any of the checks.

On February 27, 1992, First Wisconsin gave notice to Austin of its claim for breach of warranty by indicating that the checks lacked proper endorsement. First Wisconsin demanded that Austin refund to First Wisconsin the amount of the checks, a total of $273,152.88 plus interest. Austin failed to respond to this request for a refund, and Plaintiffs filed this suit.

DISCUSSION

When considering a motion to dismiss, we assume as true all factual allegations contained in the complaint and make all possible inferences in favor of the plaintiff. A motion to dismiss will not be granted unless "it appears beyond all doubt that the plaintiff can prove no set of facts in support of his claims which would entitle him to relief." With these principles in mind, we proceed to analyze Austin's motion to dismiss.[23] . . .

Count II: Negligence in the Presentment

In its second count, Great Lakes alleges that Austin was negligent and breached its duty to exercise ordinary care under 810 ILCS 5/4-202 by accepting the checks without proper endorsement and sending them for presentment to First Wisconsin. Austin contends that because the harm to Plaintiffs occurred in the acceptance of the checks by Austin without proper authorization, rather than in the presentment process, § 5/4-202 does not apply here.

Under the U.C.C., presentment means "a demand made by or on behalf of a person entitled to enforce an instrument (i) to pay the instrument made to the drawee or a party obliged to pay the instrument or, in the case of a note or accepted draft payable at a bank, to the bank or (ii) to accept a draft made to the drawee." 810 ILCS 5/3-501. Section 4-202 provides that: "A collecting bank must exercise ordinary care in . . .presenting an item or sending it for presentment." 810 ILCS 5/4-202(a)(1). Official Code Comment Two to this section states: "If the bank makes presentment itself, subsection (a)(1) requires ordinary care with respect both to the time and manner of presentment . . . If it forwards the item to be presented the subsection requires ordinary care with respect to routing (Section 4-204), and also in the selection of intermediary banks or other agents." *Id.* at cmt. 2.

Under a plain reading of Official Comment Two, *Id.*, we hold that where, as here, Austin merely forwarded the item to First Wisconsin to be presented, it is only responsible for ordinary care under § 4-202 with respect to the routing and selection of intermediary banks or other agents. *Id.* Because Austin displayed reasonable care in regard to these activities by immediately forwarding the checks to First Wisconsin, we hold that § 4-202 does not apply to the instant case.

---

[23] We have jurisdiction over this dispute based upon the diversity of the parties. The parties are here on diversity. We shall use the law of Illinois in our analysis because the injury allegedly occurred at the Austin bank located in Chicago, Illinois. [Illinois adopted Revised Articles 3 and 4 effective January 1, 1992 Ed.]

The case cited by First Wisconsin, *Northpark Nat'l Bank v. Bankers Trust Co.*, 572 F.Supp. 524, 534 (S.D.N.Y. 1983), for the proposition that this Court should be flexible in applying § 4-202 claims is not persuasive. That case addressed wrongdoing in the presentment process where the defendant bank failed to timely return a fraudulent check or send notification of having received it unpaid within the applicable U.C.C. time limits. *Id.* at 527-28. By contrast, Great Lakes argues that the exercise of ordinary care in the presentment process set out in § 4-202 extends to the acceptance of unauthorized checks. We refuse to extend the ordinary care standard this far in light of the Official Comment and the fact that other relevant U.C.C. remedies in breach of warranty exist that are more applicable to the instant situation.[24] Because these alternative remedies exist, we are not, as First Wisconsin asserts, allowing Austin to completely avoid liability by refusing to allow a negligence claim against it.

Count III: Common Law Negligence

Plaintiffs invoke the law of common law negligence against Austin in their third count. In response, Austin cites *Moorman Mfg. Co. v. National Tank Co.*, 91 Ill.2d 69, 61 Ill.Dec. 746, 753-54, 435 N.E.2d 443, 450-51 (1982), for the proposition that under Illinois law, the parties to a commercial transaction cannot recover in tort for economic losses (the "Moorman doctrine"). In *Moorman*, the plaintiff sued the company that designed, manufactured and sold him a defective storage tank, asserting damages for the cost of repair and reinforcement as well as loss of use of the tank. *Id.* The Illinois Supreme Court held that the plaintiff had suffered "a commercial loss of the type that the law of warranty is designed to protect" rather than a "sudden and dangerous occurrence best served by the policy of tort law." *Id.* The court held that its conclusion applied to cases of negligence as well as strict liability, noting that "allowing an aggrieved party to recover under a negligence theory for solely economic loss would constitute an unwarranted infringement upon the scheme provided by the U.C.C."

The Seventh Circuit has upheld *Moorman* in applying Illinois law. In *Valenti v. Qualex, Inc.*, 970 F.2d 363, 369 (7th Cir. 1992), the court held that the *Moorman* decision has been upheld consistently in Illinois and by the Seventh Circuit. The court explained that "the basic principle of *Moorman* is that the type of loss, not the defendant's conduct, is critical. When only economic loss is incurred, the plaintiff may only raise contract theories even if the defendant's alleged conduct constituted a tort as well as a breach of contract." *Id.* quoting *Bethlehem Steel Corp. v. Chicago Eastern Corp.*, 863 F.2d 508 (8th Cir. 1988). *See also Nielsen v. United Servs. Automobile Ass'n.*, 244 Ill.App.3d 658, 183 Ill.Dec. 874,881, 612 N.E.2d 526, 533 (1993) (stating that the *Moorman* doctrine applied to fire insurance policy coverage so that defendant had no duty in negligence to plaintiffs apart from their contractual undertakings).

Plaintiffs' argument is not persuasive that because the U.C.C. clearly intended that it would be supplemented by common-law principles (§ 1-103), it follows that a claim for negligence may be asserted unless a specific provision of the U.C.C. expressly overrules the common law. No section of the U.C.C. expressly displaces any common law remedy. It is by implication that an alternative remedy under the U.C.C. exists for such a factual situation that the common law is displaced on that same point. Here, First Wisconsin and Great Lakes have other remedies under the U.C.C. which they have alternatively plead in their complaint, thus showing that a common law action for negligence is unnecessary and may not be alleged here.

---

[24] *See* U.C.C. §§ 4-207 and 3-417.

We also do not accept Plaintiffs' contention that there is a need for further investigation in order to determine whether there existed a "commercial or contractual relationship" between the disputed parties, so as to invoke the *Moorman* doctrine. It is clear that the relationship is a commercial one because the transactions and damages involved in this case are financial in nature. Thus, there is nothing further to establish and Plaintiffs' negligence claim may not be properly asserted under Illinois law because of the *Moorman* doctrine.

Count IV: Breach of Warranty
Against Third Party

In Count IV, Great Lakes alleges that it is the third party beneficiary of a U.C.C. § 4-207transfer warranty owed by Austin to First Wisconsin, and thus Great Lakes is suing Austin for breach of warranty as a third party. Section 4-207 provides in relevant part that "a customer or collecting bank . . .warrants to the transferee and to any subsequent collecting bank that . . .all signatures on the time are authentic and authorized." 810 ILCS 5/4-207. Though Great Lakes is neither a customer nor a subsequent collecting bank, it relies upon a third party beneficiary theory of warranty owed by Austin to First Wisconsin. In this action, Great Lakes is the "drawer" of the checks from First Wisconsin, and First Wisconsin is the "drawee" of the checks.

Austin points to *Steinroe Income Trust v. Continental Bank N.A.*, 238 Ill.App.3d 660, 179 Ill.Dec. 671, 673, 606 N.E.2d 503, 505 (1992), in which the Illinois Appellate Court for the First District adopted the majority view that under Illinois law, a drawer may not maintain an action under U.C.C. § 4-207. *Steinroe* specifically rejected *Sun'n Sand, Inc. v. United California Bank*, 57 Cal. App.3d 125, 129 Cal.Rptr. 861 (1976), the California case representing the minority viewpoint that a drawer may maintain an action as a third party beneficiary. The *Steinroe* court based its decision in part upon the U.C.C. Comment to newly amended U.C.C. § 3-417which explicitly rejected the *Sun'n Sand* case in favor of the majority view. Ill.Ann.Stat., ch. 26, ¶ 3-417, U.C.C. Comment 2 (Smith-Hurd 1992).

Because *Steinroe* is the main case to address this issue under Illinois law, we accept its holding that a drawer, such as Great Lakes in the instant case, may not assert a third party beneficiary claim in order to maintain a breach of warranty under U.C.C. § 4-207. Plaintiffs' fourth count must therefore be dismissed.

Count V: Conversion

In Plaintiffs' fifth count, First Wisconsin alleges that Austin converted the checks in violation of prior U.C.C. § 3-419, Ill.Rev.Stat. ch. 26, § 3-419 (1961), and current U.C.C. § 3-420. 810 ILCS 5/3-420 (1992). Illinois courts do not recognize an action for conversion of intangible rights. *In re Oxford Marketing Ltd.*, 444 F.Supp. 399, 404 (N.E.Ill.1978) *citing* Janes *v. First Federal Savings & Loan Ass'n.*, 11 Ill.App.3d 631, 297 N.E.2d 255, 260 (1973). However, Illinois courts do recognize a cause of action for conversion of commercial paper, such as a check, on the theory that the intangible right is merged into the specific document. *Id.* A party pleading an action in conversion under either common law principles or U.C.C. § 3-419 must allege that it had title to or possession of the check. *In re Oxford,* 444 F.Supp. at 404-05. Under Illinois law, the elements of a cause of action for conversion under U.C.C. § 3-419 are: (1) plaintiff's ownership of, interest in, or possession of the check; (2) plaintiff's forged or unauthorized endorsement on the check; and (3) defendant bank's unauthorized cashing of the check.

Austin makes two assertions in order to dismiss First Wisconsin's conversion claim. First, it contends that because the checks represent a debt of First Wisconsin rather than an asset, First Wisconsin could not have had the requisite possession or interest in them to claim conversion. We hold that First Wisconsin's only interest in the checks at the time of the alleged wrongdoing was an obligation or debt to the payees, so that First Wisconsin did not have the requisite *possessory* interest to claim conversion. *Id.* The payees were the only ones who had the requisite possessory interest in the checks to bring a claim of conversion. *See* J. White & R. Summers, Uniform Commercial Code § 15-5, at 665 (3rd ed. 1988).

First Wisconsin's reliance on *Justus Co. v. Gary Wheaton Bank*, 509 F.Supp. 103, 106 (N.D.Ill. 1981), is misplaced because it dealt only with the drawer's rights in conversion rather than the drawee's rights and was decided before the new § 3-420 was released. The Official Comment to § 3-420 rejected *Justus*'s reasoning that a drawer is entitled to sue the depositary bank for conversion by stating that the "check represents an obligation of the drawer rather than property of the drawer" so that there "is no reason why a drawer should have an action in conversion." 810 ILCS 5/3-420, Official Comment 1. The new version of the Code thus supports Austin's contention that a drawee, like a drawer, has no valuable possessory interest in the checks and may not bring a claim for conversion.[25]

CONCLUSION

For the foregoing reasons, we dismiss with prejudice counts II, III, IV, and V of Plaintiff's complaint and give Plaintiffs leave to amend Count I by showing which party suffered damages in this suit.

§ 13.09 Liability of Drawee or Acceptor

[A] In Contract

Read: U.C.C. §§ 3-408, 3-409, 3-410, 3-413.

---

[25] This is not to say that First Wisconsin has no action against Austin for accepting money in exchange for the unauthorized checks. Under the liberal pleading standard for the Federal Rules of Civil Procedure, Rule 8(e), the facts set out in Plaintiffs' complaint seem to state an action for breach of presentment warranties under 3-417(a) and we grant First Wisconsin leave to amend its complaint accordingly.

EUROPEAN ASIAN BANK, A.G. v. G. CROHN & CO.

[The opinion appears in § 12.04[B], *supra*.]

HOTEL RIVIERA, INC. V. FIRST NATIONAL BANK & TRUST CO.

[The opinion appears in § 13.03, *supra*.]

FIRST NATIONAL BANK OF ALAMOSA v. FORD MOTOR CREDIT CO.

United States District Court, D. Colorado
748 F. Supp. 1464 (1990)

MEMORANDUM OPINION AND ORDER

NOTTINGHAM, DISTRICT JUDGE.

Plaintiff First National Bank in Alamosa's ("the Bank's") lawsuit against Ford Motor Credit Company ("Ford") is based on Ford's refusal to honor nine sight drafts presented to Ford, as acceptor or drawee, and directing it to pay a total of $93,144.86. The drafts were drawn on Ford by Clark/Cravens Alamosa Motors, Inc. (the Bank's customer and a car dealer associated with Ford Motor Company), and delivered to the Bank for collection through the commercial banking system. Alamosa Motors initiated the collection process by depositing the nine drafts into its account at the Bank between March 3, 1986, and March 10, 1986. The Bank treated the drafts as "cash items"—that is, it credited Alamosa Motors' account and permitted Alamosa Motors to have immediate use of the funds represented by that credit, as had been its practice when Alamosa Motors deposited similar drafts on prior occasions. Unfortunately, the principals of Alamosa Motors left town, literally in the middle of the night, around March 12, 1986. By the time the sight drafts (1) had been presented through the interbank collection system, (2) were dishonored, and (3) came back to the Bank, Alamosa Motors' account at the bank was overdrawn by $64,543.28. Unable to recover from Alamosa Motors, the Bank initiated this lawsuit against Ford.

The case, which defendant has removed to this court on account of the parties' diverse citizenship, involves three claims for relief. First, the Bank asserts that, when Alamosa Motors signed the sight drafts, it did so as an "agent or authorized representative" of Ford and thereby obligated Ford to honor the drafts. Second, the Bank alleges that Ford was negligent in introducing "confusing and misleading negotiable instruments" into the commercial banking system. Third, the Bank asserts a promissory estoppel claim, arguing that Ford orally promised to pay the drafts and that it has detrimentally relied on the promise by giving Alamosa Motors immediate credit for the drafts.

Ford has moved for summary judgment on all three claims for relief, and the Bank has moved for summary judgment on the third claim. These motions are now before the court for decision. The parties agree that articles three (commercial paper) and four (bank deposits and collections) of the Uniform Commercial Code (U.C.C.), enacted in Colorado as Colo.Rev.Stat. §§ 4-3-101 through 4-4-504 (1973), supply the applicable principles of law. Resolution of the motions therefore requires me, first, to discuss the commercial setting in which these drafts were used and, second, to analyze the parties' business relationship and transactions in terms supplied by the U.C.C.

I. FACTS

1. The Commercial Setting.

Ford provides blank, pre-printed drafts such as the nine at issue here to approved dealers of Ford Motor Company. The drafts are among the numerous documents used in the system by which Ford finances automobile sales to consumers. The customer who wants to buy a car on credit from a Ford Motor Company dealer enters into a retail installment sales agreement with the dealer, promising to pay the amount financed and giving the dealer a security interest in the automobile. Since dealers do not typically want to finance the sale themselves, Ford's system provides a means by which Ford assumes responsibility for financing the consumer's purchase and the dealer receives the amount financed. To use this system, a dealer does two things. First, after the consumer signs the retail installment sales agreement, the dealer assigns the agreement to Ford and sends the agreement and related documents to Ford for approval. Second, the dealer completes one of the pre-printed drafts (by paying itself or its bank the amount financed) and presents the draft for payment through the commercial banking system. Assuming that the documents are in order and that Ford agrees to finance the transaction, Ford transfers the amount financed to the dealer by honoring the sight draft. According to Ford's evidence (undisputed by the Bank), sight drafts are commonly used in the automobile industry. Their purpose is to facilitate and expedite payment to the dealer.

The nine sight drafts also contain the language "payable through . . .The First National Bank, Colorado Springs, Colorado," which is printed in the lower left-hand side of each draft. To understand how the drafts were used, this provision must be explained. Ford employed The First National Bank of Colorado Springs as its "collecting bank." *See* U.C.C. § 3-120, Colo.Rev.Stat. § 4-3-120 (1973) ("An instrument which states that it is 'payable through' a bank or the like designates that bank as a collecting bank to make presentment *but does not of itself authorize the bank to pay the instrument.*") (emphasis added). After a collecting bank such as the First National Bank of Colorado Springs receives a sight draft from a depositary bank, it contacts Ford to ask Ford if it is prepared to pay the draft. If Ford disapproves the transaction, it instructs its collecting bank to dishonor the sight draft. If it wants to pay the draft, Ford instructs the collecting bank to pay the draft and mails the collecting bank a Ford check in the amount of the draft. The collecting bank, in turn, pays depositary banks, such as First National Bank in

Alamosa, the amount of the sight draft, by means of inter-bank credits provided through the Federal Reserve system.

Dealers often execute and deposit the pre-printed Ford sight draft with their local bank as soon as the consumer sale is made. This can create problems. If the sight draft reaches Ford's collecting bank through the bank collection system before the retail installment sales agreement reaches Ford through the mails, Ford will instruct its bank not to honor the dealer's sight draft. More importantly, Ford will not honor a sight draft if the agreement and related documents are not in order, or if the dealer has failed to pay Ford the wholesale price for the car which the dealer has sold and proposes to finance through Ford.

2. The Parties' Business Relationship and Transactions.

The nine drafts in question here were used in the commercial setting described above. Each sight draft represents a separate retail consumer financing transaction. Ford dishonored seven of the drafts because Alamosa Motors had not paid Ford the wholesale price of the car which it was seeking to have Ford finance. It rejected an eighth because Alamosa Motors had not submitted to Ford the retail installment sales agreement. It rejected the ninth because the automobile in question had previously been leased, and Alamosa Motors had not paid off the retail lease account on the vehicle.

All nine instruments in question are similar. The rectangular printed forms contain the Ford corporate logo and the words "Ford Motor Credit Company" in the upper left-hand corner. There is no doubt that they are properly characterized, under the U.C.C., as "drafts," since each is an "order" directed expressly "TO Ford Motor Credit Company," as drawee, to pay the amount specified in the draft. *See* U.C.C. § 3-104(2)(a), Colo.Rev.Stat. § 4-3-104(2)(a) (1973) (negotiable instrument is a " 'draft' . . . I if it is an order"); U.C.C. § 3-102(1)(b), Colo.Rev.Stat. § 4-3-102(1)(b) (1973) ("An 'order' is a direction to pay."). Each draft is payable to the order of "Alamosa Motors, Inc.," as payee. Each is signed in the lower right-hand corner by the drawer, "Alamosa Motors, Inc." (words affixed to the draft by typewriter), acting by "Maureen Gonzales" (words affixed by manual signature), Alamosa Motors' title clerk. In other words, Alamosa Motors made the sight drafts payable to itself. On the reverse side, it indorsed each draft, "PAY TO THE ORDER OF FIRST NATIONAL BANK OF [sic] ALAMOSA; FOR DEPOSIT ONLY; ALAMOSA MOTORS, INC." It then deposited the drafts to its account at the Bank. The First National in Alamosa was thus the "depositary bank" in this case. *See* U.C.C. § 4-105(a), Colo.Rev.Stat. § 4-4-105(a) (1973) (" 'Depositary bank' means the first bank to which an item is transferred for collection."). The drafts were then presented for collection through the commercial banking system.

As I have indicated, the Bank regarded sight drafts such as those at issue here as "cash items." William Griggs, president and primary loan officer of the Bank during the relevant time period, and David E. Broyles, who held the title "senior loan officer" during the period, testified that the Bank gave Alamosa Motors immediate credit for the drafts and did not place a "hold" on the funds represented by the credit. Griggs testified that it was "the normal course of business" to give immediate cash credit to auto dealer sight drafts. In his experience as a banker in Colorado and several other states, Griggs had never previously seen a sight draft returned. Mr. Broyles testified that sight drafts from Ford were "pretty frequent" and that "we thought we had a course of dealing, that they were being accepted." He affirmed that the Bank treated the sight drafts as cash items, instead of giving only provisional settlements, admitting that "there is always an element of risk" in giving immediate credit but the bank considered the risk "minimal." He explained:

> Oh, I think that [the risk] was very minimal. We considered that it was Ford Motor Credit that wrote the check [sic], and it was the obligation of Ford Motor Credit Company. And I guess what we're saying, we're looking at the Ford Motor Credit Company backing up the instrument.

As the basis for his belief that Ford Credit would back up the instruments, Broyles cited his prior experience with sight drafts and his experience with this particular auto dealer and its predecessor. Also, Mr. Broyes stated that he remembered a conversation in the spring or summer of 1985 between President Griggs and himself. As Broyles remembered the conversation, Griggs told Broyles that he had asked Ford whether the sight drafts should be treated as "cash items" or "collection items." Ford had assured Mr. Griggs that the bank could handle sight drafts as cash items. Mr. Griggs, however, testified at his deposition that he did *not* recall having any conversations whatsoever with Ford concerning sight drafts.

II. LAW

1. First Claim for Relief—Liability on the Instruments Themselves.

Ford is not liable on these nine instruments for the simple reason that it did not "accept" the sight drafts. U.C.C. § 3-410(1), Colo.Rev.Stat. § 4-3-410(1) (1973) ("Acceptance is the drawee's *signed* engagement to honor the draft as presented. *It must be written on the draft,* and may consist of his signature alone." (emphasis supplied).) Under the U.C.C., a drawee who refuses acceptance is generally not liable *on the instrument*. U.C.C. § 3-409(1), Colo.Rev.Stat. § 4-3-409(1) (1973) ("A check or other draft does not of itself operate as an assignment of any funds in the hands of the drawee available for its payment, and the drawee is not liable on the instrument until he accepts it.") Plaintiff's remedy on the instruments is against the drawer of the drafts, Alamosa Motors. U.C.C. § 3-413(2), Colo.Rev.Stat. § 4-3-413(2) (1973) ("The drawer engages that upon dishonor of the draft and any necessary notice of dishonor or protest he will pay the amount of the draft to the holder. . ..").

The Bank seeks to avoid the conclusion that Ford is not liable on the instruments by advancing two arguments. First, it asserts that the name "Ford Motor Credit Company" is prominently pre-printed on the drafts in two places—once in the upper left-hand corner (next to the Ford logo) and once in the middle of the draft, on the left-hand side, in the for, "TO Ford Motor Credit Company." The Bank notes that Ford supplied these forms to its dealers as a means of facilitating payment to the dealers. It concludes that Ford has thus "signed" the instruments—or, at least, that the appearance of Ford's name on the instruments creates a genuine issue of material fact concerning Alamosa Motors' authority to "sign" them on Ford's behalf and therefore precludes summary judgment for Ford.

The Bank's first argument must fail because, as a matter of law under the applicable provisions of the U.C.C., it has not "signed" the instruments in question here by pre-printing its name on them in the manner described. Under the U.C.C., a party "signs" a writing when the party affixes its name or symbol to the writing "with *present intention* to authenticate" the writing. U.C.C. § 1-201(39), Colo.Rev.Stat. § 4-1-201(39) (1973) & official comment 39 (defining "signed") (emphasis supplied). *See also* U.C.C. § 3-401, Colo.Rev.Stat. § 4-3-401 (1973) & official comments 1 & 2 (no person is liable on an instrument unless the person has "signed" the instrument).

In deciding whether a party has affixed its name to an instrument with a "present intention" to authenticate the instrument, courts "must use common sense and commercial experience. . .." U.C.C. § 1-201, Colo.Rev.Stat. § 4-1-201 (1973) Official comment 39. "A typewritten or printed name on the top of the instrument, like a letterhead or billhead, . . .will rarely be found to be a signature." 4 W. Hawkland & L. Lawrence, Uniform Commercial Code Series ¶ 3-401:09 at 510 (1984). *See also Agric. Nat'l Bank of Pittsfield v. Great American Indem. Co.* 287 Mass. 414, 192 N.E. 8 (1934) (pre-Code case). In *Pittsfield*, a national insurance company pre-printed drafts, with itself as drawee, and supplied these forms to its claims agents. The claims agent signed the draft in question, but the collecting bank, upon the instructions of the insurance company's home office, refused to honor the draft. The court held that the insurance company did not "sign" the draft forms, because the mere printing and furnishing of the forms to the claims agent did not evidence an intent to authenticate the drafts.

Here, the nine drafts themselves sufficiently demonstrate, on their face, that the words "Ford Motor Company" were not placed thereon with a "present intention" to authenticate the drafts. With respect to the appearance of the words "TO Ford Motor Credit Company" on the left-hand side of each draft, it is clear on the face of each instrument that the words are directed to Ford as the "drawee" or prospective "acceptor" of the draft. A drawee's name necessarily appears on every draft, so that other parties to the instrument will know the identity of the party to whom the instrument must be presented for acceptance. To hold that the mere printing of the drawee's name on the instrument may be used as evidence of a "present intention" to authenticate the instrument would deprive the drawee of its right to accept or reject the instrument, introduce considerable uncertainty concerning the use of such instruments, and limit the usefulness of the instruments in commercial transactions. The same may be said of the Ford logo and the words "Ford Motor Credit Company" in the upper left-hand corner of each draft. Since it is clear on the face of each instrument that the instrument is a "sight draft" and that Ford is the "drawee" or prospective "acceptor," these pre-printed words amount to a letter-head or billhead and are without additional legal significance.

The point concerning the significance of the pre-printed words "Ford Motor Credit Company" on these drafts can be made by comparing them to a more common form of draft—the ordinary check. *See* U.C.C. § 3-104(2)(b), Colo.Rev.Stat. § 4-3-104(2)(b) (1973) (" 'check' . . .is a draft drawn on a bank"). Checks are commonly pre-printed with the name of the drawee bank in the place where Ford's name appears as drawee on the drafts here and the name of the account holder and prospective drawer at the top of the check. One authoritative treatise on the U.C.C. has made the point as follows:

> Comment 2 to 3-401 tells us that a person may make his signature in a variety of ways: "handwritten, typed, printed or made in any other manner." Under this broad view an imaginative plaintiff might argue that pre-printed forms (for instance, checks) with the name of a corporation or individual inscribed on them are "signed" instruments. Before one tears up all his pre-printed checks, he should consider section 1-201(39). " 'Signed' includes any symbol executed or adopted by a party with the present intention to authenticate a writing." One would be hard pressed to maintain that a party had "present intention to authenticate" whatever might later be written on a check when he ordered a batch of checks with his name printed on them.

1 J. White & R. Summers, Uniform Commercial Code, ¶ 13-2at 624 (3d ed. 1988). The pre-printed Ford sight drafts with the Ford name and corporate logo are no more a "signature" than are any

individual's preprinted personal checks, which do not ordinarily constitute the signature of either the individual or the drawee bank.

The Bank's second argument for holding Ford liable on the instruments in a variation on the first: invoking section 3-403 (Colo.Rev.Stat. § 4-3-403 [1973]), it asserts the right to prove at trial that Alamosa Motors, acting through its title clerk, Maureen Gonzales, signed the drafts as Ford's authorized agent and thereby obligated Ford on the drafts. Section 3-403 provides as follows:

> (1) A signature may be made by an agent or other representative, and his authority to make it may be established as in other cases of representation. No particular form of appointment is necessary to establish such authority.

Claiming that Alamosa Motors' authority to sign the drafts as Ford's agent or representative is a factual matter to be resolved at trial and that the matter must be resolved by taking parol evidence, the Bank argues that Ford's motion for summary judgment on the Bank's first claim must be denied.

The Bank's argument ignores the remaining parts of section 3-403 and therefore misconceives the section as a whole. As the official comments explain, a principal is not liable under section 3-403 unless the principal's name appears on the instrument. "Even though he [the agent] is authorized the principal is not liable on the instrument, under the provisions (Section 3-401) relating to signatures, *unless the instrument names him and clearly shows that the signature is made on his behalf.*" U.C.C. § 3-403, Colo.Rev.Stat. § 4-3-403 (1973) official comment 2 (emphasis supplied). If the agent signs his own name and does not name the principal or indicate that the signature is made in a representative capacity, the agent—not the principal—is obligated on the instrument. U.C.C. § 3-403(2)(a), Colo.Rev.Stat. § 4-3-403(2)(a) (1973). In such a situation, "parol evidence is inadmissible under subsection (2)(a) to disestablish [the agent's] obligation." U.C.C. § 3-403, Colo.Rev.Stat. § 4-3-403 (1973) official comment 3. In other words, the Bank may invoke section 3-403(1) and introduce parol evidence to establish Alamosa Motors' authority to act for Ford *only if* Ford is identified as the party whose name is being signed. When an authorized agent signs an instrument in a way which makes it unclear whether he intended to obligate his named principal or himself, section 3-403 provides a set of rules which enable a holder of the instrument to determine, solely by reference to the instrument itself, which of the two parties is bound; it does not provide a general warrant for a court to receive parol evidence that a named agent was acting on behalf of an unnamed principal.

Here, the nine drafts show on their face that Ford was not named as a drawer. Each draft contains two lines in the lower right-hand corner. The first is a blank followed by the pre-printed word, "DEALER." The second is a blank followed by the pre-printed word, "TITLE." The words, "Alamosa Motors, Inc.," are typed in the blank on the first line, before the word "DEALER." The manually-affixed words "Maureen Gonzales" and the typed words "Title Clerk" occupy the second line, before the word "TITLE." As the U.C.C. makes clear, "[B]y long established practice judicially noticed or otherwise established a signature in the lower right hand corner of an instrument indicates an intent to sign as the maker of a note or the drawer of a draft." U.C.C. § 3-402, Colo.Rev.Stat. § 4-3-402 (1973) official comment. The *most* that the Bank could argue from the way in which the drawee signature blocks are completed is that the word, "DEALER," in each block ambiguously suggests a signature in a representative capacity. Even so, the U.C.C. clearly states that the signature operates to bind the purported agent, not the unnamed principal, and prohibits the receipt of parol evidence *in an action brought by a holder of the instrument.*

U.C.C. § 3-403(2)(b), Colo. Rev.Stat. § 4-3-403(2)(b) (1973) & official comment 3 ("[T]he section [3-403(2)(b)] admits parol evidence in litigation between the immediate parties [the principal and agent] to prove signature by the agent in his representative capacity.").

Under section 3-403(3), then, the legal effect of the drawee signature space, as completed on each draft, is that Alamosa Motors, not Ford, is liable on the drafts as a drawer. Contrary to the Bank's argument, the fact that Alamosa Motors affixed the words, "Alamosa Motors, Inc.," instead of using its full proper corporate name, "Clark/Cravens Alamosa Motors, Inc.," is not relevant. A party's proper or full name need not be used for the words to be effective as a signature. U.C.C. § 3-401(2), Colo.Rev.Stat. § 4-3-401(2) & official comment 2.

Although the argument is not explicit, the Bank also seems to suggest that it may properly invoke section 3-403 to introduce parol evidence concerning Alamosa Motors' authority to act for Ford, because (as previously noted) Ford's name does appear elsewhere on the drafts, albeit not in the drawer signature blocks. This suggestion ignores the requirement that an alleged principal is liable for signing the instrument only if the instrument names him *and clearly shows* that the signature is made on his behalf. U.C.C. § 3-403, Colo.Rev.Stat. § 4-3-403 (1973) official comment 2. Ford's pre-printed name in the upper left-hand corner, diagonally opposite the drawer signature block, does not constitute such a showing. Neither does the appearance of its name as the drawee or prospective acceptor. Because Ford is not liable on the drafts, having neither accepted them as drawee nor signed them as drawer, and because the U.C.C. does not permit the introduction of parol evidence in these circumstances, Ford is entitled to summary judgment on the Bank's first claim for relief.

NOTES

(1) The check as a payment device is not issued in contemplation of presentment for acceptance. Rather, the check is designed to permit the payee to obtain payment of the underlying obligation and the drawee-bank is generally asked to pay or dishonor. This is the basis of the Code rule that the drawee-bank is under no obligation to certify. U.C.C. § 3-409(d).

However, in looking forward to a transaction involving payment by check, the payee may desire something other than secondary liability of the drawer. The payee may be unwilling to assume the risk that something will go wrong between the time of taking the check and clearing the check through the bank collection system. There is little justification for the holder's procuring certification. Banks resist the practice because of the possibilities of the banks' becoming liable on altered checks. The holder who desires to procure certification rather than payment could exchange the check for a cashier's check and obtain the same protection.

(2) The function served by the certified check may also be served by the use of a "personal money order."

SEQUOYAH STATE BANK v. UNION NATIONAL BANK

Arkansas Supreme Court
621 S.W.2d 683, 32 U.C.C. Rep. 213 (1981)

ADKISSON, CHIEF JUSTICE.

The only issue in this case is whether Union Bank by its own initiative can stop payment on a personal money order it had issued in exchange for a hot check and, thereby, cause Sequoyah Bank, a holder in due course, to bear the loss. Under these circumstances the loss must be borne by Union Bank which issued the negotiable instrument to be circulated in commerce.

We do not decide the question of whether the purchaser may stop payment, but we do hold that after the sale of a personal money order, the issuing bank cannot stop payment on the instrument.

A personal money order is issued with unfilled blanks for the name of the payee, the date, and the signature of the purchaser. Only the amount is filled out at the time of issue, usually by check-writer impression as was done in this case.

The Uniform Commercial Code apparently did not directly contemplate the use of money orders and made no specific provision for them. *Mirabile v. Udoh*, 399 NYS2d 869 (1977). It was recognized in *Mirabile* that it is the custom and practice of the business community to accept personal money orders as a pledge of the issuing bank's credit. We may consider this custom and practice in construing the legal effect of such instruments. See Ark Stat Ann § 85-1-103(Add 1961).

Appellee relies on the cases of *Garden Check Cashing Service, Inc. v. First National City Bank*, 25AD2d 137, 267 NYS2d 698 (1966), affd 18 NY2d 941, 223 NE2d 566, 277 NYS2d 141(1966) and *Krom v. Chemical Bank New York Trust Co.*, 313 NYS2d 810 (1970), revd 329 NYS2d 91 (AD 1972) which held that a purchaser of a personal money order may stop payment on it. However, the only cited case to specifically address the issue of whether the issuing bank, on its own initiative, may stop payment on a personal money order is *Rose Check Cashing Service, Inc. v. Chemical Bank NY. Trust Co.*, 244 NYS2d 474, 477 (1963). In holding that the issuing bank could not stop payment and therefore must suffer the loss the court stated:

> All of these differences between the instrument at issue and an ordinary check would seem to indicate that the bank would honor the order to pay no matter who signed the face of the instrument, assuming of course an otherwise valid negotiation of the instrument.
>
> . . ..
>
> In the instrument in suit, the drawer purchases the instrument from the bank. The transaction is in the nature of a sale. No deposit is created. The funds to pay the instrument immediately come within the bank's exclusive control and ownership. . ..

> The bank's contention that the instrument is a check is inconsistent with its own acts. The bank (drawee) stamped "Stop Payment" on the instrument in suit on its own order. Nowhere in the Negotiable Instruments Law is there any provision that a drawee [bank] may "Stop Payment" of a check unless ordered to do so by the drawer.

Appellee also denies liability on the instrument based upon Ark Stat Ann § 85-3-401(1) which states that "No person is liable on an instrument unless his signature appears thereon." Subdivision (2) of this same section provides that a signature may be "any word or mark used in lieu of a written signature." The authenticity of the instrument involved here is not in question. The issuance of the money order with the bank's printed name evidences the appellee's intent to be bound thereby. *Mirabile, supra.*

Appellee also relies on Ark Stat Ann § 85-3-409 for the proposition that it is not liable on the personal money order since it did not accept it. In our opinion, however, the appellee accepted the instrument in advance by the act of its issuance. *Rose Check Cashing Service Inc. v. Chemical Bank New York Trust Co.*, 252 NYS2d 100 (1964).

The personal money order constituted an obligation of Union from the moment of its sale and issuance. The fact that Union was frustrated in retaining the funds because instead of cash it accepted a check drawn on insufficient funds is no reason to hold otherwise. We note by analogy that the Uniform Commercial Code on sales Ark Stat Ann § 85-2-403(1)(b) provides that a purchaser of goods, who takes delivery in exchange for a check which is later dishonored, transfers good title to the goods.

Union placed the personal money order in commerce for a consideration it accepted as adequate and was, thereafter, liable on it. Banks are not allowed to stop payment on their depositor's checks and certainly should not be allowed to stop payment on personal money orders. See Note, *Personal Money Orders and Teller's Checks: Mavericks Under the U.C.C.*, 67 Colum L Rev 524 (1967).

Reversed.

Holt, Dudley, and Hays, JJ., dissent.

Dudley, Associate Justice. (Dissenting).

This case involves a personal money order, not a bank money order, not a certificate of deposit and not a certified check. A personal money order is for the convenience of anyone who does not have an ordinary checking account and needs a safe, inexpensive and readily acceptable means of transferring funds. The bank simply sells to the individual a check-sized form which has the amount impressed into the face of the paper, an identification number and the name of the issuing bank. No authorized representative of the bank signs the instrument. When the purchaser of the instrument decides to pass it, he dates it, enters the name of the payee and signs the instrument.

Ark Stat Ann § 85-3-104(1)(a)(Add 1961) requires that a writing be signed by the drawer or maker in order to be negotiable. Any item which is an order to pay is considered a "draft" and any draft on a bank and payable on demand is a "check." § 85-3-104(2)(a), (b). Since the only signature on a personal money order is that of the purchaser, since the instrument takes the form of an order to pay, and since it is drawn on a bank and payable on demand, it is clearly within the classification of a check. The absence of the bank's signature as a "maker" and the absence of any express "undertaking" to pay by the bank, § 85-3-102(1)(c) and § 85-3-104(2)(d) preclude a finding that the instrument is a note. Aside from "draft," "check" and "note" the only other form of negotiable instrument recognized by the Uniform Commercial Code is a "certificate of deposit" and that requires an acknowledgment that the bank will repay it. § 85-3-104(2)(c). Under these code provisions a personal money order must be classified as a check. There is no other code classification of negotiable commercial paper. § 85-3-104. For the sake of clarity in the law of commercial paper this personal money order should be classified as a check.

However, the matter of classification is not nearly as important as the issue of liability. No authorized representative of appellee bank signed this check. Section 85-3-401 states: *"No person is liable on an instrument unless his signature appears thereon."* Section 85-3-409(1) states that a check or other draft is not an assignment of funds held by the drawee (appellee Union Bank) and *the drawee is not liable until it accepts the check or draft.* Appellee did not accept this instrument. It stopped payment. The language of these statutes, a part of the Uniform Commercial Code, is unmistakable.

The majority opinion holds:

> The personal money order constituted an obligation of Union from the moment of its sale and issuance.

I respectfully submit that statement is supported by absolutely no authority and it creates an unnecessary legal quagmire. Assume that a purchaser of a personal money order has not filled in the name of the payee or has not signed the check and it is lost or stolen. The purchaser then wants to stop payment before it is negotiated to a third party. The majority has stated that it was an obligation of the bank from the moment of sale and issuance. Fairness and logic dictate that the purchaser should not be allowed to stop payment and leave the bank liable. Yet, § 85-4-403(1) provides:

> Customer's right to stop payment—Burden of proof of loss. A customer may by order to his bank stop payment of any item payable for his account but the order must be received at such time and in such manner as to afford the bank a reasonable opportunity to act on it prior to any action by the bank with respect to the item described in Section 4-303.

Comment 4 to this statute makes it abundantly clear that personal money orders are intended to be covered by this broad language.

One of the three explanations given for the holding is:

> The issuance of the money order with the bank's printed name evidences the appellee's intent to be bound thereby.

That notion will echo because the name of the drawee bank is printed on every ordinary check in circulation.

The other two explanations are that banks should not be allowed to stop payment and business custom. Both explanations are dead letters. Assume, for the sake of argument only, that banks should not be allowed to stop payment. That occurrence takes place after the sale and issuance of the instrument. The majority has held that liability attached upon issuance. Therefore this subsequent event logically cannot have any effect on liability. It very simply is not a reason for a decision that liability attached at the time of issuance. Business custom is not proven. There is not one single word in the transcript or abstract about business custom. Even if this defense had been proven it would be an estoppel defense, or a defense which accrues after the sale and, once again, it would not be a reason for a decision that liability attached at the time of issuance.

The master purpose of the Uniform Commercial Code is to clarify the law governing commercial transactions. The tragedy of this case is that both the purpose and the Code are emaciated for no reason.

I dissent.

NOTE

See U.C.C. § 3-104(f) and Comment 4.

PROBLEM 13.7

In March, plaintiff sold and delivered cement to Marshfield Sand and Gravel, Inc. ("Marshfield") and was paid by checks drawn on Marshfield's account with the Bank. Each check bore the legend "Payable at South Shore Multi-bank, Quincy, Ma." In early April plaintiff received a check for $44,166.75 as full payment for the March delivery to Marshfield. The check was deposited but returned, marked "insufficient funds." Plaintiff received Marshfield's assurances that sufficient funds existed to cover the check but was unable to verify this statement with the bank. Plaintiff redeposited the check and it was again returned. Plaintiff then spoke with an officer of the Bank and was told that Marshfield had sufficient funds but the Bank would not pay plaintiff due to an agreement among all of Marshfield's creditors. Although plaintiff claimed not to be a party to the alleged agreement, the Bank refused to honor the check. Plaintiff subsequently made futile demands for immediate payment on Marshfield and the Bank. Marshfield ceased doing business in early May and on May 26 was forced into involuntary bankruptcy.

Plaintiff claims that it was harmed by the Bank's refusal to honor the check drawn on Marshfield's account and it therefore has a cause of action against the Bank for the face value of the check. What are the rights of plaintiff against the Bank?

[B] In Tort

Read: U.C.C. § 3-420, see § 3-206(c)-(f).

FIRST NATIONAL BANK OF COMMERCE v. ANDERSON FORD-LINCOLN-MERCURY INC.

Texas Court of Appeals
704 S.W.2d 83, 42 U.C.C. Rep. 1684 (1985)

First National Bank of Commerce, Texas appeals from a judgment holding it liable for breach of contract, negligence, and conversion. Because we hold that the jury could have properly found the bank to be negligent, we affirm the trial court's judgment. However, we must remand the case for a determination of the amount of attorney's fees which can be recovered.

Jerry McKnight, a defendant below against whom a default judgment was entered, visited the bank and informed a vice-president that he planned to purchase a new truck. The next day

McKnight represented to Anderson Ford that the bank had agreed to loan him the money to buy the truck. An Anderson Ford employee testified that he phoned the bank vice-president who told the Anderson Ford employee "draft on me for $ 13,000.00," the truck's list price. However, the bank never signed a written draft. Anderson Ford delivered the truck to McKnight and issued a refund check to him for $ 1,577.00, a manufacturer's rebate. The following day the bank vice-president phoned Anderson Ford and stated that there had been a mistake and that the bank would not finance McKnight's truck purchase. Anderson Ford twice submitted a draft to the bank which the bank refused to honor.

In four points of error, the bank contends: that no enforceable contract existed between Anderson Ford and the bank; that because the bank owed no legal duty to Anderson Ford, the bank was not negligent; that the bank did not convert the truck by retaining the certificate of title; and that Anderson Ford was not entitled to an award of attorneys' fees. We hold that the jury could have properly found the bank negligent; therefore, we affirm the judgment of the trial court.

In its second point of error the bank alleges that under Tex. Bus. & Com. Code Ann. § 3.409(a) and 3.410 (Vernon 1968), it had an absolute right to dishonor the draft before written acceptance; consequently, it owed no legal duty to Anderson Ford in issuing oral drafting instructions. The bank did not become contractually liable on the draft because it did not accept the draft in writing. However, this does not preclude the bank's tort liability for its oral drafting instructions. Tex. Bus. & Com. Code Ann. § 3.409(b) (Vernon 1968) provides:

> (b) Nothing in this section shall affect any liability in contract, tort or otherwise arising from any letter of credit or other obligation or representation which is not an acceptance.

Comment 3 to this section states that a drawee who fails to accept an item may be liable in tort because of his representation that he has accepted or that he intends to accept the item. Thus, § 3.409(a) does not preclude the bank's possible liability for negligence in issuing oral drafting instructions.

The issue then becomes what duty, if any, did the bank owe to Anderson Ford when it issued the drafting instructions over the telephone. Tex. Bus. & Com. Code Ann. § 4.103 (Vernon 1968) states that a drawee bank has a duty "to exercise ordinary care" in handling items. Thus, the bank was under a legal duty to exercise ordinary care in issuing oral drafting instructions.

There are no Texas cases directly on point. In *Galaxy Boat Mfg. Co. v. East End State Bank*, 641 S.W.2d 584 (Tex. App.-Houston [14th Dist.] 1982, no writ), the court held that because a drawee bank is not liable on a check until it accepts the check in writing, the bank was not liable to the payee for obeying its customer's oral order to stop payment on a check. However, the Houston court expressly noted that there was no evidence of any representation by the bank upon which the manufacturing company could have relied.

In the instant case the jury specifically found that the bank made representations indicating to Anderson Ford an intent to accept the draft, including the oral instruction to "draft on me for $ 13,000.00." The jury further found Anderson Ford was not contributorily negligent.

Moreover, there are cases from other states decided under the Uniform Commercial Code which uphold a drawee's liability for negligence under § 3.409(b). In *Carroll v. Twin City Pontiac Used Cars*, Inc., 397 So.2d 42 (La. App.-2nd Circuit, 1981) where the drawee bank breached an oral promise to honor a draft for partial payment of the purchase price of an automobile, the court found that, although the bank was not liable on the instrument, the bank was negligent in failing to exercise ordinary care in handling the item.

In *Peoples Bank in North Fort Myers v. Bob Lincoln, Inc.*, 283 So.2d 400 (Fla. Dist. Ct. App. 1973) a bank orally informed a car dealer that a car purchaser's check would be honored, and the car dealer delivered the vehicle to the purchaser. A few days later, the bank dishonored the check. The Florida court held that, while the bank was not liable on the instrument, it was liable for negligence.

Tex. Bus. & Com. Code Ann. § 1.102(2)(c) states that one of the underlying purposes of the act is to make the law uniform among the various jurisdictions. The Louisiana and Florida statutes are identical to Tex. Bus. & Com. Code Ann. § 3.409(b) (Vernon 1968). We agree with their interpretation of § 3.409(b). While the bank was not liable on the draft, it was legally proper for the jury to find it liable for negligence.

. . ..

Because the bank owed a legal duty of ordinary care to Anderson Ford in issuing oral drafting instructions, the jury could properly have found the bank liable for negligence. Accordingly, we affirm the judgment of the trial court and remand the cause for a determination of what amount of attorney's fees are recoverable.

Affirmed.

GREAT AMERICAN INSURANCE COMPANIES v. AMERICAN STATE BANK OF DICKINSON

North Dakota Supreme Court
385 N.W.2d 460, 1 U.C.C. Rep. 2d 498 (1986)

LEVINE, JUSTICE.

American State Bank of Dickinson [American State Bank] appeals from a district court judgment in favor of Great American Insurance Companies [Great American] for conversion of a "payable through"[26] draft which Welch Rathole Service [Welch] deposited in its account at American State Bank without the endorsement of a joint payee, Ford Motor Credit Company [Ford Credit]. We reverse and remand for further proceedings.

Great American insured a truck owned by Welch and financed by Ford Credit. That insurance policy listed Welch and Ford Credit as loss payees for claims on the truck. The truck was involved in an accident, and Great American issued a $ 13,000 "payable through" draft, dated May 20,

[26] Section 41-03-20 [U.C.C. § 3-120], N.D.C.C., defines a "payable through" draft and provides:

41-03-20. (3-120) Instruments "payable through" bank. An instrument which states that it is "payable through" a bank or the like designates that bank as a collecting bank to make presentment but does not of itself authorize the bank to pay the instrument.

The drawer of a "payable through" draft is also the drawee. See Murray, *Drafts Payable Through Banks*, 77 Commercial L.J. 389 (1972) for a discussion of the use of payable through drafts. [See U.C.C. § 4-106(a).—Ed.]

1982, for the claim. The draft was made payable to the order of Welch and Ford Credit, and Great American delivered it to Welch. Ford Credit's interest in the draft was $9,712.08, and Welch's interest was $3,287.92. Welch endorsed and deposited the draft in its account at American State Bank without the endorsement of Ford Credit. On May 27, 1982, American State Bank endorsed the draft, credited Welch's account in the amount of $ 13,000, and forwarded the draft through banking channels to Great American's Bank, Provident, for payment. Provident presented the draft to Great American, and on June 3, 1982, an employee of Great American reviewed and initialed the draft in accordance with its procedure with Provident for paying payable through drafts.

Great American took possession of the truck and sold it for salvage to George Franchuk for $3,000. In December 1982, Franchuk informed Great American that Ford Credit would not release its lien on the truck because it had not been paid for its interest in the truck. Welch had filed for bankruptcy on November 5, 1982, and, in order to obtain clear title for Franchuk, Great American paid Ford Credit $9,712.08 for a release on its lien. On March 30, 1983, Ford Credit assigned Great American all its interest and rights arising out of the May 20 payable through draft.

Great American, as Ford Credit's assignee, commenced an action against American State Bank alleging that it converted the May 20 draft and that it breached its presentment warranties. Great American subsequently moved to dismiss its cause of action based on breach of presentment warranties and proceeded solely on the claim for conversion. After a bench trial, the court granted judgment against American State Bank for $9,712.08 plus interest, and costs and disbursements of $1,808.39. American State Bank appealed.

American State Bank contends that its failure to obtain the endorsement of a co-payee of a negotiable instrument does not constitute conversion under the Uniform Commercial Code [U.C.C.] because § 41-03-56(1) [U.C.C. § 3-419(1)], N.D.C.C., refers only to a forged endorsement and not a missing endorsement in defining conversion. American State Bank points out that there is no common law in North Dakota where the law is declared by statute, § 1-01-06, N.D.C.C., and that the U.C.C. may be supplemented by common law "unless displaced by the particular provisions of this title." Section 41-01-03 [U.C.C. § 1-103], N.D.C.C. American State Bank argues that § 41-03-56(1) [U.C.C. § 3-419(1)], N.D.C.C., displaces the common law for conversion of negotiable instruments in North Dakota, and it is thus not liable for conversion.

Great American counters that a collecting bank that pays a draft without the endorsement of a joint payee is liable to that joint payee for conversion under common law and also under the U.C.C. because the general principles of common law supplement the U.C.C. Section 41-01-03 [U.C.C. § 1-103], N.D.C.C. We agree.

We are not persuaded by American State Bank's argument because the particular language of § 41-01-03 [U.C.C. § 1-103], N.D.C.C., permitting common law supplementation of the U.C.C., controls the general language of § 1-01-06, N.D.C.C. See § 1-01-07, N.D.C.C. We do not believe that the common law of conversion has been displaced by the particular provisions of the U.C.C.

Although § 41-03-56(1) [U.C.C. § 3-419(1)], N.D.C.C., does not specifically provide that payment without the endorsement of a payee constitutes conversion, we agree with those jurisdictions which have supplemented the U.C.C. with common law and determined that, for purposes of conversion of a negotiable instrument, there is "no legal difference between payment of an instrument on a forged endorsement and payment on no endorsement by the payee at all."

E.g. Humberto Decorators, The. v. Plaza National Bank, 180 N.J. Super. 170, 434 A.2d 618, 619 (1981). See generally Annot., 47 A.L.R.3d 537, 540 (1973); 6 Anderson, Uniform Commercial Code § 3-419:18 (3rd Ed.).

Conversion is the wrongful exercise of dominion over the property of another in a manner inconsistent with, or in defiance of, the owner's right. We believe that payment of an instrument on a forged endorsement and payment on no endorsement by the payee both constitute the wrongful exercise of dominion over the property of another in a manner inconsistent with the owner's rights. In our view, the absence of an endorsement presents a more compelling case for conversion than a forged endorsement because a missing endorsement is easily discernible, while a forged endorsement is the result of an error in the identification of a payee. Accordingly, we hold that a bank that pays a draft without obtaining the endorsement of a co-payee may be liable to that co-payee for conversion of the draft.

Section 41-03-56(3) [U.C.C. § 3-419(3)], N.D.C.C., provides the following defense for conversion actions:

> 41-03-56. (3-419) Conversion of instrument-Innocent representative.
>
> 3. Subject to the provisions of this title concerning restrictive endorsements a representative, including a depositary or collecting bank, who has in good faith and in accordance with the reasonable commercial standards applicable to the business of such representative dealt with an instrument or its proceeds on behalf of one who was not the true owner is not liable in conversion or otherwise to the true owner beyond the amount of any proceeds remaining in his hands.

On appeal, American State Bank characterizes its conduct in accepting the draft without Ford Credit's endorsement as a "mistake." An employee of American State Bank testified that its paying the draft without Ford Credit's endorsement was not in accordance with reasonable commercial standards, and the trial court's memorandum opinion states that "American State has acknowledged that accepting the draft with a missing endorsement is not in accordance with reasonable commercial banking standards." We agree. Consequently, American State Bank may not avail itself of the defense provided in Section 41-03-56(3) [U.C.C. § 3-419(3)], N.D.C.C.

American State Bank asserts that several statutory provisions of the U.C.C. preclude its liability. The trial court ruled to the contrary. Our analysis is based upon the U.C.C. statutory scheme of liability for negotiable instruments.

The U.C.C. provides three theories of liability for negotiable instruments: (1) contract liability, (2) warranty liability, and (3) conversion liability. White & Summers, Uniform Commercial Code §§ 13-6, 13-11, 15-4(2nd Ed. 1980); Hillman, McDonnell, Nickles, Common Law and Equity Under the Uniform Commercial Code, ¶ 14.01[2] (1985).

The contractual liabilities on the instrument run against those who sign the instrument and are generally set out in §§ 41-03-50 [U.C.C. § 3-413] and 41-03-51 [U.C.C. § 3-414], N.D.C.C. An endorser's liability on the instrument is based on § 41-03-51 [U.C.C. § 3-414], N.D.C.C., and requires presentment, dishonor, and notice of dishonor before imposition of contractual liability through the recredit of an account and charge-back.[27]

In addition to contractual liability on the instrument, the transferor of an instrument makes certain presentment warranties to its transferee and a collecting bank makes those warranties

[27] The requirements for presentment, dishonor, and notice of dishonor are set forth in Sections 41-03-57 through 67 [U.C.C. §§ 3-501 through 3-511], N.D.C.C.

to the payor bank or other payor. Sections 41-03-57 [U.C.C. § 3-417] and 41-04-17 [U.C.C. § 4-207], N.D.C.C.[28] Although the contractual liability of an endorser of an instrument may be discharged by failure to make a proper presentment, to dishonor, or to give timely notice of dishonor; or because payment is final under § 41-03-55 [U.C.C. § 3-418][29] and 41-04-23 [U.C.C. § 4-213], N.D.C.C., a party in the collection chain may still be liable on the basis of a breach of one or more of the presentment warranties. White & Summers, Uniform Commercial Code, § 16-1(2nd Ed. 1980); 7 Anderson, Uniform Commercial Code, § 4-207:13 (3rd Ed. 1985); § 41-04-26 [U.C.C. § 4-302], N.D.C.C.; § 41-04-22(5) [U.C.C. § 4-212(5)], N.D.C.C.

In addition to contract liability and warranty liability, conversion liability is also available to the "owner" of an instrument. White and Summers, Uniform Commercial Code, § 15-4 (2nd Ed. 1980).

These theories of liability form the basis for according separate treatment for a forged drawer's signature and a forged endorsement in the ordinary check collection case where the drawer and drawee are different parties. Generally, a drawee bank is liable to its drawer customer for payment of a draft bearing either a forged drawer's signature or a forged endorsement. The drawee bank's liability may be limited by § 41-04-33 [U.C.C. § 4-406], N.D.C.C., which requires the drawer customer to exercise reasonable care and promptness to examine his bank statement and items to discover and notify the drawee bank of any unauthorized signatures or endorsements or alterations. In the case of a forged endorsement, the drawee generally may pass liability back up the collection chain to the party who took from the forger and, of course, to the forger himself, if available. See generally, White and Summers, Uniform Commercial Code, ch. 15(2nd Ed. 1980); *see also National Credit Union Administration v. Michigan National Bank*, 771 F.2d 154 [41 U.C.C. Rep Serv 1573] (6th Cir. 1985); *Perini Corp. v. First National Bank*, 553 F.2d 398 (5th Cir. 1977). In this respect, the U.C.C. treats a missing endorsement and a forged endorsement the same. See generally Murray, *Joint Payee Checks—Forged and Missing Indorsements*, 78 Commercial L. J. 393 (1973). In the case of a forged drawer's signature, however, liability generally rests with the drawee because the drawee will almost never have a warranty cause of action and the final payment rule will also bar a restitutionary cause of action. See generally, White and Summers, Uniform Commercial Code, ch. I 6(2nd Ed. 1980); See also *National Credit Union Administration v. Michigan National Bank, supra; Perini Corp. v. First National Bank, supra*.

In the instant case, Great American is both the drawer and drawee of the "payable through" draft. See fn. 1. Ford Credit assigned all of its interest and rights arising out of the May 20 draft to Great American. The trial court noted that:

> Ford Credit could have brought an action against either American State or Great American for conversion under NDCC Section 41-03-56 (3-419) or against Great American on the underlying obligation. Great American would have then been forced to proceed against

[28] The warranties of§ 41-04-17 [U.C.C. § 4-207], N.D.C.C., are given by bank customers and collecting banks and pertain directly to the check collection process. The warranties given by the customer or collecting bank to the payor bank or other payor are that the customer or collecting bank has good title to the item; that he has no knowledge that the signature of the drawer is unauthorized; and that the item has not been materially altered. U.C.C. § 4-207(1). The warranties of § 41-03-57 [U.C.C. § 3-417], N.D.C.C., are given by any person who obtains payment or acceptance and any prior transferor and are similar to those warranties given by a customer or collecting bank under U.C.C. § 4-207.

[29] The final payment rule of § 41-03-55 [U.C.C. § 3-418], N.D.C.C., is by its terms, not applicable to breach of warranty on presentment under § 41-03-54 [U.C.C. § 3-417], N.D.C.C.

American State for breach of its warranties. Instead, Great American paid Ford Credit and obtained an assignment of its cause of action. Although Great American had set forth an action for breach of warranties, it amended the Complaint and proceeded only on the assignment.

We agree with the trial court's assessment. Under the full range of potential theories of liability and parties available under the U.C.C., Ford Credit could have brought an action against either American State Bank or Great American for conversion under § 41-03-56 [U.C.C. § 3-419], N.D.C.C., or against Great American on its obligation under the insurance contract. If Ford Credit had proceeded directly against Great American, Great American, as drawee, could have brought an action for indemnity against American State Bank, as collecting bank, for breach of the presentment warranties and, pursuant to § 41-04-17(4) [U.C.C. § 4-207(4)], N.D. C. C., American State Bank could have asserted that its liability was discharged to the extent of any loss caused by the delay in making the claim. If Ford Credit had proceeded directly against American State Bank for conversion, we believe American State Bank could have asserted against Great American that its (American State Bank's) liability was discharged to the extent of any loss caused because Great American did not make a claim for breach of warranty within a reasonable time after Great American learned of the breach pursuant to § 41-04-17(4) [U.C.C. § 4-207(4)], N.D.C.C. Although Great American, as Ford Credit's assignee, brought the instant action for conversion and not for breach of the presentment warranties, we do not believe that assignment precludes American State Bank from asserting that its liability was limited under the provisions of § 41-04-17(4) [U.C.C. § 4-207(4)], N.D.C.C. See *Sun 'N Sand, Inc. v. United California Bank*, 21 Cal. 3d 671, 148 Cal.Rptr. 329, 582 P.2d 920(1978). That section provides:

> 4. Unless a claim for breach of warranty under this section is made within a reasonable time after the person claiming learns of the breach, the person liable is discharged to the extent of any loss caused by the delay in making claim.

American State Bank argues that the date when Great American's employee initialed the check, June 3, 1982, should be used as the date when Great American learned of the breach under § 41-04-17(4) [U.C.C. § 4-207(4)], N.D.C.C. Because Welch's account had sufficient funds to cover the draft on June 4, 1982, American State Bank contends that it should be discharged from any liability.

Our research has revealed no cases specifically addressing this issue within the context of a "payable through" draft paid over a missing endorsement.

The objective of the U.C.C. statutory scheme for check collections, and particularly the warranty provisions, is to place the loss on the wrongdoer, or because the wrongdoer is usually unavailable or unable to pay, upon the party who last dealt with the wrongdoer because that party is in the best position to verify and obtain the necessary endorsements. The policy behind the U.C.C. warranty provisions is to speed up the collection process and to remove the burden from every bank in the collection chain to meticulously check the endorsements of each item transferred, and, thus, the first bank taking an item for collection is primarily responsible for obtaining the necessary endorsements. *Federal Deposit Insurance Corp. v. Marine National Bank of Jacksonville*, 303 F.Supp. 401 (M.D. Fla. 1969). See generally Murray, *Joint Payee Checks-Forged and Missing Indorsements*, 78 Commercial L. J. 393 (1973). Thus, a drawee bank that pays an item over a missing endorsement is generally not obligated to discover that missing endorsement. *Federal Deposit Insurance Corp. v. Marine National Bank of Jacksonville, supra*; see generally Murray, *Joint Payee Checks-Forged and Missing Indorsements*, 78 Commercial L. J. 393 (1973). Consequently, in the usual check collection case involving a drawer customer and a drawee bank, a drawee bank does not "learn of the breach" within the meaning of § 41-04-17(4) [U.C.C. § 4-207(4)], N.D.C.C., when it pays an item over a missing endorsement. Additionally, in the usual check collection case, the drawer customer has certain responsibilities with regard to checking his banking statement and items for alterations or unauthorized signatures or endorsements. Section 41-04-33 [U.C.C. § 4-406], N.D.C.C.

However, the instant case involves a payable through draft in which the drawer and drawee are the same entity, and that entity is not a bank. That entity initially issued the joint payee draft and was in a position to check the draft for the necessary endorsements before paying it. See Murray, *Drafts "Payable Through" Banks*, 77 Commercial L. J. 389 (1972). Professor Murray suggests that a drawer-drawee insurance company is more able to detect a forged payee's signature on a draft by comparing the signature on the draft with the insured's signature on an insurance application form or claim form. *Id.* at 390. We need not go so far. The instant case involves a missing endorsement which is easily discernible from the face of the instrument and requires no such comparison. In such a case, a breach of presentment warranties is evident from the face of the instrument. Both logic and equity militate in favor of imposing primary responsibility on the drawer-drawee to check the very draft which it issued in the first place to the "forger."

Taking into account that, in the usual check collection case, the drawer customer has certain responsibilities for checking his statement and items and that, in the instant case, the drawer and drawee are one and the same and in a position to check the draft for missing endorsements, we believe that June 3, 1982, was the date when Great American learned, or should have learned, of the missing endorsement and the consequent breach of the presentment warranties pursuant to Section 41-04-17(4) [U.C.C. § 4-207(4)], N.D.C.C. Accordingly, we conclude that for purposes of a payable through draft with missing endorsements, the party claiming a breach of presentment warranties "learns of the breach" within the meaning of Section 41-04-17(4) [U.C.C. § 4-207(4)], N.D.C.C., when it approves the draft for payment.

In the instant case, the trial court made no finding on what was a reasonable time after Great American learned of the breach and, if a claim were not made within that time, the extent of any loss caused by the delay in making a claim.[30] Findings on these matters are necessary for a resolution of this issue and may require additional evidence on the balance in Welch's account on certain dates. Accordingly, we reverse the judgment and remand the case for further proceedings consistent with this opinion.[31]

---

30 We reject American State's argument that June 4,1982, was the appropriate date for determining the extent of loss because that would impose a stricter requirement on Great American than that provided by the midnight deadline. Section 41-04-04(1)(h) [U.C.C. § 4-104(1)(h)], N.D.C.C.

31 The other U.C.C. provisions raised by American State Bank relating to final payment, presentment, dishonor, notice of dishonor, and discharge would be applicable to a contract action but are not applicable to an action for conversion and would not preclude an action for breach of presentment warranties.

American State Bank also contends that the trial court erred in determining that laches and waiver were not applicable to this case. These issues involve the same argument as that made under § 41-04-17(4) [U.C.C. § 4-207(4)], N.D.C.C. Because of our resolution of that issue, we need not address American State Bank's argument concerning laches and waiver.

NOTE AND QUESTIONS

(1) On which of the theories of liability does the court base its decision?

(2) To the effect that a check paid over a missing indorsement is treated the same as a check paid on a forged indorsement for purposes of conversion under former U.C.C. § 3-419(1)(c), *see Boyer v. First National Bank of Kokomo, Indiana*, 476 N.E.2d 895, 40 U.C.C. Rep. 1745 (Ind. App. 1985). See U.C.C. § 3-420(a) and Comment 1.

FIRST NATIONAL BANK OF ALAMOSA v. FORD MOTOR CREDIT CO.

United States District Court, D. Colorado
748 F. Supp. 1464 (1990)

[The facts and first part of the opinion appear in § 13.09 [A], *supra*.]

2. Second Claim for Relief—Negligence.

In claiming that Ford is liable on a negligence theory, the Bank asserts that Ford has carelessly designed form instrument with the words "Ford Motor Credit Company" and "SIGHT DRAFT" prominently displayed thereon and allowed those instruments to circulate in the commercial banking system. Thus, argues the Bank, Ford has confused depositary banks and misled them into thinking that the instruments were backed up by Ford and would always be honored by Ford. Ford never told the Bank "that the drafts might not be honored by" Ford or that Ford "did not consider the drafts to be drawn by [Ford] or against [Ford] funds." *Complaint* ¶¶ 18, 19.

The Bank's negligence claim must fail, because Ford did not owe the Bank or anyone else a general duty to refrain from preparing and using instruments such as the nine at issue here. There is nothing confusing or misleading about the words "SIGHT DRAFT." "Sight drafts" and drafts "payable through" collecting banks are expressly recognized by the U.C.C., discussed in numerous court decisions, and used regularly in commerce. The significance of the term "sight" has been explained as follows: "Commercial parlance often uses the rather inexact terms of 'sight draft' versus 'time draft.' *Both terms refer to the maturity date of the draft:* A sight draft is payable on demand while a time draft is payable a certain time after acceptance by the drawee or after 'sight' ". B. Clark, The Law of Bank Deposits, Collections and Credit Cards ¶ 7.1[1] at 7-2 (1981) (emphasis supplied). *Accord*, U.C.C. § 3-108; Colo.Rev.Stat. § 4-3-108 (1973) (sight drafts are "instruments payable on demand"). Ford's evidence demonstrates (and the Bank does not dispute) that the sight draft system is widely used in the automobile industry. The reported cases also suggest that sight drafts are commonly used in other industries. *See, e.g., Drummond v. Hales*, 191 F.2d 972 (10th Cir.1951) (sight drafts used in cattle industry) (pre-U.C.C. case); *First Nat'l Bank of Dodge City v. Perschbacher*, 335 F.2d 442 (10th Cir.1964) (sight drafts used in cattle industry) (no liability for drawee absent "consent"—or "acceptance," to use U.C.C. terminology).

Similarly, the use of Ford's name on the drafts is not confusing or misleading; indeed, it would have been confusing had Ford's name not appeared on the drafts. The words, "TO Ford Motor Credit Company," clearly name Ford as the drawee and thus identify for holders of the drafts the person to whom they must be presented. As previously noted, there is no general drawee liability where the drawee has neither accepted nor signed the instrument. If the Bank was confused or misled by the drafts, it was because of its own misunderstanding of the nature of these instruments. Ford is thus entitled to judgment on the negligence claim.

§ 13.10 Liability of Guarantors and Accommodation Parties

Read: U.C.C. §§ 3-419, 3-605; see § 3-116, 3-305(d).

Until the 1960's most law schools offered a course in "Credit" or "Secured" Transactions. These courses would usually examine the three types of collateral or security available to lenders: real property, personal property and the person. Real property security consisted primarily of the study of mortgages, personal property security consisted of examining a variety of statutes dealing with conceptually different types of personal property used for financing. (*See* Note to U.C.C. § 9-102.) Use of the person as security led to an examination of the law of Suretyship.

As real property financing became more sophisticated and with the enactment of U.C.C. Article 9 relating to personal property financing, the consolidated courses disappeared from the curriculum and real and personal property security were taught in separate courses. Where did that leave Suretyship? With the exception of those instances where the person became a surety on a negotiable instrument, the answer to the question is nowhere? *See* Introduction to Permanent Editorial Board Commentary No. 11, Suretyship Issues Under Sections 3-116, 3-305, 3-415, 3-419, and 3-605 (1994).

Students are often distressed to learn that an accommodation party may appear on a negotiable instrument in any capacity. Too often they assume that one who signs as an accommodation party simply indorses or co-signs the note. The cases indicate, however, a variation in fact pattern. Sometimes the facts must be litigated in order to determine which party accommodated whom. The student should, however, appreciate the necessity of being able to recognize the suretyship relationship underlying the liability of the parties.

> Suretyship is the relation which exists where one person has undertaken an obligation and another person is also under an obligation or other duty to the obligee, who is entitled to but one performance, and as between the two who are bound, one rather than the other should perform.[32]

This definition of the surety relationship can be better stated in terms of the basic parties involved in the multiparty relationship. If *P* is the principal debtor, S is the surety who obligates himself to the obligation, and *C* is the creditor to whom the obligation is due. Assuming further that the obligation is a money obligation (which covers those obligations to be found in negotiable

[32] Restatement of Security § 82 (1941).

instruments), then suretyship can be defined as that relationship which exists where *P* and *S* are both bound to pay *C*, but as between *P* and *S*, *P* rather than S ought to pay. The key to the relationship is the fact that *S* must pay *C*, but can ultimately recover against *P*. However, *P* and *S* are severally bound to pay *C*.

It is possible to classify sureties in terms of the promise which *S* makes to *C*. If *S* makes the same promise as *P*, then S's liability is unconditional. If *S* makes the promise to pay if *P* does not, then *S*'s promise is sometimes termed secondary. The latter promise is sometimes unfortunately referred to as that of a "guarantor."[33] This terminology can be confused with U.C.C. terminology. Under former U.C.C. § 3-416 (1) and (2) a distinction was made between a guarantor of payment and a guarantor of collection. The term "guarantor of payment" meant that the signer ensured that if the instrument was not paid when due, the guarantor would pay it according to its tenor, without resort by the holder to any other party. This was similar to the liability of a maker. Collection guaranteed indicated that if not paid when due, the guarantor would pay, but only after the holder's claim against the maker or acceptor had been reduced to judgment and execution had been returned unsatisfied, or the maker or acceptor had become insolvent or it was otherwise apparent that it was useless to proceed against him. Under U.C.C. 3-419(d) the substance to the liability of the guarantor of collection is retained. However, former U.C.C. § 3-416(1) regarding the contract of the guarantor of payment is omitted from the new Article 3. From this follows the thought that any *unqualified* indorser is basically a "guarantor of payment." (UCC § 3-415) Thus, an indorser who adds the words "payment guaranteed" or the like to the instrument has the same liability as an indorser who adds no special words, and may be entitled, *inter alia*, to notice of dishonor under § 3-503. *See* PEB Commentary No. 11, Issue 5, and the revision of Comment 4 to 3-419.

This discussion does not preclude the possibility that the parties *P*, *S*, and *C* may be multiple. That is, *A* and *B* might be principal co-obligors, with S1 and S2 as co-sureties on an obligation running in favor of *C-1* and *C-2* as co-creditors.

Under basic suretyship law, the consideration which supports *P*'s promise to pay *C* will also support *S*'s promise to pay *C*. The promise of the surety must be in writing. On a negotiable instrument, a simple signature or indorsement will be a sufficient writing. In negotiable instruments terms, a surety becomes an accommodation party and the principal becomes the accommodated party. The surety test is, as mentioned, the test of who ought to pay. The test of the accommodation party is the test of who (accommodation party) has lent his name or credit for the benefit of whom (accommodated party). For clarity's sake, in the materials that follow, the following indicates the suretyship symbolism:

Principal]
Accommodated Party] *P*

C Creditor

Surety]
Accommodation] *S*
Party

There are a number of basic principles associated with the surety relationship. These principles involve the surety's remedies and the surety's defenses. How these principles operate in the context of Article 3 of the U.C.C. is treated in this section. Most of these principles are reflected in the underlying law of Suretyship, but most, are also dealt with, to some extent, in Article 3.

---

[33] *See* Simpson on Suretyship §§ 3-6 (West 1950).

Several of these rights are the rights of the surety against the principal.

Reimbursement: Reimbursement is the surety's right to have the principal pay the surety in the event that the surety pays the creditor. This right is based upon an implied promise of the principal. Where the principal obtains a surety, the law implies a promise made by the principal to reimburse the surety. This promise is implied irrespective of any express recognition of this surety's right. *See* U.C.C. § 3-419(e).

Subrogation: Probably the most potent weapon in the surety's arsenal directed at the principal is the right of subrogation. As between *P* and *S, P* ought to pay. Where *S* does pay, the surety is treated is as an assignee of the creditor's rights against P. This means, as it is often said, that a paying surety will be able to stand in the shoes of the creditor and exercise the creditor's remedies. These subrogation remedies are many. The surety may utilize any security held by the creditor and he may even assume the creditor's favored position in insolvency proceedings or before a trustee in bankruptcy of the principal. Notice that the right of subrogation arises out of the nature of the suretyship relationship and therefore is exercisable irrespective of any right of reimbursement. *See* U.C.C. § 3-419(e).

Exoneration: Exoneration is a very limited right of the surety to compel the principal to pay in order to save harmless the surety. Exoneration cannot be used by the surety as a defense against the creditor. The right of exoneration follows from the principal's duty of payment. A few states have statutes that require a creditor to first pursue a principal debtor before seeking payment from a surety. Although not a part of Article 3, they may apply to accommodation parties under the Code. A few states also follow the rule of *Pain v. Packard*, 13 Johns R. 176 (N.Y. Sup. Ct. 1816) which requires the creditor to use diligence in his efforts to collect first from the principal debtor before proceeding against the surety.

In addition to these rights, a surety may have against the principal, a surety may also have a right to *Contribution* from co-sureties. It is not uncommon for an instrument to be signed by two or more persons as accommodation parties. Usually they all sign in the same capacity and each is jointly and severally liable to the creditor. When the creditor collects from one who pays the amount of the instrument, this right of contribution comes into play and sureties are generally liable to one another for a proportionate share of the debt.

Defenses: Certain "suretyship defenses" are recognized which are based upon the general notion that the surety will be or should be discharged from his obligation to the creditor if the creditor should unilaterally increase the surety's risk. It is often said that the surety is a favorite of the law inasmuch as his promise is unsupported by consideration flowing to him. (The law has been somewhat less favoring of the modern compensated or professional surety.) Thus, generally it had been held that the surety was discharged by (a) a release of the principal, (b) a binding extension of time granted to the principal, (c) a modification of the principal's contract, or (d) a surrender or impairment of collateral or security held by the creditor. As we will see, there have been some substantial changes to Article 3 with respect to all four of these matters.

After this brief introduction to the law of suretyship, coupled with our primitive thoughts about the maker's and indorser's liability as discussed, *supra*, it should be evident that problems will be created where a surety and a principal appear as parties on a negotiable instrument. It might not be too bad if the principal appeared as a maker and the surety as a "surety," but this is not the way that commercial usage does it. Assume Principal wishes to borrow money from Creditor and Surety is to lend his name and credit to that of Principal. The obligation may appear on a negotiable note (and to use the example of a bill of exchange would be to multiply the possibilities) in any one of the following ways:

(1) Principal signs as maker of a note payable to Creditor and Surety indorses on the back. (Surety would then be an anomalous or irregular indorser because be would not be in the chain of title.)

(2) Principal and Surety could sign as co-makers payable to Creditor.

(3) Surety could sign as maker payable to Principal who would indorse payable to Creditor.

(4) Principal could sign as maker payable to Surety who would indorse to Creditor.

(5) Surety could sign as maker payable to Creditor with Principal signing on back (or not appearing on the note at all).

(6) Surety could sign payable to Principal and Principal would endorse on back to Creditor at the same time a Co-surety also signed on back.

Keeping this in mind, how do we determine if we are dealing with an "accommodation party?"

IN RE ROBINSON BROTHERS DRILLING, INC.

United States Court of Appeals
9 F.3d 871, 22 U.C.C. Rep. 2d 291 (10th Cir. 1993)

LOGAN, CIRCUIT JUDGE.

ABB Vecto-Gray, Inc. (ABB) appeals from a district court order affirming a judgment of the bankruptcy court which held that certain prepetition payments made to ABB were voidable preferences under 11 U.S.C. § 547(b). The Trustee recovered the payments pursuant to 11 U.S.C. § 550(a). On appeal from the district court's order, we review the bankruptcy court's factual findings for clear error and its legal determinations de novo, *see Clark v. Valley Federal Sav. & Loan Ass'n (In re Reliance Equities, Inc.)*, 966 F.2d 1338, 1340 (10th Cir. 1992), and reverse for the reasons explained below.

I

In January 1983, debtors and debtors' president, J.D. Holdges, jointly executed a note payable to ABB. In return for the note, and an additional cash payment from debtors, ABB dismissed a lawsuit then pending against both parties. Debtors made two payments on the note, totaling less than half of its face amount, before commencement in July 1983 of an involuntary Chapter 7 proceeding, later converted to Chapter 11. Because these payments were made more than ninety days but less than one year before the bankruptcy filing, the Trustee brought this adversary proceeding to set them aside under § 547(b)(4)(B). That section permits avoidance of preferential transfers within this time frame if the creditor benefited was an insider. Although ABB was an outsider, the Trustee alleged that debtors' obligation to ABB had been guaranteed by Hodges, an insider, when he co-made the note. On a prior appeal, we held that if Hodges served as guarantor or surety for an obligation on which debtors made prepetition payment, he could fulfill the role of benefited insider-creditor required by the statute. *See Manufacturers Leasing Corp. v. Lowrey (In re Robinson Bros. Drilling, Inc.)*, 892 F.2d 850 (10th Cir. 1989) (adopting opinion in *Lowrey v. First Nat'l Bank (In re Robinson Bros. Drilling, Inc.)*, 97 B.R. 77(W.D. Okla. 1988).

Following that earlier decision, the parties' dispute focused upon the proper characterization of Hodges' legal status with respect to the obligation owed to ABB and, thus, the nature of his relationship to debtors. In order to avoid a preferential transfer, § 547(b)(4)(B) requires a benefit to an insider-*creditor*. Therefore, the critical issue is whether Hodges is merely a co-maker who, under the circumstances here, has no contribution claim against debtors, as ABB maintains, or, as the Trustee insists, is an accommodation maker, *i.e.*, a surety who lent his name to debtors on the note, and consequently has a subrogation/reimbursement claim against them, *see* Okla.Stat. tit. 12A, § 3-415(1), (5) (1961) (effective Jan. 1, 1963) (current version at *id.* § 3-419(a), (3) (1991)). The latter claim, even though contingent, would be sufficient to confer creditor status on Hodges for purposes of § 547(b)(4)(B) under this court's earlier decision. *See Lowrey*, 97 B.R. at 80, 82.

The issue of Hodges' status as an accommodation party raises questions of both law and fact. Initially, we must determine how Oklahoma law defines accommodation parties and distinguishes them from other co-makers or endorsers. We then apply the facts in the record to that law to determine whether the Trustee established that Hodges was an accommodation party.

II

For most of this century, Oklahoma law sharply distinguished an accommodation maker from a simple co-maker by the absence of personal benefit derived from the instrument signed for the benefit of another: "An accommodation party is one who has signed the instrument as maker, drawer, acceptor, or indorser, without receiving value therefor, and for the purpose of lending his name to some other person." Okla.Stat. tit. 48, § 76 (1951); Okla.Stat. § 11323 (1931); Pkla.Stat. § 7699 (1921); Rev.L. § 4079 (1910); *see also Unger v. Willibey*, 141 Okl. 254, 284 P. 854, 855 (1929) ("The mode of distinguishing between a principal and a surety is by inquiring whether he who claims to stand in the relation of surety did or did not derive a benefit from the contract.").

Oklahoma law in effect at the time the facts of this case occurred defined an accommodation party simply as "one who signs the instrument in any capacity for the purpose of lending his name to another party to it," Okla.Stat. tit. 12A, § 3-415(1) (1961), without any reference to the matter of benefit. The state commentary to the statute explains the omission:

> The Commercial Code provision is more concise than former 48 Okl.St.Ann. § 76, and is a little broader, for it includes one who signs as surety.
>
> The Commercial Code omits the words "without receiving value therefor." Most courts have ignored this apparent requirement, and have held that one who signs as a paid accommodation party is controlled by the provisions of the NIL [*i.e.*, the Negotiable Instruments Law, including Okla.Stat. tit. 48, § 76 (1951)].

Okla.Code Comment to § 3-415(1) (1961). Oklahoma has since adopted the revised Uniform Commercial Code (UCC) section relating to accommodation parties, which states the distinction relevant to the instant case more precisely:

> If an instrument is issued for value given for the benefit of a party to the instrument ("accommodated party") and another party to the instrument ("accommodated party") signs

> the instrument for the purpose of incurring liability on the instrument *without being a direct beneficiary of the value given for the instrument,* the instrument is signed by the accommodation party "for accommodation."

Okla.Stat. tit. 12A, § 3-419(a) (1991) (emphasis added).

We do not regard the altered language in the 1961 enactment as making any change in the Oklahoma law relevant to the issue before us. Although a party lending his or her name to another on an instrument is still an accommodation maker despite being paid for rendering such service, it does not declare that one may remain an accommodation maker despite being a direct beneficiary of the instrument itself. Receiving the direct benefit of the instrument itself is contrary to the basic principle of lending one's name or credit to another (rather than using it for oneself), while accepting payment for assuming the role of surety is, by its own terms, obviously consistent with surety status. *See* 1 White & Summers § 13-14 at 660-61 & n.6 (3d ed. 1988) (recognizing that "receipt of proceeds from the instrument or other direct benefit would generally be inconsistent with accommodation status [under § 3-415(1)]," but also noting "that the surety may undertake his obligation gratuitously or for compensation without affecting his status as a surety."). The Oklahoma cases while the 1961 provision was in effect are consistent with this view.

Thus, we hold the applicable Oklahoma law is that, absent some special indication of status on the instrument, to be deemed an accommodation party one must lend his or her name to another on an instrument, for a fee or otherwise, without being the direct beneficiary of the value given for the instrument. We turn now to the facts to evaluate whether Hodges met this test.

III

Under 11 U.S.C. § 547(g), a trustee seeking to avoid an allegedly preferential transfer under § 547(b) "has the burden of proving by a preponderance of the evidence every essential, controverted element resulting in the preference." 4 Collier on Bankruptcy ¶ 547.21[5] at 547-93 (15th ed. 1993); *see, e.g, Sloan v. Zions First Nat'l Bank (In re Casteltons, Inc.)*, 990 F.2d 551, 555 (10th Cir.1993) (trustee's avoidance claim rejected because "she did not satisfy her burden of proof under § 547(b)(5)"). Consequently, the Trustee bears the burden of demonstrating that Hodges was a creditor within the meaning of § 547(b)(4)(B). To do this the Trustee must show Hodges lent his name to debtors on the note given to ABB and did not receive a direct personal benefit in return for the note.

ABB contends Hodges derived precisely the same benefit in return for execution of the note that debtors obtained—dismissal of a pending adverse legal claim. Oklahoma law recognizes that the settlement of a legitimate legal controversy, whatever its merits, provides a valid and enforceable benefit to the settling parties. The Trustee responds that Hodges' alleged settlement benefit is specious, because he actually had no liability exposure in the ABB lawsuit.

The district court held in favor of the Trustee based on the stipulated facts that debtors owed ABB the sum sought in the settled action and debtors had made the two initial payments alone. Although these facts confirm debtors' role in, and benefit obtained from, the settlement, they do not negate the evident role played, and benefit derived, by Hodges. If debtors' conceded obligation to ABB were *exclusive* of any concurrent liability on Hodges' part, these stipulations would fully support the district court's conclusion. However, there are no other facts cited by the Trustee or contained in the record indicating such exclusivity. The pertinent record, consisting of the settlement letter and note, excerpts from Hodges' deposition, and the pretrial order, contain nothing to indicate the particular nature of ABB's claim against Hodges, let alone establish the illegitimacy of that claim. The record reflects only the operative documents themselves and Holdges' testimony acknowledging that ABB was asserting liability against him individually as well as against debtors.

It is important to recognize that the Trustee not only had to satisfy, in general terms, the burden of proof imposed by § 547(g), but, given the particular circumstances involved here, also present evidence sufficient to enable the court to look behind an executed settlement and declare that the underlying claim asserted against a settling party lacked a good-faith legal foundation. This the Trustee did not do. We therefore hold that the Trustee failed to establish his entitlement to the avoidance sought under § 547(b)(4)(B). The judgment entered in the Trustee's favor must, accordingly, be *reversed.*

QUESTION

Note the Court stated that it did not regard the altered language in § 3-419(a) as making any change in former § 3-415(1). Does that mean that the decision in the case would have been the same had the new Article 3 been in effect? *See* § 3-116(b).

DAIGLE v. CHAISSON

Louisiana Court of Appeal
396 So. 2d 573, 31 U.C.C. Rep. 1032 (1981)

CULPEPPER, J.

This is a suit on a promissory note. Plaintiff Alvin Daigle, an indorser and presently the holder of the note, seeks indemnity or, in the alternative, contribution from the defendant, David Chaisson, a co-indorser. The district court rejected plaintiff's claim against defendant. Plaintiff appeals.

The principal issue is whether plaintiff; suing as an accommodation indorser who has paid the instrument, has a right of recourse against defendant, and, if so, for how much.

On March 22, 1979, Jerry Iguess made a promissory note payable to the Calcasieu Marine National Bank in the amount of $7,000 with 10% interest and attorney's fees. On the reverse side of the note appear the names of Alvin Daigle, David Chaisson and Marlene Daigle, plaintiff's wife. Under each of these names is the word "endorser." The note became due on July 20, 1979.

On May 18, 1979, Jerry Iguess, the maker of the note, filed a petition for bankruptcy listing the Calcasieu Marine Bank note as one of his items of liability. Mr. Iguess received a discharge in bankruptcy on August 9, 1979.

When the note became past due, the bank knew that Iguess had filed a petition in bankruptcy court, so the bank made demand on both Daigle and Chaisson as indorsers. Daigle testified that at this point he asked Chaisson to pay the note, but Chaisson refused. Pretending not to damage his own credit, plaintiff purchased the note from Calcasieu Marine for the sum of $7,535, of which $7,000 was the principal and the remainder was interest. He then filed the present suit against both Chaisson and Iguess for the sum of $7,535 which he paid for the note, plus legal interest thereon and a reasonable attorney's fee. In the alternative, he seeks judgment against Chaisson as co-indorser for one-half the amount he paid for the note. Iguess was later dismissed by plaintiff as a party.

After the presentation of the evidence, the district court denied plaintiff any indemnity or contribution against Chaisson. In its written opinion, the court concluded that plaintiff could not obtain contribution from a co-indorser without first seeking recourse from the maker. For the reasons which follow, we reverse.

Under the Commercial Laws, La RS 10:1–101, et seq adopted in 1975 and repealing the former Negotiable Instruments Law, an accommodation party is "one who signs the instrument in any capacity for the purpose of lending his name to another party to it." La RS 10:3-415(1). From the note itself, it is apparent that Daigle, his wife and Chaisson signed the note as indorsers. The accommodation character of the three indorsements is also clear since they do not appear in the chain of title to the note. La RS 10:3-415(4). This finding is also supported by the testimony which reflects that the names of the three indorsers were added to the instrument as additional security for the bank.

Directly above the three indorsements on the note is found the following language: ". . .the undersigned hereby jointly and severally guarantee to the Calcasieu Marine National Bank of Lake Charles, its successors, indorsers or assigns, the punctual payment at maturity of said loan;". The three indorsements on the reverse side of the note appear in a horizontal line rather than vertical. Plaintiff's indorsement is farthest to the left followed by that of Chaisson and then plaintiff's wife.

Initially, we interpret the phrase "jointly and severally" to mean that the three indorsers bound themselves in solido with the principal obligor. The common law term "joint and several" has been held synonymous with our Civil Law term "in solido." Moreover, as these parties "guaranteed" the punctual payment of the loan, the bank could proceed directly against each indorser for the whole amount without first making demand upon the maker. La RS 10:3-416(1). The Official Comment to Uniform Commercial Code, Section 3-416 states:

> An indorser who guarantees payment waives not only presentment, notice of dishonor and protest, but also all demand upon the maker or drawee. Words of guarantee do not affect the character of the indorsement as an indorsement [Section 3-202(4)]; but the liability of the indorser becomes indistinguishable from that of the co-maker.

The order of liability of indorsers is provided in La RS 10:3-414(2) as follows:

> Unless they otherwise agree, indorsers are liable to one another in the order in which they indorse, which is presumed to be the order in which their signatures appear on the instrument.

It could be argued under § 3-414(2) that since plaintiff signed farthest to the left, followed by Chaisson, on the horizontal line on which all three indorsers signed, that plaintiff indorsed first and is precluded by this section from any recourse against Chaisson. However, the presumption of § 3-414(2) may be rebutted by evidence which shows a different order or division of liability was intended or agreed to by the parties.

In the instant case, the testimony shows that Jerry Iguess and David Chaisson were business partners engaged in a welding business. The present debt was incurred to purchase land and equipment for their welding shop. Plaintiff testified that his and his wife's names were supplied to the instrument only to accommodate Iguess. Daigle testified that he had no financial interest in defendants' business, nor did he receive any of the funds borrowed. The record also shows that all three indorsements were affixed to the instrument simultaneously.

We think the circumstances surrounding the signing of the note, as well as the other factors mentioned, negate any intent on the part of the indorsers to be bound in the order in which they signed. All of the evidence in the record shows no indorser was to share a greater portion of the liability than the other co-indorser. Chaisson makes no contention to the contrary.

We thus conclude that § 3-414(2) does not bar plaintiff from seeking recourse against his co-indorsers. We find, however, no provisions in the Commercial Laws which provide for indemnification or contribution between accommodation indorsers once the presumption of § 3-414(2) has been overcome.

We are aware that in *The Work of the Louisiana Appellate Courts for the 1978-79 Term-Security Devices,* 40 La L Rev 572 at 574, the author suggests La RS 10:3-415(5) should be construed to mean that "An accommodation indorser who pays the holder may still pursue the other indorsers and the maker on the instrument and recover whatever attorney's fees, costs, and interest the note provides." The entire § 3-415 reads as follows: . . .[the Court quotes U.C.C. § 3-415].

In our view, Subsection (5) governs only the relationship between the accommodation party and the "party accommodated." The party accommodated in most cases is the maker, but it could be a prior indorser in the chain of title or another party. The rule which § 3-415(5) makes clear is that an accommodation party is not liable to the party accommodated, whoever he be, and if an accommodation party pays the instrument he has a right of recourse *on the instrument* against such party, meaning the *party accommodated.* We cannot construe Subsection (5) as meaning that where one of two or more accommodation co-indorsers agrees to be bound in solido to pay the principal obligation, as in the present case, that one of the accommodation parties can pay the instrument and sue the other accommodation parties "on the instrument" for the principal debt, interest, attorney's fees, etc.

Our construction of the statute is supported by the Official Comment under the U.C.C., § 3-415 which reads as follows:

> 5. Subsection (5) is intended to change the result of such decisions as *Quimby v. Varnum,* 190 Mass 211, 76 NE 671(1906), which held that an accommodation indorser who paid the instrument could not maintain an action on it against the accommodated party since he had no "former rights" to which he was remitted. Under ordinary principles of suretyship the accommodation party who pays is subrogated to the rights of the holder paid, and should have his recourse on the instrument.

The Comment, *Suretyship Law And Negotiable Instruments Law: The Liability Of An Accommodation Party To A Negotiable Instrument In Louisiana*, 24 Loy LR 251 at 258 also supports our position:

> Article 3 (of the U.C.C.), unlike the Negotiable Instruments Law, recognizes that an accommodation party, whether he signs the instrument as a maker or as an indorser is basically a surety. The official comments emphasize the accommodation party's suretyship nature: "He differs from other sureties only in that his liability is on the instrument and he is a surety for another party to it. His obligation is therefore determined by the capacity in which he signs." The comments continue to discuss the liability of an accommodation maker, a party not generally treated as a surety under prior law. Because the comments repeatedly refer to the accommodation party as a surety, "the drafters doubtless intended suretyship law, at least to some extent, to apply in defining the liability of the accommodation party. Because the Uniform Commercial Code does not generally purport to regulate suretyship law, the drafters in referring to the accommodation party as a surety presumably meant to refer to the state law of suretyship. What remains unclear is the extent to which state suretyship law may be used to define the liability of the accommodation party."

Having concluded the Commercial Laws contain no provisions for indemnification or contribution amongst accommodation indorsers, once the presumption of La RS 10:3-414(2) is overcome, we must look to other areas of Louisiana law which may apply to the instant case. La RS 10:1 -103 provides: "Unless displaced by the particular provisions of this title, the other laws of Louisiana shall apply."

When Daigle and Chaisson signed the note as accommodation indorsers and guarantors, they contracted to become solidary sureties for the principal debtor. La CC Article 3035, *C L T Corporation v. Rosenstock*, 205 So2d 81 (La App 4th Cir 1967). Moreover, the U.C.C. Official Comment to § 3-415 states: "an accommodation party is always a surety (which includes a guarantor), and it is his only distinguishable feature."

Our Louisiana law of suretyship expressly recognizes the right of a surety who has paid the primary debt to seek recourse from other co-sureties. . .

. . . .

For the reasons assigned, the judgment appealed is reversed and set aside. It is now ordered, adjudged and decreed that there be judgment herein in favor of plaintiff, Alvin Daigle, and against the defendant, David D. Chaisson, for the sum of $2,511, together with legal interest thereon from date of judicial demand until paid and for all costs of these proceedings both in the trial and appellate courts.

Reversed and rendered.

NOTES AND QUESTIONS

(1) Where do we find former § 3-414(2) today?

(2) Assume *A, B*, and *C* agree to stand surety for P on the same obligation. The presumption of surety law is that of co-suretyship in the event of loss. Why should that presumption be changed by the order in which *A, B* and *C* sign the back of a negotiable instrument? If *A, B* and *C* were seated around a table at the time of the execution of the agreement, what facts would control the order of indorsement? What controlled the order of indorsement in the *Daigle* case? *See* U.C.C. § 3-116, Comment 2.

(3) Did the court accord appropriate significance to the fact that Iguess and Chaisson were business partners and the debt was incurred to purchase land and equipment for *their* welding shop?

(4) Notice that as among themselves, sureties are generally liable to one another, through contribution, for a *proportionate* share of the debt. *See* PEB Commentary No. 11, Issue 4 (1994).

PEOPLES NATIONAL BANK OF MORA v. BOYER

Minnesota Court of Appeals
354 N.W.2d 559 (1984)

HUSPENI, JUDGE.

Obligee bank brought this action under a promissory note against accommodation parties who endorsed and guaranteed previous promissory notes by this obligor. The trial court ordered judgment for the respondents, and denied appellant's motion for a new trial. We affirm.

FACTS

Appellant Peoples National Bank of Mora (Peoples) is the obligee on a note signed by Donald F. Boyer. The note is a consolidation of two separate loans to Donald F. Boyer. Respondents are Donald's parents, Donald E. and Dorothy Boyer (the Boyers). They initially executed written guarantees on each of the two notes. The guarantees which are the subjects of this suit were signed in October 1977, and May 1979. The guarantees included a consent to extensions or renewals of the loans.

Each of the original loans was "renewed" several times before they were consolidated in August 1981. Each new note had as its principal the balance of the principal and unpaid interest on the old note. The Boyers did not sign guarantees on any of the "renewal" notes, nor on the consolidated note. The bank sent the Boyers three letters requesting their signatures to guarantee the new loans. The Boyers did not respond to the letters, since they understood they were no longer liable on the notes. Despite the Boyers' refusal to sign, the bank consummated the transactions with Donald Boyer, which resulted in the new notes.

The notes issued immediately subsequent to the notes guaranteed by the Boyers bore higher interest rates. The old credit and life insurance policies were cancelled, and unearned premiums credited against the unearned balance. New insurance policy premiums were added to the new balance.

The bank's records for the two loans guaranteed by the Boyers show a balance of zero on the date of the last transaction, which is the date the new loans were issued. They also carry the notation "paid loan." The payment history information on the new notes starts on the dates they were issued.

In March 1982, Donald F. Boyer filed for bankruptcy. He was subsequently discharged on this debt to the bank. The bank demanded payment from the Boyers, who refused. The bank then commenced this suit. The trial court found the Boyers discharged of liability under their guarantees because: 1) the guaranteed notes were paid and satisfied by the acceptance of the substituted notes; 2) there were material and fraudulent alterations in the additional insurance benefits; 3) a novation occurred; and 4) the final note was usurious. The bank appeals on the ground that the trial court's findings are clearly erroneous, and its conclusions not supported by the evidence.

ISSUE

Whether the two guarantees signed by Donald E. and Dorothy Boyer in 1977 and 1979 are applicable to the consolidated note issued in 1981.

ANALYSIS

The trial court initially determined that the Boyers were not liable on the guaranteed notes because those notes were paid and satisfied by acceptance of the substituted notes. As to this issue, if the notes issued subsequent to the guaranteed notes are merely renewals, the Boyers are liable on them. If they, in fact, do represent new obligations delivered in satisfaction of the previous debts, they were the sole responsibility of Donald F. Boyer, now discharged in bankruptcy.

The Minnesota Supreme Court has set out the applicable rules as follows:

> It is generally held that the mere execution of a renewal note evidences the same debt by a new promise and does not constitute a payment or discharge of the original note but operates only as an extension of time for payment. (Citations omitted) It is true that one note may be accepted in payment of another, but a new note given without any new consideration to the same person for the same sum as the old one is not generally deemed a satisfaction thereof, unless so received and accepted.

Farmers Union Oil Co. v. Fladeland, 287 Minn. 315, 319, 178 N.W.2d 254, 257 (1970). *Fladeland* involved an extension note for the principal and unpaid interest of a primary note, at the same interest rate.

Here the trial court found that the later notes did not operate "only as an extension of time for payment." *Id.* Plaintiff bank told Donald F. Boyer that the new notes were substituted for the old. The trial court found that all bank records indicated that the guaranteed notes were paid. The new notes were made with new consideration in the form of higher interest rates. New insurance premiums were charged on each new note. The bank made repeated requests for review guarantees from the Boyers.

A review of the record reveals substantial evidentiary support for the trial court's finding that the new notes were substituted in full satisfaction of the guaranteed notes. In view of our determination as to this issue, it is not necessary to address those additional factors listed by the trial court as the basis for discharging the Boyers from liability.

DECISION

Affirmed.

NOTES

(1) Review the decision in light of U.C.C. § 3-605(b) and Comment 3. Read PEB Commentary No. 11, Issue 6.

(2) Review the decision in light of U.C.C. § 3-605(c) and Comment 4.

(3) Review the decision in light of U.C.C. § 3-605(d) and Comment 5. Read PEB Commentary No. 11, Issue 3, 8, 9.

FEDERAL DEPOSIT INSURANCE CORP. v. BLUE ROCK SHOPPING CENTER, INC.

United States Court of Appeals
766 F.2d 744, 41 U.C.C. Rep. 1 (3d Cir. 1985)

O'NEILL, DISTRICT JUDGE.

Federal Deposit Insurance Corporation has brought this action on a note against Blue Rock Shopping Center, Inc., Max Ambach and his wife Rose Ambach. The district court granted summary judgment to plaintiff.

Summary judgment is, of course, proper only if there is no genuine issue as to any material fact and the moving party is entitled to a judgment as a matter of law. Moreover, the inferences drawn from the evidence submitted to the trial court must be viewed in the light most favorable to the party opposing the motion. On review, this court is required to apply the same test the district court should have used.

Viewed most favorably to defendants, the facts may be summarized as follows. On September 29, 1966, in return for a loan by Farmers Bank of the State of Delaware in the amount of $800,000, Blue Rock, by its President, Mr. Ambach, executed a Bond and Warrant in which it promised to pay Farmers $800,000 plus annual interest of 6.25 percent. The Bond was secured by a first mortgage on real estate owned by Blue Rock and located in Blue Rock Shopping Center, Wilmington, Delaware. As additional collateral, Blue Rock assigned to Farmers its interest in a lease of a warehouse located on the real estate. The payments to be made by the lessee, A.

T. C. of Wilmington, Inc., which were assigned to Farmers, coincided with Blue Rock's installment obligations to Farmers under the Bond. Payment of the rent was guaranteed by Atlantic Thrift Centers, Inc., and ultimately by Arlen Realty and Development Corporation, its corporate successor.

Settlement of the transaction was held on September 29, 1966, the day that the Bond and Assignment of Lease were signed. These documents and others were delivered to Farmers, and the proceeds were disbursed.[34] Two letters were exchanged. Farmers' letter to the attorney for Blue Rock stated:

P.S. The $800,000 Bond and Warrant is to be signed by Max Ambach and his wife, Rose.

The attorney's letter to Farmers said:

> I understand that it is your desire to have Max Ambach and Rose Ambach, his wife, individually sign the corporate bond and warrant, and consequently, I have prepared a new such bond and warrant and have forwarded it to Mrs. Ambach today for signature. When returned to me, I will then substitute this bond and warrant for the one which you presently possess.

Since the Bond sued upon is dated September, 1966, and is signed by all defendants, it is apparent that the contemplated substitution occurred.[35] The individual defendants did not receive any of the borrowed funds.

In July, 1975, Blue Rock defaulted on its obligations to Farmers. Its default was caused by the concomitant default of Arc and Arlen, who had discontinued operations at the Shopping Center. Farmers declined Blue Rock's request that it agree to a settlement proposal made by Arlen, which offered to pay $ 100,000 for the immediate termination of the lease and an additional $24,000 if the premises were not relet within a year. At the time of this request, approximately $428,000 remained due from Arlen on its guaranty of the lease. Instead, Farmers and Blue Rock executed a letter agreement in which Blue Rock assigned to Farmers all of its interest in the Arlen guaranty in consideration of Farmers' refraining from enforcement of its rights against Blue Rock arising out of the default.[36] Thereafter, in March, 1976, Farmers sued Arlen on the guaranty in the Delaware Superior Court.

On October 25, 1976, pursuant to an Assistance Agreement previously made between FDIC and Farmers, Farmers assigned to FDIC all of its interest in the Bond and Mortgage, the Assignment of Lease, and the guaranty of the lease payments.

In January, 1980, the Shopping Center was sold for $325,000 at a sheriff's sale which occurred because taxes due to the City of Wilmington had not been paid. FDIC received $188,115.33 from the proceeds of the sale, which was applied to the amount owing on the Bond. On November 12, 1982, without the consent of defendants, FDIC settled its Superior Court action against Arlen for the sum of $148,467. As a result, as of October 22, 1982, there was a deficiency balance of $523,105.71 plus interest. This suit seeks to collect the remaining debt.

The district court granted summary judgment to plaintiff and dismissed defendants' affirmative defense which asserted that FDIC's unreasonable delay in prosecuting the claim against Arlen

[34] After satisfaction of a previously existing mortgage of Blue Rock to Farmers and discharge of other corporate obligations, Blue Rock received new proceeds of approximately $50,000 from the loan.

[35] No date in September is filled in above the signatures on the Bond. The signers bound themselves "jointly and severally."

[36] Farmers reserved all of its rights including its right to proceed against the collateral.

and its unilateral settlement of the suit against Arlen constitute an impermissible impairment of collateral barring recovery in this action. The district court held that: (l) as a matter of Delaware law, § 3-606(1)(b) of the Uniform Commercial Code does not operate to discharge a co-maker of a note, as opposed to an accommodation maker; (2) because defendants do not rely upon any written agreements to prove that the Ambachs acted as accommodation makers, the FDIC should be considered a holder in due course under 12 U.S.C. § 1823(e) and any parole evidence tending to establish the Ambachs as accommodation makers would be barred; and (3) Max and Rose Ambach are co-makers, not accommodation makers, and are not discharged by virtue of § 3-606(1)(b).

The question to be resolved on this appeal is whether a co-maker of a negotiable instrument is entitled to assert the defense of unjustifiable impairment of collateral as provided by § 3-606(1)(b) of the Uniform Commercial Code. Since we hold that a co-maker with a right of recourse may assert the defense, we also will comment on the extent to which 12 U.S.C. § 1823(e) limits the evidence which the individual defendants may offer on remand.

II.

Section 3-606(1) of the Uniform Commercial Code provides that "[t]he holder discharges any party to the instrument to the extent that without such party's consent the holder . . .(b) unjustifiably impairs any collateral for the instrument given by or on behalf of the party or any person against whom he has a right of recourse."

This language extends the protection of the statute to "any party to the instrument." Nevertheless, there is a division of authority as to whether § 3-606 operates to discharge a maker of a note. Some courts have concluded that the statute must be read literally and that the words "any party" clearly include a maker or co-maker:

> There is a split of authority in other jurisdictions as to whether a maker of a note is discharged by the holder's impairment of collateral. . . . We are impressed with the clear and unambiguous language used in the statute in providing that any party to the instrument is discharged to the extent the holder unjustifiably impairs any collateral. The plain meaning of the phrase "any party" clearly would include a co–maker. No one can deny that a co–maker is a party to the instrument. Many times we are called upon to construe ambiguous provisions in the statutes and in doing so we must employ various rules of construction to arrive at the meaning of the words used. But unless we are faced with some ambiguity we should give words their plain meaning and stop there. We believe this is such a case.

Southwest Florida Production Credit Assn. v. Schirow, 388 So. 2d 338, 339 (Fla. App. 1980) (citations omitted).

Other courts look to the policy which the defense is designed to serve and reason as follows:

> At first blush, this section appears to provide a defense. However, a maker of a note, as opposed to a surety, is not entitled to invoke this defense. . . .
>
> This interpretation of § 3-606 is soundly based. The maker of a note is always primarily responsible for the debt with no recourse except against co-makers. Sureties, whether accommodation makers or endorsers . . .retain a right of recourse against the primary obligor. . .. Fairness dictates that if the risk a surety has agreed to undertake is increased through the impairment of the securing collateral by the person to whom payment is due, the surety should be discharged to the extent of impairment.

United States v. Unum, 658 F.2d at 304-305 (citations omitted).

The district court adopted the reasoning of the *Unum* court and similar state decisions, which it regarded as the majority view, and held that "Section 3-606 does not operate to discharge a co-maker on a note, as opposed to an accommodation maker." We agree with the *Unum* court that § 3-606 is meant to apply only to parties who act as sureties. We hold, however, that a co-maker who signs a note to accommodate the primary obligor and who has a right of recourse against the primary obligor is a surety who can assert the defense of § 3-606(1)(b).

Section 3-606 of the Code is derived from section 120 of the Uniform Negotiable Instruments Law, which provided for discharge, in certain circumstances, of "a person secondarily liable on the instrument. . ."[37] The Comment to the Code explains the nature and purposes of the change as follows:

Sec. 3-606.1. Draftsmen's Comment.

Prior Uniform Statutory Provision: Section 120, Uniform Negotiable Instruments Law.

Changes: reworded; new provisions.

Purposes of Changes and New Matter. To make it clear that:

1. The words "any party to the instrument" remove an uncertainty arising under the original section. The suretyship defenses here provided are not limited to parties who are "secondarily liable," but are available to any party who is in the position of a surety, having a right of recourse either on the instrument or dehors it, including an accommodation maker or acceptor known to the holder to be so. . ..

5. Paragraph (b) of subsection (1) is new. The suretyship defense stated has been generally recognized as available to indorsers or accommodation parties. . ..

It is evident from this Comment and the prior law that the draftsman of the Code used the words "any party" in place of "persons secondarily liable" to make it clear that the newly codified defense of § 3-606(1)(b) would be available to any party to the instrument who is in the position of a surety with a right of recourse. As under § 120 of the N.I.L., this party can be one who is "secondarily liable" such as an indorser. Now, however, any accommodation party, including a co-maker who has a right of recourse against the maker who posted the collateral, may claim the suretyship defenses of § 3-606[38] even though the co-maker possessing that right is jointly and severally liable to the holder on the note.[39]

---

[37] "§ 120. When Persons Secondarily Liable On; Discharged.—A person secondarily liable on the instrument is discharged:

(1) By an act which discharges the instrument;

(2) By the intentional cancellation of his signature by the holder;

(3) By the discharge of a prior party;

(4) By a valid tender of payment made by a prior party;

(5) By a release of the principal debtor, unless the holder's right of recourse against the party secondarily liable is expressly reserved;

(6) By an agreement binding upon the holder to extend the time of payment, or to postpone the holder's right to enforce the instrument, unless made with the assent of the party secondarily liable, or unless the right of recourse against such party is expressly reserved."

[38] "An accommodation party is one who signs the instrument in any capacity for the purpose of lending his name to another party to it." U.C.C. § 3-415(1).

[39] See White & Summers, Uniform Commercial Code § 13-12at 516-17:

This analysis is supported by *American Express Internat'l Banking Corp. v. Sabet*, 512 F. Supp. 463 (S.D.N.Y 1980), decided under New York's enactment of the Code, in which the court said:

> These sections defining impairment of collateral have been applied to discharge a party to a loan transaction other than the party actually pledging collateral which was subsequently unjustifiably impaired, but only when the party seeking discharge was entitled to look to the collateral for reimbursement of any payment made to the creditor, either as a result of the discharged party's position with respect to the creditor—*e.g.*, as a guarantor with a right to be subrogated to the creditor's right against the collateral . . . or as a result of the discharged party's status as co-maker or accommodation party with respect to the owner of the collateral, entitling the discharged party to contribution or indemnification from the owner. . .

Id. at 469-70 (citations omitted).

One of the authorities cited in *American Express* was *Indianapolis Morris Plan Corp. v. Karlen*, 28 N.Y.2d 30, 34, 319 N.Y.S.2d 831, 834, 268 N.E.2d 632, 634 (1971), in which the Court of Appeals of New York, per Breitel, J., noted that § 3-606 differs from the N.I.L. in that it refers to any party on the instrument and not merely to persons secondarily liable, and recognized that § 3-606 was available to individual defendants who were co-makers of a note with a corporation.[40] In that case, it was not disputed that the corporation was the borrower and that only the form of the note made the individual defendants co-makers.[41]

In light of the above analysis, we conclude that if the individual defendants were co-makers with a right of recourse they may assert the defense provided in § 3-606(1) (b) of the Code.

One with money to lend . . .may have doubts about a prospective debtor's ability to pay. In such cases he is likely to demand more assurance than the debtor's bare promise of payment. The prospective creditor can reduce his risk by requiring some sort of security. One . . .type of security takes the form of joining a third person on the debtor's obligation. A third party who thus obligates himself to answer for the debt or default of the debtor is called a surety.

Structurally, suretyship is a three party relationship involving the creditor, the principal debtor and the surety. The debtor's obligation as a borrower of money is already familiar. So, too, his obligation as a signer of a negotiable instrument. The surety's obligation is somewhat different. In effect the surety undertakes to "back up" the performance of the debtor and he thereby gives the creditor the added assurance of having another party to the obligation. It is common practice for a surety to appear on a note either as a co-maker or as an indorser. Assume for example that a father is going to be the surety on his son's contract to pay for a new car. The father may sign the note as co-maker or he may simply indorse the note. As we will see, in either case he is what the Code calls an "accommodation party" and owes the holder of the note the obligation of a maker, or of an indorser as the case may be (although he will have certain defenses not normally available to makers or indorsers against all but holders in due course without notice of his accommodation status.)

As between the surety and the debtor, it is clear that the debtor has the primary obligation to pay the debt. Since the creditor is entitled to only one performance and the debtor receives the benefit of the transaction, the surety's obligation is undertaken with the expectation that the debtor will meet his commitment to the creditor. Thus if the surety is made to pay his principal's debt, he has the right to recover from the principal. If the creditor releases the principal debtor and so deprives the surety of the right to recover from the principal by being subrogated to the creditor's rights, or if the creditor fails to perfect a security interest in collateral given by the debtor and so is unable to recover his debt out of the collateral, the surety's burden will be increased. The law assumes that the surety has not assented to such increased burdens. Consequently the law has traditionally held that conduct by the creditor which increases the surety's risk discharges the surety.

[40] The *Karlen* court held, however, that defendants had waived their rights under § 3-606.

[41] *American Express* also cited *Beneficial Finance Co. of NY v. Husner,* 82 Misc.2d 550, 369 N.Y.S.2d 975 (N.Y. Sup. Ct. 1975), which held that the right of one co-obligor on a note to contribution from another co-obligor, who owned the collateral pledged as security for the note, was a right of recourse within the meaning of § 3-606 of the Code.

With respect to the corporate defendant, we reach a different conclusion. Since the words "any party" read literally include Blue Rock, the question is not free from doubt. We are persuaded, however, by the Draftsmen's Comment to the Code and the reasoning in *Unum* and *American Express* that, absent a contrary provision, the primary obligor as among co-makers, *i.e.*, the one who posted the collateral and received the proceeds of the loan and who therefore is not a surety, remains liable to the holder for the debt incurred regardless of any impairment of collateral by the holder.

We believe that these conclusions conform to the clearly expressed intent and policy of the Code to protect any party to an instrument who is in the position of a surety with a right of recourse, but not a party who does not occupy such a position. Our conclusions require a remand for an evidentiary hearing with respect to whether the Ambachs were sureties with a right of recourse, and if they were whether they can prove that FDIC unjustifiably impaired the collateral securing the Bond.

NOTE

Read § 3-605(e), (f) and (g). *See* PEB Commentary No. 11, Issue 11; Amendment of Comment 8 to § 3-605.

TRANSAMERICA COMMERCIAL FINANCE CORP. v. NAEF

Supreme Court of Wyoming
842 P.2d 539, 21 U.C.C. Rep.2d 704 (1992)

[Transamerica sought recovery from Linda Naef for amounts due under a promissory note and guaranty she had signed for her husband's business. Both the business and the husband had filed for bankruptcy protection. Transamerica continued its action against Linda.]

We consider first the guaranty Linda Naef signed. It is readily evident that the guaranty was not a negotiable instrument; and she could not, therefore, be an accommodation party on it under the Uniform Commercial Code. The guaranty did not contain any promise or order to "pay a sum certain in money," nor was it payable "to order or to bearer." We cannot, therefore, accept Transamerica's argument that Mrs. Naef's signature on the guaranty made her an accommodation party under the Uniform Commercial Code.

Even if Mrs. Naef was not an accommodation party on the guaranty, Transamerica argues that she was an accommodation party, or even a co-maker, on the promissory note. Transamerica highlights our holding in *Lawrence v. Farm Credit System Capital Corp.*, 761 P.2d 640, 651 (Wyo.1988), that one of several signatories to a promissory note will be held liable as a co-maker even if he did not personally receive consideration for his signature. However, we believe that under the circumstances of this case, Mrs. Naef was neither a co-maker nor an accommodation party on the promissory note.

Transamerica's branch manager, Robert Wood, testified as follows during the trial:

Q: Is there any [Transamerica] practice with respect to having wives sign with a husband if the husband is the shareholder?

A: It's a common practice. Probably more often than not.

Q: And why is that?

A: A lot of it deals with the community property laws, transferring of assets, et cetera.

. . . . .

Q: [Would you have given the corporation a loan] based on Mr. Naef's financial statement alone?

A: It's possible. But I don't believe that it would have been approved, no.

Later, on cross-examination, Mr. Wood testified:

Q: Now, Transamerica never asked for a financial statement from Linda Naef, did it?

A: We received a personal financial statement from Richard Naef.

Q: Okay. But you never asked for or required a financial statement from Linda Naef, did you?

A: It's not the common practice. Married individuals are usually consolidated.

Q: You didn't know whether Mr. Naef was married based on his financial statement, did you?

A: No.

Linda Naef testified as follows concerning the signing of the promissory note:

Q: . . . Did you have some discussion or participate in some discussion with Mr. Wood prior to your signing that?

A: Yes, I did. In fact, I was sitting at my chair and he came up and wanted my signature, and I told him I had no intention of signing that thing because there was no way I could guarantee it. And he said, you don't have to. And I says, it says right on there that I have to guarantee it with a signature. And he said, that's not important. You have two weeks to take care of it.

The evidence shows that Mrs. Naef was pressured into signing the promissory note without any indication that her credit was needed to approve the loan. Although she was an officer of Teton Power Products at the time she signed, the trial court found that "[a]t the time of the signing of the documents and at all times subsequent thereto, Linda Naef owned no interest in the Defendant corporation." Not only was her signature gratuitous, it was most probably illegally obtained as a form of discrimination based on marital status. Federal Consumer Credit Protection Act, 15U.S.C. § 1691 *et seq.* (1982).

Section 1691(a) of the Federal Consumer Credit Protection Actstates that

[i]t shall be unlawful for any creditor to discriminate against any applicant, with respect to any aspect of a credit transaction—

(1) on the basis of race, color, religion, national origin, sex or *marital status* or age (provided the applicant has the capacity to contract)[.] [emphasis added]

The implementing regulations, found at 12 C.F.R. § 202.7(d)(1), state:

> Except as provided in this paragraph, a creditor shall not require the signature of an applicant's spouse or other person, other than a joint applicant, or any credit instrument if the applicant qualifies under the creditor's standards of creditworthiness for the amount and terms of the credit requested.

(12 C.F.R. § 202.7(d) provides certain exceptions from this rule, none of which are applicable here.)

In *Douglas County Nat. Bank v. Pfeiff*, 809 P.2d 1100 (Colo.App.1991), the Colorado Court of Appeals held that a wife who was sued on a note she was required to co-sign to guarantee the debts of her husband's business could state a counterclaim for discrimination based on marital status under the Equal Credit Guaranty Act. The facts of *Pfeiff* are quite similar to those of this case, and we are persuaded by its reasoning that Transamerica violated the Act in this instance.

The evidence, then, shows that Mrs. Naef had no interest in the business for which she was signing, did not wish to sign, and only signed after a Transamerica representative told her that her signature was "not important." She had no intent to be a co-maker and was told in essence that she would not be. We recognize that these elements, although they suggest misrepresentation or overreaching, would not alone be sufficient to render the promissory note unenforceable against Mrs. Naef. *Cf. Standard Finance Co., Ltd. v. Ellis*, 3 Haw.App. 614, 657 P.2d 1-56 (1983) (fact that husband assured wife that her signature was a formality and he alone would be liable on note did not make note unenforceable against co-signer wife); *Abruzzino v. Farmers' & Merchants' Bank*, 168 Ga. App. 639, 309 S.E.2d 911 (1983) (wife was liable on promissory note she signed for husband's business even though she was not actively involved in the business and did not know exactly what she was signing). Were these the only facts presented to us, we would probably have to hold that Mrs. Naef was liable as an accommodation party. However, when coupled with evidence that Transamerica acted under a blanket, illegal and unreasonable policy of requiring spousal signatures, the totality of the circumstances convince us that Mrs. Naef's signature on the promissory note cannot be enforced against her as either a co-maker or an accommodation party. Under these circumstances of misrepresentation and illegality, we will affirm the decision of the trial court for Mrs. Naef.

We hold that the trial court properly dismissed Transamerica's suit against Mrs. Naef.

NOTE

It is a deceptive act or practice within the meaning of the Federal Trade Commission Act, to obligate a surety in connection with the extension of credit without giving the surety the following notice:

NOTICE TO CO-SIGNER

You are being asked to guarantee this debt. Think carefully before you do. If the borrower doesn't pay the debt, you will have to. Be sure you can afford to pay it if you have to, and that you want to accept this responsibility.

You may have to pay the full amount of the debt if the borrower does not pay. You may also have to pay late fees or collection costs, which increase this amount.

The creditor can collect this debt from you without first trying to collect from the borrower. The creditor can use the same collection methods against you that can be used against the borrower, such as suing you, garnishing your wages, etc. If this debt is ever in default, that fact may become part of *your* credit record.

This notice is not the contract that makes you liable for the debt.

16 CFR 444.3(FTC Consumer Credit Practices Rules).

§ 13.11 Accrual of Cause of Action and Statute of Limitations

Read: U.C.C. § 3-118, 4-111, see §§ 3-416(d), 3-417(f), 4-207(3), 4-208(f).

TEPPER v. CITIZENS FEDERAL SAVINGS & LOAN ASSOCIATION

Florida District Court of Appeals
448 So. 2d 1138, 38 U.C.C. Rep. 528 (1984)

FERGUSON, J.

The sole question presented is when does the statute of limitations begin to run against a drawer in an action for wrongful dishonor of a check—on the date of issuance of the check or the date of presentment and dishonor?

Rose Tepper (appellant) was adjudicated an incompetent in December, 1982. On examination of her personal effects, a court-appointed guardian discovered a check for the sum of $6,068, dated January 4, 1974. The check was drawn to Rose Tepper by Citizens Federal Savings and Loan Association against its account with Jefferson National Bank.

On December 20, 1982, appellant's representative presented the check to the drawee bank, Jefferson National (not a party to this action), which refused payment. The representative then advised the drawer, Citizens Federal (appellee), of the dishonor. Citizens Federal orally notified appellant's representative that it would neither honor nor refund the instrument. The guardian instituted this action against the drawer on July 12, 1983.

The trial court dismissed the guardian's complaint on appellee's motion, holding that "the statute of limitations began to run on the date of issuance of the check herein sued upon, [so the] action is barred by the applicable five-year statute of limitations." We reverse upon a holding that the statute of limitations begins to run against a drawer of a check on the date of presentment and dishonor.

Although there seems to be a dearth of Florida case law on the issue presented, appellant has found all the law necessary to a correct resolution. The decision here is based upon an application of clear statutes and is supported by several treatises.

A draft is a three-party instrument whereby the drawer orders the drawee to pay money to the payee. See J. White and R. Summers, Uniform Commercial Code § 13-1(2d ed 1980). A draft is also called a check when the drawee is a bank and the instrument is payable on demand. § 673.104(2)(b), Fla Stat (1983). A drawee is not liable on the instrument until there has been an acceptance. § 673.409. The drawee may, by accepting in writing on the instrument, agree to honor it as presented. § 673.410. By contrast, a drawee may reject the instrument, as by stamping insufficient funds on a check where the drawer's deposited funds are less than the amount of the instrument. The act of accepting the instrument renders the drawee primarily liable as an acceptor. See § 673.414(1). Because there are no conditions precedent to its liability, a cause of action accrues against an acceptor in the case of a demand instrument on the date of the instrument or date of issue. § 673.122(1)(b).

The drawer, on the other hand, is only secondarily liable on the instrument, in that there are conditions precedent to liability. W. Hawkland, Commercial Paper 52 (2d ed 1979). The normal conditions precedent include presentment to the drawee, dishonor, and notice of dishonor. *Id.*; see § 673.501. Therefore, a cause of action against the drawer of a draft accrues only upon demand following dishonor of the instrument. § 673.122(3). Notice of dishonor constitutes a demand. *Id.* This latter section is clearly dispositive of the issue presented, as a cause of action against the drawer herein, Citizens Federal, thus did not accrue until appellant's representative received notice of dishonor from the drawee, Jefferson National Bank.

Florida case authority for the proposition that the statute of limitations begins to run against an issuing bank on a cashier's check at the moment of issuance, *Atlantic National Bank of West Palm Beach v. Havens*, 45 So 2d 342 (Fla 1950), is distinguishable. A cashier's check is a check on which the issuing bank acts as both the drawer and the drawee. Its own act of issuance renders the bank a drawee who has accepted the draft; thus the issuing bank becomes primarily liable as an acceptor. J. White and R. Summers, Uniform Commercial Code § 17-5(2d ed 1980). Presentment of a negotiable instrument is not necessary in order to establish liability against parties who are primarily liable. In such a case the statute of limitations begins to run on a demand instrument at the moment of issuance. W. Hawkland, Commercial Paper 42-43 (2d ed 1979). As to parties secondarily liable, however, such as the drawer herein, there is no instant liability and thus no cause of action until demand following presentment and dishonor. H. Bailey, Brady on Bank Checks § 4.12(5th ed 1979).

The distinction between a cashier's check where the issuing bank is primarily liable and other drafts, where the drawer is secondarily liable, is stated:

> [U]nder the Code, cause of action against a certifying bank or a bank issuing a cashier's check accrues on the date of the check (or date of issue if the check is undated). This means that the statute of limitations begins to run at that time and suit against the bank will be barred after the statute of limitations has run. But a cause of action against a drawer of a check does not accrue until demand following dishonor. This theoretically means that the time for bringing action against the drawer may be deferred indefinitely if there is no presentment for payment.

H. Bailey, Brady on Bank Checks § 4. 12 (5th ed 1979).

Under Florida law an action may not be deferred indefinitely in all instances; instead, a drawer will be discharged from its liability if presentment is unreasonably delayed and the drawee bank becomes insolvent during the delay. § 673.502(1)(b).

In that appellee herein was the drawer of the instrument which is the subject of this action, and therefore only secondarily liable, a cause of action did not accrue against it until after demand following presentment and dishonor on December 20, 1982. The action for wrongful dishonor of the instrument was commenced timely.

Reversed and remanded.

NOTES AND QUESTIONS

(1) Is the distinction between certified checks and personal uncertified checks still relevant? *See* U.C.C. § 3-401 (g) and (h). When will the cause of action "accrue" on an unaccepted personal check? *See* U.C.C. § 3-118(c). On a certified check? *See* § 3-118(d). On a tellers check? *See* § 3-118(d) and Comment 3.

(2) Former U.C.C. § 3-122 was entitled "Accrual of Cause of Action." This section is now omitted from the Code. *See* Comment 1 to U.C.C. 3-118. With the exceptions of § 3-118(g), §§ 3-416(d) and 4-207(e) dealing with Transfer Warranties, and §§ 3-417(f) and 4-208(f) concerning Presentment Warranties, "accrual" is given short shift. U.C.C. § 3-118 does provide an extensive statute of limitations which the former Code did not provide.

WILDMAN STORES, INC. v. CARLISLE DISTRIBUTING CO., INC.

Arkansas Court of Appeals
688 S.W.2d 748, 40 U.C.C. Rep. 1766 (1985)

COOPER, J.

Carlisle Distributing Co., Inc. delivered a check in the amount of $10,000.00 to William Paladino, who pledged the check to the appellant as security for an $8,000.00 loan (which was later repaid in full). Subsequently, the appellant delivered to Paladino a check for $8,200.00, who endorsed it over to John Carlisle in payment of past indebtedness. Some 17 months later the appellant attempted to negotiate the $10,000.00 check, but the payor bank dishonored it. The appellant then sued the appellee Carlisle Distributing Co., Inc. on the $10,000.00 check and later filed suit against John Carlisle's estate to recover the $8,200.00 he received after Paladino endorsed the appellant's check to Mr. Carlisle.

The trial court sitting without a jury dismissed the appellant's complaint, finding that the $10,000.00 check lost its character as a negotiable instrument through age. The court made no specific finding relating to the $8,200.00 check. From that decision, comes this appeal.

The appellant argues on appeal that the trial court erred in failing to grant judgment against the appellee corporation, the maker of the $10,000.00 check, after finding that the appellant was a holder in due course of the negotiable instrument. First, we note that the trial court did not make a specific finding that the appellant was a holder in due course. However, because of our disposition of this case, we need not address that issue.

The trial court ordered that the appellant's complaint be dismissed for failure of proof. In explaining its rationale for refusing to hold the appellee corporation liable on the $10,000.00 check, the court stated that the check had lost its character as a negotiable instrument through age (in the 17 months during which the appellant held the check without presenting it for payment). The trial court erred because the check did not lose its negotiability by the mere passage of time. Also, even if the check for some other reason was nonnegotiable, that fact alone would not discharge the appellee corporation from liability as the drawer of the check. It appears that the trial court misconstrued the relationship between various statutes relating to negotiable instruments, namely Ark Stat Ann, §§ 85-3-503(2)(a)(Add 1961), which prescribes the time for presenting a check for payment, after which time the check becomes stale; 85-3-601(1)(i) and 85-3-502(1)(b) (Add 1961), providing for discharge of a drawer's liability upon unexcused delay in presentment; 85-3-304(3)(c) (Add 1961), attributing notice to the purchaser of an overdue instrument; 37-209 (Repl 1962), the statute of limitations for commencing actions founded upon written instruments not under seal; and 85-3-104 (Add 1961), which sets forth the requisites of negotiability.

The drawer of a dishonored check, the appellee corporation in the case at bar, remained secondarily liable on the check until the statute of limitations ran or until its liability was otherwise discharged. The statute of limitations for instruments not under seal is five years under Ark Stat Ann, § 37-209(Repl 1962), and thus the action against the appellee corporation was not barred by limitations.

Arkansas Statutes Annotated, § 85-3-601(Add 1961), sets forth the conditions under which a party may be discharged from liability on an instrument; subsection (1)(i) deals with discharge due to unexcused delay in presentment, notice of dishonor or protest. When presentment is delayed beyond the time when it is due, the drawer of an instrument is discharged only if the conditions provided for in § 85-3-502(1)(b) (Add 1961) are present. Section 85-3-503(2)(a) (Add 1961) should not be read in conjunction with § 85-3-601(1)(i) so as to discharge the drawer of a check merely because it was stale.

We must reverse and remand this case for a new trial, since the record before us does not indicate whether or not the conditions for discharge were met and that issue was not addressed by the trial court. This court cannot act as a factfinder in cases appealed from circuit court.

The trial court made no findings as to the appellant's claim on the $8,200.00 check. Since we have reversed and remanded for a new trial as to the $10,000.00 check, the issues related to the $8,200.00 check can also be fully developed on retrial.

Reversed and remanded.

NOTES AND QUESTIONS

(1) *See* U.C.C. § 3-414(b) and (f), and Comment 2. Where did the Court find the five year statute of limitations applicable to this situation? How long would appellant have to bring an action on the $10,000 check under the U.C.C. today?

(2) Are there any circumstances under U.C.C. § 3-118 where a cause of action may never be barred?

§ 13.12 Discharge

Read: U.C.C. §§ 3-601 through 3-605.

FIRST NATIONAL BANK OF LONG ISLAND v. ROB-GLEN

New York Supreme Court, Appellate Division
101 A.D.2d 848, 476 N.Y.S.2d 161 (1984)

[The opinion appears in § 12.07, *supra*.]

QUESTIONS

What are the consequences of paying the person entitled to enforce the instrument but leaving the instrument in circulation? Are "instruments" ever discharged?

HOHN v. MORRISON

Colorado Court of Appeals
870 P.2d 513, 23 U.C.C. Rep. 2d 817 (1993)

ROTHENBERG, J.

Plaintiff, Janet E. Hohn, appeals from the judgment of the trial court entered in favor of defendant, Michael J. Morrison. Defendant cross-appeals that portion of the judgment denying his request for interest and attorney fees. We affirm in part, reverse in part, and remand with directions.

In 1978, Hohn purchased approximately 72 acres of vacant land from Morrison. As partial payment for the property, Hohn executed and delivered to Morrison a promissory note for $62,000, secured by a deed of trust (the Morrison note and deed of trust). The note was payable on a monthly basis with a balloon payment due February 1, 1988.

In exchange for the note, Morrison executed and delivered to Hohn a general warranty deed. However, her title was subject to Morrison's deed of trust (the Morrison deed of trust) and also to a prior lien, *i.e.*, a first deed of trust in favor of a third party (the Berry and Stark note and deed of trust).

Over the years, Hohn's payments to Morrison were consistently late and several of her payment checks were returned for insufficient funds. As a result, Morrison began to hold many of the checks for long periods of time before depositing them. Without Morrison's consent, Hohn then began to send her payments on a semi-annual basis.

Subsequently, and without notice to Hohn, Morrison began foreclosure proceedings. However, Hohn cured the foreclosure by sending a check for payments due.

Thereafter, Hohn again began sending her checks late and, again, several checks were returned for insufficient funds. The trial court found that both parties "ignored the provisions of the note and the agreement between them" and that both had caused a "bookkeeping nightmare."

In 1982, Morrison paid off the Berry and Stark note and received the original promissory note, deed of trust, and executed request for release of deed of trust. However, he failed to take steps necessary to release the Berry and Stark deed of trust until 1990.

In November 1987, Hohn obtained a loan commitment from a bank in order to allow her to make the balloon payment due on February 1, 1988. The bank loan to Hohn required release of the Berry and Stark deed of trust. Although she and her attorney subsequently sent Morrison letters requesting a payoff amount, he did not respond.

In January 1988, Hohn and the bank entered into an escrow agreement calling for a special account to hold the loan proceeds. In February 1988, the bank informed Morrison that the funds were being held in an escrow account and would be released to him upon presentation of a release of the Berry and Stark deed of trust, which was the second lien. Morrison did not respond to the bank's letter.

No further activity occurred until 1989, when Hohn attempted to sell the property. Although she entered into a written contract to sell, the sale did not occur because Morrison failed to provide a payoff figure.

Hohn then filed this quiet title action against Morrison and also sought damages for his failure to release both the Morrison note and deed of trust and the Berry and Stark deed of trust. Morrison filed a counterclaim seeking the balance due on the Morrison note and also seeking foreclosure on his deed of trust.

Following a bench trial, the court entered judgment in favor of Morrison in the amount of $37,824 and found that: (1) on February 1, 1988, Hohn made a full legal tender of the amount due; (2) the reason the amount was not paid was Morrison's failure to provide a payoff figure;

(3) once tender was made, Hohn was discharged from further liability for interest, costs, and attorney fees; (4) although there was a tender, there was no actual satisfaction of the indebtedness due under the note; (5) neither Colo. Sess. Laws 1987, ch. 277, § 38-35-124 at 1338-39 nor § 38-35-109(3), C.R.S. (1982 Repl.Vol. 16A) applied to the facts of this case; and (6) Hohn was not entitled to damages and attorney's fees.

The funds were subsequently deposited into the registry of the court pending this appeal. . . .

On cross-appeal, Morrison contends that the trial court erred in denying his request for interest incurred after February 1, 1988, and in denying his request for attorney fees and costs. We disagree.

Section 4-3-604, C.R.S. (1992 Repl.Vol. 2) provides: [The court quotes former § 3-604.]

At trial, the court ruled that Morrison was not entitled to interest, costs, or attorney fees after February 1, 1988 because Hohn made a legal tender on the note on that date by making the escrow funds available to Morrison. The court further ruled that the funds were not released to Morrison because he failed to provide Hohn with the requested payoff statement.

We perceive no error in the court's conclusion. The record clearly supports the court's findings that Hohn was "able and ready" to pay him and had sufficient funds set aside in the escrow to do so. This was tantamount to a tender, and, under these particular circumstances, it was sufficient to discharge Hohn from all liability for interest, costs, and attorney fees incurring after the date of tender.

That part of the judgment denying Hohn attorney fees is reversed, and the cause is remanded for further proceedings regarding such fees. The judgment is affirmed in all other respects.

RULAND and BRIGGS, JJ., concur.

FIRSTIER BANK, N.A. v. TRIPLETT

Nebraska Supreme Court
497 N.W.2d 339, 20 U.C.C. Rep. 2d 549 (1993)

FAHRNBRUCH, J.

After finding that Richard L. and Coralea J. Triplett had not fully paid a promissory note they had given for money they borrowed from FirsTier Bank, N.A., the district court for Washington County entered a $7,231.55 judgment in favor of FirsTier and against the Tripletts.

At trial and in this appeal, the Tripletts, who are husband and wife, contend that their debt was satisfied when their note was marked "paid" and mailed to them by FirsTier. The trial court found that the note was unintentionally marked "paid" and mailed to the Tripletts as a result of clerical error and without the bank's authority.

ASSIGNMENT OF ERROR

Restated, the sole issue on appeal is whether the district court erred in granting a money judgment on a promissory note that had been marked "paid" and returned to the maker.

FACTS

At trial, two original promissory notes the Tripletts gave to FirsTier was referred to as exhibits 7 and 8. Exhibit 7, dated April 17, 1986, was for $14,000. It was secured by a 1986 Toyota pickup and a 1979 Lincoln automobile and was originally due April 20, 1990. By subsequent agreement, the due date was extended to June 20, 1990. Exhibit 8, dated June 16, 1987, was for $3,500. The note was secured by a 1979 Ford van.

The Tripletts sold the Toyota, and on July 6, 1987, Richard Triplett tendered a check for $7,200 as payment on the notes to FirsTier's branch at Blair, Nebraska. At the time the check was tendered, the balance was $10,498.79 on exhibit 7 and $2,418.73 on exhibit 8.

In late July 1987, the Tripletts received a letter from FirsTier containing an original "Note and Security Agreement," exhibit 7, which was stamped "PAID . . .FirsTier Bank, N.A. Omaha, Nebraska." The stamp was signed by a clerk and hand dated "7-7-87." In November 1987, exhibit 8 was returned to the Tripletts. It also was stamped "PAID . . .FirsTier Bank, N.A. Omaha, Nebraska," and hand dated "7-7-87," but was signed by another clerk.

At trial, a bank officer testified that when a note has been paid in full, it is FirsTier's practice to send a computer-generated form letter over the original loan officer's name, thanking the customer for his or her business. He testified that the loan officer never sees or signs these letters, which he believed were signed by a clerk.

Richard Triplett testified that more than a year after receiving the last note, he received notice from FirsTier that the Tripletts still owed money on one of the notes. When FirsTier demanded payments of the note, Richard Triplett indicated to FirsTier that "the loan was paid up."

In May 1989, FirsTier sued the Tripletts for payment of the balance remaining on exhibit 7, for reformation and reinstatement of the erroneously canceled note, and for reinstatement of FirsTier's security interest.

At trial, Leonard Olson, FirsTier's vice president and manager of loan operations, testified that exhibit 7 had never been paid in full, although regular payment had been made until one large payment of $4,781.27 was made on July 6, 1987. At the time of trial, exhibit 7 had an outstanding balance of $7,231.55, representing $5,717.52 in principal plus accrued interest, which continued to accrue at a rate of 10 percent, or $1.57 per day. Olson also testified that with the payment of $2,418.73 on July 6, 1987, exhibit 8 was paid in full.

Olson testified that through clerical error, the file for exhibit 7 was pulled instead of the file for exhibit 8 and that a clerk erroneously marked exhibit 7 "paid." Olson testified that the employee who marked exhibit 7 "paid" was a loan service clerk, one step above an entry-level position. According to Olson, the loan service clerk did not have authority to release a note which had not been paid in full, and FirsTier never intended to discharge exhibit 7 without payment in full. Both Olson and Lloyd Sheve, vice president and manager of FirsTier's Blair branch, testified that only the bank's collection department could authorize the release of an unpaid note, and they testified that neither of them had ever received authorization to settle and release exhibit 7.

In spite of Richard Triplett's initial representation to FirsTier that "the loan was paid up," the Tripletts do not dispute the fact that exhibit 7 has never been paid in full. Both of the Tripletts testified that they knew the $7,200 check was insufficient to pay off the balances of both notes. Richard Triplett testified that he had made no representations to FirsTier that he was paying off both notes. He testified that he did not know whether FirsTier had made an error in releasing exhibit 7.

Instead, the Tripletts alleged that exhibit 7 was discharged pursuant to § 3-605 (Reissue 1980) by (1) intentional cancellation of the note which was not a result of a mutual mistake or a unilateral mistake caused by the Tripletts' fraud or inequitable conduct and (2) surrender of the note.

The district court made specific factual findings that

> at the time of the $7,200.00 payment by the Defendants [Tripletts] to the Plaintiff [FirsTier], the Defendants specifically acknowledged and knew that said $7,200.00 was insufficient to make payment in full on both promissory notes. . .. [T]here was no intent on the part of FirsTier Bank to release promissory note [exhibit 7] for less than payment in full thereof, there was no agreement nor consideration to support same that promissory note [exhibit 7] would be released without payment in full, the stamping of [exhibit 7] as paid in full and the return thereof to the Defendants was as a result of a clerical error, allowing said release of promissory note [exhibit 7] would result in unjust enrichment to the [Tripletts], and the individual in the clerical position stamping promissory notes for return to bank customers did not have the authority or power to authorize the release of promissory notes without payment in full thereof.

The court entered a $7,231.44 judgment, plus interest and costs, in favor of FirsTier on its first cause of action and granted no relief on the second and third causes of action. The Tripletts appealed. FirsTier did not cross-appeal.

ANALYSIS

The Tripletts claim that their debt on exhibit 7 was discharged as a matter of law under § 3-606(1) (Reissue 1980) because FirsTier marked exhibit 7 "paid" and returned it to them. FirsTier counters that a promissory note is not discharged when it is canceled as the result of clerical error by a party who has no authority to release a loan. The bank's position is that such an action does not constitute intent to cancel the maker's indebtedness and that therefore there was no discharge of the note.

Section 3-605 governed the discharge of negotiable instrument through cancellation or renunciation at all times material to this case. That statute provided in part:

> (1) The holder of an instrument may even without consideration discharge any party,
>
> (a) in any manner apparent on the face of the instrument or the indorsement, as *by intentionally cancelling the instrument* or the party's signature by destruction or mutilation, or by striking out the party's signature; or
>
> (b) by renouncing his rights by a writing signed and delivered or *by surrender of the instrument to the party to be discharged.*

(Emphasis supplied.)

Whether a promissory note is discharged pursuant to the Uniform Commercial Code when it is marked "paid" and surrendered to the maker is a question of first impression in Nebraska.

Other jurisdictions have considered the question, and their opinions are persuasive in deciding this case.

Because FirsTier both stamped exhibit 7 "paid" and surrendered it to the Tripletts by mailing it back to them, we must consider whether either of these actions by FirsTier had the effect of discharging the Tripletts' indebtedness under the note.

Subsection (a) of § 3-605(1) clearly stated that cancellation must be done "intentionally." Courts that have considered discharge of a promissory note under their states' counterparts to subsection (a) have held that cancellation must be accompanied by an *intent to discharge the maker*. . .. Such intent is not the equivalent of a clerk's stamping the note "paid" when, in fact, it has not been paid. . .. The Tripletts' assertion that the physical act of intentionally stamping exhibit 7 "paid" discharges the note as a matter of law is plainly incorrect in the absence of FirsTier's intent to discharge the Tripletts' indebtedness.

Although subsection (b) of § 3-605(1) did not specifically state that *surrender* of an instrument must be intentional in order to effect a discharge, "[t]he courts have glossed this section by requiring that surrender of the instrument be accompanied by an intent to discharge the party." 1 James J. White & Robert S. Summers, Uniform Commercial Code § 13-22at 683 (3d ed. 1988). This is consistent with the Legislature's latest revision of Nebraska's Uniform Commercial Code. Discharge by cancellation or renunciation is now governed by Neb. U.C.C. § 3-604(Reissue 1992), which replaced § 3-605 (Reissue 1980). Section 3-604(a) provides that "[a] person entitled to enforce an instrument . . .may discharge the obligation of a party to pay the instrument (i) by an *intentional* voluntary act, such as *surrender* of the instrument to the party . . .or *cancellation* of the instrument. . .." (Emphasis supplied.) This language requires that discharge be intentional, whether by cancellation *or* surrender.

All jurisdictions that have considered the issue have concluded that clerical error does not have the legal effect of canceling an existing debt or discharging an instrument. This is simply an application of the general rule that cancellation or surrender of an instrument has no effect when done by a person without authority from the holder of the instrument. A bank may recover even when its agents or officers have acted negligently, to prevent the maker of a note from retaining a gratuitous benefit to which he or she is not entitled.

Although the Tripletts, citing *J.J. Schaefer Livestock Hauling v. Gretna St. Bank*, 229 Neb. 580, 428 N.W.2d 185 [7 U.C.C. Rep. Serv. 2d 143] (1988), and *Peterson v Crown Financial Corp.*. 661 F.2d 287 [32 U.C.C. Rep. Serv. 497] (3d Cir. 1981), argue that subjective intent of the holder is irrelevant, both of these cases are distinguishable from the case at bar on their facts.

In *J.J. Schaefer Livestock Hauling,* the president and vice president of a bank satisfied promissory notes which the bank was holding by exercising the bank's right of setoff against the maker's account, to the detriment of third parties who were entitled to the funds in the account. The notes were canceled and returned to the maker. Only after the bank was compelled by legal process to reimburse the third parties did the bank attempt reformation of the notes in what was essentially a claim for indemnity against the maker. This court held that surrender of the notes discharged the obligations as a matter of law. The court adopted the rationale of *Peterson* that " parties . . .which deal regularly in negotiable instruments, ought to be held, as a matter of law, to an understanding of the implications which normal business practice assigns to intentionally cancelling [an] instrument . . . . [Citation omitted.] [S]ubjective intent not to discharge was irrelevant; mere intent to cancel was sufficient."

In *Peterson,* a lender incorrectly advised a maker, Peterson, that $499,658.85 in interest was due on his note, instead of the $860,837.57 which was actually due. Peterson paid $500,000 in interest, and a vice president of the lending institution sent him a letter thanking him for his payment and advising him that this payment represented the interest due at that time. Peterson executed a new note to replace the previous note. The lender stamped the first note "canceled" and returned it to Peterson. When the second note became due 3 years later, the lender attempted to collect the deficiency in interest from the previous note.

Construing Pennsylvania law, the U.S. Court of Appeals for the Third Circuit held that the first note was discharged as a matter of law. However, the court made it clear that this was a very narrow holding:

> In such a situation . . .the lending institution is deemed as a matter of law not to have intended that the old indebtedness survive. Subjective intent *under these circumstances* is irrelevant; *in the absence of clerical error or other mistake—neither of which is claimed here*—the lender cannot, consistent with the dictates of § 3-605, remain free to insist upon the terms of a cancelled note simply because it did not subjectively intend to alter its terms.

The court explicitly stated that an underlying obligation would not be discharged by unintentional or mistaken cancellation.

Thus, both *J.J. Schaefer Livestock Hauling* and *Peterson* are distinguishable from the present case. In *J.J. Schaefer Livestock Hauling,* the notes were intentionally canceled and surrendered by bank officers who had the authority of the holder to discharge the indebtedness. They also had no actual knowledge of the transactions and their legal ramifications. In *Peterson,* there also was no claim of clerical error. In the case at bar, FirsTier had no intention to cancel the Tripletts' indebtedness. The claimed discharge was through clerical error by an individual who had no authority to do so.

Therefore, the issue before the court is whether FirsTier possessed the requisite intent to discharge the Tripletts' indebtedness, as evidences by exhibit 7, by either cancellation or surrender of the note. Intent is a question of fact.

That exhibit 7 has never been fully paid is undisputed. Two of FirsTier's vice presidents testified that FirsTier had no intention to discharge exhibit 7 without payment in full that no one with authority to discharge exhibit 7 had done so, and that the cancellation and surrender of the note was done through clerical error. The Tripletts offered no evidence to refute this testimony.

CONCLUSION

The district court's factual finding that the note, exhibit 7, was unintentionally released through clerical error is not clearly erroneous. We hold that the unintentional cancellation and surrender of a promissory note through clerical error do not discharge the maker of the note. The district court's judgment is affirmed.

Affirmed.

GRANT, J., dissenting.

I respectfully dissent. When the promissory notes in question were made, and when payment of the notes was sought by litigation, Neb. U.C.C. § 3-605(Reissue 1980) provided, in part: "(1) The holder of an instrument may even without consideration discharge any party . . .(b) by renouncing his rights by a writing signed and delivered or by surrender of the instrument to the party to be discharged."

The evidence shows that plaintiff renounced its rights against defendants "by a writing signed and delivered" in a letter to defendants, which letter enclosed defendants' note stamped "paid." The instrument in question was surrendered to defendants.

The majority recognizes that subsection (b) of § 3-605 did not specifically state that surrender of an instrument must be intentional in order to effect a discharge. The majority, however, adopts the view of commentators and other courts that " 'courts have glossed this section by requiring that surrender of the instrument be accompanied by an intent to discharge the party.' " When language in a statute is clear, I do not believe that courts should "gloss" legislative language to reach a goal which courts guess that the Legislature desired.

By adopting Neb. U.C.C. § 3-604 (Reissue 1992) to replace § 3-605 (Reissue 1980), the Legislature recognize that the earlier act did not give lending institutions the protection that the court has afforded such institutions in this case. Section 3-605, prior to adoption of § 3-604 (Reissue 1992), provided (without glossing) that the holder of a note could discharge the maker of the note in various ways that did not require intent. Plaintiff, the holder of the note in question, so acted, without any fraud or inducement by defendants.

To permit a bank to prevail in this litigation removes much certainty in banking transactions. The resulting uncertainty is bad for lenders and borrowers. All parties to promissory notes must now wonder if a bank means that a note is paid just because the bank says that it is paid.

I would reverse the judgment, but if the judgment must be affirmed, I also question the amount of the judgment. At the time of trial, apparently, plaintiff contended that the principal sum of $5,717.52 was due. Most of any delay in repayment was caused specifically by plaintiff's actions in telling defendants that the note was paid. Under those circumstances, when the trial court did not reform or reinstate the note in question as plaintiff requested. I do not see how plaintiff is entitled to any interest as set out in the note. If judgment must he entered, it should be in the amount of $5,717.52. Granting interest on that judgment, of course, is different from, in effect, granting plaintiff prejudgment interest.

CAPORALE, J., dissenting.

I join in that portion of Judge Grant's dissent which declares that we ought not read into Neb. U.C.C. § 3-605(Reissue 1980) an intent requirement which is absent from the statutory language. Indeed, we have piously pronounced that courts may not add language to the plain terms of a statute so as to either restrict or extend its meaning. *See Wittler v. Baumgartner*, 180 Neb. 446, 144 N.W.2d 62 (1966). The fact that courts of other jurisdictions saw fit to engage in acts of judicial legislation does not license us to do the same.

QUESTION

What is "glossing?"

PEOPLES NATIONAL BANK OF MORA v. BOYER

[The opinion appears in § 13.10, *supra.*]

FEDERAL DEPOSIT INSURANCE CORP. v. BLUE ROCK SHOPPING CENTER, INC.

[The opinion appears in § 13.10, *supra.*] The materials dealing generally with the discharge of accommodation parties under U.C.C. § 3-605 are found in § 13.10 *supra.*]

WILDMAN STORES INC. v. CARLISLE DISTRIBUTING CO. INC.

[The opinion appears in § 13.11, *supra.*]

NOTES

(1) *See* U.C.C. § 3-414(f) and Comment 6. *See also* § 3-414(c) and Comment 3.

(2) *See* U.C.C. § 3-415(e) and Comment 4, concerning discharge of indorsers of checks when the check is not presented for payment, § 3-415(c) when necessary notice of dishonor is not given, and § 3-415(d) when draft is accepted by a bank after an indorsement is made.

(3) Regarding the discharge of warrantors by untimely notice of a claim for breach of the transfer and presentment warranties, *see* §§ 3-416(c) (4-207(d)) and 3-417(e) (4-208(e)).

(4) For discharge by alteration of an instrument, *see* U.C.C. § 3-407(b).

(5) For discharge by an acceptance varying a draft, *see* U.C.C. § 3-410(c).

(6) For discharge by virtue of reacquisition, *see* U.C.C. § 3-207.

HARDISON v. JACKSON

Arkansas Court of Appeals
45 Ark App 49, 23 U.C.C. Rep. 2d 136 (1994)

John Mauzy Pittman, J.

Appellees, Michael and Cathy Jackson, sued appellants for $1,200.00, which they alleged was due them on their contract to paint appellants' house. The trial court awarded appellees judgment for this amount together with $1,500.00 in attorney's fees after finding appellants had not proved their defense of accord and satisfaction. On appeal, appellants claim that the trial court erred in not holding that appellees' acceptance of appellants' check of $460.50 operated as an accord and satisfaction of their claim against appellants. They also argue that the court erred in awarding attorney's fees. Appellees contend on cross-appeal that the attorney's fees awarded them were unreasonably low. We agree with appellants and therefore reverse on appeal. Because the issue raised by appellees then becomes moot, we dismiss the cross-appeal.

On September 30, 1991, appellees submitted an oral bid of $2,450.00 to paint the inside of appellants' house. The bid was accepted by appellants, and they advanced appellees $750.00 of their fee. After appellees began painting the house, a dispute arose as to whether certain work was included within the parties' agreement and when the work was to be completed. Appellants contend they were forced to cancel an open house because the work was not completed by an October 12 deadline. Appellees argue, however, that the painting was completed by October 6. There was also a dispute regarding the quality of appellees' work and the amount of work that was included in the agreement.

On October 19, appellee Mike Jackson attended the auction of appellants' house in order to be paid the remainder of appellees' fee. Appellants' real estate agent, Larry Boling, met with Jackson and advised him that appellants refused to pay him any more money but later returned and told him that appellants had agreed to pay him $500.00. After some discussion, Jackson agreed to take appellants' check for $460.50.[42] Jackson was then given a check on which was written "Pd. in full for painting." Several days later, Jackson scratched out the "Pd. in full" notation and inserted the words "Mike Jackson payment not made in full" and cashed it.

Appellees later file suit for the $1,200.00 balance they alleged was due them under the parties' oral agreement. Appellants defended that appellees' acceptance of their $460.50 check operated as an accord and satisfaction of their claim. After a trial on the merits, the chancellor held that

[42] Although the parties agreed to a payment of $500.00, the check was written for $460.50 because certain items Jackson purchased at the auction were deducted from it.

appellants had not proved their defense of accord and satisfaction and awarded appellees judgment of $1,200.00 and attorney's fees of $1,500.00

On appeal, appellants claim appellees' acceptance of their check bearing the notation "Pd. in full for painting" is an accord and satisfaction of appellees' claim. Appellees cross-appeal that the trial court erred in not awarding them the entire $5,050.00 they claimed in attorney's fees.

An accord and satisfaction generally involves a settlement in which one party agrees to pay and the other to receive a different consideration or a sum less than the amount to which the latter is or considers himself entitled. There must be a disputed amount involved and a consent to accept less than the amount in settlement of the whole before acceptance of the lesser amount can be an accord and satisfaction, and, while it is not necessary that the dispute or controversy be well founded, it is necessary that it be made in good faith.

Generally, acceptance by a creditor of a check offered by the debtor in full payment of a disputed claim is an accord and satisfaction of the claim. *Dyke Indus., Inc. v. Waldrop, supra.* A payee is estopped to deny an account has been paid in full where, after a dispute as to the amount due, a payee accepts and cashes a check that recites it is in settlement of the account. *See Market Produce Co. v. Holland*, 183 Ark. 711, 38 S.W.2d 317 (1931), where the supreme court stated:

> It is true that, in order to constitute an accord and satisfaction, it is necessary that the offer of the payment should be made by one party in full satisfaction of the demand, and should be accepted as such by the other. But when the claim is disputed and unliquidated, and a less amount than is demanded is offered in full payment, the question as to whether the creditor in such case does so agree to accept the amount offered in full satisfaction of his demand is a mixed question of law and fact. If the offer or tender is accompanied by declarations and acts so as to amount to a condition that, if the creditor accepts the amount offered, it must be in satisfaction of his demand, and the creditor understands therefrom that, if he takes it subject to that condition, then an acceptance by the creditor will estop him from denying that he has agreed to accept the amount in full payment of his demand. His action in accepting the tender under such conditions will speak, and his words of protest only will not avail him.

Pillow v. Thermogas Co. of Walnut Ridge, 6 Ark. App. 402, 644 S.W.2d 292 [35 U.C.C. Rep. Serv. 1404] (1982), is similar to the case at bar. There, the appellee accepted a check and scratched through the notation on the check "acc in full" and wrote "check not accepted in full payment of account" and signed and cashed it. The trial judge held the appellee was entitled to judgment for the difference between the full amount he claimed and the amount paid by the check from the appellants. On appeal, this court reversed, holding that the appellee's unilateral alteration of the check was of no legal consequence and that he had the option of accepting the check as tendered or of returning it. We stated:

> [W]e hold that the acceptance by a creditor of a check offered by the debtor in full payment of a disputed claim is an accord and satisfaction of the claim. A unilateral action by the creditor in protest or an attempted reservation of rights by the alteration of a check offered as payment in full is of no legal consequence.

In 1991, these general rules concerning accord and satisfaction by use of an instrument were codified at Ark. Code Ann. § 4-3-311 (Repl. 1991), which provides in part [The court quotes U.C.C. § 3-311(a) and (b).]

In the case at bar, the chancellor found that "this dispute raised by the [appellants] was raised by [appellants] after the contract amount was due and owing," and used this finding as the basis for holding that appellants had not proved their defense of accord and satisfaction. We cannot agree that this finding is supported by the evidence. Furthermore, it is not conclusive of whether appellants proved their defense of accord and satisfaction. It is the circumstances that exist when the payment for the lesser amount is received that determine whether an accord and satisfaction has been reached. Here, it is uncontested that a dispute existed between the parties at the time appellees accepted and obtained payment of appellants' check. Both parties admitted that there was some disagreement as to what work was supposed to be performed under the contract and the time frame in which it was to be completed. Appellee Mike Jackson admitted there was some controversy as to whether appellees were supposed to paint the vents and the inside of the kitchen cabinets and that appellees were unable to finish painting the garage because there was large machinery preventing them from getting to all the walls. He also stated that, on the day he came back to wash appellants' house prior to the auction, appellant Hardison told him to leave, that the work should have been already completed, and that appellees were not getting paid.

Appellant Jack Hardison testified that appellees were supposed to paint the insides of the cabinets, that the paint job was shoddy, and that appellees left paint on the wall plugs, the stained wood, the window sills, the glass, the ceilings, the floors, and the carpet. He stated that the job was to be completed by October 12 but their equipment was still there on that date. He stated the next time he saw Jackson, on the 17th or 18th when Jackson came out to spray down the house, he told him that the house had already been sprayed and there was nothing further for appellees to do.

In reference to the $460.50 check appellants gave appellees, Hardison testified that, on the day of the auction, Jackson came to the auction and sent Larry Boling over to appellants for his money. He stated that he told Boling that Jackson had been overpaid with the $750.00 as far as he was concerned but that Boling convinced him to pay Jackson $500.00 more. He stated he gave Boling a check on which his wife had written "Pd. in full for painting" to give Jackson.

Larry Boling testified that it was explained to appellees that the house needed to be ready for the open house, that he had trouble getting Jackson to start work, that Jackson knew Mr. Hardison was not happy with the work, and that Jackson and Hardison argued every time they were together. He stated that, when Jackson came to the auction, he told him the Hardisons were not willing to pay him the full amount but he could get him $500.00 and that Jackson replied to go ahead and give him his money and he would go. He stated that Jackson did not say anything about going to court when he accepted the $460.50 check.

Jackson testified that he returned on the day of the auction and Larry Boling told him that appellants were displeased with the work, that they had an offer they would make him, and that was all they were going to pay. He stated that he told Boling that he had given appellants plenty of time to let him know if there was a problem and Boling then went to talk to appellants. He stated that Boling then returned and told him that appellants would pay him $500.00 but that was all they would pay, and that it was "either take it or leave it." Jackson testified he told Boling to tell appellants to give him the $500.00 and that Mrs. Hardison then gave him a check on which she had written "Pd. in full for painting." He stated he told Mrs. Hardison and Boling that it was not over and he was going to get the rest of his money.

On appeal, chancery cases are tried de novo on the record. Nevertheless, we will not reverse the findings of the chancellor unless they are clearly erroneous or clearly against the preponderence of the evidence. A finding is clearly erroneous when, although there is evidence to support it, the reviewing court on the entire evidence is left with a definite and firm conviction that a mistake has been committed.

Here, the uncontroverted evidence plainly shows that appellants disputed the amount they owed appellees when appellee accepted appellants' check. We therefore conclude that appellants proved their defense of accord and satisfaction and the chancellor's award of damages and attorney's fees in favor of appellees is clearly erroneous.

The judgment for damages and attorney's fees in favor of appellees is reversed and dismissed. Because appellees' cross-appeal for additional attorney's fees is predicated on their having prevailed on their contract claim against appellants, *see* Ark. Code Ann. § 16-22-308 (Supp. 1991), and we have reversed that judgment, appellees' cross-appeal is rendered moot.

Reversed on appeal; dismissed on cross-appeal.

ROBBINS and ROGERS, JJ., agree.

NOTE

ACCORD AND SATISFACTION

Under § 3-311 (1990), it is recognized that a person who is in good faith tenders a check as full satisfaction of the claim, can indeed effectuate a settlement of the dispute. If the check is sent to the proper person in the company with the proper statement, then the claim is discharged. But the person who sends the check to the person against whom the claim is asserted must prove that the instrument or accompanying written communication contained a conspicuous statement to the effect that the instrument was tendered as full satisfaction for the claim. If that is done, then the cashing of that check by the creditor represents a settlement of that dispute.

As the drafters have stated, Section 3-311 follows the common law rule with a minor variation to reflect modern business conditions. In cases covered by Section 3-311, there often will be an individual on one side of the dispute and a business organization on the other. This section is designed neither to favor the individual nor the business organization. In the first example, the person seeking accord and satisfaction is a consumer who, in paying for disputed goods that are defective, tenders a lesser amount. In the second example, an insurance company tenders an amount in settlement, seeking the accord and satisfaction. Revised Section 3-311 is based on the belief that the common law rule produces a fair result and that informal dispute resolution by full satisfaction checks should be encouraged. Thus it settles the conflicting court decisions. This new section permits one to settle disputes through the use of a negotiable instrument that contains a conspicuous statement that this is in settlement of the dispute or in full payment of it.

While there may be some cases which deal with whether the statement of full payment and settlement is conspicuous or not, conspicuous is defined elsewhere in the Code. A statement is "conspicuous" if it is so written "that a reasonable person against whom it is to operate ought to have noticed it." In most cases, a statement written on either the face of the check or on the back where indorsements are made would seem readily noticeable. Indeed, it could be put in both places to be "super-conspicuous." The validity of this general means of settling various disputes is now recognized. The creditor is precluded from taking and cashing that check and simply noting that it is not in full settlement or from simply striking and ignoring that statement and cashing the check.

While business organizations and creditors will undoubtedly quickly become aware of the law in this regard, it may be asked whether most consumers will be. In the drafter's example of the insurance company sending an individual a settlement check, marked "Payment in Full," will that person realize that this terminates his legal rights? Is it in regard to property loss, hospital expenses, personal injuries, or other consequential losses? Should there be further notice or explanation? Since many consumers will not be aware of this legal result, should there be either an amendment or separate protective legislation requiring a thorough and more conspicuous or separate notice?

---

§ 13.13 Effect of Instrument on Underlying Obligation

Read: U.C.C. § 3-310.

BERARDINI v. HART

Colorado Court of Appeals
682 P.2d 519, 38 U.C.C. Rep. 941 (1984)

KELLY, J.

Plaintiff appeals from a judgment for defendant on a claim for professional services. We affirm.

Trial was to the court on the following stipulated facts. Defendant incurred a debt of $3,883.69 to plaintiff for attorney's fees arising from plaintiff's representation of defendant between October 1975 and January 1978. In payment of the fees, defendant assigned a promissory note for $5,000 to plaintiff. As part of this transaction, plaintiff gave defendant a check for $1,701.31.

The maker of the promissory note paid plaintiff a total of only $600 before filing for bankruptcy in which proceeding the maker's debt on the note was later discharged. Plaintiff then brought suit on the note against defendant claiming an outstanding balance of $4,400.

In relevant part, the written assignment stated that:

> G. Phillip Hart, hereby assigns all right, title, and interest in and to that certain Promissory Note dated August 11, 1978 in the principal sum of $5,000. . ..
>
> The consideration for this assignment is as follows:
>
> 1. The full and complete discharge of attorney's fees to Assignee in the sum of $3,883.69.
>
> 2. Assignee's order for payment in the amount of $1,701.31.

The check from plaintiff to defendant bore the following notation:

> When cashed constitutes full and complete discharge, satisfaction, and liquidation of any and all accounts between payor and payee, including but not limited to, the purchase by assignment of a $5,000 Promissory Note from Dr. John P Dugan dated 3/1/78, to G. Phillip Hart.

The trial court entered judgment for defendant finding that "the language of the release on the back of the $1,701.31 check terminated the financial relationship of the plaintiff and the defendant."

Plaintiff's sole contention on appeal is that defendant's debt to plaintiff was discharged only to the extent of the $600 received by plaintiff from the maker of the note. We disagree.

Plaintiff contends that a limited discharge of the debt follows from § 4-3-802(1), CRS, which states:

> Unless otherwise agreed, where an instrument is taken for an underlying obligation:
>
> . . . .
>
> (b) . . .the obligation is suspended pro tanto until the instrument is due or if it is payable on demand until its presentment. If the instrument is dishonored, action may be maintained on either the instrument or the obligation. . . .

However, the rule of this statute that a negotiable instrument constitutes conditional payment is expressly subject to the condition "[u]nless otherwise agreed." Hence, if the parties agree that one of them will take an instrument in satisfaction of the debt, then the underlying obligation is discharged by acceptance of the instrument. J. White & R. Summers, Uniform Commercial Code § 13-20 at 541 (1980).

Here, the written assignment expressly stated that the consideration for the assignment of the promissory note was "the full and complete discharge of attorney's fees to Assignee in the sum of $3,883.69." This language, together with the notations upon the $ 1,701.31 check, unequivocally demonstrates that the promissory note was offered in full satisfaction of defendant's underlying obligation to plaintiff. Accordingly, acceptance of the promissory note by plaintiff discharged defendant's obligation to plaintiff. See Restatement (Second) of Contracts § 287 (1981).

Judgment affirmed.

ROY v. MUGFORD

Vermont Supreme Court
642 A.688, 24 U.C.C. Rep.2d 963 (1994)

DOOLEY, J.

Plaintiffs Denis and Helen Roy appeal from a decision of the Washington Superior Court denying them attorney's fees on their successful action to recover $20,000 due on a 1987 promissory note. Defendants are Wayne and Waldo Mugford; Peerless Granite Company, a business the Mugfords purchased from plaintiffs by stock sale; and M & W Polishing Company, another business owned by the Mugfords. Defendants cross-appeal the court's decisions to allow recovery of the $20,000. We affirm the court's award of the $20,000 plus interest, but reverse and remand for determination and award of attorney's fees.

In the fall of 1986, plaintiffs, who were then in the process of divorcing, decided to sell Peerless Granite Company in order to take advantage of favorable capital gains tax treatment that was to be eliminated after 1986. Denis Roy contacted certain local companies about buying Peerless, and defendants Mugford, who had been contemplating expanding their granite polishing business, showed immediate interest. On December 6, the Mugfords took a tour of the Peerless operation. During this visit, Helen Roy gave them computer-generated balance sheets covering the period July 1984 through November 1986. Plaintiffs explained to the Mugfords that the Peerless accounts would change through the end of December, reflecting normal operating expenses.

To expedite the sale, the parties negotiated a straight stock purchase. The purchase and sale agreement was drafted by the Mugfords' attorney. The closing took place on the evening of December 31, 1986, with plaintiffs signing over all sixteen outstanding Peerless shares, twelve owned by Denis Roy and four by Helen Roy, in exchange for consideration of $670,000. The final price was negotiated down from the plaintiffs' asking price of $700,000. Prior to this closing, the Mugfords neither requested, nor were they provided, with any financial information other than that which they received in early December. They relied, however, on advice and analysis supplied by their accountant.

Although the sale was closed on the evening of December 31, defendants did not complete their permanent financing until a second closing on January 30, 1987. During the second closing, Peerless Granite Company, by Wayne Mugford, executed a $59,000 promissory note to plaintiffs, with final payment due July 1, 1987. Like the purchase and sale agreement, this note was also drafted by defendants' attorney. The final paragraph of this note provided: "In the event of the default of this note, the maker and any endorsers hereof hereby agree to pay all reasonable attorney's fees and the costs of collection necessarily incurred."

During the day of December 31, Helen Roy drew herself a $20,000 bonus check. When she drew the check, Helen Roy was not aware that the Mugfords had decided to purchase Peerless and that the closing would occur that evening. The bonus was taken pursuant to a temporary divorce stipulation signed by Helen and Denis Roy in September. Plaintiffs had agreed that Helen would take a bonus before year end, which would be treated as salary for her, and that the bonus would then be deposited into a college tuition account for their children. Helen Roy did not disclose the bonus at the closing.

The Mugfords discovered the bonus payment three months later when Helen Roy stopped working for Peerless and was replaced by a new bookkeeper. At that time, defendants asked plaintiffs to explain the payment. Not satisfied with plaintiffs' answer, defendants withheld $20,000 from their final payment on the $59,000 promissory note and placed it in an escrow account for a time, but later withdrew the funds. Plaintiffs subsequently filed suit to recover the $20,000 withheld from the final note payment.

On appeal, plaintiffs' sole argument is that the trial court abused its discretion in failing to award attorney's fees under the promissory note. We agree and reverse and remand for calculation and award of such fees. On cross-appeal, defendants make four arguments that actually reduce to two: (1) the taking of the bonus by check, cashed after the stock was transferred to the Mugfords, violated the purchase and sale agreement as a matter of law; and (2) the court failed to make essential findings to dispose fully of defendants' affirmative defenses and counterclaims. We are not persuaded by defendants' contentions, and, therefore, we affirm judgment for plaintiffs in the amount of $20,000 plus interest. We address defendants' arguments on the underlying judgment before turning to the matter of attorney's fees.

Defendants first argue that plaintiffs breached the stock purchase agreement, requiring reversal of the trial court's judgment as a matter of law. Specifically, defendants content that when plaintiff Helen Roy wrote the $20,000 bonus check to herself on December 31, 1986, but did not deposit the check until January 6, 1987, she violated Paragraph 6 of the Stock Purchase and Sale Agreement, which states:

> All loans and indebtedness owned to DENNIS A. ROY and HELEN ROY by the [Peerless] corporation will be cancelled on the corporate books as of December 31, 1986, the date of closing.

Citing 9A V.S.A. § 3-802(1) and the accompanying commentary, defendants contend that a check is nothing more than a loan or indebtedness until presented for payment, that is, simply a conditional payment which remains suspended until presented. According to the terms of Paragraph 6, defendants' argument runs, Peerless' indebtedness to Helen Roy in the form of that $20,000 check was cancelled as of the closing and, therefore, plaintiffs breached Paragraph 6 when they took payment on a cancelled obligation from Peerless after December 31.

The short answer to defendants' contention is that payment on a check relates back to the time the check is delivered to the payee. *See Ivy v. American Roads Ins. Co.*, So. 2d 165, 166 (La.Ct.App.) ("The law is well established that a check is a conditional payment and once the check has made its commercial cycle back to the drawee bank where it is finally accepted and paid, such payment relates back to the time the check was delivered to the payee. . ..."), rev'd on other grounds, 409 So. 2d 549 [33 U.C.C. Rep. Serv. 622] (La.1981); *Regents of Univ. of New Mexico v. Lacey*, 107 N.M. 742, 744, 764 P.2d 873, 875 (1988) (payment relates back to time of delivery of check; citing 6 R. Anderson, Anderson on The Uniform Commercial Code § 3-802:19(3d ed. 1984) and collecting cases); see also *General Motors Acceptance Corp. v. Abington Casualty Ins. Co.*, 413 Mass. 583, 602 N.E.2d 1085, 1087 [18 U.C.C. Rep. Serv. 2d 1151] (1992) (underlying debt discharged when check delivered to payee and drawn on account with sufficient funds at solvent bank). In this case, payment on the $20,000 bonus check related back to the December 31, delivery date, and therefore was not a loan or debt outstanding as of the closing. As a Louisiana court has observed, the purpose of allowing payment of a check to relate back to the date of delivery

> is both logical and apparent. It is commonplace in today's highly commercialized society to discharge obligations by the use of checks. Many obligations require that payments be made timely or at certain times. Examples are installment notes, insurance premiums . . .and many others. The rule . . .protects the debtor from such claims as possible additional interest, penalties or breach of contract for untimely payment. The rule is designed to allow . . .timely payment by check . . .otherwise it would make the timeliness of payment depend upon the actions of the creditor. Thus a debtor who paid by check would not be assured that his payment was timely even though the check was delivered timely.

Ivy, 298 So. 2d at 167.

For the defendants' argument to have any merit, we would have to find that there was no agreement that the check constituted payment. *See Drew v. Chrysler Credit Corp.*, 596 F.Supp. 1371, 1376 (D.Mo. 1984) ("Where there is no agreement that the check itself shall constitute payment, a 'satisfaction' does not occur until payment of the check has actually been received.").

There is no evidence suggesting that Helen Roy did not intend that the check constitute payment of her 1986 bonus salary.

Even outside of the relation-back doctrine, defendants' argument would fail because it neglects other, more relevant sections of Article 3 of the Uniform Commercial Code. Under the Code, the check Helen Roy drew was a negotiable instrument. *See* 9A V.S.A. § 3-104 (defining negotiable instrument, including check). A check is "a draft drawn on a bank and payable on demand." *Id.* § 3-104(2)(b). In turn, instruments payable on demand "include those payable at sight or on presentation and those in which no time for payment is stated." *Id.* § 3-108. Presentment is simply the demand for payment. 1 J. White & R. Summers, Uniform Commercial Code § 13-11, at 649 (3d ed. 1988). Under the terms of § 3-503:

> (2) A reasonable time for presentment is determined by the nature of the instrument. . .. In the case of an uncertified check which is drawn and payable within the United States and which is not a draft drawn by a bank the following are presumed to be reasonable periods within which to present for payment or to initiate bank collection:
>
> (a) with respect to the liability of the drawer, thirty days after date or issue whichever is later. . ..

Helen Roy was well within the thirty-day period for presentment of the Peerless check when she deposited the check six days after its date and issue.

Returning to defendants' argument that the check was a suspended indebtedness cancelled by Paragraph 6, we find defendants' reading of § 3-802 incorrect. This section is simply "a tidying-up provision. It states the legal effects of the *underlying obligation* when one takes a negotiable instrument for that obligation, and it states the legal effects on the underlying obligation when the obligation on the instrument is discharged." 1 J. White & R. Summers, *supra*, § 13-23, at 684 (emphasis added) (footnote omitted). The underlying obligation is "the original obligation between the parties which led to issuance of the negotiable instrument. . .. In most cases, this obligation will be a contract. . .." *Id.* § 13-23, at 684-85. Here, the underlying obligation was the obligation of Peerless to pay Helen Roy a bonus as agreed by the then-owners of Peerless; the $20,000 check was a negotiable instrument given to discharge that obligation.

The discussion of suspension in § 3-802 refers not to the suspension of the negotiable instrument, but rather suspension of the right to bring an action on the underlying obligation. *See id.* § 13-23, at 685 (discussing § 3-802 and noting that "issuance of a check in the usual circumstance does not discharge the obligation but merely suspends it"). Thus, the check remains a valid instrument, and the right to sue on the obligation—here the $20,000 bonus—is suspended until and if the check is not honored by the bank to which it is presented. *See* 9A V.S.A. § 3-802 comment 3.

IN RE UNION SECURITY MORTGAGE CO.

United States Court of Appeals
23 U.C.C. Rep. 833 (6th Cir. 1994)

PER CURIAM.

Larry Stewart, plaintiff and trustee for Union Security Mortgage Company ("debtor"), appeals the district court's reversal of the bankruptcy court's order that voided the assignment of a note and deed of trust to defendant, East Tennessee Title Insurance Agency, Inc. ("ETT"). Because we conclude that debtor had an equitable interest in the note and deed of trust at the time it assigned them to ETT, we agree with the bankruptcy court that the assignment was a voidable preference under 11 U.S.C. § 547. We therefore reverse the decision of the district court.

I.

In 1989, debtor agreed to loan Philip Walker $72,867 to enable him to purchase a tract of residential real estate from Erica Collins. Debtor arranged to have ETT simultaneously close the loan transaction and the sale of Collins' home to Walker. This closing was scheduled for December 29, 1989. On that date, Walker and Collins met with the president of ETT, Myron Ely. The closing did not take place as planned, however, because, contrary to expectations, debtor had not yet provided ETT with a $72,867 check to fund the sale of Collins' home. Ely nonetheless had Collins execute the warranty deed for her property, and had Walker make both a note in the principal amount of $72,867, payable to the order of Union Security, and a deed of trust securing that note. ETT held these documents in anticipation of its receipt of the funding check from debtor.

On January 3, 1990, debtor delivered to ETT a $72,867 check payable to the order of ETT. This check was uncertified and was drawn on debtor's bank account. ETT deposited this check in its bank account and then used its own funds to pay Collins the purchase price of the home. ETT also delivered the warranty deed to Walker, and the note and deed of trust to debtor.

ETT learned on or about January 9, 1990, that debtor's bank had dishonored the $72,867 check. On January 11, 1990, ETT sued debtor in Tennessee state court, seeking a writ of possession for the note and deed of trust. ETT's action was terminated later that day, however, when debtor signed the note and deed of trust to ETT ("the assignment"). Since that time, ETT has held the note and received monthly payments from Walker.

Roughly one month later, in February 1990, debtor was the subject of an involuntary petition filed under Chapter 11 of the Bankruptcy Code. Trustee Steward thereafter commenced an action against ETT, in which he sought to avoid the assignment as a preference under 11 U.S.C. § 547. Stewart moved for summary judgment in the § 547 action. The bankruptcy court granted this motion and issued an order that voided the assignment. ETT appealed to the district court, which reversed on the basis of its holding that the assignment was not a preference. This appeal followed.

On appeal following district court review, we review a bankruptcy court decision for clear error as to findings of fact, and de novo as to conclusions of law. *XL/Datacomp, Inc. v. Wilson (In re Omegas Group, Inc.)*, 16 F.3d 1443, 1447 (6th Cir. 1994). This appeal presents only questions of law, because the facts are undisputed. . ..

ETT presents a number of arguments that the district court had no need to address. The first such argument is founded on ETT's novel conception of the exchange that took place between debtor and ETT on January 3, 1990. ETT maintains that debtor and ETT had an agreement which provided that debtor would give ETT $72,867 as consideration for ETT's transfer of the note and deed of trust to debtor. ETT notes that, under Tenn. Code Ann. § 47-3-802(1)(b), one who "takes an instrument for an underlying obligation" can maintain an action "on either the instrument or the obligation" if the instrument is dishonored. Tennessee law also provides for recision of a contract if a "failure of consideration . . .defeats the very object of the contract or concerns a matter of such grave importance that the contract would not have been executed had that default been contemplated." *James Cable Partners, L.P. v. City of Jamestown*, 818 S.W.2d 338, 343 (Tenn.App. 1991), cert. denied, 112 S. Ct. 872 (1992). Thus, according to ETT, when debtor's check was dishonored, ETT's right of recourse on the underlying obligation included a right to rescind the "agreement" pursuant to which the check was presented. Recision "involves . . .placing the parties in their prior status." *Mills v. Brown*, 568 S.W.2d 100, 102 (Tenn. 1978). Citing *Beds and More, Inc. v. Deutscher (In RE Southern Indus. Banking Corp.)*, 36 B.R. 1008 [38 U.C.C. Rep. Serv. 249] (Bankr. E.D. Tenn. 1984), ETT thus argues that its right of recision gave it equitable title to the note and deed of trust, and that the assignment accordingly did not cause it to receive more than it otherwise would have received in a Chapter 7 liquidation of debtor's assets.

ETT's argument rests upon a flawed conception of debtor's arrangement with ETT. Debtor plainly did not agree to give ETT $72,867 as consideration for ETT's "transfer" of the note and deed of trust. That debtor did not so agree is revealed by the fact that ETT never had any ownership rights in those documents, which were made out to debtor and held by ETT merely as an escrow agent. Instead, the arrangement between debtor and ETT appears to have been a more pedestrian one: in exchange for a relatively small fee, ETT agreed to make appropriate dispersals of funds and documents upon the satisfaction of certain conditions. Debtor's delivery of the $72,867 check to ETT was one of those conditions, just as Collins' delivery of the warranty deed to ETT was one of those conditions. Debtor's delivery of the check no more discharged an obligation owed by debtor to ETT than Collins' delivery of the warranty deed discharged an obligation owed by her to ETT. These deliveries were merely incident to the performance of ETT's escrow agent function. Since no obligation owed by debtor to ETT underlay debtor's delivery of the check to ETT, there was no "underlying obligation" upon which ETT could maintain an action when the check was dishonored. In the absence of such an obligation, there could be neither a "failure of consideration" nor an agreement that could be rescinded. Because the remedy of recision accordingly was unavailable to it, ETT had no right to return to the status quo as it was before the documents-for-check "exchange."[43] ETT's argument that a right of recision gave it equitable title to the note and deed of trust therefore is without merit.[44] . . .

[43] ETT's only recourse in fact was to sue debtor as the drawer of a dishonored instrument. See Tenn. Code Ann. 47-3-413(2)("The drawer engages that upon dishonor of the draft and any necessary notice of dishonor or protest he will pay the amount of the draft to the holder or to any endorser who takes it up."). Debtor apparently recognized its liability as drawer of the dishonored check, and so it settled ETT's claim by means of the assignment. In doing so, however, it singled out ETT for preferential treatment, to the detriment of its other creditors.

[44] We note that ETT's argument would be unavailing even if ETT had some recision-based right to return to the status quo as it was before the documents—for-check "exchange." Unlike the plaintiff in Beds and More, ETT had no right to the stream of payments described in the note it held in escrow, because the note was made out to debtor, not ETT. The assignment gave ETT a right to that stream of payments, and thus did more for ETT than a right of recision could have done.

---

§ 13.14 Lost, Destroyed or Stolen Instruments

Read: U.C.C. §§ 3-309, 3-312.

THOMAS C. COOK, INC. v. ROWHANIAN

Texas Court of Appeals
700 S.W.2d 672, 42 U.C.C. Rep. 899 (1985)

OSBORN, ASSOCIATE JUSTICE.

This case involves traveler's checks which were purchased in Iran and lost in New York. We reverse and remand.

About the time of the Shah's abdication in 1979, Azizollah Rowhanian left Iran and came with his daughter to the United States. Prior to his trip, he purchased $9,500.00 in traveler's checks in his name. He also purchased $20,100.00 in traveler's checks from street brokers. Since it was illegal to leave the country with more than $3,000.00 in currency, he hid all of these traveler's checks in a tape recorder when he flew out of Iran.

When he arrived in New York, he entered an elevator at the airport in order to make a change of planes. After entering the elevator he believed he was having a heart attack and stepped off the elevator, but left his tape recorder in the elevator. When the elevator returned, the tape recorder was gone. Mr. Rowhanian filed a claim with Thomas C. Cook, Inc., the party issuing the checks, for reimbursement of all of his lost traveler's checks. He was paid for those checks which he purchased in his name. The claim was denied and suit was filed for the $20,100.00 worth of checks which he had purchased from street brokers.

The appellee alleged in his amended petition that he was entitled to recover for lost instruments under the provisions of § 3.804 of the Texas Business and Commerce Code. That provision of the code states:

> The owner of an instrument which is lost, whether by destruction, theft or otherwise, may maintain an action in his own name and recover from any party liable thereon upon due proof of his ownership, the facts which prevent his production of the instrument and its terms. The court may require security indemnifying the defendant against loss by reason of further claims on the instrument.

Mr. Rowhanian testified and there was received into evidence the various "Sales Advice" from Thomas Cook, Inc. which reflect the serial numbers and denominations of the checks which were issued in May, 1979, and are now claimed to have been lost. Like all traveler's checks, these checks had a place for the owner to sign when the checks were issued and another place for a signature when the checks were negotiated. Mr. Rowhanian testified that the checks which he purchased from the street brokers and which he subsequently lost had no signatures on them. The parties stipulated the value of the lost checks was $20,100.00. The jury found Mr. Rowhanian had acquired ownership of the traveler's checks in question, that such checks were stolen or lost and that the "advices" accurately reflect the terms of the checks.

In Point of Error No. Three, the appellant attacks the legal sufficiency of the evidence to support the jury's verdict and contends the trial court erred in overruling its motion for an instructed verdict. We conclude that there is no evidence to support the answer to Special Issue No. 3. The sales advices do not reflect the actual terms of the checks and do not show that in fact there was a promise to pay when properly countersigned by the holder. Mr. Rowhanian did not testify that the lost checks contained a promise to pay the face amount of the checks when properly countersigned.

The real problem is that this case was tried on the wrong theory. Appellee pled, tried and submitted the case to the jury based upon § 3.804, Tex.Bus. & Com.Code. That provision of the code is not applicable. Section 3.804 applies to the owner of an "instrument." Section 3. 102, Tex.Bus. & Com.Code, says an "Instrument" means a negotiable instrument. Section 3. 104, Tex.Bus. & Com.Code, comment 4, says:

> Traveler's checks in the usual form, for instance, are negotiable instruments under this Article when they have been completed by the identifying signature.

Mr. Rowhanian testified these checks had not been completed and in fact had no signature of the owner on them. Therefore these checks did not qualify as "instruments" under § 3.804 and the case should not have been tried on that theory. We sustain the no evidence point of error, but since the case was tried on the wrong theory, in the interest of justice we reverse and remand for a new trial.

QUESTION

What theory do you believe Justice Osborn had in mind?

BUSTER v. GALE

Alaska Supreme Court
866 P.2d 837 24 U.C.C. Rep. 1164 (1994)

RABINOWITZ, J.

I. FACTS AND LOWER COURT PROCEEDINGS

In June 1984 James Gale, Thomas Westerhof, and Mary Westerhof (Gale and the Westerhofs) executed a deed of trust in favor of Cameron Milliron and M. Jo Milliron (the Millirons), as security for an obligation of $44,000. The signatures of Gale and the Westerhofs were notarized, and the deed of trust was recorded.

Jack Buster (Buster) argues that Gale and the Westerhofs additionally signed a deed of trust note (the note), in which they assumed the $44,000 debt to the Millirons. The Millirons assigned the note to Robert Baines and Christine Baines (the Baineses) in May 1985. The assignment was certified and recorded.

In his deposition, Robert Baines stated that after Gale and the Westerhofs had defaulted on their payments in September 1986, he "closed the escrow and took possession of the original deed of trust note."[45] Baines also stated in his deposition that he gave the note to Buster in May 1988.

The location of the note after this time is unclear. Buster testified that Robert Baines instituted an action to collect on the note in 1988, and that at that time, Buster had the original note.[46] Buster further testified that he believed that he later accidentally threw the note out "in a frenzy of housecleaning." According to Buster, all three original documents—the deed of trust, the note, and the assignment from the Millirons to the Baineses—were lost.

In May 1988, before moving from Alaska to Paris, France, the Baineses executed general powers of attorney in Buster's favor. Buster further claims that under these general powers of attorney, he assigned the note to himself "as Robert Baines' attorney-in-fact on January 16, 1990. Buster testified that he wrote this assignment on the back of the original note. Also on January 16, Buster filed a complaint against Gale and the Westerhofs to recover on the note.[47]

In December 1990, Buster met with Gale and Thomas Westerhof to discuss a settlement between the parties. Gale and Westerhof offered Buster $8,000 to settle the dispute. According to Thomas Westerhof's testimony, Buster reached into his briefcase at this point to pull out the note, and discovered that he did not have it. Buster then went home to look for the note, but was unable to find it. No formal settlement was ever reached between Buster, the Westerhofs, and Gale.

Buster states that he signed a second assignment of the note "signed by me for Christine Baines as her power of attorney" on January 23, 1991.[48] During direct examination, Buster testified that he wrote this assignment on the back of the original note. However, during cross-examination, Buster admitted that he had been unable to produce the note at the December 1990 meeting between himself, Gale, and Thomas Westerhof. Buster then stated that he must have written the January 23 assignment on the back of a copy.

In March, 1991, Buster listed Robert Baines on his preliminary witness list. Buster then deposed Baines in Anchorage in July 1991. At this deposition, Baines indicated that he then resided in London, England. When questioned about his availability for trial in Alaska in December 1991, Baines responded that he did not anticipate being in Alaska but stated: "[I]f it's necessary, well, we'll—we'll make arrangements."

---

[45] The deposition was ruled inadmissible at trial, and this evidentiary ruling is one of the issues in this appeal.

[46] Buster testified that this action was dismissed for lack of prosecution.

[47] Buster attached a copy of the note to the complaint, but he did not attach a copy of the back of the note, where the endorsement and assignment signatures allegedly were located.

[48] Buster testified: "I executed this to correct an oversight in the previous assignment of 1990 where I'd failed to note that Christine Baines was also the holder of this note . . .so I executed an assignment of whatever interest she may have also to myself."

Three days prior to the commencement of the superior court trial Buster filed a designation of deposition testimony, indicating his intent to use the Robert Baines deposition.[49] At trial, Gale and the Westerhofs objected to the use of the deposition of Robert Baines, claiming that there was no showing that Baines was unavailable. Buster testified that Robert Baines had told him, one month prior to trial, that he would be travelling in North Africa for two or three weeks, and then would be returning to London.

The superior court found that Robert Baines might be an essential witness, and that the record did not adequately reflect Baines' unavailability. The court held that Robert Baines' deposition would not be admitted, but offered a continuance of the trial: "Probably the best way to handle this would be to close all the discovery except a beefed up deposition, maybe even by phone, of Mr. Baines, although it sounds like somebody wants him to be here. I'd be willing to search for a one-day spot on the trial calendar." Both parties turned down the superior court's suggested continuance.

At trial, Buster sought to admit into evidence a document titled Plaintiff's Trial Exhibit No. 1 (Exhibit No. 1), which consisted of a copy of what was purported to be the note including the endorsements from the Millirons to the Baineses, and from the Baineses to Buster. Buster testified that at some point after he realized that the original was lost, he wrote "certified to be a true and exact copy of the original" on the copy, and signed his name.

Buster argued that under Alaska Rule of Evidence 1003, he did not have to establish the admissibility of the purported copy of the note and signature page by clear and convincing evidence. Buster further argued that Gale and the Westehofs had not contested the contents of the note or its original execution in their responses to his requests for admission. The superior court refused to admit the copy.

Gale and Thomas Westerhof testified that they recognized their signatures on the copy, but that they could not remember if the contents of the copy were the same as what they had signed. They testified that they had not retained any copies of the note in their records.[50] Gale and the Westerhofs argued that Buster's claim on the lost note was governed by former AS 45.03.804, that the appropriate standard of proof for that statute was clear and convincing evidence, and that Buster had failed to meet this burden.[51]

Upon conclusion of the non-jury trial, the superior court entered findings of fact and conclusions of law. The court found that "Jack Buster's testimony is not unworthy of belief, although his testimony lacks corroboration." In its conclusions of law the superior court stated in part:[52]

---

[49] Buster also deposed Christine Baines at the same time he deposed Robert Baines, and excerpts from the "Christine M. Baines deposition taken July 18, 1991" were included in Buster's designation of deposition testimony.

[50] An attachment to the April 1991 cross-motion for partial summary judgment filed by Gale and the Weserhofs consisted of an identical copy of the note and an endorsement page including all of the endorsements at issue except the assignment of the interest of Christine Baines.

[51] Additionally, Gale and the Westerhofs claimed as an affirmative defense that "[Buster] contracted with defendants to accept $8,000.00 in exchange for the original deed of trust note and dismissal of this action." This point was not argued with much enthusiasm at trial, and is not relevant to the appeal.

[52] In its oral opinion the superior court informed counsel for the Westerhofs and Gale that

> I've rejected your ownership argument and I've rejected your accord and satisfaction argument, decided simply on the narrow issue that [Buster] fails to meet his clear and convincing burden and therefore obtain the admission of [Exhibit No. 1], without which his case fails.

1. AS 45.03.804 provides the procedure by which the owner of a lost promissory note is to maintain an action to recover on said note.

2. Plaintiff has the burden of establishing ownership of the lost note, and the circumstances surrounding the loss of the note, followed by proving the terms and conditions of the note.

3. The applicable standard of proof to be met by plaintiff pursuant to AS 45.03.804 is the clear and convincing standard.

. . ..

5. Plaintiff has not met his burden of proof and is therefore not the prevailing party in this action.

6. Defendants are entitled to judgment in this action and plaintiff shall take nothing by way of his complaint.

Thereafter a formal judgment was entered dismissing Buster's claim for relief and awarding Gale and the Westerhofs attorney's fees of $4,430.40 and costs of $1,423,78. This appeal followed.

Three questions are presented in this appeal. First, did the superior court err in excluding Buster's purported copy of the note? Second, did the superior court err in precluding Buster's introduction of Robert Baines' deposition into evidence? Third, did the superior court err in holding that Buster had failed to prove his right to recover on the note?[53] . . ..

C. Did The Superior Court Err in Holding that Buster Failedto Present Clear And Convincing Evidence of His Right to Recover on the Note?

Our earlier holdings that the superior court erred in its refusal to admit into evidence Exhibit No. 1 and Robert Baines' deposition testimony would normally require a remand for new trial. On the other hand, review of the record persuades us that a new trial is unnecessary, since we conclude that on the basis of the evidence admitted at trial the superior court erred in holding that Buster failed to present clear and convincing evidence of his right to recover on the note. On the contrary, Buster proved all the elements of his right to recover on the note under former AS 45.03.804.

Our starting point is the well established common law doctrine that an unintentional loss of a written evidence of debt does not extinguish the rights and obligations of the parties thereto. *Bottum v. Herr*, 83 S.D. 542, 162 N.W.2d 880, 884 (1968); 52 Am. Jr.2d Lost and Destroyed Instruments § 2 (2d ed. 1970). In recognition of this principle, and the historic common law remedies afforded in law and equity to the owner of a lost instrument, the drafters of the Uniform Commercial Code provided:

> The owner of an instrument which is lost, whether by destruction, theft or otherwise, may maintain an action in his own name and recover from any party liable thereon upon due proof of his ownership, the facts which prevent his production of the instrument and its terms. The

[53] This case involves the review of both questions of law and evidentiary proceedings. The appropriate standard of review for questions of law is substitution of judgment *Langdon v. Champion*, 745 P.2d 1371, 1372 n.2 (Alaska 1987); *Guin v. Ha*, 591 P.2d 1281, 1284 n.6 (Alaska 1979). The appropriate standard of review for evidentiary decisions is abuse of discretion. *Dura Corp. v. Harned*, 703 P.2d 396, 409 (Alaska 1985). This court has stated that "[w]e will find that a trial court abused its discretion only "when we are left with a definite and firm conviction, after reviewing the whole record, that the trial court erred in its ruling.' " *Id.* at 409 (quoting *Peter Pan Seafoods, Inc. v. Stepanoff*, 650 P.2d 375, 378–79 (Alaska 1982)).

court may require security indemnifying the defendant against loss by reason of further claims on the instrument.

Former U.C.C. § 3-804 (superseded 1990).[54] At the time of the events leading to this litigation, this provision of the U.C.C. was part of Alaska statutory law. *See* former AS 45.03.804.

In order to determine whether the superior court erred in its ruling that Buster failed to prove his claim under former AS 45.03.804, we must first determine if the superior court correctly held that "clear and convincing evidence" is the appropriate burden of proof for actions under former AS 45.03.804.

Courts that have addressed this burden of proof issue under similar statutory provisions have required proof by "clear and convincing" evidence. *See, e.g., Castellano v. Bitkower*, 216 Neb. 806, 346 N.W.2d 249, 252 [38 U.C.C. Rep. Serv. 561] (1984) (stating that the appropriate standard of evidence regarding lost notes is "clear and convincing" evidence); *Lutz v. Gatlin*, 22 Wash.App. 424, 590 P.2d 359, 361 [26 U.C.C. Rep. Serv. 129] (1979) ("To establish a lost instrument, the evidence must be clear, cogent and convincing.").

Clear and convincing evidence has been characterized as evidence that is greater than a preponderance, but less than proof beyond a reasonable doubt. *Castellano* provides a useful statement of the standard, holding that "clear and convincing evidence means and is that amount of evidence which produces in the trier of fact a firm belief or conviction about the existence of a fact to be proved." 216 Neb. 806, 346 N.W.2d at 25; *see also Welton v. Gallagher*, 2 Haw.App. 242, 630 P.2d 1077, 1081 (1981), aff'd, 65 Haw. 528, 654 P.2d 1349 (1982).

We believe that the clear and convincing evidence standard adopted by the superior court is the appropriate standard of proof under former AS 45.03.804, as it provides the heightened scrutiny that is necessary to ensure that a party claiming to have lost physical control over an instrument was in fact the rightful owner of the instrument. This heightened standard should reduce the instances where multiple parties come forward to claim ownership of a missing note. While the statute envisions such a problem and accordingly provides that a court may require the posting of security to indemnify the defendant against future claimants, the heightened burden of proof serves as an additional safeguard.

We next address whether the superior court erred in its conclusion that Buster failed to present clear and convincing evidence of his right to recover on the note.

Under the provisions of former AS 45.03.804, Buster must establish (a) the facts which prevent production of the instrument, (b) the terms of the instrument, and (c) "due proof of ownership." We address these issues seriatim.

Upon review of the record we believe that Buster's uncontradicted evidence clearly and convincingly established that the note in question was unintentionally lost.[55] Similarly, study

---

[54] The official comment to this section read: [The court quotes the comment.]

Article 3 of the U.C.C. was substantially revised in 1990. *See* 2 U.L.A. 5(1991). As a result, significant changes occurred in the language of § 3-804. This section has been renumbered § 3-309, and it reads as follows: [The court quotes § 3-309(a) & (b).]

The legislature recently amended AS 45.03, adopting language which substantially conforms with the new changes in the U.C.C. *See* AS 45.03.309.

[55] In part, the record reveals the following testimony on Buster's part:

Q: "What happened to the original of the deed of trust note?

A: "I discarded the original note by error.

of the evidence persuades us that Buster clearly and convincingly established the terms of the note. We reach this conclusion for essentially the same reasons identified in our earlier discussion of the admissibility of Exhibit No. 1.[56]

Proof of Buster's ownership of the note involves the following critical links: (1) the initial promise to pay embodied in the note by Gale and the Westerhofs to the Millirons; (2) the subsequent assignment of the note by the Millirons to the Baineses; (3) proof that Buster was given general powers of attorney by the Baineses; and (4) the conveyances, through the general powers of attorney, of the Baineses' interest in the note to Buster.

We conclude that Buster clearly and convincingly proved that Gale and the Westerhofs executed a deed of trust note on June 14, 1984, in the principal sum of $44,000 to the Millirons. The unrefuted evidence also shows that the Millirons assigned their interests in the note to the Baineses in May 1985. It is also uncontradicted that the Baineses granted general powers of attorney to Buster in May 1988. Lastly, we are persuaded that the evidence in the record clearly and convincingly establishes that under the unrevoked general powers of attorney given him by the Baineses, Buster conveyed both of their interests in the note to himself. In light of the above, we hold that Buster has clearly and convincingly proved ownership of the note as well as the remaining elements of a claim under former AS 45.03.804.

The matter is reversed and remanded to the superior court with directions to vacate its judgment and award of attorney's fees and costs, and to enter an appropriate judgment for Buster under the deed of trust note. In fashioning its judgment on remand the superior court shall determine whether it will require security to indemnify Gale and the Westerhofs against loss by reason of further claims on the deed of trust note.[57]

Q: "How?

A: "I'd had a previous collection matter with Mr. Westerhof and had maintained that file just for—in case that there was some ancillary information that might be of use to me in there, and I married the two files, that is, the old file and the new file, the new file being the one that contained this particular note. And in a frenzy of housecleaning one day I decided that there was no information in the old file on Mr. Westerhof and I threw it in the garbage along with a number of other files. It wasn't until some time later that I—that I reasoned that I must have included this new file or this particular—the original to this note in that file and discarded it, because it was nowhere to be found and that's the only explanation that I have."

Buster testified further that during settlement negotiations with gale and Thomas Westerhof.

"I went back because these gentlemen were still waiting for me and I told'em I couldn't find the note and that until I could find the note or determine what happened to it, there wasn't any point in proceeding further. Then they went away, I went back and made a more thorough and careful search of all my files and records and—an exhaustive search, and couldn't find it."

[56] In addition to the evidence previously referred to we note that counsel for Gale and the Westerhofs stipulated that they signed the note and that it had a principal amount of $44,000.

[57] Our resolution of this appeal makes it unnecessary to address any other issues raised herein.

QUESTIONS

Where does one find a "clear and convincing" requirement in former U.C.C. § 3-804? In U.C.C. § 3-309? Are burdens of proof and amounts required for security correlatives?

HELMSLEY-SPEAR, INC. v. ATLANTIC BANK OF NEW YORK

New York Supreme Court, New York County
21 U.C.C. Rep. 2d 1052 (1993)

CAHN, J.

Plaintiff Helmsley-Spear, Inc. ("Helmsley-Spear") moves for an order, pursuant to CPLR 3213, granting it summary judgment in lieu of complaint against defendant in the principal sum of $35,000. Defendant Atlantic Bank of New York ("Atlantic Bank") cross moves for an order dismissing he action on the ground that plaintiff failed to bring a proper action pursuant to U.C.C. 3-804.

This action is based upon two official checks issued by Atlantic Bank payable to plaintiff in the aggregate sum of $35,000.

On or about October 1, 1992, Nick Diamond purchased two cashier's checks from Atlantic Bank which were payable to Helmsley-Spear in the sums of $20,000 and $15,000 respectively. The checks were delivered by Diamond to DeLuca, a tenant who owed money to plaintiff. Plaintiff alleges that the checks were given to it by DeLuca the tenant, for rent due. They were then endorsed by plaintiff but stolen before they could be deposited into plaintiff's account. As a result, on or about November 9, 1992, plaintiff-payee requested that Atlantic Bank issue a stop payment order on these checks.

On November 16, 1992, Nick Diamond executed an Indemnity Agreement with Atlantic Bank wherein he stated that the subject checks were stolen and requested that Atlantic Bank repay the face amount of the checks to him. He executed an Indemnification Agreement in Atlantic Bank's favor. In December of 1992, Atlantic Bank credited Diamond's account in the amount of $35,000.

Helmsley-Spear has requested that Atlantic Bank reissue official checks in the sum of $35,000 payable to it, and defendant has refused. As a result, plaintiff commenced this action to recovery $35,000 on the two cashier's checks issued by Atlantic Bank.

UCC 3-804 expressly provides, in pertinent part, as follows: "*[t]he owner* of an instrument which is lost, whether by destruction, theft, or otherwise, may maintain an action in his own name and recover from any party liable thereon upon due proof of his ownership, the facts which prevent his production of the instrument and its terms. The court *shall require security, in an amount fixed by the court not less than twice the amount allegedly unpaid on the instrument,* indemnifying the defendant, his heirs, personal representatives, successors and assigns against loss, including costs and expenses, by reason of further claims on the instrument . . ." (emphasis added). The claims which are meant and for which indemnity should be given are not the claims which may be brought by Diamond, as he clearly transferred the checks before they were lost or stolen.

The purpose of this section is to provide a method for recovering on lost instruments while protecting the bank from double liability should the original checks ultimately wind up in the hands of a holder in due course. Therefore, the statute, contrary to plaintiff's suggestion, makes the furnishing of security mandatory. (*See In the Matter of Diaz v. Manufacturers Hanover Trust Co.*, 92 Misc2d 802 [23 U.C.C. Rep. Serv. 385 (1978)]; *also see* Hawkland on U.C.C. 3-804:06, p. 125).

No issue of fact has been raised which would bar the relief plaintiff seeks. It has not been disputed that plaintiff is the payee and owner of the two checks. Atlantic Bank is therefore obligated to pay the face value of the checks to plaintiff, upon compliance with the direction to post an undertaking. *Abilities, Inc. v. Citibank*, 87 AD2d 831 [33 U.C.C. Rep. Serv. 1428] (2d dept.-1982). The fact that Atlantic Bank previously paid Diamond is immaterial, since Diamond was not the owner of the checks.

Accordingly, the motion and cross motion are granted solely to the extent that plaintiff is entitled to judgment against Atlantic Bank in the sum of $35,000, together with costs, upon posting an undertaking in the amount of $70,000 in favor of Atlantic Bank, as herein described.

The clerk may enter judgment herein.

Settle order.

QUESTIONS

Where in former U.C.C. § 3-804 do you find that a court shall require security in *twice* the amount unpaid on the instrument? In U.C.C. § 3-309? Would the facts in *Helmsley* require any security today? *See* U.C.C. § 3-312.

CHAPTER 14

BANKS AND THE CHECK COLLECTION PROCESS

§ 14.01 The Bank Customer Relationship

[A] Introduction

[1] The Role of Banks

Banks provide the pivotal link in facilitating payments of money between parties. This chapter examines three of these roles—banks as participants in the check collection process (Article 4); a related role in the facilitation of consumer electronic fund transfers (Federal Reserve Board Regulation E); and finally, the role of banks as facilitator of wholesale (commercial) wire fund transfers (Article 4A). Chapter 14 addresses both the nature of the contractual relationship that exists between a demand deposit (checking) account customer and the drawee/payor bank that maintains the account, and consumer electronic fund transactions in which checking, savings, and credit card account customers utilize electronic technology in the form of automated teller machines, debit cards, and point of sale terminals.

Chapter 15 examines the development of wholesale wire transfer technology whereby large commercial payment transactions occur between customers and their banks. The prefatory note to Article 4A governing Funds Transfers provides a useful description:

> There are a number of mechanisms for making payments through the banking system. Most of these mechanisms are covered in whole or part by state or federal statutes. In terms of number of transactions, payments made by check or credit card are the most common payment methods. Payment by check is covered by Articles 3 and 4 of the U.C.C. and some aspects of payment by credit card are covered by federal law. In recent years electronic funds transfers have been increasingly common in consumer transactions. . . .
>
> Another type of payment, commonly referred to as a wholesale wire transfer, is the primary focus of Article 4A. Payments that are covered by Article 4A are overwhelmingly between business or financial institutions. The dollar volume of payment made by wire transfer far exceeds the dollar volume of payments made by other means. The volume of payments by wire transfer over the two principal wire payment systems—the Federal Reserve wire transfer network (Fedwire) and the New York Clearing House Interbank Payments System (CHIPS)—exceeds one trillion dollars per day. Most payments carried out by use of automated clearing houses are consumer payments covered by [the Electronic Funds Transfer Act] and therefore are not covered by Article 4A. There is, however, a significant volume of non-consumer [Automated Clearing House] payments that closely resemble wholesale wire transfers. These payments are also covered by Article 4A.

> There is some resemblance between payments made by wire transfer and payments made by other means such as paper-based checks and credit cards or electronically-based consumer payments, but there are also many differences. Article 4A excludes from its coverage these other payment mechanisms. Article 4A follows a policy of treating the transaction that it covers—a "funds transfer" — as a unique method of payment that is governed by unique principles of law that address the operational and policy issues presented by this kind of payment.

As you proceed through this chapter, note the structure of each type of transaction, including both the similarities and the differences. Consider the need for two separate but similar bodies of law to govern these types of transactions.

[2] Checks and Check Collections

We are already familiar with the check as a special form of draft that is drawn on a bank. As with all drafts, the check is a three-party document in which the drawer orders a drawee/payor to pay a sum of money to a payee. While the drawee of a draft may be anyone, the drawee/payor of a check must be a financial institution. The drawer maintains a deposit relationship with the drawee/payor bank. The check functions as a basic payment device with the written item representing the drawer's instructions to the bank to direct payment of the drawer's funds to a designated payee. Because the relationship between the parties is contractual, the drawer can revoke his or her instruction at any time until the bank has "settled" on paying the item.

There are four principal sources of law governing checks and check collections. Article 3 addresses the basic questions of negotiability and deals with the rights and responsibilities of parties on checks until the items are first presented to a bank for collection or payment. Article 3 also outlines some of the rules concerning liability and remedies once a check has been dishonored. Article 4 provides the second principal source of law on checks. These statutory provisions set forth the basic rules used in the bank collection and payment process to the extent federal law does not preempt such rules. In 1990, the National Conference of Commissioners on Uniform State Laws and the American Law Institute revised Article 4 to clarify language and to incorporate modern technology and business practices. Because there is not yet a substantial body of law interpreting the revised statute, some of the cases in this section will be pre-revision cases. Although for the most part, the revisions do not change the law substantially, there are important clarifications. As you read the cases, check the statutory references carefully to see if, how, and where the revised statute changes past practice.

The third source of law governing checks is federal law in the form of the Expedited Funds Availability Act, 12 U.S.C. §§ 4001-4010, and the implementing Federal Reserve Regulation CC. 12 CFR part 229. The Act addresses bank float and mandates how soon a bank customer's deposited funds must be made available to that customer. Until the passage of the Expedited Funds Availability Act, banks placed different time limits on a customer's ability to access funds deposited into that customer's account. See 12 CFR parts 229.10-13.

The fourth and final source of law governing checks is the contractual agreement between the parties. This agreement is typically found in the customer-bank deposit account contract or in a processing agreement between or among banks. While parties have considerable power to vary applicable law by agreement, there are some important limitations. For example, a bank cannot disclaim its responsibility for either a lack of good faith in handling an account or for the bank's failure to exercise ordinary care in such handling. Regulation CC also provides that banks cannot limit the measure of damages for their failures to exercise ordinary care or to act in good faith. 12 CFR 229.37.

Generally, problems in the Article 4 area can be discussed under the following subject categories:

(1) the relationship between a bank and its deposit customer—when does the bank have a right to debit the customer's account?

(2) the relationship between a bank and a person other than the customer with whom the bank deals—when does a bank have the right to recover from a party who has been paid erroneously? and,

(3) the relationship among various banks involved in the collection process—what responsibilities and rights do banks have with respect to each other as checks deposited in one area are forwarded for collection from drawee/payor banks in other areas of the country?

[B] When A Bank May Charge Its Customer's Account

Read: U.C.C. §§ 4-102, 4-103, 4-401, 4-402, 4-303(2), and 4-403.

It is impossible to talk about the bank-customer relationship without first discussing aspects of the business of banking. A debtor-creditor relationship begins whenever a customer opens a checking account with a bank. While the deposit represents an asset for the customer, it represents an obligation for a bank. In effect, the customer has loaned the bank money that is subject to the customer's demand but which can be used by the bank for third-party loans or other investments.

Because most people do not withdraw every dollar they deposit, banks can engage in fractional reserve banking. Under this system, the bank retains only a portion of the outstanding deposit/loan of each customer and uses the larger portion of the customer's money to invest. Unlike non-banking firms, a bank's assets consist principally of financial rather than physical assets. The largest asset category for most American banks is loans. Historically, banks have earned a sizable portion of their profits from the difference between the cost of acquiring funds (deposit interest rates) and the interest earned on third-party loans (the rate spread).

Banks have a high volume of depositor claims (debts) relative to net worth (equity). Bank owners (shareholders) have far fewer dollars at risk in proportion to the total debts owed by the bank. The large majority of bank assets therefore, are funded by borrowed monies in the form of deposits rather than by shareholder investments. The short-term nature of depositor claims together with the poor ratio of net worth to depositor claims hold critical implications for both the risk exposure and liquidity of a bank's assets. Risk management for a banker means not only investigating the creditworthiness of a borrower on the asset side, but also maintaining some balance between the maturity dates for assets and liabilities. The banker must be constantly aware of the rate of customer withdrawal demands and have either cash available to meet withdrawals, or assets that can be converted easily and quickly into cash to meet customers' withdrawal demands. Bankers call the effort to match assets and maturing liabilities "hedging." Hedging often forces banks to bypass some, potentially more profitable, but less liquid (easily convertible into cash), investment opportunities for a less risky, less profitable, but more liquid venture.

The basic obligation of a bank to its deposit customer is to pay money from that customer's account to some payee when ordered by the customer to do so, provided there are sufficient funds in that customer's account. The customer's instructions usually come in the form of a check. When the bank properly pays an item, it may then charge (debit) the customer's account. The flip side of this relationship is also clear—if the customer does not order the bank to pay, then the bank has no right to pay; if the bank pays a check improperly, it cannot charge the customer's account. U.C.C. § 4-401.

A corollary to the properly payable rule concerns overdrafts. If the customer draws a check for an amount that exceeds the amount held on deposit (an overdraft), the bank is not required to pay the check. At the bank's option, it may choose to pay the item and create an overdraft on the account for which the customer will be responsible. The bank's payment on an overdraft reverses the debtor-creditor relationship and makes the customer the debtor of a bank loan. Though less concerned with the concept of properly charging a customer's account, the next case raises interesting questions concerning the debtor-creditor relationship between a bank and its customer.

IN RE ROSIN

Supreme Court of Illinois
156 Ill. 2d 202, 620 N.E.2d 368, 23 U.C.C.R. Serv. 2d 117 (1993)

JUSTICE BILANDIC delivered the opinion of the court:

This disciplinary action against respondent, Joseph Rosin, began with a two-count complaint charging that he had commingled and converted client funds, and that he also commingled and converted the interest earned on those funds. The Hearing Board found that respondent had commingled but not converted client funds; however, it did not make any findings and conclusions regarding the interest earned on those funds. The Hearing Board recommended censure. The Review Board found that respondent had commingled client funds, and that he also had converted and commingled the interest earned on those funds. The Review Board recommended censure, conditioned on respondent's paying restitution of $7,374.83 to a former client for interest earned on her funds. . . . .

Between December 1, 1981, and October 6, 1986, respondent maintained a business firm account at Bank Leumi in Chicago. Upon completion of law cases (by settlement or judgment), the satisfaction or payment was made with an insurance draft payable jointly to the client and respondent. These drafts were usually drawn on out-of-state banks. First, attorney fees and costs were deducted. Next, the client would endorse the insurance draft and simultaneously receive a settlement check for the net proceeds due to the client drawn on respondent's business firm account at Bank Leumi. Usually, the client would present respondent's check to Bank Leumi as soon as it was received.

After the insurance draft was endorsed by the client, respondent would also endorse it and deposit it into the firm business account at Bank Leumi during the regular course of business. Often, clients cashed their checks before respondent deposited the insurance draft.

In the normal course of banking practice, the insurance company draft would require approximately five business days to clear before it was credited to respondent's business firm account. Nevertheless, every client settlement check was honored when presented for payment. All business transactions of the firm were conducted through the firm account. . . . .

On several occasions, the balance in the firm account was less than the amount of an outstanding check issued to a client. The manager of Bank Leumi testified that respondent was a well-regarded customer with a $600,000 line of credit, and that he had arranged to guarantee payment of all checks written against his account regardless of the firm balance. It is undisputed that every settlement check issued by respondent to a client was promptly honored upon presentment, and that no checks were ever dishonored.

On February 1, 1983, the bank began to pay interest on funds deposited into the account. The complaint charged that respondent never informed clients that their funds had earned interest, and that the interest was retained in the firm account. In particular, on January 3, 1983, respondent issued a settlement check in the amount of $162,000 to a client, Penelope Bell, as her portion of the proceeds in a wrongful death action. Bell did not deposit respondent's check into the bank until July 25, 1983. During the seven months that Bell held the settlement check, the bank paid respondent $4,076.73 in interest on those funds.

The Review Board noted that respondent made no effort to notify Bell that interest was earned on the settlement check. According to the Review Board, respondent's failure to reimburse Bell for the interest which accrued during the seven-month period, compounded over the past nine years, resulted in a total obligation to Bell in the amount of $7,374.83. Respondent complied with the condition recommended by the Review Board, and issued a check to Bell for $7,374.83 for the earned interest. In addition, respondent has paid $5,770.74 to the Lawyers Trust Fund for the interest attributable to the settlement checks.

. . . . [W]e now address whether: (1) the overdraft protection agreement between respondent and Bank Leumi precluded respondent from converting client funds; (2) client funds were commingled in the firm account; and (3) respondent commingled and converted the interest earned on client funds.

I

Conversion has been defined by this court as "any unauthorized act, which deprives a man of his property permanently or for an indefinite time." (*In re Thebus* (1985), 108 Ill. 2d 255, 259, 483 N.E.2d 1258, 91 Ill. Dec. 623, quoting *Union Stock Yard & Transit Co. v. Mallory, Son & Zimmerman Co.* (1895), 157 Ill. 554, 563, 41 N.E. 888.) The essence of an action for conversion is the wrongful deprivation of property from the person entitled to its possession. . . . .

The Review Board found that because respondent maintained a $600,000 line of credit with the bank, client funds in his law firm account were protected and no conversion occurred. We agree.

The statutory law governing commercial paper, as applied to the facts in issue, leads to the unmistakable conclusion that respondent did not convert client funds. The settlement check issued by respondent is a negotiable instrument, for it contained an order to pay a fixed amount of money on demand to the client at the time it was issued. As set forth in section 3-202(1) of the Commercial Code, a negotiable instrument payable to order is negotiated by delivery and indorsement. As the maker of the settlement check, respondent's liability was established at the time that he signed it. When respondent signed and delivered the check to the client, he transferred to the client all rights that he had to the funds which were the subject matter of the check. In the event the check was dishonored upon presentment, the client's cause of action against respondent as maker accrued upon the date of issue. Application of the . . . Uniform Commercial Code clearly establishes that when respondent issued the settlement check, he was legally bound to transfer possession of specified funds in the firm account to the client, who, in turn, had an enforceable right to those funds.

Assuming, arguendo, that the balance in the firm account was less than the stated amount of the check when the client presented it for payment, section 4-401 of the Commercial Code explicitly provides that a bank may charge against a customer's account any item which is otherwise properly payable from that account even though the charge creates an overdraft. Moreover, section 4-401 was subsequently amended to provide that an item is properly payable if it is authorized by the customer, and is in accordance with any agreement between the customer and the bank. 4-401(a).

The testimony of the bank manager indicated that respondent was a well-regarded customer with a $600,000 line of credit, and had arranged to guarantee payment of all checks written against his account. It is undisputed that no settlement check was ever dishonored by the bank, nor had any client voiced a complaint, experienced delay, or incurred a financial loss as a result of respondent's banking arrangement. As stated, a wrongful deprivation of property from the person entitled to possession permanently or for an indefinite time is an essential element of a cause of action for conversion. . . . Such wrongful deprivation of property from the client never occurred in this case. Indeed, in the event that the insurance draft had been dishonored when it was presented by respondent, he alone would have shouldered the risk because the client had already received a check guaranteed to be collectible. . . .

Dismissed.

Chief Justice Miller, dissenting:

The respondent, Joseph Rosin, was charged . . . with commingling and converting client funds (count I) and commingling and converting interest earned on client funds (count II). The majority dismisses both counts, finding the evidence of the respondent's wrongdoing insufficient to sustain the charges against him. Unlike the majority, I believe that the allegations of the complaint were established by the record in this case, and accordingly I dissent.

The parties" evidence, which was largely stipulated, reveals that the respondent would deposit the proceeds of judgments or settlements in his firm's general business account and issue to his clients checks drawn on that account for the client's share of the award. From time to time the balance in the firm's account would fall below the amount then payable to clients. No check was ever dishonored, however, for a line of credit extended by the bank to the respondent was always more than sufficient to cover any shortfall in the account. On other occasions, clients would not immediately negotiate the checks they had received from the respondent; as a consequence, the law firm's account would be credited with interest attributable to those client funds. These arrangements formed the basis for the charges filed against the respondent.

The majority concludes that the respondent should not be found guilty of commingling client funds with his own funds because the conduct charged here preceded this court's decision in *In re Elias* (1986), 114 Ill. 2d 321, 499 N.E.2d 1327, 102 Ill. Dec. 314. The majority notes that the respondent established a separate client trust account after *Elias* "expressly clarified that it is mandatory for an attorney to establish and maintain" such an account regardless of the manner in which the attorney distributes client funds. The majority further asserts that the respondent's procedures functioned in much the same way as a separate trust account.

Contrary to the majority's view, the rule against commingling client funds was not in need of clarification prior to this court's decision in *Elias*. Disciplinary Rule 9-102(a) of the Code of Professional Responsibility provided, throughout the period relevant here:

"All funds of clients paid to a lawyer or law firm, including funds belonging in part to a client and in part presently or potentially to the lawyer or law firm, shall be deposited in one or more separate identifiable trust accounts in a bank or savings and loan association maintained in the State in which the law office is situated." 107 Ill. 2d R. 9-102(a).

Rule 9-102(a) took effect on July 1, 1980. Even before that time, however, this court had recognized the obligation of attorneys to maintain the separate identity of client funds. . . . .

This court's decision in *Elias* simply reaffirmed these principles, which at that time were expressed by Rule 9-102(a):

> It is manifest that this provision is mandatory, admitting of no exceptions for any reason. Repeatedly, this court has held that the foregoing provision embodies an unambiguous requirement that an attorney must establish and maintain a separate, identifiable trust account into which any and all funds belonging, in whole or in part, to clients are to be deposited regardless of the manner in which an attorney chooses to handle final disbursement of these funds. . . . .

The respondent's practice here of depositing the proceeds of judgments and settlements in his firm's general business account and paying clients their shares of the awards with checks drawn on that account clearly represented commingling. Clients did not receive the cash, bank drafts, or money orders mentioned by the concurring justice, but checks drawn on an account containing both the proceeds of client awards and the law firm's own operating funds. Notably, the respondent makes no challenge to the Hearing Board's and Review Board's determinations that his handling of client funds violated Rule 9-102(a). Given the clear evidence in this case, together with the respondent's acknowledgment that he was in violation of Rule 9-102(a), I would uphold the Hearing Board's and Review Board's determinations that the respondent was guilty of commingling, as alleged in count I of the complaint.

Less clear is the question whether the respondent was guilty of the conversion of client funds during the periods when the balance of the firm's account fell below the amount then belonging to clients. The respondent correctly notes that no client's check was ever dishonored, for the substantial line of credit extended to the respondent by his bank was more than sufficient to cover any overdrafts that occurred during the time in question. The majority agrees with the respondent that the existence of the line of credit effectively prevented the conversion of any client funds during that period.

Conversion is established upon a showing that the balance in an account in which client funds are being held falls below the amount then belonging to clients. . . . We have not previously considered, however, the effect of a line of credit, or other form of overdraft protection, on the operation of that general rule.

In light of the respondent's practice of immediately remitting to a client the client's share of a judgment or settlement, the balance of the respondent's business account might have innocently fallen below the total amount belonging to clients if a client happened to present his check for payment before the respondent's bank had collected the proceeds of that particular award. In certain instances, however, it appears that the account balance fell below the necessary level even after the proceeds of an award had been collected by the respondent's bank. Applying the principle that conversion occurs once the balance in the account falls below the amount of client funds being held in the account, one must conclude that conversion occurred at least on those occasions. Although the line of credit extended to the respondent by his bank would have protected clients against any loss when the respondent's commingled account was overdrawn, the line of credit would not have prevented conversion from occurring in the first instance. Of course, termination of the line of credit, for whatever reason, would have placed those client funds in jeopardy.

Count II of the complaint charged the respondent with the commingling and conversion of interest earned on client funds in his possession. The majority concludes that the respondent is not guilty of these charges. Addressing only the case of client Penelope Bell, who waited seven months to deposit a $162,000 check issued by the respondent, the majority believes that Bell was not entitled to the interest earned on that sum because she could have immediately negotiated her check yet chose not to do so. The majority emphasizes that the respondent had no role in determining when Bell finally decided to negotiate the check.

The Review Board properly found the respondent guilty of the commingling and conversion of interest earned on client funds deposited in the law firm's general business account. It is no answer to say, as the majority does, that a client must forfeit whatever right he might have to interest earned on his funds simply because he fails to immediately negotiate a check issued to him. The respondent should not have commingled client funds with his own funds in the first place, and certainly he could gain no greater right to the interest earned on client funds through that arrangement than if he had initially placed those funds in a separate trust account. Attorneys do not somehow become entitled to retain for their own use interest earned on client funds merely by commingling them with their own funds, as the respondent did here. In this State, the appropriate beneficiary of interest earned on a client's funds is the individual client himself or the Lawyers Trust Fund of Illinois, as the administrator of the interest on lawyers trust accounts (IOLTA) program. The record here shows that the respondent's firm retained the interest earned on client funds held on deposit in the firm's account. For these reasons, I believe that the allegations of count II of the complaint were established by the evidence in this case.

The respondent's primary offense was his failure to maintain a separate client trust account. Misconduct of this type creates a substantial risk of harm to clients. The applicable rules are clear and unambiguous, designed to forestall the potential problems that may arise from those activities. . . . . In the present case, however, the respondent's actions apparently were motivated by nothing more than what might be termed a "misguided sense of efficiency" . . . . Because of the line of credit extended to the respondent by his bank, none of the respondent's clients ever incurred any loss, temporary or permanent, as a consequence of the respondent's commingling and conversion of client funds. In addition, the respondent has made restitution of $7,374.83 to client Bell for the amount of interest earned by the respondent on her award; separately, the respondent has paid the Lawyers Trust Fund of Illinois the sum of $5,770.74, which represents interest earned on other client funds held by the respondent. Like the Hearing Board and the Review Board, I believe that censure is the appropriate sanction here.

COMMENTS AND QUESTIONS

Do you agree with the majority or dissent in *Rosin* on the issue of attorney liability? Should a bank bear any responsibility with respect to monitoring a law firm's account? Pre-revision article

4 contained no affirmative definition of the phrase "properly payable." Section 4-104(1)(i) provided that the phrase "includes the availability of funds for payment at the time of decision to pay or dishonor." Revised section 4-401(a) provides a more general definition of the concept.

It takes a strong person to handle someone else's money and not bother it; this case serves as a reminder of our ethical responsibilities as attorneys. Each year, more lawyers are disbarred or censured because of commingling client funds than for any other reason.

Obviously, the issue of when a bank may charge its customer's account goes beyond questions of professional responsibility. While the reproduced version of this case omits court references to article 3, you should note that the term "properly payable" under section 4-401 incorporates the applicable provisions concerning negotiable instruments under article 3, the customer's deposit account contract with the bank, as well as the provisions of article 4.

There are at least three situations where a bank has not paid according to its customer's order: (1) where the purported authorizing signature of the customer is a forgery (see U.C.C. § 3-403(a)); (2) where someone alters the amount of a check after issuance (U.C.C. § 4-401(d)(1)) and (3) where any necessary indorsement was forged (U.C.C. § 3-501(3)).

PROBLEM 14.1

On June 1, Drawee/Payor Bank sent a statement of account to its customer, Diane Drawer, accompanied by canceled checks paid by the Bank. On June 2 during her review of the statement, Drawer discovered that one of the checks paid had not been issued by her and in fact bore a forgery of her signature. She also discovered that another check, actually written by her, had been skillfully raised from $100 to $1000. Drawer immediately reported the two problem checks to her Bank and demanded that the Bank re-credit her account for the full amount of the forged check and for the $900 difference on the altered check. Must Bank re-credit Diane's account? See U.C.C. §§ 3-403, 4-401, and cf. 3-407(c). Would the result change if the forgery were that of the payee rather than the drawer? If bank paid the item over a forged payee's indorsement, could Drawer demand that the bank re-credit her account? See also, U.C.C. § 3-309.

NOTES AND QUESTIONS

(1) *Bank's Payment of an Overdraft*. Comment 1 to U.C.C. § 4-401 notes that an item is properly payable if the customer authorized the payment even where the bank's payment would result in an overdraft of the customer's account. Because it paid a customer-authorized item, the bank can treat an overdraft amount as a demand loan to the customer. Subsection 4-401(b) addresses situations where there is more than one customer who can draw on an account. The section provides that the non-signing customer should not be held responsible for an overdraft amount if that customer neither signed the item nor benefitted from the proceeds.

Query, how this section would be interpreted in a community property state where a spouse writes a check on a joint account creating an overdraft that the drawee/payor bank honors. If the check writing spouse disappears, should the bank be able to recover the overdraft amount from the other spouse?

(2) *Bank's Payment of a Postdated Check.* With today's automated processing systems, checks are usually paid without regard to the date. Under former law, the payor bank that paid an item before the check date could not charge the customer's account because it was not properly payable. Subsection (c) to § 4-401 addresses this problem by allowing banks to pay postdated items even though payment occurs before the date marked on the check. To avoid having the item charged against the account early, a customer must give the bank notice of the postdated item and describe it in such a manner so as to give the bank an opportunity to act. If, after receiving such notice, a bank charges the customer's account before the check date, the bank will be liable for loss damages, including the possibility of damages for the dishonor of subsequent items under section 4-402.

Most banks process thousands, if not millions, of checks daily. Query, even given the above protections, is it reasonable to expect a bank to ascertain whether a check is postdated?

[C] Events Terminating the Bank's Authority to Pay

Read: U.C.C. §§ 4-303, 4-403, 4-404 and 4-405.

Article 4 contains a number of statutory provisions that evolve from section 4-401's concept of properly payable. The sections are often referred to as the "four legals" because the described events help to define the necessary legal consequences surrounding a bank's non-payment (dishonor) of an item that appears on its face to be properly payable. The provisions either prohibit payment by the payor bank (mandatory dishonor), or permit the payor to refuse payment (permissive dishonor). Mandatory dishonor provisions include sections 4-401 (items not properly payable), 4-403 (stop payment orders), 4-303 (receipt of legal process), and 4-405 (death or incompetence of the drawer). Permissible dishonor provisions include section 4-303 (bank's right of setoff) and 4-404 (stale checks).

[1] Stop Payment Orders

DUNNIGAN v. FIRST BANK

Connecticut Supreme Court
585 A.2d 659 (1991)

BORDEN, ASSOCIATE JUSTICE.

In this appeal, we are called upon to define the meaning and scope of General Statutes § 42a-4-403(3)[1] of the Uniform Commercial Code (Code) as applied to the facts of this case. The defendant bank appeals, after a court trial, from the judgment of the trial court in favor of the plaintiff, the trustee in bankruptcy of Cohn Precious Metals, Inc. (Cohn), a customer of the bank. We transferred the appeal to this court pursuant to Practice Book § 4023, and we now reverse the trial court's judgment.

The plaintiff brought this action against the bank for wrongfully paying a check issued by Cohn over Cohn's valid stop payment order. The trial court determined that the plaintiff had

---

[1] General Statutes § 42a-4-403 provides as follows: "Customer's Right to Stop Payment; Burden Of Proof Of Loss. (3) The burden of establishing the fact and amount of loss resulting from the payment of an item contrary to a binding stop payment order is on the customer." [*See* revised U.C.C. § 4-403(c).]

established a loss within the meaning of § 42a-4-403(3) as a result of the bank's payment of the check and that the subrogation provisions of General Statutes § 42a-4-407[2] did not defeat the rights of Cohn. The court accordingly rendered judgment for the amount of the check. This appeal followed.

The bank claims that judgment was improperly rendered for the plaintiff because (1) as a matter of law, Cohn did not suffer a loss within the meaning of § 42a-4-403(3), and (2) the bank was subrogated to the rights of the payee of the check and of the collecting banks, pursuant to § 42a-4-407. We agree with the bank's first claim and therefore need not reach its second claim. Furthermore, it is not necessary to define the relationship between §§ 42a-4-403(3) and 42a-4-407.

The parties stipulated to the following facts. On November 8, 1978, pursuant to purchase order 1142, Lamphere Coin, Inc. (Lamphere), a trader in coins and precious metals, delivered to Cohn certain silver dollars with a unit price of $1.71 and with a total value of $27,492.07. Cohn's bookkeeper incorrectly recorded the unit price of those coins, however, as $17.10, resulting in an erroneous total value of $47,098.93. On November 9, 1978, Cohn paid Lamphere $47,098.93 by wire transfer to Lamphere's bank account, resulting in an overpayment to Lamphere by Cohn of $19,606.86. On November 10, 1978, Lamphere delivered three and one-half bags of silver dollars to Cohn pursuant to Cohn's purchase order 1145. The value of the silver dollars was $21,175. On the same day, Cohn issued two checks drawn on its account at the bank to Lamphere, one in the amount of $12,175 and one in the amount of $9,000, totaling $21,175.

Between November 10 and November 15, Cohn discovered its bookkeeper's error and, on November 14, 1978, directed the bank to stop payment on the two checks totaling $21,175 that had been issued on November 10, 1978. The bank stopped payment on the $9,000 check, but on or about November 20, 1978, the bank inadvertently honored the $12,175 check over the valid stop payment order. Cohn retained the three and one-half bags of silver dollars, but never recovered its overpayment from Lamphere. As of November 20, 1978, the date of the improper payment of the check by the bank, and at all times thereafter Lamphere owed Cohn in excess of $13,000 as a result of these transactions.

The merits of this controversy revolve around the meaning of § 42a-4-403(3), which provides that "[t]he burden of establishing the fact and amount of loss resulting from the payment of an item contrary to a binding stop order is on the customer." The bank argues that where there is good consideration for a particular check, or where the check was given as payment on a binding contract, the bank that paid the check over a valid stop payment order is not liable to its customer, because there was no "loss resulting from [its] payment . . . ." General Statutes § 42a-4-403(3). Thus, in the bank's view a customer cannot establish a loss under this provision of the code by relying on the loss of credits due the customer from prior unrelated transactions between the customer and the payee of the check. The plaintiff argues, as the trial court concluded, that whether a customer has incurred a "loss" within the meaning of § 42a-4-403(3) cannot be determined solely by focusing on the transaction underlying the particular check involved, but

[2] General Statutes § 42a-4-407 provides as follows: "Payor Bank's Right To Subrogation On Improper Payment. If a payor bank has paid an item over the stop payment order of the drawer or maker or otherwise under circumstances giving a basis for objection by the drawer or maker, to prevent unjust enrichment and only to the extent necessary to prevent loss to the bank by reason of its payment of the item, the payor bank shall be subrogated to the rights (a) of any holder in due course on the item against the drawer or maker; and (b) of the payee or any other holder of the item against the drawer or maker either on the item or under the transaction out of which the item arose; and (c) of the drawer or maker against the payee or any other holder of the item with respect to the transaction out of which the item arose."

must be determined by focusing on the entire relationship between the customer and the payee of the check. The plaintiff contends that it is unreasonable to disregard the relative positions of the parties, especially where they have demonstrated a continuing course of business dealings, where they are likely to be such credits. Under such circumstances, the plaintiff claims that focusing on a single transaction is contrary to the intent of the Code. Thus, in the plaintiff's view, Cohn would have had a good "defense" to a claim by Lamphere on the check because of the overpayment, and by paying the check the bank caused Cohn a loss within the meaning of § 42a-4-403(3).

The issue, therefore, is whether, on the facts of this case, the bank customer who sought to establish "the fact and amount of loss resulting from the payment of an item contrary to a binding stop payment order" pursuant to § 42a-4-403(3) was entitled to do so by resorting to credits from prior transactions unrelated to that for which the check was issued, or whether the customer was limited to the facts of the particular transaction for which the check was issued. We conclude that the customer was limited to the facts of the particular transaction for which the check was issued, and that § 42a-403(3) does not contemplate taking into account a loss by the customer of credits that arose from prior unrelated transactions.

We note first that, contrary to the plaintiff's suggestion, there is nothing in the stipulated facts to indicate that Cohn and Lamphere had a "continual course of business dealings." Those facts disclose only the two separate transactions occurring on November 8 and 9, 1978, and on November 10, 1978. Furthermore, this is not a case involving a revolving credit, open account or ongoing contractual relationship between the customer of the bank and the payee of the check. Thus, we need not decide whether those facts would yield a different conclusion.

Under § 42a-4-403(1), a bank customer has the right to order his bank to stop payment on a check, so long as he does so in a timely and reasonable manner, and, under § 42a-4-403(2), an oral stop payment order is binding on the bank for a limited period of time. See footnote 1, *supra*. The fact that the bank has paid the check over the customer's valid stop payment order does not mean, however, that the customer is automatically entitled to repayment of the amount of the check. Under § 4-403(3), the customer must also establish "the fact and amount of loss resulting from" the bank's improper payment.

The case law makes clear that "[t]he loss . . . must be more than the mere debiting of his account." [Citations.] The commentators agree. *See* W. Hillman, Basic U.C.C. Skills 1989, Article 3 and Article 4, p. 302; E. Peters, A Negotiable Instruments Primer (1974) p. 79; 1 J. White & R. Summers, Uniform Commercial Code (3d Ed. 1988) § 18-6, pp. 909-10. Otherwise, § 42a-4-403(3) would be superfluous. Furthermore, whether the customer has suffered such a loss is in the first instance a question of fact. [Citations.]

The cases and commentators also agree that where the check in question was supported by good consideration, or where the payee has enforceable rights against the maker based on the transaction underlying the check, the customer has suffered no loss within the meaning of § 42a-4-403(3). [Citations.] As then Professor Peters explained, it "is implicit in § 4-403(3) that if a check was issued for good consideration . . . failure to observe a stop payment order does no more than to accelerate the drawer's inevitable liability, and is therefore a defense to the payor bank." . . .

Applying these principles to the facts of this case, we conclude that as a matter of law Cohn suffered no "loss" within the meaning of § 42a-4-403(3). The check was supported by good consideration because it was issued in payment for the silver coins that Lamphere delivered to

Cohn. Furthermore, on the basis of that underlying transaction Lamphere had enforceable rights to payment by Cohn for those coins.

The plaintiff argues, however, that, although the particular check was supported by valid consideration and although there were no defenses available to it arising out of that particular transaction, the previous transaction between Cohn and Lamphere had supplied Cohn with a defense to payment of the check based on Cohn's overpayment to Lamphere. We disagree.

First, the language of § 42-4-403(3) suggests a narrower reading than would be required by the plaintiff's position.[3] Section 42a-4-403(3) places on the bank's customer the "burden of establishing the *fact and amount of loss resulting from the payment* of an item contrary to a binding stop payment order . . . ." (Emphasis added.) By contrast, § 42a-4-402, which deals with a bank's liability to its customer for a wrongful *dishonor*, as opposed to a wrongful payment, provides as follows: "A payor bank is liable to its customer for *damages proximately caused by the wrongful dishonor* of an item. When the dishonor occurs through mistake, liability is limited to actual damages proved. If so, proximately caused and proved damages may include damages for an arrest and prosecution of the customer or other consequential damages. Whether any consequential damages are proximately caused by the wrongful dishonor is a question of fact to be determined in each case." (Emphasis added.) Thus, pursuant to § 42a-4-402 the wrongfully dishonoring bank may be liable for all consequential damages proximately caused by its wrongful conduct, including damages resulting from arrest or prosecution of the customer, whereas there is a conspicuous absence from § 42a-4-403(3) of language indicating such a broad scope of liability for wrongful payment.

This difference in the scope of the language used in § 42a-4-403(3), as compared to that used in § 42a-4-402, is consistent with the notion that § 42a-4-403(3) is intended to impose a limited, rather than broad, form of liability on banks. "The trade-off for requiring banks to accept stop orders under § 4-403(1) was the limitation of their liability under §§ 4-403(3) and 4-407." E. Peters, *supra*.

The case law and commentary support this more restrictive view of the scope of § 42a-4-403(3). In determining whether a customer has established a "loss" under this section of the code, they focus on the check itself and on the transaction underlying it, and not on whether there were other prior, unrelated transactions between the maker and payee of the check. "In order to prove a loss under [§ 42a-4-403(3) of] the Code, a customer must prove he was not liable to the payee *on the check*." [Citations.] Although Cohn had an offset or counterclaim available to it with respect to Lamphere, it did not have a defense to payment of the check itself.

Finally, we find guidance in *Siegel v. New England Merchants National Bank, supra*. In that case, the court held that § 42a-4-403(3) must be read together with the subrogation provisions of § 42a-4-407. *Id.*, 386 Mass. at 678, 437 N.E.2d 218. Although we need not go that far because on the facts of this case § 42a-4-403(3) can be read independently of § 42a-4-407, we are persuaded by the holding of *Siegel* that in order to establish a § 42a-4-403(3) "loss" the customer

[3] Ordinarily we would look to the official commentary to the code for guidance in interpreting its language. Comment 2 to Connecticut General Statutes Annotated § 42a-4-403 provides: "The position taken by this section is that stopping payment is a service which depositors expect and are entitled to receive from banks notwithstanding its difficulty, inconvenience and expense. The inevitable occasional losses through failure to stop should be borne by the banks as a cost of the business of banking." This comment does not help in the resolution of the issue in this case, however, because it does not address the question of how to measure the scope of those "occasional losses through failure to stop . . . ."

must show that he had defenses to payment of the check that were good against a holder or holder in due course under §§ 42a-3-305 and 42a-3-306, as the case may be, or that he had a good defense to liability on the underlying transaction. *Id.* at 679, 437 N.E. 2d 218. None of these defenses arise from facts outside the confines of the particular check in question or the transaction underlying it.

In this case, the plaintiff seeks more than to establish a loss caused by the bank's failure to honor Cohn's stop payment order. That "loss" occurred in fact on November 9, 1978, when Cohn overpaid for the coins it had received. Rather, the plaintiff seeks to recoup a loss resulting from a prior transaction separate from and independent of the stopped check. Thus, the plaintiff's position would permit the customer to establish a "loss" based on offsets or counterclaims against the payee based on prior unrelated transactions, no matter how remote from the check in question or from the transaction underlying it. We do not believe that the intent of § 42a-4-403(3) ranges that far.

The dissent reads the commentary of Peters and of White & Summers too broadly. Although both refer to the situation, unlike the case at bar, where a customer seeks to establish a loss resulting from the dishonor of subsequent checks, neither commentator states with any confidence that the customer would prevail under § 42a-4-403(3). Peters discusses the hypothetical without coming to any conclusion other than "[w]hatever the inferences that may appropriately be drawn . . . it can hardly alter the conviction that § 4-403(3) accomplishes its purpose of severely limiting a drawer's power to stop payment." E. Peters, *supra*, 80. White & Summers do venture that they would find the bank liable, but "confess uncertainty about this conclusion, for it leaves little substance to § 4-403(3)." J. White & R. Summers, *supra*, 912. In any event, that is a case where the purported "loss" *follows* the wrongful payment and thus could arguably be said to be the result thereof, and not as in this case, where it *precedes* that payment. Furthermore, the dissent's equation of § 42a-4-403(3) to the law of causation in negligence ignores the difference in statutory language between § 42a-4-402, where that concept is incorporated, and § 42a-4-403(3), where "A factual finding must be reversed as clearly erroneous if it was based on an incorrect rule of law." [Citation.] The trial court's finding in this case that the plaintiff had established a loss within the meaning of § 42a-4-403 was so based.

The judgment is reversed, and the case is remanded with direction to render judgment for the defendant.

In this opinion CALLAHAN and HULL, JJ., concurred.

SHEA, ASSOCIATE JUSTICE, with whom GLASS, ASSOCIATE JUSTICE, joins, dissenting.

In this case it is undisputed that the drawer, Cohn Precious Metals, Inc. (Cohn), complied fully with General Statutes § 42a-4-403(1) in stopping payment on the checks it had delivered to Lamphere Coin, Inc. (Lamphere), on November 10, 1978, while unaware of the overpayment of $19,606.86 on November 9, 1978. It is also clear that, but for the negligence of the bank in paying the $12,175 check contrary to the stop payment order, Cohn could have offset its overpayment of the previous day against the value of the coins received from Lamphere on November 10, 1978. Thus, as the trial court concluded, the plaintiff trustee, on behalf of Cohn, sustained his "burden of establishing the fact and amount of loss resulting from payment of an item contrary to a binding stop payment order" by the defendant bank, as § 42a-4-403 requires.[4]

[4] On the basis of the facts before us, the trial court's award of $12,175 damages may have been excessive. The amount of the overpayment of November 9, 1978, was $19,606.86. The value of the silver dollars received by Cohn

The majority opinion does not challenge, as unsupported by the evidence, the trial court's factual finding that Cohn suffered a loss resulting from the bank's negligent payment of the $12,175 check to Lamphere, but rejects this straightforward "but for" causation analysis in favor of a narrower view of the "resulting from payment" provision of § 42a-4-403(3). The majority would restrict a bank's liability for paying a check contrary to a stop order to losses arising from the transaction in which the check was issued, such as a failure of consideration. I disagree, because there is nothing in the text of § 42a-4-403(3) or its history to support such an unjustifiable curtailment of the right of the drawer recognized by § 42a-4-403(3) to stop payment on a check for any reason, so long as the order is given to the bank in a timely and reasonable manner, as in this case. The right, of course, would be illusory without recourse against the negligent bank.

"The right to stop payment is an established right that was recognized prior to the Code. The right is absolute." J. Reitman et al., 6 Banking Law § 133.02. "If the drawer has a good defense on a check against a payee or holder, then the drawer suffers a loss when the bank wrongfully pays the check over a stop payment order." *Id.* The plaintiff trustee had the burden of proving that Cohn's loss resulted from non-compliance with the stop payment order, just as any negligence victim must prove causation. Even if the standard of causation applicable to breaches of contract should govern, reasonable foreseeability of the damages at the time the drawer and bank enter into this relationship; [Citation]; 3 Restatement (Second), Contracts § 351(1); it is evident that a bank must be deemed to foresee that its payment of a check over a valid stop payment order is likely to cause a loss to the drawer in the amount of the payment. There is nothing in § 4-403(3) that warrants a narrower approach to the issue of causation than that applicable to breaches of contract. In order to prevail against a bank that has ignored a stop payment order, "[t]he customer must show that (i) the account was debited, (ii) some other loss was suffered, if applicable, and (iii) bank's noncompliance with the stop order was the 'but for' cause." W. Hillman, Basic U.C.C. Skills 1989, Article 3 and Article 4, p. 319. As the trial court found, those criteria were satisfied by the plaintiff trustee in this case.

In adopting its constricted view of the "loss resulting from the payment of an item contrary to a binding stop payment order" provision of § 42a-4-403(3), the majority cites a plethora of authorities, none of which address the issue of whether a bank is excused from liability for failing to obey a stop payment order simply because the drawer had no defense arising out of the transaction in which the check was issued but only a right of set-off from another transaction. Most of the cases cited involve the principle that, when a bank has paid a check on which payment has been stopped, it becomes subrogated to the rights of the payee on the check. The quotation relied upon from E. Peters, A Negotiable Instruments Primer (1974) p. 79, it "is implicit in § 4-403(3) that if a check was issued for good consideration . . . failure to observe a stop payment order does no more than to accelerate the drawer's inevitable liability," is also based on the right of the bank to assert the rights of the payee on the check as a defense to an action by the drawer. Such a defense would not have been effective in this case, however, because

---

on November 10, 1978 was $21,175. Before the two checks totaling $21,175 were issued for this purchase, Cohn owed Lamphere $1568.14. That debt was discharged by the bank's erroneous payment of the $12,175 check. Thus Cohn received good consideration of $1568.14 as a result of the bank's payment and its loss is limited to the balance of the amount paid on the $12,175 check, $10,606.86.

The defendant bank has not challenged the amount of the award and, since it has fully prevailed on appeal, it is unnecessary to consider the issue further.

the drawer, Cohn, had no such "inevitable liability," given its right to set off the previous overpayment to Lamphere against the bank's claim as subrogee of Lamphere's rights on the check.

Two of the commentators relied upon by the majority refer to the situation in which a bank has wrongfully debited a customer's account after a stop payment order and this action has resulted in dishonoring for insufficient funds subsequent checks issued by the drawer with the consequence of impairing his credit. E. Peters, *supra*; 1 J. White & R. Summers, Uniform Commercial Code (3d Ed. 1988) p. 912. Although they disagree as to how this problem should be resolved under § 42a-4-403(3), they implicitly recognize that the bank's liability for failing to obey a stop payment order may well subject it to liability with respect to other transactions resulting in damages to a drawer that have been caused by the bank's oversight. The narrow concept of causation adopted by the majority cannot be reconciled with the views of these commentators.

The majority stresses the difference between the "resulting from" causation language of § 42a-4-403(3) and the more elaborate provision of § 42a-4-402 that expressly makes the bank liable for consequential damages for wrongfully dishonoring a check, including such damages as may result from the arrest or prosecution of the customer. Such a provision in § 42a-4-402 is probably necessary if liability for such damages is to be imposed because of the contract law limitation of damages to those that are reasonably foreseeable at the time of the contract. 3 Restatement (Second), Contract § 351(1). Such a provision in § 42a-4-403(3) is unnecessary to make a bank liable for the amount of a check it has paid after a stop payment order, however, because it is obvious that such a loss to the drawer from the bank's oversight is readily foreseeable.

As the majority acknowledges in a footnote, the official commentary in § 42a-4-403 takes the position "that stopping payment is a service which depositors expect and are entitled to receive from banks notwithstanding its difficulty, inconvenience and expense" and that "[t]he inevitable occasional losses through failure to stop should be borne by the banks as a cost of the business of banking." The view of the majority that a drawer should be made to bear a loss that would have been avoided but for the bank's neglect, because it did not arise from the transaction in which the check was issued, places a substantial restriction on the right to stop payment that § 42a-4-403(1) purports to give.

With respect to § 42a-4-407 and the defendant's claim to be a holder in due course, there is nothing in the record to indicate that the collecting bank ever allowed the payee to draw on the check after it was deposited. Since there is no proof that the collecting bank gave value, the defendant's claim to be subrogated to the status of a holder in due course is without foundation.

Accordingly, I dissent.

NOTES AND QUESTIONS

(1) Under Revised U.C.C. § 4-403(c), White and Summers believe that the dissent in *Dunnigan* may have the better argument. *See*, particularly, the last sentence of § 4-403(c). What is your judgment? *See* J. White & R. Summers, Uniform Commercial Code § 18-6 at 689 (4th ed. 1995).

(2) Who may order stop-payment on a check? See U.C.C. § 4-403(a) and Comment 2, plus § 4-405(b) and Comment 3. How long is a stop-payment order effective? Is an oral stop-payment order effective? U.C.C. § 4-403(b). May payment be stopped on (1) a cashier's check or (ii) a certified check? U.C.C. § 4-403 Comment 4 and U.C.C. sections cited within.

(3) What if an issuer of a cashier's check refuses payment as an accommodation to a customer and the payee stands to lose consequential damages as a result? U.C.C. § 3-411(c) and Comment 3.

(4) A woman took her fur coat to a furrier for repairs. When she went to pick up the coat, the furrier informed her that the charge was $500. The woman objected, considering the amount excessive. She was informed that the charges remained if she was to gain possession of the coat. Thinking quickly, she wrote a check payable to the furrier for $500, received the coat, then walked over to the bank and stopped payment. Is there any problem if it can be demonstrated that the lady issued the check intending to stop payment?

Assume the lady consulted you as to how to go about retrieving the coat. Do you see any ethical problems involved in counseling the procedure which the lady actually took? Note that Model Penal Code § 224.5, entitled "Bad Checks," states in part: "A person who issues or passes a check or similar sight order for the payment of money knowing that it will not be honored by the drawee, commits a misdemeanor."

(5) To what extent does inadvertence, accident or oversight constitute negligence? *See* U.C.C. § 4-103(a). It is possible to draft an exculpatory clause disclaiming liability for payment despite a stop order? Would such language disclaiming bank responsibility be effective? Consider the language contained in the following Stop Payment Order Form.

BANK COPY

PLEASE ENDEAVOR TO STOP PAYMENT ON THE CHECK DESCRIBED BELOW

OFFICE	DATE	TIME	REASON		
ACCOUNT OF				ACCOUNT NO.	
PAYABLE TO				AMOUNT $	
CHECK NO.	DATED	RECEIVED BY	DATE LETTER REC'D.	DUPLICATE NO.	DUPLICATE ISSUED

THE UNDERSIGNED AGREES TO HOLD YOU HARMLESS FOR ALL EXPENSES AND COSTS INCURRED BY YOU ON ACCOUNT OF REFUSING PAYMENT ON SAID ITEM, AND FURTHER AGREES NOT TO HOLD YOU LIABLE ON ACCOUNT OF PAYMENT CONTRARY TO THIS REQUEST IF THE SAME OCCURS DUE TO CIRCUMSTANCES BEYOND YOUR CONTROL, OR IF BY REASON OF SUCH PAYMENT ANOTHER ITEM OR ITEMS DRAWN BY THE UNDERSIGNED IS OR ARE RETURNED UNPAID FOR INSUFFICIENT FUNDS.

ACKNOWLEDGMENT IS HEREBY MADE OF THE RECEIPT OF THE NOTICE OF THE EXPIRATION WHICH TAKES EFFECT SIX MONTHS FROM THE DATE OF THIS ORDER.

FORM 828

CBT THE CONNECTICUT BANK AND TRUST COMPANY

SIGNATURE
(PLEASE SIGN AND RETURN TO BANK)

FORM 14–1 Stop Payment Order

[2] Stale Checks

Read: U.C.C. § 4-404; see §§ 3-414(f), 3-415(e) and Comment 4.

U.C.C. § 4-404 states that a bank has no obligation to pay checks (other than certified checks) that are more than six months old. A bank may charge its customer's account for a payments made on items older than six months if made in good faith. While section 4-404 was not revised, one should note that the definition of good faith has changed. *See* §§ 4-104(c), 3-103(a)(4): "Good faith means honesty in fact and the observation of reasonable commercial standards of fair dealing." *Cf.* U.C.C. § 1-201(19). Why are certified checks excluded from § 4-404?

In *RPM Pizza, Inc. v. Bank One-Cambridge*, 869 F. Supp. 517 (E.D. Mich. 1994), the plaintiff-customer claimed that defendant-bank violated the U.C.C.'s rules on payment of stale checks. After citing § 4-404 the court said:

> The term "good faith" is defined as "honesty in fact in the conduct or transaction." [§ 1-201(19).] Good faith definition is a subjective test, requiring an evaluation of the honesty of the Bank's intent, rather than its diligence . . . . Indeed, a Bank could act in good faith and still not follow accepted banking procedures.

The court concluded:

> Turning to the facts presented in this case, the Court notes that Plaintiff has been unable to offer so much a scintilla of evidence to demonstrate that the bank had noted the stale date, or the existence of an expired stop-payment order, or was in any respect less than completely unwitting when it paid the stale check. Furthermore, Plaintiff has been unable to raise a question of fact disputing the Bank's sworn allegation that its review of the check was limited to signature verification, because of its practice of signature verifications on all checks over $50,000. Therefore, Defendant's motion for summary judgment must be granted on the claim of breach of a duty of good faith.

869 F. Supp. at 520. Query, how would the revised definition of "good faith" affect this case? Can a bank in good faith pay with knowledge of an expired stop-payment order? *See* U.C.C. § 4-403(b).

[3] Death or Incompetence of Customer

Read: U.C.C. § 4-405.

The incompetence or death of a drawer raises the question of whether an item drawn before the event remains a properly payable item afterward. Section 4-405 protects the bank by providing that neither the death nor incompetence of the drawer will revoke the bank's authority to pay *until* the bank learns of the drawer's death or incompetence. Even if the bank has knowledge, it may pay or certify checks drawn on a deceased drawer's account for ten days after the date of death unless the bank receives a stop payment order from a person claiming an interest in the account. Comments 2 and 3 to section 4-405 note that so long as it acts in good faith, a payor bank has no duty to determine the validity of a claim and may simply honor the no-payment order by any one claiming an interest in the decedent's account. The effect of the statutory language then, is to give any surviving relative, creditor, or other interested party, a right to issue a stop order on items during the ten day period following a drawer's death. The section protects the bank only; thus, a person claiming an interest in the account may proceed against a payee or other recipient of a payment made by the bank if the stop order comes too late.

REPUBLIC NAT. BANK v. JOHNSON

Florida District Court of Appeals
622 So. 2d 1015 (1993)

COPE, JUDGE.

Republic National Bank of Miami appeals an adverse final judgment after a bench trial. We reverse.

Appellee Maria Johnson was a depositor at Republic National Bank. In March, 1989 she opened a checking account with a balance of $59,000. In May through July, 1989 Ms. Johnson made a series of cash withdrawals from her account at the bank. These withdrawals eventually depleted the balance in the account.[5]

Unbeknownst to the bank, during this time period Ms. Johnson's landlord had been attempting to have the Department of Health and Rehabilitative Services take action to determine Ms. Johnson's competency. However, no action was accomplished until after the withdrawals in question. On September 28, 1989 the probate division of the circuit court entered an order adjudging Ms. Johnson incompetent by reason of organic mental syndrome. At this time Ms. Johnson was 76 years old.

The Guardianship Program of Dade County, Inc., investigated the cash withdrawals that Ms. Johnson had made. The guardian was unable to locate any of the money or to ascertain what happened to it. There are some signs that Ms. Johnson was the victim of exploitation, but no facts have emerged which would yield the money or an explanation.

The guardian brought suit against Republic National Bank. The guardian contended that there were "red flags" in this case which should have alerted the bank that Ms. Johnson was not competent, or that Ms. Johnson was being exploited. After a bench trial in the probate division, the court ruled that the bank should have made some inquiry regarding the final two withdrawals, for $15,000 and $26,949, respectively. The court entered judgment for the guardian in those amounts, plus prejudgment interest. The bank has appealed.

The guardian urges that the exploitation of the elderly is a problem to which banks must be alert. The guardian argues that the circumstances in the present case were suspicious because the elderly customer withdrew large amounts of cash from a personal checking account. Also

---

[5] The transactions were:

Date	*Amount*
5/11/89	$ 2,500.00
6/14/89	$ 2,000.00
7/03/89	$ 2,500.00
7/07/89	$ 6,000.00
7/11/89	$ 5,000.00
7/13/89	$15,000.00
7/17/89	$26,949.00

In the case of the withdrawal of $26,949, Ms. Johnson used $10,000 to purchase a certificate of deposit and took the balance in cash.

said to be suspicious is the fact that the withdrawals occurred using counter checks or starter checks of the recently opened account.[6]

On the question of competency of a bank customer, the Uniform Commercial Code draws a "bright line" rule. The Code states: [U.C.C. § 4-405(1).]

The U.C.C. official comment states:

Purposes:

. . . .

> 2. Subsection [1] follows existing decisions which hold that a drawee (payor) bank is not liable for the payment of a check before it has notice of the death or incompetence of the drawer. The justice and necessity of the rule are obvious. A check is an order to pay which the bank must obey under penalty of possible liability for dishonor. *Further, with the tremendous volume of items handled any rule which required banks to verify the continued life and competency of drawers would be completely unworkable.*

Uniform Commercial Code Comment, 19B Fla. Stat. Annot. (Supp. 1993) at 204 (emphasis added) . . . . As there was admittedly no adjudication of incompetency until after the transactions in question, the bank proceeded consistently with the Uniform Commercial Code. *See* § 674.103(3), Fla. Stat. (Supp. 1992). In light of the U.C.C. provision and official comment, the bank did not have a duty to inquire into the customer's competency.[7]

The guardian argues, however, that this case is not aimed at the problem of undetected incompetency. Instead, the guardian's main concern is the problem of exploitation of the elderly through scams invented by unscrupulous con artists. According to the guardian, this is a broader problem which victimizes elderly depositors who are gullible enough to be taken in, and is not a phenomenon directed solely at persons who are incompetent.

Subsequent to the events which occurred in this case, a new statute became effective which partially speaks to the guardian's concern. The legislature added banks, savings and loan associations, and credit unions to the entities who are required to report possible exploitation of the elderly to the Department of Health and Rehabilitative Service's Central Abuse Registry.

As amended, the statute now provides that any "[b]ank, savings and loan, or credit union officer, trustee, or employee, who knows, or has reasonable cause to suspect, that an aged person or disabled adult is an abused, neglected, or *exploited person* shall immediately report such knowledge or suspicion to the central abuse registry . . . on the single state-wide toll-free telephone number." § 415.103(1)(a)(7), Fla. Stat (1991) (emphasis added). Failure to report is a misdemeanor. *Id.* § 415.111(1).

It is now the obligation of banks, savings and loan associations, and credit unions to develop compliance programs so that their officers, trustees, and employees know when they should make

---

[6] There is no evidence regarding Ms. Johnson's demeanor on the occasions in question. With regard to the withdrawals of $15,000 and $26,949, Ms. Johnson presented the documentation which was necessary for the bank to complete its Form 4789 Currency Transaction Reports. The only specific recollection bank personnel had of Ms. Johnson was when an officer assisted her on a matter relating to her account which did not involve a withdrawal. The officer stated that on that occasion Ms. Johnson was lucid and appeared to understand what she was doing.

[7] We do not mean to suggest that the bank would never have a responsibility to take steps on behalf of its customer. If, for example, the customer had a seizure or stroke or physically collapsed while on the premises, or became obviously delusional, then the bank would have to take prudent action. Here, however, the guardian argues that an inquiry should have been triggered on account of the size of the cash withdrawals.

a report on the toll free number. The guardian presented expert testimony that there are a number of "red flags" which may be indicative of exploitation. Financial institutions must give clear instructions to officers and front line employees so that they will know what should be reported to the Department, and when and how to report it.[8] It should be noted that the law places the reporting obligation not only on each bank, savings and loan association, and credit union, but also each officer, trustee, and employee individually.[9]

The guardian urges, however, that we should impose on financial institutions a broader obligation. The guardian argues that where an elderly customer seeks to withdraw large amounts of cash from a personal account, the bank has a duty to halt the transaction temporarily so that an officer can inquire into the purpose of the cash withdrawal. If the bank officer is satisfied that the customer knows what he or she is doing and is not being victimized, then the bank would allow the cash withdrawal. If the officer is not satisfied, then the authorities would be summoned for a more thorough inquiry.[10]

In essence the guardian urges us to impose a new standard of care on the bank where an elderly customer in writing a check to withdraw the customer's own funds from his or her account. The bank would be obliged to inquire into the purpose of a large cash withdrawal by an elderly customer, and would be obliged to halt the transaction if not satisfied with the explanation. This would work a significant change in the depositor-financial institution relationship, and would represent a marked departure from existing law.

If such a new mandatory duty of care is to be created, it should be brought about by the legislature after appropriate study. In that way customer rights and financial institution responsibilities can be clearly stated and clearly understood. At present we think the Uniform Commercial Code runs counter to the guardian's position. While we are entirely sympathetic to the goals articulated by the guardian and the trial court, we must reverse the final judgment. This ruling renders moot the guardian's appeal, consolidated herewith, of the denial of attorney's fees under section 45.061, Florida Statutes (1991).

One of the expert witnesses testified below that a number of banks have developed voluntary programs for attempting to detect and thwart scams directed at the elderly. Experts also testified that banks frequently attempt to dissuade elderly customers from leaving the premises with large amounts of cash, for reasons of personal safety among other things. Nothing we say here is intended to limit or discourage such voluntary measures.

As to Republic National Bank's appeal, reversed and remanded with directions to enter judgment for defendant. As to the guardian's appeal, affirmed.

---

[8] Presumably the Department of Health and Rehabilitative Services and law enforcement agencies will be available for consultation on implementation of the new statute.

[9] We express no opinion on the question whether failure to comply would result in civil liability.

[10] Although the facts of the present case are suspicious, it is unknown what the result of any such inquiry by a bank officer in this case would have been.

QUESTION

Why does U.C.C. § 4-405(b) provide a limited period after death during which a drawee bank may continue to pay checks even though it has notice? Shouldn't the section also apply if the drawer were adjudicated an incompetent?

[4] Bankruptcy of Customer

Read: U.C.C. § 4-303 and Comments 1 and 2; Bankruptcy Code § 542(c).

As we shall see later, bankruptcy law seeks to provide over-burdened debtors with a fresh start. The law provides that upon a debtor's filing a petition, all of the debtor's property becomes property of the bankruptcy estate which is administered by a trustee. A bankruptcy filing will clearly have an effect on the bank-customer relationship and what items are properly payable. What are the payor bank's responsibilities once the petition has been filed? Can the bank continue to pay items and if so, under what conditions? In *Bank of Marin v. England,* 385 U.S. 99, 87 S. Ct. 274, 17 L. Ed. 2d 197 (1966), the payor bank paid items after the drawer declared bankruptcy but before the bank received notification. The trustee claimed that the filing of the petition vested all of the drawer's property in the trustee who was the only person who could authorize payment. Because bankruptcy is an enumerated power granted to the federal government, bankruptcy law supersedes inconsistent state law. Thus, the trustee argued that the bank's discretion and authority to pay items from the drawer's account terminated with the filing of the petition. Relying upon the equitable principles, the Supreme Court concluded that the authority of the bank to pay continued until it received notice of the bankruptcy proceeding. The court noted:

> We cannot say that the act of filing a voluntary petition in bankruptcy *per se* is reasonably calculated to put the bank on notice. Absent revocation by the drawer or his trustee, or absent knowledge or notice of the bankruptcy by the bank, the contract between the bank and the drawer remains unaffected by the bankruptcy and the right and duty of the bank to pay duly presented checks remain as before.

Cf. U.C.C. § 4-405(1).

[D] Wrongful Dishonor

Read: U.C.C. §§ 4-402, 4-401(c), 4-403(c).

What happens when a bank dishonors an item that is in fact properly payable? For example, what result if the payor mistakenly determined that there were insufficient funds in a drawer's account? What if the payor improperly setoff monies in the drawer's account for money allegedly due from the drawer-customer? In both instances, the dishonor constitutes a breach of the customer-bank deposit contract. Because the customer's account is not debited, damages for wrongful dishonor are consequential and not direct. The customer does not demand that the bank re-credit customer's account. Instead, the customer may seek damages for both the economic and emotional impact of the dishonor. Section 4-402(b) provides that a payor bank is liable for "damages proximately caused by the wrongful dishonor of a item." Liability, however, is limited to the actual damages proven by the customer. Actual damages can include damages for an arrest or prosecution of the customer. The possibility of applying the "trader rule" from former law has been eliminated.[11]

The availability of consequential damages is a question of fact to be determined in each case by focusing on whether the damages are proximately caused by the wrongful dishonor. Clearly, the customer has a difficult burden of proving speculative losses caused by a wrongful dishonor. Even if the customer prevails, the dishonor will likely never give rise to punitive damages under Article 4 (punitive damages may be justified under other state law). Although the next two cases apply pre-revision section 4-402, they provide good examples of when a wrongful dishonor action is and is not warranted.

KARRER v. GEORGIA STATE BANK OF ROME

Georgia Court of Appeals
452 S.E.2d 120 (1994)

Pope, Chief Judge.

Plaintiff, Phyllis E. Karrer, appeals the trial court's grant of summary judgment for defendant, Georgia State Bank of Rome ("Bank").

On August 24, 1989, Karrer and her adult son opened a joint checking account with the Bank. At the time the account was opened, Karrer and her son signed a signature card/account agreement, which specified the terms and conditions of the account relationship. One of the specific provisions of the agreement requires that the customer, in this case Karrer, report any account problems (with some exceptions not pertinent here) to the Bank within 60 days of receipt of her statement, or else lose her right to assert the problem against the Bank.

On Wednesday, August 15, 1990, Karrer tendered a check drawn on the account, in the amount of $1,510 to Casey Construction ("Casey"). The check was signed by Karrer and dated the same day it was made out, August 15, 1990. At the time the check was tendered, Karrer admits that she knew there were insufficient funds in the account to cover the check. Karrer's checkbook ledger and the monthly bank statement issued by the Bank verify that when the check was tendered Karrer only had $836.94 in the account. additionally, at no time during August 1990 was the account balance sufficient to pay the check.

Casey also maintained a checking account with the Bank in August 1990. On Friday morning, August 17, 1990, prior to the Bank's 4:00 p.m. cut-off time, Casey deposited the check to its account at the Bank, along with another check in the amount of $55, and received $965 in cash. On Saturday, August 18, 1990, Karrer went to the main office of the Bank and for the first time notified it that she wanted to stop payment on the check. Karrer asserts that she made this decision after meeting with Casey at approximately 6:00 p.m. on Friday, August 17, 1990. Karrer claims that it was at that time she concluded that Casey's work was defective.

[11] Under the trader rule, a damage award could be made without a proof of specific damage if the customer was a business customer. See comment 1 to section 4-402.

Although Saturday is not a normal banking day for the Bank, in that the Bank does not carry on substantially all of its banking functions on that day, Karrer spoke with Nan Langford, a customer service representative at the Bank, and informed her that she wanted to stop payment on the check. Karrer claims she told Langford that if a stop-payment order could not be issued Karrer wanted to deposit sufficient funds in the account to cover the check. Langford accessed the account on the Bank's computer and informed Karrer that the check had not yet posted to the account because the account lacked sufficient funds to cover the check. Langford then contacted a Bank officer and was told that the Bank would do all that it could to stop payment on the check. At that time Karrer's stop-payment order was accepted. Additionally, Karrer claims that Langford assured her at that time that the Bank would stop payment on the check.

The stop-payment order was not implemented before the check was returned to Casey for insufficient funds. Whether the check was actually returned on Monday, August 20, 1990, or Tuesday, August 21, 1990, is disputed by the parties. The record shows, however, that the Bank, in its regular course of business, issued a notice of insufficient funds to Karrer advising her that the check had been presented, that the available balance in the account was insufficient to cover the check, and that the check had been returned. Karrer denies ever seeing this notice. The bank statement, however, issued to Karrer for the period of July 24, 1990 through August 20, 1990, shows a $15 debit to the account for an insufficient funds item. This debit was dated August 20, 1990.

On August 24, 1990, after the Bank returned the check to Casey, Casey's attorney mailed a letter to Karrer by registered mail, return receipt requested. In the letter, the attorney informed Karrer that the check had been dishonored by the Bank. The letter also notified Karrer that if she did not pay the full amount of the check to Casey within 30 days a civil action might be filed against her or a criminal action under OCGA § 16-9-20 would be initiated. The letter was returned by the postal authorities marked "Unclaimed."

Both the letter from Casey's attorney and all the mailings from the Bank to Karrer were sent to the address Karrer gave the Bank when she opened the account. It is undisputed that the address was correct as of the time of the mailings. Karrer, however, in no way responded to the notice of insufficient funds and did not notify the Bank of any problem she had after receiving her bank statement, even though she has admitted she saw the statement prior to her October 9, 1990 arrest for issuance of a bad check. Additionally, Karrer did not contact Casey and try to make the check good prior to her arrest.

The record in this case shows that from the time they opened the account, Karrer and her son never effectively reconciled their checkbooks with the bank statements provided to them by the Bank. In fact, Karrer admits that the account was an unworkable situation. The record also shows that Karrer and her son were very disorganized, to say the least, when it came to picking up their mail. Karrer has testified that many times her son would pick up the mail and simply leave it wherever he happened to be. Karrer and her son stored some of their bank records and other mail in a rented warehouse. The warehouse was not organized in any way and documents placed in it were merely placed in boxes. Karrer has admitted that upon going through the documents stored in the warehouse she found many documents she previously did not know existed.

On October 9, 1990, Casey swore out a warrant for Karrer's arrest for the issuance of a bad check. Karrer was arrested on the same day and was subsequently indicted by the Chatooga County Grand Jury. She did not communicate to the Bank any problem she had concerning the requested stop-payment order or the return of the check for insufficient funds until June 4, 1991, approximately eight months after her arrest. Even when she closed her account on February 15, 1991, she said nothing to the Bank about its handling of the check or the stop-payment order. Karrer filed suit against the Bank on August 15, 1991 alleging that the Bank's failure to stop payment on the check and the Bank's return of the check for insufficient funds were wrongful, unlawful and improper. Karrer also claimed that the Bank's actions constituted a breach of the agreement between her and the Bank. The damages Karrer complains of allegedly arise from her arrest, imprisonment and subsequent indictment for the charge of issuing a bad check. On September 5, 1991, the Bank answered, denying liability and asserting various defenses. On September 13, 1993, the Bank filed a motion for summary judgment. By order dated November 9, 1993, the trial court granted the Bank's motion. On appeal, Karrer contends that the trial court erred in granting summary judgment to the Bank. We disagree and affirm.

1. Karrer contends that when the Bank failed to process the stop payment order and returned the check to Casey for insufficient funds, the Bank committed an act tantamount to wrongful dishonor of the check, thereby subjecting the Bank to potential liability under OCGA § 11-4-402. We reject this contention.

OCGA § 11-4-402 provides as follows: "A payor bank is liable to its customer for damages proximately caused by the wrongful dishonor of an item. When the dishonor occurs through mistake, liability is limited to actual damages proved. If so, proximately caused and proved damages may include damages for an arrest or prosecution of the customer or other consequential damages. Whether any consequential damages are proximately caused by the wrongful dishonor is a question of fact to be determined in each case." In this case, the damages Karrer complains of all arise from her arrest, imprisonment and subsequent indictment and prosecution for the offense of issuing a bad check. Under OCGA § 16-9-20 "[a] person commits the offense of deposit account fraud when such person makes, draws, utters, executes, or delivers an instrument for the payment of money on any bank or other depository in exchange for a present consideration or wages, *knowing* that it will not be honored by the drawee. For the purposes of this Code section, it is prima facie evidence that the accused knew that the instrument would not be honored if: . . . (2) Payment was refused by the drawee for lack of funds upon presentation within 30 days after delivery and the accused . . . shall not have tendered the holder thereof the amount due thereon, together with a service charge, within ten days after receiving written notice that payment was refused upon such instrument." (Emphasis supplied.) *Id.*

Here, Karrer has admitted that at the time she delivered the check to Casey on August 15, 1990, she knew that her account lacked funds sufficient to cover the check. Furthermore, it is undisputed that when Casey presented the check to the Bank on August 17, 1990, there were still insufficient funds in the account. In fact, throughout August 1990, there was never enough money in the account to cover the check. Casey's attorney notified Karrer by certified mail, return receipt requested, at the address listed on the check, that the check had been drawn on insufficient funds. A review of this notice demonstrates that it complies with the notice guidelines set forth in OCGA § 16-9-20(a)(2)(A), (B). The notice was returned with the notation "unclaimed" and thus by statute is deemed sufficient and equivalent to having been received by Karrer. *See* OCGA § 16-9-20(a)(2)(A). It also is undisputed that Karrer never tendered any money to Casey after said notice was sent. All of the above constitutes prima facie evidence that Karrer knew her check would not be honored. [Citation.] This prima facie evidence alone amounts to sufficient probable cause to warrant Karrer's arrest, indictment and subsequent prosecution, all of which comprise the damages Karrer complains of here. Consequently, we conclude that the Bank cannot be held accountable for such damages in the case at bar.

Karrer's contention that she told Casey, upon presenting the check to him, that there were insufficient funds in her account to cover the check and that he should not present the check for payment until Karrer could deposit sufficient funds to her account, does not create a genuine issue of material fact in this case. OCGA § 16-9-20(h)(1) provides in relevant part that "[i]n any civil action for damages which may be brought by the person who made, drew, uttered, executed, or delivered such instrument, *no evidence of statements or representations as to the status of the instrument involved or of any collateral agreement with reference to the instrument shall be admissible unless such statements, representations, or collateral agreement shall be written simultaneously with or upon the instrument at the time it is delivered by the maker thereof."* (Emphasis supplied.) *Id.* There is no record evidence of any simultaneously written statements, representations or collateral agreements in this case. The record shows that the check was not even post-dated. Thus, Karrer's contention that she told Casey, at the time she issued him the check, that her account did not have sufficient funds to cover the check, is irrelevant to the case at bar because any such alleged statement is inadmissible. Therefore, such a contention neither creates a genuine issue of material fact to be resolved in this case, nor does it rebut the prima facie evidence of Karrer's knowing issuance of a bad check.

Furthermore, Karrer is precluded from recovery against the Bank in this case because she failed to take any steps to minimize her alleged damages (*i.e.* her arrest, indictment and subsequent prosecution). Although a bank is liable for damages proximately caused by its wrongful handling of an item, a customer has an obligation to exercise reasonable care to minimize any damage done and if the customer fails to minimize its damages, the customer is precluded from recovery against the bank. [Citation.] In this case Karrer made no effort to minimize her alleged damages. The record shows that the Bank, in its ordinary course of business, sent Karrer a notice of insufficient funds prior to her arrest. The notice advised Karrer that the check had been presented and returned. Additionally, Karrer admits that she received her bank statement for the period of July 24, 1990 through August 20, 1990. This statement also indicates that the check was returned for insufficient funds. Both the notice and the statement were mailed to Karrer's correct address. Moreover, the letter from Casey's attorney notifying Karrer that the check was returned for insufficient funds and demanding payment was also mailed to the correct address, return receipt requested. The record shows that Karrer, either intentionally or through extreme carelessness, disregarded all these mailings. She did not notify the Bank of any problem after receiving her bank statement, even though she admitted seeing the statement prior to her arrest. Karrer also failed to contact Casey and try to make the check good prior to her arrest. Based on the above, we conclude that the trial court was warranted in finding no issue of material fact concerning damages. The damages complained of by Karrer were all directly and solely related to her own admitted carelessness and general lack of fiscal responsibility. The trial court, therefore, did not err in granting summary judgment to the Bank.

2. Karrer also is barred from recovery against the Bank in this case because she failed to meet a condition precedent to bringing suit. The agreement Karrer and her son signed at the time they opened the account contains a provision which requires them to report any account problems to the Bank within 60 days of receipt of their bank statement, or else lose their right to assert the problem against the Bank. Upon review of the record it is clear that Karrer failed to assert any problem she had with the account, relative to the stop-payment order or the return of the

check to Casey for insufficient funds, within 60 days of the receipt of her bank statement for the period of July 24, 1990 through August 20, 1990. In fact Karrer did not notify the Bank of any problem she had concerning the stop-payment order or the return of the check until June 4, 1991, approximately ten months after she received the statement indicating that the check has been returned. Accordingly, Karrer has forfeited her right to challenge the Bank's actions with respect to its handling of the check. [Citation.]

Judgment affirmed.

QUESTION

Does revised U.C.C. §§ 4-402 and 4-403(c) change the result or analysis of the *Karrer* case?

TWIN CITY BANK v. ISAACS

Arkansas Supreme Court
672 S.W.2d 651, 39 U.C.C. Rep. 35 (1984)

STEELE HAYS, JUSTICE.

Twin City Bank has appealed from a judgment entered on a jury verdict against it in favor of Kenneth and Vicki Isaacs for damages sustained from the bank's wrongful dishonor of the Isaacs" checks resulting in a hold order against their account for a period of approximately four years.

On Sunday, May 13, 1979, the Isaacs discovered that their checkbook was missing. They reported the loss to Twin City promptly on Monday, May 14, and later learned that two forged checks totalling $2,050 had been written on their account and honored by the bank on May 11 and 12. The sequence of events that followed is disputed, but the end result was a decision by the bank to freeze the Isaacs" checking account which had contained approximately $2,500 before the forgeries occurred. A few checks cleared Monday morning before a hold order was issued leaving the balance at approximately $2,000. Mr. Isaacs had been convicted of burglary and the initial hold on the account was attributable to the bank's concern that the Isaacs were somehow involved with the two forged checks. The individual responsible for the forgeries was charged and convicted soon after the forgeries occurred and on May 30, 1979 the police told the bank there was nothing to connect the Isaacs with the person arrested. Two weeks later the police notified the bank a second time they could not connect the Isaacs to the forgeries. The bank maintains it continued to keep the account frozen on the advice of its attorneys. However that may be, the Isaacs were denied their funds for some four years. The Isaacs followed suit in Mid-June of 1979 for wrongful dishonor of their checks and wrongful withholding of their funds.

The jury awarded the Isaacs $18,500 in compensatory damages and $45,000 in punitive damages. The bank made a motion for a new trial pursuant to ARCP Rule 59, which was denied. From that denial the bank brings this appeal contending error on three grounds: 1) Misconduct of a juror at trial, 2) the trial court's refusal to give two requested instructions, and 3) jury error in assessing excessive damages contrary to the evidence and the law.

. . . .

On the issue of damages, the bank maintains there was insufficient evidence to support the $18,500 award for mental anguish, for loss of credit and loss of the bargain on a house, that the award of punitive damages should not have been given at all as there as not only insufficient proof of actual damages but insufficient evidence of malice or intent to oppress on the part of the bank. The bank does not challenge the sufficiency of the evidence of its wrongful dishonor, but contends only that there was no evidence to support an award of damages. These arguments cannot be sustained.

The statute upon which this suit was based in Art. Stat. Ann. § 85-4-402 . . . .

The jury was instructed that if they found the bank liable they were to fix the amount of money which would compensate the Isaacs "for any of the following elements of damage sustained which were proximately caused by the conduct of Twin City Bank: 1) Any amounts of money wrongfully held by the defendant and remaining unpaid 2) any mental anguish and embarrassment suffered by the plaintiffs 3) any financial losses sustained by the [Isaacs]."

Initially, there can be no serious question as to certain losses: the $2,000 wrongfully withheld by the bank for four years, and the value of two vehicles repossessed because the Isaacs did not have access to their funds, resulting in a loss of approximately $2,200. Additionally, after the account was frozen the bank continued to charge the account a service charge and overdraft fees on checks written before the forgeries but presented after the account was frozen. The bank does not refute these damages but argues there is no showing of any financial deprivation from loss of credit or loss of the bargain on a house the Isaacs wanted to buy, and insufficient proof of mental anguish. We find, however, that in addition to the losses previously mentioned, there was sufficient evidence to sustain damages for mental suffering, loss of credit, and sufficient demonstration of some loss attributable to the inability to pursue the purchase of a home.

Mental suffering under § 4-402 of the Uniform Commercial Code is relatively new and has not been frequently addressed by other courts, but of those a majority has allowed recovery. [Citations.] In general, the type of mental anguish suffered under § 4-402 does not need to rise to the higher standard of injury for intentional infliction of emotional distress. Wrongful dishonors tend to produce intangible injuries similar to those involved in defamation actions. [Citation.] Damages of this kind are more difficult to assess with exactness. In *Wasp Oil v. Arkansas Oil and Gas*, 280 Ark. 420, 658 S.W.2d 397 (1983) we noted the general rule that damages may not be allowed where they are speculative, resting only upon conjectural evidence, or the opinions of the parties or witnesses, but there are instances where damages cannot be proven with exactness. In *Wasp* we recognized a different rule applies when the cause and existence of damages have been established by the evidence, that recovery will not be denied merely because the damages cannot be determined with exactness. We went on to say the plaintiff in the case at bar was not trying to prove the latter sort of damage such as *mental anguish* as a result of defamation, but loss of income.

Decisions upholding recovery for mental suffering under the code have found injury resulting from circumstances comparable to this case. In *Northshore Bank v. Palmer, supra*, for example, a $275 forged check was paid from Palmer's account. After the bank knew or should have known the check was forged, it charged Palmer with the $275 check and later wrongfully dishonored other checks. Part of the actual damages awarded was attributed to mental suffering for the "embarrassment and humiliation Palmer suffered from having been turned down for credit for the first time in his life."

In *Morse v. Mutual Federal Savings and Loan*, *supra*, $2,200 was awarded for "false defamatory implications arising from temporary financial embarrassment." And in *Farmers & Merchants State Bank of Krum v. Ferguson*, *supra*, the plaintiff's account in the amount of $7,000 was frozen apparently one month for reasons not stated. The plaintiff was awarded $25,000 for mental anguish, $3,000 for loss of credit based on a denial of a loan, $5,000 for loss of time spent making explanations to creditors, and $1,500 for loss of use of his money. The court justified the mental suffering award because the dishonor was found to be with malice—the bank had failed to notify Ferguson that the account was frozen, some checks were honored while others were not, and the bank continued to withdraw loan payments due it during the entire time.

In this case, prior to the forgery incident the Isaacs" credit reputation with Twin City Bank was described by the bank as "impeccable" and the freezing of their funds had a traumatic effect on their lives. They obviously lost their credit standing with Twin City, and were unable to secure credit commercially at other institutions because of their status at Twin City. The Isaacs had to borrow from friends and family, and were left in a precarious position financially. They did not have use of their $2,000 for four years. The allegation relative to the loss of a house resulted from the dishonor of an earnest money check for a home they were planning to buy, ending prospects for the purchase at that time. Though there may have been sufficient proof of loss of the bargain on the house, as the bank argues, nevertheless this evidence was admissible as an element of mental suffering. The denial of credit contributed to some monetary loss as occurred in *Ferguson, supra*, in addition to its being a reasonable element of mental suffering as was found in *Palmer, supra.* There was also testimony that the financial strain contributed to marital difficulties leading at one point to the filing of a divorce suit. The suit was dropped but there was testimony that the difficulties caused by the bank's action caused substantial problems in the marriage. Finally, the Isaacs lost equities in two vehicles repossessed as a result of the withholding of their funds. One of these, a new van, was repossessed by Twin City in June, 1979, before a five day grace period for a current installment had expired.

We believe there was substantial evidence to support the verdict. The jury heard the evidence of the amount wrongfully withheld, the loss of two vehicles, credit loss through loan denials, loss of the use of their money for four years, the suffering occasioned by marital difficulties, the inability to acquire a home they wanted, and the general anxieties which accompanied the financial strain. We recognize that our holding today presents some conflict with pre-code law by allowing recovery without exactness of proof as to damages. In *State Bank of Siloam Springs v. Marshall, supra*, a suit based on the predecessor to § 85-4-402, we stated that the plaintiff must show the facts and circumstances which occasioned the damage and the amount thereof. However, *Marshall* itself recognized the nature of the damages in this action, and § 85-4-402, although similar to its predecessor, has additional language which impliedly recognizes mental suffering and other intangible injuries of the type noted in *Wasp, supra*, as recoverable under this statute. *See* White, Summers, *supra* § 17-4, p. 675. To the extent that exactness in proof is not required, the law as stated in *Marshall* is displaced by § 85-4-402.

The bank's objection to the award of punitive damages is threefold: a) The instruction on punitive damages was in accordance with AMI 2217, which is intended for use in negligence cases and not applicable here; b) there was not evidence that the bank acted intentionally or with malice, and c) the verdict of $45,000 was excessive. However, we address only the question of the excessiveness of the verdict, as the other points were not raised in the trial court by objection to the instruction.

In *Holmes v. Hollingsworth*, 234 Ark. 347, 352 S.W.2d 96 (1961), we noted the elements that may be considered in assessing the amount of punitive damages, recognizing that the deterrent effect has some correlation to the financial condition of the party against whom punitive damages are allowed. In view of the circumstances in their entirety presented by this case, we cannot say the amount awarded was grossly excessive or prompted by passion or prejudice.

The judgment is affirmed.

NOTES AND QUESTIONS

(1) Would revised U.C.C. § 4-402 change the result or analysis of the *Twin City Bank* case? As to punitive damages, *see* U.C.C. § 4-402 Comment 2 (last sentence), and §§ 1-203, 1-106.

(2) Does U.C.C. § 4-402 preclude an action for wrongful dishonor by a plaintiff other than the bank's customer? *See* § 4-402 Comment 5, which states in part: "Some courts have allowed a plaintiff other than the customer to sue when the customer is a business entity that is one and the same with the individual or individuals operating it. *Murdaugh Volkswagen, Inc. v. First National Bank,* 801 F.2d 719 (4th Cir. 1986)."

(3) *Time of Bank's Determination of Customer's Account Balance. See* U.C.C. § 4-402(c) and especially read Comment 4. *See* Regulation CC, 12 CFR § 229.10(a)(1).

(4) Customer has $328.12 in her account when seventeen checks totaling $664.45, are presented for payment. The checks range in amount from $5 to $75. Only three of the checks are greater than $50. Banker calls you for advice. What do you say? *See* U.C.C. § 4-303(b). What relevance does that section have to § 4-402?

[E] Duties of the Customer to the Bank

Read: §§ 4-406, 3-406.

We have seen in § 14.01[B] above that a drawee-payor bank may not charge against the account of the drawer-customer a check that is not "properly payable." Just as the bank has certain duties with respect to the customer's account, the customer also owes certain concurrent duties to the bank. A customer's failure to meet its obligations to the bank will free the bank from duties owed the customer. Section 4-406 imposes a duty on the customer to examine any bank statement promptly for forged or altered items and a duty to notify the bank if any such problems are found. The section precludes a customer from disclaiming responsibility based upon an alteration or a forged signature if the customer failed to give the payor bank notice of the unauthorized payment. In effect, section 4-406 provides payor banks with a negligence defense against customer claims under section 4-401(a).

Although not required to do so, almost invariably, payor banks provide statements of their customers" accounts. The account statement may include either a return of paid items or information sufficient to permit the customer to identify the items paid. Ordinarily, a statement showing the item number, payment amount, and date of payment will be sufficient. § 4-406(a) & (b). Subsection (c) requires the customer to examine the statement for forgeries (forged indorsements are *not* included), alterations, or any other unauthorized use. If the customer promptly notifies the bank of an unauthorized use, the customer will be protected and the bank cannot debit the customer's account for the unauthorized item paid (*i.e.*, the customer will be permitted to claim that the item was not properly payable under § 4-401(a).

If the payor can prove that its customer reasonably should have discovered the unauthorized payment and failed to notify the bank, section 4-406(d) precludes the customer from asserting the unauthorized signature against the bank if the bank can also prove that it suffered a loss by virtue of the customer's failure to give notice. Under subsection (d)(1) the question is whether the bank could have avoided or minimized the loss on an unauthorized payment (through restitution or some other remedy); if so, the customer-drawer will be responsible. Subsection (d)(2) applies to those cases where the customer failed to notify the bank and the bank pays that item and subsequent ones involving the same wrongdoer. If payment of those subsequent items occurred before the bank had notice and after the customer had a reasonable time to report the first unauthorized use (no more than 30 days after receipt of the bank statement), the customer will once again be precluded from asserting the alteration or unauthorized signatures on those subsequent items.

If the customer is precluded from claiming unauthorized payment by subsection (d) but the customer can prove that the bank failed to exercise ordinary care when it paid the item(s) and that the bank's failure substantially contributed to the loss, subsection (e) of 4-406 provides a comparative negligence test for allocating the losses between the customer and the bank. Section 4-406(e) also states that "if the customer proves the bank did not pay an item in good faith, the preclusion under subsection (d) does not apply." Like Revised § 3-406(b) which also establishes a comparative negligence standard, § 4-406(e) avoids preclusion from a failure to give notice if the customer proves that the bank paid in bad faith. See also comments to sections 3-404, 3-405, and 3-406.

Finally, irrespective of the payor's negligence or lack of ordinary care, a drawer will be precluded from asserting an unauthorized payment if the drawer did not report the unauthorized activity on the account within one year after receiving the bank statement that should have identified the unauthorized use. § 4-406(f). Subsection (f) is a statute of limitation for alterations and forged checks; it does not apply to forged indorsements, which have a three year statute of limitations under section 4-111.

NEW JERSEY STEEL CORPORATION v. WARBURTON

New Jersey Supreme Court
655 A.2d 1382 (1995)

GARIBALDI, J.

This appeal concerns the allocation of check-fraud losses under specific provisions of Articles 3 and 4 of the Uniform Commercial Code ("U.C.C."), adopted in New Jersey as *N.J.S.A.* 13A:3-406 and *N.J.S.A.* 12A:4-406. The Court must allocate those losses between a corporation whose negligence allowed the defalcation to occur and a depository-payor bank that accepted checks for deposit without following its own procedures for inspecting the endorsements on those checks. Defendant Midlantic National Bank ("Midlantic Bank") failed to discern endorsements that did not correspond to the payees as well as forged maker signatures, thus violating its duty to pay an instrument "in accordance with reasonable commercial standards" and to exercise "ordinary care." Plaintiff, New Jersey Steel Corporation ("N.J. Steel"), failed to examine its monthly statements, thus violating its statutory and contractual duty "to exercise reasonable care and promptness to examine the statements and items to discover . . . unauthorized signature or any alteration on an item."

I

Prior to 1984, defendant Rupert Warburton ("Warburton") was an employee of N.J. Steel. In 1984, Warburton formed his own independent computer consulting business that operated under the trade name of Mapics Unlimited. N.J. Steel hired Warburton as its independent computer consultant, thus allowing him access to its computerized financial and accounting systems. With that access, Warburton devised and implemented a plan to defraud N.J. Steel. Warburton's plan began with "waste checks" —blank checks that were left in N.J. Steel's computer room—and ended with deposits into accounts opened by Warburton for his personal and business use. Warburton would write those checks to fictitious payees whose names resembled, but were not identical to, the trade name of his own consulting business, which was the name on the depositing bank account. For example, he made the checks payable to "M.P.S." and "M.M. Systems," but the name of his business and corresponding bank account was "Mapics Unlimited." Warburton was the sole authorized signatory for the Mapics account. Next he would fill in an account payable that was identical to the amount of a legitimate, previously issued check. Warburton then would forge the name of one or both of the authorized signatories for N.J. Steel's account at Midlantic Bank.

He would then endorse each check with only the words "For deposit" or "For deposit only," followed by 362010144, the account number for Mapics Unlimited, rather than the account number for the payee. Indeed, the name of the fictitious payee did not appear in the endorsement; no one signed the endorsement on behalf of that payee; and the checks were not endorsed for deposit into an account in the name of the payee. The tellers then made no attempt to verify whether account 362010144 belonged to the named payee of each check. Instead, each forged check was subsequently deposited in the Mapics Unlimited account at the Rossmoor branch of Midlantic Bank, and the bank transferred funds from N.J. Steel's account to Warburton's account. Midlantic Bank, therefore, was both the payor and the depository bank for those checks.

To complete his plan, Warburton would obtain N.J. Steel's monthly statements from Midlantic Bank, remove and destroy each forged check, and replace it with the corresponding previously negotiated check. He would also adjust N.J. Steel's computer records to reflect that the only payee was that of the corresponding previously negotiated check. From November 1989 to October 1990, Warburton completed this scheme fourteen times, depositing checks with sums ranging from $19,083.40 to $64,146.98, for a personal gain of $571,931.90. N.J. Steel did not discover that loss until January 1991, whereupon it immediately notified Midlantic Bank.

One of the reasons Warburton was able to escape detection for so long was that in early 1990, he had convinced N.J. Steel to abandon its manual check-reconciliation process in favor of a computerized process he conducted himself. Previously, N.J. Steel and Midlantic Bank had entered into an account reconciliation plan that provided in pertinent part:

> The Corporation agrees it will examine its statement and items for unauthorized signatures, items paid but not issued or alterations. Failure by the Corporation to notify the Bank of any unauthorized signatures, items paid but not issued or alterations within 14 days of the Corporation's receipt of statement and items will bar the Corporation's right to assert a claim

against the Bank for subsequent unauthorized signatures, items paid but not issued or alterations, by the same person.

The Corporation understands that Midlantic will exercise reasonable care in providing the Account Reconciliation Plan described herein on behalf of the Corporation. The Corporation hereby agrees that Midlantic shall have no liability regarding any item processed with reasonable care under this agreement.

Although the corporation received all the monthly statements and canceled checks in a timely manner, N.J. Steel failed to perform a manual reconciliation or to examine its canceled items for unauthorized signatures pursuant to its agreement with Midlantic Bank.

In addition to that agreement between the parties, Midlantic Bank adopted and put into place institutional policies that governed its acceptance of customers" deposits. Midlantic Bank's Policy 5.1 provides, "For deposits containing 5 checks or less, the teller must read each endorsement to make sure that it is correct . . . . By reading endorsements, the teller is responsible for verifying endorsements on all checks deposited." Policy 5.1 also provides, "Any single check over $10,000 must be initialed by two tellers (the one accepting the deposit and another teller evidencing a thorough review of the transaction) on the back." None of the checks at issue bear such initials. Midlantic Bank's Policy 7.4 provides, "[c]hecks drawn to the order of a corporation must be deposited in an account bearing the same title and cannot be transferred by endorsement to any individual or another company."

In January 1991, N.J. Steel sued Warburton, Midlantic Bank, and other defendants seeking damages in connection with the forged checks. N.J. Steel alleged in its amended complaint that Midlantic Bank was liable under several alternative theories: strict liability for accepting and negotiating checks without properly authorized signatures (count 4); strict liability for accepting checks without proper endorsements (count 5); negligently accepting checks without properly authorized signatures (count 6); negligently accepting checks without endorsements of the named payees (count 7); and failure to act within generally accepted commercial practices in debiting N.J. Steel's account for checks having forged signatures and missing proper endorsements (count 8). Midlantic Bank asserted various affirmative defenses and cross-claims for indemnification and contribution, including that N.J. Steel's action was barred or diminished in whole or part because its loss had been caused by its own contributory or comparative negligence. In February 1991, N.J. Steel obtained a Consent Judgment against all defendants except Midlantic Bank. Subsequently, Hartford Insurance Company intervened in the action as partial subrogee and/or assignee of N.J. Steel against each defendant, including Midlantic Bank.

After extensive discovery, the case was tried without a jury. At trial an employee of Midlantic Bank testified to the bank's internal procedures for inspection of deposited checks for proper endorsements. He testified that tellers must read each endorsement if the deposit contained five or fewer checks, and must fan the checks to determine the presence or absence of endorsements if the deposit contained more than five checks. Moreover, under the same policy directive, any single check for more than $10,000 must be examined by two tellers. The witness also testified that if the account number in an endorsement on the reverse side of a check did not match the payee's account number, the teller was required to reject the check as incorrectly endorsed under Policy 5.1. N.J. Steel's expert compared the bank's institutional policies to the industry standards and concluded that the bank had been negligent because it had not followed those policies.

The trial court found that the subject checks were not properly endorsed because the endorsements did not contain the name of the payee and the checks were endorsed for deposit "into an account of one other than the [named] payee." The trial court further found that Midlantic Bank had failed to follow its own written policy and procedures concerning inspection of checks for proper endorsements: "I find that [Midlantic's policy] was not followed since a thorough review of these checks by a trained teller would have revealed the inadequacy of the endorsements." Finally, based on the testimony of N.J. Steel's expert, the trial court determined that Midlantic Bank's failure to review properly the endorsements constituted a violation of the "ordinary procedures in the banking industry" and that Midlantic Bank's acceptance of the checks without proper endorsements was a "proximate cause" of N.J. Steel's loss. The trial court, however, refused to find that Midlantic Bank had violated its Policy 7.4.

The trial court concluded that since Midlantic Bank failed to exercise ordinary care in paying the subject checks, it could not invoke *N.J.S.A.* 12A:4-406 as a defense. In assessing damages, the trial court held that plaintiff's claim with respect to the first forged check was time-barred under *N.J.S.A.* 12A:4-406(4). The trial court calculated the total damages to be $247,264.15. Finally, the trial court held that N.J. Steel was not entitled to recover prejudgment interest because of "the equities of the situation." In reaching that conclusion, the trial court found that N.J. Steel had failed to examine its account statements and thereby contributed to the perpetration of the fraud.

The Appellate Division affirmed in a *per curiam* opinion "substantially for the reasons stated by [the trial court]." We granted Midlantic Bank's petition for certification. 137 *N.J.* 166, 644 A.2d 614 (1994).

II

Although both *N.J.S.A.* 12A:3-406 and *N.J.S.A.* 12A:4-406 govern this case, we discuss first *N.J.S.A.* 12A:4-406.

12A:4-406. Customer's Duty to Discover and Report Unauthorized Signature or Alteration.

(1) When a bank sends to its customer a statement of account accompanied by items paid in good faith in support of the debit entries of holds the statement and items pursuant to a request or instructions of its customer or otherwise in a reasonable manner makes the statement and items available to the customer, the customer must exercise reasonable care and promptness to examine the statement and items to discover his unauthorized signature or any alteration on an item and must notify the bank promptly after discovery thereof.

(2) If the bank establishes the customer failed with respect to an item to comply with the duties imposed on the customer by subsection (1) the customer is precluded from asserting against the bank:

(a) his unauthorized signature or any alteration on the items if the bank also establishes that it suffered a loss by reason of such failure; and

(b) an unauthorized signature or alteration by the same wrongdoer on any other item paid in good faith by the bank after the first item and statement was available to the customer for a reasonable period not exceeding fourteen calendar days and before the bank receives notification from the customer of any such unauthorized signature or alteration.

(3) The preclusion under subsection (2) does not apply if the customer establishes lack of ordinary care on the part of the bank in paying the item(s).

The provisions of *N.J.S.A.* 12A:4-406 are to be read in conjunction with one another. *N.J.S.A.* 12A:4-406(1) establishes the customer's duty to discover and report unauthorized signatures or alterations. *N.J.S.A.* 12A:4-406(2) precludes the customer from making various assertions against the bank if the bank has established the customer's breach of that duty as outlined in provision (1). However, under *N.J.S.A.* 12A:4-406(3), a bank may assert that preclusion only if it paid the check in "good faith" and the customer is unable to establish "lack of ordinary care on the part of the bank in paying the item(s)." Therefore, provisions (1) and (2) are inoperative if the customer can establish that the bank has also been negligent. In a transaction where both parties might be negligent, the loss stemming from the combined effect of those three provisions is on the last party found negligent: the payor bank (also referred to as the drawee bank). That is made clear by the New Jersey Study Comment to *N.J.S.A.* 12A:4-406(3):

> 3. Subsection 4-406(3) makes the rules of subsections 4-406(1) and (2) inoperative if the bank, itself, has been negligent. In other words, a negligent bank cannot put the loss resulting from a forgery or the like onto the customer on the ground that the customer also has been negligent. There is no New Jersey statutory or case law precisely on point, but the rule of subsection 4-406(3) seems to be simply an application of the general rule of contributory negligence; where both the plaintiff and the defendant have been negligent, let the loss remain where it has fallen.

That comment has been cited with approval in *Faber v. Edgewater Nat'l Bank of Edgewater,* 101 *N.J. Super*. 354, 359, 244 A.2d 339 (Law Div. 1968), in which the court reasoned that "subsection 4-406(3) makes the rules regarding due diligence inoperative if the bank, itself, has been negligent. In other words, a negligent bank cannot put the loss resulting from a forgery or the like onto the customer on the ground that the customer also has been negligent." *Id.* at 359, 244 A.2d 339 (citing *N.J.S.A.* 12A:4-406 Study Comment.)

In reviewing the same U.C.C. provision in effect in New York, the New York Court of Appeals held that "[u]nder (both U.C.C. 4-406 and 3-406), when both the bank and its customer have been negligent and even when the customer is by far the more negligent party, the entire loss may still be asserted against the bank." [Citations.]

III

> 12A:3-406. Negligence Contributing to Alteration or Unauthorized Signature.
>
> Any person who by his negligence substantially contributes to a material alteration of the instrument or to the making of an unauthorized signature is precluded from asserting the alteration or lack of authority against a holder in due course or against a draw or other payor who pays the instrument in good faith and in accordance with the reasonable commercial standards of the drawee's or payor's business. L. 1961, c. 120, § 3-406.

N.J.S.A. 12A:3-406 is broader in scope than *N.J.S.A.* 12A:4-406. Under *N.J.S.A.* 12A:3-406, a customer "who by his negligence substantially contributes" to the loss is estopped from recovering against a payor bank that is required to "pay[] the instrument in good faith and in accordance with . . . reasonable commercial standards." Again, the initial loss is imposed on the customer who is negligent. However, the effectiveness of the bar to recovery is conditioned on the payor bank having acted pursuant to the reasonable commercial standards of the banking business.

Under *N.J.S.A.* 12A:3-406, the slightest contributory negligence on the part of the bank makes the defense of the customer's negligence unavailable. Donald J. Rapson, *Loss Allocation in*

Forgery and Fraud Cases: Significant Changes Under Revised Articles 3 and 4, 42 Ala. L. Rev. 435 (1991). Significantly, the comments to revised article 3, approved by the National Conference of Commissioners on Uniform State Laws and the American Law Institute in 1990, explain: "The 'substantially contributes' test is meant to be less stringent than a 'direct and proximate cause' test. Under the less stringent test the preclusion should be easier to establish." U.C.C. Revised Article 3, § 3-406 cmt 2, 2 *U.L.A.* 105 (1991). Although "reasonable commercial standards" are not defined in that section of the New Jersey law, the New Jersey Study noted that "any bank which takes or pays an altered check which ordinary banking standards would require it to refuse cannot take advantage of the estoppel." New Jersey Study Comment to *N.J.S.A.* 12A:3-406(6) (1994).

Therefore, a negligent customer may shift total liability to the payor bank by showing that the bank negligently failed to confirm to industry standards in paying the item contrary to the customer's order. At least one court has held that it is commercially unreasonable to accept for deposit a check made out to a corporate entity but endorsed for deposit to a personal account. *See In re Lou Levy & Sons Fashions, Inc. Litig.*, 988 F.2d 311, 313-14 (2d Cir. 1993) (applying New Jersey law, court found bank negligent in accepting checks with endorsements containing account number for individual account where named payee was corporation; bank therefore could not invoke drawer's negligence as preclusion under § 3-406). Another court has stated "the [payor] bank has a duty to make payment only to the payees named in its depositors' checks or to their order. Consequently, the [depository] bank as a general rule has a duty to determine the identity of the payee." [Citation.]

A lack of ordinary care on the part of the bank paying items under this provision of the U.C.C. "may be established by proof either that the bank's employees were below standard or that the bank's employees failed to exercise care in processing the items." *First Nat'l Bank & Trust Co. v. Cutright*, 189 Neb. 805, 205 N.W.2d 542, 545 (1973) (cited in U.C.C. § 3-406, at n.9). For a payor bank to escape liability, it must establish that it acted in accordance with reasonable commercial standards and exercised ordinary care. [Citations.]

IV

Pursuant to the Account Reconciliation Plan Operating Agreement that it had entered into with Midlantic Bank, and under *N.J.S.A.* 12A:4-406(1), N.J. Steel owed a duty to Midlantic Bank to examine within a reasonable time any canceled checks and account statements received and to give timely notice of any irregularities. [Citation.] N.J. Steel is not excused from that duty by having entrusted its performance to an incompetent or dishonest agent, like Warburton. [Citation.]

By its own admission, N.J. Steel was negligent in supervising Warburton. As an independent computer consultant, Warburton advised N.J. Steel to abandon its manual check-reconciliation process in favor of a computerized process that he conducted himself. In so doing, N.J. Steel put Warburton in a position to perpetuate his fraudulent plan, and then failed to perform both its statutory obligations under *N.J.S.A.* 12A:4-406(1) and its contractual duties under the account-reconciliation plan with Midlantic Bank. Thus, under the statute, N.J. Steel would be liable for the checks due solely to its duty to discover and report unauthorized signatures or alterations, if Midlantic Bank could affirmatively establish that N.J. Steel's "negligence in inspecting the statements or giving notice of the forgeries *caused* the loss." [Citation.]

However, any lack of reasonable care and promptness in the conduct of N.J. Steel "in examining its bank statements is of no weight under the statutory scheme if the bank is proven to have failed to use ordinary care in paying the items." [Citation.] N.J. Steel can shift liability solely to Midlantic Bank by proving the bank's lack of ordinary care under *N.J.S.A.* 12A:4-406(3). Under that provision, the bar to recovery by N.J. Steel from *N.J.S.A.* 12A:4-406(1) and (2) does not apply if the payor bank failed to exercise ordinary care in paying an item . . . .

Midlantic Bank is both the depository and payor bank. Because a payor bank "has a duty to make payment only to the payees named," a depositary bank "has a duty to determine the identity of the payee" of its depositor's checks. [Citations.] If it had acted only as payor bank, Midlantic Bank could have recovered from the depository bank. [Citation.] However, Midlantic Bank assumed dual roles of responsibility. Thus, Midlantic Bank's position that it has no duty to examine the checks as to the named payees is "totally unacceptable." *Hanover, supra*, 482 F. Supp. at 505. Instead, that "bank's lack of ordinary care may be demonstrated by proof that the bank's procedures were below the standard or that the bank's employees failed to exercise due care in processing the items."

The trial court found N.J. Steel had demonstrated that Midlantic Bank failed to exercise ordinary care by proof that although the bank had developed institutional procedures for deposits that would meet the appropriate standard of care, that bank's employees failed to exercise due care in following those procedures. They failed to verify the endorsement appearing on each check and to ensure that the checks were endorsed to the named payee. Midlantic Bank's own institutional policies required its tellers to check carefully the endorsements of deposits of less than five checks and to seek supplemental review from another teller with endorsements on checks for more than $10,000. Therefore, the checks at issue merited careful review by Midlantic Bank's employees because of the amounts as well as the quantity of the deposited checks. However, Midlantic Bank did not check the endorsements. Midlantic Bank accepted large checks for deposit that bore neither the business account's name as payee nor an endorsement matching the payee of the check.

Midlantic Bank failed to prove that it acted in accordance with industry standards as well as its own institutional policies. In its role as depository bank, Midlantic Bank attempted to do so only through cross-examination of experts who acknowledge that tellers and other bank personnel often interpret literally the industry standard of "Know your endorser" by ignoring institutional policies for a customer who frequented the bank and could chit-chat with the teller about his family. Although "local banking practices may be useful in determining the standard required," we refuse to find that the practices of individual tellers might provide support for minimal standards that, if actually put in place, would "amend the statutory requirements." [Citation.] Moreover, the testifying experts concluded that such common practice by tellers or other bank personnel does not comport with reasonable commercial standards. Thus, notwithstanding any prevailing local custom in the banking industry, we agree with the trial court that Midlantic Bank's tellers did not conduct a thorough review of the endorsements, which would have revealed the inconsistency between the payee and the authorized payee on the account number written as an endorsement.

Although not relied on by the lower courts in holding Midlantic Bank liable, that Warburton forged the names of the authorized signatories on all checks is undisputed. N.J. Steel's expert testified that the normal procedure for the payor bank's processor would have been to compare the maker signatures found on a quantity of checks for the corporation in question. For example, viewing thirty checks in that manner would highlight any differences or similarities in maker signatures. When more than one signature is identified on checks for one corporation, the bank's processor would then check them against the authorized signature card on file to ascertain the number of authorized signatures. Under that example, the expert concluded that any processor who used such procedures would have discovered the fraud in this case. Therefore, in addition to missing the irreconcilable differences in the endorsement account numbers and the varied but fraudulent payees, Midlantic Bank's employees also missed the unauthorized signature on each check. Thus, the expert concluded that those checks were not properly payable. Although Midlantic Bank's expert testified that the forgeries were so good that a lay person would fail to detect them, we question whether a processor in a bank is such a lay person. Based on the record, we conclude that one could find Midlantic Bank also liable to N.J. Steel for its failure to catch the forged maker signatures, under both *N.J.S.A.* 12A:3-406 and 4-406.

Midlantic Bank argues that this case is one of double forgery and asserts that under that theory, it would not be liable. *See Brighton, Inc. v. Colonial First Nat'l Bank,* 176 N.J. Super. 101, 115, 422 A.2d 433 (App. Div. 1980) (adopting rule from *Perini Corp. v. First Nat'l Bank*, 553 F.2d 398 (5th Cir. 1977), which requires double forgery cases to be treated "as if they involved forged drawer's signatures alone"), *aff'd p.c.o.b.*, 86 N.J. 259, 430 A.902 (1991). However, the record does not indicate a case of double forgery. Double forgery consists of a forged maker's signature *and* a forged endorsement. While Warburton certainly forged the names of authorized signatories of the corporation's account, his endorsement consisted of the words "For deposit only" followed by a *valid* account number for his consulting business. That endorsement was not forged. Here the problem resulted from the teller's failure to use the endorsement to compare the authorized payees of that account with the payee on the check.

In addition to the underlying facts, cases of double forgeries are problematic for a reason inapplicable to this case: a decision to treat a case as one of a forged signature results in loss to the payor bank whereas treatment by the courts as a forged endorsement shifts the loss to the depository bank on its warranty covering forged endorsements. *See* Rapson, *supra*, 42 Ala. L. Rev. at 468. As has been outlined above, Midlantic Bank is both payor and depository bank. Therefore, its argument of double forgery is confusing because liability falls on it due to its roles as a payor and a depository bank, rather than the degree of forgery involved. The rule adopted in *Brighton, supra*, is distinguishable from the present case because of the type of negligent conduct as well as the different factual scenario. [Citation.] Thus, we find that the holding of *Brighton, supra,* is inapplicable to this situation.

N.J.S.A. 12A-3-406 requires that the payor bank "pay[] the instrument in good faith and in accordance with . . . reasonable commercial standards." *N.J.S.A.* 12A:4-406(3) requires that the payor bank exercise "ordinary care . . . in paying the item(s)." Midlantic Bank failed to meet the standards of both statutes. Payor banks have a duty to ascertain the identity of the payee. While payor banks are not in a position to determine the authenticity of an endorsee's signature, they can and should verify whether the endorsement matches the payee name. The *Hanover* court explained:

> We find the [payor] bank's position that it has no duty to examine the check as to the named payee to be totally unacceptable. The [payor] bank has a duty to make payment only to the payees named in its depositors" checks or to their order. Consequently, the [payor] bank as a general rule has a duty to determine the identity of the payee.

[482 F. Supp. at 505.]

Accordingly, Midlantic Bank had a duty to examine the endorsements as the payor bank.

Given the tremendous volume of checks that must be processed by even the smallest of banks, whether sight review of checks should be required in the modern banking era is a difficult issue, but not an issue that this Court must resolve. The trial court, in finding that Midlantic Bank failed to exercise ordinary care, did not impose a general duty on all banks to inspect endorsements visually. As the trial court found, Midlantic Bank had voluntarily assumed a certain standard of care in promulgating written policies and procedures for accepting checks. Under Midlantic Bank's procedures, the patent discrepancy between the payee name and the account name required Midlantic Bank to reject the deposit or at the very least to make further inquiries about the identity of the payee. Hence, Midlantic Bank breached its duty of care when its tellers failed to follow its own official procedures. Therefore, this Court should not disturb the trial court's finding that Midlantic Bank failed to exercise ordinary care when it accepted for deposit checks that its own written procedures required it to reject.

In conclusion, Midlantic Bank failed to exercise ordinary care in paying the items at issue and thus may not invoke N.J. Steel's negligence in defense. Midlantic Bank is therefore strictly liable for paying items that were not "properly payable." Under both *N.J.S.A.* 12A:3-406 and 4-406, such negligence removes any defense that Midlantic Bank might have against N.J. Steel. Therefore, the customer's assertion of contributory negligence by the bank allows "the loss [to] remain where it has fallen" —on Midlantic Bank. Although the result might seem unjust, it is in accordance with the law governing the claims at issue as well as with the particular facts of this case where defendant bank was "doubly negligent" as a payor and depository bank to its customers. As this type of "double agent," Midlantic Bank had two opportunities to catch the fraud perpetuated by Warburton on N.J. Steel before the reconciliation agreement directed N.J. Steel to review carefully its monthly statement. Because Midlantic Bank failed to conform with commercially reasonable banking standards and to exercise ordinary care, we affirm the judgments of both the trial court and the Appellate Division.

We note that the Legislature passed and the Governor on February 15, 1995, signed into law S. 344, now L. 1995, c. 28, that revises Articles 3 & 4 of the U.C.C. and embraces the spirit of comparative negligence. However, that Act does not take effect until the first day of the first calendar month which follows the 90th day after enactment.

The judgment of the Appellate Division is affirmed.

NOTES AND QUESTIONS

(1) Do you agree with the court's decision? The last paragraph of the opinion refers to New Jersey's enactment of revised Article 4 which "embraces the spirit of comparative negligence." What result if the court had applied the revised statute?

(2) *Ordinary care and Comparative Negligence.* Under the pre-revision Code, the slightest contributory negligence by the bank made the preclusion defense of section 4-406 unavailable, even if the customer was also negligent. Revised section 4-406(e) provides for a comparative

negligence standard where there is negligence of the customer and a failure of the bank to exercise ordinary care and *both* failures contributed to a loss. In such cases the loss is allocated between the customer precluded and the bank that asserts preclusion according to the extent their respective failures contributed to the loss. Under section 4-406(e), the customer has the burden of proving that the bank failed to exercise ordinary care and that the failure "substantially contributed to the loss."

Ordinary care is defined at § 3-103(a)(7) as the "observance of reasonable commercial standards, prevailing in the area in which the person is located with resect to the business in which the person is engaged." The section specifically notes that a bank is not required to subject each item to a sight examination in order to establish ordinary care. This portion of the statute permits banks to rely on automatic processing methods without violating the duty of care owed the customer. If the customer proves that the bank did not pay the item in good faith, the customer will not be precluded from claiming that the item was not properly payable. Under such circumstances, the bank would have to re-credit the customer's account and suffer the resulting loss if the wrongdoer could not be found.

There is a very practical problem which must be faced with regard to the comparative negligence standard. How can it be made an effective remedy which can be applied? In many cases, the amount in question will not be sufficient for a consumer, or even a business, to bring legal action. Fees and legal costs would quickly surpass the amount of the check. The consumer's right without a realistic remedy is an injustice. What is to stop a bank from asserting (without sufficient basis) that the customer is primarily negligent when in fact the customer is not! The bank could then simply refuse to re-credit the customer's account or instead credit the account with some small percentage. The bank is in a position of strategic power. Even though a consumer might successfully be able to assert that the bank has violated its duty of good faith entailing both actual and punitive damages, most would not bring an action.

A more informal, less expensive, and yet neutral system should be available for resolving most bank-customer disputes. As a part of fairness, good customer relations, and as a part of its overall good faith obligation in the performance and enforcement of transactions, banks could establish procedures of mediation and arbitration. A neutrally conducted mediation, at a relatively low cost, may bring the parties to an agreement as to the solution. The comparative negligence may be so defined after reasonable discussion by both parties. If agreement cannot be reached, arbitration may be provided as an alternative. This mechanism should be built into the Code itself for bank—customer problems and an amendment in this regard would seem in order. If such a statutory amendment does not occur, then the Permanent Editorial Board should amend the comments to encourage such practices.

If there is a failure of the Permanent Editorial Board to encourage such informal dispute settlement provisions or a failure of banks to provide for them, other measures may be necessary. Legislative amendments to the Code or even separate legislation could be enacted. Another possibility is to bring negligence liability of consumers on checks more into line with the federally limited liability for lost or stolen credit cards. Thus, consumers would be liable for no more than fifty dollars maximum, and the remainder would be borne by the banks as a cost of doing business or a matter of insurance.

(3) *Section 3-406*. Section 3-406(b) uses language nearly identical to that found in 4-406 applying a standard of care to payor banks: "if the person asserting the preclusion (under 3-406(a)) fails to exercise ordinary care in paying or taking the instrument and that failure substantially

contributes to loss, the loss is allocated between the person precluded and the person asserting the preclusion according to the extent to which the failure of each to exercise ordinary care contributed to the loss." Under 3-406(b) the question is whether the bank took appropriate precautions to detect fraud on an instrument and therefore avoid paying on it.

Section 3-406(a) addresses situations of negligence before an alteration or forged signature occurs. The subsection is broader than § 4-406 and covers both forged indorsements and forged checks. It provides that "a person whose failure to exercise ordinary care substantially contributes to an alteration of an instrument or to the making of a forged signature on an instrument is precluded from asserting the alteration or the forgery against a person who, in good faith, pays the instrument or takes it for value or for collection." The question this statute raises is what precautions could the drawer have taken to avoid the fraud? If there were steps that could have been taken to avoid the problem, then the drawer will be precluded from denying responsibility on the item *unless* the drawer can prove that the bank acted dishonestly or failed to observe "reasonable commercial standards of fair dealing." Thus, the good faith standard under the section is not a negligence standard, but instead a measure of commercial reasonableness. As a practical matter, bad faith will be difficult, if not impossible, for a drawer to establish under normal check collection procedures.

(4) *Check Truncation.* Consider the following description and identification of problems; do you see other benefits or costs to truncation?

(1) Process

> . . . One of the most significant innovations in the revisions to article 4, and perhaps the most significant from the economic point of view — the authorization of check truncation. With truncation, the information on the physical piece of paper that constitutes a check is transferred to an electronic signal, and then the signal, rather than the piece of paper, is sent through the collection process. Thus, the customer never receives the check but gets only a copy of the information that was transmitted through the system. Some banks already truncate the process at its final stage by retaining checks drawn upon the payor bank. The payor then sends its customer the information rather than the check. There is nothing in the U.C.C. that prohibits truncation of this sort. We believe that this procedure provides only minor savings with respect to check collection costs. The truly significant step would be to truncate the process at its inception, that is, when the check is first deposited by the payee. This system, called *depository bank or radical truncation* (emphasis added), is impossible under the former U.C.C., which requires that the physical piece of paper be transferred from one party to another. The revisions permit depository bank truncation by providing that the information on the check constitutes an "item" for collection purposes and by declaring that truncation agreements are binding.
>
> Truncation itself may create a social equity problem. People are accustomed to receiving their canceled checks, which they use for monitoring their account(s), for their taxes, and for other record keeping purposes. If a bank offers only truncated accounts, customers may feel that they have been denied a desired and previously available service. Even if the bank offers both kinds of accounts, but charges more for the non-truncated variety, people may feel that they are paying extra for the service that was previously standard. But truncation provides a number of advantages that can be readily explained to consumers; it lowers the cost . . . ."[12] [*See* revised U.C.C. §§ 3-501(b)(1), 4-110 and Comments.]

---

[12] Rubin, *Efficiency and Equity*, 42 Ala. L. Rev. 574 (1991). Copyright © 1991 by the Alabama Law Review. Reprinted by permission.

How might check truncation effect the claims of both the customer and the bank when a problem arises? If truncation occurs at the deposit stage, does the depositary bank assume greater responsibility and potential liability? If so, at what benefit? Does truncation contribute to more or less care in check handling and processing?

§ 14.02 The Bank Collection Process

[A] The Collection Process Described

Read: U.C.C. §§ 4-105, 4-214 Comments 1 and 2.

The process by which banks collect and effect payment on negotiable instrument is governed by three primary sources of law—Article 4 of the U.C.C., regulations of the Federal Reserve Board, and contractual rules adopted through clearinghouse associations. Article 4 defines the rights between parties with respect to bank deposits and collections. As we have already seen, the statute does not regulate the terms of the bank-customer agreement or prescribe constraints that different states may choose to impose on that relationship in the interest of consumer protection. The statute also attempts to create a legal framework that recognizes both bank collection practices, especially those methods used in automated collection and truncation.

A network of banks, federal agencies, and clearinghouses exists to facilitate the handling of the more than 135 million checks that pass through the U.S. banking system daily. Federal Reserve regulations, Reserve Bank operating circulars, and clearing house rules can vary the provisions found in Article 4. Most checks are collected through interbank settlements. The depositary bank initially acquires the deposited checks and then sorts the items into three categories— "on us," "clearing house," and "transit" items. Classification of a bank as payor, collecting, depositary, or intermediary determines the legal and commercial relationship to the owner of the item and to other persons or banks involved in both the collection process and in the underlying transaction. A bank may wear more than one hat during the collection and payment process. For example, items to be collected locally are usually presented directly to the payor by the collecting bank. Nonlocal items are typically sent through an intermediary collecting bank which serves as an agent for collection. See U.C.C. §§ 4-105(4) and 4-201. Any bank that presents an item to the payor for payment is called the "presenting bank." Section 4-105(6). Given the possibility of multiple roles, it is entirely possible for one bank to be a depositary-collecting-presenting bank or an intermediary-collecting-presenting bank.

The following passage summarizes the both the categorization and collection process:[13]

> In payment for goods sold Buyer draws a check for $500 on Drawee Bank and issues it to Seller as payee. While Seller could take the check directly to Drawee Bank for payment in cash it is more likely that Seller will deposit the check in its account with its bank, Depositary Bank, for the purpose of having the check forwarded to and paid by Drawee Bank (also known as Payor Bank). § 4-105(3). This deposit is effected typically by having Payee-Seller complete a "deposit ticket" containing the following:
>
> Seller presents the check properly indorsed with the "deposit ticket" to Depositary Bank's teller. The teller furnishes a receipt indicating a credit to Seller's account. This $500 credit is "provisional." That is, if the check is not collected the credit will be revoked.

[13] Excerpt from B. Stone, Uniform Commercial Code In A Nutshell, pages 274-77 copyright (c) 1995 West Publishing Company, reprinted with permission.

Depositary Bank (§ 4-105(2)) will now seek to collect the item (§ 4-104(a)(9)), as the check is called in the process of collection:

1. *"On us" items.* If Depositary Bank (Seller's bank) is also Drawee Bank (Buyer's bank)—referred to in the collection process as Payor Bank (§ 4-105(3)), this depositary-payor bank will determine that the check is in good form (*e.g.*, not forged) and that there are sufficient funds in Buyer's account, after which the $500 is "paid" (by deducting $500 from Buyer's account and crediting Seller's account). *See* § 4-401(a). The provisional credit given to Payee-Seller is now final and Payee-Seller may withdraw the funds. More on how Payor Bank "pays" is discussed presently.

2. *"City" or "clearing house" items.* If Depositary Bank (Seller's bank) and Payor Bank (Buyer's Drawee Bank) are not the same bank but are located in the same vicinity, they may daily forward checks drawn on each other—including Buyer's $500 check—and provisionally settle by striking a balance. Example: Depositary Bank has checks in the amount of $750,000 drawn on Payor Bank; Payor Bank has checks in the amount of $650,000 drawn on Depositary Bank. Thus Payor Bank would "owe" $100,000 to Depositary Bank. Payment of this difference may be accomplished by debiting and crediting accounts.

When several banks are located in the same vicinity they may find it convenient to establish a clearing house to handle their items. § 4-104(a)(4). Here, these banks: (a) send to the clearing house the checks deposited with them but drawn on other banks and (b) receive from the clearing house checks drawn on them but which were deposited with other banks. Similar to the two-bank situation, a balance will be struck between the amount of the checks forwarded to the clearing house and the checks received from the clearing house and a *provisional settlement* made.

3. *"Country" or "transit" items.* Where the Depositary Bank and Payor Bank are not in the same vicinity more steps may be required to forward the check to Payor Bank. Thus assume a California Seller and a Maine Buyer. Seller deposits Buyer's check for collection in Depositary Bank in California. The item (check) moves through two or three California banks to the Federal Reserve Bank of San Francisco, to the Federal Reserve Bank of Boston, to Payor Bank in Maine. *See* § 4-215 Comment 2. Each bank in the process will provisionally credit the account of its transferor along the collection chain. Note that the Federal Reserve Bank fulfills a country-wide clearing house function. These typical banks in the chain are called Depositary Bank (the first bank to take the item); Collecting Bank (a bank handling an item for collection except the payor bank); Presenting Bank (a bank presenting an item except a payor bank); Payor Bank (a bank that is the drawee of a draft). § 4-105.

Upon receipt of an item Payor Bank must decide whether or not to "finally pay" it. *See* § 4-215 . . . . This is so whether the item was received over the counter ("on us") or by mail or though a clearing house. When check collection was done manually at Payor Bank the process was described as follows: "After the initial receipt the item moves to the sorting and proving departments. When sorted and proved it may be photographed. Still later it moves to the bookkeeping department where it is examined for form and signature and compared against the ledger account of the customer to whom it is to be charged [buyer-drawer]. If it is in good form [*e.g.*, no forgeries or alterations] and there are funds to cover it [and no stop payment orders, garnishments, etc.], it is posted to the drawer's account, either immediately or at a later time. If paid, it is so marked and filed with other items of the same customer. This process may take either a few hours or substantially all of the day of receipt and of the next banking day." Former § 4-213 Comment 3. In modern-day practice "process of posting" events do not occur. *See* former § 4-109. "Checks enter payor banks in large sacks with many other checks, are run through the payor bank's [electronic and mechanical] processing equipment and are charged to various accounts without human intervention." U.C.C. Hornbook § 17-5. Periodically (*e.g.*, monthly) Payor Bank will send to its customer (Buyer-Drawer) a statement of account accompanied by the canceled items. § 4-406(a).

The following diagrams of the bank collection process may be useful:

COLLECTION OF CHECKS--SCHEMATIC DIAGRAM

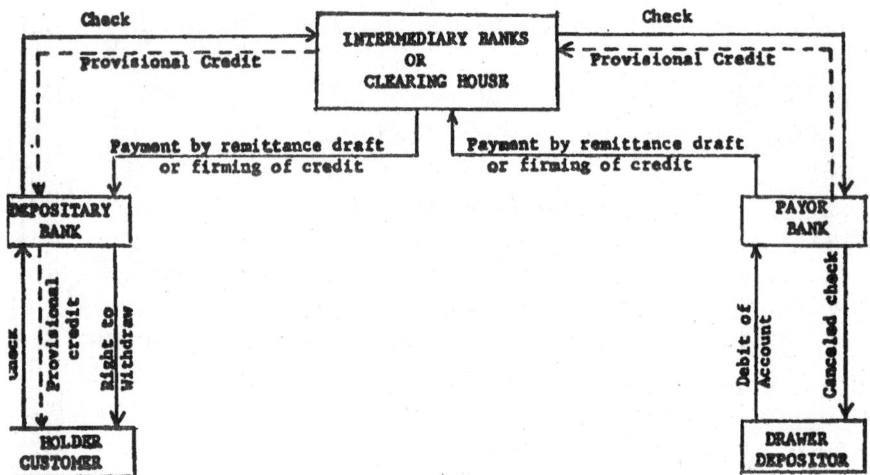

IF CHECK IS HONORED

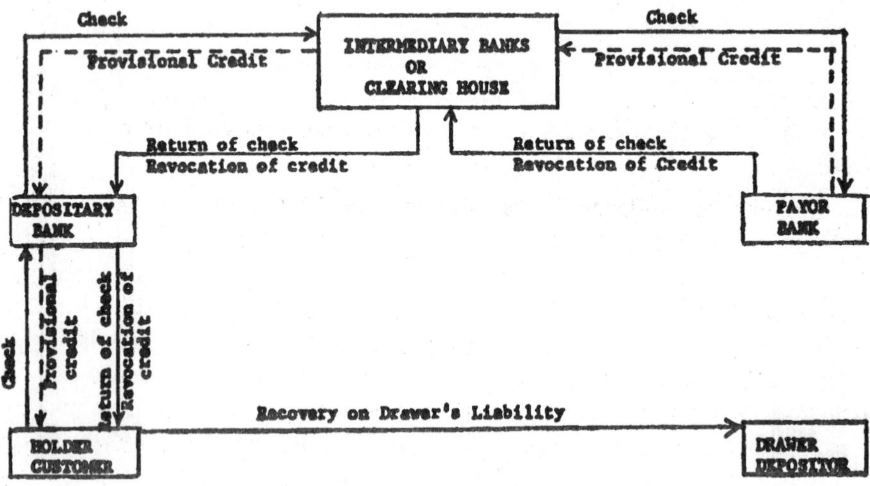

IF CHECK IS DISHONORED

FLORIDA NATIONAL BANK AT PERRY v. CITIZENS BANK OF PERRY

Florida District Court of Appeals
474 So. 2d 852, 41 U.C.C. Rep. 1348 (1985)

NIMMONS, J.

The Florida National Bank at Perry (FNB) appeals from a final judgment declaring the rights of the parties hereto relative to the method utilized by The Citizens Bank of Perry (Citizens) of presenting checks drawn on FNB which checks Citizens" customers have cashed or deposited in Citizens accounts. The final judgment also awarded damages to Citizens. We reverse.

FNB and Citizens are commercial banks located in Perry, Florida. Each business day, several hundred checks drawn on FNB are deposited in Citizens and several hundred checks drawn on Citizens are deposited in FNB. In 1966, FNB and Citizens informally agreed to a collection process which, although not provided for in Chapters 673 and 674 Florida Statutes (Florida's version of the Uniform Commercial Code), best suited the needs and collection abilities of each bank. Pursuant to the agreement, each day FNB would separate the Citizens checks it had received for that day and total the amount of the checks. An FNB employee would then bring the bundle of Citizens checks to Citizens and request payment for the checks. At the same time FNB was following this procedure, Citizens would do the same with the FNB checks it had received during the day. Because of the volume of checks involved, each bank, in the capacity of payor, agreed to forego its right to examine each item. Instead, the banks would examine each item individually after payment and, following examination, would honor the request of the other bank, as payor,[14] to return improper items to the collecting bank. In addition, FNB and Citizens agreed that it would not be necessary for each bank, as payor, to issue its bank draft in settlement for the total amount of checks presented for payment by the collecting bank.[15] Rather, the two banks would "net out" the amounts submitted and issue one check to the bank which had presented the higher amount of checks of the day. The parties were protected from loss by the terms of the agreement.

The two banks operated under that arrangement from 1966 until mid-April 1982. At that time FNB installed a centralized, computerized system for reviewing or proofing its items which enabled FNB to route its items through its system more efficiently and more economically. All items from all other banking institutions would be deposited or cashed each day at FNB and sent in a bundle to a computer center in Jacksonville for sorting and proofing. Each item would then be appropriately credited to FNB's account at its correspondent bank in Jacksonville.[16] Under this new system, FNB would no longer sort out checks, including Citizens, prior to presentment through its Jacksonville clearinghouse. FNB, therefore, terminated its informal reciprocal arrangement for the exchange of checks which it had with Citizens.

Accordingly, on March 17, 1982, FNB informed Citizens that, effective April 16, 1982, it would be presenting items through a correspondent bank in Jacksonville, and FNB suggested that Citizens might wish to make presentment in the same way.

---

[14] "Payor bank" means a bank by which an item is payable as drawn or accepted. Section 674.105(2), Florida Statutes (1981). [*See* revised § 4-105(3).]

[15] "Collecting bank" means any bank handling the item for collection except the payor bank. Section 674.105(4), Florida Statutes (1981). [*See* revised § 4-105(5).]

[16] A "correspondent bank" is a bank which has a customer or account relationship with another bank.

Notwithstanding FNB's advice concerning its termination of the agreement,[17] Citizens apparently preferred to continue the daily practice of physically carrying the bundle of checks to the latter's bank in Perry. On April 17, 1982, Mr. Sons, Citizens" vice-president and cashier, personally carried a two-inch stack of checks to FNB. Mr. Jones, FNB's cashier, reminded Sons that FNB was no longer exchanging checks with Citizens pursuant to the former arrangement as the latter had been discontinued by FNB. However, Jones advised Sons that Citizens could present them over-the-counter. To Sons" inquiry as to what that would entail, Jones advised him that each item would have to be exhibited individually and endorsed as a receipt for payment. Alternatively, Jones told Sons that Citizens could deposit the checks in the latter's account at FNB.[18] Apparently, Sons did not wish to deposit the checks in Citizens" account at FNB, and when he learned that, in order to present over-the-counter, he would be expected to exhibit and endorse each check as a receipt for payment, he departed the bank with the checks.

At some point in time—it is unclear from the record when it was first mentioned—FNB advised Citizens that it would have to charge a collection fee of $2.00 per item in order to accommodate Citizens" presentment of bundles of checks for payment over-the-counter. We do know from the trial testimony that no mention was made on April 17 when the over-the-counter presentment was attempted. The collection fee was apparently first mentioned in a subsequent letter from FNB to Citizens.

After the unsuccessful efforts to present over-the-counter on April 17, Citizens chose to present the FNB items through its correspondent bank in Jacksonville. Citizens did so from April 1982 through May 1983 at an approximate cost of four cents per item. In May 1983 Citizens decided to present its items through a Tallahassee correspondent bank which, although costing Citizens five and one-half cents per item, was less expensive in that the Tallahassee correspondent bank was able to give next-day credit on roughly 90% of the funds whereas the Jacksonville correspondent bank gave no credit on any of the funds until two days after presentment.

Citizens filed this action seeking a declaratory judgment that it was entitled, under the Uniform Commercial Code, to make over-the-counter presentment in the manner it attempted and that the conditions imposed for such presentment by FNB amounted to an improper refusal of the presentment. Citizens also sought damages by reason of charges and the loss of use of funds resulting from having to resort to another method of presentment.

After a non-jury trial, the trial court found that presentment at FNB's banking headquarters in Perry was a proper place for presentment of the subject checks and that the conditions imposed by FNB for the over-the-counter presentment constituted a denial of Citizens" rights to make such presentment. The trial court also awarded damages to Citizens for the per-item fees charged Citizens by the Jacksonville and Tallahassee correspondent banks for processing or returning FNB checks. The court, however, denied recovery of damages attributable to Citizens' claimed loss of use of funds. Citizens cross appeals the denial of this loss of use element of damages.

We disagree with the trial court that FNB refused presentment of the checks on April 17, FNB had decided to move its bank collection procedures into the 20th century. Citizens, on the other

---

[17] Understandably, no assertion has been made by Citizens that FNB was not entitled to terminate their previous arrangement for exchanging checks.

[18] This version of what occurred on April 17, 1982, is based upon Mr. Jones" testimony. Mr. Sons, the only other person to testify as to what occurred on April 17, simply testified that Jones arbitrarily refused his over-the-counter presentment. The language of the final judgment is such that it is apparent that the trial court accepted Mr. Jones" testimony given the fact that the judgment ruled against FNB on the basis of the conditions for presentment imposed by FNB as opposed to a finding that FNB simply refused the presentment.

hand, wished to perpetuate its old system for collection which it had operated by agreement with FNB for sixteen years. As one writer has noted:

> Although the U.C.C. does not prohibit over-the-counter presentment, this method is rare in the realm of bulk check processing. The U.C.C. gives express approval to the two modes of presentment common to the bank collection system; presentment by mail in the case of transit items or direct routing [footnote citation to U.C.C. § 3-504(2)(a), adopted in Florida as section 673.504(2)(a)] and presentment through the clearinghouse in the case of local items [footnote citation to U.C.C. § 3-504(2)(b), adopted in Florida as Section 673.504(2)(b)]. [*See* revised § 3-501(b)(1).] Clark, The Law of Bank Deposits, Collections and Credit Cards, Section 1.3(1)(rev. edition 1981). We do not disagree with the trial court's conclusion that Citizens was entitled to make over-the-counter presentment of the FNB checks. *See* § 674.204, Florida Statutes (1981). However, where a collecting bank chooses that method of presentment for payment of its daily accumulations in bulk, it will have to be prepared to satisfy conditions reasonably imposed by the payor bank.

Section 673.505, Florida Statutes (1981), provides: . . . [the Court cites § 673.505]. [*See* revised § 3-501(b)(2).] FNB was acting within its rights to expect individual exhibition of the checks presented over-the-counter in bulk in order to determine that each check was, in fact, an item upon which payment should properly be made. *See Peabody v. Citizens State Bank,* 98 Minn. 302, 108 N.W. 272 (1906) (individual exhibition of each item reasonably required where a number of checks were presented by a bank over-the-counter to the payor bank). We are also of the view that FNB was within its rights to require, as a condition to Citizens" over-the-counter presentment, that Mr. Sons" receipt for each of the checks.

As earlier noted, there was apparently no mention made of a per item collection charge at the time of the April 17 attempted presentment. Even assuming that we were to hold that such collection charge could not reasonably be imposed by FNB, the fact is that there is no evidence that such a charge was a factor in the failure of the attempted presentment on April 17. In fact, Citizens, although purporting to make an over-the-counter presentment, failed to make a valid presentment by reason of its refusal to satisfy the reasonable requirements imposed by FNB.

We also reject Citizens" argument that FNB was required, upon the over-the-counter presentment of the bundle of checks, to provisionally pay Citizens without requiring Sons to exhibit each check to determine at that time whether the checks were properly payable by FNB. We do not believe that where Citizens, as collecting bank, insists upon an in-bulk over-the-counter presentment that it can *require* immediate provisional payment and thus eliminate FNB's right to require individual exhibition of the items.[19]

Citizens never made a valid presentment, and the court erred in awarding damages to Citizens. Citizens never having made a valid presentment and therefore not being entitled to an award of damages, we need not treat the issue raised by Citizens in its cross appeal pertaining to the trial court's denial of its loss of use element of damages.

Reversed.

---

[19] Relative to provisional vs. final payment or settlement, *see* §§ 674.104(1)(j), 674.213 and U.C.C. Comments. [*See* revised §§ 4-104(a)(11), 4-215 and Comments.]

[B] Agency Status and Responsibility of Collecting Banks

Read: U.C.C. §§ 3-103(e), 4-105, 4-201, 4-202, 4-203, 4-204, 4-207 through 4-214.

Agents of any kind owe certain duties to their principals and to persons with whom they deal on behalf of those principals. Principals owe correlative duties to their agents. Pre-Code cases spent much time and effort in determining the relationship between a non-bank holder of an instrument and the collecting bank, whether depositary or intermediary. (*See* Comment 1 to U.C.C. § 4-201.) The Code settles the problem in favor of giving the banking system the best of two worlds. Not only do the rules permit banks to vary collection procedures by agreement between banks (see U.C.C. § 4-103), but they also provide that collecting banks act as agents of the owner of an item presented for collection. As agents, banks act only on the owner's behalf and undertake no liability as owners themselves. U.C.C. § 4-201(a). A collecting bank is not liable for the misfeasance or nonfeasance of other banks with which it deals on behalf of the owner. U.C.C. § 4-202(c). Even though a bank enjoys the status of an agent, it may also qualify for the benefits of a holder in due course. See U.C.C. §§ 4-210 and 4-211. Finally, in the event of the insolvency of a bank that is part of the collection process, the risk of loss is borne by the depositor-owner and not the depositary bank. Collecting banks are liable to the owner of an item only where the bank failed to exercise its responsibility for ordinary care in the handling of the item. U.C.C. § 4-202. The next two cases explore this aspect of the collection process.

GREATER BUFFALO PRESS, INC. v. FEDERAL RESERVE BANK

United States Court of Appeals
866 F.2d 38, cert. denied, 490 U.S. 1107 (2nd Cir. 1989)

MESKILL, CIRCUIT JUDGE:

This is an appeal from a judgment of the United States District Court for the Western District of New York, Curtin, C.J., granting the summary judgment motion of the Federal Reserve Bank of New York (Fed NY) and John T. Keane and dismissing the complaint.

. . . .

BACKGROUND

A. *Federal Reserve Banks and the Process of Check Collection*

Federal Reserve Banks play a major role in the nation's system of check collection. *See* The Comptroller General, Report to the Congress: The Federal Reserve Should Move Faster to Eliminate Subsidy of Check Clearing Operations 4 (1982) (the Federal Reserve collects over forty percent of the checks written in the United States), J. App. 935, 936; Clarke, *Check-Out Time for Checks,* 21 Bus. Law. 931, 932 (1966) (one-third of checks are sent to Federal Reserve Banks), J. App. 793, 795. The check collection process, or specifically Fed NY's participation in it, is at the center of this dispute. For that reason, we briefly examine some background. *See generally* H. Hutchinson, Money, Banking and the United States Economy 117-27 (5th ed. 1984); Baxter and Patrikis, *The Check-Hold Revolution*, 18 U.C.C.L.J. 99, 114-17 (1985), J. App. 751, 766-69.

When payment is made by means of a check, a payor draws the check against an account at his or her bank, the payor bank. Upon receiving the check, the payee will often deposit it in his or her own bank, the depositary bank. At this point, two processes must occur. First, the check itself must be physically transported from the depositary bank to the payor bank. Second, payment must be made from the payor bank back to the depositary bank.

One option available to the depositary bank is to utilize the check clearing services of the Federal Reserve System. In order to do so, the depositary bank must send the check to the Federal Reserve Bank for its district. If the payor bank is in the same district, then the Federal Reserve Bank can present the check directly to the payor bank. If the payor bank is located in a different district, the Federal Reserve Bank receiving the check will forward it to the Federal Reserve Bank for the payor bank's district. That Federal Reserve Bank will then present the check to the payor bank.

In addition to effecting the physical delivery of the check, the Federal Reserve System also serves to facilitate payment between the payor and depositary banks. After sending a check to its Federal Reserve Bank for processing, the depositary bank will receive credit for the check in its reserves account with the Federal Reserve. This credit will be given usually within one or two days, depending on how long it is expected to take the check to reach the payor bank for payment. After the check reaches the payor bank, the Federal Reserve System uses transfers of credit through an Interdistrict Settlement Fund to achieve payment.

If there is an unexpected delay in transporting the check to the payor bank, then the credit for the check will be given by the Federal Reserve to the depositary bank before payment can be received from the payor bank. This so-called "float" in effect gives the depositary bank an interest-free advance at the expense of the Federal Reserve. Thus, delays in processing not only adversely affect Federal Reserve Banks with respect to the competitive attractiveness of their check clearing services, but also result in direct economic costs, *see* Baxter and Patrikis, *supra* at 117, J. App. at 769.

. . . .

B. *The Facts Leading to This Litigation*

In 1977, the sixty-five plaintiffs-appellants were all supplier creditors of Neisner Brothers, Inc. (Neisner), a retail department store chain. The dispute in this case arises from seventy-five checks drawn by Neisner, in October and November of 1977, on its account at Lincoln First

Bank of Rochester (Lincoln) and made payable to the appellants. After receiving the checks, the appellants deposited them at their various depositary banks around the country. Greater Buffalo Press, for example, maintains that it deposited one check for $43,537.66 on November 21, 1977 and one check for $109,671.55 on November 23, 1977 in its account at Marine.

After receiving the checks, the various depositary banks forwarded them for collection to the defendant-appellee Fed NY, either directly or indirectly, through other Federal Reserve Banks. The district court accepted Fed NY's contentions as to the dates it received the checks. The court found that Fed NY received three of the seventy-five checks between November 19-22, nine of the checks between November 24-25 and sixty-three of the checks on or after November 26.

The next step in the collection process called for Fed NY's Buffalo Branch to forward the checks to the payor bank, Lincoln, for payment. The parties are in substantial agreement as to the days the checks were finally received by Lincoln, and Fed NY concedes that there were delays due to an "unprecedented" increase in the volume of checks requiring processing, Br. of Defendants-Appellants at 12. For example, the $43,537.66 check payable to Greater Buffalo Press was received by Fed NY on either November 21 or 22, but was not presented to Lincoln until December 5, J. App. at 566.

Neisner filed a petition for bankruptcy December 1, 1977. The district court found that Lincoln had begun to dishonor the checks of Neisner on November 29, but the appellants maintain that Lincoln only began to dishonor Neisner's checks after learning of the filing of the bankruptcy petition on the morning of December 1. When the checks were presented for payment, Lincoln dishonored them. The checks were returned to Fed NY, and from there back to the appellants" depositary banks. In at least some cases, a second attempt at collection was made, but the checks were again dishonored by Lincoln.

C. The Litigation

[In an omitted portion of the case the court summarizes the prolonged history of the litigation which began in January, 1978].

. . . .

DISCUSSION

. . . .

A. *Governing Law with Respect to Liability*

1. The Legal Basis for the Cause of Action

The crux of appellants" complaint is that but for Fed NY's delays in processing their checks, the appellants would have been paid because the checks would have arrived at Lincoln in time to be honored. The appellants have cited Fed NY's assurance to the public of prompt and efficient check clearing services, contending that it was all the while sitting on a mountain of checks that continuously grew faster than Fed NY could process them. They contend that Fed NY foresaw or should have foreseen the processing delays and should have either remedied the situation or warned its customers of potential problems. Instead, the appellants contend, Fed NY sought to cover up the situation.

While constantly pressing a broad censure of Fed NY's operations, the appellants" specific legal theory supporting their first amended complain remained unclear. Nearly three years after the commencement of this action, the district court was still dealing with this problem patiently, giving appellants every opportunity to replead with greater specificity . . . . More than six years later, the appellants" position remained imprecise if not evasive, characterizing their cause of action as including "basic tort and contract claims . . . including tort, fraud, conversion, breach of contract, etc." . . .

It is obvious that the appellants cannot recover against Fed NY by simply criticizing its operations. In order to survive a summary judgment motion, the appellants had to present supporting facts and arguments showing some legal basis for liability on the part of the defendants; it was not enough simply to put forth conclusory allegations of wrongdoing . . . .

We agree with the district court's approach in viewing the cause of action on this record as sustainable only by reliance on the provisions of New York's Uniform Commercial Code that deal specifically with the duties of banks in collecting and processing checks. *See* N.Y.U.C.C. §§ 4-201, 4-202 (McKinney 1964). The district court found meritless the appellants" arguments as to possible alternative theories of liability . . . . We too are unable to discern from the record any other legal basis for liability on the part of Fed NY or Keane. To the extent that the facts might support some other conceivable basis for such liability, we find that the appellants" unsubstantiated conclusory allegations of wrongdoing were properly considered by the district court to have been insufficient to survive the summary judgment motion.

2. Liability Under The New York Uniform Commercial Code

The New York Uniform Commercial Code, section 4-202(1) imposes certain duties on "collecting bank[s]." Three of these duties on a quick reading might seem relevant to the facts of this case. The Code provides:

A collecting bank must use ordinary care in

(a) presenting an item or sending it for presentment; and (b) sending notice of dishonor or nonpayment or returning an item . . . to the bank's transferor or directly to the depositary bank . . . after learning that the item has not been paid or accepted, as the case may be; and

. . . .

(e) notifying its transferor of any loss or delay in transit within a reasonable time after discovery thereof.

N.Y.U.C.C. § 4-202(1). [cf. revised § 4-202(a).] Fed NY does not contest that, as a "collecting bank," these provisions apply to its processing of checks.

This provision imposed on Fed NY a duty of ordinary care in its presentment of checks for payment. The focus of the appellants" complaint is Fed NY's delay, after having received the checks, in presenting them to Lincoln. They base their cause of action in part on the contention that Fed NY breached its duty and that the breach caused the dishonor of their checks. If applicable to this case, Fed NY would bear the burden of showing that it exercised ordinary care in processing the checks if the checks were not properly processed within the "midnight deadline." *See* N.Y.U.C.C. § 4-202(2). [cf. revised § 4-202(b).]

Section 4-202(1)(b) requires collecting banks to give prompt notification of the dishonor of checks [cf. revised § 4-202(a)(2).] This provision has no application to this case, however. Appellants have not shown or even argued that Fed NY delayed in providing notification of Lincoln's dishonor of the checks. Rather, their alleged injury stems from the dishonor itself, not from any delay in notification of the dishonor. *Cf. Washington Petroleum and Supply Co. v.*

Girard Bank, 629 F. Supp. 1224, 1226 (M.D. Pa. 1983) (allegation of injury from delayed notification of dishonor).

Section 4-202(1)(e) requires collecting banks to give prompt notice of a transferor of any "loss or delay in transit." At oral argument, the appellants relied on this section, contending that Fed NY at the very least should have alerted the appellants to the delays in the processing of their checks, thus giving them an opportunity to arrange alternative means of processing.

The appellants have not shown, and we have serious doubt as to whether they would be able to show, how a failure to warn of the delays would be causally linked to the dishonor of the checks. A trier of fact would have to question whether the appellants, armed with notice of the processing delay but without the benefit of hindsight or advance warning of Neisner's bankruptcy petition, would have either retrieved their checks from Fed NY or arranged for alternative clearinghouse services. In our review of a grant of summary judgment, however, we do not rely on these weaknesses in the appellants" case. Rather, we simply note that the appellants have no cause of action on these facts based on section 4-202(1)(e). That section applies where delays were caused by "mishaps in the mails," not to delays caused by the collecting bank's own internal processing operations, the situation present in our case . . . .

Thus, we find that the only duty created by section 4-202(1) that is relevant here is Fed NY's duty of ordinary care in the presentment of checks under section 4-202(1)(a). But, in order to recover under this section, the appellants must show more than Fed NY's breach of duty. They also must show that the duty extended to them.

Section 4-201 of the Uniform Commercial Code says: "Unless a contrary intent clearly appears and prior to the time that a settlement given by a collecting bank for an item is or becomes final . . . the bank is an agent or sub-agent of the owner of the item." As the Fifth Circuit has recognized: "The agency relationship established by § [4-201] is the only basis in the Code for determining to whom the duties imposed on collecting banks [by § 4-202(1)] run. Once that agency relationship is severed, the duties are no longer owned. More simply stated, *liability flows only from agency status." Childs v. Federal Reserve Bank,* 719 F.2d 812, 814 (5th Cir. 1983) (per curiam) (emphasis added). The appellants' cause of action thus rests solely on an agency theory, and their complaint must stand or fall on their contention that Fed NY acted as their agent.

3. The Effect of Federal Regulation J

In considering the availability to the appellants of a cause of action based on the U.C.C., we have thus far considered New York state law. As required by the Supremacy Clause, U.S. Const. art. VI, however, the state U.C.C. statutes cannot be considered in isolation but instead must be read together with applicable federal statutes and regulations . . . .

The Board of Governors of the Federal Reserve System promulgates regulations governing the operation of the Federal Reserve System. *See* 12 C.F.R. §§ 201-269b (1988). Pursuant to its authority under 12 U.S.C. §§ 248(i), 248 (o), 342, 360 (1982) and other laws, the Board of Governors has promulgated Regulation J, concerning the collection of checks. *See* 12 C.F.R. § 210.1 (1988); 14 Fed. Reserve Bull. 80 (1928). The appellants have not called into question the Board of Governors" authority to promulgate regulations, nor the propriety of the promulgation of this particular regulation . . . . Thus, as a properly promulgated substantive regulation, Regulation J must be given the force and effect of federal law . . . .

At the time the actions relevant to this litigation occurred, Regulation J said, in part:

> A Federal Reserve Bank will act only as the agent of the sender in respect of each cash item or noncash item received by it from the sender . . . . A Federal Reserve Bank will not act as the agent or the subagent of any owner or holder of any such item other than the sender. A Federal Reserve Bank shall not have, nor will it assume, any liability to the sender in respect of any such item and its proceeds except for its own lack of good faith or failure to exercise ordinary care.

12 C.F.R. § 210.6(a) (1977) (footnote omitted), J. App. at 528. In so restricting the potential liability of the Federal Reserve Banks with "the sender rule," the regulations also provided: "The term 'sender," in respect of an item, means a member bank, a nonmember clearing bank, a Federal Reserve Bank, an international organization, or a foreign correspondent." 12 C.F.R. § 210(e) (1977), J. App. at 525. The appellants do not and cannot claim to be "senders" under Regulation J. They simply do not fall within the definition of section 210.2(e).

The application of Regulation J to this case is straightforward. The appellants" cause of action against Fed NY is based entirely on the theory of it as an agent of the appellants in the check collection process. Regulation J unambiguously "severs the agency relationship" between Fed NY and the "non-sender" appellants . . . . Because Regulation J requires that Fed NY not be considered an agent of the appellants, Fed NY cannot be found to have owed the appellants any duty under N.Y.U.C.C. §§ 4-201 and 4-202.

The appellants claim that, properly interpreted, Regulation J merely defines the extent of agency of Federal Reserve Banks and does not limit their liability based on the duty of ordinary care. But the sole basis for liability on the part of Fed NY in this case is agency. Without a duty based on agency, there is no liability . . . .

We believe that this case reveals no basic inconsistency between federal Regulation J and the New York Uniform Commercial Code. While N.Y.U.C.C. §§ 4-201 and 4-202 might suggest a basis for liability here, the New York U.C.C. also provides that: "The effect of the[se] provisions . . . may be varied by agreement except that no agreement can disclaim a bank's responsibility for its own lack of good faith or failure to exercise ordinary care." N.Y.U.C.C. § 4-103(1) (McKinney 1964). [cf. revised § 4-103(a).] The reference to "agreement" is further clarified: "Federal Reserve regulations and operating letters, clearing house rules, and the like, have the effect of agreements under subsection (1), whether or not specifically assented to by all parties interested in items handled." N.Y.U.C.C. § 4-103(2). [cf. revised § 4-103(b).] Thus, "[b]y its own terms," New York law provides that Regulation J is to control the rights and duties of the parties here . . . . [*See*] *Coldwell testimony* at 117, J. App. at 951 ("The Uniform Commercial Code permits the regulations of the Board and the operating circulars of the Federal Reserve Banks to govern many of the terms and conditions for collection of checks."). By operation of Regulation J and notwithstanding the non-assent of the appellants, the depositary banks and Fed NY agreed to vary the U.C.C. provisions applicable to this case, providing that Fed NY was to act as an agent only of "senders." Fed NY's duty of ordinary care simply did not extend to the appellants, . . and thus there can be no liability under sections 4-201 and 4-202(1)(a). Nor does the limitation in section 4-103(1) of a bank's power to disclaim the duty or ordinary care aid the appellants. Because Fed NY was not an agent of the appellants, there existed no such duty to be disclaimed.

We note that even if Regulation J were not consistent with New York law here, Regulation J would preempt the inconsistent state law provisions that might otherwise provide for agency liability on the part of Fed NY. As one district court has said in examining the interplay between U.C.C. §§ 4-201, 4-202 and Regulation J:

> The provisions are in conformity when the sender of an item is also its owner; however, when the owner is a remote party, the provisions are in direct conflict. The Reserve bank is either liable to parties more remote than the sender or is not; it cannot be both. Since in this case simultaneous compliance with the federal regulation and the state statute is impossible, the federal law prevails. *Colonial Cadillac, Inc. v. Shawmut Merchants Banks, N.A.*, 488 F. Supp. 283, 286 (D. Mass. 1980); *see also Washington Petroleum and Supply*, 629 F. Supp. at 1229-30.[20]

Faced with the clear application of Regulation J, the appellants complain of unfairness and predict calamitous consequences for the future of the transferability and negotiability of commercial paper. With respect to the latter concern, we note that Regulation J is not a recent innovation, . . . and thus far we see no evidence of such dire consequences. Moreover, this limitation of the liability of Federal Reserve Banks has long been supported by sound federal policy. In establishing the Federal Reserve System, Congress showed concern for the nation's costly and circuitous check processing system. Consistent with its goal of creating an equitable and efficient system of exchange, Congress provided for the Federal Reserve to serve as a national clearinghouse for checks . . . . Soon after its creation, a major concern of the Federal Reserve was to implement federal policy by addressing the check collection problem . . . . Through their regulatory authority, the Governors of the Federal Reserve sought to establish and maintain "a direct, expeditious, and economical system of check collection and settlement of balances." . . . As noted *supra*, until the enactment of the Monetary Control Act of 1980, check clearing services were provided by Federal Reserve Banks free of charge to member banks in order to ease the burden of Federal Reserve membership . . . . Fed NY explains: "The sender rule [of Regulation J] was a natural complement to the gratuitous service, because it effectively limited the Reserve Bank's duty to exercise ordinary care to only those institutions who were receiving the gratuitous service, thereby reducing losses as well as the overall cost of the service." . . .

This understanding of the policy behind Regulation J finds support in recent changes in the Federal Reserve System. It appears that the Monetary Control act of 1980 was designed in part to improve the efficiency of the Federal Reserve System and promote competition by other banks and check clearinghouses. [Citations.] (Congress did not intend to protect competitive positions of private collection services). Such a change would undermine an existent "protectionist" policy that supports giving the Federal Reserve Banks the competitive advantage of limited liability under Regulation J. Accordingly, the Board of Governors, in 1986, amended Regulation J and repealed the sender rule in order to

> [p]ermit the owner of a check or other item who is allegedly injured by a Reserve Bank's alleged failure to exercise ordinary care or act in good faith in collecting an item to bring an action against the Reserve Bank, regardless of whether that person is a "sender" as defined in Regulation J.

51 Fed. Reg. 21740 (June 16, 1986), . . .

---

[20] Because the appellants" cause of action against Fed NY and Keane is based entirely on an agency theory under N.Y.U.C.C. §§ 4-201 and 4-202(1)(a), we need not consider whether other state law causes of action would be preempted by Regulation J . . . .

Nevertheless, this change in the law came too late to aid the appellants, whose complaint and supporting evidence must be governed by the law in place in November of 1977. Under that law, Fed NY and its Branch Manager Keane breached no duty to the appellants in this case.

. . . .

CONCLUSION

The judgment of the district court following an order granting the motion of the defendants-appellees Fed NY and John T. Keane for summary judgment and dismissing the complaint is affirmed.

NOTES

Though this case arose under old Article 4, Revised sections 4-201 and 4-202 did not change the law. Collecting banks have a duty to exercise ordinary care in returning items. If a bank fails to meet that standard of care, the bank can be liable for damages. Any damage amount will be reduced by the amount that could not have been realized had the collecting bank exercised ordinary care.[21] Section 4-202 sets a standard of ordinary care for a collecting bank and relieves collecting banks from responsibility for the failures of other banks. Does this standard leave depositors in an untenable bind? Or, is this standard the only plausible one for effectuating an efficient bank collection process? If you were a consumer advocate, what standard of care might you suggest?

REGULATION J

Federal Reserve Regulation J, 12 CFR § 210.1, only governs the collection of checks and other items through the Federal Reserve Bank System. The regulation's principal purpose J is to speed the collection process and result in final settlement more quickly. The regulation outlines additional requirements for a bank that enters into collection agreements with a Federal Reserve Bank to facilitate the processing and collection of items. Regulation J applies only where a specific item is collected through a Federal Reserve Bank. 12 CFR § 210.3. Under section 210.3, each reserve bank has the power to issue operating circulars to govern the details of that bank's handling of items. Like Article 4, Reg J also provides that Reserve Banks act only as agent or subagent of the owner of an item sent through the system for payment or collection. The regulation classifies items into cash and noncash categories and prescribes a time table for settlement and payment or rejection and return of items. "On the day a paying bank receives a cash item . . . from a Reserve Bank, it shall settle for the item such that the proceeds of the settlement are available to the Reserve Bank by the close of Fedwire [Fedwire is the funds-transfer system owned and operated by the Federal Reserve Banks that is used primarily for the transmission

[21] This liability system is not disturbed by the growth of electronic presentment. With electronic presentment an item is reduced to an electronic image and stored. The electronic image can then be submitted to the payor for payment. See U.C.C. § 4-110. The payor still has until midnight of the day following receipt to act on the item cr else the item will be classified as finally paid.

and settlement of payment orders of wholesale wire transfers] on that day, or it shall return the item by the later of the close of the paying bank's banking day or the close of Fedwire." 12 CFR § 210.9. See also §§ 210.10 through 210.14.

While Reg J provisions may supersede provisions contained in Article 4, the *Greater Buffalo* court notes that the ordinary care provisions of Reg J and those of section 4-202 conform. Do you agree? What result in the above case if the collecting bank in this case were not the Federal Reserve? Should a Federal Reserve Bank be subject to the same standards as a private bank? To higher or lower standards? Why?

SMALLMAN v. HOME FEDERAL SAVINGS BANK

Tennessee Court of Appeals
786 S.W.2d 954 (1989)

GOODARD, JUDGE.

Home Federal Savings Bank was sued by David Smallman and his wife Tommie after Home Federal charged back funds from the Smallman's checking account because a check in the amount of $703.87 deposited in their account was returned unpaid. After the charge-back 14 outstanding checks written by the Smallmans on their account were returned because of insufficient funds. The jury awarded the Smallmans $703.87, the amount of the check, and $30,000 in other damages. Both sides have appealed.

Home Federal insists on appeal that the Trial Curt erred in failing to direct a verdict as to the amount of the check and the other damages claimed to have been suffered by the Smallmans, in admitting evidence of Home Federal's net worth and in charging the jury that it might award damages for embarrassment and humiliation. The Smallmans insist that the Court erred in directing a verdict for Home Federal as to their punitive damage claim.

The facts are essentially undisputed. The Smallmans made a sale of some business inventory to Linda Petruzello, a sister-in-law of a friend of the Smallmans, for $703.87. Ms. Petruzello tendered a check dated April 18, 1985, drawn on AmSouth Bank in Alabama in that amount to the Smallmans which they deposited in their checking account at Home Federal on April 22. Home Federal then submitted the check for processing and collection. This process involved the check first going to First American National bank, then to First Tennessee Bank, then to the Federal Reserve Bank of Atlanta, then to AmSouth Bank which refused to pay the check because Ms. Petruzello's account contained insufficient funds. At some point in the return process to Home Federal the check was lost in the mail.

On July 30, slightly more than three months after it was deposited, Home Federal received a photocopy of the check and notice that the check was being returned for non-payment. It received no explanation for the delay. Believing that the check had not been processed in a timely fashion, Gary Underwood, an officer of Home Federal, embarked on a course of conduct designed to collect the check because he thought that it was just a problem among the banks that were involved in the collection process. The Smallmans were not notified of any potential problem with the check when Home Federal received the notice.

On August 30, more than four months after the check was deposited, Home Federal received a second notice that the check would not be paid and that a time delay had not occurred relative to collection but that the check had been lost in the return process to Home Federal. The dishonor notice to the Smallmans was prepared on September 5, and received on September 12 or 13 in an envelope dated September 10.

On Sunday, September 8, the Smallmans tried to withdraw cash from an automatic teller machine but the machine showed a zero balance despite a recent deposit of $900. The Smallmans testified that they had no knowledge of dishonor of the Petruzello check until September 9 when Mr. Smallman contacted Mr. Underwood at Home Federal to inquire about the zero balance on the ATM machine. It was then that Mr. Underwood informed the Smallmans that the Petruzello check had not cleared and $703.87 had been taken out of their account. The charge-back occurred on September 5.

Because of the charge-back, the Smallmans had 14 checks returned unpaid, all but two of which were written prior to the conversation on September 9 between Mr. Underwood and the Smallmans which is the point in time that the Smallmans received actual notice that the check had been returned unpaid and that their account had been charged back. The Smallmans had employed counsel on or before the date they received the written notice and notified Home Federal, in accordance with their counsel's advice, that they would be making no further deposits in their account. The account, consequently, was closed on September 20.

The Smallmans offered no proof to show that the check could have been collected had they received timely notice of dishonor.

At trial, Home Federal's motion for a directed verdict was denied. The evidence adduced included evidence of the bank's net worth which was admitted over Home Federal's objections. A verdict was rendered in favor of the Smallmans as hereinbefore stated.

We now turn to the first issue raised by Home Federal questioning whether a directed verdict should have been granted in its favor at the close of all the proof. In support of its position, Home Federal asserts that: (1) there was no evidence to show that it was negligent in handling the check; (2) even if there was proof sufficient to establish negligence, it could charge-back on the unpaid item anyway; (3) the Plaintiffs failed to establish damages within the purview of T.C.A. 47-4-103(5):

> (5) The measure of damages for failure to exercise ordinary care in handling an item is the amount of the item reduced by an amount which could not have been realized by the use of ordinary care, and where there is bad faith it includes other damages, if any, suffered by the party as a proximate consequence.

T.C.A. 47-4-202 imposes a duty of ordinary care on a collecting bank in notifying its customer of non-payment or dishonor. Also of importance here is T.C.A. 47-4-212(1)[22] which permits

[22] *47-4-212. Right of charge-back or refund.*—(1) If a collecting bank has made provisional settlement with its customer for an item and itself fails by reason of dishonor, suspension of payments by a bank or otherwise to receive a settlement for the item which is or becomes final, the bank may revoke the settlement given by it, charge-back the amount of any credit given for the item to its customer's account or obtain refund from its customer whether or not it is able to return the items if by midnight deadline or within a longer reasonable time after it learns the facts

a bank to charge-back the amount of any credit extended to a customer's account "if by its midnight deadline or within a longer reasonable time after it learns the facts it returns the item or sends notification of the facts." The midnight deadline is "midnight on its next banking day following the banking day on which it receives the relevant item or notice or from which the time for taking action commences to run, whichever is later." T.C.A. 47-4-104(1)(h).

August 30, when the copy of the check was returned a second time, was a Friday, and due to the Labor Day Holiday on September 2, the midnight deadline was Tuesday, September 3. On that date, which was the next banking day, Mr. Underwood attempted to contact AmSouth, the Bank upon which the check was drawn, to determine if the check would clear. Upon learning that it would not he decided that a charge-back was in order. The charge-back was effected on September 5.

As to Home Federal's first point under the first issue, the jury could reasonably find Home Federal was negligent in failing to notify the Smallmans of the dishonored check prior to the midnight deadline.

Apropos of T.C.A. 47-4-212(1) relative to charge-back, the authors of Anderson's Uniform Commercial Code (Volume 3, Page 261) make the following observation:

§ 4-212:6. Exercise of right.

> In order to exercise the right of charging back a credit provisionally given to its customer, the collecting bank must act before its midnight deadline. If the bank does not learn of the facts justifying such action within time to act before that deadline, it may act after the deadline has passed if it does so within a reasonable time after it learns of the facts justifying such action against its customer.

Notwithstanding the foregoing, Home Federal argues that the measure of damages is found in T.C.A. 47-4-103(5), hereinbefore set out. [cf. revised U.C.C. § 4-103(e).]

It argues that in view of the fact the Smallmans adduced no proof to show that they suffered damages because of the negligence of Home Federal they are not entitled to recover.

If the suit were predicated upon negligence other than failure to meet the midnight deadline, we would be inclined to agree. However, the real question is whether Home Federal was entitled to charge-back notwithstanding its failure to meet the midnight deadline and its failure to show it learned any facts justifying an extension thereof.

It seems clear that Home Federal's right to charge-back depends on whether the statute establishes a condition precedent or whether it defines the duty of care relative to the right of charge-back, which also would require a showing of damages by reason of the breach of the duty.

The cases which we have found disclose a split of authority. [Citations] hold that meeting the midnight deadline is a condition precedent for charging back. Two Federal cases [Citations] hold otherwise.

Our reading of the statute persuades us that the majority view above expressed is the proper one and that under the plain language of the statute the Bank is not entitled to charge-back a returned check unless it meets the requirements as to the midnight deadline.

---

it returns the item or sends notification of the facts. These rights to revoke, charge-back and obtain refund terminate if and when a settlement for the item received by the bank is or becomes final (subsection (3) of § 47-4-211 and subsections (2) and (3) of § 47-4-213). [cf. revised U.C.C. § 4-214.]

This is not intended to say, and we are not called upon to determine whether a bank would be entitled to recover from a depositor under the statute authorizing recovery against endorsers, T.C.A. 47-3-414,[23] but hold only that a bank which misses its midnight deadline is precluded from charging back against the depositor's account.

It is appropriate to discuss together Home Federal's insistence as to the other damages and the Smallmans" insistence as to their right to have the question of punitive damage determined by the jury.

The Smallmans" right to additional damages beyond the amount of the check is governed by T.C.A. 47-4-103(5), hereinbefore set out.

In answer to a question by a juror after the jury had deliberated a period of time, the Trial Court, in an attempt to describe bad faith which would entitle the Smallmans to other damages, told the jury the following:

> This law goes on and says, "Where there is bad faith, it includes other damages, if any, suffered by the Plaintiff as a proximate consequence." Bad faith—I previously defined for you good faith. Good faith under the law means honesty in fact in the conduct or transaction concerned. So, bad faith would be dishonesty or willful and wanton misconduct or intentional wrongful conduct, intentional wrongful conduct done with the knowledge that serious damage would probably result or with willful and wanton disregard of possible results.

In all deference to the Trial Court we are candid to say that the foregoing would appear to us to be a classic statement of factors justifying an award of punitive damages. We thus conclude that either the Trial Court was in error in submitting the question of bad faith to the jury or in error in not submitting the question of punitive damages.

Counsel for the Smallmans" principal assertion that they are entitled to damages for bad faith as well as punitive damages is based upon their contention that Home Federal laid in wait, so to speak, to pounce on their meager checking account after watching it for a number of days until they had made a deposit sufficient to satisfy the returned check. The fallacy of this argument is that from the date it was learned on September 3 that the check would not clear after it had been returned the second time, until it was charged back, there were sufficient funds in the account to satisfy the check.

Additionally, there are the following undisputed facts which belie any contention that Home Federal was guilty of bad faith:

1. An officer of Home Federal offered to hold the Smallmans" checks a few days to enable them to cover them with a deposit.

2. Home Federal waived all "not sufficient funds" charges against the Smallmans" account and credited their account accordingly.

3. An official of Home Federal offered to contact individuals or firms where the Smallmans" checks had been returned and explain to the recipients the circumstances surrounding their return.

We accordingly conclude the Trial Court was correct in directing a verdict as to punitive damages and that he likewise should have directed one as to damages predicated upon bad faith.

In view of our disposition of the foregoing issues, it is unnecessary that we address the other issues raised by Home Federal.

---

[23] *47-3-414. Contract of endorser—Order of liability.* [Cf. revised U.C.C. § 3-415.]

. . . .

QUESTION

One authority on the Code has suggested that revised U.C.C. § 4-214(a) rejects the holding in the *Smallman* case. Do you agree? What specific language in § 4-214(a) supports this position? Is there any language which suggests otherwise?

[C] Final Payment

Read: U.C.C. §§ 4-215, 4-301, 4-302, 4-303, & 3-418.

Once a check is deposited, the question then turns to the availability of the funds. As noted above, final payment is the "end of the line" in the collection process when provisional settlements become final. A confusing but inescapable aspect of the bank collection process under both Reg J and Article 4 is the concept of provisional settlement and final payment. From the time an item is deposited a series of provisional credits (settlements) occur as the depositary bank and each collecting bank in the chain provisionally credits the account of the forwarding party (the depositary bank provisionally credits the account of the depositor, an intermediary collecting bank provisionally credits the account of the depositary bank, etc.). This provisional settling continues until the payor bank receives the item. When the payor receives an item for collection it only has two real choices—to pay a properly payable item or, to refuse payment (dishonor) and return the item to the presenter. Any dishonor would demand a communication back through the collection system. Under Article 4, the communication of a notice of dishonor allows banks to revoke their provisional settlements. As we have already seen, a payor may have a number of reasons for dishonoring an item—there could be a stop payment order on the drawer's account; the account could be subject to some form of legal process; or, the drawer has insufficient funds in the account and the bank refuses to make an overdraft loan. Upon receiving a notice of dishonor each collecting bank has a right to charge-back the amount of any credit given for an item to that bank customer's account. See U.C.C. § 4-214 and comments 1 & 2. Despite the variety of reasons for dishonor, the overwhelming majority of presented items are, in fact, paid without problem.

Given that most items are paid, it would be unduly burdensome to require a payor bank to send a message back through the collection system *acknowledging* payment. Instead of an actual notice of payment, the Code uses the midnight deadline to create a time of presumptive settlement. The payor becomes accountable for an item if it retains that item beyond a specified point in time without settling for it. See U.C.C. §§ 4-302 and 4-213. Section 4-215 defines the concept of final payment as the end point in the collection process. Once final payment occurs, collecting banks no longer have a right to charge-back their provisional credits and the depositing customer may withdraw the funds from its bank as a matter of right. Thus, a depositary bank gets no signal from the payor that an item has been honored and paid. Provisional settlements must be revoked in a timely manner or else the settlement becomes final.

Article 4 uses midnight of the next banking day as the deadline signal to the collection system that the time has passed for any bank in the process to reverse the collection process by revoking its provisional settlement. See U.C.C. §§ 4-104(10) and 4-301. If a payor bank provisionally settles on an item, it may recover that settlement if the payor returns the item or gives notice of dishonor *before midnight of the next banking day following the payor's receipt of the item.* See also § 4-108. A payor bank becomes accountable on an item if it retains the item beyond its midnight deadline without settling it. Banks are given very limited circumstances when they may be excused for missing the midnight deadline. U.C.C. 4-109(b).

A bank is excused for missing the deadline if there has been an unanticipated and unaccountable interruption in communications or a break down of computer facilities; if there has been a suspension of payments by another bank; or, if there has been an outbreak of war. The emergency situation must be a circumstance beyond the control of the bank. Banks must meet a very high level of proof to avoid being held responsible for not meeting the midnight deadline. Courts have held that banks have a duty to provide for unforeseeable difficulties. Hence a series of back-ups are necessary rather than a single contingency measure. The midnight deadline rule has been described as a strict liability rule. Payor banks are still required to meet the midnight deadline requirement with respect to previously dishonored checks that have been re-submitted for payment. Without such an exacting rule, so the argument goes, none of the other banks in the collection process could safely assume that check has been paid. But how exacting is this rule? Consider the next two cases.

BANK LEUMI TRUST CO. OF NEW YORK v. BALLY'S PARK PLACE, INC.

United States District Court, Southern District of New York
528 F.Supp. 349, 32 U.C.C. Rep. Serv. 1542 (1981)

BRIEANT, DISTRICT JUDGE.

In this diversity action between a bank and the proprietor of a gambling casino, the court is called upon to decide where the loss or damage, as between the payee-depositor of a check known to be bad, on the one hand, and a drawee bank guilty of computer induced negligence, on the other hand, shall be imposed. The court believes that there is nothing in the Uniform Commercial Code or prior New York case law which requires the Bank to suffer the resultant damage as between the parties.

The relevant facts, stated below, are not in dispute. Plaintiff's motion for summary judgment is granted and defendant's motion for the Same relief is denied.

Defendant Bally's Park Place, Inc. ("Bally's"), is a New Jersey corporation which is the proprietor of a gambling casino located at Atlantic City, New Jersey. Plaintiff Bank Leumi Trust Company of New York ("the Bank" or "Bank Leumi"), is a commercial bank and trust company incorporated under the laws of the State of New York. The Bank had a checking account customer, one Allen Brinker, a resident of New York.

In June 1980, Brinker visited Atlantic City and took a walk on the Boardwalk, followed by a bath at Bally's. He issued a personal check drawn on his account at Bank Leumi in the amount of $60,000, payable to Bally's to cover the markers for his gambling losses.

In order to shuffle and process the vast amount of paperwork which checks of retail banking customers entail, all United States banks today process checks drawn by their customers by computer. They do this by issuing specially imprinted checks to bank customers. These pre-printed checks contain numbers along the bottom of the face of the check identifying the customer's bank, branch and account number. Such numbers are printed or "micro-encoded" in magnetic ink, which is capable of being read by computers without the intervention of human hands, eyes or minds. When such a check is then deposited by the payee with a collecting bank, the collecting bank further imprints the check with computer readable magnetic ink identifying the amount of the check. If the check has been deposited with a collecting bank out of the area of the drawee bank, as occurred in this case, the check is then processed through the Federal Reserve Bank System.

During the processing two things take place: the check is physically transferred to the drawee bank, and a credit for the amount of money due on the check is transferred by computers from the account of the maker at the drawee bank to the account of the payee at the collecting bank.

On Saturday evening, June 7, 1980 and early Sunday morning, June 8, 1980, while Brinker was gambling at Bally's, he issued several checks or markers to Bally's in return for gambling chips. Brinker had in previous months incurred debts to Bally's of $22,000, $22,100 and $40,000, which were promptly satisfied, and Bally's was therefore willing to extend him further credit. In the early morning hours of Sunday June 8, 1980, Brinker issued a single check drawn on Bank Leumi for $60,000 to Bally's to consolidate and replace the earlier smaller markers issued during Saturday night and Sunday morning.

Neither this consolidation check nor the earlier smaller checks were issued on the ordinary pre-printed, numbered and computer readable check forms provided by Bank Leumi to its customers, including Brinker. Instead, an ordinary blank form check prepared for Bally's was used. This check form showed the words "Bally's Park Place Casino Customer Check" printed on the top and Bally's logo printed on the background. The payee was pre-printed as "Pay to the Order of Bally's Park Place, Inc."[24]

On this blank check furnished by Bally's were written in ink the name of the drawee bank, its location, its American Banking Association identification number, the amount of the check and the name, address and signature of Brinker. This check was completed at two different times and its appears that two or three different persons filled in different portions of the check.[25] In one handwriting are the words "Bank of Leumi," Bank of Leumi's American Banking Association identification number, the words "Consolidation Check," the date "6-7-80," the amount, and Brinker's Printed name. In what appears to this court to be another handwriting, is Brinker's signature In the latter entry and Possibly still a third handwriting are Brinker's address

[24] The blank form check may have been used because Brinker did not have any of his preprinted Bank Leumi checks with him. Many regular gamblers follow the custom and habit of not carrying checks when gambling, so as to minimize the temptation to risk more than the cash on their person. To meet this well known practice, Bally's apparently had printed its own form of blank check for use by such customers, including Brinker.

[25] It is clear that the check was completed at two different times because the photocopy of the check sent to Brinker's named executor on July 15, 1980 does not include Brinker's address or the location of his branch of Bank Leumi (Ex B to Wohl Affidavit), yet these items appear on the check when it was microfilmed by Bank Leumi (Ex 1 to D'Amato Affidavit).

It is evident that this copy of Brinker's check was made at least twelve hours after the check was signed by Brinker in the early morning hours of Sunday, June 8, 1980, because it contains a time and date stamped by Bally's made at "June 8, 5:25 PM. '80." This copy may have been made as late as July 15,1980, when it was mailed to Wohl.

and the location of his branch of Bank Leumi. It is likely that Bally's filled out the name of Brinker's bank, his account number, Bank Leumi's identification number, the date, the amount and printed Brinker's name and gave the check to Brinker for him to sign. At some later time Bally's then added Brinker's address and the location of his branch of Bank Leumi. Since this was not a pre-printed check and since Brinker's account number and bank number were handwritten, this check was not computer readable.

On June 27, 1980, Brinker cashed in his chips for the last time, apparently leaving an insolvent estate of less than $5,000.00. Somehow, Bally's became aware of Brinker's death shortly thereafter. On July 7, 1980 Brinker's account at Bank Leumi was closed.

On or before July 15, 1980, Brinker's attorney and named executor Ronald Wohl received a call from Bally's seeking to collect the $60,000.00 from Brinker's estate. Wohl informed Bally's that there was less than $5,000.00 in the estate, that the estate would not even be able to pay Brinker's burial expenses, and that there were no funds from which to pay Bally's claim. Wohl found it surprising that Bally's extended Brinker $60,000 in credit because Brinker had been adjudicated as a bankrupt two years earlier and was generally unable to obtain credit. He had only one credit card, from Avis Rent-A-Car.

On July 15, 1980, Bally's submitted a formal claim against the estate for $60,000.00.

On Saturday, September 6, 1980, Bally's prepared a large deposit which included Brinker's check. This deposit was picked up by the armored car service for Bally's bank, the First National Bank of South Jersey (the "collecting bank"). The check was processed by the collecting bank on Monday, September 8, 1980. The check was deposited on this particular date, the 91st calendar day following the date of the check, because it is Bally's policy to wait at least 90 calendar days but less than 90 banking days after a check is drawn, to deposit it. This procedure appears to comply with the requirement of the New Jersey statute governing the granting of credit to gamblers by casinos. NJSA § 5:12-101. The fact that Bally's held the check for this length of time is relevant only insofar as it is clear that when the check was deposited, Bally's had already known for some time that the check was bad, that Brinker was dead, and that his estate was insolvent. The logical inference is that Bally's knew that it was unlikely that the check would be paid by Bank Leumi, however, it decided to deposit the check and try to collect it anyway in the hope that by some chance it might be paid.[26] In fact, this gamble paid off for Bally's, as is described below.

In any event, the delay in depositing the check is otherwise irrelevant in this action. This court does not rely on any New Jersey law or regulations which are said to permit or require this holding of the check. It need only be observed that the check was not a stale check when Bally's deposited it. See New York U.C.C. § 4-404, which establishes that a check does not become stale until it is six months old. Bally's, or any holder of a check may deposit it at any time before it becomes a stale check. Any New Jersey statutes or regulations which may provide otherwise do not exist for the protection of a drawee-bank.

Under customary and normal banking practices and procedures, when a check is received for collection, the collecting bank will promptly encode the amount credited on the check in computer

[26] Bally's claims that it "was certainly entitled to put the check to the test-by depositing it" because its management "might have thought" that the information received from Wohl, the estate's attorney and executor, was incorrect. (Memorandum of Law in support of Bally's Motion for Summary Judgment, at 13). And Bally's might have thought Bank Leumi would be negligent in discovering it was a bad check, as happened.

readable magnetic ink.[27] If the check were presented missing any of the other necessary encoded information, such as the account number or the bank identification number, the collecting bank would also encode this information. When the First National Bank of South Jersey received Brinker's check it encoded the amount of the check and also the bank identification number which had been handwritten on the check. The bank, however, failed to encode Brinker's account number which was also handwritten on the top of the check next to the bank identification number. This omission is unexplained.

Upon the arrival of the check in New York, Bank Leumi, as a part of its obligations to the collecting bank, had the duty to decide that the check be accepted and paid, or protested, and to do so by midnight of the bank's business day next following the day of receipt of the check. New York U.C.C. §§4-301,4-302,4-104(1) (h). Bank Leumi did not, however, protest the check by this deadline.

By the time the check arrived at Bank Leumi on September 9, 1980, there were no funds available to pay the check because Brinker's account had been closed for more than two months.

The normal practice at Bank Leumi and other banks is to process all incoming checks directly through a computer, without the human intervention of any employee. The computer rejects, or "spits out" those checks which it cannot process, because they are not properly or completely encoded. Brinker's check, which was missing the encoded account number, as well as a number of checks which were torn, mutilated, improperly encoded, not encoded at all, or spurious, were spit out by the computer. Such items were regularly placed in a separate basket or box by Bank Leumi employees, for future attention.

It is then the duty and practice of Bank Leumi employees to go through that basket of rejected paper, and process each of the items in the traditional and time consuming way, by hand. Bank Leumi was negligent in this regard; it failed to process the Brinker check by the protest deadline of midnight the following business day.[28] Apparently, and for unknown reasons, Bank Leumi did not protest the Brinker check until April 8, 1981, seven months later.[29] By this time, by reason of New York U.C.C. § 4-302 it was impossible for Bank Leumi to return the check to the collecting bank in New Jersey marking it "insufficient funds" or "account closed" or relying on other traditional banking procedures This delay was the product of negligence on the part of Bank Leumi. However, this negligence was in part caused by the negligent or intentional failure of the collecting bank, the First National Bank of South Jersey, (Bally's agent) to encode Brinker's account number as required by banking industry practice. The negligence on the part of Bank Leumi was readily and reasonably foreseeable. Bally's undoubtedly knew or should have known

---

[27] Oral argument of the motion was not recorded. The court takes judicial notice of the customary and normal banking practices and procedures. Rule 201, F.R. Evid.

[28] It is not clear when Bank Leumi actually discovered that there were no funds with which to pay the Brinker check, or that the check had already been paid by mistake. Bank Leumi only states that, "due to error, the draft was paid and the mistake was not immediately discovered." Bank Leumi claims that the cause of the delay was that:

> During the time in question, Bank Leumi was experiencing more than a doubling in volume of its daily transactions as a result of its purchase in July of 1980 of thirteen branches formerly operated by Bankers Trust Co. This multiple branch acquisition was an extraordinary expansion of the number of branches operated by Bank Leumi and severely taxed the bank's transaction processing resources.

(D'Amato Affidavit, at 4).

[29] Insofar as this action is concerned, it is irrelevant when Bank Leumi discovered the mistake or its cause since the midnight deadline had passed, so as to preclude protesting the check and sending it back to the Collecting Bank. As between these parties, this action was timely commenced.

that most personal checks are pre-printed with computer readable identifying numbers. It was certainly foreseeable when Bally's deposited this check in non-computer readable form, known by it to be drawn on insufficient funds as of the date it was deposited, that the drawee-bank would fail to protest and return it within the very brief time period allowed by the Code.

Accordingly, as we noted above, this court must choose whether the liability for this loss is to be imposed upon the payee of a check known to be bad on the date deposited for collection on the one hand, or the negligent drawee-bank which foreseeably failed to protest the check because it was not in computer readable form, and under the pressure of business failed to meet the midnight deadline for such protest, under New York U.C.C. § 4-302. This court believes that the loss must fall on the payee, rather than on the drawee bank. To hold otherwise would permit the maker or payee of a check simply by providing a non-computer readable form check, to set a trap for an unwary bank.

New York law is clear as between the parties, that "[a] bank paying out money on a check or note by mistake may recover back the payment from the person to whom it was made, even though the bank was negligent in making the mistake, so long as the payee does not suffer as a result of the mistake." 42 NY Jury Negotiable Instruments § 585. A bank may recover funds paid on a check by mistake, when as here the customer's account with the bank had been closed as of the date the check was presented for payment. *Manufacturers Trust Co. v. Diamond*, 17 Misc 2d 909 (App Term 1st Dept 1959). "There is no reason why a bank, merely because it is a bank, should be denied recovery of money paid by mistake in circumstances which would justify recovery by anyone else. Banks have been held entitled to relief in such situations." *Id.* at 910.

By its terms, the Uniform Commercial Code, as adopted by New York, does not alter this result. "Unless displaced by the particular provisions of this Act, the principles of law and equity, including . . . the law relative to . . . mistake shall supplement its provisions." New York U.C.C. § 1-103.

According to the New York Court of Appeals, "[u]nder the plain import of this section, nothing short of an express code provision limiting plaintiffs remedy would suffice. *Hechter v. New York Life Insurance Co.*, 46 N.Y.2d 34, 39 (1978). The commentators agree that the U.C.C. expressly preserves the common law governing mistake without alteration. Anderson, Uniform Commercial Code § 1-103:42. See New York U.C.C. § 4-407, Official Comment 5.

Bally's reliance on New York U.C.C. §§ 3-418, 4-301 and 4-302 is misplaced. These sections of the U.C.C. apply to inter-bank settlement procedures, and not to subsequent actions for restitution. A contrary reading of §§ 3-418, 4-301 and 4-302 would be inconsistent with § 1-103 which retains the common law governing mistake. It would lead to the unintended result of allowing a payee, unjustly, to retain monies improperly obtained.

Furthermore, although the death of the maker of a check or note does not terminate his liability, it does revoke the authority of the payee to collect from the drawee-bank and relegates the payee to the status of a general creditor of the estate of the deceased. The U.C.C. provides a similar result. New York U.C.C. § 4-405(1). "Under 4-405 (1) a bank's authority to handle items on its customer's account terminates when the bank learns that he had died." White & Summers, Uniform Commercial Code at 665 (2d ed 1980). Bally's, therefore, had no right to collect the check from Bank Leumi once it knew Brinker had died. On this additional ground, Bank Leumi may recover for its mistaken payment.

Bally's implies that it relied on Bank Leumi's payment of the Brinker check, and thereby forfeited its right to proceed as a creditor against Brinker's estate. (Bally's Reply Memorandum of Law, at 3). First, Bally's could not recover against Brinker's estate if, as appears, the estate was and is clearly insufficient and probably insolvent. Nor has Bally's lost its right to proceed against Brinker's estate. See New York CPLR §§ 210, 213.

Bally's submitted the Brinker check for collection knowing that the check was not on pre-printed computer readable Bank Leumi form of check, and it was therefore likely to be subject to delays in payment. Bally's also had been reliably informed that Brinker was dead and his estate was insufficient. It was therefore likely that there were insufficient funds in Brinker's Bank Leumi account, if the account still existed, from which to pay the check. Bally's also knew or should have known that it was very possible, if not likely, that the check would be paid by mistake. Bally's has not suffered through this mistake. It has lost no rights which it would have had if Bank Leumi had not paid the check by mistake, nor has it suffered any other loss because of any action of Bank Leumi.

In light of all of the above, this court finds that the burden of pursuing the estate of the maker should fall on the depositor of a check known to be worthless, rather than on the drawee-bank guilty of computer induced negligence in failing to protest the check in timely fashion.

The Clerk shall enter final judgment in favor of plaintiff Bank Leumi in the sum of $60,000.00, plus pre-judgment interest at 6% per annum from April 8, 1981; costs to be taxed.

NOTES

In *Bank Leumi*, the bank missed its midnight deadline but nonetheless avoided liability because the party initiating collection knew that the check would not be paid. Thus, a payor bank can defend an action against it based on accountability by showing that the item involved fraud. Revised Article 4-302 codifies the *Bank Leumi* holding. But what happens when there is an allegation of bad faith? Does a depositary bank that suspects fraud have a good faith duty to disclose its suspicions to the payor? Does a bank act in bad faith if it suspects a fraud and attempts to shift the loss to the other bank? The next case raises these questions and introduces us to Regulation CC. Before we begin, consider the following overview of Reg CC.

REGULATION CC AND EXPEDITED FUNDS AVAILABILITY

In 1987, Congress passed the Expedited Funds Availability Act which sought to place restrictions on the length of time banks could hold customer funds before making them available for withdrawal. 12 U.S.C. § 4001 et seq.. The promulgating regulation CC, 12 CFR §§ 229.1 et seq., has two primary subparts. Sections 229.10 through 229.21 (Subpart B) address the availability of funds. Sections 229.30 through 229.42 (Subpart C) address check return and collection. Like Reg J, the provisions of Reg CC supersede any inconsistent state law, including the Uniform Commercial Code.

Reg CC Subpart B mandates a certain availability for deposited funds, based on the nature of the items deposited. Cash deposits or electronic payments must be made available by the next business day following receipt. On the other hand, Article 4 does not require that deposited funds be made available for withdrawal at any particular time except that a cash deposit must be made available by opening time of the next banking day following the bank's receipt of the item. U.C.C. § 4-215(f). Deposits of local checks (those drawn on a payor located in the same check processing region as the depositary bank) must be made available not later than the second business day following the banking day of deposit. 12 CFR § 229.12(b). Deposits of non-local items must be made available for withdrawal not later than the fifth business day following the banking day of receipt. 12 CFR § 229.12(c).

Because the federally mandated availability schedule of Reg CC could result in a depositary bank making funds available for withdrawal before a deposited item is paid by the payor under Article 4, Reg CC provides a series of exceptions to the funds availability schedule. These exceptions allow a depositary bank to delay making funds available for withdrawal beyond the time specified in the schedule. Exceptions include: new accounts (open for 30 days or less), large deposits (in excess of $5000), re-deposited checks (those already dishonored by the payor but re-deposited by the customer), accounts with repeated overdrafts (checks presented for payment on insufficient funds on six or more banking days during the preceding six months, or, items that would overdraw an account by $5000 or more on two or more banking days during the same time period (*i.e.*, the preceding six months)), or emergency conditions (where communications or equipment facilities fail, or other circumstances beyond the control of the depositary bank). 12 CFR § 229.13. Section 229.13(e)(1) also provides an exception from the funds availability schedule for reasonable cause to doubt the collectability of an item. The required schedules do not apply "if a depositary bank has reasonable cause to believe that the check is uncollectible. . . ." The commentary to the section provides examples of situations that might constitute reasonable cause to doubt collectability. The more obvious example is notice that a check is being returned by the payor.

Subpart C to Reg CC imposes a series of return requirements that seek to expedite the return of dishonored items on an even faster basis than the midnight deadline rules articulated under Article 4. The provisions on expedited return are imposed on top of Article 4's midnight deadline, and not as a replacement. The Reg CC requirements are related to the time a dishonored item is received by the depositary bank, rather than the time a returning bank sends notice of the dishonor back through the system. Under Article 4, every collecting bank in the forward collection process (*i.e.*, the presentment of an item for payment) is an agent or subagent of the owner. U.C.C. § 4-201(a). As an agent, each bank in the forward collection process has a duty to handle the item when it is returned after a payor bank dishonors it. U.C.C. § 4-202. Because collecting banks provisionally credit accounts during the forward collection process, they will also have a direct interest in rescinding their provisional credit whenever an item is dishonored. With an item's dishonor then, Article 4 envisions the forward collection process in reverse, with each collecting bank having a duty of ordinary care that can be met only by returning the item within the bank's midnight deadline.

Reg CC modifies this return-upon-dishonor process by providing that an item need not be returned by the same route as the forward collection process. Because Reg CC makes a distinction between the forward collection and return processes, the regulation preempts Article 4's rules on provisional settlement IF the item is returned by a different route. In such an instance, preemption is necessary because a provisional settlement can not be revoked if an item were returned by a different route. The consequence of the Reg CC rule is that all settlements for checks between banks are considered final when made, both in the forward and return process. See 12 CFR §§ 229.31(c), 229.32(b), and 229.36(d). The dishonored check does not have to be returned through the same set of collecting banks, or even to the specific branch bank of the depositary bank that took the item for collection initially. Only the depositary bank has a duty to handle a returned item. 12 CFR § 229.31(d). Cf. U.C.C. 4-202(a)(2).

In essence, Reg CC makes the returning bank an agent of the payor bank and a subagent of the depositary bank rather than continuing the bank's Article 4 role as agent of the owner. The returning bank may be liable to the depositary bank and that bank's depositing customer but generally has no responsibility for the actions of other banks in the chain of collection or return. The convergence of laws governing returned items means that a payor bank which misses its Article 4 deadline by failing to return an item by midnight of the banking day after banking day following receipt, could be liable under Article 4, Regulation J, or Regulation CC. The counseling point is to remember to consult both Articles 3 and 4 as well as Regulations J and CC whenever an issue concerning check collection arises.

FIRST NATIONAL BANK IN HARVEY v. COLONIAL BANK

United States District Court, Northern District, Illinois
898 F. Supp. 1120 (N.D. Ill. 1995)

GRADY, J.

BACKGROUND

Check kiting is a form of bank fraud. The kiter opens accounts at two (or more) banks, writes checks on insufficient funds on one account, then covers the overdraft by depositing a check drawn on insufficient funds from the other account.

To illustrate the operation, suppose that the defrauder opens two accounts with a deposit of $ 500 each at the First National Bank and a distant Second National Bank. (A really successful defrauder will have numerous accounts in fictitious names at banks in widely separated states.) The defrauder then issues for goods or cash checks totalling $3000 against the First National Bank. But before they clear and overdraw the account, he covers the overdrafts with a check for $4,000 drawn on the Second National Bank. The Second National account will be overdrawn when the $4,000 check is presented; before that happens, however, the defrauder covers it with a check on the First National Bank. The process is repeated innumerable times until there is a constant float of worthless checks between the accounts and the defrauder has bilked the banks of a substantial sum of money. John D. O'Malley, *Common Check Frauds and the Uniform Commercial Code*, 23 Rutgers L. Rev. 189, 194 n.35 (1968-69). By timing the scheme correctly and repeating it over a period of time, the kiter can use the funds essentially as an interest-free loan. *Williams v. United States*, 458 U.S. 279, 281 n.1, 73 L. Ed. 2d 767, 102 S. Ct. 3088 (1982) (quoting Brief for the United States).

Check kiting is possible because of a combination of two rules found in Article 4 of the Uniform Commercial Code. Under § 4-208(1), a depositary bank may allow a customer to draw on uncollected funds, that is, checks that have been deposited but not yet paid. Second, under §§ 4-301 and 4-302, a payor bank must either pay or dishonor a check drawn on it by midnight of the second banking day following presentment. Barkley Clark, The Law of Bank Deposits, Collections and Credit Cards P 5.03[5] (3d ed. 1990). Thus when a kite is operating, the depositary bank allows the kiter to draw on uncollected funds based on a deposit of a check. The depositary bank presents that check to the payor bank, which must decide whether to pay or return the check before the midnight deadline. The check may appear to be covered by uncollected funds at the payor bank, and so the payor bank may decide to pay the check by allowing the midnight deadline to pass.

A kite crashes when one of the banks dishonors checks drawn on it and returns them to the other banks involved in the kite. Clark, *supra*. Usually, such a dishonor occurs when one bank suspects a kite. *Id*. However, an individual bank may have trouble detecting a check kiting scheme. "Until one has devoted a substantial amount of time examining not only one's own account, but accounts at other banks, it may be impossible to know whether the customer is engaged in a legitimate movement of funds or illegitimate kiting." James J. White & Robert S. Summers, Uniform Commercial Code § 17-1 (3d ed. 1988 & Supp. 1994). But each bank is usually able to monitor only its own account, and "there is no certain test that distinguishes one who writes many checks on low balances from a check kiter." White & Summers, *supra*, § 17-2. Even if a bank suspects a kite, it might decide not to take any action for a number of reasons. First, it may be liable to its customer for wrongfully dishonoring checks. § 4-202. Second, if it reports that a kite is operating and turns out to be wrong, it could find itself defending a defamation suit. White & Summers, *supra*, § 17-1 (Supp. 1994). Finally, if it errs in returning checks or reporting a kite, it may risk angering a large customer. *Id*.

FACTS

This case involves the fallout of a collapsed check kite. Two of the banks involved, First National Bank in Harvey ("First National") and Colonial Bank ("Colonial") are the parties to this litigation. The Federal Reserve Bank of Chicago (the "Reserve Bank"), through whose clearinghouse the relevant checks were processed, is also a party.

Shelly International Marketing ("Shelly") opened a checking account at First National in December 1989. The principals of Shelly also opened accounts at the Family Bank (a nonparty) in the names of Shelly Brokerage and Crete Trading around December 1990. On December 31, 1991, the principals of Shelly opened a checking account at Colonial Bank in the name of World Commodities, Inc.. Shelly and World Commodities were related companies, with the same or similar shareholders, officers, and directors. The principals of Shelly and World Commodities began operating a check kiting scheme among the accounts at the three banks in early 1991.

The main events at issue in this case took place in February 1992. The checks that form the basis of this suit are thirteen checks totalling $1,523,892.49 for which First National was the depositary bank and Colonial was the payor bank (the "Colonial checks"). Also relevant are seventeen checks totalling $1,518,642.86 for which Colonial was the depositary bank and First National was the payor bank (the "First National checks").

On Monday, February 10, Shelly deposited the thirteen Colonial checks to its First National account. First National then sent those checks through the check clearing system. That same day, World Commodities deposited the seventeen First National checks to its Colonial account.

The next day, Tuesday, February 11, the Colonial checks were presented to Colonial for payment, and the First National checks were presented to First National for payment. That day,

David Spiewak, an officer with First National's holding company, Pinnacle, reviewed the bank's records to determine why there were large balance fluctuations in Shelly's First National account. Spiewak began to suspect that a kite might be operating. He did not know whether Colonial had enough funds to cover the Colonial checks that had been deposited on Monday, February 10, and forwarded to Colonial for payment. Later that day, First National froze the Shelly account to prevent any further activity in it.

On the morning of Wednesday, February 12, Spiewak met with First National president Dennis Irvin and Pinnacle's chief lending officer Mike Braun to discuss the Shelly account. Spiewak informed the others of what he knew, and the three agreed that there was a possible kite. They concluded that further investigation was needed. The First National officers decided to return the First National checks to Colonial. First National says that the decision was made at this meeting, but Colonial says the decision was actually made the day before.

On Wednesday, First National returned the First National checks to Colonial. Under Regulation CC, a bank that is returning checks in excess of $2,500.00 must provide notice to the depositary bank either by telephone, actual return of the check, or Fed Wire before 4:00 p.m. on the second business day following presentment. First National notified Colonial by Fed Wire that it was returning the seventeen First National checks. Initially, the large item return form indicated that the reason for the return was "uncollected funds," but Spiewak changed that reason to "refer to maker."

Colonial received the Fed Wire notices at approximately 2:45 p.m. on Wednesday and routed them to its cashier, Joanne Topham. Randall Soderman, a Colonial loan officer, was informed of the large return, and immediately began an investigation. He realized that if the Colonial checks were not returned by midnight that same day, Colonial would be out the money. Returning the Colonial checks before midnight would protect Colonial from liability, but it would risk disappointing the customer. Anthony Schiller, the loan officer in charge of the World Commodities account, called World Commodities comptroller Charles Patterson and its attorney Jay Goldstein. Both assured Schiller that the First National checks were good and should be redeposited. Ultimately, Richard Vucich, Colonial's president, and Joanne Topham, Colonial's cashier, decided not to return the Colonial checks on Wednesday. They decided instead to meet on Thursday morning with Schiller to discuss the matter.

Schiller, Topham, and Vucich met on the morning of Thursday, February 13. At the conclusion of the meeting, they decided to return the thirteen Colonial checks to First National. At about 10:45 a.m., Colonial telephoned First National to say that it intended to return the Colonial checks. Colonial sent the Colonial checks back through the Reserve Bank as a return in a return cash letter. The Reserve Bank debited First National's Reserve Bank account in the amount of the Colonial checks. First National received the returned Colonial checks on Friday, February 14.

First National then resorted to the Fed's "challenge procedure" to contest the return of the Colonial checks after the midnight deadline. First National prepared and submitted to the Reserve Bank a "Sender's Claim of Late Return" form for each of the Colonial checks. The Reserve Bank processed the claim forms and credited the Reserve Bank account of First National $1,523,892.49 and debited the Reserve Bank account of Colonial in the same amount. On February 24, Colonial prepared and filed a "Paying Bank's Response to Claim of Late Return" form for each of the thirteen Colonial checks. As a consequence of the processing of the response forms, the Reserve Bank reversed the credit given to First National and the debit made to Colonial.

First National then filed this suit against Colonial and the Reserve Bank, alleging that Colonial wrongfully returned the Colonial checks after the midnight deadline and the Reserve Bank wrongfully accepted the late return. Count I of First National's amended complaint against Colonial alleges breach of warranty under Regulation CC for the late return of the checks. 12 C.F.R. § 229.34. Count II against the Reserve Bank alleges breach of warranty under Regulations CC and J for accepting the late return. 12 C.F.R. § 210.6. Count III against Colonial alleges breach of a duty of ordinary care in Colonial's return of the Colonial checks. Count IV against the Reserve Bank alleges breach of a duty of ordinary care in processing the late return. Count V against Colonial alleges breach of U.C.C. § 4-302 for Colonial's failure to return the checks by the midnight deadline. Count VI against the Reserve Bank and Count VII against Colonial allege breach of contract for each party's failure to comply with the terms of the Reserve Bank's Operating Circular No. 4 ("OC-4").

First National moved for partial summary judgment as to Count V. On August 27, 1993, this court denied the plaintiff's motion. *First Nat'l Bank in Harvey v. Colonial Bank*, 831 F. Supp. 637 (N.D. Ill. 1993). The parties now have each moved for summary judgment on all counts. Along with deciding the remaining counts, today's opinion reconsiders portions of our earlier ruling on Count V. *Avitia v. Metropolitan Club*, 49 F.3d 1219, 1227 (7th Cir. 1995).

DISCUSSION

I. Count V: Breach of U.C.C. § 4-302 Against Colonial

A. Accountability

Article 4 of the Uniform Commercial Code adopts a policy of "final payment" ; that is, a check is considered to be finally paid at some specific and identifiable point in time. § 4-215 Comment 1. Final payment is the "end of the line" in the check collection process. *Id.* Section 4-301 sets up the "midnight deadline" in the process: a payor bank which intends to return a check presented to it must do so before midnight of the next banking day following receipt of the check. §§ 4-301(a), 4-104(a)(10). If a payor bank fails to return a check before the midnight deadline, final payment occurs.

Section 4-302 spells out the payor bank's liability for its late return of an item, that is, return after the midnight deadline:

> (a) If an item is presented to and received by a payor bank, the bank is accountable for the amount of:
>
> > (1) a demand item, other than a documentary draft, whether properly payable or not, if the bank . . . does not pay or return the item or send notice of dishonor until after its midnight deadline . . . .

§ 4-302. The operative word in this section is "accountable." Courts interpreting this section have nearly unanimously concluded that § 4-302 imposes strict liability on a payor bank for failing to adhere to the midnight deadline, and makes the measure of damages the face amount of the check. In an early decision, the Illinois Supreme Court held that "accountable" means "liable" for the amount of the item. *Rock Island Auction Sales, Inc. v. Empire Packing Co.*, 32 Ill. 2d 269, 204 N.E.2d 721, 723 (Ill. 1965). The *Rock Island* court contrasted the "accountability" language in § 4-302 with the language used to specify the measure of damages in what is now § 4-103(e).[30] Section 4-103(e) makes a bank liable for failing to exercise ordinary care in the handling of a check in "the amount of the item reduced by an amount that could not have been realized by the exercise of ordinary care." § 4-103(e). The Official Comment to this section explains: "When it is established that some part or all of the item could not have been collected even by the use of ordinary care the recovery is reduced by the amount that would have been in any event uncollectible." In other words, § 4-103(e) imposes liability in the amount of the loss caused by the negligence, while § 4-302(a) imposes strict liability in the face amount of the check.

The *Rock Island* court reasoned that the special role of the payor bank in the check collection system justifies the imposition of liability regardless of negligence. The midnight deadline requires the payor bank — the bank in the best position to know whether there are funds available to cover the check — to decide whether to pay or return the check:

> The role of a payor bank in the collection process . . . is crucial. It knows whether or not the drawer has funds available to pay the item. The legislature could have considered that the failure of such a bank to meet its deadline is likely to be due to factors other than negligence, and that the relationship between a payor bank and its customer may so influence its conduct as to cause a conscious disregard of its statutory duty.

Rock Island, 204 N.E.2d at 723.

The overwhelming majority of courts that have considered the meaning of § 4-302(a) have followed the *Rock Island* court in concluding that the liability of a payor bank that fails to return a check by the midnight deadline is strict and is in the face amount of the check.

Even where the damage suffered by the payee is not caused by the lateness of the return, the midnight deadline still has been strictly enforced. For example, in *Chicago Title Ins. Co. v. California Canadian Bank*, 1 Cal. App. 4th 798, 2 Cal. Rptr. 2d 422, 424 (Ct. App. 1992), the payor bank decided to return twenty-eight checks involved in a massive check fraud scheme. The checks left the bank before the midnight deadline, but did not arrive at the clearinghouse until the next day — after the midnight deadline had passed. *Id.* at 424. The court held that the bank's return was late. *Id.* at 425. It held the bank strictly accountable for the face amount of the checks, reasoning that the bank "may be held strictly liable for its failure to return the checks by the applicable deadlines, regardless whether [the other party] demonstrated it suffered actual damage solely as a result of [the Bank's] omission." *Id.* at 426-29. . . .

But is it appropriate to enforce the accountability provision of § 4-302 where a check kiting scheme is involved? The Minnesota Supreme Court did in *Town & Country State Bank v. First State Bank*, 358 N.W.2d 387, 393-95 (Minn. 1984). There, the court held that two payor banks that held kited checks beyond the midnight deadline made "final payment" on the checks and were therefore accountable for the amounts of those checks. [Citations].

Colonial cites cases in which courts have declined to impose strict liability under other U.C.C. provisions. However, none of these other provisions contains the "accountable" language found in § 4-302. [Citations]. The reasoning of these cases, then, is simply not applicable here.

---

30 Section 4-103(e) provides:

> The measure of damages for failure to exercise ordinary care in handling an item is the amount of the item reduced by an amount that could not have been realized by the exercise of ordinary care. If there is also bad faith it includes any other damages the party suffered as a proximate consequence.

This court's prior opinion held that First National could not recover under the accountability provision of § 4-302 if it would be unjustly enriched by the recovery. § 1-103; 831 F. Supp. at 641. On the undisputed evidence presented by First National on the present motion, however, we now see that it did suffer a loss. At some point during the check kiting scheme, funds were siphoned out of the banking system, causing a deficit in First National's assets. The important point is that First National will not be unjustly enriched by recovering from Colonial. It has suffered a loss at some point, and will not experience a windfall if it recovers from Colonial.

Therefore, we conclude that Colonial is absolutely liable in the face amount of the Colonial checks for missing the midnight deadline. This does not end the analysis, however, because Colonial raises the defenses of good faith and mistaken payment to defeat strict accountability.

B. Good Faith

The general provisions of the Uniform Commercial Code state: "Every contract or duty within this Act imposes an obligation of good faith in its performance or enforcement." § 1-203. The Code defines "good faith" as "honesty in fact in the conduct or transaction concerned." § 1-201(19). Colonial argues that First National's lack of good faith defeats its § 4-302 claim of accountability, contending that First National orchestrated the events of the week of February 10 in order to cause Colonial to miss the midnight deadline for returning the Colonial checks.

The first question is whether we should even consider bad faith in this check kiting case. First National urges us to refrain from injecting notions of bad faith to reallocate the loss here. It contends that introducing the concept of bad faith will muddy the concepts of certainty and finality, which are central to the treatment of kites by Article 4. However, the U.C.C. itself, in § 1-103, injects notions of good faith into every transaction covered by it, and we cannot simply ignore the statute.

Colonial charges that First National returned the seventeen First National checks to Colonial on Wednesday, February 12, under circumstances amounting to bad faith. Colonial argues that First National deliberately caused confusion in returning the First National checks, which caused Colonial to miss the midnight deadline for the Colonial checks.

Colonial offers the following facts to show First National's bad faith. On Tuesday, February 11, Spiewak thought that a kite was taking place and together with other First National officers decided that the First National checks would be dishonored and returned to Colonial. First National returned the checks the next day, Wednesday, a day on which it is closed for business. It also notified Colonial of the return late in the day (2:45 p.m.) by Fed Wire rather than by telephone, a practice that is rarely used and less desirable than telephone notice because a wire notice may not be picked up by an employee for some time, while telephonic notice is received directly by a bank employee who can take immediate action. Finally, First National changed the reason for the return from "uncollected funds" to "refer to maker." When Colonial received the wire transmittal, it attempted to contact First National to determine why First National returned the checks "refer to maker." No one at Colonial was able to talk to anyone at First National, however, because a recorded message informed Colonial employees that First National was closed on Wednesdays. First National's endorsement stamp contains only its general telephone number, not any other telephone number that would allow telephone calls to be made even when the switchboard is closed, as is the practice at most Chicago area banks.

In short, Colonial argues that First National's failure to advise Colonial of the kite, its delay in giving notice of the return, its use of Fed Wire to give notice of the return, its return of the checks marked "refer to maker," and its return of the checks on a day when it was closed for business caused Colonial to miss the midnight deadline for the Colonial checks. These facts amount to bad faith, Colonial contends; consequently First National may not recover any losses it suffered in the kite. And, in any event, whether First National's acts constitute bad faith is an issue of fact that precludes summary judgment in favor of First National.

Colonial's argument raises specific questions about whether First National's conduct amounts to bad faith. But it also raises more general questions about banks" conduct in check kiting schemes: Does a depositary bank that suspects a kite have a good faith duty to disclose its suspicions to the payor bank? Furthermore, does a bank act in bad faith if it discovers or suspects a kite and attempts to shift the loss to the other bank by returning checks drawn on it while at the same time forwarding checks that have been deposited with it for payment?

Courts that have dealt with these issues usually take the latter two questions together, and most have concluded that a bank has no good faith obligation to disclose a suspected kite or to refrain from attempting to shift the kite loss. These were the conclusions of the Mississippi Supreme Court in the leading case of *Citizens Nat'l Bank v. First Nat'l Bank*, 347 So. 2d 964 (Miss. 1977). In *Citizens*, a check kite was operating through accounts at Citizens National Bank and at First National Bank. First National discovered the kite, and returned all checks drawn on its account that Citizens had presented. At the same time, First National presented checks to Citizens that the kiter had drawn on Citizens and deposited with First National. First National also accepted deposits by the kiter and payments by Citizens. After the kite crashed, Citizens sued First National, charging that First National converted funds belonging to Citizens. *Id.* at 966.

The Mississippi Supreme Court upheld the dismissal of the complaint, agreeing with the chancellor's opinion which stated, "I cannot find where FNB has been charged with doing anything other than acting as a prudent and careful bank should act." *Id.* at 967, 969. In holding that there was no duty on the part of First National to notify Citizens of its conviction that their mutual customer was kiting checks, the court reasoned:

> These two banks were competitors in the banking field and ordinarily banks deal with each other at arm's length. The bill does not allege any circumstances or facts that tend to show that a confidential or fiduciary relationship existed between these two banks, neither does it show that there is any requirement in the banking field that one bank notify another of its discovery of a customer kiting checks. In the absence of a fiduciary or confidential relationship, or some other legal duty, First National Bank had no duty to inform Citizens National Bank that Duran was kiting checks. This being true, we are of the opinion that First National Bank had the legal right to continue to accept for deposit checks drawn by Duran on accounts at Citizens National Bank and present those checks for payment. At the same time, First National Bank had the legal right to refuse to pay checks drawn by Duran on accounts in First National Bank and deposited in Citizens National Bank.

Id. at 967 . . . .

The facts here amount to, at most, an attempt by First National to shift the kite loss to Colonial. First, as First National points out, wire notice is a legally permissible method of notifying another bank of a large return. 12 C.F.R. § 229.33(a). In addition, First National has presented evidence that notifying other banks of large returns by wire rather than by telephone was its usual practice. . . . .

Although Colonial makes much of the fact that First National returned the First National checks marked "refer to maker" rather than "uncollected funds," the parties agree that "refer to maker" is a legally permissible reason for returning a check. And Colonial had contacted the maker, World Commodities, and its counsel, receiving assurances that the checks were good. As to First National's delay in informing Colonial of the return, it is undisputed that First National notified a Colonial employee at 9:30 a.m. on Wednesday, February 12, that it would be returning certain checks, although it notified the wrong employee and did not specify the number or dollar amounts of those checks. But First National sent the wire notice later the same day stating that seventeen checks totalling $1,518,642.86 were being returned "refer to maker." Even if, as Colonial contends, First National officers decided to return the checks on Tuesday rather than Wednesday, Colonial had notice more than twelve hours before the midnight deadline that checks drawn on the Shelly account were being returned. And even though Colonial was not able to contact First National on Wednesday, Colonial knew on that day that the First National checks were being returned and that the midnight deadline for the Colonial checks was rapidly approaching.

All of First National's conduct regarding the First National checks was proper under the applicable laws. First National had the right to present the Colonial checks for payment and the right to return the First National checks. At most, First National took advantage of these laws and regulations to attempt to shift the kite loss onto Colonial. But even if this is what happened, such conduct does not constitute bad faith.

First National and Colonial were faced with the same dilemma at the same time: a number of checks totalling a goodly sum of money drawn on the account of a customer with low collected funds balances. First National chose to return the checks unpaid, but Colonial chose to trust its customer to cover the checks. By the time Colonial realized that its decision was wrong, it was too late — the midnight deadline had passed and the checks were paid. Each bank made a business decision; First National's turned out to be the correct one.

. . . .

D. Damages

Let us return to the sticking point of the court's earlier ruling — damages. Summary judgment was denied First National because the court was not satisfied that it had been damaged, and held that it might be unjustly enriched if it were to recover from Colonial. 831 F. Supp. at 641. On this motion, First National has presented evidence showing that it has suffered a loss from the Shelly/World Commodities check kite.

At some point during the operation of the kite, the kiters siphoned funds out of the banking system, and because Colonial returned the Colonial checks to First National, the loss fell on First National.[31] Specifically, the Reserve Bank debited First National's Reserve Bank account in the amount of the return, $1,523,892.49. This caused First National to make ledger entries reflecting the debit to the Reserve Bank account and a reduction in First National's assets.[32]

---

31 The defendants present evidence that the funds were siphoned from the system during the spring and summer of 1991, before the Colonial account was even opened. But when the funds were siphoned is not the issue; such an inquiry would lead to questions about whether Colonial is at fault for the loss. As explained in the text, the relevant principles here are Colonial's liability in the face amount of the checks reduced by any amount by which First National would be unjustly enriched.

32 Had the Shelly account still been open when the Reserve Bank debited First National's account, First National says that it would have charged the debit to the Shelly account, causing an overdraft in the account. The defendants deny that First National could have charged the debit to the Shelly account because there were never any collected funds in that account. But the result is the same either way — First National took the loss.

But as we have held, Colonial's return was improperly late, and § 4-302 directs that it bear the loss here.

The next question is the amount for which Colonial is liable. Section 4-302 makes Colonial liable in the face amount of the checks. However, where the payee has mitigated its damages (as in the case of a payee bank recovering from the drawer of the check), the payor's liability is reduced by the amount mitigated. *State & Sav. Bank v. Meeker*, 469 N.E.2d 55, 59 (Ind. Ct. App. 1984). Otherwise, the payee would be unjustly enriched by the full recovery. § 1-103. In this case, then, First National is entitled to the face amount of the Colonial checks ($1,523,892.49) less any amount it recovered from Shelly, its customer.

The parties dispute how much First National recovered from its customer. In addition to the checking account, Shelly also maintained a line of credit with First National. During the months of March, April, and May 1992, First National received $676,757.30 in loan payments. First National also applied to the loan balance $42,463.38 that remained in the Shelly checking account when it was closed on February 28. The defendants say, then, that First National actually received $719,220.68 from Shelly after the kite crashed — the $676,757.30 in loan payments plus $42,463.38 that remained in the Shelly checking account.

Colonial says that First National's recovery should be reduced by $719,220.68. But Colonial has presented no evidence to refute First National's evidence that it applied the $719,220.68 to pay off the loan. This being the case, First National will not be unjustly enriched by recovering the face amount of the checks from Colonial. However, First National submits a report of Arthur Andersen & Co. saying that the funds from Shelly were sufficient to pay off the loan and reduce the loss from the kite, leaving it with an actual loss of $1,425,970.61. If First National's recovery is reduced to avoid unjust enrichment, it is entitled to recover $1,425,970.61, plus interest, which represents the face amount of the Colonial checks offset by any recovery from Shelly that exceeded the amount necessary to pay off the loan.

. . . .

II. Count III: Alleged Breach of Duty of Ordinary Care by Colonial

First National alleges that Colonial breached its duty of ordinary care with respect to its return of the Colonial checks. Regulation CC provides:

> A bank shall exercise ordinary care and act in good faith in complying with the requirements of this subpart. A bank that fails to exercise ordinary care or act in good faith under this subpart may be liable to the depositary bank, the depositary bank's customer, the owner of a check, or another party to the check. The measure of damages for failure to exercise ordinary care is the amount of the loss incurred, up to the amount of the check, reduced by the amount of the loss that the party would have incurred even if the bank had exercised ordinary care.

12 C.F.R. § 229.38(a). Under this provision, there must be a causal relationship between the bank's actions and the loss.

Colonial argues, and First National concedes, that First National could not have recovered any of the disputed $1.5 million even if Colonial had returned the Colonial checks by the midnight deadline. Because Colonial's late return did not cause First National's loss, First National cannot prevail on its claim for breach of the duty of ordinary care.

III. Count I: Alleged Breach of Warranty by Colonial

Count II: Alleged Breach of Warranty by Reserve Bank

First National alleges breach of warranty counts against both Colonial and the Reserve Bank under Regulation CC,[33] which provides:

> (a) Warranties. Each paying bank or returning bank that transfers a returned check and receives a settlement or other consideration for it warrants to the transferee returning bank, to any subsequent returning bank, to the depositary bank, and to the owner of the check, that —
>
> (1) The paying bank, or in the case of a check payable by a bank and payable through another bank, the bank by which the check is payable, returned the check within its deadline under the U.C.C. Regulation J (12 CFR part 210), or § 229.30(c) of this part;
>
> . . . .
>
> (d) Damages. Damages for breach of these warranties shall not exceed the consideration received by the bank that presents or transfers a check or returned check, plus interest compensation and expenses related to the check or returned check, if any.

12 C.F.R. § 229.34. The Commentary to Regulation CC, 12 C.F.R. pt. 229, app. E, indicates that the damages under § 229.34(d) are the warranty damages of U.C.C. § 4-207(c): "an amount equal to the loss suffered as a result of the breach . . . ." As discussed in the preceding section, First National's loss was not caused by Colonial's late return of the checks.

Despite its admitted lack of damages suffered as a result of the breach, First National contends that it may recover its attorneys fees under the provision of § 229.34(d) that allows recovery of "expenses." In Illinois, it is within the trial court's discretion to award attorney's fees as "expenses" under § 4-207(c). *Southern Provisions, Inc. v. Harris Trust & Sav. Bank*, 96 Ill. App. 3d 745, 422 N.E.2d 33, 35, 52 Ill. Dec. 352 (Ill. App. Ct. 1981). First National cites no case in which a court has ever awarded attorneys fees as "expenses" in the absence of actual damages. We cannot see why a litigant who cannot establish liability for breach of warranty because it has suffered no damages as a result of the breach should recover attorneys fees as expenses.

IV. Count IV: Breach of Duty of Ordinary Care Against Reserve Bank

Count VI: Breach of Contract Against Reserve Bank

Count VII: Breach of Contract Against Colonial

First National's remaining three counts are based upon the Reserve Bank's and Colonial's alleged failure to follow the terms of the dispute resolution procedures contained in the Reserve Bank's Operating Circular No. 4 ("OC-4"). First National alleges a breach of duty of ordinary care claim against the Reserve Bank, and a breach of contract claim against each of the defendants.

Circular OC-4 sets up the Reserve Bank's "Disputed Return Procedure." It provides that if a depositary bank believes that the paying bank has returned a check after the midnight deadline, the depositary bank may dispute the return by sending the Reserve Bank the returned check and a signed statement that the bank believes the paying bank did not return the check within the

---

[33] The claim against the Reserve Bank is brought through Regulation J, which provides:

> A Reserve Bank may be liable to the owner, to the sender, to a prior collecting bank, or to the depositary bank's customer with respect to a check as defined in 12 CFR 229.2(k). A Reserve Bank shall not have or assume any liability with respect to an item or its proceeds except for the Reserve Bank's own lack of good faith or failure to exercise ordinary care, except as provided in paragraph (b) of this section and except as provided in subpart C of part 229.

12 C.F.R. § 210.6(a)(1). This section incorporates by reference Regulation CC, including § 229.34.

midnight deadline. When the Reserve Bank receives the statement, it credits the amount of the returned check to the bank's account. It also charges the paying bank's account the amount of the check, and sends the returned check and statement to the paying bank. OC-4 P 48 (Pl. Ex. 38). Circular OC-4 further provides that the Reserve Bank will revoke the credit given to the disputing bank and recredit the paying bank if it receives a form from the paying bank that (i) states that the paying bank returned the check within the midnight deadline; and (ii) shows the banking day of receipt and the date of return, and "explains any difference in dates exceeding one banking day." *Id.* P 49.

First National contends that because the Response Forms submitted by Colonial did not contain a statement explaining why the differences in the date of receipt and the date of return exceeded one banking day, the Reserve Bank should not have processed them. But the Reserve Bank points to a provision of OC-4 which states that the Reserve Bank "assume[s] no responsibility for determining whether the paying bank returned the check within" the midnight deadline. *Id.* P 50. First National replies that this section does not absolve the Reserve Bank from following its own guidelines and ensuring that all response forms are properly and thoroughly completed. It points to an internal Reserve Bank memorandum that states:

> Reserve Banks will not examine the items in question, verify the accuracy of the information provided, or verify the statements of alleged facts to ascertain the validity of the claims in carrying out this procedure. However, the Reserve Banks should monitor the timeliness and completeness of these claim forms and respond to them within 5 business days.

Pl. Ex. 37. By accepting the Response Forms and reversing the debit to the Colonial account and the credit to the First National account, First National says the Reserve Bank caused it to suffer $1,523,892.49 in damages (plus interest and legal expenses). Because Colonial submitted the incomplete Response Forms, and the Reserve Bank processed those forms, First National seeks to hold them liable for violating OC-4.

But First National has cited no authority holding a bank liable under an operating circular on a negligence or breach of contract theory. And at least one court has concluded that operating circulars do not create any substantive rights. *Continental Ill. Nat'l Bank & Trust Co. v. Sterling Nat'l Bank & Trust Co.*, 565 F. Supp. 101, 103 (S.D.N.Y. 1983). We agree, and hold that First National may not bring either a negligence or breach of contract claim against either Colonial or the Reserve Bank for their alleged failures to follow the terms of OC-4.

CONCLUSION

For the reasons explained, plaintiff First National's motion for summary judgment is granted as to Count V of the first amended complaint and denied as to Counts I, II, III, IV, VI and VII. The Reserve Bank's motion for summary judgment is granted as to Counts II, IV and VI. Colonial's motion for summary judgment is granted as to Counts I, III and VII and denied as to Count V.

. . . .

COMMENT

The relationship between Reg CC and Article 4 is as complex as it is unsettled. Under the expedited availability rules, a depositary bank may be required to make funds available before a deposited item has been paid and the funds collected. Thus, it is possible for a depositary bank to be required to permit its customer to withdraw funds before the depositary bank receives notice of the payor bank's dishonor. As the *Colonial Bank* case notes, Reg CC provides that banks must "exercise ordinary care and act in good faith." A bank that violates these duties will be liable in damages to a depositary bank, the depositary bank's customer, or to any other party to the item. The measure of damages will be the amount of the loss, up to the amount of the check, reduced by the amount of loss that would have been suffered had the bank exercised ordinary care. In the case, First National's loss was not caused by Colonial's late return; thus, First National could not prevail on its damages claim for breach of ordinary care.

The Reg CC requirement of good faith is undefined; thus, its relationship to Article 4 is unclear. For Article 3 purposes, the Code defines good faith as honesty in fact and the observance of reasonable commercial standards of fair dealing. See U.C.C. § 3-103(a)(4). However, the general concept that presumably applies to Article 4 is found at §§ 1-201(19) and 1-203, which define good faith as "honesty in fact in the conduct or transaction concerned." The *Colonial* opinion notes that most courts have concluded that banks owe no good faith obligation to disclose a suspected kite or to refrain from attempting to shift the losses that result from a kite. Do you agree with the court's characterization? What definition would you apply to Reg CC?

[D] Warranties

Read: U.C.C. §§ 4-207, 4-208, 3-416, 3-417.

[1] Transfer and Presentment Warranties

The plaintiff in the *Colonial Bank* case also made an unsuccessful breach of warranty claim based on the deadlines warranty under Reg CC. Under 12 CFR § 229.34, every paying and returning bank that transfers a returned check and which receives settlement or other consideration for the item warrants the following matters to the bank's transferee, to any subsequent returning bank, to the depositary bank, and, to the owner of the item:

1. that the paying bank returned the item within the appropriate deadlines under Article 4, Regulation J, and Regulation CC;
2. that the paying or returning bank has authorization to return the check;
3. that the check has not been altered in any material way; and
4. that if the bank is returning a notice of return rather than the item itself, then the original item both has not and will not be returned.

Reg CC also contains a separate warranty of compliance with respect to expeditious return of an item under sections 229.30(a) and .31(a). All of the Reg CC warranties focus on transfers that occur after dishonor by a payor bank; as such, the warranties only address the return process. The warranties protect against unauthorized returns and subsequent alterations of an item that is being returned to the depositary bank.

Articles 3 and 4 of the U.C.C. contain two types of warranty provisions—transfer and presentment warranties. Warranty claims often arise when there has been some wrongdoing with respect to an item. For example, a drawee/payor that suffers a loss on an item (*e.g.*, when the drawee/payor recredits a drawer's account for an item improperly paid over a forged indorsement), can seek recovery from parties up the collection chain, presumably until liability reaches the wrongdoer. See U.C.C. §§ 3-416 and 4-207. Both section 3-416 and section 4-207 create five transfer warranties. Whenever an item is transferred, the transferor represents:

1) that as transferor, the person is someone entitled to enforce the instrument (*i.e.*, there are no unauthorized or missing indorsements that would prevent the transferor from making the transferee a person entitled to enforce the instrument);

2) that all signatures on the instrument are authentic and authorized;

3) that there are no alterations on the instrument;

4) that the instrument is not subject to a defense or claim in recoupment that could be asserted against the transferor; and,

5) that the transferor has no knowledge concerning potential difficulties that one might have in enforcing the instrument. Transferors also warrant that they have no knowledge of insolvency proceedings against an obligor on the item.

The same transfer warranties are also given by bank customers and collecting banks when an item is placed in the bank collection system. U.C.C. § 4-207. The only difference between the two sections concerns section 4-207(b) which provides that customers or collecting banks that transfer items, whether by indorsement or not, undertake to pay the item if it is dishonored. This obligation cannot be disclaimed. See Official Comment to section 4-207 and comment 5 to section 3-416.

Article 4 transfer warranties focus on the forward collection process and protect against actions of parties before an item is presented for payment. If there is an indorsement, the warranty runs with the instrument; thus, a remote holder may sue the transferror on the warranty directly. Because Article 4 envisions a mirror image process for the return of dishonored items (*i.e.*, a reverse of the forward collection system), the statute does not provide any additional warranty protection for dishonored items.

Under Reg CC, an item could be returned in a manner different from the forward collection process. In such an instance, banks handling the item for the first time would need protection. Thus, Reg CC also includes a warranty that the transferror who is returning an item has done so within Article 4's midnight deadline. Despite the different focus of the two provisions, damages under both Reg CC and Article 4 are limited to the losses suffered as a result of the breached warranty and cannot exceed the consideration received by the warrantor (the value of the item), plus expenses and loss of interest. In the *Colonial Bank* case, the court found First National's loss was caused by the kite and not by Colonial's late return of the checks.

Both Articles 3 and 4 also contain presentment warranties. See sections 3-417 and 4-208. Presentment warranties are narrower than transfer warranties. Subsection (a) states three warranties. The person obtaining payment or acceptance and a previous transferror warrant to the drawee/payor that: 1) the warrantor is a person entitled to enforce the item, 2) the item has not been altered; and 3) that the warrantor has no knowledge that the signature of the drawer is unauthorized. When making the warranty to an acceptor or payor, as opposed to a transferee, the transferor/warrantor limits the representation concerning signatures to the warrantor's knowledge, that is, the transferor has no knowledge of an unauthorized drawer's signature. This limited warranty continues the rule of *Price v. Neal* that a payor (or acceptor) who pays (or accepts an item) over a forged drawer's signature should not be able to recover that payment because the payor is in the best position to detect the forgery. The next two cases address warranties. Although the first case arose under the previous version of the U.C.C., the case provides a good illustration of the use of multiple theories for recovery in a bank collection matter. The resolution of the second case should remind you of the *Colonial Bank* case and the limitations involved with breach of warranty claims.

MATCO TOOLS CORP. v. PONTIAC STATE BANK

United States District Court, Eastern District of Michigan
614 F.Supp. 1059, 41 U.C.C. Rep. Serv. 883 (1985)

FREEMAN, DISTRICT JUDGE.

Matco Tools Corporation has brought this action against several defendants on various theories. In the portion of the lawsuit presently before the court, Matco, as the named payee on a negotiable instrument, seeks to recover the value of the instrument from Pontiac State Bank, as depository bank, under warranty and conversion theories, for accepting the instrument for deposit over an allegedly forged endorsement. Both parties have moved for summary judgment.

The material facts are largely undisputed. David Cox was a distributor of Matco Tools. Cox purchased the tools from Matco on credit and assigned to Matco a security interest in the tools and their proceeds. Cox did business under the assumed name of DMC Enterprises.

On August 16, 1980, Cox opened a commercial checking account at Pontiac State Bank under the name DMC Enterprises. At the time he opened the account, Cox presented Pontiac State Bank with a letter from Matco's Controller. That letter, on Matco Tools stationery, states:

To Whom It May Concern:

> In the normal course of business, an authorized Matco Tools Distributor, who is an independent businessman, will receive checks from his customers designating the payee as Matco, Matco Tools, Matco Man, Tool Man, etc. These checks are rightfully payable to the Distributor for amounts due him. We hereby authorize him to endorse these checks for deposit as the intended payee.
>
> Any questions regarding the above should be directed to my attention.

Very truly yours,
MATCO TOOLS CORPORATION
/s/
Dale Gillespie
Controller

Cox also obtained an endorsement stamp which states:

FOR DEPOSIT ONLY
Pay to the Order of
PONTIAC STATE BANK
MATCO TOOLS
DMC ENTERPRISES,
AUTHORIZED DISTRIBUTOR
3160-364-5

Pontiac State Bank provided Cox with deposit slips which stated "DMC Enterprises, authorized Matco Tool Distributor," and which were imprinted with the Matco Symbol.

In May 1983, a quantity of Cox's tools were stolen. Cox's insurer, The Travelers Indemnity Company, sent a settlement check in the amount of $24,960.71 to Cox. The check was payable to "David M. Cox and Matco Tools Corp." Cox endorsed the check with his own signature and the deposit stamp and deposited the check into the DMC Enterprises account at Pontiac State Bank. The money deposited was later withdrawn by Cox. Matco, named as a loss payee on the Travelers insurance policy, never received any proceeds from the insurance settlement.

Matco alleges that Cox forged Matco's endorsement on the check. Matco seeks to recover the value of the check from Pontiac State Bank under warranty and conversion theories. Matco contends that Pontiac State Bank is liable for breaching a warranty that all endorsements are authorized. U.C.C. §§ 3-417(2)(b), 4-207(2)(b) [Cf. Revised Code §§ 3-416(a)(2) & 4-207(a)(2)]. Matco also contends that Pontiac State Bank is liable for converting the check under U.C.C. § 3-419(1)(c) [Cf Revised § 3-420].

Warranty

The Uniform Commercial Code imposes certain implied warranties in connection with negotiable instruments. Matco relies upon the implied warranties imposed by § 3-41 7(2)(b) and § 4-207(2)(b). Section 3-41 7(2)(b) provides: . . . [the Court cites U.C.C. § 3-417(2)(b)].

Section 4-207(2)(b) provides: . . . [the Court cites U.C.C. § 4-207(2)(b)].

These sections have no application here. Pontiac State Bank was the depository bank in regard to the check from Travelers. Matco was one of two named payees on the check. Neither § 3-417 nor § 4-207 create any warranties which run expressly to a payee from a depository bank. The only case which addresses the issue holds that a payee may not maintain an action against the depository bank under either § 3-417 or § 4-207. No authority holds that a payee may maintain an action against a depository bank under these sections. This court will not so hold.

Since no implied warranties imposed by the U.C.C. run to Matco, Matco cannot maintain any breach of warranty action. For this reason, the court will grant Pontiac State Bank's motion for summary judgment as to plaintiff's breach of warranty claim.

Conversion

Both the Uniform Commercial Code and the common law of Michigan permit a direct action by a payee against a depository or collecting bank which forwarded an instrument bearing a forged endorsement for collection.

The relevant U.C.C. provision is § 3-419, which provides in pertinent part: . . . [the Court cites U.C.C. § 3-419(1)(c), (3)].

The first issue under this section is whether Pontiac State Bank paid the instrument over a forged endorsement. If so, the second issue is whether Pontiac State Bank is protected from liability by subsection (3) because it acted "in good faith and in accordance with the reasonable commercial standards."

A. Forged Endorsement

The parties seriously dispute whether any endorsement on the check can be considered "forged." Matco clearly gave Cox authority to endorse checks from customers. Travelers, however, was not a customer of Cox.

Section 3-401(2) provides: . . . [the Court cites U.C.C. § 3-401(2)].

Here, the check bore an endorsement stamp bearing the words "Matco Tools." This suffices as Matco's signature under § 3-401(2). Section 1-201(43) defines an unauthorized signature to mean "one made without actual, implied or apparent authority and includes a forgery." Conversely, a signature which is authorized is not a forgery. MCLA § 440.3404(1). It is clear that Cox had no express authority to endorse the check on behalf of Matco because Travelers, the drawer of the check, was not a customer of Cox.

Pontiac State Bank contends that it had no knowledge as to whether the Travelers check came from one of Cox's customers, that nothing on the face of the check put it on notice that Cox was acting beyond the scope of his authority, and that it had no duty to inquire into the underlying transaction. This argument appears relevant not to the issue of whether there was a forgery, but to the issue of whether Pontiac State Bank acted "in good faith and in accordance with the reasonable commercial standards." The court holds that Pontiac State Bank deposited the check in the account of DMC Enterprises over the unauthorized endorsement of Matco.

B. Good Faith/Reasonable Commercial Standards Defense

Pontiac State Bank raises the defense set forth in subsection (3) of § 3-419 and contends that it cannot be held liable because it no longer has any proceeds from the check in its possession and because it dealt with the check "in good faith and in accordance with the reasonable commercial standards." The threshold issue is whether Pontiac State, being the depository bank in the transaction, can assert the defense provided by § 3-419(3) [Cf. Revised § 3-420(c)]. Despite the unambiguous language of § 3-419(3), the caselaw interpreting the section constitutes one of the more bizarre chapters of the law of commercial paper.[34]

The precise language of § 3-419(3), though already quoted, bears repeating:

Subject to the provisions of this act concerning indorsements a representative, including a depository or collecting bank, who has in good faith and in accordance with the reasonable commercial standards applicable to the business of such representative dealt with an instrument or its proceeds on behalf of one who was not the true owner is not liable in conversion or otherwise to the true owner beyond the amount of any proceeds remaining in his hands.

Although this subsection appears to provide a defense to "a representative, including a depository or collecting bank," numerous courts have held that subsection (3) does not apply to suits by payees, such as Matco, against depository or collecting banks, such as Pontiac State

[34] According to Professors White and Summers, "[T]he courts have taken up § 3-419(3), and what they have done to it shouldn't happen to a dog." J. White & R. Summers, Uniform Commercial Code § 15-4, at 591 (2d ed. 1980).

Bank, for payment of checks bearing forged endorsements. There are two theories by which courts have reached this result.

One line of cases has held that a depository or collecting bank cannot be a "representative" within the meaning of this subsection. These courts have reasoned that § 4-201 makes a collecting bank an agent only of the owner of the instrument[35] and not of the forger/depositor; therefore, the bank is not acting as a representative when it deposits or pays an instrument over a forged endorsement. These courts have also relied upon the common law principle that a bank's agency status is brought to an end upon collection of the paper. This reasoning flies in the face of the language of subsection (3), which expressly provides that a representative can be a person (or bank) "who has . . . dealt with an instrument . . . on behalf [of] one who is not the true owner."

The second line of cases is equally doubtful. These courts have concluded that subsection (3) can never apply because the depository bank will always retain all the proceeds in its hands regardless of whether the forged instrument was cashed or deposited and then withdrawn. When a bank cashes a check, the reasoning goes, it pays out its own funds and retains the "proceeds" in its own hands. When the true owner brings an action against the depository bank to recover such proceeds, the owner ratifies the collection by the depository bank but does not ratify the payment of funds to the forger. Such reasoning defies common sense.

The Michigan Court of Appeals, in *Sheriff Goslin Co. v. Cawood*, 91 Mich. App. 204, 210 (1979), held that § 3-419(3) provides no defense for the depositor/ collecting bank in a suit by the owner of an instrument cashed or deposited over a forged endorsement. The court discussed the various theories by which other courts have reached the same result, but did not state which theory it was relying on. While recognizing that the body of caselaw discussed above has been criticized for its failure to follow the language of the statute, the court of appeals was persuaded by undeniably good policy reasons which support the result.

[T]he reasons which support [this body of caselaw] are clearly ascertainable. This case is a good example of the most important of these reasons. The bank here accepted for collection some 300 checks drawn by various entities on many different banks. If the payee cannot sue the depository bank directly it would be necessary to sue either the drawee bank under § 3-419(1)(c) or the drawer under § 3-804. Thus 300 lawsuits might be required where one will do under the prevailing construction of § 3-419(3). But, even then the matter would not be closed. When the drawee bank or drawer loses the suit to the payee, they in turn pass the loss to the first party to deal with the forger . . . under the warranty provisions of § 3-417.

More recent decisions from other states, however, cast doubt on the Michigan court's characterization of denial of the defense as the prevailing construction of § 3-419(3). Five more recent decisions, including three by state supreme courts hold that any construction of § 3-419(3) which denies its application to depository banks, while perhaps based on good policy reasons, violates the clear language of the section. [Citations]. The rationale of these decisions was succinctly stated by the New Jersey Supreme Court in *Knesz*:

> We are in consequence not persuaded that the underlying policy served by the common law — the recognition of a single direct action by an owner-payee against the depository or

[35] Section 4-201(1) provides in pertinent part:

> Unless a contrary intent clearly appears and prior to the time that a settlement given by a collecting bank for an item is or becomes final . . . the bank is an agent or sub-agent of the owner of the item and any settlement given for that item is provisional . . .

> collecting bank and the avoidance of circuitous or chain litigation—overrides the plain terms of § 3-419(3). That policy was undoubtedly known to the drafters of the Code. It was presumably within their contemplation when § 3-419(3) was inserted granting immunity to these banks. We are constrained to adhere to the choice made by the Legislation in its enactment. It has not been shown that this choice leads to intolerable or absurd results, a factor that would have given us pause in applying § 3-419(3) in accordance with its terms.
>
> It is possible that the burdensome circuitous litigation deplored by many commentators may be mitigated today. The "circuity argument" has been criticized as being exaggerated and inconsequential in the modern era of long-arm jurisdiction, negotiated settlements, and liberal rules of interpleader . . . . In addition, foreclosing a direct suit against a depository bank and, instead, forcing the payee to sue his drawer or the drawee bank preserves in some instances the timely presentation of appropriate defenses that would have been unavailable to a depository bank, such as that of the drawer's negligence in causing or detecting the forgery.

97 N.J. at -, 477 A.2d at 814 (citations omitted).

In this diversity action, the court is bound by the doctrine of *Erie R. Co. v. Tompkins*, 304 U.S. 64 (1938), to apply the law as announced by the Michigan Supreme Court. The court is not bound to apply a decision of the Michigan Court of Appeals if it determines that the Michigan Supreme Court would decide otherwise. The Michigan Supreme Court has not passed on the issue at bar. In view of the foregoing authority, this court is convinced that the Michigan Supreme Court would not follow the decision in *Sheriff Goslin*, but would hold that § 3-419(3) does provide a defense to a depository bank such as Pontiac State Bank. This court, therefore, holds that Pontiac State Bank can assert the good faith/reasonable commercial standards defense provided by § 3-419(3).

The next issue before the court is whether Pontiac State Bank, in accepting the check for deposit, acted "in good faith and in accordance with the reasonable commercial standards." MCLA § 440.3419(3). If Pontiac State Bank acted in good faith and in accordance with reasonable commercial standards, then Matco cannot recover against it on a conversion theory. In view of this court's rejection of the perpetually retained proceeds theory, there can be no dispute that Pontiac State Bank no longer has any of the proceeds of the check in its hands.

Good faith and adherence to reasonable commercial standards are separate elements of the defense provided by § 3-419(3). Good faith is defined in the Code as "honesty in fact in the conduct of the [sic; or] transaction concerned." MCLA § 440. 1201(19). Matco has not alleged that Pontiac State Bank failed to act in good faith, nor could the court so find since there is no evidence of dishonesty on the part of Pontiac State Bank. The only issue concerning the asserted defense, therefore, is whether Pontiac State Bank acted in accordance with reasonable commercial standards.

Matco, relying on the principle that it is usually not commercially reasonable for a bank to accept for deposit into an individual account a check naming a corporation as a payee, asks this court to take judicial notice that Pontiac State Bank did not act in accordance with reasonable commercial standards . . . . . These cases are distinguishable from the present case, however, in that they involved forgeries of the corporate payees" endorsements or endorsements by persons with no authority to endorse on behalf of the corporate payee. Here, Cox had authority to endorse some checks, *i.e.*, checks from customers, for deposit into the DMC Enterprises account. The court can locate no authority by which the court can determine as a matter of law the commercial reasonableness of Pontiac State Bank's conduct in this case.

It is undisputed that Cox had limited authority to endorse some checks payable to Matco and deposit them into the account of DMC Enterprises. It is also undisputed that the Travelers check was endorsed by Cox and stamped with the name of "Matco Tools/DMC Enterprises/Authorized Distributor." Although Cox only had authority to endorse checks payable to Matco if such checks were from customers, Pontiac State Bank's personnel were unaware of whether Travelers was a customer of Matco. They accepted the check for deposit without inquiring as to Cox's authority to endorse the Travelers check. The assistant manager of the Pontiac State Bank Walled Lake branch testified at her deposition that she believed acceptance of the check for deposit as endorsed was in accordance with reasonable commercial standards. (Cheryl Marotta dep. at 25-26).[36] The court holds that there is a genuine issue of fact as to whether Pontiac State Bank, in accepting the Travelers check for deposit, acted in accordance with reasonable commercial standards.

. . . .

Conclusion

For the reasons set forth herein, the motion for summary judgment of Pontiac State Bank will be granted in part and denied in part; the motion shall be granted as to Matco's warranty claim, but denied as to Matco's conversion claim. Matco's motion for summary judgment shall be denied. An appropriate order shall be submitted.

COUNTY OF PIERCE v. SUBURBAN BANK OF ELMHURST

U.S. District Court, N.D. Illinois, Eastern Division
815 F. Supp. 1124, 21 U.C.C.R.S. 2d 75 (1993)

Judge George M. Marovich

Memorandum Opinion and Order

The County of Pierce ("County") filed suit against the Suburban Bank of Elmhurst ("Bank") alleging breach of warranty of good title. The County claims damages of $77,147.11 as a result of the Bank's failure to obtain all endorsements on a warrant check issued by the County and deposited in an account with the Bank. The Bank moves for summary judgment claiming that the missing endorsement was not the cause of the County's loss. The Bank further claims that the County failed to give it timely notice of the missing endorsement. For the reasons set forth below, we grant the Bank's motion for summary judgment.

FACTS

The County entered into a contract for road improvements with Semia Construction Company ("Semia") on April 18, 1989. The contract was assigned to Henry Disharoon and Victor Lazzaroni on July 13, 1989. On August 14, 1989, the County issued a warrant check payable to "H.W. Disharoon & V. Lazzaroni & Semia Construction Co. Suburban Bank of Elmhurst." The County

[36] Matco makes much of the fact that manager of the Walled Lake branch testified that a teller can accept a check for deposit which is drawn on another bank without even checking to see if it is endorsed. (Christine Downing dep. at 6-7,10-11). The court finds this testimony to be largely irrelevant to the issue of whether Pontiac State acted reasonably in accepting the Travelers check for deposit; the Travelers check was endorsed, so the narrower issue is whether Pontiac State acted reasonably in failing to inquire into Cox's authority as to this particular check.

intended the check for direct deposit in the account number 4016994 of the Bank. Disharoon endorsed the instrument on his own behalf and on behalf of Semia and to be deposited in the designated account on August 24, 1989. The Bank deposited the check in the proper account — number 4106994. Lazzaroni did not endorse the instrument. Disharoon subsequently misappropriated the funds in the account and failed to pay the project creditors. The County paid the face amount of the instrument on August 29, 1989 through a clearinghouse financial institution. All warrant checks were processed electronically and were not reviewed by the County unless the warrant number, account number, and dollar amount were inconsistent. The County became aware of a problem with the check on May 9, 1990.

Although the funds were eventually diverted by Disharoon, the account was not completely depleted until the end of October, two months after the check was deposited. In September, 1989, the average account balance was $64,671.00, and on October 17, 1989, the account balance was $34,898.89. On October 31, 1989, all funds were withdrawn from the account. The County did not notify the Bank during this time that there were any problems with the account or the check.

The County did not make a claim or demand upon the Bank until the service of summons in this action on or about April 1, 1992. No claim has been made against the County by virtue of the missing endorsement.

. . . .

DISCUSSION

The County argues that the Bank violated the warranty of good title under § 4-207 of the Uniform Commercial Code by failing to obtain the endorsement of all payees on the check. 810 ILCS 5/4-207 (1992). Under § 4-207, a collecting bank warrants to a drawee bank that all endorsements on a check are valid. . . . A collecting bank which breaches the warranty is liable to a party which takes a check in good faith for damages suffered as a result of the breach. 810 ILCS 5/4-207(c) (1992). In addition, § 4-207(d) provides that a claimant must give the warrantor notice of a breach within 30 days after the claimant has reason to know of the breach. 810 ILCS 5/4-207(d) (1992).

Although the Bank's failure to obtain all endorsements on the check technically violates the warranty of good title under § 4-207, the County has not demonstrated that this failure was the cause of its damages. The check in question was deposited in account number 4016994 as intended by the County. Thus, the missing endorsement did not prevent the check from reaching the proper account. Unlike a situation in which a party endorsing a check improperly receives the funds from that check due to a bank's failure to check for proper endorsements, here, the Bank directed the funds to the proper account and once these funds were in the proper account, they were diverted. The County's damages are a result of Disharoon's misconduct rather than the Bank's failure to verify the endorsements.

A typical claim under § 4-207 is that of a payor bank which has paid a check, despite missing or false endorsements, against the collecting bank which failed to verify the endorsements . . . . Although the check had been issued to two payees, the collecting bank allowed one of the payees to deposit the check in its account with only the typewritten endorsement of the second payee. *Id.* The payor bank subsequently credited the account of the drawer, who issued a second check to the original payees. *Id.* at 450. The court held that the collecting bank was liable to the payor bank for breach of its duty under § 4-207. *Id.* at 454.

The present case differs from *First Nat'l Bank* and other cases brought under § 4-207 in one important respect. In the present case, the County admits that it designated its check for direct deposit in account number 4016994 at the Bank. Despite the Bank's technical violation in failing to obtain all endorsements, the check was deposited in the designated account. In *First Nat'l Bank*, one payee was permitted to deposit the check into its account to the detriment of the other payee. As a result, the drawee was forced to issue a second check to both payees and the payor bank was forced to reimburse the drawee for the first check.

In the present case, on the other hand, the check reached the very account for which it was designated by the County. The payee whose endorsement was absent from the check, Lazzaroni, has made no claim against the County as a result of the deposit of the check without his endorsement. The Bank's error in this case did not cause the proceeds of the check to be deposited in the wrong account. The County's loss was caused by Disharoon's misconduct after the check was deposited in the appropriate account.

When the lack of a payee's endorsement has caused no damage to the payee, drawer, or drawee, the collecting bank is not liable for damages for failing to obtain an endorsement. *Security Trust and Savings Bank v. Federal Reserve Bank*, 269 F. Supp. 893, 896 (D. Mont. 1967). The County is not automatically entitled to damages equal to the face amount of the check, rather it must show that it actually incurred damages in that amount as a result of the Bank's actions. See *Maier-Lavaty Co. v. Aetna State Bank*, 247 Ill. App. 419 (1928) (stating that the measure of the plaintiff's damages is the loss occasioned by the improper conduct of the defendant). In the present case, the Bank's technical violation of § 4-207 did not cause the plaintiff's damages. The plaintiff is therefore not entitled to collect the amount of the check from the Bank.

Because the County's claim under § 4-207 is not valid, it is unnecessary to address whether the County failed to give the Bank timely notice of the missing endorsement under § 4-207(d). It is worth noting, however, that the County did not notify the Bank of a problem with the check until over two and a half years after the check was deposited. Although a drawee bank generally has no duty to verify endorsements, *Federal Deposit Ins. Corp. v. Marine Nat'l Bank*, 303 F. Supp. 401, 403 (M.D. Fla. 1969), a party which issues and approves checks for payment should be held responsible for giving notice of a problem with one of its checks. See *Great American Ins. Cos. v. American State Bank*, 385 N.W.2d 460, 465-66 (N.D. 1986) (stating that, when a party is both the drawer and the drawee of a check, "both logic and equity militate in favor of imposing primary responsibility to check the very draft which it issued in the first place to the forger").

If the County had notified the Bank of a problem with the check within two months after the date of deposit, the Bank would have been able to substantially reduce or prevent the damages altogether. The County admits that it became aware of a problem with the check on May 9, 1990, but it did not notify the Bank until almost two years later when it filed this suit. Although the Bank may no longer have been able to mitigate damages at this time, the County was clearly remiss in its obligation to give the Bank immediate notice of a problem.

CONCLUSION

For the foregoing reasons, the Bank's motion for summary judgment is granted.

PROBLEM 14.2

On March 16, Mark Smith Cycles, Inc. ("Mark Smith") issued a check to Rick Case Motors ("Rick Case") in the amount of $50,000. Rick Case deposited the check into its account held with Bank One, Akron, N.A. ("Bank One"). Bank One then encoded the check with Magnetic Ink Character Recognition numerals ("MICR") in the amount of $5,000 instead of $50,000. MICR allows computers to mechanically read the check during the collection process.

Bank One credited Rick Case's account $5,000 and processed the check through the Cleveland Clearing House to the drawee bank, National City Bank ("NCB"). NCB's computers read the MICR and paid the check in the amount of $5,000. NCB subsequently posted the check to Mark Smith's account and debited the account $5,000.

Rick Case subsequently realized that there had been an error in the crediting of Rick Case's account and notified Bank One. Bank One then attempted to collect the $45,000 from Mark Smith's account at NCB. NCB refused to pay the remaining $45,000, because Mark Smith had previously filed a petition in bankruptcy and there were insufficient funds in the account. NCB had previously set off the amount in Mark Smith's account to satisfy an outstanding debt Mark Smith owed to NCB.

Bank One then credited Rick Case's account in the amount of $45,000 and brought this action to recover $45,000 from NCB. NCB filed a subsequent answer and counterclaim. The case was submitted to a referee on stipulated facts and evidence. The referee recommended that the trial court find in favor of Bank One and grant damages in the amount of $45,000 and costs. However, the trial court rejected the referee's report and found in favor of NCB. Bank One now appeals. What result? *See* revised U.C.C. § 4-209. (*See Bank One, Akron, N.A. v. National City Bank*, 583 N.E.2d 439 (Ohio App. 1990)).

---

[2] Encoding and Retention Warranties

Read: U.C.C. § 4-209

As the above problem indicates, there is a third type of warranty under Article 4—the encoding provisions of section 4-209. Professors White and Summers introduce the topic of encoding and retention warranties by noting that "[a]lmost always the collecting bank is the Pontius Pilate of a final payment suit; it can disclaim all responsibility. . . . Now new technologies have brought additional burdens to collecting banks." White & Summers, Uniform Commercial Code, 4th ed., § 17-6, p. 649 (1995). They are referring to the problem of misencoding the amount of an item on the Magnetic Ink Character Recognition (MICR) line.

To process the number of checks presented more efficiently, banks have adopted the practice of encoding the amount of a check on the bottom of the item. The MICR encoded information permits high-speed check sorting machines to identify the amount of a check, the Federal Reserve zone of the payor, and of course, both the payor bank and the bank customer's account. Encoding can be done by the depositary bank or by that bank's customers if they are payees of a large volume of checks (a utility company for example). Section 4-209 provides that any party who encodes information on an item after issue warrants to any subsequent collecting bank and to the payor that the information is encoded correctly. Even if the customer of a depositary bank encodes the information, § 4-209(a) requires that the bank also makes the warranty. Because encoding warranties are unique to the bank collection process, the provisions in section 4-209 have no counterpart in Article 3. A MICR encoding error by either the depositary bank or its customer might result in a $2500 check being encoded for $25,000. Because checks are most often paid by automated means according to the MICR encoding, the payor ends up paying $22,500 more than the payor can charge against the drawer's account (a properly payable amount of only $2500). In such a case, section 4-209 gives the payor a warranty claim of recourse against the encoding party, an option that might well be more appealing than the payor's pursuit of the payee as a prerequisite. It should also be noted that the reverse is also true. Thus, if a $25,000 item were encoded for $2500, and the payor could not recover by debiting the drawer's account, section 4-209 allows the payor to proceed against the party that made the encoding error.

New statutory provisions always provide interesting opportunities to construe the meaning of the statute. The next case provides one brief example.

FRANCE v. FORD MOTOR CREDIT COMPANY

Supreme Court of Arkansas
323 Ark. 167, 913 S.W.2d 770 (1996)

NEWBERN, JUSTICE.

This is a replevin case. The appellant, Harold L. France, bought a used tractor and entered an installment contract to pay the appellee, Ford Motor Credit Company (Ford Credit), for it. Mr. France tried on two occasions to prepay the full obligation, as permitted by the contract, by personal check. Because of errors which occurred in the encoding of the first check and in drawing the second one Mr. France's account was debited for only small portions of the amount due. Mr. France thereafter refused to pay the balance. Ford Credit sought to replevy the tractor. Mr. France claimed, and argues on appeal, that the obligation was "suspended" according to Ark.Code Ann. § 4-3-310 (Repl.1991) and, therefore, Ford Credit was not entitled to replevin. Mr. France also contended, and now argues, that Ford Credit's remedy is against its agent which made the encoding error and not against Mr. France. The Trial Court held replevin was proper, and we affirm.

The purchase price of the tractor was $10,035. Mr. France paid $2,000 down. The amount that remained, including finance charges, was $9,845.76. Mr. France was to make 47 monthly payments of $205.12 beginning on September 23, 1993.

Prior to the date that the first installment was due, Mr. France elected to pay the balance in full. After deducting items such as unearned interest and insurance cancellation rebate, the outstanding balance was $8,506.19. On August 11, 1993, Mr. France's spouse Connie S. France, an attorney, drew check # 2224 on their joint account at the Bank of Eureka Springs to the order of Ford Credit for that amount. As directed by the contract, the check was sent to a Dallas, Texas, address.

The address was that of a box monitored by Mellon Financial Services (Mellon). Under agreement with Ford Credit, Mellon encoded the amount of the check, using magnetic ink, in the lower right-hand corner and forwarded it to Ford Credit's depositary bank in Dallas, Texas Commerce Bank. The encoding was done incorrectly in the amount of $506.19 rather than $8,506.19 The magnetic ink encoding enables the next bank in the chain of collection to process the check mechanically.

Texas Commerce Bank processed the check mechanically, crediting Mr. France with $506.19. Mr. France's check was then forwarded to the Bank of Eureka Springs, the bank upon which it was drawn. The Bank of Eureka Springs debited the France account $506.19.

The encoding error was discovered, and on September 13, 1993, Ms. France attempted to draw a second check, # 2313, for the remaining $8,000 balance. In the place on the check where the amount is shown numerically, the figure "$8,000.00"' appeared; however, on the line where the amount is written out Ms. France wrote "Eight dollars and 00/100."

Check # 2313 was sent through the same channels as the previous check. Mellon made another error and encoded the check, not for $8,000 or for $8, but for $800. These words appear to have been stamped on the front of the check: "AMOUNT GUARANTEED TO BE," and immediately below appears the handwritten figure "8,000."

Texas Commerce Bank credited $800 to the France account with Ford Credit and sent # 2313 on to the Bank of Eureka Springs. As words prevail over numbers, Ark.Code Ann. § 4-3-114 (Repl.1991), the Bank of Eureka Springs debited the France account $8.00, and notified Texas Commerce Bank which reversed the $800.00 credit and substituted $8.00. Ford Credit thus was paid $8.00. Mr. France's account has been charged, and Ford Credit has received, a total of $514.19, leaving a balance of $7992. Ford Credit filed its complaint for replevin of the tractor on October 12, 1994. The "guarantee" was apparently ignored in the collection process.

1. Replevin

Section 4-3-310 deals with the effect of an uncertified check issued in payment of an underlying obligation such as the contract in this case. The statute, in pertinent part, provides:

4-3-310. Effect of instrument on obligation for which taken.

(a) Unless otherwise agreed, if a certified check, cashier's check, or teller's check is taken for an obligation, the obligation is discharged to the same extent discharge would result if an amount of money equal to the amount of the instrument were taken in payment of the obligation. Discharge of the obligation does not affect any liability that the obligor may have as an indorser of the instrument.

(b) Unless otherwise agreed and except as provided in subsection (a), if a note or an uncertified check is taken for an obligation, the obligation is suspended to the same extent the obligation would be discharged if an amount of money equal to the amount of the instrument were taken, and the following rules apply:

(1) In the case of an uncertified check, suspension of the obligation continues until dishonor of the check or until it is paid or certified. Payment or certification of the check results in discharge of the obligation to the extent of the amount of the check.

. . . .

As Mr. France does not contend his obligation has been discharged, the first sentence of § 4-3-310 providing for "suspension of the obligation" is all that is at issue. We have found no case or other authority which addresses the facts presented here, but the language of the statute leaves us with little doubt as to the proper resolution of this case. It does no more than recognize the uncertainty attendant upon an uncertified and unpaid check and suspends the obligation until that uncertainty is resolved. *See Cornwell v. Bank of America Nat. Trust and Sav. Ass'n*, 224 Cal.App.3d 995, 274 Cal.Rptr. 322 (1990). In this case, the two checks submitted to Ford Credit have been paid, but in amounts less than the amount owed. The suspense is over, and all are aware of the amount of Mr. France's obligation to Ford Credit which has yet to be satisfied. In this case, the statute provides no defense to the replevin action.

2. Other remedies

Mr. France contends Ark.Code Ann. § 4-4-209 (Repl.1991) provides Ford Credit a remedy against Mellon which should have been pursued rather than the replevin action against him. Section 4-4-209 provides:

> Encoding and retention warranties.
>
> (a) A person who encodes information on or with respect to an item after issue warrants to any subsequent collecting bank and to the payor bank or other payor that the information is correctly encoded. If the customer of a depositary bank encodes, that bank also makes the warranty.
>
> . . . .
>
> (c) A person to whom warranties are made under this section and who took the item in good faith may recover from the warrantor as damages for breach of warranty an amount equal to the loss suffered as a result of the breach, plus expenses and loss of interest incurred as a result of the breach. The statute provides warranties to collecting banks and payors but not to a payee such as Ford Credit.

The record does not show how the "guarantee" appeared on the check or who placed it there. Mr. France's argument assumes it to have been stamped and written on the check by Mellon and thus that it could have formed the basis of recovery by Ford Credit against Mellon. Nothing in the record suggests that Mr. France in any way guaranteed the check to be for $8,000 or was asked by Mellon or any other bank in the collection chain to do so. No authority whatever is cited for the contention that the "guarantee" limited Ford Credit's remedies against Mr. France. Nor does he cite any authority or render convincing argument that the "guarantee" resolved the conflict between the written and figure amounts on the check. Certainly the Bank of Eureka Springs and Texas Commerce Bank did not consider it to have had any effect. Absent any citation of authority or convincing argument, we decline to consider the argument. *Neal v. Wilson*, 321 Ark. 70, 900 S.W.2d 177 (1995).

Affirmed.

NOTE

RETENTION WARRANTY

Article 4 authorizes electronic presentment (§ 4-110). To effect such a presentment, item truncation will occur at some point. Section 4-209(b) recognizes the possibility of truncation and outlines a new retention warranty which provides that any party who retains an item under a truncation arrangement (either by sorting or destroying the item), warrants to subsequent banks that the truncation is in compliance with the terms of the applicable truncation agreement. Section 4-209 represents an important step in increasing the responsibilities of depositary banks in the collection process.

[E] Finality of Payment—Mistake and Restitution

Read: U.C.C. §§ 3-418 and 4-215.

Where a drawee-bank pays a check over the forged signature of the drawer, or in a situation where a payee's endorsement is forged, or where the check has been altered, the drawee-payor bank is not entitled to debit the drawer's account, absent a showing that the drawer's negligence contributed to the forgery or alteration. The question remains to what extent can a drawee-payor recover payment. In those cases where the person receiving payment is the forger, there is, of course, no problem. But what happens where the payor seeks recovery from the depositary bank? Because it is highly desirable to end a transaction on an instrument when that item is paid or accepted, both the common law of commercial paper and the Code recognized payment as final in favor of a holder in due course or a person who changed position in good faith reliance on acceptance or payment of the instrument. Section 3-418(c). Rather than reopen a matter and upset a series of commercial transactions when an objection to payment subsequently arose, the Code closed the door on the issue of payment. Claimants continued to have warranty cause of actions based on sections 3-417 and 4-208.

In *Price v. Neal*,[37] a drawee-payor sued to recover payments made over the drawer's forged signature on two bills of exchange, one of which the plaintiff payor had accepted. The theory of the action was recovery of money paid under mistake of fact to prevent unjust enrichment. In holding for the defendant, Lord Mansfield wrote:

Here was no fraud: no wrong. It was incumbent upon the plaintiff; to be satisfied "that the bill drawn upon him was the drawer's hand," before he accepted or paid it, but it was not incumbent upon the defendant, to inquire into it. Here was notice given by the defendant to the plaintiff of a bill drawn upon him: and he sends his servant to pay it and take it up. The other bill, he actually accepts; after which acceptance, the defendant innocently and bona fide discounts it. The plaintiff lies by, for a considerable time after he has paid these bills; and then found out "that they were forged" : and the forger comes to be hanged. He made no objection to them,

---

[37] 97 Eng. Rep. 871 (K.B. 1762).

at the time of paying them. Whatever neglect there was, was on his side. The defendant had actual encouragement from the plaintiff himself, for negotiating the second bill, from the plaintiff's having without any scruple or hesitation paid the first: and he paid the whole value, bona fide. It is a misfortune which has happened without the defendant's fault or neglect. If there was no neglect in the plaintiff, yet there is no reason to throw off the loss from one innocent man upon another innocent man: but, in this case, if there was any fault or negligence in any one, it certainly was in the plaintiff; and not in the defendant. There are only a handful of transactions that fall outside the *Price v. Neal* finality of payment rule. Subsection (a) to 3-418 recognizes, as an exception to *Price v. Neal*, payments by mistake. The subsection allows restitution where a drawee/payor acts on a mistaken belief that an item was not forged or payment had been stopped. The drawee/payor will be entitled to recover the funds paid or to revoke an acceptance regardless of the bank's negligence so long as the defendant is not one who either changed position in good faith reliance on the payment, or, who took the item as a holder in due course.

Comment 3 to section 3-418 provides:

> Subsection (b) covers cases of payment or acceptance by mistake that are not covered by subsection (a). It directs courts to deal with those cases under the law governing mistake and restitution. Perhaps the most important class of cases that falls under subsection (b), because it is not covered by subsection (a), is that of payment by the drawee bank of a check with respect to which the bank has no duty to the drawer to pay either because the drawer has no account with the bank or because available funds in the drawer's account are not sufficient to cover the amount of the check. With respect to such a case, under Restatement of Restitution § 29, if the bank paid because of a mistaken belief that there were funds available in the drawer's account sufficient to cover the amount of the check, the bank is entitled to restitution.

NATIONAL SAVINGS AND TRUST CO. v. PARK CORPORATION

United States Court of Appeals
722 F.2d 1303 (6th Cir. 1983)

BOYCE F. MARTIN, JR., CIRCUIT JUDGE.

In this diversity action, National Savings and Trust challenges the summary denial of its claim for restitution of $74,737.25 it mistakenly paid to Park Corporation on a bad check.

On January 8, 1980, Park Corporation contracted to sell some used mining equipment to DAI International Investment Corporation. The sales agent for the transaction was Garland Caribbean Corporation. As part of its down payment, DAI gave Garland a check for $ 75,000 drawn on its account with the plaintiff, National Savings and Trust Company. On January 16, Garland called National Savings to determine if DAI had sufficient funds in its account to cover this check. The bank said DAI did not. That same day, Garland endorsed the check over to Park Corporation. Park Corporation then sent the check to National Savings "for collection."

On January 22, Garland once again called the bank to determine if DAI had sufficient funds in its account to cover the check. Once again, the bank said DAI did not.[38] Moreover, on this

[38] There is no evidence Park was ever aware of Garland's phone conversations with the bank.

occasion, the banking employee who received the inquiry went to the bank's "platform officer" and notified him not to accept any DAI checks drawn on insufficient funds. Unfortunately for the bank, the platform officer only saw checks arriving through normal banking channels and not those coming in "for collection."

DAI's check arrived at the bank that same day. However, the employee who normally processed "for collection" checks was scheduled to work in another department that day. Prior to her departure, she did manage to open the incoming mail, including the DAI check. Her supervisor then volunteered to help out by taking the DAI check to the wire room for payment. Neither employee followed the bank's standard procedure and checked DAI's account to ensure that it held sufficient funds to cover the check. Each assumed that the other had done so. As a result, the check was paid even though DAI had only $ 263.75 in its account.

On January 28, 1980, after discovering its mistake, National Savings asked Park Corporation to return the $ 75,000. Park refused and National Savings subsequently brought this lawsuit. On motion for summary judgment by the defendant, the court found for Park on the grounds that National Savings had made an improvident extension of credit and that the bank was in a better position to know the true facts and to guard against mistakes. We disagree.

The basic law of restitution in Ohio, the state whose law controls, is summarized in *Firestone Rubber & Tire Co. v. Central Nat'l Bank of Cleveland*, 159 Ohio St. 423, 112 N.E.2d 636 (1953). The Firestone case held that money paid to another by mistake is recoverable unless the other person has changed his position in reliance on the payment. This rule applies even if the mistake was the result of negligence.

Park Corporation attempts to circumvent the holding in *Firestone* by arguing that banks are not protected by normal restitutionary principles when they pay an insufficient funds (NSF) check. There is some support for this position. *See, e.g., Spokane & Eastern Trust Co. v. Huff*, 63 Wash. 225, 115 P. 80 (1911); 7 Zollman, The Law of Banks and Banking @ 5062 (1936). Nonetheless, this rule has not been universally applied, *see, e.g., Manufacturers Trust Co. v. Diamond*, 17 Misc. 2d 909, 186 N.Y.S.2d 917, 919 (1959), and Park has not cited, nor have we been able to find, any Ohio cases adopting this rule. Moreover, it is questionable whether such a doctrine, if ever in existence, would survive the subsequent enactment of the Uniform Commercial Code in Ohio and the particular provisions applicable to the facts of the present case.

Park Corporation next argues that Firestone does not control because National Savings' payment was not a mistake but rather a knowing extension of credit. Park relies heavily on the New Jersey case of *Demos v. Lyons*, 151 N.J. Super. 489, 376 A.2d 1352 (Law Div.1977). The factual circumstances of *Demos*, however, are quite distinct from the present case. In *Demos*, the bank actually examined the customer's account, realized the customer had insufficient funds to cover the check, yet paid the check anyway. The bank did not want to embarrass its customer and it hoped that he had made a late deposit to cover the check which would appear on the next day's balance sheet. No such deposit was ever made. In our case, National Savings never intended to make good on an NSF check. The platform officer had been notified not to pay out on DAI's check. The "for collection" employees were operating under standing orders to check balances before paying a check and never to pay on an NSF check. Despite all these precautions, the check was paid. At no time, however, did the employees making the payment decision know that DAI's account had insufficient funds to cover the check.

Park's next contention is that the Uniform Commercial Code as adopted in Ohio bars restitutionary recovery for banks that pay NSF checks. This argument focuses on an apparent conflict between two provisions of the U.C.C., section 3-418 and section 4-213 [Revised § 4-215]. Section 3-418 of the Code (O.R.C. § 1303.54), which applies to all transactions involving negotiable instruments, states that "payment or acceptance of any instrument is final in favor of a holder in due course, or a person who has in good faith changed his position in reliance on the payment."[39] Because a holder in due course is simply a special type of detrimental relier, this section is basically a codification of restitutionary principles established in *Firestone*. Official Comment 3 to this section makes clear that if there is no detrimental reliance by the payee, then recovery of payment is permitted.

Park Corporation argues that another provision of the U.C.C., section 4-213 [Revised § 4-215], establishes a special non-recovery rule for banks which mistakenly pay on a bad check. Section 4-213(1) (O.R.C. § 1304.19(A)) states that "an item is finally paid by a payor bank when the bank has done any of the following, which ever happens first: (a) paid the item in cash . . . ." Cf. [Revised § 4-215]. Park contends that "finally paid" as used in this section has the same meaning as the "payment is final" language in section 3-418, namely restitutionary recovery is no longer possible. Moreover, because section 4-213 does not have the restrictive provisions which limit coverage to holders in due course or those who detrimentally rely, Park argues that section 4-213 makes a bank strictly liable as soon as it pays on an NSF check. Furthermore, U.C.C. § 4-102 provides that, in case of conflict between Articles 3 and 4, the provisions of Article 4 are to govern. Thus, Park argues, National Savings is barred from recovering the $75,000.

At first glance, Park's argument has a certain appeal. That is not surprising because it is based in large part on the work of White & Summers, whose treatise, . . . is generally considered the leading authority on commercial transactions. . . . Several courts have also reached the same conclusion. [Citations].

Nonetheless, opinion on the matter is by no means uniform. Other writers, see H. Bailey, Brady on Bank Checks § 14.20 at 14-32 (5th ed Supp. 1983); B. Clark, The Law of Check Deposits § 5.3[3] (2d ed. 1981), and other courts, [Citations], have argued that banks retain their restitutionary rights with respect to mistaken payment of NSF checks. Our own analysis of the Code convinces us that the latter group is correct and that section 4-213 does not expand the final payment doctrine to bar recovery by payor banks from payees who have not detrimentally relied. In our analysis, we rely heavily on the official Comments to sections 3-418 and 4-213. While these comments to the Code are not part of enacted law, they are a very helpful guide to construing the meaning of Code provisions. *See In re Augustin Bros. Co.*, 460 F.2d 376, 380 (8th Cir.1972).

An examination of the comments to section 3-418 makes clear both that this section was intended to apply to "the payment of overdrafts, or any other payment made in error as to the state of the drawer's account," Comment 2, and that restitutionary recovery was to be denied only when the payee had relied on the payment. "If no value has been given for the instrument, the holder loses nothing by the recovery of the payment, . . . and it is not entitled to profit at the expense of the drawee . . . ." Comment 3.

The only mention of section 4-213 occurs in Comment 5, where the Code drafters point out that the provisions of section 3-418 do not apply until payment is final as defined in section

---

39 Section 3-418 also has special exceptions not applicable here which allow banks and other acceptors and payors to recover where a check has a forged endorsement.

4-213. This comment suggests a method for resolving the apparent conflict between section 3-418 and 4-213. As the court in *Demos v. Lyons* put it, section 4-213 "is oriented toward time of payment, not legal effect of payment." 376 A.2d at 1356. The purpose of section 4-213 is "to determine when settlement for an item or other action with respect to it constitutes final payment." Comment 1, § 4-213 Section 4-213 determines when the final payment rule of section 3-418 comes into effect, not what that rule is supposed to mean. Further support for this position comes from the remaining comments to section 4-213. Comment 1 states "final payment is important" because it helps determine "priorities between items and notices, stop orders, legal process and setoffs, [because it] is the end of the line in the collection process, [and because it] is the point at which many provisional settlements become final." The remaining comments discuss such arcane banking matters as posting, provisional settlements, and midnight deadlines. At no point does any comment to section 4-213 mention the effect this section is supposed to have on the restitutionary rights of banks. Thus, it seems evident that the drafters of the Code never intended for section 4-213 to supersede section 3-418, and we can see no reason to adopt a position contrary to that intent.

As further support for our decision, we feel obliged to note that White & Summers, the authorities most relied on for the contrary proposition, now appear to have changed their minds. Professor White, in a note written for a colleague's textbook, has recanted and now supports the view that section 4-213 makes no substantive change in the law of restitution as applied to banks. See D. Epstein & J. Martin, Basic Uniform Commercial Code 514 (2d ed. 1983). Presumably the next edition of his treatise will reflect this change in thinking.

Park Corporation next contends that, even if section 3-418 controls, it is both a holder in due course and one who has changed its position in reliance on National Saving's payment and therefore should be allowed to retain the $ 75,000. We find no support in the record for either proposition. On the holder in due course issue, Park does not qualify because it did not give value for the check. It was still in possession of the machinery it had contracted to sell to DAI. Although it had promised to deliver the equipment to DAI, such an executory promise does not constitute value. U.C.C. § 3-303, Comment 3. Park Corporation is, of course, no longer required to carry out its promise because DAI has breached its agreement to pay.

As for detrimental reliance, Park contends that it paid $ 37,500 as a commission to Garland Corporation on the assumption that DAI's check was good. However, Park did not pay Garland until February 13, 1980, two weeks after National Savings had informed Park that it had paid the DAI check by mistake and that it wanted Park to return the money. Section 3-418 only makes payment by the bank Final in favor of someone who has "in good faith changed his position in reliance on the payment." Once aware of the insufficiency in funds, Park could not have "in good faith" paid Garland $ 37,500 in reliance on that check. Park also alleges it paid rent for storing the equipment and painted the equipment in reliance on the payment. There is no evidence to support these allegations.

Accordingly, the decision of the district court is reversed.

NOTE

The *Park Corporation* reasoning has been noted specifically in comment 4 to Revised 3-418. The next excerpt presents the remainder of the *Colonial Bank* case discussed previously in this Chapter. Note the court's curt address to Colonial's 3-418 argument.

FIRST NATIONAL BANK IN HARVEY v. COLONIAL BANK

United States District Court, Illinois, Northern District
898 F. Supp. 1120 (N.D. Ill. 1995)

Grady, J.

. . . .

C. Mistake and Restitution

The revised U.C.C. § 3-418 sets out rules governing restitution in the event a bank mistakenly pays a negotiable instrument. Colonial argues that the provisions of § 3-418 apply to it and override § 4-302 accountability. Section 3-418 provides:

> (a) Except as provided in subsection (c), if the drawee of a draft pays or accepts the draft and the drawee acted on the mistaken belief that (i) payment of the draft had not been stopped under Section 4-403 or (ii) the signature of the drawer of the draft was authorized, the drawee may recover the amount of the draft from the person to whom or for whose benefit payment was made or, in the case of acceptance, may revoke the acceptance. Rights of the drawee under this subsection are not affected by failure of the drawee to exercise ordinary care in paying or accepting the draft.
>
> (b) Except as provided in subsection (c), if an instrument has been paid or accepted by mistake and the case is not covered by subsection (a), the person paying or accepting may, to the extent permitted by law governing mistake and restitution, (i) recover the payment from the person to whom or for whose benefit payment was made or (ii) in the case of acceptance, may revoke the acceptance.
>
> (c) The remedies provided in subsection (a) or (b) may not be asserted against a person who took the instrument in good faith and for value or who in good faith changed position in reliance on the payment or acceptance.

§ 3-418. There was some doubt before the revision to Article 3 whether this restitution provision overrode the accountability provisions of Article 4, that is, whether a payor bank could recover for a mistaken payment even after passage of the midnight deadline. Compare *National Sav. & Trust Co. v. Park Corp.*, 722 F.2d 1303 (6th Cir. 1983) (holding that restitution for mistaken payment is available to bank that holds checks beyond midnight deadline), cert. denied, 466 U.S. 939, 80 L. Ed. 2d 464, 104 S. Ct. 1916 (1984), with *Northwestern Nat'l Ins. Co. v. Midland*

Nat'l Bank, 96 Wis. 2d 155, 292 N.W.2d 591 (Wis. 1980) (holding that restitution for mistaken payment is not available to bank that holds check beyond the midnight deadline); *State & Sav. Bank v. Meeker*, 469 N.E.2d 55 (Ind. Ct. App. 1984) (same). Official Comment 4 to the revised § 3-418 makes it clear that the right of a drawee to recover a mistaken payment is not affected by the Article 4 rules that determine when an item is finally paid. § 3-418 Official Comment 4. Therefore, Colonial's retention of the Colonial checks beyond the midnight deadline is no bar to its ability to recover a mistaken payment.

Subsection (c) of § 3-418 provides that a drawee cannot seek restitution against a person who took the check in good faith and for value or who in good faith relied on payment. In a check kiting scheme, does a depositary bank that suspects a kite take payment of checks in good faith and for value? The drafters of the revised § 3-418 take no position on this question:

> In some cases, however, it may not be clear whether a drawee bank should have a right of restitution. For example, a check-kiting scheme may involve a large number of checks drawn on a number of different banks in which the drawer's credit balances are based on uncollected funds represented by fraudulently drawn checks. No attempt is made in Section 3-418 to state rules for determining the conflicting claims of the various banks that may be victimized by such a scheme. Rather, such cases are better resolved on the basis of general principles of law and the particular facts presented in the litigation.

§ 3-418 Official Comment 3.

In order for Colonial to seek refuge under the restitution principles of the revised § 3-418, two questions must be answered. First, was Colonial's payment of the Colonial checks a payment by mistake under subsection (a) or (b)? Second, if payment was by mistake, did First National take the Colonial checks in good faith and for value, or rely on payment, so as to defeat Colonial's restitution claim as provided in subsection (c)?

Subsection (a) only applies to mistaken payments on forged checks and checks on which the drawer has stopped payment, so it has no application here. Subsection (b) is a catchall, allowing restitution where "an instrument has been paid or accepted by mistake and the case is not covered by subsection (a)." § 3-418(b). Was Colonial's retention of the Colonial checks beyond the midnight deadline payment by mistake?

Several commentators take the position that a losing bank in a check kite has made a conscious extension of unsecured credit to its customer, and has not made a "mistaken payment" under § 3-418. "The decision to allow a customer to draw against uncollected funds is basically a credit decision." Clark, *supra*, P 5.03[5]. Professors White and Summers agree:[40]

> In these cases, one bank ends the kite by dishonoring a large number of checks. After the dust has settled one bank may sue the other in restitution on the other checks previously paid. It will argue, of course, that it made payment in the mistaken belief that there were or would be sufficient funds.
>
> Is this a case in which one should allow restitution? We think not. In a typical kite it is difficult to maintain that one of the banks is more at fault than another. Moreover, the fact

[40] There is no mistake when a bank chooses to pay an instrument against uncollected funds or against an overdrawn account. Here the bank makes a conscious judgment to make a loan to its customer in the belief the customer is good for it. If the bank is mistaken about its customer's creditworthiness, that is not a payment by mistake, but rather a credit mistake and the bank has no right to restitution.

1B James J. White & Robert S. Summers, Uniform Commercial Code § 17-2 (3d ed. 1993).

that one bank has decided not to honor checks drawn against uncollected funds is not proof of its knowledge that the other bank's payment is "mistaken." It is hard to see how society is benefitted by spending a good deal of money on lawyers" fees at the conclusion of the kite, even in a fruitful attempt to shift the loss from one bank to another. All are culpable. White & Summers, *supra*, P 17-2.

Colonial does not explain why its retention of the Colonial checks beyond the midnight deadline was a payment by mistake that would put its actions within the ambit of § 4-318(b). It is undisputed that after Colonial received notice of the return of the First National checks at 2:45 p.m. on Wednesday, Colonial officers immediately began investigating the Colonial account. Randall Soderman, a Colonial loan officer, realized that Colonial had to return the Colonial checks by midnight the same day or risk losing the money. He knew that returning the Colonial checks before midnight would protect Colonial, but would risk disappointing its customer, World Commodities. Anthony Schiller, the loan officer in charge of the World Commodities account, had called World Commodities comptroller Charles Patterson and its attorney Alan Jay Goldstein. Both assured Schiller that the First National checks were good and should be redeposited. The Colonial officers decided not to return the Colonial checks on Wednesday but rather to meet on Thursday morning to discuss the matter.

It is not surprising that Colonial does not argue that these facts constitute a payment by mistake. Colonial was well aware that the midnight deadline for the Colonial checks was approaching, but deferred the decision of whether to return them until the next day. It contacted its customer and received assurances that the returned First National checks were good. Under these facts, Colonial cannot be said to have paid the Colonial checks by mistake so as to allow it to rely on the mistaken payment rules of § 3-418.

Rather than showing that it paid the checks by mistake, Colonial skips ahead to the inquiry under subsection (c), namely, whether First National took in good faith and for value or changed its position in reliance on payment. Colonial cites several cases for the proposition that a depositary bank with suspicion or knowledge of a kite that forwards checks for payment is not a holder in due course of those checks. *Farmers & Merchants State Bank v. Western Bank*, 841 F.2d 1433 (9th Cir. 1987); *Community Bank v. Ell*, 278 Ore. 417, 564 P.2d 685 (Or. 1977). (Colonial's argument is based upon cases decided under the former § 3-418, where the only question was whether the plaintiff was a holder in due course or a good faith relier on payment. But the revision to § 3-418(c) omits the "holder in due course" language in favor of "a person who in good faith took the instrument for value.") But it is unnecessary to inquire whether First National took in good faith and for value under subsection (c), because Colonial has not shown that it made a mistaken payment under subsection (b).

COMMENT

Section 3-418 is rooted in the restitutionary principle of unjust enrichment. Restitution is the primary method of recovery for checks bearing a forged drawer's signature and for payments made by the payor's mistaken belief that there were sufficient funds in the account to cover the item. There are only a small number of transactions that fall outside the final payment rule; finality occurs where payment has been made or acceptance granted to a person who took an instrument in good faith and for value or to someone who has relied to her detriment. The next case stands for the proposition that no finality principle can defeat a contrary federal policy. As you read this case, consider the power of the stated rationale for the federal policy.

FEDERAL DEPOSIT INSURANCE CORP. v. McKNIGHT

United States Court of Appeals
769 F.2d 658, 42 U.C.C. Rep. Serv. 488 (10th Cir. 1985)

MOORE, CIRCUIT JUDGE.

This is an appeal from a judgment denying plaintiffs, Federal Deposit Insurance Corporation (FDIC) and Deposit Insurance National Bank of Oklahoma City (DINB), relief on their claim for restitution of money mistakenly paid on cashier's checks issued by the insolvent Penn Square Bank, N.A. (Penn Square). The district court concluded that even though the plaintiffs established a prima facie case for restitution, their recovery was barred by the final payment rule of the Uniform Commercial Code (U.C.C.). We conclude the trial court correctly decided the question of restitution, but in applying the U.C.C. to this case, it overlooked the consequences of Penn Square's insolvency. Since those consequences placed the defendants in the position of creditors of an insolvent national bank, and since the federal law providing for liquidation of a national bank must take precedence over the U.C.C., we reverse.

This action has its genesis in a number of separate transactions negotiated by the defendants immediately prior to the closing of Penn Square. While the district court found there was no evidence that any defendant knew of Penn Square's impending failure when these transactions occurred, the proximity of the events to Penn Square's insolvency is the underlying cause of what followed. On July 1, 1982, two banking days prior to Penn Square's closing, defendant Rocket Oil Company redeemed a certificate of deposit (CD) in the face amount of $ 1.5 million for $ 1,480,273.98, taking a Penn Square cashier's check of even amount in place of cash. On the following day, defendants Pauline Oil Company and Pauline McKnight liquidated both matured and unmatured CD's and converted the proceeds to cashier's checks totaling $323,538.46. On the same day, defendant All Souls Episcopal Church redeemed two CD's and other paper and exchanged the proceeds for three cashier's checks in the aggregate of $452,527.25. All of the checks received by defendants were deposited in their own banks for collection.

At 7:00 p.m., Monday, July 5, 1982, before any of the checks were presented for payment, the Comptroller of the Currency of the United States declared Penn Square insolvent under 12 U.S.C. § 191, and appointed FDIC to act as receiver pursuant to 12 U.S.C. § 1921(c). FDIC, in turn, organized DINB as a new bank through which insured parties were to be paid. FDIC transferred to DINB funds with which to accomplish this purpose and to conduct operations.

One of the first tasks performed by FDIC employees was the programming of the bank's computer to reject any items in excess of $100,000 drawn against Penn Square accounts. This was done to avoid payment of any withdrawal in excess of the deposit insurance limits. By oversight, the program was not extended to cover cashier's checks issued by Penn Square. Before this error was discovered on July 7, all of the cashier's checks issued to defendants had been presented by the collecting bank and paid by plaintiffs. Upon discovery of these payments, this action was commenced to recover the difference between the insured amounts and the amounts actually paid.

As the facts were not in dispute, the issues were ultimately resolved on cross-motions for summary judgment. FDIC asserted that upon the date of insolvency, all outstanding and unpaid cashier's checks of Penn Square had been converted to deposits by operation of law. This contention was based upon 12 U.S.C. § 1813(1)(4), which states: "The term 'deposit' means . . . [an] outstanding . . . cashier's check, . . . issued in the usual course of business *for any purpose*" (Emphasis added.). FDIC further contended that payment of any of the cashier's checks in excess of $ 100,000, the insured amount of any deposit, was a mistake subject to restitution.

Defendants countered with many contentions, principally that they accepted the Penn Square cashier's checks in good faith and that they were thus holders in due course. Accordingly, they argued they were entitled to application of the "final payment rule," which states that payment of any instrument is final as to a holder in due course. U.C.C. § 3-418; Okla. Stat. tit. 12A, § 3-418 (1971).

After consideration of the arguments, the trial court concluded the plaintiffs made a prima facie case for restitution. The court, in effect, reasoned that 12 U.S.C. § 1813(1)(4) governed, that defendants were only entitled to payment of the insured amount, and that payment of sums of money greater than the insured amount constituted unjust enrichment. We concur with this reasoning. Yet, the court went on to conclude that since plaintiffs" claims to restitution were based on negotiable instruments, "special rules" in defense were applicable. The court then proceeded to apply the final payment rule. Holding payment of the cashier's checks constituted final payment, the court barred recovery of restitution. We disagree.

Application of the final payment rule was erroneous for a number of reasons. First, as the trial court recognized in concluding plaintiffs had made a prima facie case, the consequence of insolvency and the resultant application of the apposite portion of the Federal Deposit Insurance Act [12 U.S.C. § 1813(1)(4)] converted the cashier's checks from negotiable instruments to deposits by operation of law. Thus, the "special rules" applicable to negotiable instruments are irrelevant.

Second, and of greater importance, when the uncollected cashier's checks were finally presented, the defendants were creditors of an insolvent national bank. As such, their rights and liabilities became fixed by the National Bank Act. When that act provides a remedy, it takes precedence over state law. Here, the National Bank Act provides for the liquidation of the debts of an insolvent national bank. Accordingly, payment of the debts of Penn Square following insolvency had to have been made in compliance with the National Bank Act, not the Uniform Commercial Code.

Finally, neither the good faith of the defendants nor the source of the funds used to acquire the cashier's checks is of consequence. Despite their good faith and the origin of the funds,[41]

[41] Some defendants have argued because the money used to acquire the cashier's checks came from their deposits, the cashier's checks represented "their" money.

the defendants have been cast by law into the role of creditors,[42] and, as such, they must be treated in a circumscribed fashion.

The seminal point is the closing of Penn Square. That event not only triggered the liquidation process, but it also cast in stone the relationship of defendants to the bank. "It is well settled that the rights and liabilities of a bank and the bank's debtors and creditors are fixed at the declaration of the bank's insolvency." *American National Bank v. FDIC*, 710 F.2d 1528, 1540 (11th Cir. 1983). See also 7 Michie on Banks and Banking, Ch. 15, §§ 236, 247 (perm. ed. 1980 and supp. 1985). It is of equal certainty that the holder of a cashier's check is not entitled to preference over general creditors when the issuing bank fails before payment of the check. 10 Am. Jur. 2d Banks § 799 (Supp. 1983). Hence, when the cashier's checks were presented by the collecting bank, they represented an indebtedness subject to ratable dividends to be paid by the FDIC from the remaining Penn Square assets. 12 U.S.C. § 194.

Notwithstanding, it must also be kept in mind that the FDIC functioned as both receiver and insurer in this liquidating process. For this reason, the provisions of the Federal Deposit Insurance Act and the National Bank Act work, and must be read, conjunctivally. Therefore, in its capacity as insurer, FDIC was required to pay each of the debts represented by the cashier's checks as insured deposits in accordance with § 1813(1)(4) and 12 C.F.R. § 330.11. Payment of any sums in excess of the insured amounts, however, would be contrary to the statutory provisions for liquidation and would create a preference of the defendants over the other creditors of Penn Square. Although defendants have argued that this is an inequitable result, it is nonetheless the harsh reality and consequence of Penn Square's insolvency.

The judgment of the trial court is reversed and the case remanded for entry of judgments in favor of plaintiffs for the difference between the amounts mistakenly paid and the insured amount to which each defendant is entitled.

QUESTION

Do you agree with the court's reasoning in *McKnight*? Can you envision a case where the federal policy should be subordinate?

[42] Despite the effort made by some defendants to otherwise cast their role, this conclusion is inescapable. Even had insolvency not occurred, as holders of unpaid cashier's checks drawn on Penn Square, defendants were still creditors. We have previously made plain a cashier's check is nothing more than a debt of the bank accepted by it upon issuance. Moreover, even though defendants" banks had "paid" the checks, payment did not come from the issuing bank, Penn Square. Hence, the "payment" received by defendants was not final, and the checks were simply in the process of collection when the Penn Square insolvency occurred. Cf. U.C.C. § 3-501.

BRADFORD TRUST CO. OF BOSTON v. TEXAS AMERICAN BANK-HOUSTON

United States Court of Appeals
790 F.2d 407, 1 U.C.C. Rep. Serv. 2d 828 (5th Cir. 1986)

DAVIS, CIRCUIT JUDGE.

This diversity case presents the question of who should bear the loss flowing from a fraudulently induced $800,000 wire transfer. We must choose between the institution that honored the forged order of its customer to wire funds and the bank to whom the funds were wired which did not credit the account as directed. On cross-motions for summary judgment the district court applied the Texas comparative negligence statute, Tex. Rev. Civ. Stat. Ann. art. 2212a (Vernon Supp. 1985),[43] and apportioned the loss equally between the two parties. Both parties appeal and argue that the other party should bear the entire loss. We decline to apply comparative negligence principles and reverse the judgment of the district court. We conclude that the initial bank that honored the forged order must bear the entire loss.

I.

In an ingenious scheme, two con artists, using aliases of Hank and Dave Friedman, arranged to buy rare coins and gold bullion from Colonial Coins, Inc. (Colonial) in Houston for $800,000. The impostors informed Colonial that they would wire funds from their bank in Boston to Colonial's account at Texas American Bank-Houston N.A. (Texas American)[44] to pay for the coins. Colonial agreed and gave the Friedmans its account number at Texas American.

The impostors next sent a forged letter and stock power to Bradford Trust Company (Bradford), the agent for a mutual fund, directing the liquidation of $800,000 from the mutual fund account of Frank Rochefort. The forged order also instructed Bradford to wire the $800,000 from this account to Colonial's account in Texas American in Houston. Bradford, without following internal procedures recently instituted because of a similar scam,[45] ordered its correspondent bank, State Street Bank of Boston (State Street) to wire the funds to Texas American. The text of the transfer included the number of Colonial's account at Texas American, but stated that it was for the account of Frank S. Rochefort.[46] When the funds were received, Texas American notified Colonial that the funds had been deposited into Colonial's account. With this assurance, Colonial released the coins to the impostors.

Bradford became aware of the scam when an astonished Rochefort received notice of the withdrawal and informed Bradford that he had not authorized it. Bradford reinstated Rochefort's

---

[43] The Texas comparative negligence statute in effect at the time of this incident, Art. 2212a, was repealed by Section 1 of Acts 1985, 69th Leg. Ch. 959 and a substantially identical version enacted as § 33.001 of the Civil Practice and Remedies Code.

[44] This bank changed its name from Southern National Bank-Houston to Texas American Bank after this incident. We will refer to it throughout this opinion as Texas American.

[45] In April of 1980, Bradford was the victim of a similar fraudulent scheme. As a result, new security procedures were instituted. For transactions over $100,000, the new procedures required thorough review of the documents, shareholder confirmation when the shareholder instructed Bradford to wire the money to a person or to an address other than that on record, and approval by senior management.

[46] The wire transfer stated: "State Street Bos/Michealpiemont MCMT 5207 X 6386 Southern Hou/A/O/Frank S. Rochnefort, Jr. Acct. * 057 141." (*eds. note*: observe that "Rochefort" was misspelled.)

account and demanded that Texas American and Colonial reimburse it. Texas American and Colonial refused and this lawsuit followed. Bradford compromised its claim against Colonial, which was dismissed from the litigation. The district court, on summary judgment, applied the Texas comparative negligence statute and divided the loss equally between Bradford and Texas American. Bradford appeals, contending that Texas American should bear the entire loss because its negligence in failing to follow Bradford's order to deposit the funds in Rochefort's account was the primary cause of the loss. Texas American cross-appeals, arguing that Bradford should suffer the entire loss because Bradford dealt with the imposter, honored the forged order to pay and hence was in the best position to prevent the loss.

II.

A.

The district court, having no well-defined body of law that clearly applied to resolve the dispute in this case, relied on the Texas comparative negligence statute as authority to divide the damages between the parties. The district court cited as authority *Duncan v. Cessna Aircraft Co.*, 665 S.W.2d 414 (Tex. 1984), which applied comparative negligence principles to a strict products liability case.

Although we feel the same equitable tug the district court undoubtedly felt to apply comparative negligence principles, we are persuaded that it would be a mistake to do so in this commercial case.

The comparative negligence statute expressly extends to actions "to recover damages for negligence resulting in death or injury to persons or property. Art. 2212a, *supra*. This language clearly extends comparative negligence principles to cases of physical harm to persons and property; whether this statute was intended to apply to other types of damage is doubtful. Although it is not inconceivable that a Texas court would interpret property broadly enough to include a loss such as that at issue here, we are persuaded that a federal diversity court should not adopt such a questionable interpretation. This is particularly true where, as here, neither party to the appeal urges us to apply comparative negligence principles.

We are also influenced by our recognition that in commercial disputes between seasoned bankers and other businessmen, certainty of result is more important than in traditional tort litigation. In commercial relationships known risks can be priced or shifted to others; if disputes arise, a bright line rule results in faster, easier settlements. The principal reason for a comparative negligence rule in physical harm cases—avoiding the harsh distributional results of precluding the recovery of the slightly negligent plaintiff who has suffered a devastating loss—has considerably less force in the commercial banking world. Prosser and Keeton on The Law of Torts, § 67, p. 469 (5th ed. 1984).

B.

Having decided that the Texas comparative negligence statute does not apply to this case, we widen our search for Texas law that does apply. Unfortunately, we have found no direct authority that resolves the question. Neither the Electronic Fund Transfer Act, 15 U.S.C. § 1693(a)(6)(B), nor the Uniform Commercial Code apply. *Delbrueck & Co. v. Manufacturers Hanover Trust Co.*, 609 F.2d 1047 (2d Cir. 1979); *Evra Corp. v. Swiss Bank Corp.*, 673 F.2d 951(7th Cir.), cert. denied, 459 U.S. 1017 (1982). Other courts faced with resolving controversies relating to wire transfers have applied the U.C.C. by analogy. *Delbrueck, supra*, at 1051; *Securities Fund Services v. American National Bank and Trust Co.*, 542 F. Supp. 323 (N.D. Ill. 1982). Because of the close analogy between allocation of fraud losses in negotiable instruments and wire transfers we look to both Texas court decisions before Texas adopted the U.C.C. and the U.C.C. for guidance. Two factors emerge from these sources that are helpful in analyzing the question of who should bear the loss in this case: 1) which party was in the best position to avoid the loss; and 2) which solution promotes the policy of finality in commercial transactions?

The first factor, which party is in the best position to avoid the loss, is a principal reason underlying a number of loss allocation calls in the U.C.C. For example, it provides the essential reason for requiring the drawee bank to bear the loss if it pays on the drawer's forged signature. Tex. Bus. & Com. Code Ann. § 3.404 (Vernon 1968); *Greenville Avenue State Bank v. Lang*, 421 S.W.2d 748 (Tex. Civ. App. 1967). This is because the bank, which can verify its customer's signature, is in the best position to discover the forgery and avoid the loss. Similarly, if an endorsement on an instrument is forged, the loss is ordinarily placed on the party in the collection chain who accepted the instrument from the forger. Tex. Bus. & Com. Code Ann. § 3.405(1)(a) (Vernon 1968) and comment 3. Again, the U.C.C. recognizes that the party dealing directly with the forger has an opportunity to verify the endorser's identity and is in the best position to avoid the loss. Indeed, the common thread running through the imposter cases is to "throw the loss resulting from dealing with an imposter on the person who dealt with the imposter, and presumably, had the best opportunity to take precautions that would have detected the fraud, rather than on a subsequent holder, who had no similar opportunity." *Fair Park National Bank v. Southwestern Investment Co.*, 541 S.W.2d 266, 269-70 (Tex. Civ. App. 1976).

Bradford dealt directly with the imposter. It received the forged order directing the liquidation of Rochefort's account. If Bradford had followed procedures it had in place that called for verification of the customer's order, the loss would not have occurred. Instead of following those procedures and verifying Rochefort's order, Bradford set the fraudulent scheme into motion by liquidating Rochefort's account and wiring the funds to Texas American. Although Texas American should have recognized the discrepancy between the account number and the name of the owner of the account to whom the wire directed the funds be credited, we are persuaded that Texas American's fault was secondary to that of Bradford's. It is far from certain that the loss would have been prevented even if Texas American had noticed the discrepancy between the account number and the holder of the account and had called this discrepancy to Bradford's attention. To conclude that this action by Texas American would have avoided the loss requires us to assume that such a call to Bradford would have caused Bradford to contact Rochefort and verify his order. On the other hand, it is certain that if Bradford had called Rochefort to verify his purported order to transfer funds to Colonial this scheme would have been discovered and no loss would have been suffered.

Two wire transfer cases decided by Texas courts before the adoption of the U.C.C. follow this same reasoning. In *Western Union Telegraph Co. v. American State Bank*, 277 S.W 226 (Tex. Civ. App. 1925), an individual who identified himself as Joe Spinks, deposited two checks in American State Bank. Before the bank learned that the checks were bogus, it received a telegram from Joe Spinks requesting the bank to wire him $650. The bank instructed Western Union to wire the money to Spinks. When the bank discovered Spinks was an imposter, it sued Western Union to recover the money. The Texas Court of Appeals in reversing a judgment entered by the district court in favor of the bank stated that: "[t]he duty devolves on the Bank to identify its customers, and when they accepted the unknown as Joe Spinks, they laid the groundwork for subsequent trouble." 277 S.W at 227. In *Western Union Telegraph Co. v. Cosby*, 99 S.W.2d 662 (Tex. Civ. App. 1936), an imposter representing himself as Cosby, a business partner of Langlois, called Langlois and asked Langlois to wire him $400. Langlois, thinking it really was Cosby, ordered Western Union to send him the money. Cosby then sued Western Union to recover the money once he discovered the error. The court of appeals again reversed the district court's judgment against Western Union stating that, "where two innocent parties have been deceived, the loss must be borne by the one who primarily made such loss possible." 9 S.W.2d at 664.

For the reasons set forth above, we are persuaded that Bradford, by honoring the forged order to transmit Rochefort's funds after dealing directly with the imposter, was in the best position to avoid the loss.

We have also considered how our allocation of the loss in this case squares with the desired policy of finality in commercial transactions. The U.C.C. in § 3.418 adopted the principle established in the time honored decision of *Price v. Neal*, 3 Burr. 1355 (1762) in which the court held that a drawee who accepts or pays an instrument on the forged signature of the drawer is bound on his acceptance and cannot recover back his payment. Section 3.418 provides in part: ". . . payment or acceptance of any instrument is final in favor of a holder in due course or a person who has in good faith changed his position in reliance on the payment." Tex. Bus. & Com. Code art. 3.418 (Vernon 1968) The reporters in the official comments to this section give two justifications for adopting this rule: "The traditional justification for the result is that the drawee is in a superior position to detect a forgery because he has the maker's signature and is expected to know and compare it; a less fictional rationalization is that it is highly desirable to end the transaction on an instrument when it is paid rather than reopen and upset a series of commercial transactions at a later date when the forgery is discovered." *Id.* at comment 1.

In *Perini Corporation v. First National Bank of Habersham County*, 553 F.2d 398 (5th Cir. 1977), we considered who should bear the loss as between the drawee bank that paid on forged signatures of the drawer and the depository bank which accepted the instruments without proper endorsements. In deciding this Georgia diversity case, we resolved conflicting U.C.C. rules by relying primarily on the finality policy and concluded that the drawee bank must bear the entire loss.[47]

Assessing the loss in this case to Bradford and ending the transaction when Bradford paid under Rochefort's forged order rather than inquiring into and upsetting later transactions after the forgery was discovered clearly serves this bedrock policy of finality.

C.

Bradford urges us to find that Texas American's failure to follow Bradford's instructions in the wire transfer was the primary, overriding cause of the loss. Bradford argues that its earlier negligence in accepting the forged order of Rochefort to pay would have been inconsequential had Texas American handled the transfer with due care and in accordance with ordinary standards and practices of the banking industry. We agree with Bradford that Texas American was negligent in failing to notice the discrepancy between account number and the name of the owner of the account to which the funds were to be credited. Even if allocation of the loss depended entirely

[47] Because of a special agreement between the drawee bank and the drawer, Perini, that Perini would honor all checks bearing signatures from its checkwriting machine, the loss was diverted from the drawee bank to Perini.

upon a determination of which party was more at fault, however, this would not alter our decision to lay the loss at Bradford's feet. We are persuaded that Bradford's act in honoring the forged authorization without following its own internal procedures to verify the genuineness of the request was the primary cause of the loss. The fault of Texas American failing to note the discrepancy between the account number and the name of the owner of the account to whom the money was to be credited was less grave than that of Bradford.

Bradford argues that liability is imposed on Texas American by sub-part (b) of Regulation J of the Federal Reserve System, 12 C.F.R. § 210.56(b)(1981) which governs federal reserve wire transfers of funds. We disagree. This regulation, at most, placed a duty on Texas American to follow the instructions contained in Bradford's wire. Texas American owed this duty without regard to Regulation J and as indicated above, we agree with the district court that Texas American breached this duty and was guilty for negligence in failing to follow those instructions. For the reasons stated above, despite the negligence of Texas American, we conclude that Bradford must bear the loss. Accordingly, the judgment of the district court is reversed and the action is remanded to the district court for entry of judgment in favor of Texas American and against Bradford.

Reversed and Remanded.

§ 14.03 Documentary Drafts

Read: U.C.C. §§ 4-501 through 4-504

Revised Article 4 introduces several new provisions that effect "payable through" drafts. A payable through draft is one directed to a bank for the purpose of presentment to a third party payor (either another bank or, a nonbank payor like an insurance company). The payable through draft identifies itself as such and designates a specific bank as collection agent for purposes of presenting the item to the payor. See U.C.C. § 4-106(a). The payable through draft does not authorize the bank to pay the item but serves to identify a bank as agent. Article 4 sections 4-501 through 4-504 provide rules governing documentary drafts. A documentary draft is an item "to be presented for acceptance or payment if specified documents . . . or the like are to be received by the . . . payor before acceptance or payment . . . " See § 4-104(a)(6). Most often, payable through drafts are used in conjunction with other documentary transactions. In certain parts of the country, documentary drafts are used widely in the sale of used cars, or transfer of livestock or other commodities. The idea behind a documentary transaction is that the party presenting the draft will insist upon payment before that party releases the title documents that govern the transaction. Documentary drafts have not been subject to the same control and standardized practices that apply to checks. The provisions of Part 5 to Article 4 attempt to address this situation by providing an outline of expected behavior in a documentary transaction.

GREAT WESTERN BANK v. STEVE JAMES FORD, INC.

United States Disrict Court, Southern District, Georgia
915 F. Supp. 392 (S.D. Ga. 1996)

JOHN F. NANGLE.

Before the Court is the Motion for Summary Judgment filed by counter-defendant Great Western Bank. Fed.R.Civ.P. 56. For the reasons set forth below, the motion is granted.

I. BACKGROUND

This case arose out of an alleged check-kiting scheme that resulted in losses to both Great Western Bank ("Great Western Bank" or "Great Western") and Southeastern Bank ("Southeastern Bank" or "Southeastern"). In 1992, Derrick Musselwhite opened a checking account with Great Western which he used in his automobile broker business. From December, 1992, through April, 1993, Mr. Musselwhite conducted business with Steve James Ford, Inc. ("the dealership" or "Steve James Ford") and its officers. From May, 1993, through December, 1993, Mr. Musselwhite and James Holloway engaged in a joint venture to manage the dealership. The dealership maintained general and payroll checking accounts and new and used car floor plan financing with Southeastern Bank. From May to December, 1993, the dealership also maintained a "Steve James Ford, Special Account" at Southeastern.

Great Western maintains that, in 1993, Mr. Musselwhite and Mr. Holloway executed a check-kiting scheme. They are alleged to have deposited automobile sight drafts at the dealership's account at Southeastern. Southeastern would give them immediate credit for the deposits. After these funds were credited, Messrs. Musselwhite and Holloway are alleged to have written checks on the dealership account to Mr. Musselwhite who would deposit the checks in his account at Great Western. Great Western alleges that those funds were used to cover the funds deposited at Southeastern and money was funneled back and forth between the two banks. The check-kiting scheme was discovered in December, 1993, and resulted in losses to both Great Western and Southeastern.

Great Western brought suit against Steve James Ford, Inc., Derrick Musselwhite and James Holloway alleging, among other claims, both federal and State RICO violations. Great Western later amended its complaint and added Steve Garry James and Southeastern Bank as defendants. The claims against Southeastern were dismissed by order of this Court. Presently before the Court is Great Western's motion for summary judgment on Southeastern Bank's counterclaim which arises out of the same series of transactions.

On December 6, 1993, Steve James Ford, Inc., presented seven documentary drafts to Southeastern Bank, its depository bank. These seven drafts were signed by an authorized agent of Derrick Musselwhite in Mr. Musselwhite's name and were being used to purchase the automobiles described on the drafts from Steve James Ford. The drafts contained the language "Pay or Return Within 7 Days." The total amount of the drafts was $116,013.00. A copy of one of the drafts is attached hereto as Exhibit 1.

Upon receipt of the drafts, Southeastern Bank issued immediate credit to Steve James Ford, Inc., pursuant to the dealership's $500,000.00 credit line on drafts. On December 9, 1995, Southeastern forwarded the drafts along with a transmittal notice by mail to Great Western Bank in Orlando, Florida. The drafts were received by Great Western sometime between December 13, 1993, and December 15, 1993. On December 21, 1993, Mr. Musselwhite instructed Great Western Bank to return the drafts unpaid to Southeastern Bank. Great Western mailed the drafts to Southeastern via certified mail on December 21, 1993. They were received by Southeastern on December 29, 1993. After the kiting scheme collapsed, Steve James Ford had an overdraft of $261,638.00 in its account at Southeastern. Southeastern Bank obtained a promissory note for that amount from Steve James Ford.

Southeastern Bank brings this counterclaim against Great Western Bank alleging that it is liable for the face amount of the drafts because it did not return the drafts within the seven days provided for on the drafts. Great Western filed a motion for summary judgment on three different grounds: (1) Great Western Bank was a collecting bank, rather than a payor bank, and thus is not liable to Southeastern Bank on these drafts; (2) the promissory note was a full or partial satisfaction of Southeastern's claim against Great Western and (3) that, even if the drafts were received on December 13, 1995, return of the drafts on December 21, 1995, was within seven days because Sunday, a nonbanking day, is not counted in the computation of time.

II. DISCUSSION

. . . .

B. Payor Bank or Collecting Bank

A payor bank is "a bank that is the drawee of a draft" and is strictly liable for failure to timely return documentary drafts. Fla. Stat. Ann. § 674.105(3); Fla. Stat. Ann. § 674.302(1)(b).[48] A collecting bank "means a bank handling an item for collection except the payor bank." Fla. Stat. Ann. § 674.105(5). A collecting bank is required to seasonably notify its customer upon learning that a documentary draft has not been paid. Fla. Stat. Ann. § 674.501. Great Western argues that, even if the drafts in this case were not returned within seven days, it cannot be liable for them because it acted merely as a collecting bank. Southeastern, on the other hand, argues that Great Western was a payor bank, and thus strictly liable for the face amount of the drafts because it did not return them within seven days.

Based upon the drafts in question, the Court is unable to conclude that Great Western was the drawee of the drafts as is required for it to be a payor bank. The drafts are ambiguous as to whether Great Western was a drawee or a collecting bank. Mr. Musselwhite's name and business are listed on the left-hand side of the draft and Great Western is listed on the right-hand side of the draft. A drawee designation does not appear on any of the seven drafts. Moreover, there is no specific account number listed on the draft. See *Whitehall Packing Co., Inc. v. First National City Bank*, 55 A.D.2d 675, 390 N.Y.S.2d 189, 191 (1976)(finding that leaving blank the portion of the draft which directed the payor to charge a certain account supported a holding that bank was collecting bank).

In *Alimenta (U.S.A.), Inc. v. Stauffer*, 568 F. Supp. 674, 677 (N.D.Ga. 1983), the Court held that an ambiguity existed when the bank's name was on the left side of the draft and the customer's name on the right side of the draft because it was unclear whether the customer's name was a continuation of the account number listed under the bank's name. Likewise, in this case, it is difficult to tell from the drafts whether Great Western's name on the right side of the draft was meant to be a continuation of the drawee designation or merely the address of the collecting bank. Moreover, even if both Mr. Musselwhite's business and Great Western Bank had been designated as drawees, it would still be ambiguous as to whether the Great Western bank was a co-drawee. See *Southern Cotton Oil Co., Inc. v. Merchants National Bank*, 670 F.2d 548, 550 (5th Cir. 1982)("Where the names of both the customer and the bank were listed in the space for drawee, as in the present case, it was unclear whether the bank was the drawee.").

[48] "The liability of a bank for action or nonaction with respect to any item handled by it for purposes of presentment, payment or collection is governed by the law of the place where the bank is located. In the case of action or nonaction by or at a branch or separate office of a bank, its liability is governed by the law of the place where the branch or separate office is located." O.C.G.A. @ 11-4-102(2). The branch of Great Western Bank that is charged with untimely return of the seven drafts is in Orlando, Florida. Accordingly, Florida law applies to the counterclaim.

Accordingly, the drafts are ambiguous as to whether Great Western Bank was a drawee of the drafts.

Before the enactment of the 1990 Revision to the Uniform Commercial Code, a court would look to the surrounding facts and circumstances to determine a bank's status if the drafts were ambiguous. *Alimenta*, 568 F. Supp. at 677. In the present case, it is clear from looking at the surrounding circumstances that Great Western was a collecting bank. The Advices sent along with the drafts by Southeastern labels the drafts as an "Outgoing Collection" and states: "We mailed a collection item to the addressee." Great Western is listed as the addressee. See *id.* (holding that bank was collecting bank supported by fact that transmittal notices stated: "We enclose the described documents for collection.").

Finally, and most importantly, Great Western Bank was not authorized to pay the drafts from Mr. Musselwhite's account without his prior approval. In *Southern Cotton Oil Co., Inc. v. Merchants National Bank, supra*, the Court held that where a bank was not authorized by the buyer to charge its account for payment of the draft without prior approval, the bank was a collecting bank. *Id.* at 550. In the present case, Mr. Musselwhite testified that Great Western did not pay any documentary drafts until he was contacted, reviewed the drafts and provided funds for payment. Affidavit of Derrick Musselwhite at P 5. Sometimes the funds to pay the drafts were part of the existing funds in his Great Western account, but usually Mr. Musselwhite deposited new funds and then purchased a cashier's check from Great Western to send to Southeastern. *Id.* at P 7. The deposition excerpts of Great Western's employees supplied by Southeastern support this assertion. See Deposition of Linda Doll at 20-23, 32; Deposition of Lisa Rathel at 36-40. In this case, as in *Southern Cotton Oil Co, Inc.*, "it is clear that the [Great Western] Bank acted as a collecting bank, presenting the drafts to the buyer for payment and forwarding the payment to the seller's local bank only after receiving funds or authorization from the buyer." 670 F.2d at 550.

Southeastern Bank relies on the reasoning of *Horney v. Covington County Bank*, 716 F.2d 335 (5th Cir. 1983), to argue that Great Western Bank is not a collecting bank. In *Horney*, the Fifth Circuit, relying largely on the fact that the bank's customer's authorized agent prepared and signed the drafts, held the bank to be a payor bank. *Id.* at 338-39. Southeastern contends that because Mr. Musselwhite's authorized agent prepared and signed the drafts in this case, Great Western should be held to be a payor bank.

In a footnote, the Middle District of Florida recognized the argument that Southeastern is making. "Thus, at least in the new Fifth Circuit the determination of whether a draft listing both the bank and a customer designates the bank as a drawee is dependent upon whether the payee or the bank's customer drew the bill." *Gathercrest Ltd. v. First American Bank and Trust*, 649 F. Supp. 106, 116 n.2 (M.D.Fla. 1985), aff'd, 805 F.2d 995 (11th Cir. 1986). Southeastern's argument overlooks one crucial fact — the adoption of Fla. Stat. Ann. § 674.1061(3).

As noted above, the Uniform Commercial Code was revised in 1990. New section 4-106 provides as follows:

> If a draft names a nonbank drawee and it is unclear whether a bank named in the draft is a co-drawee or a collecting bank, the bank is a collecting bank.

Fla. Stat. Ann. § 674.1061(3). This Code Section is not consistent with the Fifth Circuit's rule, and Southeastern's argument, that the status of the drawee's bank is determined by who signed the draft. If that rule were followed, it would never be unclear whether a bank was a co-drawee or a collecting bank. This is not to say that who signed the draft cannot be considered when determining if a draft is ambiguous. Certainly, this case is a much closer one because Mr. Musselwhite's agent signed the draft. However, the adoption of § 674.1061(3) clearly shows that there is no hard and fast rule for determining payor bank/collecting bank status. Rather, the Code now provides its own "tie-breaker" in favor of collecting bank status in the case of an ambiguous draft. Given that the drafts in this case are ambiguous, this Court finds that Great Western Bank is a collecting bank notwithstanding the fact that Mr. Musselwhite's authorized agent signed the drafts. Such a result is clearly allowed under the Revised Uniform Commercial Code.

In sum, the drafts in this case are ambiguous as to whether Great Western Bank is a drawee. The Advices sent along with the drafts, and the fact that Mr. Musselwhite had to approve the drafts before they were paid, show that Great Western acted as a collecting bank. Moreover, Fla. Stat. Ann. § 674.1061(3) provides that if a draft is ambiguous as to whether a bank named with a nonbank drawee is a co-drawee or a collecting bank, it is a collecting bank. Accordingly, Great Western Bank was a collecting bank with regard to these drafts.

C. What Liability Does a Collecting Bank Have for Failure to Seasonably Return Documentary Drafts?

Having found that Great Western Bank was a collecting bank, the question then becomes what liability attaches when a collecting bank fails to seasonably return documentary drafts. Fla. Stat. Ann. § 674.202 provides that a collecting bank must exercise ordinary care in its day-to-day operations. However, § 674.202(1)(b) specifically excludes sending notice of dishonor or nonpayment of a documentary draft from those functions. Collection of documentary drafts is governed by Section 5 of Article 4 of the U.C.C. Fla. Stat. Ann. § 674.501 et seq. However, that section does not state whether a collecting bank must exercise ordinary care in seasonably returning documentary drafts or whether a collecting bank is strictly liable for failure to seasonably return documentary drafts. The distinction is an important one in this case because, if an ordinary care standard applies, Fla. Stat. Ann. § 674.103(5) provides that the only damages recoverable are those that would not have occurred had the bank exercised ordinary care. Southeastern Bank has conceded that, if § 674.103(5) applies, it cannot prove that it suffered damages because of Great Western's failure to exercise ordinary care given that Southeastern Bank gave immediate credit on the documentary drafts to its depositor, Steve James Ford. Thus, if a collecting bank is only required to exercise ordinary care in relation to the collection of documentary drafts, Southeastern Bank cannot recover any damages in this case and Great Western is entitled to summary judgment.

There is little case law on this issue. Southeastern Bank makes a plausible argument, based upon statutory construction, that a collecting bank should be strictly liable for its failure to timely return documentary drafts. Nevertheless, this Court finds that the better-reasoned approach is that a collecting bank's duty is one of ordinary care with respect to the return of documentary drafts. Nowhere in the Uniform Commercial Code does it state that a collecting bank is strictly liable for its failure to seasonably return documentary drafts. Rather, it seems more reasonable to hold that the documentary drafts were excluded from U.C.C. 4-202(b)(2) so that they could be given their own coverage in Section 5 of Article 4. The duty of ordinary care still applies to a collecting bank's collection of documentary drafts.

> [A] bank purchasing a documentary draft owed a duty to its seller to see that the documentary tender owed the buyer under the underlying sales or other transaction was in fact made, or

> that the seller was informed of the reasons why the transaction had gone awry. Since documentary drafts are usually noncash items, or items sent for collection and remittance, a failure to receive remittance within a normally expected time should trigger a duty to trace as a facet of the duty of ordinary care in sending, and at least provoke a duty of inquiry.

William D. Hawkland, J. Fairfax Leary, Jr., and Richard M. Alderman, Uniform Commercial Code Series § 4-501:01 at Westlaw pages 7-8 (1984); see also *Gathercrest Ltd. v. First American Bank and Trust*, 649 F. Supp. at 117-18 (holding that collecting bank had duty to exercise ordinary care with respect to collection of documentary draft and measuring damages under 4-103(5)). Accordingly, the Court finds that Great Western was a collecting bank and owed only a duty of ordinary care to seasonably return the documentary drafts. Great Western is entitled to summary judgment given Southeastern's admission that it cannot prove that it suffered damages because of Great Western's failure to exercise ordinary care.

III. CONCLUSION

Although the Court made preliminary findings on other issues in its December 11, 1995 order, it is unnecessary for the Court to address those issues given its ruling above. Accordingly, for the reasons set forth above,

IT IS HEREBY ORDERED that Great Western Bank's Motion for Summary Judgment on Southeastern Bank's counterclaim be and is granted.

QUESTION

Are the responsibilities for collection of documentary drafts all that different from other Article 4 provision?

§ 14.04 Electronic Fund Transfers

The cost of operating a paper-based checking system has grown just as geometrically as the volume of checks written. Current estimates suggest that the overall cost of check collection in the U.S. exceeds $12 billion annually. While technological growth has permitted banks to accommodate the more than 50 billion checks written each year, the pressures continue to mount to replace this antiquated system. In 1978, Congress enacted the Electronic Fund Transfers Act in 1978 as Title IX to the Consumer Credit Protection Act (15 U.S.C. § 1693 et seq.) as a first regulatory step to govern non-paper based transactions. In 1979, Regulation E, issued by the Board of Governors of the Federal Reserve System, was intended to implement and carry out the purpose of the Act (12 C. F. R. Part 205). The term "electronic fund transfer" (EFT) was used as a generic term describing the transfer of funds, other than a transaction originated by check, draft or similar paper instrument, initiated through an electronic terminal, telephone or computer for the purpose of ordering, instructing or authorizing a financial institution to debit or credit an account. The term includes but is not limited to point-of-sale (POS) transfers, automated teller machines (ATM) transfers, preauthorized debit and credit transactions conducted through automated clearing houses, preauthorized pay by telephone transfers, check verification and guarantee, check truncation and wire transfers (which are now covered by Article 4A). The term EFT does not include payments made by check, draft or similar paper instruments at an electronic terminal.

The purpose and rationale of the Act resulted from a finding by Congress that the use of electronic systems to transfer funds provided substantial benefits to consumers. It is the purpose of the Act to provide a basic framework establishing the rights, liabilities, and responsibilities of participants in the electronic fund transfer systems. The primary objective of the Act, however, was to provide rights for the individual consumer, and Regulation E is primarily intended to carry out that purpose. The underlying goal is to reduce the flow of paper instruments and transactions in order to eliminate or significantly reduce the time and cost involved in the collection process. While consumers may find payment by bank card more convenient than by cash or check, it is not necessarily more economical. To encourage consumer participation, most banks and merchants are not charging customers fees for POS purchases. In the not-too-distant future, the cost of the electronic transactions probably will be passed on to consumers in the same manner as fees for using automated teller machines are currently being passed. Another drawback for the consumer is the loss of float time, the days between writing a check and having it subtracted from one's account. Despite these 'negatives,' it is clear that we are moving toward a society where checks, and perhaps cash itself, will become obsolete.

The term "electronic fund transfer" refers to a wide variety of payment systems and financial transactions. Whether or not a particular transaction falls within the provisions of the Act can pose a substantial question.

KASHANCHI v. TEXAS COMMERCE MEDICAL BANK

United States Court of Appeals
703 F.2d 936 (5th Cir. 1983)

RANDALL, CIRCUIT JUDGE:

The plaintiff, Morvarid Paydar Kashanchi, appeals from a final judgment of the district court dismissing her complaint for lack of subject matter jurisdiction. The issue on appeal is whether the term "electronic fund transfer" as used in the Electronic Fund Transfer Act ("EFTA" or "the Act"), 15 U.S.C. § 1693 (Supp. V 1981), includes a transfer of funds from a consumer's account, initiated by a telephone conversation between someone other than the owner of the account and an employee of a financial institution, when that transfer is not made pursuant to a prearranged plan or agreement under which periodic transfers are contemplated. For the reasons set forth below, we affirm.

On or about February 9, 1981, the plaintiff and her sister, Firoyeh Paydar, were the sole owners of a savings account at Texas Commerce Medical Bank in Houston, Texas. On or about that date, $4900 was transferred from their account. The transfer was allegedly initiated by a telephone conversation between an employee of the bank and someone other than the plaintiff or her sister. Upon receipt of a March 31, 1981 bank statement showing the $4900 withdrawal, Firoyeh Paydar sent a letter to the bank, dated April 15, 1981, notifying the bank that the withdrawal was unauthorized.

After the bank refused to re-credit the account with the amount of the allegedly unauthorized withdrawal, the plaintiff filed this action on December 4, 1981, alleging violations by the bank of the EFTA. The district court granted the defendant's motion to dismiss on the ground that the plaintiff's cause of action was excluded from the coverage of the Act under 15 U.S.C. § 1693a(6)(E). The plaintiff timely appealed.

This is apparently the first case in which we have been called upon to interpret any of the substantive provisions of the EFTA. We begin our inquiry with the language of the statute itself, recognizing that "absent a clearly expressed legislative intent to the contrary, the plain meaning of the language is ordinarily controlling."

The parties agree that the telephonic transfer that allegedly occurred in this case falls within the broad definition of "electronic fund transfers" in the Act:

> [T]he term "electronic fund transfer" means any transfer of funds, other than a transaction originated by check, draft, or similar paper instrument, which is initiated through an electronic terminal, telephonic instrument, or computer or magnetic tape so as to order, instruct, or authorize a financial institution to debit or credit an account. Such term includes, but is not limited to, point-of-sale transfers, automated teller machine transactions, direct deposits or withdrawals of funds, and transfers initiated by telephone.

15 U.S.C. § 1693a(6). Some of what Congress has given, however, it has also taken away. Excluded from the definition of an electronic fund transfer is

> any transfer of funds which is initiated by a telephone conversation between a consumer and an officer or employee of a financial institution which is not pursuant to a prearranged plan and under which periodic or recurring transfers are not contemplated . . . . .

15 U.S.C. § 1693a(6)(E). The plaintiff concedes that the unauthorized transfer of her funds was not made "pursuant to any prearranged plan," and that it was made by an employee of the bank. The question in this case is whether the telephone conversation was between the employee and a "consumer."[49]

The Act defines a consumer as "a natural person." 15 U.S.C. § 1693a(5). If we were to apply this definition to the language in the exclusion, we would have to conclude that the withdrawal of the plaintiff's funds was excluded from the coverage of the Act since a natural person, even if the person was neither the plaintiff nor her sister, made the withdrawal. The plaintiff argues, however, that we should read the term "consumer" more narrowly in this portion of the Act; she would have us interpret the provision to exclude only transfers made by the account holder.

The plaintiff maintains that the legislative history of the Act supports her narrow reading of the exclusion. She points out that the House version of the bill used the word "holder," meaning "the individual who is recognized as the owner of the account by the financial institution where the account is held," H.R. 13007, § 903(i), 95th Cong., 2d Sess., 124 Cong.Rec. 25737 (1978),

---

[49] Relying on the Federal Reserve Board's use of the conjunction "and" in its regulations implementing the EFTA, rather than the relative pronoun "which" used in the Act, the plaintiff maintains that the test for whether a particular transfer falls within the exclusion is two-pronged. The federal regulations exclude:

> Any transfer of funds that (1) is initiated by a telephone conversation between a consumer and an officer or employee of a financial institution and (2) is not under a telephone bill-payment or other prearranged plan or agreement in which periodic or recurring transfers are contemplated.

12 C.F.R. § 205.3(e) (1982). We do not think that the difference in grammatical construction changes the nature of the exclusion.

where the Senate version, eventually adopted by Congress as the EFTA, uses the word "consumer." The plaintiff would have us infer that the Senate intended the word "consumer" to be synonymous with "holder." There is no indication in the legislative history, however, that this is what the Senate intended.[50] The only criticism leveled at the definition of consumer concerned the exclusion of corporations, particularly nonprofit corporations, from that definition. See The Electronic Funds Transfer Consumer Protection Act, 1977: Hearings on & 2065 Before the Sub comm. on Consumer Affairs of the Senate Comm. on Banking, Housing and Urban Affairs, 95th Cong., 1st Sess. 37 (1977) (Statement of Linda Hudak, Legislative Director, Consumer Federation of America).

Secondly, Congress demonstrated in other sections of the EFTA that when it wanted to limit a particular provision of the Act to an account holder, rather than to all natural persons, it was perfectly capable of adding language to do so. For example, the Act defines an "unauthorized electronic fund transfer" as an electronic fund transfer from a consumer's account initiated by a person other than the consumer without actual authority to initiate such transfer 15 U.S.C. § 1693a(11). It is a well-established principle of statutory construction that "where Congress includes particular language in one section of a statute but omits it in another section of the same Act, it is generally presumed that Congress acts intentionally and purposely in the disparate inclusion or exclusion." *United States v. Wong Kim Bo*, 472 F.2d 720, 722 (5th Cir. 1972).[51] In addition, reading "consumer" as the equivalent of "holder" would create redundancies in other portions of the Act. See, *e.g.*, 15 U.S.C. § 1693a(8).[52] "[W]ords in statutes should not be discarded as 'meaningless' and 'surplusage' when Congress specifically and expressly included them, particularly where the words are excluded in other sections of the same act." *Wong Kim Bo*,

[50] One Senate version of the bill used the words "person" and "customer" instead of "consumer." The term "person" was defined as

> an individual who is a citizen of the United States or an alien lawfully admitted for permanent residence, or a partnership, corporation, association, trust, or any other legal entity organized under the laws of a State of the United States.

The term "customer" was defined as

> any natural person who is a debit instrument patron of a debit instrument issuer who utilizes electronic fund transfer services primarily for personal, family or household purposes.

Consumer Protection Aspects of EFT Systems, 1978: Hearings on S. 2546 and S. 2470 Before the Subcomm. on Consumer Affairs of the Senate Comm. on Banking, Housing, and Urban Affairs, 95th Cong., 2d Sess. 131(1978). The Senate did not explain, however, why it chose the word consumer" and the broader definition of that word over the word "customer."

[51] The plaintiff reads the definition of an "unauthorized electronic fund transfer" as an indication that not every natural person is a consumer within the context of the EFTA. She emphasizes that the federal regulations state that the definitions apply "unless the context indicates otherwise." 12 C.F.R. § 205.2 (1982). While the plaintiff's interpretation of the unauthorized transfer definition is not without merit, her own emphasis on the importance of the context in which the language is used undercuts her argument. In a context where Congress has expressly narrowed the class of consumers to whom a specific provision in the statute applies, the more narrow definition is controlling. Congress did not, however, narrow the class of consumers to be covered by the exclusion, as it did in the unauthorized transfer section.

[52] Section 1693a(8) provides:

> the term "financial institution" means a State or National bank, a State or Federal savings and loan association, a mutual savings bank, a State or Federal credit union, or any other person who, directly or indirectly, holds an account belonging to a consumer.

15 U.S.C. § 1693a(8).

472 F.2d at 722. In short, the language of the statute would seem to exclude the transfer in this case from the coverage of the Act.

Further, the legislative history of the EFTA is consistent with the plain meaning of the language in the statute and with the presumption arising from Congress's disparate inclusion and exclusion of words of limitation. The plaintiff emphasizes that Congress designed the Act to provide a comprehensive scheme of federal regulation for all electronic transfers of funds. See H.R.Rep. No. 1315, 95th Cong., 2d Sess. 2 (1978); see also E. Broadman, *Electronic Fund Transfer Act: Is the Consumer Protected,* 13 U.S.F.L.Rev. 245 (1979). Congress undoubtedly intended the Act's coverage to be broad; the Act itself provides that its list of electronic fund transfers is not all-inclusive. 15 U.S.C. § 1693a(6). Aware that computer technology was still in a rapid, evolutionary stage of development, Congress was careful to permit coverage of electronic services not yet in existence: "The definition of 'electronic fund transfer' is intended to give the Federal Reserve Board flexibility in determining whether new or developing electronic services should be covered by the act and, if so, to what extent." S.Rep. No. 915, 95th Cong., 2d Sess. 9 (1978), U.S. Code Cong. & Admin. News 1978, pp 9273, 9411; see also National Commission on Electronic Fund Transfers, EFT in the United States, 4 (Final Rep. 1977).

Congressional concern about electronic systems not specifically mentioned in the Act was focused, however, on future and as yet undeveloped systems, not on systems that Congress had simply failed to discuss. For example, the report on the House version of the Act explained the need for flexibility in dealing with future electronic systems:

> Many aspects of electronic fund transfer systems are undergoing evolutionary changes and, thus, projections about future events necessarily involve a degree of speculation. Consequently, the appropriate approach to those new financial service concepts is, in general, to permit further development in a free market environment and, to the extent possible, in a manner consistent with the nature and purpose of existing law and regulations governing financial services.

H.R.Rep. No. 1315, *supra*, at 33. The absence of discussion about informal personal phone transfers would seem to indicate an intent not to cover these transfers, or at least an absence of congressional concern about them, in light of the extensive discussion throughout the hearings and reports of the other existing types of electronic transfers. It is highly unlikely that this silence was a result of congressional ignorance of the problem since these informal phone withdrawals presumably had been occurring since shortly after the time of Alexander Graham Bell.

The exclusion of these informal transactions was not in the House version of the EFTA, and presumably it was not in the original version of the Senate bill either since the minority report criticized the bill's coverage of incidental telephone instructions:

> In an attempt to reach the automatic telephone payments (transfers through a touch-tone telephone and computer network routing instructions to the financial institution) the Committee has also covered incidental telephone instructions by (a) depositor to a teller to make a transfer from a savings account to cover an overdraft or pay a bill.

S.Rep. No. 915, *supra*, at 24, U.S.Code Cong. & Admin.News 1978, p. 9425. Apparently, this criticism led to the inclusion in the final version of the EFTA of the exemption which is the subject of this suit. Focusing on the Federal Reserve Board's statement that phone transfers made as an "accommodation to the consumer" are not covered by the Act, 46 Fed.Reg. 46880 (1978), and the Senate minority report's discussion of telephone instructions made by a "depositor," the plaintiff would have us conclude that only transactions made as a favor to the actual account holder were excluded from the Act.

These transfers were more probably excluded, however, not because they are made as a favor to the account holder, but because of the personal element in these transfers. On the one hand, as the plaintiff points out, all phone transfers are particularly vulnerable to fraud because there is no written memorandum of the transactions; there is no signature to be authenticated. This lack of a written record was one of the factors that motivated Congress to pass the EFTA. See H.R.Rep. No. 1315, *supra*, at 2, 4. The other factor, however, was the dependency of electronic fund transfer systems on computers and the resulting absence of any human contact with the transferor. The House report explains: "Consequently, these impersonal transactions are much more vulnerable to fraud, embezzlement, and unauthorized use than the traditional payment methods." *Id.* at 2. Senator Proxmire opened the hearings on the Senate bill with the warning that "[c]omputer systems are far from infallible, and electronic fund transfers—so totally dependent on computers—will also be error prone." The Electronic Funds Transfer Consumer Protection Act, 1977: Hearings on S. 2065 Before the Subcomm. on Consumer Affairs of the Senate Comm. on Banking, Housing and Urban Affairs, 95th Cong., 1st Sess. 2 (1977); see also 124 Cong.Rec. 25731 (1978) (statement of Rep. Annunzio, bill sponsor). As one commentator explains, telephonic communications were included in the definition of electronic fund transfers in order to extend coverage over computerized pay-by-phone systems; informal non-recurring consumer-initiated transfers were excluded, however, because they are not prone to computer error or institutional abuse since they are handled on a personal basis:

> The final exemption from the purview of the EFT Act is an exclusion for nonrecurring transfers of funds that are initiated by an ordinary telephone conversation between a consumer and an officer or employee of the financial institution. In order to extend coverage over computerized "pay-by-phone" systems, the general definition of the term "electronic fund transfer" had to be broad enough to encompass transactions initiated through a telephone. Like automatic debiting of service charges and automatic crediting of interest, however, ordinary nonrecurring transfers informally initiated by a consumer's call to an officer or employee of his neighborhood bank or savings and loan association was not considered to pose a serious threat warranting the coverage and additional costs of the EFT Act. Such requests are handled on a personal basis, so the possibility of computer error or institutional abuse, believed to exist with respect to some other EFT systems, was deemed to be absent.

Brandel & Olift, *The Electronic Fund Transfer Act.— A Primer,* 40 Ohio St.L.J. 531, 545 (1979). Telephonic transfers made between a natural person and an employee of the financial institution share this element of human contact, regardless of whether the transfer is made by the account holder or someone else.

Finally, we note that the EFTA was passed because "[e]xisting law and regulations in the consumer protection area are not applicable to some aspects of the new financial service concepts." H.R.Rep. No. 1315, *supra*, at 33. See also 15 U.S.C. § 1693a. The plaintiff suggests in her reply brief that she would have no adequate legal remedy for the wrong she has suffered if she were denied relief under the EFTA. While she conceded at oral argument that she might have an action under state law for conversion or breach of contract (her deposit agreement with the bank), she maintained that a person suffering a loss resulting from the abuse of one of the other electronic fund transfer systems[53] would also have such an action under state law.

---

[53] Congress was specifically concerned with four principal types of electronic fund transfer services: (1) automated teller machines, (2) Pay-by-phone systems, (3) direct deposits and automatic payments, and (4) Point-of-sale transfers. S.Rep. No. 915, *supra*, at 2, U.S Code Cong. & Admin.News 1978, p. 9404.

The plaintiff ignores the essential difference between electronic fund transfer systems and personal transfers by phone or by check. When the bank employee allegedly agreed to withdraw funds from the plaintiff's account, he or she presumably could have asked some questions to ascertain whether the caller was one of the account holders. The failure to attempt to make a positive identification of the caller might be considered negligence or a breach of the deposit agreement under state law. When someone makes an unauthorized use of an electronic fund transfer system, however, the financial institution often has no way of knowing that the transfer is unauthorized.[54] For example, in order to make a transfer at an automatic teller machine, a person need only possess the machine card and know the correct personal identification number. The computer cannot determine whether the person who has inserted the card and typed in the magic number is authorized to use the system. What might be a withdrawal negligently permitted by the financial institution in one situation might not be a negligent action in the other.

Our analysis of both the language of the EFTA and the legislative history of the Act leads us to conclude that Congress intended to exclude from the Act's coverage any transfer of funds initiated by a phone conversation between any natural person and an officer or employee of a financial institution, which was not made pursuant to a prearranged plan and under which periodic and recurring transfers were not contemplated. Accordingly, we hold that the withdrawal of funds from the plaintiff's account is not covered by the Act even though said withdrawal allegedly was not made by either the plaintiff or her sister. The district court's dismissal of the plaintiff's action for lack of subject matter jurisdiction is

Affirmed.

QUESTION

Why was Kashanchi so enthused to be within the provisions of the Act? Might it have something to do with U.C.C. § 908, which provides that a financial institution that fails to resolve an error satisfactorily may entitle the consumer to treble damages?

NOTE

Regulation E provides that the Board shall determine, upon request of any state, financial institution or other interested party, whether the Act or the regulation preempt state laws relating to EFTs. A substantial majority of states have electronic fund transfer statutes. Only those state laws that are inconsistent with the Act and the regulation are preempted and then only to the extent of the inconsistency. A state law is not preempted when it is more consumer protective than the federal law.

The terms and conditions of electronic fund transfers involving a consumer's account must be disclosed at the time the consumer contracts for an EFT service. The disclosures must be in accord with regulations of the Board and must be readily understandable written terms which the consumer can retain. Such information must contain, if applicable, a summary of the consumer's liability for unauthorized EFTs, the telephone number and address of the person or office to be notified when the consumer believes that an unauthorized transfer has taken place, the financial institution's business days, the type of EFT that the consumer may make and any

[54] One of the purposes of the EFTA was to determine who should bear the loss for these unauthorized transfers. S.Rep. No. 915, *supra,* at 3, 5-6, U.S.Code Cong. & Admin.News 1978, pp 9405, 9407-9408. Limitations on the consumer's liability for unauthorized transfers are contained in 15 U.S.C. § 1693g.

limitations on dollar amounts or frequency of use, any charges for an EFT and a summary of the consumer's right to stop payment of a preauthorized EFT

For each electronic fund transfer initiated by a consumer at an electronic terminal, the account holder must make available to the consumer written documentation of such a transfer. The document must set forth the amount involved and the date of the transfer, the type of transfer, the identity of the account, the identity of any third party to whom the funds were transferred and the location or identification of the terminal involved.

As indicated in the *Kashanchi* case, the EFTA applies only to services used by or offered to consumers and they are defined as natural persons. As a consequence, the Act does not deal with a large number of electronic fund transfers initiated by banks or businesses, such as an automated clearing house (ACH). An ACH has been described as an association of depositary institutions operating an apparatus similar to a check clearing center for the purpose of exchanging batches or groups of paperless entries (debits and credits) and transfers of funds information. An ACH is designed to facilitate electronically routine recurring payments, such as payrolls and social security payments, insurance premium remittances, mortgage payments, and utility charges. The ACH facility processes the information on the paperless entries and distributes the payment and transfer orders in machine readable form (*e.g.*, magnetic tape or punched cards) or paper listings to the receiving institutions, which then debit or credit the accounts of participating customers.[55]

Today, ACHs perform other functions beyond those connected with preauthorized recurring payments. EFTs through a number of ACHs transfer amounts in the trillions of dollars between banks annually. In the main, the legal structure of these transactions is handled through private agreements and operating rules of the ACH and by Federal Reserve Regulation J.[56]

Procedures for resolving error are generally defined in the initial agreement for access to an electronic terminal. The Act provides for specific consumer protection requirements Where an electronic fund transfer also involves an extension of credit under an agreement between a consumer and a financial institution to extend credit when the consumer's account is overdrawn or to maintain a specific balance in the consumer's account, the financial institution must comply with the requirements of the Act rather than those in the Federal Truth & Lending Act.

Most consumers know they cannot lose more than $50 if their credit card is lost or stolen. What many do not know is that loss of an EFT card can be more costly. If an EFT card is lost or stolen, it should be reported to the bank immediately. If the notification occurs within two business days after discovery of the loss, liability for unauthorized use of the card is limited to $50. If the bank is not notified within sixty days, customers could be liable for as much as $500, if the card has been fraudulently used. Then, if the monthly bank statement shows unauthorized EFTs customers must report them within 60 days after the statement is mailed. If they are not reported, the bank may not have to return any missing money, which could include all the funds in the account and possibly more, based on any automatic overdraft coverage on the account. (15 U.S.C. § 909.)

As stated above, there are any number of EFTs in which consumers are participating that are turning us into a checkless or cashless society. Check verification and guarantee combines the electronic transfer with the "normal" check payment procedure. The customer uses the issued

---

[55] National Commission on Electronic Fund Transfers, EFT in the United States 205-207 (1977).

[56] 12 C.F.R. § 210 (1986).

card and enters a PIN (personal identification number) into the terminal installed at the merchant's place of business. The terminal determines from the data of the customer's account whether to authorize the check. If the check is approved, the check is "guaranteed" so that if the check is later dishonored for some reason, the bank will still have to stand behind the check. The significant difference between the POS and the check guarantee is the time in which the merchant is given credit. In the guarantee or verification situation a hold is placed on the cardholder's account. A credit is not given to the merchant until the paper comes back for payment through the collection process.

Preauthorized debit and credit arises when a depositor desires to have an account debited on a monthly basis for a recurring payment. This authorizes the creditor to initiate periodic debits to the account. The creditor must have the authority of the bank as well as the depositor. The depositor may authorize credits to the account as well, by requesting that wages or other benefits be directly credited to the account.

Pursuant to a preauthorized pay by telephone transfer, a consumer may use an identifying card number to pay someone from the account. The arrangement may also be used to transfer funds from one account to another.

The popularity of automated teller machines has provided the impetus for the development of electronic payment systems at retail outlets. The growth in the number of POS terminals is attributed to the development of EFT networks that allow a single retailer to accept bank machine cards from numerous institutions. ATM and POS transactions can involve single or multiple depository institutions. That is, the merchant and the consumer can both be depositors at a single institution, or they can be depositors at different or multiple depository institutions. In the single institution point-of-sale, a financial institution installs a terminal at a merchant's place of business which is programmed with the records of the consumer depositor's account. Specifically, the institution issues an accepted card to its depositor, together with a PIN which serves to identify the holder and grant access to the terminal. The system operates by the consumer taking the card to a retailer's place of business which has terminal access and punching the PIN into the computer while the merchant punches in the data regarding the particular purchase. The transaction, if approved, provides the card holder with a receipt which indicates a debiting to the account and a crediting of the merchant's account for the same amount. The multi-institutional transaction, where the customer is not a depositor at the same institution as the merchant, involves switching in the computer terminals.

If you were legislative director for a Senator looking to "add substance" to the provisions of the EFT act, what points might you suggest the Senator consider?

PORTER v. CITIBANK

New York City Civil Court
123 Misc. 2d 28, 472 N.Y.S.2d 582 (1984)

EDWARD H. LEHNER, JUDGE:

To withdraw funds from your Citibank account at any time all you need do is place your card in their machine, enter your secret code, and then push a button. So the advertisement goes. But, complains the plaintiff, on two occasions this was done, no money was received, and yet his account was charged. Thus the Court is faced with another type of dispute between man and machine, for which no precedent has been found.

Plaintiff testified that on August 23, 1983 he sought to withdraw $100 from his checking account. When no money was dispensed from the machine after the necessary buttons were pushed, he reported the fact to a bank official who stated that the matter would be investigated. A few weeks later, on September 5, plaintiff took the requisite steps to make a $200 withdrawal. When no money appeared, he then repeated the process with the same result, which he thereupon reported to management. As a result of the foregoing plaintiff's account showed one withdrawal of $ 100 and two of $200 (for a total of $ 500), which amount he seeks to recover in this action.

The witnesses employed in the branch of the bank where the machine involved was located testified that in examining it on the day after the first of the two occurrences they found the account in balance, while on the latter date there was a cash overage of $90. They further indicated that, on the average, the cash machines were out of balance once or twice per week, but never for a sum in excess of $100.

Although no reported decision has been found dealing with this type of situation, *McEvans v. Citibank, NA.*, 96 Misc.2d 142, 408 N.Y.S.2d 870 (Civil Ct., N.Y Co., 1978) involved a somewhat analogous problem There, a customer, who admitted failing to supply the bank with a deposit slip, claimed to have made a deposit by placing cash in an envelope in the cash machine. However, she received no credit because the bank denied receipt. The Court ruled in favor of the customer, but only because it found the bank negligent in failing to follow its own publicized procedures of having one person open the deposit envelopes, with a second employee observing the opening.

In *Employers Insurance of Wausau v. Chemical Bank*, 117 Misc.2d 601, 459 N.Y S.2d 238 (Civil Ct., N.Y Co., 1983), the undersigned was confronted with a situation where the plaintiff claimed to have made a deposit in the night depository for which the bank had no record. Believing the testimony of the plaintiff's witness, judgment was rendered in its favor through application of the rules of bailment. See also: *Judd v. Citibank*, 107 Misc.2d 526, 435 N.Y.S.2d 210 (Civil Ct., Queens Co., 1980) and *Ognibene v. Citibank*, 112 Misc.2d 219, 446 N.Y.S.2d 845 (Civil Ct., N.Y Co., 1981), where bank customers who were tricked into permitting others to use their bank cards were granted recovery.

As indicated in the discussion in *Employers Insurance of Wausau v. Chemical Bank, supra*, a minority of the few courts in the nation that have considered the question have declined to grant a recovery against a bank solely on the testimony of a customer that a deposit was made. This reluctance is based on the fear of fraudulent suits against these public institutions. The policy underlying this view is illustrated by the dicta in *Roscoe v. Central National Bank of Canajoharie*, 96 Misc.2d 517, 521, 409 N.Y.S.2d 189 (Sup.Ct., Schenectady Co. 1978), where it was said that it would be "sheer folly" to "permit unrestrained and unlimited suits against banks simply on the bare assertion of an individual that he made a deposit. Without subsequent discovery, there would be no way of actually knowing whether the claimed deposit was in fact made, and in such a situation, fraught with limitless opportunities for fraud, banks should not be held answerable or liable."

However, the preferable majority view is to permit recovery where the Court is convinced that the deposit was in fact made and the bank could not explain its absence. Although the bailment presumptions applicable to night deposit cases cannot be said to be applicable to the opposite situation at bar where the claim is that the withdrawal was not received, the cases are pertinent in their holdings that a Court may give credence to testimony of an undocumented deposit. Similar to the night depository customer, who is not in a position to produce any documentary evidence to establish that he made the deposit, the cash machine customer can produce nothing to show that the money was not dispensed to him.

Here we are dealing with machines which defendant's witnesses acknowledged were out of balance one or two nights a week (although not to the extent involved in this case). Such witnesses also stated their belief that at times a subsequent machine customer received money properly belonging to the prior user of the machine. Plaintiff was a rather credible witness who had no record of banking problems although he had used the machines numerous times. Under the circumstances, the Court holds that plaintiff established by a fair preponderance of the evidence that he did not receive the money for which he was charged as a result of the above mentioned transactions. Therefore, he is entitled to judgment for $500, plus interest from September 5, 1983.

In so deciding the Court is not unmindful of the possibility of fraudulent suits. However, this fear exists in many areas of the law and the history of jurisprudence has not indicated that Courts have been unable to competently (although certainly not perfectly) deal with such challenges.

NOTES AND QUESTIONS

(1) Does *Porter v. Citibank* heighten your enthusiasm for your EFT card?

(2) In the last sentence of the opinion, the court appears to assume that our legal system is not perfect. In your opinion, what is the basis for such assumption?

CREDIT CARDS

Another form of electronic transaction and payment system involves credit cards. There are two categories of credit cards: merchant cards — those designed to facilitate sales of goods or services of the particular issuer, and financial institution cards — those which provide cardholders with a line of credit that can be used to purchase goods from a variety of sellers. In the case of financial institution cards, the merchant is party to a pre-existing arrangement either directly with the issuer of the card or with an interbank system to which the issuer belongs. The merchant receives the amount of the purchase less a discount to compensate the issuer for financing the purchase. The issuer obtains compensation by obtaining the full amount from the cardholder, hence the credit risk is assumed by the issuer.

A limitation on the liability of cardholders for unauthorized use is given in the Consumer Credit Protection Act. Section 1642 bans the practice of issuing credit cards to people who did not request them. Section 1643 makes the cardholder not liable for the unauthorized use of the card. A cardholder is only liable if the card is an accepted credit card, the liability is not in excess of $50, the issuer gives adequate notice of the potential liability, the issuer notified the cardholder of a means to report theft, and the unauthorized use occurs before the issuer has been notified.

Further, under 1666i, the cardholder is given an exception to the rule that the cardholder is obligated to pay the issuer (bank) regardless of any dispute which may arise respecting the merchandise. The section allows claimants whose transactions exceed $50 and who have made a good faith attempt to obtain satisfactory resolution of the problem to assert claims and defenses arising out of the card transaction. The limitation placed on the cardholder is that the location of the initial transaction is within the same state or within 100 miles of the cardholder. Any claim which the cardholder may assert may only be as good as and no better than his claim against the merchant. Hence, the plaintiff's claim must be scrutinized to ascertain its merits.

In most instances, the rules governing payment system favor commercial practicality. However, in other instances, the rules are designed to protect the consumer, as in the case of credit cards and in fund availability.

CHAPTER 15

THE ROLE OF BANKS IN WIRE TRANSFERS

§ 15.01 Introduction

Read: U.C.C. Article 4A Prefatory Note

Each day, more than one trillion dollars is transferred electronically between business and financial institutions by wire transfers. As we have seen, payments by check are covered under both Articles 3 and 4 of the Uniform Commercial Code (U.C.C.), while many aspects of credit card transactions are covered by various state and federal laws such as the Electronic Funds Transfer Act of 1978 (EFTA),[1] and the federal Truth in Lending laws.[2] But in the case of wire transfers, legal rules were culled from four sources: (1) regulations governing the two principal wire transfer systems in the United States, the Federal Reserve wire transfer network (Fedwire) and the New York Clearing House Interbank Payments Systems (CHIPS); (2) uniform rules of various regional bank associations throughout the United States; (3) rules of the National Automated Clearing House Association on credit transfers; and (4) Federal Reserve Bank rules and operating circulars. These uniform rules covered limited technical aspects of wire transactions but failed to resolve broader issues involving such variables as the contract between the parties and the extent to which courts will make an analogy to laws governing similar types of payment mechanisms. Until recently, no consensus existed as to the rights and obligations created by the various wholesale wire transfer systems; Article 4A of the U.C.C. was designed to address the uncertainty in this area of the law by providing a uniform set of rules to protect justifiable party expectations.

In its classic form, a funds transfer occurs when a customer instructs her or his bank to deal with another bank for the purposes of immediately crediting the account of a named person (defined in the Act as a "beneficiary") with a fixed or determinable amount of money. The same type of transaction could even occur between accounts at the same bank. Article 4 dealt with only some of the issues raised by the development of computer technology and electronic communications systems. Problems arose because the "wire transfer" transaction was not a paper based transaction like those involving commercial paper under Article 3 or the bank collection system under Article 4. Article 4A uses the broader term "funds transfer" to encompass those situations in which payment orders use both existing and yet to be developed technology to effect the payment of funds to a beneficiary. While the statute defines fund transfer broadly, Article 4A excludes consumer transactions because they are governed by the Electronic Funds Transfer Act.

---

[1] 15 U.S.C. § 1693 *et seq.*

[2] 15 U.S.C. § 1601 *et seq.*

History

The following description, adopted from the *Banque Worms* case, provides some of the history of fund transfers that led to the promulgation of Article 4A.

While courts have attempted in wire transfer cases to employ, by analogy, the rules of the more traditional areas of law, such as contract law, the law of negotiable instruments and the special relations between banks, these areas are governed by principles codified in Articles 3 and 4 of the Uniform Commercial Code. Various commentators found these efforts ineffective and inadequate to deal with the problems presented . . .As pointed out by the Official Comment to Article 4A, "attempts to define rights and obligations in funds transfers by general principles or by analogy to rights and obligations in negotiable instruments law or the law of check collection have not been satisfactory." Consequently, it was concluded, . . . that a new article was needed because "[t]here is no comprehensive body of law that defines the rights and obligations that arise from wire transfers". . .

Electronic funds transfers have become the preferred method utilized by businesses and financial institutions to effect payments and transfers of a substantial volume of funds. These transfers, commonly referred to as wholesale wire transfers,[3] differ from other payment methods in a number of significant respects, a fact which accounts in large measure for their popularity. Funds are moved faster and more efficiently than by traditional payment instruments, such as checks. The transfers are completed at a relatively low cost, which does not vary widely depending on the amount of the transfer, because the price charged reflects primarily the cost of the mechanical aspects of the funds transfer (Prefatory Note to U.C.C. Art. 4A). Most transfers are completed within one day and can cost as little as $10 to carry out a multimillion dollar transaction. . . The popularity of wholesale wire transfers is evidenced by the fact that nearly $1 trillion in transactions occur each day, averaging $5 million per transfer and on peak days, this figure often approaches $2 trillion . . . .

Wholesale wire transfers are generally made over the two principal wire payment systems: the Federal Reserve Wire Transfer Network (Fedwire) and CHIPS.[4] The CHIPS network handles 95% of the international transfers made in dollars, transferring an average of $750 billion per day. . . These funds are transferred through participating banks located in New York because all of the banks belonging to the CHIPS network must maintain a regulated presence in New York. As a result, this State is considered the national and international center for wholesale wire transfers.

The low cost of electronic funds transfers is an important factor in the system's popularity and this is so even though banks executing wire transfers often risk significant liability as a result of losses occasioned by mistakes and errors, the most common of which involve the payment of funds to the wrong beneficiary or in an incorrect amount. . . Thus, a major policy issue facing the drafters of U.C.C. Article 4A was determining how the risk of loss might best be allocated, while preserving a unique price structure. In order to prevent or minimize losses, the industry had adopted and employed various security procedures, designed to prevent

[3] The Official Comment to U.C.C. 4A-102 notes that while most payments covered by Article 4A are usually referred to as "wire transfers" and involve an electronic transmission, other types of transmissions such as letter, or other written communication or oral communication, are also covered, thus the broader term "funds transfer" is used in preference to the narrower term "wire transfer." (2A ULA [Master ed.], at 147, 1990 Supp. Pamph.).

[4] CHIPS is owned and operated by the New York Clearing House Association and the Federal Reserve Bank owns and operates Fedwire, the largest American wire transfer network.

losses[5] such as the use of codes, identifying words or numbers, call-back procedures and limits on payment amounts or beneficiaries that may be paid.

As indicated above, it was the consensus among various commentators that existing rules of law did not adequately address the problems presented by these wholesale electronic funds transfers. Thus, the National Conference of Commissioners on Uniform State Laws (NCCUSL) and the American Law Institute (ALI) undertook to develop a body of unique principles of law that would address every aspect of the electronic funds transfer process and define the rights and liabilities of all parties involved in such transfers. After extensive investigation and debate and through a number of drafts, in 1989, both the NCCUSL and the ALI approved a new Article 4A of the Uniform Commercial Code. . . In 1990, the New York State Legislature adopted the new Article 4A and incorporated it into the New York Uniform Commercial Code (N.Y. U.C.C. Art. 4-A).[6] Although the new statute, which became effective January 1, 1991, may not be applied retroactively to resolve the issues presented by this litigation, the statute's legislative history and the history of Article 4A of the Uniform Commercial Code from which it is derived and the policy considerations addressed by this legislation, can appropriately inform our decision and serve as persuasive authority in aid of the resolution of the issue presented in this case. . .

Both the NCCUSL and ALI drafters of Article 4A and the New York Legislature sought to achieve a number of important policy goals through enactment of this article. National uniformity in the treatment of electronic funds transfers is an important goal, as are speed, efficiency, certainty (i.e., to enable participants in fund transfers to have better understanding of their rights and liabilities, and finality. Establishing finality in electronic fund wire transactions was considered a singularly important policy goal. . . Payments made by electronic funds transfers in compliance with the provisions of Article 4A are to be the equivalent of cash payments irrevocable except to the extent provided for in Article 4A (see, Assn of Bar of City of NY, Committee on Banking Law, Report on proposed New York U.C.C. Art. 4-A; see also, *Delbrueck & Co. v. Manufacturers Hanover Trust Co.*, 609 F.2d 1047, 1049-1051 [2d Cir.] [once an electronic fund transfer is completed and the funds released, the transaction is final and irrevocable under the CHIPS system]) (Excerpt from *Banque Worms v. Bank America International*, 568 N.Y.S. 2d 541, 570 N.E. 2d 189 (1991).

§ 15.02 The Parties

Read: U.C.C. §§ 4A-103, 4A-104

The funds transfer process begins with an "originator", the person who orders the bank to make a payment order. Article 4A defines the originator as "the sender of the first payment order

---

[5] The Official Comment to U.C.C. 4A-201 as drafted by the American Law Institute and National Conference of Commissioners on Uniform State Laws states that "it is standard practice to use security procedures that are designed to assure the authenticity of the message [and] to detect error in the content of messages. . . . The question of whether loss that may result from the transmission of a spurious or erroneous payment order will be borne by the receiving bank or the sender or purported sender is affected by whether a security procedures was or was not in effect and whether there was or was not compliance with the procedure." (2A ULA [Master ed.], at 156-157, 1990 Supp. Pamph.)

[6] The new Article 4A will regulate funds transfers other than consumer transactions governed by the Federal Electronic Fund Transfer Act of 1978 (15 USC § 1693 *et seq.*). It will not apply to consumer transactions such as check payments or credit card payments for the Federal EFTA will continue to govern these transactions. If any part of a fund transfer is covered by the EFTA, the entire funds transfer will be excluded from Article 4A.

in a funds transfer." Section 4A-104(3). Any number of senders can be involved, but only the sender of the first payment order in the chain can be the originator. The "originator's bank" is (i) the receiving bank to which the payment order of the originator is issued if the originator is not a bank, or (ii) the originator if the originator is a bank." U.C.C. § 4A-104(4). It is possible for the sender also to be the beneficiary of the payment. For example, a corporation that ordered a bank to transfer funds from one of its accounts to another at that or another bank would be both an originator and a beneficiary.

The originating bank is defined as the institution to which the sender's payment order is addressed. An originating bank may also become a sender when it carries out a sender's payment order by transmitting a second payment order to another bank requesting that payment be made to the person specified in the original sender's payment order. The process can continue in a chain of transactions, where a number of banks receive and in turn send payment orders to other banks to execute the original payment order. Each bank that receives a payment order and then issues its own payment order to effectuate the first order acts as both a receiving bank and a sender within the meaning of Article 4A.

An "intermediary bank" is any bank in the chain of the transaction other than the originator's bank or the beneficiary's bank. U.C.C. § 4A-104(2). The "beneficiary's bank" sits at the end of the funds transfer transaction; it is defined as the "bank identified in a payment order in which an account of the beneficiary is to be credited pursuant to the order or which otherwise is to make payment to the beneficiary if the order does not provide for payment to an account." U.C.C. § 4A-103(3). Article 4A awkwardly defines the beneficiary as "the person to be paid by the beneficiary's bank." U.C.C. § 4A-103(2). Perhaps a more helpful way of thinking about the definition would be to characterize the beneficiary as the person the originator intends to pay when transmitting a payment order to the receiving bank.

Article 4A defines the term "customer" as a person, including a bank, having an account with a bank or one for whom a bank has agreed to receive payment orders. The account designated by the customer as the source of funds for the payment order(s) is known as the "authorized account." If the customer does not designate an authorized account, any account of that customer at the bank will be considered an authorized account for purposes of Article 4A so long as use of that account is consistent with any restrictions previously agreed upon between the customer and the bank.

The drafters of Article 4A were persuaded by wire transfer users that the customer should be able to specify the account to be used for payment order funding since specification would be instrumental in guarding against any unauthorized use of payment orders by means of accessing other customer accounts at a bank. Where an originator instructs the bank to make payments to a certain party at regular intervals, the blanket payment instruction is treated as a separate payment order with respect to each payment made to the named beneficiary.

DONMAR ENTERPRISES, INCORPORATED v. SOUTHERN NATIONAL BANK OF NORTH CAROLINA

United States Court of Appeals
64 F.3d 944 (4th CIr. 1995)

WIDENER, CIRCUIT JUDGE:

Donmar Enterprises, Inc. (Donmar) appeals from the district court's grant of summary judgment to Southern National Bank of North Carolina (Southern National) as to Count I of

Donmar's complaint, which was predicated on Federal Reserve Board Regulation J, Subpart B, Appendix B, and dismissal of Counts II and III, which raised negligence and wrongful payment claims under state law. The district court held that a private cause of action can be maintained pursuant to Regulation J, and that Regulation J pre-empted Donmar's state law claims of negligence and wrongful payment. It granted summary judgment to Southern National as to the Regulation J claim since the requirements of Regulation J were satisfied, and along the same line, dismissed the state law counts.

I.

We recount the facts and inferences in the light most favorable to the non-moving party. Donmar, located in Florida, engages in the selling of automobile sunroofs and accessories, which involves purchasing inventory from businesses in foreign countries. In making foreign purchases, Donmar pays by converting U.S. currency to foreign currency. For this conversion, Donmar used Stephen's Trading Company (Stephen's), a North Carolina company. After a transaction in which Donmar wired funds directly into Stephen's account at Wachovia Bank in North Carolina, Donmar's president, Kal Levinson, and Stephen Selleck, Stephen's owner and president, agreed that future transfers would be handled through the defendant, Southern National, and that Donmar would be a beneficiary of Donmar's wire transfers to Southern National, which would be sent to Southern National with a Stephen's transaction code. Donmar did not have an account with Southern National, Stephen's did have. Donmar would then fax to Stephen's its authorization for the purchase of foreign currency and where it was to be transferred, and Stephen's would deliver the facsimile from Donmar to Souther National as authorization to transfer the funds. Southern National, however, was not advised of this agreement. On two occasions in 1990, Donmar caused its bank, First Union of Jacksonville, Florida (First Union) to transmit funds by wire to Southern National. On August 10, 1990, the first wire transfer was sent with the notation "ATTN INT DIV R E STC DONMAR WIRE 102 1003" and, with reference to that August 10th transfer, Stephen's sent southern National a facsimile message authorizing deposit of the funds into its account. Southern National credited the funds to Stephen's account. Seven days later, at Stephen's direction, Southern National transferred funds to a bank in Great Britain, referencing STC/Donmar No. 102-1003 as the order customer and sent Donmar confirmation of this transaction. This confirmation from Southern National led Donmar to believe that Southern National was acting pursuant to Donmar's authorization facsimile sent to Stephen's. A second similar wire transaction occurred in October of 1990, when Donmar had First Union wire money to Southern National with the notation "ATN INTL DIV REF STC DON MAR WIRE 102 1007," and Southern National, pursuant to instructions received from Stephen's credited Stephen's account and thereafter transferred funds to Great Britain. However, Selleck does not recall receiving confirmation of this wire transfer.

On February 26, 1991, Donmar authorized First Union to wire transfer $15,000 to Southern National, with the wire noting "ATTN; INTL DIV RE STC DONMAR TRANS CODE 1021011," pursuant to instructions from Stephen's to Donmar as to the notation on the wire. This $15,000 was the margin required to hold the purchase of pounds sterling 280,000. The supervisor of wire transfers in Southern National's international division, upon receipt of the $15,000 wire transfer, called Selleck of Stephen's to confirm that Stephen's was in fact the intended beneficiary of this wire transfer. Selleck confirmed the wire transfer and instructed the supervisor that it was to be credited to Stephen's account. Pursuant to instructions from Stephen's, Southern National wired this money to a bank in Pennsylvania, to be credited to the account of David A. Selleck.

On March 27, 1991, Stephen's sent a facsimile message to Donmar, requesting that it send "My USD to: Southern National Bank, Lumberton, N.C. . . Re: STC/Donmar Trans Code 102-1011." The same day, Stephen's notified Southern National that it was expecting a wire transfer of $524,276.71 from First Union, referenced as "INCOMING WIRE STC/DONMAR CODE 102-1011" and again directed Southern National to deposit funds from the wire transfer into Stephen's account. Subsequently, Donmar authorized First Union to wire the $524,276.71 to Southern National and faxed instruction to Stephen's to wire pounds sterling 200,000 to Lloyds Bank in London and to hold or sell the other pounds sterling 80,000. First Union transferred the funds to Southern National at 1:39 p.m., with the notation "ATTN INTL DIV REF SLC/DONMAR TRANS CODE 102-1011." Southern National deposited the funds to Stephen's account. Also on March 27th, pursuant to instructions from Stephen's received at 2:32 p.m., Southern National wired $524,000 to Stephen's account at Discount Corp. of New York. On March 28, Stephen's directed Southern National to wire funds in the amount of pounds sterling 200,000 to Lloyd's Bank in England, but Southern National informed Stephen's that it lacked sufficient funds to accomplish the transfer. That same day, at 11:38 a.m., Stephen's sent Donmar a facsimile message to the effect that it was unable to complete the international wire for pounds sterling 200,000 "[d]ue to capital being held for hedging transactions in Stephen's Trading account," but estimated that the transaction should be completed on April 1, 1991. Shortly thereafter, Levinson of Donmar called First Union and instructed it to contact Southern National and requested that the $524,276.71 wire transfer be returned. At 12:10 p.m. on March 28, Levinson spoke directly with an employee at Southern National and informed her that the wire transfer beneficiary line was addressed RE: STC/DONMAR, but was told that a wire addressed in that manner would not have been accepted by Southern National. At 1:26 p.m. on March 28, southern National received a wire from First Union stating that the SLC referred to in the wire transfer should have been STC, not SLC. On April 3, 1991, Southern National transferred the equivalent of pounds sterling 200,000 from Stephen's account to Donmar's British supplier's account at Lloyd's Bank, as directed by Stephen's.

While the foregoing recitation of some relevant facts may seem somewhat complicated, in actuality there is little complication. The unfamiliarity of the terms, we suggest, accounts for any apparent confusion. The following facts also stand out:

Donmar did not have and had never had an account in Southern National.

Donmar had never had an agreement with Southern National.

Donmar had never been a customer of Southern National.

Donmar never gave any direction to Southern National as to the disposition of any of the funds involved in this case until the calls from Levinson to First Union and Southern National on March 28, 1991.

Neither Stephen's nor Donmar gave any direction to Southern National to set up a joint account in their names or payable to their order.

Stephen's directed Donmar to wire the money immediately involved in this case (the $15,000 and $524,726.71) to Southern National, giving a code number to identify the transmission.

Donmar directed First Union to wire that same money involved to Southern National, using the code number given to it by Stephen's.

When the money was received at Southern National in the sum expected and with the same code number, it was deposited in Stephen's account in Southern National, as Stephen's had directed Southern National.

We find that the foregoing facts are not contradicted and support the judgment appealed from. We are of opinion there is no issue of fact in this case.

II.

Donmar claims that it lost $187,276.71 and filed a complaint seeking recovery under three counts, alleging Southern National's violation of Federal Reserve Board Regulation J, 55Fed. Reg. 40,791 (1990) (as amended Oct 5, 1990) (codified at 12 C.F.R. Part 210(Subpart B and Appendix B)); wrongful payment; and negligence. Southern National filed a motion to dismiss or for summary judgment. The district court granted summary judgment to Southern National on the Regulation J claim and dismissed the negligence and wrongful payment claims as being inconsistent with, and therefore pre-empted by, Regulation J.

Donmar raises three issues on appeal. First, Donmar claims that an issue of fact exists as to who was the beneficiary of the wire transfers and argues that both it and Stephen's were joint beneficiaries and that Southern National was obligated, pursuant to Regulation J's adoption of section 4A-404(a) of the U.C.C., to pay them as joint beneficiaries. See Part I, *supra*. Second, Donmar argues that Southern National was required to refuse to accept the wire transfer, since the designation STC/Donmar was an unidentifiable or nonexistent beneficiary under Regulation J's section 4A-207. Third, Donmar argues that the district court erred in determining that Regulation J pre-empted its state law causes of action in this case.

III.

Our review of a summary judgment is de novo. Since the provisions of Regulation J are applicable to this case, a review of those regulations and the context in which they arose is appropriate. As of January 1, 1991, the Federal Reserve Board revised Subpart B of Regulation J to apply the provisions of U.C.C. Article 4A to funds transfers handled by Federal Reserve banks. The official commentary to the U.C.C. provisions in Regulation J. Subpart B provide that the official comments to U.C.C. Article 4A, while not incorporated in Subpart B or its official commentary, may nonetheless "be useful in interpreting Article 4A." Recently, electronic funds transfers, also known as wire transfers, have become increasingly utilized by businesses and financial institutions to effect payments and transfers of a vast volume of funds. The success of funds transfer systems is predicated on speed, efficiency, high volume, low cost, certainty, and finality. The drafters of the U.C.C. considered these factors in assessing liabilities under Article 4A.

This system of pricing may not be feasible if the bank is exposed to very large liabilities in connection with the transaction. A major policy issue in the drafting of Article 4A is that of determining how risk of loss is to be allocated given the price structure in the industry.

U.C.C. § 4A-101, Prefatory Note.

IV.

Donmar contends that Regulation J does not pre-empt its state law negligence and wrongful payment claims and that the district court erred in dismissing these causes of action. In considering the preemptive effect of federal law, including federal regulations, we first look to the regulation to determine the expressed preemptive intent of the Federal Reserve Board. Regulation J itself contains a preemption standard.

> [R]egulations of the Board may pre-empt inconsistent provisions of state law. Accordingly, Subpart B of this part supersedes or pre-empts inconsistent provisions of state law. It does not affect state law governing funds transfers that does not conflict with the provisions of Subpart B of this part, such as Article 4A, as enacted in any state, as it applies to parties to funds transfers through Fedwire whose rights are not governed by Subpart B of this part.

Appendix A to Subpart B to Part 210, 12 C.F.R. § 210.25 (1995). This regulation specifies that inconsistent provisions of state law are pre-empted, while state law that does not conflict is not pre-empted, and lists as an example of a non-conflicting state law, a state law governing funds transfers that applies to parties to which the federal Article 4A does not apply. But Article 4A applies in this case.

The Official Commentary to U.C.C. section 4A-102 provides insight as to the objectives of the Federal Reserve board in adopting Article 4A:

> Before this Article was drafted there was not a comprehensive body of law—statutory or judicial—that defined the judicial nature of a funds transfer or the rights and obligations flowing from payment orders. Judicial authority with respect to funds transfers is sparse, undeveloped and not uniform. Judges have had to resolve disputes by referring to general principles of common law or equity . . . [b]ut attempts to define rights and obligations in funds transfers by general principles or by analogy to rights and obligations in negotiable instrument law or the law of check collection have not been satisfactory. . . The rules that emerged represent a careful and delicate balancing of those interests and are intended to be the exclusive means of determining the rights, duties and liabilities of the affected parties in any situation covered by particular provisions of the Article. Consequently, resort to principles of law or equity outside of Article 4A is not appropriate to create rights, duties and liabilities inconsistent with those stated in this Article.

It is apparent from the U.C.C. commentary that a uniform and comprehensive national regulation of Fedwire transfers was the goal of the Board in adopting Article 4A. Furthermore, the board has made clear that the type of state laws it considers not in conflict with Subpart B are state laws specifically governing funds transfers and parties not subject to Subpart B. Because we conclude in Part V that Southern National complied with and therefore has no liability under Subpart B, any liability founded on state law of negligence or wrongful payment would necessarily be in conflict with the federal regulations and is pre-empted.

Accordingly, we hold that any state causes of action based on negligence or unlawful payment on the facts of this case are preempted by Regulation J.

V.

Donmar argues that the notation STC DONMAR TRANS CODE 1021011 on its wire transfer dated February 26, 1991 and the notation SLC/DONMAR TRANS CODE 1021011 on its wire transfer dated March 27, 1991 indicate that STC and Donmar were joint beneficiaries of the transfer. Therefore, Donmar claims that Southern National violated section 4A-404(a) by crediting the funds to Stephen's only. Section 4A-404(a) of Regulation J provides in relevant part:

> [I]f a beneficiary's bank accepts a payment order, the bank is obliged to pay the amount of the order to the beneficiary of the order . . .

In support of its contention that an issue of fact exists as to whether Donmar was a beneficiary of the transfer and that Southern National violated this section. Donmar relies upon the affidavit of Levinson to the effect that it was his intention, by putting Donmar's name of what he refers to as the "beneficiary line" of the wire transfer, that Donmar be a joint beneficiary, along with Stephen's, of the transfer. However, Donmar submits no evidence that this cryptic reference would render Donmar a joint beneficiary of the transfer. Donmar merely states that the notations in question appeared on what Donmar calls the "beneficiary line" of the wire transfer. Donmar points to no authority or evidence of common usage within the industry to support its interpretation of the transfer order and its claimed joint beneficiary status, and we fail to see how Donmar's construction of the message can be justified, in light of the facts of this case and the Fedwire format and funds transfer practice. The format used for Fedwire has no separately designated fields for data about the originator or beneficiary of a transfer, Red to Expand Fedwire Format to Oblige New Wire Regs, Money Laundering Alert, Dec 1993, at 6, and "does not provide sufficient space for complete originator and beneficiary information," Amy G. Rudnick and Julie A. Stanton, Treasury and Fed Are Fashioning New Wire Transfer Rules, Banking Policy Report, Oct 4, 1993 at 11. While Fedwire limits remittance information to approximately 250 characters, the Federal Reserve Board has issued a policy statement encouraging financial institutions to include information on senders as well as beneficiaries on wire transfers and has proposed regulations that mandate that information. Considering this and especially in view of the complete lack of direction by Donmar to Southern National; the specific direction of Stephen's to Southern National; and Donmar's following of Stephen's directions as to the transfer, even to the code number, the only reasonable conclusion is that Southern National was justified in not considering the notation STC Donmar or STC/Donmar as designating Stephen's and Donmar as joint beneficiaries, as argued by Donmar. In sum, there is no evidence that Southern National was ever advised prior March 28, 1991, that Donmar advised that it and Stephen's were joint beneficiaries of the wire transfers; rather, the inferences from the evidence are to the contrary.

We further think that Southern National correctly identified the beneficiary of the wire transfers from First Union as Stephen's and are thus of opinion that Southern National was entitled to summary judgment on Donmar's Regulation J claims predicated on alleged violations of sections 4A-404(a) and 4A-207.

The judgment of the district court is accordingly AFFIRMED.

NOTE

The *Donmar* court concluded that the statement "STC DONMAR" did not sufficiently identify Donmar as one entitled to payment. Article 4A does not require a recipient of a funds transfer to determine whether there are one or more beneficiaries when that recipient recognizes the name of one as a depositor beneficiary. Should Article 4A have such a requirement?

---

§ 15.03 The Funds Transfer

Read: U.C.C. § 4A-206

This process begins when the sender gives the payment order to the receiving bank. See U.C.C. § 4A-104(1). The request can either be accepted or rejected, unless the bank has agreed to accept payment orders or a funds transfer system rule requires acceptance. The duties and obligations of a receiving bank do not begin until the bank chooses to accept the payment order.[7] The sender who issues a payment order (or who gives cancellation instructions or amendments) to a receiving bank should be aware that intermediaries are not liable for mis-transmission. The funds transfer system is considered an agent of the sender under Article 4A. Thus, liability for mis-transmission, if any, must be determined by resort to agency law.

The Payment Order

Article 4A's central theme is the "payment order," which begins the funds transfer process. Unlike checks, payment orders to not embody independent rights and liabilities for the payment of money. Instead, the rights and liabilities of the parties to a payment order arise out of the agreement between the parties and from the provisions of Article 4A that apply when the payment order is accepted by the receiving bank. U.C.C. §4A-209. Other than a contract outside Article 4A, the receiving bank has no duty under Article 4A to accept a payment order. U.C.C. § 4A-212. A payment order is like a draft presented to a drawee for acceptance, which may be refused, but the drawee may be liable for that refusal under an agreement with the drawer. This treatment occurs because payment orders are not like checks where there always is a prearranged account; in some funds transfer cases, banks may not want to, or cannot, extend credit to a sender.

Payment orders must possess a number of essential elements to be subject to Article 4A.[8] First, it must be an instruction given by the sender to the receiving bank to pay, or cause another bank to pay, a "fixed or determinable amount of money to a beneficiary." The drafters did not accord any special treatment to the "fixed or determinable" requirement; thus, it should be interpreted along the same lines as it is construed under Article 3. As long as the amount to be paid is calculable by some formula (*i.e.*, foreign currency conversion or interest rate specified) then the amount is fixed and determinable.

In addition to the fixed or determinable requirement, a payment order must meet several other requirements: (1) the order must state that there is no condition for payment other than the time at which it is to be made; (2) the transaction involved must be a credit transfer and not a debit transfer; and (3) it must entail an instruction transmitted by the sender directly to the receiving bank or to an agent or funds transfer system for transmittal to the receiving bank. The payment order is accepted by a receiving bank when it executes the order. U.C.C. § 4A-209. A payment order is executed when the receiving bank issues its own payment order in response to the received payment order. U.C.C. §§ 4A-301 and 4A-302. Under section 4A-301, the beneficiary's bank may accept an order by completing the transfer of funds to the beneficiary but does not and cannot execute it. Generally, acceptance by a beneficiary's bank occurs on the earliest of (i)

---

[7] The receiving bank could become liable during the pre-acceptance period if it delayed in giving notice of the bank's rejection of the payment order past the requested payment date. In such a case, the receiving bank would be liable for lost interest.

[8] Payment order is defined at 4A-103(a)(1). To avoid fraud, Article 4A has provisions dealing with the authentication of payment orders. Common law rules relating to an agent's authorization are not helpful when delivery of information is via a computer screen. Section 4A-201 describes "security procedures" as the use of "algorithms or other codes, identifying words or numbers, encryption, callback procedures, or similar security devices." Unlike the paper-based check collection system, Section 4A-201 notes that "[c]omparison of a signature on a payment order or communication with an authorized specimen signature of a customer is not by itself a security procedure." If however, a commercially reasonable security procedure has been agreed upon, the receiving bank is protected, provided that certain additional conditions, such as acceptance in good faith, are met.

certain payments or notice to the beneficiary that an order has been received, (ii) receipt of payment of the amount of the sender's order; or, (iii) the opening of the next funds-transfer business day after the payment date of the order, if the order was not rejected and funds are available for payment. See U.C.C. § 4A-209(2).

When a bank executes a payment order it incurs the following obligations under Article 4A: (1) it must issue a payment order that complies with the sender's order and follows the sender's instructions; (2) it must advise any intermediary bank involved in the funds transfer about the instructions of the original sender; (3) in cases where the sender indicates a desire for the transaction to be carried out by telephone or wire transfer, or otherwise asks for the most expeditious means of transfer, the receiving bank must employ such means and instruct any intermediary banks to do the same; and, (4) the receiving bank must transmit its payment order in sufficient time to allow payment to the beneficiary on the sender's requested payment date, if any, or as soon thereafter as is feasible. See U.C.C. § 4A-302.

If the receiving bank executes the payment order before the sender's requested payment date, resulting in payment to the beneficiary before the requested payment date, acceptance will not occur until the requested payment date. Such an occurrence would result in a loss of interest to the receiving bank. If a bank executes early, it risks cancellation of, or amendment to, the payment order by the sender. In the event of a cancellation by the sender, Article 4A does not require the sender to pay the receiving bank. Instead, the receiving bank will have to resort to common law rules of mistake and restitution to recover its money from the beneficiary it paid prematurely.

CONTINENTAL AIRLINES, INC. v. BOATMEN'S NATIONAL BANK OF ST. LOUIS

United States Court of Appeals
13 F.3d 1254 (8th Cir. 1994)

John R. Gibson, Circuit Judge.

This appeal is about the proceeds of a check for $683,505.24 which was wire transferred to the wrong company [which is] now in bankruptcy, and which party should bear the loss. Boatmen's National Bank of St. Louis, under its contractual arrangements with Continental Airlines, obtained a check payable to Continental from the Military Airlift Command in payment of Continental's transportation service to the Command. The Command placed Continental's name and a code number on the check. Boatmen's followed the code number rather than the name, and wire transferred the check proceeds to an account of First Southern Financial Corporation of Sanford in Fayetteville, North Carolina. The district court entered summary judgment in favor of Continental on its claims against Boatmen's. On appeal, Boatmen's argues that the district court erred in entering summary judgment because: (1) the exculpatory and indemnification provisions in the Remittance Processing and Wire Transfer Agreements between Continental and Boatmen's defeat Continental's claims; and (2) there are disputed questions of fact precluding the entry of summary judgment. We affirm the district court's judgment, but on grounds other than those articulated in its order.

On April 1, 1986, Continental entered into an agreement with Boatmen's (then known as Centerre Bank, N.A.) for the processing and payment of government checks from the Military Airlift Command to Continental. This service, called government lock box "Remittance

Processing," provided Continental with access to payments from the Command via next-day wire transfers. The agreement contained an indemnification and hold harmless provision.

On March 25, 1986, Boatmen's sent a letter to Continental asking Continental to send a letter of authorization to its payor office (in this case, the Command) changing the payment address to include Continental's lock box identification number. Continental sent a letter dated April 1, 1986, notifying the bank of its payment address, including its assigned lock box number, and authorizing the bank to collect payments due from the Command at Scott Air Force Base. The bank forwarded this letter to headquarters of the Command asking if the letter provided sufficient authorization from Continental. On June 30, 1986, the bank accepted a Wire Transfer of Funds Agreement from Continental, authorizing the bank to transfer funds from specific customer accounts to any other customer bank accounts. This agreement also contained an indemnification provision.

Boatmen's assigned unique lock box identification numbers, call LBIDs, to each of its remittance processing customers. Under this procedure the bank arranged for courier pickup of checks and credited the proceeds to the designated accounts. The processing arrangement between Continental and Boatmen's was straightforward. A Boatmen's courier picked up government checks payable to Continental from the Command at Scott Air Force Base in Illinois once a day. At Boatmen's request, Continental authorized the Command to place Continental's LBID on the government checks to be processed by Boatmen's. The courier delivered the checks to a Boatmen's bank in St. Louis, where Boatmen's sorted, copied, and routed the checks. Boatmen's then forwarded the original check to the Federal Reserve Bank in St. Louis for payment and sent a copy of the check to Continental. The check proceeds were then transferred, either the same or next day, to Continental's account at Chase Manhattan Bank in New York. Although Continental maintained a demand deposit account at Boatmen's, Boatmen's credited an internal account pending the wire transfer.

On August 17, 1990, Continental billed the Command $683,505.24 for transportation charges. Continental completed the section "payee's Name and Address" as follows:

Continental Airlines

CO/Boatmen's Natl Bk., St. Louis

Scott Air Force Base, IL 62225

The address did not include the LBID assigned to Continental.

On August 29, 1990, Boatmen's received a $683,505.24 check drawn by the Command payable to Continental, but containing the LBID of another government lock box customer of Boatmen's, First Southern. The Command designated the payee as: "Continental Airlines, LBID 700039 HIC." Boatmen's endorsed the check:

BOATMEN'S NATL
BANK OF ST
LOUIS MO
CREDIT PAYEE
4-3 Lock box 4-3
WITHOUT
PREJUDICE
081000032

The check was presented to the Federal Reserve Bank in St. Louis and it cleared. Relying on the LBID designated by the Command, Boatmen's processed the check for LBID 700039, not Continental's LBID 70009, and on August 30, 1990, Boatmen's wire transferred $683,505.24 to First Southern's account at a bank in North Carolina. Boatmen's also forwarded a copy of the check to First Southern.

During this same time period, Boatmen's sent "Account Batch Listings" to Continental. These statements identified the items processed, the dollar amount of the items processed, and the date of the wire transfer. The Command check was not included in these listings.

Continental notified Boatmen's in February 1991 that it had not received the $683,505.24 from the Command. On April 4, 1991, Continental sued Boatmen's to recover the amount, asserting four theories of recovery: breach of contract, final settlement under Mo. Rev. Stat. §400.4-213(3)(1986), negligence, and conversion. Boatmen's filed a counterclaim against Continental based on the indemnification provisions in the governing agreements, and also filed a third-party complaint against First Southern. Boatmen's moved for summary judgment against First Southern, and Boatmen's and Continental filed summary judgment motions against each other.

The district court granted Boatmen's motion for summary judgment against First Southern for $683,505.24. *Continental Airlines, Inc. v. Boatmen's Nat'l Bank*, No. 91-0658C(3), slip op. at 13 (E.D. Mo. Apr. 1, 1992). The district court also granted Continental's motion for summary judgment against Boatmen's for $683,505.24, and denied Boatmen's cross-motion for summary judgment against Continental based on the indemnity provisions contained in the agreements and the alleged negligence of Continental. *Id.* at 14. The court explained:

> It is apparent that the $683,505.24 was payment to Continental by [the Command] for services rendered. Accordingly, this Court will effect the return of that sum to Continental. In order to accomplish that end, the Court must engage in a reverse routing of the money from First Southern, through Boatmen's, then back to Continental.

Id. at 7.

Boatmen's filed a Motion to Amend Judgment seeking to clarify the language in the order. Boatmen's sought to amend the judgment to condition its liability to Continental upon its recovery from First Southern. Continental filed a similar motion seeking to clarify Boatmen's liability to Continental regardless of whether Boatmen's recovered from First Southern. The case was then transferred to the Honorable George F. Gunn, Jr., following Judge Hungate's retirement. The district court denied both parties' motions, explaining that the court's order:

> grants judgment against First Southern in favor of Boatmen's and therefore provides Boatmen's the opportunity to recover the entire amount that it is obligated to Continental. In all judgments, a risk exists that the prevailing party cannot recover the entire amount the Court awards. The Court will not amend the order . . . because the language of the judgment is absolute.

Continental Airlines, Inc. v. Boatmen's Nat'l Bank, No. 91-0658C(6), 1993 WL 566493, slip op. at 3 (E.D. Mo. Feb. 9, 1993). Boatmen's appeals.

I.

Boatmen's argues that the district court was seeking an equitable result, which has been frustrated by the insolvency of First Southern. Continental is not entitled to summary judgment, Boatmen's argues, because of the exculpatory in the governing agreements. Pointing to the findings of the district court that Continental agreed to accept the risk of loss and that this agreement was not against public policy, Boatmen's argues that the district court's findings are inconsistent with its entry of summary judgment for Continental. Boatmen's essentially argues that remittance processing, including the wire transfer of funds, is but one part of an arrangement to facilitate the next day wire transfer of funds.

Continental contends that the transaction giving rise to this dispute is governed by Article 3 and 4 of the Uniform Commercial Code as adopted in Missouri, and that we may affirm the judgment on this ground. Continental's argument rests on the assumption that the remittance processing procedure by which the bank obtains and endorses the check is distinct from the wire transfer transaction. From this assumption, Continental argues that Boatmen's agreement to process Command checks payable to the order of Continental qualified Boatmen's as a "depository bank" and a "collecting bank" under Mo. Rev. Stat. § 400.4-105(a) and (d)(1986). Continental concludes that as a collecting bank, Boatmen's owes Continental the full amount of the check under Mo. Rev. Stat. § 400.4-213, and as a depository bank, Boatmen's is liable for conversion under Mo. Rev. Stat. § 400.3-419.

More specifically, Continental argues that when Boatmen's received the $683,505.24 check, it acted as an agent for its customer, Continental. Mo. Rev. Stat. § 400.4-104(1)(e) ("Customer" defined as "any person having an account with a bank or for whom a bank has agreed to collect items. . ."). Continental argues further that when Boatmen's successfully collected on the check, Boatmen's became the debtor of its customer, Continental, for $683,505.24. Mo. Ann. Stat. § 400.4-201 U.C.C. cmt. 4 (Vernon 1965) ("At some stage in the bank collection process the agency status of a collecting bank changes to that of debtor, a debtor of its customer.") Thus, Continental contends that Boatmen's is liable as a collecting bank under Mo. Rev. Stat. § 400.4-213(3) which provides: "If a collecting bank receives a settlement for an item which is or becomes final. . .the bank is accountable to its customer for the amount of the item. . ."

Continental also argues that Boatmen's, in its capacity as a depository bank, is liable for conversion under Mo. Rev. Stat. § 400.3-419 for payment of the check inconsistently with a restrictive endorsement. Continental contends that Boatmen's had authority under the Remittance Processing Agreement to endorse the check "credit payee," and because "credit payee" is a restrictive endorsement, Mo. Rev. Stat. § 400.3-205, Boatmen's was obligated to credit the account of the named payee, Continental.

Boatmen's responds that because the purpose and intent of this arrangement was to facilitate the next day wire transfer of funds, Articles 3 and 4 of the U.C.C. do not apply. Boatmen's points out that Continental did not maintain a demand deposit account for credit pending wire transfer, and that the exculpatory and indemnification provisions bar recovery under Missouri common law. Second, Boatmen's cites several cases which have rejected the application of Articles 3 and 4 to issues surrounding wire transfers, as well as Article 4A of the U.C.C. (adopted in Missouri in 1992) which governs funds transfers. Mo. Rev. Stat. § 400.4A-101-400.4A-507

(Cum. Supp. 1992). Boatmen's also argues that even if Articles 3 and 4 govern this transaction, no conversion occurred because it paid the check as directed by the lock box number reflected on the check.

We are convinced that Articles 3 and 4 of the U.C.C. govern this dispute. The significant event which fixed the bank's liability was the receipt and endorsement of the check, and the check's presentation to and payment by the Federal Reserve Bank. The misdirected wire transfer was simply the method by which the bank breached its duty with respect to the check. Although Missouri did not adopt the Uniform Commercial Code Funds Transfers until 1992, and so it does not control this case, the comment to the Act states that if a check includes a payment order, or is accompanied by a payment order, "the instruction to Beneficiary's Bank is a payment order," and thus, falls under 4A of the Act, "but the check itself. . . is an instrument under Article 3." Mo. Ann. Stat. § 400-4A-104 U.C.C. cmt. 5 (Vernon Supp. 1992).

The addition of the lock box identification number on the face of the check did not change the identity of the payee. Under Mo. Rev. Stat. § 400.3-117(c), "an instrument made payable to a named person with the addition of words describing him in any manner is payable to the payee unconditionally. . ." The comment to the Missouri statute explains that "[a]ny other words of description, such as "John Doe, 1121 Main Street " are merely words of identification, and not a condition of payment. Mo. Ann. Stat. § 400.3-117 U.C.C. cmt. 3 (Vernon 1965). Contrary to Boatmen's argument, the inclusion of the lock box identification number does not convert the named payee from Continental to the lock box number. Accordingly, we reject Boatmen's argument that it paid the check in accordance with the endorsement because it credited the account corresponding to the lock box number.

Boatmen's also contends that the indemnification provisions in the Remittance Processing and Wire Transfer Agreements absolve it of any liability. The Remittance Processing Agreement contained an indemnification and hold harmless provision, protecting Boatmen's from:

> any and all claims . . . which [Boatmen's] at any time shall or may sustain or incur by reason of (a) inadvertently processing any checks contrary to the instructions or other error of judgment, made in good faith, (b) failure to perform, or perform within time schedule agreed, or properly within time schedule agreed, or properly or accurately perform any service whatsoever in connection with check processing. . . In the ordinary course of business, checks may be processed contrary to instructions, although Bank will use its best efforts to process in accordance with the Instructions.

The Remittance Processing Agreement also stated that Continental agreed "to be bound by the terms of the. . .Wire Transfer of Funds Agreement as to all funds which are to be transferred by wire transfer to [Continental]." The Wire Transfer of Funds Agreement also contained a hold harmless provision protecting the Bank from:

> any and all claims. . . arising directly or indirectly out of transfer requests or orders initiated pursuant to this Agreement or in any other way connected with the arrangements provided for herein, except for liability to Customer for direct losses (to the exclusion of any consequential or special loss or damage) occasioned by the Bank's gross negligence or lack of good faith. . .

Boatmen's argues that the agreements are enforceable because there is no showing of a lack of good faith or failure to exercise ordinary care. See Mo. Rev. Stat. § 400.4-103(1)("[N]o agreement can disclaim a bank's responsibility for its own lack of good faith or failure to exercise ordinary care."). Boatmen's argues that it acted in good faith and exercised ordinary care, citing evidence that banks generally direct check proceeds to lock box identification numbers, rather than named payees. Boatmen's argues that, at the very least, there exists a question of fact as to whether it exercised ordinary care.

Continental responds that the indemnification provisions do not protect Boatmen's from liability. In Missouri, parties may contractually allocate the risk of loss. See, *e.g.*, Mo. Rev. Stat. § 400.4-103(1); *Rock Springs Realty, Inc. v. Waid*, 392 S.W.2d 270, 272 (Mo. 1965). There are, however, two reasons why the agreements in this case do not protect Boatmen's actions. First, Boatmen's cannot disclaim failure to exercise ordinary care. See Mo. Rev. Stat. § 400.4-103(1). There are a number of cases which hold that a bank's failure to process a check consistently with a restrictive endorsement constitutes lack of ordinary care as a matter of law. See, *e.g.*, *Cairo Coop. Exch. v. First Nat'l Bank*, 228 Kan. 613, 620 P.2d 805, 809 (1980) (depository bank's failure to deposit checks according to restrictive indorsement constitutes lack of ordinary care); *Kelly v. Central Bank and Trust Co.*, 794 P.2d 1037, 1042-43 (Colo. Ct. App. 1989) (bank failed to act in accordance with reasonable commercial standards by depositing checks inscribed "For Deposit Only" to an account other than payee's). Boatmen's payment of check proceeds to a lock box other than the named payee's contradicts section 400.3-117(c) and constitutes lack of ordinary care as a matter of law.

Second, Missouri courts strictly construe indemnity contracts. Clear language is required to show that a contract of indemnity was intended to cover conditions or operations under the control of the party indemnified.

The language in the agreements before us lacks the requisite clarity needed to indemnify Boatmen's for its misdirection of the funds. Nothing in the provisions expressly requires Continental to indemnify Boatmen's if Boatmen's erroneously relied on an incorrect LBID provided by a Continental customer. Moreover, the indemnification language could be interpreted as requiring Continental to indemnify and hold Boatmen's harmless from claims of third parties because the language suggests that Boatmen's would be indemnified from any losses Boatmen's sustained. Further, although Continental asked Boatmen's to authorize the Command to place Continental's LBID number on its checks. Boatmen's forwarded the authorizing letter to the Command and never explained to Continental or the Command that the checks would be exclusively processed according to the identification number. Indeed, Boatmen's explained in its "Description of Services" that "funds are wire transferred according to instructions provided by the customer." Under these circumstances, we are persuaded that the indemnification clauses do not protect Boatmen's from liability.

Finally, Boatmen's argues that evidence of negligence by Continental and its agent, the Command, present genuine issues of material fact precluding the entry of summary judgment. Boatmen's alleges that Continental was negligent because: (1) its agent, the Command, placed the incorrect LBID on the check; (2) Continental submitted an invoice which did not include any LBID; (3) Continental failed to review and reconcile statements provided to it to discover that it had not received the check proceeds; and (4) Continental waited five months before discovering and reporting to Boatmen's that it had not received the check proceeds.

We reject these arguments. First, we are unpersuaded that the Command qualified as Continental's agent. An "essential element of an agency relationship is the principal's right to control the conduct of the agent with respect to matters entrusted to him." *Martin Coin Co. v. King*, 665 S.W.2d 939, 942 (Mo. 1984) (en banc). The record contains no evidence that

Continental had a right to control any aspect of the Command. It is true that Continental authorized the Command to place Continental's LBID on the government checks. Continental asked the Command to do so, however, at Boatmen's request, and Boatmen's never informed Continental what would happen if the Command placed the wrong number on the check. Similarly, Continental's failure to place the LBID on its invoices to the Command is not negligence. Boatmen's sent a copy of a letter from Continental dated April 1, 1986, to the Command reflecting the lock box number for Continental, and there is no evidence in the record that Continental had a duty to include the identification number in each of its invoices to the Command. As far as Continental's alleged failure to review Boatmen's statements, the statements did not show that Boatmen's had received the Command check. Thus, the only way Continental could have discovered that it had not been paid the check proceeds is if the command notified Continental. Boatmen's does not argue, nor is there any evidence, that Continental knew that the Command made the August payment.

We affirm the judgment of the district court.

§ 15.04 Scope

Read: U.C.C. §§ 4A-107, 4A-108

SHEERBONNET, LTD. v. AMERICAN EXPRESS BANK, LTD.

United States District Court, Southern District, New York
905 F.Supp. 127 (1995)

PRESKA, DISTRICT JUDGE:

Instructed by the Court of Appeals not to abstain from further determinations, I return to this case to address the remaining arguments in defendant's renewed motion to dismiss. The facts having been set out in my earlier order, as well as by the Court of Appeals, will only be summarized here. They should be considered retrospectively, in light of the seizure by the superintendent of Banks of the State of New York ("Superintendent"), as part of a worldwide seizure in July of 1991, of the New York assets of the Bank of Credit and Commerce, S.A. ("BCCI"). The collapse of BCCI and the subsequent seizure of its assets has spawned a legion of lawsuits, of which this is but one.

FACTS

Plaintiff Sheerbonnet, Ltd. ("Sheerbonnet") is a British trading company which contracted in 1990 to sell troop carriers to the Hady Establishment ("Hady"), a Saudi Arabian company. The carriers were to be used by Allied forces during the Persian Gulf War. For payment, Hady obtained an irrevocable $14,080,000 letter of credit from Banque Scandinave, in Geneva, Switzerland. Ten percent of this price was downpayment, the remainder due after delivery. After receiving the downpayment and fulfilling its obligations under the contract, Sheerbonnet awaited the balance, approximately $12.4 million, due on July 5, 1991.

Sheerbonnet requested that the payment be made through a funds transfer to its account at BCCI in London. Because Sheerbonnet was to be paid in U.S. dollars, Banque Scadinave initiated payment on July 3rd by instructing its correspondent bank in New York, Northern Trust

International ("Northern Trust"), to transfer $12.4 million to American Express Bank ("AEB") for credit to BCCI's account at AEB in New York on July 5th.

On the morning of July 5th, regulators in England and Luxembourg suspended the operations of the faltering BCCI. On the same day in the United States, the Federal Reserve Bank advised AEB and other banks of the suspension of BCCI accounts worldwide, including the seizure of BCCI's New York operations. At 9:00 a.m., the Superintendent closed BCCI's New York Agency and announced the seizure of all "business and property" of BCCI in New York.

Shortly thereafter, AEB received by wire from Norther Trust the payment order for the transfer of $12.4 million to the BCCI account at AEB in New York. Knowing the account was frozen, AEB nevertheless credited to it the $12.4 million. Because of the freeze, these assets remained in New York.

After crediting the funds to the BCCI account, AEB asserted its rights over the entire account as an off-set against debts owed to it by the insolvent BCCI. The $12.4 million is thus in AEB's control, none of this money having ever reached Sheerbonnet.

The Superintendent, pursuant to New York Banking Law § 606(4)(a), thereafter began liquidation proceedings to dispose of BCCI's assets in New York. In March of 1992, the Superintendent petitioned the Supreme Court of the State of New York ("Liquidation Court") for an order compelling AEB and several New York banks to turn over any BCCI funds held in their accounts. A settlement agreement was reached, and the Liquidation court entered a turnover Order on April 27, 1992 instructing the banks to cede BCCI funds to the Superintendent, less set-offs claimed by the banks. Upon remittance, the turnover Order provided that the banks would be "discharged from liability with respect to claims for funds of BCCI, S.A. located in New York." Having already claimed the BCCI London account as a set-off, AEB did not turn over any funds to the Superintendent.

In September of 1992, Sheerbonnet commenced suit against AEB in this Court. After motion by the defendant, I abstained from the case under the federal abstention doctrine enunciated by the Supreme Court in *Burford v. Sun Oil Co.*, 319 U.S. 315, 63 S.Ct. 1098, 87 L.Ed. 1424 (1943). That order was reversed by the Court of Appeals, and defendant now renews its motion to dismiss.

DISCUSSION

AEB has moved to dismiss the complaint on three grounds: (1) that Sheerbonnet has failed to state a claim upon which relief can be granted, under Fed.R.Civ.P. 12(b)(6); (2) that the claim is barred by a previous order of the Liquidation Court; and (3) that Sheerbonnet has failed to join an indispensable party, under Fed. R. Civ. P. 19. I will address these arguments in order. For the reasons set forth, I find each argument to be unpersuasive.

I. Failure to State a Claim

AEB has offered two reasons why Sheerbonnet's claim fails to state a legally cognizable claim. The first is that Article 4-A of the New York Uniform Commercial Code provides the exclusive remedy for the type of injury alleged, and the complaint not only ignores Article 4-A but is inconsistent with several of its provisions. The question of the exclusivity of Article 4-A as a whole, or the preclusive effect of any of its parts, has yet to be directly addressed in this Circuit. The second reason offered by AEB is that Sheerbonnet's common law claims, even it not excluded by Article 4-A, are inadequate as a matter of law. Neither position is supportable.

A. NY—UCC Art. 4-A Does Not Bar
Sheerbonnet's Claim

Effective as of January 1, 1991, Article 4-A is the latest addition to New York's Uniform Commercial Code. Its exact contours, its reach, and the implications of its various provisions have not yet been tested in state or federal courts. The provisions of Article 4-A are dense, and a preliminary discussion of their subject matter is helpful before addressing AEB's first argument for dismissal, grounded as it is on the purpose and scope of the provisions. Article 4-A governs "funds transfers" or "wire transfers." N.Y. U.C.C. § 4-A-102 (McKinney 1991). A by-product of new communications technology, funds transfers are a specialized "method of payment in which the person making the payment (the originator) directly transmits an instruction to a bank either to make payment to the person receiving payment (the beneficiary) or to instruct some other bank to make payment to the beneficiary." N.Y. U.C.C. § 4-A-104, Official Comment, at p. 561. A funds transfer is initiated by a "payment order," which is an instruction from the person making the payment to a "receiving" or "intermediary" bank to transfer the funds to the bank account of the beneficiary, normally in the "beneficiary's bank." N.Y. U.C.C. § 4-A-103. A payment order may pass through several banks on its route from the sender, or originator, to the beneficiary. A payment order must be for a fixed or determinable sum, must not state a condition for payment to the beneficiary other than time, must require the receiving bank to be reimbursed by debiting or otherwise receiving payment from the originator, and must be communicated directly to the receiving bank (as opposed to the originator's bank). See *id.* Furthermore,

> payment by the originator to the beneficiary is accomplished by providing to the beneficiary the obligation of the beneficiary's bank to pay. Since this obligation arises when the beneficiary's bank accepts a payment order, the originator pays the beneficiary at the time of acceptance and in the amount of the payment order accepted.

N.Y. U.C.C. § 4-A-406, Official Comments, at p. 623.

Most often, funds transfers are made to discharge an underlying payment obligation which arose through earlier commercial dealings between the originator (*e.g.*, a purchaser of goods or services) and the beneficiary (*e.g.*, a provider of goods or services). Insofar as they facilitate the efficient, high-speed, low-cost, national and international transfer of huge sums of money, usually between sophisticated institutional parties, funds transfers have become an integral component of large business transactions.

1. Article 4-A is not Exclusive

Article 4-A responded to the growing use of funds transactions and the absence of a "comprehensive body of law—statutory or judicial—that defined the juridical nature of a funds transfer or the rights and obligations flowing from payment orders." N.Y. U.C.C. § 4-A-102, Official Comment, at p. 559. The pastiche of laws-statutory, administrative and judicial—applied to funds transfers prior to Art. 4-A was found to be unsatisfactory. See *id.*

The drafting committee made "a deliberate decision. . . to use precise and detailed rules to assign responsibility, define behavioral norms, allocate risks and establish limits on liability, rather than rely on broadly stated, flexible principles." *Id.* AEB relies heavily on passages selected from the official commentary to support its argument that Article 4-A is the exclusive remedy for claims like Sheerbonnet's arising out of funds transfers:

> In the drafting of Article 4A, a deliberate decision was made to write on a clean slate and to treat a funds transfer as a unique method of payment to be governed by unique rules that address the particular issues raised by this method of payment. . .The[se] rules. . .represent a careful and delicate balancing of [competing] interests and are intended to be the exclusive means of determining the rights, duties and liabilities of the affected parties in any situation covered by particular provisions of the Article. Consequently, resort to principles of law or equity outside of Article 4A is not appropriate to create rights, duties and liabilities inconsistent with those stated in this Article.

N.Y. U.C.C. § 4-A-102, Official Comments, p. 559.

These passages are the foundation for AEB's conclusion that "[b]ecause Sheerbonnet has not alleged that AEB violated any provision of Article 4-A, the Complaint has failed to state a cognizable cause of action and should be dismissed." Defendant's Memorandum of Law in Support of Renewed Motion to Dismiss, at 11. AEB's conclusion is unjustified for several reasons.

On their face, the above passages fail to establish a legislative intent to preclude any and all funds transfer actions not based on Article 4-A. A desire to start on a "clean slate" implies only that in drafting the Article, the legislature was neither borrowing from related U.C.C. regulations, such as Article 4 (Bank Deposits and Collections) or Article 3 (Commercial Paper), nor from principles of common law or equity. Clearly, parties whose conflict arises out of a funds transfer should look first and foremost to Article 4-A for guidance in bringing and resolving their claims, but the article has not completely eclipsed the applicability of common law in the area. The exclusivity of Article 4-A is deliberately restricted to "any situation covered by particular provisions of the Article." Conversely, situations not covered are not the exclusive province of the Article. The legislative intent reflected here is that carefully drafted provisions, designed to bring uniformity, predictability, and finality to an increasingly important area of commercial law, are not to be side-stepped when convenient by reference to other sources of law. But where the provisions do not venture, the claimant need not turn back; he or she may seek other guides, statutory or judicial. The only restraint on the plaintiff seeking such relief is that "resort to principles of law or equity outside of Article 4A" must not be inconsistent with provisions within the Article.

Commentators uniformly recognize that Article 4-A is not a hermetic legal seal over funds transfers. See J.J. White & R.S. Summers, Uniform Commercial Code, § 1-2, at p. 132 (1993 pocket part) ("With the adoption of Article 4A, electronic funds transactions are governed not only by Article 4A, but also common law, contract, Federal Reserve rules, Federal Reserve operating letters, rules of automated clearing houses, CHIPS and Title IX of the Federal Consumer Credit Protection Act."). Professor White goes on to discuss how Article 4-A's scope questions come in two basic forms. First—as to transactions partly covered by 4-A, but also partly covered by contract, by CHIPS' rules or by Fedwire rules, or other law—which part is covered by 4A and which part by other rules? Second—as to transactions completely beyond Article 4A—which are these and what are their characteristics?" White & Summers, § 1-2, at p. 133 (1993 pocket part). As explained elsewhere, "the Drafting Committee intended that Article 4A would be supplemented, enhanced, and in some places superseded by other bodies of law. . .the Article is intended to synergize with other legal doctrines." T.C. Baxter & R. Bhala, *The Interrelationship of Article 4A with Other Law*, 45 Business Lawyer 1485, 1485. (1990) (describing eleven "points of contact" between the article and other law, including tort law).

The Article itself is replete with references to common law remedies. Many sections borrow freely from the tort concepts of "ordinary care," "reasonableness," and "the law governing mistake and restitution." See, *e.g.*, § 4-A-205(2) (the sender of an erroneous payment order who is notified by the receiving bank that the order was executed or the sender's account was debited has "a duty to exercise ordinary care. . .to discover the error"); § 4-A-404(2) (if payment order does not instruct notice from the beneficiary's bank to the beneficiary, notice may be by "any other means reasonable in the circumstances"); § 4-A-205 (if a payment order erroneously instructs payment in an amount greater than intended, the sender is not obliged to pay to the beneficiary the excess amount but the receiving bank is entitled to recover from the beneficiary "to the extent allowed by the law of mistake and restitution").

Based on the foregoing, I conclude that Article 4-A of the New York Uniform Commercial Code is not the exclusive means by which a plaintiff can seek to redress an alleged harm arising from a funds transfer.

2. Plaintiff's Allegations are not Inconsistent with Article 4-A.

Having determined that Article 4-A is not an automatic bar to electronic funds transfers claims grounded elsewhere, the remaining question is whether Sheerbonnet's common law causes of action are nonetheless inconsistent with any of the Article's provisions and therefore must be dismissed. Neither the case law nor the specific provisions argued by AEB demonstrate such inconsistency.

Typical of AEB's myopic argumentation on this point is its reliance on the New York court of Appeals decision in *Banque Worms v. Bank America Int'l*, 77 N.Y.2d 362, 568 N.Y.S.2d 541, 570 N.E.2d 189 (Ct. of App. 1991). To support its assertion that "case law also rejects Sheerbonnet's limited vision of the reach of Article 4-A," Defendant's Reply Memorandum in Support of its Motion to Dismiss, at 7-8, AEB cites the pronouncement in *Banque Worms* that the National Conference of Commissioners on Uniform State Laws and the American Law Institute "undertook to develop a body of unique principles of law that would address every aspect of the electronic funds transfer process and define the rights and liabilities of all parties involved in such transfers." *Banque Worms*, 568 N.Y.S.2d at 547, 570 N.E.2d at 195. AEB fails to recognize, however, that the issue in *Banque Worms*, taken by the Court of Appeals as a certified question from the Second Circuit, was which of two common law doctrines, "discharge for value" or detrimental reliance, would be imported into Article 4-A to remedy an erroneous electronic transfer of funds. The Court ultimately decided that the "discharge for value" rule, the product of "a myriad of cases," *id.*, 568 N.Y.S.2d at 545, 570 N.E.2d at 193, was the most appropriate supplement to Article 4-A because the most consistent with its policy goals. It reached this finding despite expressly noting that the Article did not invite an application of this judicially constructed rule:

> We believe such an application accords with the legislative intent and furthers the policy considerations underlying Article 4-A of the New York Uniform Commercial Code. Although no provision of Article 4-A calls, in express terms, for the application of the "discharge for value" rule, the statutory scheme and the language of various pertinent sections, as amplified by the Official Comments to the U.C.C., support our conclusion that the "discharge for value" rule should be applied in the circumstances here presented.

Banque Worms, 568 N.Y.S.2d at 548, 570 N.E.2d at 196. See *Banque Worms v. Bank America Int'l*, 928 F.2d 538, 541 (2d Cir. 1991) (applying the discharge for value rule to the erroneous funds transfer); see also *Gen. Elec. Capital Corp. v. Central Bank*, 49 F.3d 280 (7th Cir. 1995) (Easterbrook, J.) (following *Banque Worms* in the interest of national uniformity in the treatment of wire funds transfers). As the reasoning of our Court of Appeals and the New York Court of Appeals make clear, despite its exhaustive aspirations, Article 4-A has not completely filled the area of law surrounding funds transfers. Common law and equitable principles, where they compliment the important policy considerations of the Article and are not inconsistent with any of its specific provisions, can and should be used to resolve conflicts between parties to this type of transaction.

In *Aleo Int'l, Ltd. v. Citibank N.A.*, 160 Misc.2d 950, 612 N.Y.S.2d 540 (Sup. Ct. N.Y.Co. 1994), also relied on by AEB, plaintiff brought an action to recover funds which Citibank had transferred to a third party pursuant to instructions that the plaintiff unsuccessfully retracted. Citibank claimed not to have received the cancellation until payment had been accepted. The court dismissed the complaint, which alleged negligence, holding that "unless Citibank's failure to cancel [plaintiff's] transfer order was not in conformity with Article 4-A, plaintiff. . .has failed to state a cause of action, and this action must be dismissed." *Aleo*, 612 N.Y.S.2d at 541. In its one-page opinion, however, the court was able to refer to two provisions of Article 4-A directly applicable to the facts alleged. Reference to § 4-A-211(2) (governing cancellation and amendment of payment orders) and § 4-A-209(2) (governing acceptance of payment orders), quickly demonstrated that, because the stop transfer order was received after the payment and acceptance had occurred, cancellation was ineffective, and Citibank bore no liability. 612 N.Y.S.2d at 541. Were the allegations in this action so clearly circumscribed by applicable sections of Article 4-A, Sheerbonnet could not be heard to protest if its common law claims were dismissed on the pleadings. Aleo is an excellent example of how the underlying policies of Article 4-A—predictability, consistency, finality—are well-served by its clear and careful drafting. We are not so fortunate here.

As in *Aleo,* another recent State Supreme Court case resolved a dispute arising out of an allegedly erroneous funds transfer by reference to Article 4-A provisions directly on point. See *Southtrust Bank of Ala., N.A. v. Turkiye ve Ihracat Bankasi, A.S., et al.*, no. 116581/94 (Sup. Ct. N.Y. Co. Jan. 19, 1995). In *Southtrust,* plaintiff's bank relayed a payment order to American Express for the transfer of $500,000 to the account of a creditor of the plaintiff. The order included correct verbal instructions, but an erroneous written account number. It was into this wrong account that American Express transferred the $500,000. Neither American Express nor the holder of the account into which the funds were sent agreed to return the funds to plaintiff, who in turn sought unsuccessfully to have the funds garnished. As in our facts, American Express in *Southtrust* used the funds which it credited as a set-off against debts owed to it by the account holder. *Southtrust*, slip op. at 3-4.

The court dismissed plaintiff's complaint, based on negligence, and denied leave to amend to substitute other common law tort claims which it said were inconsistent with Article 4-A. Again the court was able to point to specific provisions with which the plaintiff's tort theories conflicted.[9] The section on point, which eclipsed plaintiff's claims no matter how they were styled, was § 4-A 207 ("Misdescription of a Beneficiary"). Clearly from the language of the section, American Express was entitled to rely on the representation of the account number as it appeared on the payment order it received, even if that number conflicted with the

[9] Prefacing its analysis by flagging the intention of Article 4-A's drafters to work off a clean slate and exclusively determine the rights and obligations of parties in situations covered by its provisions, the court goes on to say that proposed pleadings outside of Article 4-A must be scrutinized not in light of an absolute bar on their being brought (which would require no scrutiny) but rather in "light of the clear intention of the drafters of Article 4-A to limit strictiy the resort to common law and equitable principles." *Southtrust,* slip op. at 7.

accompanying description of the account. *Id.* at 10. Only because it ignored this plainly applicable and inconsistent provision was plaintiff's complaint dismissed.

Further distinguishing *Southtrust* from this case was American Express's ability to argue lack of knowledge. Plaintiff in *Southtrust* could not prove that American Express was aware of the discrepancy between the account number and its description. In the instant case, however, AEB's knowledge of the insolvency and seizure of BCCI's accounts—before accepting the Northern Trust payment order and crediting the BCCI London account—is undisputed. Nor was the sender in our case responsible for conveying an erroneous order or tardy cancellation. AEB's knowledge that the $12.4 million it was asked to receive and transfer was destined for a seized account seems relevant to its decision to accept the order and credit the frozen account, but there is no provision in Article 4-A dealing with such circumstances.

AEB fares no better in direct reliance on specific provisions of Article 4-A, three of which it argues are inconsistent with, and thus preclude, Sheerbonnet's theory of tort liability.

First, AEB argues that § 4-A-209 is both applicable and inconsistent insofar as it gives the receiving bank full discretion to accept or reject a payment order. Since it is granted full discretion, AEB argues that it would be inconsistent to impose tort liability for the acceptance of the payment order. The intent of granting this discretion is explained in the commentary, however, which stresses the receiver's ability to reject the order: "Section 4A-209 is based on a general principle that a receiving bank is not obliged to accept a payment order unless it has agreed or is bound by a funds transfer rule to do so. Thus, provision is made to allow the receiving bank to prevent acceptance of the order." N.Y. U.C.C. § 4-A 209, Official Comments, at p. 593. Section 4-A-209 is primarily devoted to describing how and when acceptance, and the liability attendant to it, occurs—not to how and when a receiving bank's discretion should be exercised. There is no indication that such discretion is meant to serve as a veil against liability for the manner in which the discretion to accept is exercised. A payment order is merely a request by the sender that the receiving bank pay or execute the order. With acceptance of an order comes certain obligations. A receiving bank may refuse requests which would expose it to unreasonable high risk of loss—as when there does not seem to be adequate funds to cover the order. It can hardly promote the purposes of Article 4-A to equate a general discretion to accept or reject payment orders with a ban on judicial inquiry into the circumstances under which that discretion was exercised and what followed its exercise.

AEB also looks to § 4-A-212 as a shield from Sheerbonnet's claims. This section governs the "Liability and Duty of Receiving Bank Regarding Unaccepted Payment Order." Specifically, AEB relies on a part of the provision which reads that, "[a] receiving bank. . .owes no duty to any party to the funds transfer except as provided in this Article or by express agreement." N.Y. U.C.C. § 4-A-212. First, in full context this section indicates that (1) no liability attaches to a receiving bank before it accepts a payment order, (2) absent an express agreement to the contrary, the receiving bank is not obliged to accept the order, and (3) the receiving bank is not an agent of any party to the funds transfer and hence, outside its acceptance of the order, owes no intrinsic duty stemming from an agency relationship. See *id.*; N.Y. U.C.C. §4-A-212, Official Comments, at p. 602; White & Summers, at § 3-5 (1993 pocket part). Second, it is not clear whether this section applies to banks that are acting as both a receiving bank and the beneficiary's bank, as AEB argues it was. Third, and perhaps most telling, § 4-A-212, governing liability for unaccepted payment orders, should be read in tandem with § 4-A-210, governing rejection of payment orders. Section 4-A-210 indicates that, if not constrained by agency principles, receiving banks cannot conduct their business with blinders on to extenuating circumstances.

Comment 1 to § 4-A-210 reads in part:

> In some cases, the receiving bank may not be able to carry out the instruction because of equipment failure, credit limitation on the receiving bank, or some other factor that makes proper execution of the order infeasible. In those cases notice of rejection is a means of informing the sender of the facts so that a corrected payment order can be transmitted or the sender can seek alternate means of completing the fund transfer.

N.Y. U.C.C. § 4-A-210, Official Comment, at pp. 595-96.

The final section relied on by AEB to bar Sheerbonnet's claim as inconsistent is § 4-A-502, governing set-offs. This section is inapplicable in light of the pleadings. AEB argues that it is expressly entitled to set off any funds credited to BCCI's account against debt owed to AEB by BCCI. It is correct in this assertion. See N.Y. U.C.C. § 4-A-502(3)(a)("if a beneficiary's bank has received a payment order for payment to the beneficiary's account. . .(a) The bank may credit the beneficiary's account. The amount credited may be set off against an obligation owed by the beneficiary to the bank. . ."). Sheerbonnet does not challenge AEB's rights to a set-off, however. Instead, it challenges AEB's preliminary decision to credit the BCCI account. As stated in Sheerbonnet's Brief on Appeal to the Court of Appeals on the issue of abstention:

> 2. The Conversion Here Was the Wrongful Credit, Not American Express's Attempted Setoff.
>
> . . .The conversion alleged by Sheerbonnet in this action is the purported crediting of funds to the BCCI London account; American Express's attempted setoff was at most the motive for the wrongful "credit," and is not even mentioned in Sheerbonnet's complaint. Reply Brief of Plaintiff-Appellant, at 12.

Whether AEB's set-off was in bad faith, as Sheerbonnet later alleged, is immaterial at this juncture. For purposes of this motion, Sheerbonnet's claim that AEB's crediting of the BCCI account was an intentionally tortious and unjustly enriching act is not inconsistent with the provisions of § 4-A-502 regarding set-offs and therefore is not barred by it.

Unlike *Aleo* or *Southtrust*, the allegations here and the circumstances giving rise to them do not fit neatly into any of Article 4-A's "precise and detailed rules." The rules of the article are transactional, aimed essentially at resolving conflicts created by erroneous instruction or execution of payment orders, whether by the originator, by an intermediary or receiving bank, or by the beneficiary's bank. A major objective is to reduce and control risks that arise in payment systems by defining when and how rights and obligations are incurred and discharged. As organized by the article, funds transfer errors fall into three main categories. Errors may occur during the issuance and acceptance of the payment order-as when a payment order is made for the wrong amount, or identifies the wrong beneficiary, or, as in *Aleo*, is untimely canceled. Errors may also occur during the execution of the payment order by the receiving bank—as when the originator's instructions are not followed, or the order is executed late, or is issued in an improper amount, or is not executed at all. Errors may also stem from payment issues—as in the obligation of the originator to pay the receiving bank, of the beneficiary's bank to pay the beneficiary, and notification of payment and discharge of duties requirements. None of these three areas, nor any of Article 4-A's miscellaneous provisions, directly addresses the allegations here.

Sheerbonnet does not complain of an erroneous instruction or execution in the processing of Northern Trust's payment order, causing it to be credited to the wrong party, or in the wrong amount, or at the wrong time. Ironically, we are here now because AEB apparently followed its instructions to the letter. Sheerbonnet argues that in light of the unprecedented and superseding seizure of BCCI, AEB's decision to credit the BCCI London account, knowing that it was frozen and knowing that AEB would use these very funds as a $12.4 million set-off against BCCI's debt to AEB, was an exercise in self-serving, tortious tunnel vision. AEB did not ask either the originator or the beneficiary how they would like to proceed in light of the seizure, nor did it confer with the Superintendent of Banks.

There is no doubt, as Sheerbonnet contends, that the global seizure of BCCI was an unprecedented event that tests the limits of Article 4-A in a novel way. More at issue is whether AEB, seizing on the seizure, unfairly capitalized on this event. As plead, it appears that AEB was at least in a position to do so, functioning as it was as both the receiving bank and the beneficiary's bank. As the receiving bank, AEB had full discretion to accept or deny the payment order; as the beneficiary's bank AEB had full discretion to off-set against debts owed to it by the beneficiary. In isolation, these two provisions of Article 4-A are clear, harmonious, and equitable. But when linked in a transaction through a single entity, and placed in the crucible of the BCCI insolvency and seizure, the clarity, harmony, and equity fracture. The separate links of the funds transfer at issue here are whole, yet the chain was broken. Sheerbonnet agreed to sell troop carriers to Hady, on the basis of an irrevocable letter of credit issued by Banque Scandanave. The carriers were delivered. Sheerbonnet had an account with BCCI in London, which it wished credited in fulfillment of the letter of credit. Banque Scandanave directed its correspondent bank in New York, Northern Trust, to credit BCCI's London account through AEB in New York. Northern Trust so instructed AEB. AEB so credited the (frozen) BCCI London account. AEB then set-off the credit against BCCI debts.

When the electronic transfer was "completed," step-by-step according to Article 4-A, only one element was missing: the seller was never paid for its goods. The irony of this was not lost on the Court of Appeals. "Thus, the money originally destined for Sheerbonnet ended up not in the hands of the buyer or seller, but of a bank whose only role was to transfer the funds." *Sheerbonnet*, 17 F.3d at 48.

A further peculiarity manifest in these facts is that under the terms of the payment order BCCI is itself the beneficiary, not Sheerbonnet. What agreement existed between BCCI and Sheerbonnet for final payment is beyond the pleadings. Thus, although in the real world Sheerbonnet was to be the "beneficiary" of the $12.4 million, in the electronic world of funds transfers it was BCCI—and that has made all the difference. When the intended beneficiary became insolvent, the normal payment process was disrupted. When AEB off-set against BCCI debts, the credit to that account initiated by Hady and destined for Sheerbonnet was effectively pulled back, as if on an electronic string, before it was within Sheerbonnet's grasp. Professor White, in a discussion of issues that could interfere with the completion of a funds transfer, calls the insolvency of one of the banks within the system during a funds transfer the "least likely of all" scenarios and "the bank equivalent of nuclear holocaust." White & Summers, § 2-1, at p. 146 (1993 pocket part). He, like Article 4-A, does not even raise the specter of the insolvency of the beneficiary itself.

As in *Banque Worms*, these circumstances, not specifically provided for in an otherwise thorough statutory scheme, demand resort to other legal principles in order to reach a fair resolution. Article 4-A is an attempt to balance competing interests, namely "those of the banks that provide the funds transfer services and the commercial and financial organizations that use the services, as well as the public interest." N.Y. U.C.C. § 4-A-102, Official Comment, at p. 559. A necessary risk taken by the drafting committee in eschewing "broadly stated, flexible principles" in favor of "precise and detailed rules" is that maneuvering among these competitors will eventually land them somewhere in between precise rules, and dependent on broader principles to resolve their conflict. This is such a case.

Article 4-A is a thorough but not exhaustive legislative treatment of funds transfers. Nevertheless, resort to judicial or other legal principles is prohibited if those principles conflict with any discrete components of the statutory scheme. Sheerbonnet's common law claims, based in tort and equity, do not conflict with any of Article 4-A's provisions. In fact, in the context of the circumstances giving rise to them, these claims compliment primary policy goals of the Article, including consistency, predictability, finality, and the fair allocation of risk. For the foregoing reasons, defendant's motion to dismiss for failure to bring this claim under Article 4-A is denied.

B. Plaintiff's Common Law Claims
Are Legally Cognizable

AEB argues in the alternative that "[e]ven if not preempted, Sheerbonnet's tort and equity causes of action should be dismissed for failure to state a cognizable claim." Defendant's Reply Brief in Support of Renewed Motion to Dismiss, at 17. AEB claims that it only did what it was instructed and entitled to do and therefore cannot have any liability as a matter of law. This approach misses the forest for the trees.

Freed from the confines of Article 4-A, Sheerbonnet's claims—conversion, tortious interference with contract, unjust enrichment—all turn in varying degrees around one narrow question: what is the standard of care that is to be exercised by a receiving bank, also serving as the beneficiary's bank, in the handling of a payment order to be credited to the seized account of an insolvent bank that is also the beneficiary of the payment order—particularly when the crediting of the frozen account will have the effect of increasing the receiving/beneficiary's bank offset against debts owed to it by the beneficiary, thus ensuring that the transferred funds will not in fact reach the beneficiary?

The absence of language in Article 4-A expressly restraining AEB from completing the transfer, and the allegedly porous restrictions attending the Supervisor's seizure of BCCI accounts no more vitiates Sheerbonnet's claims than does AEB's protestation that is was simply following orders. Plaintiff has made out a prima facie claim on each of cause of action.

II. This Action is Not Barred By The Liquidation Court's Turnover Order

AEB argues that a 1992 Turnover Order from the Liquidation Court bars the present action, presumably under the doctrine of res judicata. This argument is not supportable, and Sheerbonnet's claims are not precluded.

After seizing BCCI assets in New York on July 5, 1991, the Superintendent, exercising his powers under New York Banking Law § 606(4)(a), petitioned the Liquidation Court for an order compelling nine banks in possession of BCCI funds deposited in New York to surrender those funds. After the banks and the Superintendent reached a settlement agreement in March of 1992, notice of settlement was given and a hearing was held on the proposed settlement terms. A Turnover Order was then entered by Judge Dontzin of the New York State Supreme Court on April 27, 1992. Under the terms of the order, the banks were to turn over to the Superintendent all funds from BCCI accounts in New York, less any claimed set-offs.

The order directed that in return for remitting the BCCI funds to the Superintendent, and to overcome the banks' reluctance to do so for fear of exposing themselves to lawsuits filed by third parties claiming an interest in the funds, those banks would be "discharged from liability with respect to claims for funds of BCCI, S.A. located in New York" and

> that upon turnover by each Bank of funds pursuant to this Order, and provided that such Bank has complied fully with the terms of this Order, this Court permanently enjoins all persons and entities from asserting any claim or cause of action against such Bank for funds of BCCI, S.A. located in New York.

Turnover Order at 6.

AEB argues that the discharge and injunction ordered by the Liquidation Court bars this action. The discharge and injunction are not without limit however; they begin and end with the turnover of funds to which they correspond. There is no discharge of liability as to any monies except those turned over, and there is no injunction against any third parties except those staking a claim to the turned over funds, that is, the "funds of BCCI, S.A." As made clear by the Court of Appeals when it scrutinized the plaintiff's complaint, Sheerbonnet stakes no such claim and asks for no such monies. See *Sheerbonnet*, 17 F.3d at 49-50.

Sheerbonnet's causes of action sound in tort, in particular: conversion, unjust enrichment, and tortious interference with contract. In relief, Sheerbonnet seeks damages for AEB's allegedly faulty banking practices. In ruling that the nature of these claims did not necessitate my abstention in favor of disposition in a state proceeding, the Court of Appeals clearly separates the merits of this case from the state liquidation of BCCI's New York accounts. "Because the claims in this case are addressed to American Express' banking conduct, they do not belong in the Liquidation Court." *Id.* at 49. Rejecting AEB's argument that Sheerbonnet's tort claims should be resolved by the Liquidation Court, the Court noted that:

> the proceedings involve different subject matters and different forms of relief. . .the issues presented here-tort claims against American Express—differ from those pressed before the Liquidation Court—creditor's claims of entitlement to BCCI's assets. [citation omitted]. While the Liquidation Court is the proper forum for claims that might affect the res being administered by the Superintendent, in this case, Sheerbonnet seeks tort damages from American Express, and the outcome of its claims will have no impact on the state liquidation proceeding.

Id. at 50.

The Turnover Order is not so sweeping as to bar a claim simply because it arises out of transactions involving a frozen BCCI New York account. Sheerbonnet does argue that AEB should not have credited its $12.4 million payment from Hady to a seized BCCI account, but it does not seek to recover the funds from that account. It instead seeks damages from AEB for its allegedly tortious conduct. Thus, although due full faith and credit from this court under 28 U.S.C. § 1738, such credit is given to a state court judgment only where it is due. This action, and the remedy sought, do not fall within the scope of the order and thus are not precluded by it.

Even if this action did fall within the scope of the Turnover Order, claim preclusion would not be appropriate. A federal court must give the same preclusive effect to decisions of state courts as would other courts within that state. Under New York law, a party is precluded from raising a claim that was raised or could have been raised in a prior proceeding, when the claim arises from the same set of facts or underlying transactions. Before a claim is precluded, it must be shown that the claimant had a full and fair opportunity to litigate the matter, that there is an identity of issues and parties in the earlier and later proceedings, and that the claim was necessarily decided on the merits in the earlier action.

Without addressing the identity-of-issues and necessarily-decided-on-the-merits elements, both of which are lacking in light of the above analysis, it is clear that Sheerbonnet was also not afforded a full and fair opportunity to have its claims heard by the Liquidation Court. The Liquidation Court turnover order was the product of a settlement reached between the Superintendent and the nine banks holding frozen BCCI monies. In return for surrendering those funds, the order served as a prophylactic interpleader, providing the banks with a shield from later claims to the funds. Notice of the proposed settlement order was given, and opposition to it was invited at a settlement hearing which Sheerbonnet did not attend. As AEB notes, these "objections were carved out for a separate hearing."

Even had Sheerbonnet responded to the notice and attended the hearing, which it chose not to do, it would not have had a full and fair opportunity to litigate its tort claims—nor was the Liquidation Court a proper forum for doing so. Res judicata will not apply when "the initial forum did not have the power to award the full measure of relieve sought in the later litigation." *Davidson v. Capuano*, 792 F.2d 275, 278 (2d Cir. 1986). In the underlying action, the Liquidation Court, even if asked, was not in a position to address or provide full relief for Sheerbonnet's tort claims. Furthermore, Sheerbonnet had no cause to contest the turnover of BCCI funds to the Superintendent, since it was not making a claim to those funds.

The lack of both a full and fair opportunity to litigate and an identity of issues necessarily decided prevent a finding of res judicata even under New York's pragmatic "transactional analysis test," which bars claims that are "coterminous with the transaction or series of transactions from which the earlier claims arose." *Couri v. Westchester Country Club, Inc.*, 186 A.D.2d 715, 589 N.Y.S.2d 494, 496 (2d Dep't 192) (citations omitted). As stated above, the Turnover Order does not, and was not designed to, bar a claim simply because it is related to the seizure of BCCI assets in New York. If that were the case, the multiplicity of litigation spawned by that seizure would thereby have been swallowed in its entirety by the Liquidation Court. In light of the salient differences between this action and the Liquidation Court proceeding, a transactional analysis also fails to identify "the same gravamen of the wrong upon which the action is brought." *Reilly*, 407 N.Y.S.2d at 648, 379 N.E.2d at 175.

It can hardly be said that barring Sheerbonnet's current claim serves the primary purposes of the doctrine of res judicata: to prevent repetitive litigation, to promote judicial economy, and to provide for certainty in legal determinations.

III. The Superintendent Is Not A Necessary Party

AEB moves under Fed.R.Civ.Pro.12(b)(7) for dismissal for failure to join a necessary party pursuant to Fed.R.Civ.Pro. 19. Rule 19(a) requires joinder of a party, when joinder will not deprive the court of subject matter jurisdiction, if:

> (1) in the person's absence complete relief cannot be accorded among those already parties, or (2) the person claims an interest relating to the subject matter of the action and is so situated that the disposition of the action in the person's absence may (i) as a practical matter impair or impede the person's ability to protect that interest or (ii) leave any of the persons already parties subject to a substantial risk of incurring double, multiple, or otherwise inconsistent obligations by reason of the claimed interest.

Fed. R. Civ. Pro. 19(a).

AEB explains its evocation of Rule 19, specifically Rule 19(a)(2)(ii), as follows:

> In this action, Sheerbonnet must establish that it—and not some other party—is entitled to the funds credited to the BCCI Account. The Superintendent, however, has recovered from AEB the net balance in the BCCI Account and has challenged the setoffs taken by AEB against that Account. [citation omitted]. In light of this conflict, if the Superintendent were not joined as a party, AEB could not receive complete relief in this proceeding and would be exposed to a substantial risk of multiple liability.

Defendant's Memorandum in Support of its Motion to Dismiss, at 23.

AEB's fear of exposure to multiple and conflicting judicial determinations stems from its mischaracterization of the nature of this action. Properly characterized, this action does not require the joinder of the Superintendent for just adjudication.

As made clear by the Court of Appeals, and as discussed above, this action is not about the funds that were frozen in the BCCI New York account, nor about AEB's right as a creditor of BCCI to offset from those funds against BCCI's debt, nor about the Superintendent's right to seize, liquidate, demand the turnover of or otherwise contest the legitimacy of setoffs against BCCI funds in New York. Sheerbonnet brings this action seeking relief from allegedly tortious conduct by AEB in its banking practices, conduct which precipitated but is distinct from AEB's claimed right to a setoff, for which Sheerbonnet seeks monetary relief.

AEB states that the Superintendent "has challenged the setoffs taken by AEB against [the BCCI] Account." Defendant's Memorandum of Law in Support of its Motion to Dismiss, at 23. This statement is followed by a citation to an exhibit of a summons with notice which evidences a suit brought by AEB against the Superintendent and the New York Agency of BCCI, challenging the Superintendent's rejection of over $30 million in setoffs against BCCI funds claimed by AEB, and seeking a declaratory judgment as to its rights and entitlement to damages. If, when and to what extent AEB is entitled to offsets against BCCI funds, questions that all center around AEB's prior banking relationship with BCCI, is the gravamen of the action described. A determination in the present action as to whether AEB did or did not engage in tortious banking practices in regard to its handling of the Northern Trust payment order, and the extent, if any, of the damages sustained by Sheerbonnet because of such conduct, do not implicate the interests of the Superintendent. A determination here will neither impair or impede the Superintendent's ability to protect his interest in contesting AEB to multiple, inconsistent judicial outcomes by reason of the Superintendent's claimed interest in the BCCI offset. This action may therefore continue without the joinder of the Superintendent.

CONCLUSION

AEB's motion to dismiss is denied in all respects.

---

§ 15.05 Payment Order, Obligation, Process

Read: U.C.C. §§ 4A-212, 4A-301, 4A-302, 4A-402, 4A-403, 4A-404, 4A-405, 4A-406.

WESTON COMPAGNIE DE FINANCE ET D' INVESTISSEMENTS v. LA REPUBLICA DEL ECUADOR

Southern District, New York
1993 WL 267282 (1993)

McKenna, District Judge.

1.

Plaintiff moves (I) for an order directing defendants to return at least $704,858.12 to this jurisdiction either to be held by the Marshal subject to prejudgment attachment or such return to be conditional on entry of any judgment in plaintiff's favor, and (ii) for a stay pending appeal of this Court's Order and Memorandum of June 11, 1993 (the "June 11 Order") to the extent it affected funds held by garnishee Chase Manhattan Bank, N.A. ("Chase"). Defendant Banco Central del Ecuador ("Central Bank") cross-moves for an order compelling Chase to release $151,247.05 on the ground that such funds are immune from prejudgment attachment. Further, both plaintiff and the Central Bank have addressed the issue of the applicability of New York Commercial Code § 4-A-503, as directed in the June 11 Order at 18-19.

2.

Plaintiff in substance concedes that the $704,858.12 it would have the Court direct the Central Bank return to New York is immune from prejudgment attachment under the June 11 Order. "It is true that the $704,858.12 so transferred involved funds held for the state telephone company, as was the $161,290.08 found by the Court to be immune." (Pl.Supp.Mem. at 16.) Plaintiff argues, however, that, in removing the funds from New York, prior to the June 11 Order, the Central Bank interfered with the order of attachment granted by the Judge to whom this case was previously assigned, and that, therefore, "the monies should now be returned either as a sanction or as an equitable remedy to restore the status quo." (*Id.*)

Upon review of the parties' submissions, the Court finds that the Central Bank did not violate the order of attachment, and no sanction is warranted. Nor would the relief sought preserve the status quo in any meaningful sense. Rather, it would give plaintiff, in effect, prejudgment attachment of property of a foreign central bank held for its own account, which this Court held to be impermissible under the Foreign Sovereign Immunities Act ("FSIA") in the June 11 Order. The first branch of plaintiff's motion is, therefore, denied.

3.

This Court stayed the June 11 Order for five days "in order to allow any party to make such application as it may wish to the Court of Appeals," *id.* at 22, in the expectation that expedited review of that order would be sought. No application to the Court of Appeals appears, however, to have been sought by plaintiff, who now seeks a stay pending appeal, pursuant to Fed.R.App.P.8(a), from this Court. The Court will, however, assume that plaintiff did not understand that it was free to proceed to seek a stay in the Court of Appeals.

Four factors are relevant to whether a stay under Fed.R.App.P8(a) should be granted:

> (1) whether the movant will suffer irreparable injury absent a stay, (2) whether a party will suffer substantial injury if a stay is issued, (3) whether the movant has demonstrated "a

substantial possibility, although less than a likelihood, of success" on appeal, and (4) the public interests that may be affected.

Hirschfeld v. Board of Election, 984 F.2d 35, 39 (2d Cir.1993) (citations omitted).

Denial of a stay will, of course, injure plaintiff, to the extent that, should it recover judgment, there will be less money immediately accessible to satisfy that judgment. Whether that injury will be irreparable is less clear. The Republic of Ecuador is a member of the community of nations on good terms with the United States, with, presumably, a principled legal system, and plaintiff has not shown that, were it necessary to do so, a final judgment of a court of the United States would not be recognized, and enforced, in Ecuador.

Grant of a stay will cause injury to the Republic of Ecuador, to the extent that funds that the Court of Appeals may find not to be subject to prejudgment attachment will be unavailable to the Republic at least for a period of some months.

This Court does not believe plaintiff has shown a substantial possibility of success on appeal, but nevertheless recognizes that the June 11 Order deals with novel issues, and that the Court of Appeals may read the relevant provisions of the FSIA differently than did this Court.

The only public interest that may be affected, in this Court's view, is that of Republic of Ecuador in not losing, for a time, the use of funds not properly subject to prejudgment attachment. Perhaps there is, as well, a public interest in the relations between the United States and Ecuador that suggests at least proceeding with care when the latter nation's funds are at stake.

On balance of the above factors, this Court does not believe a stay pending appeal is warranted. Plaintiff's motion for a stay is, therefore, denied, with the exception that this order is stayed until July 19, 1993, in order to allow plaintiff to apply to the Court of Appeals for a stay pending appeal pursuant to Fed.R.App.P. 8(a), this Court now having "failed to afford the relief which the applicant requested." *Id.*

4.

The Central Bank's motion for an order directing Chase to release the sum of $151,247.05, referred to in 6 of the June 28, 1993 affidavit of Mr. Cabezas is granted. That sum is in the same category as the $161,290.08 in an account at Chase described at page 20 of the June 11 Order, and is not subject to prejudgment attachment under the FSIA.

5.

Although the parties have addressed the issue of the applicability of New York Commercial Code § 4-A-503, the Court is still unclear as to the mechanics of certain of the transactions for which Chase purportedly holds "private-source" funds on behalf of the Central Bank. Apparently, two types of transactions are reflected in those funds. First, the Central Bank acts "as the receiving or beneficiary bank" of funds transfers. In this situation, no further funds transfers are consummated; the account is "subject to an offsetting debit but without any further transfer orders." (P1.Supp.Mem. at 5.) The second type of transaction, used by the Central Bank in a hypothetical to illustrate the anticipated movement of these funds contemplates Chase acting as an intermediary bank. An originator's Australian bank, wishing to transfer funds to Ecuador, transfers funds first to the Central Bank's account at Chase in New York. Chase, in turn, wire transfers the funds to the Central Bank in Ecuador, the beneficiary's bank, where the funds are made available to the beneficiary (the "Westpac Transfer"). Only this second type of transaction may not be restrained in New York under § 4-A-503 because in this instance the New York Bank is acting as a receiving bank other than the originator's bank or the beneficiary's bank.

Article 4A of the New York Uniform Commercial Code became effective in January 1991. "For the first time 4A put into place specific rules for the regulation of funds transfers." *Manufacturas Int'l, Ltda v. Manufacturers Hanover Trust Co.*, 792 F.Supp. 180, 194 (E.D.N.Y. 1992). The parties' dispute turns on the interpretation and applicability of § 4-A-503. That section states that:

> For proper cause and in compliance with applicable law, a court may restrain (i) a person from issuing a payment order to initiate a funds transfer, (ii) an originator's bank from executing the payment order of the originator, or (iii) the beneficiary's bank from releasing funds to the beneficiary or the beneficiary from withdrawing the funds. A court may not otherwise restrain a person from issuing a payment order, paying or receiving payment of a payment order, or otherwise acting with respect to a funds transfer.

N.Y.U.C.C. § 4-A-503(McKinney 1991). That section's official comment describes the section as preventing "interruption of a funds transfer after it has been set in motion." Official Comment to § 4-A-503. A court may only restrain a funds transfer at certain stages of the operation—prior to initiation by the originator, prior to execution by the originator's bank, prior to release of funds by the beneficiary's bank, and prior to withdrawal of funds. "In particular, intermediary banks are protected."

As a preliminary matter, plaintiff contends that § 4-A-503 does not apply to the instant dispute because that section relates to injunctions, not attachments. The Court does not agree. Section 4-A-502, which addresses the rights and obligations of parties where service has been made at some point in the course of a funds transfer, provides, in pertinent part, that 'creditor process' means levy, attachment, garnishment, notice of lien, sequestration, or similar process issued by or on behalf of a creditor or other claimant with respect to an account." N.Y.U.C.C. § 4-A-502(1)(McKinney 1991). The term "creditor process" is a generic term and covers a variety of devices by which a creditor can seize an account. Official Comment to § 4-A-502. Therefore, because of the existence of the order of attachment, the contested "private-source" transactions do not automatically fall outside the scope of Article 4A as plaintiff contends. Instead, if § 4-A-503 is satisfied an order of the Court attaching "private-source" funds may issue.

As discussed above, Mr. Yepez, the Central Bank's manager of operations, stated that the Central Bank "acts as the receiving or beneficiary bank" for certain third party funds in the Central Bank's account at Chase. (Yepez Aff. 7) An order of attachment is entirely appropriate under § 4-A-503 where a bank is acting as the receiving bank, and no further transfer is contemplated. A beneficiary's bank may be restrained prior to its release of transferred funds pursuant to § 4-A-503(iii). Because the Central Bank does not dispute Mr. Yepez's characterization of its role, the Court concludes that Chase acted, at least in certain transactions, as a beneficiary's bank. Accordingly, the order of attachment is confirmed with respect to the "private-source" funds held by Chase in the account of the Central Bank, subject to submission of documentary evidence that specific funds were later to be wire transferred so that Chase is not the beneficiary's bank.

A different result obtains when Chase or any other bank acts as an intermediary bank. As described by the Central Bank, Chase acted as an intermediary bank in the Westpac Transfer. Funds transfers that are in motion are not attachable at the intermediary bank stage under § 4-A-503. Unfortunately, the parties have not described the disputed transactions in sufficient detail for the Court to determine if any bank (except Chemical Bank) was acting as an intermediary bank.

Plaintiff's reliance on the length of time that funds remain in accounts in New York as determinative of whether a bank acted as an intermediary bank is misplaced. Section 4-A-503, and its official comment, are silent as to periods of time. The $10,885.02 of "private-source" funds held by Chemical Bank, which according to plaintiff was comprised of a balance dating as far back as April 5, 1993 and which was subsequently transferred from New York on April 28, 1993 is not attachable because Chemical Bank functioned as an intermediary bank regardless of the amount of time the funds remained in New York. Chemical Bank acted as a receiving bank, but was not the originator's bank or the beneficiary's bank.

Because the parties have not adequately described the disputed funds transfers, any party wishing to vacate the order of attachment with respect to a specific transaction must present documentary evidence of the funds transfer's intended route, including intermediary bank(s) and beneficiary's bank(s). Plaintiff may, of course, present contradictory evidence.

So Ordered.

§ 15.06 Acceptance, Rejection, Cancellation or Amendment

Read: U.C.C. §§ 4A-209, 4A-210, 4A-211.

SHAWMUT WORCESTER COUNTY BANK v. FIRST AMERICAN BANK & TRUST

United States District Court, D. Massachusetts
731 F.Supp. 57 (1990)

YOUNG, DISTRICT JUDGE.

This action arises out of an error made by the plaintiff, the Shawmut Worcester County Bank ("Shawmut" or "transferor"). As is often the case with bank errors concerning money, restoring the status quo ante is somewhat more complicated than the slip that created the problem. In the instant case, Shawmut mistakenly transferred $10,000 from the account of American Optical Corporation, not a party to this action, to First American Bank & Trust in West Palm Beach, Florida ("First American" or "transferee"), purportedly for the benefit of one Fernando Degan ("Degan" or "beneficiary"), also not a party to this action, by means of an Electronic Funds Transfer System known as "Fedwire." Although Degan was the sole named beneficiary of the transfer, the payment order issued from Shawmut to First American also indicated that First American should credit account number 100 205 001 633, an account, it turns out, which is jointly held by Degan and one Joseph Merle. Shawmut discovered its error one hundred six (106) days after the mistaken transfer, credited the account of its customer American Optical the sum of $10,000.65, and asked First American to "reverse" a "previous day's" transfer, *i.e.*, credit Shawmut the amount mistakenly transferred. First American asked Merle, its customer, if he would authorize the "reversal." Merle refused. Accordingly, American told Shawmut it would not reverse the transfer. Merle has already been adjudicated liable to Shawmut for $10,000. Apparently unsatisfied, Shawmut also seeks judgment against First American and its employee Michael Woods ("Woods").

Shawmut asserts claims of conversion against First American (Count I) and Woods (Count III) in handling the transfer. Shawmut also claims that First American is liable to it for breaching a principal-agent relationship (Count V) and for negligence (Count VI). Finally, Shawmut seeks recovery under rights purportedly derived from a federal statute, the Electronic Funds Transfers Act, 15 U.S.C. sec. 1693 *et seq.*, (1982) (Counts VII, VII, X, and XI), as well as two Massachusetts statutes: Mass. Gen. Laws ch. 93A(the Massachusetts "consumer protection statute") (Count II) and Mass.Gen.Laws ch. 106 (the Massachusetts Uniform Commercial Code) (Counts XIII and XIV). First American and Woods have moved either to dismiss or for summary judgment with respect to all claims.

The first issue concerns the choice of law to be applied to the common law claims. Shawmut argues conclusorily that Massachusetts law applies. Woods and First American do not argue the point. This Court, applying the choice of law rules of the forum state as dictated by *Klaxon Co. v. Stentor Co.*, 313 U.S. 487, 61 S.Ct. 1020, 85 L.Ed 1477 (1941), here Massachusetts, concludes that Florida law applies. In Massachusetts, the choice of law in actions such as this depends on a number of factors as set forth in *Bushkin Associates, Inc. v. Raytheon Co.*, 393 Mass. 622, 473 N.E.2d 662 (1985). Here, these criteria all point toward the application of Florida law.

Woods and First American are entitled to summary judgment with respect to Shawmut's conversion theory. It is well-settled Florida law that conversion consists of an act in derogation of the plaintiff's possessory rights. The essence of a conversion claim is the wrongful deprivation of identifiable property from a person entitled to possession. The act must be unauthorized and must involve an interference with legal rights incident to ownership.

Viewing the record before the Court in the light most favorable to Shawmut and indulging all inferences favorably to Shawmut, neither First American nor its employee, Woods, effected a conversion of property owned by Shawmut when the bank, through Woods, refused to "reverse" the erroneous funds transfer made 106 days earlier. A conversion occurs at the time the defendants act in derogation of an interest in possession in identifiable goods.

No conversion took place by virtue of the acts of August 11, 1986, the day of the transfers, since First American was authorized to act, that is, to execute the payment orders issued by Shawmut. Likewise, no conversion took place on November 25, 1986, the day Shawmut first requested that First American "reverse" the erroneous transfer, because, as of November 25, Shawmut had no possessory rights in the mistaken transfer. By then the money had been "finally paid" by First American's Federal Reserve bank to First American, which extinguished Shawmut's "ownership interest" in the funds as personal property. Put another way, by November 25, 1986, there was no longer any property owned by Shawmut which was subject to conversion by First American. Therefore, Woods and First American are entitled to summary judgment with respect to the conversion counts, Counts I and III.

Shawmut's second common law claim alleges that First American breached its duties as Shawmut's agent (1) in handling the August 11 transfers and (2) in refusing to "reverse" the erroneous transfer on November 25. On August 11, First American was undoubtedly the receiving agent for its customers, Merle and Degan, for purposes of receiving the transfer and crediting the account. Shawmut, however, alleges that First American was also acting as Shawmut's agent for purposes of the transaction and it was in this capacity that First American was negligent in discharging its duties. See *Securities Fund Services, Inc. v. American Nat. Bank & Trust Co. of Chicago*, 542 F.Supp. 323, 327 (N.D.Ill. 1982) (a "corresponding bank," which regularly performs services for another in a market to which the other does not have direct access, may be an "agent" for the initiator of a wire transfer).

Shawmut claims that the pattern of dealings between the banks establishes a general agency between them, with no limiting dimension, that extended at least until November 25, one hundred six days after the August 11 transactions, and that it was within the scope of first American's duties as Shawmut's agent to "reverse" the transaction at that time. This view is not supported by the undisputed facts. The record before the Court is insufficient to establish the existence of any principal-agent relationship between Shawmut and First American. Scrutiny of all attendant facts surrounding the relationship between these banks reveals that, unlike the scenario in Securities Fund, First American was not operating as a "correspondent bank" for Shawmut. It is simply an independent bank, like Shawmut, that maintains an account with the Federal Reserve System and, like Shawmut, participates in the national Federal Reserve Wire Network ("Fedwire") facilitating electronic fund transfers between financial institutions on behalf of the financial institutions' customers. Participants in Fedwire transfers like the one in this case are bound, to be sure, to conform their conduct to the standards prescribed by Fedwire regulations. See 12 C.F.R. § 210.25-38 (Subpart B of Regulation J governs the wire transfer of credits and debit of funds and preempts all conflicting state laws and private contract provisions). A difficult hurdle that Shawmut has failed to negotiate in establishing an agency relationship is that under Regulation J the transferor bank, Shawmut, did not have the right to control First American's conduct with respect to the original crediting of the account specified in the payment order. Under Regulation J, the transferor bank, in making a request for a transfer, authorizes its Reserve Bank to debit its account for the amount of funds to be transferred and further authorizes the transferee institution's Reserve Bank to credit the same amount to the transferee bank. Any request by a transferor to interrupt the carrying out of a funds transfer must be made to the transferee's Reserve Bank, not to the transferee. Even then, that Reserve Bank is not obligated to accommodate the transferor, but may do so if the request is made in time to give the Reserve Bank a reasonable opportunity to comply, 12 C.F.R. § 210.35(a)—that is, before it makes final payment to the transferee receiving bank. This legal limitation on the powers of the purported principal is fatal to Shawmut's agency theory.

In the alternative, this Court rules that even if an agency relationship existed between a transferor bank and a transferee bank in transactions of this kind, it is necessarily circumscribed by the parties' respective obligations as set out in Regulation J. See 12 C.F.R. § 210.27(b). Any agency a transferor bank may be said to have with a transferee bank ends at the time of final payment by the transferee bank's Reserve bank, see 12 C.F.R. § 210.36, because a transferee that receives such notice agrees only to credit promptly the beneficiary's account or otherwise make the amount available to the beneficiary, 12 C.F.R. § 210.30(b). As matter of law, this is the permissible scope of the agency. At the time the transfer item is finally paid, the transferee bank becomes the beneficiary's receiving agent and any obligations as "agent" for the transferor bank re limited to crediting promptly the beneficiary's account. In this case, as First American's Reserve Bank had made final payment to it, First American was not obliged by any applicable principle of agency law to "reverse" a transaction made 106 days earlier by reaching into its client's account for the money.

Shawmut grasps at one final straw in supporting its agency theory. It claims that on August 11, 1986, First American breached its fiduciary duty as Shawmut's agent by failing to act in strict accordance with Shawmut's instructions, instead crediting a jointly held account, where only one account holder was the actual beneficiary. Shawmut claims that First American's failure to inform its principal of Merle's status as joint holder in the account number indicated on the payment order amounts to a breach of First American's fiduciary duties as an agent toward it with regard to that discrete transaction. It is undisputed that Shawmut's instructions, contained in the payment order were to credit Fernando Degan. It is also undisputed that the payment order also gave the account number to which the deposit should be made, which was the joint account of Degan and Merle. Even assuming, contrary to the conclusion that this Court reaches as matter of law above, that a jury could find an agent-principal relationship existed between Shawmut and First American on August 11, no reasonable jury would be warranted, on these facts, in concluding that First American had a duty to disclose the joint ownership of the account to which Shawmut expressly, albeit erroneously, transferred funds. Accordingly, summary judgment must enter for First American on Count V, alleging a breach of the principal-agent relationship.

Shawmut's claim based on rights allegedly secured by the Electronic Funds Transfer Act, 15 U.S.C. § 1693(1982) ("Transfer Act") is also without merit. Although the statute does indicate that a subsidiary purpose of the Transfer Act is to "provide a basic framework establishing the rights, liabilities and responsibilities of participants in [electronic funds transfer] systems," the Transfer act was primarily created for the especial benefit of consumers. 15 U.S.C. § 1693(b). The Transfer Act evidently is aimed at providing a framework of law regulating the rights of consumers as against financial institutions in electronic funds transfers. The Transfer Act contains civil remedies only for consumers, with "consumers" being statutorily defined as "natural persons." 15 U.S.C. § 1693a(5).

This dispute is between two financial institutions and there is no evidence before the Court, even after ample discovery, that First American "directly or indirectly holds an account belonging to a consumer" that conceivably might create the kind of financial institution and consumer relationship between First American and Shawmut that the Act regulates. See 15 U.S.C. sec. 1693a(8). In the absence of such evidence, it is evident that this sort of funds transfer—a garden-variety wire transfer between financial institutions—is specifically expected from Transfer Act coverage by the provisions of section 1693a(6)(B). Therefore, summary judgment must now be entered for Woods and First American on counts VII, VIII, X, and XII which allege a cause of action under the Transfer Act.

The counts that rest on the application of Massachusetts statutory law to this interbank dispute must also be dismissed. The provisions of the Massachusetts Consumer Protection act, as amended, Mass.Gen.Laws ch. 93A, § 11 (1989), preclude application of that Massachusetts statute to this dispute, since the transaction constituting the alleged unfair or deceptive act or practice—First American's refusal to act on Shawmut's belated "reversal" request—occurred in Florida. Since the conduct complained of did not occur "primarily and substantially within the Commonwealth [of Massachusetts]," this action cannot be maintained under Mass.Gen.Laws ch. 93A. The Massachusetts version of the Uniform Commercial Code has no application in the premises since Mass.Gen.Laws ch. 106, § 4-102(2) specifically states that "[t]he liability of a bank for action or non-action with respect to any item handled by it for purposes of presentment, payment or collection is governed by the law of the place where the bank is located." First American, the bank whose liability for action or non-action is at issue here, is located in Florida. Therefore, if electronic funds transfers are governed by the Uniform Commercial Code, the law of Florida and the Florida Commercial Code, Fla.Stat. chapters 671-673 (1966), applies. The Circuits that have considered the matter have uniformly concluded that the Uniform Commercial Code does not apply to Electronic Funds Transfers, except perhaps by analogy. An electronic funds transfer is not within article 3 of the Uniform Commercial Code because it is not a signed negotiable instrument. See Fla.Stat. secs. 673.3-102(1)(e); 673.3-104; 673.3-401; Mass.Gen.Laws ch 106, secs. 3-102(1)(e); 3-104; 3-401. Although the language of Article 4 could be stretched to include electronic funds transfers, they were surely not within the contemplation of the draftsmen.

What remains is the negligence claim (Count VI). The state of the common law in regard to electronic funds transfers generally and the liabilities concomitant to erroneous payment orders in particular is not yet well developed. There is no comprehensive body of law to define the rights and obligations that arise from wire transfers. More particularly, Florida decisions offer no specific guidance on the negligence issue in these circumstances.

Were it Massachusetts common law that supplied the rule of decision here, this Court could turn confidently to the American Law Institute Restatements as they so frequently guide the growth of the common law in this Commonwealth. Florida common law decisions do not, however, so frequently advert to the Restatements. This Court is not nearly so sure, therefore, that the Florida Supreme Court will follow the Restatements as adopted. Nevertheless, given the dearth of decided cases, this Court will be guided—subject to reconsideration in the manner discussed below—by the American Law Institute, Proposed Article 4A, Uniform Commercial Code, Proposed Final Draft (April 20, 1989) ("ALI Article 4A").

Shawmut argued first that First American was negligent in facilitating payment to an account number not peculiarly identified to the name of the transfer beneficiary. This is precisely the argument the Court has already considered—and rejected as matter of law—in evaluating whether First American violated any duty imposed on it as a possible agent of Shawmut. *Supra* at 61. The same result follows in the negligence context under the American Law Institute proposal. ALI Article 4A-209(3)(b) provides that duplicate transfers may be subject to cancellation if the sender discovers a mistake has been made. Section 4A-209(3) also cross references Fedwire rules, and reads, in pertinent part as follows:

> (3) Cancellation or amendment of a payment order accepted by the receiving bank is effective only if the bank agrees or a funds transfer system rule allows cancellation or amendment without agreement of the bank. . .

Fedwire rules do not permit a cancellation, "revocation," or "reversal" of a previous day's funds transfer without permission of the receiving bank. The transferee or receiving bank is under no obligation under Regulation J to comply with a request, even if the transferor provides indemnity. 12 C.F.R. § 210. Both the ALI Article 4A and the Fedwire rules recognize that even with indemnity, the beneficiary's bank may be reluctant to alienate its customer, the beneficiary, by denying the customer the funds. See ALI Article 4A-209, Comment 5. The language of section 4A-209 is permissive, not mandatory, where, as here, the funds transfer system rules do not permit cancellation without the permission of a receiving bank. Even if a receiving bank is the sender's "agent" on the day of the transfer, the regulatory framework that undergirds the parties' relationship cannot support the conclusion that the receiving bank is an agent for the sender charged with a duty broader than simply to credit promptly the beneficiary's account. The policies underlying this arrangement are even more compelling where a sending bank requests cancellation of a payment order three and one half months after the receiving bank has credited its customer's account. This Court rules that, as matter of law, a receiving bank is not negligent where it credits a payment order to the joint account as set out in the order.

Shawmut next argues that First American should have acted to prevent the reasonably foreseeable harm that proximately resulted from its negligent failure to notice that Shawmut's second payment order was a mistake and duplicative. The issue before the Court, thus, is whether First American was somehow put on notice that the transaction was so irregular that it should have investigated the circumstances prior to crediting the account a second time.

If Shawmut's own contributory negligence is put to one side for a moment, this last argument has some appeal. As a practical matter, the receiving bank probably is in a better position to recover the funds from the beneficiary, especially where the beneficiary is a customer of that bank. It thus makes sense that the risk of loss for duplicative payment orders such as the one involved in the instant case be shifted in some instances to a bank which blithely executes payment orders without exercising even ordinary care. The American Law Institute is considering this matter. See ALI Article 4A-205 permitting such a shift of the risk of loss where the sender can show that it complied with applicable security procedures and that the error would have been detected by the receiving bank had that bank complied with similar security procedures. Here, however, there is no evidence before the Court that First American failed to comply with one of its own security procedures and no evidence that the lack of a reasonable security procedure may have caused the error to have gone undetected.

Before judgment enters, however, one matter may require further consideration. In disposing of the negligence claim, the Court has relied upon ALI Article 4A. Its reasoning depends on the following conclusions, one legal and the other factual, viz:

1. that the Florida Legislature or Supreme Court will adopt or follow the American Law Institute proposal, and

2. that no applicable security procedure was followed by Shawmut and ignored by First American.

Because the parties could have no inkling that the Court would apply ALI Article 4A to this case, they have not briefed either of the above matters. Fairness requires they be given an opportunity to do so as well as the opportunity to consider whether a certification of the legal issue to the Supreme Court of Florida is appropriate. Accordingly, the parties shall have thirty (30) days from the date of this memorandum to address these issues by briefs and affidavits. Should none be received, judgment will enter for Woods and First American. Should either party brief these issues, however, the Court will reconsider the negligence point.

So Ordered.

ALEO INTERNATIONAL, LTD. v. CITIBANK, N.A.

Supreme Court, New York County
160 Misc.2d 950, 612 N.Y.S.2d 540 (1994)

HERMAN CAHN, JUSTICE

Defendant Citibank, N.A. ("Citibank") moves for an order, pursuant to CPLR 3212, granting it summary judgment dismissing the complaint. Plaintiff Aleo International, Ltd. ("Aleo") is a domestic corporation. On October 13, 1992, one of Aleo's vice-presidents, Vera Eyzerovich ("Ms. Eyzerovich"), entered her local Citibank branch and instructed Citibank to make an electronic transfer of $284,563 US dollars to the Dresdner Bank in Berlin, Germany, to the account of an individual named Behzad Hermatjou ("Hermatjou"). The documentary evidence submitted shows that at 5:27 p.m. on October 13, 1992, Citibank sent the payment order to the Dresdner Bank by electronic message. Dresdner Bank later sent Citibank an electronic message: "Regarding your payment for USD 284,563.00 DD 13.10.92 [indecipherable] f/o Behzad Hermatjou, Pls be advised that we have credited A.M. beneficiary DD 14.10.92 val 16.10.92 with the net amount of USD 284.136,16." This information was confirmed by the Dresdner Bank by fax to Citibank on July 29, 1993: "Please be advised that on 14.10.92 at 09:59 o'clock Berlin time Dresdner Bank credited the account of Behzad Hermatjou with USD 284,136.16 (USD 284,563.00 less our charges)." It is undisputed that Berlin time is six hours ahead of New York time, and that 9:59 a.m. Berlin time would be 3:59 a.m. New York time. At approximately 9 a.m. on October 14, 1992, Ms. Eyzerovich instructed Citibank to stop the transfer. When Citibank did not, this action ensued.

Article 4-A of the Uniform Commercial Code ("UCC") governs electronic "funds transfers." The Official Comment to U.C.C. § 4-A-102 states that the provisions of Article 4-A are intended to be the exclusive means of determining the rights, duties and liabilities of the affected parties in any situation covered by particular provisions of the Article. Consequently, resort to principles of law or equity outside of Article 4A is not appropriate to create rights, duties and liabilities inconsistent with those stated in this Article.

Article 4-A does not include any provision for a cause of action in negligence. Thus, unless Citibank's failure to cancel Ms. Eyzerovich's transfer order was not in conformity with Article 4-A, plaintiff Aleo has failed to state a cause of action, and this action must be dismissed.

UCC 4-A-211(2), which governs the cancellation and amendment of payment orders, provides that:

> A communication by the sender cancelling or amending a payment order is effective to cancel or amend the order if notice of the communication is received at a time and in a manner affording the receiving bank a reasonable opportunity to act on the communication before the bank accepts the payment order.

"Acceptance of Payment Order" is defined by U.C.C. 4-A-209(2), which provides that:

> a beneficiary's bank accepts a payment order at the earliest of the following times: (a) when the bank (i) pays the beneficiary. . .or (ii) notifies the beneficiary of receipt of the order or that the account of the beneficiary has been credited with respect to the order. . .

The documentary evidence shows that Hermatjou's account was credited on October 14, 1992 at 9:59 a.m. Berlin time. Thus, as of 3:59 a.m. New York time, the Dresdner Bank "paid the beneficiary" and thereby accepted the payment order. Because this payment and acceptance occurred prior to Ms. Eyzerovich's stop transfer order at 9 a.m. on that day, according to U.C.C. 4-A-211(2), Ms. Eyzerovich's attempt to cancel the payment order was ineffective, and Citibank may not be held liable for failing to honor it.

Accordingly, defendant's motion is granted and this action is dismissed.

---

§ 15.07 Mistaken or Erroneous Payments

Read: U.C.C. § 4A-205, 4A-303.

BANK OF AMERICA, N.T.S.A. v. SANATI

California Court of Appeal, Second District
14 Cal. Rptr. 2d 615, 11 Cal. App. 4th 1079 (1992)

JOHNSON, ASSOCIATE JUSTICE.

In an action for unjust enrichment, money had and received, conversion, and declaratory relief, the trial court granted plaintiff's motion for summary judgment finding defendants had no defense to plaintiff's request for restitution for an erroneous funds transfer. Defendants appeal from the adverse judgment claiming the trial court erroneously applied the common law pertaining to check and negotiable instruments instead of the law specifically pertaining to funds transfers. We affirm.

FACTS AND PROCEEDINGS BELOW

In 1963 Hassan and Fatane Sanati were married in Tehran, Iran. They lived in Iran until Mrs. Fatane Sanati moved with their two children to Los Angeles in 1983. Between 1983 and 1987 Mr. Sanati spent nearly half his time living in Los Angeles. In 1987 Mr. Sanati permanently left the United States.

When Mr. Sanati left, he arranged for payments to be made to Mrs. Sanati in Los Angeles. He instructed Bank of America in London to send interest, as it accrued monthly from an account held in his name only, to an account he held jointly at Bank of America with Mrs. Sanati in Tarzana, California. The amount of each interest payment was between $2,000 and $3,000.

On April 30, 1990, Bank of America in London erroneously sent the principal of Mr. Sanati's bank account as well as the accrued interest to the joint Sanati account in Tarzana, California. The amount of the erroneous fund transfer was $203,750. The next day Mrs. Sanati authorized her children to withdraw $200,000 from this account. These funds were then deposited into various bank accounts under Mrs. Sanati's and her children's names.

Bank of America (bank) immediately realized its error and requested reimbursement for the erroneous payment. Mrs. Sanati and her children, Babak and Haleh Sanati (collectively Sanatis or defendants) refused the bank's requests.

In July 1990, the bank filed a complaint against the Sanatis seeking restitution for the amount of the erroneous payment. Eventually Mr. Sanati's bank account in London was re-credited the amount of the principal transferred without his authority and he was dismissed as a defendant in the action. The remaining parties stipulated the funds from the erroneous transfer would be placed in a blocked account at Bank of America pending resolution of the litigation.

The bank then moved for summary judgment. The trial court denied the bank's motion in order to allow the defendants to depose Mr. Sanati to determine whether he had altered his payment instructions to Bank of American London in this instance. The trial court allowed an additional 90 days continuance for this purpose. When 90 days elapsed and Mr. Sanati had not been deposed, the bank again moved for summary judgment, claiming it was entitled to judgment as a matter of law because the Sanatis had no defense to the bank's claim for restitution.

The trial court granted the bank's motion and this appeal followed.

DISCUSSION

I. REVIEW OF THE COMMON LAW GOVERNING ERRONEOUS FUND TRANSFERS.

. . . .

. . . [U]nder the law in effect at the time of the fund transfer in this case, the general common law and equitable principles controlled. Under the law as it then existed, the bank was entitled to restitution from the beneficiaries for the amount of the unauthorized transfer despite its negligence under general legal principles of mistake and unjust enrichment.

This rule, however, was subject to certain defenses. The most widely acknowledged defense to a claim for restitution for an erroneous transfer of funds was detrimental reliance by an innocent beneficiary.

A less widely acknowledged defense to a claim for restitution was the "discharge for value" rule. (Rest., Restitution, § 14.) This defense arises where there is a preexisting liquidated debt or lien owed to the beneficiary by the originator of the payment. If the originator or some third party erroneously gives the beneficiary funds at the originator's request, and the beneficiary in good faith believes the funds have been submitted in full or partial payment of the preexisting debit or lien and is unaware of the originator's or third party's mistake, the originator or third party will not be entitled to seek repayment from the beneficiary of the erroneously submitted funds.

The ban contends California courts have not adopted this rule and therefore it should not be applied in this case. A review of the cases, however, indicates to the contrary. For example, the decision in *California Pacific Title & Trust Co. v. Bank of America NT & SA* (1936) 12 Cal. App. 2d 437, 55 P.2d 533 was specifically referred to in the reporter's notes to the Restatement of Restitution section 14 on the "discharge for value" rule as the basis for illustration six of comment (b). (See Rest., Restitution § 14, reporter's notes, p. 11)

Other California cases have invoked the principle without specifically mentioning the "discharge for value" rule. The decision in *Montgomery v. Meyerstein*, 186 Cal. 459, 199 P. 800 (1921) is one such example. In that decision the court held a plaintiff who sought to rescind a land sale contract due to fraud was not entitled to seek restitution from preexisting lienholders whose liens had been satisfied out of the sales proceeds and who were unaware of the fraud.

Thus, under existing law the bank was entitled to seek restitution for the overpayment to defendants despite its negligence, unless defendants had detrimentally relied on the additional payment without notice of the mistake or unless the defendants had applied in good faith the additional erroneous payment to a preexisting debt or lien owed to them from Mr. Sanati.

II. THE BANK WAS ENTITLED TO JUDGMENT EVEN IF THE STATUTORY PROVISIONS GOVERNING ERRONEOUS FUND TRANSFERS CONTROLLED.

On appeal defendants vigorously argue the trial court erred in applying to a fund transfer case the general common law pertaining to commercial paper and negotiable instruments. They argue the court should have applied Division 11 of the California Uniform Commercial Code which governs the consequences of an erroneous execution of a payment order. Defendants also suggest that had the court applied the new law, summary judgment would have been inappropriate because there would have been a triable issue of material fact whether defendants believed in good faith the additional erroneous payment was sent in satisfaction or discharge of a preexisting debt or lien from Mr. Sanati.

Defendants' argument fails for two reasons. First, the trial court did not err in failing to apply the new fund transfer provisions of Division ll of the California Uniform Commercial Code. The Legislature expressly stated that division only applied to fund transfers in which the originator's payment order was transmitted on or After January 1, 1991. (Stats. 1990, c. 125, § 3.) The payment order in the present case was transmitted in April of 1990. Thus, by its terms the new fund transfer provisions of the California Uniform Commercial Code did not apply to the transfer in this case.

Secondly, even if the new fund transfer provisions were applied to this case, we conclude defendants have failed to create a triable issue of material fact whether Mr. Sanati owed them a preexisting debt or lien even assuming their good faith.

Section 11303 [UCC § 4A-303] of the California Uniform Commercial Code discusses the effect of an erroneous transfer. That section merely restates existing law governing such errors and provides in pertinent part:

> (a) A receiving bank that (i) executes the payment order of the sender by issuing a payment order in an amount greater than the amount of the sender's order . . .is entitled to payment of the amount of the sender's order . . . The bank is entitled to recover from the beneficiary of the erroneous order the excess payment received to the extent allowed by the law governing mistake and restitution.

The comment to the Uniform Commercial Code which was incorporated into the comments in the California Uniform Commercial Code provides examples illustrating how this section should operate. The effect of the comment explicating this section is to expressly adopt the "discharge for value" rule found in section 14 of the Restatement of Restitution.

The relevant comment provides:

> Subsections (a) and (b) deal with cases in which the receiving bank executes by issuing a payment order in the wrong amount. If Originator ordered Originator's Bank to pay $1,000,000 to the account of Beneficiary in Beneficiary's Bank, but Originator's Bank erroneously instructed Beneficiary's Bank to pay $2,000,000 to Beneficiary's account, subsection (a) applies. If Beneficiary's Bank accepts the order of Originator's Bank, Beneficiary's Bank is entitled to receive only $1,000,000 from Originator. Originator's Bank is entitled to recover the overpayment from Beneficiary to the extent allowed by the law governing mistake and restitution. Originator's Bank would normally have a right to recover the overpayment from Beneficiary, but in unusual cases the law of restitution might allow Beneficiary to keep all of part of the overpayment. For example, if Originator owed $2,000,000 to Beneficiary and Beneficiary received the extra $1,000,000 in good faith in discharge of

the debt, Beneficiary may be allowed to keep it. In this case Originator's Bank has paid an obligation of Originator and under the law of restitution, which applies through section 1-103, Originator's Bank would be subrogated to Beneficiary's rights against Originator on the obligation paid by Originator's Bank.

Thus, under this section defendants would be entitled to retain the erroneously sent funds if in good faith they believed the funds were sent to them in satisfaction of or in discharge of a valid preexisting debt or lien.

Toward this end, Fatane Sanati asserted she had a quasi community property interest in Mr. Sanati's London bank account as well as in all other property accumulated during their marriage. In an affidavit offered in opposition to the bank's motion for summary judgment Mrs. Sanati declared:

"3. I was married to Hassan Sanati, ('husband'). . .on September 7, 1963 in Tehran, Iran where we resided until I came to Los Angeles with our two children.

"4. My husband and I lived with our children, also defendants in this action, in Los Angeles since 1983. My husband was travelling in and out of the United States and until November of 1987, he had collectively spent 22 months in California during that period.

"5. During our marriage we accumulated a substantial amount of money and real property, most of which was located in Iran and England.

"6. My husband has always kept all of the bank accounts and most of the real property, wherever situated, in his own name.

"7. Since he left in November, 1987, my children and I have been receiving interest monthly from our bank account in London, England to our account. . .at Bank of American, Tarzana branch. The account in London was opened by my husband with funds derived from our bank accounts and real property in Iran.

"8. I had asked my husband on numerous occasions to transfer the London account to me in Los Angeles. Although he had agreed to do so on several occasion he had never done it.

"9. My children and I have been virtual prisoners here and completely at my husband's mercy with regard to financial matters. For the last twenty five years, my husband has always exercised complete control over all of our marital community assets worldwide.

". . .

"11. In May, 1990, the Bank of America in London transferred the monthly interest and the entire principal of the account to my and my husband's account in Bank of American in Tarzana.

"12. I used some of these funds for the family and I removed the remainder to accounts under my control.

". . .

"17. Since the London account was transferred to our joint account in California, I have spoken to my husband via telephone. On several occasions, he agreed to keep the transferred money in our joint account under both our names. However, to this date, he has not done so.

". . .

> "19. I have filed a petition for Dissolution of Marriage at the Los Angeles Superior Court on July 2, 1990. . . The Summons and Complaint were personally served upon my husband, in Tehran, Iran, by Rosy Shahbodaghi, on September 24, 1990. I have instructed my counsel to enter his default therein. . ."

Thus, Mrs. Sanati's declaration raises a reasonable inference of a potential quasi community property interest in the funds in the London bank account held in Mr. Sanati's name alone. However, this evidence does not raise a reasonable inference of a preexisting debt or lien at the time of the transfer of the type recognized in those decisions applying the "discharge for value" rule.

For example, in *Banque Worms v. Bank America International*, (S.D.N.Y. 1989) 726 F.Supp. 940 (S.D.N.Y. 1989), *aff'd.*, 928 F.2d 538 (2nd Cir. 1991), the case upon which defendants primarily rely, the debt was a bank loan. In that case the originator had an outstanding loan for $2,000,000 from Banque Worms. On the day before the erroneous transfer, Banque Worms notified the originator it was calling the loan. The next day Banque Worms received a wire transfer for $2,000,000 from Security Pacific International Bank (SPIB), the originator's bank, and applied it to the originator's outstanding loan balance. Shortly thereafter Banque Worms received a second wire transfer from the originator's bank for $1,974,267.97 which was the amount the originator actually requested to be sent. Because it only had instructions for the latter payment, SPIB could not debit the originator's bank account for the first erroneous payment. Because Banque Worms received the payment in the good faith belief it was in response to their demand for repayment of the loan, the court held SPIB had to suffer the loss the for mistaken payment under the "discharge for value" rule.

Examples in the Restatement of Restitution describing the "discharge for value" rule describe debts that are liquidated, concrete and preexisting, not merely probable and undetermined. (*e.g.*, Rest., Restitution, § 14, com. b, illus. 1 [no restitution for proceeds erroneously used to pay existing mortgage on real estate]; illus. 2 [no restitution from city for property taxes paid on property not actually owned]; illus. 3 [no restitution where bank erroneously cashes customer's check given to payee in payment for services rendered]; illus. 4 [no restitution from judgment creditor for execution of judgment of wrong person's property.]) No decision we are aware of has applied the discharge for value rule where the debt or lien in question was anything less than an objectively verifiable, preexisting, liquidated obligation. (See Rest., Restitution, (append.) § 14 and cases collected.) Indeed, allowing the rule to apply to debts or obligations any less substantial would risk destroying the certainty of the rule and allow the exception to control its application.

Consequently, it does not appear the "discharge for value" rule can be properly invoked in a case such as this where the alleged preexisting debt or lien is at best a probable yet undetermined interest in a portion of the funds in Mr. Sanati's bank account in London.

The defendants do not contend they changed their position to their detriment in reliance on the erroneously transmitted funds. Nor do the defendants' opposition papers raise any other potential defense to the bank's action for restitution. Thus, in the absence of any viable defense, the bank was entitled to restitution from the beneficiaries for the erroneously transmitted funds. We therefore conclude the trial court did not err in finding the bank was entitled to judgment as a matter of law.

The judgment is affirmed.

---

§ 15.08 Liability for Failure to Effect a Funds Transfer

Read: U.C.C. § 4A-305.

PROBLEM 15.1

Your senior partner has asked for your ideas as to a situation in which his client, a Swiss Bank, is being sued. The plaintiff alleges that your client is liable for consequential damages because of a failure to make a requested transfer of funds. You are given the following information as facts:

> H&M Company chartered a ship, the Pandora, for one year, with an option to extend the charter for a second year, with a fixed daily rate of pay for the hire of the ship during both the initial and the option period. The agreement state that charter fees were to be paid semi-monthly "in advance." If payment was not made on time the Pandora's owner could cancel the charter. Payment was to be made by deposit to the owner's account in the Banque de Paris in Geneva, Switzerland. On the morning of April 25, 1994, H&M telephoned Conte Bank, where it had an account, to transfer $27,000 to the Banque de Paris account of the Pandora'a owner in payment for the charter hire period from April 27 to May 11, 1994. The requested telex went out to Conte's London office on the afternoon of April 25, which was nighttime in England. Early the next morning a telex operator in Conte's London office dialed your client's general telex number, which rings in the Bank's cable department. But that number was busy, and after trying unsuccessfully for an hour to engage it, the Conte telex operator dialed another number, that of a machine in your client's foreign exchange department which he had used in the past when the general number was engaged. However, your client did not receive the telex because the machine did not print it out and thus failed to comply with the payment order, and no transfer of funds was made to the account of the Pandora's owner in the Banque de Paris. On the morning of April 27, Pandora's owner cancelled the charter because of nonpayment. On May 1, Conte Bank retransmitted the telex message to your client. The next day your client attempted to deposit the $27,000 in the account of the Pandora's owner at the Banque de Paris, but the payment was refused. Pandora's owner was entitled to cancel the agreement. H&M then brought this action against your client, seeking to recover the profits that it lost because of the cancellation of the charter.

Your senior partner is unsure as to whether the court will apply common law or Article 4A? What do you think? Will the results differ?

IMPULSE TRADING, INC. v. NORWEST BANK MINNESOTA, N.A.

United States District Court, D. Minnesota
907 F.Supp. 1284 (1995)

SPENCER WILLIAMS, DISTRICT JUDGE.

FINDINGS OF FACT

1. Plaintiff Impulse Trading, Inc. ("Impulse") is a Minnesota corporation that engages in trade with companies in the former Soviet Union. Marc Stipakov is the president, sole shareholder and only employee of Impulse.

2. Impulse does it banking with Defendant Norwest Bank Minnesota, N.A. ("Norwest").

3. In January 1991, Stipakov traveled to Russia to arrange a sale of computer equipment to Ilka, a Russian corporation. Because Russian rubles are not readily convertible into Western "hard" currencies such as the dollar or pound, the parties agreed that the equipment would be paid for in Indian rupees. At the time of the agreement, Stipakov intended to open an account at the State Bank of India ("SBOI") into which the rupees would be deposited. Stipakov then planned to exchange the rupees into dollars and have them transferred to his Norwest account in the United States.

4. Upon returning to the United States, Stipakov learned that he could not open an individual account with SBOI. Consequently, he called Norwest to inquire about how the transaction could be completed.

5. Rhonda Grubbe, in Norwest's foreign exchange department, informed Stipakov that Norwest had an account with SBOI, and that he could have the rupees deposited there. Grubbe also told him that once the rupees were deposited at SBOI, Norwest could exchange them for dollars and credit Stipakov's account.

6. The funds transfer proceeded as follows. Ilka instructed its bank Vnesheconombank Bank SSSR ("Bank of Russia"), to transfer the rupees to Norwest's SBOI account. To carry out this instruction, the Bank of Russia telexed a payment order to SBOI's New Delhi office on February 26, 1991 directing SBOI to debit the Bank of Russia's account in New Delhi and to credit Norwest's account in Bombay. SBOI followed these instructions and issued a payment order crediting Norwest's account on March 11, 1991.

7. While these transactions were occurring, Stipakov called Ann Levi in Norwest's reconciliation department to alert her that he was expecting rupees to be deposited in Norwest's SBOI account. He also called back several times to ask whether the rupees had arrived.

8. Subsequently, Levi received Norwest's March 1991 bank statement from SBOI indicating that a deposit of rupees had been made to Norwest's account. Levi relayed this information to

Stipakov, who said that the rupees belonged to him. Relying on this representation, Levi called Rhonda Grubbe in Norwest's foreign exchange department and told her to exchange the rupees for dollars. Stipakov spoke directly to Grubbe and arranged to have the newly converted dollars deposited into his Norwest account.

9. Although a payment order referencing Impulse accompanied Norwest's March 1991 bank statement from SBOI, no one at Norwest who was involved in this series of transactions ever saw or relied on it.

10. In mid-1991, Stipakov arranged a similar sale to another company in Russia. The method of payment involved identical funds transfers.

11. Then, on November 1, 1991, Impulse entered into a contract to supply Petrospek, a Soviet-British joint venture located in St. Petersburg, Russia, with photocopiers and computer equipment. The contract required Petrospek to make an advance payment of 6 million rupees during the 45-day period after the contract was signed. After shipment of the goods, Petrospek would make a payment of an additional 24 million rupees. The method of transferring the funds was to be the same as for Impulse's previous transactions with Ilka.

12. Before receiving the advance payment from Petrospek, Stipakov shipped the copiers and computer equipment to Russia.

13. In late November or early December of 1991, Stipakov informed Levi to expect a deposit of approximately 6 million rupees into Norwest's SBOI account. He called back repeatedly to ask her if the money had arrived yet.

14. On November 27, 1991, SBOI debited the Bank of Russia's account in the amount of 6,053,350 rupees. On December 19, 1991, 6,054,925 rupees were deposited in Norwest's SBOI account. The difference between the two amounts resulted from foreign currency exchange rate fluctuations.

15. Thereafter, on December 28, 1991, SBOI's New Delhi office informed the Bombay office that the credit to Norwest's account "was in error". SBOI took no immediate action to remedy the error, however, and did not notify Norwest of either the credit or the later determination that the credit was in error.

16. On January 21, 1992, Levi reviewed Norwest's monthly statement from SBOI. The statement contained a credit of 6,054,925 rupees, but did not reveal the source of the credit or make any reference to Impulse. Accompanying the statement was a payment order that did not reference Impulse either.

17. Due to previous conversations with Stipakov, Levi assumed that the credit belonged to him. Based on this belief, Levi called Stipakov and informed him that his rupees had arrived. She then called Grubbe and told her to exchange the rupees and deposit dollars into Stipakov's account. Grubbe did so, resulting in a $231,929.12 credit to Stipakov's account.

18. On January 31, 1992, SBOI reversed the 6,054,925 rupee credit to Norwest's account. Levi learned of the reversal upon receiving Norwest's January 1992 SBOI bank statement. She immediately informed Grubbe and Michael Schaefer, the manager of Norwest's foreign exchange department. Schaefer told Levi to contact SBOI to determine the cause for the reversal, which she did by telex on February 26, 1992. Levi also called Stipakov to see if he was aware of any problems on the Russian end of the transaction.

19. SBOI responded to Levi's telex on March 25, 1992 by stating simply that the "deposit was in error".

20. The next day, March 26, 1992, Levi sent another telex requesting an explanation, this time to the international manager of SBOI in New Delhi. On April 29, 1992, SBOI confirmed that the December 1991 credit was a mistake, but refused to give any explanation. SBOI also informed Norwest that its account was overdrawn by 276,000 rupees.

21. Norwest later learned that transferring non-convertible rupees into accounts owned by firms and banks outside of India and Russia is forbidden by the Foreign Exchange Regulations of India and the Soviet-Indian Trade and Payment Agreement. Stipakov does not dispute this fact.

22. Norwest debited Stipakov's account for $231,929.12 on April 30, 1992 and for $2,293 in interest thereon on May 12, 1992.

23. Impulse then filed this action alleging claims against the Bank of Russia, SBOI and Norwest. Impulse did not name Petrospek as a defendant, apparently for "business reasons."

24. Subsequently, SBOI was dismissed from the case for lack of jurisdiction. The Bank of Russia has never made an appearance in this action. Impulse's remaining claims are all against Norwest.

CONCLUSIONS OF LAW

I. Introduction

1. Impulse asserts claims against Norwest for (1) violation of Article 4A of the Uniform Commercial Code ("U.C.C."), Minn.Stat. §§ 336.4A-101 et seq.; (2) wrongful setoff; (3) conversion; and (4) negligence. The Court will address each claim in turn.

II. Article 4A of the U.C.C. Preempts All of Impulse's State Law Claims As They Relate to the Funds Transfer

1. This action is governed by Article 4A of the U.C.C. which covers electronic funds transfers. Minnesota adopted Article 4A of the U.C.C. in 1991. M.S.A. § 336.4A-101 et seq.

2. The comment to Article 4A states the following:

> In the drafting of Article 4A, a deliberate decision was made to write on a clean slate and to treat a funds transfer as a unique method of payment to be governed by unique rules that address the particular issues raised by this method of payment. . . The rules that emerged represent a careful and delicate balancing of [various] interests and are intended to be the exclusive means of determining the rights, duties and liabilities of the affected parties in any situation covered by particular provisions of the Article. Consequently, resort to principles of law or equity outside of Article 4A is not appropriate to create rights, duties and liabilities inconsistent with those stated in this Article.

3. In the only case the Court has located specifically addressing the scope of Article 4A's preemption, the court found common law tort claims to be preempted by Article 4A. See *Donmar Enterprises, Inc. v. Southern Nat'l Bank of North Carolina*, 828 F. Supp. 1230, 1235-36 (W.D.N.C. 1993) (finding that Federal Reserve Board Regulation J which adopts Article 4A of the U.C.C. preempts both contradictory and duplicative causes of action for wrongful payment and negligence), *aff'd*, 64 F.3d 944 (4th Cir. 1995). Preemption is also in accord with the Minnesota courts' general interpretation of the U.C.C. as barring all common law tort claims arising out of commercial transactions except those involving personal injury.

4. Therefore, Article 4A preempts Impulse's common law claims for conversion, wrongful setoff and negligence as they relate to the funds transfer.

III. Norwest Is Not Liable to Impulse Under Article 4A.

A. The Payment Order Was Cancelled by Operation of Law.

1. If a receiving bank does not execute a payment order within five business days, the payment order is cancelled by operation of law. Minn.Stat § 336.4A-211(d). This rule was designed to prevent unexpected delayed acceptance of payment orders. See Minn.Stat. § 336.4A-211, Comment 6.

2. A receiving bank accepts a payment order when it executes the order. Minn.Stat. § 336.4A-208(a). A payment order is executed when the receiving bank issues a payment order intended to carry out the payment order received by the bank. Minn.Stat. § 336.4A-301(a).

3. A cancelled payment order cannot be accepted. Minn.Stat. §336.4A-211(d).

4. Here SBOI received a payment order from the Bank of Russia on November 21, 1991, but did not execute the order until December 19, 1991. As a result of this delay, the payment order was cancelled by operation of law, and Norwest could not have accepted it.

B. SBOI Was Forbidden By Law From Accepting the Payment Order From the Bank of Russia.

1. A receiving bank cannot accept a payment order that it is forbidden by law to receive. Minn.Stat. § 336.4A-209(c).

2. Here, both the Foreign Exchange Regulations of India and the Soviet-Indian Trade and Payment Agreement prohibit the transfer of non-convertible rupees to accounts held by firms and banks outside of Russia and India. Thus, SBOI was forbidden by law to transfer non-convertible rupees into Norwest's SBOI account, and SBOI's attempted acceptance of the payment order from the Bank of Russia was ineffective.

C. Because Norwest Never Received or Accepted a Legitimate Payment Order From SBOI Directing It to Pay Impulse, Norwest is Not Liable to Impulse.

1. Except under circumstances not applicable in this case, a beneficiary's bank receiving an electronic funds transfer is not liable to the beneficiary for those funds unless the beneficiary's bank has received and accepted a payment order. See Minn.Stat. § 336.4A-212 & § 336.4A-209(c); see also, Minn.Stat. § 336.4A-209(b)(3) & § 336.4A-210(b) (stating exceptions to this rule).

2. As discussed above, the payment order Norwest received from SBOI was ineffective because it had been cancelled by operation of law and because SBOI was forbidden by Indian law from accepting it. Therefore, Norwest is not liable to Impulse for payment, and Norwest was entitled to set off Impulse's account in the amount of the credit plus interest.

CONCLUSION

In light of the foregoing, the Court finds in favor of Norwest on all claims in this action. Let judgment be entered accordingly. The parties shall bear their own costs.

It Is So Ordered.

§ 15.09 Fraud in a Funds Transfer

Read: U.C.C. §§ 4A-201, 4A-202,4A-203, 4A-204.

GENERAL ELECTRIC CAPITAL CORPORATION v. CENTRAL BANK

United States Court of Appeals
49 F.3d 280 (7th Cir. 1995)

EASTERBROOK, CIRCUIT JUDGE.

Duchow's Marine, Inc., financed its inventory of boats with a loan from general Electric Capital Corporation (GECC), which took a security interest in the boats and the proceeds from their sale. The security interest was perfected under Wisconsin law. Duchow's Marine and its owner Roger Duchow (collectively Duchow) promised to deposit proceeds into an account from which they could be disbursed only on GECC's signature. The name on this account at Central Bank was "Duchow Marine, Inc. GE Escrow Account." Following the parties' convention, we call this the blocked account. Duchow maintained a separate account at Central Bank for revenues from other sources; we call this the regular account. In November 1990 Duchow sold a yacht to Gray Eagle, Inc., and directed the customer to remit $215,370 of the purchase price to the regular account. By issuing this instruction Duchow set out to defraud GECC.

Gray Eagle instructed its bank to make a wire transfer, giving it the number of Duchow's regular account. Gray Eagle's bank, which we call the "originator's bank" following the convention of the Uniform Commercial Code's new Article 4A, asked Banker's Bank of Madison, Wisconsin, to make the transfer on its behalf. The originator's bank performed correctly. As an intermediary bank, Banker's Bank should have relayed the payment order exactly. It didn't. Banker's Bank made the transfer by crediting Central Bank's account at Banker's Bank, but it bobtailed the instructions. Banker's Bank told Central Bank (which the U.C.C. calls the "beneficiary's bank") that the credit was for Duchow's benefit. That's all; the payment order omitted account identification. A clerk at Central Bank routed the funds to the first account she found bearing Duchow's name: the blocked account. This credit was made on November 23, 1990. Entirely by chance, Duchow's fraudulent scheme had been foiled.

But not for long. Duchow, thinking the funds were in the regular account, promptly wrote a check in an effort to spirit them away. The check appeared on the overdrawn accounts list of November 29. When contacted, Roger Duchow asserted that the money belonged in the regular account. Central Bank inquired of Banker's Bank, which on November 30 relayed the full payment order, including the number of Duchow's regular account. Without notifying GECC, Central Bank then reversed the credit to the blocked account, credited Duchow's regular account, and paid the check. When it discovered what had happened, GECC filed this diversity action seeking to hold Central Bank liable for conversion of its funds. Central Bank impleaded Duchow, but no one believes that he or his firm is good for the money; Duchow has not participated in this case. The parties agree that Wisconsin supplies the applicable law.

That the money removed from the blocked account belonged to GECC there can be not doubt. U.C.C. § 9-306. Central Bank does not deny that GECC has established the ordinary elements of conversion so much as it asserts a bankers' privilege: a beneficiary's bank following the payment order of an intermediary bank in a funds transfer should be free from liability, Central Bank insists. We may assume that this is so if the beneficiary's bank follows the original payment order. GECC does not contend that it could recover from any of the three banks (originator's, intermediary, or beneficiary's) if all three had slavishly followed a set of instructions that Gray

Eagle gave its bank, even though Duchow devised these instructions to cheat GECC. Central Bank could not be thought to "convert" funds over which it never had a right of control.

Once the funds landed in the blocked account, however, Central Bank had to make a nonclerical decision. Must it move them? Could it move them? By accepting the payment order, Central Bank incurred an obligation to credit the funds to Duchow. As it had done exactly that, crediting an account where they discharged one of Duchow's debts, Duchow had no legitimate complaint—certainly not given GECC's security interest in the proceeds. No rule of law obliged Central Bank to change the credit. Banker's Bank fouled up and may have been liable to Gray Eagle; Central Bank was in the clear. See U.C.C. §§ 4A-207(b)(2), 4A-305(b)(iii); Wis.Stat. §§ 410.207(2), 410.305(2). Seven days had passed, and credits in the banking system often become irrevocable in less time. Think of the "midnight deadline" for checks under U.C.C. § 4-301(a). Removing funds from an account bearing the title "escrow" calls for the exercise of considered discretion.

Some alterations in credits to accounts are essentially risk-free no matter what the rules of banking law say. If Central Bank had credited the account of, say, John Q. Public with the $215,000 it could have reversed the credit a week later without any risk, for Mr. Public, lacking any legal interest in the funds, could not have cried conversion or sought restitution. The bank does not need a customer's consent to make the transfer; erroneous credits are reversed every day without anyone supposing that an accidental recipient, with no interest in the funds, must be consulted. GECC's reminder that its signature was required for transactions in the blocked account is irrelevant; we deal not with a "withdrawal" but with the calculation of the proper credit. If Central Bank had credited the Duchow-GECC blocked account with $500,000 meant for Acme Widget Corp., the bank could have reversed the bookkeeping blunder without GECC's consent. U.C.C. § 4A-207. Things are dicier when the bank credits the account of someone who has a legitimate claim to the funds. If GECC had withdrawn the money on the fifth day, Central Bank could not have compelled it to make restitution, because GECC's security interest gave it the legal right to the funds. (We have more to say later on the subject of restitution.) If GECC's interest is strong enough to resist a suit for restitution if it gets to the money first, is it not strong enough to support a suit for conversion if the bank drains the account?

During 1990, when the events of this case took place, the right way to approach the last question we have posed was obscure. Article 4 of the U.C.C. concentrated on checks; courts in some states extended its provisions by analogy to wire transfers, but analogies are always imperfect—and Wisconsin's courts had not had an occasion to engage the subject at all. Some aspects of the process are governed by the federal Electronic Fund Transfer Act, 15 U.S.C. §§ 1693-1693r; others come within the gambit of Regulation J issued by the Federal Reserve or the rules adopted by the New York Clearing House Interbank Payments System (CHIPS). Transfers such as the one we consider that did not use the Fedwire or CHIPS fell into a legal limbo. Recognizing the shortcomings of Article 4 and the pastiche of ancillary rules, the American Law Institute and National Conference of Commissioners on Uniform State Laws had been drafting a wire transfer code for more than a decade. Their solution, the new Article 4A was enacted in Wisconsin in 1991, after these events. Yet because the highest court of New York has used the provisions of Article 4A to illuminate the law preceding its enactment, see *Banque Worms v. Bank America International*, 77 N.Y.2d 362, 568 N.Y.S.2d 541, 570 N.E.2d 189 (1991), the parties agree that the Supreme Court of Wisconsin would do likewise. We accept this understanding and turn to Article 4A. It soon becomes clear why the parties are so willing to have us apply a subsequently enacted statute to their transaction: Article 4A points us back to the common law of restitution.

The first question is whether the bungle at Banker's Bank produced an order that Central Bank could accept and act on—for if not the money that found its way to the blocked account belonged to central Bank rather than GECC. The answer is "yes." Section 4a-207(b)(2) provides that if the payment order received by the beneficiary's bank identifies a beneficiary both by name and by account number, and these designations are inconsistent, then:

> If the beneficiary's bank pays the person identified by name. . .no person has rights as beneficiary except the person paid by the beneficiary's bank if that person was entitled to receive payment from the originator of the funds transfer. If no person has rights as beneficiary, acceptance of the order cannot occur.

So if the payment order from Banker's Bank had included Duchow's name without further elaboration, and the number of the regular account, Central Bank still could have "accepted" the payment order by making a credit to the blocked account—for that account too is identified by Duchow's name, and GECC "was entitled to receive payment from the originator of the funds transfer." The omission of the regular account's number does not make credit to the blocked account less acceptable.

Whether a credit properly made after acceptance by the beneficiary's bank may be reversed is a subject addressed almost in passing by § 4A-303, which principally concerns a receiving bank's obligation, to the sender, to execute the payment order. (A "receiving bank" is the originator's bank and any intermediary bank that executes a payment order; a beneficiary's bank can "accept" but not "execute" a payment order. U.C.C. §§ 4A-103(a)(4), 4A-301(a) and Official Comment 1. Section 4A-303(c) provides:

> If a receiving bank executes the payment order of the sender by issuing a payment order to a beneficiary different from the beneficiary of the sender's order and the funds transfer is completed on the basis of that error, the sender of the payment order that was erroneously executed and all previous senders in the funds transfer are not obliged to pay the payment orders they issued. The issuer of the erroneous order is entitled to recover from the beneficiary of the order the payment received to the extent allowed by the law governing mistake and restitution.

Banker's Bank, a "receiving bank" in this terminology, issued to central Bank a payment order that was at least arguably "to a beneficiary different from the beneficiary of the sender's order." Central Bank completed the transfer under § 4A-207(b)(2) by crediting the blocked account. The issuer (that is, Banker's Bank) could "recover from the beneficiary of the order" (that is, Duchow and GECC to the extent of each one's interest in the blocked account) "the payment received to the extent allowed by the law governing mistake and restitution." By issuing a revised payment order with the number of Duchow's regular account, Banker's Bank attempted to recoup from GECC and make the funds available to Duchow personally. The question is whether "the law governing mistake and restitution" permitted that step. If it did, Central Bank is off the hook without needing its own shelter in Article 4A. If id did not, Central Bank is liable for conversion. See also U.C.C. § 1-103 (preserving the common law for situations not specifically addressed in the U.C.C.).

Official Comment 2 to § 4A-303 traces out the statute's implications for the case of a mistakenly large payment order ($2 million, when the originator wanted to send only $1 million):

> Originator's Bank would normally have a right to recover the overpayment from Beneficiary, but in unusual cases the law of restitution might allow Beneficiary to keep all or part of the

overpayment. For example, if Originator owed $2,000,000 to Beneficiary and Beneficiary received the extra $1,000,000 in good faith in discharge of the debt, Beneficiary may be allowed to keep it. In this case Originator's Bank has paid an obligation of Originator and under the law of restitution, which applies through Section 1-103, Originator's Bank would be subrogated to Beneficiary's rights against Originator on the obligation paid by Originator's Bank.

Banque Worms—the first case decided by any state or federal court arising out of a mistaken payment order under Article 4A, and one of a handful to date—illustrates how the system works in practice. Spedley Securities instructed Security Pacific Bank to make a wire transfer of approximately $2 million to Bank American International for the benefit of Banque Worms, to which Spedley was indebted. Security Pacific waited for Spedley to muster the funds to cover the transfer. Before Spedley had assembled the entire $2 million, it instructed Security Pacific to make the transfer to National Westminster Bank rather than to Bank America. As the result of a bookkeeping error, Security Pacific made both transfers. It asked Bank America to reverse the erroneous credit to Banque Worms; after being given an indemnity Bank America did so, but Banque Worms protested, contending that it was entitled to payment on the antecedent debt. Soon Spedley entered insolvency proceedings in Australia, leaving Banque Worms and Security Pacific to contest the entitlement under the law of restitution, with the winner to get $2 million in cash and the loser to become Spedley's creditor in bankruptcy.

New York's Court of Appeals concluded that Banque Worms was entitled to the money. It was the beneficiary of a payment order that Security Pacific had issued and Bank America had accepted. Just as Central Bank does, Security Pacific argued that the error leading to the credit was sufficient justification for reversing the transaction unless Banque Worms had relied on the credit to its detriment (which it had not). Rejecting this position, the Court of Appeals followed the "discharge for value" rule in § 14(1) of the ALI's Restatement of Restitution (1937). Section 14(1) reads:

> A creditor of another or one having a lien on another's property who has received from a third person any benefit in discharge of the debt or lien, is under no duty to make restitution therefore, although the discharge was given by mistake of the transferor as to his interests or duties, if the transferee made no misrepresentation and did not have notice of the transferor's mistake.

The discharge for value rule fit Banque Worms perfectly—and it fits our case as well. Banque Worms was Spedley's creditor; that Security Pacific made the payment by error did not oblige Banque Worms to disgorge. GECC not only was Duchow's creditor but also, by virtue of the security interest, held a lien on the proceeds. Neither Banque Worms nor GECC made a misrepresentation; neither had notice of the transferor's mistake. Although § 14 was devised for slow-moving paper transactions, the Court of Appeals thought it an apt rule for speedy wire transfers too, largely because it promotes finality in commercial transactions. Wire transfers permit recipients to draw on funds immediately, and the velocity with which funds turn over can be considerable. Exposing creditors who thought that their debts had been paid off to a lengthy period of uncertainty during which they might be required to reverse the transfer would be the equivalent of pouring molasses on the payments system. The recipient could not tell what its outstanding obligations were and would have to exercise undue caution. As the Court of Appeals saw things, a creditor should be able to treat funds credited in apparent payment of a debt as irrevocably his, unless news of the error precedes arrival of the funds. Costs of errors should be borne by those who make errors (the better to induce them to take care) rather than by innocent beneficiaries.

GECC asked the district court to follow Banque Worms. The court declined and entered judgment for Central Bank after concluding that Wisconsin does not employ the discharge for value rule. The court wrote: "Wisconsin, unlike New York, adheres to the 'mistake of fact' doctrine of restitution. Under this doctrine, money paid under a mistake of fact may be recovered back, however negligent the party paying may have been in making the mistake, unless the payment has caused such a change in position of the other party that it would be unjust to require him to refund." (Footnote omitted.) As it happens, however, New York also embraces this approach as the norm. *Banque Worms*, 568 N.Y.S.2d at 543-44, 570 N.E.2d at 191-92. It treats the discharge for value rule as an exception to its ordinary approach. So does California. See *Bank of America National Trust and Sav. Ass'n v. Sanati*, 11 Cal. App. 4th 1079, 14 Cal. Rptr. 2d 615, 618 (2d Dist. 1992). Does Wisconsin do likewise? The Supreme Court of Wisconsin has never mentioned the discharge for value rule favorably or unfavorably, and it has never cited § 14 of the Restatement of Restitution. The omission is not surprising; mistaken payments that just happen to land in the pockets of the true owner are not common. We need to know how Wisconsin would handle the rare case when it arrives.

One of Wisconsin's options is to follow New York in order to promote national uniformity in the treatment of funds transfers. Wisconsin enacted Article 4A of the U.C.C. for this very reason; we would be surprised if that state's courts decided to go it alone on ancillary issues such as the law of restitution. The Restatement of Restitution offers a national standard for the common law parallel to the national statutory benchmark of the U.C.C. When adopting § 14 as the law of New York, that state's Court of Appeals remarked that "[n]ational uniformity in the treatment of electronic funds transfers is an important goal." 568 N.Y.S.2d at 547, 570 N.E.2d at 195. Indeed it is. Funds transfers cross state and national borders, and, because New York is the nation's (and the world's) largest financial center, any transfers go through banks in New York. Uniform, known law governing these transactions (and promoting finality in payments, as the discharge for value rule does) enables banks to tailor their practices accordingly, and it produces lower costs for all customers. Wisconsin's businesses share that benefit of uniformity. Variability does not impose costs on banks; once they learn the risks, they adjust prices accordingly. Competition among financial intermediaries passes those expenses to customers. Uncertainty serves no one's interests. So our question is not whether Wisconsin might blaze a lonely path, but whether it has already done so. It hasn't.

The district court cited only one Wisconsin case: *Amalgamated Ass'n of Street Electric Ry. and Motor Coach Employees v. Danielson*, 24 Wis.2d 33, 128 N.W.2d 9 (1964) (Fairchild, J.). That opinion recites the mistake-of-fact approach and approves a detrimental-reliance qualification. It does not mention, let alone disparage, a potential discharge-for-value qualification. In Danielson a labor union that had promised a death benefit to survivors of its members paid twice after a member's death; the discharge for value rule would not have allowed the survivor to keep the second payment, and just about any rule of restitution lets the union recover the second payment, as the court in *Danielson* did. We have found the varying applications of the mistake-of-fact doctrine in Wisconsin hard to reconcile and have wondered whether that doctrine represents Wisconsin's current approach. To be more precise, what has puzzled us is the mistake-of-law corollary to Wisconsin's doctrine: that payments made under a mistaken understanding of the law may not be recovered even if the recipient has no proper claim to the money. No matter, a mistake-of-fact rule of the sort used in *Danielson* is simply beside the point when the recipient is entitled to the money.

Indeed, *Danielson* implies that Wisconsin is prepared to accept the discharge for value approach when the need arises. The opinion states the rule this way: "a payment made under a mistake of fact caused by forgetfulness may be recovered, where the person to whom the payment is made is not entitled thereto and cannot in good conscience retain it." 24 Wis.2d at 36, 128 N.W.2d at 11. Wisconsin's cases bristle with references to "equity and good conscience." Language such as this passage in Danielson suggests that judicial consciences in Wisconsin would not be troubled by permitting persons entitled to money to keep it. Illustration 3 to the Restatement's § 14 is a no-funds check. "A presents a check payable to him and for which he has paid value, drawn by B on the C bank. The bank, erroneously believing that B has sufficient funds to his credit, pays the amount of the check to A who has no notice as to the insufficiency of funds. C is not entitled to restitution from A." It is hard to believe that Wisconsin would come to a different conclusion—or that having accepted this principle Wisconsin would nonetheless repudiate the main theme of § 14. We believe that Wisconsin would adopt the discharge for value rule of § 14, and therefore that it would follow *Banque Worms*.

On reading this conclusion, the president of Central Bank may be tempted to tear out his hair in exasperation. In exchange for the few dollars it collects for a wire transfer, how can the Bank have accepted such a risk?, he may well wonder. Duchow perpetrated a fraud, and Banker's Bank bungled the payment order. Details of the law of restitution to one side, why ought this lead to liability for the beneficiary's bank, which did not know the source of the funds or GECC's security interest in them? Requiring receiving banks to inquire into the source of the funds or to research financing statements in public records would raise the costs of funds transfers and slow down a mechanism that is designed to allow the movement of huge sums within minutes. The answer is that it ought not lead to liability for the beneficiary's bank—and it would not have left Central Bank holding the bag had it taken precautions after learning of the error. Before reversing the credit in response to Duchow's request, Central Bank could have sought an indemnity agreement from Banker's Bank, and perhaps from Duchow as well. This is what happened in *Banque Worms*, where a chain of indemnities brought the costs of the error home to the responsible party. 568 N.Y.S.2d at 543, 570 N.E.2d at 191. Banker's Bank might have been unwilling to give an indemnity without its own assurances from the originator's bank and the originator itself. If asked for assurances, Gray Eagle would have learned that it was a pawn in Duchow's fraud, which would have come to light. Even the absence of an indemnity does not necessarily leave Central Bank with the loss. On paying GECC, Central Bank will be subrogated to all of GECC's rights against Duchow. See U.C.C. § 4A-303 Official Comment 2. It is, after all, Central Bank's customer Duchow who devised this scam and made off with the money, and it was Banker's Bank's error that put Central Bank in this pickle. Central Bank must pay GECC; whether Central Bank may be made whole remains to be seen.

Reversed.

CHAPTER 16

AN INTRODUCTION TO SECURED TRANSACTIONS

§ 16.01 Introduction

[A] Importance and General Use

Secured transactions represent a key means of economic expansion because the concept provides people with a mechanism for unlocking the inherent value in various items of personal property. The possibility of lending on a secured basis encourages banks, insurance companies, and finance companies, to offer credit at lower interest rates because the presence of "securing" collateral minimizes the credit risk. A borrower's failure to repay a loan gives the secured lender the right to repossess that collateral, without judicial process, if the lender can retake the property without breaching the peace. Once the lender seizes the collateral it may sell the property and apply the proceeds against the borrower's outstanding loan balance.

Article 9 of the Uniform Commercial Code applies to any transaction "intended to create a security interest in personal property or fixtures including goods, documents, instruments, general intangibles, chattel paper or accounts . . ." U.C.C. § 9-102(1). U.C.C. § 1-201(37) defines the phrase "security interest" as "an interest in personal property or fixtures which secures payment or performance of an obligation." Article 9 prescribes the procedures necessary to create and maintain a security interest between the secured party and the debtor. A secured party who follows the necessary steps for providing notice to third parties who might be potential claimants on the property will gain rights superior to those parties. These rights become important in two situations: (1) when the debtor fails to perform some contractual obligation (default); and (2) when the debtor enters bankruptcy.

[B] General Use

For manufacturers and other sellers of goods, secured credit provides benefits at both the production and sales stages. To secure working capital, manufacturers often give financiers security interests in the raw materials that they use to construct a product (inventory). Not only may the security interest exist in inventory, but it also may continue in the material through the various stages of manufacturing into the finished product. The financier's security interest may even attach to the proceeds the manufacturer receives upon sale of the finished product. In addition, many manufacturers use equipment and accounts receivable as additional forms of collateral to obtain operating funds.

Wholesalers frequently use secured credit when selling goods to retailers. Like the manufacturer, a wholesaler takes a security interest in the very goods which go to create the buyer-retailer's inventory. Even though the retailer sells the goods, the wholesaler's security interest extends to the amount the retailer receives upon disposition. The wholesaler can also structure the arrangement to cover replacements in inventory through the use of an after-acquired property clause.

The seller who takes a security interest in goods assures herself that there will be something of value to seize should the buyer fail to meet its contractual obligation. A secured transaction gives buyers the opportunity to acquire goods and take possession of them before payment. Thus, secured transactions result in more credit for consumers as well.

[C] History

The statutory provisions governing secured transactions represent the culmination of a half century of effort to provide a unitary approach to the variety of security devices used by creditors and debtors to create security interests. Exploration of these pre-Code security devices provides a better understanding of the full scope of Article 9's provisions. This historical overview also serves as an introduction to the basic terminology of the Code.

The *pledge* was the earliest form of the secured transaction for personal property. Under the concept, the debtor provided the creditor with physical possession of some piece of property, which the creditor kept until the debtor satisfied the obligation. The pledge, first formally recognized under Roman Law, was used by a number of early traders and societies. Medieval merchants and moneylenders also used the pledge. The creditor's physical possession of the collateral protected the lender against other parties who might claim an interest in the property.

The pledge concept provided a lender with the maximum possible protection against a debtor's default. Unfortunately, pledging also meant that only tangible items of personal property (chattels) could be used as collateral to borrow money. The common law pledge also resulted in the debtor relinquishing possession of property. Clearly, there were many types of potential collateral that the debtor would not want to surrender to a creditor.

Another type of security device at early common law was the *real property mortgage.* With this type of land transaction the debtor offered the lender real estate as security for a loan. In most instances, the debtor continued in possession of the land. The creditor (mortgagee) recorded its interest in a specific location under the debtor's name. Potential creditors could check the record to determine if the land was already encumbered by another even though the debtor maintained possession. Although this idea was not extended to the concept of movable items (goods) for several centuries, the real property mortgage served as the basis for later developments in non-possessory secured transactions in goods.

The dawn of the industrial revolution led to the development of non-possessory secured interests in personal property. New methods of production, coupled with an increase in commercial activity, brought about a heightened demand for credit and for devices to secure such credit. In his landmark treatise on secured transactions, Professor Grant Gilmore noted this development:

> Until early in the nineteenth century the only security devices which were known in our legal system were the mortgage of real property and the pledge of chattels. Security interests in personal property which remained in the borrower's possession during the loan period were unknown. A transfer of an interest in personal property without delivery of possession was looked on as being in essence a fraudulent conveyance, invalid against creditors and purchasers. (This principle, common to both sales law and security law, dates from at least 1601 and the decision in *Twyne's Case.*) Since the principle maintained itself for over two hundred years-few

rules of law enjoy so long a run-we must conclude that it corresponded to the needs of its time.

As the primary source of credit for early industrial companies, banks demanded assurances of repayment beyond the contractual promise and real estate collateral that had been utilized previously. As industrialization progressed, personal rather than real property became the principal repository of wealth. The mortgage on Blackacre could no longer support the merchant's insatiable demand for credit and the banker's demand for security. Even the medieval institution of the pledge proved insufficient in accommodating the need for collateral. Although stock certificates and bonds could be pledged, more obvious forms of value like the equipment of a factory, the rolling stock of a railroad, or the inventory stock of the merchant could not be used. Property that could not be pledged because it had not been used in the borrower's business represented a nearly inexhaustible source of prime collateral for loans. Developing some mechanism to unlock this store of value became a key goal for bankers and merchants alike.

Two of the earliest non-possessory security devices were the *chattel mortgage* and *conditional sale.* The chattel mortgage device evolved as a simple extension from real property mortgage law. Under the chattel mortgage, a seller of goods received a mortgage from the buyer who was allowed to possess the goods. To ensure against the debtor-buyer's misappropriation of the goods, the seller recorded its security interest to make the seller's claim valid against third parties. The seller both retained title and held an equitable lien on the property until full payment occurred. The non-purchase money security interest in equipment and consumer goods represents the modern equivalent of the chattel mortgage.

The idea of a seller's retaining title to goods was known as a *conditional sale.* Although the buyer had possession and the right to use the goods, the law recognized title as remaining with the seller until the buyer paid the debt in full; in effect, the seller conditioned the passing of title to the goods on the buyer's payment. One problem with the conditional sale was the different requirements for enforcing the seller's interest. Some jurisdictions applied the same notice requirement as that for chattel mortgages, while other jurisdictions required an entirely different third party notification system. Thus, it was quite possible that a seller could lose its priority claim to property because notice of the conditional sale failed to meet the prescribed requirements. Conditional sales also applied only to goods; the creditor's security interest applied only to the debt that arose under the sales contract. Reservation of title to goods under § 2-401(1) represents today's equivalent of the conditional sale.

Even though the security devices noted above reached a variety of transactions, gaps in coverage remained. The comment to U.C.C. § 9-101 notes that "in many states, for example, a security interest could not be taken in inventory or a stock or trade although there was a real need for such financing." It was often difficult to maintain valid secured interests when goods went through a manufacturing process. Similarly, it was not clear how one might take a secured interest in intangible property.

Other mechanisms were developed in an attempt to cover secured interests in inventory. One such device was *field warehousing.* If the collateral was of such a nature that it would be imprudent for the creditor to possess (or risky to leave in the debtor's possession), the parties could arrange to store the collateral in a warehouse. The warehouse operator would issue a negotiable warehouse receipt (known as a document of title) which had to be surrendered before the warehouse operator would release the goods. The debtor could then pledge the warehouse receipt to the creditor as collateral. See generally, §§ 7-201 and 7-202.

With field warehousing, the warehouse operator went to the location of the goods (usually the debtor's facility) and physically set the goods apart from other items of the debtor. The field warehouser would issue a receipt which noted that the goods were under the warehouser's control and not that of the debtor. The field warehouse receipt would then be pledged to the creditor. Once the debtor repaid the debt, the warehouse receipt was returned to the debtor who could surrender it for the goods.

Still another type of pre-code security device for inventory was the *trust receipt.* Under this strained use of trust law, a debtor persuaded a creditor to buy goods from a manufacturer. The creditor would surrender the goods to the debtor only after: 1) the creditor filed notice in an appropriate location describing the purchase money lending transaction, and noting the lender's intent to enter repeated transactions involving goods that changed nature while in the debtor's hands; and, 2) the debtor signed a receipt acknowledging that, in taking receipt of the goods, the debtor operated as the creditor's trustee. When the debtor-trustee sold goods, the proceeds went to the creditor-entruster to pay off the obligation. Trust receipt financing was also known as *floor planning*—the creditor provided the financing necessary to stock the debtor's floor with inventory for sale. This type of arrangement frequently occurred in the automobile industry. It was available only where the inventory could be identified easily and separately. Today's equivalent is the purchase money security interest in inventory. See § 9-312(3).

Another security device related to the trust receipt was the *factor's lien.* The word "factor" originally meant a selling agent who helped finance the debtor's business. The factor loaned money against inventory the debtor currently owned. The factor's lien interest had to be filed in a central location to protect the factor against other claimants on the inventory. A major drawback to the factor's lien arrangement was the limitation of the lien to existing inventory; the lien did not extend to changing inventory, a debtor's after-acquired property. The modern analogy to the factor's lien is the non-purchase money security interest in inventory already in the debtor's possession. See generally, § 9-312(5).

One of the last forms of security device to develop was *accounts receivable financing.* Accounts are intangible forms of collateral—there are no physical items of property or pieces of paper that necessarily represent the debt owed; accounts simply represent a right to receive payment. Despite the lack of a tangible item of property, the idea of an account representing an item of value was inescapable. Some creditors were willing to make loans secured only by the debts owed the borrower. The accounts were assigned to the creditor who could then seek to collect from the account obligors should the assigning debtor fail to pay its obligation. Accounts financiers often met judicial hostility when seeking to enforce their interests where the accounts receivable financing was secret or where the debtor was left in control of the accounts and proceeds.

Courts found it unfair to hold account debtors responsible to the accounts financier where the account debtor paid its creditor instead of the accounts financier who had been assigned the obligation. Filing notice of a security interest became essential for any type of non-possessory secured interest. By recording its security interest in a certain type of property, the secured creditor placed potential third party claimants on notice of the secured party's prior claim.

The multitude of security interests and conflicting rules governing them gave rise to a crying need for legal reform. Filing systems varied for different types of collateral from state to state. There were different notice requirements for chattel mortgages and conditional sales. If the instrument labeled as a conditional sale was later determined by the court to be a chattel mortgage, the instrument would be invalid because it was not filed as a chattel mortgage. Courts also held a particular hostility toward security interests in a debtor's after-acquired property because such arrangements tying up the debtor's assets were presumed unconscionable.

The drafters of the Code confronted the confusion of a multitude of security devices, judicial hostility, and an over-emphasis on technicalities, by examining the assumptions on which those old principles rested. The drafters made a major decision that there should be a single security interest encompassing the past forms of security such as the chattel mortgage, conditional sale, bailment, lease, and trust receipt. These past forms would, in effect, be abolished and a new legal device called the security interest would be created.

In creating a single secured interest, the drafters eliminated the traditional distinctions of the past. The concept of title ceased to be the crucial determinant of whether one continued to hold a secured interest and what one's rights were as to third parties. This radical simplification treated the law of secured transactions in a more functional, rather than formal, manner. See Comment to U.C.C. § 9-101. The further history of secured interests is essentially the history of the Uniform Commercial Code. First enacted in Pennsylvania in 1952, the Code subsequently became law in most states during the late 1950s and early 1960s. By the mid-1960s, the Uniform Commercial Code with Article 9 on secured transactions, was virtually the law of the land.

During the 1960s and 1970s, conflicts arose between the Uniform Commercial Code and the Bankruptcy Code. The rights of secured creditors collided with bankruptcy concepts of debtor rehabilitation and the efforts of bankruptcy trustees to assert rights that would benefit the debtor's unsecured creditors. The Bankruptcy Reform Act of 1978 resolved a number of these problems.

The period of the late 1960s and early 1970s also witnessed the rise of consumer protection legislation. During this time a number of federal and state consumer protection laws were enacted. At times, that legislation either overrode or conflicted with the rights of secured parties. The impact of consumer protection statutes will be noted throughout this part of the book.

As this book goes to press in 1977, members of the American Law Institute are reviewing a new and completely reorganized draft of Article 9. While the process of ultimately translating a draft into uniform legislation will take a few years, you should be aware of some of the issues that the Institute has been working on.

The proposed draft expands the scope of Article 9 in several respects. For example, the proposed new draft would include deposit accounts as forms of personal property capable of serving as original collateral. The draft includes most sales of general intangibles for money due or to become due.[1] The draft also proposes to expand Article 9 to include insurance policies and certain tort claims. Under the current draft choice of law rules would be changed for most types of collateral to the law of the jurisdiction where the debtor is located (i.e., organized as a corporate entity). Rules on perfection, default, and enforcement are also expanded and clarified in the new draft. The draft expands the definition of proceeds. Perhaps most importantly, the draft includes several new rules governing priority disputes between parties.

Despite the wide array of proposed changes, the proposed draft still leaves many issues unresolved. Should Article 9 include additional provisions designed to protect consumers? Should the priority scheme be modified further? Should Article subordinate perfected security interests to the rights of certain classes of unsecured creditors? Is the treatment of future advances

[1] Current Article 9 includes sales of accounts and chattel paper, but not sales of general intangibles for the payment of money.

satisfactory? As you proceed through the remaining chapters, keep these and other questions firmly in mind, recognizing that the law governing secured transactions remains a dynamic and ever–evolving realm.

[D] Types of Collateral

As noted above, the U.C.C.'s solution to the variety of security devices was to create one set of rules for all consensual security interests in personal property and fixtures whether tangible property or not. Article 9 distinguishes among types of transactions on functional rather than formal lines.

The Code divides collateral into 10 types: money, chattel paper, documents, instruments, accounts, general intangibles, consumer goods, equipment, farm products, and inventory. See §§ 9-103, 105, 106, and 109; see also § 1-201(24) and Comment 5 to § 9-102.

The ten types of collateral can be grouped into three specific categories: GOODS, INTANGIBLES, AND PURE INTANGIBLES. The goods category includes tangible items like equipment, inventory, farm products, and consumer goods. See § 9-109. Intangibles are items that come in the form of pieces of paper which represent abstract rights. This group includes documents, chattel paper, money, and instruments (both securities under § 8-102 and negotiable instruments under § 3-104). See § 9-106. The third category, pure intangibles, include items that are abstract and theoretical in concept. Such items consist of accounts and general intangibles like goodwill, patents, copyright, and trademarks. See § 9-106. The collateral categories directly relate to the type of third-party notice (perfection) a secured party must give others so as to protect that creditor's security interest.

PROBLEM 16.1

Johnson is the treasurer of a small tool manufacturing company. She shows you, as outside counsel, the company's most recent balance sheet set forth below. Johnson asks your advice on whether any of the corporation's assets may be used for collateral to secure a working capital loan that she hopes to negotiate with Local Bank. Please advise.

XYZ TOOL COMPANY, INC.
Balance Sheet December 31, 1996

		(In thousands)
Current Assets		
	Cash	150
	Investment Securities	75
	Accounts receivable (less allowance for bad debt:$100,000)	900
	Inventories	1,100
	Total current assets	2,225
Fixed Assets		
	Land	350
	Building (less mortgage payable:$220,000)	600
	Machinery	1,300
	Office Equipment	100
		$2,350
	(less accumulated depreciation)	(450)

XYZ TOOL COMPANY, INC.
Balance Sheet December 31, 1996

Net fixed assets	$1,900
Prepayment of expenses; Deferred charges	150
Intangibles (goodwill, patent, trademark)	200
Cash value of life insurance	100
	450
TOTAL ASSETS	$4,575
LIABILITIES	(in thousands)
Current Liabilities	
Accounts payable	$1,535
Notes payable	1,005
Accrued expenses payable	400
Income tax payable	150
Total current liabilities	3,090
Long-term Liabilities	
Mortgage bonds (10% interest, due 1998)	400
Debenture (12% interest, due 1999)	500
Total long-term liabilities	900
Total Liabilities	3,990
SHAREHOLDERS' EQUITY	(in thousands)
Capital Stock	
Common Shares ($5.00 par value; 100,000 authorized)	
75,000 issued and outstanding	375
Retained earnings	210
Total Shareholders' Equity	585
TOTAL LIABILITIES AND SHAREHOLDERS' EQUITY	$4,575

[E] Types of Transactions

Any lending transaction provides a benefit to the borrowing debtor. Secured lending occurs in two specific instances—purchase money and non-purchase money. The brief descriptions below may be helpful to your understanding a number of often-litigated issues surrounding Article 9.

[1] Purchase Money Security Interests

The purchase money security interest facilitates a borrower's purchase of collateral. The Code defines a purchase money security interest as a security interest that "is taken or retained by the seller of the collateral to secure all or part of its price." U.C.C. § 9-107(a). Purchase money interests can also arise where a finance company or lender "gives value to enable the debtor to acquire rights in or the use of collateral if such value is in fact so used." U.C.C. § 9-107(b).

One of the policies behind permitting this special type of security interest focuses on the idea that the party advancing credit or money provides the debtor a new asset of value. Since the asset acquired is one that the debtor would not have but for the advance, the purchase money security party should have priority over other creditors who might lay claim to that particular asset. Without purchase money security protection, sellers and lenders might refuse credit to borrowers who already had other secured creditors. Because a single lender might monopolize the credit relationship and endanger the business enterprise, the priority given to purchase money security interests promotes the continuance of business by enabling debtors to deal with more than a single lender. The purchase money security interest therefore, tends to promote commerce. In the case of consumer goods, purchase money credit can be extended to buyers without substantial assets. The priorities surrounding purchase money transactions will be discussed later. For now it is important to note that the Code gives purchase money security interests priority over non-purchase money security interests and over security interests with after-acquired property clauses.

[2] Non-Purchase Money Security Interests

Creditors also extend secured credit in non-purchase money situations. In these cases, the creditor takes a security interest in existing property of the debtor. For example, a creditor may lend to a business and secure the loan by taking an interest in existing factory assets. Consumers may also seek a general loan from a finance company which takes a security interest in the debtor's currently owned property. The security interests taken under these types of loans would not be purchase money. The mechanics of security interest creation and perfection for both purchase money and non-purchase money transactions are, for the most part, similar. As noted above, the Code provides the purchase money creditor with priority over non-purchase creditors. To obtain that priority, the purchase money creditor must take certain steps to notify non-purchase money creditors of the "loan-to-buy" transaction. Even though the Code does not employ the phrase "non-purchase money security interest," it may be helpful to think of the concept in this comparative manner.

[F] Settings for Secured Transactions Issues

[1] General Setting (Non-Bankruptcy)

Secured transaction cases generally arise as either a battle between claimants to collateral in a non-bankruptcy setting or, as a trustee challenge to a party's claimed secured status in bankruptcy. In the non-bankruptcy setting, the issues are tried in state courts. The court's task is to resolve the complaint by applying the principles of law that come from the state's specific enactment of Article 9. The cases typically pit one creditor against another creditor, or one creditor against a purchaser of the collateral. At times, the case may involve issues which have arisen between the debtor and the secured creditor.

The cases between two creditors often arise because one creditor claims that its secured interest is superior to the other's secured interest. If the debtor is unable to pay and disposition of the debtor's property can satisfy only one of the creditors, the secured interest that is superior will get paid first. Subordinate creditors often get little or nothing once the senior secured party receives payment. In some instances, the conflict arises between a party who has financed a debtor's acquisition of property and another creditor who has loaned money to the same debtor. Both creditors have provided credit to the debtor and both claim an interest in the same type of collateral. In most of these cases, the second creditor will attempt to prove that the first creditor's security interest is invalid. For example, Creditor #2 will claim that Creditor #1's security interest in the goods is invalid because of a defect in Creditor #1's acquisition of the security interest. Creditor #2 may claim that the proper form of agreement has not been used or that it has not been properly signed. In other situations, Creditor #2 might claim a superior interest because #2 recorded its security interest first. Creditor #2 might also claim a superior security interest because Creditor #1 filed in the wrong place, and therefore failed to give third parties (like #2) proper notice of #1's interest. Consequently, Creditor #2 will claim that Creditor #1 does not have a valid security interest.

Sometimes one party will claim ownership rights in the goods and allege that those rights are superior to the ones claimed by the secured creditor. For example, the lessor of goods may be involved in a conflict with a creditor of the lessee who has loaned money to the lessee and who took a security interest in goods similar to the leased goods. At other times, a purchaser of some form of collateral will claim ownership rights superior to the secured party. Examples of these priority battles will be discussed in Chapter 18.

In cases between the secured party and the debtor, a number of issues may arise out of the security agreement as a contract. For example, a secured party may assert that the debtor defaulted under the terms of the security agreement. Because Article 9 does not define the term "default", the court must interpret the term as used in the security agreement. In another situation, the secured party may assert that the debtor has damaged or mistreated the collateral in violation of a provision in the security agreement which required proper maintenance. In still other cases, the secured party may allege that the debtor improperly removed the secured property from the location mentioned in the agreement without notifying the secured party.

Typically, the secured party claiming breach of contract will assert its rights by repossessing the property. Because Article 9 permits self-help repossession, many secured parties assume that they will not be required to litigate over the debt. Litigation over self-help remedies has abounded, however. Section 9-503 authorizes repossession only if it can occur without a breach of the peace. A debtor or another creditor of the debtor might challenge the manner in which the secured party gained possession of the property. Debtors and other creditors might also litigate the commercial reasonableness of the repossessing creditor's resale of the property. See § 9-504. Even when repossession and resale occurs smoothly, there may be a court question concerning the debtor's deficiency liability—is the debtor still responsible for the difference between the proceeds the creditor received on resale of the property and the amount of the debt? As noted earlier, all of these cases will be tried in state court under the specific Article 9 enactment in that jurisdiction.

[2] Bankruptcy Setting

In a bankruptcy case, the issues related to secured transactions are tried within the federal bankruptcy court system. Often, the issues are related to Article 9 and are similar to those tried in the non-bankruptcy setting. At times however, the issues may be directly related to federal bankruptcy law. In some those cases, Article 9 concepts clash with those of bankruptcy law. Our main concern in these materials is with the U.C.C. Article 9 issues, even where the case arises in a bankruptcy setting. We provide the following brief description of the bankruptcy system to give you a better understanding of how bankruptcy and Article 9 issues are inter-related.

Both secured and unsecured creditors find themselves in bankruptcy court when the debtor is unable to pay a debt and files a petition in bankruptcy. The goal of bankruptcy law is to provide debtors with a fresh start. Individuals, partnerships, or corporate debtors may file bankruptcy petitions. If granted relief, the bankrupt debtor will be able 1) to reorganize credit obligations or, 2) to obtain a discharge of certain obligations. In some cases, a creditor will join with several other creditors to force the debtor into bankruptcy by filing an involuntary petition. Whether voluntary or not, filing bankruptcy means that the bankrupt debtor's property will be "rounded up" in order to arrange for an equitable distribution of the property to the bankrupt debtor's creditors.

The actual marshalling of a bankrupt's property is supervised by the bankruptcy court alone; even if a creditor began an action in state court before the petition, bankruptcy law stays all actions against the bankrupt and places total supervision of the bankrupt's affairs in the hands of the bankruptcy court.

The bankruptcy court hears only bankruptcy cases. Bankruptcy judges are appointed by the Federal Circuit Court of Appeals and serve a term of fourteen years (in contrast to the Federal District Court judges, who serve for life). Bankruptcy court appeals proceed directly to the Federal District Court. In most cases, the bankruptcy court judge appoints a trustee to marshall the debtor's property. The trustee seeks to accumulate as much property of the debtor as possible in order to obtain a large estate for the ultimate distribution to all creditors. In appointing the trustee, the judge will generally consider the nature of the case and select an individual with adequate knowledge and experience for the post.

While the trustee generally represents the interests of all creditors, the officer is primarily concerned with protecting the interests of unsecured, general creditors because they have no claim to specific property of the debtor. The trustee in bankruptcy may attack any interest that favors one creditor at the expense of other creditors if there is some reasonable basis. For example, the trustee may assert that the secured creditor did not acquire a valid security interest. If the trustee succeeds in its challenge, the secured creditor loses its status as a secured party who would ordinarily get the full amount of the security. A creditor who loses its secured status becomes an unsecured claimant who must share the bankruptcy estate with all others who are similarly situated. In challenging a party's claimed, secured status, the trustee may assert a number of different bases for avoiding the interest.

One of the most frequently asserted bases for avoiding a creditor's interest is the "strong-arm clause" of section 544(a) of the bankruptcy code. Under this section, the trustee receives the status of a hypothetical lien creditor. Section 9-301(b) of the U.C.C. provides that lien creditors have priority over unperfected parties. Thus, if the trustee can establish that a creditor's security agreement was invalid or that the public notice of the security interest was improperly recorded, the trustee will prevail over the creditor under section 544(a). The trustee will then utilize section 550(a) of the bankruptcy code to recover the property and return it to the bankruptcy estate for the benefit of the estate.

If property was leased to a now-bankrupt debtor, the trustee may assert that the alleged lease was not a true lease, but instead a security agreement which, for one reason or another, should be found invalid. By attacking the priority of the secured interest "disguised" as a lease, the trustee may again force the creditor to share the property with all unsecured general creditors. Thus, many of the issues that arise in a non-bankruptcy setting may also arise in a bankruptcy law setting.

The trustee has other tools available to challenge the validity of a security interest. At times, the trustee may assert that the transfer was fraudulent or preferential. There are specific bankruptcy provisions which govern the trustee's ability to avoid on these bases. This variety of avoidance powers will be discussed in chapter 20.

[G] Inter-relationship of Issues

While the cases throughout these chapters dealing with secured transactions have been selected and edited primarily to emphasize a particular point or Code section, it becomes readily apparent that often there are a number of issues and Code sections involved within each case. Indeed, very often there will be some issues in regard to matters covered by various sections found in several chapters. The case below illustrates this type of inter-relationship. Even though the case involves a relatively simple plot and factual setting, it contains interesting issues as to what constitutes a security agreement (Chapter 16); how should a creditor perfect its security interest as against others and what happens when there is a problem in the system (Chapter 17); and who has priority with respect to the collateral (Chapter 18). With a slight change or additional fact, issues from Chapters 19 (Default), 20 (Security Interests in Bankruptcy), and 21 (Advanced Questions of Scope) could be implicated. The case provides a "preview" of some things to come on your "bus ride" through the subject of Secured Transactions (which hopefully will be a better one than Mr. Simplot's).

SIMPLOT v. WILLIAM C. OWENS, M.D., P.A.

Idaho Court of Appeals
805 P.2d 477, 14 U.C.C. Rep. Serv. 2d 892 (1990)

BURNETT, JUDGE.

This case presents the saga of a bus, a buyer, a bureaucratic bungle, a secured party and a seller who dropped out of sight. The issues on appeal concern a dispute between the buyer and the secured party. We are asked to decide (1) whether there is a valid security interest in the bus; (2) whether this interest was timely perfected; (3) whether the perfection was later invalidated; and (4) whether, in any event, the buyer acquired the bus free of any security interest as a buyer in the ordinary course of business. The district court resolved all these questions in favor of the secured party. We affirm.

The facts are undisputed. In March, 1985, Dr. William C. Owens, acting as trustee of the pension and profit sharing plans created by his professional corporation, loaned $25,000 to Chester Howard. The loan was evidenced by two promissory notes. To secure the notes, Howard endorsed the certificate of title of his 1956 G.M.C. bus and delivered the certificate to Owens. On August 26, 1985, Howard sold the same bus to Don J. Simplot for $45,000, to be paid in installments. Simplot paid the last installment on January 22, 1986. He then took possession of the bus and received a bill of sale from Howard. The bill of sale recited that the bus was free from all liens and encumbrances. Simplot asked for the certificate of title, but Howard told him it was lost. Simplot requested that the Idaho Department of Transportation conduct a title search. He also applied for a transfer of title. His application was stamped "received" by the Department on May 2, 1986.

Meanwhile, in April, 1986, Owens approached Howard and demanded payment of the loan. No payment was made. On May 5, 1986, Owens applied for a certificate of title showing Howard as the owner and Owens as a lienholder. On May 7, despite the fact that Simplot's application was pending, the Department issued Owens the requested title. On May 20, the Department also issued a certificate of title to Simplot, designating him as the owner and showing no liens or encumbrances. Sometime thereafter, Howard notified Simplot that Owens was claiming a security interest in the bus. At Simplot's request, the Idaho Department of Transportation held a hearing to determine the parties' respective interests. The Department concluded that Simplot owned the bus, but that the title was encumbered by Owens' lien.

Simplot then filed this action, claiming ownership free of liens and seeking an award of damages against Howard. Howard could no longer be found. He was served by publication and a default judgment eventually was entered against him. With respect to the dispute between Simplot and Owens, the district judge upheld the Department's determination that Owens was a lienholder. Simplot has appealed.

I

Simplot first argues that Owens never had a valid security interest in the bus. He contends that the promissory notes given by Howard to Owens did not contain language sufficient to create such an interest.

The question is governed by our decision in *Idaho Bank & Trust Co. v. Cargill*, Inc., 105 Idaho 83, 665 P.2d 1093 (Ct. App. 1983). There we held that a security interest is not enforceable against the debtor or a third party unless certain requirements are met. An enforceable security interest requires a "security agreement signed by the debtor containing a description of the collateral" if the collateral is not in the possession of the secured party. *Id.* at 87, 665 P.2d at 1097. No particular words are needed to create a security interest; the agreement need not even contain the term "security interest" to be valid. However, there must be language in the instrument which (1) leads to the conclusion that it was the intention of the parties to create a security interest and (2) identifies the collateral. *Id.*

Here, each promissory note contained the words "SECURITY: 1956 GMC Bus." As we have noted, Howard also endorsed his motor vehicle certificate of title to the G.M.C. bus on the line labelled "transfer of title." He then delivered the certificate to Owens. Upon this evidence, we agree with the district court that a valid security interest was intended and created.

II

Simplot next argues that Owens' security interest was not perfected before he purchased the bus from Howard. This argument requires us to determine which statutory scheme—the Vehicle Titles Act or Article Nine of the Uniform Commercial Code—applies to this case. The Legislature has provided that the Idaho Vehicle Titles Act exclusively governs the perfection of security interests in motor vehicles, unless the vehicles are held in inventory for sale. See I.C. §§ 28-9-302(3)(b) and 49-512. Here, the bus was a second-hand vehicle. Nowhere does the record suggest Howard was a used car dealer. Therefore, the bus was not inventory held for sale. The perfection of Owens' security interest was governed by the Vehicle Titles Act.

The Act provides that a security interest in a motor vehicle is perfected upon the filing of an application, with supporting documents and payment of the filing fee, for issuance of a certificate of title showing the secured party as a lienholder. I.C. § 49-510. The Act also provides that the purchaser of a motor vehicle acquires no legal right to the vehicle until a certificate of title is issued to him. I.C. § 49-503. Here, Owens completed the application process on May 5, 1986. Simplot was not issued a certificate of title until May 20. Because Owens perfected his security interest before Simplot acquired any legal right to the bus, the perfection was timely.

We acknowledge that the existence of a timely perfected security interest may be hard for Simplot to accept. After all, he applied for a certificate of title on May 2. It is not his fault that the certificate did not issue until May 20. Neither is it easy to understand why his certificate, when it finally did issue, showed no lienholder. However, these bureaucratic errors do not alter the statutes governing motor vehicle titles and security interests, as applied to this case. The underlying lesson here is that if a buyer, having received no certificate of title from the seller, parts with his money before obtaining a certificate of title from the Department of Transportation, he runs the risk of being unpleasantly surprised at some point by the discovery of a perfected security interest.

III

Simplot next argues that even if the perfection was timely, it was invalidated when the certificate of title was issued to Owens, naming his corporation as the lienholder and Howard as the owner. Strictly speaking, Owens' corporation was not a party to the security agreement; rather, the secured party was, collectively, the pension and profit-sharing plans, formed by Owens' corporation.

The purpose of listing a lienholder's interests on a certificate of title is similar to the policy behind Article Nine's requirement that financing statements be filed of record. That purpose is to provide inquiry notice to third parties. See, *e.g.*, I.C. § 28-9-402(1) and U.C.C. § 9-402 Official Comment 2. We think the purpose was served here. Simplot has not shown how he was prejudiced by a technical discrepancy in the name of the lienholder on the certificate of title issued to Owens. We hold that the description of the lienholder on the certificate of title was sufficient to place on inquiry notice anyone who saw the certificate or who obtained a title search by the Department. The discrepancy did not invalidate the perfection of the security interest.

IV

Simplot finally contends that even if Owens has a properly perfected security interest, Simplot is protected from that interest, under I.C. § 28-9-307(1), as a buyer in the ordinary course of business. We disagree. As noted above, this case involves the sale of a motor vehicle which was not held in inventory. Consequently, it is governed by the Vehicle Titles Act and not by Article Nine. Idaho Code § 28-9-307(1) does not apply. The Vehicle Titles Act contains no provision extending special protection to buyers in the ordinary course of business.

An argument for protection could be made by analogy to Article Nine, but such an argument would founder upon the provision in the Vehicle Titles Act that a buyer acquires no interest in a vehicle until he has been issued a certificate of title. I.C. § 49-503. In *Lux v. Lockridge, 65 Idaho 639, 150 P.2d 127 (1944)*, our Supreme Court interpreted this statute to mean that a buyer who had not been issued such a title could not be deemed a bona fide purchaser for value. In any event, an analogy to Article Nine would be unavailing because a buyer in the ordinary course of business must have purchased the goods from "a person in the business of selling goods of that kind." I.C. § 28-1-201(9). There is no evidence in the record to suggest that Howard was in the business of selling motor vehicles. Therefore, Simplot was not a buyer in the ordinary course of business.

Neither would an analogy to Article Nine be helpful in order to invoke the protection extended by I.C. § 38-9-307(2) to purchasers of consumer goods. This protection exists only if the buyer lacks knowledge of the security interest and the secured party has not filed a financing statement prior to the purchase. Here, of course, Owens did not file a financing statement but he did file the documents required to perfect a security interest in a motor vehicle under the Vehicle Titles Act—and he did so before Simplot acquired a legally cognizable interest in the bus. We conclude that Simplot does not qualify by analogy for the protection of I.C. § 28-9-307(2).

Accordingly, we affirm the district court's judgment upholding the Department's determination that Simplot owns the bus, subject to Owens' lien. Costs to respondent, Owens. Although Owens has requested attorney fees under I.C. § 12-121, we cannot say that this appeal was frivolous, unreasonable or without foundation. Therefore, the parties shall bear their own attorney fees.

WALTERS, C.J., and SWANSTROM, J., concur.

NOTE

The collateral in *Simplot* was a used bus. Where goods are mobile, effecting and maintaining a security interest can be difficult. Because of the ease of mobility with motor vehicles, neither local nor statewide notice of a creditor's security interest provides adequate information to third parties. In most states, mobile goods are subject to some type of motor vehicles law. The drafters of Article 9 recognized the potential for conflicts between a state's motor vehicle law and the law governing secured transactions. Where the collateral is a motor vehicle or some other type of good covered by a certificate of title, the Code provides that a security interest is perfected by notation on the certificate of title. Perfection is therefore controlled by the certificate of title rather than by the law of the state where the security interest arose. See § 9-103(2).

Despite this meshing of two separate laws, problems can still arise where: 1) the property is removed from the state issuing the certificate of title; or 2) a sale to a non-business buyer occurs. The key to the concept of perfection is public notice. If a security interest is not noted on the certificate of title when an automobile is moved to a different state, parties in the second state are NOT put on notice. Although Mr. Simplot made such an argument, the court rejected his claim. Simplot presents a good overview of the importance of the security interest concept and the consequences that flow from it. While we will return to certificates of title in Chapter 17, let us now turn to the non-motor vehicle context of security interest creation.

§ 16.02 The Security Agreement: Creating a Security Interest

Read: U.C.C. § 9-203.

[A] General Form

The secured transaction relationship begins with the creation of the security interest. Security interests are consensual agreements between the debtor and creditor; as such, they are pure contractual arrangements. There is no particular requirement as to the form of a security interest other than the contract creating the interest. This contract is known as a security agreement. Article 9 keeps formal requirements for a valid security agreement to a minimum: a writing which contains the debtor's signature, and which describes the collateral. Section 9-203 requires two additional events before a security interest becomes effective between the creditor and debtor—first, the creditor must provide some type of value to the debtor (the concept of value is broader than the common law concept of consideration); and second, the debtor must have rights in the collateral that will serve as security. When all of these requirements occur, the security agreement becomes enforceable between the parties and is said to "attach." See Comment 1 to § 9-203. In essence, the section 9-203 requirements ensure that the debtor and creditor have reached a mutual, and enforceable, agreement to create a security interest. For a discussion of the history and policy implications surrounding section 9-203, see *King, Policy Decisions and Security Agreements Under the Uniform Commercial Code, 9* Wayne L. Rev. 957 (1963).

Most security agreements contain a number of terms setting forth the rights and obligations of both the creditor (*e.g.*, Seller or Loan Company or Bank) and the debtor (Buyer or Borrower). Standard form/model security agreements are readily available to parties seeking to enter a secured transaction. A typical security agreement is set forth below. As you read this form, examine it carefully and determine where you might wish to improve it. Does the document say what was intended? Is it redundant? Are there different types of security arrangements that might suggest a simpler or a more complex form? What are the dangers associated with each choice?

SECURITY AGREEMENT:[2]
CONSUMER GOODS AND EQUIPMENT

. . . Debtor, and . . . Secured Party, with address as they appear with their signatures below, agree as follows:

I. Creation of Security Interest. Debtor hereby grants to Secured Party a security interest in the Collateral described in Paragraph II to secure the performance or payment of the Obligations of Debtor to Secured Party under Paragraph III.

II. Collateral. The Collateral of this Security Agreement is . . . . of the following description: . . . .

III. Debtor's Obligations.

A. Obligation to Pay. Debtor shall pay to Secured Party the sum or sums evidenced by the promissory note or notes executed pursuant to this Security Agreement in accordance with the terms of the note or notes.

B. Additional Obligations.

(1) Protection of Collateral. The Collateral

(a) Will be used primarily . . . . unless Secured Party consents in writing to another use, and

(b) Will not be misused or abused, wasted or allowed to deteriorate, except for the ordinary wear and tear of its intended primary use, and

[2] Copyright © 1986 from Willier & Hart, Bender's Uniform Commercial Code Service, Forms and Procedure, Form 9-1. Copyright permission obtained.

(c) Will be insured until this Security Agreement is terminated against all expected risks to which it is exposed and those which Secured Party may designate, with the policies acceptable to Secured Party and payable to both Secured Party and Debtor, as their interests appear, and with duplicate policies deposited with the Secured Party, and

(d) Will be kept at . . . . where Secured Party may inspect it at any time, except for its temporary removal in connection with its ordinary use or unless Debtor notifies Secured Party in writing and Secured Party consents in writing in advance of its removal to another location.

(2) Protection of Security Interest.

(a) The Collateral will not be sold, transferred or disposed of or be subjected to any unpaid charge, including taxes, or to any subsequent interest of a third person created or suffered by Debtor voluntarily or involuntarily, unless the Secured Party consents in advance in writing to such charge, transfer, disposition or subsequent interest, and

(b) Debtor will sign and execute alone or with Secured Party any Financing Statement or other document or procure any document, and pay all connected costs, necessary to protect the security interest under this Security Agreement against the rights or interests of third persons, and

(c) Debtor will reimburse Secured Party for any action to remedy a default which Secured Party elects pursuant to the terms of Paragraph VI.

IV. Secured Party's Obligations. Secured Party hereby sells the Collateral and shall transfer possession of the Collateral to Debtor on 19. . for the purpose of . . . .

V. Default. Misrepresentation or misstatement in connection with, noncompliance with or nonperformance of any of Debtor's Obligations or Agreements under Paragraphs III and VIII shall constitute default under this Security Agreement. In addition, Debtor shall be in default if bankruptcy or insolvency proceedings are instituted by or against the Debtor or if Debtor makes any assignment for the benefit of creditors.

VI. Secured Party's Rights and Remedies.

A. Secured Party May Assign this Security Agreement, and

(1) If Secured Party does assign this Security Agreement, the Assignee shall be entitled, upon notifying the Debtor, to performance of all of Debtor's Obligations and Agreements under Paragraphs III and VIII, and Assignee shall be entitled to all of the rights and remedies of Secured Party under this Paragraph VI, and

(2) Debtor will assert no claims or defenses he may have against Secured Party against the Assignee except those granted in this Security Agreement, and

B. Upon Debtors' Default, Secured Party may exercise his rights of enforcement under the Uniform Commercial Code in force in . . . . at the date of this Security Agreement and, in conjunction with, addition to or substitution for those rights, at Secured Party's discretion, may

(1) Enter upon Debtor's premises to take possession of, assemble and collect the Collateral or to render it unusable, and

(2) Require Debtor to assemble the Collateral and make it available at a place Secured Party designates which is mutually convenient, to allow Secured Party to take possession or dispose of the Collateral, and

(3) Waive any default or remedy any default in any reasonable manner without waiving the default remedied and without waiving any other prior or subsequent default.

VII. Rights and Remedies of Debtor. Debtor shall have all of the rights and remedies before or after default provided in Article 9 of the Uniform Commercial Code in force in . . . . at the date of this Security Agreement.

VIII. Additional Agreement and Affirmations.

A. Debtor Agrees and Affirms.

(1) That information supplied and statements made by him in any financial or credit statement or application for credit prior to this Security Agreement are true and correct, and

(2) That no financing statement covering the Collateral or its proceeds is on file in any public office and that, except for the security interest granted in this Security Agreement, there is no adverse lien, security interest or encumbrance in or on the Collateral, and

(3) That the addresses of Debtor's residence and place or places of business, if any, are those appearing below his signature, and

(4) That, if Debtor is also Buyer of the Collateral, THERE ARE NO EXPRESS WARRANTIES UNLESS THEY APPEAR IN WRITING SIGNED BY the SELLER AND THERE ARE NO IMPLIED WARRANTIES OF MERCHANTABILITY OR FITNESS FOR A PARTICULAR PURPOSE IN CONNECTION WITH THE SALE OF THE COLLATERAL.

B. Mutual Agreements.

(1) "Debtor" and "Secured Party" as used in this Security Agreement include the heirs, executors or administrators, successors or assigns of those parties.

(2) If more than one Debtor executes this Security Agreement, their Obligations under this Security Agreement shall be joint and several.

(3) The law governing this Secured Transaction shall be that of the State of . . . . in force at the date of this Security Agreement.

EXECUTED IN TRIPLICATE THIS . . . . DAY OF . . . . 19. ..

Secured Party ____________________

Address:

Debtor's Signature ____________________

Debtor's Residence:

Debtor's Address (Chief Place of Business):

Addresses of other places of Debtor's business:

[B] Sufficiency of Writing

Read: U.C.C. §§ 1-201(46), 9-203 and 9-402.

Even though the requirements for creating a security interest are minimal, there are times when the party claiming secured status fails to meet those minimum standards. How should the law address such failures? Should a creditor be able to assert a secured claim against a debtor when no formal security agreement was ever signed, but where other documents tend to show an intent to create a security interest? Compare the next two cases.

IN RE MODAFFERI

Bankruptcy Court, Southern District of New York
45 B.R. 370, 40 U.C.C. Rep. Serv. 268 (1985)

HOWARD SCHWARTZBERG, BANKRUPTCY JUDGE.

This creditor, Peg-Leg Productions, Inc., desires to get a leg up on the unsecured creditors of the above-captioned debtors and asserts that it holds a perfected secured claim by virtue of the debtors' written promissory note and the subsequent filing of U.C.C.-1forms with the appropriate offices in Rockland County and New York State. On the other hand, the trustee in bankruptcy in this Chapter 7 case argues that Peg-Leg Productions does not have a leg to stand on as a secured claimant because its position is flawed by the absence of a security agreement, as required under Article 9 of the Uniform Commercial Code, § 9-203.

FACTS

1. On December 13, 1982, the debtors borrowed $ 10,000 from Peg-Leg Productions in exchange for their written promissory note to repay that amount to Peg-Leg Productions, upon demand at the latter's offices in New City, New York, with interest at the rate of ten percent per annum, payable on a quarterly basis. The note was silent as to the existence of any collateral to secure payment.

2. One month later, on January 14, 1983, Peg-Leg Productions filed a financing statement, Form U.C.C.-1, in the appropriate filing office in Rockland County, New York. The financing statement was signed by the debtor, Joseph Modafferi, and the president of Peg-Leg Productions. The debtor listed on the financing statement was Joseph Modafferi, C.P.A. His office address was also specified. Item 5 of form U.C.C.-1states that the financing statement covers the following property: "All office equipment, furniture and all accounts payable." A similar form U.C.C.-1was filed by Peg-Leg Productions five months later, on June 21, 1983, with New York State.

3. On December 27, 1983, the debtors filed with this court their joint voluntary petition in bankruptcy pursuant to Chapter 7 of Title 11, United States Code.

4. Peg-Leg Productions filed a proof of claim in this case as a secured claimant on the basis of the December 13, 1982 promissory note it received for the $ 10,000 loan and the subsequent

filing of U.C.C.-1forms, which referred to the office equipment, furniture and accounts receivable of the debtor, Joseph Modafferi.

5. The debtors did not sign any document specifically referred to as a security agreement other than the promissory note and the form U.C.C.-1which was signed by the debtor, Joseph Modafferi.

DISCUSSION

Having failed to obtain from the debtors a signed separate security agreement containing a description of collateral for the purpose of creating a security interest, Peg-Leg Productions has no kick coming when the debtors' trustee in bankruptcy objects that Peg-Leg Productions does not hold a secured claim in this case.

It is fundamental that three requirements must be met for a security interest to be valid and enforceable against both the debtor and third parties: the debtor must sign a document describing the collateral, the security interest must attach and the interest must be perfected. *Allegaert v. Chemical Bank*, 657 F.2d 495, 503 (2d Cir. 1980); NY U.C.C. § 9-203(1)(McKinney Supp. 1984-1985). Section 9-203(1) states in pertinent part that "the security interest is not enforceable . . . unless . . . the debtor has signed a security agreement which contains a description of the collateral. In contrast to a financing statement which merely places creditors on notice that further inquiry is prudent, the security agreement embodies the intentions of the parties. *Commercial Trading Company, Inc. v. Bassin (In re Laminated Veneers Co., Inc.)*, 471 F.2d 1124, 1125 (2d Cir 1973). Consequently," [u]nless the grant of a security interest is contained in the security agreement, there is no security interest." *In re Marta Cooperative*, Inc., 74 Misc. 2d 612, 614, 344 N.Y.S. 2d 676, 678 (N.Y. Nassau County Ct 1973).

The foregoing authorities and a literal reading of U.C.C. § 9-203(1)are not dispositive of the issue in this case, namely, whether a financing statement taken together with an earlier signed promissory note, silent as to the existence of collateral, satisfy the writing requirement for the creation of a security interest. The two-fold purpose of the writing requirement was explained by the First Circuit Court of Appeals in *In re Numeric Corp.*, 485 F.2d 1328, 1331(1st Cir 1973), as follows:

> The draftsmen of the U.C.C. ascribed two purposes to [the writing] requirement. One purpose was evidentiary, to prevent disputes as to precisely which items of property are covered by a secured interest. See Uniform Commercial Code § 9-203, Comment 3; *J.K Gill Co. v. Fireside Realty Inc.*, 262 Ore. 486, 488, 499 P.2d 813 (1972). The second purpose of the signed-writing requirement is to serve as a Statute of Frauds, preventing the enforcement of claims based on wholly oral representations. See Uniform Commercial Code § 9-203, Comment 5.

The strong weight of authority is of the view that although it is not necessary to present a separate, formal document entitled "security agreement" to establish a valid security interest, a standard form financing statement, standing alone, does not constitute a security agreement. Indeed, official comment 2 to U.C.C. § 9-402 explains that the financing statement alone "indicates merely that the secured party who has filed may have a security interest in the collateral described."

It is clear that where a standard financing statement is presented to establish a valid and enforceable security interest, there must be some further documentation corroborative of the debtor's intent to pledge collateral. Thus, in *In re Numeric, the First* Circuit sustained a claim of security after examining a financing statement together with a resolution passed by the debtor's board of directors authorizing the debtor to grant a security interest in the same collateral listed in the notice on file. 485 F.2d at 1328. Similarly, in *In re Bollinger Corp.*, 614 F.2d 924, 928-29 (3rd Cir. 1980), the Third Circuit Court of Appeals upheld a security interest where, in addition to a financing statement, the parties exchanged letters constituting their course of dealing which clarified the debtor's pledge of collateral. Other cases have found valid security agreements where a financing statement was coupled with a letter from the debtor which described the collateral [court-cited cases omitted]. . . . In each of these cases, the debtor's intent to grant a security interest was manifested in written form. It therefore appears that in the absence of a "security agreement" denominated as such, some language reflecting a desire to grant a security interest must be contained within the documents offered to establish a security agreement under U.C.C. § 9-203. As the court stated in *Mitchell v. Shepherd Mall State Bank*:

> The fact that the parties signed and filed a financing statement which covered inventory, accounts receivable and contract rights, in addition to equipment, furniture, and fixtures, is of no consequence to our decision. The function of a financing statement is to put third parties on notice that the secured party who has filed it may have a perfected security interest in the collateral described. *Absent language which would constitute the debtor's grant of a security interest, a financing statement cannot serve as a security agreement.*

458 F.2d 703-04. [court-cited cases omitted] (citing *Mitchell* with approval and dismissing claim for security interest where financing statements contained no "granting" language); (financing statements usually do not contain necessary grant of a security interest); (financing statement form could not qualify as a security agreement due to lack of evidence of debtor's intent to grant security interest in property); (financing statement, though signed by the debtor and describing the collateral, did not create a security interest where there was no grant of such).

One recent bankruptcy court decision has noted that there is no statutory or case law supporting or contradicting the positions taken in *In re Numeric* and *In re Bollinger* where supplementary documentation was relied upon to support financing statements and uphold Security interests. Notwithstanding the deference displayed to these decisions by Judge Duberstein in Countrywide Metal Finders, Inc. v. Coffee Cupboard, Inc. (*In re Coffee Cupboard Inc.*), 33 B.R. 668, 671-72(Bankr. E.D. N.Y. 1983), it was held that an array of documents including a financing statement signed by the debtor did not constitute a written expression of present intent to create a security agreement. In another case decided in this circuit, a district court has concluded that boilerplate language in a promissory note that did not refer to a financing statement describing the collateral was insufficient to grant a security interest.

An examination of the evidence in this case reveals no written expression by the debtor granting a security interest. The financing statement presented by Peg-Leg Productions, signed by one of the debtors, merely lists the covered collateral; it contains no "granting" language and therefore fails to demonstrate a present intent to pledge collateral. Notwithstanding the policy expressed by the drafters of the U.C.C. that its terms be construed liberally, see § 1-102(1), this court is constrained to find that the debtor did not grant a security interest to Peg-Leg Productions based on the evidence presented. The goal of liberal construction does not dispense with the requirements of U.C.C. § 9-203. This point was expressed in *In re Broggard Auto Broker's* Inc., 11 U.C.C. Rep. Serv. (Callaghan) 402, 404 (Bankr. S.D. Fla. 1972) as follows:

> Although there is a direction above that the code is to be liberally construed, the further provision in regard to making the law uniform puts a restriction on such a direction. A line must be drawn somewhere. If each court or each jurisdiction went along its merry way waiving

> one or more specific requirements of the act in order to liberally construe the act, there would probably be a complete lack of uniformity. Furthermore, it is not the security agreements that are to be liberally construed, it is the act.

Accord *Shelton v. Erwin*, 472 F.2d at 1120. The U.C.C.'s requirements for the creation of a security interest are simple and clearly set forth. It is not unreasonable to require that a creditor who seeks to obtain priority over other creditors comply with these minimal requirements as a condition for being accorded such favored treatment. *Mitchell v. Shepherd Mall State Bank*, 458 F.2d at 704.

Even if this court were to overlook the lack of "granting" language in the documents proffered by Peg-Leg Productions, there is another reason to deny this creditor secured status. This is not a case where the promissory note refers to collateral or a financing statement so that there are two documents indicative of an intent to create a security agreement. Instead, the promissory note in this case is silent as to the existence of any collateral. Furthermore, the requirement that there be a nexus between the note and financing statement is absent in that the latter fails to state that it secures the indebtedness acknowledged by the debtors in the December 13, 1982 promissory note. The significance of the nexus between the note and financing statement was set forth by the court in *Needle v. Lasco Industries, Inc.* as it rejected a claim of security:

> There is a second reason why the financing statement here cannot be considered a security agreement. While the collateral is described, there is no indication of the obligation for which it is security. For all that appears from the writing, the obligation secured may have been a loan . . . which was subsequently repaid. . . . A security interest is collateral "which secures payment or performance of an obligation" and the security agreement is effective only "according to its terms between the parties . . . against creditors." At a minimum the "terms" must recite the obligation secured.

10 Cal. App. 3d at 1108, 89 Cal. Rptr. at 595-96 (citations omitted). The financing statement presented by Peg-Leg Productions does not on its face recite that it secures the $ 10,000 obligation evidenced by the December 13, 1982 note and therefore, it does not qualify as a Security agreement under Article 9 of the U.C.C..

CONCLUSIONS OF LAW

1. Peg-Leg Productions does not have a validly perfected secured claim against the office equipment, furniture and accounts payable belonging to the debtor, Joseph Modafferi by reason of the promissory note signed by both debtors and the subsequently filed financing statement, form U.C.C.-1, which was signed by Joseph Modafferi and the President of Peg-Leg Productions.

2. The bankruptcy trustee's objection to secured status for Peg-Leg Productions under the claim filed by the latter, is sustained.

MADDOX v. FEDERAL DEPOSIT INSURANCE CORPORATION

Bankruptcy Court, Western District of Texas
92 B.R. 707, 9 U.C.C. Rep. Serv. 2d 333 (1988)

MEMORANDUM OPINION

LARRY E. KELLY, CHIEF JUDGE.

. . . .

I. FACTS

Maddox began the process of obtaining from National Bank of Texas a 90% guaranteed SBA (Small Business Administration) loan on November 29, 1985 by submitting a Business Loan Application. Various exhibits and attachments within this application were signed by Maddox. Once a decision was made by the National Bank of Texas, Austin, Texas (hereafter "the Bank") to grant an SBA loan to Maddox, Maddox signed on March 18, 1986 (i) a promissory note in the original face amount of $52,000.00 (hereafter "Note"), (ii) an Authorization and Loan Agreement (hereafter "Loan Agreement") and a Lessor's Agreement between Maddox as lessee and Michael Kelch as lessor (hereinafter "Lessor's Subordination Agreement"). On March 19, 1986 Maddox signed and delivered to the Bank a U.C.C.-1Financing Statement (hereafter "U.C.C.-1"). On May 27, 1986 Maddox signed and delivered to the Bank a Resolution of Corporate Board—Authority to Procure Loan (hereafter "Corporate Resolution"). No separate document entitled "Security Agreement" was ever signed by Maddox with the intent to grant a security interest to the Bank by that single document. The parties have agreed and stipulated that if the existence of a security agreement cannot be determined from the above-listed documents, none exists.

With regard to the subjective intent of the parties at the time of the execution of the above-listed documents, the parties have stipulated as follows:

1. At the time of the loan Maddox understood the loan to be secured.

2. To obtain the loan Maddox intended to comply with the requirements of the Bank and the SBA by granting a security interest in the collateral described on the U.C.C.-1.

The Note was funded only to the extent of $49,814.26. At some point prior to June, 1987, the National Bank of Texas, Austin, Texas failed, and the FDIC as receiver became its successor in interest. The FDIC is the legal owner and holder of the Note and the security interest securing same.

On June 2, 1987, Maddox filed for protection under Chapter 153 of the Bankruptcy Code. On February 16, 1988 Maddox filed the Adversary Proceeding now before the Court to determine the validity of FDIC's security interest.

There is no dispute as to the following requirements of Tex.Bus. & Com. Code § 9.203, and the Court finds and rules that (i) value had been given by the Bank in the amount of $49,814.26 and (ii) at all relevant times Maddox owned the collateral and had rights in it.

The language from the loan documents relied upon by the parties which evidence the existence of a security agreement is as follows:

> PROMISSORY NOTE: The Collateral, and each part thereof, shall secure the indebtedness and each part thereof. The covenants and conditions set forth or referred to in any and all instruments of hypothecation constituting the Collateral are hereby incorporated in this Note as covenants and conditions of the undersigned with the same force and effect as though such covenants and conditions were fully set forth herein. . . . page 1
>
> Upon the non-payment of the indebtedness, or any part thereof, when due, whether by acceleration or otherwise, Holder is empowered to sell, assign, and deliver the whole or any part of the Collateral at public or private sale. . .. [continues with extensive list of holder's rights with regard to the collateral] . . . page 2
>
> LOAN AGREEMENT
>
> 3. Terms of Loan . . .
>
> c. Collateral:
>
> 1. First lien evidenced by Security Agreement(s) and U.C.C.-1filing(s) on all a. equipment (excluding titled motor vehicles) b. inventory c. accounts receivable now owned and hereafter acquired.
>
> 2. Prior to first disbursement the appropriate U.C.C. lien searches must be made to determine Lender's priority of lien.
>
> UCC-1 Describes parties as "debtor" and "secured party". Contains a complete description of all collateral.
>
> LESSOR'S SUBORDINATION AGREEMENT
>
> Lessor subordinates to all liens securing the note, until payment in full, every lien or claim against any or all of the property hypothecated as collateral for the indebtedness in favor of "Bank/SBA" hereinabove referred to . . .

II. DISCUSSION OF LAW

The sections of the Texas version of the Uniform Commercial Code that govern the Court's opinion are:

1. § 9.203(a)(1) which described the formal requisites of a security agreement;
2. Comments 1 and 5 to § 9.203 which elaborate on the purpose and function of the formal requisites of § 9.203(a)(1);
3. § 9.105(a)(12) which defines a security agreement;
4. § 1.201(3) which defines "agreement"; and
5. § 9.402 which states that a security agreement can be a financing statement.

The only requirements for the enforceability of a non-possessory security interest are (a) a writing, (b) the debtor's signature, and (c) a description of the collateral. Tex.Bus. & Com.Code § 9.203(a)(1) and Comment 1 thereto. Applying the plain meaning of the statute it would appear that here an enforceable security interest was created. Unfortunately, one of the first courts to interpret this section enunciated what has come to be known as the "express grant rule." *American Card Company v. H.M.H. Co.*, 97 R.I. 59, 196 A.2d 150 (1963). In that case the court examined a standard form U.C.C. statement alone which the lender asserted was sufficient of itself to constitute a security agreement. The American Card court applied the Rhode Island version of (i) U.C.C. § 9-203 setting forth the formal requirements for a security agreement and (ii) U.C.C. § 9-402 which states that some security agreements are sufficient as a financing statement if filed. It concluded that a financing statement, absent an agreement therein, cannot be treated as the equivalent of a security agreement. At one point, the court expresses this holding as "[S]ince the financing statement filed here contains no such grant [i.e., debtor's grant of a security interest] it does not qualify as a security agreement." *American Card Company v. H.M.H. Co.*, 97 R.I. 59, 196 A.2d 150 (1963).

Most commentators and many courts, even those which have not followed American Card, have taken the holding of this case to mean that no financing statement can serve as a security agreement and that there must be a document in which debtor expressly grants a security interest. Grant Gilmore writes in his classic work on security interests:

> In *American Card Co. v. H.M.H. Co.*, the discrepancies between § 9-203 and § 9-402 led the Rhode Island court to an unfortunate decision. To secure a debt, H.M.H. agreed to give the card company a security interest in certain tools and dies. The card company filed a financing statement which complied in all respects with the § 9-402 requirements. In an equity receivership, the card company was denied status as a secured creditor on the ground that the debtor had not signed a "security agreement" in addition to the financing statement. The court noted that a security agreement, if executed, could have been filed as a financing statement (if it met the additional requirements of § 9-402) but concluded that the reverse was not true: "it is not possible for a financing statement which does not contain the debtor's grant of a security interest to serve as a financing statement." Certainly, nothing in § 9-203 requires that the "security agreement" contain a "granting" clause. The "9-402 financing statement contained all that was necessary to satisfy the § 9-203 statute of frauds as well as being sufficient evidence of the parties' intention to create a security interest in the tools and dies. No doubt the court would have upheld the security interest if the debtor had signed two pieces of paper instead of one. The § 9-402 provision that a short financing statement may be filed in place of the full security agreement was designed to simplify the operation. The Rhode Island court gives it an effect reminiscent of the worst formal requisites holding under the nineteenth century chattel mortgage acts. Grant Gilmore, Security Interests in Personal Property § 11.4 (1965).

In fact, the holding of American Card need not be read so broadly. The American Card court merely held that some financing statements (those in which "nowhere in the form is there any evidence of an agreement") are not sufficient as security agreements, not that no financing statement can ever be sufficient as a security agreement. American Card, supra.

In this case, we have before the court not a mere standard form U.C.C. statement, but several documents from which the FDIC urge us to find "evidence of an agreement". As pointed out by the FDIC, the composite document rule is the rule in most circuits which have addressed this question. *Matter of Miller*, 545 F.2d 916 (5th Cir.1977); *Matter of Numeric Corp.*, 485 F.2d 1328 (1st Cir.1973); *Matter of Bollinger Corporation*, 614 F.2d 924 (3rd Cir.1980) (a well reasoned opinion which surveys and attempts to reconcile the existing law on the subject); . . .

The Composite Document Rule is that there need not be a separate document labeled "Security Agreement" but rather all relevant loan documents may be examined to determine whether a security agreement exists, i.e., a security interest has been granted. An often unstated corollary to the Composite Document Rule is that the "evidence of agreement" can be that the documents examined would not have been written, signed or worded as they are unless a security interest was granted. That is, a security agreement is found by necessary implication rather than by express grant. The Ninth Circuit has found sufficient evidence of a security agreement by the mere fact that a sufficient financing statement is prepared, signed by the debtor and filed. After all, why would a debtor and lender go to the trouble to perfect a security interest that had not been created? *In re Amex-Protein Development Corp.*, supra. The First, Third, Fifth, and Seventh Circuits have taken the middle ground and required more evidence from other documents but no formal words of grant. The Fifth Circuit has stated:

> The principal test for determining whether a transaction is to be treated as a security interest is: "[i]s the transaction intended to have effect as security?" *Id.* § 9.102 (Comment 1 [to U.C.C. § 9-102]). No formal wording is required; we are to examine the substance of the documents, in light of the circumstances of the case. *Matter of Miller*, 545 F.2d 916 (5th Cir.1977).

Maddox cites a Texas case, *Mosley v. Dallas Entertainment Company*, Inc., 496 S.W.2d 237 (Tex. Civ. App.—Tyler 1973, writ dism'd) for the proposition that no grant of a security interest may be found by implication. Mosley is not controlling, however, for three reasons. First, in Mosley the creditor argued that a standard form U.C.C.-1 financing statement alone was a sufficient security agreement. The Court found the U.C.C.-1 insufficient because it "fails to contain any language showing the alleged debtor granted the creditor (appellee) an interest in the collateral," Mosley, supra 240. The situation here is factually distinguishable since more documentation than a mere U.C.C.-1 exists. Second, Maddox reads the holding of Mosley too broadly. As in American Card, the court held that the evidence before it (a standard form U.C.C. statement) contained insufficient evidence of a security agreement, not that the grant of a security interest can never be determined by necessary implication. Third, the creditor in the Mosley case attempted to prove the existence of a security by oral testimony. This the court properly refused to allow. Mosley, supra at 240. As stated by comment 5 to U.C.C. § 9-203:

> 5. The formal requisites stated in this Section are not only conditions to the enforceability of a security interest against third parties. They are in the nature of a Statute of Frauds. Unless the secured party is in possession of the collateral, his security interest, absent a writing which satisfies subsection (1)(b), is not enforceable even against the debtor, and cannot be made so on any theory of equitable mortgage or the like.

Maddox also cites the case of *Martin Grinding & Machine Works*, 793 F.2d 592 (7th Cir.1986) for the proposition that neither oral nor written evidence outside a formal security agreement can be used to expand the scope of the interest actually granted in a formal written signed security agreement (which both parties concede is missing entirely in this case). Here Maddox demonstrates either disingenuousness or an understandable confusion between the Statute of Frauds and the Parol Evidence Rule. The parol evidence rule applied in *Martin Grinding* does not allow oral evidence or prior written evidence to vary the terms of a written agreement which the court has determined the parties intended as the full and final expression of their agreement. In *Martin Grinding* there was a written security agreement granting a security interest in four broad categories (machinery, equipment, furniture, fixtures). The financing statement covered these categories and inventory and accounts receivable. Because of the parol evidence rule, the written financing statement could not be used to vary the terms of the written security agreement. *Martin Grinding & Machine Works*, 793 F.2d 592 (7th Cir. 1986). In the case before the Court, there is no single written agreement which the parties intended as the full and final expression of their agreement. Thus *Martin Grinding* and the parol evidence rule are inapplicable.

It is evident that no conditions are imposed on the security agreement other than it create a security interest. The definition of agreement provided by the Uniform Commercial Code as enacted by Texas provides additional guidance for establishing the existence of an agreement in this case:

> "Agreement" means the bargain of the parties in fact as found in their language or by implication from other circumstances including course of dealing or usage of trade or course of performance as provided in this title (Sections 1.205 and 2.208). Whether an agreement has legal consequences is determined by the provisions of this title, if applicable; otherwise by the law of contracts (Section 1.103). . . .

The statute of frauds, as applied in *Mosley* is applicable. *Mosley* correctly held that parol evidence is not admissible to vary the terms of a written financing statement (which terms in that case were not sufficient to evidence the existence of a security agreement). However, *Mosley* is not inconsistent with the application of the Composite Document Rule. In this case the Court has been presented with several written documents from which the FDIC asks it to glean evidence of the existence of a security agreement. On the basis of the foregoing Findings of Fact and Conclusions of Law it is the decision of this Court that there is sufficient evidence in these written documents of the existence of a security agreement and that such an agreement exists, is enforceable against the debtor and is enforceable against third parties due to its perfection on March 19, 1986.

A separate judgment of even date has issued affirming the FDIC's security interest in the property of the debtor, Maddox described in the U.C.C.-1 filed March 19, 1986.

NOTES AND QUESTIONS

(1) Can the different results in *Modafferi* and *Maddox* be reconciled? Both cases demonstrate that first year contracts is not something a student can tuck away in the recesses of her mind. Section 9-203 serves as a Statute of Frauds provision for Article 9—the parties must put the substance of their agreement in a writing. In most instances, that writing serves to explain the parties' commitment. The *Modafferi* decision demonstrates the consequence of a creditor's failing to obtain a signed security agreement—the creditor will not be afforded secured status and will therefore have no security interest in a debtor's property. The Composite Document Rule adopted by the Maddox court puts cracks in the writing requirement; should the court have done so?

(2) Both *Modafferi* and *Maddox* cite I*n Re Bollinger Corp.*, 614 F.2d 924 (3d Cir. 1980). In *Bollinger* there was a detailed financing statement filed by the creditor and signed by the debtor; however, the parties never managed to have the debtor execute a security agreement. Like *Maddox*, the *Bollinger* court found various executed documents that reflected the necessary party

intention to create a security interest. In reaching its decision, the *Bollinger* court considered the debtor's promissory note, the financing statement, and a group of letters which demonstrated a course of dealing between the parties. The court held that those documents, construed together, provided the minimum formal requirements demanded by § 9-203(1)(b). All of the documentation that the court relied upon made reference to a security agreement that was to be delivered later; despite the fact that no such document was ever delivered, the court found the § 9-203 requirements satisfied. Perhaps the *Bollinger* decision could be justified by the facts: 1) no third parties were injured by the failure to execute a formal security agreement; and 2) there was no dispute between the immediate parties as to the existence of the secured relationship. Are the facts of *Maddox* more or less like those in *Bollinger*?

(3) The *Modafferi* case goes against the weight of most court decisions since *Bollinger* by refusing to recognize the composite document rule. If courts can meet the requirement by finding additional evidence of party intent, has the Statute of Frauds outlived its usefulness? Which approach provides greater certainty and stability in secured transactions?

COMPARING SECURITY AGREEMENTS AND FINANCING STATEMENTS

The security agreement and financing statement serve two distinct purposes. The security agreement represents the contractual agreement between the debtor and creditor. As one court noted, the security agreement serves two principal objectives:

> One purpose was evidentiary, to prevent disputes as to precisely which items of property are covered by a secured interest. The second purpose of the signed-writing requirement is to serve as a Statute of Frauds, preventing the enforcement of claims based on wholly oral representations. . . . A writing or writings, regardless of label, which adequately describes the collateral, carries the signature of the debtor, and establishes that in fact a security interest was agreed upon, would satisfy both the formal requirements of the statute and the policies behind it.

In Re Numeric Corp., 485 F.2d 1328, 13 U.C.C. Rep. 416 (1st Cir. 1973).

The financing statement, on the other hand, serves the limited purpose of placing third parties who might deal with the debtor, on notice that another person might have an interest in the debtor's property. Given this limited purpose, the formal requirements for a financing statement are even more minimal than those for a security agreement. The basic requisites for a financing statement are noted in § 9-402(1):

> A financing statement is sufficient if it gives the names of the debtor and the secured party, is signed by the debtor, gives an address of the secured party from which information concerning the security interest may be obtained, gives a mailing address of the debtor and contains a statement indicating the types, or describing the items of collateral. A financing statement may be filed before a security agreement is made or a security interest otherwise attaches. . .. A copy of the security agreement is sufficient as a financing statement if it contains the above information and is signed by the debtor. . ..

While a copy of a security agreement can be filed as a financing statement if it meets the requirements, the normal practice is to file a simple form containing only the required information. Consider the following simple statutory form which is set forth at § 9-402(3):

> A form substantially as follows is sufficient to comply with subsection (1):
>
> Name of debtor (or assignor) ______________________

Name of secure party (or assignee) ______________________

Address ______________________

1. This financing statement covers the following types (or items) of property:

   (Describe) ______________________

2. (If collateral is crops) The above described crops are growing or are to be grown on:

   (Describe Real Estate) ______________________

3. (If applicable) The above goods are to become fixtures on

   (Describe Real Estate __________ and this financing statement is to be filed [for record] in the real estate records. (If the debtor does not have an interest of record) The name of a record owner is _______

4. (If products of collateral are claimed) Products of the collateral are also covered.

   (use whichever is applicable)

____

Signature of Debtor (or Assignor)

____

Signature of Debtor (or Assignee)

The Composite Document Rule provides that a standard form financing statement, taken alone, cannot be considered sufficient as a security agreement. A detailed financing statement, coupled with other documentation that reflects party intention to create a security interest, could however, suffice as a security agreement.

Given the minimal requirements established by section 9-203, does the Composite Document Rule make a mockery of the importance of careful drafting? Or, is the rule a proper example of a court's refusal to apply form over substance?

[C] Parol Evidence

Read: U.C.C. § 2-202.

Since the security agreement is a simple contract, various contract rules concerning the agreement apply. One question that arises occasionally is whether extrinsic evidence may be introduced to expand the collateral description under the agreement. In In Re Swearingen, 27 B.R. 379, 35 U.C.C. Rep. 962 (Bankr. D. Kan. 1983), the security agreement failed to list a mobile home as collateral even though the certificate of title (for present purposes, the equivalent of a financing statement) noted the lien on the home. The creditor asked the court to accept parol evidence that the parties intended to include the mobile home as collateral, but had inadvertently omitted it from the security agreement. The court found the security agreement complete and unambiguous and thus refused to permit the evidence. The court noted that the parties' intent was immaterial and that the secured party should simply have been more thorough in filling out the security agreement.

In *Rempa v. La Parte Production Credit Association*, 444 N.E.2d 308, 35 U.C.C. Rep. Serv. 1646 (Ind. Ct. App. 1983), the security agreement and financing statement were signed in blank and later filled in by the secured party. The debtor claimed that certain collateral was not intended to be included in the security agreement and wanted to introduce evidence to support its position. The court held that the security agreement was a reflection of the underlying contract of the parties and permitted parol evidence to explain the underlying agreement.

If no formal security agreement exists, can parol evidence be introduced to establish that the parties intended specific documents to function as the security agreement? In *Krieger v. Hartig*, 11 Wash. App. 898, 527 P.2d 483, 15 U.C.C. Rep. Serv. 938 (1974), the court held that the existence of a security agreement was a question of fact and that the parol evidence rule did not apply; thus, extrinsic evidence was permitted.

[D] Signature of Debtor

Read: U.C.C. § 1-201(39).

The Code provides that the security agreement must be signed by the debtor. This requirement assumes that the presence of the debtor's signature assures that the debtor intended to grant a security interest. The Code does not require that the debtor's signature be acknowledged or witnessed.

Although there is no requirement that the security agreement be signed by the secured party, general principles of contract law suggest that a secured party's signature is advisable if only to demonstrate the existence of a contract between the parties.

BAYSTATE DRYWALL, INC. v. CHICOPEE SAVINGS BANK

Massachusetts Supreme Judicial Court
429 N.E.2d 1138, 32 U.C.C. Rep. Serv. 1315 (1982)

WILKINS J.

We are concerned with whether the defendant Chicopee Savings Bank (bank) held an enforceable security interest in a motor vehicle. The bank argues that its claim is superior to the claim of the plaintiff which sold the motor vehicle on execution to satisfy its judgment against the vehicle's owner. A judge of the District Courts ruled for the bank, and the plaintiff claimed a report. The Appellate Division of the District Courts dismissed the report on a ground we find to have been inappropriate. The case is before us on the plaintiff's appeal. We rule in favor of the bank.

We summarize the significant facts contained in the report. In June, 1976, Josephine I. Tessier borrowed $5,478 from the bank. She signed a promissory note and security agreement that stated that a specifically described 1976 Oldsmobile Cutlass Supreme automobile was security for the loan. The bank issued a check payable to Josephine I. Tessier and Reiter Oldsmobile. Mrs. Tessier's husband Gerard purchased the vehicle, using the proceeds of the loan to pay for the vehicle, and title was placed in his name only. The title certificate listed him as the owner and listed the bank as a lien holder under a chattel mortgage. Gerard authorized Josephine to use the motor vehicle as collateral and to execute the necessary documents to create the bank's security interest. This case arises because Gerard did not sign the security agreement, and, as far as the report shows, he did not give the bank directly any written statement that as owner of the vehicle he acknowledged the bank's security interest.

In January, 1978, about eighteen months later, the plaintiff recovered judgment against Gerard in the amount of $ 1,817.84 in an action brought in the Springfield District Court. Pursuant to an execution, the motor vehicle was sold in March, 1978, for $3,400. The plaintiff paid the bank $2,831.73 for the release of the bank's alleged lien on the motor vehicle. When, on the delivery of a copy of the security agreement, the plaintiff discovered that Gerard had not signed the security agreement, the plaintiff made demand on the bank for the return of the $2,831.73. The bank declined to pay the amount demanded, and the plaintiff commenced this action seeking to recover it.

A security interest is not enforceable against the debtor or third parties unless certain conditions are met. G.L. c. 106, § 9-203(1), as appearing in St. 1957, c. 765, § 1. Where the collateral is not in the possession of the secured party, as is the case here, three conditions must be met before a security interest in the collateral can attach. There must be a proper security agreement signed by the debtor and containing a description of the collateral (G.L. c. 106, § 9-203[1][b]); the debtor must have rights in the collateral; and value must be given (G.L. c. 106, § 9-204[1]). When these three requirements for the attachment of a security interest are fulfilled, the security interest then only becomes fully enforceable if it is perfected by recording or by following some similar procedure.

The plaintiff grants that certain of these conditions are met. However, the plaintiff argues that, if Gerard was a debtor for the purposes of § 9-203(1), he did not sign a security agreement and that Josephine, by her execution of the security agreement, did not have rights in the collateral so as to create a security interest in the motor vehicle. We conclude that Gerard (as well as Josephine) was a debtor for the purposes of § 9-203(1)(b), and, consequently, the bank's purported security interest is enforceable against the plaintiff only if Gerard has "signed a Security agreement which contains a description of the collateral."

We regard Gerard as a "debtor" for the purposes of § 9-203(1), because in these circumstances a "debtor" includes the owner of the collateral, even if he is not obligated on the debt. See G.L. c. 106, § 9-105(1)(d), defining a debtor and set forth in the margin. The provisions of G.L. c. 106, § 9-203, deal with the collateral; thus under G.L. c. 106, § 9-105(1)(d), the owner of the collateral, Gerard, is a debtor for the purposes of determining rights in the collateral. This conclusion is supported by the decisions of courts which have dealt with this question in similar circumstances.

We turn then to the question whether Gerard signed a security agreement sufficient to create a security interest. It is not necessary that Gerard have signed a formal security agreement, if there were documents which collectively established an intention to execute a security agreement by the grant of a security interest in the motor vehicle. *In the Matter of Numeric Corp.*, 485 F.2d 1328, 1331 (1st Cir. 1973). The two purposes of the Signature requirement are to prevent disputes over which items of property are covered by a security interest and to serve as a statute of frauds. *Id.* A "Security agreement" is "an agreement which creates or provides for a security interest." G.L. c. 106, § 9-105(1)(l). An "agreement" is "the bargain of the parties in fact as found in their language or by implication from other circumstances." G.L. c. 106, § 1-201(3).

We must, therefore, look to what agreement or agreements exist and whether Gerard signed any document which with other documents constitutes a security agreement. There was a security agreement signed by Josephine. She signed it with Gerard's understanding and assent, and the inference is clear the purpose of the loan was to obtain funds so that Gerard could purchase the motor vehicle. Although Gerard did not sign that agreement, it is admitted that Josephine did sign it with his authority but not in his name. But for the absence of Gerard's signature, the formal security agreement is adequate in all respects to create an enforceable security interest in favor of the bank. If Gerard signed a separate acknowledgment of the existence of the security interest, we think the security interest properly attached (see G.L. c. 106, § 9-204(1)), as appearing in St. 1957, c. 765, § 1) and is enforceable.

Although the report does not contain an application signed by Gerard for the issuance of a certificate of title showing the bank's Security interest, the inference is fairly warranted that he signed such an application. The record contains a certificate of title in Gerard's name showing the bank's lien. Under G.L. c. 90D, § 21, inserted by St 1971, c. 754, § 1, "[a] security interest in a vehicle for which a certificate of title is issued under [G.L. c. 90D] is perfected by the delivery to the registrar of . . . an application for a certificate of title containing the name and address of the lienholder." The owner must execute the application to name the lienholder. G.L. c. 90D, § 22(a). We think, therefore, that the record reasonably shows that Gerard signed an application disclosing the bank's interest in the collateral.

We accept the view, generally held, that a security interest in a motor vehicle cannot be created just by completing the process prescribed by a "certificate of title" statute, nor does a reference to a lien stated on a title certificate alone constitute a security agreement. A debtor need not, however, sign a document designated "security agreement" in order to satisfy the code requirement that the debtor sign a Security agreement.

[The court cites cases showing that a combination of documents may meet the requirement. For example: promissory note, financing statement and correspondence; financing statement and a director's resolution; financing statement and letter where debtor wrote "agreed," a financing statement and letter; and a promissory note and financing statement.]

On the basis of these principles, we conclude that the combination of (1) the security agreement signed by Josephine with Gerard's authority and (2) his written acknowledgment of the existence of the Security interest, stated in his application for a title certificate to the motor vehicle, constituted a security agreement signed by the debtor for the purposes of permitting enforcement of the security interest in favor of the bank. There was a clear indication of the security interest both on the security agreement and on the title certificate, and the application for the title certificate was a document signed by Gerard acknowledging the existence of the Security interest. No creditor or other third party could reasonably have been misled. See *Casco Bank & Trust Co. v. Cloutier*, supra at 1230-1231. Although the procedures followed by the bank are hardly recommended practices, the bank's security interest did attach and was perfected before the plaintiff acquired any rights in the motor vehicle.

Entry of judgment for the defendant was correct, and the order of the Appellate Division dismissing the report is affirmed.

So ordered.

NOTES

(1) Often, the parol evidence rule excluding evidence of the parties' intent will not apply to the case of signatures. Courts will admit evidence of intent where the interpretation of a signature is at issue. *See e.g.,* In *re Mid-Atlantic Piping Products of Charlotte, Inc.,* 24 B.R. 314, 35 U.C.C. Rep. 618 (Bankr. Ct. W.D.N.C. 1982).

(2) Debtor signs a security agreement. A photocopy of the agreement is filed as a financing statement. Is the financing statement (the photocopy) properly signed? See *Sommers v. International Business Machines*, 640 F.2d 686, 30 U.C.C. Rep. 1757 (5th Cir. 1981). See also U.C.C. § 9-402(1).

[E] Sufficiency of Security Agreement's Collateral Description

Read: U.C.C. § 9-110.

IN RE: TECHNO PRODUCTS, INC. EISEN v. UNITED STATES

United States Bankruptcy Court, Northern District of Ohio
129 B.R. 487, 15 U.C.C. Rep. 2d (1991)

DAVID F. SNOW, BANKRUPTCY JUDGE.

. . . .

The Debtor contends that Messrs. Green and Estrate (collectively the "Employees") are not secured creditors because they failed to perfect the security interests allegedly granted to them by the Debtor prior to its initiation of this Chapter 151 proceeding. At the December pretrial it was agreed by the parties (and the Internal Revenue Service—the paramount secured creditor) that the Employees' status as secured or unsecured appeared to depend on whether their failure to file financing statements with the Secretary of State of Ohio was fatal to their claim as secured creditors.

Discussion

Harold Green worked for the Debtor as a commission salesman and was owed some $47,000 evidenced by three promissory notes at the time that his employment ceased shortly before the Chapter 151 filing. According to the Employees' brief, these three notes were "each secured by a Uniform Commercial Code Financing Statement providing a name, address and signature of the Debtor and Creditor as well as the following description of the collateral: [a]ll corporate assets to the amount of [the amount of each particular debt]." Mr. Estrate was also employed by the Debtor. His employment continued until terminated in connection with Mr. Eisen's sale of the business. His claims also arise out of unpaid salary and are evidenced by the Debtor's promissory notes and by financing statements substantially identical to those of Mr. Green. Each of the Employees' financing statement was duly filed for record with the Recorder for Cuyahoga County, but no filing was made with the Secretary of State of Ohio.

But even if the Employees' failure to file their financing statements with the Secretary of State were not fatal, it appears doubtful that their papers created a valid security interest under Ohio law. It appears that there was no security agreement as distinguished from the financing statements described above. According to *Silver Creek Supply v. Powell*, 36 Ohio App. 3d 140, 521 N.E. 2d 828 (1987) a financing statement may not serve as a security agreement. Under this authority no security interest was every created. But even if the hurdle were surmounted, it has been held generally that language such as that used in the Employees' financing statements is inadequate to create a valid security interest. *In re Swanson*, 104 B.R. 1 (Bankr. C.D. Ill. 1989), the court noted that a description of the purported collateral as "all personal property" was plainly insufficient under section 9-110 of the Uniform Commercial Code (O.R.C. § 1309.08). Likewise, "all corporate assets" which appears in these financing statements is too general to reasonably identify the purported collateral.

Therefore, it appears that the Employees' security interests, if any, in the debtor's assets were not perfected and are not enforceable against the Debtor's trustee. Consequently, the Employees have no secured interests in the proceeds of the sale of those assets.

IN RE SRJ ENTERPRISES, INC. NBD PARK RIDGE BANK v. SRJ ENTERPRISES, INC.

United States Bankruptcy Court, N.D. Ill., E.D.
151 B.R. 198, 22 U.C.C. Rep. Serv. 2d 1181 (1993)

MEMORANDUM OPINION

RONALD S. BARLIANT, BANKRUPTCY JUDGE.

The Debtor, SRJ Enterprises, Inc., sold all of its automobile dealership assets free and clear of all liens, with any valid liens attaching to the sale proceeds. Part of the sale proceeds included $177,569.88 for "parts". Success National Bank of Lincolnshire filed a motion for partial summary judgment to declare its security interest in the parts proceeds superior to all other liens. For the reasons stated below, this Court has denied Success' motion.

I. UNCONTESTED FACTS

The relevant facts of this dispute are simple. The Debtor financed the operation of its dealership with the proceeds of loans from NBD Park Ridge Bank and Success. Both NBD and Success perfected security interests in the Debtor's assets. NBD filed first. NBD's security agreement provides:

> (a) "Inventory" means new and used motor vehicles now owned or hereafter acquired by Dealer which are held for sale or lease, . . ., together with all of the proceeds thereof, including, but not limited to, cash or its equivalent, accounts receivable, factory receivables and contract rights. . .
>
> (c) "Collateral" means all Inventory, property described in paragraph 5(e) of this Agreement, and other property from time to time subject to the security interest herein provided for, including but not limited to all proceeds of every kind of any such Inventory and property.
>
> . . .
>
> 5(e) Dealer grants to Bank a security interest in, and agrees and acknowledges that Bank shall continue to have a security interest in, all of the furniture, fixtures, equipment, tools, machinery,

accessories, appliances, accounts receivable (including, but not limited to, factory receivables), contract rights and any other personal property of Dealer now owned or hereafter acquired, and in all of the proceeds thereof.

Success' security agreement, similar to NBD's, provides:

2.01 Collateral shall mean (a) all Accounts, Accounts Receivable, and Contract Rights of Debtors, whether now or hereafter existing or acquired; . . . (c) all furniture, fixtures (trade or otherwise), goods, parts, accessories, equipment (excluding motor vehicles), machinery, Inventory, raw materials and work in progress or finished goods of Debtors, whether now or hereafter existing or acquired, . . .; (d) all general intangibles; and (e) all proceeds and products of the foregoing.

. . . .

2.03 Inventory shall mean all goods held by Debtors, or either of them, for sale or lease, or furnished by Debtors, . . ., but excluding interests in motor vehicles.

II. ANALYSIS

Success clearly has a lien on "parts"; but, NBD filed first. The issue then is whether NBD's lien covers "parts" even though the word "parts" is not used. The parties make much of the esoteric Article 9 question of whether a collateral description of "all personal property" is too broad to satisfy § 9-110, 9-203 and 9-402.[3] See generally J. White and R. Summers, Uniform Commercial Code, § 24-4 (3rd Ed. 1988). But this is not a situation where the gray areas and nuances of the Commercial Code need be examined.

Section 9-110 provides: "[f]or the purposes of this Article any description of personal property or real estate is sufficient whether or not it is specific if it reasonably identifies what is described." 810 ILCS 5/9-110 (1992) (emphasis added). If NBD's entire description of collateral reasonably identifies "parts", no further inquiry is required.

Section 9-203 requires that an enforceable security agreement contain a "description" of the collateral, as defined by § 9-110. See 810 ILCS 5/9-110, 5/9-203 (1992). The description of collateral in NBD's security agreement is not ambiguous.[4] NBD, the Debtor's floor-planning financier, took a blanket security interest in the Debtor's personal property-the language covers several specific types of collateral and contains a catch-all for any other type of personal property. The Commercial Code requires reasonable identification, not exactitude. Therefore, in this case, the listing of several specific types of automobile dealership property (including "accessories"), coupled with a protective clause for any other kind of personal property not listed, reasonably identifies "parts". See generally *Midkiff Implement Co. v. Worrall*, 116 Ill. App.3d 546, 71 Ill.

[3] Notwithstanding Success' protestations to the contrary, NBD's collateral description is not "all personal property". Rather, it covers "all other personal property", a clause that must be read together with the remainder of the collateral description.

[4] Success' attempt to create a question of "intent" also must fail. Success claims that: (1) the NBD security agreement expressly adopted all Commercial Code definitions, (2) the Commercial Code definition of "inventory", if unaltered, could include "parts" and (3) NBD's definition of "Inventory" purposely varies from the Commercial Code definition and does not encompass "parts". In addition to the fact that Success' security agreement also classified "parts" separate from "inventory", the first essential premise to Success' argument is incorrect. NBD's security agreement specifically defines "Inventory" and then provides that "[a]ll other terms" shall have Commercial Code meanings. This is the second example of Success reading the word "other" out of NBD's security agreement . . .

Dec. 655, 451 N.E.2d 623 (Ill. App. 4th Dist. 1983). Ejusdem generis, the venerable canon of contract construction, buttresses this conclusion.

The financing statement also must contain a reasonable identification of collateral. 810 ILCS 5/9-110, 5/9-402 (1992). The function of a financing statement is "only to provide enough notice so that other creditors will make further inquiry to determine the nature and extent of security interests in the debtor's collateral." *Chrysler Credit Corp. v. Knebel Chevrolet-Buick*, 976 F.2d 1012, 1014 (7th Cir. 1992), quoting *Citizens Nat'l Bank v. Wedel*, 489 N.E.2d 1203, 1208 (Ind. App. 1986). NBD's financing statement tracks the language of paragraph 5(e) of its security agreement. No reasonable creditor could read the entire description of NBD's collateral and definitively conclude that the Debtor's parts were unencumbered. At the least, a prudent lender seeking a prior lien on parts would ask NBD and seek a release or subordination agreement from NBD.

For the foregoing reasons, this Court has denied Success' motion for partial summary judgment.

QUESTION

Can the results in the *Park Ridge Bank* and *Techno Products* cases be reconciled? Do you agree with the Park Ridge court that § 9-110 allows very broad descriptions? Should the statute be interpreted narrowly? What are the implications of such a decision?

PROBLEM 16.2

Your client, LM Bank, Ltd., has made some large loans to the new Olympiad Shoe Store and taken a security interest "in all its inventory." Bank client also properly filed a financing statement. The Olympiad Shoe Store did very well initially with the impending Olympic games and other major sports events, later it was unable to sell many of its sport shoes and became insolvent. The other creditors are now contesting the security interest of your client claiming that the description is inadequate. What is the Code criteria and what arguments would you make? Olympiad's other creditors argue that even if the court holds the description to be adequate, the security interest applies only to the inventory current at the time the loan was made, and not to any future inventory. How should the court decide?

[F] Rights in Collateral

Until this point, we have focused principally on § 9-203(1)(a)'s requirements for creating a valid security agreement. Section 9-203(1)(c) provides that the security interest does not become effective (*i.e.*, "attach") unless the debtor also has rights in the collateral. In many debtor-creditor relationships, the creditor checks to see if other persons might claim interests in potential collateral before finalizing the arrangement and advancing funds. Article 9 permits such action because a filed financing statement only serves to place others on notice that there might be a claim on certain property of a debtor. The real secured transaction relationship begins only after all of the 9-203 requirements are met and the security interest attaches. Frequently, the last event to occur before attachment is the debtor's acquisition of rights in collateral.

Article 9 does not define the phrase "rights in the collateral". A debtor who has less than full or complete ownership of collateral may nonetheless have sufficient rights in collateral to create a security interest. Where the line between ownership and mere possession should be drawn is a conceptual quagmire. Courts find rights in collateral through many different theories; agency, fraud, and estoppel are some examples.

The debtor can obtain such power by traditional bodies of law as noted in U.C.C. § 1-103 or through specific Code provisions. In *Swets Motor Sales, Inc. v. Pruisner*, 236 N.W.2d 299 (Iowa 1975), Swets sold cars to Pruisner, a retailer. Swets took a security interest in the cars sold to Pruisner. Pruisner had also given a security interest in all of its inventory presently owned or to be acquired in the future, to the Chrysler Corporation as another supplier of cars (this type of all-encompassing security interest is known as a floating lien; see § 16.03 infra). Pruisner paid for the Swets cars with bad checks. Swets sought a court declaration that its interest was superior to Chrysler's because Pruisner allegedly had no rights in collateral to grant Chrysler a security interest in the cars Swets sold to Pruisner. The Iowa Supreme Court held that § 2-403(1)(b) (now § 2-403(2)) gave Pruisner the "power" to pass good title to a good faith purchaser even where Pruisner paid for the items with a bad check. Because Pruisner had the power to convey voidable title under Article 2, the court found that he had sufficient rights in the collateral to grant Chrysler a valid security interest.

We will study more about rights in collateral when we discuss priorities in Chapter 17. For now, note that the concept is an elusive one. Consider the following case and whether the phrase "rights in collateral" appropriately describes the idea.

TRUST COMPANY BANK v. The GLOUCESTER CORPORATION

Massachusetts Supreme Judicial Court
643 N.E.2d 16, 419 Mass. 48, 25 U.C.C. Rep. Serv. 2d 62 (1994)

GREANEY, JUSTICE.

The facts in this case are undisputed. On December 19, 1991, Sigma International, Inc. (Sigma), agreed to sell seafood to the Gloucester Corporation (Gloucester). On January 16, 1992, Sigma delivered to Gloucester under the agreement a quantity of scallops worth $143,391. The invoice from Sigma stated that the sale was "pending FDA release," and included a payment term of "net 30 days from FDA release date." The invoice also assigned Sigma's rights in Gloucester's account to the plaintiff, Trust Company Bank. On January 24, 1992, the defendants, Fleet National Bank and Cooperative Central Raiffeisen-Boerenleenbank, B.A., banks which held duly perfected security interests in all of Gloucester's tangible and intangible personal property, including after-acquired property, determined that Gloucester was in default, and seized and liquidated all of Gloucester's inventory, including the scallops.

The plaintiff commenced an action in the Superior Court against Gloucester and the defendants. As far as now relevant, the plaintiff sought to recover damages from the defendants for conversion of the scallops. On that claim, the defendants moved for summary judgment under Mass.R.Civ.P. 56(b), 365 Mass. 824 (1974), contending that they had enforceable security interests in all of Gloucester's assets pursuant to G.L. c. 106, § 9-203 (1992 ed.).[5] It was undisputed that the

[5] General Laws c. 106, § 9-203 (1992 ed.), provides in part as follows: "(1) Subject to the provisions of [three statutes which are not applicable to this case], a security interest is not enforceable against the debtor or third parties

defendants had met the requirements of § 9-203(1)(a) and (b), and the defendants maintained that they were entitled to judgment, as matter of law, on the requirement contained in § 9-203(1)(c), namely that, under the sales agreement between Gloucester and Sigma, Gloucester had acquired "rights in the collateral." A judge of the Superior Court denied the defendants' motion for summary judgment, and they moved for reconsideration. The plaintiff opposed the defendants' motion for reconsideration, and filed its own motion for summary judgment pursuant to Mass.R.Civ.P. 56(a), 365 Mass. 824 (1974). The judge allowed the defendants' motion for reconsideration, and, after reconsideration, allowed the defendants' motion for summary judgment. The plaintiff has appealed from the judgment in favor of the defendants, and we transferred the case to this court on our own motion. We now affirm the judgment.

The plaintiff argues that the defendants' security interests could not attach to the scallops, and thus were subordinate to its rights as Sigma's assignee, because Gloucester could not acquire "rights in the collateral" under G.L. c. 106, § 9-203(1)(c), before obtaining "FDA release" of the scallops. We disagree.

The term "rights in the collateral" is not defined in the Uniform Commercial Code, and there is no relevant Massachusetts case law discussing the term. Authority from other jurisdictions, however, has defined the term broadly. While a debtor's mere possession of goods usually is not enough to satisfy the "rights in the collateral" requirement of § 9-203(1)(c), "[t]he cases generally hold . . . that where a debtor gains possession of collateral pursuant to an agreement endowing him with any interest other than naked possession, the debtor has acquired such rights as would allow [a] security interest to attach" under § 9-203. . . . Consistent with this standard, it has been held that, a debtor's possession of goods with contingent rights of ownership, gives the debtor "rights in the collateral." . . . If the goods are entirely owned by a third party, mere acquisition of possession by the debtor will not be enough. But there are intermediate cases in which the debtor acquires less than full ownership and courts hold that this is enough for attachment [to the extent of the value of the rights]. It follows that almost any "rights in the collateral" will suffice under 9-203."[6]

The delivery of the scallops by Sigma to Gloucester pursuant to their sales agreement gave Gloucester "rights in the collateral" for purposes of G.L. c. 106, § 9-203(1)(c). Those rights arose under art. 2 of the Uniform Commercial Code governing sales.[7] General Laws c. 106, §2-501(1) (1992 ed.), recognizes that, from the moment goods are identified to a contract of sale, the buyer has "a special property and an insurable interest." Here, the scallops had been delivered pursuant

---

with respect to the collateral and does not attach unless: (a) the collateral is in the possession of the secured party pursuant to agreement, or the debtor has signed a security agreement which contains a description of the collateral and in addition, when the security interest covers crops growing or to be grown or timber to be cut, a description of the land concerned; (b) value has been given; and (c) the debtor has rights in the collateral."

[6] The plaintiff relies on *In re McFarland*, 131 B.R. 627 (Bankr.E.D.Tenn.1990), aff'd without opinion, 943 F.2d 52 (6th Cir.1991), to support its argument that, the defendants' security interests could not attach prior to "FDA release" of the scallops. The *McFarland* case involved the sale of two automobiles that was contingent on the purchasers receiving financing. The court held that the purchasers did not acquire sufficient rights in the collateral, even though they drove off in the automobiles after the parties had signed the contract. *Id.* at 631–632. This case, however, is inapposite because, under the sales contract, the purchasers were not entitled to even possessory rights in the automobiles. *Id.* Rather, they received possession of the collateral only because the dealer, for whatever reason, allowed them to have the automobiles before financing was obtained.

[7] When the security interest relates to a sale of goods, art. 2 determines whether a debtor has rights. See 8 Anderson, Uniform Commercial Code § 9-203:44, at 688 (3d ed. 1985); *Johnson v. Conrail-Amtrak Federal Credit Union,* 37 U.C.C. Rep. Serv. (Callaghan) 933, 942 (D.C. Super. 1983); *Manger v. Davis*, 619 P.2d 687, 690 (Utah 1980).

to an agreement of sale that made sale and payment subject to inspection by a government agency. That condition, if not satisfied, might have relieved Gloucester of its obligation to pay, but the condition did not negate the existence of an actual sales agreement between Gloucester and Sigma.[8] Gloucester had acquired a degree of control and authority over the scallops as well as "a special property and an insurable interest" in them under § 2-501(1). These incidents were sufficient to allow the defendants' security interests to attach to the scallops and to make the plaintiff's rights subordinate to the defendants' liens in the absence of the plaintiff having a perfected purchase money security interest. See G.L. c. 106, §§ 9-107, 9-303, 9-312(3) (1992 ed.). We view this result as comporting with the goal of art. 9, to promote efficiency and certainty in secured financing transactions. See Official Comment to § 9-101, 3 U.L.A. 60-61(Master ed. 1992). Otherwise, if a buyer, like Gloucester is determined to lack "rights in the collateral," a creditor's valid security interest covering the goods constituting the collateral could be "defeated by the sort of hidden-title subterfuge the Code was intended to prevent." . . ..

Judgment affirmed.

COMMENT

Can you think of a different definition to explain the concept of rights in collateral? How would you revise the Code to illustrate the concept? Perhaps the phrase "rights in collateral" is really misleading; all a debtor need have is the "power" to create a security interest.

[G] Possession of Collateral as a Security Agreement Alternative

The Code makes an exception to the writing requirement in cases where the collateral remains in possession of the secured party or creditor. The reason for the exception is that the evidentiary need for a written record is much less where the collateral is in the possession of the creditor. However, it is rare that the creditor retains possession. Generally, the debtor prefers to keep possession of the collateral for the debtor's own purposes. We will explore possession of collateral in subsequent chapters.

§ 16.03 After-Acquired Property

Read: U.C.C. § 9-204(1),(2).

The secured creditor may not only take a security interest in existing property of the debtor, but may also obtain an interest in property the debtor acquires at a later date. The security device which permits the creditor to tie up property in this fashion is called an after-acquired property clause. After-acquired property clauses are also known as "floating liens" because the security interest (lien) applies to (floats over) any property the debtor has at a given time.

---

[8] The role of title is not significant to the analysis. The Uniform Commercial Code emphasizes that the concept of "title" is immaterial to whether a security interest attaches. See the Official Comment to § 9-101, 3 U.L.A. 60-61(Master ed. 1992). In addition, G.L. c. 106, § 2-401(1) (1992 ed.), provides that "[a]ny retention or reservation by the seller of the title (property) in goods shipped or delivered to the buyer is limited in effect to a reservation of a security interest."

The Code does not define the term "after-acquired property." Consequently, such a clause may be drafted in broad fashion requiring only some reasonable identification of the property covered. After-acquired property clauses may be used with various types of collateral but are absolutely essential for inventory. Without the use of such a clause, a creditor's security interest would extend only to inventory a debtor held at the start of a loan; that existing inventory would disappear as the debtor sold inventory and replaced it with new inventory. Without an after-acquired property clause, the secured creditor would be left with little or no collateral even though the debtor maintained a relatively constant level of inventory. Use of the clause allows creditors to look to future assets of the debtor in default — to satisfy an obligation that goes into default. One example of an after-acquired property clause follows: "All inventory and stock in trade of the XYZ Pharmacy, consisting of drugs, pharmaceutical, patent medicines, toiletries, novelties, and all other products offered for sale by the debtor, whether now in the possession of the debtor or hereafter acquired by way of replacement, substitution or addition." In terms of after-acquired property, descriptive terms such as replacement, substitution, or addition, or a more general term of "all after-acquired property" should generally be adequate. If a valid after-acquired property clause exists in a security agreement, no further action on the part of the secured party is necessary for the lien to reach similar types of property held by the debtor.

Given the power of after-acquired property clauses to provide a creditor with the opportunity to tie up a debtor's future property, it goes without saying that the potential for abuse of such clauses exists. It doesn't take a genius of a creditor to ask, "why not include an after-acquired property clause in every financing deal?" Indeed, most commercial arrangements include this type of security device, thus providing a form of monopoly relationship with a debtor. The word "monopoly" frightens many people, including judges and lawmakers. Courts often monitor after-acquired property clauses with respect to reasonableness. The drafters of the Code limited the power of such clauses by prohibiting their use in security arrangements for consumer goods. Subsection 2 of § 9-204 provides that "[n]o security interest attaches under an after-acquired property clause to consumer goods . . . when given as additional security unless the debtor acquires rights in them within ten days after the secured party gives value."

Query, does this limitation succeed in limiting a creditor's monopoly power over a debtor? What consequenses flow from such a creditor monopoly?

§ 16.04 Future Advances

Read: U.C.C. § 9-204(3).

Commercial borrowers frequently need more money to operate. Often, they return to the original lender seeking such additional financing. In anticipation of such long-term relationships, many creditors will insert language in the original loan documents and security agreement which provides that any future loan will be secured by the original collateral. The Code recognizes the validity of these future advance clauses. Just as the after-acquired property clause enables a creditor to reach additional collateral, the future advance clause permits that creditor to secure future loans to the debtor with the original collateral. Such clauses may provide for mandatory future advances or for optional ones; such advances will be effective against intervening creditors. The economic status of the debtor may be unpredictable and the lender may not want to commit to mandatory future advances. The unpredictability of both the lender and borrower's economic condition and other opportunities may also militate against such a firm commitment. Like the after-acquired property clause, the future advance provision enables the creditor to go a long way toward monopolizing the credit relationship with the debtor. Should the law seek to limit the use of such clauses? What dangers are associated with the future advance clause?

In addition to understanding the function of the after-acquired property clause or floating lien, one might better analyze the cases by noting some history and policies.

King, POLICY DECISIONS AND SECURITY AGREEMENTS UNDER THE UNIFORM COMMERCIAL CODE

9 Wayne L. Rev. 957 (1963)[9]

One of the major battles has centered around the floating lien, and some of the attributes of allowing the security interest to apply to after-acquired property. The exact content of the floating lien is not a subject of general agreement. Like the six Hindustani blind men who examined the elephant, it means different things to different persons. Speaking generally, however, it "floats" over a particular portion of the debtor's business where goods flow in and out or over goods in the process of change. Thus, the lien or secured interest floats over the shifting stock of goods, and is of extreme importance in the manufacturing area where the secured interest must follow the collateral through changing stages of development manufacture, and sales. While the floating lien has many aspects, the after-acquired property allowance is perhaps the key one. Under such a clause, a secured interest may be kept in a shifting stock of inventory in which goods are constantly going through the process of being acquired or sold. Further, many of the objections voiced against the floating lien are in fact objections to the after-acquired property aspects of it. Therefore, both the floating lien and after-acquired property clauses are considered in this portion. Other provisions of the Code which indirectly relate to the floating lien problem, such as the problems of dominion and control and future advances will be discussed later in light of the specific struggles centered around them.

While the battle has become more intense in recent years, its roots may be found in the bias of 19th century courts against the floating lien. One of the main bases of this opposition rested upon the conceptualistic notion that one could not pass title to what one did not then own. This argument found support in early cases which expressed the view that a conveyance of property not in existence at the time of the conveyance is "void at law" simply because there is nothing to convey. In order to alleviate the harshness of this rule, some courts permitted principles of equity to operate and hence gave certain protection to the party with a security interest in after-acquired property. Some jurisdictions, however, never accepted this theory where intervening creditors existed.

Another slightly more sophisticated argument, however, was soon to be advanced by opponents of the lien. This centered around the economic argument that the secured interest party thereby forced the debtor to tie up all of his assets and hence held a monopoly over his credit. A closely related criticism of the floating lien concerned its effect on other creditors. It has been observed that at least part of the wide-spread prejudice of the past century against the floating lien was

---

the feeling of the courts, often inarticulate, that a cushion of free assets should be preserve for other creditors.

On the other side, advocates of the floating lien have fought this judicial prejudice and the arguments of its opponents. Perhaps the brunt of the attack favoring the floating lien has been the necessity of having an instrument which fits the needs of business. Thus, it has been argued that legal provisions favoring floating liens on inventory and accounts receivable enable business without much capital to get started, facilitate expansion of existing businesses, and permit temporary financing of seasonal goods purchases in advance. Further, the filing of statements as a practical matter is not feasible in light of the multiplicity of acquisitions and sales.

One of the early decisions of the drafters of the Code was to validate the use of after-acquired property clauses. Thus, in the 1950 draft many provisions are found which recognize such clauses as being a legitimate legal device. While it does this in a somewhat indirect manner in the text, the comments to the Code make clear the intent of the drafters. This position continued in the 1952 draft, which first became law in Pennsylvania.

Perhaps one of the most effective points made by the advocates of the floating lien was that under the Code there would be no tendency towards a complete monopoly through the floating lien since a second lender could enter the picture provided it was a purchase money security interest transaction. Credit for the debtor, therefore, is not completely cut off and he is able to finance the acquisition of new purchases in order to effectively carry on his business. The purchase money security interest is thus one limitation on the floating lien and takes priority over it.

A lesser, but noteworthy battle was fought in the area relating to future advances. While the validity of future advance clauses has generally been recognized by statute or case law, certai problems existed in relation to the rights of subsequent lenders or creditors. In most cases i has been held that future advances made after the execution of recording of a subsequent secure interest-but without actual notice of it-take precedence. But considerable difference of judici opinion exists where it is not mandatory in the agreement that the lender make future advance

On one hand, it was contended that the future advance made under an optional clause shou not be given priority over the intervening creditor. Several reasons were given. One was very conceptualistic argument that the secured party making the optional future advance sho not expect the "benefits of a contract which, from prudential or other considerations, they unwilling to make, and did not make until after the rights of other parties had intervened." U this rationale, the future advance is a "new debt" and should be treated as a new contract. Anc argument related to the burden of searching the records. Some courts feel that there is no re why the secured party making the future advance should not have to examine the recor see if there is any intervening encumbrance. They are of the opinion that this burden is negli and affords the secured party adequate protection.

On the other hand, it has been argued that the intervening lender or creditor may searc record and hence obtain notice of the possibility of future advances, therefore the interv creditor should not be given priority.

More significantly, however, the advocates of the optional future advance clause have their argument upon the business utility of such clauses. While it may be known that some will be needed by the debtor in the future, the amount may be quite uncertain. Moreov particular economic or business status of the debtor may be unpredictable and the original may hesitate to obligate himself in advance. Nevertheless, the optional future adva economic advantages since often the interest rate and financing charges on loans covered by such clauses will be less than those connected with Separate loans whenever additional funds are needed.

The drafters of the Code took a position which validated the future advance clause and permitted it to be effective as against intervening creditors even though optional. It is expressly provided that the security agreement "may include future advances . . . whether or not the advances or value are given pursuant to commitment." The drafters took cognizance of the judicial decisions opposing the optional future advance and placing specific restrictions as to amount and time on it, and rejected this body of law. The Code's validation of the optional future advance clause tends to make financing easier and makes the floating lien concept a more effective device. Not only can a changing stock of goods be covered under the security agreements, but advances in the future, which may later be found necessary to supplement the original loan, can be made without losing priority. It is clear that the general policy of the drafters favoring the floating lien was a major reason for its inclusion.

The optional future advance clause is an important legal device with which the lawyer should become familiar. It makes it possible for the lender to make an original loan which can later be supplemented should the need arise. Neither definite times nor amounts are required. The optional advances need only be mentioned in a clause of the original agreements. For purposes of priority, the future advance relates back to the original security agreement date. One word of caution, however, should be added. The purchase money security interest will have priority over the security interests of the future advances. This, however, is consistent with the general policy of the Code favoring purchase money security interests and also prevails in the area relating to after-acquired property.

Consider Professor King's comments when reading the following case.

IN RE STANNISH
STANNISH v. COMMUNITY BANK OF HOMEWOOD-FLOSSMOOR

Bankruptcy Court, Northern District of Illinois
24 B.R. 761, 35 U.C.C. Rep. Serv. 235 (1982)

ROBERT L. EISEN, BANKRUPTCY JUDGE.

This matter came to be heard on Community Bank of Homewood-Flossmoor's motion for summary judgment as to the secured status of three loans extended to the debtors, Michael Stannish and Margaret Stannish, by Community Bank and one by General Finance Corporation. The court having carefully considered the memoranda filed by the parties, and being fully advised the premises, does hereby find Community Bank to have a valid secured claim in the value the 1981 Pontiac Phoenix and a valid unsecured claim for the excess, if any . . ..

FINDINGS OF FACT

Community Bank holds three separate debt instruments signed by the debtors. The first instrument entitled a "Check Credit Account Agreement," was dated May 1, 1976. It created a line of credit which could be drawn upon by the debtors with special checks. The line of credi also provided coverage for checking account overdrafts. The balance due on this agreement was $ 1,454.20 on January 4,1982, the date on which the debtors filed their Chapter 7 petition.

The second instrument is a note and security agreement, dated July 21, 1980. This instrument reflects a purchase money loan of $3,600.00, plus credit insurance premiums. The instrument is also a security agreement, identifying a new 1980 Pontiac Phoenix as collateral. The agreement contains the following relevant language in number three of its terms and conditions:

> Debtor(s) agrees that Holder shall have, and there is hereby created in favor of Holder a security interest in the Collateral described herein to secure (I) the payment of the debt evidenced hereby, . . . and (iv) all other past, present and future, direct or contingent liabilities of Debtor(s) to Holder. The Holder shall have the right of set-off against any deposits and other sums which may now or in the future be owing by the Holder to the Debtor(s).

As part of the explanatory language on the first page of the agreement, the following is found after the words "Security Interest":

> This loan is secured by a security interest created under this Security Agreement in the property described above which security interest may attach to any accessions thereto. In addition to the foregoing security the Holder has a security interest for the payment of all obligations due it in all property and assets of Debtor(s) which are in the possession or control of Holder and a right of set-off or lien on any deposit or sums now or hereafter owed by Holder to Debtor(s). Holder has a security interest in the proceeds and the unearned premiums in any insurance required or purchased. This security agreement will secure future or other indebtedness.

The title to the Phoenix is in the possession of Community Bank which is listed as the first lien-holder on the face of the title. The balance at the time of the bankruptcy filing was $2,768.39. Debtors continued to make monthly payments of $ 112.23 as of the time the motion for summary judgment was filed on June 8, 1982 and therefore, the balance due was decreasing each month.

The third instrument is an installment note, dated August 9, 1980, for a $ 1,000.00 loan to debtors. The balance due on this note at the time of the petition was $654.46.

On November 24, 1980, General Finance Corporation loaned the debtors $2,233.87 which was also secured by the Phoenix automobile. General Finance is listed on the car's title as the second lienholder.

DISCUSSION

The issue before the court is whether Community Bank may use the value of the car in excess of the amount owed the bank on the purchase money loan to set off unpaid amounts remaining on other loans extended from Community Bank to the debtor.

The note and security agreement for the purchase money loan on the car contains language as quoted above which secures prior amounts owed and future advances with the collateral securing the purchase money loan. This clause, referred to as a "dragnet" clause is commodity found in security agreements and is not favored under Illinois law. . . . Dragnet clauses will be upheld, however, where no ambiguity exists and will be interpreted according to the language used. The law presumes the parties intended the agreement to mean what the language clearly imports.

The Uniform Commercial Code provides that a secured agreement may cover future advances without an additional agreement. Code § 9-201 states that "Except as otherwise provided by this Act a security agreement is effective according to its terms between the parties, against purchasers of the collateral and against creditors." Ill Rev. Stat. 1981, ch. 26 § 9-201. Section 9-204 provides that such a security agreement may secure "future advances or other value whether or not the advances or value are given pursuant to commitment." Illinois Rev Stat 1981, Ch 26, § 9-204(3).

In a situation similar to the one at issue here, the Second Circuit applied the Commercial Code and similar New York state common law to find that a dragnet clause in a chattel mortgage extended the value in mortgagor's equipment to security for the note as well as for payments of any obligation or liability due or to become due whether existing or subsequently arising. The security agreement encompassed a contemporaneously made real estate bond and mortgage and hence, also covered debt arising from default on foreclosure of the real estate mortgage. Thus, the mortgagee was entitled to priority over federal tax liens as a result of the dragnet clause.

The Second Circuit based its holding on the character and priority of the debtor's debts on relevant state common law and statutes. The specific clause at issue, which is similar to the clause before this court was found to be clear and unambiguous and therefore would be effective and sufficient to put a subsequent creditor on notice. *Id.* at 1213.

In the present case, the language found in the Note and Security Agreement is also clear and unambiguous. The language of the agreement clearly states that: "[t]he Holder shall have the right of set-off against any deposits and other sums which may now or in the future be owing by the Holder to the Debtor(s)"; and in the explanatory portion of the agreement, that "[T]his Security Agreement will secure future or other indebtedness." General Finance Corporation, the subsequent creditor, clearly was or should have been on notice of the Bank's position when it read the note and security agreement which listed the 1980 Pontiac Phoenix as collateral. As a result, General Finance Corporation's position is junior to the bank's in all respects. General Finance should have realized that it did not have a reasonable chance of recovering on its loan to the debtors. The language of the agreement made it clear that Community Bank could use the automobile as security for any past or future advances it made to the debtor.

. . . .

CONCLUSIONS OF LAW

It is well established that clear and unambiguous security agreement clauses extending the collateral to secure past and future advances are valid under common law and the Uniform Commercial Code. Clearly, the clause in question here was clear and unambiguous and provided sufficient notice to the subsequent creditor, General Finance, that their security interest in the 1980 Pontiac Phoenix was secondary to any other obligations the debtor owed to Community Bank.

. . . .

Therefore, it is hereby ordered that defendant's motion for summary judgment is granted as defendants have a valid security in the Pontiac Phoenix and have priority over any interest held by General Finance in the same collateral.

NOTE

In *Stannish,* the future advance clause was clear. What result if the future advance is not so clear cut? Assume that a debtor has several dealings with a particular creditor. If the original loan documentation contains a broad future advance clause, can all of the debts associated with the various dealings be covered by the future advance language (*i.e.*, does the creditor become a secured party as to all of the debts owed it via the future advance clause?)? What if the security agreement contains NO future advance clause, but a perfected secured party nonetheless makes an additional advance? Is that advance secured? See § 9–312(7). There are a number of other questions generated by the use of future advance and after-acquired property provisions. We will address some of those issues in subsequent chapters.

§ 16.05 Goods in Process and Proceeds

Read: U.C.C. §§ 9-315& 9-306.

Under U.C.C. § 9-315, a security interest may be taken in goods at any stage in the production process. The interest follows the goods through manufacturing and attaches to the final product. In addition, the secured party has a security interest in the identifiable proceeds of any sale or disposition of the covered collateral. U.C.C. § 9-306. While the security agreement's description of collateral may be drafted to include proceeds, even if there is no mention of proceeds, the Code makes coverage automatic, so long as the proceeds are identifiable. U.C.C. § 9-306(2). There are several theories for permitting a secured party's interest to reach proceeds: (1) the property was received in substitution and the security interest therefore attached to it; (2) the proceeds were held by the debtor in trust for the secured party; or (3) the debtor held the proceeds as an "agent" of the secured party. Under any of these theories, so long as the secured party can trace its original security interest to specific proceeds, she may claim an interest in them, even as against a trustee in bankruptcy.

§ 16.06 Secured Interests, Freedom of Contract, and Limitations on Such Freedom

Read: U.C.C. § 1-102(3).

The doctrine of freedom of contract remains a basic principle of the Code. As stated in U.C.C. § 1-102(3):

> (3) The effect of provisions of this Act may be varied by agreement, except as otherwise provided in this Act and except that the obligations of good faith, diligence, reasonableness and care prescribed by this Act may not be disclaimed by agreement but the parties may by agreement determine the standards by which the performance of such obligations is to be measured if such standards are not manifestly unreasonable.

Though the doctrine is a basic principle, it may be limited by general principles of good faith and fair dealing. In addition, the unconscionability principle set forth in Article 2 of the Code dealing with the sale of goods may be applied by analogy to secured interests in Article 9. The same policies of preventing oppression and harsh terms are present in the secured transaction context. Consider the following case as one example.

K.M.C. CO. INC. v. IRVING TRUST CO.

United States Court of Appeals
757 F.2d 752 (6th Cir. 1985)

CORNELIA G. KENNEDY, CIRCUIT JUDGE.

Irving Trust Company (Irving) appeals from a judgment entered against it in this diversity action for breach of a financing agreement. K.M.C. is a Tennessee corporation headquartered in Knoxville and engaged in the wholesale and retail grocery business. In 1979, Irving and K.M.C. entered into a financing agreement, whereby Irving held a security interest in all of K.M.C.'s accounts receivable and inventory and provided K.M.C. a line of credit to a maximum of $3.0 million, increased one year later to $3.5 million at a lower rate of interest, subject to a formula based on a percentage of the value of the inventory plus eligible receivables. On March 1, 1982, Irving refused to advance $800,000 requested by K.M.C. This amount would have increased the loan balance to just under the $3.5 million limit. K.M.C. contends that Irving's refusal without prior notice to advance the requested funds breached a duty of good faith performance implied in the agreement and ultimately resulted in the collapse of the company as a viable business entity. Irving's defense is that on March 1, 1982, K.M.C. was already collapsing, and that Irving's decision not to advance funds was made in good faith and in the reasonable exercise of its discretion under the agreement. . ..

III. Liability

Irving contends that the Magistrate erred in instructing the jury with respect to its obligations under the financing agreement, that K.M.C. failed to sustain its burden of showing that Irving acted in bad faith and that the jury's verdict was against the weight of the evidence. We conclude that the jury instructions were not in error and that the jury's verdict was supported by substantial evidence.

A. Instructions

The essence of the Magistrate's instruction to the jury was that there is implied in every contract an obligation of good faith; that this obligation may have imposed on Irving a duty to give notice to K.M.C. before refusing to advance funds under the agreement up to the $3.5 million limit; and that such notice would be required if necessary to the proper execution of the contract, unless Irving's decision to refuse to advance funds without prior notice was made in good faith and in the reasonable exercise of its discretion. Irving contends that the instruction with respect to notice gave undue emphasis to K.M.C.'s theory of the case and was an erroneous explanation of its contractual obligations, in that the decision whether to advance funds under the financing agreement was solely within the bank's prerogative. It reasons further than an implied requirement that the bank provide a period of notice before discontinuing financing up to the maximum credit limit would be inconsistent with the provision in the agreement that all monies loaned are repayable on demand.

As part of the procedure established for the operation of the financing agreement, the parties agreed in a supplementary letter that all receipts of K.M.C. would be deposited into a "blocked account" to which Irving would have sole access. Consequently, unless K.M.C. obtained alternative financing, a refusal by Irving to advance funds would leave K.M.C. without operating capital until it had paid down its loan. The record clearly established that a medium-sized company in the wholesale grocery business, such as K.M.C., could not operate without outside financing. Thus, the literal interpretation of the financing agreement urged upon us by Irving, as supplemented by the "blocked account" mechanism, would leave K.M.C.'s continued existence entirely at the whim or mercy of Irving, absent an obligation of good faith performance. Logically, at such time as Irving might wish to curtail financing K.M.C., as was its right under the agreement, this obligation to act in good faith would require a period of notice to K.M.C. to allow it a reasonable opportunity to seek alternate financing, absent valid business reasons precluding Irving from doing so. Hence, we find that the Magistrate's instructions were an accurate statement of the applicable law. See *Wells v. Alexander*, 130 N.Y. 642, 29 N.E. 142, 143 (1891) ("[I]f a notice was requisite to its proper execution, a covenant to give such notice will be inferred, for any other construction would make the contract unreasonable, and place one of the parties entirely at the mercy of the other." (citations omitted)); cf. U.C.C. § 2-309 comment 8 ("[T]he application of principles of good faith and sound commercial practice normally call for such notification of the termination of a going contract relationship as will give the other party reasonable time to seek a substitute arrangement.").

Irving cites *Grandin Industries, Inc. v. Florida National Bank*, 267 So.2d 26 (Dist. Ct. App. Fla. 1972), and *Midlantic National Bank v. Commonwealth General, Ltd.*, 386 So.2d 31 (Dist. Ct. App. Fla. 1980), for the proposition that it had no legal obligation to advance funds under the financing agreement. These cases are distinguishable on a number of grounds. First, in neither case did the Florida court consider the possibility of a good faith limitation on the bank's discretion. Nor is it clear that the exercise of absolute discretion under the agreements in question conferred on the banks the same power over the continued existence of the debtors as in the instant case. Second, in neither case had there been a consistent and uninterrupted course of dealing between the parties over an extended period of time as in the instant case. It does not appear that the agreement in *Grandin* established any specific line of credit or eligibility formula, or that the ongoing financing of a high volume, capital intensive business was contemplated. *Midlantic* involved a line of credit secured by personal certificates of deposit, for which there was no written agreement and which was merely supplementary to numerous loans already outstanding from the bank to the debtor. Finally, we note that the Irving-K.M.C. agreement is governed by New York law. To the extent that our decision may be inconsistent with *Grandin* and *Midlantic*, we find them not to be controlling.

Nor are we persuaded by Irving's reasoning with respect to the effect of the demand provision in the agreement. We agree with the Magistrate that just as Irving's discretion whether or not to advance funds is limited by an obligation of good faith performance, so too would be its power to demand repayment. The demand provision is a kind of acceleration clause, upon which the Uniform Commercial Code and the courts have imposed limitations of reasonableness and fairness. See U.C.C. § 1-208; *Brown v. AVEMCO Investment Corp.*, 603 F.2d 1367, 1375-80 (9th Cir. 1979). The Magistrate did not err in refusing the requested charge on the demand provision.

Irving did not object to the good faith portion of the Magistrate's instruction. Nevertheless, on appeal it suggests for the first time that before liability can be imposed, the proof must establish not only abuse of discretion but also bad faith, which it defines as synonymous with dishonesty. Even if such an argument were timely at this stage in the proceedings, which it is not, none of the cases cited by Irving are on point. In *Awrey v. Progressive Casualty Insurance Co.*, 728 F.2d 352 (6th Cir. 1984), and *Gordon v. Nationwide Mutual Insurance Co.*, 30 N.Y.,2d 427, 334 N.Y.S.2d 601, 285 N.E.2d 849 (1972), the courts held that a showing of actual bad faith would be necessary in the limited situation in which an insured sought to impose liability on an insurer on excess of policy limits. In fact, in *Gordon* the court specifically restates the familiar principle that "[i]n every contract "there exists an implied covenant of good faith and fair dealing" (*Kirke La Shelle Co. v. Armstrong Co.*, 263 N.Y. 79, 87, 188 N.E. 163, 167)." 30 N.Y.2d at 437, 334 N.Y.S.2d at 608, 285 N.E.2d at 856. . ..

Irving contends that the sole factor determinative of whether it acted in good faith is whether it, through its loan officer Sarokin, believed that there existed valid reasons for not advancing funds to K.M.C. on March 1, 1982. It quotes *Blaine v. G.M.A.C.*, 82 Misc.2d 653, 655, 370 N.Y.S.2d 323, 327 (1975), for the proposition that under applicable New York law, it is the bank's "actual mental state" that is decisive. The Magistrate observed that there was competent evidence that a personality conflict had developed between Sarokin and Butler of K.M.C. He suggested that the jury may have concluded that Sarokin abused his discretion in refusing without notice to advance funds despite knowing that he was fully secured because of his disapproval of Butler's management philosophy.

Were the outcome of this case solely dependent upon Sarokin's subjective state of mind, we might feel constrained, despite the conclusions of the Magistrate above, to hold that the evidence was insufficient to support the verdict. However, to a certain extent the conduct of Irving must be measured by objective standards. While it is not necessary that Sarokin have been correct in his understanding of the facts and circumstances pertinent to his decision not to advance funds for this court to find that he made a valid business judgment in doing so, there must at least be some objective basis upon which a reasonable loan officer in the exercise of his discretion would have acted in that manner.[10] The court in *Blaine* did state that:

> [T]he test as to the good faith of the creditor in accelerating under an insecurity clause is a matter of the creditor's actual mental state and this is not negatived by showing there was no basis for the creditor's belief, *Sheppard Federal Credit Union v. Palmer* [408 F.2d 1369 (5th Cir. 1969)], supra, and it is immaterial whether the information upon which the creditor based his determination was in fact not true or the creditor was negligent in not examining to determine whether it was true. *VanHorn v. Van de Wol*, Inc., 6 Wash. App. 2d 959, 497 P.2d 252 (1972).

370 N.Y.S.2d at 327. However, this definition followed the court's statement that "[t]he criterion for permissible acceleration . . . has the dual elements of (1) whether a reasonable man would have accelerated the debt under the circumstances, and (2) whether the creditor acted in good faith." *Id.* (citation omitted). There is ample evidence in the record to support a jury finding that no reasonable loan officer in the same situation would have refused to advance funds to K.M.C. without notice as Sarokin did on March 1, 1982.

---

10 While the appellee suggests in its brief that the Magistrate charged the jury on a wholly subjective standard, we do not read the charge that way. The jury was charged "that what is important *in connection with the requirement of good faith* is the actual mental state of the officers and agents of Irving Trust." The definition of an arbitrary and capricious decision that followed, as one "having no rational basis," is consonant with our analysis.

James Kuharski was executive vice president and manager of secured lending activities for Irving, and two levels above Sarokin in Irving's management hierarchy. Kuharski acknowledged that Irving owed its clients a duty of good faith, that it was not a policy of Irving to terminate financing without notice, and that if Sarokin believed that Irving was adequately secured he would not have been acting in accordance with that duty of good faith to have refused without notice to advance funds to K.M.C.

William Calloway was president of the Park National Bank in Knoxville, which was the depository bank for K.M.C.'s "blocked account" and a 20% participant with Irving in the financing agreement. He also acknowledged that he believed that there is a duty of good faith from a banker to his client that would require a period of notice prior to termination of financing if a loan was well secured. He testified further that on March 1, he believed that the loan to K.M.C. was fully secured as to both interest and principal, and that any reasonable banker looking at the loan would agree that it was fully secured.

Gerald Connolly was an attorney in Milwaukee, Wisconsin, one of whose clients was a large wholesaler named Gateway Foods. In response to a call from Butler on March 1, Gateway's president requested that Connolly assist K.M.C. in any way he could. Connolly testified that pursuant to that request he called Sarokin, who acknowledged in their conversation that Irving was adequately secured and that terminating financing would destroy K.M.C., and that Sarokin ultimately agreed to advance the funds requested by K.M.C., in part to give Connolly the opportunity to come to Knoxville and evaluate K.M.C. for the purpose of acquisition by Gateway Goods. Connolly testified that he called Irving the next day enroute to Knoxville and was told by a subordinate that Sarokin had changed his mind about advancing funds, and that in a telephone conversation that night Sarokin stated that he had changed his mind and decided to "proceed with his game plan."

In fact, counsel for Irving conceded in his summation to the jury that the bank was adequately secured on March 1, 1982. He argued, however, that what is important is not the amount of security, but the capacity of the debtor to pay back the loan. The jury was entitled to find that a reasonable notice period would not change the ability of K.M.C. to pay the loan. The nature of the security was such that the loan would rapidly be paid down on demand. Irving's quarterly audits and other memoranda regarding K.M.C. consistently stated that the strength of its position was in the inventory, which was readily marketable. As late as two months before the events in question, the quarterly audit had concluded that even in the event of a liquidation of the company no loss would be sustained by Irving.

Generally, there was ample evidence in the record from which the jury could have concluded that March 1 simply was not that unusual a day in the history of the relationship between Irving and K.M.C. Such factors as payables and receivables, cited by Sarokin as the basis for his conclusion that K.M.C. was in a state of financial collapse, were closely monitored by Irving. Moreover, three days later, on March 4, Sarokin agreed to advance $700,000 to K.M.C., increasing its outstanding balance to $3.3 million. While the evidence was in conflict whether K.M.C.'s overall financial condition was deteriorating or improving, there is ample evidence belying Irving's characterization that on March 1, Sarokin was faced with a sudden crisis of unprecedented proportions. On this basis alone, the jury could have found that Irving did not fulfill its obligation of good faith performance to K.M.C. when it cut off financing without prior notice.

Irving also argues that it was entitled to a directed verdict on the ground that Sarokin reasonably believed that even if he advanced the $800,000 requested on March 1, K.M.C.'s checks to its suppliers would bounce in significant number and amount and K.M.C. would fold anyway. The events of March 1 were triggered by K.M.C.'s request the previous Friday for an extension of its line of credit to $4 million. Sarokin testified that he believed that K.M.C. would have required this extension, in addition to its request for $800,000 up to its $3.5 million line, to cover all of its outstanding checks. The evidence was substantially in conflict on whether with the $800,000 all of K.M.C.'s checks would have been honored when presented. The jury, by its verdict, resolved this fact issue in favor of K.M.C. In awarding damages to K.M.C. it found that Irving's breach caused K.M.C.'s injury. Irving does not object that the jury was improperly charged on causation. It necessarily follows from the jury's award of damages to the plaintiff that it found that checks would not have bounced. There was ample evidence in the record from which the jury could have so found. However, the question of whether checks in fact would have bounced is distinct from the question of whether Sarokin reasonably could have believed that they would bounce. On the record before us we do not think that the jury could find that Sarokin could not reasonably have held such a belief. Therefore, the question that we must address is whether such a belief in itself would constitute a valid business reason for Irving to refuse to advance the funds requested by K.M.C. without prior notice. We hold, on the particular facts before us, that it would not.

Whether or not the $800,000 requested would have been sufficient to cover all of K.M.C.'s outstanding checks, Sarokin's abrupt refusal to advance funds to K.M.C. on March 1 amounted to a unilateral decision on his party to wind up the company. If Sarokin had agreed to advance the $800,000 but no more, and checks still had bounced, we would have a different case. But, given that Sarokin knew or should have known that the bank was adequately secured, and that if adequately secured it was Irving's policy that some period of notice would be due before financing was denied, Sarokin's action could only be justified if in some way he reasonably believed that it was necessary to protect the bank's interests. There was ample evidence—in particular, the conclusion of Irving's auditors that no losses would be sustained by the bank in the event of liquidation, and Sarokin's decision on March 4 to advance almost the full amount requested just three days earlier, despite the fact that K.M.C. was in much worse condition because of the intervening damage to its credit standing—from which the jury could have concluded that Sarokin had no such reason in mind and hence that his action was arbitrary and capricious.

Finally, Irving contends that even if a period of notice were required, it would be unreasonable to impose upon it an obligation to continue financing K.M.C. for the length of time that would have been necessary to arrange alternative financing or a sale of the company. If Irving had given K.M.C. 30 days, 7 days, even 48 hours notice, we would be facing a different case.[11] However, no notice was given. Until Sarokin told Butler on the phone the afternoon of March 1 that the $800,000 requested would not be advanced, not even Calloway of the Park Bank or Lipson, who had been sent down to Knoxville by Sarokin the previous Friday to gather information, both of whom lunched with Butler immediately before the call to New York, had any inkling that Sarokin might act as he did. Based upon the reasoning above, whether alternative financing could have been found or a sale arranged is pertinent to causation rather than whether Sarokin acted reasonably and in good faith, and there was ample evidence in the record from which the jury could find that either would have been possible.

---

[11] If during that period a tentative commitment was made with respect to a sale or alternative financing, since either of those once completed would result in the immediate repayment of Irving's loan, it might well be that it would be arbitrary and capricious for Irving to terminate financing at the expiration of the notice period if that period was insufficient to permit completion of the contemplated transaction.

* * *

The judgment is affirmed.

COMMENT

The *K.M.C.-Irving Trust* case may represent the high water point in applying the concept of good faith to lender liability questions. As you study the remaining cases in this text ask yourself how far should the good faith-bad faith concept be extended. Would a creditor that acquires a security interest in property be more or less susceptible to a debtor's claims of bad faith? If so, when, and under what circumstances? Although the *K.M.C.* decision remains good law, the case has been criticized by a number of courts and may well be limited in its reach. Do you agree with the court's finding? Why or why not? Should K.M.C.'s changed financial circumstances have been considered differently? What could Irving Trust have done to protect itself once K.M.C.'s fortunes began to decline? Would any change in the lending arrangement amount to bad faith once the debtor encountered financial difficulty?

CHAPTER 17

PERFECTION

§ 17.01 Introduction

Read: U.C.C. §§ 9-301 through 9-306.

This chapter introduces the various ways in which one can claim or challenge a secured party's preferred creditor status. While the security agreement protects the creditor's rights with respect to the debtor, frequently there are a number of potential third party claimants. The creditor needs to take legal steps to protect its security interest against such third parties. Under the Code, protection of one's security interest is called "perfection." Perfection represents the legal steps taken by a secured party to give public notice to other, potential claimants on a debtor's property that the secured party will attempt to claim a higher interest. These steps are explained in sections 9-302 through 9-306.

The idea of perfection denotes the time when a creditor's security interest becomes good against other persons claiming an interest in property of the debtor. The act of perfecting puts others on inquiry notice that property of the debtor may be subject to another's claim. A perfected security interest usually suggests that the creditor has rights superior to other claimants, irrespective of whether those claimants are other creditors, the trustee in bankruptcy, or even persons who purchased property of the debtor that was subject to the security interest. Perfection shields the secured party against possible conflicting claims, interests, or rights in a debtor's property as collateral.

Despite the considerable advantage that can be gained by a secured creditor's perfecting its security interest, it should be noted that perfection is not synonymous with absolute protection. Sometimes the secured party will lose, even though it has done everything the Code requires. Section 9-307(1), for example, subordinates a fully perfected security interest in inventory to the claim of a buyer in the ordinary course of business. The rationale for subordination is that the secured party remains protected because its security interest attaches to whatever the debtor-seller received upon the disposition of inventory.

§ 17.02 Methods of Perfection

There are three basic methods of perfecting security interests—filing a financing statement with a public recorder's office, physical possession of the collateral by the secured party, and automatic perfection for certain types of collateral. For most types of property, filing or taking possession are alternative methods of perfection. However, because of the nature of certain types of collateral, perfection can occur in only one way for those categories of collateral. For example, the filing of a financing statement is the only method of perfection available for accounts receivable, contract rights, and all forms of intellectual property (general intangibles). With these types of collateral, there is nothing tangible for a secured party to possess; filing is essential.

On the other hand, physical possession is the only method of perfection available where money, letters of credit, or negotiable instruments serve as collateral. With these types of property, possession is necessary because the debtor-owner could use the collateral to the detriment of the secured creditor if the items remained in the debtor's hands (the debtor could sell the negotiable instrument to a bona fide purchaser, pledge either the negotiable instrument or the letter of credit a second time, or, simply spend the money). Such use would defeat the secured party's interest by eliminating the very property that was to serve as collateral. By taking possession, the secured party removes the debtor-owner's ability to use collateral in a manner contrary to the secured party's interest.

In the case of security interests in other types of collateral however, possession is generally not practical. Most often, the debtor will want possession of the collateral. For example, the secured party's retaining possession of a business debtor's inventory, manufacturing equipment, or fixtures, like heating and air conditioning units, would hinder the debtor's operations. In purchase money situations, the very purpose of the credit is to allow a debtor to buy and have possession of the property purchased. Consequently, most secured transactions will involve the filing of a financing statement.

While filing and possession are the normal methods of perfection, occasionally the Code recognizes a different type of filing act as a proper method of perfection. In most instances, this different act is authorized by another statute. One example that will be explored subsequently is the perfection of a security interest in a motor vehicle. Often, perfection can be achieved by an appropriate notation on a motor vehicle certificate of title. See § 9-302(3)(b)(c).

There is a third method of public notice—automatic perfection— which only applies to specific types of collateral. A purchase money security interest in consumer goods becomes perfected automatically at the time the transaction occurs. The purchase money creditor does not have to file a financing statement or retain possession of the consumer goods to be perfected against most claimants. See § 9-302(1)(d). Automatic perfection is not as ideal as it seems, however. Section 9-307(2) presents one important exception to the rule concerning automatic perfection in consumer goods. The section provides that a purchase money secured party will still lose out to a second consumer who buys the consumer goods from the consumer-debtor unless the secured party filed a financing statement.

In addition to automatic perfection for consumer goods, sections 9-304(4) and (5) give automatic but temporary perfected status to security interests in instruments and negotiable documents. Under section 9-304(4), no public notice of an interest need be given to perfect a security interest in these types of collateral for a period of 21 days from the time of attachment if the security interest arises for new value under a written security agreement. See also, § 1-201(44). This limited automatic perfection covers those situations where a debtor needs temporary possession of the collateral in order to transfer or deliver property effectively. Another example of temporary automatic perfection occurs where a stockbroker provides a secured "day loan" to a customer. Under this type of arrangement, the loan will be paid the next day, requiring either possession or filing to perfect the broker's secured status would be unduly onerous for both the creditor and any filing office involved.

Subsection 9-304(5) states that a security interest remains perfected for 21 days without the secured party's filing a financing statement where the secured creditor has a perfected security interest in an instrument, negotiable document of title, or goods held by a bailee under a non-negotiable document, but turns over that collateral to the debtor for purposes of storing, shipping, manufacturing, processing, selling or exchanging the collateral. Once again, the rationale for the subsection is that the secured party's surrender of the collateral is temporary, limited, and necessary.

With any secured transaction, the first step is to classify the collateral. The type of collateral involved in the transaction bears directly on the method of perfection required.

§ 17.03 Perfection by Possession

Read: U.C.C. §§ 9-302(1)(a), 9-304(1), 9-305, and 8-321.

[A] Generally

The secured party's obtaining actual possession of a debtor's property as collateral for a loan is one of the oldest forms of secured transaction (commonly known as a pledge). Not only does the creditor's possession of collateral serve to satisfy the formality requirements for creating a security interest (in the absence of a written security agreement), but it also serves to perfect the security interest against third parties. If the secured party retains possession of collateral, then future, potential creditors will not be misled into believing that the debtor had property that could be pledged to them free from any claims by other creditors. U.C.C. § 9-305 lists the following types of collateral as property for which possession constitutes a permissible method of perfection: goods, money, instruments (other than certificated securities), negotiable documents, chattel paper, and letters and advices of credit.[1] The section also requires that the secured party, the secured party's agent, or a bailee have actual possession of the collateral in order to perfect.[2] Although these requirements seem straightforward, some controversies still arise concerning § 9-305. Consider the following cases.

IN THE MATTER OF THE RETURN OF PROPERTY IN STATE v. PIPPIN: NATIONAL PAWN BROKERS UNLIMITED LOAN SYSTEMS v. OSTERMAN, INC.

Wisconsin Court of Appeals
176 Wisc. 2d 418; 500 N.W.2d 407 (1993)

Before Eich, C.J., Gartzke, P.J., and Dykman, J.

Gartzke, P.J.

National Pawn Brokers and Hull Loan Systems ("pawnbrokers") appeal from a circuit court order returning jewelry to Osterman, Inc. The jewelry was evidence in a trial on criminal charges against Donald Pippin. He had obtained it from Osterman, a retail jeweler in Madison, Wisconsin, by paying with a bad check and then pawned it to [pawnbrokers] in Minnesota. Both sides claim

[1] Security interests in money or instruments (other than certificated securities or instruments that are part of chattel paper) can be perfected *only* by possession. See § 9-304(1).

[2] Perfection can occur at any time during the debtor-creditor transaction. One example that many people miss occurs when a secured party repossesses collateral upon a debtor's default. If the secured party was unperfected at the time of default, the security interest becomes perfected upon the creditor's seizure of the collateral.

a security interest in the jewelry. We hold that the pawnbrokers' security interest [is] prior to Osterman's. We reverse.

. . . .

I. FACTS

The pertinent facts are undisputed. On November 24, 1990, Pippin purchased the jewelry from Osterman in Madison. The purchase price was $39,750.38. Pippin signed three documents in connection with the sale. The first was a credit application. It provides personal information regarding Pippin, including his Menomonie, Wisconsin, address and describes the jewelry. The second was a sales agreement. It describes the items sold, the purchase price, the amount paid by check and the balance payable under a "Super Charge" agreement. It provides,

> The balance due on this purchase is payable in installments under my credit plan contract and security agreement which is incorporated herein by reference. I agree that seller shall retain ownership of the items so purchased until entire balance is fully paid . . ..

The third was a "Super Charge Retail Charge Agreement," by which Pippin agreed that in consideration of the sale,

> A security interest in each item of goods purchased hereunder and the proceeds thereof shall remain with Seller until the unpaid balance directly relating to each such item of goods purchased is fully paid. Buyer will not dispose of the goods . . . or encumber them without written consent of Seller . . . until Buyer has fully paid for them.

Pippin paid Osterman $30,000 by check, and agreed to pay the balance in installments. The check was drawn on a closed account. On November 27, 1990, he pawned some of the jewelry to National in Bloomington, Minnesota, for a $6,995 loan and on November 30, 1990, he pawned the remaining items to Hull in Minneapolis for a $2,076.04 loan. He signed a promissory note and security agreement with Hull. No written security agreement with National is of record.

On December 6, 1990, a criminal complaint issued in Dane County, Wisconsin, charging Pippin with violating sec. 943.24(2), Stats. (1989-90), issuing a check payable for more than $500, intending it not be paid. Having learned that Pippin had pawned the jewelry, the Madison police requested the Minnesota police to obtain a search warrant directed to the pawnbrokers' businesses. The Minnesota police did so, and on December 11, 1990, they seized the jewelry from the pawnbrokers and turned it over to the Madison police the next day. On December 13, 1990, the Madison police delivered the jewelry to Osterman but retook it the next day for use as evidence at the criminal trial. Pippin was convicted.

On December 26, 1990, the pawnbrokers petitioned the Dane County Circuit Court for Dane County, Wisconsin, for return of the jewelry. On February 12, 1991, Osterman also petitioned for its return, and on February 14, filed a financing statement in the office of the Wisconsin Secretary of State and in the offices of the Dane and Dunn County Registers of Deeds. On July 25, 1991, the pawnbrokers petitioned the Minnesota court which issued the search warrant for return of the jewelry to that court. On August 13, 1991, the Dane County Circuit Court entered the order before us on appeal, and on October 22, 1991, the Minnesota court denied the pawnbrokers' petition to it because they had chosen to litigate the matter in Wisconsin.

. . . .

III. PAWNBROKERS' SECURITY INTERESTS ATTACHED TO THE JEWELRY

A security interest "is not enforceable against the debtor or third parties with respect to the collateral and does not attach" unless the debtor signed a security agreement containing a description of the collateral or the collateral is in the possession of the secured party pursuant to agreement, value was given, and "the debtor has rights in the collateral." U.C.C. § 9-203(1), sec. 409.203(1), Wis. Stats., and Minn. Stat. § 336.9-203(1).

Osterman asserts that the third requirement — the debtor has rights in the collateral — has not been met for the pawnbrokers' security interests to attach to the collateral. Osterman relies on the sales agreement which provides that Osterman retains ownership of the jewelry until the purchase price is fully paid, and on its security agreement which prohibits Pippin from disposing of the jewelry without Osterman's consent.

Article 9 of the Uniform Commercial Code does not define "rights in the collateral." Because Osterman's transaction with Pippin was a sale, Article 2 determines whether he had such rights. 8 R. Anderson, Uniform Commercial Code, sec. 9-203:44, at 688 (1985) (footnote omitted).

Osterman's sales agreement and security agreement do not affect Pippin's rights in the collateral. The debtor's "rights" in the collateral do not depend on whether the debtor has title to it. "Each provision of this Article with regard to . . . rights . . . applies irrespective of title to the goods . . .." U.C.C. § 2-401, sec. 402.401, Wis. Stats., and Minn. Stat. § 336.2-401; see also U.C.C. § 9-202, sec. 409.202, Wis. Stats., and Minn. Stat. § 336.9-202.

Article 2 converts Osterman's retention of title into a security interest. "Any retention or reservation by the seller of the title (property) in goods shipped or delivered to the buyer is limited in effect to a reservation of a security interest." U.C.C. § 2-401(1), sec. 402.401(1), Wis. Stats., and Minn. Stat. § 336.2-401(1). The attempted prohibition of sale in Osterman's security agreement is part of its security interest.

. . . .

Pippin had voidable title to the collateral because he procured it by a dishonored check. That was the rule at common law and is the rule under Article 2. 2 Hawkland, sec. 2-403:03, at 869-70. *Hudiburg Chevrolet, Inc. v. Ponce*, 17 Wis.2d 281, 285-86, 116 N.W.2d 252, 255 (1962). "A person with voidable title has power to transfer a good title to a good faith purchaser for value. When goods have been delivered under a transaction of purchase the purchaser has such power even though . . . (b) the delivery was in exchange for a check which is later dishonored . . .." U.C.C. § 2-403(1), sec. 402.403(1), Wis. Stats., and Minn. Stat. § 336.2-403(1). Pippin therefore possessed the power to transfer title to a good faith purchaser for value.

Possessing the power under U.C.C. § 2-403(1) to transfer good title to a good faith purchaser for value, Pippin had the power and the right to transfer a security interest to a creditor, including an Article 9 secured party. *In re Samuels & Co.*, 526 F.2d 1238, 1243 (5th Cir. 1976) (en banc) (per curiam). Consequently, Pippin's rights in the collateral were sufficient to allow attachment of a security interest. *Id.*

. . . .

IV. PAWNBROKERS' SECURITY INTERESTS REMAIN PERFECTED

The pawnbrokers acquired their security interests and perfected them by possession in Minnesota. The law of that state determines whether those interests remained perfected on

February 14, 1991, when Osterman perfected its security interest by filing a financing statement. U.C.C. § 9-103(1)(b), sec. 409.103(1)(b), Wis. Stats., and Minn. Stat. § 336.9-103(1)(b). If the pawnbrokers' security interests remained perfected, those interests have priority over Osterman's under the law of both Minnesota and Wisconsin

. . . .

"A security interest in . . . goods . . . may be perfected by the secured party's taking possession of the collateral. . .. A security interest is perfected by possession from the time possession is taken without a relation back and continues only so long as possession is retained, unless otherwise specified in this Article. . .." U.C.C. § 9-305, sec. 409.305, Wis. Stats., and Minn. Stat. § 336.9-305. The parties cite no Minnesota case that discusses whether a security interest perfected by possession remains perfected when police seize the collateral pursuant to a search warrant.

Although it authorizes perfection by the secured party's taking possession of the collateral, the Code does not define "possession." Without a definition, "possession" is protean and ambiguous.

Throughout the law, "possession" is a notoriously slippery concept; age-old property law recognizes and distinguishes among constructive possession, physical possession, actual possession, mere custody, and a host of other similar notions. . .. In the course of the hundreds of decisions which have dealt with its meaning, the word "possession" has taken on a wonderfully plastic form and has accommodated itself to the needs of the real property law, the law of consignment, insurance, and the criminal law. The drafters of the U.C.C. were aware of this history, and they wisely declined the futile task of defining possession in the Code. . .. We are left, therefore, with several hundred years of cases and with the policy of Article Nine to help us define the word possession. 2 White & Summers, Uniform Commercial Code, sec. 24-12, at 350-51 (3rd ed. 1988).

We therefore analyze "possession" in U.C.C. § 9-305, sec. 409.305, Wis. Stats., and Minn. Stat. § 336.9-305, in light of the reason why a security interest may be perfected by possession of the collateral.

In his discussion of perfection by possession, Professor Gilmore states:

> The requirement that a secured party take possession of his collateral — or at least effectively remove it from his debtor's possession and control — in order to perfect his interest dates from the beginning of legal history. . .. The basic idea is that the secured creditor must do something to give effective public notice of his interest; if he leaves the property in the debtor's possession and under his apparent control, the debtor will be given a false credit and will be enabled to sell the property to innocent purchasers or to induce other innocent persons to lend money to him on the strength of his apparently unencumbered assets.

1 G. Gilmore, Security Interests in Personal Property, sec. 14.1, at 438 (1965) (footnote omitted).

White and Summers comment that "possession (particularly by one known to be in the lending business) is a perfectly sound indication of a security interest." White & Summers, sec. 24-12, at 347-48. They add that:

> the pledge, like automatic perfection of security interests in consumer goods, facilitates secured financing in small-sum transactions. Pawnbrokers make numerous small loans. Requiring a financing statement for each such transaction might seriously curtail the availability of informal

loans or significantly increase the cost of such credit to those least able to bear increased costs. *Id.* at 348.

The notice function of possession by the secured creditor persuades us that police seizure does not interrupt that possession under U.C.C. § 9-305. Third parties know the police make no claim to own the property they seized pursuant to a warrant. For that reason, we are satisfied that seizure from the pawnbrokers did not interrupt their possession for purposes of U.C.C. § 9-305, sec. 409.305, Wis. Stats., and Minn. Stat. § 336.9-305. . ... The discussion by White and Summers of a bankruptcy case, *In re Republic Engine and Manufacturing Co.*, 3 U.C.C. Rep. Serv. (Callaghan) 655 (Bankr. N.D. Ohio 1966), convinces us that this should be the law.

In *Republic Engine*, after the sheriff levied on the debtor's equipment, a creditor (who was also the debtor's landlord) locked the doors of the building in which the equipment was located. When the debtor filed bankruptcy, the creditor surrendered possession of the equipment to the sheriff. White and Summers reject the bankruptcy court's holding in Republic Engine that the creditor's "surrender of possession to the sheriff subsequent to the lockout dissolved any perfection which he might have had during the time the goods were locked up on the premises. . .. Secured creditors should be encouraged to cooperate with law enforcement officers. Moreover, possession by the sheriff will deter further reliance on the collateral by third parties." White & Summers, sec. 24-12, at 352-53.

Far from cooperating with the Minnesota police, the pawnbrokers refused to surrender the collateral, and that resulted in the warrant and seizure. But depriving the pawnbrokers' security interests of perfection merely because the police seize the collateral under a warrant will hardly encourage future cooperation by creditors with the police.

Because possession is not interrupted when law enforcement officers levy on the collateral, possession should be deemed continuous even if the police seize it. In *Waterhouse v. Carolina Limousine Mfg., Inc.*, 96 N.C. App. 109, 384 S.E.2d 293 (N.C. App. 1989), Waterhouse levied execution on its debtor's property in possession of the debtor's creditor, Southwestern, who asserted that it had perfected its security interest in the collateral by possession under U.C.C. § 9-305. The trial court concluded that the levy interrupted Southwestern's possession but nevertheless ruled that its security interest had priority over Waterhouse's interest. The North Carolina Court of Appeals reversed, not on the merits, but because of a standard of appellate review.

However, the Waterhouse court expressed its view of the merits in dicta. The court described the trial court's conclusion regarding interruption of possession as a "misapprehension of applicable law." *Id.* at 295. The court said, "In one case remarkably similar to the instant case the court found that a creditor who had perfected his security interest in goods by possession had priority over the sheriff who, at a later date, levied on the goods for delinquent personal property taxes of the debtor. *Walter [E.] Heller & Company v. Salerno*, 168 Conn. 152, 362 A.2d 904 (1975)." *Waterhouse*, 394 S.E.2d at 295. The *Heller* court held that when the plaintiff perfected its security interest in the debtor's collateral, and the defendant later attempted to levy on the collateral, the plaintiff's interest was prior to the defendants. 362 A.2d at 907.

V. CONCLUSION

Because Pippin had a right in the jewelry purchased by a bad check from Osterman's, the pawnbrokers' security interests attached to the jewelry, they perfected their security interests by possession, and that possession was not interrupted, for purposes of U.C.C. § 9-305, sec. 409.305, Wis. Stats., and Minn. Stat. § 336.9-305, when Osterman perfected its security interest. The interests of the pawnbrokers have priority over Osterman's interest. For that reason, the trial court erred when it ordered that possession of the collateral, the jewelry, be granted to Osterman's. On remand, the trial court shall enter judgment giving possession to the pawnbrokers. . ..

NOTE

Despite its unusual fact pattern, *Osterman* represents a good discussion of the general principles concerning both security interest attachment and perfection by possession. Do you agree with the court's decision that possession was uninterrupted? What arguments would you make against that construction on appeal? The next case examines a more common example of perfection by possession and demonstrates that the manner of possession may influence whether that possession qualifies the creditor as a perfected secured party.

KALK v. SECURITY PAC. BANK WASHINGTON, N.A.

Washington Court of Appeals
866 P.2d 1276; 23 U.C.C. Rep. Serv. 2d 655 (1994)

J. Scholfield

. . . .

Marjorie Kalk and her mother, Marjorie Worsham, owned three certificates of deposit (CD's) as joint tenants with right of survivorship. The first two CD's, purchased from Seattle Trust in 1982, were in the face amounts of $ 20,000 and $ 55,000, respectively. Each CD stated, "This certificate is not transferable except on the books of Seattle Trust." The third CD was purchased from Rainier National Bank (Rainier Bank) in 1983, in the face amount of $ 100,000, and stated it was a "non-negotiable time certificate of deposit." All three CD's were payable to Marjorie Worsham or Marjorie Kalk, and all three designated Worsham and Kalk as joint tenants with right of survivorship. The record does not reflect whose funds were used to purchase any of the CD's.

On January 12, 1983, Worsham signed a Rainier Bank security agreement, pledging the $100,000 Rainier Bank CD as collateral for a loan by Rainier Bank to William Argo.[3] Argo was Worsham's accountant. Argo invested the loan proceeds into Pacific Wood Products, a company he established.

On June 14, 1989, Worsham signed a security agreement to Security Pacific Bank Washington (the Bank), the successor to Rainier Bank. Worsham assigned the two Seattle Trust CD's in the

---

[3] By signing the security agreement, Worsham agreed to "[deliver] and [grant] to the Bank a Security Interest" in the $ 100,000 CD as security for the Bank's loan to William Argo, including all renewals.

aggregate amount of $ 75,000 to the Bank as security for another loan to Argo.[4] The Bank took possession of each of the CD's covered by the two security agreements. Kalk did not sign either of the security agreements, nor was she aware of them.

Worsham died March 9, 1990. The Bank renewed the loans to Argo in late March 1990. On December 11, 1990, the Bank informed Argo he was in default on the loans and claimed ownership of the secured CD's. Kalk, as the surviving joint tenant owner of the CD's, was not notified of Argo's default or the Bank's intent to claim the CD's.

Kalk sued the Bank on a number of theories. On cross motions for partial summary judgment, the trial court granted Kalk's motion, concluding that Kalk owned the certificates free of the Bank's security interests at the moment of Worsham's death. The Bank appeals the order and judgment awarding Kalk the face value of the three CD's plus interest.

Perfected Security Interest

The Bank contends it had a perfected security interest in the three CD's, pursuant to the Uniform Commercial Code (U.C.C.), RCW 62A. Kalk argues the U.C.C. does not apply. Kalk's contention is not supported; we agree with the Bank. First, the security agreements are clearly "intended to create a security interest." RCW 62A.9-102(1)(a). Moreover, even if the security agreements constitute a "pledge" as Kalk contends, Article 9 "applies to security interests created by contract including pledge, [and] assignment . . ." RCW 62A.9-102(2).

Nor are these transactions excluded by RCW 62A.9-104(l), as Kalk contends. That section provides that Article 9 does not apply "to a transfer of an interest in any deposit account (subsection (1) of RCW 62A.9-105), except as provided with respect to proceeds . . ." RCW 62A.9-105(1)(e) defines a "deposit account" as a demand, time, savings, passbook or like account maintained with a bank, savings and loan association, credit union or like organization, other than an account evidenced by a certificate of deposit[.] Thus, U.C.C. Article 9 applies to this transaction involving certificates of deposit.

To determine if the Bank had a perfected security interest, we must categorize the collateral, determine if a security interest attached and, if so, if the Bank perfected a security interest.

Collateral

Characterizing CD's for purposes of Article 9 is a question of first impression in Washington. Although there is authority to the contrary, a CD is an instrument. An instrument is a negotiable instrument (defined in RCW 62A.3-104), or a certificated security (defined in RCW 62A.8-102) or any other writing which evidences a right to the payment of money and is not itself a security agreement or lease and is of a type which is in [the] ordinary course of business transferred by delivery with any necessary indorsement or assignment[.] RCW 62A.9-105(1)(I). None of the three CD's at issue is negotiable, and none is a certificated security. However, each is clearly a writing which evidences a right to payment of money. Moreover, a CD is not a security agreement or lease, and it is transferred in the ordinary course of business by delivery with an endorsement. In fact, these CD's were not endorsed, but Worsham did not intend to transfer them — she intended to pledge them.

---

[4] This security agreement provided that Worsham's pledge of the two CD's was "security for the payment . . .of all promissory notes executed by William Argo . . .now, in the past or in the future and all renewals, modifications or extensions thereof . . .".

. . . .

Perfection

"A security interest in money or instruments . . .can be perfected only by the secured party's taking possession . . ." RCW 62A.9-304(1). The Bank had possession of all three CD's at all relevant times. Therefore, the Bank had a perfected security interest in the three CD's. The only question remaining is what effect, if any, Worsham's death had on the Bank's perfected security interest.

Effect of Worsham's Death

As with the characterization of CD's, this is a question of first impression in Washington, and there is a split of authority among other courts which have considered the issue.

Representative of one view is *In re Certificates of Deposit Issued by Hocking Vly. Bank of Athens Co.*, 58 Ohio St. 3d 172, 569 N.E.2d 484 (1991), relied on by the trial court here. In that case, a husband and wife purchased six CD's, with a face value of $10,000 each, payable to the husband or wife as joint tenants with right of survivorship. The husband and wife subsequently both signed a security agreement pledging their interest in one of the CD's as collateral for a loan to them. The following year, the husband alone received five additional loans from the bank, and individually signed five security agreements pledging the remaining five CD's as collateral. The husband died prior to the loans' maturity dates, and the bank and surviving wife each claimed ownership of the five CD's individually pledged by the husband. The Supreme Court of Ohio held that when only one joint tenant with the right of survivorship to a certificate of deposit signs a security agreement and pledges the certificate as collateral to secure his or her loan, and such joint tenant dies before the loan is satisfied, the joint tenant survivor(s) is entitled to the entire amount of the certificate, as the bank's interest is extinguished upon the death of the debtor joint tenant. *Hocking*, at 174. The court characterized the husband's interest in the CD's as an "ownership interest [limited] to his lifetime subject to divestment on his death." *Hocking,* at 174. Several other states agree with this approach.

The other view, rejected by the trial court here, is that a perfected security interest survives a pledging joint tenant's death, and that the surviving joint tenants take ownership subject to the security interest. This view is represented by *Bridges v. Central Bank & Trust Co.*, 926 F.2d 971 (10th Cir. 1991). In that case, one of five joint owners with right of survivorship pledged a CD as collateral for a loan solely to him. The lending bank perfected its security interest by possessing the CD. After the pledgor's default, the lending bank demanded payment of the CD by the issuing bank, which surrendered the funds. The remaining joint tenants sued the issuing bank for breach of contract and conversion. The Tenth Circuit Court of Appeals held that an instrument arguably held in joint tenancy and nominated in the alternative under Kansas law can be effectively unilaterally pledged in full by one of the co-owners as security for a loan and later redeemed by the secured creditor in foreclosure. *Bridges*, 926 F.2d at 974.

The trial court here distinguished *Bridges* because the *Bridges* court relied on a specific Kansas statute "which made an instrument that used the conjunction 'or' as opposed to 'and' a negotiable instrument." Actually, the *Bridges* court relied on that statute, which is similar to RCW 30.22.140, for the proposition that a CD payable to joint tenants in the alternative is "payable to any one of them" and thus any one of them with possession of the CD could cash the CD in or pledge it in its entirety. *Bridges*, at 973 n.2.

The trial court here also distinguished *Heffernan v. Wollaston Credit Union*, 30 Mass. App. Ct. 171, 567 N.E.2d 933 (1991), which the Bank relied on. Heffernan and Dore opened a joint savings account payable to either of them, with a right of survivorship. Dore subsequently pledged part of the balance of the account as collateral for a car loan. Dore died before the loan was due; after the due date, the bank transferred the amount due from the joint account, and the surviving joint tenant sued. The Massachusetts court found that a "party to a Massachusetts joint bank account . . .has the right to withdraw all the funds in a joint account, or any portion of them." *Heffernan,* at 177. The court concluded that "the authority to create a security interest, equitable or otherwise, is included within the ordinary and reasonable meaning of the authority to assign or transfer." *Heffernan*, at 179.

We find the reasoning of the Ohio Supreme Court in the *Hocking Valley Bank* case unpersuasive when applied to the facts and law of the case before us. *Hocking* followed case law holding the rights of a survivor paramount to a bank's security interest "when the bank fails to encumber the interest of all joint tenants." *Hocking*, at 173-74. The bank prevailed in respect to the one CD where both the husband and the wife signed the security agreement.

In this State, there is clear statutory authority for one joint owner to withdraw or pledge all funds on deposit. RCW 30.22.140; RCW 30.22.040(17), (14). The *Hocking* court reasoning cannot prevail in the face of the Washington statutory scheme, which also provides that payment to a depositor shall constitute a complete release and discharge of the financial institution from all claims for the amounts so paid regardless of whether or not the payment is consistent with the actual ownership of the funds . . .. RCW 30.22.120. As previously discussed, payment to a depositor includes "pledge[s] of sums on deposit by a depositor." RCW 30.22.040(14).

In light of the Washington statutory scheme, we find the reasoning of *Bridges v. Central Bank & Trust Co., supra*, and *Heffernan v. Wollaston Credit Union, supra*, more persuasive.

The trial court's grant of partial summary judgment to Marjorie Kalk is reversed.

NOTE

An instrument is any writing that embodies some underlying set of rights. Section 9-105(1)(i) supplies a definition of the term "instrument" which includes any writing that evidences a right to payment of money, any negotiable instrument, or certificated, corporate security. Ownership rights follow the possession of the instrument. A pledge of the instrument therefore transfers the rights and value embodied by the document. The *Kalk* case represents a consistent application of this principle. The decision demonstrates that possession is the *only* method of perfection for instruments.

The real issue in the case is what interest did the bank have when it took possession of the certificates of deposit? A majority of jurisdictions hold that although one joint tenant may unilaterally pledge property, surviving cotenants take the property or account funds free of the pledge at the moment of the debtor joint tenant's death. Thus, the bank has only a lifetime interest in the pledged property.

[*Ed. note*: In 1995, the *Kalk* decision was reversed by the Washington Supreme Court on non-U.C.C. grounds holding that the death of the pledging joint tenant extinguished the security interest and that the surviving joint tenant's survivorship interest was not subject to the security interest. ". . . the Bank knew of Kalk's ownership interest when her mother pledged the CD's; similarly, the Bank was aware of Kalk's survivorship interest when it renewed the loans following Worsham's death. By comparison, Kalk was uninformed and unwitting. The Bank could have protected itself at all times by requiring Kalk's signature. The majority rule appropriately balances a bank's control and access to information against the joint tenant's ownership of deposited funds. We hold that Worsham's death extinguished the Bank's security interest and therefore, Kalk should receive the CD's free of the Bank's encumbrance." 126 Wash. 2d 346, 352.]

PROBLEM 17.1

Betty borrows $10,000 from Larry and signs a paper acknowledging the obligation. Assume that the writing does not satisfy the requirements for an instrument under U.C.C. § 9-105(1)(i). Does Larry's retaining possession of the writing constitute possession sufficient for him to claim perfected secured party status? See § 9-106. Would your answer change if the writing were found to be a negotiable promissory note?

For a good discussion analyzing the rationale of the perfection by possession rule, see Ebron, *Perfection by Possession in Article 9: Challenging the Arcane But Honored Rule*, 69 Ind. L. J. 1193 (1994).

[B] Investment Securities (Stock)

Read U.C.C. § 9–115 and prefatory note to Article 8

The rules concerning security interests in stock differ from other types of collateral. The original version of Article 8, drafted in the 1940s, was based on the assumption that possession and physical delivery if certificates was essential. Traditionally, ownership of securities was evidenced by actual possession of the certificates and changes were accomplished by delivery of the certificates. Transfer of securities in the traditional certificate–based system was a complex and labor–intensive process. The problems associated with processing the paperwork for securities transfers ultimately led to the development of electronic systems for recording ownership of securities and transfers of ownership. In 1978, amendments to Article 8 of the Uniform Commercial Code were approved to establish a set of rules that would permit the evolution of uncertificated securities.

The system of securities holding envisioned by the 1978 amendments differed from the traditional system for securities transfer in that changes in ownership could be evidenced by record changes n the records of the issuer. Instead of surrendering an indorsed certificate for registration of transfer, an instruction would be sent to the issuer directing it to register the transfer. Unfortunately, this type of system has not yet developed. Individual investors who wish to be recorded as registered owners on an issuer's books still obtain and hold the physical stock certificate. However, the certificates representing the largest portion of the shares of publicly traded companies are not held by the beneficial owners, but by clearing corporations. More than 4/5s of all of the trading in publicly held companies is executed through broker–dealers who are participants in a limited purpose trust system known as The Depository Trust Company. Settlement of securities trading under DTC occurs not by delivery of certificates or by registration of transfer on the records of the issuers (or their transfer agents). Instead, computer entries are made in the records of the clearing corporations and securities intermediaries. By handing all securities over to a common depository, various deliveries upon trading or even pledging can be eliminated. Transfers can be accomplished by adjustments to the DTC accounts. Greater processing efficiency was achieved through the creation of a separate corporation, the National Securities Clearing Corporation, which nets all receive and deliver transactions among participants daily, Thus, entries only need to be made once at the end of each day.

The traditional paper–based system and the uncertified system contemplated by the 1978 amendments are described as "direct" securities holding systems because the beneficial owners have a direct relationship with the issuer of the securities. The DTC depository system is an "indirect" holding system because the issuer's records do not show the identity of all beneficial owners. Instead, most securities are recorded in the issuer's records as belonging to a depository. The depository's records in turn show the identity of the banks or brokers who are its members, and the records of these securities intermediaries show the identity of the specific customer–owners. Because the 1978 amendments failed to take these points into account, Article 8 was again revised in 1994.

Revised Article 8 uses the simple concepts of the traditional direct holding system and applies them to indirect holding system. The phrase"security entitlement" provides the starting point for recognizing the rights and property interests of holders of financial assets. The revised Article 8 also removed provisions governing security interests in securities from the article entirely. Rules on security interests in investment securities are now set out in Article 9 rather than Article 8. The changes in Article 9 conform to the new concept of a security entitlement. The changes also go beyond to establish a simplified structure for the creation and perfection of security interests in investment securities, whether held directly or indirectly. All of these rules are set forth in one section of Article 9, section 9–115.

The revised Article 9 rules continue to adhere to the principle that a security interest in a security represented by a certificate can be perfected by a possessory pledge. The revised rules do not require that all security interests in investment securities take place through the conceptual structure of a common law pledge. Under the revised rules, a security interest in securities can be created under 9–203 in the same fashion as a security interest in any form of property—by agreement between the debtor and secured party. There is no requirement of a transfer, delivery, or other similar physical (or metaphysical) action, for the creation of an effective security interest.

Section 9–115(4) outlines the methods of perfecting a security interest in investment securities. The basic rule is that a security interest may be perfected by "control." The concept of control is defined in Article 8 at section 8–106. Obtaining control means taking the steps necessary to place a lender in a position where it can have the collateral sold *without* additional cooperation from the debtor/securities owner. Thus, for a certificate security, a lender obtains control by taking possession of the certificate along with any necessary indorsement. For securities held through a securities intermediary, the lend obtains control in either of two ways. First, the lender obtains control if it becomes an entitlement holder; that is, if the securities position is transferred to an account in the lender's own name. A second method of obtaining control involves the securities intermediary agreeing to act on instructions from the secured party to dispose of the positions, *even though* the debtor/securities owner remains entitled as the holder. Such an arrangement serves to give the lender control even though the debtor retains the right to trade and to exercise other rights of an entitlement holder.

Except where the debtor is a securities firm itself, the filing of a financing statement would also provide an acceptable method of perfection. The filing of a financing statement does not, however, provide the same degree of protection as obtaining control because the priority rules provide that a secured party who obtains control has priority over a secured party who does not obtain control. Read the official comments to section 9–115 carefully.

The following case applies the 1978 version of Article 8. As you read it, consider whether the results or analysis would differ under section 9–115.

FIRST BANK OF IMMOKALEE v. ROGERS NK SEED COMPANY

District Court of Appeals of Florida, Second District
637 So.2d 11, 23 U.C.C. Rep. Serv. 2d 558 (1994)

ALTENBERND, Judge.

The First Bank of Immokalee (First Bank) appeals an order declaring that its security interest in certain stock owned by Precision Agricultural Products, Inc. (Precision), is inferior to the judgment lien of Rogers NK Seed Company (Rogers). We conclude that First Bank's security interest under section 678.321, Florida Statutes (1989), is superior to Rogers' judgment lien. Accordingly, we reverse the order on appeal.

Precision borrowed $200,000.00 from First Bank on July 30, 1990. To secure this obligation, Precision signed a security agreement listing 50,000 shares of ATNN Inc. and 118,000 shares of Non-Invasive Monitoring Systems, Inc., as collateral. First Bank did not file the security agreement in the method used to perfect a security interest in many types of personal property. See § 679.302, Fla. Stat. (1989). Because the stock was in the possession of Precision's broker, F.N. Wolf & Co., Inc. (F.N. Wolf), First Bank wrote to F.N. Wolf on July 30, 1990, and advised that Precision had assigned these shares of stock as collateral for the loan. The letter enclosed a copy of the promissory note and the security agreement. A few days later, F.N. Wolf sent a reply, refusing to "hold the securities in trust for anyone other than our client," but offering to assist in a physical transfer of stock certification if that was the desire of Precision. First Bank apparently did not respond to this letter.

In January 1992, Rogers obtained a judgment in the amount of $291,359.37 against Precision. In supplementary proceedings, Rogers discovered the existence of these publicly listed stocks held by Precision's broker and began efforts to sell them to satisfy its judgment. First Bank then intervened in the supplementary proceedings to establish the priority of its security interest.

After evidentiary hearing, the trial court ruled that First Bank's security interest was not perfected because the security agreement had not filed and because First Bank had failed to take possession of the stock as suggested by F.N. Wolf. Accordingly, it ordered that the stock be sold and that Rogers have a first priority to the proceeds of the sale. The stock was sold for approximately $150,000.00, and the proceeds have been deposited into the court's registry pending this appeal.

Security interests in stock are perfected under rules that do not apply to most other types of property. Section 678.321(1), Florida Statutes (1989), provides that a security interest in stock in enforceable and can attach only of the security interest is "transferred" to the secured party or its designee pursuant to a provision of section 678.313(1). "A security interest so transferred pursuant to agreement by a transferor who has rights in the security to a transferee who has rights in the security to a transferee who has given value is a perfected security interest. . ." § 678.321(2), Fla.Stat. (1989). Although such a security interest is subject to the provisions of chapter 679, no filing is required to perfect the security agreement. § 678.321(3)(a), Fla.Stat. (1989); cf. Finiziov. Shubow, 557 So.2d 640 (Fla. 4th DCA 1990)(agreement pledging securities to secure payment of final judgment gave judgment creditor an enforceable security interest).

Thus, to resolve this case, one must determine when the security interest was "transferred" to First Bank. Section 678.313(1)(h), Florida Statutes (1989), provides, in pertinent part, that the "transfer" of such a security interest occurs

> at the time a written notification. . . (which may be a copy of the security agreement). . . is received by:
>
> 1. A financial intermediary on whose books the interest of the transferor in the security appears;

By definition, F.N. Wolf is a "financial intermediary." § 678.313(4), Fla.Stat. (1989).

It is undisputed that the First Bank provided F.N. Wolf with a copy of the signed security agreement with its notification letter on July 30, 1990. Thus, a transfer of the security interest in the stock occurred when F.N. Wolf received the written notification. Cf. In re Southmark Corp., 138 B.R. 820 (Bankr. N.D. Tex. 1992) (perfection occurred when financial intermediary received notice of pledge agreement).

Despite its efforts in the reply, F.N. Wolf had no ability to decline or prevent the transfer that resulted from its receipt of the notification. As explained in the Official Reasons for the 1977 Change to the Uniform Commercial Code:

> Subparagraph (h), limited to the transfer of a security interest, deals with the situation where a security interest, pursuant to written agreement, is perfected by notice to a bailee under Section 9–305. Unlike a transfer under subparagraph (d), (e) or (f) of subsection (1), Section 9–305 does not require confirmation or acknowledgment by the controlling party, but only the receipt of notice. Subparagraph (h) provides that a transfer is effective when notice is received and further identifies the party to be notified.

Section 9–305 provides:

> If such collateral other than goods covered by a negotiable document is held by a bailee, the secured party is deemed to have possession from the time the bailee receives notification of the secured party's interest.

Thus, the reply from F.N. Wolf did not alter the date upon which First Bank perfected its security interest in this stock. Because the judgment was recorded long after that date, First Bank's security interest has priority over Rogers' judgment lien.

Reversed and remanded.

CAMPBELL A.C.J., and SCHOONOVER, J., concur _____

Application under 1978 Version of Article 8

Ordinarily, shares of stock are held either by the share owner or by that owner's broker. If the stock collateral is in the possession of a third person who acts as the agent of the secured party, possession by that third party is considered to be possession by the secured party. The Code deems the secured party to have possession from the time the agent/bailee receives notification of the secured party's interest. See comment 2 to § 9–305.

Section 9–305 excludes certificated securities from the listing of collateral that may be perfected by a secured party's taking possession. Perfection for investment securities is covered under Article 8. Under U.C.C. § § 8–321(1),(2) and 8–313(1)(a) a security interest will be perfected at the time the secured party or a person designated by the secured party acquires possession of the certificated security by transfer from the debtor. Comment 2 to § 8–321 notes that "an appropriate transfer will result not only in an enforceable security interest but also in one that is perfected. Under this section, an unperfected security interest in a security cannot be created."

With uncertificated securities, U.C.C. § § 8–321, 8–313(1)(b), and 8–108 indicate that a security interest will be perfected at the time the pledge is registered to the secured party or to a person designated by that secured creditor. Registration occurs by having the debtor, as registered owner of the uncertificated security, issue an instruction to the issuer that the secured party's interest be recognized. U.C.C. § 8–308(4). The secured party may be listed as a registered owner or as a registered pledgee. If the secured party is registered as an owner, the creditor has a right to vote the shares and to receive dividends like any other stockholder. If the secured party is a registered pledgee, the debtor–stockholder as the registered owner continues to have all the rights of an owner except the power to order a transfer. U.C.C. § 8–207(3). Under § 8–108, there can be no more than one registered pledgee at a given time. The concept of a registered pledge permits the secured party of uncertificated shares of stock to have the same ability to prohibit a debtor's transfer of uncertificated stock as the secured party pledgee of certificated stock (who has possession of the stock certificate). The one difference between the rights of a pledgee of uncertificated stock and the pledgee of certificated stock is that the certificated stock pledgee does not receive dividends or other distributions. Even though the secured party is in possession of the stock certificated as collateral, a pledgee of certificated stock, the secured party is still not recognized by the company issuing the stock as an owner entitled to a distribution is not recognized as the registered pledgee of an uncertificated security, however, is eligible to receive distributions from the stock because the company that issued the stock has a record of the pledgee's interest. U.C.C. § 8–207.

PROBLEM 17.2

In March, Block, the president and a director of Heinicke Co., brought 25,000 shares of to–be–issued Heinicke stock for $250,000. In May, Block assigned all of the stock to Bergman as security for a loan. Unfortunately, the Stock Exchange's approval of the Heinicke stock issue was delayed. Heinicke was notified of the Block–Bergman transaction and the company agreed to register the stock in Block's name but to deliver the certificates to Bergman. Thinking that he was registered as a pledgee, Bergman assigned the stock to Exchange National Bank as a collateral for a loan. By the time the Stock Exchange approved the stock issue in January of the next year, other creditors of Block had the certificates seized in the day the stock was issued. Bergman and Exchange National claimed priority over the other creditors by arguing that Heinicke Co. operated as their agent even though the stock had been issued to Block. You sit as a clerk to the judge hearing this case – who should prevail? Can perfection by possession occur where stock has not yet been issued? See § § 9–305 and 9–9-304. If Bergman and Exchange National had a valid but unperfected security interest in stock that was to be issued, could either ro both have perfected the interest by filing a financing statement for unissued stock as a general intangible? If so, what result when the stock was finally issued and the method of perfection became possession? Does application of § 9–115 change the result?

§ 17.04 Perfection By Filing

Read U.C.C. § 9–302 §9–304.

As noted above, perfection by filing is the most frequently used technique. A secured creditor's filing to perfect ensures [that other creditors have an opportunity to discover the security interest]. The secured creditor records her interest by filing a financing statement with the appropriate public authority. The secured party's perfected status becomes effective at the time a financing statement is filed in the appropriate office. In most instances, once a secured creditor files, she will be able to claim a higher interest in the property than other, subsequent claimants.

Article 9's system creates a notice filing system—the financing statement simply puts parties on notice that the parties named in the document are, or expect to be, engaged in financing transactions which may cover certain types of property as collateral. Notice filing differs from transaction filing systems where the filed document is a copy of the actual contract outlining the entire transaction. A notice filing system recognizes that in many debtor–creditor transactions, the parties contemplate a long–term relationship with the parties entering a series of transactions over time. Under a notice system there is no need to file each separate security agreement; third parties are put on notice and must seek additional information before entering into a transaction with the debtor. One of the major disadvantages of a notice system is that filing provides little details about the particular financing transaction—it does not state the amount of debt secured by the collateral, and may only identify the actual collateral in a generalized fashion. Despite these limitations, the system works well for secured transactions because it provides enough general information to serve for further inquiry, Section 9–208 recognizes the subsequent, potential creditor's need for additional information and provides a system whereby that potential second creditor may have the debtor compel the first secured party to confirm the debt owed and the collateral securing that debt. Once the potential second creditor receives such information, the creditor may then make an informed decision about whether to extend credit to the debtor.

[A] Basic Filing Systems

Read: U.C.C. §§ 9-401 and 9-402.

Section 9-401 of the U.C.C. offers jurisdictions a choice of several filing systems. The jurisdiction's choice will be affected by: 1) policy considerations related to filing, 2) the accessibility of a central filing office to debtors, creditors, and other interested parties within the jurisdiction, and 3) its choice as to the importance of local filing offices and a central filing office within their filing system. The basic choices offered by the Code are central filing, local filing, and dual filing.

The system of central filing offers a number of advantages. Filing need occur in only one office; typically, that location is the office of the Secretary of State in the jurisdiction where the collateral will be located. Central filing eliminates the question of where a secured party should file. Searches against the records are more convenient because only one office needs to be checked. This system is also particularly well-suited to the smaller state where access to a central filing office is not difficult. Even in larger states there are advantages to a central filing system. Companies engaged in business on a national scale may find it easier to check a centralized filing record. The first alternative of section 9-401(1) provides the version most oriented toward central filing. Given the possibility of establishing a centralized computer filing system with terminals throughout a state, the central filing system should gain in importance during the next few years. Despite the benefits of ease and inexpensive access to information, not all states have adopted a system of centralized filing.

Alternative 2 to section 9-401(1) rests on the assumption that some filings, other than real property-related filings, should be local. Local filing occurs when a secured party files a financing statement in the office of a designated official in the county where the debtor resides and the collateral sits. If the debtor is not a resident of the county where the collateral is located, the financing statement must be filed with a similar official in the county where the collateral does sit. Security interests in certain types of collateral—consumer goods, farm products, accounts, contracts, general intangibles arising from farm sales, and equipment used in farming operations—can be perfected through local filing. The rationale for local filing in these instances is that such sales are often local in nature and the credit extended to debtors is usually through local financing. Security interests in personal property attached to real estate (fixtures) and crops must also be perfected by filing in the county where the real estate is located. In all other cases, filing should be made centrally with the Secretary of State. Even though the emphasis is on local filing for certain collateral, it is somewhat of a misnomer to term this second system "local filing." Filings for inventory, equipment, documents of title, chattel paper, accounts, contract rights, and general intangibles must still be made centrally.

The third alternative filing system under 9-401(1) is a dual system of local and central filing. Alternative 3 outlines the same filing locations as in alternative 2, except that in the last category (all other cases), filing must be made with both the secretary of state and the county of the debtor's place of business or residence. This dual system carries with it the inconvenience and expense of filing in two places; it also creates risks regarding proper filing in both places. Further, the period before the secured interest becomes perfected might be prolonged. The advantage to the system is that for most items local records may be checked instead of having to check the central records. The development of a centralized computer filing system would significantly reduce this advantage. The ease with which such central records could be checked by interested parties within local offices would greatly lessen the need for separate local records. For a recent article examining the underlying principles and criticizing the notice filing system, see James J. White, *"Managing the Paper Trail": Evaluating and Reforming the Article 9 Filing System: Reforming Article 9 Priorities in Light of Old Ignorance and New Filing Rules*, 79 Minn. L. Rev. 529 (1995).

[B] Specialized Filing Systems

Read: U.C.C. §§ 9-302(3), (4).

In addition to the systems above, security interests in certain types of collateral may be exempt from filing altogether under the Code. In these cases, there is a specialized system covered by another statute. Security interests and other liens may be checked through that system. Certificate of title statutes are the most notable non-Article 9 system. These statutes cover cars (when sold as consumer goods and not as inventory) and other motor vehicles. Similarly, there are other statutory provisions in some jurisdictions relating to boats and aircraft. Article 9 of the Code recognizes these various systems and makes certain exceptions. Sometimes where aircraft, copyrights, or trademarks are involved, the creditor may choose to file under both the Code system and a separate system.

§ 17.05 Filing Errors Generally

Read: U.C.C. §§ 9-402 and 9-403.

A number of problems may arise under recording or filing requirements. Many of these problems are primarily related to the actual act of filing a financing statement. For example, the question of precisely when a perfected security interest takes effect may be important in some situations. Does the secured party's interest become perfected when the financing statement is presented to the filing officer or at some later date? What happens if there are errors in the filed financing statement? What if some of the filing requirements are not met—suppose, for instance, the signature of either the secured party or the debtor is missing? If the debtor changes residency, does the secured party's perfected status follow? What happens if the collateral is moved? Each of these situations can cause problems in the filing system that must be addressed.

The law can take either of two approaches in dealing with filing system errors. One method would be to adopt a formalistic approach, requiring strict conformity to the requirements. This strategy would mean that when a mistake occurred in the financing statement, the erring party must suffer. Under this rigid approach, the mistake would render the filing ineffective and the secured party would consequently lose its priority claim on the property to other claimants or creditors.

A second approach would be to emphasize the underlying policy considerations for filing. To what extent should the court consider the general notice nature of the filing system as opposed to giving detailed notice? Was the error of such a nature that third party notice did not occur? Did the other party know of the secured interest despite the improper filing? This method would also consider whether the filing error actually resulted in a loss to another party. It would also take into account the fact that mistakes are certain to occur in volume financing and filing.

§ 17.06 Errors in the Instrument

Read: U.C.C. § 9-402(7).

[A] Generally

One problem that may arise in any filing system is an error in the financing statement. Most of the complaints about errors in the instrument arise when other creditors contest the secured party's claim. The debtor and creditor in a secured transaction rarely raise such issues because they have a direct contractual relationship outlining their responsibilities.

As noted earlier, the principal purpose of the financing statement is to provide notice to third parties that there is a secured interest involving certain property of a debtor. Those third parties have the burden of inquiring further about the details of the underlying transaction. In most instances a potential secured creditor will search the filing records to determine what property of the debtor might be encumbered before making the decision to lend. Filing errors obviously inhibit a third party's ability to check the records and find a secured party's notice filing. But do all errors damage a third party in the same fashion? The drafters of the Code believed that a secured party's financing statement should remain effective despite minor errors if it substantially complied with the requirements for third party notice and if the errors were not seriously misleading. See § 9-402(8). Unfortunately, the Code provides little guidance for determining whether an error is seriously misleading.

IN RE SPIRIT OF THE WEST, INC.

Bankruptcy Court, Middle District of Pennsylvania
164 B.R. 34(1993)

OPINION AND ORDER

JOHN J. THOMAS, BANKRUPTCY JUDGE.

Before this Court is an issue under the Uniform Commercial Code, Article 9-402(7), cited in Pennsylvania as 13 Pa.C.S.A. § 9402(g).

The material facts are not disputed. Spirit of the West, Inc. is a corporation primarily engaged in the retail sale of western apparel, shoes, and related items. Stipulation Nos. 3 and 4. On June 1, 1991, the corporation filed for relief under Chapter Eleven of the United States Bankruptcy Code. Stipulation No. 10.

This controversy arises out of a series of transactions that pre-dated the bankruptcy.

In June of 1989, Northeastern Bank of Pennsylvania ("NEB") made a loan to Grover E. Conklin III ("Conklin") and Patricia A. Krisovitch ("Krisovitch"), individually and trading as Spirit of the West, a partnership, in the amount of Ninety-Five Thousand Dollars ($95,000.00) secured by a mortgage on real estate owned by Conklin and a security interest in the inventory of the partnership. Stipulation No. 4. On or about September 8, 1989, NEB loaned Twenty-Five Thousand Dollars ($25,000.00) to the individuals in the form of a line of credit for Spirit of the West. The line of credit was secured by the prior security interest duly perfected by filed financing statements. Stipulation No. 6. On or about June of 1990, the Debtor was incorporated and the assets of the partnership were conveyed to the new corporate entity. Stipulation No. 7.

After incorporation, American Business Credit ("ABC") made a loan of One Hundred Fifty-Five Thousand Dollars ($155,000.00) to Grover E. Conklin III, now the principal shareholder of the Debtor. This loan was secured by a mortgage on the real estate owned by Mr. Conklin and by a security interest in the corporate inventory. Stipulation No. 8.

Although the September 8, 1989 NEB note was marked "paid" sometime in September of 1990, a new note, purportedly renewing the line of credit from NEB in the amount of Twenty-Five Thousand Dollars ($25,000.00), was executed on or about October of 1990. Bank Exhibit No. 1.

The issue presented by the parties can be set forth as follows: Is the security interest of NEB in the inventory of Grover E. Conklin III and Patricia A. Krisovitch, individually and trading as Spirit of the West, superior to the position of ABC, which filed its financing statement against Spirit of the West, Inc.?

Both parties focus on 13 Pa.C.S.A. § 9402(g) as being the controlling statute on the issue. That statute reads as follows: Sufficiency of name of the debtor.—A financing statement sufficiently shows the name of the debtor if it gives the individual, partnership or corporate name of the debtor, whether or not it adds other trade names or the names of partners. Where the debtor so changes his name or in the case of an organization its name, identity or corporate structure that a filed financing statement becomes seriously misleading, the filing is not effective to perfect a security interest in collateral acquired by the debtor more than four months after the change, unless a new appropriate financing statement is filed before the expiration of that time. A filed financing statement remains effective with respect to collateral transferred by the debtor even though the secured party knows of or consents to the transfer.

The parties have correctly pointed out the importance of analyzing Section 9402(g) in deciding the efficacy of the financing statements on record. Nevertheless, in the Court's opinion, the parties have "placed the cart before the horse" in not first establishing what security agreement, if any, binds the corporation.

The parties have stipulated that Spirit of the West, Inc. executed a security agreement in inventory in favor of ABC. Stipulation No. 8. A copy of that agreement has been attached to ABC's answer.

On the other hand, NEB has neither alleged nor established that there was any security agreement between itself and the debtor corporation. Neither has it alleged nor established that the corporation was an alter ego of the individual owners or the former partnership.

Section 9201 of the Uniform Commercial Codestates: "A security agreement is effective according to its terms between the parties, against purchasers of the collateral and against creditors." 13 Pa.C.S.A. § 9201.

NEB does not have a security agreement with the Debtor corporation. The Bank's allegation that it is a superior claimant to ABC must necessarily rely on the binding effect of its financing statement on all transferees of the collateral. This does not appear to be in dispute. The parties appear to acknowledge that NEB had the principal security interest in Spirit of the West, the partnership. Since that inventory was transferred on or about June of 1990 to the corporation at the time of its formation, it would continue in that collateral as provided by the last sentence of Section 9402(g).

Nevertheless, it is important to note that the Uniform Commercial Code specifically does not address the issue of the effectiveness of a financing statement with respect to collateral acquired after the incorporation. 2 James J. White & Robert S. Summers, Uniform Commercial Code (3rd ed. 1988) at pg. 386.

NEB, in its Brief, relies on *In re Darling Lumber, Inc.*, 56 B.R. 669(Bankr. E.D. Mich. 1986) as authority for the proposition that a secured creditor is not required to file a new financing statement whenever a Debtor changes from a proprietorship to a corporation. Unlike the present case, the secured creditor in *Darling Lumber* had a security agreement with both the partnership and the corporation. *Id.* at pg. 670.

NEB also relies on *Interfirst Bank of Abilene, N.A. v. Lull Mfg.*, 778 F.2d 228 (5th Cir. 1985) for the proposition that the incorporation of an entity using the same name is not seriously misleading within the meaning of Section 9402(g). Again, this Court notes that the secured creditor in *Interfirst Bank* had security agreements with both the proprietorship and the successor corporation. *Id.* at pg. 231.

NEB cites also the case of *Borg-Warner Acceptance Corporation v. Bank of Marin*, 36 Cal. App. 3d 286, 111 Cal. Rptr. 361 (1973). That Court found that a financing statement filed against the partnership Loch Lomond Yacht Sales was effective against the corporation Loch Lomond Yacht Sales, Inc. and therefore, was not "seriously misleading." No mention in that case was made of whether or not appropriate security agreements were executed by the partnership and/or corporation. That case did note that the "purpose of filing a financing statement . . . is to give an existing or prospective creditor the opportunity to inform himself of whether, and of the extent to which, an existing or prospective debtor has encumbered his assets and to govern himself accordingly in dealing with the debtor." *Id.* at pg. 288, 111 Cal.Rptr. 361.

Assuming that a filing against Spirit of the West, a partnership, is adequate to give notice to the creditors of Spirit of the West, Inc.—notice of what? At best, the creditors of Spirit of the West, Inc., the debtor herein, would make inquiry of NEB and discover that there was no security agreement with the Debtor corporation.

The facts of this case bear a remarkable similarity to those facts that were addressed in the case of *In re Scott*, 113 B.R. 516 (Bankr. W.D. Ark. 1990).

In *Scott*, the Bank of Yellville ("Bank") had a security agreement with Shannon D. Scott and his wife Patricia R. Scott d/b/a K/C Audio/Video Center of Camden. The said security interest encumbered inventory, receivables, machinery, equipment, furniture and fixtures. Subsequent to the execution of that security agreement, the Debtors formed a corporation identified as "K.C. of Camden, Inc.." K.C. of Camden, Inc. executed a security agreement in favor of Borg-Warner which granted a security interest in all inventory. The Bank argued that the Uniform Commercial Code Article 9-402(7), which is identical to the Pennsylvania statute at issue in the case before us, allowed its security interest to attach to collateral acquired after incorporation. Application of section 9-402(7) to property acquired by the corporation under these facts is difficult because a security interest cannot be created under Article 9 unless the debtor has signed a security agreement in favor of the secured party, value has been given and the debtor has rights in the collateral. (Citations omitted.) A security interest in inventory is perfected when a valid financing statement, signed by the debtor, is properly filed. (Citation omitted.) In this case no security agreement was executed by the corporation in favor of the Bank and no value was extended by the Bank to the corporation. Although the last sentence of section 4-9-402(7) permits the continued perfection of a security interest in collateral which is transferred to a new entity, new property acquired by the transferee corporation is, by definition, not collateral transferred by a debtor. Whether or not a financing statement is misleading so as to render a filing ineffective would appear to be legally irrelevant if there is no underlying security interest to perfect. *Id.* at p. 520.

Spirit of the West, the partnership, has more than effected a name change to Spirit of the West, Inc. They have actually transferred the collateral to another entity.

Just as this Court did in the similar case of *Just for Kids, Inc.*, 150 B.R. 123 (Bankr. M.D. Pa. 1992), we hereby hold that the specific collateral transferred by the Spirit of the West, the partnership, to the corporate Debtor remains encumbered by the Bank, but NEB's security interest cannot attach to newly acquired corporate assets, which would appear to be subject to the first lien of ABC.

NOTES AND QUESTIONS

(1) Compare *Spirit of the West* with *In re Rentclub, Inc.*, 149 B.R. 699(Bankr. M.D. Fla. 1993). In *Rentclub* the court found the original financing statement seriously misleading after the debtor changed its name from "Tampa Rentclub, Inc." to "Rentclub, Inc." When the creditor failed to file a new financing statement within the four-month window, the court found that the creditor had a perfected security interest only as to secured property that debtor owned at the end of the four-month period. The creditor had only an unperfected security interest in any property acquired by debtor after that date. The court's test for "seriously misleading" turned on factual considerations and the effect on potential creditors of the debtor's name change. What other bases could the court have considered? Were there any it *should* have considered?

(2) In *In re Paramount International, Inc.*, 154 B.R. 712(Bankr. N.D. Ill. 1993), the court held that a secured creditor's original financing statement was not rendered seriously misleading after debtor changed its name from "Paramount Attractions, Inc." to "Paramount International, Inc." Since the debtor's business address remained the same after the name change and the debtor was authorized to use its former corporate name as a trade or street name, such a change was not seriously misleading for purposes of § 9-402(7). Thus, the creditor's security interest in debtor's accounts receivable remained valid. The court stated that the test for determining whether a name change was "seriously misleading" depended upon whether a "reasonably diligent" searcher would be able to discover the financing statement after the name change. What types of steps must a searcher take to satisfy the reasonable diligence standard?

[B] Name and Spelling Errors

Read: U.C.C. § 9-402.

DISTRICT OF COLUMBIA v. THOMAS FUNDING CORP.

District of Columbia Court of Appeals
593 A.2d 1030 (1991)

BELSON, J.

This is an appeal from the trial court's ruling that the assignee of an account had an interest in the account that took priority over an Internal Revenue Service lien on the account. We hold that the financing statement filed by the assignee was insufficient to perfect its security interest because it did not correctly set forth the name of the assignor taxpayer. Therefore, we reverse.

I.

Silverline Building and Maintenance Company contracted with the District of Columbia in December 1983 to perform janitorial services in two office buildings occupied by the District of Columbia. At approximately the same time, Silverline entered into a factoring arrangement with Thomas Funding Corporation in which Silverline assigned its right to payment pursuant to its contracts with the District to Thomas Funding in exchange for money Silverline received from Thomas Funding that Silverline used as working capital. Silverline notified the District of the assignment by letter and directed the District to make payments to Thomas Funding on Silverline's invoice to the District. This practice continued on a monthly basis through September 1984. In addition, Thomas Funding filed a financing statement with the Recorder of Deeds on January 4, 1984, covering "all now owned and hereafter acquired accounts, contract rights . . .general intangibles of the debtor." The financing statement, however, inadvertently identified the debtor as "Silvermine Building Maintenance Co.," mistakenly substituting the letter "m" for the second letter "l" in the word "Silverline." Until October 1984, the District had paid Thomas Funding the amount due Silverline under the janitorial service contracts.

In April and May of 1984, the Internal Revenue Service made assessments against Silverline for unpaid federal income taxes totalling $ 22,370.19. On October 5, 1984, the IRS filed a notice of tax lien against Silverline with the Recorder of Deeds and served the District with notice of tax levy against any property or rights to property belonging to Silverline. At that time, the District owed $ 18,747 on the janitorial service contracts for work performed during September 1984. Instead of paying the amount owed under the contracts to Thomas Funding, the District paid this amount to the IRS on January 1, 1985.

Thomas Funding brought suit against the District for the amount due under the Silverline contracts, $18,747. The District asserted in its answer that its honoring of the IRS levy discharged it of any obligation to Thomas Funding, but nevertheless filed a third-party complaint against the United States. The trial court granted the United States's motion to dismiss because the nine-month statute of limitations for a suit for wrongful payment to the IRS had run. On cross motions for summary judgment, the trial court awarded Thomas Funding $ 18,747, plus costs and post-judgment interest. The trial court found that Silverline had no property rights in the assigned accounts, but instead its rights had been transferred to Thomas Funding. Furthermore, the trial court concluded that the misspelling of the debtor's name in the financing statement was a minor error, which could not have misled the District because the District had actual notice of the assignment.

II.

. . . .

The law of the District of Columbia has recognized generally that parties to contracts may assign their contractual rights. *Flack v. Laster*, 417 A.2d 393, 399 (D.C. 1980) ("The right to assign is presumed, based upon principles of unhampered transferability of property rights and of business convenience.") However, most assignments of accounts are governed by Article 9 of the District of Columbia's Uniform Commercial Code. D.C. Code § 28:9-101 to 28:9-507 (1981 & Supp. 1990). The United States Court of Appeals for the District of Columbia Circuit, applying District of Columbia law, has held that when the Uniform Commercial Code does not apply to a particular situation, general contract principles govern. . .. Thus, we must determine whether the assignment between Silverline and Thomas Funding is one included under Article 9 of the Code and, if so, what results from the application of Article 9 to the transaction involved here.

Thomas Funding contends that Article 9 does not apply to the transaction between it and Silverline because the transaction effected a sale of Silverline's entire interest in the accounts rather than the creation of a security interest. However, Article 9 applies not only to any transaction which is intended to create a security interest in accounts, but also to any sale of accounts. D.C. Code § 28:9-102(1)(Supp. 1990). The drafters of the Uniform Commercial Code expressed concern that transactions involving the sale of accounts would be indistinguishable from transactions involving accounts as security, and thus they included both types of transactions within the scope of Article 9:

> An assignment of accounts . . . as security for an obligation is covered by subsection (1)(a) [of section 9-102]. Commercial financing on the basis of accounts . . .is often so conducted that the distinction between a security transfer and a sale is blurred, and a sale of [accounts] is therefore covered by subsection (1)(b) [of section 9-102] whether intended for security or not, unless excluded by Section 9-104. The buyer then is treated as a secured party, and his interest as a security interest.

Unif. Commercial Code § 9-102, 3 U.L.A. 76, 79(1972) (official comment 2). Certain transactions involving accounts are excluded from the scope of Article 9 because, by their nature, they have nothing to do with commercial financing Transactions. Unif. Commercial Code § 9-104, 3 U.L.A. 143, 147(1972) (official comment 6). Those transactions excluded from the scope of Article 9 are the sales of accounts as part of a sale of a business, an assignment of an account for the purpose of collection only, a transfer of a right to payment to one who is also obligated to perform under the contract, and a transfer of a single account in satisfaction of a preexisting debt. D.C. Code § 28:9-104 (f)(Supp. 1990).

The assignment of accounts in the case at hand was part of a factoring arrangement, a frequently used means of commercial financing that the drafters of the Uniform Commercial Code clearly contemplated would fall within the scope of Article 9. Because we find that the assignment of accounts is within the scope of Article 9, we must look to the provisions of Article 9 to determine the rights of the parties involved.

Under Article 9, the account debtor is authorized to pay the assignor until the account debtor receives notification that the amount due has been assigned and that payment is to be made to the assignee. D.C. Code § 28:9-318 (3)(Supp. 1990). If thereafter the account debtor continues to pay the assignor, the debtor will remain liable to the assignee for the same amount. . .. The obligation of the account debtor is not discharged by the "wrongful payment" to the assignor. Clearly, as between the assignor and the assignee, the assignor has no right to payment from the account debtor once notice is given and a demand is made. D.C. Code § 28:9-318 (3).

The District, in this case, received notice of the assignment and received a request that payment be made to Thomas Funding instead of Silverline. Consequently, under the provisions of Article 9, Silverline would have no right to payment from the District. See *id.*

. . . .

To be a perfected security interest, the security interest must have attached and the secured party must have taken the applicable steps required for perfection. D.C. Code § 28:9-303 (1)(1981). Attachment of the interest generally occurs when the debtor has signed a security agreement which contains a description of the collateral, the secured party has given value, and the debtor has rights in the collateral. D.C. Code § 28:9-203 (1) (Supp. 1990). Perfection generally may be achieved by either filing a financing statement or obtaining possession of the collateral.

D.C. Code §§ 28:9-302 (1), 28:9-304 (1), 28:9-305(Supp. 1990). However, perfection of an interest in accounts must be achieved by filing. D.C. Code § 28:9-302 (1)(Supp. 1990); Unif. Commercial Code § 9-302, 3 U.L.A. 364, 369 (1972) (official comment 5) ("filing is thus the only means of perfection contemplated by this Article"). The drafters of the Uniform Commercial Code noted that "the filing requirement of this section applies both to sales [of accounts] and to transfers thereof for security." Unif. Commercial Code § 9-302, 3 U.L.A. at 369 (official comment 5). In fact, the drafters further commented that "any person who regularly takes assignments of any debtor's account should file" to perfect his or her security interest. *Id.* It follows from the foregoing that an assignment that falls within the scope of Article 9 which is not perfected leaves a property interest in the assignor against which a third party lien creditor, such as the IRS, can attach a lien. . ..

In this case, Thomas Funding filed a financing statement that was intended to cover the accounts of Silverline. However, the financing statement named the debtor as "Silvermine Building Maintenance Co." Thus, we must determine whether Thomas Funding obtained a perfected security interest by filing a financing statement that misspelled Silverline's name.

Article 9 adopts a system of "notice filing," requiring only a simple notice, the financing statement, to be filed, rather than the security agreement itself. D.C. Code § 28:9-402 (1)(Supp. 1990); see Unif. Commercial Code § 9-402, 3A U.L.A. 45, 51(1972) (official comment 2). The Recorder of Deeds is required to index the financing statement according to the name of the debtor. D.C. Code § 28:9-403 (4)(Supp. 1990). Thus, a prime requisite of the sufficiency of a financing statement is that it set forth the debtor's name. D.C. Code § 28:9-402 (1). Whether a financing statement that misspells the debtor's name substantially complies with this requirement depends upon whether the misspelling is a minor error which is not seriously misleading. D.C. Code § 28:9-402 (8)(Supp. 1990). As the drafters of the Uniform Commercial Code noted, section 9-402 (8) "is in line with the policy of this Article to simplify formal requisites and filing requirements and is designed to discourage the fanatical and impossibly refined reading of such statutory requirements in which courts have occasionally indulged themselves." Unif. Commercial Code § 9-402, 3A U.L.A. at 54 (official comment 9). With this in mind, we must look to the facts of this case to determine whether the misspelling of the debtor's name in this case is so seriously misleading that it renders the financing statement ineffective.

An indication of the seriousness of the misspelling here is the fact that the Recorder of Deeds certified that no financing statement against Silverline had been filed. The Recorder of Deeds, or any other person searching the records, likely would not have found the financing statement filed by Thomas Funding because of the misspelling of Silverline's name. There is some chance that because "Silvermine" would be near "Silverline" in alphabetical order, a person searching the records would happen upon it. But it would not be obvious to the beholder that "Silvermine" is merely a misspelling of Silverline. We are persuaded that a financing statement filed under the name "Silvermine" essentially fails to give notice of the security interest in the accounts receivable of Silverline. Moreover, the fact that the District had actual notice of the assignment of the accounts has no bearing on whether the financing statement is effective in this case because our focus is upon whether Thomas Funding perfected its interest to preclude other creditors, *e.g.*, the IRS, from stepping in front of it.

We hold that the misspelling of Silverline's name as "Silvermine" is an error so seriously misleading as to render the financing statement ineffective for purposes of putting a third party on notice that Silverline had given Thomas Funding a security interest in the accounts. Other courts have ruled similarly. See *Reisdorf Bros., Inc. v. Clinton Corn Processing Co.*, 130 A.D.2d 951, 516 N.Y.S.2d 375, 375 (4th Dep't 1987) (misspelling of debtor's own name and his d/b/a name was so seriously misleading as to render financing statement ineffective); *Bank of North America v. Bank of Nutley*, 94 N.J. Super. 220, 227 A.2d 535, 538-39 (1967) (financing statement misspelled Kaplan as Kaplas); *In re Brawn*, 6 U.C.C. Rep. Serv. 1031, 1037-39 (Bankr. D. Me. Sept. 18, 1969) (financing statement misspelled Brawn as Brown); *National Cash Register Co. v. Valley Nat'l Bank*, 5 U.C.C. Rep. Serv. 396, 396-97 (N.Y. Sup. Ct. June 3, 1968) (financing statement misspelled Borgwald as Boywald). But see *Beneficial Finance Co. v. Kurland Cadillac-Oldsmobile, Inc.*, 57 Misc. 2d 806, 293 N.Y.S.2d 647, 649 (N.Y. Sup. Ct. 1968) (financing statement misspelled debtor's first name as Shelia instead of Sheila was obviously a minor error), rev'd on other grounds, 32 A.D.2d 643, 300 N.Y.S.2d 884 (2d Dep't 1969). See generally Annotation, Sufficiency of Designation of Debtor or Secured Party in Security Agreement or Financing Statement Under U.C.C. § 9-402, 99A.L.R.3d 478, 534-36 (1980). Because we conclude that the misspelling renders Thomas Funding's security interest unperfected, we hold that Silverline retained an interest in the accounts in the sense that any lien creditor of Silverline could attach its lien to the assigned accounts to satisfy its judgment.

. . . .

Reversed.

NOTES

(1) *Silvermine vs. Silverline*. In the instant case, the filed financing statement contained a misspelling of the assignor's (taxpayer's) name. The court found the misspelling sufficiently serious because the filing officer certified that no financing statement against the taxpayer had been filed. Do you agree? Is the "seriously misleading" standard a workable one?

(2) What effect would a computerized recording system have on the concept of "seriously misleading"? In the case of *In re Tyler*, 23 B.R. 806, 34 U.C.C. Rep. Serv. 1428 (1982), the debtor changed its name from "Tri-State Moulded Plastics, Inc." to "Tri-State Molded Plastics, Inc." The creditor did not file an amended financing statement because the name change was so slight. However, because the filing system was computerized, even a slight variation in the spelling of the name would make retrieval of the file impossible. Citing the need to treat other creditors fairly, the court ruled that the name change was seriously misleading:

> . . . any intelligent human seeing both names would be expected to investigate both. It is difficult to conceive of a more insignificant change, and there is no reason HNB should have had reason to believe refiling was necessary. . . . The result in this case is harsh for the creditor, but an opposite result negates the noticing system. 34 U.C.C. Rep. Serv. at 1433-4.

The result in *Tyler* suggests that U.C.C. § 9-402(7)is incompatible with a computerized filing system. Do you agree? Compare *In re Thriftway Auto Supply, Inc.*, 159 B.R. 948, 22 U.C.C. Rep. Serv. 29 (W.D. Okla. 1993) aff'd 39 F.3d 1193 (10th Cir. 1994), where the court held that use of the debtor's trade name in a financing statement fell within a recognized exception for such use. The court noted that either the particular indexing system in place must provide an inquirer with flexibility in its search, or the trade name must be "very close" to debtor's legal name. The court found the county's computerized indexing system gave the second creditor the necessary flexibility and that the creditor's search was simply insufficient.

(3) An incorrect address on a financing statement is dealt with in essentially the same manner as an incorrect name. The court will examine whether the wrong address significantly impeded the giving of notice to prospective creditors. The circumstances of each case will control whether an incorrect address is seriously misleading. In *Teel Construction v. Lipper Inc.*, 11 U.C.C. Rep. Serv. 2d 667 (Va. Cir. Ct. 1990), the court noted that the failure to include any address in a financing statement would be fatal to perfection; however, where the debtor's address was deficient in some other way, the issue of sufficiency was a question of fact. The court considered the difficulty an interested party would encounter in attempting to contact or identify the debtor at such an incorrect address. Because the interested party had knowledge of the debtor's actual location, the court held that the incorrect address contained in the financing statement did not unduly harm the party, and therefore should not serve to prevent perfection of the creditor's security interest. If you had been the judge, would you have decided differently? Why or why not?

[C] Missing Signatures

Read: U.C.C. §§ 9-401 and 9-402.

Section 9-402(1) requires that the financing statement be signed by the debtor. Usually, this requirement will be satisfied by the debtor's longhand, personal signature. However, the word "signed" is defined quite broadly as any symbol executed or adopted by the party with a present intention to authenticate a writing. See § 1-201(39). The comment to that section provides that "authentication may be printed, stamped or written . . .and in appropriate cases may be found in a billhead or letterhead." A number of issues may arise concerning the signature requirement. For example, if a creditor files a financing statement as to collateral for which the filing has lapsed, is it necessary for the debtor to sign the new financing statement? See *In re Tebbs Const. Co. Inc.*, 39 B.R. 742, 38 U.C.C. Rep. Serv. 1400 (Bankr. E.D. Va. 1984) (held: the debtor's signature was not necessary where the parties stipulated that the financing statement was a refiling).

Most courts strictly enforce the signature requirement of U.C.C. § 9-402(1). Thus, even where a security agreement signed by the debtor was stapled to the unsigned financing statement, the security interest was held to be unperfected. See *In re Pischke*, 32 U.C.C. Rep. Serv. 349, 11 B.R. 913 (Bankr. E.D. Va. 1981). Does the *Pischke* holding follow the provisions of U.C.C. § 1-102(1) assuming that the purpose of filing is to give notice? In certain instances, section 9-402(2) permits a secured party to sign a financing statement instead of the debtor. Is such an exception good policy? Why or why not? See comment 4.

In cases involving multiple debtors, must each debtor sign the financing statement? In *In Re Hammons*, 23 U.C.C. Rep. Serv. 1077, 438 F. Supp. 1143 (D. Miss. 1977), the court found the signature of one partner sufficient where both partners had signed the security agreement. The court observed: "A financing statement is intended to provide notice only, it is not intended to have the legal sufficiency of a security agreement or other contract." In cases where the debtor and the owner of the collateral are not the same person, it may be necessary for both to sign the financing statement so as not to mislead creditors of the owner. See *General Motors v.*

Washington Trust Co. of Westerly, 24 U.C.C. Rep. Serv. 211 (R.I. Sup. Ct. 1978), where a husband's signature was held insufficient where his wife was the record owner of the collateral (a Cadillac).

Where a wife testified to a pattern of conduct in which her husband assumed responsibility for the collateral in question (farm equipment), the husband's signature was held sufficient in his capacity as her agent. *In re Kinney*, 34 U.C.C. Rep. Serv. 305, 16 B.R. 664 (Bankr. W.D. Mo. 1981). In the *Kinney* case, the court said ordinarily one spouse may not encumber property to secure an individual debt without the consent of the other. Thus, in a subsequent similar case, the same court held the omission of the wife's signature fatal to perfection despite the fact that she had signed all notes and security agreements. *In re Davison*, 36 U.C.C. Rep. Serv. 717, 29 B.R. 987 (Bankr. W.D. Mo. 1983) The court distinguished *Kinney*: "In *Kinney* the wife testified that her husband handled all the commercial matters. She was not required to sign the security agreement nor was she even fully aware the tractor involved had been pledged. This is not the case with the Davisons. Betty Davison signed all the security agreements and notes. . .. If Marvin Davison suddenly presumed to act as Betty's agent in signing the financing statement there should be some evidence of such agency on the face of that document." . Do you agree with the court's reasoning in these cases? Would the application of the doctrine of implied consent have yielded the same result?

In *Hobart Corporation v. North Central Credit Services, Inc.*, 628 P.2d 842, 31 U.C.C. Rep. Serv. 1481 (Wash. Ct. App. 1981), the court reversed a summary judgment that was granted in favor of Hobart. In two separate contracts, Hobart sold meat cutting equipment to Dean Nielson who was doing business as Country Market. U.C.C. § 9-402(1) requires that the signature of the debtor and the addresses of both parties be included on a financing statement. At the bottom of the first financing statement was typed: "Country Market" and at the bottom of the second was typed: "Dean Nielson, d/b/a Country Market." The appellate court found these to be seriously misleading because individuals operate sole proprietorships under names other than their own, and the only acceptable name to achieve basic notice to creditors is the individual's proper name. The court also found nothing on either financing statement to indicate that the debtor had adopted a typed name as his signature. Do you agree?

§ 17.07 Improper Place

Read: U.C.C. § 9-401(2).

IN RE SCHOENFELD
CHECKETT v. SCHOENFELD

United States Bankruptcy Court, Western District, Missouri
111 B.R. 832, 12 U.C.C. Rep. 2d 574 (1990)

ARTHUR B. FEDERMAN, BANKRUPTCY JUDGE.

Plaintiff bankruptcy trustee filed this action seeking a determination that defendant does not hold a perfected security interest in certain assets of the debtor. The Court finds for the Plaintiff. On January 14, 1987, the debtor, Dr. Roger Harold Schoenfeld, borrowed $4,000.00 from his father, defendant, Roger P. Schoenfeld. In exchange, the debtor signed a promissory note as well as a security interest in the debtor's gun collection. The determination of the perfection of the security interest in this case is complicated by the fact that the city of Joplin, Missouri, is located within two counties — Jasper County and Newton County. The father attempted to perfect such security interest by filing U.C.C.-1financing statements with the Secretary of State and with the Recorder of Deeds of Jasper County, Missouri. The U.C.C.-1 filed by the father lists an address for the debtor which was his office in Newton County, Missouri. The security agreement states that the guns will be kept at such address.

The Trustee contends that the U.C.C.-1filings were not sufficient to perfect the lien. Missouri law provides for the perfection of security interests in consumer goods by the filing of a financing statement ". . . in the office of the Recorder of Deeds in the county of the debtor's residence or if the debtor is not a resident of this state then in the office of the Recorder of Deeds in the county where the goods are kept. . ." (R.S. Mo. § 400.9-401(1)(a)). In his response, the father contends that his son was a resident of Jasper County on the date the financing statement was filed and that, therefore, the lien was validly perfected. While not referred to in his answer, the father at trial also offered evidence to show, in the alternative, that the lien was perfected by possession as to a substantial number—and apparently the most valuable—of the guns. Missouri law provides that a secured party can perfect a security interested in goods by possession. R.S. Mo. § 400.9-305 reads in part as follows:

> A security interest in letters of credit and advices of credit (subsection (2)(a) of section 400.5-116), goods, instruments, money, negotiable documents or chattel paper may be perfected by the secured party's taking possession of the collateral. . .. A security interest is perfected by possession from the time possession is taken without relation back and continues only so long as possession is retained, unless otherwise specified in this article. The security interest may be otherwise perfected as provided in this article before or after the period of possession by the secured party.

The evidence at trial showed that on January 14, 1987, the debtor did own a house in Jasper County, Missouri. However, the evidence showed that in September of 1986, he had moved his furniture and other personal belongings to Miami, Oklahoma, to the house of Kay Francis Walker, whom he married on January 10, 1987. A child of he and Ms. Walker, born on January 24, 1987, was issued a birth certificate stating both parents to be residents of Miami, Oklahoma. Ms. Walker testified that such certificate was based on information provided by Dr. Schoenfeld. The debtor and Ms. Walker remained married until September 25, 1987. During the period immediately before and after the grant of the security interest to the defendant, Ms. Walker testified that the debtor either stayed at her house or, on evenings when he worked late, at his office, which is located in Joplin, Newton County, Missouri. In fact, she testified that after August, 1986 there was no bed or other furniture at the Jasper County home. The debtor himself testified that at various other times he lived at his office and that accommodations were available at such office. On February 3 or 4, 1987, the debtor and Ms. Walker purchased a residence in Newton County, Missouri using the $4,000 lent from the debtor's father as the down payment.

The debtor agrees that almost all his household goods were moved to Oklahoma in August or September, 1986 but contends that he kept a pallet and some changes of clothes at the Jasper County address for when he worked late or had a disagreement with his new wife. He acknowledges that water service to the Jasper County home was turned off prior to January, 1987, but says that electrical service was maintained. However, as the trustee points out, the amount of electricity actually used in late 1986 and early 1987 is nowhere near that which would be used if the house had been occupied.

From the evidence, it is obvious that the debtor did not reside in Jasper County, on January 14, 1987. He either lived in Newton County or, more likely, in Oklahoma. If in Newton County, the U.C.C.-1 should have been filed there, but was not. If in Oklahoma, the U.C.C.-1 should have been filed in the county in which the goods were kept as of the date the security interest was granted.

The question of where the goods were kept is also related to the father's claim of a possessory lien. At trial, both the debtor and his father testified that certain of the guns were kept in the father's possession. The debtor testified that he kept them there because his father had a safe at his house in which the guns could be stored, and also that he kept them there because he periodically went hunting on his father's farm. His father testified that the guns were brought to him "as part of the loan process" in order to prepare the list attached to the financing statement. (Tr. 44) The father's residence is in St. Louis, Missouri, and his farm is near St. Louis, in Owensville. Neither is located in Jasper County, Missouri. Therefore, at least as to the guns in the father's possession, the financing statement was not properly filed in the county where such guns were kept, and the lien granted to him in these guns was not perfected.

That leaves two questions. Does the father have a possessory lien on the guns held by him? And did the father's U.C.C. filing in Jasper County perfect a lien on the guns not in his possession — that is, were those guns kept in Jasper County?

As to the claimed possessory lien, such lien did not exist. The purpose of the perfection requirement is to give notice to all current and potential creditors that the property is being used as collateral and cannot be repledged. See *In re Copeland*, 531 F.2d 1195 (3rd Cir. 1976). The mere fact that one person holds property of another does not create a lien. Copeland noted that if the debtor or "an individual closely associated" with him holds the collateral this would not sufficiently alert prospective creditors that the debtor's property is encumbered. See *In re Rolain*, 823 F.2d 198 (8th Cir. 1987). Here, the property was certainly held by someone close to the debtor — his father. No one testified that the guns were given to the father for the purpose of perfecting a lien. In fact, the parties intended to perfect the lien by the U.C.C. filing. The debtor gave the guns to his father for safekeeping or convenience, and had free and unfettered access to such guns while in his father's possession. When the debtor wanted to go hunting, he went to his father's house and got a gun. In fact, the father testified that by August, 15, 1989 he had only seven of the guns in his possession; the rest had been taken back by the debtor for his own use. The debtor himself testified that most of the guns remained in his father's possession only until he moved into the Newton County residence in August 1987 (Tr. 68). Any perfected lien the father may have had was erased when the debtor took a gun back. But it cannot be argued that any such possessory lien ever existed, since the father did not exercise dominion and control over such guns as against the debtor.

The final issue is whether the father perfected a lien on any of the other guns, not in his possession, by the U.C.C. filing in Jasper County. That issue turns on where the goods were kept as of January 14, 1987, assuming the debtor lived in Oklahoma as of that date. The debtor testified that he kept some of such guns at his office, in Newton County, some in his cars, and some at the house in Jasper County. (Tr. 69) His ex-wife testified that guns were moved to Oklahoma along with his other possessions in 1986. (Tr. 25) His father said he saw certain guns at the Jasper County residence at one time (Tr. 38), but did not testify that he had even been in such residence after 1986. A former employee of the debtor testified that the debtor kept some guns in his car. (Tr. 6) No witness testified as to which guns in particular were stored in Jasper County, the car, the office, or Oklahoma. In defense of a turnover action, a party attempting to prove that it has a perfected lien on assets of the debtor must prove each and every element necessary to perfect such a lien. See *In re Pester*, 845 F.2d 1476, 1486 (8th Cir. 1988). While the defendant did prove that the financing statement was filed in Jasper County on January 14, 1987, he has failed to prove which particular guns were kept in such county on that date. In fact, the evidence demonstrated that most of the guns were kept elsewhere as of that date.

Based upon the above and foregoing, the Court finds that any security interest held by the defendant is not perfected and that the guns referred to herein must be turned over to the Trustee within 10 days of the date of this Order. This Order is not intended to restrict the debtor's ability to claim lawful exemptions as to the guns which are to be turned over to the Trustee.

NOTE

Schoenfeld demonstrates that if a financing statement is not filed in the appropriate office, the security interest will not be perfected. However, it is possible that an improperly filed statement could provide a secured party with some protection. As you read the following case, recall the purposes of the filing system—to provide certainty and to eliminate controversies over whether someone had knowledge of a prior filing. To the extent that U.C.C. § 9-401(2) raises questions about a party's knowledge concerning a filed statement, is it inconsistent with the basic principle that the first properly filed financing statement should have priority?

AFFILIATED FOOD STORES, INC. v. FARMERS AND MERCHANTS BANK OF DES ARC, ARKANSAS

Supreme Court of Arkansas
300 Ark. 450, 780 S.W.2d 20, 10 U.C.C. Rep. 2d 1473 (1989)

NEWBERN, JUSTICE.

In this appeal we must decide which of two parties was first to perfect its security interest in the inventory of a grocery store and is thus entitled to the proceeds of the sale of the inventory to satisfy a debt. Our holding is that the creditor which was the first to file with the office of the secretary of state prevails.

On November 1, 1986, Bill Rogers sold a grocery store named "Scotty's Affiliated Foods" to Bob Davis d/b/a Bob's Supermarkets of Arkansas, Inc., (Bob's). Davis changed the store's name to "Bob's Thriftway." Rogers paid off his account with the appellant, Affiliated Food Stores, Inc., (Affiliated), the company which had supplied the store's inventory. On November 3, 1986, Davis signed a security agreement with Affiliated giving it a security interest in the new inventory he then purchased for the store. On November 4, 1986, Davis signed an agreement with the appellee, Farmers and Merchants Bank of Des Arc, Arkansas, giving the bank a security interest in the inventory of the store. The agreement showed the name of the borrower to be Bob's Supermarkets of Arkansas, with a Little Rock address. The bank had loaned Davis $62,083.64, including its finance charge, as purchase money to assist Davis in purchasing the store. On November 7, 1986, Affiliated supplied inventory to the store, thus giving value in accordance with its agreement with Davis.

On November 7, 1986, the bank filed its financing statement and security agreement with the Prairie County Circuit Clerk. On November 18, 1986, Affiliated filed its financing statement with the Prairie County Circuit Clerk. On November 19, 1986, Affiliated filed its financing statement with the secretary of state's office. On November 25, 1986, the Bank filed with the secretary of state's office.

Thereafter, Bob's became insolvent, and the parties caused the inventory to be sold. Money from the sale of the inventory, in the amount of $44,748.00, was deposited in the registry of the court. The underlying action was brought by the bank for replevin and to have a receiver appointed. Because the bank received credit for the sale of other items in which the bank held a secured interest, the bank's maximum claim against the fund resulting from the sale of inventory was reduced to $26,688.49. Affiliated was, by agreement of the parties, paid $18,059.51 from the fund. The $26,668.59 remaining in the registry of the court was the object of the competing security interests.

In his order, the trial court held that the bank was entitled to the money. The court noted that priority was to be determined by the "first to file" provision of Ark.Code Ann. § 4-9-312(5) and (6) (Supp.1989). The court recognized that perfection of a security interest in inventory, Ark.Code Ann. § 4-9-401(1)(c) (1987), requires filing with the office of the secretary of state and provides for local (county) filing if the debtor does business in only one county. Although it was found that Bob's operated stores in more than one county, the court held that the local filing with the Prairie County Circuit Clerk was sufficient because, "this store (Scotty's) was operated as a separate entity, had been assigned a separate account number, and was billed separately by Affiliated Foods." The bank thus prevailed because it had been the first to file in the county where the store was located.

1. The filing requirement

The subject of section 4-9-401 is "[t]he proper place to file in order to perfect a security interest. . . ." Subsections (a) and (b) deal with security interests in specific items such as farm equipment, farm products, timber, and minerals. Subsection (c) provides, in relevant part:

> In all other cases, in the office of the Secretary of State and in addition, if the debtor has a place of business in only one county of this state, also in the office of the clerk of the circuit court and ex officio recorder of such county. . . .

The bank's filing with the circuit clerk on November 7, 1986, would have perfected its security interest only if it had also filed with the secretary of state and if Bob's had been doing business only in Prairie County.

We find no authority in support of the trial court's apparent conclusion that, because Affiliated kept separate billing records for Scotty's or Bob's Thriftway, that Bob's could be considered to be doing business only in Prairie County. Even if that conclusion were supportable, the bank would not have been entitled to priority on the basis of a first filing. It had not complied with the first requirement of filing with the office of secretary of state until November 25, 1986, which was after Affiliated had filed with both the office of the secretary of state and the Prairie County Circuit Clerk. Although the first filing was by the bank, the bank was not the first to file correctly which, in these circumstances, is required in order for it to have priority over Affiliated, which was the first to file correctly. B. Clark, The Law of Secured Transactions § 3.8[1] (Cumm. Supp. No. 3, 1987). See also J. White and R. Summers, Uniform Commercial Code, § 25-4(2nd ed. 1980).

If the bank is to prevail, it must be on a basis other than its contention that it filed correctly and filed first.

2. Knowledge and good faith

The bank argues that, due to its first filing with the circuit clerk, Affiliated had knowledge of its security interest in the inventory and thus the filing with the circuit clerk was sufficient, citing *In re Davidoff*, 351 F. Supp. 440 (S.D.N.Y. 1972). In that case, in which New York law was applied, it was held that a creditor who had actual knowledge of a prior security interest could not defeat the prior interest on the basis that the prior interest was filed improperly. In the case now before us there is no evidence that Affiliated had actual knowledge of the bank's interest.

Nor do we agree that Ark. Code Ann. § 4-9-401(2) (1987) supports the bank's argument that its incorrect filing prevails because it was made in good faith against a person "who has knowledge of the contents of such financing statement." In the parlance of the Uniform Commercial Code, "knowledge of the contents" means actual rather than constructive knowledge. *First State Bank v. United Dollar Stores,* 571 P.2d 444 (Okla. 1977); J. White and R. Summers, *supra*; § 23-15, B. Clark., The Law of Secured Transactions Under the Uniform Commercial Code § 3.8[1] (1980).

. . . .

Conclusion

The authorities we have cited, (see particularly B. Clark, *supra*, § 3.8[1]), make it clear that in the circumstances presented here priority as between two secured interests depends on the outcome of the race to file correctly. Affiliated was the first to file correctly. The case is reversed and remanded for orders consistent with this opinion.

NOTES

(1) In *Duquoin National Bank v. Vergennes Equipment, Inc.*, 599 N.E. 2d 1367 (Ill. App. 1992), a secured party sought to gain priority over a Bank based on its good-faith filing of a financing statement in an improper location. The court rejected the party's claim under § 9-401(2) because the Bank's interest arose prior to the party's misguided filing. In the court's view, § 9-401(2) offers protection for filings made in improper locations against subsequent security interests in the same collateral after the improper filing. The court found that the section could not be used to usurp priority from a secured party whose interest arose prior to the improper filing.

(2) How are the concepts of good faith and knowledge similar? How are they different? Does § 9-401(2) increase fairness at the expense of certainty? Which result is better to have if both cannot be achieved at the same time? For a good discussion of the knowledge requirement, see *In re Nemko, Inc.*, 136 B.R. 334 (Bankr. E.D.N.Y. 1992) (held: priority given to first creditor where the second creditor had actual knowledge of the first creditor's improper filing).

§ 17.08 Errors By the Filing Officer

Read: U.C.C. §§ 9-403 through 9-407.

PEOPLES NATIONAL BANK OF ROCKLAND COUNTY v. WEINER

Supreme Court, Appellate Division, Second Department
129 A.D.2d 782, 514 N.Y.S.2d 772, 3 U.C.C. Rep. Serv. 2d 1615 (1987)

Before THOMPSON, J.P., and BROWN, EIBER and SPATT, JJ.

Memorandum by the Court.

. . . .

This action arises out of a secured transaction in which the plaintiff loaned Speedcraft Auto Parts, Inc. (hereinafter Speedcraft) $60,000 and in return received as collateral a security interest in Speedcraft's inventory and equipment. The plaintiff was represented in the transaction by the defendant Stanley Weiner, an attorney, and he in turn retained the defendant McCall Abstract Corp. (hereinafter McCall) to conduct the title searches on the collateral and to file the U.C.C. financing statements with the proper authorities. On August 12, 1977, the day following the closing, McCall delivered the financing statement to the office of the Rockland County Clerk for filing and on that same day, mailed a copy of the financing statement, together with a check for the filing costs, to the office of the Secretary of State. McCall received no return receipt; its check for the filing fees was never returned or negotiated and no completed copy of the financing statement was returned.

Subsequently, approximately one month later, Speedcraft filed for bankruptcy and during the course of those proceedings, it was discovered that the plaintiff's financing statement had never been filed with the Secretary of State, and as a result, the plaintiff lost its status as a secured creditor and was relegated to the status of a general unsecured creditor.

In this action, the plaintiff seeks partial summary judgment on the issue of liability on the ground that the defendants breached their duty to ensure that the financing statement was properly filed.

We agree with the plaintiff that it was entitled to partial summary judgment on the issue of liability as there are no issues of fact to be determined and no meritorious defenses (CPLR 3212[b]; *Northway Mall Assocs. v. Bernlee Realty Corp.*, 90 A.D. 2d 739). We reject the defendants' contention that they perfected the plaintiff's security interest by merely mailing the financing statement. Mere mailing does not constitute "[p]resentation" to the filing officer pursuant to U.C.C. 9-403 (1). We find that a financing statement must be received by the filing officer before it is presented and that evidence of receipt is required.

U.C.C. 9-403 (1)states that "[p]resentation for filing of a financing statement and tender of the filing fee or acceptance of the statement by the filing officer constitutes filing under this Article." The defendants erroneously equate "acceptance" with "receipt" and argue that receipt is not required because either presentation or receipt constitutes filing. The defendants confuse the filing officer's performance of duty, *i.e.*, acceptance, with receipt of the document. Acceptance is not the equivalent of receipt. Acceptance is not necessary to filing while receipt is. "[T]he contemplation of the U.C.C. is that filing be effective regardless of whether the officer receiving the controlling documents makes the right gestures of acceptance." (*Matter of Flagstaff Food-Service Corp.*, 16 B.R. 132, 135). The *Flagstaff* rule reflects the proposition that the party presenting the financing statement shall not bear the risk that the filing officer will not properly perform his duty (see, *In re May Lee Indus.*, 380 F. Supp. 1, *aff'd*, 501 F.2d 1407). It is self-evident that the filing officer cannot carry out the duty to record or index a financing statement if the statement is not received.

Moreover, prior to adoption of U.C.C. 9-403 (1) receipt was required. The New York annotations to the U.C.C. indicate that the rule of U.C.C. 9-403 (1)is directly in accord with New York law, citing *In re Labb* (42 F. Supp. 542). *In re Labb* is explicit on the issue, stating that a document is filed "when it is delivered to the proper officer, and by him received, to be kept on file" (*In re Labb, supra*, at 543; *Presidents & Directors of Manhattan Co. v Laimbeer*, 105 N.Y. 578). In addition, at least one other jurisdiction has identified receipt of the financing statement as the operative moment for perfection of a security interest (see, *In Re Poteet v. United Bank of Chattanooga*, 5 B.R. 631, 635 ["receipt of the financing statement and the fee by the filing officer is 'filing' " of a financing statement under U.C.C. 9-403(1)]).

We reject the defendants' further contention that the presumption of mail delivery can satisfy the evidentiary requirement of receipt. The presumption is inadequate in two respects. First, in order to establish priorities, the time as well as the fact of receipt must be established (see, *In Re Mutual Board & Packaging Corp.*, 342 F.2d 294). The purpose of U.C.C. 9-403(1) is not only to absolve the secured party of responsibility for errors or omissions by the filing officer in matters such as indexing, but also " 'to render certain the time when filing will be deemed to have occurred' " (*In Re Poteet v. United Bank of Chattanooga, supra*, at p. 635, quoting *In Re Brawn*, 6 U.C.C. Rep. Serv. 1031, 1037). Filing occurs upon receipt, not mailing (see, *Security Discount Assoc. v. Lynmar Homes Corp.*, 13 A.D. 2d 389, 216 N.Y.S. 2d 543.

If the presumption of mail delivery were not deficient in this regard, it would nevertheless face a second obstacle to establishing receipt by the filing officer. "A letter shown to have been properly addressed, stamped and mailed is presumed to have been delivered in the due course of mail. The presumption is said to be based upon the probability that officers of government will perform their duty" (Richardson, Evidence § 80, at p. 55 [10th ed., Prince]). A conflict of presumptions arises if a statement is not recorded or indexed but is presumed received. The necessary inference is that the filing officer failed to perform his or her duty, in clear conflict with the presumption of regularity, namely, that he did perform his duty. Thus, the presumption of delivery is in conflict with the presumption of regularity, and both should be disregarded (Richardson, Evidence § 94, at p. 70 [10th ed, Prince]).

Having concluded that mailing does not constitute filing under the U.C.C., it is clear that the defendants' duty to the plaintiff did not terminate upon mailing. The defendants were under an obligation to ascertain whether the mailed documents were received by the filing officer. Their failure to do so for a period of approximately one month, which resulted in the plaintiff's loss of its secured status in a bankruptcy proceeding, was so unreasonable as to constitute negligence as a matter of law (see, *Andre v. Pomeroy*, 35 N.Y. 2d 361, 362 N.Y.S. 2d 131, 320 N.E. 2d 853). Given the critical nature of lienholder status and priorities depending upon not only the day, but the hour of presentation and filing (see, *Security Discount Assoc. v. Lynmar Homes Corp.*, 13 A.D. 2d 389, 216 N.Y.S. 2d 543, supra), the defendants should have acted after sufficient time has elapsed for the documents to have been received, recorded and returned by the filing officer, to insure that those documents had indeed been received and recorded.

We have considered the defendants' remaining contentions and find them to be without merit. . ..

NOTES AND QUESTIONS

(1) Satisfaction of § 9-403(1) requires more than the presentment and tendering of a fee or acceptance of the statement by the filing officer. As a threshold matter, the documents offered as a financing statement must contain the requisite components or be rejected by the filing officer. Thus, where a creditor's documentation failed to include the collateral's tax identification number, the filing officer was under a statutory duty to reject the papers, and the creditor's security interest could not be perfected. See *In re C.J. Rogers Inc.* 150 B.R. 413(E.D. Mich. 1993).

(2) May the state filing officer be liable for negligence in carrying out ministerial and statutory duties? What, if any, limits should be placed on any recovery granted? In *Borg-Warner Acceptance Corp. v. the Secretary of State*, 731 P.2d 301 (Kan. 1987), a secured creditor sought damages as compensation for the harm caused by the negligence of employees of the secretary of state in failing to disclose to the creditor the existence of a prior security interest in collateral which the creditor was investigating through the central office. The court sided with the creditor, and approved a damages award of $70,622, a steep penalty for the employees' negligence. Was the amount awarded excessive or a reasonable and exemplary amount?

(3) The speaker of the state senate has asked you to comment on a proposal to create a state insurance fund to cover filing officer mistakes. The senator suggests that such an amendment to the U.C.C. could be funded by adding a nominal amount to the filing fee. Your opinion? Misconduct by filing officers is examined by Professors Adams and Nickles in their article, *Amending the Article Nine Filing System to Meet Current Deficiencies,* 59 Mo. L. Rev. 833 (1994). Although the authors do not address the creation of a state insurance fund to compensate for mistakes of filing officers, they do offer proposals which will attempt to define the roles and duties of filing officers within the filing system more clearly.

§ 17.09 Errors as to Classification

Read: U.C.C. §§ 9-109 and 9-110.

IN RE PIPES

United States Bankruptcy Court, Western District Missouri
116 B.R. 154, 12 U.C.C. Rep. Serv. 2d (1990)

FRANK W. KOGER, CHIEF JUDGE.

ITT Financial Services, Inc. (hereinafter ITT) filed its proof of claim in this proceeding as a secured claim. The Trustee has objected thereto. The Honorable Karen M. See, on December 13, 1989, allowed ITT 10 days to file an amended claim. This was accomplished by ITT and it is this amended allegedly secured claim that the Trustee suggests should be allowed as unsecured.

The roots of the difference between the Trustee and ITT go back to 1963 when the Missouri legislature, in its collective and infinite wisdom, adopted the so-called dual filing system for financing statements pertaining to business property. Such a system, while in the distinct minority, requires filing both with the Secretary of State and the Recorder of Deeds of the obligor's county of business location if business property is the claimed collateral. On the other hand, if the claimed collateral is consumer goods, farm products, or farm equipment the filing is required in the county of the obligor's residence only.

The question then becomes how the collateral in this case is defined or characterized. The trustee asserts that the collateral herein (mechanic's tools) should be classified as business equipment. ITT says that the tools are consumer goods. Unfortunately, collateral does not spring onto or from the printed page of a security agreement with a scarlet label upon its forehead. The same items can often be a) inventory; b) business equipment; c) consumer goods; or d) farm equipment. The nature of the label to be applied depends on the use to which the equipment is put. The main factor most courts have used as the measuring rod to determine which category the item falls into has been the use to which the pledging owner reasonably makes of the item.

Consider a simple wooden stool. If that given stool is in the possession of a dealer in furniture who is trying to sell same, it would be inventory; but if that same dealer in furniture actually used the stool to sit on while he is waiting for customers or to stand on while changing light bulbs in his showroom, it would be business equipment. If the stool was in the dealer's home and he sat on it at home or stood on it to change light bulbs in the home, it would be consumer goods. Finally, if our furniture dealer were also a farmer and sat on the same to milk his cow (or goat), the stool might conceivably be classified as farm equipment.

In the Missouri filing system, the first two examples would require dual filing of U.C.C.-1's to perfect a security interest. The latter two examples would require only a local filing (and might not require any filing if the security interest were a purchase money security interest).

Based on the foregoing, how should we classify the tools? The schedules indicate that debtor Keith Roy Pipes was a mechanic and he and his wife operated a service station where gasoline and oil were sold and minor repairs performed. On creditor's collateral list the tools were listed and valued as follows:

"Mechanics Tools & Top/Bottom Chest Mac Tools — $5,000.00."

The Court finds that these were not the typical hand tools found at the typical residence and used to effect typical household repairs, carpentry, plumbing and all the other chores performed by typical homeowners. Instead these were extensive and expensive hand tools used in the debtors' business of repairing motor vehicles at the debtors' place of business for financial reward. ITT asserts that this was a consumer loan and the Court finds no disagreement with that assertion. However, the fact that ITT calls the loan a consumer loan does not mean that the collateral for the loan has to be considered consumer goods. ITT's denomination of the loan does not control the classification of the collateral. The tools in question should wear the label of business equipment and not consumer goods. It was incumbent upon ITT not only to recognize the proper label at the time of the loan, but to follow the statutory requirements for perfection of their security interest in said property if they wished to achieve perfection sufficient to defeat the Trustee's position as a hypothetical, perfected lien creditor.

The Motion of ITT Financial Services to modify the Order Disallowing Claim #7 as a secured claim is denied since ITT did not file U.C.C.-1's with the Secretary of State to perfect a security interest in business equipment.

The foregoing Memorandum Opinion constitutes Findings of Fact and Conclusions of Law as required under Rule 7052, Rules of Bankruptcy.

So Ordered.

RAINIER NATIONAL BANK v. SECURITY STATE BANK

Washington Court of Appeals
59 Wash. App. 161, 12 U.C.C. Rep. Serv. 2d 822 (1990)

WILLIAMS, JUDGE PRO TEM.

Security State Bank appeals from a summary judgment determining the plantation grown Christmas trees are not "crops" pursuant to chapter 62 A.9 RCW (U.C.C. Article 9) but rather that Christmas trees are part of the realty. The trial court then held that Rainier National bank had a perfected security interest prior to Security State Bank's security interest. Security State Bank argues that Christmas trees are crops and that its perfected security interest should take priority. We agree with Security State Bank, and reverse.

On January 2, 1981, Fred and Evelyn Wall leased property in Thurston County to Ronald Ritter for 10 years for the purpose of growing Christmas trees. On January 29, 1982, Ritter d/b/a/ Ritter Spraying Co. entered into security agreements with Rainier National Bank (Rainier Bank). The security agreements listed collateral as follows:

> All accounts, contract rights, chattel paper, general intangibles or other rights to payment now or hereafter arising out of business of borrower.
>
> All inventory including but not limited to trees and tree planting equipment of borrower, all accounts, contract rights, chattel paper, general intangibles, documents and equipment, including parts, accessories and accessions thereto; all as now or hereafter owned by borrower or arising out of borrower's business.

The security agreements were properly filed and the security interests perfected. Ritter later entered into a security agreement with Security State Bank (Security Bank), which listed as collateral as follows:

> All crops and farm products and natural increases thereof now growing or to be grown including all proceeds, accounts receivable or contract rights arising from the sale of such crops. All crops and farm product after they have been severed or removed including but not limited to Christmas trees.

Security Bank perfected its security interest on June 4, 1985. Ritter then defaulted on his loans precipitating this dispute regarding the characterization of the Christmas trees which were growing on the property Ritter had leased.

The trial court, in a letter opinion, determined that Christmas trees are not crops for Article 9 purposes. The trial court based that conclusion on the reasoning that the term "crops" is not intended to apply to farm products that are not harvested on a yearly basis and that immature Christmas trees are part of the realty. As a result, the trial court gave priority to Rainier's security agreement covering the realty of leasehold interest. The trial court then entered its order for summary judgment. Rainier Bank later obtained a decree of foreclosure over Ritter's lease including the Christmas trees, which was sold.

I

Rainier Bank argues that the issue of whether the Christmas trees are "crops" or realty is moot because the decree of foreclosure only foreclosed upon the rights to the lease or use of the realty. However, the trial court had determined that the Christmas trees were a part of the realty. As a result, in foreclosing upon the realty, the trial court also foreclosed upon the Christmas trees pursuant to its decision on summary judgment. Furthermore, Rainier Bank admits that the purchaser of the foreclosed lease also obtained the existing Christmas trees. Therefore, the issue not moot.

II

In reviewing the trial court's decision to grant summary judgment, this court engages in the same inquiry as the trial court. *Honz v. State*, 105 Wash.2d 302, 311, 714 P.2d 1176 (1986). A motion for summary judgment should be granted if there is no genuine issue as to any material fact and the moving party is entitled to a judgment as a matter of law. C.R. 56(c); *Hontz*, 105 Wash.2d at 311, 714 P.2d 1176. The parties do not contest the facts, only the legal conclusions resulting therefrom. Therefore, summary judgment was appropriate.

U.C.C. Article 9 applies to "any transaction (regardless of its form) which is intended to create a security interest in personal property or fixtures including goods. . ." RCW 62A.9-102(1)(a).

> "Goods" includes all things which are movable at the time the security interest attaches or which are fixtures (RCW 62A.9-313) . . . "Goods" also includes standing timber which is to be cut and removed under a conveyance or contract for sale, the unborn young of animals and *growing crops*. (Emphasis added). RCW 62A.9-105(h).

The term "crops" is not defined by the U.C.C. as a general rule, where a term is not defined in the statute, the term must be accorded its plain and ordinary meaning unless a contrary intent appears. *Dennis v. Department of Labor & Indus.*, 109 Wash. 2d 467, 480, 745 P.2d 1295 (1987). "Crop" is defined as "a plant or animal or plant or animal product that can be grown and harvested extensively for profit or subsistence." Webster's Third New International Dictionary 540 (3d ed. 1969). These Christmas trees are plants grown and harvested extensively for profit and, therefore, are a crop for purposes of U.C.C.

Rainier Bank's argument that only annually harvested plants constitute crops is unpersuasive. Although many plants mature and are ready for harvesting annually, the speed in which a plant matures does not change its characterization as a crop.

Rainier argues that Christmas trees constitute fixtures. The true criterion of a fixture is the united application of these requisites: (1) Actual annexation to the realty, or something appurtenant thereto; (2) application to the use or purpose to which that part of the realty with which it is connected is appropriated; and (3) the intention of the party making the annexation to make a permanent accession to the freehold. *Lipsett Steel Prods. Co. v. King Cy.*, 67 Wash. 2d 650, 652, 409 P.2d 475 (1965).

Although the first two criteria are met in this case, the parties to the security agreement knew that Ritter did not intend to leave the trees as permanent fixtures, but rather to harvest the trees upon maturity. As a result, the trees are not fixtures.

III

Rainier Bank's argues that its financing statement covering inventory includes the growing Christmas trees. However, RCW 62A.9-109(3) provides in pertinent part as follows:

Goods are . . .

(3) "farm products" if they are crops . . .

If goods are farm products they are neither equipment nor inventory. RCW 62A.9-109.

Because Rainier characterized its collateral as inventory, it necessarily did not include the growing Christmas trees which are farm products or crops and, therefore, does not have a perfected security interest in the Christmas trees. As a result, Security Bank's perfected security interest has priority.

Reversed.

COMMENT

If Christmas trees don't grab your fancy, consider whether longhorn cattle are inventory or equipment. In *Morgan County Feeders, Inc. v. McCormick*, 836 P.2d 1051 (Colo. App. 1992), the court presents a thoughtful analysis of the differences between the two terms (the primary difference being the length of use of the good). The court classified the cattle as equipment because they were used principally for recreational cattle drives on the ranch, rather than for purposes of immediate/ultimate sale or lease. See § 17.11[A], *infra.*

IN RE FRAZIER
COOKEVILLE PRODUCTION CREDIT ASSOCIATION v. FRAZIER

United States Bankruptcy Court, Middle District of Tennessee
16 B.R. 674, 33 U.C.C. Rep. Serv. 1150 (1981)

PAUL E. JENNINGS, BANKRUPTCY JUDGE.

Debtors own and operate an agriculture nursery and landscaping business in DeKalb County, Tennessee under the name of Frazier Brothers Nursery. From that evidence and pleadings it appears that Cookeville Production Credit Association (PCA) extended credit to the debtors on a number of occasions. PCA alleges debtors' total indebtedness to PCA as of February 9,1981 was $33,338.95. PCA further alleges that it has a valid and perfected security interest in the following items owned by the debtors: all nursery stock, all tractors, all farm equipment, all nursery equipment, one 1979 pickup 4 speed vehicle, one 530 Case backhoe, one 12 horsepower Gravely tractor with equipment, one trailer to haul backhoe, one tractor plow, one row cultivator, one 24 disc and one 1980 Chevrolet Luv vehicle. Alleging inadequate protection of its security interest, PCA instituted Adversary Proceeding No. 281-0400 requesting modification of the automatic stay and abandonment of the above-described property.

Also in dispute is whether the description contained in the security agreements are sufficient to comply with TCA § 47-9-110. . .. Thus, the courts are left with a case by case determination of whether a particular description "reasonably identifies what is described."

In the instant case, the documents describe the disputed collateral as follows:

> all nursery stock
>
> all tractors
>
> all farm equipment
>
> all nursery equipment
>
> one 1979 pickup 4 speed vehicle
>
> one 530 Case backhoe
>
> one trailer to haul backhoe
>
> one tractor plow
>
> one row cultivator
>
> one 24 disc

This court finds the above descriptions to be sufficient to reasonably identify the collateral as required by TCA § 47-9-110. It is not necessary to use the classifications of goods as defined in TCA § 47-9-109 as long as the language used reasonably identifies the collateral.

The description of the real estate is also subject to the reasonable identification test of TCA § 47-9-110. The real estate was described as follows:

> All of the above described crops are or will become located on the farm land owned (rented) by *Edward Frazier and all various farms in DeKalb County*, Tennessee. (Emphasis signifies handwritten words in original).

Testimony by the debtors indicated that although all of the nursery business was conducted on 10 acres of land, the debtors do own several farms in DeKalb County. The court finds that the above description reasonably identifies on what property defendant's collateral was or might be located, that is, on any of the farms owned or rented by Edward Frazier in DeKalb County, Tennessee. Although a legal description of each parcel of land would have been the best description of the land, the description given is sufficient.

Having found PCA to have a valid and enforceable security interest in the described collateral, the last issue presented for resolution is whether that security interest was properly perfected by the filing of the financing statement in DeKalb County, the county of the debtors residence and of the real property on which the debtors' nursery was located. TCA § 47-9-401 dictates the filing requirements for perfection of security interests and, in pertinent part, provides:

> The difficulty of classifying the nursery stock is that the debtors' occupation is a mixture of farming operations as well as business operations. The debtor testified that he grows some of the plants used in his nursery business and that he also buys some stock. Debtor testified that he is engaged in a "continual growing process" because it often takes from one to seven years for the seedlings that he sets out to reach a salable size. Of course, the length of growing time depends upon the particular type of plant. This cultivation process of tending and caring

for the trees, shrubs and plants is obviously a farming operation and the products of this farming operation are farm products.

. . .However, that part of the nursery stock which is mature and is available for sale by the nursery-man is inventory within the definition of TCA § 47-9-109(4).

Therefore, the court finds PCA is properly perfected as to that nursery stock which is still in the ground and has not yet matured. This stock is farm products-crops. Mature stock is inventory and as to that, PCA is not perfected.

Debtors assert that even if the nursery stock is found to be crops, PCA's security interest does not attach in after acquired nursery plants pursuant to TCA § 47-9-204(4). . .. Clearly, PCA does not have a security interest in the crops which were acquired or planted after May 11, 1979, the security agreement having been executed on May 11, 1978. However, some, if not most, of the plants which the nursery had in the ground (and which are considered farm products by this court) are still in the growing process and thus PCA's security interest in those plants, trees and shrubs continue, at least until the trees, plants, and shrubs reach maturity and removed for sale. Thus, the court determines that PCA has a validly perfected security interest in these plants, trees and shrubs which were acquired prior to May 11, 1978, and which were still in the cultivation process at the time of the debtors' filing in bankruptcy. Trees, plants, and shrubs in the crop category as above discussed and acquired after May 11, 1979, are not covered as they became crops more than one year after execution of the security agreement.

There is no question that the tractors, farm equipment, nursery equipment, 1979 pickup 4 speed vehicle, 530 Case backhoe, trailer to haul backhoe, tractor plow, row cultivator, and 24 disc are equipment. The issue is whether this equipment was bought or used primarily in connection with the debtors' landscaping or nursery business operation (requiring filing with the Secretary of State) or the debtors' farming operation (requiring filing with the DeKalb County Register's Office). . .. Debtors insist that the nursery stock is inventory and that all of the other items listed as collateral are equipment which required filing in the Secretary of State's office. Debtors admitted that PCA's security interests in the 1980 Chevrolet Luv vehicle and the one 12 horsepower Gravely tractor with equipment are validly perfected. PCA's lien on the 1980 Chevrolet Luv truck was noted on its title and filed with the Tennessee Secretary of State. Apparently, the debtors admit that the Gravely tractor is farm equipment and thus properly perfected by filing in DeKalb County. PCA argues that the nursery stock is farm products and the rest of the collateral is farm equipment and, thus, the proper place for filing was in the DeKalb County Register's Office.

TCA § 47-9-109 classifies goods into four categories: consumer goods, equipment, farm products, and inventory. These classes are mutually exclusive in that the same property cannot at the same time and to the same person, be in different classes. In borderline cases the principal use of the property is determinative. These categories are important in determining the correct place to file a financing statement in order to perfect a security interest. . . ..

Debtors testified that the 530 Case backhoe and trailer to haul it are used exclusively for landscaping and excavation. Debtors stated that the backhoe is used to pick up and haul debris and to level ground and is not used in connection with the growth of any crops. Based upon this uncontroverted testimony, the court finds that the backhoe and trailer used to haul the backhoe are business equipment and therefore PCA is not properly perfected as to those items.

Clearly, the tractor plow, row cultivator, and 24 disc are farm equipment insofar as they are used in the cultivation process of the nursery stock referred to infra. PCA is properly perfected as to those items. There was no testimony concerning the use of the tractors, farm equipment, nursery equipment or 1979 pickup 4 speed vehicle. . .. Therefore, it appears the burden was on the debtors to prove that PCA was not a secured creditor. Debtors have not met this burden with respect to the tractors, farm equipment, nursery equipment and the 1979 pickup 4 speed vehicle. Therefore, the court must find that these items of collateral are farm equipment and PCA's security interests in these items are properly perfected.

Accordingly, it is the determination of the court that PCA is a secured creditor with respect to the following items of collateral:

1. nursery stock which was acquired prior to May 11, 1979, and which was still in the cultivation stage on the date of the Debtors' filing in bankruptcy;
2. tractor plow;
3. row cultivator;
4. 24 disc;
5. tractors;
6. farm equipment;
7. nursery equipment; and
8. 1979 pickup 4 speed vehicle.

PCA's lien upon the following items of collateral is declared void:

1. nursery stock herein designated as inventory;
2. nursery stock acquired after May 11, 1979, and which is still in the cultivation stage;
3. 530 Case backhoe; and
4. trailer to haul backhoe.

An appropriate order will be entered.

---

§ 17.10 Automatic Perfection

Read: U.C.C. §§ 9-304(4), (5), (6), 9-302(1)(d), 9-107, and 9-307(2).

The third method of perfection under the Uniform Commercial Code is "automatic perfection." Usually, the secured party must file a financing statement or take possession of the collateral to perfect her interest. With automatic perfection, the secured party's act of entering into the transaction provides her with perfected creditor status; no formal steps are necessary—the debtor may retain possession of the goods and the creditor need not record her interest by filing. The most important type of automatic perfection applies to purchase money security interests taken during sales of consumer goods. A consumer good is any item bought or used primarily for personal, family, or household purposes. If either the seller of a consumer good or another person who gives the value that enables the debtor to acquire the goods, takes a security interest in those items, that interest is perfected automatically under § 9-302(1)(d).

A primary reason for the drafters giving automatic perfection to this class of goods was the fact that other methods may not be commercially feasible. Often, consumer transactions involve small amounts of money and low profit margins for the financier. The inconvenience and costs of filing may outweigh the advantages. Thus, an appliance retailer who sells a refrigerator to a consumer on credit and retains a security interest in the refrigerator is automatically perfected.

While the principle of automatic perfection is relatively simple and easy to utilize, some complications arise. The goods involved must satisfy the Code definition of consumer goods under § 9-109(1). Suppose that a consumer buys a refrigerator on credit for use in her office. If the appliance retailer relies on its purchase money security interest being automatically perfected, the retailer will not have a perfected security interest because the refrigerator is, by virtue of its use, "equipment" and not a "consumer good."

Similarly, a finance company which advances money for the purchase of consumer goods can obtain automatic perfection by engaging in the transaction. If however, the consumer borrows the money to make the purchase and then uses it for something other than consumer goods, there is no automatic perfection even if the consumer buys the refrigerator with other funds at a later date. The purchase money advanced must actually be used for the purchase of the consumer item. Given this prospect, most finance companies that make loans for consumer purchases do so by making the check payable to the seller, or payable to buyer and seller jointly. Either method ensures that the advance is in fact purchase money.

IN RE LOCKOVICH

United States District Court, W.D. Pennsylvania
124 B.R. 660, 14 U.C.C. Rep. Serv. 2d 605 (1991)

MEMORANDUM OPINION

LEE, DISTRICT JUDGE.

Gallatin National Bank (Gallatin) appeals the order of the United States Bankruptcy Court for the Western District of Pennsylvania denying Gallatin's Motion for Relief from Automatic Stay, and invalidating Gallatin's lien on property in the estate. 105 B.R. 297.

The facts at issue are not in dispute. On or about August 20, 1986, John J. Lockovich and Clara Lockovich, his wife (Debtors), purchased a 22 foot 1986 Chapparel Villian III boat from the Greene County Yacht Club for $32,500.00. Debtors paid $6,000.00 to Greene County Yacht Club and executed a "Security Agreement/Lien Contract" which set forth the purchase and finance terms. In the Contract, Debtors granted a security interest in the boat to the holder of the Contract. Gallatin paid to the Yacht Club the sum of $26,757.14 on Debtor's behalf, and the Contract was assigned to Gallatin.

Gallatin filed financing statements in the Greene County Prothonotary's Office and with the Secretary of the Commonwealth of Pennsylvania. Greene County was the county in which Gallatin was located, but Debtors were residents of Allegheny County. The filing of the financing statements, therefore, was ineffective to perfect the security interest in the boat.

The Debtors defaulted under the terms of the Security Agreement to Gallatin by failing to remit payments as required. Before the Gallatin could take action, Debtors filed for relief under Chapter 11 of the Bankruptcy Code. Gallatin filed a Motion for Relief from the Automatic Stay, seeking to enforce their rights pursuant to the Security Agreement.

On October 2, 1989, the Bankruptcy Court denied Gallatin's Motion for Relief from the Automatic Stay, holding that Gallatin failed to perfect its security interest in the boat and, therefore, was an unsecured creditor in the Chapter 11 bankruptcy. As a holder of an unperfected security interest, Gallatin's right to the boat was inferior to that of the debtor-in-possession, a hypothetical lienholder pursuant to 11 U.S.C. § 544. *General Electric Credit Corporation v. Nardulli & Sons, Inc.*, 836 F.2d 184, 192 (3rd Cir. 1988).

The issue on appeal is whether Gallatin must file a financing statement to perfect its purchase money security interest in the boat. Gallatin's position is that the boat is a consumer good as defined by the Pennsylvania Uniform Commercial Code, 13Pa.C.S.A. § 1101-9507 (Code). Because the boat was a consumer good subject to a purchase money security interest, Gallatin contends it was not required to file a financing statement in order to perfect its security interest. For the reasons below stated, we reverse the decision of the Bankruptcy Court and find that Gallatin has a valid security interest in the boat.

To perfect a security interest in collateral under the Code, 13 Pa.C.S.A. § 9401, a secured party must file a financing statement in the offices of the Secretary of the Commonwealth and the Prothonotary of the county in which the debtor resides. Under 13 Pa.C.S.A. § 9302, the Code permits several exceptions to the general rule depending upon the type of collateral. Section 9302(a)(4) provides as follows: "(a) General Rule—A financing statement must be filed to perfect all security interests except the following:. . ... (4) a purchase money security interest in consumer goods; but filing is required for a motor vehicle required to be registered."

There are three significant problems in determining automatic perfection of purchase money interests in consumer goods. First, what is a purchase money security interest? Second, what are "consumer goods"? Third, can massive and expensive items qualify as consumer goods? See James J. White and Robert S. Summers, Uniform Commercial Code, West Publishing Company, Second Edition, § 23-7 (1980).

A purchase money security interest is defined as one: (1) taken or retained by the seller of the collateral to all or part of its price: or (2) taken by a person who by making advances or incurring an obligation gives value to enable the debtor to acquire rights in or the use of collateral if such value is in fact so used. 13 Pa.C.S.A. § 9107. It is undisputed in the instant case that the security interest held by Gallatin was a purchase money security interest, therefore the first hurdle has been cleared.

Goods are divided into four classes under 13 Pa.C.S.A. § 9109(1): (1) consumer goods; (2) equipment; (3) farm products; and (4) inventory. Comment 5 to such section provides that goods not covered by one of the definitions in § 9109 are to be treated as equipment. "Goods" are defined as "consumer goods" if they are used or bought for use primarily for personal, family or household purposes. The goods are not classified according to design or intrinsic nature, but according to the use to which the owner puts them. Debtors have never maintained that the boat was used for anything other than for their personal use.

The question remaining for this Court is whether a $32,500.00 watercraft can be properly classified as consumer goods under § 9302. Pennsylvania's appellate courts have yet to consider such issue. Because the Pennsylvania Supreme Court has not spoken to the question, this Court must predict how the Supreme Court would resolve the above issues if presented with the specific facts of this case. A Court of Common Pleas in Erie County, Pennsylvania, however, has held that a thirty-three (33) foot motor boat is not a consumer good. *Union National Bank of Pittsburgh v. Northwest Marine, Inc.*, 27 U.C.C. Rep. Serv. 563, 62 Erie Co. L.J. 87 (1979). Though a lower court case is entitled to "some weight," it is not controlling. *Carpenters Health and Welfare Fund of Philadelphia and Vicinity v. Kenneth R. Ambrose, Inc.*, 727 F.2d 279, 283 (3rd Cir.1983).

It is apparent from the opinion of the Bankruptcy Court, and from the opinion of the court in Northwest Marine, that those courts perceive a void in the Code which does not address the problem of secret liens on valuable motorboats. The court in Northwest Marine stated that this void was "best filled by interstitial law-making by the court" until the Legislature acts to bridge the gap. *Union National Bank of Pittsburgh v. Northwest Marine, Inc.*, 62 Erie Co.L.J. at 90.

We disagree. Determining what is a consumer good on an ad hoc basis leaves creditors with little or no guidelines for their conduct. Under the clear mandate of the Code, a consumer good subject to exception from the filing of financing statements is determined by the use or intended use of the good; design, size, weight, shape and cost are irrelevant. Should a millionaire decide to purchase the Queen Mary for his personal or family luxury on the high seas, under § 9109 of the Code, the great Queen is nothing but a common consumer good. There need be no debate as to cost, size or life expectancy. Creditors must be confident that when they enter into a commercial transaction, they will play by the rules as written in the Code.

The Bankruptcy Court was also persuaded by Pennsylvania's history of disfavoring secret liens. It is undisputed that the Code's exemption of consumer goods from the burden of filing breeds the emergence of secret liens on such goods. Such secret liens, however, do not imperil the commercial world. Although the security interests described in paragraph (a)(4) of § 9302 are perfected without filing, § 9307(b) provides that unless a financing statement is filed certain buyers may take free of a security interest even though perfected. 13 Pa.C.S.A. § 9307(b) reads as follows:

> In the case of consumer goods, a buyer takes free of a security interest even though perfected if he buys without knowledge of the security interest, for value and for his own personal, family or household purposes unless prior to the purchase the secured party has filed a financing statement covering such goods.

This allows a secured party to file a financing statement, though one is not required for perfection, in order to insure that all buyers take subject to his security interest. At the same time, purchasers of consumer goods, who intend to maintain the characterization of such goods as consumer goods, are protected from hardships created by secret liens.

The Bankruptcy Court was also interested in protecting the reasonable expectations of subsequent creditors and purchasers. As above noted, a subsequent purchaser who intends to use the goods for personal, family or household purposes is protected by § 9307(b). A subsequent purchaser with resale as its intent, such as the boat dealer in Northwest Marine, or a subsequent creditor, are, or should be, sophisticated in commercial dealings. They are charged with the knowledge of the contents of the Code, and should conduct themselves accordingly. A boat dealer is certainly aware when dealing with a consumer on the trade-in of a boat, that such boat could conceivably be subject to a purchase money security interest capable of perfection without filing. Likewise, a subsequent creditor is aware of the perils associated with accepting collateral which can clearly be subject to a secret lien.

Creditors, subsequent creditors and subsequent purchasers under the Code have options available to them that lend appropriate protection. To determine what protections are available to them "by interstitial law-making by the court" is more likely to defeat the intended simplification, clarification, and modernization of the law governing commercial transactions.

The court in *Northwest Marine* likened motor vehicles to motorboats. The Bankruptcy Court thought the comparison appropriate. Such finding may be appropriate, however it does not legitimately bring motorboats within the motor vehicle exception of § 9302(a)(4). Motor vehicles and motorboats are comparable in that, if held for personal use, both are classified as consumer goods under the Code. Section 9302(a)(4) specifically provides that when the consumer good is a motor vehicle, which is required to be registered, a secured creditor must file a financing statement. No such requirement is imposed for motorboats or any other consumer goods.

There are two legislative solutions to the problem. One is to explicitly require the filing of security interests in motorboats.[5] The other approach, as done in some states, is to limit the value to which the exemption applies.[6] Durable, valuable "consumer goods" upon which a creditor is likely to rely for collateral, encompasses more than motorboats or mobile homes. If motorboats or other expensive items are to be excluded from the dictates of § 9302(a)(4), either via specific exemptions or a fixed ceiling price for consumer goods below which no financing statements are required, such determinations are necessarily for the Pennsylvania Legislature.

This Court, therefore, holds that Chapparel Villian III is a consumer good, and pursuant to 13 Pa.C.S.A. § 9302(a)(4) a financing statement was not required to be filed by Gallatin to perfect the security interest in the boat. Gallatin has a valid security interest in the boat and under 11 U.S.C. § 362(d), is entitled to relief from the automatic stay.

An appropriate order shall follow.

PROBLEM 17.3

Breakiron had a revolving charge account with Wards, a local department store. The charge account contract provided:

> Except for motor vehicle purchases, Wards will retain a purchase money security interest as permitted by law in each consumer good purchased under this agreement until such consumer good, together with related FINANCE CHARGE, is paid for in full. Wards will not claim a security interest or other lien in any property.

Breakiron purchased a television on credit from Wards. The charge slip stated that "[t]his purchase is subject to the terms of my credit agreement with you. You will retain a security interest in this merchandise until it is paid for in full." Breakiron subsequently files for protection in bankruptcy and seeks to have the television exempted from the bankruptcy estate. Breakiron contends that Wards' method of applying payments to the total balance due on the account causes the company to lose its original, automatically perfected purchase money security interest. You are law clerk to the judge deciding this case. What do you recommend? See In Re Breakiron, 32 B.R. 400, 37 U.C.C. Rep. Serv. 257 (Bankr. W.D. Pa. 1983).

---

[5] California requires a filing for a "boat required to be registered." See Cal. Com. Code § 9302(1)(d). Michigan requires a filing for a "vehicle, mobile home, or watercraft for which a certificate of title is required by the laws of this state." See Mich. Comp. Laws § 440.9302(1)(d), Mich. Stat. Ann. § 19.9302(1)(d).

[6] Kansas ($1,000.00), Maryland ($1,500.00), Colorado ($250.00) and Wisconsin ($250.00) have imposed purchase price limitations above which automatic perfection is not allowed.

SOUTHTRUST BANK OF ALABAMA v. BORG-WARNER ACCEPTANCE CORP.

United States Court of Appeals
760 F.2d 1240, 40 U.C.C. Rep. Serv. 1601 (11th Cir. 1985)

TUTTLE, SENIOR CIRCUIT JUDGE:

Borg-Warner Acceptance Corporation ("BWAC") appeals from a decision of the district court denying its motion for summary judgment and granting summary judgment to Southtrust Bank ("the Bank") in a diversity suit. The Bank filed a declaratory judgment action to ascertain which of the parties has priority in the inventory of four debtors, Molay Brothers Supply Company, Inc., Gulf City Distributors, Inc., Standard Wholesale Supply Company and Crest Refrigeration, Inc. These debtors, which are no longer in existence, defaulted on obligations they owed to one or the other party.

Both the Bank and BWAC have perfected security interests in the inventory of the debtors. In each case, the Bank filed its financing statement first. BWAC contends that as a purchase money lender it falls within the purchase money security interest exception to the first to file rule and therefore is entitled to possession of the inventory. The Uniform Commercial Code (U.C.C.) as adopted in both Alabama and Georgia, provides in pertinent part:

> A security interest is a "purchase money security interest" to the extent that it is: (a) Taken or retained by the seller of the collateral to secure all or part of its price; or (b) Taken by a person who by making advances or incurring an obligation gives value to enable the debtor to acquire rights in or the use of collateral if such value is in fact so used.

Ala.Code § 7-9-107 (1975); O.C.G.A. § 11-9-107 (1981).

BWAC engages in purchase money financing. Here, BWAC purchased invoices from vendors who supplied inventory items to the debtors in question. The security agreements between BWAC and each of the debtors contained the following provision:

> In order to secure repayment to Secured Party of all such extensions of credit made by Secured Party in accordance with this Agreement, and to secure payment of all other debts or liabilities and performance of all obligations of Debtor to Secured Party, whether now existing or hereafter arising, Debtor agrees that Secured Party shall have and hereby grants to Secured Party a security interest in all Inventory of Debtor, whether now owned or hereafter acquired, and all Proceeds and products thereof.

The term "Inventory" was defined as "all inventory, of whatever kind or nature, wherever located, now owned or hereafter acquired . . .when such inventory has been financed by Borg-Warner Acceptance Corporation."

BWAC and the debtors employed a scheduled liquidation arrangement to reduce the debt owed BWAC. Under this arrangement a debtor was permitted to pay a percentage of the invoice each month, without regard to whether the item was actually sold. If an unpaid item was sold, then the remaining inventory served as collateral to secure the unpaid balance.

The key issue for decision by this Court is whether inclusion of an after-acquired property clause and a future advances clause in BWAC's security agreements converted its purchase money security interest (PMSI) into an ordinary security interest.

The district court held that inclusion of after-acquired property and future advances clauses ("the clauses") in the security agreement converted BWAC's PMSI into an ordinary security interest. The court relied on In re Manuel, 507 F.2d 990 (5th Cir.1975) (holding, in a consumer bankruptcy context, that PMSI must be limited to the item purchased at time of the agreement and cannot exceed the price of that item); In re Norrell, 426 F. Supp. 435 (M.D. Ga.1977) (same); and In re Simpson, 4 U.C.C. Rep. Serv. 243 (W.D.Mich.1966) (inclusion of future advances clause in security agreement for farm equipment destroys PMSI).

BWAC argues that the cases relied on by the court are distinguishable. First, BWAC notes that almost all the cases following the "transformation" rule (*i.e.*, inclusion of the clauses transforms a PMSI into an ordinary security interest) are consumer bankruptcy cases. It argues that the rationale of those cases, which is to protect the consumer, does not apply in commercial cases such as the case at bar. See In re Mid-Atlantic Flange, 26 U.C.C. Rep. Serv. 203, 208 (E.D.Pa.1979). BWAC argues that the policy considerations in a commercial setting, promoting commercial certainty and encouraging credit extension, do not support the application of the transformation rule. According to BWAC, applying the transformation rule to inventory financiers would require them to police inventory constantly and to see that inventory corresponds on an item-by-item basis with debt.

The Bank argues that the transformation rule is not a product of special bankruptcy considerations, and that if the drafters had intended to limit the rule to consumer transactions, they would have said so, as they did in other sections of the Code. The Bank contends that a holding that inclusion of the clauses destroys a PMSI would not have a serious negative effect on inventory financiers. It points out that such financiers could retain priority by obtaining a subordination agreement from the first-to-file creditor.

We see no reason to limit the holding of *In re Manuel* to consumer bankruptcy cases. In that case, the Fifth Circuit stated:

> A plain reading of the statutory requirements would indicate that they require the purchase money security interest to be in the item purchased, and that, as the judges below noted, the purchase money security interest cannot exceed the price of what is purchased in the transaction wherein the security interest is created. . ..

Id. at 993. Nothing in the language of U.C.C. § 9-312(3) or § 9-107 distinguishes between consumer and commercial transactions or between bankruptcy and nonbankruptcy contexts. We see no policy reasons for creating a distinction where the drafters have not done so.

Second, BWAC contends that the cases supporting the transformation rule involve situations in which the clauses were actually exercised, *e.g., Manuel* (agreement covered pre-existing debt); *Simpson* (future advances actually made). BWAC argues that mere inclusion of the clauses does not void a PMSI. *In re Griffin*, 9 Bankr. 880 (Bankr.N.D.Ga.1981) (when creditor is seller, mere existence of unexercised future advances clause does not destroy PMSI); *Mid Atlantic Flange* (same). We need not reach the issue of whether mere inclusion of unexercised future advances and after-acquired property clauses voids a PMSI because we find that BWAC exercised the clauses here. After entering the security agreements with the debtors, BWAC regularly purchased inventory for the debtors and now claims that the debtors' BWAC-financed inventory secures these purchases. This is an exercise of the future advances clause. Similarly, BWAC claims as collateral not only the inventory purchased at the time the security agreements were entered, but all BWAC-financed inventory. This is an exercise of the after-acquired property clause. We hold, therefore, that BWAC's exercise of the future advances and after-acquired property clauses in its security agreements with the debtors destroyed its PMSI.

We note, as did the district court, that BWAC retains a security interest in the goods. It merely loses its priority status as a purchase money secured lender. The concept of the floating lien under the U.C.C. remains intact. We hold, merely, that such a floating lien is inconsistent with a PMSI. A PMSI requires a one-to-one relationship between the debt and the collateral.

BWAC's final argument is that the court should adopt a "to the extent" rule, based on the literal language of U.C.C., § 9-107:

> A security interest is a "purchase money security interest" *to the extent that* it is . . .(b) Taken by a person who by making advances or incurring an obligation gives value to enable the debtor to acquire rights in or the use of collateral if such value is in fact so used. (emphasis added.)

Some courts have held that the clauses, even if exercised, do not invalidate a PMSI if there is some method for determining the extent of the PMSI. For example, in *In re Staley*, 426 F. Supp. 437 (M.D.Ga. 1977), the court held that the PMSI was valid because the security agreement specified that payments be allocated first to items bought first. Thus, it was easy for the court to ascertain which items had been fully paid for and hence no longer served as collateral. Here, however, nothing in the contract or in state law allocates payments to particular items of inventory. BWAC, in fact, claims all BWAC-financed inventory as its collateral without regard to payments made by the debtors. We agree with the court in *In re Coomer*, 8 B.R. 351, 355 (Bankr. E.D. Tenn. 1980), that

> Without some guidelines, legislative or contractual, the court should not be required to distill from a mass of transactions the extent to which a security interest is purchase money.

Unless a lender contractually provides some method for determining the extent to which each item of collateral secures its purchase money, it effectively gives up its purchase money status.

Because we hold that BWAC's exercise of the after-acquired property and future advances clauses in its security agreements voided its PMSI, we need not reach the other issues raised by the Bank. We also do not reach the issue raise by BWAC concerning the district court's reference to proceeds from sales of the inventory being held "in trust." Whether the proceeds are held "in trust" is relevant only to the issue of damages. The district court entered final judgment only on the claim for declaratory relief and referred the damage claim to a magistrate. Because no final judgment has been entered as to damages, that issue is not properly before this Court.

Affirmed.

NOTES

(1) The transformation rule, taken from the *Southtrust* case remains a controversial decision. The net effect of the rule is to render priority to purchase money creditors only where each sale

can be treated as a separate transaction. Before this case, most observers believed that a purchase money financer would lose to an inventory financer who filed a financing statement on the debtor's inventory before the purchase money party filed. This situation would leave the purchase money secured party with a priority claim on only the inventory remaining in the debtor's hands at the time of default. *Southtrust* raises doubt as to even the unsold inventory. The court's reliance on consumer cases involving § 522(f) of the bankruptcy code and § 9-302(1)(d) seems entirely misplaced in this case where two sophisticated commercial financers are involved. The court's suggestion that a purchase money financer could protect its interest by acquiring an intercreditor subordination agreement is good theoretical advice but worth very little in reality because there is no incentive for the first-to-file party to subordinate its interest.

(2) Although "automatic" perfection takes place in regard to consumer goods and serves as protection against subsequent creditors, it does not give the secured creditor protection against a subsequent consumer purchaser. When the appliance store retailer sells a refrigerator to a consumer on credit and takes a purchase money security interest, the retailer's security interest is automatically perfected and will prevail over any creditors of the consumer who may also claim an interest in the refrigerator. But if the consumer sells the refrigerator to a second consumer who buys without knowledge of the security interest, for value and for personal, family, or household purposes, the purchasing consumer prevails over the purchase money secured party *unless* that purchase money creditor filed a financing statement prior to the sale to the buyer. See comment 3 to § 9-307(2). If the retailer had perfected through filing instead of through "automatic perfection," the retailer would prevail over the buyer.

(3) There are other limits on the application of the automatic perfection rule. For example, there can be no automatic perfection for motor vehicles that must be registered. Security interests in motor vehicles can be perfected either by filing or by notation on the certificate of title. Consumer goods become fixtures when the collateral becomes so attached to the real estate as to be considered a part of the real property. The secured party with an interest in fixtures must file a fixture financing statement with the local real estate recorder's office to achieve priority over other real property interest holders. See § 9-313(4)(a). Thus, even though a refrigerator is to be used for personal, family, or household purposes, if local law considers the refrigerator so attached to the property as to become a fixture, a purchase money security interest in the appliance can be perfected only by filing the fixture financing statement. In such an instance, the automatic perfection created by section 9-302 will not operate to protect a fixture purchase money secured party. Conflicts between secured parties and others who claim interests in real estate will be discussed more fully in chapter 3.

(4) One last note: most standard security agreements and loan documentation for inventory financing provide that the creation of any second creditor lien or encumbrance on secured property constitutes an event of default under the lending arrangement with the first creditor. In most security agreements, a default permits the secured creditor to accelerate the loan and demand the entire amount due and payable immediately. Thus, it is quite possible that the first-to-file secured party could call a loan if the debtor even attempted to enter into a purchase money arrangement with another creditor. Given this situation, does § 9-312(3) have any meaningful commercial significance?

[A] Automatic Perfection and Isolated Assignments of Accounts

Article 9 governs the assignments of accounts since most assignments involve a financing arrangement. U.C.C. § 9-102(1)(b). However, some assignments or sales of accounts are not part of a commercial financing transaction. In such instances, these assignments are not covered by Article 9. Examples of assignments excluded from the scope of Article 9 include assignments that arise out of the sale of a business, assignments for collection purposes, assignment and delegation of duties, wage assignments, and assignments in satisfaction of a preexisting debt.

When an assignment is governed by Article 9, the secured party as assignee must generally take steps to perfect its interest by filing. However, if an assignment of accounts represents an isolated or insignificant transaction, section 9-302(1)(e) provides that no filing is necessary to perfect. Although the language of the section focuses on whether the assignment represents a significant portion of the debtor's outstanding accounts, Official Comment 5 to the section states that the subsection seeks to save casual assignments from becoming invalid. Given the language of the statute and the comment, two tests have developed. The following case discusses those two tests.

IN RE FORT DODGE ROOFING CO.

United States Bankruptcy Court, Northern District of Iowa
50 B.R. 666 (1985)

MEMORANDUM

It is the contention of the Trustee in Bankruptcy that the transfer of accounts receivable from Fort Dodge Roofing Co. to Stetson Building Products Corp. on May 7, 1982, was not an absolute transfer of the accounts to Stetson Building Products Corp. The court agrees with the Trustee, given the nature of the transactions involved. At the time of the assignment, Stetson was owed on open account in excess of $170,000.00 by Fort Dodge Roofing. Stetson informed the Debtor that it would not continue to provide materials to the Debtor on open account unless arrangements were made on the past due open accounts.

Fort Dodge Roofing Co. agreed to transfer seven accounts to Stetson. This transfer was accomplished via an instrument denominated as an assignment. On its face, the assignment appears to be absolute in form. After the assignment was made, Stetson did not adjust its books to decrease the amount owed to it by Fort Dodge Roofing and in fact claimed that after the transfer was made, Fort Dodge Roofing was still indebted to it in the amount of $170,000. There is no record regarding any credits to the account of Fort Dodge Roofing for any payments made to Stetson on the other assignments to Stetson. The court is perplexed by the fact that no credit was made to the account of Fort Dodge Roofing owed to Stetson after the transfer was made. Therefore, the court concludes that even though Stetson acted as the owner of the account, the transfer was in reality merely a transfer of a security interest in the accounts rather than an outright transfer of the ownership to Stetson.

Having successfully avoided the first obstacle in his path to claim the account receivable owed by Malta High School, the Trustee falters in light of the second obstacle placed in its path by Stetson. Stetson claims that even if the transfer of the accounts receivable was merely a transfer of a security interest in the accounts receivable, that it was not required to perfect that security interest as it falls within a recognized exception to the requirement that perfection of security interests be accomplished by filing a financing statement. Stetson cites the following exception set forth in the Iowa Code § 554.9302(1)(e):

A financing statement must be filed to perfect all security interests except the following:

(e) An assignment of accounts which does not alone or in conjunction with other assignments to the same assignee transfer a significant part of the outstanding accounts of the assignor. . . . Code of Iowa (1985).

The court has reviewed Iowa case law, a task which is relatively simple given that no cases exist, and concludes that Stetson's interpretation of the cited code section is correct. Stetson cites an annotation found in 85 A.L.R. 3d 1050 entitled, When is Filing of Financing Statement Necessary to Perfect an Assignment of Accounts Under U.C.C. § 9-302(1)(e). This annotation explains in great detail the provisions of said section and points out that the courts have utilized two basic tests to determine whether filing a financing statement is necessary to perfect a security interest in accounts receivable. These tests are:

casual and isolated transactions test; and

percentage of accounts test.

The casual and isolated transactions test is based upon the comments found to § 554.9302(1)(e) wherein the drafters of the Uniform Commercial Code stated:

The purpose of the subsection (1)(e) exceptions is to save from ex post facto invalidation casual or isolated assignments: some accounts receivable statutes have been so broadly drafted that all assignments, whatever their characteristic or purpose, fall within their filing provision. Under such statutes many assignments which no one would think of filing may be subject to invalidation. The subsection (1)(e) exceptions go to that type of assignment. Any person who regularly takes assignments of any debtor's accounts should file. In this connection, § 9-104(f) which excludes certain transfers of accounts and contract rights from the article should be consulted.

In the case at bar, the president of Stetson testified that on only one previous occasion had Stetson accepted an assignment of accounts receivable. That was approximately two years before accepting the assignment in the instant case. Since Stetson is not involved in the commercial lending business, it appears that its acceptance of assignments of accounts receivable is indeed an isolated and casual transaction such that it would fall within the casual and isolated transaction test derived from the comments quoted above.

In a similar fashion, a percentage test has been utilized by numerous courts as has been set forth in the ALR annotation cited above. Under the percentage test, courts have found that transactions in which 40 percent of the accounts receivable were transferred constitutes a significant part of the outstanding accounts of the assignor. 85 A.L.R. 3d at 1053. Conversely, courts have generally held that assignments did not constitute a "significant percentage" of the total accounts where the assignments in question ranged anywhere from 5 percent to 16 percent of the assignor's total accounts. 85 A.L.R.3d at 1054. In this context, Stetson argues that at most the accounts assigned to it constituted 6.2 percent of the accounts receivable of Fort Dodge Roofing Co. at the time the assignment was made. Stetson further argues that accounts receivable should not be the sole measure utilized in determining the percentage in application of the percentage test. Rather, Stetson argues that contract rights and/or work in progress should also be added to the accounts receivable to determine the denominator to be used in determining what percentage of the assignor's accounts have been transferred.

This court makes no comment on the above argument inasmuch as only 6.2 percent of the accounts receivable were transferred. The court concludes that 6.2 percent is not a significant percentage of the accounts receivable and therefore Stetson meets the percentage test to qualify for the exception to filing a financing statement.

CONCLUSION

This court concludes that although the assignment of accounts receivable was not an absolute transfer of those accounts to Stetson Building Products, the assignment was one which fits within the enumerated exception to the requirement of filing a financing statement to perfect a security interest. The test which the Iowa Supreme Court might choose to apply is inapposite inasmuch as Stetson proved its case under both tests. The court finds that the Trustee's argument that $52,000 is a significant sum is unpersuasive in light of the total accounts receivable of Fort Dodge Roofing at the time the transfer was made.

Therefore, the court concludes that Stetson Building Products is a creditor having a properly perfected security interest in the account in question.

NOTES

(1) Do you agree with the court's decision? Some courts have combined the two tests to prohibit an assignee from avoiding the filing requirement if the assignee receives a large proportion of the debtor's accounts, even though the transaction is isolated. *Query:* What result if the debtor was Sears and the one percent of accounts totaled $100 million?

(2) Under subsections 9-302(1)(c) and (1)(g), assignments of beneficial interests in trusts and assignments for the benefit of creditors are other examples of assignments that do not require the filing of a financing statement.

[B] Temporary Automatic Perfection

The Code also provides that no filing is necessary to perfect certain security interests for temporary periods of time. U.C.C. § 9-302(1)(b). The temporary perfected status arises at certain stages of transactions involving instruments, negotiable documents, and proceeds from collateral. Section 9-304(4) provides the secured party with automatic perfection in instruments or negotiable documents for a period of 21 days from the date the security interest attaches. The attached security interest must arise out of a transaction for new value under a written security agreement. The basic reason for the exception is to provide lenders some flexibility in making very short-term loans based on such collateral. To require either a filing or possession of collateral for such short-term transactions would be burdensome for the parties and would "clutter" the filing records. Thus, while security interests in instruments may only be perfected by possession, a short-term security transaction will be perfected for the 21 day period without possession. Though it may seem counter-intuitive to some readers, it should be understood that bankers and other lenders often make loans for brief periods of time. To illustrate, consider the following example:

> Under a written agreement dated June 1, Blackmon's Bank & Trust loans $100,000 to a debtor for fifteen days. BBT takes a security interest in negotiable promissory notes owned by the

debtor but does not take possession of the notes. Because the transaction ends within the automatic perfection time period, BBT's security interest is perfected without its physical possession of the collateral because the interest arose under a written security agreement for new value and attached on June 1.

Temporary automatic perfection also makes sense at another stage of some secured transactions. At times, a perfected secured party may wish to release the collateral to the debtor for some limited purpose. Because the debtor has possession of the collateral during this time, the secured party's perfected status would be jeopardized if the collateral was of a type that had to remain in the secured party's possession to perfect. To resolve this situation, section 9-304(5) of the Code creates a special 21-day period of automatic perfection for instruments, negotiable documents, and goods in the possession of a bailee (*i.e.*, a bailee other than the party who issued the negotiable document). The 21-day "grace" period begins to run from the date the secured party releases the collateral to the debtor. Examples include:

(a) A bank's issuing a letter of credit secured by documents, then releasing those documents to the customer to enable that customer to get the goods through customs.

(b) A bank's issuing a letter of credit for its customer, agreeing to pay for goods when a negotiable bill of lading arrives; the bank may pay for the goods and release the bill of lading to the customer who takes delivery of the goods, resells them, and repays the bank.

(c) A debtor is borrowing from the bank and giving a security interest in warehoused goods. The debtor gives the bank negotiable warehouse receipts, but borrows the receipts to claim the goods once it has made a contract to resell the goods. In such a case, the debtor must deliver the warehouse receipts to the buyer (possession of the receipts affords the buyer the right to gain access to the goods); with the money obtained from the sale, the debtor then pays the bank.

(d) A bank holding commercial paper as collateral releases it to another bank for purposes of presentment, collection, or renewal.

In each of the above situations, the automatic perfection period arises only if the secured party's release of collateral occurs for one of the special purposes set forth in section 9-304(5)(a) or (b).

[C] Proceeds

Section 9-306(3) of the Code provides a third type of temporary, automatic perfection. Under that section, if a security interest in collateral is perfected, the security interest continues in proceeds from the sale or disposition of the collateral for ten days following the debtor's receipt of the proceeds. If the security interest in proceeds is to continue beyond the 10-day period, the secured party may have to take additional steps to assure that the interest remains continuously perfected. We will discuss the concept of proceeds more fully in the next chapter.

§ 17.11 Methods of Perfection for Various Types of Collateral

Read: U.C.C. § 9-102, Comment 5.

The three methods of perfection—filing, possession, and automatic perfection—serve as a basic framework for legal analysis and decision-making under Article 9. Security interests in certain types of collateral may be perfected by one or more of these methods. Some people prefer to think of perfection in terms of the type of collateral. The following cases illustrate some of the special rules surrounding various types of collateral. Since cases involving questions of perfection often also raise issues of priority, both perfection and priority issues may be seen in most cases.

[A] Equipment

Read: U.C.C. §§ 9-109(2), 9-302, 9-305.

Goods used in a business are classified as equipment. The designation "equipment" is a veritable catchall classification that is often used to classify collateral that does not fall into other categories. As such, a security interest in equipment can be perfected through possession or filing. Perfection through possession is rarely practical since the debtor usually requires use of the equipment. With certain types of equipment collateral (mobile goods), perfection can occur by notation on a certificate of title. The possibility of multiple perfection methods may create problems for the secured creditor. As you read the following case, consider whether there are legitimate reasons for having more than one type of perfection mechanism for equipment. What are the benefits and the costs of multiple methods of perfection?

MORGAN COUNTY FEEDERS, INC. v. McCORMICK

Colorado Court of Appeals, Div. III
836 P.2d 1051, 18 U.C.C. Rep. Serv. 2d 632 (1992)

Opinion by JUDGE ROTHENBERG.

. . . .

In 1990, Morgan County Feeders, as a secured creditor, obtained a default judgment against Neil Allen for $1,461,019. Morgan County Feeders attempted to garnish 45 longhorn cows and one bull that were in the possession of Roy Creamer. Creamer contested the garnishment, and Morgan County Feeders filed a post-judgment motion for issuance of a writ of garnishment and to join third-persons who also claimed an interest in the cattle. The court granted Morgan County Feeders' motion. The parties then stipulated to the sale of the cattle, and the proceeds were placed in the registry of the court pending a hearing.

At the hearing, Morgan County Feeders claimed a priority in the proceeds based on its perfected security interest arising from a security agreement with Allen, which, in part, contained an after-acquired property clause. McCormick claimed an interest in the proceeds based on an oral agreement with Allen to buy the cattle.

After making extensive findings of fact and conclusions of law, the trial court entered judgment in favor of Morgan County Feeders, finding that the 45 longhorn cattle were "equipment" and not "inventory" under the Uniform Commercial Code and that Allen had no authority to dispose of the longhorn cattle free of Morgan County Feeders' perfected security interest. Accordingly, the court awarded Morgan County Feeders the sale proceeds minus certain costs owed to Creamer. McCormick is the only party that has appealed the judgment.

I.

McCormick first contends that the trial court erred in determining that the cattle purchased by Allen were equipment, rather than inventory. We disagree.

Under the Uniform Commercial Code, "goods" are defined as, "all things which are moveable at the time the security interest attaches. . .." Section 4-9-105(1)(h), C.R.S. (1991 Cum. Supp.). Goods are classified under four major types which are mutually exclusive. These include: consumer goods; equipment; farm products; and inventory. See § 4-9-109, C.R.S.

Here, the parties agree that the cattle constitute "goods" under the Uniform Commercial Code. They further agree that the cattle are not "farm products." Thus, the remaining issue surrounding the cattle is whether they should be designated as inventory or equipment. The distinction is important because buyers of inventory in the ordinary course of business take free of perfected security interests. See § 4-9-307(1)(a), C.R.S. (1991 Cum.Supp.); § 4-1-201(9), C.R.S.

Section 4-9-109(2), C.R.S., provides that goods are equipment: if they are used or bought for use primarily in business (including farming or a profession) . . . or if the goods are not included in the definitions of inventory, farm products, or consumer goods. In contrast, § 4-9-109(4), C.R.S., provides that goods are inventory: if they are held by a person who holds them for sale or lease or to be furnished under contracts of service or if he has so furnished them, or if they are . . . materials used or consumed in a business. Inventory of a person is not to be classified as his equipment.

In ascertaining whether goods are inventory or equipment, the principal use of the property is determinative. Section 4-9-109, C.R.S. (Official Comment 2). The factors to be considered in determining principal use include whether the goods are for immediate or ultimate sale and whether they have a relatively long or short period of use in the business. Section 4-9-109, C.R.S. (Official Comment 3); *First Colorado Bank & Trust v. Plantation Inn, Ltd.*, 767 P.2d 812 (Colo. App. 1988).

Goods used in a business are equipment when they are fixed assets or have, as identifiable units, a relatively long period of use. They are inventory, even though not held for sale, if they are used up or consumed in a short period of time in the production of some end product. *First Colorado Bank & Trust v. Plantation Inn, Ltd., supra.*

The classification of "goods" under § 4-9-109 is a question of fact, and therefore, the trial court's classification must be upheld if there is support in the record for that determination. . . .

At trial, the court determined that the longhorn cattle were "equipment" and not "inventory" because: Allen did not acquire or hold them for the principal purpose of immediate or ultimate sale or lease. . .. Instead, the cattle were to be used principally for recreational cattle drives . . .. While Allen might have occasionally leased the cattle to other entrepreneurs, it was his intention to utilize the cattle principally in his own recreational business. . .. Thus, the court concluded that McCormick bought the cattle subject to Morgan County Feeders' security interest.

Although we recognize that the classification of cattle as "equipment," rather than "inventory," is highly unusual, we also recognize that the evidence presented to the trial court disclosed unusual circumstances, and we conclude that the record supports the court's classification.

Allen testified that his purpose for purchasing the longhorn cows was to use them on cattle drives and that these cows have a relatively long period of use in comparison to rodeo calves and feeder cattle. Several other witnesses also testified that Allen had stated his intent to use the longhorn cows for recreational cattle drives. Thus, the trial court was justified in rejecting McCormick's contention that the cattle were purchased only for rodeos. And, it did not err in finding that, under these unique circumstances, the cattle should be classified as "equipment."

. . . .

The judgment is affirmed.

CRISWELL and RULAND, JJ., concur.

NOTE

Do you agree with the court's classification? Are there other factors the court should have considered? In classifying goods as either equipment or inventory, courts have held that the test is the owner's use of the goods. The debtor's stated intended purpose, at the time that the security interest attaches, defines the nature of the goods.

[B] Inventory

Read: U.C.C. §§ 9-109(4), 9-302.

Goods are inventory if they are held by a person who holds them for sale, lease, or under a service contract to others. Inventory may include raw materials, work in progress, or materials used during the course of a business. The Code's definition of inventory suggests that items which are turned over or replaced with some regularity fit the classification. Consider that definition in the next two cases.

IN RE DUPONT FEED MILL CORPORATION

Southern District of Indiana
121 B.R. 555, 13 U.C.C. Rep. Serv. 2d 1287 (1990)

BARKER, DISTRICT JUDGE.

. . . .

I. Background.

The case below was submitted to the bankruptcy court on stipulated facts. In addition, the bankruptcy court made further findings of undisputed fact in ruling on the cross motions for summary judgment. The court's findings reveal that on December 2, 1981, a Promissory Note in the principal amount of $300,000 was executed and delivered to Wells Fargo by Dupont Feed. The Note was signed, "Dupont Feed Mill Corporation, by William Wildman, President." On April 12, 1982, Dupont Feed executed a "Continuing Security Agreement" in favor of Wells Fargo which granted a security interest in:

> All accounts, deposit accounts, accounts receivable, chattel paper, instruments, documents, and general intangibles as defined in the California Uniform Commercial Code—Secured Transactions (collectively called rights to payments), now existing at any time or hereafter arising

> from the conduct of the Debtor's business (whether they arise from the sale, lease, or other disposition or inventory or from performance of contracts services, manufacture, construction, repair or otherwise), ... together with a security interest in all inventory, goods held for sale or lease or to be furnished under contract of service, goods sold, leased or furnished, raw materials, component parts, work in progress or materials used or consumed in Debtor's business (hereinafter called inventory) now or at any time hereafter, and prior to the termination hereof, owned or acquired by Debtor where ever located,. . .. and all products thereof (hereinafter called products), whether in the possession of Debtor, warehousemen, bailers, or other persons and whether located at Debtor's place of business or elsewhere, together with whatever is receivable or received when any of the foregoing or the proceeds thereof are sold, collected, exchanged or otherwise disposed of, whether such disposition is voluntary or involuntary, including without limitation all rights to payment, including returned premiums, with respect to any insurance relating to any of the foregoing, and all rights to payment with respect to any cause of action affecting or relating to the foregoing (hereinafter called the "proceeds"). . ...

This Security Agreement was signed "Dupont Feed Mill Corporation, by William Wildman, President." The Security Agreement stated that the obligations secured all present and future indebtedness of Dupont Feed to Wells Fargo. Wells Fargo filed a financing statement on this security agreement with the County Recorder of Jefferson County on June 17, 1982 and with the Indiana Secretary of State on June 28, 1982.

In August, 1983, Wildman, through his attorney, contacted Rushville to inquire about receiving a $100,000 loan to purchase the Arlington Ag-Center ("Arlington"). This property was to be purchased by Wildman in his individual capacity. In the course of requesting the loan, Wildman issued a personal financial statement to Rushville. On September 26, 1983, Rushville agreed to loan Wildman $100,000 for the mortgage on the property. In addition to the loan to purchase the Arlington property, Wildman requested a loan from Rushville for operational expenses on the business. In this regard, Rushville agreed to extend a line of credit for $150,000 to William and Sandra Wildman d/b/a Arlington Ag-Center. Wildman testified that he orally informed Wells Fargo that Rushville would be financing his acquisition of Arlington.

On September 30, 1983, Dupont Feed executed a Demand Note to Wells Fargo in the principal amount of $725,000. Moreover, on December 31, 1983, Dupont Feed executed another Demand Note to Wells Fargo in the principal amount of $2,000,000.

On October 27, 1983, Wildman received title to the Arlington property and personally executed a mortgage note payable to Rushville for $100,000. Subsequently, Wildman leased the Arlington property to Dupont Feed.

On December 29, 1983, a Promissory Note in the amount of $150,000, payable to Rushville, was executed as follows: "Arlington Ag-Center: by William Wildman." On the same day, a cashiers check in the amount of $136,023.06 was issued to "William Wildman and Bergdon Company." Also on December 29, 1983, Wildman and his wife executed a Continuing Guaranty to Rushville, stating the debt being guaranteed was the debt of "William Wildman—Arlington Ag-Center," at a maximum amount of $250,000.

On February 9, 1984, Rushville filed a financing statement with the Recorder of Rush County, Indiana. The financing statement listed "Arlington Ag-Center" as the Debtor, and further stated that it covered "all inventory, accounts receivable, equipment, furniture and fixtures located at Arlington Ag-Center."

The parties have stipulated that Arlington is a branch location of Dupont Feed and is not a separate corporation.

On September 10, 1984, Dupont Feed filed its Chapter 11 Petition. Arlington was listed as an asset, while Wells Fargo and Rushville were listed as creditors.

Thereafter, on or about December 17, 1984, Rushville filed a financing statement with the Indiana Secretary of State's office covering the inventory of the Dupont Feed. In December, 1984 and January, 1985, Rushville took possession of and sold Arlington's fertilizer for the sum of $95,000 and credited Debtor's account that amount.

An adversary proceeding was commenced on January 29, 1985 by Rushville filing a complaint against Wildman d/b/a Arlington Ag-Center, Dupont Feed, Ted R. Todd as Trustee for Dupont Feed, and Wells Fargo. On April 8, 1985, Wells Fargo filed a counterclaim against Rushville for conversion, asking for compensatory and punitive damages. In October of 1985, Rushville filed a Motion to Dismiss its claim against Wildman, which was granted in December, 1986. In September of 1986, the trustee petitioned the bankruptcy court to approve the assignment of his "strong arm" powers to Wells Fargo. The record is not clear as to whether the bankruptcy judge ever signed the approval order.

The bankruptcy court determined that the sole issue was whether Rushville or Wells Fargo was entitled to the proceeds of the sale of the fertilizer. By determining that the fertilizer was inventory and that Wells Fargo was the first to file its financing statement securing its interest in that inventory, the bankruptcy court found in favor of Wells Fargo and granted its motion for summary judgment.

Both Rushville and Wells Fargo appeal the bankruptcy court's grant of summary judgment in favor of Wells Fargo. Rushville argues that the bankruptcy court erred when it found that the fertilizer in question was "inventory." Instead, it argues that the fertilizer was a "farm product." Such a characterization, Rushville argues would have validated its financing statement filed in Rush County, thereby perfecting its security interest in the fertilizer.

. . . .

II. Analysis

A. Perfected Security Interests.

The existence of a properly perfected security interest is a question of state law. *Matter of Martin Grinding & Machine Works, Inc.*, 793 F.2d 592 (7th Cir.1986). Indiana law governing the attachment and perfection of security interests is found in the Uniform Commercial Code ("the U.C.C.") as adopted by Indiana Code §§ 26-1-9-101 et seq.

1. Characterizing The Collateral

As an initial matter, Rushville challenges the bankruptcy court's determination that the collateral was inventory. Rushville asserts that the fertilizer is a "farm product." While such a characterization might seem logical and could possibly validate its Rush County financing statement, it is not supported by the terms of the U.C.C.[7]

---

[7] Indiana Code § 26-1-9-401(1)provides that: The proper place to file in order to perfect a security interest is as follows: (a) When the collateral is . . . farm products . . ., then in the office of the county recorder in the county of the debtor's residence. . ..

The fertilizer at issue does not fall within the statutory definition of "farm products." Indiana Code § 26-1-9-109(3) states that goods are "farm products" if they are: crops or livestock used or produced in farming operations or if they are products of crops or of livestock in their unmanufactured states (such as ginned cotton, wool-clip, maple syrup, milk and eggs), and if they are in the possession of a debtor engaged in raising, fattening, grazing or other farming operations. By definition, fertilizer cannot be deemed a "farm product"—it is neither a crop nor a product of a crop used in farming.[8] Instead, fertilizer, particularly potash, is composed of minerals. Rushville's citation to the Encyclopedia of Chemical Technology demonstrates that it is aware that "[t]he potash industry is essentially a mining and beneficiation industry." *Id.* p. 77. Consequently this court affirms the characterization of the fertilizer as inventory, because it was held primarily for sale or lease. Ind. Code § 26-1-9-109(4).

2. Erroneous Filing

The only proper place to file a financing statement for inventory is with the Indiana Secretary of State's office. Ind. Code § 26-1-9-401(1)(c).

Rushville filed its financing statement listing a security interest in all of Arlington's "inventory, accounts receivable, equipment, furniture and fixtures" with the Rush County Recorder.[9] "Arlington Ag-Center" was listed as the debtor on this financing statement. Rushville seeks to convince this court that since it filed a financing statement covering Arlington's inventory with the Rush County Recorder's Office in February, 1984, it should fall within the terms of the Erroneous Filing provision in the U.C.C.[10] See Ind. Code § 26-1-9-401(2). However, Rushville's argument is again misguided.[11] The statute provides:

> A filing which is made in good faith in an improper place or not in all of the places required by this section is nevertheless effective with regard to any collateral as to which the filing complied with the requirements of I.C. 26-1-9. . . . Ind. Code § 26-1-9-401(2).

This provision requires that if the improper filing was made in good faith, it is effective only for the collateral for which it is properly filed. Consequently, the Rush County filing might have been sufficient for Arlington's equipment, farm products and accounts, if Arlington can be considered a "farming operation." See Ind. Code § 26-1-9-401(1)(a). However, since a financing statement covering a security interest in inventory can only be filed with the Secretary of State's

---

[8] In addition, there is no evidence in the record to support the proposition that Arlington was engaged in "farming operations." Instead, there is evidence in the record that Arlington was in the business of selling, among other things, fertilizer.

[9] Rushville eventually filed a financing statement with the Secretary of State in December, 1984, but this was after Dupont Feed filed for bankruptcy and in violation of the automatic stayimposed by 11 U.S.C. § 362(a).

[10] Rushville's arguments on this point contradict its actions. The Rush County financing statement listed the debtor as "Arlington Ag-Center" without specifying whether this was an assumed business name. If, as Rushville claims, it made its loan to Wildman in his individual capacity, then it should have listed the debtor as "Wildman," not "Arlington Ag-Center." On the other hand, if Rushville was dealing with Arlington as a corporation, as would seem evident by its financing statement, then it did not file in all the proper places. Section 9-401(1)(a) specifies that "if the debtor is a corporation [file] in the office of the county recorder in the county where the principal place of business, and in the office of the secretary of state. . .."

[11] The court would be remiss if it did not point out that even if Rushville did fall within the Erroneous Filing Provision, its priority date would be February, 1984. Wells Fargo, however, filed in June of 1982. Therefore, Wells Fargo would still have a superior lien on the inventory, under Ind.Code § 26-1-9-312(5) (the first to file or perfect rule).

office, Rushville's filing with the Rush County Recorder was invalid and can not be validated by the erroneous filing provision. See, *Citizens State Bank v. Peoples Bank*, 475 N.E. 2d 324, 328 (Ind. App. 1985).[12]

In contrast, Wells Fargo filed a financing statement with the Indiana Secretary of State's office in June of 1982. The security agreement entered into between Dupont and Wells Fargo granted a security interest in Dupont Feed's "inventory now or at any time hereafter, and prior to the termination hereof, owned or acquired by Debtor where ever located. . . ." Because the parties stipulated that Arlington was "a branch location and not a separate corporation," Wells Fargo's security interest in Dupont's inventory "where ever located" includes the fertilizer located at Arlington. As a result, Wells Fargo's security interest became perfected in June, 1982. Since it was the first to file, it has priority over other secured creditors as to the same collateral. Ind. Code § 26-1-9-312(5).

In addition, Rushville makes an argument in an effort to convince this court that Wells Fargo's filing under "Dupont Feed" was misleading and therefore erroneous. Essentially Rushville argues that it would not have been alerted to Wells Fargo's prior interest in the inventory because, had it searched the records, it would have searched under "Arlington," not "Dupont Feed." According to Rushville, to reward this type of behavior would be contrary to public policy. The court, however, can only assume that the reason Rushville is making this argument in terms of public policy is because it failed to check the files as a prudent creditor would have done.[13] To reward the carelessness of Rushville in this situation also would not be a good policy.[14]

. . . .

[Eds. note—HELD: Creditor's erroneous filing of financing statement for debtor's inventory with county recorder, rather than with Secretary of State as required by Indiana law, could not be validated by erroneous filing provision of Uniform Commercial Code.]

---

12 In addition, Rushville fails to fall within the second provision of § 9-401(2) wherein an erroneously filed financing statement nevertheless is effective against any other secured party who has knowledge of the contents of the financing statement. See, *Citizens State Bank v. Peoples Bank*, 475 N.E. 2d 324 (Ind. App. 1985). It appears that this provision was inserted into the U.C.C. to protect secured parties who filed earlier, albeit partially erroneous, financing statements. If a second secured party knew of the erroneously filed financing statement, then that second party could not take advantage of the first secured party's good faith mistake.

13 Although a search under Wildman or Arlington would have revealed no connection to Dupont, it would have been prudent to protect Rushville's rights.

14 Rushville was in the better position to avoid this entire situation by asking for more information regarding Wildman's connection with Dupont and its connection with Arlington. To impose such an obligation on a bank extending a $250,000 loan is not too great a burden.

THRIFT, INCORPORATED v. A.D.E., INC.

Indiana Court of Appeals
454 N.E.2d 878 (1983)

ROBERTSON, P.J.

Thrift, Incorporated (Thrift) appeals the trial court's judgment which held that its security interests in three automobiles had not attached. The trial court ruled the automobiles were not inventory of a third party, Devers Auto Sales (Devers) and found in favor of the original seller, A.D.E., Inc. (A.D.E.).

We reverse.

A.D.E. is an Indiana corporation which engages in the sale of motor vehicles in Indianapolis. Thrift is also an Indiana corporation and one of its activities includes the financing of motor vehicles intended for resale. Devers was an automobile dealer in Evansville involved in the acquisition, purchase, and resale of motor vehicles.

Devers obtained inventory financing from Thrift which perfected its security interests in Devers's inventory by filing a financing statement with the Secretary of State pursuant to Article 9 of the Uniform Commercial Code, Ind. Code 26-1-9-101 et seq. The financing statement included a security interest in Devers's after acquired inventory. On February 18, 1981, A.D.E. entered an agreement to sell three automobiles to Devers. In order to prevent Devers from making a return trip to Evansville, A.D.E. gave Devers possession of the three vehicles and Devers agreed to pay A.D.E. $20,335 on February 23, 1981. Thrift advanced Devers $17,975 and executed a trust receipt agreement which purported to give Thrift a security interest in the motor vehicles. Devers tendered checks to A.D.E. on February 23, 1981, which were dishonored for insufficient funds.

The parties stipulated that Devers did not receive express permission to encumber, use, sell, or dispose of the automobiles until the sale from A.D.E. was completed. A.D.E. retained title to the vehicles at all times and did not give Devers any bills of sale or odometer verification statements regarding the vehicles. Devers mixed the automobiles with the other vehicles on its lot. There was no evidence that the vehicles were prepared or offered for sale prior to Devers's default on its financing agreement with Thrift on March 9, 1981. Upon default, Thrift took possession of Devers's inventory, including the three automobiles in question. Thrift demanded the titles of these vehicles from A.D.E., and A.D.E. demanded the return of the vehicles. This action followed with judgment entered in favor of A.D.E.

The trial court examined the provisions of Ind Code § 26-1-9-204 and ruled that Thrift's security interests did not attach because Devers did not obtain any rights in the collateral. The trial court found that A.D.E. had a superior interest in the automobiles because it had retained the certificates of title and that Devers was a mere possessor or bailee of the vehicles. The trial court held that the three automobiles did not constitute inventory and thus, perfection of A.D.E.'s security interests had been accomplished by noting a valid lien on the certificates of title. The trial court also found that Thrift failed to inquire about the certificates of title prior to advancing funds to Devers.

The provisions of Ind Code § 26-1-9-302 control when a financing statement is required. This section indicates the filing provisions of Article 9 are still applicable to motor vehicles which are "inventory held for sale."

A.D.E. does not contest this interpretation of the statute, but argues the trial court correctly concluded that the vehicles did not constitute inventory. The classification of goods is contained in Ind.Code § 26-1-9-109. An examination of the comments regarding this section is very helpful. Comment 2 states that the classes of goods are mutually exclusive such that the goods can only be characterized as belonging in one of the four classes at the same time by the same person.

A characterization that the automobiles are consumer goods fails because Devers was engaged in the business of buying and selling motor vehicles, and the automobiles were not being used for personal, family, or household purposes. The determination which remains is whether the automobiles held by Devers constituted equipment or inventory. Comment 3 is dispositive of this question because it indicates that the principal test to determine whether goods are inventory is that they are held for immediate or ultimate sale. Although A.D.E. and Devers may have intended that Devers not encumber the vehicles for immediate sale until A.D.E. was paid, the facts clearly indicate that Devers held the automobiles for ultimate sale. Thus, the vehicles constituted inventory.

A.D.E. also argues that Thrift's security interest did not attach. Under the U.C.C., a party can only claim a security interest in property when the debtor has signed a security agreement, and the agreement contains a description of the collateral. The security interest does not attach to the collateral until there is an agreement that it attach, value is given, and the debtor has rights in the collateral. It is not contested that Thrift and Devers had an agreement describing the collateral or that value had been given, but A.D.E. does argue that Devers did not have rights in the collateral.

A.D.E. argues Devers merely had possession of the automobiles and did not have any rights in the collateral because A.D.E. retained the titles. A.D.E. supports its argument with the evidence that Devers did not have permission to sell or encumber the automobiles, nor did Devers receive bills of sale or odometer verification statements. A.D.E. directs our attention to *Gicinto v. Credit Thrift of America, No. 3, Inc.*, (1976) 219 Kan. 766, 549 P.2d 870, where the opinion distinguished cash sales from credit transactions and found in favor of an automobile dealer who had retained the titles to motor vehicles after transferring the vehicles to another automobile dealer. *Gicinto* is distinguishable from the present situation because the secured party in *Gicinto* stipulated that its security interest was unperfected. Furthermore, the present case does not involve a cash sale as A.D.E. contends. Devers was not obligated to pay A.D.E. until February 23, 1981, which was five days after Devers received the automobiles. In *Central National Bank of Mattoon v. Worden-Martin, Inc.*, (1980) 413 N.E.2d 539, the Appellate Court of Illinois faced similar facts and ruled such an arrangement constitutes a credit sale. While A.D.E. correctly notes that mere possession of goods by a debtor does not establish rights in the collateral, *Cain v. Country Club Delicatessen, Inc.*, (1964) 25 Conn. Supp. 327, 203 A.2d 441, we believe Devers acquired an interest in the three automobiles.

The passage of title pursuant to an Article 2 transaction is contained in Ind Code § 26-1-2-401(1). . . . Moreover, the decision of *First National Bank of Elkhart County v. Smoker*, (1972) 153 Ind. App. 71, 286 N.E. 2d 203, is dispositive on the issue of when the debtor obtains rights in the collateral. The decision held:

> [W]hen the debtor acquires possession of the collateral under a contract, he has acquired such rights in the collateral as to allow the security of his creditor to attach to the collateral, and this is true regardless of who may be deemed to have title to and ownership of such collateral.

153 Ind. App. at 81. In the present case, Devers acquired an interest in the collateral when it received possession of the automobiles from A.D.E. pursuant to their contract. Thus, Thrift's secured interest attached at that time. This result is in full accord with the holding of *Central National Bank of Mattoon v. Worden-Martin, supra*, which also found in favor of a secured party where a debtor, automobile dealer, acquired possession of motor vehicles pursuant to a contract from another automobile dealer who retained the titles to the vehicles.

A.D.E. argues the *Smoker* decision is distinguishable because *Smoker* involved cattle and not motor vehicles where priority interests are determined by notation of liens upon the certificates of title. However, as this opinion stated previously, motor vehicles held as inventory are not subject to these provisions. *National Bank and Trust Co. of South Bend v. Moody Forra's, supra.* A.D.E. also argues the present case is distinguishable because A.D.E. and Devers did not intend for the titles to pass until A.D.E. received payment from Devers. In *Smoker*, the buyer and seller had an oral agreement to delay the passage of title until a specified time after delivery, which was in accordance with the custom and usage of the industry. We rejected this argument and found in favor of the secured creditor, holding that the cattle became a part of the buyer's inventory upon coming into his possession pursuant to a contract. We remain unpersuaded that the present case is distinguishable from Smoker.

The final argument A.D.E. presents is that Thrift, with reasonable diligence, could have protected itself by inquiring about the titles to the automobiles. While this assertion is true, it is also quite clear that A.D.E. could have taken precautions to protect its interest. A.D.E., as an automobile dealer, must certainly be aware that other dealers have financing arrangements which are secured by the dealers' inventory. A fundamental policy of Article 9 of the U.C.C. is to discourage secret liens, *Matter of Maplewood Poultry Co.* (Bankr. D. Me. 1980) 2 B.R. 550. A contrary decision would undercut this fundamental policy.. . .

The judgment is reversed. . . .

NOTES

(1) Both *Dupont Feed* and *Thrift* demonstrate the importance of proper classification and filing for inventory. In *Dupont*, the creditor's improper filing resulted in its subordinate position. In *Thrift*, the debtor sought to avoid the creditor's security interest by claiming that the creditor failed to note its interest on the certificate of title. The court properly classified the cars as inventory which required a central filing. If the cars had been sold to companies as equipment

or to consumers as consumer goods, perfection would have to occur under the filing provisions found in certificate of title statutes.

(2) Be careful not to lump all items used in a business as inventory; if the items will be used during the course of business and not held for sale to others, such goods will be classified as equipment. Consider, for example, a leasing business—are the leased goods inventory or equipment? What if the leasing company also uses certain goods in performing similar work for others on its own account?

(3) Although perfection in inventory can be achieved by filing, a purchase money inventory financer must also give notice to all parties who have prior security interests in inventory in order to have priority under U.C.C. § 9-312(3). The omitted portion of *Dupont Feed* discusses purchase money priority. We will take up that subject in the next chapter.

[C] Accounts Receivable

Read: U.C.C. § 9-106 and 9-302(1)(e).

The term "account" is defined at U.C.C. § 9-106 as "any right to payment for goods sold or leased or for services rendered which is not evidenced by an instrument or chattel paper, whether or not it has been earned by performance." Normally, perfection of accounts may occur only by filing since accounts are pure intangibles and cannot be possessed. The proper place for filing is the state in which the debtor's place of business is located. If the debtor has more than one place of business, filing should be made in the state where a business debtor has its chief executive office or where a non-business debtor resides. See U.C.C. § 9-103(3)(b), (c), and (d).

THORP COMMERCIAL CORP. v. NORTHGATE INDUSTRIES, INC.

United States Court of Appeals
31 U.C.C. Rep. 801 (8th Cir. 1981)

MCMILLIAN, CIRCUIT JUDGE.

Franklin National Bank (the Bank) appeals from an order of the District Court for the District of Minnesota granting summary judgment to Thorp Commercial Corp. (Thorp) dismissing the Bank's counterclaim against Thorp for conversion. The conversion counterclaim arose out of Thorp's collection of proceeds from accounts receivable of a third party (the debtor, Northgate Industries, Inc.) who was indebted to both the Bank and Thorp. The Bank argues that the district court erred in holding that the Bank's claim to a security interest in certain of the debtor's accounts receivable failed as against Thorp because the Bank had not filed an adequate financing statement before Thorp perfected its own security interest in the accounts receivable. For the reasons discussed below, we reverse the district court's judgment and remand for further proceedings consistent with this opinion.

At issue in this appeal are security interests taken by both the Bank and Thorp in accounts receivable of a debtor, Northgate Industries, Inc., a firm engaged in repair of structures damaged by fires or other casualties. On May 13, 1971, the Bank lent the debtor $6,500 and under a security agreement took a security interest in collateral including all of the debtor's accounts receivable and proceeds. The security agreement indicated that ongoing financing arrangements were contemplated, because the security agreement purported to secure payment of all indebtedness existing or to be created afterward. The Bank duly filed with the Minnesota Secretary of State on May 21, 1971, a financing statement describing the collateral as "assignment accounts receivable" and "proceeds." On July 21, 1971, the Bank lent the debtor an additional sum of over $8,000; by May 4, 1972, the debtor had fully repaid both loans to the Bank, but the financing statement was not modified or withdrawn.

Meanwhile, on April 2, 1972, Thorp set up its financing arrangement with the debtor by entering into a security agreement covering certain collateral, including the debtor's accounts receivable and specifying coverage of both existing accounts and accounts which would be subsequently acquired. Thorp filed a financing statement identical to its security agreement two days later.

Subsequently, both the Bank and Thorp made further loans to the debtor. Prior to the business failure of the debtor, Thorp collected about $685,000 in repayment of its advances and apparently was owed as much as $ 100,000 more by the debtor; the Bank seems to have advanced a smaller amount, but as much as $60,000 of the debtor's indebtedness to the Bank appears to remain unpaid. On two occasions the Bank filed additional financing statements, one in July, 1972, describing the collateral in relevant part as "Assignment A/C Rec," and one in February, 1973, describing the collateral in relevant part as "All accounts receivable now or herein-after acquired." The Bank, however, never withdrew or modified its 1971 financing statement.

The present case is part of litigation that arose out of the failure of the debtor's business. At the time of the failure the debtor owed substantial sums to both the Bank and Thorp. Thorp commenced a lawsuit against the Bank and others alleging common law fraud and violations of federal securities laws arising in part out of alleged improper relationships between officers of the Bank and the debtor. The Bank filed a counterclaim against Thorp for conversion. The counterclaim is based on a theory that Thorp had converted funds it received from the debtor, because the funds belonged to the Bank, which claimed a prior perfected security interest in the proceeds of the debtor's accounts receivable by virtue of its 1971 agreement and financing statement.

The district court dismissed the Bank's counterclaim because in its view the 1971 financing statement covered only accounts receivable in existence at the time and not accounts receivable subsequently created. The Bank has not disputed that Thorp also had a perfected security interest in the debtor's accounts receivable on the basis of Thorp's April, 1972, security agreement and financing statement securing collateral including the debtor's accounts. Under Article 9 of the Uniform Commercial Code (UCC), which Minnesota has adopted, Minn Stat Ann § 336.9-101 et seq. (West 1966 & Supp. 1981) (all statutory references are to Minn Stat Ann), where two creditors hold security interests in the same collateral of the kind involved in this case (a significant portion of the debtor's accounts receivable), the creditor which first perfects its security interest by filing a financing statement has the prior interest, regardless of the time of the creation of the security agreement. §336.9-312(5). Thorp contended, and the district court agreed, that the 1971 financing statement filed by the Bank did not cover any accounts receivable coming into existence subsequent to the date the statement was filed. Thorp's April, 1972, financing statement would then be the earliest one covering the debtor's accounts receivable; therefore, Thorp would have the prior interest in the accounts and the Bank's conversion claim would fail. The district court certified its decision as a final order under Fed. R. Civ. P. 54(b), and this appeal followed.

The U.C.C. provisions governing secured transactions in the financing of accounts receivable set up a system designed to facilitate arrangements by which a debtor may obtain ongoing financing by using a significant portion of its accounts receivable as collateral. The creditor's security interest in the accounts receivable "attaches" when the debtor signs a valid security agreement covering the collateral, § 336.9-203(1); the security interest is "perfected" when the creditor files a financing statement giving notice of the security interest, § 336.9-302. Cf. § 336.9-302(i)(e) (no financing statement required to perfect a security interest in an assignment of less than a significant portion of the debtor's outstanding accounts). Both the security agreement and financing statement may cover ongoing financing arrangements; once such an ongoing security arrangement attaches and is perfected, the creditor's interest in the accounts may be secured as collateral for future as well as past advances, see *Thorp Finance Corp. v. Ken Hodgins & Sons*, 73 Mich. App. 428, 251 N.W. 2d 614 (1977), despite the rollover process of closing of the debtor's existing accounts and opening of new accounts that were not in existence at the time the arrangement was set up.

The security agreement and financing statement have different functions under the U.C.C. The security agreement defines what the collateral is so that, if necessary, the creditor can identify and claim it, and the debtor or other interested parties can limit the creditor's rights in the collateral given as security. The security agreement must therefore describe the collateral. The financing statement, on the other hand, serves the purpose of putting subsequent creditors on notice that the debtor's property is encumbered. The description of collateral in the financing statement does not function to identify the collateral and define property which the creditor may claim, but rather to warn other subsequent creditors of the prior interest. The financing statement, which limits the prior creditor's rights vis-a-vis subsequent creditors, must therefore contain a description only of the type of collateral. One corollary to this principle is that, as between two creditors with security interests in the accounts receivable of the same debtor, the first to provide notice by filing a financing statement has priority. Moreover, the financing statement may be filed before the security agreement is made without affecting the first to file rule of priority.

Because the purpose of the financing statement is to warn subsequent creditors rather than to identify the collateral, the U.C.C. makes clear that the collateral need not be specified in the financing statement but may be described by "type." The U.C.C. commentary makes clear that it is ordinarily not expected that the financing statement itself will tell a subsequent creditor what collateral is already covered by a prior security interest. "The notice itself indicates merely that the secured party who has filed may have a security interest in the collateral described. Further inquiry will be necessary to disclose the complete state of affairs."

The district court failed to focus upon whether the financing statement contained an adequate description of the type of collateral so that a subsequent creditor would reasonably make further inquiry; Instead, the district court considered whether the financing statement adequately described the collateral itself. The district court found great significance in the word "assignment" and reasoned that "assignment accounts" could only refer to specific accounts listed in the security agreement or actually transferred in some other way prior to the filing of the financing statement. In the district court's view, the words "assignment accounts receivable" would not be adequate to cover future accounts receivable under §336.9-110, which provides, "[A]ny description of personal property . . .is sufficient whether or not it is specific if it reasonably identifies what is described."

But, as noted above, the U.C.C. requires a description of only the type of collateral, not the collateral itself, in the financing statement to perfect a security interest. Under §336.9-110, a description of the collateral in a financing statement "is sufficient whether or not it is specific if it reasonably identifies" the type of collateral. The drafters of the U.C.C. contemplated that the financing statement would need to give only enough description of the collateral to induce a subsequent creditor to make further inquiries. The description "reasonably identifies" the type of collateral, therefore, if it would reasonably induce further inquiry.

The district court's approach, however, has support under a line of cases in which courts have largely ignored the function of a financing statement to suggest further inquiry about the collateral. A split in authority exists in this area. For example, one court has held that a financing statement describing the collateral as "accounts receivable" did not cover accounts created after the financing statement was filed, reasoning that some subsequent creditors may have been misled by the failure to specify subsequently created accounts and that the prior creditor could easily have made the financing statement clearer. Other courts have, however, considered financing statements describing the collateral as "accounts receivable" or "accounts" as adequate to cover accounts created subsequent to the filing of the financing statement.

A substantial theoretical difference seems to underlie these inconsistent results. Under one view a financing statement adequately covers collateral if it reasonably puts a subsequent creditor on notice of a need for further inquiry about the possibility that the collateral is subject to a prior security interest. The reasonableness of the notice would depend on balancing such factors as the difficulty of making further inquiry against factors such as the likelihood the type of collateral described in the financing statement might include the collateral which interests the subsequent creditor.

Under the second view of Article 9, a financing statement suffices to perfect a security interest in collateral if the financing statement itself contains a reasonable description of the collateral. The determination of reasonableness involves balancing such factors as the ease with which the prior creditor could make the description of the collateral more precise or clearer against factors like the danger that a subsequent creditor might fail to recognize that the collateral is covered. *E.g., In re Middle Atlantic Stud Welding Co., supra*, 503 F.2d 1133 (explicitly weighing these factors).

The district court in deciding the instant case relied upon an Oklahoma case involving similar facts which adopted this second view of financing statements. In *Georgia-Pacific Corp. v. Lumber Products Corp.*, 590 P.2d 661 (Okla. 1979), a financing statement covering "assignment accounts receivable" was held inadequate to perfect a security interest in accounts receivable other than those specifically assigned by the debtor to the secured party. The court in Georgia-Pacific found that the words "assignment accounts receivable" were reasonably descriptive of only an assignment of specific listed accounts receivable and held that the words did not "reasonably identify the collateral as all accounts receivable." *Id.* at 664. Although the opinion does not elaborate on the factors which determine whether the description reasonably identifies the collateral, the Oklahoma court did not consider whether it would have been reasonable for subsequent creditors to make further inquiries about what the financing statement covered, but rather considered what was described in the financing statement itself.

The approach of the Oklahoma court in the Georgia-Pacific case and other courts which requires that the financing statement by its own terms describe the collateral cannot be supported under Article 9. Article 9 simply does not require that the financing statement describe anything more than the type of collateral and leaves to interested parties the burden of seeking more information. Ultimately, such a requirement for a description of the collateral itself in a financing statement would eliminate the distinction between the financing statement and the security agreement, because the only way for a creditor to make sure that the financing statement describes the collateral would be to use the same description which identified the collateral in the security agreement setting up the security interest. Indeed, the district court suggested in the instant case that the "optimum practice" is for the creditor "to describe the collateral in the financing statement exactly as it appears in the security agreement." Such a requirement was rejected by the drafters of the U.C.C. who specifically commented,

> the financing statement is effective to encompass transactions under a security agreement not in existence and not contemplated at the time the notice was filed, if the description of collateral in the financing statement is broad enough to encompass them. Similarly, the financing statement is valid to cover after-acquired property . . .whether or not mentioned in the financing statement.

One central purpose of allowing a broad financing statement is to allow a creditor that envisions an ongoing financing arrangement to protect the priority of its interest by filing at an early date a notice to third parties which will cover the existing arrangement and broad range of potential future modifications. By requiring a description of the collateral in the financing statement itself, courts would destroy this flexibility.

The Minnesota courts have not addressed the precise question before us. In a case involving similar questions, however, the state supreme court explained,

> [o]nce a financing statement is on file describing property by type, the entire world is warned, not only that the secured party may already have a security interest in property of that type. . ., but that it may later acquire a perfected security interest in property of the same type acquired by the debtor in the future.
>
> . . .
>
> . . .The code very simply and briefly provides for a notice-filing procedure with a minimum of information required to be publicized in a filed financing statement. All that is required is a minimal description, and it may be by type or kind. The statement need not necessarily contain detail as to collateral, nor any statement of quantity, size, description or specifications, or serial numbers. No preciseness is required with respect to whether the collateral exists at the time of filing or is to be acquired thereafter. . . .

Minnesota thus appears to be one of the jurisdictions which has adopted the first view discussed above, that a financing statement covers the collateral in question if it merely makes it reasonable for a subsequent creditor interested in the collateral to make further inquiries.

The Minnesota Supreme Court's reasoning seems fundamentally inconsistent with the Oklahoma court's decision in *Georgia-Pacific Corp. v. Lumber Products Co., supra*, 590 P.2d 661. If the financing statement covers not only existing security interests in the type of collateral described but also security interests which may arise in the future, then a financing statement covering "assignment accounts receivable" would cover any assignment of the debtor's accounts receivable that might exist or be made in the future. The word "assignment" might mean a specific assignment of named accounts receivable but is broad enough to refer to a general assignment of all the debtor's accounts receivable, including those acquired in the future. A subsequent creditor, faced with notice that a security interest may exist or be created in any or all of the debtor's accounts, would certainly have reasonable grounds for inquiring further before relying on any of the debtor's accounts for collateral. We conclude that under Minnesota law applying the U.C.C. the financing statement covering "assignment accounts receivable" was adequate to perfect the Bank's security interest in accounts acquired subsequent to the filing of the financing statement, whether or not there was a specific assignment of particular accounts.

In reaching this conclusion we do not overlook the district court's concern that a creditor should not benefit from use of a misleading or overreaching financing statement. The notice filing concept has a primary purpose of facilitating ongoing financing arrangements not merely by the first creditor on the scene but also subsequent creditors. The requirement for filing a financing statement provides notice, at least theoretically, to subsequent creditors of what assets may already be encumbered by prior creditors. The financing statement would not provide notice where the description of collateral is misleading, for example, if the description were simply wrong or if the description seemingly would not cover the collateral but contained coverage under some hidden ambiguity that could not be considered reasonable notice. Even assuming the words "assignment accounts receivable" could be interpreted narrowly to refer to a single assignment of specific accounts receivable, the words also have an obvious alternative broad meaning; in the present case notice filing has served its purpose of alerting subsequent creditors to the need for further inquiry. The U.C.C. puts the burden on the subsequent creditor to seek clarification.

Accordingly, the judgment of the district court is reversed and the case is remanded for further proceedings consistent with this opinion.

NOTE

Review the material on Isolated Assignment of Accounts and *Fort Dodge Roofing* in the previous section on temporary automatic perfection (§ 17.10[A]).

[D] Instruments and Money

[1] Instruments

Read: U.C.C. §§ 9-105(1)(i), 9-304, and 9-305.

U.C.C. § 9-105(1)(i) supplies a broad definition of instruments which includes negotiable instruments under Article 3 (checks, drafts, and promissory notes), corporate securities under Article 8 (stock), and "any other writing which evidences a right to payment of money and is not itself a security agreement or lease and is of the type which is in the ordinary course of business transferred by delivery with any necessary endorsement or assignment." Because these items represent the basic elements of commercial life, the Code provides that possession is necessary to perfect an interest in any of these items. U.C.C. § 9-304(1).

IN RE ALLEN

United States Bankruptcy Appellate Panel for the Ninth Circuit
134 B.R. 373, 16 U.C.C. Rep. Serv. 2d 1165 (1991)

JONES, BANKRUPTCY JUDGE:

The bankruptcy court granted summary judgment for the bankruptcy trustee in an adversary suit asserting strong-arm powers, holding that a secured party had failed to perfect its security interest in a note and deed of trust by failing to take possession of the instruments. The secured party appeals. We reverse and remand.

BACKGROUND

Debtors Arthur and Peggy Allen ("the Allens") owned a half-interest in certain real property in Maricopa County, Arizona. On June 25, 1986, the Allens sold their half-interest to the Krejci and Smets Partnership ("Partnership"), taking a note ("Note") in the amount of $570,000.00 as partial payment. The Note was secured by a Deed of Trust and Assignment of Rents ("Deed of Trust"). Under the Deed of Trust, the Partnership was the trustor, the Allens were the beneficiaries, and Title U.S.A. Company of Arizona ("TCA") was the trustee.

TCA was the collection agent for the Debtors in connection with the Note and Deed of Trust pursuant to an account servicing agreement dated July 1, 1986. Pursuant to the agreement, TCA took possession of the Note and Deed of Trust.

On August 5, 1986, the Allens assigned their interest in the Note and their beneficial interest under the Deed of Trust to Casa Grande Cotton Finance Company ("Casa Grande") through an Assignment of Beneficial Interest Under Deed of Trust ("Assignment"). The Assignment was delivered to TCA on the date of execution and recorded with the Maricopa County Recorder's Office on August 18, 1986.

After the Allens filed for bankruptcy, Casa Grande asserted its interest in the proceeds from the Note and Deed of Trust. The bankruptcy trustee, Stanley W. Fogler ("Fogler"), filed an adversary proceeding asserting his strong-arm powers pursuant to the United States Bankruptcy Code, 11U.S.C. § 544(1988) ("§ 544"). Fogler argued that Casa Grande never properly perfected a security interest in the Note and Deed of Trust. Fogler moved for and was granted summary judgment. Casa Grande appeals. We reverse and remand.

. . . .

DISCUSSION

The bankruptcy trustee, as hypothetical lien creditor, has the power to avoid unperfected security interests under § 544. Fogler argues that Casa Grande failed to take possession of the Note and Deed of Trust and thereby failed to perfect pursuant to Ariz. Rev. Stat. Ann. § 47-9304(A)(1988) ("A.R.S."), which reads in part: "A security interest in money or instruments . . . can be perfected only by the secured party's taking possession [of the collateral]."

Casa Grande argues that it perfected its security interest in the Note and Deed of Trust by recording pursuant to Arizona real property law, and that the U.C.C. possession requirement is inapplicable under the instant facts. Even though Casa Grande is wrong on these points, there are factual issues raised by A.R.S. § 47-9305 which preclude the granting of summary judgment against Casa Grande on the issue of perfection.

Whether the U.C.C. Applies

The Uniform Commercial Code has been adopted in Arizona. A.R.S. § 47-1101. Article 9 generally does not apply to the "creation or transfer of an interest in or lien on real estate, including a lease or rents thereunder." A.R.S. § 47-9104(10). But there are several exceptions to this rule, notably Comment 4 to U.C.C. § 9-102 which makes Article 9 applicable to "realty paper." The following is a simplification of the illustration from Comment 4: X mortgages his real estate to Y. Y gives X's note and the real estate mortgage to Z as security for a loan. Article 9 does not apply to the mortgage transaction between X and Y, but it does apply to the transaction between Y and Z.

The Y and Z transaction in the illustration is identical to the instant facts, showing that Article 9 applies in the instant case.

What the U.C.C. Requires for Perfection

Because the instant transaction includes two instruments, (1) a note (usually perfected by possession), and (2) a deed of trust (usually perfected by recording), some courts have been confused as to how to achieve perfection. The note appears to be merely "realty paper," while the deed of trust appears to be a legitimate "realty interest." One court found that the note was perfected by possession under the U.C.C., while the deed of trust was perfected by recording under state law. *In re Maryville Sav. & Loan Corp.*, 743 F.2d 413 (6th Cir. 1984), supplemented in, 760 F.2d 119 (6th Cir.1985). This result produces the worst of both worlds according to one commentator.

The better approach is to require no action to be taken with regard to the deed of trust, but instead to concentrate on the note. Promissory notes are instruments. Security interests in instruments can only be perfected by possession. A.R.S. § 47-9304(A); *In re Staff Mortgage & Inv. Corp.*, 550 F.2d 1228, 1230 (9th Cir. 1977) (recording of an assignment in instruments is not enough to perfect).

Possession

Casa Grande never had physical possession of the Note and Deed of Trust. TCA had physical possession.[15] Even so, Casa Grande could argue that it obtained "constructive" possession (possession by a bailee or an agent) through TCA pursuant to A.R.S. § 47-9305:

> If [a security interest in instruments] is held by a bailee, the secured party is deemed to have possession from the time the bailee receives notification of the secured party's interest . . .. Comment 2 to § 9-305 adds: Possession may be by the secured party himself or by an agent on his behalf: it is of course clear, however, that the debtor or a person controlled by him cannot qualify as such an agent for the secured party. . ..

Bailment and Agency

Thus, § 47-9305 allows for two forms of "constructive" possession: (1) through a bailee, or (2) through an agent. However, courts vary in the legitimacy they lend to the different forms. . . .Some courts require that the holder of the instruments be within the secured party's exclusive control. Other courts are satisfied by a showing that the holder is not within the debtor's exclusive

[15] Possession, a slippery term with roots in age-old property law, is never defined in the U.C.C. 2 White & Summers, *supra* note 2, § 24-12 at 350. The Ninth Circuit has held that only "actual" possession will suffice to satisfy U.C.C. § 9-305. and that "constructive" possession is not enough. *Staff Mortgage*, 550 F.2d at 1230. Nevertheless, the *Staff Mortgage* court allowed "actual" possession to be achieved by an agent or a bailee. *Id.* Other courts refer to this kind of "actual" possession as "constructive" possession.

control,[16] so long as the holder has notice of the secured party's interest. Arizona falls into the latter category.

Under Arizona law, a bailee is neither under the debtor's nor the secured party's exclusive control, but acts more like an escrow.[17] Under facts substantially identical to those in the instant case, the Arizona Court of Appeals in *Mur-Ray Management Corp. v. Founders Title Co.* reversed a grant of summary judgment against a secured party, finding that a title company acting as servicing agent pursuant to an escrow agreement with a debtor, with notice of the assignment to the secured party, was an independent bailee. *The Mur-Ray* court found that the title company's notice of the assignment was evidence that it was not wholly controlled by the debtor. *Mur-Ray*, 819 P.2d at 1008.

Control

On motion for summary judgment, the moving party has the burden to show absence of material issues of fact and entitlement to judgment as a matter of law. *E.g., Celotex Corp. v. Catrett*, 477 U.S. 317, 106 S.Ct. 2548, 91 L.Ed.2d 265 (1986). But Fogler failed to present any evidence to show who controlled TCA as a matter of fact. Furthermore, pursuant to *Mur-Ray* and the cases cited by it, Fogler was required to show that the Allens had exclusive control over TCA in order to meet both prongs of his burden on motion for summary judgment. Absent such a showing, and in light of Fogler's admission that the Assignment was delivered to TCA thereby creating "a reasonable inference that the title company was not controlled by the debtor alone," a triable issue remains and the motion for summary judgment should have been denied. See *Mur-Ray*, 819 P.2d at 1008.

CONCLUSION

Accordingly, we reverse the judgment of the bankruptcy court and remand for further proceedings consistent with this opinion.

COMMENT

The court does a good job describing the dilemma a creditor faces when using both a promissory note and a deed of trust to provide security for a financing transaction. For deeds of trust, the proper method of perfecting an interest is recording the deed in the appropriate office where the property is situated. However, because promissory notes qualify as negotiable

[16] Possession gives notice of an interest in collateral, while non-possession makes an alleged interest suspect. 2 White & Summers, . . .,§ 24-12 at 347. Possession by a third party, and perhaps more importantly lack of possession by the debtor, gives notice to potential creditors that the debtor's interest in the collateral may be restricted. An independent third party possessor will not automatically be regarded as an instrumentality or agent of the debtor. *Copeland*, 531 F.2d at 1204-05; *In re Van Kylen*, 98 B.R. 455, 467 (Bankr. W.D. Wis. 1989).

[17] An escrow agent serving both parties can qualify as a bailee/agent under U.C.C. § 9-305. *In re Cedar Rapids Meats, Inc.*, 121 B.R. 562, 571(Bankr. N.D. Iowa 1990) (citing *Copeland*, 531 F.2d at 1203-04); see also *In re Rolain*, 823 F.2d 198, 199 (8th Cir. 1987); *In re O.P.M. Leasing Servs., Inc.*, 46 B.R. 661, 670 (Bankr. S.D.N.Y. 1985).

instruments, the only method of perfection is possession. The *Allen* court suggests that the better approach is to disregard the deed of trust and "instead to concentrate on the note." Do you agree? Do the costs of recording the deed of trust and taking possession of the promissory note outweigh the degree of certainty created by requiring specific acts for each type of item?

[2] Money

Read: U.C.C. §§ 1-201(24), 9-305.

A security interest in money can be perfected only through possession. While this seems relatively simple, some problems may still arise. For example, is money in an escrow account a contract right with a security interest perfected only by filing; or, is it money with the security interest perfected only by possession? Is money in an escrow account in one's possession? In the case of *In re O.P.M. Leasing Services, Inc.*, 46 B.R. 661, 40 U.C.C. Rep. Serv. 1422 (S.D.N.Y. 1985), the court rejected the argument that the escrow account was a general intangible and that filing was required. Instead, the court found the collateral to be money, and that the element of possession was present. Like the *Allen* court, the *O.P.M. Leasing* court pointed out that one may have possession of money through a bailee. According to the court, actual possession by the creditor's agent or bailee would serve to notify prospective third party creditors that the debtor did not have unfettered use of this collateral. Does the same logic apply in other instances?

IN RE VISCOUNT FURNITURE CORP.

United States Bankruptcy Court, Northern District Mississippi
133 B.R. 360, 15 U.C.C. Rep. Serv. 2d 1315 (1991)

David W. Houston, III, Bankruptcy Judge.

On consideration before the court are the applications for compensation and reimbursement of expenses filed by the law firms of Stennett, Wilkinson and Ward and Knight and Knight, P.A.; objections to said applications, as well as, a motion for the disgorgement of retainers filed by the Office of the United States Trustee; and the court having heard and considered same hereby finds as follows, to-wit:

. . . .

II.

The law firms of Stennett, Wilkinson, and Ward and Knight and Knight were employed by the debtor on November 25, 1988. Stennett, Wilkinson, and Ward received a retainer in the sum of $13,000.00, and Knight and Knight received a retainer in the sum of $7,500.00. The debtor filed its voluntary Chapter 11 bankruptcy case on December 2, 1988, and the two law firms filed their disclosures of compensation pursuant to 11 U.S.C. § 329, setting forth their respective retainers. The bankruptcy case was converted from Chapter 11 to Chapter 7 on September 12, 1989.

As a result of a motion filed by the U.S. Trustee to compel compliance with a previous order of this court, the law firms filed their applications for compensation and reimbursement of expenses. The application of Stennett, Wilkinson, and Ward was filed on August 16, 1990, and requested the following:

Attorneys' fees	$16,990.00
Expenses	3,429.80

Total	$20,419.80

The application of Knight and Knight was filed on March 25, 1991, and requested the following:

Attorneys' fees	$ 8,567.50
Expenses	122.68
Total	$ 8,690.18

The U.S. Trustee filed an objection to the aforesaid fee applications, alleging among other things that the employment of the law firms to represent the debtor had never been approved by the court. The U.S. Trustee also filed a motion requesting the court to order the disgorgement of the retainers which had been previously paid to the law firms.

Responding to the objections, on March 25, 1991, the law firms filed a joint motion requesting the court to approve their employment to represent the debtor, nunc pro tunc, November 25, 1988. Since there was no objection to this motion and in reliance on *Matter of Triangle Chemical's Inc.*, 697 F.2d 1280 (5th Cir. 1983), the court entered an order approving the employment on June 25, 1991.

Now that the amounts of compensation have been approved, the court must decide how these fees and expenses can be paid, particularly since the bankruptcy case has been converted to Chapter 7 subsequent to the time that most of the compensation was earned.

. . . .

IV.

The first issue that must be resolved is the status of the retainers paid to the law firms. Judge Eugene R. Wedoff in *In re McDonald Bros. Const., Inc.*, 114 B.R. 989 (Bankr. N.D. Ill. 1990), presented a thorough analysis of three types of retainers. Excerpts from his opinion are set forth as follows:

a. "Classic" Retainers:

. . . a "classic "retainer fee' arrangement" is one in which a "sum of money [is] paid by a client to secure an attorney's availability over a period of time," so that "the attorney is entitled to the money regardless of whether he actually performs any services for the client." . . ..

Classic retainers have been explained both as payment "to bind the attorney from representing another" and simply as payment "for accepting the case.". . . Whatever the explanation, however, an essential characteristic of the classic retainer is that it is entirely earned by the attorney upon payment, with the client retaining no interest in the funds.

. . .. To the extent that a classic retainer is paid to a bankruptcy attorney prepetition, the attorney only disclosed the payment pursuant to § 329 of the Code. Because the debtor holds no interest in a classic retainer, it does not become part of the estate and no fee application is required before the attorneys use the retainer funds.

b. "Security" Retainers:

[This] . . . type of retainer agreement between debtors and their attorneys provides that the retainer will be held by the attorneys to secure payment of fees for future services that the attorneys are expected to render. Under such a "security retainer," the money given to the debtor's attorneys is not present payment for the future services. Rather, the retainer remains the property of the debtor until the attorney "applies" it to charges for services actually rendered; any unearned funds are turned over by the attorneys. This type of retainer is recommended in Burnstein, Collier Bankruptcy Compensation Guide, Para. 2.03 at 2.14 (1989):

> [T]he agreement should provide that: (1) the retainer is deemed a trust fund, subject to deposit in the firm's client account . . .; (2) any interest accrual on the retainer amount are added to the retainer; (3) the firm has a right to apply against the retainer amount all accrued time charges and reimbursable costs at a monthly basis upon the submission to the client of detailed statements of such time charges and reimbursable costs . . .; and (4) if either of the client or the firm notifies the other party in writing of its decision to terminate the agreement, the balance of the retainer amount may be applied to all accrued but unpaid charges . . . and any remainder will be returned . . .

c. "Advance" Payment Retainers:

. . . [Is] one in which the debtor pays, in advance for some or all of the services that the debtor is expected to perform on the debtor's behalf. This type of retainer differs from the security retainer in that ownership of the retainer is intended to pass to the attorney at the time of payment, in exchange for the commitment to provide the legal services.

Id. at pages 997-1000.

The comment to Rule 1.5 of the Mississippi Rules of Professional Conduct, which specifically deals with fees, allows an attorney to require advance payment of a fee. However, this comment, read in conjunction with Rule 1.16(d), also requires the attorney to return any unearned portion of the advance payment to the client. The two Rules make no distinction between a retainer and a fee paid in advance. Correlating the two Rules of Professional Conduct with the analysis of the three types of retainers found in *In re McDonald*, leads this court to the conclusion that a "security retainer" is permissible in the State of Mississippi.

V.

A "security retainer" is established when the attorney receives and holds the client's money as a pledge, in the form of a possessory security interest, that the attorney's fees will be paid when earned.

The Uniform Commercial Code expressly allows a possessory security interest in money. Subject to the applicability of the Mississippi Statute of Frauds, security agreements related to collateral in the possession of the secured party are not required to be in writing. See, § 75-9-203(1)(a), Miss. Code Ann. A financing statement is not required to be filed since a security interest in money can only be perfected by possession. See, § 75-9-305, Miss. Code Ann. See also, In re McDonald, 114 B.R. at 999.

Although no written employment contracts between the two law firms and the debtor have been produced, the court is of the opinion that, subject to the two issues which will be addressed below, the payment and retention of the respective retainers without further action created security agreements and valid security interests in favor of the law firms in the retainers. Each requirement set forth in § 75-9-203(1)(a), (b), and (c), Miss. Code Ann., has been met. Perfection of the security interests was achieved by the law firms' continuous possession of the debtor's funds.

[The] extent of the security interests . . . is limited to the fees actually earned, *i.e.*, those approved herein by the court. In re Burnside Steel Foundry Co., 90 B.R. 942, 945. n.1 (Bankr. N.D. Ill 1988) speaks to this point as follows:

[I]f the retainer is of the security type . . ., ownership of the retainer remains in the debtor even after the petition is filed . . . Thus, on the filing of the petition, the security retainer becomes property of the estate under 11 U.S.C. § 541(a)(1). . . In such a case, the right to keep the retainer ultimately turns on the *filing and approval of a fee application under section 330 of the Code.* (emphasis added) Although the funds comprising the retainers are considered still to be the property of the debtor's estate, the law firms' security interests in the retainers extend to the respective amounts approved by the court as allowed claims. In this case, the compensation approved for the law firm of Stennett, Wilkinson, and Ward, i.e., $18,464.30, is secured to the extent of its retainer in the sum of $13,000.00. The compensation approved for Knight and Knight, i.e., $6,567.68, is secured to the extent of $5,758.93 [$6,567.68 — ($750.00 + $58.75)]. The balance of the Knight and Knight retainer must be refunded to the bankruptcy estate as set forth hereinbelow. . . . Without the retainers, the fees and expenses approved for Stennett, Wilkinson, and Ward and Knight and Knight would ordinarily be classified as Chapter 11 U.S.C. § 503(b). . . . Because the law firms did obtain pre-petition retainers, the effective conclusion concerning the payment of their allowed compensation is set as follows: Stennett, Wilkinson, and Ward may immediately apply its retainer of $13,000.00 against its allowed claim of $18,464.30. The balance of the claim in the sum of $5,464.30 is to be treated by the Chapter 11 administration expense claim in his final report and accounting. Knight and Knight, may immediately apply $5,758.93 of its prepetition retainer in the total sum of $7,500.00 against its allowed claim in the sum of $6,657.68. The balance of the prepetition retainer in the sum of $1,741.07 must be refunded to the Chapter 7 trustee within thirty days of the date of the entry of the order which will be filed contemporaneously with this opinion. The balance of the allowed compensation in the sum of $808.75 is to be treated by the Chapter 7 trustee as a Chapter 7 administrative expense claim in the final report and accounting.

[E] Chattel Paper and Documents

Read: U.C.C. §§ 9-105(1)(b) and Comment 4, 9-304(1), 9-305 and 9-308 and Comment 1.

[1] Chattel Paper

Chattel paper consists of a writing or writings which evidence both a monetary obligation and a security interest in, or a lease of, specific goods. U.C.C. § 9-105(b). There can be two elements to chattel paper: 1) a writing that evidences the debtor's monetary obligation; and 2) a writing that evidences the lease of, or a security interest in, the specific goods that secure the monetary obligation (sometimes the same writing). In sharp contrast to security interests in instruments and money which require possession for perfection, a security interest in chattel paper may be perfected by filing or possession. Because the documents that comprise the chattel paper are so closely associated with the rights they represent, the physical transfer of chattel paper transfers the ownership of those rights. Consequently, chattel paper can be pledged and perfection can take place either by the secured party's filing a financing statement or by taking possession. Chattel paper often consists of installment purchase contracts and security agreements or leases, and promissory notes. Under U.C.C. § 9-105 and Comment 4, the "rules applicable to chattel paper, rather than those relating to instruments, are applicable to the group of writings (contract plus note) taken together." We will review more on chattel paper in the next chapter.

[2] Documents

Read: U.C.C. §§ 9-105(1)(f), 9-302, 9-304, 9-305.

The Code defines a document as a record of title to some form of property. Documents include bills of lading, warehouse receipts, dock warrants and receipts, orders for the delivery of goods, and any other item which is recognized in the regular course of business as sufficient evidence that the person in possession of the document has the right to receive and dispose of both the document and the goods it covers. Generally, a bailee issues a document of title when it receives possession of goods from a party. Negotiable documents of title may be perfected by filing. The negotiable document controls accessibility to the goods; perfection with respect to the document automatically carries over to the goods.

With non-negotiable documents, the security interest resides in the goods themselves and not in the documents. Filing as to the goods or possession of them by either the creditor or a bailee will perfect a security interest. The issuance of either a non-negotiable bill of lading which designates the secured party as consignee, or a non-negotiable warehouse receipt with delivery to be made to the secured party (and notice sent to the warehouse as bailee) constitutes possession.

[F] General Intangibles

Read: U.C.C. §§ 9-106 and 9-302.

A general intangible is any personal property other than goods, accounts, chattel paper, documents, instruments, or money. The concept is a catchall category covering miscellaneous contract rights and personal property that may become collateral. Examples include goodwill, literary rights, rights to performance, copyrights, trademarks, and patents. The next two cases demonstrate the breadth of the general intangibles classification.

IN THE MATTER OF INFORMATION EXCHANGE, INC.
DABNEY v. INFORMATION EXCHANGE

United States Bankruptcy Court, Northern District of Georgia
98 B.R. 603, 8 U.C.C. Rep. Serv. 2d 823 (1989)

W. DRAKE, BANKRUPTCY JUDGE.

This case is before the Court on a motion for relief from the automatic stay filed by John C. Dabney, Jr. on February 16, 1989. At the hearing on the motion on March 14, 1989, the Court took the matter under advisement, and the parties have submitted letter briefs and a stipulation of facts which can be summarized as follows.

The debtor was in the business of collecting, sorting, storing, and reselling public legal record information by use of a computer program and database.

Dabney is an attorney who was hired to represent the debtor in a suit by the previous owner of the debtor's business who sought to recover the balance of the purchase price called for in the transaction for the sale of the business assets. During the course of the representation, Dabney was provided with magnetic computer tapes which included a copy of the debtor's program and database. The trustee concedes for present purposes that the debtor gave Dabney an oral security interest in the magnetic tapes to secure the payment of attorney's fees.

The trustee holds another copy of the program and database which is subject to a first priority security interest held by Capital South Group, Ltd., to secure a claim in excess of $83,000.00. The trustee opposes Dabney's motion because the return to the secured creditor and the benefit to the estate from the sale of the database would be reduced if Dabney is also able to sell a copy.

Dabney asserts that he holds a valid attorney's lien pursuant to O.C.G.A. §§ 15-19-14(a) and (b). The trustee argues that Dabney's attorney's lien claim is preempted by 11 U.S.C. § 542(e) and that any lien or oral security interest held by Dabney is voidable under § 544.

O.C.G.A. § 15-19-14(b)provides for an attorney's lien on any recovery obtained in a lawsuit. Such a lien on funds does not appear to be involved in this case, and, in any event, the trustee can avoid the lien arising under § 15-19-14(b) if the lien is not recorded as permitted by § 15-19-14(d). See *In re Burnham*, 12 Bankr. 286 (Bankr. N.D. Ga. 1981).

As to Dabney's attorney's lien claim pursuant to § 15-19-14(a) on the property of his client in Dabney's possession, this Court has examined Formal Advisory Opinion No. 87-5 (86-R1) which was issued by the Supreme Court of Georgia on September 26, 1988 and which was cited by both parties. While some language in the Advisory Opinion indicates that the magnetic tapes in question in this case are within the type of property to which an attorney's lien will attach, the Opinion clearly advises that an attorney may not to the prejudice of the client withhold the client's papers or properties as security for unpaid fees. In this case, Dabney's retention of his client's tapes prejudices the client, and, in turn, this estate, by jeopardizing the sale of the property or reducing the amount to be realized from such sale.

Furthermore, 11 U.S.C. § 542(e) provides for the turnover of property subject to an attorney's lien when the attorney is adequately protected. See *In re Beef N' Burgundy, Inc.*, 21 Bankr. 69 (Bankr. N.D. Ga. 1982). The Court agrees with the trustee that the tapes held by Dabney should be turned over to the estate pursuant to § 542(e). The value of Dabney's lien claim is adequately protected by virtue of the lien attaching to any proceeds of the sale of the property.

Finally, as to Dabney's assertion that he holds an oral security interest perfected by possession of the collateral, it is true that O.C.G.A. § 11-9-203(1)(a) permits the creation of a security interest to arise by possession rather than by a signed security agreement. However, perfection of the security interest is a different matter. A security interest in letters of credit, goods, instruments, money, negotiable documents, or chattel paper may be perfected by possession of the collateral pursuant to O.C.G.A. § 11-9-305. As to security interests which cannot be perfected by possession pursuant to § 11-9-305, a financing statement must be filed in order to perfect the security interest as required by § 11-9-302(1)(a).

The Court is of the opinion that the collateral in which Dabney claims a security interest is a "general intangible" as defined by § 11-9-106, which is not included within the listed types of collateral in which security interests can be perfected by possession pursuant to § 11-9-305. Although security interests in "goods" or tangible personal property may be perfected by possession, it is not the computer tape itself which is actually in issue here but the information and programming which is recorded on the tape. That is, the tape in and of itself is of little value; it is the information copied on the tape which is claimed as collateral. Because such information is a general intangible, Dabney can only perfect his security interest in the collateral by filing a financing statement.

This conclusion is buttressed by the consideration of the rationale behind permitting perfection by possession for some types of property. If a secured party has possession of a tangible item of collateral belonging to a debtor, this possession serves as a substitute for a filed financing statement by giving third parties notice of the likely existence of a security interest. Here, Dabney's mere possession of a copy of the debtor's program provides no notice to third parties that Dabney holds a security interest in the program itself or in all existing copies. Therefore,

Dabney's oral security interest could not be perfected by possession and is unperfected. The security interest is therefore subject to avoidance by the trustee under 11 U.S.C. § 544.

Accordingly, it is Ordered that the motion for relief from the automatic stay filed by John C. Dabney, Jr. is Denied; and it is

Further Ordered that Dabney shall turn over to the trustee all copies of the debtor's magnetic tapes in his possession within five (5) days from the date of entry of this Order.

It Is So Ordered.

IN RE ROMAN CLEANSER CO.

United States Bankruptcy Court Eastern District of Michigan
43 B.R. 940, 39 U.C.C. Rep. Serv. 1770 (1984)

George Brody, Bankruptcy Judge.

Roman Cleanser Company was a Michigan corporation engaged in the business of manufacturing, packaging and marketing a variety of items including "Roman Cleanser" and other household cleaning products. In connection with the business, the corporation employed the following federally registered trademarks:''Roman," registration number 912,017, originally registered on June 8, 1971; "Easy Monday," registration number 992,277, originally registered on September 3, 1974; "Romay," registration number 936,235, originally registered on June 20, 1972; and "Roman Cleanser," registration number 233,087, originally registered on September 20, 1927.

On November 15, 1983 Patterson Laboratories, Inc. (Patterson) entered into an agreement with Roman Cleanser Company to purchase all of Roman Cleanser's "machinery and equipment related to the manufacture of chemicals" for $175,000.00 and to loan $350,000.00 to the debtor. The agreement also provided that "[i]n the event of default by Roman, Patterson shall be entitled to and Roman grants to Patterson an exclusive perpetual license entitling Patterson to sell chemical products under all Roman owned trademarks/trade names and labels; . . ." On February 9, 1984, Roman Cleanser Company (debtor) filed a voluntary bankruptcy petition under chapter 11 pursuant to 11 United States Code § 301. On August 8, 1984, the case was converted to a proceeding under chapter 7. 11 U.S.C § 1112. After the petition in bankruptcy was filed, Patterson filed a complaint for declaratory judgment contending that it was the owner of the debtor's trademarks by virtue of the debtor's default under the November, 1983 agreement. This claim was contested by the trustee. Subject to a determination by the court as to the respective interests of the estate and Patterson in the trademarks, the federally registered trademarks, formulas and customer lists were sold by the trustee to Michlin Chemical Corporation for $180,000.00 and the claim of Patterson was transferred to the proceeds of sale. After the sale, National Acceptance Company of America (NAC) filed a motion to intervene, which was granted, contending that it had a security interest in the trademarks and that its interest was senior to any interests of either the estate or Patterson. Both the trustee and Patterson challenge the validity of NAC's security interest. This opinion deals solely with the question of the validity of NAC's security interest. The facts are not in dispute.

On January 18, 1978, the debtor executed a loan and security agreement granting NAC a security interest "in and to all of Roman Cleanser's then owned and thereafter acquired goods, equipment, and general intangibles and the proceeds thereof as collateral for the payment of all indebtedness and liabilities then existing or thereafter arising of Roman Cleanser to NAC." (NAC's Statement of Position, page 2). NAC filed a financing statement with the Michigan Secretary of State, pursuant to the Michigan Uniform Commercial Code. Mich Comp. Laws § 440.9401 (1979). Sometime prior to the filing of the petition, NAC released its security interest in the vehicles, machinery, and equipment.

The trustee initially contends that to perfect a security interest in a federally registered trademark a creditor must file a conditional assignment with the United States Patent and Trademark Office and since NAC did not do so, its security interest is unperfected. Surprisingly, there are no cases that address this Issue.

Article 9 of the Michigan Uniform Commercial Code sets forth a comprehensive scheme for the regulation of security interests in personal property and fixtures. The basic scope of this article is found in MCL § 440.9102(1).

The term "general intangibles" is defined in MCL § 440.9106 as "any personal property (including things in action) other than goods, accounts, chattel paper, documents, instruments, and money." The Official U.C.C. Comments state that the term "general intangibles" includes "[m]iscellaneous types of contractual rights and other personal property which are used or may become customarily used as commercial security. Examples are goodwill, literary rights and rights to performance. Other examples are copyrights, trademarks and patents, except to the extent that they may be excluded by Section 9-104(a)."

Trademarks are defined under federal law as "any word, name, symbol or device or any combination thereof adopted and used by a manufacturer or merchant to identify his goods and distinguish them from those manufactured or sold by others." Trademarks are valuable property rights. 1 J. McCarthy, Trademarks and Unfair Competition, § 2.8 p. 75 (2d ed 1984); also compare, *Trade-Mark Cases*, 100 US 82, 92 (1879) (property right) with, *A. Bourjois & Co. v. Katzel*, 260 US 689, 691 (1922) potentially great value). They are clearly general intangibles within the meaning of Article 9. *Heine-Geldern v. ESIC Capital, The. (In re Magnum Opus Electronics, Ltd.)*, 19 U.C.C. Rep. Serv. (Callaghan) 242 (Bankr. S.D. N.Y. 1976). However, a finding that trademarks are general intangibles does not necessarily mean that the perfection of a security interest in such marks is governed by the Uniform Commercial Code.

The current federal trademark law, commonly referred to as the Lanham Act, is found at 15 U.S.C. § 1051 et seq. It is derived from legislation originally enacted in 1946.

. . . .

The question, therefore, is whether 15 U.S.C. § 1060 is a statute which "specifies a place of filing for a security interest different" from that in the Uniform Commercial Code. For the reasons set forth below, this court concludes that the Lanham Act does not do so.

Trademark cases distinguish between security interests and assignments. An "assignment" of a trademark is an absolute transfer of the entire right, title and interest to the trademark. "In order for a transfer of rights in a trademark to constitute a sale or assignment, thereby vesting title to the trademark in a party, the transfer must be absolute and must relate to the entire rights in the trademark." The grant of a security interest is not such a transfer. It is merely what the term suggests-a device to secure an indebtedness. It is a mere agreement to assign in the event of a default by the debtor. "[T]he rule is well established that a mere agreement for the future assignment of a trademark is not an assignment of either the mark itself or the good will attached to it." Since a security interest in a trademark is not equivalent to an assignment, the filing of a security interest is not covered by the Lanham Act. Accordingly, the manner of perfecting a security interest in trademarks is governed by Article 9 and not by the Lanham Act.

Rule 2.185 which provides that "[o]ther instruments which relate to such marks may be recorded in the discretion of the Commissioner" does not require a different result. Initially, it is to be noted that the recordation of other instruments relating to marks is permissive only. More importantly, the regulation is invalid, if in fact it intended to suggest that a security interest is embraced within the term assignment" and therefore subject to filing under the Lanham Act. Section 1123 of title 15 states that "The Commissioner shall make rules and regulation, not inconsistent with law, for the conduct of proceedings in the Patent and Trade Mark Office." Rules promulgated by a government agency are subject to the limitations imposed by the specific legislation pursuant to which the regulations are issued. . .. Since the Lanham Act provides merely for the filing of assignments, the attempt to provide for the filing of other documents has no legal effect.

The Official Comment to § 9104 of the Uniform Commercial Code is also illuminating. The Comment states that the filing provision contained in the Federal Copyright Act, 17 U.S.C. §§ 28, 30 (current version 17 U.S.C. § 205(1982)) and the Patent Act, 35 U.S.C. § 47 (current version 35 U.S.C. § 261 (1982)) "are recognized as the equivalent" to filing under Article 9. The failure to include the Trademark Act in the Comment suggests that the drafters of the Uniform Commercial Code were of the opinion that the reference to "assignments" in the Lanham Act did not embrace security interests. A similar inference may be drawn from an examination of Professor G. Gilmore's comprehensive and scholarly treatise, Security Interests in Personal Property (1965). Professor Gilmore devotes a chapter to a discussion of the perfection of security interests subject to federal statutes. Nowhere in that chapter is there any reference to the Lanham Act nor any requirement that a security interest in trademarks is to be perfected under federal law.

The Uniform Commercial Code provides a simple mechanism for obtaining and perfecting security interests in personal property. Understandably, the Code defers to federal legislation if such legislation accomplishes the same purpose. However, unless federal preemption is clearly established, the Code procedures should continue to apply. Commentators who address the question admit that 15 U.S.C. § 1060 presents problems of construction and does not clearly establish a method for perfecting a security interest in trademarks. J. McCarthy, in his treatise on trademarks and unfair competition states: "Until either the U.C.C. or the Lanham Act is clarified the courts should treat either federal or state recordation of a conditional security assignment as sufficient to perfect such a security." Bernstein and Patinkin advise a similar approach:

> Although it appears that perfection of a security interest in a trademark is governed by the U.C.C., it is nevertheless recommended that if a particular trademark is otherwise subject to the federal trademark statute, the secured party should also record a document with the Patent and Trademark Office, in accordance with the procedures set forth in 15 U.S.C. § 1060, describing the secured party's security interest.

Not only is there lack of agreement as to whether § 1060 provides for the recordation of security interests with respect to trademarks but, additionally, the commentators who assume that a

Lanham Act filing is required, do not agree as to what documents are to be filed. Some commentators suggest that the filing of a conditional or collateral assignment suffices. Others suggest that the creditor, in addition to the filing of a conditional assignment, must file a security agreement. At least one commentator suggests a more complicated procedure:

> One approach, therefore, would be an agreement to assign the trademarks in the future, conditioned upon a default as defined in the underlying security agreement. This agreement to assign can be part of the mortgage indenture (or, as Article 9 of the Uniform Commercial Code calls it, "security agreement") and can also include an irrevocable power of attorney to the mortgagee or "secured party" to execute the assignment on behalf of the debtor in the event of a default, should the latter fail or refuse to execute and deliver the assignment.
>
> Such a security agreement to assign should be recorded in the United States Patent and Trademark Office so that third parties would be put on notice that the debtor's trademarks are subject to a security interest or lien under the agreement.

All commentators apparently agree that the relationship between 15 U.S.C. § 1060 and Article 9 "is an extremely treacherous area, one where the fit. . .is uneasy at best." B. Clark, *supra* p 11. Given this uncertainty, there is no justification for holding that Code-perfected security interests are not valid.

The terms "assignment" and "security interest" are terms of art with distinct and different meanings. If Congress intended to provide a means for recording security interests in trademarks in addition to assignments, it would have been simple to so state. However, for whatever reasons, Congress did not do so. A plausible reason surfaces. Congress was concerned with protecting the public from the deceptive ruse of trademarks. See discussion *infra*. A security interest in a mark does not grant the secured creditor the right to use the mark absent default by the debtor. A security interest in a trademark, therefore, cannot lead to public deception. Thus, there was no reason to provide for the filing of security interests. It may be that all transactions with respect to federally registered trademarks should be controlled by federal law. However, it is not for a court to adopt a policy not spelled out in the legislation it is construing. For the foregoing reasons, the Article 9 filing perfected NAC's security interest in the collateral which included the debtor's trademarks, formulas, and customer lists.

Neither the trustee nor Patterson question that NAC has a valid and perfected security interest in the formulas and customer lists. NAC, therefore, had a perfected security interest in the assets sold to Michlin. NAC's security interest is not subject to attack by the trustee as an assignment in gross.

An appropriate order is to be submitted for entry.

[G] Fixtures

A fixture is an item of personal property so incorporated into real estate that an interest in the property arises under real estate law. State law outside the U.C.C. determines whether an item of property is a fixture. Adverse claimants on fixtures may include the holder of an Article

9 security interest, a mortgage lien creditor, a judgment lien creditor, or even an owner of the property. The drafters of the Code created a special, separate filing requirement in local real estate records for items that become fixtures. The fixture requirement is less cumbersome than the traditional real estate mortgage recording requirement. Although the next case is complicated procedurally and factually, it provides a good example of the difficulties associated with perfecting a security interest in fixtures.

IN RE MATTER OF CLIFF'S RIDGE SKIING CORP.

United States Bankruptcy Court, Western District of Michigan
123 B.R. 753, 13 U.C.C. Rep. Serv. 2d 1309 (1991)

JAMES D. GREGG, BANKRUPTCY JUDGE.

INTRODUCTION

In this contested matter, three creditors are fighting over sale proceeds from a ski chairlift. Although the parties have attempted to settle this matter, this has not been possible. The court will therefore grapple with the issues and render a decision.

The issues presented are many. Was the chairlift a fixture? Which creditor has, or creditors have, a valid and perfected mortgage interest or security interest in the chairlift and the proceeds? Does one of the creditors have a perfected purchase money security interest in the chairlift and the proceeds? What is the priority of the creditors' respective interests? Did one creditor validly subordinate its interest to another creditor? Is there a circular priority problem? If so, how should it be resolved?

PROCEDURAL BACKGROUND

On October 28, 1987, Cliff's Ridge Skiing Corporation, ("Debtor"), filed for relief under chapter 11 of the Bankruptcy Code. 11 U.S.C. §§ 101-1330. On January 4, 1988, the case was converted to a chapter 7 case. The Debtor's assets were sold, after notice and hearing, pursuant to a court order dated July 28, 1988. The sale proceeds were distributed to secured creditors, or retained by the estate, pursuant to a court order dated December 27, 1988. One of the assets sold was a Riblet chairlift-2 place, No. 6470, 75 HP electric drive ("chairlift"). The sale proceeds received from the chairlift were $422,500.00. These proceeds were placed in an interest-bearing escrow account pending a court determination as to creditors' entitlement to the proceeds.

Three creditors, First National Bank & Trust Company of Marquette ("First National"), Cliffs Ridge Development Co. ("Cliff's Ridge Dev."), and First of America Bank-Marquette, N.A., formerly known as Union National Bank & Trust Company of Marquette ("FOA"), each assert they are legally entitled to the escrowed proceeds and the interest earned therefrom. The chapter 7 trustee received notice of this proceeding. The trustee's counsel has informed the parties and the court that the bankruptcy estate now makes no claim to the chairlift proceeds.

. . ..

FACTS

On July 24, 1980, FOA loaned Cliff's Ridge Dev. the sum of $300,000 pursuant to a note. (Exh. A.) Repayment of this indebtedness was secured by Cliff's Ridge Dev. executing a mortgage and a security agreement each dated July 24, 1980. (Exhs. B and C.) The mortgage was properly perfected by recordation with the Marquette County Register of Deeds on August 1, 1980. The mortgage language granted FOA an interest in certain real property owned by Cliff's Ridge Dev. together with "all improvements now or hereafter created on the property . . . and all fixtures now or hereafter attached to the property, all of which, including replacements and additions thereto, shall be deemed to be and remain a part of the property covered by this mortgage." The security interest which granted FOA an interest in all tangible and intangible personal property of Cliff's Ridge Dev. was perfected by the filing of a financing statement with the State of Michigan, Secretary of State, U.C.C. Division on July 29, 1980. No fixture filing was made with the Marquette County Register of Deeds.

The indebtedness owed to FOA, which is secured by its mortgage, has not been fully satisfied. FOA is now owed an amount which is greater than the escrowed chairlift proceeds and the interest earned therefrom. (Stipulated Statement of Facts, ¶ 2.)

During summer or early fall of 1981, Cliff's Ridge Dev. entered into discussions with Brown, a prospective purchaser, regarding a sale of all of Cliff's Ridge Dev.'s assets. A Preliminary Sales Agreement was properly and validly executed by Brown and Cliff's Ridge Dev. in November, 1981. (Exh. F; Brown Deposition, p. 6; Stipulated Statement of Facts, ¶ 7.) All rights and duties pursuant to this agreement was subsequently assigned to the Debtor. (Stipulated Statement of Facts, ¶ 7.) After execution of the sales agreement, but before closing of the sale, the Debtor operated the ski hill with the cooperation of a principal of Cliff's Ridge Dev. (Brown Deposition, p. 6.) On February 4, 1982, the Debtor assumed Cliff's Ridge Dev.'s obligations owed to FOA. (Exh. GG.)

The Debtor determined it was advisable to purchase an additional chairlift and purchase was discussed with a principal of Cliff's Ridge Dev. (Brown Deposition, p. 7.) In April or May, 1982, the Debtor contacted Breckenridge Ski Area to purchase the chairlift on a case-on-delivery basis. (Stipulated Statement of Facts, ¶ 12.) The price paid for the chairlift by the Debtor was $65,000. In addition, the Debtor paid $10,000 for shipping, $7,500 for engineering, and approximately $80,000 for erection of the chairlift. The Debtor paid the shipping and engineering costs at, or shortly after, the time they were incurred. (Stipulated Statement of Facts, ¶ 16.) The parties agree the other terms of the sale are not now known; no sale documents were introduced into evidence.

The chairlift was delivered in August, 1982. The erection of the towers for the chairlift commenced in September, 1982, with the concrete pads having been poured prior to the erection. The erection of the towers was completed by November 15, 1982. The cable was strung during the latter part of November, 1982 and was spliced on December 2, 1982. The chairlift was tested with the chairs in place on December 7, 1982. The State of Michigan certified the chairlift for operation on December 23, 1982. (Stipulated Statement of Facts, ¶ 11.) The chairlift was specially engineered and modified for a slope on the ski hill real property. Although the chairlift is attached to the real property, it can be severed form the real property, removed and sold. (Stipulated Statement of Facts, ¶ 16.)

After delivery of the chairlift, and sometime during the erection of the chairlift, the Debtor sought financing from the Economic Development Corporation for the County of Marquette ("EDC"). On or about September 10, 1982, the Debtor submitted its project Plan to the EDC. (Exh. G.) The Project plan stated that the Debtor intended to (1) purchase Cliff's Ridge Dev.'s real property, (2) expand the ski hill by constructing the chairlift, (3) finance the project through the issuance of revenue notes in the amount of up to $175,000, (4) obtain financing from First

National, and (5) secure repayment by granting a security interest in the chairlift improvement. Local government entities each considered the request that the Debtor's project Plan be approved at various meetings or hearings, (Exhs. H, I, J, K, L, M, N, O, P, Q, and R.) At an EDC meeting on November 22, 1982, the Debtor's Project Plan was approved and the EDC representatives were authorized to sign the loan documents. (Exh. S.) No evidence exists at this time that Cliff's Ridge Dev. had any actual knowledge of the Debtor's request to have its Project Plan approved by the EDC. (Stipulated Statement of Facts, ¶ 9.) Based upon the record, the court finds that Cliff's Ridge Dev. also lacked any implied knowledge of the Debtor's Project Plan.

On November 22, 1982, Cliff's Ridge Dev. conveyed its ski hill real property to the Debtor pursuant to a warranty deed. (Exh. F.) The deed given to the Debtor was subject to the prior mortgage granted by Cliff's Ridge Dev. to FOA dated July 24, 1980. (Stipulated Statement of Facts, ¶ 6.) Also on November 22, 1982, the Debtor granted Cliff's Ridge Dev. a mortgage respecting the ski hill real property. The mortgage was properly perfected by recordation with the Marquette County Register of Deeds on November 23, 1982. The mortgage states it is "a second mortgage, the prior mortgage of [FOA] for the SBA debt described in said preliminary sales agreement, this mortgage being specifically subordinate to said mortgage". The mortgage does not contain any express language granting Cliff's Ridge Dev. an interest in the debtor's fixtures, whether then owned or after acquired. Rather, the mortgage only grants an interest in the conveyed real property together "with the hereditaments and appurtenances thereunto belonging or in anywise appertaining." (Exh. F.)

The indebtedness owed to Cliff's Ridge Dev. which is secured by its mortgage, has not been fully satisfied. Cliff's Ridge Dev. is now owed and amount which is greater than the escrowed chairlift proceeds and the interest earned therefrom. (Stipulated Statement of Facts, ¶ 2.)

On December 13, 1982, the Debtor, the EDC and First National executed a Loan Agreement. In that agreement the Debtor guaranteed "all of the duties, obligations, undertakings and liabilities" of the EDC under the agreement. (Exh. T.) The Loan Agreement provides, inter alia, that (1) First National will loan $175,000 to the EDC to be used to purchase the chairlift, (2) First National will receive a perfected security interest in the chairlift, (3) the note evidencing the loan will be a nonrecourse note with respect to the EDC but a recourse obligation with respect to the Debtor, and (4) as a condition precedent to the loan, FOA will subordinate any security interest it might claim with respect to the chairlift collateral to First National. The agreement also includes a representation that the Debtor has, or will obtain, good and marketable title to the chairlift except for liens disclosed to First National. At the time of this Loan Agreement, the parties apparently failed to recognize that Cliff's Ridge Dev. might claim an interest in the chairlift pursuant to its prior mortgage.

Although the loan transaction closing was to have been concluded on an earlier date, the loan transaction was consummated on December 13, 1982 in accordance with the Loan Agreement and other documents executed by the parties thereto. (Stipulated Statement of Facts, ¶ 11.) The EDC executed and gave First National a Limited Obligation Economic Development Revenue Note in the amount of $175,000. (Exh. U.) The Debtor executed a Security Agreement which granted the EDC an interest in the chairlift. (Exh. V.) The EDC executed and gave First National an Assignment of Security Agreement. (Exh. W.) Two principals of the Debtor, and their respective spouses, each executed and gave First National a Guaranty Agreement which guaranteed payment of the Debtor's loan obligation. (Exh. W.) Also on December 13, 1982, the EDC, First National, FOA and the Debtor entered into a Subordination Agreement. (Exh. X.) That agreement states in pertinent part:

> [I]n consideration of the premises and to induce [First National] and the EDC to accept a security agreement and note and also in consideration of $1.00 paid to [FOA], the receipt whereof is hereby acknowledged, [FOA] agrees with [First National] and EDC that a security agreement to be held by EDC and [First National] and covering [the chairlift] shall be prior to and superior to any claims of [FOA] with respect to [the chairlift], and [FOA] does hereby subordinate its security interest in [the chairlift] to the interest of [First National] and the EDC as their interest may appear.

Cliff's Ridge Dev. was not a party to the Subordination agreement and there is no evidence that Cliff's Ridge Dev. knew of this agreement prior to, or at the time, the agreement was executed. At the time the EDC loan documents were executed, the Debtor had a legal right or interest in the chairlift, (Stipulated Statement of Facts, ¶ 11.) The Debtor executed, and First National and the EDC filed, three financing statements regarding First National's assigned security interest in the chairlift collateral.

First, on December 14, 1982, a financing statement, intended as a fixture filing, was filed where mortgages are recorded with the Marquette County Register of Deeds. (Exh. CC.) The EDC is listed as the secured party and First National is shown as the assignee. The real property description is attached to the financing statement. The financing statement states, "The goods are to become fixtures on 11/24/82". On November 5, 1987, a continuation statement was filed with the Marquette County Register of Deeds. (Exh. DD.)

Second, on December 15, 1982, a financing statement, intended as a fixture filing, was filed with the Michigan Secretary of State, Uniform Commercial Code Section. (Exh. Z.) This financing statement was identical to that filed with the Marquette County Register of Deeds and again stated the "goods are to become fixtures on 11/24/82". On November 12, 1987, a continuation statement was filed with the Secretary of State. (Exh. BB.)

Third, on December 15, 1982, a financing statement, designated as a "Non-Fixture Statement", was filed with the Michigan Secretary of State, Uniform Commercial Code Section. (Exh. Y.) The chairlift is identified on the financing statement. On November 12, 1987, a continuation statement was filed with the Secretary of State. (Exh. AA.)

Cliff's Ridge Dev. did not consent in writing to First National's security interest or otherwise disclaim an interest in the chairlift as a fixture. The Debtor did not have the right to remove the chairlift as to Cliff's Ridge Dev. (Stipulated Statement of Facts, ¶ 7.)

Pursuant to the loan transaction, proceeds were disbursed to the Debtor on December 17, 1982, in the amount of $100,000. (Exh. EE.) On December 23, 1982, another disbursement was made to the Debtor in an amount which appears to be $49,864.39. (Exh. FF; this exhibit is somewhat illegible and the amount of this loan disbursement is uncertain.) No evidence or stipulated fact disclosed whether the remaining loan proceeds were ever disbursed to the Debtor. The indebtedness now owed to First National, secured by the security interest respecting the chairlift, exceeds the value of the escrowed chairlift proceeds and the interest earned therefrom. (Stipulated Statement of Facts, ¶ 2.)

. . .

Under governing Michigan law, all requirements of the three-part test to determine whether personal property has become a fixture have been met. The court concludes that the chairlift in dispute is a fixture.

Creation and Perfection of an Interest in Fixtures.

Under Michigan law, there are two methods by which a creditor may create and perfect an interest in fixtures. A creditor may utilize procedure under Michigan real estate law. Alternatively, a creditor may take a security interest in a fixture and perfect that interest under the Uniform Commercial Code as adopted in Michigan ("U.C.C.").

Article 9 of the U.C.C. allows the creation of an interest in fixtures pursuant to state real estate law.[18] Prior to adoption of the U.C.C., Michigan law was well-settled that once a fixture is annexed or attached to realty, the fixture became part of the realty and title to the fixture is subject to a real estate mortgage. See, *e.g., Wilson v. Union Guardian Trust Co. (Petition of Johns-Manville Sales Corp.)*, 88 F.2d 520 (6th Cir. 1937) (chattels annexed to realty became permanent fixtures and part of the realty covered by a mortgage); *Whitaker-Glessner Co. v. Ohio Savings Bank & Trust Co.*, 22 F.2d 773 (6th Cir. 1927) (machinery attached to realty held to be a fixture covered by mortgage); *Wood Hydraulic Hoist & Body Co. v. Norton*, 629 Mich. 341, 257 N.W. 836 (1934) (equipment was a fixture and component part of building; it was included in mortgage security); *Studley v. Ann Arbor Savings Bank*, 112 Mich. 181, 70 N.W. 426 (1897) (machinery attached permanently to realty will be treated as fixtures covered by mortgage).

As stated in *Kent Storage Co. v. Grand Rapids Lumber Co.*, 239 Mich. 161, 164-165, 214 N.W. 111, 112-113 (1927): "It is a salutary rule that whatever is affixed to a building by an owner in complement, to facilitate its use and occupation in general, becomes a part of the realty, though capable of removal without injury to the building." Accord, *Wood Hydraulic Hoist & Body Co. v. Norton*, 269 Mich. at 346, 257 N.W. 836. When a fixture becomes complemental to real property, it becomes a permanent accession and becomes part of the realty; the fixture becomes part of the security with regard to any existing mortgage. *Sequist v. Fabiano*, 274 Mich. 643, 646 265 N.W. 488, 489 (1936). A mortgage covers fixtures even when they are not expressly mentioned in the mortgage. *Tyler v. Hayward*, 235 Mich. 674, 676, 209 N.W. 801, 802 (1926) (equipment installed on realty became fixtures and held to be covered by subsequent deed or mortgage without special mention in the conveyance).

Once a mortgage creates an interest in fixtures under Michigan real estate law, the interest must be perfected. Perfection under state real estate law is accomplished by recordation of the mortgage in the county where the real property is located. Mich. Comp. Laws Ann. §§ 440.9401(1)(b); 53.145; 565.1; 5465.23.

The second method by which a security interest in fixtures may be created and perfected is under the U.C.C. without reference to state real estate law. A "security interest" is defined very broadly to mean "an interest in personal property or fixtures which secures repayment of an obligation." Mich. Comp. Laws Ann. § 440.120(37). Article 9 of the U.C.C. applies "[t]o any transaction (regardless of its form) which is intended to create a security interest in personal property or fixtures. . . ." Mich. Comp. Laws Ann. § 440.9102(1)(a).[19]

Except in instances when a secured party is in possession of collateral in accordance with an agreement, creation and attachment of a valid security interest require: (1) the debtor to sign an agreement which adequately describes the collateral, (2) value to be given, and (3) the debtor

[18] Mich. Comp. Laws Ann. § 440.9313(3) states: "[t]his article does not prevent creation of an encumbrance upon fixtures pursuant to real estate law."

[19] As discussed herein, the U.C.C. method of obtaining an interest in fixtures is non-exclusive, an interest in fixtures may be obtained under state real estate law. Mich. Comp. Laws Ann. § 440.9313(3).

to have rights in the collateral. Mich. Comp. Laws Ann. § 440.9203(1). The security interest attaches when all three events take place, absent an explicit agreement to postpone the attachment. Mich. Comp. Laws Ann. § 440.9203(2). Cf. *West. Dist. of Mich. Trustees, Inc. v. First of America Bank-Ludington (In re Pierce)*, 63 B.R. 740, 741(Bankr. W.D. Mich. 1986) (holding once attachment of security interest occurs under U.C.C. § 9-203 the attachment is not affected by the debtor's subsequent modification of the collateral).

To perfect a personal property interest in a fixture, and be accorded proper priority, a financing statement must be filed.[20] Mich. Comp. Laws Ann. § 440.9302(1)(d). To be sufficient, a financing statement must: (1) state the names of the debtor and secured party, (2) be signed by the debtor, (3) provide the address of the secured party to allows inquiry about information regarding the security interest, (4) provide the mailing address of the debtor, and (5) contain a statement setting forth types or describing items of collateral. Mich. Comp. Laws Ann. § 440.9402(1). In addition, a financing statement covering fixtures or goods to become fixtures must: (6) state that it covers this type of collateral; (7) recite it is to be recorded in the real estate records; (8) contain a description of the real estate where the fixtures are located or to be located, which is sufficient to provide constructive notice under state real estate mortgage law; and (9) if the debtor does not have an interest of record in the real estate, the owner or record must be disclosed. Mich. Comp. Laws Ann. § 440.9402(5).

The financing statement which covers fixtures, or goods to become fixtures, must be filed where a mortgage on the real estate would be recorded. Mich. Comp. Laws Ann. § 440.9401(21)(b). In Michigan, an interest in real estate is properly recorded at the register of deeds in the county in which the real estate is located. Mich. Comp. Laws Ann. §§ 53.145; 565.1; 565.23. When a sufficient financing statement is filed in the proper place, a "fixture filing" occurs. Mich. Comp. Laws Ann. § 440.9313(1)(b). After a proper fixture filing, a secured party has a perfected interest in the fixtures and may enforce its security interest against other persons according to designated priorities. Mich. Comp. Laws Ann. § 440.9313(4), (5), (6) and (7).

Under the U.C.C., a mortgage may be effective as a fixture filing from the date of its recordation provided four specified requirements are met, including that the mortgage describes the goods by "item or type". Mich. Comp. Laws Ann. § 440.9402(6)(a). An issue exists whether this U.C.C. subsection mandates that a mortgage creating an interest in fixtures under state real estate law must contain a sufficient description of the fixtures, or the goods to become fixtures, by "item or type". At the hearing, some argument was made that if a mortgage fails to include such a description, no valid interest in fixtures can be created under the state real estate law. The court has been unable to discover any reported case which addresses this issue.

As discussed above, an interest in fixtures, or goods which become fixtures, may be created under state real estate law, or under the U.C.C. State real estate law creates real property interests in fixtures while the U.C.C. allows creation of personal property interests in fixtures. The U.C.C. establishes priorities resolving conflict between these distance legal creatures on "turbulent waters . . . with difficulty". White & Summers, Uniform Commercial Code 1151(3rd ed. 1988).

A "sufficient" fixture filing requires a "statement indicating the types or describing the items of collateral." Mich. Comp. Laws Ann. § 440.9402(1). A complying mortgage filed in lieu of a financing statement must also contain, among other things, a description of goods "by item

[20] Although the filing of a financing statement is not required when automatic perfection occurs or the secured party has possession of the collateral, those exceptions are not germane to this matter.

or type". Mich. Comp. Laws Ann. § 440.9402(6). The U.C.C. requires, whether a fixture filing is accomplished by filing a financing statement or recording a complying mortgage, the information included must be the same. However, the U.C.C. also permits a valid security interest in fixtures to be created under state real estate law. Mich. Comp. Laws Ann. § 440.9313.(3).

The U.C.C. requirement that the type or items of collateral be adequately described applies only to the creation and perfection of personal property interests in fixtures under the U.C.C.; this U.C.C. requirement does not apply to creation and perfection of real property interests in fixtures under state real estate law. U.C.C. law and state real estate law are separate and distinct methods by which interests in fixtures are created and perfected. The court therefore rejects any argument that the collateral must be explicitly described by item or type in a mortgage which otherwise creates an interest in fixtures under state real estate law.

Do the Creditors Hold a Valid Interest in the Chairlift and the Proceeds?

FOA's mortgage on the real property where the chairlift was affixed was granted on July 24, 1980; the mortgage was properly recorded on August 1, 1980. The mortgage granted FOA an interest in the real property together with "all improvements now or hereafter created on the property . . . and all fixtures now or hereafter attached to the property, all of which, including replacements and additions thereto, shall be deemed to be and remain a part of the property covered by this mortgage."

When a fixture becomes complemental to real property, it becomes a permanent accession and the fixture becomes part of the security with regard to any existing mortgage. *Sequist v. Fabiano*, 274 Mich. at 646, 265 N.W. at 489. The language in FOA's prior recorded mortgage is sufficient to create and perfect its interest in the chairlift fixture under state real estate law. FOA retained its interest in the proceeds pursuant to this court's order whereby valid liens would attach to the proceeds of the sale. 11 U.S.C. §§ 363(e); 361(2); cf. Mich. Comp. Laws Ann. § 440.9306.

Cliff's Ridge Dev.'s mortgage on the real property where the chairlift was affixed was granted on November 22, 1982; the mortgage was properly recorded on November 23, 1982. The mortgage itself recognizes FOA's prior mortgage and states Cliff's Ridge Dev.'s interest is subordinate to FOA's prior mortgage. Cliff's Ridge Dev.'s mortgage grants an interest in the real property together "with the hereditaments and appurtenances thereunto belonging or in anywise appertaining." There is no language in the mortgage relating to "fixtures". An "appurtenance" is an "article adapted to the use of the property to which it is connected, and which was intended to be a permanent accession to the freehold." Black's Law Dictionary 94 (5th Ed. West Publishing Co. 1979). An "appurtenance" is equivalent to a "fixture".

A mortgage covers fixtures even when they are not explicitly mentioned in the mortgage. *Tyler v. Hayward*, 235 Mich. at 676, 209 N.W. at 802. If the chairlift became connected to the real property after the grant of Cliff's Ridge Dev.'s mortgage, Cliff's Ridge Dev. has an interest in the chairlift; the appurtenance or fixture becomes part of the security with regard to any existing mortgage. *Sequist v. Fabiano*, 274 Mich. at 646, 265 N.W. at 489. On the other hand, if the chairlift became connected to the real property before the grant of the mortgage, the chairlift would be covered by the subsequent mortgage without a special mention in the mortgage. *Tyler v. Hayward*, 235 Mich. at 209 N.W. at 802. Therefore, under state real estate law, Cliff's Ridge Dev. has an interest in the chairlift. Cliff's Ridge Dev. also has an interest in the proceeds from the chairlift sale in accordance with the court's prior order. 11 U.S.C. §§ 363(e); 361(2); cf. Mich. Comp. Laws Ann. § 440.9306.

On December 13, 1982, the Debtor granted the EDC a security interest in the chairlift. On the same date, the EDC assigned its security interest to First National. As of December 13, 1982, the Debtor had signed a security agreement which described the collateral and rights in the collateral. On December 17, 1982, First National made its first loan disbursement of $100,000 to the debtor. Since there was no agreement to postpone attachment of the security interest, First National's attachment of the security interest occurred on December 17, 1982. Mich. Comp. Laws Ann. § 440.9203(2).

On December 14, 1982, a financing statement regarding the chairlift was filed where mortgages are recorded with the Marquette County Register of Deeds. The form of the financing statement meets all the necessary requirements under the U.C.C. Mich. Comp. Laws Ann. § 440.9402(1) and (5). A sufficient financing statement regarding the chairlift fixture was filed in the proper place and a "fixture filing" occurred. Mich. Comp. Laws Ann. §§ 440.9313(1)(b); 440.9401(1)(b). First National therefore holds a perfected personal property interest in the chairlift under the U.C.C. It now also holds an interest in the sale proceeds pursuant to this court's prior order. 11 U.S.C. §§ 363(e); 361(2); cf. Mich. Comp. Laws Ann. § 440.9306.

If these were the only facts and law to be applied, the court would now easily apply the U.C.C. priority rules and determine entitlement to the sale proceeds. Unfortunately, sorting out commercial security transactions is not always so simple.

Is the Chairlift a Fixture?

Mich. Comp. Laws Ann. § 440.9313(1)(a) states: "Goods are 'fixtures' when they become so related to particular real estate that an interest in them arises under real estate law." Uniform Commercial Code § 9-313(1)(a) is "unhelpful" and "it is merely an invitation to read the real estate statutes and the local case law on what is an what is not a fixture." White & Summers, Uniform Commercial Code 1153 (3rd ed. 1988).

In Michigan, whether personal property becomes a fixture and thereby part of realty is determined by a three-part test: (1) is the property annexed or attached to the realty, (2) is the attached property adapted or applied to the use of the realty, and (3) is it intended that the property will be permanently attached to the realty? *Colton v. Michigan Lafayette Bldg. Co.*, 267 Mich: 122, 126, 255 N.W. 433, 434 (1934); *First Mortgage Bond Co. v. London*, 259 Mich. 688, 691, 244 N.W. 203, 204 (1932); *Peninsular Stove Co. v. Young*, 247 Mich. 580, 582, 226 N.W. 225, 226 (1929); *Moris v. Alexander*, 208 Mich. 387, 390-391, 175 N.W. 264, 265 (1919). The three-part test remains valid under current Michigan law. *Velmer v. Baraga Area Schools*, 430 Mich. 385, 394, 424 N.W. 2d 770, 774 (1988) (addressing whether a milling machine not bolted to the floor may constitute a fixture and a dangerous condition of a building within the public building exception to governmental immunity).

In this case, FOA and Cliff's Ridge Dev. each assert the chairlift is a fixture, was annexed to the realty, and is therefore subject to their respective prior recorded mortgages. FOA and Cliff's Ridge Dev. each implicitly assert that the three-part test has been satisfied. First National does not seriously dispute that the chairlift is a fixture. This court must therefore determine whether the chairlift is a fixture.

The chairlift was attached to the realty. Concrete pads were poured in the realty prior to the erection of the chairlift. Towers were then bolted to the concrete pads, cables were strung, and about 100 chairs were attached to the cables. (Brown Deposition, pp. 19-20; Stipulated Statement of Facts, ¶ 11.) The parties have stipulated that "chairlifts are part of ski hills but can be severed from the ski hills and sold." (Stipulated Statement of Facts, ¶ 16.) The court finds the chairlift was annexed or attached to the real property.

The parties have stipulated that the chairlift was engineered to be erected on the realty and the chairlift was specially modified to be attached to the realty. (Stipulated Statement of Facts, ¶ 16.) The court finds the chairlift was adapted to the ski hill real property for its use and purposes.

Very little testimony exists whether the parties intended to permanently affix the chairlift to the real estate. (Brown Deposition, pp. 25-28.) In the project plan, and other documents relating to the Debtor's request to obtain EDC financing, it is stated that the loan was intended to finance "construction" and "installation" of the chairlift "improvements" to the realty. (Exhs. G, I, J, K, Q and R.) Final approval of the requested financing was conditioned upon conveyance of the realty from Cliff's Ridge Dev. to the Debtor. (Exh. H.) In two financing statements dated December 14 and December 15, 1982, filed by First National, it is stated, "The goods are to become fixtures on 11-24-82." (Exhs. Z and CC.) No other evidence regarding intent has been introduced by any party. Under Michigan law, attachments to realty to facilitate its use become part of the realty and, if done by the owner, are presumed to be permanent. *McTevia v. Pullman, Inc., (In the Matter of Mahon Industrial Corp.)*, 20 B.R. 836, 839-840 (Bankr. E.D. Mich. 1982). Based upon the preponderance of the evidence, the court finds the Debtor intended to permanently affix the chairlift to the realty.

Under governing Michigan law, all requirements of the three-part test to determine whether personal property has become a fixture have been met. The court concludes that the chairlift in dispute is a fixture.

[H] Crops, Livestock, and Farm Products

Read: U.C.C. §§ 9-109(3) 9-302, 9-401(1), 9-312(2), and 9-307.

Growing crops present novel challenges for the Code's notice mechanism for perfection. Because crops sprout from the land, the Code provides that the financing statement must contain a description of the particular real estate where the crops are located if a secured party is to perfect its interest. The description need not be as detailed as that for a real estate mortgage; but, as the following case demonstrates, a secured party's failure to describe the real estate may leave the creditor unperfected.

IN RE BOGETTI
BOGETTI & SONS v. BANK OF AMERICA

United States Bankruptcy Court, Eastern District of California
162 B.R. 289(1993)

J.W. HEDRICK, JR., BANKRUPTCY JUDGE.

MEMORANDUM DECISION

This matter comes before the court on complaint of debtor Robert Bogetti & Sons (the "Partnership") against Bank of America ("Bank") to determine the extent, validity, and priority of lien claimed by Bank. Evidence and arguments were presented at trial on September 24, 1993, after which the matter was taken under submission.

BACKGROUND

For several years prior to filing Chapter 11 bankruptcy in December 1992 and during the pendency of this case, the Partnership has engaged in farming operations. The Partnership's primary operations are growing beans on thirteen parcels of land located in San Joaquin and Stanislaus Counties. Bank asserts to have a $ 2.0 million perfected security interest in beans and proceeds of beans grown by the Partnership for the 1989 through 1992 crop years presently stored or on account with independent third-party agricultural cooperatives.

In June 1990, Bank agreed to loan up to $ 1.7 million to the Partnership on a revolving note to fund farming operations. In August 1991, the debt was renewed and restructured, and a new revolving note with a maximum loan amount of $ 2.0 million was executed by the parties.

Both notes were secured by identical form security agreements provided by Bank and signed by general partners of the Partnership. These security agreements were signed on the same date as the revolving notes and secured payment of debts incurred under the revolving notes and all other pre-existing or future debt incurred by the Partnership. The description of the collateral after the granting language was in printed form and provided in relevant part as follows:

> A. All farm products of whatsoever kind or nature, including all crops now growing or hereafter to be grown or timber to be cut on that certain real property described below; and also including all livestock and supplies used or produced in farming operations.
>
> B. . ...
>
> C. All present and future accounts, chattel paper, documents, notes, drafts, instruments, contract rights, general intangibles and returned goods.
>
> D. All proceeds and products of the foregoing.

The security agreements referenced five parcels of land with legal descriptions attached as exhibits A through E.

Concurrent with execution of the June 1990 revolving note and security agreement, the parties executed financing statements which Bank filed with the Secretary of State and with the recorder's offices in San Joaquin and Stanislaus Counties. The financing statements were printed forms approved by the Secretary of State. Item 6 provided in printed form as follows:

> This FINANCING STATEMENT covers the following types of items of property in which Debtor grants to Secured Party a security interest. . ..

Under item 6, Bank typed in a description of collateral which for the most part restated the collateral granted in the security agreement except for including a reference to after-acquired farm products which did not appear in the security agreements.

> All crops now being grown or hereafter grown on real property described as follows: See Exhibits A, B, C, D, and E attached hereto and made a part hereof, all farm products of whatsoever kind and nature now owned or hereafter acquired by debtor. All present and future accounts, chattel paper, documents, notes, intangibles and returned goods. All proceeds and products of the foregoing.

Descriptions of the five parcels reference in the security agreement were attached as Exhibits A through E.[21]

---

[21] Bank amended its June 1990 financing statements twice—in July 1991 and November 1991. The July 1991 amendment amended item 6 to include rights to payment on a contract between debtor and Rhodes Bean and Supply Company.

By December 16, 1992, when the Partnership filed Chapter 11, it owed $1,989,622.67 in principal and $164,889.32 in interest for a total debt under the secured revolving notes of $2,154,511.99.

Assets on the date of filing listed in the Partnership schedules included beans and proceeds from the sale of beans harvested in 1989, 1991, and 1992 from all thirteen parcels farmed by the Partnership. The 1989 and 1991 crop was stored with Rhodes Bean and Supply Company ("Rhodes"). Under the Partnership's agreement with Rhodes, upon harvest the beans were trucked to Rhodes processing facilities where the beans were clean, bagged, and made ready for sale. Under normal procedures, Rhodes would sell the beans and account to the Partnership for the proceeds after deducting costs, fees, and/or commissions. The 1992 crop was stored at a Vernalis, California, warehouse ("Vernalis Warehouse") owned by independent third parties which apparently operated under a cooperative agreement similar to the Partnership's agreement with Rhodes.[22] In addition to the stored crop, Vernalis Warehouse owed the Partnership $ 69,000 on account from bean sales.

The Partnership presented testimony of general partner Robert Bogetti that the 1992 crop and proceeds were not property of the Partnership, but rather individual property of Robert Bogetti. Mr. Bogetti testified that he had hired the Partnership for the 1992 crop year to work as a "contract farmer" only, and the Partnership had no interest in the crops. Bank offered evidence rebutting Mr. Bogetti's testimony including that the Partnership had made draws for 1992 crop production cost in February 1992 and that the Partnership had consistently been treated as sole owner of the crop in 1989, 1990, and 1991, and as debtor-in-possession in 1993. The court takes judicial notice of the schedules filed by the Partnership (submitted under penalty of perjury) that the Partnership owned the 1992 crop and crop proceeds. Although the schedules have not been formally amended consistent with Mr. Bogetti's testimony, the Partnership filed a declaration by Mr. Bogetti in connection with a cash collateral motion in February 1993 that the crop and crop proceeds were individual rather than Partnership property.

Bank relies on its security documents and evidence of Partnership ownership in the 1992 crop to assert a perfected security interest in all the Partnership's 1989, 1991, and 1992 bean crop and crop proceeds. The Partnership contests the Bank's assertions and argues that since the bean crop is now held as "inventory" rather than "crops" or "farm products," Bank's security agreement does not extend a security interest in any of the beans stored and held for sale with third parties. Alternatively, the Partnership contends that if Bank's security documents are sufficient to sustain a security interest in the stored beans, such security interest is limited to the crops harvested from the five parcels described in the security agreements. The Partnership additionally argues that none of the 1992 crop is subject to any security interest because it is individual property of Robert Bogetti.

DISCUSSION

The nature, extent, and validity of Bank's security interest in Partnership property is governed by state law. *Butner v. United States*, 440 U.S. 48, 59 L. Ed. 2d 136, 99 S. Ct. 914 (1979). Resolving the dispute at hand requires the court to look to California law on contracts and the

---

The November amendment was identical to the language in the June 1990 financing statement except that it added "general intangibles" where previously it provided only for "intangibles."

[22] Evidence regarding the contractual relationship between the Vernalis Warehouse and the Partnership was not extensively developed or disputed.

Uniform Commercial Code as adopted by the California Legislature. The ultimate questions are whether Bank has a security interest on the Partnership's beans and proceeds and whether such interest is perfected sufficient to defeat the section 544 "strong arm" powers of the debtor-in-possession to avoid unperfected interests. To resolve these questions requires the court to determine (1) what property Bank's security interest attached to, (2) whether Bank's security interest was properly perfected, and (3) if Bank had a perfected security interest, whether such interest continued to the date the Partnership filed bankruptcy.

Attachment

Section 9203 of the California Commercial Codesets forth the basic requirements for attachment and enforceability of security interests:

> [A] security interest is not enforceable against the debtor or third parties with respect to the collateral and does not attach unless all of the following are applicable:
>
> (a) The collateral is in the possession the secured party pursuant to agreement, or the debtor has signed a security agreement which contains a description of the collateral and in addition, when the security interest covers crops growing or to be grown or timber to be cut, a description of the land concerned.
>
> (b) Value has been given.
>
> (c) The debtor has rights in the collateral.

Cal. Com. Code § 9203(1) (West 1990). Section 9203(2) continues to specify that absent contrary agreement "attachment occurs as soon as all of the events specified in subdivision (1) have taken place . . .." Cal. Com. Code § 9203(2) (West 1990).

The parties do not dispute whether value has been given, but do dispute the adequacy or interpretation of the collateral descriptions and whether the Partnership had rights in certain of the claimed collateral. To determine what property is subject to Bank's security interest, the court will specifically address the issues raised concerning the language of the security agreements with reference to property of the Partnership estate existing at the time of execution of the security agreements.

1. 1991 Bean Crop from Five Parcels Identified in Security Agreements.

The security agreements provided a grant of security interest in "crops growing or to be grown." Consistent with the requirements of section 9203(1) that a security interest in crops growing or to be grown include a description of the land, descriptions of five Partnership farming parcels were referenced and attached to the security agreements.

Based on the clear language of the security agreements, Bank obtained an enforceable security interest on any crops that were growing or to be grown on the five identified properties from the date the first security agreement was executed in June 1990. This category of goods indisputably includes the 1991 crop grown on the five described parcels.

The Partnership raises a curious argument that even though Bank's security interest may have attached to the 1991 crop from the five identified parcels, the security interest "unattached" when the crop was harvested and sent to Rhodes for cleaning, bagging, and marketing. The basis of the Partnership's argument is that once the beans were delivered to Rhodes, they became "inventory." Since Bank's security agreement did not include "inventory," the security interest is alleged to have been lost. The Partnership cites California Commercial Code provisions, code comments, and case law purporting to establish that once "farm product," such as a harvested crop, comes into the possession of a non-farmer for sale or marketing, it becomes inventory; and, unless the security agreement references inventory, no security agreement is created or retained in those goods.

The authority cited by the Partnership does not, however, support the argument advanced. There is no question that the 1991 bean crop was covered by the "growing crops or crops to be grown" language of the security agreements. That the beans later became "farm product" once severed from the land and may have become "inventory" when trucked to Rhodes for processing and sale does not affect attachment or enforceability of Bank's security interest. Security agreements are required to define the rights of the debtor and secured party in identified collateral. Once a security interest attaches to described collateral, subsequent transmutations as to classification under section 9109 do not defeat that security interest. The Partnership has cited no relevant authority supporting its contention and ignores basic precepts of secured transactions that a security interest once attached to identified property continues in that property notwithstanding changes debtor's use of the property or even, in some circumstances, sale to third parties. See, *e.g.*, Cal. Com. Code § 9306 (West 1990) (a security interest continues in collateral notwithstanding sale, exchange or other disposition thereof); Cal. Com. Code § 9401(3) (West 1990) (perfected security interest continues in goods notwithstanding change in debtor's use of collateral).

Based on the foregoing, the court determines that Bank's security agreements created a valid and enforceable security interest in the Partnership's 1991 bean crop from the five parcels described in the security agreements.

2. 1989 Bean Crop.

As the Partnership emphasized in its argument regarding the 1991 crop, the subclassifications of goods in section 9109 are mutually exclusive, and without proper identification, there can be neither an enforceable security interest nor perfection. See Cal. Com. Code § 9109 (West 1990) California Code and Uniform Code cmts. Bank's security agreement included "farm product," but did not include "inventory." Bank contends that the 1989 crop was "farm product" when the security agreements were executed. The Partnership contends the 1989 crop was "inventory" and not subject to Bank's security interest.

The evidence at trial established that immediately upon harvest, the 1989 bean crop was trucked to Rhodes for cleaning, bagging, and marketing. Thus, at the time the security agreements were executed in June 1990 and August 1991, the 1989 beans had already been harvested and were stored at Rhodes.

For harvested crops to be classified as "farm products," they must be "in the possession of a debtor engaged in raising, fattening, grazing or other farming operations." Cal. Com. Code § 9109(3) (West 1990). The code comments are specific that when crops come into the possession of a third party for marketing or sale, the crops cease to be "farm products" and become "inventory."

When crops or livestock or their products come into the possession of a person not engaged in farming operations they cease to be "farm products." If they come into the possession of a marketing agency for sale or distribution or a manufacturer or processor as raw materials, they become inventory. Cal. Com. Code § 9109 (West 1990) Uniform Code cmt. 4.

Notwithstanding the clear language of the code and comments, a split of authority has developed that certain degrees of constructive possession where crops are stored with third parties for sale may satisfy the possession requirement to cause harvested crops held by a third party for sale to remain "farm products." California courts have not addressed this issue, and Bank urges the court to adopt the analysis of the court in *In re Roberts*, 38 Bankr. 128 (Bankr. D. Kan. 1984), which appears to the seminal case developing this split. Similar to this case, the farmer in Roberts harvested his grain crop and stored it with an independent storage facility. The court first noted that "possession" was not a term defined in the code. The court then cited several commentators supporting a final conclusion that as long as the farmer has some indicia of ownership such as a negotiable or non-negotiable receipt for the stored crops, the crops remained in the farmer's possession and could continue to be classified as "farm products."

This court cannot accept the *Roberts* court's analysis. First, the facts are distinguishable or incomplete in an important respect. In *Roberts*, it was either unclear or a fact that the storage facility did not market the farmer's grain. In this case, there is no question that the Partnership's agreement with Rhodes includes a duty on Rhodes' part to market and sell the beans. Second, although "possession" is not a defined term, the comments strongly suggest that "possession" means actual possession. Uniform comment 4 quoted above states that crops become "inventory" when they come into possession of a marketing agency for sale. Use of the word marketing agency assumes constructive possession and ownership of the farmer. Finally, the court feels strongly that certainty is fostered by interpreting language literally. Accepting "constructive possession" as "possession" would add an undesired "gray" area in determining goods classifications which are routinely relied upon by debtors and creditors to be mutually exclusive. These terms should be given plain "black and white" meanings to the extent possible.

Based on the foregoing, the court determines that Bank's security agreements did not create a security interest in any of the Partnership's 1989 crop currently stored at Rhodes or Vernalis Warehouse.

3. 1991 Bean Crop from Eight Parcels not Described in the Security Agreements.

Bank concedes that attachment or perfection of a security interest in growing crops or crops to be grown requires descriptions of the real property to be attached to the security agreement. Bank also concedes that when the August 1991 security agreement was executed, all of the Partnership's 1991 crop was yet to be harvested. Notwithstanding, Bank contends to have a security interest in the entire 1991 crop based on having rights to "after-acquired farm products." Bank asserts that when the 1991 crop was severed from the ground in the harvest, it became "farm product" and Bank's security interest attached.

Bank urges this court to determine its security interest in after-acquired farm products based on two grounds. First, Bank emphasizes that the financing statement filed in June 1990 contained an explicit reference to after-acquired farm products. This financing statement also contained language granting a security interest and was signed by partners of the Partnership. Accordingly, Bank claims that all requirements for a valid security agreement were met, and the financing statement should be determined to have expanded the security interest to include after-acquired farm products. Second, Bank argues that the granting language in the security agreements should be construed to include after-acquired farm products because they referenced "all farm products of whatsoever kind or nature."

a. Financing statement expanding security interest.

Contrary to Bank's argument that the June 1990 financing statement expanded the scope of its security interest set forth in the security agreement, a financing statement is overwhelmingly held ineffective to expand the collateral described in a security agreement. Courts following this general rule typically offer similar rationales—two of which repeatedly appear.

The first rationale concerns differences between the function and purpose of a security interest and that of a financing statement. A security agreement is an agreement describing the property in which the debtor has conveyed a security interest to the creditor. The code comments emphasize that it is in the nature of a statute of frauds designed to establish whether a security interest in fact exists and its scope or extent. Cal. Com. Code § 9203 (West 1990) Uniform cmt 5. By contrast, a financing statement is not designed to define or create contractual rights and is merely a notice and perfection tool. A financing statement is publicly filed. It perfects a creditor's interest vis-a-vis subsequent lien creditors and allows interested parties to obtain fuller information before entering into transactions with the debtor. The description of collateral in a financing statement may be, and is often, more expansive than the security agreement to ensure that perfection and notice is unquestioned in the collateral specifically described in the security agreement. Accordingly, where disputes arise as to what collateral is covered by a security interest, courts limit their inquiry to what is described in the security agreement even though the financing statement may describe additional collateral. See, *e.g., Northwest Acceptance Corp. v. Lynnwood Equipment, Inc.*, 841 F.2d 918, 921 (9th Cir. 1988) (security agreement rather than financing statement defined extent of security interest); *In re Martin Grinding & Machine Works, Inc.*, 793 F.2d 592 (7th Cir. 1986) (broader description of collateral in a financing statement is ineffective to extend a security interest beyond that stated in the security agreement).

The second recurring rationale is that a financing statement is generally not intended to be a security agreement and, as a result, usually lacks intent or granting language sufficient to create a security interest. Without this specific intent shown by language granting a security interest, the financing statement is simply ineffective to create one. See, *e.g., Shelton v. Erwin*, 472 F.2d 1118 (8th Cir. 1973) (financing statement is merely evidence of creation of a security agreement and is usually not itself a security agreement); *In re John Oliver Co.*, 129 Bankr. 1 (Bankr. D. N.H. 1991) (statement "to cover my interest up to $ 250,000.00" in financing statement was insufficient to create security interest); *In re Mack*, 93 Bankr. 695 (Bankr. D. N.D. 1988) (security agreement giving creditor security interest in growing crops was unenforceable for lack of land description even though financing statement contained statutorily sufficient description).

Bank would have the court ignore the first rationale described above and determine, with respect to the second, that the language in the financing statement was sufficient to create a security interest. The court is unwilling to do either.

The secured loan between Bank and the Partnership was documented in a standard manner with three documents signed by the Partnership: a revolving note, a security agreement, and a financing statement. Each of these documents was clearly identified on its face, and there was clearly no question as to what the parties intended by each one. The Partnership and, especially, Bank knew the purpose and function of each of these documents. With the purposes of these documents in mind, the Partnership and Bank would have looked exclusively to the security agreement to define Bank's collateral. In addition, while Bank would be extremely interested in crafting the collateral description in the financing statement to preserve its rights vis-a-vis other lien creditors, the Partnership would have little incentive to review it carefully. Where a transaction contains such standard documentation, the court is extremely unwilling to determine that an otherwise complete and unambiguous security agreement was intended by the parties to be supplemented or corrected by a financing statement that "re-granted" an additional security interest.

Additionally, the court is not persuaded that the language asserted by Bank to have granted a security interest actually does so. The printed language relied on by Bank provides as follows:

> This FINANCING STATEMENT covers the following types or items of property in which Debtor grants to Secured Party a security interest.

In this sentence, the purported granting language appears to be a mere "tag on" to clarify that debtor has granted a security interest in the property, not that the debtor is presently granting a security interest. Contrasted to the language clearly intended to create a security interest in the security agreements, this purported granting language pales.

> As security for the payment by ROBERT BOGETTI AND SONS, A PARTNERSHIP ("Borrower") to SECURITY PACIFIC NATIONAL BANK ("Bank") of a Promissory Note executed by Borrower in favor of Bank, dated June 5, 1990, for $ 1,700,000.00 . . .Borrower hereby grants to Bank a security interest in the following "Collateral". . ..

The court concedes, however, that Bank's argument may have some merit had there not been a contemporaneously executed security agreement. Several courts have liberally construed less than clear granting language in a financing statement to create a security interest where there is no formal security agreement between the parties. See, *e.g., Morey Machinery Co., Inc. v. Great Western Industrial Machinery Co.*, 507 F.2d 987 (5th Cir. 1975) (financing statement with the words "Secured hereby" stamped on top of it was sufficient to create a security agreement); *Little v. County of Orange*, 31 N.C. App. 495, 229 S.E.2d 823 (1976) (as long as writing contains language which makes and evidences bargain, it does not matter that it is not denominated a security agreement). This authority should, however, be strictly limited to the factual context in which all of the cases found by the court arose—namely, where there was no formal security agreement, and the secured party was struggling on the basis of one or more contract theories to establish a security interest using the financing statement as written evidence of a security agreement.

b. "All farm products" language.

Section 9204 provides that a security agreement may provide for a security interest in after-acquired collateral. Unless specifically provided for, however, a security interest attaches only to the collateral described and in existence at the time the security agreement is executed.

As discussed above, the security agreements did not include a clause describing after-acquired farm products. Nevertheless, Bank contends the language of the security agreements providing for a grant of a security interest in "all farm products of whatsoever kind or nature" created a security agreement in after-acquired farm products. Bank relies on a well-developed line of authority that where a security agreement provides for a security interest in "all inventory" or "all accounts" or similar broad language, the security interest includes after-acquired inventory and accounts.

Bank has, however, cited no case extending this line of authority beyond inventory and accounts receivable. As emphasized recently by the Ninth Circuit in *Stoumbos v. Kilimnik*, 988 F.2d 949 (9th Cir. 1993), this line of authority is based on the assumption that the parties realize that inventory and accounts receivable are in a constant state of turnover and "no creditor could reasonably agree to be secured by collateral that would vanish in a short time in the normal course of business." *Id.* at 955 In *Stoumbos*, the court refused to extend this line of authority to a security interest in "equipment" which it determined was not a category of goods subject to constant turnover.

"Farm products" is a broad subcategory of goods which includes crops, livestock, and supplies used or produced in farming operations. Cal. Com. Code § 9109(3) (West 1990). Although there are conceivably some items included in "farm products" that may, like inventory or accounts receivable, "vanish" and be replaced in a short period of time in the normal course of business, such turnover has not been shown by Bank to be so constant that a creditor would reasonably expect to secured by after-acquired farm products. Indeed, some farm products, such as livestock, may remain in the farmer's possession for substantial periods without replacement. Accordingly, the court is not willing to extend the line of authority cited by Bank to include "farm products."

Based on the foregoing, Bank has no security interest in the 1991 bean crop or crop-proceeds from the eight parcels not identified in the security agreements.

4. 1992 Crop and Crop Proceeds

The Partnership takes a rare position for a debtor-in-possession that certain property is not property of the estate—namely, the 1992 bean crop and proceeds. This position is less shocking, however, since the Partnership is alleging that the crop is the personal property of general partner Robert Bogetti.

The Partnership submitted no documentary evidence supporting its contentions, and the only evidence was the testimony of Robert Bogetti. Mr. Bogetti testified to the effect that, in 1992, he individually owned the crop on all thirteen parcels previously farmed by the Partnership. He further testified that he hired the Partnership to "custom farm" the 1992 crop. This testimony, however, is not credible.

The Partnership had farmed the parcels in question in 1989, 1990, 1991, and 1992, and continues to farm the parcels in 1993 as debtor-in-possession. For each of these years, except 1992, the Partnership claims to own the bean crop. No business reason is given for the change in ownership of the crop where the Partnership continued to farm the parcels, and Mr. Bogetti merely claims that he decided to own the crops for 1992 and hire the Partnership as a contract farmer. The only reason the court can infer for Mr. Bogetti's decision is that Mr. Bogetti and the Partnership are seeking to defeat Partnership lien claimants. This inference is supported by credible evidence that the Partnership does indeed own the 1992 bean crop.

First, the Partnership's schedules as originally filed show the Partnership as owning the 1992 crop subject to Bank's security interest. The Partnership's bankruptcy petition was filed on or about December 16, 1992. The only schedules ever filed in the case were dated January 29, 1993, and filed together with a verified amendment to the creditor matrix and a verified schedule of current income and current expenditures. The schedules have never been amended. Attached to the schedules was a financial statement dated November 30, 1992, showing as assets unsold harvested crops worth $ 1,494,968.00. Included in that sum are crops from 1989, 1991, and 1992. The amount shown for 1992 is $ 411,390.00.

Second, the Partnership filed a declaration of Robert Bogetti which contained an Exhibit A further admitting that at least some of the 1992 crop was subject to the Bank lien. Although this declaration was later contradicted by a supplemental declaration of Mr. Bogetti that he owned none of the 1992 crop, the court considers the declaration, like Mr. Bogetti's current testimony to be suspect.

Finally, the Bank introduced bank statements showing that the Partnership drew funds on its revolving credit line in February 1992 for 1992 crop financing. As a contract farmer, the

Partnership would have had no legitimate reason or purpose to draw funds for crop financing unless it owned the 1992 crop.

Having reviewed the documents hereinabove referred to, and having heard the testimony and observed the demeanor of Mr. Robert Bogetti, and having weighed all of the other evidence, the court finds and concludes that the 1992 crop and the proceeds thereof are assets of the Partnership's estate and not the property of Robert Bogetti individually. The treatment to be accorded the liens of the Bank regarding the 1992 crop is the same as that accorded Bank liens as to the 1991 crop.

Perfection

Even though Bank's security interest has attached as previously described, Bank must have an adequate and properly filed security interest to defeat the debtor-in-possession's section 544 "strong arm" powers. In this case, the Partnership does not challenge Bank's financing statements as to adequacy or place of filing. The Partnership does, however, appear to challenge the continuing validity of Bank's perfection based on changes in the classification of the goods covered by the security agreements after Bank's security interest attached—specifically from crops and farm products, which was covered by Bank's security agreement, to inventory, which was not.

The California Commercial Code appears to directly address this issue and indicates that a properly perfected security interest continues in goods notwithstanding the fact that the debtor's use of the goods (and consequently its classification under the code) changes.

> A filing which is made in the proper place in this state continues effective even though the debtor's residence or place of business or the location of the collateral or its use, whichever controlled the original filing, is thereafter changed. Cal. Com. Code § 9401(3) (West 1990).

In addition, even though ignoring section 9401(3), the court in *Robins v. Product Credit Ass'n (In re Walkington)*, 62 Bankr. 989 (Bankr. W.D. Mich. 1986), recognized the policy of the Uniform Commercial Code that perfected security interests should not be defeated merely because the debtor's use of the goods and the goods characterization under the code changes.

Based on the foregoing, the court determines that Bank's security interest remained perfected in the Partnership's bean crop notwithstanding any classification changes subsequent to attachment of Bank's security interest.

Conclusion

Counsel for the Partnership is directed to prepare findings of fact, conclusion of law, and judgment consistent with the above memorandum decision. These documents shall be served on opposing counsel. Absent objection after 10 days, the order shall be signed and entered.

Farm products present special problems because of the intervention of other federal statutes like the Food Securities Act. The next case demonstrates how the F.S.A. could come into consideration.

FARMERS & MERCHANTS STATE BANK v. TEVELDAL

Supreme Court of South Dakota
524 N.W.2d 874 (1994)

SABERS, JUSTICE.

Bank and feed supplier claim priority in competing security interests in hogs owned by farmer and the proceeds therefrom. Feed supplier appeals summary judgment in favor of Bank. We affirm.

Facts

Farmers & Merchants State Bank (Bank) and Kevin Teveldal d/b/a Kevin's Livestock Management Service (Teveldal) claim priority of competing security interests in hogs owned by Gary Haiar (Haiar) and in the proceeds of sale. On January 7, 1991, Bank filed a financing statement with the South Dakota Secretary of State and perfected a security interest in Haiar's farm products, including beef cattle, dairy cattle and hogs.

Teveldal provided Haiar with hog feed in the amount of $24,358.96 from September 3, 1991 to May 24, 1992. Bank claims it released $32,710.00 to Haiar from August 9, 1991 to June 12, 1992 so that Teveldal could be paid for supplying feed. When Haiar did not pay for the feed, Teveldal telephoned the Secretary of State's office to inquire whether any security interest existed in Haiar's hogs. He was told that the Bank had a security interest in beef and dairy cattle under the farm products section of the Effective Financing Statement list (EFS), which Congress required in the Food Security Act (FSA).[23] Teveldal filed a Financing Statement with the Secretary of State on August 4, 1992, perfecting a security interest in 600 head of Haiar's hogs to secure payment of debt of $26,852.04.

Between August 6 and August 14, 1992, some of Haiar's hogs were sold at the John Morrell Meatpacking Company (Morrell) in Sioux Falls, S.D. Morrell issued two checks totalling $5,257.37 to Bank, Teveldal, and Haiar as joint payees. Teveldal refused to release his claim to the checks. The Bank took possession of the remaining hogs and they were sold by the Bank for $35,319.18.[24]

Bank brought suit to determine the priority of the competing security interests in the hogs and the proceeds from the sale to Morrell. Teveldal counterclaimed, claiming his right to the proceeds based on a superior perfected security interest. The trial court denied both parties' first motions for summary judgment on April 14, 1993. The trial court granted Teveldal leave to amend his counterclaim to include a claim for $ 26,852.04 for feed supplied to Haiar for the hogs. Teveldal claimed that if Bank's interest were deemed superior there would be unjust enrichment

---

[23] The FSA mandated the central filing system for farm products, 7 U.S.C. § 1631, and, as a result, the EFS codes were created. See Form U.C.C.-1(South Dakota Secretary of State, 1987 revision)

[24] Bank's brief claims the State required them to take possession of the hogs or the State would take them. It appears that Gary Haiar was involved in the Wessington Springs Puppy Farm which had neglected animals which caused them serious health problems. Haiar allegedly had been neglecting and mistreating the hogs. Twenty feeder pigs and three sows died but the remainder were saved. Bank claims it was required to take possession of the hogs to feed and nurse them back to health. Once they became marketable, they were sold by Bank.

because supplying feed helped the hogs survive. The court held that Bank had the first perfected security interest in Haiar's hogs.

In addition to the written description of the collateral on form U.C.C.-1, the holder of a security interest in farm products is to designate the products by a code number for EFS purposes under the FSA. Bank provided the codes for beef and dairy cattle but not for hogs. The trial court held that Bank was perfected despite its failure to enter the code for hogs under the EFS. The trial court also held that Teveldal was not a "buyer" protected by the FSA, 7 U.S.C. § 1631(c)(1). Both parties moved for summary judgment. The trial court granted summary judgment in favor of Bank on Bank's claim for the sale proceeds and against Teveldal on his counterclaim for the price of the feed.

Whether Bank's failure to comply with the EFS code numbering system destroys perfection of its security interest as against a secured supplier of feed?

Each party claims a superior perfected security interest in Haiar's hogs. Under SDCL 57A-9-312(5)(a), the first security interest perfected is superior to all competing claims. Since Bank perfected first, we must determine whether Bank's failure to list the EFS code for hogs destroyed perfection of its security interest and whether the FSA protects Teveldal.

Under SDCL 57A-9-402(8), "[a] financing statement substantially complying with the requirements of this section is effective even though it contains minor errors which are not seriously misleading." Bank included in its description of collateral "all cattle, hogs, sheep & wool now owned or hereafter acquired, together with natural increase from said livestock." Plaintiff's Exhibit A. Bank included the EFS code numbers for beef cattle and dairy cattle, but not for hogs.

In *First Bank v. Eastern Livestock Co.*, 837 F. Supp. 792 (S.D. Miss. 1993), the court considered the sufficiency of a collateral description in a financing statement under the EFS. The court found no case under the FSA, so it resorted to the U.C.C. for precedent. *Id.* at 799. The court held that:

> the majority of courts addressing the adequacy of financing statements under the U.C.C. have held that a financing statement, in order to perfect a security interest, need not specifically identify the property which is the subject of a security interest; rather, it is sufficient if the description would put a reasonably prudent prospective lender or buyer on notice that the collateral sought to be purchased or encumbered might be the subject of a preexisting security interest. *Id.* (citations omitted).

"[T]he financing statement is designed only to provide general notice or warning that certain collateral might already be encumbered[.]" *Production Credit Ass'n v. Bartos*, 430 N.W.2d 238, 241 (Minn.App. 1988). Therefore, the financing statement need not provide all information but only that information which states that a transaction has taken place and that details may be obtained from the address shown. *First Bank*, 837 F. Supp. at 799.

A majority of courts have adopted the view that a description is sufficient if it "merely provides notice of the need for additional inquiry." *United States v. Southeast Mississippi Livestock Farmers Ass'n*, 619 F.2d 435, 438 (5th Cir. 1980). Here, Bank's financing statement provided general notice that Bank held a security interest in Haiar's hogs. Teveldal should have conducted a search more thorough than a mere EFS code inquiry. The omission of the code number in the EFS section did not render Bank's financing statement insufficient. The formal requirements for a financing statement were met, SDCL 57A-9-402 (1), and the Bank's filing constituted perfection of its security interest in Haiar's hogs. SDCL 57A-9-303(l).

Teveldal places too much reliance upon a telephone call to the Secretary of State. "The secretary of state is not responsible for accuracy and completeness of the information furnished verbally in response to a telephone request." SDCL 57A-9-407.1. Teveldal did not ask for a computer printout which would have shown the Bank's interest was perfected in hogs as well as cattle. A reasonable inquiry by requesting a printout would have shown the hogs were also covered under the financing statement. Teveldal could have received a copy of the entire financing statement prior to supplying the feed, thereby precluding the need for this lawsuit. SDCL 57A-9-403(9), 57a-9-407(3).

Even though Bank perfected its security interest, Teveldal claims he is a "buyer in ordinary course" protected under the FSA, 7 U.S.C. § 1631. The FSA provides "a buyer who in the ordinary course of business buys a farm product from a seller engaged in farming operations shall take free of a security interest created by the seller, even though the security interest is perfected[,] and the buyer knows of the existence of such interest." 7 U.S.C. § 1631(d). Under SDCL 57A-l-201(9), a "buyer in ordinary course" is a person "who in good faith and without knowledge that the sale to him is in violation of the ownership rights or security interest of a third party in the goods[,] buys in ordinary course from a person in the business of selling goods of that kind[.]" The FSA deleted the "good faith and without knowledge" requirement to protect buyers even though they know of the existence of a perfected security interest. *Lisco State Bank v. McCombs Ranches, Inc.*, 752 F. Supp. 329, 334 (D.Neb. 1990). Prior to the FSA, a buyer of farm products could be liable to the seller/debtor and to the party holding a security interest in the farm products. 7 U.S.C. § 1631(a) (2); see SDCL 57A-9-307; Lisco, 752 F. Supp. 329. Under the FSA, buyers of farm products are not exposed to liability for double payment.[25] 7 U.S.C. § 1631(d); *Sanborn Cty. Bank v. Magness Livestock Exch.*, 410 N.W.2d 565, 566 n.1 (S.D. 1987).

"Buying" does not include receiving goods or documents of title under a preexisting contract as security "for or in total or partial satisfaction of a money debt," SDCL 57A-1-201(9), thereby excluding "attaching creditors and others who take goods in satisfaction of preexisting debts" from the definition of a "buyer in ordinary course." 2 J. White & R. Summers, Uniform Commercial Code, § 26-13, at 533, n.2 (3rd ed. 1988). Teveldal did not obtain a security interest in Haiar's hogs until after he had supplied feed. Therefore, it was a preexisting debt. A creditor who receives a security interest for a preexisting debt is not a "buyer in ordinary course." *Id.*, § 26-13, at 533, nn. 2-3.

Other than eliminating double payment liability for a "buyer in ordinary course" in farm products, Congress did not intend to preempt state law relating to the creation, perfection, or priority of security interests. 9 C.F.R. § 205.202; *Food Services of Am. v. Royal Heights*, 69 Wash. App. 784, 850 P.2d 585, 588 (1993). Teveldal erroneously argues that he is a buyer in

[25] The FSA also protects commission merchants and selling agents from incurring double payments for any farm products sold on commission on behalf of a seller of farm products. 7 U.S.C. § 1631(g)(1).

"Commission merchant 15 any person "engaged in the business of receiving any farm product for sale, on commission, or for or on behalf of another person." 7 U.S.C. § 1631(c)(3). A "selling agent" is "any person, other than a commission merchant, who is engaged in the business of negotiating the sale and purchase of any farm product on behalf of a person engaged in farming operations." 7 U.S.C. § 1631(c)(8).

Teveldal claims to be a "selling agent" protected under the FSA. However, he did not engage in the business of negotiating or selling the hogs; he only supplied feed. The FSA does not protect a creditor taking a security interest in farm products. See 7 U.S.C. § 1631.

the ordinary course, deserving protection under the FSA. Obviously, Teveldal was not a buyer. He was a seller and supplier of feed. Therefore, he is not entitled to protection under the FSA. The trial court correctly concluded that Teveldal was not a "buyer" protected under the FSA.

We have considered Teveldal's other arguments and determine them to be without merit.

Affirmed.

MILLER, CHIEF JUSTICE, and WUEST, AMUNDSON and KONENKAMP, JUSTICES, concur.

[I] Minerals, Oil, Gas, and Timber

Read: U.C.C. §§ 9-103(5) and Comment 8, 9-105 and 9-402(2); compare § 2-107.

The perfection of security interests in timber, minerals, oil, and gas presents certain unique problems. If the minerals are still in the ground, they are generally considered part of the real estate and any security interest must be in a real estate instrument itself and properly recorded as such. Under U.C.C. § 9-103(5), the law of the particular state where the wellhead or minehead is located controls. Because ownership and lease interests in various types of minerals may differ as to their classification in terms of real and personal property, particular state law should be consulted. Under U.C.C. § 9-105(4), minerals are excluded from the definition of goods until extracted; no Article 9 security interest can attach until that time. Once minerals are extracted however, security interests are subject to Article 9's provisions and perfection generally takes place by filing under § 9-402. In a few states, a mortgage or security interest in minerals will be classified as a chattel mortgage; if so, a security interest could be perfected by filing for a general intangible. See Coogan, Hogan, Vagts, Secured Transactions Under the Uniform Commercial Code, Vol. 1B, § 16.15.

A financing statement covering timber to be cut or removed under a contract or conveyance must be filed locally in the office where a real estate mortgage would be recorded. The Code classifies the timber as goods and therefore the rules of Article 9 apply. Filing for perfection would occur under U.C.C. § 9-402, which requires a description of real estate. Generally, timber not subject to such a contract or conveyance would still be classified as real estate and not subject to Article 9.

§ 17.12 Multistate Transactions and Choice of Law Rules

Read: U.C.C. § 9-103 and Comments.

What happens when a secured transaction involves more than one state? Should the financing statement be filed in the state where the debtor resides, in the state where the collateral currently sits, or where it ultimately will be located? What is the effect on a secured party's interest if the debtor removes the collateral from one state to another? Which state's law governs the perfection of various security interests? Under § 1-105(1), there is a general U.C.C. rule that the parties involved in a contract may, by agreement, determine the law that is to govern their relationship, so long as the transaction "bears a reasonable relation" to the law of the jurisdiction selected. Because most secured transactions cases involve disputes between a secured party and third persons rather than the contracting parties, the general rule of § 1-105 has a limited application. Given the wide scope of modern business, choice of law problems often arise in secured transactions. The Code provides a detailed outline on how to handle conflict of law disputes at section 9-103. The categories are based on the nature of the collateral involved, and suggest which state's law should serve as the focal point for giving notice to third parties.

[A] Documents, Instruments, and Ordinary (Non-mobile) Goods

For these types of collateral, subsection (1) of § 9-103 provides that the law of the state where the collateral is located controls perfection questions. This basic conflicts test is known as the "situs" or "location" rule. To illustrate, consider the following example: XYZ Company owns production plants in Missouri, Iowa, and Florida. XYZ gives a security interest in manufacturing equipment located in the Iowa plant to Fifth National Bank of Chicago as collateral for a working capital loan. If Fifth National files a financing statement in Iowa, it will have a perfected security interest because the equipment is located in Iowa. If the bank were to file in any other location, it would have an unperfected security interest.

If collateral is to be moved from one state to another, the situs test provides little help unless there is a specific time at which the test can be applied. The Code sets forth three rules— **the last event, 30 day, and 4 month rules**—to resolve such perfection questions. Under the *last event rule* the initial issue of perfection is governed by the law of the state in which the collateral is located when the last event occurs on which a claim of perfected or unperfected status is based. Put in a different way, the last event rule asks the secured party to explain how it acquired a perfected security interest. The Code looks to the last time-related element associated with perfection and determines where the goods were located as of that time. The law of the jurisdiction where the goods were located when that last event took place controls the issue of perfection. U.C.C. § 9-103(1)(b).

Sections 9-203 and 9-302(1) combine to require four events before a claim for perfection may be made: first, there must be a written security agreement between the debtor and secured party; second, the creditor must give the debtor some type of value for the security interest; third, the debtor must have acquired rights in the collateral; and fourth, the secured party must have given public notice of its security interest. While these four events may occur in any order, all four must occur before a claim of perfection can be sustained (unless perfection is automatic). Thus, the last event test focuses on the location of goods when the last event before perfection was made. Usually, this event is the filing of a financing statement. However, any other aspect of creating a perfected security interest could be the last event. For example, with after-acquired property the last event would be the debtor's acquiring rights in the after-acquired collateral. In the illustration above, if Fifth National Bank had taken a security interest in XYZ's existing and subsequently acquired equipment in Iowa and Missouri, but had filed only in Iowa, FNB would have no claim to either existing or acquired equipment located in Missouri because there was no filing in Missouri. For the existing equipment in Missouri, the last event would be the location of the equipment when FNB filed; for after-acquired equipment the last event would be XYZ's acquisition of rights in the collateral and Missouri would still be the proper location. The key to the last event rule is understanding that most non-mobile goods rarely change location. Thus, non-mobile goods are lumped together with documents and instruments (which a prudent creditor would possess to perfect). Perfection with non-mobile goods should therefore be in the place where located. § 9-103(1)(b).

The *thirty-day rule* relates to purchase money security interests in non-mobile goods where attachment is in one state but where the parties intend to remove the collateral to another jurisdiction within 30 days after the debtor receives possession. In such instances, section 9-103(1)(c) provides that the law of the destination state applies. Thus, a purchase money creditor/seller should file in the state where the creditor understands that the goods will be located. If the goods reach the destination state within 30 days, the seller's filing there would perfect its status.

The thirty day test is a limited rule because it applies only to purchase money transactions: the lender and debtor must "understand" that when the security interest attaches, that the goods are intended for another state. Finally, the goods must actually reach the intended destination state within the 30 day period or the purchase money secured creditor loses its perfected status (if the collateral has not been taken to the destination state within the 30-day period, the place of perfection would again be governed by the basic location test of the last event rule on the thirty-first day). To apply the thirty-day rule to a transaction between Fifth National Bank and XYZ, assume that FNB agrees to lend XYZ money to buy a new piece of equipment from a seller in Missouri. If the parties understand that XYZ intends to place the equipment in its Florida plant, the proper place for FNB to file is Florida. A filing there will perfect FNB's interest so long as the goods actually reach the state of Florida by the end of the 30 day period.

PROBLEM 17.4

Assume that the transaction between Fifth National and XYZ fits within the 30-day rule of § 9-103(1)(c). XYZ receives the loan, purchases the equipment, and takes possession of it in Missouri on July 1, and promptly ships the items to Florida. The equipment arrives in Florida on July 10. On July 15, a judgement creditor of XYZ's obtains a judgement and execution lien on the property in Iowa. FNB files financing statement with the Florida Secretary of State's office on July 20. If the judgement creditor challenges FNB's status, who prevails? See §§ 9-103(1)(c) and 9-301(1)(b).

Of course, some debtors can be devious; a creditor could lose its perfected, secured party status if the debtor does not deliver the property to the destination state within the 30 day period. Secured creditors are also at risk if a debtor removes collateral from the jurisdiction where the creditor held a perfected interest. If collateral is brought into and kept in a second state, the secured party's filing in the first state does not put third parties on notice in the second state. If collateral location rules were applied, the law of the second state would govern the issue of perfection. The drafters of the Code believed that secured creditors in such situations should have an opportunity to trace collateral taken into another state; thus, they created a *four-month rule.* Section 9-103(1)(d) gives secured creditors who were properly perfected in one state a four-month grace period to take whatever steps are necessary under a second state's law to perfect a security interest in the property removed to the new state. If some further action is required to perfect an interest in the collateral under the law of the second state, section 9-103(1)(d)(i) provides that the security interest lapses at the end of the four month period unless the secured creditor takes appropriate action to perfect. The secured party would be deemed to have an unperfected security interest against a person who purchased the property after it was removed to the second state. However, if the secured party took appropriate action before the four-month period expired, section 9-103(1)(d)(ii) continues the secured party's perfected status.

ROCKWELL INTERNATIONAL CREDIT CORP. v. VALLEY BANK

Idaho Court of Appeals
707 P.2d 517, 41 U.C.C. Rep. Serv. 1803 (1985)

BURNETT, J.

We are asked to determine the priority of competing security interests in collateral moved from one state to another. The district court ruled that a security interest held by Rockwell International Credit Corporation was prior to a security interest held by Valley Bank. For reasons explained below, we reverse.

The facts are undisputed. Valley Bank has a general security interest in "all equipment" of a debtor known as Curtis Press. Rockwell International Credit Corporation has a purchase money security interest in a particular item of equipment acquired by the debtor. Both security interests were duly perfected in Idaho. The instant controversy arose after the debtor moved the equipment to Wyoming and then defaulted in the obligations owed to both creditors.

The Uniform Commercial Code, as amended in 1972, has been adopted in both Idaho and Wyoming. U.C.C. § 9-103(1)(d), codified at I.C. § 28-9-103(l)(d) and at Wyo. Stat. § 34-21-903(a)(iv), provides [the Court cites U.C.C. § 9-103(1)(d)(i)]. In this case, the Wyoming statute required Rockwell and Valley Bank to re-perfect their security interests within four months after the collateral entered that state. For reasons not germane here, neither creditor did so. After this period had expired, Valley Bank located the equipment and re-perfected its security interest by taking possession of the collateral. See U.C.C. § 9-305. Rockwell then belatedly re-perfected its security interest by filing a continuation statement with the Wyoming Secretary of State. When Rockwell asked Valley Bank to relinquish the equipment, the bank declined. This litigation ensued.

Ordinarily, a purchase money security interest, such as the one held by Rockwell, would enjoy priority over the general security interest in "all equipment" held by Valley Bank. See U.C.C. § 9-312(4). But when collateral moves across state lines, it puts security interests at risk. As recited in U.C.C. § 9-103(1)(d), if a security interest is not re-perfected within four months, it "*becomes unperfected at the end of that period and is thereafter deemed to have been unperfected* as against a person who became a *purchaser* after removal (Emphasis added.)

Here, the parties have devoted much effort to debating whether Valley Bank was a "purchaser" as to whom Rockwell's security was "deemed to have been unperfected. . . "The district court treated this as the dispositive question in this case. The court held that although secured creditors could be "purchasers" under the statute, Valley Bank was not such a "purchaser" in Wyoming because it had already acquired its lien against the collateral in Idaho. Therefore, concluded the court, Rockwell retained its priority against Valley Bank.

However, we think the court's reasoning misapprehends the plain language of the statute. As we read 9-103(1)(d), failure to re-perfect within four months carries two distinct consequences.

First, the security interest "becomes unperfected" at the end of the four-month period. Second, it is "deemed to have been unperfected" during the same period as against any person who became a "purchaser" after the collateral was moved. These consequences are textually joined by the conjunctive term "and." The first consequence is prospective; the second is retroactive. If a security interest is not re-perfected within four months, the first consequence is that it becomes unperfected in the future as against the claims of all other secured creditors, regardless of whether they are "purchasers." It remains unperfected until re-perfection occurs. The second consequence is that the security interest also is deemed to have been unperfected as against the claims of"purchasers" during the elapsed four-month period. The second consequence cannot be obviated by tardy re-perfection. See generally J. White & R. Summers, Handbook of The Law Under The Uniform Commercial Code, § 23-18(c) (2d ed. 1980).

The first consequence governs this case. When Rockwell failed to re-perfect within four months, its security interest became unperfected not merely as to purchasers but as to any holder of a competing security interest. Valley Bank held such an interest. Of course, its interest, like Rockwell's had become unperfected by operation of § 9-103(1)(d). But Valley Bank thereafter was the first to re-perfect its interest, doing so by taking possession of the collateral before Rockwell filed with the Secretary of State. Valley Bank's actual knowledge of Rockwell's perfected security interest in Idaho did not relieve Rockwell of its statutory duty to refile in Wyoming. United States v. Handy and Harman, 750 F.2d 777 (9th Cir. 1984). See I*n re Miller*, 14 U.C.C. Rep. Serv. 1042 (Bankr. D. Or. 1974). Valley Bank, in essence, won the re-perfection race and in so doing, it elevated its security interest from a subordinate position to a superior one.

The judgment of the district court is reversed. Costs to appellant, Valley Bank. No attorney fees on appeal.

WALTERS, C.J., and SWANSTROM, J., concur.

QUESTION

What result if the security interest was unperfected in the first state when the collateral was brought into the destination state?

[B] Accounts, General Intangibles and Mobile Goods

The location tests found in section 9-103(1) only apply to items of collateral which have both a physical presence and relatively stable location. If goods are mobile[26] and normally used in more than one jurisdiction, the location test proves unworkable. Since the location of mobile goods is expected to change, a choice of law rule based on location would confuse rather than assist third parties dealing with a debtor. Similarly, intangible collateral has no physical presence or location; thus, the situs rules of 9-103(1) cannot be applied. The drafters of the Code recognized this fact and created a different set of perfection rules for mobile goods, accounts, and general intangibles. Under section 9-103(3), the debtor's location becomes the primary focus for choosing which state's law to apply.

---

[26] "Mobile goods" are defined as equipment normally used in more than one jurisdiction, such as vehicles, trailers, rolling stock, airplanes, shipping containers, road building and construction machinery, and commercial harvesting machinery. Such items are considered mobile goods even if they are not classified by Article 9 as equipment, if the items represent inventory leased or held for lease to others by the debtor. This definition of mobile goods does not include items that would be subject to certificate of title statutes under U.C.C. § 9-103(2).

Typically, a debtor's location is his or her place of business or the chief executive office, if the debtor has more than one place of business. Under this definition, it is possible for a corporate debtor to be incorporated in one state and "located" in another. For example, a debtor incorporated in Delaware but with its chief executive office in St. Louis would be deemed located in Missouri. If a debtor is located in a foreign country which has no provision for recording a security interest, the location of the debtor's principal executive office in the U.S. governs the requirements for filing. If the debtor does not have a principal office in the U.S., perfection for accounts can be achieved by the secured party's giving notification to the account debtor.

Where a debtor who has given a security interest in accounts, general intangibles, or mobile goods, changes location to another state (*i.e.*, moves residence, office, or chief executive office), section 9-103(3)(e) provides a four-month rule similar to that for ordinary goods. Under the provision, a security interest perfected in the former state of location remains perfected for four months after the debtor moves. After that time, the security interest becomes unperfected, unless the secured party has taken appropriate steps to perfect its interest in the new location state.

IN RE GOLF COURSE BUILDERS LEASING

United States Court of Appeals
768 F.2d 1167, 41 U.C.C. Rep. Serv. 1010 (10th Cir. 1985)

KERR, DISTRICT JUDGE

. . . .

The appellant, John B. Jarboe, Trustee for the bankrupt, Golf Course Builders Leasing, Inc., appeals from the decision of the district court reversing the ruling of the United States Bankruptcy Court for the Northern District of Oklahoma.

The facts of the case are not in dispute and many facts were stipulated in the bankruptcy pretrial order. Golf Course Builders Leasing, Inc. (GCB) was incorporated in Colorado in 1975 and later became domesticated to do business in Oklahoma on May 6, 1977 in connection with the filing of an unrelated lawsuit there. GCB was established by its sole shareholder, Lew Hammer, for the purpose of leasing heavy equipment to another corporation owned mainly by Hammer, Lew Hammer, Inc. (LHI). LHI was engaged in the business of general contracting and landscaping of golf courses.

The golf course landscaping business soon became unprofitable, but the heavy equipment which GCB leased was adaptable to mining operations. GCB began using the equipment for coal mining in Oklahoma in September of 1976. At that time, the equipment was moved to Oklahoma on the mineral lease sites, with the exception of two pieces of equipment still located on a previous job site in Idaho. This equipment, too, was later moved to Oklahoma for use in the coal mining operations.

In October of 1976, after mining operations had commenced, Lew Hammer and GCB obtained a loan from the United Bank of Denver (bank) in the amount of $50,000, providing to the bank as security an interest in GCB's accounts receivable. In January of 1977, Hammer, on behalf of GCB, obtained further financing from the bank, executing a $750,000 promissory note. In March 1977, another promissory note was executed to the bank for $50,000. The notes were secured by accounts receivable and inventory belonging to GCB. This inventory consisted mainly of "mobile goods" and "mobile equipment," as characterized by the Uniform Commercial Code.

The funds were intended to be used in purchasing additional equipment for the mining operations and financing statements were timely filed by the bank in Colorado. On September 13, 1977 the bank filed additional financing statements in Oklahoma; however, on September 19, 1977 an involuntary bankruptcy petition was filed by GCB creditors seeking that GCB be declared bankrupt.

Pursuant to an agreement entered into in August of 1977 between GCB and Petroleum Reserve Corporation, GCB sold its equipment in October of 1977, with proceeds totaling $710,070.50. These proceeds were placed with the bank in accordance with a court approved stipulation. The proceeds from GCB's receivables amounted to $77,900, which the trustee held after collection. The trustee filed a complaint in bankruptcy court alleging that the bank was not entitled to the proceeds from the sale of the mobile equipment because it had not perfected its security interest in Oklahoma until after it had become aware of GCB's insolvent status.

With regard to the perfection of a security interest under the Uniform Commercial Code of both Colorado and Oklahoma, the provision concerning the conflict of laws on "mobile goods" is identical for each state. That language provides:

> (2) If the *chief place of business* of a debtor is in this state, this Article governs the validity and perfection of a security interest and the possibility and effect of proper filing with regard to general intangibles or with regard to goods of a type which are normally used in more than one jurisdiction (such as automotive equipment, rolling stock, airplanes, road building equipment, commercial harvesting equipment, construction machinery and the like) if such goods are classified as equipment or classified as inventory by reason of their being leased by the debtor to others. Otherwise, *the law* (including the conflict of laws rules) *of the jurisdiction where such chief place of business is located shall govern*. If the chief place of business is located in a jurisdiction which does not provide for perfection of the security interest by filing or recording in that jurisdiction, then the security interest may be perfected by filing in this state.

Okla. Stat. tit. 12A, § 9-103(2)(1972); Colo. Rev. Stat. § 4-9-103(2)(1973) (emphasis added).

The bankruptcy court in construing Okla. Stat. tit. 12A, § 9-103(2), held that the "chief place of business" of GCB was Oklahoma, and that, therefore, Oklahoma was the proper place for filing financing statements and perfecting the bank's security interests in the mobile goods. Thus, the Colorado filings by the bank were ineffective. Further, the bankruptcy court held that the filings made by the bank in Oklahoma only a few days before bankruptcy proceedings were instituted constituted a voidable preference since the bank had reasonable cause to believe GCB was insolvent at the time.

Other portions of the bankruptcy court's holding concerning other security interests are not before this court on appeal.

The district court in reversing the decision of the bankruptcy court, found that the determination of "chief place of business" under § 9-103(2) was a question of law and that the bankruptcy court had erred in finding GCB's "chief place of business" to be Oklahoma. The district court held that as Colorado was GCB's "chief place of business," the bank had properly perfected its security interests in Colorado and should, therefore, have been adjudged a secured creditor. The district court never reached the voidable preference issue.

. . . .

We agree with the district court that here the determination of GCB's "chief place of business" is a question of law, there being no dispute as to the facts. Furthermore, we conclude that the bankruptcy court erred in its legal conclusion that Oklahoma was the "chief place of business" because it misconstrued § 9-103(2), thus failing to apply the correct legal standard.

The bankruptcy court relied heavily and almost solely on the "volume of business" test set forth in *Tatelbaum v. Commerce Investment Co.*, 257 Md. 194, 262 A.2d 494 (1970), 7 U.C.C. Rep. Serv. (Callaghan) 406 (1970), in concluding that Oklahoma was GCB's "chief place of business." In *Tatelbaum*, the court determined that "chief place of business" under Maryland's § 9-401 relating to the recordation place of financing statement was analogous to that under § 9-103 and that it meant the place where the corporate debtor conducted the greatest volume of business activity. *Tatelbaum*, 262 A.2d at 498. The bankruptcy judge, after reviewing the facts, concluded that GCB conducted its greatest volume of business in Oklahoma and that Oklahoma was, therefore, the "chief place of business."

In the present case, it is undisputed that GCB's volume of business was greatest in Oklahoma. However, we agree with the district court's reliance on the Ninth Circuit case of *In re J. A. Thompson & Son, Inc. v. Shepherd Machinery Co.*, 665 F.2d 941, 949-950 (9th Cir. 1982), that volume of business may be a factor but it cannot be the only factor in determining "chief place of business."

The official comments to code section 9-103 are important in providing guidance as to what the drafters of the code intended as the "chief place of business" for multi-state operators. The official comment by the drafters of the Uniform Commercial Code § 9-103, comment 3 provides in part:

> "Chief place of business" does not mean the place of incorporation: *it means the place from which in fact the debtor manages the main part of his business operations. This is the place where persons dealing with the debtor would normally look for credit information, and is the appropriate place for filing.* The term "chief place of business" is not defined in this Section or elsewhere in this Act. Doubt may arise as to which is the "chief place of business" of a multi-state enterprise with decentralized, autonomous regional offices. A secured party in such a case may easily protect himself at no great additional burden by filing in each of several places. Although under this formula, as under the accounts receivable rule stated in subsection (1), there will be doubtful situations, the subsection states a rule which will be simple to apply in most cases, which will make it possible to dispense with much burdensome and useless filing, and which will operate to preserve a security interest in the case of non-scheduled operations.

(emphasis added).

. . . .

The undisputed facts of this case demonstrate that during the period of GCB's operations, Lew Hammer maintained the office for LHI at 2385 South Lipan Street, Denver, Colorado. From this office Hammer largely conducted the business of GCB. Hammer conducted much of the negotiations and business transactions for GCB from this Denver office, spending only an average of two days per week in Oklahoma supervising the mining operations there. There was no permanent office in Oklahoma for GCB. Rather, temporary office locations existed at each mine site; these temporary office locations in turn moved with the mining operations. All officers and directors of GCB were located in Colorado, and on the Oklahoma domestication certificate, Lew Hammer was named as the registered agent, listing his home address in Colorado.

All the financial records of GCB were maintained at the Denver office, including accounts receivables and invoices. Invoices were paid by the Denver office, even though at times they may have first been sent to a mine site office for approval by the mining supervisor. The payroll of GCB was prepared in the Denver office and forwarded to the mine site offices in Oklahoma. All monthly, quarterly, and annual reports were prepared at GCB's office in Denver and all of GCB's accountants were located in Colorado. GCB acquired all of its liability and worker's compensation insurance through the Denver office and much of the equipment owned by GCB was purchased or leased by Hammer through the Denver office.

Applying this two-fold inquiry, we agree with the district court that the conclusion to be drawn from these facts is that GCB's place of management and executive office was in Colorado. Furthermore, creditors seeking information would have likely looked to Lew Hammer, the president and key manager of GCB, who mainly worked and lived in Colorado and had access to GCB's financial records in Colorado.

We hold that Colorado was GCB's "chief place of business" and that the district court was correct in so concluding. Thus, the bank properly perfected its security interests in the "mobile goods" or equipment in Colorado. It is, therefore, unnecessary to reach the voidable preference issue concerning the filings made in Oklahoma.

The decision of the district court is, therefore,

Affirmed

NOTE

The one category of accounts to which section 9-103(3) does not apply is an account that results from the sale of minerals, oil, or gas from a wellhead or minehead. In these cases, the law of the state where the minehead or wellhead is situated applies. See U.C.C. § 9-103(5). The financing statement covering such collateral must contain a description of the real estate and must be filed locally. This special rule applies when a security interest attaches to minerals prior to, or upon, extraction, and to the accounts created by a sale of such minerals. The reasons for this rule are explained in Official Comment 8 to § 9-103.

[C] Chattel Paper

Because of its hybrid nature, chattel paper presents a different conflict of law problem. Recall that chattel paper is a special type of collateral which has characteristics attributable to both ordinary goods and to accounts or general intangibles. Under section 9-105(1)(b), chattel paper means a writing or writings that evidence both a monetary obligation and a security in, or lease of, specific goods. Should the rules of perfection be governed by the location of the goods or the location of the debtor? Section 9-103(4) combines the rules of location for security interests in chattel paper. If a security interest in chattel paper is to be perfected by filing, the law of the state where the debtor is located (the debtor's residence, place of business, or chief executive office) governs perfection. If perfection of chattel paper occurs by possession, the law of the place of location governs perfection.

[D] Uncertificated Investment Securities

U.C.C. § 9-103(6) states that the governing choice of law rules for uncertificated investment securities are those of the jurisdiction where the issuing business is organized. To illustrate, assume that the issuer of uncertificated stock is incorporated in New York, but has its principal office in Illinois. If the owner of the stock, who lives in Iowa, grants a security interest to a lender located in Ohio, the law of New York governs the perfection or nonperfection of the Ohio lender's security interest.

If the stock is represented by a certificated security, the law governing perfection as to instruments governs. See U.C.C. § 9-103(1).

[E] Certificates of Title

In some cases, collateral involved in multiple state transactions is covered in part by Federal Acts, *e.g.* aircraft, or by state certificate of title laws. Many states have certificate of title statutes which cover a wide range of mobile goods such as automobiles, motorcycles, trailers, mobile homes, boats, and tractors. Security interests in goods covered by such statutes usually require notation of the creditor's interest on the certificate of title as a condition of perfection. Creditors therefore perfect their Article 9 security interests by complying with the certificate of title statutes rather than by filing a financing statement. See U.C.C. § 9-302(3). Under section 9-103(2)(b), the law of the state issuing the certificate governs perfection. Two problems arise with this requirement: 1) removal of the goods to a different state; and 2) sales to non-business buyers.

Since the key to perfection is public notice, the failure to note a security interest on the certificate of title when a vehicle is moved to a different state, results in insufficient notice to parties in the second state. Generally, when a vehicle moves to a new state, the expectation is that the new certificate of title will reflect liens on the vehicle from the old state and thus provide third parties with notice. However, not all states have certificate of title laws. Further, some states do not require notation of liens as a means of perfection.

Under section 9-103(2)(b), the law of the state issuing a certificate of title governs perfection. Where a security interest is noted on the certificate of title, the secured party's interest is perfected by the notation and remains perfected even if the property is removed to another jurisdiction. The law of the state issuing the certificate continues to govern so long as the certificate of title is not surrendered and the vehicle is not registered in that new jurisdiction. If the goods are registered in the new state, the secured party has four months after removal to take appropriate steps in the new jurisdiction to record its interest. If the secured party fails to take action within the four months, the creditor loses its perfected status. See Comment 4(c) to § 9-103.[27]

If a security interest is perfected other than by notation on the certificate of title (non-certificate state) and the property is moved to a different state which issues a "clean" certificate of title—one that does not show the creditor's security interest— the secured party's perfected status in the original state will be lost four months after the vehicle was removed from the original jurisdiction unless the creditor takes action within the four months to perfect in the second state. U.C.C. § 9-103(2)(c).

---

27 As a practical matter, whenever a clean certificate of title is issued by the state of removal, the secured party will have difficulty getting its interest noted on the certificate, absent cooperation from the debtor, who now has a clean certificate of title. In such cases, the secured party may be forced to perfect within the four-month period by repossessing the property.

Where a security interest is perfected in any manner (by notation on a certificate of title or by filing) and the property is removed to another state which issues a "clean" certificate of title, the creditor's security interest will be subordinate to the rights of a nonprofessional buyer (someone who is not a dealer) who gives value and purchases the property without knowledge of the security interest. This rule applies without regard to the four-month period. See U.C.C. § 9-103(2)(d) and Comment 4(e). The protective rule for non-business buyers does not operate in situations where property is brought into a certificate state and the state issuing the clean certificate indicates that the vehicle *may* be subject to a security interest in another state. Such an indication provides sufficient warning to such non-business buyers. In such a case, the four-month rule would apply and the secured party may take the necessary steps to perfect its interest in the new jurisdiction during that four month period.

TRANS CANADA CREDIT CORP. v. KOSACK

Superior Court of Pennsylvania
404 Pa. Super. 401, 590 A.2d 1295 (1991)

KELLY, J.

In this opinion, we are called upon to determine whether the plaintiff-appellee's security interest in an automobile which was perfected in Canada remained superior to that of defendant-appellant who subsequently purchased and resold the automobile without notice of the foreign security interest. We find that the foreign security interest is valid and superior over the interests of the defendant-appellant pursuant to 75 Pa.C.S.A. § 1132(c)(2)(ii).

The facts have been succinctly set forth by the trial court as follows.

The Plaintiff, a Canadian Corporation, lent money to DiCicco and secured its interest in the loan proceeds with a chattel mortgage. By the terms of the chattel mortgage, the Plaintiff could take immediate possession of the vehicle upon either DiCicco's removal of the vehicle from Canada or DiCicco's sale or transfer of vehicle. DiCicco later removed the vehicle from Canada and obtained a Pennsylvania Certificate of Title on or about April 14, 1987[,] which did not have an endorsement indicating Plaintiff's lien as an encumbrance on the vehicle. The title certificate in Pennsylvania did, however, bear a notation indicating that the vehicle was an "out of state" vehicle.

On May 16, 1987, DiCicco sold the secured vehicle to the Defendant, a Pennsylvania automobile broker and dealer for over forty years. Kosack subsequently resold the vehicle at an interstate auto auction.

. . . .

Not until January of 1988 did Plaintiff make application in Pennsylvania pursuant to 75 Pa.C.S.A. 1132(c)(2)(ii) to perfect its security interest. This allows a security interest to be perfected in the Commonwealth of Pennsylvania before or after the expiration of a four month period within which an out-of-state lien might otherwise be perfected under the laws of the jurisdiction where the motor vehicle was located when the secured interest attached. Thus, Plaintiff styles this filing in January of 1988 a "reperfection" of the security interest. Tr.Ct.Op. at 2-3.

Trans Canada Credit Corporation, Ltd., plaintiff-appellee, after several demands made to Richard Kosack d/b/a Family Motors, defendant-appellant, which were refused, filed the instant action demanding $ 4875.00, the uncontested fair market value of the automobile at the time defendant-appellant re-sold the automobile at an auto auction. A nonjury trial resulted in a verdict in favor of defendant-appellant. Upon consideration of post-trial motions, the trial court granted judgment non obstante veredicto in favor of plaintiff-appellee.

In this timely appeal, defendant-appellant raises the following two issues for our consideration.

I. DID THE APPELLEE HAVE A PERFECTED SECURITY INTEREST WITHIN THE MEANING OF 75 PA.C.S. SECTION 1132(C)(2)(ii) AT THE TIME THE VEHICLE IN QUESTION WAS SOLD BY THE APPELLANT?

II. DID THE TRIAL COURT ERROR [sic] IN GRANTING A JUDGMENT NOT WITHSTANDING THE VERDICT?

Defendant-appellant's Brief at 3. After a careful review of the applicable authorities, the parties' briefs, the record and the well-reasoned opinion of the Honorable Bernard S. McGowan, we affirm the first issue on the basis of the trial court opinion as set forth below.

Plaintiff's position is that 75 Pa.C.S.A. 1132(c)(2)(ii) in literal terms provides:

> (ii) If the name of the lienholder is not shown on an existing certificate of title issued by that jurisdiction, the security interest continues perfected in this Commonwealth for four months after a first certificate of title of the vehicle is issued in this Commonwealth, and, thereafter if, within the four-month period, it is perfected in this Commonwealth. The security interest may also be perfected in this Commonwealth after the expiration of the four-month period in which case perfection dates from the time of perfection in this Commonwealth.

Plaintiff argues that where an out-of-state lien is not shown on the existing certificate of title, a security interest continues perfected in the Commonwealth for four months after a first certificate of title of the vehicle is issued in the Commonwealth regardless of whether the security interest holder applies for its perfection before or after the expiration of the four months. The Defendant argues that Plaintiff, not having perfected it in four months, can only have it perfected from the time of actual application.

The Canadian title proffered to the Commonwealth for retitling indisputably did not note the encumbrance of Plaintiff's interest from Canada.

However, as Plaintiff points out, there was a notation on the Pennsylvania title which Defendant acknowledged to be an indication through the letter code "F" that the Pennsylvania title was derived from a prior out-of-state title which should have placed Defendant on inquiry notice. Defendant was a dealer in automobiles for some forty years and was not unsophisticated in the matter of auto titles and security interests.

The plain language of the statute gives an absolute and unconditional four-month period within which an out-of-state security interest, if the same were perfected under the law of the jurisdiction where the vehicle was located when the security interest attached, continues perfected in the Commonwealth of Pennsylvania for four months following a Pennsylvania issuance of title.

By reason of the foregoing recited dates, it is clear that Trans Canada's security interest was perfected during the period of time that DiCicco sold the vehicle to the Defendant and at the time when the Defendant sold the vehicle at the Butler auto auction. The law of Ontario which is the applicable out-of-state law does not require notice of an encumbrance to be noted on the

Ontario title. To the contrary, under Ontario law, the interest is perfected when a financial statement is registered. The Defendant does not contest Plaintiff's statement that the Canadian security interest was perfected whenever a financing statement was filed with the appropriate authorities in Canada. With Canada not requiring a further notation of an encumbrance on a certificate of title to an automobile, this case is identical with a case decided under virtually the exact provisions of the Uniform Commercial Code containing the same provisions as the aforementioned § (c)(2)(ii). This case concerned a four month unconditional grace period for an out-of-state lienholder with a perfected security interest in the foreign state to have his lien considered perfected in the state to which the vehicle is removed.

In *IAC, Ltd. v. Princeton Porsche-Audi*, 75 N.J. 379, 382 A.2d 1125 (1978), the New Jersey Supreme Court held that the four-month grace period was absolute and unconditional when the Defendant was a dealer in automobiles rather than an innocent consumer purchasing for value. The exact same result is dictated under 75 Pa.C.S. 1132(c)(2)(ii).

Counsel for either party at the time of the case or thereafter was unable to cite any Pennsylvania cases touching on this issue. At Post Trial Argument, the case of *IAC, Ltd. v. Princeton Porsche-Audi, supra,* was cited to the Court as being precisely on point. The reasoning of the New Jersey Supreme Court is persuasive. If the title to an automobile originates in a jurisdiction where there is no requirement that a perfected security interest appear on the face of the title and the automobile is brought into another jurisdiction and a new certificate of title issued showing no security interest, the holder of the security interest continues to have a perfected security interest for four months from the date of issuance of a new title. It is of no moment that the security holder did not perfect its interest until after the four month period expired. The purpose of the Statute is to give the security interest holder a four month period to recover the auto without being foreclosed by the defense of a bona fide purchase for value. This is particularly appropriate when a title indicates a predecessor title of foreign origination. The purpose of this foreign title notation can only be to alert a purchaser that reliance cannot be placed on the absence of an encumbrance of the fact of the present title or that further inquiry as to the foreign title of organization should be made. This is particularly so when the purchaser is a dealer in automobiles and not an unsophisticated consumer. Tr.Ct.Op. at 3-7.

. . . .

In conclusion, we affirm defendant-appellant's first contention on the reasoning of the trial court opinion as adopted herein, and we affirm the entry of the judgment n.o.v.

Judgment Affirmed.

PROBLEM 17.5

Miles purchased a car from a Chrysler Corporation dealership in New Hampshire. The certificate of title properly reflected Chrysler's security interest. Miles then took the vehicle into New York and obtained registration and license plates, but no certificate of title from that state. Five months later, Miles files for creditor protection in bankruptcy. The trustee challenges

Chrysler's claimed security interest. You are the judge, how do you decide? See U.C.C. § 9-103(2)(b) and *In re Males*, 999 F.2d 607 (2d Cir. 1993).

CHAPTER 18

PRIORITIES

§ 18.01 Introduction

Read U.C.C. §§ 9-201, 9-301 and 9-312.

Priority issues represent the heart of secured transactions. When a debtor encounters financial difficulties, that debtor's creditors will often rush to seize the debtor's property. More often than not, the debtor does not have enough property to satisfy the claims that creditors might make. In many instances, creditors will claim property in which other parties also claim an interest. Where competing claims to collateral exist, which claimant should prevail and on what basis? Section 9-201 states the general rule concerning the validity of security agreements: secured parties prevail against purchasers of collateral and against other creditors. Section 9-301 provides a broad exception to this general rule: lien creditors will have superior rights in collateral over unperfected secured parties.[1] U.C.C. § 9-301(1)(b).

Part three of Article 9 also provides various rules for determining priority in certain types of collateral. These rules recognize three basic categories of competing claimants: 1) lien creditors (see U.C.C. § 9-301); 2) buyers in the ordinary course (see U.C.C. §§ 9-306 and 9-307); and 3) other Article 9 secured parties (see U.C.C. §§ 9-312 and 9-306 through 9-316).[2] Under the Code, the priorities of creditors are based upon several factors including the types of interests in collateral, the specific collateral, the time the interest was taken, and the time the claimant perfected the interest. Although the rules of priority have provided quite a degree of certainty, there are some basic policy issues that remain open questions. The Code structure gives the first party to file, superior claims on the debtor's property. U.C.C. § 9-312(5). Because omnibus security agreements can be, and often are, entered into, some critics of Article 9 argue that the first creditor has the potential for unfairly monopolizing a debtor's access to credit. These critics note that meritorious claims may go unrewarded because a secured creditor relationship exists. As you proceed through the chapter, consider this tension between economic efficiency and fairness. Could a better balance be created?

---

[1] A lien creditor is anyone with an interest in, or charge against, property to receive payment of a debt or performance of an obligation. Lien creditor status can arise by judicial process, by statute, or by agreement. Article 9 applies to consensual lien agreements. Recall that section 544(a) of the Bankruptcy Codegrants a statutory, hypothetical lienholder status to the trustee in bankruptcy. Judicial lienholder status arises whenever a party obtains a judgment against another and seeks to seize property to satisfy the court's remedy award.

[2] Other possible claimants recognized by other sections of Article 9 and non-U.C.C. law include unsecured creditors, real property lienholders claiming an interest in fixtures, consignors, and the federal government.

§ 18.02 First in Time Rule

Read U.C.C. § 9-312(5).

One of the basic principles of a filing system is that the first secured party to file should prevail. The party who claims a subsequent interest in property has notice of the prior interest from the filing and may decide to assume the risk of making a loan as a junior creditor. A second-to-file party, a later creditor, or a later trustee in bankruptcy, may seek to have the first creditor's filing invalidated because of a deficient security agreement, an inadequate collateral description, a defective financing statement, or because the first party filed in the wrong place. Invalidation of the first creditor's earlier interest would, of course, elevate the later party's claim. The next case provides a rather long discussion of the simple concept of priority to the first party to file. The case also explains some of the ways in which a party will seek to challenge another secured creditor's claimed priority.

UNITED STATES v. BRANCH BANKING & TRUST CO.

United States District Court, E.D. North Carolina
11 U.C.C. Rep. Serv. 2d 351 (1990)

FOX, DISTRICT JUDGE.

This is a civil action in which the United States of America, on behalf of the Farmers Home Administration ("FmHA"), seeks damages for the conversion of property in which it claims a perfected security interest, specifically, a 1980 Model 1486 International Harvester tractor and a Model 2020 John Deere tractor. The defendant, Branch Banking and Trust Company ("BB&T"), claims a purchase money security interest in the subject collateral and further asserts that it did not convert the same since its security interests had priority over the security interests held by FmHA. Hence, the case focuses on the priority to be accorded conflicting security interests held by FmHA and BB&T in the two tractors.

Discovery in this case ended November 3, 1989. The plaintiff filed its motion for summary judgment on November 17, 1989. BB&T filed its cross-motion for summary judgment on November 30, 1989. The matter is now ripe for disposition.

UNDISPUTED FACTS

Between 1972 and 1985, Mr. and Mrs. Ralph L. Ginn ("the Ginns"), residents of Greene County, North Carolina, borrowed substantial sums of money from FmHA. Over this thirteen year period FmHA loaned the Ginns the aggregate sum of $264,510.00. The Ginns furnished FmHA numerous financial statements in connection with said loans.

On January 20, 1977 FmHA filed a financing statement executed by the Ginns, in the Greene County Public Registry, said financing statement stating "Collateral is or includes Crops & Equipment." Statements of continuation of said financing statement were filed on September 11, 1981, January 18, 1982, March 28, 1983, and March 29, 1983.

Beginning in 1983, the Ginns turned to BB&T for a portion of their financial requirements. Mr. Ralph M. Becton was the loan officer at BB&T who responded to the Ginns' loan requests. In 1983 BB&T made its first loan to the Ginns, who executed their first promissory note to BB&T

evidencing the same. At that time, Mr. Becton visited their home in order to verify their county of residence. He visually inspected the home and the roads leading to and from it. Additionally, Mr. Becton visited the Wayne County, North Carolina, Register of Deeds and located financing statements filed against property belonging to the Ginns. Based upon this information, Mr. Becton mistakenly believed the Ginns to be residents of Wayne County, and determined that financing statements evidencing BB&T's security interest in the Ginns' property should be filed with the Wayne County Register of Deeds.

On February 16, 1984, FmHA and the Ginns executed a security agreement wherein the Ginns granted to the former a security interest in all farm equipment whether then owned or after acquired. An additional statement of continuation of the 1977 financing statement was filed in Greene County on the same date. It is this security agreement under which FmHA claims a security interest in the two tractors subsequently acquired by the Ginns as hereinafter discussed.

On October 25, 1984, the Ginns executed and delivered a second promissory note to BB&T in the amount of $15,500.00. They used the proceeds of this loan to purchase a 1980 Model 1486 International Harvester tractor from J & L Tractor Company. In a security agreement executed on the same date, the Ginns gave BB&T a security interest in the tractor as collateral for the loan. The financing statement reflecting such security interest was filed, improperly, with the Wayne County Register of Deeds, on October 31, 1984.

During 1984 and 1985, the Ginns furnished financial statements to FmHA in connection with their FmHA loans. In the course of such negotiations, Mr. Ginn told Mr. Moses H. Ramsey, the Assistant County Supervisor of FmHA, that BB&T had a lien on the Model 1486 International Harvester tractor and that he was making payments to BB&T on a loan incurred to purchase the same. Mr. Ginn's affidavit is corroborated by a FmHA financial statement which he signed in December, 1984, which notes under the section labelled "Liens on Chattels and Crops" that BB&T had a lien on a tractor, that the final due date of the debt secured by the lien was December 31, 1987, that the annual installment was $6,901.00, and that the unpaid balance was $15,740.00. In addition, FmHA was furnished a financial statement dated May 20, 1985, which under Section K, labelled "Debt Repayment," lists the lien on the International Harvester tractor by BB&T.

On January 8, 1985, the Ginns executed and delivered a promissory note to BB&T in the amount of $19,350.00. They used a portion of these loan proceeds to purchase a 1970 Model 2020 John Deere tractor from Dick Smith Equipment Company. In a security agreement executed on the same date, the Ginns gave BB&T a security interest in this tractor as collateral for the loan. The stated purpose of the second loan made to the Ginns (as evidenced by a notation on the promissory note evidencing the same) was to "pay off note 02 and furnish $3,300 for purchase of tractor." Business Loan Presentation, Defendant's Exhibit C. The reference "note 02" implicitly is a reference to the Ginns' second note evidencing the October 25, 1984, loan made by BB&T to the Ginns. The financing statement reflecting BB&T's security interest was filed, improperly, on January 17, 1985, with the Wayne County Register of Deeds.

Mr. Ginn and his wife filed a Chapter 7 bankruptcy petition on April 9, 1986. On May 29, 1986, an order was entered lifting the automatic stay and allowing BB&T to proceed against its security interest in the two tractors along with other equipment. An order to abandon these two tractors was made by the trustee of the bankruptcy estate on July 11, 1986. Pursuant to these orders, BB&T had the 1980 Model 1486 International Harvester and 1970 Model 2020 John Deere tractors sold for $9,000.00 and $2,300.00 respectively during the first week of September 1986.

. . . .

N.C. Gen. Stat. § 25-9-312(5)(a)[UCC § 9-312] (1988) provides that:

> (5) In all cases not governed by other rules stated in this section (including cases of purchase money security interests which do not qualify for the special priorities set forth in subsections (3) and (4) of this section), priority between conflicting security interests in the same collateral shall be determined according to the following rules:
>
> > (a) Conflicting security interests rank according to priority in time of filing or perfection. Priority dates from the time a filing is first made covering the collateral or the time the security interest is first perfected, whichever is earlier, provided that there is no period thereafter when there is neither filing nor perfection.

A security interest in equipment is "perfected" when it has "attached" and when a financing statement has been filed. See N.C. Gen. Stat. § 25-9-302 [U.C.C. § 9-302] and 9-303(1). A security interest "attaches" when "(a) the collateral is in the possession of the secured party pursuant to agreement, or the debtor has signed a security agreement which contains a description of the collateral . . .and (b) value has been given; and (c) the debtor has rights in the collateral." N.C. Gen. Stat. § 25-9-203(1)[UCC § 9-203]. A financing statement describing the collateral may be filed before the security interest attaches, N.C. Gen. Stat. § 25-9-402(1)[UCC § 9-402], and in this case the security interest "is perfected at the time it attaches." N.C. Gen. Stat. § 25-9-303(1)[UCC § 9-303].

In the instant case, FmHA first filed a financing statement, executed by the Ginns, which states that "Collateral is or Includes Crops & Equipment," in the Greene County Public Registry, on January 20, 1977. FmHA filed continuation filing statements regularly, the last on February 16, 1984. FmHA's January 20, 1977 financing statement, as continued, was thus effective until February 16, 1989. See N.C. Gen. Stat. § 25-9-403. While FmHA's February 1984 security agreement contained an after-acquired property clause, covering "[a]ll farm and other equipment," neither its January 20, 1977, financing statement nor its subsequently filed statements of continuation (including that of February 16, 1984) disclosed, per se, that its collateral included the same. If FmHA's 1977 financing statement as continued was sufficient at law to include the after-acquired Model 2020 John Deere tractor, FmHA's security interest therein was perfected upon the Ginns' acquisition of the tractor in January 1985 (*i.e.*, (a) upon the debtor's acquisition of rights therein, (b) value therefor having been given by FmHA for a security interest therein, (c) the tractor being covered by the February 16, 1984, security agreement's after-acquired property clause, and (d) the 1977 financing statement having been filed prior thereto.) As FmHA's priority ranks "according to priority in time of filing or perfection" under N.C. Gen. Stat. § 25-9-312(5)(a)[U.C.C. § 9-312], its priority would date from January 20, 1977, the date it filed the first financing statement covering the Ginns' equipment.

However, BB&T contests the relevance of the foregoing, correctly noting that a later perfected purchase money security interest in collateral other than inventory may take priority over a prior perfected security interest in the same collateral. See N.C. Gen. Stat. § 25-9-312(4)[U.C.C. § 9-312]. BB&T's January 8, 1985, transaction with the Ginns qualifies as a purchase money security interest because BB&T gave "value to enable the debtor to acquire rights in or the use of [the] collateral". N.C. Gen. Stat. § 25-9-107(b)[U.C.C. § 9-107]. BB&T, however, did not properly perfect its purchase money security interest in the collateral, because it did not file the financing statement in the county of the debtors' residence. See N.C. Gen. Stat. § 25-9-401(1)(a)[U.C.C. § 9-401]. Thus, nothing else appearing, the priority of BB&T's purchase money security interest in the Model 2020 John Deere tractor falls under the general priority rule of N.C. Gen. Stat. § 25-9-312(5)(a)[U.C.C. § 9-312]. See J. White & R. Summers, Uniform Commercial Code, Vol. 2, § 26-5, at 515 (if the purchase money lender fails to comply with Subsection (4) of § 9-312, priority is "clearly governed" by Subsection (5)) (footnote omitted). Therefore, if FmHA's January 20, 1977, financing statement, as continued, was sufficient to include after-acquired equipment (notwithstanding its failure explicitly to identify the same) the priority of FmHA's perfected security interest would date back to January 20, 1977. In such event, FmHA's security interest in the tractor would have priority, because BB&T's January 8, 1985, purchase money security interest was never perfected.

Whether or not after-acquired property of the type identified as collateral in a financing statement must be identified, per se, in order to have a validly perfected security interest therein, is apparently a question of first impression under North Carolina law.

The applicable law is found in N.C. Gen. Stat. § 25-9-402(1) [U.C.C. § 9-402], which provides that:

> (1) A financing statement is sufficient if it gives the names of the debtor and the secured party, is signed by the debtor, gives an address of the secured party from which information concerning the security interest may be obtained, gives a mailing address of the debtor and contains a statement indicating the types , or describing the items, of collateral
>
> . . . .

Thus, a creditor can either give a detailed description of each item of collateral, "if it is convenient for him to do so," or he can "list the collateral by types if he so chooses." In the *Matter of H.L. Bennett Co.*, 588 F.2d 389, 393 [25 U.C.C. Rep. Serv. 284] (3d Cir.. 1978). "Equipment," as designated in the FmHA financing statement, is a "type" of personal property defined in N.C. Gen. Stat. § 25-9-109(2)[U.C.C. § 9-109].

By authorizing filing under "types,"

> This section adopts the system of notice filing which proved successful under the Uniform Trust Receipts Act. What is required to be filed is not, as under chattel mortgage and conditional sales acts, the security agreement itself, but only a simple notice which may be filed before the security interest attaches or thereafter. The notice itself indicates merely that the secured party who has filed may have a security interest in the collateral described. Further inquiry from the parties concerned will be necessary to disclose the complete state of affairs. Section 9-208 provides a statutory procedure under which the secured party, at the debtor's request, may be required to make disclosure . . . .
>
> However, even in the case of filings that do not necessarily involve a series of transactions the financing statement is effective to encompass transactions under a security agreement not in existence and not contemplated at the time the notice was filed, if the description of collateral in the financing statement is broad enough to encompass them. Similarly, the financing statement is valid to cover after-acquired property and future advances under security agreements whether or not mentioned in the financing statement —.

N.C. Gen. Stat. § 25-9-402[U.C.C. § 9-402], Amended Official Comment [sic; "Draftsmen's Comment to the 1972 Official Text"] 2. See also *Evans v. Everett*, 279 N.C. 352, 183 S.E.2d 109 [9 U.C.C. Rep. Serv. 769] (1971) (N.C. Gen. Stat. § 25-9-402 [U.C.C. § 9-402] adopts a system of notice filing).

"An overwhelming majority of cases have held that a Code category such as . . .equipment is alone enough to cover after acquired property of the same type." J. White & R. Summers, *supra*, at 381 (footnote omitted). See also R. Anderson, Uniform Commercial Code, Vol. 8, § 9-204:10, at 704-05 (3d ed. 1985) ("[T]here is no requirement that the financing statement contain an after-acquired property clause, and the priority of the security interest in after-acquired property is not affected by the omission of such a clause from the financing statement.") (footnote omitted). The rationale behind this majority rule is the same rationale expressed *supra*, in Amended Official Comment [sic; "Draftsmen's Comment to the 1972 Official Text"] 2 to N.C. Gen. Stat. § 25-9-402: [U.C.C. § 9-402] "[b]ecause the Code authorizes a filing under 'types', it already imposes the burden on the searcher to determine exactly what property is covered." J. White & R. Summers, *supra*, at 381.

Moreover, this liberal construction toward the validity of the financing statement is supported by Amended Official Comment [sic; "Draftsmen's Comment to the 1972 Official Text"] 5 to N.C. Gen. Stat. § 25-9-204. . . .:

> The effect [of] after-acquired property and future advance clauses in the security agreement should not be confused with the use of financing statements in notice filing. The references to after-acquired property clauses and future advance clauses in Section 9-204 are limited to security agreements. This section follows Section 9-203, the section requiring a written security agreement, and its purpose is to make clear that confirmatory agreements are not necessary where the basic agreement has the clauses mentioned. This section has no reference to the operation of financing statements. The filing of a financing statement is effective to perfect security interests as to which the other required elements for perfection exist, whether the security agreement involved is one existing at the date of filing with an after-acquired property clause or a future advance clause, or whether the applicable security agreement is executed later . . . . Indeed, Section 9-402(1) expressly contemplates that a financing statement may be filed when there is no security agreement. There is no need to refer to after-acquired property or future advances in the financing statement. . . .

While the Comments are not binding, they should be given "substantial weight" in interpreting the legislative intent of the Code. *In re Bristol Assocs., Inc.*, 505 F.2d 1056 [15 U.C.C. Rep. Serv. 561] (3d Cir. 1974). This court concludes that the Official Comments make it quite clear that "the legislature did not intend that an after-acquired provision be necessary in the financing statement to have a validly perfected security interest in property of the 'type' set forth in the financing statement which is purchased subsequent to the filing." *In re Taylor*, 45 B.R. 643, 646 [41 U.C.C. Rep. Serv. 1832] (Bankr. M.D. Pa. 1985).

The court thus holds that FmHA's 1977 financing statement and the statements of continuation thereof were sufficient to give notice to a third party creditor that it should contact the secured party—FmHA—to inquire as to the extent of the security interest. Had BB&T contacted FmHA in January 1985 (when it negotiated the promissory note and security agreement with the Ginns which enabled them to purchase the Model 2020 John Deere tractor), it would have discovered that FmHA's February 16, 1984, security agreement with the Ginns contained an after-acquired property clause covering equipment. Therefore, a perfected security interest existed in favor of FmHA in favor of the Model 2020 John Deere tractor, and BB&T had constructive notice of FmHA's security interest even though the description of collateral in the financing statement and continuation statements did not include an after-acquired equipment clause. . .. . .Thus, FmHA's security interest in the Model 2020 John Deere tractor, for which a filing was first made on January 20, 1977, has priority over BB&T's unperfected purchase money security interest of January 8, 1985, under N.C. Gen. Stat. § 25-9-312(5)(a)[U.C.C. § 9-312].

There is, however, another statutory provision in the Code which BB&T seeks to use to avoid this result. If BB&T can prove that, notwithstanding its erroneous filing, FmHA had "knowledge" (which N.C. Gen. Stat. § 25-1-201(25)[UCC § 1-201] defines as "actual knowledge") of the contents of BB&T's January 8, 1985, financing statement, then BB&T's concomitant purchase money security interest would have a perfected status as against FmHA's security interest, N.C. Gen. Stat. § 25-9-401(2), [UCC § 9-401] and would have special priority under N.C. Gen. Stat. § 25-9-312(4)[UCC § 9-312], as discussed *supra*. (The "knowledge" element of the statute is the only element contested by the parties. FmHA does not argue that BB&T's filing was not "made in good faith.")

There is a range of authority as to the minimum level of knowledge short of reading the document that will satisfy the actual knowledge standard. See, *e.g., Franklin Nat'l Inv. Corp. v. American Swiss Parts Co.,* 42 Mich. App. 211, 201 N.W.2d 673 [11 U.C.C. Rep. Serv. 877] (1972) (where one creditor told another creditor that the collateral in question was being financed; held, sufficient to give "knowledge of the contents of any financing statement filed by [the financier]"); *United States v. Waterford No. 2 Office Center,* 246 Ga. 475, 271 S.E.2d 790, 791 [29 U.C.C. Rep. Serv. 1680] (1980) ("Knowledge of the claim of a security interest is not equivalent to knowledge of the contents of the financing statement.") (cite omitted). Whether the party must have actually observed the financing statement to be bound by it is not clear. However, most jurisdictions agree that mere knowledge of a security agreement is inadequate. But see *In re Davidoff,* 351 F. Supp. 440 [11 U.C.C. Rep. Serv. 609] (S.D.N.Y. 1972). This issue apparently is another issue of first impression in North Carolina.

As an initial matter, the court notes that § 9-401(2) contemplates (1) filing of a financing statement somewhere; and (2) knowledge by a subsequent secured party of the contents of such financing statement, not merely that a security interest exists. *Citizens State Bank v. Peoples Bank,* 475 N.E.2d 324, 329 [40 U.C.C. Rep. Serv. 1549] (Ind. App. 1 Dist. 1985). A security interest is not the same thing as a financing statement. Had the legislature intended for knowledge of a security interest to be the same as knowledge of the contents of a financing statement it could have said so. "Section 9-301(1)(b) of the 1962 Code shows us the drafters knew how to say 'knowledge of the security interest' when that was what they meant to say." White & Summers, *supra,* at 368.

Next the court notes that a creditor's general knowledge that a debtor has a relationship with or financing with another creditor is insufficient to constitute the "knowledge" required under § 9-401(2) of the Uniform Commercial Code("UCC.") *In re County Greene Ltd. Partnership,* 438 F. Supp. 693 [23 U.C.C. Rep. Serv. 168] (W.D. Va. 1977). The statute clearly requires more. See Amended Official Comment [sic "Draftsmen's Comment to the 1972 Official Text"] 5 to N.C. Gen. Stat. § 25-9-401[UCC § 9-401] and N.C. Gen. Stat. § 25-1-201(25) [UCC s 1-201] (knowledge means "actual knowledge").

BB&T relies on several cases which have liberally construed § 9-401(2), especially *First State Bank in Talihina v. United Dollar Stores,* 571 P.2d 444 [23 U.C.C. Rep. Serv. 230] (Okla. 1977), and would have the court adopt such a standard. Although professing to eschew any reliance on a "constructive knowledge" standard, the Oklahoma court goes on to state that "reason to have actual knowledge" is sufficient "knowledge" under § 9-401(2). *Id.* at 448. The United States, in its memorandum of law in opposition to defendant's motion for summary judgment at 9-10, argues that "the acceptance of such a standard would convert the actual knowledge standard into a constructive knowledge standard. To say that a creditor had'reason to have actual knowledge' of the contents of an improperly filed financing statement is quite different from saying that the creditor had actual knowledge of the contents of that improperly filed financing statement."

The court accepts this argument. Furthermore, the court believes that adoption of the amorphous *Talihina* standard would be tantamount to equating "knowledge" with "notice." N.C. Gen. Stat. § 25-1-201(25) [UCC s 1-201] states that:

> A person has notice of a fact when
>
> (a) he has actual knowledge of it; or
>
> (b) he has received a notice or notification of it; or
>
> (c) from all the facts and circumstances known to him at the time in question he has reason to know that it exists.

The subsection further states: "A person 'knows' or has 'knowledge' of a fact when he has actual knowledge of it." *Id.*

The definition of "notice" under the statute is thus broader than that of "knowledge" because of the inclusion of clause (c). The *Talihina* standard reads clause (c) into the definition of "knowledge," a result which is contrary to the text of § 1-201(25). The court declines to adopt this liberal construction of the statute, which it believes is an unwarranted departure from the plain English of the text of the U.C.C.

This court, in declining to accept the broad view of what constitutes "knowledge" under § 9-401(2), does not hold that examination of the improperly filed financing statement, per se, is necessary. Rather, it holds "knowledge" to equate to actual awareness of such information that would have been gleaned from an examination of the improperly filed financing statement (had such examination occurred) as would be sufficient to accord the filing party a perfected security interest had proper filing occurred. This standard imposes upon the party which has misfiled its financing statement the burden of proving actual knowledge on the part of the other party of the same information that such party would have obtained had he examined the financing statement properly filed. Such knowledge of the contents of the financing statement would generally include the names of the debtors and creditors and an adequate description of the collateral. *In re Mistura, Inc.*, 705 F.2d 1496, 1499 [36 U.C.C. Rep. Serv. 329] (9th Cir.. 1983).

The court thus adopts a fairly rigid adherence to the Code language of § 9-401(2). Not only is this approach faithful to the plain English of the U.C.C., it also has a beneficial policy result, as was succinctly stated by the Court of Appeals of Georgia in *Tuftco Sales Corp. v. Garrison Carpet Mills,* Inc., 158 Ga. App. 674, 282 S.E.2d 159, 162 [31 U.C.C. Rep. Serv. 1775] (1981) (citations omitted):

> Although strict adherence to the Code requirements may at times lead to harsh results, efforts by courts to fashion equitable solutions for mitigation of hardships experienced by creditors in the literal application of statutory filing requirements may have the undesirable effect of reducing the degree of reliance the market-place should be able to place on the Code provisions. The inevitable harm doubtless would be more serious to commerce than the occasional harshness from strict obedience. . . ..

Moreover, "[s]upport for a stingy construction emerges from the history of the provision." White & Summers, *supra*, at 367. As professors White and Summers point out:

"The question of the effectiveness of a misfiled mortgage or deed has been with us for years. The second sentence of Comment 5 to 9-401 tells us that the drafters at least had those cases in mind when they were preparing subsection (2): The subsection rejects the occasional decisions that an improperly filed record is ineffective to give notice even to a person who knows of it[.] Under prior versions of 9-401(2) knowledge of the filing sufficed. In 1956, however, the current requirement of knowledge of the contents of the financing statement was substituted." *Id.*

In the instant case, BB&T has not provided any evidence demonstrating that FmHA had actual knowledge of the information contained in the misfiled January 8, 1985, financing statement reflecting BB&T's purchase money security interest in the Model 2020 John Deere tractor. Indeed, Mr. Ginn, in his affidavit of November 25, 1989, states that he "cannot recall at this time whether I told Mr. Ramsey [the FmHA Assistant County Supervisor] about my purchase of the John Deere 2020 tractor." Mr. Ramsey, in his affidavit of December 18, 1989, states that he does "not recall any mention of the John Deere Model 2020 and a review of the Farmers Home Administration records does not reflect any information regarding this tractor during the above mentioned period and until well after the bankruptcy of Ralph L. Ginn and Evelyn S. Ginn."

Since BB&T is without evidence that FmHA had actual knowledge of the contents of BB&T's improperly filed financing statement listing the Model 2020 John Deere tractor prior to the perfection of FmHA's security interest therein, such improperly filed financing statement is ineffective as against FmHA. Accordingly, FmHA's prior perfected security interest in the Model 2020 John Deere tractor has priority. See N.C. Gen. Stat. § 25-9-312(5)(a)[UCC § 9-312].

. . . .

CONCLUSION

. . . . FmHA's prior perfected security interest has priority over BB&T's security interest. Although BB&T had a purchase money security interest in the Model 2020 John Deere tractor, BB&T has not demonstrated that FmHA had actual knowledge of the contents of its improperly filed financing statement. Therefore, FmHA's prior perfected security interest has priority over the later unperfected purchase money security interest of BB&T in the Model 2020 John Deere tractor.

NOTES

(1) The general rule of section 9-312(5)(a) gives special effect to filing. The rule also recognizes the fact that perfection may take place by possession or by temporary automatic perfection. Indeed, it is possible for a secured party to be perfected by one method which is then followed by another. So long as there is a continuity in the secured party's perfected status, priority will be determined by the earliest date. Comment 5 to § 9-312 provides a few illustrative examples:

A. SP #1 files a financing statement identifying the debtor and collateral on February 1. SP #2 files against the same debtor and collateral on March 1. SP #2 advances money against the collateral on April 1. SP #1 advances against the same collateral on May 1. SP #1 has priority even though SP #2's advance occurred earlier and was perfected at the time it was made. It makes no difference whether or not SP #1 knew of SP #2's interest or not when #1 made the advance.

B. #1 and #2 advance money against the same collateral. The collateral is in the debtor's possession and neither secured party's interest was perfected at the time the advances were made. The secured party who first perfects (by filing or by taking possession) will take priority.

C. SP #1 has a temporarily perfected security interest in negotiable documents that are in the debtor's possession under § 9-304(4) or (5). On day number five, SP #2 files and thus acquires a perfected security interest in the same document. On day number ten, SP #1 files. #1 has priority because she perfected first, and has maintained continuous perfection.

(2) Section 9-312(5)(b) provides a residual rule where both claimants fail to establish perfected secured party status: "so long as conflicting security interests are unperfected, the first to attach has priority."

---

§ 18.03 Purchase Money Security Interests

Read: U.C.C. § 9-107.

[A] Generally

The purchase money security interest is a key feature in the priority structure under the Code. A security interest is purchase money if it is taken by the seller of the goods, or by a third party who has loaned the debtor money that enables the debtor to acquire the very property that serves as collateral for the loan. Because the purchase money secured party provides new value to the debtor, the Code gives the perfected purchase money security interest priority over prior, perfected security interests. The item being purchased through such a credit arrangement adds to the debtor's property without diminishing any of the earlier secured party's interests. In addition, purchase money priority allows the debtor to avoid a monopoly creditor situation by tying up all of its future assets and capacity to make purchases with the first creditor. The purchase money security party must perfect its interest in order to enjoy this preferred status.

[B] Non-Inventory

Read: U.C.C. § 9-312(4).

A purchase money security interest in collateral other than inventory receives priority over an earlier perfected security interest in the same collateral so long as the purchase money creditor perfects its interest within ten days of the time the debtor obtains possession of the collateral. There is no requirement that the purchase money secured party be without notice or knowledge of another's security interest; the purchase money creditor takes priority even if she knows of another's interest. See Comment 3 to § 9-312. A number of states have extended the 10-day grace period for purchase money perfection to 20 days (as in the next case). Irrespective of the time period, section 9-312(4) gives the purchase money creditor additional time to acquire priority after the debtor takes possession of the collateral.

CITIZENS NATIONAL BANK OF DENTON v. COCKRELL

Supreme Court of Texas
850 S.W.2d 462, 19 U.C.C. Rep. Serv. 2d 1205 (1993)

PHILLIPS, CHIEF JUSTICE.

The issue in this case is whether a seller of equipment timely filed financing statements reflecting his purchase money security interest. To decide this question, we must determine when the purchaser received possession of the equipment. We conclude that as a matter of law the purchaser's control over the equipment after sale constituted "possession" within the meaning of Tex. Bus. & Com. Code § 9.312(d), and we therefore reverse the judgment of the court of appeals for the seller against a competing creditor. 802 S.W.2d 319.

Respondent John H. Cockrell, Jr. owned a mini-blind manufacturing business in Dallas, Texas. On August 1, 1985, he executed a written agreement for the immediate sale, assignment, and transfer of the business and its assets, including merchandise, leases, and fixtures, to Kevin and Richard Sydnor. Cockrell promised to pay all business debts incurred prior to August 1, but he was to be paid all accounts receivable that had accrued as of that date. The Sydnors paid Cockrell $ 5,000 cash and signed a promissory note in the principal amount of $ 130,000. To secure payment of the note, the Sydnors agreed to grant Cockrell a security interest in the transferred assets.

The Sydnors began operating the mini-blind business on August 1, assuming the lease on the warehouse where the equipment was located on that date. However, Cockrell also participated in the day-to-day operations and had access to the equipment until early October. Cockrell testified that he was concerned about relinquishing control of the equipment to the Sydnors while there were still orders in process for which he was responsible, as it was only through successful completion of these orders that he could fulfill his contractual obligation to pay for the debts incurred prior to August 1. For this reason, and to assist the Sydnors in becoming familiar with the manufacturing process, he and two of his employees remained involved with the work in the warehouse, and Cockrell retained a set of keys and continued to use an office three doors away.

During the first few days in October, the Sydnors told Cockrell that, from collecting receivables on Cockrell's behalf, they were able to make the payment due to the business's major supplier for raw material purchases. Cockrell testified, "We had a moment of great joy when they made the first major hurdle. And at that point, then, we were ready to give them possession of the equipment." On October 3, Cockrell turned over to the Sydnors his set of keys to the warehouse. On or about the same day, Cockrell testified, he and the Sydnors executed the security agreement and signed the financing statement. Cockrell filed the financing statement with the Secretary of State on October 7, 1985.

Prior to making this agreement, the Sydnors had become indebted to Provident Bank of Denton on a promissory note in the original amount of $ 40,000, backed by a security interest in all equipment then owned or thereafter acquired by the Sydnors. Provident Bank had filed a financing statement covering this security interest on May 9, 1985. When the Sydnors acquired rights in the mini-blind equipment by purchasing the business from Cockrell, Provident Bank's security interest attached to the collateral and became perfected. See Tex. Bus. & Com. Code Ann. §§ 9.203(a,b), 9.303(a) (Vernon 1991). The note and security interest were subsequently purchased by Petitioner Citizens National Bank of Denton (the Bank).

After assuming complete control of the mini-blind business on October 3, the Sydnors defaulted in their obligations to the Bank. The Bank foreclosed on the equipment and sold it to a third party.[3] Cockrell then brought this suit against the Bank, claiming that since his security interest had priority, the Bank's foreclosure and sale amounted to conversion of the property. Although Cockrell concedes that the Bank's security interest attached and became perfected prior to perfection of his security interest on October 7, 1985, he asserts the priority accorded to a purchase money security interest. See *id.* §§ 9.107, 9.312(d). Section 9.312(d) gives a purchase money security interest priority over a conflicting security interest "if the purchase money security interest is perfected at the time the debtor receives possession of the collateral or within 20 days thereafter." The decisive question in this case is whether the perfection of Cockrell's security interest on October 7, 1985, was within 20 days after the Sydnors "received possession" of the equipment.

The case was submitted to a jury, which answered all questions favorably to Cockrell, including this question:

> Do you find that John H. Cockrell, Jr., filed notice of his security interest with the Secretary of State of the State of Texas at the time that the Sydnors received possession of the collateral or within 20 days thereafter?
>
> ANSWER: "Yes" or "No."
>
> Answer: yes

The charge contained no definition of the term "possession," as the trial court sustained an objection to Cockrell's request for an instruction that possession was "the detention and control of the property for one's use and enjoyment either as owner or as the proprietor of a qualified right of property to the exclusion of all other persons."

The trial court granted the Bank's motion for judgment n.o.v., holding that there was no evidence of probative force to sustain the jury's answer to the question quoted above. The court of appeals reversed the trial court's judgment, concluding that "possession" in section 9.312(d) "means that condition of facts under which one can exercise power over property at his pleasure to the exclusion of all other persons." 802 S.W.2d at 323. Because under this definition there was sufficient evidence to support the jury's answer, and because the Bank had not attacked any of the other jury findings, the court of appeals rendered judgment for Cockrell in accordance with the jury verdict, awarding $ 44,705 for the reasonable market value of the equipment on the date of sale and $ 15,000 in exemplary damages for the Bank's wanton disregard of Cockrell's rights. We granted the Bank's and the FDIC's application for a writ of error.[4]

---

[3] There was also testimony at trial indicating that the Sydnors failed to pay Cockrell, but the Bank foreclosed on the equipment before Cockrell took any formal action.

[4] On March 8, 1990, while the case was pending before the court of appeals, the Comptroller of the Currency declared the Bank insolvent and appointed the FDIC as receiver. The court of appeals then added the FDIC as an appellee in the case.

The term "possession" is not defined in the Uniform Commercial Code, and we have found no decision specifically addressing whether "possession" under section 9.312(d) must be exclusive. Most of the cases construing the phrase "at the time the debtor receives possession of the collateral" have arisen when the debtor has had use of the collateral prior to sale or prior to execution of a security agreement. In *Mark Products U.S., Inc. v. InterFirst Bank Houston, N.A.*, 737 S.W.2d 389 (Tex. App.—Houston [14th Dist.] 1987, writ denied), for example, the plaintiff initially sold equipment to the purchaser on an unsecured basis and, after the buyer had in the interim procured a loan against the equipment from the defendant bank, the seller obtained from the buyer a promissory note for the balance of the purchase price and a security interest in the equipment. When the equipment was sold to satisfy the bank's security interest, the seller-financier sued the bank, asserting a first-priority security interest under section 9.312(d). The seller argued that the twenty-day grace period did not begin to run when the goods were delivered, because until execution of the security agreement, the purchaser was not a "debtor" in possession of "collateral."

Rejecting this argument, the court held for the bank, observing that "where there is no . . . notice of record [of a conflicting security interest] and where the debtor has been in possession for more than twenty days, a creditor may rely upon mere possession of the collateral as sufficient evidence of ownership and extend credit without further inquiry." *Id.* at 393. The court criticized the seller's argument as "seriously undermining the importance of physical delivery in determining the priority of a purchase money security interest." *Id.*

In so deciding, the court was consistent with a number of other decisions that have resolved comparable issues by focusing on the date physical control of the collateral was transferred, rather than on the date the formalities of the transaction were completed or the conditions of the contract attendant to delivery were fulfilled. See, *e.g.*, *In re Automated Bookbinding Services, Inc.*, 471 F.2d 546, 551-53 (4th Cir.. 1972) ("possession" began when crates containing equipment arrived at buyer's plant, not when seller subsequently completed installation required by sales contract's terms of delivery); *In re Vermont Knitting Co.*, 98 B.R. 184, 188-89 (Bankr. D. Vt. 1989) (debtor possessed equipment once it arrived at business premises, even though it had not been set up for use); *In re Henning*, 69 B.R. 348 (Bankr. N.D. Ill. 1987) (grace period began when cattle were delivered to ranch, not when debtor signed promissory note or security agreement). See also *James Talcott, Inc. v. Associates Capital Co.*, 491 F.2d 879, 882-83 (6th Cir.. 1974) (debtor's initial possession of equipment under lease, not exercise of option to purchase, commenced grace period for filing). There are, however, several contrary decisions, see, *e.g.*, *Brodie Hotel Supply, Inc. v. United States,* 431 F.2d 1316 (9th Cir.. 1970); *In re Miller*, 44 B.R. 716, 720 (Bankr. N.D. Ohio 1984); *Commerce Union Bank v. John Deere Industrial Equipment Co.*, 387 So. 2d 787, 791 (Ala. 1980), including one Texas case. See *State Bank and Trust Co. of Beeville v. First National Bank of Beeville*, 635 S.W.2d 807, 809 (Tex. App.—Corpus Christi 1982, writ ref'd n.r.e.).

Of course, these cases do not resolve the issue before us; many of them, including Mark Products, turn more on the meaning of "debtor" or "collateral" than on the meaning of "possession," which is critical here.[5] Nonetheless, as these cases discuss the policy considerations that underlie section 9.312(d), they are useful in deciding whether or not the "possession"

[5] Cockrell argues not that the twenty-day grace period commenced on October 3 because that was when the security agreement was signed, but that it commenced on October 3 because it was not until then that the Sydnors had complete possession of the equipment.

contemplated by section 9.312(d) is limited to complete and exclusive possession. In rejecting the proposition that "possession" did not occur until the knitting machines covered by the security interest were connected to computers and set up for use, *Vermont Knitting* noted that "Article 9 is a notice statute" which "simplified many of the more rigid and complex formalities of pre-Uniform Commercial Code law and made the information contained in the lien files of recording entities more accessible." *Vermont Knitting,* 98 B.R. at 189. To make the grace period triggered by "possession" dependent upon the seller's performance of instalation work, the court noted, could allow the seller to "manipulate that time to the detriment of other creditors and quite possibly avoid Article 9's filing requirements altogether." *Id.*

The court in *Automated Bookbinding* was driven by similar concerns in choosing physical possession as the touchstone over contractually defined "tender of delivery":

> The ostensible ownership exercised through possession is demonstrated through simple physical control. One who controls the collateral possesses it, and leads others to believe it is his.
>
> . . . .
>
> Tender of delivery is a sales concept . . .which binds a buyer and seller to contractual conditions. It affects their rights against each other. It would be a serious error to allow those private conditions to affect the carefully defined rights of creditors under Article 9.
>
> . . . To define "possession" as requiring completion of tender of delivery terms would permit a secured creditor to . . .avoid the filing requirement indefinitely. *Automated Bookbinding,* 471 F.2d at 552-53.

Under these cases, "possession" in section 9.312(d) is interpreted in light of the impression conveyed to an observer not involved in the transaction, not according to private limitations contained in the contract between the buyer and seller. As commentators have noted, the U.C.C. drafters' choice to have the purchase money priority rule turn on "possession," rather than on when the debtor obtains "rights" in the collateral (see § 9.203(a)(3)), indicates a desire that the commencement of the grace period be easily ascertainable. See 1B Peter Coogan, William Hogan, Detlev Vagts, & Julian McDonnell, Secured Transactions under the Uniform Commercial Code § 19.02[3][a], at 19-36 (1987).

The definition of "possession" adopted by the court of appeals implicates these same concerns. During August and September, the equipment was located in the warehouse that had become the Sydnors' place of business, used for the business that the Sydnors were then managing, and operated by employees of the Sydnors. If, despite this ostensible possession, the Sydnors were not in "possession" within the meaning of section 9.312(d) because Cockrell and two of his employees retained access to the warehouse, then section 9.312(d) "possession" acquires a meaning different from the simple physical control that to outside parties suggests ownership rights.[6] Since the duration of Cockrell's supervision of the business was a matter of agreement between him and the Sydnors, the court of appeals' interpretation would also allow some manipulation of the grace period by the parties to the transaction, frustrating Article 9's scheme.

The purpose of the twenty-day grace period (which in most states is only ten days) is to enable the financier to keep its priority even when the debtor-purchaser demands immediate delivery

[6] In this case, of course, the Bank was not a creditor who lent money in reliance on the Sydnors' apparent possession of the property for more than twenty days during August and September. However, in construing section 9.312(d) we must consider other types of situations to which it could apply.

of the goods. See 2 Grant Gilmore, Security Interests in Personal Property § 29.5, at 800 (1965). That purpose is not thwarted by requiring the financier to file within twenty days of delivery even if, as here, the nature of the transaction requires the financier to maintain some control over the collateral beyond that twenty-day period.

Another consideration in interpreting section 9.312(d) is that, to the extent possible, "possession" in that section should be given a meaning harmonious with its use in other parts of Article 9. This consideration arguably weighs against our holding today, because with regard to a secured party's perfection by possession under section 9.305, it has been stated that possession must be "unequivocal, absolute and notorious." *Hutchison v. C.I.T. Corp.*, 726 F.2d 300, 302 (6th Cir.. 1984); *Transport Equipment Co. v. Guaranty State Bank,* 518 F.2d 377, 381 (10th Cir.. 1975); *Greenbush State Bank v. Stephens,* 463 N.W.2d 303, 308 (Minn. App. 1990).

However, given the facts and rationale of those decisions, we do not believe that our holding gives a conflicting meaning to "possession." All of those cases involved a secured party who acquired less thorough and, more important, less visible possession of the collateral than the Sydnors did. In *Transport Equipment Co.,* the creditor contended that simply by having its employees present on the debtor's premises preparing to remove the collateral on the morning before a competing creditor filed a financing statement, it had perfected its interest by possession. *Transport Equipment Co.,* 518 F.2d at 380-81. In Hutchison, the collateral was likewise located on another entity's business premises, but the creditor claimed that its interest had been perfected by possession because it had a night watchman "keep an eye on the equipment." *Hutchison,* 726 F.2d at 301. Finally, in *Greenbush State Bank,* the tractor that was the subject of the security interest was shared by the secured party and the debtor, and moved between their two farms. *Greenbush State Bank,* 463 N.W.2d at 308.

In deeming the secured party's possession insufficient in each case, the courts relied, as we have, on the need for sufficient possession to alert other potential creditors to the secured party's interest. We do not believe that, if presented with a secured party exercising the degree of dominion that the Sydnors did, these courts would still have concluded that the notice function had not been fulfilled. Indeed, since the *Transport Equipment Co.* court concluded that a possessory interest somewhat comparable to Cockrell's (*i.e.*, employees on the debtor's business premises) was insufficient to give notice, we think the case supports our conclusion that notwithstanding Cockrell's employees the Sydnors had ostensible control sufficient to constitute "possession." The *Transport Equipment Co.* decision, in fact, relied heavily on *Automated Bookbinding.*

For the foregoing reasons, we think that the court of appeals erred in limiting "possession" in section 9.312(d) to a power over property exercisable to the exclusion of all other persons. Moreover, we do not see any other basis on which the jury verdict can be sustained. That the equipment was in the Sydnors' place of business beginning on August 1, 1985 was undisputed. It was similarly uncontested that the equipment was used in the Sydnors' business during the succeeding months, and Cockrell presented no evidence to suggest that the equipment was in some manner set aside or specially labeled to denote his purchase money interest in it. Because this undisputed evidence establishes the Sydnors' "possession" under section 9.312(d) as we conclude that section must be read, there is no evidence to support the jury finding that the Sydnors received possession within twenty days of October 7, 1985. The trial court's judgment n.o.v. was correct.

In light of our disposition of this point of error, we do not reach the FDIC's further contention that federal law exempts it from the award of exemplary damages imposed by the court of appeals.

We reverse the judgment of the court of appeals and render judgment that Cockrell take nothing from the Petitioners.

[C] Inventory

Read: U.C.C. § 9-312(3).

A purchase money security interest in inventory prevails over conflicting interests if it is perfected at the time the debtor receives possession of the collateral and notification is given to any prior security interest holder. There is no grace period for filing in the case of the inventory purchase money security interests; the interest must be perfected *before* the debtor receives possession. A creditor can easily achieve proper perfection by filing a financing statement in advance of the transaction, a step permitted under the Code. For example, a financing statement could be filed a week in advance of the creditor's giving value and/or yielding possession of the collateral. Perfection of inventory before possession avoids misleading prior secured creditors who may have floating lien interests in inventory. Such floating lien interests attach as soon as the debtor receives possession. Thus, to avoid confusion about which creditor has the superior interest, the Code requires the purchase money secured party, as subsequent secured party, to have its interest recorded before the debtor takes possession.

In the case of the inventory, the Code also requires the purchase money secured party to notify all other secured creditors of the security interest before the debtor receives possession of the collateral. The notification requirement protects earlier secured parties from unwittingly making future advances in anticipation of a floating lien interest attaching to the debtor's property. There is nothing the secured party can do with the notification, other than to reassess the debtor as a credit risk now that a second secured party has become involved. Comment 3 to U.C.C. § 9-312 points out that "typically the arrangement between an inventory secured party and his debtor will require the secured party to make periodic advances against incoming inventory or periodic releases of old inventory as new inventory is received." It is possible that a "fraudulent debtor may apply to one security interest holder for an advance even though he has already given a security interest in the inventory to another secured party." By requiring notification, the risk to others engaging in inventory financing diminishes.

IN RE DANIELS

United States Bankruptcy Court Western District of Oklahoma
35 Bankr. 247, 37 U.C.C. Rep. Serv. 967 (1993)

RICHARD L. BOHANON, BANKRUPTCY JUDGE.

The matter for determination arises from a motion made by ITT Diversified Credit Corporation for a decision as to its priority status regarding conflicting security interests. The matter has been fully briefed by all parties and the facts are not controverted. Due to a thorough stipulation of facts there remains only the sole question of whether a letter of notification sent by American Bank of Commerce to ITT complied with 12A O.S. 1981 § 9-312.

In January, 1982 the debtor entered into two wholesale financing and security agreements with ITT Diversified Credit Corporation for the purpose of purchasing boats, motors and related accessories for his business operation known as Daniels Marine, Inc. ITT was granted a security interest in several items listed as exhibits and made a part of the record. ITT properly perfected its security interest in these items by filing the necessary financing statements.

The Small Business Administration through the American Bank of Commerce subsequently loaned Daniels Marine, Inc., certain sums of money and in return was granted a security interest in the inventory and equipment. In July, 1981 the American Bank of Commerce forwarded to all known creditors of Daniels Marine, Inc., a letter regarding their security interest in said inventory and equipment. That letter provides in pertinent part:

> Gentleman:
>
> The American Bank of Commerce has taken, or plans to take a security interest in the following equipment located at the customers place of business at Longtown, Oklahoma, mailing address Highway # 9, Eufaula, Oklahoma: All machinery & equipment; inventory; accounts receivable; automotive equipment, furniture & fixtures now owned or hereafter acquired; All Used boats and motors now owned or hereafter acquired including but not limited to: [listing numerous items with specific descriptions and serial numbers].
>
> /s/ John Freeman

ITT admits that it received the subject letter and raises no question regarding time of receipt, description of the collateral or other points beyond the issue raised by this proceeding.

In April of 1982, pursuant to an order of this Court, the Small Business Administration conducted a foreclosure sale of property in which it claimed a security interest pursuant to agreements with the debtor as previously set forth. Among the property sold at the foreclosure sale were certain items in which both ITT and the Small Business Administration, through the American Bank of Commerce, claimed a security interest.

This proceeding raises a novel and interesting question regarding the perfection of a purchase money security interest in inventory and is a case of first impression. We are asked to decide the priority among conflicting security interests in the same collateral. Our inquiry begins with the Uniform Commercial Code and Oklahoma's adoption of the 1972 amendments to the pertinent section, 12A O.S. 1981 § 9-312:

> (3) A perfected purchase money security interest in inventory has priority over a conflicting security interest in the same inventory and also has priority in identifiable cash proceeds received on or before the delivery of the inventory to a buyer if:
>
> (a) the purchase money security interest is perfected at the time the debtor receives possession of the inventory; and
>
> (b) the purchase money secured party gives notification in writing to the holder of the conflicting security interest, if the holder had filed a financing statement covering the same types of inventory (i) before the date of the filing made by the purchase money secured party, or (ii) before the beginning of the twenty-one day period where the purchase money security interest is temporarily perfected without filing or possession (subsection (5) of Section 9-304); and
>
> (c) the holder of the conflicting security interest receives the notification within five (5) years before the debtor receives possession of the inventory; and

(d) the notification states that the person giving the notice has or expects to acquire a purchase money security interest in inventory of the debtor, describing such inventory by item or type.

In the instant case the notification letter from American Bank of Commerce to ITT did not literally track the specific language of 12A O.S. 1981 § 9-312(3)(d) in that it only states "[the bank] has taken, or plans to take, a security interest . . . ." and makes no mention of a "purchase money security interest." ITT urges that failure of the bank to state the taking of a purchase money security interest in the notification is insufficient to meet the standards prescribed by law, and therefore the bank may not be afforded priority status which it otherwise would acquire. On the other hand, the bank argues the letter was sufficient to put ITT on notice even though it did not contain the words "purchase money" since there could have been no other reason for sending the notice nor did the letter contain any misleading information.

. . . .

Some recognition must be given to the policy and commercial reasons why purchase money security interests receive special priority. The drafters of the Code realized the impact upon commercial flow which would result should a debtor be strangled by a prior secured creditor. Such a creditor by not providing additional funds could cripple a debtor's commercial operation. The debtor, on the other hand, would be hamstrung in receiving other financing since another creditor would have no collateral protection. The purchase money security interest rescued the debtor from this commercial impasse. In their treatise, Handbook On The Uniform Commercial Code, the authors explained this policy rationale:

> The debtor needs some protection from a creditor who has filed a financing statement with respect to his goods, but who is unwilling to advance additional funds. If such a debtor can find a lender willing to finance a new line of merchandise, the purchase money provisions enable him to give that new lender a first claim on the new merchandise notwithstanding a prior filing by another creditor. Thus, the purchase money provisions give the debtor somewhat greater bargaining power and at least theoretically enlarge his ability to get credit. J. White & R. Summers, Handbook On The Uniform Commercial Code, § 25-5 at 1043 (2d ed. 1980).

Consequently, there is a strong policy statement which supports the operation of the purchase money interest which should not be interrupted for the sake of mere technical conformity. Moreover, it is generally accepted that the U.C.C. provisions should be liberally construed in order to promote the underlying policies and purposes of the Code. Compare 12A O.S. 1981 § 1-102 (liberal construction to permit commercial expansion). Conversely, we are unable to identify any policy or purpose which would be served by a literalist statutory reading of 12A O.S.1981 § 9-312.

As for the specific notification provisions of 9-312, resort must be made to the reasons for its mechanics. These are best explained by the draftsmen's comments to the 1972 official text:

> The reason for the additional requirement of notification is that typically the arrangement between an inventory secured party and his debtor will require the secured party to make periodic advances against incoming inventory or periodic releases of old inventory as new inventory is received. A fraudulent debtor may apply to the secured party for advances even though he has already given a security interest in the inventory to another secured party. The notification requirement protects the inventory financier in such a situation: if he has received notification, he will presumably not make an advance; if he has not received notification (or

> if the other interest does not qualify as a purchase money interest) any advance he may make will have priority. Since an arrangement for periodic advances against incoming property is unusual outside the inventory field, no notification requirement is included in subsection (4).

See U.C.C. Report. Serv. (Callaghan) § 9-312 at 167 (1977) (citing U.C.C. Art. 9 Draftsman's Comment To 1972 Official Text).

It is clear from these comments that the notice provision was for the protection of the prior secured creditor. The first creditor would be alerted not to make further advances since another inventory financier could usurp his prior secured position. If this written notice requirement is essentially accomplished, the linguistical technique of how it is accomplished becomes of little importance. Indeed the drafters of section 9-312 specifically directs the reader to the definitional cross references of "give notice" and "knowledge" found in section 1-201. These sections clearly provide that:

> (25) A person has "notice" of a fact when
>
> (a) he has actual knowledge of it; or
>
> (b) he has received a notice or notification of it; or
>
> (c) from all the facts and circumstances known to him at the time in question he has reason to know that it exist
>
> (26) A person "notifies" or "gives" a notice or notification to another by taking such steps as may be reasonably required to inform the other in ordinary course whether or not such other actually comes to know of it.

We do not feel that the reference to the section 1-201 definitions in 9-312 are to be discarded as mere surplusage. Rather, we think these definitional terms are to be equally applied to 9-312 when the circumstances so demand in order to promote the underlying policies of the U.C.C. We think this is one such circumstance. Here we are not dealing with simply garden variety consumers untrained in the commercial world. These parties are sophisticated commercial entities in the business of commercial lending and financing. The letter received by ITT, although not containing the magic words "purchase money", did contain terms which clearly indicate a purchase money interest. The use of the terms "furniture or fixtures now owned or hereafter acquired" and "boats and motors now owned or hereafter acquired" should be clear indicators to a sophisticated commercial entity that a purchase money transaction is at hand. This conclusion is buttressed by the fact that in no other situation excepting a purchase money interest is another creditor required to forward any notice to the prior secured party. This is not to say that as a matter of commercial courtesy or for communication purposes creditors may not provide such notices to each other. However, such practices should not confuse the issue at hand in view of the totality of circumstances which exist here.

In light of what we have stated we do not see how ITT could have been misled or confused by the notification letter not having stated "purchase money" among its terms. To reach any other conclusion would be contrary to reason and militate against the very policy of having purchase money security transactions. Moreover, a literal reading of 9-312 while serving no policy interest or purpose would ignore the referenced definitional terms of notice and the liberal construction of the Code. Therefore, in light of all the facts and circumstances known to ITT we find the absence of the terms "purchase money" in the notice forwarded to ITT to be de minimus. However, we feel that our conclusion and holding necessarily must be limited to the facts of this particular case.

Accordingly, for all the above cited reasons we hold that pursuant to the purchase money security interest in the debtor's inventory that the American Bank of Commerce obtained priority secured status;

Further, that the American Bank of Commerce and the Small Business Administration are entitled to the proceeds of the sale of the debtor's inventory items;

Further, that the motion of ITT to determine priority status be and hereby, is denied.

QUESTIONS

(1) Do you agree with the court's decision? How difficult is it to use specific words of purchase money to describe a transaction? What benefits would occur if there were an express requirement that words of purchase money be used?

(2) The statutory provision for purchase money security interests in inventory does not grant a grace period. Why? What are the characteristics which distinguish non-inventory collateral from inventory collateral for purposes of purchase money treatment?

(3) Purchase money priority problems can also arise in situations where a creditor takes a security interest in present and future accounts of a debtor and a different creditor takes a purchase money interest in that debtor's inventory. When the debtor sells inventory, anything received upon sale constitutes proceeds. Proceeds can consist of accounts, chattel paper, or payments by cash or check. In the case of accounts proceeds, which secured party has priority, the accounts financier or the inventory purchase money party? Section 9-312(3) gives priority to the inventory purchase money creditor but restricts that priority to "identifiable cash proceeds received on or before the delivery of the inventory to a buyer." Even if the purchase money creditor filed after the accounts financier, the purchase money financier has priority with respect to cash proceeds that can be identified specifically. See U.C.C. § 9-306(1). Because accounts are non-cash proceeds from inventory sales, priority in such collateral goes to the accounts financier who filed earlier. Thus, in cases other than that of the purchase money inventory financier and identifiable cash proceeds, the first to file rule of section 9-312(5) applies. Subsection (6) of 9-312 states that for purposes of the first to file rule, the date of perfection for the collateral also constitutes the date of filing for proceeds. See Official Comment 8 to section 9-312 for examples. Despite this apparent resolution of a thorny problem, questions can still arise concerning the appropriate treatment between accounts and inventory. What result if a creditor claims purchase money priority in an account directly?

MBANK ALAMO NATL. ASSN. v. RAYTHEON CO.

United States Court of Appeals
886 F.2d 1449, 10 U.C.C. Rep. Serv. 2d 35 (5th Cir. 1989)

REAVLEY, CIRCUIT JUDGE

MBank Alamo National Association ("MBank") and E.I. DuPont de Nemours Company, Inc. ("DuPont") pressed this conversion action against Raytheon Company ("Raytheon"), claiming that Raytheon collected certain accounts receivable, in which MBank and DuPont had security interests superior to those of Raytheon. Raytheon's defense was that it had a purchase money security interest in the accounts receivable. Concluding that Raytheon had no purchase money security interest in the accounts, the district court held that Raytheon's security interests were subordinate to those of MBank and DuPont, and granted MBank's and DuPont's motions for summary judgment. We affirm.

I. Background

MBank and DuPont entered various security agreements with Howe X-ray ("Howe"). By January 10, 1983, in accordance with these agreements, both DuPont and MBank held perfected liens in Howe's present and future accounts receivable. MBank also held a perfected security interest in Howe's present and after acquired inventory.

Beginning in January 1983, Raytheon, an x-ray equipment manufacturer, entered a series of transactions with Howe who was one of its distributors. Raytheon agreed to ship x-ray equipment to Howe after Howe contracted with one of its customers for the sale, delivery, and installation of certain Raytheon equipment. In exchange, Howe agreed to assign the specific accounts receivable to Raytheon. Subsequent to the assignments, Raytheon filed financing statements in specific accounts receivable of Howe. Between July 1983 and December 1984, Raytheon collected over $ 850,000.00.

By November 1984, Howe had defaulted on its obligations to MBank and DuPont. MBank and DuPont, pursuant to their security interests, demanded payment from Raytheon from the accounts receivable that it had collected. Raytheon refused, claiming that it had a purchase money security interest ("PMSI") in the accounts receivable and that its interests were therefore superior to those of MBank and DuPont.

In addition to its contention that it had a PMSI in the accounts receivable, Raytheon claimed that even if it did not have a PMSI in those accounts, MBank waived its security interest in the accounts. The district court granted MBank's and DuPont's motions for summary judgment, deciding that Raytheon had no PMSI in the accounts receivable and that Raytheon had not raised an issue of MBank's alleged waiver.

Raytheon appeals the district court's determination that it did not have a PMSI in the accounts receivable. In the alternative, Raytheon contends that if our construction of the PMSI statutory provisions excludes the Raytheon — Howe transaction, the ruling should not apply to this case under the doctrine of nonretroactivity. Raytheon also appeals the district court's finding that Raytheon failed to produce sufficient evidence of waiver to overcome MBank's motion for summary judgment.

II. Analysis

A. Purchase Money Security Interests

The rules governing the rights of creditors are set out in Chapter 9 of the Texas Business and Commerce Code ("Code"), which essentially adopted the provisions of the Uniform Commercial Code — Secured Transactions. See Tex.Bus. & Com.Code Ann. § 9.101 et seq. (Vernon 1989). These provisions were enacted "to provide a simple and unified structure within which the immense variety of present-day secured financing transactions can go forward with less cost and with greater certainty." § 9.101, 1972 Official U.C.C. Comment. In keeping with these goals, rules were enacted prioritizing conflicting security interests in the same property.

The general rule provides that the first perfected security interest to be filed has priority and other perfected interests stand in line in the order in which they were filed. See § 9.312(e). PMSIs are excepted from the first-to-file rule and take priority over other perfected security interests regardless of the filing sequence. § 9.312(c), (d). The district court found that Raytheon did not fall within the PMSI exception, that MBank had priority as the first to file, under § 9.312(e)(1), and that DuPont takes second priority since it filed next.

Raytheon claims the district court erred by not recognizing its priority in the accounts receivable as a PMSI under § 9.312(d).[7] Section 9.312(d) provides that "[a] purchase money security interest in collateral other than inventory has priority over a conflicting security interest in the same collateral or its proceeds if the purchase money security interest is perfected at the time the debtor receives possession of the collateral or within 20 days thereafter."

As a threshold matter, Raytheon must establish that it meets the statutory definition of a PMSI. Raytheon contends that it fits the statutory requirements of a PMSI under § 9.107(2), which provides:

> A security interest is a "purchase money security interest" to the extent that it is
>
> . . . .
>
> (2) taken by a person who by making advances or incurring an obligation gives value to enable the debtor to acquire rights in or the use of collateral if such value is in fact so used.

To meet these requirements Raytheon must show: (1) that it gave value; (2) that the value given enabled Howe to acquire rights in the accounts receivable; and (3) that the accounts receivable qualify as collateral within the meaning of the statute.

The value requirement is satisfied by any consideration sufficient to support a simple contract. See *Thet Mah and Assoc. v. First Bank of North Dakota,* 336 N.W.2d 134, 138 (N.D. 1983); § 1.201(44)(D) (Vernon 1968). Assuming arguendo that Raytheon gave value by extending credit to Howe in exchange for Howe's promise to assign the accounts receivable to Raytheon, see *Thet Mah,* 336 N.W.2d at 138, Raytheon has failed to satisfy the other two requirements.

To create a PMSI, the value must be given in a manner that enables the debtor to acquire interest in the collateral. This is accomplished when a debtor uses an extension of credit or loan money to purchase a specific item. See *Ingram v. Ozark Prod. Credit Assoc.,* 468 F.2d 564, 565 (5th Cir.. 1972); *In re Dillon,* 18 Bankr. 252, 254 (Bankr. E.D. Cal. 1982) (PMSI lien attaches to item actually purchased); Jackson & Kronman, *Secured Financing and Priorities Among Creditors,* 88 Yale L.J. 1143, 1165 (1979) (PMSI priority limited "to loans that can be traced to identifiable, discrete items of property.").

The collateral at issue here is the accounts receivable. In an attempt to force its interest into the PMSI mold, Raytheon has characterized the transaction as follows: "Raytheon, by agreeing to extend credit on its equipment, enabled Howe X-Ray to enter into subsequent contracts of sale with its customers, thereby acquiring rights in the contract accounts which, upon the specific

---

[7] Raytheon claims a PMSI in the accounts receivable and not in the inventory. Raytheon cannot claim a PMSI in this inventory because it did not comply with § 9.312(c)(2), which requires a PMSI holder to notify in writing the holder of a conflicting security interest in the same inventory.

advance and delivery of equipment, blossomed into a right to the collateral accounts receivable." Raytheon, however, cannot force this transaction to fit. To accept this characterization, we would have to close our eyes to the true nature of the transaction.

Raytheon, in essence, is claiming that it advanced x-ray machines to Howe on credit, which then enabled Howe to purchase accounts receivable from its customers. This, however, does not comport with our view of commercial reality. While, as Raytheon suggests, it may be theoretically possible to create a PMSI in accounts receivable by advancing funds for their purchase, see *Northwestern Nat'l Bank Southwest v. Lectro Systems,* 262 N.W.2d 678, 680 (Minn. 1977); Gilmore, *The Purchase Money Priority,* 76 Harv. L. Rev. 1333, 1372 (1963), the same cannot be done by advancing x-ray machines. We view this as a two-step transaction in which Raytheon first advanced machines to Howe for retail sale and, once these machines were sold, Howe then assigned the accounts receivable to Raytheon. Through the credit advance, Howe acquired an interest in the machines, not the accounts receivable. Raytheon's credit advance, therefore, did not enable Howe to acquire an interest in the accounts receivable, as collateral within the meaning of the statute.

Additionally, in its characterization of the transaction, Raytheon is attempting to benefit from the PMSI's preferred status in a manner that was not contemplated by the U.C.C. drafters. PMSIs provide an avenue for heavily burdened debtors to obtain credit for specific goods when creditors who have previously loaned money to the debtor may be unwilling to advance additional funds. Jackson & Kronman, *Secured Financing and Priorities Among Creditors,* 88 Yale L.J. 1143, 1145 & n. 9 (1979). By giving a PMSI holder a priority interest in the specific goods purchased, there is some incentive for a lender to advance funds or credit for the specific transaction. The scope of a PMSI holder's preferred interest, however, is specifically limited by the Code.

Under § 9.312(c), a PMSI inventory is limited to that inventory or to "identifiable cash proceeds received on or before the delivery of the inventory to a buyer. . . ." The drafters noted that general financing of an inventory business is based primarily on accounts resulting from inventory, chattel paper and other proceeds. § 9.312, Official U.C.C. Reasons for 1972 Change comment (4). Reasoning that "accounts financing is more important in the economy than the financing of the kinds of inventory that produce accounts, and [that] the desirable rule is one which makes accounts financing certain as to its legal position," *id.*, they specifically excluded accounts resulting from the sale of inventory from the protections of a PMSI. Thus, financing statements that are filed on a debtor's accounts take precedence over any subsequent claim to accounts as proceeds of a PMSI in inventory. Additionally, to protect lenders who make periodic advances against incoming inventory, the PMSI holder is required to notify other secured parties before it can take priority. § 9.312(c)(2); see *id.*, 1972 Official U.C.C. Comment 3.

The priority scheme, however, differs in the context of collateral other than inventory. Under § 9.312(d), a PMSI in collateral other than inventory entitles the holder to a superior interest in both the collateral and its proceeds regardless of any intervening accounts. The differing entitlement to proceeds is due to differences in the expectations of the parties with respect to the collateral involved.

Collateral other than inventory generally refers to equipment used in the course of business. See *id.*, Official U.C.C. Reasons for 1972 Change comment (4); Gilmore, *The Purchase Money Priority,* 76 Harv. L. Rev. 1333, 1385 (1963). Since, unlike inventory, "it is not ordinarily expected that the collateral will be sold and that proceeds will result, [the drafters found it] appropriate to give the party having a purchase money security interest in the original collateral an equivalent priority in its proceeds." § 9.312, Official U.C.C. Reasons for 1972 Change comment (3).

Howe's business primarily involved the sale of inventory, which included the Raytheon x-ray machines. See § 9.109(4). The accounts receivable are proceeds resulting from the sale of the machines. MBank and DuPont took security interests in the accounts receivable, in accordance with their expectation that sale of the inventory would generate the accounts. If we were to accept Raytheon's argument that it holds a PMSI in Howe's accounts receivable, we would be giving Raytheon a priority interest in the proceeds of inventory, in direct contravention to the express intent of the drafters. Additionally, Raytheon would have successfully avoided the notice requirements of § 9.312(c)(2).

Raytheon argues, however, that the policies underlying PMSIs actually favor recognizing Raytheon's priority interest in Howe's accounts. It points out that Howe could find no other source of financing besides Raytheon and that "MBank and DuPont benefitted by the financing arrangements because the extension of [credit] by Raytheon helped Howe X-ray stay in business thereby servicing its debts." Raytheon also contends that if the Code is interpreted to limit the security interests of creditors, such as Raytheon, to a mere promise of repayment and the grant of a PMSI in inventory, a "valuable source of credit" to similarly encumbered debtors would "dry up." This is because the risk of default is too great in the face of prior liens on the debtor's accounts.

The Code itself, however, answers this argument. The drafters were apparently well aware that the failure to extend a PMSI holder's priority status to the resulting accounts would provide less incentive for inventory financiers to provide credit. See § 9.312, 1972 Official U.C.C. Comment 8. Yet, they did not extend the protections of a PMSI and merely noted that "many parties financing inventory are quite content to protect their first security interest in the inventory itself, realizing that when inventory is sold, someone else will be financing the accounts and the priority for inventory will not run forward to the accounts." *Id.* The drafter's recognition of the problem and the statutory favoring of accounts financing demonstrate that the drafters were not overly concerned that this source of financing would "dry up."

Additionally, Raytheon had alternative means of securing its right to receive payment. Besides obtaining a PMSI in the inventory by complying with the § 9.312(c)(2) notice requirements, it could have entered subordination agreements with MBank and DuPont on the specific accounts resulting from the sale of Raytheon's x-ray machines. It also could have sold the machines to Howe's customers who would have paid Raytheon directly, with Howe receiving a commission on the sale. If Raytheon had followed either of these courses, it would not have subverted the notice and filing requirements of the Code. As this transaction goes beyond that contemplated by the PMSI provisions, we decline "to expand the scope of special protection afforded a purchase money security interest, lest in so doing we defeat the underlying purposes of the Code: to bring predictability to commercial transactions." *Mark Prod. U.S., Inc. v. Interfirst Bank Houston, N.A.*, 737 S.W.2d 389, 393 (Tex.App. — Houston [14th Dist.] 1987).

Since Raytheon did not have a PMSI in Howe's accounts receivable, the first-to-file priority rules govern. See *Ford Motor Credit Co. v. First State Bank of Smithville,* 679 S.W.2d 486, 487 (Tex. 1984). As the last to file, Raytheon's interest is subordinate to those of MBank and DuPont.

. . . .

. . . . The district court properly granted the motions for summary judgment. . . . The judgments for MBank and DuPont are AFFIRMED.

GOLDBERG, CIRCUIT JUDGE, dissenting:

What we confront today is another nettle in the thicket of the Texas Uniform Commercial Code. A thorny question of statutory interpretation that could cause scratch and abrasion if not reconnoitered under the illumination provided by the Texas Supreme Court. After examining the relevant statutes and commentaries, however, I believe that the majority has not construed the code as would the Texas Supreme Court in the face of the same problem. So because the scratch of a thorn may cause infection if not properly treated, I must respectfully DISSENT.

The nettle of this case is whether an account receivable should be considered "collateral" in the words of the purchase money security interest statute so that the purchase money interest has priority over a security interest previously perfected in an identical account. My belief is that accounts receivable are an appropriate form of collateral because they can be used to invigorate marginal businesses. I would thus hold that Raytheon established a purchase money security interest in the specified accounts of Howe x-ray.

I. THE FACTS

Both MBank and DuPont had loaned money to Howe, a dealer in medical equipment including expensive x-ray machines. To guard themselves against the possibility that Howe would default on these loans, MBank, whose loan was made before DuPont's, perfected a security interest in Howe's accounts receivable then existing and subsequently arising and also perfected a similar security interest in Howe's inventory. DuPont's security interest was also perfected in Howe's accounts receivable then existing and subsequently arising but was filed after MBank's interest.

While the MBank/DuPont loans were outstanding, Raytheon entered into a series of transactions with Howe. Each transaction was executed according to a preexisting distribution agreement which allowed Howe to contract with customers for the sale of Raytheon x-ray machines. Under this agreement, Raytheon promised to supply an x-ray machine to Howe in exchange for Howe's promise to assign the account receivable that arose from the sale of the machine to Raytheon. Raytheon gave notice of its security interest in each account by filing a financing statement within the applicable 20 day period after the creation of the account. The structure of this agreement between Howe and Raytheon arose because Howe had begun to experience difficulty in obtaining additional financing and was spiraling down toward bankruptcy, its final fate.

II. DISCUSSION

Before I get involved in the details of Raytheon's purchase money security interest, however, a momentary step back is in order to scan the general landscape of security interests. As a general observation, the usual method for growth in the area of commercial law has been the daring creativity of a company pushing out beyond the boundaries of "normal practice" in response to business exigencies. The history of trust receipts, the factor's liens, and the eventual adoption of Article 9 of the Uniform Commercial Code illustrates this general observation in the area of security interests. See G. Gilmore, Security Interests in Personal Property, Ch. 1-8 (1965).

"The idea which the draftsmen [of Article 9] started with was that the system of independent security devices [developed in different area of commerce] had served its time; that the formal differences which separated one device from another should be scrapped and replaced with the simple concept of a security interest in personal property; that all types of personal property, whether held for use or for sale, should be recognized as available for security." *Id.* at 290. . . .

Article nine was thus intended to be a flexible statute that could respond to divergent commercial needs.

The facts of this case present exactly the type of problematic situation which demands a creative solution. Raytheon, as a manufacturer of expensive x-ray equipment, often does not seek out customers itself but instead uses local distributors such as Howe to make sales. But Howe had to borrow money for it to function as a merchant of medical equipment. MBank and DuPont provided this money protecting themselves by with security interests in the collateral Howe had available, Howe's present and future accounts receivable and inventory. This type of security interest in a borrower's intangibles such as accounts receivable is extremely common. The key to who has priority is to determine who filed the security interest in the collateral first. First in time, first in line goes the rhyme.

The problem with this situation is that a manufacturer will not loan or give a heavily indebted merchant any goods to sell on credit because once the merchant sells the goods, the banker, not the manufacturer, will have priority in the resulting accounts under the first in time first in line principle. Raytheon would thus not advance any x-ray machines to Howe because MBank and DuPont would have priority in any accounts that arose from the sale of the machines. Yet it is these very sales which would enable Howe to make profits to pay off its loans to MBank and DuPont. So how does an indebted merchant, who is unable to pay a manufacturer for goods that the merchant must sell to service the banker's loan, stay in business? Often what occurs is a scenario where the banker's loan is not paid, the merchant goes out of business, and the manufacturer loses an opportunity to distribute its goods on the market.

Article 9 provides a solution: the purchase money security interest. This device, with its root in the Railroad Car Trusts of the Nineteenth Century, has priority over security interests filed earlier because of its specific transaction oriented function. *Id.* at 743-53 (citing *U.S. v. New Orleans R.R.,* 79 U.S. (12 Wall.) 362, 364-65, 20 L. Ed. 434 (1871) (pre *Erie* commercial case giving priority to the later in time party)). The purchase money security interest operates outside the notice principle which favors early interest holders over later ones. Notice is not the driving force behind the purchase money security interest.

It was this purchase money device that allowed Howe an opportunity to continue doing business to the benefit of MBank, DuPont and Raytheon. Howe did not have enough money to purchase a $ 140,000 x-ray machine for inventory but Raytheon would not advance a machine on credit to Howe. A creative alternative was necessary. Raytheon agreed to advance a machine to Howe in exchange for Howe's enforceable purchase order or account receivable. Raytheon thus used the account as a vehicle to ensure Howe's payment for the machine. It was a creative solution to the meeting of two creditors, a manufacturer of expensive equipment, and a heavily indebted retailer, that allowed commerce to continue to flow.

But for the law to recognize this creativity, it must be determined whether Raytheon has complied with the elements of the Texas purchase money security interest statute. Admittedly this arrangement does not present a paradigmatic purchase money security interest, but I believe that creativity, when in harmony with the statutory requirements, should be encouraged.

. . . .

C. THE COLLATERAL REQUIREMENT

The thorny question in this case centers on whether accounts receivable should be considered collateral for the purpose of a purchase money security interest under Section 9-107(b). To my mind, Raytheon has jumped this hurdle.[8]

Under section 9.105(a)(3), which is listed in the definitional cross references of section 9.107, collateral is defined as "the property subject to a security interest and includes accounts and chattel paper which have been sold. . . ." Moreover, under section 9.106, which is also listed in the definitional cross references of section 9.107, "account means any right to payment for goods sold or leased or for services rendered which is not evidenced by an instrument or chattel paper, whether or not it has been earned by performance." The comment to 9.106 states that the section is referring to "ordinary commercial accounts receivable." By reading these two definitional sections in tandem, it is clear that an account receivable can be collateral for the purposes of a purchase money security interest under section 9.107.

---

[8] MBank and DuPont argue that Raytheon does not have purchase money security interest in the accounts receivable of Howe. They contend that the proper way to characterize the transaction between Raytheon and Howe is to view Raytheon as having advanced credit to Howe. This credit, the argument continues, allowed Howe to purchase inventory from Raytheon in the form of the x-ray machine. Thus, according to MBank and DuPont, the x-ray machine served as collateral to secure the advance of the credit from Raytheon. Howe then sold the x-ray machines to its customers. The sales created accounts receivable which Howe assigned to Raytheon.

The implication of MBank and DuPont's characterization of the transaction between Raytheon and Howe is that MBank and DuPont have priority in the accounts receivable over Raytheon because Raytheon would not be able to claim a valid purchase money security interest. Raytheon would not be able to claim a purchase money security interest under section 9.312(d) because this section requires that the interest be taken in collateral other than inventory. Section 9.312(d) states that "A purchase money security interest in collateral other than inventory has priority over a conflicting security interest in the same collateral or its proceeds if the purchase money security interest is perfected at the time the debtor receives possession of the collateral or within 20 days thereafter."

Raytheon would thus have to claim a purchase money security interest under another section because according to MBank and DuPont, the collateral in the transaction was inventory. The purchase money security interest would have to be justified under section 9.312(c) which applies to purchase money security interests in inventory. Section 9.312(c)(2) requires "the purchase money secured party [to give] notification in writing to the holder of conflicting security interests if the holder has filed a financing statement covering the same type of inventory." Raytheon, however, failed to give any notice to MBank or DuPont and could not, therefore, establish a valid purchase money security interest under this section.

Because Raytheon would be precluded from claiming a purchase money security interest under section 9.312(c) or section 9.312(d), MBank and DuPont would have priority over Raytheon in the accounts receivable of Howe under section 9.312(e). Section 9.312(e) states that "conflicting security interests rank according to priority in time of filing or perfection." Therefore, because both MBank and DuPont filed notice of their claims prior to Raytheon, they would have superior interests under section 9.312(e).

This analysis, however, suggested by MBank and DuPont begs the question. The question is whether Raytheon established a purchase money security interest in the accounts receivable of Howe not whether Raytheon properly perfected a purchase money security interest in the inventory of Howe. The analysis of whether Raytheon properly perfected a security interest in the inventory of Howe assumes that MBank and DuPont's characterization of the transaction is correct. But the very question to be decided is how to characterize the transaction for the purposes of defining a purchase money security interest. Nothing in the code mandates that Raytheon to claim a purchase money security interest in Howe's inventory. Raytheon claimed a purchase money security interest in the accounts receivable of Howe. The question is thus whether accounts receivable may be considered collateral for the purposes of a purchase money security interest.

There is, however, no other authority to our knowledge that expressly states that accounts receivable should be considered collateral for the purpose of a purchase money security interest. The Supreme Court of Minnesota has suggested that a purchase money security interest in accounts could validly arise. See *Northwestern National Bank Southwest v. Lectro Systems,* 262 N.W.2d 678, 680 (Minn. 1977) ("This is not a case in which funds were advanced and used for purchase of a receivable."). And, Professor Grant Gilmore, one of the original drafters of article 9, has stated in his treatise on security interests, that the purchase money concept might apply to intangible property in occasional cases. G. Gilmore, I Security Interests in Personal Property, 781 (1965) ("There seems to be no reason, however, why the term 'collateral' should have other than its normal meaning: the purchase-money concept may thus, in an occasional case, apply to intangible property. . . .").

MBank and DuPont have asserted that accounts receivable should not be considered collateral for the purpose of defining a purchase money security interest under Section 9.107(2). Their argument, adopted by the majority, is that because accounts receivable financing has been accorded a special importance by the Texas Uniform Commercial Code, its legal position should not be made less certain by the operation of Sections 9.107(2) and 9.312(d). Once a security interest has been created under section 9.107(2), section 9.312(d) grants it special status. Section 9.312(d) states that "a purchase money security interest in collateral other than inventory has priority over a conflicting security interest in the same collateral or its proceeds if the purchase money security interest is perfected at the time the debtor receives possession of the collateral or within 20 days thereafter."

. . . .

Because of the operation of section 9.312(d), however, the first party to file notice of a security interest in an account would not necessarily have priority under section 9.312(e)(1). Section 9.312(d) would grant priority over any interest filed previously in the same account if purchase money status in the account was first established under section 9.107. The legal position of accounts receivable financing might thus be made less certain if a purchase money security interest could be claimed in accounts receivable under section 9.107(2). Diminished certainty could result in the sense that the first party to file notice of its interest in an account under section 9.312(e) would be uncertain as to whether it had priority in the account or whether another party has priority because the latter established purchase money status in the same account under 9.107(2).

MBank and DuPont argue that this uncertainty in the legal position of accounts receivable financing should be prohibited because of the special importance accorded to accounts receivable financing under the code. They find this importance in the history of section 9.312(c) which prohibits the establishment of purchase money security interests in accounts receivable, derivatively, as proceeds of inventory. The argument points out that this prohibition was created due to the importance of accounts receivable financing in the economy. Based on these premises, the argument concludes that the possibility of a purchase money security interest in accounts receivable under section 9.107(2) should also be prohibited. The fallacy of this logic, however, is that it equates the value of accounts receivable as applied to a problem that arose in the area of inventory financing with the values behind the section 9.107 purchase money security interest.

The argument thus rests upon MBank and DuPont's interpretation of section 9.312(c). Section 9.312(c) provides that "a perfected purchase money security interest in inventory has priority over a conflicting security interest in the same inventory and also has priority in any identifiable cash proceeds received on or before the delivery of inventory to a buyer."

. . . .

Section 9.312(c) offered a solution to this conflict. It states that a prior right to the inventory of a debtor does not confer a prior right to any proceeds that arise from the sale of the inventory except for identifiable cash proceeds. There is no prior right to accounts receivable as proceeds from the sale of the inventory. Under this section, it would not be possible to establish a purchase money security interest in inventory and then claim a purchase money security interest in any of the accounts that arose from the sale of that inventory. This exclusion of accounts receivable as proceeds of inventory under section 9.312(c) rests upon the assumption that accounts receivable financing is more important in the economy than the financing of the types of inventory that produce accounts when sold.

MBank and DuPont thus argue that a purchase money security interest in accounts receivable should not be permitted under section 9.107(2) because a purchase money security interest in accounts receivable may not be claimed derivatively as proceeds of the sale of inventory under section 9.312(c). However, when this argument is examined in light of the policy interests underpinning section 9.107(2), the argument's core assumption, the importance of accounts receivable financing in the economy, dictates precisely the opposite result.

The most important policy justification for a purchase money security interest under section 9.107(2) is the protection that it gives to a debtor who is unable to raise additional funds to remain in business. Creditors who have previously loaned money to the debtor and taken a security interest in the debtor's goods may be unwilling to advance additional value or funds. These additional funds, however, could enable a debtor to purchase goods, make sales, and in turn, generate profits. Profits which could not only be used to create more business, but also, to allow the debtor to pay off the creditor's loans. The purchase money security provisions thus enable a leveraged debtor who is able to find a new lender to give that new lender a first claim on the new collateral purchased notwithstanding a prior filing by another creditor.

The arrangement between Raytheon and Howe exemplifies the use of accounts receivable to advance the policy rationale behind the purchase money security interest. It was the use of the accounts receivable by Raytheon as collateral for the x-ray machines that allowed Howe to continue to do business. The additional business that Howe was able to generate with the advance of the x-ray machines, at minimum, gave Howe an additional opportunity to stay in business. This opportunity was a benefit to creditors such as MBank and DuPont whose loans would not be repaid unless Howe had the ability to generate profits. It also demonstrates the importance of accounts receivable financing in another forum, the creation of purchase money security interests.

The use of accounts receivable as collateral in this case also benefitted MBank and DuPont as creditors because the consequences of an unpaid account were relatively greater to Raytheon. Raytheon, MBank and DuPont would each have been harmed if Howe's customers failed to pay their accounts. If an account receivable were to remain unpaid, Raytheon would lose the entire value of the x-ray machine advanced to Howe. In contrast, it is unlikely that the failure of one account would drive Howe into bankruptcy so that Howe would be unable to repay MBank and DuPont. Yet it is this additional risk taken by Raytheon which allowed Howe a profit that could be used to fund its business to the advantage of MBank and DuPont.

Finally, any obligation imposed on MBank and DuPont to determine whether Howe was using its accounts receivable to collateralize purchase money security transactions is diminished in two respects. First, as stated, it is these very purchase money transactions that allowed Howe an additional opportunity to service its debts to these creditors. Second, MBank and DuPont as creditors had already established relationships with Howe. In future transactions, it would not have been difficult for them to ascertain whether Howe was using any accounts to collateralize purchase money transactions with other creditors and draft the loan contracts accordingly.

To my mind, Raytheon has established a valid purchase money security interest under section 9.107(2) of the Texas Uniform Commercial Code. The x-ray machine advanced by Raytheon constituted the value that enabled Howe to acquire accounts receivable, the collateral, for the purposes of section 9.107(2). As such, this case should be reversed and remanded, where the issue of waiver could be examined with a headlight's incandescence and the retroactivity issue appropriately explored. I therefore respectfully DISSENT.

NOTES

Is Judge Goldberg's dissent persuasive? What problems do you foresee with extending purchase money protection to accounts?

CONSIGNMENTS

Read: U.C.C. §§ 9-114 and 2-326.

Some inventory financing is done through consignment, a method of entrusting goods by one person to another in a bailment for sale arrangement. The owner of goods, as consignor, entrusts the items to an agent, the consignee, to facilitate a sale of those items for the owner. If unable to sell the goods, the consignee may return them to the consignor who always maintains control over the terms of sale. Under Article 2 of the Code, a consignment is considered a sale or return arrangement. See § 2-326(1)(b).

Problems arise when the consignee's creditors lay claim to the consigned goods because the items look like inventory of the consignee. If in reality, the consignment is a security transaction, Article 9 governs and the consignee's creditors may prevail over the consignor based on sections 9-301 and 9-312. However, if the transaction is classified as a true consignment, the owner/consignor will have priority and section 2-326(3) will determine the priority dispute NOT Article 9. Under § 9-114, a priority dispute between an existing creditor with a perfected security interest in inventory (including after-acquired property) and a later consignor will be resolved in favor of inventory secured creditor unless the consignor notified existing creditors according to the provisions of § 2-326(3). The consignor must give the same notice to the debtor's inventory secured parties that the consignor would have to give had the transaction been a secured transaction instead of a consignment. The drafters of the Code required an intent test—if the parties intended a true consignment, then only section 9-114 of Article 9 applies. Under U.C.C. § 9-114(2), a consignor of goods who failed to comply with the notice requirement would be subordinated to "a person who would have a perfected security interest in the goods if they were the property of the debtor."

Identifying a true consignment is difficult. Usually with a true consignment, the consignee does not have an established place of business for dealing with the particular type of goods. If the consignee does have an established business, the property must be listed so as to inform the public that the goods held do not belong to the consignee. A true consignment is neither a sale nor a security device, instead, it is merely a marketing mechanism by which the owner markets certain goods to the public.

GEORGIA-PACIFIC CORP. v. WALTER E. HELLER & CO., SOUTHEAST, INC.

Florida District Court of Appeal, First District
37 U.C.C. Rep. Serv. 735 (1983)

Appeal from the Circuit Court for Duval County. Before Mills, Thompson and Wigginton, JJ.

Per Curiam.

Georgia Pacific Corporation appeals a final judgment in favor of Walter E. Heller & Co., et al., permitting Heller recovery of the value of certain property converted by Georgia Pacific in the amount of $11,321.00 plus interest. The issue for our review is whether the total business relation involving these parties and a bankrupt entity was a transaction encompassed within the Florida Uniform Commercial Code, § 672.326, Florida Statutes. No published Florida cases deal directly with the specific question before us and therefore we resort to authorities from other jurisdictions for assistance. The trial judge in this case, Judge Thomas D. Oakley, considered those authorities and favored the parties and this court with a well-reasoned and erudite judgment which we adopt as our own. That order provides as follows:

This cause came on for trial before the court without a jury.

The facts are not in dispute. In December of 1976, Georgia Pacific Corporation ("Defendant") entered into a contract with Bill Amos Brokerage Co., Inc. ("Bill Amos"), whereby Defendant agreed to consign stock to Bill Amos. The contract provided that the risk of loss for merchandise shipped to Bill Amos would pass to Bill Amos upon delivery of the merchandise by a carrier.

The contract contained numerous references to the term "consigned merchandise" and provided that Bill Amos would assist the Defendant in any reasonable manner to protect the interest of Defendant "in this consignment transaction including, but not limited to, execution (of) financing statement, posting of signs under a sign law, and otherwise." The Defendant took no action to perfect its interest in goods shipped to Bill Amos by the filing of a U.C.C.-1financing statement.

At the time Bill Amos entered into the agreement with the Defendant, Bill Amos operated a warehouse facility located in Jacksonville, Florida, at which Bill Amos was engaged in business as a wholesale food and grocery distributor, broker and merchant, dealing in food products and grocery items, including paper products.

Subsequent to the execution of the agreement, Defendant consigned merchandise to Bill Amos consisting of paper products such as paper towels, tissue and the like.

The Defendant shipped paper products to Bill Amos primarily to facilitate the sale of such products to military commissaries located in the State of Florida. When Bill Amos would ship consigned merchandise to a commissary, it would file a report with Defendant indicating that the delivery had been accomplished. The Defendant then invoiced the commissaries and received payments directly from the commissaries for the paper products delivered. Bill Amos received a commission from the Defendant representing 8% of the total sale price.

On August 2, 1977, Plaintiff's predecessor in interest, First National Heller-Factors, entered into an Inventory Loan Security Agreement and an Accounts Financing Security Agreement with Bill Amos. First National Heller-Factors obtained and filed U.C.C.-1financing statements covering all "accounts, contract rights, chattel paper and general intangibles, all inventory. . ." The financing statements also covered the proceeds of collateral.

On September 15, 1978, First National Heller-Factors assigned to Plaintiff Walter E. Heller & Company Southeast, Inc. ("Plaintiff"), all of its right, title and interest in the Inventory Loan Security Agreement, the Accounts Financing Security Agreement, and the financing statements in question.

On September 15, 1978, and at all material times thereafter, Bill Amos was indebted to Plaintiff in an amount in excess of $500,000.

On January 22, 1979, Bill Amos filed a voluntary petition in the United States Bankruptcy Court, For the Middle District of Florida, pursuant to Chapter XI of the Bankruptcy Act.

Shortly after the filing of the bankruptcy petition, the Defendant entered upon the premises of Bill Amos to reclaim the merchandise that had been consigned by Defendant to Bill Amos. The Defendant expected to find in excess of 1,400 cases of paper products. In fact, the Defendant located and removed from the Bill Amos facility consigned inventory consisting of 390 cases of goods, valued at $ 11,321.00.

Plaintiff contends that the removal of such goods by the Defendant was in derogation of the Plaintiff's superior rights to possession as a secured creditor and as such constituted conversion. Plaintiff argues that either the transaction constituted a consignment intended as security within the meaning of § 671.201(37), Florida Statutes, or was a sale or return transaction governed by the provisions of § 672.326, Florida Statutes. . . .

Defendant contends that the transaction was not a consignment intended as security. Defendant further contends that the paper products consigned to Bill Amos were not delivered "for sale" and that as such the provisions of Section 672.326(3), Florida Statutes, are inapplicable. Defendant relies primarily upon the case of *Walter E. Heller & Company Southeast, Inc. v. Riviana Foods, Inc.*, 648 F.2d 1059 [31 U.C.C. Rep. Serv. 881] (5th Cir. 1981).

The *Riviana* case, like the instant case, arose out of the Bill Amos bankruptcy proceeding. As in the instant case, the contractual agreement between Riviana and Bill Amos made no express provision for the sale of Riviana's goods by Bill Amos. Nonetheless, Riviana conceded, as the evidence indicates herein, that Bill Amos operated a place of business under its own name at which it dealt in food and grocery products. Riviana also admitted, as is admitted by the Defendant herein, that it took no steps whatsoever to evidence its retained ownership interest in the goods shipped by Riviana to Bill Amos and held at the Bill Amos facility.

In the *Riviana Foods* case, the United States District Court, For the Middle District of Florida, granted Riviana's motion for summary judgment in an unpublished opinion. The Court determined that the transaction between Riviana and Bill Amos was not a deemed sale or return under

§ 672.326(3), Florida Statutes. The United States Court of Appeals for the Fifth Circuit subsequently affirmed this opinion per curiam at 648 F.2d 1059.

A principal issue in the *Riviana* case, as in the instant case, was whether the goods had been delivered by Riviana to Bill Amos "for sale," since no express authority had been conferred upon Bill Amos to sell.

The *Riviana* case has been criticized as an incorrect interpretation of § 2-326(3) of the Uniform Commercial Code. See Brown, *U.C.C. Section 2-326(3): Creditor Protection in the Deemed Sale or Return Transaction,* 32 Case Western Reserve Law Review 904. This court does not agree with the decision reached in the *Riviana* case.

The legislative history with respect to § 672.326(3), Florida Statutes, indicates that a consignee's creditors are to be protected from secret reservations in ostensible ownership situations. Official Comment 2, § 672.326, Florida Statutes.

Section 672.326(3), Florida Statutes, was enacted for the purpose of protecting the creditors of a merchant who is the apparent owner of goods located at the place of business of the merchant.

In the case of *Manufacturer's Acceptance Corporation v. Penning's Sales, Inc.,* 487 P.2d 1053 [9 U.C.C. Rep. Serv. 797] (Wash. App. 1971), a paint manufacturer shipped an inventory of paint to itself in care of a paint store under an agreement with the store owner by which the paint manufacturer reserved title to the paint which the store owner was to hold in a storage area at the rear of the paint store, subject to the manufacturer's order to ship the paint to one of the paint manufacturer's dealers in the area. For this service, the paint store was paid 6% of the amount of each order shipped or delivered to a dealer of the paint manufacturer. The paint store conducted a retail paint sales business in the front portion of the store.

The paint manufacturer contended that the agreement was simply a warehousing agreement, and that as such the goods could not be subjected to the claims of Manufacturer's Acceptance Corp., which held a perfected security interest in the inventory of the paint store. The court held that the transaction was a sale or return within the meaning of § 2-326 of the Uniform Commercial Code, since the paint store was dealing in goods of the kind involved in the inventory stored on the premises. The court went on to point out that the paint manufacturer had not rendered the sale or return provision inapplicable by establishing one of the three exceptions contained in § 2-326 (3) of the Uniform Commercial Code.

The decision in *Manufacturer's Acceptance Corp. v. Penning's Sales, Inc., supra,* demonstrates that the Uniform Commercial Code disregards the intended character of the transactions between the parties and treats a transaction as a sale or return when goods are delivered to a person who maintains a place of business at which he deals in goods of the kind involved under any name other than that of the person making delivery. See 1 Anderson, Uniform Commercial Code, § 2-326:6.

In the case of *General Electric Co. v. Pettingell Supply Co.,* 199 NE 2d 326 [2 U.C.C. Rep. Serv. 184] (Mass 1964), General Electric delivered electrical fixtures to Pettingell Supply Company. Pursuant to the agreement between the parties, Pettingell could sell to certain customers who purchased for their own use and was also authorized to make deliveries under contracts for sale entered into between General Electric and certain distributors of General Electric.

The court held that § 2-326(3) of the Uniform Commercial Codewas applicable, and that as such the creditors of Pettingell had a superior right to possession of the goods.

The agreement between Defendant and Bill Amos refers to consigned merchandise. Although Defendant has argued that the transactions in question were only storage and warehousing agreements, the court, in *In re Novak, supra*, after finding that the correspondence between the parties referred to the goods as "consigned stock" and "consigned inventory," held that use of the term "consigned" would be deemed to have the meaning associated with a general commercial transaction. The court stated:

> The term "consignment" used in a commercial sense, ordinarily implies an agent, and denotes that property is committed to the consignee for care or sale. [*Id.* at p.202]

Just as the existence of an undisclosed interest in goods does not prevent passage of title pursuant to § 672.403(2), Florida Statutes, neither should a hidden interest prevent the enforcement of a security interest in goods delivered "for sale," whether the sale was to be made by the supplier or by the person to whom the goods were consigned.

Just as in *Vonins*, Bill Amos was providing a component part of the total sales transaction, for which it was paid a percentage of the overall consideration. The consignment of paper goods by Defendant to Bill Amos was to facilitate sales transactions and was thus "for sale" within the meaning of § 672.326(3), Florida Statutes.

In the instant case, the Defendant delivered possession to a consignee, Bill Amos, who was engaged in the business of selling goods of the type consigned by Defendant, and the Defendant failed to give public notice of any retained interest in the goods.

It should further be noted that although Bill Amos had no express authority to sell or otherwise dispose of merchandise consigned to it by the Defendant, the Defendant found that in excess of 1,000 cases of merchandise were missing when it attempted to retrieve its consigned goods. Although there is no direct evidence as to what has become of the goods, it is clear that as a dealer of goods in the kind involved Bill Amos could have passed good title to the goods pursuant to the provisions of § 672.403, Florida Statutes.

Furthermore, it is obvious from the provisions of the contract between the Defendant and Bill Amos, a contract prepared by Defendant, that the Defendant was aware that some action was required to protect its interest in the consigned merchandise. Certainly, the Defendant was in the best position to protect itself. It could have done so by storing its products with a party who did not deal in food and grocery items. It could have done so by complying with the Article 9 filing requirements. The Defendant failed to protect its own interests and, as such, had an unperfected interest in the consigned goods, subordinate to the perfected security interest of Plaintiff.

The removal of goods by the Defendant was in derogation of Plaintiff's superior rights to possession of the inventory as a secured creditor and as such, constituted conversion. See 12 Fla. Jur. 2d, Conversion and Replevin, Sections 6 and 17. See also *Fletcher v. Dees*, 101 Fla 402; 134 So 234 (1931). As such, Plaintiff is entitled to recover the reasonable market value of the property converted, together with interest thereon. 12 Fla. Jur. 2d, Conversion and Replevin, Section 20.

In the instant case, the value of the goods removed by Defendant from the warehouse of Bill Amos was $11,321.00. Plaintiff is entitled to a final judgment in that sum, together with interest at the rate of 6% per annum from January 22, 1979 through June 30, 1982, and at the rate of 12% per annum from July 1, 1982, through the date hereof. Based on the foregoing, it is

Ordered and adjudged that Plaintiff, Walter E. Heller & Company Southeast, Inc., do have and recover of and from the Defendant, Georgia Pacific Corporation, the sum of $11,321.00, together with interest thereon in the amount of $3,264.17, and costs of this action in the amount of $41.00, for a total sum of $14,626.17, for which let execution issue.

In adopting the trial court's opinion we, as did the trial judge, decline to follow the decision of the Fifth Circuit Court of Appeals in *Riviana* and rely instead on the better reasoned view of the authorities cited herein.

Affirmed.

MILLS, THOMPSON and WIGGINTON, JJ., concur.

NOTES

(1) Unless a consignment is intended as security, reservation of title by the consignor is not a security interest. Nevertheless, a consignment sale is subject to the provisions on consignment sales under section 2-326. This means that in most instances, compliance with Article 9's filing provisions is necessary in order to protect the consignor's interest. Thus, even though most consignments are not intended as security and are therefore not subject to the provisions of Article 9, they may still be subject to filing requirements. See also, *In re Great American Veal, Inc.*, 59 B.R. 27, 1 U.C.C. Rep. Serv. 2d 565 (1985).

(2) In *General Electric Co. v. Pettingell Supply Co.* (cited in *Heller*), the plaintiff/consignor argued that U.C.C. § 2-326d id not apply to contracts that established only a principal-agent relationship. The court disagreed with the novel argument and observed that U.C.C. § 2-326(3) states, in part: "The provisions of this subsection are applicable even though an agreement purports to reserve title to the person making delivery until payment or resale or uses such words as 'on consignment' or 'on memorandum.' " Does the word "resale" in that subsection allow the inference that the goods must first be sold to the consignee? The primary consideration for the courts dealing with this issue is whether goods were delivered for sale. Thus, any retention of title by the consignor will be given little weight where it has been determined that the goods were delivered "for sale or return."

(3) Unlike goods held on consignment, which may require filing to protect the owner's interest, goods held for processing into a manufactured product are not subject to any mandatory filing requirements of Article 9. See *Medomak Canning Co. v. William Underwood Co.*, 25 U.C.C. Rep. Serv. 473 (D. Me. 1977).

PROBLEM 18.1

A mobile home manufacturer consigns ten mobile homes to its dealer. The dealer subsequently grants a security interest in the mobile homes to a credit corporation. The manufacturer then retakes possession of the mobile homes. The credit corporation brings suit to recover damages for conversion. What result? See *General Electric Credit Corp. v. Town & Country Mobile Homes, Inc.*, 574 P.2d 50, 22 U.C.C. Rep. Serv. 1255 (Ariz. Ct. App. 1977).

PROBLEM 18.2

Finance Company has a perfected security interest in Retailer's inventory. Supplier agrees to ship goods to Retailer on consignment. Supplier files a proper financing statement and notifies Finance Company of the consignment arrangement. Retailer then notifies Supplier of financial difficulties and requests that Supplier postpone shipment. Two years pass before Supplier ships the goods. Retailer sells the goods. Payment is accepted in the form of a promissory note. Retailer defaults. Finance Company takes possession of Retailer's entire inventory. What rights does Supplier have?

[D] Crops

Read: U.C.C. § 9-312(2).

The Code provides a special form of purchase money protection for creditors who extend new value which enables a debtor to produce crops during a production season. The protection is limited, however. Under section 9-312(2), a later, perfected secured party obtains priority over the earlier perfected secured party only if the purchase money advance was made within three months of the time when the crops became growing crops and the debt to the prior secured party became due more than six months prior to that time. Knowledge of the first security transaction does not affect a secured party's rights. This rule resolves priority conflicts between lenders who advance monies against current crop production and prior secured parties who also claim an interest in such crops. Thus, even though a farmer may be in default on a prior loan, she will be able to use current crop production as collateral for a new loan.

PRODUCTION CREDIT ASSN. OF THE MIDLANDS v. FARM & TOWN INDUS.

Supreme Court of Iowa
518 N.W.2d 339, 23 U.C.C.R. Serv. 2d 1246 (1994)

ANDREASEN, JUSTICE.

This appeal involves the determination of the validity of and the priority of competing creditors' liens on a debtor's 1991 and 1992 corn crops and proceeds. *[Eds. note: we have chosen only to reproduce the portion of the case discussing the 1992 crop]* . . . .

I. Background and Factual Proceedings.

On August 10, 1990, McGraw Farms, a partnership consisting of Dale McGraw and Verle McGraw, along with Dorothy McGraw and Roxanne McGraw (collectively McGraw) entered into a loan restructure agreement with Production Credit Association of the Midlands (PCA). As part of the agreement McGraw granted PCA a security interest in "all crops now growing or hereafter planted or grown . . .whether harvested or unharvested; all stored crops wherever kept; all products of crops growing, to be grown, or stored . . . ." The security agreement extended to all proceeds and products of the described collateral. PCA filed a financing statement to perfect its security interest.

Farm & Town Industries, Inc. (FTI), a licensed grain dealer, contracted in August 1991 to buy a total of 20,000 bushels of corn then growing from McGraw. In September PCA sent written notice of its security interest in McGraw's crops to FTI. Pursuant to the contracts McGraw delivered the corn to FTI in October. FTI drafted a crop proceeds check representing payment under the contracts, jointly payable to McGraw and FTI. FTI then canceled that check and applied the proceeds to McGraw's outstanding balance. FTI later reissued a check made payable to McGraw and PCA. The check was not delivered.

On January 14, 1992, the McGraw partnership filed a petition under chapter 12 of the United States Bankruptcy Code.[9] PCA filed a motion to dismiss the bankruptcy case. In April McGraw filed a motion for authority to obtain credit or to incur debt under section 364 of the bankruptcy code. See 11 U.S.C. § 364(d)(1988). On May 12 the bankruptcy court granted McGraw's motion and authorized FTI to extend credit to enable McGraw to produce a 1992 crop. The court's order granted FTI "a first security interest in the 1992 crop and any proceeds thereof . . . ."

Following a June 23 hearing on PCA's motion to dismiss, the bankruptcy court dismissed McGraw's chapter 12 case. See 11 U.S.C. § 1208(c)(1), (9). McGraw appealed the dismissal. The dismissal order was silent on the matter of FTI's section 364(d) lien. The court later denied, on procedural grounds, two motions by FTI to expand the dismissal order to preserve its priority lien on the 1992 crop. FTI took no appeal from either ruling. McGraw's appeal of the dismissal order was later denied as untimely.

On July 6, PCA filed a petition in Iowa district court to foreclose on certain mortgages and security interests it held against McGraw. PCA sought to establish that its claims to McGraw's property were superior to all other creditors, including FTI.

PCA subsequently filed a motion for partial summary judgment against FTI asserting that its security interests in both McGraw's 1992 and 1991 crops and proceeds took priority over FTI's claims. After a hearing on the motion, the district court made a calendar entry granting summary judgment in favor of PCA on both counts. FTI then filed a motion under Iowa Rule of Civil Procedure 179(b) to alter or amend the ruling and to find that its liens on both crops took priority over PCA's interests. PCA resisted FTI's motion and also filed a rule 179(b) motion asking the court to set forth its findings of fact and conclusions of law.

Later the court issued a written decision denying FTI's motion and affirming summary judgment for PCA. The court found that (1) the bankruptcy court's dismissal of McGraw's chapter 12 case vacated FTI's security interest in the 1992 crop and (2) PCA's interest in the 1991 crop proceeds was prior and superior to FTI's unsecured claim. FTI appeals.

On appeal FTI argues that (1) dismissal of the bankruptcy case did not vacate the court-authorized lien on McGraw's 1992 crop; (2) its security interest in the 1992 crop is enforceable and superior to PCA's security interest under Iowa law; (3) the McGraw partnership is liable for the debt incurred during the pendency of the chapter 12 case; and (4) as a buyer in the ordinary course of business it takes the 1991 proceeds free of PCA's interest. Further discussion of the facts will be detailed in the course of our analysis of the legal issues presented.

. . . .

[9] Congress created chapter 12 bankruptcy in 1986 for the benefit of "family farmers." See Pub. L. No. 99-554, 100 Stat. 3105 (1986) (codified as amended at 11 U.S.C. §§ 1201-1231(1988)). "Chapter 12 was designed to afford another avenue of reorganization for those farm debtors who had no hope of meeting the stricter adequate protection and confirmation standards of chapter 11." 9B Am. Jur. 2d Bankruptcy § 2717, at 415 (1991).

III. 1992 Crop.

Secured transactions are governed by Article 9 of the Uniform Commercial Code (U.C.C.). See Iowa Code §§ 554.9101-.9507(1991). Priority among conflicting security interests in the same collateral is generally determined by the time of the filing or perfection. *Id.* § 554.9312(5). Here the parties initially agree that before McGraw filed its chapter 12 petition, PCA possessed a prior security interest in McGraw's 1992 crop pursuant to the terms of the August 1990 loan restructure agreement. They also agree that on May 12, 1992 the bankruptcy court granted FTI a superior lien on the same crop and proceeds.

The court's order authorized McGraw to obtain credit from FTI in the amount of $ 50,000 in order to procure inputs to produce the 1992 crop. When certain conditions are met section 364(d) of the bankruptcy code allows the court to "authorize the obtaining of credit or the incurring of debt secured by a senior or equal lien on the property of the estate that is subject to a [prior] lien." 11 U.S.C. § 364(d)(1). Relying on this order FTI extended credit to McGraw and McGraw in turn executed a credit agreement, a security agreement, and an assignment of proceeds and loss payable agreement securing FTI's lien on the 1992 crop and proceeds. The security agreement provided that it was "subject to and limited by the U.S. Bankruptcy Court and Orders of the Bankruptcy Court . . . ." FTI also filed a financing statement to perfect its security interest.

. . . .

B. Application of State Law.

PCA argued, and the district court agreed, that state law was not relevant because the bankruptcy dismissal completely voided FTI's security interest. Thus, PCA did not address the relative priorities of the security interests under state law.

A leading authority on bankruptcy law comments on the relevance of state law in this context:

> The most difficult question for the parties to the transaction, and particularly the non-debtor party, is to determine the extent to which normal, *i.e.*, non-bankruptcy, documentation practices should be followed. If, for example, the lien authorized under section 364(c) is one which, absent bankruptcy, must be perfected by recording to be valid or prior against competing interests, such action should not be necessary as long as the bankruptcy proceeding is extant . . . . What, however, would the result be if the case is dismissed? Unless the court for cause orders otherwise, under section 349(b) (3), dismissal re-vests property of the estate in the entity in which the property was vested immediately before the commencement of the case. While the dismissal should be conditioned upon protection of the rights of parties . . .this may be scant protection after the case has been dismissed . . . . The better practice is for the lender to fully document its loan and to comply with applicable non-bankruptcy recording statutes.

2 Collier P 364.04, at 364-11 to 364-12. We believe that under these circumstances it would be inequitable to deprive a secured creditor of an interest otherwise enforceable under state law. See *Kucera*, 123 B.R. at 855. Therefore, we must determine the rights as between these competing creditors under Iowa commercial law.

C. Iowa Code Section 554.9312(2).

We find the record clear that FTI fully complied with statutory requirements for filing and perfection of its security interest in the 1992 crop. Although PCA's security interest was perfected much earlier, FTI claims that its lien takes priority under Iowa Code section 554.9312(2).

Under Article 9 of the U.C.C., purchase-money security interests generally take priority over conflicting security interests in the same collateral. See Iowa Code § 554.9312(3), (4). Loans for the purchase of seed and other supplies for crop production are forms of purchase-money financing. Crop loans are treated differently from purchase-money loans. *Id.* § 554.9312(2). Section 554.9312(2) provides:

> A perfected security interest in crops for new value given to enable the debtor to produce the crops during the production season and given not more than three months before the crops become growing crops by planting or otherwise takes priority over an earlier perfected security interest to the extent that such earlier interest secures obligations due more than six months before the crops become growing crops . . ., even though the person giving new value had knowledge of the earlier security interest.

Like other purchase-money provisions, we believe this statute must be applied to "maximize the protection given to the creditor who is actually financing the production of the [current] crop." *In re Bossingham*, 49 B.R. 345, 352 (Bankr. S.D. Iowa 1985).

It is undisputed that FTI extended $50,000 credit in May of 1992 making it possible for McGraw to produce a 1992 crop. FTI's security interest was for new value and was given within three months of planting. See, *e.g., Bossingham*, 49 B.R. at 351; *McCoy v. Steffen*, 227 Neb. 72, 416 N.W.2d 16, 18 (Neb. 1987).

Over the years PCA made a number of loans to McGraw. On September 1, 1991, McGraw failed to pay an installment of $43,046.85 due under several notes and the 1990 loan agreement. McGraw also failed to pay an installment due on October 1 of $45,119.62. Because McGraw failed to cure the default PCA declared the entire obligation due in December.

The term "due" in section 554.9312(2) has been interpreted as overdue. See *Salem Nat'l Bank v. Smith,* 890 F.2d 22, 23-24 (7th Cir. 1989); 13 Neil E. Harl, Agricultural Law § 118.02[3], at 118-38 to 118-39 (1993). Applying this provision we find that two of McGraw's installments to PCA were due more than six months before the 1992 crop was planted. *Salem Nat'l Bank,* 890 F.2d at 24 (crop production lender has priority to the extent that installment payments are overdue). Therefore, under section 554.9312(2) FTI's purchase-money security interest in the 1992 crop takes priority over PCA's security interest.

. . . .

V. Disposition.

We hold that the bankruptcy court's dismissal of McGraw's chapter 12 case did not void FTI's security interest in McGraw's 1992 crop under state law. Under Iowa Code section 554.9312(2)FTI's security interest takes priority over PCA's interest in the 1992 proceeds. . . ..

Accordingly, we affirm the court's grant of partial summary judgment concerning the 1991 proceeds . . . .

[E] Retaining or Losing Character

One of the problem issues surrounding purchase money transactions is the continuing nature of the purchase money interest when the original loan is refinanced through renewal or consolidation with another obligation of the debtor. There is a split of authority concerning the treatment to be afforded such re-financing cases. One line of cases holds that a purchase money security interest is automatically "transformed" into a non-purchase money interest when the proceeds from a re-financing are used to satisfy the original note. Under this theory, the collateral secures either an antecedent debt, or something more than the purchase money price; either way, interest is no longer purchase money. See *e.g., In Re Keeton*, 161 B.R. 410 (Bankr. S.D. Ohio 1993) and In *Re Faughn*, 69 B.R. 18(Bankr. E.D. Mo. 1986).

A second line of cases articulates a "dual status" rule. This line of cases rejects the all-or-nothing approach in favor of a situation-by-situation analysis. Security interests are not automatically destroyed by re-financing or consolidation; instead, the creditor's interest may become part purchase money and part non-purchase money. The dual status rule derives from the language of § 9-107, which provides that an interest is purchase money "to the extent" that it is taken to secure the purchase price of collateral. Consequently, the theory provides that a purchase money security interest under an original note remains purchase money in a consolidation or re-financing, to the extent the security interest is taken to secure the purchase price of the collateral. See *e.g.,* In *Re Short*, 170 B.R. 128, 24 U.C.C. Rep. Serv. 2d 1020 (Bankr. S.D. Ill. 1994) and *In Re Parsley*, 104 B.R. 72 (Bankr. S.D. Ind. 1988). As you read the following case, consider which rule gives greater effect to the substance of a re-financing transaction.

IN RE IONOSPHERE CLUBS, INC.

United States District Court, Southern District New York
123 B.R. 166, 13 U.C.C. Rep. Serv. 2d 1276 (1991)

SWEET, DISTRICT JUDGE.

A number of financial institutions holding promissory notes of Eastern Airlines have appealed from a ruling of the Bankruptcy Court, *In re Ionosphere Clubs, Inc*., 112 B.R. 78 (Bankr. S.D.N.Y. 1990), that certain security interests which they hold in equipment owned by Eastern Airlines, Inc. ("Eastern") are not exempted form the automatic bankruptcy stay. For the following reasons, the decision of the Bankruptcy Court is reversed.

The Parties

The appellants include a group of European Banks that lent money to Eastern to finance its purchase of a number of Airbus aircraft ("the Airbus Lenders"), the first National Bank of Boston ("FNBB") as trustee under an indenture of mortgage which secures the loans, and Lazard Brothers & Co., Ltd. ("Lazard"), the holder of a number of other notes from Eastern.

Eastern is a corporation engaged in the business of providing air transportation service in interstate and foreign commerce. Eastern's principal place of business and its corporate headquarters are located in Miami, Florida. Eastern filed its petition under Chapter 22 of the Bankruptcy Codeon March 9, 1989, and currently operates as a debtor-in-possession pursuant to §§ 1107(a) and 1108 of the Code.

Statutory Scheme

The filing of a bankruptcy petition ordinarily stays all actions by creditors of the debtor, including any action by a secured creditor to take possession of its collateral. 11 U.S.C. § 362. One exception to this provision is created by § 1110, which permits a secured creditor to enforce its rights to take possession of the debtor's property if the creditor has a particular type of security interest in a particular type of property. Aircraft owned by air carriers are one such type of property. A creditor who possesses a "purchase-money equipment security interest" ("PMESI") in the property is allowed to bypass the automatic stay and to take possession of the property in the event of default by the debtor. Section 1110 also provides a limited extension of time in which the debtor may elect to cure the default and to continue to make current payments in order to prevent the creditor from taking possession of the collateral. The Second Circuit has held that once § 1110's explicit conditions are met, a court may not impose further conditions on a creditor's exercise of the rights which the statute provides. *In re Air Vermont, Inc.*, 761 F.2d 130, 134 (2d Cir.. 1985).

Proceedings Below

In May 1989, shortly after it filed its petition, Eastern moved for a declaration that a number of its credit agreements with various lenders were not subject to § 1110. The Airbus Lenders were the only parties to oppose that motion and to cross-move for a declaration that § 1110 required Eastern to continue to make payments on the loans or to surrender the collateral. FNBB, as trustee of the indenture which secured the loan, and Lazard, as holder of other notes secured by the same indenture, joined in opposing Eastern's motion and in the cross-motion. Eastern's motion was granted and the Airbus Lenders' cross-motion was denied in a memorandum opinion issued March 30, 1990, *In re Ionosphere Clubs, Inc., supra*, 112 B.R. 78.

The Facts

The loans and corresponding security arrangements which are the subject of this dispute are set forth in two sets of documents: the Indenture of Mortgage dated October 1, 1963, as supplemented, modified, and restated, between Eastern and FNBB as Trustee and successor by merger to the Old Colony Trust Company ("the Indenture"), and two Credit Agreements, one executed in 1978 and one in 1981 ("the Credit Agreements").

The Indenture was created in 1963 by Eastern as a means of collateralizing loans which it had taken out and which it planned to take out in the future. It grants each lender a security interest in the form of a primary mortgage on a "floating collateral pool" consisting of aircraft, aircraft engines, and various spare parts owned by Eastern ("the Collateral Pool"). The mortgage is held by FNBB as trustee of all of the lenders. The actual property in the pool changes over time as old property is removed from the pool and new property is added, subject to various limitations of the Indenture and the oversight of the trustee. All of the loans issued pursuant to the Indenture are secured by all of the property in the Collateral Pool, so that if Eastern defaults on any one of the loans FNBB may take possession of any or all of the property in the Collateral Pool, and to use that property to pay off all of the loans "ratably to the persons entitled thereto without discrimination or preference." The trustee holds the mortgage in the Collateral Pool "for the ratable benefit and security of each and every" lender, "without preference, priority or distinction."

The Credit Agreements set forth the specific terms of the loans which are the focus of this appeal. The Airbus Lenders extended credit to Eastern to enable it to finance the purchase of twenty-three Airbus Aircraft, fourteen under the loan made in 1978 and nine more under the 1981 agreement (collectively, "the Aircraft"). In 1978, the loans totalled $247 million, with another $221 million in 1981. Both the 1978 and 1981 loans were evidenced by a separate series of notes issued for each individual Aircraft ("the Notes"). Both agreements provided that the Aircraft would become part of the Collateral Pool, and that the indenture would secure payment of the loans. In addition, the Credit Agreements specified that if Eastern elected to remove any of the Aircraft from the Collateral Pool, it would be immediately required to prepay the outstanding amount of the note associated with that Aircraft. Because such prepayment would constitute a payment required under the Credit Agreements, a refusal to prepay would constitute a default under the terms of the Indenture.

Both the Indenture and the two Credit Agreements are governed by New York state law.

Prior to filing its bankruptcy petition, Eastern had sold twelve of the Aircraft which had been purchased with the proceeds of the 1978 loan and had prepaid the Notes associated with those Aircraft. Thus, as of the petition date there were eleven Aircraft remaining in the Collateral Pool. Eastern's outstanding indebtedness on the Notes associated with these Aircraft amounted to $95.8 million, while the market value of the property in the Collateral Pool totalled $820 million. At that time Lazard held all of the remaining loans secured by the Indenture ("the Non-Airbus Loans"), which had a total outstanding value of $118 million. After filing its petition, Eastern ceased making any payments on all of the loans secured by the Indenture.

The Airbus Lenders assert that this default, combined with § 1110, permits FNBB to seize the Aircraft and sell them. Under the Indenture's terms, the proceeds of such sale would be applied equally and ratable to all loans secured by the Collateral Pool, not just to the Notes held by the Airbus Lenders. Thus, because the Airbus loans constitute less than half of the total outstanding loans subject to the Indenture, if the appellants' cross-motion were successful the Airbus Lenders would receive less than half of the proceeds from the repossession and sale of Aircraft.

Since filing the motion at issue here, Eastern has sold the remaining Aircraft pursuant to orders providing that the sales were without prejudice to the rights of the parties to this appeal under § 1110 and that the proceeds of the sales would be held in escrow and would be deemed the equivalent of the Aircraft for the purposes of this dispute.

Discussion

1. Standard of Review

The Bankruptcy Court's decision is subject to de novo review in this Court. For the most part, the facts are not in dispute, and appellants challenge only the legal conclusions of the Bankruptcy Court. *Brunner v. New York State Higher Educations Services Corp.*, 831 F.2d 395, 396 (2d Cir.. 1987); *In re Beker Industries Corp.*, 89 B.R. 336, 342n. 5 (S.D.N.Y. 1988). Because the Bankruptcy Court's decision was based primarily on interpretation of the parties' written agreements, the issues raised in this appeal present questions of law. *In re Topco, Inc.*, 894 F.2d 727, 738 (5th Cir. 1990).

2. The Airbus Lenders' Standing

At the outset, Eastern claims that the Airbus Lenders themselves have no security interest in any property in the Collateral Pool, because the only party with the power to seize property in the pool is FNBB, the trustee under the Indenture. However, § 1110 by its own terms applies to situations in which a trustee holds the security interest for the benefit of the actual creditor, thus the fact that FNBB is the party which holds the power to seize the collateral does not defeat the appellants' claims.

3. Section 1110

a. PMESI

There is no dispute that the Aircraft are equipment of the type subject to § 1110. The next question to be answered is whether the security interest in the Aircraft which is created by the Indenture and the Credit Agreements is a PMESI. Although the application of § 1110 depends almost entirely on whether a security interest is or is not a PMESI, the Bankruptcy Code offers no definition of the term. The appellants assert, and the Bankruptcy Court agreed, that a PMESI may be defined by reference to the definition of all purchase-money security interest ("PMSI") contained in § 9-107 of the U.C.C. Eastern opposes this view, claiming that the addition of the term "equipment" in § 1110 reflects a congressional intent to distinguish the type of interest at issue there from a standard PMSI. However, Eastern offers no alternative definition of the term.

The appellants' contention is adopted, that a PMESI is simply a PMSI, as defined by § 9-107, in one of the limited types of "equipment" covered by § 1110. Therefore, as both parties agree that the Aircraft are such equipment, the question reduces to whether the security interest in the Aircraft created by the transaction are PMSIs.

b. PMSI

Section 9-107 specifies that:

A security interest is a "purchase money security interest" to the extent that it is

(a) taken or retained by the seller of the collateral to secure all or part of its price, or

(b) taken by a person who by making advances or incurring an obligation gives value to enable the debtor to acquire rights in or the use of collateral if such value is in fact so used.

Eastern does not dispute that the Airbus Lenders gave present consideration—the Airbus loans—in exchange for security interests in the Aircraft. The Airbus Lenders undeniably took whatever security interest they acquired as security for those loans, not to secure any pre-existing obligations of Eastern. Nevertheless, the Bankruptcy Court held that no PMSI could have been created because the Aircraft were "taken as collateral securing the antecedent debt owed to the other lenders." 112 B.R. at 83. This conclusion was based on the statement that "[t]he general rule is if collateral secures debt other than its own price, it is not a PMSI." *Id.*

However, the only authority cited in support of this "rule" concerned situations in which the "debt other than its own price" was a debt owed to the same creditor as the one seeking PMSI status. See *In re Norrell,* 426 F. Supp. 435, 436 (M.D. Ga. 1977); *In re Manuel,* 507 F.2d 990 (5th Cir.. 1975). Moreover, as discussed *infra*, the more modern trend is to recognize that only the security interest which secures the non-purchase price debt is not a PMSI, but the interest which secures the purchase price dept retains its PMSI character. See, *e.g., Pristas v. Landaus of Plymouth, Inc.,* 742 F.2d 797, 800 (3d Cir.. 1984). Under this approach, the relevant question is whether the financing party takes an interest in the collateral as security for the purchase price obligation, not whether the purchased property also serves or will serve as collateral for other debts of the purchaser.

Therefore, the fact that the Aircraft became part of the Collateral Pool subject to the Indenture does not take the transaction outside the scope of § 9-107. At least at the time the loans were made, the Airbus Lenders possessed PMSIs in the Aircraft.

. . . .

d. Add-on clauses

The Bankruptcy Court also concluded that even if PMSIs had at one time been created in the Aircraft, they had been destroyed by the fact that the Aircraft were placed into the Collateral Pool and the Airbus Lenders received a mortgage in the entire pool under the terms of the Indenture. 112 B.R. at 84-86. This approach relies on the "transformation rule," which states that "[a] PMESI is destroyed when PMESI collateral is co-mingled with non-PMESI collateral." 112 B.R. at 84.

The general problem of analyzing loans which are secured by collateral other than or in addition to property which is purchased with the loan proceeds is addressed in McLaughlin, *"Add On" Clauses in Equipment Purchase Money Financing: Too Much of a Good Thing,* 49 Ford. L.Rev. 661 (1981). In this article, then-Professor McLaughlin discussed the various types of "add on" clauses which can affect purchase money security agreements. "Debt add on" clauses seek to use the purchased property to secure debts in addition to the purchase price, such as pre-existing debts from the purchaser to the seller/financier, or debts created after the property is acquired. "Collateral add on" clauses extend the lender's security interest to collateral other than the purchased property. Finally, "debt collateral add on clauses" apply additional collateral to secure the purchase money debt and use the purchased property to secure debt other than that used for the purchase.

As the article explains, at the time of its publication several courts had adopted the position that an add on clause in a security agreement was enough to destroy any PMSI created by the agreement. See, *e.g., In re Simpson,* 4 U.C.C. Rep. Serv. 243 (Bankr. W.D. Mich. 1966) (denying PMSI because of collateral add on clause); *In re Manuel,* 507 F.2d 990 (5th Cir.. 1975) (debt collateral add on clause destroyed PMSI). However, at least one New York court had rejected the view that the presence of a collateral add on clause would defeat a creditor's claim to have a PMSI. *National Cash Register Co. v. Mishkin's 125th St., Inc.,* 65 Misc.2d 386, 389, 317 N.Y.S.2d 436, 440 (N.Y. Civ. Ct. 1970) ("Defendant had a purchase money interest [as] defined in Section 9-107 U.C.C.There is no basis for holding that the nature of its interest has been changed because it included an after-acquired property provision.").

Professor McLaughlin pointed out that the language of § 9-107, particularly the fact that it defined a PMSI as a security interest "to the extent" that it secures a purchase price debt, suggested that a security interest could have both PMSI and non-PMSI components. He concluded that, provided it is possible to determine what portion of the security interest secures purchase price dept, the existence of a "collateral add on" or a "debt collateral add on clause" should not eliminate the PMSI character of the interest. 49 Ford. L. Rev. at 691-92, 696.

This rule has been referred to as the "dual status" rule, because it allows a security interest to have both the status of a PMSI, to the extent that it is secured by collateral purchased with loan proceeds, and the status of a general security interest, to the extent that the collateral secures obligations unrelated to its purchase.

The important point here is that it is the security interest which has the dual status, not the loan which it secures. To the extent that the security interest gives the creditor the right to seize the collateral because of a default on the purchase price obligation, it is a PMSI, and to the extent that it allows seizure because of defaults on other loans, it is non-PMSI. If a dual status creditor is permitted to take priority in possession of the collateral because of a PMSI, the proceeds of sale of the collateral may only be applied to satisfy the purchase price debt. Any surplus would be returned to the debtor, to be held for the benefit of all creditors who held non-purchase money security interests in the collateral.[10]

This scheme requires that the debtor's payments be clearly allocated to each of its obligations, so that a default can be clearly traced to a particular loan. The creditor holding that loan would then have PMSI priority in whatever collateral was purchased with that loan, but only general secured creditor status with respect to the other collateral securing the loan. See 49 Ford. L.Rev. at 691-99.

Of course, where the obligations are owed to different creditors, there is not problem in allocating payments to each individual loan. The only complexity arises when the debtor takes multiple loans from a single creditor to finance multiple purchases, with each loan secured by security interests in all of the purchased property.[11] In this event, the debtor might make a single periodic payment to the creditor rather than separate payments on each loan. In the event of default, the creditor must be able to determine how much is outstanding on each loan, to determine how much of a PMSI exists in each of the purchased items. Provided that there is some method for doing so, the creditor retains its preferred standing with respect to the collateral. See 49 Ford. L.Rev. at 694; *Pristas, supra*, 742 F.2d at 801.

After discussing both the transformation rule and the dual status rule, the Bankruptcy Court stated that the dual status rule had been adopted by only a "minority of courts," and was inapplicable to this case because there was "no scheme to allocate between collateral and debts." 112 B.R. at 84, 85. In fact, the appellants have cited twelve cases decided since 1981 in which courts have chosen to follow Professor McLaughlin's analysis and to apply the dual status rule rather than the transformation rule. *See Pristas, supra*, 742 F.2d 797.

The Bankruptcy Court's conclusion that there is no method of allocating Eastern's payments on the Notes to the particular loans is incorrect. Each series of Notes represents the loan used to finance the purchase of one individual Airbus. Payments on the Notes reduce the outstanding amount of the loan by a predefined amount, and correspondingly reduces the extent to which the security interest in the Aircraft is PMSI.[12]

As of the date of the petition, the $95.8 million outstanding on the Notes was secured by a general security interest in the entire $820 million worth of property in the Collateral Pool. Only a small portion of that security interest would qualify as a PMSI, namely that portion of the interest in each individual Aircraft which represented the unpaid balance of the Notes associated wit that Aircraft. If any of the Aircraft had a value which was less than the outstanding purchase

---

[10] Thus the Bankruptcy Court's statement that "the PMESI cannot exceed the price of what is purchased", 112 B.R. at 86, is correct. Nevertheless, a creditor may very will possess a PMSI in collateral whose value exceeds the amount of the loan made to purchase it, such as when a buyer obtains financing for only a fraction of the purchase price.

[11] This situation typically arises in consumer credit cases. See, *e.g.*, *Pristas v. Landaus of Plymouth, Inc., supra*, 742 F.2d 797 (3d Cir. 1984); *In re Manuel, supra*, 507 F.2d 990; *In re Staley*, 426 F. Supp. 437 (M.D. Ga. 1977).

[12] In this respect, the relative sophistication of the parties leads to a situation less complex than the typical consumer credit case, in which the consumer's account is "simplified," often to the consumer's detriment, by consolidating the loans into a lump sum payment which is not clearly allocated to the purchase price of each separate piece collateral.

dept, the PMSI would cover the entire Aircraft. To the extent that an Aircraft's value exceeded the unpaid balance, the security interest in that Aircraft would be a general security interest. See, *e.g.*, McLaughlin, *supra*, 49 Ford. L.Rev. at 694-95.

Therefore, the Airbus Lenders possessed a PMSI in the Aircraft at the time of the loans in question, and the purchase money quality of the security interest is not eliminated by the fact that the debt was secured by other collateral in addition to the Aircraft. Because the Aircraft are the type of property specified in § 1110, the interests here qualify as PMESIs and thus § 1110's exemption from the automatic stay applies.

COMMENT

The difficulty with the dual status rule lies with determining the extent of a purchase money interest after a re-financing or consolidation. When purchase money loans are consolidated with non-purchase money debt and payments have been made, some method of applying payments between the purchase money and non-purchase money portions is necessary. Some courts deny purchase money status if the parties failed to specify a method of calculation. See *e.g., Coomer v. Barclays American Financial, Inc (In re Coomer)*, 8 B.R. 351, 353-54 (Bankr. E.D. Tenn. 1980). Other courts apply a "first in, first out" method. See *e.g., In Re Clark*, 156 B.R. 693 (Bankr. S.D. Fla. 1993).

Given the problems with both the transformation and the dual status rules, which policy would you adopt if you were a judge in a jurisdiction of first impression?

[F] Simultaneous Purchase Money Security Interests

What happens when there are multiple purchase money security interests in the same collateral? How should a priority battle be resolved? Simultaneous purchase money transactions can occur when the debtor obtains part of the purchase price from a lending institution and part from a seller who finances the remainder. Assume, for example, that a credit union issues a check to the purchaser in return for an executed security agreement granting an interest in a specified automobile. Next, the auto dealer executes a conditional sales contract to finance the remainder of the purchase price. Since the car is to be used for consumer purposes, neither A nor B files a financing statement. In *Framingham U.A.W. Credit Union v. Dick Russell Pontiac, Inc.*, 7 U.C.C. Rep. Serv. 252 (Mass. App. 1969), the court found superior rights in the security interest taken by the auto dealer: ". . . the plaintiff credit union could not possibly obtain an interest in the collateral supposedly securing its loan unless and until defendant, the owner, was willing to put an interest in the collateral in Willis' hands under the conditional sale. Thus presumably it would not be willing to do without retaining an interest in the collateral superior to all other interests therein."

The *Framingham* case seems subject to criticism on a number of points. Is the court on firm ground in holding that the dealer's security interest "attached" (U.C.C. § 9-204) before that of the Credit Union? Didn't the dealer have such knowledge to assume that the Credit Union would have a security interest? There are at least three solutions to the problem posed: (a) order of filing controls; (b) the secured parties' share pro rata; and (c) the first to extend value should succeed. Which of these approaches finds the best support in the Code?

§ 18.04 Purchasers of Collateral

Read: U.C.C. §§ 9-307, 9-308, and 9-309.

There are a number of factors that should be considered when addressing priority disputes between buyers of collateral and secured parties. First and foremost is the question of whether the security interest is, in fact, perfected? If the security interest is unperfected, section 9-301 provides the basis for inquiry. The Code distinguishes rights among three types of purchasers of collateral. See U.C.C. § 9-301(1)(c). The buyer of collateral in the ordinary course of business, other than farm products, receives the greatest protection. Transferees in bulk are the least favored type of buyer, while buyers not in the ordinary course receive an intermediate form of protection. To prevail over an unperfected security interest under section 9-301(1)(c), such buyers must give value, receive delivery of the collateral both without knowledge of the security interest, and before that interest becomes perfected. Unless these requirements are met, the unperfected, secured party will prevail. To illustrate, consider a bank that has a valid but unperfected security interest in all of a debtor's inventory of microwave ovens. Assume that the debtor sells the entire inventory to Michael, who gives value for the goods on July 1. If Michael takes delivery of the collateral on July 11, Michael will prevail if he had no knowledge of bank's security interest prior to receiving delivery. But if the bank perfected its interest on July 10, and Michael took delivery the next day, bank's security would be superior.

If the security interest is perfected, or if § 9-301 fails to define the rights of the particular transferee, sections 9-307, 9-308, and 9-309 provide specific priority rules for certain types of collateral. Thus, if the merchant debtor above sold a microwave oven to Lauren on July 1 before the contract with the bank, section 9-307(1) would apply to determine the priority.

[A] Buyers of Goods

Read: U.C.C. §§ 9-301(1)(a), 9-307, 2-403, and 1-201(9).

A creditor with a perfected secured interest in goods has priority over a buyer who purchases goods from the debtor unless the secured party authorized the debtor to sell the goods, or unless the buyer is a buyer in the ordinary course of business. See section 9-306(2). Under section 9-307(1), the ordinary course buyer takes free of the perfected security interest created by the buyer's seller even though the buyer knows of the security interest's existence. Thus, the inventory purchaser is protected from one who has a security interest in the inventory; the inventory secured party remains protected because it has a continuing interest in the proceeds received upon the sale. While many courts rely on section 9-307(1) to protect the buyer of inventory, most inventory cases should be decided under section 9-306(2). In most cases, parties expect inventory to be sold. Typically, the secured party has authorized inventory sales by the debtor either explicitly or implicitly.

Thus, the secured party relinquishes its security interest in the goods sold under section 9-306(2). Section 9-307(1) should come into play only when a debtor's authorization to sell was subject to certain conditions that were not met in a particular transaction.

AIRCRAFT TRADING & SERVICES v. BRANIFF, INC.

United States Court of Appeals
819 F.2d 1227, 3 U.C.C.R. Serv. 2d 1297 (2nd Cir. 1987)

MINER, CIRCUIT JUDGE:

BACKGROUND

In December 1982, ATASCO, a Panamanian company engaged in the business of selling and leasing aircraft and aircraft engines, sold a jet aircraft engine to Northeastern Airlines ("Northeastern"), a commercial airline carrier. The purchase price of the engine was $412,344. The sales agreement provided that Northeastern would pay ATASCO $36,000.00 as a down payment, with the balance to be paid in 36 equal installments of $10,454.00, due monthly, beginning in March 1983. Northeastern's obligation to pay the debt was secured by a chattel mortgage dated December 31, 1982, held by ATASCO. The chattel mortgage provided that Northeastern would be in default if it (1) failed to pay any note when due; (2) disposed of the engine before all payments were made; or, (3) was subject to bankruptcy proceedings.

Northeastern paid the monthly installments on the engine through January 10, 1985, but has made no payments since then, and is now in bankruptcy. The balance due on the engine is $135,902 plus interest. ATASCO failed to record the chattel mortgage with the FAA, as required under 49 U.S.C. § 1403(c), until March 1985.

On November 28, 1984, Northeastern agreed to sell the aircraft containing the engine subject to ATASCO's chattel mortgage to Braniff, a commercial airline carrier. Northeastern, in its bill of sale to Braniff, represented that it was conveying good and marketable title for both the aircraft and the engine. Braniff, which was planning to sell this aircraft immediately to William Condren, a private individual, checked the FAA records for prior claims or liens upon the aircraft or its parts, and found no record of any encumbrances. After the sale to Braniff was consummated, Braniff filed the bill of sale with the FAA on November 30, 1984. On December 7, 1984, Braniff sold the aircraft to Condren after Condren also checked the FAA records for a prior claim. Condren subsequently filed his bill of sale.

In early February 1985, Condren leased the aircraft, with an option to buy, to IAL. The lease was not filed with the FAA as required by 49 U.S.C. § 1403. ATASCO finally filed its chattel mortgage with the FAA in March of 1985. In April of 1985, IAL learned of ATASCO's chattel mortgage when Condren notified IAL of ATASCO's interest by letter. Nevertheless, in late July or early August of 1985, after procuring a copy of ATASCO's chattel mortgage directly from the FAA, IAL exercised its option to buy the aircraft. That bill of sale was filed with the FAA on August 5th.

ATASCO brought suit for conversion, replevin, and forfeiture against Braniff, Condren and IAL. ATASCO's central contention before the district court was that its rights were superior to those of IAL because its chattel mortgage was filed prior to IAL's filing, and IAL had actual knowledge of the terms of the instrument when it exercised its option to purchase. The district court granted summary judgment in favor of IAL, Condren, and Braniff, noting that if the only transaction at issue were the sale to IAL, then ATASCO might prevail. However, the district court ruled that, because of the intermediate transfers to Braniff and Condren prior to ATASCO's filing of the chattel mortgage, Braniff received good title and passed good title to Condren, who in turn passed good title to IAL.

DISCUSSION

A. The Federal Aviation Act

Under the Federal Aviation Act, an interest in aircraft or aircraft engines, including a chattel mortgage, see 49 U.S.C. § 1403(a), is not valid against an innocent third party[13] "until such conveyance or other instrument is filed for recordation in the office of the Secretary of Transportation." 49 U.S.C. § 1403(c). Federal law thus requires recordation with the FAA to perfect a security interest in an aircraft engine. The district court, relying on the language and purpose of 49 U.S.C. § 1403, concluded that Congress must have intended intervening conveyances to render invalid the late recordation of a security interest in an aircraft engine. Therefore, the court denied plaintiff's motion for summary judgment and granted defendants' cross-motion for summary judgment.

The district court interpreted section 1403(c) of the Act to mean that a security interest in an aircraft engine is void unless filed with the FAA before the engine is conveyed again. This reading misinterprets the phrase "until such conveyance or other instrument is filed," 49 U.S.C. § 1403(c). The district court's construction effectively replaces "until" with "unless," and reads into the statute a timely filing requirement. "The use of the word 'until' . . . rather than "unless' indicates that mere delay . . . [is] not enough to cause forfeiture." *Washingtonian Pub. Co. v. Pearson,* 306 U.S. 30, 39, 83 L. Ed. 470, 59 S. Ct. 397 (1939) (rejecting argument that failure promptly to register copyright precluded infringement claim, where Copyright Act of 1909 provided that no action could be maintained "until" registration requirements were complied with).

The purpose of section 1403 is "to create "a central clearing house for recordation of titles so that a person, wherever he may be, will know where he can find ready access to the claims against, or liens, or other legal interests in an aircraft.' " *Philko Aviation, Inc. v. Shacket,* 462 U.S. 406, 411, 76 L. Ed. 2d 678, 103 S. Ct. 2476 (1983) (quoting Hearings on H.R. 9738 before the House Committee on Interstate and Foreign Commerce, 75th Cong., 2d Sess. 407 (1938) . . .

. . . .

Under the teaching of *Philko Aviation,* the first to perfect by filing with the FAA is not necessarily assured priority. *Philko Aviation,* 462 U.S. at 413. Rather, because section 1403 requires recordation to validate or perfect the security interest, federal law will only determine priority where the security holder has not recorded his interest. *Id.* An interest that intervenes before a creditor perfects under section 1403 does not necessarily extinguish the creditor's subsequently recorded security interest. In such a situation, a court must look to state law to determine priority. See *South Shore Bank v. Tony Mat,* Inc., 712 F.2d 896, 899 (3d Cir. 1983) (state law determines priority where buyer of airplane eventually recorded ownership with FAA after bank with intervening security interest brought suit).

[13] Section 1403(c) invalidates an unfiled interest in an aircraft as against "any person other than the person by whom the conveyance or other instrument is made or given, his heir ordevisee, or any other person having actual notice thereof. . . ." 49 U.S.C. § 1403(c).

In the case before us, although both Braniff and Condren purchased the engine and filed with the FAA prior to the time that ATASCO filed and perfected its interest,[14] ATASCO eventually did file and perfect in March of 1985. Therefore, state law determines priority as between ATASCO and Braniff and Condren, and as between ATASCO and IAL. All parties concede that New York's Uniform Commercial Code applies to determine priority in this case. We therefore turn to an analysis of the New York U.C.C., particularly Article 9, to determine how ATASCO's late perfected security interest should be treated.

B. The Uniform Commercial Code

1. Buyer in the Ordinary Course of Business

Appellees contend that, under New York's Uniform Commercial Code section 9-307(1), Braniff was a buyer in the ordinary course of business who could subsequently convey the engine free of ATASCO's security interest. Section 9-307 provides:

> (1) A buyer in ordinary course of business . . .takes free of a security interest created by his seller even though the security interest is perfected and even though the buyer knows of its existence. N.Y. U.C.C. Law § 9-307(1) (McKinney 1964). It generally is recognized that the purpose of section 9-307(1) is to protect the buying public where the secured party finances inventory that is sold to the public by the debtor in the regular course of the debtor's business. J. White & R. Summers, Uniform Commercial Code § 25-13, at 1067 (2d ed. 1980); N.Y. U.C.C. Law § 9-307 practice commentary 1 (McKinney 1964).

Under section 9-307(1), if Braniff were a buyer in the ordinary course of business, it would "take free" of the security interest created by its seller, Northeastern, extinguishing ATASCO's interest, whether or not ATASCO subsequently perfected. Section 9-307(1) thereby provides an exception to the general rule, codified in section 9-306(2), that "a security interest continues in collateral notwithstanding sale, exchange or other disposition thereof unless the disposition was authorized by the secured party." N.Y. U.C.C. Law § 9-306(2) (McKinney Supp. 1987).

A buyer in the ordinary course of business is defined as "a person who in good faith and without knowledge that the sale to him is in violation of the ownership rights or security interest of a third party in the goods buys in ordinary course from a person in the business of selling goods of that kind . . . ." N.Y. U.C.C. Law § 1-201(9) (McKinney Supp. 1987). This definition requires, inter alia, that the buyer in ordinary course buy from a seller who ordinarily sells similar goods. ATASCO argues that Northeastern, an airline carrier, was not in the business of selling airplanes, and therefore Braniff was not a buyer in the ordinary course of business. Appellees counter that it is a practice in the airline industry for airlines periodically to sell off airplanes and therefore Northeastern sold the plane to Braniff in the ordinary course of business.

Northeastern evidently was selling jets and engines to upgrade its fleet, which may be a practice in the industry. However, under New York law, whether a sale is an ordinary sale of similar goods turns on whether the goods sold are classified as capital equipment or as inventory. In *Hempstead Bank v. Andy's Car Rental Sys.*, 35 A.D.2d 35, 312 N.Y.S.2d 317 (2d Dept. 1970), the court held that a rental company's used car sales were not in the ordinary course of business, even though such sales are common in the industry, because the used cars were capital equipment

[14] The date of perfection of a security interest in aircraft generally is held to coincide with the date that the security interest is filed for recordation. *In re Gelking*, 754 F.2d 778, 780 (8th Cir.), cert. denied, 473 U.S. 906, 105 S. Ct. 3529, 87 L. Ed. 2d 653 (1985).

of the leasing company and not inventory. Accord *Sindone v. Farber,* 105 Misc. 2d 634, 432 N.Y.S.2d 778 (Sup. Ct. 1980). IAL's reliance on *Tanbro Fabrics Corp. v. Deering Milliken, Inc.,* 39 N.Y.2d 632, 350 N.E.2d 590, 385 N.Y.S.2d 260 (1976), is misplaced. In *Tanbro Fabrics* the unfinished textiles sold off by a converter were inventory and not capital equipment. Therefore, the sale was in the ordinary course of business, a result that accords with the *Hempstead Bank* holding. See 69 Am. Jur. 2d Secured Transactions § 469, at 328 (1973) ("a buyer of collateral that is classified as equipment will rarely if ever be a buyer in ordinary course of business, even where the debtor makes it a regular practice to sell used or obsolescent equipment at regular intervals").

Northeastern's aircraft and engines clearly were capital equipment. See N.Y. U.C.C. Law § 9-109(2) (McKinney 1964). Therefore, we hold that the sale to Braniff was not in the ordinary course of business, and section 9-307(1) does not extinguish ATASCO's security interest. We note that neither Condren nor IAL attempts to establish status as a buyer in the ordinary course of business. Even if Condren or IAL qualified as a buyer in the ordinary course of business, however, they would be unable to avail themselves of section 9-307(1) protection because section 9-307(1) applies only to security interests created by the buyer's seller. Here, Northeastern created the security interest and therefore Braniff was the only party in a position to invoke section 9-307(1) in its own right.

2. Priority Between ATASCO and Braniff & Condren

We now turn to a determination of the strength of ATASCO's claim as against Braniff and Condren. Section 9-301(1) provides that:

> (1) an unperfected security interest is subordinate to the rights of . . .
>
> (b) a person who becomes a lien creditor before the security interest is perfected;
>
> (c) in the case of goods, instruments, documents, and chattel paper, a person who is not a secured party and who is a transferee in bulk or other buyer not in ordinary course of business . . . to the extent that he gives value and receives delivery of the collateral without knowledge of the security interest and before it is perfected.

N.Y. U.C.C. Law § 9-301(1) (McKinney Supp. 1987. Both Braniff and Condren bought without knowledge of ATASCO's security interest and before it was perfected. Therefore, as buyers not in the ordinary course of business, their respective rights to the engine were superior to ATASCO's, by application of section 9-301(1)(c).

It is critical to note for the discussion that follows that ATASCO's unperfected security interest, though subordinate, continued to exist. Section 9-301(1) explicitly provides that "an unperfected security interest is subordinate" to the rights of certain buyers and lien creditors. The language of subordination indicates that the secured party's rights live on, although junior to the buyer's rights. Contrast the language of section 9-307 — "[a] buyer in ordinary course . . .takes free of a security interest created by his seller" — which terminates the secured party's interest for all time. Some courts seemingly ignore the subordination language of section 9-301(1) and state that a senior buyer "takes free" of an unperfected security interest, see, *e.g., United States v. Handy & Harman,* 750 F.2d 777, 780-81 (9th Cir. 1984); *In re Miguel,* 30 Bankr. 896, 898 (Bankr. E.D. Cal. 1983), but those cases do not involve subsequent buyers and apparently use the phrases "takes free" and "has priority over" interchangeably. One commentator has suggested that the U.C.C. drafters intended that an unperfected security interest terminates upon subsequent sale of the collateral to a buyer not in the ordinary course of business, but that an unperfected security interest subject to a senior lien continues. D. G. Carlson, *Death and Subordination Under Article 9 of the Uniform Commercial Code: Senior Buyers and Senior Lien Creditors*, 5 Cardozo L. Rev. 547, 553-57 (1984). We decline, however, to interpret section 9-301(1) in a manner that would give "subordinate" two different meanings in the same sentence depending upon the particular subsection that is relevant to the case at bar — section 9-301(1)(c) (buyers not in the ordinary course of business) or section 9-301(1)(b) (lien creditors). Rather, we are convinced that a plain reading of the statute requires that "subordinate" be given consistent meaning within section 9-301, and that the difference in phrasing between sections 9-301(1) ("is subordinate") and 9-307 ("takes free") is to be given effect, notwithstanding cases that use language of termination interchangeably with language of subordination.

3. Shelter Provision of Article 2, Sales

Appellees argue that if Braniff and Condren are buyers not in the ordinary course of business, their priority over ATASCO's security interest under section 9-301(1) would pass to IAL with the conveyance. Relying on the shelter provision of Article 2, Sales, section 2-403, appellees assert that Braniff conveyed title to Condren, and Condren conveyed that title to IAL, subject at most to ATASCO's subordinated unperfected security interest. Section 2-403 provides that:

> (1) [a] purchaser of goods acquires all title which his transferor had or had power to transfer except that a purchaser of a limited interest acquires rights only to the extent of the interest purchased.

N.Y. U.C.C. Law § 2-403(1) (McKinney 1964). Appellees have directed us to no authority for their assertion that the shelter provision of Article 2 may be applied to immunize transferees from a buyer who is protected under section 9-301(1)(c). It is a novel theory that we believe must fail.

Appellees' reliance on *In re Gary Aircraft Corp.*, 681 F.2d 365 (5th Cir. 1982), is misplaced. In *Gary Aircraft*, the secured party contended that it was entitled to possession of an aircraft because the last purchaser in the chain of sale was not a purchaser for value without notice, and therefore could not escape the secured party's interest as a buyer in the ordinary course of business. Rejecting that analysis, the Fifth Circuit held that the last purchaser was not subject to the secured party's interest because an intervening purchaser qualified under section 9-307 as a buyer in the ordinary course of business. That special status of the intervening purchaser extinguished the security interest in the collateral such that a subsequent sale could not resurrect it, and the last purchaser therefore prevailed.

New York law is in agreement. See *Marine Midland Bank, N.A. v. Smith Boys, Inc.*, 129 Misc. 2d 37, 41, 492 N.Y.S.2d 355, 358 (Sup. Ct. 1985) (if any party in the chain of title takes free of the security interest under section 9-307, "all succeeding buyers likewise take free of the security interest"). However, this is a narrow exception to the general rule stated in section 9-306(2) that a security interest in collateral continues upon the sale of the collateral unless the sale was authorized by the secured party. *Id.* at 43, 492 N.Y.S.2d at 360. The case before us does not fall within this narrow exception because ATASCO's security interest was not extinguished, but merely subordinated, by the sale to Braniff: Braniff did not "take free" of ATASCO's interest under section 9-307; it took subject to ATASCO's subordinated claim. See T. M. Quinn, Uniform Commercial Code Commentary and Law Digest para. 9-306[A][2], at 9-169 (1978) ("Anyone dealing with the collateral deals with it subject to the continuing security interest.").

As the Fifth Circuit recognized in *Gary Aircraft,* "the rule is that section [2-403(1)] is not available to save one who buys when the seller's title is subject to a security interest but who does not qualify under section [9-307]" for preferred status as a buyer in the ordinary course of business.[15] *Gary Aircraft,* 681 F.2d at 377. See *Commercial Credit Equipment Corp. v. Bates,* 159 Ga. App. 910, 285 S.E.2d 560 (1981). But see *Executive Financial Services, Inc. v. Pagel,* 238 Kan. 809, 715 P.2d 381 (1986) (buyer in the ordinary course of business may prevail on "entrustment" theory under section 2-403(2) and (3) even though he could not prevail under section 9-307(1)). Similarly, in *National Shawmut Bank v. Jones,* 108 N.H. 386, 388, 236 A.2d 484, 486 (1967), the court recognized section 9-307 as the only provision of Article 9 "under which a buyer of goods can claim to take free of a security interest where a sale, exchange or other disposition of the collateral was without consent of the secured party. . . . Article 9-306(2) gives the court no leeway to create any other exceptions to its dictates." Accord *Matteson v. Harper,* 297 Ore. 113, 117, 682 P.2d 766, 769 (1984). See J. White & R. Summers, Uniform Commercial Code § 25-15, at 1073 (2d ed. 1980).

We find further support for this rule in other sections of the U.C.C. Section 9-306(2) provides for continuance of a security interest upon sale of the collateral "except where this Article otherwise provides." We interpret this clause as expressly limiting exceptions to those found within Article 9. Moreover, section 2-402(3)(a) specifies that "nothing in this Article shall be deemed to impair the rights of creditors of the seller . . . under the provisions of [Article 9]." We conclude that the general scheme of the U.C.C. contemplates that a security interest is to be governed by Article 9, unimpaired by Article 2. See *National Shawmut,* 108 N.H. at 389, 236 A.2d at 486; *J. I. Case Credit Corp. v. Foos,* 11 Kan. App. 2d 185, 188-89, 717 P.2d 1064, 1067 (1986); *Carlson, supra,* at 550 n.9 & 556 ("section 2-403 does not contemplate the destruction of unperfected security interests"); *Anderson, supra,* § 9-102:9, at 453. Furthermore, the drafters of the U.C.C. explicitly provided shelter elsewhere in Article 9. See N.Y. U.C.C. Law § 9-302(2) (McKinney Supp. 1987) ("If a secured party assigns a perfected security interest, no filing under this Article is required in order to continue the perfected status of the security interest against creditors of and transferees from the original debtor."). "Their failure to do so in section 9-301(1)(c) should be taken as significant." *Carlson, supra,* at 558.

Finally, we note that the U.C.C. does not require a security interest to be filed immediately or promptly, Anderson, *supra,* § 9-302:20, at 77-78, although it is the most prudent course for a cautious lender. Delay in perfection does not preclude perfected status at a later time upon filing. While the secured party's interest may be subordinated to interests of others arising prior to filing, "he can, of course, file, even after a delay, and protect himself against interests arising subsequent to such filing." 53 N.Y. Jur. Secured Transactions § 175, at 152 (1967); 69 Am. Jur. 2d Secured Transactions § 422, at 271 (1973); Anderson, *supra,* § 9-301:9, at 29-30. The rule appellees urge us to adopt effectively would freeze a secured party's priority status as of the time of the first intervening conveyance: If one failed to file a security interest the day of the sale, the buyer could, by immediately reselling, forever destroy the security interest. While appellees urge that their rule would result in an increment of certainty in such transactions, we believe that such an extreme result would discourage lenders from taking security interests and would thereby inhibit commerce. The U.C.C. does not attempt to remove all uncertainty from secured transactions. It provides automatic perfection in certain situations, see N.Y. U.C.C. Law

---

15 IAL purchased with knowledge of ATASCO's security interest after ATASCO filed and perfected its claim. Therefore IAL cannot invoke protection in its own right under section 9-301(1)(c).

§§ 9-302(1)(b) (10-day automatic perfection for documents, proceeds), 9-302(1)(d) (purchase money security interest in consumer goods), & 9-304(4) (21-day automatic perfection for certain instruments) (McKinney Supp. 1987), and allows a filing to relate back to the time of attachment in others, see N.Y. U.C.C. Law §§ 9-103(1)(d), 9-103(3)(e) (McKinney Supp. 1987) (in multistate transaction, secured party has four months to file in state to which collateral has been removed). The U.C.C. aims to balance the competing concerns of protection for secured lenders and encouragement of trade.

4. Priority Between ATASCO and IAL

Having determined that ATASCO's security interest was not extinguished by the subsequent conveyances to Braniff and Condren, we now address the priority in the engine as between ATASCO and IAL.

At the time the engine was conveyed from Northeastern to Braniff and then to Condren, ATASCO's claim was subordinate to Braniff's and Condren's under section 9-301, as discussed above, because it was unfiled and unperfected. However, ATASCO eventually did file and perfect its security interest, and therefore section 9-301, which determines priority where an interest is unperfected, has no bearing on the issue of priority as between ATASCO and IAL, who have competing perfected interests in the engine.

Section 9-312(5)(a), the catch-all priority section of Article 9, governs conflicts between competing perfected interests:

> Conflicting security interests rank according to priority in time of filing or perfection. Priority dates from the time a filing is first made covering the collateral or the time the security interest is first perfected, whichever is earlier, provided that there is no period thereafter when there is neither filing nor perfection. N.Y. U.C.C. Law § 9-312(5)(a) (McKinney Supp. 1987).

As previously discussed, section 1403 of the Federal Aviation Act requires filing with the Secretary of the FAA to perfect an interest in an aircraft engine. Therefore, time of filing is identical to time of perfection in the case before us. Under section 9-312(5)(a), the first to file an interest with the FAA will rank first in priority. It is undisputed that ATASCO filed its chattel mortgage with the FAA in March 1985, and IAL filed its interests on August 5, 1985. Therefore, under the first to file or perfect rule of section 9-312(5)(a), ATASCO's security interest in the engine has priority over IAL's interest. We therefore reverse the district court's grant of summary judgment in favor of IAL and the denial of ATASCO's motion for summary judgment as against IAL, and remand the case for a determination of damages.

. . . .

CONCLUSION

For the reasons stated above, we reverse the district court's grant of summary judgment in favor IAL. We affirm the district court's grant of summary judgment for Braniff and Condren, on the grounds herein stated. We reverse the denial of ATASCO's summary judgment motion as against IAL, and remand for a determination of damages and entry of judgment.

SEARS CONSUMER FINANCIAL CORP. v. THUNDERBIRD PRODUCTS

Court of Appeals of Arizona, Division One, Department C
166 Ariz. 333, 802 P.2d 1032, 12 U.C.C.R. Serv. 2d 675 (1990)

GERBER, J.

Sears Consumer Financial Corporation (Sears) appeals from summary judgment entered in favor of Thunderbird Products (Thunderbird). The issues presented concern allocating liability under the Uniform Commercial Code (U.C.C.) between parties who were innocently unaware of the other's dealings with a boat in which each thought it had the primary interest.

HISTORY

Thunderbird Products, an Indiana corporation, manufactures and sells motor boats. In late 1985, Thunderbird sold a 1986 Formula F 25PC 25-foot cabin cruiser (the boat) to Glen Canyon Marine, a boat dealer in Page, Arizona, for it to sell at retail. ITT Commercial Finance (ITT) financed the sale to Glen Canyon Marine. ITT filed a blanket U.C.C. financing statement signed by Glen Canyon Marine as debtor.

When Glen Canyon Marine went out of business in 1986, Thunderbird bought ITT's interest in the secured debt on the boat. Thunderbird thereafter engaged D & J Marine and RV Services (D & J), also in the business of selling new and used boats in Page, to repossess the boat from Glen Canyon Marine and temporarily store it on Thunderbird's behalf.[16] While Thunderbird knew that D & J was in the boat sales business, Thunderbird did not authorize D & J to sell the boat but only to store it.

D & J nonetheless displayed the boat for public sale. On September 12, 1986, it entered into an agreement to sell it to Eugene Abernathy for $ 57,240.00. Sears agreed to lend Abernathy $ 40,000.00 to complete his purchase of the boat. Neither Abernathy nor Sears had knowledge of Thunderbird's claim to the boat. Abernathy created a purchase money security interest in the boat in favor of Sears. As part of the same transaction, D & J's general partners executed an "Indorsement" on the payment order form issued by Sears, warranting that D & J had delivered to the appropriate state agency the applications and fees necessary to secure a proper recording of Sears' lien on the boat as a valid first lien. Although Sears paid the $ 40,000.00 loan proceeds to D & J, the documents necessary to perfect Sears' purchase money security interest in the boat were never filed.[17] D & J delivered neither the boat nor a certificate of title to Abernathy. D & J paid none of the sales proceeds to Thunderbird.

The boat continued to sit in storage at Page. Unaware of the transactions between D & J and Abernathy and assuming continued ownership of the boat, Thunderbird took possession of it from D & J in October 1986 and stored it elsewhere in Page until February 1987. Thunderbird then transported the boat back to its factory in Indiana and resold it to Renton Marine Center

[16] It is unclear from the record whether Thunderbird accepted the boat in satisfaction of the debt owed by Glen Canyon Marine.

[17] Sears conceded early in this litigation that its purchase money security interest in the boat "remained unperfected" due to D & J's failure to file the necessary documents. We accordinglytake that as a given fact on appeal. However, under U.C.C. § 9-302(1)(d) [A.R.S. § 47-9302(A)(4)], a purchase money security interest in a consumer good is perfected automatically without the filing of a financing statement.

in Trenton, New Jersey. Abernathy subsequently defaulted on his Sears loan. Sears then looked to the boat for its security. Only then did it discover that Thunderbird had previously repossessed it.

In January 1988, Sears brought this action against Thunderbird for conversion. With some justification, each party portrayed itself in the trial court as an innocent interest holder wronged by the other's unauthorized interference in the course of its security interest in the boat. Sears and Thunderbird filed cross-motions for summary judgment. After argument, the trial court ruled for Thunderbird without stating any reasons. Sears timely appealed.

RIGHT OF SECURED PARTY TO MAINTAIN
ACTION FOR CONVERSION OF COLLATERAL

Thunderbird contends that Sears lacked a sufficient possessory interest in the boat to maintain a conversion action against Thunderbird. Thunderbird argues that Arizona follows the rule that a financier arranging the purchase of goods does not thereby obtain a possessory interest sufficient to maintain an action for conversion. Thunderbird also argues that Sears cannot maintain an action for conversion against Thunderbird because Sears' only legitimate objective is to collect its debt from Abernathy.

Conversion is an act of wrongful dominion or control over personal property in denial of or inconsistent with the rights of another. *Huskie v. Ames Bros. Motor & Supply Co.,* 139 Ariz. 396, 402, 678 P.2d 977, 983 (App.1984). A common law action for conversion may be brought by one who had the right to immediate possession of the chattel at the time of the alleged conversion. Restatement (Second) of Torts § 243 (1965), comment b; W. Prosser and W. Keeton, The Law of Torts (5th ed. 1984) § 15. According to Prosser and Keeton, one entitled to immediate possession includes "a chattel mortgagee or conditional seller after default." *Id.* at 104. Under Article 9 of the U.C.C., a secured party has sufficient possessory interest to bring a conversion action when the party's debtor defaults. Under U.C.C. § 9-503, a secured party "has on default the right to take possession of the collateral."

Secured parties may bring conversion actions against third parties who interfere with their rights in collateral. In *Empire Fire & Mar. Ins. Co. v. First Nat. Bank of Ariz.,* 26 Ariz.App. 157, 546 P.2d 1166 (1976), the court stated that in order to bring an action for conversion, the plaintiff must be entitled to immediate possession of the property. Conversion is an offense against possession of property. *Id.* at 159, 546 P.2d at 1168. On default, a secured party has the right to take possession of the collateral. Id. Even if Thunderbird's repossession of the boat from D & J did not convert Sears' interest in the boat, its continued control of the boat after Abernathy defaulted constituted conversion.

This result is not new. A purchase money secured party has a right to recover damages for conversion when the seller's inventory financier takes possession of the collateral from the seller's premises and sells it. *Rex Financial Corp. v. Mobile America Corp.,* 119 Ariz. 176, 580 P.2d 8 (Ct. App. 1978). . . .

. . . .

DID THUNDERBIRD'S ENTRUSTMENT EXTINGUISH
ITS SECURITY INTEREST IN THE BOAT?

Sears argues that Thunderbird's perfected security interest in the boat was extinguished pursuant to U.C.C. § 2-403(2) when D & J sold the boat to Abernathy. Section 2-403(2) provides:

> Any entrusting of possession of goods to a merchant who deals in goods of that kind gives him power to transfer all rights of the entruster to a buyer in ordinary course of business.

U.C.C. § 2-403(3) defines "entrusting" as follows:

> "Entrusting" includes any delivery and any acquiescence in retention of possession regardless of any condition expressed between the parties to the delivery or acquiescence and regardless of whether the procurement of the entrusting or the possessor's disposition of the goods have been such as to be larcenous under the criminal law.

U.C.C. § 1-201(9) provides:

> "Buyer in ordinary course of business" means a person who in good faith and without knowledge that the sale to him is in violation of the ownership rights or security interest of a third party in the goods buys in ordinary course from a person in the business of selling goods of that kind . . . .

In response, Thunderbird argues that because Sears itself does not meet the definition of "buyer in ordinary course" and Abernathy is not a party to this suit, Sears has no right to invoke the entrustment doctrine of U.C.C. § 2-403(2).

We disagree with Thunderbird. Rather than claiming that it is a buyer in ordinary course from D & J, Sears bases its conversion claim on the distinct theory that Thunderbird's security interest was extinguished by operation of § 2-403(2) when D & J sold the boat to Abernathy in the ordinary course of business. As a result, only Sears had a security interest in the boat when Thunderbird repossessed it. Thunderbird responds that because D & J did not create Thunderbird's security interest, D & J's sale of the boat to Abernathy had no effect on this original security interest under Article 9. See U.C.C. § 9-307(1) (providing that buyer in ordinary course "takes free of a security interest created by his seller . . . ."). Thunderbird concludes that its perfected security interest therefore prevailed over Sears' unperfected purchase money security interest in the same collateral. See U.C.C. § 9-302(2) (perfected security interest remains perfected after assignment); U.C.C. §§ 9-301(1)(a) and 9-312 (unperfected security interest subordinate to perfected security interest).

We thus have to determine whether Article 2 or Article 9 of the U.C.C. governs these facts. U.C.C. § 9-307(1) does not apply to these facts because it extinguishes only a security interest created by the seller. It provides:

> A buyer in ordinary course of business (subsection (9) of section 1-201) other than a person buying farm products from a person engaged in farming operations takes free of a security interest created by his seller even though the security interest is perfected and even though the buyer knows of its existence.

Contrary to the thrust of Thunderbird's answering brief, Sears does not contend on appeal that Thunderbird's security interest was extinguished pursuant to § 9-307(1). We consider § 9-307(1) only as it bears on the interpretation of U.C.C. § 2-403(2). We must now determine whether § 2-403(2) applies.

The authorities are split on whether U.C.C. § 2-403(2) operates to extinguish an Article 9 security interest. Even the noted commentators James J. White and Robert S. Summers, authors of Uniform Commercial Code (3d ed. 1988), are unable to agree. Section 26-16 of their treatise states in part:

> Section 2-403 is the Article 2 analogue to 9-307. It, like 9-307, is a bona fide purchase provision designed to protect good faith purchasers from certain prior interests. In certain respects, 2-403

> is more generous to subsequent purchasers than is 9-307. So the question: May a subsequent purchaser disappointed under 9-307 fall back on 2-403 and argue that it renders him superior to a prior security interest? We believe the answer is no, and we think that the cases holding to the contrary are in error.

Id. at 544. Footnote 2 to this passage, however, states in part: "One of your authors, having been convinced by the analysis of one of his student assistants, disagrees with White and would read 2-403 broadly to protect the innocent purchaser." *Id.* at 544 n. 2.

With respect to entrustment by secured parties, Professor Summers offers the better view. It is certainly true that when a secured party is not in control of the collateral and does not acquiesce in its entrustment to a merchant who deals in goods of that kind, the sale to a buyer in the ordinary course of the merchant's business should not affect the secured party's rights in the collateral. However, where the secured party itself entrusts the collateral, or acquiesces in its entrustment as occurred here, § 2-403(2) governs. "Where one of two innocent parties must suffer through the act or negligence of a third person, the loss should fall upon the one who by his conduct created the circumstances which enabled the third party to perpetuate the wrong or cause the loss." *Al's Auto Sales v. Moskowitz,* 203 Okla. 611, 224 P.2d 588, 591 (1950); see also *Mercer v. Braziel,* 746 P.2d 702 (Okla.App.1987).

Comment 2 to § 2-403 supports the view that § 2-403(2) applies to entrustment of collateral by a secured party. It states in part:

> As to entrusting by a secured party, subsection (2) is limited by the more specific provisions of section 9-307(1), which deny protection to a person buying farm products from a person engaged in farming operations.

According to Professor White, this comment supports the view that § 2-403(2) is inapplicable to disputes between secured creditors and subsequent purchasers. See 2 White and Summers, Uniform Commercial Code (3d ed. 1988) § 26-16, at 545. We interpret it differently. By interpreting § 9-307(1) as excepting from the general protection of § 2-403(2) buyers of farm products entrusted by a secured party to persons engaged in farming operations, the comment appears to recognize that other entrusting by secured parties is subject to the rights of buyers in ordinary course under § 2-403(2).

Thunderbird argues that U.C.C. § 9-306(2) precludes the application of § 2-403 to an Article 9 security interest. U.C.C. § 9-306(2)provides:

> Except where this article otherwise provides, a security interest continues in collateral notwithstanding sale, exchange, or other disposition thereof unless the disposition was authorized by the secured party in the security agreement or otherwise, and also continues in any identifiable proceeds including collections received by the debtor. (Emphasis added).

Thunderbird argues that because § 2-403(2) is not part of Article 9, it has no effect on a security interest in entrusted collateral.

This reasoning does not apply to entrustment by a secured party. Comment 3 to § 9-306 states in part:

> In most cases when a debtor makes an unauthorized disposition of collateral, the security interest, under prior law and under this article, continues in the original collateral in the hands of the purchaser or other transferee. That is to say, since the transferee takes subject to the security interest, the secured party may repossess the collateral from him or in an appropriate case maintain an action for conversion. Subsection (2) codifies this rule.

This comment indicates that the drafters of Article 9 intended § 9-306(2) to address only transfers of collateral by debtors or their transferees. Contrary to Thunderbird's argument, § 9-306(2) does not override § 2-403(2) when the entrustment is by a secured party.

Thunderbird contends that U.C.C. § 2-403(2)i s inapplicable here and that this controversy must be resolved exclusively under the provisions of Article 9. In support of this view, Thunderbird relies on § 2-403(4), which provides:

> The rights of other purchasers of goods and of lien creditors are governed by the articles on secured transactions (Article 9), bulk transfers (Article 6) and documents of title (Article 7).

Section 2-403(4), however, does not apply because Sears is not a lien creditor. Section 9-301(3) provides:

> A "lien creditor" means a creditor who has acquired a lien on the property involved by attachment, levy or the like and includes an assignee for benefit of creditors from the time of assignment, and a trustee in bankruptcy from the date of the filing of the petition or a receiver in equity from the time of appointment.

In addition, § 2-403(4) states that the "rights of other purchasers of goods . . . are governed by . . . (Article 9)." This language indicates that purchasers other than those covered in § 2-403 are governed by Article 9.

Likewise § 2-402(3) does not apply to this case. Section 2-402(3) provides:

> Nothing in this article shall be deemed to impair the rights of creditors of the seller . . .under the provisions of the article on secured transactions (Article 9) . . . .

In this case, Thunderbird was a secured creditor of Glen Canyon Marine and not of D & J, the seller of the boat. Section 2-402(3) therefore does not prevent extinguishment of Thunderbird's security interest pursuant to § 2-403(2).

The better reasoned and factually similar cases hold § 2-403(2) applicable to entrustment by a secured party. See *In re Woods*, 25 B.R. 924 (Bankr.E.D.Tenn.1982); *Executive Financial Serv., Inc. v. Pagel,* 238 Kan. 809, 715 P.2d 381 (1986). As the court stated in *Executive Financial Services,*

> Typically, the entruster and the holder of the security interest are separate entities with the security holder not involved in the entrustment. In such a case the security interest would continue in the goods because under [U.C.C. § 2-403(2)] only the "rights of the entruster" would be transferred. Here, however, the security holder is the entruster and its rights as such are transferred to the buyer.

Id. 715 P.2d at 387.

CONCLUSION

Judgment for Thunderbird is reversed and the trial court is instructed to enter judgment for Sears.

Our conclusion is consistent with the basic goal of the U.C.C. to protect good faith purchasers. See *Martin v. Nager,* 192 N.J. Super. 189, 469 A.2d 519 (1983). A major aim of the U.C.C. is to facilitate the merchantability of property. *Riverside Nat. Bank v. Law,* 564 P.2d 240 (Okla.1977). In this case, Thunderbird, as a secured party, entrusted possession of the boat to D & J, a merchant dealing in this kind of goods. Under the explicit language of § 2-403(2),

Thunderbird unwittingly thereby gave D & J the power to transfer all Thunderbird's rights in the boat to Abernathy. D & J exercised that power by selling the boat to Abernathy in the ordinary course of its business. The sale by D & J to Abernathy extinguished Thunderbird's perfected security interest in the boat. Accordingly, Thunderbird at that point lost any legal right to repossess it, though not, of course, its own claim for conversion against D & J. Sears acquired the right to possession of the boat under its purchase money security interest with Abernathy. Thunderbird's repossession of the boat constituted conversion of Sears' interest even though Thunderbird acted without knowledge of Sears' interest. As between these two innocent parties, U.C.C. § 2-403(2) places liability on the party whose conduct first allowed this boat to set sail on this uncharted voyage.

NOTES

(1) The *Thunderbird* court cited the dispute between Professors White and Summers in their treatise on the Uniform Commercial Code. White takes the view that priority disputes between secured creditors and subsequent purchasers must be governed exclusively by Article 9 and that a subsequent purchaser who is disappointed under U.C.C. § 9-307 cannot fall back on section 2-403 by suggesting that the section renders the purchaser superior to the prior security interest. Summers believes that section 2-403 should be read broadly to protect the innocent purchaser. Which view do you support?

(2) The Food Security Act of 1985, 7 U.S.C. § 1631(d) preempts the Code and other state statutes on security interests in farm products. Section 1631(d) provides that ". . . a buyer who in the ordinary course of business buys a farm product from a seller engaged in farming operations shall take free of a security interest created by the seller, even though the security interest is perfected; and the buyer knows of the existence of such interest." Thus, under this federal law, the buyer in the ordinary course of business of farm products prevails over a prior, perfected secured party.

If the secured party is heavily engaged in financing which makes it advisable to take security interests in farm products, it may still take some preventive measures to protect its interest. It may require the debtor to "furnish to the secured party a list of the buyers, commission merchants, and selling agents to or through whom the person engaged in farming operations may sell such farm product." The act also requires commission merchants or selling agents of farm products to register with the Secretary of State in states with centralized filing systems so that the secured party may give them notice of the security interest.

PROBLEM 18.3

Bank finances a car for A. Bank's security interest is not noted on the certificate of title due to an error of the licensing agency. A transfers the car to B, a car dealer and assigns B the certificate of title. B sells the car to C for C's personal use. Between the bank and C, who has the right to the car? Why? See *Quinn v. Scheu*, 675 P.2d 1078 (Ore. Ct. App. 1984).

[B] Buyers of Instruments, Documents, and Securities

Read U.C.C. § 9-309.

Purchasers of instruments, documents, and securities receive special protection under other provisions of the Code. Because purchasers include secured parties, a secured party who is a holder in due course of an Article 3 negotiable instrument that is not part of chattel paper, a bona fide purchaser of an investment security or, a holder to whom an Article 7 negotiable document of title has been negotiated duly, will have a special priority in the collateral that is unqualified by Article 9. For example, a bona fide purchaser of a corporate security takes the security free of any adverse claim under U.C.C. § 9-115. U.C.C. § 9-309 also makes it clear that the protected status afforded such a purchaser receive continues under Article 9 irrespective of other provisions in Article 9 that might be interpreted as giving the secured party a superior claim.

IN RE JOE MORGAN, INC.
UTILITY CONTRACTORS FINANCIAL SERVICES INC. v. AMSOUTH BANK, N.A.

United States Bankruptcy Court, Southern District of Alabama
130 B.R. 331, 15 U.C.C. Rep. Serv.2d 1367 (1991)

ARTHUR B. BRISKMAN, BANKRUPTCY JUDGE.

This matter came on for hearing on the Complaint of the Plaintiff, Utility Contractors Financial Services, Inc., for determination of priority of its claim against the estate of the Debtor, Joe Morgan, Inc., and distribution of proceeds from the collection of accounts receivable of the Debtor. The Defendant, Sunburst Bank, counterclaimed for distribution of proceeds from the collection of accounts receivable by the Trustee and AmSouth Bank, and declaration of a prior perfected security interest of the Defendant, Sunburst Bank. The Plaintiff, Defendant and Trustee stipulate the validity of the first lien of the Defendant, AmSouth Bank, and the satisfaction of their debt from the proceeds of the Debtor's accounts receivable.

After due consideration of the pleadings, affidavits, arguments of counsel, testimony and briefs subsequently submitted, this Court finds and concludes as follows:

FINDINGS OF FACT

The Debtor, Joe Morgan, Inc. ("JMI"), executed and delivered to Sunburst Bank ("Sunburst") a promissory note and security agreement to Sunburst for $100,000.00 with interest on October 14, 1988. On October 27, 1988, JMI executed a second promissory note and security agreement for $300,000.00 with interest. JMI delivered a third promissory note and security agreement to Sunburst for $407,043.43 with interest on December 9, 1988.

On March 15, 1989, Sunburst filed with the Secretary of State of Alabama a security agreement and financing statement including "[a]ll of debtor's accounts, whether now existing or hereafter arising or acquired, whether or not earned by performance; all chattel paper owned by debtor or arising from conversion of accounts covered by the security agreement, whether now existing or hereafter arising or acquired . . . ." JMI delivered to Sunburst a fourth promissory note and security agreement on May 22, 1989 for $399,910.00 with interest. The May 22, 1989 note was a renewal and extension of JMI's three previous notes to Sunburst secured by the financing statement filed with the Alabama Secretary of State on March 15, 1989.

In March 1989, Joe Morgan, ("Morgan") President of JMI, met with Robert Watters ("Watters"), Vice President of Utility Contractors Financial Services, Inc., ("UCON") to discuss UCON's possible purchase of JMI's accounts receivable. UCON was a factor which purchased receivables at a five percent discount of their face value from utility company contractors. UCON collected the factored receivables form the account debtors. All payments collected by UCON from the account debtors were made by check.

UCON began to purchase JMI's accounts receivable in March or April 1989. JMI did not inform UCON of Sunburst's prior security interest in JMI's accounts receivable. The proceeds from the sale of the Debtor's accounts were initially deposited by wire transfer into JMI's account with South-Trust Bank, and after June 1989, in JMI's operating account with Sunburst.

In April 1989, Watters accompanied Morgan to a meeting with John Turner, an officer at AmSouth Bank ("AmSouth"). AmSouth held a first lien on JMI's accounts receivable which was superior to Sunburst's interest. The validity of AmSouth's superior interest in JMI's account proceeds is not disputed. At the meeting with Turner, Watters became aware of JMI's outstanding loan from AmSouth, AmSouth's security interest in JMI's receivables and AmSouth's refusal to loan JMI any additional funds.

Watters first learned of Sunburst's security interest in JMI's accounts receivable on July 17, 1989 at a meeting with Morgan and Doug McCrory, Senior Vice President of Sunburst. Sunburst had been unaware of UCON's factoring of JMI's accounts receivable until this meeting, and was informed that UCON would not continue factoring JMI's receivables after August 1, 1989.

Watters discussed U.C.C. filing requirements with two attorneys and received conflicting advice about the necessity of searching U.C.C. records for prior security interests in accounts receivable and filing a financing statement. After the meeting with Morgan and Doug McCrory, Watters filed a financing statement covering JMI's accounts receivable with the Secretary of State of Alabama on July 19, 1989.

Sunburst and UCON representatives met to discuss JMI's need for working capital on July 20, 1989, and agreed that UCON should continue to factor JMI's accounts receivable until August 1, 1989 on the following conditions: 1) the funds received by JMI would be used to cover payroll; and 2) JMI would generate new receivables in an amount greater than the amount being factored. Based on this understanding, UCON continued to factor JMI's accounts receivable.

The Debtor filed a Chapter 11 petition on September 13, 1989. Shortly before JMI's bankruptcy petition, AmSouth notified and instructed JMI's account debtors to submit payment of their accounts to AmSouth. Pursuant to successive cash collateral orders of this Court, the proceeds collected were used to retire AmSouth's secured debt of $634,071.66 in principal and $19,674.63 in interest. The Debtor converted to a Chapter 7 proceeding on February 16, 1990. This Court ordered AmSouth to continue to collect and hold the proceeds from accounts for the Trustee pending further order of the Court.

UCON factored $1,428,706.27 in JMI's accounts receivable from April 14, 1989 to July 12, 1989. UCON factored $837,195.42 of JMI's accounts from July 20, 1989 to August 31, 1989. UCON factored a total of $2,511,481.01 in JMI's accounts receivable and collected $2,099,209.56. The amount owed UCON for accounts purchased but uncollected is $412,271.45. As of the date of its filing on September 13, 1989, JMI owed Sunburst $399,910 in principal and $15,613.44 in interest. UCON filed a complaint to establish the priority of its claim in the proceeds held by AmSouth and Sunburst counterclaimed to assert its rights in the proceeds.

CONCLUSIONS OF LAW

I. Pre-July 17, 1989 Accounts

UCON is a holder in due course under § 7-9-309 of the Code of Alabama (1975) and therefore has priority over Sunburst's prior security interest. Section 7-9-309 provides: "[n]othing in this article limits the rights of a holder in due course of a negotiable instrument (section 7-3-302) . . . and such holders or purchasers take priority over an earlier security interest even though perfected. Filing under this article does not constitute notice of the security interest to such holders or purchasers."

Section 9-309 of the Uniform Commercial Code protects a holder in due course against the claim of a prior perfected security interest. In *Thorp Commercial Corp. v. Northgate Indus., Inc.*, 490 F. Supp. 197 (D. Minn. 1980), rev'd on other grounds, 654 F.2d 1245 (8th Cir. 1981), a debtor gave a security interest in its accounts receivable to a primary secured party. Subsequently, the debtor paid a secondary secured party by endorsing checks paid by account debtors on the accounts receivables which were the subject of the primary security interest. The court held that if the secondary secured party met the requirements of a holder in due course, it would have priority over the primary secured party under § 9-309. *Id.* at pp. 203-204. Similarly, a Texas state court in *Dallas Bank & Trust Co. v. Frigiking, Inc.*, 692 S.W.2d 163 (Tex. Ct. App. 1985) allowed a second-in-time secured party to assert its holder in due course status against a prior security interest and keep payments made by check from the debtor. See also *Citizens Valley Bank v. Pacific Materials Co.*, 263 Or. 557, 503 P.2d 491 (1971).

The Permanent Editorial Board for the Uniform Commercial Code recently issued a supplementary commentary elaborating on § 9-309.[18] The Board explains:

> The operation of this section can be seen when two secured parties have a perfected security interest in an account, chattel paper, or general intangible and the secured party that does not have priority receives a payment by check directly or indirectly from the account debtor. If the recipient takes the check under circumstances that give the recipient the rights of a holder in due course (Section 3-302), then the recipient's security interest in the check will take priority over the competing security interest and the recipient will be entitled to keep the payment.

Proposed Commentaries of the Permanent Editorial Board for the U.C.C., 3 U.L.A. 1990Supplement, pp. 258-59.

Section 7-3-302 of the Code of Alabama (1975) defines a holder in due course as a holder who takes an instrument: 1) for value; 2) in good faith; and 3) without notice that it is overdue or has been dishonored or of any defense against or claim to it on the part of any person. The checks received by UCON from JMI's account debtors were taken for value, in good faith, and without knowledge of Sunburst's prior security interest. Therefore, UCON stands as a holder in due course against Sunburst's prior security interest as to JMI's accounts receivable factored before July 17, 1989.

II. Post-July 17, 1989 Accounts

Sunburst's acquiescence in July 1989 to the factoring agreement between UCON and JMI estops Sunburst's assertion of its security interest in the proceeds held by AmSouth. Under the

---

[18] Alabama has not adopted the Board's new commentary.

doctrine of equitable estoppel, a promise which the promisor should reasonably expect to induce action or forbearance of a definite and substantial nature on the part of the promisee, and which does cause such action or forbearance, is binding if injustice can be avoided only by enforcement of the promise. *Mazer v. Jackson Ins. Agency,* 340 So.2d 770, 772-73 (Ala. 1976). Equitable estoppel results when: 1) the actor, with knowledge of the true facts, communicates information in a misleading way by word, conduct or silence; 2) the other party relies upon the communication; and 3) the other party would be harmed materially if the actor is later permitted to assert any claim inconsistent with his earlier conduct. *Ex parte Baker,* 432 So.2d 1281, 1285 (Ala. 1983) (citing *Mazer,* 340 So.2d at 773).

Sunburst's officials agreed to allow UCON to factor JMI's accounts receivables in order to allow JMI to cover its payroll expenses and remain in business on condition that the proceeds collected be applied to payroll expenses and that JMI generate more accounts than UCON factored. Relying on Sunburst's agreement, UCON continued to factor JMI's accounts receivable until JMI filed its bankruptcy petition. Therefore, Sunburst is estopped from asserting its prior perfected security interest against UCON's interest in the proceeds of JMI's account after 17, 1989.

SUMMARY

UCON's claim in the proceeds of JMI's accounts receivable for $412,272.45 has priority over Sunburst's previously perfected security interest. UCON's complaint for distribution of proceeds from the collection of accounts receivable is due to be granted. Sunburst's counterclaim for distribution of proceeds from the collection of accounts receivable collected by the Trustee and AmSouth and declaration of priority of a perfected security interest held by Sunburst Bank is due to be denied.

[C] Buyers of Chattel Paper

Read: U.C.C. § 9-308.

The protection of purchasers of instruments, documents, and securities under section 9-309 is closely related to the protection afforded purchasers of chattel paper and instruments. Section 9-308 resolves conflicts between a subsequent purchaser of chattel paper and a prior secured party by giving the purchaser priority *only if* the purchaser provided new value and took possession of the chattel paper in the ordinary course of the purchaser's businesses. If a purchaser meets these requirements, section 9-308 establishes two rules. Under subsection (a), the purchaser receives priority over the prior perfected security interest only if the purchaser acted without knowledge of the prior secured party's interest. Subsection (b) does not require such innocence. If the prior secured party's claim to the chattel paper is "merely as proceeds of inventory subject to a security interest," then the purchaser of the chattel paper will have priority, "even though he knows that the specific paper or instrument is subject to the security interest." The expression "merely as proceeds" means that the original secured party did not rely upon the possibility that there would be proceeds in the form of chattel paper when the original advance occurred. See U.C.C. § 9-306.

AMERICAN STATE BANK v. AVCO FINANCIAL SERVICES

California Court of Appeal, Fourth District, Division 2
139 Cal. Rptr. 658, 532 P.2d 558 (1977)

McDaniel, Associate Justice.

This case was presented to the trial court on a stipulated set of facts upon which extensive findings were made. To summarize the findings, Western Travel Center, Inc. (dealer), was in the business of selling recreational vehicles (motorhomes) and in discounting to banks conditional sales contracts covering such vehicles. Defendants Avco Financial Services of the United States, Inc., and Westinghouse Credit Corporation (flooring lenders) held security interests in the dealer's resale inventory of motorhomes by reason of the filing of U.C.C.-1 financing statements covering that inventory. At the outset, these security interests extended to two motorhomes, the proceeds of sale of which are the subject of this litigation.

Fairfield, the president of the dealer, entered into fraudulent schemes with Jackson and McCullough which included sham sales of a motorhome to each. All the paper work in the form of credit applications and conditional sales contracts were fixed up showing Jackson and McCullough as conditional purchasers of the respective motorhomes and as having made down payments of $1,269.75 and $1,450. However, neither of them had made the down payment or ever took delivery.

Nevertheless, the dealer took the two conditional sales contracts to plaintiff American State Bank (bank) who accepted assignment of them without recourse and paid the dealer $8,044 and $8,409. A report of sale was submitted to DMV by the dealer, and the motorhomes were registered to show Jackson as the registered owner of one and McCullough as the registered owner of the other. The bank appeared as legal owner of both on the California Ownership Certificates (pink slips).

Fairfield did make a few payments on the conditional sales contracts but eventually they lapsed into default. For reasons not fully explained by the record, the motorhomes were seized and impounded by the police about seven months after the pink slips were issued. The flooring lenders and the bank agreed that the motorhomes should be sold and the priority of the competing security interests and hence the right to the proceeds of such sales be determined in a declaratory relief action.

In that action the trial court held for the bank, concluding that this result was called for by section 9307 of the Commercial Code and "California Case Law." The flooring lenders appealed.

Briefly stated, the appeal by the flooring lenders challenges the application of section 9307 mainly because the findings, according to these defendants, do not support a conclusion that the plaintiff bank was a buyer of the motorhomes "in ordinary course of business." We agree.

The findings clearly establish that there was no valid sale or even transfer of possession to Jackson and McCullough, and although there is no California case precisely elaborating on the definition of a "[b]uyer in ordinary course of business" as set forth in section 1201, subdivision (9), a fair reading of the text writers and the California Code comments leads to the conclusion that "business" as used in the "course of business" language of that section means the seller's business. If this interpretation is correct, then the sham sales by the dealer to Jackson and

McCullough did not amount to the kinds of transactions which invoke the operation of section 9307, subdivision (1).

As one of its contentions, the bank argues that because the dealer never transferred title to Jackson and McCullough and then assigned the purported conditional sales contracts to the bank, that it (the bank) acquired title to the motorhomes and hence was a buyer in the ordinary course of business. This, it argues, put the bank in a position to enjoy the operation of section 9307, subdivision (1). This also was the conclusion of law reached by the trial court. The difficulty we have with this view of the case is that banks are not in the business of buying motor vehicles; they are in the business of lending money. Accordingly, although it is not necessary to our ultimate disposition of the appeal, it is our view that banks which variously finance retail purchases of motor vehicles by others, and end up appearing as the legal owners thereof on the pink slips issued by the DMV for those motor vehicles, are not "buyers in ordinary course of business" as defined in section 1201, subdivision (9) and as used in section 9307, subdivision (1).

However, the trial court reached a further conclusion of law which in effect stated that as between the flooring lender and the bank which "purchased legal title [to the collateral] from a dealer," the bank takes free of any security interest in the collateral running in favor of the flooring lender. In reaching this conclusion, the trial court can be taken as invoking section 9308 which reads,

> [a] purchaser of chattel paper . . . who gives new value and takes possession of it in the ordinary course of his business has priority over a security interest in the chattel paper . . . (a) Which is perfected under Section 9304 (permissive filing and temporary perfection) or under Section 9306 (perfection as to proceeds) if he acts without knowledge that the specific paper or instrument is subject to a security interest; or (b) Which is claimed merely as proceeds of inventory subject to a security interest (Section 9306) even though he knows that the specific paper or instrument is subject to the security interest.

The application of section 9308 has not yet been the subject of appellate review in California, but it has in several other states which have enacted the Uniform Commercial Code and particularly the language of section 9308 as it appears on California's statute books. The competing priorities dealt with in this section usually collide in situations where the dealer gets into financial difficulty and for a variety of reasons will have the collateral or its proceeds in his possession thereby precipitating a contest for the collateral or its proceeds between the flooring lender who held a security interest in the collateral before its retail sale and the bank who financed the retail sale.

In the several cases which have come to our attention where this issue has been presented, the courts have applied the equivalent of California's section 9308 and held for the bank which financed the retail purchase. Such a case was *Rex Financial Corp. v. Great Western Bank & Trust* (1975), 23 Ariz.App. 286, 532 P.2d 558. To summarize the facts in *Rex* using the same generic terms as we have been using, there was a flooring agreement between the dealer and the flooring lender who had a perfected security interest in the dealer's inventory of mobilehomes. Four mobile homes were sold by the dealer to retail purchasers in the regular course of the dealer's business and the sales were covered by conditional sales contracts. These contracts were sold and assigned to the bank in the regular course of the bank's business for current value paid to the dealer. To quote from the opinion, "[u]fortunately, the dealer did not use these funds to pay off its outstanding loans owed to the [flooring lender]." (*Id.* at p. 560.) It further appears that in this case the bank even had knowledge of the security interest claimed by the flooring lender.

In deciding *Rex*, the court was first concerned with whether the conditional sales contracts involved were "chattel paper" as defined by Arizona Revised Statutes, section 44-3105(A)(2), which is substantially the same as California section 9105, subdivision (b).

The court had no difficulty in deciding that the documents involved came within the definition, and clearly, in the case before us, on their faces the conditional sales contracts presented to the bank by the dealer were chattel paper as defined in section 9105, subdivision (b).

The next subsidiary issue in *Rex* was to determine the meaning of the statutory language "in the ordinary course of his business." The court rejected a contention that what was meant was a practice which should have been followed and not the practice of this particular purchaser of chattel paper. We agree; otherwise the use of the word "his" would have no significance. Digressing briefly to the case before us, the evidence will support an inference that the bank purchased the two conditional sales contracts in the ordinary course of its business.

This brought the *Rex* court to the final issue which required an application of the equivalent of section 9308, subdivision (b), namely

> [a] purchaser of chattel paper . . . who gives new value and takes possession of it in the ordinary course of his business has priority over a security interest in the chattel paper . . . [w]hich is claimed merely as proceeds of inventory subject to a security interest (Section 9306) even though he knows that the specific paper . . . is subject to the security interest.

In the case before us, there was no finding on the factual issue of whether the bank had knowledge that the conditional sales contracts were subject to the security interest of the flooring lender. However, for purposes of our decision, we shall presume such knowledge on the part of the bank, either actual or constructive, because of the flooring lender's U.C.C.-1 filing on which was checked "Box A," the proceeds of collateral. In its analysis of the operation of this statutory provision, the *Rex* court took the position that the more likely or probable expectation of the flooring lender in making its loans to the dealer was a reliance upon the collateral itself before its retail sale, and then on the cash proceeds of such sale rather than on any chattel paper that might be generated from time to time on the sales of collateral.

The opinion reads, should such reliance have been different, "Rex could have protected itself by requiring all security agreements executed on sale of the mobile homes to be turned over immediately to Rex, or if sold, that all payments for the security agreements (chattel paper) be made to itself." (*Rex Financial Corp. v. Great Western Bank & Trust, supra,* 23 Ariz.App. 286, 532 P.2d 558, 561.) On this reasoning it upheld the judgment of the trial court in favor of the bank.

We concur with the analysis and reasoning in *Rex* and hold that where there is financing of resale inventory and a security interest therein perfected by a U.C.C.-1 filing, and where an item of inventory (here motorhomes) is sold on conditional sale and that contract is purchased for new value by a bank in the ordinary course of its business, and where the bank takes possession of the contracts, section 9308 operates to give the bank's security interest in the chattel paper priority over that of the flooring lender who financed that inventory . . . .

The foregoing analysis and citation of authority is something of a nod to orthodoxy in dealing with a case of first impression, for it perhaps would have been enough to observe that the result we have reached was clearly indicated by the straightforward language of section 9308 which requires no extended interpretation and which obviously reflects the custom, practice, and usage of the mercantile community followed in thousands of transactions each day from Crescent City and Alturas to San Ysidro and Calexico.

The reader who is primarily interested in the precedential impact of this opinion in the application of section 9308 generally need go no further. However, for the benefit of the litigants here involved, certain factual aspects of the record unraveled some loose ends which we must tie up.

The first such question to be resolved is whether the result reached should be different because of the fraudulent schemes concocted by Fairfield which operated to prevent Jackson and McCullough from becoming buyers in ordinary course of business and which in turn precluded there being any valid chattel paper in the hands of the dealer. Stated otherwise, suppose Fairfield had continued to make the payments to the bank on the two conditional sales contracts, and suppose, because of the dealer's default vis-a-vis the flooring lender, that the latter had seized the dealer's inventory, including the two motorhomes here involved; under such facts Jackson and McCullough could under no theory have successfully asserted any rights to the motorhomes as against the flooring lender. With this the situation, what should be the result if as here the contest were instead between the bank which bought the chattel paper and the flooring lender? This precise question was discussed in *Chrysler Credit Corporation v. Sharp, supra,* 56 Misc.2d 261, 288 N.Y.S.2d 525. In the cited case, Mrs. Sharp purported to purchase a 1963 Chevrolet from the dealer. A credit application was made to Chrysler Credit Corporation (bank) to finance the purchase. A loan of $1,710 was approved, and a conditional sales contract signed by Mrs. Sharp and endorsed by the dealer to the bank. The bank then paid the loan proceeds to the dealer who deposited them with Marine Midland Trust (flooring lender). The conditional sales contract recited that Mrs. Sharp had made a $443 down payment. In fact, she had not, having arranged with the dealer to bring the money in after receiving an income tax refund. This arrangement also required that she allow the Chevrolet to remain in the dealer's possession until she brought in the money. Immediately upon payment of the loan proceeds, the bank completed the U.C.C.-1 filing necessary in New York to perfect its security interest in the Chevrolet. So far so good, but before Mrs. Sharp could bring in the down payment, the flooring lender with legal justification closed in on the dealer, seizing all the automobiles on its lot, including the 1963 Chevrolet. It was sold by the flooring lender along with the remaining dealer inventory. When the bank learned of this, it sued the flooring lender for the proceeds of the sale of the Chevrolet.

In its initial treatment of the case, the court dealt with the section 9308 issue upon the assumption that Mrs. Sharp was a buyer in ordinary course of business and decided in favor of the bank. At the conclusion of its opinion the court addressed itself to the question of whether a different decision should have been reached if the irregularities of the transaction had the result of characterizing Mrs. Sharp other than as a buyer in ordinary course of business, *i.e.,* had the result of the dealer's selling chattel paper which misrepresented the facts to the bank. The court determined, even if such were the fact, that it would not make any difference, and its reasoning is expressed where it said

> [i]f there is a usage of trade which exposes an entruster on floor plan to certain risks, these are risks against which he can guard by audits and accounting procedures or he can refuse to knowingly expose himself to the risk with the particular dealer. To fail to place the exposure of such risk with the entruster in such situation would make it impossible for retail finance companies to do business with any dealer unless the entruster were directly a participant. (*Id.* at p. 534.)

An eminent scholar in the field, Professor Robert H. Skilton, writing in the Wisconsin Law Review, deals with the same question couched in somewhat different terms when he asks whether the bank who purchases chattel paper from the dealer must establish that the purchaser who executed the chattel paper be a buyer in the ordinary course of business and thus himself entitled to take free under section 9307 before the bank in turn can claim the benefit of section 9308. In his comments, Professor Skilton refers to the flooring lender as F-One and the bank as F-Two, and states:

> [u]nless F-Two should have visited the dealer's premises before taking the chattel paper, to discover whether the car was still there—usually a profitless thing to do—or unless we say that F-Two should check with every buyer directly before it takes the chattel paper, there is nothing that F-Two did or failed to do that should make its position of priority dependent on the kind of buyer Mrs. Sharp was. The question posed by section 9308 is what is, or should be, the ordinary course of business for a retail financer like F-Two. Did F-One bear the risk of its dealer-debtor misconduct, in case his dealer-debtor sold to a buyer in ordinary course, as far as F-One's rights against F-Two are concerned? Yes, says section 9308. It's not too much to say that F-One's risk versus F-Two should likewise extend to the case where B[uyer] is, unknown to F-Two[,] not a buyer in ordinary course, since F-One already bears the burden of knowing his dealer and keeping an eye on him. (Wisc. L. Rev. (1974) 1, 85.)

In our view, this analysis comports with the modern objectives of the Uniform Commercial Code and the directives for its application as set forth in section 1102. In other words, what is presented here is not a case where the bank has dealt with and derived its rights through the buyer, but rather where it has dealt with and derived its rights through the seller. In such instance the risk of dereliction by the seller (dealer) is, for policy reasons, more logically placed on the flooring lender than on the bank. Accordingly, the result which we have reached, based upon the application of section 9308, is not affected by the fact that Jackson and McCullough were not buyers in ordinary course of business as contemplated by section 9307.

That brings us to the necessity of closing the gap between the prior rights in the chattel paper and the proceeds of the sale of the two motorhomes. Section 9308 by its terms deals with security interests in chattel paper. At the outset of the transactions under review, the security interest of the flooring lenders was in the two motorhomes, and it was the motorhomes which remained in the hands of the dealer and were impounded by the police. One might ask how the phony conditional sales contracts metamorphosed into something which provided the basis for the bank to compete successfully for the motorhomes. Parenthetically, this was the actual focus of the contest, for the agreement to sell and then resolve the right to the proceeds was a mutual undertaking reached after the real dispute arose over the right to possession of the motorhomes.

In dealing with this aspect of the case, section 9306, subdivision (2) is of some help. It provides, "[e]xcept where this division otherwise provides, a security interest continues in collateral notwithstanding sale, exchange or other disposition thereof unless the disposition was authorized by the secured party in the security agreement or otherwise, and also continues in any identifiable proceeds including collections received by the debtor." The unstated counterpart of this provision is that the security interest does not continue in the collateral if there is consent to its disposition by the debtor (dealer).

The record does not disclose any express authorization by the flooring lenders which would permit the dealer to dispose of the collateral. However, both U.C.C.-1 financing statements by which the flooring lenders perfected their security interests had "Box A" checked, the one which extends the effect of the filing and perfection to proceeds of the collateral. In a situation of this kind, it has been held that the extension of the security interest to proceeds has impliedly authorized the debtor to dispose of the collateral. (*McFadden v. Mercantile-Safe Deposit & Trust Co.,* 260 Md. 601, 273 A.2d 198, 207.) As stated in *Commercial Credit Corp. v. National Credit Corp., supra,* 251 Ark. 541, 473 S.W.2d 876,

> [e]ven if National [flooring lender] had perfected its security interest in the automobile . . . Mathews [dealer] . . . was authorized by National to sell the automobile involved in the case. It would thus appear that when Mathews sold the automobile to Edgerson [buyer in ordinary course of business] . . . National's security interest would no longer have followed the automobile but would have only continued in the "proceeds" of the sale going to Mathews. The proceeds of the sale going to Mathews included the conditional sales contract [chattel paper] executed by Edgerson . . . while such proceeds were in the possession of Mathews. Mathews sold Edgerson's contract to Commercial [bank] . . . and . . . National's security interest would not have followed the chattel paper into the hands of Commercial, but would have continued in the proceeds [money] Mathews received from Commercial in the sale of the chattel paper . . . (*Id.* at p. 880.)

We read the sense of this to mean that when there is a consent to dispose of the collateral, either express or by implication (arising from a check in "Box A" of the U.C.C.-1), that the debtor-seller (dealer) actually has a kind of power of defeasance or substitution over the security interest as originally perfected in the tangible collateral. Thus if he subjects that collateral to a conditional sales contract and the buyer walks out with the goods, the security interest moves on to that contract in the hands of the dealer. Parenthetically, this represents a particular application of section 9307. However, if the dealer does not carry his own contracts and discounts them to the bank, then the bank, when it pays new value, takes a prior security interest in that contract as against the flooring lender per force of section 9308, and the latter's security interest moves on to the proceeds in the hands of the dealer. Thereafter, the rights in the chattel paper control the disposition of the tangible property which was the original collateral.

With these the legal consequences of a regular transaction, if the factual circumstances are sufficiently scrambled so that the original tangible collateral (motorhomes) falls back into the possession of the flooring lender and it turns out that the chattel paper was phony, what is to prevent the flooring lender from insisting that its security interest in the tangible collateral was never divested and that it has a prior right to possession of the tangible collateral? We think the answer to that question must be rationalized just as Professor Skilton did the buyer-in-ordinary-course-of-business issue. In other words, the effective functioning of the mercantile community in this area requires that those institutions financing retail purchases by means of the purchase of chattel paper be entitled to rely on the represented validity of that paper unless they have such knowledge as to preclude their being bona fide purchasers. The same reasons for placing the risk on the flooring lender, if the dealer absconds with the funds received from the bank that it was bound to pay to the flooring lender, should apply to the set of facts before us where the sales were dummied up from the start. Parenthetically, in the reasoning which underlies it, this result parallels the well-established rule in the negotiable instruments field that a drawee who has paid a bill of exchange or check on which the drawer's or maker's signature has been forged cannot recover the payment from a holder in good faith for value and without fault. (*United States v. Chase Nat. Bank,* 252 U.S. 485, 494, 40 S.Ct. 361, 64 L.Ed. 675.) Beyond that, it may be too elementary to observe, but, once this step has been taken to recognize that chattel paper, although irregular in its inception, can become valid and enforceable in the hands of a bona fide purchaser (just as can a forged bill of exchange), it necessarily follows that the right to possession of the tangible property subject to the chattel paper is dictated by the terms thereof.

In summary then, once a dealer has launched even irregular chattel paper in the mercantile stream and into the hands of a bona fide purchaser, chattel paper which covers tangible property which once was collateral of the dealer's financing party, the chattel paper becomes the collateral and the rights in that chattel paper control and represent the power to dispose of the tangible property upon default of the obligation stated in the chattel paper. This is the expectation under which the mercantile community operates, and the law should reflect it.

The judgment is affirmed.

§ 18.05 Proceeds

Read: U.C.C. §§ 9-306, 9-312(5)(6) and Comment 8.

Proceeds includes whatever the debtor receives upon the sale, exchange, collection, or other disposition of collateral. U.C.C. § 9-306(1). With certain exceptions, the secured party's interest continues in the collateral unless that secured party authorized disposition. The interest also continues in any identifiable proceeds that the debtor might have received, including the proceeds from proceeds. Thus, the secured party may claim an interest in both proceeds and collateral in order to satisfy the debt obligation. See U.C.C. § 9-306(2). Although parties may agree that proceeds will not be covered by the security interest, section 9-203(3) provides that a secured party has an interest in proceeds even if the security agreement is silent on the issue.

Section § 9-306(3) states that a security interest in proceeds is continuously perfected if the interest in the original collateral was perfected. The security interest in proceeds becomes unperfected ten days after the debtor receives the proceeds unless the secured party perfects an interest in the proceeds by filing a financing statement covering them or by taking possession. See § 9-306(3)(a),(b), and (c).

IN RE SPRINGFIELD CASKET CO., INC.

United States Bankruptcy Court
21 B.R. 223, 34 U.C.C. Rep. Serv. 305 (1982)

CHARLES A. ANDERSON, BANKRUPTCY JUDGE.

. . . .

FINDINGS OF FACT

On 2 January 1981, the parties entered into a Note whereby the Bank loaned Debtor "$23,853.60 with interest from the date due at the rate of 21 per cent per annum and at the legal maximum rate per annum after maturity until paid." The term of the Note was one year. The Note also contained a consensual security agreement, as follows:

> As collateral security for the payment hereof, and of any and all other indebtedness of us, or any of us, to the holder hereof present and future, hereby grants a security interest unto said bank in the following property: All existing accounts receivable & which will come into

existence and all proceeds arising therefrom. All inventory now owned or hereafter acquired and all products and all proceeds arising therefrom. (Payments of $1,000.00 shall be made monthly on 10th of each month beginning Feb. 10, 1981 with balance due at maturity.) Interest rate shall be 1 percent above base rate which may be adjusted from time-to-time as base rate of Security National Bank & Trust Co. changes.

The Bank perfected its security interest by an earlier filing of a financing statement on 17 December 1974; and the filing of a continuation statement on 22 August 1979. Note ORC §§ 1309.21 and 1309.40. The financing statement described the collateral as follows: "All of Debtor's inventory now owned or hereinafter acquired and all products and all proceeds arising therefrom." The court notes that the proper perfection of the Bank's security interest is not in dispute. The court also notes that neither the Debtor nor the Trustee have contested the amount alleged due on the underlying transaction, or the validity of either the security agreement, financing statement, or continuation statement.

Debtor filed its Petition in this court under 11 U.S.C. Chapter 7 on 10 September 1981, and scheduled the Bank as a creditor in the amount of $18,356.94, and accounts receivable in the aggregate amount of $ 15,547.00. The instant dispute stems from the Trustee's collection of two of the accounts, reported to the court in the amount of $5,957.59 collected from Littleton Funeral Home on 6 October 1981, and $1,320.00 from Ohio Casket Co. on 23 October 1981. In its memorandum, the Bank further contends that the Trustee has possession of additional undeposited checks totaling $71,224.94. The court notes, however, that these additional checks are not documented by the record, and that the matter was presented for determination of the proper distribution of only the two accounts described above. The court, therefore, will consider the proper disbursement of only the $7,277.59 of proceeds from the two above-described accounts, hereinafter referred to as the subject accounts.

The basic dispute regarding the accounts is whether the Bank's financing statement is defective by "omission" of the classification, "accounts receivable," from the description of collateral in the financing statement, argued by the Trustee as rendering the Bank's interest in the subject accounts unperfected, and thus allowable only as an unsecured claim. See 11 U.S.C. § 544, and ORC §§ 1309.20, 1309.21, and 1309.39. In response, the Bank contends that the subject accounts receivable constitute "proceeds," as that term is used in ORC § 1309.25(A) [U.C.C. § 9-306], and are thus properly perfected by the financing statement which does include the term, "proceeds of inventory," in the description of the collateral. To the contrary, the Trustee argues that, since the terms, "accounts" and "proceeds," have separate statutory definitions, ORC §§ 1309.01(A)(15) and 1309.25(A), respectively, a finding that the terms are synonymous would "violate the rules of statutory construction." In addition, the Trustee contends that the subject accounts "are not actually the proceeds of the collateral because the accounts arose from a finished product after application of showroom and sales service." The Trustee further argues, in the alternative, that the proceeds are not "proceeds of the inventory," as described in the financing statement, but are proceeds of the accounts receivable, and thus not perfected by the financing statement filing. ORC § 1309.39 . . . .

DECISION AND ORDER

I

The parties do not dispute that the Bank possesses a valid security interest in the inventory (caskets) and the sales proceeds, and that the security agreement also recites Debtor's accounts receivable, ORC § 1309.14(A) [U.C.C. § 9-203]. The initial question presented to the court, therefore, is whether the Bank's interest in the proceeds of subject accounts receivable received by the Trustee from pre-bankruptcy sales is perfected, so as to be enforceable against the Trustee in Bankruptcy. See 11 U.S.C. § 544 and ORC § 1309.20(A)(2) and (C).

Under the facts at bar, the proper means of perfection of the Bank's interest is the filing of a financing statement, ORC § 1309.21. In this case, the Bank has duly filed a financing statement, (ORC § 1309.38) and the court notes that the fact that the financing statement predated the parties' security agreement does not alter the effectiveness of the financing statement. ORC § 1309.39. The narrow legal issue at bar, therefore, is whether the Bank's financing statement contains a "statement indicating the type, or describing the items, of collateral," so as to "reasonably identify" the subject accounts for purposes of ORC Chapter 9. ORC §§ 1309.08, and 1309.39(A).

The Bank essentially argues that the subject accounts constitute "proceeds of inventory," and are thus properly described in the Bank's financing statement. ORC § 1309.39(A). The Trustee contends that "accounts" should not be classified as "proceeds" because such determination would be violative of the "statutory scheme" which separately defines the terms, precluding finding that they are "synonymous." ORC §§ 1309.01(15) and 1309.25(A) [U.C.C. § 9-306].

It is the determination of the court that the Bank has properly perfected its security interest in the subject accounts by the description of the accounts as "proceeds of inventory." To begin with, the character of inventory is not changed by actions taken to retail the inventory. Hence, for purposes of Article Nine, goods remain inventory, though transformed from their component parts into a finished product retailed with a "showroom and sales service," as long as the goods are held for "immediate or ultimate sale." Official Comment to ORC § 1309.07. In addition, although, as argued by the Trustee, "proceeds" and "accounts" are not synonymous; proceeds" are defined in ORC § 1309.25 to include accounts receivable as a subclass within the class of "non-cash proceeds." ORC § 1309.25(A).

Thus, those accounts receivable which were received in "exchange" for Debtor's inventory as retailed are adequately described in the Bank's financing statement, ORC § 1309.25(A), as would be statutorily presumed in Ohio even had the Bank omitted "proceeds" from the description of collateral. ORC § 1309. 14(C), effective in Ohio on 1 January 1979. Further, filing of a separate financing statement to cover proceeds is unnecessary if the proceeds are "collateral in which a security interest may be perfected by filing in the office or offices where the financing statement (for the original collateral) has been filed as is the case instanter." ORC § 1309.25(C)(1).

In the event of insolvency, state law specifically recognizes the continuing perfection of a security interest in "identifiable non-cash proceeds and in separate deposit accounts containing only proceeds." ORC § 1309.25(D)(1). In the case sub judice, the Trustee contends that the monies in his possession are technically proceeds of proceeds," (*i.e.* proceeds of the subject accounts rather than Debtor's inventory), and thus not perfected by the bank's financing statement. It is the opinion of this court that the character of the proceeds should be determined by their status at the time of the filing of the bankruptcy petition, at which time the instant proceeds were accounts in which the Bank possessed a perfected security interest as discussed above. The court further notes, however, that, regardless of a change in form of the proceeds, as long as the proceeds remain identifiable, (as the instant monies are), conversion of proceeds from accounts receivable to cash should not operate to obviate perfection in the "proceeds of the proceeds." ORC § 1309.25(D)(1) and (2).

. . . .

It is hereby ordered, adjudged and decreed that the Bank's interest in the subject accounts receivable, held by the Trustee in the amount of $7,277.59, is deemed to be a secured claim.

. . . .

CHEMICAL BANK v. MILLER YACHT SALES

New Jersey Superior Court, Appellate Division
173 N.J. Super. 90, 413 A.2d 619, 28 U.C.C. Rep. Serv. 1160 (1980)

KOLE, J.

Jean Muller bought in New York a 1975 32-foot Luhrs motorboat (Luhrs) for a cash sales price of $29,000, which was financed by Chemical Bank (Chemical). The retail installment contract-security agreement was assigned to Chemical on June 15,1976. Within 10 days thereafter and after receipt of the boat by Muller, Chemical filed two financing statements, one in tile Nassau County Clerk's Office, New York, since the boat was to be stored in Nassau County, and one in the New York City Registrar's Office, New York, as Muller lived in New York City. Neither of these financing statements was signed by Muller. In the security agreement he did not give Chemical express authorization to file them without his signature.

A salesman from Miller Yacht Sales (Sales), of New Jersey was approached at the New York boat show in January 1977 by Jean Muller, who represented himself to be Lawrence J. Millen. Millen wanted to buy a 36-foot Marine Trader motorboat (Marine Trader) from sales. Negotiations continued for several months.

On August 26, 1977 Sales sold in New Jersey the Marine Trader to Millen for a cash price of $47,500. Millen gave a cash down payment of $2,000 and was given a trade-in allowance of $22,500 on the Luhrs. Central Jersey Bank & Trust Company (Jersey Bank) financed the balance of the purchase price and was assigned the retail installment contract as security.

Sales took possession of the Luhrs in New Jersey by a bill of sale dated August 26, 1977 and resold it to someone in Florida on October 3, 1977 for $17,000.

In August 1977 Jean Muller defaulted on his payments to Chemical. Chemical claims that the balance due under its financing arrangement is $34,474.68. In letters of November 4, 1977 to Sales and Jersey Bank, Chemical advised that this amount was the "gross balance" due. However, in a letter of November 15, 1977 to Muller, the debtor, Chemical informed him that the "entire net balance of $21,976.11 is now due and payable on or before November 22, 1977."

Chemical notified Sales of its security interest in the Luhrs by telephone on November 2 or 3, 1977 and was informed of the sale of the Luhrs to a third party and the sale of the Marine Trader to Lawrence Millen. By two letters dated November 4, 1977, Chemical informed Sales and Jersey Bank that it claimed a valid security interest in the Luhrs and demanded immediate possession of the Luhrs or full payment on its financing contract. In its letter to Jersey Bank it also referred to the Marine Trader and its awareness that the Luhrs had been used as a trade towards the Marine Trader (in which Jersey Bank had a security interest) and that Jersey Bank was about to repossess the vessel in which it had its security interest. Chemical suggested that the lines of communication remain open between the banks so that neither would suffer financial loss.

Despite Chemical's communications, Jersey Bank repossessed the Marine Trader when Millen defaulted under the terms of its security agreement and sold it at public sale in December 1977. Efforts to locate Lawrence J. Millen, a/k/a Jean Muller were unsuccessful.

After trial the judge denied Chemical any relief by way of damages against Sales or Jersey Bank. He found that under the Uniform Commercial Code (U.C.C.) Chemical had a valid perfected security interest in the Luhrs without the filing of a financing statement that was superior to and valid as against any security or other interest that Sales had therein. He found, further, that Chemical could not recover conversion damages against Sales or Jersey Bank "independent of its rights under Article Nine of the Uniform Commercial Code." He determined that since Sales no longer had the Luhrs in its possession, the fact that it sold the Luhrs did not give rise to a claim against it for conversion of the Luhrs under Article Nine; but rather the Marine Trader should be considered the proceeds of the disposition of the Luhrs. He held that Chemical's financing statements did not give it a perfected security interest in the Marine Trader—the proceeds of the Luhrs—and, accordingly, its interest was subordinate under Article Nine to Jersey Bank's perfected purchase money security interest in that boat. He asserted that those statements wrongfully indicated that they were authorized to be filed without the debtor's signature thereon. As a result Chemical was denied a money judgment in conversion against both Sales and Jersey Bank but Chemical was declared to have a valid superior interest in the Luhrs as against the interest of Sales therein. Chemical appeals from the ensuing judgment.

Chemical argues that it is entitled to damages from Sales for Sales' conversion of the Luhrs boat and damages from Jersey Bank for its conversion of the proceeds of the Luhrs boat, the Marine Trader.

Except as otherwise indicated below, the rights of the parties here are governed by the law of New York where the Security agreement relating to the Luhrs was made and where the Luhrs was then located.

As used hereafter, the New York U.C.C. (McKinney) will be referred to as N.Y. U.C.C.. Unless otherwise indicated, all references to provisions of § 9 [sic; Article 9] will relate to N.Y. U.C.C..

We hereafter hold that the Luhrs is consumer goods and that, accordingly, a financing statement was not required to be filed to perfect Chemical's purchase money Security interest therein. § 9-302(1)(d). We note that § 9-302(1)(d), mandating filing of a financing statement to perfect a security interest in a motor vehicle required to be licensed or registered, does not apply to boats. See, N.Y. Veh. and Traf. Law (McKinney) Art 48 § 2251(6); Art 46, §§ 2104, 2101(n); Chapter 62A, § 159. We also note that there was no requirement that the Luhrs be registered or the security interest therein filed with the Federal Government under the Ship Mortgage Act of 1920, 46 U.S.C. § 921 et seq. Additionally, the evidence discloses that in fact no such registration or filing was effected as to the Luhrs. Hence, the secured transaction here involved is subject to § 9 [Article 9] of N.Y. U.C.C..

Marine Trader

Chemical claims that it is entitled to a judgment against Jersey Bank for conversion of the proceeds of the Luhrs, *i.e.* the Marine Trader for which the Luhrs was given as part payment.

In the circumstances of this case considerations of fairness and equity satisfy us that the awarding of such relief in favor of Chemical is not justified. See, *Kaplan v. Walker*, 164 NJ Super. 130 (App. Div. 1978); *Muir v. Jefferson Credit Corp., supra.*

Thus, we believe that in this case the term "proceeds," as defined in § 9-306(1), should not be interpreted as covering the Marine Trader, even though by definition it includes whatever is received when collateral is exchanged or otherwise disposed of and may consist of property other than cash.

The purchase price of the Luhrs was $29,000. It was used as a down payment on the much more substantial Marine Trader, the purchase price of which was $47,500. Jersey Bank financed $23,000 of that purchase price remaining after the trade-in. In the rather extraordinary circumstances here, its relationship to the Luhrs was so attenuated and remote that it reasonably cannot be considered as having financed the "proceeds" of that boat. It is accordingly inappropriate to conclude that as against Jersey Bank the Marine Trader represented the proceeds of the smaller boat so that Chemical's perfected security interest in the Luhrs attached to the Marine Trader as "proceeds" thereof. Jersey Bank's purchase money security interest in the Marine Trader was a continuing one until it was fully paid under its security agreement and in our view that interest was superior to any claim which Chemical could assert against that boat as "proceeds."

Even if, however, the Marine Trader is considered proceeds of the Luhrs, Chemical is not entitled to damages against Jersey Bank for conversion by reason of the sale of the Marine Trader.

We express no opinion as to whether under the facts here, pursuant to § 9-402(2)(b), Chemical's rights in the proceeds represented by the Marine Trader might have been vindicated by the award of conversion damages against Jersey Bank simply by reason of its filing of financing statements in New York. Neither in its brief nor on oral argument before us was that contention raised by Chemical. Instead, in connection with its rights against Jersey Bank and the proceeds represented by the Marine Trader, Chemical relied on the fact that the financing statements were properly filed under § 9-402(2)(c). Accordingly, we treat the issue here as thus framed.

Moreover, Chemical chose to file under § 9-402(2)(c) rather than (b) to protect its interest in the proceeds of the Luhrs. It should be bound by this choice.

§ 9-306(3)(a) provides that the security interest in proceeds is a continuously perfected security interest if the interest in the original collateral was perfected but it becomes unperfected 10 days after receipt of the proceeds by the debtor unless, among other things, a filed financing statement covering the original collateral also covers proceeds. As indicated, the financing statements filed by Chemical in New York were filed under § 9-402(2)(c), a provision apparently appearing only in the N.Y. U.C.C.. It does not appear in the New Jersey version of the U.C.C. See, NJSA 12A:9-402(2). Under § 9-402(2)(c) a financing statement is sufficient although it is signed only by the secured party when it is filed to perfect a security interest in collateral under a security agreement signed by the debtor and authorizing the secured party to file a financing statement. That section further provides, however, that such a financing statement must state that it is filed in accordance with a security agreement signed by the debtor and authorizing the filing of a statement by the secured party.

Although each of the financing statements filed by Chemical provides that it covers the Luhrs and the proceeds thereof, Chemical checked the provision of the statement which indicates that it is filed without the debtor's signature to perfect a security interest in collateral under a security agreement "signed by debtor" authorizing the secured party to file the statement. It did not check the provision that it was filed without such signature to perfect a security interest in collateral "which is proceeds of the original collateral described" in which a security interest was perfected (i.e. § 9-402(2)(b)). It is undisputed that the security agreement signed by the debtor in fact did not authorize the secured party alone, Chemical, to file the financing statements.

Chemical argues that we should imply such authority from the security agreement itself. Such implication would contravene § 9-402(2)(c), which contemplates an express authorization by the debtor that the statement be filed without his signature. The significance of strict compliance with this "New York variation" from the U.C.C. is emphasized by the Practice Commentary of Professor Homer Kripke set forth in the Comment to § 9-402 and § 9-312. He states that use of this provision should not become routine, for the debtor has a great interest in a properly limited financing statement, and that a debtor can protect himself against loss of borrowing sources by refusing to sign a financing statement in which the collateral is described more broadly than in accordance with the intent of the parties. Of course, § 9-402(2)(c) precludes the debtor from having any control of the financing statement filed if appropriate prior authority has been given by him.

Even though the foregoing commentary emphasizes the debtor's rights, an issue not present in this case, we have concluded that the same strict compliance with § 9-402(2)(c) was required in this case where Chemical, as a secured party, seeks refuge in that provision to protect its rights in the Marine Trader as proceeds of the Luhrs under § 9-306(3)(a). Under the facts of this case, we do not consider this deficiency merely to be an erroneous but substantial compliance with the requirements of § 9-402(2)(c). Rather, the error was seriously misleading and thus not saved by § 9-402(5). Cf. *Bank of No. America v. Bank of Nutley*, 94 NJ Super. 220 (Law Div 1967).

We note that here it would have been virtually impossible for Jersey Bank to have discovered Chemical's claimed rights in the proceeds of the Luhrs by virtue of the financing statements filed by Chemical, even if Jersey Bank had searched the records in New York. Thus, the name used by the debtor in the Chemical security agreement was different from that which he used when he transacted business in connection with Jersey Bank's security interest in the Marine Trader. To hold that Chemical may obtain rights in the Marine Trader as proceeds, notwithstanding its misleading representation in the financing statements that it had authority to file them without the debtor's signature, is to place a further unwarranted road block with respect to the protection of the rights of Jersey Bank, an innocent good faith purchase money security lender, in the claimed proceeds. It would benefit Chemical at the expense of Jersey Bank without any legal or business justification.

Accordingly, we hold that each of the financial statements filed by Chemical was fatally defective as to proceeds in erroneously stating that it could be filed without the debtor's signature because he authorized such filing. Chemical thus failed to protect its security interest in the Marine Trader as the proceeds of the Luhrs. § 9-306(3). It had no right or interest in the Marine Trader superior to that of Jersey Bank with which the latter interfered. Jersey Bank is thus not liable to it for conversion of that boat.

We add that even if the New York financing statements were not defective, it would appear that the failure of Chemical to perfect its claimed security interest in the proceeds represented by the Marine Trader by filing a financing statement here within four months of the Luhrs' arrival in New Jersey serves to defeat any rights that it may assert against Jersey Bank with respect to the Marine Trader. The Luhrs came into New Jersey on or about August 26, 1977 and, within four months thereafter, by early November 1977, Chemical was aware of that fact. Although Chemical was not required to file a financing statement here within that four-month period to perfect its security interest in the Luhrs, it would appear that such filing in New Jersey was required at least within that period to perfect its claimed security interest in the Marine Trader as the proceeds of the Luhrs.

We have considered the other arguments advanced by Chemical and find them to be without merit.

QUESTIONS

Is this decision technical? Was Jersey Bank an innocent good faith purchase money secured party? Should commercial parties be expected to make inquiries with due diligence? Why or why not?

IN RE S & J HOLDING CORP

United States Bankruptcy Court, Southern District of Florida
42 B.R. 249, 39 U.C.C. Rep. Serv. 668 (1984)

JOSEPH A. GASSEN, BANKRUPTCY JUDGE.

This matter came before the court on April 24, 1984, upon the Motion of A.M. June, Inc., for relief from stay or for adequate protection.

The debtor's business is primarily in operating video games. The issue in this case comes down to whether or not the creditor has a valid, perfected security interest in the cash revenues generated by the video game machines and vending machines.

The debtor executed a security agreement covering "[a]ll of the assets of Shazamm Enterprises, Inc., including without limitation all. . . equipment,. . . inventory, . . . accounts receivable, contract rights, intangibles, video games, cigarette machines, coin changes, [sic] and any and all other personal property or assets owned and used by the debtor in its business wherever located as well as any and all personal property hereinafter acquired." The same items were listed on the financing statement which was filed with the Secretary of State, and the debtor also checked the box which provides "Products of collateral are covered."

First, the court concludes that the cash obtained through the machines is not proceeds of other collateral which might have automatic perfection under Florida Statute § 679.306. Proceeds which are protected under § 679.306 are defined in Section (1): " 'Proceeds' includes whatever is received upon the sale, exchange, collection, or other disposition of collateral or proceeds." The video game equipment is collateral under the security agreement in question. But the cash which is generated through that equipment is not received from the sale of the collateral, but rather, through the use of it. It is more analogous to income generated through the use of, for example, construction equipment, which is given as collateral. The fact that the money was earned through the use of the collateral does not make it "proceeds" subject to the protection of § 679.306.

The fact that the financing statement stated that "products" of collateral are also covered is of no significance at all. Only the property specifically defined in § 679.306 is given any unique protection, and the money here does not fit within the definition.

Although the money in question is not "proceeds" it might have been included as collateral standing on its own. However, the only item which might apply to it is "intangibles." The court concludes that this is an insufficient description to cover the revenue from the machines.

For a security agreement to attach there must be "a security agreement which contains a description of the collateral," Florida Statute § 679.203(1)(a). And "any description of personal property. . . is sufficient whether or not it is specific if it reasonably identifies what is described. . ." The cases interpreting the "reasonably identified" provision have been fairly strict. Language such as "all property of the undersigned of every name and nature whatsoever" and "all other personal property" is clearly too broad. Greater particularity in the description of the collateral is required in the security agreement than in the financing statement, and the description should have sufficient detail that third parties could reasonably identify the particular assets covered.

Applying these standards, the court concludes that "intangibles" is not specific enough to reasonably identify the cash revenues from the video and vending machines. But it may also be inaccurate, as discussed below with regard to the perfection issue.

Assuming that the security agreement was sufficient to constitute an agreement between the parties that the security interest would attach to the cash revenues, the court concludes that the secured creditor was not perfected. Florida Statute § 679.304(1) provides that a Security interest in money can be perfected only by the secured party's taking possession except as provided in other sections which are not applicable here. See also Coogan, Kripke and Weiss, "Money and Deposit Accounts as Primary Collateral" in The Outer Fringes of Article 9: Subordination Agreements, Security Interests in Money and Deposits, Negative Pledge Clauses, and Participation Agreements, 1C Bender's U.C.C. Serv. § 23.09 (P. Coogan and J. McDonnell ed. 1984).

Because A.M. June, Inc. does not have a perfected security interest in the cash revenues from the video and vending machines in the debtor's business it loses priority to the debtor-in-possession. Therefore it is

Ordered and adjudged that the motion of A.M. June, Inc. for relief from stay or for adequate protection is denied.

PROBLEM 18.4

Bank provides working capital to a Debtor and takes a security interest in all of the debtor's inventory. Debtor's warehouse is located in North Carolina, but its chief executive office is located in Virginia. If Bank filed its financing statement in North Carolina, does the Bank have a perfected security interest? If Debtor sells its inventory to various retailers on open account, can Bank claim an interest in the accounts as proceeds? If the Bank can claim such an interest in accounts, is that interest perfected? Would the Bank prevail over a second creditor who took a security interest in Debtor's accounts after Bank filed, but who instead filed in Virginia? Would the result change if the second creditor filed as to accounts first?

PROBLEM 18.5

(2) XYZ Appliances borrowed $250,000 in working capital from ABC Bank which took a security interest in all of XYZ's inventory now owned or subsequently acquired. XYZ sold a

washing machine and dryer to Peter for $1500 under an installment sales contract which specifically reserved a security interest in the machines for XYZ. The dealer then sold a big screen television to Martha for $2500. Martha put $500 down and gave XYZ an unsecured promissory note for the remainder. XYZ then sold both contracts to Elizabeth's Finance Company. To facilitate the sale, XYZ assigned all of its rights to EFC. If both Peter and Martha default on their obligation, who prevails in a priority battle, ABC Bank or EFC? See U.C.C. §§ 9-308, 9-309, and 9-312(5).

§ 18.06 After-Acquired Property Priority

Read: U.C.C. §§ 9-204, 9-312(5) and Comment 6.

Section 9-204(1) permits a creditor to claim a security interest in a debtor's after-acquired property. This right is particularly important in inventory financing because of the rapid turnover of collateral. In fact, the after-acquired property clause makes the security interest in shifting inventory or goods possible. Because lien floats from the original security agreement and financing statement to after-acquired property, it receives priority over subsequent creditors. Sales of inventory often give rise to accounts; new inventory is often purchased with the proceeds from an inventory sale. With the after-acquired property clause, it is possible for a creditor to subject new collateral to the secured creditor's interest without the parties entering a new security agreement. Because the application of after-acquired property priority can work a severe hardship on other parties, the Code provides for several exceptions.

First, such an interest is not allowed in consumer goods except to the extent that the debtor acquires the property within ten days after the giving of value by the creditor. This rule protects the consumer against oppressive agreements that tie credit availability to a single lender. For similar reasons, after-acquired interests in crops are limited to one year, or the application of the clause must be in conjunction with a land purchase or improvement. Under section 9-307(1), buyers in the ordinary course of business also prevail over the after-acquired interest.

The major exception to the priority of the after-acquired property clause occurs where the later security interest is a purchase money security interest. As discussed earlier, the purchase money secured party receives priority because that new creditor contributes to the debtor's assets in the form of particular property that would probably not be available unless the purchase money creditor could be given priority. Recall that under section 9-312(3), the purchase money security interest in inventory collateral has priority over an after-acquired property clause only if certain requisites are satisfied. The security interest must be perfected when the debtor obtains possession of the collateral and notification must be given to the person with the earlier security interest. Once these requisites are satisfied, the purchase money security interest in inventory takes priority over a prior perfected party with an after-acquired property clause.

BOATMEN'S BANK OF PULASKI COUNTY v. SMITH

United States Bankruptcy Court, Western District of Missouri
29 B.R. 690, 36 U.C.C. Rep. Serv. 685 (1983)

JOEL PELOFSKY, BANKRUPTCY JUDGE.

In this adversary proceeding Boatmen's Bank of Pulaski County, hereinafter Bank, filed two pleadings. In one the Bank alleged that it loaned money to debtors based on financial statements which were materially false. In the other it sought relief from the stay alleging that debtors had converted the collateral. The Bank also sought in this second pleading a determination that the debt was not dischargeable. Both pleadings were filed by the Clerk as a single action.

Thereafter the Bank filed another petition in this same action adding Farmers Home Administration, hereinafter FmHA, as an additional party defendant. In this petition the Bank sought a determination of priorities as between it and FmHA as to certain collateral and for other relief. The Bank also filed Count II to a complaint, precisely which of the three then pending being unknown, again naming debtors and FmHA as defendants, seeking a determination of priorities and asking that the proceeds of the sale of cattle repossessed by FmHA be used to satisfy the Bank's debt.

Debtors answered the first two petitions by general denial. They filed no response to any other pleading. FmHA answered the so-called Count II by asserting the perfection and priority of its security instruments.

A hearing was held. Debtors appeared in person and by counsel. The Bank and FmHA appeared by counsel and representatives. Evidence was introduced and the matter taken under advisement.

The evidence shows that debtor Lloyd Smith was borrowing money from the Bank's predecessor in 1970. In August of 1976 the Bank took a security interest in "All livestock now owned and after acquired." No significant amount of money was advanced to debtors at this time. There is no evidence that debtors had any livestock in August of 1976. In March of 1979 debtors borrowed money from FmHA and executed a security agreement in favor of FmHA identifying cattle and hogs as collateral. Just prior to the advance a financing statement was filed and designated as security, inter alia, ". . . proceeds and products thereof: (a) . . . livestock . . . ." Debtors deposited the funds in their account at the Bank and purchased the cattle and hogs called for in the security agreement.

During the period June 1981 through January 1982 debtors borrowed $20,222.59 from the Bank. During the period from April 17, 1981 through January 1982 debtors gave the Bank four financial statements. Debtors gave a statement in September of 1980 but this, the court finds, is too remote in time to be of probative value except that it also, as do the others, omits any reference to the FmHA debt. On August 24, 1981 the Bank filed a continuation statement of its 1976 U.C.C. filing.

According to an affidavit filed by FmHA, an agent searched the U.C.C. filings in Pulaski County on September 1, 1981 and found no continuation filing by the Bank. In late September 1981, debtors executed a security agreement in favor of FmHA identifying cattle and hogs as collateral. No financing statement was filed in connection with this security agreement. In March of 1982 FmHA foreclosed its security interest in the cattle and sold them, applying the proceeds against the loan. Debtors filed for relief under Chapter 7 of the Code on March 18, 1982, after the foreclosure. This adversary was filed shortly thereafter.

Section 400.9-312, R.S. Mo. 1969, deals with "[p]riorities among conflicting security interests in the same collateral."

Section 400.9-109(3) R.S. Mo. 1969 classifies goods as "[f]arm products" if they are ". . . livestock . . . used . . . in farming operations. . .If goods are farm products they are neither equipment nor inventory."

The evidence shows that FmHA filed its financing statement prior to the funds being paid to debtor. Debtor used a substantial part of the money to purchase pigs and cattle. The purchases were made within two months of the advance. The purchase money security interest therefore was perfected when debtors received the collateral.

Debtors were engaged in farming at all times herein set out and § 400.9-109(3) excludes, therefore, these animals from the definition of inventory. The question of priority of creditors consequently is determined by reference to § 400.9-312(4). That section does not require notice to a creditor holding a prior filing in the same product with an after acquired clause and allows the creditor making a purchase money advance to have priority over the creditor holding "after acquired" rights. Thus, in May of 1979, FmHA had a priority in the purchased cattle over the claim of the Bank.

In its brief the Bank concedes that FmHA had a purchase money security interest in the collateral until September 27, 1981. The Bank argues that the security agreement dated September 28, 1981, destroyed that status and gave FmHA a security interest for an antecedent debt, thus restoring the Bank to its first filed priority status. There is no evidence that FmHA released its first security agreement or U.C.C. filing or advanced new funds in return for execution of this September, 1981 security agreement. No financing statement was filed in connection with the 1981 security agreement.

There was no testimony explaining the 1981 agreement. It would appear that it was taken after the FmHA agent ran a lien search and discovered, or so it seemed, that the Bank lien had expired. The 1981 agreement may have been taken to identify the then existing security.

There are a number of reasons why execution of the 1981 security agreement is immaterial. The Bank had filed a continuation statement and the court so finds. The Bank is not charged with FmHA's failure to discover such a filing or the apparent failure of the Recorder to index or file. The Bank continued to occupy a secured position in some respects. Nonetheless, as to the purchased cattle, FmHA's purchase money position was a priority without regard to the prior Bank filing and needed no subsequent action to maintain that priority even if the Bank's filing had lapsed.

The court concludes that execution of the 1981 security agreement, without more, is of no significance. The 1979 agreement was perfected and not altered by the subsequent agreement.

The Bank also contends that the FmHA security agreement loses its purchase money character and priority as to cattle produced from those purchased. Calves which are bred are not purchased. They are "after acquired" in a general sense. The FmHA security agreement also covers all increases. The question then is whether cattle bred from security for a purchase money security interest are themselves purchase money security.

Section 400.9-107, R.S. Mo. 1969, defines a purchase money security interest as one taken by a person who by making advances . . . gives value to enable the debtor to acquire rights in or the use of collateral if such value is in fact so used." Here there is no question that debtors used the FmHA advance to purchase cattle which they used for their benefit. The advance ultimately, through a natural process, also enabled debtors to have the use of calves, *i.e.,* the products of the purchase money collateral.

The Uniform Commercial Code enables a security interest to follow collateral even if it is transformed. See § 400.9-314, R.S. Mo. 1969, as to rules concerning accessions and § 400.9-315, R.S. Mo. 1969, as to rules concerning commingled or processed goods. But these statutes, while preserving a security interest, do not resolve the issue as to whether the interest retains its purchase money character but there are clear suggestions that the character remains unchanged. See, for example, § 400.9-31 5(1)(b) which provides that a financing statement covering goods "also covers the product into which the goods have been manufactured, processed or assembled." See also *Holzman v. L.H.J. Enterprises, Inc.*, 476 F.2d 949 (9th Cir. 1973) where the court held that inventory purchased from the sale of inventory subject to a purchase money security interest retained the character of purchase money security.

The purchase money security interest as an exception to the rules of priority of filing allows the creditor to have a security interest in identified collateral which it enabled the debtor to obtain. While such collateral may be transformed, as through manufacturing, it does not expand through its own effort. Cattle do (ignoring the biological act). The purchase money security interest is maintained by keeping the collateral intact or tracing the proceeds. Cattle as collateral expand by natural process.

In a case styled *In re Ingram*, 11 U.C.C. Rep. Serv. 605 (5th Cir. 1972) the court held a security interest in progeny of leased cattle was not a purchase money security interest because the creditor only enabled the debtor to acquire "rights in and use of the breeder stock" and not the progeny. The suggestion in § 400.9-204, R.S. Mo. 1969 is that since the debtor had no rights in unconceived progeny at the time the security agreement was executed, no security interest could attach and therefore the creditor acquired no rights in such unconceived animals.

The purchase money security interest priority is an exception to the general rule and should be construed narrowly even though the application to a cattle situation is inexact. Compare *Index Store Fixture Co. v. Farmers' Trust Co.*, 536 S.W.2d 902 (Mo. App. 1976). It must be remembered, in support of a narrow reading, that even the natural process of herd growth does not proceed without assistance not provided by the purchase money creditor. The result could be different if the evidence showed that some part of the purchase money collateral was sold and new animals purchased, but that is not the case here. Similarly this could be a variation if the calves only replaced cattle that had died. Again, while the herd has diminished here, there is no evidence that diminution occurred from the aging process.

The court concludes, therefore, that the purchase money security interest does not apply to the calves. FmHA is entitled to the proceeds of the sale of those cattle which retained purchase money character at the time of foreclosure but the Bank is entitled to the proceeds from the sale of any others.

The evidence shows that debtors purchased 19 cows and 20 pigs with the FmHA loan. FmHA sold 13 cows and 7 calves. Debtors owned no pigs at the time of the foreclosure. There is no evidence as to disposition of the other cows. The sale price was not allocated among the animals, although it appears that all of the cows could have been part of the purchase money herd. The parties are directed to confer and to advise the court whether a further hearing would be necessary to resolve the issue of allocation.

The court also reserves the question of the nondischargeability of the debt to the Bank until the issue of allocation is resolved. Further evidence may be necessary on that question.

—

§ 18.07 Future Advances

Read: U.C.C. §§ 9-204(3), 9-301(4), 9-312(5) and (7) and Comment 7.

As with after-acquired property, it is possible to provide that a security interest will cover future advances made by a creditor. Such advances normally have the same priority as advances made at the time the initial loan took place. To avoid having such a provision give priority over all subsequent creditors, the drafters of the Code outlined a priority rule at section 9-301(4). The secured creditor receives absolute priority for advances made prior to the time another person becomes a lien creditor, and for 45 days afterward. At the end of the 45-day period, the secured creditor has priority only when the advance is made without actual knowledge of the subsequent creditor's lien interest, or, when the advance occurs pursuant to a commitment that was entered into without knowledge of the other creditor's lien. See also U.C.C. § 9-105(1)(k).

FIRST NATIONAL BANK & TRUST v. SECURITY NATIONAL BANK

Oklahoma Supreme Court
676 P.2d 837 (1984)

. . . .

LAVENDER, JUSTICE:

At issue is the priority, inter se, of two creditors claiming a security interest in the same collateral under Part 3, Art. 9 of the Oklahoma Commercial Code-Rights of Third Parties; Perfected and Unperfected Security Interests; Rules of Priority (12A O.S.1981 § 9-309, et seq.).

The essential facts for determination of the issues on appeal are as follows:

On November 22, 1980, The Weather Station, Inc. (Weather Station) borrowed $30,000 from Security National Bank and Trust Company of Norman (Security) and gave Security a note and a security interest in all furniture, fixtures, equipment, inventory, accounts receivable and proceeds then owned by Weather Station or thereafter acquired. The security interest agreement further provided:

> This security interest is given to secure: (1) payment (of the note with interest when due); (2) future advances to be evidenced by like notes to be made by Bank to Debtor at Bank's option; (3) all expenditures by Bank for taxes, insurance, repairs to and maintenance of the Collateral and all costs and expenses incurred by Bank in the collection and enforcement of the note and other indebtedness of Debtor; and (4) all liabilities of Debtor to Bank now existing or hereafter incurred, matured or unmatured, direct or contingent, and any renewals and extensions thereof and substitutions thereof.
>
> Uniform Commercial Code notice was duly and timely filed.

On August 25, 1980, the indebtedness was fully paid, but no termination statement was filed by Security, and none was demanded by Weather Station.

On April 10, 1981, Weather Station borrowed $41,056.56 from Security and gave Security interest in four vehicles. Lien entry forms were timely and duly filed with the Oklahoma Tax Commission.

While the $41,056.56 indebtedness was outstanding and unpaid, Weather Station Successively borrowed from First National Bank and Trust Company of Norman, Oklahoma (First) as follows:

January 25, 1982, $40,000 to purchase equipment;

March 1, 1982, $20,000 and

March 21, 1982, $30,000, giving First a security interest on the latter two loans in the property covered by Security's initial security interest agreement. All of the First loans were duly and promptly recorded in accordance with Oklahoma's Uniform Security Code (UCC). No part of the indebtedness to First has been paid.

On June 1, 1982, Security loaned Weather Station $30,000 and received a security interest in all furniture, fixtures, equipment and accounts receivable of Weather Station. Notice was duly and timely filed under U.C.C. On June 15,1982, Weather Station repaid $20,000 and executed a new promissory note on the same date in the sum of $10,000. The note for $10,000 has not been paid.

On February 10,1983, the court below, after trial, determined that Security's position as a creditor is prior to that of First, and rendered judgement accordingly.

First appeals.

Priority between conflicting security interests in the same collateral is governed by Art. 9 of the Oklahoma Uniform Commercial Code (12A O.S.1981 § 9-101, et seq.) . . . .

Since the security interest of both Security and First were perfected by filing, our inquiry on appeal is directed to whether the "future advances" provisions of Security's financing statement of November 22, 1980, insures Security a first priority position as against First's subsequently filed security interest in the same collateral.

A security agreement under U.C.C. is a contract. . . . .

In *Blue v. H-K Corp.*, Okla. App., 629 P.2d 790 (1981), the Oklahoma Court of Appeals held (791):

> A creditor may obligate the collateral to cover future advances or other value in the initial security agreement. § 9-204(5). However, the security agreement must by its language indicate that the collateral is intended to cover future advances.

In the case at bar, Security's security agreement of November 22, 1980, clearly and unequivocally purports to bind the collateral with "all liabilities of Debtor to Bank now existing or hereafter incurred, matured or unmatured, direct or contingent, and any renewals and extensions thereof and substitutions thereof." A clearer manifestation of an intent to bind all future indebtedness which may be owing by Weather Station to Security is difficult to imagine.

First urges, however, that payment by Weather Station of the November 22, 1980, indebtedness in effect terminated the security interest of Security despite the fact that no termination statement was filed or requested by Weather Station, and despite the fact that the April 10, 1981, indebtedness of Weather Station, secured by four vehicles was outstanding and unpaid at the time First perfected its security agreement of January 25, 1982, thus (First argues) placing First's perfected security interests in a position prior to that of Security. We disagree.

. . . .

In *Texas Kenworth v. First Nat. Bank of Bethany, Okla.*, 564 P.2d 222 (1977) we held (227): Unless a written demand by the debtor sent to the creditor, pursuant to 12A O.S. 1971 § 9-401, makes a demand, there is no duty on behalf of the creditor to file a release or termination statement. Conversely, there is no duty on the part of the debtor to make a written demand. Since there is no duty to file a release or termination statement, unless requested, and since there is no duty to make such a request, we attach no significance to the fact that no release or termination statement was filed.

In *State Bank of Young America v. Vidmar Iron, Minn.*, 292 N.W.2d 244 (1980), *Texas Kenworth* was cited with approval and followed (249), the Minnesota Supreme Court further holding that where, as here, the creditor continued to incur additional debts after the original debt was paid, the "future advances" clause of the security agreement thereafter remained valid and covered a renewal note and additional loans made by debtor in favor of creditor.

The doctrine of relation back has been incorporated in the U.C.C., thus giving future advances made while a security interest is perfected the same priority enjoyed with respect to the first advance. 12A 1981 § 9-312(7).

The question thus becomes one of determining whether Security's original perfected financing statement was in fact terminated or extinguished prior to First's perfecting its financing statement, since the failure to issue, or the creditor's failure to request and record a termination statement is not determinative.

Since the U.C.C. offers no specific guidance as to when a "future advances" clause in a financing statement terminates where the financing statement is silent as to its duration, we conclude that its prospective duration must be determined by the intention of the parties as in other cases involving the law of mortgages generally.

In *Safe Deposit & Trust Co. v. Berman* (CA 1, 1968), 393 F.2d 401, it was suggested that failure on the part of a debtor to demand a termination statement may be evidence of an intention that the security interest was to continue beyond the original obligation and to cover future advances secured by the same collateral. In the absence of a statute justifying an inference that a mortgage is dead once there is no debt momentarily existing, no such inference necessarily follows under the common law.

Here, the creditor (Security) did not deliver a termination statement to the debtor (Weather Station), nor did the debtor demand one. Approximately seven months following the payment of the original indebtedness, further secured financing of four vehicles was entered between Weather Station and Security, and while the original financing statement remained perfected and unreleased of record. First, with record notice of the existing financing statement containing its "dragnet" clause, perfected its subsequent financing covering the same collateral as was covered in Security's financing statement. We hold that Security's position was prior to that of First in the collateral both as to Security's original financing statement, and as to Security's subsequent financing statement on the same collateral.

Security next urges that whether future liabilities fall within a security agreement's future-advances clause is determined by whether the debts are of the same class as the primary obligation and in contemplation of the parties at the time the agreement was executed, relying upon *Security Nat. Bank v. Dentsply Professional, supra,* [617 P.2d 1340] (1345-1346) so stating.

We are not here concerned with whether the debts are of the same class as the primary obligation for the reason that the parties to this cause so stipulated, and the uncontroverted evidence adduced at trial disclosed that both debts were working capital and for the same purpose.

We therefore turn to the question of whether the future advances were within the contemplation of the parties at the time the original financing statement agreement was executed.

In *Kimbell Foods, Inc., v. Republic Nat. Bank* [(CA 5th, 1977) 557 F.2d 491 (498), aff'd, 440 U.S. 715, 99 S. Ct. 1448, 59 L. Ed. 2d 711 (1979)] the Court of Appeals applied Texas law in addressing this precise issue. There the Court said (496):

> The language of the contract, unless ambiguous, represents the intention of the parties. The intent deduced from this objective matter, is controlling. (Citations omitted.) Testimony as to . . . subjective intent in receiving the future advance clause was a classic violation of the parol evidence rule and clearly inadmissible.
>
> The district court compounded this error by failing to consider the truest test of the parties' intention, the words of the contract clearly providing that the security agreement should cover future indebtedness.
>
> That Oklahoma law comports with that of Texas on this issue is clear.

The language of the future-advances clause being clear, unambiguous and unequivocal, that it was within the contemplation of the parties that future advances be covered by the original financing statement, no further inquiry may be made.

Security, having intervened in First's suit seeking a court order for possession of the collateral and its sale, and having established its prior right to that of First to the possession of the secured collateral and prior right to the proceeds from the sale of the collateral, Security was the prevailing party within the meaning of 12 O.S. 1981 § 1580, and, as such, was entitled to recover a reasonable attorney fee from First to be set by the trial court to be taxed and collected as costs. The order of the trial court denying Security's motion for attorney fees is reversed.

The parties having stipulated that the reasonable value of Security's attorney fees is the sum of $ 1,750, said sum is hereby taxed as costs against First and in favor of Security.

BARNES, C.J., and HARGRAVE, OPALA and WILSON, JJ., concur.

SIMMS, V.C.J., and HODGES, J., dissent.

---

§ 18.08 Fixtures

Read: U.C.C. § 9-313.

Fixtures present one of the most complicated issues under the Code. Most Article 9 priority contests involve two or more persons asserting interests in collateral under personal property law. The claimants derive their lien interests from consent between or among the parties or from a judicial determination. The possible claimants on a fixture not only include judgment lienholders and Article 9 security holders, but also persons whose interests arise under real estate law (mortgage lien creditors or owners).

A fixture is an item of personal property that becomes so incorporated into real estate that an interest in it arises under real property law. The U.C.C. provides a separate filing mechanism for personal property that become fixtures—because the goods are affixed to the real estate, filing should be made in the office of the county where real estate records are filed. By making such a filing, the interest of the fixture secured party takes precedence over subsequent purchasers of the real estate, creditors who obtain subsequent liens on the property, and creditors who make sale advances. This priority also extends over subsequent purchasers at foreclosure sales. But what exactly is a fixture?

IN RE HAMMOND

United States Bankruptcy Court Eastern District of Tennessee
38 B.R. 548, 38 U.C.C. Rep. Serv. 659 (1984)

RALPH H. KELLEY, BANKRUPTCY JUDGE.

The debtors objected to claims 1 and 2 filed by Agristor Credit Corporation as secured claims. The debtors contend that the claims are unsecured because Agristor failed to perfect its security interests by filing financing statements in the correct place. 11 U.S.C. § 544(a); Tenn. Code Ann. § 47-9-301(1)(b)& (3).

Agristor filed financing statements in McMinn County, Tennessee, where the silos and unloaders are located. This was the correct place of filing to perfect the security interests if the silos and unloaders are "fixtures." Tenn Code Ann § 47-9 401(1)(b). The debtors contend, however, that the silos and unloaders are "farm equipment." Perfection of a security interest in farm equipment requires filing in the county where the debtor resides. Tenn Code Ann. § 47-9-401(1)(a). The parties agree that the debtors reside in Polk County, Tennessee.

The question, then, is whether the silos and unloaders are "fixtures" subject to a perfected security interest or "farm equipment" in which Agristor's security interest is unperfected.

The parties agreed to allow the court to decide on a written record.

The debtors bought one silo and unloader from Southern Harvestore Company in 1976. The debtors bought the other silo and unloader from Volunteer Harvestore Systems in 1978. "Harvestore" is the name of the manufacturer or a brand name used by the manufacturer. The sales contracts were combined installment sale contracts and Security agreements.

Both contracts contain the following provision:

> The Collateral shall be used primarily for business, shall at all times be and remain personalty, shall remain severable from the above-described premises (or any other premises) and shall not be or become fixtures as part of the premises irrespective of their use or manner of attachment to the premises, and are not and shall not become subject to the claims of any holder of superior title to the premises or to any encumbrances heretofore or hereafter placed on the premises by Buyer or assigns. . . . Buyer shall, at Seller's request, procure the execution of Fixtures Disclaimers by all persons with interests in the premises and shall pay all the filing or recording costs whenever filing or recording is deemed by the Seller to be desirable.

The contracts also provided that on default the seller would have all the remedies allowed by the Uniform Commercial Code. Those remedies include repossession and resale. Tenn Code Ann §§ 47-9-503 & 47-9-504. The contracts were assigned to Agristor.

Each silo is 20 feet in diameter by 80 feet high. Both silos and both unloaders were installed on the debtors' farm in McMinn County.

The parties introduced into evidence portions of the deposition of Agristor's district manager, James H. Ashby, II.

He described the construction of Harvestore silos. The first step is the pouring of a round concrete foundation. The depth of the foundation depends on the local footing requirements, but in all cases about 5 feet of the foundation is above ground. The bottom metal sheets are bolted to this part of the foundation. The builders then construct the top of the silo by assembling the "tub" sheet and attaching the roof to it. The next step is to raise the completed portion on jacks. The builders then use four or five curved metal sheets to make another vertical Section of the silo. They jack up the completed portion and repeat the process until the silo is completed. They also install vertical stiffeners at the bottom and horizontal stiffeners on the sides. The bottom is welded into the silo in sections.

The metal side sheets have glass fused on the inside. A tight sealer like glue is used on the seams inside the silo and around the bolts.

A silo can be taken down by repeating the process in reverse. The silos are not easy to take down. The sealer on the seams has to be broken carefully in order to avoid separating the glass liner from the metal sheet. The liner cannot be replaced, but a new sheet can be substituted for a damaged one. A crew of four or five men would take four or five days to take down a 20' X 80' silo. Agristor does not have work crews that can do this, but the Harvestore dealers do.

Mr. Ashby also testified about the re-use of used silos. There is a market for used Harvestore silos. They are put up and can be taken down the same way all across the country. They are re-sold or released through the Harvestore dealers. People in the business know that used silos can be bought and will contact dealers about buying them. When a used silo is put up, it is put up in warrantable condition. Damaged parts are replaced. Used silos have generally had a good re-sale value, about 75% to 80% of the price of a new silo of the same size.

Discussion

Outside of bankruptcy, the security agreements would control in any dispute involving only the debtors and Agristor. The court would have to conclude that the goods are farm equipment and Agristor's security interests are unperfected. However, the conclusion would make no difference. If no third party's rights were involved, perfection of the Security interest would make no difference to Agristor's right to repossess the goods. This proceeding is different because the debtors can assert the rights of a hypothetical third party-a judgment lien creditor under Bankruptcy Code § 544. See also 11 U.S.C. §§ 1106 & 1107.

A judgment lien on the real property would not give the debtors priority over Agristor because it perfected its security interests in the goods as fixtures. Tenn Code Ann § 47-9-313. Therefore, the debtors contend that the silos and unloaders are farm equipment and Agristor's unperfected security interest is inferior to the judgment lien given by the Bankruptcy Code. Tenn Code Ann § 47-9-301.

What is a fixture? A fixture is an odd creature of the law. It has two distinguishing characteristics. First, it is so firmly attached to real estate that it is considered a "permanent" improvement and subject to the claims of anyone with an interest in the real estate. Second, it is so loosely attached to real estate that for financing purposes it retains some of its characteristics as a chattel.

This paradox has led to a common kind of dispute. One person claims the fixture as part of the real estate and another claims the fixture itself as personal property. Which person has the superior claim is determined under § 9-313 of the Uniform Commercial Code (UCC). Tenn. Code Ann. § 47-9-313. That section essentially leaves the question of whether goods are fixtures to Tennessee law other than the U.C.C.

Whether goods are fixtures is said to depend on (1) annexation to the real property, (2) intention of the parties and (3) removal without substantial injury to the realty.

"Annexation" to the realty is a threshold test for determining whether the goods in question might be a fixture. . . . Are the goods sufficiently attached that they might be considered a permanent improvement to the realty? The silos and unloaders easily pass the annexation test. They may be fixtures.

The next consideration is the "intention of the parties." When a third party is involved, the courts are not limited to considering their contract in determining the intention of parties. A third party is not likely to know what the contract provides, and the courts generally look to more objective criteria. Nevertheless, the contract is some evidence of the parties' intent.

In this case, the debtors as judgment lien creditors are arguing that the contract correctly states their intent and Agristor's intent that the silos and unloaders not become fixtures. The contract at least shows Agristor's intent that the goods not become fixtures while Agristor's security interest continues. A provision like this is meant to protect collateral from the claims of persons with an interest in the realty. The contract could not control their rights but the secured party could point to it as evidence of the debtors' intent that the goods not become fixtures. Certainly Agristor should not be allowed to deny a provision of the contract meant for its benefit. The court thus concludes that Agristor is bound by the contract and cannot deny that the silos and unloaders are equipment. The result is that the court need go no further. Agristor's security interest is unperfected.

However, assuming that Agristor can deny the contract, the court would still conclude that the silos and unloaders are equipment rather than fixtures.

The size of these silos, the manner in which they are attached, and the fact that they were annexed by the owner of the land all suggest that they were meant to be permanent improvements. On the other hand, there is an established market for used silos and unloaders of this kind. People involved in agricultural businesses know that this kind of silo can be moved from one farm to another. These silos are essentially like large grain bins often used on farms.

This court has held that grain bins were fixtures but those bins were part of a feed mill. *In re Mayfield,* cited above. The Tennessee Supreme Court held that for tax purposes certain grain bins were not fixtures. . . . The Arkansas Supreme Court held in one case that large grain bins were fixtures. . . . In that case, however, the expert witness testified that grain bins were seldom moved. He knew of only two that had been moved and they had not been set on concrete foundations. On the other hand, silos like these are regularly dismantled, repossessed and resold. Even though dismantled and removed, the silos have substantial resale value. People in agricultural businesses realize that silos like these may be moved. Finally, in *McCarthy v. Bank,* the court held that a 20' X 60' Harvestore silo like the ones in question was not a fixture. 423 A.2d 1280, 31 U.C.C. Rep. Serv. 1462 (Pa. Super. 1980).

The final consideration is whether removal would substantially injure the realty. Obviously the land would be worth more for dairy or livestock farming if it had the silos and unloaders but that is not the controlling fact. If the silos were removed, the concrete foundations would be difficult to remove so that the land could be used for other purposes. The foundations would, however, be available to use for new silos. Thus, the proof was not clear as to how removal of the silos would affect the use or value of the land.

The court concludes that the silos and unloaders are not fixtures or in the alternative, that Agristor cannot deny that they are equipment as provided in the contract. Accordingly, the court will enter an order allowing Agristor's claims as unsecured. . . . .

NOTES AND QUESTIONS

(1) The question of whether specified goods are fixtures, as the *Hammond* case demonstrates, may depend largely on the facts of the case. Should the intent of the parties weigh more heavily in the determination rather than whether removal would injure the property? A questionable decision regarding this determination is *Sears Roebuck and Co. v. Detroit Federal S. & L. Ass'n*, 79 Mich. App. 378, 262 N.E.2d 831, 23 U.C.C. Rep. Serv. 494 (1977). Detroit Federal (the bank) perfected a security interest in the form of a mortgage in all materials required in the construction and equipping of a condominium project. The security agreement referred to "all uninstalled materials on site and all stores, refrigerators, dishwashers, disposals etc." Subsequently, Sears perfected a security interest in refrigerators, stores, dishwashers, disposals etc. under a conditional sales contract. The mortgage agreement with the bank included a provision securing an interest in after-acquired property. Rather than decide the case on the basis of priorities between a security interest in fixtures and an interest in real estate, the court considered priorities between a secured interest in inventory and a purchase money interest. It was certainly questionable whether the bank had ever extended new value, as well as, whether the goods in question qualified as inventory. What result would this case yield under the tests suggested in *Hammond*? Under U.C.C. § 9-313?

(2) In *Motorola Communications and Electronics, Inc. v. Dale*, 665 F.2d 771, 32 U.C.C. Rep. Serv. 1656 (5th Cir. 1982), the lessee of real estate affixed a radio transmission tower to the property by bolting it to a concrete slab. Based on this annexation to realty, the district court held that the tower had become a fixture, and thus, became the landowner's property when the lessee defaulted on his rent. Motorola had not made a fixture filing required to protect its security interest in the tower. The appellate court reversed, reasoning that in determining whether something becomes a fixture, the greatest weight must be given to the intention of the party who performs the annexation. Here, Motorola's agreement with the lessor stated that the tower would not be considered as part of the real estate. Would this approach be proper in a case not involving a landlord-tenant relationship?

Fixture priority rules are found at section 9-313. Unfortunately, that section does not provide a complete definition of a fixture; state law outside the U.C.C. determines what constitutes a fixture.[19] The basic rule states that an encumbrancer or owner of real estate to which a fixture is attached prevails over the claim of a secured party unless a contrary rule appears elsewhere in section 9-313. Sub-sections 9-313(4), (5), and (6) detail specific exceptions which give the fixture secured party priority. Under § 9-313(4)(a), a purchase money fixture party receives protection against a prior owner or encumbrancer of real estate if the fixture secure party makes a fixture filing within 10 days of the time the goods become fixtures, and if the debtor has an interest in the real estate. The subsection only protects purchase money secured, fixture claimants against *prior* real estate interests. Non-purchase money security interests in fixtures are subordinated to prior claims.

All fixture security interests prevail over persons claiming a subsequent realty interest. Under subsection (4)(b) of § 9-313, priority follows the order of perfection or recording. Thus, in a priority dispute between a fixture claimant and a subsequent encumbrancer or owner of real estate, the first to file or perfect wins, provided the debtor has an interest of record in the property (record ownership or possession). Because notice must be given to possible real estate claimants, the fixture secured party must meet the requirements of section 9-402 for filing and describe the real estate onto which the fixture attaches (a fixture filing). If the fixture secured party fails to describe the realty, the secured party will be unperfected under section 9-313.

A non-fixture filing can still provide the fixture secured party with some protection under section 9-313(4)(c) and (d). Under subsection (4)(c), a fixture security interest in collateral that is either readily removable factory or office machines, or readily removable replacements of domestic appliances that are consumer goods, can be perfected by either a fixture filing, or by any other method of perfection. The justification for this rule is that a real estate claimant is not likely to be misled if such an interest did not appear in the real estate records because the encumbrancer or owner would know that the collateral was of the type that was readily removable. The exception is a very narrow one because the collateral must be found to be a fixture under state law, it must be readily removable, and the collateral must be of a specific type (factory or office machines or, replacement domestic appliances).[20]

Similarly, subsection (4)(d) to § 9-313 provides another narrow exception in which a non-fixture filing will give a secured party some protection. Under this provision, a fixture secured party prevails over the creditor who has a lien on the real estate by virtue of a legal or equitable

---

[19] There is one exception: section 9-313(2) specifies that no matter what non-Code law provides, "no security interest exists under this Article in ordinary building material incorporated into an improvement on land." In this type of situation, the validity and perfection of a security interest will be governed exclusively by real estate law.

[20] To illustrate, consider the case of a purchase money creditor under section 9-312(4) who sells a large item of equipment to the debtor and files with the secretary of state on the equipment. If the debtor incorporated the equipment into its factory by removing a wall and bolting the equipment into the concrete, subsection (4)(c) would not protect the purchase money creditor against either prior or subsequent real estate interests because the collateral was not readily removable.

proceeding, *if*, perfection occurred *before* the lien arose. The rule is very similar to the one found in section 9-313(4)(b); the rules differ because under (4)(b), the fixture claimant must have made a fixture filing. Under (4)(d), a non-fixture filing would protect the secured party.

FIRST NATIONAL BANK OF HAYES CENTER v. ROSE

Nebraska Supreme Court
213 Neb.. 611, 330 N.W.2d 894, 35 U.C.C. Rep. Serv. 1335 (1983)

CAPORALE, J.

Plaintiff-appellant, First National Bank of Hayes Center (Bank), appeals from the denial of its motion for summary judgment and the granting of the motion for summary judgment filed by defendants-appellees, Vincent W. Rose and Lucile I. Rose, husband and wife. We reverse.

The plaintiff Bank urges the trial court erred in determining that its security interest did not attach to the items in question prior to the time they became fixtures and therefore did not defeat the Roses' claim to such items.

The Roses sold a 1,200-acre farm to Mr. and Mrs. Cary W. Leonard pursuant to a land contract dated April 23,1976. The Leonards paid the Roses $80,000 toward the purchase price of $330,000. Subsequently, Mr. Leonard arranged with Sargent Irrigation Company for the drilling and installation of an irrigation well with pertinent equipment, including the items in question: a pump, bowl, well column, and gear head. On or about April 27,1976, Mr. Leonard signed a promissory note, a financing statement, and a Security agreement in favor of the Bank in exchange for a loan of $54,000. The financing statement and security agreement each covered, among other things, all farming and irrigation equipment. The financing statement was filed in the office of the Lincoln County clerk on April 29, 1976, but the security agreement was not filed in the office of the Lincoln County register of deeds until September 18, 1979. According to Mr. Rose, the well was drilled in April 1976 and the items in question were delivered to the farm and installed during the spring of 1977. Because the Leonards were unable to meet the payment schedule set forth in the land contract, they and the Roses, on or about July 21, 1978, entered into an agreement modifying the land contract. Under the terms of this modification agreement the Leonards paid $15,580 rather than the $23,420 due May 1, 1978; agreed that if the revised payment schedule was not met on November 1, 1978, the Roses were to keep all payments previously made to them; the quitclaim deed executed by the Leonards would be delivered by the escrow agent to the Roses; and the Leonards would vacate the property on or before March 1, 1979. The Leonards defaulted and the quitclaim deed was delivered to the Roses during the first part of November 1978; the Roses took possession of the land on which the well was located on or about March 1, 1979. An effort by Sargent Irrigation Company during the latter part of November 1978 to pull out the pipe was successfully thwarted by Mr. Rose. Thereafter, the plaintiff Bank brought this action to replevin the items in question and to recover damages. Subsequently, the Bank moved for a summary judgment that it was entitled to possession of the items in question. That motion was overruled by the trial court. The Roses also filed a motion for summary judgment, the precise nature of which we cannot determine because, although the Bank's praecipe calls for such, it is not found in the transcript. However, the Roses' notice of hearing on a summary judgment motion and the judgment from which the plaintiff Bank appeals are contained in the transcript. That judgment dismisses all of the Bank's claims relevant to this appeal against the Roses.

The rights of the parties are controlled by the Uniform Commercial Code as adopted in Nebraska. The first question to be determined is when plaintiff Bank acquired a security interest in the items in question. Neb. U.C.C. § 9-204(1)(Reissue 1971), now found generally at Neb. U.C.C. § 9-203(1)(Reissue 1980), provided then as follows: "A security interest cannot attach until there is agreement (subsection (3) of section 1-201) that it attach and value is given and the debtor has rights in the collateral. It attaches as soon as all of the events in the preceding sentence have taken place unless explicit agreement postpones the time of attaching."

The agreement element was met by the execution of the security agreement on April 27, 1976. The value requirement was met by the plaintiff advancing to Mr. Leonard the amount of the loan. Therefore, the only element which remains for consideration is at what time the debtor Leonard acquired rights in the collateral, for that is the time which determines when plaintiffs security interest "attached," that is to say, came into existence. Although there is dictum in *Tillotson v. Stephens*, 195 Neb. 104, 237 N.W.2d 108 (1975), which may suggest otherwise, when the collateral consists of goods purchased by the debtor, the sales article of the Uniform Commercial Code determines when the debtor has acquired rights in the collateral. . . . *Tillotson* was concerned not with the question of when a security interest attached but, rather, with the priority of claims as between parties to a conditional sales contract and a subsequent purchaser of realty for value.

. . . .

Since the items in question could not be affixed to the realty until after delivery, even if installation were to have taken place immediately thereafter, it necessarily follows that in this instance plaintiffs security interest came into existence prior to the time the items were attached to the realty and thus became fixtures. See, also, *Wood Chevrolet Co. v. Bank of the Southeast*, 352 So 2d 1350 (Ala. 1977), holding that delivery controlled when title passed to certain automobiles.

The foregoing conclusion makes necessary that we determine the priority between plaintiff's claim and the Roses' claim. . . . Accordingly, plaintiff's security interest takes priority over the claim of the Roses unless the Roses come within any one of the exceptions contained in § 9-313(4). They clearly obtained no subsequent lien by judicial proceedings. Nor did they make any subsequent advances; the evidence establishes that the Leonards made a payment to the Roses in exchange for a modification of the land contract. The question then becomes solely whether the Roses are subsequent purchasers for a value. The delivery of the quitclaim deed to them did not create in them any interest in the realty which they did not already own. It merely terminated the equitable lien of the Leonards in the realty, who had in fact lost such by being in default. Delivery of the quitclaim deed simply fulfilled the bargained-for procedural shortcut to clear the Roses' title in and to the land. See *O'Hara Plumbing Co., Inc. v. Roschynialski*, 190 Neb. 246, 207 N.W.2d 380 (1973), holding that a land contract vendee has an equitable interest in the land. Unlike the purchaser at the foreclosure sale in *Tillotson v. Stephens,* 195 Neb. 104, 237 N.W.2d 108 (1975), the Roses were not subsequent purchasers for value; consequently, the security interest of the plaintiff Bank is superior to the claim of the Roses.

Each party filed a motion for summary judgment. The pleadings, together with the depositions and affidavits received in evidence, show there is no genuine issue as to any material fact and establish that the plaintiff Bank, rather than the Roses, is entitled to judgment as a matter of law. Under such circumstances the plaintiff Bank's motion for partial summary judgment should have been sustained and the motion of the Roses overruled.

The judgment of the lower court in favor of the defendants Rose dismissing the claim of the plaintiff Bank is reversed and the cause remanded for further proceedings in accordance with this opinion.

NOTES AND QUESTIONS

(1) Under a retail installment contract, personal property which is to be attached to the real estate may, by agreement, retain the classification of personal property. In such case, the goods to be attached become an "accession." Note that the form of financing statement under U.C.C. § 9-402 does not provide the distinction between fixtures and accessions. The lack of such a distinction in the financing statement may have serious consequences. See *Babson Credit Plan, Inc. v. Cordele Production Credit Ass'n.,* 24 U.C.C. Rep. Serv.. (Ga. App. 1978).

(2) Bank has a security interest in a mobile home as assignee of a conditional sales contract. The mobile home is installed on premises where X holds a real estate mortgage. Did Bank's security interest attach before the mobile home became a fixture? Is the time of perfection of Bank's security interest material? See *Hartford Nat'l Bank & Trust v. Godin*, 398 A.2d 286, U.C.C. Rep. Serv. 398 (Vt. 1979).

U.C.C. § 9-313(5) provides a waiver and removal provision. Under the subsection, a fixture secured party will prevail over an encumbrancer or owner of real estate if: (1) the owner or encumbrancer consented to the security interest in writing; (2) the owner or encumbrancer disclaimed an interest in the goods as fixtures; or, (3) the debtor had a right to remove the goods as against the owner or encumbrancer. A good example of this last situation can be seen where a debtor buys a mobile home and places that home on leased property. Assume that the seller retained a security interest in the mobile home as personal property. If the mobile home were considered a fixture under state law, the seller would need to make a fixture filing within ten days of the home's attachment to the land to preserve its rights. If the seller failed to make such a filing, its rights would be subordinate to those of the owner. However, under § 9-313(5)(b), the seller would have priority over the owner because the debtor would have a right to remove the collateral from the leased property.

Section 9-313(6) provides a special rule for construction mortgages. A construction mortgage is a type of purchase money mortgage; it secures an obligation incurred for the building of an improvement on land including the acquisition cost of such land. Often, a construction mortgagee and a purchase money secured party with an interest in fixtures will compete for the same collateral. Ordinarily in such a case, section 9-313(4)(a) would give the purchase money fixture party priority. This result would unfairly prejudice the expectation of a construction mortgage lender who believed that it would receive a security interest in all usable collateral by virtue of its prior real estate filing (this would include the land, any buildings on it, and any fixtures attached to it). Subsection (6) subordinates the purchase money fixture party's priority given under section 9-313(4)(a) if the construction mortgagee recorded its interest prior to the time the goods became fixtures, and only if the goods became fixtures during the course of construction. It goes without saying that this degree of protection is limited. Furthermore, the fixture secured party can still prevail if it can successfully invoke some other provision of section 9-313(4) or (5).

If there is a default and enforcement of the security interest is necessary, the Code provides that the fixture secured party may remove the fixture provided that she reimburse the owner or mortgagee of the real property for any physical injury caused by the removal. U.C.C. § 9-313(8). Because the fixture secured party might fail to make necessary repairs, or to provide reimbursement for such repairs, the owner or encumbrancer may refuse permission for the removal unless the fixture secured party provides adequate security.

---

§ 18.09 Accessions

Read: U.C.C. § 9-314.

The fixture priority rules of section 9-313 apply when an item of personal property becomes affixed to a parcel of real property. When items of personal property are combined, a similar potential for conflict arises between parties. As between two claimants, who should prevail, the person claiming an interest in a component part, or the person claiming an interest in the larger unit? If the component part retains its own identity, it will be considered an accession and the rules found in section 9-314 will determine priority. Subsection (1) of § 9-314 gives priority to the holder of a security interest in the accession if the interest attaches before the property is installed. Consider the accession claim in the following case.

IN RE AZTEC CONCRETE, INC.

United States Bankruptcy Court, Southern District of Iowa
136 B.R. 535, 17 U.C.C. Rep. Serv. 2d 288 (1992)

RUSSELL J. HILL, BANKRUPTCY JUDGE.

ORDER ON MOTION FOR RELIEF FROM STAY
AND DETERMINATION OF LIEN STATUS

. . . .

FINDINGS OF FACT

1. On March 30, 1989, Ford Motor Company issued a certificate of origin for a new 1989 Ford model LT 8000 Truck, vehicle identification number (VIN) 1FDZU82AXKVA 38398. This vehicle was transferred to Boyer Ford Trucks, Inc. (Boyer Truck), Minneapolis, Minnesota, by use of the certificate of origin.

2. Boyer Ford transferred this truck to McNeilus Trucking & Manufacturing (McNeilus), Dodge Center, Minnesota, a dealer, which mounted an 8 yard mixer (hereinafter "the mixer") on the truck.

3. On June 20, 1989, the vehicle, with mixer, was transferred to Aztec Concrete by McNeilus. The certificate of origin was then endorsed to show Aztec Concrete as the purchaser and Concord Commercial Corporation (herein "Concord") as the lienholder. This vehicle was then ready for titling.

4. On June 21, 1989, Debtor executed a security agreement in favor of Concord wherein Debtor borrowed and agreed to pay back $ 68,650.00, plus interest, from Concord. Debtor gave Concord a security interest in the truck and mixer.

5. On June 28, 1989, a financing statement was filed with the Secretary of State. This financing statement listed Aztec Concrete as a debtor with Concord as the secured party on the truck and mixer.

6. On July 14, 1989, Debtor's president, Rosalie J. McCoy, prepared an Iowa Application for Certificate of Title for the truck. This application identified Circle Business Credit, Inc., as holding the first security interest.

7. On the basis of this application a Certificate of Title was issued on July 14, 1989, for said vehicle. The Certificate of Title identified Aztec Concrete as the owner and Circle Business Credit, Inc., as the holder of the first and second security interest in said vehicle.

8. Upon discovery of this mistake Concord protested and the Circle Business Credit security interest was released on October 24, 1990.

9. Unknown to Concord and on October 19, 1990, Debtor's attorney, Mike Christensen, placed another lien on the truck. Concord commenced legal proceedings against Mike Christensen to compel the release of this lien.

10. On January 22, 1991, an Involuntary Chapter 7 Petition was filed against Debtor.

11. On January 25, 1991, Debtor's president made application to the Iowa Department of Transportation that the security interest of Concord be noted upon the Certificate of Title. Mike Christensen released his first lien and on January 28, 1991, the Certificate of Title was noted to show Concord as holding the first security interest in the truck and Mike Christensen as holding the second security interest.

12. An Order for Relief was entered on May 1, 1991.

DISCUSSION

Concord requests the court exercise its equitable powers to grant relief from stay to allow Concord to foreclose and enforce its security interest in the truck or, in the alternative, allow Concord to foreclose and enforce its security interest in the mixer as a matter of law. The trustee objects to Concord's motion and asks the court to make a finding that the lien held by Concord is invalid and to void the lien pursuant to 11 U.S.C. § 549. At issue then is whether and to what extent Concord holds a perfected lien in the property at issue. For the reasons stated below, the court determines that Concord's lien is subject to avoidance by the Trustee under 11 U.S.C. § 549 and Concord's motion for relief shall be denied.

. . . .

THE TRUCK

Concord concedes that it failed to perfect its lien in the truck pursuant to Iowa Code § 321.50 before Aztec was forced into bankruptcy. Iowa Code § 321.50 provides for the notation of security interests in vehicles subject to the Iowa certificate of title law. The application for a lien notation pursuant to § 321.50 was not submitted to the treasurer until January 25, 1991. The lien was not noted on the title until January 28, 1991. Thus, Concord's lien in the truck was unperfected as of January 22, 1991, the date of the bankruptcy filing.

The court declines to accept Concord's invitation to find its lien perfected under its equitable powers, since Iowa law is clear on the proper method for perfection of a security interest in a vehicle. It is a creditor's responsibility to ensure that its interest is properly perfected. Section 321.50 is written in such a way as to provide notice to the lienholder that its lien is properly perfected. Section 321.50(3) expressly provides that upon the notation of the security interest upon the certificate of title, the county treasurer shall then mail the certificate of title to the first secured party as shown on the certificate of title.

THE MIXER

The court now turns its attention to whether Concord has a perfected interest, not subject to the trustee's § 549 avoidance powers, in one MTM 8-1/2 yard mixer body attached to the truck in which Concord failed to perfect its interest by notation on the vehicle's certificate of title. The following pertinent facts are reiterated. The truck with mixer was sold to Aztec as one assembled unit. The certificate of origin indicated Concord's security interest in the truck; however, when the truck was brought to Iowa and registered, Concord's lien was not noted on the Iowa certificate of title. Thus, Concord's interest in the truck was unperfected. Concord did, however, file a financing statement indicating its interest in the "Truck with One (1) MTM 8-1/2 Yard Mixer." An involuntary petition was filed against Aztec on January 22, 1991 and the court entered an order for relief on May 1, 1991. On or about January 25, 1991, an application for notation of lien was made and Concord's security interest in the truck was noted on the truck's title on January 28, 1991.

Concord argues that under Article 9 it has a perfected interest in the mixer, which is not subject to the trustee's § 549 avoidance powers. Arguing that the mixer is a "good," under I.C. § 554.9105(1)(h), and "equipment," under I.C. § 554.9109(2), Concord claims the mixer is an "accession," I.C. § 554.9314(2) & (3), to which its security interest attached after the mixer was mounted on the truck. This interest was perfected, argues Concord, under §§ 554.9314 and 554.9401(1)(c) when a financing statement covering the truck with mixer was filed June 28, 1989.

The trustee argues that the mixer is an integral part of the vehicle and, therefore, Concord cannot have a separate security interest in the mixer. The trustee has cited a number of cases from other jurisdictions to support her position that a security interest in the mixer could have attached and have been perfected only under certificate of title law.

Statutory law contemplates situations in which security interests are given in vehicles by means of the certificate of title provisions and, if property is attached to a vehicle by a supplier-installer, the supplier-installer can perfect, by means of the U.C.C., a security interest in the item it has supplied or installed. See, *e.g.*, Iowa Code § 554.9314(2) (1991) (providing for security interest in accessions); *Omaha Standard, Inc. v. Nissen*, 187 N.W.2d 721 (Iowa 1971) (doctrine of accession did not nullify supplier's reservation of title to truck body, hoist, and accessories); see generally 2 G. Gilmore, Security Interests in Personal Property, § 31.1 at 837 (Little, Brown & Co. 1965). In such cases, the supplier-installer of the property maintains its interest in the property provided it has complied with all statutory requirements.

Likewise, courts seem to have little difficulty finding that a creditor perfecting its interest in property attached to a vehicle by means of certificate of title notation does not lose its interest in the attached property when it is separated from the vehicle. See, *e.g., Mack's Used Cars & Parts v. Tennessee Truck & Equip.*, 694 S.W.2d 323 (Tenn. Ct. App. 1985) (security interest in truck by notation on certificate of title extended to wrecker assembly that was bolted to truck).

No case law, however, deals with the situation before the court now: a situation where a creditor has attempted but failed to perfect its interest in a cement truck by means of timely noting its interest on the title, but where the creditor did file a financing statement purporting to cover the truck and attachments.

This court holds that, pursuant to Iowa Code § 554.9302(3), a truck with equipment attached prior to sale, without retention of a separate interest in its parts (as in the case of a supplier/installer), is subject only to Iowa Code § 321.50 (certificate of title security interest notation provision). In arriving at this conclusion the court finds that the mixer is an integral part of the cement truck, which was registered under the Iowa certificate of title law.

Courts have used the following factors to determine whether a component has become an accession of the property to which it is attached:

1) whether the component was intended to be a permanent attachment;

2) the relative ease/difficulty in detaching the affixed property;

3) whether the act of detaching the affixed property would result in damage to the vehicle;

4) the manner and extent to which the property is affixed;

5) the relationship the affixed property bears to the property to which it is affixed; and

6) the degree to which the component is a standardized part, its interchangeability. . . . .

7) the purpose and use for which the annexation has been made and the relation and use of the party making it and whether the component and chassis are united in the prosecution of a common enterprise;

8) whether the chattel is united to the materials of another and whether the combined materials form a joint product; and

9) whether the components were annexed before delivery of the trucks to the debtor, and the debtor purchased the completed units from a single seller, granting a security interest in the assembled units.

See 694 S.W.2d at 326-27.

Applying these factors to the facts in this case indicates that the mixer body is an integral part of or an accession to the truck. It appears that the mixer body was intended to be a permanent attachment to the cement truck. See *Crown Concrete Co. v. Conkling,* 247 Iowa 609, 611, 75 N.W.2d 351, 352 (Iowa 1956) (finding mixers mounted on trucks constitute a permanent, integral part of such trucks and as such were not subject to a separate personal property tax). It would also appear that it would take a fair amount of time and effort to separate the mixer from the vehicle. *Id.* (finding it would take two men a day and a half to remove a mixer from a cement truck). No evidence exists in the record to indicate whether separation would damage the vehicle, or the manner and extent to which the property is affixed. While it would also appear that the truck will run without the mixer body attached, it would no longer be a cement truck, the truck's raison d'etre. To what degree the mixer body is a standard part is unknown and does not seem particularly probative. The "vehicle" and the mixer body are united in the prosecution of a common enterprise—mixing cement. See *Crown Concrete,* 247 Iowa at 611, 75 N.W.2d at 352; *In re Lyford,* 22 Bankr. 222, 224 (Bankr. D. Me. 1982) (log loader, jake brake, tag axle and truck were united in the prosecution of transporting logs). Finally, the intent of the parties can be gleaned from the fact that the mixer body was annexed before delivery of the truck to the debtor and the debtor purchased the cement truck as a complete unit. The "intent" here being the parties' intention to give a security interest in the cement truck as a whole, as opposed to the parties' general intention to enter into a security arrangement. Cf. *Omaha Standard,* 187 N.W.2d at 724 (the Iowa court does not explain which intent should be ascertained).

This case should be distinguished from the case of the supplier/installer. The supplier/installer of or a lender for a particular part of the whole as opposed to the whole still should resort to Iowa Code § 554.9314 (1991). The crucial factors in the case at hand are that the cement truck was sold to Aztec as a whole unit and the parties intended a security interest in the whole unit, which failed. For example, if Aztec bought a truck with Concord financing, then later bought a mixer with Concord financing and attached it to the truck, then a U.C.C. filing could perfect Concord's interest in the mixer.

The risk in holding that Concord's interest in the truck or the mixer is perfected might be to encourage "secret liens," a modern day equivalent to *Twyne's Case,* 3 Co. Rep. 806, 76 Eng. Rep. 809 (Star Chamber, 1601) (holding that retention of possession by seller of goods was a badge of fraud). The basic idea of perfection is that a secured creditor must do something to give effective public notice of its interest; otherwise the debtor may be given false credit and will be able to sell property to innocent purchasers or to induce other innocent persons to lend money on the strength of apparently unencumbered assets. See 1 G. Gilmore, Security Interests in Personal Property, § 14.1 at 438 (Little, Brown & Co. 1965). A creditor, albeit not the most diligent creditor, might have lent Aztec money relying on the fact that no security interest was indicated on the truck's certificate of title. In measuring the value of the cement truck as security, it is likely such a creditor would have included the mixer body in its calculations as to the value of the whole cement truck. The fundamental question then in this case is whether credit risk would be easier or harder to calculate by virtue of this court's holding. This court believes its holding will make the calculation of credit risk more certain in this type of circumstance.

ORDER

IT IS ACCORDINGLY ORDERED that Concord's motion for relief is denied.

IT IS FURTHER ORDERED that Concord's lien in the cement truck including the attached mixer is avoidable under the trustee's 11 U.S.C. § 549 powers in accordance with the opinion above.

NOTES

(1) Are accessions synonymous with accessories? Could tires on a car be classified as an accession? What about propeller blades for an airplane? See *In Re Fields*, 56 B.R. 149, 42 U.C.C. Rep. Serv. 1476 (Bankr. S.D. Ohio 1985) and *In Re Tacoma Aviation Center, Inc.*, 35 U.C.C. Rep. Serv. 298 (W.D. Wash. 1982). How much weight should party intention carry in making the determination? Is intention even relevant? Why or why not?

(2) X took a purchase money security interest in refrigerator units to be installed in truck trailers. A year later, X took a security interest in the trailers together with all accessions thereto. Y knew of X's prior interest. What result? See *IDS Leasing Corp v. Leasing Associates, Inc.*, 590 S.W.2d 607, 27 U.C.C. Rep. Serv.. 1441 (1979).

(3) Section 9-314(3) subordinates any unperfected, pre-installation security interest in an accession to three types of claimants: (1) a subsequent purchaser for value; (2) a subsequent judgment lien creditor; and (3) a prior, perfected secured party who makes subsequent advances. These parties receive priority only if the purchase took place, the lien was obtained, or the subsequent advance was made without knowledge of the secured party's security interest in the accession, and before the secured party perfected that interest. To illustrate, consider the case of Lauren who buys a computer under a retail installment contract from a dealer who retains a perfected Article 9 security interest. After the warranty expires, the hard drive on the machine needs to be replaced. Lauren buys a new hard drive from a second dealer who perfects its security interest securing the purchase price before installing the hard drive. If Lauren then sells the computer to Michael a few months later, the second dealer would prevail over Michael. What result if the second dealer never perfected? Would the second dealer prevail over Michael? What if the original seller still claimed an interest in the computer—would the second dealer prevail over the original seller?

§ 18.10 Commingled Goods

Read: U.C.C. § 9-315.

Recall that with accessions, the item should be capable of removal to fit within section 9-314. It is quite possible for an item of personal property to be processed in such a manner as to cause that item to lose its original identity. The item cannot be removed or identified separately—sheet metal used in the manufacture of a robot, for example. U.C.C. section 9-315(1) provides that a perfected security interest in goods continues in the commingled mass. Under section 9-315(2) all recognized security interests rank equally. It is unimportant that the various components were added to the whole at various stages in the manufacturing process. Priority is determined by the ratio of the cost of the components in which each secured party has a security interest to the total cost of the commingled mass. Calculating such a ratio may be close to impossible. Both fortunately, and inexplicably, there are no cases which shed light on that portion of the statute. The following case demonstrates the limits of the commingling concept.

IN RE McDOUGALL

United States Bankruptcy Court, Western District of Pennsylvania
60 B.R. 635,1 U.C.C.R. Serv. 2d 563 (1986)

BENTZ, WARREN W., BANKRUPTCY JUDGE.

The dispute arose out of an adversary proceeding filed by Meadville Production Credit Association ("Meadville") to determine the validity of its security interest in certain proceeds.

A hearing was held on April 4, 1986 on the Trustee's Motion for authorization to settle the claim of Meadville and objections filed thereto by a general creditor, Agway Petroleum Credit ("Agway").

The facts are not in dispute. The debtors borrowed money from Meadville on May 21, 1984. Meadville had a duly perfected security interest in growing crops, including certain grain, as a result of a financing statement filed with the Prothonotary of Mercer County on May 21, 1984, and a security agreement dated May 21, 1984.

The debtors subsequently purchased cattle and fed the cattle with grain which was the subject matter of the aforesaid security interest.

Prior to the filing of the within bankruptcy petition, the Debtor sold certain of the cattle; that sale is not here in issue. After the filing of the within bankruptcy petition, the remaining cattle were sold and the Trustee holds the proceeds.

The question for this court is whether the duly perfected security interest of Meadville in the grain/crops continued into the cattle and ultimately the proceeds of the sale of the cattle. We hold it did not.

Meadville's position is that it is protected by the Uniform Commercial Code as adopted in Pennsylvania at 13 Pa. C.S.A. § 9315 et seq. Section 9-315 provides:

> (a) General rule. If a security interest in goods was perfected and subsequently the goods or a part thereof have become part of a product or mass, the security interest continues in the product or mass if:
>
> > (1) the goods are so manufactured, processed, assembled or commingled that their identity is lost in the product or mass; or
> >
> > (2) a financing statement covering the original goods also covers the product into which the goods have been manufactured, processed or assembled.

The issue, with virtually identical facts, has been previously addressed by the Colorado Court of Appeals. In *First National Bank of Brush v. Bostron*, 39 Colo. App. 107, 21 U.C.C. Rep. 1475, 564 P2d 964 (1977), an agricultural credit association held a valid perfected security interest in "all feed now owned or hereafter acquired, all crops now growing or to be grown, proceeds and products of collateral."

The Court focused its attention on the meaning of the words "product" and "mass" as those terms are used in the Colorado's identical counterpart to § 9-315 of the Pennsylvania Code. The court concluded that cattle are neither a product nor mass as those terms were contemplated by the drafters of the Uniform Commercial Code, that once consumed by the cattle, the feed lost its identity and ceased to exist, and that the feed is not manufactured, processed, assembled, or commingled as provided in the Code, when it is eaten by cattle. We have not been directed to any persuasive interpretation of that section which would support Meadville's position.

We concur with the Colorado Court and hold that a security interest in feed or grain does not continue into cattle which consume the feed or the proceeds of such cattle upon their sale. Accordingly, Meadville must be treated as a general unsecured creditor. Meadville's requested relief is denied; the objection of Agway Petroleum Credit to the Trustee's motion to settle and compromise is sustained; and the within Adversary Proceeding is dismissed.

It is so ORDERED.

NOTES

(1) Though the security interest continues, under U.C.C. § 9-315, in the "mass or entity" with which the goods are commingled, the goods must still exist in some sense. In accord, *Farmers Cooperative Elevator Co. v. Union State Bank*, 409 N.W.2d 178, 180 (Iowa 1987) (hogs were not proceeds of their feed). Should the concept of commingled goods ever apply to feed or other agricultural products? For example, what result if the creditor had a security interest in cattle that became leather handbags?

(2) P held a security interest in debtor's "inventory, work in process, raw materials, stock in trade, and all after-acquired inventory and proceeds therefrom." After an intercompany transfer of the debtor company's assets, P took a new promissory note from the acquiring company, including an agreement subordinating it to the prior security interest. The acquiring company's assets were subject to D's Security interest. What result? See *First Security Bank of Utah v. Zions First Nat'l Bank*, 537 P.2d 1024, 17 U.C.C. Rep. Serv. 858 (Utah 1975).

(3) Sections 9-314 and 9-315 overlap in their coverage. Comment 3 to section 9-315(1)(b) provides a good example of the overlap. The comment states that the section not only applies to readily identifiable and removable goods like flour, sugar and eggs, but also to cases where such items are assembled into cake mix as a commingled product. According to the comment, a secured party can elect to come under section 9-314 and take a security interest in the item of property as an accession by filing a financing statement covering the collateral. But, the secured party may also file a financing statement covering the product into which the goods were manufactured. In the case where the secured party filed noting an interest in the final product, the creditor loses its priority in the added item of collateral but takes a security interest in the completed mass. Perhaps it would have been more sensible to have § 9-314 cover the case in which property added was identifiable and removable and section 9-315 to cover only cases where the added product lost its identity. What do you think?

§ 18.11 Liens

[A] Statutory: Liens by Operation of Law

Read: U.C.C. § 9-310.

Many people provide services that add value to or help preserve goods. Mechanics repair automobiles; jewelers repair necklaces. Often, laws outside the U.C.C. give such persons a lien interest in the items repaired or serviced. Such liens are created by statute or by case law, and continue only as long as the person performing the services retains possession of the item. Liens "by operation of law" sometimes conflict with secured interests. For example, does the bank which has loaned money for the purchase of a truck and has taken a security interest in the truck have priority over a repair shop that fixes the truck and asserts a mechanic's lien unless paid?

Section 9-310 gives a service lienholder priority over a prior and perfected security interest if: (1) the service occurs in the ordinary course of the servicer's business; (2) the servicer retains possession of the goods; and (3) the applicable state statutes do not expressly subordinate the servicer's claim to that of an Article 9 security interest.

ITT COMMERCIAL FINANCE CORP. v. MADISONVILLE RECAPPING CO., INC.

Kentucky Court of Appeals
793 S.W.2d 849, 14 U.C.C. Rep. Serv. 2d 268 (1990)

HOWARD, JUDGE.

In this case, the appellant appeals from a judgment of the Webster Circuit Court upholding the findings of fact and conclusions of a special commissioner in which mechanic's liens were determined to have priority over a purchase money security interest. The facts in this case are largely undisputed.

Coal Exchange of Kentucky, Inc. operated a strip mine in Webster County, Kentucky, and all of its equipment was in that county. Coal Exchange, however, has a registered office in Jefferson County, Kentucky.

In September of 1985, the appellee, Madisonville Recapping Company, Inc., performed repairs on and supplied tires for a Michigan loader owned by Coal Exchange. The bill for the repairs and tires was $10,260.62. At about that same time, the appellee, Watson Brothers Industries, Inc., provided services and parts totaling $5,616.00 for repair of the Coal Exchange's loader. Partly because the loader was so large, these repairs were performed at the mining site in Webster County.

Because no payment was made, Madisonville Recapping filed a mechanic's lien against Coal Exchange on December 4, 1995. On December 20, 1985, Watson Brothers asserted its mechanic's lien against Cola Exchange. On December 30, 1985, Cola Exchange filed for bankruptcy in the United States Bankruptcy Court, Western District of Kentucky, and an automatic stay was issued.

The appellant, ITT Commercial Finance Corporation, claimed a purchase money security interest in the loader. On the appellant's motion, the bankruptcy court lifted the stay in order that the appellant could pursue its state court remedies.

Madisonville Recapping filed a complaint on November 5, 1986, against Coal Exchange, Watson Brothers and the appellant. Coal Exchange was subsequently dropped as a party and the only question was the interests of the parties in the loader. The record does not contain any details on this point, but the appellant evidently repossessed and sold the loader.

On April 20, 1988, the special commissioner issued his findings of fact and conclusions of law. The special commissioner concluded that Madisonville Recapping and Watson Brothers had properly perfected their liens and these liens took priority over the appellant's alleged security interest. The special commissioner's findings and conclusions were sustained by the trial court on August 24, 1988.

The appellant first argues that Madisonville Recapping did not have a valid lien.

The lien statement relied upon by the special commissioner was filed by Madisonville Recapping in Webster County. KRS 376.440 requires the lien statement to be filed in the county "in which the owner of the equipment, machine, machinery or motor resides," unless the owner is a non-resident, then the lien statement must be filed in the county where the equipment or machinery is being kept or used.

The appellant argues the question of where a corporation "resides" is answered by KRS 355.9-401(e) which provides as follows: "A corporation organized under KRS Ch.'s 271A, 273 or 274 shall be deemed a resident of the county in which its registered office is located, as set forth in its most recent corporate filing with the Secretary of State which officially designates its current registered office." The difficulty with applying KRS 355.9-401(e) to the instant case is that it was not in effect in December of 1985. The statute gives no indication that it is to be applied retroactively. A statute will not have retroactive effect unless such intent is clearly expressed in the statute. *Roberts v. Hickman County Fiscal Court,* Ky., 481 S.W.2d 279 (1972).

The special commissioner, in finding the filing of the liens in Webster County was proper, relied on *Wheeler v. Burgess*, 263 Ky. 693, 93 S.W.2d at 353, the Court stated that "[a] person may have many residences but can have but one domicile." The Court in *Wheeler, supra,* however did not address the specific issue of where a corporation resides.

National Cash Register Co. v. K.W.C. Inc., 432 F.Supp. 82 (E.D. Ky. 1977), involved an appeal from the bankruptcy court and the sole question was whether a corporation's residence under the Uniform Commercial Code was the location of its registered office or the location of its principal place of business. In *National Cash Register, supra*, a corporation was doing business only in Kenton County, Kentucky, and its articles of incorporation listed its address as Campbell County. National Cash Register filed a financing statement in Kenton County on some equipment purchased by the corporation. The corporation subsequently filed bankruptcy.

The Court in *National Cash Register, supra*, pointed out that Kentucky had not yet adopted a provision like what is now KRS 355.9-401(e), although the drafters of the uniform act had proposed such an amendment. The Court then reviewed Kentucky tax and venue cases, the policies underlying the U.C.C. and the wording of the then-existing statute. The Court then concluded that the residence of a corporation under the U.C.C. was the place set by the articles of incorporation, not its principal place of business. We believe this result is well reasoned.

KRS 376.440, however, is not part of the U.C.C. But many of the factors discussed in *National Cash Register, supra*, apply to this case. The transactions involved were commercial in nature and the policies concerning the need for certainty and clarity are the same in both. The Court in *National Cash Register, supra*, pointed out that if the residence was the principal place of business and the corporation had a number of places of business located in different counties, creditors would have difficulty determining which was the "principal" place of business. This reasoning would certainly apply to liens. Therefore, we believe a corporate owner resides for purposes of KRS 376.440 in the county where his registered office is located.

As a result of our holding on this issue, Jefferson County, not Webster County, was the corporate residence of Coal Exchange. Madisonville Recapping did not properly perfect its lien.

The appellant next contends that a purchase money security interest takes priority over a non-possessory statutory lien.

KRS 355.9-310 provides as follows:

When a person in the ordinary course of his business furnishes services or materials with respect to good subject to a security interest, a lien upon goods in the possession of such person given by statute or rule of law for such materials or services takes priority over a perfected security interest unless the lien is statutory and the statute expressly provides otherwise.

The trial court relied on *Corbin Deposit Bank v. King,* Ky., 384 S.W.2d 302 (1964), in concluding that the liens prevailed over the purchase money security interest. The Court in *King, supra*, based its decision on KRS 355.9-310. However, the lienholder had possession of the motor vehicle at issue in *King, supra,* until the holder of the security interest removed it pursuant to a court order. Possession was not an issue in *King, supra*, and it is not dispositive of the case at bar.

The interpretation of KRS 355.9-310 urged by the appellant is certainly justified by its language. The statute uses the language "goods in possession" of a lienholder. The courts have a duty to construe a statute literally unless to do so would lead to an absurd or wholly unreasonable conclusion. *Bailey v. Reeves, Ky.*, 662 S.W.2d 832 (1984). Requiring possession for KRS 355.9-310 to be effective would not lead to an absurd or wholly unreasonable result.

When the words of a statute are clear and unambiguous and express the legislative intent, there is no need for construction and the statute must be accepted as written. *Griffin v. City of Bowling Green,* Ky., 458 S.W.2d 456 (1970). KRS 355.9-310 is clear and unambiguous in its requirement of possession by the lienholder.

In addition, it is stated in Leibson and Nowka, The Uniform Commercial Code of Kentucky § 8.4(D)(7) as follows:

> If the statute creating the lien does not defer to a security interest, section 9-310 gives the lien priority over a security interest so long as the repairman maintains possession of the goods. If the repairman voluntarily relinquishes the goods without taking payment, the lien is subordinate to the security interest.

A similar view is expressed in 69 Am.Jur.2d, Secured Transactions § 509.

Watson Brothers argues that possession should not be required in cases such as this one where the machinery was so large that repair on the owner's premises was necessary. Watson Brothers maintain that if possession is required, under KRS 355.9-301, then repairmen of large mining or construction equipment would not have the same protection as others.

Without discussing any possible merit to the Watson Brother's argument, we note that the plain meaning of a statute cannot be ignored by the courts simply because another interpretation might be considered to state a better policy. *Board of Education of Nelson County v. Lawrence,* Ky., 375 S.W.2d 830 (1963).

In his findings of fact and conclusions of law, the special commissioner referred to the appellant's "alleged" security interest. Thus, the special commissioner never found that the appellant had a perfected security interest and nothing in the record shows that. Essentially, what the special commissioner did was conclude that even if the appellant had a security interest, the lien had priority and it could not prevail at trial. Thus, the appellees were given a summary judgment. Consequently, on remand, the appellant would need to produce sufficient evidence of its claimed security interest or again lose on summary judgment or perhaps a directed verdict.

The judgment is reversed and remanded for further proceedings consistent with this opinion.

All concur.

PROBLEM 18.6

Dominion Bank provided Leah with the purchase money to buy an automobile. Bank filed a financing statement covering the car. Leah drove the car without engine oil and blew the engine. She took the car to Auto House to have a new engine installed. A week later, she took delivery of the repaired car after promising Auto House that she would pay them at the end of the following week when she was paid. Leah failed to make the promised payment. Under state statutory law, Auto House had a lien interest in the automobile to secure the value of any services rendered. In a priority contest, Auto House claims that its interest is superior to Dominion under section 9-310. Who prevails? Would your answer differ if Auto House still retained possession of the car? Are there other provisions of Article 9 that could apply? For instance, could the new engine be considered and accession under § 9-314? Could it be considered a commingled good under section 9-315? Which statutory section provides the greatest protection?

[B] Federal Tax Liens

The tax lien performs the same general function for the federal government that consensual and statutory liens provide for other creditors. The tax lien enables the government to liquidate a taxpayer's property efficiently and thus satisfy that party's tax obligation. Failure to pay taxes due lead to a delinquency assessment which section 6321 of the Internal Revenue Coderecognizes as a lien in favor of the United States. See generally, 26 U.S.C. § 6321 et. seq. The lien applies to all property belonging to the taxpayer and it continues until the tax liability is satisfied. If a taxpayer has failed to pay taxes, it is also quite likely that that person has also failed to pay other creditors who might assert interests in the taxpayer's property. In general, the tax lien has priority over all third-party claimants, except persons who have choate liens before the federal tax lien arises or, those who are protected by the Federal Tax Lien Act of 1966.

Tax liens arise without public notice after the government makes a tax assessment and a demand for payment, and the taxpayer fails to pay that obligation. The creation of a tax lien does not require public notice filing. However, section 6323(a) of the Internal Revenue Code provides that a tax lien "shall not be valid as against any purchaser, holder of a security interest, mechanic's lienor, or judgment lien creditor until notice thereof which meets the requirements of subsection (f) has been filed by the Secretary or his delegate." Thus, even though the tax lien arises after assessment and nonpayment, it does not become valid against third parties until a notice of tax lien has been filed. Section 6323(f). Notice of the tax lien must be filed in the office designated by state law. If state law does not designate a place for filing, the government must file its notice in the office of the clerk for the federal district court in the district where the property is located. The location for real property is the physical location of the property. The location of personal property is deemed to be the residence of the taxpayer at the time the notice is filed. The tax lien notice filing is effective for a period of six years and can be extended by refiling within a one year period thirty days after the expiration of the original six year period.

Historically, all interests in a taxpayer's property acquired after the assessment date will be subordinate to the tax lien. The Federal Tax Lien Act of 1966 changed prior law by subordinating the govenment's tax lien with respect to certain prior Article 9 secured claimants. The Act sets forth a set of basic priority rules based upon a first-in-time-first-in-right principle. Thus, a prior choate lien will have priority if the lien is perfected, the identity of both the lienor and the property is established. If the lien is inchoate, it will be subordinate to the tax lien even if it were acquired *before* the tax assessment date. See section 6323(a).

Sections 6323(c) and 6323(d) specifically address Article 9 security interests in after-acquired property and future advances. Under section 6323(c), the secured party attains priority in property acquired by the taxpayer after the notice of tax lien is filed if: 1) the secured party obtained the security interest and perfected it before the federal tax lien was filed; 2) the collaeral was commercial financing security (accounts, chattel paper, or inventory, but not equipment); and 3) the property was acquired within forty-five days of the federal tax lien filing. Both sections 6323(c) and 6323(d) apply to future advances made after a notice of tax lien is filed. Under these sections, the future advance receives priority over the federal tax lien if the secured party had obtained and perfected its security interest before the federal tax lien was filed and if the extension of credit occurred witin forty-five days of the federal tax lien's filing, or before the creditor obtained knowledge of the filing, whichever occurred first. The future advance priority is not limited to "commercial financing security."

Some authorities question whether the choate lien doctrine has any effect given the broad scope of section 6323. Arguably, to the extent that the section does not apply, the choate lien doctrine might still have some application. The basic point under both the statute and the common law doctrine is that there are some limits to the ability of the federal government to assert priority over all property of a taxpayer/debtor. Though unusually long, the following case provides a good example of the interplay between the federal tax lien statute and Article 9.

METROPOLITAN NATL. BANK v. UNITED STATES

United States Court of Appeals
901 F.2d 1297 (5th Cir. 1990)

JOLLY, CIRCUIT JUDGE.

The United States appeals from the district court's judgment holding that the United States' perfected tax lien, filed against three parcels of real property owned by the taxpayer, Weaver & Sons, Inc., was not entitled to priority over the interests claimed in the property by the appellees, Metropolitan National Bank (the "Bank"), James M. Oberlies, and Robert E. Ryan. 716 F. Supp. 946. We hold that the appellees were not entitled to priority under section 6323(a) of the Internal Revenue Code, and we therefore reverse the judgment of the district court and remand the case for further proceedings.

I

The facts were stipulated by the parties. On February 23, 1978, Weaver & Sons, Inc. (the "taxpayer"), by its president, S. Albert Weaver, executed a deed of trust in favor of First State Bank and Trust, the predecessor of appellee Metropolitan National Bank. The deed of trust recited that the taxpayer was indebted to the Bank in the amount of $400,000, and listed certain real property owned by the taxpayer located in Gulfport, Mississippi, as security for the indebtedness. The deed of trust designated Robert L. Taylor as trustee for the lender, and Robert L. Taylor, in his capacity as a notary public, acknowledged the signature of the grantor's president. The deed of trust was filed and recorded by the Chancery Clerk's office in Harrison County, Mississippi on February 24, 1978.

On February 23, March 2, March 9, March 16, and June 2, 1987, assessments were made against the taxpayer for unpaid federal withholding, Federal Insurance Contributions Act (FICA), and Federal Unemployment Tax Act (FUTA) taxes. Notices of the federal tax liens resulting from these assessments were enrolled with the Harrison County Chancery Clerk's office on May 7 and August 27, 1987. The unpaid balance of these assessments totaled $195,621.61, plus interest and statutory additions to tax.

The taxpayer defaulted in payment of its obligation to the Bank, and subsequently filed a Chapter 7 bankruptcy petition. Although none of the papers relating to the taxpayer's bankruptcy are contained in the record before us, the appellees' brief states that the taxpayer's bankruptcy petition was filed on August 19, 1987 and that the Internal Revenue Service ("IRS") filed a proof of claim dated November 24, 1987. At the time the taxpayer defaulted, it owed $268,833.55 on the loan secured by the deed of trust.

On March 8, 1988, the taxpayer executed a corrected deed of trust in favor of the Bank's predecessor institution in the amount of $400,000, secured by the subject property. The corrected deed of trust was properly acknowledged and recorded in the Harrison County Chancery Clerk's office on March 9, 1988.

The bankruptcy court lifted the automatic stay, authorizing the Bank to repossess and foreclose upon the subject property. Notices of foreclosure were posted in the county courthouse, published in the local newspaper, and sent to the IRS by certified mail. A nonjudicial foreclosure sale was held on April 19, 1988, at which the Bank, for $103,600, and appellee Robert E. Ryan, for $31,000, each purchased a portion of the subject property. Thereafter, the Bank conveyed a portion of the property it had purchased in the foreclosure sale to appellee James M. Oberlies. The IRS took no action to stop the foreclosure, or to prevent the sale of the property to the Bank or to Ryan and Oberlies.

II

The appellees brought this action against the United States under 28 U.S.C. § 2410, seeking to quiet title to the property. The United States counterclaimed, joining the taxpayer as an additional defendant, seeking to foreclose its federal tax liens against the subject property and to collect $195,621.65, the outstanding tax liability of the taxpayer. On cross motions for summary judgment, the district court granted summary judgment in favor of the appellees. The district court held that the original deed of trust was improperly acknowledged and that, even though the deed of trust was recorded, because the defect in the acknowledgment was apparent on the face of the deed, the recordation of the deed did not provide constructive notice to subsequent creditors that the property was encumbered. Nevertheless, the court held that, even though the deed was improperly acknowledged and should not have been recorded, the deed "provided actual notice to anyone who cared to review the records of the Chancery Clerk." The district court did not hold, however, that agents of the United States had in fact reviewed the county records prior to filing the notices of federal tax liens against the taxpayer, or that the United States possessed any information sufficient to place it on "inquiry notice" of the deed. Finally, the district court concluded that the United States' tax lien was not entitled to priority over the Bank's interest because, under state law, the Bank held equitable title to the property by virtue of the original defective deed of trust, and the United States had actual notice of such equitable title. Thus, when the Bank foreclosed upon the property in the non-judicial sale, the district court held that the United States' junior tax lien was extinguished under the provisions of Internal Revenue Code section 7425(b). The United States appeals.

III

A

Under 26 U.S.C. § 6321, the amount of a delinquent taxpayer's liability constitutes a lien in favor of the United States upon all of the taxpayer's property and rights to property, whether real or personal. The lien imposed by § 6321 is effective from the date of assessment of the tax, and continues until the liability is satisfied or becomes unenforceable by reason of lapse of time. 26 U.S.C. § 6322. The question whether and to what extent a taxpayer has "property" or "rights to property" to which the tax lien attaches is determined under the applicable state law. *United States v. Rodgers*, 461 U.S. 677, 683, 103 S. Ct. 2132, 2137, 76 L. Ed. 2d 236 (1983). It is undisputed in this case that the taxpayer owned, or had rights to, the subject property to which the federal tax liens attached.

Once it has been determined under state law that the taxpayer owns property or rights to property, federal law controls for the purpose of determining whether an attached tax lien has priority over competing liens asserted against the taxpayer's property. *Rodgers,* 461 U.S. at 683, 103 S. Ct. at 2137. "When a third party also claims a lien interest in the taxpayer's property, the basic priority rule of 'first in time, first in right' controls, unless Congress has created a different priority rule to govern the particular situation." *Texas Commerce Bank-Fort Worth, N.A. v. United States,* 896 F.2d 152 (5th Cir. 1990). Section 6323 of the Internal Revenue Code, as amended by the Federal Tax Lien Act of 1966, governs the validity and priority of federal tax liens imposed by § 6321 against "certain persons." The appellees rely on the special priority rules of subsection (a) of § 6323, which provides, in pertinent part, that a federal tax lien shall not be valid against any "holder of a security interest" until notice of the tax lien has been filed. Thus, the respective priorities with respect to federal tax liens and competing claims that are protected under § 6323(a) are dependent upon which claim is perfected "first in time." Both parties agree that, if the Bank was a "holder of a security interest" at the time the United States filed its federal tax liens, the appellees' interests are entitled to priority over the federal tax liens and that the tax liens were thus extinguished in the foreclosure sale.

The definition of "security interest" is found in 26 U.S.C. § 6323(h)(1):

> The term "security interest" means any interest in property acquired by contract for the purpose of securing payment or performance of an obligation or indemnifying against loss or liability.

A security interest exists only when the lienholder satisfies two requirements:

> (A) if, at such time the property is in existence and the interest has become protected under local law against a subsequent judgment lien arising out of an unsecured obligation, and (B) to the extent that, at such time, the holder has parted with money or money's worth.

Because the subject property is in existence and the Bank parted with money in return for the deed of trust, the Bank's interest in the subject property by virtue of the original deed of trust is entitled to priority over the subsequently filed federal tax lien under § 6323(a) if, as a result of filing the original deed of trust, the Bank is "protected under local law against a subsequent judgment lien arising out of an unsecured obligation." 26 U.S.C. § 6323(h)(1). The United States argues that the district court erred in holding that the Bank is a "holder of a security interest" within the meaning of § 6323(a) because the Bank's interest was not protected under Mississippi law against a subsequent judgment lien arising out of an unsecured obligation, and thus, there was no security interest in existence, within the meaning of § 6323(h)(1), at the time of the filing of the federal tax liens.

B

Because the corrected deed of trust was not filed until after the federal tax liens were filed, the issue before us is whether the Bank held an interest under the original deed of trust that was protected under Mississippi law against a subsequent judgment lien arising out of an unsecured obligation.

Under § 6323(h)(1), a security interest exists only if "the interest is protected under local law against a subsequent judgment lien arising out of an unsecured obligation." The House Committee Report states with reference to § 6323(h)(1) that:

> [A] security interest becomes protected against a subsequent judgment lien on the date on which all actions required under local law to establish the priority of the security interest against such a judgment lien have been taken, or, if later, the date on which all such actions are deemed effective, under local law, to establish such priority.

H.R. Rep. No. 1884, 89th Cong., 2d Sess. 49 (1966).

As we explain below, our examination of the relevant Mississippi cases and statutes convinces us that the Bank's interest under the original deed of trust would not have been entitled to protection against a subsequent judgment lien arising out of an unsecured obligation unless such a judgment lien creditor had actual notice or knowledge of the defectively acknowledged deed of trust.[21]

(1)

Under Mississippi law, all deeds of trust are "void as to all creditors and subsequent purchasers for a valuable consideration without notice, unless they be acknowledged or proved and lodged with the clerk of the chancery court of the proper county, to be recorded. . . ." Miss.Code Ann. § 89-5-3 (1972). "But as between the parties and their heirs, and as to all subsequent purchasers with notice or without valuable consideration, said instruments shall nevertheless be valid and binding." *Id.* In *Burkett v. Peoples Bank of Biloxi*, 225 Miss. 291, 294, 83 So.2d 185, 187 (1955), the Mississippi Supreme Court held that this statute "applies with as much force to a creditor obtaining a lien by judgment as it does to a subsequent purchaser or encumbrancer; and creditors without notice and subsequent purchasers for value without notice are on the same footing and are protected to the same extent."

---

[21] Other courts have taken two different approaches in determining the kind of protection Congress contemplated that a security interest must have in order to be "protected under local law against a subsequent judgment lien." One line of cases applies the "subjective knowledge lien creditor test," and places the United States in the shoes of a subsequent judgment lien creditor. Under those cases, if the United States obtains actual or constructive knowledge of the competing nonfederal interest prior to filing its federal tax liens, and if, under local law a judgment lien creditor is protected only if he is without actual or constructive knowledge of a prior interest, the tax lien is not entitled to priority over the nonfederal interest. See, *e.g., United States v. Ed Lusk Constr. Co.*, 504 F.2d 328, 331 (10th Cir. 1974); *United States v. Trigg*, 465 F.2d 1264, 1268-69 (8th Cir. 1972), cert. denied, 410 U.S. 909, 93 S. Ct. 963, 35 L. Ed. 2d 270 (1973). The other line of cases applies a "hypothetical judgment lien creditor test" that focuses on the protection state law gives to the security interest against other hypothetical lien creditors. Under that test, the question is whether the security interest is protected under local law against any hypothetical judgment lien creditor that might arise, whether or not the government has knowledge of the competing nonfederal interest. See, *e.g., Dragstrem v. Obermeyer*, 549 F.2d 20, 25-27 (7th Cir. 1977). We do not need to decide which test should apply in this case. The district court applied the "subjective knowledge" test, and both parties have assumed the applicability of that test in their presentation of the case to this court.

A deed of trust is not eligible for recordation unless it is properly acknowledged, and an instrument that does not contain a proper acknowledgment does not impart constructive notice to creditors or bona fide purchasers, pursuant to Miss. Code Ann. § 89-3-1(1972):

> [A] written instrument of or concerning the sale of lands . . .shall not be admitted to record in the clerk's office unless the execution thereof be first acknowledged or proved, and the acknowledgment or proof duly certified by an officer competent to take the same in the manner directed by this chapter; and any such instrument which is admitted to record without such acknowledgment or proof shall not be notice to creditors or subsequent purchasers for valuable consideration.

It is undisputed, and the district court correctly held, that the original deed of trust dated February 23, 1978 was improperly acknowledged by the trustee named in the deed. See *Holden v. Brimage,* 72 Miss. 228, 229-30, 18 So. 383, 383 (1894) (an acknowledgment to a trust deed taken before an officer who is himself trustee therein, with power to sell to pay debts, is void and does not entitle the deed to be recorded). Under Mississippi law neither a grantee designated by a deed of trust, nor the trustee designated to act for the grantee, can properly acknowledge a deed of trust.

Under Mississippi law, the taking of an acknowledgment is a judicial or quasi-judicial rather than a ministerial act, and . . . this act cannot be performed by a grantee in the deed, or by one who, though not a grantee, is the procuring cause of the conveyance or has a financial or beneficial interest in the transaction. . . .

It would be against public policy to permit a grantee, mortgagee, or trustee, or other person beneficially interested in the transaction to take an acknowledgment to an instrument in which he is named as a party or has a beneficial interest. The object of the law is to prevent the perpetration of fraud, and the policy of the law seems to be that the officer taking the acknowledgment must not be in such relationship to the grantee that there shall exist any temptation for the officer to do aught but his duty impartially. *Mills v. Damson Oil Corp.,* 686 F.2d 1096, 1102-03 (5th Cir. 1982) (quoting 1 Delvin on Real Estate and Deeds, § 477d (3d Ed. 1911)). The acknowledgment taken by the trustee in this case was thus void.[22] *Jones v. Porter,* 59 Miss. 628 (1882) (where the acknowledgment of a grantor was taken by the husband of the grantee, who was the procuring cause of the conveyance, the acknowledgment was void). Because the acknowledgment was void, the deed of trust was not eligible for recordation and, even though the deed was recorded, it nevertheless did not impart constructive notice to creditors under Miss.Code Ann. § 89-3-1. See also *Holden v. Brimage,* 72 Miss. at 229-30, 18 So. at 383; *Wasson v. Connor,* 54 Miss. 351, 352-53 (1877) (where grantee acknowledged grantor's signature, "the deed never having been legally acknowledged, [it] was, of course, improperly recorded, and it afforded notice to nobody").

In *Mills v. Damson Oil Corp.*, this court stated that "it is well settled in Mississippi that constructive notice is not imparted to bona fide purchasers by recording a defectively acknowledged deed." 686 F.2d at 1103-04 (citing *Ligon v. Barton,* 88 Miss. 135, 40 So. 555 (1906); *Elmslie v. Thurman,* 87 Miss. 537, 40 So. 67 (1905); *Smith v. McIntosh,* 176 Miss. 725, 170 So. 303 (1936)). The court noted, however, that the cited cases, as well as most of the other cases that describe the nature of the defect involved, concern patent defects, *i.e.,* "defects which

[22] Although the acknowledgment was void, it does not follow that the deed itself was void. Pursuant to Miss.Code Ann. § 89-5-3, a deed that is neither acknowledged nor recorded is "nevertheless valid and binding" as between the parties and their heirs, and as to all subsequent purchasers (and creditors) with notice or without valuable consideration.

are apparent on the face of the acknowledgment." *Mills,* 686 F.2d at 1104. The defect in *Mills* was "entirely latent" because there was "nothing in the deed or its acknowledgment to indicate that the named grantee, Lurline Daws, and S.B. Daws, who took the acknowledgment, were related to each other, or, indeed, that either was married." *Id.* Because only one Mississippi case, *Roebuck v. Bailey,* 176 Miss. 234, 166 So. 358 (1936), discussed the effect of a latent defect in an acknowledgment on bona fide purchasers, and because in that case the Mississippi court recognized a potential distinction between latently and patently defective acknowledgments, this court certified the following question to the Mississippi Supreme Court:

> Whether a defectively acknowledged and recorded deed imparts constructive notice if the defect in the acknowledgment is entirely latent?

Mills, 686 F.2d at 1114. The Mississippi Supreme Court answered "yes." *Mills v. Damson Oil Corp.,* 437 So.2d 1005, 1006 (Miss. 1983).

Nothing in the Mississippi Supreme Court's answer to the certified question in *Mills* casts any doubt on the cases involving defectively acknowledged deeds in which the defects are patent. Those cases hold that the recording of such defectively acknowledged deeds does not impart constructive notice to bona fide purchasers. See *Mills,* 686 F.2d at 1103-04 and cases cited therein; see also *Cotton v. McConnell,* 435 So.2d 683 (Miss. 1983) (a deed with a defective acknowledgment is not eligible for recordation, and is not effective as to third parties, under § 89-3-1, but it is wholly effective between the parties to it). The original deed of trust in this case names Robert L. Taylor as trustee, and Robert L. Taylor acknowledged the signature of the grantor. Thus, it is clear that the defect in the acknowledgment is patent, and the district court correctly held that the deed did not give constructive notice to subsequent bona fide purchasers and creditors. We therefore conclude that, under Mississippi law, the recordation of the defectively acknowledged deed of trust did not impart constructive notice, and thus did not protect the Bank's interest under the deed of trust against a subsequent judgment lien creditor in the absence of actual notice to such a subsequent judgment lien creditor.

(2)

The district court held that, although the recordation of the defective deed did not impart constructive notice, it could impart actual notice "to anyone who cared to review the records of the Chancery Clerk." The district court then held that the United States did have actual notice, apparently because IRS agents could have discovered the deed by reviewing the county land records. The United States argues that the district court's holding that the United States had actual notice of the deed is unsupported by the record, and contends that the district court confused the notion of constructive notice with actual notice in its holding that actual notice is imparted to third parties by the mere recordation of a defective deed of trust.

Under Mississippi law, a prior deed, whether recorded or unrecorded, is good against a subsequent purchaser or creditor with actual notice of it. *Dixon & Sharkey v. Lacoste,* 9 Miss. 70, 107 (1843). In addition, a recorded deed that is not acknowledged is valid against "one who sees upon the record and reads an instrument improperly recorded, because not acknowledged or proved as required by law." *Woods v. Garnett,* 72 Miss. 78, 16 So. 390, 391 (1894). In order to have "actual notice," a party must be "aware of the nature and purposes of the deed." *Bass v. Estill,* 50 Miss. 300, 306 (1874). Actual notice is defined by Black's Law Dictionary (5th ed. 1979) as "such notice as is positively proved to have been given to a party directly and personally, or such as he is presumed to have received personally because the evidence within his knowledge was sufficient to put him upon inquiry."

The appellees contend, and the district court held, that the United States had actual notice because the deed was recorded and could have been located had the United States searched the records. This argument confuses the concepts of actual notice and constructive notice. The mere recording of a deed does not provide actual notice to strangers to a transaction who are not in possession of facts that would place them on inquiry notice. Rather, the primary purpose of recording is to impart constructive notice.

The appellees contend, however, that the United States had a "duty to inquire" because its agents had knowledge of sufficient facts to place it upon inquiry notice to check the title to the subject property. "Inquiry notice," as recognized in Mississippi, arises when a party has actual notice or knowledge of facts that would lead a reasonably prudent person to question the sufficiency of title to property. *E.g., Burkett v. Peoples Bank of Biloxi,* 225 Miss. 291, 83 So.2d 185, 188 (1955). A party who has inquiry notice "is charged with notice of all those facts which could or would be disclosed by a diligent and careful investigation." *Id.* Under Mississippi law, a party is not on inquiry notice from the mere recordation of a deed evidencing an interest in property. *C & D Investment Co. v. Gulf Transport Co.,* 526 So.2d 526, 530 (Miss. 1988).

In support of their position that the United States had a duty to inquire, the appellees argue, without any citation of authority, that the fact that the taxpayer had not paid its taxes should have provided notice to the United States that the title to any property owned by the taxpayer would be subject to other liens or problems. We disagree. The fact that the taxpayer was delinquent in its federal tax obligations created no inferences concerning the taxpayer's title to any particular property and falls short of the type of information necessary to place the United States on inquiry notice. We also reject the appellees' argument that the taxpayer's filing of a petition in bankruptcy should have led the United States to conduct an investigation that would have resulted in the discovery of the Bank's deed of trust. We need not consider whether the taxpayer's filing of its bankruptcy petition was sufficient to put the IRS on inquiry notice because the record contains absolutely no factual support for the appellees' argument. For example, the record does not indicate when the United States received notice of the filing of the bankruptcy petition, or whether it received such notice prior to the filing of its federal tax liens.

We conclude that the record does not support the district court's holding that the United States had actual notice of the defective deed of trust. The record contains no evidence indicating that the United States was aware of the deed of trust prior to the time it filed its federal tax liens, or that it possessed any knowledge of circumstances that would have put it on inquiry which, if pursued, would have led it to actual knowledge of the defective deed of trust. Although the district court's statement that the defective deed of trust could give actual notice "to anyone who cared to review the records of the Chancery Clerk" is correct as far as it goes, there is no evidence that any agent of the United States reviewed the records of the Harrison County Chancery Clerk, and, under the facts in the record, the United States did not have inquiry notice of the existence of the deed.

(3)

The district court further held that the defectively acknowledged deed of trust gave the Bank "equitable title" sufficient to defeat the claims of "a subsequent purchaser or party coming after the document in question, who has notice of the questionable document." Even if we assume that the defectively acknowledged deed of trust gave the Bank "equitable title," the United States, as we have already noted, did not have notice of the defectively acknowledged deed of trust.

We reject the appellees' argument that, when the defectively acknowledged deed was recorded, the United States received constructive notice of the Bank's equitable interest because, as we have already held, the recordation of the defectively acknowledged deed did not impart constructive notice to subsequent creditors under Mississippi law. We therefore conclude that, under Mississippi law, the Bank's interest in the property under the defectively acknowledged deed of trust was not "protected by state law against a subsequent judgment lien creditor." The district court therefore erred in holding that the Bank is a "holder of a security interest" with respect to the property within the meaning of 26 U.S.C. § 6323(h)(1). Thus, the Bank is not entitled to the protection of § 6323(a).[23]

C

The district court's holding that the federal tax lien was extinguished in the foreclosure sale of the property under the provisions of 26 U.S.C. § 7425(b) is based on its erroneous conclusion that the tax liens were junior to the Bank's lien. As we have already held, the Bank's lien did not prime the federal tax liens. Section 7425(b) provides that, even if the government's lien is inferior under state law, it will not be discharged by the foreclosure sale unless the proper type of notice is given to the *United States. Myers v. United States,* 647 F.2d 591, 596-97 (5th Cir. 1981). It is undisputed that the United States was properly notified of the foreclosure sale by the Bank. Thus, the sale has "the same effect with respect to the discharge or divestment of

[23] In *Aetna Ins. Co. v. Texas Thermal Industries, Inc.*, 591 F.2d 1035, 1038 (5th Cir. 1979), this court held that the Federal Tax Lien Act of 1966 was intended to supplant the federal common law with respect to "tax lien priority questions as to which that statute provides an unambiguous federal answer." In *Texas Commerce Bank — Fort Worth, N.A. v. United States,* 896 F.2d 152, 161 n. 8 (5th Cir. 1990), however, another panel of this court has recently noted that there is an apparent conflict between *Aetna* and two earlier decisions of this court, *Rice Investment Co. v. United States,* 625 F.2d 565, 572 (5th Cir. 1980) and *Texas Oil & Gas Corp. v. United States,* 466 F.2d 1040, 1053 (5th Cir. 1972), cert. denied sub nom., *Pecos County State Bank v. United States,* 410 U.S. 929, 93 S. Ct. 1367, 35 L. Ed. 2d 591 (1973). In *Rice* and *Texas Oil,* the court, after concluding that nonfederal liens were not entitled to priority under the Tax Lien Act of 1966, proceeded to examine the question of priority under pre-1966 common law. We note that *Aetna* involved a nonfederal lien that was clearly entitled to priority under the Tax Lien Act and in that respect may be distinguishable from the nonfederal liens involved in *Rice* and *Texas Oil.*

In the case before us, the statute provides a nonambiguous federal answer to the priority. It is unnecessary for us to resolve any conflict between *Aetna, Rice,* and *Texas Oil* in this case because, even if we examine the question of priority under pre-1966 federal common law, the answer is the same. Pre-1966 federal common law requires that the competing nonfederal lien be not only first in time but "choate" as well. A nonfederal lien is choate when "the identity of the lienor, the property subject to the lien, and the amount of the lien are established beyond any possibility of change or dispute." *Rice Investment*, 625 F.2d at 568. The question whether a lien has acquired sufficient substance and has become so perfected as to defeat a later-arising or later-filed federal tax lien is governed by federal law. *Id.*

Although the deed of trust identifies the lienor and describes the property subject to the lien, the amount of the lien was not established "beyond all possibility of change or dispute" at the time the notices of tax liens were filed. The deed of trust secured not only the $400,000 loan, but also "such future and additional advances as may be made to the grantor," as well as "all debts, obligations, or liabilities, direct or contingent, of the grantor . . .to the beneficiary, whether now existing or hereafter arising at any time before actual cancellation of this instrument on the public records of mortgages and deeds of trust, whether the same be evidenced by note, open account, over-draft, endorsement, guaranty or otherwise." Because the deed of trust had not been cancelled at the time the IRS filed the notices of tax liens, the amount of the Bank's lien, under the express terms of the deed of trust, was subject to a "possibility of change or dispute" and thus was not perfected, or "choate," under pre-1966 federal common law.

such lien . . .of the United States, as may be provided with respect to such matters by the local law of the place where such property is situated." 26 U.S.C. § 7425(b)(2). As this court held in *United States v. Boyd,* 246 F.2d 477, 483 (5th Cir.), cert. denied, 355 U.S. 889, 78 S. Ct. 261, 2 L. Ed. 2d 188 (1957), under Mississippi law, a nonjudicial sale, with proper notice to the United States, cuts off the government's lien only if the tax lien is junior to the nonfederal lien being foreclosed. See also *Peoples Bank & Trust Co. v. L & T Developers, Inc.*, 434 So.2d 699 (Miss. 1983). We therefore hold that the district court erred in concluding that the senior tax liens of the United States were discharged by the Bank's nonjudicial foreclosure sale.

For the foregoing reasons, the judgment of the district court is REVERSED, and the case is REMANDED to the district court for further proceedings. . . . .

COMMENT

The tax people cometh but they do not always win. As the *Metropolitan National* case notes, the Internal Revenue Code § 6323(a), 26 U.S.C. § 6323(a), states that the lien imposed under section 6321 will not be valid against any holder of a security interest unless notice of that interest has been filed. The implied harshness of the provision is tempered by section 6323(c) which gives the IRS priority over a holder of a prior perfected security interest in accounts receivable only to a limited extent. The prior perfected secured party has priority for the first 45 days after the IRS notice. Thus, the IRS only gains priority beginning with the 46th day after it properly recorded the tax lien. All accounts receivable earned after that day will inure to the IRS until the lien is satisfied. See *e.g., In Re Thomas Communications*, 161 B.R. 621, 627-8 (Bankr. S.D. W. Va. 1993).

[C] Maritime Liens

IN RE STERLING NAVIGATION CO., LTD.

United States District Court, Southern District of New York
31 B.R. 619 (1983)

This is an appeal by the shipowner, A/S Gerrards ("Gerrards"), from a decision of the Bankruptcy Court granting summary judgment to the Trustee of the estate of Sterling Navigation Co. ("Sterling"), on a motion to declare invalid a shipowner's maritime lien on subfreights which had not been perfected under Article 9 of the New York Commercial Code ("Article 9 of the Code"). The shipowner in that action appeals the Bankruptcy Court's decision and cross moves for summary judgment pursuant to Rule 56, F.R. Civ. P. It contends that its maritime lien on subfreights is not subject to Article 9 and would thus have priority over the Trustee without the need to file, *i.e.* perfect under that Article. The case appears to be one of first impression.

On December 13, 1974, Gerrards and Sterling entered into a charter party agreement in which Sterling as charterer agreed to hire the M/S Regal, Gerrards' ship, for at least thirty-three months. Under the charter agreement, Sterling was to use the ship to transport merchandise and was to pay Gerrards at an agreed hire rate semi-monthly in advance.

The charter contract utilized was the New York Produce Exchange Form which allowed Sterling to trade the vessel world-wide within Institute warranty limits. Some of the standard provisions were altered, however, Clause 18, which granted the owner a lien on all subfreights, was retained. That section stated in relevant part: ". . . the Owners shall have a lien upon all cargoes and all subfreights . . . . due under this Charter . . . ."

. . . It is undisputed that this lien was never perfected by Gerrards.

Pursuant to the charter agreement, Gerrards delivered the M/S Regal to Sterling on January 1, 1975, in Kawasaki, Japan. Thereafter, Sterling entered into two sub-charter agreements; the first on June 27, 1975, with the Bangladesh Agricultural Development Corporation ("Development Corporation") for the carriage of a cargo of urea to Bangladesh, and the second on July 8, 1975, with A. Halcoussis Shipping Ltd. ("Halcoussis") to transport grain to Bangladesh. Trustee's Brief in Support of its Motion at 4. The agreement with the Development Corporation provided that the United States Agency for International Development ("AID") would issue a letter of commitment agreeing to pay Sterling for the urea freight. Trustee's Statement under Local Rule 3(g) at para. 6.

Sterling defaulted on the charter for hire on September 1, 1975. As a consequence, Gerrards withdrew the M/S Regal from Sterling, but only after the grain and urea cargoes had been delivered as scheduled. On October 17, 1975, Gerrards exercised its maritime lien on the subfreights under Clause 18, by serving notices of lien on the Peoples Republic of Bangladesh and on AID in Washington, D.C. Gerrards then brought an enforcement action on the lien in the District Court for the District of Columbia. That same day, October 28, 1975, Sterling filed a Chapter XI petition in this District. It was adjudicated a bankrupt on December 17, 1975. . . .

. . .[T]he freights due for the carriage of the urea and grain cargoes were paid to the Bankruptcy Court and there held in an interest bearing account pending a determination of priority and ownership of the funds.

Against this factual backdrop, the Bankruptcy Court held that Article 9 of the Code as amended in 1977 governed Gerrards' maritime lien on subfreights and that its failure to file, in accordance with the procedures therein, destroyed its claim for priority over the Trustee.

. . . .

. . . My basic disagreement with the Bankruptcy Judge is with his conclusion that the shipowner's maritime lien was subject to Article 9's filing requirement.

. . . .

Gerrards asserts that as a matter of federal maritime law, the owner's contractual maritime lien in subfreights is superior to the Trustee's non– maritime lien, and that the purpose of the 1966 amendments was to clarify the filing requirements for the assignment of ship charters, since for perfection purposes, the charters could arguably be considered chattel paper, accounts, general intangibles or contracts. Moreover, Gerrards contends that a ship charter is like a true lease and that therefore, with the exception of the assignment of that interest as security, the charter and the lien on subfreights would be excluded from Article 9. Thus, it concludes that the lien is perfected without being filed pursuant to the terms of Article 9. Gerrards staunchly opposes the suggestion that contractual maritime liens are subject to Article 9, both due to the historical priority of the shipowner's lien on subfreights over a Trustee's non-maritime lien, and because of the absence of any indication in the legislative history that the drafters of the Code intended to disturb those traditional priorities.

. . . The Trustee also argues that a maritime lien cannot be perfected unless filed as required by Article 9, and that if the legislature had intended to exclude maritime liens on subfreights from Article 9, it would have specifically done so, as was done with a true lease, see, N.Y. [Uniform Commercial Code] § 1-201(37) (McKinneys 1964), and an interest in real estate, *id.* § 9-104(j). Finally, he contends that regardless of whether the legislative history spoke only of assignments of ship charters, the intent of the drafters was not to limit the scope of §§ 9-106 and 9-105(1)(b), nor to alter the plain language of the statute.

Bankruptcy Judge Ryan adopted the Trustee's view and held that under Section 9-106 "rights under a charter" included maritime liens. Thus construing the statute narrowly, the court held that Gerrards' lien on subfreights was a separate and distinct security interest, and was therefore subject to the filing requirements of Article 9.

Determination

Prior to the 1966 amendments to Sections 9-106 and 9-105(1)(b), the shipowner's lien on subfreights had priority over the Trustee in bankruptcy without perfection.

The leading case is *In re North Atlantic & Gulf Steamship*, [204 F. Supp. 899 (S.D.N.Y. 1962) aff'd sub. nom., *Schilling v. AIS DIS*, 320 F.2d 628 (2d Cir. 1963)] in which this court held that where the owner's lien on subfreights arose prior to the time of filing the petition in bankruptcy, the shipowner's security interest in the freights was superior to the trustee's lien. The owner's lien "arose" when the vessel was loaded with cargo. Similarly at issue was Clause 18 of the New York Standard Produce Exchange Form, which as here provided: ". . . That the Owners shall have a lien upon all cargoes, and all subfreights for amounts due under this Charter."

In finding for the shipowner, the court stated:

Thus the owner's lien on subfreights earned by a vessel, for hire due under its charter, which has been asserted by notice to a shipper from whom the earned subfreights are due, is not void under § 67, sub. a . . . It is a maritime lien arising out of maritime contract and is not 'obtained by . . . legal or equitable process or proceedings.' It is valid and enforceable against the trustee.

In *Diana Co. Maritima*, [280 F. Supp. 607 (S.D.N.Y. 1968)] this court reaffirmed that position:

Section 67(a) of the Bankruptcy Actneither applies to nor invalidates contractual, common law, equitable and statutory liens . . . No legal or equitable process or proceeding is required for the creation of a maritime lien on subfreights . . . the maritime lien in the present case arose out of the charter party . . .—a maritime contract . . .—and is therefore, not 'obtained' by legal or equitable process or proceeding . . . . The maritime lien on all the subfreights presently held by the Court is therefore, valid as against the Trustee under any and all provisions of the Bankruptcy Act.

Id. at 614-15. In line with this reasoning are the conclusions of Grant Gilmore, co-author of The Law of Admiralty (1957, 2d ed. 1975), who in an opinion letter submitted on behalf of Gerrards stated that for the purpose of Article 9 a ship charter was like a true lease and as such did not come under the filing provisions of Article 9. He viewed the Article as applicable only to the transfer of the charter or its ancillary rights as security.

In light of the seeming unquestioned priority of the shipowner's lien on subfreights as against the Trustee before the 1966 amendments, it would seem logical to assume that had the desire been to effect a major change in maritime law by requiring the filing of the owner's security interest, it would have been clear from the plain language of the statute or at least noted, if only cryptically, in the legislative history. Instead, a careful perusal of the Code and of the Drafter's Official Comments to the 1966 amendments to Sections 9-105(1)(b) and 9-106 find them barren of any such suggestion.

The reasons given for the 1966 amendments to Section 9-105 were that:

> Many types of *ship financing* based on *assignment of a charter* involve international transactions and there are numerous executed copies of the charter . . . . Application of this rule would require the parties to change traditional practices in order to control all executed copies. Moreover, it is desirable to treat all types of ship charters alike, and some cannot be deemed chattel paper. This amendment and the related amendment to 9-106 make it clear that ship charters are "contract rights" (emphasis added).

Similarly, the comments interpreting the amendments to Section 9-106 address solely the question of the assignment of ship charters, and in particular the potential problems created where there are ancillary rights to the payment of money provided for in the charter assignment. The Board concluded:

> These ancillary rights if considered in the abstract, might be thought to be "general intangibles," since they do not themselves involve the payment of money; but it is not the intent of the Code to split up the rights to the payment of money and its ancillary supports and thereby multiply the problem of *perfection of assignments*. Therefore, all . . . . rights of the owner in a ship charter are to be perfected as "contract rights." (emphasis added).

Reference in 9-106 to the perfection of "unearned rights in a ship charter" is likewise directed to the subsequent assignment of those rights—

> It has been found advisable to distinguish rights earned from rights not yet earned for several reasons. The recognition of the "contract right" as collateral in a security transaction makes clear that this Article rejects any lingering common law notion that only rights already earned *can be assigned*. Furthermore, in the triangular arrangement following assignment, there is reason to allow the original parties—assignor and account debtor—more flexibility in modifying the underlying contract before performance. It will, however, be found that in most situations the same rules apply to both accounts and contract rights. The application of the same rules to rights under ship charters, whether earned or unearned, is assured by the last sentence of the Section: such rights are contract rights without regard to the general definitions. (emphasis added) *Id.*

. . . .

Thus, every reference to and explanation of the amendments points to the conclusion that their purpose was to provide uniformity in the perfection of assignment of ship charters. This result is further mandated by the Board's express desire not to "change traditional practices" in regard to ship financing, and the undisputed pre-Code rule that a contractual maritime lien on subfreights had priority over a trustee's lien in bankruptcy.

It is not the place of the courts to attribute an intention to the legislature where one is not clearly expressed. *Banzhaf v. FCC,* 132 U.S. App. D.C. 14, 405 F.2d 1082, 1089 (D.C. Cir. 1968), cert. denied sub nom., *National Broadcasting Co., Inc. v. FCC*, 396 U.S. 842, 24 L. Ed. 2d 93, 90 S. Ct. 51 (1969). Accordingly, I find that the shipowner's maritime lien on subfreights will have priority over the trustee's lien in bankruptcy without filing under Article 9.

. . . .

Accordingly, the decision of the Bankruptcy Court is reversed.

CHAPTER 19

DEFAULT

§ 19.01 Introduction

Read: U.C.C. § 9-501

Perhaps the one area of greatest concern for a seller or financier is the set of remedies available if the debtor cannot repay her obligations. The rights of a secured party after default represents the very core of secured transactions; a security interest is only as good as the creditor's ability to enforce it. Part five of Article 9 outlines the procedures for enforcing a security interest in cases of default. The Code attempts to find a balance between the interests of the creditor to collect the obligation owed, and those of the debtor, who has a strong interest both in keeping the collateral and in avoiding any unnecessarily burdensome liability that might be associated with debt collection and default.

The basic Code remedy is similar to that of foreclosure in real property mortgage cases: the secured party may obtain possession of the collateral, sell the property, and use the proceeds of the sale to satisfy the obligation. Although there are other remedies such as maintaining a lawsuit on the underlying contractual obligation, or seeking specific and stipulated remedies aimed at other forms of collateral, the cost and relative ease of creditor self-help repossession of tangible personal property makes this remedy the most frequently sought measure once a debtor defaults.

§ 19.02 Default

The term "default," important as it is, is not defined in the Code. Freedom of contract is the prevailing rule and the contracting parties may specify what events constitute default. Generally, a default occurs whenever a debtor fails to tender an obligation due; such a failure entitles the creditor to an appropriate remedy.

The security agreement may also include terms other than non-payment which may be deemed to be a default if violated. Some security agreements provide that a default will occur if the creditor deems itself insecure as to probability of forthcoming payments by the buyer. Because courts view such provisions with scrutiny, the exercise of creditor rights pursuant to an insecurity clause are ripe with danger. Other examples of events of default include the debtor's failure to maintain the property, a failure to keep property insured, or the removal of collateral from the governing jurisdiction. As with all contract provisions, terms of default are subject to general Code principles concerning good faith, unconscionability, and reasonableness.

Since any breach of a security agreement could constitute a default, questions concerning creditor practices have arisen over the particular enforcement of certain security agreements. Most security agreements are conceived and drafted by secured parties. The drafters of the Uniform

Commercial Code sought to solve some of those problems by providing basic limits on the ability of parties to alter certain obligations contractually. These limits seek to set forth a system which is satisfactory to both the creditor and the debtor by requiring that the creditor obtain and dispose of property in a commercially reasonable manner. At the same time, the Code protects the debtor by setting up certain safeguards. The following obligations cannot be altered by party agreement, except as specified in the particular Code provision:

1. The secured party must conduct any sale of collateral in a reasonably commercial manner. The provisions regarding notice of a sale cannot be varied. U.C.C. §§ 9-507, 9-504(3).

2. The secured party must account to the debtor for any surplus obtained from a sale of collateral. Surplus is any amount over and above that required to pay off the debt, any interest, and allowable expenses such as the cost of the sale. U.C.C. §§ 9-502(2), 9-504(2).

3. If the collateral is consumer goods, the property must be sold under certain circumstances unless the debtor agrees, *after default*, that the secured party may keep the collateral in satisfaction of the debt. U.C.C. § 9-505(2).

4. If the secured party elects to keep the collateral as satisfaction of the obligation, the debtor is entitled to notice of that decision and may nevertheless require a sale. This right to force a sale cannot be waived in the security agreement or in any manner *before* default. U.C.C. §§ 9-505(1).

5. The debtor has a right to redeem collateral 1) before the collateral has been sold; 2) before a contract for the sale of the collateral has been made; or 3) before the secured party has accepted the collateral in satisfaction of the obligation. U.C.C. §§ 9-501, 9-506.

Despite the Code's careful drafting, a secured party still runs a risk in pursuing self-help remedies because certain conduct could be construed to constitute a waiver of rights. If, for example, a secured party ignores a default which is later cured by the debtor, the secured party may not be able to rely on the same type of default to justify a repossession on a subsequent occasion. Similarly, if the secured party misleads a debtor as to whether there is a default, or about the creditor's intention to act upon a default, the secured party may be estopped from acting on the default. Although Article 9 does not deal with waiver or estoppel explicitly, U.C.C. § 1-103 provides that general principles of law and equity apply. These supplemental principles include both waiver and estoppel. The following case is illustrative.

MERCEDES-BENZ CREDIT CORP. v. MORGAN

Supreme Court of Arkansas
312 Ark. 225, 850 S.W.2d 297, 20 U.C.C.R. Serv. 2d 705 (1993)

GLAZE, J.

This tort of conversion case was commenced by Dr. Jerry Morgan after his 1984 Porsche had been repossessed by Mercedes-Benz Credit Corporation (MBCC). Morgan purchased the Porsche from Riverside Motors and afterwards, Riverside assigned the purchase installment contract to MBCC. Under the contract, Morgan was to make a payment of $253.37 on the first day of each month for forty-eight months commencing March 1, 1990. Morgan was indisputably late in his payments, and on March 22, 1991, MBCC decided to exercise its right under statutory law and the parties' contract to self-help repossession. MBCC peacefully and without incident gained possession of the Porsche on April 8, 1991. Following repossession, Dr. Morgan brought his account current. MBCC then offered to return the Porsche to Morgan, but he refused, choosing instead to file this conversion action against MBCC.

Prior to trial, MBCC moved for summary judgment which the trial court denied. The parties tried the case to a jury which returned a verdict for Dr. Morgan in the sum of $11,900.00. MBCC filed motions for directed verdict and for judgment notwithstanding the verdict, all of which were denied. The trial court also awarded attorney's fees to Morgan. MBCC brings this appeal arguing the trial court erred in denying its motions for directed verdict and judgment notwithstanding the verdict and in awarding Morgan attorney's fees.

Morgan proceeded below on two theories, namely (1) he was not in default when MBCC decided to repossess Morgan's car, and alternatively (2) if Morgan was in default, MBCC had established a course of dealing by accepting late payments, so MBCC was required to put Morgan on notice that it would no longer allow late payments and would require strict compliance with the parties' contract. Both of these theories were presented to the jury, and if Morgan is correct on either argument, we must affirm.

As to Morgan's first point, our review of the record shows he was clearly in default at the time MBCC repossessed Morgan's car. Morgan makes much of the argument that MBCC had miscalculated the receipt of his late February 1 and March 1, 1991 payments. He showed MBCC had misapplied his February 1 payment to the wrong account and mistakenly delayed in crediting this payment to Morgan's correct account until April 15, 1991. Morgan argued MBCC had actually accepted his late February 1 payment well in advance of its declaring Morgan in default. Morgan also claimed that MBCC had accepted his late March 1 payment on April 1, 1991. In both cases, Morgan asserts his account was current prior to MBCC's repossession of Morgan's car on April 8, 1991.

Although the record appears to support Morgan's argument as to his February and March payments, the evidence also reflects he still was late on his payment due on April 1, 1991, which was not received by MBCC until on or about April 11, 1991 — several days after MBCC repossessed Morgan's car. In sum, we conclude MBCC is correct in its argument that Morgan was, indeed, in default when it regained possession of Morgan's car. That being so, MBCC argues it was not liable for conversion.

. . . .

The *Herring* case, however, is not controlling here because it does not address Morgan's second theory or argument. In other words, while the *Herring* case correctly upheld a seller's or secured creditor's right to repossess collateral when a debtor is in default, the *Herring* court was not confronted with the argument Morgan makes here — where the secured creditor (MBCC) routinely accepts a debtor's (Dr. Morgan's) delinquent payments, does the creditor waive strict compliance with the parties' contractual payment and enforcement provisions, at least until the creditor notifies the debtor that strict compliance will be expected henceforth?

Morgan's theory argued below and on appeal is well-grounded in legal authority. In pre-code cases, this court adhered to the principle that acceptance of late payments waives strict compliance with contract terms specifying time of payments. See *Commercial Credit Co. v. Ragland,* 189 Ark. 349, 72 S.W.2d 226 (1934); *General Motors Acceptance v. Hicks,* 189 Ark. 62, 70 S.W.2d

509 (1934); see also *Ford Motor Credit Co. v. Waters,* 273 So.2d 96 (Fla. Dist. Ct. App. 1973) (where seller of automobile had consistently accepted late payments from the buyer, who had made more than half of the thirty-six monthly payments when the vehicle was repossessed at time buyer was two months behind, the court held the seller's conduct led buyer to believe late payments would be accepted and therefore buyer had a right to be notified, prior to repossession, of any modification of such conduct, and in absence of such notice, buyer was entitled to recover for wrongful repossession.)

Professor Steve H. Nickles thoroughly discussed in his article, *Rethinking Some U.C.C. Article 9 Problems,* the foregoing principle concerning the effect of a creditor's acceptance of late payments as follows:

> A similar case involves a secured party who has regularly accepted late payments but eventually decides to repossess when the debtor fails to make the next payment on time. A clause in the security agreement usually gives the creditor the right to declare the contract in default if any payment is delinquent. When sued by the debtor, the secured party argues that this contract language entitled him to repossess despite the established pattern of accepting late payments and foregoing repossession. The courts typically hold that "an established course of dealing under which the debtor . . . makes continual late payments and the secured party . . . accepts them does not result in a waiver of the secured party's right to rely upon such a clause in the agreement authorizing him to declare a default and repossess the chattel." But "a secured party who has not insisted upon strict compliance in the past . . . must, before he may validly rely upon such a clause to declare a default and effect repossession, give notice to the debtor . . . that strict compliance with the terms of the contract will be demanded henceforth if repossession is to be avoided. By his course of dealing the secured party has, in effect, waived the right to repossession based on defaults in making timely payments. The secured party must then reinstate the right by giving the debtor notice that strict compliance with the contract is now expected before a late payment can justify repossession. In many of these cases such notice has not been given, and the secured party is found liable for wrongful repossession.

34 Ark. Law Rev. 1, 137 (1980-81).

In the present case, Dr. Morgan made only one timely payment of the fourteen monthly payments required prior to MBCC having repossessed Morgan's automobile. The thirteen late payments ranged from a few days to more than thirty days delinquent from the due date required under the parties' agreement. MBCC's personnel had contacted Morgan concerning his delinquent payments, but no one at MBCC ever informed Morgan that MBCC intended to commence strict enforcement of its rights under their contract. The record shows that shortly before it repossessed Morgan's Porsche on April 8, 1991, MBCC had again accepted another late payment (March) on April 1, 1991, and it also accepted Morgan's delinquent April payment on April 11, 1991. In fact, MBCC even tendered the car's return to Morgan when Morgan became current on his account. Clearly, a jury, under the above authority, could have found that (1) MBCC, by its course of dealing, had waived its right to repossession based on its having repeatedly accepted late payments, and (2) in order to reinstate its right under the parties' contract, MBCC was required to give Morgan notice that MBCC expected strict compliance in future dealings. If MBCC failed to give such notice in these circumstances, it would then not have the right to declare a default and repossess its collateral.

At this point, we note that the secured party's liability for wrongful repossession is usually based on the common law rule of conversion. See Nickles, 34 Ark. L. Rev. at p. 139. The *Hicks* case previously cited was such a repossession case where this court upheld a buyer-debtor's claim that the creditor committed conversion when the creditor wrongly took possession of her refrigerator. Conversion is the exercise of dominion over the property in violation of the rights of the owner or person entitled to possession. *Herring,* 267 Ark. 701, 589 S.W.2d 584. As discussed above, MBCC failed to reinstate its right under the parties' contract to declare default and to repossess its collateral for late payments. As a consequence, its repossession of and exercise of dominion over Morgan's automobile in these circumstances sufficiently supported the jury's finding of conversion.

Before leaving this point, we acknowledge MBCC's reliance on *Westlund v. Nelson*, 7 Ark. App. 268, 647 S.W.2d 488 (1983). MBCC argues that Westlund stands for the proposition that acceptance of a late payment precludes acceleration because of the lateness of that payment, but is not a waiver of the right to accelerate when default occurs in a subsequent installment. See *Rawhide Farms v. Darby,* 267 Ark. 776, 589 S.W.2d 210 (Ark. App. 1979). Thus, MBCC concludes that, while it may have accepted thirteen late payments from Morgan, Morgan was still delinquent in his last April 1 payment, and under the *Westlund* rationale, MBCC could declare default and enforce its rights under the parties' contract by repossessing Morgan's car.

First, we note that MBCC never argued *Westlund* below either in support of its directed verdicts or its motion for judgment notwithstanding the verdict. MBCC relied simply on the fact that Morgan was in default, and under the holding in Herring, it had the right to repossess Morgan's car. On the other hand, Morgan, as discussed above, argued, when opposing MBCC's directed verdict motions and during his closing argument, that by accepting late payments, MBCC had established a course of dealing which required MBCC to notify Morgan that it expected future payment to comply with the parties' contract. Morgan, without objection, argued this theory to the jury and emphasized that MBCC never gave Morgan such notice and therefore it had no right to repossess Morgan's car when it did.

In sum, MBCC simply failed to object or attack the legal soundness of Morgan's course of dealing argument below, nor did it argue that the principle in *Westlund* should control over Morgan's theory. Neither the trial court nor the jury was apprised of the legal argument MBCC now advances for the first time on appeal.[1] Because substantial evidence was presented that Morgan never received notice from MBCC that it would henceforth require prompt payments under the parties' contract, the jury could have readily determined MBCC wrongfully repossessed Morgan's vehicle when it did. This is especially true since MBCC continued its pattern of accepting late payments from Morgan by accepting his late April 1 payment on April 11, 1991, and offering to return Morgan his car. We note further that it was MBCC's burden to demonstrate error and having failed to do so, we must affirm. *Jenkins v. Goldsby*, 307 Ark. 558, 822 S.W.2d 843 (1992).

. . . .

For the reasons above, we affirm the jury verdict entered in Morgan's behalf . . ..

---

1 We further acknowledge the existence of a "non-waiver/no oral modification" cause in the Retail Installment Contract. However, MBCC failed to present any argument as to that clause's effect upon the parties' course of dealing. Mindful of a split of authority, See *Tillquist v. Ford Motor Credit Co.*, 714 F. Supp. 607 (D. Conn. 1989); Barkley Clark, The Law of Secured Transactions Under the Uniform Commercial Code, para. 4.01[3] (2d.ed. 1988); Ronald Anderson, Uniform Commercial Code, § 9-503:14 (3d.ed. 1985 & Supp. 1991), we refrain from deciding this issue until it is properly raised and argued in an appropriate case.

NOTE

In *Van Bibber v. Norris*, 419 N.E.2d 115, 31 U.C.C. Rep. Serv. 1522 (Ind. 1981), the Indiana Supreme Court evaluated the effect of a "nonwaiver" clause in a security agreement. In *Van Bibber*, Norris brought an action against AFNB for damages resulting from the wrongful repossession of his mobile home and the loss of its contents. The trial court held that AFNB, as a result of continual acceptance of late payments, waived its right to enforcement of the acceleration and repossession terms of the default section of the agreement.

The relevant portion of the agreement stated:

> No waiver by the seller of any default shall be effective unless in writing, nor operate as a waiver of any other default nor of the same default on a future occasion.

The general rules applicable to secured transactions have been summarized as follows:

> [T]he secured party may not ordinarily establish a pattern of accepting time payments which may be slightly late and then suddenly insist on strict compliance with time provisions and declare a forfeiture; in such case, where the parties have treated the time clause as waived with respect to some payments, the secured party, in order to avail himself of the right of forfeiture for failure to make subsequent payments on time, must give reasonable, definite and specific notice of his changed intention.

This rule generally does not consider the impact of a non-waiver clause on the secured party's rights. The *Van Bibber* court ruled that,

> [s]ome courts have considered it to be jury question whether acceptance of late payments amounts to a waiver of the non-waiver clause. *Smith v. General Finance*, (1979) 243 Ga. 500, 255 S.E. 2d 14. We consider this approach to be illogical, since the very conduct which the clause is designed to permit—acceptance of late payment—is turned around to constitute waiver of the clause permitting the conduct.
>
> We believe the correct approach is that
>
> [U]nder an installment . . .contract providing that waiver of any default shall not be deemed a waiver of any other or subsequent default, the acceptance of late payments . . .does not constitute a waiver of the secured party's right to demand that payments be made according to contract provisions, or to declare a default and repossess. . ..
>
> 79 *C.J.S. Supp.* Secured Transactions § 100 (1974). . ..
>
> Another approach is to hold that since a security agreement is to be enforced according to its terms, an agreement containing a non-waiver and non-modification clause gives the secured party the right to take possession of the collateral without notice upon default.
>
> We believe the latter approach better serves the purpose of Ind. Code § 26-1-9-503, and carries out the terms to which Norris agreed. If the nonwaiver clause preserves the secured party's right to demand strict compliance, and the debtor's failure to comply with the terms

would otherwise give rise to the secured party's right to repossession without notice, then, we believe, the right to repossess without notice is similarly preserved.

As this court said in analyzing the general concept of waiver:

"[T]he vendor may waive strict compliance with the provisions of the contract by accepting overdue or irregular payments, and having so done, equity requires the vendor give specific notice of his intent that he will no longer be indulgent and that he will insist on his right of forfeiture unless the default is paid within a reasonable and specified time. (Citations omitted.)"

It follows that where the vendor has not waived strict compliance by acceptance of late payments, no notice is required to enforce its provisions.

Since the secured party here is in the same position, by virtue of the non-waiver clause, as one who never accepted a late payment, we conclude that no notice was required before it could proceed with its contract remedies. 31 U.C.C. Rep. Serv. at 1527-9.

Do you agree with the analysis given by the court? Cf., *Dyersburg Production Credit Assn. v. Kile*, 42 U.C.C. Rep. Serv. 1842 (Tenn. Ct. App. 1986), where the court held that despite a 20-year relationship between a farmer and Dyersburg, there was no 'course of dealing' waiver of the security agreement provision for notification prior to sale of livestock collateral. In resolving the issue in favor of the creditor Dyersburg, the court found that "the express terms of an agreement will control when their construction is inconsistent with the course of dealing by the parties." Do these cases swing the pendulum too far in favor of creditors?

PROBLEM 19.1

Shelton bought a mobile home from Logan's Mobile Home Company. The contract called for monthly installments of $350. Shelton granted Logan's a security interest in the home to secure the debt. The dealer assigned its rights under the contract to another party who in turn sold it to Westinghouse. Shelton made 20 of the 60 monthly payments before defaulting. Of the 20 payments Shelton made, 16 were late. Westinghouse accepted each late payment. When Shelton failed to make the 21st installment, Westinghouse called the debt due in full in accordance with the contract and requested a writ of replevin for the mobile home. The trial court granted possession to Westinghouse. Shelton counterclaimed for wrongful conversion, claiming that the Westinghouse acceptance of late installments constituted a waiver of the default provision. What result? If you were law clerk to the judge deciding this case, what other information might you seek before making a recommendation to your judge? See *Westinghouse Credit Corp. v. Shelton,* 645 F.2d 869 (10th Cir. 1981). Would your answer change if the Westinghouse security agreement also contained an insecurity clause?

§ 19.03 Acceleration of Payments

Read: U.C.C. § 1-208.

Security agreements typically provide that upon default, the secured party may accelerate the debt and demand that all payments are due immediately. Instead of simply owing for one month, the borrower now owes the entire amount. The Code provides that the exercise of such a right shall be in good faith. Section 1-201(19) defines good faith as "honesty in fact in the conduct or transaction concerned." Professors White and Summers have described this standard as lying "somewhere between a strict objective test (reasonable prudent person) and a thoroughly subjective one (whim). The drafters apparently intended an objective standard." White & Summers, Uniform Commercial Code (4th ed. 1995) § 25-3, p. 904. Consider the following two cases.

CLAYTON v. CROSSROADS EQUIPMENT COMPANY

Supreme Court of Utah
655 P.2d 1125, 34 U.C.C. Rep. Serv. 1448 (1982)

HOWE, J.

The plaintiff, David D. Clayton, brought this action against the defendants Crossroads Equipment Company (Crossroads) and John Deere Company (Deere) seeking damages and possession of two John Deere combines which he alleged they wrongfully repossessed from him. The trial court, sitting without a jury, awarded the plaintiff $27,400 representing the amount he had paid on the combines, and $100 nominal damages for "unlawful detention." Plaintiff was also awarded $20,000 punitive damages against Deere. Crossroads and Deere were awarded the combines as their interest appeared, and Crossroads was awarded a set-off against the plaintiff in the amount of $1,413 and attorney's fees of $750 for money he owed to Crossroads on an open account. Defendants appeal.

On October 7, 1977 the plaintiff purchased a John Deere combine from Crossroads for $47,250. Plaintiff signed a contract marked "Retail Installment Contract, Security Agreement" which provided for a down payment of $18,900, an initial installment payment of $4,352 due on July 1, 1978, and equal payments of $3,793 every six months thereafter commencing January 1, 1979, until the balance was paid. Crossroads assigned this contract to Deere's branch office in Portland, Oregon for financing and it was accepted.

On May 15, 1978 plaintiff purchased a second combine on terms similar to those of the first purchase. The total purchase price was $54,470 minus a discount of $10,000. Plaintiff paid down $8,500 cash and gave a promissory note for $3,000 for the balance of the required down payment of $11,500. The first installment of $4,880 was due on July 1, 1978 and payments thereafter were to be made at six-month intervals. This contract was also submitted for assignment to Deere at Portland for financing but Deere refused to accept it.

Plaintiff used both combines to harvest crops for farmers. He traveled from state to state to work and had 14 years of experience as a contract harvester. In early August of 1978 he brought both combines back to Utah in search of harvesting work. He had hoped to harvest barley for Ivin Barlow, president of Crossroads. When plaintiff arrived in Utah, however, he discovered that Barlow's barley crop was overrun with weeds and was not yet ready for harvest.

Plaintiff then had the combines serviced by Crossroads together with some warranty work. On September 21, 1978 he commenced leaving with them intending to travel to Illinois where he had arranged to harvest corn. Crossroads had earlier informed the plaintiff that he could not take the second combine from the Crossroads lot since Deere had refused to accept the contract for financing which left the combine without insurance coverage. When Ivin Barlow discovered that the plaintiff had taken both combines and was leaving town he attempted to overtake him. On his way, he stopped to enlist the help of Deputy Sheriff Wayne Holt. When Deputy Holt and Barlow caught up with plaintiff, he had already been stopped by Barlow's son, Les. Les Barlow had observed the plaintiff leaving and had pulled his pickup across the path of the 1978 combine which was being driven by Bill Miles, an assistant of the plaintiff. After a roadside discussion between the men, the officer took temporary possession of the keys to the two trucks on which the combines were loaded. Later that day Deere requested Crossroads' assistance in further detaining the 1977 combine. The two combines were moved to Crossroads' lot. Plaintiff did not pursue obtaining their possession at that time but later brought this action.

Plaintiff was awarded damages of $27,400 against both defendants plus punitive damages of $20,000 against Deere because of its improper repossession. He also recovered nominal damages of $100 for slander, false arrest, or "unlawful detention." Possession of the combines was given to the defendants. Crossroads was awarded a set-off of $1,413 which plaintiff owed to it on his open account, together with reasonable attorney's fees of $750.00 for collection services.

The broad issues which we consider material to the resolution of this appeal are:

1. Whether the "Retail Installment Contract, Security Agreement" executed pursuant to the purchase of the 1978 combine was in full force and effect on September 21, 1978, the date of repossession.
2. Whether the combines were wrongfully repossessed.
3. Whether the trial court's award of damages was proper.
4. Whether the trial court erred in awarding plaintiff punitive damages against Deere.

I. THE 1978 CONTRACT

One of the defenses raised by the Answer of Crossroads was that at the time the contract for the purchase of the second combine was entered into in May 1978, it was orally agreed between the parties that the contract would not be carried by Crossroads but that the purchase would have to be financed by John Deere as was the first contract, or by someone else. Thus the contract was subject to either a condition precedent to its taking effect, or was subject to a condition subsequent which would terminate it if the parties were unable to find financing. The trial court made no finding on this issue although by implication it found that the contract was in effect when the repossessions took place in September 1978.

We find this defense to be meritorious. Both the plaintiff and Ivin Barlow testified that financing of the second contract was necessary and much of their testimony concerned the efforts of the parties to obtain financing. The contract was twice submitted to Deere's Portland branch office for acceptance for financing, but Deere refused to accept it. Contact was made with Borg-Warner for financing but without success. Plaintiff and Barlow even discussed the possibility of a lease arrangement between them. Finally, the matter culminated when the combines were in the shop of Crossroads in September 1978 for warranty work and servicing. It is uncontroverted that Barlow insisted that since financing had not been obtained, the combine should be left there in the possession of Crossroads, or that the plaintiff pay an additional $10,000 on the purchase price. Plaintiff admitted that on the morning of September 21, 1978 he spent several hours making telephone calls from Crossroads in an attempt to raise additional money to pay on the combine. It was only after he failed in that effort that he decided to take possession of the combine and transport it to Illinois where he claimed to have work awaiting him.

The parties had made efforts from May until September 21, 1978 to obtain financing. Since they had been entirely unsuccessful in obtaining it, Barlow had the legal right to take possession of the combine because the condition of financing had not been met. In view of the uncontroverted status of the evidence in this regard, the judgment against Crossroads must be reversed and the case remanded to the trial court for the purpose of amending the Findings of Fact accordingly, and for the purpose of the court making a determination of how much, if any, of the $8,500 which the plaintiff had paid on the machine should be returned to him.

II. THE REPOSSESSION OF THE 1977 COMBINE

The next question presented is whether the 1977 combine was wrongfully repossessed. In the sales contract, there is a provision that:

> In the event of the default (as defined on the reverse side hereof), holder may take possession of the GOODS and exercise any other remedies provided by law.The event of default with which we are here concerned is recited on the back of the agreement as follows:
>
> This note shall be in default . . . if for any reason the holder of this note deems the debt or security unsafe, and in any such event the holder may immediately and without notice declare the entire balance of this note due and payable together with all expenses of collection by suit or otherwise, including reasonable attorney's fees.

The validity of such a contractual provision is not in dispute. Section 70A-1-208, U.C.A. (1953), provides that such provisions shall be construed to mean that the secured party shall have the power to exercise the remedies provided for "only if he in good faith believes that the prospect of payment or performance is impaired." The defendants could, therefore, accelerate the contract (note) and repossess the combine only in a good faith belief that the debt or their security was about to become impaired. See *State Bank of Levi v. Woolsey*, Utah, 565 P.2d 413 (1977).

"Good faith" is defined by § 70A-1-201(19), U.C.A. (1953), as "honesty in the fact in the conduct or transaction concerned." The obvious purpose of requiring that a secured party act in good faith is to impose the basic obligation of fair dealing, and to protect the purchaser from the mere whim or caprice of the secured party. In the instant case the trial court found that no cause or reason existed on September 21, 1978, the date of the repossession, for Deere to feel any less secure than it did at the time the 1977 (first) contract was entered into between the parties. The court further found that nothing had occurred during the interim to make the plaintiff less credit worthy and concluded that Deere had acted in bad faith in repossessing the combine, particularly because the plaintiff was then current with his payments.

Deere assails this finding and conclusion primarily on the ground that when it investigated the plaintiff's credit at the time the second contract was submitted to it for acceptance of financing, it obtained information from its branch office in Dallas, Texas (where the plaintiff had formerly dealt) that he was a poor credit risk. The difficulty with Deere's position is that the record fails to establish that the transactions and events which formed the basis for the derogatory credit report from the Dallas office occurred after October 1977 when Deere accepted the first contract. Deere, without much investigation, had accepted the plaintiff as a credit risk on the 1977 contract.

It would be highly inequitable to allow Deere to change its mind once it had accepted that contract simply because it subsequently conducted a more thorough investigation; it is unfair to put the buyer in default based upon information which was apparently available in one of Deere's own branch offices at the time that it had accepted plaintiff. Under pre-U.C.C. law, it was held that "insecurity" clauses contained in chattel mortgages and other security agreements were meant to apply to possible changes in conditions or circumstances, or new developments affecting the mortgagee's security. . . .. Facts that would justify the mortgagee's taking possession "must arise from the acts of the parties or changes in values occurring subsequent to the execution of the mortgage." . . .. Neither has Deere cited nor have we found any cases which have been decided under the U.C.C. on this point; but, no reason is apparent why the law should be any different now. . . ..

This is not a case where the plaintiff's credit had deteriorated after the contract had been accepted by Deere. On the contrary, the plaintiff had made all required payments to date on the 1977 combine. Furthermore, a representative of Deere had met in June 1978 with the plaintiff to collect an overdue payment which plaintiff made to him. He indicated to the plaintiff that he would use his effort to induce Deere to accept the second contract. We therefore affirm the trial court's finding that Deere failed to act in good faith, based upon its finding that there was no substantial change in his credit standing between the time of the execution of the 1977 sales agreement and the time the defendants repossessed the combine.

Deere further contends that it was justified in deeming the debt and security unsafe because the plaintiff had declared his intent to take the combine to Illinois. The contract provided that it would be kept in Riverside County, California. The U.C.C. financing statement had been filed only in that state. This contention is also unavailing. Deere's own witnesses contradicted each other as to whether plaintiff's announced intention to take the combine to Illinois was a factor in its determination to repossess the combine. John Hubbard, manager of financial services in the Portland office, testified that while he did not object to the machine being brought to Utah for warranty work, he did object to it being taken to Illinois and this was one factor in his decision to repossess it. D.D. Sommerfield, assistant to Hubbard, testified that Deere would have repossessed the combine irrespective of the events of September 21, 1978. A note which Sommerfield made following a telephone conversation with the plaintiff in June 1978 bears out that repossession was considered by him at that early date. Deere was obviously shaken by the adverse credit information it had received from its Dallas office and as Sommerfield admitted, it was foregone that Deere would have to repossess the 1977 combine, but he did not know just when it would take place. In view of this conflict in the testimony of Deere's own representatives and in view of all of the evidence, the trial court was not compelled to believe and to find that Deere exercised its repossession rights because the plaintiff announced his intention to take the combine to Illinois.

Moreover, the record establishes that Deere did not advance this as a reason at the time of the repossession. Les Barlow, who actually stopped the plaintiff from leaving, testified that Hubbard had telephoned him and told him that Deere had decided to repossess the combine pursuant to the "insecurity" provision and had called his attention to that provision in the printed form. Barlow then, apparently at Hubbard's request, pointed out this provision to the plaintiff as the basis for the detention of the combine. There was no evidence that the plaintiff was ever informed by Barlow or anyone else that Deere objected to the combine being taken out of the state. Had that reason been advanced by Deere or its agent, Barlow, Plaintiff would have had the opportunity to have taken the combine and returned to his home in Riverside County, California.

III. THE DAMAGES

Deere next complains that the trial court erred in awarding the plaintiff as damages the amounts he had paid on the combine. We find no error in this regard. In *Even Odds, Inc. v. Nielson,* 22 Utah 2d 49, 448 P.2d 709 (1968) we stated that the desired objective in computing damages and fashioning a remedy is to evaluate a loss suffered by the most direct and practical method which could be employed. It appears that allowing Deere to retain the combine which it had earlier repossessed in addition to compensating the plaintiff for his investment in the combine, was the most direct method of providing relief to the plaintiff. In *Keller v. Deseret Mortuary Co.,* 23 Utah 2d 1, 455 P.2d 197 (1979) we held that a non-breaching party to a contract should receive an award which will put him in as good a position as he would have been in had there been no breach. That appears to be exactly what the trial court attempted to do. The combine had been repossessed by Deere and had been in its possession for several months at the time of trial. Allowing Deere to retain possession of the combine and compensating plaintiff for his investment therein was not an unreasonable method of fixing damages. In fixing damages the trial court is vested with broad discretion and the award will not be set aside unless it is manifestly unjust or indicates that the trial court neglected pertinent elements, or was unduly influenced by prejudice or other extraneous circumstances. *Aerospace Realty v. Tooth, Ltd.,* Colo. App., 539 P.2d 1314 (1975).

It is true, as pointed out by Deere, that the plaintiff did not seek rescission of the contract in his complaint but sought damages for loss of use both in his complaint and at trial. However, Deere has not shown how it was prejudiced by the trial court's action in adopting a different measure of damages. Plaintiff testified that based on past experience, he could have earned approximately $43,000 after expenses with the two combines for the harvesting which he had already contracted for in the fall of 1978. He was, of course, unable to perform the harvesting after the repossession. Had the trial court compensated him for the loss of use, of one combine, the amount of the award could have been, based upon plaintiff's testimony, in excess of the $18,900 which the trial court awarded him on the rescission and restitution theory.

(Two justices have dissented to this part of the opinion, but a 2 to 2 vote works an affirmance of the trial court.)

IV. THE PUNITIVE DAMAGES

Deere contends there is no basis in the evidence for the award by the trial court of $20,000 punitive damages against it. Deere assails that court's findings that it (1) conceived a scheme to extract from the plaintiff as much money as possible and to then repossess the combine, and (2) that Ivin Barlow enticed the plaintiff to come to Utah and bring his machines upon a false promise that he had crops to harvest. Without discussing these points in detail, if we assume the validity of Deere's argument, there is other competent evidence which amply supports the award of punitive damages.

We have already concluded in Part II that there is evidence to sustain the trial court's finding that the repossession by Deere was not made in good faith. It should also be observed that the repossession came during the harvest season when the plaintiff had considerable work scheduled. The loss of the combine was more egregious at that time than it would have been at any other time of the year. The repossession, if allowed, would have probably resulted in the loss of plaintiff's equity. Section 70A-1-106, U.C.A. 1953 provides that punitive damages may not be had "except as specifically provided in this act or by other rule of law." It is well established in the jurisprudence of this state that punitive damages may be awarded when the proof supports a finding that the defendant's conduct was wilful or malicious. . . .. Specifically, in a case involving the repossession of goods, the United States Court of Appeals for the 10th Circuit in *Klingbiel v. Commercial Credit Corp.*, 439 F.2d 1303 (1971) approved an award of punitive damages upon a showing by the plaintiff of "such gross neglect of duty as to evince a reckless indifference of the rights of others on the part of the wrongdoer, and an entire want of care so as to raise the presumption that the person at fault is conscious of the consequences of his carelessness" quoting from *Watkins v. Layton,* 182 Kan. 702, 324 P.2d 130 (1958). In *Klingbiel,* the defendant creditor had repossessed the plaintiff's automobile without notice which was required by the terms of the contract. An award of punitive damages was upheld. See the cases collected at 35 A.L.R. 3d 1044 (1971) which the annotator states support the award of punitive damages where the repossession was under an ostensible claim of right, but the creditor acted with gross negligence, recklessness or oppressiveness. See also 69 Am. Jur. 2d § 653 Secured Transactions (1973) to the same effect. In view of the trial court's finding of bad faith, and of all the evidence, we find no error in the award of punitive damages in the instant case. Cf. *Calhoun v. Universal Credit Co.,* 106 Utah 166, 146 P.2d 284 (1944) where we reversed an award of punitive damages in a repossession case, finding that the conversion was not made in bad faith.

The judgment below is affirmed except as modified herein and the case is remanded for further proceedings consistent with this opinion. Each party shall bear his or its own costs.

STEWART, JUSTICE, concurring.

OAKS, JUSTICE: (Concurring and Dissenting). I concur in Justice Howe's opinion, except for Part III, damages.

When Deere wrongfully repossessed the 1977 combine, the buyer was not in default. Consequently, the Uniform Commercial Code provisions regulating the rights of the parties upon the debtor's default are inapplicable. The sole statutory provision applicable to the rights of a debtor who is not in default is § 70A-9-507(1), which is either inapplicable to the facts of this case or cumulative of the common-law remedy elected by the debtor.

In this case, the buyer (debtor) elected an action for wrongful repossession of goods sold under contract, an intentional tort which, if proven, would entitle the buyer to a tort measure of damages, including punitive damages. . . .. However, the compensatory relief awarded by the trial court and approved by Justice Howe's opinion in this case was comparable to the relief that would be given under the legal remedy of recision for a material breach of contract: Deere keeps the combine and the buyer recovers all of the amounts he has paid.

The trial court's broad discretion in fixing damages cannot justify the compensatory damages awarded in this case for three reasons: (1) A plaintiff cannot elect one theory or remedy in his complaint and proof at trial and then obtain relief only appropriate to another and inconsistent theory or remedy. . .. (2) Even the remedy of recision requires that the plaintiff's recovery be reduced for benefits received, in this case the reasonable value of the use of the combine during the time he possessed it. . . .. (3) Punitive damages are only recoverable for a "tortious invasion of the chattel holder's interest," . . . and therefore cannot be an element of damages accompanying the contract remedy of recision for a mere breach of contract. . ..

I would therefore vacate the award of compensatory damages and remand with directions to redetermine plaintiff's damages on the existing record on the basis of the loss the plaintiff suffered from the wrongful action of Deere, with appropriate adjustment for the disposition of the collateral since it was repossessed. In the alternative, the award of punitive damages should be vacated and plaintiff's recovery as compensatory damages of the amounts he had paid should be reduced by the value of his possession of the combine. . . ..

GREENBERG v. SERVICE BUS. FORMS INDUS.

United States Court of Appeals
882 F.2d 1538, 9 U.C.C. Rep. Serv. 2d 841 (10th Cir. 1989)

PER CURIAM.

Service Business Forms Industries, Inc. (Service Business) and Service Computer Forms Industries, Inc. (Service Computer), defendants, appeal the district court's order granting plaintiffs partial summary judgment on their claim for recovery of an accelerated debt allegedly due under Service Business' promissory note. The district court determined that there were no material issues of fact as to Service Business' default under the terms of the promissory note and that plaintiffs properly exercised their right to accelerate the unpaid principal balance and accrued interest. On appeal, defendants contend there are genuine issues of fact regarding each of its defenses.

Plaintiffs are co-trustees of the Mal Greenberg Testamentary Trust (the Trust). On October 29, 1982, plaintiffs entered into a stock redemption agreement with Service Computer, a Nevada corporation presently owned and operated by Carolyn and Laurance Wolfberg. The Wolfbergs are the sister and brother-in-law of Robert Greenberg (Greenberg), a plaintiff and a trustee of the Trust. Under the stock redemption agreement, the Trust transferred all the shares it owned in Service Computer back to the company in exchange for $102,000. Of this amount, $2,000 was to be paid at closing and $100,000 was to be paid pursuant to the promissory note at issue here.

Pursuant to the stock redemption agreement, Service Business, an affiliate of Service Computer which is also operated by the Wolfbergs, executed a $100,000 promissory note on October 29, 1982, the closing date of the stock redemption agreement. The note provided for annual payments to be calculated on a twenty-year amortization schedule with full payment to be made on the tenth anniversary of the note's execution. The note further stated that the Trust had the option to accelerate the debt and demand full payment if Service Business defaulted on any of its obligations under the note. The note did not specify a specific due date for the annual payments. In addition to this written agreement, Service Business alleged that Greenberg promised to execute a disclaimer of any interest he had as a beneficiary under the Trust. Greenberg denied that he ever made such an agreement.

By April, 1986, Service Business had made only one payment on the note, in the amount of $ 5,000. As a result of further negotiation between the parties, Greenberg executed a written disclaimer in favor of Service Computer under which Greenberg disclaimed any interest he might have through inheritance in the family jewelry. The disclaimer was conditioned on Service Business' payment of all past due amounts owing under the promissory note and upon its "timely payment" of all future installments. The disclaimer also failed to designate a specific date for the future annual payments. Thereafter, Service Business paid $ 43,231.86 on June 26, 1986, which included partial payment of the 1986 installment. On November 6, 1986, not having received the payment from Service Business which they considered due on October 29, 1986, plaintiffs sent Service Business a notice of their intention to accelerate payment of the note. On November 14, 1986, and again on October 29, 1987, Service Business tendered payment of the installment amount owing, calculated as of the anniversary date of the note. On both occasions, plaintiffs refused to accept the payments.

Plaintiffs brought this action to recover the accelerated amount of the principal and accrued interest under the note. In its answer, defendants raised several defenses, including waiver, estoppel, and lack of default under the terms of the note. Defendants also filed a counterclaim, alleging failure of consideration by virtue of Greenberg's refusal to execute a disclaimer of any interest in the Trust funds. Plaintiffs moved for summary judgment and, after a hearing, the district court granted partial summary judgment in their favor. The court found that the terms of the contract clearly designated the payments to be due on October 29th of each year, by virtue of the date of the note's execution and the fact that annual payments were calculated on the basis of a twenty-year amortization. The court further held that there were no material issues of fact as to waiver, estoppel, or default and found that Business Service had defaulted on its payment obligations, that the Trust had the right to accelerate the balance owing upon default, and that the Trust properly exercised its right to accelerate. The court ruled, however, that there were material issues of fact regarding the issue of whether Service Business received full consideration for the stock redemption agreement with the Trust because Greenberg allegedly failed to issue a disclaimer of any interest as beneficiary under the Trust. This last issue was presented to the jury, which returned a verdict in favor of Greenberg and the Trust.

On appeal, Service Business contends that there are several genuine issues of fact which precluded the granting of partial summary judgment. First, Service Business contends that it did not default on its obligations under the note because the document did not specify a date on which payment was due, and argues under Oklahoma law that payment was thereby due within a reasonable time. We disagree. Oklahoma statute dictates that contracts are to be interpreted according to the intent of the parties at the time the instrument was executed. Okla. Stat. tit. 15, §§ 152, 153 (1981). Intent must be determined by construing the contract as a whole, and the court must construe the contract so as to give effect to each provision. *Amoco Prod. Co. v. Lindley,* 609 P.2d 733, 741 (Okla. 1980). The language of the note setting the date of final payment as October 29, 1992, and the method for calculating the amount of annual payments clearly indicate that the parties intended that payments were to have been made on the anniversary date of the note.

Second, Service Business asserts that plaintiffs did not accelerate the note in good faith. Service Business claims the duty of good faith arises both under the Uniform Commercial Code (UCC), Okla.Stat. tit. 12A, § 1-208 (1981), and under the common law doctrine of good faith in the performance of a contract. Section 1-208 provides:

> A term providing that one party . . .may accelerate payment or performance or require collateral or additional collateral "at will" or "when he deems himself insecure" or in words of similar import shall be construed to mean that he shall have power to do so only if he in good faith believes that the prospect of payment or performance is impaired. The burden of establishing lack of good faith is on the party against whom the power has been exercised.

Id.; see also *Mitchell v. Ford Motor Credit Co.*, 688 P.2d 42, 44-45 (Okla. 1984) (acceleration by a secured party). In finding that plaintiffs properly exercised their power of acceleration, the district court implicitly found that the good faith requirement set forth in § 1-208 does not apply to notes that permit acceleration at the option of the holder upon default by the debtor. We agree.

The only Oklahoma case we have located which addresses the question of whether the good faith requirement under the U.C.C. applies to acceleration on default clauses is *Knittel v. Security State Bank, Mooreland, Okla.*, 593 P.2d 92 (Okla. 1979). The case did not directly address the issue; however, it upheld a challenged jury instruction which stated that the good faith requirement under § 1-208 did not apply to an acceleration on default clause. *Id.* at 97. Because a court must determine whether a challenged jury instruction properly states the applicable law, . . . it logically follows that *Knittel* supports the position that the U.C.C. good faith requirement does not apply to acceleration on default clauses.

Several states have similarly held that the U.C.C. good faith requirement is not applicable when the acceleration clause is based on an event in the debtor's complete control. . .. Because of the ruling in *Knittel* and the general consensus in other jurisdictions, we conclude that Oklahoma would not apply the good faith requirement in § 1-208 to the acceleration on default clause at issue in this case.

Service Business also claims that plaintiffs failed to perform their contract in good faith under common law equitable principles. Service Business relies on *Brown v. AVEMCO Inv. Corp.*, in which the Ninth Circuit applied the common law doctrine of good faith to a due-on-lease clause contained in a security agreement executed in conjunction with a promissory note.[2] 603 F.2d at 1375-79. In reversing a jury verdict in favor of the creditor, the court noted that, under Texas law, acceleration clauses are designed to protect a creditor from conduct or events that jeopardize or impair the creditor's security. *Id.* at 1376. The court held that the jury should have been instructed on the issue of the creditor's good faith in exercising the due-on-lease clause when evidence existed that it inequitably desired to take advantage of a technical default, not because it in good faith feared its security was impaired. *Id.* at 1379. This decision was based on Texas case law which clearly mandated that equitable considerations should be applied when a creditor exercises an optional right to accelerate for the sole purpose of receiving the entire payment rather than for the purpose of protecting its debt. *Id.* We must determine whether Oklahoma would likewise impose an equitable duty on a creditor to not use the power of acceleration when its security is not impaired.

The Oklahoma Supreme Court has ruled on two occasions that an acceleration clause contained in a mortgage will not be enforced where the conduct of the mortgagee has been unconscionable or inequitable. *Continental Fed. Sav. & Loan Ass'n v. Fetter,* 564 P.2d 1013, 1019 (Okla. 1977); *Murphy v. Fox,* 278 P.2d 820, 826 (Okla. 1955). In *Continental,* the court denied a bank's request to accelerate and foreclose on a mortgage based on a due-on-transfer clause when the bank refused to consent to a transfer solely because the mortgagor would not pay a substantial transfer fee. The transfer fee was an additional condition unilaterally imposed by the bank and was not

[2] Under the security agreement, the creditor, AVEMCO, had the option to accelerate the entire debt if the debtor leased the property, an airplane, without its written consent. In 1973, the debtor leased the airplane to a third party and also executed an option to purchase. The debtor sent notice of the agreement to AVEMCO. Two years later, the lessee exercised its option to purchase and tendered full payment of the remainder owing under the promissory note. AVEMCO, after two years of inaction, refused the tendered payment and instead exercised its option to accelerate under the due-on-lease clause but also demanded an additional sum for the cost of insurance premiums. After the debtor refused to pay the additional amount, AVEMCO repossessed the airplane and sold it for a higher profit. 603 F.2d at 1369.

contained in the original mortgage agreement. The court held the bank's conduct in demanding additional payment was unconscionable and denied its requested relief. 564 P.2d at 1019.

In *Murphy,* the court refused to permit a mortgagee to accelerate the maturity of a promissory note because the court found that the mortgagee had attempted to hinder timely payment by the mortgagor and had encouraged its default. 278 P.2d at 824. The court determined that this conduct was motivated solely by the mortgagee's desire to accelerate the maturity of the entire debt and held that the technical default of tendering late payment of taxes was insufficient to justify acceleration when the mortgagee had acted unconscionably. *Id.* at 826.

According to our reading of these cases, whether the Oklahoma court permits acceleration depends on the conduct of the mortgagee and whether he has dealt fairly with the debtor or has acted oppressively or unconscionably. This view is consistent with that of several other jurisdictions. See *Phipps v. First Fed. Sav. & Loan Ass'n*, 438 N.W.2d 814, 819 (S.D. 1989) (an acceleration clause will be enforced absent fraud, bad faith, or other conduct on part of the mortgagee which would make it unconscionable to enforce the clause); *Key Int'l Mfg., Inc. v. Stillman,* 103 A.D.2d 475, 480 N.Y.S.2d 528, 530 (1984) (absent some element of fraud, exploitative overreaching or unconscionable conduct by the creditor, the court should enforce an acceleration clause), aff'd as modified, 66 N.Y.2d 924, 489 N.E.2d 764, 498 N.Y.S.2d 795 (1985); *Bowen v. Danna,* 637 S.W.2d at 564 (a court in equity can relieve a debtor from the hardship of acceleration based on accident, mistake, fraud, or inequitable conduct of the creditor). . ..

Nothing in the record warrants an application of these equitable principles in the instant case. Plaintiffs did not exercise their option to accelerate after a considerable delay. Nor did the default concern a technical, secondary obligation such as payment of taxes.[3] Rather, the default violated the essence of the written agreement, timely payment of principal and interest. Finally, no evidence was presented that Greenberg attempted to hinder or otherwise cause the default so as to make his conduct unconscionable. Defendants had complete control over the event which triggered plaintiffs' right to accelerate. The mere fact that the plaintiffs' interest might not have been in jeopardy, without some misconduct on the part of the plaintiffs, does not warrant a refusal to enforce an acceleration clause which was a bargained-for element of the contract between the parties. Under the circumstances of this case, we conclude that there are no material issues of fact under the applicable Oklahoma law regarding the enforceability of the acceleration clause and the issue of good faith.

Service Business also asserts that plaintiffs waived their right to accelerate through their prior acceptance of late payments. Ordinarily, prior acceptance of late payments only waives the right to accelerate as to those past installments. *McGowan v. Pasol*, 605 S.W.2d 728, 732 (Tex. Civ. App. 1980). When a creditor establishes a prior course of dealing in accepting late payments, the creditor is estopped from declaring total debt due on future defaults. *Id.* Estoppel does not apply, however, when the obligor gives the debtor notice that the terms of the agreement will be enforced in the future. . .. Because Service Business or its officers received adequate notice by virtue of the disclaimer executed in April, 1986, that the trustees demanded all future payments to be made timely, no material issue of fact exists on the issue of waiver.

---

[3] In *Murphy,* the court discussed several cases from other jurisdictions which considered a technical default to be a failure to comply with a secondary obligation such as payment of taxes or assessments as opposed to a default on payment of principal or interest. See 278 P.2d at 825. Generally, these cases consider a default in payment of a principal or interest payment to be a substantial breach rather than a technical default. See *e.g., Graf v. Hope Bldg. Corp.,* 254 N.Y. 1, 171 N.E. 884, 885-86 (1930).

. . . .

The judgment of the United States District Court for the Western District of Oklahoma is AFFIRMED.

NOTES

Which case presents the better analysis and application of U.C.C. § 1-208? Are there flaws in either court's logic? Do you agree with Professors White and Summers that an objective standard of good faith should apply to acceleration clauses? Should the debtor be able to prove that the secured party did not act in good faith by simply establishing that the secured party did not observe *reasonable* commercial standards? Or, should the debtor have to prove that the secured party did not have an *honest belief* that there was an impairment in its security? The Code definition of good faith is "honesty in fact." Some courts have interpreted this language to mean that the test is a subjective one and that the honest belief or insecurity of the secured party controls. What *should* the Code require as a condition for acceleration based on insecurity?

§ 19.04 Taking Possession

Read: U.C.C. § 9-503; see also § 9-502(1).

If there is a breach of the security agreement, the secured party has a right to take the collateral from the debtor, or to render equipment inoperative, or to require under a clause in the security agreement that the debtor assemble the collateral and make it available to the secured party. The taking of possession is often called "repossession" since it can involve a re-taking of goods by a seller who had the items originally, and who provided credit.

Whether there has been a default of a single payment or the total amount, the secured party has a right to take possession of the goods. In taking possession, the Code provides that this may be done without any additional process "if this can be done without breach of the peace." The underlying purpose is to permit the secured party to take the goods without the expense of any legal proceeding or action in cases where there will not be any difficulty.

Under some agreements, the secured party may require the debtor to assemble the collateral and make it available to him at the designated place. In this situation, the collateral usually consists of a number of items from different places. Businesses or commercial activity are usually involved. Such a provision is validated by the Code.

Where heavy equipment is the collateral, repossession of the secured interest property may not be the most feasible means of enforcement. In such situations, the Code permits a secured party to render the equipment unusable through the removal of a part or other similar means. It also permits a secured party to dispose of the collateral by private or public sale on the debtor's premises.

One purpose of U.C.C. § 9-503 is to permit the seller to retake the goods where there is either consent or acquiescence to the retaking. In such circumstances, it may be to the benefit of both parties. The creditor saves the costs and time connected with a more formal or judicially authorized repossession. Self–help repossession also ultimately benefits the borrower since it reduces the costs reflected in a deficiency judgment.

In other situations, however, there may be a dispute as to the underlying contract or security agreement. The debtor may assert that he is not in default. He may have some defenses based on the quality of the goods or on other conduct of the seller or lender. In such cases, the debtor may be unwilling to give up possession of the goods. Disputes may arise as to whether a "breach of peace" has occurred in the self-help repossession by the creditor. The courts have been faced with considering what actually constitutes a "breach of peace."

DAVENPORT v. CHRYSLER CREDIT CORP.

Court of Appeals of Tennessee, Middle Section
818 S.W.2d 23, 15 U.C.C. Rep. Serv. 2d 324 (1991)

KOCH, JUDGE.

This appeal stems from the repossession of a new automobile shortly after its purchase. The buyers filed an action in the Circuit Court for Montgomery County seeking statutory and punitive damages. The trial court, sitting without a jury, found that the repossession was proper and awarded the creditor a $6,774 deficiency judgment on its counterclaim. The debtors have appealed, asserting that the automobile should not have been repossessed and that the repossession was carried out improperly. We find that the repossession was carried out improperly and, therefore, reverse the judgment.

I.

Larry and Debbie Davenport purchased a new 1987 Chrysler LeBaron from Gary Mathews Motors on October 28, 1987. They obtained financing through Chrysler Credit Corporation ("Chrysler Credit") and signed a retail installment contract requiring them to make the first of sixty monthly payments on or before December 8, 1987.

The automobile developed mechanical problems before the Davenports could drive it off the dealer's lot. Even before their first payment was due, the Davenports had returned the automobile to the dealer seven times for repair. They were extremely dissatisfied and, after consulting a lawyer, decided to withhold their monthly payments until the matter was resolved.

Chrysler Credit sent the Davenports a standard delinquency notice when their first payment was ten days late. The Davenports did not respond to the notice, and on December 23, 1987, Chrysler Credit telephoned the Davenports to request payment. Mrs. Davenport recounted the problems with the automobile and told Chrysler Credit that she would consult her lawyer and "would let them know about the payment." After consulting the dealer, Chrysler Credit informed Mrs. Davenport that it would repossess the automobile if she did not make the payment.

Chrysler Credit telephoned the Davenports on December 30, 1987 because their first payment was three weeks late. Mr. Davenport told Chrysler Credit that he had turned the matter over to his lawyer and that he was not going to make the payment. Chrysler Credit telephoned again on January 7, 1988. On this occasion, Mrs. Davenport stated that their lawyer had instructed them to make the payment, and Chrysler Credit requested her to send the payment to its Brentwood office.

Chrysler Credit telephoned the Davenports one last time on January 13, 1988. It had still not received their first payment, and their second payment was five days past due. Mrs. Davenport insisted that she had mailed one payment[4] and added that she "was not responsible for the mail." Before hanging up abruptly, she also stated that she did not intend to make any more payments "on the advice of her attorney." At this point, Chrysler Credit determined that the Davenports were in default and requested American Lender Service Company to repossess the car.

Employees of American Lender Service arrived at the Davenports' home on the evening of January 14, 1988. They informed the Davenports that they were "two payments in default" and requested the automobile. The Davenports insisted that they were not in default and, after a telephone call to their lawyer, refused to turn over the automobile until Chrysler Credit obtained the "proper paperwork." The American Lender Service employees left without the car.

Before leaving for work the next morning, Mr. Davenport parked the automobile in their enclosed garage and chained its rear end to a post using a logging chain and two padlocks. He also closed the canvas flaps covering the entrance to the garage and secured the flaps with cinder blocks. When the Davenports returned from work, they discovered that someone had entered the garage, cut one of the padlocks, and removed the automobile.

American Lender Service informed Chrysler Credit on January 18, 1988, that it had repossessed the automobile. On the same day, Chrysler Credit notified the Davenports that they could redeem the car before it was offered for sale. The Davenports never responded to the notice. Instead of selling the automobile immediately, Chrysler Credit held it for more than a year because of the Davenports' allegations that the automobile was defective. In July, 1989, Chrysler Credit informed the Davenports that the automobile had been sold and requested payment of the $6,774 deficiency.

II.

We need not tarry long with the Davenports' claim that Chrysler Credit had no basis to repossess the automobile or to accelerate their debt. We disagree. The proof supports the trial court's conclusions that Chrysler Credit had a legal right to initiate repossession procedures.

The Davenports were already two months delinquent when Chrysler Credit decided to repossess the automobile. In fact, they had not made a single payment since they bought the automobile despite Chrysler Credit's repeated requests. Even through Chrysler Credit had warned them of the risk of repossession, the Davenports steadfastly refused to make their monthly payments until their complaints about the automobile were resolved.

The Davenports' dissatisfaction with their automobile did not provide them with a basis to unilaterally refuse to honor their payment obligations in the retail installment contract. At the time the repossession took place, the Davenports had not requested rescission of the contract, attempted to revoke their acceptance of the automobile, pursued their remedies under the "lemon law," or taken any other formal steps to resolve their dispute with the dealer concerning the

[4] Chrysler Credit received the Davenports' first payment on January 18, 1988 and the second payment on January 23, 1988. Even though the check for the second payment was dated January 8, 1988, its envelope was post-marked January 21, 1988.

automobile. The Davenports' conduct gave Chrysler Credit an adequate basis to consider the loan to be in default and to decide to protect its collateral by repossessing the automobile.

III.

We now consider whether the repossession of the Davenports' automobile was consistent with Tenn. Code Ann. § 47-9-503(1979). The trial court determined that it was, relying on *Harris Truck & Trailer Sales v. Foote,* 58 Tenn. App. 710, 436 S.W.2d 460 (1968). We disagree, but only because *Harris Truck & Trailer Sales v. Foote* improperly restricts the scope of the protection Tenn. Code Ann. § 47-9-503 affords to buyers of consumer goods.

A.

Tennessee has long recognized that secured parties have a legitimate interest in obtaining their collateral from a defaulting debtor. Prior to the Uniform Commercial Code, secured parties could repossess collateral either with or without the assistance of the courts. *Rice v. Lusaky Furniture Co.*, 167 Tenn. 202, 205, 678 S.W.2d 107, 108 (1934). If they chose to proceed without judicial assistance, they were required to obtain the debtor's consent. *Nashville Auto Sales Co. v. Wright,* 26 Tenn. App. 326 329, 171 S.W.2d 834, 835 (1943)., and to proceed without a breach of the peace. *Morrison v. Galyon Sales Co.,* 16 Tenn. App. 394, 397, 64 S.W.2d 851, 853 (1932).

The General Assembly preserved the secured parties' self-held remedies when it enacted the Uniform Commercial Code in 1963. It also preserved the requirement that repossessions must be accomplished without breach of the peace. Tenn. Code Ann. § 47-9-503 states in this regard that "[i]n taking possession a secured party may proceed without judicial process if this can be done without breach of the peace or may proceed by action."

B.

Tennessee's version of the Uniform Commercial Code does not define "breach of the peace." Like the U.C.C.'s drafters, the General Assembly decided that this task should be left to the courts. *Riley State Bank v. Spillman,* 242 Kan. 696, 750 P.2d 1024, 1029 (1988); 2 J. White & R. Summers, Uniform Commercial Code § 27-6(3d ed. 1988) (hereinafter "White & Summers"). Thus, it falls to us to determine what types of conduct the General Assembly intended to proscribe when it decided in 1963 that repossessions must be accomplished without a breach of the peace..

Our role in construing status is to ascertain legislative intent and then to carry it out. *Westinghouse Elec. Corp. v. King,* 678 S.W.2d 19, 23 (Tenn. 1984), cert. denied, 470 U.S. 1075, 105 S.Ct. 1830, 85 L.Ed.2d 131 (1985); *Dorrier v. Ark,* 540 S.W.2d 658, 659 (Tenn. 1976). As we go about our task, we must take care not to unduly restrict the statute's coverage or to expand it beyond its intended scope. See *United States. v. Bacto-Unidisk,* 394 U.S. 784, 800-01, 89 S.Ct. 1410, 1419, 22 L.Ed.2d 726, reh. denied, 395 U.S. 954, 89 S.Ct. 2013, 23 L.Ed. 2d 473 (1969).

The courts have many interpretational techniques available to them. We may conduct a textual analysis, giving the words in the statute their natural and ordinary meaning. *State v. Williams,* 690 S.W.2d 517, 529 (Tenn. 1985). We may analyze the statute in light of other related statutes. *Westinghouse Elec. Corp. v. King,* 678 S.W.2d at 23; *Coleman v. Acuff,* 569 S.W.2d 459, 461 (Tenn. 1978). We may also analyze a statute in light of earlier judicial interpretations of the statute itself or similar statutes. . ..

No one interpretational tool is inherently more preferable to the others. Thus, the courts should bring all applicable rules of construction to bear in order to elucidate a statute's meaning. *O.H. May Co. v. Anderson,* 156 Tenn. 216, 219, 300 S.W.12, 14 (1927).

C.

Any modern interpretation of the "breach of the peace" restriction in Tenn. Code Ann. § 47-9-503 must take into consideration (1) the Uniform Commercial Code's own rules of construction, (2) the Code's intent to adopt the common law where appropriate, and (3) this court's decision in *Harris Truck & Trailer Sales v. Foote,* 58 Tenn. App. 710, 436 S.W.2d 460 (1968).

The Uniform Commercial Code contains its own rules of construction. Tenn. Code Ann. § 47-1-102(2). . .. We cannot achieve the Code's objective of uniformity by ignoring other jurisdictions' construction of uniform laws. See *Holiday Inns, Inc. v. Olsen,* 692 S.W.2d 850, 853 (Tenn. 1985). While we should not blindly follow precedents from other jurisdictions, we should seriously consider them and should adopt them when they are harmonious with this State's public policy.

Statutes do not alter the common law any further than they expressly declare or necessarily require. *In re Deskins' Estates,* 214 Tenn. 608, 611, 381 S.W.2d 921, 922 (1964); *Linder v. Metropolitan Life Ins. Co.,* 148 Tenn. 236, 243-44, 255 S.W. 43, 45 (1923). Thus, courts will give statutory terms their well-recognized common law meaning as long as doing so is consistent with the remainder of the statute and is harmonious with its general purpose.

. . . .

Section 9-503 of the Uniform Commercial Code does not embody new rights or obligations. *Salisbury Livestock Co v. Colorado Cent. Credit Union,* 793 P.2d 470, 473 (Wyo. 1990). The Code's drafters used the phrase "breach of the peace" because they intended to codify the common law's restrictions on self-help. . ..

There is a dearth of Tennessee authority concerning the meaning of "breach of the peace" as it appears in Tenn. Code Ann. § 47-9-503. The only reported case, decided over twenty years ago, involved the repossession of an unoccupied truck that the owner had left in a third-arty's open parking lot. This court held:

> We think the legislative intent in the enactment of T.C.A. section 47-9-503, in using the words "if this can be done without breach of the peace", contemplated that the breach of the peace there referred to must involve some violence, or at least threat of violence. *Harris Truck & Trailer Sales v. Foote,* 58 Tenn. App. at 718, 436 S.W.2d at 464.

We have determined that the *Harris* court improperly narrowed the scope of Tenn. Code Ann. § 47-9-503 by requiring that a repossession must be accompanied by violence or a threat of violence in order to be considered a breach of the peace. Its interpretation of "breach of the peace" is inconsistent with the common law and with the Supreme Court's earlier interpretations of the term.

D.

The term "breach of the peace" is a generic term that includes all violations or potential violations of the public peace and order. . . .. It includes all unlawful acts and acts of public indecorum that disturb or tend to disturb the public peace or good order. *State ex rel. Thompson v. Reichman,* 135 Tenn. 685, 700-01, 188 S.W. 597, 601 (1916) ("*Reichman II*"); *Galvin v. State,* 46 Tenn. (6 Cold.) 283, 294 (1869).

While breaches of the peace frequently involve offenses against individuals, they also include offenses against the public at large or the State. *Reichman II,* 135 Tenn. at 702, 188 S.W. at 602. The term "peace" means

> The tranquility enjoyed by citizens of a municipality or community where good order reigns among its members, or, that individual sense of security which every [person] feels so necessary to his [or her] comfort, and for which all governments are instituted. *Reichman II,* 135 Tenn. at 701, 188 S.W. at 601.

Offenses against individuals, generally criminal offenses, must be accompanied by violence or a threat of violence in order to be considered a breach of the peace. However conduct that is "incompatible with the tranquility and good order which governments are organized to maintain" need not involve violence or a threat of violence in order to be considered a breach of the peace. *Reichman II,* 135 Tenn. at 702, 188 S.W. at 602.

We can find no support the *Harris* court's decision to circumscribe Tenn. Code Ann. § 47-9-503 by limiting "breach of the peace" to its criminal context. The Code's drafters intended the term to have a broader meaning. . .. Thus, neither violence, the threat of violence, nor personal confrontation is necessary in order for a secured party's conduct to amount to a breach of the peace under Tenn. Code Ann. § 47-9-503. . ..

E.

Secured parties may repossess their collateral at a reasonable time and in a reasonable manner. See Restatement (Second) of Torts § 183 (1976). Thus, determining whether a particular secured creditor's conduct amounts to a breach of the peace requires a review of the reasonableness of the secured party's conduct in light of the facts of the case.

Professors White and Summers have recommended that the inquiry should take into consideration (1) where the repossession took place, (2) the debtor's express or constructive consent, (3) the reactions of third parties, (4) the type of premises entered, and (5) the creditor's use of deception. See White & Summers § 27-6, at 575-76.

Public policy favors peaceful, non-trespassory repossessions when the secured party has a free right of entry. *Trevino v. Castellow Chevrolet-Oldsmobile, Inc.,* 680 S.W.2d 71, 74 (Tex. Ct. App. 1984). However, forced entries onto the debtor's property or into the debtor's premises are viewed as seriously detrimental to the ordinary conduct of human affairs. . .. Accordingly, courts have consistently found that repossessions accomplished by breaking locks or cutting chains are inconsistent with the Uniform Commercial Code. *Laurel Coal Co. v. Walter E. Heller & Co.,* 539 F. Supp. 1006, 1007 (W.D. Penn. 1982) (chain on fence cut); *Henderson v. Security Nat'l Bank,* 72 Cal. App. 3d 764, 140 Cal. Rptr. 388, 3891 (1977) (garage door lock broken); *Riley State Bank v. Spillman,* 750 P.2d at 1030 (locksmith opened locked door); *General Elec. Credit Corp. v. Timbrook,* 291 S.E.2d at 385 (door lock on mobile home broken).

The courts have also disapproved of repossessions in which the secured party or its agent entered the debtor's closed premises without permission, *Oaklawn Bank v. Baldwin,* 289 Ark. 79, 709 S.W.2d 91, 92 (1986) (no entry through gates, doors or other barricades); *Raffa v. Dania Bank,* 321 So.2d 83, 85 (Fla. Dist. Ct. App. 1975) (no entry into home or other closed building);

Bloomquist v. First Nat'l Bank, 378 N.W.2d at 86 (entry through broken window), and repossessions causing damage to the debtor's property. *Ford Motor Credit Co. v. Herring,* 267 Ark. 201, 589 S.W.2d 584, 586 (1979); *Quest v. Barnett Bank,* 397 So.2d 1020, 1024 (Fla. Dist. Ct. App. 1981). These decisions, and others like them, have prompted Professors White and Summers to observe that "a breach of the peace is almost certain to be found if the repossession is accompanied by the unauthorized entry into a closed or locked garage." See White & Summers § 27-6, at 577 n.11.

F.

Self-help procedures such as repossession are the product of a careful balancing of the interests of secured parties and debtors. On one hand, secured creditors have a legitimate interest in obtaining possession of collateral without resorting to expensive and sometimes cumbersome judicial procedures. On the other hand, debtors have a legitimate interest in being free from unwarranted invasions of their property and privacy interests. . ..

Repossession is a harsh procedure and is, essentially, a delegation of the State's exclusive prerogative to resolve disputes.[5] Accordingly, the statutes governing the repossession of collateral should be construed in a way that prevents abuse and discourages illegal conduct which might otherwise go unchallenged because of the debtor's lack of knowledge of legally proper repossession techniques. *Steichen v. First Bank Grand,* 372 N.W.2d 768, 773 (Minn. Ct. App. 1985).

American Lender Service's repossession of the Davenports' automobile was not accompanied by violence or the threat of violence because the Davenports were not at home at the time. However, Chrysler Credit and American Sender Service do not dispute that they obtained the automobile by entering a closed garage and by cutting a lock on a chain that would have prevented them from removing the automobile. Despite the absence of violence or physical confrontation, entering the closed garage and cutting the lock amounted to a breach of the peace. Thus, unlike the trial court, we find that the manner in which the Davenports' automobile was repossessed was inconsistent with the requirements Tenn. Code Ann. § 47-9-503 places on secured parties who are repossessing collateral from defaulting debtors.

NOTES

(1) What alternative did the "repo people" have in *Davenport*? What about the debtor? Should the courts articulate a debtor's "zone of expected privacy"? For example, if property is kept within such a zone, the creditor could exercise repossession only with notice and the debtor's consent. What acts would constitute effective notice of either the creditor's intent to repossess or the debtor's expected no-seizure zone? A padlocked garage doesn't seem to be a difficult case. However, should a creditor be prohibited from self-help repossession if a debtor offers resistance in a less tangible way?

[5] See *Fuentes v. Shevin,* 407 U.S. 67, 93, 92 S.Ct. 1983, 2000-01, 32 L.Ed.2d 556 (1972); *Hilliman v. Cobado,* 499 N.Y.S.2d at 614.

In *Williams v. Ford Motor Credit Co.,* 674 F.2d 717 (8th Cir. 1982), the creditor repossessed an automobile at 4:30 a.m. from one Cathy Williams, a mother of two small children who lived in a house trailer. Williams's former husband, who had been required by the divorce court to make payments on the car, defaulted on the obligation and then signed a voluntary repossession authorization. Ms. Williams knew of the default and was in the process of trying to get her former husband to resume payments. When she heard noise outside her trailer, Williams emerged to find two repo men towing her car away. She managed to catch the men's attention and told them that she was attempting to bring the payments up to date. When the men were unmoved, Williams asked if she could remove her personal effects from the car. The men gave her the personal items and then drove off with the car, "without further complaint from Williams." A jury awarded Williams $5000 in damages for conversion, but the trial court entered a judgment notwithstanding the verdict, holding that no reasonable jury could find a breach of the peace under the facts. The Eighth Circuit affirmed the judgment n.o.v. decision, noting that the repossession did not present a situation likely to provoke violence. Would the result have been different if Ms. Williams had simply shouted "stop!"? For an interesting twist on resisting repossession see *James v. Ford Motor Credit,* 842 F. Supp. 1202 (D. Minn. 1994) (held: specific objection revoked any ability of creditor to repossess car on debtor's property without debtor's consent; however, no breach of peace where car repossession occurred in a public parking lot).

(2) Does repossession after an act of resistance constitute a breach of the peace even when there is no contact or confrontation between the repossessor and the debtor at the time and place of repossession? Consider the following excerpt from *Wade v. Ford Motor Credit Co.,* 668 P.2d 183 (Kan. Ct. App. 1983):

> . . . Wade entered into an automobile retail installment contract on August 9, 1979, for the purchase of a 1979 Ford Thunderbird automobile. The contract was assigned to Ford which advanced $ 6,967.75 enabling her to purchase the car. Pursuant to the terms of the contract, Ford had a security interest in the car which had been fully perfected. Wade contracted to pay Ford forty-eight equal monthly installments of $ 194.52 commencing September 8, 1979. Wade was late with these payments right from the start. The following illustrates her payment record:
>
> | Payment Due: | Payment Made: |
> |---|---|
> | September 8, 1979 | September 17, 1979 |
> | October 8, 1979 | October 23, 1979 |
> | November 8, 1979 | January 18, 1980 |
> | December 8, 1979 | February 14, 1980 |
> | January 8, 1980 | March 4, 1980 |
>
> No other payments were made.
>
> On December 6, 1979, Ford mailed Wade a notice of her default and of her right to cure the default. . .. It was returned to Ford several days later marked "Return to sender, moved, left no address." Wade had moved and not notified Ford of a new address. . ... The trial court found that Ford had complied with the statutory notice requirements precedent to repossession.
>
> Collection efforts continued after the mailing of the above notice. After communication with Wade, a payment was received and promises of additional payments were made. With the account still in arrears, Ford assigned it on February 4, 1980, to the Kansas Recovery Bureau, a subsidiary of Denver Recovery Bureau, as independent contractors to repossess the car.

On or about February 10, 1980, in the early afternoon, David Philhower, an employee of Kansas Recovery Bureau, located the car in the driveway of Wade's residence. He had a key for the car, so he unlocked the door, got in and started it. Philhower then noticed an apparent discrepancy between the serial number of the car and that listed in his papers. He shut the engine off, got out and locked the car door. At that time Wade appeared at the door of her house. Philhower told her that he had been sent there by Ford to repossess the car, and she replied that he was not going to take it because she had made the payments on it. She invited him in the house to prove her claim, but was unable to locate the cancelled checks and receipts for the payments made. Philhower told her of the serial number discrepancy, and stated that he was not going to take the car until he confirmed the number, and advised her to contact Ford to straighten out the problem.

Wade then told him that if he came back to get the car that she had a gun in the house, which she had obtained because of several burglaries in the area, and she would not hesitate to use it. She then called a representative of Ford and stated she had a gun and that if she caught anyone on her property again trying to take her car, that "I would leave him laying right where I saw him."

Ford then received two more payments, the last being received March 4, 1980. On March 5, 1980, Ford reassigned the account to Kansas Recovery Bureau for repossession. In the early morning hours of March 10, 1980, at around 2:00 a.m., Philhower made another attempt to repossess the car from the driveway of Wade's residence. This time he was successful. Wade heard a car "burning rubber" at around 2:00 a.m., looked out the window, and discovered her car missing. There was no confrontation between Wade and Philhower, since Wade was not even aware of the fact her car was being repossessed until after Philhower had safely left the area in the car. Upon calling the police, Wade was informed that her car had been repossessed. Philhower had informed the police just prior to the repossession that he was going to recover the car in case they received reports of a prowler.

Wade subsequently brought an action against Ford for wrongful repossession, conversion and loss of credit, and sought both actual and punitive damages, along with attorney fees. Ford filed a counterclaim for breach of contract, seeking the deficiency of $2,953.44 remaining after the car was sold at public auction. . ..

The trial court found that Ford had breached the peace in repossessing Wade's car. . . .. the trial court emphasized Wade's lack of consent to the repossession and stated:

> [I]n no way did she consent at no time did she consent to the peaceful recovery of the security, namely, one automobile that she kept and maintained on her private property, namely, that of her residence. The plaintiff, having threatened Mr. Philhower, the recovery agent, with bodily harm through the use of a lethal weapon known as a revolver, having informed Mr. Philhower never to enter her property again, otherwise she would shoot him. So, that being the last communication between Philhower and the plaintiff, at a later date when it was a month or so later, I don't recall since this hearing was seven months ago, Mr. Philhower, after that initial confrontation at 2:00 o'clock in the morning, 1:00 in the morning, quietly entered this private property, in effect, in this Court's opinion, taking the law in its own hands, come what may.

. . . These facts violate every principle of civilized procedures that is understood as to why we have the courts and why we have the law to avoid confrontations between parties to avoid dangers to life, limb, and property. It's an orderly process that we seek to serve in this case.

The trial court also emphasized the potential for violence brought on by Wade's threats made during the first repossession attempt. A breach of the peace may be caused by an act likely to produce violence. The facts presented in this case do not, however, rise to that level. A period of one month elapsed between the repossession attempts. During that period, Wade and Ford were in communication and two payments were made. We find the potential for violence was substantially reduced by the passage of this time. Moreover, the actual repossession was effected without incident. The time of the repossession was such that in all likelihood no confrontation would materialize. In fact, Wade was totally unaware of the repossession until after Philhower had successfully left the premises with the car. We therefore find that as a matter of law there was no breach of the peace in the repossession of Wade's car.

The trial court's judgment finding a breach of the peace is reversed, and the case is remanded for a modification of the award of damages in accordance with this opinion.

Do you agree with the appeals court decision in *Wade*? Both *Wade* and *Williams* involved repossession in the early hours of the morning. Stirring around a person's residence at night seems to be an occasion ripe with peril. How would you react to a court-crafted "per se" rule prohibiting repossessions between dusk and dawn so as to prevent possible acts of violence?

(3) What result if the creditor assumes a disguise as a means of tricking the debtor into surrendering possession?

In *Stone Machinery v. Kessler*, 1 Wash. App. 750, 463 P.2d 651 (1970), the secured party located the collateral (a tractor) in a neighboring state. When the debtor threatened violence if the creditor attempted repossession, the creditor contacted the local sheriff and asked the officer to accompany the creditor. After looking over the contract and security agreement, the sheriff agreed to accompany the repo people to the debtor's location. The sheriff was in uniform, wore a badge, and carried a sidearm. Upon arrival, the sheriff informed the debtor that the creditor had a right to repossess, "[w]e come to pick up the tractor." The debtor asked whether the sheriff had proper papers to take the tractor and the sheriff answered "no." The debtor protested the repossession but offered no physical resistance because he didn't think he could ignore an order from a sheriff.

Though the peace officer was a government official, he had no authority to repossess. Thus, even though the creditor and the sheriff acted to prevent the possibility of the threatened violence, the court found that the sheriff actively participated in the seizure and held for the debtor. The effect of the sheriff's presence "was to prevent the defendant . . . from exercising his right to resist by all lawful and reasonable means a non-judicial take-over."

(4) Not all refusals to surrender property are inappropriate. Keep in mind that there may be some situations where the debtor may deny that it is in default, or may have a legal defense against the attempted repossession. In such cases, the debtor may be unwilling to surrender possession of the goods.

(5) *A Bankruptcy Note*. Once a debtor files a petition for bankruptcy, an automatic stay puts a "freeze" upon the property, and repossession by the security interest holder is no longer possible. Any attempt to repossess would be in contempt of court. The automatic stay prevents creditors

from rushing in and taking the debtor's assets and provides for orderly administration in bankruptcy.

§ 19.05 Constitutional Considerations

Read: Fourteenth Amendment, U.S. Constitution.

There have been several constitutional challenges to self-help repossession. During the 1970s, there were four United States Supreme Court decisions on the constitutionality of state prejudgment creditor remedies. Those cases fashioned guidelines on what judicial procedures under state law could be made available to creditors in their efforts to seize a debtor's assets extra-judicially. The concern over procedural due process carried over to Article 9 with debtor challenges to secured creditor repossession under section 9-503. Most courts rejected the due process argument because self-help usually does not involve state action—a prerequisite for due process review. Nevertheless, some debtors continued to raise denial of due process claims. The next case provides a useful discussion of the issue.

DEL'S BIG SAVER FOODS, INC. v. CARPENTER COOK, INC.

United States District Court, Wester District of Wisconsin
603 F. Supp. 1071, 40 U.C.C. Rep. 1924 (1985)

CRABB, CHIEF JUDGE.

. . . .

FACTS

Before December of 1983, plaintiffs Burdell and Janice Robish owned and operated Del's Big Saver Foods, Inc., a retail grocery store. In July of 1983, in order to finance their business, the plaintiffs individually and as officers of their incorporated store, signed a note and security agreement, giving defendant Carpenter Cook Company, a subsidiary of defendant Farm House Foods Corporation, a security interest in "all furniture, fixtures, equipment, now owned or hereafter acquired by the borrower, together with all inventory . . . [and] the proceeds from the sale thereof."

On December 6, 1983, the defendant law firm of Doyle, Ladd & Philips, P.C. filed a complaint in the Circuit Court of Vilas County, Wisconsin on behalf of defendant Carpenter Cook, alleging among other things that Burdell and Janis Robish had repeatedly defaulted on their note, that Carpenter Cook had a security interest in some of the Robishes' property, and that pursuant to Wis. Stats. § 409.503 (Wisconsin's Commercial Code), Carpenter Cook was entitled to possession of the property. Along with the complaint, defendant Carpenter Cook submitted an affidavit in support of its motion for possession of the secured property. In the affidavit, Philip Strohl, an officer of Carpenter Cook, stated that the Robishes had defaulted repeatedly on their loan and had breached other covenants of the security agreement. Strohl asserted that the collateral would deteriorate in the hands of the Robishes. Also, Strohl stated the value of the collateral and its location. Defendant Carpenter Cook submitted to the court a $100,000 indemnity bond issued by defendant United States Fidelity & Guaranty Company.

On December 6, 1983, the day the complaint was filed in the Vilas County court, the state trial judge issued an order granting defendant Carpenter Cook immediate possession of the collateral, the right to operate the Robishes' store as a going concern, and the right to use the proceeds from the sale of the collateral "in the operation of the store." That same day, defendant Strohl, as agent for defendant Carpenter Cook, with the aid of the defendant law firm, obtained certification of the order from the deputy clerk of the Circuit Court of Vilas County. Members of the defendant law firm then proceeded to plaintiffs' store, claiming that if plaintiffs did not turn over possession of the store, the county sheriff would be summoned pursuant to the court order to serve the documents and remove the plaintiffs bodily. In response to these demands, plaintiffs turned over the premises to defendant Carpenter Cook.

Plaintiffs had no notice of defendant Carpenter Cook's intent to take possession of the store, or of the court proceedings to gain possession, until the order was presented to them on December 6, 1983. Plaintiffs would not have relinquished possession of the store but for the court order signed by the circuit judge.

OPINION

. . . In sum, plaintiffs have alleged two causes of action: (1) that in concert with defendants Carpenter Cook (through its agent Strohl) and Doyle, Ladd and Philips, the state trial judge applied Wisconsin's repossession procedures in violation of plaintiffs' due process rights; and (2) that these same defendants intentionally damaged plaintiffs' business reputation in violation of state law. Plaintiffs alleged no cause of action against defendant United States Fidelity & Guaranty Company and its motion to dismiss will be granted.

Plaintiff's Claim under 42 U.S.C. § 1983

Before a plaintiff can prevail on a claim brought pursuant to 42 U.S.C. § 1983, he must prove (1) that the defendant has deprived him of a right secured by the Constitution or the laws of the United States; and (2) that the defendant has deprived him of this right under color of state law. *Adickes v. S.H. Kress & Co.*, 398 U.S. 144, 26 L. Ed. 2d 142, 90 S. Ct. 1598 (1970).

I. Deprivation of a Constitutional Right

Plaintiffs contend that the state judge's application of Wis. Stats. § 409.503 to them deprived them of their Fourteenth Amendment right to due process because their property was taken without notice or an opportunity to contest the repossession. Plaintiffs cite the line of Supreme Court cases beginning with *Sniadach v. Family Finance Corp.*, 395 U.S. 337, 23 L. Ed. 2d 349, 89 S. Ct. 1820 (1969) and culminating in *North Georgia Finishing, Inc. v. Di-Chem, Inc.*, 419 U.S. 601, 42 L. Ed. 2d 751, 95 S. Ct. 719 (1975), for the proposition that it is a denial of due process for a creditor to repossess property upon ex parte application to a court without giving the debtor notice or an opportunity to contest the taking. Not surprisingly, the defendants cite those same cases to support their claim that plaintiffs in this case have not been denied their constitutional rights.

1. Due Process Precedent

Sniadach arose out of a challenge to a Wisconsin statute permitting a creditor to freeze the debtor's wages upon application to the clerk of the state court without affording the debtor notice or an opportunity to be heard. The United States Supreme Court ruled that in the context of wages a debtor's property may not be taken without notice and a prior hearing. *Sniadach v. Family Finance Corp.,* 395 U.S. at 340-342.

In *Fuentes v. Shevin,* 407 U.S. 67, 32 L. Ed. 2d 556, 92 S. Ct. 1983 (1972), the Court reviewed a state procedure under which a creditor could obtain a prejudgment writ of replevin through a summary process of ex parte application to a court clerk, upon the posting of a bond for double the value of the property to be seized. The Supreme Court held that these state replevin procedures were unconstitutional because they deprived the debtor of notice and an opportunity to be heard before his property was seized. *Id.* at 96. The Court explained that even though the debtor had access to certain post-deprivation remedies, those remedies were only "another factor to weigh in determining the appropriate form of hearing, [and were] not decisive of the basic right to a prior hearing of some kind." *Id.* at 86.

In *Mitchell v. W.T. Grant Co.,* 416 U.S. 600, 40 L. Ed. 2d 406, 94 S. Ct. 1895 (1974), the Court retreated from its position in *Fuentes*. In *Mitchell*, the Court was reviewing provisions of the Louisiana Code of Civil Procedure that made available to a lien holder a writ of sequestration to forestall waste or alienation of the encumbered property. Although the writ was obtainable on the creditor's ex parte application, without notice to the debtor or an opportunity for a hearing, the writ would issue only upon a detailed affidavit by the creditor and only upon a judge's authorization after the creditor had filed a sufficient bond. The debtor could seek immediate dissolution of the writ, which had to be ordered unless the creditor proved the grounds for issuance (existence of the debt, lien, and delinquency), failing which the court could order return of the property and assess damages in the debtor's favor. The Court found that the Louisiana procedures satisfied the requirements of the due process clause despite the fact that they permitted an ex parte deprivation of property: the statutory scheme decreased the likelihood of an erroneous pre-hearing deprivation because the creditor had to present detailed factual allegations to a judicial officer before a sequestration order could be issued, *Id.* at 616-617, and statutory procedures did not effect a final deprivation of property because the debtor had an immediate right to a post-seizure hearing. *Id.* at 609-610. From this, the Court concluded that because the statute provided certain pre-deprivation procedures designed to reduce erroneous deprivations, and because the deprivation was only temporary, the Louisiana procedures effected a constitutional accommodation of the interests of debtors and creditors. *Id.* at 607.

Finally, in *North Georgia Finishing, Inc. v. Di-Chem, Inc.,* 419 U.S. at 601, the Supreme Court examined a Georgia statutory scheme that permitted a creditor to obtain a writ of garnishment issued by a court clerk on an affidavit containing only conclusory allegations and that permitted the debtor to dissolve the garnishment only by filing a bond with the court. The Court held that the garnishment of the debtor's bank account was unconstitutional because there were no pre-deprivation protections as in *Mitchell,* and because the debtor was not entitled to an immediate hearing after seizure to dissolve the writ. *Id.* at 607.

From these cases, I conclude that in creditor repossession or garnishment cases, the due process clause requires either (1) that the debtor be provided a hearing before his property is taken, or (2) that the debtor be provided certain pre-seizure procedural safeguards, coupled with a prompt post-deprivation hearing before final judgment. Those pre-seizure safeguards need not include a hearing, but must include a deprivation order issuable only by a judicial officer based upon detailed factual allegations provided by the party seeking possession.

In this case, since I must accept as true plaintiffs' allegation that they did not receive a hearing prior to the seizure of their property, I can grant defendants' motion for summary judgment only if I am satisfied that plaintiffs had the benefit of the requisite pre-deprivation procedures and the right to a post-deprivation hearing pending final judgment.

2. Wisconsin Procedures

The plaintiffs base their claim on what they contend is the state judge's unconstitutional application of Wis. Stats. § 409.503. That section, which corresponds to § 9.503 of the Uniform Commercial Code, gives a secured creditor the right to take possession of a defaulting debtor's secured property. It provides that "in taking possession a secured party may proceed without judicial process if this can be done without breach of the peace or may proceed by *action*." (Emphasis added.) Since the defendants Carpenter Cook, Philip Strohl, and Doyle, Ladd & Philipps resorted to the courts to seize plaintiffs' property, they proceeded "by action." Plaintiffs' claim is that the state judge misapplied the "by action" method of repossession by permitting a deprivation which fell short of plaintiffs' right to due process.

The text of the U.C.C. and the Official Comments to § 9-503 fail to provide any guidance to the meaning of "by action." However, the courts and commentators agree that "by action" refers to the applicable state's replevin procedures.

It appears that the 1977 revisions of the Wisconsin replevin procedures were drafted specifically in response to the Supreme Court's holdings in *Mitchell* and *North Georgia Finishing*. The pre-seizure requirements set out in those cases are satisfied by the provision in the Wisconsin replevin procedures that an order directing a return of the property may be issued only by a judge or other judicial officer and only after the creditor has submitted a verified complaint or affidavit containing several detailed allegations specified in the statute. Also, the replevin statutes provide that at any time the debtor may request a hearing before the judge for vacation or modification of the possession order "for any sufficient cause." Wis. Stats. § 810.05. Moreover, the statutes make it clear that the ex parte seizures merely provide for delivery before final judgment.

3. Application of § 409.503 and Chapter 810

The undisputed facts of the seizure in this case reveal that the state court judge did not deprive plaintiffs of their constitutional rights. Carpenter Cook's state court affidavit and complaint incorporated by exhibit into the Robishes' complaint in this case establish that defendants complied with Wis. Stats. § 810.02. Thus plaintiffs cannot contend that the judge abridged their pre-seizure rights. Also, because the judge merely granted an order for possession, rather than entering a final judgment, plaintiffs had an opportunity to seek an immediate post-seizure hearing. Whether plaintiffs exercised their right to a hearing is irrelevant to this discussion. The due process clause guarantees only the "right to an opportunity to be heard . . . [and thus] . . . no hearing need be held unless the [debtor], having received notice of his *opportunity*, takes advantage of it." *Fuentes v. Shevin,* 407 U.S. at 92 n. 29 (emphasis in original). Because the judge complied with the plaintiffs' pre-seizure procedural rights and did not deny them a post-seizure hearing, plaintiffs cannot prevail on their claim that their due process rights were violated.

. . . .

ORDER

IT IS ORDERED that defendants' motion to dismiss this case is GRANTED. Plaintiffs' motion to strike the reply brief of defendants Doyle, Ladd and Philips, P.C. is DENIED.

NOTE

(1) In *Penney v. First Nat'l Bank of Boston,* 385 Mass. 715, 433 N.E.2d 901; 33 U.C.C. Rep. Serv. 433 (Mass. 1982), Bank took possession of the debtor's collateral, a commercial fishing boat, after demanding full payment on four separate occasions. Bank refused debtor's offer of late payments and failed to give the debtor notice of its intention to seize the boat. Bank had also attached the real property of a guarantor on debtor's note. The bank chose not to proceed further against the guarantor but instead sold the boat at a public auction for $13,500. Because he did not receive notice before the bank's seizure, debtor was unable to recover lobster pots left at sea. Debtor sued the bank claiming a denial of due process and seeking damages resulting from the Bank's allegedly wrongful seizure of the boat. The bank counterclaimed for the balance due on the notes with interest, costs and attorney's fees. The court found in favor of the bank, holding that there was no state action and that a secured party has the right to repossess collateral upon default without giving the debtor notice of its intent to seize the property. The court noted that under section 9-501(2), the secured party has this right even though the contract was silent on the point.

Penney also serves to remind us that a secured party's rights are cumulative under section 9-501(1). Bank could have sought a personal judgment against the debtor and seized any of Penney's general assets to satisfy the debt. Bank could have also foreclosed on the equipment collateral, or pursued the guarantor. Nothing in the Code prohibits a creditor from choosing among these remedies or in fact pursuing all of them at the same time, so long as the total amount recovered does not exceed the amount owing along with any costs associated with collection. If those remedies failed to make the secured party whole, the creditor could also seek a deficiency judgment against the debtor.

One final note about *Penney*—the Bank not only prevailed as to the appropriateness of its repossession and subsequent deficiency suit, but it also won a judgment against Penney for its attorneys' fees. Virtually all security agreements contain provisions imposing collection costs upon the debtor; such provisions include attorney's fees. In bringing his case, Penney not only ended up losing the boat and his means of earning a living (the lobster pots), but he also lost his figurative, economic shirt because he had to pay Bank of Boston's lawyers!

§ 19.06 The Secured Party's Choices—Retention or Resale?

Read: U.C.C. §§ 9-504, 9-505.

[A] Generally

After obtaining possession of the collateral, the secured party has two alternatives: 1) sell the collateral and use the proceeds to satisfy the obligation (see § 9-504); or, 2) within certain limits, keep the collateral in satisfaction of the obligation (§ 9-505(2)). In some instances, retention of collateral may be best for both parties. For example, retention seems a better alternative if the expected return on the collateral is low and the costs associated with collection and sale are high. With retention, the secured party also saves some of the costs associated with foreclosure.

The secured party may also be able to arrange a loan workout agreement in some cases. Under such an arrangement, retention of collateral satisfies the major portion of a debt; any remainder would be covered under a new lending agreement. In still other instances, the creditor may wish to lease rather than retain or sell the property.[6]

In most cases however, the secured party will derive the greatest advantage by repossessing and then selling the collateral. The secured party may use as much of the proceeds from a disposition as necessary to satisfy the debtor's obligation of collateral. The key aspect in the disposition of collateral is that the type of sale conducted by the secured party must be commercially reasonable. See U.C.C. § 9-507(2). The sale may be public (auction) or private; the property may be sold as a single unit or in parcels; the sale can be for cash or credit and may be conducted at any time or place—but the sale must be *reasonable*. If the sale is conducted in a manner recognized by the marketplace (the property is sold at a price recognized by some acknowledged market, or the sale takes place in a manner that conforms with the commercial practices of dealers in that type of collateral), the sale will be deemed prima facie reasonable.[7]

[B] Notice Requirements

[1] Retention of Collateral

If the secured party elects to keep collateral, the creditor must give notice of its intention. The creditor must notify the debtor (unless the debtor has waived the right to notice after default occurred) and any other secured party who has filed or of whom the retaining creditor has knowledge. The parties have twenty-one days to object to the creditor's proposed retention of collateral. If no party objects, the secured party may keep the collateral and the debtor's obligation will be discharged. A creditor who retains collateral has no right to seek a deficiency judgment. If any party with a right to notice does object to the secured party's retaining collateral, the secured party **must** sell the collateral. See U.C.C. § 9-505(2).

In the case of consumer goods, if the debtor has paid sixty percent of either the cash price in a purchase money transaction, or the loan amount in a non-purchase money transaction, the creditor **must** sell the collateral. The creditor has no ability to keep the consumer goods collateral if the debtor has paid at least sixty percent (unless the debtor has waived this right after default). § 9-505(1). Not only must there be a sale in these circumstances, but the sale must also be made within 90 days from the time of repossession.

---

6 Though rare, a secured party may also decline pursuit of the collateral and instead sue on the underlying debt. If the collateral is of little value or if the debtor is a solvent entity, the creditor may well choose to establish liability through a judicial proceeding rather than through self-help collection under Article 9. If property is recovered by judicial process, the rules governing the sale will come from non-U.C.C. state law. Early secured transactions cases held that the secured party waived her security interest by proceeding on the underlying debt. Section 9-501(1) rejects the idea of a secured party election. The remedies provided under part 5 of Article 9 are cumulative. The secured party may pursue any number of debt satisfaction methods in an effort to make the creditor whole.

7 Although judicial approval is not needed to conduct a sale, if a creditor obtains court recognition, there is a conclusive presumption of reasonableness.

LAMP FAIR, INC. v. PEREZ-ORTIZ

United States Court of Appeals
888 F.2d 173, 9 U.C.C. Rep.Serv. 2d 1388 (1st Cir. 1989)

BREYER, CIRCUIT JUDGE.

Does Article 9 of the Uniform Commercial Code permit a secured creditor, over the objection of the debtor, both to retain collateral for the creditor's own use and also to obtain a deficiency judgment? We believe that, in the circumstance of the present case, the answer is "no." Accordingly, we reverse the judgment of the district court.

I.

RELEVANT BACKGROUND FACTS

The plaintiff in this diversity case, Lamp Fair, Inc., sold its store to the defendant, Pedro Perez Ortiz, and Perez Ortiz failed to pay the full price. Lamp Fair then repossessed the store, kept it, and sued Perez Ortiz for the "deficiency" between Lamp Fair's valuation of the store and what Perez Ortiz still owed. A Security Agreement between the parties provides that Connecticut law governs. Connecticut has enacted the Uniform Commercial Code, Conn. Gen. State. §§ 42a-9-501 et seq., (see attached Statutory Appendix), and so we must interpret the relevant provisions of that Code to determine whether or not Lamp Fair can obtain a deficiency.

To be more specific, we take the following factual background as relevant to this appeal:

a. On July 1, 1985, Pedro Perez Ortiz and Lamp Fair, Inc., made a contract. Perez Ortiz bought Lamp Fair's lighting fixture store located in Orange, Connecticut. Perez Ortiz promised to pay $327,000; in return he received furniture, fixtures, equipment, inventory, goodwill, and covenants not to compete.

b. Perez Ortiz paid Lamp Fair $50,000 at the time of the sale. He signed notes promising to pay the remaining $277,000 over time. He and Lamp Fair also signed a Security Agreement, intended to make certain that Perez Ortiz would pay this money. The Security Agreement gave Lamp Fair a secured interest in the store as collateral for the notes.

c. After a few months had passed, Perez Ortiz decided he could not, or would not, pay the additional money he owed under the contract and notes. On December 26, 1985, he returned the store—inventory, fixtures, and all—to Lamp Fair.

d. Lamp Fair immediately began to operate the store. In January 1986 Lamp Fair sent Perez Ortiz a bill for $131,000, which, it said, represented the difference between a) the money Perez Ortiz still owed under the contract and notes, and b) the value of the store and inventory, which he had returned.

e. Perez Ortiz refused to pay the $131,000. Lamp Fair then brought this suit.

After a trial before a magistrate, the district court entered a judgment in Lamp Fair's favor and against Perez Ortiz for $65,000. Both sides now appeal.

II

THE LAW

Perez Ortiz argued at trial that his return of the store in December, and Lamp Fair's acceptance of the store, amounted to a rescission of the July contract. That is to say, it amounted to an agreement between the parties that Lamp Fair would accept the store back and, in return, would forgive Perez Ortiz's still outstanding debt. The magistrate found, however, that there was no such rescission or new agreement. He found that Lamp Fair, while accepting the store, did not promise to forgive any still outstanding debt. The magistrate's conclusion on this issue was not "clearly erroneous," and we accept it as lawful. See Fed. R. Civ. P. 52(a).

If there was no rescission of the contract, however, the original contract, notes and, in particular, the Security Agreement govern the legal relation between the parties. The Security Agreement set out what would happen if Perez Ortiz defaulted on his obligation to pay the remainder of the purchase price (as he did). It provided that Lamp Fair could require Perez Ortiz to assemble the collateral, and that Lamp Fair could then take possession of it (i.e., the store), which is just what happened. The Agreement also provided that Lamp Fair would have "all the remedies of a Secured Party under the Uniform Commercial Code of Connecticut." In light of this last statement in the Agreement the magistrate should have looked to the Uniform Commercial Code (as adopted by Connecticut) to determine whether or not Lamp Fair was entitled to more than it had already received—the $50,000 down payment, the monthly payments through December, and the returned store. The magistrate failed to do this. We have examined Connecticut law ourselves, however, and we conclude that Lamp Fair cannot recover a deficiency.

A.

Article 9 of the Uniform Commercial Code sets forth the remedies available to a secured party. It gives a secured party, such as Lamp Fair, three basic options after default. See 2 J. White and R. Summers, Uniform Commercial Code 570 (3d ed. 1988). Each of these options, while permitting the creditor under some circumstances to obtain the collateral, contains safeguards to assure the debtor that the secured party will not take unfair advantage of the situation and that the value of the collateral will be fairly ascertained.

1. *Judgment.* The secured party may simply sue on the note itself; that is to say, he "may reduce his claim to judgment . . . by any available judicial procedure." U.C.C. § 9-50(1); Conn. Gen. Stat. § 42a-9-501(1). At a judicial sale of the debtor's property (which would not be governed by the Code), the secured party may buy the collateral himself, and he can look to the debtor's other property to satisfy any remaining debt. U.C.C. § 9-501(5), § 9-501 comment 6. A secured party choosing this option may take possession of the collateral prior to obtaining judgment, but only to preserve it as security for the debt. *Kimura v. Wauford,* 104 N.M. 3, 715 P.2d 451, 453 (1986). He does not own the collateral; he may use it only "for the purpose of preserving the collateral or its value" for future disposition. U.C.C. § 9-207(4); *Wade v. Sport Concession Enterprises,* Inc., 138 Ga. App. 17, 225 S.E.2d 488, 489 (1976). It would be "unfair to the debtor to allow a creditor to take possession at all, if the creditor never intended to dispose of the security." *Kimura,* 715 P.2d at 454.

Lamp Fair cannot look to this "judgment option" to support its claim to a "deficiency judgment," because Lamp Fair did not choose this option. The record makes clear that Lamp Fair has not sought a judicial sale of the store, nor did Lamp Fair take possession of the store simply for the purpose of preserving it or its value for future disposition. Rather, Lamp Fair intended to keep the store for its own use, and to obtain a deficiency judgment as well.

2. *Retention.* The secured party's second option after default is to "retain the collateral in satisfaction of the obligation." U.C.C. § 9-505(2). The Code makes clear however, that retention of the collateral normally completely satisfies the debt; the secured party must abandon any claim for deficiency (unless the debtor signs a written statement permitting such a claim, which Perez Ortiz did not do). U.C.C. § 9-505, comment 1; 2 J. White and R. Summers, Uniform Commercial Code 585; *Tanenbaum v. Economics Laboratory, Inc.,* 628 S.W.2d 769, 771 (Tex. 1982). The Code also states that the secured party must give notice of its intention to retain the collateral in satisfaction of the obligation, so that the debtor may object to retention and demand that the collateral be sold. Lamp Fair did not give this notice; it did not consciously choose this option.

3. *Disposition.* Section 9-504 sets forth the secured creditor's remaining option. It says that he "may sell, lease or otherwise dispose of any or all of the collateral . . . by public or private proceedings." After doing so, he must "account to the debtor for any surplus," and "the debtor is liable for any deficiency." Every aspect of the disposition must be "commercially reasonable." In addition, the secured creditor must give the debtor notice of when the sale or other disposition will take place. The secured creditor can buy the collateral himself at any "public sale," but he cannot buy it at a "private sale" unless the collateral is "of a type customarily sold in a recognized market or . . . the subject of widely distributed standard price quotation." U.C.C. § 9-504(1)-(3). These rules in part seek to protect the debtor, for they help prevent the creditor from acquiring the collateral himself at less than its true value or unfairly understating its value to obtain a greater-than-warranted deficiency judgment. 2 J. White and R. Summers Uniform Commercial Code 590, 599 (3d ed. 1988); 1A P. Coogan, W. Hogan, D. Vagts & J. McDonnell, Secured Transactions Under the Uniform Commercial Code § 8.04(2)(c) at 8-97, § 8.06(2) at 8-123 (1989); *Ocean National Bank of Kennebunk v. Odell,* 44 A.2d 422, 425 (Me. 1982).

B.

Given these provisions of Connecticut law, Lamp Fair, in our view, cannot both retain the collateral and also obtain a deficiency judgment. We can reach this conclusion through either of two alternative lines of reasoning.

First, the majority of courts that have dealt with this issue would simply hold that Lamp Fair's conduct in retaining and operating the store on a permanent basis brings the transaction within the scope of the § 9-505(2) "retention option," irrespective of whether or not Lamp Fair consciously chose to invoke this option. See, *e.g., Shultz v. Delaware Trust Co.,* 360 A.2d 576, 578 (Del. Super. 1976) (retention of collateral for five years may be found to be in satisfaction of obligation despite secured party's protestations to the contrary); *Millican v. Turner,* 503 So.2d 289, 291 (Miss. 1987) (adopting "majority position" that creditor who retains collateral for unreasonably long period is deemed to have retained in satisfaction); *Swanson v. May,* 40 Wash. App. 148, 697 P.2d 1013, 1015-16 (1985) (same); *Schmode's, Inc. v. Wilkinson,* 219 Neb. 209, 361 N.W.2d 557, 559 (1985) (secured party who used collateral for nearly three years elected to retain in satisfaction); *Haufler v. Ardinger,* 28 U.C.C. Rep. Serv. 893, 896-97 (Mass. App. 1979) (use of collateral for 38 months is election to retain barring deficiency); *In re Boyd,* 73 B.R. 122, 124-25 (Bankr. N.D. Tex 1987) (use of collateral for three months deemed retention in satisfaction). See also 2 J. White and R. Summers, Uniform Commercial Code 588. These courts reason that the Code intends "to put the creditor to an election to either sell the repossessed collateral pursuant to section 9.504 or to retain the collateral in complete satisfaction of the debt pursuant to section 9.505." *Tanenbaum v. Economics Laboratory, Inc.*, 628 S.W.2d at 771-72 (creditor who retained and then scrapped collateral deemed to have retained in satisfaction of debt). The secured creditor cannot both avoid a more "objective," market-based, valuation of the collateral and also obtain an additional "deficiency judgment" remedy (unless the debtor expressly consents).

We note, however, that a minority of courts, including the Second Circuit in a rather different context, have written that § 9-505(2) does not apply when the secured creditor, wishing it not to apply, does not fulfill its procedural prerequisites (*i.e.*, does not give notice). See *Warnaco, Inc. v. Farkas,* 872 F.2d 539, 544-45 (2d Cir. 1989) (Winter, J.) (predicting Connecticut would not follow cases applying § 9-505(2) where creditor did not give written notice of intent to retain collateral in satisfaction of debt); *S. M. Flickinger Co. v. 18 Genesee Corp.*, 71 A.D.2d 383, 423 N.Y.S.2d 73, 76 (1979); *In re Nardone*, 70 B.R. 1010, 1016-17 (Bankr. D. Mass. 1987). In effect, these courts have refused to "force" § 9-505(2) upon an unwilling secured creditor. Since Lamp Fair wishes to obtain a deficiency judgment, it is such an "unwilling creditor."

Our second, alternative, line of reasoning would accept this minority view; it would start from *Warnaco*'s premise that § 9-505(2)'s "retention option" does not apply because an unwilling Lamp Fair did not give the required notice. Following this line of reasoning, we should note that the transaction must fall within the scope of the remaining "disposition option." This option, under § 9-504, does permit a creditor to obtain a deficiency judgment. But, regardless, Lamp Fair failed to satisfy § 9-504's preconditions for obtaining such a judgment because Lamp Fair did not "sell, lease or otherwise dispose" of the store. Lamp Fair did not hold a "public sale," at which it could have bid for the collateral. Nor could it have purchased the collateral itself by means of "private sale," for the store is not of the "type customarily sold in a recognized market or . . . the subject of widely distributed standard price quotations." And, whatever the meaning of the words "otherwise dispose of," they do not include permanent retention of the collateral for the secured party's own use. *Appeal of Copeland,* 531 F.2d 1195, 1207 (3d Cir. 1976). Cf. *National Equipment Rental, Ltd. v. Priority Electronics Corp.*, 435 F. Supp. 236, 240 (E.D.N.Y. 1977) (repossession and conversion to own use by plaintiff's agent not "disposition" under § 9-504, so § 9-505 applies); Black's Law Dictionary 423 (5th ed. 1979) (defining "disposition" as "transferring to the care or possession of another . . . parting with alienation of, or giving up property"). (Consider, as well, the contrasting use of "disposition" in section 9-504 and "retention" in section 9-505. *Copeland,* 531 F.2d at 1207.)

We concede that this last point (that § 9-504 does not foresee a creditor's both retaining the collateral (without public or private sale) and obtaining a deficiency judgment) is not absolutely clear in the Code. Conceivably, one could argue the contrary by pointing out that the Code elsewhere gives a remedy to a debtor when a secured creditor holds his collateral and will not dispose of it. (To be specific, § 9-507(1) says: "it is established that the secured party is not proceeding in accordance with the provisions of this part disposition may be ordered or restrained on appropriate terms and conditions.").

One might reason that where the creditor keeps the collateral and where the debtor does not use § 9-507(1) to force its disposition, the creditor then may proceed under § 9-504 to collect a deficiency judgment. (In any such proceeding the creditor might have to overcome a special "rebuttable presumption" that the collateral was worth at least as much as the debt. *Savings Bank of New Britain v. Booze,* 34 Conn. Supp. 632, 382 A.2d 226, 228-29 (1977) (creating "presumption" as a penalty for creditor's failure to fulfill § 9-504's notice requirements); *Connecticut Bank and Trust Company, N.A. v. Incendy,* 207 Conn. 15, 540 A.2d 32, 38 (1988) (adopting *Booze*).) This retention-plus-deficiency-judgment-plus-presumption theory does not strike us as a very plausible analysis of § 9-504, however. And, we have found only one court that has taken this last-mentioned course, allowing a deficiency judgment (while imposing a "rebuttable presumption") where the creditor simply retained the collateral. *S. M. Flickinger Co. v. 18 Genesee Corp.* 71 A.D.2d 382, 423 N.Y.S.2d 73, 76 (1979) (court divided 3-2). Every other case we have found has denied the creditor the deficiency judgment. See, *e.g., H.V. Funding, Inc. v. Ernest Varkas & Sons, Inc.,* 140 Misc. 2d 587, 531 N.Y.S.2d 484, 486 (1988) (agreeing with *Flickinger* dissenters and denying deficiency). The Third Circuit, for example, has said that to permit a deficiency judgment "would contravene the Code's mandate that an effective election to retain the collateral results in a complete discharge of the underlying obligation," *Appeal of Copeland,* 531 F.2d at 1207, a mandate that permits the credit to obtain a deficiency judgment only with the "collateral valuation" safeguards that a "commercial reasonable" sale under § 9-504 or a judicial sale make possible.

We need not decide which alternative line of reasoning Connecticut would follow, whether Connecticut would hold 1) that § 9-505(2) governs, or 2) that the transaction falls within the scope of, but fails to meet the necessary prerequisites of, § 9-504. Either way the law denies Lamp Fair its deficiency judgment. We can predict with reasonable assurance, *Meredith v. Winter Haven,* 320 U.S. 228, 236-38, 64 S.Ct. 7, 11-13, 88 L.Ed. 9 (1943), that Connecticut would follow one or the other of these paths to this result. Therefore the judgment of the district court must be

Reversed.

COMMENT

Judge (now Justice) Breyer's opinion provides a good summary of the secured party's available remedies under Article 9. If the secured party obtains title to repossessed collateral and then seeks to recover a deficiency judgment, there must be some mechanism for assessing the amount of the deficiency claim. The seller's act of using repossessed goods in its business is not the type of reasonable disposition the drafters of § 9-504(3) envisioned. The repossessing secured party is not the owner of collateral and therefore cannot become the owner without following procedures designed to appraise the collateral and to protect any potential equity the debtor may have in the property.

[2] Notice of Disposition

The reasons for requiring a secured party to dispose of repossessed collateral is simple—to realize and to apply as much value as possible so that the secured party will be paid and the debtor can benefit from any surplus. In theory, this goal can best be achieved by authorizing the secured party to determine how and when the disposition should be made. The Code affords the creditor some flexibility in this regard—the disposition can be by sale, lease, or any other commercially reasonable method. Because the debtor has the most direct interest in any disposition of collateral, section 9-504(3) requires the creditor to give the debtor notice. Unless the collateral is perishable, the creditor must provide the debtor with notice of a proposed public sale within a reasonable time before the sale is to take place. If the proposed sale will be a private transaction, the creditor must give notice within a reasonable time before the secured party enters the contract to sell.

With the exception of consumer goods, a creditor's notice of sale for all other types of collateral must be given to both the debtor and to any other secured party who has notified the secured party of a claim or interest in the collateral. If the collateral is consumer goods, the creditor need notify only the debtor. A debtor can waive the right to notice, but waiver can occur only after default.

CHITTENDEN TRUST CO. v. ANDRE NOEL SPORTS

Supreme Court of Vermont
159 Vt. 387, 621 A.2d 215, 20 U.C.C. Rep. Serv. 2d 710 (1992)

JOHNSON, J.

This is an interlocutory appeal from two superior court orders, one granting summary judgment in favor of defendant debtors and guarantors as to whether plaintiff Chittenden Trust Company (CTC) has the right to obtain a deficiency judgment following its failure to provide notice of the sale of repossessed collateral, and the other dismissing remaining claims that sought damages based on, among other things, allegations that defendants fraudulently transferred some of the collateral after they had defaulted on their loan. We affirm the court's refusal to allow CTC a deficiency judgment, but reverse its decision to dismiss all the remaining claims.

Defendants, various individual and corporate debtors and guarantors who import, distribute and retail exclusive alpine ski clothing and accessories, executed two promissory notes in June of 1984 evidencing two loans from CTC totaling approximately $800,000. Defendants defaulted on the loans, and in January of 1987, CTC filed suit and secured a writ of attachment on defendants' inventory, accounts receivable, fixtures, and equipment. CTC repossessed some ski apparel pursuant to the writ, but after months of intermittent discussion, the parties failed to agree on how to liquidate the merchandise.

On November 4, 1987, CTC informed defendants that it would pursue the sale of the goods beginning the week of November 2, 1987, and that notification of the specific sale times and places would follow as soon as they were available. On December 23, 1987, the bank informed defendants that a sale of the collateral had been advertised and was being conducted at a certain location. The sale had begun approximately one month earlier, and an enclosed advertisement indicated that the sale would continue through Christmas. CTC netted about $35,000 from the sale of the merchandise.

Eventually, defendants moved for summary judgment, claiming that plaintiff had failed to provide them with proper notice of the sale. The trial court granted the motion, concluding that the notice was improper, and, that therefore, CTC was absolutely barred from obtaining a deficiency judgment. Following a hearing, the court also granted defendants' motions to dismiss the case on the ground that CTC's remaining claims were derivative of, and ancillary to, the deficiency action. The court then stayed further proceedings concerning pending counterclaims, and certified the following questions for this appeal:

> 1. Did the trial Court err in ruling that on the state of the record hereby presented plaintiff, Chittenden Trust Company, as a secured party, was barred from pursuing its claim for a deficiency judgment against defendant debtors on the grounds that it failed to give defendants prior notification of the time and place of the sale of repossessed collateral in accordance with 9A V.S.A. § 9-504(3)?

. . . .

On appeal, CTC argues (1) that the court erred by granting summary judgment because there are disputed facts concerning whether notice was required in this instance; (2) that even if notice was required, this Court should abandon or narrow the absolute-bar rule it adopted in a prior decision; . . ..

I.

CTC's first argument is without merit. A secured party must give "reasonable notification of the time and place of any public sale" of repossessed collateral unless the collateral (1) "is perishable or threatens to decline speedily in value" or (2) "is of a type customarily sold on a recognized market." 9A V.S.A. § 9 — 504(3). The first exception is applicable where a "quick resale of the collateral would better serve the debtor's interests" and "the time consumed in giving notice might have disastrous consequences" due to the possibility of a sharp price decline. J. White & R. Summers, Uniform Commercial Code § 25-12, at 1222 (3d ed. 1988). This exception rarely applies to chattels. *Rock Rapids State Bank v. Gray,* 366 N.W.2d 570, 573 (Iowa 1985).

The reasoning behind the "recognized market" exception is that "the debtor does not need the protection against a self-dealing or dishonest creditor because independent market forces set the sale price which is presumptively "commercially reasonable.' " J. White & R. Summers, *supra,* at 1222. This exception generally applies to widely traded stocks, bonds or commodities sold in recognized markets, where the prices are fixed and therefore not subject to manipulation by the secured party. *Id.; Hertz Commercial Leasing Corp. v. Dynatron, Inc.*, 427 A.2d 872, 876 (Conn. Super. Ct. 1980); *Ocean Nat'l Bank of Kennebunk v. Odell*, 444 A.2d 422, 425-26 (Me. 1982); see generally Annotation, *Nature of Collateral Which Secured Party May Sell or Otherwise Dispose of Without Giving Notice to Defaulting Debtor Under U.C.C. § 9-504(3),* 11 A.L.R.4th 1060 (1982).

We conclude, as a matter of law, that neither of these exceptions applies in this instance, where no material facts are in dispute. See *Wheeless v. Eudora Bank,* 509 S.W.2d 532, 534 (Ark. 1974) (court held, as matter of law, that used car did not meet either exception). As noted, the repossessed collateral in this case was outdated, high-fashion ski and sports apparel. The prices for the individual garments were set by the bank or its agent, not by a recognized market. Furthermore, CTC had possession of the collateral for over six months without giving proper notice of its sale. See *Rock Rapids State Bank,* 366 N.W.2d at 573 (because collateral was not sold until three weeks after it was turned over to bank, bank failed to show urgency that would preclude proper notice). Notwithstanding CTC's arguments as to the "volatile" nature of the collateral, the continuing negotiations with defendants over how to deal with the collateral, and the nature of the sale, a reasonable factfinder must conclude that proper notice was required here.

II.

Next, CTC asks us to overrule or limit our holding in *Chittenden Trust Co. v. Maryanski,* 138 Vt. 240, 246-47, 415 A.2d 206, 210 (1980), that reasonable notice is a condition precedent to recovery of a deficiency judgment. We decline to do so.

Neither the Uniform Commercial Code (Code) nor its predecessor, the Uniform Conditional Sales Act (Sales Act), provided a specific remedy for a secured party's failure to notify a debtor of the sale of repossessed collateral, and the vast majority of courts have declined to limit the debtor's remedy to that provided by § 9-507(1). See 9A V.S.A. § 9-507(1) (debtor is entitled to seek recovery of loss caused by secured party's failure to comply with Code provisions); *Liberty Bank v. Honolulu Providoring, Inc.,* 650 P.2d 576, 581 (Haw. 1982) (minority view that § 9-507(1) is debtor's exclusive remedy "has been generally criticized"). The Court in *Maryanski* adopted the "absolute bar" rule, which it stated was the majority rule, because it is in accord with prior Vermont case law under the Sales Act, see *General Acceptance Corp. v. Lyons,* 125 Vt. 332, 336, 215 A.2d 513, 516 (1965), and because strict compliance with the notice requirement is not unreasonable considering that it is one of the few specific requirements in the Code relating to the sale of collateral. *Maryanski,* 138 Vt. at 246-47, 415 A.2d at 210. CTC argues that this decision is inconsistent with subsequent decisions of this Court, the overwhelming majority of other jurisdictions, and the policies and provisions of the Code. We disagree.

This Court has consistently, and recently, reaffirmed the principle, first articulated in *Maryanski,* that a secured party cannot recover any deficiency from a debtor or guarantor absent reasonable notice. See, *e.g., Vermont Indus. Dev. Auth. v. Setze*, 157 Vt. 427, 430, 600 A.2d 302, 304-05 (1991); *Vermont Nat'l Bank v. Hamilton*, 149 Vt. 477, 480, 546 A.2d 1349, 1351 (1988). Further, notwithstanding CTC's arguments to the contrary, recent decisions by this Court have not undermined the *Maryanski* holding.

In *Allard v. Ford Motor Credit Co.,* 139 Vt. 162, 422 A.2d 940 (1980), decided approximately seven months after *Maryanski,* a debtor brought an action for conversion and unlawful disposition of collateral against the secured party that repossessed and sold his car without giving him notice. This Court held that, in the absence of actual damages, the debtor's recovery was limited to the minimum specified in 9A V.S.A. § 9-507(1). *Id.* at 164, 422 A.2d at 942 (citing § 9-507(1)). This holding merely stands for the proposition that when a debtor brings a separate affirmative action against a secured party for illegal disposition of collateral, and there are no actual damages, the debtor's recovery is limited by § 9-507(1). *Allard* says nothing about defense of a secured party's action to recover a deficiency judgment. See *First State Bank of Morrilton v. Hallett,* 722 S.W.2d 555, 556 (Ark. 1987) (majority position is that § 9-507 is a separate affirmative action by a debtor to recover damages and is not applicable to a creditor's action to recover a deficiency judgment, which depends on whether the creditor has complied with statutory notice and disposition requirements). The nature of the actions and the underlying facts in the other Vermont cases cited by CTC are even more remote than those in *Allard.*

. . . .

The law of this state, both before and after adoption of the Code, has been to deny deficiency judgments in situations where the creditor has failed to provide reasonable notice of the sale of repossessed collateral. This rule is simple, certain, and easily administered, and it provides greater incentive for creditors to comply with § 9-504(3), which seeks to give debtors an opportunity to protect their interests by taking part in the sale of the collateral. Although we recognize that there are policy considerations and statutory arguments that favor the rebuttable-presumption rule, they are not so compelling as to persuade us to abandon our long-held rule. See J. White & R. Summers, *supra,* § 25-19, at 1245-46 (stating statutory arguments that can be made for either rule); *Westgate State Bank v. Clark,* 642 P.2d 961, 968 (Kan. 1982) (listing arguments supporting each rule). There may be rare instances where the nature of de minimis violations makes invocation of the rule inappropriate, see, *e.g., Barnhouse v. Hawkeye State Bank,* 406 N.W.2d 181, 185-86 (Iowa 1987) (deficiency judgment not barred where bank sold a bucket of bolts and a broken engine analyzer to bystanders as it was seizing collateral), but this case does not present such an instance. Therefore, the court's first certified question is answered in the negative.

. . . .

The superior court's denial of a deficiency judgment and dismissal of claims on the note are affirmed. . . .

NOTES

(1) Courts treat the failure to give reasonable notice differently. Some courts treat the lack of notice as giving rise to a presumption that the fair market value of the collateral equals the unpaid balance of the outstanding debt. *First Galesburg Nat'l Bank & Trust Co. v. Joannides,* 103 Ill.2d 294, 469 N.E.2d 180, 39 U.C.C. Rep. Serv. 18 (1984). Other courts simply bar recovery of a deficiency judgment, even if the collateral was disposed of in a commercially reasonable manner in every other respect. *Commerce Bank of St. Louis v. Dooling*, 875 S.W.2d 943, 23 U.C.C. Rep. Serv. 2d 640 (Mo. App. 1994). Should the burden of notice be a sliding scale, dependent upon the value of the collateral? What would be the consequences if a scale was adopted?

(2) The statutory requirements for reasonable notice also differ depending on whether the sale is public or private. Notice of a public sale must state the time and place of the sale, whereas notice of a private sale need only state the time of the sale. *See Beard v. Ford Motor Credit Company,* 41 Ark. App. 174, 850 S.W. 2d 23 (1993).

(3) In *Ford Motor Credit Co. v. Thompson Machine,* 649 A.2d 19 (Me. 1994), the court held that the notice provisions of U.C.C. § 9-504(3) applied to guarantors as well as to debtors. The court also found that the guarantor's right to notice could not be waived in advance of default. "We agree with the majority of jurisdictions that have held that guarantors are 'debtors' covered by [§ 9-105(1)(d)] on the strength of the broad language "the person who owes payment or other performance of the obligation secured. " Compare *Steinberg v. Cinema N' Drafthouse Systems,* 28 F.3d 23 (5th Cir. 1994) (under Texas law, the guarantor may waive the right to a commercially reasonable sale; notice provides a type of collateral-preserving function that is diminished in the case of a guarantor who should be left to assess his own interest).

(4) Creditors with prior or conflicting security interests are also entitled to notice under U.C.C. § 9-504(3). A secured party's failure to notify other creditors may result in those creditors receiving exemplary damages. *See e.g., Bara v. White Oak State Bank*, 28 B.R. 366, 39 U.C.C. Rep. Serv. 1688 (S.D. Ohio 1982).

PROBLEM 19.2

Debtor was notified of the sale of repossessed collateral. The notification stated that no bid below a specified amount would be accepted. The debtor did not attend the first attempted sale. Several months later the secured party accepted a bid $11,000 lower thaN the minimum stated in the notification. Under these circumstances, is the debtor estopped from a defense of improper notice in an action by the secured party for a deficiency judgment? See In re Lucas, 35 U.C.C. Rep. Serv. 1688, 28 B.R. 366 (S.D. Ohio 1982).

[C] Disposition: Commercially Reasonable Sale

The dual requirements of section 9-504(3) of "reasonable notification" and a "commercially reasonable" disposition of collateral have been the most litigated issues under Article 9. The guiding premise of section 9-504 is allowing the secured party flexibility in deciding the best method of resale so long as others in the trade regard the method as a prudent procedure.

The secured party bears the burden of establishing notice and commercial reasonableness. Section 9-507(2) provides that commercial reasonableness can be established conclusively, if the secured party obtains approval for the disposition in a judicial proceeding. The time and cost of a court action however, will often dissuade the creditor from pursuing legal action to establish the reasonableness of a sale. The drafters of the Code recognized this likelihood and provided that a commercially reasonable sale occurs whenever a secured party sells collateral either: 1) in the usual manner in a recognized market for property of that type; 2) at the current price of property in a recognized market; or 3) in conformity with the regular commercial practices of dealers in that type of property. The fact that a better price could have been obtained does not, in and of that fact alone, imply that the sale was commercially unreasonable. In their treatise on commercial transactions, Professors White and Summers categorize commercial reasonableness case law into six general areas. Even though there are clearly many more categories of cases on the subject, the following list provides a useful beginning of some of the main considerations effecting commercial reasonableness:

1. cases where the sale took place too soon after notice or too long after repossession.

2. cases involving poor advertising—notice was not given with an eye toward informing the best market for the best buyers.

3. situations where the sale was conducted in a less desirable geographic location or at a time and place different than that given in the notice.

4. instances where prospective bidders did not have the opportunity to inspect the collateral.

5. situations where the secured party failed to clean or repair collateral prior to sale. See J. White & R. Summers, Uniform Commercial Code (4th ed. 1995) § 25-10, pp. 928-929. The next three cases discuss commercial reasonableness as a concept. As you read them, consider whether a meaningful statutory definition is even possible; also consider both the basis for an attack on the validity of a sale and the desired result if a sale was found to be unreasonable.

CROSBY v. REED

United States Bankruptcy Appellate Panel of the Ninth Circuit
176 Bankr. 189, 25 U.C.C.R. Serv. 2d 1032 (1994)

RUSSELL, BANKRUPTCY JUDGE:

The debtors filed an objection to an amended proof of claim filed by a secured party after the secured party foreclosed on the collateral eight months after repossession. The debtors assert, in an effort to bar the secured party from obtaining a deficiency judgment, that the secured party elected to retain the collateral in satisfaction of the obligation and that the sale was not conducted in a "commercially reasonable" manner after an eight month delay. The bankruptcy court overruled the objection. The debtors appeal. We AFFIRM.

I. FACTS

On July 14, 1989, the appellees, Douglas and Gayle Reed ("Reeds") sold the Palomino Room, a bar/restaurant well known in Red Bluff, California to the debtors/appellants, Ralph and Beverly Crosby ("Crosbys") and third parties Joseph Dean and Brenda Eitzen ("Eitzens") for $351,000.[8]

The Reeds retained the master lease for the premises and granted a sub-lease to the Crosbys and Eitzens. Pursuant to the sale, the Crosbys and Eitzens paid $116,000 in cash and signed two promissory notes for the remaining $235,000. A security agreement was also executed, securing both notes with "all stock in trade and goodwill of . . .the Palomino Room . . .and the . . . fixtures and equipment[.]"

The Crosbys and Eitzens assigned their interest in the Palomino Room to the Crosby/Eitzen California Partnership, d.b.a. Palomino Room ("partnership"). The partnership defaulted on the notes and in May 1990 the Reeds obtained a state court judgment against the partnership, the Crosbys and the Eitzens for $264,359.75.

In December 1990, the Reeds were granted relief from the automatic stay to foreclose on the collateral securing their judgment. Prior to vacating the premises, the existing inventory was valued at $11,916.15.

The Reeds reopened and began operating the restaurant in mid-December, 1990, and had an appraisal conducted in January 1991. The appraised value of the fixtures and equipment was $40,290.55.

In August 1991, the Reeds published a notice of a public auction, in which the stock in trade, the fixtures and equipment of the Palomino Room were to be sold pursuant to the security

[8] The sales price was allocated as follows:

Fixtures and Equipment	50,000
Goodwill	5,000
3 year covenant not to complete	205,000
Leasehold interest	50,000
Liquor License	25,000
Inventory	16,000
	351,000

agreement. The sale was conducted by a licensed auctioneer. The Reeds were the only bidders at the sale, and purchased all of the assets with a credit bid of $40,000.

In October 1993, the Crosbys and the Chapter 7 trustee filed objections to the Reeds' amended claim for the deficiency. The bankruptcy court held a hearing on the objection.

The bankruptcy court ruled in favor of the Reeds, overruled the objection and valued the Reeds' claim at $231,315.53. The bankruptcy court also noted that if there were sufficient assets to pay all claims in full, then the Reeds would also be entitled to interest on the principal from February 1991. The Crosbys timely filed a notice of appeal.

II. ISSUE

. . . B. Whether the sale of a secured creditor's collateral is commercially reasonable when the sale was conducted eight months after repossession.

III. STANDARD OF REVIEW

. . . Classification of collateral under the Uniform Commercial Code is a question of law reviewed de novo. *In re Newman,* 993 F.2d 90, 93 (5th Cir. 1993). A finding by the bankruptcy court that a sale is "commercially reasonable" is a finding of fact and will be upheld by a reviewing court unless it is clearly erroneous. *Ingersoll-Rand Fin. Corp. v. Miller Mining Co., Inc.,* 817 F.2d 1424, 1427 (9th Cir. 1987).

IV. DISCUSSION

. . . .

2. Good Faith and Commercial Reasonableness

California Commercial Code § 9504(3)provides in pertinent part:

> A sale . . . of collateral may be . . . at any time and place and on any terms, provided the secured party acts in good faith and in a commercially reasonable manner. Cal. Comm. Code. § 9504(3) (West 1994 Supp.)

a. Good Faith

In exercising a power of sale, the secured party must act in good faith and safeguard the interests of the debtor. The secured party must exercise reasonable care and diligence to obtain a reasonable price. *Faivret v. First Nat'l Bank in Richmond,* 160 F.2d 827, 831 (9th Cir. 1947).

Here, the Reeds acted in good faith by conducting a public sale with a licensed auctioneer. In addition, the Reeds obtained appraisals shortly after repossession and they credit bid the appraised value of the restaurant. Thus, based on the evidence before us, the Reeds acted in good faith.

b. Commercial Reasonableness

In surveying differing state views on this issue, one learned treatise has stated:

> Generally, the courts which have considered the question have held, either expressly or by necessary implication, that the determination of whether a secured party has disposed of repossessed collateral in a commercially reasonable manner, as required by U.C.C. § 9-504(3), should be based on a consideration of all relevant factors in each individual case, with emphasis

being given to the aggregate of circumstances rather than to specific details taken in isolation, and that the factors of manner, method, time, place, and terms, mentioned in the statute, are to be viewed as necessary and interrelated parts of the whole transaction. Richard C. Tinney, *Annotation, What is "Commercially Reasonable" Disposition of Collateral Required by U.C.C. § 9-504(3),* 7 A.L.R.4th 308, 316 (1981).

Although repeatedly used in the California Commercial Code, the term "commercially reasonable" is not specifically defined therein. However, case law has developed which provides some insight into those instances in which a sale is considered unreasonable. *Ingersoll-Rand,* 817 F.2d at 1427. Seventeen factors can be derived from the case law, each of which are of equal weight and should be applied in determining whether a sale of collateral is "commercially unreasonable."[9] The factors are:

1. Choice of public or private sale;
2. Sale at wholesale or retail price;
3. Sale as unit or in parcels;
4. Price realized on foreclosure sale;
5. Price realized on subsequent sale;
6. Time of sale;
7. Place of sale;
8. Solicitation and receipt of bids;
9. Publicity;
10. Appraisal;
11. Sale with or without repair;
12. Familiarity with type of property;
13. Judicial approval of disposition;
14. Secured party's purchase of collateral;
15. Sale of bankruptcy debtor's property;
16. Sale on or at price current in recognized market or in accordance with reasonable commercial practices; or
17. Other factors.

Several of the above factors apply to the present case. The Reeds held a public sale, which was conducted by a licensed auctioneer. The Crosbys assert that the eight month delay between repossession and the sale barred any deficiency. We disagree. As previously stated, the above factors are applied in the aggregate, with each factor given equal weight. Here, it does not appear that an eight month delay was "commercially unreasonable." The Crosbys did not offer any evidence that the delay caused a decline in value or any other type of prejudice.

The fact that the Reeds obtained an appraisal also indicates that the sale was "commercially reasonable." See *In re Cummings,* 147 Bankr. 738, 745 (Bankr. D.S.D. 1992) (holding sale was commercially unreasonable when creditor did not take an inventory and failed to obtain an appraisal prior to the sale). The Reeds had all of the equipment appraised shortly after

[9] This summary is based on Richard C. Tinney's annotation at 7 A.L.R.4th 308 (1981).

repossession; the equipment was valued at $40,290, with a salvage value of $7,970. At the auction sale, the Reeds bid $40,000 for all of the assets being sold. This is a further indication that the sale was "commercially reasonable."[10]

We therefore hold that when a secured party retains collateral after repossession, and that retention does not cause the debtor any prejudice or decline in value, the secured party may conduct a sale of the collateral within a reasonable time period. Under these facts, the eight month period of time which elapsed before the public sale was conducted was "commercially reasonable" under § 9504(3).[11]

V. CONCLUSION

The Crosbys have failed to prove that there was an election to retain the collateral in satisfaction of the obligation by the Reeds. Proper notice was given under § 9504(2)(b) informing the Crosbys of the public sale of the collateral. The covenant not to compete was not part of the security agreement since it was not included in such agreement. The sale was conducted in a "commercially reasonable" manner. Accordingly, we AFFIRM.

QUESTIONS

Do you agree with the court's decision? If a lapse of eight months does not constitute an unreasonable amount of time before disposition, how much time would have to elapse before commercial unreasonableness could be found? Are the seventeen factors listed by the court merely variations of Professors White and Summers's five general categories?

---

[1] Public or Private Proceeding?

Some courts have held that the failure to conduct a private rather than a public sale can lead to a commercially unreasonable disposition. Article 9 does not define public or private disposition. Generally, a private sale is not open to the public and does not require some type of general advertisement. When a secured party contemplates a private sale, the creditor must nevertheless contact enough potential buyers so that there is some probability that a real valuation by a private auction market can occur. The creditor's failure to contact enough potential buyers may lead a court to conclude that the sale was commercially unreasonable.

When a foreclosing creditor contemplates a public sale of collateral, notice of the proposed sale should also be distributed to a broad enough cross-section of the public to ensure a reasonable

[10] The Crosbys were treated very fairly by the Reeds. At the time of the foreclosure sale, the lease on the premises had lapsed and it was clear that the Crosbys had no buyer for what was left of the business. Indeed, the credit bid of $40,000 for the inventory was far greater than the salvage value of $7,970 which would have been the value of the inventory to any other purchasers.

[11] Because we find the sale was held in a "commercially reasonable" manner, we need not decide whether the prior Commercial Code § 9504 or the present Commercial Code § 9504 that became operative on January 1, 1991 applied to the sale. However, it appears that the result would have been the same under either version.

possibility of competitive bidding. Although some forms of publicity are extended to the public, the advertising will not always produce a commercially reasonable sale.

FORD & VLAHOS v. ITT COMMERCIAL FINANCE CORP.

Supreme Court of California
8 Cal. 4th 1220, 885 P.2d 877, 36 Cal. Rptr. 2d 464, 25 U.C.C. Rep. Serv. 2d 630 (1994)

MOSK, J.

This case presents a narrow question of law: whether the California version of Uniform Commercial Code section 9-504, subdivision (3), definitively limits a secured party's duty to advertise the sale of collateral merely to placing a legal notice in a newspaper. We conclude it does not, and therefore reverse the Court of Appeal's judgment and remand the case for consideration of the secured party's other claims of error.

Defendant secured party lent plaintiff debtor money to buy a Lockheed Hercules C-130A aircraft and acquired a purchase-money security interest in it. The parties agreed that California law would govern the security agreement.

Plaintiff defaulted on the loan and was notified by defendant that it would repossess the aircraft. On August 26, 1987, defendant informed plaintiff it would hold a public sale of the C-130A on September 3 at Chandler, Arizona.

On August 28, 1987, defendant advertised the sale's time and place in the Arizona Republic, a newspaper of general circulation in Maricopa County, Arizona, where Chandler is located. The advertisement stated that the United States Department of State would have to approve "the purchaser and the secured party's right to bid [on] and purchase" the aircraft. But the advertisement apparently inadvertently omitted the information about whom to contact to qualify as a bidder. That error caused defendant to place a corrected advertisement in the Phoenix (Arizona) Gazette on September 2.

Defendant, the sole bidder at the auction, bought the C-130A the next day for $1 million. After the sale defendant's agent advertised the aircraft in Trade-A-Plane. The agent testified that Trade-A-Plane is "the Bible of aircraft sales in this country." In March 1988 defendant agreed to sell the C-130A to African Air Trans, Inc., for $1,525,000, eventually, according to defendant, receiving $1,487,000 from that company.

Plaintiff sued for improper disposition of the collateral and defendant cross-complained for a deficiency plaintiff allegedly owed after credit for the $1 million foreclosure-sale bid.

The trial court found the aircraft's sale commercially unreasonable because accompanied by insufficient publicity and hence the subject of too few bids. The court also found the notices of sale "legally insufficient" for various reasons. The court's statement of decision recited:

> The only notice of the auction was the Arizona Republic newspaper ad placed in the auction section of the newspaper. The ad contained an incomplete sentence regarding qualifications to purchase.
>
> The Court finds that a correction appeared in the Phoenix Gazette on September 2, 1987, one day prior to the auction.

The Court finds that there was no evidence that the Arizona Republic or Phoenix Gazette were publications circulated among or read by potential purchasers of this Aircraft.

The Court finds that no publicity for the September auction sale was given in aviation trade journals, such as Trade-A-Plane. . ..

The Court concludes that publication of a notice for the September 3 auction of this Aircraft in the Phoenix Gazette was legally insufficient to satisfy [California Uniform Commercial Code section] 9504 in that it did not conform to the five-day time requirement of the statute.

The Court finds that the Arizona Republic notice affirmatively stated that pre-qualification as a bidder was necessary.

The Court concludes that the omission of any contact name or telephone number to obtain pre-qualification information rendered the wording contained in the Arizona Republic notice legally insufficient under [California Uniform Commercial Code section] 9504. . ..

The Court finds that, other than the newspaper notices, Defendant ITT made no efforts to contact potential purchasers regarding the September 3 auction.

The Court finds that Defendant ITT had available to it the resources of an aircraft broker . . . who knew potential aircraft buyers and the means of publicity to announce aircraft auctions. . ..

The Court concludes that Defendant ITT did not conduct the auction sale on September 3, 1987 in good faith and in a commercially reasonable manner as required by [California Uniform Commercial Code section] 9504. . ..”

With regard to the collateral's value, the court ruled, “based on . . . expert opinion testimony . . ., that the fair market value of the Aircraft on the date of sale, September 3, 1987, was $3.8 million.”

On the basis of that valuation, the court set plaintiff's damages at $3.8 million, but granted defendant an offset of $996,050, a figure representing the sum of plaintiff's debt to defendant and defendant's expenses in repossessing, refurbishing and selling the aircraft. The ensuing judgment netted plaintiff $2,803,950.

The Court of Appeal reversed the judgment in part. As relevant here, the majority decided the Legislature had created a “safe harbor” in California Uniform Commercial Code section 9504, subdivision (3)—unlabeled statutory references are to this code—whereby satisfying the statute's notice requirement precluded any challenge to the sale's commercial reasonableness on the basis of inadequate publicity. The majority wrote, “ITT [defendant] contends that by specifying the time and manner for notice of a public sale, our Legislature intended to establish a bright-line rule to prevent disputes over the ‘reasonableness’ of pre-sale publicity. This contention is supported by the legislative history of section 9504(3).” Thus, the majority reasoned, “Compliance with the letter of section 9504(3) creates a safe harbor against claims that the publicity for a public sale was inadequate.” Acknowledging that “there may be situations . . . where such a limited notice would seem less than fair,” the majority stated in essence that any complaints should be addressed to the Legislature. The majority thus rejected the reasoning of *American Business Credit Corp. v. Kirby* (1981) 122 Cal.App.3d 217, 221 [175 Cal.Rptr. 720], and *Clark Equipment Co. v. Mastelotto, Inc.* (1978) 87 Cal.App.3d 88, 96-97 [150 Cal.Rptr. 797], “cases that have suggested, contrary to our conclusion, that a single, timely newspaper notice might not be sufficient," because those cases "did not consider section 9504(3)'s legislative history, or address whether the statute's notice provisions were meant to conclusively establish what is required to publicize an auction of collateral."

The dissent declared that the majority's bright-line rule was unfounded. Citing the cases mentioned above, the dissent observed that, "In each of these cases the court treated adequate notice and adequate publicity to be commercially reasonable as two distinct inquiries. Adequate notice, that is notice which met the minimum requirements of the subdivision, did not define the scope of commercially reasonable publicity or advertising." The dissent continued, "In my view the specific notice requirements imposed by the section define the minimum notice which must be given. I do not, unlike the majority, construe notice to be coextensive with publicity. The duty to publicize a sale adequately arises from the general duty of the creditor to act'in a commercially reasonable manner.' What is commercially reasonable publicity must turn on the specific circumstances of what the collateral is and how it is to be sold. . . .. The published notice given here was not, standing alone, commercially reasonable publicity for the sale of a multimillion dollar aircraft."

Because the Court of Appeal majority concluded that the Legislature had conclusively defined the publicity required for a sale of foreclosed collateral, it did not address defendant's other claims of error, including contentions regarding the court's calculation of the aircraft's value, its valuation of defendant's expenses attendant to repossessing and selling the aircraft, and its asserted refusal to find that plaintiff was not the real party in interest.

. . . .

Defendant contends that the references to notice in subdivision (3) of section 9504 conclusively define the publicity required for a public sale of foreclosed collateral. Defendant reasons that because it met the statute's notice requirements, the court could not properly find the sale commercially unreasonable for want of sufficient publicity. In sum, it contends the Court of Appeal majority correctly understood the meaning of section 9504, subdivision (3).

We interpret the California Uniform Commercial Code otherwise. As we will describe, notice on the one hand, and publicity or advertising on the other, are separate but related concepts under the California Uniform Commercial Code. (We define advertising broadly as all efforts to alert possible buyers to an impending sale, including professionally designed displays in public media and flyers or brochures circulated to a narrower audience.)

. . . .

By its plain terms, section 9504, subdivision (3), provides that the secured party is to "act[] in good faith and in a commercially reasonable manner" when auctioning foreclosed personalty. (See also § 1203). The term "commercially reasonable" is again articulated, and is partially defined, in section 9507, subdivision (2), which provides in relevant part, "The fact that a better price could have been obtained by a sale at a different time or in a different method from that selected by the secured party is not of itself sufficient to establish that the sale was not made in a commercially reasonable manner. If the secured party either sells the collateral in the usual manner in any recognized market therefor or if he sells at the price current in such market at the time of his sale or if he has otherwise sold in conformity with reasonable commercial practices among dealers in the type of property sold he has sold in a commercially reasonable manner."

. . .

Read together, sections 9504, subdivision (3), and 9507, subdivision (2), cast considerable doubt on the Court of Appeal majority's view that as long as the statutory notice requirements are met, the publicity attending a sale of foreclosed collateral is deemed to be commercially reasonable. Section 9507 provides that property sold by methods a responsible dealer would utilize is sold in a commercially reasonable manner. A dealer in the type of property repossessed here—a valuable airplane—surely would advertise its auction in the relevant market by, for example, informing brokers, placing reasonably prominent announcements in recognized trade journals, or contacting individuals or entities known to be seeking an airplane of the type for sale. . .. To be sure, nowhere does subdivision (2) of section 9507 explicitly state that failing to sell collateral of this type as would a responsible dealer makes the sale commercially unreasonable. But it is difficult to read the law any other way with regard to the valuable type of collateral at issue here. (See *Canadian Commercial Bank v. Ascher Findley Co.* (1991) 229 Cal.App.3d 1139, 1149 [280 Cal.Rptr. 521] ["A commercially reasonable disposition is presumed to be in good faith and at the greatest possible market rate."].)

And yet defendant's interpretation of section 9504, subdivision (3), would simply nullify section 9507, subdivision (2), whenever complying with the former statute's formal notice requirements would not yield the kind of publicity a responsible dealer would generate to sell a chattel of the type foreclosed. We cannot conclude that the Legislature meant to provide that a sale's advertising is commercially reasonable as long as the bare requirements of formal notice are met, even if, to sell the type of collateral involved, a responsible dealer would employ more extensive advertising than placing a legal notice in agate type in an obscure newspaper. Publicity is much too important to a proper sale of foreclosed collateral for such a hypothesis to be commercially viable. For advertising is sine qua non to attendance at an auction, and as then-Presiding Justice Panelli explained in *Ford Motor Credit Co. v. Price* (1985) 163 Cal.App.3d 745, 751 [210 Cal.Rptr. 17], "Common sense tells us that the larger the attendance at a public sale of collateral, the more likely it is that there will be competitive bidding. Competitive bidding helps to assure that the purchase price approximates the fair market value of the property and also prevents a [secured party] from exaggerating his deficiency by underbidding." Hence, "[o]ne of the most important elements of commercial reasonableness is the duty to surround the sale with publicity sufficient to attract a 'lively concourse of bidders.' " (*Westgate State Bank v. Clark* (1982) 231 Kan. 81 [642 P.2d 961, 970].)

The importance of advertising as an element of commercial reasonableness was emphasized in *Villella Enterprises, Inc. v. Young* (1988) 108 N.M. 33 [766 P.2d 293], the facts of which are similar to those the trial court found here. "We are particularly concerned with the minimal effort exerted by Villella to notify the public of the sale. Notice of sale should be given to a 'public' reasonably expected to have an interest in the collateral and should be "published in a manner reasonably calculated to assure such publicity that the collateral will bring the best possible price from competitive bidding of a strived-for lively concourse of bidders.' [Citations.] Villella placed an ad only in the Health City Sun, a weekly legal periodical, two weeks prior to the sale. No evidence was produced that the Health City Sun is the type of publication that would reach prospective bidders for the assets of a bar business. [Citations.] Neither is there any indication that Villella contacted the individuals who had offered . . . to purchase [the business] . . . even though he was aware of their identities." (766 P.2d at p. 297; see also *Commercial Credit Equipment v. Parsons* (Mo.Ct.App. 1991) 820 S.W.2d 315, 323; *Farmers Equipment Company v. Miller* (1972) 252 Ark. 1092 [482 S.W.2d 805, 809-810]; *Levers v. Rio King Land & Inv. Co.* (1977) 93 Nev. 95 [560 P.2d 917, 920].)

The foregoing reasoning clearly applies to the sale of an airplane. (*Dynalectron Corporation v. Jack Richards Aircraft Co.* (W.D.Okla. 1972) 337 F.Supp. 659, 662-663.) "Although [secured party] offered testimony that it gave notice of the sale orally to all major airplane brokers in the United States, the judge disbelieved this testimony, and we cannot say he was clearly wrong to do so. So far as appears, all [secured party] did in the way of notice was to place an inconspicuous ad in one publication of the used-aircraft trade . . .. There was testimony that a serious effort to interest potential buyers would have required a more conspicuous ad plus advertising in other trade publications as well. The fact that no one showed up for the sale except [secured party] is consistent with the fact that [it] made little effort, on this occasion anyway, to sell the plane." (*Contrail Leasing Partners v. Consolidated Airways, supra,* 742 F.2d at p. 1099.)

. . . .

The purpose of notice to the debtor and to other secured creditors under the California Uniform Commercial Code is to alert them that their interests may be extinguished very soon. This concept derives from the venerable American legal rule that a private creditor must give formal legal notice before selling a debtor's property at public auction. . . Because a nonjudicial foreclosure sale is a "summary sale" . . . elementary fairness to the debtor requires that it, other interested parties, and the public receive formal notice so as to protect the debtor from another's self-dealing or an unfairly low auction price

. . . .

In contrast to notice, one purpose of which is to alert the debtor and other secured creditors to take steps to protect their interests, possibly including locating bidders for their collateral, the purpose of requiring adequate advertising of a foreclosure sale is to force the secured party to ensure the auction is well attended by legitimate bidders, so that the highest commercially reasonable price for the collateral will be obtained.

But a prime purpose of notice by publication is to provide notice of the auction to the public *i.e.,* to advertise, in the broad sense of that term, the sale. "Whereas the official text provides only for 'reasonable [notification],' the legislation adopted in California explicitly sets out the requirements for notice both to the debtor and to the general public when a public sale is to be held." (*Ford Motor Credit Co. v. Price, supra,* 163 Cal.App.3d 745, 750.) Hence, there will surely be sales of foreclosed personalty for which the advertising requirement will be wholly satisfied by giving notice by publication as specified in section 9504, subdivision (3).

Failure to comply strictly with the notice-by-publication requirement is fatal to a contention of compliance with section 9504, subdivision (3). (*Ford Motor Credit Co. v. Price, supra,* 163 Cal.App.3d at pp. 750-751.) Thus, the minimum advertising required to make the publicity aspect of a sale of foreclosed collateral commercially reasonable is the notice given by publication. But if placing the required legal notice is not a commercially reasonable method of informing potential buyers of the sale's time and place, the sale will fail to meet the requirements of subdivision (3) of section 9504.

In this case, substantial evidence supported the trial court's conclusion that the Phoenix newspapers, with their limited circulation, did not provide a forum likely to bring bidders and a fair price for the foreclosed aircraft, and the sale hence was commercially unreasonable. (See *General Elec. Credit v. Durante Bros., etc.* (1980) 79 A.D.2d 509 [433 N.Y.S.2d 574, 576] [""the newspaper selected for advertising was clearly not the most appropriate one for reaching the intended market."].)

. . . .

The Court of Appeal's judgment is reversed and the cause is remanded to consider defendant's other claims.

WAINWRIGHT BANK & TRUST v. RAILROADMENS FEDERAL SAV. & LN.

806 F.2d 146, 4 U.C.C. Rep.Serv.2d 1295 (7th Cir. 1986)

COFFEY CIRCUIT JUDGE.

. . . .

I.

There is no dispute as to the facts. Robert H. Wilson and Samuel L. Dowden, third-party plaintiffs-appellants ("plaintiffs" or "appellants") were the founders of the Golden Manor Corporation, an Indiana corporation financed with a $350,000 loan from Wainwright Bank & Trust Company ("Wainwright"), and the third-party defendant-appellee, the United States Small Business Administration ("SBA"). The Golden Manor Corporation loan, approved in the amount of $350,000, was secured with the appellants' personal guarantees and personal real estate mortgages on property located in Hamilton County, Indiana. Real property was purchased with the loan for the purpose of operating a restaurant named the Golden Manor.

In 1979, the restaurant owned by the appellants, after a short period in operation, encountered financial difficulties resulting in the Golden Manor Corporation becoming insolvent and defaulting on the loan. On July 7, 1979, the Automatic Sprinkler Corporation filed suit in the Hamilton (Indiana) Superior Court to collect a debt owed by the Golden Manor Corporation. The SBA, the State of Indiana, and Topics Newspaper, Inc. were named as co-defendants to answer for the claims asserted against the Golden Manor Corporation. On August 16, 1979, Wainwright assigned its interest in the mortgages and personal guarantees executed by the Golden Manor Corporation to the SBA. On November 28, 1979, the United States acting for and on behalf of the SBA, cross-claimed against the Golden Manor Corporation, the State of Indiana, and Topics Newspaper, Inc. to foreclose on the SBA's mortgage on the real estate of the Golden Manor Corporation. On April 20, 1981, the United States was awarded judgment on its cross-claim in the sum of $322,732.83 plus interest accruing to the date of judgment together with a decree of foreclosure on the mortgages.

During this same approximate time period, several events involving the property of the Golden Manor Corporation took place. On October 17, 1979, the Hamilton County Circuit Court appointed a Receiver for the Golden Manor Corporation, and approximately four months later, on February 8, 1980, gave the Receiver the authority to appraise and to proceed to attempt to sell the Golden Manor Corporation's property. The appraisal valued the real property at $420,000 and the personal property at $25,325.

The Receiver, though diligent in his efforts to locate a private buyer for the property over a ten-month period, received but two offers. One was rejected as patently insufficient. The Receiver recommended approval of the other offer from Fred Spottsville, Jr., M.D. (the "Spottsville offer"). The SBA, on January 29, 1981, rejected the Spottsville offer, primarily on the basis of an inadequate debt-to-net-worth ratio of Dr. Spottsville and his personal corporation.

On April 20, 1981, the Hamilton Superior Court rendered judgment in favor of the SBA allowing them to foreclose on the property of the Golden Manor Corporation. The SBA then requested that the Sheriff of Hamilton County publish a notice of foreclosure sale in a public newspaper of general circulation (the Noblesville Daily Ledger) for three days, May 28, June 4 and June 11, 1981. Notices of the sale were also posted in three public places in Hamilton County, and at the door of the Hamilton County Courthouse in Noblesville, Indiana in compliance with the Indiana Code.

An appraisal conducted by the SBA on June 29, 1981 valued the real property of the Golden Manor Corporation at $315,000. On July 9, 1981, a public sale was held and the Sheriff of Hamilton County sold the real property at the door of the Hamilton County Courthouse, Noblesville, Indiana, to the highest bidder, the SBA, for the sum of $235,000. On October 1, 1981, the personal property of the Golden Manor Corporation likewise was sold to the highest bidder at a public auction for $8,575.

On March 15, 1983, the appellants filed a third-party complaint against the SBA. The appellants alleged that the SBA breached its contractual obligation of good faith dealing in refusing to permit the assumption of the loan by Dr. Spottsville. The case was removed from the Boone County Superior Court to the United States District Court for the Southern District of Indiana. The district court granted summary judgment in favor of the SBA pursuant to Fed.R.Civ.P. 56(c). *Wainwright Bank & Trust Co. v. Railroadmens Federal Savings & Loan Assoc. of Indianapolis,* No. IP 83-417-C, Slip Op. (S.D.Ind. May 25, 1984).

The appellants appeal the grant of summary judgment to the SBA raising what amounts to one primary issue containing two sub-issues. The appellants argue that a genuine issue of material fact existed regarding whether the SBA's sale of the real and personal property was commercially reasonable. Whether summary judgment was properly granted depends on (1) whether there was a genuine issue of material fact concerning the commercial reasonableness of the SBA's choice of a public auction over a private sale, and (2) whether there was a genuine issue of material fact concerning the commercial reasonableness of the SBA's manner of the public sale.

. . . .

The appellants argue that the district court erred in granting summary judgment because there were important factual issues in dispute concerning whether the sale by the SBA was commercially reasonable, both in the SBA's choice of a public over a private sale and in the manner of conducting the public sale.

. . . .

III.

The appellants argue that a genuine issue of material fact existed regarding the SBA's choice of holding a public auction rather than a private sale. In particular, they argue the SBA's rejection of the Spottsville offer was commercially unreasonable. Sec. 26-1-9-504(3) of the Indiana Code (regarding a secured party's right to dispose of collateral after default) provides:

> Disposition of the collateral may be by public or private proceedings and may be made by way of one or more contracts. Sale or other disposition may be as a unit or in parcels and at any time and place on any terms, but every aspect of the disposition including the method, manner, time, place and terms must be commercially reasonable.

In deciding whether the SBA acted commercially reasonable both in choosing a public over a private sale and in the manner of the public sale, we are required to consider the aggregate of the circumstances. *C.I.T. Corp. v. Lee Pontiac, Inc.,* 513 F.2d 207, 210 (9th Cir.1975).

The appellants do not contest the fact that the Receiver made a diligent effort for some ten months to sell the property to a private buyer. Only two offers were received—Dr. Spottsville's being the only one of any possible merit.[12] Although the Receiver approved the Spottsville offer, the SBA determined that it was unacceptable from a commercial business point of view.

The appellants argue that in rejecting the Spottsville offer, the SBA acted commercially unreasonably. The appellants emphasize several aspects of the Spottsville offer that if, analyzed individually, would cast the offer in a favorable light: (1) the offer ($415,000) was near the appraised value of the real property ($420,000); (2) the offer was made by a young, practicing physician and cardiologist with an existing medical practice presumably with his best income producing years ahead of him; (3) the offer was substantially higher than the other firm offers received by the Receiver;[13] and (4) the offer would have avoided a forced liquidation sale.

Despite the fact that there may have been some merit to Dr. Spottsville's offer, the SBA's decision to reject Dr. Spottsville's offer was a sound financial business decision and commercially reasonable in view of the myriad of questionable factors surrounding the offer. The district court found that the SBA relied upon the following facts in deciding not to accept the Spottsville offer: the doctor's total net worth at the time of the offer was $9,503; he had only $3,500 in cash on hand or in the bank, an amount that was far short of the $41,251.31 needed to close; the doctor apparently had no stocks, bonds or real property which could be pledged as collateral and whatever life insurance he had was previously pledged to secure a prior loan; the doctor's yearly income was $43,000 but his annual obligations were over $18,500; and the offer was contingent upon the assumption of the SBA loan (approximately $374,000) and the securing of additional financing in the amount of $360,000. *Wainwright Bank & Trust Co. v. Railroadmens Federal Savings & Loan Assoc. of Indianapolis,* No. IP 83-417-C, Slip Op. at 4-5 (S.D.Ind. May 25, 1984).

Based on what it deemed to be sound lending practices, the SBA properly refused to consent to the sale to Dr. Spottsville as it considered him an unsatisfactory credit risk at that particular time placing special emphasis on the doctor's debt-to-net-worth ratio of 9 to 1, and the 4.7 to 1 ratio for the doctor's personal corporation. The district court found the SBA's rejection of the

---

[12] The first offer was at a figure substantially less than the appraised value and was rejected.

[13] This argument rings somewhat hollow since the one and only other private offer was rejected outright.

Spottsville offer appropriate: "The financial condition of the offeror renders ludicrous third-party plaintiff's claim that the SBA was unreasonable in rejecting the offer to purchase the property." *Id.* at 5.

We agree with the district court's finding that Dr. Spottsville's offer lacked a proper financial foundation. Although the doctor was a relatively young man who could reasonably be expected to have significant earning potential in the future, his financial resources were clearly inadequate to assume a loan of the size in issue at the time he made the offer (approximately $374,000): his net worth was a mere $9,503; he had only $3,500 readily at hand—far short of the $41,251.31 needed to close; and his yearly income was $43,000 which was partially offset by the sum of $18,500 in annual obligations. In addition, the doctor's ability to secure the necessary additional $360,000 in financing even with prior SBA approval was, in our opinion, based on pure speculation. We hold the action of the SBA in proceeding with a public auction was both commercially reasonable and proper.

IV.

The appellants also argue that a genuine issue of material fact exists regarding whether the manner of public sale was commercially unreasonable. The disposition of collateral "including the method, manner, time, place and terms must be commercially reasonable." I.C. 26-1-9-504(3).

The appellants argue that the forced public sale by the SBA was marred by several deficiencies: the SBA knew of the specialized nature of the property, yet made no attempt to reach the best market available to sell the property; the advertising of the sale was limited to a very narrow market (Hamilton County, Indiana) and to the minimum required by statute; the SBA made no attempt to seek out potential buyers of restaurants; a professional auctioneer was not retained to sell the real property; the sale of the real property was held at the door of the Hamilton County Courthouse rather than at the site of the real property, thereby depriving potential buyers of the opportunity to view it at the time of sale; and, lastly, the actual price was substantially below the appraised value.

The cases cited by the appellants in support of their argument that the manner of public sale was commercially unreasonable are distinguishable. In *United States v. Willis,* 593 F.2d 247 (6th Cir.1979), as opposed to the situation in the present case, the government held a public auction despite the existence of two outstanding firm offers to buy the property on sale for five times the price realized on the public sale. In *United States v. Conrad Publishing Co.,* 589 F.2d 949 (8th Cir.1978), the public sale involved specialized printing equipment while in the present facts the sale of real property predominated. *Connex Press, Inc. v. International Airmotive, Inc.,* 436 F.Supp. 51 (D.D.C.1977), aff'd without opinion, 574 F.2d 636 (D.C.Cir.1978) is similarly distinguishable. In *Connex Press,* the foreclosed property was a luxury airplane purchased by the secured party, a dealer in aircraft.

The district court, in its August 30, 1985 memorandum opinion responding to the appellants' motion to alter or amend its grant of summary judgment, stated: "The third-party plaintiffs also contend that the public sale that was held was commercially unreasonable because of the manner in which it was conducted. However, it is undisputed that notice of the sale of the real estate at issue was published in the Noblesville Daily Ledger (a public newspaper of general circulation in the county of the real estate's situs) once each week for three consecutive weeks, well in advance of the sale. Notices of the sale were also posted in three public places in Hamilton County plus at the door of the Hamilton County Courthouse in Noblesville. The real estate was then sold, in the traditional manner, to the highest bidder by the Hamilton County Sheriff on the County Courthouse steps of the county in which the real estate is located. Additionally, the personal property was sold at a well advertised auction." *Wainwright Bank & Trust Co. v. Railroadmens Federal Savings & Loan Assoc. of Indianapolis,* No. IP 83-417-C, Slip Op. at 4 (S.D.Ind. Aug. 30, 1985).

We strongly agree with the district court's conclusion that the manner of public sale was clearly commercially reasonable. The SBA completely complied with what was required by Indiana law, I.C. 32-8-16-1.[14] Notice of the sale was published in the Noblesville Daily Ledger for three weeks, well before the sale. Notice was posted as required in three public places in Hamilton County and on the door of the Hamilton County Courthouse. The decision to pursue the public sale came only after ten months of efforts by the Receiver to arrange for a private sale. The eventual price paid by the SBA for the real property was approximately 75% of the SBA's appraisal value. In sum, in viewing the aggregate set of circumstances, the appellants' arguments fail to convince us that the district court's finding that the manner of sale was commercially reasonable is clearly erroneous.

V.

After a review of the record and each of the appellants' arguments regarding the commercial unreasonableness of the choice of a public over a private sale and the manner of the public sale, we hold that the district court's decision in granting summary judgment was proper. Affirmed.

NOTES

(1) If a secured party fails to establish whether a sale of collateral was commercially reasonable, a presumption arises that the value of the collateral equaled the amount owed by the debtor. Usually the question is one for the jury. The evidence presented in support of commercially reasonable resale will often involve the common practices used by dealers in goods of that kind. Consider the case of a truck, originally purchased at retail, which, upon reposession, was sold by the secured party through a dealership in the process of liquidating its inventory. How could such a sale fail to meet the commercially reasonable standard? See *Ford Motor Credit Co. v. Jackson*, 126 Ill.App.3d 124, 466 N.E.2d 1330, 39 U.C.C. Rep. Serv. 743 (1984).

(2) In *Pippin Way, Inc v. Four Star Music Company, Inc.*, 29 U.C.C. Rep. Serv. 343 (N.D. Tenn. 1979), the court examined the commercial reasonableness of a sale of Four Star's "Catalogue" that included all copyrights, royalties, and other interests in musical compositions.

[14] I.C. 32-8-16-1 requires that in advertising the public sale: (d) [t]he sheriff shall advertise . . . once each week for three [3] successive weeks in a daily or weekly newspaper of general circulation printed in the English language and published in the county where the real estate is situated. The first publication shall be made at least thirty [30] days before the date of sale.

. . . .

(e) The sheriff also shall post written or printed notices thereof in at least three [3] public places in the township in which the real estate is situated and at the door of the courthouse of the county.

In the sale of this unique item, the seller never obtained an independent appraisal, never actively solicited bids and received only a few bids, never attempted to ascertain the proper market for such an item, and eventually sold it for a promissory note without earnest money or any requirement that the buyer account for earnings or profits, despite the fact that the buyer had the unrestricted freedom to rescind the sales contract and cancel all its obligations. The court found that the aggregate of these circumstances represented a clear divergence from the accepted standards of commercial reasonableness. The court also found that the buyer, as a merchant, should have known that this was not a commercially reasonable sale and was not, therefore, a good faith purchaser.

(3) The issue in *General Electric Credit Corporation v. Durante Brothers & Sons, Inc.*, 30 U.C.C. Rep. 760 (N.Y. App. Div. 1980), was whether a creditor, by failing to dispose of collateral after default in a commercially reasonable manner, forfeited its right to a deficiency judgment completely, or whether it forfeited its rights to the extent of a fair and reasonable value of the collateral. The court concluded that the creditor was entitled to a deficiency judgment based on the fair and reasonable value of the collateral.

[2] Secured Party as Buyer of Collateral

Not only can the secured party arrange for the sale of repossessed collateral, but the creditor can also bid on the property during the disposition sale. The drafters of the Code recognized the danger of a secured creditor's self-dealing in a private sale. Section 9-504(3) generally prohibits secured parties from purchasing property from themselves through a private sale. However, the section permits a secured party to purchase collateral in a private sale if the property is of a type customarily sold in a recognized market or of a type that is subject to a set of recognized, widely distributed price quotations. Section 9-504(3) also provides that the secured party may purchase from herself at a public sale. In the case of a public sale, it is especially important for the creditor to take all necessary steps to ensure that the sale is, in fact, a public one. Usually, the safest method of ensuring a public sale classification involves the hiring of a professional auctioneer who will auction the collateral after generating publicity sufficient to stimulate competitive bidding.

§ 19.07 Debtor's Remedies

[A] Generally

Sections 9-504 through 9-507 combine to provide the debtor with certain rights during a default and subsequent foreclosure on collateral. Section 9-507(1) makes a general reference to the debtor's right to recover from the secured party "any loss caused by a failure to comply" with Part 5 of Article 9. Unfortunately, the Code does not specify what consequences might occur if there is noncompliance under § 9-504(3). Perhaps the most common consequence of noncompliance (either insufficient notice of disposition, or a commercially unreasonable sale) is the debtor's ability to resist a creditor's deficiency action. Generally, under section 9-504(2), a debtor is liable for any shortfall from a sale of collateral that yields an amount less than the secured claim plus expenses. Many of the previous cases in this chapter arose when a debtor challenged a creditor's claim for a deficiency amount.

However, if a debtor discovers that a secured party is about to make a commercially unreasonable sale, the debtor can seek injunctive relief to restrain the transaction. Injunctive relief can be an important remedy for the debtor because a resale purchaser can often acquire good and proper title even if the sale was commercially unreasonable. U.C.C § 9-504(4) provides that the person who buys property at a public sale takes the debtor's title free from both the secured party's lien and all junior liens if the purchaser has no knowledge of any defects in the sale and if the purchaser did not buy the property in collusion with anyone associated with the sale. If the disposition involved a private sale, the purchaser takes title free from both the debtor's and other creditors' claims if the purchaser acted in good faith. See comment 4, U.C.C. § 9-504.

Because common law causes of action and remedies are available under Article 9, an aggrieved debtor may also be able to assert claims in tort for punitive damages. In addition, the debtor has the power to resist a creditor's retaining consumer goods in satisfaction of an obligation. If the debtor has paid sixty percent of the cash price or sixty percent of a loan secured by consumer goods, the secured party must resell the goods within 90 days and account for the proceeds. U.C.C. § 9–505(2).

RUDEN v. CITIZENS BANK AND TRUST COMPANY OF MARYLAND

Court of Special Appeals of Maryland
99 Md. App. 605, 638 A.2d 1225 (1994)

MOYLAN, JUDGE.

. . . .

Facts

The Rudens purchased a 35-foot Cheoy Lee sailboat in 1980 for $85,000. They financed $67,000 of the purchase price with People's Security Bank. In 1982, they leased the boat to James Morris. Morris kept the boat in a marina located on Hilton Head Island, South Carolina.

In 1984, the Rudens refinanced the boat with Citizens Bank and Trust Company of Maryland (Bank). The Rudens executed a Consumer Loan Note and Security Agreement in which they promised to pay to the order of the Bank the principal sum of $58,883.50 plus interest by making monthly payments. Morris was still leasing the boat from the Rudens at that time.

In February, 1985, Morris was two months behind in his payments. Additionally, the Rudens discovered that the boat was no longer located on Hilton Head Island, South Carolina. They became concerned. Subsequently, the boat was found in Miami, Florida. Morris's lease was terminated and the boat was seized by the U.S. Marshal in connection with a civil maritime action instituted by the Rudens in the United States District Court for the Southern District of Florida. Allied Marina, a marina located in Miami, Florida, acted as the substitute custodian for the boat.

The Rudens continued to make monthly payments to the Bank until August, 1986, when they could no longer do so. By a certified letter dated October 10, 1986, the Rudens were notified by the Bank that, because they had failed to make the required monthly payments, the boat would be repossessed on or after October 20, 1986 unless all defaults were cured by that date. In November, 1986, the Bank had the boat appraised, and it was valued at $45,000 by an appraiser.

Subsequently, the Rudens were informed by letter that the boat was repossessed on December 9, 1986 and that it continued to be stored at Allied Marina in Miami, Florida. The letter explained that they may redeem and retake possession of the boat during a 15-day period prior to its sale at public auction. At that time, however, the boat, apparently unbeknown by the Bank, was still in federal custody.

The Rudens were notified of the time, date, and location of the public sale and received copies of advertisements placed in The Washington Post and The Miami Herald. A public sale was held on January 27, 1987. The bidding opened at $35,000, but no bids were made. The Bank "bought" the boat for $35,000, but the sale was never consummated. Because the boat had been in federal custody when the Bank attempted to sell it at a public auction, the repossession and subsequent public sale were invalid.

After learning that the boat had been and was no longer in federal custody, the Bank officially notified the Rudens that the boat was being repossessed and that it intended to dispose of the boat. On March 16, 1987, the Rudens were informed by letter that the boat was being sold at private sale on or after April 1, 1987. The boat was sold to a third party for $12,500.00 and the sale was consummated on July 8, 1987. By a letter dated July 16, 1987, the Bank notified the Rudens that their boat was sold on July 8, 1987 and that they were responsible for the deficiency balance. The sale price, however, was stated as being $35,000.

The Bank filed its Complaint in November, 1987 in the Circuit Court for Anne Arundel County. The case was tried before a jury on September 1, 2, and 3, 1992. The Bank requested that judgment in its favor be entered in the amount of $100,888.01, which included the deficiency, interest, and attorney's fees. The jury returned a verdict in favor of the Bank in the amount of $75,753.00. This appeal resulted.

Creditor's Entitlement to a Deficiency Judgment

A. Compliance With § 9-504(3): Deficiency Award Automatic

When the sale is conducted with full compliance with the requirements of § 9-504(3), the sale price will be considered to be the true value of the collateral and any deficiency will be awarded automatically to the creditor.[15] Md.Code Ann., Com.Law § 9-504 (1992). In terms of compliance with § 9-504(3), there was no issue in this case with respect to the giving of adequate notice. The issue in dispute was the commercial reasonableness of the sale. The circuit court instructed the jury, with regard to commercial reasonableness:

> In determining whether the sale was held in a commercially reasonable manner, for the purposes of a deficiency judgment, the burden of proof is on the Plaintiff, on the bank, who has brought suit. The fact that a better price could have been obtained by a sale at a different time or in a different method from that selected by the secured party is not, of itself, sufficient to establish that the sale was not made in a commercially reasonable manner. If the secured party either sells the collateral in the usual manner in any recognized market or if he sells at the price current in such market at the time of the sale, or if he has otherwise sold in conformity with reasonable commercial practices among dealers in the type of property sold, he has sold in a commercially reasonable manner. If you find the sale was held in a commercially reasonable manner and you have found that there is reasonable notification given to the Defendant, then you must return a verdict in favor of the Plaintiff against the Defendant.Thus far, the judge's instruction was absolutely correct.

[15] If, on the other hand, there is a surplus beyond the amount necessary to satisfy the debt and the reasonable expenses of repossessing and disposing of the collateral, the creditor must account to the debtor for such surplus.

B. Noncompliance: What Is the Sanction?

At that point, the trial judge went on to instruct the jury as to what it should have done in case it found the sale to have been commercially unreasonable. As to any damages that might have resulted from the failure of the Bank to conduct the sale of the boat in a commercially reasonable manner, the judge advised:

If you find that the sale was not held in a commercially reasonable manner, your job is not finished because you must determine to what extent the Defendant has been damaged by the failure to hold the sale in a commercially reasonable manner. To determine the effect of a sale which was not held in a commercially reasonable manner, you must determine from the evidence presented what sale price would have resulted from a commercially reasonable sale. . .. If the price which would have been obtained at a commercially reasonable sale is higher than that which was actually obtained, you must subtract the difference from the Plaintiff's demand and return a verdict in favor of the Plaintiff in the reduced amount

. . . .

The Rudens contend that the circuit court's instruction as to damages that may result from the Bank's failure to conduct the sale in a commercially reasonable manner was in error. They argue that failure to meet the requirement of a commercially reasonable sale under § 9-504(3) totally bars the recovery of a deficiency judgment in any amount and, therefore, the circuit court's instruction was in error. We disagree.

It is clear that § 9-504(3) requires both 1) that the sale of the collateral be conducted in a commercially reasonable manner and 2) that reasonable notice be given to the debtor. Section 9-504 does not, however, explicitly address the consequences of a secured party's failure to meet either of those requirements.

C. Sanction # 1: Deficiency Judgment Absolutely Barred

Courts across the country have approached the problem in essentially three different ways. Some jurisdictions absolutely bar a secured party's recovery of any deficiency judgment for failure to comply with the requirements of § 9-504. They do so regardless of whether the noncompliance was the failure to give notice or the failure to conduct the sale in a commercially reasonable manner. The rationale invigorating that position was well articulated by *Leasco Data Processing Equip. Corp. v. Atlas Shirt Co.,* 66 Misc.2d 1089, 323 N.Y.S.2d 13, 16 (N.Y.City Civ. Ct. 1971):

> It surely has meaning that the very section [9-504] that affirms the right to a deficiency judgment after sale of a repossessed article also describes in simple and practical terms the rules governing dispositions as well as the pertinent notice requirements. If a secured creditor's right to a deficiency judgment were intended to be independent of compliance with those rules, one would surely expect that unusual concept to be delineated with clarity. The natural inference that the right depends upon compliance is forcefully underlined by the joining of the two provisions in one section. . ...

D. Sanction # 2: Burden on Debtor to Qualify for Set-Off

A second approach traditionally allowed the secured creditor to recover a deficiency judgment notwithstanding noncompliance with § 9-504(3), subject only to a reduction or set-off for damages suffered by the debtor. . . ..

. . . .

Under that second approach, the creditor did not automatically suffer any sanction at all for his noncompliance. The full burden was placed on the debtor to establish the fair market value of the collateral. Only when he had done so was he then entitled to a set-off for the difference between the sale price actually realized and the fair market value of the collateral, to wit, the price it should have brought if it had been sold in a commercially reasonable way. That difference would be used, as a set-off, to reduce the amount of the deficiency.

In fashioning an appropriate sanction, courts were initially faced with that starkly bipolar choice between two extremes. On the one hand, noncompliance would absolutely bar a creditor from any deficiency judgment, no matter how relatively minor the impact of the noncompliance and no matter how unduly harsh the total bar to a deficiency might be. On the other hand, the only apparent alternative inflicted virtually no penalty whatever on the creditor for noncompliance but, rather, allocated to the debtor the burden of establishing the prejudice that he may have suffered from such noncompliance. 2 James J. White & Robert S. Summers, Uniform Commercial Code, § 27-19, at 631 (3d ed. 1988) described this dichotomy:

> On one end of the scale, *Skeels* in Pennsylvania and now *[First State Bank of Morrilton v.] Hallett* [291 Ark. 37, 722 S.W.2d 555 (1987)] in Arkansas stand clearly and unequivocally for the proposition that a creditor who violates the provisions of Part Five of Article Nine loses his right to a deficiency. At the other extreme, some states expressly allow the creditor a deficiency judgment, subject to set-off for whatever loss the debtor can prove as a result of the improper sale.

In rejecting both extremes, the Supreme Court of Appeals of West Virginia, in *Bank of Chapmanville v. Workman,* 185 W.Va. 161, 406 S.E.2d 58 (1991), focused its critical gaze initially on the "absolute bar" approach, observing, 406 S.E.2d at 64:

> Under the "absolute bar" rule, any secured creditor who is found to have disposed of the collateral in a commercially unreasonable manner is absolutely barred from seeking a deficiency judgment. There are several problems with this rule. First, it is a judge-made punitive provision. . ..
>
> . . . .
>
> Second, there is absolutely no support in the wording of the U.C.C. for the "absolute bar" rule. Third, the "absolute bar" rule involves a forfeiture, and the law generally disfavors forfeitures. Fourth, the amount of the penalty bears no relation to the degree of commercial unreasonableness of the secured creditor's conduct, but depends solely upon the amount of the deficiency. That is, a creditor who is owed a deficiency of one million dollars can be penalized more for slightly commercially unreasonable conduct than a thoroughly abusive creditor who is left with a deficiency of one hundred dollars. . . ..

It then turned its analytic scrutiny on the opposite extreme, the "set-off" rule, observing, 406 S.E.2d at 64-65:

> At the other extreme, under the "set-off" rule, the creditor collects a deficiency judgment, subject only to whatever statutory damages are awarded to the debtor on a counterclaim under U.C.C. 9-507(1). . . The main problem with this rule is that the debtor has the burden of proving his losses under U.C.C. 9-507, and will usually have a hard time proving that

the fair market value was higher than what the collateral actually sold for at the repossession sale. In many cases, the secured creditor's commercially unreasonable behavior (*e.g.*, lack of adequate notice to the debtor) will have greatly hindered the debtor's ability to prove his damages. (citation omitted).

E. Sanction # 3: The Middle Position

More recently, a middle position has emerged which has softened the harsh bipolarity of the earlier choice. In *Bank of Chapmanville v. Workman,* it is not surprising that West Virginia, after roundly criticizing the two extremes, as noted above, opted for the third, newer, and middle position: Courts around the country have chosen from among the following three rules: (1) the "absolute bar" rule; (2) the "set-off" rule; and (3) the "rebuttable presumption" rule. The "rebuttable presumption" rule appears to have become the majority rule, and is the soundest of the three. (footnote omitted). 406 S.E.2d at 64.

. . . .

After twenty years of adherence to the "absolute bar" position, the Supreme Court of Georgia, in *Emmons v. Burkett,* 256 Ga. 855, 353 S.E.2d 908 (1987), abandoned the "absolute bar" rule in favor of what has come to be called the "rebuttable presumption" rule. As 2 James J. White & Robert S. Summers, Uniform Commercial Code § 27-19, at 627 (3d ed. 1988) has explained, "According to this rule, the creditor who fails to give notice or conducts a commercially unreasonable sale can still recover a deficiency if he rebuts the presumption that the value of the collateral was equal to the debt." *Emmons v. Burkett,* 353 S.E.2d at 911, held that:

> . . . the rebuttable-presumption rule, by placing the burden on the creditor to show the propriety of the sale and making him liable under [9-507] for any injury to the debtor, provides an adequate deterrent to an improper sale on the part of a creditor, and adequately protects the debtor's interest, without arbitrarily penalizing the creditor.

The decided trend, nationwide, is toward the "rebuttable presumption" rule as state after state has rallied under that banner. . . ..

. . . .

F. The Maryland Case Law: Failure of Notice

Before we may proceed to make a policy choice, of course, we must determine what freedom of movement is permitted us by stare decisis. On two occasions, the Court of Appeals has squarely held that the failure of a creditor to comply with the provisions of § 9-504(3) will operate as an absolute bar to the creditor's recovery of a deficiency judgment. *First Nat'l Bank v. DiDomenico,* 302 Md. 290, 487 A.2d 646 (1985); *Maryland Nat'l Bank v. Wathen,* 288 Md. 119, 414 A.2d 1261 (1980).

. . . .

Wathen and *DiDomenico* establish unmistakably that in Maryland the failure of a creditor to comply with the notice requirement of § 9-504(3) will operate as an absolute bar to the obtaining of any deficiency judgment against the debtor. Beyond that, however, the field is yet unplowed. In neither *Wathen* nor *DiDomenico* did the Court of Appeals give any thought (it was not called upon to give any thought) to the appropriate sanction in the case of a creditor's noncompliance with any provision of § 9-504(3) other than the notice requirement.

G. The Maryland Law: Commercial Unreasonableness

That rationale of *Wathen* and *DiDomenico*, whatever its force in the no-notice context, does not necessarily support totally barring the recovery of a deficiency judgment in the different context of a secured party's failure to conduct the sale of the debtor's collateral in a commercially reasonable manner. As result of a secured party's conduct in that regard, the debtor may still, of course, be damaged. That damage, however, can be quantified in monetary terms. Equity does not logically require, therefore, that the debtor be completely relieved of total responsibility for any deficiency, as he would be in the case of non-notice. Thus, we reject the Rudens' argument that a secured party should be totally barred from recovering any deficiency judgment if its conduct as to the sale of the collateral is found to be commercially unreasonable.

. . . .

In making a conscious policy choice between the "rebuttable presumption" approach and the "set-off" approach as an alternative to an absolute bar, we conclude that the "rebuttable presumption" rule represents a fair accommodation between the legitimate interests of the debtor and the residual interests of even a creditor whose actions have not necessarily been commercially reasonable and is, therefore, the preferred approach. This was the position taken by the Supreme Court of Kentucky in *Holt v. Peoples Bank of Mt. Washington,* 814 S.W.2d 568 (Ky.1991). It weighed the two alternatives to an absolute bar and concluded that the "rebuttable presumption" rule was a better approach:

> "The second and third approaches described by Professors Leibson and Nowka [*Eds. note*: D. Leibson and R. Nowka, The Uniform Commercial Code of Kentucky, § 8.6(G)(2) (1983)] are substantially the same except as to the allocation of the burden of proof. In our view, the second approach is preferable. It begins with a presumption that the collateral is worth at least the amount of debt it secures and the burden is cast upon the secured party to prove that its commercial unreasonableness did not result in diminished proceeds, or if it did, by what amount. Upon failure of the secured party to prove that its conduct did not diminish the proceeds, the presumption that the collateral is of sufficient value to satisfy the debt would control and the claim for deficiency would be forfeited. If, in such circumstances, a secured party is unwilling to depend entirely upon the view, if any, that its conduct did not result in diminished proceeds, it may present evidence as to the amount of damage it caused and such sum will be deducted from the deficiency. To avoid application of the presumption that the collateral is of sufficient value to satisfy the debt, a secured party whose conduct has been found to be commercially unreasonable must prove that its conduct did not cause damage or if it did, by what amount." 814 S.W.2d at 571.

As part of this widespread trend toward the "rebuttable presumption" rule, Massachusetts, in *Shawmut Bank, N.A. v. Chase,* 34 Mass. App. Ct. 266, 609 N.E.2d 479 (1993), was even more persuasive: Massachusetts has rejected the forfeiture approach. The issue whether Massachusetts would adopt the rebuttable presumption or the set-off approach was expressly left open. . .. As between two approaches, we think the rebuttable presumption approach, which has more widespread acceptance elsewhere, is fairer. Generally, the facts concerning any sale of collateral are peculiarly within a creditor's knowledge, and a debtor who has not been notified of such sale would be at a disadvantage in trying to prove the extent of the resulting loss. Moreover, it seems more appropriate, and more likely to encourage compliance, to place the burden of proof on the party who failed to live up to the requirements of the Code than on the innocent party. (citations omitted). 609 N.E.2d at 483.

. . . .

There was no dispute that: 1) the Bank held a public sale in an attempt to sell the Rudens' boat on January 27, 1987; 2) bidding opened at $35,000, but no bids were received; 3) the public sale was a nullity because the boat was still in federal custody; and 4) the boat was sold in a private sale to two men from Florida for $12,500. It is further uncontroverted that a letter was sent to the Rudens in July, 1987 incorrectly stating that the boat had been sold for $35,000, the amount of the opening bid at the public sale.

The confusion that generated the controversy surrounds the documentation that was prepared by a documentation company to comply with Coast Guard regulations and to complete the transfer of title to the two purchasers of the boat after the private sale had taken place. Evidence was offered that the documentation company prepared two sets of bills of sale: one to the Bank for Thirty-Five Thousand Dollars ($35,000) and one to the purchasers for Twelve Thousand Five Hundred Dollars ($12,500).

The documentation company, to be prepared for any contingency, had prepared two sets of documents. One set, however, was meaningless because it related to the aborted sale in January, 1987, that turned out to be an utter nullity. Out of 1) the Bank's uncontrovertedly incorrect letter to them in July, 1987, and 2) the meaningless set of documents prepared by the documentation company that referred only to a nullity, the Rudens have concocted some convoluted theory that the Bank purchased the boat and thereby violated the provisions of § 9-504(3). In a mental sleight-of-hand that we are confessedly not quick enough to follow, the Rudens are attempting somehow to spin a factual reality out of two undisputed unrealities.

The actual evidence in the case showed indisputably that there was only one valid sale. The first sale, a public sale in which bids were opened at $35,000, was a nullity. The second sale, a private sale, was the only valid sale, and uncontradicted evidence, in the form of a written contract and a check, established that the boat was sold to two purchasers for $12,500. There was no support in the evidence for the requested instruction. We find no error.

Private Sale Not Foreclosed

The Consumer Loan Note and Security Agreement signed by the Rudens stated, in its pertinent part, that:

> (4) Repossession and Sale of Collateral: If I default, I will deliver the Collateral to you, or you can repossess it without either notice to me or any court proceedings. In either event, you have the right to (but are not required to) sell the Collateral at public sale to reduce the amount owed to you by me. If the amount of the sale proceeds are not enough to pay all amounts owed under this Note and Security Agreement (including any costs which you incur for insurance, repossession, storage, repair or sale of the Collateral), you have a right to obtain a deficiency judgment against me for the balance which is still owed. . . .

The Rudens contend that the contract did not authorize the Bank to sell the boat at a private sale. They argue that the Bank's statement that it had the right to sell the boat at public sale is a waiver of its 9-504(3) right to sell the boat at either a public or a private sale. Thus, the Rudens assert that the circuit court erred in failing to instruct the jury that the Bank was not entitled to a deficiency judgment if it sold the boat at a private sale.

The trial court found that the Bank did not waive its rights under 9-504(3). We agree. The contract states that, although the Bank is permitted to sell the boat at a public sale, it is not required to do so. The contract does not explicitly state that the Bank is permitted to sell the boat at a private sale, but neither does it affirmatively waive the Bank's statutory right. The words "but are not required to" leave open the possibility that another type of sale is contemplated and permitted. We see no error.

. . . .

Judgment Affirmed; Costs to Be Paid by Appellants.

DAVENPORT v. CHRYSLER CREDIT CORP.

Court of Appeals of Tennessee, Middle Section
818 S.W.2d 23, 15 U.C.C. Rep. Serv. 2d 324 (1991)

[See § 19.04, *supra,* for facts of this case.]

IV.

The question of damages remains since we have determined that the manner in which Chrysler Credit repossessed the Davenports' automobile was improper. The Davenports put on little proof of actual damage and have been unable to articulate an intelligible theory of recovery. Even so, they have demonstrated that they are entitled to the minimum statutory penalty authorized in Tenn. Code Ann. § 47-9-507(1)(1979).

A.

The Davenports' lawsuit challenged Chrysler Credit's decision to consider them in default and the manner in which American Lender Service repossessed their automobile. It did not take issue with the commercial reasonableness of Chrysler Credit's disposition of the automobile after it had been repossessed. These acts, according to the Davenports, entitled them to (1)"compensatory damages for the amount paid on the vehicle," (2)"damages for conversion as provided in T.C.A. 47-9-507(1)," (3)"[t]wenty [f]ive [t]housand [d]ollars in punitive damages, and (4) damages for injury to their credit reputation.

The Davenports' proof of damages is almost non-existent. While they proved that Chrysler Credit had accepted one of their payments, Chrysler Credit proved that it had credited this payment to their account. While they proved that they had been denied credit on other occasions, Chrysler Credit proved that the Davenports had a spotty credit history. They proved that American Lender Service cut a lock but neglected to prove the lock's value. They also proved that removing the automobile had caused some negligible cosmetic damage to their gravel driveway.

B.

Secured parties who do not abide by Tenn. Code Ann. §§ 47-9-501-507 (1979 & Supp. 1990) expose themselves to a broad array of civil, and perhaps criminal, consequences. See White & Summers § 27-16, at 617. Tenn. Code Ann. § 47-9-507(1) provides that :

> [I]f it is established that the secured party is not proceeding in accordance with the provisions of this Part disposition may be ordered or restrained on appropriate terms and conditions. If the disposition has occurred, the debtor or any person entitled to notification or whose security interest has been made known to the secured party prior to the disposition has a right to recover from the secured party any loss caused by a failure to comply with the provisions of this Part. If the collateral is consumer goods, the debtor has a right to recover in any event an amount not less than the credit service charge plus ten percent (10%) of the principal amount of the debt or the time price differential plus ten percent (10%) of the case price.

The statute applies not only to situations involving the wrongful disposition of collateral but also to wrongful repossessions. See *Lee County Bank v. Winson*, 444 So.2d 459, 463 (Fla. Dist. Ct. App. 1983); *Randolph v. Franklin Investment Co.*, 398 A.2d 340, 349 (D.C. App. 1979); White & Summers § 27-18, at 622.

Tenn. Code Ann. § 47-9-507(1)'s remedies are not intended to be exclusive and, in fact, are cumulative to other remedies available to debtors under state law. Thus, for example, seeking the relief provided in the statute will not preclude seeking to bar a deficiency judgment if the secured party disposes of the collateral in a commercially unreasonable manner.[16] *Atlas Thrift Co. v. Horan*, 27 Cal. App. 3d 999, 104 Cal. Rptr. 315, 321 (1972); *Christian v. First Nat'l Bank*, 531 S.W.2d 832, 843 (Tex. Civ. App. 1975).

The Uniform Commercial Code's drafters included the statutory penalty for consumer goods in Section 9-507(1) because they believed that compensatory damages would not be a sufficient deterrent in the average consumer case. See White & Summers § 27-18, at 623. They intended that the statute would provide the minimum recovery for consumers who prove that a secured party did not proceed in accordance with the Uniform Commercial Code. See 9 R. Anderson, Anderson on the Uniform Commercial Code § 9-507:21(1985).

In cases involving consumer goods, debtors are entitled to recover the statutory penalty without regard to their actual loss or their ability to prove that they have been damaged at all. *Gulf Homes, Inc. v. Goubeaux*, 136 Ariz. 33, 664 P.2d 183, 186 (1983); *First Nat'l Bank v. DiDomenico*, 302 Md. 290, 487 A.2d 646, 650 (1985); *Erdmann v. Rants,* 442 N.W.2d 441, 443 n.1 (N.D. 1989); *First City Bank v. Guex,* 677 S.W. 2d 25, 29 (Texas 1984). Thus, other than proof that the secured party's conduct was inconsistent with the Uniform Commercial Code, the debtor need only prove the terms of the transaction. See 9 R. Anderson. Anderson on the Uniform Commercial Code § 9-507:11 (1985).

We have no reported cases in Tennessee dealing with the imposition of Tenn. Code Ann. § 47-9-507(1)'s minimum penalties. However, this court has, in at least three unreported cases,

[16] A secured party who disposes of collateral in a commercially unreasonable manner runs the risk of losing any deficiency judgment it might obtain because of the rebuttable presumption that the value of the collateral equals the amount of the debt. *Investors Acceptance of Livingston, Inc. v. James Talcott,* Inc., 61 Tenn. App. 307, 330, 454 S.W.2d 130, 141 (1969).

recognized that the remedy is available to debtors who prove that the secured party's conduct was contrary to the Uniform Commercial Code. . . ..

C.

The Davenports have never challenged the commercial reasonableness of Chrysler Credit's disposition of their automobile, and we have already concurred with the trial court's finding that Chrysler Credit was justified in repossessing the automobile and accelerating the debt because the Davenports were in default. Accordingly, the Davenports are only entitled to recover their damages stemming directly from the manner in which American Lender Service repossessed their automobile.

The Davenports' only proof concerning these damages is a broken lock and minor, cosmetic damage to their driveway. They are not entitled to recover for damage to their credit reputation because Chrysler Credit did not wrongfully accelerate their debt and because the proof showed that they had other credit problems. Thus, the Davenports are entitled to recover only Tenn. Code Ann. § 47-9-507(1)'s minimum penalty.

For similar reasons, we have determined that Chrysler Credit should not forfeit its deficiency judgment. It did not act improperly by determining that the Davenports were in default, and its disposition of the automobile has not been challenged. Thus, as in cases involving the wrongful disposition of collateral, the Davenports are entitled to set off the deficiency judgment by the amount of their Tenn. Code Ann. § 47-9-507(1) damages. The record contains sufficient proof to enable us to calculate the parties' damages. Thus, we need not require the parties or the trial court to go to the time and expense of doing so on remand.

The calculation of the Davenports' Tenn. Code Ann. § 47-9-507(1) damages should be based on the original amount of the debt. See White & Summers § 27-18, at 623. The retail installment contract states that the Davenports financed $15,243.65 and that the total finance charges were $5,203.15. Accordingly, the Davenports' Tenn. Code Ann. § 47-9-507(1) damages were $6,728.[17] Chrysler Credit's deficiency after the sale of the Davenports' automobile was $6,774. Granting the Davenports a $6,728 credit against the deficiency, Chrysler Credit is entitled to a $46 judgment against the Davenports.

D.

The final issue concerns the Davenports' request for punitive damages. We have determined that the Davenports are not entitled to punitive damages under the fact of this case.

A party is entitled to punitive damages only if it recovers actual damages, *Liberty Mut. Ins. Co. v. Stevenson,* 212 Tenn. 178, 180, 368 S.W.2d 760, 761 (1963); *Solomon v. First Am. Nat'l Bank,* 774 S.W. 2d 935, 943 (Tenn. Ct. App. 1989), and if the defendant's conduct amounts to fraud, malice, oppression, gross negligence, or outrageous conduct. *Moorehead v. J. C. Penney,* 555 S.W. 2d 713, 718 (Tenn. 1977); *Inland Container Corp. v. March,* 29 S.W.2d 43, 44-45 (Tenn. 1975); *Blank v. Smith,* 197 Tenn. 683, 687, 277 S.W.2d 377, 379 (1955).

The Davenports have not proved that they were actually damaged by the manner in which their automobile was repossessed. Chrysler Credit's and American Lender Service's actions in this case did not amount to outrageous conduct, fraud, or oppression, especially in light of the tolerant standard contained in *Harris Truck & Trailer Sales v. Foote.*

[17] $5,203.15 (credit service charge) + $1,524.37 (10% of $15,243.65) = $6,727.52.

Like Tenn. Code Ann. § 47-9-507(1)'s minimum penalty, punitive damages are intended to serve as a financial penalty to deter similar acts in the future. *Huckeby v. Spangler,* 563 S.W.2d 555, 558-59 (Tenn. 1978). We need not penalize Chrysler Credit twice. Since we have already imposed the statutory minimum penalty, we need not assess punitive damages as well.

V.

We reverse the trial court's judgment dismissing the Davenports' complaint and remand the case for the entry of an order consistent with this opinion. We tax the costs in equal proportions against the Davenports and Chrysler Credit Corporation, and their respective sureties, for which execution, if necessary, may issue.

LEWIS and CANTRELL, JJ., concur.

[B] Debtor's Right to Redeem

Read: U.C.C. §§ 9-506.

Section 9-506 gives the debtor a right to buy back repossessed property by tendering to the secured party all of the obligations secured by the collateral. This amount includes the secured creditor's expenses in repossessing, storing, preparing for, and arranging the sale. The amount would also include any attorneys' fees, legal, or other expenses provided for in the security agreement. Redemption must occur before the secured party enters a contract to dispose of the collateral or before the secured party elects to retain the collateral in satisfaction of the obligation. The debtor can execute a written waiver of the right to redeem after default (section 9-501(3) operates to prevent any waiver or alteration of the right to redemption before default).

U.C.C. § 9-506 also allows other secured parties of the debtor to redeem. Why? Given this power, is there a real prospect of creditor collusion? If there is such a prospect, should the Code provide protection for unsuspecting debtors? How would you draft such protective measures?

[C] Mandatory Resale

Read: U.C.C. § 9-505.

In the case of consumer goods, where sixty percent or more of the purchase price of the goods has been paid, the Code provides for a mandatory disposition through sale rather than permitting a retention of the goods by the secured party. U.C.C. § 9-505(1). In situations where there has been a relatively large down payment, a default at an early point (before the sixty percent of the price has been paid), and where the goods are still in very good condition, it might be profitable for the secured party simply to exercise the remedy of retaking the goods. The secured party could then resell the items independent of any other remedy. Abuses could occur if the repossessing creditor resold the same goods several times to persons likely to default and thereby reap a considerable profit.

The Code gives the secured party only two choices if the debtor has paid sixty percent of the cash price before defaulting on a consumer good. First, the creditor may resell the goods in accordance with Code procedures. If the secured party takes possession and fails to resell the goods within fifty days, the debtor may recover in conversion under section 9-507(1). Under that section, a debtor may recover any loss caused by the creditor's failure to comply with part five of Article 9; this cause of action could include claims for punitive damages. The debtor also has a right to recover 1) the credit service charges assessed on the account plus ten percent of the principal amount of the debt; or, 2) the time price differential plus ten percent of the cash price. Even though the loss may not be shown by virtue of the creditor's failure to comply with the Code, the secured party could be found liable for this minimum amount.

Second, after default the secured party can obtain a waiver of rights from the debtor renouncing or modifying any rights to a mandatory resale. U.C.C. § 9-505(1). If the debtor can obtain a discharge of an obligation by waiving mandatory resale, it may be to the debtor's advantage to allow the creditor to keep the property even though more than sixty percent of the purchase price had been paid. Courts are generally suspicious of creditor over-reaching in default cases and may review such agreements or waivers critically. In some instances courts require the creditor to show: 1) how a debtor would benefit by waiving rights under such an agreement and 2) that the debtor has not suffered any significant loss by virtue of the waiver.

QUESTION

If you were advising the Article 9 drafting committee about changes to sections 9-504 and 9-507 concerning the debtor's remedies what suggestions would you make? Would a statutory litany of examples of commercially unreasonable behaviors help? Should the consumer debtor be granted greater or lesser remedial powers?

§ 19.08 Consumer Protection: The Uniform Consumer Credit Code

[A] Introduction

Critics of Article 9's approach to consumer defaults asserted that a creditor's disposition sale might not produce fair value because of the limited resale market for most types of consumer items. These critics accurately noted that other than the provisions prohibiting waiver before default and the mandatory sale provisions for consumer goods under section 9-505(1), the U.C.C. was relatively neutral with respect to consumer protection. Article 9 recognized the principle of freedom of contract and attempted to provide the greatest latitude possible to the contracting parties. Unhappy with the Code's approach, consumer advocates successfully lobbied for the creation of a special statute governing consumer credit transactions.

[B] The U.C.C.C. Approach: Freedom of Contract Limited

The Uniform Consumer Credit Code (U.C.C.C.) begins with the premise that a consumer cannot generally waive rights and benefits under the Act. Section 1.107 specifically addresses waiver or other variation: "except in settlement of a bona fide dispute, a consumer may not agree to forego rights or benefits under this Act". Compare U.C.C. §§ 1-102(3) and 9-501(3).[18] In addition, the U.C.C.C. defines default[19] and restricts the ability of credit sellers to recover deficiencies.

---

[18] Waiver or other variation is specifically provided for in some sections, such as Section 5.204(4) on rescission. In the absence of such a provision, waiver or agreement to forego must be part of a settlement, and settlements are subject to review as provided in this section.

[19] Section 5.109 provides:

[Default]

An agreement of the parties to a consumer credit transaction with respect to default on the part of the consumer is enforceable only to the extent that:

(1) the consumer fails to make a payment as required by agreement; or

(2) the propsect of payment, performance, or realization of collateral is significantly impaired; the burden of extablishing the prospect of significant impairment is on the creditor.

Section 5.103 divides credit sales (including purchase money consumer loans made by a lender who is related to the seller) into two classes based on a specified break-off point of $1750.

§ 5.103 [Restrictions on Deficiency Judgments in Consumer Credit Sales]

(1) This section applies to a consumer credit sale of goods or services and on a consumer loan in which the lender is subject to claims and defenses arising from sales and leases (Section 3.405). A consumer is not liable for a deficiency unless the creditor has disposed of the goods in good faith and in a commercially reasonable manner.

(2) If the seller repossesses or voluntarily accepts surrender of goods which were the subject of the sale and in which he has a security interest, the consumer is not personally liable to the seller for the unpaid balance of the debt arising from the sale of a commercial unit of goods of which the cash sale price was $1750 or less, and the seller is not obligated to resell the collateral unless the consumer has paid 60 per cent or more of the cash price and has not signed after default a statement renouncing his rights in the collateral.

(3) If the seller repossesses or voluntarily accepts surrender of goods which were the subject of the sale but in which he has a security interest to secure a debt arising from a sale of goods or services or a combined sale of goods and services and the cash price of the sale was $1750 or less, the consumer is not personally liable to the seller for the unpaid balance of the debt arising from the sale, and the seller's duty to dispose of the collateral is governed by the provisions on disposition of collateral (Part 5 of Article 9) of the Uniform Commercial Code.

(4) If the lender takes possession or voluntarily accepts surrender of goods in which he has a purchase money security interest to secure a debt arising from a consumer loan in which the lender is subject to claims and defenses arising from sales and leases (Section 3.405) and the net proceeds of the loan paid to or for the benefit of the consumer were $1750 or less, the consumer is not personally liable to the lender for the unpaid balance of the debt arising from that loan and the lender's duty to dispose of the collateral is governed by the provisions on disposition of collateral (Part 5 fof Article 9) of the Uniform Commercial Code.

(5) For the purpose of determining the unpaid balance of consolidated debts or debts pursuant to open-end credit, the allocation of payments to a debt shall be determined in the same manner as provided for determining the amount of debt secured by various security interests (Section 3.303).

(6) The consumer may be held liable in damages to the creditor if the consumer has wrongfully damaged the collateral or if, after default and demand, the buyer has wrongfully failed to make the collateral available to the creditor.

(7) If the creditor elects to bring an action against the consumer for a debt arising from a consumer credit sale of goods or services or from a consumer loan in which the lender is subject to claims and defenses arising from sales and leases (Section 3.405), when under this section he would not be entitled to a deficiency judgment if he took possession of the collateral, and obtains judgment:

(a) he may not take possession the collateral, and

(b) the collateral is not subject to levy or sale on execution or similar proceedings pursuant to the judgment.

(8) The amounts of $1750 in subsections (2), (3) and (4) are subject to change pursuant to the provisions on adjustment of dollar amounts (Section 1.106).

Under section 5.103, if the selling price is below the $1750 break-off point, the secured creditor has no right to a deficiency and the creditor does not have to worry about the commercial reasonableness of the property resale. A creditor's repossession thus functions like a strict foreclosure; the secured party retains any surplus; the creditor must choose between repossession and a suit on the debt, but cannot pursue both remedies. U.C.C.C. § 5.103(2).

For amounts greater than $1750, the secured party may proceed under the rules of U.C.C. § 9-504 and recover a deficiency, if the circumstances permit. To illustrate, consider the case of a consumer who buys a used car on credit for $10,000 and gives the seller a security interest to secure the debt. Assume that the debtor defaults and the seller repossesses. If the seller resells the car for $7500 then seeks a deficiency judgement for the remainder, the seller will prevail if there are no violations under section 9-504. Section 5.103 of the U.C.C.C. does not restrict the seller because the selling price would be above the break-off point.

If the auto had a cash sales price of $1500 and the debtor defaulted, the repossessing creditor would not be required to resell the car. However, the creditor would be precluded from seeking a deficiency judgment, even if a subsequent resale failed to produce an amount sufficient to satisfy the entire claim. If the debtor had paid $900 of the $1500 purchase price at the time of default, section 5.103(2) obligates the creditor to make a resale because the debtor paid more than sixty percent of the outstanding obligation. If the resale yielded a surplus, the creditor would be obligated to account to debtor. But if the resale resulted in a deficiency, the creditor would be prohibited from suing to recover the deficiency under the U.C.C.C.

As one might expect, the break-off point of section 5.103 represented a compromise between the consumer advocates who argued that there should be no deficiency, and the pro-creditor forces who advocated for no limitations at all. Deficiency claims always include resale costs, attorneys fees, and the like — these extra costs become a substantial penalty for the debtor when the value of the collateral is small. As both collateral and the amount financed become larger, the costs associated with deficiency claims become less significant.

QUESTION

How much *real* protection does the U.C.C.C. provide? The statute does not expressly preclude a creditor's levying on other assets of a debtor as a means of satisfying a deficiency. While the spirit of the Uniform Consumer Credit Code would seem to prevent a creditor from making such a levy, the absence of a statutory direction demonstrates that there can be a substantial gap in the protection afforded such debtors. Consider the next case.

UNION NATIONAL BANK OF WICHITA v. SCHMITZ

Court of Appeals of Kansas
18 Kan. App. 2d 403, 853 P.2d 1180, 21 U.C.C.R. Serv. 2d 403 (1993)

LEWIS, J.:

This action was commenced by Union National Bank (UNB) against Clifford J. Schmitz (defendant) for the recovery of a deficiency judgment in the amount of $2,087.97. The trial court concluded that UNB's sale of a repossessed vehicle was not commercially reasonable and denied it a deficiency judgment. UNB appeals from that decision. After careful review, we reverse the decision of the trial court and remand with directions.

The original lawsuit was filed as a limited action, and the evidence offered by UNB to sustain its burden of proof was also limited. UNB called one witness, an assistant vice-president. The evidence indicated that the defendant had borrowed $4,662.40 from UNB to purchase a 1983 Buick automobile from a local dealer.

The documents required the defendant to pay $194.97 per month on the note purchased by UNB. The defendant failed to do so on a regular basis and, in time, was in default. UNB sent the defendant a right to cure notice, which was apparently ignored. An unsuccessful attempt was made to work something out on payments. When this failed, the defendant voluntarily surrendered the vehicle in question to UNB.

After it had been in possession of the vehicle for some period of time, UNB sent another notice to the defendant advising him that the property would be sold at private sale at any time after a specified date. This same notice advised the defendant that he had the right to redeem the collateral at a stated figure. The defendant was also advised by this notice that he would be held responsible for any deficiency balance remaining after the sale of the vehicle. The vehicle was sold without further notice to the defendant.

The witness called by UNB described the vehicle as being in a "rough" condition when repossessed and in "fair to poor shape." The witness testified that the paint was faded, it was dented with some rust, the interior visors were missing, and the driver's seat was shredded. In order to prepare the vehicle for sale, UNB spent $15 having it washed and vacuumed.

The vehicle was sold at the Mid-America Auto Auction. This auction was described by the UNB witness as a dealer-only auction, which was held every week on Thursday. The UNB witness testified that the auction was well known to dealers in the Wichita area and was well attended by dealers. It was explained that bidding at the auction was on a competitive basis and that UNB retained the right to reject any and all bids. The vehicle voluntarily surrendered by the defendant was sold at this auction for $920, minus a $75 sale fee, and the witness for UNB testified, "I believe it was the fair value of the car at the time."

The defendant offered no evidence. The defendant was present in person during the trial of the matter but did not retain counsel. He did testify briefly but offered nothing substantial to contradict the testimony of the plaintiff's witnesses. If the defendant had a particular objection to what took place, it appears that his complaint was that the vehicle did not sell for as much money as he thought it was worth. The defendant has not filed a brief with this court.

The trial court, after hearing the evidence, held that the plaintiff had not sustained its burden of proof to show that the sale of the vehicle was commercially reasonable. The court then denied the plaintiff's prayer for a deficiency judgment. There are no findings set out by the trial court, and we must take its rationale from comments made on the record. Of those comments,the following reveals the court's reasoning on the issue:

> This vehicle was then sent to a public auction which was, however, restricted to automobile dealers and effectively precluding the defendant from making a bid or from any other nonautomobile dealer from making a bid and effectively restricting the price which could be obtained for a wholesale price.
>
> Therefore, the vehicle, the Court finds, was not reasonably exposed on the retail market; and, accordingly, the Court finds that the plaintiff has failed to sustain his burden of proving that the sale was conducted in a commercially reasonable manner.

The only issue on appeal is whether the trial court erred in its conclusion that the sale of the automobile by UNB was not commercially reasonable.

STANDARD OF REVIEW, BURDEN OF PROOF, ETC.

This is a consumer credit transaction and is governed by the Kansas Uniform Consumer Credit Code (UCCC) K.S.A. 16a 5-103 of the U.C.C.C provides in part:

> (1) This section applies to a deficiency on a consumer credit sale of goods or services and on a consumer loan in which the lender is subject to defenses arising from sales (section 16a-3-405); a consumer is not liable for a deficiency unless the creditor has disposed of the goods in good faith and in a commercially reasonable manner.

It should come as no surprise that our Supreme Court has interpreted the emphasized language quite literally. In this state, it is settled law that in proceedings governed by the U.C.C.C a debtor is not liable for a deficiency judgment as a matter of law unless the goods have been disposed of in good faith and in a commercially reasonable manner. . .. It is apparent in this case that the plaintiff is not entitled to a deficiency judgment unless the trial court erred in its conclusion that the sale was not commercially reasonable.

Although the U.C.C.C controls this factual situation, it does not define what is or is not commercially reasonable.

> "As the Kansas Comment reveals, in consumer credit transactions involving default, the Kansas Uniform Consumer Credit Code governs. However, when the U.C.C.C is silent on consumer default, then the U.C.C. provisions on default (K.S.A. 84-9-501 et seq.) are to be applied. Consequently, as the U.C.C.C does not define what is a commercially reasonable disposition of repossessed collateral in a consumer credit transaction, courts may refer to U.C.C. decisions in determining what is a commercially reasonable disposition of collateral." *Medling v. Wecoe Credit Union,* 234 Kan. 852, 863, 678 P.2d 1115 (1984).

The net result is that, while this is a case controlled by the U.C.C.C, our principal references from this point forward will be the U.C.C. and cases decided under that code.

The first question we must resolve is the manner in which it is determined whether a disposition is or is not commercially reasonable. This process has been defined by our courts as to be one of a question of fact:

> "Unfortunately, the U.C.C. does not specifically define the term 'commercially reasonable.' Because the statutory definition of a commercially reasonable sale is vague, the cases generally hold that a factual determination as to whether a sale was commercially reasonable must depend on the particular facts of each case. See *Hall v. Owen Co. State Bank, et al.*, 175 Ind. App. 150. We agree that the determination of the issue whether a sale was held in a commercially reasonable manner is a question of fact to be determined in each particular case by the trier of fact, and that, in an action for a deficiency judgment, the secured creditor has the burden of proof to show that the disposition or sale of the collateral was made in a commercially reasonable manner." *Westgate State Bank v. Clark*, 231 Kan. at 91.

> The commercial reasonableness of a sale of collateral by a secured creditor is a question of fact to be determined by the trier of fact. The creditor has the burden of proving commercial reasonableness. . .."

It is well established that whether a particular disposition was done in a commercially reasonable manner is a question of fact to be determined by the trier of fact. The burden of proving that collateral was disposed of in a commercially reasonable manner is placed upon the secured creditor — in this case, UNB.

In the ordinary case, the standard of review of this court would be to determine whether the findings of the trial court are supported by substantial competent evidence. *Medling v. Wecoe Credit Union*, 234 Kan. at 866.

DEALER ONLY WHOLESALE AUCTION

The method utilized to dispose of the collateral in this case was a well-known, regularly scheduled, dealer-only wholesale auction. The trial court's findings that this sale was commercially unreasonable are so broad that they virtually declare any dealer-only wholesale auction to be not commercially reasonable. In deciding this issue, the trial court focused solely on the nature of the auction and the price received for the vehicle. The trial court's decision, if allowed to stand, would mean that a dealer-only wholesale auction could not be commercially reasonable. This is not the law, and the trial court erred in reaching this conclusion.

We conclude that a dealer-only wholesale auction may be commercially reasonable and that the trial court erred in finding that it cannot be commercially reasonable. We reach this conclusion not because the decision is not supported by substantial competent evidence but because the trial court focused on the wrong factors in reaching its decision.

The trial court reasoned that the sale was not commercially reasonable because it was restricted to dealers only and the defendant could not bid. There is no support in the law for such a conclusion.

> "The duty to give notice of the sale of repossessed collateral is defined by K.S.A. 84-9-504(3), which provides in relevant part as follows:
>
> > 'Unless collateral is perishable or threatens to decline speedily in value or is of a type sold on a recognized market, reasonable notification of the time and place of any public sale or reasonable notification of the time after which any private sale or other intended disposition is to be made shall be sent by the secured party to the debtor, if he has not signed after default a statement renouncing or modifying his right to notification of sale. In the case of consumer goods no other notification need be sent.'
> >
> > The statute clearly distinguishes between the type of notice which must be given when the secured creditor selects a private as opposed to a public sale. Only if the sale is public need the debtor be given notice of where and when the sale will take place. As to a private sale, the creditor must inform the debtor of the date after which the sale will be made." *Garden Nat'l Bank v. Cada,* 241 Kan. 494, 496, 738 P.2d 429 (1987).

The Supreme Court in the *Cada* decision concluded that a dealer-only auction, such as that involved in the instant matter, was a private sale.

> "In the instant case, Mrs. Cada's automobile was sold at a wholesale car dealer's auction in Denver, Colorado. Only a limited class of persons, car dealers, were entitled to participate at the sale. As Mrs. Cada or members of the public could not participate in the auction, notice of the time and place of the sale would have served little purpose." 241 Kan. at 497.

It is clear that the Kansas Supreme Court has recognized the validity of a dealer-only auction. Since this auction has been determined to be a private sale, the debtor not only has no right to bid, he need not even be given notice of the time and place of such sale. Reasoning by analogy, it becomes apparent that the fact that the defendant was precluded from making a bid is irrelevant in determining whether the sale was commercially reasonable. The trial court erred in concluding that, since the defendant could not bid, the sale was not commercially reasonable.

The trial court also focused on the fact that the auction was a "wholesale" auction in finding that it was not commercially reasonable. Indeed, the court seems to say that a vehicle must be exposed to the retail market or the sale is not commercially reasonable. This conclusion also has no support in the law of this state.

The essential difference between a "retail" and a "wholesale" auction is the price for which the goods will be sold. Obviously a wholesale price is by definition somewhat lower than a retail price. The focus on the price received is much too narrow.

As pointed out under these circumstances, reliance may be had on the U.C.C. in order to determine commercial reasonableness under the U.C.C.C. K.S.A. 84-9-507(2) provides in relevant part:

> The fact that a better price could have been obtained by a sale at a different time or in a different method from that selected by the secured party is not of itself sufficient to establish that the sale was not made in a commercially reasonable manner. If the secured party either sells the collateral in the usual manner in any recognized market therefor or if he sells at the price current in such market at the time of his sale or if he has otherwise sold in conformity with reasonable commercial practices among dealers in the type of property sold he has sold in a commercially reasonable manner.

In *U.S. v. Cox*, 731 F. Supp. 1023, 1025-26 (D. Kan. 1990), the defendants argued that the sale was not commercially reasonable because the price received was inadequate. The federal district judge cited K.S.A. 84-9-507(2) and held: "Nonetheless, the fact that a better price might have been obtained if the sale had been conducted in a different manner does not by itself establish that the sale was commercially unreasonable." . . .

. . . .

We think it apparent from the decisions and the statutes cited that the mere fact collateral is sold at wholesale and not "exposed to the retail market" is not in and of itself sufficient to render a sale commercially unreasonable. The trial court in the instant matter erred in reaching this conclusion.

In the final analysis, the determination of whether a sale was commercially reasonable is a complex question which requires the consideration of many factors. For instance, in *Prairie State Bank v. Hoefgen,* 245 Kan. at 249, the Supreme Court indicated that "[t]he passage of time is but one factor to consider in the determination of whether a sale is commercially reasonable." In *Westgate State Bank v. Clark,* 231 Kan. at 91, our Supreme Court . . . set out nine factors to be considered by the court in determining the commercial reasonableness of a disposition. 231 Kan. at 92-95. . ..

The nine factors as set forth and discussed in the *Westgate* decision are: (1) The duty to clean up, fix up, and paint up the collateral; (2) public or private disposition; (3) wholesale or retail disposition; (4) disposition by unit or in parcels; (5) the duty to publicize the sale; (6) length of time collateral held prior to sale; (7) the duty to give notice of the sale to the debtor and competing secured parties; (8) the actual price received at the sale; and (9) other factors.

The trial court in this case did not apply all of the *Westgate* factors. It focused only on the nature of the sale and the fact that the vehicle was not exposed to a "retail market." The trial court did not consider the "aggregate of circumstances" as required, and this was error.

We hold that the trial court erred in holding that a dealer-only wholesale auction is per se not a commercially reasonable manner in which to dispose of collateral.

We emphasize that we do not hold here that such a sale is per se commercially reasonable. We hold only that it is not per se commercially unreasonable. The determination of whether such a sale is commercially reasonable must be made on a case-by-case basis considering the Westgate factors and the aggregate of circumstances shown. The decision of the trial court in the instant matter was much too narrowly focused.

The burden of proving that a sale is commercially reasonable is placed upon the secured party. It is apparent that, in order to prove this fact, counsel must be prepared to touch on all of the *Westgate* factors which apply. A failure to do so may result in a record which is insufficient to prove the commercial reasonableness of a particular disposition.

WAS THIS SALE COMMERCIALLY REASONABLE?

The next question is whether, based on the record, the sale in this particular case was commercially reasonable. The record in this action is skimpy. It is apparent that counsel for UNB proved only the bare essentials. The defendant was not represented by an attorney, and this factor may have led to a false belief that the proof required was only that of a barebones nature. We think such a belief to be misplaced.

Although the record is skimpy, we conclude the plaintiff did focus on a number of the *Westgate* factors. The testimony of the witness called by UNB was uncontradicted by the defendant. The defendant appears not to question notice given or even necessarily the manner in which the vehicle was sold. He has not chosen to file a brief with this court, and, as near as we can tell from the brief comments made by the defendant on the record, he was only unhappy with the price received. Based on the uncontradicted testimony of the witness for UNB, we hold that there was adequate proof the sale in this case was commercially reasonable.

We have held the trial court erred in focusing too narrowly on the nature of the sale and on the price received. When those elements are considered along with the other facts shown and considered in the aggregate, the record shows a commercially reasonable sale and there is no evidence to the contrary. While the evidence is certainly lacking in details and specificity, it is totally uncontradicted and sufficient to prove that the sale was commercially reasonable. We hold that the trial court erred in concluding the sale in this case was not commercially reasonable. We reverse that decision and remand with instructions to enter a deficiency judgment in favor of the plaintiff and against the defendant.

Reversed and remanded.

§ 19.09 Rights of Junior Creditors

A junior creditor is one who claims a secured interest subsequent to that of a prior perfected secured party. With personal property, secured parties with junior interests in property have few rights. This situation is a sharp contrast to protection afforded junior creditors of real property where the foreclosing senior mortgagee would join junior mortgagees in a judicial foreclosure, or notify junior creditors of an extra-judicial sale. Under Article 9, a junior secured party has a right to receive notification of the senior secured party's intention to dispose of collateral *only if* the senior secured party received prior written notice of the junior creditor's interest. § 9-504(3). If the senior creditor has such notice, then the junior creditor can share in the proceeds of disposition to the extent that disposition nets more than the amount due and owing to the senior creditor. The junior creditor may also recover damages from the senior secured party for wrongful disposition, if the senior had notice of the junior's claim. The following case discusses the pitfalls that can await a junior creditor who fails to give notice.

LOUIS ZAHN DRUG CO. v. BANK OF OAK BROOK TERRACE

Illinois Appellate Court

95 Ill. App. 3d 435; 420 N.E.2d 276; 50 Ill. Dec. 959; 31 U.C.C. Rep. Serv. 1207 (1981)

NASH, J.

In this appeal we consider whether plaintiff, a junior secured creditor, has stated a cause of action pursuant to sections 9-504(1)(c) or section 9-507(1) of the Uniform Commercial Code (Ill. Rev. Stat. 1979, ch. 26, pars. 9-504(1)(c) and 9-507(1)) against defendant, a senior secured creditor, and others, to recover damages for the alleged improper disposition of the collateral which secured their respective loans to the debtor.

Plaintiff, Louis Zahn Drug Co., commenced this action in the circuit court of Du Page County in which it filed a five-count complaint against defendant, Bank of Oak Brook Terrace, and others. The case was subsequently removed to the United States District Court for the Northern District of Illinois, which dismissed counts 3 and 4 brought under Federal law, and remanded the remainder of the case to the circuit court of Du Page County. Defendant's motion to dismiss counts 1, 2 and 5 of the complaint was granted by the trial court and plaintiff appeals.

In count 1 plaintiff alleged that prior to June 6, 1977, defendant, Bank of Oak Brook Terrace (Bank) loaned $25,000 to George Meringolo and GJM Enterprises, Inc. (debtor). According to a financing statement filed on June 6, 1977, the loan was secured by a security interest in "inventory, fixtures, equipment now owned or hereafter acquired [by the debtor]." On December 20, 1977, plaintiff loaned $82,282.82 to the debtor and, according to a financing statement filed on January 9, 1978, plaintiff was given a security interest in

> All fixtures, furnishings, fittings, utensils, tools and equipment, signs, prescription records and files, stock in trade, inventory, pharmaceuticals, drugs, sundry products, lease hold improvements, accounts receivable, proceeds, franchises, contract rights, good will, assignment of store lease, including, but not limited to, all other goods, wares, merchandise furniture, fixtures, equipment, appliances, prescriptions and miscellaneous items, now existing or hereafter acquired by debtor . . . .

The debtor subsequently defaulted on the obligations to both plaintiff and defendant.

After the debtor defaulted, plaintiff attempted to find purchasers for the business and defendants, Harold Schapiro and Donald Warsaw (Buyers), expressed an interest in purchasing it for $70,000. Plaintiff alleged that prior to October 20, 1978, it entered "into negotiations with the defendant [Bank], with an intent to obtain a settlement of the first lien position of the defendant [Bank] . . . by way of verbal and written communications with said Bank. . . . " At about the same time, plaintiff began negotiations with defendant American National Bank & Trust Co., as Trustee (Trustee), which held legal title to the debtor's premises, and its rental agent, defendant Triangle Management Co., in order to assure that the Buyers would be able to obtain a lease of the premises. James Guido was alleged to be the beneficial owner of the premises and also a major shareholder and chairman of the board of the defendant Bank. Plaintiff alleged it also received another offer to purchase the business for $100,000 and then invited the Buyers to reconsider their previous bid. When plaintiff did not hear from them, it resumed its attempts to consummate a sale of the business to the high bidder.

Plaintiff alleges that on October 30, 1978, the bank had, without notice to plaintiff, obtained a renunciation of rights in the collateral from the debtor and sold the entire inventory, assets, fixtures and equipment of the debtor's business for $70,000 to others. The complaint asserts that the sale was commercially unreasonable "in that, among other things, a higher price could have been obtained" and that the Bank, the Buyers, and Triangle Management Co. "did enter into a conspiracy" to defraud plaintiff. Plaintiff further alleged that the Bank had failed to exercise good faith in its dealings with plaintiff concerning the sale, in failing to give notice of it, and in failing to disclose the relationship between the Bank, the beneficiaries of the trust under which title to the premises was held, and Triangle Management Co. Plaintiff also alleged that although the Bank had received payment in full for its loan, it had refused to account for the balance of the funds received or to pay over any excess amount to the plaintiff. Plaintiff prayed that the sale be held commercially unreasonable and that damages be awarded pursuant to section 9-507(1) of the Uniform Commercial Code (Ill. Rev. Stat. 1979, ch. 26, par. 9-507(1)).

. . . .

Section 9-504(1) of the Uniform Commercial Codedescribes a secured party's right to dispose of collateral after default and provides that the proceeds of the disposition shall be applied first (a) to the expenses incurred, then (b) to satisfaction of the principal indebtedness secured, and then (c) to

> ". . . the satisfaction of indebtedness secured by any subordinate security interest in the collateral if written notification of demand therefor is received before distribution of the proceeds is completed. . . ." (Ill. Rev. Stat. 1979, ch. 26, par. 9-504(1)(c)). With certain exceptions not pertinent here
>
> ". . . notification shall be sent to any other secured party from whom the secured party [who is making the disposition] has received (before sending his notification to the debtor or before the debtor's renunciation of his rights) written notice of a claim of an interest in the collateral. . . ." (Ill. Rev. Stat. 1979, ch. 26, par. 9-504(3).)

Section 9-504(3) further provides that the "[s]ale or other disposition may be as a unit or in parcels and at any time and place and on any terms but every aspect of the disposition including the method, manner, time, place and terms must be commercially reasonable." The Code also provides a remedy if a secured party fails to proceed in accordance with its provisions in the disposition of collateral:

> "If it is established that the secured party is not proceeding in accordance with the provisions of this Part disposition may be ordered or restrained on appropriate terms and conditions. If the disposition has occurred the debtor or *any person* entitled to notification or *whose security interest has been made known to the secured party prior to the disposition* has a right to recover

from the secured party any loss caused by a failure to comply with the provisions of this Part. . . ." (Emphasis added.) (Ill. Rev. Stat. 1979, ch. 26, par. 9-507(1).)

Thus, in seeking to impose liability upon a secured party under the remedies provided by section 9-507, plaintiff must allege facts showing it is "a person entitled to notification" or that its security interest was "made known" to defendant prior to disposition of the collateral.

The essential question presented by defendant's motion to dismiss the complaint in the trial court and by the arguments of the parties on appeal is whether plaintiff, as a secondary secured party, must allege it gave notice in writing to defendant in order to proceed under section 9-507, or whether allegations that plaintiff's security interest was otherwise "made known" to defendant before disposition are sufficient.

Plaintiff relies upon the allegations in the complaint that plaintiff and defendant Bank had negotiated in an attempt to settle the Bank's first lien against the collateral and did so by both written and verbal communications. It contends that by these means plaintiff's security interest was made known to defendant prior to sale of the collateral giving plaintiff standing to now assert the sale was commercially unreasonable and to seek damages pursuant to section 9-507. Defendant contends, however, that a secondary secured party such as plaintiff may not complain about any aspect of the sale of the collateral unless it has given written notice of its claim or interest before sale and plaintiff's complaint failed to allege it did so.

Prior to the 1972 amendments of article 9 of the Uniform Commercial Code, a secured party wishing to dispose of collateral was under a duty to give notice to any person who had a security interest in the collateral who had filed a financing statement with the Secretary of State. (Ill. Ann. Stat., ch. 26, par. 9-504, Illinois Code Comment, at 341 (Smith-Hurd 1974); Ill. Rev. Stat. 1971, ch. 26, par. 9-401(1)(c).) He was also required to give notice to any other person known to him to have a security interest in the collateral. (Ill. Ann. Stat., ch. 26, par. 9-504, Illinois Code Comment, at 341 (Smith-Hurd 1974).) Under the 1972 amendments the notice requirements were eased to the extent that a selling secured party need not notify other secured parties of a proposed disposition of collateral unless such parties had first given him written notice of a claim of interest in the collateral. (Ill. Rev. Stat. 1979, ch. 26, par. 9-504(3); Ill. Ann. Stat., ch. 26, par. 9-504, Illinois Code Comment, at 341 (Smith-Hurd 1974).) It necessarily follows that a subordinate secured party who has failed to give the requisite written notice of his claim cannot be heard to complain if he is not notified in advance of the disposition of the collateral and may not seek satisfaction of his indebtedness from the proceeds of the disposition pursuant to section 9-504(1)(c). See *Kolton v. K & L Furniture & Appliances, Inc.* (1979), 82 Ill. App. 3d 868, 875, 403 N.E.2d 478, 484.

It does not necessarily follow, however, that the failure of a subordinate secured party to give written notice of a claim of interest in the collateral forecloses him from contesting the commercial reasonableness of the sale and seeking damages if proven. While the amendments to section 9-504(3) eased the notice requirements of the selling secured party, the provisions of section 9-507(1) giving a secured party whose security interest has been "made known" to the selling secured party an action for damages was not affected by the amendments. We note that the commentators to section 9-507 have reasoned that its language "whose security interest has been made known" to the other secured party may be read to mean "made known in writing," but that is not what it says. (Ill. Ann. Stat., ch. 26, par. 9 — 507, Illinois Code Comment, at 359 (Smith-Hurd 1974).) Had the legislature intended that an action for damages was to be limited to subordinate secured parties whose interest had been made known to the selling secured party "in writing," as it did so limit their rights under section 9-504(1)(c), it could easily have done so. The legislature clearly chose, however, to retain the existing remedy in favor of other secured parties whose interest was made known to the selling party prior to disposition of the collateral. Those subordinate secured parties who have given written notice of their claim against the collateral are entitled to receive notice of its proposed disposition and also to satisfaction of their claim from any surplus in the proceeds. The remedy sought by plaintiff arises after disposition and is granted to the debtor, any person entitled to notification (being those who have given written notice of their claim), or (any person) whose security interest has been made known to the selling party. If, as urged by defendant, the remedy extends only to those secured parties in the third category who have given notice in writing, it would be redundant as such parties are already included within the second category.

One of the purposes of the Code requirement that a sale of collateral be conducted in a commercially reasonable manner is to protect the interests of other secured parties. The selling party is not required to search out and give notice of an intended disposition to all other secured parties, but as to those from whom it had received written notice of their claim of an interest in the collateral prior to the time distribution of the proceeds has been completed, the holder of the subordinate security interest would be entitled to seek satisfaction of its indebtedness from any surplus remaining of the proceeds of sale after payment or expenses and the primary indebtedness.

In the event the subordinate secured party has not given the notice required by section 9-504(3), then he would not be entitled to receive the notice provided by that section from the principal secured party. As we have noted, however, the subordinate secured party is not without remedy, as section 9-507(1) provides that any person whose security interest has been made known to the secured party prior to disposition of the collateral may recover for losses caused by a failure to comply with the Act.

Under somewhat analogous circumstances, this court in *Blackhawk Production Credit Association v. Meridian Implement Co.* (1980), 82 Ill. App. 3d 93, 402 N.E.2d 277, considered the rights of a secured party holding a subordinate security interest where the party with the superior security interest retained the collateral in full satisfaction of the debtor's obligation to it. Under section 9-505(2) (Ill. Rev. Stat. 1979, ch. 26, par. 9-505(2)) if a secured party retains the collateral in satisfaction of its obligation, it is required to send notice to any other secured party from whom it has received written notice of a claim of an interest in the collateral, and if another secured party objects in writing within 21 days thereafter, the collateral must be disposed of under section 9-504. In *Blackhawk* we held that a secured party was not authorized by section 9-505 to retain collateral in satisfaction of unsecured as well as secured debts and, therefore, the failure of the holder of a subordinate security interest to serve written notice on the senior secured party prior to the repossession of the collateral did not preclude his recovery since his security interest was made known to the senior secured party before the subsequent sale of the collateral. The wrongful disposition of the collateral in that case which gave rise to a claim under section 9-507(1) was the sale of the collateral after the primary secured party had received notification of the interest of the junior secured party.

Similarly, it has been said that mere knowledge by the selling secured party of the interest of another secured party in the collateral is sufficient to subject him to liability under section 9-507(1), if he fails to dispose of the collateral in a commercially reasonable manner. See *Liberty National Bank & Trust Co. v. Acme Tool Division of the Rucker Co.* (10th Cir. 1976), 540 F.2d 1375, 1382.

We conclude that a subordinate secured party's security interest in the collateral need not be made known in writing to the selling secured party in order to challenge a disposition under section 9-507 on the grounds it was commercially unreasonable where the interest was otherwise made known to the secured party prior to disposition.

While plaintiff does not and need not allege that its security interest was made known to the Bank in writing in order to maintain an action under section 9-507, its complaint must set forth facts which if proven show that the selling secured party had been informed of plaintiff's interest prior to the disposition of the collateral. It may not be inferred from plaintiff's allegation that it negotiated with the Bank seeking to settle the Bank's first lien that the Bank became aware of plaintiff's junior secured status. A complaint will not withstand a motion to dismiss under section 45 of the Civil Practice Act unless it at least minimally alleges facts setting forth the essential elements of a cause of action (*Kolton v. K & L Furniture & Appliances, Inc.* (1980), 82 Ill. App. 3d 868, 403 N.E.2d 478). . ..

. . . .

The trial court dismissed the complaint finding it lacked necessary allegations that plaintiff had given written notice to the Bank of its claim of an interest in the collateral. As we have determined written notice is not required to preserve a remedy pursuant to section 9-507(1), the court erred in dismissing counts I and V on that ground. Defendants did not attack the sufficiency of the allegations of these counts under section 45 of the Civil Practice Act (Ill. Rev. Stat. 1979, ch. 110, par. 45), however, and will be given an opportunity to do so on remand. A complaint should not be dismissed unless it clearly appears that no set of facts can be proved which will justify a recovery . . ., and plaintiff may wish to amend its complaint in an effort to supply the deficiencies we have discussed.

For these reasons the judgment of the trial court will be reversed and the cause remanded for further proceedings in accordance with the views expressed herein.

Reversed and remanded.

COMMENT

A junior secured party bargains for an interest in the debtor's equity. If the senior creditor sells the property for an amount less than the real value, the junior creditor is injured to the extent that the debtor's equity in the property would be reduced. Even though it may have lost an interest in the collateral, a junior creditor still has rights against the debtor on the debt. If the senior secured party has violated section 9-504(3) in making a commerically unreasonable sale by accepting too low a price, the junior secured party under section 9-507(1) may recover from the senior creditor the amount of any surplus that would have been obtained through a commercially reasonable sale. The Article 9 study committee has recommended that section 9-507(1) be revised to afford all junior creditors a remedy, and not just those creditors who notified the senior creditor. The recommendation only indirectly gets at the heart of the junior creditor's problem—ensuring the highest value possible from a disposition sale. See also *River Valley State Bank v. Peterson,* 154 Wis2d, 453 N.W.2d 193 (1990), *Ramsey v. Ernoko, Inc.*, 74 Ohio App.3d 749, 600 N.E. 2d 701 (1991), and *Georgia-Pacific Corp. v. First Wisconsin Fin'l Corp.*, 805 F.Supp. 610, 19 U.C.C. Rep. Serv. 2d 1237 (N.D. Ill. 1992). Are there other ways to protect the interests of junior creditors? Should the junior creditor's interests be considered at all?

CHAPTER 20

SECURITY INTERESTS IN BANKRUPTCY

§ 20.01 Introduction — Non-Bankruptcy Approaches

We have already seen the impact of bankruptcy law on various aspects of the secured transaction relationship in previous chapters. Each year, more than one million bankruptcy petitions are filed. In many of those cases, a debtor became insolvent. Section 1-201(23) of the U.C.C. describes an insolvent person as someone who has either ceased to pay his or her debts in the ordinary course of business, or someone who cannot pay his or her debts as they become due. When a debtor becomes insolvent, some form of insolvency proceeding usually ensues. Such proceedings may be instituted under either state or federal law. If the debtor chooses to use state law, there are four basic alternatives: composition, extension, assignments for the benefit of creditors, and state receivership appointments. Before examining the security interest in bankruptcy, consider non-bankruptcy approaches to a problem debt.

In a composition, creditors agree to accept a lesser payment amount in full satisfaction of a debt. An extension is a contract between the debtor and two or more creditors in which the creditors agree to extend the debtor's time for payment of an obligation. In many instances a debt settlement will involve both a composition and an extension; in essence, an agreement to accept less over a longer time. Composition agreements are governed by principles of contract law rather than specific state debtor-creditor laws, thus, the composition arrangement must have consideration to be effective. Courts have found consideration in the agreements among creditors to reduce their claims to lesser amounts. Thus, there can be no composition between a debtor and a single creditor; to be effective, the agreement must have at least two creditors participating.

There is no requirement that all of a debtor's creditors agree to a composition. Creditors who do not agree are not affected by the composition arrangement. The debts owed to those creditors remain outstanding for the full amounts. In a similar fashion, there can be different treatment even among the creditors who do agree to a composition. Creditor A can agree to be paid a higher or lower proportion of the debt owed than Creditor B. The common law does not condemn preferences so long as no creditor receives any secret and additional consideration.

A third type of non-bankruptcy proceeding is the assignment for the benefit of creditors. Under this arrangement the debtor voluntarily transfers her assets to a person who serves as trustee to liquidate the assets and distribute the proceeds to creditors. If a debt problem reaches state court, those courts have the power to appoint a receiver to handle the debtor's business in the same manner as an assignee. The assignee or receiver takes all legal title to the property transferred; there can be no reservation of an interest in the debtor. U.C.C. § 9-301(3) provides that the assignee for the benefit of creditors and the receiver have lien creditor status from the time of the assignment; this provision implies that the assignee and receiver have priority over an unperfected security interest under section 9-301(1)(b). If a creditor has a perfected security interest in property before an assignment for the benefit of creditors is made or a receiver is appointed, the secured creditor continues to have priority over the assignee or receiver's lien interest.

The duties of either the assignee or receiver are the same — each is accountable to the creditors as a trustee. Consent of the creditors is not a condition precedent for either appointing a receiver or making an assignment for the benefit of creditors. Most assignments for the benefit of creditors are regulated by state statutes that are similar to the federal bankruptcy law — the assignment must be recorded, schedules of the assigning debtor's assets and liabilities must be filed, and notice must be given to the creditors.

In problem debt situations there are a number of reasons why a debtor might prefer a non-bankruptcy proceeding. Composition and extension agreements permit the debtor to continue operating without the stigma that often attaches to a bankruptcy filing. An assignment for the benefit of creditors provides flexibility, informality, and frequently results in higher liquidation prices. In addition, the costs of administration under these non-bankruptcy approaches are typically lower than those associated with a bankruptcy case.

Because the secured creditor can tie up all of a debtor's property outside bankruptcy, many secured creditors become intractable over the prospect of loan restructuring when a debt becomes a problem. Some of these creditors mistakenly believe that their security interests in property will protect them in both non-bankruptcy and bankruptcy cases. Consequently, some creditors minimize the importance of working out a debt plan with the debtor. Ironically, by refusing to consider non-bankruptcy alternatives, some creditors ultimately force their debtors into bankruptcy — a situation which can have far-reaching effects on the Article 9 secured creditor. Examples of such effects include: delays in the secured creditor's realizing on collateral; the debtor's continued use, lease, or sale of collateral; a loss of priority in collateral to a post-petition creditor; elimination of the secured party's ability to claim an interest in after-acquired property under a floating lien arrangement; and, the return of already-repossessed property. The next section briefly describes how some of these effects can arise.

§ 20.02 The General Nature of Bankruptcy — What Can Happen To the Secured Creditor's Interest?

The traditional aim of bankruptcy is to provide a debtor with a fresh financial beginning. Bankruptcy law is codified in Title 11 of the U.S.C.A., which has eight substantive chapters:

Chapter 1: General Provisions, Definitions, and Rules of Construction

Chapter 3: Case Administration

Chapter 5: Creditors, the Debtor, and the Estate

Chapter 7: Liquidation

Chapter 9: Adjustment of the Debts of a Municipality

Chapter 11: Reorganization

Chapter 12: Adjustment of the Debts of a Family Farmer With Regular Annual Income

Chapter 13: Adjustment of the Debts of an Individual With Regular Income

Chapters 1, 3, and 5 generally apply in all bankruptcy proceedings. Chapters 7, 9, 11, 12, and 13 address specific rules for different types of bankruptcy cases. A bankruptcy case begins when a petition for relief is filed by or against a debtor in bankruptcy court. The bankruptcy court has broad jurisdiction over all of the debtor's property, regardless of location. Most requests for relief come under chapter 7's liquidation provisions, or chapter 11's outline for a business debtor's reorganization. This chapter will only address cases under chapters 7 and 11.

Under Chapters 7 and 11 there are five steps to the bankruptcy process. With Chapter 7 liquidations, the five steps are: commencement, collecting property, reducing property to cash, distributing the proceeds, and determining whether a discharge should be granted. For business reorganizations under Chapter 11 the five steps are: commencement, continued operation of the business after commencement, the formulation of a debt rehabilitation plan, creditor acceptance of the rehabilitation plan, and court confirmation of the plan.

[A] Case Commencement

A bankruptcy case begins with the filing of a petition for relief in the bankruptcy court. BRA § 301. Generally, the debtor pays a fee and files a voluntary petition under chapters 7, 11, 12, or 13.[1] There are also certain instances where the creditors of a debtor may file an involuntary petition against a debtor under chapters 7 or 11. Section 303 of the Bankruptcy Code provides that there must be at least three creditors with unsecured claims totalling $10,000 or more in order to file an involuntary petition. If a debtor has fewer than twelve unsecured creditors, a single creditor with an unsecured claim of $10,000 can file an involuntary petition. In a voluntary case, the order for bankruptcy relief occurs at the time the petition is filed. In involuntary cases, the order for relief comes after the debtor has had an opportunity to file an answer. If the debtor does not file an answer, the bankruptcy court will order relief. BRA § 303(h). However, if the debtor timely answers an involuntary petition, the court can only adjudicate the debtor as bankrupt if one of two grounds for involuntary relief can be established. The two bases for involuntary relief are: 1) the debtor is generally not paying debts as they come due; or 2) within 120 days of the petition filing, a general receiver, assignee, or custodian takes possession of substantially all of the debtor's property. With involuntary petitions, the order of relief against a debtor usually occurs several weeks after the filing.

[B] The Trustee in Bankruptcy and Property of the Estate

The next event after a bankruptcy filing is a meeting of the creditors where a trustee is elected. BRA § 341. In every chapter 7 liquidation case, the bankruptcy court appoints a private citizen to serve as trustee of the bankruptcy estate; if the creditors have elected a particular trustee, the court will usually affirm that selection. The trustee is essentially a creature of federal law who acts as a representative of general, unsecured creditors. The trustee has the responsibility of marshalling all of the bankruptcy estate's property and reducing that property to money to pay off creditors on a pro rata basis. BRA § 704(1). In a Chapter 11 case, the debtor ordinarily retains possession of the estate property and assumes most powers of the trustee. See BRA § 1107. The bankruptcy court still has the power to appoint a trustee in a reorganization case if the court believes that such oversight is warranted. Where no trustee is appointed, the court can designate an examiner to oversee the handling of estate property by the debtor-in-possession.

Section 541(a) of the Bankruptcy Code provides that the commencement of any case creates an estate comprised of "all legal or equitable interests of the debtor in property." Property of

[1] The filing fee for a Chapter 7 bankruptcy is $90 and $500 for a Chapter 11 case. 28 U.S.C.A. § 1930(a). The bankruptcy court may dismiss a case for non-payment of fees.

the estate therefore, includes any property, *whether subject to a security interest or not.* As representative of the bankruptcy estate, the trustee has complete power over all property once a case begins. The Bankruptcy Code requires the turnover of all the debtor's property to the trustee, even if a secured creditor has repossessed under U.C.C. § 9-503. BRA § 542(a).

Returning repossessed property is most important in reorganization cases. Section 542(a) compels the turnover of or an accounting for, "property that the trustee may use, sell, or lease under section 363 . . . . unless such property is of inconsequential value or benefit to the estate." The Bankruptcy Code does not explain what it means by the phrase "inconsequential value." The interest of the bankrupt estate could include the debtor's pre-bankruptcy right to redeem property under U.C.C. § 9-506, or the right to any surplus produced by a forced sale under section 9-504. Thus, if either the debtor-in-possession or the trustee concludes that some value to the estate could be derived by returning repossessed property, either party could demand a turnover.

SPS TECHNOLOGIES, INC. v. BAKER MATERIAL HANDLING CORPORATION

United States District Court, Eastern District of Pennsylvania
153 Bankr. 148 (1993)

DALZELL, J.

SPS Technologies, Inc. ("SPS") filed this action against Baker Material Handling Corporation ("Baker") seeking to collect an $114,929.58 account receivable (the "Baker Receivable") that Baker owed to a third party, E.C. Campbell, Inc. ("ECC"). SPS, a secured creditor of ECC, levied on the account on October 11, 1991, but when ECC filed for Chapter 11 bankruptcy about three weeks later, Baker paid the receivable to ECC's estate instead of to SPS.

SPS alleges in its complaint that Baker's payment of the account receivable to ECC constituted both a breach of contract and a violation of the Virginia Commercial Code. SPS also alleges that Baker aided and abetted a fraudulent conversion of the Baker Receivable because Baker's allegedly illegal payment to ECC made it possible for ECC to distribute a large portion of the receivable to persons and entities other than ECC's secured creditors.

Both SPS and Baker have filed motions for summary judgment. The pivotal issue these motions present is whether the receivable constituted property of ECC's bankruptcy estate. If the receivable was part of the estate, Baker was correct to pay it to ECC, but if it was not, Baker should have paid SPS. For the following reasons, we conclude that the receivable constituted part of ECC's estate. We will therefore grant Baker's motion and deny SPS's motion.

I. BACKGROUND

The parties have stipulated to the facts necessary to decide this motion. See Stipulation of Facts, filed January 15, 1993. SPS sold goods to ECC on an open account in connection with a material handling system ECC was installing. As a result, ECC became indebted to SPS in the amount of $602,223.00. After ECC failed to make timely payments on this debt, SPS and ECC memorialized the debt on November 6, 1990 by executing a "Settlement Agreement" and a "Confessed Judgment, Commercial Note and Security Agreement." The security agreement gave SPS a security interest in all of ECC's assets, including the company's accounts receivable.

In September of 1991, SPS notified ECC that ECC had defaulted on its payment obligations under the security agreement. SPS, knowing that Baker owed ECC at least $114,929.58, levied on that account on October 11, 1991 by notifying Baker to direct all future payments on the account to SPS.

On October 30, 1991, ECC filed a bankruptcy petition under Chapter 11 of the United States Bankruptcy Code with the United States Bankruptcy Court for the Eastern District of Virginia, Alexandria Division. On that same day, ECC's counsel wrote to Baker's Vice-President of Finance and Accounting to inform him both that ECC had filed for bankruptcy and that "an automatic stay was imposed . . .against any and all creditors . . .of [ECC] attempting to assert any rights or claims against [ECC's] receivables." Exhibit D to SPS's motion for summary judgment ("SPS's motion"). ECC's counsel instructed Baker to "immediately disburse all funds due and owing to [ECC]." *Id.* Baker responded on November 7, 1991 by wiring $114,929.58 to ECC.

SPS subsequently sent Baker two letters, dated February 19, 1992 and May 18, 1992, contending that "turnover of the payment to ECC without court order determining the relative rights of the parties violated SPS's perfected secured interest in the account payable to ECC", and demanding that Baker immediately pay the account receivable to SPS. February 19, 1992 letter, Exhibit E to SPS's motion. In spite of these communications, Baker has yet to pay any portion of the Baker Receivable to SPS. By letter dated December 10, 1991, however, ECC's counsel forwarded SPS a check in the amount of $20,000.00 which ECC represented was part of the proceeds of the Baker Receivable.

II. DISCUSSION

. . . .

When a debtor files for Chapter 11 bankruptcy, section 542 of the Bankruptcy Coderequires that custodians of "property of the [debtor's] estate" deliver that property to the estate. See 11 U.S.C. § 542(a). Section 541 of the Code defines property of the debtor's estate to include "all legal or equitable interests of the debtor in property as of the commencement of the case." 11 U.S.C. § 541(a)(1). Generally, a debtor's legal or equitable interests are determined by the application of non-bankruptcy law. See 4 Collier on Bankruptcy § 541.02, at 541-10-10 (5th ed. 1988).

The Supreme Court addressed the question of whether a debtor has "legal or equitable interests" in property that a secured creditor has seized in *United States v. Whiting Pools, Inc.,* 462 U.S. 198 (1983), and held that "the reorganization estate includes property of the debtor that has been seized by a creditor prior to the filing of a petition for reorganization." *Id.* at 209-10. The Supreme Court reached this conclusion after surveying the legislative history of sections 541 and 542, and determining that Congress intended the debtor's estate to be inclusive rather than exclusive in order to "facilitate the rehabilitation of the debtor's business." *Id.* at 204. The Court also remarked, however, that the turnover provision "may" not apply if a levy or seizure transfers "ownership" of the property to the creditor. *Id.* 462 U.S. at 210.

Several Bankruptcy Courts have tried to limit the *Whiting Pools* holding (that a debtor's estate includes the debtor's property that a creditor levied upon pre-petition) to cases involving tangible property. These courts contend that the *Whiting Pools* opinion did not contemplate levies on intangible property because it focused on debtors' ownership interests that are unique to tangible property[2] and was grounded in the policy consideration that tangible assets are less valuable when sold for scrap than when returned to debtors for ongoing business use. See, *e.g.*, 126 Bankr. at 772.

Although the Supreme Court spent a portion of its opinion discussing issues exclusive to tangible property levies, we do not believe that it intended to limit the impact of its decision to cases involving tangible property. The reason that the Supreme Court granted certiorari in *United States v. Whiting Pools, Inc.*, 674 F.2d 144 (2d Cir. 1982) (Friendly, J.) ("*Whiting Pools I*"), was to resolve a conflict between *Whiting Pools I,* which held that levied-upon tangible property was property of a debtor's estate, and a Fourth Circuit decision, *Cross Electric Co. v. United States,* 664 F.2d 1218 (4th Cir. 1981), which held that levied-upon intangible property was not part of a debtor's estate. See 462 U.S. at 203.

If the Supreme Court believed, as some bankruptcy courts believe, that intangible property was subject to markedly different treatment than tangible property, it would not have found *Cross Electric* and *Whiting Pools I* to conflict and would not have granted certiorari in order to "resolve this conflict in an important area of the law under the new Bankruptcy Code." 462 U.S. at 202. As the Court of Appeals for the Eleventh Circuit noted in *In re Challenge Air Int'l, Inc.,* 952 F.2d 384 (11th Cir. 1992):

> Had the Supreme Court intended to restrict its holding to situations involving tangible saleable property, it either would have not recognized a conflict between *Cross Electric* and *Whiting Pools I* and refused to grant certiorari, or it would have, at the very least, indicated that no conflict existed between the two decisions in view of the different types of property involved.

Id at 386-7. We therefore believe that the *Whiting Pools* decision controls the outcome of both cases involving intangible property and those involving tangible property.

Nevertheless, we cannot ignore the Supreme Court's comment that the turnover provision "may" not apply if a levy transfers ownership of the levied-upon property to the creditor. We cannot assert that *Whiting Pools* requires all property seized pre-petition to be included in the property of the debtor's estate. Instead, we believe that *Whiting Pools* creates a presumption that all property levied upon pre-petition is included in the debtor's estate, and unless the creditor can show that the levy completely transferred ownership of the property to the creditor, leaving the debtor with no remaining interest, the property must be returned to the estate. We do not believe that such a transfer occurred here.

Whether a debtor who has filed for bankruptcy has "legal or equitable interests" in property is determined by state law. See *In Re Nejberger*, 934 F.2d 1300, 1302 (3d Cir. 1991). SPS and Baker agree that Virginia law applies to their controversy. Virginia has adopted both Article Nine and Article Two of the Uniform Commercial Code ("UCC").

The Court of Appeals for the Ninth Circuit has greatly assisted our analysis with its opinion in *In re Contractor's Equipment Supply Co.,* 861 F.2d 241 (9th Cir. 1988), an opinion in which the court assessed a debtor's interest in a levied-upon account receivable under the U.C.C. As

[2] A levy on tangible property is not complete until the property is sold and reduced to cash. See *Whiting Pools*, 462 U.S. at 212. Until the property is sold, the debtor has two identifiable interests in that property. See *In re Professional Technical*, 71 Bankr. at 949. First, the debtor has a right to redeem that property at any time prior to sale by paying the total debt owed. *Id.* Second, the debtor has the right to any surplus received upon the sale of the property. *Id.*

In re Contractor's Equipment explains, an Article Nine transaction involving an account receivable can entail either a sale of an account or a grant of a security interest in an account. *Id.* at 245 (citing *Major's Furniture Mart, Inc. v. Castle Credit Corp.*, 602 F.2d 538, 542 (3d Cir. 1979)); see also U.C.C. § 8.9-102(1). The type of transaction involved determines whether the debtor retains any interest in the subject account receivable when a creditor forecloses on it. 861 F.2d at 245. If the transaction involved a sale, which the U.C.C. tells us entails a passage of title, see U.C.C. § 8.2-106(1), the debtor is only entitled to any surplus or liable for any deficiency if the parties' agreement so provides. U.C.C. § 8.9-502(2). If the transaction involved a security interest, however, the U.C.C. states that the debtor is without exception entitled to any surplus and liable for any deficiency. *Id.* As the statute attests, the creditor's right to levy on the account is simply a "collection right"; it is not a right to transfer of ownership. U.C.C. § 8.9-502. We are therefore compelled to conclude that a levy on an account in which the creditor holds a security interest does not entail the passage of title, in contrast to what occurs in a sale. See 861 F.2d at 245. In any case, the debtor's right to any surplus from the account receivable is an identifiable post-levy "legal or equitable interest" which brings the account into section 541's definition of "property of the estate."

Moreover, under the U.C.C., a debtor has the right to redeem its collateral "at any time before the secured party has disposed of collateral or entered into a contract for its disposition . . .by tendering fulfillment of all its obligations secured by the collateral." U.C.C. § 8.9-506. Because "collateral" includes accounts receivable, see U.C.C. § 8.9-105, a debtor has a right to redeem its levied-upon accounts before the creditor collects on them. This right to redeem the accounts is also a "legal or equitable interest" rendering the accounts property of the estate under section 501 of the Bankruptcy Code.[3]

SPS argues that, on the facts of the instant case, ECC's right to redeem and right to surplus are insufficient to bring the Baker Receivable into ECC's estate. Specifically, SPS points out that there is no surplus in the instant case because ECC owes over $300,000 to SPS and the account in dispute amounted to only $144,949.58. Similarly, because the debt ECC owes to SPS is so much greater than the value of the Baker Receivable, SPS argues that it is unrealistic to contend that ECC would ever choose to redeem the account. Therefore, SPS maintains that ECC had no exercisable right to surplus or right to redeem.

This argument, however, is the same argument the Supreme Court rejected by overruling *Cross Electric* in *Whiting Pools.* In *Cross Electric*, the Court of Appeals for the Fourth Circuit noted that the debtor had "indicated no intention of redeeming" the levied-upon account, that "it would be incredible that [the debtor] would pay a tax of over $40,000 in order to redeem an account

[3] SPS asserts that a debtor's right to redeem accounts receivable must terminate upon levy because a rule extending the right to redeem until the account debtor pays the account to the levying creditor would render the creditor a hostage to the account debtor. Although we understand SPS's concern, we find that, in the absence of evidence that the debtor and account debtor have improperly colluded to deprive the levying creditor of its rightful property, we cannot justify divesting debtors of their right to redeem property prior to disposition.

SPS does allege that Baker purposefully withheld payment to SPS because it was a supplier to one of ECC's contracts and hoped that paying ECC the Baker Receivable would enable ECC to complete that contract. SPS, however, has provided us with no support for this bald allegation of intent. ECC, on the other hand, has submitted the deposition testimony of Hermann Kling, a corporate officer of Baker who, along with Baker's president, made the decision to pay the receivable to ECC. Kling testified that he made the decision to pay ECC on the advice of counsel and that the decision was in no way motivated by Baker's desire to sustain its contractual relationship with ECC. See Excerpt from Kling's deposition, Baker's Reply to SPS's Opposition to Baker's Motion for Summary Judgment at 11-12.

of approximately $5,500", and that there was no "possible likelihood of any surplus arising out of the sale or liquidation of the account levied upon." 664 F.2d at 1221. On this basis, the Fourth Circuit concluded that:

> since it is thus plain that the trustee is in no position to exercise any of the limited rights it may have to redeem the property levied upon there was no authority . . .to "dissolve" the . . . levy or to order the delivery of the account levied upon . . . to the trustee and the [creditor] is entitled to collect the account pursuant to its levy.

Id. Because we believe that the Supreme Court necessarily rejected this reasoning when it affirmed *Whiting Pools I,* we will not adopt *Cross Electric's* reasoning here. Instead, we hold that ECC's right to redeem the Baker Receivable and its right to any surplus in the receivable, even if they are rights that ECC could not, or would not, assert in the instant situation, are sufficient to render the account "property" of ECC's estate and subject to turnover under section 542 of the Bankruptcy Code.

We are comfortable with this decision because SPS remains entitled to adequate protection of its interest under § 363 of the Bankruptcy Code. See 11 U.S.C. § 363(e). Moreover, as *In re Challenge Air* noted, "the *Whiting Pools* decision authorized turnover of the debtor's property held by the [secured creditor] to maximize the estate in order to facilitate the debtor's reorganization." 952 F.2d at 387. Our decision "simply requires [SPS] to seek protection of its interest according to the congressionally established bankruptcy procedures, rather than by withholding the seized property from the debtor's efforts to reorganize." *Whiting Pools*, 462 U.S. at 213.

III. CONCLUSION

We therefore find that although SPS had levied on the Baker Receivable before ECC filed for bankruptcy, the receivable was "property of the estate" and the Bankruptcy Code required Baker to pay the account to ECC. Under these circumstances, we cannot hold Baker liable either for improper payment or for aiding and abetting ECC's allegedly improper payment of the proceeds to unsecured creditor.

We will therefore grant SPS's motion for summary judgment and deny Baker's motion for summary judgment.

NOTES

(1) Do you agree with the court's decision to include the Baker receivable as property of the bankruptcy estate? How likely was it that ECC would have been able to redeem? The court finds that no harm would come to SPS by virtue of its decision because SPS was entitled to adequate protection. How would you provide such protection?

(2) In *In Re Alcom America Corp.*, 154 B.R. 97 (Bankr. D.C. 1993), the debtor received financing from ABC which took a security interest in Alcom's contracts with the Spanish government for the purchase of ethanol. When the debtor defaulted, ABC repossessed a supply of ethanol and arranged to sell it to a third party under a F.O.B. contract dated March 9, 1984. A week later, Alcom filed for bankruptcy. The trustee argued that ABC's actions violated the automatic stay and that the property should be turned over to the estate. ABC claimed that the Alcom had completely divested itself of any rights in the ethanol before the bankruptcy petition. The court found that the sale was completed before the debtor filed its petition. ABC had a valid

security interest in the ethanol because its contract right constituted a general intangible under U.C.C. § 9-106. Because the ethanol was substituted for the debtor's contract rights, the ethanol became proceeds of those rights. The court held that under section 9-506, the debtor lost the right to redeem the collateral when ABC entered the contract to dispose of the collateral and that the trustee had no power to upset a valid disposition sale.

[C] The Automatic Stay

Commencement of a bankruptcy case automatically stays any action a secured party might take against a debtor or that debtor's property. B.R.A. § 362(a). The secured creditor may not collect the debt, repossess the collateral, seek to enforce a judgment, make a setoff, or even perfect a security interest, once the bankruptcy petition has been filed. Under B.R.A. § 362(c)(1), the stay continues until the property ceases to be property of the estate or when the case is closed, dismissed, or where the debtor receives a discharge from liability.

BRA § 362(d)(2) provides that a secured creditor may seek relief from the automatic stay if: 1) the debtor has no equity in the collateral, and 2) the property is not necessary for an effective reorganization. The stay will terminate 30 days after a request is made unless the court takes some other action. Subsections (e) and (f) of section 362 provide for both a preliminary hearing and a final hearing on the request for relief. The court can continue the stay or grant relief under certain circumstances. The party requesting relief from the stay bears the burden of proof on the issue of the debtor's equity in the property, while the party opposing relief has the burden of proof on all other issues. BRA § 362(g).

A secured creditor can also seek relief from the stay if the creditor's interest in the property is not adequately protected. The concept of adequate protection is discussed at section 361 of the Bankruptcy Code. The statute protects the secured party's interest by permitting the bankruptcy court to require the trustee to make periodic cash payments to the secured creditor to the extent of any decrease in the value of the property while it is a part of the bankruptcy estate. Section 361 also permits additional or replacement liens as well as other types of relief that will result in the creditor's receiving the "indubitable equivalent" of the interest in collateral. The Bankruptcy Code does not define the phrase "indubitable equivalent"; thus, the facts of each particular case become important in determining whether a creditor's interests are adequately protected. The next two cases provide examples of the scope of the automatic stay and creditor claims for relief from the stay.

IN RE BUILDING 62 L.P.

United States Bankruptcy Court for the District of Massachusetts
132 Bankr. 219 (1991)

WILLIAM C. HILLMAN, UNITED STATES BANKRUPTCY JUDGE

This matter came before the Court at an evidentiary hearing on the Motion of BayBank Harvard Trust Company ("BayBank"). BayBank requests relief from the automatic stay pursuant to 11 U.S.C. §§ 362(d)(2) and (d)(1). Building 62 Limited Partnership ("Debtor") objects to the requested relief and states that the property in question, Building 62, is necessary for an effective reorganization.

The Debtor is a limited partnership with one general partner and five limited partners. It is the lessee under a 65-year lease with the Boston Redevelopment Authority ("BRA") of a leasehold interest in the property known as Building 62 in the Charlestown Navy Yard. On July 8, 1988 BayBank advanced $4,350,000.00 to the Debtor for the purposes of renovating Building 62. As security for the loan, the Debtor granted to BayBank a Construction Leasehold Mortgage, Security Agreement, and Assignment (the "Mortgage") with respect to its leasehold interest. The loan is also secured by an assignment of the subleases between the Debtor and the tenants of Building 62.

On January 1, 1990, the Debtor entered into a five year lease with the Massachusetts General Hospital ("MGH"). MGH occupies 70% of Building 62. BayBank further agreed to advance $1,650,000.00 to the Debtor on May 2, 1990 for the purposes of fitting-out the area to be occupied by MGH. Prior to the second advance, the Debtor and BayBank attempted to restructure the loan. These negotiations were not successful. On February 15, 1991, MGH began to withhold rent due to the Debtor's failure to reimburse MGH for tenant improvements.

On May 8, 1991, BayBank notified the debtor that, pursuant to the rights provided in the Mortgage, it was taking possession of Building 62. BayBank hired Congress Realty to manage Building 62. On May 17, 1991, the Debtor filed for relief under Chapter 11 of the Bankruptcy Code. BayBank filed a Motion for Relief From the Automatic Stay on May 28, 1991. The Debtor timely objected to the Motion. As of this date, the Debtor has not filed a plan of reorganization.

At a hearing on September 16, 1991, the Debtor explained the provisions of its proposed plan of reorganization. The general partner of the Debtor stated that by October 15, 1991 MGH would resume rental payments because MGH has recouped the expenses it has incurred to make tenant improvements. According to its expert, Gerald Katz, the Debtor intends to use some of this income to develop a marketing plan to attract new tenants to fill the 30% of the building that is presently vacant. The Debtor hopes to have the building 90% occupied within eight to twelve months. Because the Charlestown Navy Yard is currently under a BRA development plan, Katz expects that the Debtor will be able to rent out the space. The Debtor, he stated, has not been able to rent out the space in the months since the filing only because the Debtor does not have possession of the building. The Debtor has been attempting to lease Building 62 since July of 1988.

Mr. Katz stated at the hearing that if the spaces are leased, the value of Building 62 will increase. The expenses, he said, will not so increase. Because of this increased value, the Debtor expects to attract investors to the project. These investors will receive a substantial equity interest in the partnership. The Debtor stated that the limited partners will voluntarily give up their current equity position to further the reorganization.

Due to the increase in value of the property after it is fully leased and the additional funds received from an investor, the Debtor also anticipates being able to procure a mortgage of $2.8 million. With the mortgage and the money from the investors, the Debtor expects to pay BayBank's secured claim of $3.4 million upon confirmation. Additionally, the new loan and additional monies will fund the plan and pay a dividend to the unsecured creditors.

According to this plan, BayBank will hold an unsecured deficiency claim. The claim will be far greater than the other unsecured claims. Nevertheless, the Debtor states that the Bank will not be treated unfairly because all unsecured creditors will receive a dividend. The Debtor intends to place the unsecured claims of BayBank, the trade creditors, and the limited partners into separate classes. Having three classes, the Debtor expects at least one vote in favor of the plan.

The Debtor lastly explains that the plan, in the event that any of the partners retain an interest in the Debtor, will not violate the "absolute priority rule" because it will fall under the "new value" exception.

DISCUSSION

A party is entitled to relief from stay under 11 U.S.C. § 362(d)(2) if the debtor does not have any equity in the property and the property is not necessary to an effective reorganization. The burden is on the creditor to establish that the debtor does not have any equity in the property. § 362(g). After the creditor establishes the lack of equity, the burden of proof then shifts to the debtor to show that the property is necessary for an effective reorganization. *Id.*

The debtor's burden of proof to show that the property is necessary for an effective reorganization depends upon the point in time when the debtor is asked to present the prospects for reorganization. *United Savings Ass'n v. Timbers of Inwood Forest Associates, Ltd.*, 484 U.S. 365, 375-376, 98 L. Ed. 2d 740, 108 S. Ct. 626 (1988). If the debtor is required to establish the prospects for an effective reorganization at an early stage in the proceedings the burden on the debtor is not as great as it would be in the later stages of the proceedings. *In re Wasserman*, 122 Bankr. 839, 844 (Bankr. D. Mass. 1991). This principle is not the case, however, if within the exclusive period to file a plan the debtor lacks any realistic prospect of effective reorganization. *Timbers,* 484 U.S. at 375-376.

The parties agreed at the hearing on September 16, 1991 that the value of the property is $3.4 million. BayBank's claim is $5,767,086.07 plus accrued interest. Accordingly, the debtor has no equity in the property. The issue before the Court, therefore, is whether the debtor has met his burden of proof in showing that the property is necessary for an effective reorganization.

The Supreme Court has stated that what § 362(d)(2)(B)

> . . . requires is not merely a showing that if there is conceivably to be an effective reorganization, this property will be needed for it; but that the property is essential for an effective reorganization that is in prospect. This means . . . that there must be a reasonable possibility of a successful reorganization within a reasonable time. *United Savings Ass'n v. Timbers of Inwood Forest Associated Ltd.*, 484 U.S. 365, 375-76, 98 L. Ed. 2d 740, 108 S. Ct. 626 (1988).

Based on the language of *Timbers* and cases in this District, this Court will apply the *Timbers* "feasibility" test. *In re North Carver Pine Corporation*, 69 Bankr. 616, 620 (Bankr. D. Mass. 1987); *In re Park West Hotel Corp.,* 64 Bankr. 1013, 1023 (Bankr. D. Mass. 1986); *In re Jug End in Berkshires, Inc.,* 46 Bankr. 892, 902 (Bankr. D. Mass. 1985).

There are few cases in this district which address the "feasibility" test. In one, the debtor failed the test because it did not present that which the court determined was necessary to reorganize, namingly, any purchasers or investors willing to buy or invest in the property. *In re Jug End in Berkshires,* 46 Bankr. 892, 902 (Bankr. D. Mass. 1985). In another, the court found that the debtor met the test not because it met the requirements of § 1129,[4] rather, that it showed a

[4] 11 U.S.C. § 1129 states in part:

(a) The court shall confirm a plan only if all of the following requirements are met:

(1) The plan complies with the applicable provisions of this title . . .

(3) The plan has been proposed in good faith and not by any means forbidden by law . . .

(7) With respect to each impaired class of claims or interests-(A) each holder of a claim or interest of such class . . .accepted the plan; or . . .will receive or retain under the plan on account of such claim or interest property of a value, as of the effective date of the plan, that is not less than the amount that such holder would receive . . .if the debtor were liquidated.. (B) if section 111(b)(2) applies . . .

reasonable possibility of meeting the requirements of that section. *In re Ledgemere Land Corp.*, 125 Bankr. 58, 65 (Bankr. D. Mass. 1991). For the purposes of § 362(d)(2)(B), another court held that the plan "must avoid statutory flaws that would prohibit confirmation . . . the debtor must prove that the things which are to be done after confirmation can be done as a practical matter." *In re Wasserman,* 122 Bankr. 839 (Bankr. D. Mass. 1991).

In a case factually similar to this case, the court provided the following list of requirements that the debtor needed to demonstrate in order to meet its burden under § 362(d)(2)(B):

1. The debtor must be moving meaningfully to propose a plan;

2. The plan must provide that the lender's allowed secured claim would be valued and payable from the debtor's net operating income generated by its property or the ability to propose a plan based on the infusion of new capital, sale, or other viable means;

3. The plan must have a realistic chance of confirmation;

4. Without deciding the issue with the same scrutiny as a confirmation hearing, the debtor's proposed plan must not be obviously unconfirmable;

5. The reorganization must occur in a reasonable period of time. In this regard the factors to look at are:

a. the negotiations among the parties;

b. the amount of time that the debtor has been in possession and operating the business;

c. the length of time since the expiration of the exclusivity period.

In re Ashgrove Apartments of DeKalb County Ltd., 121 Bankr. 752 (Bankr. S.D. Ohio 1990).

This Court recognizes, as did the court in *Ashgrove Apartments,* that a list such as the one above is illustrative and not all-inclusive. The factors are meant to provide an outline of considerations.

The debtor in the case at bar filed for reorganization on May 17, 1991. As the exclusivity period has only recently expired, this Court will apply a more lenient standard. *In re Wasserman,* 122 Bankr. 839, 844 (Bankr. D. Mass. 1991). Nevertheless, the Debtor has failed to meet its burden.

Under *Ashgrove,* the Court must first look whether the Debtor is moving meaningfully to propose a plan. The Debtor explained that it is moving towards a plan but that there are still many conditions to be met. The Debtor first relies on the renewal of the rental income from MGH. It does not have confirmation from MGH that the rent is forthcoming. Nonetheless, with this unassured income, the Debtor proposes to begin a marketing plan to attract new tenants. As a result of the marketing plan, it expects that it will lease out the remaining 30% of its building within the next six to twelve months. While the Court appreciated the Debtor's testimony regarding the development plans in the Navy Yard, it still must take into consideration the same testimony that described the current 17% vacancy rate in Boston, the arrival of two new vacant office buildings on the horizon, and the fact that the Debtor has been attempting to lease out the space for over two years.

---

(10) If a class of claims is impaired under the plan, at least one class of claims that is impaired under the plan has accepted the plan, determined without including any acceptance of the plan by an insider . . .(b)(1) . . .the court on request of the proponent of the plan, shall confirm the plan notwithstanding the requirements of such paragraph if the plan does not discriminate unfairly . . .with respect to each class of claims or interests that is impaired . . . *Id.*

The Debtor expects that if it leases 90% of the building, the overall value of the building will increase to $4,100,000.00. The increased occupancy, according to the Debtor, will not result in increased expenses. With a higher occupancy rate, it also anticipates the arrival of a new investor. The Debtor stated that, although an investment in the Debtor would be risky, it would be able to entice a new investor because of the increased value and by offering the investor equity in the partnership. The Debtor made only vague references to possible investors and did not present any investors to the Court. Accordingly, although the Debtor is moving toward a plan it is not moving meaningfully because there are too many obstacles it must overcome.

In addition, the Debtor must demonstrate that the proposed plan provides that the lender's allowed secured claim would be valued and payable over time from the debtor's net operating income generated by its property or the ability to propose a plan based on the infusion of new capital, sale, or other viable means. The Debtor clearly contemplates the showing of the latter requirement.

The Debtor states that by confirmation, it will have the funds to pay the secured claim of BayBank. The Debtor, however, does not have a commitment for new funds and its ability to procure such funds relies on a host of variables. The Debtor relies on investors without explaining who these investors will be. It does not intend to sell the lease. The Debtor has not produced any other viable means. Accordingly, the Debtor has likewise not met the second requirement of *Ashgrove.*

Ashgrove also requires that the plan not be patently unconfirmable. The Debtor, contrary to the assertion of BayBank, is not required to presently demonstrate that the plan will meet all of the confirmation requirements set out in § 1129. *In re Ledgemere Land Corp.*, 125 Bankr. 58, 65 (Bankr. D. Mass. 1990). The Debtor must, however, show that the plan is capable of being confirmed.

To confirm the plan, the Debtor relies on a future ruling by this Court that the unsecured claims can be placed in separate classes pursuant to *In re Greystone III Joint Venture*, 102 Bankr. 560 (Bankr. W.D. Tex. 1989), aff'd *In re Greystone*, 127 Bankr. 138 (D.C. W.D. Tex. 1990). It also relies on a future ruling regarding the absolute priority rule and the "new value" exception. The Court in *Ashgrove* stated that "unsettled legal issues relating to confirmation disputes will not be decided in the context of a relief from stay." *Ashgrove*, 121 Bankr. at 757. This Court finds, however, that the Debtor's reliance on favorable rulings on three major issues of law is unwarranted.

Such issues outstanding indicate that the plan is, at the present time, unconfirmable.

Lastly, *Ashgrove* requires a showing that the debtor show that the proposed plan can be met within a reasonable period of time. In this regard, the court found telling the presence or absence of negotiations among the parties, the presence or absence of good faith efforts by the parties to reach a consensual solution, and the length of the case. The Debtor has been in Chapter 11 since May. There has been an absence of negotiation between the principal parties in interest and an absence of the parties to reach a solution in good faith. Many of the contingencies, according to the Debtor, are not going to be realized for eight to twelve months. Accordingly, the Debtor has not met the requirements as set forth in *Ashgrove.*

In *Wasserman,* the court reviewed a proposed plan that likewise had a low value for a secured claim and both an expectation of increased value due to new leases and subsequent refinancing. The court found that these elements indicated that the plan was clearly unconfirmable. The court denied relief, however, because new leases were substantially in progress, the plans of reorganization were the subject of negotiation, and the debtors were sophisticated business people. *Wasserman,* 122 Bankr. at 844. The court conditioned the continuing stay for 75 days in the event that the debtor did not obtain confirmation. In the case at bar, new leases are speculative and there is no negotiation regarding a plan. Therefore, even a conditioned stay is unwarranted.

The Debtor has made a valiant attempt to meet its burden but unfortunately, rather than presenting the Court with a reasonable prospect of reorganization, it demonstrated what is commonly known as terminal euphoria. On that basis the Debtor has failed to meet its burden under § 362(d)(2)(B). The Court will not address the alternate grounds for Relief set forth in Baybank's Motion. The Motion for Relief from Stay is granted.

IN RE CAROLINA UTILITIES SUPPLY COMPANY, INC.

United States Bankruptcy Court for the District of South Carolina
118 Bankr. 412 (1990)

BISHOP, BANKRUPTCY JUDGE.

Before the court is the debtor's motion to use cash collateral pursuant to 11 U.S.C. § 363. First Factors Corporation ("First Factors" or "the Bank") objects and contends that the financing arrangement between First Factors and the debtor under their "Factoring Contract and Security Agreement" was a factoring agreement ("sale") as to specific accounts or invoices rather than a loan secured by these accounts. First Factors also asserts that since it purportedly purchased and acquired the debtor's accounts receivable, collections on such accounts receivable are not property of the estate under § 541 of the Bankruptcy Code. Further, if the Court finds that the proceeds of such accounts receivable are property of the estate, First Factors submits that it is not possible for the Court to provide it with adequate protection under § 361.

FINDINGS OF FACT

1. On June 3, 1988, the debtor and the bank entered into an agreement entitled "Factoring Contract and Security Agreement." The agreement was guaranteed by a number of the shareholders of the debtor pursuant to certain personal guarantees attached to the agreement.

2. At the March 22, 1990 hearing, Douglas H. Rogers Vice President of First Factors, testified as follows:

a. The Bank claims an ownership interest in all pre-petition accounts receivable of the debtor purchased by the bank.

b. The Bank retains full recourse against the debtor on the accounts.

c. The Bank is owed approximately $280,000.00, and has a valid security interest in receivables of the debtor totalling approximately $800,000.00.

d. When an invoice from the debtor is "assigned" to the Bank, the Bank does not pay the debtor anything for the invoice. Instead, the Bank (1) receives the invoice, (2) charges the debtor a "factoring fee" of .75% of the amount of the invoice, (3) deducts 20% of the amount of the invoice and applies it to a "reserve" account of the debtor, and (4) "advances" the remaining 80% of the invoice to the debtor, and charges the debtor interest at the prime rate plus 2% on the funds so loaned. If payment is not received by the Bank on the invoice assigned, the amount of the invoice is first charged against the reserve account of the debtor and to the extent the reserve account is not sufficient to cover the accounts, the Bank would seek recovery from the debtor or the personal guarantors.

e. If the debt were paid in full, then the bank would claim no interest in the remaining accounts receivable of the debtor. Once the $280,000.00 debt is paid, the debtor is then the undisputed owner of the remaining $480,000.00 worth of accounts receivable.

f. There are differences between a factoring contract and an accounts receivable financing contract and these differences were enumerated by this witness.

3. Though it is undisputed that the Bank is claiming an ownership interest in approximately $800,000.00 of accounts receivable, the Bank could not adequately explain why it would return the remaining accounts to the debtor once the $280,000.00 debt was satisfied if in fact it owns these pre-petition accounts.

4. The statements on the accounts receivable prepared by the Bank show that the amount of each invoice "assigned" to the Bank is the exact amount that the Bank shows as the potential risk to the debtor.

5. The debtor's president summarized the aging of the accounts, grouping them as follows:

0-30 days	$224,000.00
30-60 days	$234,000.00
60-90 days	$194,000.00
90-120 days	$166,000.00
Over 120 days	$342,000.00

He further stated that approximately $394,000.00 in accounts are over 60 days past due and are "ineligible accounts" under the Bank's formula for making advances. Another $27,000.00 in accounts are less than 60 days past due but are disputed. Another $137,000.00 in accounts are less than 60 days past due but are owed by the same customers who owe accounts which are more than 60 days past due. He stated that when these categories are subtracted from the total accounts, the Bank is left with "good accounts" of around $242,000.00 while it has advanced to the debtor about $282,000.00, leaving a deficit of approximately $40,000.00.

6. The debtor has collected and retained post petition approximately $335,000.00 in proceeds from factored invoices.

ISSUES

1. Whether the document entitled "Factoring Contract and Security Agreement" entered into between the Bank and the debtor constitutes a sale of specific account receivables of the debtor or creates and reflects a loan secured by these accounts?

2. If the court finds that the agreement is a secured loan and the accounts are therefore cash collateral, is the Bank adequately protected?

CONCLUSIONS OF LAW

. . . .

On the basis of the testimony presented at the hearing, arguments of counsel, a review of the record, and after applying the elements considered by the courts in . . . ., it is clear to this court that the relationship between the parties is actually one of debtor and secured party (loan) and not that of grantor and grantee (sale) as to the specific accounts. Therefore, the debtor is the owner of the accounts receivable and the Bank claims and has a security interest therein. The accounts receivable are property of the estate within the meaning of 11 U.S.C. § 541, and cash collateral within the meaning of 11 U.S.C. § 363.

Having found that the specific accounts receivable are cash collateral, the second issue before the court is whether the bank is adequately protected.

The debtor has suggested that the personal guarantee of its officer should constitute adequate protection to First Factors in this case. While it has been held that a guaranty secured by mortgages on two pieces of real property with substantial value may constitute adequate protection [*In re T.H.B. Corp.*, 85 Bankr. 192, 19 Collier Bankr. Cas. 2d (MB) 419 (Bankr. D. Mass. 1988)], Collier states that guaranties do not usually afford adequate protection. "The idea of a third-party guarantee as adequate protection is of very dubious validity since an unsecured guarantee would hardly be the 'indubitable equivalent' of collateral. An acceptable alternative might be a letter of credit issued by a responsible financial institution." 3 Collier Bankruptcy Practice Guide § 41.06(3) (1989). There is no evidence in the record about Mr. Poole's financial condition and even if there were, an unsecured guaranty of a principal of the debtor offers little or no protection to the Bank.

Also, the debtor has openly violated the prohibitions of § 363 of the code by its post petition use of proceeds in which the bank has an interest without its consent and this action is an element considered by this court on the issue of adequate protection.

For all the above reasons, the bank is not adequately protected by debtor's use of cash collateral and this use is hereby denied.

[D] Property Abandonment by the Trustee

The bankruptcy trustee also has the power to abandon any property of the estate that is burdensome or of inconsequential value to the estate. BRA § 554(a). The trustee must provide the bankruptcy court with notice of intent to abandon the property. The court must then conduct a hearing before abandonment will be permitted. The bankruptcy court may also order abandonment of property upon the request of a party in interest. BRA § 554(b). Secured parties often request abandonment where the value of the collateral is less than the secured debt. If the trustee abandons property or the court grants relief from an automatic stay, a secured creditor can proceed under the remedial provisions of part five of Article 9 of the U.C.C.

[E] Determination of Secured Status

If a debtor fails to redeem collateral, or if the secured party cannot obtain relief from the automatic stay or persuade the trustee to abandon property, the creditor will need to participate in the bankruptcy case. Under BRA § 506, the court may allow a "claim of a creditor secured by a lien on property in which the estate has an interest." If the value of the collateral is greater than the secured debt, the trustee will likely choose to sell the property under section 363 and retain the surplus for the estate. In such a case, section 506(b) provides that the secured party is entitled to full payment of the secured debt, interest, and the reasonable costs noted in the security agreement. When the collateral is worth less than the secured debt, the secured party may file a proof of claim as an unsecured creditor for the amount of the debt that exceeds the value of the collateral. BRA § 506(a). Although secured creditors can file proof of claims in bankruptcy, they are not required to do so. In *Dewsnup v. Timm*, 116 L. Ed.2d 903 (1994), the Supreme Court held that secured creditors have the right to ignore their debtors' bankruptcies unless someone sues them and serves them with process. If the secured creditor ignores the bankruptcy and no one challenges the creditor's interest, the lien passes through bankruptcy unaffected. In most cases the trustee in bankruptcy will demand evidence of the secured party's status whether a proof of claim is filed or not. Typically, the trustee carefully examines such evidence in order to determine whether to challenge the claim. Section 546(a) gives the trustee up to two years from the date of trustee appointment to challenge a secured claim.

[F] Use, Sale or Lease of Collateral

Section 363 of the Bankruptcy Code provides for the sale of collateral by the trustee. In most cases, the sale must be authorized by the secured party or by the bankruptcy court. If the court approves a trustee's proposed sale of collateral, the court must ensure that the interests of the secured creditors are adequately protected. Such a sale typically provides the purchaser with a title free and clear of any other interest. Section 363 also authorizes the use or lease of collateral by the estate.

In limited cases, upon the bankruptcy court's approval, a trustee may borrow on behalf of the bankruptcy estate, securing estate property as collateral. Normally, a party who makes a secured loan to the trustee will have rights subordinate to those of a prior perfected secured party in the property. Section 364(d) of the Bankruptcy Code provides that a borrowing trustee can grant a super-priority to a new lender. This super-priority will prevail over the rights of the prior, perfected secured party to the extent the secured party receives adequate protection for its interest. Generally, this type of borrowing only takes place where the trustee or a debtor-in-possession continues to operate a debtor's business (most frequently, in Chapter 11 cases).

[G] Limitations on Floating Liens

We have previously discussed the secured creditor's use of after-acquired property clauses in commercial credit transactions. While after-acquired clauses are expressly permitted under Article 9 at section 9-204, the power of such clauses are cut off in bankruptcy under section 552(a). That provision states that a security agreement entered into before the commencement of a case does not reach property acquired after the commencement of the case other than proceeds.

To illustrate the operation of section 552(a), consider the case of the Creditor who makes a loan to Debtor on September 1. Creditor obtains and perfects a security interest in all of Debtor's inventory. The security agreement contains an after-acquired property clause. On November 1, Debtor acquires additional inventory. On November 5, Debtor files for bankruptcy reorganization under Chapter 11 and continues in possession of the business. On December 1, the Debtor-in-possession acquires additional inventory. Because Debtor acquired the last inventory after the petition in bankruptcy, Creditor's floating lien will not reach that property. Creditor's interest would apply to both the September 1 inventory and to that acquired on November 1. If Debtor sold the November 1 inventory on December 5, section 552(b) would recognize Creditor's security interest in the post-petition proceeds because those funds came from a sale of pre-petition collateral which was subject to the Creditor's floating lien. The next case further develops this example.

IN RE BUMPER SALES

United States Court of Appeals
907 F.2d 1430, 11 U.C.C. Rep. Serv. 2d 1044 (4th Cir. 1990)

CHAPMAN, CIRCUIT JUDGE.

This appeal stems from the district court's affirmance of the bankruptcy court's order granting to the appellee/cross-appellant Marepcon Financial Corporation (Marepcon), t/a Norshipco Financial Corporation (Norshipco), a post-petition security interest in the inventory, receivables and other assets of debtor Bumper Sales, Inc. (Bumper Sales), to the detriment of appellant/cross-appellee Unsecured Creditors' Committee (the Committee). We affirm.

I

In order to expand its inventory of car and truck bumpers, Bumper Sales borrowed from Marepcon, a small asset-based lender whose trade name is Norshipco, about $510,000 in the form of two promissory notes, one for $110,000 dated December 8, 1987, and another for $400,000 dated March 9, 1988. In return, Bumper Sales agreed to give Marepcon a security interest in "all of . . .[Bumper Sales'] inventory, accounts receivable, contract rights, furniture, fixtures and equipment, general intangibles, now owned or hereafter-acquired and the proceeds from said collateral," as stipulated by the parties.

To perfect its security interest, Marepcon filed three financing statements in the Circuit Court of the City of Norfolk and with the State Corporation Commission. The first was filed in April 1987, and showed Marepcon as secured party against all of Bumper Sales' "inventory or the proceeds thereof now owned or hereafter-acquired." The second was filed in November 1987, and showed Norshipco as secured party against "all accounts receivable, inventory and general intangibles and the proceeds thereof now owned or hereafter-acquired." The third was filed in December 1987, and showed Norshipco as secured party against "all accounts receivable, inventory, general intangible, furniture, fixtures and equipment now owned and hereafter-acquired." A fictitious name certificate indicating that Norshipco is a trade name for Marepcon was filed in the Circuit Court of Norfolk and with the State Corporation Commission in July, 1987.

When Bumper Sales filed for Chapter 11 bankruptcy on July 22, 1988, the principal remaining due to Marepcon was $499,964.88. At that time, the value of Bumper Sales' inventory, which consisted solely of finished bumpers, was $769,000. Bumper Sales continued to operate the business as debtor-in-possession. On August 12, 1988, Bumper Sales' counsel, Jonathan L. Hauser, wrote to Ronald M. Gates of Marepcon, stating that he assumed that our [Bumper Sales'] previous understanding with Mr. Waters [the former Executive Vice President of Marepcon] remains, *i.e.*, that [Bumper Sales] may continue to use the cash collateral subject to the security interest of Norshipco Financial Corporation [Marepcon] in the ordinary course of business, so long as it continues to keep . . .[Marepcon's] loan current and complies with all of the other usual covenants contained in the loan documents.

In other words, Marepcon consented to Bumper Sales' use of the cash proceeds of pre-petition inventory and accounts to finance post-petition inventory. No order conditioning such use of cash collateral on the grant of a post-petition lien in the collateral was entered.

However, on August 19, 1988, Bumper Sales' owner and president, Joel B. Campbell, and Bumper Sales' counsel, Mr. Hauser, met with Joseph R. Mayes, counsel for the Committee, and had the following exchange:

> Mr. Mayes: Q. What arrangements have been made with Norshipco [Marepcon] for the use of cash collateral?
>
> Debtor (Mr. Campbell): A. We've provided them with security.
>
> Mr. Mayes: Q. Is this cash collateral arrangement in effect or about to come into effect?
>
> Mr. Hauser: A. Yeah. I've discussed it with counsel and basically so long as the terms and so long as we provide them with certain information, they'll be reasonably happy.
>
> Mr. Mayes: Q. Will there be a post petition lien in effect?
>
> Mr. Hauser: A. Yes. Most assuredly. The parties stipulated that, during the post-petition period, Bumper Sales did not borrow any outside funds or incur any outside debt; that Bumper Sales used only Marepcon's cash collateral — the cash proceeds of inventory secured under Marepcon's security interest — to finance new inventory; and that Bumper Sales would not have been able to reorganize without the use of the cash collateral.

On March 31, 1989, Marepcon filed a Motion to Condition Use, Sale or Lease of Collateral and Proceeds, declaring a claim of $500,000 against Bumper Sales and asserting a security interest in Bumper Sales' inventory, accounts receivable, general intangibles, furniture, fixtures, equipment, and proceeds. The motion sought adequate protection for this security interest. The Committee filed an objection to the motion challenging the proper perfection of Marepcon's security interest and contending that any post-petition lien had been lost by Marepcon's failure to condition use of the collateral. The bankruptcy court held that Marepcon had a valid and properly perfected security interest in Bumper Sales' pre-petition inventory and receivables, among other assets, and their proceeds, and that this security interest continued post-petition to the extent of Marepcon's unpaid claim. As a result, the court granted Marepcon a lien on Bumper Sales' pre-and post-petition collateral. The U.S. District Court for the Eastern District of Virginia affirmed the bankruptcy court, and the Committee appeals.

II

We address first Marepcon's contention (in its cross-appeal) that the Committee lacks standing to contest Marepcon's motion to condition use of the cash collateral. Section 1109(b) of the Bankruptcy Codestates that:

> [a] party in interest, including the debtor, the trustee, a creditors' committee, an equity security holders' committee, a creditor, an equity security holder, or any indenture trustee, may raise and may appear and be heard on any issue in a case under this chapter.

11 U.S.C. § 1109(b)(1988). . . .

The Committee is clearly a "party in interest" under the express language of Section 1109(b). Unfortunately, the Code does not explain the difference between a "case," in which the Committee plainly may intervene, and an "adversary proceeding," in which the Committee has a debatable right to intervene. However, it is apparent that this dispute is a case, not an adversary proceeding. First, the purpose of this motion — to condition the use of cash collateral — is not cited in the list of adversary proceedings set forth in Rule 7001 of the Bankruptcy Rules. While it is arguable that this is a proceeding "to determine the validity, priority or extent of a lien or other interest in property," that was not the original purpose of the motion. Moreover, the motion's focus on this issue does not justify turning the motion into an adversary proceeding, given Congress's intent under Section 363 to allow the court to handle such issues expeditiously so as to minimize any delay that may harm a debtor-in-possession or trustee who needs the use of cash collateral to continue operations. Finally, Bankruptcy Rule 4001(d) allows the court to approve a motion for approval of an agreement for the use of cash collateral, even though a creditors' committee's objection may raise issues pertaining to the extent of a lien or interest in property. It would be inconsistent with this rule to require an adversary proceeding in this case, which invokes the same kind of issues.

Second, Marepcon initiated this dispute by filing a motion on March 31, 1989, pursuant to Section 363(e) of the Bankruptcy Code. However, Rule 7003 of the Bankruptcy Rules requires that an adversary proceeding be commenced with the filing of a complaint. This indicates that the parties and the court did not consider this to be an adversary proceeding. Marepcon cannot argue now that it is one in order to thwart the Committee's right to intervene in the case. Third, the express language of Section 363(e) states that a hearing is optional, whereas an adversary proceeding by definition involves a hearing; thus, the mere possibility of the lack of a hearing under a Section 363(e) motion seems to preclude its characterization as an adversary proceeding. Therefore, we find that this is a "case" under Section 1109(b) and hold that the Committee has standing to be heard. See 3 Collier Bankruptcy Practice Guide, para. 41.04 at 41-11 (1990) ("The cumbersome adversary proceeding mechanism is not required under section 363.").

. . . .

IV

We now address the crux of the Committee's appeal: whether Marepcon has a security interest in Bumper Sales' post-petition assets. This issue is partly answered easily, because the Committee does not contest that Marepcon holds a security interest in the pre-petition collateral (*i.e.,* that held as of the bankruptcy filing on July 22, 1988) remaining in Bumper Sales' hands at the time of Marepcon's motion for adequate protection on March 31, 1989. It was stipulated that the total amount of inventory at the time of the filing was $769,000. Mr. Waters, the former Executive Vice President of Marepcon, testified that the total cost of goods sold, and hence total amount of inventory released, during this period was at most $464,000 and at least $168,000, making the inventory remaining at the time of the motion between $305,000 ($769,000 − $464,000) and $601,000 ($769,000 − 168,000). Adding the undisputed value of pre-petition equipment of $74,000 and pre-petition receivables of $11,215.57, Marepcon's security interest extends to at least $390,215.57 ($305,000 + $74,000 + $11,215.57) of Bumper Sales' post-petition assets. Given that Marepcon's total claim against Bumper Sales amounts to $486,957.69, the remainder of this opinion is devoted to the issue whether the $96,742.12 balance is secured.

The Committee maintains that Marepcon's security interest does not cover Bumper Sales' post-petition inventory and accounts, because Section 552(a) of the Bankruptcy Code invalidates the operation of after-acquired clauses in bankruptcy. Section 552(a) states as follows:

> Except as provided in subsection (b) of this section, property acquired by the estate or by the debtor after the commencement of the case is not subject to any lien resulting from any security agreement entered into by the debtor before the commencement of the case.

11 U.S.C. § 552(a)(1988). This subsection was "designed to facilitate the debtor's 'fresh start' by allowing the debtor to acquire post-petition assets free of pre-petition liabilities" and thereby

offer "post-petition accounts receivable and inventory as collateral" to new creditors. *In re Photo Promotion Associates, Inc.*, 53 B.R. 759, 763(Bankr. S.D.N.Y. 1985).

In response, Marepcon asserts that Section 552(b), which carves out an exception to Section 552(a), applies:

> (b) Except as provided in section[] 363 . . .of this title, if the debtor and an entity entered into a security agreement before the commencement of the case and if the security interest created by such security agreement extends to property of the debtor acquired before the commencement of the case and to proceeds . . .of such property, then such security interest extends to such proceeds . . .acquired by the estate after the commencement of the case to the extent provided by such security agreement and by applicable nonbankruptcy law, except to any extent that the court, after notice and a hearing and based on the equities of the case, orders otherwise.

11 U.S.C. § 552(b)(1988). Marepcon correctly explains that, according to Section 552, "proceeds coverage, but not after-acquired property clauses, are valid under title 11." *In re Gross-Feibel Co., Inc.*, 21 B.R. 648, 649(Bankr. S.D. Ohio 1982) (quoting 124 Cong. Rec. H11, 097-98 (Sept. 28, 1978) (remarks of Rep. Edwards); S17,414 (Oct. 6, 1978) (remarks of Sen. DeConcini)). Marepcon contends that its security interest extends to Bumper Sales' post-petition inventory and accounts because they are proceeds of Bumper Sales' pre-petition inventory and accounts, pointing out that Bumper Sales' post-petition inventory was financed solely by the proceeds of its pre-petition inventory and accounts.

The issue before us, then, is whether Bumper Sales' post-petition inventory and accounts are after-acquired property or proceeds. In order to determine the applicability of the exception in Section 552(b), we must undertake a four-part inquiry. First, is there a pre-petition security agreement that by its terms extends to Bumper Sales' pre-petition inventory, accounts and proceeds? Second, did Bumper Sales receive the proceeds of the pre-petition inventory and accounts after the filing of the petition? Third, is Bumper Sales' post-petition inventory second generation proceeds of pre-petition inventory and accounts, and are Bumper Sales' post-petition accounts proceeds of post-petition inventory? Fourth, did Marepcon's consent to Bumper Sales' use of the proceeds of pre-petition inventory and accounts to purchase post-petition inventory destroy Marepcon's security interest?

Under the first inquiry, it is clear that Marepcon has a security interest that was created before Bumper Sales filed its petition for bankruptcy and that covers inventory, accounts and proceeds. Under the second inquiry, the parties do not deny that Bumper Sales received the proceeds of pre-petition inventory after the filing of the petition. Thus, the basic factual prerequisites of Section 552(b) are met.

Under the third inquiry, we encounter difficulties in construing the Bankruptcy Code, because Section 552(b) fails to establish the parameters of "proceeds." Two interpretations are possible. One infers from the absence of a Code definition and from Section 552(b)'s language limiting any security interest "to the extent provided by . . . applicable nonbankruptcy law" that Congress intended to defer to state law, *i.e.*, to the U.C.C. See 4 Collier on Bankruptcy para. 552.02 at 552-11 (8th Ed. 1989). The other interpretation relies primarily on the legislative history stating that "the term "proceeds' is not limited to the technical definition of that term in the U.C.C., but covers any property into which property subject to the security interest is converted." H.R. Rep. No. 95-595, 95th Cong., 1st Sess. 377 (1977). This view encourages a broader coverage of proceeds than in the U.C.C. See, *e.g.*, 2 Norton Bankr. L. and Prac. § 38.03 at 38-2 (1981) (proceeds includes "property into which the pre-petition property is converted, property derived from the pre-petition property, and income from the prepetition property that is acquired by the estate after the commencement of the case."). However, we believe that Section 552(b)'s express reference to "nonbankruptcy law" should take priority over a vague and isolated piece of legislative history. We also note that the judicial creation of a definition for "proceeds," broader post-petition than pre-petition, would produce arbitrary and potentially inequitable results. As a result, we hold that the U.C.C.'s definition and treatment of proceeds applies to Section 552 of the Bankruptcy Code. . . .

Turning to the U.C.C., we start with Section 9-306(2), which states that a security interest in collateral continues in any proceeds of such collateral: "Except where this title otherwise provides, a security interest . . .continues in any identifiable proceeds including collections received by the debtor." Va. Code Ann. § 8.9-306(2)(1950). Section 9-306(1) explains what is included: " 'Proceeds' includes whatever is received upon the sale, exchange, collection or other disposition of collateral or proceeds. . . . Money, checks, deposit accounts, and the like are 'cash proceeds.' " Va. Code Ann. § 8.9-306(1)(Supp. 1989). Thus, the funds received by Bumper Sales from the sale of its inventory and collection of accounts are cash proceeds, and Marepcon's security interest in Bumper Sales' pre-petition inventory and accounts continues in the cash proceeds, so long as they are identifiable. But there is no doubt that the cash proceeds are identifiable, because the parties have stipulated that Bumper Sales used only these cash proceeds to finance its operations during bankruptcy. Since only these proceeds were used, they are conclusively identifiable.

However, Sections 9-306(3) and (4), expanding on Section 9-306(2)'s requirement that the proceeds be identifiable, place limits on a secured party's rights in proceeds. The Committee argues that Section 9-306(4) applies to this case, asserting that the proceeds of Bumper Sales' inventory were commingled with other funds in Bumper Sales' debtor-in-possession account and that Marepcon's failure to provide evidence indicating the amount of proceeds received by Bumper Sales within twenty days of the filing destroys its security interest in the proceeds. But the Committee overlooks the ample and well-reasoned precedent holding that Section 9-306(4) "governs the extent of a creditor's interest in commingled proceeds only up to and including the instant of commencement of the insolvency proceedings." *In re Hugo*, 58 B.R. 903, 907 (Bankr. E.D. Mich. 1986). As a result, Section 9-306(4) "specifically deals with the cases in which funds are commingled prior to filing bankruptcy . . .[and not to] cases in which funds are commingled after filing." *In re Turner*, 13 B.R. 15, 22 n. 1 (Bankr. D. Neb. 1981). Since any proceeds claimed under Section 552(b) are received after the filing, Section 9-306(4) is per se inapplicable. See also *In re Heims*, 65 B.R. 112, 116 n. 4 (Bankr. N.D. Iowa 1986); *In re SMS, Inc.*, 15 B.R. 496, 500 (Bankr. D. Kansas 1981). Moreover, to hold that Section 9-306(4) is applicable "would have a chaotic effect upon existing liens on property of the type customarily taken by lenders to operating businesses," because any proceeds of pre-petition collateral received after the filing would not be covered by a pre-petition security agreement. *In re Aerosmith Denton Corp.*, 36 B.R. 116, 118 (Bankr. N.D. Tex. 1983). Thus, we decline to apply Section 9-306(4).

Consequently, we believe that Section 9-306(3) is the proper approach to analyzing whether a security agreement extends to post-petition proceeds of pre-petition collateral. We feel that this section avoids an overly technical definition of proceeds (such as in Section 9-306(4)) that the legislative history expressly rejects. Moreover, the use of this section ensures that a creditor's security interest in proceeds receives the same treatment both before and after a filing for bankruptcy. Finally, this section will not thwart the "fresh start" ambitions of the Code, because the debtor-in-possession will still be able to encumber assets that are not proceeds of pre-petition collateral.

Under Section 9-306(3)(b), a security interest in proceeds remains perfected twenty days after receipt by the debtor if "a filed financing statement covers the original collateral and the proceeds are identifiable cash proceeds." In this case, we have already shown that Marepcon has a security interest in the pre-petition inventory and accounts and that the cash proceeds of such inventory and accounts are identifiable. As a result, Marepcon has a security interest in the cash proceeds. However, Bumper Sales subsequently used the cash proceeds to finance new inventory, which was both after-acquired property and proceeds. This presents an apparent conflict between Section 552(a), which cuts off after-acquired property clauses, and Section 552(b), which continues security interests in proceeds. Professor Clark describes this collision and offers a solution:

> What happens when the proceeds or final products are sold by the estate and the cash is used to manufacture new inventory, particularly in a rehabilitation proceeding? A literal reading of § 552 would suggest that the general rule applies and the floating lien is cut off. In other words, a bright line is drawn between first-generation proceeds and after-acquired property. Such a result, however, could completely deprive the secured party of his pre-petition perfected security interest. Therefore, the term "proceeds" should be read broadly — as in U.C.C. § 9-306— to include after-acquired property, at least where inventory and accounts are concerned and there is no improvement in position. This is nothing more than a post-petition substitution of collateral.

Clark, The Law of Secured Transactions under the Uniform Commercial Code, para. 6.6[3] at 6-47 (1980).

We agree that Section 552(b) covers second generation proceeds, even if they are in the form of inventory, because such proceeds are clearly contemplated by the U.C.C. Section 9-306(1) states that proceeds includes the proceeds of proceeds: " 'Proceeds' includes whatever is received upon the sale, exchange, collection or other disposition of collateral or proceeds." Va. Code § 8.9-306(1)(Supp. 1989). As a result, "after-acquired property will frequently qualify as second-generation proceeds, as when a dealer sells an appliance and reinvests the cash proceeds in new inventory." Clark, The Law of Secured Transactions Under the Uniform Commercial Code, para. 10.1[2] at 10-4 (1980). The fact that Section 552(a) denies the validity of after-acquired property clauses in bankruptcy does not affect this reasoning. Accordingly, the courts have held that, when a secured party has a pre-petition security interest in a crop in Year 1, its security interest extends to the post-petition proceeds of that crop as well as to the post-petition crop in Year 2 and its proceeds if the Year 2 crop is financed with the proceeds of the Year 1 crop. . . . The only requirement is that the second generation proceeds be traceable to the original collateral, which, as discussed above, the parties have stipulated is true in this case. Therefore, we hold that Marepcon has a properly perfected security interest in Bumper Sales' post-petition inventory as well as in any post-petition accounts and cash generated therefrom.[5]

Under the fourth inquiry, the Committee argues that Marepcon's consent to Bumper Sales' use of the proceeds to purchase inventory destroyed Marepcon's security interest in the proceeds.

---

[5] Our holding is further supported by the fact that Marepcon's security interest in post-petition inventory does not prejudice the Committee in any way, again because the post-petition inventory was produced entirely with the proceeds of Marepcon's pre-petition collateral, not with any of the debtor's unencumbered assets to which the Committee, as unsecured creditors, might have had a claim in bankruptcy.

In particular, the Committee claims that Marepcon's consent precludes its right to trace proceeds under Section 9-306(2) of the U.C.C. In effect, the Committee argues that Marepcon's failure to condition its consent on the grant of a post-petition lien on Bumper Sales' inventory under Section 363 precludes its security interest in the post-petition inventory and the proceeds thereof. We disagree.

Section 9-306(2) states that:

> a security interest continues in collateral notwithstanding the sale, exchange, or other disposition thereof unless the disposition was authorized by the secured party in the security agreement or otherwise, and also continues in any identifiable proceeds including collections received by the debtor.

Va. Code Ann. § 8.9-306(2)(Supp. 1989). Therefore, under Section 9-306(2), a secured party's authorization may nullify its security interest in the collateral, so long as "there is a clear manifestation of the secured party's intent that the collateral be transferred free and clear of its security interest." *In re Southern Properties, Inc.*, 44 B.R. 838, 843 (Bankr. E.D. Va. 1984) (interpreting the Virginia version of U.C.C.); *In re Brubaker*, 57 B.R. 736, 740 (Bankr. W.D. Va. 1986) (interpreting the Virginia version of U.C.C.).

However, the authorized disposition of the collateral has no effect on the secured party's security interest in the proceeds of the disposition: "The secured party remains protected because the Code provides that its security interest will continue in the proceeds of the sale of the collateral." *In re Southern Properties*, 44 B.R. at 842-43. See also *In re Cullen*, 71 B.R. 274, 279 (Bankr. W.D. Wis. 1987) ("[A] security interest in proceeds continues in accordance with the express language of U.C.C. § 9-306(2) regardless of a secured party's consent to sale of the collateral."); *In re Mid State Wood Prods. Co.*, 323 F. Supp. 853, 857 (N.D. Ill. 1971) ("Section 9-306(2) of the Code expressly reserves the right to proceeds notwithstanding authorization to sell the primary collateral. Whether the sale was authorized . . . in no manner affects [the secured party's] interest in the retained proceeds."). In this case, Marepcon is claiming only an interest in the proceeds of the use of the cash collateral, *i.e.*, the post-petition inventory and its proceeds, not the cash collateral itself. Thus, Section 9-306(2) preserves Marepcon's security interest in the post-petition inventory, regardless of Marepcon's consent to Bumper Sales' use of the cash collateral.

The Committee's argument under Section 363 is premised on the fact that Section 552(b) is expressly subject to the provisions of Section 363 of the Code. This section deals in part with the use of cash collateral, which includes the proceeds of property subject to a pre-petition security interest; under this definition, the cash proceeds of Bumper Sales' pre-petition inventory and accounts secured by Marepcon are cash collateral. In particular, the Committee claims that Marepcon consented to the use of its cash collateral pursuant to section 363(c)(2), which states that a debtor may not use cash collateral without the secured party's consent. The Committee insists that Marepcon's failure to seek a court order conditioning the use of cash collateral under Section 363(e) is fatal to its claim.

However, we see nothing in Section 363 that alters the rule established under Section 9-306 of the U.C.C. by requiring a secured party to obtain a court order to preserve rights in the proceeds of cash collateral. Indeed, Section 363 deals with the antecedent issue whether the debtor may even use the cash collateral in the first place, an important determination because the use of cash collateral "may involve a complete consumption of the [secured party's] collateral." 3 Collier Bankruptcy Practice Guide, para. 41.04 at 41-13 (1990). However, Section 363 does not concern the issue whether the debtor's use affects the secured party's interest in the proceeds of the cash collateral. The latter issue depends on the application of Section 9-306. As a result, Marepcon's consent to Bumper Sales' use of the cash collateral under Section 363(c)(2) does not affect Marepcon's security interest in the proceeds of the cash collateral. Of course, Marepcon could have prevented the litigation of this issue by seeking a court order under Section 363(e), but Marepcon did not lose its security interest by failing to do so. . . .

AFFIRMED.

NOTE

The court makes two points in the case. First, under BRA § 552(a), a secured creditor loses its security interest in inventory acquired post-petition unless the exception found in section 552(b) applies. Subsection (b) extends a creditor's pre-petition security interest to the proceeds of a debtor's pre-petition collateral. In *Bumper Sales*, the question was whether post-petition inventory constituted after-acquired property or proceeds. Obviously, money received from a post-petition sale of pre-petition inventory or a post-petition collection of pre-petition accounts, should be considered proceeds under section 552(b). The question for the *Bumper Sales* court was whether the protection given under section 552(b) extended to second generation inventory — new property purchased with the proceeds from pre-petition collateral? Since the Bankruptcy Code does not define proceeds, the court avoided applying the U.C.C. definition by relying on "applicable non-bankruptcy law" to find that the secured creditor had a properly perfected security interest in both the post-petition inventory and post-petition accounts. The case is unusual because the parties stipulated that *Bumper* had only used the proceeds from Marepcon's collateral to purchase new inventory. In most cases, the secured party will not be able to identify the proceeds so clearly. The creditor would be forced to trace the proceeds; if the debtor had commingled proceeds cash with other funds, the creditor might well lose, especially if, as in this case, there was a substantial delay before assessing rights to the proceeds.

The second point made by the *Bumper Sales* court is that consent to the use of cash collateral does not constitute a waiver of the creditor's right to assert a security interest in collateral purchased with cash collateral. In most cases a secured claimant would seek adequate protection for a security interest at the outset of a bankruptcy case. Because Marepcon waited nine months before making a claim, the creditors' committee asserted that the delay amounted to a waiver of any claim concerning the use of the cash collateral.

[H] Property Exemptions

In the case of an individual's bankruptcy, Section 522(b) permits the debtor to exempt certain property from the property of the estate. The list of exempt property is detailed at section 522(d). However, most debtors will not be able to utilize the section's federal exempt property list. The section is only available to individual debtors who reside in states that have not enacted "opt out" legislation under section 522(b)(1). Under that section, a state legislature has the power to enact legislation precluding its residents from electing the federal exempt property scheme under the Bankruptcy Code. Most states have passed such opt out legislation; thus, the typical individual debtor in bankruptcy will exempt property based on the more favorable state laws of the debtor's domicile. Like the Article 9 rules prohibiting waiver of rights before default, the Bankruptcy Code expressly addresses the effect of a debtor's contracting away her or his exemptions — the contract has no effect under section 522(e).

The Bankruptcy Code does not deal with the problem of a debtor's converting non-exempt property into exempt property on the eve of bankruptcy. To illustrate, consider the case similar to *Bumper Sales* — a debtor who withdraws money from a bank account and uses the funds to purchase a new home. Under most exemption laws (both state and federal), a homestead is exempt property — the individual debtor will be able to keep possession of the exempt property. Both the legislative history and case law indicate that such "bankruptcy estate planning" would result in a permissible conversion, even though some courts have withheld a discharge from a Chapter 7 debtor under section 727(a)(2).

Section 522(f)(2) creates a narrow exception that is important for secured creditors — the debtor may avoid security interests that are *non-purchase money*, *non-possessory*, and which involve *only certain types of collateral.*[6] The property includes items that are held primarily for the personal, family, or household use of the debtor; on professional books and other tools of a debtor's trade; and on professionally prescribed health aids for a debtor. The section applies in every individual bankruptcy case but is narrow in its scope because all three requirements must be satisfied. The section is aimed at transactions in which a creditor seeks to secure a debt by taking a security interest in household goods or other necessities already owned by the debtor. In many of these cases, the "new" collateral may be worth more to the debtor than any resale value; thus, the very threat of foreclosure gives the creditor great power over the debtor. To discourage this type of manipulative act, Congress subordinated such interests to the debtor's exemption power. Section 522(f) does not totally avoid judicial liens and security interests; instead, the statute permits avoidance only to the extent necessary to preserve the exemption. Thus, if a debtor's equity in property is greater than the exemption, the creditor's lien or security interest remains a valid charge on the nonexempt portion of the equity in the property.[7] Although the cases in this chapter revolve around business debtors, it is important to understand some of the considerations an individual debtor must make as well.

[I] Effect of Discharge on Secured Claims

Once the issue of exempt and non-exempt property has been addressed, the trustee in a Chapter 7 case will liquidate the non-exempt property and then distribute the cash proceeds to general claimants on a pro rata basis. BRA § 704. Upon distribution, the debtor looks to the bankruptcy court for a discharge of liability for remaining debts. Only individual debtors are eligible to receive a discharge under Chapter 7. If the debtor is a corporation, liquidation strips the entity to a shell — it has no assets but still owes debts.

The bankruptcy discharge only excuses the individual debtor from certain debts. Section 727(a) outlines ten exclusive grounds for the bankruptcy court's withholding a discharge. Most of the grounds deal with aspects of debtor dishonesty. Unless the trustee or a creditor can establish one of those ten objections, the debtor in a Chapter 7 case will receive a bankruptcy discharge. A discharge in bankruptcy only relieves the debtor from any further personal liability for certain types of debts. Section 523(a) details ten types of debt that are excepted from discharge. Certain tax claims, debts resulting from money obtained by false pretenses, or by use of false financial

[6] Under subsection 522(f)(1) a debtor may avoid judicial liens on any exempt property.

[7] If the debtor cannot avoid a creditors' security interest under section 522(f), the debtor can still extinguish the interest by redeeming the property. To redeem, the debtor must pay the secured creditor the value of the encumbered property. To illustrate, consider the case of a debtor who owes a used car dealership $5,000. The dealer has a security interest in debtor's Volkwagon Jetta which is valued at $3,500. In bankruptcy, the debtor can eliminate the dealer's security interest by paying the dealer $3,500. BRA § 722.

statements, and liability for willful torts are examples of debts which will not be subject to a Chapter 7 discharge. If a debt falls into one of the ten categories, the section bars the debtor from receiving relief on that obligation.

While the sections are similar in nature, the section 727(a) objections to discharge differ from the section 523(a) exceptions to discharge. If an objection to a discharge can be established under section 727(a), all creditors may attempt to collect the unpaid balance of their claims from the debtor. If however, a creditor establishes an exception to discharge under section 523(a), only that creditor may attempt to collect the unpaid portion of its claim from the debtor; all other pre-petition claims remain discharged. Proof of an objection to discharge therefore benefits all creditors while proof of an exception to discharge benefits only the creditor who establishes the exception.

The bankruptcy discharge does not wipe out the debt; instead, it eliminates the creditor's ability to look to the debtor to account for the obligation. A creditor can look to other parties such as guarantors and insurers, where the obligation on the debt remains unaffected. Similarly, a discharge in bankruptcy does not eradicate liens; secured creditors can still look to collateral not retained by the bankruptcy estate for sale, use, or lease.

Corporate debtors can receive a discharge only under Chapter 11. In a reorganization case, the debtor-in-possession proposes a plan to pay creditors all or part of the amounts owed. The payment proposal will be based on currently available assets or future revenue. Section 1123 outlines both the mandatory and the permissive provisions for a Chapter 11 plan. Although the plan can provide for payments over a long period of time, most rehabilitation plans propose to pay unsecured claimants over a 5 to 7 year period. A Chapter 11 plan may alter the rights of secured and unsecured creditors, as well as those of corporate shareholders. Under Chapter 11, the goal of reorganization is the creation of a viable rehabilitation plan that will provide the debtor with sufficient debt relief or restructuring so as to allow the continued operation of the business. Under section 1122(a), claims can be separated into various classes. Each member of a segregated class must be treated in a "substantially similar" fashion.

Although Chapter 11 contemplates a consensual restructuring of a debtor's financial obligations, not every claimant must consent to approve the plan. Chapter 11 introduces the concept of "impairment" of a claim or interest. Under section 1124 a class of claims will be deemed "impaired" (and therefore classified as rejecting a rehabilitation plan) unless the legal, equitable, and contractual rights of the claimant are left unaltered; or, unless there is a cash payment to the claimant equal to the allowed amount of the claimed debt. To avoid classification of a class as impaired, many debtors will classify all small claims as one class and then propose to pay those claims in full. Any claim that receives full cash payment is not impaired and is deemed to have accepted the rehabilitation plan. To avoid unreasonable or unfair proposals, the Bankruptcy Code requires a debtor seeking reorganization to propose a plan which, at minimum, promises to pay creditors at least as much as those creditors would have received had there been a liquidation proceeding under Chapter 7. BRA § 1129(a)(7).

A class of creditor claimants will be deemed to have accepted a plan when more than one half in number and at least two thirds in amount of the allowed claims actually voting on the plan approve it. Approval of a Chapter 11 plan involves both creditor acceptance and court confirmation. A rehabilitation plan can be confirmed by the bankruptcy court only if all classes of impaired claims vote to accept. Section 1129(a) outlines eleven requirements for confirmation. If the 11 requirements are met, the bankruptcy court must confirm the plan. Plans accepted by less than every class can still be confirmed but only if the additional requirements of section 1129(b) are fulfilled. Section 1129(b), known as the "cram down" provision, requires that at least one impaired class of claims accept the plan; that the plan does not discriminate unfairly; and, that the plan is fair and equitable. A comprehensive consideration of the cram down provisions of section 1129(b) is beyond the scope of this basic text and should be reserved for a specific course in bankruptcy. Most Chapter 11 cases are confirmed under § 1129(a) but only after considerable bargaining. Secured parties are in a strong position to bargain because most are the only members of a class; consequently, the secured creditor as a class of claimant can bar confirmation of a plan until the debtor pays a substantial portion of the debt. If the secured party refuses to accept a plan, cram down under section 1129(b)(2)(A) can occur, but only if the secured party receives the economic value of its secured claim under the plan.

Confirmation of a rehabilitation plan means that the plan governs the debtor's performance obligations. The confirmed plan binds both the debtor and the debtor's creditors and shareholders whether those parties accepted the plan or not. BRA § 1141(a). Confirmation also operates as a discharge of any remaining debt under section 1141(d). To illustrate, consider the plan of a debtor corporation who owes $500,000 to Bank. If the bankruptcy court confirms the debtor's reorganization plan which proposes to pay Bank $300,000, the remaining $200,000 of the debt has been discharged. The grounds for denying a discharge in a Chapter 11 case are different from the grounds for denying a discharge under Chapter 7. The Chapter 11 debtor will be denied a discharge only if: 1) the plan provides for liquidation of all or substantially all of the estate property; 2) the debtor does not engage in business after consummation of the plan; and, 3) the debtor would be denied a discharge if the case arose under Chapter 7.

§ 20.03 The Trustee's Avoidance Powers

[A] The Strong Arm Clause of Section 544(a)

There are a number of provisions in the Bankruptcy Code that permit a trustee to avoid various lien interests. Throughout the past four chapters, we have seen the effect of one of the most important powers — the trustee's strong arm powers under section 544(a). The statute permits the trustee to act like a hypothetical lien creditor and set aside any transfer of an interest in property as voidable if state law permits such avoidance. Section 9-301(1)(b) subordinates the rights of an unperfected secured creditor to those of a lien creditor. By cloaking the trustee in bankruptcy with the powers of a hypothetical lien creditor, section 544(a) combines with U.C.C. § 9-301(1)(b) to empower the trustee to invalidate any unperfected security interest or unrecorded real property mortgage. Once the interest is invalidated, the trustee can relegate that unperfected, secured creditor to general claimant status, sell the collateral, and use the proceeds to satisfy unsecured claims, rather than satisfying just the claim of the unperfected secured creditor.

Nearly all Chapter 7 cases are filed by the debtor. Most debtors liquidate their property before filing a bankruptcy petition. These debtors convert their assets to cash and pay creditors, or, they convert assets into exempt property. In roughly 95 percent of Chapter 7 cases, all of the assets of the estate are fully encumbered by security interest and liens at the time of filing. The system has a built-in incentive for trustees to seek avoidance because avoidance of an interest brings property back into the estate. Without avoidance, many trustees will not be paid. The next case provides an example of section 544(a) at work.

IN RE NEWMAN

United States Court of Appeals
993 F.2d 90, 20 U.C.C. Rep. Serv. 2d 1377 (5th Cir. 1993)

REYNALDO G. GARZA, CIRCUIT JUDGE:

West Loop Savings Association ("West Loop") appeals from an adverse summary judgment entered by the district court, which held that West Loop held an unperfected security interest in an annuity contract assigned by the debtor Bobby Lynn Newman ("Newman"). The court held that the annuity contract was a general intangible and, as a result, a financing statement was required to be filed with the secretary of state in order to complete perfection. West Loop contends that the annuity contract is not a general intangible, but an instrument and, therefore, its security interest was perfected upon delivery. We agree with the district court that the annuity contract is a general intangible and, therefore, the case is in all respects AFFIRMED.

BACKGROUND

West Loop is a creditor in Newman's bankruptcy. West Loop had loaned Newman an amount in excess of $166,000. As security for the loan West Loop received an assignment of an annuity contract issued by Manufacturers Life Insurance Company ("MLIC"). However, West Loop neglected to file a financing statement with the Texas Secretary of State.

This action started when appellee Knostman, the trustee, filed an adversary proceeding in the bankruptcy court under Section 544 of the Bankruptcy Code. While it was undisputed that West Loop held a security interest in the annuity, it was disputed as to whether West Loop had perfected its security interest in the annuity.

West Loop argued that the certificate was an instrument, which is automatically perfected upon delivery. However, the court held that the certificate was a general intangible, and West Loop had failed to perfect its assigned interest. The court noted the definition of a general intangible, which reads: "any personal property (including things in action) other than goods, contracts, chattel paper, documents, instruments and money." Tex.Bus. & Com.Code § 9.106.

The bankruptcy court reasoned that the annuity contract is not "of a type which is in the ordinary course of business" transferred by delivery. Tex.Bus. & Com.Code § 9.105(a)(9) (one of the requirements for "instrument" status). The annuity contract states:

> [an] assignment does not bind us until we receive it at one of our offices; we are not responsible for its validity or its effects; it should be filed with us in duplicate; we will return a copy.

The court determined that this language precludes delivery of the writing together with an assignment as an effective transfer of rights and, thus, it concluded that the certificate was not an instrument. Because the certificate was found to be a general intangible, and West Loop did not file a financing statement it held an unperfected security interest, which was trumped by the trustee under Section 544(a)(1). West Loop appealed to the district court.

On appeal, the district court properly narrowed the issue as to whether the annuity contract was an instrument or a general intangible. The court noted that the definition of instrument in this case came down to two elements. The annuity contract must: (i) evidence a right to the payment of money; and (ii) be of the type which is in the ordinary course of business transferred by delivery with an endorsement or assignment. Tex.Bus. & Com.Code 9.105(a)(9).

The district court reasoned that the annuity contract did not evidence a right to payment of money to the person in possession of the certificate. The court focused on the contractually specified method of changing the beneficiary. It found that possession of the certificate alone without following the method of changing the beneficiary did not entitle the transferee to receive annuity payments.

The court further elaborated that delivery of the certificate alone is insufficient to confer rights in the assignee until, MLIC receives notice of the assignment. Therefore, it concluded that "this is not the type of writing which is transferred by delivery with an assignment in the ordinary course of business." Therefore, the district court affirmed the bankruptcy court on the ground that the annuity contract was a general intangible. West Loop appeals.

DISCUSSION

The only issue to be confronted on appeal is: did West Loop perfect its security interest in the annuity contract it received from the debtor, Newman. This issue reduces to the classification of the annuity contract. If the contract is a general intangible, then West Loop perfected its security interest in the annuity; however, if the contract is an instrument, then West Loop did not perfect its security interest. We find that the contract is a general intangible and, thus, West Loop had to file a financing statement with the secretary of state in order to perfect its security interest. As a result of West Loop's failure to file a financing statement, they now hold an unsecured interest in the annuity.

. . . .

General Intangible or Instrument

The U.C.C. defines a general intangible merely by stating what is not a general intangible. A general intangible is essentially a bundle of rights such as those inherent in a franchise, a chose in action, a copyright, or an annuity . . . .

There is a dearth of case law on the classification of general intangibles. In fact, most of the cases focus on the difference between an account and a general intangible. See, *e.g., In re Slippery Rock Forging, Inc.,* 99 Bankr. 679, 681 (Bankr.W.D.Pa.1989) (settlement of preference action found not to be account and by default general intangible). In two of the cases that were faced with the issue of general intangible versus instrument, the courts in each instance tersely concluded that the bundle of rights in question were general intangibles. See *In re ESM Government Secs., Inc.,* 812 F.2d 1374, 1377 (11th Cir.1987) (right to payment of funds from repurchase of GNMAs was not an account or instrument and thus general intangible); *Union Inv., Inc. v. Midland-Guardian Co.,* 30 Oh.App.3d 59, 506 N.E.2d 271, 273 n. 2 (1986) ("Without a detailed explanation of our reasons, we find that the [promissory] note . . . is a general intangible").

Perhaps the only substantive confrontation with the instrument versus general intangible classification occurred in *Coral Petroleum. See Coral Petroleum,* 50 Bankr. at 837-39. In *Coral Petroleum,* Bankruptcy Judge Manuel Leal concluded that a promissory note was an instrument. See *id.* at 838. Interestingly, the creditor in *Coral Petroleum* sought to have the note classified as a general intangible in order to have a perfected security interest because it did not possess the note, but had filed a financing statement. See *id.* at 835. Conversely, herein West Loop seeks to have the annuity classified as an instrument because it has possession, but did not file a financing statement.

Coral Petroleum approached the problem in a pragmatic manner. The court concluded that the test for determining whether a writing is transferable in the ordinary course of business hinges on what professionals would ordinarily do to transfer such an interest. *Id.* at 838 (citing Harris, *Non-negotiable Certificates of Deposit: An Article 9 Problem,* 29 U.C.L.A.L.Rev. 330, 372 (1981)). The court reasoned that if professionals would attach significance to possession of the writing and treat certain collateral as an instrument, then the law should likewise treat the collateral similarly. See *id.*

After carefully reviewing the record, we find no indication that this or any other annuity is transferred in the regular course of business by endorsement. In an instance such as this, where precise categorization is unclear, it seems to this court that a finding of general intangible is warranted. The cases indicate that collateral such as certificates of deposit and promissory notes are instruments because professionals attach significance to their possession. However, interests such as Keogh Plans and the contractual right to receive insurance are treated as general intangibles because they are not customarily transferred by delivery with endorsement. These annuities are general intangibles because based upon the "reasonable professional standard" outlined in *Coral Petroleum* there is no indication that they are regularly traded by delivery or that possession of the annuity certificate confers the right to payment.

In a vacuum, if left to formulate our own test for distinguishing between a general intangible and an instrument, our benchmark would begin with the definition of an instrument. Section 9.105(a)(9) defines an "instrument" as "any other writing which evidences a right to the payment of money and is not itself a security agreement or lease and is of a type of which is in the ordinary course of business transferred by delivery with any necessary indorsement or assignment." Tex.Bus. & Com.Code § 9.105(a)(9). Because the annuity contract in question: (i) does not evidence a right to payment on its face; and (ii) is not ordinarily transferred by delivery, it is not an instrument.

Further, it appears from the face of the contract that possession alone is not enough to confer the right to payment. The Certificate reads:

> Protection of Payments. If you choose someone other than yourself to receive payments, that payee cannot commute, assign, or encumber the payments unless that right was granted when the payee was chosen. The same is true if the beneficiary chooses someone else to receive the payments. The trustee contends, and we agree, that based upon this language possession is irrelevant to the right to receive payments. The trustee also asserts that the certificate expressly contemplates that persons other than the owner of the annuity contract, or the possessor of the certificate, may receive payments. This contention is buttressed by reading the provision entitled "currency and place of payment," which conspicuously omits any requirement of possession. We agree with the lower court and conclude that possession of the certificate alone does not convey the right to receive payments.

Further, the court below noted that the annuity contract provided that any assignment was not binding on MLIC until it received a copy of the assignment. Consequently, the court concluded that "the delivery of the writing together with the assignment is not sufficient to transfer the rights conferred by the annuity certificate. Rather, the extra step of notice and delivery is required."

West Loop argues that the language in the annuity contract merely governs the rights of MLIC vis a vis Newman. They argue that "the language quoted by the bankruptcy court has nothing to do with the transfer of what the law requires, but only with MLIC's claimed rights." West

Loop also contends that the steps of notice and delivery apply equally in the event that a financing statement was required and that failure in that instance would not impair their perfection.

The principal case that West Loop relies on is *First Nat'l*. To be sure, *First Nat'l* does lay out a tripartite test needed for instrument status. The test reads as follows: (i) a writing; (ii) that evidences a right of payment; and (iii) is transferred by delivery with assignment. The appellants tersely contend that the test is met in the instant case.

First Nat'l, however, involved a certificate of deposit. There is extensive case law holding that a certificate of deposit is an instrument. See, *e.g.*, *Smith*, 805 F.2d at 285. *First Nat'l* held that the certificate of deposit was an instrument despite the fact that on its face it was "non-negotiable." Really, the case does not appear to help here because it merely establishes the difference between a negotiable instrument and an instrument. Rather, in the present case we are faced with a choice between instrument and general intangible. In any event, West Loop has failed to prove that this annuity contract is transferred by delivery with assignment in the ordinary course of business.

CONCLUSION

The annuity contract that Newman assigned to West Loop was a general intangible. The annuity contract is a general intangible principally because after applying the reasonable professional test outlined in Coral Petroleum, we conclude that professionals do not attach significance to the possession of the annuity certificate itself. Moreover, the language of the annuity contract does not contemplate that the annuity is an instrument. Consequently, we find that West Loop holds an unperfected security interest in the annuity contract, and we AFFIRM the district court's summary judgment in favor of the trustee.

NOTES

(1) In a 1993 law review article published in the Loyola Law Review, Professor James J. White, one of the leading commentators on Article 9, proposed the repeal of U.C.C. section 9-301(1)(b) based on reasons of fairness and efficiency. White's premise is that nothing in section 544(a) gives the trustee "an independent right under federal law to strike down an unperfected security interest." Since the trustee's rights are derivative from state law, White argues that the real competitor for the unperfected security interest is not the trustee, but instead the unsecured creditor whose debtor is in bankruptcy. Since U.C.C. section 9-201 provides that a security agreement is effective "between the parties against purchasers of the collateral and against creditors", White believes that the trustee should not have the power to upset the security arrangement between the debtor and creditor by challenging the creditor's perfected status. By repealing section 9-301(1), state legislatures would eliminate a preference given to "non-reliance creditors" — general creditors who do not rely on filing records when they lend, and who therefore, should not be protected against the secured creditor who took the extra step of acquiring a security interest, but who failed to take a final step of perfecting that interest. See, James J. White, *Revising Article 9 to Reduce Wasteful Litigation,* 26 Loy. L.A. L. Rev. 823 (1993).

Another U.C.C. scholar argued that Professor White's proposal would primarily benefit banks, commercial lenders, and finance companies at the expense of unsecured claimants such as environmental damage claimants, trade creditors, tort victims, and unpaid employees. See Lynn LoPucki, *The Unsecured Creditor's Bargain,* 80 Va. L. Rev. 1887 (1994). What do you think?

(2) Trustees are rarely appointed in Chapter 11 cases. Usually, the debtor exercises the discretion of a trustee as debtor-in-possession. If the debtor-in-possession succeeds in avoiding a secured creditor's lien, the secured party's status converts to unsecured and the creditor's leverage in approving a rehabilitation plan is limited. Debtors-in-possession often have reasons for not seeking to avoid interests in bankruptcy. In many instances, the debtor corporation gave a security interest to persons with whom the corporation has ongoing business relations (an owner or manager, for example). Because the debtor-in-possession is a fiduciary, the failure to bring an action to avoid an interest can constitute a breach of duty and an abuse of discretion. In such instances, some bankruptcy courts permit the unsecured creditor's committee to sue in place of the debtor-in-possession.

(3) In limited situations sections 546(b) and 362(b)(3) of the Bankruptcy Code permit a secured creditor to perfect its security interest after the filing of a petition. Perfection post-petition defeats the rights of the trustee under section 544(a). One example of this retroactive effect is U.C.C. § 9-301(2). A purchase money security interest perfected by filing within ten days of the debtor's taking possession of the collateral, cannot be avoided by the trustee even if the debtor goes into bankruptcy before the filing.

NOTE ON SECTION 554(b)

Like the previous section, BRA § 544(b) does not create any new substantive right in the trustee. The section provides that the "trustee may avoid any transfer of an interest of the debtor in property or any obligation incurred by the debtor that is voidable under applicable law by a creditor holding an unsecured claim . . . ." The trustee can only assert already-existing rights that individual unsecured creditors might assert. The right to set aside a transfer may have its origin in either state or federal law. In most cases, a trustee will claim a right arising under some state law provision. Typically, the relevant state law involves fraudulent conveyance law; consequently, more about section 544(b) will be discussed later in this chapter.

[B] Preferential Transfers

Read: Section 547 of the Bankruptcy Code

The common law and most state laws permit insolvent debtors to treat some creditors more favorably than other creditors by paying the preferred creditors more than the others. A few states have enacted the Uniform Fraudulent Transfers Act which makes some types of preferences avoidable. See U.F.T.A. § 5(b). Under state law, a diligent creditor may obtain more favorable status against an insolvent debtor by proceeding to judgment and by executing against the debtor's property. Bankruptcy law takes a different position from state law and permits the trustee to avoid any preferential payment, or any voluntary or involuntary transfer by an insolvent debtor in favor of certain creditors. Section 547(b) prescribes five elements of a preference; the trustee can void any transfer of property of the debtor if she can establish:

1) the transfer was to or for the benefit of a creditor;

2) the transfer was made on or for the account of an "antecedent debt" owed by the debtor prior to the time of transfer;

3) the debtor was insolvent at the time of the transfer; (section 547(f) creates a rebuttable presumption that the debtor was insolvent during the 90 days immediately preceding the date

of filing of the petition.)[8]

4) the transfer was made within 90 days before the filing of the petition in bankruptcy, or, in the case of an insider[9] the transfer was made within one year before the date of the filing of the petition; and,

5) the transfer has the effect of increasing the amount that the transferee would receive in a Chapter 7 liquidation case. If the trustee succeeds in avoiding a transfer as preferential, the property will be transferred back to the bankruptcy estate. The following two cases illustrate the applications of section 547(b).

IN RE WESLEY INDUSTRIES, INC.

United States Court of Appeals
30 F.3d 1438 (11th Cir. 1994)

BARKETT, CIRCUIT JUDGE:

Robert Galloway ("Trustee"), Trustee for Wesley Industries, Inc. ("Debtor"), appeals the district court's denial of his request to void and recover a transfer that Debtor made from its cash collateral account to First Alabama Bank ("First Alabama") between 90 days and one year prior to Debtor's filing for bankruptcy. First Alabama cross-appeals the lower court's decision granting the Trustee's request to void and recover transfers, or the proceeds of transfers, of a real estate mortgage and of a security interest in various items of personal property including machinery, equipment, and inventory, that Debtor also conveyed to First Alabama between 90 days and one year prior to bankruptcy.

We affirm the district court's decision to void and permit recovery of the transfers, or proceeds therefrom, of the real estate mortgage and of the security interest. We also affirm the decision denying the recovery of the transfer from the Debtor's cash collateral account.

I.

In 1986, approximately four years prior to filing for bankruptcy, Debtor, a corporation producing agricultural chemicals, established a lending relationship with First Alabama. First Alabama provided Debtor with working capital loans, which Debtor secured with inventory and accounts receivable. The security agreement provisions of various draw notes that Debtor executed and delivered to First Alabama governed the loans.

On May 25, 1989, the parties renewed and consolidated four draw notes into a Consolidated Note. Concurrent with the execution of the Consolidated Note, Debtor granted First Alabama additional security in the form of a security interest in machinery, equipment, furniture, fixtures, office equipment, raw materials, finished goods, work-in-process, goods in transit, licenses, distribution rights, patents, copyrights, trade secrets, cash and all books, records and computer software evidencing the property. Debtor also granted First Alabama a mortgage upon real property in Talladega County, Alabama.

---

[8] Section 101(32) provides a balance sheet test for insolvency. . . the sum of the debtor's debts (liabilities) is greater than all of the debtor's property (assets), based upon a fair valuation.

[9] Section 101(31) includes in the definition of insider relatives of an individual debtor, partners of a partnership, and directors, officers, or other control persons of a corporation.

In conjunction with the Consolidated Note, Debtor established a revolving line of credit cash collateral account. Debtor deposited all proceeds it collected from accounts receivable into this cash collateral account, and from it made payments to First Alabama of principal and interest on the Consolidated Note.

On February 21, 1990, Debtor filed a voluntary Chapter 11 bankruptcy petition and the Bankruptcy Court for the Southern District of Alabama granted relief. On October 23, 1990, the bankruptcy court ordered the case converted to a Chapter 7 proceeding, naming appellant Galloway as Trustee. This adversary proceeding arises from the Trustee's attempt to recover the three transfers that Debtor made to First Alabama between 90 days and one year prior to filing its Chapter 11 petition: (1) the additional security; (2) the mortgage upon Debtor's real property in Talladega County, Alabama; and (3) the payments from Debtor's cash collateral account.

II.

Pursuant to 11 U.S.C. § 547(b), a trustee may recover payments made within the 90 days preceding the filing of a bankruptcy petition. This provision allows a trustee to avoid any improper tactics that debtors and preferred creditors may employ in anticipation of a bankruptcy filing. Section 547(b)(4)(B) extends this 90-day window to a full year where the payment is to or for the benefit of an insider. All of the transfers involved in this appeal occurred more than 90 days but within one year before the filing of the bankruptcy petition. Thus, pursuant to § 547(b)(4)(B), to be subject to the avoidance powers of the Trustee, the Debtor must have made the transfers to or for the benefit of a creditor who was an insider at the time of the transfer.

Although First Alabama, the transferee in this instance, was not an insider, the transfers indirectly benefitted insider Jack Boykin, Debtor's president, director and majority stockholder, who personally guaranteed First Alabama's loans to the Debtor. Thus, we initially must decide whether transfers to non-insider creditors that benefit insider-guarantors extend the preference period from 90 days to one year pursuant to 11 U.S.C. § 547(b)(4)(B). This is a question of first impression in this circuit.

In *Levit v. Ingersoll Rand Financial Corp. (In re V.N. Deprizio Construction Co.),* 874 F.2d 1186 (7th Cir.1989), the Seventh Circuit became the first court of appeals to address the one-year reachback period of § 547(b)(4)(B) in the context of an insider-guarantor. In *Levit,* commonly referred to as *Deprizio,* a trustee filed adversary proceedings against various creditors — none of whom were insiders of the debtor — seeking to recover payments that the debtor made within one year, but more than 90 days before filing for bankruptcy. The court reasoned that although the creditors were not themselves insiders, the payments that debtor made to these "outside" creditors were for the benefit of guarantors of the loans who were insiders of the debtor. The payments benefitted the insiders because every dollar the debtor paid to an outside creditor reduced the insiders' exposure by the same amount.

Following *Deprizio,* all other courts of appeals that have decided this issue have agreed with the Seventh Circuit's analysis, concluding that insider-guarantors are creditors of the debtor because they hold contingent claims against the debtor that become fixed when they pay the outsider-creditors whose claims they guarantee. Thus, these courts have held that trustees may recover transfers that a debtor makes to a non-insider creditor between 90 days and one year prior to filing for bankruptcy where such transfers benefit an insider-guarantor.

We are persuaded by this reasoning and likewise hold that the preference-recovery period is one year when the transfer produces a benefit for an inside creditor who is a guarantor. Thus, we reject First Alabama's argument on cross-appeal that Boykin, as guarantor, is not a creditor, and affirm the district court's decision voiding the real estate and security interest transfers.

III.

Having adopted the *Deprizio* rationale, we likewise find that the district court correctly decided that the transfer from the cash collateral account was subject to the Trustee's avoidance power. This resolution, however, is not dispositive as to this transfer, because notwithstanding that it occurred during the applicable avoidance period, First Alabama asserts two defenses provided under 11 U.S.C. § 547(c): the "ordinary course of business exception," *id.* § 547(c)(2); and the "floating lien exception," *id.* § 547(c)(5). Neither the bankruptcy court nor district court addressed whether § 547(c)(2) provides a defense in this instance because they granted relief under § 547(c)(5). Because we affirm the resolution of this matter under § 547(c)(5), we likewise find it unnecessary to address § 547(c)(2). Section 547(c)(5) provides in pertinent part:

(c) The trustee may not avoid under this section a transfer —

(5) that creates a perfected security interest in inventory or a receivable or the proceeds of either, except to the extent that the aggregate of all such transfers to the transferee caused a reduction, as of the date of the filing of the petition and to the prejudice of other creditors holding unsecured claims, of any amount by which the debt secured by such security interest exceeded the value of all security interests for such debt on the later of —

(A) . . .

(ii) with respect to a transfer to which subsection (b)(4)(B) of this section applies, one year before the date of the filing of the petition . . . .

The Bankruptcy Reform Act of 1978 ("the Act") established that a lender's perfected security interest in property later acquired independently by the debtor might not be insulated from preferential attack. Section 547(c)(5) of the Act carves out an exception for inventory or accounts receivable that protects the transfer of a security interest in after-acquired property, *i.e.*, a "floating lien," provided that the creditor does not improve its position within the vulnerable period prior to bankruptcy. This exception:

permits a creditor with, say, a "floating lien" on the "receivables" of such a company to maintain that lien as the specific accounts receivable are paid off, and replaced by new ones, without fear that a future bankruptcy trustee will mount a preference attack on new accounts receivable arising during the "preference" period . . . . Insofar as the grant of a security interest in the new collateral (receivables or inventory that comes into existence during the preference period) improves the creditor's position (compared to his position at the beginning of the preference period), the grant of security constitutes a preference to the extent of the improvement. *Braunstein v. Karger (In re Melon Produce, Inc.)*, 976 F.2d 71, 75 (1st Cir.1992) (citation omitted). The bankruptcy judge recognized that the secured transaction at issue in this case was a "floating lien." We adopt this determination and now apply the "improvement in position" test.

To determine whether a creditor improves its position, the factfinder must compare the amount of debt outstanding to the value of collateral securing the debt (*i.e.*, inventory and accounts receivable) at the beginning and end of the appropriate preference period. *Roemelmeyer v. Walter*

E. Heller & Co., Southeast, Inc. (In re Lackow Bros., Inc.), 752 F.2d 1529, 1531-32 (11th Cir.1985). At each point in time, the difference between debt outstanding and collateral is deemed a "deficiency." There is no "improvement in position" so long as the deficiency at the beginning of the preference period is equal to or smaller than the deficiency at the end of the preference period.

If on February 21, 1989 (the date one year prior to Debtor's filing for bankruptcy), the amount of First Alabama's deficiency was greater than it was on the date of filing, the Trustee could recover the payments Debtor made from its cash collateral fund to First Alabama. If, however, the amount of the deficiency was smaller, reflecting no relative improvement in position, then § 547(c)(5) provides First Alabama with a complete defense to the Trustee's attempt to avoid the cash collateral transfers.

The bankruptcy judge applied the "improvement in position" test by calculating the deficiency at the two relevant points in time. The bankruptcy court found that on February 21, 1989, First Alabama's collateral was valued at $363,048, securing an obligation of $1,300,000. The court determined the deficiency on that date to be $936,952. The court then looked to the date the Debtor filed the bankruptcy petition and found that on February 21, 1990, First Alabama's collateral was valued at $70,442, securing an obligation of $1,034,815 and resulting in a $964,373 deficiency. Applying the "improvement in position" test, the bankruptcy judge found an increase in the amount of the deficiency between the two relevant points in time.

It is clear from these numbers that First Alabama did not improve its position with regard to the cash collateral account during the one year immediately preceding the Chapter 11 filing to the prejudice of the debtor's unsecured creditors. The amount by which the debt exceeded the value of the collateral increased rather than decreased during this time . . . . Bankruptcy Opinion at 10.

Discovering no error in the factual findings of the lower courts, and no abuse of discretion, we affirm the judgment of the district court in its entirety.

NOTES

(1) *Insider Preferences.* The *Wesley Industries* court adopts the reasoning of *Levit v. Ingersoll Rand,* 874 F.2d 1186 (7th Cir.1989). *Levit* was one of the first cases to examine the issue of insider preferences. The Seventh Circuit considered sections 547 and 550 of the Bankruptcy Code independent and unrelated provisions. Under *Levit,* once a court finds a 547(b) preferential transfer, the analysis should then turn to section 550 to determine the possible, responsible parties. The "to or for the benefit of a creditor" language of section 547(b)(1) contemplates three party transactions in which a debtor makes a transfer to Creditor 1, but the act of the transfer provides a benefit to Creditor 2. Under section 550, a party responsible need not be the same party who received preferential transfer; the section permits recovery from any actual transferee. In *Levit,* the court held that the payment to a non-insider creditor provided a "benefit" to an insider creditor even though the transfer occurred more than ninety days before the debtor's bankruptcy filing. The consequence of the the *Levit* finding extends beyond insider guarantors and could effect other secured creditors.

Consider, for example, the case of a business debtor that has two secured creditors C1 and C2, both of whom have security interests in the debtor's equipment; C1's interest is prior to C2. Debtor owes C1 $100,000 and C2 $200,000. The equipment is worth $150,000. If debtor makes a $50,000 payment on the C1 debt, that payment is not preferential with respect to C1 because C1 was a fully secured creditor. The transfer is preferential with respect to C2 because the C1 payment would reduce C1's bankruptcy claim on the equipment and correspondingly increase C2's secured claim (from $50,000 to $100,000). The trustee could use section 550 to recover the $50,000 preference from either C1 or C2.

(2) *Exceptions Under Section 547(c).* The *Wesley Industries* case also introduces section 547(c) of the Bankruptcy Code which provides that certain transactions, although preferential, **cannot** be avoided by the trustee. The statutory section lists seven basic exceptions to the trustee's preferential transfer avoiding powers. If a transfer comes within one of the following exceptions, the trustee cannot invalidate the transfer even though each of the section 547(b) elements is present:

1) transfers that are substantially contemporaneous exchanges for new value. This provision protects transactions where a creditor takes a security interest or receives a payment and waits several days to perfect or to deposit and collect the check used to make payment.

2) transfers that are ordinary course payments of debts. Section 547(c)(2) only protects absolute transfers (*i.e.*, payments, not security interests) that are routine bill payments. Both the debt and the payment must be in the ordinary course of both the debtor and the creditor's financial affairs. The exception protects most sellers on open trade terms if those sellers are paid within a reasonable time after a sale.

3) enabling loans. Under 547(c)(3), the interest of a purchase money secured creditor who gives the debtor new value that permits the debtor to acquire real or personal property cannot be avoided if the creditor perfects within 10 days after the debtor receives possession of the collateral.

4) advances made by a creditor after a preferential transfer takes place. Section 547(c)(4) protects a creditor who, after receiving a preferential transfer, then extends further unsecured credit to the debtor. Under this section the sequence of events is critical — the additional extension of credit must occur **after** the preferential transfer.

5) certain floating liens. Section 547(c)(5) creates a limited exception from preference attack. In the *Wesley Industries* case the court discusses this section with respect to proceeds. A perfected security interest in inventory, receivables, or the proceeds from either, will not be subject to a preference attack if the secured party did not improve its position in relation to that of unsecured claimants during the 90-days preceding the bankruptcy filing (or the 1 year period for insiders). There are seven steps involved in this section's test: i) determine the amount of the debt on the the date of the bankruptcy petition; ii) determine the value of the debtor's property that is subject to the security interest (accounts, inventory or both); iii) subtract (ii) from (i); iv) calculate the amount of the debt owed 90 days before the bankruptcy petition; v) determine the value of the debtor's encumbered property 90 days before the petition; vi) subtract (v) from (iv); vii) compare the result of (iii) with that in (vi). If (vi) is greater than (iii), then there is a preference that can be avoided.

6) statutory liens that cannot be avoided under section 545 are excepted from preference attack. Since Article 9 security interests are consensual liens, this section would not affect a secured claimant.

7) transfers involving consumer debts less than $600 are also not subject to a preference attack.

The remaining cases in this chapter discuss section 547(c) exceptions.

IN RE COHEE

United States Bankruptcy Court, Middle District of Tennessee
178 Bankr. 154 (1995)

J. TRAUGER

This matter is before the court upon the motion for summary judgment filed by defendants Resource Bancshares Mortgage Group and Freedom Mortgage Corporation. For the reasons set forth below, the motion will be denied.

FACTS

On March 8, 1994, the debtors executed a note and deed of trust in favor of defendant Freedom Mortgage Corporation, which was simultaneously assigned to defendant Resource Bancshares Mortgage Group. The deed of trust states that "Borrower owes Lender" $71,152, and that, except for encumbrances of record, "Borrower is lawfully seized of the estate hereby conveyed." The note contains debtors' promise to pay $71,152 plus 8 percent interest "in return for a loan received from Lender." Interest is to be charged "from the date of disbursement of the loan proceeds by Lender" (on the loan already "received," according to this document, by the debtors). Nothing in either document indicates that debtors' obligations were conditional upon receipt of the loan proceeds or anything else.

Also, on March 8, the debtors and a "Settlement Agent," whom the parties orally stipulated was an agent of the defendants, signed a HUD Settlement Statement (including an Addendum) prepared for the defendants by Lehman Land Title. The Settlement Statement reflected that the loan proceeds were to be used to refinance debtors' existing mortgage with AmSouth and that actual disbursement of the funds to AmSouth would occur on March 31, 1994. The Settlement Statement also included debtors' representation that it was "a true and accurate statement of all receipts and disbursements made on my account or by me in this transaction." The Settlement Agent represented that the document was "a true and accurate account of the funds which were received and have been or will be disbursed by the undersigned as part of the settlement of this transaction."

The loan proceeds were disbursed to AmSouth on March 31, 1994. Resource Bancshares recorded the deed of trust on April 11, 1994. Debtors filed a Chapter 7 bankruptcy petition on May 24, 1994, and the Chapter 7 trustee commenced this adversary proceeding to recover a preferential transfer on July 18, 1994. The case was converted to Chapter 13 on September 1, 1994, and the Chapter 13 trustee was permitted to be substituted as plaintiff by Order entered on January 11, 1995.

THE ISSUE

The trustee as plaintiff asserts that the recording of the deed of trust constitutes a preferential transfer under § 547(b) of the Bankruptcy Code. Under that section, the trustee has the burden of proving that there was a transfer of an interest of the debtor in property:

-to or for the benefit of a creditor;

-on account of an antecedent debt owed by the debtor before such transfer was made;

-made while the debtor was insolvent;

-made on or within 90 days before the filing of the petition;

-that enabled the creditor to receive more than it would receive in a hypothetical Chapter 7 liquidation if the transfer had not been made.

11 U.S.C. §§ 547(b) and (g). The parties filed written stipulations that the transfer at issue meets all of the above elements except the antecedent debt requirement.

The defendants contend that the transfer was not on account of an antecedent debt and that it was actually a contemporaneous exchange for new value protected under § 547(c)(1). Under that section, the defendants have the burden of proving that the transfer was intended by the debtor and the creditor to be a contemporaneous exchange for new value and, in fact, was a substantially contemporaneous exchange. 11 U.S.C. §§ 547(c)(1) and (g).

When the transfer is the perfection of a security interest, courts look to § 547(e)(2) to determine both of these issues. See *In re Arnett*, 731 F.2d 358, 363 (6th Cir. 1984); Norton Bankruptcy Law and Practice 2d, § 57:13 at 57-64 and 65 (1994). That section provides in pertinent part that, for purposes of § 547, a transfer is made —

(A) at the time such transfer takes effect between the transferor and transferee, if such transfer is perfected within 10 days; [or]

(B) at the time such transfer is perfected, if such transfer was perfected after such 10 days. If the transfer falls within this 10-day "safe harbor" it is not avoidable, both because is not on account of an antecedent debt, see § 547(b)(2), and because it is a substantially contemporaneous exchange under § 547(c)(1). *Arnett,* 731 F.2d at 364.

In this case, there is no question that the transfer of the deed of trust was perfected on April 11, when the deed of trust was recorded. The problem is determining when the transfer "took effect" between the parties, so as to trigger the running of the 10-day period. The defendants assert that it took effect on March 31, when the loan was funded. If this is true, perfection occurred within 10 days and the transfer is deemed to have been made on March 31. Because the transfer and the tendering of new value would be deemed to have occurred on the same day, there would be no antecedent debt and the exchange would in fact be substantially contemporaneous. The parties have stipulated that if the effective date of the transfer was March 31, the defendants did not receive a preferential transfer.

The trustee asserts, however, that the transfer took effect on March 8, when the deed of trust unconditionally conveyed to the lender a security interest in the property and when the debtors unconditionally promised to pay money to the lender pursuant to a note. If this is true, perfection occurred outside the 10-day period and thus the transfer would not relate back to the earlier date. The transfer would be deemed "made" on April 11, 34 days after it took effect between the parties. The transfer would therefore be preferential because it was on account of an antecedent debt and was not a contemporaneous exchange.

ANALYSIS

The defendants assert that the disbursement of the loan proceeds was a condition precedent to the debtors' obligations under the note and deed of trust. Until those funds were disbursed to AmSouth, the deed of trust was inoperative as a conveyance and could not "take effect" between the parties.

In support of their argument, the defendants rely upon *In re Pitman*, 843 F.2d 235 (6th Cir. 1988). In that case, the buyer in a seller-financed real estate sale executed a sales contract, note and mortgage on July 12, 1984. The seller accepted the sales contract on September 14 and subsequently executed a warranty deed to the buyer, which was recorded along with the deed of trust on October 16 and mailed to the debtor thereafter. The Sixth Circuit held that the buyer's transfer of the mortgage occurred contemporaneously with the transfer of the warranty deed and thus was not a preferential transfer.

The court reasoned that, despite the execution of the mortgage document in July, "the transfer of the mortgage interest was not complete, and it could not 'take effect' until the condition — the passing of clear title — was performed by the seller." *Id.* at 240. A significant factor in the court's holding was § 547(e)(3), which provides that, for purposes of § 547, "a transfer is not made until the debtor has acquired rights in the property transferred" — in other words, "the transferor must acquire the property interest in question before he can be considered to have transferred it." *Id.* at 238. The court rejected the lower courts' conclusion that the transfer of the mortgage interest "took effect" when the contract of sale was accepted by the seller, noting that under applicable state law (Kentucky), "a purchaser has no liability to pay or convey a mortgage to a seller . . . until the seller conveys title." *Id.* at 239.

The trustee distinguishes *Pitman* on its facts, noting that, in this case, the debtors had title to the property at the time they executed the deed of trust. The trustee relies instead on *In re Petrewsky,* 147 Bankr. 27 (Bankr. S.D. Ohio 1992), in which the court held that the debtor's obligation to pay arose when the debtor signed a note and security agreement on an automobile, not a week later when the lender paid the purchase price to the auto dealer. *Id.* at 30. Apparently based upon an examination of the documents, the court emphatically stated that "there is nothing in this record to show that the obligation of the debtor to pay his note was conditioned on that advance [to the dealer]." *Id.* Because the lien was not perfected until 13 days after the unconditional promissory note and security agreement were signed, it did not fall within the 10-day period of § 547(e)(2) and thus was not protected from avoidance by § 547(c)(1). *Id.*

Among the authorities cited in the *Pitman* opinion was the following statement from Osborne, Mortgages (1951), § 26:

> In an executory contract by E to lend or perform in some other way and to receive security in return for M's promise to borrow and repay or pay, the property is intended to be security for the obligation to pay or repay and only to the extent of such duty. Until the loan is made or the other stipulated performance is given, no duty to pay or repay arises. Since it was this duty which was intended to be secured, no equitable mortgage will arise until E makes the agreed upon performance. E's performance is a condition precedent either to specific performance of a promise to give a mortgage or to giving effect to an agreement that property be held, or operate presently, as security.

The defendants rely on this language for their argument that the transfer in this case did not come into existence until the date the loan proceeds were disbursed. In context, however, the quoted passage appears to have less to do with when an obligation arises than whether it arises at all. The passage is from the chapter on equitable mortgages, which discusses what obligations parties may have to each other in the absence of an enforceable written mortgage.

Here, however, we have a written mortgage, which is dealt with differently in this treatise. In the chapter on mortgages securing future advances, Osborne notes that "making the advances is a condition precedent to performance of the promise [to repay]; it is not necessary to its existence." Osborne, *supra,* § 114 at 179. That section goes on to contrast mortgages for future advances with those involving after-acquired property. While the latter mortgage cannot create a security interest until the debtor actually acquires the property to be transferred, "in a mortgage to secure future advances, . . . the property mortgaged is owned at the time and a present legal security interest is transferred by a validly executed and recordable conveyance." *Id.* at 180.

Another recognized treatise applies this future advances rule to facts similar to those in this case, noting that it is common in modern real estate transactions for the mortgage to be executed and recorded prior to the actual disbursement of loan proceeds. In such circumstances, the mortgage comes into existence before the proceeds are disbursed:

> Because the [loan] application and commitment [by the lender] have created an obligation to make the loan before the mortgage is recorded, there is sufficient debt created to make the mortgage valid. The mortgage debt already exists and it is not necessary that the actual advance of the committed funds has occurred.

3A Powell, Law of Real Property P 442[3] at 37-67. See *id.* P 441.3 at 37-55 (commitment letter approving loan application creates a binding contract to make a mortgage loan). Under this analysis, the validity of the deed of trust between the debtors and the lender was not conditioned upon disbursement of the loan proceeds, which the lender was already committed to do.

Support for this conclusion is also found in Tennessee law, which governs this transaction and is relevant in construing § 547(e)(2)(A). See *Pitman,* 843 F.2d at 239-40. Under Tennessee law, a deed (including a deed of trust) must comply with certain formalities, first to pass title and then to constitute notice to third parties. To be effective between the parties, a deed must be executed and delivered to the grantee. *Brevard v. Neely,* 34 Tenn. 164, 169 (1854); *Estate of Atkinson v. Allied Fence,* 746 S.W.2d 709, 711 (Tenn. Ct. App. 1988). "The delivery of a deed which has been knowingly executed with the intention of transferring title completes the transaction so far as the title is concerned and vests title in the grantee." *Mast v. Shepard,* 56 Tenn. App. 473, 408 S.W.2d 411, 413 (Tenn. Ct. App. 1966) (quoting 7 Thompson on Real Property (Perm Ed.), Sec. 4110, pp. 555-559). Acknowledgment or proof by witnesses is necessary to recording of the deed, but not to the passing of title between the parties; "the very moment the deed is signed by the maker, and delivered to the [grantee], or to someone for him, whether the same is acknowledged or witnessed or not, the title passes absolutely and unconditionally to the [grantee] without more." *Leadford v. Leadford,* 3 Tenn. Civ. App. 502, 508 (1912). See 6A Powell, *supra,* P898[2] at 81A-76 (deed becomes effective as of the date of delivery).

Delivery is a question of the intention of the parties, which may be inferred from the circumstances. *Estate of Atkinson,* 746 S.W.2d at 712. The delivery must be such as to deprive the grantor of power to recall the deed. *Id.; Brevard,* 34 Tenn. at 170. Possession of the deed by the grantee is prima facie evidence of delivery, absent opposing circumstances. *Estate of Atkinson,* 746 S.W.2d at 712.

The proof here dictates the conclusion that the executed deed of trust was "delivered" to the defendants on March 8, 1994. That was the date on which the defendants' agent (the same person who signed the HUD Settlement Statement), as notary, witnessed the signatures of the debtors on the deed of trust. This document states that it was prepared by Freedom Mortgage Corporation, one of the defendants, and, at paragraph 15, that "Borrower shall be given one conformed copy of this Security Instrument." The defendants' agent had possession of the deed of trust on March 8 after the debtors as borrowers signed it, when she notarized their signatures on it. The next two acts, recording it and providing a copy to the borrowers, were the responsibility of the lender, and there is no reason to believe that the lender would not have kept possession of the original.

This is prima facie evidence of delivery, and no "opposing circumstances" present themselves. Under the *Atkinson* case, delivery of the deed of trust took place on March 8 and, under Tennessee law, that was the effective date of the transfer. The defendants did not perfect their security interest within 10 days of that date and, therefore, there was no substantially contemporaneous exchange.

ALTERNATE GROUND FOR DECISION

An alternate basis for the court's decision is found in the legislative history to § 547, which indicates that the phrase "takes effect between the transferor and the transferee" is intended to be synonymous with the concept of attachment of a security interest under the U.C.C. See *In re McFarland,* 131 Bankr. 627 (E.D.Tenn. 1990) (citing H.R. Rep. No. 595, 95th Cong., 1st Sess. 213, reprinted in 1978 U.S.Code Cong. & Admin. News 5787, 5963, 6173), aff'd mem. 943 F.2d 52 (6th Cir. 1991).

Under Tennessee's version of the U.C.C., a security interest attaches only after three requirements are met:

(1) the secured party has possession of the collateral or the debtor has signed a security agreement describing the collateral;

(2) value has been given by the secured party; and

(3) debtor has rights in the collateral.

T.C.A. § 47-9-203(1). T.C.A. § 47-1-201(44) defines "value" to include "a binding commitment to extend credit or for the extension of immediately available credit" and "any consideration sufficient to support a simple contract."

Courts construing similar U.C.C. sections in other states have held that "value" may be given prior to the actual disbursement of loan proceeds if the lender has previously incurred a binding obligation to extend credit. See, *e.g., U.S. v. Cahall Bros.,* 674 F.2d 578 (6th Cir. 1982) (Ohio law) ("the actual disbursement of the loan proceeds at a later date would not constitute value . . . since [creditor] would merely be tendering money to [debtors] pursuant to a preexisting-existing legal duty"); *In re Air Vermont,* 45 Bankr. 817 (D.Vt. 1984) (Vermont law) (secured party gave value as of date documents were executed); *State Bank & Trust Co. of Beeville v. First National Bank of Beeville,* 635 S.W.2d 807, 33 U.C.C.RS 1775 (Tex. App. 1982) ("the promissory note represented a binding loan commitment, a promise on the part of [creditor] to extend credit to the debtor, which constituted 'value' given").

Although not yet adopted in Tennessee, the Uniform Land Security Interest Act provides rules similar to U.C.C. Article 9 for land transfers. See 3 Powell, *supra,* P 442[1] at 37-63. Under the ULSIA, a mortgage takes effect between the parties upon completion of the same three requirements — a signed writing identifying the property, value given by secured party, and debtor having rights in the collateral. *Id.* In this case, those requirements were met on March 8. The debtor already had rights in the collateral (this was a second mortgage on his house), the defendants made a binding commitment to make the loan, and the debtors signed the deed of trust. Thus, the transfer of the deed of trust "took effect" between the parties on March 8, 1994.

CONCLUSION

For all of the above reasons, the court finds that the transfer of the deed of trust took effect between the parties 34 days before it was perfected by recording. The transfer was thus on account of an antecedent debt created at the March 8 closing and does not constitute a substantially contemporaneous exchange for new value under § 547(c)(1). Defendants' motion for summary judgment must therefore be denied.

For the reasons stated in the Memorandum filed herewith, the defendants' motion for summary judgment is DENIED.

NOTE

The *Cohee* court based its decision on two different rationales. First, the court held that where the debtor had title and right to transfer at the time of execution, the mortgage should be deemed transferred at the time the deed of title was properly executed and delivered, not when the funds were actually dispensed. Alternatively, the court found that the phrase "takes effect" should be interpreted as synonymous with the concept of attachment under Article 9. Recall that attachment occurs when the secured party is in possession of the collateral, value has been given, and the debtor has rights in the collateral. The *Cohee* court found all these steps to have occurred on March 8, thereby placing the transaction outside the ten-day safe harbor of section 547(e)(2). Which of the alternative reasons do you find more persuasive? Why?

IN RE AUSMAN JEWELERS, INC.

United States Bankruptcy Court, Western District of Wisconsin
177 Bankr. 282 (1995)

ROBERT D. MARTIN, BANKRUPTCY JUDGE.

Ausman Jewelers, Inc. ("Ausman") filed for chapter 11 bankruptcy on May 22, 1992. The case was converted to chapter 7 on July 12, 1993. Prior to filing, Ausman paid $4,330.39 to Aetna Finance Company d/b/a ITT Financial Services ("Aetna") for the benefit of two of its customers. The chapter 7 trustee seeks to recover the payment as a preference. After a trial on December 8, 1994, I held the transfer to be an avoidable preference under 11 USC § 547 and invited further briefing on whether Aetna was an initial transferee from whom recovery could be had under 11 USC § 550(1994).

Ausman sold jewelry pursuant to a "90-Day Same-As-Cash" program ("the program") under which customers could pay for merchandise up to 90 days after the date of sale without paying interest. Customers utilizing the program would sign contracts evidencing their intent to pay within 90 days of the purchase date. Ausman was paid the price of the merchandise as soon as it delivered the signed contracts to Aetna.

In December 1991, two customers purchased merchandise totaling $4,330.39 under the program. By virtue of their contracts, the customers agreed to pay Aetna for the price of the merchandise. The customers returned the merchandise to Ausman within a short time after purchase and were promised a refund of the purchase price. Ausman, however, was financially unable to refund cash immediately and instead agreed to pay the customers' contractual obligation to Aetna. In March 1992, Ausman paid Aetna the total amount the two customers owed. Almost three months later, Ausman filed bankruptcy.

Sections 547 and 550 of the Bankruptcy Code are independent and require two steps to recover a preference claim. *Levit v Ingersoll Rand Financial Corp.*, 874 F.2d 1186, 1194 (7th Cir 1989). The transfer must be avoidable under 11 USC § 547 and the party from whom payment is being sought must be responsible for payment under 11 USC § 550(a).

Section 547 requires six elements be shown to avoid a transfer. The trustee must show that: a transfer of the property of the debtor to or for the benefit of a creditor, for or on account of antecedent debt, while the debtor is insolvent, within 90 days preceding the petition, and the creditor has received more than what the creditor would have received under chapter 7. *Matter of Smith*, 966 F.2d 1527 (7th Cir 1992). Aetna affirmatively claimed the payment was in the ordinary course of business and excepted from the class of avoidable preferences.

I

Aetna argues that the transfer did not diminish the estate. *Matter of Smith,* 966 F.2d 1527, 1535 (7th Cir 1992) ("Courts, have also long held that to be avoidable, transfers must result in a depletion or diminution of the debtor's estate."). Creditors are not harmed by a transfer of property not belonging to the debtor as the amount they would share in the distribution of the debtor's estate would not be diminished. *In re Hartley,* 825 F.2d 1067, 1070 (6th Cir 1987). The principal factor in determining if the estate has been diminished is the extent the debtor owned or controlled the transferred property. *Id.* As was held following trial, the evidence in this case shows that the funds used by Ausman to pay Aetna were in Ausman's general account. The funds were never segregated from the other funds, nor were they earmarked for Aetna.

When the customers returned the merchandise without receiving an immediate cash refund, a new debtor-creditor relationship was created between Ausman and the two customers. By accepting Ausman's offer to pay Aetna, the customers chose to be paid indirectly at a time in the future. They extended credit to Ausman for the price of the returned merchandise. Ausman's payment, although made to Aetna, was made for the benefit of selected creditors, the customers. No debtor-creditor relationship existed at any time between Aetna and Ausman.

Ausman used funds obtained from unknown sources (possibly from resale of the returned jewelry, although there is no evidence of it) for the benefit of two of its creditors. By using these funds for the sole benefit of the two creditors, the Ausman estate was diminished and other unsecured creditors were injured to the extent they were deprived of their share of the $4,330.39.

II

Payments made in the ordinary course of business are among the categories of transfers excepted from avoidance. See 11 USC § 547(c)(2)(1994). The ordinary course of business exception requires that the payment was on account of debt incurred in both the creditor's and debtor's business, the payment was made and received in the ordinary course of the involved parties' business, and the payment was made according to ordinary business terms. *In the Matter of Tolona Pizza Products Corp,* 3 F.3d 1029, 1031 (7th Cir 1993). The burden of proof under § 547(c) lies with the party from whom recovery is being sought. 11 USC § 547(g)(1994).

At trial, Aetna presented no evidence that the transfer was in either Ausman's or the customers' ordinary course of business. Nor was there any evidence that the transaction was ordinary for the industry as a whole. See *Matter of Tolona Pizza Products Corp.*, 3 F.3d at 1033 ("The creditor must show that the payment received was made in the ordinary business terms in the industry."). The only evidence produced at trial was the sole testimony of Richard Ausman, president of debtor, that Ausman's standard practice was to refund cash to customers who returned merchandise. Aetna, therefore, did not meet its burden of proof with regard to the applicability of the ordinary course of business exception.

III

Aetna asserts that the trustee may not recover from Aetna as it is not the entity for whose benefit such transfer was made. That is not the issue.

Under § 550(a)(1), a trustee is provided a choice of from whom to recover a preference. *Bonded Financial Services v European Amer. Bank,* 838 F.2d 890, 895 (7th Cir 1988). A trustee either may recover from "the initial transferee of such transfer" or from "the entity for whose benefit such transfer was made." 11 USC § 550(a)(1). "Section 550(a)(1) recognizes that debtors often pay money to A for the benefit of B; that B may have indeed arranged for the payment . . .; that but for the payment B may have had to make good on the guarantee or pay off his own debt; and accordingly that B should be treated the same way initial recipients are treated." *Bonded Financial*, 838 F.2d at 896. This is almost the exact situation in our case. Ausman paid money to Aetna for the two customers so that they would not have to pay it. Thus, the trustee may recover either from the customers, as the entity for whose benefit the transfer was made, or the initial transferee. In order to recover from Aetna, the trustee must establish that Aetna is the initial transferee.

The Bankruptcy Code does not define "initial transferee." Case law suggests an initial transferee is the first party exercising "dominion over the money or other asset" or "has the right to put [the property] to one's own use." *Bonded Financial*, 838 at 893. In our case, when Aetna was paid, it was able to do with the received funds whatever it wished. It was the "initial" party to exercise control over the transferred funds. Thus Aetna was the initial transferee of the funds. Because Aetna was the initial transferee of the funds, it is responsible to the trustee for the repayment of the preference.

The result of recovering the transfer from Aetna may be, inter alia, the resurrection of an obligation from the two customers to Aetna for the payment on the contracts. The customers are not parties to this action and pursuit of them by Aetna, if undertaken at all, must therefore be the subject of a separate action, presumably in a different court. None of this precludes entering judgment in favor of the trustee against Aetna in this adversary proceeding. Judgment should therefore be ordered, consistent with the findings of fact and conclusions of law contained herein.

IT IS HEREBY ORDERED that Ausman Jewelers' $4,330.39 payment to Aetna Finance Company be avoided as a preference and that the total payment be recovered from Aetna under 11 USC § 550(a) because it is the initial transferee of the avoided transfer.

NOTES

(1) *Ausman* is a good application of sections 547 and 550 despite the sparse discussion concerning what constitutes a transfer in the ordinary course of business. The court first determined that the payments were avoidable preferences. Under Section 550, the trustee can recover from either the party for whose benefit the transfer was made or from the initial transferee.

Aetna was the initial transferee because it was the first party to receive the funds and because it had control over them. Does allowing the trustee to recover against Aetna strike justice, and if so, for whom? The court seems to stretch a bit under the "resurrection theory." Is Ausman guilty of conversion?

(2) As previously discussed, courts treat section 550 separate from and independent of section 547. See *Levit v. Ingersoll Rand*, 874 F.2d 1186 (7th Cir. 1989). The important phrase of section 550 is ". . . for the benefit of the estate." This provision allows the trustee in bankruptcy to go after and recover any qualified transferee regardless of whether the action helps a specific creditor who provided the basis for the underlying claim. This principle codifies a long standing axiom first expressed in *Moore v. Bay*, 284 U.S. 4 (1931) (holding that a chattel mortgage was void in bankruptcy, providing all creditors with the benefit of the avoidance, whether or not they had rights under the state law).

(3) The Code also seeks to protect second generation transferees who take property: 1) for value; 2) in good faith and, 3) without knowledge of the voidability of the transfer. Section 550(b). The second generation transferee may recover from the initial (first) transferee even if that transferee acted in good faith and without knowledge of the voidability of the transaction. Section 550(a). The transferee will be given protection in the form of a lien in the bankrupt's estate if the conditions of section 550(d)(1) are met.

IN RE McLAUGHLIN

United States Bankruptcy Court, Western District of Wisconsin
183 Bankr. 171 (1995)

ROBERT D. MARTIN, UNITED STATES BANKRUPTCY JUDGE.

Susan McLaughlin wanted to purchase a new mobile home from Steenberg Homes ("Steenberg"). The purchase was to be funded in part by financing available through Steenberg. Security Pacific Housing Services ("SPHS") conditionally agreed to accept from Steenberg an assignment of McLaughlin's retail installment contract. After the assignment, SPHS would receive the contract payments and hold a lien on the purchased mobile home. On April 27, 1994 McLaughlin signed a retail installment contract and security agreement with Steenberg and made a down payment. McLaughlin also signed a motor vehicle title application so that the lien she agreed to provide could be perfected. (Def. Ex. 7.)

On May 12, 1994, McLaughlin took delivery of the new home and began to reside in it. Steenberg promptly forwarded the required paperwork to SPHS. The papers had been received by SPHS when, on May 20, 1994, an employee of SPHS telephoned McLaughlin to determine her satisfaction with the home. After this conversation, the retail sales contract and security agreement were modified by the SPHS employee changing the due date of the first installment payment from June 1, 1994 to June 15, 1994. The revised agreement was dated May 15, 1994.

On May 31, 1994, SPHS accepted the assignment of McLaughlin's installment sale contract and security agreement. On June 1, 1994, SPHS mailed a check to the manufacturer, Liberty Homes, for the amount due from Steenberg in exchange for the Manufacturers Statement of Origin ("MSO"). After receiving the MSO on June 10, 1994, SPHS forwarded it and the application for registration to the motor vehicle department. The application was received by the department on June 13, 1994 and a title showing the SPHS security interest was issued on July 2, 1994.

On July 21, 1994, McLaughlin filed for chapter 7 bankruptcy. The trustee moved to avoid the SPHS security interest as the fruit of a preferential transfer. A trial was held on March 29, 1995. At its conclusion, I made a preliminary holding that SPHS' security interest was perfected by a preferential transfer and that the ordinary course of business exception to a preferential transfer did not apply because, inter alia, there were irregularities in the transaction as it was handled by SPHS.

By signing the security agreement on April 27, 1994, McLaughlin created a security interest in favor of Steenberg. Wis Stat § 409.105(m) (1993-94). However, the security interest was not enforceable against McLaughlin or any third party until it "attached." Attachment requires that the creditor give value and the debtor have rights in the collateral. Wis Stat § 409.203 (1993-94). Steenberg gave value and McLaughlin gained rights in the collateral when the mobile home was delivered to her possession on May 12, 1994. See *Chambersburg Trust Co. v Eichelberger,* 403 Pa. Super. 199, 588 A.2d 549, 552 (Pa Super Ct 1991). The security interest then became enforceable against McLaughlin, but it could still be primed or defeated by third parties until it was perfected.

When the security interest attached, the contract had yet to be assigned to SPHS. Under the terms of the security agreement, Steenberg was the secured party. Steenberg did not perfect the security interest on its own behalf and it remained unperfected until an application for title was delivered to the motor vehicle department on June 13, 1994. Wis Stat § 342.19(2) (1993-94). Nothing in Wisconsin law deems the perfection to relate back to an earlier date.

Section 547(b) requires six elements be shown to avoid a transfer as a preference. "The trustee must show that: a transfer of the property of the debtor to or for the benefit of a creditor, for or on account of antecedent debt, while the debtor is insolvent, within 90 days preceding the petition, and the creditor has received more than what the creditor would have received under chapter 7." *In re Ausman Jewelers* 177 Bankr. 282, 284 (Bankr WD Wis 1995); see also *Matter of Smith,* 966 F.2d 1527 (7th Cir 1992). Each of these elements has been met in this case.

Cases have widely held that giving a security interest in property constitutes transfer of property of the debtor. See *In re Melon Produce,* 976 F.2d 71, 74 (1st Cir 1992). When a security interest is not perfected within 10 days after it becomes enforceable, the date of perfection is the date of the transfer. 11 USC § 547(e)(2)(B)(1994); in the present case, June 13, 1994. McLaughlin is presumed to have been insolvent because the transfer occurred within 90 days of her bankruptcy filing. 11 USC § 547(f)(1994). The transfer was to SPHS, which by then was a creditor of McLaughlin on account of an antecedent debt. When the home was delivered, McLaughlin had an obligation to pay for it. The questioned transfer took place 32 days later. Finally, SPHS does not dispute that it received more than what it would have received under chapter 7 without the transfer.

Section 547(c) of the Bankruptcy Code provides that certain transactions, although preferential, cannot be avoided by the trustee. The first exception claimed by SPHS, that for ordinary course of business, has already been denied. SPHS also contends that either 11 USC § 547(c)(1), the contemporaneous exchange exception, or 11 USC § 547(c)(4), the new value exception, applies to these facts. On the evidence as presented, neither section applies.

The contemporaneous exchange exception provides:

(c) The trustee may not avoid under this section a transfer—

(1) to the extent such transfer was—

(A) intended by the debtor and the creditor to or for whose benefit such transfer was made to be a contemporaneous exchange for new value given to the debtor; and

(B) in fact a substantially contemporaneous exchange. 11 USC § 547(c)(1).

The parties do not dispute that McLaughlin and SPHS intended the transaction to be contemporaneous. Rather, they disagree on whether the transfer was "in fact" contemporaneous.

The trustee argues that perfection of the security interest was not contemporaneous because it did not occur within 10 days of its creation. Several courts outside of this circuit have so held. *See Matter of Tressler,* 771 F.2d 791 (3d Cir 1995); *In re Davis,* 734 F.2d 604 (11th Cir 1984); *In re Arnett,* 731 F.2d 358 (6th Cir 1984); *Matter of Vance,* 721 F.2d 259 (9th Cir 1983).

However, the Seventh Circuit follows a different rule. In *Pine Top Ins. v Bank of America Nat. Trust & Sav.,* 969 F.2d 321, 328 (7th Cir 1992), the court rejected the proposition that to be contemporaneous in fact, a transfer must occur within 10 days of it becoming effective. "The modifier 'substantial' makes clear that contemporaneity is a flexible concept which requires a case by case inquiry into all of the relevant circumstances (*e.g.,* length of delay, reason for delay, nature of the transaction, intentions of the parties, possible risk of fraud) surrounding an allegedly preferential transfer." *Id* at 329. Thus, the particular facts of the present case must be examined.

After accepting the assignment on May 31, 1994, SPHS took immediate steps to perfect its security interest. SPHA paid Liberty Homes to obtain an MSO and, after receiving it, immediately applied to the motor vehicle department for a title. The actual process of perfecting the security interest was completed as soon as possible after SPH started it.

However, the process of perfection was not initiated until 19 days after the security interest attached. From May 12, 1994 to May 31, 1994, neither Steenberg nor SPHS attempted to perfect a security interest in the home. SPHS claims that it could not have perfected the security interest prior to May 31, 1994. However, the evidence suggests that SPHS had all of the information necessary to approve the transaction on May 18, 1994 (Def. Ex 26) and probably sooner. At trial, SPHS' sales manager testified that all of the required information to finalize the transaction was in SPHS' possession within the first two weeks of May. At any time thereafter, SPHS could have finalized its acceptance and initiated the perfection process.

SPHS has offered little justification for its delay. Rather, it focused on events occurring after May 31, 1994. To the extent that SPHS presented evidence to justify its delay, it conflicted with other evidence. At trial, SPHS' sales manager testified that SPHS employees were too busy to initiate the process earlier. However, SPHS' internal purchase log shows that in similar transactions occurring around the same time as McLaughlin's, SPHS took steps to perfect their security interest much more quickly following telephone audits. For an example, inter alia, the telephone audit for account number 72201253 occurred on May 25, 1994 and SPHS purchased the contract on the same date. (Def. Ex. 31.) The telephone audit for account number 72201255 occurred after McLaughlin's, yet that contract was purchased before McLaughlin's. SPHS has not provided a reasonable explanation as to why the McLaughlin transaction took as long as it did.

As the party from whom recovery is being sought, SPHS has the burden of proof in establishing that an exception to the avoidance of a preferential transfer exists. 11 USC § 547(g)(1994). Because there has been little evidence presented concerning the days from May 18 until May 31, 1994, SPHS has not sustained its burden of proof. When those 13 days are part of the 32 days that elapsed from attachment to perfection of SPHS' interest, perfection cannot be said to be contemporaneous.

SPHS next contends that the new value exception in § 547(c)(4) applies. That section provides:

> (c) The trustee may not avoid under this section a transfer— . . .
>
> (4) to or for the benefit of a creditor, to the extent that, after such transfer, such creditor gave new value to or for the benefit of the debtor; (A) not secured by an otherwise unavoidable security interest; (B) on account of which new value the debtor did not make an otherwise unavoidable transfer to or for the benefit of such creditor.

11 USC § 547(c)(4)(1994). SPHS argues that it advanced new value to McLaughlin which allowed her to purchase the home. However, SPHS' reliance on the new value exception is misplaced. This exception only applies to creditors who have received avoidable preferences and thereafter make further loans to the debtor. 11 USC § 547(c)(4)(A)(1994); Robert E. Ginsberg & Robert D. Martin, Bankruptcy: Text, Statutes & Rules (1993). The exception allows a creditor to set off the amount of post-preference advances that are both unsecured and unpaid on the petition date against any amounts the creditor must return to the trustee under the preference provision. In our case, SPHS is not seeking set off nor did it advance any unsecured funds after the security interest was perfected. Thus, the exception is not applicable.

If a preference is voidable, the trustee may recover from either the initial transferee (or the entity for whose benefit the transfer was made) or any immediate or mediate transferee of the initial transferee under 11 USC § 550. At the very least, SPHS was Steenberg's immediate transferee by virtue of being first recipient of the security interest's perfection. It could also be argued that SPHS was the entity for whose benefit the transfer was made. Under either characterization, the trustee in this case may recover against SPHS.

Having determined that a preferential transfer has taken place to which there is no applicable exception and that recovery may be had against SPHS, the inquiry must be directed to the appropriate remedy. Section 550(a) provides:

> (a) Except as otherwise provided in this section, to the extent that a transfer is avoided under section 544, 545, 547, 548, 549, 553(b), or 724(a) of this title, the trustee may recover, for the benefit of the estate, the property transferred, or, if the court so orders, the value of such property.

When a preferential transfer is avoided, the plain language of § 550(a) allows the trustee to recover the property transferred or its value. However, the section does not offer any guidance in determining which remedy the trustee should receive. . . .

Generally, where the record contains no or conflicting evidence of the market value of the transferred property, the courts have ordered that the property be returned. See *In re King Arthur Clock Co., Inc.,* 105 Bankr. 669, 672 (Bankr SD Ala 1989); *In re General Industries, Inc.,* 79 Bankr. 124, 135 (Bankr D Mass 1987); *In re Handsco Distributing, Inc.,* 32 Bankr. 358, 360 (Bankr SD Ohio 1983); *In re Vann,* 26 Bankr. 148, 149 (Bankr SD Ohio 1983). "Where the property is unrecoverable or its value diminished by conversion or depreciation, courts will permit the recovery of value." *Classic Drywall,* 127 Bankr. at 877. However, if the market value of the property can be readily determined and would work a savings for the estate, the trustee may recover value rather than the property. *International Ski,* 119 Bankr. at 657. The market price at the time of transfer is the proper measure of § 550 damages. *Id* at 659.

In the present case, the transferred property is recoverable and there has been no allegation that the value of the property has diminished. In April, 1994, the mobile home's purchase price was $38,160 plus tax. McLaughlin paid a $7,000 down payment, leaving a debt of $31,160 plus tax in April 1994. This, plus any accrued interest, is the maximum value of SPHS' lien in the property.

The value of the lien is related to the market price of the home. Other than the purchase price, no party has provided any evidence of the mobile home's value. The purchase price may or may not be the home's market value. See *King Arthur Clock,* 105 Bankr. 669, 672 (Bankr SD Ala 1989). Ascertaining the value of a mobile home differs from determining the value of the machinery and supplies returned in *International Ski.* In *International Ski,* 119 Bankr. at 659, the debtor had returned machinery for which it had not yet paid. In exchange, the creditor credited the debtor what the debtor had agreed to pay for the goods. The court determined this amount to be the value of the property. *Id.* Presumably, the creditor could easily resell the goods which the debtor had returned to another buyer for the same price the debtor had agreed to pay. However, unlike the goods in *International Ski*, the mobile home had been used for approximately one month before the transfer took place, a seller may not be able to find a buyer willing to pay the same price that McLaughlin did.

In any event, the value of SPHS' lien cannot be readily determined on the evidence produced. Therefore, the trustee is entitled to recover the lien but not money damages equal to its value. An order may be entered transferring the lien on McLaughlin's mobile home from SPHS to the trustee and requiring SPHS to take whatever steps are required to accomplish that transfer.

IT IS HEREBY ORDERED that Security Pacific Housing Services' lien in the mobile home of Susan A. McLaughlin be avoided as a preferential transfer.

IT IS FURTHER ORDERED that the lien be transferred to the trustee and that Security Pacific Housing Services take whatever steps are required to accomplish that transfer.

NOTE

In *McLaughlin*, the trustee attacked the financier as having received a voidable transfer of an interest. The court unravels the credit arrangement that provided the debtor shelter because the transaction was not in fact, a contemporaneous event. Is this decision justifiable? Does it tip the balance of power toward the trustee too far? Compare the court's interpretation of "contemporaneous" with the definition crafted in *Cohee*; are they the same?

IN RE IRFM, INC.

United States Court of Appeals
52 F.3d 228 (9th Cir. 1995)

BEEZER, CIRCUIT JUDGE:

Robert P. Mosier, Chapter 7 Trustee, appeals the district court's grant of summary judgment in favor of creditor Ever-Fresh Food Company ("Ever-Fresh"). Mosier filed this action seeking recovery of $ 72,895.17 in preferential transfers from the Debtor, IRFM, Inc., to Ever-Fresh. The district court, affirming the bankruptcy court, held that Ever-Fresh was entitled to a full new value offset under section 547(c)(4), notwithstanding the fact that the new value did not remain unpaid. . . .

I

IRFM was a retail grocery with several stores in the Southern California area. The grocery specialized in selling high quality fresh meats and produce to its customers, and charged the customers accordingly. IRFM expanded its operations to other areas of Southern California where the demand for high quality, high priced groceries was not great. As a result, IRFM suffered substantial losses.

Ever-Fresh was a supplier of fresh cheese and dairy products to IRFM. Ever-Fresh delivered the goods to IRFM on a weekly basis. IRFM often paid Ever-Fresh for these goods more than seven days after delivery, frequently writing one check for a series of invoices, and not in accordance with the terms of payment or industry standards.

In July, 1988, IRFM filed a voluntary Chapter 11 bankruptcy petition. This petition was converted to one under Chapter 7 in October 1989. The appointment of Mosier as trustee became final in November 1989.

During the ninety day period immediately prior to bankruptcy, IRFM and Ever-Fresh engaged in the following transactions:

CHECK DATE	PAYMENT AMOUNT	GOODS SHIPPED
April 25	$ 18,475.86	
		$ 18,849.16
May 2	$ 18,095.66	
		$ 33,063.18
May 11	$ 16,197.93	
		$ 16,197.93
May 16	$ 14,492.91	
		$ 17,280.78
May 23	$ 18,056.21	
		$ 20,590.11
May 30	$ 18,420.07	
		$ 23,056.79
June 6	$ 18,922.37	
		$ 17,436.51
June 13	$ 23,479.03	
		$ 15,967.54
June 20	$ 17,127.20	
July 22		$ 113,566.47
	$ 163,267.24	$ 276,008.47

Mosier filed this action in bankruptcy court seeking to avoid and recover $72,895.17 of the payments made by IRFM to Ever-Fresh under 11 U.S.C. § 547. Mosier calculated this amount by first subtracting the total amount of the payments, $163,267.24, from $253,639.31, the amount he calculated as the total new value given by Ever-Fresh. The remainder, $90,372.07, Mosier argues is the amount of new value which remained "unpaid" at the time of bankruptcy and may be retained by Ever-Fresh. Mosier then subtracted this "unpaid" new value from the $ 163,267.24 in payments made by IRFM. Mosier contends that the resulting $72,895.17 is paid new value and may be avoided.[10]

[10] In computing the amount he seeks to avoid, Mosier erroneously states that the total amount of new value given was $ 253,639.31. As the table indicates, the amount of new value given was actually $ 276,008.47. Using this figure and Mosier's method of calculating the allegedly avoidable amount, we arrive at an amount of "unpaid" new value

The bankruptcy court, Judge John Ryan, rejected this argument and held that Ever-Fresh was entitled to a new value offset for the entire $163,267.24. In reaching this conclusion, the bankruptcy court held that new value need not remain unpaid. *In re IRFM, Inc.,* 144 Bankr. 886 (Bankr. C.D. Cal. 1992). The district court affirmed this decision and granted summary judgment in favor of Ever-Fresh. Mosier now appeals.

. . . .

III

A trustee is empowered to challenge every transfer made by a debtor to a creditor during the ninety day period immediately prior to the filing of a bankruptcy petition. 11 U.S.C. § 547(b). This avoidance power enables the trustee to protect the estate of the debtor and to ensure an equitable distribution among the unsecured creditors.

Once the trustee has established that a transfer is a preference, a creditor may assert a defense to the preference under 11 U.S.C. § 547(c). Ever-Fresh contends that it is entitled to a "new value" defense under section 547(c)(4). Ever-Fresh asserts that after each preferential transfer, it gave IRFM new value and thus may retain the transfers by IRFM. Mosier argues that in order to qualify for a new value defense a creditor must prove (1) the new value was given to the debtor after the preferential transfer; (2) that the new value is unsecured; and (3) that it remain unpaid. Ever-Fresh has satisfied the first two elements. The parties contest the operation of the third.

For support of his position, Mosier relies upon language in cases to the effect that new value must remain unpaid. While this is the literal holding of these cases, these cases did not intend to reach the result urged by Mosier in this case.[11] More importantly, Mosier's argument is contrary to both the language of section 547(c)(4) and the legislative history of the Bankruptcy Code. The following analysis of the language of section 547(c)(4) demonstrates why Mosier's position is erroneous.

---

of $ 112,741.23 and an allegedly avoidable amount of $ 50,526.01. At a hearing in the bankruptcy court on this issue, Mosier conceded that the $ 276,008.47 figure was correct and also conceded that the preference amount was approximately $ 50,000. Mosier's miscalculation is irrelevant to our decision, however, because we hold that Ever-Fresh is entitled to a full new value offset.

[11] The result which Mosier urges may be best understood by an example. Assume IRFM made a preferential transfer of $50,000 to Ever-Fresh sixty days prior to filing bankruptcy. Subsequent to this transfer, Ever-Fresh gave IRFM new credit valued at $ 100,000. If bankruptcy were filed on this day, Ever-Fresh would be able to successfully assert a new value defense and retain the $50,000 transferred by the debtor. However, if one week before bankruptcy IRFM made another transfer to Ever-Fresh of $50,000, under Mosier's rule, Mosier would be able to avoid the entire $100,000 transfer by the debtor. This result follows because none of the new value remains "unpaid."

Under this rule, Mosier may "double count" the second preferential transfer. First, Mosier may properly avoid the second $50,000 transfer because Ever-Fresh transferred no new value subsequent to this preference. Second, Mosier may also use this second transfer to "pay" for the new value, allowing Mosier to recoup the first $50,000 which had previously been subject to a valid new value defense.

At oral argument, Mosier argued that this was not the result urged. However, by totaling new value, subtracting the preferential transfers and then allowing a new value defense for only the amount left "unpaid," this is the exact result that would occur.

A

Section 547(c)(4) of the Bankruptcy Code provides:

The trustee may not avoid under this section a transfer which–

(4) to or for the benefit of a creditor, to the extent that, after such transfer, such creditor gave new value to or for the benefit of the debtor -

(A) not secured by an otherwise unavoidable security interest; and

(B) on account of which new value the debtor did not make an otherwise unavoidable transfer to or for the benefit of such creditor[.]

Courts and commentators agree that the exception contains two key elements. First, the creditor must give unsecured new value and, second, this new value must be given after the preferential transfer. See *In re Fulghum Constr. Corp.,* 706 F.2d 171, 172 (6th Cir.) cert. denied, 464 U.S. 935 (1983). The majority of courts have also adopted a short hand approach to section 547(c)(4)(B) and hold that section 547(c)(4) contains a third element, that the new value must remain unpaid. The Eighth Circuit recently followed this approach in *In re Kroh Bros. Dev. Co.,* 930 F.2d 648, 653 (8th Cir. 1991) (creditor who has been paid for the new value by the debtor may not assert a new value defense). See also *In re New York City Shoes, Inc.,* 880 F.2d 679, 680 (3d Cir. 1989); *In re Jet Florida Sys., Inc.,* 841 F.2d 1082, 1083 (11th Cir. 1988); *In the Matter of Prescott,* 805 F.2d 719, 731 (7th Cir. 1986).

The rationale for this position is (1) if new value has been repaid by the debtor, the estate has not been replenished and; (2) the creditor is permitted the double benefit of a new value defense and the repayment of the new value. See *Kroh Bros.,* 930 F.2d at 652. However, focusing only on the issue of whether the new value is unpaid may lead to some absurd results, as Mosier's position demonstrates. As a result, an emerging trend has developed where a few courts have reached the contrary result and hold that new value need not remain unpaid. See *In re Ladera Heights Comm. Hosp., Inc.,* 152 Bankr. 964, 968 (Bankr. C.D. Cal. 1993).

However, an even more recent trend has developed where courts and commentators have rejected the short hand approach and have undertaken a more thorough analysis of the language of section 547(c)(4)(B). These cases reason that the numerous decisions focusing on the narrow issue of whether the new value remains unpaid are incomplete and inaccurate. *In the Matter of Toyota of Jefferson, Inc.,* 14 F.3d 1088, 1093 n.2 (5th Cir. 1994); *In re PNP Holdings Corp.,* 167 Bankr. 619, 629 (Bankr. W.D. Wash. 1994); *In re Check Reporting Servs., Inc.,* 140 Bankr. 425, 431-34 (Bankr. W.D. Mich. 1992).

According to this view, the proper inquiry directed by section 547(c)(4)(B) is whether the new value has been paid for by "an otherwise unavoidable transfer." *In the Matter of Toyota of Jefferson,* 14 F.3d at 1093 n.2. This inquiry follows the *Kroh Bros.* rationale that a creditor should not get double credit for an advance of new value. However, instead of barring the new value defense altogether anytime new value has been repaid, this approach allows the new value defense if the trustee can recover the repayment by some other means.

This analysis fully comports with the statute's plain language. While the phrase "the debtor did not make an otherwise unavoidable transfer" is complicated, it is not ambiguous and its meaning is easily discernible. See *Check Reporting Servs.,* 140 Bankr. at 434-36 (conducting an exhaustive analysis of the phrase "did not make an otherwise unavoidable transfer"). As one commentator has explained:

> If the debtor has made payments for goods or services that the creditor supplied on unsecured credit after an earlier preference, and if these subsequent payments are themselves voidable as preferences (or on any other ground), then under section 547(c)(4)(B) the creditor should be able to invoke those unsecured credit extensions as a defense to the recovery of the earlier voidable preference. On the other hand, the debtor's subsequent payments might not be voidable on any other ground and not voidable under section 547, because the goods and services were given C.O.D. rather than on a credit, or because the creditor has a defense under section 547(c)(1), (2), or (3). In this situation, the creditor may keep his payments but has no section 547(c)(4) defense to the trustee's action to recover the earlier preference. In either event, the creditor gets credit only once for goods and services later supplied.

Vern Countryman, *The Concept of a Voidable Preference in Bankruptcy,* 38 Vand. L. Rev. 713, 788 (1985) (footnotes omitted) (quoted in *In the Matter of Toyota of Jefferson, Inc.,* 14 F.3d at 1092-93).

We agree with this analysis and hold that a new value defense is permitted unless the debtor repays the new value by a transfer which is otherwise unavoidable.

B

In addition to its consistency with the language of the statute, this approach meets the policy underlying preference actions. *Check Reporting Servs.,* 140 Bankr. at 437. The purpose of section 547 is twofold. First, enabling a trustee to avoid preferential transfers allows the trustee to secure equality of distribution among the unsecured creditors by preventing a debtor from benefiting a particular creditor on the eve of bankruptcy. Second, the new value exception encourages creditors to continue to do business with financially troubled debtors, with an eye toward avoiding bankruptcy altogether. *Id.*

The rule for which Mosier argues would discourage creditors from having any dealings with a financially troubled debtor. For instance, Ever-Fresh could have sold the goods to another purchaser and been able to retain the payment for those goods. Instead, Ever-Fresh would not only be required to forfeit all payments made by IRFM during the preference period, but Ever-Fresh would also lose the new value extended to the debtor. Mosier's rule also makes the creditor worse off vis-a-vis the other creditors. By refusing to permit the creditor to receive some benefit for the transfer of new value, the proposed rule would put the creditor in a worse position than those creditors who chose not to deal with the debtor.

IV

We must now decide the proper calculation of the new value offset. The district court adopted the following approach:

CHECK DATE	PAYMENT AMOUNT	GOODS SHIPPED	PREFERENCE
April 25	$ 18,475.86		$ 18,475.86
		$ 18,849.16	
May 2	$ 18,095.66		$ 18,095.66
		$ 33,063.18	
May 11	$ 16,197.93		$ 16,197.93
		$ 16,197.93	
May 16	$ 14,492.91		$ 14,492.91
		$ 17,280.78	

CHECK DATE	PAYMENT AMOUNT	GOODS SHIPPED	PREFERENCE
May 23	$ 18,056.21		$ 18,056.21
		$ 20,590.11	
May 30	$ 18,420.07		$ 18,420.07
		$ 23,056.79	
June 6	$ 18,922.37		$ 18,922.37
		$ 17,436.51	$ 1,485.86
June 13	$ 23,479.03		$ 24,964.89
		$ 15,967.54	$ 8,997.35
June 20	$ 17,127.20		$ 26,124.55
July 22		$ 113,566.47	$ 0.00
	$ 163,267.24	$ 276,008.47	$ 0.00

This calculation results in a full new value defense for Ever-Fresh and we accept it as correct. This approach is derived from *In re Thomas W. Garland, Inc.*, 19 Bankr. 920 (Bankr. E.D. Mo. 1982). Under this method, subsequent advances of new value may be used to offset prior (although not immediately prior) preferences. A creditor is permitted to carry forward preferences until they are exhausted by subsequent advances of new value.

The rationale behind this method is twofold. First, it encourages creditors to do business with financially troubled debtors. A creditor will be more likely to continue to advance new value to a debtor if all these subsequent advances may be used to offset a prior preference. If a second advance of new value carries no benefit, the creditor will be unlikely to make it. *In re Meredith Manor, Inc.*, 902 F.2d 257, 259 (4th Cir. 1990). Second, this approach recognizes the fluid nature of ongoing commercial activity where a creditor looks to a debtor's entire repayment history, instead of one isolated transaction, to decide whether to advance new credit. *Id.*

. . . .

We adopt the *Garland* approach with a few additional requirements that are necessary given our holding in section III.

First, to calculate the new value defense, consideration must be given to whether an increment of new value has been paid for by something other than an avoidable transfer. If so, this increment of new value may not be included in calculating the amount of the new value defense.

Second, assurance must be given that the creditor will not attempt to obtain double credit for a transfer. This requirement may be satisfied by disallowing a creditor from asserting a separate section 547(c) defense against a preference when the creditor has already used section 547(c)(4) to offset that preference.

Applying these requirements to the present case, we affirm the district court's award of the full new value offset to Ever-Fresh. Under the *Garland* test where new value may offset more than the immediately prior preference, the resulting preference amount is zero. Second, the parties agreed that all transfers by IRFM which are challenged by Mosier are preferences under 547(b). Therefore, none of these transfers are "otherwise unavoidable." Finally, because Ever-Fresh has been granted a new value offset for each of these preferential transfers, no other preference defense is available for these same transfers.

V

The preference section of the Bankruptcy Code requires that new value must not be repaid by an otherwise unavoidable transfer. Because the parties agree that the transfers made in this case are preferences under section 547(b), they are not "unavoidable." We conclude that Ever-Fresh is entitled to a new value defense for the entire amount of preferential transfers made by IRFM.

AFFIRMED.

[1] Security Interests in Inventory and Accounts

Read: BRA § 547(c)(5).

Section 547(c)(5) allows a floating lien on a debtor's inventory to be protected from preference attack so long as the security received does not exceed the value of the inventory advance to the debtor. To allow protection of an inventory supplier makes logical sense. We want to encourage a supplier to provide the debtor with inventory that can be sold in most instances. If the debtor is cut off from receiving any supplies, the law would inevitably force an already-struggling business into bankruptcy. By allowing the debtor access to inventory financing, the Bankruptcy Code provides a basis for the business to remain operational, thus giving the firm the greatest chance to survive. Consider the following case.

IN RE EBBLER FURNITURE & APPLIANCES, INC.

United States Court of Appeals
804 F.2d 87 (7th Cir. 1986)

FLAUM, CIRCUIT JUDGE.

This suit involves an issue of first impression in this circuit. We are asked to define the word "value" as used in 11 U.S.C. § 547(c)(5). We affirm the bankruptcy court and district court in their use of "cost" as the proper measurement in this case. However, we remand this case for further proceedings to determine the precise amount of the preference payment that the defendant received.

I.

The present action is by the trustee in bankruptcy under 11 U.S.C. §§ 547(b) and (c)(5)(1986), to recover preference payments received by the defendant. Ebbler Furniture and Appliance, Inc. ("Ebbler"), filed a voluntary petition for relief pursuant to the Chapter 7 liquidation provisions of the Bankruptcy Code.

The appellant, Alton Bank & Trust Co. ("the Bank"), was the inventory financier for Ebbler. Although the security agreement is not in the record, it appears that the security agreement granted the Bank a security interest in Ebbler's inventory, and accounts receivable. The record is unclear as to whether the security interest covered proceeds and whether it was properly perfected.

The bankruptcy court made the following factual findings. Purchases made by the debtor within ninety days prior to bankruptcy totaled $170,911.33. The cost of goods sold during the ninety day period equaled $214,065.19. The ending inventory, as of the date of filing bankruptcy, was $67,000.00. The cost of the beginning inventory ninety days prior to the filing of the bankruptcy was calculated by the bankruptcy court in the following manner:

> cost of goods sold ($214,065.19) + ending inventory ($67,000.00) — purchases $170,911.33) = beginning inventory ($110,153.86). The bankruptcy court also found that there were $19,000 worth of accounts receivable, subject to the Bank's security interest. These receivables were added to beginning inventory. The bankruptcy court then concluded:

> 12. On the basis on [sic] the foregoing figures, the creditor Bank received a preference as described in 11 U.S.C. § 547(c)(5) of approximately $75,000.00, *i.e.*, the difference between what the Bank received on account of the debt it was owed ($204,571.61), less the debtor's beginning inventory ($110,000.00) and its accounts receivable ($19,000).

In re Ebbler Furniture & Appliances, Inc., No. 84-0150 (Bankr. S.D. Ill. 1985) (unpublished order).

The bankruptcy court noted that a discrepancy existed in the amount of $15,000 as to the value of the ending inventory. Consequently, the bankruptcy court reduced the preference by $15,000.00, and found a preference of $60,000.00.

Beginning approximately three to four months before filing its petition, Ebbler conducted a going out of business sale. Ebbler ceased doing business on November 30, 1983. At that time Ebbler was indebted to the Bank in the amount of $50,000 and had $67,000 in inventory (valued on a cost basis). The Bank repossessed $50,000 worth of inventory and sold it at cost applying the $50,000 proceeds to the debt.

Finally, and perhaps most important for purposes of this appeal, the bankruptcy court determined that the parties "were relying on the cost basis of the inventory in evaluating the security for the indebtedness." *Id.*

II

A.

When a court reviews a bankruptcy court decision on appeal, the court must adopt the bankruptcy court's findings of fact unless clearly erroneous. *In re Kimzey*, 761 F.2d 421, 423 (7th Cir. 1985); *In re Evanston Motor Company, Inc*., 735 F.2d 1029, 1031 (7th Cir. 1984). The clearly erroneous rule does not apply to review of the bankruptcy court's conclusions of law. *In re Kimzey,* 761 F.2d 421, 423 (7th Cir. 1985).

This case involves a mixed question of fact and law. The definition of value in § 547(c)(5) is a legal question, which depends on factual determinations made by the bankruptcy court. The factual determinations are subject to the clearly erroneous standard; but the manner in which these factual conclusions implicate the legal definition of value is subject to a de novo review. We note, however, that by deferring to these initial factual determinations, subject to review by the district courts, we are not abdicating our role as the reviewer of the definition of value adopted by the lower courts.

B.

The issue presented is the interpretation of "value" as used in § 547(c)(5) of the Bankruptcy Code. Section 547(c)(5) applies to situations where a secured creditor does not have sufficient collateral to cover his outstanding debt. Subparagraph five (5) codifies the "improvement in position test" and overrules an earlier line of cases such as *Grain Merchants of Indiana, Inc. v. Union Bank & Savings Co.,* 408 F.2d 209 (7th Cir.), cert. denied, 396 U.S. 827, 24 L. Ed. 2d 78, 90 S. Ct. 75 (1969). Section 547(c)(5) prevents a secured creditor from improving its position at the expense of an unsecured creditor during the 90 days prior to filing the bankruptcy petition. See generally 4A Collier on Bankruptcy para. 547.41, p. 547-133 (15th ed.).

The first step in applying section 547(c)(5) is to determine the amount of the loan outstanding 90 days prior to filing and the "value" of the collateral on that day. The difference between these figures is then computed. Next, the same determinations are made as of the date of filing the petition. A comparison is made, and, if there is a reduction during the 90 day period of the amount by which the initially existing debt exceeded the security, then a preference for section 547(c)(5) purposes exists. See generally 4A Collier on Bankruptcy para. 547.41. The effect of 547(c)(5) is to make the security interest voidable to the extent of the preference. *Id.* at p. 547-134. Of course, if the creditor is fully secured 90 days before the filing of the petition, then that creditor will never be subject to a preference attack. *Id.*; see also *Matter of Missionary Baptist Foundation*, 796 F.2d 752, 760 n.11 (5th Cir. 1986).

C.

The language of section 547(c)(5), the "value of all security interest for such debt," was purposely left without a precise definition. See generally H.R. No. 595, S.Rep. No. 989, 95th Cong., 2d Sess., reprinted in 1978 U.S. Code Cong. & Ad. News, 5787, 6176; N. Cohen, *"Value" Judgments: Account Receivable Financing and Voidable Preferences Under the New Bankruptcy Code,* 66 Minn. L. Rev. 639, 653 (1982) (hereinafter "Cohen"); *In re Beattie*, 31 Bankr. 703, 714 (W.D.N.C. 1983). Furthermore, it has been persuasively argued that the other Bankruptcy Code sections' definitions of "value" would not be useful for section 547(c)(5) purposes. Cohen, *supra,* at 651-654. Thus, the only legislative guidance is "that we are to determine value on case-by-case basis, taking into account the facts of each case and the competing interests in the case." *Matter of Lackow Bros., Inc.*, 752 F.2d 1529, 1532 (11th Cir. 1985), citing H.R. Rep. No. 545, 95th Cong., 1st Sess. 356 (1977) reprinted in 1978 U.S. Code Cong. & Ad. News 5787, 6312.

The method used to value the collateral is crucial in determining whether or not the bank received a preference. The Bank urges that we adopt an "ongoing concern" value standard, which, in this case, would be cost plus a 60% mark-up. The Bank relies on *Lackow Bros., supra,* as authority for the use of this definition of value. We find *Lackow Bros.* readily distinguishable. There, the only evidence of value before the court was ongoing concern value. As the Eleventh Circuit stated: "The only evidence in the record of value for the ninetieth day prior to the filing of the bankruptcy is the ongoing concern value; therefore, this is the only standard of valuation that can be applied to determine if Creditor's position improved. . . ." *Lackow Bros.* at 1532.

Another view as to how value should be defined is proposed by Professor Cohen. He proposes an after-the-fact determination of value. In his article discussing accounts receivable, Cohen argues that the courts should look at the actual manner in which the collateral was liquidated, *i.e.* cost or ongoing concern. Whatever method is used to dispose of the collateral, Cohen argues, should be used to value the collateral 90 days before the filing of the bankruptcy petition. Cohen, *supra,* at 664. At least one circuit has found Cohen's reasoning useful, though not necessarily adopting it as a rigid rule. *Matter of Missionary Baptist Foundation*, 796 F.2d 752, 761-62 (5th Cir. 1986).

In *Missionary Baptist Foundation, supra*, the appellate court remanded to the district court for factual determinations as to whether or not the bank improved its position during the preference period. *Id.* at 761. The court noted, however, that merely remanding for factual findings may not be sufficient in light of the ambiguous meaning of "value" in section 547(c)(5). Id. at 761-62. The Fifth Circuit quoted with approval Cohen's admonition of an individualized approach in defining value and his hindsight solution of the problem. We follow the Fifth Circuit's lead and hold that under Section 547(c)(5) value should be defined on a case by case basis, with the factual determinations of the bankruptcy court controlling.

D.

In the present case, we affirm the bankruptcy court's use of cost as the method for valuing the collateral for 547(c)(5) purposes. The bankruptcy court found that the parties were using a cost basis for valuing the security. Furthermore, when the Bank removed inventory with a cost of approximately $50,000, about a week before the petition was filed, Ebbler was given credit for that amount — $50,000. We do not find the bankruptcy court's factual findings so clearly erroneous as to warrant reversal. *In re Kimzey*, 761 F.2d 421, 423 (7th Cir. 1985).

Using these factual findings the bankruptcy court applied cost as the legal definition of "value." We affirm the use of this definition as applied to these facts.

III.

We remand to the bankruptcy court, however, for a determination as to the amount of the preference. The bankruptcy court found, weighing the conflicting evidence, that a preference of $60,000 existed. It is not clear why the bankruptcy court did not consider the $43,000 in cash which the debtor had in hand at the time of filing the bankruptcy petition.

The bankruptcy court held that the Bank had a security interest in the inventory and accounts receivable. The bankruptcy court's opinion is silent as to whether or not this security agreement covered cash proceeds, and whether or not the $43,000 in actuality was cash proceeds of the inventory. It must also be determined if these interests were properly perfected. The only evidence in the record is Mr. Ebbler's testimony that all the proceeds from sales of inventory were deposited into an account at the Bank. The bank statement shows that on the 90th day prior to the bankruptcy the account contained $43,000. Depending on the court's findings on these issues an adjustment downward in the amount of the preference might be appropriate.

IV.

For the reasons set forth, we affirm the use of cost as a basis for defining value in section 547(c)(5) of the Bankruptcy Code. We remand, however, for a determination as to how the debtor's cash on hand affected the preference amount.

EASTERBROOK, CIRCUIT JUDGE, Concurring.

This case involves the meaning of "value" under 11 U.S.C. § 547(c)(5). I join the court's opinion, which concludes that the statute does not require bankruptcy judges to use one universal definition. The history of condemnation litigation shows that a single definition of "value" is not within judicial grasp. Still, we need not leave bankruptcy judges and litigants adrift. Security interests must be appraised with some frequency in bankruptcy litigation. The greater the uncertainty in the legal rule, the harder it is to settle pending cases. "Anything goes" is not a durable rule. The parties cannot know their entitlements until bankruptcy, district, and appellate courts have spoken. One important function of appellate courts is to provide additional clarity, when that is reasonably possible. It is possible here. The bankruptcy judge did better than to avoid an abuse of discretion. He decided the case correctly.

"Value" is defined for a purpose, which sets limits on the admissible standards of appraisal even though it does not govern all cases. Section 547(c)(5) requires the court to find whether the secured creditor improved its position at the expense of other investors during the 90 days before the filing of the petition in bankruptcy. This calls for two appraisals, one on the day of filing and one 90 days earlier, using the same method each time, to see whether there was an improvement in position. The only standard that might plausibly be used in this case is wholesale cost of goods, because that is the only standard that could have been applied on both dates.

Wholesale cost is also the appropriate standard as a rule because wholesale and retail goods are different things. A furniture store, a supermarket, or the manufacturer of a product (the three situations are identical) uses raw materials purchased at wholesale to produce a new item. In the retailing business, the difference between the wholesale price and the retail price is the "value added" of the business. It is the amount contributed by storing, inspecting, displaying, hawking, collecting for, delivering, and handling warranty claims on the goods. This difference covers the employees' wages, rent and utilities of the premises, interest on the cost of goods, bad debts, repairs, the value of entrepreneurial talent, and so on. The increment of price is attributable to this investment of time and other resources. The Bank does not have a security interest in these labors. It has an interest only in its merchandise and cash on hand. The value of its interest depends on what the Bank could do, outside of bankruptcy, to realize on its security. See Thomas H. Jackson, *Avoiding Powers in Bankruptcy,* 36 Stan. L. Rev. 725, 756-77 (1984). What it could do is seize and sell the inventory. It would get at most the wholesale price — maybe less because the Bank would sell the goods "as is" and would not offer the wholesaler's usual services to its customer. The Bank does not operate its own furniture store, and if it did it would still incur all the costs of retailing the goods, costs that would have to be subtracted from the retail price to determine the "value" of the inventory on the day the Bank seized it. Cf. *Contrail Leasing Partners, Ltd. v. Consolidated Airways, Inc.,* 742 F.2d 1095, 1101 (7th Cir. 1984); Uniform Commercial Code § 9-504(1)(a).

To give the Bank more than the wholesale value is to induce a spate of asset-grabbing among creditors, which could make all worse off. If the Bank gets the whole increment of value (from wholesale to retail) during the last 90 days, other creditors may respond by watching the debtor closely and propelling it into bankruptcy when it has a lower inventory (and therefore less "markup" for the Bank to seize). The premature filing may reduce the value of the enterprise. There are other defensive measures available to creditors. The principal function of § 547(c)(5) is to reduce the need of unsecured creditors to protect themselves against the last-minute moves of secured creditors. It would serve this function less well if goods subject to a security interest were appraised at their retail price.

Too, the Bank's security interest does not reach the "going concern" value of the debtor; it had security in the goods, not in the firm. To value the inventory in a way that reflects "going concern" value is to give the Bank something for which it did not contract. At all events, this wrinkle does not make a difference. If Ebbler had been sold as a going venture 90 days before the filing of the bankruptcy petition, the buyer of the business would have paid only wholesale price for Ebbler's inventory. If Ebbler had been at the peak of health, the buyer would have paid no more for inventory. A buyer would not have paid retail, because it would have had to invest the additional time and money necessary to obtain the retail price. So whether Ebbler is valued as a defunct business or as a going business sold to a hypothetical buyer on the critical date, wholesale is the right valuation, because it reflects the price that a willing buyer would pay after arms'-length negotiation. (The "going concern" value of Ebbler is reflected in its name, reputation, customer list, staff, and so on — things in which the Bank did not have a security interest.)

To put this differently, a willing buyer of a flourishing retail or manufacturing business will not pay more than the wholesale price for inventory of goods or parts on hand, because this buyer could purchase the same items on the market from the original sellers. Why pay Ebbler $500 for a sofa when you can get the same item for $200 from its manufacturer? Nothing would depend on whether Ebbler planned to stay in business. The court therefore properly does not allow the outcome of this case to turn on the fact that Ebbler chose a Chapter 7 liquidation rather than a Chapter 11 reorganization. Chapter titles are of little use in valuing assets under § 547(c)(5). A "liquidation" may be a sale of the business en bloc as an ongoing concern, and a "reorganization" may be a transition from one line of business to another.

The difference between the wholesale and retail prices of the inventory is the compensation that the other factors of production — the employees, landlords, utilities, etc. — obtain for their services. To appraise Ebbler's inventory at "retail" is to award to the Bank the entire value of the work done during the last 90 days by these other creditors of Ebbler. It is to allow the Bank to improve its position at their expense. Because a valuation at "retail" would produce exactly the consequence that § 547(c)(5) is designed to avert, the bankruptcy court wisely chose to appraise the goods at wholesale. The court leaves to another day the question whether retail price is ever an appropriate measure of value under § 547(c)(5). The observation that the bankruptcy court has leeway, however, does not imply that the court's discretion should be exercised without reference to the function of § 547(c)(5) and the limits of the security interest.

NOTE

The opinions of Judges Flaum and Easterbrook present contrasting views on how inventory should be valued for purposes of section 547(c)(5). Judge Flaum believes that the drafters of the Bankruptcy Code intentionally left the term "value" without a specific definition. Such a situtation would force courts into a case-by-case analysis of the facts surrounding the calculation of value. However, determining the measuring device for value (whether wholesale cost or ongoing concern should be used) may have a significant effect in determining whether a preferential transfer did occur. Once a measuring value has been decided upon, in order to compute whether a preference has indeed occurred, one needs to ascertain both the amount of the loan outstanding 90 days prior to the bankruptcy filing and the "value" of the collateral on that day. The difference between these figures is then computed. The same determinations are made with respect to the loan and collateral value as of the date of the bankruptcy filing. If the value of the collateral in relation to the outstanding debt balance has increased during the 90-day period, a preferential transfer has occurred and section 547(c)(5) cannot protect the beneficiary of that transfer from an avoidance action by the trustee.

Judge Easterbrook believes that wholesale cost was the only standard that could be applied in the case because any use of retail value would necessarily include value added from the debtor's general assets. To permit the bank to capture such value would amount to a diversion of unencumbered assets from unsecured creditors to the bank as a secured party. Which judge presents the more workable approach?

[2] Proceeds

IN RE GUARANTEED MUFFLER SUPPLY

United States Bankruptcy Court, Northern District of Georgia
5 Bankr. 236 (1980)

A.D. KAHN, UNITED STATES BANKRUPTCY JUDGE.

Before the court is Plaintiff/Trustee's motion for "judgment on the pleadings regarding the specific issue of law whether the application of Ga. Code § 109A-9-306(4)(d)(1962) shall be limited by National Bank of Georgia's having to trace the proceeds from the disposition of each piece of [property in which NBG holds a valid security interest]." The court will interpret the Trustee's motion to constitute a request for a ruling that would limit a secured party's proceeds claim under U.C.C. § 9-306(4)(d) to those proceeds which are appropriately identified as having been collected upon disposition of property which is validly encumbered by the secured party's lien. For the reasons outlined below, the court is inclined to grant the Trustee's request.

As explained more fully by court order entered November 27, 1979 (reported at 1 B.R. 324, 27 U.C.C.Rep. 1217), the relationship between the above-named parties was initiated in 1976 when Defendant National Bank of Georgia (NBG) took a security interest in all inventory and accounts owned by a predecessor partnership of the corporate Bankrupt. Some two years later, after the corporation was formed and the assets of the old partnership were transferred to the new entity, Defendant Hamilton took a security interest in all inventory and accounts of the newly formed corporation.

In March of 1979, the corporation filed a petition in bankruptcy, but the lien-holding Defendants and the Trustee could not resolve their conflicting claims to property of the estate. The Trustee, therefore, commenced the above-styled proceeding to resolve the conflict.

Although Defendant Hamilton's lien on property of the estate is subordinate to those claims which NBG validly asserts to the same property (see U.C.C. § 9-312(5) and order entered February 6, 1980), the court made clear in its November 1979 order that NBG's lien on property of the estate is limited to the following: (1) partnership accounts and inventory which survived until the date of bankruptcy; (2) proceeds collected by the partnership upon sale of the accounts and inventory; and (3) proceeds collected by the now bankrupt corporation upon its sale of partnership property encumbered by NBG's lien. These limitations are imposed upon NBG's lien because NBG failed to obtain a security interest in property of the corporate entity and because no party has urged the court to pierce the corporate veil.

Of tremendous practical significance is the fact that NBG may assert a lien on property which is alleged to constitute proceeds only after it is shown that the property is indeed the fruit obtained upon disposition of NBG's collateral. This requirement is otherwise known as the requirement that proceeds be "identifiable." Ga. Code Ann. § 109A-9-306(1962); *In Re Guaranteed Muffler Supply Co., Inc.,* 1 B.R. 324, 328, 27 U.C.C.Rep. 1217, 1223 (Bk.Ct.N.D.Ga. 1979); *Howarth v. Universal C.I.T. Credit Corp.,* 203 F. Supp. 279, 1 U.C.C. Rep. 515 (W.D.Pa. 1962). See especially *In Re Guaranteed Muffler Supply Co., Inc.,* 27 U.C.C. Rep. 1228 (Bk.Ct.N.D.Ga. 1980).

Since NBG's claim to property of the estate is largely rooted in U.C.C. Article 9proceeds theory, the court declared in its November order that the general U.C.C. restrictions placed upon proceeds rights should apply not only to NBG's claims to proceeds collected by the partnership, but also to NBG's claims to proceeds collected by the corporate Bankrupt, (otherwise known as the "transferee's proceeds"). One such restriction discussed in the order was the one found in U.C.C. § 9-306(4)(d)(1962) which "eliminates secured parties' rights in cash proceeds which are on hand as of the date of a bankruptcy unless a secured party can show that the cash was collected within ten days before bankruptcy or that the cash was not mingled with [non-proceeds] cash." *In Re Guaranteed Muffler Supply Co., Inc.,* 1 B.R. 324, 329, 27U.C.C.Rep. 1217, 1224 (Bk.Ct.N.D.Ga. 1979).

That characterization of the nature of U.C.C. § 9-306(4)(d) implicitly answers the question posed by the Trustee's motion. The court's view of § 9-306(4)(d) as a provision which RESTRICTS secured parties' claims to proceeds is an implicit rejection of any interpretation of § 9-306(4)(d) through which secured parties obtain greater lien rights than they would in the absence of § 9-306(4)(d).

Admittedly, at least one court has taken the position that U.C.C. § 9-306(4)(d) "gives the secured creditor a perfected security interest in the entire amount [of cash proceeds] deposited [or received] by the debtor within ten days before bankruptcy without limiting the interest to the amount that can be identified as the proceeds from the sale of the creditor's collateral." *In Re Gibson Products of Arizona,* 543 F.2d 652, 655 (9th Cir.), cert. denied 430 U.S. 946, 97 S. Ct. 1583, 51 L. Ed. 2d 794 (1976). The *Gibson Products* court elaborated on its position by stating that "with respect to the funds that are not the creditor's proceeds, the creditor has no security interest except that conferred by U.C.C. Section 9-306(4)(d)." *Id.* at 655.

It is this court's position that the *Gibson Products* view misinterprets the language and logic of the U.C.C. proceeds section. Although the *Gibson Products* court ultimately relied upon bankruptcy preference law to invalidate that portion of the secured party's claim to proceeds conferred solely by § 9-306(4)(d), this court is of the opinion that there is absolutely no conflict between § 9-306(4)(d) and the Bankruptcy Act. Accord *Fitzpatrick v. Philco Finance Corp.,* 491 F.2d 1288 (7th Cir. 1974). To create a false conflict in this circumstance is not only to raise complicated questions involving the meaning of a preferential "transfer," but also to cause unnecessary argument about the extent to which portions of the U.C.C. are to be invalidated as disguised state priorities or voidable statutory liens. See *In Re Dexter Buick — GMC Truck Co.*, 2 B.R. 242 (Bk.Ct.D.R.I. 1980).

The point of departure between the position taken by this court and the Ninth Circuit *Gibson Products* panel is rooted in conflicting views about the very nature of secured parties' rights to proceeds. Such rights are obtained by authority of U.C.C. § 9-306(2), which states that an article nine lien "continues in collateral notwithstanding [an unauthorized] sale, and also continues in any identifiable proceeds . . . ." This important provision makes proceeds claims, by definition, depend upon a showing that the property claimed is identified as the fruit of a sale or other disposition of the original collateral. Thus, a right to proceeds of any kind, whether in bankruptcy or not, arises out of the language of § 9-306(2); the limitations upon "cash proceeds" listed in § 9-306(4)(d)(ii), therefore include, by definition, the identifiability limitations which apply to all claims made to all proceeds. To require that proceeds claims be so limited is consistent with the fact that the exercise of lien rights is confined to specific property which the debtor has chosen to make available as a surrogate for his own performance.

Accordingly, the Trustee's motion is hereby GRANTED. No secured party in this proceeding may claim property of the estate on the basis of U.C.C. article nine proceeds theory unless the property is shown to have been collected upon the disposition of property in which the secured party held a valid lien.

NOTE

The logic of *Guaranteed Muffler* remains sound. In order to collect proceeds, it is fair to force a creditor to show that the proceeds are from the property that the creditor actually secured. The holding of *Guaranteed* is straightforward: no secured party may claim property of the estate on the basis of an U.C.C. Article 9 proceeds theory, unless the property is shown to have been collected upon the disposition of property in which the secured party held a valid lien.

[C] Fraudulent Transfers

Read: Section 548 of the Bankruptcy Code

Section 548 allows the trustee to avoid transfers that might tend to hinder, delay, or defraud any party to whom the debtor has an obligation. The trustee has the power to seek recovery under either section 548, or, to proceed under section 544(b) which authorizes the use of state fraudulent transfer law. In reality, the choice of statutes is often meaningless; the text of section 548 is substantially similar to that found in the Uniform Fraudulent Transfer Act. Given that most states laws reflect the influence of the Uniform Act, significant differences in avoidance powers are usually not provided by section 548.

Despite the similarity of state law provisions on fraudulent transfers and section 548, it is still necessary to talk briefly about how section 548 operates. Like state fraudulent conveyance law, section 548(a) reaches transfers that are made by the debtor with the actual and subjective intent of defrauding creditors. Section 548(a)(1) corresponds to section 7 of the Uniform Fraudulent Conveyances Act and empowers the trustee in bankruptcy to invalidate transfers made with the actual intent to hinder delay or defraud creditors. Because there is rarely any direct evidence of actual fraudulent intent, one typically establishes that intent through circumstantial evidence. Section 548(a)(2) may be of greater practical significance because it provides for the avoidance of transfers where the debtor receives less than a "reasonably equivalent value" and either (i) the debtor became insolvent because of the transaction; or, (ii) the debtor's capital position was or became unreasonably small because of the transaction; or, (iii) the debtor intended to incur or believed that s/he would incur debts beyond her/his ability to pay. Subsection (a)(2) therefore, carves out a set of transfers that are *constructively fraudulent.*

Establishing a constructively fraudulent conveyance obviously turns on the adequacy of the consideration given to effect the transfer. Establishment also depends upon the financial position of the debtor, even more so than the intention of the debtor. Section 548(a)(2) has been increasingly applied to a host of business transactions that have little to do with debtor intention.

Examples of transactions found to be subject to the trustee's avoidance powers under section 548(a)(2) include foreclosure sales, leveraged buyouts, and intercorporate guarantees. In *Durrett v. Washington National Insurance Co.,* 621 F.2d 201 (5th Cir. 1980), the court held that a non-judicial foreclosure sale, which complied fully with state law, could be a fraudulent conveyance under section 548. The trustee presented evidence that the price received at foreclosure sale was less than 70% of the market value of the property.[12] Section 3(b) of the Uniform Fraudulent Transfers Act attempts to avoid the *Durrett* percentage analysis by stating a conclusive, statutory presumption: "a person gives reasonable equivalent value if the person acquires an interest of the debtor in an asset pursuant to a regularly conducted, noncollusive foreclosure sale or execution of a power of sale . . ."Comment 5 to UFTA § 3 states that the foreclosure sale after a debtor's default is the "safest way of establishing the fair market value of the collateral." Do you agree? Are there problems with assuming that a foreclosure sale nets market value? How would you define market value in the face of the relatively overwhelming evidence that the prices received at a foreclosure sale are not nearly as high as those produced by privately negotiate sales? The next case presents a *Durrett* issue.

[12] The actual amound paid for the property was $115,400, 57.7% of the "fair market value" of $200,000.

IN RE BUNDLES

United States Court of Appeals
856 F.2d 815 (7th Cir. 1988)

RIPPLE, CIRCUIT JUDGE.

In this appeal, we must decide whether a debtor in bankruptcy may set aside under section 548(a)(2) of the Bankruptcy Code (the Code), 11 U.S.C. § 548(a)(2)(Supp. IV 1986), the sale of his personal residence upon foreclosure of the mortgage. The bankruptcy court and the district court held that he could not. We reverse and remand for further proceedings.

I

Background

A. Statutory Background

Section 548 of the Code provides in pertinent part:

§ 548. Fraudulent transfers and obligations

(a) The trustee may avoid any transfer of an interest of the debtor in property, or any obligation incurred by the debtor, that was made or incurred on or within one year before the date of the filing of the petition, if the debtor voluntarily or involuntarily —

. . . .

(2)(A) received less than a reasonably equivalent value in exchange for such transfer or obligation; and

(B)(i) was insolvent on the date that such transfer was made or such obligation was incurred, or became insolvent as a result of such transfer or obligation; . . . . 11 U.S.C. § 548(a)(2)(Supp. IV 1986).

This provision sets forth four elements that must be established before a debtor may set aside a transfer of property. These are: (1) the debtor had an interest in the property transferred; (2) the debtor was insolvent at the time of the transfer or became insolvent as a result of the transfer; (3) the transfer occurred within one year of the filing of the bankruptcy petition; and (4) the transfer was for less than a "reasonably equivalent value." The parties agree that the debtor has established each of these elements except the last. Therefore, the only issue before us is whether the debtor received less than a reasonably equivalent value for the property in question.

B. Facts

The facts are stipulated. The debtor-appellant Donald Eugene Bundles has maintained a residence in Indianapolis, Indiana since 1964. Sometime in 1984 and 1985, due to various financial and health problems, Mr. Bundles was unable to meet his mortgage payments. On March 4, 1985, the mortgagee, Indiana National Bank (INB), commenced an action in state court seeking foreclosure of Mr. Bundles' residence. On July 10, 1985, the state court entered a default judgment against Mr. Bundles in the amount of $4,696.46. In addition, an IRS tax lien against the real estate was reduced to a personal judgment against Mr. Bundles in the amount of $2,666. A sheriff's sale of Mr. Bundles' residence was scheduled and held on September 11, 1985, after proper notice and in compliance with Indiana foreclosure law. As of this date, Mr. Bundles was insolvent. The property was purchased at the sale by William J. Baker for $5,066.80. The value of the property at this time was $15,500. On September 12, 1985, Sheriff James L. Wells of Marion County executed a deed to Mr. Baker conveying Mr. Bundles' residence to him. The deed to the property was recorded on September 24, 1985.

On September 25, 1985, after the foreclosure and sale of his residence, Mr. Bundles filed a voluntary petition under Chapter 13 of the Code. Thereafter, on November 14, 1985, he filed a complaint in the bankruptcy court to set aside the foreclosure sale as a fraudulent conveyance. The complaint named as defendants Mr. Baker, the purchaser of his home; INB, the foreclosing mortgagee; and James C. Wells in his official capacity as the Sheriff of Marion County, Indiana.

C. The Bankruptcy Court Opinion

Under section 548, as we have noted already, a debtor in bankruptcy may set aside a transfer of his property as a fraudulent conveyance if he received less than a reasonably equivalent value for the property. In this case, the bankruptcy court held that Mr. Bundles had received a reasonably equivalent value for his home and therefore denied his complaint to set aside the transfer. The bankruptcy court determined that "any avoiding effect accorded a low purchase price by Section 548(a)(2)(A) is misplaced and overbroad with respect to regularly conducted, non-collusive foreclosure sales." *Bundles v. Baker (In re Bundles),* 61 Bankr. 929, 936 (Bankr. S.D. Ind. 1986), aff'd, 78 Bankr. 203 (S.D. Ind. 1987). Therefore, the court held that the sale price obtained at a regularly conducted, non-collusive foreclosure sale should be presumed to constitute a reasonably equivalent value under section 548(a)(2)(A). *Id.*

In reaching this conclusion, the bankruptcy court focused primarily on legislative history and legislative intent. First, the court examined the legislative history of the Bankruptcy Amendments and Federal Judgeship Act of 1984 (BAFJA). Although the court found that the plain language of the amended statute allows avoidance of foreclosure sales, it nonetheless determined that this language conflicted with the obvious intent of the drafters of the amendments. This intent, the court concluded, was to "preserve rather than avoid regularly conducted, non-collusive foreclosure sales." *Id.* at 934.

Second, the court examined the historical roots of section 548. It noted that section 548 developed from the English law of fraudulent conveyances dating back to a 1570 statute enacted by the Parliament of Queen Elizabeth I. *Id.* at 935. The purpose of fraudulent conveyance law was "to prevent the debtor from taking deliberate action to hinder, delay, or defraud his creditors." Alden, Gross, and Borowitz, *Real Property Foreclosure as a Fraudulent Conveyance: Proposals for Solving the Durrett Problem,* 38 Bus. Law. 1605, 1605 (1983). As a result, fraudulent conveyance law originally focused solely on the debtor's subjective intent to defraud his creditors. American adaptation of this law in the Code, however, extended its reach "to cases where the objective result of the transaction is detrimental to creditors, whether or not the debtor actually intended such detriment." *Id.* at 1605-06 (footnote omitted). Despite the shift in American bankruptcy law from focus on subjective intent to focus on objective results, the bankruptcy court concluded that "Section 548(a)(2) [was] designed to produce . . . the same substantive results as the Statute of 13 Elizabeth [*i.e.,* to invalidate only transfers made with actual intent to defraud]." *Bundles,* 61 Bankr. at 935 (quoting Zinman, Houle & Weiss, *Fraudulent Transfers According to Alden, Gross, and Borowitz: A Tale of Two Circuits,* 39 Bus. Law. 977, 991 (1984) (footnote omitted)).

D. The District Court Opinion

The district court reached a similar result as the bankruptcy court albeit by a somewhat different route. The district court held that "the reasonable equivalency standard should be . . . irrebuttably satisfied where property is sold at a regularly conducted, non-collusive foreclosure sale to a third party purchaser and where the deed to the property is executed and recorded before the debtor filed his bankruptcy petition." *Bundles v. Baker (In re Bundles),* 78 Bankr. 203, 208 (S.D. Ind. 1987). Unlike the bankruptcy court, the district court limited its holding to the facts before it; the court applied the irrebuttable presumption only to the situation where the property was sold to a third-party purchaser and declined to decide whether the same irrebuttable presumption would apply if the mortgagee had purchased the property at the foreclosure sale. The district court reasoned that this limitation is justified on the theory that, where the property is sold to a third party, the sale is more likely to have been the result of competitive bidding thereby assuring that a fair price was given. *Id.* at 208-10.

In reaching this result, the district court reviewed the legislative history of the BAFJA and determined that it was inconclusive. *Id.* at 206. Therefore, instead of focusing on statutory interpretation, the district court directed its attention to the policy concerns raised by the parties. The policy issue, in the court's view, was one of defining the proper relationship between federal bankruptcy law and nonbankruptcy state law. This relationship has been addressed by the Supreme Court in *Butner v. United States,* 440 U.S. 48, 59 L. Ed. 2d 136, 99 S. Ct. 914 (1979). The district court interpreted *Butner* as counseling that courts should not use section 548, or any other provision of the Code, "to alter existing property interests under state law absent an overriding federal interest." *Bundles,* 78 Bankr. at 209. In this case, the court determined, both state foreclosure law and federal fraudulent conveyance law seek to protect creditors. The court continued that state foreclosure law achieves this goal by maximizing the likelihood of competitive bidding at foreclosure sales. As a result, the court concluded, there is no overriding policy underlying section 548 that would justify intervening and changing the rights of creditors as established under state law. *Id.*

II

Discussion

We must interpret the phrase "reasonably equivalent value" as applied to a foreclosure sale. Our task is complicated by the fact that reasonably equivalent value is not defined in section 548 or in any other provision of the Code. The courts addressing this issue have expressed a variety of viewpoints. Nevertheless, two basic lines of authority, each espousing a different interpretation of reasonably equivalent value as that term is used in section 548(a)(2)(A), have developed. We begin by reviewing the cases on either side of this difference of opinion among the courts.

A.

The two seminal cases in this area are *Durrett v. Washington National Insurance Co.*, 621 F.2d 201 (5th Cir. 1980), and *Lawyers Title Insurance Co. v. Madrid (In re Madrid)*, 21 Bankr. 424 (Bankr. 9th Cir. 1982), aff'd on other grounds, 725 F.2d 1197 (9th Cir.), cert. denied, 469 U.S. 833, 83 L. Ed. 2d 66, 105 S. Ct. 125 (1984). Their precise holdings have ultimately come to be less important than the analytical approach that each has fostered in subsequent cases. Courts have interpreted *Durrett* as standing for the position that reasonably equivalent value in the foreclosure context should be determined as a set percentage of the fair market value of the property, with 70 percent being the appropriate benchmark. Similarly, courts have interpreted

Madrid as representing the position that the sale price obtained at a regularly conducted, noncollusive foreclosure sale should be presumed conclusively to be the reasonably equivalent value for purposes of section 548(a)(2)(A). Bankruptcy courts have followed both approaches. . . . The bankruptcy court and the district court in this case both followed *Madrid.* Because of the influential impact of *Durrett* and *Madrid* on subsequent judicial interpretation of section 548(a)(2)(A), a more thorough discussion of these two cases is in order.

Durrett was decided under section 67(d) of the former Bankruptcy Act, 11 U.S.C. § 107(d), which employed the term "fair consideration" rather than "reasonably equivalent value." In reversing the trial court's determination that a sale price of 57.7 percent of the fair market value of the property on the date of the foreclosure sale was a fair equivalent, the Fifth Circuit stated that it had been unable to locate a decision of any court that approved a transfer for less than 70 percent of the market value of the property. *Durrett,* 621 F.2d at 203. The court's reference to 70 percent has led other courts and commentators to read that opinion as establishing a fixed percentage mark — the so-called "*Durrett* 70 percent rule." However, the Fifth Circuit's actual approach in *Durrett* is one of simply analyzing the question of reasonably equivalent value in terms of whether the foreclosure sale price is some acceptable percentage of the fair market value of the property.

Durrett is certainly not without its critics. In *Madrid,* a bankruptcy panel of the Ninth Circuit was the first court to reject *Durrett's* percentage rule and to articulate a different standard. The *Madrid* court noted that the only case cited by the Fifth Circuit in support of its holding involved a voluntary transfer of real property by the debtor corporation to the mother of the principal stockholder of the debtor corporation. 21 Bankr. at 426 (the case was *Schafer v. Hammond,* 456 F.2d 15 (10th Cir. 1972)). The *Madrid* court opined that, "however valid it may be to hold that less than 70 percent of fair market value is not a fair equivalent for a private transfer to an insider, application of that standard to regularly conducted public sales is questionable." *Id.* Its own research, the court observed, did not reveal any cases, other than the Fifth Circuit's decisions in *Durrett* and *Abramson v. Lakewood Bank & Trust Co.,* 647 F.2d 547 (5th Cir. 1981) (per curiam), cert. denied, 454 U.S. 1164, 71 L. Ed. 2d 320, 102 S. Ct. 1038 (1982), where a non-judicial foreclosure sale was set aside on fraudulent conveyance grounds. Furthermore, the *Madrid* court was concerned that the *Durrett* approach would alter radically state foreclosure law under which the mere inadequacy of price is usually insufficient to upset a foreclosure sale. *Id.* at 427. Consequently, the court reasoned that "the law of foreclosure should be harmonized with the law of fraudulent conveyances." *Id.*

Based on the above analysis, the *Madrid* court held that "the consideration received at a non-collusive and regularly conducted foreclosure sale" should be presumed to be the reasonable equivalent value for purposes of section 548. *Id.* Applying this holding to the facts before it, the *Madrid* court upheld a foreclosure sale where the debtor received a price between 64 and 67 percent of the market value of the property at the time of the sale. The bankruptcy panel's opinion in *Madrid* was affirmed by the Ninth Circuit on different grounds. 725 F.2d 1197 (9th Cir. 1984). Nevertheless, its reasoning has been followed, as we have noted already, by several bankruptcy courts, and recently was adopted in dictum by the Sixth Circuit in *In the Matter of Winshall Settlor's Trust,* 758 F.2d 1136, 1139 (6th Cir. 1985) ("the better view is that reasonable equivalence for the purposes of a foreclosure sale under § 548(a)(2)(A) should be consonant with the state law of fraudulent conveyances").

B.

We begin our analysis, as did the bankruptcy court and the district court, with the language of the statute. Section 548(a)(2)(A) provides that a transfer of the debtor's property may be set aside if it is transferred for less than a reasonably equivalent value. It makes no distinction between sales that do and sales that do not comply with state law. If we take the statute at its face value, we must conclude that its unambiguous language requires the reviewing court to make an independent assessment of whether reasonable equivalence was given.

Our analysis of the statutory language is not altered by the legislative history of the BAFJA. This legislative history, consisting of an exchange between two Senators recorded after the BAFJA was passed, indicates only that the amendments were not intended to resolve the so-called "*Durrett* issue." Furthermore, one of the proposed amendments to the BAFJA dealt specifically with the *Durrett-Madrid* debate and adopted the *Madrid* irrebuttable presumption rule. This amendment, however, was not included in the bill that ultimately became law. Accordingly, we believe that the most reasonable interpretation of the legislative history is that Congress did not legislate an irrebuttable presumption in the case of mortgage foreclosure sales.

Nevertheless, INB urges us to adopt state foreclosure law as the federal rule of reasonable equivalence under section 548. Under INB's theory, if a low sale price does not vitiate a foreclosure sale under state law, the bankruptcy court should not permit the reasonable equivalence standard in section 548 to produce such a result. INB's argument is similar to the position adopted by the district court. The district court held that state law should be used in fashioning a federal rule; INB appears to argue that the state rule for setting aside a foreclosure sale should be itself controlling, see Appellee's (INB) Br. at 16-17. INB relies, as did the district court, on the Supreme Court's opinion in *Butner v. United States,* 440 U.S. 48, 54, 59 L. Ed. 2d 136, 99 S. Ct. 914 (1979), in support of its argument that state law should be controlling here. In *Butner,* the issue was whether the right to rents collected during the period between the mortgagor's bankruptcy and the foreclosure sale of the mortgaged property should be determined by a federal rule of equity or by state law. The Court held that, where Congress has not exercised its power to establish laws governing bankruptcies, state law should be applied.

Butner is inapposite to this case. Here, Congress has not left the determination of property rights to state law. Rather, Congress has enacted a federal rule defining when a foreclosure sale may be set aside in bankruptcy. The *Butner* Court expressly recognized as much when it said:

> The constitutional authority of Congress to establish "uniform Laws on the subject of Bankruptcies throughout the United States" would clearly encompass a federal statute defining the mortgagee's interest in the rents and profits earned by property in a bankrupt estate. But Congress has not chosen to exercise its power to fashion any such rule. The Bankruptcy Act does include provisions invalidating certain security interests as fraudulent, or as improper preferences over general creditors. Apart from these provisions, however, Congress has generally left the determination of property rights in the assets of a bankrupt's estate to state law.

Id. at 54 (footnotes omitted). In an accompanying footnote, the Court listed 11 U.S.C. § 107(d)[of the old Bankruptcy Act] [presently codified at § 548(a) of the Code] as an example of a provision in which Congress has established a federal property rule for bankruptcy. *Id.* at 54 n.8. Accordingly, we must reject the view that state law, either directly or as the federal rule of decision, should determine the outcome of a bankrupt's complaint under section 548(a)(2)(A).

Here, Congress has set forth a federal standard. We must give effect to that congressional will, however ambiguous its manifestation.

We realize that much of the debate over this issue has centered on policy considerations that favor one result over the other. However, " the meaning of a statute must, in the first instance, be sought in the language in which the act is framed, and if that is plain, and if the law is within the constitutional authority of the law-making body which passed it, the sole function of the courts is to enforce it according to its terms. " *Central Trust Co. v. Official Creditors' Comm. of Geiger Enters.*, 454 U.S. 354, 359-60, 70 L. Ed. 2d 542, 102 S. Ct. 695 (1982) (per curiam) (quoting *Caminetti v. United States*, 242 U.S. 470, 485, 61 L. Ed. 442, 37 S. Ct. 192 (1917)). It is beyond our scope of review to consider the policy implications of permitting the debtor to set aside the foreclosure of his home. Any change deemed desirable on policy grounds should be addressed to Congress rather than to this court. Our duty is simply to interpret the language of the statute. . . .

Implying an irrebuttable presumption would be inconsistent with that language. Such a reading, in effect, creates an exception to the trustee's avoiding powers under section 548(a)(2)(A) — an exception not otherwise found in the statute — for property sold at a foreclosure sale. See *In re Madrid*, 21 Bankr. at 428 (Volinn, J., dissenting) ("By concluding that a regularly conducted sale in the absence of collusion satisfies the 'reasonably equivalent value' test, the majority has excised vital language from § 548 in order to create an exception to the statute where a forced sale of the debtor's property is involved."); *Richardson v. Gillman (In re Richardson),* 23 Bankr. 434, 446 (Bankr. D. Utah 1982) ("fixing an irrebuttable presumption of reasonable equivalence for non-collusive, regularly conducted public sales proscribes the factual inquiry into 'reasonable equivalence' which Section 548(a)(2) was designed to facilitate"). Moreover, an irrebuttable presumption has the effect of reading good faith into section 548(a)(2)(A); as long as the sale is conducted in good faith and in accordance with state law, the sale price is conclusively presumed to be a reasonably equivalent value. This result is inconsistent with section 548(a)(2)'s purpose of permitting the trustee to avoid transfers as constructively fraudulent, irrespective of the parties' actual intent. See *Richardson*, 23 Bankr. at 447; 4 L. King, Collier on Bankruptcy para. 548.02 at 548-28, para. 548.03 at 548-49 (15th ed. 1988); Ehrlich, *Avoidance of Foreclosure Sales As Fraudulent Conveyances: Accommodating State and Federal Objectives*, 71 Va. L. Rev. 933, 956 (1985). Finally, an irrebuttable presumption renders section 548(a)(2) merely duplicative of other Code provisions, such as section 548(a)(1) (permitting avoidance for actual intent to defraud) and section 544(b) (permitting avoidance where state law would allow it), see *Richardson,* 23 Bankr. at 447 ("insofar as *Madrid* permits an attack under Section 548 on the good faith of a foreclosure sale, it merely duplicates rights which the trustee already has under the law of most states through Section 544(b)"). We therefore conclude that section 548(a)(2)(A) establishes a federal basis — independent of state law — for setting aside a foreclosure sale.

C.

Having determined that there is a federal statutory basis for avoiding a foreclosure sale under section 548(a), we are confronted with the problem of defining that federal standard. As Justice Brandeis once observed, "value is a word of many meanings." *Missouri ex rel. Southwestern Bell Tel. Co. v. Public Serv. Comm'n,* 262 U.S. 276, 310, 67 L. Ed. 981, 43 S. Ct. 544 (1923) (Brandeis, J., concurring). A good example of this observation is in the Code where value is defined differently throughout. For instance, section 522(a)(2) refers to "fair market value as of the date of the filing of the petition," 11 U.S.C. § 522(a)(2)(Supp. IV 1986), and section 506(a) refers to value "determined in light of the purpose of the valuation and of the proposed disposition or use of such property," 11 U.S.C. § 506(a)(1982). The definition of value found in section 548 is not very useful for our purposes. It defines value as "property, or satisfaction or securing of a present or antecedent debt of the debtor, but does not include an unperformed promise to furnish support to the debtor or to a relative of the debtor . . . ." 11 U.S.C. § 548(d)(2)(A)(Supp. IV 1986). If anything is clear from the various uses of the word "value" in the Code, it is that Congress did not mean fair market value when it used the term reasonably equivalent value. On the other hand, Congress' conscious use of a federal standard suggests that it did not believe that the expedient of relying entirely on state foreclosure law would protect adequately federal interests. "State law's sanction of exchanges in foreclosures which are not reasonably equivalent gives effect to state contract and foreclosure policy but may overlook the interests of other creditors of the debtor." *In re Richardson*, 23 Bankr. at 447.

In our view, in defining reasonably equivalent value, the court should neither grant a conclusive presumption in favor of a purchaser at a regularly conducted, noncollusive foreclosure sale, nor limit its inquiry to a simple comparison of the sale price to the fair market value. Reasonable equivalence should depend on all the facts of each case. This middle ground has been adopted by several of the bankruptcy courts. See, *e.g., General Indus. v. Shea (In re General Indus.),* 79 Bankr. 124 (Bankr. D. Mass. 1987); *Adwar v. Capgro Leasing Corp. (In re Adwar),* 55 Bankr. 111 (Bankr. E.D.N.Y. 1985); *Ruebeck v. Attleboro Sav. Bank (In re Ruebeck),* 55 Bankr. 163 (Bankr. D. Mass. 1985); *First Fed. Sav. & Loan Ass'n v. Hulm (In re Hulm),* 45 Bankr. 523 (Bankr. D.N.D. 1984); *In re Richardson,* 23 Bankr. at 448; see also *In re Madrid*, 21 Bankr. at 428 (Volinn, J., dissenting) (arguing that the concept of reasonably equivalent value requires that the trial court examine the consideration received in a foreclosure sale in the factual context of a particular case and concluding that the price paid at a regularly conducted foreclosure sale should be given, at best, a strong presumption of adequacy).

The implementation of this approach requires case-by-case adjudication. In determining whether property was sold for reasonably equivalent value, the bankruptcy court must, of course, be mindful constantly of the purpose of section 548's avoiding powers — to preserve the assets of the estate. See *Martin v. Phillips (In re Butcher),* 58 Bankr. 128, 130 (Bankr. E.D. Tenn. 1986); *In re Richardson,* 23 Bankr. at 447. This consideration requires that, in determining reasonably equivalent value, the court must focus on what the debtor received in return for what he surrendered. See *In re Butcher,* 58 Bankr. at 130; *Meister v. Jamison (In re Jamison),* 21 Bankr. 380, 382 (Bankr. D. Conn. 1982). Consequently, it is appropriate to consider, as a starting point, the fair market value. However, the fact that the sale was the result of a foreclosure rather than an arm's length transaction between a willing buyer and a willing seller is also of considerable importance. Therefore, the bankruptcy court must focus ultimately on the fair market value as affected by the fact of foreclosure. As a practical matter, the foreclosure sale price is the only means of measuring the effect of foreclosure on the value of the property. Indeed, in usual circumstances, it would be appropriate to permit a rebuttable presumption that the price obtained at the foreclosure sale represents reasonably equivalent value. However, the bankruptcy court also must examine the foreclosure transaction in its totality to determine whether the procedures employed were calculated not only to secure for the mortgagee the value of its interest but also to return to the debtor-mortgagor his equity in the property. The bankruptcy court therefore must consider such factors as whether there was a fair appraisal of the property, whether the property was advertised widely, and whether competitive bidding was encouraged.

The inquiry outlined in the foregoing paragraph is necessarily a fact-specific one; it will require the bankruptcy court to draw upon its expertise in evaluating the economic forces at play in a specific case. Once that determination is made, we must accord it great deference. On the other hand, we shall expect the bankruptcy court, while recognizing that it alone has the responsibility to determine whether the transaction meets the federal standard of reasonably equivalent value, to accord respect to the state foreclosure sale proceedings. While the sale price determined in the foreclosure proceeding cannot be considered conclusive with respect to the issue of federal law before the bankruptcy court, it is an important element in the analysis of that question.

Conclusion

We hold that the sale price at a regularly conducted, noncollusive foreclosure sale cannot automatically be deemed to provide a reasonably equivalent value within the meaning of section 548(a)(2)(A). We therefore reverse the judgment of the district court and remand to the bankruptcy court for further proceedings not inconsistent with this opinion.

REVERSED AND REMANDED.

NOTES

(1) *Bundles* requires an independent judicial review of a foreclosure sale, even if regularly conducted. How much weight should the reviewing court give to the fact that the price will always be negatively influenced by the fact this is a foreclosure sale on the courthouse steps? Will the price always be too low? Does *Bundles* recognize that fact, and simply require that the price, although low, cannot be unreasonably low? Would the outcome in *Bundles* change if the trustee had proceeded under section 547?

(2) The buyer in *Bundles* occupied the same weak position as the buyer in *Durrett.* Was it professionally irresponsible for the lawyer to stipulate that the property was worth more than three times the amount received at foreclosure? Is the "reasonble equivalent value" language of section 548 the same as "fair market value"? Why or why not?

(3) The purpose of section 548 is to preserve the assets of an insolvent debtor's estate; the statute does not make distinctions between sales that do and do not comply with state law. It would be inconsistent with the statutory language for the court to create a non-rebuttable presumption in favor of the sales price. The *Bundles* court thus agrees with the *Durrett* rationale but rejects the mechanical 70% test. For another opinion rejecting the *Durrett* rationale, see *In re Madrid,* 725 F.2d 1197 (9th Cir. 1984).

(4) Leveraged buyouts can also create fraudulent transfer problems under section 548. Assume, for example that Bank makes a loan to Michael enabling him to acquire the Chicago Bulls Corporation and franchise. To secure this loan, Michael grants a security interest in all of the Bulls' organization assets. If the Bulls' Corp. subsequently files for bankruptcy, the trustee in bankruptcy may be able to avoid the lien on the team's assets because the company made a transfer of its assets to Bank and received no consideration for the transfer. The issue for the bankruptcy court would be 1) whether the change in ownership of the Bulls Corp. was of value to the company; and 2) whether the value was the reasonble equivalent of what the Bulls Corp. transferred.

PROBLEM

Fifth Bank & Trust makes a $1,000,000 loan to the L&M Corporation. Assume that the loan is guaranteed by Lauren Co., a wholly owned subsidiary of L&M Corp. If Lauren Co. subsequently files for bankruptcy, FBT will be able to look only to L&M for satisfaction of the obligation. If Lauren Co.'s guarantee would have made the company insolvent, can the trustee avoid Lauren Co.'s guarantee as a fraudulent transfer under § 548(a)(2)? Do you see the trustee's possible argument? Did L&M receive reasonably equivalent value? Did Lauren receive any indirect benefit from the loan to L&M? See *Matter of Xonics Photochemical, Inc,*. 841 F.2d 198 (7th Cir. 1988).

CHAPTER 21

PROBLEMS OF ADVANCED SCOPE

§ 21.01 Article 9's Boundaries

Read: U.C.C. §§ 9-101, 9-102, 9-104

There are an array of interesting issues when one tries to articulate the scope of Article 9. Which transactions are covered by Article 9 and which ones are not? Courts encounter problems of scope with fixtures, bailments, real property interests, and setoffs.

The policy rationale for Article 9 is stated in the Official Comment to § 9-101:

> The growing complexity of financing transactions forces us to keep piling new statutory provisions on top of our inadequate and already sufficiently complicated nineteenth-century structure of security law. The results of this continuing development are, and will be, increasing costs to both parties and increasing uncertainty as to their rights and the rights of third parties dealing with them.
>
> The aim of this Article is to provide a simple and unified structure within which the immense variety of present-day secured financing transactions can go forward with less cost and with greater certainty.
>
> Under this Article the traditional distinctions among security devices, based largely on form, are not retained; the Article applies to all transactions intended to create security interests in personal property and fixtures.

In *Klinger v. Pocono International Raceway, Inc.,* 433 A. 2d 1357, 31 U.C.C. Rep. Serv. 1223 (Pa. Super. Ct. 1981), the court wrote

> [t]he Code is meant to be comprehensive and flexible, and to free the law from artificial distinctions restricting the rational conduct of commercial financing. The existence of subdivisions of personal property in the Code should not obscure the fact that under § 9-102, an Article Nine security interest could be taken in *any personal property* not specifically excluded by § 9-103 or § 9-104. [emphasis supplied].

Unfortunately, identifying the scope of Article 9's application is not as easy as these quotes suggest.

IN RE M. VICKERS, LTD.

United States District Court, D. Colo.
111 B.R. 332, 11 U.C.C. Rep. Serv. 2d 655 (1990)

KANE, SENIOR DISTRICT JUDGE.

The issue in this appeal is whether the profits derived from the motel business are "rents," and therefore an interest in real property, or "accounts," and therefore an interest in personalty. Super 8 Motels, Inc. appeals the bankruptcy court's determination that motel profits are rents and that Super 8 did not properly perfect its security interest in such rents although it had filed a financing statement encumbering the contract rights, accounts receivable and bank accounts of the debtor, M. Vickers, Ltd. The majority of courts addressing this issue have concluded that such profits are personalty and not an interest in real property. Therefore, I reverse.

I. Facts.

The facts of this case are undisputed. In 1983 and 1985, Mr. and Mrs. Burton Vickers purchased three motels located in Lamar, Gunnison, and Canon City, Colorado. In May, 1985, Mr. Vickers obtained a loan from H.F.C. Commercial Realty, Inc. The loan was secured by a Deed of Trust and an Assignment of Rents for each of the motel properties. H.F.C. also took a security interest in the structures, chattels, rents and profits of the properties. The Deeds of Trust, the Assignments and the U.C.C.-1 financing statements were filed on May 6 and May 7, 1989 with the County Recorders in the respective counties where the motels were located.

In September, 1985, Mr. Vickers obtained another loan from Super 8 Motels, Inc. As collateral for this loan, Super 8 took a security interest in the contract rights, accounts receivable, and bank accounts of the three motels. Super 8 filed its U.C.C.-1 financing statements to this effect on September 16 and 17, 1989 with the respective County Records and with the Colorado Secretary of State.

Mr. Vickers obtained still another loan in February, 1986 from the Mid-America Mortgage Company. As a condition to this financing, Mid-America required the Vickers to transfer their interest in the motels to the Debtor, M. Vickers, Ltd., a limited partnership of which Mr. Vickers was the sole general partner. The partnership then executed a Second Deed of Trust and Security Agreement on the motel properties and an Assignment of Rents. These documents were filed with the County Recorders on February 10, 1986. U.C.C.-1 financing statements covering the rents and profits of the motels were filed thereafter. On September 30, 1986, Mid-America transferred its interest in the Vickers' loan to the Alpine Federal Savings and Loan Association.

On September 1, 1987, M. Vickers, Ltd. filed for bankruptcy . . . .

Super 8 claimed that its interest in the funds in the account was superior to H.F.C.'s because the funds in the account could not be secured by H.F.C.'s assignment of rents since the profits derived from the hotel business are "accounts" under U.C.C. and not "rents." Consequently, since Super 8 properly perfected its interest in accounts of M. Vickers, Ltd. by filing a U.C.C.-1 financing statement with the Secretary of State, it had priority. Alternatively, Super 8 argued that the funds could be considered both "rents" and "accounts" and that, even if H.F.C. could have perfected its interest through foreclosure of its recorded assignment of rents, Super 8 perfected its interest first. The bankruptcy court rejected both of Super 8's arguments, finding that the funds in the accounts were rents and that H.F.C. had the priority interest. Super 8 now appeals. Since the facts in this case are undisputed and the issues presented are legal in nature, my review is de novo. *First Bank v. Mullet (In re Mullet)*, 817 F.2d 677, 679 (10th Cir. 1987).

II. Issues.

A. Characterization of Motel Profits.

The issue of which secured creditor has the priority security interest in the debtor's cash collateral account is controlled by Colorado Law, since the situs of the account is Colorado. *Butner v. United States,* 440 U.S. 48, 54-57, 99 S.Ct. 914, 917-19, 59 L.Ed.2d 136 (1979); *Chaussee v. Morning Star Ranch Resorts Co. (In re Morning Star Ranch Resorts),* 64 B.R. 818, 821 (Bankr. D. Colo. 1986). Under § 9-104(j) of the Colorado Uniform Commercial Code (UCC), Colo. Rev. Stat. § 4-9-104(j)(1974), "an interest in or a lien on real estate, including a lease or rents thereunder" is excluded from the provisions of Article 9 of the U.C.C. Hence, "if the money in the account represents an interest in real estate, in the form of rents, then any security interest in the funds under Article 9 of the Colorado Commercial Code (U.C.C.) is invalid. Alternatively, if the account balance represents the proceeds of accounts receivable, then the funds are personalty and not properly the subject of an assignment of rents." Bankruptcy Court Order at 7.

The term "rent" is not defined in the U.C.C., and there is no Colorado statute or case law directly construing this term in the context of Article 9 of the U.C.C. Nevertheless, the bankruptcy court concluded that motel profits are "rents" under Colorado law. The court relied primarily on three cases to reach this conclusion. In *Peterson v. Oklahoma City Housing Authority,* 545 F.2d 1270, 1274 (10th Cir. 1976), the Tenth Circuit defined the term "rent" as "compensation or income which the owner of land receives from a tenant for the use or occupation of the land." *Peterson* involved an attempted class action by the tenants in a low-rent housing project who were contesting the City's requirement that they provide security deposits. *Peterson* is not helpful in this context, since it involved a clear-cut landlord-tenant relationship, and not the characterization of motel proceeds.

The second case cited by the bankruptcy court was *Phillips v. Webster*, 162 Colo. 315, 426 P.2d 774 (1967). In *Phillips,* the issues before the court were whether a receiver was properly appointed for a motel property going through foreclosure, whether the receiver's final report should have been approved by the court and how the net profits generated during the receivership should be distributed. On the final issue, I differ with the bankruptcy court's interpretation of the holding of this case. The bankruptcy court stated,

> The Colorado court did not directly address the proper characterization of the payments collected from the motel patrons. It did, however, approve the trial court's disposition of the payments collected during the receivership in which the trial court awarded the payment to the creditor that held the assignment of rents. Hence the Colorado court apparently considered the payments received from motel patrons to be rents arising from the use of real property and therefore subject to an assignment of rents.

Bankruptcy Court Order at 8-9. Contrary to the bankruptcy court's reading of *Phillips,* the Colorado court awarded the profits to the record owner of the property after the foreclosure, Mr. Phillips, and not to the creditors/ mortgagees, Mr. and Mrs. Webster. See 426 P.2d at 777, 778. Thus, the court in *Phillips* did not implicitly recognize that motel profits could be subject to an assignment of rents, and in any event, did not address the merits of the issue in this case.

The third case upon which the bankruptcy court relied in *Chaussee v. Morning Star Ranch Resorts (In re Morning Star Ranch Resorts,* 64 B.R. 818(Bankr. D. Colo. 1986). In *Morning Star Ranch,* a lender with a deed of trust on the debtor's motel property (which included an assignment of rents clause) moved for a temporary restraining order to prevent the debtor from using the profits generated by the motel. The bankruptcy court in *Morning Star Ranch* reviewed applicable bankruptcy and Colorado law regarding the perfection of an assignment of rents post-bankruptcy. The court concluded that the creditor's filing of a § 546(b) notice to claim an interest in rents and profits was the equivalent of a motion for an appointment of a receiver, that the creditor had therefore perfected his interest in such rents, and that the creditor was entitled to a temporary restraining order limiting the debtor's use of the cash collateral. *Id.* at 820-22. It is clear that the *Morning Star Ranch* court simply assumed that the profits generated by the hotel were subject to the assignment of rents, without considering whether they were an interest in real or personal property. *Morning Star Ranch* is therefore of limited assistance in answering this question . . . .

Several federal courts have addressed the characterization of hotel profits under the laws of other states. The leading case in this area is *United States v. PS Hotel Corp.*, 404 F. Supp. 1188 (E.D. Mo.), aff'd, 527 F.2d 500 (8th Cir. 1975). the issue in *PS Hotel Corp.* was very similar to the case at bar. Two creditors claimed that they had a priority interest in the profits of the hotel. One claimed its interest under an assignment of rents clause in a lease, and the other under an Article 9 financing statement covering accounts receivable. In holding for the Article 9 secured creditor, the court stated:

> Section 400.9-104 [of the Missouri Commercial Code] excludes from the Secured Transactions Article various listed transactions, one of which is "the creation or transfer of an interest in or lien on real estate, including a lease or rents thereunder."

Defendants have cited us to no case which construes this section, particularly as applied to a pledge of accounts receivable of a motel or hotel business to secure payments due under a lease. In our judgment, the statutory exclusion was not intended to apply to such accounts receivable, and the language of the statute cannot reasonably be construed to include them. This case does not involve an instrument conveying an interest in or lien on real estate. And as concerns the words "rents thereunder," what is referred to are the rents payable to the lessor under the provisions of a lease, not charges made by the lessee for services it provides to its patrons, even though those services include furnishing rooms in the leased premises for the use of its guests. Hence, the mere fact that the lease and lease amendment [containing the assignment of rents clause] were recorded as instruments affecting real estate does not affect the priority of plaintiff's security interest in the accounts receivable. *Id.* at 1192. The Eighth Circuit then affirmed this decision with little discussion of its merits. 527 F.2d at 501.

Since *PS Hotel Corp.,* at least four other courts have addressed this question. Each has concluded that hotel room charges are not rents, and that these charges are accounts which are secured under Article 9 of the U.C.C. For example, in *Victor Savings & Loan Association v. Grimm (In re Greater Atlantic & Pacific Investment Group, Inc.),* 88 B.R. 356, 359 (Bankr. N.D. Okla. 1988) (citations omitted), the court reasoned,

> As a general rule, ". . . guests in a hotel . . . are mere licensees and not tenants, and . . . they have only a personal contract and acquire no interest in realty . . . the relation is not that of landlord and tenant, for, notwithstanding the guest's occupancy, it is the house of the innkeeper[.]" It follows that a hotel guest's payment to the innkeeper for lodging is in the nature of a payment under contract or on account, *i.e.,* an "account receivable."

At common law, "rents" are "something which a tenant renders out of the profits of the land which he enjoys[.]" Since motel guests have no interest in motel realty, guests do not, strictly speaking, pay "rent." . . . Payments by motel guests resemble payments under contract or on account much more nearly than lease payments or "rent." No reason appears why the contractual term "rent" should be read so broadly as to include "accounts receivable."

Although *PS Hotel Corp.* and *In re Greater Atlantic* were decided under Missouri law, the common-law principles espoused in these cases apply here . . . .

The bankruptcy court attempted to distinguish *PS Hotel* by noting that the hotel in that case "provided patrons with food and liquor in addition to providing rooms . . . . In the case at bar the Debtor's motels provide patrons with room and access to vending machines only. The account balance is composed solely of room revenues and does not include any vending machine revenue." Bankruptcy Court Order at 7. To rely on this kind of distinction in other cases would have absurd results. Any time a creditor wished to secure an interest in hotel room rental profits as collateral, it would be required to assess the level of services provided by the hotel. If the hotel provided many services other than simply letting rooms, the creditor would file under Article 9. If few services were provided, the creditor would record an assignment of rents. But in the lacuna in between, the creditor could never be certain what method to use to secure his interest.

The more practical approach is a bright-line rule. The only cases which have directly considered this issue have concluded that motel profits are personalty, and may be secured by an Article 9 financing statement. While the question is dependent on state law, there is little indication that Colorado state law differs significantly from the law of the states under which other courts have ruled. Furthermore, the recent decision by the Colorado Court of Appeals in *Investment Hotel Properties, Ltd. v. City of Colorado Springs* provides a strong indication that the rental of guest rooms is considered personalty under Colorado law as well. Consequently, Super 8's perfected security interest in the accounts receivable and contract rights of M. Vickers takes priority over H.F.C.'s interest under the assignment of rents since it was properly perfected by filing with the Secretary of State. See Colo. Rev. Stat. § 4-9-401(1974). Likewise, the description of Super 8's security interest as "contract rights, accounts receivable and bank accounts" was sufficiently specific to give notice to other creditors of its interest. See *id.* § 4-9-402(1) (Supp. 1989). The decision of the bankruptcy court is REVERSED.

QUESTION

The *Vickers* court follows the majority of courts in finding that room rental receipts constitute personal property rather than realty. Do you agree with the decision? What factors might lead a court to conclude that motel rents should be classified as realty rather than personalty?

When working with transactions governed by a federal statute, one must remember that to the extent such statute does not explicate party rights, the transaction is subject to the provisions of state law under Article 9. Comment 1 to U.C.C. § 9-104 provides that "[a]lthough the Federal Copyright Act contains provisions permitting the mortgage of a copyright (17 U.S.C. § 28, 30) such a statute would not seem to contain sufficient provisions regulating the rights of the parties and third parties to exclude security interests in copyrights from the provisions of this Article." Compare comment 8 to section 9-302(3); it seems to us that this comment conflicts with U.C.C.

§ 9-104(a). If the drafters indeed intended what they said in the comment, it is possible that a creditor might need to file notice of its security interest in intellectual property in both federal and state offices. Consider the next case.

IN RE 199Z, INC.

United States Bankruptcy Court, Central District of California
137 Bankr. 778, 17 U.C.C.R. Serv. 2d 598C (1992)

JOHN E. RTAN, BANKRUPTCY JUDGE.

Memorandum of Decision

I. Introduction

A. Factual Background and Procedural History

199Z, Inc., a California corporation ("199Z" or "Debtor") entered into an asset purchase agreement dated as of February 5, 1990, with 1200 Valencia, Inc., a California corporation ("Valencia"), Ocean Pacific Sunwear, Ltd., a California limited partnership ("OP") (collectively, "Defendants"), and Republic Factors Corp., a California corporation ("Republic"). Valencia is the general partner of OP. Pursuant to this asset purchase agreement, Defendants sold and 199Z purchased assets associated with the trademarks "JIMMY'Z" and "WOODY LOGO" ("Trademark Assets"). In exchange for the Trademark Assets, 199Z gave Defendants a total purchase price of $6,346,183.00, consisting of $500,000.00 cash and promissory notes for $2,300,000.00 and $3,346,183.00. As security for the promissory notes, 199Z executed a security agreement in favor of OP encumbering all of 199Z's business, goodwill, trademarks and assets ("Security Agreement").

To perfect this security interest, 199Z (1) recorded a Memorandum of Security Agreement in the U.S. Patent & Trademark Office (the "Patent Office") on April 2, 1990; and (2) filed a U.C.C.-1 Financing Statement in the Office of the Secretary of State of California on June 4, 1990 ("June U.C.C.-1"); and (3) filed an amended U.C.C.-1 Financing Statement in the Office of the Secretary of State of California on November 1, 1990, including a U.C.C.-2 amendment to the June U.C.C.-1 ("November U.C.C.-2").

The November U.C.C.-2 resulted from the discovery of an error in the June U.C.C.-1. The June U.C.C.-1, in the section describing the property covered by the U.C.C.-1, states "See Attachment A hereto." Attachment A states:

Exhibit A

> The personal property in which [OP] as Debtor, grants a security interest to Republic Factors Corp., as Secured Party, includes, but is not limited to, all of the following, whether now owned or hereafter acquired:
>
> 1. Trademarks. Any and all trademarks, trade names or trade styles, registered or recognized in the United States of America or in any state or territory therein or in any foreign country, excluding the trademark, tradename [sic] and trade styles of "JIMMY'Z" and "WOODY LOGO"; and
>
> 2. Property. All of debtor's presently existing and hereafter acquired goodwill (whether associated with and identified by the Trademarks or not), ...

Obviously, "Exhibit A" refers to an agreement between OP and Republic, and not to the Security Agreement between Debtor and Defendants. The corrected exhibit to the November U.C.C.-2 states:

Personal Property

> The personal property in which 199Z, Inc., as Debtor, grants a security interest to [OP], as Secured Party, includes, but is not limited to, all of the following, whether now owned or hereafter acquired:
>
> 1. Trademarks. Any and all trademarks, trade names or trade styles, registered or recognized in the United States of America or in any state or territory therein or in any foreign country; and
>
> 2. Property. All of debtor's presently existing and hereafter acquired goodwill associated with and identified by the Trademarks, business . . . .

On November 10, 1990, OP declared that all sums due to it under the asset purchase agreement were immediately payable. A foreclosure sale was noticed and held, at which OP purchased the assets encumbered by the Security Agreement through a $1,000,000.00 credit bid.

An involuntary petition under Chapter 7 of the Bankruptcy Codewas filed against 199Z on December 6, 1990. On January 14, 1991, Debtor filed a Notice of Consent to Entry of Order for Relief and Election to Convert to Case Under Chapter 11. This Court entered an order converting the case to a case under Chapter 11 on January 24, 1991. On Debtor's motion, this Court entered an order converting the case to a case under Chapter 7 on April 16, 1991. James J. Joseph (" Trustee") was appointed as the acting Chapter 7 Trustee for the estate of 199Z on May 10, 1991.

B. The Adversary Complaint and Motion for Partial Summary Judgment

On October 22, 1991, Trustee filed an adversary complaint against Defendants and Republic. The adversary complaint alleged causes of action for avoidance and recovery of preferential transfers, fraudulent misrepresentation, negligent misrepresentation, breach of contract, accounting, damages, turnover and injunctive relief. The preferential transfer upon which Trustee bases his adversary complaint is the transfer allegedly created by the filing of the November U.C.C.-2.

On December 23, 1991, Defendants moved for partial summary judgment on that element of the Trustee's preferential transfer cause of action specified under 11 U.S.C. § 547(b)(5). Defendants claim that the filing of the November U.C.C.-2 did not result in the Defendants' receiving more than they would otherwise have received in a distribution under Chapter 7, and that therefore the Trustee cannot establish this element of his cause of action for avoidance and recovery of preferential transfer. Specifically, Defendants argue that the filing of the November U.C.C.-2 did not operate to perfect OP's security interest in the Trademark Assets.[1] Therefore, Defendants argue, the filing of the November U.C.C.-2 "was without effect and did not enable the Defendants to receive more than the Defendants would get in a case under chapter 7 of title 11 if the transfer had not been made."[2]

---

[1] Defendants wish to avoid a determination that the November U.C.C.-2 operated to perfect their alleged security interest in the Trademark Assets, because that filing occurred within the preference period under § 547.

[2] The language of their pleadings notwithstanding, Defendants appear to be arguing that the filing of the November U.C.C.-1 did not constitute a transfer, either in addition to or in place of their argument that the filing did not enable them to receive more than they would receive through an ordinary Chapter 7 distribution.

II. Discussion

A. Contentions of the Pleadings

Defendants present various alternative arguments in support of their contention that the November U.C.C.-2 was without effect. The meritorious arguments among these can be summarized as follows:

(1) that the filing of the June U.C.C.-1 perfected the transfer of the security interest in the Trademark Assets to OP, notwithstanding the erroneously attached "Exhibit A";

(2) that the November U.C.C.-2 was only an amendment of the June U.C.C.-1 and did not "destroy the priority of the secured party in previously perfected collateral [sic]."; and

(3) that OP's security interest in the Trademark Assets was perfected by the filing of a Memorandum of Security Interest with the Patent Office.

In opposition, Trustee contends as follows:

(1) A security interest in a trademark must be perfected by a filing in accordance with the requirements of the U.C.C. and not by a filing with the Patent Office:

(A) The Lanham Act provides only for the filing of "assignments" and not "security interests;" and

(B) An "assignment" is not a "security interest" under the Lanham Act.

Trustee's "Statement of Genuine Issues" is deficient: it does not refer to any evidence supporting the Trustee's contention that a genuine issue remains to be litigated. As such, Defendants correctly point out, Trustee has offered no evidence in opposition to the motion. This Court finds that no material issue of fact remains to be litigated, and therefore an analysis of the legal issues presented follows.

B. Analysis

Federal Bankruptcy Rules of Procedure Rule 7056 incorporates Federal Rules of Civil Procedure Rule 56 by reference in adversary actions. Rule 56 states that the Court shall grant summary judgment or summary adjudication of issues where the evidence presented demonstrates that no genuine issue of material fact exists and that the moving party is entitled to judgment as a matter of law. (See *Anderson v. Liberty Lobby,* 477 U.S. 242, 247-248, 91 L. Ed. 2d 202, 106 S. Ct. 2505 (1986).)

The dispositive legal issues which Defendants present for decision are more coherently stated:

(1) How is a security interest in trademarks, trade names and trade style properly perfected?

(2) Do Defendants have a perfected security in the Trademark Assets?

(1) Perfection of Security Interest in Trademark Assets: Federal Law

The Uniform Commercial Code provides for perfection of a security interest through filing a financing statement conforming with its requirements with the appropriate Secretary of State. In this manner, a security interest in "general intangibles" can be perfected. The Uniform Commercial Code Official Comment to § 9106 ("Definitions: 'Account;' 'General Intangibles' ") states:

> The term "general intangibles" brings under this Article miscellaneous types of contractual rights and other personal property which are used or may become customarily used as

> commercial security. Examples are goodwill, literary rights and rights to performance. Other examples are copyrights, trademarks and patents, except to the extent that they may be excluded by Section 9-104(a). *Id.*

In turn, § 9104 provides:

> This Article does not apply
>
> (a) to a security interest subject to any statute of the United States, to the extent that such statute governs the rights of parties to and third parties affected by transactions in particular types of property; . . . *Id.*

Further, Section 9-302(3)(a) states that a filing under that section is not

> necessary or effective to perfect a security interest subject to . . . a statute or treaty of the United States which provides for a national or international registration . . . or which specifies a place of filing different from that specified in [Article Nine] for filing of the security interest. *Id.*

Defendants argue that, regardless of the sufficiency of either the June U.C.C.-1 or the November U.C.C.-2, their claimed security interest should be deemed perfected through their filing with the Patent Office. As authority for this proposition, Defendants direct the attention of the Court to *National Peregrine, Inc. v. Capitol Federal Savings & Loan of Denver (In re Peregrine Entertainment, Ltd.),* 116 Bankr. 194, 16 U.S.P.Q.2D (BNA) 1017 (C.D. Cal. 1990) ("*Peregrine*"). In *Peregrine,* Judge Kozinski held that the Copyright Act preempted state law provisions with respect to the perfection of security interests in copyrights, and that a creditor seeking to perfect a security interest in copyrights must file the appropriate documents with the U.S. Copyright Office and not with the Secretary of State. While many of the characteristics of copyright supporting federal preemption of state law, as outlined by Judge Kozinski, are equally applicable to trademarks (such as a unique federal interest in the subject matter as shown through comprehensive federal legislation, promotion of uniformity, and lack of situs of the personal property because of its incorporeal nature), one critical distinction exists between the federal legislation at issue in *Peregrine* and the Lanham Act trademark legislation. The Copyright Act provides expressly for the filing of any "mortgage" or "hypothecation" of a copyright, including a pledge of the copyright as security or collateral for a debt. *Peregrine,* 116 Bankr. at 198-199. The Lanham Act, however, provides expressly only for the filing of an assignment of a trademark, and the definition of "assignment" does not include pledges, mortgages or hypothecations of trademarks.

Trademark cases distinguish between security interests and assignments. (Citations omitted.) An "assignment" of a trademark is an absolute transfer of the entire right, title and interest to the trademark. (Quotation and citation omitted.) The grant of a security interest is not such a transfer. It is merely what the term suggests — a device to secure an indebtedness. It is a mere agreement to assign in the event of default by the debtor. (Quotation and citation omitted.) Since a security interest in a trademark is not equivalent to an assignment, the filing of a security interest is not covered by the Lanham Act. *Roman Cleanser Co. v. National Acceptance Co. of America (In re Roman Cleanser Co.,* 43 Bankr. 940, 225 U.S.P.Q. (BNA) 140 (Bankr. E.D. Mich. 1984). Had Congress intended that security interests in trademarks be perfected by filing with the Patent Office, it could have expressly provided for such a filing, as it did in the Copyright Act. "If Congress intended to provide a means for recording security interests in trademarks in addition to assignments, it would have been simple to so state. However, for whatever reasons, Congress did not do so." *Id.* at 946. This Court finds this distinction dispositive. Although there is no reported appellate decision precisely on point, this Court cannot find as a matter of law that the federal preemption for the purposes of perfecting security interest in copyrights set forth in *Peregrine* applies equally to the perfection of security interests in trademarks.[3] This conclusion is harmonious with those reached in the reported decisions of other bankruptcy courts. See *Creditors' Committee of TR-3 Industries, Inc. v. Capital Bank (In re TR-3 Industries),* 41 Bankr. 128, 131 (Bankr. C.D. Cal. 1984); *Roman Cleanser Co. v. National Acceptance Company of America (In re Roman Cleanser Co.),* 43 Bankr. 940, 944 , 225 U.S.P.Q. (BNA) 140 (Bankr. E.D. Mich. 1984). Accordingly, the recordation of the Memorandum of Security Agreement in the Patent Office did not perfect Defendants' security interest in the Trademark Assets. Therefore, I shall next consider whether Defendants properly perfected their security interest in the Trademark Assets under California law.

(2) Perfection of Security Interest in Trademark Assets: California Law

Defendants contend that they perfected their claimed security interest in the Trademark Assets by filing the June U.C.C.-1 with the Office of the Secretary of State of California, because the June U.C.C.-1 meets the formal requisites of a financing statement under California law even though the erroneous exhibit was attached. Defendants argue that the erroneous exhibit was "not seriously misleading" within the meaning of Cal. Comm. Code § 9402(8).

Cal. Comm. Code § 9402 sets forth the formal requisites of financing statements. § 9402(1) provides in relevant part:

> A financing statement is sufficient if it gives the names of the debtor and the secured party, is signed by the debtor, gives an address of the secured party from which information concerning the security interest may be obtained, gives a mailing address of the debtor, and contains a statement indicating the types, or describing the items, of collateral. *Id.*

§ 9402(8) provides in relevant part:

> A financing statement substantially complying with the requirements of this section is effective even though it contains minor errors which are not seriously misleading. *Id.*

From the plain language of § 9402(1) the financing statement must contain (A) a description of (B) the property of the debtor in which the secured party has an interest. Yet Defendants argue that the June U.C.C.-1 is "not seriously misleading" under § 9402(8) because the exhibit attached to it, describing an agreement between OP and Republic Factors and not an agreement between OP and Debtor, is merely a "minor error." According to Defendants, an interested party reviewing the June U.C.C.-1 would notice that the exhibit was a mistake, and therefore would be obligated to inquire regarding the substance of the actual security agreement between Debtor and OP.

A review of the applicable case law, however, compels a different conclusion. Taking Defendants' argument to its logical conclusion, Defendants could have attached a copy of the front page of The Los Angeles Times to the June U.C.C.-1 and the financing statement would be effective: interested third parties reviewing the June U.C.C.-1 would be on notice that there was a mistake and that they must inquire into the true substance of the underlying security

[3] This result is not altered by the fact that, as in this case, the Patent Office accepts the filing of documents memorializing the granting of a security interest in a trademark. The Lanham Act gives the Patent Office the discretion to accept various documents not expressly described in the Act; it does not, however, expressly provide for the filing of documents memorializing pledges of trademarks, as the Copyright Act does for hypothecations of copyrights.

agreement. However, the Commercial Code and the cases interpreting it require more. To be effective, a financing statement must reasonably describe the property of the debtor in which the secured party claims an interest.

The requirements of § 9402 are not to be read so broadly that they are read out of existence. The Ninth Circuit has stated:

> As we have said, § 9402 is to be read liberally: "only the most basic description of property deemed to be collateral for an Article 9 security interest was contemplated [by § 9402] insofar as it might indicate to an interested third party that possible prior encumbrances might exist with respect to prospectively contemplated collateral." *Biggins v. Southwest Bank,* 490 F.2d 1304, 1307-08 (9th Cir. 1973). However, as we recently noted, § 9402 is not a nullity; the statute does require a financing statement to contain a reasonable description of the encumbered property. See *In re Softalk Publishing Co., Inc.,* 856 F.2d 1328, 1331 (9th Cir. 1988). *Gill v. U.S. (In re Boogie Enterprises, Inc.),* 866 F.2d 1172, 1174 (9th Cir. 1989) ("Personal property" was an insufficient description of collateral to satisfy the requirements of the Commercial Code).

In a case remarkably similar to the case at bar, and cited in the above quotation, a financing statement was filed with the California Office of the Secretary of State where, in the section designated for description of collateral, the financing statement read: "See Attached." A separate sheet of paper was attached reciting:

> Debtor hereby grants [secured party] a security interest in all of the following types or items of property ("Collateral" herein) in which the debtor now has or hereafter acquires any right, title, or interest, or rights present and future, . . . and all increases therein and products and proceeds thereof. Proceeds include but are not limited to inventory, returned merchandise, accounts, accounts receivable, chattel, paper, general intangibles, insurance proceeds, documents, money, goods, equipment, instruments, and any other tangible or intangible property arising under the sale, lease or other disposition of collateral:

Nothing followed the colon. *Webb Co. v. First City Bank (In re Softalk Publishing Co., Inc.),* 856 F.2d 1328, 1329 (9th Cir. 1988). In *Softalk,* the Ninth Circuit agreed with the Bankruptcy Court and with the Bankruptcy Appellate Panel in concluding that the filing of that financing statement was ineffective to perfect the claimed security interest because the financing statement contained an inadequate description of the collateral. "[A] financing statement that contains no description of collateral at all is insufficient to perfect a security interest and may not be cured pursuant to subsection 9402(8)." *Id.* at 1331. The Ninth Circuit explained:

> One of the section 9402 requisites provides that a financing statement must contain a statement identifying or describing the collateral. See Cal. Comm.Code § 9402(1). This statement need not be specific, see Cal. Comm.Code § 9110, and it may contain minor errors that are not seriously misleading, see Cal. Comm.Code § 9402(8), but its existence is mandatory, see Cal. Comm.Code § 9402(1). As the BAP observed, "since the U.C.C. has reduced the formal requisites of a financing statement to a minimum, there can be no acceptable excuse for failure to comply with its provisions." *Id.* (citation omitted).

The Ninth Circuit further specifically rejected the contention that Defendants raise in this case that the financing statement should put interested third parties on inquiry notice only, and is not misleading if it fails to describe the collateral at all:

> Perhaps, realistically speaking, no statement of collateral at all is necessary to put a potential third party lender on notice of possible encumbrances. Nevertheless, the drafters of the

> U.C.C. and the California legislature decided that financing statements must contain a statement of collateral. This decision imposes a substantive requirement on secured parties to include in their financing statements a statement of collateral that is somehow meaningful. *Id.* at 1332.

In this case, the attachment to the June U.C.C.-1 failed completely to describe the collateral of the Debtor in which OP claimed a security interest. Therefore, the June U.C.C.-1 was ineffective to perfect a security interest in any collateral of Debtor, including the Trademark Assets. See *Webb Co. v. First City Bank (In re Softalk Publishing Co., Inc.),* 856 F.2d 1328, 1329 (9th Cir. 1988). Since this Court concludes that the June U.C.C.-1was ineffective to perfect OP's claimed security interest in the Trademark Assets, Defendants' contentions that the November U.C.C.-2 amended a duly perfected security interest arising from the June U.C.C.-1 have no validity.

III. Conclusion

Neither the filing with the Patent Office nor the filing of the June U.C.C.-1 perfected the claimed security interest of OP in the Trademark Assets. Therefore, Defendants' motion for partial summary adjudication, which depends on a duly perfected security interest through either of these filings, is denied.

This memorandum of decision constitutes the Court's findings of fact and conclusions of law. Counsel for the Trustee shall lodge and serve a proposed order denying partial summary adjudication consistent with this memorandum of decision.

COMMENT

The confusion regarding the proper place to file security interests in copyrights and patents suggests that the safest approach is to file both in federal and state offices. *Note:* Should the court adopt a harmless error approach when determining whether a description of collateral is adequate? Given the purpose of filing (notice), why should a secured party who has attempted to follow the system be punished for a slight descriptive error, especially if no one ever detrimentally relied on the inappropriate filing?

§ 21.02 Leases

Read: U.C.C. § 1-201(37)

The classic and re-occurring example of advanced problems of scope under Article 9 is the lease/security agreement issue. One test that courts use to determine the nature of the transaction is a residual value test. This approach requires a factual determination by the courts whether the transaction results in a leasehold of value to be returned by the lessee. If the object of the lease is returned with value remaining, it is a lease and under Article 2A. If not, it was a conditional sale under the purview of Article 9. Since a complete understanding of Article 9 facilitates resolution of scope problems, it is important to review the provisions of Article 9 already studied. The cases in this chapter are designed to build upon those previously studied provisions and to illustrate just how difficult describing the scope of Article 9 can be.

Before the U.C.C.'s enactment, many creditors managed to avoid certain filing requirements and default provisions for conditional sales and chattel mortgages by structuring what was in fact a lending transaction as a lease. Because any installment credit arrangement involving collateral can be structured as a lease, such arrangements applied to both consumer goods and business equipment deals. By structuring the transaction as a lease, the creditor/lessor retained ownership of the property; if the lessee defaulted, the lessor could simply reclaim its property. Provisions for public notice and proper repossession upon default simply did not apply.

Security Interest v. "True Lease". Under § 1-201(37) an agreement that purports to be a lease may be a true lease or it may create a security interest. If the arrangement creates a security interest, the transaction is governed exclusively by Article 9 and filing requirements apply. If the agreement is a true lease, Article 2A governs the transaction. Thus, Article 9 may apply to transactions that appear to be leases. This situation arises because any secured installment credit sale can be recast in the form of a lease. To avoid filing and default requirements, some creditors attempt to structure a secured transaction as a lease. The buyer receives possession of the goods as lessee. In such an arrangement, the lessee's payments over the term of the lease are about equal to the installment purchase price of the goods. At the end of the term the lessee who has made all the rental payments is either entitled to keep the goods or may be given an option to purchase them at a nominal price. Section 1-207(37) conclusively presumes that this type of lease is intended as security. An option to purchase for nominal or no consideration, however, makes a lease one intended as a security only when it necessarily arises upon compliance with the terms of the lease. *Matter of Marhoefer Packing Co.,* 674 F.2d 1139 (7th Cir. 1982). In contrast, an essential characteristic of a "true lease" is that there be something of value to return to the lessor after the term. Consider the next case.

[A] Leases with Options

IN RE THE ANSWER—THE ELEGANT LARGE SIZE DISCOUNTER, INC.

United States Bankruptcy Court, Southern District of New York
115 B.R. 465 (1990)

HOWARD SCHWARTZBERG, BANKRUPTCY JUDGE.

Greyhound Financial Corporation ("Greyhound") a financial institution engaged in the business of making commercial loans to business entities, including the Chapter 11 debtor in this case, Virginia Specialty Stores, Inc. ("Debtor"), has moved for an order pursuant to 11 U.S.C. § 361, 365 and 503 of the Bankruptcy Code for alternative relief. Greyhound seeks an order (1) requiring the Debtor to pay certain pre-petition equipment lease rents; (2) ordering the payment of accrued post-petition rents as an administrative expense of the Debtor's estate; (3) requiring the Debtor to provide adequate protection to Greyhound, and (4) fixing a time within which the Debtor must assume or reject the leases entered into between the Debtor and Greyhound.

The Debtor resists Greyhound's motion on the ground that the leases are not "true" leases, but are, instead, security financing agreements which need not be assumed or rejected under 11 U.S.C. § 365.

FINDINGS OF FACT

1. On November 27, 1989, the Debtor and some of its affiliated entities each filed with this court voluntary petitions for relief under Chapter 11 of the Bankruptcy Code and have remained in possession of their assets and continue to manage their businesses as Debtors in possession in accordance with 11 U.S.C. § 1107 and 1108.

2. The Debtor and its affiliate entities operate a chain of retail stores throughout the nation for the sale of clothing and wearing apparel for large size women.

3. Greyhound Financial Corporation is engaged in the business of financing commercial enterprises and providing funds for the acquisition of capital and equipment pursuant to written documents, including Equipment Lease Agreements.

4. Commencing in the Fall of 1985, the Debtor sought to obtain from Greyhound approximately $2,500,000.00 to finance the Debtor's acquisition of computer hardware and software equipment, furniture, fixtures, custom designed trade fixtures, display racks, cash wrap counters with office cubicles and other trade fixtures for use in the Debtor's retail stores.

5. In order to establish the availability of financing from Greyhound, the Debtor paid a 1% fee to obtain a written commitment letter. The commitment fee was non-refundable.

6. On September 30, 1985, October 25, 1985, and April 12, 1986, the Debtor and Greyhound executed documents entitled "Executory Lease Agreements" whereby Greyhound, as Lessor, agreed to lease to the Debtor as lessee, the computer equipment and trade fixtures which the Debtor proposed to purchase from third party vendors for installation in the Debtor's various retail units. The agreements provide that the rental payments made by the Debtor will be net to Greyhound. Therefore, the Debtor was responsible for the payment of all sales, use and other taxes with respect to the acquisition of the equipment from the various vendors. Additionally, the Debtor agreed to look solely to the various vendors for any claims based on the quality or condition of the equipment, their performance, merchantability of fitness for use, and further agreed not to assert any such claim, offset or defense against Greyhound.

7. The Debtor did not acquire any of the computer equipment or trade fixtures from Greyhound, but purchased these items independently from third party vendors, without any consultation, notice, or input involving Greyhound. Indeed, the software system which the Debtor acquired for its computer system was licensed by the software supplier exclusively to the Debtor and could not be transferred to any other entity.

8. The mainframe computer hardware which the Debtor purchased has an eight year technological life span, with four years remaining. The computer equipment currently has a $330,000.00 fair market value in place on the Debtor's premises but, if removed from the debtor's premises, the computer equipment would be worth approximately $110,000.00, exclusive of the cost of removal or the expense to install the computer equipment elsewhere.

9. The Debtor's Chief Financial Officer testified that the Debtor never contemplated returning any of the computer equipment at the end of the term of the contract with Greyhound because the computer equipment was regarded as essential to the ongoing operations of the Debtor. It was not economically feasible to ever consider a return of the computer equipment.

10. Approximately three-fourths of the funds which the Debtor obtained from Greyhound were applied to the purchase of trade fixtures, many of which were custom designed for the Debtor's stores.

11. Under the documents in question, the Debtor is obligated to make monthly payments to Greyhound in the approximate amount of $40,970.00. The rental payments are based on the current Treasury Bill rate for funds. If the Treasury Bill rate rises the payments required under the Debtor's written agreements with Greyhound also rise accordingly.

12. The written agreements provide that the Debtor shall have an option, at the conclusion of the term, to purchase the equipment at the then fair market value. However, the computer

equipment is subject to declining technological obsolescence. The trade fixtures will also have substantially reduced values over cost because many of the items were custom designed for the Debtor's stores.

13. The Debtor was in default under the written agreements with Greyhound prior to the filing of its Chapter 11 petition. As of this month, the Debtor owes approximately $286,440.00 to Greyhound under these agreements, of which $20,500.00 was owed pre-petition. The Debtor's principal post-petition indebtedness to Greyhound is in excess of $208,746.29, following the Debtor's payment of $20,472.57 to Greyhound on January 17, 1990.

14. The Debtor continues to use the computer equipment and trade fixtures listed in its agreements with Greyhound, and has made no further payments to Greyhound, although the equipment is declining in value due to wear and tear and technological obsolescence. Greyhound's interest in the equipment is eroding and its rights are being prejudiced. The Debtor continues to use and enjoy the use of the equipment without adequately protecting Greyhound's interests.

DISCUSSION

Once again a court is called upon to decide whether or not a transaction entered into between sophisticated commercial entities whereby one party provides the funds to enable the other party to acquire and operate tangible business property constitutes a "true" lease as to the property in question, or an advance of funds to enable the other party to acquire and operate the property which then serves as the collateral for the advance of funds and which may be acquired by the user at the end of the contractual term by the exercise of a purchase option. As in the case of a magic show, the parties to the transaction use numerous devices to create an illusion which may take on all sorts of appearances to the audience, depending upon who is the beholder. The language may have one meaning for tax depreciation purposes, another significance for judgment creditors, a different appearance for those concerned with the issue of risk of loss, and still another meaning for determining the duration of the economic use and need for the property. Considerable judicial and counsel time has been expended in litigating which factors were more significant than others in the written documents executed by the parties in determining the appropriate label to be given to the transaction. Conversely, in some cases certain factors are not treated as significant, even if they are expressly included in the agreement. Thus, the 1987 Official Text of the U.C.C. proposed for Arizona, the state whose laws the parties agreed should apply to the interpretation of their written agreements, has expressed that certain provisions in an agreement need not mean that it constitutes a security agreement rather than a lease. A transaction does not create a security interest merely because it provides that (a) the present value of the consideration the lessee is obligated to pay the lessor for the right to possession and use of the goods is substantially equal to or is greater than the fair market value of the goods at the time lease is entered into, (b) the lessee assumes risk of loss of the goods, or agrees to pay taxes, insurance, filing, recording, or registration fees, or service or maintenance costs with respect to the goods, (c) the lessee has an option to renew the lease or to become the owner of the goods, (d) the lessee has an option to renew the lease for a fixed rent that is equal to or greater than the reasonably predictable fair market rent for the use of the goods for the term of the renewal at the time the option is to be performed, or (e) the lessee has an option to become the owner of the goods for a fixed price that is equal to or greater than the reasonably predictable fair market value of the goods at the time the option is to be performed. Arizona U.C.C. Official Comment § 1-201(37) (1978).

Greyhound reasons that the documents relating to the computer equipment and fixtures used by the Debtor and financed by Greyhound do not create a security interest because of the existence of the following provisions: (a) The Debtor is obligated to return the Equipment at the end of the Lease term unless it exercises its purchase options; (b) The Debtor's option to purchase the Equipment is exercisable at fair market value and not less; (c) The consideration required for the Debtor to become the owner of the property is substantial; (d) The bargain between the Debtor and Greyhound does not involve the taking of a security interest; (e) Greyhound's remedies upon the Debtor's default are (i) to enforce performance by appropriate court action or to recover damages; (ii) to terminate the Debtor's rights under the Lease and/or (iii) to take possession of the Equipment and recover damages. Greyhound does not have the right under the Lease to the usual remedy that would accrue to a secured party: the acceleration and recovery of the underlying debt.

The factor which Greyhound reasons is most significant is the existence of a purchase option at fair market value of the computer equipment and custom fixtures in place at the Debtor's premises. Courts have held that if a document contains a purchase option that allows the user to purchase the equipment only at its fair market value, it is presumptively a "true" lease. See *In re Celeryvale Transport, Inc.*, 822 F.2d 16 (6th Cir.1987). In *National Can Services Corp. v. Gateway Aluminum Co.,* 683 F.Supp. 719 (E.D.Mo.1988) it was held that an agreement to lease recycling equipment constitutes a "true" lease because the user was obligated to return the equipment at the conclusion of the lease if it did not exercise its option to purchase the equipment at fair market value, despite the fact that the user paid the taxes, assumed all maintenance and repair costs, and assumed the risk of loss or damage to the equipment. The filing of a U.C.C. Financing Statement as a precautionary measure was not a critical factor in barring a determination that a "true" lease was involved. Similarly, an option to purchase farm equipment at the fair market value of the equipment at the time the option was exercised was regarded as significant in finding a "true" lease in *In re Cress,* 106 B.R. 246 (D. Kan. 1989). The right to purchase the equipment by the exercise of a purchase option at fair market value was also critical to finding a "true" lease in other cases. See *In re Aspen Impressions, Inc.,* 94 B.R. 861 (Bankr. E. D. Pa. 1989); *In re Triple B Oil Producers, Inc.,* 75 B.R. 461 (Bankr. S. D. Ill. 1987); *In re Air Vermont, Inc.,* 44 B.R. 440 (Bankr. D. Vt. 1984). On the other hand, in *In re Beker Indus. Corp.,* 69 B.R. 937 (Bankr. S.D.N.Y. 1987), it was observed that the option to purchase used telephone equipment at fair market value was illusory in the absence of evidence that there was a market for used telephone equipment. Nor was the existence of an option to purchase at fair market value dispositive when the agreements conferred on the user the essential attributes of ownership in *In re Catamount Dyers, Inc.,* 43 B.R. 564 (Bankr. D. Vt. 1984).

Another significant factor in determining whether or not a lease or a security agreement is involved is the objective intention of the parties. The court must determine from the language in the agreement and the facts and circumstances underlying the transaction, whether or not the parties objectively intended to enter into a "true" lease or a security agreement. *In re O.P.M. Leasing Services, Inc.*, 23 B.R. 104 (Bankr.S.D.N.Y.1982). In arriving at the intentions of the parties from the facts in each case, the inclusion of an option to purchase at fair market value does not of itself rule out the existence of a security agreement, especially if the property is dependent upon advances in technology so that due to obsolescence or special use, the property is useless to others at the end of the agreement term. In such case, the court will more likely find that the transaction is a security device and not a "true" lease. *Pacific Express, Inc. v. Teknekron Infoswitch Corp. (In re Pacific Express, Inc.),* 780 F.2d 1482 (9th Cir.1986). Where the property or equipment in question has substantially reduced value at the end of the contract term, especially where the property is custom designed for the specific needs of the user so that any reversionary interest claimed by the financing party is significantly less at the end of the contract term, the document will be more indicative of a security interest rather than a "true" lease. See *In re Leasing Consultants, Inc.*, 351 F.Supp. 1390 (E.D.N.Y.1972), aff'd, 486 F.2d 367 (2d Cir.1973).

In the instant case, the Debtor purchased computer equipment and fixtures which were custom designed for its various stores throughout the county only after first obtaining a written loan commitment from Greyhound. The Debtor obtained funds from Greyhound and then purchased the computer and store fixtures from various third-party vendors. Greyhound did not inspect any of the equipment before purchase and acquired no documents of title for the equipment other than a U.C.C. Financing Statement. The full risk of loss and maintenance of the equipment was borne by the debtor. The fixtures purchased for the various stores operated by the debtor were custom designed for the Debtor's operations. There was no evidence that these fixtures had any significant value to other potential users. The computer equipment was subject to obsolescence as new technology comes on to the market. Indeed, the present market value of the computer equipment in place, which was stated to be approximately $330,000.00, was reduced to approximately $110,000.00 off the Debtor's premises, excluding the cost of removal and the cost of installation elsewhere. Greyhound had no input with respect to the selection and purchase of the computer equipment and fixtures and merely advanced the funds to the Debtor for their acquisition, subject to the issuance of a commitment loan agreement and the receipt of U.C.C. Financing Statements.

All of the facts and circumstances in this case lead to the inescapable finding that Greyhound financed the Debtor's equipment and fixture needs and did not have any ownership interest in the computer equipment and fixtures other than as collateral under a security agreement, for which Greyhound was entitled to receive monthly payments calculated to produce a return to Greyhound for the cost of the funds it advanced to finance the equipment.

Although the parties referred to the written arrangement as an "Equipment Lease Agreement", it is clear that their transaction was actually a disguised security arrangement whereby Greyhound simply advanced funds for the debtor's purchase of equipment from third party vendors, which then served as security for Greyhound's loans. Where a business entity purchases equipment directly from third party vendors without any selection or input from the funder, and where the purchaser is totally responsible for taxes, maintenance and loss or damage to the equipment and the equipment was never shipped by or to the funder, the transaction should be regarded in reality as a financing arrangement. *Sierra Diesel Injection Service v. Burroughs Corp.*, 890 F.2d 108, 115-16 (9th Cir.1989). The fact that the debtor has an option to purchase the equipment at a fair market value which is substantially less than the original cost, and that such value will continue to decline as a result of technological obsolescence, will not obscure the economic realities of the relationship between the parties.

ADEQUATE PROTECTION

Because Greyhound has a financial interest in the collateral which it financed and which is currently being used by the Debtor, Greyhound is entitled under 11 U.S.C. § 363 to obtain an order which "shall prohibit or condition such use . . . as is necessary to provide adequate protection of such interest." Manifestly, the market value of the computer equipment is declining as a result of technological obsolescence. Additionally, the custom designed store fixtures will decline in value with age and use. Greyhound reasons that the monthly payments required under the written documents executed by the Debtor constitute adequate protection for the use of Greyhound's collateral and its loans, especially since Greyhound is not the owner of the equipment and has no realistic equity in the property to serve as an equity cushion. In these circumstances, Greyhound is entitled to an order directing the debtor to pay all past-due post-petition amounts called for under its agreements with the Debtor within thirty days from the date of the order. In the absence of such payment, Greyhound may proceed to foreclose upon its secured interest, unaffected by the automatic stay imposed under 11 U.S.C. § 362(a) which will be deemed lifted for enforcement purposes.

CONCLUSIONS OF LAW

2. Greyhound's motion for an order directing the Debtor to pay post-petition Equipment Rents, and fixing a time within which the Debtor must assume or reject the so-called Equipment Leases is denied because the written documents in question are disguised security agreements and not "true" leases assumable, or rejectable under 11 U.S.C. § 365

3. Greyhound is entitled under 11 U.S.C. § 363 to an order prohibiting or conditioning the Debtor's continued use of the equipment in question unless the Debtor pays all past-due post-petition amounts called for under the Agreements in question within thirty days from the date of the order to be entered in this matter.

4. In the event that the Debtor fails to pay Greyhound as ordered, Greyhound may proceed to foreclose upon its secured interest and the automatic stay imposed under 11 U.S.C. § 362(a) shall be lifted for such purpose.

SETTLE ORDER on notice.

NOTES

(1) *Benefits.* One of the benefits of having a lease instead of a security interest involves bankruptcy proceedings. If a transaction can be classified as a true lease, then the asset returns to the lessor. But, if the arrangement receives classification as a security agreement, the trustee in bankruptcy receives the collateral to distribute to general creditors because the secured party would have failed to perfect its interest in a timely fashion.

(2) *Nominal?* Issues arise as to when the amount of an option to buy or renew is nominal. Should the term "nominal" be defined as fair market value at the time the option arises, fair market value as anticipated by the parties when the lease is signed, or some other method if measuring residual value?

(3) *Residual value v. Full payout lease.* If the lessor retains residual value, then it is a lease. What if the lessee pays during the time frame of the lease an amount equal to or greater than the fair market value of the object? Is this analogous to the lessor not retaining residual value, so it should be considered a security agreement? See Comment 37 to § 1-201, which states that a full pay out lease is not a per se security agreement.

(4) *Factors.* U.C.C. § 1-201(37) indicates the facts of each case determine the resolution of the lease/security agreement issue. However, in *In re Aspen Impressions, Inc.*, 94 B.R. 861 (Bankr. E.D.Pa., 1989), the court set out factors to aid in distinguishing the two. The parties agreed to lease a printing press for seven years. The total payments equaled a 17% return for the lessor.

The court noted the following factors are: (1) does the lessee have to insure items for a value equal to the amount of the rent payments; (2) does the lessee have the risk of loss; (3) does the lessee have to pay taxes, repair or maintain the objects; (4) do acceleration and resale provisions exist in the agreement in the event of default; and (5) are the goods easily removed as fixtures. In *Taylor Rental Corp. v. Ted Goodwin Leasing, Inc.*, 38 U.C.C. Rep. Serv. 577, 584 (Mont. 1984) the court noted additional factors:

> In analyzing the facts of the case as a whole to determine whether the leases were intended as security, significant factors include but are not limited to: (1) whether the lessee acquires any equity in the property; (2) whether the lessee is required to bear the risk of loss; (3) whether the lessee is responsible for all charges and taxes; (4) whether the rent may be accelerated; (5) whether the equipment was purchased specially for lease to this lessee; (6) whether the lessee must provide insurance; and (7) whether the lessor disclaims all warranties. (Citations omitted).

These cases emphasize that courts should not rely solely on these factors as conclusive but use them in relation to the facts and to determine the intent of the parties. Are there additional factors you think a court should consider? Would an economic realities test improve matters if the test incorporated all of the above plus a subjective judicial analysis of the transaction? Do you foresee problems with such an approach?

(5) With Article 2A on leasing, the distinction between "true" leases and leases intended as security is preserved with regard to filing. Rather than choosing an alternative solution which required all leases to be filed in order to give notice to subsequent creditors, the lease need be filed only if it is one intended as security. The comments to U.C.C. § 1-201(37) notes that "the task of sharpening the line between true leases and security interests disguised as leases continues to be a function of this section." Since the lessor has not parted with title, she is entitled to full protection against the lessee's creditors and the trustee in bankruptcy.

In light of the U.C.C.'s general de-emphasis on title, one may well question why it should be so important in this context. Article 9 provides for the optional filing of leases and it could easily be made mandatory, as it has in at least one Canadian province which has adopted Article 9 with this modification. The authors believe that such a move would also end the uncertainty and endless litigation as whether a transaction is a true lease or a security interest in disguise. What do you think?

[B] Open-end Leases

IN RE OTASCO, INC.

United States Bankruptcy Court, Northern District of Oklahoma
111 Bankr. 976, 11 U.C.C. Rep. Serv. 2d 1262 (1990)

WILSON, BANKRUPTCY JUDGE

Wheels, Inc. brought an adversary proceeding for declaratory judgment against Otasco, Inc. to determine priority of conflicting interests in certain motor vehicles or their proceeds. The issue is whether a written agreement concerning these vehicles and purporting to be a lease should be treated as an unperfected security agreement. The matter has been submitted for decision on stipulations, briefs and oral argument. Upon consideration thereof, the Court finds, concludes and orders as follows.

FINDINGS OF FACT

Wheels, Inc. ("Wheels") "is an Illinois corporation with its principal place of business in Des Plaines, Illinois. Wheels is in the business of leasing automobiles to businesses," Pre-trial Order p. 2, para. II (1).

Otasco, Inc. ("Otasco") "is a Nevada corporation with its principal place of business in Tulsa, Oklahoma. Otasco is in the business of retail sales of tires, accessories, and other goods," Pre-trial Order p. 2, para. II (2).

"On February 2, 1984, Wheels entered into an agreement with Otasco (the 'Agreement'), which governed the terms under which Otasco, from time to time, would obtain motor vehicles from Wheels," Pre-trial Order p. 3, para. II (6). A copy of the Agreement is admitted as exhibit 1 appended to the pre-trial order.

The Agreement is designated "Lease" and identifies Wheels as "Lessor" and Otasco as "Lessee." para. 14 of the "Lease" is entitled "Ownership" and recites in pertinent part as follows: "It is expressly agreed that the Lessee by virtue of this lease acquires no ownership, title, property, right, interest, (or any option therefor) in any leased motor vehicle save as herein provided . . . ."

The Agreement provides that "Lessee hereby leases one motor vehicle for delivery as specified by Lessee and other motor vehicles as may hereafter be ordered by Lessee . . . . with the Lessee to have possession and right to use said motor vehicles . . . .," Agreement para. 1, subject to minimal use restrictions, Agreement para. 4. The Agreement imposes all burdens and expenses of licensing, registration, taxes, fees, fines and penalties, maintenance and replacement, insurance, and liability for use in connection with the operation of leased vehicles on the Lessee, paras. 4, 5, 7, 8, 11. Lessee may mark the vehicles with its own insignia, Agreement para. 9. The Agreement imposes no duties on Lessor except delivery of each vehicle at the inception of the lease, and acceptance, disposition and accounting of and for each vehicle at termination of the lease, as discussed below.

The Agreement provides that "each motor vehicle shall be leased for an initial term of 12 months from the date of the delivery of such vehicle to Lessee and thereafter for successive 12 month renewal terms; provided that Lessee shall have the right to cancel any vehicle at any time after the end of the first 12 months of the initial lease term for such vehicle by giving written notice of such cancellation to the Lessor . . . .," Agreement para. 12. No provision in the Agreement permits the Lessor to cancel once a vehicle has been leased; but "either Lessee or Lessor may terminate the obligation to lease additional or replacement vehicles at any time upon written notice to the other party," Agreement para. 12. The parties expected continuation beyond the initial 12-month term (as admitted in oral argument). There is no express limit to the possible number of "successive 12 month renewal terms," Agreement para. 12; nor is there any express option to purchase at any particular time.

The Agreement provides that "The monthly rental for each motor vehicle shall be computed on the basis of the rider hereto attached marked 'Rental Schedule' and made a part hereof, and is intended to include the Reserve accrued for the estimated depreciation of the leased vehicle," Agreement para. 2. The "Rental Schedule" reads in its entirety as follows:

RENTAL SCHEDULE

(Rider attached to and made a part of this lease.)

The monthly payment for each vehicle shall be computed as follows:

RENTAL

The rental shall be computed on the stipulated cost of the vehicle at the rates shown below for the period of rental indicated:

1st – 12th Month 2.9928%

13th – 24th Month 2.7428%

25th – 36th Month 2.4629%

37th – 48th Month 2.2329%

49th – 50th Month 2.0987%

Provided, however, that at no time will the rental be less than a minimum of $ 3.00 per month.

AMORTIZATION ACCOUNT:

2.00% per month of the stipulated cost of each vehicle for the duration of the contract for such vehicle or until a total of 100% of the stipulated cost shall have been paid, whichever occurs first.

It is anticipated that at the end of the maximum term herein prescribed, the vehicle will have only scrap value and if for any reason the Lessee desires to continue to operate the vehicle the Lessee agrees to pay to the Lessor a monthly rental of $ 3.00 during such extended period.

The rental hereinabove specified may be changed on notice from the Lessor to the Lessee but only as it affects vehicles delivered after the effective date of change cited in said notice.

The Agreement further provides as follows:

3. LESSEE ACCOUNT. The Lessor, upon receipt of a leased motor vehicle from the Lessee after the termination of the lease of said motor vehicle, will proceed to sell said motor vehicle at wholesale on the best terms available for cash, in the discretion of the Lessor (the net amount received from the sale of the motor vehicle to the Lessor to the final completion of the sale thereof being called the "Net Proceeds"). If the Net Proceeds plus the amount accrued for the Reserve for said motor vehicle (the "Total Recovery") is in excess of the "stipulated cost" of the motor vehicle, then the amount of such excess shall be promptly credited to the Lessee by the Lessor. If the Total Recovery is less than the "stipulated cost" of the motor vehicle, then the Lessee shall promptly pay such deficiency to the Lessor; provided that in the event of any such sale the Lessor shall guaranty to Lessee that the Net Proceeds shall at least equal (a) the following percentages of the fair value of the vehicle as of the beginning of the 12 month period during which the date of termination occurs:

Percentage Period Initial 12 month period of lease 20% each subsequent 12 month period 30% less, in any case, (b) the amount of any loss or damage to be insured or borne by Lessee under Section 5 or 11 hereof. As an alternate to sale of the vehicle by the Lessor, the Lessee may, at its option, on 30 days written notice to the Lessor, arrange for the sale of the vehicle for the account of the Lessee (but not to the Lessee), without the services of the Lessor, providing payment is first made to the Lessor by or on behalf of the Lessee of the remaining book balance for said vehicle, and any charges accrued to the Lessor on said vehicle to said date.

It is stipulated that "The 'amount accrued for the Reserve of said motor vehicle' referred to in Paragraph 3 of the Agreement is calculated on the Rental Schedule under the heading 'Amortization Account,' " Pre-trial Order p. 5, para. II (11).

The "stipulated cost" referred to above is not expressly defined anywhere in the agreement. However, the Agreement provides that "at the beginning of each month, the Lessor shall render a monthly invoice to the Lessee for all payments due to the Lessor for all motor vehicles theretofore delivered to the Lessee, and the Lessee agrees to make prompt payment thereof. The Lessor will also render to the Lessee details of the 'stipulated cost' together with the term of the lease thereof, the rental rate and charges of all motor vehicles delivered to the Lessee," Agreement para. 2.

At the end of the lease term, "the Lessor will render efficient service in sale or disposal of the leased motor vehicle to obtain the largest net return for the Lessee," Agreement para. 6.

On November 6, 1988, Otasco filed its petition for relief under 11 U.S.C. Chapter 11 "Otasco is operating its business and remains in possession of its property as debtor and debtor in possession," Pre-trial Order p. 2, para. II (3).

On July 11, 1989, Wheels filed its complaint herein seeking declaratory judgment that the Agreement is a true lease which Otasco must assume or reject; or, in the alternative, that Wheels has a perfected security interest in the "leased" vehicles. Otasco answered, and asserts that the Agreement is not a true lease, is intended as security, and that Wheels' security interest has not been perfected.

The matter was set for trial on December 11, 1989. However, on that date, the parties filed their "Agreed Pre-Trial Order," reciting stipulated facts, stating that "no other facts are in dispute" and no further evidence would be offered, and announcing that "the parties intend to file cross-motions for summary judgment on the legal issues involved," Pre-trial Order p. 7, para. IV. The Court thereupon ordered that briefs, if any, must be filed on or before December 18, 1989, and scheduled oral argument for December 19, 1989.

"As of the date of th[e] Pre-Trial Order, Otasco had in its possession 21 motor vehicles which it obtained from Wheels. These 21 motor vehicles and the States of origin of their respective certificates of title are as follows:

Vehicle I.D. #	Year Make	State of
Title 2G2AF19X1G9274515	1986 Pontiac	Oklahoma
1G2AF19X3GT246689	1986 Pontiac	Oklahoma
1G2AF19X1GT248053	1986 Pontiac	Oklahoma
2G2AF19XXG9273797	1986 Pontiac	Oklahoma
1G2AF19XOGT246343	1986 Pontiac	Georgia
2B4FK41G7GR798422	1986 Dodge	Oklahoma
2G2AF19XOG9274778	1986 Pontiac	Oklahoma
1G2AF51W1HT275488	1987 Pontiac	Tennessee
1G2AF51W8HT279621	1987 Pontiac	Louisiana
3G1AW51W9JS509008	1988 Chevrolet	Kansas
2B4FK4133JR580322	1988 Dodge	Tennessee
1GCER14GHS110304	1987 Chevrolet	Oklahoma

Vehicle I.D. #	Year Make	State of
2G2AF51W1H9265373	1987 Pontiac	Arkansas
2G2AFS1WXH9248796	1987 Pontiac	Georgia
1G2AG51WXHT283909	1987 Pontiac	Texas
1G2AFS1W3JT254356	1988 Pontiac	Georgia
1G2AF51W3JT254390	1988 Pontiac	Kansas
1G2AF51W1JT254372	1988 Pontiac	Oklahoma
1G2AF51W1JT254386	1988 Pontiac	Louisiana
2B4FK4131JR750886	1988 Dodge	Oklahoma
2B4FK4134JR748470	1988 Dodge	Oklahoma

Pre-Trial Order, pp. 3-4 para. II (7). "All of the vehicle titles list Wheels as the owner, but the titles do not list Wheels as a lienholder," Pre-Trial Order, p. 4 para. II (8). So far as appears from the record, no lien entry forms were ever delivered to the Oklahoma Tax Commission, pursuant to 47 O.S. § 1110, as to any of the vehicles herein.

Some of these vehicles have been or are to be sold, and the proceeds escrowed; Otasco is making scheduled payments on the rest, Pre-Trial Order pp. 4-5, para. II (9), (10).

On December 14, 1989, Wheels filed its Trial Brief. Otasco filed no brief. On December 19, 1989, at oral argument, counsel for Otasco stated that he was unaware that Wheels had filed its brief, and that in order to conserve estate funds he had chosen to rely on oral argument. After oral argument, counsel for Otasco waived any further opportunity to file his brief. The oral argument was no mere ritual exercise, but served as an effective supplement to the written record.

Any "Conclusions of Law" which ought more properly to be "Findings of Fact" are adopted and incorporated herein by reference.

CONCLUSIONS OF LAW

This is a core proceeding under 28 U.S.C. § 157(b)(2)(K), (O) 11 U.S.C. § 541(a)(1), § 544(a)

I. WHETHER LEASE IS INTENDED AS SECURITY

Wheels seeks declaratory judgment that certain vehicles were leased by Wheels to Otasco, and are therefore owned by Wheels as lessor and are not part of Otasco's bankruptcy estate under 11 U.S.C. § 541(a)(1) Otasco argues that the purported "lease" should be treated as a secured sale, and therefore the vehicles are owned by Otasco and are property of Otasco's bankruptcy estate, subject to Wheels' security interest. Further, that said security interest is unperfected and inferior to Otasco's interest pursuant to 11 U.S.C. § 544(a), § 1107(a) Otasco's position depends upon the combined effect of 11 U.S.C. § 541(a)(1) which gives Otasco's bankruptcy estate certain ownership rights as successor in interest to the debtor, and § 544(a), which gives Otasco's bankruptcy estate certain priority rights enjoyed by a particular class of creditor as against other, lesser creditors. But as a first step, it must be determined whether Otasco has any ownership rights, and whether Wheels should be treated as a mere creditor. Resolution of this issue in turn requires interpretation and evaluation of the parties' "lease" Agreement.

The Agreement provides that it shall be interpreted according to the laws of the State of Illinois. Wheels is an Illinois corporation; but Otasco is an Oklahoma corporation, most of the vehicles are titled in Oklahoma, and this Court sits in Oklahoma. Wheels asserts that this Court, as a Federal court sitting in Oklahoma, must apply the choice of law rules of the state of Oklahoma;

that Oklahoma courts use the Restatement 2nd rules for choice of law; and that under those rules, the parties' choice of law governs, unless there is no reasonable connection between their choice and the forum State or some fundamental policy of the forum State would be infringed.

Wheels' assumption that this Court must automatically apply Oklahoma's choice of law rules is not well founded. Although Wheels' assertion might be well taken in a Federal diversity case, this is not a diversity case.

In cases where items of property are scattered through several states, or where legal relations governed by varying state laws are affected by the trustee's status under the section 544(a), problems of the conflict of laws are certain to arise. Although some courts have appeared to think that a bankruptcy court is obliged to apply the conflict-of-laws rules of the state of the forum, the more supportable view is that the bankruptcy court should be free to exercise for itself the choice of applicable state law. In any event, the tendency of the courts is to treat the law of the situs of property at the commencement of the case as governing to the extent that section 544(a) refers to non-bankruptcy law, 4 Collier on Bankruptcy (15th ed. 1989) para. 544.02 pp. 544-13, 544-14. The whereabouts of all of these vehicles at the commencement of this case is not shown. The situs of chattels subject to documents of title is debatable.

However, if the Court does not automatically adopt Oklahoma's choice-of-law rules, the Court must determine whose choice-of-law rules it should adopt, or must fashion its own as a matter of Federal bankruptcy case law. Here, Otasco does not argue the point; and the Court sees no particular reason why the parties' choice of law should not govern. The applicable substantive law will be Uniform Commercial Code Sections 1-201(37) and 9-201(1)(a), enacted in identical form in both Illinois and Oklahoma (until recent amendment of § 1-201(37) in Oklahoma, see below), concerning "leases" intended as security, a subject on which there are no published opinions of the Supreme Courts of either Illinois or Oklahoma. Wheels offers a decision by a Bankruptcy Court sitting in Illinois, *In re Loop Hospital Partnership*, 35 Bankr. 929 (B.C. N.D. Ill. 1983), but cites no authority which would make this decision binding on this Court. The court in *In re Loop Hospital Partnership,* cites, among other non-Illinois authorities, an opinion from this District, *In re Tulsa Port Warehouse Co., Inc.*, 4 Bankr. 801 (D.Ct. N.D. Okla. 1980) aff'd, 690 F.2d 809 (10th Cir. 1982), and the Court of Appeals of this Circuit, U.S. for *Eddies Sales and Leasing, Inc. v. Federal Insurance Co.,* 634 F.2d 1050 (10th Cir. 1980). This Court, the District Court of this District, and the Court of Appeals of this Circuit, have developed considerable case law on the subject of leases vs. security agreements under Oklahoma's pre-1988 version of Uniform Commercial Code § 1-201(37) Under these circumstances, this Court will therefore proceed to interpret and analyze this "lease" Agreement under the law of the State of Illinois, but construing Illinois statutes with reference to comparable statutes in other States and case law thereunder.

Effective November 1, 1988, the State of Oklahoma amended its version of Uniform Commercial Code § 1-201(37) in conjunction with Oklahoma's enactment of Uniform Commercial Code Article 2A The amendments themselves are said to "clarify" prior law, and to that extent might be read back into prior transactions, as was done in *In re Cole: Woodson v. Ford Motor Credit Co.,* 100 Bankr. 561 (B.C. N.D. Okla. 1989). Wheels urges this Court to follow *In re Cole*, and interpret the lease Agreement herein in light of Oklahoma's new amended version of Uniform Commercial Code § 1-201(37) Even though the amendments purport to "clarify" the prior Uniform Commercial Code text, they certainly are meant to alter some caselaw interpreting and applying that prior text. To that extent these amendments do change prior law.

For that reason, this Court has already refused to read these amendments back into prior leases even under Oklahoma law, *In re Thompson,* 101 Bankr. 658 (B.C. N.D. Okla. 1989). This Court certainly will not attempt to interpret an Illinois statute in light of a later Oklahoma statute which has not been enacted in Illinois. This Court will confine itself to that version of the Uniform Commercial Code existing in Illinois, its counterpart in other States, and caselaw thereunder.

The general nature of an inquiry into whether a purported lease should be treated as a secured transaction was explained at length in *In re Breece,* 58 Bankr. 379, 382-383 (B.C. N.D. Okla. 1986) and summarized in *In re Harvey,* 80 Bankr. 533, 537 (B.C. N.D. Okla. 1987), and need not be repeated here.

However, a summary review of this Agreement's provisions and operation (as set forth in more detail in the "Findings of Fact" above) is appropriate.

The Agreement herein has a 12-month "initial" term, renewable thereafter every 12 months, apparently without limit unless the lessee cancels (although the lessor may refuse to provide any further new or replacement vehicles). It was admitted at oral argument that the parties expected continuation beyond the initial 12-month term. The rental and amortization schedules appended to the Agreement indicate that the parties contemplated a normal term of 50 months. During this term, for all practical purposes the lessee would treat the "leased" vehicles as its own.

At termination, whether after the initial 12 months, or after any subsequent 12-month period, or after 50 months, or at any other time, the "leased" vehicle must be sold, by either lessor or lessee. The sale proceeds are added to the "Reserve," and the total is credited against "stipulated costs." Neither "Reserve" nor "stipulated cost" are clearly defined in the Agreement; but "stipulated cost" appears to be arbitrarily fixed by the lessor, and the "Reserve" accrues as a percentage of "stipulated cost" which over 50 months would equal 100% of "stipulated cost." If the sale proceeds plus Reserve exceed stipulated cost, the excess is credited to the lessee. If the sale proceeds plus Reserve are less than stipulated cost, the deficiency must be paid by the lessee. Accordingly, the express purpose of the sale is "to obtain the largest net return for the Lessee," Agreement paragraph 6.

After "maximum term," also not defined but bearing some relationship to the 50-month maximum rent and amortization periods, "it is anticipated that . . . . the vehicle will have only scrap value" and the lessee has an option: lessee may allow the vehicle to be sold as described above, or the lessee may "continue to operate the vehicle" for "a monthly rental of $ 3.00 during such extended period."

The rent paid during the 50-month term is based on the stipulated cost of each vehicle. Over 50 months, the rent would total 129.3742% of stipulated cost.

A transaction purporting to be a lease will be deemed a secured transaction if "a purchase option exists and it or other items in the 'lease' permit the 'lessee' to become full owner by merely paying no or nominal consideration after complying with its terms." *In re Fashion Optical, Ltd.: Steele v. Gebetsberger,* 653 F.2d 1385, 1388 (10th Cir. 1981).

This Agreement contains no express purchase option. Otasco argues that there is an "implied" or disguised purchase option, in that: (1) lessee may terminate at any time, upon termination the vehicle must be sold, and nothing in the Agreement prohibits lessee from buying the vehicle itself; and (2) after 50 months, lessee can keep a vehicle indefinitely for only $ 3.00 per month, or can then have the vehicle sold and pocket all of the sale proceeds. Otasco points out that the lessee must be entitled to all of the sale proceeds, because the rental and amortization schedules ensure that the stipulated cost is entirely paid off after 50 months, so there is nothing against which sale proceeds must be offset. This appears to be a correct reading of the Agreement. Therefore, this Agreement does contain a purchase option, despite the draftsman's efforts to conceal the same. The question is whether such purchase option permits the lessee to buy the vehicle for "no or nominal consideration."

"The percentage that [the] option purchase price bears to the list price, especially if it is less than 25%, is to be considered as showing the intent of the parties to make a lease as security," *In re Fashion Optical, Ltd.*, 653 F.2d at 1389.

The Agreement itself posits that, after 50 months, the vehicle will have only scrap value. The actual list price of vehicles does not appear, nor do any estimates in dollars of their scrap value. It seems highly probable that any motor vehicle's scrap value must be far less than its list price when the vehicle is new — far less even than 25% of list price. Therefore, this purchase option price would be for "nominal consideration." Unfortunately, such prices and values are not in evidence. Under the circumstances, the Court has no choice but to continue its inquiry.

Option purchase price may be "nominal" regardless of any percentage of list price, "where the terms of the lease and option to purchase are such that the only sensible course for the lessee at the end of the lease term is to exercise the option and become the owner of the goods," *In re Fashion Optical, Ltd.*, 653 F.2d at 1389.

Here, after 50 months lessee can either sell the car to another and pocket the proceeds, buy the vehicle, or continue to use the vehicle for "rent" of $ 3.00 per month. Rather than accumulate a fleet of old, worn-out cars, Otasco is very likely to sell the vehicles to others and pocket the proceeds. The Lessee therefore might well refuse to exercise its option to become the owner of the goods themselves. The Court cannot say that "the only sensible course for the lessee . . . . is to exercise the option and become the owner of the goods."

The Court strongly suspects that the option purchase price is "nominal" yet the Court must conclude that Otasco has failed to demonstrate the point by admitted evidence.

In *In re Loop Hospital Partnership*, it is said that "It is this court's opinion that the express or implied option plus a nominal fair market value are both necessary to create a security interest," *Loop Hospital,* 35 Bankr. at 934. That statement appears to be dictum, and is not followed by this Court, since it unduly restricts the fact-specific inquiry called for by U.C.C. § 1-201(37) and is contrary to other authorities cited immediately below. In any event, the Loop Hospital case is distinguishable, as is discussed in due course below.

"If the option does require greater than nominal consideration for full ownership, a true lease is usually found," *In re Fashion Optical, Ltd.*, 653 F.2d at 1389. However, "usually" does not mean invariably. "Thus, even though nothing in the 'lease' may permit purchase at nominal consideration, the 'lease' will still be deemed one intended as security if the facts otherwise expose economic realities tending to confirm that a secured transfer of ownership is afoot," *id.*, citing *In re Tulsa Port Warehouse Co.*, 4 Bankr. 801, (N.D. Okla. 1980) aff'd, 690 F.2d 809 (10th Cir. 1982). This Court reviewed and analyzed the *Tulsa Port* doctrine at length in *In re Breece, supra,* and applied it in *In re Harvey, supra,* and recently in *In re Thompson, supra.* Those principles must now be applied herein. In those cases, secured transactions were shown by: (1) the concentration of all incidents of ownership of the vehicles, save bare legal title, in lessee; (2) the effect of termination provisions, which established an equity in the vehicles in lessee and removed any reversionary interest from lessor; (3) economic equivalence of the transactions with secured sales or loans.

Here, "as a practical matter, the lessee [holds] all the incidence of ownership except bear legal title," *In re Breece,* 58 Bankr. at 387 (quoting *Tulsa Port,* 690 F.2d at 812). In this respect, the Agreement herein is equivalent to a secured transaction.

Here, the termination provisions are of an "open-end" type in which the vehicle must be sold, the sale proceeds are credited against lessee's monetary obligation, any excess is credited to lessee, and any deficiency is made up by lessee. Thus, the lessee bears the risk of loss or the expectation of gain upon disposition of each vehicle. Such provisions indicate an equity in the lessee, and therefore a lease intended as security, *In re Breece, supra*, and *In re Tulsa Port, supra.*

Here, where the vehicle must be sold, and the sale is essentially for the benefit of the lessee, there is no true lease-like reversion in the lessor. From the outset of the "lease," the lessor gives up any expectation of recovering the vehicles themselves, and any expectation of recovering their value beyond a set amount. Upon sale, of course, the lessor will cease to hold even bare legal title to the vehicle. "It is indeed a curious 'lease' whose termination, rather than restoring full ownership to the lessor, extinguishes whatever ownership had remained in the lessor during the lease term," *In re Breece,* 58 Bankr. at 385 n.4. In this respect also, the termination provisions of this Agreement indicate a lease intended as security.

"The final test is whether the transactions are economically equivalent with secured sales or loans — if so, they are to be treated as such. This test calls for evaluation of the real-world operation of these leases, including all the factors discussed so far, considered not separately but in combination . . . .," *In re Thompson, supra.*

Despite lack of actual sale prices and such dollar amounts in evidence, and despite the apparently calculated obscurity of lease terms such as "reserve" and "stipulated cost," the economic effect of this Agreement can be inferred from the contractual provisions themselves. Lessor will get "stipulated cost" plus 29.3742% over 50 months — the same amounts even if the lease term ends earlier than 50 months — and the right to take back the car, sell it, and deduct those amounts if the lessee does not pay. Lessor irrevocably gives up any other rights in the vehicle at the inception of the "lease" and cannot take the vehicle back unless the lessee defaults. The lessee gets a vehicle which he can treat as his own, and either keep as long as he likes or sell when he likes, provided he pays the lessor the pre-determined cost plus 29.3742%, either by installment or from sale proceeds or by paying off the balance in a "balloon" payment at term end. Such an arrangement is indistinguishable from a secured sale.

In *In re Loop Hospital Partnership, supra,* the court held that a lease of hospital equipment was a true lease because there was no option to purchase (not even an implied option), the lease term apparently ended after only five years, there was no evidence to indicate that the property's useful life was exhausted or that the parties intended any continuation of the lease, lessee was required to return the property to lessor, and there was no evidence to indicate that the property or its value would in any manner be retained by the lessee. That case is clearly distinguishable on its facts from the situation herein.

The Court concludes that this Agreement is not a true lease but is intended as security. As such, it must be treated as a secured transaction. Lessor's interest in this vehicle is not an ownership interest but a security interest.

This discussion may be closed, and the next subject introduced, with this observation:

It is a bit mystifying that drafters continue to churn out such sham leases—apparently even fooling themselves into believing they need not file—especially since unrelated benefits of the lease characterization, such as tax benefits, have largely disappeared, James A. Martin, "*Secured Transactions*," 19 Wayne Law Review 598, 611-612 (1973); and see *In re Thompson,* 101 Bankr. 658, 675 (B.C. N.D. Okla. 1989).

II. WHETHER THE SECURITY INTEREST IS PERFECTED

Wheels proposes that, "even assuming that the lease is one intended for security, the listing of Wheels as owner on the certificates of title is sufficient to perfect Wheels' security interest," for the reason that: "Wheels's [sic] denomination as owner on the motor vehicles' Certificates of Title puts third parties on notice of Wheels' interest. As a result, Wheels has substantially complied with the procedure for perfection of a security interest under Oklahoma law," Wheels' brief p. 14.

In this Chapter 11 case, Otasco is a debtor-in-possession, 11 U.S.C. § 1101(1) there is no trustee. However, the debtor-in-possession's powers are derived from those of a trustee, 11 U.S.C. § 1107(a) In the following discussion, reference to "the trustee" includes the debtor-in-possession.

Where a "lease" is intended as security, the "lessee" has in fact bought the chattel and is the true owner of it. When the "lessee" enters bankruptcy, his ownership interest in the chattel becomes property of his bankruptcy estate, 11 U.S.C. § 541(a)(1) This interest, in turn, is legally managed and represented by the estate's trustee (or debtor-in-possession), 11 U.S.C. § 323, § 1107(a) — in effect, his ownership interest is inherited by his bankruptcy trustee. The trustee's basic duty is to allocate the Debtor's assets among the Debtor's creditors. This proceeding is analogous to an equity receivership and is inherently equitable in nature. As a rule, "equality is equity," and the ideal rule of distribution of assets in satisfaction of pre-petition claims is that all creditors are given equal *(i.e.,* pro rata) shares of the available assets or their proceeds, 3 (Pt. 2) Collier on Bankruptcy para. 60.01, 743 (14th ed. 1978); 4B Collier on Bankruptcy para. 70.45, 557-558 (14th ed. 1978); Report of the Commission on the Bankruptcy Laws of the United States, July 1973, Pt. 1 p. 213-218; H.R.Rep.No. 95-595 at 178. There are some exceptions to the ideal rule of equal distribution, which exceptions permit some creditors to receive more than their pro rata share of available assets, at the expense of the other creditors. For reasons stated in the preceding sources, such exceptions are not favored. For example, creditors with security interests in specific items of estate property naturally attempt to reserve such collateral items for themselves, in spite of the trustee's attempts to liquidate the items and divide the proceeds equally among all creditors. Under some circumstances, such "selfish" creditors' efforts are allowed to succeed.

Although the trustee inherits the debtor's interest in property, the trustee's right (if any) to keep specific items of collateral as against the "selfish" claims of secured creditors is determined by giving the trustee certain creditor's rights. Under the former Bankruptcy Act, the trustee shall have as of the date of bankruptcy the rights and powers of: (1) a creditor who obtained a judgment against the bankrupt upon the date of bankruptcy, whether or not such a creditor exists, (2) a creditor who upon the date of bankruptcy obtained an execution returned unsatisfied against the bankrupt whether or not such a creditor exists, and (3) a creditor who upon the date of bankruptcy obtained a lien by legal or equitable proceedings upon all property, whether or not coming into possession or control of the court, upon which a creditor of the bankrupt upon a simple contract could have obtained such a lien whether or not such a creditor exists, Act Sec. 70c (quoted in 4A Collier on Bankruptcy 4 (14th ed. 1978)). This provision, first introduced in 1910, has been called the "strong arm clause" of the bankruptcy laws. It was said to confer upon the trustee "a status with the consequent capacity to act, just as if he were in actuality a creditor of the kind to which the provision refers," 4B Collier on Bankruptcy para. 70.46, 559 (14th ed. 1978). Of the kinds of creditors mentioned in Act § 70c, the most important was the judicial lien creditor. "The term 'lien creditor' will generally be used as a shorthand expression . . . to denote the status conferred upon the trustee by the strong-arm clause," *id.* at para. 70.45, 560 n.12. The "strong-arm clause" appears in the present Bankruptcy Code as 11 U.S.C. § 544(a) which provides in pertinent part as follows:

> The trustee shall have as of the commencement of the case, and without regard to any knowledge of the trustee or of any creditor the rights and powers of, or may avoid any transfer of property of the debtor or any obligation incurred by the debtor that is voidable by —
>
> (1) a creditor that extends credit to the debtor at the time of the commencement of the case, and that obtains, at such time and with respect to such credit, a judicial lien on all property on which a creditor on a simple contract could have obtained such a judicial lien, whether or not such a creditor exists; . . . .The trustee is not himself a judicial lien creditor; but Federal law directs that he be treated as if he were one, for purposes of ascertaining the strength and priority of his claim to collateral as against other creditors. The rights of lien creditors to goods such as motor vehicles as against other secured creditors are determined by the commercial laws of the various States, and nowadays by the State versions of the Uniform Commercial Code. These state laws are, in effect, adopted by Federal law for bankruptcy purposes. The state commercial laws are adopted by Federal law merely to provide a convenient rule for fixing the trustee's rights and priorities as against certain creditors. One merely inserts the trustee onto the ladder of creditor priorities at the prescribed level — that of the lien creditor as of the date of bankruptcy — and observes whether he is higher or lower than the creditor(s) in question. If the trustee has higher priority, he has prior claim to the collateral and can liquidate it for the benefit of all creditors of the bankruptcy estate. If the trustee has lower priority, he must acknowledge the prior claim to the collateral of the secured creditor in question. In practice, the trustee will surrender the collateral or its value to the particular secured creditor, and the other creditors of the bankruptcy estate get no part of the value of that particular item. Since the trustee is not himself a lien creditor, yet has rights equivalent to one, he is spoken of as an "ideal", "hypothetical" or "artificial" lien creditor.

"The trustee in bankruptcy . . . by force of law, stands here as the ideal creditor, irreproachable and without notice, armed cap-a-pie with every right and power that is conferred by the law of the state upon its most favored creditor who has acquired a lien by legal or equitable proceedings," *In re Waynesboro Motor Co.,* 60 F.2d 668, 669 (D.Ct. S.D. Miss. 1932). "In effect, as of the date of bankruptcy, the trustee has the whole bundle of rights by virtue of his purely hypothetical status," 4B Collier para. 70.50, 614 (14th ed. 1978). It is Federal law which gives the trustee the status of a lien creditor, though State law determines what the rights enjoyed by creditors of that status shall be.

And what are the rights and powers of a judicial lien creditor? State laws, and in particular the original Uniform Commercial Code § 9-301(3), drew a distinction between lien creditors without knowledge of prior security interests, and lien creditors with knowledge of prior security interests. The former had priority over prior unperfected security interests; the latter did not. (For present purposes, no distinction need be attempted between "knowledge" and "notice," or "actual" versus "inquiry" knowledge or notice, etc. See U.C.C. Secs. 1-201(25), 9-301(1)(b), and *U.S. v. Ed Lusk Const. Co., Inc.*,, 504 F.2d 328 (10th Cir. 1974).)) The whole purpose of giving a bankruptcy trustee lien creditor status was to provide a means of determining his priority as against secured creditors-but which lien creditor status, "without knowledge" and prior, or "with knowledge" and inferior, is inured to the trustee? Given the purpose and intended operation of the "strong-arm clause," it was held "obvious that the words 'without notice' are embodied by necessary implication in the language of the Act," *Matter of Ford-Rennie Leather Company,* 2 F.2d 750, 756 (D.C. Del. 1924); see generally, 4B Collier on Bankruptcy para. 70.53, 636-38 (14th ed. 1978) and cases cited on p. 636-637 n. 10. It followed that perfected security interests had priority over bankruptcy trustees; but bankruptcy trustees had priority over unperfected security interests.

This simple scheme was muddled in practice by some unfortunate misconceptions. A bankruptcy trustee is not a mere assignee of creditors, but an officer empowered by Federal law to act in furtherance of Federal purposes. Yet, certain authorities insisted on treating this Federal officer as if he had no rights of his own, but was merely a representative of a particular assortment of actual creditors of a bankrupt. According to this theory, the trustee's powers were no greater than the sum of the rights and powers of the actual group of creditors which he "represented" in bankruptcy; hence, where the bankrupt's creditors were all "with knowledge" of a secured transfer, it was proposed that the bankruptcy trustee himself must be a "lien creditor with knowledge" and accordingly must lack priority even over unperfected security interests.

Under many, if not most, state statutes relating the recordation of various instruments of transfer, it is the rule that before a creditor is permitted to prevail over an unrecorded transfer by virtue of his own lien through legal process or other status sufficient under the particular law, the creditor must achieve such status without actual notice of the unrecorded security interest. The Uniform Commercial Code renders an unperfected security interest subordinate to the claims of intervening lien creditors without notice, in § 9-301(1)(b), and by definition in Subsection (3) includes the trustee in bankruptcy within the term lien creditor. That subsection goes on to provide that unless "all creditors had knowledge of the security interest such a representative of creditors [*e.g.,* the trustee] is a lien creditor without knowledge even though he personally has knowledge of the security interest." This would mean that if all creditors did have such a knowledge, it would be imputed to the trustee, as a matter of state law. Accordingly, the question has occasionally arisen as to whether or not the fact that all the creditors of the bankrupt had actual notice of the transfer in question has any bearing on the trustee's rights under the strong-arm clause. At first blush this seems to call for a quick and obvious answer . . . . But a few courts have exhibited some confused thinking on the matter, hence an analysis of the problem is in order.

A number of factors have contributed towards the difficulty of solution: the general principle in bankruptcy that the trustee represents the creditors of the estate has tended to make some courts forget the hypothetical or artificial status accorded the trustee under the strong-arm clause . . . . even after the amendment of 1910 first added the strong-arm clause to the Act it was difficult for a number of small courts to dispel the former notion that the trustee was always bound by the rights of some actual creditor of the estate . . . . a few courts found it difficult to accept the implications of the Bankruptcy Act that the distributees of the proceeds of a recovery by the trustee should include creditors who could not have recovered by nonbankruptcy law . . . .

With these factors in mind, it is easier to understand those decisions that have held in effect that before the trustee can prevail under the § 70c . . . . he must represent at least one creditor who did not have actual notice of the transfer sought to be avoided. It is impossible to reconcile such a holding with the now well settled principles concerning the trustee's status under § 70c. As demonstrated previously, the trustee is accorded an "ideal" status — he is the "perfect" creditor who has complied with all requirements necessary under the applicable law for a lien by legal or equitable process. He has such status irrespective of whether there are actually any such creditors in existence. He acquires his status from the Act, not from the creditors of the estate . . . . the fact that distribution may go to those that could not themselves have avoided the transfer has no bearing on the trustee's recovery or his status, for he recovers for the benefit of all and not on behalf of any one creditor or group of creditors. Consequently, the better reasoned cases have held that the trustee under § 70c has the status of a creditor without notice, and thus there is no necessity for demonstrating that he does or does not represent at least one actual creditor without notice . . . . Since the trustee has the ideal status of a creditor without notice, the question merely is one whether or not such a creditor could prevail under state law. 4B Collier on Bankruptcy para. 70.53, 634-637 (14th ed. 1978).

[Uniform Commercial Code § 9-301(3),] implies an attempt to impute knowledge to a trustee in bankruptcy, if all the creditors he represents had knowledge of the security interest. If the attempt . . . . is successful then an unperfected security interest would prevail against a trustee in bankruptcy under . . . . § 70c . . . . as long as all creditors had knowledge of it. It is not likely that the attempt will be successful because it does not conform to the language, intent and interpretation of § 70c. As stated previously . . . . the trustee is accorded an "ideal" status by § 70c; he is the "perfect" creditor who has complied with all requirements to obtain a judicial lien. He acquires his status from the Bankruptcy Act, not from the creditors of the estate. The better reasoned cases have held that the trustee under § 70c has the status of a creditor without notice; and thus there is no necessity for proving that he does or does not represent at least one actual creditor without notice, as § 9-301(3) would seem to require.

The language in § 9-301(3) is not in line with the weight of authority construing § 70c and should not be permitted to override it. *Id.*, at para. 70.62A[9] 727-728. In sum, it was "Congressional intent to keep the trustee free of knowledge as a matter of law," *id.* On occasion, courts deprived bankruptcy trustees of lien creditor status because all of the bankrupt's creditors had or should have had knowledge of an unperfected security interest. This either disregarded the "obvious" intent of the Bankruptcy Act, or allowed the State Commercial Codes to overrule the Federal Bankruptcy Act in violation of the Supremacy Clause of the United States Constitution, and was patently in error. Most courts declined so to contradict the Federal Bankruptcy Act and the Supremacy Clause, and allowed bankruptcy trustees to exercise lien creditor rights as a matter of the trustee's own status qua trustee, whether or not lien creditors without knowledge could actually occur in any particular bankruptcy case.

If any uncertainty remained, it should have been eliminated by enactment of the Bankruptcy Code in 1978. Section 544(a) expressly provides that the bankruptcy trustee "shall have" the rights and powers of a lien creditor "without regard to any knowledge of the trustee or of any creditor."

Since lien creditors themselves do not rely on any knowledge of prior security interests in obtaining their judgment liens, it made little sense to deny any of them lien creditor priority status based on the extent of their knowledge of prior unperfected security interests. Accordingly, the Uniform Commercial Code itself was amended to delete from § 9-301(1)(b), (3) the references to "knowledge." This removed any conflict between the Uniform Commercial Code and the bankruptcy laws on this point. As the U.C.C. now stands, lien creditor status is not affected by any knowledge of prior unperfected security interests.

Within the limits of the present discussion, it can accurately be said that the Bankruptcy Code cares nothing for notice, and neither does the modern Uniform Commercial Code.

To the extent Wheels' argument would revive the ancient heresy, and impute creditors' "notice" to the bankruptcy trustee or debtor-in-possession acting under the "strong-arm clause," such argument must be emphatically rejected.

Since Wheels cannot use "notice" to demote the debtor-in-possession from judicial lien creditor status, Wheels attempts instead to use "notice" to promote itself to perfected secured creditor status. The effect is much the same: either way, the fact that all actual creditors would have had notice is said to deny priority to the debtor-in-possession who has no notice. Wheels' subtle variation on the old heresy does involve some additional factors and principles of law, and so must be examined and dealt with on its own terms. Instead of U.C.C. § 9-301(1)(b), (3) Wheels relies on U.C.C. 9-402(8) and its rule of "substantial compliance."

Pursuant to Uniform Commercial Code § 9-302(1) security interests must be perfected by filing a financing statement meeting the requirements of § 9-402, except as otherwise provided. One of the exceptions is 12A O.S. § 9-302(1)(h),

> (h) A security interest in a vehicle as defined in Section 23.2b of Title 47 of the Oklahoma Statutes for which a certificate of title may be properly issued by the Oklahoma Tax Commission, except as otherwise provided for in Section 23.2b of Title 47 of the Oklahoma Statutes, which in-turn appears duplicative of the provisions of 12A O.S. § 9-302(3), which provides in pertinent part as follows:

The filing of a financing statement otherwise required by this article is not necessary or effective to perfect a security interest in property subject to:

> . . . .
>
> (b) a statute of this state that provides for central filing of, or that requires indication or delivery for indication on a certificate of title or, any security interests in the property, but, during any period in which collateral is inventory held for sale by a person who is in the business of selling goods of that kind, the filing provisions of Sections 9-401 et seq. of this title apply to a security interest in that collateral created by him as debtor; . . . .

12A O.S. § 9-302(4) further provides:

> Compliance with a statute or treaty described in subsection (3) of this section is equivalent to the filing of a financing statement pursuant to the provisions of this article, and a security interest in property subject to the statute or treaty can be perfected only by compliance with such statute or treaty except as provided for in Section 9-103.1 of this title on multiple state transactions.

The statute referred to in 12A O.S. § 9-302(3), (4) is part of the Oklahoma Vehicle License and Registration Act, formerly 47 O.S. § 23.2b, now 47 O.S. § 1110, which provides in pertinent part as follows:

> A. 1. Except for a security interest in vehicles held by a dealer for sale or lease . . . . a security interest, as defined in Section 1-201 of Title 12A of the Oklahoma Statutes, in a vehicle as to which a certificate of title may be properly issued by the Oklahoma Tax Commission shall be perfected only when a lien entry form prescribed by the Commission,

and the existing certificate of title, if any, or application for a certificate of title and manufacturer's certificate of origin containing the name and address of the secured party and the date of the security agreement and the required fee are delivered to the Commission or to a motor license agent . . . . The filing and duration of perfection of a security interest, pursuant to the provisions of Title 12A of the Oklahoma Statutes, including, but not limited to, Section 9-302 of Title 12A of the Oklahoma Statutes, shall not be applicable to perfection of security interests in vehicles as to which a certificate of title may be properly issued by the Commission, except as to vehicles held by a dealer for sale or lease . . . . In all other respects Title 12A of the Oklahoma Statutes shall be applicable to such security interests in vehicles as to which a certificate of title may be properly issued by the Commission.

2. Whenever a person creates a security interest in a vehicle, such person shall surrender to the secured party the certificate of title or the signed application for a new certificate of title, ... and the manufacturer's certificate of origin. The secured party shall deliver the lien entry form and the required lien filing fee within ten (10) days as provided hereafter with certificate of title or the application for certificate of title and the manufacturer's certificate of origin to the Commission or to a motor license agent. If the lien entry form, the lien filing fee and the certificate of title or application for certificate of title and the manufacturer's certificate of origin are delivered to the Commission or to a motor license agent within ten (10) days after the date of the lien entry form, perfection of the security interest shall begin from the date of the execution of the lien entry form, but, otherwise, perfection of the security interest shall begin from the date of the delivery to the Commission or to a motor license agent.

3. a. For each security interest recorded on a certificate of title, or manufacturer's certificate of origin, such person shall pay a fee of Ten Dollars ($ 10.00), ... Upon the receipt of the lien entry form and the required fees with either the certificate of title or an application for certificate of title and manufacturer's certificate of origin, a motor license agent shall, by placement of a clearly distinguishing mark, record the date and number shown in a conspicuous place, on each of these instruments . . . .

5. Any person creating a security interest in a vehicle that has been previously registered in the debtor's name and on which all taxes due the state have been paid shall surrender the certificate of ownership to the secured party. The secured party shall have the duty to record the security interest as provided in this section and shall, at the same time, obtain a new certificate of title which shall show the secured interest on the fact of such certificate of title.

6. The lien entry form with the date and assigned number thereof clearly marked thereon shall be returned to the secured party . . . .

7. The Commission shall have the duty to record the lien upon the face of the certificate of title issued at the time of registering and paying all fees and taxes due on such vehicle.

B. 1. A secured party shall, within fifteen (15) business days after the satisfaction of such security interest, furnish directly or by mail a release of a security interest to the Commission and mail a copy thereof to the last-known address of the debtor. If the secured party fails to furnish such release as herein required, the secured party shall be liable to the debtor for a penalty of One Hundred Dollars ($ 100.00) and, in addition, any loss caused to the debtor by such failure . . . .

C. The Commission shall file and index certificates of title so that at all times it will be possible to trace a certificate of title to the vehicle designated therein, identify the lien entry form, and the names and addresses of secured parties, or their assignees, so that all or any part of such information may be made readily available to those who make legitimate inquiry of the Commission as to the existence or nonexistence of security interest in the vehicle.

These provisions may be summarized as follows: under Oklahoma law, security interests in motor vehicles are perfected not by filing financing statements pursuant to 12A O.S. § 9-302(1), 9-401 et seq., but only by delivery of a lien entry form and payment of the required fee to the Oklahoma Tax Commission. The secured creditor must, in effect, identify itself as such by submitting a lien entry form designating the secured creditor as such; pay the prescribed fee therefor; release the security interest in due course, or owe certain penalties to the debtor; and provide such information in the lien entry form as will permit the Oklahoma Tax Commission to answer any request as to whether a particular vehicle is subject to a security interest. These requirements must be met whether the vehicle is new or not, and regardless of what may or may not appear on any certificate of title. The lien entry form is required in addition to any certificate of title or application therefor. It is the lien entry form which will cause the Oklahoma Tax Commission to note the lien as such on the certificate of title, to index it accordingly, and thus enable it to ascertain, on request, whether any particular vehicle is subject to a security interest. This method is exclusive—if it is not complied with, there is no perfection, *Liberty Nat'l Bank & Trust Co. of Okla. City v. Garcia,* 686 P.2d 303 (Okla. 1984), *In re Thompson,* 101 Bankr. 658 (B.C. N.D. Okla. 1989), *In re Breece,* 58 Bankr. 379 (B.C. N.D. Okla. 1986), *In re The Chief Freight Lines Co.,* 37 Bankr. 436 (B.C. N.D. Okla. 1984), *In re Haning,* 35 Bankr. 242 (B.C. N.D. Okla. 1983). For an exception specified by statute, see 12A O.S. § 9-103.1; *In re Foster*, 611 P.2d 232 (Okla. 1980); *In re B & S Motor Freight, Inc.,* 59 Bankr. 259 (B.C. N.D. Okla. 1986).

U.C.C. § 9-402 , prescribes the requirements of a financing statement, and para. (8) thereof provides that "A financing statement substantially complying with the requirements of this section is effective even though it contains minor errors which are not seriously misleading." Since Section 9-402 deals only with financing statements, it has no necessary application to methods of perfection other than financing statements (such as certificates of title, lien entry forms, and other devices required by State motor vehicle laws in lieu of financing statements). The motor vehicle laws themselves may call for strict compliance with their requirements, or they may permit deviations comparable to the treatment of financing statements in Section 9-402. How liberally a motor vehicle act should be read depends, in the last analysis, on the motor vehicle act itself, and not on Section 9-402(8). For example, if a motor vehicle act authorized by 12A O.S. § 9-302(1)(h), (3)(b) expressly stated that "Compliance with this Act is strictly required regardless of 12A O.S. § 9-402(8)," then strict compliance with its terms would be required. A similar legislative intent might be implied by various provisions of the motor vehicle act, even if not expressly stated. The point is that Section 9-402 applies of its own force only to financing statements and need not apply in any way to non-financing-statement devices. No court is justified in jumping to the conclusion that any particular motor vehicle act must be read in light of Section 9-402(8). This is expressly stated in 12A O.S. § 9-302(4), and is suggested by the limited adoption of "the filing provisions of Sections 9-401 et seq." by 12A O.S. § 9-302(3)(b).

As noted above, 47 O.S. § 110(A)(1) provides in part that "the filing and duration of perfection of a security interest, pursuant to the provisions of Title 12A of the Oklahoma Statutes, including, but not limited to, Section 9-302 of Title 12A of the Oklahoma Statutes, shall not be applicable to perfection of security interests in vehicles . . . . except as to vehicles held by a dealer for sale or lease. In all other respects Title 12A of the Oklahoma Statutes shall be applicable to such security interests in vehicles . . . ." The statutory language is ambiguous: it might be read to forbid application of 12A O.S. § 9-402(8) to perfection of security interests in vehicles; or it might be read to require application of 12A O.S. § 9-402(8) to perfection of security interests in vehicles. In *In re Hembree: Woodson v. General Motors Acceptance Corp.,* 635 P.2d 601 (Okla. 1981) and *In re Cook: Woodson v. Ford Motor Credit Co.,* 637 P.2d 588 (Okla. 1981), the Oklahoma Supreme Court held that 12A O.S. § 9-402(5), now (8), did apply to the Oklahoma Motor Vehicle Act's provisions prescribing the method of perfecting security interests in motor vehicles. Those opinions do not mention the ambiguous language of the Motor Vehicle Act itself, nor take account of either the express provisions of 12A O.S. § 9-304(2) or the negative implication of 12A O.S. § 9-302(3)(b). But they are the Oklahoma Supreme Court's latest word on the matter, and will be followed by this Court.

The purpose of U.C.C. Section 9-402(8) is made clear by the draftsmen's comments on the U.C.C. official text, carried over without change (except for renumbering of the subsection) from the comments on the original subsection 9-402(5), as follows:

> Subsection (8) is in line with the policy of this Article to simplify formal requisites and filing requirements and is designed to discourage the fanatical and impossibly refined reading of such statutory requirements in which courts have occasionally indulged themselves. As an example of the sort of reasoning which this subsection rejects, see *General Motors Acceptance Corporation v. Haley,* 329 Mass. 559, 109 N.E.2d 143 (1952).

In the cited case, General Motors Acceptance Corporation ("GMAC") filed a "statement of trust financing receipt" intended to protect its security interest in various items of collateral. The debtor or "trustee's" correct name was " E. R. Millen Co., Inc." The statement named the trustee "E. R. Millen Company," was signed by " E. R. Millen Trustee," and included the trustee's correct address and a correct description of the collateral. The trial court held the statement fatally defective because it did not contain the trustee's correct name. On appeal, GMAC argued that the statute merely requires that the trustee be so designated that a creditor or other interested person would not be misled as to the identity of the trustee; and here, it is said, no one could be deceived because of the resemblance of name, the identity of address, and the description of the goods acquired by the trustee, *GMAC,* 109 N.E.2d at 146. Nevertheless, the Massachusetts Supreme Court affirmed the trial court—a ruling which certainly merits the U.C.C. draftsmen's description as "fanatical and impossibly refined."

The purpose of Section 9-402(8), then, is to validate financing statements which contain essentially complete and correct information, save for "minor errors" of the sort appearing in *GMAC v. Haley, e.g.*, variances among "Inc.," "Co." and "Company," and other such trivial inaccuracies of commission or omission which do not render the financing statement essentially false or do not "amount to substantial non-compliance," 49 Op. Atty. Gen. Md. 476 (1984), 2 U.C.C.R. 108, 110. Whether errors are "minor" or are "seriously misleading" depends on the facts of each case, *In re Strickland*, 94 Bankr. 898 (B.C. N.D. Miss. 1988), *In re Service Lawn & Power, Inc.,* 83 Bankr. 515 (B.C. E.D. Tenn. 1988), *First Agri Services, Inc. v. Kahl,* 129 Wis. 2d 464, 385 N.W.2d 191 (Ct.App.Wis. 1986), *In re Mount,* 5 U.C.C.R. 653 (D.Ct. S.D. Ohio 1968); and on factors such as good faith, commercial reasonableness, the substantive purpose of actual notice to creditors, the actual harm or lack of harm from deviations, and the need for enforcement of uniformity and regularity in compliance with statutory directives. The latter policy is especially important where the U.C.C. intermeshes with other laws, *In re Mount,* 5 U.C.C.R. at 655.

Oklahoma cases are few but are generally in accord. *Consolidated Equipment Sales, Inc. v. First State Bank & Trust Co. of Guthrie,* 627 P.2d 432 (Okla. 1981) is digested in Oklahoma Statutes Annotated under 12A O.S. § 9-402(8), but actually deals with sufficiency of description of collateral under § 9-402(1) and does not mention § 9-402(8) at all. *In re Hembree: Woodson, Trustee v. General Motors Acceptance Corp.,* 635 P.2d 601 (Okla. 1981) validated a lien entry form which was not signed by the secured party, noting that such signature was not specifically required by the statute, 47 O.S. § 23.2b, and "it is conceded that the secured party is in full compliance with all other requirements and the form has been properly filed," *Hembree,* 635 P.2d at 604. *In re Cook: Woodson, Trustee v. Ford Motor Credit Co.,* 637 P.2d 588 (Okla. 1981) validated a lien entry form which "contains all of the statutorily required information" but also included "an 18-day error in the notation of the date" of the security agreement, *Cook,* 637 P.2d at 590. The court cited with approval other rulings that total omission of an item specifically required by statute was a "major" and not a "minor" error, and that "major" error constituting "substantial failure to comply with the statutory requirement" was not excused by § 9-402(8); see *In re Cook, supra,* 637 P.2d at 590, citing *In re Benson,* 3 U.C.C.R. 272 (D.Conn. 1966) and *In re Vielleux,* 5 U.C.C.R. 277 (D.Conn. 1967).

In the case now before this Court, the certificates of title misname the secured party as the "owner," do not contain the real owner's name or address at all, and do not disclose the existence, let alone the date, of any security agreement. These misstatements and omissions are not inadvertent but are deliberate and intentional, committed in furtherance of a scheme to misrepresent the true nature of the transaction between these parties and the role (and in that sense, at least, the "identity") of the secured party herein. Such intentional deviations from accuracy are not "errors" at all, in the usual sense of that word indicating mistakes or accidents. Since they are not "errors," they are not excused by Section 9-402(8), whether or not they are "minor." But if they are "errors," they are not "minor" ones. They are not comparable to the trivial slip-ups, equivalent to slight misspellings, in *GMAC v. Haley*. It is true that a persistent searcher might find in these certificates, read against a background of extrinsic evidence (*i.e.,* prior knowledge that the vehicles are in Otasco's hands), some hint of the existence, name and whereabouts of a disguised secured party. This alone does not convert major omissions into "minor" ones. According to Wheels, if a fault is not invariably fatal, then it isn't even serious. In any event, whatever is on the certificates of title, it must be observed that no lien entry form was ever delivered, or even attempted to be delivered, to the Oklahoma Tax Commission, and so of course the fee required therefor was never paid. According to Wheels, the total nondelivery of a lien entry form is "substantial compliance" with a statute requiring delivery of a lien entry form as a condition of perfection in no uncertain terms. If all this is "substantial compliance," it would seem that just about anything short of a certificate of title in blank must be "substantial compliance."

This is in essence what Wheels proposes. According to Wheels, there is enough information on the certificate of title (never mind how it got there) to suggest to a diligent inquirer (who already knows the extrinsic fact that the vehicles are actually in Otasco's hands) that something is amiss and that further inquiry is appropriate (and to direct inquiries to the proper place, Wheels' offices). Wheels says the mere giving of such information, however inaccurate or incomplete, constitutes perfection. In other words, says Wheels, notice is perfection. Wheels' approach, if approved, would demolish the U.C.C.'s policy of encouraging routine compliance with clear, simple, statutorily-prescribed methods of achieving perfection. It would do likewise to the Oklahoma Motor Vehicle Act's policy of enabling the Oklahoma Tax Commission to determine, by resort to lien entry forms, whether or not a given vehicle is subject to a security interest (since the Oklahoma Tax Commission cannot be expected to make reliable answer to the query whether some vehicle is subject to a security interest, if such answer depends on extrinsic evidence combined with implications or suggestions that may or may not arise from the face of the title absent any lien entry form). It is true that perfection is meant to give notice, but notice alone does not give perfection. Only perfection gives perfection. Perfection means giving such notice as is required by law, in the manner and to the extent prescribed by law. Nothing else will suffice to accomplish perfection. Here, Wheels may have given notice, of some sort, in some manner, in some degree. But Wheels certainly has not followed the procedure prescribed by 47 O.S. § 1110 as the "only" method by which Wheels could give such notice as would accomplish perfection. In *Liberty National Bank & Trust Co. of Oklahoma City v. Garcia,* 686 P.2d 303 (Okla. 1984), the Oklahoma Supreme Court held that it is delivery of a properly filled out lien entry form, and not notice of this or that, which accomplishes perfection of a security interest in a motor vehicle.

All things considered, the doubtful good faith of a secured creditor masquerading as a "lessor;" the complete omissions and misleading partial entries on the certificate of title; the total failure to deliver, or even attempt to deliver, a lien entry form as specifically required by statute; the intentional character of these acts and omissions; and the commercial unreasonableness of this attempt to turn a simple, forthright disclosure into a guessing game, the Court concludes that Wheels' noncompliance with 47 O.S. § 1110 is not "minor," is "seriously misleading," and does not rise to the dignity of "substantial compliance" under 12A O.S. § 9-402(8).

Given its systematic and extensive noncompliance with the statutory requirements for perfection, Wheels cannot be taken seriously when it claims "substantial compliance" with the statutory perfection requirements. Wheels simply did not perfect, and did not even attempt to perfect. Rather, Wheels concocted a procedure which, Wheels proposes, is the functional equivalent of perfection, because this improvised procedure gives somewhat the same notice as would be given by perfection. Wheels wants its do-it-yourself alternative to perfection treated as if it were "the real thing." Such a principle, if once admitted, would demolish the U.C.C.'s perfection scheme. But, in any event, in bankruptcy Wheels' attempted substitute for perfection fails. Despite all Wheels' machinations in "giving notice," the bankruptcy Trustee, as a matter of Federal law, has no notice. And, as discussed above, any attempts to smuggle notice to the Trustee into the Bankruptcy Code must fail. Since Wheels' interest is an unperfected security interest of which the bankruptcy Trustee has no notice, Wheels' interest is inferior to that of the Trustee.

Wheels cites *In re Circus Time, Inc.,* 641 F.2d 39 (1st Cir. 1981) to the contrary, and observes that

> The overwhelming majority of other courts that have decided this issue have adopted the First Circuit's rationale in *In re Circus Time* and have held that substantial compliance with Certificate of Title Acts by the listing of the lessor/seller as the owner on the certificate of title is sufficient to perfect a security interest in a motor vehicle. See, *e.g., In re Load-It Inc.,* 774 F.2d 1077 (11th Cir. 1985) (applying Georgia law); *In re National Welding of*

Michigan, Inc., 61 Bankr. 314 (W.D. Mich. 1986); *In re Carraway,* 65 Bankr. 51 (Bankr. E.D.N.C. 1986) (dictum); *In re Yeager Trucking,* 29 Bankr. 131 (Bankr. D. Colo. 1983); *In re McCall,* 27 Bankr. 106 (Bankr. W.D.N.Y. 1983); *In re Loague,* 25 Bankr. 940 (Bankr. N.D.Miss. 1982); *In re Coors of the Cumberland Inc.,* 19 Bankr. 313 (Bankr. M.D.Tenn. 1982); *In re Trivett,* 12 Bankr. 373 (Bankr. E.D.Tenn. 1981) (applying Indiana law),

Wheels' brief p. 17. To this list may be added *In re Thummel: Kirtley, Trustee v. General Motors Acceptance Corporation et al,* 109 Bankr. 447, (N.D. Okla. 1989).

To the extent that *In re Circus Time, Inc.,* and its progeny, conflict with the views herein expressed, those cases would seem to deviate from the weight of authority under the former Bankruptcy Act, to disregard the Supremacy Clause and/or the express command of 11 U.S.C. § 544(a) to exaggerate the intended operation of U.C.C. § 9-402(8) and to confuse notice with perfection. To that extent, such cases are not persuasive and will not be followed by this Court. In any event, *In re Circus Time, Inc.*, is distinguishable in this respect: the State laws involved in *In re Circus Time, Inc.,* required notation of information on the face of certificates of title (not delivery of lien entry forms) to accomplish perfection; the secured creditor in *In re Circus Time, Inc.,* had managed to get at least some entries onto the face of the certificate of title, and the issue was whether such entries, though inaccurate and incomplete, "substantially complied" with the perfection requirements. In the present case, delivery of lien entry forms (not notation on the face of the title) is the sole means of perfection. There has been no delivery of any lien entry forms whatever in this case.

In *In re Thummel,* the Court, on the strength of an unduly expansive reading of *In re Hembree, supra,* and *In re Cook, supra,* held as follows:

> In light of these cases, the Court finds that GMAC's action in obtaining a certificate of title listing it as "owner" of the Vehicle gave notice to interested parties of its interest in the Vehicle so that no third party could be prejudiced by GMAC's failure to have its lien noted on the title. Therefore, under Oklahoma law, GMAC substantially complied with the requirements for perfecting its security interest, and the Court finds that such security interest is perfected. In reaching this conclusion, the Court respectfully declines to follow the decision of Judge Wilson in *In re Thompson [supra],* in which Judge Wilson concluded that "a security interest in a motor vehicle is perfected solely by delivery of a lien entry form to the Oklahoma Tax Commission . . . ." See *Thompson* at 677 . . . . It is not clear whether Judge Wilson considered the argument that lessors in *Thompson* had "substantially complied" with Oklahoma perfection requirements since there is no discussion of that issue. *In re Thummel*, slip opinion at 11. The ruling in *In Re Thompson,* 101 Bankr. 658 (B.C. N.D. Okla. 1989), that "a security interest in a motor vehicle is perfected solely by delivery of a lien entry form to the Oklahoma Tax Commission" merely paraphrases the language of the Oklahoma Motor Vehicle Act, Thompson, 101 Bankr. at 677. Courts are not at liberty to "decline to follow" the positive command of statutes. And total nondelivery of a lien entry form is total noncompliance with the statute; total noncompliance cannot be passed off as "substantial compliance." For these reasons, this Court respectfully declines to follow *In re Thummel.*

Wheels calls this result "inequitable," Wheels' brief p. 19. From a bankruptcy standpoint, Wheels' failure to perfect results in distribution of the proceeds of these vehicles among all creditors (including Wheels) pro rata, a highly equitable result. In attempting to keep these proceeds to itself, it is Wheels which seeks to deflect the usual course of equity. The precise issue presented is not a matter of "pure" bankruptcy law; and the Uniform Commercial Code's perfection provisions are legal and not equitable in nature. Wheels has not shown circumstances raising an estoppel or other equitable obstruction to the normal operation of the Uniform Commercial Code's perfection requirements. Wheels, which has deliberately misrepresented its status as a secured creditor, is in no position to demand any extraordinary interventions of equity in its behalf. Under such circumstances, equity follows the law. Wheels has simply failed to do what the law requires to accomplish perfection. Therefore, Wheels must suffer the consequences prescribed by the law for failure to perfect. The result satisfies both equity (in bankruptcy) and law (in the Uniform Commercial Code). AND IT IS SO ORDERED.

NOTES

(1) *Open-end v. closed-end leases.* Under an open-end lease the relationship between the lessee and lessor does not end at the termination of the lease. Instead, the lessee returns the goods to the lessor, and the lessor sells the goods, paying the lessee for any surplus and recapturing from the lessee any deficit. A closed-end lease directs the lessee to return the goods at the end of the lease, thereby terminating the relationship. Which seems more reliable? See *In re Tulsa Port Warehouse Co.*, 690 F.2d 809 (10th Cir. 1982), for a case indicating courts scrutinize open-end leases more rigorously for indicia of a security interest.

(2) *Erroneous Categorization.* The effect of a lessor erroneously categorizing its interest can be disastrous. If a court determines the parties intended a security agreement, and the lessor failed to file, the trustee relegates the lessor to the status of unsecured creditor. See § 9-301(1)(b) discussing lien creditor's superiority to unsecured parties.

(3) *Permissive Filing?* Does the lessor have any method of protecting its interest in the event a court determines the parties created a security interest? Official Comment 2 to § 9-408 indicates the lessor can permissive file to protect itself in such an event. Filing under this provision does not indicate the intention of the parties, so it protects the lessor from becoming an unsecured party. Given the small fee required, is it sound advice to encourage most of your clients to file even when they believe the transaction to be a lease?

§ 21.03 Fixtures

Read: U.C.C. § 9-313

Although Article 9 does not apply to real property transactions, it does specifically apply to real property transactions involving fixtures. U.C.C. § 9-313 A security interest may be created in goods which are fixtures or may continue in goods which become fixtures. U.C.C. § 9-313(2)

What goods are fixtures? Intuitively explained, "a fixture can . . . be defined as a thing which, although originally movable . . . , by reason of its annexation to, or association in use with land, [is] regarded as part of the land. The law of fixtures concerns those situations where the chattels annexed still retains a separate identity, in spite of annexation, for example a furnace or a light fixture." Brown, The Law of Personal Property 514-515 (3d ed. W. Raushenbush 1975). The Code recognizes three categories of goods: (1) those which retain their chattel character entirely and are not part of the real estate; (2) ordinary building materials which have become an integral part of the real estate and cannot retain their chattel character for purposes of finance; and (3) an intermediate class which has become real estate for certain purposes, but as to which certain financing may be preserved. This third and intermediate class is the primary subject of this section. Thus, the Code specifically excludes ordinary building materials that are incorporated into an improvement on land. Whether other goods integrally incorporated into the real estate are fixtures is determined by state law, which varies widely among jurisdictions.

How to Perfect: Fixture Filing. The term "fixture filing" emphasizes that when a filing is intended to give priority advantages against real estate interests, the filing must be in the office where a mortgage on the real estate would be filed. U.C.C. § 9-313 The filing must also comply with the additional requirements in § 9-402(1) & (5).

Priority: Perfected Security Interest in Fixtures vs. Encumbrancer or Owner of Real Estate. As a general rule of priority, a fixture filing gives the fixture secured party priority as against other real estate interests; that is, the first to file or record prevails. Official Comment 9-313(4)(b). The principal exception to this general rule of priority occurs in the area of purchase money security interests. The purchase money secured party will receive priority as against a prior recorded real estate interest, if that the purchase money secured party filed its interest as a fixture filing in the real estate records before the goods became fixtures, or within 10 days thereafter. Official Comment 9-313(4)(a). A special exception to the usual rule of priority based on precedence in time is in favor of holders of security interests in "readily removable" factory and office machines and "readily removable" replacements of domestic appliances which are consumer goods. In the case of these goods, the security interest can be perfected by any method permitted by this Article before the goods become fixtures. U.C.C. § 9-313

Perfection of Consumer Goods. Consumer goods automatically perfect under § 9-302(1)(d). Does the lessor holding removable consumer goods always have a perfected interest?

Traditional Test v. Institutional Doctrine. The traditional test focuses on the intention of the parties as indicated by the nature of the article affixed, circumstances and mode of the party affixing the article, and purpose for affixing the article. The institutional doctrine, on the other hand, focuses on whether the article is permanently essential to the completeness of the structure or use. If removal of the article would cause permanent damage to the structure or inhibit its use, the article is permanent. See *In re Corrugated Box Corp.*, 249 F.Supp. 56 (D.N.J. 1966). Remember to consult state law on the issue, since § 9-313(1) provides that state law determines the character of goods and when such goods become fixtures.

IN RE GAIN ELECTRONICS CORPORATION

United States Bankruptcy Court for the District of New Jersey
117 Bankr. 805, 13 U.C.C. Rep. Serv. 2d 265 (1990)

STEPHEN A. STRIPP, UNITED STATES BANKRUPTCY JUDGE.

First Fidelity Bank, N.A., North Jersey (hereinafter "FFB") has moved for a declaration of rights in the proceeds of sale of certain assets of the debtor. Movant FFB and respondent MDFC Equipment Leasing Corporation (hereinafter "MDFC") both claim entitlement to said proceeds. There are two issues. The first issue is whether FFB is estopped from claiming such entitlement. If FFB is not estopped, then the second issue is whether or not the assets in question were fixtures or improvements. If they were fixtures or improvements, FFB is entitled to the sale proceeds. If they were not fixtures or improvements, MDFC is entitled to the sale proceeds. This shall constitute the Court's finding of facts and conclusions of law.

I.

Gain Electronics Corporation (hereinafter "Gain" or "debtor") was in the business of manufacturing computer chips. For that purpose it leased premises at 22 Chubb Way, Branchburg, New Jersey from Pivot Realty Company Limited Partnership (hereinafter "Pivot). On January 29, 1986 Pivot entered into an agreement with FFB for a loan of $ 7.5 million for construction of the subject premises. On January 31, 1986 FFB recorded a mortgage securing the loan in the Somerset County Clerk's Office. The mortgage granted FFB a lien on the subject real property and on:

> . . . . all fixtures affixed to the same, or intended to be and also all equipment and improvements now in, upon or which may hereafter be installed or placed in or upon the same, adopted to or necessary for the complete and comfortable use, enjoyment or occupancy thereof, all of which shall be considered as real estate for all purposes to all persons.

In addition, U.C.C.-1 financing statements were filed with the Somerset County Clerk on January 31, 1986 and with the Secretary of State on February 5, 1986 granting FFB a lien on:

> . . . . all items of personal property owned by [Pivot] including, but not limited to . . . . all other equipment and machinery, tools, appliances, fittings, fixtures and building materials of any kind and whether or not affixed to the realty located at the premises.

Pivot and Gain had entered into their lease on November 27, 1985. Section 2.02 of the lease provided in pertinent part as follows:

> Title to all fixtures and improvements installed by Tenant [Gain] and paid for by the Landlord [Pivot] in the course of constructing the Clean Facility [the subject premises] shall become, upon installation, and shall remain the property of the Landlord; title to all other fixtures and improvements installed by Tenant, but not paid for by Landlord, shall remain the property of the Tenant during the term of this Lease, and shall revert to the Landlord upon the Expiration Date or sooner termination of this Lease except for all semiconductor processing equipment which shall remain the property of the Tenant, removable at any time.

As additional collateral for FFB's construction loan, Pivot assigned all of its rights in the lease to FFB on January 29, 1986. The assignment was recorded in the Somerset County Clerk's Office on January 31, 1986.

As a result of the foregoing, FFB perfected a first lien on all fixtures and improvements on the subject premises.

On July 30, 1987, MDFC leased certain semiconductor processing equipment to Gain for use on the subject premises. As security for its obligations under the lease, Gain gave MDFC a security interest in all of Gain's equipment and proceeds thereof. U.C.C.-1 financing statements perfecting MDFC's security interest in the equipment were filed with the Secretary of State on July 10, 1987. As a result, MDFC obtained a first lien on Gain's equipment.

II.

Gain filed a petition for relief under chapter 7 of the Bankruptcy Code on January 2, 1989. An involuntary petition was filed against Pivot, and an order for relief was entered on February 23, 1989. Both before and after the bankruptcy petitions, the parties attempted to sell Gain as a going concern to maximize the value received for its assets, but those efforts were unsuccessful. FFB then obtained title to the real property from Pivot's trustee. By order of June 21, 1989 MDFC obtained relief from the automatic stay and abandonment of the Gain estate's interest in the equipment leased by MDFC to enable MDFC to sell it to Boeing and Advantest Corporation (hereinafter "Boeing").

After consummation of that private sale, MDFC and Gain's trustee agreed to sell the remaining collateral which had been ordered abandoned to MDFC, together with other equipment belonging to the estate, at an auction sale on August 29, 1989. On July 26, 1989 the notice of sale required by Bankruptcy Rule 2002(a)(2) was sent to all of Gain's creditors. FFB received the notice. It provided that any objections to the auction sale had to be filed by August 21, 1989.

On August 25, 1989 FFB moved on one day's notice to MDFC for an order enjoining the auction which was scheduled for two business days thereafter. FFB claimed that it realized belatedly that MDFC proposed to sell three assets which FFB argues are fixtures or improvements: An Onan Amber Energy System Generator Model 150 ("the generator"); a Sullair Vacuum System Model SCSFR 2200-2 s/n 056-8496 ("the vacuum system"); and a Deionized Water System with fiberglass storage tank, RO filter system, ultrafilter system and assorted pumping system ("the water system"). The Court denied FFB's application to enjoin the auction, and instead directed that the proceeds of the sale of the three items in question would be held in escrow by the trustee pending resolution of the issue of entitlement to the proceeds.

At the auction FFB was the high bidder for the vacuum system at $3,500. and the water system at $45,000. A third party was the high bidder for the generator at $10,000. The trustee is holding the aggregate sale proceeds of $58,500 in escrow pending further order of the Court.

III.

MDFC notes that FFB did not object to MDFC's motion for relief from the automatic stay and abandonment of assets including the disputed items, which was granted by order of June 21, 1989. FFB also failed to file a timely objection to the auction. MDFC argues that those facts bar FFB's claim to the disputed items under principles of equitable estoppel, judicial estoppel and finality of judgments.

MDFC relies primarily on *Oneida Motor Freight, Inc. v. United Jersey Bank,* 848 F.2d 414 (3rd Cir.) cert. denied, 488 U.S. 967, 109 S. Ct. 495, 102 L. Ed. 2d 532 (1988). In *Oneida,* the debtor/plaintiff had breach of contract and tort claims against the secured creditor/defendant. However, the existence of the claims was never disclosed during the bankruptcy case. They were not scheduled as assets. They were not asserted at the time of entry of several orders adjudicating the bank's rights, including orders determining the extent and validity of the bank's lien and the amount of its debt, which was paid in full during the case. The debtor's claims were not disclosed in its plan of reorganization or in the disclosure statement filed in connection with the plan, which the bank voted to accept. Nor was there any mention of the claims in the order confirming the plan. The debtor filed suit against the bank seven months later.

The Court of Appeals for the Third Circuit affirmed the District Court's dismissal of the case. The Court of Appeals held that the debtor violated its duty under Bankruptcy Code § 1125 to disclose the existence of the claims in its disclosure statement. The Court also stated:

> We can assume that revealing the potential action may also have impacted upon the bank's decision to enter into the stipulation establishing the extent and validity of its lien against Oneida and to vote for confirmation. The practical effect of a successful prosecution of Oneida's claim would be to require the bank to make restitution of the amount realized

> on its bankruptcy claim, since Oneida's present action calls into question the bank's right to collect its secured debt. This would also constitute a successful collateral attack on the bankruptcy court's order confirming the reorganization plan. In such circumstances, employment of equitable estoppel is required to preserve the integrity of the earlier proceedings, particularly where, as here, the creditors have reasonably acted in reliance upon the assumed finality and integrity of those adjudications. *County Fuel Company v. Equitable Bank Corporation,* 832 F.2d 290 (4th Cir. 1987).

In order to preserve the requisite reliability of disclosure statements and to provide assurances to creditors regarding the finality of plans which they have voted to approve, we hold that under the facts here present Oneida's failure to announce this claim against a creditor precludes it from litigating the cause of action at this time. *Id.* at 418.

The Court of Appeals held that Oneida's claims against United Jersey Bank were barred by equitable estoppel for three reasons: first, Oneida breached its duty to disclose the claims in its disclosure statement; second, the bank relied to its detriment on Oneida's failure to disclose the claims at various points in the case; and third, to recognize the claims would constitute a successful collateral attack on the order confirming the plan.

Comparison of those factors with this case reveals that Oneida was quite different from this case. A creditor with a lien claim has no duty to disclose such claim, or to dispute priorities, on a motion by another creditor to vacate the automatic stay and for abandonment. Vacating the automatic stay means only that the movant can pursue its rights outside of the bankruptcy court. *In re Winslow,* 39 Bankr. 869, 871 (Bkrtcy. N.D. Ga. 1984). Abandonment means only that the bankruptcy estate has no further property interest in the assets in question. *In re Caron,* 50 Bankr. 27, 31-32 (Bkrtcy. N.D. Ga. 1984). As FFB correctly notes, granting such relief to one lienholder does not constitute any adjudication of the lien priorities. Hence FFB violated no duty to MDFC by failing to object to MDFC's motion to vacate the stay and for abandonment. Because relief from the automatic stay and abandonment do not constitute an adjudication of the priority of competing liens, FFB's motion is not a collateral attack on the order granting MDFC's motion to vacate the automatic stay and for abandonment.

Most importantly, MDFC has neither alleged nor shown how it relied to its detriment on FFB's failure to assert its claim. Detrimental reliance was one of the primary reasons for the holding in Oneida, and it is one of the elements which must be proven to establish the affirmative defense of equitable estoppel. *Heckler v. Community Health Services,* 467 U.S. 51, 59, 81 L. Ed. 2d 42, 104 S. Ct. 2218 (1984).

For the same reasons, the doctrine of judicial estoppel does not apply here either. Oneida and the other cases which MDFC cites in support of its estoppel arguments are distinguishable.

IV.

MDFC also argues that FFB's motion essentially seeks to reopen or modify the Court's order of June 21, 1989 granting MDFC relief from the automatic stay and abandonment. MDFC asserts that this motion does not comply with the standards set forth in Bankruptcy Rule 9024 incorporating Federal Rule of Civil Procedure 60(b) and cases thereunder. This argument is without merit for several reasons.

First, the order of June 21, 1989 grants relief from the automatic stay and abandonment of certain equipment listed on Exhibit A to the verified application of Michael D. Platt, Esq. in support of MDFC's motion. The disputed items were not listed on Exhibit A, which apparently contained only the equipment MDFC leased to Gain. The disputed items were instead on Exhibit B, which apparently was other equipment in which MDFC had a security interest. Thus the order of June 21, 1989, which was drafted by MDFC's attorneys, does not deal with the disputed items. FFB cannot be seeking a reopening or modification of an order which didn't address the items in question at all.

Second, the stated purpose of the order is to permit the sale of certain equipment to Boeing, and these items weren't among those sold to Boeing.

Third, as previously stated, vacating the automatic stay and abandonment do not constitute an adjudication of lien priorities, and such adjudication was not put in issue by MDFC's motion. Therefore, even if the order had granted relief as to the disputed items, it would not have disposed of the issue on this motion.

For these reasons, FFB's motion does not seek to reopen or modify the order of June 21, 1989 and MDFC's opposition on that basis must fail. The Court therefore does not have to address the question of whether FFB's motion would meet the standards of F. R. Civ. P. 60(b)

V.

The generator, vacuum system and water system in question were installed by Gain during construction of the premises. FFB alleges that they were all "physically bolted and annexed to the premises." MDFC does not dispute that the generator was affixed by bolts to a concrete slab, which the purchaser at the auction cut to remove the generator. MDFC alleges that the motors, tanks and filters for the water system and vacuum system "simply sat on the floor of the warehouse." MDFC admits that those systems also included extensive piping systems. However, MDFC alleges that most of the piping hung from ceiling rafters or ran outside of, rather than within, the walls of the facility.

Bankruptcy Rule 9017 incorporates F. R. Civ. P. 43, subsection (e) which provides that when a motion is based on facts not appearing of record the court may hear the matter on affidavits of the parties. The details regarding the extent to which the items in question were affixed to the premises were not of record prior to FFB's motion. Hence FFB had an obligation to present affidavits regarding those matters, which it failed to do. MDFC did present such affidavits. The Court therefore finds that the material facts regarding the extent to which the subject items were annexed to the premises are as alleged and admitted by MDFC in the preceding paragraph of this opinion.

As noted in Section I above, FFB had a perfected first lien on Gain's fixtures and improvements, and MDFC had a perfected first lien on Gain's equipment. The parties do not dispute that if the items in question are fixtures or improvements, the sale proceeds belong to FFB, and if the items were equipment, the proceeds belong to MDFC. The dispute is over the correct definitions of fixtures and improvements.

VI.

N.J.S.A. 12A:9-313(1)(a) states that "goods are 'fixtures' when they become so related to particular real estate that an interest in them arises under real estate law." The Official Comment to this section adds that " . . . . goods integrally incorporated into the real estate are clearly fixtures."

Readily removable factory machines can become fixtures. N.J.S.A. 12A:9-313(4)(c) However, neither N.J.S.A. 12A:9-313 nor any other provision of Title 12A specifies the criteria for determining the point at which goods "become so related to particular real estate that an interest in them arises under real estate law." N.J.S.A. 12A:9-313(8) does provide that a secured creditor who removes fixtures "must reimburse any encumbrancer or owner of the real estate who is not the debtor and who has not otherwise agreed for the cost of repair of any physical injury . . . .," but there is no guidance in the statute as to the relationship of the question of injury to the definition of fixtures.

Prior to the adoption in 1981 of the present version of N.J.S.A. 12A:9-313 the New Jersey courts had used two alternative tests for determining whether an item was a fixture, the "traditional test" and the "institutional doctrine."

Under the "traditional test," intention is the dominant factor. A chattel becomes a fixture when the party making the annexation intends a permanent accession to the freehold . . . . Under the "institutional doctrine," the test is whether the chattel is permanently essential to the completeness of the structure or its use. A chattel is a fixture if its severance from the structure would cause material damage to the structure or "prevent the structure from being used for the purposes for which it was erected or for which it has been adapted." [citations omitted] *In re Park Corrugated Box Corp.,* 249 F. Supp. 56, 58 (D. N.J. 1966).

However, when the present version of N.J.S.A. 12A:9-313 was adopted, it was the intention of the drafters that it would abrogate the institutional doctrine. Official Comment, *supra,* para. 9. That was confirmed in *City of Bayonne v. Port Jersey Corporation,* 79 N.J. 367, 376, 399 A.2d 649 (1979). MDFC argues that City of Bayonne also implicitly rejects the traditional test of intention as well.

City of Bayonne dealt with the question of whether certain giant cranes were real or personal property for purposes of taxation under N.J.S.A. 54:4-1 et seq. or 54:11A-1 et seq. Under N.J.S.A. 54:11A-2(b)(2) goods and chattels are personal property unless they are "so affixed to real property as to become part thereof and not to be severable or removable without material injury thereto." The New Jersey Supreme Court held in *City of Bayonne* as follows:

> We conclude, therefore, that the exclusion of "goods and chattels so affixed to real property as to become part thereof and not to be severable or removable without material injury thereto" appearing in N.J.S.A. 54:11A-2 should, looking solely to the language of the statute, be taken to mean only those chattels the removal of which will do irreparable or serious physical injury or damage to the freehold. *Id.* at 378.

Admittedly, *City of Bayonne* interpreted different statutes than N.J.S.A. 12A:9-313 However, the purpose was the same, *i.e.,* determining whether goods had become so affixed to realty as to lose their character as personalty. No reason is apparent from review of the statutes or otherwise for using one test for purposes of taxation and a different test for purposes of competition between private interests. Moreover, the definition in *City of Bayonne* is consistent with the suggestion in the Official Comment to 9:313 that goods are fixtures when they become "integrally incorporated into the real estate." Also, *City of Bayonne* relied heavily on N.J.S.A. 12A:9-313 its legislative history and learned treatises on it to reject the institutional doctrine for purposes of both taxation and article 9, without even suggesting that the distinction between realty and personalty should differ depending upon whether the question arose under Title 54 or Title 12A of the New Jersey statutes. Lastly, having the same test for all purposes serves a salutary public purpose of uniformity and avoidance of confusion. For all of these reasons, the Court concludes that the test for determining whether an item is a fixture is that stated in *City of Bayonne, i.e.*, will its removal cause irreparable or serious physical injury or damage to the freehold. For the same reasons, the Court agrees with MDFC that *City of Bayonne* implicitly rejects the subjective traditional test of intention in favor of the objective test of irreparable or serious physical injury or damage.

The burden of proof rests upon the party who asserts the affirmative of an issue. 29 Am. Jur. 2d Evidence § 127. Since FFB asserts that the items in question are fixtures, it therefore has the burden of proving that they are. FFB has not met that burden. As to the generator, it was bolted down, and was removed by simply cutting the bolts. MDFC alleges, and the Court finds, that "the ends of the bolts can easily be removed or filed down, leaving the premises completely restored and undamaged." The vacuum system and water system present a closer question. However, the motors, tanks and filters simply sit on the floor of the warehouse, and the pipes run outside rather than inside the walls and ceiling. The Court finds that FFB has not met its burden of proving that removal of these items would cause irreparable or serious physical injury or damage to the premises. The Court therefore holds that the subject items were not fixtures.

VII.

As previously noted, FFB has a perfected first lien on improvements as well as fixtures. The term "improvement" is not defined by Title 12A. However, the case of *Parker v. Wulstein,* 48 N.J. Eq. 94, 96, 21 Atl. 623 (Ch. 1891), states:

> The word "improvement" may be said to comprehend everything that tends to add to the value or convenience of a building or a place of business, whether it be a store, manufacturing establishment, warehouse or farming premises. It certainly includes repairs of every description. It necessarily includes much more than the term "fixtures." Indeed, so far as I am able to understand, it is difficult to conceive any additions made to a building by a tenant for his own convenience in the conduct of the business which may not properly be included in the term "improvements."

Parker v. Wulstein was followed in *In re Herold,* 57 F. Supp. 359 (D. N.J. 1943), aff'd, 145 F.2d 236 (3rd Cir. 1944). In *Herold,* the debtor was a tenant under a lease that had the following clause:

> That no alterations, additions or improvements shall be made in or to the premises without the consent of the Landlord in writing, under penalty of damages and forfeiture, and all additions and improvements made by the Tenant shall belong to the Landlord. *Id.* at 360.

There was a dispute over whether a lighting system which had been installed by the tenant/debtor was property of the debtor or the landlord. The court held:

> [the above] clause is clearly determinative of the rights of the parties, and it is unnecessary to resort, as did the referee, to the law of fixtures to ascertain the meaning of its unequivocal language . . . . The lighting system, of which the lighting fixtures were an integral part, was an "improvement" within the meaning of the lease, and became the property of the Petitioner (the landlord) upon its installation. [citations omitted] *Id.*

MDFC relies on *Altman v. Anderson,* 151 Ariz. 209, 726 P.2d 625 (Ariz. App. 1986), which has a different view:

> We think the best approach, at least under the facts before us, is to recognize that the word "improvement" has no definite and fixed meaning, that it is a relative and comprehensive

term whose meaning in a particular case must be ascertained from the context and the subject matter of the instrument in which it is used.

This Court holds that the term "improvement" has the meaning stated in *Parker v. Wulstein,* for three reasons. First, *Parker v. Wulstein* is a New Jersey case. Second, the definition in *Parker v. Wulstein* is close to the dictionary definition of the term. Third, it is an objective test. To the extent that *Altman v. Anderson* expresses a different view, this Court declines to follow it.

Since the items in question were additions made by Gain to the building in the conduct of its business which tended to add to the value or convenience of the building to Gain, the Court holds that they were improvements. FFB therefore is entitled to the sale proceeds.

CONCLUSION

To summarize, the Court holds the following:

1. The doctrines of equitable estoppel and judicial estoppel do not bar FFB's claim.
2. FFB has not sought to modify or reopen the Court's order of June 21, 1989.
3. The items in question are not fixtures.
4. The items in question are improvements.
5. FFB is entitled to the proceeds of sale.
6. Any arguments raised by the parties and not addressed above have been considered and determined to be without merit. FFB is to submit an order consistent with this opinion under the five-day rule.

§ 21.04 Real Property Interests

Section 9-104 states, "this article does not apply, except to the extent that provision is made for fixtures in section 9-313, to the creation or transfer of an interest in or lien on real estate, including a lease or rents thereunder. In contrast, section 9-102(3) states, "the application of this article to a security interest in a secured obligation is not affected by the fact that the obligation is itself secured by a transaction or interest to which this article does not apply." A difficult question raised by these conflicting statements is whether the U.C.C. applies to security interests taken in promissory notes secured by real estate mortgages. If Article 9 applies to the promissory note secured by the real property, then the only way to perfect is by possession. If, however, Article 9 does not apply to the promissory notes, then recording in a real estate office will be enough to perfect the mortgage and possession would not be required for perfection. Courts have split on the issue of whether a mortgage can exist separately from the note it secures. See *In re Maryville*, 743 F.2d 413 (6th Cir. 1984) (concluding that Article Nine applies to the plaintiff's security interest but only in the promissory notes themselves); *Army National Bank v. Equity Developers, Inc.*, 245 Kan. 3 (1989) (holding Article Nine governs the collateral assignment of the real property interests, mortgages).

IN RE WISTON XXIV LIMITED PARTNERSHIP

United States District Court
147 B.R. 575 (D. Kansas. 1992)

SAFFELS, DISTRICT JUDGE.

This matter is before the court on the appeal taken by Balcor Pension Investors V ("Balcor") from an order of the Bankruptcy Court for the District of Kansas. The bankruptcy court denied Balcor's claim that post-petition rents accruing to the debtor, Wiston XXIV Limited Partnership ("Wiston") constitute cash collateral pursuant to 11 U.S.C. § 363(a) and that Balcor's interest in the rents withstands the bankruptcy trustee's avoiding powers.

Facts

Wiston is a Kansas limited partnership. Its primary asset is an apartment complex located in Overland Park, Kansas, known as Villa Medici Apartments. Balcor, an Illinois limited partnership, loaned Wiston $10,850,000 on November 23, 1987, in exchange for Wiston's Secured Promissory Note, Mortgage and Security Agreement, and Assignment of Leases and Rents. Both the mortgage and the assignment were recorded with the Johnson County Register of Deeds on November 30, 1987.

Three years later, in December 1990, Wiston defaulted on the note. On February 19, 1991, Balcor accelerated the outstanding balance on the note, terminated Wiston's contractual right to use the rents generated by the apartment complex, declared that all rents were to be held in trust for Balcor, and demanded payment to Balcor of all rents then in Wiston's possession or thereafter received by Wiston.

On March 1, 1991, Wiston filed a voluntary petition under Chapter 11 of the Bankruptcy Code Wiston remained in possession of the apartment complex and other assets of the bankruptcy estate, subject to the bankruptcy court's approval of its operating budgets. On the same day the petition was filed, Wiston also filed a Motion for Order Authorizing Use of Cash Collateral, seeking authority to use rental income from the apartment complex for its ongoing operating expenses. Balcor immediately filed a motion to segregate and sequester rents pursuant to 11 U.S.C. § 363(c)(4) and § 546(b) claiming a perfected senior lien in the rents and giving notice of its claim that the rents constituted its cash collateral. On April 2, 1991, the bankruptcy court ordered Wiston to make a monthly accounting of all operating expenditures to Balcor, and ordered segregation of all rents generated by the property in excess of the court-approved operating budget, prohibiting the debtor from using such funds except by order of the court. Wiston subsequently submitted proposed operating budgets to the bankruptcy court for approval, to which Balcor filed objections.

On November 8, 1991, Balcor filed a motion for relief from the automatic stay imposed by 11 U.S.C. § 362 Balcor also claimed it held a perfected security interest in the post-petition rent income from the apartment complex notwithstanding the filing of the bankruptcy petition. A hearing on Balcor's motion for relief from stay was held on January 23, 1992.

In an order dated April 21, 1992, the bankruptcy court held that the security interest in rents was not perfected as of March 1, 1991, the date the bankruptcy petition was filed, and hence Balcor's security interest in the post-petition rents was subject to the avoiding powers of the bankruptcy trustee under 11 U.S.C. § 544(a)(2) The court also concluded that the rents were not Balcor's cash collateral. See *In re Wiston XXIV Limited Partnership,* 141 B.R. 429, 432 (Bankr. D. Kan.1992) . Balcor appeals from this interlocutory order.

Jurisdiction

Wiston argues that this appeal is premature since the order of the bankruptcy court was not stayed pursuant to Bankruptcy Rule 8005 and the bankruptcy proceeding has not terminated.

However, a Rule 8005 stay is discretionary, and is not a prerequisite to an appeal. Further, 28 U.S.C. § 158(a) grants the district court jurisdiction to hear appeals from interlocutory orders of bankruptcy judges with leave of the court.

Apparently on the assumption that the order appealed was a final order, Balcor filed a timely notice of appeal pursuant to Bankruptcy Rule 8001(a) and 8002(a) without an accompanying motion for leave to appeal as required by Rule 8001(b) for interlocutory orders. Because the bankruptcy court's order from which Balcor appeals did not resolve all of Balcor's adversary claims to the bankruptcy estate, particularly the primary contested issue of whether Balcor was entitled to relief from the automatic stay, this court finds that it is not a final order appealable as of right. See, *e.g., In re Durability, Inc.,* 893 F.2d 264, 266 (10th Cir.1990) (appropriate "judicial unit" for finality purposes in bankruptcy is the particular adversary proceeding or discrete controversy); *In re Louisiana World Exposition, Inc.,* 832 F.2d 1391, 1396 (5th Cir.1987) (each adversary proceeding and contested matter should be considered a separate judicial unit for purposes of determining finality) (quoting 1 Collier on Bankruptcy 3.03, at 3-157 (L. King 15th ed. 1987)).

Although D. Kan. Rule 710(a)(2) provides that leave to appeal interlocutory orders is to be sought by filing an application for leave to appeal, subsection (a)(4) provides that the timely filing of a notice of appeal shall be deemed a timely and proper application for leave to appeal. See also Bankruptcy Rule 8003(c) The record on appeal includes each of the items required by Rule 710(a)(2) for an application for leave to appeal. The court also finds that the issue presented in this appeal is a significant question of law in the bankruptcy context, which has not been considered at the appellate level on the basis of property rights under Kansas law. The court therefore deems the timely notice of appeal a proper application for leave to appeal, and by this order the court grants Balcor leave to appeal.

Scope of Appellate Review

Since the order of the bankruptcy court determined an issue of law on undisputed facts, review by this court is de novo. See, *e.g., Virginia Beach Federal Savings and Loan Ass'n v. Wood,* 901 F.2d 849, 851 (10th Cir.1990).

Analysis

In a bankruptcy proceeding, property interests are determined on the basis of state law. *Butner v. United States,* 440 U.S. 48, 55, 99 S.Ct. 914, 918, 59 L.Ed.2d 136 (1979). State law varies considerably with regard to the perfection of a mortgagee's interest in rents and the permissible methods by which such an interest may be perfected while the automatic stay of bankruptcy is in effect. See, *e.g., United States v. Landmark Park & Associates,* 795 F.2d 683, 686 (8th Cir.1986), and cases cited therein. Because the real property at issue in this case is located in Kansas, the law of Kansas applies to determine the property rights of Balcor to the rents generated by the mortgaged property. *Butner,* 440 U.S. at 54, 99 S.Ct. at 918.

In Kansas, a mortgage is not a conveyance; a mortgagee acquires only a lien securing the mortgagor's indebtedness. See *Mid-Continent Supply Co. v. Hauser,* 176 Kan. 9, 269 P.2d 453, 457 (1954); *Hall v. Goldsworthy,* 136 Kan. 247, 14 P.2d 659, 660 (1932); *Missouri Valley Investment Co. v. Curtis,* 12 Kan. App. 2d 386, 745 P.2d 683, 685 (1987); K.S.A. 58-2301. A mortgagor is entitled to use and possession of the premises, together with income generated from the property, until his right is divested by appropriate judicial proceedings, or at least until a receiver is appointed to take possession after foreclosure proceedings begin. *Caldwell v. Alsop,* 48 Kan. 571, 573, 29 P. 1150, 1151 (1892), quoted in *Hall v. Goldsworthy*, 14 P.2d at 661; see *Mid-Continent Supply Co.,* 269 P.2d at 458 (where mortgages contained no assignment of rents and profits, mortgagor remained entitled to rents and profits so long as he retains possession; but if receiver appointed following foreclosure, receiver takes possession of rents and profits to be held for benefit of parties in interest). The "lien theory" of the mortgage relationship, followed in Kansas, is the majority rule in the United States. Randolph, *The Mortgagee's Interest in Rents: Some Policy Considerations and Proposals,* 29 Kan. L. Rev. 1, 14 (1980) [hereinafter "Randolph"].

Under Kansas law, an assignment of rents to secure payment of a mortgage debt is deemed part of the mortgage, and is enforceable only in accordance with the law relating to the foreclosure of mortgages. *Hall v. Goldsworthy,* 14 P.2d at 661; cf. *First Federal Savings and Loan Ass'n v. Moulds,* 202 Kan. 557, 451 P.2d 215, 219 (1969) (right to possession and to rents and profits of property being foreclosed is in defendant owner and except for waste, is absolute); *Capitol Building and Loan Ass'n v. Ross,* 134 Kan. 441, 7 P.2d 86, 87 (1932) (mortgagor's right to possession of property during redemption period includes right to rents and profits, which cannot be waived by any provision of the mortgage); *Mid Kansas Federal Savings and Loan Ass'n v. Zimmer,* 12 Kan.App.2d 735, 755 P.2d 1352, 1355 (1988) (separate assignment of rents, executed at same time as note and mortgage, is subject to statute prohibiting waiver of redemption in any mortgage instrument).

Although the assignment creates a lien or security interest in favor of the assignee just as a mortgage creates a lien on behalf of the mortgagee, under Kansas case law the assignee is "entitled to the benefit of the contract" only after he takes action in court to reduce the rents to his possession or control. *Hall v. Goldsworthy,* 14 P.2d at 661. "Any proper procedure which would empower the court to control the rents and profits would be sufficient to vest the mortgagee with the title thereto . . . ," including appointment of a receiver. *Id.* at 661-62; see also *Holton Building and Loan Ass'n v. Gibson,* 139 Kan. 829, Syl. P, 33 P.2d 138 (1934) (right to benefit of rent assignment does not accrue until such rents have been subjected to possession of mortgagee by proper action in courts). While the assignee must take court action or the equivalent to obtain title to the rents, thereby divesting the assignor of his entire interest therein, the court is unaware of any Kansas case that requires the assignee to take court action in order to perfect a security interest in rents.

In this court's view, the court procedure envisioned in *Hall* necessary to "entitle" the assignee to rents is analogous to the state foreclosure proceeding that is the prerequisite to enforcing the mortgagee's interest in the real property. The mortgagee/assignee has a property right in the realty and rents whether or not he has taken action to "foreclose" his property right by any "proper procedure" as described in *Hall.* See *In re Foxhill Place Associates,* 119 B.R. 708, 712 (Bankr.W.D.Mo.1990) (applying Kansas law) (enforcement of creditor's rights in rents describes the process taken to realize or possess the rent revenues and is distinct from the process of perfecting the security interest).

Applying Kansas law to the facts of this case, Balcor held a security interest in the rents prior to the filing of the bankruptcy petition by virtue of the assignment of rents granted in conjunction with the mortgage in 1987. Kansas law does not require court action such as appointment of a receiver in order to create a security interest in rents assigned by the mortgagor; the agreement between the parties creates the security interest. See *Hall v. Goldsworthy,* 14 P.2d at 661; cf.

Cates v. Musgrove Petroleum Corp., 190 Kan. 609, 376 P.2d 819, 821 (1962) (appointment of receiver does not determine any rights nor destroy any liens; receiver merely becomes assignee of insolvent, and takes possession subject to all valid liens existing upon the property at time of appointment), cited in *Maxl Sales Co. v. Critiques, Inc.*, 796 F.2d 1293, 1297 n. 2 (10th Cir.1986). Although the assignment granted Wiston a limited right to use the rents, Balcor expressly terminated that right pursuant to the demand letter issued on February 19, 1991. This court construes the demand letter as Balcor's initial step in enforcing its security interest in the rents, but it was not sufficient to comply with the requirements of Kansas case law in order to take constructive possession of the rents before the filing of the petition in this case. Consequently, the court finds that Balcor is not entitled to possession of the rents unless and until it takes action to empower the state court to control the rents and profits, such as by appointment of a receiver.

Nevertheless, at the time the bankruptcy petition was filed on March 1, 1991, Balcor certainly held an interest in the rental income by virtue of the assignment and demand, even though it had not instituted any court proceeding to divest Wiston of its rights to the rental income. Although in effect the assignment was initially conditioned upon the mortgagor's default since it granted Wiston a license to collect and use the rents absent default, it became unconditional on February 19, 1991, when Balcor terminated Wiston's license to use the rents. See *Army Nat'l Bank v. Equity Developers, Inc.*, 245 Kan. 3, 774 P.2d 919, 932 (1989) ("assignment passes all of the assignor's title and interest to assignee, and divests assignor of all right of control over the subject matter of the assignment") (quoting *Patrons State Bank & Trust Co. v. Shapiro*, 215 Kan. 856, 861, 528 P.2d 1198 (1974)). It follows that the pre-petition rents constitute "cash collateral" as defined by 11 U.S.C. § 363(a) which reads: (a) In this section, "cash collateral" means cash, negotiable instruments, documents of title, securities, deposit accounts, or other cash equivalents whenever acquired in which the estate and an entity other than the estate have an interest and includes the proceeds, products, offspring, rents or profits of property subject to a security interest as provided in section 552(b) of this title, whether existing before or after the commencement of a case under this title.

The specific issue in this appeal, however, is whether rents accruing after the filing of the petition constitute "cash collateral." As a general rule, property acquired by the bankruptcy estate or by the debtor after the commencement of the case is not subject to any lien resulting from any security agreement entered into by the debtor before the filing of the petition. 11 U.S.C. § 552(a) However, § 552(b) carves out an important exception to the general rule. Subject to several other provisions of the Bankruptcy Code, if a preexisting security agreement between the debtor and a secured party grants a security interest in property acquired pre-petition and to rents or profits of that property, then the security interest extends to such rents and proceeds acquired post-petition to the extent provided by such security agreement and by applicable non-bankruptcy law. 11 U.S.C. § 552(b) see Randolph, *supra,* at 45 (interpreting § 552(b)). Hence, Kansas law determines whether the Balcor's security interest in Wiston's apartment complex extends to post-petition rental income from the complex. If so, Balcor's security interest created by the assignment of rents extends to rents accruing post-petition, which would therefore fall within the definition of "cash collateral."

Under Kansas law, an assignment of rents as security for a mortgagee is valid as to rents accruing after default and before the beginning of the statutory redemption period. See *Holton Building & Loan Ass'n v. Gibson,* 139 Kan. 829, 33 P.2d 138 (1934); *Missouri Valley Investment*

Co. v. Curtis, 12 Kan. App. 2d 386, 745 P.2d 683 (1987) (citing *Hall v. Goldsworthy*). Therefore, Balcor's security interest extends to rental income from the mortgaged property that accrues post-petition, until the beginning of the statutory redemption period, if any.

The exception embodied in 11 U.S.C. § 552(b) as to after-acquired property, however, is expressly subject to the avoiding powers of the bankruptcy trustee as set forth in § 544. Under § 544, the bankruptcy trustee or debtor-in-possession may set aside any security interest not perfected prior to the filing of the bankruptcy petition, and state law determines whether and when the interest has been perfected. See *Virginia Beach Federal Savings and Loan Ass'n v. Wood,* 901 F.2d 849, 852 (10th Cir.1990); *In re Casbeer,* 793 F.2d 1436, 1440 (5th Cir.1986) (citing *Butner v. United States,* 440 U.S. 48, 55, 99 S.Ct. 914, 918, 59 L.Ed.2d 136 (1979)).

Under Kansas law, a security interest in rents is perfected by recording the assignment of rents with the recorder of deeds. *In re Foxhill Place Associates,* 119 B.R. at 712 (citing *In re Cherry Creek,* No. 89-10481, slip op. at 10 (Bankr.D.Kan.1990) (unpublished) and *Federal Home Loan Mortgage Corp. v. Nazar,* 100 B.R. 555, 558 (D.Kan.1989) (applying federal rule applicable to federal lenders)); cf. *Army Nat'l Bank v. Equity Developers, Inc.,* 245 Kan. 3, 774 P.2d 919, 928 (1989) (recording statutes were intended to protect mortgagor and those dealing with the underlying land); *National Bank of Tulsa v. Warren,* 177 Kan. 281, 279 P.2d 262, 265 (1955) (assignment to lender of production payments from oil and gas leases as security for loan was a conveyance of interest in land, amounting to a mortgage). Under the recording statutes, "[e]very instrument in writing . . . whereby any real estate may be affected, . . . may be recorded in the office of register of deeds . . . ." K.S.A. 58-2221. Every such instrument so recorded is deemed to impart notice to all persons of the contents, and all subsequent purchasers are deemed to purchase with notice. K.S.A. 58-2222, 58-2223. Since Balcor recorded the assignment with the Johnson County Register of Deeds in November 1987, this court finds that the security interest in rents was properly perfected well before the filing of Wiston's bankruptcy petition. Therefore, under 11 U.S.C. § 544(a) the bankruptcy trustee's rights are subject to Balcor's interest in the rents, which was perfected by recording in 1987.

Balcor's security interest in post-petition rents under § 552(b) is therefore protected against the strong-arm powers of the trustee and the debtor-in-possession under § 544(a). However, the exception set forth in § 552(b) is also subject to § 363, which defines "cash collateral" and prohibits the trustee or debtor-in-possession from using cash collateral except upon agreement of the entity holding an interest therein or upon authorization of the court following notice and a hearing. See 11 U.S.C. § 363(a), (c)(2) In this case, Balcor has not agreed to permit the use of rents by the trustee or Wiston, the debtor-in-possession.

Contrary to the holding of the bankruptcy court below, the court finds that the definition of "cash collateral" in 11 U.S.C. § 363(a) covers the post-petition rents in this case. Having determined that Balcor held a perfected security interest in the real property prior to the filing of the petition, the rents derived from the property constitute "cash collateral" under § 363. See *supra* pp. 580-81 (quoting § 363(a)).

The Bankruptcy Code imposes limitations on the use of cash collateral in § 363(c)(2), which reads as follows: (2) The trustee may not use, sell, or lease cash collateral under paragraph (1) of this subsection unless— (A) each entity that has an interest in such cash collateral consents; or (B) the court, after notice and a hearing, authorizes such use, sale, or lease in accordance with the provisions of this section. Since Balcor did not consent to Wiston's use of the rents, the only remaining question is whether the Bankruptcy Court's disposition of the rents complied with § 363(c)(2)(B).

Following notice and a hearing held March 14, 1991, the bankruptcy court permitted Wiston, as debtor-in-possession, to use the rents for court-approved operating costs of the apartment complex, and ordered sequestration of any excess rent income. In subsequent orders, the bankruptcy court has apparently continued to permit Wiston use of the rents to the extent of the reasonable and necessary operating expenses of the real property. The reasoning underlying the bankruptcy court's orders appears to be consistent with the purpose of Chapter 11 bankruptcy proceedings to enable the debtor an opportunity to reorganize and pay off its debts. See, *e.g., Matter of Winshall Settlor's Trust,* 758 F.2d 1136, 1137 (6th Cir.1985). It is also consistent with Kansas law favoring the equitable right of redemption, during which period the debtor has a right to possession of the real estate as well as the rents generated by the property. See, *e.g., Capitol Building and Loan Ass'n v. Ross,* 134 Kan. 441, 7 P.2d 86, 87 (1932). However, because the bankruptcy court erroneously determined that Balcor did not hold a perfected interest as of the date the bankruptcy petition was filed and that the rents in this case did not constitute "cash collateral," it did not reach Balcor's contention that adequate protection had not been afforded the cash collateral as required by § 363. This court therefore remands this matter to the bankruptcy court for further proceedings consistent with this memorandum and order.

IT IS BY THE COURT THEREFORE ORDERED that the appellant is granted leave to appeal.

IT IS FURTHER ORDERED that the appellant's motion to expedite the appeal (Doc. 8) is hereby denied.

IT IS FURTHER ORDERED that the holding of the bankruptcy court that appellant's interest in the rents was not perfected as of the date the bankruptcy proceeding was commenced and that the rents therefore do not constitute cash collateral is hereby reversed, and the matter is remanded to the bankruptcy court for further proceedings consistent with this memorandum and order.

§ 21.05 Interests Excluded From Article 9

[A] Subrogation

Article 9 applies to security interests created by contract. Rights of subrogation, although growing out of a contractual setting and often articulated by the contract, do not depend on a grant in the contract. Instead, subrogation is an equitable remedy that permits courts to avoid injustice. Therefore, subrogation rights are not “"security interests" within the meaning of Article 9. *Jacobs v. Northeastern Corp.,* 416 Pa. 417 (Pa. 1965). Filing under the Code is unnecessary to preserve the priority of a surety's right of subrogation over the rights of a trustee in bankruptcy. *Canter v. Schlager,* 358 Mass. 789 (1971).

**INTERFIRST BANK DALLAS, N.A. v.
UNITED STATES FIDELITY AND GUARANTY COMPANY**

Court of Appeals of Texas, Fifth District, Dallas
774 S.W.2d 391 (1989)

ROWE, JUSTICE.

NCNB Texas National Bank (Bank), as successor in interest to Interfirst Bank Dallas, N.A., appeals from a judgment which determined that United States Fidelity and Guaranty Company (USF & G) had a superior right to certain funds owed by various prime contractors to certain related subcontractors (Wallace). In six points of error, Bank complains that the trial court erred in concluding that: (1) Wallace forfeited its rights to funds still held by the prime contractors because Wallace committed a material breach of contract by not satisfying claims of all laborers and materialmen; (2) USF & G, as subrogee of the prime contractors, had priority over Bank to the withheld funds; (3) USF & G, as subrogee of lien claimants with unperfected laborers' and materialmen's liens, had priority over Bank to the funds; (4) certain lien claimants had perfected their liens under applicable state law; (5) the terms of USF & G's payment bonds were incorporated into Wallace's subcontracts; and (6) USF & G was entitled to a $30,000.00 reimbursement for its costs and expenses incident to bond claim handling on the International Pavilion Project. For the reasons given below, we modify the trial court's judgment by deleting the $30,000.00 award for reimbursement and, as modified, affirm.

General Background

The issue presented in this case is whether USF & G's subrogation rights in certain funds are superior to Bank's perfected security interest in accounts receivable. The funds in dispute are undisbursed progress payments and retainages withheld by the prime contractors under various bonded subcontracts. This complicated case proceeded to trial on stipulated facts. As an appellate court, we are bound by the facts as expressly stipulated by the parties. See *Geo-Western Petroleum Dev., Inc. v. Mitchell,* 717 S.W.2d 734, 736 (Tex.App.—Waco 1986, no writ); *Trinity Universal Ins. Co. v. Bellmead State Bank,* 396 S.W.2d 163, 172 (Tex.Civ.App.— Dallas 1965, writ ref'd n.r.e.).

On October 16, 1981, USF & G and Wallace entered into a Master Surety Agreement. This agreement provides for USF & G to issue payment bonds on all Wallace subcontracts and secures USF & G's interest by subrogating it to all Wallace's rights in the subcontracts. All of the bonds issued under the Master Surety Agreement require USF & G to pay laborers and materialmen without regard to the perfection of liens. All bonded subcontracts between Wallace and the various prime contractors provide that final payments thereunder are not due until all lienable claims of laborers and materialmen have been satisfied. The subcontracts clearly reflect that Wallace was to use funds due from the prime contractors to pay for labor and materials being incorporated into the various projects. The subcontracts do not, however, expressly incorporate USF & G's contractual subrogation rights.

By documents dated December 16, 1981, Bank made loans to Wallace to provide operating capital for its construction business. In exchange, Wallace granted Bank a security interest in its accounts and the proceeds of its accounts. Bank properly perfected this security interest. It is clear that Wallace was to devote all funds advanced by Bank to completing the subcontracts according to their terms. Moreover, the Master Surety Agreement was already in place when Bank first advanced funds to Wallace on December 16, 1981, and Bank was familiar with these contractual undertakings as they occurred. Indeed, payment bond coverage on all Wallace subcontracts was an integral feature of Bank's loan commitments.

On August 6, 1984, Wallace filed voluntary bankruptcy. The bankruptcy court entered an order dated September 6, 1984, directing that all payments owed to Wallace under the bonded subcontracts be made to USF & G. On July 30, 1986, the bankruptcy court entered an order directing Wallace to abandon to Bank all its remaining accounts receivable. This order further provided that "this order shall not prejudice or otherwise affect any rights which any sureties may assert as to any of the accounts receivable so abandoned in which they may assert an interest." Thus, the bankruptcy court released the funds from the debtors' estates without determining whether Bank or USF & G had a superior right to such funds.

At the time of its bankruptcy, Wallace had failed to pay in full its obligations to laborers and materialmen under the subcontracts. Accordingly, USF & G was called upon to satisfy these unpaid obligations under the terms of its bonds. The total of these unpaid obligations exceeded the amount of retainages available under the subcontracts. USF & G contends that it is entitled to apply the retainages to help satisfy Wallace's unpaid obligations. Bank argues that it has a superior right to such funds by virtue of its perfected security interest in accounts receivable.

Four Allen Center Project, Houston, Texas

On April 30, 1982, Carl P. Wallace Company, Inc., entered into a subcontract with Texas Construction, Inc., the prime contractor, whereby Wallace agreed to provide all labor and materials necessary for the installation of plumbing for the Four Allen Center Project. On that same date, USF & G, as surety, and Wallace, as principal, executed a subcontract labor and material bond and subcontract performance bond in favor of the prime contractor. On the date of the bankruptcies, the prime contractor owed Wallace $121,144.47—$86,833.49 in progress payments and $34,310.98 in retainage withheld pursuant to the subcontract. Also as of that date, Wallace owed several subcontractors for labor and materials.

The prime contractor notified USF & G that Wallace had defaulted under its subcontract and made demand upon USF & G pursuant to the payment bond. USF & G paid the claims of the Wallace subcontractors pursuant to its bond obligations. Only one of the subcontractors had perfected a mechanics' lien in the amount of $772.00. The rights of the other subcontractors to perfect liens had expired prior to the dates upon which USF & G received notice of, or paid, the claims. The prime contractor then paid USF & G the entire $121,144.47 balance remaining in the Wallace subcontract. Bank has made demand for $120,372.47, which represents the $121,144.47 balance less the $772.00 paid to the perfected lien claimant.

Buena Vista Palace Hotel Project, Buena Vista, Florida.

On September 8, 1981, Carl P. Wallace Company, Inc., entered into a subcontract with the prime contractor, Pavarini Construction Company, whereby Wallace agreed to furnish all labor and materials necessary for the installation of a heating, ventilating, and air conditioning system and plumbing for the Buena Vista project. On September 16, 1981, USF & G, as surety, and Wallace, as principal, executed a subcontract labor & material bond and a subcontract performance bond in favor of the prime contractor. Wallace had completed the performance of the work under its subcontract before its bankruptcy. There was a balance remaining with the prime contractor in the Wallace subcontract in the sum of $88,053.48, which represented retainage withheld pursuant to the terms of the subcontract.

Three subcontractors to Wallace were owed for materials and labor as of the date of bankruptcy. The prime contractor notified USF & G of the money owed to these subcontractors and USF & G paid the claims in full. None of these subcontractors had perfected a mechanics' lien relating to the project. In fact, the rights of each of these subcontractors to perfect a mechanics' lien expired prior to the dates upon which USF & G received notice of, or paid, their claims. The prime contractor paid USF & G the $88,053.48 balance remaining in the Wallace subcontract. Bank has made demand for this balance.

Farmers Insurance Building Project, Columbus, Ohio

On January 31, 1983, Huffman-Wolfe Company (Wallace) entered into a subcontract with HCB/Peck Contractors, the prime contractor, to provide all labor and materials necessary to furnish and install certain mechanical work for the Farmers Insurance Building. USF & G, as surety, and Wallace, as principal, issued a subcontract labor & material bond and a subcontract performance bond in favor of the prime contractor on February 1, 1983. As of the date of the bankruptcies, certain items of contract, corrective, and warranty work required under the subcontract remained unfinished. At that time, there was a balance remaining in the Wallace subcontract with the prime contractor in the sum of $328,618.75, which represented $39,899.75 in progress payments and $288,719.00 in retainage withheld pursuant to the terms of the subcontract. Also as of that date, certain subcontractors to Wallace were owed for labor and materials furnished pursuant to their subcontracts.

On September 12, 1984, the prime contractor transmitted to USF & G the sum of $187,394.00 from the balance which remained in the subcontract. USF & G distributed this money to Wallace's unpaid subcontractors. The prime contractor incurred $31,030.25 in expenses in completing the contract. After deducting the $187,394.00 paid to USF & G and the $31,030.25 for the prime contractors' expense in completing the subcontract obligations, the balance remaining in the Wallace subcontract totaled $110,194.50.

Three of the Wallace subcontractors paid by USF & G did not perfect mechanics' liens. In fact, the rights of each of these three subcontractors to perfect a mechanics' lien expired prior to the dates upon which USF & G received notice of, or paid, their claims. One of these materialmen filed an untimely mechanics' lien which was released in exchange for payment by USF & G. Four subcontractors timely filed and perfected mechanics' liens relating to the Farmers Project in the amount of $79,588.00. There is insufficient evidence, however, to determine whether some of the other subcontractors had perfected mechanics' lien rights.

Bank asserts a claim to $107,806.00 of the $187,394.00 previously paid to USF & G and to the $110,194.50 balance in the Wallace subcontract. Bank does not assert priority to the $79,588.00 paid to perfected lien claimants or to the $31,030.25 expended by the prime contractor to complete the project. As a result of competing claims to this sum, USF & G and Bank agreed that the $110,194.50 contract balance held by the prime contractor would be paid to Winstead, McGuire, Sechrest & Minick as escrow agent to be held in escrow until entitlement to the funds was agreed by settlement or awarded by final judgment. This money is currently held in the escrow account.

Ohio State Life Insurance Project, Columbus, Ohio

On January 31, 1983, The Huffman-Wolfe Company (Wallace) entered into a subcontract with the prime contractor, HCB/Peck Contractors, whereby Wallace agreed to provide all labor and materials and services necessary to furnish and install certain mechanical work for the Ohio State Insurance Project. USF & G, as surety, and the Wallace Company, as principal, executed a subcontract labor & material bond and a subcontract performance bond in favor of the prime contractor on February 1, 1983. As of the date of the bankruptcies, there was a $176,079.02 retainage balance remaining in the Wallace subcontract which the prime contractor had withheld pursuant to the terms of the subcontract. Wallace owed certain subcontractors for labor and materials so the prime contractor made demand upon USF & G that it perform pursuant to its payment bond on the project.

On September 12, 1984, the prime contractor transmitted $132,429.00 to USF & G from the balance which remained in the subcontract with Wallace. The prime contractor incurred costs and expenses in the sum of $33,844.52 in completing the contract. After deducting the $132,429.00 paid to USF & G and the $33,844.52 for the prime contractor's expense in completing the subcontract obligations, the balance remaining in the Wallace subcontract totaled $9,805.50.

Three of Wallace's subcontractors timely filed and perfected liens relating to the Ohio State Project in the amount of $58,003.88. The other subcontractors paid by USF & G failed to timely file and perfect mechanics' and materialmen's liens. Bank asserts a claim to the $9,805.50 balance in the Wallace subcontract with the prime contractor on the Ohio State Project. As a result of competing claims to this sum, the prime contractor, USF & G, and Bank entered into a compromise settlement agreement whereby the parties agreed that the $9,805.50 would be paid to Winstead, McGuire, Sechrest & Minick as escrow agent to be held in escrow until such time as entitlement to such funds was agreed by settlement or awarded by final judgment. Bank also asserts a claim to $64,619.62 of the $132,429.00 previously paid to USF & G by the prime contractor. Bank does not assert a claim to the remainder of $58,003.88 which USF & G paid to satisfy perfected lien claimants.

International Pavilion Project, New Orleans, Louisiana

On December 2, 1982, Carl P. Wallace, Louisiana, entered into a subcontract with the prime contractor, J.A. Jones Construction Company, whereby Wallace agreed to furnish all labor and materials necessary for the installation of certain mechanical work for the International Pavilion Project. On December 10, 1982, USF & G, as surety, and Wallace, as principal, executed a subcontract payment bond and a subcontract performance bond in favor of the prime contractor. As of the date of the Wallace bankruptcies, Wallace had completed the performance of the work under its subcontract on the International Pavilion Project. At that time, there was a balance remaining in the Wallace subcontract of $327,554.55.

On the date of the bankruptcies, Wallace owed various subcontractors and suppliers $548,745.46 for materials and labor, including $91,200.00 owed to Grinnell Fire Protection Systems Company. The prime contractor paid Grinnell $27,700.00, and Grinnell timely filed and perfected a mechanics' lien in the amount of $63,500.00 for the balance. USF & G paid the claims of some of the Wallace subcontractors totalling $122,455.66, including a $63,500.00 payment to Grinnell in exchange for a release of Grinnell's timely perfected mechanics' and materialmen's lien.

Bank does not assert a claim to the $27,700.00 paid by the prime contractor to Grinnell. Deducting this sum, the balance remaining in the Wallace subcontract totals $299,854.55, which represents $129,016.65 in progress payments and $170,837.90 in retainage. Through declaratory judgment actions, USF & G and Bank have each asserted a claim to the retainage still held by the prime contractor. Bank has conceded, however, that USF & G has a superior right to the $63,500.00 paid to Grinnell in exchange for a release of its lien.

Surety's Rights to Equitable Subrogation

USF & G has not sought to legally enforce any contractual rights, but instead has relied upon the doctrine of equitable subrogation. Based upon the stipulated facts, the trial court filed the following conclusions of law with respect to USF & G's claim:

Upon satisfaction of Wallace's debts and subcontract obligations to the prime contractors, USF & G is subrogated to the position and rights of . . . the defaulting contractor Wallace. USF & G's rights of subrogation are equitable principals [sic] and do not depend upon an assignment, a lien, or contract.

Subrogation is said to be of two types: conventional and legal. The latter type is often referred to as equitable subrogation. This type is not dependent upon contract but arises by operation of law or by implication in equity to prevent injustice. For purposes of Texas law, equitable subrogation has been defined as "a legal fiction by force of which an obligation, extinguished by payment made by a third person, is treated as still subsisting for his benefit" or "the procedure by which the equitable rights of one person are worked out through the legal rights of another." *Texas Co. v. Miller,* 165 F.2d 111, 115 (5th Cir.1947); see also 73 AM. JUR. 2d Subrogation §§ 2 & 3 (1964); 83 C.J.S. Subrogation § 3 (1953). Application of the doctrine is said to be "the purest of equities," and the courts of Texas are said to be particularly hospitable to it. *Yonack v. Interstate Sec. Co.,* 217 F.2d 649, 651 (5th Cir.1954). The doctrine has been widely applied, both as to governmental and private projects, where the obligation of a contractor under a construction contract is backed by payment bonds issued by a commercial surety. *E.g., Pearlman v. Reliance Ins. Co.,* 371 U.S. 132, 141, 83 S.Ct. 232, 237, 9 L.Ed.2d 190 (1962); *Trinity Universal Ins. Co. v. United States,* 382 F.2d 317, 320-21 (5th Cir.1967); *Trinity Universal Ins. Co. v. Bellmead State Bank,* 396 S.W.2d 163, 168 (Tex. Civ. App.—Dallas 1965, writ ref'd n.r.e.); see also Cushman, *The Surety's Right of Equitable Priority to Contract Balances in Relation to the Uniform Commercial Code,* 39 Temp. L. Q. 239 (1966).

In *Trinity Universal Ins. Co. v. Bellmead State Bank*, a case involving a private construction contract, this Court addressed the proper disposition of conflicting claims to retainage asserted by a surety, which had discharged the obligation of its principal, and by a garnishing bank creditor of the contractor. Chief Justice Williams on that occasion, in holding that the surety was entitled to priority over the bank in the retainage, justified the holding on the following principles of subrogation: That a surety has an independent right growing out of its relationship as such to require the retainage to be applied to contract obligations is well settled by the courts, both federal and state . . . . It is further well-settled in our law that the surety whose funds go to discharge contractor's obligations is thereby subrogated to the rights of the owner to apply the contract balances to the completion of the project in payment of bills incurred in that connection . . . . Simply stated, the right of subrogation of the surety is founded solely upon the equitable principle of having paid, pursuant to a bound obligation so to do, what in equity should have been paid by the contractor . . . . *Id.* at 168.

It is established that as the assignee of a perfected security interest in the accounts and proceeds of a contractor, a lender is entitled to the same right to the funds as his assignor. See Tex.Bus. & Com.Code Ann. § 9.106 (Vernon Supp. 1988). Such an assignee cannot, however, take greater rights than his assignor. See Tex.Bus. & Com.Code Ann. § 9.318(a) (Vernon Supp. 1988). Here, it is clear that when Wallace granted Bank a security interest in its accounts receivable, Wallace's rights were already subject to USF & G's subrogation rights in the event that Wallace failed to satisfy its obligations under the various contracts.

On each project, Wallace's contract with the respective prime contractor expressly required payment of all subcontract suppliers' bills as a condition of completion of the contract obligations. Similar contract language was construed in *Corpus Christi Bank and Trust v. Smith,* where the supreme court held that such a retainage provision was intended to provide incentive for the contractor to finish the project, provide completion funds in case the contractor abandoned the project, and provide funds to remedy defects. 525 S.W.2d 501, 504-05 (Tex. 1975). As a result, the retainage provision does not make the laborers and materialmen third party beneficiaries or deprive the contractor of an interest in the retainage. Thus, Bank's position as assignor of Wallace clearly prevails over the position of laborers and materialmen having no perfected liens. *Id.* at 505; see *Citizens Nat'l Bank v. Texas & Pacific Ry. Co.,* 136 Tex. 333, 340-41, 150 S.W.2d 1003, 1007 (1941).

Because of the holding in the *Corpus Christi* case, USF & G cannot defeat Bank's claim to the retainages simply by paying off the laborers and materialmen and thereby succeeding to their rights. USF & G can defeat Bank's claim only by establishing that, because of the posture of the parties, equitable considerations dictate that the retainages be utilized in the first instance to help defray the surety's obligations of satisfying all lienable claims of laborers and materialmen, whether perfected or not. Directly impacting these equitable considerations is the legal issue of whether the traditional right of a surety to equitable subrogation survived the enactment of the secured transactions provisions of Article Nine of the Uniform Commercial Code.

Effect of U.C.C. on Surety's Subrogation Rights

Although there is some minor difference of opinion on this legal issue, the majority rule clearly appears to be the one which was sanctioned by Justice Robert Braucher in his definitive analysis of the subject in *Canter v. Schlager,* 358 Mass. 789, 267 N.E.2d 492 (1971). According to Justice Braucher's analysis, a surety's subrogation rights are not security interests within the purview of Article Nine. *Id.* at 494. This being the case, the promulgation of the U.C.C. and the enactment of its progeny (such as the Texas Business and Commerce Code) do not adversely affect the pre-Code subrogation rights traditionally afforded to sureties. *Id.*; see 2 White & Summers, Uniform Commercial Code § 23-6 (3d ed. 1988) (surety's subrogation rights not a security interest); accord *National Shawmut Bank v. New Amsterdam Casualty Co.,* 411 F.2d 843, 847 (1st Cir.1969). Further, it necessarily follows from Braucher's analysis that a surety's right to equitable subrogation is not adversely affected by the lack of perfection of lien claimants' rights if the surety is obliged to satisfy all lienable claims of laborers and materialmen, whether perfected or not.

The overwhelming and essentially unanimous post-U.C.C. decisions have held that the interest of a surety, such as USF & G, continues to be superior to the claim of a contract assignee, such as Bank. *Transamerica Ins. Co. v. Barnett Bank,* 540 So.2d 113, 117 (Fla.1989).

For the above reasons, it now becomes apparent that, although each of Bank's first five points of error may technically be well taken, such points do not singularly or collectively entitle Bank to priority in the retainages. With respect to the first point, even if Wallace had substantially performed all four subcontracts, Wallace's failure to meet the "final payment" prerequisite of satisfying all lienable claims for labor and materials would entitle the surety to priority in the retainages. With respect to the second point, although the prime contractor might not itself be legally entitled to pay the retainages directly to laborers and materialmen with unperfected liens, the surety's priority in the retainages is not dependent upon such rights of the prime contractor.

With respect to the third point, although laborers and materialmen with unperfected liens may have no direct rights in the retainages, the surety's priority therein is not dependent upon such rights by these claimants. With respect to the fourth point, the surety's priority in the retainages is not dependent upon the perfection of liens by laborers and materialmen since the surety was obliged to satisfy all lienable claims regardless of perfection. With respect to the fifth point, the surety's priority in the retainages is not dependent solely upon the express contractual agreements appearing in its principals' subcontracts; the symbiotic relationship existing between the prime contractor, its subcontractor, its subcontractor's surety, and its subcontractor's lender is of controlling importance. Accordingly, Bank's first five points of error are overruled.

With respect to Bank's sixth point, the surety is by Bank's concession entitled through subrogation to recoup the $63,500.00 paid on the lien claim of Grinnell Fire Protection System. The surety is not entitled, however, to recover the stipulated $30,000.00 costs and expenses related to its processing of bond claims on the International Pavilion Project. To the extent this recovery of costs and expenses is dependent upon contract, it fails because of the surety's lack of a perfected security interest in the contract rights of its principal. To the extent it is dependent upon subrogation, it fails because a surety's subrogation rights cover only the amount it has paid to discharge its principal obligation. *Phipps v. Fugua*, 32 S.W.2d 660, 663 (Tex. Civ. App.—Amarillo 1930, writ ref'd). Accordingly, Bank's sixth point of error is sustained.

Having overruled Bank's first five points of error and having sustained Bank's sixth point of error, we modify the trial court's judgment by removing the $30,000.00 award in favor of USF & G for costs and expenses related to its processing of claims on the International Pavilion Project. As so modified, we affirm the trial court's judgment.

BURNETT, JUSTICE, DISSENTING.

I dissent. I arrive at a different result by relying on controlling Texas law. The majority's reliance on the equitable principles enunciated in *Trinity Universal Ins. Co. v. Bellmead State Bank*, 396 S.W.2d 163 (Tex. Civ. App.—Dallas 1965, writ ref'd n.r.e.), is misplaced because USF & G's right to equitable subrogation did not arise until payment. Thus, for the reasons discussed herein, it is second in time to NCNB's perfected legal right.

In *Trinity Universal*, the surety took over the project when the contractor became financially unable to continue. As a public relations matter, the contractor continued to issue checks to the subcontractors. However, the account on which the checks were drawn was funded by the surety. Prior to the surety's deposits, the contractor contacted the owner and released its claim to all rights to amounts due under the contract, assigned its interests to the surety and requested that the owner pay the surety. Thus, the owner made progress payments to the surety instead of the contractor. Before the final progress payments and retainages were disbursed to the surety, Bellmead State Bank, as a creditor of the contractor, served the owner with garnishment papers seeking the funds still held by the owner. Interestingly, the contract between the owner and contractor specifically provided "[n]o payments shall be due while the [contractor] is in default in respect of any of the provisions of this proposal." *Trinity Universal*, 396 S.W.2d at 166. Thus, pursuant to the contract, upon default the contractor had no entitlement to the funds pursuant to the express language of the contract.

Bellmead State Bank asserted that the surety must rely on the unfiled assignment from the contractor which was subordinate to the bank's status as a judgment lien creditor under article 260-1 (the predecessor to the present Texas U.C.C.). However, the court disagreed and stated as follows: The stipulation [of facts] expressly provided that the fund herein involved represented the retained percentages due under the contract. When the stipulation is reviewed within its four corners, we think there was such a default on the part of the contractor as contemplated by the agreement and that the Surety's independent rights to the fund is founded on its suretyship relationship as such. The rights of the surety in this case, as revealed by the stipulation of facts, does not depend upon an independent assignment, . . . therefore we are not here concerned with the application of [the U.C.C.]. *Trinity Universal*, 396 S.W.2d at 168. Thus, the court expressly refused to apply the predecessor to the U.C.C. and appears to have relied upon the express contract language under which the contractor forfeited any rights to money after a default despite any partial performance.

However, the *Trinity Universal* court then went on to discuss a surety's "independent right growing out of its relationship as such to require the retainage to be applied to contract obligations." *Id.* As noted by the majority, the court justified its decision in favor of the surety by stating: The rights of the Surety in this case are based upon its payment of the debt of another . . . . Simply stated, the right of subrogation of the Surety is founded solely upon the equitable principle of having paid, pursuant to a bound obligation so to do, what in equity should have been paid by the contractor. *Trinity Universal,* 396 S.W.2d at 168. It is this dicta upon which the majority so heavily relies. However, the facts in *Trinity Universal* reveal that the surety had expended the funds before Bellmead State Bank's interest attached. Thus, the "equitable principle of having paid" found in that case requires that NCNB's interest take priority over USF & G's claim for the reasons further discussed herein.

Equitable subrogation is the substitution of one party in the place of another, so that he who is substituted succeeds to the rights of the other in relation to the debt. *McBroome-Bennett Plumbing, Inc. v. Villa France, Inc.*, 515 S.W.2d 32, 36 (Tex.Civ.App.—Dallas 1974, writ ref'd n.r.e.); 53 Tex.Jur.3D Subrogation § 1 (1964). Texas courts in particular have been partial to this "pure equity" and have often stated: The doctrine of subrogation is always given a liberal interpretation and is broad enough to include every instance in which one person, not acting voluntarily has paid a debt for which another was primarily liable and which in equity and good conscience should have been discharged by the latter. *McBroome-Bennett,* 515 S.W.2d at 36; *Independence Indemnity Co. v. Republic Nat'l Bank & Trust Co.*, 114 S.W.2d 1223 (Tex. Civ. App.—Dallas 1938, writ dism'd); *Constitution Indemnity Co. v. Armbrust,* 25 S.W.2d 176, 180 (Tex.Civ.App.—San Antonio 1930, writ ref'd); *Galbraith-Foxworth Lumber Co. v. Long,* 5 S.W.2d 162, 167 (Tex. Civ. App.—Dallas 1928, writ ref'd). Courts apply equitable subrogation on behalf of an insurer to prevent an injustice such as double recovery for an insured. *Ortiz v. Great Southwestern Fire and Casualty Ins.,* 597 S.W.2d 342, 343 (Tex.1980).

However, it is undisputed that under Texas law, this right of equitable subrogation, which is not dependent on an assignment or contract clause, arises upon payment by an insured under indemnity insurance. See, *e.g., Ortiz,* 597 S.W.2d at 344 (fire insurance).

Assuming in the instant case that USF & G has an equitable right to subrogation, under controlling Texas law, it arose upon payment. The majority concedes that USF & G's claim to subrogation is not contractual and therefore did not arise by virtue of the Master Surety Agreement executed prior to the Bank's loan. In the stipulated facts before the trial court, USF & G admitted that the Bank had loaned the money to Wallace and perfected its lien before USF & G paid any of the materialmen. Thus, USF & G's subrogation claim would be second in time to the Bank's right to payment secured by its interest in Wallace's accounts receivable. Accordingly, the Bank should prevail under the "first in time is the first in right" rule. See *United*

States v. City of New Britain, 347 U.S. 81, 85, 74 S.Ct. 367, 370, 98 L.Ed. 520 (1954); *Diversified Mortgage Investors v. Lloyd D. Blaylock General Contractor, Inc.,* 576 S.W.2d 794, 807 (Tex.1978). It is also well established that as between competing legal and equitable claims, the legal claim generally prevails. See *Anderson v. Waco State Bank,* 92 Tex. 506, 49 S.W. 1030 (1899). (A prior equitable right does not prevail over a subsequently acquired legal claim provided the legal claim holder was without notice of the pre-existing equitable right). Contrary to the majority's assertions, an injustice would occur if USF & G prevailed in this case under a misapplied theory of equitable subrogation. The proper logic is simple—the Bank expended its funds first and perfected its lien. USF & G could have protected its position by insisting that the mechanics and materialmen file liens as a prerequisite to payment, whether or not such liens were required by contracts with Wallace. This would have insured a right of recourse against the owner of the property. Instead, USF & G seeks to gain an advantage in equity after failing to protect its rights at law. In recognizing the obligations of an insurance company, the Texas Supreme Court has stated that "the loss should be borne by the insurer for that is a risk the insured has paid it to assume." *Ortiz,* 597 S.W.2d at 344.

Performance Under the Contract by Wallace

In its first point of error, the Bank asserts that the trial court erred in concluding that, since the Wallace companies did not pay certain claims of subcontractors on the projects, Wallace committed a material breach under its contracts with the prime contractors and therefore had no entitlement to the funds which remain owed to Wallace under those subcontracts to the extent which subcontractors were not paid. Thus, the trial court held that the Bank, as assignee of a security interest in Wallace's accounts receivable, had no interest in those funds. I agree with the Bank's contention that the trial court erred in concluding that Wallace, and thus its assignee Bank, had no claim to the funds. Accordingly, I would sustain point of error number one for the following reasons.

It is established that as the assignee of a perfected security interest in the accounts and proceeds of a contractor, a lender is entitled to the same right to the funds as his assignor. See Tex.Bus. & Com.Code Ann. § 9.106 (Vernon Supp.1988). However, such an assignee cannot take greater rights than his assignor. See Tex.Bus. & Com.Code ANN. § 9.318(a) (Vernon Supp.1988).

USF & G argues that the trial court properly found that Wallace's failure to pay certain of its subcontractors on each of the projects constitutes a material breach and that therefore, Wallace had not substantially performed. On each project, Wallace's contract with the respective prime contractor expressly required payment of all subcontractor supplier bills as a condition of completion of the contract obligations. However, similar contract language was construed in *Corpus Christi Bank and Trust v. Smith,* 525 S.W.2d 501, 505-06 (Tex.1975), where the Texas supreme court held that such a retainage provision was intended to provide incentive for the contractor to finish the project, provide completion funds in case the contractor abandons the project, and provide funds to remedy defects. *Corpus Christi,* 525 S.W.2d at 504-05. The *Corpus Christi* court determined that the retainage provision did not, as argued by USF & G, make the materialmen third party beneficiaries or deprive the contractor of an interest in the retainage. Thus, the bank's secured claim was not defeated. *Id.* at 505; *See Citizens Nat'l Bank v. Texas & Pacific Ry. Co.,* 150 S.W.2d 1003, 1007 (Tex.1941); *East Texas Bank and Trust Co. v. Mid-South Contractors, Inc.,* 451 S.W.2d 782 (Tex.Civ.App.—Tyler 1970, no writ); *Scarborough v. Victoria Bank & Trust Co.,* 250 S.W.2d 918 (Tex.Civ.App.—San Antonio 1952, writ ref'd).

Under Texas law, when a contractor has substantially performed, he is entitled to recover the full contract price less the cost required to remedy the defects. However, the burden is on the contractor to introduce evidence which may be used to measure the amount of the deduction. *Vance v. My Apartment Steak House,* 677 S.W.2d 480, 481-82 (Tex.1984); *BPR Construction & Engineering, Inc. v. Rivers,* 608 S.W.2d 248, 249-50 (Tex.Civ.App.—Dallas 1980, writ ref'd n.r.e.). In the instant case, Wallace has substantially performed and the Bank makes no claims to contract funds used to complete the projects or remedy defects.

With regard to the Four Allen Center Project, the stipulated facts reveal that Wallace performed all of its contract obligations with the exception of the air balancing work. However, the parties did not stipulate nor is there any evidence in the record that any funds were expended to remedy this alleged defect. The balance remaining in the Wallace contract was $121,144.47. Of this total, the Bank does not claim priority to the portion used to pay the $772 mechanics' and materialmen's lien filed against the project. However, under the theory of substantial performance, I would hold that Wallace and therefore the Bank as its assignee, is entitled to the difference of $120,372.47 which was paid to USF & G by the prime contractor on September 12, 1985. Likewise, on the Buena Vista project, Wallace had fully performed its contract obligations. Thus, the Bank as Wallace's assignee is entitled to the entire contract balance of $88,053.48 which was paid by the prime contractor to USF & G.

On the Farmer's Project, Wallace had not completed certain items of contract, warranty or correction work. The stipulated facts reflect that the prime contractor incurred $31,030.25 in expenses in completing Wallace's contract obligations. The amount of the contract balance after deducting these costs of completion was $297,588.50. The Bank does not claim priority to the $79,588 which was expended to satisfy the claims of the perfected materialmen's lien claimants. I would hold that the Bank, by virtue of its perfected security interest in Wallace's accounts receivable, is entitled to $218,000.50, which includes the $110,194.50 held in escrow.

Similarly, on the Ohio State Project, Wallace substantially completed its subcontract obligations subject to certain contract, corrective and warranty work. The stipulated facts reveal that the prime contractor expended $33,844.52 to finish the job. After deduction of completion costs, the balance remaining on the contract was $142,234.50. The Bank does not claim the $53,003.88 paid to satisfy the perfected mechanics' and materialmen's lien claimants. I would hold that under the substantial performance doctrine, the Bank is entitled to the remaining balance, $89,425.12 of which was paid to USF & G and $9,805.50 which is held in the escrow account.

All the work required under the contract with the prime contractor was performed by Wallace on the International Project. Neither the prime contractor nor USF & G expended any funds for completion. The contract balance due totals $299,854.55 after deduction of the $27,700 paid by USF & G to release a perfected mechanic's lien. I would hold that the Bank has a right to the $299,854.55 balance remaining by virtue of its full performance. Thus, I would hold that the Bank has priority over USF & G to that amount as the holder of a perfected security interest.

Surety's Rights as Subrogee to Owner

In its second point of error, the Bank argues that the trial court erred in holding that as subrogee to the prime contractors, USF & G, as surety, has a superior right to the balance owed on the Wallace subcontracts to the extent necessary to pay Wallace's material and labor claimants, whether or not they possessed valid mechanic's liens. I would sustain point of error number two for the reasons discussed herein.

Federal cases have long held in favor of the surety on an equitable subrogation theory. These cases involve United States government contracts and performance bonds required by federal statutes on federal government jobs. The federal cases stress various viewpoints which are not relevant to private litigants in a state justice system. One such viewpoint is that the surety ought to win because it directly helped the United States by completing construction work under a government construction contract, whereas the Bank was but a money lender whose only equity arose when it could show its money was actually used to pay labor and materials which discharged obligations for which the surety would otherwise have been liable.

The federal cases hold that in paying labor and materialmen, the surety becomes subrogated to their rights. However, these cases do not recognize that those laborers and materialmen had no legal rights against the United States as owner. Under state law, contractors who deal with individuals or private entities may seek protected status through compliance with mechanics' and materialmen's lien statutes. See, *e.g.,* Tex. Prop. Code Ann. ch. 53 (Vernon 1984). Unlike a situation where a government entity is the owner, a contractor or subcontractor on a private project who has properly perfected a lien may demand payment from the owner of the property. *Id.* at § 53.083. Under the Federal Miller Act, the labor and materialmen only had rights against the payment bond surety and against the contractor, whose payment the surety had guaranteed.

The Federal cases also hold that by completing the performance of a defaulting contractor, the surety became subrogated to the contractor's rights. However, these cases do not recognize that the defaulting contractor had only the conditional right to receive sums earned under the contract from the owner and that the contractor may have made a valid assignment of those sums under state law. The federal courts also have held that the surety, by performing under its bond, became subrogated to the rights of the United States, as owner. These holdings stretch the equitable subrogation theory rather thin in view of the fact that the purpose of the surety bond was to comply with the Federal Miller Act. The purpose of that Act was to give laborers and materialmen protection which they would not otherwise have had under state mechanics' lien statutes because the United States government is immune from the execution of state liens. These holdings further ignore the fact that the United States, as owner, had the right under government construction contracts to receive performance by the contractor and, under the surety's bond, had the right to have the contractor's performance guaranteed by the surety. Additionally, the United States, as owner, had only the duty to pay money for performance but had no right to receive money to which right the surety could, by performing the contractor's duties, become subrogated.

Under Texas law a contractor who enters a public works contract with the state must obtain specific performance and payment bonds. Tex.Rev.Civ.Stat.Ann. art. 5160 (Vernon 1987). Pursuant to article 5160, any such contractor who abandons performance forfeits any claim to further proceeds under the contract until the contractor pays all costs of completion. *Id.* at sec. E. Thus, courts have held that a bank with a perfected security interest in the contractor's accounts receivable likewise has no claim to any progress payments or retained percentages which remain unpaid when the contractor abandons the project. *First Hutchings-Sealy Nat'l Bank v. Aetna Casualty,* 532 S.W.2d 114 (Tex.Civ.App.—Houston 1975, writ ref'd n.r.e.); *Deer Park Bank v. Aetna Ins. Co.,* 493 S.W.2d 305 (Tex.Civ.App.—Beaumont 1973, no writ); *Travelers Indemnity Co. v. Snyder Nat'l Bank,* 361 S.W.2d 926 (Tex.Civ.App.—Eastland 1952, writ ref'd n.r.e.).

This statute has been strictly construed to allow a surety, as subrogee to the owner, to prevail over a bank with a security interest even if the surety signs a subordination agreement with the bank. *Travelers Indemnity,* 361 S.W.2d at 926. However, as with the Federal Miller Act, the purpose of this article is to protect laborers and materialmen who had worked on or supplied materials for construction of public improvements and whose valid claims could not be enforced by procuring a lien upon the property. *Allis-Chambers Mfg. Co. v. Curtis Elec. Co.,* 259 S.W.2d 918, 921 (Tex.Civ.App.— Austin 1953), reversed in part on other grounds, 153 Tex. 118, 264 S.W.2d 700 (1954).

Accordingly, despite urging by USF & G, I would decline to follow federal precedent or apply article 5160 to private projects. Instead, I consider it in the best interest of the law of the State of Texas to decide the issues in this case based on our understanding of controlling state law as discussed with regard to point of error one. Accordingly, I would sustain the Bank's second point of error.

Surety's Rights as Subrogee to Materialmen

In its third point of error, the Bank maintains that the trial court's judgment was in error because USF & G, as subrogee to the rights of the materialmen and labor claimants, does not have a superior right to the subcontract balances by virtue of a trust or equitable lien on the funds. In order for an express trust to be created, the settlor must manifest an intention to create a trust in reasonably certain terms. Tex.Trust Code Ann. § 112.002 (Vernon 1986). None of the various Wallace subcontracts contain any evidence of intent to create trusts for the benefit of the mechanics and materialmen. In the absence of such intent, a court should not impose a trust. *Spiritas v. Robinowitz,* 544 S.W.2d 710 (Tex. Civ. App.—Dallas 1976, writ ref'd n.r.e.).

Alternatively, USF & G also urges that a statutory trust arose in favor of the mechanics and materialmen. Under Texas law, Construction payments are trust funds . . . if the payments are made to a contractor or subcontractor or to an officer, director, or agent of a contractor or subcontractor, under a construction contract for the improvement of specific real property in this state. Tex.Trust Code Ann. § 162.001 (Vernon 1984). However, this chapter expressly does not apply to a lender. Tex. Trust Code Ann. § 162.004(a) (Vernon Supp.1986); *Republic Bank Dallas, N.A. v. Interkal, Inc.,* 691 S.W.2d 605, 607 (Tex.1985). In the absence of an ambiguity, we must follow the clear language of the statute. *Id.* Consequently, under the plain language of the statute, the Bank's priority over the materialmen as a secured creditor is not defeated.

Since the contracts themselves do not manifest an intent to create a trust and the statutory trust contemplated in section 162.004 does not apply to a lender, I conclude that no trust arose in favor of Wallace's mechanics and materialmen. A subrogee has no greater rights in relation to a debt than his subrogor. *Insurance Co. of North America v. Fredonia State Bank,* 469 S.W.2d 248, 252 (Tex. Civ. App.—Tyler 1971, writ ref'd n.r.e.). Accordingly, USF & G as subrogee to the mechanics and materialmen, cannot properly assert a superior claim to the funds by virtue of a trust or equitable lien. I would sustain point of error three.

Kirk Williams and Kahoe Air's Liens

In point of error four, the Bank asserts that there is insufficient evidence to determine and therefore, USF & G failed to prove, that Kirk Williams had timely filed and perfected a valid mechanic's lien on the Farmers Project and that Kirk Williams and Kahoe Air timely filed and perfected valid mechanics' liens on the Ohio State Project. The only issue involved pertains to the existence of properly filed and perfected mechanics' liens on projects in Ohio.

The parties do not dispute that Ohio law applies as to the perfection of these liens. See *Duncan v. Cessna Aircraft Co.,* 665 S.W.2d 414, 420-21 (Tex.1984). Ohio law requires strict compliance with the procedural steps necessary to create a mechanic's lien. *M.J. Kelly Co. v. Haendiges,* 397 N.E.2d 416, 417-18 (Ohio Ct.App.1978). Also, the party which seeks the benefit of the lien bears the burden to plead and prove compliance with the procedures. See *Seybold v. Pitz,* 101 Ohio App. 316, 136 N.E.2d 666, 669 (1955). The Ohio mechanic's lien statute states that specific information must be included in the affidavit including the amount due, property description, name of the owner, and names and addresses of the lien claimant and prime contractor. The affidavit must also be verified. This affidavit must be filed within a specified time and endorsed by the recorder with the date and hour of filing. The statute expressly provides that no exemptions apply to the recording provision. Ohio Rev.Code Ann. § 1311.06 (1988).

A thorough review of the record reveals that none of the liens through which USF & G claims an interest were in evidence. Although the parties stipulated that Williams and Kahoe Air filed liens, there is insufficient evidence for us to conclude that their liens are valid under the Ohio law. Thus, these lien claimants are general unsecured creditors of Wallace who have no priority over the Bank. I would sustain point of error four.

Relationship of Surety Bonds and Subcontracts

In point of error five, the Bank maintains that the trial court was in error when it concluded that the terms of USF & G's payment bonds are "read into and incorporated in" the Wallace subcontracts, that the failure to pay for all labor and materials was a material default under the bond terms and that therefore, Wallace had no interest in the contract balances to which the Bank's lien could attach.

Under general contract principles, the primary concern of the courts is to give effect to the intentions of the parties as expressed in the instruments. *Ideal Lease Service, Inc. v. Amoco Production Co.,* 662 S.W.2d 951, 952-53 (Tex. 1984). In the face of an unambiguous provision, the court must give effect to the contract as written. *Id.; Sun Oil Co. v. Madeley,* 626 S.W.2d 726, 728 (Tex. 1981).

Each of the Wallace subcontracts specifies what documents form the contract and the bonds are not included in the list. Additionally, each subcontract contains a clause which states that the subcontract constitutes the entire agreement of the parties. I would conclude that the agreements are unambiguous and thus the bond provisions are not incorporated into the Wallace subcontracts. I would sustain point of error five.

International Project—Costs and Expenses

In point of error six, the Bank maintains that with respect to the International Project, there is no evidence to support the trial court's decision that USF & G is entitled to $30,000 in expenses for the settlement of the claims under the bonds, together with costs and expenses incurred to recover the contract funds. The stipulated facts provide that the amount of expenses incurred by USF & G was $30,000. With regard to entitlement to that amount, USF & G relies on an indemnity clause from the master surety agreement executed by Wallace and the prime contractor before the Bank acquired its security interest.

I would hold that this claim for fees in the Louisiana suit is premature because the suit is still pending. Additionally, under my analysis USF & G would not prevail in this lawsuit. Thus,

I would hold that the evidence is insufficient to support the award of attorney's fees. I would sustain the Bank's sixth and final point of error.

I would reverse the trial court's judgment and render judgment for the Bank. As the prevailing party, I would hold that the Bank is entitled to the stipulated attorneys' fees in the amount of $74,043.06.

In summary, in accordance with my dissenting opinion, I would reverse the judgment of the trial court in favor of appellee United States Fidelity and Guaranty and render judgment that appellant NCNB, recover from appellee United States Fidelity and Guaranty Company as follows:

1. The principal sum of $674,285.87 inclusive of the amount held in escrow by agreement of the parties;
2. prejudgment interest at the annual rate of ten percent (10%) from July 30, 1986 to March 21, 1988, the date of the trial court's judgment;
3. stipulated attorneys' fees in the amount of $73,043.06;
4. costs incurred by appellant in the trial court and of this appeal; and,
5. post-judgment interest at the annual rate of ten percent (10%) per annum on the above principal, interest, fees and costs from March 21, 1988, the date of the trial court's judgment, until paid.

With regard to the balance which is held by the prime contractor on the International Project in Louisiana, I would grant appellant's request for declaratory relief and hold that NCNB has priority over United States Fidelity and Guaranty Company to the balance due Carl P. Wallace of Louisiana on August 6, 1984, less any costs expended to complete Wallace's obligations under the subcontract and less the amount necessary to release any perfected mechanics' and materialmen's liens on the project by Wallace's subcontractors.

QUESTION

Which side prevents the better rationale, the majority or the dissent?

PROBLEM 21.1

Your client, the All Nations Insurance Company, has issued performance and payment bonds to insure payment of debts if the general contractor of a major sky scraper building runs into any problems. Unfortunately, only 50 of the proposed 110 stories in the building were completed before All Nations took over the project, completed construction, and paid off all the suppliers of material and labor. Now that the building is completed, there are payments coming in regularly from a tenant, the All Nations Trade Towers Association Company. Your company believes that it is entitled under the bond to these payments, but other creditors are now asserting that your client's interest was a secured interest and that it had failed to file under Article 9. By contrast your company is contending that Article 9 is not applicable since it is enforcing equitable rights of subrogation which exists under Surety Law. The other creditors contest this and say that your client's rights are contractual under the bond and hence are consensual secured interest subject to Article 9 filing. What are your client's rights?

[B] Subordination

Under a subordination agreement, one unsecured creditor may have agreed that its debt shall be subordinate to the debt of another unsecured creditor. Subordination agreements are enforceable in bankruptcy. Bankruptcy Code § 510(a) A subordination agreement, however, does not come within the scope of the U.C.C. Moreover, a subordination agreement differs from conventional security interests in that it does not affect any other creditor except those who have subordinated their claims. See § 1-209, § 9-316.

[C] Set-off

A set-off is the netting of a debt owed by the depositor to the bank against the bank's debt owed back to the depositor. U.C.C. 9-104(i) seems to exclude any consideration of the right of setoff from Article 9. Moreover, a security interest in a deposit account is also outside of Article 9, § 9-104(1). The issue of whether the right to setoff is excluded from article 9 arises, however, when one examines section 9-105(1)(e) which provides that accounts evidenced by a certificate of deposit are not deposit accounts. Furthermore, section 9-306 states that in certain situations bank accounts constitute proceeds and will be governed by Article 9.

IN RE OTHA C. JEAN & ASSOCIATES

United States Bankruptcy Court, E.D. Tennessee

152 B.R. 219 (1993)

RALPH H. KELLEY, CHIEF JUDGE.

This adversary proceeding has become a dispute between USBI on one side and the two banks on the other side. USBI hired the debtor, Jean & Associates, as a subcontractor. After filing bankruptcy, Jean & Associates billed USBI about $99,000 for work done under the contracts. USBI asserts a claim against Jean & Associates for about $476,000 in overpayments under earlier contracts. USBI argues that it can set off the $99,000 it owes to Jean & Associates against the $476,000 that Jean & Associates owes to it.

The banks share a perfected security interest in the general intangibles and accounts of Jean & Associates. They argue that their security interest gives them the right to the $99,000 ahead of any set-off rights that USBI may have. The banks have filed a motion for summary judgment. USBI has filed its own motion for summary judgment.

The banks argue that their security interest has priority because § 553 of the Bankruptcy Code disallows set-off by USBI. 11 U.S.C.A. § 553 (West 1979 & Supp. 1992). Section 553 generally preserves the right to set off mutual pre-bankruptcy debts. If a creditor could collect a pre-bankruptcy claim against the debtor by setting off a pre-bankruptcy debt to the debtor, § 553(a) preserves the creditor's right of set-off, subject to some restrictions.

This implies another general rule: a creditor cannot collect its pre-bankruptcy claim by setting off its post-bankruptcy debt to the debtor. *Paris v. Transamerica Ins. Group (In re Buckley & Associates Ins., Inc.),* 67 B.R. 331, 334 (Bankr. E.D. Tenn.1986) rev'd on other grounds 78 B.R. 155 (E.D.Tenn.1987) The banks argue that this rule prevents set-off by USBI; USBI's claim against Jean & Associates arose pre-bankruptcy, but USBI's $99,000 debt to Jean & Associates arose post-bankruptcy.

USBI argues that § 553 is irrelevant. The bankruptcy trustee might use § 553 to prevent the set-off for the benefit of the bankruptcy estate, but the banks cannot use it solely for their benefit. Since the outcome of this dispute will not affect the debtor or the bankruptcy estate, it should be decided as if there were no bankruptcy.

The rule that the banks rely upon follows a basic principle of bankruptcy law: a creditor cannot collect its unsecured pre-bankruptcy claim by taking, solely for its benefit, property that the debtor acquires after the beginning of the bankruptcy case. Property acquired by the debtor post-bankruptcy must be used for the benefit of all unsecured creditors or for the debtor's benefit in reorganizing or for the debtor's fresh start. 11 U.S.C.A. §§ 524, 541, 727, 1123, 1129, 1141, 1207, 1222, 1225, 1227, 1306, 1322, 1325 & 1327 (West 1979 & Supp. 1992). See *MNC Commercial Corp. v. Joseph T. Ryerson & Son, Inc.,* 882 F.2d 615 (2d Cir.1989); *Prudential Ins. Co. v. Nelson,* 101 F.2d 441 (6th Cir.1939), cert. den. 308 U.S. 583, 60 S.Ct. 106, 84 L.Ed. 489 (1939) (decided under prior bankruptcy statutes).

Denying USBI the right of set-off will not increase the money available in the bankruptcy case to pay all unsecured claims. It will not give Jean & Associates use of the money for reorganization or for a fresh start. Of course, if set-off is allowed, USBI will collect a large portion of its claim, even though other creditors with pre-bankruptcy unsecured claims may collect less or nothing at all in the bankruptcy case. However, the payment to USBI would come from an asset, USBI's debt to Jean & Associates, that is not available to pay the other pre-bankruptcy unsecured claims.

The court agrees with USBI. Allowing set-off will not violate the reasons behind the rules expressed or implied by § 553(a). Denying set-off under § 553 will give the banks an advantage based on bankruptcy law for no reason related to the bankruptcy case. The banks should not get a windfall because Jean & Associates happened to file bankruptcy. The result should be controlled by the law that would control outside of bankruptcy. *MNC Commercial Corp. v. Joseph T. Ryerson & Son, Inc.,* 882 F.2d 615 (2d Cir. 1989). The court concludes that § 553(a) does not bar set-off by USBI. This brings the court to the banks' argument on priority under state law.

The banks make a three-step argument. First, USBI's right to set-off is a security interest under Article 9 of the Uniform Commercial Code (the U.C.C.). Second, priority must be determined by Article 9's rules for priority between security interests. Third, priority is determined by the rules in § 9-312, and under those rules, the bank's perfected security interest has priority over USBI's unperfected security interest. Tenn.Code Ann. § 47-9-312 (1992).

At least one case supports the banks' argument. *Atlantic Kraft Corp. v. Gibson Group, Inc. (In re Gibson Group, Inc.),* 126 B.R. 759 (Bankr. S.D. Ohio 1991). In that case the court held that a creditor with a security interest in an account receivable was not an "assignee" under U.C.C. § 9-318 Tenn.Code Ann. § 47-9-318 (1992). It also held that an account debtor's right of set-off against the debtor was a security interest. This court disagrees.

A creditor's right of set-off is not an Article 9 security interest. Section 9-104 of the U.C.C. provides that Article 9 does not apply to a right of set-off. Tenn. Code Ann. § 47-9-104(j) (1992). Professor Grant Gilmore, one of the drafters of Article 9, thought that the exception should have been left out: "Of course a right of set-off is not a security interest and has never been confused with one; the statute might as appropriately exclude fan dancing." However, banking groups lobbied to have the exception put in so that a bank's right to set off a customer's account could not be mistaken for a security interest. 1 Grant Gilmore, Security Interests in Personal Property § 10.7 at 315-316 (Little Brown 1965).

Though a right of set-off is not a security interest, the exception in § 9-104 is worded too broadly. It says that Article 9 does not apply to a right of set-off. It would have been more accurate to say that a right of set-off is not a security interest but may be dealt with by some provisions of Article 9.

In particular, § 9-318 appears to apply to this dispute, except for the problem with the meaning of "assignee." Article 9 usually refers to a creditor with a security interest as a "secured party," but for some unknown reason, § 9-318 uses the term "assignee" instead of "secured party." Tenn.Code Ann. § 47-9-105(m) (1992); Tenn.Code Ann. § 47-9-318(1) (1992).

At one point, Professor Gilmore described the debtor as the assignor and the secured party as the assignee under § 9-318. 2 Grant Gilmore, Security Interests in Personal Property § 41.10 at 1116 (Little Brown 1965). A creditor who takes an assignment of accounts or general intangibles to secure a debt is a secured party. Tenn.Code Ann. §§ 47-1-201(37), 47-9-102, 47-9-104 & 47-9-105(m) (1992). The court believes that the converse is true; a secured party with a security interest in accounts or general intangibles is the assignee under § 9-318.

The courts have generally applied § 9-318 this way without mentioning the change in terminology. See, *e.g., Barclays American Business Credit, Inc. v. Paul Safran Metal Co.,* 566 F.Supp. 254 (N.D.Ill.1983); *Michigan Milk Producers Ass'n v. Bancroft Milk Products, Inc. (In re Bancroft Dairy, Inc.),* 10 B.R. 920 (Bankr. W. D. Mich. 1981); *Bank of Kansas v. Hutchinson Health Services, Inc.,* 13 Kan.App.2d 421, 773 P.2d 660 (1989), aff'd 246 Kan. 83, 785 P.2d 1349 (1990); *James Talcott, Inc. v. H. Corenzwit & Co.,* 76 N.J. 305, 387 A.2d 350 (1978).

The court concludes that "assignee" under § 9-318 includes a secured party with a security interest in accounts or general intangibles. Section 9-318 determines priority between USBI's right of set-off and the banks' security interest.

In two other cases the courts applied the priority rules under § 9-312, instead of § 9-318, to deny set-off, but those cases can easily be distinguished. In both cases the account debtor wanted to set off someone else's claim against the debtor. *MNC Commercial Corp. v. Joseph T. Ryerson & Son, Inc.,* 882 F.2d 615 (2d Cir. 1989); *Bank Leumi Trust Co. v. Collins Sales Service, Inc.,* 47 N.Y.2d 888, 419 N.Y.S.2d 474, 393 N.E.2d 468 (N.Y.1978).

Under the general rule in § 9-318(1)(a), USBI's defenses under the contracts that gave rise to the $99,000 debt would have priority over the banks' security interest in the $99,000 debt. Tenn.Code Ann. § 47-9-318(1)(a) (1992); *Patton v. McHone,* 822 S.W.2d 608 (Tenn.App.1991).

There is an exception to this rule when the contract between the account debtor (USBI) and the debtor (Jean & Associates) waives the account debtor's defenses as to an assignee (the banks). As far as the court knows, the later contracts between USBI and Jean & Associates do not contain a waiver of defenses by USBI.

The general rule of § 9-318(1)(a) appears not to apply for another reason. USBI's claim against Jean & Associates for the overpayments arose under the earlier contracts, not the later contracts that gave rise to the $99,000 debt. Nevertheless, USBI argues that the general rule in § 9-318(1)(a) should apply. USBI bases this argument on a clause in the later contracts. It says that USBI can set off a debt under the later contracts against any claim it has against Jean & Associates.

The court does not agree with USBI's argument. The earlier contracts and the later contracts are not the same contract for the purposes of § 9-318(1). The clause that USBI relies upon does not make the separate contracts into one contract. The clause only puts into writing USBI's right to set off claims under different contracts. *Paris v. Transamerica Ins. Group (In re Buckley &*

Associates Ins., Inc.), 67 B.R. 331, 334 (Bankr.E.D.Tenn.1986) rev'd on other grounds 78 B.R. 155 (E.D. Tenn.1987)

This brings the court to § 9-318(1)(b). Priority under § 9-318(1)(b) depends on (1) when USBI's overpayment claim against Jean & Associates accrued, and (2) when USBI received notification of the banks' security Interest. Tenn.Code Ann. § 47-9-318(1)(b) (1992).

The banks perfected their security interest by filing a financing statement. However, the filing of the financing statement was not notification to USBI of the security interest. *Chase Manhattan Bank v. State,* 40 N.Y.2d 590, 388 N.Y.S.2d 896, 357 N.E.2d 366 (N.Y. 1976).

The court cannot grant summary judgment to either side under § 9-318. The undisputed facts do not show when USBI was notified of the banks' security interest. The parties also have not argued the question of when USBI's overpayment claim accrued. With respect to § 9-318, there are genuine issues of material fact. Fed. R. Bankr. Proc. 7056 (West 1984).

USBI has raised the point that Alabama law may control. The court has examined the Alabama statutes and cases; they lead to the same result. Ala.Code Ann. §§ 7-1-201(37), 7-9-102, 7-9-104 & 7-9-105 (1992); *Lawson State Community College v. First Continental Leasing Corp.,* 529 So.2d 926 (Ala.1988), overruled on other grounds, *Berner v. Caldwell,* 543 So. 2d 686 (Ala. 1989).

The court reserves ruling on other arguments raised in the summary judgment motions. The court will enter an order denying summary judgment.

CHAPTER 22

INVESTMENT SECURITIES

§ 22.01 Sale of Investment Securities

The General Comment to the UCC states: "The concept of the [Code] is that 'commercial transactions' is a single subject of the law notwithstanding its many facets." After reciting certain facets of the commercial transaction (*e.g.,* sales, negotiable instruments, secured transactions), the Comment concludes: "Obviously, every phase of commerce involved is but a part of one transaction, namely, the sale of and payment for goods."

With respect to the inclusion of investment securities within the Code, the Comment relates:

> If, instead of goods in the ordinary sense, the transaction involved stocks or bonds, some of the phases of the transaction would obviously be different. Others would be the same. In addition, there are certain additional formalities incident to the transfer of stocks and bonds from one owner to another.

Read: U.C.C. §§ 8-101, 8-102(1)(a) and (b) (8-102(a)(4),(15),(18)(1994)).

In several respects, the sale of investment securities under Article 8 can be likened to the sale of goods under Article 2. For instance, § 8-319 (1978) was a statute of frauds provision relating to contracts for sale of investment securities. This section conformed to the policy of U.C.C. § 2-201 relating to the sale of goods. Section 8-113 (1994), however, states: "A contract . . . for the sale or purchase of a security is enforceable whether or not there is a writing signed or record authenticated by a party against whom enforcement is sought . . . ." The Comment explains: "With the increasing use of electronic means of communication, the statute of frauds is unsuited to the realities of the securities business . . . ."

With respect to remedies, § 8-107(2) (1978) provided that a seller in certain instances may recover the price of securities if a buyer failed to pay the price as it became due. This conformed to the policy of § 2-709(1) relating to the sale of goods. Also, § 8-314 (1978) dealt with certain aspects of performance. "Revised Article 8 [1994] deletes these provisions on the theory that inclusion of a few sections on issues of contract law is likely to cause more harm than good since inferences might be drawn from the failure to cover related issues. The deletion of these sections is not, however, intended as a rejection of the rules of contract law and interpretation that they expressed." Prefatory Note to Revised Article 8, Revision Note 8.

In seeking relevant contract law, do not forget that U.C.C. § 1-102 Comment 1 approves reasoning by analogy: "[Courts] have recognized the policies embodied in an act as applicable in reason to subject matter which was not expressly included in the language of the act . . . . They have done the same where reason and policy so required, even where the subject-matter had been intentionally excluded from the act in general." In this vein § 2-105 Comment 1 provides:

> "Investment securities" are expressly excluded from the coverage of this Article. It is not intended by this exclusion, however, to prevent the application of a particular section of this Article by analogy to securities (as was done with the Original Sales act in *Agar v. Orda*, 264 N.Y. 248, 190 N.E. 479, 99 A.L.R. 269 (1934)) when the reason of that section makes such application sensible and the situation involved is not covered by the Article of this Act dealing specifically with such securities (Article 8).

See also U.C.C. §§ 2-313 Comment 2, 8-107 Comment 2 (1978).

§ 22.02 Investment Securities as Negotiable Instruments

[A] Issuance, Transfer and Registration of Transfer

Several sections of Article 8 deal with the certificated security as a negotiable instrument. U.C.C. § 8-105(1)(1978). Accordingly, Article 8 may be appropriately compared with Article 3, Negotiable Instruments, *i.e.,* drafts and notes.

A simplified set of transactions with regard to stock will give a basic orientation to the process of (1) issuance, (2) transfer and (3) registration of transfer. References are to the 1994 Revised Article 8. For example, M Corporation issues (U.C.C. § 8-201(a)) a certificated security, *i.e.,* a stock certificate. U.C.C. § 8-102(a)(4) and (15), cf. § 3-104 (functional test vs. formal test). It is signed by authorized corporate officials and also signed by the corporation's transfer agent and registrar. The transfer agent and registrar, by signing, enter upon certain warranties, *e.g.*, that the certificate is genuine. U.C.C. § 8-208. The certificate is delivered to shareholder A, in registered form in the name of A. U.C.C. § 8-102(a)(13); cf. §§ 3-104(a)(1), 3-109(b). The name of A is registered on M Corporation's books so as to entitle A to dividends, etc.

B concludes a contract for purchase of the certificate from A, no stockbrokers being involved in the transaction. A indorses in blank either on the back of the certificate or on a separate paper, often referred to as a stock power. U.C.C. §§ 8-102(a)(11), 8-107(a)(1), 8-304(a); cf. §§ 3-204(a), 3-205. *See also* § 8-304(b), cf. § 3-203(d). A by the indorsement assumes no obligation that the issuer, M Corporation, will honor the security. U.C.C. § 8-304(f); cf. §§ 3-415(a), 7-505. A does enter upon certain transfer warranties to B, *e.g.,* that the certificate is genuine. U.C.C. § 8-108(a); cf. §§ 3-416(a), 7-507. In addition A will have its signature guaranteed by its bank, *e.g.*, the bank warrants that the signature is genuine. U.C.C. § 8-306(a) and (h). A delivers the certificate to B. *See* U.C.C. §§ 8-301(a), 8-304(c).

Although B is the owner of the certificate, it will wish to have the transfer registered on the books of the corporation so as to be entitled to vote at shareholder's meetings, receive dividends, etc. *See* U.C.C. § 8-307. B, in presenting the certificate for registration of transfer, may make certain presentment warranties. U.C.C. § 8-108(f); cf. § 3-417. M Corporation will satisfy itself that the preconditions to registration of transfer have been met (U.C.C. § 8-401), cancel the old certificate registered in the name of A, and issue a new certificate registered in the name of B.

The following is a diagram of these transactions:

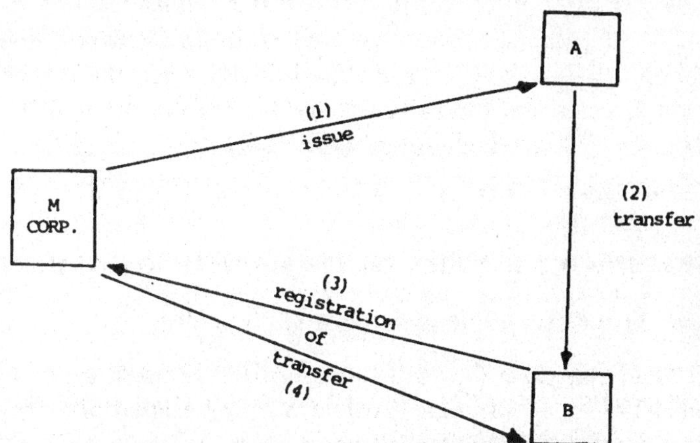

Diagram of Stock Transfer Registration Transaction

When brokers are involved, the transaction can be far more complex though the fundamentals of transfer remain. Typically, a buyer of stock will not even know who its seller is. All the buyer knows is that it placed an order with its broker and some time later a certificate registered in its name was received. In fact, in the first instance, seller's broker and buyer's broker may not have determined a definite seller for a definite buyer, as securities are fungible (U.C.C. § 1-201(17)). For example, seller's broker may have engaged to deliver/transfer 1,500 shares of XYZ Corp. to buyer's broker and buyer's broker, on the other hand, has engaged to deliver/transfer 500 shares of XYZ Corp. to seller's broker, these shares representing several transactions. Consequently, the delivery/transfer will be accomplished by seller's broker delivering/transferring the balance of 1,000 shares to buyer's broker. *See* U.C.C. §§ 8-301(a), 8-304(c).[1]

[1] Former § 8-107(1)(1978) stated that "a person obligated to transfer securities may transfer any certificated security of the specified issue in bearer form or registered in the name of the transferee."

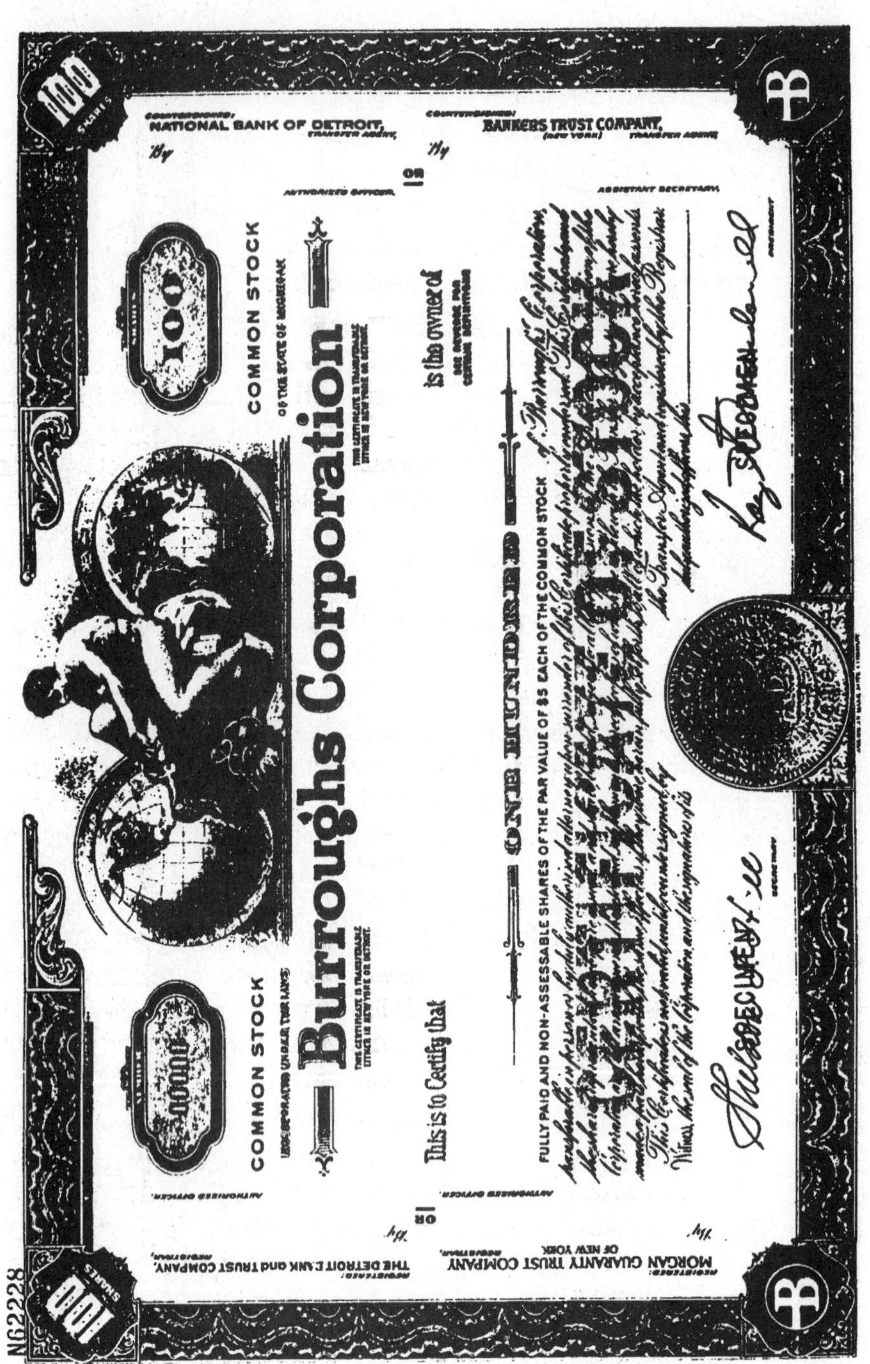

Burroughs Corporation Stock Certificate

The following abbreviations, when used in the inscription on the face of this certificate, shall be construed as though they were written out in full according to applicable laws or regulations:

TEN COM —as tenants in common

TEN ENT —as tenants by the entireties

JT TEN —as joint tenants with right of survivorship and not as tenants in common

UNIF GIFT MIN ACT— .... Custodian ....
(Cust) (Minor)
under Uniform Gifts to Minors
Act ....
(State)

Additional abbreviations may also be used though not in the above list.

For value received, ________ *hereby sell, assign and transfer unto*

PLEASE INSERT SOCIAL SECURITY OR OTHER IDENTIFYING NUMBER OF ASSIGNEE

____

PLEASE PRINT OR TYPEWRITE NAME AND ADDRESS OF ASSIGNEE

____

____

____ *Shares*

of the capital stock represented by the within Certificate, and do hereby irrevocably constitute and appoint ____

____ *Attorney to transfer the said stock on the books of the within named Corporation with full power of substitution in the premises.*

Dated, ________________

____

NOTICE: THE SIGNATURE TO THIS ASSIGNMENT MUST CORRESPOND WITH THE NAME AS WRITTEN UPON THE FACE OF THE CERTIFICATE IN EVERY PARTICULAR, WITHOUT ALTERATION OR ENLARGEMENT, OR ANY CHANGE WHATEVER.

____

THIS SPACE MUST NOT BE COVERED IN ANY WAY

Burroughs Corporation Stock Certificate (Reverse)

ASSIGNMENT SEPARATE FROM CERTIFICATE

For Value Received ______________________________

hereby sell, assign and transfer unto ______________________________

______________________________ (__________) Shares of the $5.00 par value Common Stock of Burroughs Corporation, a Michigan Corporation, standing in ______________________________ name on the books of said Corporation represented by Certificate No. ______________________________ herewith and do hereby irrevocably constitute and appoint ______________________________ attorney to transfer the said stock on the books of the within named Corporation with full power of substitution in the premises.

Dated __________________ ______________________________

IN PRESENCE OF

SIGNATURE GUARANTEED

____

____

The signature(s) of the person(s) executing this assignment should correspond with the name(s) as written upon the face of stock certificate(s) and should be guaranteed by a Bank or Trust Company.

Assignment Separate From Certificate

[B] Adverse Claims: Rights Acquired by Purchaser

Read: U.C.C. §§ 8-302, 8-303(1994); cf. §§ 3-302, 3-306.

A person having the rights of a holder in due course takes free of a claim to the instrument. Similarly, a "protected purchaser" acquires its interest in a security free of any adverse claim. U.C.C. §§ 3-306, 8-303. (Under the 1978 Code the "protected purchaser" was referred to as a "bona fide purchaser." § 8-302(3) (1978).) The leading case of *Turnbull v. Longacre Bank*, 163 N.E. 135 (1928), and cited in U.C.C. § 8-207 Comment 2 (1978), illustrates. There, Stockbroker gave stock certificates issued by Corporation(s) to a messenger to deliver to certain other brokers. The certificates were indorsed in blank. The messenger stole the certificates which came into the possession of Brinkman. Brinkman pledged the certificates to Longacre Bank as security for a loan. The loan was never paid. Thereafter, Stockbroker learned the stolen certificates were in the possession of Bank and brought an action against Bank and in the complaint asked that Bank be restrained from transferring the certificates or from seeking to have the certificates presented to Corporation for registration of transfer. Bank answered the complaint and set up as a defense that it was entitled to retain possession of the certificates as a purchaser for value without notice. The court responded:

> It is unnecessary for us to decide whether at common law the defendant bank might retain the stolen certificates as pledgee. Elements of negotiability of certificates of corporate stock, lacking at common law, have been supplied by article 6 of the Personal Property Law (Consol. Laws, c. 41) the Uniform Stock Transfer Act. Title to a certificate may be transferred by delivery of the certificate indorsed in blank (section 162). It is provided by section 166 that—
>
> > The delivery of a certificate to transfer title in accordance with the provisions of section one hundred and sixty-two is effectual; except as provided in section one hundred and sixty-eight, though made by one having no right of possession and having no authority from the owner of the certificate or from the person purporting to transfer the title.
>
> Section 168 provides that—
>
> > If the delivery of a certificate was made (c) without authority from the owner, . . . the possession of the certificate may be reclaimed and the transfer thereof rescinded, unless: (1) The certificate has been transferred to a purchaser for value in good faith without notice of any facts making the transfer wrongful . . . .
>
> Here the evidence and findings establish that the Longacre Bank is a purchaser for value and without notice of any facts making the transfer wrongful. It is evident that under the provisions of the Personal Property Law the possession of an innocent purchaser for value of certificates of stock indorsed in blank is fully protected. In that respect, though delivery was made by one who, being a thief, had himself neither right of possession or authority to transfer title, such certificates possess the attributes of negotiable instruments. The bank has acquired title to the certificates as pledgee. The plaintiffs may reclaim the certificates only by payment of the debt for which they are security.

163 N.E. at 137. This result would be confirmed by U.C.C. §§ 8-302, 8-303(1994); *see* § 9-506.

[C] Issuer's Defenses

Read: U.C.C. §§ 8-202, 8-205, 8-206(1994); cf. §§ 3-305(a) and (b), 3-403, 3-406, 3-407.

The right of a holder in due course to enforce the obligation of a party to pay a negotiable instrument is subject to certain "real defenses" but is not subject to "personal defenses" or "claims in recoupment." U.C.C. § 3-305(b). One of the personal defenses is want or failure of consideration. U.C.C. § 3-305(b) and Comment 2. Similarly, most defenses of an issuer of a certificated security are ineffective against a purchaser for value without notice of the particular defense. U.C.C. § 8-202.

The leading case of *Bankers' Trust Co. v. Rood*, 233 N.W. 794 (Iowa 1930), is illustrative. There, Monarch Company issued a stock certificate for 188 shares to W.B. Rood. Rood did not pay cash but rather he gave his note. Subsequently, Rood pledged the certificate to Bankers' Trust Company for the purpose of securing a loan. A portion of the loan ($36,000) was never paid and Rood became insolvent. As a result Bankers' Trust foreclosed on the Monarch stock belonging to Rood.

Monarch asserted that Rood received no interest in the stock and, consequently, Bankers' Trust obtained nothing through the action of Rood in attempting to pledge such stock. This assertion was based on Iowa Code Supp. § 1641 which stated in part: "[N]o corporation . . . shall issue any certificate . . . of shares of . . . stock . . . until the corporation has received the par value thereof . . . . The . . . stock of any corporation issued in violation of the . . . provisions hereof shall be void."

The Iowa Supreme Court affirmed for appellee Bankers' Trust stating in part:

> Previous consideration has been given by this court to section 1641 . . . of the foregoing statutes. [Citations.] Our conclusion upon each occasion was that the word "void," used in said section, means "voidable" in fact. The section, it was held in the above-cited cases, is for the benefit of the corporation. A note given for stock is collectible, although compliance has not been made with this section of the statute. While considering these statutes, we said in *Sherman v. Smith*: . . . "We are of the opinion that when the statutes are read together, as they should be, it was not the legislative intention to make stock issued under the condition at bar ipso facto void, but to make violations of this chapter a cause for having the stock canceled at the suit of the Attorney General, and to inflict other punishments for the violation, which, however, do not include that the stock issue shall be void instead of voidable."
>
> When considering the same legislation, the Circuit Court of Appeals, in the Eighth Circuit, declared: . . . "The purpose of the legislators in enacting the statute [the sections of the . . . Code above quoted] was to secure to the corporation payment for its stock in money or its equivalent to an amount equal to the par value of the stock. That object will be attained more successfully and certainly if the stock issued in violation of the statute is held to be voidable than if it is adjudged to be absolutely void. If it is held to be voidable, the corporation may avoid it, if its full value is not paid when demanded, and, on the other hand, may secure that value if the purchaser is willing to pay for it. If it is held to be utterly void, it can recover nothing for the stock it has sold, and must return that which it has received . . . ."
>
> Returning now to the case at bar, it is found that the stock in question was issued by the appellant corporation to W.B. Rood, in consideration for his note. Under the authority of the foregoing cases, the stock thus issued was voidable by a suit of the Attorney General, and

probably by action of the corporation itself. However, before the corporation exercised the power of declaring the stock void, W.B. Rood, for a full and a valuable consideration, pledged the same with the appellee Bankers' Trust Company. Thereby the rights of a third person have intervened. Appellees declare that the intervening third person was an innocent purchaser of this stock and therefore obtained the same for the purposes of the security without any subjection to the appellant's claims because the latter issued the stock, delivered it to W.B. Rood, and thus authorized him to go out into the world and borrow money upon such security.

For the purposes of the present discussion, it will be assumed that the appellee Bankers' Trust Company loaned the money and took the security without any knowledge of appellant's equities. Thus it is apparent that the appellant in effect perpetrated a fraud upon the Bankers' Trust Company because the stock was issued and W.B. Rood received an apparent certificate therefor, although the cash consideration had not been given. Contrary, then, to appellant's previous action, it now seeks to say that W.B. Rood, regardless of the certificate, does not own the stock because he did not pay therefor. No matter what appellant pretended before, it now says that the appellee Bankers' Trust Company must suffer loss for the reason that the stock was not paid for originally. Although appellant extended an invitation to the world, including the appellee Bankers' Trust Company, to deal with W.B. Rood and buy or accept the stock as collateral security, yet the appellant now would repudiate its actions and representations in that regard and hide behind the statute aforesaid for protection against an innocent pledgee for value. Obviously appellant cannot thus conduct itself.

Corporation stock is not negotiable paper, but it possesses many characteristics of negotiability: for instance, such certificates of stock may be transferred by proper indorsement, etc. Business necessity demands that transfers of these stock certificates be sustained unless unsurmountable legal barriers prevent. Estoppel against the corporation issuing the stock is the principle applied to protect the innocent transferee thereof. [Citations.]

. . .

It is not necessary to further quote from the authorities, for sufficient already appears to indicate the care with which courts must proceed before they exercise their power to declare such stock transfer of no validity. Here there is presented a case where the corporation, before it had exercised its option to declare its issuance of the stock void, permitted the holder of such stock to pledge the same to an innocent transferee for a valuable consideration. The stock not being void from its inception, but only voidable, it is apparent that the corporation has estopped itself from exercising the statutory opinion. [Citation.]

There is no new theory in the pronouncement of law above made. Frequently officers of corporations have caused the institution financial loss or estopped it by fraud or misconduct. In the case at bar, as before said, the appellee Bankers' Trust Company was a transferee for value in good faith, and we at this place assume without notice of any infirmity in the stock. Consequently, the transferee is entitled to have the stock transferred to it upon the corporate records. [Citation.] Also the appellee Bankers' Trust Company may, if it desires, sell the stock at foreclosure sale, and the purchaser thereof likewise will be entitled to have the stock transferred upon the corporate record. When thus transferred, the then holder of such stock will be entitled to demand and receive dividends, vote the stock, and otherwise engage in the corporate activities . . . .

233 N.W. at 797-99. The Code would affirm this result. *See* U.C.C. § 8-202(b)(1994). This case was cited in Comment 4 to U.C.C. § 8-202 of the 1972 Code which stated in part:

> Many jurisdictions have . . . statutory requirements that unless substantial value is received by the issuer for the security it shall be void. This Article follows the better case law and validates securities in the hands of bona fide purchasers where the provisions are statutory . . . .

[D] Merger

M Corporation issues (U.C.C. § 8-201) a security represented by a stock certificate to A who indorses and delivers it to B. U.C.C. § 8-301(a). To register the transfer B must present the certificate to M. U.C.C. § 8-401. To be a "protected purchaser" B must obtain control of the certificate. U.C.C. §§ 8-303(a)(3), 8-106(a) and (b). A creditor of B who wants to attach or levy upon the certificated security must cause it to be seized. U.C.C. § 8-112(a), cf. § 7-602. *See also* U.C.C. §§ 8-204, 8-209. To pledge a certificated security the pledgee must acquire possession of the certificated security. U.C.C. § 9-115(4)(a); see §§ 9-115(1)(e) and (f)(i), 8-106(a) and (b), 8-301(a)(1). These are manifestations of the concept of merger, that is, the claim of B is so merged into the paper evidencing the claim that the paper is treated as if it were the claim itself. Cf. U.C.C. §§ 3-602(a), 3-301(i), 1-201(20); § 7-403.

§ 22.03 Security Interests in Investment Securities

The 1994 U.C.C. Article 9, Secured Transactions, applies to security interests in "investment property," which means, inter alia, a "security," whether certificated or uncertificated, or a "security entitlement," or a "securities account." U.C.C. §§ 9-115(1)(f), 8-102(a)(15) and (17), 8-501(a). Thus revised Article 8 reflects both a direct holding system and an indirect holding system. Section 9-115 Comment 2 explains:

> The distinction between the direct and indirect holding systems plays an important role in the rules on security interests in securities. Consider two investors, X and Y, each of whom owns 1000 shares of XYZ Co. common stock. X has a certificate representing 1000 shares and is registered on the books maintained by XYZ Co.'s transfer agent as the holder of record of those 1000 shares. X has a direct relationship with the issuer, and receives dividends, distributions, and proxies directly from the issuer. In Revised Article 8 terminology, X has a direct claim to a "certified security." If X wishes to use the investment position as collateral for a loan, X would grant the lender a security interest in the "certified security." . . . XYZ Co. might not issue certificates, but register investors such as X directly on its stockholder books. In that case, X's interest would be an "uncertificated security." . . . By contrast to these direct relationships, Y holds the securities through an account with Y's broker. Y does not have a certificate and is not registered on XYZ Co.'s stock books as a holder of record. Rather, Y holds the securities through a chain of securities intermediaries. Under Revised Article 8, Y's interest in XYZ common stock is described as a "securities entitlement." If Y wishes to use the investment position as collateral for a loan, Y would grant the lender a security interest in the "securities entitlement."

In explaining the evolution of the indirect holding system the Prefatory Note to Revised Article 8 at I, C comments:

> If one examines the shareholder records of large corporations whose shares are publicly traded on the exchanges or in the over the counter market, one would find that one entity — Cede & Co. — is listed as the shareholder of record of somewhere in the range of sixty to eighty per cent of the outstanding shares of all publicly traded companies. Cede & Co.

> is the nominee name used by The Depository Trust Company ("DTC"), a limited purpose trust company organized under New York law for the purpose of acting as a depository to hold securities for the benefit of its participants, some 600 or so broker-dealers and banks. Essentially all of the trading in publicly held companies is executed through the broker-dealers who are participants in DTC, and the great bulk of public securities — the sixty to eighty per cent figure noted above — are held by these broker-dealers and banks on behalf of their customers. If all of these broker-dealers and banks held physical certificates, then as trades were executed each day it would be necessary to deliver the certificates back and forth among these broker-dealers and banks. By handing all of their securities over to a common depository all of these deliveries can be eliminated. Transfers can be accomplished by adjustments to the participants' DTC accounts.

It is suggested that you read the entire Prefatory Note.

PROBLEM 22.1

Sara Shareholder has a certificate representing 1000 shares and is registered on the books maintained by XYZ Co.'s transfer agent as the holder of record of those shares. To secure a loan from Bank, Sara grants to Bank a security interest in the 1000 shares. How may a security interest in the shares be perfected? U.C.C. § 9-115(4); see §§ 9-115(1)(e), 8-106(a) and (b), 8-301(a).

PROBLEM 22.2

In Problem 22.1 suppose XYZ Co. does not issue certificates but registers Sara Shareholder directly on its stockholder books. In this case Sara's interest would be an uncertificated security. How may a security interest in the 1000 shares be perfected? U.C.C. § 9-115(4); see §§ 9-115(1)(e), 8-106(c), 8-301(b).[2]

NOTES

(1) *Indirect Holding System.* For discussion of security interests in "security entitlements" and "securities accounts," see U.C.C. § 9-115 Comment 4 (1994).

[2] Please note that former Article 8 (1978) had detailed provisions concerning "registered pledges" of uncertificated securities. *See, e.g.*, U.C.C. §§ 8-108, 8-408(1978) and 15 West's Legal Forms § 57.6 — Forms 1-3 (2d ed. 1985). Revised Article 8 adopts a new system of rules that make it unnecessary to have special statutory provisions for registered pledges of uncertificated securities. *See* Prefatory Note to 1994 Revised Article 8 at IV, B, 5.

(2) *Priority Rules*. U.C.C. § 9-115(5) and (6) specifies the priority rules for conflicting security interests in the same investment property. *See* § 9-115 Comment 5 and illustrative examples. *See* U.C.C. §§ 9-116, 8-511.

FIRST BANK OF IMMOKALEE v. ROGERS NK SEED COMPANY

District Court of Appeal of Florida
637 So.2d 11 (1994)

ALTENBERND, JUDGE.

The First Bank of Immokalee (First Bank) appeals an order declaring that its security interest in certain stock owned by Precision Agricultural Products, Inc. (Precision), is inferior to the judgment lien of Rogers NK Seed Company (Rogers). We conclude that First Bank's security interest under section 678.321, Florida Statutes (1989), is superior to Rogers' judgment lien. Accordingly, we reverse the order on appeal.

Precision borrowed $200,000.00 from First Bank on July 30, 1990. To secure this obligation, Precision signed a security agreement listing 50,000 shares of ATNN Inc. and 118,000 shares of Non-Invasive Monitoring Systems, Inc., as collateral. First Bank did not file the security agreement in the method used to perfect a security interest in many types of personal property. *See* § 679.302, Fla. Stat. (1989). Because the stock was in the possession of Precision's broker, F.N. Wolf & Co., Inc. (F.N. Wolf), First Bank wrote to F.N. Wolf on July 30, 1990, and advised that Precision had assigned these shares of stock as collateral for the loan. The letter enclosed a copy of the promissory note and the security agreement. A few days later, F.N. Wolf sent a reply, refusing to "hold the securities in trust for anyone other than our client," but offering to assist in a physical transfer of stock certification if that was the desire of Precision. First Bank apparently did not respond to this letter.

In January 1992, Rogers obtained a judgment in the amount of $291,359.37 against Precision. In supplementary proceedings, Rogers discovered the existence of these publicly listed stocks held by Precision's broker and began efforts to sell them to satisfy its judgment. First Bank then intervened in the supplementary proceedings to establish the priority of its security interest.

After an evidentiary hearing, the trial court ruled that First Bank's security interest was not perfected because the security agreement had not been filed and because First Bank had failed to take possession of the stock as suggested by F.N. Wolf. Accordingly, it ordered that the stock be sold and that Rogers have a first priority to the proceeds of the sale. The stock was sold for approximately $150,000.00, and the proceeds have been deposited into the court's registry pending this appeal.

Security interests in stock are perfected under rules that do not apply to most other types of property. Section 678.321(1), Florida Statutes (1989), provides that a security interest in stock is enforceable and can attach only if the security interest is "transferred" to the secured party or its designee pursuant to a provision of section 678.313(1). "A security interest so transferred pursuant to agreement by a transferor who has rights in the security to a transferee who has given value is a perfected security interest . . . ." § 678.321(2), Fla. Stat. (1989). Although such a security interest is subject to the provisions of chapter 679, no filing is required to perfect the security agreement. § 678.321(3)(a), Fla. Stat. (1989); *cf. Finizio v. Shubow*, 557 So. 2d 640 (Fla. 4th DCA 1990) (agreement pledging securities to secure payment of final judgment gave judgment creditor an enforceable security interest).

Thus, to resolve this case, one must determine when the security interest was "transferred" to First Bank. Section 678.313(1)(h), Florida Statutes (1989), provides, in pertinent part, that the "transfer" of such a security interest occurs at the time a written notification . . . (which may be a copy of the security agreement) . . . is received by:

1. A financial intermediary on whose books the interest of the transferor in the security appears;

. . . .

By definition, F.N. Wolf is a "financial intermediary." § 678.313(4), Fla. Stat. (1989).

It is undisputed that First Bank provided F.N. Wolf with a copy of the signed security agreement with its notification letter on July 30, 1990. Thus, a transfer of the security interest in the stock occurred when F.N. Wolf received the written notification. *Cf. In re Southmark Corp.*, 138 B.R. 820 (Bankr. N.D. Tex. 1992) (perfection occurred when financial intermediary received notice of pledge agreement).

Despite its efforts in the reply, F.N. Wolf had no ability to decline or prevent the transfer that resulted from its receipt of the notification. As explained in the Official Reasons for the 1977 Change to the Uniform Commercial Code:

> Subparagraph (h), limited to the transfer of a security interest, deals with the situation where a security interest, pursuant to written agreement, is perfected by notice to a bailee under Section 9-305. Unlike a transfer under subparagraph (d), (e) or (f) of subsection (1), Section 9-305 does not require confirmation or acknowledgment by the controlling party, but only the receipt of notice. Subparagraph (h) provides that a transfer is effective when notice is received and further identifies the party to be notified.

Section 9-305 provides:

> If such collateral other than goods covered by a negotiable document is held by a bailee, the secured party is deemed to have possession from the time the bailee receives notification of the secured party's interest.

Thus, the reply from F.N. Wolf did not alter the date upon which First Bank perfected its security interest in this stock. Because the judgment was recorded long after that date, First Bank's security interest has priority over Rogers' judgment lien.

Reversed and remanded.

CAMPBELL, A. C. J., and SCHOONOVER, J., CONCUR.

QUESTION

What result under 1994 Revised Article 8? *See* U.C.C. §§ 9-115, 9-203 and Revision Note 2 (Prefatory Note to Revised Article 8 at IV, B, 2).

CHAPTER 23

LETTERS OF CREDIT

§ 23.01 Background

[A] Introduction

Read: U.C.C. §§ 5-102, 5-103(1)(a); Revised §§ 5-102(a)(10), 5-103(a).

PROBLEM 23.1

Suppose a client asks you for advice on how to resolve the following problem. Your client, Clayton "Paris" Molinero, operates an exclusive gift shop in Duluth, Minnesota that deals in rare, often exotic gifts from around the world. Clayton has recently been contacted by Stephen Ryder, a large supplier of quality English goods, in particular split cane bamboo fly rods. Clayton is convinced he could sell a large quantity of these rods. He wishes to establish a working relationship with Stephen Ryder so that he may buy other luxury items from him in the future. Stephen Ryder, however, is apprehensive about sending several of the high priced rods across the Atlantic without any knowledge of Clayton's credit worthiness. Stephen also wishes to avoid the high cost and frustration of investigating the financial stability of an overseas businessperson. Stephen has indicated that he has dealt with Clayton's bank, Hayes' First International in St. Paul, Minnesota on several previous occasions.

Clayton, in return, has worries of his own. He is concerned that simply wiring the money to an account in London would be temerarious and put him in jeopardy if Stephen Ryder should ship shoddy merchandise, or worse, not ship anything at all. There is nothing to guarantee Stephen's performance, and the last thing a retailer from Duluth wants is to try and recoup lost payments in a foreign country. Clayton is curious if there is a payment mechanism that would allow Stephen Ryder the security he requires without forcing Clayton to send a check off with no guarantee that Stephen will send the fly-rods. Is there a possible solution that will appease both Clayton and Stephen?

A significant risk for the seller relates to whether the buyer will accept the goods and pay for them. What if the buyer refuses to honor the draft drawn upon him by the seller? The seller, of course, will still control the goods, but the goods are now probably in the buyer's city. The seller may suffer heavy losses in seeking to sell the goods located there. The seller wants

 (Pub.244)

assurances *before* it ships that someone responsible has assumed the payment obligation. This is where the letter of credit is utilized.

A "letter of credit" or "credit" is "an engagement by a bank or other person made at the request of a customer. . .that the issuer will honor drafts or other demands for payment upon compliance with the conditions specified in the credit." U.C.C. § 5-103(1)(a) [revised § 5-102(a)(10). In its usual form, a letter of credit is a written promise by a bank on behalf of its customer, who is a buyer of goods, to pay the beneficiary, the seller of the goods, in accordance with the terms and conditions of the promise. Such terms usually include presentation to the issuer of the seller's draft for the price, an order bill of lading properly indorsed, and an inspection certificate and insurance policy covering the goods. Credits of this type are denominated "documentary letters of credit."

The use of the letter of credit grows out of the mutual needs of sellers and buyers of goods who are at a distance from one another, and who are unwilling to rely upon the credit or the bare promises of the other. It enables the seller, before it ships goods to the buyer, to know that its draft for the price will be paid, and that a bank is lending its credit to the buyer to guarantee that payment is in fact made. On the buyer's side, through the condition of the letter of credit that the draft must be accompanied by an order bill of lading, insurance policy and inspection certificate relating to the goods, it assures the buyer that upon payment of the draft it will obtain control over the goods it has contracted for. Thus, the seller substantially diminishes the "credit risk" that the buyer will not pay for the goods, and the buyer reduces materially the "goods risk" that the seller will not deliver the goods the buyer has paid for, or that the goods will not conform to the contract, or that they will be damaged in transit after the risk of loss has passed to the buyer (although, as we shall see in this chapter, these risks are not entirely eliminated).[1]

As a starting point, study the following overview of the letter of credit transaction:[2]

The letter of credit transaction involves legal relations between (1) the customer (Buyer) and the beneficiary (Seller); (2) the issuer (Buyer City Bank) and the customer (Buyer); (3) the issuer (Buyer City Bank) and the beneficiary (Seller). § 5-103 Comment 3 [revised § 5-102 Comments]. These relationships arise per the following sequence:

1. *The underlying sales transaction.* Seller and Buyer enter into a contract for sale of goods with the following form of letter of credit term:

It is agreed that Buyer shall, within ______ days after the date of this agreement, establish with the Buyer City Bank an irrevocable letter of credit in the amount of the purchase price, naming Seller as beneficiary. The terms and conditions of the letter shall provide that Seller will present to the Buyer City Bank the following documents on or before ______ 19____:

---

[1] Letters of credit are not limited to sale of goods transactions. In addition to the documentary letter of credit, there is the "traveler's letter of credit," by which the issuing bank undertakes to pay drafts, up to a specified total, drawn when the letter of credit is presented to its correspondent banks. Such credits are drawn in so-called "circular form," whereby the correspondent bank paying the draft makes a notation upon the back of the letter as to the amount of each draft; drafts will be honored in this fashion until the amount of the credit is exhausted. The Code calls these "notation credits." § 5-108 (omitted as obsolete under 1995 Revised Article 5). Also, banks have found frequent use of letters of credit in many transactions other than the sale of goods; these are described as "clean" credits because they are not conditioned upon the presentation of documents such as bills of lading. See § 23.02 below for discussion of the "standby letter of credit" which represents an obligation to the beneficiary on the part of the issuer to make payment on account of any default by the customer in the performance of an obligation.

[2] Excerpt from B. Stone, Uniform Commercial Code In A Nutshell, pp. 516-521; copyright © 1995 West Publishing Company, reprinted with permission.

a. Commercial invoice

b. Ocean bill of lading adequately describing goods sold under this agreement.

c. Consular invoice

d. Inspection certificate issued by ______

e. Certificate or policy of insurance governing goods described in this agreement.

Any confirmation of the letter of credit shall be by the Seller City Bank.

U.C.C. § 2-325 applies to letter of credit terms and states that: A letter of credit is required to be irrevocable; delivery to seller of a proper letter of credit suspends buyer's obligation to pay; failure of buyer seasonably to furnish a letter of credit is a breach of the contract for sale. See U.C.C. § 5-103, Comment 1 [revised § 5-103 Comments].

Note that the underlying transaction above involved the sale of goods per Article 2. However, the underlying transaction may involve the sale of investment securities (per Article 8), the transfer of [negotiable instruments] (per Article 3), the transfer of documents of title (per Article 7), or be a transaction intended to create a security interest (per Article 9). § 5-103, Comment 3 [revised § 5-103 Comments].

2. *The Buyer (customer) [applicant] and Buyer City Bank (issuer) transaction.* Buyer applies to Buyer City Bank for a letter of credit and a letter of credit agreement is entered into. Per this agreement Buyer City Bank agrees to issue an irrevocable letter of credit to Seller; Buyer agrees to pay the bank a sum for this service and to reimburse immediately the bank for payment made under the credit. § 5-114(3) [revised § 5-108(i) Comments]. If the bank is to lend money to Buyer on a security basis (trust receipt financing, now Article 9 security agreement, see § 9-102(2)), Buyer will obtain the bill of lading without paying for the goods, but Buyer City Bank will obtain a purchase money security interest in the bill and the goods.

Note well: Buyer City Bank (issuer) must honor a draft which complies with the terms of the credit *regardless* of whether the goods or documents conform to the underlying contract for sale. § 5-114(1) [revised § 5-108(a) Comments]. Buyer City Bank's obligation to Buyer (customer) includes good faith and observance of any general banking usage but does not include liability or responsibility for performance of the underlying contract for sale between Buyer (customer) and Seller (beneficiary). § 5-109(1)(a) [revised § 5-108]. The basic obligation of Buyer City Bank is to examine the documents with care so as to ascertain that on their face they appear to comply with the terms of the credit. § 5-114(2) [revised § 5-109(a)].

Thus we see that a letter of credit is essentially a contract between the issuer (Buyer City Bank) and the beneficiary (Seller) and is recognized by Article 5 as independent of the underlying contract between the customer (Buyer) and the beneficiary (Seller). In view of this independent nature of the engagement, the issuer is under a duty to honor the drafts which in fact comply with the terms of the credit without reference to their compliance with the terms of the underlying contract. § 5-114, Comments 1 and 2 [revised § 5-108 Comments]. See UCP Arts. 3, 4.

The above rules rest on the following assumptions: Issuer (Buyer City Bank) has had no control over the making of the underlying contract or over the selection of the beneficiary (Seller); the issuer receives compensation for a payment service rather than for a guaranty of performance; the small charge for the issuance of a letter of credit ordinarily indicates that the issuer assumes minimum risks as against its customer; normally an issuer performs a banking and not a trade function. § 5-109, Comment 1 [revised § 5-108 Comments].

3. *The Buyer City Bank (issuer) and Seller (beneficiary) transaction.* Pursuant to the agreement with Buyer, Buyer City Bank issues an irrevocable letter of credit naming Seller as beneficiary. As we have observed, this is essentially a contract between Buyer City Bank and Seller and is independent of the underlying contract between Buyer and Seller. See §§ 5-102 through 5-106 [revised §§ 5-103 through 5-106]. The key language of the credit states:

> We hereby agree with the drawers, endorsers and bona fide holders of drafts drawn under and in compliance with the terms of this credit that such drafts will be duly honored on presentation to the drawee.

The credit is forwarded to Seller City Bank (the *advising* bank) which advises Seller that Buyer City Bank has issued the letter of credit in favor of Seller. The advising bank does not assume any obligation to honor drafts drawn under the credit. §§ 5-107(1), 5-103(1)(e) [revised §§ 5-107(a), 5-102(a)(4)]. If Seller City Bank is a *confirming* bank, the bank becomes directly obligated on the credit as though it were the issuer. §§ 5-107(2) and Comment 2, 5-103(1)(f). (Seller may not wish to rely on an engagement of a bank in distant Buyer City without an engagement from Seller's local bank.)

Seller now has assurance that Buyer City Bank will honor drafts upon compliance with the conditions specified in the credit, namely, the presenting of the following documents to the bank: the draft(s), commercial invoice, bill(s) of lading, consular invoice, inspection certificate, certificate of insurance. See §§ 2-320, 2-503, 2-504, 2-509, 3-106(a), 7-304.

4. *Performance.* Seller now performs Seller's obligations. Seller procures the appropriate inspection and insurance certificates; Seller delivers the goods to Carrier and receives appropriate bills of lading; Seller draws a draft on Buyer City Bank (or Buyer); Seller prepares and procures appropriate invoices. These documents are forwarded to Seller City Bank which sends the documents to Buyer City Bank. (Seller warrants to Buyer City Bank that the necessary conditions of the credit have been complied with an addition to warranties arising under Articles 3, 4, 7.) § 5-111 [revised § 5-110].

Buyer City Bank is thus called on to honor the draft drawn under the credit. Its duty is to examine the documents with care so as to ascertain that on their face they appear to comply with the terms of the credit. § 5-109(2) [revised § 5-108]. This may take time and § 5-112 [c.f. revised § 5-108(b)] gives the bank until close of the third banking day following receipt of the documents to make its decision. Cf. § 3-502(c). Thus Buyer City Bank must now determine whether the documents comply with the terms of the credit:

(1) If the documents do comply and Buyer City Bank (issuer) dishonors the draft, the bank is liable to Seller (beneficiary). §§ 5-114(1), 5-115 [revised §§ 5-108(a), 5-111].

(2) If the documents do not comply and Buyer City Bank (issuer) honors the draft, the bank is liable to Buyer (customer). § 5-109(1), (2) [revised § 5-108]. See § 5-114(2), (3) [revised §§ 5-108, 5-109].

The question of when the documents in fact and in law do or do not comply with the terms of the credit is not covered by Article 5 (which deals with some but not all of the rules and concepts of letters of credit). § 5-102(3) and Comment 2 [revised § 5-101 Comment] . . . [See § 23.01[D] below.]

Assuming that the documents comply with the terms of the credit and that Buyer City Bank honors the draft and obtains the documents, Buyer City Bank is entitled to reimbursement from

Buyer. § 5-114(3) [revised § 5-108(i)]. See § 2-707 and Comment. When Buyer reimburses the bank, Buyer obtains the bill of lading and presents the bill to Carrier and gets the goods.

Now study the diagram and explanation of the numbered steps:

Use of Documentary Letter of Credit in Sale of Goods

The following diagram illustrates the use of the documentary letter of credit in a transaction involving the sale of goods:

1. Contract for sale of goods from S to B, containing letter of credit term.

2. B applies to Issuing Bank for letter of credit, and B and Issuing Bank enter into letter of credit agreement—See Form 23-1.

3. Issuing Bank issues letter of credit and forwards it to Advising [or Confirming] Bank—See Forms 23-2, 23-3.

4. Advising [or Confirming] Bank issues Advice [or Confirmation] of Credit to S—See Forms 23-4, 23-5.

5. S secures insurance policy covering the goods while in transit.

6. S has goods inspected (by Inspection Agency designated in letter of credit) and secures inspection certificate — See Form 23-9.

7. S delivers goods to Carrier and receives negotiable bill of lading covering the goods.

8. Carrier transports goods to destination.

9. S draws draft upon Issuing Bank [or B] for purchase price, insurance and freight, and forwards draft and documents (bill of lading, insurance policy, and inspection certificate) to Advising [Confirming] Bank. (If Bank is Confirming Bank, S will receive payment at this point; if Advising Bank, S may receive immediate credit as the draft is forwarded to Issuing Bank for collection.)

10. Advising [Confirming] Bank sends draft and documents to Issuing Bank.

11. Issuing Bank examines draft and documents, and if in compliance with the letter of credit, remits payment to Advising [Confirming] Bank.

12. Advising Bank remits payment to S, deducting any credit already advanced to S upon the draft. (If Confirming Bank, S has already received payment under 9 above.)

13. B pays the amount of the draft to Issuing Bank and receives the documents (and the draft, if B is drawee).

14. B turns bill of lading over to Carrier and receives the goods.

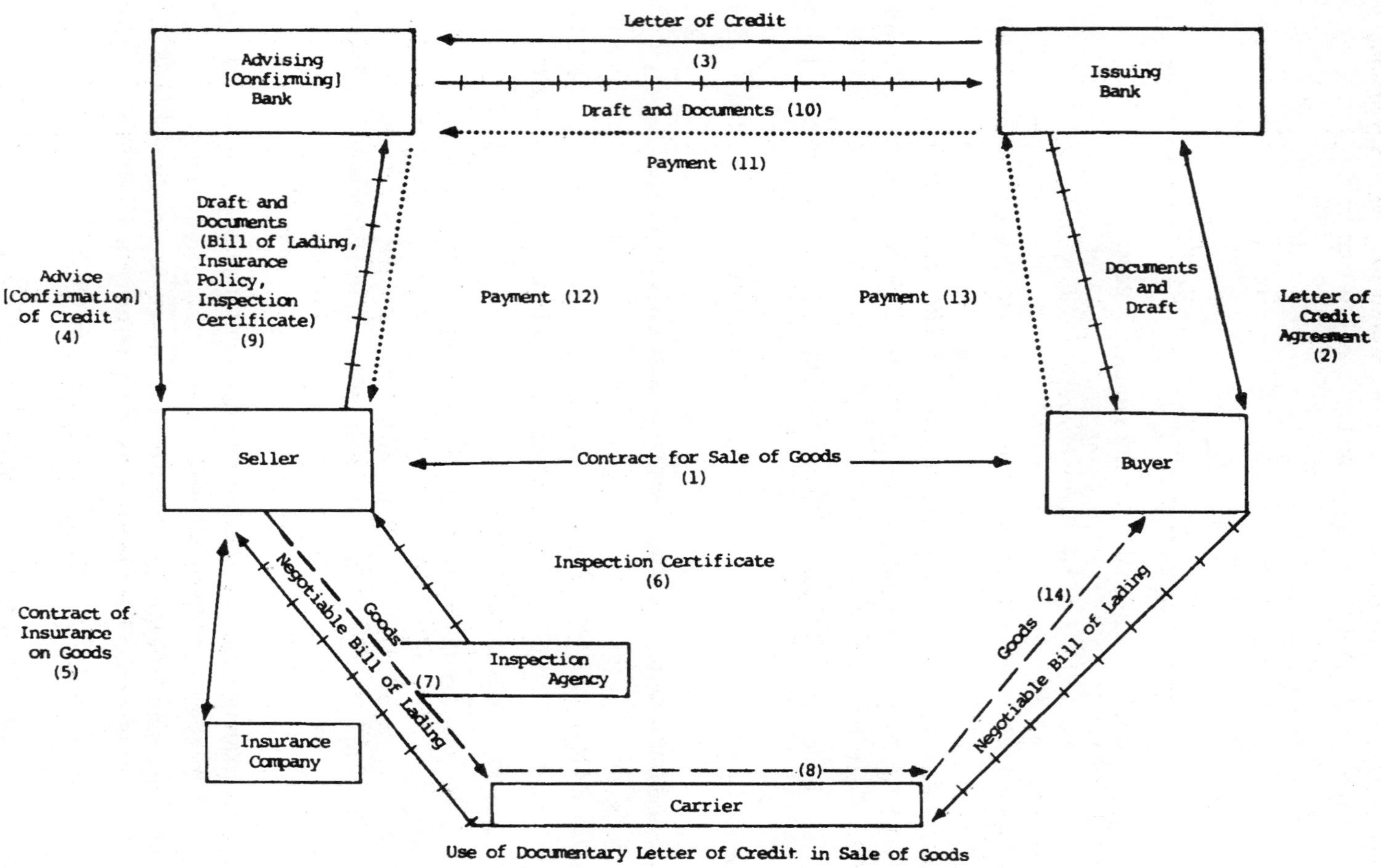

Use of Documentary Letter of Credit in Sale of Goods

Form 23-1: Commercial Letter of Credit Application and Agreement

Commercial Letter of Credit Application and Agreement

Comerica Bank-Detroit

SPECIMEN

To: Comerica Bank-Detroit
International Department
Post Office Box 858
Detroit, Michigan 48231

Number ______________ (Bank use only)

Date ______________

Please issue an irrevocable Letter of Credit (the "Credit") and either:

□ notify through your correspondent by □ airmail, □ brief cable, full details by airmail or □ cable full details;

□ airmail directly to beneficiary; or □ return to us for airmailing to beneficiary; as follows:

Advising Bank	For Account of (Applicant)
In Favor of (Beneficiary)	Amount —Drafts must be negotiated or presented to drawee on or before— (Expiration Date)

Available by drafts at sight or ______________ drawn, at your opinion, on you or your correspondent for ______________ % of the Invoice value.

When accompanied by the following documents, as checked:

Check Documents Required

□ Commerical Invoice in ________ copies
□ Customs Invoice in ________ copies
□ Airway Bill consigned to **Comerica Bank-Detroit** dated not later than ________, bearing evidence that freight is **Collect/Prepaid.**
□ Full set of **On Board** Ocean Bills of Lading issued to order of **Comerica Bank-Detroit, Michigan. Marked** ______________ **notify and marked freight: Collect/Prepaid.**
□ Bills of lading must show that the merchandise has been loaded on board the vessel named in the bills of lading not later than ______________
□ Marine
Insurance Policy and/or Certificate in negotiable form covering: ______________
□ Air
______________ (Specify war risks, S.R.C.C., etc.)
□ Insurance effected by ourselves. We agree to keep insurance coverage in force until this transaction is completed.
□ packing list in ________ copies □ weight list in ________ copies
□ Other documents ______________

Covering: Merchandise described in the invoice as: (Mention commodity only in generic terms omitting details as to grade, quality, etc.)

______________ Price Basis ______________ (Specify F.O.B., C & F, FAS, etc.)

Shipment From:

To:

Partial Shipments □ Permitted □ Prohibited
Transshipments □ Permitted □ Prohibited

□ Special Conditions: ______________

Shipping documents for custom house entry are to be sent by you to ______________

We warrant that no shipment involved in this Application is in voilation of U.S. Treasury Foreign Assets Control or Cuban Assets Control Regulations.

In consideration of your opening at the request of the undersigned a Commercial Letter of Credit, in accordance with the foregoing application, the undersigned hereby agrees as follows:

F1314 (4-83)

1. As to drafts or acceptances under or purporting to be under the Credit, which are payable in United States Currency, we agree: (a) in the case of each sight draft, to reimburse you at your head office at **Detroit, Michigan**, on demand, in lawful money of the United States of America, the amount paid on such drafts, or, if so demanded by you, to pay you at your said office in advance in such money the amount required to pay such draft; and (b) in the case of each acceptance, to pay to you, at your said office, in lawful money of the United States of America, the amount thereof, on demand but in any event not later than one business day prior to maturity, or, in case the acceptance is not payable at your said office, then on demand but in any event in time to reach the place of payment in the course of the mails not later than one business day prior to maturity.

2. As to drafts or acceptances under or purporting to be under the Credit, which are payable in currency other than United States Currency, we agree: (a) in the case of each sight draft, to reimburse you, at your said office, on demand, the equivalent of the amount paid, in lawful money of the United States of America, at the rate of exchange then current in **Detroit** for cable transfers to the place of payment in the currency in which the draft is drawn; (b) in the case of each acceptance, to furnish you, at your said office, on demand, but in any event in time to reach the place of payment in the course of the mails not later than one business day prior to maturity with first class bankers' demand bills of exchange to be approved by you for the amount of acceptance, payable in the currency of the acceptance and bearing our endorsement, or, if you so request, to pay you, at your said office, on demand, the equivalent of the aceptance in lawful money of the United States of America, at the rate of exchange then current **Detroit** for cable transfers to the place of payment in the currency in which the acceptance is payable. Demand shall be considered made as of the time you leave same at, or send or telephone same to the respective addresses of mine or ours and a demand made on one of us shall fix the exchange rate as to all of us.

3. We also agree to pay you, on demand, a commission at the rate of

per cent (%),

on such part of the Credit as may be used, and, in any event, a minimum commission of and all charges and expenses paid or insured by you in connection therewith, and interest where chargeable.

4. We hereby recognize and admit your security interest in and an unqualified right to the possession and disposition of (a) all property shipped under or pursuant to or in conection with the Credit or in any way relative thereto or to the drafts drawn thereunder, whether or not released to any of us on trust or bailee receipt or otherwise; (b) all shipping documents, warehouse receipts, policies or certificates of insurance and other documents accompanying or relative to drafts drawn under the Credit; (c) the proceeds of each and all of the foregoing, until such time as all the obligations and liabilities of us or any of us to you at anytime existing under or with reference to the Credit or this agreement, or any other credit or any other obligation or liability to you, have been fully paid and discharged; (d) all deposits (general or special) and credits of ours with you and any claims by us against you at any time existing; an (e) any additional property in which we have granted a security interest to you, which we agree to convey on your demand; all as security for any such obligations and liabilities; and that all or any of such property and documents, and the proceeds of any thereof, coming into the possession of you or any of your correspondents, may be held and disposed of by you as herein provided; and the receipt by you, or any of your correspondents, at any time of other security, of whatsover nature, including cash, shall not be deemed a waiver of any of your rights or powers therein recognized.

5. We agree from time to time to execute in your favor security agreements in the nature of trust receipts in any form acceptable to you for any property released by you to any of us, to sign and deliver to you financing statements in any form acceptable to you and to pay related filing fees.

6. Except insofar as instructions have been heretofore given by us in writing expressly to the contrary, we agree that you and any of your correspondents may receive and accept as "Bills of Lading" under the Credit, any documents issued or purporting to be issued by or on behalf of any carrier which acknowledge receipt of property for transportation, whatever the specific provision of such documents, and that the date of each such document shall be deemed the date of shipment of the property mentioned therein; that you may receive and accept as documents of insurance either insurance policies or insurance certificates; and that any such bill of lading issued by or on behalf of an ocean carrier may be accepted by you as an "Ocean Bill of Lading" whether or not the entire transportation is by water.

7. Except insofar as instructions have been heretofore given by us in writing expressly to the contrary, we agree that partial shipments or shipments in excess of quantity called for in the Credit may be made under the Credit and you may honor the relative drafts; and that if the Credit specifies shipments in installments within stated periods, and the shipper fails to ship in any designated period, shipments of subsequent installments may nevertheless be made in their respective designated periods and you may honor the relative drafts.

8. We agree that in the event of any extension of the maturity or time for presentation of drafts, acceptances or documents,or any other modification of the terms of the Credit, at the request of any of us, with or without notification to the others, or in the event of any increase in the amount of the Credit at your request,this agreement shall be binding upon us with regard to the Credit so increased or otherwise modified, to drafts, documents and property covered thereby, and to any action taken by you or any of your correspondents in accordance with such extension, increase or other modification.

9. The users of the Credit shall be deemed our agents and we assume all risks of their acts or omissions. Neither you nor your correspondents shall be responsible: (a) for the existence, character, quality, quantity, condition, packing, value, or delivery of the property purporting to be represented by documents; (b) for any difference in character, quality, quantity, condition, or value of the property from that expressed in documents; (c) for the validity, sufficiency or genuineness of documents, even if such documents should in fact prove to be in any or all respects invalid, insufficient, fraudulent or forged; (d) for the time, place, manner or order in which shipment is made; (e) for partial or incomplete shipment, or failure or omission to ship any or all of the property referred to in the Credit; (f) for the character, adequacy, validity, or genuineness of any insurance; (g) for the solvency or responsibility of any insurer, or for any other risk connected with insurance; (h) for any deviation from instructions, delay,

default or fraud by the shipper or anyone else in connection with the property or the shipping thereof; (i) for the solvency, responsibility or relationship to the property of any party issuing any document in connection with the property; (j) for delay in arrival or failure to arrive of either the property or any of the documents relating thereto; (k) for delay in giving or failure to give notice of arrival or any other notice; (l) for any breach of contract between the shippers or vendors and ourselves or any of us; (m) for failure of any draft to bear any reference or adequate reference to the Credit, or failure of documents to accompany any draft at negotiation, or failure of any person to note the amount of any draft on the reverse of the Credit or to surrender or take up the Credit or to send forward documents apart from drafts as required by the terms of the Credit; each of which provisions, if contained in the Credit itself, it is agreed may be waived by you; (n) for any use which may be made of this Credit or for any acts or omissions of the beneficiary(ies) in connection herewith; or (o) for errors, omissions, interruptions or delays in transmission or delivery of any messages, by mail, cable, telegraph, wireless or otherwise, whether or not they be in cipher; nor shall you be responsible for any error, neglect, or default of any of your correspondents; nor shall you be responsible for errors in translation or for errors in interpretation of technical terms, nor shall you be responsible for any consequences arising from causes beyond your control; and none of the above shall affect, impair, or prevent the vesting of any of your rights or pwers hereunder. We shall protect you and any other drawee in paying any draft dated on or before the expiration of any time limit expressed in the Credit regardless of when drawn and when or whether negotiated. We are responsible to you for all obligations imposed upon you with respect to the Credit or the relative drafts, documents property. In furtherance and extension and not in limitation of the specific provisions hereinbefore set forth, we agree that any action taken by you or by any correspondent of yours under or in connection with the Credit or the relative drafts, documents or property, if taken in good faith, shall be binding on us and shall not put you or your correspondent under any resulting liability to us; and we make like agreement as to any inaction or omission, unless in breach of good faith.

You shall not any way be liable for any failure by you or anyone else to pay or accept any draft or acceptance under this Credit resulting from any censorship, law, control or restriction rightfully or wrongfully exercised by any de facto or de jure domestic or foreign or agency or from any other cause beyond your control or the control of your correspondents, agents, or sub-agents or for any loss or damage to us or wnyone else resulting from any such failure to pay or accept all such risks being expressly assumed by us and we agree to indemnify and hold you harmless from any claim, loss, liability or expense arising by reason of any such failure to pay or accept.

10. We agree to procure promptly any necessary import, export or other licenses for the import, export or shipping of all property shipped under or pursuant to or in connection with the credit and to comply with all foreign and domestic governmental regulations in regard to the shipment of such property or the financing thereof, and to furnish such certificates in that respect as you may at any time require, and to keep the property adequately covered by insurance satisfactory to you, issued by companies satisfactory to you, and to assign such policies of insurance to you, or to make the loss or adjustment, if any, payable to you, at your option; and to furnish you if demanded with evidence of acceptance by the insurers of such assisngment.

11. Each of us agrees at any time and from time to time, on demand, to deliver, convey, transfer, or assign to you, as security for any and all of his and/or our liabilities hereunder, and also for any and all other liabilities, absolute or contingent, due or to become due, or held or to be held by you, whether created directly or acquired by assignment, tort, or otherwise, which are now or may at any time hereafter be owing by him or us or any of us (whether jointly, severally, jointly with any other or others, independently or otherwise) to you, additional property of a value and character satisfactory to you, or to make such payment as you may require. Each of us agrees that the balance with you existing from time to time of any deposit account (whether general or special or for any specific purpose) of him or us or in which he or we may have an interest and any claim of any of us against you existing from time to time and all property belonging to him or us, or in which he or we may have an interest, including power of hypothecation or disposition, now or hereafter in your possession or custody (all remittances and property to be deemed left with you as soon as put in transit to you by mail or carrier) for any purpose (including safekeeping or pledge for any liability of him or us) whether or not such property is in whole or in part released to any of us on security agreement in the nature of a trust or bailee receipt, are hereby made security and subject to a lien for any and all such liabilities of him or us or any of us. Any property so held as collateral may be transferred to and/or registered in the name of your nominee and to do so before or after the maturity of any of the obligations or liabilities hereunder without notice to us.

12. Each of us agrees that (a) upon his or our failure at all times to keep a margin of security with you satisfactory to you, or (b) upon the non-payment or non-fulfillment of any liabilities or obligations of any of us when they shall become due or be made due, or (c) upon his or our death, or (d) upon the insolvency of, or upon the application for the appointment or the appointment of a receiver of any of us or of any or all of the property of, or (e) upon an assignment for the benefit or creditors by any of us, or the filing by or against any of us of a voluntary or involuntary petition in bankruptcy or a voluntary or involuntary petition pursuant or purporting to be pursuant to any present or future acts or regulations of any jurisdiction on the subject of bankruptcies or relief of debtors or any amendments of any such acts or regulations, whether or not relating to bankruptcy, or (f) upon the issuance of any warrant of attachment or any attachment against the credits or property of him or us, or (g) upon the taking possession by any public official having regulatory powers over any of us of the property of any of us for the purpose of conserving his or our assets, or (h) upon the failure of the undersigned promptly to furnish satisfactory additional collateral then any and all such liabilities and/or obligations of any of us shall become and be immediately due and payable, without notice, presentment, demand of payment or protest, all such being hereby waived, and notwithstanding any credit or time allowed to any of us or any instrument evidencing such liabilities or otherwise. You are hereby authorized and empowered at your option at any time without notice to appropriate and apply to the payment of any such liabilities any and all moneys or other property or proceeds thereof, now or hereafter in your hands, on deposit or otherwise, for account of, to the credit of, or belonging to any of us (whether said deposit is general, or special or for any specific purpose including safekeeping or pledge for any liability of any of us) whether any of said liabilities and/or obligations are then due or not due. Each of us expressly authorizes you upon the nonpayment or non-fulfillment of any liabilities of any of us when they shall become due or be made due, to sell, without demand, advertisement or notice to us or any of us, all of which are hereby expressly waived, any or all property of every description securing any liabilities of any of us, arrived or to arrive, at private sale or at public auction or at brokers' board or exchange or otherwise, at your option, in such parcel or parcels, at such time or times, at such place or

places, either for cash or credit or future delivery and otherwise upon such terms and conditions as you may deem proper, and to apply the net proceeds of such sale or sales, together with any balance of deposits and any sums credited by or due from you to any of us in general account or otherwise, to the payment of any and all such liabilities. If any such sale be at brokers' board or exchange, or at public auction, you may yourself be a purchaser at such sale, free from any right of redemption, which we and each of us hereby expressly waive and release. Demands or calls for collateral on, or any notices to me or us respectively may be made or given by you by leaving same at the respective addresses given below or the last known address of mine or ours, provided you in writing, respectively or by sending or telephoning same to either such address, with the same effect as if delivered to me or us in person. In the event of the sale or other disposition of such property, you may apply the proceeds of any such sale or disposition first to the satisfaction of your reasonable attorney's fees, legal expenses and other costs and expenses incurred in connection with your retaking, holding, preparing for sale, and selling of the property. Each of us agrees that with or without notification to any of us, you may exchange, release, surrender, realize upon, release on trust receipt to any of us, or otherwise deal with any property by whomsoever pledged, mortgaged, or subjected to a security interest to secure directly or indirectly any of the obligations hereunder or for which any of the undersigned may be liable. Notice of acceptance of this agreement is waived.

We will bear and pay all expenses of every kind (including all charges for legal services) of the enforcement of any of your rights therein mentioned or of any claim or demand by you against us, or of any actual or attempted sale, exchange, enforcement, collection, maintenance, retention, insurance, compromise, settlement, release, delivery on security agreemnt in the nature of a trust receipt, or delivery of any such security, and of the receipt of proceeds thereof, and will repay to you any such expenses incurred by you.

13. You shall not be deemed to have waived any of your options, powers or rights (including those hereunder) unless you or your authorized agent shall have signed such waiver in writing. No such waiver, unless expressly as stated therein, shall be effective as to any transaction which occurs subsequent to the date of such waiver, nor as to any continuance of a breach after such waiver. No segregation or specific allocation by you of specified collateral against any liability shall waive or affect any lien of any sort against other securities or property or any of your options, powers or rights (including those hereunder).

14. The word "property" as used in this agreement includes goods, merchandise, securities, funds, choses in action, and any and all other forms of property, whether real, personal or mixed and any right or interest therein. Property in your possession shall include property in possession of any one for you in any manner whatsoever. Your options, powers and rights specified in this agreement are in addition to those otherwise created. 15. You may assign or transfer this agreement, or any instrument(s) evidencing all or any of the aforesaid obligations and/or liabilities, and may delivery all or any of the property then held as security therefor, to the transferee(s), who shall thereupon become vested with all the powers and rights in respect thereto and you shall thereafter be foreever relieved and fully discharged from any liability or responsibility with respect thereto. This agreement shall be binding upon the undersigned, there heirs, executors, administrators, successors and assigns of undersigned, and shall inure to the benefit of, and be enforceable by, you, your successors, transferees and assigns. If this agreement should be terminated or revoked by operation of law as to the undersigned, the undersigned will indemnify and save you harmless from any loss suffered by you in acting prior to receipt of notice in writing of such termination or revocation.

16. That, except as otherwise expressly provided in this agreement or as oyou and the undersigned may otherwise expressly agree with regard to, or proir to your issuance of this credit, the "Uniform Customs and Practice for Documentary Credits (1974 Revision), International Chamber of Commerce Brochure 290" shall in all respects be deemed a part hereof as fully as if incorporated herein and shall apply to this credit. If this agreement is signed by one individual, the terms "we", "our", "us", shall be read throughout as "I", "my", "me", as the case may be. If this agreement is signed by two or more parties, it shall be the joint and several agreement of such parties. In addition, the laws of the State of Michigan shall govern all aspects of this agreement.

____
Firm Name

____
Address

____
Authorized Signature

Irrevocable Documentary Letter of Credit

IRREVOCABLE DOCUMENTARY

LETTER OF CREDIT NO. 1234 September 1, 1986

Overseas Export Co.

4321 Nathan Road

Kowloon, Hong Kong

Gentlemen

We hereby authorize you to draw on Comerica Bank, Detroit, Michigan 48264, for the account of Detroit Import Co., 1911 Smith St., Detroit Michigan 00000 up to the aggregate amount of U.S. $45,000.00 (Forty Five Thousand and 00/100 Dollars).

The credit amount is available to you by your drafts on us at sight for 100% of invoice cost bearing the clause: "Drawn under Comerica Bank Documentary Credit No. 1234", accompanied by:

Commercial invoice in triplicate covering: "10,000 Ceramic Ashtrays", CIF, New York.

Insurance certificate or policy covering all risks including war risks.

Full set clean onboard ocean bills of lading consigned to order of Comerica Bank marked "Notify Customs Brokers of Detroit, 321 W. Fifth Street, Detroit, Michigan and "Freight Prepaid" evidencing shipment from Hong Kong to any United States West Coast Port for final delivery to Detroit, Michigan.

Bills of lading must show that the merchandise was loaded on board the vessel named in the bills of lading not later than October 10, 1985.

Partial shipments are prohibited. Transhipment is permitted.

Advising bank's charges, if any, and negotiation charges are for your account. Negotiating bank is authorized to forward all documents in one airmail.

The amount of each draft negotiated must be endorsed on the original credit by the negotiating bank.

We hereby agree with drawers, endorsers and bonafide holders of drafts drawn under an in compliance with the terms of this credit that such drafts will be duly honored on due presentation to the drawees if negotiated on or before October 25, 1986.

Except so far as otherwise specified, this documentary credit is subject to the Uniform Customs and Practice for Documentary Credits (1983 Revision), International Chamber of Commerce Publication 400.

____

(Authorized Signature)

Form 23-2: Irrevocable Straight Credit[3]

[Bank]

CABLE ADDRESS _______ *[Address]*
Irrevocable Straight Credit *[Date]*

MAIL TO:

[Beneficiary]
[Address]

All drafts drawn must be marked:
[Bank] Ref. No.: 0000000
Opener's Reference No:

Dear Sirs:

At the request of:

[Customer/Account Party]

and for the account of *[Customer/Account Party]* we hereby open in your favor our Irrevocable Credit, numbered as indicated above, for a sum or sums not exceeding a total of U.S. $ _______ available by your drafts [at SIGHT] on us subject to the following:

Expiration Date:

Trans shipment: [*not allowed*]

Partial shipment: [*not allowed*]

Ship from: [*Seller's Port*]

Ship to: [*Buyer, Country*]

and accompanied by the following documents:

1. [*Ocean bills of lading*].
2. [*Insurance certificates*].
3. [*Customs invoice combined with certificate of origin*].
4. [Etc.].

This letter is to accompany all draft(s) and documents. When presenting your draft(s) and documents or when communicating with us please make reference to our reference number shown above.

We hereby agree to honor each draft drawn under and in compliance with the terms of this credit, if duly presented (together with the documents specified) at this office on or before the expiration date.

The credit is subject to the Uniform Customs and Practice for Documentary Credits, 1993 revision, ICC Publication No. 500.

Yours very truly,
[*Signature of Issuer*]

---

[3] Excerpt from 15 *West's Legal Forms*, pages 392-393; copyright © 1985 West Publishing Company, reprinted with permission.

Form 23-3: Irrevocable Negotiation Credit[4]

[Bank]

CABLE ADDRESS ________ *[Address]*
Irrevocable Negotiation *[Date]*
Credit

MAIL TO:

[Beneficiary]
[Address]

All drafts drawn must be marked:
[Bank] Ref. No.: 0000000
Opener's Reference No:

Dear Sirs:

At the request of:

[*Customer/Account Party*]

and for the account of [*Customer/Account Party*] we hereby open in your favor our Irrevocable Credit, numbered as indicated above, for a sum or sums not exceeding a total of U.S. $ _______ available by your drafts [at SIGHT] on us subject to the following:

Expiration Date:

Trans shipment: [*not allowed*]

Partial shipment: [*not allowed*]

Ship to: [*location*]

Latest shipping date:

and accompanied by the following Documents:

1. [*Ocean bills of lading*].
2. [*Insurance policy or certificate*].
3. [*Commercial invoice*] .
4. [*Etc.*].

This letter is to accompany all draft(s) and documents. When presenting your draft(s) and documents or when communicating with us please make reference to our reference number shown above.

We hereby engage with the drawer, endorsers and bona fide holders that each draft drawn under, and in compliance with, the terms of the said credit, and accompanied by the above-specified documents will be duly honored if NEGOTIATED on or before the expiration date.

The credit is subject to the Uniform Customs and Practice for Documentary Credits, 1993 revision, ICC Publication No. 500.

Yours very truly,
[*Signature of Issuer*]

---

[4] Excerpt from 15 *West's Legal Forms*, pages 394-395; copyright © 1985 West Publishing Company, reprinted with permission.

Form 23-4: Uncomfirmed Cover Letter—Advise of Credit

Export - Unconfirmed Cover Letter

Comerica Bank
International Banking Department
Post Office Box 64858
Detroit, Michigan 48264

Date ____________________

Mail To

Beneficiary

Our Advice Number ____________________

Correspondent's Number ____________________

We are informed by our correspondent that they have issued their Irrevocable Credit in your favor. Our correspondent's original credit is attached. A copy of it is being held by us.

Correspondent

This advice conveys no engagement or obligation on our part - however, our correspondent's credit is irrevocable on their part.

Documents must conform strictly with the terms of the enclosed credit. If you are unable to comply with its terms, please promptly communicate with us or your customer with a view to having the conditions changed.

Drafts when presented, must clearly specify the number of this advice, and be presented to us in the form prescribed on the attached original credit.

Please include one extra copy of your commercial invoice for our records.

This advice is subject to the Uniform Customs and Practice for Documentary Credits (1974 Revision) International Chamber of Commerce Publication 290.

F1932 (1 84)

Form 23-5: Confirmed Cover Letter — Confirmation of Credit

Export-Confirmed Cover Letter

Comerica Bank
Post Office Box 64858
Detroit, Michigan 48264

Mail To

Beneficiary

Date____________________

Our Confirmed Advice No.____________________

Our Correspondent's No.____________________

We are informed by our correspondent that they have issued their Irrevocable Credit in your favor for $ expiring at our counters. Our correspondent's original credit is enclosed and a copy of it is being held by us.

Correspondent

Account

At the request of our correspondent, we confirm their Irrevocable Credit and engage with you that all drafts drawn under and in compliance with the terms of this credit will be duly honored.

Drafts when presented must clearly specify the number of this credit and be presented to us with the original credit and amendments, if any. Drafts are to be completed in the form prescribed.

Documents must conform strictly with the terms of this credit. If you are unable to comply with these terms, please communicate with us, or your customer, with a view to having the conditions changed.

This credit is subject to the Uniform Customs and Practice for Documentary Credits (1974 Revision) International Chamber of Commerce Publication 290.

Please include one extra copy of your Commercial Invoice for our records.

International Banking Department

____
Authorized Signature

F1931 (11-82)

Form 23-6: Amendment to Documentary Credit

Comerica Bank
International Banking Department
Post Office Box 64858
Detroit, Michigan 48264

Swift: DBTDUS33
Telex: 23-5393

7

Amendment to Documentary Credit No. __________________ Dated ________

Advising Bank	Amendment Number __________ Date __________
Beneficiary To	□ This refers to our cable of today through the Advising Bank □ This Amendment is forwarded to the Advising Bank by Air Mail
Applicant	This Amendment is to be considered part of the Letter of Credit described above and must be attached thereto.

Dear Sirs:
The above described Credit is amended as follows:

All Other Terms and Conditions remain unchanged.

The advising Bank is requested to inform the beneficiary of this amendment. Sincerely, Comerica Bank __________ Issuing Bank's Authorized Signature	Advising Bank's Notification Place, Date, Name and Signature of Advising Bank

F1685 01 (11-82)

Form 23-7: Commercial Invoice*

[*Name and Address of Seller*]

CUSTOMER ORDER NO. NUMERO DE PEDIDO DEL CLIENTE	SELLER ORDER NO. NUMERO DE PEDIDO DE SELLER	SHPT. NO. DESPACHO
EXPORT SALES DEPT. CABLE ADDRESS	SELLER INVOICE DATE FECHA DE LA FACTURA	

SOLD TO VENDIDO A	OF DE
TERMS PLAZOS	FAS/
IMPORT LICENSE LICENCIA DE IMPORTACION	LETTER OF CREDIT CARTA DE CREDITO

MARKS AND CASE NUMBERS MARCAS Y NUMEROS DE CAJA		QUANTITY SHIPPED CANTIDAD EMBARCADA	DESCRIPTION OF GOODS DESCRIPCION DEL MATERIAL	SELLING PRICE / PRECIO DE VENTA UNIT UNIDADES	 TOTAL TOTAL

Form 23-8: Consular Invoice*

Nº

República Dominicana

FACTURA CONSULAR OFICIAL

________________19____

FACTURA de mercancías embarcadas por ______________________ a bordo del ______________________ nombrado ___ su capitán ___ dirigidas al puerto de ___
(Clase y Nacionalidad, del Buque)

a la consignación de ______________ por cuenta y orden de ______________

Marca	Número Marca	Número de Bultos	Clase de Bultos	CONTENIDO	Cantidad	Peso en Kilos		VALORES		Países de Origen de las Mercancías
						Bruto	Neto			

Juramos y declaramos: Que las marcas, números de bultos, contenido de los mismos en lo que respecta a su peso, Vista y registrada bajo el número____________cantidad y clase de mercancias y el valor de éstas aquí consignadas, son exactas.

19 19

Lugar Fecha Firma Lugar Fecha Cónsul

*** Excerpt from 15 West's Legal Forms, page 418; copyright © West Publishing Company. Reprinted with permission.**

Form 23-9: Inspection Certificate[5]

[*Letterhead*]

To [*name and address of buyer*]:

RE: Order No. 00000

Gentlemen:

We certify that we have examined [*describe goods*] comprising the above order and find them to be [*specify,quantity, quality, etc., of goods*] as specified in said order.

Yours very truly,
[*Signature of Inspection Certificate Issuer*]

[B] Applicable Law: U.C.C. and Uniform Customs

U.C.C. Article 5 deals with letters of credit. It is the first substantial effort at codification of the law relating to letters of credit, but it should be noted that it expressly disclaims that it is all-encompassing: "This Article deals with some but not all of the rules and concepts of letters of credit as such rules or concepts have developed prior to this act or may hereafter develop." U.C.C. § 5-102(3) [revised § 5-101 Comment]

Prior to the promulgation of the Code, there was practically no legislation relating to letters of credit. For example, the only explicit provision in the United States Code relating to letters of credit is found in Section 615 of Title 12 of the United States Code, giving national banks the "power . . .to issue letters of credit."[6] The law was almost wholly case law, based originally upon common law principles and the custom of merchants, and traceable to an early date. However, with the great expansion of the use of letters of credit in the twentieth century, banking institutions in the various nations felt a need for a concise statement of the basic rules applicable to letters of credit. This culminated in 1933 in the adoption of the Seventh Congress of the International Chamber of Commerce of the "Uniform Customs and Practice for Commercial Documentary Credits." The Uniform Customs have been widely adopted by banks, and have been revised since 1933, most recently in 1993.

Because of the widespread use of the Uniform Customs by banks engaging in documentary letter of credit transactions, it was strongly argued that Article 5 of the Code was unnecessary. A major effort was made in New York to delete Article 5 entirely from the Code as adopted in that state; and while the opponents of Article 5 did not entirely succeed, they did accomplish a part of their goal through the addition of a new Subsection (4) to the New York version of Section 5-102:

> Unless otherwise agreed, this Article 5 does not apply to a letter of credit or a credit if by its terms or by agreement, course of dealing or usage of trade such letter of credit or credit is subject in whole or in part to the Uniform Customs and Practice for Commercial

[5] Excerpt from 15 West's Legal Forms, p. 419; copyright © 1985West Publishing Company. Reprinted with permission.

[6] For discussion of letters of credit and bank regulations, see J. Dolan, The Law of Letters of Credit, Ch. 12 (2d ed. 1991).

Documentary Credits fixed by the Thirteenth or by any subsequent Congress of the International Chamber of Commerce.[7]

Articles 1-4, 6, 9, 13, and 37c of the 1993 Uniform Customs for Documentary Credits (UCP) are summarized:

Article 1 applies to documentary credits (including standby letters of credit) where the UCP is incorporated into the text of the credit, viz., "The credit is subject to the Uniform Customs and Practice for Documentary Credits (1993 Revision), ICC Publication No. 500."

Article 2 defines a credit to mean any arrangement whereby an "issuing bank" acting on the instructions of an "applicant" (customer) is to make payment to the "beneficiary" against stipulated documents, provided that the terms and conditions of the credit are complied with.

Article 3 states that credits are separate transactions from the sales contracts on which they may be based and issuers are in no way concerned with or bound by these contracts.

Article 4 observes that issuers deal with documents and not with goods to which the documents relate.

Article 6 reverses the prior UCP by asserting that in the absence of an indication whether a credit is revocable or irrevocable, it is deemed to be irrevocable.

Article 9 states that an irrevocable credit constitutes a definite undertaking of the issuing bank, provided (1) the stipulated documents are presented to the issuing bank and (2) the terms and conditions of the credit are complied with.

Article 13 sets forth the standard for examination of documents: (1) Banks must examine all documents stipulated in the credit with reasonable care to ascertain whether or not they appear on their face to be in compliance with the terms and conditions of the credit. (2) Compliance shall be determined by international standard banking practice as reflected in the UCP. (3) Documents which appear on their face to be inconsistent with one another will be considered as not appearing on their face to be in compliance.

Article 37c provides that the description of the goods in the commercial invoice must correspond with the description in the credit. In all other documents, the goods may be described in general terms not inconsistent with the description in the credit. This article affirms *Laudisi v. American Exch. Nat. Bank*, 239 N.Y. 234, 146 N.E. 347 (1924) (The credit referred to Alicante Bouchez Grapes, the invoice specified Alicante Bouchez grapes, but the bill of lading said "grapes." The bank honored the draft; the court upheld the bank stating that taken together, the documents were adequate.)

The current version of the Uniform Customs and Practices for Documentary Credit, issued by the International Chamber of Commerce is entitled I.C.C. Publication No. 500 (1993). The U.C.P. becomes the governing law in any letter of credit that incorporates it as such. Because the U.C.P. is more detailed and is more familiar to international businessperson, many letters of credits opt for the U.C.P. over the U.C.C. The New York Article 5 provision states for a statutory preference of the U.C.P. as a default rule. See N.Y. Uniform Commercial Code § 5-102(4).

[7] See N.Y.— McKinney's Uniform Commercial Code § 5-102(4). See also, Code of Ala. 1975, § 7-5-102(4); Vernon's Ann.Mo.Stat. § 400.5-102(4).

See J. Dolan, The Law of Letters of Credit, ¶ 4.06, "The Code and the Uniform Customs" (2d ed. 1991).

The U.C.C. and the U.C.P. are similar in most regards, and Revised Article Five represents a conscious effort by the drafters to align the U.C.C. with its foreign cousin in areas of divergence. An important example of the new similarities, is Revised § 5-108(c) which provides that the issuer is precluded from asserting a discrepancy not stated in its timely notice. Under the prior U.C.C., there was no requirement that the issuer provide any explanation as to why the letter of credit demand had been denied. This new provision brings the Revised Article parallel to the U.C.P.

[C] Requirements

Read: U.C.C. §§ 5-102 and 5-104; Revised §§ 5-103, 5-104.

TRANSPARENT PRODS. CORP. v. PAYSAVER CREDIT UNION

United States Court of Appeals
864 F.2d 60, 7 U.C.C. Rep. Serv. 2d 832 (7th Cir. 1988)

EASTERBROOK, CIRCUIT JUDGE.

Uncertain of the difference between a line of credit and a letter of credit, the president of Paysaver Credit Union signed this document on the Credit Union's letterhead:

Transparent Products Corporation
Bensenville, IL. 60101
RE: Thomas Wells

Gentlemen:

> We hereby establish our letter of credit at the request of Thomas Wells of 1003 South 23rd Avenue, Maywood and of Titan Tool of 1315 South 3rd Avenue, Maywood up to the aggregate amount of fifty-thousand dollars ($50,000).

At the time Paysaver signed this document, Titan Tool owed Transparent some $33,000 on open account credit for plastics. Titan wanted to buy another $61,000 worth, but Transparent had balked unless Titan's creditworthiness could be assured. Wells, an employee of Titan who had a $50,000 certificate of deposit with Paysaver, procured this document. Transparent apparently deemed it insufficient assurance of payment and did not sell additional goods to Titan. Some 13 months later Titan, then a debtor in bankruptcy, still had not paid the original $33,000. Transparent demanded that Paysaver make good the debt. Transparent believes that the document guarantees Titan's general debts; Paysaver believes that the document is a mishmash with no legal effect.

The district court concluded after a trial (at which the president of Paysaver allowed that he did not understand how letters of credit differed from lines of credit) that the document is a letter of credit. The court then held, in part on the basis of the intent underlying Paysaver's decision to send the document, that Transparent's delay in making a demand equitably estopped it from collecting. The injection of such considerations into the enforcement of letters of credit is unprecedented and would be most unfortunate. The district court did not find that Transparent deceived Paysaver or otherwise induced detrimental reliance on an unkept promise; it found only that Transparent tarried unduly. Letters of credit are designed to provide assurance of payment and could not serve that purpose if the beneficiary risked being denied payment for withholding a demand "for too long" while attempting to collect from the primary debtor. We need not consider, however, whether principles of estoppel are forever beyond the pale when dealing with letters of credit, for Paysaver defends its judgment on the ground that the document is not one.

Letters of credit facilitate commercial transactions by providing the assurance of a reliable party that a debt will be paid quickly and with no fuss. Letters often provide that the issuer will pay on presentation of shipping documents, relieving the seller of the risk of nonpayment (or delayed payment) while shifting to the buyer the risk that the goods will be defective and it will need to pursue the seller. Standby letters of credit do not contemplate immediate payment by the issuer but serve as assurance if the debtor does not pay. Guarantee letters of credit serve a role similar to more conventional guarantees of debt, but with the promise that the issuer will pay on demand rather than balk and precipitate litigation to determine whether the underlying debt was due (a common event when guarantees are issued by officers or shareholders of the debtor), and with the additional benefit of enabling banks to stand behind their customers' transactions when they are forbidden to issue straight guarantees. See generally Cassondra E. Joseph, *Letters of Credit: The Developing Concepts and Financing Functions,* 94 Banking L.J. 816 (1977). In any of these cases, the issuer specifies conditions under which payment will be made. The Uniform Commercial Code defines "credit" by reference to these conditions. The definition has two stages. Section 5-102, Ill. Rev. Stat. ch. 26 para. 5-102, establishes the scope of Article 5 (governing letters of credit), and § 5-103(1) defines "credit": 5-102. Scope. (1) This Article applies

(a) to a credit issued by a bank if the credit requires a documentary draft or a documentary demand for payment; and

(b) to a credit issued by a person other than a bank if the credit requires that the draft or demand for payment be accompanied by a document of title; and

(c) to a credit issued by a bank or other person if the credit is not within subparagraphs (a) or (b) but conspicuously states that it is a letter of credit or is conspicuously so entitled.

5-103. Definitions. (1) In this Article unless the context otherwise requires

(a) "Credit" or "letter of credit" means an engagement by a bank or other person made at the request of a customer and of a kind within the scope of this Article (Section 5-102) that the issuer will honor drafts or other demands for payment upon compliance with the conditions specified in the credit. A credit may be either revocable or irrevocable. The engagement may be either an agreement to honor or a statement that the bank or other person is authorized to honor.

Transparent relies on § 5-102(1)(c), observing that the document conspicuously calls itself a "letter of credit". (A statement is "conspicuous" if it is "so written that a reasonable person against whom it is to operate ought to have noticed it." U.C.C. § 1-201(10). Paysaver, which wrote this short letter, had to notice its own words.) But § 5-102(1)(c) applies only to "a credit", and under § 5-103(1)(a) a "credit" is an "engagement" to "honor drafts or other demands for payment upon compliance with the conditions" stated. The document Paysaver signed does not engage to do anything, under any conditions.

Sections 5-102 and 5-103, taken together with §§ 5-104 and 5-105 (saying that there are no formal requirements), show that a letter of credit need not be supported by consideration or contain any magic words or expiration date. They show with equal force that a letter of credit is an "engagement" to pay on the occurrence of specified events or the presentation of specified documents. A document engaging to do nothing and mentioning no events is simply a stray piece of paper. (A document labeled a "letter of credit" is a "guarantee" if its terms are the elements of guarantees and not letters of credit.)

The title controls only when the document contains the terms appropriate to the substance of such an instrument. The letter Paysaver signed is no different in principle from a pumpkin on which "$50,000" and "letter of credit" had been stenciled. Just as calling a sports car a "principal residence" will not permit the owner to take the deduction for interest under the tax laws, so calling a pumpkin a "letter of credit" will not make it one. This harmonizes our views with *Board of Inland Revenue v. Haddock*, in which String, J., concluded that a cow bearing the words "To the London and Literary Bank, Ltd.: Pay to the Collector of Taxes, who is no gentleman, or Order, the sum of fifty-seven pounds (and may he rot!). L 57/0/0", was a negotiable instrument.[8] The judge observed that the writing included all the terms necessary for negotiability, and that the cow could be endorsed over to any willing holder.

Insistence on having terms—a concrete "engagement"—is not mere pedantry. Letters of credit give assurance of payment; to promote the reliability of the device, courts do not look beneath the surface of the documents to discover side agreements, plumb the intent of the parties, and the like. Yet only such a detour could flesh out the document written by Paysaver. If this letter were viewed as an ordinary contract, it would be unenforceable on the ground that the undertaking is hopelessly indefinite. A document too vague to be enforced as a contract is an implausible candidate for an Article 5 letter of credit.

Consider what is missing. One item is the term most important to any letter of credit: specification of the circumstances requiring the issuer to pay. Transparent believes that the document commits Paysaver to make good Titan's existing debt. Yet letters of credit to guarantee payment of prior debts are rare. One could see the document alternatively as an undertaking to make good on any new transaction, such as the $61,000 sale under discussion. A letter with this meaning would not stand behind the $33,000 accrued debt. Only speculation or a detailed inquiry into oral negotiations—both anathema in letter of credit transactions—could supply the missing term. Contrast *Bank of North Carolina, N.A. v. Rock Island Bank*, 570 F.2d 202 (7th Cir. 1978) (holding an undertaking to be a letter of credit because it contained detailed terms on which payment would occur).

Another missing or confusing item is the customer. The document is captioned "RE: Thomas Wells". Wells was an employee of Titan and not indebted to Transparent. Counsel for Transparent conceded at oral argument that it had no claim against Wells personally. Only the recitation that the document was issued "at the request of" Titan in addition to that of Wells offers support for application to Titan's transactions. If we must choose between reading the document as standing behind Wells or standing behind Titan, where the former is what the caption says and the latter is a felony (given limitations on credit unions' activities, 12 U.S.C. § 1757), the choice is simple. Transparent balked (as well it should) when asked whether a document saying something like "at the request of Exxon Corp., we undertake to assume the obligations of Titan Tool" would allow Transparent to invoke the letter of credit to collect a debt due from Exxon. Transparent suggested that we dip beneath the surface of this document to see that the negotiations leading to its issuance grew out of commercial dealings between Transparent and Titan, but we

[8] This enlightening case does not appear in the official reports, perhaps because it is the invention of A.P. Herbert, Uncommon Law 201-06 (1935), but given what does appear in the official reports, *Board of Inland Revenue v. Haddock* has its attractions.

have explained already why courts do not consider parol evidence when evaluating letters of credit.

The document is silent or obscure on every significant question. Such writings do not promote certainty in commercial transactions. Why a credit union put the words "letter of credit" to a document is beyond us; perhaps the National Credit Union Administration ought to have a few words with the management at the Paysaver Credit Union. Whatever this document may be, it is not a "credit" under §§ 5-102 and 5-103 of the U.C.C.

AFFIRMED

NOTES

(1) The drafters of Revised Article Five have noted that nearly $250 billion of letter of credit financing occurs in the United States annually. It is thus surprising that the U.C.C. requires no formalities for creation of a letter of credit other than 1) a writing 2) that is signed by the issuer. A well drafted letter of credit will contain much more than the statutory minimum. As in all contracts, a skillfully crafted letter of credit will clearly express each parties intentions.

(2) *Letters of credit may be revocable or irrevocable.* See § 5-103 and 5-106 [revised §§ 5-102, 5-106 Comment]. A revocable letter of credit is similar to an illusory promise—issuer may revoke or modify the letter with out notice, or consent of either the customer or beneficiary. § 5-106(3) [revised § 5-106(b)]. Practitioner's query: Why would anyone ever accept a revocable letter of credit? An irrevocable letter of credit can be modified or revoked only with the consent of the customer; once the beneficiary receives the letter or the advice of letter, modification or revocation permitted only with beneficiary's consent. § 5-106(1) and (2) [revised § 5-106(a) and (b)]. Note that Article 6 of the U.C.P. provides that credits which do not explicitly state the status of a letter of credit clearly are deemed revocable. Can you hypothesize why a bank would find it advantageous to argue for a letter of credit being governed by the U.C.P. when all documents are silent to the governing law and the bank is aware that the customer is having financial difficulties? Why should the U.C.P. default rule favor that a letter of credit is "revocable?"

[D] Obligation of Issuer

Issuer's Responsibility for Performance of the Underlying Sale Contract. We have established from previous discussion that the issuer of a documentary letter of credit is generally in the banking business, and does not intend to become involved either as buyer or seller with reference to the goods transaction underlying the issuance of the credit. Performance of the sales contract is not the issuer's concern; it is only obligated under its agreement with its customer to honor the beneficiary's draft if the terms of the credit are met. Again, insofar as the documents accompanying the draft are concerned, the issuer must make a sufficient examination to ascertain that the documents are regular and appear to comply with the terms of the letter of credit, but does not become responsible for the genuineness of the documents themselves. All of this is made explicit in U.C.C. § 5-109(1), (2) [revised § 5-108]. Further, the issuer has no concern with the conformity of goods or documents to the underlying sale contract.[9] Several of the Articles of the Uniform Customs, 1993 revision, pertain to the issuer's duties in this regard. See Articles 2-4, 9 and 13.

---

[9] "An issuer must honor a draft or demand for payment which complies with the terms of the relevant credit regardless of whether the goods or documents conform to the underlying contract for sale. . ." U.C.C. § 5-114(1) [revised § 5-108(a)].

Compliance of Documents with the Terms of the Credit: Strict versus Substantial Compliance. Although the issuer generally need not be concerned with the goods but only with the documents, it nevertheless must determine whether the documents tendered by the seller comply with the terms of the credit. If the documents fail to comply, and the issuer pays the draft, it breaches its contract with the customer-buyer (U.C.C. § 5-109(1), (2); see § 5-114(3)) [revised §§ 5-108, 5-109]; on the other hand, if they in fact do comply but the issuer dishonors the draft, it is liable to the beneficiary-seller (U.C.C. §§ 5-114(1), 5-115) [revised § 5-108(a), 5-111].

One of the important areas *not* covered by Article 5 revolves around the question of "when documents in fact and in law do or do not comply with the terms of the credit." § 5-102(3) and Comment 2 [cf. § 5-108]. Therefore, we must look to case law and the Uniform Customs (UCP).[10]

Professor Kozolchyk remarks:[11]

> One of the most often quoted and influential judicial statements in letter of credit law was made by Lord Sumner in the 1927 English case of *Equitable Trust Co. of New York v. Dawson Partners* [(1927, 27 Ll.L. Rep. 49, 52 (H.L.).]: "There is no room for documents which are almost the same or which will do just as well." In other words, the issuing bank's verification has to be governed by a strict standard which excludes deviations, however slight, from the customer's instructions and from the credit terms.

The major justification for this strict standard is that the successful utilization of commercial letters of credit depends on the trustworthiness of the promises made by the issuing banker to the customer and the beneficiary. Unless those promises are kept inviolate they are not likely to be relied upon by either party. A less apparent justification relates to the nature of the banking business. Banks are not normally interested in becoming involved in the underlying transactions as would be required if documents were to be checked for facts other than their apparent or formal regularity, or if their regularity had to be established by resorting to evidence extrinsic to the letter of credit transaction.

> Nevertheless there is an economic if not a physical limit to the diligence required from a bank when checking formal or apparent regularity. As stated by an experienced banker, if an absolutely perfect tender were the required standard, very few tenders would qualify. . . .
>
> One of the realities of "living" letters of credit law is that customers have a marked propensity to find deviations from strict compliance whenever there is a sharp drop in the market price of the goods purchased from the seller beneficiary. Such deviations are not too difficult to find given the large number of words and clauses normally involved in documentary credits.
>
> Courts in major trading centers have become aware of this propensity and are, therefore, less insistent upon strict compliance. This attitude became apparent to this author . . .when comparing court decisions in different jurisdictions and legal systems on objections to strict compliance. Courts were inclined to take more seriously a banker's objection of noncompliance raised against a beneficiary's tender of documents than a customer's objection raised against the issuing bank's verification. . . . The second question posed in the introduction to this

---

[10] See, e.g., UCP Arts. 9, 13, 37c summarized at § 23.01[B] above.

[11] From Vol. IX, International Encyclopedia of Comparative Law, Chapter 5 by B. Kozolchyk at §§ 5-148 and 5-149, 5-155 and 5-156 (1978)." Compliance with the terms of a letter of credit is not like pitching horseshoes. No points are awarded for being close." *Fidelity Nat'l Bank v. Dade County*, 371 So. 2d 545, 546 (Fla.Dist.Ct.App. 1979).

subchapter can therefore be answered in the affirmative. There are differences in the application of the standard of strict compliance and they depend upon the parties involved in the controversy and the plaintiff's or defendant's relationship to the issuing bank. . . .

In *J.H. Rayner & Co. v. Hambro's Bank, Ltd.* [1943] 1 K.B. 37, B contracted to purchase Coromandel groundnuts from S, and secured a letter of credit requiring bills of lading covering "a shipment of about 1400 tons Coromandel groundnuts." S presented its draft with an invoice describing Coromandel groundnuts, but a bill of lading covering "machine-shelled groundnut kernels." It was understood in the trade that "Coromandel groundnuts" and "machine shelled groundnut kernels" were the same commodity. The issuing bank refused to pay the draft, claiming the bill of lading to be nonconforming to the terms of the credit. S brought suit against the bank, but the court upheld the bank's refusal.[12]

In *Courtaulds North America, Inc. v. North Carolina National Bank*, 528 F.2d 802, 806 (4th Cir. 1975), the bank denied liability chiefly on the assertion that the draft did not agree with the letter's conditions, viz., that the draft be accompanied by a "Commercial invoice in triplicate stating [inter alia] that it covers. . .100% acrylic yarn"; instead, the accompanying invoices stated that the goods were "Imported Acrylic Yarn." The court held for the bank and concluded:

> Had Bank deviated from the stipulation of the letter and honored the draft, then at once it might have been confronted with the not improbable risk of [buyer Adastra] bankruptcy trustee's charge of liability for unwarrantably paying the draft moneys to the seller, Courtaulds, and refusal to reimburse Bank for the outlay. Contrarily, it might face a Courtaulds claim that since it had depended upon Bank's assurance of credit in shipping yarn to Adastra, Bank was responsible for the loss. In this situation Bank cannot be condemned for sticking to the letter of the letter.

BEYENE v. IRVING TRUST CO.

United States Court of Appeals
762 F.2d 4, 40 U.C.C. Rep. 1811 (2nd Cir. 1985)

KEARSE, CIRCUIT JUDGE.

Plaintiffs Dessaleng Beyene and Jean M. Hanson appeal from a final judgment of the United States District Court for the Southern District of New York, Morris E. Lasker, Judge, dismissing their complaint seeking damages for the alleged wrongful refusal of defendant Irving Trust Company ("Irving") to honor a letter of credit. The district court granted Irving's motion for summary judgment dismissing the complaint on the ground that, since the bill of lading presented to Irving misspelled the name of the person to whom notice was to be given of the arrival of

[12] Restatement, Second, Contracts § 221, Illustration 9 is based on this case. The section concludes: "Bank is not bound to honor drafts accompanied by bills of lading covering 'Machine-shelled groundnut kernels.' See Uniform Commercial Code § 5-109(1)(c)."

the goods and thereby failed to comply with the terms of the letter of credit, Irving was under no duty to honor the letter of credit. On appeal, plaintiffs contend, inter alia, that the mere misspelling of a name should not relieve a bank of its duty to honor a letter of credit. We agree with the district court that the misspelling in this case was a material discrepancy that relieved Irving of its duty to pay the letter of credit, and we affirm the judgment.

FACTS

The material undisputed facts may be stated briefly. In March 1978, Beyene agreed to sell to Mohammed Sofan, a resident of the Yemen Arab Republic ("YAR"), two prefabricated houses. Sofan attempted to finance the purchase through the use of a letter of credit issued by the Yemen Bank for Reconstruction and Development ("YBRD") in favor of Beyene. YBRD designated Irving as the confirming bank for the letter of credit and Irving subsequently notified Beyene of the letter's terms and conditions. Beyene designated the National Bank of Washington ("NBW") as his collecting bank.

In May 1979, NBW sent Irving all of the documents required under the terms of the letter of credit. Thereafter, Irving telephoned NBW to inform it of several discrepancies in the submitted documents, including the fact that the bill of lading listed the party to be notified by the shipping company as Mohammed Soran instead of Mohammed Sofan. The NBW official contacted testified at deposition that Irving never waived the misspelling discrepancy and continued to assert that it was a discrepancy, though it undertook to request authorization from YBRD to pay the letter of credit despite the discrepancy. Such authorization was not forthcoming, and Irving refused to pay.

Plaintiffs instituted the present suit seeking damages for Irving's failure to pay the letter of credit. Irving moved for summary judgment dismissing the complaint on a variety of grounds. The district court, in an opinion reported at 596 F Supp 438 (1984), granted the motion on the sole ground that the misspelling of Sofan's name in the bill of lading constituted a material discrepancy that gave Irving the right to dishonor the letter of credit. This appeal followed.

DISCUSSION

On appeal, plaintiffs contend principally that (1) the district court's ruling is unsound as a matter of precedent and of policy, and (2) Irving should be required to pay the letter of credit on grounds of waiver and estoppel. We find merit in none of plaintiffs' contentions. We need discuss only the first.

The nature and functions of commercial letters of credit have recently been explored by this court, see *Voest-Alpine International Corp. v. Chase Manhattan Bank*, N.A., 707 F2d 680, 682-83 (2d Cir 1983); *Marino Indus.tries Corp. v. Chase Manhattan Bank*, N.A., 686 F2d 112, 114-15 (2d Cir 1982), and will not be repeated in detail here. The terms of a letter of credit generally require the beneficiary of the letter to submit to the issuing bank documents such as an invoice and a bill of lading to provide "the accredited buyer [with] some assurance that he will receive the goods for which he bargained and arranged payment." H. Harfield, Bank Credits and Acceptances 57 (5th ed 1974). The issuing bank, or a bank that acts as confirming bank for the issuer, takes on an absolute duty to pay the amount of the credit to the beneficiary, so long as the beneficiary complies with the terms of the letter. In order to protect the issuing or confirming bank, this absolute duty does not arise unless the terms of the letter have been complied with strictly. Literal compliance is generally "essential so as not to impose an obligation upon the bank that it did not undertake and so as not to jeopardize the bank's right to indemnity from its customer." Voest-Alpine International Corp. v. Chase Manhattan Bank, 707 F2d at 683; see H. Haffield, Letters of Credit 57-59 (1979).

While some variations in a bill of lading might be so insignificant as not to relieve the issuing or confirming bank of its obligation to pay, see, *e.g.*, H. Harfield, Bank Credits and Acceptances 75-78, we agree with the district court that the misspelling in the bill of lading of Sofan's name as "Soran" was a material discrepancy that entitled Irving to refuse to honor the letter of credit. First, this is not a case where the name intended is unmistakably clear despite what is obviously a typographical error, as might be the case if, for example, "Smith" were misspelled "Smithh." Nor have appellants claimed that in the Middle East "Soran" would obviously be recognized as an inadvertent misspelling of the surname "Sofan." Second, "Sofan" was not a name that was inconsequential to the document, for Sofan was the person to whom the shipper was to give notice of the arrival of the goods, and the misspelling of his name could well have resulted in his nonreceipt of the goods and his justifiable refusal to reimburse Irving for the credit. (Indeed, the record includes a telex from Beyene, stating that Sofan had not been notified when the goods arrived in YAR and that as a result demurrage and other costs had been incurred.) In the circumstances, the district court was entirely correct in viewing the failure of Beyene and NBW to provide documents that strictly complied with the terms of the letter of credit as a failure that entitled Irving to refuse payment.

Plaintiffs do not contend that there was any issue to be tried as to the fact of the misspelling of Sofan's name. Their assertions that Irving waived the admitted discrepancy or was estopped from relying on it were not supported sufficiently to withstand a motion for summary judgment and were properly rejected by the district court for the reasons stated in its opinion, 596 F Supp at 439-41.

CONCLUSION

The judgment of the district court is affirmed.

NOTE

Letter of Credit Update 11-12 (August, 1985) comments on the *Beyene* case:[13]

> Quoting from *Marino Industries v. Chase Manhattan Bank, N.A.*, 686 F. 2d 112 (2d Cir. 1982), the district court concluded that "a single discrepancy, including one involving the misspelling of a party's last name, is sufficient to excuse a confirming bank from paying the proceeds of a letter of credit." *Beyene*, 596 F. Supp. 438 at 441.
>
> On appeal, the Second Circuit affirmed. "We agree with the district court that the misspelling in this case was a material discrepancy that entitled Irving to refuse to honor the letter of credit . . . . The district court was entirely correct in viewing the failure of Beyene and NBW to

[13] Copyright © 1985 by James E. Byrne. Reprinted by permission.

provide documents that strictly complied with the terms of the letter of credit as a failure that entitled Irving to refuse payment."

The Second Circuit's decision may muddy the waters of strict compliance even more. Despite its ruling that the district court was correct in granting summary judgment, the opinion is less clear as to the state of the doctrine of strict compliance.

The district court held that the discrepancy was sufficient to justify dishonor regardless of its materiality. According to its understanding of the law, "a confirming bank need not ascertain the magnitude of each discrepancy before its obligation to pay is relieved. Under the rule of 'strict compliance,' Irving did not have to scrutinize the underlying transaction between Beyene and Sofan, nor did it have to establish whether the misspelling of an Arab name was a meaningful mistake or find that it was a major error before it could claim that a discrepancy in the documents existed." *Beyene*, 596 F. Supp. 438 at 442.

The Second Circuit, however, clearly looked at whether the mistake was material and concluded that it was. Whatever one may think of its reasoning, the court drew upon the facts, as indicated in the quotation above, to justify its conclusion that materiality existed. Oddly enough, it perceived the position of the district court to be that there was a material discrepancy.

Whatever the courts may say, then, it would appear that not just any discrepancy will do, there must be some indication that it was material.

From the beneficiary's viewpoint, the entire scenario looks like a catch-22. According to Beyene's attorney, William L. Borden, the error was made by the Baltimore steamship company and noticed by the freight forwarder and collecting bank when the documents were assembled for presentation. At that time, Beyene contended, they determined that the discrepancy was too minor to bother correcting.

Sound like grounds for an action against the local bank? Beyene thought so and sued both the issuing bank and the collecting bank, figuring that one would be responsible. Because the action was brought in D.C., however, it was held that there was no jurisdiction over the issuing bank under the applicable long arm statute. Hence, the instant action in New York. The action against the collecting bank proceeded but Beyene was unable to produce Irving as a witness to prove that the bank's alleged error in judgment caused its loss because the D.C. rules in effect provided no means of process by which Irving could be compelled to testify.

"It is an example of how little people can get terribly hurt under this system," said attorney Borden in an interview. "As a result of a petty error of which he had no knowledge and as to which the two banks blame each other, both are exonerated and the small businessman is stuck with a crushing loss." Will Beyene utilize letters of credit again? "Not soon," exclaimed Borden.

AMERICAN COLEMAN CO. v. INTRAWEST BANK OF SOUTHGLENN, N.A.

United States Court of Appeals
887 F.2d 1382, 10 U.C.C.R. Serv. 2d 1361 (10th CIr. 1989)

BARRETT, SENIOR CIRCUIT JUDGE.

After examining the briefs and the appellate record, this panel has determined unanimously that oral argument would not materially assist the determination of this appeal. See Fed.R.App.P. 34(a); Tenth Cir. R. 34.1.9. The cause is therefore ordered submitted without oral argument.

In this diversity case, the American Coleman Company (American Coleman), plaintiff below, appeals from the district court's order granting summary judgment on behalf of the defendant below, Intrawest Bank of Southglenn, N.A., the predecessor to the United Bank of Southglenn, N.A. (Bank). The court dismissed, with prejudice, American Coleman's action for damages for an alleged wrongful dishonor of a request for payment pursuant to a letter of credit.

In 1984, American Coleman sold some real property located in Littleton, Colorado, to James E. Gammon (Gammon) and the South Santa Fe Partnership (the Partnership) and took a note secured by a first deed of trust on the property. The note and deed of trust were dated November 16, 1984, but not recorded until November 21, 1984. The terms of the repayment of the note required Gammon and the Partnership to post a letter of credit, of which American Coleman would be the beneficiary. The Bank, on behalf of its customer, Gammon and Associates, established a "Clean, Irrevocable Letter of Credit" in amount of $250,000 in favor of American Coleman. It was dated February 15, 1985, and was to expire on November 15, 1986. In consideration, the Bank received from Gammon a letter of credit fee and a second deed of trust on the Littleton property under a reimbursement contract whereby Gammon was to repay Bank for all payments made by Bank to American Coleman pursuant to the letter of credit. The letter of credit arrangement, once established, is often referred to as a statutory obligation on the part of the issuer (Bank) to honor drafts drawn by the beneficiary (American Coleman) that comply with the terms of the letter of credit. The transaction is separate and independent from the underlying business transaction between the beneficiary (American Coleman) and the Bank's customer (Gammon and Associates) which is contractual in nature. A letter of credit is not an evidence of indebtedness; it is merely a promise by a bank to lend money under certain circumstances.

The Bank was to make funds available to American Coleman pursuant to its sight drafts to be accompanied by the "original Letter of Credit and your signed written statement that Jim Gammon and Associates is in default on the Note and Security Agreement dated November 21, 1984, between American Coleman and Jim Gammon and Associates." (R., Vol. I, Tab 2, Exh. A). The above reference to a note and security agreement dated November 21, 1984, was an error, inasmuch as no such documents ever existed. The record does not resolve the dispute relative to the party responsible for the error. However, on November 16, 1984, Gammon and

Associates executed and delivered to American Coleman a note in the principal sum of $1,037,500 secured by a first deed of trust on the Littleton property sold which were recorded on November 21, 1984.

Thereafter, on December 31, 1985, and on May 16, 1986, American Coleman requested payments of $75,000, respectively, under the letter of credit. Both of these requests included the original letter of credit and the specific default language previously referred to, *i.e.*, "Jim Gammon and Associates is in default on the Note and Security Agreement dated November 21, 1984, between American Coleman and Jim Gammon and Associates." (R., Vol. I, Tab 5, Exhibits A and B). Thus, a balance of $100,000 remained available to be drawn on under the letter of credit when on November 13, 1986, American Coleman tendered to Bank a sight draft in amount of $100,000 with the following statement appended thereto:

> The American Coleman Company informs you that Jim Gammon and Associates is in default on the Note and Security Agreement dated November 21, 1984, and the Promissory Note dated November 16, 1984, between American Coleman and Jim Gammon and Associates.

(R., Vol. I, Tab 2, Exh. B).

Bank formally dishonored the draft on November 17, 1986, two days after the letter of credit expired because (1) the amount requested was in advance of any default, and (2) no default could occur until November 16, 1986. Bank did not give as a reason for dishonor the fact that the wording of American Coleman's request was not in strict compliance with the terms of the letter of credit.

In the district court, both parties moved for summary judgment, agreeing that there was no genuine dispute of material fact relative to Bank's liability for its dishonor of American Coleman's request of November 13, 1986, for the balance of funds under the letter of credit. Bank contended that the fact that the note was not then in default constituted a valid ground for dishonor and, further, that dishonor was proper because American Coleman's request was not in strict compliance with the terms of the letter of credit. American Coleman argued that Bank should be estopped from raising the defense of strict compliance because Bank had not asserted this defense at the time of dishonor. Further, should Bank not be estopped, American Coleman contended that its request for funds was in strict compliance with the terms of the letter of credit. In considering the cross-motions for summary judgment, the district court relied upon the pleadings, the briefs, affidavits and other documentation.

The district court found/concluded that Bank was not estopped from raising the defense of strict compliance and that American Coleman's request of November 13, 1986, was not in strict compliance with the terms of the letter of credit. The court did not reach the issue whether the original reason given by the Bank, i.e., that the note was not yet in default, was a valid ground for dishonor.

On appeal, American Coleman contends that the district court's decision was erroneous, contrary to law, and an abuse of discretion in the court's holdings that: (1) the note was not yet in default, (2) the demand was not in strict compliance, technically or literally, with the terms of the letter of credit, (3) the Bank was not estopped from raising lack of strict compliance as a reason for dishonor, and (4) the beneficiary (American Coleman) was not misled, and could not have cured the defect because Bank was allowed, pursuant to C.R.S. § 4-5-112(1)(a), to defer payment or dishonor for three banking days.

No contention is raised on appeal that substantial issues of material fact existed, precluding summary judgment under Rule 56(a) Fed R.Civ.P. Even so, it is our duty to examine the record on appeal to determine whether any genuine issue of material fact pertinent to the ruling remains and, if not, whether the district court properly applied the substantive law. And in making this evaluation, pleadings and documentary evidence must be construed liberally and in favor of the party opposing the motion. We are satisfied that no genuine issues of material fact remained when the district court granted summary judgment. Finally, in our de novo review, we have recognized different degrees of deference we must give to the interpretations and applications of state law by a resident federal judge sitting in a diversity action (some deference, great deference, clearly erroneous). We shall proceed under the "some deference" standard.

I.

American Coleman argues that the district court was clearly erroneous in finding/concluding that the Note of November 16, 1984, was not yet in default when the November 13, 1986, demand for payment was made by American Coleman upon Bank. The record shows, however, that the district court made no such finding.

It is true that after the draft of November 13, 1986 was submitted Bank did inform American Coleman that it would not fund the letter of credit because the Note was not in default and could not be in default until November 16, 1986. Because this was the only ground relied upon by Bank to dishonor the draft, American Coleman argued, unsuccessfully, that Bank should be estopped from raising the defense of strict compliance in the district court action because it failed to assert the issue of nonconformity at the time it dishonored the draft.

The district court plainly did not find/conclude that the Note of December 16, 1984, was in default. In the district court's Memorandum Opinion and Order of December 17, 1987, the court stated:

> Since I conclude that the bank is not estopped from raising the defense of strict compliance, and since I further find that American Coleman's request for funds was not in strict compliance with the terms and conditions of the letter of credit, I need not reach the issue of whether the original reason given by the bank (that the note was not yet in default) was a valid ground for dishonor.

(R., Vol. I, Tab 6, p. 5).

II.

American Coleman contends that the district court erred in holding that the doctrine of strict compliance required American Coleman, as beneficiary of the letter of credit from Bank, as issuer, to literally and technically adhere to the requirements of the letter of credit. The district court found/concluded:

> In the present case, it is clear that American Coleman's request for payment presented November 13, 1986 was not in technical or literal compliance with the terms of the letter of credit. American Coleman's reference to two different notes could easily have caused the bank's documents examiner some confusion. Accordingly, because I conclude that the rule of strict compliance, as it is applied in Colorado, requires literal compliance with the terms and requirements set forth in the letter of credit, and there was no such literal compliance in this case. . . .

(R., Vol. I, Tab 6, p. 13).

The district court recognized that many courts refuse to allow an issuing bank to dishonor a demand for payment when the nonconformity between the language contained in the draft or demand and the terms contained in the letter of credit is trivial or technical. *Id.* at 9. The court observed that the Colorado Supreme Court has not as yet ruled on the distinction between traditional strict compliance versus substantial compliance, and particularly so where the deviation is "as minor and technical as in this case." *Id.* at 13. Even so, based upon *Colorado National Bank v. Board of County Commissioners*, 634 P.2d 32, 40 (Colo. 1981) ("To maintain the commercial vitality of the letter of credit device, strict compliance with the terms of the letter of credit is required"); *Guilford Pattern Works, Inc. v. United Bank of Boulder*, 655 F. Supp. 378, 379-80 (D.Colo. 1987) ("Colorado courts have held that in order to maintain the commercial validity of the vehicle of letters of credit, strict compliance with the terms and conditions is necessary."), and other cases and authorities, the district court reasoned that the Colorado Supreme Court "would shun the non-standard of substantial compliance and would require literal and technical adherence to the requirements of the letter of credit." (R., Vol. I, Tab 6, p. 13). We agree.

C.S.R. § 4-5-114(1) provides:

> An issuer must honor a draft or demand for payment which complies with the terms of the relevant credit, regardless of whether the goods or documents conform to the underlying contract for sale or other contract between the customer and the beneficiary. The issuer is not excused from honor of such a draft or demand by reason of an additional general term that all documents must be satisfactory to the issuer, but an issuer may require that specified documents must be satisfactory to it.

In *Raiffeisen-Zentralkasse Tirol v. First National Bank*, 671 P.2d 1008 (Colo.App. 1983), the court held that the obligation of the issuer of a letter of credit to honor the letter is wholly separate from the beneficiary's compliance with the terms of the underlying contract and is dependent solely on the terms and conditions contained in the letter of credit. This separation is supportive of the rule laid down in *Colorado National Bank v. Board of County Commissioners, supra,* that strict compliance with the terms of a letter of credit is required to maintain the commercial vitality of the letter of credit device. Failure on the part of Bank to oversee careful compliance with the terms of the letter of credit would have prohibited Bank from collecting the funds paid to the beneficiary (American Coleman) from its customer, the Partnership (Jim Gammon and Associates). See *Philadelphia Gear Corp. v. Central Bank*, 717 F.2d 230 (5th Cir.), reh'g denied, 720 F.2d 1291 (5th Cir. 1983). The duty of the issuing Bank is ministerial in nature, confined to checking the presented documents carefully against what the letter of credit requires. Marino Industries *Corp. v. Chase Manhattan Bank, N.A.*, 686 F.2d 112 (2d Cir. 1982).

The district court found that the language in American Coleman's draft of November 13, 1986, referring to "The Note and Security Agreement dated November 21, 1984, and the Promissory Note dated November 16, 1984, between American Coleman and Jim Gammon and Associates" was not in strict compliance because of the extra language that was included. (R., Vol. I, Tab 6, pp. 5-6). We agree.

It has been observed that most courts apply the "strict compliance" standard which leaves "no room for documents which are almost the same or which will do just as well." A minority of the courts hold that a beneficiary's "reasonable" or "substantial" performance of the letter of credit's requirement will do. However, no matter how one reads the cases, strict compliance endures as the central test. White & Summers, Uniform Commercial Code, Third Edition (1988),

Vol. 2, § 19-5, p. 31. The authors state that cases applying the "reasonable" or "substantial" compliance standard "are so few and their notion so inherently fuzzy that they give little or no clue as to what might be 'reasonable' or 'substantial' compliance." *Id.*

While it is apparent from the cases that minute discrepancies which could not possibly mislead a document examiner are usually disregarded, this does not constitute a retreat from the strict compliance standard applicable in this case inasmuch as the district court found that "American Coleman's reference to two different notes could easily have caused the bank's documents examiner some confusion." (R., Vol. I, Tab 6, p. 13). We agree.

We hold that the district court did not err in applying the strict compliance standard. We reject American Coleman's argument that reference in the November 13, 1986, draft to the second note was mere "surplusage." The apparent existence of two promissory notes supports the district court's finding that Bank could have been misled by American Coleman's November 13, 1986, draft. American Coleman's contention that Bank could not have been misled by the draft because Bank drafted the letter of credit is without support in this record. The deposition testimony of American Coleman representative Joseph E. McElroy demonstrates that American Coleman's attorney assisted in drafting the letter of credit (R., Vol. I, Tab 4, Exh. F). There is no other evidence in the record on appeal relative thereto.

III.

American Coleman contends that the district court was clearly erroneous in holding that Bank was not estopped from raising the defense of lack of strict compliance as a reason for its dishonor of the November 13, 1986, draft.

The district court recognized that in Colorado the general rule is that "when an issuer of a letter of credit formally places its refusal to pay upon specified grounds, it is held to have waived all other grounds," quoting from *Colorado National Bank v. Board of County Commissioners*, 634 P.2d 32, 41 (Colo. 1981). However, the district court relied upon that same case for the proposition that the waiver-estoppel rule "is limited to situations where the statements have misled the beneficiary who would have cured the defect but relied on the stated grounds to its injury." *Id.* at 41.

The district court relied on *Colorado National Bank v. Board of County Commissioners*, supra, for its ruling that Bank was not estopped from raising a ground for dishonor in defense of suit brought by American Coleman even though it failed to state such ground at the time of dishonor.

In *Colorado National Bank v. Board of County Commissioners*, the letter of credit provided for a 15-day sight draft. However, the beneficiary submitted a demand draft on the day the letter of credit was to expire. Bank gave several reasons for dishonor, but did not rely upon the fact that the beneficiary had presented a demand draft in lieu of the required 15-day sight draft. Even so, the court held that the bank was not estopped from raising this ground in defense of the suit because the non-conforming demand draft was presented on the same day that the letter of credit expired. The court observed that under C.R.S. § 4-5-112(1)(a) a bank called upon to honor a draft or demand for payment under a letter of credit may defer payment or dishonor until the close of the third banking day following receipt of the documents. Thus, the court reasoned that the beneficiary could not have cured the defect since any subsequent presentment would have been untimely. Accordingly, the beneficiary could not have detrimentally relied on the bank's failure to state the discrepancy as a ground for dishonor.

We agree with the district court's conclusion that the facts of the instant case are quite similar to those in *Colorado National* and that American Coleman cannot be said to have detrimentally relied on Bank's failure to state the strict compliance discrepancy as one ground for dishonor, and that Bank is not estopped from raising the doctrine of strict compliance in its defense. November 13, 1986, was a Thursday. Three banking days thereafter would extend to November 18, 1986, just one day after Bank gave formal notice of dishonor. American Coleman could not have submitted another draft before the note expired. C.R.S. § 4-5-112(1) provides, in pertinent part:

A bank to which a documentary draft or demand for payment is presented under a credit may without dishonor of the draft, demand or credit (a) defer honor until the close of the third banking day following receipt of the documents. . . .

American Coleman insists that the letter of credit in this case is clearly denominated a "clean" letter of credit as distinguished from a "documentary" letter of credit and that, accordingly, the three-banking-day rule does not apply. We agree that this statute applies only to a documentary draft or demand for payment. We disagree with American Coleman's contention that simply because the letter of credit here was denominated "Clean Irrevocable Letter of Credit" (R., Vol. I, Tab 2, Exh. A), it was treated by the parties as such.

C.R.S. § 4-5-103(1)(b) defines a "documentary draft" or a "documentary demand for payment" as one honor of which is conditioned upon the presentation of a document or documents. "Document" is defined therein as any paper, including invoice, certificate, notice of default, and the like. In the case at bar, American Coleman was required under the terms of the letter of credit to present the original letter of credit (a document) and a notice of default (a document) with each draft. American Coleman's effort to restrict the definition of "documentary draft" to documents of title or shipping invoices must fail.

We Affirm.

NOTES

(1) Is the strict compliance doctrine required to ensure consistency and predictability in letters of credit, or is it a stubborn throwback to inflexible Blackstonian principles that ignore the realities of the business world? Is it fair for a bank to avoid paying an obligation it voluntarily assumed because of an innocent and insignificant error, such as the misspelling of a word in a bill of lading, or the improper invoice number? Or is the presentment of complying documents something so basic that an exacting standard should be a hurdle for payment? Some commentators have eloquently argued for the adoption of a "substantial performance" or "harmless error" standard to govern when a beneficiary attempts to draw on imperfect documents.

(2) The Revised U.C.C., although explicitly recognizing the strict compliance rule (Revised § 5-108), tempers the harsh results of a beneficiary's minor mistake by allowing a refusing bank only one shot to reject a substantially complying note. A diligent beneficiary will submit a request to honor a letter of credit several days in advance of any expiration date on the letter of credit. If the issuing bank refuses to honor the draft, however, it must do so within seven days and it must explain all defects at that time (except fraud), or be barred from asserting them later. See Revised § 5-108(c) (requiring a bank to provide timely notice of any discrepancies). Therefore, a beneficiary should be given enough time to clean up all actionable and objectionable blemishes of a presentment. Does the Revised U.C.C. strike an appropriate balance between predictability and equity?

PROBLEM 23.2

Assume the above structure of Revised Article 5 has been adopted in Minnesota. The letter of credit extended by the Hayes' First National Bank is set to expire on 12/01/97. Stephen Ryder has sent three dozen of the finest bamboo rods to Clayton Molinero. Stephen presents all necessary documents to the Hayes' Bank on 11/28/97, anticipating that the paperwork is in strict compliance. A keen-eyed bank clerk notices on 11/29/97 that the required bill of lading refers to the fly rods as "three dozen split cane rods." Hayes' Bank could refuse to honor the draft based on this discrepancy. Given that the line of credit is about to expire, is the Bank allowed to wait until 12/04/97 before providing Stephen notification of errors in the paper work (and thus avoiding all obligations under the letter of credit), or does the U.C.C. "within a reasonable time" standard require Hayes' Bank to provide Stephen with enough time to reasonably cure the documents?

BANK OF COCHIN LTD. v. MANUFACTURERS HANOVER TRUST CO.

Southern District of New York
612 F. Supp. 1533; 41 U.C.C. Rep. Serv. 920 (1985)

CANNELLA, D.J.:

FACTS

Bank of Cochin Limited ["Cochin"], an Indian corporation and the issuer of letter of credit BB/VN/41/80, commenced this diversity action against Manufacturers Hanover Trust Company ["MHT"], a New York corporation that acted as the confirming bank on the letter. Cochin seeks recovery of the amount paid by MHT, thereafter debited to Cochin's account at MHT, on drawings negotiated in New York between MHT and St. Lucia Enterprises, Ltd. ["St. Lucia"]. Codefendant St. Lucia, a purported New York corporation and the letter of credit beneficiary, has perpetrated a large fraud on both banks and nonparty customer Vishwa Niryat (Pvt.) Ltd. ["Vishwa"]. Unfortunately, St. Lucia has vanished and the Court must decide whose shoulders will bear the scam.

The parties agree on the salient events and have presented essentially identical and uncontroverted statements of fact pursuant to Rule 3(g) of the Civil Rules for the Southern District of New York. On February 8, 1980, in Bombay, India, Vishwa requested Cochin to issue an irrevocable letter of credit covering up to $798,000 for the benefit of St. Lucia. The letter was to have expired on April 15, 1980 and covered the anticipated shipment and purchase of 1,000 metric tons of aluminum melting scrap consisting of aluminum beverage cans.[14]

---

[14] Vishwa's application for documentary credit required that St. Lucia supply the following documents and shipment conditions as a prerequisite to payment:

Six copies of signed invoices;

One set of clean shipped on board bills of lading;

Notification of shipment to Vishwa;

A maritime insurance policy covering civil unrest, marine and war risks;

A certificate of United States origin in triplicate;

A certificate of analysis from "LLOYDS" [sic] [of London] ["Lloyd's"] confirming the quantity, quality and shipment of the aluminum scrap;

On February 14, 1980, Cochin requested MHT to supply financial information on St. Lucia. MHT responded by telex the following day that St. Lucia did not maintain an MHT account and that a thorough check of normal credit sources did not reveal any "pertinent" information. On February 22, Cochin conveyed the terms and conditions of the letter of credit to MHT by telex and requested MHT to advise "St Lucia Enterprises Ltd" of the establishment of the letter and to add MHT's confirmation.[15] The letter of credit was issued subject to the Uniform Customs and Practice for Documentary Credits (1974 Revision), Int'l Chamber of Commerce, Pub. No. 290 ["UCP"].[16]

On February 25, MHT mailed its written advice of the letter of credit establishment to St. Lucia and confirmed the amended letter on February 29.[17] Cochin amended certain terms of the letter on four occasions in March and April 1980. MHT mailed its advices of these amendments to St. Lucia from March to May and sent copies to Cochin, which were received without comment.[18] The final amended letter of credit contained the following relevant terms and conditions:

Shipment by conference or first class vessel;

Shipment by a non-Pakistani vessel.

15 The documentary and other requirements for the letter of credit set forth in Cochin's telex included:

Sight drafts of the invoice value in duplicate;

Six copies of the signed invoices showing that the aluminum was covered under notice 44-ITC(PN) 79;

One set of clean shipped on board bills of lading to the order of Cochin;

A certificate of United States origin in triplicate;

A certificate of analysis of the aluminum from Lloyd's;

Shipment from a United States port to Bombay;

A marine insurance policy issued by a first class insurance company; A packing list in triplicate;

One set of nonnegotiable documents to be sent directly to Vishwa immediately after shipment documented by a "cable advise" to Vishwa;

Shipment by conference or first-class vessel.

16 The UCP was revised effective October 1, 1984. UCP, Int'l Chamber of Commerce, Pub. No. 400 (1983). It is axiomatic that the Court must ordinarily apply the law in effect at the time it renders its decision. See *Thorpe v. Housing Authority of Durham*, 393 U.S. 268, 281, 21 L. Ed. 2d 474, 89 S. Ct. 518 (1969); *Byrne v. Buffalo Creek Railroad Co.*, 765 F.2d 364, slip op. at 4726 (2d Cir. 1985). The letter of credit was, however, governed by the 1974 UCP pursuant to its express terms. See *Marine Midland Grace Trust Co. v. Banco del Pais,* S.A., 261 F. Supp. 884, 886 n.1 (S.D.N.Y. 1966). Although the application of the 1983 UCP would favor MHT, see *infra,* it would not alter the Court's decision on the motions.

17 MHT's February 25 form advice listed correctly all the letter of credit conditions. On February 26, MHT requested information from Cochin on the first class insurance company and an explanation as to what documentation was needed to ascertain compliance with shipment by conference or first class vessel. See UCP art. 14(b) (1974) (rejecting usage of "first class" to describe issuers of documents), art. 22(b) (1983) (same). Cochin responded on February 28 by amending the letter of credit insurance clause to require that St. Lucia send a cable to Oriental Fire and General Insurance Co. ["Oriental"] citing cover note 429711. Cochin also requested that the shipping company or Lloyd's certify that the shipment was made by first class or approved vessel. The cable and certificate were to be submitted with the other documents. MHT accurately relayed this information to St. Lucia in its February 29 confirming telex.

18 Cochin sent telexes to MHT on March 3, March 15, March 27 and April 29 amending the letter to reflect that shipment should be made from a port in western Europe and extending the shipping date to May 31 and the letter of credit expiration date to June 15. The inspection clause was also changed to allow a certificate of analysis from Lloyd's or any international agency. Additionally, Cochin requested that St. Lucia produce a certificate that it had duly complied with all terms of the letter of credit.

MHT accurately conveyed these amendments to St. Lucia by written advices dated March 10, March 31, April 8 and May 2. The March 31 advice incorrectly identified the Oriental cover note as 4291, which MHT had properly

a. Sight drafts of the invoice values;

b. Six copies of the signed invoices;

c. One set of clean shipped on board bills of lading;

d. A west European certificate of origin;

e. A certificate of analysis of the aluminum scrap from Lloyd's of London ["Lloyd's"]or another international testings agency;

f. Shipment from a west European port to Bombay;

g. A maritime insurance policy, cover note 429711, to be confirmed by St. Lucia's cable to Oriental Fire and General Insurance Co. ["Oriental"];

h. A packing list in triplicate;

i. One set of nonnegotiable documents to be sent to Vishwa and a confirming cable to Vishwa;

j. A certification from Lloyd's or the shipping company that the ship was a first class or approved non-Pakistani vessel;

k. St. Lucia's certification that it had complied with all terms of the letter of credit;

l. Shipment by May 31, 1980; and

m. Letter of credit expiration on June 15, 1980.

The aluminum was allegedly shipped on May 29, 1980 from Bremen, West Germany to Bombay on the M/V Betelguese. On June 2, St. Lucia established an account at a Manhattan office of Citibank, N.A. ["Citibank"], the collecting bank, in the name of St. Lucia Enterprises, Ltd. On June 9, St. Lucia presented MHT with documents required by the letter of credit and ten sight drafts amounting to $796,603.50,[19] payable to St. Lucia Enterprises. The documents included five copies of the invoices, a clean shipped on board bill of lading, a St. Lucia certification that the aluminum was of west European origin, a certificate of analysis by an international Dutch materials testing agent, a telex confirmation of a telephone message to Oriental that the aluminum had been shipped to Bombay pursuant to cover note 4291, a packing list in triplicate, a St. Lucia certification that one set of nonnegotiable documents had been sent to Vishwa and that Vishwa had been advised by cable, certifications from the shipping company that the M/V Betelguese was an approved first class Panamanian vessel, and a St. Lucia cover letter specifying the documents submitted and requesting payment from MHT. The St. Lucia letter and certifications were on the letterhead of "St. Lucia Enterprises" and were signed by "D Agney".

MHT compared the documents against the requirements of the letter and determined that they complied with all the terms and conditions. On June 13, MHT negotiated the drafts and issued a check for $798,000 payable to St. Lucia Enterprises. The check was indorsed St. Lucia Enterprises Ltd. and was deposited in the Citibank account on June 17, 1980. Citibank collected the check from MHT through normal banking channels. MHT debited Cochin's account for

designated as 429711 in its February 29 confirming advice. Notwithstanding MHT's allegation that Cochin cited cover note 4291, Cochin accurately used cover note 429711 in its telex amendments of February 28 and March 27. Each form of advice sent to St. Lucia and Cochin contained a beneficiary box with the following address: St. Lucia Enterprises, 210 Fifth Avenue, Suite No. 1102, New York, N.Y. 10010.

[19] Invoice 36C was for $79,121.70; invoice 36D was for $79,321.20; invoice 36F was for $79,560.60 and invoices 36A, 36B, 36E, 36F, 36G, 36H, 36I and 36J were each for $79,800.

$798,000 on June 13. MHT sent a copy of its payment advice, the drafts and documents to Cochin by registered air mail on June 13. Unfortunately, Cochin apparently did not receive these documents until June 21. As it turned out, St. Lucia shipped nothing to Vishwa. The documentation submitted to MHT was fraudulent in every regard; indeed, the bills of lading, quality certification and vessel certification were issued by nonexistent corporations. St. Lucia received payment on the letter of credit and Cochin has been unable to locate any party connected with the fraudulent scheme.

Cochin sent a telex to MHT on June 18, inquiring whether St. Lucia had presented documents for negotiation. MHT responded by telex on June 20 that it had paid St. Lucia $798,000 on June 13 and had forwarded the documents to Cochin at that time. On June 21, Cochin sent the following telex to MHT:

> We acknowledge receipt of the documents [sic] Stop We find certain discrepancies [sic] in the same Stop kindly do not [sic] make payment against the same until we telex you otherwise Stop.

On June 23, MHT replied to Cochin's telex as follows:

> Reference your telex June 21 credit BB VN 4180 our 500748 Stop We note your telex fails to give reason for [sic] rejection documents as required UCP Article 8 Stop According our records documents fully complied credit terms and beneficiary already paid therefore we cannot accept your refusal of documents.

By telex dated June 27, Cochin informed MHT of alleged defects in the documents apparently uncovered by Vishwa: (1) St. Lucia's cable to Oriental showed the wrong insurance cover note number of 4291 instead of 429711; (2) St. Lucia did not submit "proof" that a set of nonnegotiable documents and confirming cable had been sent to Vishwa; (3) only one set of documents showed the original certificate of origin whereas the rest included only photocopies; and (4) the invoice packing list and certificate of origin were not duly authenticated. Cochin also noted (5) the overpayment of $1,396.50. MHT credited Cochin's account for $1,396.50 and notified Cochin by telex on June 30.

By telex dated July 3, Cochin asked MHT to recredit its account for $796,603.50 and advised MHT that it was returning the letter of credit documents. Cochin also cited an additional discrepancy that (6) MHT had negotiated documents for St. Lucia Enterprises but that the letter of credit was established for St. Lucia Enterprises Ltd. On July 4, Cochin informed MHT by telex that the documents negotiated by MHT contained the following additional defects: (7) only five signed copies of the commercial invoices, rather than six, were forwarded and (8) documents were signed by "D Agney" without specifying his capacity at St. Lucia.

MHT responded by telex of July 14 that Cochin had failed to timely and properly specify the alleged documentary variances as required by article 8 of the 1974 UCP. The telex also noted that Cochin had failed to promptly return the documents or advise MHT that Cochin was holding the documents at MHT's disposal as required by the UCP. MHT asserted in a telex dated July 16 that it still had not received certain documents from Cochin. The parties exchanged additional telexes confirming and denying that payment was proper. Cochin's Rule 3(g) statement adds the additional allegations that (9) St. Lucia failed to indicate the documents submitted in drawing against the letter of credit, and (10) the shipping company certificate fails to indicate the vessel registration number.

DISCUSSION

Letter of credit liability cases are particularly appropriate for judicial resolution without trial because they present solely legal issues. See *Dulien Steel Prod., Inc. v. Bankers Trust Co.,* 298 F.2d 836, 837 (2d Cir. 1962); *Transamerica Delaval Inc. v. Citibank, N.A.,* 545 F. Supp. 200, 203 (S.D.N.Y. 1982). The parties do not dispute the essential facts and agreed in pretrial conference to present joint summary judgment motions. This case raises novel and unsettled issues of letter of credit law concerning confirming bank liability to an issuing bank for wrongful honor of a letter of credit. The law, however, is sufficiently chartered to require summary judgment for MHT.

A letter of credit is a financing mechanism designed to allocate commercial credit risks whereby a bank or other issuer pays an amount of money to a beneficiary upon presentment of documents complying with specified conditions set forth in the letter. The beneficiary, typically the seller of goods to a buyer-customer, uses the letter to substitute the credit of the issuer for the credit of its customer. The customer applies for the letter of credit, specifies the terms of the letter and promises to reimburse the issuer upon honor of the beneficiary's draft. The letter of credit is thus an engagement by the issuer to the beneficiary to cover the customer's agreement to pay money under the customer-beneficiary contract. The reliability and fluidity of the letter of credit are maintained because the issuing bank is concerned exclusively with the documents, not the performance obligations created by the customer-beneficiary contract. Not a contract, the letter of credit has been best described as "a relationship with no perfect analogies but nevertheless a well defined set of rights and obligations." 1 A. Lowenfeld, International Private Trade § 5.53 at 103 (1977); see B. Kozolchyk, Letters of Credit, in 9 Int'l Encyclopedia of Comparative Law ch. 5 at 137-40 (1979) (negotiable instrument concept).

The central issue presented by this case is whether St. Lucia's demand for payment from MHT was in compliance with the conditions specified in the letter of credit. Cochin's action for wrongful honor is based upon its assertion that MHT's payment was improper because the documents submitted by St. Lucia did not comply with the letter. Neither the UCP nor the Uniform Commercial Code ["UCC"] specify whether a bank honoring a letter of credit should be guided by a standard of strict compliance or substantial compliance with the terms of the letter.

The great weight of authority in this jurisdiction, and elsewhere, holds that an issuing or confirming bank is usually obligated to honor the beneficiary's draft only when the documents are in strict compliance with the terms of the letter of credit. See H. Harfield, Bank Credits and Acceptances, 73-74 (5th ed. 1974) (a "basic principle" of letter of credit law is that "the beneficiary must strictly comply with the terms of the credit to compel performance by the bank. . . . 'There is no room for documents which are almost the same, or which will do just as well' ") (quoting *Equitable Trust Co. v. Dawson Partners,* [1927] 27 Lloyd's List 49, 52); G. McLaughlin, Commercial Law, N.Y.L.J., May 8, 1985 at 30 n.18 (strict compliance standard is "the prevailing view in the United States"). Thus, New York courts have traditionally held that letter of credit law requires a beneficiary to strictly comply with the conditions of the letter. Additionally, this Court has previously held that "[a] bank's obligation in a letter of credit transaction is defined by the contract between the bank and its customer. It is obliged to pay only if the documents submitted strictly comply with the essential requirements of the letter of credit." *Corporacion de Mercadeo Agricola v. Pan American Fruit & Produce Corp.,* Memorandum Decision at 4-5, 75 Civ. 1611 (JMC) (S.D.N.Y. Apr. 13, 1976), quoted in *Corporacion de Mercadeo Agricola v. Mellon Bank,* 608 F.2d 43, 48 n.1 (2d Cir. 1979). This principle of strict compliance has been recently reaffirmed by the Second Circuit and the New York Court of Appeals. See *Beyene v. Irving Trust Co.,* 762 F.2d 4, 6 (2d Cir. 1985) ("In order to protect the issuing or confirming bank, this absolute duty [of payment to the beneficiary] does not arise unless the terms of the letter have been complied with strictly."); *Voest-Alpine Int'l Corp. v. Chase Manhattan Bank, N.A.,* 707 F.2d 680, 682 (2d Cir. 1983) ("The doctrine of strict compliance with the terms of the letter of credit functions to protect the bank which carries the absolute obligation to pay the bank which carries the absolute obligation to pay the beneficiary."); *Marino Indus. v. Chase Manhattan Bank, N.A.,* 686 F.2d 112, 114 (2d Cir. 1982) (" The essential requirements of a letter of credit must be strictly complied with by the party entitled to draw against the letter of credit, which means that the papers, documents and shipping descriptions must be as stated in the letter. ") (quoting *Venizelos, S.A. v. Chase Manhattan Bank,* 425 F.2d 461, 465 (2d Cir. 1970)); *United Commodities-Greece v. Fidelity Int'l Bank,* 64 N.Y.2d 449, 455, 478 N.E.2d 172,, 489 N.Y.S.2d 31, 33 (1985) ("New York requires strict compliance with the terms of a letter of credit, rather than the more relaxed standard of substantial compliance.")

Courts and commentators have noted, however, that New York appears to maintain a bifurcated standard of compliance. This approach calls for a strict compliance standard when the bank is sued by the beneficiary for wrongful dishonor but allows for a substantial compliance test when the bank is sued by the customer for wrongful honor. The stated rationale for the bifurcated standard is that it accords the bank flexibility in reacting to "a cross-fire of pressures . . .especially in times of falling commodity prices," J. White & R. Summers, Handbook of the Law Under the Uniform Commercial Code, § 18-6, at 731-32 (quoting State of N.Y. Law Revision Comm'n, Study of Uniform Commercial Code: Article 5-Documentary Letters of Credit, at 66 (1955), by limiting the liability burden on the bank, which might otherwise be caught between the "rock of a customer insisting on dishonor for highly technical reasons, and the hard place of a beneficiary threatening to sue for wrongful dishonor." B. Clark, The Law of Bank Deposits, Collections and Credit Cards, para. 8.5[4], at 8-48 (1981).

MHT correctly asserts that Cochin was its "customer" in this transaction and therefore argues that a substantial compliance standard should be used to test its review of St. Lucia's documents. Although the ultimate customer, Vishwa, may be barred from a direct action against the confirming bank because of the absence of privity (confirming bank has "relation" with issuing bank, not customer),[20] it is undisputed that MHT owes a duty of care to Cochin, see UCP art. 7 (1974), art. 15 (1983). The question then is whether the bifurcated standard applies in a lawsuit by the issuing bank against the confirming bank.

The bifurcated standard is designed to permit the bank to retain flexibility in dealing with simultaneous customer pressure to reject and beneficiary pressure to accept. This discretion ostensibly preserves the bank's ministerial function of dealing solely with documents and the insulation of the letter of credit from performance problems. The difficulty with applying a

---

[20] The UCP suggests the better view, however, that there is a duty running from the confirming bank to the ultimate customer. See UCP art. 12(a) (1974), art 20(a) (1983) ("Banks utilizing the services of another bank for the purpose of giving effect to the instructions of the applicant for the credit do so for the account and at the risk of [such applicant]."); art. 12(c) (1974), art. 20(c) (1983) (customer indemnification of the confirming bank); see also *Pubali Bank v. City Nat'l Bank,* 676 F.2d 1326, 1329-30 & n.5 (9th Cir. 1982) (warranty and tort liability); *Instituto Nacional de Comercializacion Agricola (Indeca) v. Continental Ill. Nat'l Bank & Trust Co.,* 530 F. Supp. 279, 282-85 (N.D. Ill. 1982) (negligence and fraud); Dann, *Confirming Bank Liability in Letter of Credit Transactions: Whose Bank Is It Anyway?,* 51 Fordham L. Rev. 1219, 1238-53 (1983) (recommending creation of liability through extension of UCC and UCP provisions, negligent misrepresentation and warranty theory).

bifurcated substantial compliance standard to actions against a confirming bank is reflected in the realities of commercial transactions. An issuing bank's good faith discretion is most required when its customer seeks to avoid payment by objecting to inconsequential defects. Although the bank should theoretically take comfort from a substantial compliance test if it honors the beneficiary's drafts over its customer's protests, the bank would usually not want to exercise its discretion in favor of the beneficiary for fear that its right to indemnify would be jeopardized or that its customer would break off existing banking relationships. Accordingly, the looser test of compliance does not in practice completely remove the issuer from its position between a rock and a hard place, but has a built-in safety valve against issuer misuse if the documents strictly comply with the letter.

A confirming bank, by contrast, is usually in relatively close geographical proximity with the beneficiary and typically chosen by the beneficiary because of past dealings. Although the confirming bank should not want to injure purposely its relationship with the issuing bank, the confirming bank would usually be somewhat biased in favor of the beneficiary. Additionally, the confirming bank is not in privity with the ultimate customer, who would be most likely to become dissatisfied if a conflict is resolved by the confirming bank. A biased issuing bank that in bad faith uncovers "microscopic discrepancies", N.Y. U.C.C. Study at 66, would still be forced to honor the letter if the documents are in strict compliance. A biased confirming bank, however, can overlook certain larger variances in its discretion without concomitant liability. A safety mechanism against confirming bank misuse is therefore not present and it would be inequitable to let a confirming bank exercise such discretion under a protective umbrella of substantial compliance. Moreover, the facts of this case do not warrant the looser standard. MHT was not faced with a "cross-fire of pressures" or concern that a disgruntled "customer" would refuse reimbursement because Cochin had sufficient funds on deposit with MHT. The Court also notes that the bifurcated substantial compliance standard is only a suggested approach by courts and commentators and has not actually been followed by New York courts.[21] Finally, in *Voest-Alpine*

[21] In discussing New York's bifurcated standard, courts and commentators have mistakenly cited each other and the following cases as support for the proposition that New York courts use a bifurcated approach:

In *Bank of Montreal,* the New York Court of Appeals applied a strict compliance standard when it denied recovery in an action by the issuing bank for reimbursement from its customer who claimed that the bank wrongfully honored the letter of credit. The Court held that the draft advices describing shipments as "bales of hemp" were insufficient to comply with the letter of credit condition for invoices and bills of lading of "bales manilla hemp". In *Atterbury Bros.,* the plaintiff bank successfully sued its customer for reimbursement. The Court acknowledged that the bank took a "risk" by paying pursuant to shipping documents issued to "A. James Brown" when the letter of credit specified "Arthur James Brown". The parties, however, conceded that the intended person signed the documents. The "conclusive" point on the issue of "casein" versus "unground casein" was resolved by an "estoppel" against the customer because it had examined the documents prior to the bank's payment. The remaining objections, characterized as "afterthoughts", were dismissed on grounds of laches and because there was no possibility that a missing certificate could have misled the paying bank. See, *e.g., Beyene v. Irving Trust Co.,* 596 F. Supp. 438, 442 n.8 (S.D.N.Y. 1984), aff'd, 762 F.2d 4 (2d Cir. 1985). In *North American,* Judge Medina granted summary judgment to the bank against the beneficiary under a "strict compliance" standard. In *Chairmasters,* the court granted summary judgment to the defendant bank under the basic tenet that the bank's obligation to review documents for compliance is totally separate from the underlying transaction. In *Marine Midland,* Judge McLean ruled that letter of credit conditions must be "strictly complied" with by a beneficiary. In *Far Eastern,* the Ohio court used a strict compliance standard, but cited *Marine Midland* as the sole case law authority for its dictum discussion of the New York bifurcated standard, which was the initial judicial recognition of this approach. Similarly, in *Data General,* the Connecticut court cited only *Far Eastern* and *Marine Midland* for its dictum footnote comment on the development of "two different standards". Finally, in *Transamerica Delaval,* citing only *Far Eastern* as case law support, a New York court for the first time discussed the bifurcated standard. The court applied a substantial

Int'l Corp. v. Chase Manhattan Bank, N.A., supra, the Court implied that confirming bank actions should be judged under a strict standard in wrongful dishonor as well as wrongful honor actions. It ruled that if the confirming bank waived material discrepancies in the drafts, the confirming bank would not be entitled to reimbursement from the issuing bank, which timely discovered the mistakes, because "the issuing bank[] was entitled to strict compliance." 707 F.2d at 686. Accordingly, the Court finds that an issuing bank's action for wrongful honor against a confirming bank is governed by a strict compliance standard.

An analysis of the ten listed variances suggests that MHT failed to pick up two discrepancies not strictly complying with the letter of credit terms. The first alleged defect concerns St. Lucia's cable to Oriental using the wrong cover note number of 4291 instead of 429711. The insurance was procured by Vishwa and the cable was intended to give notice to Oriental of the shipment by quoting the proper cover note. The failure to provide the correct cover note was not inconsequential as the mistake could have resulted in Oriental's justifiable refusal to honor Vishwa's insurance policy. This mistake may appear immaterial on its face, but in *Beyene v. Irving Trust Co., supra,* 762 F.2d 4, slip op. at 3617-19, the Second Circuit affirmed the dishonor of a letter of credit on the sole ground that the misspelling of Mohammed Sofan as Mohammed Soran on the bill of lading constituted a material discrepancy.

The alleged noncompliance with conditions (2), (3), (4), (8), (9) and (10) is unsupported. These provisions were not explicitly required by the letter of credit. Nothing in the letter indicates that these requirements, some of which were essentially satisfied by the submitted documents, were implicit conditions for payment. If Vishwa or Cochin wanted additional protection, they could have requested it and so informed MHT.

The overpayment and overdebiting of $1,396.50, the fifth alleged error, is a mathematical mistake. Although this sum was reimbursed, it indicates that the documents were not carefully reviewed by MHT. It does not, however, affect whether or not the underlying documents were in compliance with the letter.

The sixth defect is that the payment was made on documents presented by St. Lucia Enterprises despite the fact that the letter of credit was established for St. Lucia Enterprises, Ltd. The result is similar to that caused by the deviation of the Oriental cover note. Although there does not appear to be any difference between the two entities, it is not clear that the "intended" party was paid. The difference in names could also possibly be an indicia of unreliability or forgery.

The seventh alleged defect is that only five copies of the documents, rather than six, were submitted to MHT. This deviation is similar to a hypothetical error not affecting strict compliance posited in *Beyene v. Irving Trust Co., supra,* 762 F.2d 4, at 6 ("Smith misspelled as Smithh"). These types of variances may be allowable "if there is no possibility that the documents could mislead the paying bank to its detriment." *Flagship Cruises, Ltd. v. New England Merchants Nat'l Bank,* 569 F.2d 699, 705 (1st Cir. 1978); see *Beyene v. Irving Trust Co.,* 596 F. Supp. 438, 442 n.8 (S.D.N.Y. 1984), aff'd, 762 F.2d 4 (2d Cir. 1985). The Court finds that the failure

compliance standard in a lawsuit by a customer against its issuing bank for wrongful honor. The customer used vague language as to what would constitute a proper demand for payment under the letter, necessitating the ruling that it would have been "unreasonable for [the customer] to insist upon strict compliance." This result is better viewed not as an adoption of the bifurcated approach, but as the use of a strict compliance test with the "corollary" that letter requirements must be "explicit" and that all ambiguities should be construed against the party formulating the language in the letter. See *Marino Indus. v. Chase Manhattan Bank, N.A., supra,* 686 F.2d at 115 (all ambiguities construed against the issuing bank in an action for wrongful dishonor by the beneficiary).

to provide a sixth set of identical documents could not have misled the bank and therefore, it does not violate the strict compliance standard.

In the final analysis, only the variances as to the Oriental cover note and the name St. Lucia Enterprises, Ltd., appear not to comply strictly with the letter of credit conditions. The inquiry is not ended at this point because courts in this Circuit have applied concepts of equitable waiver and estoppel in cases of issuer dishonor. Application of estoppel has been premised upon discoverable nonconformities that could have been cured by the beneficiary before the expiration of the letter, but were not raised by the issuing bank until its dishonor. The banks were estopped from asserting the variances because of previous assurances to the beneficiary of documentary compliance or because of silence coupled with the retention of nonconforming documents for an unreasonably long time after the beneficiary had submitted its drafts for payment.

Application of waiver has been predicated upon situations in which the issuer justifies dishonor on grounds later found to have been unjustified. In these instances, all other possible grounds for dishonor are deemed to have been waived. Waiver of nonconforming documents can also be found from statements by officials of the issuing bank or from customer authorization.

The quid pro quo for the application of a standard of strict compliance is that there be minimal obligations implicating waiver and estoppel defenses on the party benefiting from the literal compliance review. The UCP expressly provides that an issuer has the obligation to immediately notify the beneficiary by "expeditious means" of any reason for noncompliance and the physical disposition of the disputed documents. UCP art. 8(e) (1974), 16(d) (1983). The UCP also implicitly invites cure of any documentary deficiencies apparent before the letter of credit expiration by issuer notification to the beneficiary. See Thier, *Letters of Credit: A Solution to the Problem of Documentary Compliance,* 50 Fordham L. Rev. 848, 873-76 (1982) (advocating imposition of affirmative obligations on all parties to the letter). In the context of this case, "an equitable approach to a strict compliance standard demands that the issuer promptly communicate all documentary defects to the beneficiary [or confirming bank], when time exists under the letter to remedy the nonconformity." *Id.* at 873. The Court finds that Cochin is precluded from claiming wrongful honor because of its failure to comply with the explicit notice and affirmative obligation provisions of the UCP and its implicit duty to promptly cure discoverable defects in MHT's confirming advices to St. Lucia.

The issuing bank must give notice "without delay" that the documents received are (1) being "held at the disposal" of the remitting or confirming bank or (2) "are being returned" to the second bank. UCP art. 8(e) (1974), art. 16(d) (1983). An issuing bank that fails to return or hold the documents for the second bank is precluded from asserting that the negotiation and payment were not effected in accordance with the letter of credit requirements. UCP art. 8(f) (1974), 16(e) (1983); see *Manufacturer's [sic] Hanover Trust Co. v. Westport Bank & Trust Co.,* Ruling on Cross-Motion for Summary Judgment at 9-10, B-83-17 (TPS/TFGD) (D. Conn.) (issuing bank precluded from pursuing a strict compliance defense for wrongful dishonor because of its "crucial" failure to give "formal notice" that documents were being held for beneficiary despite a retrospective assertion that the documents were always available for inspection), endorsement approval, B-83-17 (TFGD) (D. Conn. 1983). The UCP also directs that an issuing bank intending to claim noncompliance shall have a "reasonable time" to examine the documents after presentment and to determine whether to make such a claim. UCP art. 8(d) (1974), art. 16(c) (1983). The revised UCP allows explicitly for the imposition of the 16(e) sanction for failure to comply with the "reasonable time" provision as well; however, this interpretation is not clear under the parties' explicit choice of law, the 1974 UCP.

Neither the 1983 UCP nor the 1974 UCP defines what constitutes a "reasonable time" to determine if the documents are defective or notice "without delay" that the documents are being held or returned. When the UCP is silent or ambiguous, analogous UCC provisions may be utilized if consistent with the UCP. The UCC provides for a period of three banking days for the issuer to honor or reject a documentary draft for payment. N.Y. U.C.C. § 5-112(1)(a)(McKinney's 1964) (issuer-beneficiary relationship). The letter of credit was issued subject to the 1974 UCP but it is silent as to what law governs its terms. Cochin cites to Indian statutes interpreting a "reasonable time" as a factual question depending on the nature of the negotiable instrument and the usual course of dealing. Under the circumstances of this case, however, it appears that under New York's comparative interest choice of law approach, New York UCC law would apply.

Cochin's failure to promptly notify MHT that it had returned the documents or that it was holding them at MHT's disposal thus violates the UCP. Cochin's telex of June 21 states that there are certain discrepancies in St. Lucia's documents, but Cochin did not advise MHT that it was returning the documents to MHT until the July 3 telex. The "reasonable time" three-day period should be the maximum time allowable for the notification "without delay" requirement. Because June 21, 1980 was a Saturday, Cochin should have complied with its notice obligations no later than June 26. The passage of an additional week before compliance precludes Cochin from asserting its wrongful honor claim. Moreover, it was not until June 27 that Cochin first specified any reason for its dishonor argument, and the St. Lucia Enterprises, Ltd. omission was not noted until July 4.

Cochin proposes that its failure to timely notify MHT was not violative of UCP or letter of credit policy because it caused no additional loss to MHT. Cochin argues that the defects were in any case incurable by the time Cochin received the documents, because St. Lucia had disappeared with the letter of credit proceeds. Although the UCP is not explicit, the Court finds that these provisions should be applied identically to an issuing bank's obligations to a confirming bank after the latter's honor of a demand for payment. Cochin's contention ignores the expectation in the international financial community that the parties will live up to their statutory obligations and is at odds with the basic letter of credit tenet that banks deal solely with documents, not in goods. Cochin's argument would defeat the letter of credit's function of being a swift, fluid and reliable financing device. Cf. *Voest-Alpine Int'l Corp. v. Chase Manhattan Bank, N.A., supra,* 707 F.2d at 684-85 (rejecting contention that a waiver analysis was inappropriate because the defects were "incurable").

Finally, the two documentary discrepancies could have been anticipated by Cochin and were curable before the demand for payment. Cochin received a copy of MHT's incorrect March 31 advice to St. Lucia, which mistakenly listed the insurance cover note as 4291. Similarly, Cochin received copies of all of MHT's advices to St. Lucia, which omitted the "Ltd." from the corporate name. Cochin had sufficient notice and time to correct MHT's confirming defects to St. Lucia and is therefore estopped from asserting them. Although MHT failed to strictly comply with the letter requirements, Cochin's failure to perform its affirmative obligations precludes an action for wrongful honor under the UCP and by letter of credit estoppel.

CONCLUSION

Accordingly, for the foregoing reasons, plaintiff's motion for summary judgment is denied, Fed. R. Civ. P. 56(a), and defendant's motion for summary judgment is granted, Fed. R. Civ. P. 56(b).

The Clerk of the Court is directed to dismiss the complaint and prepare and enter Judgment for defendant MHT.

PROBLEM 23.3

Under the Revised U.C.C., there is no longer an issue as to whether the issuing bank may accept documents that are not in complete compliance of the letter of credit requirements. Revised § 5-108 requires the bank to dishonor a presentation that does not strictly comply with the terms of the letter of credit. Is that a wise change?

NOTE

(1) Revised *U.C.C. § 5-108.* This section states that (1) an issuer shall *honor* a presentation that appears on its face *strictly* to comply with the terms and conditions of the letter of credit; (2) with two exceptions, an issuer shall *dishonor* a presentation that does not appear so to comply. Whether there has been a strict compliance is determined by the standard practice referred to in Section 5-108(e), viz., "[a]n issuer shall observe standard practice of financial institutions that regularly issue letters of credit." (Determination of the issuer's observance of that standard practice is a matter of interpretation for the court.)

The Reporter's Comments to an earlier version of this section state:

> The section adopts the standard of strict compliance, but strict compliance does not mean slavish conformity to the terms of the letter of credit. By adopting reasonable commercial standards (the norm established by reasonable document checkers in commercial banks) as a way of measuring strict compliance, it indorses the conclusion of the court in *New Braunfels Nat. Bank v. Odiorne*, 780 S.W.2d 313 (Tex. Ct. App. 1989) (beneficiary could collect when draft requested payment on "Letter of Credit No. 86-122-5" and letter of credit specified "Letter of Credit No. 86-122-S" holding strict compliance does not demand oppressive perfectionism).
>
> The section also indorses the result in *Tosco Corp. v. Federal Deposit Insurance Corp.*, 723 F.2d 1242 (6th Cir. 1983). The letter of credit in that case called for "drafts drawn under Bank of Clarksville Letter of Credit Number 105". The draft presented stated "Drawn under Bank of Clarksville, Clarksville, Tennessee letter of Credit No. 105." The court correctly found that despite the change of upper case "L" to a lower case "l" and the use of the word "No." instead of "Number," and despite the addition of the words "Clarksville, Tennessee," the presentment conformed.
>
> By adopting the standard and endorsing the *New Braunfels* and *Tosco* cases, the section rejects the standard that commentators have called "substantial compliance."

Uniform Commercial Code, Revised Article 5, Letters of Credit, § 5-114 Comments (April 10, 1992 Draft) [see revised § 5-108 Comment 1].

New Braunfels at 316-17 states:

> Most commentators agree that maintaining the integrity of the strict compliance rule is important to the continued usefulness of letters of credit as a commercial tool. *See, e.g.*, McLaughlin, *On the Periphery of Letter-of-Credit Law: Softening the Rigors of Strict Compliance*, 106 Banking L.J. 4 (1989); Dolan, *Strict Compliance with Letters of Credit: Striking a Fair Balance*, 102 Banking L.J. 18 (1985). That does not mean, however, that strict compliance demands an oppressive perfectionism. For example, one noted commentator has

recognized a logical distinction between discrepancies that relate to the business of the underlying transaction and those that relate to the banker's own business:

> The strict-compliance rule rests on the judgment that issuers should not be forced into the position of determining whether a documentary discrepancy is significant. The rule assumes that issuers are not in a position to know whether discrepancies matter to the commercial parties. Nothing in that assumption requires courts to absolve issuers from knowing the significance of discrepancies for their own business; while it is consistent with the strict-compliance rule to say that an issuer should not be charged with knowledge of whether an air bill, rather than an ocean bill, covering computer components is a significant defect, it is not consistent with the rule to say that a bank issuer is absolved from knowing whether the abbreviation of the word "number" to "No." in the legend on a draft is a significant defect. Banks presumably know nothing about the shipment of computer components, but they know a great deal about legends on drafts—legends that credits require, usually because the banks insist on them.

J. Dolan, The Law of Letters of Credit ¶ 6.03, at S6-4 (Supp. 1989) (footnotes omitted).

Compare revised U.C.C. § 5-108 with Articles 13 and 37(c) of UCP 500.

[E] Obligations of Advising or Confirming Bank

Read: U.C.C. § 5-107.

The issuing bank may send the letter of credit directly to the beneficiary. More commonly, however, it will forward the credit to a banking institution at the beneficiary's location, which will then act as an "advising" or "confirming" bank. If the second bank is to act as an advising bank, its duty is to advise the beneficiary of the issuance of the credit, and its terms. It will then act as a collecting bank to receive the beneficiary's draft and documents and forward them to the issuing bank for payment. Such advising bank acts solely as an agent, and does not itself become obligated upon the credit; it is responsible only for the accuracy of its statements to the beneficiary (U.C.C., § 5-107(1)) [revised § 5-107(a)].

The second bank may in addition lend its obligation to the credit by "confirming" it. The beneficiary may have insisted upon this, being unwilling to rely only upon the credit of the distant issuing bank, and desiring the commitment of a bank closer at hand. U.C.C. § 5-107(2) provides: "A confirming bank by confirming a credit becomes directly obligated on the credit to the extent of its confirmation as though it were its issuer and acquires the rights of an issuer." [See revised § 5-107(a).]

As to liability of advising and confirming banks under UCP 500, see Articles 7 and 9.

NOTES AND QUESTIONS

(1) *Confirming Bank. In Barclays Bank D.C.O. v. Mercantile National Bank*, 481 F.2d 1224, 1227-32 (5th Cir. 1973), Mercantile addressed the following letter to Barclays:

Mercantile National Bank
70 Broad Street, N.W.
Atlanta, Georgia 30303

June 1, 1970

Barclays Bank Limited D.C.O.
200 Park Avenue
New York, N.Y. 10017

Gentlemen:

We are enclosing an irrevocable letter of credit issued by Allied Mortgage Consultants, 127 Peachtree Street, N.E., Atlanta, Georgia dated June 1, 1970, in the amount of $400,000.00 in your favor for the account of Bay Holding Company Limited.

We can unconditionally confirm this is a valid letter of credit and that they have at all times sufficient funds to honor this commitment.

We hereby confirm the letter of credit and undertake to honor any drafts presented to us on or before expiration date of the letter of credit in accordance with the terms and conditions of said letter of credit.

Very truly yours
Carl M. Harris
/s/
Executive Vice President

CMH/ac

The court made a preliminary determination and said:

With this preliminary determination aside, we are now in a position to confront the central legal issue—whether Mercantile can confirm this credit which was issued by a non-bank [Allied Mortgage Consultants]. This issue arises as a result of the definition of a confirming bank in § 5-103(1)(f).

A "confirming bank" is a bank which engages either that it will itself honor a credit already issued by another bank or that such a credit will be honored by the issuer of a third bank.

. . . .

Having determined that the general purposes of the U.C.C. will be advanced by applying the Code to this case, we turn to the more precise question of whether the policies underlying Article 5 would be furthered by applying a rule which is not specifically articulated there, but which is nonetheless developed by analogy to specifically codified rules. Section 5-102(3) is the ready and definite answer to this question. This section reads:

> (3) This Article deals with some but not all of the rules and concepts of letters of credit as such rules or concepts have developed prior to this Act or may hereafter develop. The fact that this Article states a rule does not by itself require, imply or negate application of the same or a converse rule to a situation not provided for or to a person not specified by this Article.

Even considering the admonition in § 1-102(1) that the Code should be liberally construed in light of its general purposes and policies, the above-quoted section is somewhat unique in that it expressly contemplates court-managed expansion of the principles contained in Article 5. The drafters recognized that, although letters of credit have been used for a number of years, their use was "primarily as a financial adjunct to a contract for the sale of goods." The drafters believed that as innovative businessmen became more familiar with the credit device its use — particularly in domestic business circles — would in all likelihood increase. The rules codified in Article 5 are only the foundation from which courts must develop, by analogy, new concepts to meet novel and diverse uses of the letter of credit.

We have just this type of situation, a new and different use of a letter of credit, before us in the instant case. Rather than using some other financing tool the parties involved in the real estate venture here chose the letter of credit as a device for securing $350,000 in working capital for Bay Holding Company. Reasoning by analogy, we believe that if a bank becomes directly liable under § 5-107(2) by confirming a credit issued by another bank, then a bank which confirms a non-bank credit is also directly liable on that credit under the same section. We reach this conclusion notwithstanding that the operative facts here do not seem to fit within the literal definition of a confirming bank in § 5-103(1)(f). Mercantile has offered no other reason which militates against this conclusion. Moreover, no other provisions of Article 5 cast doubt on the propriety of holding that a bank may confirm a non-bank credit under the Uniform Commercial Code. This conclusion affords a liberal construction to the Code, and it will facilitate the continued and expanding use of the letter of credit as a financing tool in the hands of the business planner. Finally, it is expressly ordained by § 5-102(3) because "[t]he fact that this Article states a rule does not by itself require, imply or negate the application of the same . . . rule to a situation not provided for or to a person not specified by this Article."

Standby letters of credit are discussed at § 23.02 below.

(2) *Advising Bank. Sound of Market Street, Inc. v. Continental Bank International,* 623 F. Supp. 93 (E.D. Pa. 1985), rev'd, 819 F.2d 384 (3d Cir. 1987), involved an action by a beneficiary against an advising bank for failure to advise of the issuance of a letter of credit in a timely manner. (Held: For advising bank. There was no privity between advising bank and beneficiary. Beneficiary should recover its damages from the customer/applicant/account party not from advising bank.)

(3) *Indemnities for Particular Defects.* Illustration 10 to Restatement, Second, Contracts § 220 is based on *Dixon, Irmaos & Cia, Ltd a. v. Chase Nat'l Bank,* 144 F.2d 759 (2d Cir. 1944), *cert. denied*, 324 U.S. 850(1945). In the illustration a bank in New York City (Chase), issues to a seller (a Brazilian exporter) a letter of credit promising a payment on presentation of

documents including a "full set of bills of lading." By a general banking usage in New York City, banks accept less than a full set in such cases if there is a guaranty by a responsible New York bank (Guaranty Trust Company) in lieu of the missing part. The illustration states that unless otherwise agreed, the usage is part of the contract. The illustration then cites U.C.C. § 5-109. (See § 5-113 and Comment 4, § 2-323(2)(b) and Comment 2.) [Section 5-113 was omitted under revised Article 5. The rationalw is that indemnities are covered by other contract law.]

For a criticism of the *Dixon* case, see Backus and Harfield, *Custom and Letters of Credit: the Dixon, Irmaos Case,* 52 Colum. L. Rev. 589 (1952). In support of *Dixon*, see Honnold, *Letters of Credit, Custom, Missing Documents and the Dixon Case: A Reply to Backus and Harfield,* 53 Colum. L. Rev. 504 (1953). See also J. Dolan, The Law of Letters of Credit, ¶ 4.07, "Role of Custom and Usage" (2d ed. 1991).

[F] Fraud in the Letter of Credit Transaction

Read: U.C.C. § 5-114(1), (2), (3); Revised § 5-109.

Throughout the chapter we have stressed the independence principle as an underlying foundation necessary to the stability and predictability of a letter of credit transaction. There is one limited exception to the above rule, an issuing bank has a discretionary privilege to dishonor a letter of credit where its customer has provided it with notice of fraud, forgery or other defects not apparent on the face of the documents. Note that the issuing bank may still pay on a draft that the customer has warned it about, so long as the payment was in good faith. But what is good faith if the issuing bank is fully cognizant of real fraud? The inclusion of the words, ". . . a court . . . may enjoin such an honor" at the tail end of § 5-114(3) has provided a doorway of judicial intervention that many customers have attempted to pass. When can a customer successfully block the payment of a letter of credit?

We know that an issuer of a letter of credit must honor a draft or demand for payment which complies with the terms of the credit regardless of whether the goods or documents conform to the underlying contract for sale.

UNITED BANK, LTD. v. CAMBRIDGE SPORTING GOODS CORP.

New York Court of Appeals
41 N.Y.2d 254, 392 N.Y.S.2d 265, 360 N.E.2d 943 (1976)

GABRIELLI, JUSTICE.

On this appeal, we must decide whether fraud on the part of a seller-beneficiary of an irrevocable letter of credit may be successfully asserted as a defense against holders of drafts drawn by the seller pursuant to the credit. If we conclude that this defense may be interposed by the buyer who procured the letter of credit, we must also determine whether the courts below improperly imposed upon appellant buyer the burden of proving that respondent banks to whom the drafts were made payable by the seller-beneficiary of the letter of credit, were not holders in due course. The issues presented raise important questions concerning the application of the law of letters of credit and the rules governing proof of holder in due course status set forth in article 3 of the Uniform Commercial Code. . . .

In April, 1971 appellant Cambridge Sporting Goods Corporation (Cambridge) entered into a contract for the manufacture and sale of boxing gloves with Duke Sports (Duke), a Pakistani corporation. Duke committed itself to the manufacturer of 27,936 pairs of boxing gloves at a sale price of $42,576.80; and arranged with its Pakistani bankers, United Bank Limited (United) and The Muslim Commercial Bank (Muslim), for the financing of the sale. Cambridge was requested by these banks to cover payment of the purchase price by opening an irrevocable letter of credit with its bank in New York, Manufacturers Hanover Trust Company (Manufacturers). Manufacturers issued an irrevocable letter of credit obligating it, upon the receipt of certain documents indicating shipment of the merchandise pursuant to the contract, to accept and pay, 90 days after acceptance, drafts drawn upon Manufacturers for the purchase price of the gloves.

Following confirmation of the opening of the letter of credit, Duke informed Cambridge that it would be impossible to manufacture and deliver the merchandise within the time period required by the contract, and sought an extension of time for performance until September 15, 1971 and a continuation of the letter of credit, which was due to expire on August 11. Cambridge replied on June 18 that it would not agree to a postponement of the manufacture and delivery of the gloves because of its resale commitments and, hence, it promptly advised Duke that the contract was canceled and the letter of credit should be returned. Cambridge simultaneously notified United of the contract cancellation.

Despite the cancellation of the contract, Cambridge was informed on July 17, 1971 that documents had been received at Manufacturers from United purporting to evidence a shipment of the boxing gloves under the terms of the canceled contract. The documents were accompanied by a draft, dated July 16,1971, drawn by Duke upon Manufacturers and made payable to United, for the amount of $21,288.40, one half of the contract price of the boxing gloves. A second set of documents was received by Manufacturers from Muslim, also accompanied by a draft, dated August 20, and drawn upon Manufacturers by Duke for the remaining amount of the contract price.

An inspection of the shipments upon their arrival revealed that Duke had shipped old, unpadded, ripped and mildewed gloves rather than the new gloves to be manufactured as agreed upon. Cambridge then commenced an action against Duke in Supreme Court, New York County, joining Manufacturers as a party, and obtained a preliminary injunction prohibiting the latter from paying drafts drawn under the letter of credit; subsequently, in November, 1971 Cambridge levied on the funds subject to the letter of credit and the draft, which were delivered by Manufacturers to the Sheriff in compliance therewith. Duke ultimately defaulted in the action and judgment against it was entered in the amount of the drafts, in March, 1972.

The present proceeding was instituted by the Pakistani banks to vacate the levy made by Cambridge and to obtain payment of the drafts on the letter of credit. The banks asserted that they were holders in due course of the drafts which had been made payable to them by Duke and, thus, were entitled to the proceeds thereof irrespective of any defenses which Cambridge had established against their transferor, Duke, in the prior action which had terminated in a default judgment. . . .

The trial court concluded that the burden of proving that the banks were not holders in due course lay with Cambridge, and directed a verdict in favor of the banks on the ground that Cambridge had not met that burden; the court stated that Cambridge failed to demonstrate that the banks themselves had participated in the seller's acts of fraud, proof of which was concededly present in the record. The Appellate Division affirmed, agreeing that while there was proof tending to establish the defenses against the seller, Cambridge had not shown that the seller's acts were "connected to the petitioners [banks] in any manner." . . .

We reverse and hold that it was improper to direct a verdict in favor of the petitioning Pakistani banks. We conclude that the defense of fraud in the transaction was established and in that circumstance the burden shifted to petitioners to prove that they were holders in due course and took the drafts for value, in good faith and without notice of any fraud on the part of Duke (Uniform Commercial Code, § 3-302).

This case does not come before us in the typical posture of a lawsuit between the bank issuing the letter of credit and presenters of drafts drawn under the credit seeking payment (see, generally, White and Summers, Uniform Commercial Code, § 18-6, pp. 619-628). Because Cambridge obtained an injunction against payment of the drafts and has levied against the proceeds of the drafts, it stands in the same position as the issuer, and, thus, the law of letters of credit governs the liability of Cambridge to the Pakistani banks.[22] Article 5 of the Uniform Commercial Code, dealing with letters of credit, and the Uniform Customs and Practice for Documentary Credits promulgated by the International Chamber of Commerce set forth the duties and obligations of the issuer of a letter of credit.[23] A letter of credit is a commitment on the part of the issuing bank that it will pay a draft presented to it under the terms of the credit, and if it is a documentary draft, upon presentation of the required documents of title (see Uniform Commercial Code, § 5-103). Banks issuing letters of credit deal in documents and not in goods and are not responsible

[22] Cambridge has no direct liability on the *drafts* because it is not a party to the drafts which were drawn on Manufacturers by Duke as drawer; its liability derives from the letter of credit which authorizes the drafts to be drawn on the issuing banks. Since Manufacturers has paid the proceeds of the drafts to the Sheriff pursuant to the levy obtained in the prior proceeding, it has discharged its obligation under the credit and is not involved in this proceeding.

[23] It should be noted that the Uniform Customs and Practice controls, in lieu of article 5 of the code, where, unless otherwise agreed by the parties, a letter of credit is made subject to the provisions of the Uniform Customs and Practice by its terms or by agreement, course of dealing or usage of trade (Uniform Commercial Code, § 5-102, subd.[4]). No proof was offered that there was an agreement that the Uniform Customs and Practice should apply, nor does the credit so state (cf. *Oriental Pacific* [U.S.A.] *v. Toro It to Dominion Bank*, 78 Misc.2d 819, 357 N.Y.S.2d 957). Neither do the parties otherwise contend that their rights should be resolved under the Uniform Customs and Practice. However, even if the Uniform Customs and Practice were deemed applicable to this case, it would not, in the absence of a conflict, abrogate the precode case law (now codified in Uniform Commercial Code, § 5-114) and that authority continues to govern even where article 5 is not controlling (see White and Summers, *op. cit.*, pp. 613-614, 624-625). Moreover, the Uniform Customs and Practice provisions are not in conflict nor do they treat with the subject matter of section 5-114 which is dispositive of the issues presented on this appeal (see *Banco Tornquist, S. A. v. American Bank & Trust Co.*, 71 Misc.2d 874, 875, 337 N.Y.S.2d 489; *Intraworld Ind. v. Girard Trust Bank*, 461 Pa. 343, 336 A.2d 316, 322; Harfield, Practice Commentary, McKinney's Cons & Laws of N. Y., Book 62 1/2, Uniform Commercial Code, § 5-114, p. 686). Thus, we are of the opinion that the Uniform Customs and Practice, where applicable, does not bar the relief provided for in section 5-114 of the code.

[New York § 5-102(4) reads:

(4) Unless otherwise agreed, this Article 5 does not apply to a letter of credit or a credit if by its terms or by agreement, course of dealing or usage of trade such letter of credit or credit is subject in whole or in part to the Uniform Customs and Practice for Commercial Documentary Credits fixed by the Thirteenth or by any subsequent Congress of the International Chamber of Commerce.]

for any breach of warranty or nonconformity of the goods involved in the underlying sales contract (see Uniform Commercial Code, § 5-114, subd. [1]; Uniform Customs and Practice, General Provisions and Definitions [c] and article 9. . . . Subdivision (2) of section 5-114, however indicates certain limited circumstances in which an issuer *may* properly refuse to honor a draft drawn under a letter of credit or a customer may enjoin an issuer from honoring such a draft.[24] Thus, where "fraud in the transaction" has been shown and the holder has not taken the draft in circumstances that would make it a holder in due course, the customer may apply to enjoin the issuer from paying drafts drawn under the letter of credit (see 1955 Report of N.Y. Law Rev., Comm., vol. 3, pp. 1654-1659). This rule represents a codification of precode case law most eminently articulated in the land mark case of *Sztejn v. Schroder Banking Corp.*, 177 Misc. 719, 31 N.Y.S.2d 631, Shientag, J., where it was held that the shipment of cowhair in place of bristles amounted to more than mere breach of warranty but fraud sufficient to constitute grounds for enjoining payment of drafts to one not a holder in due course. . . . Even prior to the *Sztejn* case, forged or fraudulently procured documents were proper grounds for avoidance of payment of drafts drawn under a letter of credit (Finkelstein, Legal Aspects of Commercial Letters of Credit, pp. 231-236-247); and cases decided after the enactment of the code have cited *Sztejn* with approval.

. . . .

. . .The evidentiary facts are not disputed and we hold upon the facts as established, that the shipment of old, unpadded, ripped and mildewed gloves rather than the new boxing gloves as ordered by Cambridge, constituted fraud in the transaction within the meaning of subdivision (2) of section 5-114. It should be noted that the drafters of section 5-114, in their attempt to codify the *Sztejn* case and in utilizing the term "fraud in the transaction," have eschewed a dogmatic approach and adopted a flexible standard to be applied as the circumstances of a particular situation mandate. It can be difficult to draw a precise line between cases involving breach of warranty (or a difference of opinion as to the quality of goods) and outright fraudulent practice on the part of the seller. To the extent, however, that Cambridge established that Duke was guilty of *fraud* in shipping, not merely nonconforming merchandise, but worthless fragments of boxing gloves, this case is similar to *Sztejn*.

If the petitioning banks are holders in due course they are entitled to recover the proceeds of the drafts but if such status cannot be demonstrated their petition must fail. . . .

In order to qualify as a holder in due course, a holder must have taken the instrument "without notice . . .of any defense against . . .it on the part of any person" (Uniform Commercial Code, § 3-302, subd. [1], par. [c]). Pursuant to subdivision (2) of section 5-114 fraud in the transaction is a valid defense to payment of drafts drawn under a letter of credit. Since the defense of fraud in the transaction was shown, the burden shifted to the banks by operation of subdivision (3) of section 3-307 [§ 3-308(b) (1990)] to prove that they were holders in due course and took the drafts without notice of Duke's alleged fraud. As indicated in the Official Comment to that subdivision, when it is shown that a defense exists, one seeking to cut off the defense by claiming the rights of a holder in due course "has the full burden of proof by a preponderance of the total evidence" on this issue. This burden must be sustained by "affirmative proof" of the requisites of holder in due course status (see Official Comment, McKinney's Cons. Laws of N. Y., Book 62 1/2, Uniform Commercial Code, § 3-307, p. 212). It was error for the trial court to direct a verdict in favor of the Pakistani banks because this determination rested upon a

[24] [Here the court cites § 5-114(2).]

misallocation of the burden of proof, and we conclude that the banks have not satisfied the burden of proving that they qualified in all respects as holders in due course, by any affirmative proof.

. . . .

Accordingly, the order of the Appellate Division should be reversed, with costs, and the petition dismissed.

NOTES

(1) *Injunctive Relief.* In *Enterprise International, Inc. v. Corporation Estatal Petrolera Ecuatoriana*, 762 F.2d 464, 471-74 (5th Cir. 1985), the court addressed the issue of injunctive relief in international letter of credit cases. The most relevant of the court's opinion is as follows [footnotes omitted]:

In order to secure a preliminary injunction, the movant has the burden of proving four elements: "(1) a substantial likelihood of success on the merits; (2) a substantial threat of irreparable injury if the injunction is not issued; (3) that the threatened injury to the movant outweighs any damage the injunction might cause to the opponent; and (4) that the injunction will not disserve the public interest."

. . . .

In considering whether to grant or deny preliminary injunctive relief, the district court "must remember that a preliminary injunction is an extraordinary and drastic remedy," and that "[t]he movant has a heavy burden of persuading the district court that all four elements are satisfied. Thus, if the movant does not succeed in carrying its burden on any one of the four prerequisites, a preliminary injunction may not issue and, if issued, will be vacated on appeal. When the movant fails to prove that, absent the injunction, irreparable injury will result, therefore, the preliminary injunction should be denied.

Federal courts have long recognized that, when "the threatened harm is more than de minimis, it is not so much the magnitude but the irreparability that counts for purposes of a preliminary injunction," In short, "[t]he key word . . .is *irreparable*," and an "injury is 'irreparable' only if it cannot be undone through monetary remedies." Thus, "[t]he possibility that adequate compensatory or other corrective relief will be available at a later date, in the ordinary course of litigation, weigh[]s heavily against a claim of irreparable harm." The absence of an available remedy by which the movant can later recover monetary damages, however, may also be sufficient to show irreparable injury.

Federal courts have consistently applied these principles to the issuance of preliminary injunctions in cases involving international letters of credit, and, consonant with them, have refused to enjoin the honoring of international letters of credit when, absent such injunctive relief the movants would have suffered only monetary loss, for which adequate remedies at law were available.

Most of the preliminary injunctions that have been issued in such cases were justified on the basis of the inadequacy of legal remedies in Iranian courts after that country's revolution in 1979 and the taking of the United States citizens as hostages, Thus, in *Itek Corp. v. First National Bank, Rockwell International Systems, Inc. v Citibank, NA., and Harris Corp. v. National Iranian Radio & Television*, for example, the First, Second, and Eleventh Circuits found that any resort to Iranian courts to recover the movant's monetary loss, should the preliminary injunction be denied, would be futile and that the existence of the Iran-United States Claims Tribunal did not "ameliorate the likelihood of irreparable injury."

In settings other than the Iranian crisis, however, when it has been shown that foreign courts provide a legal remedy or, at worst, that access to foreign courts is speculative, injunctive relief has been refused. Even in some cases related to and arising after the Iranian revolution, however, federal courts have refused to grant preliminary injunctive relief, finding that "[t]he 'unsettled situation in Iran' [was] simply insufficient to release any party from obligations under the letter of credit," that, even if resort to the Iranian courts was futile, an adequate remedy at law was available in federal court under the Foreign Sovereign Immunities Act, and that the political turmoil in Iran did not permit a federal court "to write into the letter of credit an excusing condition which the parties themselves did not adopt."

This reluctance to grant preliminary injunctive relief in international letter of credit cases is well founded in policy and business practice as well as in equity. The obligations created by a letter of credit are "completely separate from the underlying transaction, with absolutely no consequence given the underlying transaction unless the credit expressly incorporates its terms." This principle of independence provides the letter of credit with one of its "peculiar values," assurance of payment, and makes it "a unique device developed to meet the specific demands of the market place." Indeed, the "financial value of the letter of credit promise is predicated upon its degree of legal certainty."

These features of letters of credit are of particular importance in international transactions, in which sophisticated investors knowingly undertake such risks as political upheaval or contractual breach in return for the benefits to be reaped from international trade. As the First Circuit noted in *Itek Corp.*:

> The very object of a letter of credit is to provide a near foolproof method of placing money in its beneficiary's hands when he complies with the terms contained in the letter itself . . . Parties to a contract may use a letter of credit in order to make certain that contractual disputes wend their way towards resolution with money in the beneficiary's pocket rather than in the pocket of the contracting party.

Thus, in this context, the requirements for preliminary injunctive relief, including the showing of a substantial threat of irreparable injury if the injunction is not issued, are to be strictly exacted so as to avoid shifting the contractual allocation both of the risk of loss and the burden of pursuing international litigation.

(2) *Revised U.C.C. § 5-109*. Recall that revised § 5-108 requires an issuer to honor a presentation that appears on its face strictly to comply with the terms and conditions of the letter of credit. But what if a required document is forged or materially fraudulent, or honor of the presentation would facilitate a material fraud by the beneficiary on the *issuer* or *applicant*? In these cases the issuer is required to honor the presentation *if* honor is demanded by four categories of innocent persons, e.g., holders in due course of drafts drawn under the credit taken after acceptance by the issuer, confirmers that have honored their confirmation in good faith. If the above conditions are not met, the issuer (acting in good faith) *may honor* or *dishonor* the presentation. Revised § 5-109(a). Assume, for example, it is the defrauder-seller-beneficiary that

is demanding honor of the draft by the issuer. If the applicant claims that honor of the presentation would facilitate a material fraud by the beneficiary on the issuer or applicant, a court may temporarily or permanently enjoin the issuer from honoring the presentation *only if* the court finds that:

(1) the relief is not prohibited under the law applicable to an accepted draft or deferred obligation incurred by the issuer;

(2) a beneficiary, issuer, or nominated person who may be adversely affected is adequately protected against loss that it may suffer because the relief is granted;

(3) all of the conditions to entitle one to the relief under the law of this State have been met; and

(4) on the basis of the information submitted to the court, the applicant is more likely than not to succeed under its claim of forgery or material fraud.

Revised § 5-109(b), cf. U.C.C. § 5-114(2) (1990).

INTRAWORLD INDUS. v. GIRARD TRUST BANK

Supreme Court of Pennsylvania
461 Pa. 343; 336 A.2d 316; 17 U.C.C. Rep. Serv. 191 (1974)

ROBERTS, J.

This appeal requires us to review the trial court's denial of a preliminary injunction to restrain honor of a draft under an international letter of credit. A precise statement of the facts, which are complex, is necessary for a proper understanding.

On February 11, 1972, a lease was executed by Intraworld Industries, Inc., a corporation[25] headquartered in Wilkes-Barre, Pennsylvania, and Paulette Cymbalista, a citizen of Switzerland and resident of Italy. Cymbalista agreed to lease to Intraworld the Hotel Carlton, a luxury hotel located in St. Moritz, Switzerland, for a term of 15 years at an annual rental of 800,000 Swiss francs, payable in semi-annual installments.[26] The lease provided that Intraworld was required to prepay the rent for the initial 18-month period. Intraworld was also obligated to procure, within the first 100 days of the term, a performance bond in the amount of $500,000.00 "to insure to lessor the payment of the rent."[27]

Intraworld entered into possession of the hotel on May 1, 1972. Shortly thereafter, Intraworld assigned its interest in the lease to its subsidiary, Vacanze In Paradiso Hotels, S.A., a Swiss corporation.[28]

---

[25] Intraworld is incorporated in either Pennsylvania or Delaware; the record is unclear on this point.

[26] The lease contained a formula for the adjustment of the annual rental with respect to changes in the value of the Swiss franc. At the time of the execution of the lease, the annual rental was approximately equivalent to $200,000.00.

[27] The record does not establish whether Intraworld performed its obligation to procure a performance bond.

The lease also provided: "This agreement shall be governed by the Swiss law. The competent forum shall be in Saint Moritz Court."

[28] For convenience we will refer to the lessee as Intraworld.

At a later time,[29] Intraworld and Cymbalista executed an addendum to the lease (to which the parties have referred by its German title "Nachtrag"). The Nachtrag cancelled Intraworld's obligation to procure a performance bond and substituted a duty to provide letters of credit issued by "the Girard Trust Company of Philadelphia" in order to guarantee rental payments one year in advance. Two letters of credit were specifically required, each in the amount of $100,000.00, maturing in November, 1973, and May, 1974, to secure the rent due at those times. After each rental payment, Intraworld was to provide a new letter of credit "in order that the lessor remains secured one years [sic] rent in advance." The Nachtrag also provided:

> In the event the lessee should not fulfill its obligation to pay, so that the letter of credit must be used, . . .then the lessor can terminate the lease immediately without further notice. In this case, the lessor retains the rent paid or guaranteed for the following year as a stipulated penalty for non-performance of the contract from the lessee, in doing so the lessor retains the right to make a claim for additional damages not covered by the stipulated penalty.

On September 1, 1972, Intraworld and the Girard Trust Bank, Philadelphia, entered into an agreement to provide the letters of credit required by the Nachtrag. Girard agreed to "issue a letter of credit . . .in the amount of $100,000 under which the Lessor may draw a sight draft on [Girard] for payment of the sum due under said lease (a) on November 10, 1973 and (b) May 10, 1974. Under the terms of such letter of credit, payments will be made if the Lessor presents a draft as provided in such letter of credit. Each such letter of credit will expire . . .on the twentieth day after the payment under said lease is due."[30]

In accordance with the agreement, Girard issued two irrevocable letters of credit on September 5, 1972. Each authorized Cymbalista to draw a draft on Girard in the amount of $100,000.00 if Intraworld failed to pay the rent when due.[31]

---

[29] The record does not establish the exact date.

[30] The agreement also provided: "This agreement shall be construed in accordance with the law of the State of Pennsylvania and the Acts of Congress of the United States affecting transactions under the provisions hereof."

[31] "IRREVOCABLE LETTER OF CREDIT

NO. 35798

Date: September 5, 1972" Amount: $ 100,000.00.

"Beneficiary: Paulette Cymbalista
c/o Carlton Hotel
St. Moritz, Switzerland

"For account of: Intraworld Industries, Inc.
116 South Main Street
Wilkes Barre, PA 18701

"Madam:

"You are hereby authorized to draw on us at sight the sum of One Hundred Thousand and 00/100 Dollars United States Currency ($ 100,000.00) due on November 10, 1973 under a lease, a copy of which is attached to both Beneficiary's copy and Bank's copy of this letter of credit as Exhibit 1, available by your draft for said amount, accompanied by:

"1. Simple receipt for amount drawn.

"2. A signed statement of the drawer of the draft to the effect that the drawer is the lessor under said lease and that the lessee thereunder has not paid the installment of rent due under said lease on November 10, 1973 within 10 days after said installment was due and payable.

"This credit expires on November 30, 1973.

"Drafts under this credit must contain the clause 'drawn under Credit No. 35798 of Girard Trust Bank, dated September 5, 1972.'

In the summer of 1973, the relationship between Cymbalista and Intraworld began to go awry. Norbert Cymbalista, Paulette's husband, visited the hotel in August and, after discussions with the manager, became very concerned over the hotel's financial condition. He discovered that there were unpaid bills in excess of $100,000, that all telephone and Telex communications had been cut off for nonpayment of bills, and that the filing of mechanics liens against the hotel was imminent. After a trans-Atlantic telephone call, the Cymbalistas travelled to the United States within several days of Norbert's discoveries to attempt to resolve the hotel's difficulties with Intraworld. However, as Norbert testified, "I tried to reach [the president of Intraworld] innumerable times by telephone and each time his secretary answered that he would call me back and he never did. I stayed a whole month in the United States trying continually to reach him and it was never possible."

On August 20, 1973, apparently while the Cymbalistas were in the United States, their Swiss counsel sent a letter to Intraworld reciting the unpaid bills, erosion of the Carlton's reputation, and internal corporate difficulties (apparently of Intraworld's Swiss subsidiary). It concluded:

> Based upon [Swiss law] and in reference to the provisions of the Lease Contract, we herewith extend to you a final time limit up to September 15, 1973 in order to:
>
> (a) to pay all due debts,
>
> (b) to supply the necessary means to safeguard proper management of the business,
>
> (c) to complete the Board of Directors according to the law.
>
> Within this time limit you must prove to the Hotel Owners that the aforementioned measures have been effectuated. Should you [fail to?] comply with this demand within the time-limit, the Lease Contract will be regarded as void.

Intraworld's Swiss counsel replied to the August 20 letter (but this reply is not in the record). Finding this reply unsatisfactory, Cymbalista's Swiss counsel answered on September 18, 1973:

> As [Intraworld] did not comply with our demand within this time-limit, we regard the leasing contract as terminated effective from 15 September 1973.
>
> . . . From now on, the proprietor will have direct and sole control over the hotel real estate respective to the hotel management.[32]

Further correspondence was exchanged by Swiss counsel, including, apparently, a demand on November 3 for the rent due in November. On November 7, 1973, Intraworld's Swiss counsel wrote to Cymbalista's counsel:

> You state on behalf of the lessor that [Intraworld] has the obligation to pay . . .rent by November 1. My client [Intraworld], who is presently in close contact with their American Bank [Girard], however have [sic] informed me that the payment of the rent can be made up to November 10 . . . My client informed me further that accordingly these payments shall

---

"Girard Trust Bank hereby agrees with the drawers, endorsers and bona fide owners of the bills drawn strictly in compliance with the terms of this credit that the same will be duly honored upon presentation.

"Except so far as otherwise expressly stated, this credit is subject to the uniform customs and practices for documentary credits (1962 revision), International Chamber of Commerce Brochure No. 222."

Credit No. 35799 was identical to 35798, except that it applied to the rent due on May 10, 1974, and expired on May 30, 1974.

[32] Both letters were originally written in German. The translations which we have quoted were introduced by Intraworld in the trial court without objection by any party.

be legally undertaken by the "Girard Trust Bank" . . . [M]y client cannot agree with your position according to which the lease contract can be considered as terminated either because of [Swiss law] or because of the terms of the lease agreement. . .

That letter was followed on November 9, 1973, by another from Intraworld's counsel to Cymbalista's counsel in which he stated:

> If the transfer of the rent from the United States should not be made in timely fashion, your client [Cymbalista] is at liberty to obtain payment by way of the guarantee contracts [*i. e.,* letters of credit]. In any event, there exist the two guarantee contracts, valid until November 30, 1973 and May 30, 1974, respectively, in order to preserve the rights of your client.[33]

The rent due on November 10, 1973, was not paid by Intraworld. Accordingly, on November 21, 1973, Cymbalista's American counsel presented to Girard a draft drawn on Girard for $100,000.00 under Credit No. 35798. The draft was accompanied, all parties agree, by documentation that conformed to the terms of the credit. In his letter to Girard, Cymbalista's counsel stated:

> Your attention is directed to correspondence dated November 7 and November 9, 1973, copies of what are attached, in which Swiss counsel representing the Lessee invites the Lessor to draw upon the Letters of Credit; our client, as Lessor, takes the position that the lease . . .has terminated for various reasons, including the failure timely to pay the amount due pursuant to the "Nachtrag" . . . .

Girard informed Intraworld on November 21 that it intended to honor the draft. Intraworld immediately filed an action in equity in the Court of Common Pleas of Philadelphia seeking injunctive relief prohibiting Girard from honoring the draft. Cymbalista filed a petition to intervene, which was granted by the trial court.

The November action was terminated on December 6, 1973, by agreement of all parties. Pursuant to the agreement, Girard placed $100,000.00 in escrow with a Swiss bank, with entitlement to that fund to be determined by the courts of Switzerland.

The situation remained unchanged for about six months. The rent due on May 10, 1974, was not paid. On May 21, 1974, Cymbalista's American counsel presented to Girard a draft for $100,000.00 under Credit No. 35799, accompanied by conforming documentation. Girard immediately advised Intraworld that it intended to honor the draft.

On May 24, Intraworld filed this equity action in the Court of Common Pleas of Philadelphia. It sought preliminary and permanent injunctions restraining Girard from honoring Cymbalista's draft under the letter of credit. The court issued a preliminary restraining order and set a date

33 Intraworld's Swiss counsel's letters were also in German. The record is confusing on the issue of translation. Apparently, Cymbalista offered two translations of each letter as exhibits in the trial court; exhibits 1(T) and 3(T) are translations of the November 7 letter, 2(T) and 4(T) of the November 9 letter. One set of translations was prepared by Girard, although it is unclear which one is Girard's. The other set seems to have been prepared by an associate of Cymbalista's American counsel. The confusion was compounded when an officer of Girard was cross-examined by Cymbalista's counsel. The witness was requested to read exhibit 4(T) into the record. What he actually read, as stenographically recorded in the notes of testimony, corresponds to the document in the record labelled 2(T). At the close of the trial, Intraworld's counsel objected to the admission of 2(T). However, Intraworld's counsel failed toobject when the officer of Girard read 2(T) into the notes of testimony. In any event, we find the differences between the translations to be immaterial. The translations we have quoted are exhibits 1(T) and 2(T).

for a hearing. Cymbalista again petitioned for leave to intervene, which the court granted on May 29.

After the filing of additional pleadings, including preliminary objections and an amended complaint, a hearing was held and testimony taken on May 30 and 31, 1974. On July 11, the trial court issued a memorandum and decree in which it denied a preliminary injunction. Intraworld has appealed to this Court.[34] We affirm.

At the outset we note the limited scope of our review:

> In *Pa. P. U. C. v. Alleg. Co. Port Auth.,* 433 Pa. 495, 499, 252 A.2d 367 (1969), we stated that: "It has long been the rule in this Court that on an appeal from a decree, whether granting or denying a preliminary injunction, we will not inquire into the merits of the controversy, but will, instead, examine the record only to determine if there were any apparently reasonable grounds for the actions of the court below. [Citing cases.] Moreover, we will not 'pass upon the reasons for or against such action unless it is plain that no such grounds existed or that the rules of law relied on are palpably wrong or clearly not applicable . . . .' " *Credit Alliance Corp. v. Philadelphia Minit-Man Car Wash Corp.,* 450 Pa. 367, 370-71, 301 A.2d 816, 818 (1973).

Another preliminary matter is a determination of what law we are to apply. Each of the three parties before us has, by agreement, assumed obligations to the others, and each agreement has specified a different controlling law. The lease agreement between Intraworld and Cymbalista provided that it would be "governed" by the law of Switzerland. Cf. Restatement (Second) of Conflict of Laws § 187 (1971); see also *id.* § 189. Intraworld and Girard specified that their agreement would be "construed in accordance with" the law of Pennsylvania. In its letter of credit, Girard stated that its engagement was "subject to" the Uniform Customs and Practice for Documentary Credits (International Chamber of Commerce, 1962 revision).

It is clear that the law of Switzerland does not apply to the question whether the honor of a draft by Girard should be enjoined. While questions of the rights and obligations of the parties to the lease are involved, the action sought to be enjoined would not occur in Switzerland and the party sought to be bound is not located there. See Gewolb, *The Law Applicable to International Letters of Credit,* 11 Vill.L.Rev. 742, 753-54 (1966).

Girard's obligations to Cymbalista are "subject to" the Uniform Customs and Practice. However, the UCP "is by definition a recording of practice rather than a statement of legal rules," and therefore does not purport to offer rules which govern the issuance of an injunction against honor of a draft. Harfield, *Practice Commentary,* N.Y.U.C.C., § 5-114 (McKinney's Consol.Laws, c. 38, 1964).

All parties have briefed and argued the case on the assumption that the Pennsylvania Uniform Commercial Code[35] controls, and with this assumption we agree. See 12A P.S. § 1-105(1); Restatement (Second) of Conflict of Laws § 6(1) & comment a.; *Dynamics Corp. of America v. Citizens and Southern National Bank,* 356 F.Supp. 991, 997 (N.D.Ga.1973); Gewolb, *The Law Applicable to International Letters of Credit,* 11 Vill.L.Rev. 742, 753-54 (1966). In particular the applicable law is Article 5 of the Code. That article specifically states that it applies "to a credit issued by a bank if the credit requires a documentary draft or a documentary demand

[34] Appellate Court Jurisdiction Act of 1970, Act of July 31, 1970.

[35] Act of October 2, 1959, P.L. 1023, § 1-101 et seq., amending Act of April 6, 1953, P.L. 3, 12A P.S. § 1-101 et seq. (1970).

for payment . . . ." 12A P.S. § 5-102(1)(a). Since Cymbalista's draft on Girard was required by the letter of credit to be accompanied by a receipt and "signed statement that the drawer is the lessor under said lease and that the lessee thereunder has not paid the installment of rent due," the credit clearly "requires a documentary draft." See 12A P.S. §§ 5-102, comment 1; 5-103(1)(b). It is also clear that the credit was issued by a bank. Finally, the letter of credit that is the object of this controversy is a "credit" within 12A P.S. § 5-102(1)(a). The definition is found in 12A P.S. § 5-103(1)(a):

> "Credit" or "letter of credit" means an engagement by a bank . . .made at the request of a customer and of a kind within the scope of this Article (Section 5-102) that the issuer will honor drafts . . .upon compliance with the conditions specified in the credit. . . .The engagement may be either an agreement to honor or a statement that the bank or other person is authorized to honor.

The letter of credit here includes an agreement by Girard to honor drafts drawn in compliance with the credit. The credit was issued at the request of Intraworld as "customer," see 12A P.S. § 5-103(1)(g). Because it was issued by a bank and requires a documentary draft, it is "of a kind within" section 5-102. Thus, we conclude that Article 5 by its term governs the controversy before us.

Letters of credit have long served as a financial device in international sales of goods.[36] The primary purpose of a letter of credit is to provide assurance to the seller of goods, (*i.e.,* the "beneficiary," see 12A P.S. § 5-103(1)(d)) of prompt payment upon presentation of documents. A seller who would otherwise have only the solvency and good faith of his buyer as assurance of payment may, with a letter of credit, rely on the full responsibility of a bank. Promptness is assured by the engagement of the bank to honor drafts upon the presentation of documents.

The great utility of letters of credit flows from the independence of the issuer-bank's engagement from the underlying contract between beneficiary and customer. Long-standing case law has established that, unless otherwise agreed, the issuer deals only in documents. If the documents presented conform to the requirements of the credit, the issuer may and must honor demands for payment, regardless of whether the goods conform to the underlying contract between beneficiary and customer. Absent its agreement to the contrary, the issuer is, under the general rule, not required or even permitted to go behind the documents to determine if the beneficiary has performed in conformity with the underlying contract. Accord, Uniform Customs and Practice for Documentary Credits, General Provisions & Definitions c. (International Chamber of Commerce, 1962 revision).

This principle of the issuer's right and obligation to honor upon presentation of conforming documents has been codified in 12A P.S. § 5-114:

> (1) An issuer must honor a draft or demand for payment which complies with the terms of the relevant credit regardless of whether the goods or documents conform to the underlying contract for sale or other contract between the customer and the beneficiary. . . .
>
> (2) Unless otherwise agreed when documents appear on their face to comply with the terms of a credit but a required document . . .is forged or fraudulent or there is fraud in the transaction

[36] For an illustration of the operation of a letter of credit in an international sales transaction, see J. White & R. Summers, Handbook of the Law under the Uniform Commercial Code § 18-1(1972); and see *Kingdom of Sweden v. New York Trust Co.,* 197 Misc. 431, 441, 96 N.Y.S.2d 779, 788 (Sup.Ct.1949).

. . .

(b) in all other cases as against its customer, an issuer acting in good faith may honor the draft or demand for payment despite notification from the customer of fraud, forgery or other defect not apparent on the face of the documents but a court of appropriate jurisdiction may enjoin such honor.

Intraworld seeks to enjoin honor under 12A P.S. § 5-114(2)(b)on the basis that there is "fraud . . .not apparent on the face of the documents." It points to what it believes are two respects in which Cymbalista's demand for payment and supporting documentation are false and fraudulent, although conceding that the documents on their face conform to the credit. First, it contends that Cymbalista's statement (as required by the credit) that "lessee . . .has not paid the installment of rent due under said lease on May 10, 1974," is false and fraudulent because, after Cymbalista purported to terminate the lease in September, 1973, Intraworld was not obligated to pay rent and because the statement failed to disclose the termination of the lease. Second, it argues that the demand is fraudulent because Cymbalista is not seeking rent at all (as, Intraworld contends, she represents in the documents) but rather the "stipulated penalty" pursuant to the Nachtrag.

In light of the basic rule of the independence of the issuer's engagement and the importance of this rule to the effectuation of the purposes of the letter of credit, we think that the circumstances which will justify an injunction against honor must be narrowly limited to situations of fraud in which the wrongdoing of the beneficiary has so vitiated the entire transaction that the legitimate purposes of the independence of the issuer's obligation would no longer be served. A court of equity has the limited duty of "guaranteeing that [the beneficiary] not be allowed to take unconscientious advantage of the situation and run off with plaintiff's money on a pro forma declaration which has absolutely no basis in fact." *Dynamics Corp. of America v. Citizens and Southern National Bank,* 356 F.Supp. 991, 999 (N.D.Ga.1973).

The leading case on the question of what conduct will justify an injunction against honor is *Sztejn v. J. Henry Schroder Banking Corp.,* 177 Misc. 719, 31 N.Y.S.2d 631 (Sup.Ct.1941). In that case as here, the customer sought an injunction against the issuer of a letter of credit restraining honor of a draft drawn by the beneficiary. The customer had contracted to purchase a quantity of bristles from the beneficiary and arranged to have the issuer issue a letter of credit in favor of the beneficiary. The credit required that the draft be accompanied by an invoice and bill of lading.

The beneficiary placed fifty cases of merchandise on a steamship and obtained a bill of lading describing the material as bristles. The beneficiary then drew a draft and presented it, along with the required documents, through a collecting bank. The customer's complaint alleged that the material shipped was not bristles as described in the documents, but rather "cowhair, other worthless material and rubbish [shipped] with intent to simulate genuine merchandise and defraud the plaintiff . . . ."

The collecting bank moved to dismiss the complaint for failure to state a cause of action. The court, assuming the pleaded facts to be true, denied the motion. The court recognized that the issuer's obligation was independent from the underlying contract between customer and beneficiary. That independence is predicated, however, on the genuineness of the documents. The court noted:

> This is not a controversy between the buyer and seller concerning a mere breach of warranty regarding the quality of the merchandise; on the present motion, it must be assumed that the seller has intentionally failed to ship any goods ordered by the buyer.

177 Misc. at 721, 31 N.Y.S.2d at 634. When the beneficiary has intentionally shipped no goods at all, the court held, the documentation was not genuine and therefore the predicate of the independence of the issuer's engagement was removed.

We conclude that, if the documents presented by Cymbalista are genuine in the sense of having some basis in fact, an injunction must be refused. An injunction is proper only if Cymbalista, comparable to the beneficiary in *Sztejn,* has no bona fide claim to payment under the lease. *Dynamics Corp. of America v. Citizens and Southern National Bank*, 356 F.Supp. 991, 999 (N.D.Ga. 1973). Of course, neither the trial court nor this Court may attempt to determine Cymbalista's actual entitlement to payment under the lease. Such is not the proper standard for the grant or denial of an injunction against honor. Moreover, questions of rights and obligations under the lease are required by the lease to be determined under Swiss law in the court of Switzerland. See *Dynamics Corp. of America v. Citizens and Southern National Bank, supra.*

On this record, we are unable to conclude that Intraworld established that Cymbalista has no bona fide claim to payment or that the documents presented to Girard have absolutely no basis in fact. Intraworld's argument rests on the basic premise that the lease was terminated in September, 1973. From this premise Intraworld asserts the falsity of Cymbalista's representations that she is the lessor and that the rent was due and unpaid. However, Intraworld did not attempt to prove to the trial court that, under Swiss law, Cymbalista's attempted termination was effective. In fact, Intraworld's Swiss counsel informed Cymbalista's counsel on November 7, 1973, that Intraworld "cannot agree with your position according to which the lease contract can be considered as terminated . . . ." Counsel added that Cymbalista was "at liberty to obtain payment by way of" the letters of credit. Thus, Intraworld failed to prove that, under Swiss law, Cymbalista had no bona fide claim to rent under the lease despite Intraworld's repudiation of termination.

Intraworld's argument that Cymbalista fraudulently concealed the purported termination from Girard is unpersuasive. When presenting the draft and documents to Girard in November, 1973, Cymbalista's American counsel candidly admitted that "our client, as Lessor, takes the position that the lease has terminated . . .for various reasons . . . ." In addition, Girard was a party to the first equity action and its counsel joined the agreement which terminated that action. Cymbalista could reasonably have assumed in May, 1974, that Girard was fully aware of the positions of both Intraworld and Cymbalista.

Intraworld's further contention that Cymbalista's demand was fraudulent in that she was not seeking "rent" at all but the "stipulated penalty" pursuant to the Nachtrag is more substantial but, under scrutiny, also fails. It argues that payment under the credit was permitted only for "rent," and that Cymbalista (as she concedes) was in fact seeking the "stipulated penalty," which is not "rent." Intraworld concludes that Cymbalista was fraudulently attempting to draw under the credit for satisfaction of an obligation not secured by the credit. There are two flaws in this argument.

First, we are not persuaded that the credit was issued for payment of "rent," narrowly defined, only. The letter of credit authorized Cymbalista to draw "the sum . . . due . . . under [the] lease," without specifying that the "sum due" contemplated was only "rent." The letter required that a draft must be accompanied by Cymbalista's statement that "the lessee . . . has not paid the installment of rent due under said lease." This is not equivalent to a limitation on availability of the credit only for nonpayment of rent; in fact, such nonpayment of rent is precisely the condition which triggers Cymbalista's entitlement to the "stipulated penalty." In short, Intraworld has failed to persuade us that the letter of credit was not available to Cymbalista for satisfaction of the "stipulated penalty."

Second and more important, the Nachtrag does not, in our view, create the sharp distinction between "rent" and "stipulated penalty" that Intraworld hypothesizes. It provides that "[i]n the event the lessee should not fulfill its obligation to pay, so that the letter of credit must be used," then the lessor was entitled to terminate the lease and "retain the rent paid or guaranteed [by the letters of credit] for the following year as a stipulated penalty for non-performance of the contract . . . ." Because Intraworld did fail to pay the rent due on November 10, 1973, and May 10, 1974, Cymbalista could reasonably and in good faith have concluded that she had the right to draw on the credit for the "rent . . .guaranteed for the following year."

Whether Intraworld was in fact obligated to pay the rent nonpayment of which triggered Cymbalista's right to retain the "rent guaranteed" by the credit or whether Cymbalista is not entitled to the "stipulated penalty" for some other reason are questions to be decided under Swiss law in the courts of Switzerland. We hold only that Intraworld failed to establish that Cymbalista lacked a bona fide claim to the "rent . . .guaranteed . . .as a stipulated penalty" or that her demand under the credit lacked some basis in fact. Therefore, her documented demand was not shown to be fraudulent because she was seeking satisfaction of the "stipulated penalty."

In summary, we are unable to conclude on this record that Intraworld succeeded in proving that Cymbalista had no bona fide claim for payment under the lease and that her documented demand had absolutely no basis in fact. Accordingly, it is clear that there is an apparently reasonable ground for refusing an injunction.

In addition, Intraworld alleged in its complaint and contends in this Court that Girard's decision to honor Cymbalista's draft was not formed in good faith.[37] Intraworld asserts that Girard's bad faith constituted an additional ground justifying an injunction. It is clear that an issuer of a letter of credit must act in good faith, see 12A P.S. §§ 5-114(2)(b), 5-109(1). However, we are not persuaded that issuer bad faith is a circumstance justifying an injunction against honor; in most if not all instances of issuer bad faith, it would seem that a customer would have an adequate remedy at law in a claim against the issuer or a defense against the issuer's claim for reimbursement. In any event, in this case Intraworld has failed to prove the existence of bad faith on the part of Girard. It was proved no more than that Girard failed to resolve the dispute over the rights and obligations of the parties to the lease in Intraworld's favor. This Girard was not obligated to do. Its obligations included a careful scrutiny of the documents, but once it determined that the documents conformed to the requirements of the credit, it bore no responsibility for the performance of the lease obligations or the genuineness of the documents. 12A P.S. § 5-109(1)(a) & (2). It would, we think, place an issuer in an intolerable position if the law compelled it to serve at its peril as an arbitrator of contract disputes between customer and beneficiary.

> The question between the customer and the bank which issues the letter of credit is whether the documents presented with the draft fulfill the specific requirements, and if they do . . ., the bank has the right to pay the draft no matter what may be the defects in the goods which have been shipped. The bank is not obliged to assume the burdens of a controversy between

[37] See 12A P.S. § 1-201(19); cf. 12A P.S. § 2-103(1)(b).

the beneficiary and customer and incur the responsibility of establishing as an excuse for not paying a draft that the customer's version is the correct one.

Laudisi v. American Exchange National Bank, 239 N.Y. 234, 243, 146 N.E. 347, 350 (1924).

Finally, Intraworld contends that the trial court erred in refusing to permit it to examine Norbert Cymbalista as on cross-examination as an adverse[38] or hostile witness. We need not decide whether the trial court erred, because it is clear that no prejudice whatsoever resulted. Intraworld claims that, if it had been permitted to cross-examine Norbert, his testimony would have established that Cymbalista's demand was for the stipulated penalty. Brief for Appellants at 15. Cymbalista conceded in the trial court and admits in this Court that her demand was for the "stipulated penalty." Therefore, we conclude that, because what Intraworld would have attempted to prove was admitted by Cymbalista, it was not prejudiced by the claimed error of the trial court.

Decree affirmed. Each party pay own costs.

FEDERAL DEPOSIT INSURANCE CORPORATION v. PLATO

United States Court of Appeals
981 F.2d 852 (5th Cir. 1993)

KING, J.

The Federal Deposit Insurance Corporation (FDIC) appeals from the district court's judgment against the FDIC as plaintiff and for Richard Plato and Henry Vanderkam (d/b/a the McMicken Group) as counter-plaintiffs. We reverse in all significant respects and remand to the district court.

I.

In 1985, Plato, Vanderkam, and Richard Fuqua[39] ("the buyers"), all attorneys, began negotiations with C.E. Vetco Services, Inc. (C.E. Vetco), to purchase an oil coating facility in Houston, Texas. On March 20, 1985, the parties entered into a tentative agreement to agree.[40] In an addendum to this preliminary agreement, the buyers agreed to post a $350,000 irrevocable standby letter of credit[41] in favor of C.E. Vetco as earnest money for the proposed purchase.

[38] See Act of May 23, 1887, P.L. 158, § 7, as amended by Act of March 30, 1911, P.L. 35, § 1, 28 P.S. § 381(1958).

[39] Fuqua was originally a party to this action, but has since filed bankruptcy and was dismissed.

[40] The letter agreement stated that "the parties agree to enter into an agreement to buy and sell the [herein] described assets . . . subject to mutual agreement" of the terms to be negotiated in the buy and sell agreement.

[41] A standby "letter of credit" is a common means of contingent financing. Such an arrangement involves a buyer contracting with a financial institution, whereby the institution will serve as a guarantor of a certain amount of money in a transaction between the buyer and a third-party seller. If the buyer breaches his agreement with the seller, the seller may seek payment from the institution. See generally *FDIC v. Philadelphia Gear Corp.,* 476 U.S. 426, 427-428, 106 S. Ct. 1931, 1932-1933, 90 L. Ed. 2d 428 (1986) (discussing standby letter of credit transaction); Arnold & Bransilver, *The Standby Letter of Credit,* 10 U.C.C.L.J. 272 (1978); Note, *FDIC v. Philadelphia Gear: A Standby Letter of Credit Backed By a Promissory Note is not a Deposit,* 41 U.Miami L.Rev. 357 (1986).

A letter of credit transaction actually consists of three distinct contracts: (i) the underlying purchase-and-sale agreement between buyer and seller; (ii) an application for the letter of credit filed with the financial institution by the buyer, *i.e.,* a contract between the bank and buyer; and (iii) the letter of credit itself, a contract between the bank

The buyers obtained financing for the letter of credit from Commonwealth Bank (Commonwealth), a Texas institution. The buyers completed and signed an application for the letter of credit in the amount of $350,000 on April 29, 1985. Commonwealth approved the application and C.E. Vetco was listed as the beneficiary of the letter of credit, which was to be in force through June 24, 1985. The letter of credit contained the following condition precedent: Commonwealth would pay C.E. Vetco $350,000 if C.E. Vetco presented the letter of credit and certified that the buyers had failed to comply with the terms of the March 24th agreement to agree. The buyers also signed a blank promissory note for $350,000, executed a related security agreement, and provided various assets as collateral. It was the mutual understanding of Commonwealth and the buyers that the bank was authorized to complete the blank promissory note in the event that C.E. Vetco properly presented the letter of credit for payment.

The next day, on April 30, 1985, the parties finalized their negotiations and entered into a purchase and sale agreement. The parties agreed to close the deal on or before June 24, 1985. Notably, Vetco, Inc., the parent corporation of C.E. Vetco, was substituted in place of its subsidiary as the named seller in the agreement.[42] Included in the final agreement was a provision similar to the one in the agreement to agree, which referred to a $350,000 letter of credit. This provision, however, referred to a letter of credit on behalf of Vetco, Inc., rather than C.E. Vetco, even though the latter was the only named beneficiary in the March 20th agreement to agree and the April 29th letter of credit.[43]

Sometime after April 30, 1985, Commonwealth—at the request of an official of Vetco, Inc., William Becker—altered certain terms of both the application and letter of credit itself. The beneficiary of the letter of credit was changed from C.E. Vetco Services, Inc., to Vetco, Inc. Commonwealth also changed the terms of the condition precedent in the application for the letter of credit: rather than requiring C.E. Vetco to present the letter of credit and certify that the buyers had breached the March 20th agreement to agree, the altered letter of credit required Vetco, Inc. to present the letter of credit and certify that the buyers were in breach of the April 30th purchase and sell agreement. These changes were in keeping with the substitution of Vetco, Inc. for C.E. Vetco as the named seller in the final purchase and sell agreement. Furthermore, the expiration date was changed from June 24, 1985, to June 28, 1985. A comparison of the original and altered versions of the two letters of credit indicates that Commonwealth simply whited out the altered portions of the original letter and typed over them.[44]

In the following months, the buyers failed to carry through with their obligations set forth in the purchase and sale agreement. On June 24, 1985, Vetco, Inc. responded by presenting the letter of credit to Commonwealth for payment. After Vetco, Inc. certified that the buyers had

---

and seller, whereby the bank will pay a certain amount of money to the seller in the event that the buyer fails to pay the seller in breach of the underlying contract between the buyer and seller. See *Bank of Cochin Ltd. v. Manufacturers's Hanover Trust Co.,* 612 F. Supp. 1533, 1537 (S.D.N.Y.1985), aff'd, 808 F.2d 209 (2d Cir.1986).

[42] In both the agreement to agree and the final purchase and sale agreement, the authorized representative and signatory for both parent and subsidiary was William Becker.

[43] The parties apparently considered the April 29th letter of credit to apply jointly to the parent and subsidiary. The purchase and sale agreement recited that a letter of credit "has been delivered to Seller," obviously referring to the letter executed the previous day.

[44] The parties are in dispute whether Commonwealth's alteration of the letter of credit was authorized by an agent of the buyers. The parties also are in dispute whether Commonwealth mailed copies of the altered letter of credit to the buyers. The buyers contend that they not only did not authorize the alteration, but also were entirely unaware that any alteration had occurred until many months after it took place.

breached the purchase and sale agreement, Commonwealth paid Vetco, Inc. $350,000 according to the terms of the altered letter of credit. Commonwealth then unilaterally completed the promissory note that the buyers had signed in blank. The buyers initially did not dispute the propriety of Commonwealth's payment of the letter of credit and consequent activation of the promissory note. Indeed, over the next few months, the buyers actually made numerous payments on the note. They also executed an extension of the loan in the form of a second promissory note.[45] However, by early 1986, the buyers fell behind in their payments and eventually defaulted on the note. At the time of the default, Vanderkam had paid the sum of $134,419, which included the liquidation of his collateral. Commonwealth also possessed Plato's collateral, 50,000 shares of preferred stock issued by Tejas Oil and Gas, Inc.

Commonwealth proceeded to file suit in Texas state court for the unpaid balance of the second promissory note. It was at this point that the buyers claim that they first discovered that Commonwealth had altered the original letter of credit. The buyers proceeded to file a counterclaim against Commonwealth for return of the payments made on the note and for return of all remaining collateral that had been pledged as security for the letter of credit. On April 29, 1989, Commonwealth was declared insolvent and the FDIC was appointed as receiver. All non-performing assets, including the buyers' $350,000 promissory note, were assigned to the FDIC in its corporate capacity. The FDIC was also substituted as plaintiff and counterdefendant in Commonwealth's pending state court suit against the buyers. The FDIC subsequently removed the action to federal court. In addition to its claim for the unpaid balance of the note, the FDIC also sought quantum meruit damages, claiming that the buyers had been unjustly enriched by Commonwealth's five-day extension of the expiration of the letter of credit.

After a two day bench trial, the district court entered judgment against the FDIC on its claims and for the buyers on their counterclaims. The district court found that Commonwealth, without authorization from the buyers, had materially altered the original application and letter of credit, which absolved the buyers of liability for their default on the promissory note. The district court also rejected the FDIC's contention that the buyers ratified the altered application and letter of credit by making payments on the promissory note; in this regard, the court specifically found that the buyers made the payment without any knowledge that any alteration had occurred. The court also held that the FDIC was not entitled to quantum meruit damages under well-established equity principles; the court imputed Commonwealth's "unclean hands" to the FDIC. Finally, the district court summarily rejected the FDIC's argument that it should prevail under either the holder-in-due-course or *D'Oench Duhme* doctrines. The court not only entered a "take nothing" judgment for the FDIC on its claim, but also ordered the FDIC to pay Vanderkam $134,419 and return Plato his 50,000 shares of stock. The court thereafter denied the FDIC's joint motion, pursuant to Federal Rules of Civil Procedure 59 and 60, for relief from judgment and a new trial.

II.

On appeal, the parties have raised myriad issues relating to liability and damages with respect to the FDIC's claims and the buyer's counterclaim. Because we believe that the district court committed error by summarily rejecting the FDIC's assertion of the *D'Oench Duhme* doctrine,[46]

---

[45] The renewal note was essentially identical to the first note, save the amount of payment and date of execution.

[46] See *D'Oench Duhme & Co. v. FDIC,* 315 U.S. 447, 62 S. Ct. 676, 86 L. Ed. 956 (1942). 12 U.S.C. § 1823(e) is the statutory analogue of the *D'Oench Duhme* doctrine. While related, the two are considered distinct. See *FDIC*

we need not address the bulk of issues on appeal, as our holding regarding *D'Oench* is dispositive of them.[47] Because we reverse the district court as a matter of law, we need not address any of the court's fact-findings that are challenged by the parties on appeal.

The district court rejected the FDIC's invocation of *D'Oench* with the following conclusory statement: "*D'Oench Duhme,* involving attempts by borrowers to avoid payment of promissory notes by asserting oral side agreements with the lender, is clearly inapplicable to the case at bar." The FDIC argues that the district court misunderstood *D'Oench.* The FDIC specifically contends not only that this case does in fact involve an "oral side agreement," but also that even if it did not *D'Oench* would still apply. We agree on both counts.

We have carefully examined the buyers' original and altered applications for the letter of credit filed with Commonwealth, as well as the two promissory notes (the first signed in blank by the buyers and later filled in by Commonwealth) and the security agreement governing the collateral provided to secure the promissory note. Nowhere in the applications is there any cross-reference to any promissory note. Indeed, the extensive boilerplate language appears to constitute a discrete bilateral contract between the applicant and the bank; no promissory note is contemplated by its terms. Furthermore, nowhere in the promissory notes or security agreement is there a cross-reference to either the applications for the letter or credit or the letter of credit itself. In particular, the promissory note simply states that it is "for value received"; it also contains standard boilerplate governing repayment and default. The security agreement likewise contains boilerplate and simply states that the $350,000 of indebtedness being secured with collateral was for the purpose of "personal indebtedness."

Thus, the promissory notes are facially distinct from the applications for the letter of credit. Cf. *FDIC v. Philadelphia Gear Corp.,* 476 U.S. 426, 428, 106 S. Ct. 1931, 1933, 90 L. Ed. 2d 428 (1986) ("Although the face of the note did not so indicate, both Orion and Penn Square understood that nothing would be considered due on the note, and no interest charged by Penn Square, unless Philadelphia Gear presented drafts on the standby letter of credit after nonpayment by Orion."). The only nexus between the promissory note and security agreement, on the one hand, and the application and letter of credit, on the other hand, is a parol agreement between Commonwealth Bank and the buyers entered into at the time that the application for the letter of credit was submitted in April 1985. While a strong case can be made that Commonwealth and the buyers mutually understood that the promissory note applied only to the letter of credit transaction, such a claim is simply not actionable under *D'Oench* and § 1823(e), which mandate that such collateral agreements must be in explicit written form.[48] As has been repeatedly

---

v. McClanahan, 795 F.2d 512, 514 n. 1 (5th Cir.1986). For purposes of this appeal, however, the two are interchangeable. The relevant portion of § 1823(e), that also finds expression in the common law doctrine, is as follows: "No agreement which tends to diminish or defeat the right, title, or interest of the [FDIC] in any asset acquired by it under this section . . . shall be valid against the corporation unless such agreement (1) shall be in writing. . . ."

[47] We note that *D'Oench* may serve not only as a sword but also as a shield for the FDIC: that is, the doctrine may be invoked by the FDIC not only in its capacity as a plaintiff suing to recover on a note or contract—the validity of which is disputed by the opposing party—but also in defeating a claim asserted against the FDIC. In the instant case, the FDIC invokes *D'Oench* both offensively and defensively.

[48] Similarly, we recognize that, if this were an action between Commonwealth and the buyers, principles of law specifically governing the relationship between a lending institution and an applicant for a letter of credit perhaps would dictate a different result. See, *e.g., Philadelphia Gear Corp. v. Central Bank,* 717 F.2d 230, 236 (5th Cir.1983) (discussing the doctrine of "strict compliance" in litigation concerning letters of credit, citing White & Summers, Uniform Commercial Code § 18.7at 742-43 (1972)). However, such principles have their origin in state commercial law, which is preempted by the federal doctrine embodied in *D'Oench, Duhme* and § 1823(e). See *D'Oench,* 315 U.S. at 473-74, 62 S. Ct. 676 at 686-87, 86 L. Ed. 956.

recognized, the common rationale of *D'Oench* and § 1823(e) is to facilitate to the maximum degree the FDIC's ability to assess the condition of an insolvent bank solely based on its written records. "The doctrine means that the government has no duty to compile oral histories of the bank's customers and . . . officers." See *Bowen v. FDIC,* 915 F.2d 1013, 1016 (5th Cir.1990). In this case, FDIC auditors found a promissory note that made no reference to any other agreement. Because the promissory note was facially unrelated to the letter of credit transaction, *D'Oench* forecloses any claim by the appellees that the promissory note is invalid.

Alternatively, even if we were to agree with the appellees that no unrecorded, oral agreement is at issue in the instant case, there is an alternative reason for reversing the district court on *D'Oench* grounds. As the FDIC correctly contends, the district court erred by limiting *D'Oench to* "oral side agreements." In its expansive evolution since 1942, the *D'Oench* doctrine and its statutory analogue have been applied to a wide variety of circumstances besides collateral oral agreements not evident in a failed bank's records. See *FDIC v. Hamilton,* 939 F.2d 1225, 1228 (5th Cir.1991); see generally, Note *Borrower Beware: D'Oench, Duhme and Section 1823 Overprotect the Insurer When the Bank Fails,* 62 S.Cal.L.Rev. 253 (1988). While most of that evolution has occurred in the lower courts, even the Supreme Court has applied *D'Oench* and § 1823(e) to tortious conduct committed by a failed financial institution. See *Langley v. FDIC,* 484 U.S. 86, 108 S. Ct. 396, 98 L. Ed. 2d 340 (1987) (failed bank's fraudulent misrepresentation and inducement trumped by *D'Oench*). In fact, the Supreme Court implied that only a species of tort actually rendering a contract void ab initio—*e.g.,* "fraud in the factum"—would prevent a court from applying *D'Oench.* See *id.* at 94. Plato and Vanderkam argue that "fraud in the factum" occurred in the present case.

We disagree.[49] Commonwealth's actions consisted of the alteration of the buyer's application and the letter of credit. While possibly a "material" alteration,[50] Commonwealth's unilateral changes hardly were injurious to the buyers. The substitution of Vetco, Inc. as the letter's beneficiary—merely substituting the parent corporation for its subsidiary—and the corresponding change in the condition precedent were simply nominal alterations contemplated by the express language of the purchase and sale agreement. Furthermore, the extension of the expiration date by five days in no way prejudiced the buyers.[51] It is not as if Commonwealth's alterations increased the amount or terms of repayment. Appellees appear to be clinging to a technicality in the hope of extinguishing their otherwise lawfully incurred debt.

Furthermore, even if Commonwealth's actions did constitute "material alteration" as that term is commonly understood, numerous courts, including this court, have addressed the question of whether *D'Oench* or § 1823(e) is operative when a failed financial institution materially altered, or wrongly augmented, the terms of a partially completed instrument or document. Such cases have relied on a well-recognized component of the larger *D'Oench* doctrine—that when a party

---

[49] We note that appellees did not make this argument below; therefore, they may not properly advance this claim for the first time on appeal. See *Lindsey v. FDIC,* 960 F.2d 567, 572 (5th Cir.1992) ("The Lindseys argue that even if title did pass to MBank upon foreclosure, . . . MBank committed real fraud, or fraud in the factum. The Lindseys did not raise this claim below. This Court will not address an issue raised below for the first time on appeal. . . ."). Thus, we reach the merits of this claim only in the alternative.

[50] See, *e.g.,* Tex.Bus. & Com.Code, § 3.407 (Vernon's 1992). Adopting the U.C.C. definition, the Texas statute defines "material" alteration as including a change in "the number or relation of the parties."

[51] Indeed, that extension is the basis of the FDIC's quantum meruit claim, which seeks to disgorge an unjust enrichment to the buyers. We also note that the alteration was in fact insignificant in that Vetco, Inc. presented the letter of credit on June 24, 1985, which was the last day it could have done so under the original agreement.

"lent himself" to a scheme that could mislead federal bank examiners, whether or not done unwittingly, he cannot circumvent *D'Oench* by arguing that the failed bank wrongly altered or augmented an incomplete instrument which he signed. See *D'Oench,* 315 U.S. at 460, 62 S. Ct. at 680; *Caporale,* 931 F.2d at 2 ("By signing blank notes, the Caporales 'lent themselves' to a scheme that could mislead bank examiners."); *McClanahan,* 795 F.2d at 515 (same). In the instant case, the buyers—all sophisticated attorneys—should have foreseen the consequences of signing a blank promissory note.[52]

III.

Accordingly, we REVERSE not only the district court's entry of a take-nothing judgment on the FDIC's claim, but also the court's order that the FDIC must return to Vanderkam the $134,419 that he had previously paid on the note and return to Plato his 50,000 shares of stock given as collateral. We AFFIRM the district court's judgment on the FDIC's claim only insofar as it refused to award quantum meruit damages. We REMAND for the entry of judgment (including, if and to the extent allowed under law, interest, costs, and attorneys fees). Costs of this appeal shall be borne by the appellees.

ROSE DEVELOPMENTS v. PEARSON PROPERTIES, INC.

Court of Appeals of Arkansas
38 Ark. App. 215, 832 S.W.2d 286, 19 U.C.C. Rep. Serv. 2d 55 (1992)

MAYFIELD, J.

Rose Developments appeals from the order of the circuit court which permanently enjoined the drawing on, or honor of, a letter of credit, pursuant to Ark. Code Ann. § 4-5-114(2)(b) (Repl. 1991), on the finding that appellant had committed fraud.

On December 6, 1988, appellee Pearson contracted with the appellant Rose to provide material and labor in connection with the construction of building "K" in a condominium project known as Solomons Landing Project. The amount of the contract was $458,200.00. In lieu of a performance bond, Pearson delivered an irrevocable letter of credit in the amount of $25,000.00 to secure its performance under the contract. The letter of credit authorized Rose to draw up to $25,000.00 available by "your drafts at sight" accompanied by an authorized statement that Pearson (d/b/a Homes, Inc.) had failed to perform its obligations as required under the terms

[52] We briefly note two other issues raised on appeal that are not disposed of by our application of the *D'Oench* doctrine in this case. First, FDIC argues that the district court erred in refusing to award the FDIC quantum meruit damages in addition to its contract claim on the promissory note. The FDIC specifically argues that the buyers were unjustly enriched on account of the five-day extension of the expiration date. We agree with the district court that restitutionary damages were not appropriate. The buyers did not request that extension and, according to the evidence at trial, the buyers were not even aware of the extension until well after the altered letter of credit had expired. Commonwealth's officious actions are not a proper basis for this type of equitable relief. Additionally, we note that it appears that there was no enrichment of any type based on the alteration of the expiration date from June 24, 1985, to June 29, 1985, as Vetco, Inc. presented the letter of credit on June 24th—the last valid day under the original letter of credit.

Another issue we must briefly address concerns Vanderkam and Plato's claim that the trial court failed to award them attorneys' fees under the Equal Access to Justice Act, 28 U.S.C. § 2412(d). Because the Act only applies to a "prevailing party," *id.* § 2412(d)(1)(A), our reversal renders this particular claim moot.

and conditions of its construction contract and the original of the letter of credit. Under the terms of the letter of credit, drafts had to be drawn and negotiated no later than July 15, 1989. Subsequently, buildings "E" and "L" were made addendum to the original contract. The only change was an increase in the price.

On July 5, 1989, S. Brooks Grady, Sr., Vice-President of Rose, stated in a letter to First National Bank (Bank) that "Homes, Inc. has been working on our job at Solomons Landing in Maryland since November 1988. We have been very satisfied with their work, and they are presently working on our third building." On July 15, 1989, the letter of credit was extended until January 12, 1990, for the purpose of working on buildings "E" and "L".

On December 4, 1989, the Bank was notified that Homes, Inc., had failed to perform its obligations as required under the terms and conditions of its construction contract and immediate payment of $25,000.00 was requested under the letter of credit.

On December 12, 1989, Pearson filed a petition for a temporary restraining order against Rose and the Bank alleging among other things that the draft was fraudulently presented upon misrepresentations by Rose, and alternatively that "Ark. Code Ann. Section 4-5-114 specifically grants the Court authority to enjoin the honor of a draft or demand based on 'fraud, forgery, or other defect not apparent on the face of the documents.' "

On December 13, 1989, the court granted the petition. Subsequently, the Bank filed an answer admitting its obligation to honor the draft drawn against the letter of credit unless enjoined by the court and tendered a cashier's check for $25,000.00 to the clerk of the court for safekeeping until further orders.

After a hearing, held May 31, 1990, the trial court found Rose had committed fraud which should prevent it from drawing on the letter of credit and permanently enjoined the Bank from honoring the draft and Rose from drawing on the letter of credit.

A letter of credit is a three-party arrangement involving two contracts and the letter of credit: 1) the underlying contract between the customer and the beneficiary, in this case between Pearson and Rose; 2) the reimbursement agreement between the issuer and the customer, in this case between First National Bank and Pearson; and 3) the letter of credit between the issuer and the beneficiary, in this case between First National Bank and Rose. The significant part of this arrangement is the "independence principle" which states that the bank's obligation to the beneficiary is independent of the beneficiary's performance on the underlying contract. 2 J. White & R. Summers, Uniform Commercial Code § 19-2 (3d ed. 1988). "Put another way, the issuer must pay on a proper demand from the beneficiary even though the beneficiary may have breached the underlying contract with the customer." *Id.* at 8. "It is not a contract of guarantee. . .even though the letter fulfills the function of a guarantee." *Id.* at 9.

The letter of credit involved in this case is a standby letter of credit which has been characterized as a "back-up" against customer default on obligations of all kinds. *Id.* § 19-1, at 4. Such letters function somewhat like guarantees because it is the customer's default on the underlying obligation that prompts the beneficiary's draw on the letter. *Id.* at 4. The risk to the issuer is somewhat greater than in a commercial letter of credit in that the commercial letter gives the issuer security in goods whereas the standby letter gives no ready security, and the banker behaves as a surety. *Id.* at 6. The standby letter of credit is somewhat akin to a performance bond in that:

> In place of a performance bond from a true surety, builder (customer) gets his bank (issuer) to write owner (beneficiary) a standby letter of credit. In this letter, issuer engages to pay

> beneficiary-owner against presentment of two documents: 1) a written demand (typically a sight draft) which calls for payment of the letter's stipulated amount, plus 2) a written statement certifying that customer-builder has failed to perform the agreed construction work.

Id. at 4. One difference between the standby letter of credit and the surety contract is that the standby credit beneficiary has different expectations.

In the surety contract situation, there is no duty to indemnify the beneficiary until the beneficiary establishes the fact of the obligor's nonperformance. The beneficiary may have to establish that fact in litigation. During the litigation, the surety holds the money and the beneficiary bears most of the cost of delay in performance.

In the standby credit case, however, the beneficiary avoids that litigation burden and receives his money promptly upon presentation of the required documents. It may be that the account party has in fact performed and that the beneficiary's presentation of those documents is not rightful. In that case, the account party may sue the beneficiary in tort, in contract, or in breach of warranty; but during the litigation to determine whether the account party has in fact breached his obligation to perform, the beneficiary, not the account party, holds the money. J. Dolan, The Law of Letters of Credit, at 1-18, 1-19 (2d ed. 1991).

Letters of credit are governed by the "Uniform Commercial Code-Letters of Credit," Ark. Code Ann. § 4-5-101 through 117 (Repl. 1991). Section 4-5-114(1) provides that an issuer must honor a draft which complies with the terms of the relevant credit regardless of whether the goods or documents conform to the underlying contract between the customer and the beneficiary. However, the issuer does not have an absolute duty to honor a draft authorized by the letter of credit. An exception is provided by § 4-5-114(2) which provides that an issuer need not honor the draft if "a required document does not in fact conform to the warranties made on negotiation or transfer of a document of title (§ 4-8-306) or of a certificated security (§ 4-8-306) or is forged or fraudulent or there is fraud in the transaction." Section 4-5-114(2)(b) provides that in all other cases as against its customer an issuer may honor the draft despite notification from the customer of fraud, forgery, or other defect not apparent on the face of the documents but a court of appropriate jurisdiction may enjoin such honor.

On appeal, it is argued that the trial court erred in finding the appellant committed fraud which would prevent it from drawing on the letter of credit. Appellant admits that courts have allowed injunctions for "fraud in the transaction" but argues an injunction is proper only if there is no bona fide claim to payment, and the wrongdoing of the beneficiary has so vitiated the entire transaction that the legitimate purposes of the independence principle would no longer be served. See *Intraworld Industries, Inc. v. Girard Trust Bank,* 336 A.2d 316 (Pa. 1975); *Sztejn v. Henry Schroder Banking Corp.,* 31 N.Y.S.2d 631 (1941). Appellant contends that Pearson has established only that there may be a dispute as to some of the "back charges". (Back charges have to do with material and labor that needs or needed to be performed, that Pearson was supposed to be responsible for, but appellant had to take over.)

Appellees agree the only issue on appeal is whether appellant committed fraud which would justify the issuance of the injunction and argue the injunction was proper. Appellee Pearson contends that in December 1989 or January 1990 it received a number of back charges dating as far back as December 1988; that it had never previously received these charges; that appellant, while in possession of documents it claimed were back charges, wrote a letter to obtain an extension of the letter of credit stating it was "very satisfied with the work of Homes, Inc.";

and that appellant knowingly misrepresented the facts in order to obtain an extension of the letter of credit.

In support of its argument, appellee Pearson cites *W.O.A. Inc. v. City National Bank of Fort Smith, Ark.,* 640 F. Supp. 1157 (W.D. Ark. 1986), and *Shaffer v. Brooklyn Park Garden Apartments,* 250 N.W.2d 172 (Minn. 1977). Those cases, however, involved false certification accompanying drafts for payment and have no application here. In *City National Bank* the appellant intentionally misrepresented the state of affairs when, though it had been paid, it presented drafts for payment under a letter of credit. That case relied on *Roman Ceramics Corp. v. Peoples National Bank,* 714 F.2d 1207 (3d Cir. 1983), which held that a beneficiary who tenders a draft knowing that its certification of nonpayment by the buyers is false, is guilty of fraud in the transaction. Similarly, *Shaffer* involved a situation where letters of credit guaranteed payment of certain promissory notes. The issuer received documents which appeared to comply with the presentation requirements under the letters of credit; however, the certifications which stated the customers had defaulted on their loans were false.

In the instant case, the certification stated that "Homes, Inc., has failed to perform its obligations as required under the terms and conditions of their construction contract." At trial, Robert Pearson III, Vice-President of Homes, Inc., testified they did not allege that there were forgeries "or anything like that" involved in the demand for payment on the letter of credit. Pearson admitted the letter of credit was to protect appellant in the event Pearson did not pay for labor, materials and other supplies that might be incorporated into the structure; that there were outstanding materialmen's and laborers' liens against the project; and that some of those liens were for materials, labor, and supplies that were the responsibility of Pearson. Pearson testified his allegation of fraud was based on the contention that he had been billed for work outside his contract and that Rose had called upon the letter of credit based upon certain back charges. Pearson said the majority of the back charges were unacceptable, but acknowledged that 10% of the charges were legitimate.

Appellee Bank admits this case does not involve forgery or "other defect not apparent on the face of the documents". John Thornton, Executive Vice-President of the Bank, testified he would not have extended the original letter of credit without Rose's statement that the jobs were being done in a satisfactory manner. Appellee Bank argues that none of the back charges, that predated the extension of the letter of credit, were mentioned in appellant's letter which induced the Bank to extend the letter of credit. And the Bank contends that Rose's fraud can be categorized as both egregious and intentional and that the injunction was a proper statutory remedy.

The narrow question to be decided by this court is whether the evidence will support a finding that there was "fraud in the transaction." Our research has revealed no Arkansas cases containing a definition of "fraud in the transaction" as used in the section of the Uniform Commercial Code that is involved in this case. Some courts have held that fraud in the transaction must be of such an egregious nature as to vitiate the entire underlying transaction so that the legitimate purposes of the independence of the bank's obligation would no longer be served. Other cases and writers have suggested intentional fraud should be sufficient to obtain injunctive relief in letter of credit cases. Professor Symons concludes "a proper definition of fraud will necessarily encompass and be limited by the requirement of scienter: that there be an affirmative, knowing misrepresentation of fact or that the beneficiary state a fact not having any idea about its truth or falsity, and in reckless disregard of the truth." *Symons, supra* at 379. It has also been suggested that the lesson to be learned from this section of the Uniform Commercial Code (Ark. Code Ann. § 5-4-114(2)

(Repl. 1990), is that a court should seldom enjoin payment under a letter of credit on the theory that there is fraud in the documents or fraud in the underlying transaction. See 2 J. White & R. Summers, Uniform Commercial Code § 19-7(Supp. 1991).

From our consideration of the law and the evidence in this case, we think the trial court erred in enjoining payment under the letter of credit. In the first place, we do not believe appellant's general statement "we have been very satisfied with their work" is sufficient for a finding of fraud. At the time this statement was made, appellant had extended Pearson's contract for building "K" to include buildings "E" and "L", and it seems obvious that appellant's statement was truthful or appellant would not have extended the contract. Also, the testimony shows that the total amount of the contract for building "K" was $458,200.00 and that the back charges which pre-date the statement complained of totalled only approximately $1,944.81. We do not believe the existence of back charges in that small amount supports a finding that appellant committed fraud when it said "we have been very satisfied with their work."

As to the argument that appellant's fraud consisted of billing for work that was outside its contract and other disputed back charges, Robert Pearson III testified his allegation of fraud was that the letter of credit was being called upon because appellant said that based upon "these back charges" they were still owed money, but Pearson testified that as far as "these back charges" are concerned "the majority of them are unacceptable." Pearson testified appellant was claiming a total of $50,000.00 to $60,000.00 in back charges on a project which totaled over $1.2 million. This is simply a contract dispute relating to back charges which may have to be resolved in litigation. However, as explained in Dolan, supra, in the standby letter of credit case "the beneficiary avoids that litigation burden and receives his money promptly" and during the litigation "the beneficiary, not the account party, holds the money."

When we apply the law to the evidence in this case, we think it was clearly erroneous to find that appellant committed fraud that should prevent it from drawing on the letter of credit; therefore, it was error to grant permanent injunctive relief to appellee Pearson and prevent the Bank from honoring the draft drawn on the letter of credit.

Reversed and remanded for any necessary proceedings consistent with this opinion.

§ 23.02 Standby or Guaranty Letters of Credit

We have seen the commercial letter of credit used in connection with the purchase and sale of goods. This letter of credit gave assurances to a seller that it would receive payment for sale of its goods. A "standby letter of credit" can be utilized in a sale of goods transaction or other transactions. A standby letter of credit is basically a letter of credit which represents an obligation to the beneficiary on the part of the issuer to make payment on account of any *default* by the account party/customer in the performance of an obligation. See J. Dolan, The Law of Letters of Credit, ¶¶ 1.04, 1.05, 1.06 and 3.06 (2d ed. 1991).

A seller may use a standby arrangement to support sales. "Under this plan, the seller invoices the buyer directly and draws under the standby credit only if the buyer fails to honor the invoice. This invoice credit may be clean; that is, it may be payable against a draft alone, or it may require the beneficiary to submit the invoices and a certificate reciting that they are unpaid. Unless the buyer fails to pay the invoice, the seller-beneficiary will not draw on the credit." J. Dolan, The Law of Letters of Credit 1-30 (2d ed. 1991).

A standby credit can be used to give assurance to a buyer that seller will perform its obligation to transfer and deliver the goods to the buyer. See, e.g., *KMW Int'l v. Chase Manhattan Bank,*

27 U.C.C. Rep. 203 (2d Cir. 1979): Chase to pay Iran bank on behalf of Iran buyer of telephone poles from KMW seller upon receipt by Chase of Iran bank's

> authenticated cable certifying [that] the amount drawn is the amount you have been called upon to pay Khuzestan Water and Power Authority, P.O. Box 13, Ahwaz, Iran, under your guarantee issued at the request of KMW International due to nonperformance by KMW International under the terms of Khuzestan Water and Power Authority purchase order #4229 dated August 1, 1978. . . .

Other illustrations of standby (or guaranty) letters of credit are:

1. *Construction Contract.* Letter of credit issuer agrees to honor drafts drawn by Park District if the following document is furnished: "[Y]our signed statement dated January 5, 1974 and presented on that date that your drawing is in connection with failure by McCoy Enterprises, Inc. to construct two tennis courts in Westminster, Colorado on or before January 5,1974." (*Hyland Hills Metropolitan Park & Rec. Dist. v. McCoy Enterprises, Inc.*, 554 P.2d 708 (Colo. App. 1976).)

2. *Employment Contract.* Issuer will pay up to $ 70,000 in the event of default. "Drafts presented under this credit must be accompanied by a signed affidavit of [professional football player] stating that the Chicago Football Club, Inc. . . . has not paid [football player] for a scheduled football game by Tuesday of the following week." (*Beathard v. Chicago Football Club, Inc.*, 419 F.Supp. 1133 (N.D. Ill. 1976).) In *Beathard* the credit was revocable. Under UCP 500, Article 7, if a credit doesn't indicate whether it is revocable or irrevocable, it is deemed to be irrevocable. Also, revised U.C.C. § 5-106 states that a letter of credit is revocable only if it so provides.

3. *Lease.* Issuer authorized lessor to draw draft on issuer if draft accompanied by "signed statement of the drawer . . . to the effect that the drawer is the lessor under said lease and that the lessee thereunder has not paid the installment of rent due (*Intraworld Industries, Inc. v. Girard Trust Bank*, 336 A.2d 316 (Pa. 1975).)

4. *Loan Guaranty.* Issuer to honor drafts drawn by mortgagee-creditor upon presentation of affidavit that certain closing costs were not paid. (*Mid States Mtg. Corp. v. National Bank of Southfield*, 77 Mich. App. 651, 259 N.W.2d 175 (1977).) *See also*, *Brown v. United States National Bank*, 371 N.W.2d 692, 41 UCC Rep. 1765 (1985).

5. *Charter Air Service Contract.* Beneficiary (Westates) is to furnish airplanes and crews for customer/applicant's (Charter One's) charter air service; customer/applicant is to pay a monthly fee to beneficiary. The issuer's letter of credit read: "the credit is available to you [Westates] by your drafts on us at sight accompanied by: Dated notarized copy of the ten (10) day notice described in [Westates/Charter One contract]." (This is a default notice under the contract's special "default" provision.) *Ground Air Transfer, Inc. v. Westates Airlines, Inc.*, 899 F.2d 1269, 11 UCC Rep. 2d 177 (1st Cir. 1990).

See J. Dolan, The Law of Letters of Credit, ¶ 1.06, "Frequent Uses of Standby Credit" (2d ed. 1991).

Functionally, there is little difference between a standby and a regular letter of credit. The main distinction between the two types of letters is that parties to a transaction expect a standard letter of credit to be drawn on, where as a standby letter of credit there is a condition other than shipment of goods that must occur before payment on the letter is made to the beneficiary.

Because the standby letters of credit often serve as a guarantee, the independence principle becomes strained in many relationships. Customers frequently rely on their banks to deny honoring documents presented; imploring the financial institution to find any nonconformity in the documents. Equitable issues arise where a surreptitious party to a contract fraudulently draws on a standby letter of credit. Should an issuing bank have a duty to investigate the underlying transaction when it is serving as a guarantor of performance?

COLORADO NATIONAL BANK OF DENVER v. BOARD OF COUNTY COMMISSIONERS OF ROUTT COUNTY

Supreme Court of Colorado
634 P.2d 32; 31 U.C.C. Rep. Serv. (Callaghan) 1681 (1981)

Chief Justice Hodges delivered the Opinion of the Court.

We granted certiorari to review the court of appeals' decision affirming a district court's judgment holding the petitioner, the Colorado National Bank of Denver (the Bank), liable for the face amounts of three letters of credit it issued to secure the completion of road improvements by its customer, the Woodmoor Corporation (Woodmoor). *Board of County Commissioners of Routt County v. Colorado National Bank of Denver,* 43 Colo. App. 186, 607 P.2d 1010 (1979). We reverse the judgment as to letters of credit No. 1156 and No. 1157, and affirm the judgment as to letter of credit No. 1168.

Woodmoor planned to develop a mountain recreation community in Routt County, Colorado (the County), to be known as Stagecoach. Early in 1973, Woodmoor obtained plat approval from the Routt County Board of County Commissioners (the Commissioners) for several Stagecoach subdivisions. Pursuant to section 30-28-137, C.R.S. 1973 (1977 Repl. Vol. 12), and county subdivision regulations, approval of three of these subdivision plats was conditioned upon Woodmoor's agreement to provide a bond or other undertaking to ensure the completion of roads in accordance with the subdivision design specifications. Accordingly, subdivision improvements agreements were executed between Woodmoor and the county.

At Woodmoor's request, the Bank issued three letters of credit to secure Woodmoor's obligations under the agreements. The first two letters of credit, No. 1156 and No. 1157, were issued January 23, 1973 in the respective amounts of $158,773 and $77,330 bearing expiry dates of December 31, 1975. The third letter of credit No. 1168 was issued March 7, 1973 in the amount of $113,732 bearing an expiry date of December 31, 1976. The face amounts of the letters of credit were identical to the estimated costs of the road and related improvements in the respective subdivision improvements agreements. The County was authorized by each letter of credit to draw directly on the Bank, for the account of Woodmoor, up to the face amount of each letter of credit. Each letter of credit required the County, in order to draw on the letters of credit, to submit fifteen-day sight drafts accompanied by:

> A duly-signed statement by the Routt County Board of Commissioners that improvements have not been made in compliance with a Subdivision Improvements Agreement between Routt

County and the Woodmoor Corporation dated [either January 9, 1973 or March 7, 1973] and covering the [respective subdivisions] at Stagecoach and that payment is therefore demanded hereunder.

Woodmoor never commenced construction of the roads and related improvements. On December 31, 1975, the expiry date of letters of credit No. 1156 and No. 1157, the County presented two demand drafts to the Bank for the face amounts of $158,773 and $77,330. The demand drafts were accompanied by a resolution of the Commissioners stating that Woodmoor had failed to comply with the terms of the subdivision improvements agreements and demanded payment of the face amounts of the letters of credit. On January 5, 1976, within three banking days of the demand,[53] the Bank dishonored the drafts. The Bank did not specifically object to the County's presentation of demand drafts rather than fifteen-day sight drafts as required by the letters of credit.

On December 22, 1976, the County presented the Bank with a demand draft on letter of credit No. 1168 which was accompanied by the required resolution of the Commissioners. The Bank dishonored this draft because of the County's nonconforming demand, viz., that a demand draft was submitted rather than a fifteen-day sight draft. On December 29, 1976, the County presented a fifteen-day sight draft to the Bank. This draft was not accompanied by the resolution of the Commissioners. On December 31, 1976, the Bank dishonored this draft.

The County sued to recover the face amounts of the three letters of credit plus interest from the dates of the demands. The Bank answered the County's complaints alleging several affirmative defenses. The fundamental premise of the Bank's defenses was the assertion that the County would receive a windfall since it had not expended or committed to spend any funds to complete the road improvements specified in the subdivision improvements agreements.

The County filed a motion in limine seeking a determination by the trial court to exclude evidence concerning matters beyond the four corners of the letters of credit and the demands made on the letters of credit. The bank replied by filing a cross-motion in limine seeking a ruling that it would not be precluded at trial from offering evidence outside the four corners of the letters of credit. The trial court, after extensive briefing by the parties and a hearing, granted the County's motion to limit the admissibility of evidence to the letters of credit, documents and drafts presented thereunder, the demands on the letters of credit, and the Bank's refusals to honor the County's demands for payment.

The remaining issues were whether the County's demands conformed to the letters of credit or, if not, whether the Bank had waived nonconforming demands, and whether interest ought to be awarded. The parties agreed on a stipulated set of facts concerning these remaining issues. The Bank did, however, make an offer of proof as to the rejected affirmative defenses. The Bank would have attempted to prove that the subdivisions in question remained raw, undeveloped mountain property for which there was no viable market and that the County had neither constructed, made commitments to construct, nor planned to construct the roads or other improvements described in the subdivision improvements agreements secured by the letters of credit. These allegations were disputed by the County.

The trial court entered judgment against the Bank for the face amounts of the letters of credit plus accrued interest at the statutory rate from the date of the County's demands. Costs were

---

[53] Under section 4-5-112(1)(a), C.R.S. 1973, a bank called upon to honor drafts under a letter of credit may defer until the close of the third banking day following receipt of the documents.

awarded in favor of the County. The Bank's motion for new trial was denied, and the Bank appealed.

The court of appeals affirmed the judgment of the trial court ruling that standby letters of credit are governed by article 5 of the Uniform Commercial Code, section 4-5-101 et seq., C.R.S. 1973, and that an issuer must honor a draft or demand for payment which complies with the terms of the relevant credit regardless of whether the goods or documents conform to the underlying contract. The court of appeals affirmed the trial court's refusal to consider any evidence regarding the County's alleged windfall. The court of appeals also held that any defects in the form of the county's demands were waived by the Bank.

I.

We first address the question whether the trial court properly limited the evidence to be presented at trial to the letters of credit, the demands by the County, and the Bank's replies to the demands. The Bank has continually asserted during each stage of this action that it ought to be permitted to show that the County will receive a windfall if the County is permitted to recover against the letters of credit. The Bank requested an opportunity to prove that the County will utilize the funds it would receive in a manner other than that specified in the road improvements agreements. Fundamentally, the Bank seeks to litigate the question of the completion of the purpose of the underlying performance agreements between Woodmoor and the County. This the Bank cannot do.

An overview of the history and law concerning letters of credit is useful in the consideration of this issue. The letter of credit arose to facilitate international commercial transactions involving the sale of goods. Today the commercial utility of the letter of credit in both international and domestic sale of goods transactions is unquestioned and closely guarded. In recent years, the use of the letter of credit has expanded to include guaranteeing or securing a bank's customer's promised performance to a third party in a variety of situations. See *First Empire Bank—New York v. Federal Deposit Insurance Corp.,* 572 F.2d 1361 (9th Cir.), cert. denied 439 U.S. 919, 99 S. Ct. 293, 58 L. Ed. 2d 265 (1978). This use is referred to as a standby letter of credit. Article five of the Uniform Commercial Code governs both traditional commercial letters of credit and standby letters of credit. *East Bank of Colorado Springs v. Dovenmuehle,* 196 Colo. 422, 589 P.2d 1361 (1978).

Three contractual relationships exist in a letter of credit transaction. Underlying the letter of credit transaction is the contract between the bank's customer and the beneficiary of the letter of credit, which consists of the business agreement between these parties. Then there is the contractual arrangement between the bank and its customer whereby the bank agrees to issue the letter of credit, and the customer agrees to repay the bank for the amounts paid under the letter of credit. See also section 4-5-114(3), C.R.S. 1973. Finally, there is the contractual relationship between the bank and the beneficiary of the letter of credit created by the letter of credit itself. The bank agrees to honor the beneficiary's drafts or demands for payment which conform to the terms of the letter of credit. See generally sections 4-5-103(1)(a) and 4-5-114(1), C.R.S. 1973; White and Summers, Uniform Commercial Code § 18-6(2d ed. 1980).

It is fundamental that the letter of credit is separate and independent from the underlying business transaction between the bank's customer and the beneficiary of the letter of credit. "The letter of credit is essentially a contract between the issuer and the beneficiary and is recognized by [article 5 of the Uniform Commercial Code] as independent of the underlying contract between the customer and the beneficiary . . . . In view of this independent nature of the letter of credit engagement the issuer is under a duty to honor the drafts for payment which in fact conform with the terms of the credit without reference to their compliance with the terms of the underlying contract." Section 4-5-114, Official Comment 1, C.R.S. 1973.

The independence of the letter of credit from the underlying contract has been called the key to the commercial vitality of the letter of credit. The bank must honor drafts or demands for payment under the letter of credit when the documents required by the letter of credit appear on their face to comply with the terms of the credit. Section 4-5-114(2), C.R.S. 1973. An exception to the bank's obligation to honor an apparently conforming draft or demand for payment, see *Foreign Venture Ltd. Partnership v. Chemical Bank,* 59 App. Div. 2d 352, 399 N.Y.S. 2d 114 (1977), is when a required document is, inter alia, forged or fraudulent, or there is fraud in the transaction. Section 4-5-114(2). The application of this narrow exception is discussed in detail later in this opinion.

As mentioned above, letters of credit have recently come to be used to secure a bank's customer's performance to a third party. When a letter of credit is used to secure a bank's customer's promised performance to a third party, in whatever capacity that might be, the letter of credit is referred to as a "guaranty letter of credit," see *East Bank of Colorado Springs v. Dovenmuehle, supra*; Verkuil, *Bank Solvency and Guaranty Letters of Credit, supra,* or a "standby letter of credit," Arnold & Bransilver, *The Standby Letter of Credit—The Controversy Continues, supra,* 12 C.F.R. § 7.1160(1980). Standby letters of credit are closely akin to a suretyship or guaranty contract. The bank promises to pay when there is a default on an obligation by the bank's customer. "If for any reason performance is not made, or is made defectively, the bank is liable without regard to the underlying rights of the contracting parties." Verkuil, *Bank Solvency and Guaranty Letters of Credit, supra* at 723.

While banks cannot, as a general rule, act as a surety or guarantor of another party's agreed performance, see generally Lord, *The No-Guaranty Rule and the Standby Letter of Credit Controversy,* 96 Banking L. J. 46 (1979), the legality of standby letters of credit has been uniformly recognized. *E.g., United Bank of Denver v. Quadrangle, Ltd.,* 42 Colo. App. 486, 596 P.2d 408 (1979). What distinguishes a standby letter of credit from a suretyship or guaranty contract is that the bank's liability rests upon the letter of credit contract rather than upon the underlying performance contract between the bank customer and the beneficiary of the letter of credit.

The utilization by banks of standby letters of credit is now wide-spread, although some commentators suggest that bankers may not appreciate the legal obligations imposed by the standby letter of credit. Where the bank issues a standby letter of credit, the bank naturally expects that the credit will not be drawn on in the normal course of events, *i.e.,* if the customer of the bank fulfills its agreed-upon performance, then the credit will not be drawn upon. This expectation of the bank must be compared to the bank's expectation with respect to a traditional letter of credit issued as a means of financing a sale of goods. In the latter situation, the bank expects that the credit will always be drawn upon. See Arnold & Bransilver, *The Standby Letter of Credit—The Controversy Continues, supra*; Note, *Letters of Credit: Injunction As A Remedy For Fraud In U.C.C. Section 5-114, supra.* It has been suggested that bankers may be lax in considering the credit of a customer with respect to issuing a standby letter of credit to secure the integrity of its customer to complete an agreed-upon performance, since it could be easily assumed by the bank that demand for payment would never be made. See Harfield, *The Increasing*

Domestic Use of the Letter of Credit, supra at 258-59. See also, Note, *Guaranty Letters of Credit: Problems and Possibilities,* 16 Ariz. L. Rev. 823, 832 (1974). One solution suggested by many commentators is that the issuing bank treat a standby letter of credit like an unsecured loan. Harfield, *Increasing Domestic Use of the Letter of Credit, supra*; Verkuil, *Bank Solvency and Guaranty Letters of Credit, supra*; Note: *Guaranty Letter of Credit: Problems and Possibilities, supra.* National Banks issuing standby letters of credit are subject to the lending limits of 12 U.S.C. § 84 (1976).[54]

We now turn to a discussion of the present case, and why the Bank cannot introduce evidence beyond that directly relating to its contract with the County. As discussed above, the letters of credit, and the Bank's obligations thereunder, are separate and independent from the underlying subdivision improvements agreements between Woodmoor and the County. The fact that the letters of credit issued by the Bank are standby letters of credit does not alter this general rule. The Bank is bound by its own contracts with the County.

Each of the letters of credit prepared and issued by the Bank in this case sets forth specifically the condition for payment, *i.e.,* that Woodmoor failed to make the improvements in conformance with the respective subdivision improvements agreements. Had the Bank desired additional conditions for payment, such as the actual completion of the road improvements prior to payment under the letters of credit, it could have incorporated such a condition in the letters of credit. To demand payment under the letters of credit, the County was only required to submit a "duly-signed statement by the [Commissioners] that improvements have not been made in compliance with [the] Subdivision Improvements Agreement[s]. . . ."

The Bank cannot litigate the performance of the underlying performance contracts. "Performance of the underlying contract is irrelevant to the Bank's obligations under the letter of credit." *West Virginia Housing Development Fund v. Sroka, supra* at 1114 (W.D. Pa. 1976). Likewise, the question of whether the beneficiary of the letter of credit has suffered any damage by the failure of the bank's customer to perform as agreed is of no concern.

The Bank argues that it is entitled to dishonor the County's drafts under section 4-5-114(2), C.R.S. 1973. This section provides:

> Unless otherwise agreed, when documents appear on their face to comply with the terms of a credit but a required document . . . . is forged or fraudulent or there is fraud in the transaction:
>
> (a) The issuer must honor the draft or demand for payment if honor is demanded by a negotiating bank or other holder of the draft or demand which has taken the draft or demand under the credit and under circumstances which would make it a holder in due course . . . . and in an appropriate case would make it a person to whom a document of title has been duly negotiated . . . . or a bona fide purchaser of a security . . . .; and
>
> (b) In all other cases, as against its customer, an issuer acting in good faith may honor the draft or demand for payment despite notification from the customer of fraud, forgery, or other defect not apparent on the face of the documents; but a court of appropriate jurisdiction may enjoin such honor.

[54] 12 U.S.C. § 84 (1976) provides that a national bank may not lend more than ten percent of its capital funds to any one customer. Traditionally, standby letters of credit did not fall within the aegis of this statute as they were considered contingent liabilities, and thus not reflected in a bank's balance sheet; however, the modern view, as codified in 12 C.F.R. § 7.1160 (1981), is that letters of credit are actual liabilities of a bank which must be included when calculating the marginal reserve required under this statutory provision. See Verkuil, *Bank Solvency and Guaranty Letters of Credit, supra.*

Under this section, the issuer of a letter of credit may in good faith honor a draft or demand for payment notwithstanding notice from its customer that documents are forged or fraudulent, or there is fraud in the transaction. The issuer may, however, be enjoined from honoring such drafts or demands for payment. Impliedly, the issuer may also refuse to honor such drafts or demands for payment when it has been notified by its customer of these defects. Section 4-5-114, Official Comment 2, C.R.S. 1973; *Siderius, Inc. v. Wallace, supra.*

In this case, the Bank has not argued, nor can it reasonably assert, that the documents presented by the County are forged or fraudulent. The Bank has not challenged the authenticity of the drafts and demands for payment by the County or the truthfulness of the statements that the requirements of the underlying subdivision improvements agreements have not been fulfilled. The Bank does assert, however, that there has been fraud in the transaction on the basis that the funds the County would receive would be utilized by the County other than to pay for the completion of the road improvements.

Fundamentally, "fraud in the transaction," as referred to in section 4-5-114(2), must stem from conduct by the beneficiary of the letter of credit as against the customer of the bank. See generally White and Summers, Uniform Commercial Code § 18-16 (2d ed. 1980). It must be of such an egregious nature as to vitiate the entire underlying transaction so that the legitimate purposes of the independence of the bank's obligation would no longer be served. "It is generally thought to include an element of intentional misrepresentation in order to profit from another . . . ." *West Virginia Housing Development Fund v. Sroka, supra.* This fraud is manifested in the documents themselves, and the statements therein, presented under the letter of credit. *Dynamics Corporation of America v. Citizens & Southern National Bank, supra; Shaffer v. Brooklyn Park Garden Apartments,* 311 Minn. 452, 250 N.W. 2d 172 (1977). One court has gone so far as to say that only some defect in these documents would justify a bank's dishonor. *O'Grady v. First Union National Bank of North Carolina,* 296 N.C. 212, 250 S.E. 2d 587 (1978).

In this case, the Bank has not asserted that there is fraud in the transaction between Woodmoor and the County, nor can it reasonably make such an argument. No facts have been pled to establish fraud which vitiated the entire agreement between the County and Woodmoor. No fraud has been asserted by the Bank's offer of proof which would entitle it to dishonor the County's drafts and demands for payment. See *West Virginia Housing Development Fund v. Sroka, supra; Mid-States Mortgage v. National Bank of Southfield, supra.* Thus, the trial court properly granted the County's motion in limine excluding all evidence beyond the four corners of the letters of credit, the demands thereunder, and the Bank's replies.

II.

We next consider whether the drafts and demands for payment by the County complied with the terms of the letters of credit, or if not, whether the Bank waived any nonconforming demands.

The Bank was obligated to examine the documents "with care so as to ascertain that on their face they appear[ed] to comply with the terms of the credit . . . ." Section 4-5-109(2), C.R.S. 1973. To maintain the commercial vitality of the letter of credit device, strict compliance with the terms of the letter of credit is required. If the drafts or demands for payment on their face complied with the terms of the letters of credit, the Bank was obligated to honor the drafts. Section 4-5-114(1), C.R.S. 1973. See also, *e.g.,* Annot., 35 A.L.R. 3d 1404 (1971).

In this case, the Bank promised to pay the County, for the account of Woodmoor, upon the County's presentation of fifteen-day sight drafts accompanied by a "duly-signed statement by the Routt County Board of Commissioners that improvements have not been made in compliance with [the respective Subdivision Improvements Agreements.]" In order to determine whether the County's drafts and demands for payment complied with the terms of the letters of credit, we must analyze the drafts on the first two letters of credit numbers 1156 and 1157 separately from the drafts on the third letter of credit number 1168.

Letters of credit No. 1156 and 1157 bore expiry dates of December 31, 1975. On that date, the County presented two demand drafts to the Bank in the full face amounts of the respective letters of credit. The drafts were accompanied by, as required by the letters of credit, a resolution of the Commissioners stating that Woodmoor failed to comply with the terms of the underlying subdivision improvements agreements and demanded payment under the terms of the respective letters of credit. On January 5, 1976, within three banking days of the demand, the Bank dishonored the drafts. The Bank did not object to the County's presentation of demand drafts as opposed to fifteen-day sight drafts.

A demand draft is not the same as a fifteen-day sight draft. A fifteen-day sight draft provides the issuer an additional period of time not conferred by a demand instrument to examine the draft and determine whether the conditions of payment, if any, have been fulfilled. Thus, the County's demand did not strictly conform to the terms of the letters of credit. Accord, *Bounty Trading Corp. v. S.E.K. Sportswear, Ltd., supra.*

The Bank did not, however, object to the form of the demands by the County. As a general rule, when an issuer of a letter of credit formally places its refusal to pay upon specified grounds, it is held to have waived all other grounds for dishonor. *Barclays Bank D.C.O. v. Mercantile National Bank, supra; East Bank of Colorado Springs v. Dovenmuehle, supra; Siderius, Inc. v. Wallace Co., supra.* "However, the application of the rule confining an issuer to its stated grounds for dishonor is limited to situations where the statements have misled the beneficiary who could have cured the defect but relied on the stated grounds to its injury . . . ." *Siderius, Inc. v. Wallace Co., supra* at 862.

In this case, the County did not present its drafts and demands for payment on the letters of credit until the final day of their vitality. The Bank then had three banking days before it was required to honor or dishonor the drafts and demands for payment. Within this period the Bank dishonored the drafts. The County could not have cured the defect since the presentment would have then been untimely. Consequently, the County did not detrimentally rely on the Bank's failure to state as one ground for its dishonor of the drafts that the County presented demand instruments rather than fifteen-day sight drafts. Accordingly, since the County could not have cured its nonconforming demand, we therefore hold that the Bank did not waive its objections to the County's nonconforming demands on letter of credit numbers 1156 and 1157.[55] Therefore, the Bank is not liable on these letters of credit.

---

[55] The County also asserts that long before the expiry dates of the letters of credit the Bank notified the County that the Bank would only honor drafts for amounts the County had actually expended on improvements before the expiry dates of the letters of credit. The County argues that the Bank anticipatorily repudiated its obligations under the letters of credit and consequently waived subsequent nonconforming demands by the County.

The sole substantiation in the record before us for this allegation of fact is contained in the Defendant's [Bank's] response to Plaintiff's [County's] request for production of documents and interrogatories, signed by one vice president of the Bank:

> Interrogatory # 3. Please state in what way you believe that the plaintiff has waived any rights it may have to assert any claim against you under letters of credit numbered 1156 and/or 1157.

Letter of credit number 1168 bore an expiry date of December 31, 1976. On December 22, 1976, the County presented the Bank with a demand draft on this letter of credit accompanied by a resolution by the Commissioners that Woodmoor had not fulfilled its obligations on the underlying subdivision improvements agreement. The Bank timely dishonored this draft on the basis, inter alia, that the County submitted a demand draft rather than a fifteen-day sight draft. The County cured this defect by presenting a fifteen-day sight draft to the Bank on December 29, 1976. This fifteen-day sight draft was not accompanied by the required resolution of the Commissioners. On December 31, 1976, the Bank sent the County a letter notifying the County that this draft had also been dishonored.

The same rules of strict compliance discussed above must be applied to determine whether the County's drafts and demands for payment complied with the terms of letter of credit number 1168. The County's first draft on letter of credit number 1168 was nonconforming since it was submitted as a demand instrument rather than a fifteen-day sight draft. On December 29, 1976, the County presented a fifteen-day sight draft which cured this defect. While the County failed to attach the required statement and demand for payment by the Commissioners with the fifteen-day sight draft, it was not required to do so. The County was merely curing a prior nonconforming demand. The two demands, taken together, consequently strictly complied with the terms of the letter of credit. The Bank therefore wrongfully dishonored this draft and demand for payment.

We reverse the judgment as to letters of credit No. 1156 and No. 1157, and affirm the judgment as to letter of credit No. 1168. This case is returned to the court of appeals for remand to the trial court for the entry of judgment in consonance with the views expressed in this opinion.

Justice Lohr concurring in part and dissenting in part.

I concur in part I of the majority opinion and in that portion of part II which treats letter of credit number 1168 and affirms the court of appeals' opinion upholding the district court's judgment against the Colorado National Bank of Denver (Bank) on that letter of credit. I dissent to that portion of Part II which reverses the judgment against the Bank on letters of credit numbers 1156 and 1157. I would affirm the decision of the court of appeals in its entirety.

The majority finds that the Bank justifiably dishonored letters of credit numbers 1156 and 1157 because the draft presented by Routt County (County) did not strictly comply with the terms of the credit. See section 4-5-114(1), C.R.S. 1973. Because I conclude that this was an improper application of the rule of strict compliance to a non-material term of the letters of credit, I respectfully dissent.

As the majority indicates, the prevailing rule requires strict compliance with the terms of a letter of credit. But the rule of strict compliance is not dictated by the language of the controlling

---

> Answer: . . . . The Bank notified the Board well in advance of the expiry dates of the letters of credit of the Bank's position that it should make payments under the letters of credit only prior to their expiry date and only as the Board incurred or committed to incur expenses for the particular improvements called for in the Subdivision Improvements Agreements . . . .

No other portion of the record substantiates or clarifies this statement. Nor do the parties' stipulated facts refer to this question of fact. We cannot conclude from this answer to the County's interrogatories that the Bank anticipatorily repudiated its obligation to honor drafts under letter of credit numbers 1156 and 1157. The Bank merely indicated that it should not be required to honor drafts unless the County had incurred or committed to incur expenses to complete the road improvements not that it would not honor the County's drafts unless this condition had been met. "Anticipatory repudiation centers upon an overt communication of intention or an action which renders performance impossible or demonstrates a clear determination not to continue with performance." Section 4-2-610, Comment 1, C.R.S. 1973.

statute, Uniform Commercial Code -Letters of Credit, sections 4-5-101 to 117, C.R.S. 1973 (1980 Supp.). Section 4-5-114(1), C.R.S. 1973, merely requires that the issuer honor a draft or demand for payment "which complies with the terms of the relevant [letter of] credit . . . ." Specifically, the code does not state whether strict compliance is necessary or "substantial performance" is sufficient. It was apparently a conscious decision of the drafters of the uniform act which is the source of our statute to leave this question unresolved. See J. White and R. Summers, Uniform Commercial Code, section 18-6at 729 (1980).

The prevailing view stated by the majority not only lacks statutory mandate but also has not been uniformly accepted. A minority position has been adopted by a number of courts, rejecting a formalistic application of the rule of strict compliance where this would not be consistent with the policies underlying the use of letters of credit. As stated by Judge Coffin in *Banco Espanol de Credito v. State Street Bank and Trust Co.,* 385 F.2d 230 (1st Cir. 1967), cert. denied 390 U.S. 1013, 88 S. Ct. 1263, 20 L. Ed. 2d 163 (1968):

> But we note some leaven in the loaf of strict construction. Not only does haec verba not control absolutely [citation omitted], but some courts now cast their eyes on a wider scene than a single document. We are mindful, also, of the admonition of several legal scholars that the integrity of international transactions (*i.e.,* rigid adherence to material matters) must somehow strike a balance with the requirement of their fluidity (*i.e.,* a reasonable flexibility as to ancillary matters) if the objective of increased dealings to the mutual satisfaction to all interested parties is to be enhanced. See *e.g.,* Mentschicoff, *How to Handle Letters of Credit,* 19 Bus. Lawyer 107, 111 (1963). *Banco Espanol de Credito v. State Street Bank and Trust Co., supra,* at 234.

Other cases have also recognized that non-material variations from the terms of a letter of credit do not justify the issuer in dishonoring a draft or demand for payment.

In the instant case, the majority found that the County's submission of a demand draft rather than the fifteen-day sight draft required by the letters of credit rendered the presentment defective.[56] In my opinion this is the sort of non-material, technical condition which should properly be treated under a standard of substantial rather than strict compliance.[57]

There is no danger that the Bank would be misled by the use of the demand draft, nor did the use of that draft place the Bank at risk by providing a basis for its customer Woodmoor to refuse reimbursement. In this context, the Bank's contention is no more than a technical defense which frustrates equity without furthering the policies and purposes underlying the use of letters of credit.

I am not unmindful of the need for certainty in letter of credit transactions, where a bank's function is designed to be primarily ministerial, see, *e.g., Far Eastern Textile, Ltd. v. City National Bank and Trust,* 430 F. Supp. 193, 196, 197 (E.D. Ohio 1977). However, I believe that upholding the County's claim in this case would require only a limited but beneficial exception to the general rule of strict compliance. The alleged nonconformance did not relate to the underlying transaction. Rather, the nonconformity concerned only a provision designed to assure the Bank adequate time to review and consider the adequacy of the demand for payment. Thus, I would hold only that

---

[56] Although I conclude that substitution of a demand draft for the fifteen-day sight draft required by the letters of credit does not excuse the Bank from all liability, this is not to suggest that the County could demand immediate payment. As noted *infra,* the Bank had a right to insist upon the fifteen-day review period, and the County could not unilaterally impair that right.

[57] It is of interest on the issue of materiality that the Bank made no mention of the fact that the drafts were demand drafts in its letter of January 5, 1976, dishonoring the drafts and stating its reasons.

non-material defects, independent of any requirements relating to the underlying transaction, do not excuse the duty to honor a letter of credit.[58] This would avoid placing the issuer in the undesirable position of choosing between a suit by the beneficiary of a letter of credit and the risk of refusal of reimbursement by the customer who obtained that letter, while simultaneously avoiding the assertion of a technical defense to defeat payment where that payment would not place the issuer at risk.

Of course, the Bank was free in this case to inform the County that the demand draft was improper and that payment would be made as if a fifteen-day sight draft had been submitted. The County could not unilaterally deprive the Bank of the fifteen-day period for payment prescribed by the letter of credit. But the Bank should not be able to elevate a minor nonconformance into a total exoneration from liability. Neither existing law nor sound policy requires this result.

I would affirm the decision of the court of appeals.

Justice Rovira joins in this opinion.

FDIC v. PHILADELPHIA GEAR CORP.

Supreme Court of the United States
476 U.S. 426, 106 S. Ct. 1931, 90 L. Ed. 2d 428 (1986)

JUSTICE O'CONNOR delivered the opinion of the Court.

We granted certiorari to consider whether a standby letter of credit backed by a contingent promissory note is insured as a "deposit" under the federal deposit insurance program. We hold that, in light of the longstanding interpretation of petitioner Federal Deposit Insurance Corporation (FDIC) that such a letter does not create a deposit and, in light of the fact that such a letter does not entrust any noncontingent assets to the bank, a standby letter of credit backed by a contingent promissory note does not give rise to an insured deposit.

I

Orion Manufacturing Corporation (Orion) was, at the time of the relevant transactions, a customer of respondent Philadelphia Gear Corporation (Philadelphia Gear). On Orion's application, the Penn Square Bank, N.A. (Penn Square) issued a letter of credit for the benefit of Philadelphia Gear in the amount of $145,200. The letter of credit provided that a draft drawn

[58] That holding would not be inconsistent with those cases requiring strict compliance with letter of credit requirements necessary to ensure that a substantive condition precedent to payment has been met. See, *e.g., Courtaulds North America, Inc. v. North Carolina Nat. Bank, supra* (packing lists which were attached to invoices accompanying draft by beneficiary and which stated that the shipment was 100% acrylic yarn did not satisfy requirement that invoices specify shipment was 100% acrylic yarn); *Far Eastern Textile, Ltd. v. City National Bank and Trust, supra* (requirement that principal sign purchase orders evidencing underlying transaction not satisfied by the signature of an agent on those orders). When the disputed condition relates to the underlying transaction, a standard of strict compliance may well be preferable. Thus, if the nonconformance had related to the requirement that the County certify Woodmoor's failure to construct the agreed-upon improvements a different question would be presented. In this respect, it is not necessary to apply the rule of substantial compliance as broadly as some courts have. See, *e.g., U.S. Industries, Inc. v. Second New Haven Bank, supra* (failure to certify expressly that payment for goods had been demanded as required by letter of credit excused where other documents satisfied the purpose of this requirement).

upon the letter of credit would be honored by Penn Square only if accompanied by Philadelphia Gear's "signed statement that [it had] invoiced Orion Manufacturing Corporation and that said invoices have remained unpaid for at least fifteen (15) days." App. 25. Because the letter of credit was intended to provide payment to the seller only if the buyer of the invoiced goods failed to make payment, the letter of credit was what is commonly referred to as a "standby" or "guaranty" letter of credit. See, *e. g.*, 12 CFR § 337.2(a), and n. 1 (1985) (defining standby letters of credit and mentioning that they may " 'guaranty' payment of a money obligation"). A conventional "commercial" letter of credit, in contrast, is one in which the seller obtains payment from the issuing bank without looking to the buyer for payment even in the first instance. See *ibid.* (distinguishing standby letters of credit from commercial letters of credit). See also Verkuil, *Bank Solvency and Guaranty Letters of Credit,* 25 Stan. L. Rev. 716, 717-724 (1973); Arnold & Bransilver, *The Standby Letter of Credit — The Controversy Continues,* 10 U. C. C. L. J. 272, 277-279 (Spring 1978).

On the same day that Penn Square issued the standby letter of credit, Orion executed an unsecured promissory note for $145,200 in favor of Penn Square. App. 27. The purpose of the note was listed as "Back up Letter of Credit." *Ibid.* Although the face of the note did not so indicate, both Orion and Penn Square understood that nothing would be considered due on the note, and no interest charged by Penn Square, unless Philadelphia Gear presented drafts on the standby letter of credit after nonpayment by Orion. 751 F.2d 1131, 1134 (CA10 1984). See also Tr. of Oral Arg. 32.

On July 5, 1982, Penn Square was declared insolvent. Petitioner FDIC was appointed its receiver. Shortly thereafter, Philadelphia Gear presented drafts on the standby letter of credit for payment of over $700,000 for goods delivered before Penn Square's insolvency. The FDIC returned the drafts unpaid. 751 F.2d., at 1133-1134.

Philadelphia Gear sued the FDIC in the Western District of Oklahoma. Philadelphia Gear alleged that the standby letter of credit was an insured deposit under the definition of "deposit" set forth at 12 U. S. C. § 1813(l)(1), and that Philadelphia Gear was therefore entitled to $100,000 in deposit insurance from the FDIC. See 12 U. S. C. § 1821(a)(1) (setting forth $100,000 as the maximum amount generally insured by the FDIC for any single depositor at a given bank). In apparent hopes of obtaining additional funds from the FDIC in the latter's capacity as receiver rather than as insurer, respondent also alleged that terms of the standby letter of credit allowing repeated reinstatements of the credit made the letter's total value more than $145,200.

The District Court held that the total value of the standby letter of credit was $145,200, App. B to Pet. for Cert. 20a, 28a-30a; that the letter was an insured deposit on which the FDIC was liable for $100,000 in deposit insurance, *id.*, at 37a-43a; and that Philadelphia Gear was entitled to prejudgment interest on that $100,000, *id.*, at 43a. The FDIC appealed from the District Court's ruling that the standby letter of credit backed by a contingent promissory note constituted a "deposit" for purposes of 12 U. S. C. § 1813(l)(1) and its ruling that Philadelphia Gear was entitled to an award of prejudgment interest. Philadelphia Gear cross-appealed from the District Court's ruling on the total value of the letter of credit.

The Court of Appeals for the Tenth Circuit reversed the District Court's award of prejudgment interest, 751 F.2d, at 1138-1139, but otherwise affirmed the District Court's decision. As to the definition of "deposit," the Court of Appeals held that a standby letter of credit backed by a promissory note fell within the terms of 12 U. S. C. § 1813(l)(1)'s definition of "deposit," and was therefore insured. Id., at 1134-1138. We granted the FDIC's petition for certiorari on this aspect of the Court of Appeals' ruling. 474 U.S. 918 (1985). We now reverse.

II

Title 12 U. S. C. § 1813(l)(1) provides:

The term "deposit" means —

(1) the unpaid balance of money or its equivalent received or held by a bank in the usual course of business and for which it has given or is obligated to give credit, either conditionally or unconditionally, to a commercial . . .account, or which is evidenced by . . .a letter of credit or a traveler's check on which the bank is primarily liable: Provided, That, without limiting the generality of the term "money or its equivalent," any such account or instrument must be regarded as evidencing the receipt of the equivalent of money when credited or issued in exchange for checks or drafts or for a promissory note upon which the person obtaining any such credit or instrument is primarily or secondarily liable . . . .

Philadelphia Gear successfully argued before the Court of Appeals that the standby letter of credit backed by a contingent promissory note constituted a "deposit" under 12 U. S. C. § 1813(l)(1) because that letter was one on which the bank was primarily liable, and evidenced the receipt by the bank of "money or its equivalent" in the form of a promissory note upon which the person obtaining the credit was primarily or secondarily liable. The FDIC does not here dispute that the bank was primarily liable on the letter of credit. Brief for Petitioner 7, n. 7. Nor does the FDIC contest the fact that the backup note executed by Orion is, at least in some sense, a "promissory note." See Tr. of Oral Arg. 7 (remarks of Mr. Rothfeld, representing the FDIC) ("It was labeled a note. It can be termed a note"). The FDIC argues rather that it has consistently interpreted § 1813(l)(1) not to include standby letters of credit backed only by a contingent promissory note because such a note represents no hard assets and thus does not constitute "money or its equivalent." Because the alleged "deposit" consists only of a contingent liability, asserts the FDIC, a standby letter of credit backed by a contingent promissory note does not give rise to a "deposit" that Congress intended the FDIC to insure. Under this theory, while the note here may have been labeled a promissory note on its face and may have been a promissory note under state law, it was not a promissory note for purposes of the federal law set forth in 12 U. S. C. § 1813(l)(1).

The Court of Appeals quite properly looked first to the language of the statute. Finding the language of the proviso in § 1813(l)(1) sufficiently plain, the Court of Appeals looked no further. But as the FDIC points out, the terms "letter of credit" and "promissory note" as used in the statute have a federal definition, and the FDIC has developed and interpreted those definitions for many years within the framework of the complex statutory scheme that the FDIC administers. The FDIC's interpretation of whether a standby letter of credit backed by a contingent promissory note constitutes a "deposit" is consistent with Congress' desire to protect the hard earnings of individuals by providing for federal deposit insurance. Since the creation of the FDIC, Congress has expressed no dissatisfaction with the FDIC's interpretation of "deposit"; indeed, Congress in 1960 adopted the FDIC's regulatory definition as the statutory language. When we weigh all these factors together, we are constrained to conclude that the term "deposit" does not include a standby letter of credit backed by a contingent promissory note.

A

Justice Holmes stated that, as to discerning the constitutionality of a federal estate tax, "a page of history is worth a volume of logic." *New York Trust Co. v. Eisner,* 256 U.S. 345, 349 (1921). Although the genesis of the Federal Deposit Insurance Act may not be quite so powerful a substitute for legal analysis, that history is worthy of at least a page of recounting for the light it sheds on Congress' purpose in passing the Act. Cf. *Watt v. Alaska*, 451 U.S. 259, 266 (1981) ("The circumstances of the enactment of particular legislation may persuade a court that Congress did not intend words of common meaning to have their literal effect").

When Congress created the FDIC, the Nation was in the throes of an extraordinary financial crisis. See generally F. Allen, Since Yesterday: The Nineteen-Thirties in America 98-121 (1940); A. Schlesinger, The Crisis of the Old Order 474-482 (1957). More than one-third of the banks in the United States open in 1929 had shut their doors just four years later. Bureau of the Census, Historical Statistics of the United States: Colonial Times to 1970, pt. 2, pp. 1019, 1038 (1976). In response to this financial crisis, President Roosevelt declared a national banking holiday effective the first business day after he took office. 48 Stat. 1689. Congress in turn responded with extensive legislation on banking, including the laws that gave the FDIC its existence.

Congress' purpose in creating the FDIC was clear. Faced with virtual panic, Congress attempted to safeguard the hard earnings of individuals against the possibility that bank failures would deprive them of their savings. Congress passed the 1933 provisions "[in] order to provide against a repetition of the present painful experience in which a vast sum of assets and purchasing power is 'tied up.' " S. Rep. No. 77, 73d Cong., 1st Sess., 12 (1933). The focus of Congress was therefore upon ensuring that a deposit of "hard earnings" entrusted by individuals to a bank would not lead to a tangible loss in the event of a bank failure. As the chairman of the relevant Committee in the House of Representatives explained on the floor:

> [The purpose of this legislation is to protect the people of the United States in the right to have banks in which their deposits will be safe. They have a right to expect of Congress the establishment and maintenance of a system of banks in the United States where citizens may place their hard earnings with reasonable expectation of being able to get them out again upon demand. . . .
>
> . . . .
>
> [The purpose of the bill is to ensure that] the community is saved from the shock of a bank failure, and every citizen has been given an opportunity to withdraw his deposits. . . .
>
> . . . .
>
> The public . . .demand of you and me that we provide a banking system worthy of this great Nation and banks in which citizens may place the fruits of their toil and know that a deposit slip in return for their hard earnings will be as safe as a Government bond.

77 Cong. Rec. 3837, 3838, 3840 (1933) (remarks of Rep. Steagall). See also *id.*, at 3913 (remarks of Rep. Keller) ("[We must make] it absolutely certain that . . .any and every man, woman, or child who puts a dollar in any bank can absolutely know that he will under no circumstances lose a single penny of it"); *id.*, at 3924 (remarks of Rep. Green) ("It is time that we pass a law so secure that when a man puts his money in a bank he will know for sure that when he comes back it will be there"). To prevent bank failure that resulted in the tangible loss of hard assets was therefore the focus of Congress' effort in creating deposit insurance.

Despite the fact Congress revisited the deposit insurance statute in 1935, 1950, and 1960, these comments remain the best indication of Congress' underlying purpose in creating deposit insurance. The Reports on the 1935 amendments presented the definition of "deposit" without any specific comment. The floor debates centered around changes in the Federal Reserve System made in the same bill, not on deposit insurance. Indeed, in light of the fact that instruments denominated "promissory notes" seem at the time to have been considered exclusively uncontingent, see, *e. g.*, 16 Fed. Res. Bull. 520 (1930) (Regulation A) (defining promissory note as an "unconditional promise to pay [a sum certain in dollars] at a fixed or determinable future time"); *Gilman v. Commissioner,* 53 F.2d 47, 50 (CA8 1931) ("The form of these [contingent] instruments referred to as 'promissory notes' is very unusual"), it is unlikely that Congress would have had occasion to refer expressly to contingent notes such as the one before us here even if Congress had turned its attention to the definition of "deposit" when it first enacted the provision treating "money or its equivalent."

The legislative history of the 1950 amendments is similarly unhelpful, as one would expect given that the relevant provisions were reenacted but unchanged. The Committee Reports on the 1960 amendments likewise give no indication that the amendments' phrasing was meant to effect any fundamental changes in the definition of deposit; those Reports state only that the changes are intended to bring into harmony the definitions of "deposit" used for purposes of deposit insurance with those used in reports of condition, and that the FDIC's rules and regulations are to be incorporated into the new definition.

Congress' focus in providing for a system of deposit insurance — a system that has been continued to the present without modification to the basic definition of deposits that are "money or its equivalent" — was clearly a focus upon safeguarding the assets and "hard earnings" that businesses and individuals have entrusted to banks. Congress wanted to ensure that someone who put tangible assets into a bank could always get those assets back. The purpose behind the insurance of deposits in general, and especially in the section defining deposits as "money or its equivalent," therefore, is the protection of assets and hard earnings entrusted to a bank.

This purpose is not furthered by extending deposit insurance to cover a standby letter of credit backed by a contingent promissory note, which involves no such surrender of assets or hard earnings to the custody of the bank. Philadelphia Gear, which now seeks to collect deposit insurance, surrendered absolutely nothing to the bank. The letter of credit is for Philadelphia Gear's benefit, but the bank relied upon Orion to meet the obligations of the letter of credit and made no demands upon Philadelphia Gear. Nor, more importantly, did Orion surrender any assets unconditionally to the bank. The bank did not credit any account of Orion's in exchange for the promissory note, and did not treat its own assets as increased by its acceptance of the note. The bank could not have collected on the note from Orion unless Philadelphia Gear presented the unpaid invoices and a draft on the letter of credit. In the absence of a presentation by Philadelphia Gear of the unpaid invoices, the promissory note was a wholly contingent promise, and when Penn Square went into receivership, neither Orion nor Philadelphia Gear had lost anything except the ability to use Penn Square to reduce Philadelphia Gear's risk that Philadelphia Gear would go unpaid for a delivery of goods to Orion.

B

Congress' actions with respect to the particular definition of "deposit" that it has chosen in order to effect its general purpose likewise lead us to believe that a standby letter of credit backed by a contingent promissory note is not an insurable "deposit." In 1933, Congress amended the Federal Reserve Act to authorize the creation of the FDIC and charged it "to insure . . .the deposits of all banks which are entitled to the benefits of [FDIC] insurance." § 8, Banking Act of 1933, ch. 89, 48Stat. 168. Congress did not define the term "deposit," however, until the Banking Act of 1935, in which it stated:

"The term 'deposit' means the unpaid balance of money or its equivalent received by a bank in the usual course of business and for which it has given or is obligated to give credit to a commercial, checking, savings, time or thrift account, or which is evidenced by its certificate of deposit, and trust funds held by such bank whether retained or deposited in any department of such bank or deposited in another bank, together with such other obligations of a bank as the board of directors [of the FDIC] shall find and shall prescribe by its regulations to be deposit liabilities by general usage . . . ." § 101, Banking Act of 1935, ch. 614, 49 Stat. 684, 685-686.

Less than two months after this statute was enacted, the FDIC promulgated a definition of "deposit," which provided in part that "letters of credit must be regarded as issued for the equivalent of money when issued in exchange for . . .promissory notes upon which the person procuring [such] instruments is primarily or secondarily liable." See 12 CFR § 301.1(d) (1939) (codifying Regulation I, rule 1, Oct. 1, 1935), revoked after incorporation into statutory law, 12 CFR 234 (Supp. 1962).

In 1950, Congress revisited the provisions specifically governing the FDIC in order to remove them from the Federal Reserve Act and place them into a separate Act. See Act of Sept. 21, 1950, ch. 967, 64 Stat. 874. The new provisions did not modify the definition of "deposit." In 1960, Congress expanded the statutory definition of "deposit" in several categories, and also incorporated the regulatory definition that the FDIC had employed since 1935 into the statute that remains in force today. See *supra*, at 430 (quoting current version of statute).

At no point did Congress disown its initial, clear desire to protect the hard assets of depositors. See *supra,* at 432-435. At no point did Congress criticize the FDIC's longstanding interpretation, see *infra*, at 438, that a standby letter of credit backed by a contingent promissory note is not a "deposit." In fact, Congress had reenacted the 1935 provisions in 1950 without changing the definition of "deposit" at all. Compare 49 Stat. 685-686 with 64 Stat. 874-875. When the statute giving rise to the longstanding interpretation has been reenacted without pertinent change, the "congressional failure to revise or repeal the agency's interpretation is persuasive evidence that the interpretation is the one intended by Congress." *NLRB v. Bell Aerospace,* 416 U.S. 267, 275 (1974). Indeed, the current statutory definition of "deposit," added by Congress in 1960, was expressly designed to incorporate the FDIC's rules and regulations on "deposits." As Committees of both Houses of Congress explained the amendments: "The amended definition would include the present statutory definition of deposits, and the definition of deposits in the rules and regulations of the Federal Deposit Insurance Corporation, [along] with . . .changes [in sections other than what is now § 1813(l)(1)]." H. R. Rep. No. 1827, 86th Cong., 2d Sess., 5 (1960); S. Rep. No. 1821, 86th Cong., 2d Sess., 10 (1960) (same). Congress, therefore, has expressly incorporated into the statutory scheme the regulations that the FDIC devised to assist it in determining what constitutes a "deposit" within the statutory scheme. Under these circumstances, we must obviously give a great deal of deference to the FDIC's interpretation of what these regulations do and do not include within their definition of "deposit."

C

Although the FDIC does not argue that it has an express regulation excluding a standby letter of credit backed by a contingent promissory note from the definition of "deposit" in 12 U. S. C. § 1813(l)(1), that exclusion by the FDIC is nonetheless longstanding and consistent. At a meeting of FDIC and bank officials shortly after the FDIC's creation, a bank official asked whether a letter of credit issued by a charge against a customer's account was a deposit. The FDIC official replied:

> " 'If your letter of credit is issued by a charge against a depositor's account or for cash and the letter of credit is reflected on your books as a liability, you do have a deposit liability. If, on the other hand, you merely extend a line of credit to your customer, you will only show a contingent liability on your books. In that event no deposit liability has been created.' " Transcript as quoted in *FDIC v. Irving Trust Co.,* 137 F.Supp. 145, 161 (SDNY 1955).

Because Penn Square apparently never reflected the letter of credit here as a noncontingent liability, and because the interwoven financial instruments at issue here can be viewed most accurately as the extension of a line of credit by Penn Square to Orion, this transcript lends support to the FDIC's contention that its longstanding policy has been to exclude standby letters of credit backed by contingent promissory notes from 12 U. S. C. § 1813(l)(1)'s definition of "deposit."

The FDIC's contemporaneous understanding that standby letters of credit backed by contingent promissory notes do not generate a "deposit" for purposes of 12 U. S. C. § 1813(l)(1) has been fortified by its behavior over the following decades. The FDIC has asserted repeatedly that it has never charged deposit insurance premiums on standby letters of credit backed by contingent promissory notes, and Philadelphia Gear does not contest that assertion. See Tr. of Oral Arg. 42. Congress requires the FDIC to assess contributions to its insurance fund at a fixed percentage of a bank's "deposits" under 12 U. S. C. § 1813(l)(1). See 12 U. S. C. §§ 1817(a)(4), (b)(1), (b)(4)(A). By the time that this suit — the first challenge to the FDIC's treatment of standby letters of credit backed by contingent promissory notes — was brought, almost $100 billion in standby letters of credit was outstanding. See Board of Governors of the Federal Reserve System, Annual Statistical Digest 71 (1983); FDIC, 1983 Statistics on Banking (Table 110F). The FDIC's failure to levy premiums on standby letters of credit backed by contingent promissory notes therefore clearly demonstrates that the FDIC has never considered such letters to reflect deposits.

Although the FDIC's interpretation of the relevant statute has not been reduced to a specific regulation, we conclude nevertheless that the FDIC's practice and belief that a standby letter of credit backed by a contingent promissory note does not create a "deposit" within the meaning of 12 U.S.C. § 1813(l)(1) are entitled in the circumstances of this case to the "considerable weight [that] should be accorded to an executive department's construction of a statutory scheme it is entrusted to administer." *Chevron U.S.A. Inc. v. Natural Resources Defense Council, Inc.,* 467 U.S. 837, 844 (1984). As we have stated above, the FDIC's interpretation here of a statutory definition adopted wholesale from the FDIC's own regulation is consistent with congressional purpose, and may certainly stand.

III

Philadelphia Gear essentially seeks to have the FDIC guarantee the contingent credit extended to Orion, not assets entrusted to the bank by Philadelphia Gear or by Orion on Philadelphia Gear's behalf. With a standard "commercial" letter of credit, Orion would typically have unconditionally entrusted Penn Square with funds before Penn Square would have written the letter of credit, and thus Orion would have lost something if Penn Square became unable to honor its obligations. As the FDIC concedes, deposit insurance extends to such a letter of credit backed by an uncontingent promissory note. See Tr. of Oral Arg. 8 (statement of Mr. Rothfeld, representing the FDIC) ("If this note were a fully uncontingent negotiable note that were not limited by any side agreements, it would be a note backing a letter of credit within the meaning of the statute"). See also *id.,* at 17-18. But here, with a standby letter of credit backed by a contingent promissory note, Penn Square was not in possession of any of Orion's or Philadelphia Gear's assets when it went into receivership. Nothing was ventured, and therefore no insurable deposit was lost. We believe that, whatever the relevant State's definition of "letter of credit" or "promissory note," Congress did not by using those phrases in 12 U. S. C. § 1813(l)(1) intend to protect with deposit insurance a standby letter of credit backed only by a contingent promissory note. We thus hold that such an arrangement does not give rise to a "deposit" under 12 U. S. C. § 1813(l)(1).

Accordingly, the judgment of the court below is reversed, and the case is remanded for further proceedings consistent with this opinion.

Reversed and remanded.

JUSTICE MARSHALL, with whom JUSTICE BLACKMUN and JUSTICE REHNQUIST join, dissenting.

There is considerable common sense backing the Court's opinion. The standby letter of credit in this case differs considerably from the savings and checking accounts that come most readily to mind when one speaks of an insured deposit. Nevertheless, to reach this common-sense result, the Court must read qualifications into the statute that do not appear there. We recently recognized that even when the ingenuity of businessmen creates transactions and corporate forms that were perhaps not contemplated by Congress, the courts must enforce the statutes that Congress has enacted. See *Board of Governors, FRS v. Dimension Financial Corp.,* 474 U.S. 361, 373-375 (1986). Congress unmistakably provided that letters of credit backed by promissory notes constitute "deposits" for purposes of the federal deposit insurance program, and the Court's attempt to draw distinctions between different types of letters of credit transactions forces it to ignore both the statute and some settled principles of commercial law. Here, as in *Dimension,* the inflexibility of the statute as applied to modern financial transactions is a matter for Congress, not the FDIC or this Court, to remedy.

It cannot be doubted that the standby letter of credit in this case meets the literal definition of a "deposit" contained in 12 U. S. C. § 1813(l)(1). It is "a letter of credit . . .on which the bank is primarily liable . . .issued in exchange for . . .a promissory note upon which [Orion] is primarily or secondarily liable." The Court, however, holds that the note in this case, whether or not it is a promissory note under the Uniform Commercial Code (UCC) and Oklahoma law, is not a promissory note for purposes of the Federal Deposit Insurance Act. We should assume, absent convincing evidence to the contrary, that Congress intended for the term "promissory note" to derive its meaning from the ordinary sources of commercial law. I believe that there is no such evidence in this case.

The Court justifies its restrictive reading of the term "promissory note" in large part by arguing that Congress would not have wanted to include in that term any obligation that was not the present equivalent of money. The keystone of the FDIC's arguments, and of the Court's decision, is that Orion did not entrust "money or its equivalent" to the bank. The note in this case, however, was the equivalent of money, and the Court's reading of Congress' intent is therefore largely irrelevant.

FDIC concedes, as it must, that Congress has determined that a promissory note generally constitutes money or its equivalent. Moreover, that statutory definition comports with economic reality. Promissory notes typically are negotiable instruments and therefore readily convertible into cash. The FDIC argues, and the Court holds, that the promissory note in this case is "contingent" and therefore not the equivalent of money. However, while the FDIC argues strenuously that Orion's note is not a promissory note in the usual sense of the word, one could more plausibly state that it is not a "contingent" obligation in the usual sense of that word. On its face the note is an unconditional obligation of Orion to pay the holder $145,200 plus accrued interest on August 1, 1982. It sets out no conditions that would affect the negotiability of the note, and therefore is fully negotiable for purposes of the UCC, U.C.C.§ 3-104(1)(1977); Okla. Stat., Tit. 12A, § 3-104(1)(1981).

The Court therefore misses the point when it states that at the time of the original banking Acts, the term "promissory note" was not understood to include a contingent obligation. Ante, at 434. The note at issue in this case is an unconditional promise to pay, and satisfies all the requisites of a negotiable promissory note, either under the UCC or the common law as it existed in the 1930's. The only contingencies attached to Orion's obligation arise out of a separate contract. As to such contingencies, the law was well settled long before 1930:

> "[In] order to make a note invalid as a promissory note, the contingency to avoid it must be apparent, either upon the face of the note, or upon some contemporaneous written memorandum on the same paper; for, if the memorandum is not contemporaneous, or if it be merely verbal in each case, whatever may be its effect as a matter of defence between the original parties, it is not deemed to be a part of the instrument, and does not affect, much less invalidate, its original character." J. Thorndike, Story on Promissory Notes 34 (7th ed. 1878) (footnotes omitted).[59]

It is far from a matter of semantics to state that while Orion and the bank may have an oral understanding concerning the bank's treatment of Orion's note, that note itself is unconditional and equivalent to money. The Court correctly observes that the bank would have breached its oral contract had it attempted to sue on the note; nevertheless, Orion would have had separately to plead and prove a breach of contract in that case, because parol evidence that the contract between the parties differed from the written instrument would have been inadmissible in the bank's action to collect the debt. See *American Perforating Co. v. Oklahoma State Bank*, 463 P. 2d 958, 962-963 (Okla. 1970). Similarly, should the note have found its way into the hands of a third party, Orion would have had no choice but to honor it, again being left with only the right to sue the bank for breach of the oral contract. Orion's entrustment of the note to the bank was not, therefore, completely risk free.

The risk taken on by Orion may not differ substantially from the risk assumed by one who hands over money to the bank to guarantee repayment of funds paid out on a letter of credit. The bank typically undertakes to put such cash collateral into a special account, where it never enters into the general assets of the bank. See U. C. C. § 5-117, comment (1977). Should the bank cease operations, the customer will enjoy a preference in bankruptcy, entitling it to receive

---

59 We would have a very different case if the conditions put upon Orion's obligation to the bank were reflected on the face of the note, as they were in *Allen v. FDIC*, 599 F. Supp. 104 (E.D. Tenn. 1984), appeal pending, No. 85-5003 (CA6), a case raising the same issue as the present one. Because such a note is not negotiable, it is much more plausible to argue that Congress would not have considered it "money or its equivalent." The note in this case, however, is in no sense a contingent note.

its money back before general unsecured creditors of the bank are paid. U. C. C. § 5-117; Okla. Stat., Tit. 12A, § 5-117(1981). Like Orion, then, that hypothetical customer has little to fear absent misconduct by the bank or a third party. If the federal deposit insurance program should not protect Philadelphia Gear, therefore, it probably should not protect any holder of a letter of credit, whether commercial, standby, funded, or unfunded.[60] That, however, is clearly a matter for Congress to determine.

While the Court purports to examine what Congress meant when it said "promissory note," in fact the Court's opinion does not rest on any special attributes of Orion's note. Rather, the Court rules that when an individual entrusts a negotiable instrument to a bank, that instrument is not "money or its equivalent" for purposes of § 1813(l)(1) so long as the bank promises not to negotiate it or collect on it until certain conditions are met. That is a proviso that Congress might have been well advised to include in the Act, but did not. I therefore dissent.

NOTES

(1) Note that a standby letter of credit often is simply a performance bond. Why would a party demand a standby letter of credit in lieu of a performance bond?

(2) Does the introduction of a standby letter of credit influence your approval/rejection of the complete compliance doctrine?

PROBLEM 23.4

An excited Clayton Molinero calls you on the phone with yet another financing problem. Because business has been booming (in part, due to the cane rods) Clayton plans to expand his retail floor space and has contracted with Spellman & Wu Construction, Inc. to have the work done. Spellman & Wu are known for its low prices, and unfortunately, sometimes, low quality workmanship. Clayton would like to structure a payment framework allowing Spellman and Wu to be paid at three stages of the construction process, provided that at each stage the work completed meets an inspection by an independent third party. What do you suggest to Clayton? Is possible solution a standby letter of credit?

---

§ 23.03 "Trust Receipt" Secured Financing of Buyer

Review the diagram above at page 23.01[A]. Note step 13 where "B pays the amount of the draft to Issuing Bank and receives the documents (and the draft, if B is drawee)." But what happens if B doesn't wish to pay for the goods at this point? In that situation, "trust receipt" financing can be arranged. Issuing Bank will deliver the documents to B in exchange for B signing trust receipts whereby Issuing Bank is given a security interest in the bill of lading and the goods

[60] It seems odd that Philadelphia Gear's status as an insured depositor should depend on the terms of the repayment agreement between Orion and the bank. Ordinarily, Philadelphia Gear would be indifferent to the agreement between Orion and the bank, and might not even be aware of the terms of that agreement. The Court, therefore, is not necessarily bringing greater rationality to this area of the law by creating distinctions between types of letters of credit for purposes of federal deposit insurance coverage.

represented thereby. If B defaults, Issuing Bank as a secured party can "foreclose" on the collateral. This "trust receipt" financing is now governed by Article 9 Secured Transactions. See U.C.C. § 9-102(1)(a) and (2). An example of this transaction is found in Comment 2 to § 9-303.

> A bank which has issued a letter of credit honors drafts drawn under the credit and receives possession of the negotiable bill of lading covering the goods shipped. Under Sections 9-304(2) and 9-305 the bank now has a perfected security interest in the document and the goods. The bank releases the bill of lading to the debtor for the purpose of procuring the goods from the carrier and selling them. Under Section 9-304(5) the bank continues to have a perfected security interest in the document and goods for 21 days. The bank files before the expiration of the 21 day period. Its security interest now continues perfected for as long as the filing is good. The goods are sold by the debtor. The bank continues to have a security interest in the proceeds of the sale to the extent stated in Section 9-306.
>
> If the successive stages of the bank's security interest succeed each other without an intervening gap, the security interest is "continuously perfected" and the date of perfection is when the interest first became perfected (i.e., in the example given, when the bank received possession of the bill of lading against honor of the drafts). If however, there is a gap between stages—for example, if the bank does not file until after the expiration of the 21 day period specified in Section 9-304(5), the collateral still being in the debtor's possession — then, the chain being broken, the perfection is no longer continuous. The date of perfection would now be the date of filing (after expiration of the 21 day period); the bank's interest might now become subject to attack under Section 60 of the Federal Bankruptcy Act [now Bankruptcy Code § 547] and would be subject to any interests arising during the gap period which under Section 9-301 take priority over an unperfected security interest.

---

§ 23.04 Secured Financing of Seller: Transfer and Assignment

Read: U.C.C. § 5-116 and Revised §§ 5-112, 5-114; cf. §§ 2-210, 9-318.

We have seen the letter of credit used to assure seller that it will receive *payment* for the sold goods. The letter of credit can also be used as a device to assist the *financing* of seller. For example, suppose seller wishes to purchase from its supplier goods which it has agreed to sell to buyer. The problem is that supplier may not sell to seller on unsecured credit. Seller, as beneficiary of the letter of credit, can use the letter to obtain the necessary financing:

1. The seller-beneficiary might transfer its rights and duties under the letter of credit to its supplier. U.C.C. § 5-116(1) [revised § 5-112], see § 2-210.

2. The seller-beneficiary might transfer its prospective right to the proceeds of the letter of credit to a financier as security for a loan. U.C.C. § 5-116(2) [revised § 5-114].

3. The seller-beneficiary might use the letter of credit to procure the issuance of a second letter of credit in favor of its lender or supplier ("back-to-back" letters of credit).

For discussion of these matters, see J. White and R. Summers, Handbook of the Law Under the Uniform Commercial Code § 26-12(4th Practitioner's Ed., 1995). See also, J, Dolan, The Law of Letters of Credit, Ch. 10 (Transfer and Assignment) (2d ed. 1991).

The corresponding provisions of the Uniform Customs, 1993 Revision, are Articles 48 and 49. See Reviseed U.C.C. §§ 5-112, 5-113, 5-114.

§ 23.05 Letters of Credit in Bankruptcy

IN RE COMPTON CORP.

United States Court of Appeals
831 F.2d 586 (5th Cir. 1987)

JERRE S. WILLIAMS, CIRCUIT JUDGE

This is a bankruptcy preference case in which a bankruptcy trustee seeks to recover a transfer made via a letter of credit for the benefit of one of the debtor's unsecured creditors on the eve of bankruptcy. The bankruptcy court and the district court found there to be no voidable preference. We reverse.

I. Factual Background

In March 1982, Blue Quail Energy, Inc., delivered a shipment of oil to debtor Compton Corporation. Payment of $585,443.85 for this shipment of oil was due on or about April 20, 1982. Compton failed to make timely payment. Compton induced Abilene National Bank (now MBank-Abilene) to issue an irrevocable standby letter of credit in Blue Quail's favor on May 6, 1982. Under the terms of the letter of credit, payment of up to $585,443.85 was due Blue Quail if Compton failed to pay Blue Quail this amount by June 22, 1982. Compton paid MBank $1,463.61 to issue the letter of credit. MBank also received a promissory note payable on demand for $585,443.85. MBank did not need a security agreement to cover the letter of credit transaction because a prior 1980 security agreement between the bank and Compton had a future advances provision.[61] This 1980 security agreement had been perfected as to a variety of Compton's assets through the filing of several financing statements. The most recent financing statement had been filed a year before, May 7, 1981. The letter of credit on its face noted that it was for an antecedent debt due Blue Quail.

On May 7, 1982, the day after MBank issued the letter of credit in Blue Quail's favor, several of Compton's creditors filed an involuntary bankruptcy petition against Compton. On June 22, 1982, MBank paid Blue Quail $569,932.03 on the letter of credit after Compton failed to pay Blue Quail.

In the ensuing bankruptcy proceeding, MBank's aggregate secured claims against Compton, including the letter of credit payment to Blue Quail, were paid in full from the liquidation of Compton's assets which served as the bank's collateral. Walter Kellogg, bankruptcy trustee for Compton, did not contest the validity of MBank's secured claim against Compton's assets for the amount drawn under the letter of credit by Blue Quail. Instead, on June 14, 1983, trustee Kellogg filed a complaint in the bankruptcy court against Blue Quail asserting that Blue Quail had received a preferential transfer under 11 U.S.C. § 547 through the letter of credit transaction. The trustee sought to recover $585,443.85 from Blue Quail pursuant to 11 U.S.C. § 550.

Blue Quail answered and filed a third party complaint against MBank. On June 16, 1986, Blue Quail filed a motion for summary judgment asserting that the trustee could not recover any

[61] A future advances clause in a security agreement subjects the specified collateral to any future loan made by the creditor in addition to the current loans.

preference from Blue Quail because Blue Quail had been paid from MBank's funds under the letter of credit and therefore had not received any of Compton's property. On August 27, 1986, the bankruptcy court granted Blue Quail's motion, agreeing that the payment under the letter of credit did not constitute a transfer of debtor Compton's property but rather was a transfer of the bank's property. The bankruptcy court entered judgment on the motion on September 10, 1986. Trustee Kellogg appealed this decision to the district court. On December 11, 1986, the district court affirmed the bankruptcy court ruling, holding that the trustee did not establish two necessary elements of a voidable transfer under 11 U.S.C. § 547. The district court agreed with Blue Quail and the bankruptcy court that the trustee could not establish that the funds transferred to Blue Quail were ever property of Compton. Furthermore, the district court held that the transfer of the increased security interest to MBank was a transfer of the debtor's property for the sole benefit of the bank and in no way benefitted Blue Quail. The district court therefore found no voidable preference as to Blue Quail. The trustee is appealing the decision to this Court.

II. The Letter of Credit

It is well established that a letter of credit and the proceeds therefrom are not property of the debtor's estate under 11 U.S.C. § 541. When the issuer honors a proper draft under a letter of credit, it does so from its own assets and not from the assets of its customer who caused the letter of credit to be issued. *In re W.L. Mead*; In *re M.J. Sales.* As a result, a bankruptcy trustee is not entitled to enjoin a post petition payment of funds under a letter of credit from the issuer to the beneficiary, because such a payment is not a transfer of debtor's property (a threshold requirement under 11 U.S.C. § 547(b)). A case apparently holding otherwise, *In re Twist Cap., Inc.,* 1 Bankr. 284 (Bankr. Fla. 1979), has been roundly criticized and otherwise ignored by courts and commentators alike.

Recognizing these characteristics of a letter of credit in a bankruptcy case is necessary in order to maintain the independence principle, the cornerstone of letter of credit law. Under the independence principle, an issuer's obligation to the letter of credit's beneficiary is independent from any obligation between the beneficiary and the issuer's customer. All a beneficiary has to do to receive payment under a letter of credit is to show that it has performed all the duties required by the letter of credit. Any disputes between the beneficiary and the customer do not affect the issuer's obligation to the beneficiary to pay under the letter of credit.

Letters of credit are most commonly arranged by a party who benefits from the provision of goods or services. The party will request a bank to issue a letter of credit which names the provider of the goods or services as the beneficiary. Under a standby letter of credit, the bank becomes primarily liable to the beneficiary upon the default of the bank's customer to pay for the goods or services. The bank charges a fee to issue a letter of credit and to undertake this liability. The shifting of liability to the bank rather than to the services or goods provider is the main purpose of the letter of credit. After all, the bank is in a much better position to assess the risk of its customer's insolvency than is the service or goods provider. It should be noted, however, that it is the risk of the debtor's insolvency and not the risk of a preference attack that a bank assumes under a letter of credit transaction. Overall, the independence principle is necessary to insure "the certainty of payments for services or goods rendered regardless of any intervening misfortune which may befall the other contracting party." *In re North Shore*, 30 B.R. at 378.

The trustee in this case accepts this analysis and does not ask us to upset it. The trustee is not attempting to set aside the post petition payments by MBank to Blue Quail under the letter of credit as a preference; nor does the trustee claim the letter of credit itself constitutes debtor's property. The trustee is instead challenging the earlier transfer in which Compton granted MBank an increased security interest in its assets to obtain the letter of credit for the benefit of Blue Quail. Collateral which has been pledged by a debtor as security for a letter of credit is property of the debtor's estate. *In re W.L. Mead*, 42 B.R. at 59. The trustee claims that the direct transfer to MBank of the increased security interest on May 6, 1982, also constituted an indirect transfer to Blue Quail which occurred one day prior to the filing of the involuntary bankruptcy petition and is voidable as a preference under 11 U.S.C. § 547. This assertion of a preferential transfer is evaluated in Parts III and IV of this opinion.

It is important to note that the irrevocable standby letter of credit in the case at bar was not arranged in connection with Blue Quail's initial decision to sell oil to Compton on credit. Compton arranged for the letter of credit after Blue Quail had shipped the oil and after Compton had defaulted in payment. The letter of credit in this case did not serve its usual function of backing up a contemporaneous credit decision,[62] but instead served as a back up payment guarantee on an extension of credit already in jeopardy. The letter of credit was issued to pay off an antecedent unsecured debt. This fact was clearly noted on the face of the letter of credit.[63] Blue Quail, the beneficiary of the letter of credit, did not give new value for the issuance of the letter of credit by MBank on May 6, 1982, or for the resulting increased security interest held by MBank. MBank, however, did give new value for the increased security interest it obtained in Compton's collateral: the bank issued the letter of credit.

When a debtor pledges its assets to secure a letter of credit, a transfer of debtor's property has occurred under the provisions of 11 U.S.C. § 547. By subjecting its assets to MBank's reimbursement claim in the event MBank had to pay on the letter of credit, Compton made a transfer of its property. The broad definition of "transfer" under 11 U.S.C. § 101(50) is clearly designed to cover such a transfer. Overall, the letter of credit itself and the payments thereunder may not be property of debtor, but the collateral pledged as a security interest for the letter of credit is.

Furthermore, in a secured letter of credit transaction, the transfer of debtor's property takes place at the time the letter of credit is issued (when the security interest is granted) and received by the beneficiary, not at the time the issuer pays on the letter of credit. *In re Briggs Transportation Co.*, 37 Bankr. 76, 79 (Bankr. Minn. 1984). *In re M.J. Sales, supra* (transfer of pledged collateral occurs not when bank forecloses on it, but when it is pledged.)

The transfer to MBank of the increased security interest was a direct transfer which occurred on May 6, 1982, when the bank issued the letter of credit. Under 11 U.S.C. § 547(e)(2)(A), however, such a transfer is deemed to have taken place for purposes of 11 U.S.C. § 547 at the time such transfer "takes effect" between the transferor and transferee if such transfer is perfected within 10 days. The phrase "takes effect" is undefined in the Bankruptcy Code, but under Uniform Commercial Code Article 9 law, a transfer of a security interest "takes effect" when the security interest attaches. Because of the future advances clause in MBank's 1980 security agreement with Compton, the attachment of the MBank's security interest relates back to May 9, 1980, the date the security agreement went into effect. The bottom line is that the direct transfer of

[62] As was the case in *In re W.L. Mead, Inc.*, *In re Leisure Dynamics*, *In re North Shore & Central Illinois Freight Co.*, and *In re M.J. Sales*, all *supra*.

[63] The letter of credit was dated May 6, 1982, and noted that it covered delivery of Oklahoma Sweet crude oil during March 1982.

the increased security interest to MBank is artificially deemed to have occurred at least by May 7, 1981, the date MBank filed its final financing statement, for purposes of a preference attack against the bank.[64] This date is well before the 90 day window of 11 U.S.C. § 547(b)(4)(A). This would protect the bank from a preference attack by the trustee even if the bank had not given new value at the time it received the increased security interest. MBank is therefore protected from a preference attack by the trustee for the increased security interest transfer under either of two theories: under 11 U.S.C. § 547(c)(1) because it gave new value and under the operation of the relation back provision of 11 U.S.C. § 547(e)(2)(A). The bank is also protected from any claims of reimbursement by Blue Quail because the bank received no voidable preference.

The relation back provision of 11 U.S.C. § 547(e)(2)(A), however, applies only to the direct transfer of the increased security interest to MBank. The indirect transfer to Blue Quail that allegedly resulted from the direct transfer to MBank occurred on May 6, 1982, the date of issuance of the letter of credit. The relation back principle of 11 U.S.C. § 547(e)(2)(A) does not apply to this indirect transfer to Blue Quail. Blue Quail was not a party to the security agreement between MBank and Compton. So it will not be able to utilize the relation back provision if it is deemed to have received an indirect transfer resulting from the direct transfer of the increased security interest to MBank. Blue Quail, therefore, cannot assert either of the two defenses to a preference attack which MBank can claim. Blue Quail did not give new value under § 547(c)(1), and it received a transfer within 90 days of the filing of Compton's bankruptcy petition.[65]

III. Direct/Indirect Transfer Doctrine

The federal courts have long recognized that "to constitute a preference, it is not necessary that the transfer be made directly to the creditor." *National Bank of Newport v. National Herkimer County Bank,* 225 U.S. 178, 184, 32 S. Ct. 633, 635, 56 L. Ed. 1042 (1912). "If the bankrupt has made a transfer of his property, the effect of which is to enable one of his creditors to obtain a greater percentage of his debt than another creditor of the same class, circuity of arrangement will not avail to save it." *Id.* To combat such circuity, the courts have broken down certain transfers into two transfers, one direct and one indirect. The direct transfer to the third party may be valid and not subject to a preference attack. The indirect transfer, arising from the same action by the debtor, however, may constitute a voidable preference as to the creditor who indirectly benefitted from the direct transfer to the third party.

This is the situation presented in the case before us. The term "transfer" as used in the various bankruptcy statutes through the years has always been broad enough to cover such indirect transfers and to catch various circuitous arrangements. *Katz v. First National Bank of Glen Head,* 568 F.2d 964, 969 n. 4, (2d Cir.), cert. denied, 434 U.S. 1069, 98 S. Ct. 1250, 55 L. Ed. 2d 771 (1978). The new Bankruptcy Code implicitly adopts this doctrine through its broad definition of "transfer."[66] Examining the case law that has developed since the *National Bank of Newport*

[64] Tex. Bus. & Com. Code Ann. § 9.312(g) specifies that for purposes of priority among competing secured parties, the security interest for a future advance has the same priority as the security interest for the first advance. Conflicting security interests rank according to priority in time of filing or perfection. Tex. Bus. & Com. Code Ann. § 9.312(e)(1).

[65] Nor does Blue Quail have the protection of the 11 U.S.C. § 547(c)(2) "ordinary course of business" preference exception. Getting a standby letter of credit issued to cover a debt several weeks past due does not constitute ordinary course of business.

[66] "Transfer" means every mode, direct or indirect, absolute or conditional, voluntary or involuntary, of disposing of or parting with property or with an interest in property, including retention of title as a security interest and foreclosure

case yields an understanding of what types of transfers the direct/indirect doctrine is meant to cover.

In *Palmer v. Radio Corporation of America,* 453 F.2d 1133 (5th Cir. 1971), a third party purchased from the debtor a television station for $40,000 cash and the assumption of certain liabilities of the debtor, including unsecured claims by creditor RCA. This Court found the direct transfer from the debtor to the third party purchaser constituted an indirect preferential transfer to creditor RCA. We found that the assumption by the third party purchaser of the debt owed by the debtor to RCA and the subsequent payments made there-under constituted a voidable transfer as to RCA. The court noted that such indirect transfers as this had long been held to constitute voidable preferences under bankruptcy laws. 453 F.2d at 1136.

Although the *Palmer* court did not elaborate its reasoning behind this holding, such reasoning is self evident. A secured creditor was essentially substituted for an unsecured creditor through the transfer of the television station to the third party purchaser and the assumption of the unsecured debt by the purchaser. The third party purchaser was in effect secured because it had the television station. Creditor RCA would receive payments directly from the solvent third party without having to worry about its original debtor's financial condition. The original debtor's other unsecured creditors were harmed because a valuable asset of the debtor, the television station, was removed from the debtor's estate. The end result of the *Palmer* case was that the third party's payments on the RCA debt were to be made to the debtor's estate instead of to RCA. RCA would then recover the same percentage of its unsecured claim from the estate as the other unsecured creditors.

In *In re Conrad Corp.,* 806 F.2d 610 (5th Cir. 1986), we found a voidable indirect transfer on facts similar to those of *Palmer v. Radio Corporation of America.* In the *Conrad* case, the debtors bought several restaurants from the Burtons in exchange for an unsecured promissory note. A third party in turn purchased the restaurants from the debtors and assumed the payments to the Burtons on the promissory note. Relying on the analysis of the *Palmer* case, we held that the transfer of the restaurants by the debtors in exchange for a simultaneous assumption of the Burton debt by the third party benefitted the Burtons and constituted a voidable indirect transfer as to the Burtons.

We observed that as a result of executing the assumption of debt agreement, the debtors transferred to the Burtons the debtors' right to receive from the third party so much of the sales price for the restaurants as was needed to reimburse the Burtons on their unsecured note. Once again a secured creditor, in effect, was substituted for an unsecured creditor by the transfer, and a depletion of the debtor's estate occurred. We held that the trustee of the debtor could recover from the Burtons the payments made by the third party to the Burtons and that the Burtons would recover only their proportionate share of the value of the unencumbered assets of the debtor along with the other unsecured creditors.

There are a number of federal cases in the other circuits supporting the holdings and reasoning in our direct/indirect doctrine cases. In *Aulick v. Largent,* 295 F.2d 41 (4th Cir. 1961), a third party endorsed the debtor's antecedent obligation to one of the debtor's unsecured creditors in exchange for the transfer of some stock within the preference time period. The creditor eventually received payment from the third party who in turn retained the pledged stock. The Fourth Circuit

---

of the debtor's equity of redemption. 11 U.S.C. § 101 (50). See also the Notes of the Committee on the Judiciary under 11 U.S.C. 101 ("The definition of transfer is as broad as possible.")

held that while the direct transfer of the stock to the third party to secure the contingent liability of the endorsement was not voidable because it was a transfer for consideration presently furnished, the indirect transfer to the unsecured creditor via the third party endorser was a voidable preference. The creditor in *Aulick* made the same argument that Blue Quail makes in the case at bar. The creditor claimed that the payment to it by the third party endorser came from the endorser's personal funds and thus the payment did not deplete the debtor's estate. Therefore one of the essential elements of a voidable preference was lacking.

The court rejected this argument relying on *National Bank of Newport.* The *Aulick* court found there to be two transfers arising from the pledge of stock to the third party, one direct and one indirect, and then collapsed them, in effect, into a single one for a preference attack against the indirect transferee creditor. The court noted that if the debtor had delivered the shares of stock directly to the unsecured creditor as security for the antecedent debt, the creditor would have clearly received a voidable preference. The court held that such a result could not be avoided by indirect arrangement.[67] "Preferences obtained by indirect or circuitous arrangements are to be struck down just as quickly as those obtained by direct arrangements." 295 F.2d at 52.

In *Virginia National Bank v. Woodson,* 329 F.2d 836 (4th Cir. 1964), the debtor had several overdrawn accounts with his bank.[68] The debtor talked his sister into paying off $8,000 of the overdrafts in exchange for an $8,000 promissory note and an assignment of some collateral as security. The debtor's sister made the $8,000 payment directly to the bank. The $8,000 technically was never part of the debtor's estate. The court, however, held that the payment of the $8,000 by the sister to the bank was a preference as to the bank to the extent of the value of the collateral held by the sister. The court noted that the measure of the value of a voidable preference is diminution of the debtor's estate and not the value of the transfer to the creditor.

In the *Woodson* case the sister was secured only to the extent the pledged collateral had value; the remainder of her loan to her brother was unsecured. Swapping one unsecured creditor for another unsecured creditor does not create any kind of preference. The court held that a preference in such a transaction arises only when a secured creditor is swapped for an unsecured creditor. Only then is the pool of assets available for distribution to the general unsecured creditors depleted because the secured creditor has priority over the unsecured creditors. Furthermore, the court held that the bank and not the sister had received the voidable preference and had to pay back to the trustee an amount equal to the value of the collateral.

A slightly different indirect transfer was involved in *In re Mercon Industries, Inc.,* 37 Bankr. 549 (Bank. E.D. Penn. 1984). In that case a debtor paid off a non-insider unsecured creditor within one year of the filing of the bankruptcy petition on a debt guaranteed by insiders of the debtor. The payment to the creditor had the effect of releasing the insider guarantors from contingent liability on the debt, thereby benefitting the insiders. The court held that releasing an insider guarantor from contingent liability is a beneficial transfer to the guarantor for purposes of 11 U.S.C. § 547.

---

[67] Apparently the bottom line in the *Aulick* case was that the creditor and not the third party endorser was ultimately liable for the preferential transfer. This is the way the preference provisions are supposed to work; it was the creditor, after all, and not the endorser who was preferred. It should also be noted that there would have been no preference attack against the creditor had not the endorser received the assignment of stock from the debtor to secure its contingent liability on the endorsement. It is the substitution of a secured creditor for a general unsecured creditor that constitutes the voidable transfer as to the unsecured creditor. This is a common theme underlying the direct/indirect cases and applies with equal force to the case at bar.

[68] Unsecured antecedent debts.

The court in *Mercon* viewed the payment to the non-insider creditor as effecting two transfers under the Bankruptcy Code because of the secondary liability of the guarantors on the debt. The court held that while the direct transfer from the debtor to the non-insider creditor in satisfaction of the primary debt may not be a voidable preference (if it was made over 90 days of filing), the court found that the indirect transfer to the insider guarantors extinguishing their contingent liability (and their contingent unsecured claim for reimbursement) was a separate voidable transfer under 11 U.S.C. § 547. Such an indirect transfer is voidable if it occurred within one year of filing pursuant to § 547(b)(4)(B). Furthermore, the court held that because the Bankruptcy Code "dictates that there are two transfers rather than one, liability of the guarantors under § 547(b) need not be predicated on a finding of an avoidable transfer to [the non-insider creditor], since a finding of liability on one transfer is independent of the other, rather than derivative." 37 B.R. at 552. The court held that the insider guarantors, and not the non-insider creditor, were ultimately liable for this preference.[69]

IV. The Direct/Indirect Doctrine in the Context of a Letter of Credit Transaction

The case at bar differs from the cases discussed in Part III *supra* only by the presence of the letter of credit as the mechanism for paying off the unsecured creditor. Blue Quail's attempt to otherwise distinguish the case from the direct/indirect transfer cases does not withstand scrutiny.

In the letter of credit cases discussed in Part II *supra*, the letters of credit were issued contemporaneously with the initial extension of credit by the beneficiaries of the letters. In those cases the letters of credit effectively served as security devices for the benefit of the creditor beneficiaries and took the place of formal security interests. The courts in those cases properly found there had been no voidable transfers, direct or indirect, in the letter of credit transactions involved. New value was given contemporaneously with the issuance of the letters of credit in the form of the extensions of credit in the form of the extensions of credit by the beneficiaries of the letters. As a result, the 11 U.S.C. § 547(c)(1) preference exception was applicable.

The case at bar differs from these other letter of credit cases by one very important fact: the letter of credit in this case was issued to secure an antecedent unsecured debt due the beneficiary of the letter of credit. The unsecured creditor beneficiary gave no new value upon the issuance of the letter of credit. When the issuer paid off the letter of credit and foreclosed on the collateral securing the letter of credit, a preferential transfer had occurred. An unsecured creditor was paid in full and a secured creditor was substituted in its place.

The district court upheld the bankruptcy court in maintaining the validity of the letter of credit issued to cover the antecedent debt. The district court held that MBank, the issuer of the letter of credit, could pay off the letter of credit and foreclose on the collateral securing it. We are in full agreement.

But we also look to the impact of the transaction as it affects the situation of Blue Quail in the bankrupt estate. We hold that the bankruptcy trustee can recover from Blue Quail, the beneficiary of the letter of credit, because Blue Quail received an indirect preference. This result preserves the sanctity of letter of credit and carries out the purposes of the Bankruptcy Code

[69] See also *In re Deprizio Construction Co.*, 58 Bankr. 478 (N.D. Ill. E.D. 1986) (case with similar facts and a similar holding). This case also described the bankruptcy courts' equitable powers under 11 U.S.C. § 550 to preclude a trustee from recovering from innocent creditors who were the initial direct transferees of a voidable indirect preference.

by avoiding a preferential transfer. MBank, the issuer of the letter of credit, being just the intermediary through which the preferential transfer was accomplished, completely falls out of the picture and is not involved in this particular legal proceeding.

MBank did not receive any preferential transfer–it gave new value for the security interest. Furthermore, because the direct and indirect transfers are separate and independent, the trustee does not even need to challenge the direct transfer of the increased security interest to MBank, or seek any relief at all from MBank, in order to attack the indirect transfer and recover under 11 U.S.C. § 550 from the indirect transferee Blue Quail.

We hold that a creditor cannot secure payment of an unsecured antecedent debt through a letter of credit transaction when it could not do so through any other type of transaction. The purpose of the letter of credit transaction in this case was to secure payment of an unsecured antecedent debt for the benefit of an unsecured creditor. This is the only proper way to look at such letters of credit in the bankruptcy context. The promised transfer of pledged collateral induced the bank to issue the letter of credit in favor of the creditor. The increased security interest held by the bank clearly benefitted the creditor because the bank would not have issued the letter of credit without this security. A secured creditor was substituted for an unsecured creditor to the detriment of the other unsecured creditors.

We also hold, therefore, that the trustee can recover under 11 U.S.C. § 550(a)(1)the value of the transferred property from "the entity for whose benefit such transfer was made." In the case at bar, this entity was the creditor beneficiary, not the issuer, of the letter of credit even though the issuer received the direct transfer from the debtor. The entire purpose of the direct/indirect doctrine is to look through the form of a transaction and determine which entity actually benefitted from the transfer.[70]

The fact that there was a prior security agreement between the issuing bank and the debtor containing the future advances clause does not alter this conclusion. As we pointed out in Part II *supra*, this prior security agreement gave MBank an additional shield from preferential attack because of the relation back mechanism of 11 U.S.C. § 547(e)(2)(A). 11 U.S.C. § 547(e)(2)(A), however, does not avail Blue Quail to shield it from a preferential attack for the indirect transfer. The indirect transfer to Blue Quail occurred on May 6, 1982, when the letter of credit was issued and the increased security interest was pledged. This was the day before the involuntary bankruptcy petition was filed. For purposes of 11 U.S.C. § 547, a transfer of Compton's property for the benefit of Blue Quail did occur within 90 days of the bankruptcy filing. The bankruptcy and district courts erred in failing to analyze properly the transfer of debtor's property that occurred when Compton pledged its assets to obtain the letter of credit. This transfer consisted of two aspects: the direct transfer to MBank which is not a voidable preference for various reasons and the indirect transfer to Blue Quail which is a voidable preference.

All of the requirements of 11 U.S.C. § 547(b) have been satisfied in the trustee's preferential attack against Blue Quail. There was (1) a transfer of Compton's property for the benefit of Blue Quail (2) for an antecedent debt owed by Compton (3) made while Compton was insolvent[71]

[70] We have found only one prior case that has fully addressed the application of the direct/indirect doctrine in the context of a letter of credit transaction. *In re Air Conditioning, Inc. of Stuart,* 55 Bankr. 157 (Bankr. S.D. Fla. 1985), affirmed in part, reversed in part 72 Bankr. 657 (S.D. Fla. 1987) (currently on appeal to the Eleventh Circuit). In a carefully and thoroughly reasoned opinion, the court reached the same conclusion we reach in this case.

[71] There is a presumption that a debtor is insolvent at least 90 days prior to its bankruptcy filing. 11 U.S.C. § 547(f).

(4) within 90 days before the date of the filing of the petition (5) that enabled Blue Quail to receive more than it would receive under a Chapter 7 liquidation.[72] The net effect of the indirect transfer to Blue Quail was to remove $585,443.85 from the pool of assets available to Compton's unsecured creditors and substitute in its place a secured claim for the same amount.

The precise holding in this case needs to be emphasized. We do not hold that payment under a letter of credit, or even a letter of credit itself, constitute preferential transfers under 11 U.S.C. § 547(b) or property of a debtor under 11 U.S.C. § 541. The holding of this case fully allows the letter of credit to function. We preserve its sanctity and the underlying independence doctrine. We do not, however, allow an unsecured creditor to avoid a preference attack by utilizing a letter of credit to secure payment of an antecedent debt. Otherwise the unsecured creditor would receive an indirect preferential transfer from the granting of the security for the letter of credit to the extent of the value of that security. Our holding does not affect the strength of or the proper use of letters of credit. When a letter of credit is issued contemporaneously with a new extension of credit, the creditor beneficiary will not be subject to a preferential attack under the direct/indirect doctrine elaborated in this case because the creditor will have given new value in exchange for the indirect benefit of the secured letter of credit. Only when a creditor receives a secured letter of credit to cover an unsecured antecedent debt will it be subject to a preferential attack under 11 U.S.C. § 547(b).

V. Liability of MBank for the Preferential Transfer

Blue Quail has no valid claim against MBank for reimbursement for any amounts Blue Quail has to pay the trustee under the trustee's preference claim, just as the trustee has no preference challenge against MBank. Blue Quail received the preferential transfer, not MBank. MBank gave new value in exchange for the increased security interest in its favor. Thus, it is insulated from any assertion of a voidable preference. The bank in no way assumed the risk of a preference attack by issuing the letter of credit. For these reasons, we affirm the district court's dismissal of Blue Quail's request to proceed against MBank for reimbursement.[73]

In addition, the trustee may not set aside the $1,463.61 fee Compton paid MBank to issue the letter of credit. This payment is not a preferential transfer. MBank has fully performed its duties under the terms of the letter of credit and has earned this fee. The services MBank rendered in issuing and executing the letter of credit constitute new value under the 11 U.S.C. § 547(c)(1) preference exception.

VI. Conclusion

Blue Quail Energy received an indirect preferential transfer from Compton Corporation on May 6, 1982, one day prior to the filing of Compton's bankruptcy petition. We reverse the district court and render judgment in favor of Trustee Kellogg against Blue Quail Energy, Inc. in the amount of $585,443.85 plus interest to be fixed by the district court pursuant to 11 U.S.C. §§ 547, 550. The district court's dismissal of Blue Quail's claim against MBank for reimbursement is affirmed.

---

[72] There was undisputed evidence below that the other unsecured creditors of Compton would receive less than fifty cents on the dollar for their unsecured claims.

[73] The liability of MBank to Blue Quail in the event of this Court's finding a preferential transfer to Blue Quail is interrelated with the Trustee's preference challenge against Blue Quail. The briefs of Blue Quail and Trustee Kellogg both addressed this issue.

Reversed in Part, Affirmed in Part, and Remanded.

NOTE

The *Compton* court refused to allow a creditor to secure payment of an unsecured antecedent debt by utilizing a letter of credit. Always alert of the independence principle, the court wrote, "The holding of this case fully allows the letter of credit to function. We preserve its sanctity and the underlying independence doctrine . . . Our holding does not affect the strength or proper use of letters of credit. When a letter of credit is issued contemporaneously with the extension of credit, the creditor beneficiary will not be subject to a preferential attack under the direct/indirect doctrine elaborated in this case because the creditor will have given new value in exchange for the indirect benefit of the secured letter of credit." Do you agree that this case does not infringe on the independence doctrine? How is an issuing bank suppose to evaluate whether a transaction will violate the direct/indirect doctrine presented in this case?

TABLE OF CASES

[Principal cases appear in solid capitals. Cases cited or discussed by the authors in lower case type. References are to sections.]

[Principal cases appear in solid capitals. Cases cited or discussed by the authors in lower case type. References are to sections.]

[Principal cases appear in solid capitals. Cases cited or discussed by the authors in lower case type. References are to sections.]

[Principal cases appear in solid capitals. Cases cited or discussed by the authors in lower case type. References are to sections.]

H

I

J

K

L

[Principal cases appear in solid capitals. Cases cited or discussed by the authors in lower case type. References are to sections.]

[Principal cases appear in solid capitals. Cases cited or discussed by the authors in lower case type. References are to sections.]

[Principal cases appear in solid capitals. Cases cited or discussed by the authors in lower case type. References are to sections.]

T

U

V

W

X

[Principal cases appear in solid capitals. Cases cited or discussed by the authors in lower case type. References are to sections.]

Z

TABLE OF UNIFORM COMMERCIAL CODE

[References are to sections.]

[References are to sections.]

[References are to sections.]

[References are to sections.]

[References are to sections.]

[References are to sections.]

[References are to sections.]

[References are to sections.]

[References are to sections.]

[References are to sections.]

INDEX

[References are to sections.]

A

B

[References are to sections.]

[References are to sections.]

C

[References are to sections.]

D

[References are to sections.]

[References are to sections.]

[References are to sections.]

G

H

[References are to sections.]

I

L

[References are to sections.]

[References are to sections.]

[References are to sections.]

[References are to sections.]

[References are to sections.]

[References are to sections.]

S

[References are to sections.]

[References are to sections.]

T

U

V

[References are to sections.]